BARR ST.
CLINTON ST.
MAIDEN LANE
CASS ST.
WATER ST.
EWING ST.

Volume 2

John D. Beatty
Editor of Volume 1

Phyllis Robb
Editor of Volume 2

M.T. Publishing Company, Inc.
P.O. Box 6802
Evansville, Indiana 47719-6802
www.mtpublishing.com

Graphic Designer for Patrons:
Elizabeth A. Dennis

Graphic Designer for Family Biographies:
Alena L. Richards

Indexing by M.T. Publishing Staff

Library of Congress Control Number:
2006932057

ISBN: 1-932439-44-7

Printed in the United States of America

Volume 1
1816-era Fort image on seal from an original drawing by Historian Bert J. Griswold.
Inside Front Cover: Detail from "A Map of Fort Wayne" by Noble E. Brainerd, 1933. (Courtesy of the *Fort Wayne News Sentinel.*)
Inside Back Cover: "Map of the City of Fort Wayne and Vicinity" (Klaubrech & Menzel, 1855.)

Volume 2
Courthouse image on seal from an original drawing by Brentwood Tolan, provided by the Court House Preservation Trust.
Inside Front Cover: "Panoramic View of the City of Fort Wayne, Allen County, Indiana, 1880"
Inside Back Cover: "Business Section, City of Fort Wayne" (Nirnstein's National Realty Map. ca. 1950s.)

Book Committee

Kathryn Bowen Bloom	Co-Chair & Organizations Chair
William C. Lee	Co-Chair
G. Stanley Hood	Vice Chair
John D. Beatty	Narrative History Chair
Phyllis Robb	Administrative & Editing Co-Chair Family History Co-Chair
Margery Graham	Administrative & Editing Co-Chair Family History Co-Chair
Matt Henry	Marketing Chair
Judith Obear Bunn	Financial Chair
Adrienne Mauer	Business History Co-Chair
Thomas E. Castaldi	Business History Co-Chair
Linda Churchward	Religious Congregations Chair
Patty Martone	School Organizations & Institutions Co-Chair
Leanne Mensing	School Organizations & Institutions Co-Chair
Lois Snouffer	Memorials & Tributes Chair

Table of Contents

Introduction

A Century of Change

In Volume II of the Allen County History Book, the residents of Allen County were invited to tell us their stories - the stories of their families, businesses, organizations, schools, and churches. These stories mirror the history of the county as found in the narrative history, Volume I. When reading their stories, future generations will have a unique window into the everyday lives of citizens of Allen County, Indiana, in the Twentieth Century.

The Twentieth Century in Allen County was one of tremendous change. Allen County evolved from a largely rural county with a number of small villages and one large city, Fort Wayne, into one large metropolitan area which is spreading out from the city into the countryside. Many of the small towns are growing, and along the highways between Fort Wayne and these towns, the farm fields are being replaced with shopping centers, businesses, and subdivisions of new homes. New places of worship have been built, and older ones have either enlarged or relocated to better accommodate their congregations. New schools are being built to accommodate the new population centers, and some old schools have closed. Some original Fort Wayne businesses have left the county, and new businesses have opened.

Allen County residents were anxious to tell their stories. Of special interest are the stories of family homesteads and businesses that existed through much of the century. Families were constantly adapting to change, as evidenced by the family histories. We learned that Allen County roots run deep. In addition to submissions within the county, we received submissions from all over the state of Indiana, and from twenty-three states. The histories tell of long-time residents who moved elsewhere to follow new opportunities, and of newcomers, including many immigrants, who moved into the county. We read about minority groups who stood up for their rights and took their place in the community. Allen County has indeed been blessed by the great diversity of its citizens, and we thank them all for sharing their stories.

The Process

The process we followed to prepare this volume for publication may be of interest to future generations. We distributed a brochure inviting citizens to tell us about their families, businesses, organizations, school and places of worship, or to offer a tribute to a particular person. We set a deadline of about eight months, which we had to extend twice to allow all interested parties the time to write their histories. At the final deadline, the material arrived in large quantities, and filled many boxes. It took us about five months after the final deadline to process all the submissions. Most of the material came typed, with pictures included. A few submissions were hand-written. Perhaps fifteen percent of the total material came email. Many people delivered submissions to our office, located in the Genealogy Department of the Allen County Public Library. Sometimes people brought us precious photos and and asked us scan them in the office.

Judy Bunn, Margery Graham and Kathryn Bloom and I met numerous times to decide how to set up a proper procedure and a database on our laptop computer to keep track of all the material (which eventually filled a large four-drawer file cabinet). We held several training sessions for chairpersons, and developed written procedures. The publication was a volunteer endeavor, and it would be impossible to guess how many hours the many volunteers spent over the months we worked on the book. Many people helped with this process, and they are mentioned in the first volume. Their help is greatly appreciated. I especially want to thank all the chapter chairpersons who are named in this volume, Rev. Luther Strasen who did a large amount of editing, Judy Bunn, who entered all transactions into the computer and handled the funds, and Kathryn Bloom who was at the history book office almost every day doing whatever was needed.

We provided the publisher with digital text files and photographs or good quality scanned images. In order to accomplish this, we copied the original submissions and gently edited the copies for consistency in handling dates, abbreviations, numbers, etc., and spelling and grammatical errors. We edited as little as possible in order to allow the authors to "speak in their own voices." The typed stories were changed to digital form by scanning the original typed sheets with optical character recognition software and making any necessary changes. In this way, we developed the material you find in this volume.

The Greatest Generation

The histories in this volume, in large part, tell the story of that "greatest generation," the World War II generation, and their families, businesses, religious congregations, organizations and schools. The lifespan of this "greatest generation" covered most of the Twentieth Century. They were born during or just after World War I, grew up in the 1930s during the Great Depression, served in the armed forces or supported the war effort at home during World War II, married and raised their families whom they instilled with good values and a work ethic. These are the people who worked their family farms, went to work in the factories, started businesses, educated their children, were active in their religious congregations, local schools and organizations, and dealt with the rapid social and technological changes of the past century. We treasure their stories and owe them a great debt of gratitude. Because of their efforts and sacrifices, Allen County moves into the Twenty-first Century with hope and confidence.

Phyllis Robb

Allen County Businesses

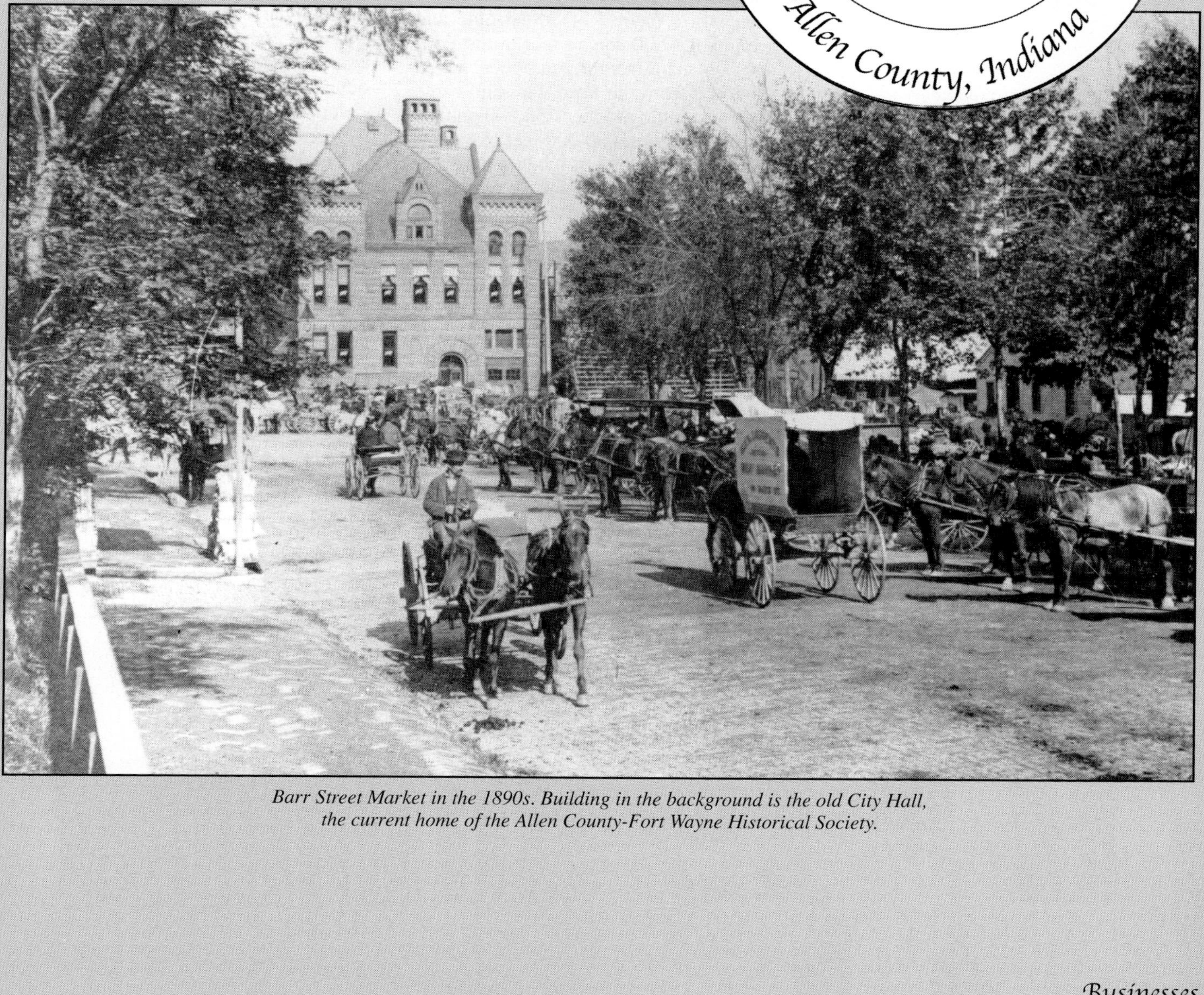

Barr Street Market in the 1890s. Building in the background is the old City Hall, the current home of the Allen County-Fort Wayne Historical Society.

Essex Group, Inc.

Essex Group, Inc., celebrated its 75th year of business in 2005. It is the largest manufacturer of magnet wire/winding wire in North America, and one of the largest in the world. Few companies in the wire and cable industry can point to a record of almost uninterrupted growth such as Essex has enjoyed since its inception in the early 20th century.

It's a far different company today from when it started in February 1930, in Detroit.

Addison Holton

Detroit Debut

Essex Wire Corporation was organized in Detroit by the late Addison E. Holton and a group of investor friends. They acquired the wire and cable assets of the Ford Motor Company, which had been established in 1924 to produce wire assemblies. Under the agreement, Holton, who had been head of a Detroit auto finance operation, Holton & Company, and a director of Anaconda Wire & Cable, leased part of Ford's Highland Park facility to supply wire harnesses for the Model A.

It is believed that the 1930 'Essex' logo was suggested by Roy Chapin, a co-investor in the company and former president of the Hudson Motor Company, manufacturer of the Essex automobile. It was not exactly a humble beginning. Incorporated on February 15, 1930, Essex began with a payroll of 700 people and occupied 125,000 square feet in the Ford plant. The manufacturing facilities, which it inherited from the Ford wire and cable operations, could produce 250,000 pounds of bare copper wire; 90,000 feet of battery cable; 24,000 pounds of magnet wire and over a million conductor feet of rubber insulated wire every day.

Despite the fact that it was a depression year, Ford spent more than $60 million for capital expansion in 1930 and by the end of the year, more than four million Model As had rolled down the company's assembly lines – each one supplied with wire from the Essex Wire Corporation.

Holton, like Ford, ignored the economic contractions that was going on in the country and pushed ahead with expansion. The first acquisition was the Redinger, Ball and Morris Manufacturing Company (RBM) in Logansport, Indiana, which made simple electrical switches and battery cut-outs for the auto industry.

Looking for additional markets for the magnet wire capabilities of the Highland Park plant, Holton teamed up with William J. Shea, a sales representative to the electrical industry centered in St. Louis. Shea did such a good job of selling magnet wire that the Detroit facilities could not keep pace with the orders. Shea stayed with the company for 30 years, retiring in 1960 when he was vice chairman, special assignments.

In 1932, Essex purchased the then idle Indiana Rubber and Insulated Wire Company in Jonesboro, near Marion, Indiana. That company was founded in 1890. The company was famous for its Paranite brand of building wire. It also produced lamp and heater cords insulated with crude rubber and later with a saturated cotton braid.

The Jonesboro plant had no rod making equipment (this was not to be added until 1939) and bought its requirements on the outside. Insulated wire made in Detroit was shipped to Logansport for making into wire assemblies. The same truck also carried bare wire to Jonesboro for processing into building wire. The trucks then returned to Detroit with completed wire harnesses and building wire.

Dudlo Building

Foothold In Fort Wayne

Looking for additional manufacturing capacity, Essex first moved into the Fort Wayne area in 1936 when it acquired 38,000 square feet of the former facilities of the Dudlo Manufacturing Corp., a company that had pioneered magnet wire production, but was an early victim of the depression. Much of the wire machinery was still in place and in good shape despite three years of inactivity. Essex was able to quickly put 50 people to work in the reactivated plant area under the direction of Herman Arber who had headed up the coil-winding department for Dudlo before General Cable closed its operations in 1933.

For those not familiar with the Dudlo Manufacturing Co., it might be helpful to provide a capsule history of that enterprise because of its with Essex, the part is played in the development of Fort Wayne as the magnet wire and diamond die capital of the world and its role as a nurturing ground for other wire and cable businesses.

Sammy Chapin

Dudlo operations began in 1910 by inventor George A. Jacobs, who had previously been employed by the Fort Wayne Works of General Electric. Jacobs was a native of Dudley, Massachusetts, and a graduate of Worcester Polytechnic Institute. While working for Sherwin Williams in Cleveland, he developed a successful enameling product that would make obsolete the tedious process of winding fine wire with cotton. Jacobs formed a partnership with his father-in-law, William E. Mossman and his son, B. Paul Mossman, both leading businessmen in Fort Wayne. In 1910, he started a company in Cleveland called Dudlo (the "dudl" from Dudley, Mass., and the "o" from Ohio) to make the enamel. His father-in-law, W. E. Mossman, persuaded him to relocate to Fort Wayne and in 1912 operations started there in a 50' X 100' shed on Wall Street on a lot owned by Mossman. Like Essex, the company became a big supplier to the Ford Motor Company (in 1920 it shipped five million ignition coils to Ford) prospered and employed 7,000 people. At its peak, Dudlo shipped some 2½ million tons of wire products yearly and took delivery of ten freight cars of copper each day. It merged with several other companies in 1927 to create a new entity called General Cable, became the Fort Wayne plant of General Cable in 1930, and closed down its operations in Fort Wayne in 1933 just 21 years after its beginnings. From Dudlo (besides General Cable) came the beginnings of Rea Magnet Wire and Inca Manufacturing Co. (which later became a part of the Phelps Dodge Copper Products) as well as many of the wire die companies now located in Fort Wayne.

Expansion of Essex continued with the Detroit Wire Assembly Division making wire assemblies and RBM manufacturing related components. By 1937, Essex' business volume at Ford had grown to $7 million (from $1.5 million in 1932) making it Ford's 12th largest supplier. At the time, Essex had 2,000 production employees and was operating two eight-hour shifts per day.

The Second Decade

By the 1940's, after the first decade of its existence, Essex possessed a remarkably broad product line featuring production of industrial staples such as electrical relays, coils, switches and electrical wire assemblies for the construction industry, magnet wires for electrical motors, transformers, generators and the like; plus the production of small transformers for communications; and general purpose wires, power cords and cord sets for electrical equipment manufacturers.

In 1942, Walter Probst, a law graduate of the University of Michigan, left his private practice in Detroit to become Essex's full-time legal counsel.

During World War II, Essex produced thousands of miles of field telephone wire for the Army's Signal Corps., millions of transformers which were incorporated into communications gear, plus entirely new types of electrical wire assemblies for the B-24 bomber assembled by Ford at its plant at Willow Run, Michigan. For it's efforts, Essex was awarded the prestigious "E" Award by the Secretary of War.

After World War II, Essex continued to add more companies and products to its roster. It participated in the postwar boom in the household appliances supplying electrical wires, circuitry switches, controls and systems and during the '50's, it was busy producing more wiring for the auto industry which was developing more and more sophisticated systems.

With expansion, Essex created its own air force, to tie together its many plant facilities. To do this Addison Holton recruited a dynamic woman named Sammy Chapin. Sammy was a highly experience WASP pilot during the war, qualified in every type of military aircraft. She was the daughter of automobile mogul Roy Chapin, one of the co-founders of the Essex company. She bought six surplus fighter trainer planes, delivering them to selected plant sites, and each including a parachute for the plant manager. Under Sammy's leadership, Essex aviation grew quickly. The company even sponsored a hot, P-51 fighter racing plane, which Sammy flew. Eventually the corporate air force would include a customized Boeing 737, the first sold to a customer other than an airline.

In 1952, Paul W. O'Malley, an engineering graduate of Pennsylvania State University and also a graduate of the University of Michigan law school began his career with Essex when he joined the legal staff of the company in Detroit, serving there for two years before being made director of engineering and moving to Fort Wayne.

Walter Probst

Probst To President

In 1959, Walter Probst, who was then executive vice president with 17 years with the company, was made president, succeeding Holton, who continued as company chairman and chief executive officer. Probst is credited with instituting new financial control procedures throughout all of Essex operations. He also introduced comprehensive reorganization programs and established Fort Wayne as the company headquarters.

In 1962, after 32 years with the company he had founded, Addison Holton retired and Walter Probst moved to chairman and chief executive officer while retaining the title of president.

During the next few years, in order to provide a deeper penetration within existing markets, the company began the manufacturing of electrical insulation materials as well as electrical and electronic magnetic controls and systems.

Going Public

In 1965, Essex, which then consisted of seven divisions operating 44 plants and 27 warehouses, went public and the symbol "EXC" was added to the New York Stock Exchange. Now 35 years old, the company had yearly sales of approximately $355 million, earnings of $17 million and employed nearly 16,000 persons.

That same year the company opened a new wire assembly plant in Canada, and established a Communications Divisions (now the Telecommunications Products Division) with the acquisition of a 290,000 square feet plant in Decatur, Illinois, formerly occupied by Western Electric. With this move, Essex entered into its first large-scale production of all types of communication cables for general commercial use. It also expanded building wire facilities at Anaheim, California, and Topeka, Kansas, and wire assembly operations made Essex the first manufacturer to produce electrical products on a national basis and in every geographical marketing region.

The next year, O'Malley, then 45 and a group vice-president, was elected president. Probst remained chairman and chief executive officer of the company with then sales of approximately $450 million annually. Under O'Malley's direction, the company launched bold manufacturing and marketing programs. Telephone, electronic and coaxial cables joined the roster of Essex products. So did integrated circuits, modules, sensors and activators for electronic applications. The company increased its production of electrical circuitry components and wire products. Strong inroads were made into maintenance and repair areas including automotive, appliance, electrical, electronic and gas equipment after markets.

In the spirit of aggressive new marketing, Essex sponsored a Grand Prix race team in 1965 and 1966, in concert with Ford, hiring a top rookie race driver, Skip Scott, and using the dynamic Ford 427 Shelby Cobra, the GT-40, and the new Mustang GT350. Competing on the

Shelby Cobra

United Technologies Truck

Grand Prix circuit, at tracks like Sebring, Daytona, LeMans and Bridgehampton, the Essex team drivers were among the most renowned anywhere.

Also in 1966, Essex started a 175,000 square foot copper and aluminum magnet wire plant in Vincennes, Indiana, as well as a 200,000 square foot plant in Bennettsville, South Carolina, and a 180,000 square foot aluminum wire and cable plant in Paducah, Kentucky.

Active In Acquisitions

Over the next three years Essex expanded tremendously in a flurry of acquisitions. In 1967, Essex acquired Boyne Products, headquartered in Detroit along with its subsidiary (Triangle Products, Inc. of Roseville, Michigan), a company which operated five plants in Michigan and manufactured electrical devices for the auto industry. Also that same year, Stevens Manufacturing, with plants at Mansfield, Ohio, and Renfrew, Ontario, and its product lines, including disc and strip thermostats including gas and electrical appliances, was acquired.

While Essex was acquiring other companies, there were some large industrial concerns watching Essex with an eye towards a possible merger. Some of the companies that came courting included Noranda Mines, Ltd. of Canada, The Chicago and Northwestern Railroad, Cerro Corp. and U.S. Plywood Champion Paper. Essex was not absorbed by any of these companies and continued to add companies to its fold.

With all these new operations, many of them with product lines other than wire, the name Essex Wire Corporation became somewhat misleading and was changed to Essex International, Inc. in 1968.

Fourteen companies, more than one a month, joined the Essex fold in 1969. The list included Fort Wayne Tool & Die, Inc.; Suflex Corp.; Insulation Corp.; Neon Products, Inc.; Macallen Co.; C.W. Bohren Transport, Inc.; Northland Industrial Plastics; Backstay Welt Co.; Gas Appliance Supply Corp.; Diatemp, Inc.; and the consumer products line of Casco Products Corp. These companies provided enlarged markets in the plastics, electrical insulation, electrical and gas controls, CATV and transportation industries.

All the growth, however, was not by acquisition. In 1969, Essex completed construction of a 100,000 square foot copper remelt operation at Three Rivers, Michigan, capable of processing 150 tons of copper scrap per day. Shortly thereafter, Essex also started its own continuous casting operations to produce copper rod. It already had a continuous aluminum billet and rod plant in Boonville, Indiana, and this made it more self-sufficient in two basic metal products. Essex constructed several continuous casting units for copper rod and wire built to its own design.

Other projects completed were a new 230,000 square foot communications wire plant in Chester, South Carolina; and expansion of manufacturing facilities in Bennettsville, South Carolina, and doubling of the size of the Wire & Cable Division plant at Columbia City, Indiana, from 120,000 to 240,000 sq. ft. A new electronics products plant at Pittsburgh also began prototype production of integrated circuits for potential use in Essex-developed computerized energy distribution and automated control systems for automobiles. Overseas, an auto harness facility was completed in Londonderry, Northern Ireland and a new plant went on line in St. Thomas, Ontario, Canada, to produce flexible printed circuits.

By 1970, now 40 years old, Essex had over 90 plants, about 26,000 employees and yearly sales of approximately $592 million. The company's continuing expansion programs had nurtured a broad group of additional products including total circuitry and control systems for appliances, air conditioning, heating, refrigeration and gas fired equipment. Other items included high voltage power cables for electrical utilities, industrial power networks and mining operations.

Making A Merger

After being wooed by a number of prestigious firms and having negotiations break down in each case, Essex finally was acquired by another company. On February 4, 1974, Essex joined United Aircraft Corp., East Hartford, Connecticut, as a wholly owned subsidiary. Essex had sales of $845 million and net earnings of over $40 million. It employed some 28,000 persons in its ten divisions and operated over 100 plants in 17 states, the UK, Canada and Mexico and had 30 warehouses in

22 states and Canada. At that time about 58 percent of its sales income came from wire products, 22 percent from electrical switch and control devices, 10 percent from metal and plastic fabricated parts, 5 percent from transportation and 6 percent from all others.

The merger, valued at around $320 million, gave Essex a broader technical base from which to grow and gave United Aircraft (later to become United Technologies) more non-military oriented products. At that time both Probst and O'Malley were elected to United's board of directors. About a year after the merger, on March 1, 1976, Essex International changed its name to Essex Group, Inc.

In December 1974, Walter Probst, 60, who had been with the company 32 years, 12 as chairman and chief executive officer, retired from Essex. Paul O'Malley, then 53, added the title of chairman and chief executive officer to that of president. In 1978, Peter L. Scott, president of the United Technologies' Norden Systems Division, assumed added responsibility as president and O'Malley continued as company chairman.

In the mid-seventies, Essex engineers, joining a partnership with Amana, developed the world's first digital touch-plate control. Essex wire and cable also powered Busch Stadium in St. Louis, the Living Seas Pavilion at Walt Disney World, and Colorado's Beaver Creek Ski Resort.

In December 1979, Scott was named head of UTC's newly formed Electronics Group as UTC executive vice president. James A. O'Connor, an Essex veteran since 1949, succeeded Scott as president of Essex Group. On January 4, 1984, John M. Bruce, former president of the Automotive Products Division of United Technologies Automotive, was named president of Essex Group. Bruce was named chief executive officer on August 1, 1984, and chairman on January 15, 1985, and assumed control for nearly a decade.

To take advantage of a different type of growth opportunity, Essex joined with home centers and consumers, and entered the "Do-It-Yourself" marketplace in 1982, allowing the public to make the choice for Essex wire and cable.

Also, in the early 80s, Essex expanded into the European market with the acquisition of ISOLA wire and cable plants in Switzerland, France and Italy.

Continued Changes

In 1988, an investor group, including Essex management, moved Essex once again into private ownership and the company flourished. During the 1990s, Essex management began to focus on international markets and on product quality issues. Many Essex operations were awarded the prestigious ISO 9000 and QS-9000 worldwide quality certifications, proving Essex was comprised of many successful teams of hardworking employees. Essex also began an aggressive campaign of capital investment, positioning Essex for continued success going forward.

Essex was repeatedly recognized for its excellence in every area of its operation. Especially in the early 1990s, when the Essex employees of both Kendallville, Indiana and Franklin, Tennessee, received the "Mark of Excellence" award from General Motors' Delco-Remy company. Many other Essex plants have received similar recognitions from other prestigious customers.

John M. Bruce

In 1992, the direction of the company was transferred to Stanley C. Craft, who had been named president of Essex Group in 1991. Essex employees throughout the organization immersed themselves in personal computer technologies to enhance decision-making and communications. The value of the employees was stressed, with everything from wellness programs to encouraging involvement in community service activities. Essex also began an aggressive campaign of capital investment for cost reduction and capacity increases, that has positioned the company for future continued success. Ownership of the company then changed in 1992, with majority ownership transferring to Bessemer Holdings. Bessemer would retain ownership for the next five years.

Essex continued its legacy of growth through a series of acquisitions by joining forces with some successful companies. Brownell-Electro, an industry-leading distributor of electrical wire, cable and related products, was followed by BICC Phillips, a Canadian distribution operation for building wire and cable, and in late 1996, Triangle Wire and Cable, a major manufacturer of building and industrial wire and cable products, joined the Essex family.

To guide Essex into the twenty-first century, 30-year company veteran Steve Abbott was named president and CEO in 1996. After serving as an Essex engineer, plant manager, director of engineering and division president, Abbott brought with him a straightforward vision for Essex: to be a prosperous, growth-oriented company.

In April of 1997, Essex management once again took the company public on the New York Stock Exchange, continuing in the tradition of success and excitement in the corporation's history. In early 1998, Finolex Essex Industries Limited began producing copper rod at their recently constructed joint venture continuous casting facility in Goa, India. In addition, Essex acquired the BICC Connollys magnet wire manufacturing business and the related Temple wire and electrical insulation distribution business, both based in the United Kingdom. Finally, Active Industries, a fabricator, converter and distributor of electrical insulation materials, products and services, joined the Essex family.

A Superior Acquisition

In February of 1999, Essex Group was acquired by Atlanta-based Superior Telecom. The combined companies with revenues of $2.4 billion, became the largest wire and cable manufacturer in North America and one of the largest producers of wire and cable in the world. Following the merger, Steven Abbott became president and CEO of Superior. Executive Vice President Charles McGregor, was named President of the Industrial Group, while Dennis Kuss, Vice President & General Manger of the Building Wire Unit was named President of the Electrical Wire Group. A few months later, Greg Schriefer was named President of the Superior Essex Industrial Group. Schriefer was a long-time Essex employee who held numerous sales and operations positions with the company. In July of 1999, Bill Evans was named President of the Superior Essex Elec-

Stanley C. Craft

Steve Abbott

Essex Group

trical Wire Group. Management changes also occurred in the Industrial Group with the appointment of Christopher L. Mapes as president.

In 2000, production of Magnet Wire began in a 280,000 square foot facility in Torreon, Mexico. A state-of-the-art facility, Torreon is located halfway between Juarez and Mexico City and provides a two-day delivery to most Mexican cities. The Torreon plant was constructed to provide more capacity for Magnet Wire production and to handle the demand from the growing number of maquiladora manufacturing facilities located throughout Mexico.

Management changes occurred in 2001 with the appointment of Harold Karp as President of the Electrical Products business. Prior to the appointment, Karp had been Senior Vice President of Manufacturing for Superior Essex Communications Group in Atlanta.

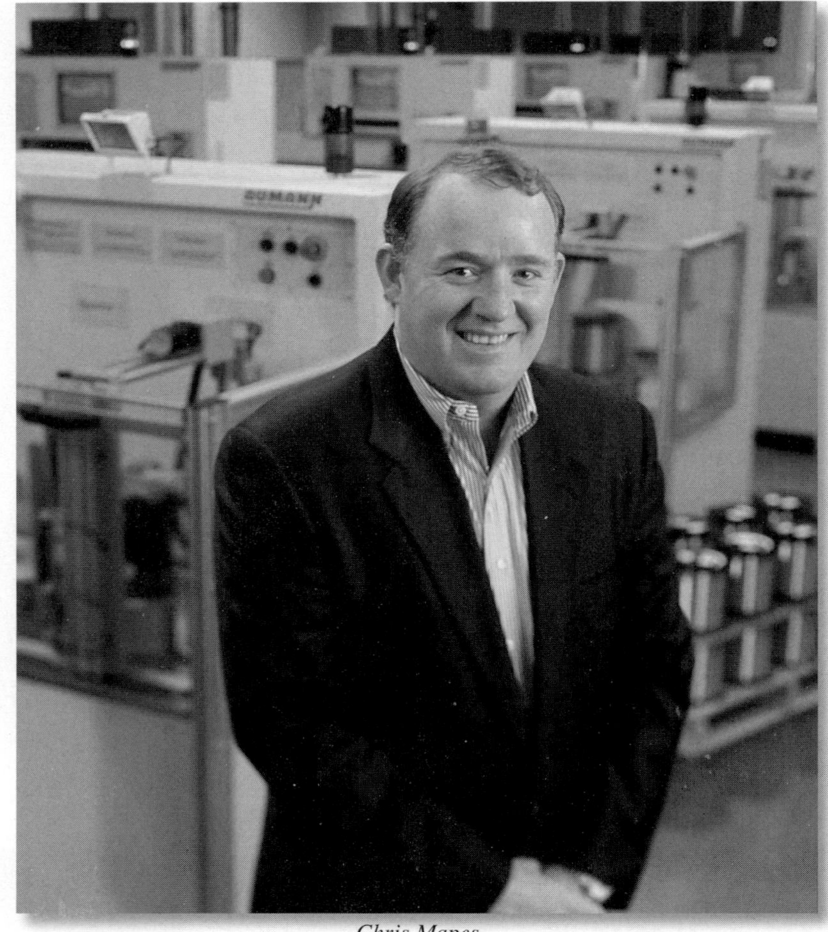

Chris Mapes

New Beginnings

Economic changes in the early part of the new millennium caused Essex Group, Inc. to make changes to the company structure. In 2002, the former Electrical Wire Group of Essex was sold to the Alpine Group (who was the holding company for Superior Telecom). The former wire and cable division, now called Essex Electric Products, moved from the Wall Street facility to the Standard Federal building on Main Street in downtown Fort Wayne in the summer of 2004.

In August of 2002, H. Patrick Jack became President of the Essex Group, Inc. Jack came to Essex from Aristech Chemi-

Torreon, Mexico Magnet Wire plant

cal Corporation, where he was President and Chief Operating Officer.

Acquisitions have continued, most recently with the purchase of the customer base and inventory of the former Nexans facility in LaGrange, Kentucky, in the fall of 2004.

Friend To The Community

Essex Group Inc. and its employees, has been a long-time supporter and sponsor of many Fort Wayne area events and organizations. This includes the American Cancer Society's Relay for Life, The American Cancer Society's Links for Life, the Vera Bradley Classic, Junior Achievement, Study Connection, the Heritage Trail, the Fort Wayne Philharmonic, Leadership Fort Wayne, and the American Red Cross.

Growing Strong

In the 75th year of operation, Essex Group, Inc. continues to grow, both domestically and internationally and is a significant contributor to the success of parent Superior Essex, headquartered in Atlanta. Stephen Carter, CEO of Superior Essex, commented on the company's continued strong performance:

"Building on our strong existing platform, we continue to look for opportunities to grow our business and add value for our shareholders. In our magnet wire business, we have just announced two separate strategic geographical expansion opportunities. In China, we plan to construct a greenfield facility that could eventually grow to 44 million pounds of annual capacity, or about $90 million of revenues at today's copper prices. We expect the first phase of capacity, about 12 million pounds, to be on line in mid-2006, with an additional 12 million pounds expected to be operational shortly thereafter. We are very optimistic about achieving profitable utilization rates by initially partnering with our North American customers who have migrated to China

We have also announced our plans to expand geographically into the European magnet wire market by combining our U.K. operations with Nexans, the largest magnet wire producer in Europe, with Superior Essex maintaining majority control of the combined entity. The extended reach of these two transactions, if consummated, will give us significant positions in the three largest magnet wire markets in the world: North America, China and Europe."

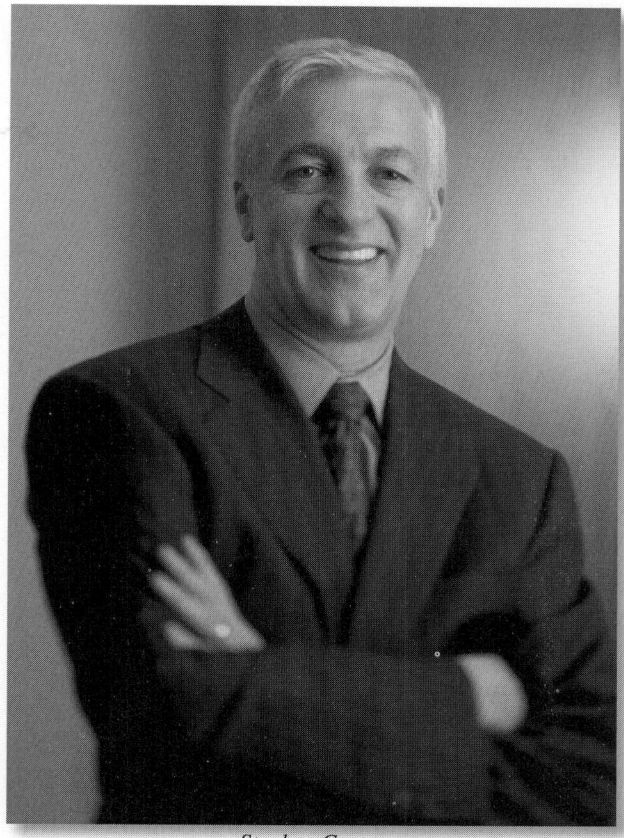

Stephen Carter

Essex Group, Inc. continues to be the North American leader in the production of Magnet Wire and in the distribution and fabrication of electrical insulation through the Essex Brownell channel.

H. Patrick Jack

Lincoln's First 100

An Enduring Legacy

The Lincoln National Life Insurance Company opened for business with a good name and four employees — three agents and a stenographer — in September 1905 in Fort Wayne, Ind. Thirty-three Fort Wayne businessmen had signed the company's articles of incorporation the previous May, and the State of Indiana chartered the new insurance enterprise on June 12.

Amid the stir of controversy that gripped the big, established insurers at the time, Lincoln's founders envisioned a new insurance enterprise — one based on dependability and honesty. "A life insurance company at which no one could ever point the finger of scorn," one of them later recalled.

COMPANY NAME GETS FAMILY APPROVAL

Perry Randall, a Fort Wayne attorney and entrepreneur, suggested the name "Lincoln," insisting that the integrity of a life insurance company was its most important asset.

Randall believed that the name of Abraham Lincoln would powerfully convey the spirit of integrity that the founders envisioned for the new company. The board of directors agreed.

Arthur Hall, the company's secretary and general manager, wrote to the 16th president's only surviving son, Robert Todd Lincoln, in late July 1905 to ask for a photograph of his father to be used on the company stationery.

Robert Todd Lincoln's reply came within a week, on August 3, 1905. His letter stated simply:

"Replying to your note of July 28th; I find no objection whatever to the use of a portrait of my father upon the letterhead of such a life insurance company named after him as you describe; and I take pleasure in enclosing you, for that purpose, what I regard as a very good photograph of him."

Arthur Fletcher Hall was instrumental in founding Lincoln National

THE LINCOLN MUSEUM PRESERVES THE LIFE AND LEGACY OF ABRAHAM LINCOLN

In 1928, Arthur Hall, then president of Lincoln National Life, decided to expand the company's association with Abraham Lincoln by establishing the Lincoln Historical Research Foundation.

Hall hired Dr. Louis A. Warren, a Lincoln scholar, to bring the foundation to life. The beginning of the museum's research collection began in 1929 with the acquisition of one of the largest collections of books in the United States about Abraham Lincoln. Other acquisitions of books and artifacts followed, and The Lincoln Museum was opened to the public in 1931.

The Lincoln Museum is now the world's largest museum dedicated to the life and times of Abraham Lincoln. Museum programs include the permanent exhibit *Abraham Lincoln and the American Experiment,* temporary exhibits, lectures, and special events.

STRONG LEADERSHIP SETS LINCOLN'S COURSE

Lincoln Life struggled for survival during the first several years. Within six years, however, Hall's tireless leadership had set Lincoln on its way to success, and the company had already begun to assume a respected position of expertise among fellow insurers and regulators.

In 1911, Lincoln reported $6.5 million of life insurance in force, with $250,000 in premium income and $750,000 in assets. With the arrival of Franklin Mead, the company's first actuary and an innovative businessman, Lincoln moved into the reinsurance business in 1912. At the time, most reinsurers were in Europe, so Lincoln was virtually a reinsurance pioneer in the United States.

LINCOLN LIFE EXPANDS AT A RAPID PACE

Lincoln made its first acquisition in 1913 —Michigan State Life —which helped to expand its distribution system and the company's assets to more than $25 million by 1915. Pioneer Life was acquired in 1917 and Merchant's Life in 1928. Even during the Great Depression, Lincoln acquired three companies, adding more than $250 million of insurance in force to the company's ledger.

By the time the Great Depression began in 1929, Lincoln's insurance in force had grown to $660 million. Of the 55 insurance companies organized in 1905, only 11 were still in business in 1929.

In 1951, just four years before Lincoln Life celebrated its Golden Anniversary, the company acquired the Reliance Insurance Company of Pittsburgh, Pa. At the time, the transaction was the largest of its kind in the life insurance industry in the United States.

No other insurance company matched the expansion of The Lincoln National Life Insurance Company during its first 50 years. From 1905–1955, Lincoln Life grew to become the ninth-largest life insurance company in the United States.

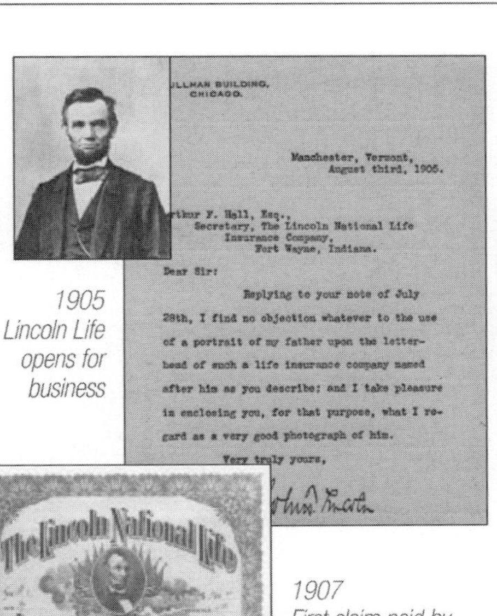

LLMAN BUILDING,
CHICAGO.

Manchester, Vermont,
August third, 1905.

thur F. Hall, Esq.,
Secretary, The Lincoln National Life
Insurance Company,
Fort Wayne, Indiana.

Dear Sir:

Replying to your note of July 28th, I find no objection whatever to the use of a portrait of my father upon the letter-head of such a life insurance company named after him as you describe; and I take pleasure in enclosing you, for that purpose, what I regard as a very good photograph of him.

Very truly yours,

1905 Lincoln Life opens for business

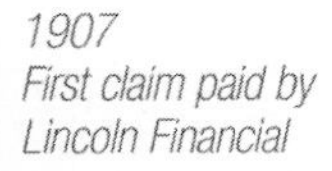

1907 First claim paid by Lincoln Financial

1908 Henry Ford manufactures the first Model T

1911 Lincoln Life boasts $6.5 million of insurance in force and more than three-quarter-million dollars in assets, impressive numbers for a new company with a small sales force

1929 Stock Market crashes; Great Depression begins

1930 Lincoln is sufficiently strong to survive the Great Depression with no layoffs

1944 Allied forces invade the beaches in Normandy, France

FORMATION OF LINCOLN NATIONAL CORPORATION CREATES ONE OF THE FIRST HOLDING COMPANIES IN THE INSURANCE INDUSTRY

Lincoln National Corporation was formed in 1968, and Lincoln Life became part of the Lincoln family of companies. Growth continued, spurred by a corporate culture that rewards creativity, gives opportunity a chance, and believes that success is derived from a diverse and talented workforce.

In many ways, the corporation's most dramatic transformation has taken place over the past 15 years. In that time, Lincoln National Corporation realigned its business operations and divested its employee benefits, property-casualty, and reinsurance operations. It also added Delaware Investments to the family of Lincoln companies, as well as the group tax-deferred annuity business from UNUM Corporation, the individual life insurance and annuity businesses of CIGNA Corporation, and the domestic individual life insurance operations of Aetna to Lincoln's life and annuity operations.

These aggressive endeavors have transformed Lincoln National Corporation into a nationally recognized financial services enterprise under a new marketing name, Lincoln Financial Group.

HELLO FUTURE

Today, Lincoln Financial Group is helping redefine retirement. The company understands that retirement is no longer an end or destination. Rather, it's a transition into a new life — a life with opportunities and advantages that have never existed before.

As we embrace the opportunities of the next 100 years, Lincoln Financial Group remains steadfast in the company's commitment to conducting business in the same spirit demonstrated by Abraham Lincoln himself — with honesty and integrity. They are values that made Lincoln a revered American, and Lincoln Financial Group one of the most enduring and fiscally sound financial services organizations in the United States.

SOUND AS THE POLICIES OF HONEST ABE
The LINCOLN NATIONAL LIFE INSURANCE COMPANY
FORT WAYNE, INDIANA
CHICAGO GENERAL AGENT
OTTENHEIMER SONS
WILLOUGHBY TOWER

1955 Lincoln celebrates its "Golden Jubilee," beginning the year as the ninth-largest life insurance company in the United States

PHILANTHROPY REFLECTS CORPORATE SHARED VALUES

Lincoln Financial Group's corporate public involvement activities are a vivid reflection of its shared values. The Lincoln Financial Group Foundation guides the giving efforts of Lincoln's corporate family, specifically funding three areas:

- Arts and culture
- Education
- Human services

Each year, the corporation sets aside 2% of its pretax earnings for philanthropy.

Besides making corporate monetary contributions, Lincoln employees also are very involved with community activities. Many serve as volunteers to help improve the quality of life where they live and work.

The foundation works diligently with a variety of community nonprofit organizations to identify the projects and programs that have an enduring effect on the people and communities these organizations serve. Working side by side with local organizations gives Lincoln the added strength it needs to make its philanthropic efforts as effective as possible.

1960 John F. Kennedy elected president

1968 Lincoln National Corporation is formed, creating a family of companies and one of the first holding companies in the insurance industry

1969 Neil Armstrong is the first man on the moon

1973 Lincoln enters the investment management business

LINCOLN:
THE CONSTITUTION AND THE CIVIL WAR TRAVELING EXHIBIT STOPS IN FORT WAYNE

In 2006, The Lincoln Museum hosted *Lincoln: The Constitution and the Civil War,* a 2,500-square-foot traveling exhibition sponsored by Lincoln Financial Group.

Developed in 2005 by the National Constitution Center in Philadelphia, and produced in association with The Lincoln Museum, the exhibit highlights how Lincoln's leadership and constitutional vision steered the nation through its most turbulent years and into a future that forever changed America.

Neither a traditional biography of Abraham Lincoln nor a conventional exhibit on the Civil War, *Lincoln: The Constitution and the Civil War* explores how one individual, deeply committed to the belief that citizens can make a real difference, exercised leadership at a pivotal time of crisis for the nation, the Constitution and the course of freedom worldwide.

The traveling exhibit made stops in Philadelphia, Fort Wayne, and Hartford, Conn., during its year-and-a-half-long itinerary.

1983 Lincoln surpasses the milestone of $100 billion of insurance in force

1984 Apple introduces the first personal computer

1995 Lincoln expands its investment management strength with the acquisition of Delaware Management Holdings, Inc.

1998 A new marketing name, "Lincoln Financial Group," is introduced, beginning the corporation's rise as a nationally recognized financial services company

Lincoln Financial Group
BATTLE AT BIGHORN
WOODS vs GARCIA

2000 Lincoln begins 6-year entitlement of ABC Sports' annual prime time golf special, featuring Tiger Woods

2001 Lincoln Financial Distributors is formed as the wholesaling distribution organization of Lincoln Financial Group

2001 Terrorists attack the World Trade Center

2002 Lincoln announces its agreement to name Philadelphia Eagles' new stadium Lincoln Financial Field

2005 Lincoln celebrates 100th anniversary

2005 Lincoln launches marketing campaign that highlights the retirement revolution. New tagline Hello future.℠ is introduced

Hello future.℠

Like many American companies, OmniSource Corporation began as one man's dream – the dream for a life of freedom and opportunity. A dream that was common to immigrants who came to America in the early twentieth century. Born in Berezen, a small Russian village near Minsk, Irving Rifkin escaped certain death in the Russian army, and as a teenager, made his way alone to America. While he was glad to leave the hardship and persecution of Bolshevik Russia behind, he also left behind his family and everything he had known.

When young Rifkin stepped off the boat in New York City, he hoped to find a better life than the one he left behind. Arriving in 1920, practically penniless and unable to speak the language, he had to find a way to survive. He started with odd jobs, and quickly learned to speak and understand English. He worked as a dishwasher and short order cook, saving his money. He eventually bought the delicatessen where he worked, but struggled through the Great Depression, barely supporting his young family. After trying his hand in the vending machine business, in 1941 he decided to take a chance that would set the course for the rest of his life.

His wife, May, had a relative in Lima, Ohio, who was in the surplus business which bought and sold equipment, scrap metal, paper, rags, and even animal hides. Irving took to the business quickly. His industrious nature and sharp mind was well suited for a trading business. It offered the challenge and opportunity he sensed would be right for him.

After just a year in the business, Irving decided he wanted to work for himself – to control his own future. "My Dad was a highly motivated person," said his son Leonard. "He had all the entrepreneurial qualities that you need to start and build a business from nothing. He had an iron will and his spirit could never be broken."

Rifkin borrowed enough money to buy a stake-bed truck and rented a small garage in Lima. His first goal was simple – to provide for his family. He went to filling stations, farms, back alleys, and metal shops buying scrap metals and waste paper, and selling wiping rags and steel. He sorted metals in the garage at night, then sold copper, brass, iron, and steel to dealers or foundries during the day. To earn extra money, he put tires on the front of his truck and offered roadside tire service.

Irving Rifkin

His efforts brought in more business, and Rifkin soon realized that he needed help to manage things. He offered his brother-in-law, Irving Walters, a partnership interest. They knew and trusted each other, plus May and her sister could be reunited. Walters agreed, and soon moved his family from New York to Lima to begin his new career.

They moved from the garage to a small shop where customers could bring scrap to sell. They bought anything of value; scrap metal, surplus, rags, bottles, and old newspapers. Rifkin did the outside sales attracting new customers and accounts, while Walters worked the shop and kept the books. As the country geared up for war, scrap recycling became a national issue, which helped the small business prosper.

Always ambitious, Rifkin believed it was time to take another step forward and buy a scrap yard. He found one for sale in Fort Wayne, Indiana. The yard was in a good location, at 127 North Clinton Street (now in Headwaters Park), and had an established scrap metal and waste paper business. The owner, Gambrath, wanted to retire, so Rifkin and Walters agreed to buy the scrap yard.

The two men pooled every dime they had, but it was not enough. They borrowed $7,500 from a relative, which gave them just enough to buy Gambrath's yard and make down payments on homes for each family. When they decided to make the move to Fort Wayne in 1943, they had no idea the tiny scrap yard they named Superior Iron & Metal would someday become one of the largest scrap recycling companies in North America!

In the early 1940s there were more than 30 scrap dealers in Fort Wayne, and competition was fierce. The war effort was in full swing, so people recycled everything from tinfoil to scraps of fabric. The city's industrial base consisted of big military suppliers like International Harvester, General Electric, and Magnavox, as well as smaller manufacturers, most of whom generated scrap. Rifkin and Walters worked seven days a week to keep up. Demand for scrap was strong and business was good enough to repay their loans and build some reserves.

An investment in scrap processing equipment was the next logical move. This would allow Superior Iron & Metal to handle more volume, increase the value of their scrap, and ship directly to steel mills. They partnered with another dealer to purchase a baler and formed Fort Wayne Scrap Baling, located on the east side of town.

In 1950, they had a bitter dispute with the partner and sold their interest in Fort Wayne Scrap Baling. They moved Superior Iron & Metal north of the river to North Calhoun Street. The new yard had room to grow and was adjacent to main line railroad tracks. Convinced that processing equipment was becoming essential, they installed their own baler, competing head-to-head with Fort Wayne Scrap Baling.

Leonard Rifkin, Irving's son, joined the company in 1956, after graduating college and completing his military service. His business education and two years of law school brought a new perspective to the company. Leonard was ambitious and competitive like his father, and would lead the next phase of business growth.

The early 1960s were the hardest times in the company's history. In 1961, differences between the Rifkins and Walters resulted in a split of the assets that nearly forced Superior Iron & Metal under. "We ended up with the company, but had to take on a tremendous amount of debt," said Leonard. "At that time, business wasn't very good. Cash flow was a daily struggle and every penny was important. The accountants predicted that we would go broke within a year."

Employees and owners alike worked longer hours for reduced pay, just to keep the company alive. Leonard's business acumen and discipline helped to extricate the company from this difficult period. He built a series of key strategic relationships with customers and banks, giving the company

consistent outlets for its scrap, and the financial backing it needed to survive.

In the mid-'60s, Irving's son-in-law from Chicago, Barry Dorman, came into the business, and eventually became a partner. Like everyone else, he learned the basics of the business; working the yard and the metal room, and buying and selling scrap. Under Irving and Leonard's tutelage, he focused on nonferrous metals, and helped drive the company's growth in that area. Years later, Barry decided to sell his interest and leave the company to invest in other ventures.

In 1969, the company expanded into the trash business. San-A-Tainer was one of the early providers of containerized service for commercial and industrial trash removal. It was a logical extension of the scrap business, with common customers and equipment. The company also established a revolutionary trash recycling facility where recyclables were sorted, metals reclaimed, and waste was incinerated. During this period, however, large public waste conglomerates were buying up smaller trash haulers, and in 1973, Leonard sold San-A-Tainer to one of the consolidators. Proceeds from the sale provided the capital and liquidity necessary to strengthen the balance sheet, paving the way for expansion in the scrap business.

Acquisitions became part of Superior's growth strategy in 1974 when Leonard negotiated the purchase of a local scrap dealer, Wayne Iron & Metal. From 1974-2004, the company made 24 acquisitions, buying scrap processors throughout Indiana, Ohio, and Michigan, and eventually expanding into the Southeast with investments in Georgia, the Carolinas, and Florida. After the Wayne Iron & Metal purchase, Superior bought Bremen Iron & Metal in South Bend (1976), and then Kripke-Tuschman Industries in Toledo, Ohio (1979). In the mid-'70s, the company also developed a business "briquetting" borings and turnings from machining operations. Production started with a plant in Warsaw, Indiana, which was soon followed by facilities in Fort Wayne and then Defiance, Ohio. The Defiance plant is still in full operation today.

During this same period, Leonard's three sons joined the company. Danny, the oldest, started full-time in 1977, while Rick began his career a year later. Marty, the youngest, followed in 1985 after completing law school. All three of "the boys," as they are still called by longtime employees, learned the business from the ground up. As kids they worked weekends and summers, raking the driveways, sweeping floors, and sorting brass. All three started full-time in the yards sorting iron, picking trucks, and running the baler. This was followed by similar training in every facet of the business. "We had to prove ourselves, like everyone else," said Danny, now president of OmniSource. "An executive spot was never guaranteed. We were required to learn every job and to respect the efforts of our people. In turn, we had to earn their respect based on our actions, not our name."

The early '80s again brought difficult times for the business and the Rifkin family. The deep industrial recession hit the scrap industry very hard, and the business struggled. Total employment had to be reduced, and all salaried staff took pay cuts to help out. At the same time, Leonard's wife Norma, succumbed to cancer at age 52, and within a matter of weeks, Irving Rifkin also passed away. As in the past, the family's resolve and support from dedicated employees made it possible to weather the storm.

As the economy emerged from recession, the business also recovered. Growth in ferrous scrap brokerage and nonferrous metal trading was the impetus to consolidate under one name, which was changed to OmniSource Corporation in 1983. The company also continued to acquire scrap companies in Indiana and Ohio, buying yards in Auburn, Indiana (1984), and its longtime rival in Fort Wayne, Levin & Sons in 1987. In Ohio, the company added yards in Mansfield (1986), Lima (1988), and St. Mary's (1989).

By 1990, OmniSource had become a large regional scrap processor. Annual sales exceeded $300 million, shipments approached one million tons, and the company operated ten facilities in Indiana and Ohio, plus three nonferrous brokerage offices. It had grown well beyond a small family business. The family enlisted its team of senior executives and managers to develop a strategy for future growth. The group developed a plan to restructure the company, and formalized a strategy to define and accomplish new goals. As a result, the '90s began a period of tremendous growth and expansion for OmniSource.

In 1990, the company pioneered a new concept, "Scrap Management," with Chrysler Corporation as its first client. Under the direction of Tom Tuschman in Toledo, a fee-based, "open book" agreement was developed in which OmniSource would invest, build, and manage on-site baling facilities at Chrysler plants, plus market the scrap and administer the total program. The arrangement was a success for both, and initiated a relationship that is still in place today. Since then, the company has applied the principles of scrap management to generators across all metalworking industries, managing over 1,000 facilities for more than 200 industrial companies.

In 1992, the company embarked on another exciting venture—the formation of a new steel company and the construction of a new steel mill. Leonard, Danny, and John Marynowski (now an executive vice president of OmniSource) approached Keith Busse, a Nucor vice president, with an idea to build a new steel mill in northeastern Indiana. Busse and two Nucor managers, Mark Millett and Dick Teets Jr., had gained notoriety for building and operating a new mill in Crawfordsville, Indiana. The mill employed a new technology that was lower in cost than traditional methods, and relied on scrap as its primary raw material. Busse had become disillusioned with Nucor and was interested in a new opportunity.

The business concept was simple. OmniSource would supply the scrap; Keith and his team would provide the management and operating expertise; and Heidtman Steel, a Toledo-based customer of OmniSource, would sell much of the output. The group worked nights and weekends to develop the business plan, but needed to secure investors and financing to raise the $300 million of capital required to proceed.

Leonard and Danny spent almost a year lining up bankers and investors for the new enterprise, a daunting task since both management and Heidtman wanted to remain anonymous until investors were found. They persisted, and eventually found an investment bank (Society Bank) and two key investors (GE Capital and Bain Capital) to make the concept a reality, and Steel Dynamics, Inc. (SDI) was formed in late 1993. By the end of 1995, Busse, Millett, and Teets had built the new mill near Butler, Indiana and started production.

OmniSource, in turn, had established a new agency division and set about the task of sourcing a million tons per year of scrap for the new mill. This provided an opportunity to expand the company's brokerage business and enter new markets.

In the mid-'90s, the investment world became interested in scrap supply, as more electric furnace mills, like Nucor and SDI, were built. Venture capital investors were attracted to a few public scrap companies that were attempting a roll-up style consolidation. Although the Rifkins received a substantial offer to sell OmniSource, they believed that a sale would not serve the best interests of its employees, and that the long-term responsibility to these people was more compelling than the offer on the table. This turned out to be the right decision. All of the consolidators ended up in bankruptcy within a few years.

In the face of consolidation, acquisitions became a larger part of the company's growth strategy. From 1998–2004, the company made ten acquisitions, and turned away dozens more. "It was important to stick to our core strategy, to expand concentrically from our primary operations during that period," commented Danny, who negotiates every acquisition. "The companies we acquired fit clearly into our long-term strategy, and were quickly integrated into our structure."

In addition to this aggressive approach to acquisitions, the company also moved into new technologies and products. In 1995, the company designed and built a heavy media facility in Fort Wayne called Recovery Technologies. The process recovers metals from the waste stream of automobile shredders, and then further separates various metals. As a means to add value to its aluminum business, in 1998, the company also built a secondary aluminum smelter in New Haven, Indiana called Superior Aluminum Alloys (named for the original scrap company). The facility converts scrap aluminum into specification aluminum ingot.

Shortly after the turn of the century, the company began a growth initiative in the Southeast, following the migration of steel, automotive, and heavy manufacturing to the region. A former scrap yard in Athens, Georgia was purchased and renovated in 2001, and two years later, a collection and transfer yard was opened in Spartanburg, South Carolina.

In 2004, the southeastern operations were merged into a joint venture with Carolinas Recycling Group (CRG). Headquartered in Spartanburg, South Carolina, CRG now represents the company's business interests in the southeastern U.S., employing 350 people at ten locations in the Carolinas and Georgia. Later that same year, Danny, Rick, and Marty worked together to acquire Admetco, one of the largest nonferrous scrap processors in the country, also located in Fort Wayne. The purchase immediately increased the company's nonferrous volume by 20% and was fully integrated within the first year.

Through the ups and downs of a cyclical business, OmniSource has maintained a steady growth path and developed a solid financial base. The company remains privately held by the Rifkin family, with Leonard and his sons managing the enterprise. Leonard currently serves as chairman, Danny is president, and Rick and Marty are executive vice presidents. There are several other executives involved in managing various segments of the business, too. "This is a large company," said Marty. "We have nonfamily members in key positions here with a lot of authority. We have always believed that placing the most capable person in the right spot is in the best interest of the company, and therefore the family."

The Rifkins say that the company's success is really dependent on the efforts of every employee, in every position. They strive to maintain a culture that emphasizes the family values of hard work, integrity, perseverance, and respect. "Our employees are part of our family," said Rick. "We want everyone who works for us to have a better life because of the strength of our company. We feel an obligation to watch out for their welfare and security as part of owning the business."

Over the years, they have demonstrated that these values are real. Employee savings plans, loans, counseling, and tuition programs have been in place for years. Children of employees are eligible for college scholarships, and the company provides English and math courses to employees that wish to participate. To honor Irving Rifkin's legacy, immigrants from Eastern Europe, Latin America, Mexico, and Asia, are given jobs and assistance with resettlement. The company also supports a wide range of philanthropic and community activities, and encourages employees to participate in the communities in which it operates.

In the 62 years since Irving Rifkin borrowed enough money to start Superior Iron & Metal, his company has grown from a two-man operation with sales of $50,000 into one of the largest scrap recycling businesses in North America. Today, OmniSource and its affiliates employ over 2,000 people in more than 45 locations. The company recycles 7 million tons per year of ferrous scrap and almost a billion pounds of nonferrous metals, with annual sales of almost $2 billion dollars.

Irving Rifkin's hope for freedom and opportunity has become a reality greater than he ever imagined. It typifies the quintessential American dream, a story forged out of steel and three generations of endless determination.

(l. to r.) Marty, Leonard, Danny, and Rick Rifkin.

The Birth Of Cable TV

A binder three inches thick with pages printed on both sides carries the history of the development of cable television channels for the people of northeast Indiana. Three photo albums stuffed with newspaper clippings reveal the struggle to implement that plan.

By the people, For the people

In 1968, local advertising agency head John Bonsib became convinced that the development of cable television should be based on original programming. Prior to that time, all cable systems (known then as CATV) were used solely to transmit existing TV signals to areas where television stations' transmitter broadcasts could not reach – over mountains, thick outcroppings of limestone, and forested areas.

Having spent the previous 25 years in advertising, Bonsib knew that the future of cable should be in developing original programming. There were and are so many meaningful and wonderful stories about the successes or needs of people, yet these were largely ignored by television owners who saw their dollars growing only in news and sports broadcasts.

By 1970, Bonsib recruited several people who agreed with his concepts, including his wife, Pat, future mayor Graham Richard, Bill Turnley and Pat Yoder. By 1973, they had learned of the concerns of many people not only in Indiana but also in New York, California, Washington and many other venues.

The group formed the Citizens Council for Programming Development with the underlying foundation that cable should contain and endorse channels for and by the people. When Citizens Cable TV won the right to lay cable in Allen County, and later in Fort Wayne and other towns, these systems carried five channels for the use of the people.

The group made plans for big things to happen when it established Citizens Cable in Allen County. The only significant population base outside of Fort Wayne in the county was in the town of New Haven, and in the Canterbury Green apartment complex, its first foray into the city. The group set up a sales office in the apartment complex and Pat Bonsib drove up and down every street in New Haven to get correct street addresses for customers.

The company incorporated and attracted the interest of more investors, including Rod Howard, Tom Teetor and Tom Eckrich, who all served on the first board of directors. Later, Leonard Rifkin, Dick Waterfield, Sr., Robert Howard, and Roger Kryder became investors. First Chicago Bank also became a major investor.

Happiness Is . . . a Cable Franchise

John Bonsib and his wife, Patricia, stand and cheer amid flying papers Thursday night in the Fort Wayne City Council chamber as the council's fifth and deciding vote was announced giving Citizens Cable of Fort Wayne Inc. the franchise to provide the city with cable television service. Bonsib is president of Citizens, which will be affiliated with Cox Cable Communications of Atlanta, Ga. Story on Page 1B. Staff Photo By John Stearns.

Give Technology A Head Start

Unlike many big-city systems that started with engineering and cable for eight to 10 channels, Citizens designed a 36-channel system with Magnavox, which included underground cable as well as several miles engineered for two-way transmission. Several doctors took advantage of the two-way transmission capability. Board member Roger Kryder, an early computer genius, developed a workable computer system for the young company.

The Magnavox system was the company's first, and the build-out was exciting and exasperating, as no one had ever worked with it before. Also exciting and exasperating was selling cable in the county; because Allen County is largely flat, there was never thought to be a need for a cable system.

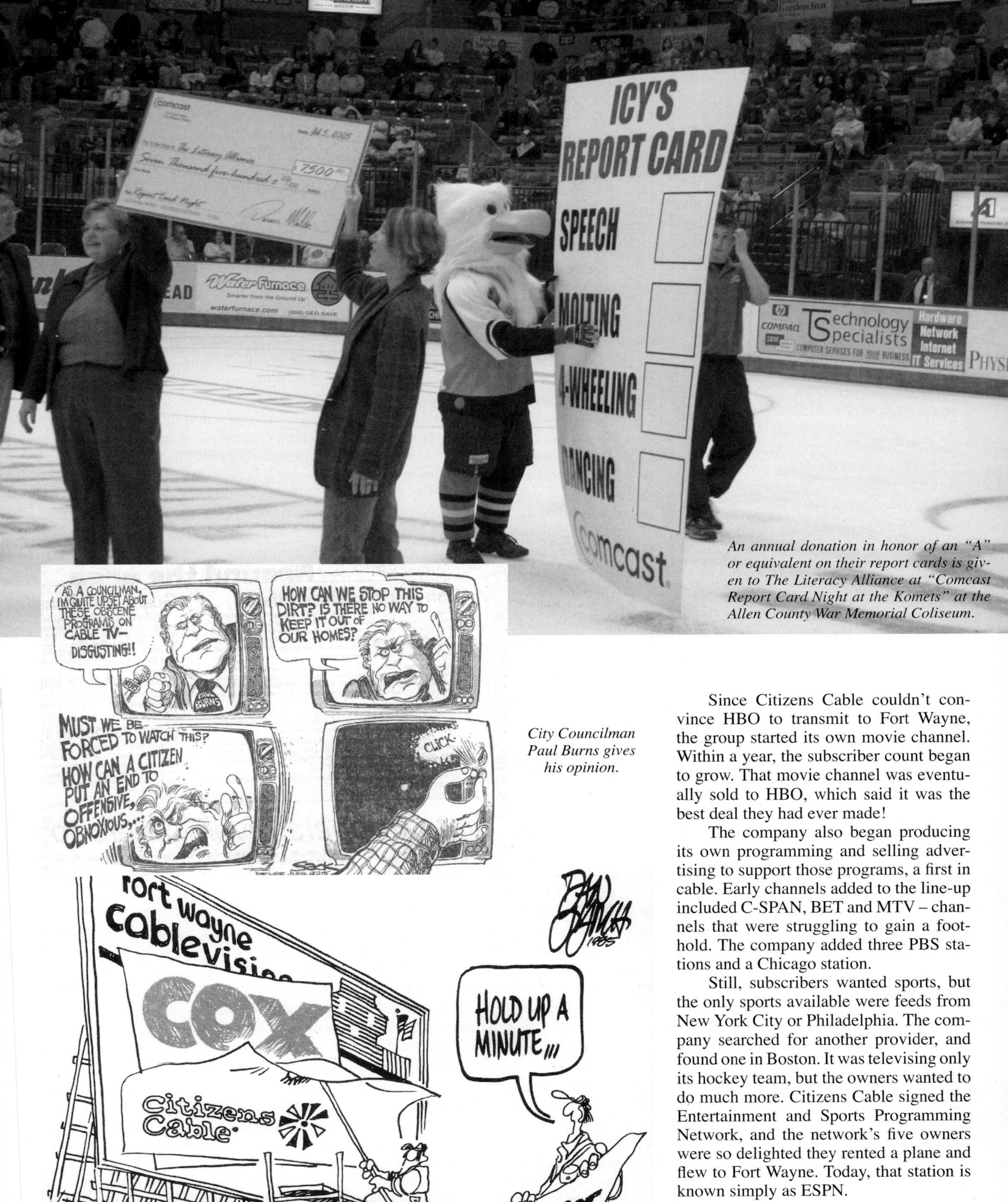

An annual donation in honor of an "A" or equivalent on their report cards is given to The Literacy Alliance at "Comcast Report Card Night at the Komets" at the Allen County War Memorial Coliseum.

City Councilman Paul Burns gives his opinion.

Announcing the Comcast purchase.

Since Citizens Cable couldn't convince HBO to transmit to Fort Wayne, the group started its own movie channel. Within a year, the subscriber count began to grow. That movie channel was eventually sold to HBO, which said it was the best deal they had ever made!

The company also began producing its own programming and selling advertising to support those programs, a first in cable. Early channels added to the line-up included C-SPAN, BET and MTV – channels that were struggling to gain a foothold. The company added three PBS stations and a Chicago station.

Still, subscribers wanted sports, but the only sports available were feeds from New York City or Philadelphia. The company searched for another provider, and found one in Boston. It was televising only its hockey team, but the owners wanted to do much more. Citizens Cable signed the Entertainment and Sports Programming Network, and the network's five owners were so delighted they rented a plane and flew to Fort Wayne. Today, that station is known simply as ESPN.

Cracking The Fort Wayne Market

While the company was thriving in the county, it had yet to crack Fort Wayne. Not until Mayor Bob Armstrong begin pressuring the city council to take action in the fall of 1975 did they consider expanding into the city. By that time, the company had very little cash remaining, so it went public, listing itself on the newly formed NASDAQ stock exchange.

With that infusion of cash, the company bought new equipment, erected a 325-foot tower and a huge satellite dish which was installed on the top of the company's New Haven office building. In 1976, the company merged with Cox Cable from Atlanta and in May 1976, Citizens Cable won the Fort Wayne franchise. Cox would pay 100 percent of the city's system, at $500,000 while Citizens held 20 percent of the ownership and the company continued to operate under the Citizens Cable name. If things didn't work out, Citizens would be able to buy out Cox's 80 percent interest.

In 1977, the city's system began with an unheard of 19 channels. Meantime, the county system continued to expand into Aboite Township. But trouble soon arrived. General Electric announced it was going to buy Cox. Moreover, the Cox system wasn't integrated with the county system: the two crews, one for the city and one for the county, were housed separately and weren't cooperating. Despite attempts to reconcile the situation, Citizens Cable was forced to take Cox to court. GE backed out and bought the NBC television network instead. In February of 1985, Citizens Cable settled the federal lawsuit, purchasing Cox Cable Fort Wayne, Inc. at a price of $333 per customer, about $9.75 million. To this date, that is the lowest price paid for an existing cable system.

By 1985, the Citizens Cable owners decided it was time to sell. Sixteen companies lined up to bid for Citizens Cable's 47,000 customers. And what started with an initial investment of $25,000 was sold for $62 million to Comcast Cable.

The Comcast Era

Comcast Cable is a division of Comcast Corporation. Founded in 1963 by Ralph Roberts, Daniel Aaron and Julian A. Brodsky, Comcast has grown from a single cable television operation serving 1,200 customers to one of the world's leading communication companies, focused on broadband cable and programming content.

Seeing the potential of community-based television systems, Ralph J. Roberts, Daniel Aaron and Julian A. Brodsky purchased a 1,200-subscriber cable system in Tupelo, Mississippi in 1963. Six years later, the company was renamed Comcast Corporation (from American Cable Systems) and incorporated in Pennsylvania.

In 1972, Comcast entered the stock market with its first public stock offering. The stock is traded on the NASDAQ Stock Market. By 1986, the year after it acquired Citizen Cable in Fort Wayne, Comcast doubled in size to 1,200,000 cable customers with the purchase of 26 percent of Group W Cable.

Headquartered in Philadelphia, Comcast is now one of the leading communications, media and entertainment companies in the world. The company serves more than twenty-one million U.S. customers and has a presence in twenty-two of the top twenty-five U.S. metropolitan areas.

Comcast's local office is at 720 Taylor Street, a building reconstructed in 1993 to house the company's growing number of employees. Diane Christie was the first general manager in Fort Wayne, while Damon Miller serves as general manager in 2005.

With an annual payroll of more than $6 million to its more than 200 employees, the franchise also pays five percent of its gross local revenue to the City of Fort Wayne as part of its franchise fee. In 2005, that amount was more than $1.7 million.

Since its initial investment in Fort Wayne, the local franchise has expanded its offerings to include dozens of specialty channels, designed to appeal to every interest. It has also taken the lead in installing $40 million in fiber optic transmission lines, and improved the production of local access services.

As of 2005, Comcast offered five local access channels for local government, citizens and educational institutions. Included in its local programming offerings is "Comcast Newsmakers," a four and a half minute interview program inserted on CNN Headline News. Guests include elected officials, community leaders, and directors of local non-profit agencies. More than 100 segments, valued at $12,000 each, were produced in 2004.

Comcast is also part of a new technology, ACENet, which links all computer systems in local schools to provide information and educational opportunities to local schoolchildren. ACENet (Allen County Education Network) serves as a high-speed education collaboration network among the partners to provide multimedia content from both within member sources, and from contracted educational sources both around the nation and internationally. The mission of ACELINK, which has a dedicated content coordinator, is to expand access, share resources, overcome limitations, increase expertise and ignite opportunities for learning with emerging technology among the ACENet partner districts and beyond.

Providing basic cable, Digital Cable and high-speed Internet services, Comcast has long been an innovator in communications technology. With Comcast Digital Cable, customers have more programming choices than ever before. Comcast Digital Cable offers customers the opportunity to enjoy more than 250 channels, including dozens of commercial-free premium movie channels as well as dozens of commercial-free music channels. Comcast Digital Cable includes an interactive, on-screen program guide and remote control that allows viewers to quickly and easily choose programs and movies by category or channel, and parental control features to help prevent children from viewing inappropriate programs.

With ON DEMAND, Comcast's video-on-demand service, Comcast Digital Cable customers select from more than 3,000 programs using their existing Digital Cable converter and watch them at any time. Customers can rewind, fast forward and pause programs, and can store most selections for up to 24 hours from the time of ordering, so they can watch programs whenever and however often they like.

Comcast's High-Definition Television (HDTV) service takes customers' viewing experience to a new level, offering HDTV programming from their local broadcast stations as well as national networks.

Digital Video Recorder (DVR) service from Comcast lets customers digitally record, store, and enjoy their favorite programs, so they never have to miss their favorite shows. DVR service from Comcast also brings customers the ability to pause and rewind "live" television.

With Comcast High-Speed Internet Service, customers can enjoy 100% Pure Broadband© with speeds up to four times as fast as 1.5Mbps DSL. They also receive an always-on connection, and a broadband portal with "click-and-play" video, personalized news, music, games, and much more.

And in late 2005, Comcast launched telephone service in Fort Wayne. Comcast Digital Voice uses an advanced technology called Voice over Internet Protocol (VoIP) to transmit voice data over Comcast's privately owned network. The service works with customer's existing phone equipment, doesn't require an Internet connection or PC, and includes 12 advanced calling features (Voice Mail, Call Waiting, Caller ID, etc.) at no extra charge. Customers can make unlimited local and long distance calls for one low monthly price.

Deister Machine Company, Inc.

1912 photograph of the employees and the original Deister Machine Company, Inc. plant at 1933 East Wayne Street, Fort Wayne, Indiana. Emil Deister is on the far left.

Born in Germany in 1872, Emil Deister founded Deister Machine Company, Inc. in 1912.

As a family-owned business for nearly a century, Deister Machine Company, Inc. plays an integral part within Allen County business history, and an even greater role in the current and future contributions of Indiana's manufacturing sector. Deister's high-quality line of feeding, scalping and screening equipment is preferred by the world's largest producers of aggregate, coal, and mineral rock products – the precious resources required to build and maintain our cities, communities, streets and highways.

One of the few companies left in its industry to resist conglomerate buyouts or foreign investors, Deister Machine Company, Inc. is rich in a history that began prior to World War I and continues into the new millennium, still guided by a family management that professes old-world traditions of workmanship, dedication to its employees, technological advancement and a solid business philosophy of putting the customer first. Each piece of equipment is designed and customized to meet specific customer needs, an aspect that is critical to the cost-efficient processing of varying materials within the aggregate industry.

The United States produces over 2 billion tons of aggregates per year. Heavy equipment, as in the line of Deister vibrating screens, is used to process natural aggregate materials according to specifications needed for a variety of end products from asphalt and concrete mixes to bricks, wallboard, roofing tiles and more. In layman's terms, vibrating screens act as large sifters. Material such as stone, sand or gravel is conveyed onto the screen where it's shaken back and forth over layers of wire meshing, eventually being separated into different sizes.

From its first year in operation to the present, Deister Machine Company remains a proud contributor to the local, state and national economy. In 1912, the company employed twenty-four laborers and accrued sales of nearly $100,000. While as of the year 2000, it supported more than 240 skilled employees with reported sales topping $30 million. Each year, Deister donates five percent of its income to charitable, cultural and religious organizations.

Irwin F. Deister, Jr., chairman, and E. Mark Deister, president, represent the family's third generation at the company's helm. Their coveted tradition of quality and customer satisfaction began with their grandfather, Emil Deister, the company's founder.

Born in Germany in 1872, Emil Deister migrated to the United States with his parents in 1878 and settled on a farm in Gar Creek, near Woodburn, Indiana. After several years working on the farm and completing the sixth grade of elementary school, Emil began working as a stable boy at the John Bass estate, now the site of St. Francis University. Within a few years he rose to the position of staff manager. In 1893, at the age of 21, he began his career as a lathe operator with the Bass Foundry & Machine Co. of Fort Wayne.

Throughout his career with Bass, during which he had risen to the position of draftsman and erecting engineer in 1905, Emil Deister took up the study of ore separation. Eventually, he would patent his own equipment, starting with a centrifugal separator that extracted gold from mercury amalgam, and continuing on to develop ore separating tables.

Deister Management Team

Irwin Deister, Jr.
Chairman

E. Mark Deister
President

Richard M. Deister
Director of Parts, Service and Customer Relations

Greg Wood
Director of Manufacturing and Production

Joe Schlabach
Director of Marketing and Sales

He built his first separating table in his basement on Fort Wayne's Baker Street near the Pennsylvania Railroad Station. Upon completion, he took his invention to Arizona, where he begged space from mill owners for its demonstration. Successful and armed with orders for the new equipment, Emil returned to Fort Wayne to set up business in 1906, as the Deister Concentrator Company. The first tables were manufactured in Louis Sipe's machine shop on Superior Street, with woodwork being done in a barn nearby.

This differential-motion ore separating table had riffles attached to its surface. The riffles collected the heavier ore particles and conveyed them in one direction toward a collector, while water washing across them carried the lighter impurities away. The table is praised in Taggert's Handbook of Ore Dressing, the official textbook at many mining schools, as the first serious competition to the only other kind of ore separating table available at the time.

In 1912, Emil sold his interests in Deister Concentrator Company and established Deister Machine Company. It is interesting to note that upon the founding of Deister Machine Company, the new owners of Deister Concentrator Company tried to stop Emil from using the Deister name in business. The Indiana Supreme Court ruled in Emil's favor in 1920, a case that is still used as a legal precedent.

Deister Machine Company began manufacturing operations at 1933 East Wayne Street in Fort Wayne, its current location. The original building, a 5,500 square-foot plant, is still in active use amidst a total operation that today spans more than 315,000 square feet. Emil also rented a two-room office on Calhoun Street beginning in July of 1912 for the sum of $14.00 per month.

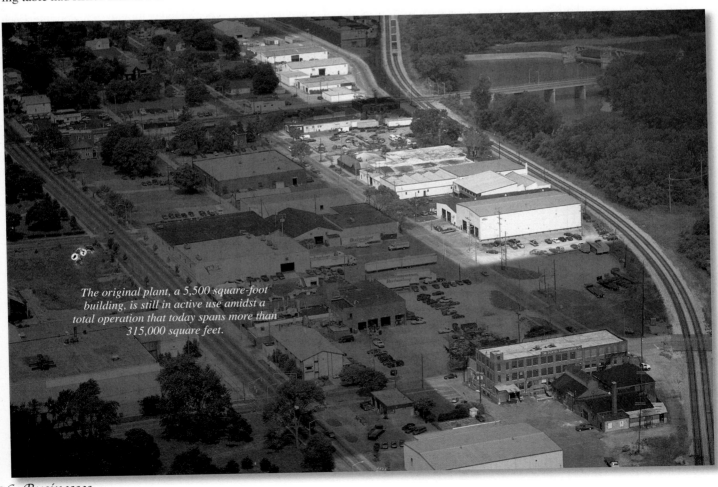

The original plant, a 5,500 square-foot building, is still in active use amidst a total operation that today spans more than 315,000 square feet.

This 3 ½ deck, 6' x 20' sizing screen is just one of sixteen Deister screens in use in a 3-million-ton-per-year Ohio dredging operation.

By 1913, the company had already expanded internationally with representation in London. However, that office was closed in 1914 as World War I swept across Europe.

Deister's London sales manager was ordered to sell or store the office furniture and return home. His Atlantic Ocean crossing was made most uncomfortable by the fact that just days before, a German cruiser sank two British ships and chased a passenger boat en route to England. In addition to the London office, the company maintained a New York City office until the mid-1950s to handle all exports of the concentrating tables.

Until World War II, Deister Concentrator Company and Deister Machine Company operated as competitors. However, in 1926, upon the request of its customers, Deister Machine Company began manufacturing vibrating screens for the separation of materials according to particle size, a process needed to meet state, federal, and industrial specifications.

In 1933, Deister introduced a special screen for sizing the aggregate used in hot-mix asphalt plants. Subsequently, the company added vibrating feeders and foundry equipment, including shakeouts, compaction tables, reclaimers and oscillating conveyors. Products varied in the 1930s and 1940s to meet the economics and sociology of the times with water softeners being produced during the Great Depression. Battery test stands meeting U.S. military standards were manufactured during World War II.

Today, Deister Machine Company, Inc. focuses entirely on its core business, providing feeding, scalping and screening equipment to the aggregate and mining industry. This equipment is used in all 50 states, Canada, and in many countries throughout Latin America, Europe and Asia.

In fact, an independent survey commissioned by the trade magazine, *Rock Products*, ranked Deister as number one in all of five categories: overall product quality, innovative product features, value for the price, product reliability and performance, and technical support.

That reputation has attracted customers known as the biggest aggregate producers in the business – corporations such as Martin Marietta, Vulcan Materials, Hanson Building Materials America, Lafarge, I.M.I. and others. Many of these top producers purchase Deister equipment exclusively and in volume. For example, Deister's largest customer has purchased more than 1,000 Deister vibrating screens and feeders since 1950.

These customer relationships, developed over years of intense support, consultation and service have resulted in ongoing improvements in the design, engineering and customization of Deister feeding and screening equipment – never more important in an era when material specifications are tightening and producers are searching for the means to remain profitable in an increasingly competitive business environment.

In addition, Deister Machine Company, Inc. supports the industry by being active participants in a variety of key organizations. Today, Irwin F. Deister, Jr. and E. Mark Deister are life members of the board of the National Stone, Sand & Gravel Association (NSSGA), both having served as chairman of its Manufacturers and Services (M & S) Division. Most recently, Deister Director of Marketing and Sales Joe Schlabach took the helm as M & S Division chairman. Deister Machine Company, Inc. is also a member of the Indiana Manufacturers Association, the Indiana Chamber of Commerce and the Greater Fort Wayne Chamber of Commerce.

Each generation of Deister leadership continues to build upon its impressive performance history. Founder Emil Deister served as its president and general manager from 1912 until his death in 1961. Enter the second generation: Irwin F. Deister, Sr., son of the founder, joined the company in 1925, eventually succeeding his father as president and chairman until his death in 1988. His brother, Emil Deister, Jr., was with the company from 1926 until his death in 1984, having served as chairman after his father's death. And, enter the third generation: Irwin F. Deister, Jr., son of Irwin, Sr., joined the company in 1951 and is now its chairman, while E. Mark Deister, son of Emil, Jr., has been active since 1963 and is the current president. Irwin and Mark act as co-chief executive officers, each owning fifty percent of the shares, and together forming the board of directors.

For Deister Machine Company, Inc., quality is its history. Its products are designed to integrate with all components of the production system, while delivering maximum performance and productivity. In fact, some of the earlier models of Deister vibrating screens are still in operation due to their rugged construction and continued high efficiency.

It is no accident that certain companies earn their place in history and others fleetingly come and go. Deister is a manufacturer whose success is based upon innovation, customer commitment and a dedication to its community. Certainly, Deister Machine Company, Inc. is a leader in its industry and in Allen County business history.

Do it Best Corp.
(Formerly known as HWI)

Do it Best Corp. is truly a great American success story. What began with little more than an idea in 1945 has grown into a multi-billion dollar company. Its success is due to a unique tradition of hard work, innovation, and determination.

Do it Best Corp., formerly known as Hardware Wholesalers, Inc. (HWI), began as the vision of Arnold Gerberding. Born in Fort Wayne, Indiana, in 1900, Gerberding worked in the hardware business from the time he graduated from Central High School in 1919. Working as a buyer, he faced many challenges and frustrations getting products at good prices and competing with the popular and rapidly growing catalog and retail chains like Sears, Roebuck and Co. and Montgomery Ward.

He was always looking for a way to improve his store's pricing and was impressed by the local farm co-ops. Co-ops were based on a simple idea: many stores buying together could get better deals from vendors than if they bought separately. Investigating this type of idea within the hardware and home improvement industry, Gerberding discovered that several regional co-ops had already been established and were experiencing success. In the late 1930s, he immersed himself in developing the concept for a new co-op that would serve independent retailers in the Midwest. Not only would independent hardware stores become members of the cooperative, they would be the company's shareholders as well. The profits made by the co-op would be returned to the members as a yearly rebate.

Arnold Gerberding

Do it Best Corp.

Once he had developed his idea for the company, Gerberding began approaching retailers to generate interest in getting it off the ground. After getting some positive responses, he quit his job and started contacting prospective members for the new company. For the company to move forward, Gerberding had to find retailers who were willing to pay $1,000 to join the co-op. So he went out on the road and met with independent retailers throughout Indiana, Ohio, and Michigan.

One of the first retailers he met with was C.A.E. Rinker, owner of Rinker's Hardware in Anderson, Indiana. Gerberding stopped by Rinker's store at 4 p.m. and was asked to wait because Rinker was too busy to meet with him. An hour later, Rinker closed the store and was planning to go home without talking with Gerberding. Gerberding asked Rinker if there was a place to eat in town, and Rinker ended up inviting Gerberding to eat dinner with his family—where they spent hours talking about the idea for the new company. Later that evening, Gerberding was invited to spend the night at Rinker's house. The next morning, Rinker signed his store

Hardware Wholesalers Warehouse

Don Wolf

Mike McClelland

as one of the charter members of the company. "I met a man I never knew late in the afternoon," Rinker remembered. "I invited him to my house for dinner, had him stay all night, provided breakfast in the morning, and invested $1,000 in a company I didn't even know existed." Such was the power of Gerberding's enthusiasm and persuasion that became the cornerstone for the company's success.

Seven retailers met on June 28, 1945, at 840 Hayden Street in Fort Wayne to formally incorporate as Hardware Wholesalers, Inc. The first board of directors was elected and was formed entirely of co-op members—a tradition that remains to this day. The first annual meeting of the HWI shareholders was held in November 1945. There were ninety-six members, and the decision was made to start operations as soon as possible.

In February 1946, HWI purchased ten acres of property on Nelson Road in New Haven. Due to federal restrictions on building after World War II and shortage of building materials, construction did not begin until August 1947 and was not completed until May 1948. In the meantime, HWI located its offices at 229 East Main Street in downtown Fort Wayne, where Freimann Square is now located. A storage space next door was used as a warehouse. When that space became too small, additional warehouse spaces were found on Hayden Street and Holten Avenue.

Right from the start, staff were taught to focus on increasing efficiency, keep a watchful eye on expenses, and continuously improve operations. Fixtures in the newly opened Nelson Road facility were built from scrap lumber, and an old barn on the property was taken apart and the lumber used to build storage racks. This spirit of keeping costs low and efficiency high still drives the company to this day.

The first buying market was held in 1946 at the Catholic Community Center using a 66- by 90-foot auditorium for displays. In attendance were sixty members who viewed displays from twenty-five vendors. Early markets were held in the warehouse; later they were moved to a tent in the parking lot. As the markets grew, they moved to the Allen County War Memorial Coliseum. Finally, in 1975, the markets moved to the Indiana Convention Center in Indianapolis, where they have been held ever since.

Gerberding was a big believer in using incentives to increase volume. In 1948, he started the one-order-a-week club. At that time, members would purchase in large quantities four or five times a year. Gerberding believed that retailers could be more profitable if they would order once a week. They could sell more items and would have less resources tied up in inventory. While this practice is a standard procedure today, at that time it was truly innovative.

By the mid 1950s, HWI was an established, rapidly growing regional cooperative. Membership had increased threefold, boasting more than 200 independent hardware and lumber retailers. HWI continued to add major product lines, recruit members, and expand membership services. Although most co-ops simply distributed product, HWI was one of the first in the industry to offer training programs for its members to improve their sales and merchandising skills.

Getting products to members in a timely fashion and in good condition was critical. In 1955, HWI added a private truck delivery system that provided members with lower cost freight and scheduled deliveries so they could promise delivery to their customers. The first fleet was made up of two 16-foot trucks. The drivers were local taxi cab drivers who made deliveries when they were off duty.

Another advancement for HWI was its entrance into the computer age. HWI installed its first computer, an IBM 1401, in 1964. Although the 8K of memory it was equipped with is minuscule by today's standards, it was an amazing amount of capacity for handling data in its day. The computer streamlined operations for ordering, payroll, and pricing.

After building HWI from merely an idea to a major company in the hardware distribution industry, founder Arnold Gerberding retired in 1967. The growth that occurred in this time was phenomenal. HWI's sales went from $171,000 in 1946 to more than $35 million in 1967. In the late 1960s, HWI faced challenges from discount and chain stores. To keep the company growing and moving forward, HWI turned to Don Wolf as its second president.

Don Wolf had been with HWI since 1947, when he began work in the warehouse building shelves out of used lumber. Don believed more than one distribution center was needed in order to keep the co-op viable. In 1971, HWI opened its first distribution center outside of Fort Wayne in Cape Girardeau, Missouri. Today, there are eight centers located in Missouri, Ohio, Illinois, New York, South Carolina, Texas, Nevada and Oregon. These centers made it possible for HWI to grow from a small, two-car garage company in downtown Fort Wayne to a national operation that serves members all over the country and around the world.

One of the most important facets of HWI's growth in the 1970s was the emergence of home center stores. In the 1970s, all the hardware stores looked the same, no matter if you were in an HWI store, or one from Ace or True Value. HWI decided to differentiate its stores with the Do it center® concept, which revolutionized the way home centers looked. The Do it center concept used bright colors and signs to create a warm and exciting atmosphere for customers and employees. The stores looked bigger, and products were easier to find. So overwhelming was the response to the new stores that in 1985, the *National Home Center News* reported that "HWI can legitimately lay claim to igniting the resurgence in hardware retailing, and even its co-op competitors concede its Do it center program has been a rousing success."

Another notable accomplishment of Don Wolf was his leadership in charitable involvement. He was one of the co-founders of the Fort Wayne and Northeastern

Indiana chapter of Big Brothers/Big Sisters and served as the president of the national board of directors of Big Brothers/Big Sisters of America. Wolf was the founder of the Study Connection Program, a volunteer-based effort to provide tutors for young people in need. This nationally acclaimed program is now being duplicated in communities across America. His legacy of volunteerism continues today. The company supports Habitat for Humanity, Junior Achievement, and the United Way; holds blood drives for the Red Cross; and assists with the PBS pledge drive.

HWI's second transition in leadership came when Mike McClelland succeeded Don Wolf as president in 1992. McClelland came to HWI in 1974 and gained extensive experience in personnel and marketing during his tenure. His focus on getting the most done in the least amount of time was a key element of his leadership of the company. In 1995, McClelland hired IBM and Purdue University to conduct a survey of the membership to determine what they needed to grow and be successful. The result of that survey was the Do it Best Vision, which provided more than thirty new or enhanced programs and services to HWI members.

In 1998 HWI combined with Our Own Hardware, a move that brought together the two most member-focused co-ops in the industry. The histories of both co-ops are closely intertwined: When Arnold Gerberding was researching co-ops in the hardware industry, he talked with George Hall, the founder of Our Own Hardware, to get ideas.

As a result of this combination and a general change in the nature of its business, HWI changed its name to Do it Best Corp. to tie together all its members, truck fleet, store designs, and advertising.

In 2002, Mike McClelland retired, and Bob Taylor took over as president. Taylor grew up working in his family's chain of hardware stores in Virginia Beach, Virginia, eventually becoming the president of Taylor's Do it Center®. Remarked one member, "It solves the problem the other co-ops are struggling with—the whole notion of a detached leadership that hasn't walked a mile in my shoes." In today's competitive marketplace, developing successful retail strategies and programs for members is just as important as distributing products. Taylor's vast experience, both as a retailer and former chairman of the board, continue to sharpen the retail focus of the co-op.

Today, Do it Best Corp. is the fastest growing co-op in the industry with sales approaching $3 billion and rebates to members totaling more than $107 million. It is Indiana's largest privately owned business. Do it Best Corp. is the only full-service member-owned distributor of hardware, lumber, and building materials products in the industry, serving 4,100 members in all fifty states and forty-five countries. The service and dedication of its 1,600 employees still exemplify the member-first philosophy established by founder Arnold Gerberding.

Do It Center

Bob Taylor

ICON International

Customcraft Store

Six decades ago, one wouldn't have known that a simple, unassuming presence would evolve into a multi-national powerhouse responsible for the images of hundreds of the world's most important companies.

Yet ICON Exhibits has always been adaptable. From its roots from a plastic fabricator to its current incarnation as the foundation for companies' images across the globe, ICON has always been at the cutting edge of image development.

ICON has its roots in CUSTOMCRAFT, a company founded in Fort Wayne in 1946 to build everything from gun turrets for aircraft to custom furniture for homes and offices. As its reputation for quality craftsmanship grew, so did the scope of its projects. Soon, CUSTOMCRAFT earned recognition as a one-of-a-kind innovator, a trait that positioned it to produce one-of-a-kind custom exhibits for trade shows and museums.

A New World

Upon their return from service during World War II, Robert Federspiel and Norman Bell started the company in a small storefront on Broadway in Fort Wayne in 1946. Designing and producing historic restorations, custom cabinetry and commercial display fixtures, they named their venture CUSTOMCRAFT, suggesting the artisan nature of their products and capabilities. It was one of the first companies to fabricate with the new material known as Plexiglas.

As its reputation for quality craftsmanship grew, CUSTOMCRAFT continued to catch the attention of designers seeking attention to the details of good design. During the 1950s, CUSTOMCRAFT produced cabinets for some homes designed by Frank Lloyd Wright.

During the 1960s, CUSTOMCRAFT focused its energies on display cases for department stores, custom installations of bank lobbies and retail outlets and small trade show exhibits.

A Culture of Innovation

Innovation and inspiration merged again in the 1970s as CUSTOMCRAFT took on unique exhibit projects for museums, corporate interiors and sets for theaters.

In 1979, Michael V. Parrott purchased CUSTOMCRAFT and became the company's seventh employee. In addition to a modest investment, he brought his previous management experience in the custom furniture industry and his interest in event marketing. Parrott initially retained the CUSTOMCRAFT name but shifted the company's focus to the design, production and servicing of exhibits for corporate trade shows.

He later changed the company name to ICON Incorporated and shifted its focus to the design and production of trade show exhibits. The company soon became the main supplier of these products to companies throughout Indiana, which were using this new marketing medium.

In 1981, ICON created and produced ExhibitPak®, the industry's first self-contained modular exhibit made from vacuum-formed plastic parts. This very successful product helped nurture the company's culture of innovation.

Three years later, in 1984, ICON created a new division, DISPLAYSOURCE, to distribute pre-manufactured portable displays that complemented the larger custom exhibits produced by the CUSTOMCRAFT Division. DISPLAYSOURCE was expanded in 1993 with a sales office and showroom in Indianapolis. Portable displays have since become trade show staples, and ICON remains a major distributors of Nimlok, one of the industry's leading brands.

Because of its diverse production capabilities, ICON created the PLASTICWORKS Division in 1986 to distribute and fabricate plastic materials. This division was sold in 1991 to Meyer Plastics of Indianapolis.

In 1990 ICON was selected from among many other companies to engineer and produce a technologically advanced exhibit system to exclusive use by United Technologies. Today, UT uses the system throughout the world and ICON serves as the central U.S. "depot" for the system's deployment.

With its selection to produce a proprietary exhibit system for a major multinational corporation, in 1990, ICON changed its name to ICON International to better reflect its growing reputation. This proprietary system set a new standard for versatile application of exhibit properties.

In 1992, for its client BASF, ICON patented ExZact®, a modular aluminum panel system based on a patented connector which cut costly trade show set-up time by as much as 50 percent. ExZact® established ICON as a leading industry innovator and continues to provide a key competitive advantage. In 1993, ExZact®won the "Best Product of the Year" award from the International Exhibitors Association.

In 1996, ICON launched ExpoDeck®, a lightweight structural system for building multi-level exhibits. First used for a 10,000-sqare-foot exhibit for Magnavox, ExpoDeck® won a prestigious international design award and established itself as one of the best decking systems in the world. ExpoDeck® is a lightweight structural system for building double-deck exhibits, incorporating its patented its QuicOnex® deck connector. This product has grown to become the industry leader for large, multi-story exhibits.

ICON Campus

Challenging Times

Faced with capacity limitations, ICON merged with Hamilton Displays in Indianapolis in 1997. The merger was dissolved a year later due to cultural differences, although ICON kept some of its production in Indianapolis.

Magnavox Exhibit

Because of the widespread popularity of its patented exhibit systems products, ICON created its HIGHMARK TechnologiesDivision in 1998 to market to the exhibit design and production community. It closed the Indianapolis facilities and consolidated all production on its Fort Wayne campus late in 1999.

Also in 1999, ICON became a part owner of Sho-Link, a major industry cooperative specializing in installation and dismantling services for the event industry. ICON was also asked to take on responsibility for several major permanent exhibits at museums in Indiana. The success with these projects led to a renewed commitment to the planning, design, fabrication and installation of museum exhibits.

In 2000, ICON introduced "Trade Show-in-a-box," program for "turnkey outsourcing" of logistically complex corporate programs involving multiple properties and events. Also in that year, ICON launched its first website, ICONlink, and a major rental program for exhibitors, ICONrent.

That year, ICON also patented its QuicOnex® deck connector and consolidated all of its facilities on its Fort Wayne campus at 8333 Clinton Park Drive. The multi-plant campus necessitated restructuring the company into two divisions, ICON Exhibits and HIGHMARK Technologies.

In March, 2002, it acquired the assets of JT Unlimited, a small California company with additional graphics production capabilities and established ICON West, an exhibit service center based in the San Francisco Bay area.

In 2005, ICON's ExpoDeck® product was named one of the "Best Product of the Year" by *Start Magazine*. ICON Exhibits started its Museum Services Division in 2005 as well.

And in 2006, ICON will celebrate 60 years in business, a fine achievement for a company in an industry that characterized by instability.

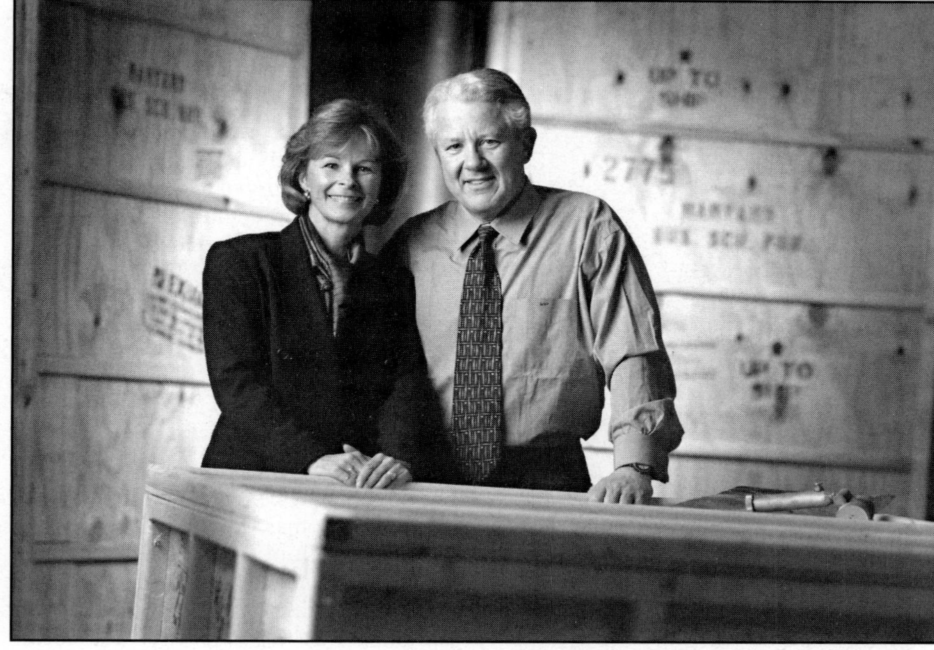

Kathy and Mick Parrott

Developing That Special Image

Producing a unique image for each of its clients has been ICON's privilege – and its challenge. Said ICON President Michael Parrott, "Exhibit design is evolving from traditional 'nuts and bolts' approaches to more experiential environments with bold systems-based architecture, dramatic visual elements, sensory atmospherics using light, sound and electronic stimuli, and live demonstration that is both educational and entertaining."

What ICON attempts to do with each assignment is to capture the essence of each client in a multi-media exhibit that provides viewers with the proper amount of information about each client without overwhelming attendees with stimuli. The company has been lauded for its work with world-class designers to create one-of-a-kind museum showcases at the Lincoln and John Dillinger museums in Indiana. The company has also designed numerous corporate lobbies, showrooms, and visitor centers, and has developed interactive exhibits for schools and science museums across the country.

ICON considers itself fortunate to be a part of expanding America's knowledge of its past through its numerous historical exhibits across Indiana and the country.

Despite the negative impact of terrorism on business travel, trade show and event marketing continues to capture the greatest share of the marketing expenditures worldwide in the early 21st century. Even with the advent and fast growth of Internet marketing, businesses large and small continue to invest in ways to enhance the personal face-to-face marketing experience.

To meet their rapidly changing needs, many exhibitors are opting for custom rental exhibits rather than making large capital investments in owned properties.

Increasingly, museum exhibitry is being targeted at younger audiences where interactivity has become an important tool for communicating and educating. ICON International has evolved to meet these ever-changing needs.

ICON International offers full-service design, production, graphics, event support, and exhibit property management services. The company lends its years of trade show and design creativity to every project.

"We use the latest materials and lighting techniques, along with the most exciting graphics, to create memorable messages," said Parrott.

Such excellence has been recognized through the numerous awards ICON and its clients have received in recent years, including dozens of "Best of Show" awards from the International Exhibitors Association and other industry groups.

With its systems technology, internal graphics production, large rental capabilities and culture of innovation, ICON International is positioned well to meet the challenges of the 21st century and beyond.

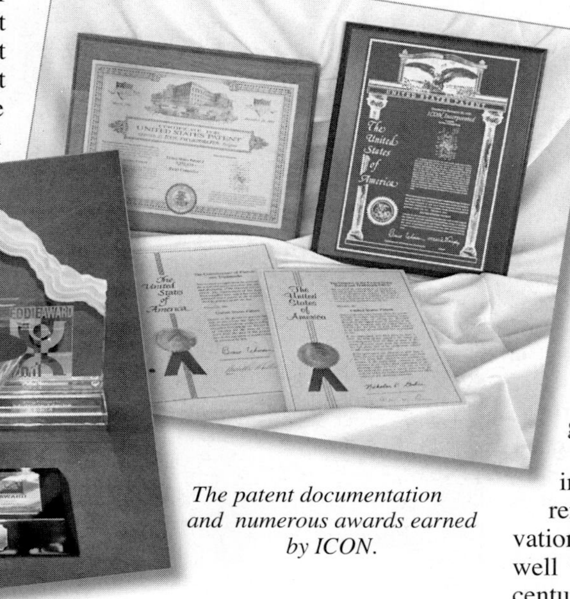

The patent documentation and numerous awards earned by ICON.

Rea Magnet Wire

George A. Jacobs

Had it not been for the inventiveness of a young man and the support of that young man's father-in-law, Fort Wayne might be a very different place today. Indeed, the entire world might not be as technologically advanced as it is.

That young man was George A. Jacobs, inventor of a special insulating process that allowed copper wire to be manufactured in extremely fine gauges. That innovation led to the development of high-speed electric motors that powered everything from the Model T to the space shuttle, and to the creation of Rea Magnet Wire, one of Fort Wayne's leading manufacturing companies.

The Early Days: Dudlo Company

A native of Dudley, Massachusetts, Jacobs and his wife, the former Ethel Mossman of Fort Wayne, developed the enamel insulation for magnet wire in 1907. Jacobs was working for Sherwin-Williams in Cleveland, Ohio at the time, but formed the Dudlo Company to continue work on the process. Ethel's father, William E. Mossman, offered his son-in-law a factory for his experiments if the couple would return to Fort Wayne, which they did.

Dudlo soon developed a "tiny black box" – automotive ignition coils that powered the Model T Ford. From 1917 to 1927, millions of ignition coils were shipped from Fort Wayne to the Ford Company – some five million in 1920 alone, enough to fill eighteen railroad cars.

During World War I, Dudlo provided wire used in military trucks, X-ray machines, telephones and anti-submarine devices. After the war, Dudlo's business increased regularly and by 1929, the employee base had grown to 6,500. The company was also producing components for radios, phonographs and loudspeakers.

The Depression Ends Dudlo, gives birth to Rea Magnet Wire

Dudlo had grown from one tin shed in 1911 to twelve departments by 1926. In 1927, it was part of a $50 million merger with several other wire and cable companies. The result of the merger was named the General Cable Corporation.

Though the future appeared bright, discontent was brewing in the Dudlo sector of General Cable. George Jacobs, whose invention started the business, resigned in 1928 and formed a new company, Inca Manufacturing, the next year. Victor Rea was named Works Manager of Dudlo after Jacobs' resignation.

Inca Manufacturing was later acquired by Phelps Dodge in 1930, and Jacobs remained for several more years before moving to California because of his wife's poor health. He died in 1945.

Meanwhile, due to the continuing financial woes of the Great Depression, General Cable closed the Dudlo plant in 1933 and relocated all manufacturing operations to Rome, New York.

Victor Rea

Rea Magnet Wire – A "Gamble with Destiny"

Victor Rea resigned from General Cable Corp. in 1932, just a few months before the company closed the Fort Wayne Dudlo plant. Shortly afterward, he, along with Jay Boeshore and Edward Snyder, announced they were forming Rea Magnet Wire. To finance the new company wasn't easy: it was 1933, the worst year of the Great Depression. Rea, Boeshore and Snyder had to borrow against their own capital – life insurance policies, stocks

Early Dudlo Facility

and bonds and mortgages on their homes. "We had to make sacrifices and gamble with destiny," Boeshore later wrote.

The gamble paid off. Victor Rea contacted his old clients and was able to get commitments. The fledgling company leased the Woodward Engineering Building at 3600 East Pontiac Street, for $500 a month, with the option to buy at $25,000, which it did in 1935. The company's headquarters remain there today.

The new company received its first order in October 1933 from Jefferson Electric Company for 10,000 pounds of 38 gauge enameled wire on three-inch spools. Quality products and ensuring customer satisfaction were Victor Rea's top priorities. Personal service to customers ensured repeat business, and the company thrived.

Rea Magnet Wire was considered one of the best places to work in Fort Wayne. In 1954, President Samuel Rea (son of Victor) established a fixed formula for figuring the profit-sharing bonuses, which won the company a national award. Other employee benefits included group health insurance, hospitalization, life insurance and pension plans.

On August 21, 1954, Victor Rea suffered a heart attack and died. His son Samuel Rea was elected President, and he began adding to the Sales Department and strengthening the areas of Engineering, Research and Development. The company's growth through the 1950s led to the 1959 construction of its first manufacturing plant outside Fort Wayne: the $1.2 million, 100,000-square-foot facility in Lafayette, Indiana. In 1957, the company built a warehouse in Somerville, N.J. to facilitate delivery of products to New England.

The Alcoa Years

In 1959, Rea Magnet Wire was doing development work with the Aluminum Company of America (Alcoa), and in January 18, 1960, the aluminum conglomerate purchased Rea Magnet Wire. Samuel Rea and his brother David resigned later that year, ending the Rea family's tenure of managing the company that continues to bear their name. Longtime sales manager (also a former Dudlo employee) Robert L. "Bob" Whearley was named President in late 1960.

Alcoa consolidated its research, development and sales of aluminum sheet and foil strip for electrical conductors at the Fort Wayne plant. Rea also coordinated all of Alcoa's activities for round copper magnet wire, round aluminum magnet wire and aluminum sheet and foil strip conductors. Rea perfected a process of removing burrs from aluminum strips and began successfully producing precision slit aluminum strip for low voltage windings of distribution transformers.

Rea continued to lead the nation in production of fine magnet wire. In October 1961, seventy-five pounds of Rea's ultra-fine wire were launched into space aboard the Midas IV satellite and scattered into the atmosphere. The resulting belt of 350 million copper wire fibers helped enable communications between any two points on Earth by reflecting radio waves. Rea wire was also used in the United States missile program and the space program.

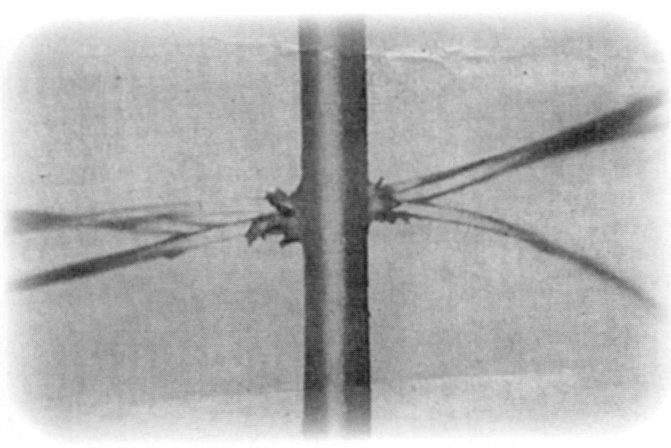

In 1962, Alcoa financed the construction of a new plant on Adams Center Road in Allen County. The plant served as a central depot for warehousing and shipping, using the first computer controlled inventory retrieval system in the magnet wire industry.

Several presidents oversaw the company in the ensuing years. Allen Sheldon, Rea's Executive Vice President, was named President in December 1964, to replace the retiring Whearley. James L. McKinley succeeded Sheldon in 1965, and he oversaw construction of an Alcoa-financed and Rea-operated plant in Laurinburg, North Carolina. That plant was designed to be able to draw, anneal and coat wire all in one operation.

In 1965 and 1967, the Lafayette plant was expanded, and in 1970, obsolete equipment was replaced and electrical systems updated. In 1974, Rea, through Alcoa, purchased General Cable Corporation's Buena Vista, Virginia, plant for $4 million. In 1975, the company, seeking to diversify into wire-related product, purchased Dixie Wire and Professional Electrical Products (PEP) of Nashville, Tennessee.

James McKinley retired in 1973 and Alcoa sent George Haymaker to become Rea Magnet Wire's President. He was the first president not to come from Rea's own ranks. Haymaker was succeeded in 1976 by Don Whitlow, who in turn was succeeded by Charles Ligon in 1979; and James "Jim" Vann in 1982.

By the early 1980s, Alcoa shifted many of the Fort Wayne general magnet wire production operations to the Lafayette plant. In 1981, a Special Products Group was formed in Fort Wayne, and given the responsibility for products other than film-insulated wire, such as tape and fibrous magnet wire, tin-lead and tinned wire, bunched wire and de-reeling equipment.

In 1983, Rea continued its expansion, purchasing Algonquin Industries of Guilford, Connecticut. And in 1984, Rea Magnet Wire produced a new record in profits, with $100 million in sales.

A Return To Private Ownership

Early in 1985, Alcoa decided to sell Rea, Algonquin and PEP industries. All offers for the three companies were below their appraised value, and in the end, Rea Magnet Wire President Jim Vann along with Bill Gorman (Algonquin's Vice President), and Rea managers Ron Foster and Bill Wyatt were able to purchase Rea and Algonquin (Alcoa had decided to keep PEP Industries.).

By 1986, the Rea plant was back in private hands, and eliminating the company's debt was the top priority. The four men decided to shutter the Buena Vista, Virginia, plant after a devastating flood. That plant's equipment was divided between the Laurinburg, North Carolina, and Lafayette plants. In 1988, Rea joined forced with Fujikara Ltd. and created Texas Magnet Wire Co, based in El Paso, Texas.

Rea's management company became Rea Wire Industries, Inc., in 1988, an umbrella organization over the three business units: Rea Magnet Wire, Rea Engineered Wire Products and Algonquin Industries. That structure still exists but is now known as Rea Magnet Wire Company. Ron Foster became President of Rea Magnet Wire in 1988, Bill Gorman remained as President of Algonquin and in 1989, Larry Bagwell came from Alcoa and became President of Rea Engineered Wire Products.

By 1993, Rea streamlined its operations by selling both Texas Magnet Wire and the Laurinburg plant, and closed the Adams Center Road facility. With its remaining debt paid off, Rea overhauled the Pontiac Street and Lafayette facilities.

In 1995, Jim Vann retired as chief executive officer of Rea, and was succeeded by Ron Foster. Foster retired in 1997 and was succeeded by Larry Bagwell, who is Rea's current chairman and CEO.

Although retired from daily activities, Rea's shareholders remain committed to growing the company and developing the employees. In 1998, Rea constructed a state-of-the-art magnet wire facility in Las Cruces, New Mexico. In 2001, Rea purchased Hanover Manufacturing, located in Ashland, Virginia, from Alcoa. This was followed in 2003 by an acquisition of Southwire Specialty Products Division (SSP) located in Osceola, Arkansas. Beginning in 2003, Rea also began to diversify internationally, to support their North American customers who were building plants in China. Rea formed a joint venture with Tongling Jingda of China, China's largest manufacturer of magnet wire. The joint venture, known as Jingda-Rea, operates state-of-the-art magnet wire plants in the cities of Nanhai (north of Hong Kong) and Tianjin (southeast of Beijing).

Today, Rea Magnet Wire employs over 800 people, with seven plants located in North America and two plants located in China. It is the third-largest producer of magnet wire and other specialty products in the world.

Riegel's, Inc.

Al Riegel and Frank Bougher, 1895, southwest corner of Calhoun and Columbia, the Kaiser Palace Saloon.

The Red Front Cigar store was founded September 14, 1874, by proprietor John Carl. Mr. Carl's business was located at the northeast corner of Main and Calhoun Street. The building also housed the Milton Place Saloon. The saloon would later be run by Joe Riegel, Al's brother. Carl sold the business to Joseph Getz. Getz operated the Corner Cigar store between the years 1891 and 1905. According to the *Journal Gazette*, Al Riegel purchased the cigar store January 12, 1905.

Aloysius (Al) L. Riegel was born October 4, 1863. He came to Fort Wayne at the age of nineteen in 1883. He became partners in business with Frank E. Bougher opening the Kieser Palace Saloon in the 1890s as one of many businesses and developments together. The two men were more than just partners; they were also brother-in-laws. They each married the other's sister. Al married Irene Bougher and Frank E. Bougher married Emma Riegel.

Al and Irene (Bougher) Riegel had no children of their own. They had one daughter, Claire Riegel, whom they adopted from one of Al's siblings.

(l. to r.) Irene Bougher Riegel, Frank Bougher, Emma Riegel Bougher, and Aloysius Riegel.

Al Riegel owned and developed many other properties as well, including: the New Riegel Building on West Jefferson which housed the International Business College in 1916, the first fire-proof theater equal in size to the Embassy Theater, and the Edgewater Arms apartments on Edgewater. Al even had a second Al Riegel Cigar Store which he opened at the corner of Calhoun and Lewis Streets, which was part of the Cooney Bayer Building. He sold it a year later to a brother in-law by the name of Hills. Hills later changed the name to Hill's Cigar store. The partnership with Frank E. Bougher appears to split sometime after Al acquired the Cigar store. Frank Bougher bought the Home Billiard Room, located at 120 West Berry Street, near the Anthony Hotel, a 7,500 square foot pool hall and saloon which just so happened to stock cigars from Al Riegel's Cigar Store.

Al Riegel died at the age of 74 on July 11, 1938. He died on his front porch at 620 West Berry Street of a heart attack while watering his lawn after returning home from his store. At the time of his death, Mr. Riegel was considered to be one of Fort Wayne's most prominent businessmen. Oddly enough, Al's partnership with F. E. Bougher continues today. Aside from the many properties that bear their names together, the two men and their wives are buried together in the mausoleum at the Catholic cemetery on Lake Avenue.

The two most significant changes for the business were the renovation of the building at the transfer corner (Main and Calhoun Streets) that occurred in 1919, and the move to its present location at 624 South Calhoun Street, in 1967. The first change came as a result of prohibition, when the saloon (owned by Perry Stuart) located directly north of the building on Calhoun Street closed. This building that housed the saloon was owned by the Steckbeck family. Al and his nephews leased the land from the Steckbecks, and razed the two buildings, digging a new foundation and building a new three-story building in its place, all the while continuing the daily operation of the business without closing for a single day. The new Rigel structure (1919-1967), which itself was a landmark structure for the center of our city is still a prominent icon to the existing business and many of its patrons and included a twenty-eight stool double horseshoe luncheon counter and a kitchen in the basement. This building was the hub of the transfer corner. The controller for the trolley cars would shout down from the second floor when the cars were to depart on time. The newsstand, which still operates in the downtown location, was a place of attraction.

(l. to r.) Frank A. Bougher, George Kuntz, Al Riegel, Virgil Roy, Frank Christie, and Fred Fry, 1919

(l. to r.) Cigar Salesman, Frank A. Bougher and Al Riegel.

Mr. Riegel never missed an opportunity to create attractions to bring patrons into the business. He sold tickets to fights, circuses, and racing events. At one time Riegel's gave advertising tokens for the trolley especially made with stamping on them. The largest tactic he used was to give his customers a ticket that gave them a single chance at winning either a General Electric radio or a Ford Model A automobile. The store never closed until the last Trolley had departed around midnight. Only after the street was completely empty would Al turn off the light above the door. The second change for the Cigar Store came as a result of the construction of the City County Building, which was completed in 1969. The city claimed eminent domain for the 100 block of West Main Street, including the 600 block of South Calhoun. All the existing businesses on the block relocated and the entire block was leveled for the development of the new government building. Riegel's moved directly across the street to 624 S. Calhoun Street where it still operates today. To date there are three Riegels' Pipe and Tobacco stores. The other two locations are Georgetown Square Shopping Center on East State

Boulevard, open in 1975 and 6412 West Jefferson Blvd, Covington Plaza buying out an existing tobacco store in 2002.

At the time of Al Riegel's death, two nephews, Frank Aloysius Bougher and George Kuntz, with whom he had been associated with the Riegel's Cigar Store for over thirty years became the Riegel's Cigar owners. Frank A. Bougher (1892-1975) came to work for his Uncle Al in 1906. He was the son of William H. Bougher of Delphi, brother of Frank E. Bougher. He married Mauriece McLaughlin in 1929 two months before the Wall Street stock market crash. Frank A. Bougher owned Riegels with his cousin George until George died in 1958. Mr. Frank A. Bougher purchased George Kuntz remaining interest in 1960 from George's widow.

Frank A. Bougher came to Fort Wayne from Delphi, Indiana, to join the Railroad. Upon his arrival he lodged with his uncle Frank E. and Emma (Riegel) Bougher. Al hired him to work at the cigar store instead. Al Riegel paid him $5.00 a week, half of which Al kept to invest, teaching the younger Frank the lifetime skill of saving and managing money. Frank Bougher suffered a heart attack the day after Christmas, December 26, 1974. He fell in the store and died less than two weeks later on January 5, 1975. He was 83 years old.

Two of Frank's three children, F. Thomas Bougher and William H. Bougher, came to work in their adolescent years during the 40s. William H. Bougher, Frank's youngest, gained principle control in 1974 when F. Thomas moved to San Diego to own a tavern. Margaret Ann Bougher married Thomas Jehl in 1954. Tom Bougher later returned to Fort Wayne and spent his remaining years at the Riegel counter. He died October 21, 1994 at the age of 62.

William Bougher, born November 3, 1933, has carried on the tradition and tutelage of the Riegel business with his children. Bill married Barbara in 1959.

Together they have eight children and are currently expecting their twenty-first grandchild. Five of the six male children have put in their share of time at Riegel's Pipe and Tobacco. The Riegel-Bougher connection has lasted four generations and soon possibly a fifth. This rarity of a business lasting over 131 years and more than one hundred years by the same family is a very rare find indeed – especially in the tobacco industry. Riegel's ranks among this nation's ten oldest cigar stores.

What does not effectively come out in this particular history is the real history of the people behind these retail leaders. Riegel's Pipe and Tobacco's longevity is greatly due to the sacrifices of the individuals that have labored for the company without a lot of fanfare. For prosperity Riegels would like to thank a few of those here. Don Romary, Red and Clark Philly, Donald Tracey, Mabel Corville, Jonathan Walters, Dennis Hills and Anthony Hills and most especially Mr. John Minnich – Riegel's Manager since 1976.

Transfer Corner

Allen County Public Library

What Happened When

1816 The first Indiana Constitution provides for libraries.

1824 Allen County is "laid off" or created and Fort Wayne chosen as county seat.

1824 $500.00 set aside for library in Allen County from monies received from the proceeds of the sale of town lots as provided for by the first Indiana Constitution.

1841 The list of books held by the library appears in the *Fort Wayne Sentinel* and includes such titles as *Nicholas Nickleby*, *Spy*, *Lord Byron's Works*, *Don Quixote*, and *Plutarch's Lives*.

1855 The working Men's Institute forms in Fort Wayne and the Young Men's Literary Society merges with it, providing a library for men.

1859 Wayne Township library is listed in *City Directory* at Berry and Calhoun.

1867 Working Men's Institute moves to the Allen County Courthouse.

1881 D.N.Foster and Col. R.S. Robertson held the state legislature pass legislation to levy taxes to establish and maintain libraries.

1887 Emerine J. Hamilton Reading Room for Women established.

1892 Women's Club League petitions for a library.

1894 Library Room set aside in City Hall.

1895 January 28 - library opens with 3,606 volumes in City Hall, 117 books from the Women's Club League; 800 from the Allen County Teachers' Associations; 1,028 from the high school including the Working Men's Institute, 247 donated documents; 1,414 purchased documents.

1895 January 29 - Mrs. Susan Hoffman, Head Librarian begins circulating books at ten in the morning.

1898 Miss Margaret Colerick is appointed Head Librarian after the death of the second Head Librarian, Mrs. Clara Fowler.

1898 Board purchases Brackenridge home at Wayne and Webster for $14,000 and the library remains there until 1901.

1901 Women's Club League petitions Andrew Carnegie for a grant of money to erect a new and more adequate building, but is refused on the first try. The second successful petition is accompanied by an endorsement from the mayor and moves Carnegie to offer $75,000.00 if the city will provide the site and at least $7,000.00 annually for maintenance.

1901 Library moves to its temporary home in the Electron (Standard) Building on Berry Street.

1902 Library adds 150 books in German to the collection.

1904 Carnegie library formally opens. Total building cost is $110,000.00 and building site is $14,750.00. There was a cost overrun and Carnegie sends an additional $15,000.

1907 Children's Department opens.

1912 First branch opens on South Calhoun Street. This was later to be known as the Shawnee Branch.

1912 Business and Municipal Department opens. Later the name is changed to Business and Technology.

1915 Orders Department opens.

1916 Extension Department organizes to serve factories, fire stations and hospitals.

1917 Cataloging Department is created.

1919 Little Turtle branch opens at Sixth Street and Wells.

1920 Petitions circulate in county to secure and extend library services to county residents.

1920 Woodburn branch opens.

1921 Monroeville and New Haven Branches open.

1922 Pontiac Branch opens.

1923 Service to county residents begins. Fort Wayne Public Library becomes Public Library of Fort Wayne and Allen County.

1923 Harlan deposit collection becomes Harlan Branch.

1925 Largest library meeting ever held in state of Indiana is held in Fort Wayne. It is a meeting of Indiana, Michigan, and Ohio librarians and trustees.

1927 Publicity Department is created.

1927 Tecumseh Branch opens.

1928 Adult Circulation Department has a collection of 37,493 books.

1929 First bookwagon hits the streets.

1933 Claude Bowers, noted author, former Fort Wayne resident, and Ambassador to Spain decries the drastic budget cuts for the Fort Wayne library. He states that the Fort Wayne library is "more responsive to reading needs of the community than the libraries of New York City..."

1935 Adult Circulation Department splits into the Reference Division and the Circulation Division.

1935 Rex Potterf becomes Head Librarian complete with national controversy.

1944 Main Library expansion begins with the purchase of the Hollywood Building on Washington. This building becomes known as "The Annex" and houses the general library administration offices.

1948 Record Department opens.

1952 The Young Adult Department opens in the basement of the Main Library.

1959 Rex Potterf retires.

1960 Fred Reynolds becomes Head Librarian.

1961 Original Genealogy Department opens with Dorothy Lower in charge.

1963 Reference Division answers 4,785 questions

1963 Library receives first class status from the state of Indiana.

1965 In August the Main Library moves to temporary quarters in the old Purdue Extension Building at Jefferson and Barr while the "new structure" goes up on Webster and Wayne. Books are packed in cardboard beer cartons for the move.

1968 Books are repacked in beer cartons for the summer move back to the "new structure" at Wayne and Webster, Dedication of the 173,500 square foot, $3,000,000.00 building is August 21.

1968 Talking Books Department opens.

1970 Waynedale opens.

1972 Hessen Cassel and Georgetown branches open.

1973 New Shawnee branch opens.

1977 Construction of the new addition to the Main Library begins.

1979 Fred Reynolds retires.

1979 Robert Vegeler becomes Library Director.

1980 January 1st the Public Library of Fort Wayne and Allen County officially becomes the Allen County Public Library by act of the state legislature.

1980 Board names Rick J.Ashton Library Director when Robert Vegeler retires.

1981 Grand opening for the Main Library 55,000 square foot addition is January 18.

1982 ACPL becomes a Cooperating Collection of The Foundation Center in New York.

1982 First Summer Reading Program for young adults held at the Main Library.

1983 Sunday hours at the Main Library begin in January.

1983 Readers' Services Department is created by joining the "old" Readers' and the Reference Department.

1984 Award winning Adult Basic Reading Center opens as part of Readers' Services.

1985 Rick J. Ashton leaves to become Library Director at Denver, Colorado.

1985 Steven Fortriede is acting director.

1985 90th birthday party held. An estimated 5,500 people eat 2,731 pizzas, the largest carryout order ever made at that time. Noble Roman's, Coca-Cola and WMEE-FM contribute to the success.

1986 Jeffrey Krull is hired as the new Library Director after a national search.

1986 CLSI is awarded automation contract to computerize library circulation.

1988 Library "goes live" with new automation system.

1990 Repairs and limited renovations performed at several library facilities; two new branches (Aboite and Dupont) constructed.

1995 Dupont Branch expands.

1997 Library board and staff begin system wide space needs analysis for all library facilities.

2001 Allen County taxpayers approve bond financing of $84 million library expansion project.

2002 Main Library plans move to temporary site at 200 East Berry.

2003 Ground is broken for branches in Woodburn, New Haven, and Monroeville.

2003 February grand opening is held at the temporary quarters at the Renaissance Square.

2003 Shawnee Branch re-opens after renovation. Woodbum and New Haven Branches have grand opening celebrations.

(Timeline by Laurabelle Hibbets McCaffery March 17, 2004 Some dates varied in different accounts of the same event. Dates that were most consistent are used. Sources used included, but were not limited to: Articles from the *Fort Wayne Journal Gazette*, *Fort Wayne News-Sentinel*; Documents written by Rick J. Ashton, Margaret M. Colerick, Paul Deane, Jr., Steven Fortriede, Betty Henning, Laurabelle Hibbets McCaffery, Fred J. Reynolds, Robert H. Vegeler, Virginia G. Williams; Allen County Public Library publications; Griswold, Bert J. *Pictorial History of Fort Wayne*. Vol.l.; This material was edited by Rosanne Coomer.)

Library Expansion And Renovation Project

In 1997 the library initiated a space needs assessment for the entire county-wide library system. Decades of steady growth in the demand for library services, coupled with the effects of new technologies, had placed obvious strains on aging buildings. The main library and many branches were becoming seriously overcrowded, as Internet workstations, word processors, and printers competed for limited space with books, magazines, and audiovisual media.

In November of 1998 the library board held a series of community meetings at the main library and several branches to gather citizens' opinions on library facilities, and to hear their views on space needs for the future. Using information obtained at these meetings, plus growth projections for library services and collections, and comparative data from other leading libraries, the library administration began to develop a capital improvement plan. The goal underlying the entire planning effort was, and remains, to make sure that the Allen County Public Library's facilities have adequate and appropriate space to serve our community at a high standard of excellence for at least the next twenty years.

Carnegie Library

Present Library

During 1999 the library administration developed preliminary proposals to construct several new branches that would replace existing, severely overcrowded branches; to expand and renovate several other under-sized branches; to renovate or update the remaining branches; to significantly expand and renovate the main library; and to provide adequate parking at all library locations. By the end of 1999 architects had been selected for all proposed projects. All local firms were selected for the branch projects; for the main library, a local firm was teamed with a nationally known firm with extensive experience designing large libraries and other civic structures.

Throughout the year 2000 architects worked to develop design solutions for their respective projects. In designing the main library expansion, library officials and architects consulted with representatives of other proposed downtown development projects to share information and ensure that the library's plans would complement and enhance other improvements in the downtown area. As word about the library's plans spread through the community, there was a growing awareness of the potential of the main library expansion to excite the imagination of the community and spark a renaissance for the city's downtown.

On April 26, 2001, architects presented their reports to the library board. The bold vision for the library's future, represented by the architects' schematic designs for major improvements through the library system, received strong editorial support by both newspapers. A series of community open house meetings, scheduled during the month of May, was announced by the board. The purpose of these meetings: to provide an opportunity for Allen County residents to get a closer look at the proposed projects, ask questions, and share ideas. The board will consider this feedback in making its decisions on how to proceed.The cost of the Allen County Public Library expansion project will be paid for through the issuance of bonds. These bonds will be funded from various sources including county option income taxes, state excise taxes and other miscellaneous revenues. However, the majority of the funding will be derived from property tax revenues. The library, being a county-wide institution, has a broad tax base. Since the taxes will be spread across the entire county, the impact on any individual property owner will be minimized. Some have questioned the need for physical libraries in the age of digital information. But all the evidence we have gathered in studies of the library's facility needs has led us to conclude that the library, as a place, will be even more highly valued in the future than it is today.Our new and expanded libraries will do much more than store books. They will provide an environment in which people and ideas in all formats can come together. This environment will foster intellectual exploration and the pursuit of knowledge.We are social creatures and we crave human interaction. Our libraries will be the social and intellectual anchors of our community, essential gathering places that will never be replaced by Internet chat rooms, web sites or other "virtual" environments.

Certified Burglar and Fire Alarm Systems

Certified Burglar and Fire Alarm Systems was founded in 1925 by Sylvester Koch. As of 2005, Sylvester's work ethic and goals are still being carried on by his wife Evelyn and son Steve. This family owned and operated company also has the distinction of being one of the twenty-five Charter Members of the National Burglar and Fire Alarm Association. The company's notable logo, the bright red six-pointed star, was designed by Koch to capture the eye and to instill confidence in potential Certified clients. Providing peace of mind for both residential and commercial customers was always the number one priority – and still is.

Mr. Koch initially trained with a large security company located in Chicago, Illinois. After training was completed, Sylvester returned to Fort Wayne, Indiana, to establish his own company. In 1925, Certified Alarm began operating out of Koch's home. Sylvester's future wife, Evelyn Stodgill, began working with him in 1938. She served as secretary and dispatcher for burglar and fire alarms installed by Mr. Koch and one other technician. In the late 50s, the Kochs moved to their new home on Capitol Avenue and the business went with them. In 1968, some aspects of the company were operated out of a small office/warehouse building on Calhoun Street. By the mid-70s, Certified had outgrown its home base and moved to the old Rogers Markets' office at 520 West Jefferson Boulevard. As the company continued to grow significantly, Certified purchased the corner lot on Jefferson Boulevard and Ewing Street, along with Dr. Hoard's Podiatry Office building. Groundbreaking for the new building was in 1986 during Win Moses' term as mayor. The current location of Certified Burglar and Fire Alarm Systems is 402 West Jefferson Boulevard in Fort Wayne, Indiana.

Sylvester Koch married Evelyn Stodgill in 1942. Shortly after, he was drafted. Because she had helped him with Certified during their courtship, Evelyn was able to run the company in his absence. She answered alarms on a 24/7 basis and even handled service calls at midnight with her trusty tool kit. After Sylvester returned from the Army in 1945, she resumed her duties as "office manager". In 1947, their only son Steven was born. Unfortunately, Mr. Koch was diagnosed with cancer in 1957. After his death in 1959, Evelyn and one serviceman, Charles Oberlin, managed to maintain the business for her son's future. In 1963, Evelyn Koch married Raymond Hafft and he later joined the business.

After graduation from Concordia High School in 1965, Steve decided to take some time to determine his future. After stints at a landscaping company, Rogers' Markets and Bercot-Gibson Construction, Koch elected to pursue electrical engineering in college. After graduation he joined the family business as an alarm technician. (Steve insists, however, that he often accompanied his father on service calls when he was nine years old; it was his job to hold the meter.) Steve Koch has worked in every aspect of the business including installation, repair, sales and management. Steve doubled the client base to over two thousand customers shortly after he began in sales during the mid-80s. Today, he and Evelyn oversee eleven full- and two part-time employees. The total combined years of service is over two hundred and sixty-five years. Mother and son both admit that the loyalty and dedication of the employees are important factors in the company's longevity and reliability. The *Journal Gazette's* first Quarter Century Club inductee was Tom, a Certified Alarm technician who has been with the company for other

Certified Alarm Office at 520 W. Jefferson Boulevard.

Current location of Certified Alarm Office at 402 W. Jefferson Boulevard.

thirty-five years. Certified's Central Station supervisor is Cheryl, who is another thirty-plus year employee. Evelyn, too, still logs over thirty hours every week and will turn ninety in April of 2006. She is very proud to be the only woman president/owner of a security company in the Allen County area.

Growth in the security industry has been extraordinary, especially in the past twenty years. More sophisticated electronics and computer advancements allow consumers to have an even greater peace of mind at a reasonable price. The following comparisons are some examples of changes that have occurred. Long ago intrusions were announced by clanging bells; now piercing sirens alert the police and burglars. Batteries used to be very bulky and needed to be replaced frequently. Today small rechargeable batteries power systems even during an AC failure. Not too many years before, alarm systems were turned off and on with a lock and key. Current touchpad stations can arm and disarm systems with a code as well as bypass zones. They even can have remote access capabilities. Photocells and floor trapwires used to be the primary ways to provide interior protection; however, today's infra-red motion sensors detect intruders immediately yet still allow cats and dogs the freedom to roam. Window foil protected most storefronts and some residences in the past. Currently both commercial and residential customers can use discreet glassbreak detectors that sense frequency of breaking glass during burglary attempts in window areas. Finally, alarm equipment used to be homemade. Although the systems were effective, they were large and obtrusive. With recent increased technology, state-of-the-art equipment is virtually "burglar proof" and aesthetically pleasing in any environment.

Certified Burglar and Fire Alarm Systems is dedicated to providing customers with the best equipment, reliable services and knowledgeable employees. Certified also has a commitment to continue monitoring its alarm systems at the on-site Central Station in downtown Fort Wayne, Indiana. Local monitoring is critical to emergency response times. Most national companies, on the other hand, rely on regional stations that are always out of state. Certified dispatchers pride themselves in knowing all the accounts so that the appropriate agency can be notified quickly and accurately in the event of a break-in, fire, or other type of emergency.

Steve Koch & Evelyn Hafft

Besides providing a wide range of security and fire alarm systems for homes, businesses, industries, and educational institutions, Certified Alarm also offers cellular radio backup, CCTV systems, door entry and card access systems, sprinkler monitors, environmental sensors, driveway alerts and medical transmitters.

Certified Burglar and Fire Alarm Systems has a strong eighty year history with the people of Allen County and neighboring counties as well. The owners agree that the future may bring even more dramatic technological advancements, but the service to Certified's customers will always be the number one priority.

Harris Water Conditioning

Harris Water Conditioning has served Allen County and the surrounding tri-state area since 1946. As they have progressed through the years, so has their name. Initially known as "Harris Culligan" (1946 to 1965), then "Bob Harris Soft Water" (1965 to 1977), and now "Harris Water Conditioning" (1977 to present); they have remained passionate in their ability to sell, rent, install, and service various water softening products.

Three brothers, Paul, Bob, and Bus Harris, took a chance on further developing the concept of soft water as World War II concluded. At that time, softening water was conceived as a service that was exclusively rented. Cast iron tanks filled with zealite were portably installed and exchanged each month. Freshly regenerated tanks were delivered back to the home as a regular service and the exhausted tanks taken back to be cleaned and exchanged again. This sequence enabled their business to further develop routine service routes that were paid for monthly. Thus, the birth of rental exchange tanks in greater Allen County was born.

Bob (age 18), "Bus" Richard (age 16) and Paul Harris (age 21) on August 19, 1932.

As time passed, the brothers began to develop other interests. Around 1964, Paul and Bus opted out of their shares of interest in the business to pursue other ventures. Paul's health started to decline, while Bus began to operate heavy machinery for much of the road development at that time.

Bob felt it was best to sell his shares as well, enabling the sale to reach fruition. This, however, wouldn't thwart Bob's passion for the water industry. Consequently, it gave him the impetus to continue with something of his very own. He relocated closer to his Harlan home and decided on the friendly confines of Grabill adjacent to the bank on Main Street. Initially known as "*Rainsoft of Allen County*," Bob's business became "*Bob Harris Soft Water*" upon incorporating May 11th, 1965.

Bob provided many more years of successful service with his own unique version of water treatment and customer service. Going out-to-eat with customers, inviting them to the lake, or even taking them for a ride in his '57 Thunderbird were all part of Bob's unique way of celebrating his patrons.

Tragically, the lean, 5' 11" vegetarian's life was cut short on the evening of January 4, 1977. Bob received a call early that evening alerting him there was a potential problem at his business. He arrived that evening to find it engulfed in flames. Bob collapsed at the scene, experienced a massive heart attack, and could not be revived. He was 62 years old.

Bob's widow Mary and son Tom had to become more active in the business to facilitate its survival. After several months of maintaining rentals, sales, and service, from their homes, they felt it in their best interest to sell the business. So in July of 1977, a contract was reached that allowed Dan Ulrich to purchase *Harris Water*. Dan was a Huntington County native who had worked for *Bechtold Soft Water* in South Whitley throughout the 1970s. He had actively been searching for a business when he met Tom. Dan met the criteria that Mary and Tom were looking for in a buyer and took over that summer. Dan sought and received permission to change the name officially to *Harris Water Conditioning, Inc.* He also reestablished a business home in the old Grabill Hatchery building. After several years of improvising with temporary accommodations, a permanent home was established. In 1985, a new 5,000 square foot building was erected on lot #1 in Grabill's Industrial Park. It continues to be the home for *Harris Water*.

One of Dan's biggest risks and possibly his greatest success was his decision to become an exclusive dealer of the non-electric, Ohio-based, Kinetico water softener. This concept of softening water with a softener that used no electricity, measured water, and regenerated only when absolutely necessary, has revolutionized the water industry. Today, demand water softeners are a staple for any potential consumer desiring the most elemental efficiencies in water treatment.

In 1983, Dan's successes with Kinetico products, through successful sales and productive in house rent-to-own financing, propelled Kinetico, Inc. to offer Dan a corporate position at their Newbury, Ohio, office. Dan's acceptance of this position, as undefined as it was at the time, would later result in a promotion to National Sales Manager, and ultimately, Vice-President of Sales for *Kinetico*, moving his residence to Chardon, Ohio in 1984. Dan began to see his business decline after moving 200 miles away. It lacked a hands-on, vested owner to guide and manage the business. This resulted in Dan hiring Rick Harris, who would begin his tenure with *Harris Water* on May 28, 1986.

Rick was the grandson of Bus, and great nephew of Bob. Upon completing an Associates degree from Indiana University/Purdue University, Indianapolis, he began his career as a salesman. He helped open a Harris satellite store in Huntington on April 1, 1988. On July 18, 1992, Rick was given the opportunity to become a vested owner of *Harris Water*.

Rick has continued to passionately pursue promoting Kinetico products. It is his desire to continue the reputation that Paul, Bus, and Bob Harris, along with Dan Ulrich, had worked so hard to create. As pioneers in the water treatment industry, it is Rick's goal to provide *Harris Water* customers with clean, quality water and to further this rich tradition of being the water treatment leader in Northeast Indiana. *Submitted by Rick Harris and authenticated by Mary Harris Hartzell.*

May 8, 1983, Harris Water Conditioning's temporary home was in the old Grabill Hatchery.

Harris Water Conditioning moved into this new facility on November 29, 1985.

Labov & Beyond, Inc.

Beginnings

Those unfamiliar with the story always find it surprising that the LaBov & Beyond of today—a Fort Wayne-based, 60-employee-plus marketing firm serving blue-chip corporations worldwide—had its genesis in a one-man operation. But truth can be stranger than fiction, especially where one man's vision is involved.

From the beginning, founder Barry LaBov sought to make LaBov & Beyond a company that would be known for its ethical practices, inspired creativity and extraordinary people. He launched the firm in 1981 from his own 1,000-square-foot home without a business loan. Soon he secured clients not only from among local businesses but also from companies national and international in scope—companies like Wendy's and Disney.

For the first seven years, Barry funneled all of his salary back into the business. It was in 1987, as he took on other employees, that he moved his operations into a larger home on Spy Run Avenue. Key partners in those days accepted salaries far below their market value with the understanding that things would get better. It was a profound leap of faith, but one that paid off. Today, LaBov & Beyond remains debt-free, financially strong and stable. It even provides key employees the opportunity to own a stake in the company.

Equally impressive is the abiding strength of its client relationships. An early testament to this is the 1992 honor accorded Barry LaBov by Ernst & Young: Indiana Start-Up Entrepreneur of the Year. (In 2002, Ernst & Young again presented Barry with an Entrepreneur of the Year award.)

Barry LaBov, founder and president of LaBov & Beyond; twice honored by Ernst & Young as Indiana Entrepreneur of the Year; author of numerous business books; respected speaker, strategist and futurist in the area of Field Relationship Management

Growth And Development

Key to LaBov & Beyond's growth was the 1992 acquisition of North American Van Line's marketing department. The mover had actually requested the acquisition when it approached LaBov & Beyond about becoming its Agency of Record. When the transaction was completed, LaBov & Beyond had gained considerable new video, print and multimedia capabilities.

In 1993, LaBov & Beyond purchased and moved into a new 16,000-square-foot office building at 609 East Cook Road, on Fort Wayne's north side. A new era had begun.

It was around this time that the company set about seriously analyzing its client base. Barry and his partners realized that the company's best clients all had one thing in common: a dealer/distributor or an internal sales/representative network. LaBov & Beyond determined that handling these types of clients exclusively would be its niche.

Major companies soon started asking LaBov & Beyond to be a strategic marketing partner in managing their dealer/distributor or internal sales/representative network communications. After careful review of all this would entail, the term Field Relationship Management was chosen by LaBov & Beyond to describe its niche.

Another groundbreaking event occurred in 1994, when the company created and conducted the first People's Automotive Challenge for Volkswagen of America. It gave consumers the opportunity to test-drive a Volkswagen Passat as well as competitive vehicles and compare not only specific features and benefits, but also the overall experience. The People's Automotive Challenge garnered LaBov & Beyond much recognition from the automotive industry and launched the company into major event management.

In order to facilitate more effective, face-to-face contact with its growing num-

LaBov & Beyond's second base of operations—which Barry and his staff moved into in 1987, after six years of running the fledgling company from Barry's own 1,000-square-foot home

609 E. Cook Road – LaBov & Beyond's current home since 1993.

ber of clients nationwide, LaBov & Beyond placed employees on site at client locations as far afield as Auburn Hills, Michigan, Indianapolis, Indiana, and Portland, Oregon. The company also opened its own Auburn Hills office facility in 2001.

As the new millennium got underway, LaBov & Beyond was developing considerable expertise in handling clients in industries as far-ranging as automotive, consumer electronics, petroleum, recreational vehicles, tires, transportation and trucking, to name a few. Its services had grown as well to include advertising, audio production, distance learning and other types of training, event management, marketing, multimedia presentations, print campaigns, strategic planning, video production and Web design.

Innovation And Inspiration

LaBov & Beyond has won—and continues to win – many awards for its innovative, entrepreneurial spirit and its achievements.

Among LaBov & Beyond's innovations are:

• RCA's Center for Retail Support, the consumer electronics industry's first Web site exclusively for dealer salespeople (with over 25,000 registered users)

• Freightliner's Destination – Success Magazine, a central part of the first manufacturer-sponsored owner-operator education program in the trucking industry

• Volkswagen DriversFest, a manufacturer-sponsored national festival for automotive customers

• Brand Specialist Programs for Audi, Newmar RV and Freightliner Trucks, the first dealer salesperson training and recognition programs focusing on one specialist at each retail location

• The People's Challenge, a customer-perceptions-based competitive comparison event that became a "first" not only for the automotive industry, but also for the RV, fire-hose nozzle and electronics industries

• The Umbrella Series, a collection of agency-written books, plays and Web-site presentations that address the challenges of maintaining effective corporate-to-dealer/distributor relationships

The list of honors LaBov & Beyond has been accorded to date for its creativity includes numerous Addy, Flame, Summit, Telly, Webby and other industry awards.

Giving Back To The Community

Though its scope has become increasingly national and international, LaBov & Beyond is known and respected throughout the Fort Wayne area for embracing many opportunities to help non-profit organizations and charities. Its contributions have entailed not only monetary and other gifts, but also lending its skills in graphic design, strategic planning, video production and Web design. Barry LaBov has donated generously of his own time and expertise, even serving as a board member for a number of organizations. The only reward that LaBov & Beyond has accepted is the reward that counts the most: a sense of fulfillment arising from the knowledge that it has helped make a difference.

LaBov & Beyond supports a number of community organizations, including but not limited to Children's Hope; Daybreak Children's Shelter; Fort Wayne Rescue Mission; The Greater Fort Wayne Chamber of Commerce; Indiana University Purdue University Fort Wayne; Lifeline Youth & Family Services; The Mental Health Association in Allen County; The Michigan Animal Society; and Unity Performing Arts Foundation.

Among the many national and regional organizations LaBov & Beyond helps are The American Cancer Society; The American Heart Association; Ariel – A Ministry of Proclamation (South Carolina); Cystic Fibrosis Foundation; The Leukemia & Lymphoma Society; The Salvation Army; Sisters of Life, Sacred Heart of Jesus Convent (NYC); and Vera Bradley Classic.

In 1999, Barry and his wife, Carol, set up The Barry and Carol LaBov Foundation as another venue for charitable giving. One of its major efforts, "Orchestrating Possibilities in Northeast Indiana," was conducted in February 2005. It brought together a number of Fort Wayne-area business leaders, challenging them to find new solutions to the community's most pressing and recurrent needs.

Always Moving Forward

LaBov & Beyond is distinguished by its unique blend of passion, strategic thinking, niche focus and know-how. This is what has led so many of the world's finest corporations to seek it out as a supplier and partner.

Over the years, the company has won hundreds of awards for creativity. It has received numerous business awards. And it has frequently gained positive media attention. While pleased with all this, LaBov & Beyond is most excited about the story it has yet to write with its clients. It promises to be an amazing adventure.

Lassus Brothers Oil

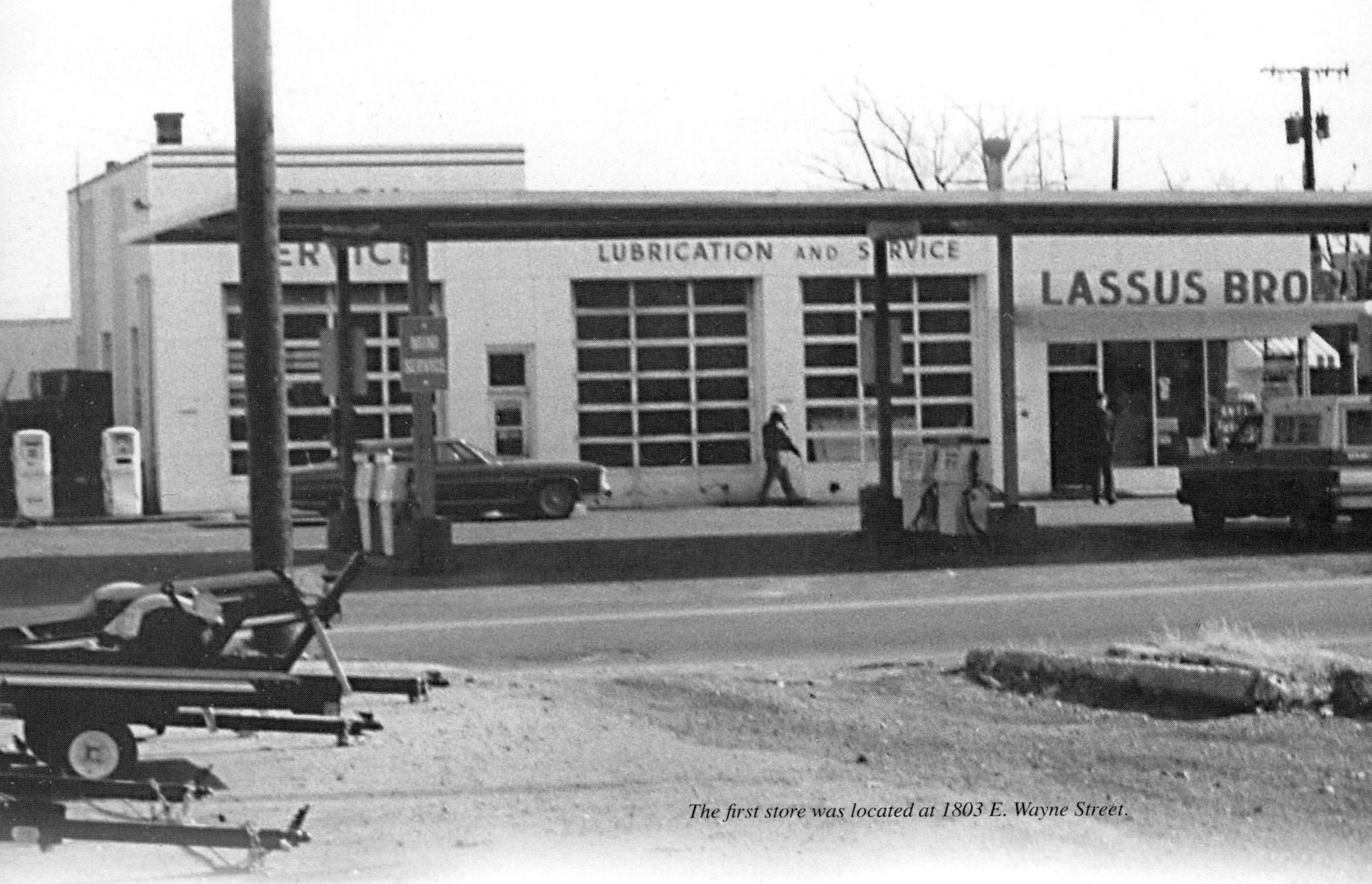

The first store was located at 1803 E. Wayne Street.

Lassus Brothers Oil evolved in 1925, when August Lassus decided to sell his coal business in order to build a gas station at one of Fort Wayne's busiest intersections. Within three years he turned the reins over to his three sons Elmer, August Jr., and William, who added gas stations around town, hired mechanics to service cars, and eventually created a wholesale fuel oil distribution division.

In 1960, Elmer's son, Jon F. Lassus, and his cousin, Bill Yarnelle, (who eventually sold his interest to Jon F.) joined the company. Their additions were most welcomed as Lassus Brothers Oil operated six very busy service stations at the time.

The 1970s provided many changes. In 1972, August Lassus, Jr. retired and Jon Lassus became president. In 1973, Bill Lassus retired and Bill Yarnelle became company vice president and with Elmer Lassus retiring in 1974 a second generation of successful management came to an end.

Under the direction and leadership of Jon F. Lassus, the Lassus Brothers Oil Co. began expanding their retail gasoline business and targeting new fuel markets, including diesel, heavy commercial-grade oil and wholesale gasoline. Additionally, even more service stations were added, thus, the stage was set for yet another successful Lassus Business venture – the Handy Dandy convenience store chain.

Lassus Handy Dandy began its convenience food store operations in 1980 as a response to a need in the community. Though Fort Wayne had offered consumers the separate services of gas stations, food stores, and sundry retailers, no retailer had offered a variety of specific items in convenient locations, available at convenient hours. The Lassus Family recognized Fort Wayne as a prime market for convenience stores.

Lassus Handy Dandy leadership is now with the fourth generation of Lassus sons - Todd, Jon R. and Greg - as well as Jon F. Lassus, who remains the company's CEO and chairman of the board.

Lassus Brother Oil Inc., owner of one of Northeast Indiana's largest independent gasoline suppliers and owner of Lassus Handy Dandy convenience stores, was awarded the 2004 Fort Wayne's Large "Business of the Year". The awards were chosen from nominations submitted by Chamber of Commerce members. The selection criteria included company growth and community involvement in 2004.

At present, with the ever changing market, Lassus Brothers Oil is working on developing new locations and constantly upgrading existing convenience stores by providing a larger variety of products ranging from car washes, ATM machines, and improved choices in food selections.

Lassus Family: Greg Lassus, Vice President; Jon R. Lassus, Vice President; Todd Lassus, President; Jon F. Lassus, CEO and Chairman of the Booard

Store #39 Lassus Handy Dandy at Scott Road and Illinois Road featuring Elmo's Subs and Pizzas and Higher Grounds Coffee.

Lupke Rice Associates

When Gustav Lupke left East Prussia for the United States he was hoping for a better life, perhaps even a life with a future. Like most immigrants he had the American dream. What he found was the life that most immigrants found. The cheap land was gone and his farm experience qualified him only as a common laborer, a helper to the more skilled masons who were building the brick structures that lined Fort Wayne's streets. He was a good looking young man and soon found a young woman willing to share his rather limited future prospects. To this union nine children were born. The oldest was Walter Herman Lupke.

Walter was a bright boy and did well in the Concordia Grade School. Both German and English came easily, but his first love was arithmetic. He did well in grade school and would have done well in high school, but the family needed help and Walter went to work. His first real job was at Doehrman's Grocery. First he stocked shelves and swept floors, but soon he was serving the customers. He could speak with them in either German or English and always added their bill correctly. It was a good job, but it didn't pay well. There was an opening at Berghoff Brewery. It was a man's job with a man's pay. You filled cases with bottles of freshly brewed beer and then loaded them on to the waiting wagons. It was hard work and exploding bottles caused terrible cuts. It was a man's job but it wasn't a career.

Machinists were skilled workers. They were respected in the community. Walter wanted that kind of advancement. He started as an apprentice, but one day he found another man at his machine. The foreman was a kindly man who said quite simply, "Walter you will never make a machinist." Young Walter asked for his check and joined the ranks of the unemployed. By now he was past high school age, but he could still go to business school. Perhaps he could learn to be a bookkeeper. He enrolled and found that his skill with numbers put him at the top of the class. He looked forward to receiving his certificate, but before finishing his training a job opened at the Citizens Trust Company. It wasn't the bank job he had hoped for. It was a job keeping the books of the insurance department. He was a little disappointed but was happy to be back working and helping to support his family.

Record keeping in a 1917 insurance agency was done by hand. Policies were typed. The books were kept by hand with pen and ink. Most of the policies provided fire insurance on dwellings or household goods. If you wanted windstorm coverage you purchased a separate windstorm policy. Each policy was recorded on the "Account Current" for the appropriate company. The bookkeeper recorded the insured's name, the policy number, the policy term, the premium, the commission and the amount due the company. At the end of the day everything had to balance. Good bookkeepers could finish their work by mid afternoon. Walter was a good bookkeeper. He spent his extra time reading the rating books and in a few months he was the office expert on rating. He liked insurance and was very good at his job. The year after he was hired he was named the Manager of the Insurance Department.

(l. to r.) Foreground: Duane E. Lupke, Walter H. Lupke, Sr., and Walter H. Lupke, Jr. on October 18, 1967.

It has been said that Fort Wayne was one third German Lutherans, one third German Catholics and one third everything else. Walter was good with the German Lutherans. What was needed was a good Catholic. That need was answered by Leo O'Brien. Leo was Catholic, gregarious and a born "good fellow". His coat pocket bulged with cigars which he passed out freely. He joined every fraternal order that would have him and after a firm handshake he was your friend for life. Leo never carried a rate book or quoted a premium. He would simply tell a new customer that "Walter takes care of that and you can count on the premium being absolutely right".

The team of Lupke & O'Brien became the insurance department of the Citizens Trust. The Trust Company was impressed with Walter. He had good potential and management offered him the position as Bank Secretary. Walter was flattered by the offer and seriously considered it, but he liked insurance and politely turned the offer down. The decision was a good one.

The year 1919 was a big year for Walter H. Lupke. He was the insurance department manager and he was making enough money to ask a handsome young woman from New Haven to become his wife. Lucy Viola Bell came from an old New Haven family. Her Grandfather's family had purchased the site of the town from a man named Samuel Hanna. They cleared the land, platted the lots and named the town after the town in Connecticut that had been near their home. The couple was married in Concordia Lutheran Church on Anthony Boulevard in June of that year. The marriage was a good one and lasted for just over fifty years.

The decade that followed brought growth to Fort Wayne and to Lupke & O'Brien, but the good years ended in 1929. The Citizens Trust Company, like many of its peers, found that solid businesses could not meet their loan payments. Loans went into default and depositors could not be paid. The bank went into receivership. Lupke & O'Brien continued to operate under the supervision of the Receiver. As part of the bank liquidation the insurance agency was put up for sale. The Lupke & O'Brien partnership was the only bidder and the Department Managers became the agency owners.

In 1936 the partnership of Walter Lupke and Leo O'Brien was ended by the death of Leo O'Brien. The "inside man" became not only the technician but also the outside salesman. The name remained unchanged for the next ten years and the cliental remained loyal to the organization and the service it provided.

The depression was severe in the Midwest, but it did not cause the economic meltdown that was experienced in Europe. Communism became a real threat in Germany. Its opposition came from the National Socialists under an Austrian Veteran named Adolph Hitler. In 1939 the world once again was rocked by war. The United States seemed very far from the troubles of Europe and the panzers of Germany rolled over the forces of Poland, France and England. On a peaceful Sunday in December while Fort Wayne enjoyed a performance of Handel's Messiah the forces of Imperial Japan destroyed the Pacific fleet and drew the United States into World War II.

The year 1942 was the year the United States became a nation at war. The young men of Fort Wayne were called into service and the empty desks were filled by women. The Insurance business had always been a man's business. Women were stenographers and secretaries. When they married they were expected to become housewives and mothers. Now the retired typists were called back to fill their husbands' shoes. They were no longer just clerical. They had to become agents and underwriters. The industry was witnessing a major social change from which it would never withdraw. At Lupke & O'Brien wives took over their husbands' business, old agents, ready to retire, continued to work and the burden of war risk insurance was handled for the commercial clients. Coverage was written for factories producing secret War material without even the most basic underwriting information. Insurance was needed and companies wrote it and never knew what they were covering.

All Wars end and when they end there is a long period of recovery. The returning veterans included a young artillery officer Lt. Walter H. Lupke Jr. He had a Chemical Engineering degree from Purdue, but he was married with a young daughter and needed a job. Insurance was close and immediate and he immersed himself in self education that ultimately included both the CPCU and CLU designations. The agency had continuity. There was someone to continue the agency when Walter Sr. retired. A few years later, after another unwanted war the second son Duane E. Lupke followed his brother into the agency. The second son had chosen to study insurance at Indiana University and after completing the mandatory two years of experience received his CPCU designation.

In 1967 Walter H. Lupke Sr. celebrated his 50th year in the Insurance industry and retired. It was marked with a bittersweet retirement party attended by dozens of company friends who had done business with the Lupke organization for many years. Lupke's failing health was obvious to all and two years later he passed into history.

Businesses constantly change and in 1972 a friendly competitor became a partner. Edward Rice had started his insurance career on his own and without that first customer. By 1972 he was well known in the community and respected as a successful businessman. His continued growth required the support of a larger organization. Lupke Insurance Agency, Inc. adopted the name Lupke Rice Associates.

As the years passed continuation once again became a question. Fortunately Stanford Rice chose insurance as a career and joined his father in the agency. The future was even more secure when David Lupke and his sister Andrea also chose to join the agency. Today Lupke Rice Associates is one of the few locally owned insurance brokerages left in the community. One by one the local competitors have been purchased by banks or out of town organizations. With each sale the city has lost a part of its history and a portion of its vigor. Like the loss of local industry it is a development to be regretted.

(l. to r.) Duane Lupke, David Lupke, and Stan Rice, 2006.

National City Bank - Fort Wayne National Bank

•1933 – March: Old-First closes after run by fearful depositors. May: Attorneys James M. Barrett, Jr. and Fred A. Shoaff spearhead campaign to form new bank. August: Stock sale begins to raise capital for a new Fort Wayne bank. October 28, Charter 13818 is approved. October 30, New bank opens with total assets of $5,584,422 and 5 employees; Fred S. Hunting named president.

•1935 – A cash dividend of 30 cents a share is paid to stockholders; employees receive a Christmas gift payment of $10.

•1937 – Employees seek to organize a union, President Hunting reiterates pledge to treat all employees fairly and urges staff to "be loyal and true to stockholders."

•1941 – U.S. enters WWII; Hunting becomes chairman of the board, Wendell C. Laycock named president.

•1943 – Bank celebrates ten year anniversary; Old-First conservatorship ends with all creditors paid in full plus 10% interest.

•1944 – Accident hits bookkeeping department, six people - including three bank employees - killed, six others seriously injured.

•1945 – WWII ends; bank sponsors "News on NBC" program.

•1947 – More than one million new businesses started nationally in past year; Hunting retires, remains on board as chairman.

•1951 – Bank opens first modern banking office at Calhoun and Rudisill; Hunting dies at age 84; Time and Temperature service starts.

•1953 – Bank is 20 years old; total assets are $78,691,506; almost 45,000 individual and business accounts; 957 shareholders, 13 directors, 19 officers, 128 employees.

•1957 – Employee profit sharing plan introduced; Southeast banking office at Anthony and McKinnie opens.

•1958 – Bank celebrates 25 years in business; 100 bank shares would now have grown to 420 with $840 in dividends paid; electronic bookkeeping is introduced.

•1960 – Bank reaches milestone of $100 million in total assets; bank makes first acquisition, Woodburn State Bank.

•1963 – Russell M. Daane becomes president, Laycock becomes chairman; bank now 310th largest in nation and sixth largest in Indiana.

•1966 – Bank acquires First Citizen's State Bank of Monroeville; President Daane announces plans for new bank building; Laycock retires.

•1968 – Paul Shaffer becomes president and chief administration officer; Daane remains chairman of the board and chief executive officer; Three Rivers Festival starts with city funding.

•1970 – Daane retires and Shaffer becomes president and chairman; bank moves into new 26 story building.

•1972 – Deposits pass $200 million mark; bank introduces 24-hour, 7-day automatic teller machine service.

- •**1977** – One-third of bank's 443 employees now work at branch offices where more than 60% of all bank business is conducted; bank creates new Three Rivers Festival major event, the Fireworks Finale off the top of the bank building.
- •**1978** – Bank reaches half-billion in assets milestone.
- •**1982** – 100-Year Flood results in Fort Wayne becoming the "City that Saved Itself."
- •**1983** – Bank celebrates 50th anniversary; Fort Wayne named "All American City." 1985 - Banking laws change to allow cross-county and out-of-state bank ownership.
- •**1986** – Bank announces acquisitions of Churubusco State Bank, The Auburn State Bank and Citizen's State Bank of Waterloo.
- •**1987** – Jackson R. Lehman becomes president and chief administrative officer; bank's assets reach $1.2 billion; acquisitions of Old-First National in Bluffton and Exchange Bank of Warren.
- •**1988** – Bank acquires the $260 million First National Bank of Warsaw and its ten offices.
- •**1990** – Bank acquires Trustcorp bank office and renames it First National Bank of Huntington; national savings and loan bailout adds an additional $600,000 to bank's operating costs, but the bank scores record gains.
- •**1991** – Lehman named CEO following Shaffer's retirement; M. James Johnston becomes new president and chief administrative officer; 48,000 square foot Operations Center opens. .
- •**1992** – Corporation's average daily assets pass $2 billion mark.
- •**1996** – Corporation acquires Valley American Bank and Trust of South Bend and its 20 offices; Lehman retires and is succeeded by Johnston as chairman, Stephen R. Gillig is named president of the Corporation and Thomas E. Elyea named president of Fort Wayne National Bank.
- •**1998** – National City Bank of Cleveland acquires Fort Wayne National Corporation which reports average daily assets of $3.4 billion and 1,531 employees; National City pledges to establish a $5 million local foundation to continue the civic work of the bank.

Information taken from *Fort Wayne National Bank – A 20th Century History*, compiled by Susan Burns.

65
FORT WAYNE NATIONAL BANK
30-floor Office Building Planned for Downtown
in Indiana
new downtown office building—possibly
aled today with the filing of legal papers
cated at Calhoun and Berry sts., west of
the tallest in the State of Indiana. It was
Fort Wayne National Bank and Central
major tenants of the building.
attorney with the law firm of Shoaff, Kee-
lest-building distinction to Fort Wayne. The Lincoln National Bank Tower was the state's tallest for many years until completion of the Indianapolis City-County Building several years ago. The Indianapolis building is
Russ Ready To Sign Pact With France
Envoy Says Treaty Possible During Visit by DeGaulle
PARIS (UPI) —Soviet Ambassador Valerian Zorin said today Moscow is ready to conclude a treaty of alliance or non-aggression with France at any time such a treaty is acceptable to President Charles de Gaulle.
Such a treaty would bring France closer than ever to the Soviet Union and would further strain ties between de Gaulle and his NATO allies.
Zorin said the Soviet Union is perfectly ready to conclude such an alliance during de Gaulle's trip to the Soviet Union in June.

The News-Sentinel

On July 6, 1833, Fort Wayne residents flocked to the offices of *The Sentinel* while two men in the office applied ink to a plate of type on an old printing press. They inserted a clean sheet of paper, pulled the lever on the hand-operated press, then removed the first copy of the first newspaper printed in Fort Wayne. They gave copies of *The Sentinel* – direct ancestor of *The News-Sentinel* – to the waiting crowd.

Starting *The Sentinel* was a calculated gamble in the future of Fort Wayne. In 1833 the city had only 300 residents. The canals and railroads that helped spur the city's development hadn't been built. There wasn't a paved road in town, no large church steeples on the skyline, no mayor, no carriages on the streets and no cookstoves in the homes.

Before those developments, Fort Wayne had a newspaper. The reason *The Sentinel* appeared on the scene so early in the city's history is that six local businessmen had enough faith in their town to instigate the founding of the paper.

Those six men – who were Fort Wayne's first entrepreneurs – had names that read like a city street map: Henry Rudisill, Lewis G. Thompson, Joseph Holman, C. Ewing, Allen Hamilton and Francis Comparet. They banded together and asked two Indianapolis printers to come here to start *The Sentinel*. They offered to loan the men $500 to buy a press and set up the business, and risk nothing but a year's labor. If the newspaper wasn't a success, ownership of the press would revert to the six men.

The printers, S.V.B. Noel and Thomas Tigar, eventually rejected the offer, but they must have been convinced the idea was worthwhile. Noel and Tigar set up *The Sentinel* with their own money, buying a second-hand press in Indianapolis and hauling it here on a six-day trek across swollen rivers and muddy roads.

Although no copies of that paper have survived, historians record that the first edition contained a reprint of the *Declaration of Independence* and a description of the Fourth of July celebration of 1833. Most of the news was reprinted from newspapers in cities such as Cincinnati, Toledo and Indianapolis, which had served previously as the only source of news for the area.

Timeline Of The News-Sentinel

1833 The first issue of *The Sentinel* is published by S.V.B. Noel and Thomas Tigar.

1861 *The Sentinel* becomes *The Daily Sentinel*

1865 *The Daily Sentinel* is sold to owners of *The Times*. The two papers are merged into *The Fort Wayne Times and Sentinel.*

1866 *The Times and Sentinel* is sold and becomes *The Democrat.*

1873 *The Democrat* is sold and renamed *The Sentinel.*

1874 *The Fort Wayne Daily News* begins publishing.

1892 C.F. Bicknell buys *The Sentinel.*

1918 *Fort Wayne Daily News and The Sentinel* are merged to create *The News-Sentinel* under Bicknell.

1920 Bicknell dies; Oscar Foellinger becomes president.

1926 *The News-Sentinel* moves into new building at Washington and Barr streets.

1936 Oscar Foellinger dies and his daughter, Helene Foellinger, becomes president and publisher.

1950 *The News-Sentinel and The Journal-Gazette* form Fort Wayne Newspapers Inc. to operate their advertising, circulation, accounting, promotion and mechanical departments.

1957 *The News-Sentinel* moves to its current offices at 600 W. Main Street.

1980 Knight-Ridder purchases *The News-Sentinel.*

1982 *The News-Sentinel* wins the Pulitzer Prize for local reporting for coverage of the flood.

1991 *The News-Sentinel* is redesigned with an emphasis on local news.

1992 Scott McGehee is named publisher of *The News-Sentinel* and president and chief executive officer of Fort Wayne Newspapers.

1996 *The News-Sentinel*'s Web site is launched.

1997 The teal edition of *The News-Sentinel* is introduced. It is aimed at readers ages 19-34.

1998 *The News-Sentinel* introduces Tributes, doubling the space for obituaries and presenting them in a more dignified way.

2001 Mary Jacobus is named publisher of *The News-Sentinel* and president and chief executive officer of Fort Wayne Newspapers.

The Sentinel was the first newspaper in town, but Fort Wayne grew so rapidly several other publications came here in the next decades. By the end of the century the city was served by six daily newspapers. *The Sentinel*'s competitors included *The News*, *The Gazette*, *The Journal*, and two German language newspapers, *Staats Zeitung* and *Freie Press.*

The Sentinel remained neutral in politics for nearly a year, at which time Noel sold his interest to Tigar. Under the latter's management, *The Sentinel* became a Democrat newspaper politically. Tigar sold *The Sentinel* to George W. Wood in 1837 and the paper became a champion of Whig policies.

In 1840, *The Sentinel* was sold to I.D.G. Nelson, who returned the editorial leanings to the Democrat interests. Nelson held *The Sentinel* for one year before selling it back to its founder, Tigar.

From the beginning, *The Sentinel* was published with "considerable regularity" until January 1, 1861, when Tigar issued the first edition of the *Daily Sentinel.* Tigar retired in 1865 after selling the *Daily Sentinel* to W.H. Dills and I.W. Campbell who owned *The Times*. *The Times* and *The Gazette* were the other two newspapers operating in Fort Wayne at the time Tigar retired. Dills and Campbell merged their two papers under the name of the *Fort Wayne Times and Sentinel.*

On January 15, 1866, Dills and Campbell sold the *Times and Sentinel* to E. Zimmerman and Eli Brown who changed the newspaper's name to *The Democrat*. Between that date and January 30, 1873, several individual companies directed *The Democrat*. In 1873, however, the firm of Dumm and Fleming (R.D. Dumm and William Fleming) restored the name of *The Sentinel* to the newspaper. In April, 1874, a corporation known as The Sentinel Publishing Company was formed to manage the newspaper. In 1877, Fleming became the sole proprietor of *The Sentinel*. Fleming owned the newspaper until April 16, 1879, when he sold it to William Rockhill Nelson and Samuel E. Morss.

Nelson and Morss sold *The Sentinel* to Edward A.K. Hackett on August 1, 1880. They then left Fort Wayne to found the *Kansas City Star.* Hackett held *The Sentinel* until his death. The

News Publishing Company took over *The Sentinel* from Hackett's estate and combined it with the *Fort Wayne News* under its present name, *The News-Sentinel*.

The first edition of *The News-Sentinel* appeared on January 1, 1918.

The *Fort Wayne Daily News* was started on June 1, 1874, by William D. Page and Charles F. Taylor. The *Fort Wayne Daily News* became known as 'the people's paper' because of its local interest emphasis. It remained politically unaffiliated until 1892 when a company headed by C.F. Bicknell purchased it. The paper then became a strong advocate of Republican policies. Bicknell was in charge at the time *The Sentinel* was taken over by the News Publishing Company, and remained in charge of the merged newspapers until his death in 1920.

On Bicknell's death, Oscar G. Foellinger became president and general manager of the News Publishing Company. He directed *The News-Sentinel* until his death October 8, 1936. Upon his death, his daughter, Helene R. Foellinger, became publisher of *The News-Sentinel* and president of the News Publishing Company. At age 25, she was the youngest publisher in the nation and one of the few women to lead a newspaper.

On March 3, 1950, Miss Foellinger also became president of Fort Wayne Newspapers, Inc., an agency corporation formed when Fort Wayne's two daily newspapers, *The News-Sentinel* and *The Journal-Gazette*, became partners in a merger of business and mechanical departments. *The News-Sentinel* and *The Journal Gazette* continue to be separately owned and separately edited papers.

In 1957, *The News-Sentinel* and *The Journal-Gazette* news departments and the Fort Wayne Newspapers business, advertising, marketing, circulation and production departments moved into their current office building at 600 West Main Street, Fort Wayne, Indiana 46802.

On February 20, 1980 Helene Foellinger announced that an agreement had been reached to sell *The News-Sentinel* to Knight Ridder Newspapers Inc. The sale became final April 9, 1980 and *The News-Sentinel* became the thirty-fourth newspaper in the Knight Ridder group. Miss Foellinger continued as publisher of *The News-Sentinel* while Phil deMontmollin, former president of the *Lexington Herald* and *Lexington Leader*, (also Knight-Ridder newspapers), became president and chief executive officer of Fort Wayne Newspapers, Inc. Miss Foellinger remained as publisher of *The News-Sentinel* until her retirement on October 13, 1981. Peter Ridder and Rick Sadowski followed deMontmollin as president and CEO of Fort Wayne Newspapers in the mid-1980s and early 1990s, but Knight Ridder did not name another publisher for *The News-Sentinel* for more than a decade. Ironically, the next on-site publisher of *The News-Sentinel* was a woman, Scott McGehee, who was given the additional responsibility and title of publisher of *The News-Sentinel* when she was named president and CEO of Fort Wayne Newspapers in 1992. Upon McGehee's retirement, Mary Jacobus took over as president and CEO of Fort Wayne Newspapers and publisher of *The News-Sentinel* in 2001.

Important Dates In News-Sentinel History

- January 1833 - Six Fort Wayne entrepreneurs invite two Indianapolis printers to start *The Sentinel*, Fort Wayne's first newspaper.
- July 6, 1833 - The first copy of *The Sentinel* was printed.
- June 1874 - The first copy of *The Daily News* was printed.
- January 1, 1918 - Fort Wayne's two evening papers - *The Sentinel* and *The Daily News* - merged, creating *The Fort Wayne News and Sentinel*.
- February 20, 1980 - Helene Foellinger, publisher of *The News-Sentinel*, announced her decision to sell the newspaper to Knight-Ridder Newspapers Inc. for $36 million.

O'Brien & Sanderson

In post WWII Fort Wayne, when jobs were few but diligence and perseverance were flush, a home-grown success story was born. Fort Wayne natives and good friends, Ray E. Sanderson and Robert O'Brien together took a risk – on an industry that hedged bets on risks. Sanderson, a graduate of the International Business College, and O'Brien, a Notre Dame University graduate, had both been working for Lupke & O'Brien Insurance Agency. Sanderson had earned experience there for nine years, and O'Brien, son of the principal owner Leo O'Brien, for three years. In early 1946 after the death of Leo O'Brien the two decided to start their own venture. They knew Fort Wayne was ripe for an agency that could offer a variety of insurance lines for varying risks. And so, armed with a combined 12 years' experience and a company motto that seemed appropriate for the times and venture, "We stand between you and loss", the aptly named O'Brien & Sanderson became Fort Wayne's newest independent insurance agency. With a commitment to service and roots firmly planted in Fort Wayne, O'Brien & Sanderson opened its Berry Street doors on July 1, 1946, representing many large nationally-known stock, fire and life insurance companies.

"They saw an opportunity and took a risk," says Morrie Sanderson, son of Ray and President of O'Brien & Sanderson for thirty years before its sale to Toledo-based Hylant Group in 2000. "I can honestly say that fifty-five years later when we sold O'Brien & Sanderson to Hylant Group, it was my Dad's and Uncle Bob's founding principles and their unwavering commitment to people, both clients and employees, that remained."

Morrie and Ray at the 40th Anniversary Open House.

When the fledgling O'Brien & Sanderson opened its doors in mid-1946 its principal owners seized opportunities where available, staying true to the agency's motto. By 1957 they had grown the company to $75,000 in revenues, had four full-time employees, and through a pro-active approach to customer service had firmly planted themselves in the Fort Wayne and regional business scene.

In 1960, Sanderson's son, Morse ("Morrie"), a recent graduate of Bowling Green State University joined the 14-year old company. "They couldn't really afford another executive salary at the time," recalls Morrie. "But the industry was undergoing some significant changes that allowed us to seize untapped opportunities." The major changes were the adoption of a direct billing procedure, where an insurance company would send an invoice directly to the customer; and a new line of insurance known as Homeowners' Insurance, both of which revolutionized the way insurance companies did business. Homeowners policies gave significant additional coverage while direct billing offered lower premiums. O'Brien and Sanderson tasked Morrie to help capitalize on these changes. He spent his first five years at O'Brien and Sanderson making evening house calls -- lots of them – and convincing the home owners to convert fire policies to Homeowner's policies. That, coupled with the conversion to the direct bill method, kept Morrie gainfully employed. While other local agencies were slow to adopt, O'Brien and Sanderson embraced these changes aggressively, giving the company a competitive edge over other agencies in the region.

By 1965, Homeowners insurance was successfully enveloped into the O'Brien and Sanderson personal insurance mix, allowing the company to expand more vigorously in to the commercial insurance lines area, then only 25-percent of its overall business. It was the beginning of significant change for O'Brien & Sanderson.

In 1971 Robert O'Brien died, leaving Ray Sanderson to run the business. Ray maintained the company's name and continued the focus on its commercial lines business. By 1975, O'Brien and Sander-

Morse Sanderson

Ray E. Sanderson
Founder

Robert L. O'Brien
Founder

son was 11 employees strong and boasted $350,000 in revenues, sharing both personal and commercial line success. It was then that Ray stepped down as President and Morrie assumed the role, shepherding the company through the next 30 years of growth and prosperity.

By 1986 O'Brien and Sanderson was a dynamic leader in the insurance industry in Fort Wayne and regionally. O'Brien & Sanderson celebrated its 40th year serving nearly 3,000 individual clients and over 400 business and professional clients throughout Indiana and in 12 other states. Its commercial lines business had flipped from 25-percent of the company's business in 1971 to nearly 75-percent in 1986, making it a regional leader in providing business insurance. Still an independent insurance company, O'Brien and Sanderson distinguished itself among its competitors as a risk-taker – a company willing to embrace technology and adopt processes and automation that would continue to make it better. "We were enjoying great success, but I still wanted to improve," says Morrie. "I recall looking in the yellow pages and counting over 200 insurance listings in the Fort Wayne area. It was a competitive landscape and we needed to figure out a way to run our company as a business, not as an insurance agency. That was going to set us apart."

O'Brien & Sanderson did just that over the next 20 years, streamlining its functions and employing forward-thinking, motivated employees. Of those new employees was Morrie's son, John Sanderson, who joined the company in 1993 as an automation expert. Under John's supervision, O'Brien and Sanderson converted to a paperless system and adopted the process of computer-based quotes. These changes quickly placed the company ahead of its peers in automation. "Our success after that are a direct result of John's contribution," says Morrie.

When O'Brien and Sanderson celebrated its 50th anniversary in 1996, the company had 13 employees, including Morrie's two other children, Chris and Jill, and revenues exceeded $1million. O'Brien & Sanderson was a company with sophisticated market knowledge, accessibility and credibility.

When Morrie chose to sell O'Brien and Sanderson to the internationally-respected Hylant Group in 2000, it wasn't because he wanted to retire. Much like his father and O'Brien felt over 55 years ago, and like he experienced over his 30-year tenure as President, Morrie just wanted to make it better. At the time of the sale, O'Brien & Sanderson was a $1.5 million revenue company with over 75-percent of its business coming from commercial clients. Hylant Group, a Toledo-based insurance company with 70 years of insurance experience, had the resources to make it better. "They could invest in staff and really raise the bar," says Morrie. "Their strength in the marketplace combined with an unfaltering focus on people is what allowed me to sell O'Brien and Sanderson with confidence. I knew my Dad and Uncle Bob's commitment to people would continue."

Today, Morrie serves as Chairman and Chief Operating Officer at Hylant Group in Fort Wayne. Jill, the only Sanderson child to remain in the insurance business, serves as Account Executive. Hylant Group's revenues in Fort Wayne have quadrupled in the five years since its purchase of O'Brien & Sanderson in 2000.

"The Hylant Group's Fort Wayne success carries with it my grandfather's and father's commitment to people and relationships," says Jill. "Just like my grandfather before him, my Dad has incomparable credibility, contacts and knowledge in this market. His role is as critical to our success today as it was 30 years ago."

Asphalt Drum Mixers, Inc.

Asphalt Drum Mixers, Inc. was incorporated on August 3, 1983. ADM, Inc. evolved from Panco, Inc. founded in 1967 by Wayne and Linda Boyd. The primary product of Panco was electric control panels for The Wayne Pump Company, Central Soya, Peter Eckrich, General Electric and American Electric Power. By 1983, Panco was primarily manufacturing asphalt plants. Because of the different product emphasis, Panco, Inc. was dissolved and ADM, Inc. was established.

ADM was founded and is currently headquartered in Huntertown, Indiana. Michael G. Devine is President with Mark Simmons serving as Vice-President and General Manager.

The Company started with twelve employees and has employed as many as seventy, but fifty seems to be the optimum number. From its inception, the Company profits have been shared by owners with employees. Each employee is individually graded according to his/her responsibility level, incentive, attendance, and years of service. This year more than 90% of full-time employees' profit share will equal or exceed their annual salary.

To date, over 700 road building units have been sold by ADM. The plants are located throughout North and South America as well as Africa, Russia , Australia and Indonesia.

ADM employees with owners, Wayne and Linda Boyd – Dylon Allen, Rex Barrett, Timm Bilger, Jr., Cathy Boren, Mark Bower, James Browning, Lynn Brown, Stave Crabill, Jason Delcamp, Michael Devine, P. Timothy Dice, Jeff Dunne, Todd Dunne, Ben Freck, Dennis Koch, Ralph Lahrman, Tony Lawyer, Jim Lawyer, Jim Maggart, Larry Martin, Jason Messmann, Mike Munro, Chadd Neace, Jon Nei, Eric Ott, Ryan Ott, Greg Parsons, Jon Patti, Mark Pfeiffer, Charlie Rasler, Aaron Reaser, Doyle Rhodes, Robert Semprini, Steve Shawd, Mark Simmons, Dean Timmerman, Ray Wagner, Chris Warner, Nathan Warner, Don Wine, and Phil Wyatt. The following employees are not pictured in the photograph: Carlos Cardenas, Rolando Haddad, Don Holbrook, Keith Hults, Dennis Jordan, Calvin Krieger, James Scott Owens, Jeff Riecke, Larry Schaeffer, and Gary Warner.

Baker & Daniels LLP

When Partner Reed Silliman looks back at the last few decades at Baker & Daniels, he sees a firm that has adapted to the changing needs of an increasingly global marketplace without abandoning its core principles and hometown roots.

As such, Silliman sees a firm that offers the community the best of two worlds in a number of ways: It's the product of a merger between two law firms that have been in operation since the 19th century, but it's a decidedly 21st century organization; it's big enough to meet the corporate and banking law and commercial litigation needs of Indiana's leading corporations, and yet focused enough to serve individual clients; it's part of a statewide organization with offices reaching as far as Washington, D.C., and China, but it continues to play a key role in the lives and commerce of Allen County.

In short, Baker & Daniels is a firm that's familiar with both the corridors of power as well as the hallways of the Allen County courthouse. And regardless of the arena in which it's operating, the firm remains committed to one objective: unmatched client service.

"We strive to distinguish ourselves by providing a level of service that is respectful of and responsive to the clients we are fortunate to have," Silliman says. "That has always been the driving force behind our success."

Baker and Daniels

A Long Allen County Presence

In Fort Wayne, Baker & Daniels ties its lineage back to 1881, when Judge William J. Vesey first hung out his shingle. Vesey's practice grew, evolved and changed names through 1981, when the firm then known as Shoaff, Keegan, Baird and Simon merged with Parker, Hoover, Keller and Waterman to become Shoaff, Parker & Keegan.

The result of that merger was a powerhouse Allen County firm that had played a key role in the creation, development and growth of leading area businesses and continued to provide legal services to some of the city's largest employers. A full-service firm with an emphasis on corporate and business law, Shoaff, Parker & Keegan provided counsel to a long list of manufacturers, retailers, wholesalers, real estate developers and professional services organizations that included Central Soya Co., Tokheim Corp., Lincoln National Corp. and General Electric Co.

Having been involved in some of these companies since their early days, Shoaff, Parker & Keegan grew with them to meet their growing needs. As those companies expanded nationally and even globally, the law firm added to its capabilities as well, equipping itself to meet these companies' daily legal needs as well as to provide counsel on such matters as initial public offerings, mergers, acquisitions, sales and leadership changes.

Silliman says the best outcome of having such an impressive client list and expanding services was the firm's ability to continually add to its greatest resource, the professionals who practice there. "The fact that we've been able to grow and attract and retain some of the best and the brightest in our profession means we have a population of resources that we otherwise wouldn't have had," he says.

A Win-Win Merger

Almost two decades before Judge Vesey opened his law practice, a future U.S. vice president opened his own law office in Indianapolis. Thomas A. Hendricks, who later served as the No. 2 man in Grover Cleveland's administration, teamed with former Indiana Attorney General Oscar Hord to start Hendricks & Hord, the foundation for Baker & Daniels, one of the state's largest legal practices.

Today, Baker & Daniels provides a full range of business and legal counsel to clients across the state, throughout the nation and around the globe. With offices stretching from South Bend to Beijing, the firm boasts a client list that includes Fortune 500 companies, regional businesses, nonprofit organizations, local governments and individuals. These include such firms as Cummins Inc., Eli Lilly and Co., Kimball International, Lilly Endowment, Rolls-Royce North America Inc., WellPoint Inc. and Zimmer Inc.

In the mid 1980s, the leaders of both Shoaff, Parker & Keegan and Baker & Daniels recognized that their firms were at crossroads. Shoaff, Parker & Keegan needed to grow in order to continue to compete, and Baker & Daniels wanted to expand into northern Indiana. When the firms collaborated on a project for a public company headquartered in Allen County, they discovered another factor that made a merger practical: The firms shared a commitment to delivering unparalleled client service. In 1986, they joined forces.

Today, Allen County citizens and businesses continue to enjoy the fruits of that merger: A local firm with global resources and an ongoing passion for client service. Long a key player in the growth and development of the community and its most dynamic businesses, Baker & Daniels has positioned itself to provide the legal counsel for the companies and community of tomorrow.

Barrett & McNagny LLP

James M. Barrett (right) formed Aldrich & Barrett with Charles H. Aldrich in 1876. Phil McNagny (left) joined the firm in 1925, and it became known as Aldrich, Barrett & McNagny.

Fort Wayne's history is tied to Barrett & McNagny LLP one of the oldest and largest law firms in Northeast Indiana. For more than 129 years, the firm has worked to promote its clients, many of them Fort Wayne business leaders and community organizations, to the pinnacle of success.

In 1876, James Madison Barrett joined Charles Aldrich to form Aldrich & Barrett. In 1925, Phil McNagny joined the firm, which then became know as Aldrich, Barrett & McNagny.

In 1987, the firm officially moved to its current location on Berry Street in a building that is as much a part of Fort Wayne history as Barrett & McNagny. Once known as the Elektron Building, it was built in 1895, and is listed today in the National Historic Registry. From 1898 to 1902, it served as the Allen County Courthouse. In1904, the building housed the Allen County Public Library while a permanent library was under construction. Lincoln National Life Insurance Company adopted the Elektron Building as its headquarters from 1912 to 1923.

One of Barrett & McNagny's greatest assets is a history in Fort Wayne that dates back more than 129 years. Doing business so long in the city makes the firm's attorneys better able to understand the local marketplace and assist their clients.

Today, Barrett & McNagny LLP continues to play an important role in Fort Wayne's development. Since its founding, the law firm has helped establish and sustain many of the area's leading businesses and public institutions. Barrett & McNagny works primarily with clients from the business community, including banks, utilities, insurance companies, health care providers, manufacturers, and media companies together with many small and medium-size companies. These clients are located mainly in Fort Wayne, northern Indiana, and western Ohio, although several have operations worldwide.

Barrett & McNagny LLP offers its clients a full range of legal services. Specialty areas include business and real estate; employment and labor relations; employee benefits; environmental, estate planning and administration; finance, securities, and taxation; health care; intellectual property, litigation and dispute resolution; media and communications; and bankruptcy and creditors' rights.

The firm assists companies as they form new businesses; buy and sell real estate; finance development; solve employment problems; comply with environmental laws and other state and federal regulations; execute retirement plans and health plans; protect copyrights and trademarks; collect debts; and resolve business disputes and conflicts through negotiation, arbitration, trials, and appeals. Its attorneys also provide personal legal services, including adoptions, wills, trust and estate planning and administration.

Barrett & McNagny LLP remains committed to its clients by offering specialized legal services. The firm recruits attorneys with the expectation that they will develop a specialty and become expert in a particular area of law. By developing this expertise, the firm can better serve the diverse needs of its clients. Clients discover that Barrett & McNagny provides them efficient, affordable, high-quality legal representation, continuing the tradition of excellence the firm has developed.

Just as Barrett & McNagny LLP has contributed to Fort Wayne's growth, so too has Fort Wayne helped mold the firm into what it is today. Fort Wayne is a community with good people and good values, which translates into good business practices. It is a privilege to do business with the people who live and work in this community.

The attorneys and other personnel at Barrett & McNagny LLP take active roles in the community, many of them volunteering as leaders in various organizations. The firm also supports the community through donations of pro bono legal time, and each year it selects different ways to support various community organizations.

Barrett & McNagny's leadership extends into the legal community as well. Throughout the firm's history, it has had various attorneys serve as the president of the Indiana State Bar Association, as well as other offices at the national, state, and local levels.

The challenge for the future is to maintain the high standards and quality that have been a Barrett & McNagny LLP tradition. Through that commitment, the legal needs of the firm's clients will be well served.

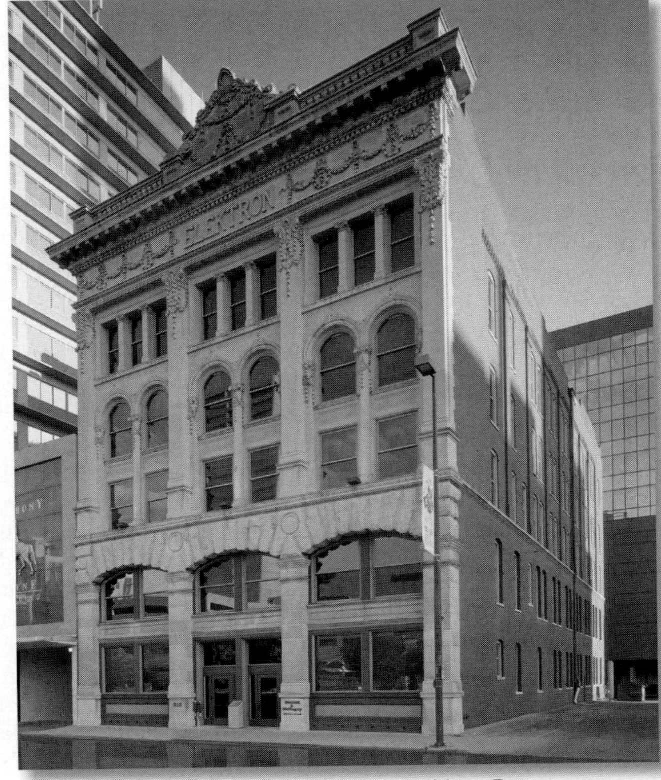

Once known as the Elektron Building, Barrett & McNagny's office was built in 1895.

Carl Schwieters established the Belmont Liquor Store in 1933, following the repeal of prohibition. At the corner of Lewis and Calhoun Streets, which is now the site of the Grile Administration Building, Carl also added a restaurant called the Flagship. The restaurant closed in 1960. Tom Druley, looking for a business opportunity, purchased the Belmont from Carl in 1971. Tom was 31 years old. His father and brother owned their own businesses and he wished to do the same. Tom received a degree in marketing from Indiana State University, worked three years as a buyer for Wolf & Dessauer, and five years in management for General Telephone.

In 1975, the City of Fort Wayne by right of eminent domain forced Belmont from the Lewis Street location. This same year Druley purchased stores at Southgate Plaza and Decatur Road. In 1979, he bought Frank Miller Liquors at Northcrest Shopping Center. Since 1975, Belmont has maintained a retail, business office, and warehouse at 1118 South Harrison Street. Today the city is again forcing the Belmont to move for the expansion of the convention center. West State Plaza became the site of a Belmont in 1983. Clarence Brase Liquors, with three locations, was purchased in 1984, and the Maplecrest store was added that same year. Benefit wine tasting began at this time, the first to aid the Museum of Art. The seventeenth wine tasting to benefit Northeast Indiana Public Radio took place in the spring of 2005.

The Belmont expanded to the South Bend–Mishawaka area in 1989, with five stores that have grown to eight. The current total of Belmont retail outlets in northeast Indiana is twenty-five employing 180 people. Druley will always point out that his people are the key. Gary Gardner, as operations manager, has been with the corporation for 32 years. Another long-term employee who contributes greatly is John Coffman, the wine buyer. All employees are trained in customer relations and product knowledge. Store managers rotate through the stores to gain experience and establish consistency. Clair, Tom's daughter, joined the company in 1993, training first as a clerk, then store manager. Clair has a degree in psychology from Purdue University and a MBA from the University of Saint Francis. To date Clair has performed every job to make the sale happen from unloading delivery trucks to changing out a computer. She is currently Vice President and will succeed her father as President of Belmont Beverage Stores in 2006. Tom will remain as CEO.

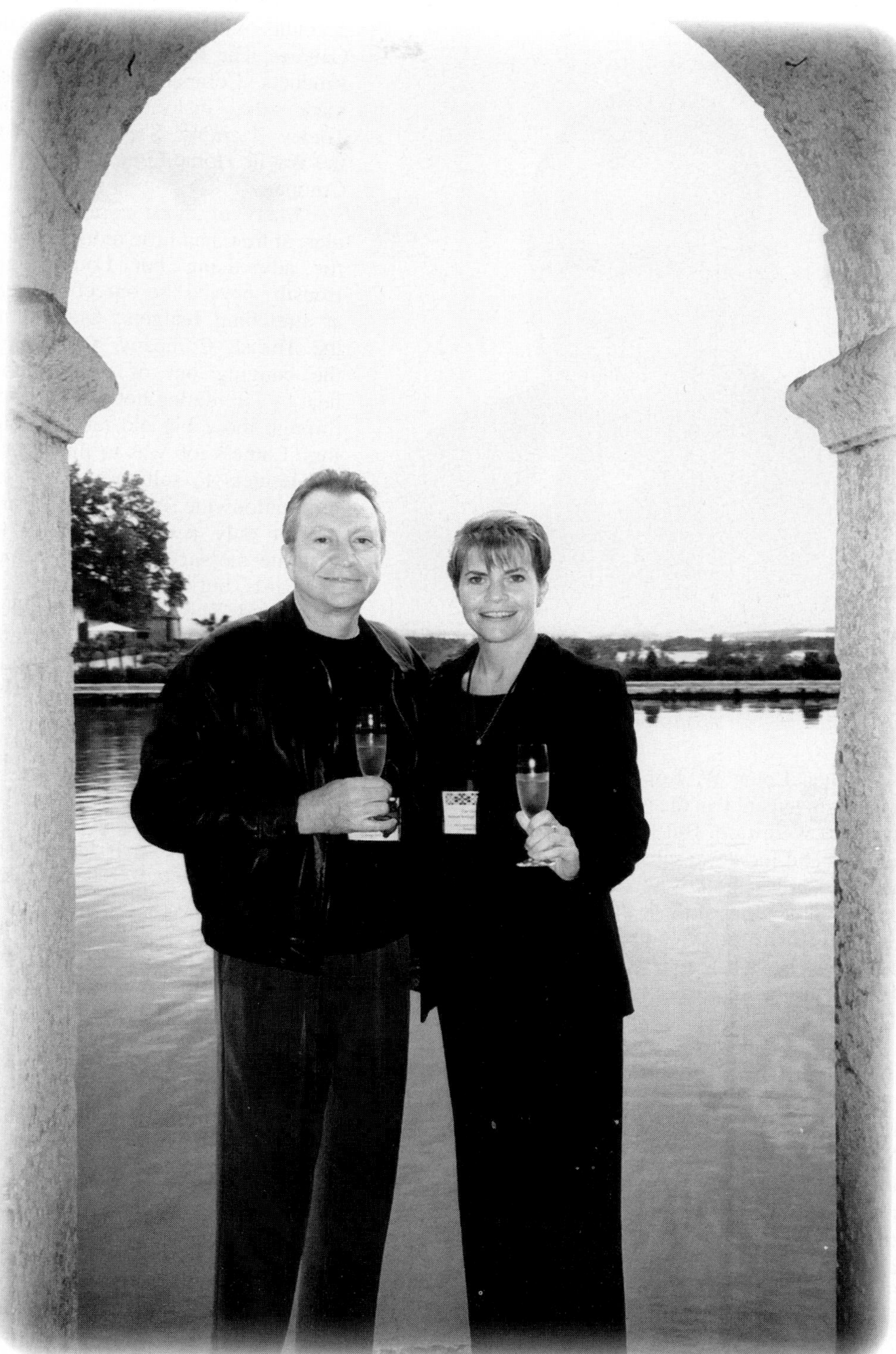
Tom Druley and Clair Druley selecting wine in Portugal in 2004.

Bonsib, Inc.

Louis Bonsib in 1947.

When Louis W. Bonsib opened his advertising agency in the mid-1920s, such agencies were rare. But he soon brought success and lucrative sales to many Indiana companies and it is a tribute to his ingenuity that many of those companies are represented in this volume. Born March 10, 1892, Bonsib graduated from I.U. in 1916. During his senior year, he edited The *Arbutus*, the University's yearbook, which gave him experience in photography, engraving and printing. He then went to work for the Indianapolis Engraving Company, serving clients along the Wabash River, often suggesting creative ideas for their advertising. These companies were so pleased with his input that they convinced Bonsib to start his own company.

Drawn to Fort Wayne because of its location between three major markets - Chicago, Detroit and Cleveland, Louis opened Bonsib, Inc. in the First National Bank Building in 1924, offering "Advertising and Sales Counsel." He brought many of his engraving clients with him: the H. A. Thrush Company in Peru; B. Walter Company, Wabash Filing Supplies, and Ford Meter Box Company in Wabash; Huntington Laboratories, and the Nurre Mirror Company in Bloomington. Before long Bonsib acquired new accounts with Lady Wayne Candies, The Juvenile Wood Products Company (which made the historic Little Toidey Training Seat) and the Wayne Home Equipment Company.

Many of those companies, at first, had little money for advertising but Louis Bonsib proved resourceful at stretching budgets. One, the Thrush Company, took the banging out of steam heat by circulating hot water through those big old radiators. Louie's job was to find wholesalers to sell the system nationwide. At first, the budget only permitted him to write messages on penny postcards, but he got the job done and Thrush achieved national success.

Bonsib had a knack for finding the right word or turn of phrase that could engage the buyer's imagination. When Wayne Home Equipment developed an oil burner for furnaces, Bonsib touted it as a solution to what he called coalatosis, the endless shoveling of dusty coal. Soon, many homeowners were converting to oil heating. An offshoot became The Wayne Pump Company which developed the first gasoline pump that could measure both volume and price. An inveterate reader, Louis named it the computing pump, a word he found in the dictionary that was little known at the time. In another Wayne Pump ad, he coined the phrase "Fill 'er up" which became part of our everyday language.

He also saw opportunity in popular culture. One of Bonsib's earliest clients was a wagon wheel maker named Rastteter who had expanded his operation to include wooden folding chairs. At that time, contract bridge was growing rapidly in popularity and it was competing with baseball to become America's national pastime. Bonsib convinced Rastteter to create a "bridge set" combining four chairs with a folding table. Bonsib took the sets to New York where he hired several outstanding bridge players, including renowned player Ely Culbertson to sit on the stage of the new Roxy Theater and play cards at Rastetter's bridge set. He got stores along Fifth Avenue to feature it in their windows. Sales soared.

In the 1940s, Louis Bonsib began taking his sons into the business. The first was Louis, Jr., known as Bill. However, as World War II started, Bill decided to enter the Army Air Force. Later he moved to Denver starting his own agency.

A second son John, following military service, worked for a major advertising agency in New York City where he gained considerable expertise in using the newly emerging medium of television. Returning to the Fort, that experience proved a boon as WKJG- TV, and others went on the air in the1950s. Under John's guidance, Eckrich became a major sponsor of Hilliard Gates sporting events. Shortly viewers were singing one of the area's first singing commercials: "E-C-K-R-I-C-H spells Eckrich. Eckrich, the house of fine meat specialties!"

Under John the advertising agency became the largest in Indiana, serving numerous clients: North American Van Lines, Rea Magnet Wire, Starcraft, Raker House Trailers, General Homes, Lincoln National Bank, McMillen Feed Mills, and Franklin Electric, and other long term clients.

By the 1970s, things began to change in the Bonsib agency. John left to build Fort Wayne's first cable company. Other members of its highly creative staff, trained by their tenure at Bonsib, left to take major positions at large agencies around the country. Then Dick Bonsib took the helm. With his wife Gretchen serving as his chief financial officer, he rebuilt the agency, renaming it Bonsib Inc. Marketing Services.

In 1975, he acquired a new client based on a marketing strategy which included a business plan. The Selmer Company was the leading manufacturer of band instruments for the rapidly growing rock music industry. Dick's use of business plans created a new strategy for Magnavox, which enabled the company to sell TV sets for use in the rapidly expanding hotel-motel business. Dick expanded the company from about 10 in 1972 to 45 by 1992. In addition to the Fort Wayne office, he had set up an office in Indianapolis to reach into the vast resources of that market.

After a long battle with Parkinson's disease, Dick died in May 2003, bringing to an end the long and successful role that the Bonsib family played within the local, state and national advertising scene.

Albert Neuenschwander, co-founder of Brotherhood Mutual, stands in front of the Eli Hoffman House at the corner of Wayne and Broadway in Fort Wayne. One of the city's most stately homes when it was built in 1887, Hoffman House was used as Brotherhood Mutual's corporate office from 1942 to 1950.

One of the nation's leading insurers of churches and related ministries grew from the dream of two Allen County men. Businessman Albert Neuenschwander and his pastor, the Rev. Aaron Souder, believed it would be good for the Defenseless Mennonite Church of North America to follow the example of other Mennonite groups in associating to provide protection from fire and storm losses.

In 1917, the denomination approved the organization of the Brotherhood Aid Association of the Conference of the Defenseless Mennonite Church of North America. The denomination is now called the Fellowship of Evangelical Churches. In its first year, the association brought in $943.93 and recorded $481.31 in assets. The association recorded 188 policies at its first annual meeting in 1918.

For its first two decades, the association wrote only fire insurance policies for Mennonites. Its first home office was a 20' x 40' room in the Grabill Post Office. In 1935, the association was incorporated as Brotherhood "Mutual" Insurance Company of the Conference of the Defenseless Mennonite Church of North America. Its charter allowed it to insure buildings and personal property against loss from such perils as fire, wind, earthquake, snow, sleet, invasion, insurrection, riot, and war.

By 1939, the company needed more space for its home office, and it relocated to Fort Wayne, a predominantly German city of about 115,000 people. In 1940, the Church of the Nazarene became the first non-Mennonite denomination to affiliate with it. The name was shortened to Brotherhood Mutual Insurance Company in 1944, and in 1953, the A.M. Best Company, an independent analyst of insurance companies, gave Brotherhood Mutual its first rating, an "A."

Introducing a homeowner policy in 1957 marked Brotherhood Mutual's entrance into the casualty business. Four years later, the company passed the $1 million mark in annual premium. In 1965, it introduced an insurance package designed specifically for churches.

The year 1965 proved a crucial one for Brotherhood Mutual. The company nearly went bankrupt after 30 tornadoes on Palm Sunday tore through the Indiana communities of Berne, Goshen, and Marion, causing more than $1 million worth of damage to Brotherhood Mutual policyholders. The company's reserves totaled only $1.4 million. The company managed to pay its losses by recovering money from reinsurance and selling some of its assets.

After Paul A. Steiner became president in 1971, Brotherhood Mutual took several steps to become more competitive. It added a mobile homeowners policy, a personal automobile policy, a church vehicle policy, and pastoral counseling liability coverage. In 1980, the company moved into its present headquarters at 6400 Brotherhood Way, which expanded in 1995. New management systems and five-year plans for profitability and growth helped to increase policyholder surplus twentyfold from the 1970s to the 1990s. During this period, the company also recruited large, independent agencies with the experience and resources to specialize in church insurance.

James A. Blum became president and CEO in 1995, and the company has continued to expand under his leadership. In 1999, it introduced Passport to Ministry®, a groundbreaking product that combines insurance coverages and travel assistance services for both short-term and long-term mission trips. MinistryFirst®, its main product, offers property and liability coverage for churches, camps, schools, colleges, daycare centers, and other Christian ministries.

The company's Web site, www.brotherhoodmutual.com, offers hundreds of free risk management articles for churches and related ministries. There, church leaders can learn about the importance of performing background screens on workers and link to a site providing discounted screening services. The Web site also offers resources for churches that can help them deal with everything from hiring employees to preventing child sexual abuse.

By early 2005, Brotherhood Mutual was licensed in all 50 states and the District of Columbia. It employed more than 200 people in Allen County and was represented by more than 400 agents from 160 independent agencies nationwide.

Over 88 years, the company grew from a fire protection association for one denomination into a comprehensive property and casualty insurance company. The original 188 active policies have become nearly 70,000 and the company's assets are now worth more than $250 million.

As the 21st century unfolds, Brotherhood Mutual is poised to continue building on its history of product innovation, financial stability, and service excellence for America's churches and related ministries.

Brotherhood Mutual's corporate offices are located just off Interstate 69 in north Fort Wayne.

Busak+Shamban

The W.S. Shamban Company was founded in 1952 by William Shamban and Henry Traub in Culver City, California. Providing products for industrial sealing and bearing systems, the company was known for its quality manufacturing and its high customer service levels. The company opened its second location on Meyer Road in Fort Wayne in 1958. In the early 1960s, it moved this facility to a new building located at 2531 Bremer Road in New Haven, Indiana.

The company grew throughout the decades that followed, acquiring additional manufacturing locations throughout the United States and opening regional sales offices to better serve their customers. These acquisitions allowed the company to diversify its product lines and sell into new industries.

In 1992, the W.S. Shamban Company was acquired by European-owned Busak+Luyken. The resulting company was named Busak+Shamban. The Busak+Shamban Americas division headquarters and a manufacturing plant are still located in its facility on Bremer Road.

In 1997, Busak+Shamban expanded its Fort Wayne facility, building a 43,000 sq. ft. addition. Named the HAT Center after co-founder Henry A. Traub (HAT), this new facility houses the Busak+Shamban Americas headquarters as well as a corporate research and development laboratory.

In 2003, Busak+Shamban became a part of the Trelleborg group, retaining its established business name. Trelleborg is a global industrial group with annual sales of approximately $3 billion with about 21,000 employees in 40 countries. The head office is located in Trelleborg, Sweden.

Mostrecently,in2004,Busak+Shamban opened its Logistics Center Americas at 3410 Meyer Road in Fort Wayne, Indiana. The 24,000 square-foot facility houses administrative offices, the Busak+Shamban Americas Great Lakes Marketing Company, and the logistics center warehouse. When fully stocked, the LCA will house thousands of SKUs and use the latest in warehouse management technology, including bar coding and RF scanning, to assist in productively and accurately fulfilling customer orders.

Today, Busak+Shamban has grown to be an international network of over 60 facilities worldwide. They include manufacturing sites, materials and development laboratories, and design and application centers.

Busak+Shamban Research and Development Centers (R&D) are engaged in material and product development. The company maintains a database of over 2,000 material formulations, and works to develop new compounds that meet the needs of its customers. The R&D group developed high-performance polymers for the most demanding conditions with temperature extremes from -425°F to 617°F. The company's Fort Wayne R&D laboratory houses a variety of testing equipment to prove seal performance over time as well as materials testing equipment to determine performance characteristics of material formulations.

With 30 strategically located manufacturing sites worldwide, Busak+Shamban is committed to best-practice techniques and cost-effective manufacturing. Its fully integrated production facilities ensure the highest quality standards, from design and compound formulation through to product manufacturing, final assembly and shipping. The company's Fort Wayne manufacturing plant achieved its first ISO 9001 certification in 1994 and its original AS9100 certification in 2004.

Busak+Shamban's president is Claus Barsøe. Mr. Barsøe has been active within the company since 1985, and was a key figure in the merger of Busak+Luyken with W.S. Shamban. Prior to becoming president in 2003, he managed the sales, research and development, logistics, and marketing divisions in Europe. The President of Busak+Shamban Americas is Tim Callison. Mr. Callison joined W.S. Shamban in 1986 as its manufacturing managers of the Newbury Park, California production facility. Prior to becoming the divisional president in 2003, Tim served in a variety of production, engineering, sales and marketing capacities.

The company's core business – developing sealing systems – has not changed over its more than fifty year history. Busak+Shamban provides over 40,000 sealing and polymer products for a variety of industries including: automotive, aerospace, mechanical engineering, stationary hydraulics, mobile hydraulics, pneumatics, fluid power engineering and electrical engineering, chemical industry, process engineering, food and pharmaceutical industries, semiconductor/chip manufacturing, oil and gas equipment, sanitary and heating technology, as well as medical engineering.

Busak+Shamban At A Glance

- Part of Trelleborg Sealing Solutions, a business area of the Trelleborg Group
- Company-owned Research and Development Centers in Europe and America
- 30 company-owned manufacturing plants worldwide
- Quality Certifications: ISO 9001, QS 9000, VDA 6.1
- Company-owned polytetrafluor-ethylene- and polyurethane-development
- Company-owned elastomer development
- More than 2000 material formulations
- Worldwide distribution network

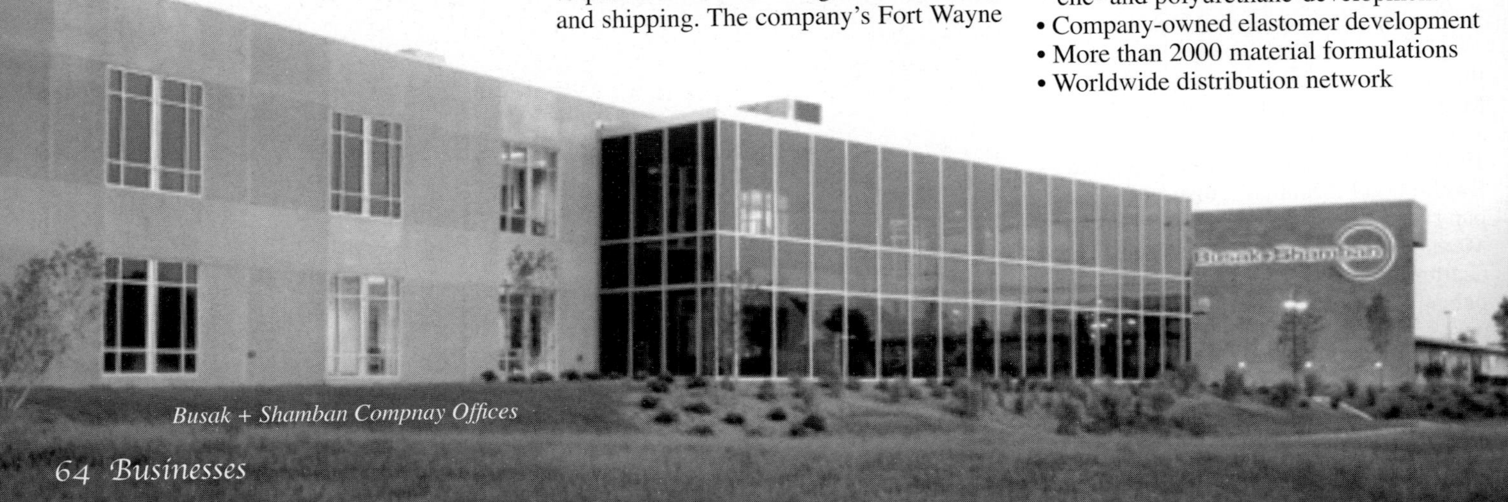

Busak + Shamban Compnay Offices

Cap n' Cork

After the repeal of Prohibition in 1933 Argire Lebamoff began selling beer and wine from a building next to his grocery, the Liberty Grocery, located on Piqua Avenue (now South Clinton). Working long hours at the Liberty Gourmet and Liquor store, George learned his dad's work ethic. "Don't stand around," he always said. "Stay busy: wash windows, wash floors, clean the shelves. Talk to the customers, find out what they want. Move and rotate the stock, make it attractive. If you want to get ahead, you've got to work hard; then you can play hard."

When George first met Rosemary Tsiguloff, age 17, at St. Nicholas Orthodox Church, he was smitten. George was older, having been to college and the service. Rosie's mother and George got along well, but her dad was unsure about the age difference. But, during Rosie's senior year, she became seriously ill with mononucleosis and was in bed for two weeks. George visited often during that time, and her father began to like George a little better. Then, when they became engaged, he wanted them to marry as soon as possible. They married on February 20, 1955. On returning from their honeymoon, George's father loaned him the money to buy the inventory for the liquor store behind his grocery. Rosie helped at the store and did the bookkeeping.

In 1958 George opened a second store, Variety Liquors, on U.S. 27 on the north edge of the city. On the roof of the store was a big billboard with a caricature of George smoking a cigar. While not able to advertise prices at that time, he advertised to "let George do it" if you were having a party. George credits his father and father-in-law both with being a great help to him in the early days; both had words of wisdom.

With the liquor business increasing, George had the resources to expand into other areas of the city, eventually owning six small stores: Liberty, Variety, and four Lebamoff's locations - on East State, Lafayette, Bluffton Road, and North Anthony Boulevard. In 1964 he had the opportunity to open a store in the new Glenbrook Mall shopping center. He incorporated Lebamoff Enterprises, DBA Cap n' Cork, and would eventually use that name for all of the stores.

George Spahiev was married to George's sister Marie, and he became manager of Variety Liquors. George's older brother Ilia, known as "Louie," managed the Bluffton Road store. George Spahiev managed Variety Liquors for nearly nine years. One day in 1972 a kid on drugs came in and demanded the money. George reached in the register and gave him about $50, telling him it was all he was getting. The kid became angry and told George he wanted all the money. George grabbed him and tried to take the pistol. They struggled and the gun went off, hitting George in a main artery. George was taken to Parkview Hospital, where he died about three hours later. He and Marie had one son, Gregory. That was a tragedy in the family, a boy without a father, Marie without a husband. The kid was caught and is still in prison.

Grand opening at Coldwater store, May of 1980, Andy, Tom, and John.

Photo taken from the December 1989 Business Digest *(l. to r.) Nick Lebamoff, Joe Doust, Andy Lebamoff, and John Lebamoff.*

In 1975 Lebamoffs opened Indiana's largest and most modern liquor "super store," a 5,000 square-foot corner building with a full basement at the Georgetown Square shopping center. George sold his small stores at this time. The store was decorated in a plush 1890s theme, with hardwood floors and an underground wine cellar. Customers came from all over the Midwest to shop at the store, a new concept in alcoholic beverage retailing. Louie Spahiev became the manager at Georgetown.

In 1980 they built the second largest liquor store in Indiana, the Cap n' Cork at 5430 Coldwater Road, more than 10,000 square feet. Around this time, George's boys and several of their friends began to help in the stores with the cleaning and vacuuming. In 1983 two more stores were added, on Broadway, and at Times Corners. Daughter Debbie married Joe Doust who came into the business. Debbie also worked at the Geogetown store as office manager. In 1989 they opened the Casual Gourmet, a grocery/bakery/deli next door to a new Cap n' Cork at 4520 Lima Road.

A major factor in Cap n' Cork's success has been the assistance of so many loyal employees, some with them 25 years or more. In 1995, when he was 68, George Lebamoff retired and sold the business to son Andy and son-in-law Joe. They have expanded the operation to fourteen Cap n' Cork locations in the Fort Wayne area, and they are the largest beer and wine retailer in Indiana. George taught his children about business just as his father taught him: The customer is always right; don't argue. Don't fix the problem; resolve the problem. They've shown that theirs is a respectable business, with people who care about providing good service.

Crossroads Flowers

In 1960, a dream became a budding time for Bill and Vivian Cearbaugh and Crossroads Flowers became a reality. They opened for business at 6221 Meyer Road. Many people said that they were too far out of the city to make it work, but they decided to give it their best shot. The store was 4½ miles from Crescent and Anthony, which at that time was the closest shopping center. Crossroads started in a very small way, but in a year they began to have people aware that it was a budding business. At that time, Meyer Road was a two-lane, stone-covered road but word got out and people began calling in orders. In five years the business had grown until they were doing a lot of weddings for young brides.

That was a great steppingstone. In 1965, the business moved into a remodeled two-car garage. In 1973, the store had grown enough that the Cearbaugh family made the big decision to move out of their home and make it a full service florist shop. How exciting the day was when they made the transition! It wasn't too long until they realized they needed more room and made an addition of a full service plant room. The business is still growing and in 1995, a large display area was added to the front of the store.

There had been talk for many years that the two-lane road should be wider. The name of the road was then changed from Meyer Road to Maplecrest Road. Maplecrest Road was widened even more. In front of Crossroads it is now a five-lane road. All this time Crossroads continued to grow and needed to hire more staff to be able to serve the community more efficiently. Bill and Vivian's middle child, Malinda, was the first employee of Crossroads and has been with the company all these years. She is now Malinda Cearbaugh-Bennett and her own middle daughter, Stephanie Bennett-Bass, is the head designer for the company. In 2004, Stephanie became accredited with the prestigious American Institute of Floral Designers (AIFD).

Crossroads has been a good influence in our community. One of the things they are proudest of is the number of young people they have been able to train to be good employees no matter what field they entered after getting a college degree. Crossroads has also sponsored St. Joe Center Little League for boys and girls for more than 25 years. They have also enjoyed supporting Charis House by donating more than $10,000.00 from proceeds of their Beanie Baby sales. The staff at Crossroads Flowers enjoys seeing to it that the women and their families at Charis House get flowers throughout the year. They make similar contributions to Hope Alive and Samaritan House. You can hear their sponsorship on the local Christian Radio Stations. They have sponsored WBCL for more than 20 years and WFCV for more than 15 years.

Vivian and Malinda have served in all positions of the local Tri-State Allied Florist Association. Vivian has been very active in several social groups like Toastmasters, SCORE, Optimist and Garden Club. Malinda actively makes donations to Grace Community Outreach and Charis House and enjoys donating her quilts to local fundraisers as well. Vivian Cearbaugh-Gordon and Malinda Cearbaugh-Bennett have taught more than 30 years for IPFW's Continuing Education program. It has given young and older people an opportunity to be introduced to the world of flowers. Some came hoping to beautify their own homes and others wanted to be employed at a flower shop. On a rare occasion, some had dreams of creating their own new floral business. Vivian and Malinda have had the excitement of seeing the dreams of some of their students come true. They are training the fourth generation too. Vivian's great granddaughter's, Alivia (4) and Madaline (2) Currington, have learned to love flowers and are eager to come to the flower shop and make bouquets. *Submitted by Malinda Bennett.*

Crossroads Flowers, 1974.

Crossroads Flowers, 2001.

Daisy Wheel & Ribbon Co., Inc.

The national recession of 1980-1982, was especially painful in Fort Wayne, Indiana. Allen County's largest employer, International Harvester, laid off thousands and eventually closed its production facility in Fort Wayne leaving 10,000 people, including Ronald Dearing, without a job. The devastating recession made it even more difficult for these 10,000 workers to find employment.

Although many Harvester UAW (United Auto Workers) members believed in Harvester's future strength and growth, Ron grew concerned about his job security having worked for Harvester for eleven years. As a result, he began to seek a more secure future within small business. Ron's fear became reality when he was laid off in 1981. While in their early thirties, Ron and his wife, Linda, cared for their three young daughters by cashing in their life insurance policies, working part-time jobs and using their savings to survive. In order to pursue his desire of becoming a small business owner and controlling his own destiny, Ron immediately traveled to California to learn about word and data processing supplies from his brother-in-law, Stephen Baer. Linda's father, William C. Baer, gave the couple money for some initial inventory. In October 1981, Ron and Linda opened Daisy Wheel Ribbon Company as a woman-owned small business. In December of 1982, the business was incorporated.

Ron and Linda began Daisy Wheel in a spare room in the basement of their home with no customer base and very little capital. They began calling on Fort Wayne businesses at a time long before computers and printers were on every home and office desk. Typewriter ribbons and daisy wheels, the first printing elements for the original word processors, made up a large percentage of the company's sales.

In the early 1980s, volume printing was done on dot matrix printers, and Ron's mechanical knowledge enabled him to develop a process for remanufacturing cartridge printer ribbons The printer cartridge itself was re-used many times; Ron replaced the worn out ribbon with new inked ribbon each time the cartridge was remanufactured using equipment he designed and made himself.

In order to keep Daisy Wheel competitive in the severe economic downturn, Ron and Linda opted to not receive a salary for two years, choosing instead to reinvest in their business. Daisy Wheel outgrew the basement and in 1986, the couple leased a much larger space on Gettysburg Pike in southwest Fort Wayne. This new location provided more space for offices, inventory such as laser, fax, and copier toner, diskettes and computer accessories, and a much larger remanufacturing area which allowed Daisy Wheel to grow.

Since its inception over twenty years ago, Daisy Wheel & Ribbon Co., Inc. has been a leader in providing brand name and remanufactured computer supplies to the Fort Wayne area. Printer technology has continually changed over the last quarter century, and new products have been added to the compatible product line of laser, ink jet, and fax cartridges. Daisy Wheel has grown with these technological advances and has recycled tens of thousands of plastic printer cartridges.

Ron and Linda learned from Harvester's collapse in Allen County, and, in 1985, Daisy Wheel joined The Greater Fort Wayne Chamber of Commerce to support locally owned, small businesses. Unlike large companies whose profits funnel to corporate headquarters outside Fort Wayne, small businesses keep their profits in the community, making Fort Wayne a better place to live and raise a family.

Perhaps the biggest challenge for Daisy Wheel over the years has been the perception that big superstores deliver the lowest prices; that small businesses cannot compete. Daisy Wheel has survived and competed for twenty-five years with a mixture of hard work, quality products, competitive prices, personalized service, and product knowledge.

In 1992, John Mozzone joined Daisy Wheel while completing his bachelor's degree in marketing at IPFW. Today he is vice president of sales keeping Daisy Wheel profitable and thriving.

Daisy Wheel is located at 2727-1 Lofty Drive, Suite #1, Fort Wayne, Indiana, and celebrates its twenty-fifth anniversary in October, 2006. (*Submitted by Linda Dearing*)

E. Harper and Son Funeral Home

E. Harper & Sons Funeral Home at US 930 E.

E. Harper & Sons Funeral Home at 939 Main Street.

The oldest business in continuous operation in New Haven and the oldest family-operated funeral home in Allen County, the E. Harper and Son Funeral Home provides families of this area with a caring homelike atmosphere born of the experience of four generations with deep roots in this family-centered, church-oriented community in east Allen County.

Edward Harper (1855-1928), a second generation son of Scots-Irish William Harper of County Tyrone, Ireland, purchased the funeral home in March 1889 from Brent Lovell. Lovell, a cabinet maker as was Harper, had owned the business located at the corner of Middle and Broadway Streets since 1872. Harper embalmed in the deceaseds' homes until 1910 when he moved to 1244 Summit Street where he was able to install more modern embalming equipment. He built most of the caskets himself using purchased hardware for embellishment.

Emmet Edward Harper (1884-1958) associated with his father in the business in 1902 which then became E. Harper and Son Funeral Home. In 1924 he moved the business to 939 Main Street, a two-story brick Italianate former boarding house, where he and his family lived on the second floor. His wife, teacher Fannie Golden Greenawalt Harper ((1889-1980) held a funeral director's license and was an active partner. Three of their six children, George, Homer, and Stanley, became licensed upon graduation from mortuary science institutions. George (1910-1954) helped his father and retained his license until his death. Stanley (1926-) worked in the business from 1948-1971 as a funeral director and embalmer.

Homer Hugh Harper (1923-) joined his father in business upon discharge from the US Navy in 1946, attending Blackburn College and graduating from the Indiana College of Mortuary Science. In 1947 he married Erna Verle Van Hoek (1924-1987) who was a partner in the family corporation. The family of four (Kristine, Gregory, Lisa and Mitchell) lived above the business on Main Street which underwent remodeling in 1953 to expand the chapel, offices and add more modern conveniences as well as additional parking. The family also maintained an ambulance service until 1979. Sons Greg and Mitch were the first in Allen County to become licensed emergency medical technicians. Homer remains a well known figure in the town and active in the community affairs and the business into his 80s, retiring in 2004.

Gregory Lee Harper (1950-) became a full partner in the family business in 1974, helping with everyday tasks and on college weekends while he was growing up. He attended Hanover College and IUPUI and graduated from the Indiana College of Mortuary Science in 1974. In 1981 an expanded new modern facility was opened at US 930 E and Werling Road, the former site of the Schnelker farmstead. Currently the business has five full time employees, including wife Janel Gruelach Harper as a pre-need counselor and business manager, Cindy Myers, licensed embalmer and funeral director and Susan Norton, administrative assistant.

Of growing up in the business, Greg Harper says, "The funeral business was a way of life. Our parents' attitude was always 'How can we be of service?' and that carried over into our thinking about business and the community." Harper's offers funeral trust or insured funeral pre-planning through "The Family Choice Plan". This unique family-owned business remains committed to meeting the needs of the families of Allen County.

Ellison Bakery, Inc.

Ellison Bakery, Archway "Home Style Cookies".

Ellison Bakery began in a one and a half car garage at the country home of Leonard and Marie Ellis on the Ellison Road, Fort Wayne, Indiana. It was the summer of 1945, and Don Ellis, the second of ten children, (See Leonard and Marie Ellis Family) had been employed as a baker for five years. It was always his dream of starting his own bakeshop. He purchased a donut fryer, Blodgett Oven, Hobart Mixer and the necessary utensils. His father built the vital worktables, dry ingredient bins, proof box, and installed the equipment.

Don's dream, which was to be just the first of a life-long fulfillment for the entire family, was ready for a practice run. Cake donuts were the first item and all the neighborhood kids were on hand to sample that first batch. The first few years Don's schedule was to bake all night, freshen up, and deliver his product to the groceries and restaurants in the area. After a few hours of sleep the process would be repeated, six days a week.

The business blossomed and brother, Bill, joined Don and later brother, Dick, took over the delivery routes. It continued to prosper and a larger shop was needed. A building was erected at Homestead Road and U.S. 24, (Ellisville) which included a restaurant, service station, mini grocery, garage, and later a motel was added. Don moved his bakeshop to the new location in November 1948. The restaurant, service station, grocery and garage opened in April 1949. The entire family became involved at this point and each filled in wherever needed as the business was open 24/7, except Christmas day.

In the fall of 1949, Don and his father were approached with a franchise offer, accepted, and began making, "just cookies". It was just a few short years and the "new" building was getting short of space. Property was purchased at Baer Field and a new plant with state of the art equipment was built in 1964. Ellison Bakery Inc. produced Archway Cookies for over fifty years, serving the franchised areas of Indiana, Wisconsin and Kentucky.

Archway National Office of Battle Creek, Michigan, has purchased the original franchise, and today (2005), just specified varieties of the Archway brands are made at the Baer Field plant. Ellison also produces special formulated cookies and various flavors of crunch, which are used on ice cream novelty items nation wide

Ellison Bakery, Inc., is now under the leadership of the third and fourth generation of the Ellis family. *(Submitted by James A. Ellis.)*

Ellison Bakery, Inc.

Fort Wayne Children's Zoo

The Fort Wayne Children's Zoo is internationally recognized for its innovative displays, award-winning animal exhibits, and well-manicured grounds. Local residents embrace the zoo as a great place to spend a sunny afternoon. But this world-renowned zoo had humble beginnings.

In 1952, 54 acres were added to Franke Park to establish a nature preserve, where monkeys, bears, wildcats, deer, mountain goats, raccoons, foxes, porcupines, pheasants, ducks, swans, and an American eagle were displayed. The popularity of the nature preserve encouraged local officials to consider building a full-fledged children's zoo.

By 1962, the planned exhibits included an Indian Village, a prairie dog colony, mammal dens, hoofed animal areas, and Noah's Ark. The zoo would be run by a staff of three, with seven employees added during the summer months.

Plans in hand, the city's Board of Park Commissioners appointed a 65-person Advisory Committee to foster interest in the zoo and raise money.

Fort Wayne rallied behind the project. Within three years, the committee raised $350,000 and secured $200,000 in donated materials and services.

By 1963, preliminary site work was underway. Local tradesman donated their time while "zoo boosters" from age two to 12 collected pennies to buy an elephant. Community groups sponsored animal exhibits.

Earl B. Wells was hired in 1964 to supervise the new Children's Zoo – a position he held until his retirement in 1994.

On July 3, 1965, the 5½ acre Fort Wayne Children's Zoo opened to the public. Attendance that first day was 6,000. From the start, the zoo was one the nation's few self-supporting zoos, earning all revenue from admissions, rides, and concessions.

The Fort Wayne Zoological Society was established in 1966 as a nonprofit organization to assist in the development and growth of the zoo.

By 1967, Amos, a rare bonobo (pygmy) chimpanzee, was the zoo's most popular resident. He rapidly became the zoo's mascot and goodwill ambassador.

In 1969 the Zoomobile program visited every third grade classroom in Allen County. This educational program grew from visiting 50 classrooms in 1969 to nearly 400 in 2004. Programs like this only increased the zoo's popularity.

In 1971, plans were unveiled for the African Veldt. The Veldt would use architectural elements, such as thatch-roofed huts and stick fences, to "immerse" visitors in the African theme when it opened in 1976.

1976 also marked the first Christmas Time at the Zoo, a tradition that continued through 1994.

Meanwhile, zoo animals visited playgrounds, nursing homes, and hospitals.

Earl Wells, Founding Director

Zoo education programs grew to include tours, presentations, and a weekly "Zoo's Who" television program. The Zoological Society became one of the largest in the nation, with a membership of 6,186 families.

In 1979, another tradition came alive: the Great Zoo Halloween. Thousands of pumpkins were carved and painted for this event.

By 1982 there were about 550 animals in the zoo, with 12 permanent staff and 50 seasonal workers. Nearly 100 volunteers helped where needed.

A survey of area school children determined the theme for the zoo's next major addition, the Australian Adventure. More than $2.5 million was raised to build the exhibit.

The 1987 opening of the Australian Adventure was the year's crowning event. The zoo broke all attendance records, and received a prestigious award from the professional zoo community.

In the early 1990s, the Fort Wayne Children's Zoo received a flurry of national recognition. Mentions in *Cosmopolitan* magazine, the *New York Times*, *Child* magazine, and ABC's Good Morning America brought unprecedented publicity to the zoo. In a survey, zoo visitors rated their zoo experience 9.6 out of 10. The zoo generated more than $14 million annually in tourism dollars for the community.

Conserving endangered species is part of the zoo's mission. In 1990, the zoo sponsored a project in Indonesia to protect five species of rare monkeys and apes. Nearly 15,000 students raised funds to "adopt" an acre of rain forest.

From this project came the idea for the zoo's next major expansion. Zoo officials detailed plans for the Indonesia Rainforest display in 1992. Within a year, the zoo had raised $5.5 million.

The first phase of the exhibit, a domed rain forest jungle, opened in 1994. Orangutan Valley, the second phase, opened in 1995, followed by Tiger Forest in 1996.

Interest in the zoo soared, and attendance topped 540,000 visitors. The zoo again was honored with awards from professional colleagues and zoos. Veteran zoo employee Jim Anderson took over as zoo director.

The late 1990s and early 2000s saw a new animal and display every year –worms, rattlesnakes, Sea Lion Beach, the Indiana Family Farm—growth in education programs, increased involvement in conservation efforts, and more than 12,000 families in the Zoological Society. The zoo covered 38 acres, housed more than 1,500 animals and employed 45 people year round, with another 100 workers added in the summer.

Bringing people and animals together and fostering an appreciation of wildlife has been the Fort Wayne Children's Zoo's mission – from its humble beginnings as a nature preserve to its current status as a world-class zoological facility.

Fort Wayne Medical Laboratory
1905—2005

Original location at 347 West Berry Street.

The Fort Wayne Medical Laboratory (FWML) was founded in 1905 by Dr. Bonnelle W. Rhamy. Dr. Rhamy was a graduate of the Fort Wayne College of Medicine (Indiana's first medical school). He was the first to provide surgical pathology services in Fort Wayne and first to perform a Wasserman test (for syphilis) in Indiana.

During the 1920s Dr. Rhamy was joined by chemist Paul Adams. Adams received the first certificate in Medical Technology from the American Society of Clinical Pathology.

Dr. Rhamy organized a regional group of physicians with the skills to provide a variety of medical tests. To do so, he developed relationships with outlying hospitals and physicians from as far away as Richmond and Plymouth, Indiana.

In the early years, the FWML office was located in the Medical Center Building at 347 West Berry Street in downtown Fort Wayne. FWML occupied an office adjoining that of Fort Wayne Radiology. The two shared a reception area but were separate businesses.

During the 1930s Dr. Rhamy brought several associate pathologists on staff and began to supervise laboratory services at Fort Wayne Methodist Hospital (now Parkview Hospital). Dr. Karl Schlademan came on board as an associate pathologist in 1948, and worked at FWML until his retirement in 1985. When Dr. Rhamy died in 1950, Dr. William Van Buskirk of Fort Wayne Radiology took over major ownership of FWML.

Upon Dr. Van Buskirk's death in 1952, Dr. Schlademan became owner of FWML. Dr. Charles Frankhouser joined FWML in 1955 and he and Dr. Schlademan began an association that would last for 30 years. In 1982 Dr. Frankhouser became owner of FWML and Laboratory Director for Parkview Hospital. Dr. Frankhouser retired in 1990 with 35 years of service.

A Century Of Firsts

In 1979, in partnership with Parkview Hospital, FWML established Fort Wayne's first electron microscopy service. FWML also developed the capacity to perform other new tests to serve patients across northeast Indiana. These include: flow cytometry (a better way to classify lymphoma, leukemia and other malignancies); and Focal Point (an automated Pap smear screen that significantly reduced the incidence of false negatives and the need for repeat testing).

In 1982 FWML moved from downtown Fort Wayne to its current location in the Parklake Medical Office Building, at 2470 Lake Avenue. Around that time, the group's leaders made the decision to change the organization from a combined anatomic and clinic laboratory to a dedicated anatomic laboratory. This move allowed FWML to provide more comprehensive services in cytology and surgical pathology.

As of 2005, FWML employs seven board-certified pathologists: Dr. Robert Burkhardt, Dr. Blandine Bustamante, Dr. Seung Soo Kim, Dr. S. Sage Lee, Dr. R. Craig McBride, Dr. Darryl Smith (who serves as president) and Dr. Y. Karen Wan. FWML employs a support staff of 19 people. The company provides medical directorships, cytology and surgical pathology services to nine area hospitals, surgical centers and physician's offices.

FWML's pathologists teach at the Medical Technology School at Parkview Hospital. For 15 years the pathologists were the major contributors to the Pathology Education program at the IU Medical School, Fort Wayne Campus. FWML's members share a history of active participation in the local medical society. Both Dr. Frankhouser and Dr. Lee are past presidents.

"Our 100th anniversary gives us a reason to reflect on how far the Fort Wayne Medical Laboratory has come," said Dr. Smith, president. "Our goal is always to give the best services to our patients and physicians. We want to keep our services in Fort Wayne for another 100 years."

Current location at Park Lake Medical Building on Lake Avenue.

Fort Wayne Orthopaedics, L.L.C.

The mission of the physicians and staff of Fort Wayne Orthopaedics (FWO) is to provide quality, cost-effective, patient-oriented care to the people of northeastern Indiana, northwestern Ohio, and southern Michigan. Fort Wayne Orthopaedics Musculoskeletal Institute is located in Fort Wayne at 7601 West Jefferson Boulevard and includes physician offices with a centrally located x-ray department, physical therapy and rehabilitation, an MRI unit, and an outstanding outpatient surgery center with 23-hour recovery beds. The Medical Staff is made up of 17 orthopaedic surgeons, four physical medicine and rehabilitation physicians, and four podiatrists.

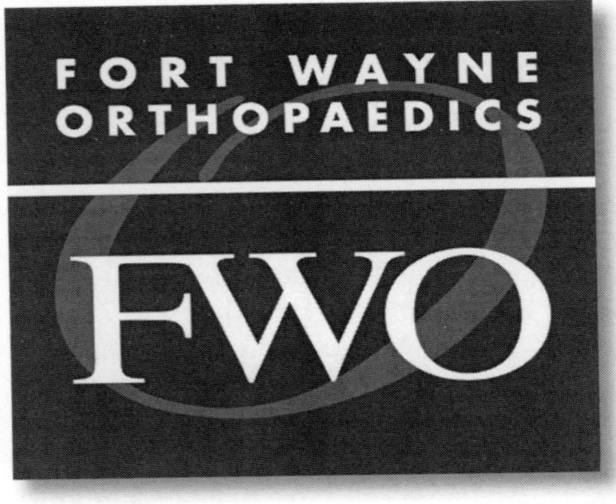

FWO grew from roots established by Dr. Richard Stauffer and Dr. Wayne Glock, who practiced together from 1946 to 1949, at which time Dr. Stauffer started his own medical practice. Dr. Glock was joined by Dr. Fred Brown in the late 1940s and Dr. Frederick Mackel in 1950, establishing Orthopaedic Surgeons Inc., which was first located in the Lincoln Tower building, then moved to the Fairfield Manor building. They later built the Ortho Manor building at Pontiac and Fairfield near the original Lutheran Hospital campus. That office now houses the Boys and Girls Club. Orthopaedic Surgeons grew with the additions of Dr. Philip Hershberger, Dr. Robert R. Shugart, Dr. James Buchholz, Dr. Michael McArdle and Dr. Jerry Mackel.

Dr. Robert Kimbrough joined Dr. Stauffer in 1951. They set up practice on the 7th floor of the old Medical Center Building on Ewing Street and worked primarily at Lutheran Hospital and St. Joseph Hospital. In 1957 the first orthopaedic operation on the first day of surgery at Parkview Memorial Hospital occurred when Dr. Stauffer and Dr. Kimbrough nailed a hip. During the early years, Dr. Kimbrough and Dr. Fred Brown established an orthopaedic training program. The Orthopaedic Residency Program has educated many outstanding orthopaedic specialists and continues today with 10 orthopaedic residents annually.

FWO was formed in 1983 when Dr. James Buchholz and Dr. Michael McArdle, who had been affiliated with Orthopaedic Surgeons, Inc., joined State Street Orthopaedics, whose members were Dr. Kimbrough, Dr. Stauffer, Dr. Michael Arata and Dr. Ronald Caldwell. In 1984 FWO merged with Dr. Gilbert Bierman of South Wayne Orthopaedics and constructed a new facility at 320 East Superior just across from Hall's Old Gas House Restaurant. FWO continued to grow with the additions of Dr. David Almdale, Dr. Steven Fisher, Dr. Barry Liechty, Dr. Jerald Cooper and Dr. Robert M. Shugart. The group was joined by Dr. Robert R. Shugart and Dr. Jerry Mackel when Dr. Frederick Mackel retired. The East Superior Building was FWO's main campus until moving to their state-of-the art Musculoskeletal Institute at 7601 West Jefferson Boulevard in July, 1994. The growth of FWO since moving to the Jefferson campus has been no less than amazing with 25 physicians and a staff of over 225.

On January 8, 1998, a first in the State of Indiana occurred in FWO's Ambulatory Surgery Center at the West Jefferson campus when Dr. Steven Fisher performed the first total knee replacement done in an ambulatory surgery center in Indiana. Since that time many more total knee replacements have been done at the Surgery Center, and total hip replacements have been done in the Surgery Center since early 1999.

The physicians at FWO have been very active in medical education and research. In addition to participating in the Orthopaedic Residency Program for a number of years, FWO promotes medical education in conjunction with The Stauffer Kimbrough Foundation, a non-profit organization founded in 1998 by the physicians of FWO. The Foundation promotes and facilitates scientific research in orthopaedics and supports education, scholarships and community outreach. Several FWO patients and physicians remain active in various ongoing research studies.

In order to meet the needs of the growing Fort Wayne community, in June, 2004, FWO opened an office at 2514 East Dupont Road. FWO also serves surrounding communities with clinics at Angola, Auburn, Kendallville, LaGrange, Peru, Topeka, Warsaw and the Jorgensen YMCA.

The physicians and staff at FWO look forward to contributing to the health and well-being of the residents of Fort Wayne and surrounding communities. They are committed to providing compassionate care of the highest quality getting patients back into the game, back to work, and back to normal day-to-day activities as quickly as possible.

Don R. Fruchey, Inc.

Don Fruchey had minimal financial resources when he founded the company, but his determination and his ability to attract highly skilled people built Don R. Fruchey, Inc. into one of the larger specialty contractors in the Midwest.

Fruchey established the company in May of 1950. His original vision was to be a small but successful steel erection contractor. "Our goal was to be one of the best, not one of the biggest, companies between Chicago and Cleveland," says Fruchey, who retired in 1980. Over the years, however, the company grew much more than he had anticipated.

During the early part of their history, the company primarily erected steel and precast concrete for new buildings and bridges. In the 1960s, Don R. Fruchey, Inc. erected the 3,606-foot-long Interstate 75 Expressway Bridge in Toledo, Ohio, the Riverfront Stadium in Cincinnati, Ohio and the City-County Building in Fort Wayne. And recently, after erecting the original Allen County Public Library in Fort Wayne, the company just erected the building's expansion.

The company evolved as it grew. Eventually, industrial equipment installation and plant maintenance services became the backbone of the company.

Fruchey's sons, Robert and David, now run the company as president and vice president, respectively. His daughter, Donna, and grandsons, Ryan and Adam, also work for the company, which is headquartered in a renovated, historic inn that once served travelers on the Wabash-Erie Canal.

Diversified Industrial Services

Don R. Fruchey, Inc. is a single source supplier for its customers, who are located mainly in the Midwest, although projects take place across the country. Its industrial services are diversified to meet customer needs. These include equipment installation, steel construction, custom steel fabrication, specialized hauling and equipment warehousing.

Don R. Fruchey, Inc. installs equipment for all types and sizes of industry from foundries to auto assembly to food processing. This work can demand a high level of precision skill and knowledge. A project can range from installing just one machine or to moving an entire industrial facility. In one unique project, involving 96 truckloads of equipment, an entire foundry was completely transferred from California to Arkansas.

Don Fruchey

The company's steel construction projects involve new building construction, as well as modifications to existing buildings.

PWC Fabrication, a division of Don R. Fruchey, Inc., offers a modern shop, a broad range of equipment and a team of skilled fabricators. PWC fabricates everything from structural steel to industrial furnaces to complicated conveyor systems.

Industrial equipment has become increasingly sophisticated and expensive over the years. To transport it, Don R. Fruchey, Inc. has a team of dedicated drivers and a fleet of specialized tractors and trailers.

The company's warehousing facilities can act, for example, as a holding area for equipment awaiting installation. Crating and equipment modification can be provided. Warehousing facilities currently consist of 75,000 square feet on site and 80,000 square feet of third party space.

Installation Press

Co-worker Loyalty

Because the work it performs is so specialized, Don R. Fruchey, Inc. relies on a highly skilled team of co-workers. Robert Fruchey believes its co-workers set the company apart: "Their sophistication and their knowledge of the type of work we do are unparalleled in the industry." That is a crucial component for success in an industry where clients are trimming their engineering support.

Typically, Don R. Fruchey, Inc. maintains co-worker base of 100 to 150 people. That number fluctuates, depending on the number of current projects. One consistent element that speaks volumes is co-worker loyalty to the company. "We have three generations of families working here," says Don Fruchey.

Safety is a major focus for the company and its co-workers. The goal is to create a workplace that is injury free.

Co-workers also take pride in the equipment that defines Don R. Fruchey, Inc. The company maintains a fleet of equipment and tools that can meet nearly every need. This includes everything from hydraulic gantries to precision leveling/alignment tools to a computer controlled burning table at PWC. "We have an excellent maintenance facility to supply our craftsmen and customers with safe; dependable equipment," David Fruchey says.

A More Technical Future

As Robert Fruchey looks to the future, he envisions more growth for the company, as it forms relationships with new customers. He also anticipates offering even more technical and computer support from all areas of the company, as well as more training to keep co-workers current with advancing technologies.

Building On Success

In the year 2005, Don R. Fruchey, Inc. celebrated its 55th anniversary. While remembering past achievements, the focus will remain on the goals that have served us well for 55 years. Excellent customer service and solid employment for its people will continue to be the foundations for a prosperous future. www.donrfruchey.com

F. W. Toenges and Sons, Inc.

Frederick William Toenges

John Toenges

Arthur Toenges

In 1878, Frederick William Toenges emigrated from Germany where he had worked as a shoe cobbler. He settled in Fort Wayne, Indiana, and continued working as a cobbler. Frederick soon recognized that retailing would be more rewarding and in 1891, established a shoe store at 112 Maumee Avenue. In 1886, he married and he and his wife, Elise, had ten children. Two of his sons, John and Arthur, joined their father in the business. Grandfather Frederick died in 1930, and John and Arthur carried on the business. In 1942, Arthur's son, Fred W. Toenges, began working in the store after school and on weekends even though he was only 14 years old. John died in 1946, and Fred W. became a full-time employee after graduating from high school.

Fred W. wanted to continue his education and enrolled in Indiana University's Fort Wayne campus to study business and then transferred to Purdue University to study engineering while still working 60 hours a week at the shoe store. The engineering courses later helped him in understanding the biomechanics of the foot and lower extremities. However, in 1951, Fred was drafted and spent 1952-1953 in Korea during the war. While home on Christmas leave he married Maureen Calder and during his absence was replaced at the store by his wife. Upon his discharge from the Army, Fred decided that he wanted to be "the best shoe man" in Fort Wayne and began his quest to learn everything he could about feet and how to care for them. Fred's quest led him to Ball State University where a pilot course in "Pedorthics" was being offered. Pedorthics is the design, manufacture, modification and fit of foot wear, including foot orthosis to alleviate foot problems caused by disease, overuse, congenital defect or injury. After Ball State he attended Temple University, Northwestern Medical University's School of Orthotics and Prosthetics, New York University and twice studied at the United States Hospital at Carville, Louisiana, under the direction of Dr. Paul Brand. At the latter he learned how to care for diabetic patients with peripheral neuropathy. He also studied biomechanics, gait deficiency problems, anatomy and body planes as part of his education so he could fill doctor's prescriptions in an educated and professional manner.

While continuing his studies, Fred also started to expand the shoe business and opened his first branch store in 1959, on East State Boulevard. That was followed by stores on West State Boulevard, South Anthony Boulevard, and children's stores in Glenbrook Mall and Covington Plaza. Fred also became president of the Pedorthic Footwear Association as well a president of the Board for Certification in Pedorthics. He was asked to serve on the National Board of the Diabetic Association and while there co-authored a physicians' manual for the care of the diabetic foot. He has also had articles published in the *Clinics in Podiatric Medicine and Surgery* on children's foot problems. Fred also worked at Lutheran Hospital's Crippled Children's Orthopedic Clinic and St. Joe Hospital's Diabetic Clinic. He continues to work at Northeast Orthopedics Foot and Ankle Clinic under the direction of Dr. Scot Karr.

Fred soon realized that he needed a large facility where he could incorporate pedorthics, a repair shop for modifying and repairing shoes, a children's and family shoe store and technical equipment for diagnosing foot problems. He purchased property at 2415 Hobson Road and built a 10,000 plus square foot building which now houses all that. Fred has four certified, licensed Pedorthists and 36 employees to care for any and all feet and foot problems. Fred has introduced Teck Scan into the business, an innovative computer system for floor reaction testing that is generally found only in large clinics such as Mayo Clinic and gait analysis laboratories. Fred closed the other five stores and now has only the Hobson Road store and another smaller facility in Muncie, Indiana where there is a full time Pedorthist on staff.

Fred considers the "High Light of My Career" was to be chosen by the Olympic Committee as one of 11 Certified Pedorthists (out of 1,800) to serve athletes from all nations at the 2004 Olympics in Athens, Greece. While there, he cared for the foot problems of athletes from 15 different countries as well as coaches and other volunteers.

During all of the above, Fred and Maureen managed to raise three children, two girls and one boy. Son Ross, who is a Certified Prosthetist, is now assuming the responsibilities of continuing his great grandfather' s legacy into the future, hopefully for another 114 years.

Fred and Ross Toenges.

Grinsfelder Associates Architects

Grinsfelder's principal architects, (l. to r.) Alan R. Grinsfelder, Edward J. Welling, Thomas P. Farny and Richard P. Rajchel.

Grinsfelder's offices at 903 West Berry Street.

Designing The Future

Now in its 40th year, Grinsfelder Architects was founded in 1965. At that time, the business was known as simply "Alan Grinsfelder, Architect," and was located in downtown Fort Wayne in the Gettle Building (now known as the Courtside Building), at the corner of Calhoun and Berry.

At the time, Alan Grinsfelder served as the head of the architectural construction technology program at IPFW, and as a member of the city plan commission. He devoted the remainder of his time to the practice, with the assistance of a part-time student.

Shortly thereafter, a partner, Gerry McArdle, came to work for the practice full-time, and they added a secretary, another architect, and a new name: "Grinsfelder McArdle Architects." In 1968, the firm moved to their present location in the historic West Central Neighborhood at 903 West Berry Street. And in 1971, Alan left IPFW to work full-time at this growing practice.

A few of Grinsfelder's earliest projects included the design of Foellinger Outdoor Theatre, which had burned down in 1970, and the Senior Center, located at 111 West Main Street. Other early projects included the design of the Phelps Dodge Offices and Allen Dairy facility. In addition, they specialized in work with local housing authorities in surrounding counties.

In the late 1970s and early 1980s, more partners were added to the firm: Mike Poorman, Richard Wismer, and Tom Boardman, and the firm once again changed their name to "Grinsfelder Wismer Boardman and Associates."

In the 1980s, more changes came about that evolved into the firm of today: existing partners left for other cities or to form their own firms, and Ed Welling and Tom Farny joined the firm, where they continue as partners today. In addition, the firm received its current name, "Grinsfelder Associates Architects."

Currently, the firm boasts four partners (Grinsfelder, Welling, Farny, and most recent addition Rick Rajchel) and a staff of eight.

Over these past 40 years, Grinsfelder has continued to specialize in public and not for profit work in Fort Wayne and surrounding communities. A few recent projects have included Headwaters Park, the WBNI/WBOI studios, WFWA PBS 39 studios, the DeKalb County Courthouse restoration, and the conversion of the former Angola and Decatur High Schools into vibrant community centers.

Grinsfelder has made a name as a community partner, becoming actively involved in the historical restoration and development of our community. They have become highly respected as a leading member of Fort Wayne's architectural community, receiving many awards and accolades locally and nationally.

In addition, they strive to make every project a priority, always assigning a principal architect to each project to ensure its highest priority and success. Grinsfelder receives their highest marks from past clients in the areas of service, client satisfaction, and goal and budget reaching.

Restoring The Past

In addition to running a successful practice for 40 years, Grinsfelder has also been proud to continually renovate and restore the 1890s home that is now their primary office space.

The Neo-Jacobian or Queen Anne Style house, located at 903 West Berry in Fort Wayne's historic West Central neighborhood, is the perfect home for this architectural firm, as it ties into their history of restoration and historic preservation.

The home originally dates back to 1838, when Isaac Parry purchased the land for $50 and commissioned builders to build a 34' long, 18' wide, 1½ story high home with a piazza for $1,525.

Unfortunately, by the end of the 1800s, the original Greek revival structure built in 1839 was either destroyed or torn down, and the present Neo-Jacobean house (of the 1890s architectural style) was erected by the Ward family.

Horatio Ward was a prominent citizen of Fort Wayne who was recognized as pioneer in the crockery business in this section of the state. He had a store on Columbia Street that advertised "imported china, glassware, house furnishing goods and paper hangings."

In later years, during the ownership of Herbert E. Atkinson, the property was used as a fraternity house (Alpha Gamma Upsilon, 1951-1953) and the West Berry Rest Home (1954-1965) until it came to be owned by Grinsfelder, who renovated the inside to blend the contemporary with the 1890 Neo-Jacobean style for his present office.

The Neo-Jacobean style places great emphasis on verandas, as well as posts, railings and grills that are relatively slender and frail. Also known as the Queen Anne tradition, the home presents a picturesque and visually varied composition. This is evident in irregularity of the plan as well as multiple roof planes, and the variety of materials and details used on the surface of the house; including brick, terra cotta, shingle, clapboard and half timbering.

Other characteristics true to this style include the fancy stripwork gables, arched windows, fishscale shingles, rooftop cresting, and decorative woodwork.

With its historical beauty preserved for the future, it is only fitting that this historic treasure of Fort Wayne's yesterdays is used to create the architectural masterpieces of our tomorrows.

Hagerman Construction Company

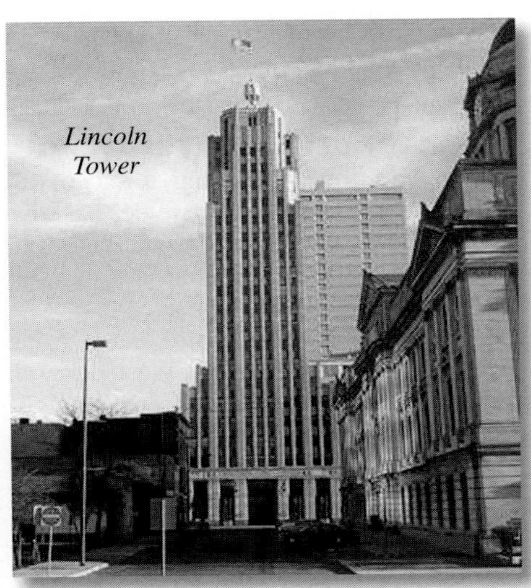
Lincoln Tower

One cannot look at the skyline of Allen County without seeing the handiwork of one of the oldest continuing construction firms in Indiana. Nor, indeed, can one look at the skyline in Indianapolis, Muncie or West Lafayette without seeing that same impact.

Hagerman Construction Corporation is one of the oldest and finest construction traditions in the Midwest, with nearly a century of experience in constructing some of Indiana's most recognized facilities, including Indiana's first skyscraper, the Lincoln Tower in Fort Wayne.

A Family Tradition

Hagerman Construction Corporation spans four generations in the same family. Founded in 1908 in Fort Wayne, Indiana by brothers-in-law William C. Hagerman and Frederick C. Buesching, the company was first known as Buesching-Hagerman Construction.

The company gradually grew in size because of the owners' commitment to quality and customer satisfaction. This commitment led to the construction of the Fort Wayne Lincoln Tower in 1930 that stood as Indiana's tallest building for 30 years.

In 1934, the company name was changed to Hagerman Construction and was incorporated in 1948. During this period, William's sons Ted and Pete assumed leadership, and many years later the mantle was passed when Ted's son Mark became president in 1978. Under his leadership the company continues its commitment to quality and customer satisfaction. While strengthening services to clients in the Midwest, the company has also expanded service to customers across the country.

In 1990, Hagerman Construction opened an office in Indianapolis to meet the ever- increasing needs of the Central Indiana construction market. Jeff Hagerman, Mark's son and the fourth generation of Hagerman's involved in the business, serves as Executive Vice President of Hagerman Construction and manages the Indianapolis office.

Merger Brings More Growth

Hagerman Construction acquired Geupel DeMars of Indianapolis in July 1998, and today functions as an industry leader in providing construction management services under the banner of GDH, LLC.

Geupel DeMars traces its roots to 1927 when an Indianapolis contractor formed the Carl M. Geupel Construction Company. Richard B. DeMars joined the company in 1951 and began pioneering a new delivery system called construction management, a tradition which GDH continues. Before merging with Hagerman, Geupel DeMars completed such significant Indianapolis landmarks as the corporate campus of Eli Lilly and Company, the Artsgarden, Lilly Biotechnology Center, National City Center, the Children's Museum, Circle Centre Mall, Methodist Hospital and the Indianapolis Zoo. Additionally, GDH has completed several significant Indianapolis renovations at the City Market, Hilbert Circle Theater, the Indiana Roof Ballroom, Soldiers and Sailor Monument and the Indianapolis International Airport.

Coliseum

Building Indiana

Over the years the company has helped develop some of the most interesting and spectacular buildings in Indiana.

Hagerman has compiled an impressive list of significant projects over nine decades. It includes such projects as Standard Federal Plaza and Memorial Coliseum in Fort Wayne. The firm also built the City-County Building, Freimann Square, the Performing Arts Center, Northcrest Shopping Center, Perfection Biscuit Co. and various buildings on the campuses of Indiana Tech, Concordia Seminary and IPFW. Hagerman completed the renovation and expansion of North Side and South Side high schools as well. Some of its landmark projects that no longer exist include Wolf & Dessauer Department Store and Southtown Mall.

South Side High School

Athletic facilities built by Hagerman include the Ball State University basketball arena and Victory Field in Indianapolis, home of the Triple-A baseball Indians, to name a few. In addition, the construction firm completed the recent renovation of the Memorial Coliseum, which included the dramatic "raising of the roof" witnessed by many Allen County residents.

The firm has also built medical facilities in Indianapolis for Indiana University, Riley and Wishard hospitals, in addition to Lutheran, St. Joseph and Parkview hospitals in Fort Wayne and Ball Memorial Hospital in Muncie.

Hagerman now employs approximately 400 people, generates cost estimates for over $400,000,000 in projects per year, and constructs approximately $150,000,000 in new facilities each year.

Hagerman Construction provides the latest in construction technology and state-of-the-art equipment in the hands of superbly trained craftsmen. Regardless of the project delivery system desired by a client, the firm delivers value-added results on all of its projects. Hagerman Construction is proud to represent Allen County as it continues its tradition of fine craftsmanship throughout the state of Indiana.

C. Henry Steel, Inc.

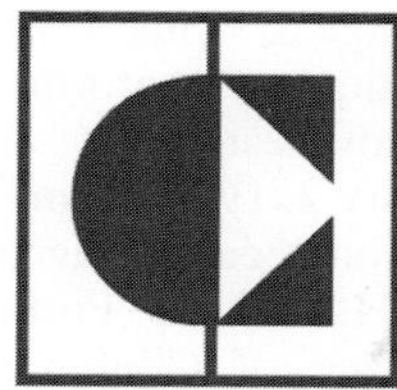

C ▸ HENRY ▸ STEEL

What do race car drivers, art students and farmers have in common? C. Henry Steel, seller of discounted steel.

Located at 1702 Winter Street, C. Henry Steel sells everything from a single scrap of metal to trainloads of discounted steel to some 4,000 customers in 15 states and Canada. Owners Chris and Carolyn Henry say the business's growth since its founding in 1999 has been astounding. In 2004, the business earned about $5 million selling more than 10,000 tons of steel.

"We are living a dream," Chris said. "We're very blessed."

The company buys and then resells steel from steel mills and service centers. Chris Henry said he purchases odd lengths, overruns and lots from auctions or business liquidations. He then resells the metal to whoever needs it.

"We have no minimums," he said. "If someone needs a little piece for an art class, or a farmer needs some to weld a fence, we'll sell it to them. I really try not to get away from the small buyers, because that's where I started out. Besides, maybe that guy might grow up and become a big customer someday!"

Steel Dynamics Inc. is another big customer for C. Henry Steel. The company is able to purchase SDI's secondary material, such as flat roll steel and structural piece like I-beams and then resell that material at a deep discount.

"I sell my material for about half what anyone else does," Chris said. "The cost savings for my farmers and my retail people are significant."

C. Henry Steel is nothing if not a family business. Chris and Carolyn have been together since they were teenagers and will celebrate their 15th wedding anniversary in 2005. Together they co-own C. Henry Steel, with Carolyn working in the office, alongside her sister, Lynn Graves, the company's office manager. And Chris's brother Karl Henry works out of C. Henry Steel's satellite office at the Steel Dynamics mill in Columbia City, Indiana. But it's clear that Chris and Carolyn Henry have something special.

"Everything I ever had I owe to Carolyn," Chris said. "She's been such a blessing to me. She has been so supportive – without that, I don't know what I would have."

That sense of family responsibility carries over into the business's efforts to help the community. As Chris said, "where there's privilege, there's responsibility," and so C. Henry Steel sponsors a Little League team in Leo, where Chris and Carolyn live. When called upon, the business lends a hand for area food banks and other causes.

"We're just in the steel business," Chris said. "It's been a great couple of years."

Home Loan Bank

On March 22, 1893, when the State of Indiana was 77 years old and Fort Wayne was only 43 years old, a group of German immigrants found they had something in common. While they had minimal incomes, they also had dreams of owning a home to build a secure future for their families. Then, 66,689 people lived in Allen County.

At number 1820 on the west side of South Calhoun Street, on the mezzanine balcony, the Teutonia Building Loan and Savings Association was born. The organizers served as the initial board of 11 directors. They were: G. Max Hoffmann, President; August M. Schmidt, Vice-President; Otto Herbst, Secretary; George Motz, Treasurer; Chas. A. Hans; Jacob J. Kern; Frederick E.W. Scheimann; John Rabus; Charles W. Jacobs; Louis Schirmeyer; and Henry A. Wiese. Additional organizers were John C. Heller and Fred Kayser.

The mortgage amounts generally were the $200.00 to $1,500.00 range. However, the smallest loan granted in 1893, was $50.00. Monthly salaries approved for corporate secretary was $40.00 and treasurer $15.00. $5.00 for the monthly office rent included fuel and lights. Notice of the first Annual Meeting was set for March 13, 1894, and was advertised in the German and English languages in all newspapers, *Daily News*, *Daily Journal*, *Daily Staats Zeiting* and *Daily Freie Presse*. Annual Meeting was held in the Philharmonic Hall Club Rooms on North Calhoun Street for a $5.00 charge for the evening meeting use. Seven members of the Association, absent at the March 18, 1896, Third Annual Meeting, were not excused and the secretary was instructed to collect a fine of $1.00 from each. This practice continued for the next several Annual Meetings.

New by-laws were adopted November 12, 1903, whereby all proceedings were to be conducted in English, but the German language shall have same privilege and all proceedings translated from one language to the other. The home office relocated to 132 East Berry Street, followed by a public Grand Opening held Saturday, December 9, 1916, with carnations for the ladies and cigars for the gentleman callers. June 4, 1918, the Board adopted the name change to Home Loan and Savings Association to conform with then present day American ideas.

On January 2, 1923, Home Loan purchased 1,000 one-cent postage stamps for $10.00 from H.W. Baals, Postmaster (the southeast corner of Clinton and Berry was the location of the main post office). Mr. Baals later served as Mayor of Fort Wayne. Nearly all financial institutions in Indiana were passing on paying interest on customer's deposits. Home Loan Savings omitted the June 30, 1932, interest to conserve their resources, a Depression trend that was nation-wide.

1962 Officers (l. to r.) Seated: Edmund A. Bittler, Chairman and Hazel Calvin Vice-President. Standing: W. Paul Wolf, Secretary-Treasurer and Paul E. Hess, President.

On January 17, 1937, Hazel Calvin was named Assistant Secretary-Treasurer, the first lady officer. Federal insurance of accounts on the deposits was approved at Washington, D.C. on October 21, 1937. On September 10, 1945, Paul E. Hess became a director then the eighth president from 1962 to 1970. William J. Hess, a director, died January 2, 1946, and Hazel Calvin assumed his secretary and managing officer positions.

On July 11, 1960, began the remodeling of 132-134 East Berry Street merging the two buildings into one lobby with Sylvester Horstman as contractor, costing $54,736.

W. Paul Wolf joined the Home Loan July 1, 1960, as assistant secretary treasurer after serving three years as one of Indiana's bank examiners. In 1962, he was elected a director to fill a vacancy due to the death of Joseph Voors of Voors Coal & Oil Company. Mr. Wolf was elected President and Chief Executive Officer in 1970, and became Chairman of the Board in 1991. During the 1970s and 1980s, locally, three life insurance companies, three commercial banks, and three federally insured savings institutions disappeared, while the Home Loan Bank expanded by opening branches, ultimately ten offices. On October 15, 1985, in the wake of federal deregulation of the banking industry, Home Loan changed its operation to the Home Loan Savings Bank. Updated again on September 15,1992, the name was changed to Home Loan Bank. Home Bancorp, an Indiana corporation, was established March 29, 1995, as a holding company for its principal subsidiary, Home Loan Bank.

Home Loan Bank's 100 years of business in Fort Wayne was celebrated at a party March 28, 1993, a Sunday afternoon, at the Memorial Coliseum's Exposition Center. The bank's 66 staff members were present to help make the day a memorable one. The bank expected about 3,000 people. Approximately 7,000 turned out for the birthday party. A limited edition, custom design letter opener in antique brass was given to the loyal customers. Other prizes, food and drawings for color TV sets every 15 minutes were pleasant surprises to those in attendance. Home Loan was the first and only Fort Wayne bank to celebrate a centennial anniversary.

During Wolf's tenure, Home Loan Bank assets grew from $10 million on July 1, 1960, to $420 million when he retired October 15, 1999. His understudy, Senior Vice President, Matthew P. Forrester, resigned October 15, 1999, to become the CEO and President of River Valley Bank, Madison, Indiana. Old Kent Financial Corp of Grand Rapids, Michigan, acquired Home Loan Bank's holding company, the Home Bancorp, in October 2000. Fifth Third Bancorp, in turn, bought Old Kent, in April 2001. *Submitted by W. Paul Wolf.*

Hoosier Metal Recycling, Inc.

If it weren't for Hoosier Metal Recycling, nearly 10 million soda pop and beer cans might be littering the fields and streets of Allen County.

That's how many aluminum cans are turned in to the modest warehouse located at 2222 West Coliseum Boulevard each year, says company owner Kurt Henry.

Add those 10 million cans to the 300,000 tons of other various scrap metals recycled there, and you'll see what kind of a service the company provides.

Discarded appliances, old heating ducts, copper wire, coils of various black cables are sorted into different bins by Hoosier Metal Recycling's 10 employees as a steady stream of people come in with garbage bags full of cans. The cans are poured onto a conveyor belt which deposits them into a crusher, grinding them into bins with a deafening roar.

"It's the sound of money," Kurt laughs. "Seriously, (can recycling) provides a living for a lot of our customers."

The business opened in 2000, handling non-ferrous metals such as copper, brass and aluminum. In 2003, it began accepting ferrous metals (iron). The company receives metal from both people off the street and from industrial accounts. The business has large receptacles which it places on-site at its approximately 150 industrials within a 60-mile radius of Fort Wayne. Those industries load the bins with scrap metal from manufacturing processes. When the bins are full, they are returned to the Coliseum Boulevard site, where workers sort the scraps of metal into classifications and then resell them to area foundries such as Steel Dynamics, where they're melted and turned into new products.

Though the business is only five years old, it's already has revenues of nearly $5 million annually. And Kurt Henry believes in sharing the wealth. The company supports Little League baseball and helps churches and other charities by offering them a higher price per pound for the cans they collect than regular retail customers.

"I'm proud that we provide an environmental service," Kurt says. "I like being in this business for that reason. You'd be surprised how many appliances would be left out in the alleys if we didn't buy them. And we provide a living for a lot of families in this town." *Submitted by Kurt Henry*

(l. to r.) Pat Kelly, Bob Tipsord, Corey Richardson, Omar Restrepo, Jim Meyers, Jerry Tulk, Ray Jackson and Kurt Henry.

The Partners of Hunt Suedhoff Kalamaros LLP

HUNT SUEDHOFF KALAMAROS LLP

ATTORNEYS AT LAW

www.hsk-law.com

<u>FORT WAYNE</u>
Post Office Box 11489
803 S. Calhoun St, 9TH Floor
Fort Wayne, IN 46858-1489
(260) 423-1311
FAX (260) 424-5396

<u>SOUTH BEND</u>
Post Office Box 4156
120 W. LaSalle Ave., 12TH Floor
South Bend, IN 46634-4156
(574) 232-4801
FAX (574) 232-9736

○ADMITTED IN MICHIGAN AND INDIANA

P. MICHAEL MILLER
ROBERT E. KABISCH
DAVID A. STEWART
ARTHUR G. SURGUINE, JR.
THOMAS C. EWING
MICHAEL D. MUSTARD
THOMAS F. COHEN*
BRANCH R. LEW
JAMES J. SHEA, SR.
SCOTT L. BUNNELL
DANE L. TUBERGEN
ROBERT D. WOODS*
KEVIN W. KEARNEY*
PHILIP E. KALAMAROS***/○

CAROLYN M. TRIER
KATHLEEN A. KILAR
BRIAN L. ENGLAND**
LYNN E. KALAMAROS*
N. JEAN SCHENDEL
TIMOTHY W. DEGROOTE
STEPHEN E. DEVER
LINDA A. POLLEY
CAROL A. VOGEL*
DANIEL J. PALMER
LYLE R. HARDMAN*
— —
THOMAS R. HAMILTON*
CHARLES H. BASSFORD*

KEITH C. DOI*
PETER J. BAGIACKAS*
JASON C. CUSTER
ORFEJ P. NAJDESKI
MELISSA G. HAWK
DEANNE M. VOLHEIM*
KEVIN R. LESLIE**
ANDREW S. WILLIAMS
STEVEN S. HAND
MARCUS P. HENDERSON**
ANDREW R. WOLF***
ELIZABETH A. JOSEPH**

LEIGH L. HUNT
(1899-1975)
WILLIAM E. BORROR
(1932-1989)
EDWARD N. KALAMAROS
(1934-1996)
CARL J. SUEDHOFF, JR.
(1925-2005)
CAROLYN W. SPENGLER
(RETIRED)

<u>OF COUNSEL</u>

J. SCOTT FANZINI***/○

<u>INDIANAPOLIS</u>
6323 S. East Street
Indianapolis, IN 46227
(317) 784-4966
FAX (317) 784-5566

<u>MICHIGAN</u>
Post Office Box 46
608 Pleasant Street
St. Joseph, MI 49085-0046
(269) 983-4405
FAX (269) 983-5645

*SOUTH BEND OFFICE
**INDIANAPOLIS OFFICE
***MICHIGAN OFFICE

The history of HUNT SUEDHOFF KALAMAROS LLP, is really the story of two law firms. The first, HUNT SUEDHOFF, dates back to the 1940s. At that time, the firm's founder, Fort Wayne Attorney Leigh L. Hunt, earned a reputation as an outstanding and effective trial lawyer. In 1950, Mr. Hunt opened his own law firm, concentrating on civil litigation. Through the years, as the firm grew, it became widely recognized for the expertise of its attorneys.

The second story begins in South Bend, Indiana, where, in 1960, Attorney Edward N. Kalamaros created the firm of KALAMAROS & ASSOCIATES. This firm also developed a heavy concentration in civil litigation and the idea of combining traditional work ethic with modern technology and contemporary techniques to serve its clients. Through the years, it too became known for its outstanding service and talented attorneys.

In 2000, the two firms with so much in common, joined forces. This solidified HUNT SUEDHOFF KALAMAROS LLP as one of the premier law firms in northern Indiana with one of the state's largest civil litigation practices. As regional defense counsel for more than 40 insurance companies, the firm represents businesses and individuals in Indiana and Michigan, including lawsuits involving product liability, medical malpractice, personal injury, worker's compensation, property damage, insurance fraud and insurance coverage disputes. The firm regularly serves as defense counsel for the State of Indiana, the City of Fort Wayne, and numerous other cities, counties and other governmental entities within Indiana and in Michigan.

The firm also provides health care law services to a wide variety of clients including some of the largest health care groups and hospitals, in Indiana, for medical malpractice defense, risk management, and guidance on regulatory issues and compliance. Additionally, the firm provides services related to the business aspects of medical and dental health care practice.

In meeting the legal needs of both individuals and companies, HUNT SUEDHOFF KALAMAROS LLP, has attorneys specializing in the areas of estate planning, probate administration, corporate, partnership and other business organizations, employment issues, commercial transactions and family law. The firm works extensively in the fields of mediation, arbitration and conflict resolution for corporate and individual clients.

As lawyers who are recognized as leaders in their fields, members of the firm are frequently called upon to participate in the training of other lawyers in various workshops and seminars sponsored by such groups as the National Institute for Trial Advocacy, the National Business Institute, the American College of Trial Lawyers, the American Inns of Court, Defense Trial Counsel of Indiana and the Indiana Continuing Legal Education Forum.

HUNT SUEDHOFF KALAMAROS LLP, currently consists of forty lawyers and more than thirty paralegals and legal assistants, with offices located in Fort Wayne, South Bend, Indianapolis, and St. Joseph, Michigan. Various members of the firm are admitted to practice in the state courts of Indiana, Michigan, and the United States District Courts located within Indiana and Michigan, the United States Court Of Appeals for the Seventh Circuit, and the Supreme Court of the United States.

Hylant

It's difficult to imagine a Toledo, Ohio-based company finding its way in to a Fort Wayne, Indiana History Book. But when you consider the Hylant Group's (HG) meteoric Fort Wayne success since purchasing the Fort-Wayne-based O'Brien & Sanderson Insurance Company (OBSI) in 2000 and Benefits Consultants Insurance (BCI) in 2001, it's easy to see why the company and its local staff and clients are so gung-ho about Fort Wayne. And why it's making history here.

The Hylant Group's success story started in 1935 when Hylant-MacLean, Inc. insurance agency opened its doors in Toledo, Ohio. Founded by Toledo residents Edward P. Hylant and John MacLean, the agency offered commercial, personal and life insurance to its clients. In 1942 when Edward died, John MacLean shepherded the company through the next decade, growing its arsenal of products and continuing to serve local clients. A young Robert Hylant, son of Edward, joined the company in 1946, and in 1957 after the retirement of John MacLean, became President and Chief Executive Officer. At the time, the company's premium volume was $135,000.

Robert Hylant was determined to grow his agency, and in 1960 with the addition of staff, agents, and products, Hylant-MacLean listed over $ 1,000,000 in premium volume. But with growth comes change. Busting at the seams, the agency needed new offices and a more sophisticated look, so in 1970 it moved to a more centrally located space in downtown Toledo. That same year, Robert's son, Patrick, joined the company, which by then boasted premium volume at over $3,000,000.

In 1982, after the retirement of Robert, Patrick became President of Hylant-MacLean, Inc. That same year he sold the company to Dana Corporation with the intention of eventually buying it back. And he did only three years later with partner Scott Stewart. In 1987, Hylant-MacLean opened its first office outside Toledo in Troy, Michigan, and then another in Cleveland, Ohio in 1989. New offices and acquisitions meant newspaper headlines. Patrick was quoted in the local Toledo paper restating the company's founding principles, "Since 1935 Hylant-MacLean has continually taken steps to expand services, improve services, and broaden geographic areas to which they are delivered... At Hylant-MacLean we pride ourselves in meeting needs for today and in anticipating needs for the future."

Hylant Group

With these beliefs in his back pocket, Patrick pursued growth with a vengeance, opening additional offices and founding several offshoots of Hylant-MacLean to better serve its rapidly growing list of clients. By 1990, Hylant-MacLean had $110,000,000 in premium volume and found itself on two prestigious published lists, including the *Top 50 Independent Insurance Brokers* in the nation and the *Top 100 Largest Brokers of U.S. Business*, an annual list published by Business Insurance.

Over the next 10 years, Hylant-MacLean opened offices in Columbus, Cincinnati, and Portland, Maine. Additionally, it formed Hylant Administrative Services, Hylant Specialty Programs, Hylant Broker Services, and Hylant Consulting Services. In 2000, the newly-named Hylant Group made its entry in to Fort Wayne, purchasing O'Brien & Sanderson Insurance and placing itself at the forefront of Fort Wayne insurance agencies. At the time of the merger, OBSI had 13 employees. Morrie Sanderson, former Owner and President of OBSI, remained as Chief Operating Officer and Chairman. During the transition, Sanderson provided valuable management skills and critical stability, allowing HG to implement new policies and strategies so they could effectively grow in the area.

New to Fort Wayne, but not to HG, was Kevin Brennan, the only HG transplant from Toledo, who assumed the role of President and Chief Executive Officer. In 2001, HG merged with Fort Wayne-based Benefit Consultants (BCI), which added a great client base and 17 more employees, including BCI owners Pat Sullivan and Leigh Smith, now Vice Presidents at HG.

Under Brennan's leadership and surrounded by a management team of Sanderson, Sullivan and Smith, HG embraced its community both civically and economically. In 2003, it was named Small Business of the Year by the Fort Wayne Chamber of Commerce. Since its merger with OBSI in 2000, HG in Fort Wayne has nearly quadrupled its revenues. In 2005, HG was 58 people strong with 90-percent of its revenues coming from commercial insurance lines. According to Brennan, its success is tied to its philosophy, "People are our most important asset and resource." And with a clear vision for the future and the right investment in those resources, HG is positioned to be the City and the region's (Indiana, Michigan and Ohio) largest insurance agency by 2006. Insurance Business placed it at #27 on its 2005 list of *Top 100 Largest Brokers of U.S. Business*. That bodes well for its employees, its customers, and for Fort Wayne, a City that embraces Hylant Group. It may be only five years old, but it's hardly a newcomer when you consider most of its employees, managers and clients come from Fort Wayne, all of whom are ready to help place Hylant in Fort Wayne's history pages.

Max Irmscher

Tom Irmscher

Max Irmscher and Sons was founded in 1892 by Max Irmscher, Sr., the great-grandfather of the current owner, Thomas A. Irmscher. Max was originally a journeyman bricklayer who came to this country from Saxony, Germany and began his business as a sole proprietorship out of an office on Liza Street in Fort Wayne. In the early 1900s, Max changed his focus from masonry work to general contracting. Max moved his offices in the 1930s to the old First National Bank Building, which Irmscher built. In the 1950s, Max Irmscher and Sons moved their offices once more to their current location, 1030 Osage Street in Fort Wayne, and changed their name to Irmscher and Sons. Always looking for an opportunity to expand their knowledge, Irmscher and Sons changed their focus in the 1970s and 1980s to construction management. In the 1980s Irmscher and Sons changed their name to Irmscher, Inc., paving their way into the design/build market in the 1990s.

Currently, Irmscher, Inc. is prepared to handle all sizes and types of institutional, industrial, commercial, and healthcare construction, construction management, general contracting, and design/build projects. While the company has performed work nationally, the majority of their clients are based in the Great Lake States of Indiana, Illinois, Michigan, Ohio, and Wisconsin, affording them an intimate knowledge of the construction labor, construction technology, and material suppliers in these areas. The result is their ability to perform in such a manner as to retain the reputation for integrity and responsibility their company has developed throughout its one hundred and thirteen years in the industry.

The current owner, Tom Irmscher, has been in the construction industry for more than 36 years. He graduated from Purdue University with a Bachelor's Degree in Management and a Minor in Civil Engineering. Among Tom's many affiliations, both professional and community, are the Associated General Contractors of Indiana, the Building Contractors Association, the Northeast Indiana Construction Advancement Foundation, Big Brothers/Big Sisters, Christian Business Mens Committee, Indiana Student Leadership Forum, and Junior Achievement. Tom believes that the driving force behind any success the company may have is in developing and maintaining mutually rewarding relationships with employees, subcontractors, and clients. They strive for superior quality, skill, and integrity within all levels of the corporation.

Among the many projects Irmscher, Inc. has been involved with over the years, several stand out: the Fort Wayne Filtration Plant, the Embassy Theatre, North Side High School, the old First National Bank Building, the Verizon Building, Brotherhood Mutual, Saint Joseph Hospital, the Scottish Rite Cathedral, and the Wolf & Dessauer Department Store, which Irmscher later renovated for Lincoln Financial Corporation.

Brotherhood Mutual

Northside High School

Jann's Power Gym

Est. 1983
2728 Brooklyn Avenue
Fort Wayne, Indiana 46802
432-5227

Jann Prince's brother, Gary Schmeling, suggested to her in 1980 to try weightlifting. A mere three years later, at age 33, Jann Prince became the first woman in the history of Fort Wayne to win a title in the 114 pound weight class in the men's division of the Fort Wayne City Powerlifting Championship. With this distinction, Jann founded Jann's Power Gym in the spring of 1983. Jann held the State Champion title for seven years. Simultaneously, she and her coach, Kurt Babb, a thirty-three time state powerlifting titleholder, promoted powerlifting through Jann's Power Gym and their affiliation with the American Drug-Free Powerlifting Association (ADFPA). An "Elite" status power-lifter, Kurt was one of the founding fathers of powerlifting in the Fort Wayne area.

From the beginning, Jann's Power Gym insisted on a drug-free atmosphere where anabolic steroids are never permitted. Through years of competition, the gym members held state, regional and national titles and records. The gym members ran many local and state championships promoting the sport of drug-free powerlifting. The female lifters received much publicity, as weightlifting was new to the female gender. Four years of Run Jane Run Championships drew lifters of world status, bringing light to the potential of female athletes.

Jann's Power Gym was also unique in that it introduced Special Olympics to the sport of drug-free lifting. Many special needs participants have received well deserved recognition for their efforts. Notable lifters to emerge from Jann's Power Gym were Lisa Kimmey (Elite status, 139# wt. class 400# deadlifter), David Osborn (114# men's 400# squatter, 235# bench press), Ethel Folkes (International Elite status lifter), Ted Striverson (242# wt class, world masters champion bench presser), and Kurt Babb (Elite status lifter, coach, sport promoter.) Jann Prince was also a National Champion holding many state records for over a decade including 280# squat, 160# bench, and 300# deadlift.

Jann's Power Gym trained and promoted several National Champion teenage lifters. Representing Jann's Power Gym, Jann Prince served as the state chairperson for ADFPA Powerlifting for four years and served as International Referee for the ADFPA for many years.

As steroids (the competition) became more prevalent, Jann's Power Gym was affected by this dangerous sports trend. Though Jann's Power Gym ended its years of dominance in the local scene of powerlifting promotion and competition, it still operates to serve an emerging new breed. Jann decided in 1988 to redirect the focus of the gym and her coaching skills to the everyday lifter wanting strength for everyday use. Certified by the National Strength and Conditioning Association and The American College of Sports Medicine, the gym is home to nearly thirty students in a one-on-one setting geared towards better health and strength.

Today the gym looks much as it did in the early days with plaques and trophies adorning the walls. It's mission, however, reflects the times and also addresses today's greatest concern: obesity. Jann's Power Gym remains dedicated to helping people enrich their lives by incorporating weightlifting into a healthy lifestyle.

Jann Prince

Keefer Printing Company, Inc.

Keefer Printing – 1915

Keefer Printing - 2005

Keefer Printing Company was established in 1914 by James H. Keefer who had previously been the publisher of a weekly newspaper in Wells County since 1890. He moved his family, which included seven children, to Fort Wayne in 1914 and opened a small "job shop" at 921 Broadway (a sight which later became a well known restaurant named Manochio's). At this time the company's main business was to print stationary, posters, theatre programs, tickets and virtually any small printing job.

In 1926, the company was officially incorporated and moved it's location to 714 West Washington Boulevard to accommodate more equipment and larger print orders.

James H. Keefer retired in 1930 and his oldest son, J. Ver Keefer, took over the business. Two other sons of James H. Keefer, Mark and Max, were also involved in the business at that time. The method of printing during these years was letterpress printing and in the 1950s there began to be a change to what was referred to as "offset printing" or lithography. The company was very involved in producing company newspapers such as the *Harvester News* for International Harvester and the *GE News* for General Electric Company. Other notable customers in these years included Allied Mills Wayne Feeds Inc., Wayne Pump Company and the Fort Wayne Komets hockey club. The building was expanded twice during these years because of the need for more space.

J. Ver Keefer passed away in October of 1960 and his only son, James M. Keefer became owner and president. The 1960s and 1970s saw the changeover almost totally to lithographic printing and, because of that development, saw the installation of several new offset presses at the company. The company's focus changed to printing more brochures and catalogs which entailed more color printing. It was during this era that the company developed business relationships with more of the area's most established companies such as Lincoln Life Insurance Co., LML Corp., Fort Wayne Philharmonic, Mutual Security Insurance Co., Container Corp., and several others. In 1983 the company purchased it's first large format two-color press which greatly enhanced its ability to produce fine color printing and because of this, added many fine advertising agencies to it's customer list such as Ferguson Advertising, Bonsib Advertising, Asher Agency and Caldwell Van Riper. In the late 1980s it became necessary once again to add additional space to the building because of rapid growth.

In 1991, Richard F. Keefer became president and owner of the company and continues to this day. After the purchase of a six-color press that year, the company once again shifted it's focus, this time to multi-color high quality printing. This resulted in greatly increased volume and the addition of still more large customers such as Biomet, Physicians Health Plan and ChromaSource. In 2002, the company moved from its location on Washington Boulevard which had 15,000 square feet of space to it's present location at 3824 Transportation Drive which has 43,000 square feet of space and room to expand.

Over the many years of its existence, Keefer Printing Company has supported many of the area's most important charities and organizations such as Big Brothers-Big Sisters, CANI, SCAN, the Mad Anthony's, Turnstone and others.

Currently in it's fourth generation of ownership, it is hoped that a fifth generation will someday take over the company. Patrick R. Keefer has indicated his desire to enter the business upon his graduation from Indiana University in 2007.

Korte Does It All

Had it not been for the encouragement of a church friend, Jerry Korte might not be "doing it all" today. "When I was in high school or even before, a guy from my church, Dale Ehle, had me working in his shop," as a 14-year-old electrician, Korte remembered. "I kind of took a liking to it." From that humble beginning, Korte established his business, Korte Electric, in March, 1965, working out of an office in his garage. His first client was Star Homes, a customer he's kept for 40 years.

In 1968, he began wiring heat pumps for heating contractors; then expanded into the heating and cooling business. He'd moved his offices by then into the Maplewood Shopping Center. By 1975, Korte began offering commercial wiring as a service, and in 1978, the growing company built offices at 10920 Stellhorn Road in New Haven. In 2005, the company began expanding their office and warehouse space at the Stellhorn Road location. In 1984, the business grew again, this time adding heating and air conditioning service. By 1989, Korte branched into offering plumbing services and in 1993, he began installing home security services. The following year, the business began installing home audio and entertainment systems and central vacuuming systems.

Korte said the expansions in the range of services his business offers just came naturally. "We do a lot of new homes for contractors," he explained, so it just made sense to increase the services they could provide. For example, the audio-visual wiring "goes in at the same time we do the rough wiring." Offering such a wide range of services gives customers plenty of options with one contractor.

Korte ensures that his employees, now numbering 115, are trained in the latest technology to keep up with the trends. Those employees are loyal, as well. Six employees have more than 20 years of service, and 14 have more than 10 years of service with the company. Mike Rekeweg has almost 40 years of service, having started as an 18-year-old electrician in October, 1965. Greg Forbing, also an electrician, started in 1971 at the age of 18, and Kelli Witte was hired in 1979 at the age of 20 to manage the purchases of heating equipment. Korte's wife, Judy, son Dave and daughter Julie are all employed with the business. Dave Korte, who started in 1979 as a warehouse helper and parts deliveryman, worked as an apprentice for HV AC and electrical jobs. He passed the electrical journeyman's test in 1990 and began supervising residential electricians two years later. In 1993, Dave began installing security systems and setting up monitoring contracts for customers, and the following year he began installing audio and home entertainment systems, as well as central vacuuming systems. By 2000, Dave became vice president of Outside Operations. Kevin Kratzman began working at Korte Electric in 1994 in plumbing sales and marketing after selling a lawn and landscape contracting business he'd owned since 1986. By 1997, Kevin took over as the company's controller, and helped develop the company's advertising campaign and jingle. Now vice president of Inside Operations, he is married to Julie Korte.

The business grew so much that in 1996, Jerry and his wife Judy made the difficult decision to merge the businesses with ARS of Memphis, Tennessee. Jerry said the decision was part of a trend in his industry at the time, but after the company was sold again, this time to ServiceMaster, he decided to buy it back. In 2000, he and his son Dave, and son-in-law, Kevin Kratzman, purchased the family business back and renamed it Korte Does It All.

These days, Jerry Korte is still involved in the business, though he and Judy try to take their retirement in bits and pieces. "We've been in it so long, I just couldn't pull up and leave," he said with a laugh. "Besides, I've got to have something to do." Jerry is proud of his business. After 40 years, he noted, he still serves his first customer, Star Homes. "You have to grow with your customers, and service what you install," he said. "I don't want to be the biggest, I want to be the best. I want to take care of our customers."

Kevin Kratzman, Jerry Korte, and Dave Korte, December, 2003.

Originally started as two businesses by two brothers, Lancia Homes grew into one of Fort Wayne and northeast Indiana's leading homebuilders.

Lancia Homes has developed a reputation as a production builder with the custom touch. The company's focus has evolved to single-family homes for first-time and move-up buyers, with 2005 prices from $105,000 to more than $200,000.

In addition to single-family homes, Lancia Homes has also developed and built condominium-style townhomes and villas. The company has also built a few commercial projects including the Lancia Office Centre on Lima Road in northwest Fort Wayne. The company's headquarters have been at the Lima Road location since 1991.

Company founders and brothers Jim and Floyd Lancia are originally from Weirton, West Virginia. Jim started Windsor Builders in 1975, following relocation to Fort Wayne from the Pittsburgh area. Floyd founded Burlington Homes in 1977. In the early 1980s the national and local economies suffered, including the housing market, while Jim and Floyd served as trim carpenters and continued to build homes.

In 1982, Jim and Floyd built their first condo-style townhomes with the Sawmill Woods project in northeast Fort Wayne. That was followed by Springmill Woods southwest and The Communities of Chadwick in the northeast corner of the city. Lancia also introduced back-to-back fourplex condo-style townhomes to Fort Wayne. These homes can be found in Sawmill Woods, Springmill Woods and Springfield Glen.

Windsor Builders and Burlington Homes were separate companies until combining in 1987 to form Lancia Construction. Known as the "Builder of Fine Homes" and later the "Professional Builder With the Personal Touch." Lancia first made its name as a builder of starter homes. Later it transitioned to primarily first- and second-time move-up homes.

In the 1990s, the second generation of Lancias came into the business with Floyd's son Matthew and Jim's son Jamie.

In 2001, the company officially became Lancia Homes, adopting a new look and slogan of "We're Built Better." Lancia, however, retained its personal touch with homeowners and suppliers and its professional outlook and attitude.

In 2003, Lancia Homes pulled the greatest number of residential building permits, 263, in northeast Indiana and had the greatest total dollar volume of more than $36 million in construction.

Lancia Homes has maintained memberships in the Home Builders Association of Fort Wayne, Indiana Builders Association, National Association of Home Builders, Greater Fort Wayne Chamber of Commerce and the Northeastern Better Business Bureau. Jim and Floyd each served as president of the HBA of Fort Wayne.

The company has supported local charities including Erin's House for Grieving Children, Make-A-Wish Foundation of Indiana, Junior Achievement, Red Cross, Leukemia and Lymphoma Society and Habitat for Humanity.

Over the years, Lancia Homes participated in the Home Builders Association of Fort Wayne's Parade of Homes. Lancia has built parade homes in Oak Borough, Lofton Woods, Hillsboro, Whispering Meadows, Hearthstone, Millstone and La Cabreah.

Not limiting itself to building homes, Lancia has specialized in developing entire subdivisions. Neighborhoods exclu-

Windsor Builders, Inc.
Burlington Homes inc.

sively featuring Lancia homes include: Fall Creek, Summerfield, Winchester Ridge, Seven Oaks, Oak Glen, Timberon, Springfield, Springfield Villas, Hickory Pointe, Walnut Creek, Shadow Ridge, New Haven's CastleRock, Kendallville's Arvada Hills, Huntertown's Turnberry at Willow Run, Ravenswood and Sycamore Lakes.

Today Jim and Floyd Lancia operate two companies, Lancia Homes Inc. and Springmill Woods Development Corp. Lancia Homes Inc. accounts for the construction end of the business. Springmill Woods Development Corp. handles the land development portion of homebuilding.

Jim and Floyd Lancia also own Waterford Enterprises LLC, the rental affiliate of Lancia Homes. Waterford Enterprises owns two apartment-home communities, Crosspointe and Waterford Park, as well as houses and townhomes available for rent.

In 2005, Lancia Homes had more than 20 full-time employees in addition to dozens of subcontractors.

The Lancia Homes management team taken in 2003.
(l. to r.) Floyd Lancia, Jamie Lancia, Jim Lancia, Matt Lancia, and Ron Abbott.

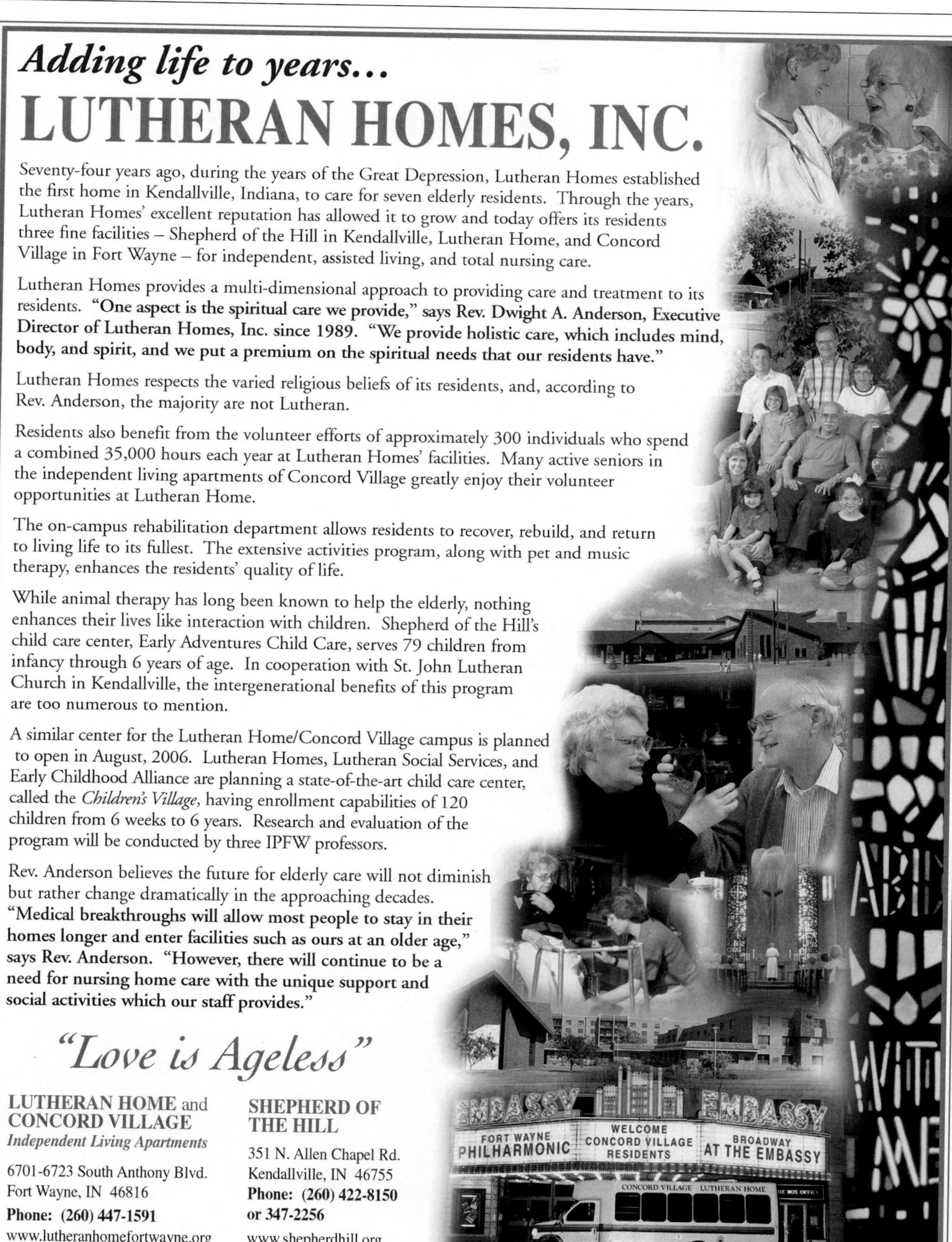

Adding life to years...
LUTHERAN HOMES, INC.
Seventy-four years ago, during the years of the Great Depression, Lutheran Homes established the first home in Kendallville, Indiana, to care for seven elderly residents. Through the years, Lutheran Homes' excellent reputation has allowed it to grow and today offers its residents three fine facilities – Shepherd of the Hill in Kendallville, Lutheran Home, and Concord Village in Fort Wayne – for independent, assisted living, and total nursing care.
Lutheran Homes provides a multi-dimensional approach to providing care and treatment to its residents. "One aspect is the spiritual care we provide," says Rev. Dwight A. Anderson, Executive Director of Lutheran Homes, Inc. since 1989. "We provide holistic care, which includes mind, body, and spirit, and we put a premium on the spiritual needs that our residents have."
Lutheran Homes respects the varied religious beliefs of its residents, and, according to Rev. Anderson, the majority are not Lutheran.
Residents also benefit from the volunteer efforts of approximately 300 individuals who spend a combined 35,000 hours each year at Lutheran Homes' facilities. Many active seniors in the independent living apartments of Concord Village greatly enjoy their volunteer opportunities at Lutheran Home.
The on-campus rehabilitation department allows residents to recover, rebuild, and return to living life to its fullest. The extensive activities program, along with pet and music therapy, enhances the residents' quality of life.
While animal therapy has long been known to help the elderly, nothing enhances their lives like interaction with children. Shepherd of the Hill's child care center, Early Adventures Child Care, serves 79 children from infancy through 6 years of age. In cooperation with St. John Lutheran Church in Kendallville, the intergenerational benefits of this program are too numerous to mention.
A similar center for the Lutheran Home/Concord Village campus is planned to open in August, 2006. Lutheran Homes, Lutheran Social Services, and Early Childhood Alliance are planning a state-of-the-art child care center, called the Children's Village, having enrollment capabilities of 120 children from 6 weeks to 6 years. Research and evaluation of the program will be conducted by three IPFW professors.
Rev. Anderson believes the future for elderly care will not diminish but rather change dramatically in the approaching decades. "Medical breakthroughs will allow most people to stay in their homes longer and enter facilities such as ours at an older age," says Rev. Anderson. "However, there will continue to be a need for nursing home care with the unique support and social activities which our staff provides."
"Love is Ageless"
LUTHERAN HOME and CONCORD VILLAGE
Independent Living Apartments
6701-6723 South Anthony Blvd.
Fort Wayne, IN 46816
Phone: (260) 447-1591
www.lutheranhomefortwayne.org
SHEPHERD OF THE HILL
351 N. Allen Chapel Rd.
Kendallville, IN 46755
Phone: (260) 422-8150
or 347-2256
www.shepherdhill.org
EMBASSY
FORT WAYNE PHILHARMONIC
WELCOME CONCORD VILLAGE RESIDENTS
BROADWAY AT THE EMBASSY
CONCORD VILLAGE · LUTHERAN HOME

MARTIN RILEY architects/engineers

The firm of Martin Riley began as a very modest and humble organization in 1986. It consisted of partners, Victor Martin, John Riley and Luther Mock. Both Mr. Martin and Mr. Riley were Registered Architects while Mr. Martin was also an Interior Designer and Mr. Riley a Registered Roof Consultant. The firm worked primarily in architectural design and roof consulting.

The firm's first office was in a Victorian style house at 806 West Washington Boulevard in the West Central Neighborhood of Fort Wayne, Indiana. As the firm grew they moved to a building in the 100 block of West Wayne Street, continuing their focus on architectural and roof design. Martin Riley continued to grow and after renovating new space moved to 222 West Berry Street, occupying the first floor of the Odd Fellows Lodge Building.

In 1996, the firm, along with others, formed a new corporation and purchased the Baker Street Train Station. After a complete renovation of the east and west wings of the building, Martin Riley moved into the renewed space in December of 1996. At that time, renovation of the Grand Concourse was delayed while historic renovation plans were developed and funding acquired for the restoration task.

By October of 2002, the entire Baker Street Station had been restored and renovated. The east and west wings were converted into first class office space and the Grand Concourse developed into reception and meeting space that hosts upward to 150 events per year. As a result of this renovation, the Station has received numerous awards for historic renovation and innovation. Locally, the Station received an ARCH award and an American Institute of Architects award for Historic Preservation. The Station also received a regional AIA Historic Renovation Award and it was recognized with an Innovative Business Award from *Inside Indiana*.

Major areas of renovation included recreating the decorative plaster found on the barrel vaulted ceiling, opening the stained glass clerestory windows, recreating the decorative railroad clock surrounds, restoring marble and terrazzo floors and repainting the ornate plasterwork in historical colors. Nearly 50 years of neglect were reversed with the work that was completed in 2002. During the renovation process, the building was put on both the State of Indiana and the National Register of Historic Places.

Presently the firm of Martin Riley has an architectural group, an interior design group and a full engineering staff working in mechanical, electrical and civil engineering. The firm also has a group that specializes in building exteriors--roofs, masonry and building envelope design and problem remediation. The firm has continued to grow and, in the intervening years, Jack Daniel came on as a partner who now has responsibility for the architectural group, as did Chris Baker who has responsibility for the building exteriors group.

Baker Street Community Association

The Baker Street Community Association grew directly out of the group that purchased the station in 1996. This is a not-for-profit group put together to operate and maintain the historical Grand Concourse of the Baker Street Station and help other not-for-profit organizations make use of the facility for special events. Central to the Association's formation were Don Steininger, Stephen Williams, Chris Rupp and Victor Martin. As a side bar, the group also collects railroad memorabilia, particularly railroad items used or associated with railroad activity in the Fort Wayne and surrounding area. The Association archives material and many items are on display in the Grand Concourse.

Recognition must be given to the original community association who had the vision and will to make the restoration of the Baker Street Station a reality. This group includes Robert A'Hearn, Dennis Becker, Pastor Richard G. Frazier, Joyce Glock, Steven Glock MD, Ann Golm, The Honorable William C. Lee, Dennis Mahuren, Victor Martin, Carol Roberts, Christine Rupp, Walter Sassmannshausen, Mary Scrogham, Donald B. Steininger, the late Sharon Stellhorn and Stephen Williams.

Ongoing restoration of the Grand Concourse continues as items original to the building or items that incorporate the heritage of the building are located and returned to the Station. Items such as the neon sign that directed passengers to the street and waiting taxis, the ornate wooden clock surrounds and the restoration of the historic railroad clocks at both the north and south exits of the Grand Concourse.

The Association encourages not-for-profit groups to utilize the space. Examples include a youth ministry group who uses the Concourse for services on a weekly basis. Another example that has turned into an annual function is the lighting of the Christmas Tree for Hospice. These lights stay on the entire month of December and the group uses the building at its convenience.

Through the work of the Association, history is preserved and the community is enriched by the work of not-for-profit groups who make use of the historic Baker Street Station.

Train Station – Baker Street Station

Maumee Valley Veterinary Clinic P.C.

Dr. David F. Nahrwold, as owner, along with his wife, Elaine, opened Maumee Valley Veterinary Clinic at 22904 Tile Mill Road in Woodburn, Indiana, on 8-20-1987, which also corresponds to their 10th wedding anniversary. Dr. Nahrwold is a 1978 graduate of Purdue School of Veterinary Medicine. For the first year following graduation, he was employed at Shelbyville Animal Clinic in Shelbyville, Indiana. Following that year, he and his wife moved to North Manchester, Indiana, eventually becoming a partner in that practice. During this time, their two daughters were born, Elisabeth and Stephanie. This partnership was not sustained, and was ended amicably. God's hand was at work because this motivated the Nahrwold's to look for a potential veterinary practice, which was within close distance to a Lutheran elementary school for their young family.

For a little over a year, while trying to discern the next move, Dr. Nahrwold split his time with two growing practices, Stellhorn Veterinary Hospital in Fort Wayne, and Honneger Animal Clinic in Ossian. During the latter half of this time, he and his family moved to Woodburn in anticipation of buying an existing practice there. Dr. Nahrwold started to serve a few of the local livestock owners there also, among which Melvin Rekeweg, Bob Buuck, Wayne Horman and Bruce Brenneke were the first dairies and Darwin Werling and Richard and David Hartmann were the first swine operations.

Late 1986 once again blessed Dr. Nahrwold and his wife with another child, Seth. At this time it was becoming apparent that if they wanted to remain in this community and to send their children to Woodburn Lutheran School, they would need to start their own veterinary clinic. James Bridge of Bridge Manufacturing offered the young couple the corner of his own business lot to place a clinic. Working also through Jim, Dr. Nahrwold ordered a custom made 14 x 70 building brought in and placed on a foundation, which remains the present building in 2005. From a conviction borne out of experience and scriptural admonition, the young couple's endeavor was to undertake this project without debt. Having been blessed with just enough capital from the prior partnership, and by doing much of the labor themselves, this conviction became a reality. One of the desires of the Nahrwolds was to be able to play background Christian music in the office, and by owning their own practice, they put this into effect, which continues to the present day.

The early emphasis of Maumee Valley Veterinary Clinic was to serve the livestock owners in the area, especially building a practice that specialized in swine consultation and computerized records. At the same time additional dairies were added and the pet practice also increased. Over the ensuing ten years, however, there was a major shift occurring in agriculture and soon many of the thriving livestock operations ceased to exist. Again, in God's Providence, by preparing Dr. Nahrwold to switch to an emphasis of small animal, his early professional career had prepared him well.

Dr. Nahrwold has been blessed with long-standing and faithful employees. Currently, besides his wife, Julanne Molitor, Deb Richeson, Linda Lengacher, and Jeannette Giangrande share part-time support in the practice and all have been with the practice for several years.

Dr. Nahrwold strives to serve his clientele with modern technology in current methods of medicine and surgery, at small town affordability. In accomplishing this, Dr. Nahrwold offers technologies that few others in the Fort Wayne area offer, including videoscopy and blood pressure monitoring on regular basis for his patients.

Just recently he has added to his computerized practice a program that only about 200 veterinary practices in the entire nation enjoy. This program allows him to enter examination results during the exam in front of the client, and it will print out a plan of action and treatment options for each abnormality. He can update these options as he comes back from continuing education conferences to continually give his clients up to date medical information. Otherwise, many good ideas are laid aside when returning from such continuing education due to the hustle and bustle of the normal daily activities.

A drug formulary program allows him to enter a pet's specific information to obtain accurate dosages, potential side effects and any incompatibilities that could be encountered.

Currently, daughter Elisabeth is a called teacher at Lutheran High in New Orleans; Stephanie is doing her clinicals in the bachelor of nursing program at IUPUI; and Elaine enjoys her first love as a part-time music teacher at Ascension Lutheran School as well as being office manager at the Clinic.

Seth aspires to gain admittance into the Purdue School of Veterinary Medicine and to eventually join his father in practice at Maumee Valley Veterinary Clinic in Woodburn, Indiana. *Compiled by David F. Nahrwold DVM*

Mayflower Mills 1889-1970

Harry E. Bash

Mayflower Mills was established in 1889. The incorporators were Joseph Hughes, Charles S. Bash, J. W. Orr, and Peter D. Smyser. The business was located at 120 W. Columbia Street in Fort Wayne and was primarily in the flour milling business but also produced ground flaxseed and specialized in recleaned flax in the early years of the business. The business immediately prospered and in 1890 they bought the building which, up to that time, they had occupied as tenants. The business continued to increase and in 1892 it acquired the adjoining building at 118 W. Columbia Street plus additional frontage of twenty feet. In 1894, they began the process of demolishing and rebuilding on the site. At the end of that process, they occupied a modern five story brick structure 110 feet deep with 50 foot frontage on W. Columbia Street and trackage in the rear of the building, abutting the Nickel Plate railroad. The new facility had 33,000 square feet of floor space.

In 1900, Mayflower Mills bought out the Bond Cereal Mills, and in 1905 acquired the adjoining property of S. Bash and Company on which was located a grain elevator. The firm had no difficulty in raising capital because of its great success. The shareholders in 1906 were Nora Bash Hughes, Charles S. Bash, Flora Orr Bash, Peter D. Smyser, Harry E. Bash, and J. W. Orr.

In the early years, and through much of its history, Mayflower Mills produced product for the retail market. Some of their early retail product names included "Silver Dust," "Vienna," "Eclipse," and "Triumph." The "Silver Dust" product name continued through most of the history of the business. The business also developed special items such as their celebrated "Chicken Feed" and "Scratch Feed" which were sold under the trade names of "Admiral" and "Bon Ton." After acquiring the Bond Cereal Mills by purchase, they added to their product line "Bond's Whole Wheat Flour," "Bond's Boston Brown Bread Flour," "Bond's Gluten Flour," and "Bond's Graham Flour." By 1915, its leading brands were "Silver Dust," "Maysill," "Newveno," and "Carnoso," and an export brand known as "Mayflower Patent." "Mayflower Patent" sold very well to foreign buyers. On May 21, 1911, the business suffered a devastating fire which for a time threatened the very heart of the business district in Fort Wayne. The fire started within the Mill property from some unknown cause about 9 o'clock on the morning of that day, and within a few hours the entire plant of the corporation was wiped out and nothing but a heap of ruins remained. A neighboring milling concern, the Volland Milling Company, located at 114 W. Columbia Street, only a few doors east of the destroyed plant, was contemplating going out of business and the Mayflower Mills management immediately leased that facility and resumed business there so that the devastating fire hardly caused the business to skip a beat.

The management of Mayflower Mills began planning for a new facility which was constructed on approximately four acres located on Leesburg Road near the crossing of the Nickel Plate and Grand Rapids and Indiana railways. The new facility was the most modern that could be built at the time. Its capacity included a daily output of seven hundred barrels of Standard Flour, two hundred barrels of Special Flours, twenty tons per day of special concentrated feeds, and seventy five barrels of ground flaxseed. The elevator had a storage capacity of fifty thousand bushels. By 1965, the daily output had been increased to 3,200 hundred weight of flour and the storage capacity increased to 250,000 bushels.

By the late 1920s Harry E. Bash had bought out the other shareholders. He served as president until his death in 1938.

David W. Bash

Harry's sons, Harry Edward, Jr., Robert, and David managed the business after Harry Sr.'s death. David served as president from 1958 until the business closed in 1970.

Over most of its history, Mayflower Mills manufactured for both the retail trade and institutional bakeries. After World War II, the flour milling industry began to change significantly due to the growth of the large national brands. By the end of the 1950s it had virtually ceased manufacturing for the retail trade. Its name brands at that point still included "Silver Dust," "Snow Goose" and "Martha Wayne." During World War II, when bleaching products were in short supply it was facetiously suggested that "Snow Goose" should be renamed "Grey Goose." By the 1960s the focus of the business shifted to manufacturing flour for export through government foreign aid programs, particularly to Central and South America. The firm still catered to some institutional bakers such as Somers Bakery and Perkins Pancake Houses. A longshoreman's strike in New Orleans in the late 1960s was a severe blow to the business because it simply cut off the foreign aid export market for a couple of months. Due primarily to health problems of top management, the business closed in 1970.

Mayflower Mills c. 1965.

D.O. McComb & Sons Funeral Home

By 1925, Fort Wayne was changing with innovation, expansion, and progress. The busiest commercial downtown area was shifting from Columbia, Berry, and Main Streets over to Wayne, Washington, and Jefferson Streets. The first municipal airport, Paul Baer Airport (Smith Field) was opening. After a hard hit from the flu epidemic of 1918-1919, Lincoln National Life had survived and moved into its now permanent headquarters on Harrison Street. Fort Wayne had gone from 86,549 residents in 1920 to approximately 100,747 residents. Growth was everywhere!

David O. McComb

David O. McComb had been serving as Superintendent of Allen County Schools since 1913. His passion was education and since the beginning of his teaching career in 1912, he had not only made an impact in the lives of his students, but also throughout the entire community. "Uncle Dave" as his students called him, had formed and served as the first president of the Northeastern Indiana Teachers' Association, obtained the first Agricultural Agent for Allen County, and inaugurated the Allen County Library system. But for all of these major accomplishments, none may have personally touched the lives of Fort Wayne's people as did founding the D.O. McComb & Sons Funeral Home.

Fort Wayne already had 27 funeral homes in the community. These funeral homes only served certain niches and all were connected to some other type of industry. Dave's friend, Mr. Conroy, posed the question, "Dave, have you thought about what you want to do when you retire from the superintendent position?" Thus, the idea for a family owned funeral home was born.

D.O. McComb & Sons Funeral Home originally opened as Conroy-McComb Funeral Home in a store front facility on the corner of East Lewis and Lafayette Streets. In 1928, after Conroy's death, the funeral home was moved to Dave's personal residence at 1140 Lake Avenue, which still today remains the Lakeside location. Dave had purchased the home shortly after the great flood of 1913 when the house withstood water rising three feet above the first level of the home. Since Dave's vision was to provide funeral service with a family atmosphere, the move here made sense.

In 1938 Fort Wayne's population was almost up to 118,400. It had been two years since David O. McComb had passed away and six years since his sons, James and Walter A. McComb Sr. took over the business. The Lakeside facility added another chapel, and the McComb family began to offer a "no-fee basis" ambulance service. This service would be an integral part of Fort Wayne community through 1978.

In 1940, Walter McComb's Sons, Walter A. McComb Jr. and David O. McComb joined the family business. Fort Wayne seemed to have reached the peak of its progress with hundreds of businesses prospering around the district centering on Calhoun Street. Even though Fort Wayne's economy would begin a decline after this decade, this began the era of our greatest expansion. In 1958 major construction to the Lakeside facility produced the structure that is there today. In 1974 Foster Park was opened at 6301 Fairfield Avenue. In 1982 Maplewood Park was opened at 4017 Maplecrest Road. In 1985 Dilgard & Cline funeral home in Auburn was purchased, and the McComb, Dilgard, & Cline location at 502 North Main Street opened. In 1987, Terra Services Inc., and Estate Security General Insurance Agency, Inc. were incorporated. In 1995 Pine Valley Park was opened at 1320 East Dupont Road, and the Mungovan & Sons Funeral Home was purchased at 2114 South Calhoun Street. In 1999 the end of a great century in Fort Wayne's history saw the final construction of chapels to date as Covington Knolls was opened at 8325 Covington Road.

The beginning of a new century had arrived in 2000. Douglas M. McComb and David W. McComb, the sons of Walter A. Jr., had been working in the family business since their teens in the 1970s. Between 2000 and 2002, the Lakeside location added an arrangement center, and the administrative offices were remodeled. A fourth company, General Buying Group, Inc. d/b/a Premier Preneed was also incorporated. Today, 2005, the children of Doug and Dave McComb prepare to carry on the family business.

A great deal has changed about both Fort Wayne and D.O. McComb & Sons Funeral Home. The seed of excellent family service that was planted by David McComb has not changed. Maybe it's that Walt's office was his grandmother's bedroom or maybe it is that Doug's uncle was born in the office he now works. Maybe it is the family spirit that lives in the 106 employees now working here. Whatever it is, this family vision has helped over 57,417 Fort Wayne families walk through a difficult experience. It is our sincere wish that this level of excellence based on a mission embracing family values continues well into the next century.

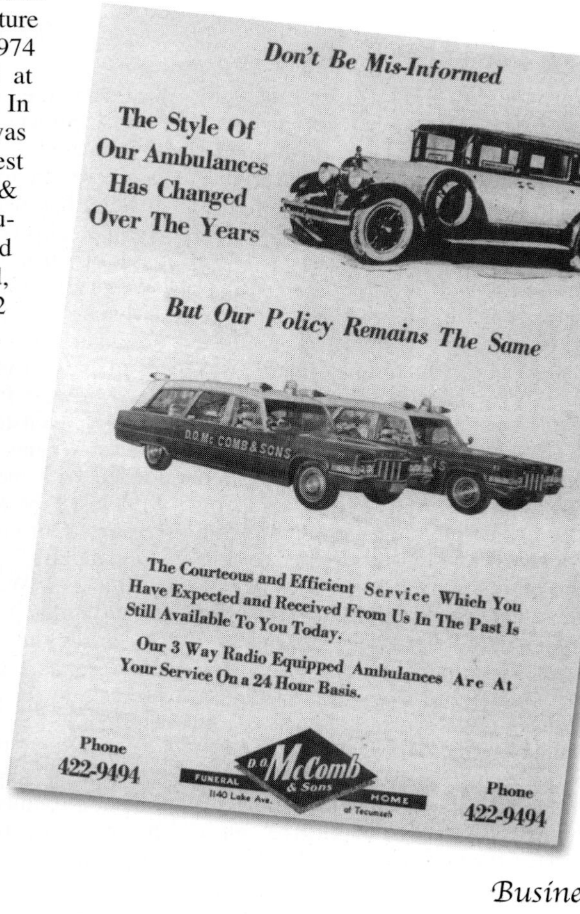

Midwest Pipe and Steel

Jerome F. Henry, Jr. (left) and Melvin Krel.

You wouldn't think, to look at him, that Jerome F. Henry Jr., got his start hauling trash in the back of a beat-up old pickup truck. Today, in his comfortable office, he commands the $100 million a year Midwest Pipe & Steel, along with a host of other business enterprises.

Yet on the wall in his office is a picture of that beat-up old pickup truck, one that he remembers spending 18 hours a day, loading and unloading by hand.

"My mom answered the phone for me when I was in school," taking hauling orders for the fledgling entrepreneur. He worked nights in a steel mill and started hauling trash and construction scrap on the side. Over time, he learned the scrap metal business and then graduated to selling steel products.

The eldest of 17 children, Henry had "the advantage, the privilege of poverty. I respect every dollar." The son of a social worker, he knew he would have to make his own way in the world.

Henry started Midwest Pipe & Steel Inc. in the early 1970s with his then-partner, Melvin Krel, on Banks Avenue off Freeman Street. Henry bought Krel out in 1975. Later, the business moved to Winter Street and then to the old Fruehauf site on Pontiac Street. The businesses offices are now located on East Berry Street.

For more than 25 years, Midwest Pipe & Steel has been supplying a wide variety of steel products to an ever-increasing base of customers across the Midwest. "We're all about metals here," Henry said. "We manufacture, sell and distribute metal products ... from unfabricated raw materials to angle iron to steel beams."

Midwest Pipe & Steel sells to some 500 active customers in a 200-mile radius of Fort Wayne. Every day, a dozen trucks loaded with metal leave the city, hauling Midwest Pipe & Steel products across the region. "Our customer base has expanded dramatically," he noted. "Once we only sold in Fort Wayne. Now we're in excess of 200 miles."

And the types of products have changed as well, he added. "Customers are asking for a more diverse inventory," he said.

Midwest Pipe & Steel specializes in the sale of angles, bars, channels, cold-finished rounds and squares, H-beams, I-beams, pipe, sheets and tubing in virtually any length or weight.

"Our customers are very precious to us," he continued. "We take them and their needs very seriously."

Henry, 54, a lifelong Fort Wayne resident, employs about 50 people at Midwest Pipe & Steel. Among them are Don Wright, vice president and sales manager, and Laura Smith, vice president of purchasing. Both have been with Midwest Pipe & Steel for more than 20 years.

The business has also been active in the community. Henry has served on a number of non-profit boards and commissions, and has been active in supporting Bishop Luers High School, Big Brothers/ Big Sisters and the Carriage House, which supports people with mental illnesses. And he's helped support other local entrepreneurs start their own businesses through his venture capital sideline.

His business philosophy is simple: "We have a passion to serve others the way we want to be served." His advice to others? "You should cut your own path through life." That's advice he's given to his five children, none of whom work with him. "I want them to find their own way." Just as he did in his beat-up old pickup truck.

Murphy Insurance, Inc.

Murphy Insurance, Inc., 626 Broadway, New Haven, Indiana was founded in 1934 on a challenge and a packet of mail order supplies. Founder Harold DeWitt Murphy

(1909-2000) was working at International Harvester (Navistar) and living in Fort Wayne. His father, Robert Ross Murphy, was a part-time agent for Farmers' Mutual Liability Company (which later became Meridian Mutual and still later became State Auto Insurance Company). Robert told Harold that he could probably sell a lot of insurance if he tried. Harold thought about it briefly. He then wrote to the company asking if they would like to have another agent in the area. Company forms and supplies were received by return mail. Harold was in the insurance business! Agent licensing was not required in 1934. Harold and his wife, Dorothy Daisy (Ewing) (1913-1994), moved to the Broadway location in 1937. This site served as the business location, as well as their family home, until 1979. The business continues at this same location.

Thomas J. Murphy (1945-), one of Harold and Dorothy's four children, decided during his early high school years that he would join his father in the insurance business. Tom graduated from New Haven High School in 1963 and began his college education with only that in mind. With a B.S. degree in General Business Administration from Ball State University in 1967, Tom and his father, Harold, formed a partnership. In 1972, Tom received his Chartered Life Underwriter (CLU) designation. He was the youngest person in Allen County to achieve that rank at that time.

Harold retired from the business at the end of 1975. In an August, 1985 newspaper interview, Harold said the biggest change that he had seen in insurance business was its complexity. He said that when he started selling insurance, it was fairly simple to figure and quote a policy cost by figuring it in his head. By 1985, it took thick manuals full of charts and figures to quote a policy and cost.

Tom's wife, Susan J. (Smith) (1945-), began working part time in the business primarily as the bookkeeper. Susan also obtain her Property/Casualty Insurance License and has continued to keep her license active. The Life Underwriter's Training Council (LUTC) designation was awarded to Tom in July, 1973. In 1986, he was awarded the Certified Insurance Counselor (CIC) designation. Murphy Insurance partnered, in 1987, with a much larger Fort Wayne based property/casualty insurance agency known as the Stewart-Brimner Group. This partnership provided Murphy Insurance with many additional markets and the ability to insure almost any type and size of insurance risk.

In 1994, Murphy received his securities license and became a "Register Investment Advisor" in 1998. Murphy Insurance was recognized as the "Business of the Year" in 1993 by the New Haven Chamber of Commerce, and on Apri1 23, 2003, Lieutenant Governor, Joseph Kernan, presented Murphy Insurance the "Half-Century Business" Award for contributions to the economic growth and prosperity of Indiana. (www.murphvinsurance.net)

Thomas L. Murphy and Harold DeWitt Murphy, August 12, 1989.

Northeast Indiana Public Radio, Inc.

Northeast Indiana Public Radio (NIPR) is the listener-supported community licensee for two stations among the 620 public radio stations nationwide: WBOI-FM 89.1's 50,000 watt signal broadcasts National Public Radio (NPR) news and jazz to thirteen counties in northeast Indiana and northwest Ohio; WBNI-FM transmits a twenty-four hour classical music service with 2,000 watts at 91.3 FM from its Orland transmitter site in Steuben County, Indiana; and 10 watts at 88.7 FM on its Fort Wayne-based translator frequency. Broadcasts integrate locally produced and nationally acquired programs into schedules that seek to serve the needs and interests of its listeners. Each station's audio is heard on the internet– www.nipr.fm

Operations are supported by a paid staff of twelve and the contributions of over 200 volunteers annually. This depth of broadcasting service has been achieved through three qualities: consistent community participation; dynamic response to challenge; and a vision to embrace the future.

Community participants were part of NIPR's first broadcast heard on WIPU-FM July 8, 1978, from a 500 square feet studio in the basement of Helmke Library on the campus of Indiana University-Purdue University Fort Wayne (IPFW). The official "Friends of WIPU," formed five months later, augmented the staff of four. The fledgling station of 4,000 watts was heard five hours a day, five days a week. Within nine months, a growing group of volunteers valuing classical music carried the station to ten-hour days, with twelve on Saturday. When IPFW could no longer fund the collegiate enterprise, the Friends incorporated in July 1981 as Public Broadcasting of Northeast Indiana, (PBNI), and formed a board of directors. PBNI, Inc. emerged, and, with FCC approval in January 1982, transformed the call letters to WBNI on March 16, 1982. Through the dedication of volunteers and on-air hosts, WBNI broadcast Monday-Sunday from 8 a.m. to 2 a.m. The broad community connection was formalized in 1982 with the founding of a community advisory board. Today, volunteers continue to serve in capacities from staffing the reception desk and maintaining the recording library to producing and hosting music and information programs In 2004, NIPR's volunteers provided over 1,500 hours of support valued at more than $100,000.

IPFW's funding cut in 1981 resulted in the Friends' incorporation of the station. Dramatically, as the station's first words were spoken under the WBNI call letters from Helmke Library at 3:45 p.m. on March 16, 1982, floodwaters forced the station off the air. The Friends moved the studios to the YWCA Villa complex on Wells Street and began immediate operation. The first grant for equipment facilitated the power increase from 4,000 to 31,000 watts in 1984. The board approved its first long-range plan the next year, and, in 1986, WBNI-FM was certified to receive federal support from the Corporation for Public Broadcasting. That same year the station became a member of National Public Radio and American Public Radio, adding national news and performance programs to the schedule.

This symbol, adopted in 2002, reflects the combined public service provided by WBNI and WBOI across northeast Indiana.

The station's programming and operational challenges were met through inventive adaptability, commitment to growth, and the capacity to a blend of vision and energy of professionals and volunteers. Subsequently stability was provided through the longevity of general managers, only three over twenty-five years. George Went, in 1978, was followed by Tim Singleton, who headed operations from 1980-1986. Bruce Haines joined WBNI from the Muncie public radio affiliate in 1987. In partnership with station's trustees, staff, volunteers, and community support, WBNI-FM began twenty-four hour broadcasting in 1989; initiated simulcasting from WBKE-FM at Manchester College in North Manchester in 1991; increased power from 31,000 to 50,000 watts and built a new facility in 1994 through the first capital campaign; dedicated the Harriet A. Parrish Performance Studio for local music and community programming production (1997); initiated simulcasting from WEAX-FM at Tri-State University in Angola (1999); established WBOI in 2002; and expanded programming to a new level of variety and sophistication.

WBOI-FM 89.1 converted to high-definition (HD) broadcasting in 2005. Providing a clear audio transmission quality, HD receivers display song and artist information, weather and traffic alerts, as well, as "multicasting" more than one audio service at the same dial position. WBOI now offers three listening options at 89.1 FM: WBOI 1 (WBOI's present programming); WBOI 2 (WBNI's classical music service); and WBOI 3 (all jazz programming).

Throughout NIPR's history, the management, staff and board have involved the community, envisioned the future and acted with courage. Listeners continue to benefit each week from NIPR's heritage that is based upon a distinguished tradition of values and a commitment to excellence. Support NIPR with a contribution by calling 260/452-1189, located at 3204 Clairmont Court, Fort Wayne, Indiana 46808.

Old Fort Supply Company, Inc.

For nearly a century Old Fort Supply Company has been a major factor in the building construction market in the city of Fort Wayne and surrounding areas. On May 13, 1914, seventeen masonry and plastering contractors pooled their resources to organize the firm. Starting with a modest $20,000 in capital, a horse and five employees, Old Fort opened its offices in a framed building at 705 Clay Street that also doubled as a warehouse.

A subject of discussion in the company board meetings in early years was the health of its horse and how much the company was spending for the animal's food. Only four years after it was founded, Old Fort had need for more space. Additional common stock was issued and a three story brick building at 709 -711 Clay Street, home of the former City Carriage Works, was purchased and remodeled to meet Old Fort's requirements.

F. E. Schouweiler came to Old Fort Supply in 1923 as a bookkeeper and became Manager in 1928 and was elected President in 1935. Those were extremely difficult times for during the depths of the Depression, in 1930 and 1931, the company was reduced to only three men, a driver, a yard man, and Mr. Schouweiler who served as manager, bookkeeper and salesman. But with bulldog tenacity, Old Fort Supply hung on, doing $39,000 in sales during even the darkest of those years.

After 31 years the headquarters on Clay Street was closed, due to the railroad elevation being put in place, which took over a good portion of the yard. In December 1959 the company moved into newly constructed buildings at 2013 South Anthony Boulevard adjacent to its ready mix concrete plant and warehouse facilities.

Old Fort Supply Company has been a by-word among contractors and builders throughout the state for many years. The company became one of the largest clay products distributors in the State representing major brick manufacturers from many different parts of the country.

The company has consistently represented many widely known products and manufacturers such as Majestic Fireplace Company, Modernfold Doors and Operable Walls, garage doors and operators, Belden Brick, construction tools and hundreds of building specialties.

In 1966 due to wide diversity in product lines and services, the company name was changed to Old Fort Industries, Inc. In September of 1970, Old Fort Industries sold its building supply division to two of its senior employees Alen G. Wyss and Wm. J. Rudolph and the company name once again became Old Fort Supply Company, Inc. The office was moved to its current location at 2000 Wayne Trace. At that time there were 19 employees that had been with the Company over 25 years and 30 that had been employed more the 10 years. Mr. Wyss, the new President stated, "Our biggest asset is our employees. We can't say enough about our people. People are important - we really care about others besides ourselves. You must have credibility. If you tell someone you'll do something, then that's the way is has to be."

Mr. Wyss and Mr. Rudolph continued to own and operate Old Fort Supply Company, Inc. until 1994 when Mr. Donald L. Menze of Fort Wayne purchased the Company. Mr. Menze has owned and operated Old Fort Supply Company since that time. The company has added a new location and showroom in North Fort Wayne at 919 Production Road under the name of Old Fort-Stonewall to better serve its many customers. The Company also has a location in Goshen, Indiana under the name of Modern Masonry.

Mr. Menze continues to lead his company in the direction it has always followed: to help build a better city by providing high quality products, premium service, and an excellent and dedicated sales staff with many years of experience in the building profession.

One of the strongest points in Old Fort Supply Company's sales staff is their ability to work closely with local and area architects, home builders, and commercial contractors to assist them in the selection of the materials they need to create beautiful and functional buildings.

Throughout Old Fort's history the common ingredient has been change. Change is necessary to meet the building market's needs for new products, new equipment, and new convenient locations. But one constant goal has remained all these years... our customers are our main concern. As long as our service to them remains strong, our future is secure.

Old Fort Supply Company, Inc., 2000 Wayne Trace.

Patterson Riegel Advertising, Inc.

Patterson Riegel Advertising, Inc.
200 East Main Street Suite 710
Fort Wayne, IN 46802

Facing his 30th birthday, Matt Henry made a momentous decision. He left a prestigious job with a solid employer and struck out on his own.

The year was 1988, and Henry, who was heading the external communications department of St. Joseph Hospital, knew if he was ever to make it on his own, that was the time.

His older brother, Jerome F. Henry Jr., helped him get the financing to start his own marketing firm, Patterson Riegel Advertising. Today, Matt Henry, 46, is sole owner of Patterson Riegel, which is a full-service advertising and marketing firm.

"We specialized initially in desktop publishing," he recalled. "We were riding the wave of the new industry created when personal computers were made available."

From strategic planning to crisis management, Patterson Riegel addresses a full slate of marketing needs for its clients.

"Our clients may need a brochure every three years or so, but they also need to stay in the public eye," he said. "Public relations is another service for our clients."

The firm helps its clients identify their marketing needs, determines the target markets (such as print publications, TV or radio advertising, or collateral materials), develops an advertising campaign, and evaluates the effectiveness of each campaign.

Patterson Riegel takes its name from Matt Henry's maternal and paternal great-grandmothers, respectively. As one of 17 children of Jerome and Marganelle Henry Sr., Matt, the father of five children with his wife Anne, wanted to stay away from the Henry moniker when choosing a name for his business. For his business logo, he incorporated a lion taken from the Riegel family crest. To Matt, the lion represented everything his company stood for: courage, honor, integrity, leadership, and pride. Today, these traits are integrated into every facet of the Patterson Riegel agency. The business helps support local charities, including Big Brothers/Big Sisters and The History Center.

(l. to r.) Matt Henry, Tina Tackett, John Foreman, and Amy Manes.

From media buying for clients as diverse as Korte Does It All and Fort Wayne Neurological Center to business-to-business advertising for a variety of industries such as Steel Dynamics, Nucor Vulcraft and National Tube Form, Patterson Riegel specializes in finding diverse solutions for its clients.

A recent addition to the services the firm offers has been specialty advertising, in the form of customized apparel, caps, pens, and incentive and promotional items. From hats to mouse pads, Patterson Riegel can incorporate a company's logo and message into virtually any item.

"That was a natural evolution for us," Matt said. "It's pretty big business."

Patterson Riegel's four full-time employees are supplemented by a variety of contract employees. Matt in particular relies on John Foreman, the firm's managing director, who oversees all day-to-day operations of the business. Foreman handles all production and scheduling for the firm's many projects and clients, Matt noted.

The company's office manager, Tina Tackett, handles "traffic" for the firm's media buys and oversees the specialty advertising division. Tackett also is instrumental in keeping the office organized and running smoothly.

The business was first located on Calhoun Street and then moved to the old Buckner building at the intersection of Fulton Street and Washington Boulevard (now home to the Charis House of the Fort Wayne Rescue Mission). Later, Patterson Riegel moved onto The Landing in historic downtown Fort Wayne. As the business grew, however, Matt realized he needed more space, and in November 2004, the firm moved into the seventh floor of the Standard Federal Plaza on Main Street. From his 7th floor corner office, Matt has a commanding view of downtown Fort Wayne, from the Bloomingdale neighborhood where he grew up to the banks of the St. Mary's River at Headwaters Park.

Matt admitted that he spends a lot of time looking out the windows as he contemplates strategies for his clients.

"My philosophy is no matter what you do in business, you need to do what you love," Matt said. "If you do what you love, the business will come." *Submitted by Matt Henry*

Physician & Surgeons Exchange / Schaefer's Anserphone Inc.

In 1925, a young woman named Florence Schaefer started a company that has continued into the 21st century. She recognized the power of a new technology - "telephones" - and exploited a niche market that has expanded along with the technology that powered it.

Physician & Surgeons was started in a house on Columbia Avenue, moving then to Standard Federal Plaza Building and then to its current location, 418 East Berry Street, in the late 50s. Florence Schaefer along with four other employees kept the phone lines open 24 hours a day, because of the doctors and companies needing the 24-hour 7-day service. The population of Allen County at that time was 130,523.

But a woman owning a business in the 1920s was an unusual thing. Florence had been a teller at a local bank when two of her brothers, Joe and Frank Schaefer, got involved in the burgeoning "telephone" business. Frank Schaefer installed telephone lines and serviced them, while Joe worked in the finance department of a telephone company in Saudi Arabia. The two brothers could see how fast the industry was growing and could see there was a need for people to answer telephones.

For many years, Physician & Surgeons Exchange served as the sole answering service for Fort Wayne's doctors. The company expanded to commercial business, such as fire alarm system for Huntertown, emergency call service for local blood banks, burglar alarms systems and even served for a time as the Western Union office for Fort Wayne.

In 1975 the company operated seven cord switchboards that held 100 accounts each, employing 21-25 people to keep the boards running 24 hours a day. Physician & Surgeons Exchange made a practice of hiring women and people with disabilities to fill operator positions. The tradition continues today.

When a caller needed a doctor, they were to write down the complete message by hand on yellow tablets- these were kept for one year. The company collected stacks and stacks of yellow tablets. When a caller sought to speak with one of the commercial accounts, the switchboard operator could either connect the call or take a message and then relay it to the account, as they called in. Messages were written by hand and were kept on file for six months.

Margery Gligor was hired in 1950 as a switchboard operator after hearing about the company from her sister-in-law. Twenty-three years later, she bought it. Florence Schaefer, who died on August 8, 2001, had retired in the late 1960s, and her brother Ben ran the company until his death in January 1973. Margery ran the business through some trying times.

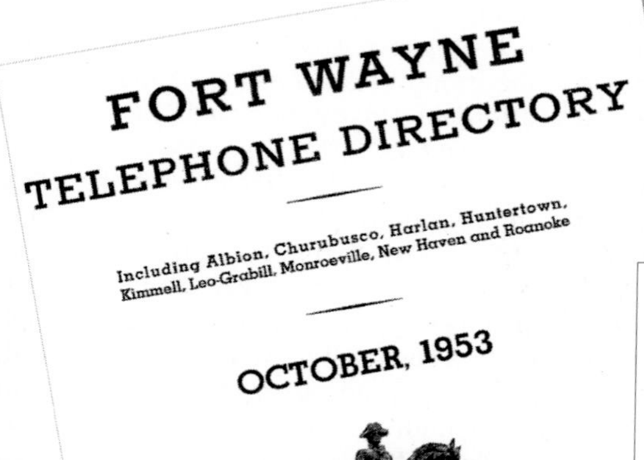

FORT WAYNE
TELEPHONE DIRECTORY
Including Albion, Churubusco, Harlan, Huntertown, Kimmell, Leo-Grabill, Monroeville, New Haven and Roanoke
OCTOBER, 1953
Emergency Fire and Police Calls....See Page 1
Other Important Information..See Pages 2 to 4
THE HOME TELEPHONE AND TELEGRAPH CO.
FORT WAYNE 2, INDIANA

Cover of 1953 Telephone Directory

Physicians' Exchanges

Physicians & Surgeons Exchange Inc
Downtown 200 Standard.........Anthony-9125
South 3105 S Calhoun...........Harrison-3301

PHYSICIANS & SURGEONS EXCHANGE INC

To Reach Your
DOCTOR
Call A-9125
Day or Night
Downtown 200 Standard.......Anthony-9125
South 3105 S Calhoun........Harrison-3301

Ad from 1953 Telephone Directory

Current Owner Nick Radu proudly notes that the lines have never been shut down. "We've been open 24 hours, seven day a week since 1925," he said. "In 1978 during the blizzard, the National Guard brought us in on snowmobiles so we could keep the phone lines open." They were sleeping on cots, on the floors, and anywhere they could, using Coleman lanterns for light.

Physician & Surgeons Exchange Incorporated a DBA of commercial accounts under Schaefer's Anserphone Inc./Anserphone Inc. Schaefer's Anserphone was at the forefront of communication technology. It brought the first fax machine to Fort Wayne in the 1960s. And it provided doctors with their first pager system in the 1970s. And it provided an InfoLine containing more than 80 different tapes of health topics, giving people ready access to information on health conditions.

By 1988, Margery Gligor decided to retire, so she turned the business over to one of her sons, Nick Radu. Nick has overseen the switch from analog lines to digital technology, and the switch to paperless messaging. The company now employs 10 people servicing between 300 and 400 accounts. While Schaefer's Anserphone continues to serve many of Fort Wayne's physicians through its Physicians and Surgeons Exchange division, it is also diversifying into becoming a call center for other businesses, Nick said. "The calls come to us and we distribute them to where they need to go," he said. "We can schedule real estate showings, private airline times - pretty much anything - and we can do it over the Internet, by fax and by email."

The company also provides live answering service, wake up service; voice mail, alpha paging, digital paging, Internet paging, fax message delivery, e-mail message delivery, multi-caller connection and pager sales and service.

The building that houses Physician & Surgeons Exchange/Schaefer's Anserphone Inc. has an interesting history itself. It was built circa 1880 and was owned by Lena and Emma Weber, who sold it to Feichter Realtors in the late 1940s, who sold it to Physician & Surgeons Exchange in 1975. "There's a whole lot of interesting stories in this building," Margery said with a smile.

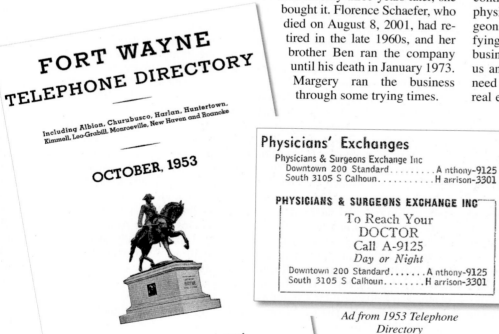

Professional Federal Credit Union

Herb Banet, Treasurer, 1967

Professional Federal Credit Union Main Branch, 1710 St. Joe River Road.

In December of 1933, seven pioneering friends and colleagues - Noel H. Whitten, Robert H. Wyatt, Meredith C. Aldred, Sadie Bacon Hatcher, A.M. Yoder, J.H. Hines, and Virginia Kinnaird - collectively invested $25,000 to form what was then Fort Wayne Teachers Credit Union (membership was extended to other Fort Wayne teachers). By taking this step, they created a not-for-profit, member-owned financial institution that has provided for its members' needs for over 70 years. Fort Wayne Teachers Credit Union was initially located in the homes of its elected treasurers. In 1958, the credit union's name was changed to Fort Wayne Community Schools Employees Credit Union. Then in 1965, when the credit union reached $1 million in assets, it was granted a federal charter as Fort Wayne Community Schools Federal Credit Union. The first office building was constructed in 1969 on Spy Run Avenue after the credit union reached $2 million in assets, and additional branches were added as growth continued. By 1973, FWCS Federal Credit Union had doubled its assets and membership reached 2,600. This increase in membership helped make it possible to open a branch in Bluffton in 1976.

By 1980, the credit union opened two more Fort Wayne offices on the south and west sides of the city and began construction on the new Main Branch located at 1710 St. Joe River Drive. In 1982, a merger with Uniserv Credit Union started to further diversify its sponsor groups. Sponsor groups affiliate themselves with a credit union so that their employees or volunteers are able to become members. The year 1984 brought a milestone when the credit union reached $25 million in assets. Then in 1986, the credit union changed its name from FWCS Federal Credit Union to Professional Federal Credit Union and diversified to include even more sponsors besides school corporations. A year later, the credit union opened a branch in Angola.

Professional Federal Credit Union began the 1990s merging with the DeKalb County Schools Employees Federal Credit Union and the KW Employees Federal Credit Union. With these mergers, Pro Fed gained an Auburn branch, which in 1992 was moved to a location in Auburn Cord Plaza. These mergers contributed to the considerable growth in assets and membership over this decade. In 1991, a Kendallville location opened its doors. Another Fort Wayne branch on the east side of town was opened in 1994, and a Columbia City location opened in 1997. The newest Fort Wayne location, on Dupont Road, opened in 1999. The same year, the Main Branch expanded to accommodate the growing administration staff, and to remodel the branch. Finally, Professional Federal opened its eleventh northeast Indiana location in Decatur in the fall of 2000. The Auburn Branch and Fort Wayne West Branch relocated to new buildings in 2004. The credit union planned to relocate their Columbia City Branch and Fort Wayne East Branch and remodel their Fort Wayne South Branch in 2005. At the end of 2004, Professional Federal had over 44,000 members and over $238 million in total assets.

The credit union also had over 150 employees and served nine Northeast Indiana counties: Adams, Allen, DeKalb, Huntington, LaGrange, Noble, Steuben, Wells, and Whitley with a total of 11 branch locations. Professional Federal offers its members a full line of products and services to meet all of their financial needs. The credit union began offering VISA Classic and Gold credit cards in 1982, Touch-Tone Teller in 1987, and Pro Fed Online Internet Banking in 1999. Other member services include savings and checking accounts, IRAs, ATMs, VISA checking cards, personal and auto loans, business loans, and first and second mortgages. An additional service is Pro-Fed Financial Advisors. Founded in 1987, the group offers a range of high quality, affordable investment and life insurance alternatives.

Pro Fed also implements the credit union philosophy of "People Helping People" by making community service a top priority. Annually, employees and members participate in various charitable causes such as the March of Dimes Walk America, fund raising for Riley Hospital for Children, the United Way's Day of Caring, Scott's Cancer Day, and Blood Drives for the American Red Cross. Pro Fed also annually awards the Carroll R. Phillips' Scholarship to five college students in honor of Mr. Phillips, Chairman of Professional Federal's Board of Directors for 28 years.

Barbara Berghoff, Professional Federal's president and CEO, celebrated her 35th anniversary with the credit union in 2004. When she started it was Fort Wayne Community Schools Federal Credit Union, and there were only three employees. Since then she has held nearly every position at the credit union, and in 1997, she became president and CEO.

R&C Fence, Inc.

Listen to Don Roop and his brother Dave and you'll hear a trace of the soft twang of their Kentucky hometown. Don't let Dave kid you that the two are just lucky that their business, R&C Fence, Inc., does well. Make no mistake: these two have figured out how to make their family business work.

"I don't like the internal stuff, the paperwork and all," Dave, the company's secretary/treasurer/general manager, readily admits. "Working with the people in the back end, the guys in the field, that's what I like." And president Don is the inside man, keeping track of the 1,200 projects the company handles in a year.

But had there not been a strike at the B.F. Goodrich plant in 1970, R&C Fence might not exist today. Dave and Don were working the night shift at Goodrich when the strike was called. Along with their friend Curt Collins, they subcontracted with Calho Fence putting in fences, just to make ends meet while the strike lasted.

Except that when the strike ended, the calls for fencing didn't.

"One call would lead to two more," Don recalls. "So we looked to make some more money and got involved in buying materials in Indianapolis. We ran a little ad in the newspaper," and the calls kept coming.

"We worked at Goodrich from midnight to 8 a.m. and then installed fencing during the day," he added. "We didn't get much sleep."

By 1974, it was decision time: take the fencing business full-time, or quit it altogether. Curt decided he didn't want to leave Goodrich, so the brothers bought him out but kept the "C" in the name because it was established in the customers' minds.

Money was tight, the brothers said. They had been working out of Don's home, with materials stored in the garage, when they were able to buy property at 4822 Avondale Drive, off Pettit and Lafayette Avenues. In 1975, gross sales were just $59,000.

"It was a risk as to whether we'd be able to feed our families," Don says.

But work was steady, and the company grew. At first, they just installed residential chain link or wooden fencing. Later, they added vinyl-coated chain link fence and began designing their own wooden products. Then they began installing fencing for commercial accounts. By 1986, they had added a retail store on Old Decatur Road offering picnic tables and patio furniture, and in 1988, added a second retail store in the Village of Coventry. That year, the company also began selling a winter line of products including billiard tables, game tables and game room furniture.

By 1989, they had outgrown their Avondale location, so they broke ground on a new combination retail and fence operation at 3326 Engle Road, opening in February 1990, where they currently operate. The company phased out its patio furniture in the mid-1990s and the gameroom items in 2003, adding Rainbow Playsets in 1998 instead.

By 2004, R&C Fence did $4.2 million in commercial and residential fencing jobs and in retail sales of Rainbow playground equipment and Goalrilla basketball goalposts. Over the years, they've also added ornamental fencing, security gates and access controls to their product line. The company concentrates its work in Indiana, Illinois and Kentucky.

The Roops' business philosophy is simple: offer a good, quality product with good service. Be the leader in the market.

"Give this community a fence company they've never had before," adds Dave, "with quality, service and craftsmanship."

The company employs 30 regular workers, a number that swells to around 45 in the busy summer season. Don's daughter Robin Willis serves as controller, and his son Don Jr. has been in sales for 18 years. Other longtime employees include Jim Raleigh, store manager with 19 years service; Pam Kruse, office manager and accounting, with 19 years service; Glen Moser, maintenance, with 18 years; and Darrel Scheumann, production foreman, with 17 years.

R&C Fence has long been involved in the American Fence Association, which it joined in 1976. Don was the Indiana/Kentucky Chapter president for five years. Dave served as AFA president and has been on the national Board of Governors and on the AFA's board of directors for the past six years.

The company has also been active in ensuring the youth of Allen County have fun. They've donated playsets and other items for fundraisers for SCAN and the Autism Society. They sponsor bowling leagues, baseball leagues and the Boys and Girls Club and Junior Achievement.

The brothers have come a long way from their Pineville, Kentucky, roots. There were ten children in their family, and their father was a coal miner. Both boys worked in the mines when they were just 15. Quipped Don, the career options in Kentucky were limited.

"It was either coal mining or bootlegging, and neither of them had a future!"

R&C Fence – Avondale Drive facility

R&C Fence – Engle Road facility

ROBY HOOD & MANGES
LAW • FIRM

Personal Injury Is Our Only Business

Roby Hood and Manges Law Firm was founded in 1983 as Roby and Hood Law Firm. The firm was founded by Daniel A. Roby and G. Stanley Hood. Roby and Hood was the first law firm in Fort Wayne to concentrate 100% of its practice on Plaintiffs personal injury law. Daniel A. Roby and G. Stanley Hood received their undergraduate degrees from Indiana University Bloomington where they were members of Acacia Social Fraternity. Both Roby and Hood received Doctor of Jurisprudence degrees from Indiana University School of Law in 1966.

Daniel A. Roby is a native of Chesterfield, Indiana, and is a graduate of Anderson High School, Anderson, Indiana. He is a past president of the Indiana Trial Lawyers Association and has received numerous state and national law honors including Trial Lawyer of the Year and the Lifetime Achievement Award of the Indiana Trial Lawyers Association. He has written many articles on various areas of trial practice and has served as a lecturer at numerous legal seminars.

G. Stanley Hood was born in Fort Wayne, Indiana, and is a graduate of South Side High School. He was a founding member and first president of the South Side High School Alumni Association, Inc., and is the author of *South Side High School The First Seventy-Five Years* published in 1996. He previously served as Associate City Attorney for the City of Fort Wayne and Allen County Deputy Prosecuting Attorney.

In 1992, Thomas A. Manges joined the law firm as an associate, and became a name partner in 2004. Thomas A. Manges was born in Fort Wayne, Indiana, and is a graduate of South Side High School. He received his undergraduate degree at Hanover College and a Doctor of Jurisprudence Degree from the Indiana University School of Law. He serves on the Board of Directors of the Indiana Trial Lawyers Association and has written and lectured on various topics relating to trial practice.

The offices of the law firm were located at One Commerce Building, 127 West Berry Street in Fort Wayne from 1983 until 1990. In May of 1990, the firm moved to its present location at Suite 520 Standard Federal Plaza, 200 East Main Street, Fort Wayne, Indiana. Roby Hood and Manges holds the highest rating possible from Martindale Hubbell Law Directory and is listed in the Bar Register of Preeminent Lawyers.

Daniel A. Roby, Thomas A. Manges, and G. Stanley Hood.

Rogers "Friendly" Markets

Pontiac Store in 1953.

Harry Rogers receives Fort Wayne Hall of Fame Award, pictured with son William (far right) and John A.'s children)

W.W., Harry, and John A. Rogers.

Rogers Markets, Inc. was incorporated in the fall of 1944. However, the grocery store history of the Rogers Family started much earlier.

W.W. Rogers' grocery experience started circa 1917 with Hoosier Stores Corporation in Fort Wayne (watch that the name Hoosier will resurface many years later). Harry E. Lowery (W.W. Rogers' brother-in-law) hired W. W. as Vice President and General Manager along with Virgil J. Roy, Secretary-Treasurer...John A. Krebs, Produce Manager...and Robert M. Roy, Meat Department Manager. Together, they operated 44 grocery/meat stores in Fort Wayne and the area. Forty-four stores each about 12-feet wide by 40 feet long. Not a small feat in those days since fax machines, cell phones, or any other of our modern day conveniences, had even been imagined. Later, Kroger would come along and buy all 44 stores. Call it opportunity, or call it fate, W.W. joined Kroger, moved to Detroit and became General Manager of the Detroit branch of the Kroger Company from 1927 through 1944, supervising 400 stores. It was a great place to start raising sons: Harry, John and Charles.

But in 1944 W.W. had a great idea. He decided to leave a promising career as General Manager with the Kroger Company...return to Fort Wayne where there were already 350 neighborhood markets to do what?...open one more grocery store.

W.W. and sons Harry and John opened the first Rogers store on the corner of Jefferson and Webster streets. Son Charles broke the chain and became a food broker in Fort Wayne introducing the city to many national brands not previously experienced by the populace at that time in history. Two years later, W.W. had another vision. Introduce Fort Wayne to what many people believed was a vision of the future: the city's first "Supermarket," at the corner of Pontiac and Smith Streets. W.W. believed that "Customer Service and Satisfaction" were what was needed to build a place in the grocery business...Rogers "Friendly" Markets was born. Rogers would grow and change as the market demanded. Stores would open, be remodeled, move and change. Several corners in Fort Wayne would host a Rogers Market at one time or another. Between the years of 1946 to 1995 Rogers could be found in Fort Wayne, Kendallville, Waynedale, Leo, and Roanoke. As previously written in a 1969 news article featuring W.W. Rogers: "No man builds a business. He builds an organization, and the organization builds the business." The employees of Rogers "Friendly" Markets, helped make the business what it was. The customers were drawn to the helpful, friendly customer service.

As time marched on a certain evolution of format took place. Superstores were built, small convenience stores would emerge. In fact, The Rogers Company operated many different formats including: Rogers Markets, City Market, Cub Foods, Food Express and Hoosier Foods. Each store was marketed differently to meet the demands of an ever-changing community. Through it all The Rogers Company became a major player in the communities it served, owning and operating 15 stores and employing a work force of over 1,300 at its peak. W.W.' grandchildren began working for the company in the 1960s: William (son of Harry), John W., Joyce, Thomas, David, Michael, Carol and Joe (children of John A.) all worked for the company at one time or another.

Nothing stays the same! As Fort Wayne grew and prospered, it became an attractive arena for much larger companies. As in many other cases, the intrusion of "huge" corporations caused the elimination of smaller locally owned businesses. Rogers Markets was the last local major grocery chain to succumb to the "huge corporations." The result was that in 1995 the Company sold the majority of its store operations to SuperValu Inc., a large Minneapolis based food wholesaler, that had previously purchased Scott's Foods and the Maloley's stores (both had been locally owned and Rogers main competitors).

The Rogers Company retained all real estate assets; the Company had begun purchasing shopping centers in 1965. Rogers still owns and operates one grocery store in Roanoke, called Hoosier Foods. It was decided to revive the name that W.W. Rogers started with in 1917. Michael Rogers, W.W.'s grandson, operates the store.

Today Rogers Markets operates as a group of affiliated companies that develop and manage buildings and neighborhood shopping centers in Allen and Huntington counties: The Rogers Company, Rogers Family Properties, Time Corners Properties and Dupont Crossing LLC. Third generation family members operate the companies: Bill (son of Harry), John, Thomas and Michael (sons of John A.) Rogers, along with long time employee, Roberta Davis, Operations Manager.

While the Companies have evolved in a different direction than when Rogers Markets Inc. was started, "Customer service and satisfaction" are still the major concerns of all involved.

Root's Camp & Ski Haus/Root's Outdoor Outfitters

Jack Root spent his twelfth birthday joining Boy Scout Troop 40 at Forest Park Methodist Church. That relationship continued for 26 years; during his last 15 years as Scout Master he had 65 active scouts in his troop. He made an Eagle Scout out of Fort Wayne Mayor Graham Richard and many other top scouts. Jack and one of his assistants were awarded the Silver Beaver award, one of Boy Scouts' hightest honors. With this background, his love for the outdoors is understandable.

Jack Root's work early in life was as a postal clerk, COD window clerk, and administering Civil Service exams. A fellow postal clerk casing mail came across a 5x7 color post card of a neat little camping trailer which weighted only 285 pounds. It could be pulled by a Volkswagon, as well as be made into a utility trailer. It set up as a camper for five to six people in sixty seconds. Jack was impressed and dropped a postcard to Heilite Company of Lodi, California, asking for information. Less than a week later he received an airmail special delivery letter offering him a unit at a discount if he would find an interested dealer and show the unit. It was a new and very well made product. Jack said to his wife, "Maybe this would make us a nice part time job!" Since he could only afford one unit and needed two, he sold the second one to a doctor friend who loved to stream fish; that way, they could display one set up and furnished plus have one to demonstrate its quick set up time.

With two other couples, Mr. and Mrs. Gene Dennis and Mr. and Mrs. Dick Chrzan, they took the two trailers to the second annual Fort Wayne Sport Vacation and Boat Show. One was placed on display while the other was used to show off the speed of set-up time. With a large clock on the wall, they demonstrated how the trailer could be set up in sixty seconds. At this time there was nothing like it, and they sold 17 units at this first show. The Roots rented a building on South Clinton Street across from the old Sears store. Customers continued asking for advice on other camping supplies. Remembering his 26 years in Scouting, Jack would say 'look for this, or that.' Finally he realized nobody understood and specialized in camping equipment. Jack and his wife sold their home and looked long and hard for a north location near the new Coliseum where they knew they would be spending time showing the trailers. It took six months befriending an old recluse who owned the site at 6844 North Clinton before he agreed to sell. Roots built one of the first of five camping centers in the U.S. in 1957. They lived above the store for seven years building the camping business.

Toward the end of the first year selling Heilites, customers suggested having a weekend with other Heilite owners. A jamboree was held the weekend after Labor Day each year. The first year there were 16 units, and it built up to over 100 units with 500 people and a police escort caravaning to parks within 100 miles of Fort Wayne. They had ox roasts, church services, hay rides, and games for young and old. They had a ball!

After several years of not doing much in the winter, and having several employees to pay, they looked around and realized they could also go into the downhill and cross country ski business. After Roots got into the ski business in the mid 1960s, customers asked about a ski trip. Since they were so successful with caravaning camping trips, they decided to see if they could help their ski customers with trips. Jack came up with the idea of promoting the "Spirit of Skiing," with the purpose, especially, of attracting new people into the sport. They searched out a nice ski area within three hours of Fort Wayne with good rental equipment and lots of ski instructors. The goal was to see that new skiers had a ski lesson and lots of fun, and came home in one piece - no broken bones. Fort Wayne's 50,000 watt radio station, WOWO, agreed it would be a great winter promo. They promoted it over the air, and Roots took care of all the details of registration, buses, equipment, and dinner on the way home. It was a great success! The first year they had six buses, then for many years, ten to twelve buses, and finally 20 buses, all on a one day ski trip. Over one half of all Fort Wayne skiers got their first taste of skiing on a Root's WOWO or Root's MAGIC ski trip. The trips were offered for forty years in a row. In 1986 Roots was awarded the Midwest Ski Retailer of the Year, the most prestigious award by Ski Industries of America. Only four of these awards were presented each year, and today they no longer give these awards. After about ten years of Michigan ski trips, customers asked about ski trips to Europe. For twelve years Roots arranged European ski trips with 25 to 80 people on each trip. They skied in six different countries, made many, many great friends, and satisfied customers. After those twelve years, they traveled to the western United States for another twelve years.

In 1974 a customer came into the store and asked, "When did you start making shoes and boots?" Root's sold ski boots, hiking shoes, moccasins, etc., but did not make them. The customer had been to Florida and saw Root's Shoes! Jack asked if they seemed well made, and he said "Oh, yes, they are beautiful!" Several months later Jack saw a national ad for Roots Natural Footwear from Toronto. He wrote them on his Root's letterhead saying, "You might find my name interesting." A few days later, Jack got a phone call from the president of Roots. He did find the name interesting and asked about the lines Fort Wayne's Root's handled. He said all their stores were Roots National Franchised Footwear stores, but this situation was unique. He flew Jack to Toronto to discuss the possibilities. As they toured the plant, lots of heads turned when they said, "This is Mr. Root." Jack was the only Root involved; they picked the name because it seemed natural, like a tree root. Fort Wayne's Root's sold a lot of Roots moccasins, hikers, and shoes. This same company produced all the olympic wear for U.S. olympic teams.

It has been almost fifty years of wonderful experiences for customers within a 100 mile radius of Fort Wayne. Jack says he would be remiss not to mention the wonderful staff that were employed all through these years: Phyllis, Jayne, Ilene, Bob, Carl, Kirk, and Chad. He is proud of the four key people and himself, pictured on the front sign stating 170 years at Root's Camp & Ski.

Three years ago Chad and Missy A'Hearn bought the business, now Root's Outdoor Outfitters, now moving to Root's Corners, Cook and Coldwater Roads. The Beat Goes On!

Rousseau Brothers DeSoto Plymouth Dealer

Rousseau Brothers, DeSoto Plymouth Dealers

The automobile firm of Rousseau Brothers was founded as a partnership in 1922 at the corner of Fifth and Harrison Streets by two brothers, Albert W. Rousseau and James H. Rousseau. The firm was in the business of selling and servicing new and used cars. The body shop was located on Goshen Road near St. Marys Avenue.

The first new car franchise was with the Elgin Motor Car Company, and was held for most of the first year. In 1923 the Elgin franchise was relinquished and the Hudson-Essex contract was acquired. This venture lasted for nearly eight years, when in 1931, Rousseau Brothers became the distributor and local dealer for Chrysler Corporation as a DeSoto-Plymouth dealer. The dealership handled nine counties in northeastern Indiana and was responsible for the establishment of many dealerships in this area.

Due to many economic and business changes brought about by World War II, the distributorship concept was cancelled and in 1948, Rousseau Brothers became a direct dealer in this area for DeSoto-Plymouth. The partnership of Albert and James Rousseau added a third partner: Edward Stouder as controller in 1937. In 1940 Richard Rousseau, son of Albert, was added as the fourth partner. Richard Rousseau had joined the firm in 1931 in the service department and later in the body shop located on Goshen Road.

James Rousseau died in 1948 and shortly after, Ed Stouder died, leaving just two partners. In 1950, Edwin J. Rousseau, son of Albert, became a partner. After his education and military commitments, he completed the Chrysler Corporation dealer management school and joined his father and brother in active management of the business. Richard then became the president and was in charge of the service and body shops' operations. Ed was made Vice-President and general manager. Albert retired but retained his share of the business.

After learning that Chrysler Corporation was going to discontinue production of the DeSoto, the business was sold to Poinsatte Motors in December of 1959. Most of the Rousseau Brothers employees and department heads were hired by Bill and Steve Poinsette at the new Poinsette Motors business on North Harrison. Some of the long-time employees were: Charlie Pierce, Rink Mills, Ralph Hubler, Bob Whitehouse, Howard "Red" Howell, Otto Knisple, Bob Kratzman, Carl Kratzman, Tom Pontius, Dean Sharp, Herb Brennan, Bob and Delilah Blaising, Monte Miller, Bud Strait, John Thompson, Gordon "Doc' Howell, and Bid Scott. Rousseau Brothers was recognized as one of the top 20 DeSoto-Plymouth dealers in the country. Most of that recognition was because of Albert Rousseau's leadership and the 55 outstanding employees.

After the sale of the business, and following the inclination of former family members, Richard and Ed entered the real estate business with Richard choosing property management and Ed pursuing a career in real estate sales, appraisals and property management. Ed combined his newly chosen field with serving the public in local government for a span of 40 years. He served as a city councilman, county councilman and county commissioner. *Submitted by Ed and Marilyn Rousseau*

St. Joseph Hospital

For more than 135 years, St. Joseph Hospital has been providing quality healthcare to the residents of Fort Wayne. In the 1860s, Bishop Henry Luers, the first bishop of Fort Wayne, realized the need for a hospital in Fort Wayne, so he began searching for German-speaking sister nurses and a building in which to house the hospital. Years before, William Rockhill had built a 65-room hotel at the corner of Broadway and Main Streets, which, unfortunately for Rockhill, proved a financial failure. Bishop Luers approached the county to help him buy the hotel, but when the request was denied, he turned to members of his flock who helped him buy the building for $52,000. In the meantime, Sister Katherine Kasper, founder of the Poor Handmaids of Jesus Christ, sent seven sisters to Fort Wayne in August 1868 to start a school. Shortly after the school's opening, three sisters were installed in their new home at St. Joseph and the hospital doors opened for the first time May 4, 1869. The first patient arrived four days later, and the first operation, a gall stone removal, was performed by Isaac Rosenthal, MD, August 23 of that same year. Fees for hospitalization were $3 to $5 per week. The first physician resident began practice at the hospital in 1876, and in 1878, the Poor Handmaids purchased the building. A smallpox epidemic hit in 1881, and the sisters consented to care for smallpox patients in the county's "pest house." Soon after, St. Joseph's built a small hospital, St. Rochus, for patients with contagious diseases such as tuberculosis. In 1896, the first elevator was installed at St. Joseph Hospital, and in 1900, the hospital was annexed into the city of Fort Wayne. On March 7, 1914, the first baby was born in the newly opened obstetrics unit. The first medical staff was organized by Maurice Rosenthal, MD, in 1919. Dr. Rosenthal was elected president, and Henry O. Brueggeman, MD, was elected secretary and treasurer. A total of 33 physicians were members of the medical staff. In 1918, St. Joseph's was named the designated hospital for flu patients, and the St. Joseph Hospital School of Nursing opened that same year. The first graduating class produced seven nurses in 1921. In 1928, the St. Joseph Hospital School of Nursing was built for $122,905.

In 1922, the sisters moved the motherhouse to Donaldson, Indiana, which freed rooms for patients, and the convent at the hospital was remodeled and became the St. Joseph Home for the Aged. In 1926, the rate for a hospital room was $3.45 a day. Of the hospital's 220 beds, 43 patients were paid in full, 141 were partially paid and 36 were receiving free care. In 1929, the original Rockhill Hotel was demolished after 61 years as a hospital, and two new structures were built with the main entrance off Berry Street, where it remained until 1966. In 1952, St. Joseph Hospital cared for 136 polio patients on its dedicated polio floor. In 1966, a nine-story wing was constructed on Broadway, along with a four-story structure on Van Buren Street that housed a chapel, an updated delivery unit and a laboratory. In 1974, the St. Joseph Regional Burn Center opened, and in 1999, the center was verified by the American College of Surgeons, becoming one of only 170 similar burn centers in North America. In 1981, the first lay administrators were installed, and in 1982, the first open-heart surgery was performed. Today, St. Joseph Hospital, a member of the Lutheran Health Network, is a progressive hospital, completely renovating its obstetrics department in 2005 and its emergency department in 2003. The hospital is also well known for its accredited sleep disorders center and its orthopedics, cardiology, wound care and hyperbaric programs. St. Joseph Hospital also prides itself on its inpatient and outpatient surgery, home care, rehabilitation, behavioral health and seniors programs.

Sauder Feeds

Sauder Feeds is the oldest continually operating business in Grabill Indiana. Founded in 1920 by J. H. Sauder as a hatchery, the firm then known as Sauder's Farm Hatchery, produced baby chickens for area poultry and broiler growers. In the mid 1970s the hatchery burned and incubating equipment was not replaced.

Sauder Feeds Fleet

Through the years the emphasis of the business had moved to feed manufacturing. Founder J. H. Sauder, built the original feed plant in 1930. The plant was rebuilt in 1965 following the loss of the original mill to a devastating fire. Soon re-named Sauder Feeds, the firm weathered the financial losses from fires by belt tightening and careful management. Employees and customers helped the firm weather these hard times. In 2005 Sauder Feeds celebrated 85 years of continuous service to the agricultural community of the tri-state area.

This business is owned and operated by the fourth generation of the Sauder family. Carlton Sauder, president and son of the founder, plus grandson Jerry I. Sauder, vice president and general manager, are the current management team. Jerry's wife, Kathy, serves as controller while great grandson Joshua Sauder works as a bulk truck driver for the firm.

Sauder Feeds can formulate and manufacture feeds for cattle, pigs, horses, and poultry plus specialty feeds for rabbits, guinea pigs, game birds, ducks, llamas, ostriches and rheas. as well as pet foods. Sauder clients include large livestock operations and small family farm flocks and herds. The pelleting equipment of Sauder Feeds allows for customized feed production for clients with unusual feed ration requirements. Carlton Sauder does much of the formulation for these unique products with the assistance of various consultants.

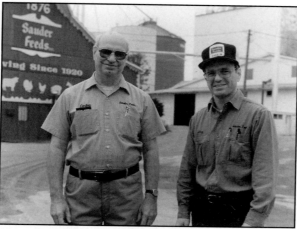

Carlton and Jerry Sauder
President and Vice-President of Sauder Feeds

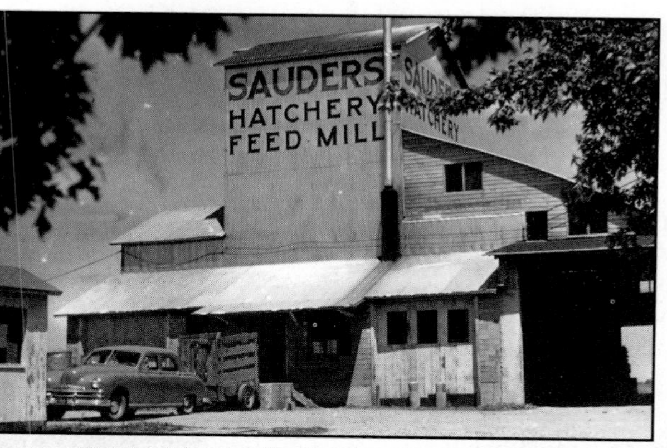

Original Sauder Feeds Plant destroyed by fire in November 1965.

Sauder Feeds has storage capacity for corn plus grain drying equipment. This allows for the production of over 400 tons of complete feed per week with a fleet of six trucks for delivery to farm customers. Over twenty-five employees keep the operation running smoothly.

The firm also operates Sauder Trucking, a trucking company that hauls agricultural products within the tri-state area. Sauder Eggs, a caged layer operation leased and operated by Sauder Feeds, produces over 100,000 dozen eggs per year.

Consistent ownership, innovative management, plus the ability to adapt to change have kept Sauder Feeds healthy through its long history. Service to customers, a well formulated product, along with courteous delivery service are the basis for Sauder Feeds ability to survive in a changing agricultural climate.

Sauder Feeds Plant in Grabill.

Stellhorn Photo

(l. to r.) Paul Saalfield, founder of Stellhorn Photo, with daughter Susan and wife Dee.

Original Stellhorn One Hour Photo site on Stellhorn Road.

In the late nineteen seventies the very fastest area residents could have a roll of film developed was four to five days, and that was through an express service provided through small parking lot huts called "Fotomat." Most folks waited the standard seven-eight days by having their film processed through drug stores with the service provided by another local company.

The founder of what would soon become Stellhorn One Hour Photo, Paul Saalfield, not only did not like the time wait for his family photos, but had no control over the quality provided. Paul was the Sales Manager for a company in Decatur called Pace Arrow Motor Homes. "I couldn't complain to anyone in the drug store in Decatur about how terrible many of my pictures were developed. Flash shots of my girls were most often all washed out. Photography was my hobby and I knew I hadn't done anything wrong when I snapped the picture" he said.

In 1980 after several years of yearning to leave the corporate world and begin a small business Paul made the decision to leave. Because the market in Decatur was too small he decided to move to Fort Wayne and begin his family high quality photo processing business. He noticed the beginning of an accelerated film process in California called "one hour photo." He thought this process could be what he was looking for to act as a "hook" to bring people into his store because of the lightening speed of service, and when they picked up their photos let them notice how every single photo was processed the very best they could have.

After the process decision was made, the next step was location. There was this abandoned gasoline station for sale on Stellhorn Road. He immediately decided this was where his business would be located. Next he would need to come up with a name. He recalled from his marketing classes at Tri State in Angola that a business should try to incorporate what the company does in its name. "Stellhorn One Hour Photo" would describe both what the company did and where it was located. Initially there were only two employees, plus Paul and his wife Dee. At this time there was no thought that the company would grow to many locations in Fort Wayne an in addition a location north in Angola. Because customers equated "Quality Processing" to the name "Stellhorn", each time a new location opened the name remained the same.

For several years Stellhorn enjoyed exclusivity in the city with the "one hour" concept. Eventually others duplicated it including the competition.

The concept of processing customer's film at the same location "one hour/on site" of where it was submitted became so popular that in the late '90s there were a total of 43 one hour photos in Allen county.

Saalfield was very well sought after for his ability to teach residents how to take better pictures through his community service offerings to service groups. It has been often said, family photos found in Allen County photo albums since 1980, are so much better than photos found in albums in any other county in the entire country all because of Saalfield and his Stellhorn Photo business.

Through years of his reputation of offering advice at his counters and through the various civic group luncheons Saalfield was strongly sought after. His manner of keeping his presentation simple yet entertaining evolved from film camera usage to digital camera usage in 2003. Thousands of adult students paid their $19.95 to learn his tips and picture taking techniques. People would come from as far away as Evansville, and Toledo to experience this two-hour live class.

Requests began pouring in for a taped video of the class presentation. These requests were from former students who could only remember a handful of the hundreds and hundreds of picture taking tips Saalfield presented. Saalfield worked with the local TV affiliate of PBS to record his two-hour presentation. Hundreds of copies were sold to former students of the live class. Extra copies were purchased as gifts for loved ones across the country. Many senior citizen relatives given digital cameras were intimidated with the technical aspects of their digital camera. Soon the recorded two-hour class on VHS or DVD was a very popular holiday gift to older relatives living in Florida and Arizona. The awareness of this instructional video spread throughout the country and into Canada. National distribution of this "Better Pictures from your Digital Camera" DVD class, presented new and different challenges to the employees of Stellhorn Photo, and has aided a bit on keeping Fort Wayne, Indiana on the map,

Chuck Surack
President, CEO – Sweetwater Sound, Inc.

How do you go from 4-track recording studio to the nation's leading retailer of professional recording and music equipment? Fort Wayne native and Sweetwater president Chuck Surack has the answer!

Surack founded Sweetwater as a recording studio in Fort Wayne in 1979. The business was located in Surack's home on Getz Road, and later moved to Bass Road. Initially the fledgling company focused on providing recording services to local and national artists and businesses.

Two things prompted the leap from recording studio to music retailer. The first was Surack's frustration with finding a reliable, knowledgeable music retailer. Prices were outrageous, and after-sale technical service and support for the sophisticated electronics he used were non-existent.

Then, in the early 1980s, the revolutionary Kurzweil K250 appeared. This groundbreaking keyboard gave musicians access to realistic orchestral and other sounds, opening new possibilities for music composition and performance. Surack created his own sound library for the keyboard, and quickly gained recognition as an expert at programming the instrument. Renowned musicians such as Stevie Wonder, Kenny Rogers, and other top names began consulting with Surack, purchasing K250 factory options and upgrades through him. Recognizing the industry's need for a new dependable, customer-oriented approach to sales, Sweetwater became a Kurzweil dealer to fulfill these requests.

As Surack's expertise became known and the industry became more sophisticated, customers returned again and again for product advice. The company began representing more product lines, and Sweetwater's emphasis shifted from recording studio to music retailer. A new building was constructed on Bass Road and was expanded four times to keep up with the skyrocketing growth of the company. But even that wasn't enough, as the company quickly grew to over 200 employees. In late 2005, Sweetwater began the process of moving to their new headquarters at Kroemer Road and U.S. Highway 30. The 38,000 square foot building with additional state-of-the-art distribution center, rich-media auditorium, and technical training center on a 13-acre property allow for Sweetwater's massive projected growth: 120 additional full-time employees and $150 million in annual sales by 2009.

Today, Sweetwater is recognized as one of the most successful and fastest-growing music retailers in the nation. The company has been named to *Inc.* magazine's list of the 500 fastest growing private companies three years in a row, and has received the *Music Inc.* magazine REX Award for excellence in retailing. The company has earned dozens of other awards from magazines, manufacturers, and rep firms.

The company takes a customer-oriented relationship-based approach to sales. Sweetwater recruits the best from the industry to serve as sales engineers. These professionals come from around the nation to Fort Wayne, bringing with them years of experience in live sound and recording. Each sales candidate receives extensive training on music and audio technology, and must pass a battery of exams before being conferred with the title "Sales Engineer." New and veteran sales engineers continue to receive training on a daily basis, keeping them current with the ever-changing technology.

Sweetwater's world-class Service, Technical Support, and Shipping departments emphasize customer service as the primary goal. Employees earn industry-topping salaries and use innovative tools and systems to perform their tasks. The company's entire focus is directed toward providing an incomparable customer experience, resulting in unparalleled customer loyalty.

The recording studio branch of the company has grown as well, and is an integral part of the company. Sweetwater Productions operates from a state-of-the-art studio, featuring three world-class rooms, with a top-of-the-line digital recording system and console, and a beautiful seven-foot Yamaha grand piano.

All of Sweetwater's marketing is handled in-house, with dedicated print and Internet staff. Innovations include the company's website, www.sweetwater.com. launched in 1995, which receives millions of hits monthly. The site, hailed by *Electronic Musician* magazine as one of the nine best online resources for musicians, has more than 63,000 pages of information, videos, demos, technical support information, and more. *SweetNotes*, a bimonthly newsletter, reaches hundreds of thousands of customers. In 1997, Sweetwater introduced *inSync*, the industry's first daily electronic newsletter. Sweetwater's 340-page *ProGear Directory* is published three times annually, and is widely acclaimed as the industry's leading source of information on music technology.

Sweetwater is firmly committed to the Fort Wayne community. Among the many causes the company sponsors are the Fort Wayne Philharmonic and its Young Artist Competition, Foundation for the Arts and Music in Elementary Education (FAME), Embassy Theatre Foundation, Easter Seals, Junior Achievement, WBNI WBOI radio, Fort Wayne Children's Zoo, Fort Wayne Children's Choir, and numerous school music programs.

Surack has ambitious plans for Sweetwater's future. "From our beginnings as a home studio to our current status as a leading retailer, our focus has always been on the customer," he states. "By maintaining that focus, we will be able to meet the challenge of continuing growth and success."

Sweetwater Studio A – featuring the Digidesign D-Control integrated console.

Tourkow, Crell, Rosenblatt & Johnston
Attorneys At Law

The law firm of Tourkow, Crell, Rosenblatt & Johnston has been located at Suite 814 Anthony Wayne Building in Fort Wayne since 1964. They were one of the first tenants in the newly constructed downtown office building. The firm was founded by Frederick R. Tourkow who began his law practice in Fort Wayne in 1946 following his discharge from the United States Army Air Corps. Fred served with distinction during World War II and attained the rank of major.

In 1950 Fred Tourkow founded the law firm of Tourkow & Dennis with offices in the Gettle Building in downtown Fort Wayne. Fred's partner was Gerald Dennis who eventually became general counsel for the Montgomery Ward Life Insurance Company located in Chicago. Fred Tourkow's legal career spanned more than six decades ending with his death in 2004. During that time he engaged not only in the practice of law but also formed the Great Northern Life Insurance Company in 1953 and owned and operated New Haven Wire & Cable Company. In the mid-1950s the firm became Tourkow, Dennis & Danehy when Jack D. Danehy became a partner. Jack practiced with the firm in excess of 40 years until his retirement in the 1990s.

In 1956 Ruth Hammer joined the firm as Fred's legal assistant and office manager. She served the firm for an outstanding 45 year period ending with her retirement in 2001. When the firm moved to its present location in 1964 Marvin S. Crell was a partner and the firm was known as Tourkow, Danehy & Crell. Marvin Crell began practicing law in 1957 and is still a name partner. G. Stanley Hood joined the firm in 1966 followed by Ronald K. Gehring in 1970. In 1974 the firm became known as Tourkow, Danehy, Crell, Hood & Gehring. It continued under that name until 1980 when it became Tourkow, Danehy, Crell, Hood & Rosenblatt. By this time Joshua I. Tourkow, son of Fred Tourkow, and Stanley L. Rosenblatt had become partners. Josh Tourkow joined the firm in 1973 followed by Stan Rosenblatt in 1975. Both Josh and Stan are name partners.

The firm adopted its present name of Tourkow, Crell, Rosenblatt & Johnston in the late 1980s when Douglas E. Johnston became a partner. Doug joined the firm in 1983. James C. Yankosky joined the firm in 2000 and became a partner in 2003. Other members of the firm are M. Bruce Scott and John D. Cowan.

For more than half a century the law firm of Tourkow, Crell, Rosenblatt & Johnston has rendered the highest degree of legal services to the families of Fort Wayne and northeastern Indiana. In addition to their downtown office, the firm maintains satellite offices in Waynedale, Monroeville, Garrett, and Decatur.

(l. to r.) Top: James C. Yankosky, M. Bruce Scott, Marvin S. Crell, Stanley L. Rosenblatt. Bottom: John D. Cowan, Joshua I. Tourkow, Douglas E. Johnston

Tower Bank

In 1997 a group of 14 community leaders responded to the bank mergers that had melded the local banks into large impersonal entities by establishing a Board of Directors for a new bank holding company that would offer a bank to truly serve the needs of this community. To lead the bank, the Board recruited Donald F. Schenkel, a prominent and respected Fort Wayne banking professional. A news conference was held in July 1998 to announce the formation of a new bank. The Board determined early on that the bank would be publicly held. This, in the Board's view, reflected the desire for a true community bank.

The early days of the bank's formation were challenging with many in the community casting doubt on the bank's ability to obtain a charter, issue its initial public stock offering and open its doors. "We did not listen to the nay sayers," remarked Don Schenkel. "We stayed with our conviction that this kind of bank would be needed and welcomed. We kept our focus on achieving the milestones, one by one."

In a sign of their faith in the bank's management, the directors contributed $760,000 of their own funds to start the bank. With the decision to locate in the Lincoln Tower, the name Tower Bank was selected. The bank's mission and vision statements, developed in October 1998, contained a real passion for service to customers, fellow employees, shareholders, and the community. These principles differentiated the bank and gave it a clear purpose from the outset.

In December 1998 the Department of Financial Institutions gave approval to Tower Financial Corporation to operate Tower Bank. On January 19, 1999, the FDIC gave approval to insure deposits of Tower Bank, and on January 22, 1999 the bank's charter was approved.

Support for the idea of Tower Bank abounded with the public sale of stock in January 1999, which was over subscribed and resulted in the generation of more than $25 million in operating capital for the bank—the largest amount ever raised to that point by a *de novo* (startup) bank in the Midwest. The public could now trade Tower Financial Corporation on the OTC Bulletin Board.

On February 19, 1999, Tower Bank opened for business with a focus on areas of the community that the bank felt had been underserved: nonprofit organizations, small businesses and the private banking market. Individual customer needs for retail services received as much respect from the bank as those of larger corporate clients. Tower Bank added investment management and trust services in October 1999, promising equal service for any trust regardless of its size. "Our bank was founded on the principles of diversity, teamwork and service," said Schenkel, "and we respect the uniqueness of each and every customer." Tower attracted the best and brightest core group of bankers, and the bank's 19 original employees developed the company's service standards that called for each employee to take personal responsibility for customer satisfaction.

Channeling funds back into serving customers, the bank still achieved assets in excess of $100 million its first year. Within the first ten weeks of trust department operations, the bank's trust assets had grown to $32 million. By October 2000 trust assets exceeded $100 million. In May 2000 the bank opened its first branch office on Dupont Road. The bank introduced telephone and online banking in fall 2000, and the bank's website, www.towerbank.net, went live in January 2001.

Rapid growth continued for the bank with three additional branch offices established: Scott Road in February 2001, Lahmeyer Road in September 2002, and Waynedale in January 2004. Tower Financial Corporation stock became available on NASDAQ in September 2001. In August 2002 the bank successfully completed a $15 million secondary offering to raise additional capital to support the company's growth. Tower Bank continued to develop and offer many unique and convenient products and services including courier banking, free interest-bearing checking for homeowners, health savings accounts, and the exclusive Something Perfect CD.

In July 2004 Tower integrated its private banking, trust and investment services into a single unit and then rounded out its wealth services with the introduction of Tower Investment Services, a full-service brokerage operation. By year-end 2004 Tower ranked fourth among all Allen County banks in deposit market share with $386 million in deposits. In just five years, more than four million common shares of Tower Bank stock were held and Tower employed more than 130 team members. By mid-year 2005 Tower crossed the $500 million mark in assets. The rapid growth surprised many competitors. "We built on a foundation of character," said Schenkel. "We've always believed in returning time, talent and treasury to the community. And it's paid off for everyone."

Tower Bank possesses a heritage rich in service to its hometown. With its entrepreneurial spirit, Tower Bank will continue to provide leadership for the betterment of Fort Wayne and show its deep appreciation for the diversity the community offers.

Tower lobby

Tower Bank Building

WBCL Radio Network

In 1975, the administration of Fort Wayne Bible College was looking toward the future. Under the leadership of President Timothy Warner and Director of Public Relations Robert Weyeneth, an application was made to the Federal Communications Commission for a radio station.

Mr. Mike Heuberger, an experienced radio pioneer from Minnesota, was hired to lead the venture. Numerous "dessert coffees" were held to raise the $100,000 needed so that WBCL could begin debt-free. On January 12, 1976, WBCL Radio signed on the air.

The 50,000 watt station, broadcasting at 90.3 FM, was the first full-time Christian radio station in Fort Wayne. The station served a large radius of listeners from Fort Wayne to Van Wert on the east, Warsaw on the west, Angola on the north, and Hartford City on the south. Tower space was rented on Coliseum Boulevard.

College officials requested the call letters WBCR for "Bible College Radio," but those call letters were not available. WBCL became an excellent alternative as it provided the slogan "We Broadcast Christ's Love."

WBCL began with two full-time employees and four part time employees in the lower level of the Fort Wayne Bible College's administration/classroom building on the south side of Rudisill Boulevard. Today there are 20 full-time and eight part-time employees.

Programming included Christian music from a large library of long-playing albums. Teaching and preaching programs were received on reel-to-reel tapes from national speakers. Over the years, LPs were replaced by CDs, but ultimately all music and programs have been computerized.

Char Binkley, Instructor at Fort Wayne Bible College, joined the staff part-time to host a daily radio talk show. Topics of interest were discussed by both local panelists and national authors. What began as a 25-minute program soon was increased to a 55-minute program to allow time for listener phone participation. Now nearly thirty years later, "Mid Morning" remains a listener favorite.

For many years, WBCL produced a children's show, "*Kids' Kaleidoscope*," which aired on Saturday mornings. Offshoots of that radio show were community activities with WBCL's hosting of a Fishing Derby at Franke Park and a Peanut Hunt on the Fort Wayne Bible College campus.

In 1978, the radio station began sponsoring A Day Away for Ladies, featuring speakers and workshops on pertinent topics. Over thirty thousand women attended throughout the twenty-two years that A Day Away was held.

Sponsoring concerts, hosting special events, and participating in community activities made it easy for listeners and air personalities to meet one another. One of the saddest days in the life of the station was on December 8, 1995, when the station's beloved morning announcer, Jeff Carlson, was killed instantly in an automobile accident.

In 1981, M&R Enterprises built a new 500-foot tower on Butler Road in Fort Wayne. They rented space to WBCL at one dollar per year for 20 years. Then they sold the tower to WBCL and gifted the five acres to the radio station.

By 1986, the radio station had outgrown its space in the administration/classroom building and needed a home of its own. Dedicated listeners pledged $600,000 during a two day on-air fundraiser to build the 6,000 square foot facility. On June 1, 1997, new state-of-the-art studios and offices were occupied on campus on Rudisill Boulevard. Included was a broadcast studio for the Mid-Morning talk show, which allows room for a studio audience.

In 1992, a 20,000 watt station was added in Northwest Ohio; and in 1997, a 6,000 watt station was added near Lima, Ohio. A translator was later added in Muncie Indiana; and, with these additions, the name became The WBCL Radio Network.

In 1992, Fort Wayne Bible College merged with Taylor University of Upland, Indiana, and the ownership of the WBCL Radio Network was transferred to Taylor University. In 1998, WBCL launched its website, streaming its programming 24/7 around the world.

In 2004, WBCL erected a 700-foot tower at the Butler Road site to replace the aging 500-foot tower. This increased the coverage area to north of Angola and to the west of Shipshewana. Again, faithful listeners underwrote the. $320,000 cost of the tower so it could be erected debt-free.

The WBCL Radio network is non-commercial, supported by its listeners. A yearly fundraiser, known as Sharathon, is held each January. Listeners pledge donations to cover the annual expenses of the network. The first Sharathon goal for WBCL was $65,000; as the network has expanded, the goal has grown to $1,360,000 annually.

The WBCL Radio network has won numerous awards, including National Religious Broadcasters Radio Station of the Year, NRB Radio News Station of the Year, and Indiana Medium Market Radio News Station of the Year. Several awards have been received for the numerous community and international outreach projects which WBCL has sponsored including the collecting of thousands of new coats, boots and shoes for the street children of Romania.

Wolf Corporation

Orphaned and penniless when he came to the United States in 1871, Paul E. Wolf was like many immigrants – an enterprising young man with a dream. Wolf came to the new country from Germany, seeking work and a better life. He traveled to Fort Wayne, Indiana, contacting a distant relative who worked there. Wolf had served as an apprentice upholsterer in Germany, and he hoped to apply those skills in the U.S.

Although unable to find work in Fort Wayne, he secured a position manufacturing mattresses for the Crane Co. in Chicago. A few years later, however, the infamous Chicago fire destroyed his livelihood. Wolf moved back to Fort Wayne, where he established the Paul E. Wolf Co. This new company included a furniture store, an upholstery repair shop, a carpet business and a tent and awning operation. More significantly, Wolf began making mattresses of husk, straw and excelsior (wood shavings) in a rented building in downtown Fort Wayne. Over time, the mattress operation grew to become the largest share of the company's business.

As the mattress business expanded, Wolf added more space to the original factory in 1885, literally in the backyard of his family's homestead. (With 13 children, he had plenty of potential help!) He employed some of his sons in the business when they were young: Erwin, just out of grade school, helped at the factory and even did some selling, and Robert became active in company management.

A tragic fire struck the building in the early 1900s, consuming the entire structure and all the equipment. Even without insurance (often the case at the time), Wolf rebuilt the facility, bought new machines and kept supplying his customers.

In 1905, the company added a garnett machine, which produces cotton batting of various lengths, widths and weights. This addition launched Wolf into the cotton-felt business, which later expanded into fiber padding. The new business quickly saw strong demand, and Wolf began supplying natural fiber batts and pads to the furniture industry and mattress manufacturers.

As early as 1913, Erwin Wolf and the leaders of other bedding companies began to meet in Chicago to discuss establishing a national association dedicated to improving the industry. Their vision took roots in the founding of a national associate, which exists today as the International Sleep Products Association. Since the association's founding, Wolf family members have been active in its work, often in a leadership role.

Wagon of Mattresses – circa 1885.

As years passed, changes in leadership occurred at the company. In 1932, Erwin and Robert became general manager and secretary respectively of the company. After World War II, Erwin's sons Richard and Donald joined the business. In 1955, Richard became general manager, while Donald became treasurer and factory superintendent.

In 1976, Richard's son Tony started working for the company. A former high school teacher, Tony began learning the business on the road selling to customers. He drove thousands of miles, calling on many furniture stores. He recalls that his family made it clear that if he wanted a place for himself at the company, he would have to create it.

With continued expansion came the need for a larger, more efficient factory operation. In 1988, the company (by then called the Wolf Corporation) moved to its current location at 3434 Adams Center Road in Fort Wayne. Located on a 16-acre plot of land, the building is a state-of-the-art facility with a modern, spacious showroom. The adjoining 95,000-square-foot factory is twice the size of the former facility.

In 1993, Wolf took its first futon mattress to market, expanding its product line. The product took off almost immediately as futons soared in popularity. Today, Wolf is one of the largest futon makers in the country, with more than 75 employees and an outstanding reputation for quality. The company's futon product line is currently headlined by Aerolife™, a unique blend of cotton and heavy-denier polyester that results in greater loft and comfort, but with 30% less weight.

A diversified corporation, Wolf continues to supply an expanded variety of natural and synthetic fiber batts and pads for the mattress, furniture and other industries, and is an independent manufacturer of innerspring bedding. Wolf has positioned itself for continued growth by being innovative in its product development in an effort to meet the ever-changing needs of buyers.

The tradition of family ownership, already more than a century and a quarter in the making, is expected to continue at Wolf Corporation. Since the company was founded, the Wolf family has overseen production, assuring the highest levels of quality in their products.

President Tony Wolf explains that family ownership has made it possible for the company to grow and prosper: "Our family has always been blessed to have somebody who cared enough to go on to another generation. The company has always taken a long view of things. Surviving is not in our lexicon, but thriving is."

Sweet Dreams
Since 1873

Agnes Morningstar
Real Estage Broker & Property Management, Inc.

AGNES MORNINGSTAR

REAL ESTATE BROKER & PROPERTY MANAGEMENT, INC.

Prior to 1990 Agnes Morningstar was a broker for 17 years managing VA and FHA foreclosures. She already owned a rental property, but later purchased many more. People flock to Agnes Morningstar's office because of service. Her company motto is "Stability First." Tenants feel very secure when they know she is there for them.

Some rental property owners do not have proper funds to support their properties, but Agnes always services the property and deducts from the rents when paid. Landlords/owners of properties that are at their wit's end contact the office hoping to be helped out of a financial problem. They are unable to fix their properties enough to rent, so they end up in Agnes's office. Some they can help, but with others they can only sympathize. When she acquires new properties, she checks them to find any mechanical or hazardous conditions, and uses independent contractors to prep the properties. Most of the contractors have been with her for 32 years. This is the key to her business: Always try to make tenants comfortable and happy. Some tenants have been with the company approaching 20 years.

The business also lists owner's properties to sell on the Multiple Listing Service if they need to dispose of their properties for any reason.

She has added more personally owned properties during the last fifteen years, and has a Rent-to-Own program should one of the tenants be interested.

All management properties are reported to NCE and their rules are followed as they apply without hesitation. The firm manages for people as far away as Australia, but most properties are in this area.

She is a member in good standing of FWAAR and BBB.

Baker's Hide-A-Way

Baker's Hide-A-Way

We started barbering in January of 1966 at 1208 East State Boulevard. We bought a shop called Weaver's Barber Shop. It had four chairs but only enough business for two. It became evident in about a year that we had to get further training to take care of the incoming long hair trend. The barber union furnished this training. In a few more years we were trained by a franchise trainer, who had special cuts and products. Business picked up pretty well after that.

In 1976, it became necessary for us to move. We set up a two chair shop at 1224 East State Boulevard. Bob Barker has had two partners in the 40 years in business; one was here 28 years and the other 12 years.

We have been involved in the State Street activities over the years. We always help put up Christmas decorations, be it Christmas trees or banners. We also attend the various Christmas parties.

We were able to purchase the building in 1985 and have had some good luck with it. Currently, State Street is trying to redo itself to attract more and different types of businesses.

Gone are Buschbaum Drugs, Scott's Grocery, Hanna Paint and Dr. Whiteleather, and many more that were here for many years.

We have many neighborhood people and people who work in the area as our customers, some travel some distance. Barbers are scarce these days and we do a good business. *Submitted by Bob Baker, Barber*

Beckman Lawson, LLP Lawyers

BECKMAN LAWSON LLP
Attorneys at Law

The law firm of Beckman Lawson, LLP originated in 1953, when Fredrick Beckman joined Louie Dunten. Dunten was a 1914 graduate of the law school at the University of Michigan. Beckman was a 1949 graduate of the Indiana University, Bloomington, School of Law. Jack Lawson joined Dunten and Beckman following his graduation in 1960 from the Valparaiso University School of Law.

From time to time, lawyers joined the firm and others left. Dunten retired in 1970 and died in 1976. In 1990, the two original lawyers, Beckman and Lawson, merged with Neil Sandler and Howard Sandler and James Federoff. The firm also had a resident partner, Stephen Snyder, and an office at Syracuse, Indiana. Snyder is now full-time counsel for Fort Wayne Community Schools and is of-counsel for the firm. Douglas Miller and Neil Sandler are now retired and also of-counsel.

The current partners of the firm are Jack Lawson, Howard Sandler, John Brandt, Robert Nicholson, Craig Patterson, Wendy Davis, Edward Ormsby, Patrick Hess, Mark Witmer, and Matthew Elliott. Associates are Brian Heck, Mark Bloom, Michael Story, Andrea Dick and Jeremy Reidy.

In addition to Beckman, Neil Sandler, Miller and Sweet, Richard Blaich and Gary Johnson are of-counsel to the firm.

BKD Fort Wayne Office

The Fort Wayne office had its inception on April 1, 1964, when Larry Rignanese started his own firm as a sole practitioner. He acquired part of an accounting practice from a CPA practitioner who wanted to downsize his practice to pursue other interests. The annual gross billings of the portion of the practice that Rignanese acquired was estimated to be approximately $40,000.

Also in 1964, Larry Drees left the same large accounting firm from which Rignanese had started (Coopers) and started his own sole proprietorship, R.L. Drees & Co.

The growth of Rignanese's firm was rapid. On November 1, 1965, Ralph Schannen and Chet Horn joined Rignanese as partners and the firm of Rignanese, Schannen & Horn was formed. Schannen and Horn were individuals with whom Rignanese had previously worked in a well known and highly regarded Fort Wayne accounting firm (Coopers).

Drees' firm expanded in 1967 when two additional partners joined him and his firm became Drees, Robinson and Perugini. In 1985, Robinson left and the firm became Drees, Perugini & Co.

Both firms continued to grow and the staff continued to expand. Included in the staff that was hired by Rignanese was John Harris who subsequently became a partner in the firm Rignanese, Schannen, Horn & Harris.

In order to accommodate the needs of these two growing firms, they felt that they needed the resources of a larger firm. Accordingly, they merged into the firm of Geo. S. Olive & Co. with Rignanese, Schannen, Horn & Harris merging on October 1, 1969 and Drees, Perugini & Co. merging in June 1991. The partners of both firms were admitted as partners in Geo. S. Olive & Co.

On January 1, 1984, the Fort Wayne firm of Haslacher, Marx & Co. was merged into the Fort Wayne office of Geo. S. Olive & Co. In 1986, the accounting practice of Gene Bailey was also merged into the Fort Wayne office of Geo. S. Olive & Co.

In June 1998, the name of the firm was changed from Geo. S. Olive & Co. to Olive LLP and on June 1, 2001 Olive merged with Baird, Kurtz & Dobson to become BKD, LLP.

The BKD Fort Wayne office now has over 50 employees, with many of them being graduates of local colleges and universities. Many of the current partners are third, fourth and even fifth generation Fort Wayne families.

BKD Metro Building

Bonahoom & Bonahoom, LLP, Attorneys At Law

(l. to r.) Joseph G. Bonahoom, Otto M. Bonahoom, and Robert E. Rhee.

In October, 1956, Otto M. Bonahoom joined Frank Celarek under the name Celarek and Bonahoom. In January, 1970, Bonahoom, Howard Chapman and Paul McNellis formed a partnership which lasted until 1986 when Bonahoom, Chapman, McNellis and Michaels merged with Barrett & McNagny at which time Joseph Bonahoom became an associate.

In 1995, Otto and Joseph withdrew as partners from the Barrett firm and formed Bonahoom & Bonahoom, LLP. Bonahoom & Bonahoom soon employed Robert Rhee as an associate and concentrated its practice in Elder Law, Estate Planning & Administration, Business Succession Planning, Business Entities and consultation for business transactions.

In 2005, Joseph also became a Sports Business Agent. He currently serves as attorney for the Fort Wayne City Council and has since 1995. He is a past president of The Boys and Girls Club of Fort Wayne and is currently President of the Board of Crossroads.

From 1995 to 2003, Otto created, produced and hosted "*The Elder Angle*", a one-hour live talk show every Saturday morning on WGL Radio. In 2004, the show became a half-hour live talk show on WFWA TV every fourth Wednesday of each month. The Elder Angle featured guest interviews on topics of interest to the senior segment of society.

Robert E. Rhee, attorney and CPA, of Hispanic descent and fluent in the Spanish language is proficient in Elder and Business law and a leader in the Hispanic community serving as treasurer of the Hispanic Chamber of Commerce. He is also treasurer of Samaritan's House.

As the senior partner of Bonahoom, Chapman & McNellis, Otto represented Northill Corporation which developed Canterbury Green Apartments and Marketplace as well as many other apartment and office complexes. Canterbury Green consists of over 2,000 units, an executive golf course, clubhouse and fitness center spread over more than 170 acres. Otto and Howard Chapman represented Citizens Cable which was awarded the cable TV franchise by the Fort Wayne City Council and in successful litigation with Comcast Cable which now owns the franchise.

Throughout his career, Otto was active in the Indiana State Bar Association serving on the Board of Governors as Treasurer, as a board member of the Indiana Continuing Legal Education Forum and as President of the Indiana Bar Foundation. He was President of the Allen County Bar Association and a member of the American Bar Association. He was elected Joint State Representative for Allen and Whitley Counties for the 1963-64 term and was appointed Probate Commissioner of Allen County serving from 1965 to 1975.

Eilbacher Fletcher LLP

The law firm of Eilbacher Fletcher, LLP took shape in June of 2004. Eilbacher Fletcher is the product of the merger of the practices of Fletcher & Niemann, LLP and four attorneys from Eilbacher Scott, PC. The firm practices primarily in the area of civil litigation. As of September of 2005, the lawyers of Eilbacher Fletcher were Lee Eilbacher, Martin Fletcher, Alan VerPlanck, Jim Fenton, Kate Brogan, Dan McNamara, Patrick Proctor, and David Bailey.

Fletcher & Niemann was founded in January of 2002 by Martin Fletcher and Scott Niemann. In July of 2003, Dan McNamara and David Bailey joined the firm. Like Eilbacher Fletcher, Fletcher & Niemann's practice was primarily dedicated to civil litigation.

Eilbacher Scott was founded in 1997 by Lee Eilbacher, Harry Scott, Alan VerPlanck, Jim Fenton, and Dan Skekloff. Patrick Proctor joined the firm in January of 2004. Eilbacher Scott's practice was focused in the areas of civil litigation and bankruptcy. The founding members of both Eilbacher Scott and Fletcher & Niemann were well-regarded, veteran attorneys when they started their respective firms.

The lawyers of Fletcher & Niemann and the litigators of Eilbacher Scott began discussing a merger of their practices in early 2004. The merger became effective on June 1 of that year. The new firm, consisting of Messrs. Eilbacher, Fletcher, VerPlanck, Fenton, McNamara, Proctor, and Bailey, began its practice on the fourth floor of the Courtside Building on Calhoun Street in downtown Fort Wayne. Kate Brogan became Eilbacher Fletcher's eighth lawyer when she joined the firm in June of 2005.

Martin Fletcher, in Eilbacher Fletcher's office at 803 South Calhoun in the courthouse building.

Fast Print, Inc.

Fast Print was officially opened for business in 1975 by Carolyn Cline. Her brother, Dan Metzger, joined her in 1979 and later became a partner.

The first location at 3215 East State occupied 800 sq. ft. and was one block east of the current site. Original equipment included one press, one copier, and one platemaker. Typesetting (now considered desktop publishing) was done using a strike-on Varityper. Fast Print grew from two to five employees at that location and as sales volume increased requiring more equipment, it was decided that more space was needed. In June, 1986 they moved two blocks west to 2828 East State and expanded to 2,000 sq. ft. The business growth continued from the increased customer base, services offered, equipment, and personnel. In May 1992 they again needed to relocate for more space and found the way into the current 5,500 sq ft. location at 3050 East State.

As with most business that have experienced growth over the past 30 years, the computer and equipment technology have had the greatest impact on the way printed products are produced. While Fast Print has grown and expanded to multiple presses, copiers, color copiers, digital platemaking, large format, e-mail, and web sites, the commitment to providing quality products, offering personalized service, and a strong desire to continue building on relationships with current and new customers will always be the foundation for success at Fast Print.

Grabill Hardware

Grabill Hardware, Do It Best.

In the late 1920s, a young man from the Grabill community, Abner Gerig, was teaching school. During the school Christmas vacation, Homer Klopfenstein, the local hardware store owner, asked Abner to help him take inventory of the hardware store. That short-term job sparked an interest in retail hardware sales for Abner.

Mr. Klopfenstein soon asked Abner if he would like to buy the hardware business. Abner's father, Daniel Gerig, was willing to finance his son. The Gerig father and son team began operating Grabill Hardware in 1930. Beginning a new business during The Great Depression was certainly challenging. When they started, a $20 sales day was pretty good. Their merchandise came in by train, "The Wabash Local," and they often took the merchandise directly from the freight cars. They also picked up some items in Fort Wayne in their Model A Ford truck.

The business continued to grow and in the 1950s, Abner joined a cooperative, Hardware Wholesalers Inc. (Do It Best Corp). The ability to stock a larger variety of merchandise and have a weekly delivery of products improved their service to the community with hardware needs. In 1972, Abner's stepson, Claude Schrock, joined him in the business.

Four years later in 1976, Grabill Hardware was completely destroyed by fire. The Amish community responded with cleaning up the debris that week. A month later the store re-opened in the old lumberyard building while they built their new store. Less than a year later they celebrated the "Grand Opening" in the new building.

Claude's son and Abner's grandson, Leonard Schrock, has now joined the Grabill Hardware management team. In 2005, Grabill Hardware is celebrating its 75th anniversary. Abner Gerig has retired but still remains interested in the business and can give good, grandfatherly advice at his 97 years of age.

Hyde Brothers Book Sellers

Hyde Brothers Book Sellers

Genteel is no longer one of the terms Joel and Sam Hyde would be likely to use in describing the business of buying and selling used books. The notion of owning a bookstore had its source in the brothers' college days. Sam in Bloomington, Joel on the West Coast became avid accumulators of large libraries on limited budgets. When their midlife career dissatisfaction became acute it seemed natural for them to focus on a business that built upon the skills and knowledge they had acquired in their avocation.

In the 1980s the seeds of the business idea grew. After looking at several bookstores on the market in the area and talking to many more or less successful operators in the business, Joel and Sam decided to start from scratch, and to own any location they might occupy. They began stockpiling books in earnest, filling garages and various buildings with auction buys, rummage shop acquisitions and garage sale purchases. Their quest for a high-traffic location finally settled on 1428 Wells Street, where the former grocery/reptile parlor/mattress warehouse sold at auction in November, 1989.

As time and finances permitted, the brothers upgraded and remodeled the building, then transferred tens of thousands of books to newly built shelves. On July 1, 1992 Hyde Brothers, Booksellers opened its doors to a small crowd of eager shoppers. Those first days were primitive-problems solved as they arose and opportunities pursued as they developed.

The past years have been exciting. The bookstore has grown, first filling the main floor to the rafters, then the back room, basement, and with the acquisition of the adjoining building, a major expansion to the south. Four employees join the brothers in processing the never ceasing stream of books. For many customers, the most memorable addition is that of Katy, the permanent-resident bookstore cat. The recent challenge of the internet has led to international sales and a widening variety in the available merchandise.

Leeper's Lawn Service, Inc.

Leeper's Lawn Service, Inc. was established in 1984 by Chris Leeper being majority owner and president and John Leeper minority owner and secretary/treasurer with no working interest. When established, the business provided basic lawn maintenance services to residential and business properties. It started with one full time employee, Chris, and one part time employee along with one truck. After being in business one year, and doing about $35,000.00 in sales, the owner was very frustrated and agreed to sell the business but then backed out after giving it much thought. The business then began its second year and grew extremely fast over the next few years. Cory Leeper joined the business in 1989 and became a minority owner. He is now the Vice President. Cindy Leeper, wife of Chris, came on board in 1990 as the office Manager and is still in that capacity today. As the company grew, it expanded its services from the original focus to include all landscape bed maintenance and landscape design and installation.

The company's lawn maintenance focus became targeted to large condominium complexes and the landscape focus was on residential landscape and design along with any commercial project that fit its scope. Some of the maintenance projects include Headwater's Park, many large condominium complexes and several hundred residential and commercial properties. Some of the landscape projects included Fort Wayne International Airport, two phases of Headwater's Park, along with many other commercial and residential projects. In 1995, John Leeper became an employee of the business and was in charge of a couple large condominium accounts.

Velma Leeper, wife of John Leeper, also joined the business in 1999 and became the office secretary. In 2003, Cory Leeper bought out John Leeper's interest in the business and became 25 percent owner and Chris Leeper was 75 percent owner. At the end of 2004, Velma Leeper retired and John Leeper became semi-retired working fewer hours to allow him to work on his golf game and travel with his wife.

Many other key employees came on board over the years that are still an important part of the operation today. Those include Jeff Hoehn, Manager of the Lawn Care Division, Travis Double, Assistant Manager of the Lawn Care Division, Walter Dobbins, Manager of the Landscape Division, Larry Bennett, Assistant Manager of the Landscape Division and Greg Waikel, Manager of the Lawn Maintenance Division. As of 2005, the company's 22nd year, there are 13 full time employees, 40 part time employees, 26 trucks and many trailers, skidloaders, mowers and other equipment.

The sales have expanded from the original $35,000.00 to approximately $2.5 million in 2004. The company has had several locations over the years. It started in the garage of Chris' parents house. After one year the company started renting space at a storage place on Ardmore Avenue. Its next location was a rented building on Lakeview Drive. They stayed there until 1988 when Chris and Cindy bought a house and 7.5 acres at 8200 Lower Huntington Road. A building and parking lots were built and the business moved to that site and operated for the next eleven years. In 1999, the business bought 2.5 acres in Waynedale at 3108 Lower Huntington Road. A 6000 square foot building was built along with parking lots to serve as its current location.

Over the years, it had made several equipment and truck purchases to a current fleet of 26 trucks, trailers, skidloaders, mowers, tractors and other miscellaneous equipment.

Moss & Harris

MOSS & HARRIS, LLP
110 WEST BERRY STREET - SUITE 1800
P.O. BOX 10839
FORT WAYNE, INDIANA 46854-0839

TELEPHONE (260) 422-1589

FAX (260) 422-1594

LINDY G. MOSS
WILLIAM E. HARRIS
KIRBY G. MOSS
PARKER L. MOSS

Of Counsel:
MICKEY M. MILLER

MARTIN P. TORBORG
(1910-1999)

JERRALD A. CROWELL
(1933-1997)

The name is relatively new, but the law firm Moss & Harris dates back to 1926 when it was founded by Clyde Reed, Samuel Cleland, and Abe Ackerman. As one might expect, the firm has seen many changes over the years, some of which have brought the firm full circle.

In the law firm's early years the emphasis was on trial work – both Cleland and Ackerman were prominent trial lawyers. Martin Torborg can remember doing little else when he joined the firm as an associate in 1935. "When I came into the firm I did almost nothing but prepare cases for trial, on both sides of the litigation – mostly tort litigation, automobile accidents, and that sort of thing," he said.

Ackerman and Cleland were also heavily involved in politics, the latter once running for congress. "They were more political than we've ever been since," Torborg said. "I, personally have steered away from politics altogether."

After Torborg became a partner in 1942 and Cleland's death in 1948 (Ackerman had died in 1936), Reed and Torborg not only ended the firm's political activities, but also moved away from trial work. "Neither Reed nor I was much interested in trial work," Torborg said.

Reed died in 1958. Four years later, Torborg made Lindy Moss and Mickey Miller partners in the firm.

William Harris and Michael Yates became partners, in 1967 and respectively. Later the firm merged with Jerrald Crowell's practice, whose office was next door on the 18th floor of the Fort Wayne National Bank Building.

In 1979 Kirby Moss joined the firm, followed in 1984 by Parker Moss, and Mickey Miller and Martin Torborg retired in about 1985. Jerrald Crowell died in 1997.

Around 1990 David Long joined the firm as a partner. In recent years Yates and Long have left the firm, leaving as the current active partners Lindy Moss, William Harris, Kirby Moss, and Parker Moss.

North Side Plumbing & Heating Co., Inc.

North Side Plumbing & Heating Co., Inc. was founded in 1929 by John R. Hartman. The Great Depression of 1929 soon followed but North Side Plumbing was able to survive, even with gas rationing, by John R. hopping on the trolley to get to his customer's homes. His wife, Mildred, assisted with the billing and accounting for over 50 years.

The company celebrated its 75th anniversary in 2004 and still operates from its original location at 2234 North Clinton Street, Fort Wayne. When John R. Hartman entered politics in 1960, his son, John D. succeeded him as president of the company. Third generation John D. Hartman Jr. followed in 1998. John D.'s wife, Sharon, is also involved in management in the company.

North Side Plumbing employs 24 and its staff of journeymen plumbers is respected in the plumbing industry for their in-home plumbing repair and bath remodeling experience and expertise. The company also has an over the counter parts department that carries the most complete stock of plumbing repair parts in the area. The company also does light commercial service and installation, installs and repairs hot water/radiant heating systems, does drain and sewer cleaning, and employs a design and bath remodel team. The company makes approximately 6,000 service calls a year. Their fleet of large green service trucks are fully stocked and readily recognized in the community.

North Side Plumbing and Heating Company, Inc., 2234 North Clinton Street

Phil's Hobby Shop

Phil's Hobby Shop at 3112 North Clinton Street.

Philip and Kathryn Gieseking started the hobby business in 1975. It all started with the purchase of a building at 1722 Lake Avenue in Fort Wayne a few blocks from their house. The building needed quite a bit of internal remodeling in preparation for the opening day in December. With Kathy's help and dedicated employees the business grew to become the best stocked and well known hobby shop for miles around. Philip was employed at the Magnavox company as an electrical engineer until he retired in 1992.

Able to devote full time to the business, he looked at expanding the business. In 1992 he purchased an existing hobby shop in Defiance, Ohio which is 47 miles east and named it also Phil's Hobby Shop. He worked that store with the assistance of local help. Philip's son Steven joined the family business in 1996. With creative ideas he managed the Defiance store bringing in new business and growth. With Defiance doing well, now managed by Chris Bercaw, Steven was able to turn his attention to helping more at the home store at 1722 Lake Avenue.

Steven has been concentrating on developing sales through the internet. This exposure is bringing in customers world wide. Steven has also improved and expanded our web site - philshobbyshop.com. Seeing the need for a larger store, Philip purchased property at 3112 North Clinton Street in 2001.

With more inventory, a large parking lot, and a good location, more customers are shopping at Phil's Hobby Shop. In 2003 the two buildings east of the Lake Avenue store were purchased for further expansion. Now with three Phil's Hobby Shops, Philip and Kathy are looking forward to further growth in sales and profit.

Plastic Composites Corporation

Plastic Composites Corporation (PCC) was started in 1957 in a three car garage near Wells Street. Originally Maritime Plastics, the company's product was a mono-hull sailboat named the Inland Cat. This was one of the country's earliest Fiberglass Reinforced Plastic sailboats and was designed by the company's incorporators, Norman G. Bell and John R. Larimore. The business was successful, and the Inland Cat became the personal sailboat of choice at many northern Indiana lakes, including particularly Lake George (where, in 2005, it still is).

Because sailboats were difficult to sell in the Indiana winters, the company began doing Custom Molding of fiberglass products for other industrial companies. One of the first difficult projects was the molding of full-scale display models of the Talos missile, which success led to orders for parts for the actual missile. Another major early customer was the large truck manufacturing business of International Harvester. The name of Maritime Plastics was changed to Plastic Composites Corporation (PCC) to reflect the business's transition from a sailboat manufacturer to a full fledged professional fiberglass composites manufacturer.

Mobile Aerial Towers (MAT) in Fort Wayne manufactured truck-mounted aerial manlifts (cherry pickers) (under the name Hi-Ranger) for the utility industry. In 1959, Lester Myers, who was the Chief Engineer for MAT, and John Larimore designed an insulated fiberglass upper boom that would allow electrical workers to work safely on or near energized high voltage electrical lines. This new insulated "bucket truck" quickly revolutionized the electric utility industry transmission and distribution operations, as linemen could now quickly and efficiently reach and work safely on electrical lines without having to climb poles. A refinement soon after resulted in a fiberglass section in the lower boom that would serve as an insulator for people on the ground that might touch the manlift device. To this day (2005), the same insulation concepts are used in the very large bucket truck industry. The Hi-Ranger was so successful that a large part of PCC's business became the production of booms and buckets for the Hi-Ranger.

Because of Larimore's continued desire for new products and production processes, he became one of the most successful pioneers in the US in the use of the Resin-Transfer-Molded process for making fiberglass composite products.

In 1982, ownership of PCC was transferred to Craig Keoun who had moved to Fort Wayne from Dallas with his then employer and wanted to stay in Fort Wayne. The company continued to develop additional processes, molding presses, testing facilities and buildings in order to serve a growing number of diverse national and international customers. In 1992, PCC lost the production of the Hi-Ranger fiberglass because of the sale of the Hi-Ranger to one of its competitors, which had their own fiberglass production operations. As a result, PCC went into the aftermarket business for fiberglass replacement parts (booms, buckets, guards, and accessories) for most brands of bucket trucks. That business grew and prospered. In 2003, Keoun sold the Custom Molding business of PCC and continued the Bucket Truck aftermarket parts business.

Schaab Metal Products, Incorporated

Schaab Metal Products, Incorporated, is a wholesale distributor of light gauge sheet metal used in the construction industry. It also carries a variety of finished goods consisting of gutters, registers, pipe, fittings, and ventilation products for new home and light to medium commercial HVAC installations. The company currently serves contractors in a seventy mile radius of Fort Wayne utilizing four delivery trucks. The business also has a shop that can produce many items that are not normally stocked in the area.

Although the business was incorporated in 1985, it has a long history in the Fort Wayne area. The company was founded as Schaab Roofing & Supply in Monroeville, Indiana, circa 1907 by John A. Schaab, his son Alfred E. Schaab, and son-in-law J. Claude Weirman. Ownership today consists of descendants, in-laws, and key employees. Originally the business specialized in roofing and gutter sales as well as light manufacturing.

After the company moved to its current downtown Fort Wayne location in 1913, they began to add other product lines to their offerings, among these were: furnaces (which were later dropped), pipe, registers, and related accessories. To facilitate the growing inventory, the business had to increase its warehouse space from 15,000 square feet to over 55,000 square feet. This was accomplished through acquisition of neighboring buildings and the construction of two steel buildings as well as the use of every "nook and cranny" available.

Over the years, the business and its buildings, have survived numerous floods, several name changes, a fire in 1947, and a large increase in competitors. While nobody can predict the future, it is evident that Schaab Metal Products, Incorporated will be there.

Schaab Metal Products, Inc.

Wayne Hardware Company

Wayne Hardware was a wholesale hardware company, which was part of the downtown Fort Wayne business community for over one hundred and twenty years. Wayne grew out of a company called Prescott Brothers who sold both wholesale and retail. They were organized in 1862 and were located on West Columbia Street. In 1897 G.W. Seavey became a partner and later took over the management from Prescott. The store then became Seavey Hardware and Company. It was then located on West Main Street until it moved to 614 South Harrison Street, at the corner of Harrison and Pearl streets.

Wayne Hardware Company

In 1914 they were licensed to operate as a wholesale and retail store. In 1919 Frank Cutshall acquired the real estate and business from Mr. Seavey's son Walter and the business became known as Wayne Hardware. The retail part of the business was discontinued. In 1930 they added a branch in South Bend, Indiana. Over the years Wayne Hardware sold not only hardware and builder's hardware but major and small appliances, sporting goods and toys. The largest part of their business was distribution of Zenith Electronics.

The Cutshall family purchased majority stock and took over control of the company. The downtown building was sold and Wayne Hardware became Wayne Distributing Company in 1986. The Company moved, for a couple of years, to Southwest Fort Wayne, to a building on Arden Drive. Wanting a more central location for the company's distribution area, Wayne Distributing Co. moved to Indianapolis. After being a Zenith distributor for 65 years, Zenith was acquired by L.G. Electronics, a Korean manufacturer. Since Zenith represented the majority of Wayne's business they were forced to liquidate in 1997. *Submitted by Doris Grandos.*

Old Established Locally Owned Area Restaurants Still Serving After All These Years

Nine Mile, Hwy. 27 S. and Flatrock Road, Poe - Est. 1837 as a stage coach stop between Decatur and Fort Wayne

Powers Hamburger Shop, 1402 South Harrison, Fort Wayne - Est. 1940

Oyster Bar, 1830 South Calhoun, Fort Wayne - Est. 1888 by Ferdinand Oetting, took the name, Oyster Bar, in 1954

Three Kings, 14832 First Street, Hoagland - Est. 1946

The Kitchen Table, formerly known as Baileys, 15315 Lima Road, Huntertown - Est. 1952

The Rib Room, 1235 East State Boulevard, Fort Wayne - Est. 1957

Henrys Restaurant, 536 West Main, Fort Wayne - Est. 1959

Coney Island Weiner Stand, 131 West Main Street, Fort Wayne - Est. 1914

Halls Original Drive In, 1502 Bluffton Road, Fort Wayne - Est. 1946, now one of 17 area locations run by the Hall family

Acme Bar, 1105 East State Boulevard, Fort Wayne - Est. 1941

Billys Bar, Old U.S. 30, Zulu, - Est. in the present location in 1947 by Lawrence "Weiny" Reuille after his Zulu tavern burned. Named Billys Bar in 1982.

Allen County Places Of Worship

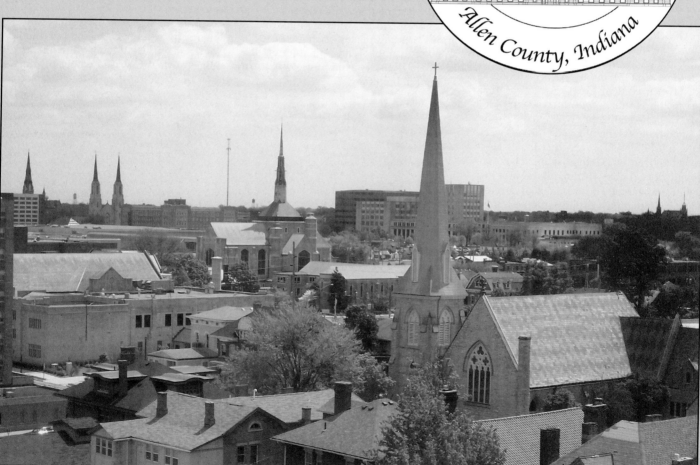

View of downtown Fort Wayne church spires looking east from the helicopter pad atop St. Joseph Hospital, Main Street and Broadway. (Photo by Phyllis Robb, May 2006.)

First Wayne Street United Methodist Church

1828 - Present
300 East Wayne Street - Fort Wayne, Indiana

There is a continual change of cells in the human body so that in the course of years it becomes completely new, yet the personality abides. So the passing years witness a complete change in the membership of a church. Whether the "personality" abides depends upon the degree to which the new generation catches the spirit of the older generation and, with equal enthusiasm, follows Jesus. – Rev. Edwin R. Garrison, 1949 Centennial Celebration, Wayne Street Methodist Church

Beginnings

The roots of First Wayne Street United Methodist Church are deep and firmly planted in the early most history of Fort Wayne, as faith's development among the early pioneers kept pace with Fort Wayne's growth from settlement to town to city. In true Wesleyan tradition – first came the class and society, then the circuit, and lastly, the organized church.

The first Methodist family reported to have arrived in Fort Wayne was that of Joseph Holman, who arrived in 1823. Mr. Holman had been given charge of the United States General Land Office. A year later a brother of Joseph, Rev. James Holman, a licensed Methodist preacher, arrived. Rev. James Holman lived in a log cabin and farmed on a parcel of ground located in that part of the settlement then known as Nebraska, on the north bank of the St. Mary's River. In this log cabin Rev. James Holman preached to the settlers of the community every Sunday.

The available records of early Methodism in Fort Wayne are not entirely in agreement as to how and when the first mission was established. This is in part due to the fact that the Indiana Conference was not organized until 1832. While Fort Wayne was officially under the control of the Illinois Conference between 1824 and 1832, the Ohio Conference was also involved in Methodism's early development in Indiana. At the annual meeting of the Ohio Conference, held at Steubenville in August, 1818, Allen Wiley was appointed to the Whitewater Charge. Allen Wiley became a prominent and influential member of the Ohio and Illinois Conferences. He was given his first appointment as a presiding elder by the Illinois Conference in 1828. This appointment was to the Madison District, which included the former Whitewater Circuit, and extended north to include Fort Wayne.

The Fort Wayne Mission was organized in 1828, as Fort Wayne Methodists came under Allen Wiley's supervision as presiding elder. However, there is no known record of appointments for the years 1828-29.

Historian William Warren Sweet in volume IV of his *Religion on the American Frontier*, published by the University of Chicago Press in 1946, wrote: On October 6, 1830, the Illinois Conference in the annual session approved the following: "On motion, resolved that Fort Wayne and its vicinity be, and same is hereby, constituted a station to be denominated the Fort Wayne Mission, and that it be attached to the Madison District." Nehemiah B. Griffith was appointed the pastor.

The growing congregation shared various meeting places—schoolhouses, a carpenter's shop, a cabinet shop, and the old Court House – as prelude to its own first church building.

A Historical Record by Alfred S. Johns, written in 1901, records that during the pastorate of James Harrison, who was appointed in 1835 for one year, an attempt was made to build a church on the south side of West Main Street, between Webster and Ewing Streets. A frame structure was partially completed but came to a standstill for lack of funds. Later, a roof was added, but again the money ran short, and the project was finally abandoned.

Berry Street Chapel of the Methodist Episcopal Church

A small church building, The Berry Street Chapel of the Methodist Episcopal Church, was erected in 1840 at the corner of Harrison and West Berry Streets—the same year Fort Wayne was incorporated as a city.

Burgeoning growth resulted in the congregation being divided by the Annual Conference in 1849, with all members residing west of Harrison Street forming a new congregation.

Berry Street Methodist Episcopal Church – 1885

Wayne Street Methodist Episcopal Church

The newly organized congregation was first known as West Charge but later changed its name to Wayne Street Methodist Episcopal Church. The congregation first met in the chapel of the Fort Wayne Female College established by the Methodist Conference in 1846. It was located at the end of Wayne Street, facing College Street. In 1852, as young men were admitted to the college, it was thereafter commonly known as the Methodist College. In later years the college reorganized and moved to Upland, Indiana, where it became Taylor University.

The Wayne Street Methodist Episcopal Church built its first building, 35 by 50 feet in size, on two lots on the southwest corner of Wayne and Broadway Streets in 1850. In 1871 a new brick building was built on the site of the old frame church and the first organ was installed in the same year. It had to be pumped by hand by the janitor, concealed behind a curtain. In 1896 the church was remodeled and enlarged.

The First Methodist Episcopal Church

"The Berry Street Chapel of the Methodist Episcopal Church" changed to "Berry Street Methodist Episcopal Church" in 1851. In 1858, the need for a larger church became apparent. Subscription lists were passed and an architect was employed, but progress was slow, and it was not until 1864 that the new church building was completed.

Continued growth led to the Berry Street Methodist Episcopal Church congregation relocating to the corner of Wayne and Lafayette Streets with the laying of the First Methodist Episcopal Church cornerstone in 1902. Following the Uniting Conference in 1939, the word "Episcopal" was dropped, and following the union with the Evangelical-United Brethren Church in 1968, the corporate name became, First United Methodist Church.

In 1954, new facilities, Wesley Hall and Gettle Memorial Chapel, were added.

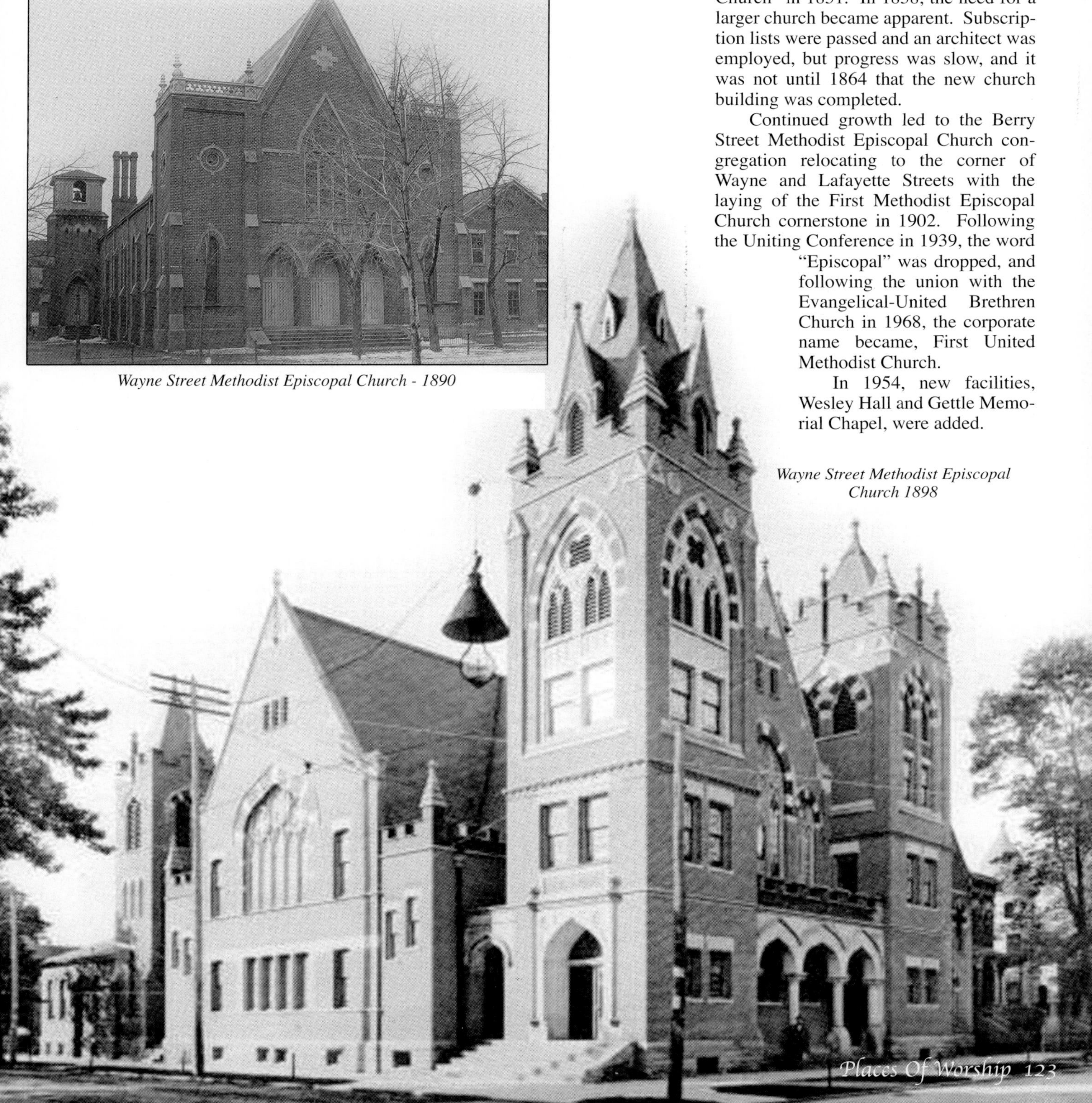

Wayne Street Methodist Episcopal Church - 1890

Wayne Street Methodist Episcopal Church 1898

Together Again

The First and Wayne Street congregations reunited on Sunday, June 23, 1968, in an inspiring service. On that Sunday, worship services began at 10:00 a.m. in the separate churches. After a short opening, each congregation left its church home to march to meet the other congregation. The First Methodist Church members marched west on Wayne Street to Harrison Street, where the members of Wayne Street Methodist Church, coming east on Wayne Street, met them. Then the united congregation moved north on Harrison to the Van Orman Hotel—located on the northwest corner of Berry and Harrison Streets—the very site at which the Berry Street Methodist Episcopal Church once stood.

The sermon for this Union Sunday was preached by Bishop Richard Raines as one of his last official acts before retirement. The ballroom of the Van Orman Hotel was filled to overflowing by members, who listened with both hope and humility to the bishop's statement that these two congregations were setting a historic precedent which would serve as an example for other congregations over the whole country.

The reunited congregation worshiped from 1968-1972 in the Wayne Street United Methodist Sanctuary, while a new First Wayne Street United Methodist Church Sanctuary was planned and built on Wayne Street frontage just west of the First United Methodist Church's Wesley Hall and Gettle Chapel.

First Methodist Episcopal Church – 1905

First Methodist Episcopal Church's Wesley Hall and Gettle Memorial Chapel - 1955

First Wayne Street United Methodist Church

A Striking Architectural Edifice Built to the Glory of God

On February 4, 1973, the First Wayne Street Congregation met at 9:30 a.m. at the Wayne Street United Methodist Church site. Here a short service of farewell was held. Then, led by a torch bearer, who carried the light from the altar candles of the old church to light the new, the pastors, choir, and congregation marched to 300 East Wayne Street for the first service in the First Wayne Street United Methodist Church.

Bishop Ralph T. Alton, Resident Bishop of the Indiana Area of The United Methodist Church, led services for the consecration of the new building on Sunday, February 11, 1973.

The First Wayne Street United Methodist Church chose to remain a downtown church and to build an architecturally striking edifice at the heart of the city, dedicated to serving Christ. Four bronze bells, cast in Holland, were hung in the prominent church tower. The faceted stained glass windows remain outstanding features of the building. Those on the south present key scenes from the creation of the world to Christ's resurrection. The west windows portray the Holy Spirit's work in the formation and shaping of the Christ's church, showing such varied scenes as the stoning of Stephen, Luther's nailing the ninety-five theses to the door of the Wittenberg Castle Church, Francis Asbury as a circuit rider, and, finally, clasped brown and white hands symbolizing the Methodist unification of 1939. In 1974, a magnificent organ, built by Rudolph Von Beckerath of Hamburg, Germany, was installed.

175th Celebration

The birthplace of Methodism in Fort Wayne, First Wayne Street United Methodist Church celebrated its 175th Anniversary in the fall of 2003 with a weekend of events: On Friday evening, November 7, the sanctuary choir presented a concert in celebration of the church, performing three Glorias (by Vivaldi, Bass, and Rutter) with orchestra. On Saturday evening, November 8, a celebration dinner was held in the Appleseed Room at the Memorial Coliseum, at which former pastors reminisced. On Sunday morning, November 9, Bishop R. Sheldon Duecker, Bishop in Residence, preached an inspiring and challenging message titled, "Let's Celebrate," taking Hebrews 11:29-12:2—Examples of Faith—as his text. In his message he said: For the past 175 years there have been persons in this congregation who sought God's vision for this church. The finger of God reached out and touched their hearts and minds. They responded to that spark of divine power… This congregation has had a glorious past. We celebrate it today. But we must do more than look to the past. We must also celebrate the future… We are the saints God has chosen to shape the future of First Wayne Street United Methodist Church. Bishop Duecker closed his message quoting the last verse of "Christ Loves the Church":

Christ needs the church, to live and tell his story, to praise his love and marvel at his trust, till, bathed in light, awakened from the dust, we walk with God, alive in grace and glory.

Our Present

We are a cosmopolitan downtown congregation drawing membership from the greater Fort Wayne Metropolitan Area. Our members and constituents comprise a rich tapestry in theological perspective, culture, education, occupation, and socio-economic background. We honor our rich Wesleyan Heritage with serious, yet open theological reflection. Our mission is to develop disciples. Music has always been central to the worship of God and First Wayne Street United Methodist Church considers it a privilege to offer the Lord the very best in harmony and praise.

Our Future

Our vision for the future of First Wayne Street United Methodist Church is that God is calling us to remain a vibrant congregation, sharing the good news of God's love in Jesus Christ at the heart of the city; transforming the hearts and minds of people; and preparing each Christian for an active role in God's Kingdom.

First Presbyterian Church

First Church Building 1837-1847

In 2005-06, First Presbyterian Church is celebrating its 175th anniversary. On July 1, 1831, five women and two men presented certificates of membership from their churches in the East to the Rev. James Clute, officially organizing First Presbyterian. Afterwards, they elected two men as ruling elders. The next day the elders were ordained during worship, and the pastor and elders constituted themselves as the church session and examined and received five more members. By the time Chute's three-week visit to Fort Wayne concluded, more than 44 signatories of several denominational backgrounds had pledged financial support to his salary, and Chute agreed to be pastor to this frontier town of about 300 residents. Prior to the founding of First Presbyterian, the only continuing religious ministry in Fort Wayne was the Sunday school founded by James Hanna in 1825 which became the nucleus of the new congregation.

John Ross, a Presbyterian minister who visited Fort Wayne five times between 1822 and 1826, found no promise for planting the Gospel here. Chute's estimate, which, like Ross', took account of the concentrations of Indians, traders, speculators and canal laborers without religious background, though not so pessimistic, was cautious. Chute took to the challenge and developed a multi-faceted ministry. He organized a choir, conducted a Wednesday evening prayer meeting, taught a weekly Bible class, founded a tract society for monthly distribution of literature, established a reading room on religion, temperance and morality, preached at as many as seven sites in the countryside and maintained an active home visitation program until death terminated his ministry on December 28, 1835.

At that time the congregation was still shuffling among temporary quarters. It moved to its own building in the fall of 1837. The first church building, located on the south side of Berry Street, east of Lafayette Street, was a white, wooden structure 40 feet square, elevated several feet to accommodate the James Hanna-founded Sunday school on the lower level. Above was a large belfry and a small spire. The move coincided with the arrival of the Rev. Alexander T. Rankin and the depression of 1837. As the depression worsened, work on the canal ceased, and, in 1840, the American Home Missionary Society cancelled its subsidy for Rankin's salary. As a result, the congregation experienced difficulty meeting its debt and its salary obligations. Rankin's salary was still in arrears when he resigned in 1843, in part for pecuniary reasons. But during his pastorate the congregation had increased numerically, spiritually and in ethical awareness, and had firmly enough aligned with the Old School side of the Presbyterian Church that it rebuffed the direct intervention of Henry Ward Beecher to win the congregation for the New School side in 1844. The foundation of First Presbyterian had matured and strengthened in such ways that it conditioned its future for the long term.

Under the Rev. William Caldwell Anderson, who served an interim pastor during the Beecher onslaught and the organization of the Second Presbyterian Church which called Henry Ward Beecher's brother Charles to be its pastor, First Presbyterian became a more activist congregation with attention to new member outreach. His successor, the Rev. Hugh Sheridan Dickson (1844-1847), a popular preacher and lecturer, also developed the congregation. So, in 1845 the congregation laid the cornerstone for a new church building, a Colonial-style building at the southeast corner of Clinton and Berry Streets. Because lagging contributions slowed construction, the building was not completed and dedicated until 1852. At 40 by 75 or 80 feet with a basement and a spire 150 feet high, the Church was praised as an imposing addition to the Fort Wayne scene.

In 1863, the congregation decided to enlarge this building by the addition of a wing and renovated the rest of the building (commonly referred to as the third building). Fort Wayne had grown to more than 9,000, and First Presbyterian's growth justified doubling the pews from 320 to 640.

A devastating fire, December 16, 1882, left First Presbyterian homeless until the education wing of the new church building was completed in October 1885. Sunday school was held at the Second Presbyterian Church, and for a short time the congregation worshiped at the Circuit Court Room of the Court House. From April 1883 to October 1885, the congregation worshiped at the Achduth Vesholom Congregation without charge, a charitable act that forged a lasting ecumenical relationship. The fourth building, for which land was purchased at the northeast corner of Clinton and Washington Streets, was 100 feet wide and 134 feet long, of modified Gothic design with seating for 750 worshipers. The exterior was yellow Michigan sandstone; the roof was slate. The 220 foot steeple (completed March 1893) was the highest in the city. The first services in the sanctuary occurred May 1, 1886. The building served until the 1950s when the fifth and current building was constructed.

Second Church Building 1847-1863

When the Rev. George Allison (1935-1949) was nearing retirement, he posed some questions to the congregation: Among them: "Is First Church doing the most it can for the Kingdom of God?" "Is it making the most effective use of its choice location near the heart of the city?" "Is it adapting to the new opportunities and limitations imposed by a modern city?" The congregation took the question seriously and appointed a committee to study the mission of the Church. The final report became the basis for programs of ministry to the parish, the neighborhood and the community that revitalized the congregation and increased the influence of First Presbyterian here and elsewhere for a generation and beyond.

Even before First Presbyterian had called Allison's successor, it started a $1,000,000 building fund in order to construct a church building appropriate to the seven-day-a-week ministry that was envisioned. Shortly after the congregation called the Rev. John W. Meister in 1950 to lead the growing congregation in its newly defined mission, the goal was raised to $2,000,000 and planning began for an extensive complex, completed in stages between 1954 and 1967 – the Christian education facility in 1954, the Sanctuary and offices in 1956, the McMillen Chapel in 1958, the Fellowship Hall in 1963, and McKay Hall and Foyer, the theater and the gallery in 1967 – at a cost of $8,000,000. The current church building, erected at the corner of Wayne and Webster Streets, is a Georgian colonial building that is dignified and welcoming. Its grace and simplicity realized the planners' principles that the church buildings be "as functional as they are beautiful" and that they "symbolize God's place in our lives" by utilizing only the best construction techniques and materials. The steeple, at 177 feet, soars in the center of the city; the elongated sanctuary with vaulted ceilings and seating for 700 in boxed pews evokes quiet and reverence. The custom brick exterior and the rich woods of the interior are testimony to styling and craftsmanship that glorifies God. The limited use of stained glass in the chancel and in the chapel, in contrast to the clear glass windows that ring these worship spaces, reminds that the church is a sacred place in a secular world.

As the Sessions refined its interpretation of the new mission, it recognized that although the task of the Church – to create creators of a Christ-like fellowship and society – remained unchanged, the modern Church would have to nurture the parish, the neighborhood and the community "without such allies as strong family life and the Sabbath." The advent of suburbs and transient populations, the Session concluded, had sundered the family as "the unit of Christian worship and nurture," and the Sabbath had become "the victim of modern industrialism and of commercialized recreation." Current conditions required contemporary facilities, innovative programs and scheduling and expanded professional talent to fulfill the mission. The new building was well conceived for the administration and operation of the seven-day-a-week, church-centered programming led by expert and creative ministerial teams recruited by the Rev. Meister.

Meister (1950-1967) grouped the extensive staff into teams of ordained and non-ordained personnel by competence and training to provide professional leadership in Parish Mission, Parish Education, Parish Life and Parish Music. The Ministry of Parish Mission determined the philosophy, planning and organization of the mission of the Church and its worship. The Ministry of Parish Education provided educational opportunities for parishioners of all ages Sundays and weekdays and evenings and in various formats and organizations such as classes, discussion groups, activity groups, summer camps and Cub Packs and Scouts. The Ministry of Parish Life was responsible for evangelistic efforts, involvement of new members in the life of the parish and nurture of parishioners through personal counseling, pastoral visits and social activities. The Ministry of Parish Music was responsible for choral and instrumental music in worship, in education for all age levels and in special concerts.

Third Church Building 1864-1882

The term "Parish" encompassed the membership, the neighborhood and the community. Program participation was never restricted to members, and some programs were designed for neighborhood and community participation. The nursery and kindergarten programs, the personal counseling services and the weekday, social and activity program for seniors were open to the neighborhood and community. The congregation sponsored an Alcoholics Anonymous group, raised volunteers to combat illiteracy, advertised its music concert series in the press and created a national organ playing competition. In 1968, First Presbyterian founded the West Central Neighborhood Association, a social service ministry to the nearby low-income, elder-populated neighborhood. With the advent of the gallery and the theater in 1968, First Presbyterian greatly expanded its community arts ministry through exhibitions and theater productions. And as its benevolent budget increased to almost one-third of the operating budget, more and more of the world became its parish.

The extensive array of professionally-directed programs was conducted in well-planned and well-equipped facilities. Space included age-appropriate and activity-appropriate classrooms with technology support, meeting rooms, bookstore, lounges of various sorts and capacities, music rehearsal room, kitchens and small and large dining spaces. The sanctuary's Aeolian Skinner organ, installed in 1956, is a gem. The 330-seat theater with lobby doubling as an art gallery is a professionally-designed and equipped space with orchestra pit, shop and dressing rooms. The entire plan was projected in the course of the 1950s as the professional staff was recruited and the respective ministerial teams were constituted and identified strategies for winning the people of Fort Wayne to Christian fellowship and service. The mainline Protestant denominations experienced exceptional growth in the two decades following World War II. The growth of First Presbyterian was even greater as it increased from 1,100 in 1950 to about 3,600 in 1970.

From its beginnings First Presbyterian attracted outstanding pastoral and lay leadership; pious, charitable and reform-minded men and women who believed that Christian witness extended beyond the fellowship of the membership to concern for the welfare of others and to advocacy of social reform. The founding pastor, James Chute, was a temperance advocate. Alexander T. Rankin also was a "fearless advocate" of temperance and an equally courageous anti-slavery advocate. In the 1840s and 1850s, First Presbyterian founded elementary and male and female high schools that operated until Presbyterians and others decided that the public schools had attained sufficient quality to educate the citizenry. To enlarge the Christian fellowship, First Presbyterian supported the founding of Third Presbyterian Church in 1868 and Bethany Presbyterian Church in 1894. In 1871, the women of First Presbyterian formally organized the Missionary Society to raise funds for international

Fourth Church Building 1886-1955

missions. First Presbyterian manifested a "community consciousness and a world-awareness" from its earliest days. It was never parochial in its interest or mission.

First Presbyterian also subscribed early to the view that a "congregation adores God by means of music and other arts." Its successive church buildings were more commanding and elaborate. In 1845, it installed an organ. Organs were not allowed in Congregational and Presbyterian churches until early in the nineteenth century. Installation of a reed organ in the simple First Presbyterian Church was a frontier novelty. In 1845, First Presbyterian already had a reputation for excellent choir with a paid director hired in 1839. Also in pursuit of the goal of excellence in honor of God, the congregation employed the male Hayden Quartet from 1889 until the 1920s.

In the post-Meister years, First Presbyterian continued to minister to the membership, the neighborhood and the community. The West Central Ministry became a multi-site operation supported ecumenically by downtown congregations. In the 1970s, under the leadership of the Rev. George Mather (1971-1986), First Presbyterian instituted the Samaritan Program to train lay persons in pastoral care ministry, hired a full-time Minister of Drama, conducted a prison ministry at Chain-O-Lakes Correction Center, administered a refugee resettlement program and began a congregation of Koreans who became an integral part of the Church with the calling of a Korean Associate Pastor in 1981. Town Hall meetings with nationally known lecturers were popular along with many educational opportunities for all ages and men's and women's support groups. In the 1990s, under the leadership of the Rev. Richard C. Hutchison (1988-2000), First Presbyterian initiated a contemporary-style worship service and developed a number of additional lay pastoral care ministries, notably the Stephen Ministry program, Christ Care groups, marriage enrichment programs, new men's and women's support groups and the prayer chain.

Emphasis upon ministries to the membership during the Hutchison years did not displace ministries to the neighborhood and the community. First Presbyterian has continuously supported national ecumenical ministries such as the National Council of Churches and local nondenominational agencies such as Associated Churches of Fort Wayne. It has participated in pulpit exchanges with Protestant, Roman Catholic and Jewish congregations; it has participated in union communion, Thanksgiving and Holy Week services; and in 1994 it raised funds to support a Russian student to study at St. Vladimir's Russian Orthodox Seminary in New York. The congregation has maintained an emphasis on Peacemaking through study groups, public discussion and Session resolutions on the nuclear arms race. Civil rights has been another priority with emphasis, in recent years, upon the issues of abortion and homophobia. In 1987, the congregation stated a pro-choice position and also declared itself an open and affirming congregation. Through its substantial benevolent budget it still supports a wide array of local, national and international missions, much of its support directed through denominational auspices. It continues to identify new community services. Recent ones include weekday childcare and serving as in Interfaith Hospitality Network host congregation for families experiencing temporary homelessness.

Today, First Presbyterian is still a downtown city church; its membership comes from various neighborhoods and suburbs; and it is demographically diverse. Though it is still big, like other mainline Protestant congregations, it is smaller. Membership is about 1,300. The membership may be less affluent; it is definitely aging. Recently, under the leadership of the Rev. James B. Wooten (called in 2000), First Presbyterian restored its professional staffing to the 1960-70s level. Many of the staff are new. They are engaged in identifying strategies of ministry for the new modernity of the 21st century "Parish."

Current Church Building 1956

St. Mary Mother of God Catholic Church
Fort Wayne

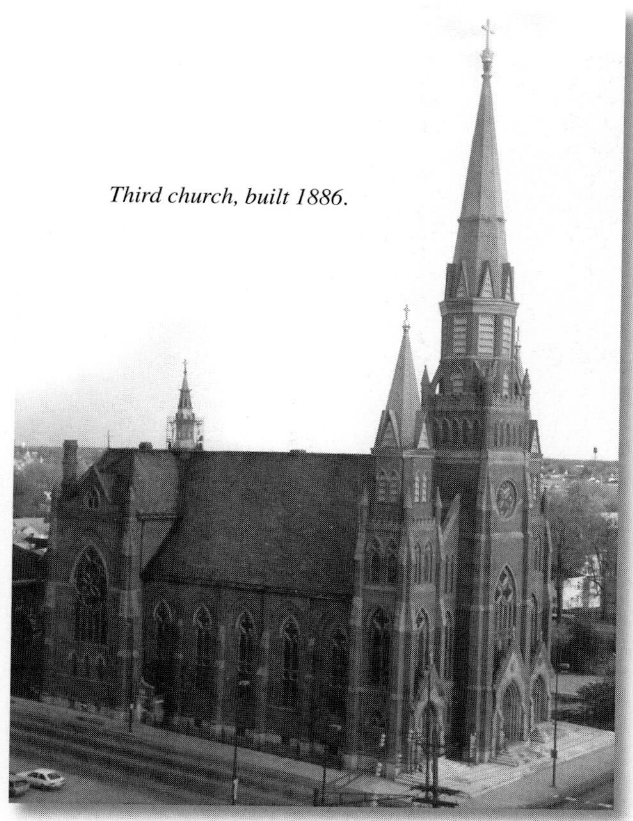
Third church, built 1886.

In 1848 thirty German families felt the need to hear the word of God in their native language. They had been attending St. Augustine, now the Cathedral of the Immaculate Conception, and the only Catholic Church in Fort Wayne at the time. They petitioned Bishop de St. Palais of Vincennes for permission to form their own parish. When this was granted, they secured lots at the corner of Lafayette and Jefferson Streets. Five men, Bernard Meyer, Nicholas Jostvert, Henry and Lucas Hoevel and Bernard Voors, mortgaged their farms to raise the $1700.00 needed for the land. Fr. Edward Faller, who had been Fr. Julian Benoit's assistant at St. Augustine, was named pastor of the first German-speaking parish in Fort Wayne.

The first church council consisted of Fr. Faller, Joseph Summers, H. Rekers, Martin Noll, G. Fox, B. Rekers, Lorenz Mayer, Ulrich Rehne and Herman Engelert. Lorenz Mayer used his team of horses to excavate for the foundation and in the construction of the 32 foot x 64 foot brick building.

In August of 1848, the work was interrupted by a cholera epidemic. The church was completed in November. On the 29th of the month, the thirty charter families moved in solemn procession from St. Augustine to the new building which was dedicated to the greater honor and glory of God under the tutelage and the title of Mutter von Gott, Str. Maria. A small one-story frame house was erected to serve as pastoral residence. A schoolhouse that had served the German children was moved from Calhoun Street a year later and placed behind the rectory.

The rapidly growing German congregation soon outgrew the modest size church.

In 1857 Thomas Lau drew up the plans and was awarded the contract for the brickwork and the woodwork for a new church structure. Plastering was to be done by N. Meyer and Nicholas Alter. Inside finish work went to Herman Wilking, George Link, and Henry Pranger. The bricks were purchased for $4.00 per thousand from Samuel Lillie. Edward Smith donated the sand. B. H. Schnieders owned one horse and borrowed another.

Lorenz Mayer again donated a team, as did B. Trentman and Joseph Zimmerman. Fr. Faller was chairman of the building committee, which consisted of Bernard Trentman, John Trentman, Herman Nierman, Martin Noll and B. H. Schnieders. Also in the year 1857, Fort Wayne and the 42 counties north of Indianapolis were designated a diocese and John Henry Luers was appointed its first bishop.

Bishop Luers laid the cornerstone in the summer of 1858. Before the church was completed Fr. Faller was transferred to New Albany, Indiana and Fr. Joseph Weutz was named pastor. On November 2, 1859, the church was completed at a cost of $30,000.00 and was rededicated by Bishop John Henry Luers to Mutter von Gott, Str. Maria. Henry Monning and Fr. Weutz traveled the country seeking donations to help retire the large debt. The spire was completed in 1871.

Many improvements in school buildings followed. In 1862 a new two-story brick school for boys was constructed on the corner of Lafayette and Jefferson. The same year, a brick combination school and convent, on Lafayette Street next to the church, was occupied by the girls and the Sisters of Providence, who taught the girls for three years. The School Sisters of Notre Dame replaced them in 1865.

Fr. Joseph Rademacher served as the third pastor of the parish from 1872 through 1880. He was later ordained Bishop of Nashville, Tennessee and would return still later as Bishop of Fort Wayne. Fr. John H. Oechtering replaced Fr. Rademacher in July of 1880.

The second St. Mary's Church served its members well until January 13, 1886 when, for some unknown reason, the boiler in the basement that supplied the steam heat exploded. The concussion was felt throughout the city. The blast killed Antoine Evans, the sexton, who was the only person who may have known the cause of the disaster. One of the large main doors was blown from its hinges and instantly killed Alberta Willard, a 13 year old who happened to be walking past the church. There was no fire but the structural damage was so severe that the church and the rectory had to be torn down.

The Catholics of Fort Wayne and much of the general population of the city, in an out-pouring of generosity, contributed to a fund to replace the church. Six months after the disaster, Bishop Joseph Dwenger laid the cornerstone of the third St. Mary's Church.

An immense throng attended the event. The elegant new structure was designed by S. M. Lane of Cleveland, and built at the cost of $75,000.00, with another $30,000.00 for furnishings.

The new church, completed in December 1887, was a 68 feet by 195 feet, red brick American gothic structure with gold sandstone trim. It featured three steeples. The center steeple soared to a height of 237 feet, the tallest one in the city. The boiler was judiciously placed in a separate building. The oak frame of the church was designed so that if the beams fell, they would not pull down the walls. The frame supported an elegant Gothic interior, which featured a white marble altar with gold augmentation flanked by marble angels holding lamps. The church had 32 large stained glass windows, one, among other scenes, portrayed the events in the life of St. Mary, Mother of God. The

St. Mary's Boys School

St. Mary's Girls School

church could seat 930 people. A new two-story brick rectory was constructed behind the church on Jefferson Street in 1886.

Fr. Oechtering was not only the pastor of the new church, but also the designer of the windows and the magnificent altar. He was highly educated, having been sent to college at the age of 14 years. He studied seven years in college and university before beginning his priestly preparation. He was ordained for the diocese of Fort Wayne in 1869 at the age of 28 and came to America the same year. He was named a Monsignor and in 1888, Immovable Rector of St. Mary's by Bishop Dwenger; in 1903, Vicar General of the Diocese by Bishop Alerting; and in 1905, Domestic Prelate of His Holiness Pope Pius X. Msgr. Oechtering wrote several treatises on Socialism and Capital and Labor. He wrote original dramas in classical style. Some of the titles were *Hermenegild*, *William Tell* and *King Saul*. He wrote a comedy: *The Living Statue, and a farce: The Discovery of America.* His *Catechism of Church History* was in common use in the area. He also served the diocese in several other capacities. Msgr. Oechtering was pastor for 47 years. In 1927 he retired at the age of 82 and moved back to his native country. He lived into his 90s in Riesenbeck, Germany and died there January 10, 1942.

Education in general and education of children in the Catholic faith was a priority of the parish from the beginning. The School Sisters of Notre Dame served the parish, teaching in the schools, for 98 years. The 1862 Girls School and Convent was torn down and replaced by a new 65 foot by 75 foot school and adjoining 55 foot by 40 foot convent in 1891. In 1896 Msgr. Oechtering and St. Mary's saw a need to prepare their students for business opportunities in Fort Wayne. They opened the first Commercial High School, which graduated many students well prepared to succeed. A much larger Boys School was constructed in 1903 across Lafayette Street from the church, on the corner of Jefferson Street, to replace the one built in 1862. The first floor contained six classrooms. The second floor contained a magnificent hall with a stage and a dining room. The basement had a meeting and recreation room, a gymnasium, bowling alleys, billiards, library and baths. Around this time there were over 500 students in the school.

Fr. George Hasser was Mgr. Oechtering's assistant for 12 years and succeeded him as pastor in 1927. He served in that capacity until 1935 when he asked to be relieved of his duties because of a persistent throat infection. Fr. Edward Miller was his assistant.

Msgr. J. Nicholas Allgeier followed Fr. Hasser as pastor. He had been born and raised in St. Mary's parish. Fr. Allgeier found it necessary to replace the heating plant and make many improvements on the property, including redecorating the interior of the church.

Msgr. Allgeier celebrated his patron saint on St. Nicholas' Day, December 6th, by passing out giant candy canes to all the children in the school. His assistants were Fr. V. J. Rosenthal and Fr. James Gertsbauer. Fr. Allgeier retired in 1963 after 28 years as pastor and remained in residence until his death in 1972. Sadly he had to close St. Mary's School the year he retired due to low enrollment and financial problems. The Commercial School was closed with the opening of Central Catholic High School in the fall of 1938. With Msgr. Allgeier's retirement, Fr. Ralph Larson was appointed pastor and served for 6 years, resigning in 1969.

Fr. Thomas Patrick O'Connor was appointed pastor of St. Mary's in 1970, by Bishop William McManus. He was raised in Gary, Indiana where his father worked in the steel mills. The parish to which he was now assigned was on busy traffic arteries in the inner city, surrounded by many people in need. Fr. O'Connor was always aware of the needy. He began sharing peanut butter sandwiches with the hungry out of his kitchen. By 1975 he officially opened St. Mary's Soup Kitchen. The charitable operation, providing soup and other foods, moved to the basement of the church late that year. In 1976, Fr. Tom was instrumental in forming the Matthew 25 Health Clinic which was opened across Jefferson Street from the church. In 1979, the Dental Clinic joined the Health Clinic.

In the 1980s, the church needed repairs on the roof, the windows, and the walls. Boilers also needed to be replaced with a gas heating system. A great deal of money was needed for these ongoing repairs. The costs became manageable when 300 families set out on a fundraising venture. Their efforts were rewarded when they raised \$500,000 towards the cost of the project.

On September 2, 1993, St. Mary's suffered another disaster. The steeple of the church was struck by lightning. The Plexiglas installed over the stained glass windows, to keep them from being damaged, prevented the firemen from getting the water to the fire. Ironically a measure taken to preserve the church ended up destroying it. The community could only watch helplessly. Although the building had to be completely demolished, the spirit of the faithful remained strong. As Fr. O'Connor watched in disbelief, his immediate thoughts were focused on the people who depended on the soup kitchen. The next day, volunteers and parishioners were distributing sandwiches from Fr. O'Connor's kitchen in the church parking lot.

On the following Sunday, Mass was celebrated from a makeshift altar on Fr. Tom's back porch. That day Bishop John D'Arcy promised the worshipers that St. Mary's would be rebuilt. It took a long time to decide what form the new church would take, considering the needs of the faith community and the larger community surrounding the church. Father Tom often referred to the parish, during the almost six years without a church building, as "nomads roaming in the desert." St. Mary's gratefully accepted St. Paul's Catholic Church's offer and attended Mass in their church. Parish meetings were held wherever a meeting place was available.

In accordance with their philosophies, Fr. Tom, St Mary's parish, and Bishop John D'Arcy, decided to build a more modest church with better facilities for services to the community. Therefore half of the insurance settlement from the fire was placed in the St. Mary's Heritage Fund. Since 1998, the fund has given 1.5 million dollers to support the needy, youth, minorities, ecumenism and evangelism. St. Mary's parish also supports Miss Virginia Mission House and the former East Side/West Side, now named Wellspring, through Fr. Tom's "Bells of St. Mary's" tuition grants, awarded to children to enable them to attend Catholic school. Not all recipients are Catholic. A source of pride is the formal sit-down Thanksgiving dinner that the parish serves to approximately 1,200 people. Another annual community meal is served on Ash Wednesday, which includes Lenten bean soup. Christmas is celebrated by making up food and gift boxes and distributing them to approximately 500 families each year.

Father Tom O' Connor's work was not only appreciated locally. In 1993, just before the fire, the Catholic Church Extension Society named him as the recipient of the Lumen Christi (Light of Christ) Award, as one "who put his faith to work through spiritual and social outreach to the residents of his inner-city parish." They also presented $25,000.00 to the diocese in his name to aid St. Mary's after the fire.

Bishop John M. D'Arcy broke the ground for the fourth St. Mary's Church on Sunday, March 2, 1997. The previous church was a grand Gothic structure and a widely appreciated landmark built for the glory of God. The design of the new church makes it very apparent that the purpose of this building is not just to serve God but also our fellow man. The new church is more modern. A modest sized tower has now replaced the large, Gothic steeple. The interior is unique. As visitors enter, they are greeted by the baptismal fountain, which flows near the main entrance in the large gathering hall. The new sanctuary is smaller with a personal quality. It seats some 250 people. There are also spacious meeting rooms. The church offices are housed in a separate wing with the Soup Kitchen. The "State of the Art" kitchen, which serves 1500 people a day, occupies 5000 square feet. Over the years, as needed, the diocese had acquired properties in the block surrounding the church. After the fire, the last house was obtained from a generous elderly parishioner. With reconstruction, St. Mary's building and parking lot occupied the full city block. A new rectory was built on Madison Street across the street from the church.

In 2002, Father Thomas O'Connor struggled in his fight against cancer and heart problems. His inability to offer Mass forced the parish to rely on the diocesan priests to take up the duties. Father, The Eternal Irishman, lost the battle on his patron saint's day, St. Patrick's Day, 2004. On August 16, 2004, the heartbroken parish opened their arms to the new pastor, Father Phillip Widmann, who is also pastor of St. Peter's parish.

St. Mary's has been blessed with members attracted from all over the area. The church is truly a melting pot in the American Tradition with a diverse congregation dedicated to the service of their fellow man. The people who worship within its walls, tempered by disasters and loss, continue 157 years of their Catholic heritage.

Fourth and current St. Mary's Church.

Bahá'í Community of Fort Wayne

The first Bahá'í group formed in Fort Wayne in 1940. By 1943, the first Bahá'í institution, the Local Spiritual Assembly of the Bahá'ís of Fort Wayne formed with the election of Maye and George Worthington, Lydia and Philip Schott, Pauline Roth, Worthy Strauser, Lulu Trenchet, Ruth Dietel, and Florence Caley.

The Fort Wayne Bahá'í community hosted, in 1966, a major proclamation. It was an event with the two-fold purpose of acquainting residents with the tenets of their faith and increasing the spirit of cooperation in diversity. Officially declaring it Bahá'í Week (November 11-20), Mayor Harold Zeis stated in his city proclamation the societal good will evident in --"increasing the spirit of cooperation amongst different religions, races, and economic groups." Some of the most prominent Bahá'ís in the United States were featured speakers: Dr. David Ruhe, Professor of Preventive Medicine at Iowa University; Dr. Daniel Jordan, Rhodes Scholar, Chicago University; Mrs. Jane McCants, A.M. Atlanta University; Col. Salvatore Pelle, U.S. Army; William Maxwell, M.A. Harvard University; and Mrs. Joy Earl, formerly of the University of Japan. In the Mezzanine of the Keenan Hotel, speakers spoke on perspectives of: science, education, civilization, world order, and unity. They were interviewed on local programs by Reid Chapman, Ken Kurtz, Ann Colone, Rol Smith, and Dick Rice; they also spoke at several high schools. The following year a Bahá'í youth convention was held in Westfield, which attracted youth from as far away as Texas. In the 1990s, several regional Bahá'í youth workshops (e.g. Indiana Dawnbreaker's Bahá'í Youth Workshop and Detroit Bahá'í Youth Workshop) performed at Fort Wayne youth centers and parks.

Bahá'í Community gathering 1940s.

Bahá'í meeting in the 1950s. (l. to r.) Seated: Lydia Schott and Pauline Roth. Back: Lola Graftmiller, Mr. Aker, Philip Schott, Vera Aker, and Mildred Holmes.

In addition to striving to develop a distinctive Bahá'í community, Bahá'ís have joined with other area faiths in matters of social justice, such as in prayer vigils and civil rights marches; Bahá'ís have served on the Mayor's Circle of Faith council and Church Women United's Interfaith committee. There have been collaborations with I.P.F.W's Women's Studies, 3R's International Village, the Y.M.C.A., the History Center, Black Expo, and 'Instant of Cooperation' ; participated in the City's 9/11 observance, 'Random Acts of Kindness' programs, and Faith Based Initiative. They sponsor drives for homeless shelters, literacy, and food banks. They have welcomed to the city such renowned Bahá'í artists as Kevin Locke, Dizzy Gillespie, Margaret Danner, Red Grammer, and Seals & Crofts.

In 2001, several area Bahá'ís joined thousands of their fellow co-religionists in Haifa, Israel for the official ceremonial opening of the Terraces of the Shrine of the Bab on Mount Carmel, which was televised live around the world, including in Fort Wayne, on public access channels.

Race Unity Day & World Religion Day, special event days on the Bahá'í calendar, have been celebrated here for many decades. In 1951, the first Fort Wayne observance of World Religion Day (initiated nationally in 1950) was held at the Bahá'í Center, 219 East Berry Street, in the Aldine Building, where Robert Hopkins, chair of the L.S.A. explained that "the purpose of the day [is] to foster the Bahá'í principle of spiritual unity as the path to world order." Race Unity Day, (initiated in 1957), has been commemorated here for years. In 2004, over 200 came out to an international children's fest to celebrate racial and cultural diversity at a Bahá'í sponsored Race Unity Day event held at Reservoir Park.

Right photo: *February 2000 - Intercalary Days - Community Party held at the Aboite Community Center. During Intercalary Days (February 26 to March 1 inclusive) Bahá'ís throughout the world prepare for the Fast, share hospitality, donate to charities, and give presents.*

August 23, 1993 - Lorraine (Peace Queen) and Howard Menking (Peace Ambassador) share methods of how to build a peaceful world with children at the Three Rivers Montessori School.

1970's Bahá'í Conference

Left photo: *1991 Children's classes presented the play, "The Seed"*

Above photo: *1990s Marsha Smiley with Philip and Elizabeth Helser man a Bahá'í booth in Walb Union, at an I.P.F.W. event celebrating diversity.*

1990's Three Rivers Festival Parade

Left photo: *June 6, 1997-During Race Unity Weekend Glynn Hines, host of WJFX Foxy Forum, interviewed Carol Butler, Public Information Officer, Dr. Bill Smits, Hoda and Kemba Thomas Mazloomian (author of "To Dine with the Blameless Ethiopians").*

1993 50th Anniversary commemoration of the Local Spiritual Assembly held at the Community Center on Main Street.

Concordia Lutheran Church

Historically Speaking By James Ackmann

The Gospel of Jesus Christ has been preached and taught at Concordia for over 100 years. Here is the story of those blessings of God and the response of His people.

Concordia Evangelical Lutheran Church was spawned by St. Paul's Lutheran Church in downtown Fort Wayne. The reason for Concordia's establishment was the need for "schooling closer to home," rather than having students make the long trip, usually on foot, to St. Paul's on the corner of Barr and Madison.

On August 6, 1899, the Eastern District of St. Paul's was granted permission to organize as an independent congregation. The following month it was resolved to erect a combined church and school building at the corner of Fletcher and Alliger Streets. Three weeks later the newly organized congregation adopted the name "Concordia." On dedication day, April 29, 1900, the new building, constructed at a cost of $9000, was filled to overflowing for three services.

The Reverend August Lange, St. Paul's pastor for its Eastern District since 1896, was called as Concordia's first pastor. The congregation numbered 727 souls

"Engaging People

and 447 communicant members. The parish school was opened in April of 1900, with Martin Pohlmann and Viola Kolby as its first teachers, and an enrollment of 136 pupils.

In June of 1900, Concordia joined the Missouri Synod. The congregation grew so rapidly that in just 3 ½ years it was resolved to build a new church edifice on South Anthony Boulevard. The building, with a seating capacity of more than 1000, cost $30,700.

The school was also growing rapidly. Therefore, in 1914, four new classrooms were added.

A pastoral change occurred when, after 22 ½ years at Concordia, Pastor Lange resigned, and Pastor Walter Klausing of South Whitley was called and installed.

The Golden Anniversary celebration was held on May 21, 1950. At that time the congregation was one of the largest in the Synod, with a total of 2285 souls.

After a period in which four different vicars assisted, the growth of the congregation necessitated the calling of an assistant pastor in 1954, a former vicar, the Reverend Osmar Lehenbauer. When the following year, Pastor Klausing died, at the age of 63 after 33 years of service to Concordia, Pastor Lehenbauer and Professor Erwin Schnedler served as associate pastors.

By this time school enrollment had reached 273, with seven full-time and two part-time teachers. In 1956 Mr. Vernon Schumacher took over the reins as its principal.

By 1956 the congregation purchased its present 20 acre site on Lake Avenue at a cost of $59,000. On January 22, 1961, a beautiful new school of brown brick and Indiana limestone was dedicated. Church services were soon held both at South Anthony and in the school gymnasium.

An important language development was also taking place. In 1957 weekly German services were reduced to twice a month. Later they were held quarterly as late as 1970.

Pastor Lehenbauer accepted a call at the end of 1967, and was succeeded by Pastor Henry Schroeder, who left Concordia in 1970. After an extended vacancy, Pastor Lowell Thomas accepted a call to Concordia. The congregation held its final service on South Anthony on August 30, 1970. The original church building was turned over to the Indiana District. The church then became Shepherd of the City Lutheran Church.

On Lake Avenue, a new church building arose, depicting the life of Christ, from the building style of ancient Bethlehem to a small hill topped by the three crosses of the bell tower. The bells were from the "Old Concordia" steeple (original cost $956). The new church building was dedicated on September 22, 1974, at a cost of $600,000, with a seating capacity of 500-700 people.

In 1980 two classrooms and a new music room were added to the school. Pastor George Black replaced Pastor Thomas in March of 1984. On September of 1994 Pastor Black accepted a call to Utica, Michigan. Mr. Randy Einem became principal in 1989, leading a faculty of 12 teachers. The enrollment was 283 students. In 1988 a preschool, under the leadership of Mrs. Kayleen Bredemeyer, was established. Mrs. Bredemeyer retired in 1998 after ten years of service.

On July 12, 1992, Ellen Luepke accepted the position of Director of CARE Ministries. On August 13 Pastor Karl Frincke was installed as Senior Pastor.

In June of 1997 Mr. Shawn Meyer was contracted to serve as full-time youth director. He left in August of 1998 and was succeeded by Mr. Doug Croucher.

A $1.6 million expansion was begun in July of 1998, which added a new multipurpose room to the church, six new classrooms, a school administrative suite, renovation to the kitchen, restrooms and nursery and handicapped accessible entrances.

Mr. Robert Boyd was welcomed as school principal in 2000. He now leads a staff of 28 in grades preschool to eighth.

A contemporary service was begun in January of 2002 in the school gym. Attendance has steadily increased in this popular addition. In 2002 the church offices were extensively remodeled, and a new music room was added.

In January of 2004, a second pastor, Reverend Kevin Wendt was welcomed. The new church courtyard and a Children's Garden were added in 2004 also.

Staff changes in 2005 included: calling Reverend Doug Croucher as a third pastor, and, on Ellen Luepke's retirement, she was replaced by Kim Pape as director of CARE Ministries.

Concordia Church and School, by God's grace, remains a vital, vibrant, and dedicated instrument in the mission of spreading the Gospel of Jesus Christ at home and abroad. With 2300 souls, 1700 communicants and school enrollment of over 400 students, Concordia looks back in respect and forward in hope and joy.

With Jesus"

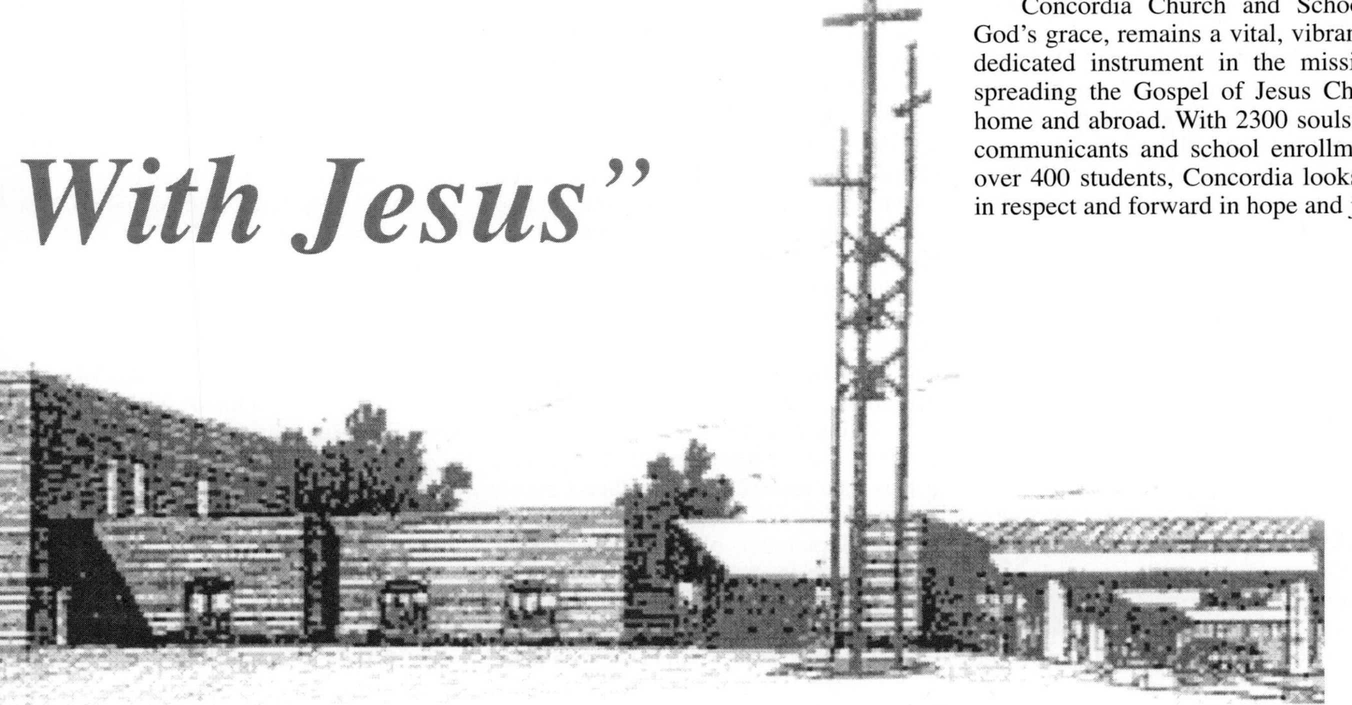

Emmanuel Lutheran Church

Emmanuel - God With Us!

Emmanuel, "God With Us" - This was the name selected for a new congregation to be located to the west of Fort Wayne in August 1867. 138 years have passed since this group of believers moved from St. Paul's, its mother church, to the 900 block of West Jefferson, established a two-room school and planned for a church on that site.

On February 9, 1868, the Emmanuel congregation unanimously resolved to build a church. Later that month, the building committee advised the congregation to build a brick church for $26,000. When asked if they had considered a frame building, the committee answered that a brick church would be cheaper than a frame building in the long run. It was resolved to build a brick church with a seating capacity of 1,100 people. A 185 foot steeple was to be erected atop a sanctuary built in the "St. Andrew's Cross" pattern. This new building would be the only one of its kind in the United States. The final report of the building committee showed that the church with all the furnishings cost $34,039.83; $65.00 more than the first estimate.

Emmanuel congregation joined the Missouri Synod, and Rev. Stubnatzi served as Central District president. The Synodical Conference in July 1876, (of which Pastor Stubnatzi was vice-president) met at Emmanuel. At this conference, a resolution was passed to begin mission work among the "American Indians and Negroes." Pastor Stubnatzi died suddenly on Sunday, September 12, 1880, and the church and the Lutheran community mourned his loss.

In 1880, Rev. Charles Gross of Buffalo, New York, accepted a call to serve as pastor. His first action, upon his installation as Emmanuel's pastor, involved coming to grips with a language problem, for now there were demands for services in German and English. Pastor Gross urged the starting of an English mission, a move which paved the way for Redeemer congregation.

In 1903, following the resignation of Pastor Gross due to ill health, Emmanuel called Rev. William E. Moll. In December of 1903, the congregation suspended paragraph "2,G" of the congregational constitution which stipulated that the pastor should at all times preach in German. It was then resolved to introduce English services.

In September of 1933, Rev. Fred Heidbrink was installed by Pastor Moll who had submitted his resignation due to failing health. During the years of the "Great Depression," churches and schools both felt the bite of hard times. A pivotal decision was made to continue the school's ministry, establishing Christian Education as a firm priority of the congregation. Not only was the choice made to stay in the education business, steps were also taken to ensure growth.

First, a school bus was purchased to bring students from outlying areas to school. Second, a kindergarten was established in 1941. This step also marked a milestone as the first woman teacher in Emmanuel's history, Miss Edna Grotelueschen, would join the staff. From that time, women staff members have served with great dedication and grace.

Rev. Heidbrink's resignation for health reasons in 1954 brought a call to Rev. Walter M. Schoedel as pastor. He was no stranger to Emmanuel as he had served as part-time pastor since 1950. During the Schoedel years, the congregation continued its promise to preach the Word at home and actively support mission efforts throughout the world.

In 1962, Emmanuel and St. Michael Lutheran Churches joined forces to form Emmanuel-St. Michael Lutheran School. The partnership was accompanied by a $208,000 building project which included a gym/auditorium, meeting room with kitchenette, stage, showers, and three classrooms.

In 1968, Emmanuel joined other west side churches to form the West Central Neighborhood Committee (today known as Wellspring); an organization ministering to the social and spiritual needs of the residents of the area.

In 1971, members of Emmanuel boldly upset a 103-year tradition when the newly created congregational assembly elected three women to office: Miss Sally Hoefelmeyer, Secretary; Mrs. George (Harriet) Visnovsky, Director of Community Relations; Mrs. Max (Marge) Boyer, Director of Parish Life.

Pastor Schoedel accepted a call to Concordia Lutheran Church, Kirkwood, Missouri, in 1971. For the first time in its ministry, Emmanuel experienced a long vacancy. During this period, leadership came from Deaconess Orluske, Vacancy Pastor Charles Tuschling, and a newly-constituted Board of Directors.

As in our nation, 1967-1977 was also a time of strife and questioning for the church. This era saw ideas of leadership, morality, and personal rights and responsibilities put to the test. The Lutheran Church-Missouri Synod was also divided over many difficult issues. As with many LCMS congregations, the turmoil in the Synod during these years had a significant emotional impact on Emmanuel congregation.

During this period, three pastors served Emmanuel – each devoted to the Gospel of Christ, each with a different approach to the issue of the day. Rev. Fred Stennfeld served Emmanuel from 1971-1975. Pastor Stennfeld built his staff around his assistant, Rev. Ronald Janssen and Deaconess Janice Orluske. Of particular importance was his moderate stand in the "Liberal-Conservative" battle raging in the Synod.

In 1975, Pastor Stennfeld accepted a call to serve as the chaplain at Lutheran Hospital. Team ministry continued when Rev. Ronald Janssen accepted the congregation's call as pastor. As Deaconess Janice Orluske had left to continue her education at Yale University, Hildegard Fritsch became Lay Assistant in the area of Women's Ministry, another first for Emmanuel congregation. Another person added to Pastor Janssen's ministry team was Arthur Klausmeier as Director of Christian Education. The Rev. Werner Wadewitz also served as Assistant to the Pastor. In 1981, Richard L. Bultemeyer was called as Minister of Christian Education and Arthur Klausmeier began his ministerial studies at Concordia Seminary. Upon ordination, Klausmeier was installed as Associate Pastor in 1982.

A gifted preacher, Rev. Janssen moved the congregation with his sermons. His administrative skill built a strong team which proved a valuable asset as Pastor Janssen soon faced significant health issues. Pastor Janssen taught the congregation not only from the pulpit, but also through his suffering.

Emmanuel congregation called Rev. Arthur Klausmeier as pastor in 1983. The following period was one of growth in both the church and school. At Emmanuel-St. Michael School, the quality of its faculty and program of Christian education began to attract the children of members and non-members alike.

Mr. Bultemeyer continued to serve as Minister of Christian Education, and Dr. Herbert Nuechterlein carried on his long and faithful ministry as choir director and organist. In 1990, Miss Linda Fiedler joined the Emmanuel staff as Parish Assistant.

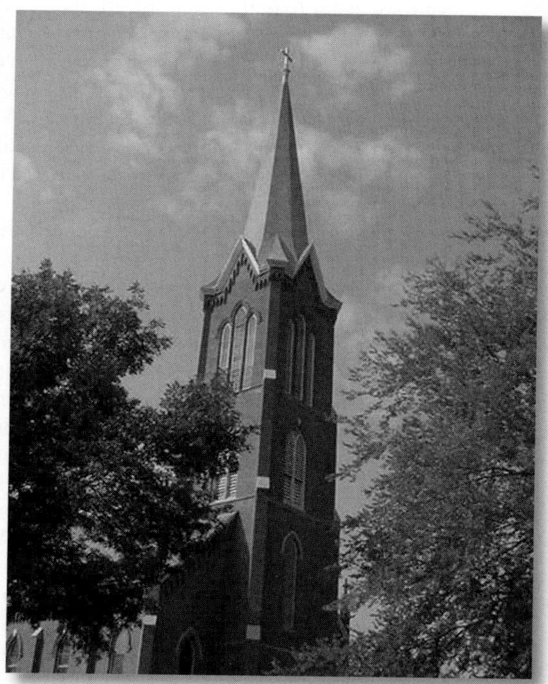

Emmanuel Lutheran Church
917 West Jefferson Boulevard, Fort Wayne

From 1982-1991, Elmer O'Keefe volunteered to serve as Lay Minister to senior members. This was another first for Emmanuel. Again another strong ministry team had come together to serve God's purposes.

In the 1990s, Emmanuel congregation supported the newly formed Aboite Lutheran Mission in the southwestern suburbs of the city. In addition, financial support was given to Shepherd of the City, Fort Wayne, and Peace, Greencastle, Indiana. These efforts continued the outreach tradition which began with Emmanuel's daughter congregations: Emmaus, Redeemer, and Bethlehem Suburban.

Rev. Klausmeier left the pastorate at Emmanuel to join the staff of The Lutheran Foundation in 1998. Once again the call to serve as pastor went to a man who had performed in other capacities at Emmanuel. This time it was Arnold Piering, who had been the eighth grade teacher in the school before entering the Seminary.

Again a team was formed around Pastor Piering. Thomas Eggold, who had been called to serve as the Director of Youth and Family Ministry from the teaching field, entered Concordia Seminary and was then assigned to a vicarage at Emmanuel. Continuing the rich history of female parish workers, Mrs. Lana Hille served as the Director of Care Ministries, and Mrs. Karen Schoenefeld joined the staff as the Early Childhood Administrator.

In 1999-2000, the congregation went through the process of developing a new constitution and plan for ministry. It also recommitted to the West Central Neighborhood both physically and spiritually. Beautiful new gardens, playground equipment, the replacement of the church doors with those of the style of the 1867 originals, and continued maintenance of the property all reflected this decision.

When Thomas Eggold completed his vicarage and course work in 2003, he was ordained and called to serve as Associate Pastor at Emmanuel. In 2004, Rev. Gene Brunow joined the staff as the Visitation Pastor, adding yet another valuable team member to this active ministry.

The new millennium brought with it an expanded music ministry and new worship opportunities complementing the rich traditional hymns and liturgy that had served Emmanuel congregation for so many years. Even with all of these changes, the Word of God remains the center of congregational life and is presented in a variety of ways to make it meaningful to people of all ages and cultural backgrounds. By God's grace, Emmanuel is alive in mission.

Though Emmanuel Lutheran Church is nearing a century and a half of Christian teaching and Gospel centered worship at 917 West Jefferson Boulevard, it is in no way old or out of touch with the present. Through its church and school, and the witness of its members, Emmanuel continues to be a presence in the community, a place of assistance and care, and most importantly a family of faith. "Emmanuel" truly is a vivid example of "God With Us." *Author: Mr. Walter "Skip" Sassmannshausen Editor: Reverend Thomas A. Eggold*

First Baptist Church

First Baptist Church on West Jefferson

Our Present Church 1950

The first church of any faith or creed in Fort Wayne was the Baptist church begun as a mission to the Indians by the Reverend Isaac McCoy and his wife Christiana, in May 1820. The McCoys were hesitant to come to Fort Wayne believing that the work would be more successful if located further from the influence of the white community with its alcohol and gambling. They finally agreed to come following a strong invitation from Miami Chief Richardville and the local Indian Agent William Turner.

The work was begun in the decommissioned military fort. It served as home for the family, which included six of his own children and six Indian foster children; school for the community's children, and worship center. The McCoy's were welcomed by both the white and Indian communities. Though McCoy remained in Fort Wayne only a little over two years, several significant "firsts" occurred during his brief tenure.

Community worship began the very first Sunday he occupied the fort. Turner's wife, Ann (Ahpezahquah, granddaughter of Little Turtle), was the first convert. She was followed by her sister, Rebekeh Hackley (Pemesahquah). On June 18, 1820, Rebekeh became the first person to be baptized into the Christian faith in Fort Wayne.

McCoy wrote the first music ever written here, a hymn commemorating the baptism of Rebekeh. The baptism took place just below the confluence of the St. Joseph and St. Mary's Rivers near the current Columbia Street Bridge. The hymn recounts how this river, which had been the scene of a bloody battle in October 1790, was now the symbol of the washing of baptism in the blood of the Lamb, bringing salvation rather than death. "Glad Tiding" is certainly the first hymn and probably the first song of any kind written in and about Fort Wayne.

McCoy established a school in the fort and within a week the school had enrolled ten English students, six French, eight Indians and one African American. The school grew and prospered under the tutelage of Johnston Lykens. In addition to the basic courses, the school taught mechanical trades and agriculture. The school increased to fifty scholars over the next two years.

On August 3, 1822, having been joined by a minister, two schoolteachers and a blacksmith, McCoy's mission was established and chartered as a church. The Potawatomi Baptist Mission Church was constituted, and the Articles of Faith were signed by: Isaac McCoy, Christiana McCoy, Giles Jackson, Benjamin Sears, Jr., John Sears, Ann Turner, Johnston Lykens, Wiskehelaehqua (a Delaware Indian woman), Jesse Cox (an African American), and May Sears.

Because of the prevalence of typhus, the interference of a portion of the white community which preyed upon the Indians with alcohol and gambling, and the death of the Indian agent, William Turner, the McCoys felt they were compelled to open a field elsewhere.

Acting under the orders of the Baptist Triennial Convention, the McCoys left Fort Wayne on December 9, 1822 to establish another mission station near what is now Niles, Michigan.

After McCoy's departure, it would be 17 years before those interested in Baptist work would be able to obtain the services of a pastor. There is no doubt that the seeds of Baptist mission and witness were successfully planted by the efforts of McCoy, even though his energies were focused on the needs of the Indians, and the French and American residents were not invited to affiliate with his fledgling congregation. It was as a result of the efforts of those "left behind" when McCoy moved his work to the Niles, Michigan area that a permanent church was finally re-chartered in 1837 and has continued to serve the city since that time.

On January 14, 1837, several Baptists met and resolved to be constituted into a church with the aid of Elder John Tisdale. On February 8, 1837, they met again, and Elder Tisdale was appointed to draft a constitution and make a report to the group on the first Saturday in March.

On March 4, 1837, they met in Alexander McJunkin's schoolhouse and unanimously adopted a declaration of Faith and a Church Covenant thereby organizing themselves into "The Fort Wayne Regular Baptist Church." The charter members were: Richard Worth, Elizabeth Worth, John Fairfield, Jane Fairfield, William Worth, Sarah Swop, Hanna Worth, Miriam Sawtelle, Ann Archer, and Elizabeth Morgan.

The church continued to worship in the school with a "parade" of short-term pastors. In the winter of 1841-42, the increased size of the congregation, as well as the rental fee for the school induced the congregation to build its own meetinghouse. Under the leadership of the Reverend William Gildersleeve, the congregation doubled in size, and with the receipt of a gift of land from the Hon. Samuel Hanna, a building was erected. The property was known as "Clay Hill," 514 East Washington Street.

Six years later the building was moved to the west side of Clinton Street between Wayne and Berry streets. This meetinghouse was a frame building and provided a seating capacity of about 300. The building did not have a steeple, nor did it have any windows in the front. The only break in the front was a double door. A transom was located above the doorway. The church had a vestibule with a door to each side leading in the assembly room. There were four windows on each side. Two wood stoves provided the heat and coal oil lamps the lighting. There was a Reed organ, and the Baptismal Fount was the nearby Maumee River. This building served the congregation until 1868.

A new brick structure was erected at 228 West Jefferson following the Civil War. Under the spiritual leadership of the Rev. G.L. Stevens, the congregation had grown to almost 200 members. Despite the difficult financial times which existed following the war, the congregation was able to pay off the note in full within six years. It cost $25,917.49 to construct this modest Gothic structure; the building was called "The Tabernacle of the People" and was dedicated on August 16, 1868.

This building underwent a number of remodeling projects over the years; the most impressive occurred in 1889 during the pastorate of the Rev. Stephen A. Northrup. The Gothic building received a significant face-lift and became Romanesque in its appearance. The building was also enlarged at that time and continued to serve the congregation until December 28, 1947.

The church continued to grow, and by 1923 it had outgrown the Jefferson Street building. A capital funds program was begun to purchase new land and build a new building. The lot immediately to the west of the building was purchased in 1925. Soon after, $45,000 was raised in contributions and pledges toward construction of a new building. In 1929 the nation was plunged into the "Great Depression," and despite the depression, it was paid off completely in 1932. By 1935 the church was once again debt-free; but the Depression was still a reality, and in its wake came World War II and the ration years that followed. This, too, passed, and the church began to look to the future once more.

During these years at "Clay Hill" and at the Jefferson street location, the church grew in both membership and ministry. The Sunday school was organized in 1842 and contributed to the development and planting of additional Baptist churches across the years. In 1890 the South Wayne Mission was organized. A lot was purchased and Deacon A.C. Weaver donated "Glenwood Chapel" in 1892. This branch school became what is now South Wayne Baptist Church. In June 1911, the Oliver Street School was organized. This school developed into Immanuel Baptist Church. A branch school in the Bloomingdale neighborhood, 1914, became the Greenlawn Baptist Church. As World War II was ending, Fort Wayne's north side was growing and a group from First Baptist started Memorial Baptist Church.

The Rev. Dr. L.E. Olsen became pastor in March 1945. A lot on the northeast corner of West Wayne and Ewing was purchased in July of the year, and in August 1946 the property on Jefferson Street was sold with the occupancy right of eighteen months granted to the congregation. Government restrictions on building materials made immediate construction of a new edifice impossible. The church entered into a contract with the Fort Wayne campus of Purdue University and took rented quarters in the University Center, where it remained for two years. During this interim, everything required for Sunday school, choir, and morning worship was transported each week to the University Center by the members from their homes. Wayne Street Methodist Church graciously allowed the use of their building facilities for funerals, weddings and mid-week services. They also allowed the First Baptist Church to conduct its business meetings in their building during this time period.

It soon became obvious that the property on West Wayne Street was inadequate both in size and in parking. A larger lot was purchased at 2323 Fairfield Avenue in July 1948.

Ground was broken for the new building on January 23, 1949, and work was begun on construction of the Colonial style building currently serving the congregation.

On May 15, 1949 the cornerstone was laid. This date was chosen because it coincided with the 129th anniversary of the beginning of Isaac and Christiana McCoy's ministry in this city. On January 8, 1950 the building was dedicated and worship was celebrated for the first time. The Rev. Dr. L.E. Olsen led the church throughout these often difficult years of transition.

The church continued to grow and require additional space for its ministries. In 1955 the Adjoining Cutshall property and mansion were purchased and provided space for the pastor's study, church offices, classrooms, and receptions until the completion and enlargement of the existing facility in 1967.

In 1963 the congregation was able to burn the mortgage. The church was then being pastored by the Rev. Dr. Phillip Philbrook, who had come in 1960. His would be the longest and one of the most meaningful pastorates in the church's illustrious history. On July 15, 1965 ground was broken for the current educational unit, administrative offices and enlargement of the sanctuary. This new and expanded facility was dedicated on January 22, 1967. In April 1969 a beautiful stained glass window designed by Thomas McMahan and constructed by City Glass was dedicated. The window depicts the six primary missions of the church: Fellowship, Service, Teaching, Preaching, Worship and Witnessing. It contains a central motif depicting Isaac McCoy witnessing to the Indians.

Under Philbrook's pastoral leadership, the congregation grew to 800 members. The tradition of church planting continued as the congregation participated in both finances and personnel in the establishment of Faith Baptist Church. The church also provided major leadership and support in the establishment of the first Hispanic Baptist Church in Fort Wayne. Rev. Philbrook retired in 1987 and continues ministry with cancer survivors in his new home in Wisconsin.

In the seven years that followed Philbrook's tenure, the church struggled to find itself and redefine its leadership and ministry goals in the community. Seven interim pastors and two-full time pastors would attempt to find the "new ground" for the church as it moved away from almost three decades of steady leadership. A further challenge came from the out-migration of people from the inner city – as the suburbs flourished, they stripped the church of almost one-half of its membership base.

In 1994 the Rev. Dr. William Deans came to serve as interim minister and assist the congregation in refocusing for the Twenty-first Century in a greatly changed community. The Fairfield Avenue building to which the church had moved in 1950 was no longer a white, middle class neighborhood. The nearby elementary school had sixteen different language groups, and the community had become a mix of Latino and Asian immigrants seeking to find their place in America.

Following an extensive search for pastoral leadership, the Search Committee recommended Dr. Deans as Senior Pastor in December of 1994. He held this position until his retirement in June 2004.

During Dr. Dean's tenure, weekday ministries began to focus on the neighborhood children in after-school enrichment programs of art, drama, and music. Fort Wayne is home to the largest Burmese community in the U.S., and First Baptist now hosts the Fort Wayne Burmese Christian Fellowship, a worshiping fellowship. The weekday program has given major focus to providing an English immersion program for the Burmese elementary students at Fairfield Elementary. This has been a joint ministry with the ABC/USA Board of National Ministries.

Just as time marches on, so does the First Baptist Church. The congregation remains a dedicated and enthusiastic community who adhere to "The Articles of Faith" as strongly as did those who signed it in 1822: "And being united together upon the foregoing plan, we deem it our duty to walk in all the commandments and ordinances of the Lord blameless, which that God may enable us to do, let every member at all times fervently pray." Thus this church, through the years united together and with fervent prayer, continues its commitment to south central Fort Wayne, "Sharing the Heart of Christ in the Heart of the City."

Harlan United Methodist Church

Our present Church sits on lovely wooded acreage on the west edge of Harlan at 16434 Highway 37. The beautiful, contemporary, pale brick structure with a large, single lighted stained glass window serves as a welcoming beacon to all who pass by. It was a proud dream come true for a small congregation of approximately 100 people when it was built out of necessity for bathrooms, parking space and classrooms in 1975. The former, outdated 1881 church at the corner of Stopher Road and Highway 37 was no longer practical. There was a two-story "annex" behind that church (which was sold and remains today as a private home on Stopher Road). It served as a parsonage and later as classrooms with its MYF "Upper Room" meeting site. Still, the 1881 red-brick two-story Church was traditionally beautiful with its many large stained glass windows, cathedral ceilings and charming balconies. It too had once been the dream of another hopeful congregation, and it was a bittersweet day for their ancestors and many of the present congregation when that church was torn down and its windows auctioned off in 1974. (While being removed, those windows were stolen and then recovered through the efforts of [then] Pastor Lynn Soughan. Details are in the Church history album.)

The church history began in 1838 when Harlan was known as "Maysville." There were two separate Methodist congregations then: The Methodist Protestant and the Methodist Episcopal Churches. The Protestant Church was begun at New Haven with a branch organizing at Cuba Corners just one mile west of Harlan in 1851. In 1854 during the pastorate of Rev. David Pattree, a frame church building 30 by 40 feet, costing $500, was erected and moved to Maysville. It was replaced in 1878 by another small frame structure erected on Water Street two blocks North of Highway 37, on the east side. The parsonage for this church still stands and is privately owned. A photo of this church, torn down in 1941 after the two churches joined, is at the church in the Church album.

The Methodist Episcopal Church was organized when Rev. True Pattee began preaching in Springfield Township to a small class who met in the Maysville School House (see details in album). In 1854 the First M.E. Church building was erected directly west of the Old Maysville Cemetery on Highway 37. An interesting written account of a former member, Mrs. Nettie Minnick (who lived to be over 100), remembered that the 24 by 40 feet one-room structure had a "stove in the center that made you too hot when you were near and too cold when you were away from it. The men and boys sat on one side and the women folks sat across the aisle on the other side." She tells of "revivals", the horseback riding preacher, of being married and "sparked" in the church, and other interesting details. This building was later moved and used as a business and storage building at its location just south of the present-day post office on Water Street. A photo of this old church was taken in the 1970s just before it was torn down, and is displayed in the Church album. In 1881 the previously described two-story red brick M.E. church was erected at a cost of $6000, raised through the sale of Maysville Cemetery lots and donations. The contents of the tin box placed behind the 1881 limestone cornerstone was opened on September 4, 1974 (see album photos), and revealed damp, ruined, tin-type photos, paper clippings, coins, etc. These are put on display once a year when we celebrate our church history. Many still remember that 1975 spring day when a police escort led our congregation as we proudly marched the half mile west along Highway 37 behind a flaming torch symbolically taken from the "old church and transferred to the new." The original 1881 cornerstone, a rose stained glass window, and a large oil painting of "Christ Knocking on the Door" (which hung on the wall behind the alter and shows up in many old wedding photos) were saved from the old church and are on display in our Lynn Soughan Fellowship Hall. Although our present sanctuary is contemporarily furnished, we cherish two antique alter chairs, an original pulpit, and candlesticks from the old church. Our youth "hang out" around a basement fireplace which is made from the original red bricks of the 1881 church. Someday a future congregation will undoubtedly open our 1975 cornerstone and find that it contains such items as a last issue of a Sears Catalog, letters, photos, coins, history, personal letters, jewelry and medals, etc.

Harlan United Methodist Ministers were: 1880-J. H. McMahan; 1881-1883 H. C. Meyers, Wm. J. James (Lay Preacher, for 6 months); 1883-1885 I. W. Singer; 1886-1887-J. A. Beaty; 1888-1889 T. F. French; 1890-A. H. Curris;1891- A. C. Gerard; 1892-1896 Lewis Reeves; 1897-1901 L. C. Zimmerman; 1902- C. A. Luse; 1903-1905 W. E. Ingalls; 1906- J. L. Hutchins; 1907-1908 Preston Polhemus; 1909-1910 J. B. Cook; 1911-1913 F. V. Westhafer (last 6 months of 1913-S. I. Zechiel); 1914-1916 S. I. Zechiel; 1916-1917 E. E. Wright; 1918-1925 L. G. Carnes; 1921-1923 J. 0. Hochstedler (multi-church charge); 1924-1927 C. E. Smith (multi-church charge); 1926- R. S. Brown (multi-church charge); 1927- Lynn Young (multi-church charge); 1928-E. P. White; 1929- Lloyd N. Alden; 1930- E. P. White; 1931- H. E. Burk; 1932-1933 E. S. Morford; 1934-1935 H. D. Stackhouse; 1936- E. A. Overton; 1937-1938 L. E. Clayton; 1938-1939 L. N. Alden; 1939-1942 S. M. Bell (merge with the Methodist Protestant Church); 1942 L. B. Sharp; 1942-1943 W. P. Thorn; 1943-1945 Olin E. Lehman; 1945-1947 Bruce Pearson; 1948 F. S. Young (Student Pastor); 1949 Harley Davis (Student Pastor); 1950 D. R. Salisbury; 1949-1957 G. R. Brittenham; 1957-1958 Stanley Newenschwander; 1958-1961 Russell Rasmussen; 1961-1963 Gene Critchfield; 1963-1964 Gordon Klopenstein; 1964-1968 Stanley Tobias; 1968-1970 Richard Applegate; 1970-1972 R. Larry Smith; 1972-1973 Larry Swartz; 1973-December 1984 Lynn Soughn; December 1984-1990 Patrick Fulbright; 1990-November 1993 Wm. L. Dunfee; December 1993-2001 Hugh Rohrer; 2001 to present 2005-Doug Davies.

Presently, we offer Sunday morning Church and Sunday School, and a more informal "Saturday Night Live" service. The Junior and Senior High Youth are a strong asset who continue to reach out with mission projects at home and away. They are a great help with the Summer Bible School and community-wide Easter Egg Hunt. Our Mission Statement is: "Harlan United Methodist Church shall share the love of Jesus Christ, by word and action, within our church, our families, our parish, our community, and our world." We have strong leaders and a generous congregation that help fulfill that mission. Our building provides an area Food Pantry and a meeting place for the Girl Scouts and the Greater Harlan Business Association. Each year we support our community by working the Harlan Days Doughnut Tent and offering our parking lot as a shuttle point for Harlan Days and the Grabill Country Fair. We hold annual Fish and Chicken Dinners to raise money for Church Missions. We collect coats for, and sponsor, needy families at Christmas. Our Fall Fest/ Christmas Bazaar and Golf Outings help support church and building projects. We recently installed a new "Sight and Sound System" with technology that supports the hearing impaired. We continue to support many worthy causes such as Homeless Shelters, Habitat For Humanity, and local and foreign missionaries. Once again, we are facing a need for more space and 2005 finds us planning a new "Phase I" addition! Our 2005 membership is 175, with many other active supporters. In recent years we have become surrounded by new housing and we look forward to welcoming all of the new families to "come as you are" into our church. *Submitted by Marquita Hertig, Historian*

Harlan United Methodist Church

St. Charles Borromeo Catholic Church

Reed and Trier Roads
Fort Wayne

St. Charles Borromeo Church was established in June 1957 by Bishop Leo A. Pursley. Father Edward I. Hession, now Monsignor Hession, was named the first pastor. In January 1958, Humbrecht Associates completed plans for the first church, school and all-purpose room. Michael Kinder & Sons was awarded the contract and the building was completed in December 1958. The first Mass was celebrated on Christmas Day that year. The new pews for the church were delayed because of a fire on the shipping dock. Parishioners were seated on metal folding chairs for this special occasion.

Fr. Robert Dombrowski was appointed the first assistant at St. Charles followed by Fr. Walter Bly. Since then, the following priests have served at St. Charles: Fr. Victor Lisek, Fr. John F. Pfister, Fr. Eugene Koers, Fr. Richard P. Hire, Fr. Barry C. England, Fr. William Sullivan, Fr. Paul A. Anandam, Fr. James A. Shafer, Fr. Michael Buescher, Fr. Laurence Tippmann, Fr. Steven Morrison, Fr. James W. Koons, Fr. Stephen E. Colchin, Fr. Timothy A. Wrozek, Fr. Matthew S. Kafka, Fr. Patrick F. Fras, Fr. Ronald Ramenaden, Fr. Michael Heintz, Fr. Polycarp Fernando, Fr. Christopher J. Young, Fr. John Klimczyk, and Fr. Gabriel Coelho. The pastor of St. Charles is now Msgr. John N. Suelzer. Assistants at the present time are Fr. Christopher Smith and Msgr. Peter Kumaraki.

Deacons who served the parish were Fr. Robert Rossi, O.S.C., Fr. William Sullivan, Fr. Gary Sigler, Fr. James Blume, Scott Schnelker, Dan Soley, Fr. James Shafer, Fr. Timothy Wrozek, Stanislaus Kos, Fr. Michael Heintz, Fr. Christopher Young, Louis McDougall and Fr. Christopher Smith.

In September 1959 St. Charles School opened with an enrollment of 247 students. Additional facilities were added in the 1960s and a new wing with six classrooms for first and second graders was added in 1978. The architect for this project was Martindale, Tourney, Gibson, Inc. and Weigand Construction Company constructed the new addition. There are now 764 students in the school in grades kindergarten through eight. The kindergarten program is held off-site at Our Lady of Good Hope Church on St. Joe Road and was started in 1999.

As the parish grew, so, too, did the parish Religious Education Program. In 1968, over 600 children came to school in the evening for their religious preparation. This program has been directed by Fr. Dombrowski, Fr. Lisek, Mr. Jack Schenkel, Sr. Barbara Mueller, O.S.F., Sr. Joan Mosher, O.S.F., Mrs. Margaret Kruse, Sr. Christina Fuller, O.S.F. and Mrs. Kathy Monagle; and is now under the direction of Sr. Patricia Ann Murray, O.S.F. A program for preschool children was started in the late 1960s under the direction of Mrs. Leanne Mensing. Mrs. Anita Carter succeeded her and the program is now directed by Mrs. Kathy Dougherty.

In the early 1960s, a convent was built for the sisters serving St. Charles. The Order of Franciscan Sisters of the Sacred Heart, whose motherhouse is in Frankfort, Illinois, has served the parish from the beginning. School principals at St. Charles have been Sr. M. Anna Skobe, Sr. Marie Meyer, Sr. Theresa Renninger, Sr. Elaine Teders, Sr. Judith Plumb, Sr. Deborah Suddarth, Mrs. Sandra Koziol and Sr. Genevieve Raupp as co-principals, and Mrs. Michelle Hittie. The current

St. Charles Borromeo Church in 1958.

St. Charles Borromeo Church in 2005.

principal is Mr. Robert Sordelet with Sr. Genevieve as Assistant Principal.

On December 28, 1963 a tragic fire caused considerable damage to the church, school and cafeteria. The charred cross at the main entrance of the present church is a reminder of this great tragedy. Holy Mass was celebrated at the Coliseum on that Sunday and continued at Bishop Dwenger High School for several months during the rebuilding process.

In March 1969, a new parish was established at Our Lady of Good Hope Church on St. Joe Road. Many members of St. Charles became parishioners at Our Lady of Good Hope when the new boundaries were set.

In the mid 1970s, St. Charles outgrew the original church and a new church, capable of seating 1400 worshipers, was built. Schenkel & Schultz, Inc. were the architects and Weigand Contruction Company was the building contractor for the new facility. The new church was formally dedicated by Bishop Leo A. Pursley on January 25, 1976. The first Mass was celebrated on Christmas Eve, December 24, 1975. Nearly 2000 parishioners crowded the church for Mass.

Directors of Music and organists serving St. Charles over the years have been Richard Eykholt, Sue Golembiewski, Katy Carroll Parson, Tom Farwell, Brother Walter Duguay, Thomas McNerney, Paul Crawford, David Simon, Judy Throm, Patricia Usina, Deborah Rendon and Jeremy Hoy. The current Director of Music & Liturgy is Karen Hope and the organist/pianist is Marie Andorfer.

Mr. Kevin DePrey was appointed Pastoral Minister in 1980 and Sr. Kathy Morrissey, O.P., is now the present Pastoral Minister, having served since 1982.

Upon Fr. Hession's retirement in 1986, Fr. John N. Suelzer was appointed pastor of St. Charles. Fr. Hession had served the parish for 29 years.

In the Spring of 1991, a Long Range Planning Committee was formed to determine a long term plan for the parish. Sixty parish organizations were surveyed to identify the needs. Parishioners were also contacted for their input. A master plan was established and a family life center, to be named the Hession Parish Center, was determined as the highest priority. A fund-raising effort was begun and the "Building Our Vision" pledge campaign brought a very generous response of 3 million dollars with which to begin the project. Ground was broken for the new facility in June 1996. The building was completed in September, 1997 and the dedication of the Hession Parish Center with 35,000 square feet for all types of gathering took place on September 7, 1997. Architects for this project were Moake Park Group, Inc. and Weigand Construction Company was the general contractor. Included in this building project were the renovation of the Religious Education office, the parish library and the new Youth Ministry Center.

In October, 1995, Fr. Hession and Fr. Suelzer were invested as Prelates of Honor with the title of Monsignor by Bishop John M. D'Arcy at a formal ceremony held at the Cathedral of the Immaculate Conception.

Construction began in July, 2005 to build a new parish rectory. Building was completed in February, 2006. The former rectory will be used solely for offices and meetings.

St. Charles Borromeo Church is the second largest parish in the Diocese of Fort Wayne-South Bend and is located on 17 acres at the corner of Reed and Trier Roads in northeast Fort Wayne. Over 2,500 families are now registered in the parish with an actual member count of over 7,800. Masses are held daily at 6:15 and 8:30 a.m. and 7:00 p.m. Monday through Friday. On Saturday, Mass is celebrated at 8:00 a.m. and 5:00 p.m. Sunday Masses are at 7:30, 9:00 and 11:00 a.m. and 5:00 p.m. People of all faiths are welcome to attend St. Charles.

The 50th Anniversary of the founding of the parish will be celebrated in 2007 along with the Diocese's 150th Anniversary. The Parish Pastoral Council plans a year-long celebration.

St. John Evangelical Lutheran Church

St. John Evangelical Lutheran Church, 729 West Washington Boulevard, Fort Wayne, Indiana was officially organized on October 2, 1853 with the name German Evangelical Lutheran, St. Johannes Church.

The founding fathers all attended the only Lutheran Church in Fort Wayne, St. Paul, but were uncomfortable with the German dialect spoken there, along with other differences, and decided to form their own congregation. These included: George Riethmiller, Heinrich Beck, Michael Ehrman, Michael Baumer, George Kiefhaber, John Braun, Michael Mueller, Tobias Hueber, Matthias Strodel, Johann Riedmiller, Michael Koehler and George True. The trustees for this newly formed congregation, August Deitten, August Reiting and Michael Miller, acquired the first land in the name of the congregation for $350 on June 8, 1853. Additional adjoining lots were acquired over the years, eventually encompassing most of the city block. This has been continuously occupied by the congregation since then.

Drawing of the first church building, reproduced from the 50th Anniversary Book (privately printed).

Reverend Christian Hochstetter, serving in Konigen, Germany, offered his services as Pastor and arrived by canal boat in Fort Wayne on August 11, 1853. He began holding Sunday services, in a recently constructed one-story, one room frame building 20 ft. x 35 ft., near the southeast corner of Van Buren and Washington, facing Van Buren. Plans for a school were initiated with Pastor Hochstetter serving as teacher, and on October 2, 1853 a Constitution was adopted.

One of the "firsts" for the congregation was the baptism of infant Matthias Mueller, son of Michael and Barbara Mueller, born January 21, 1854 and baptized January 29, 1854. The first wedding was of Martin Koehnlein and Rosine Helm on January 15, 1854. The first funeral was for George August Axler, thirteen month old child of Gottlieb and Marie Axler.

The original records of the church, (births, deaths, marriages, and confirmations), written in German, were copied by the Allen County Public Library and are in the Genealogy Department.

August 27, 1854, William Buergers was hired as the first non-preacher teacher of the school with a salary of $100. Tuition for one child was $2.50 per year; two children of the same family, $4; and three children or more, $5. He taught for 6 months and was replaced by J. M. Koch. (85 years later, Dorothy Schirm now Rodewald and a member of St. John's, signed a teaching contract for 1939-40 with an annual salary of $1000). Pastor A. Kleinegees served from October 1, 1854 to September 20, 1857. Rev. Hugo B. Kuhn served from March 1858 to April 1861. Rev. Baumann was installed April 12, 1861 and remained until about 1868.

The second church building built in 1861 and dedicated in October 1862, was brick with a wooden steeple. It measured 50 ft. x 80 ft. with the interior being 28 ft. high, and cost $885.12. The original church faced Van Buren Avenue but the new one faced Washington Boulevard and is the footprint of the current building.

A five acre plot adjoining the City Cemetery, (now McCulloch Park) was purchased as the church cemetery in early 1864. Later that same year the congregation purchased six acres on Maple Avenue for a cemetery and sold the first plot. Plots were offered for 5 cents a square foot. Small graves cost $1.50; large ones were $3. In 1872 there were neighborhood objections to the cemetery and they successfully sued to have the deceased removed. These were re-interred in the third and present cemetery on Engle Road. On November 9, 1879, a society was formed for the protection of the newly-buried, and a watch tower was built for guards to watch for grave robbers.

Rev. Johannes Kucher served as Pastor from October 25, 1868 until February 18, 1890.

St. John, Lake Township Church was founded in 1877 with the assistance of Pastor Kucher and St. John's congregation.

In 1882, the church building underwent extensive remodeling with an addition added and the present three bells were placed in the steeple. The school continued to prosper, and by 1888 it employed two teachers and had two school rooms in a two-story brick building east of the church.

Rev. H. P. Dannecker was installed, May 1, 1890 as the sixth pastor and served until January 1, 1924.

In 1891, lots were purchased on the corner of John and Pontiac Streets and with financial support and 21 members from St. John's, Grace Evangelical Lutheran Church was established, later moving to its present location on Anthony Boulevard.

By 1895 the school boasted 200 pupils, and a third teacher, Adolph Oelke, joined teachers Stumpf and Scharmann with an annual salary of $500. A larger school was soon planned and on December 5, 1897 the new building was dedicated. This third school was a two-story brick with four large school rooms and an assembly hall in the second story. Costing nearly $15,000, it was considered the most modern school building in the city. All classes were conducted in English except its Religion and German Language classes, which were taught in German.

Church services were held in both English and German, and gradually attendance at the German services declined. In 1907 the church was incorporated and the name changed to Evangelical Lutheran, St.

John's Church. At the outbreak of World War I, all classes in German were terminated.

About 1909 a new parsonage was built on the northeast corner of Washington and Van Buren. (After being sold in 1948, the building was a boarding house and nursing home. Currently it is a business with a private residence upstairs).

Pastor E. J. Boerger became the seventh pastor on May 11, 1924, serving until 1946.

In 1928, in commemoration of the 75th Anniversary of the church, the entire structure was remodeled and enlarged. This included two transepts with large decorative glass windows.

Rev. William Streng began service on May 18, 1947, remaining until 1951.

A mission project in 1950 was Bethany Lutheran Church on Engle Road. Land adjacent to the cemetery was donated to this parish, as well as financial assistance, by the congregation.

By the 1950s there were four teachers at the school, each responsible for two grades in one room.

Rev. F. E. Schoenbehm was installed January 6, 1952, and remained until October 1955.

To celebrate the Centennial Anniversary in 1953, the church interior was remodeled with the removal of the side balconies and redecorated with a new altar and chancel furniture, as well as with new light fixtures (all still being used today).

Rev. Carl H. Amelung became the ninth Pastor on January 8, 1956, staying until his retirement on December 31, 1976.

Dedication for the fourth (and current) school was held January 21, 1961, with a sculpture by Marshal Fredericks depicting Christ and the Children added in 1962. Changes in the school building over the years include new classrooms and a computer room. It continues to give superior Christian educational opportunities for grades K-8, and currently has an enrollment of about 105, with room for an additional 45 students.

In 1970, ending a 25 year tradition of assisting in training future Pastors, St. John installed Assistant Pastor Harold Heidegger. Other Assistant Pastors have been Rev. Dan Meuschke, O. Wayne Shelksohn and Rev. Chris Sanderson. In 2003-4 the Minister training tradition was revived with Vicar Kurt Simerman.

Pastor Thomas A. Herbon was installed as Senior Pastor on February 20, 1977, remaining until July 1980. A Son of the congregation, Rev. William Weiss, retired from the Mission field and served as visitation Pastor from 1981-1987.

Rev. John Pannkuk was installed February 15, 1981 and remained until his retirement in September 2000. Rev. E. Dean Windhorn served as interim Pastor for 10 months.

The Rev. Dr. Frederick W. Meuter III became the 12th Pastor in September of 2001.

In 2003 St. Johns celebrated its 150th Anniversary with a year of special events and guest Homilists, including former Sons of the congregation as well as former Vicars and Pastors.

Currently in 2005, Pastor Meuter continues his service. Vicar Wendy Piano, Organist Myra Schmidt, School Principal Jake Morrow, and eight full and part-time teachers, as well as other support staff and volunteers, are involved in the daily activities of the parish. Additional information regarding St. John Church and School can be obtained at: www.stjluth.com

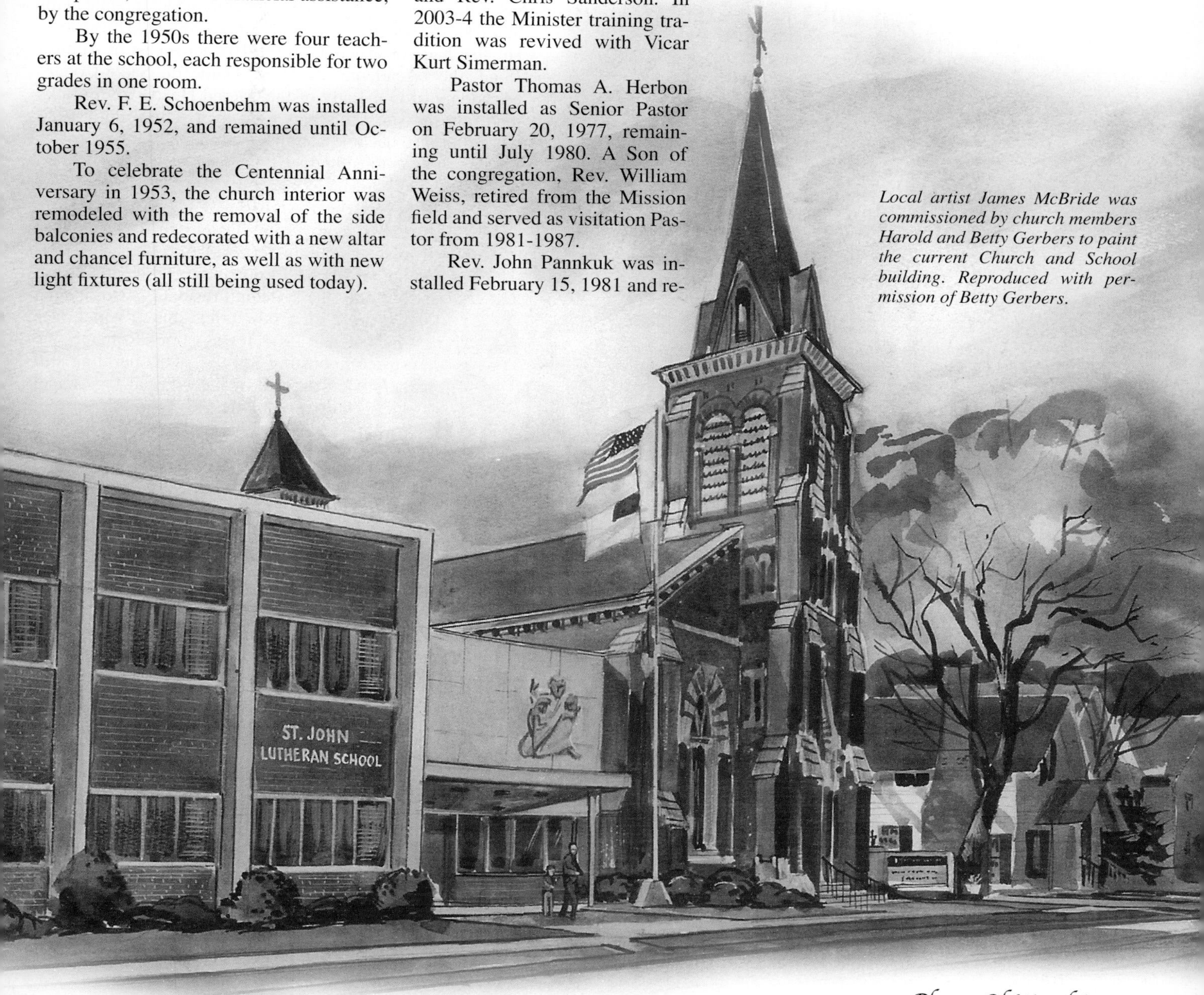

Local artist James McBride was commissioned by church members Harold and Betty Gerbers to paint the current Church and School building. Reproduced with permission of Betty Gerbers.

Saint Vincent De Paul Catholic Church

First Saint Vincent Church

Second Saint Vincent Church

In the 1830s, a group of French families emigrated from the province of Alsace-Loraine in eastern France. They settled about six miles north of Fort Wayne in what is now Washington Township, Allen County, Indiana. The region became known variously as "New France," "Académie," and "St. Vincent's." One of the French residents, Isidore Pichon, established a Catholic society (1839) which met in his home where the notable French missionary, Fr. Julien Benoit, said the first mass in the region.

In 1846, a log chapel was built on the east side of Auburn Road at the junction with Wallen Road. In 1854 it was replaced by a second log church on the west side of a two acre plot donated by Pichon. Space was also provided for a graveyard. The small community was serviced by Benoit or by Father August Bessonies until 1856 when Fr. Francis Deschamps was appointed the first resident pastor.

In 1861, the fourth pastor, Fr. Auguste Adam, supervised the construction of a new church made of white clapboard siding with an octagonal spire surmounted by a cross. He also had constructed, on the 105-acres east of Auburn Road, the "Académie de Notre Dame du Sacré-Coeur" (Academy of Our Lady of the Sacred Heart) from bricks made on the site. This was used as a school until 1936 when the site became a minor seminary for the Crosier Fathers (now a housing district).

From 1870-1897, St. Vincent's was served by the visiting Fathers of the Holy Cross from Notre Dame. In 1897, it was placed again under resident pastors. In 1901, Father Michael Louen, the eighteenth pastor, but only the sixteenth resident pastor, began the drive for a new brick church which was dedicated in 1904. It was a brick Romanesque structure costing $11,970. This building still stands on the site of the original log chapel and is now used by the Boy Scouts.

St. Vincent's Church 1861

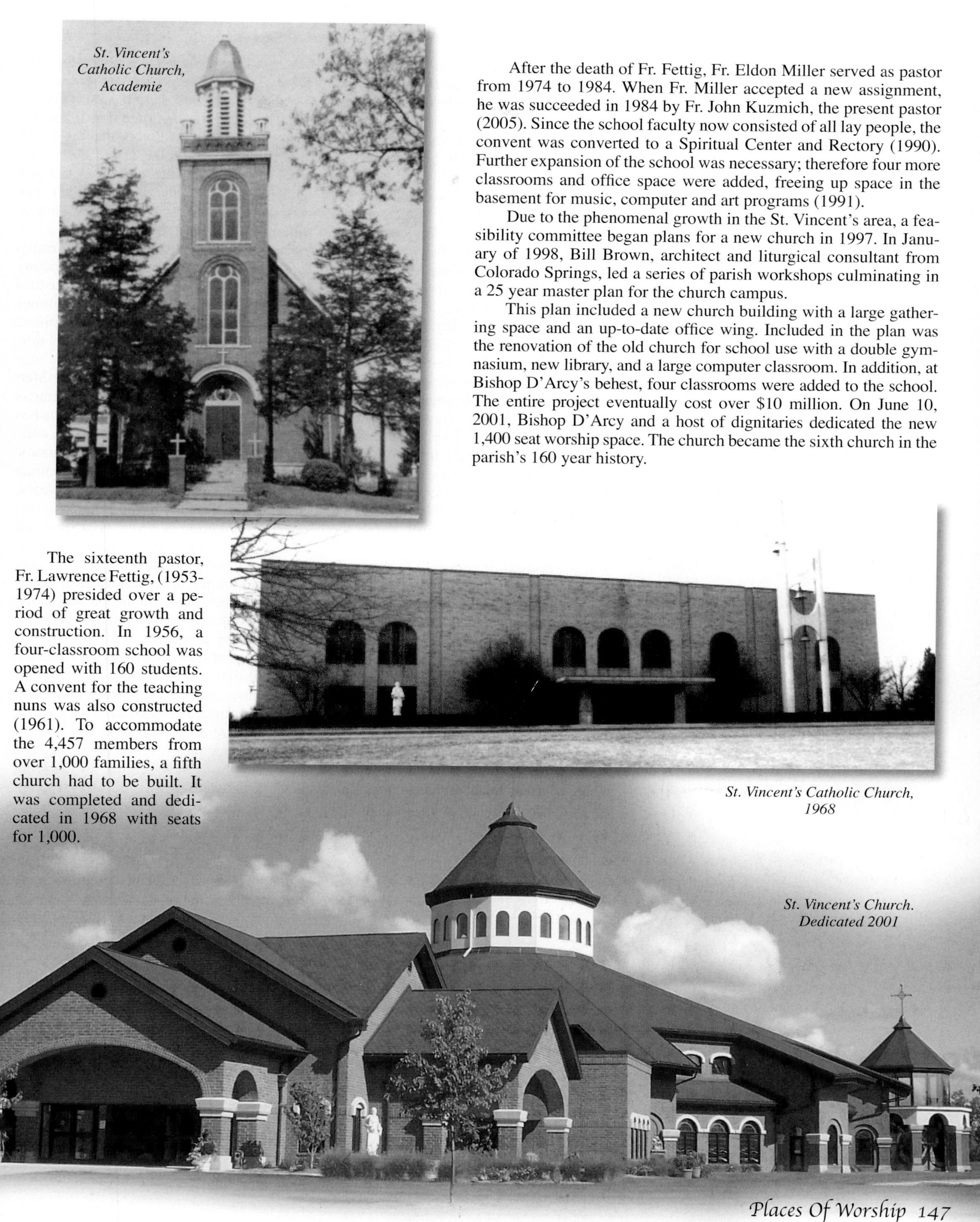

St. Vincent's Catholic Church, Academie

After the death of Fr. Fettig, Fr. Eldon Miller served as pastor from 1974 to 1984. When Fr. Miller accepted a new assignment, he was succeeded in 1984 by Fr. John Kuzmich, the present pastor (2005). Since the school faculty now consisted of all lay people, the convent was converted to a Spiritual Center and Rectory (1990). Further expansion of the school was necessary; therefore four more classrooms and office space were added, freeing up space in the basement for music, computer and art programs (1991).

Due to the phenomenal growth in the St. Vincent's area, a feasibility committee began plans for a new church in 1997. In January of 1998, Bill Brown, architect and liturgical consultant from Colorado Springs, led a series of parish workshops culminating in a 25 year master plan for the church campus.

This plan included a new church building with a large gathering space and an up-to-date office wing. Included in the plan was the renovation of the old church for school use with a double gymnasium, new library, and a large computer classroom. In addition, at Bishop D'Arcy's behest, four classrooms were added to the school. The entire project eventually cost over $10 million. On June 10, 2001, Bishop D'Arcy and a host of dignitaries dedicated the new 1,400 seat worship space. The church became the sixth church in the parish's 160 year history.

The sixteenth pastor, Fr. Lawrence Fettig, (1953-1974) presided over a period of great growth and construction. In 1956, a four-classroom school was opened with 160 students. A convent for the teaching nuns was also constructed (1961). To accommodate the 4,457 members from over 1,000 families, a fifth church had to be built. It was completed and dedicated in 1968 with seats for 1,000.

St. Vincent's Catholic Church, 1968

St. Vincent's Church. Dedicated 2001

Trinity English Evangelical Lutheran Church

Rooted in the Gospel of Jesus Christ and located in downtown Fort Wayne, Trinity English Evangelical Lutheran Church offers a wide variety of opportunities to grow in the Christian faith.

As a congregation of the Evangelical Lutheran Church in America, Trinity stands for the following:

A life of faith in the Triune God: God the Father, Son and Holy Spirit – the Creator, Redeemer and Sanctifier of the world; **A life** of new beginnings through Jesus' death and resurrection, love and forgiveness; **A life** of love and grace that reflects our oneness with God and each other in Christ; **A life** of humble thanksgiving that worships the Lord, serves our neighbor, and cares for God's creation; **A life** of peace and joy in the salvation that Christ has won for us over sin and death and the discipleship to which we have been called as children of God.

First Trinity Church

Trinity English Lutheran Church was founded on April 16, 1846 by Henry Rudisill. He and his young family came to Fort Wayne from Lancaster, Ohio on Christmas Day 1829. Being a devout Lutheran, Rudisill established the first German Lutheran congregation in Fort Wayne in 1837. However by 1846, he along with 16 other members of that congregation, decided to form an English-speaking Lutheran congregation and, thus, Trinity English came into being. Although the desire for an English-speaking Lutheran congregation was a prominent factor in founding Trinity English, differences of doctrine and worship practices also led to its formation. These differences led Trinity English to become a part of the Evangelical Lutheran Church in America and its predecessor bodies.

Trinity English has been blessed with three church homes. The first was on the south side of Berry Street just to the east of the present old City Hall Historical Museum. It was a 40-foot square, white-framed church that had housed First Presbyterian Church and was purchased from them in 1846. In 1863, plans proceeded for the construction of a new church building at the southeast corner of Clinton and Wayne Streets. The property was purchased from Allen Hamilton, and the new church was dedicated on March 27, 1864. Trinity English's current building is on the southwest corner of Wayne and Ewing Streets. Bertram Grosvenor Goodhue, considered one of the best modern Gothic architects in America, drew the plans for the building. Construction began in March 1924; and on December 13, 1925 Trinity's new Gothic home was dedicated.

The church bell that rang from Trinity English's first church home is still ringing at its current church home, making it the oldest bell in continuous use in northeastern Indiana. Also, the church is blessed with two pipe organs and a Chapel that was dedicated along with a new church school building in 1956.

A unique fact of history of Trinity English Lutheran Church is that the congregation had only three senior pastors for 130 years of its history: Dr. Samuel Wagenhals, 1868-1920; Dr. Paul Krauss, 1920-1967; and Dr. Richard Frazier, 1967-1999.

The Wagenhals era introduced three new elements in the life of the congregation. First, it introduced what was to become a long-standing tradition in the congregation of stable and long tenured pastoral leadership. This was in marked contrast to the pastoral leadership of the early years. Second, Dr. Wagenhals' leadership introduced the tradition of strong preaching and attentive pastoral care. Finally, the Wagenhals era saw the introduction of a very strong commitment to benevolence activity. These new elements in the life of the congregation also remain important today.

To these principles, the Krauss years added another three elements. First Krauss' personal dynamism was one of the dominant themes of this era and was a major factor in the tremendous growth of the congregation in size and vitality. Second, Krauss took the principles of good preaching and pastoral care to new heights. In the latter area, he showed great facility for developing programs outside of the worship service that engaged the interest of the congregation and created great energy and a sense of commitment on the part of his parishioners. Finally, Krauss took the commitment to benevolence activity to a higher level.

The Frazier years built on all of these principles and added a strong commitment to greater diversity and lay involvement in the governance of the congregation, particularly a significantly expanded role for women. Pastor Frazier's concept of team ministry has permitted even greater attention to pastoral care and during his time as senior pastor, Trinity English called its first woman pastor.

Today, team ministry continues under the leadership of the Dr. Frederick Hasecke (1999-present), with meaningful worship services; compassionate giving; and dynamic programs that lead children,

2002

Fred and Walter

Sunday School

Adult Education

youth, and adults to give thanks to God for God's saving grace. Worshippers actively participate in worship as readers, choristers, dramatists, liturgical dancers, and instrumentalists. The Music Department offers concerts and performances by internationally renowned artists, and the Drama Department provides opportunity for members of all ages to perform in the Trinity Theater or as a part of worship in the Nave and Chapel. The Education Department provides opportunities for young and old to grow in their faith through Sunday Church School, adult forums, Vacation Bible School, as well as weekly classes. Youth and Family Life provides social, sports, and service activities for youth, couples, and singles to grow closer together in their faith.

Trinity English is also a Stephen Ministry congregation that daily reaches out to persons in need. Workshops and seminars offer caregiver and grief support; healing services provide solace and comfort as members work through challenging times; prayer ministers offer prayer intercessions for those in both trying and thankful situations; eucharistic ministers bring the sacrament of Holy Communion to those unable to come to church; Stephen ministers provide listening ears and helping hands for those who may be in crisis; deacons and deaconesses take altar flowers to members in hospitals or nursing care facilities; and caring individuals are "on call" for informal visits in person or, if preferred, by telephone. No matter what the need, Trinity English reaches out with loving care, fulfilling Christ's admonition to "love one another."

From its beginning, Trinity English Evangelical Lutheran Church has been a congregation that is dedicated to sharing the Gospel of Jesus Christ with the world, and it invites everyone to be a part of this engaging and faith-filled ministry.

Monroeville United Methodist Church

In 1848 Arthur Bradly, from Decatur Work, organized a society and preached in the log cabin home of Thomas Meeks. Charter members were the John Barnharts, the William Ratledges, the Jesse Fosters, and the Meeks; with Thomas Meeks appointed as Class Leader. This small group grew in size and continued as a class under various circuits whose names and formations changed with regularity. Finally in 1869 the name of the circuit was permanently changed to Monroeville Circuit.

By the close of Rev. Smith's pastorate (1852-53), the society had become self supporting and felt that it could exist on its own. Rev. Smith received a salary of $150.00 a year. On these salaries pastors couldn't afford buggies, and they traveled over their circuits on horseback.

Under Reverend Smith's pastorate the church grew in numbers, and worship was moved from private dwellings to the Jones School. The Jones School was a log cabin large enough to hold the whole congregation and all the children in the neighborhood.

Then in 1859 the worshipers moved into a frame building called the Small School, located at the junction of South Street and Liberty Road.

The Civil War brought dissenting opinions among members of the congregation and there was some falling off of the membership during this time. But once the war was over, the church began to flourish again and many new souls were added. This new growth soon had the congregation looking for a larger building. John Barnhart donated a lot; and under the leadership of Rev. A. Curry, a frame structure was erected in 1865 on the north side of Monroeville at a cost of $1,600.00.

In 1889 the membership reached two hundred and the church began to think about building again. Over the next five years, no action was taken. Then in 1894 Rev. W. E. Murray took up the project with renewed energy. A lot was secured on South Street, subscriptions started, and the members "took hold of the task". Success crowned their efforts and the cornerstone was laid for a new building on August 30, 1895.

The Laying of the Cornerstone Celebration was conducted by Rev. F. Simpson, presiding elder of the Fort Wayne District of the Northern Indiana Conference. Board members were John Meeks, S. J. Montgomery, John Alleger, W. A. Waterman, and A. H. Anderson.

1897 Monroeville Methodist Church

Made of brick with a slate roof, the church's interior was divided into four rooms: an auditorium 36 by 55 feet, a Sunday school or lecture room with seating capacity of 200; a classroom 11 by 23 feet; and a kitchen 10 by 11 feet. Auditorium seating was circular, with a seating capacity of 350 when folding doors between auditorium and lecture/classroom were opened up.

The pulpit and choir loft sat on a raised platform, on the west side of the auditorium; with the entrance to the auditorium through a door on the southeast corner of the church. The cost of the building was $8,000.00 with new organ and interest payments still to come.

Reverend Murray was followed by Reverend Charles Tinkham, and the task of planning the Dedicatory Service fell on his shoulders. Preceding the Service itself, there had been a whole week of evening church services with a different, former pastor preaching at each service.

Then on Sunday, June 27, 1897 Reverend David Moore, D.D. from Cincinnati, Ohio preached the Dedicatory Service.

During Rev. Tinkham's ministry, the amount paid on the debt was $2,343.00, leaving a deficit of only $215.00. Thirty-five new members were added to the church, and the average attendance in Sunday School grew to 300. The pastor's salary was now $680.00 a year.

In 1904 the Methodist charge consisted of Monroeville, Pleasant Grove, and Woodland Churches with Rev. George W. Martin as pastor. During Rev. Martin's tenure (1904-06), the Methodist Congregation completed a new parsonage located just west of the church. The cost of the parsonage was $2,000.00, with no debt left upon completion.

Woodland was transferred to the Bobo Circuit in 1919. Around that same time, a tornado struck and leveled the Pleasant Grove Church. Choosing not to rebuild, most of the Pleasant Grove congregation joined the Monroeville Church.

Improvements on the church were begun in 1923 (approximate cost, $7,800.00). On October 14th, District Superintendent Rev. George Martin preached the dedicatory sermon and "secured" the $2,600.00 still needed to cover the cost of improvements. Improvements included a basement under the building, new entrance to the basement, new heating system, installation of indirect lighting, walls repainted, new cement walks on the east side of the building, and improvements made to the street out front.

On June 15 and 16, 1927 the Epworth League Convention of the Fort Wayne District was held in the Methodist Episcopal Church of Monroeville. The Monroeville Orchestra provided music for the convention programming.

The 1938-39 merger of the Methodist, Methodist Episcopal, and Methodist Protestant Churches brought the three churches together under the name of "Methodist Church." Then in 1968 the Methodist Church united with the Evangelical United Brethren Church and became today's "United Methodist Church."

In 1940 the Women's Home Missionary Society and the Ladies Aid Society merged under the name of Women's Society of Christian Service, or W.S.C.S. On September 11, 1940, 45 women from the Monroeville Church posed for their pictures as newly installed Charter Members of W.S.C.S. The Charter Study Committee included: Lois Sidell, Grace Cook, Ferrol VanBuskirk, and Margaret Guenin.

In 1954 Rev. William Meddock introduced a remodeling program for the interior of the church sanctuary. The improvements cost $25,000.00 and included a new asphalt tile floor; new oak pews and pulpit furniture; new overhead lights; and a divided chancel, with a center aisle. The Service of Consecration for the newly remodeled sanctuary was held on September, 23, 1956.

Under the Pastorate of Rev. Walter Meecham, a new parsonage was completed in 1965. Then before Rev. Meecham could move in with his family, he was transferred to a church in Fishers, Indiana; and the Summer Clarks became the first family to occupy the new parsonage. The old parsonage was remodeled and served as a Health Center for Migrant Workers until it was demolished in 1968.

On June 24, 1990, the Fort Wayne District met with the church membership to vote on plans for a building addition and renovation to the existing church. Much time and hard work had gone into the planning, with the entire congregation being consulted on each phase of plan development. At this June 24th meeting, 92 percent of those present voted to go ahead with the building plan!

With only $100,000 in hand, a target date of March 1, 1991 was set by the Capital Fund Committee to raise the remaining $300,000 needed, before construction work could begin. The target date was met and on Sunday, March 17, 1991 Pastor Dave Cornwell presided over a gala Ground Breaking Ceremony for the new addition.

The building addition was completed in late October, and the Service of Consecration held on Sunday, October 27, 1991. Former pastor, Reverend Stephen Holdzkom, was the guest speaker.

Members named to the Building Committee were: Zenda Beucler, Joe Clem, Max Clem, Susan Harless, Cindy Hoffman (Secretary), Burt Huebner, Joel Huebner, Gordon Jackson (Treasurer), Dan Lovinger (Chairman), Mel Myers, Bruce Palmer, Harold Robison, Dean Smith, Byron Webster, and Pastor David Cornwell.

Members of the Design Sub-Committee were: Dianne Clem (Secretary), Susan Harless, Ken Harris, Cindy Hoffman, Burt Huebner, Sally Huebner, Helen Leibert, Lois Lovinger, Cindy Middleton, Arlene Ogle, Dan Snyder (Chairman), and Rich Tobias.

The new addition doubled the congregation's space ... adding 3,900 square feet to the first floor, and 3,400 square feet of basement space. The upper floor was divided into four Sunday school classrooms, a large gathering room, kitchenette, and two new restrooms. Three new entry ways and a ramp for the handicapped were added to the front and back of the building. The approximate cost of construction was $535,000.

In 1995 Pastor Sandy Knepple led the congregation in a celebration of the 100th anniversary of the original (1895) building. The highlight of the day was the 'Opening of the Box in the Cornerstone'.

In 1996 a three stop elevator was installed to access the new and old basements, at an approximate cost of $60,000.

On September 28, 1997, the church celebrated its '150th Birthday as a Congregation,' and the 'Burning of the Mortgage on the New Addition.' In preparation for the celebration, walls had been repainted, new carpet laid in the sanctuary, and restoration completed on the old stained glass windows.

During the morning of the 28th, the past was revisited during Sunday School and morning services were conducted by Superintendent Larry Ray. Then everyone enjoyed an old fashioned 'box lunch' in the new basement.

Early afternoon was given over to entertainment for all ages, including games for kids, viewing historical displays in the basement, and listening to a real German band in the Gathering Room. Then at 2:30 p.m. everyone went to the sanctuary for the 'Burning of the Mortgage ...' otherwise known as 'Zero Indebtedness.' The total cost, including elevator, was $648,125.

Speakers from the church were Reverend Sandy Knepple, Steve Clem, and Dan Lovinger. Guests were Rev. and Mrs. Summer Clark; and guest speaker, Dick Lyndon, as 'Head of the NIC Committee on Church Growth.' The day ended with the cutting of the birthday cake made by Shirley Beard, in the new shape of the church.

Today's members of the church salute all of those who have gone before them, grateful for their many acts of selfless love and devotion to the church.

1991 Monroeville United Methodist Church

Agape Church of the Brethren

Pleasant Hill Church

Agape Church of the Brethren was born out of a dedicated group of people with an abundance of faith, hope and love. In fact, they chose the name "Agape" because it means "love", and theirs was a nurturing fellowship proclaiming the love of Jesus Christ.

What began in 1853 as a group of Brethren families moving from Miami County, Ohio to Allen County, Indiana, became the cell of believers which has multiplied and grown into the current 150 member congregation meeting in a first-class facility set in 10 acres of well-landscaped, attractive grounds.

In the 1853 group were Jeremiah Gump and his brother, Jacob Gump who organized several Brethren churches in this area. One of these was Pleasant Hill German Baptist Brethren (later CoB) Church, located four miles East of Churubusco in Allen County. The meetinghouse was built in 1875. Jeremiah Gump served as the original presiding elder and minister. This congregation continued to meet at the Churubusco location until 1968 when members felt a need to move from this rural area to a new, growing part of Allen County.

During this decisive time in the life of Agape, a group of 8-10 people met consistently for prayer at the Huntertown Library under the leadership of Ivan and Dorothy Fry. Years later, Ivan remarked that he "heard the Holy Spirit better than at any other time in his life", and felt sure this group of Brethren believers was headed in the right direction.

In 1968 this group stepped out in faith and formed the Agape Church of the Brethren, building a house church on Carroll Road. As anticipated, the congregation quickly outgrew the Carroll road facility and in late 1982 land was obtained from the Northern Indiana District (CoB), and through prayer and faith ground was broken for the nucleus of the present worship facility on Lima Road. Many Agape members emptied their savings accounts in order to fund the new church facility. The dedication of the new church took place on March 20, 1983. Pastor Dave Albright led the congregation during this time of growth and building. Subsequent pastors were John Glick and Sid Gauby.

In slightly more than another decade, expansion was again necessary. In 1999 a new fellowship hall was added, as well as offices and a kitchen area. This addition was dedicated on October 8, 2000. At this time Keith Simmons was called to lead the church. Agape Church of the Brethren continues to grow, looking forward in faith and reaching out in love to its members, the community and the world.

Present Agape Church

Aldersgate Church

Aldersgate Church was the outgrowth of two surveys which pointed to a need for a Methodist Congregation on the west side of Fort Wayne. Byron Stroh, the District Superintendent, appointed an investigation committee and it was from this committee that a new congregation was formed. The first worship service was held at Anthony Wayne School on February 23, 1958, and the name "Aldersgate" was chosen to commemorate the site in London where John Wesley experienced one of his conversion experiences in which he said his "heart was strangely warmed." On Palm Sunday, March 30, 1958, the church was chartered and the Reverend John Hunt was appointed the first pastor. There were a total of 132 charter members.

About the same time, 6 ½ acres of land at the "top of the hill" on Getz Road between Maurane Drive and Wilkie Drive was purchased. There were two houses on the property. One was converted for office space and the other was used as a parsonage. A temporary structure that could be used for worship was constructed on site and used for worship for the first time on June 15, 1958. Two hundred sixty persons were in attendance. However, fire totally destroyed this facility on March 4, 1959. A charred cross was found in the ashes, and erected on site with the promise that "Aldersgate will build again." Two additional acres of land were secured.

A building committee was quickly formed and plans for a new structure began immediately. A Fellowship Hall and Education unit were constructed and first used on June 26, 1960. Many members and friends gave sacrificially for this project. The whole community became involved in an annual event called "The Ox Roast" in which as many as 2,000 people were served a roast beef dinner. Proceeds went to the new building. In 1963, the Reverend Harold Bachert became pastor. A building committee was formed in 1964 to begin consideration for the construction of a nave. In 1965, the Reverend Robert Bickel was appointed senior pastor. Construction of classrooms and the nave were finished in 1968. Aldersgate's membership had grown to 600.

In 1971, the Reverend Carl Baker was appointed pastor and a new parsonage was constructed on West Hill Road. In 1974, Dr. Hilbert Berger was assigned to Aldersgate. Classroom space was sorely needed. A "third phase" of construction was undertaken. On April 1, 1977, a church library, conference room and three large classrooms were added. Membership grew to 760 and a strong emphasis on giving – especially for the sake of others – was instituted. The Aldersgate Nursery School, one of the best in the area, was formed and a strong music emphasis emerged.

In 1985, Dr. Brian Witwer was assigned as senior pastor. The issue of classroom space emerged anew as the congregation continued to grow. On April 21, 1991, eight new classrooms, a fellowship lounge, courtyard and music room were added and extensive renovation throughout the building was undertaken. Concern for a larger nave was also raised. It was during this time that Aldersgate recognized a specific need to emphasize the importance of making Christian community central to its identity in response to increasing individualism in the culture. And a new orientation to community needs emerged. The Aldersgate facilities were made available to community groups and organizations.

In 1996, construction began on a new nave and lower level complex. The old nave was renovated to include classrooms, fellowship area, and a chapel and music suite. The new state of the art facility was completed and consecrated on November 23, 1997. A renewed emphasis on the arts followed the opening of the new nave with its striking 18 by 37 foot faceted glass window featuring the risen Christ overlooking the Fort Wayne skyline.

At the end of the century, Aldersgate continues to be a vibrant and intentionally mainstream congregation serving southwest Allen County. The membership has grown to over 1,200 people. The Aldersgate community is a vital witness to the grace of God for all persons, service to the less fortunate, and a beacon of vital Christianity.

Aldersgate Church 2000

Aldersgate Church 2000

Aldersgate Church 1958

Anthony Wayne First Church of God

Present church

The Anthony Wayne First Church of God is affiliated with the Churches of God in North America General Conference. The denominational founder, Rev. John Winebrenner, organized the first congregation of the Churches of God in Harrisburg, Pennsylvania in 1825.

Anthony Wayne Church was established in 1946 as a mission church of the Indiana Eldership of the Churches of God. Much of the planning and inspiration for the church founding came from the late Mrs. Eva Shook. The first meeting place was a temporary building then part of the Anthony Wayne School (now Canterbury Elementary School). Property was then purchased at the present location, corner of South Bend Drive and Getz Road in Southwest Allen County, and the first services were held in a basement church. In January 1955, with a membership of seventeen adults, a Chapel was completed and dedicated. The Richard and Wilma Rousseau family were of the originating seventeen adults that began the church. We are pleased and proud to say that Wilma still attends regularly and is active in our church activities.

The church began to grow with the community and by 1957, plans were underway for the present worship and educational facilities. A ground breaking service was held on Easter Sunday, April 17, 1960, with construction beginning immediately.

The present facilities, consecrated May 21, 1961, consist of a Chapel, offices, seventeen classrooms, the sanctuary seating approximately 500, a parlor, nursery room and fellowship hall. The Burning of the Mortgage was held Sunday, January 11, 1981.

Presently we have services Sundays at 9:00 A.M., including Junior Worship, Youth Bell Choir, Sunday school and Wednesday Morning and Evening Bible Studies, a Dare to Care Program, and an Evening Youth Program. We are an active church with a ladies meeting the first Tuesday of each month and a sewing group the last Tuesday of each month. A Nursery School began in 1963 under Pastor Paul Sago. A Mission House was built so that our community may have access to clothing and food.

The Pastors that have served Anthony Wayne Church are Tom Douglas, Alva Klopenstein, Gail Dunn, Paul Sago, Richard Wilkin, Alvin Rockey, Harry Cadamore, Stephen Dunn, Karl Reutz, and presently, Jerry Blanchard.

We live to worship and to serve – Our mission statement reminds us: "Anthony Wayne Church is a Family of God, dedicated to bringing His Word to people and their families, inviting them to Christ, equipping them as disciples, and sending them out to serve God, our community and the world."

Our Vision

That the people at Anthony Wayne Church and those we reach out and touch would have: A growing LOVE and COMMITMENT to Jesus Christ. A growing LOVE and COMMITMENT to the Body of Christ. A growing LOVE and COMMITMENT to share Christ with the world.

Basement church

First Complete church 1955

Arcola United Methodist Church

The original circuit class at Arcola United Methodist Church had eight members. In December 1870, the trustees were Francis Sweet, John R. Ross, Elias Hine, John Meiser, Benjamin Heister, Emanuel Prill and F. Enniand. In the spring of 1871 construction of a new frame church building, 38 feet by 55 feet, began. Construction began in the ministry of the Rev. J. C. McLin and was dedicated by the Rev. A. Marine. The final cost was $1,600.00. The building is used today with a few changes. By 1876 two classes, Heiser's School and Kelsyville (now Jefferson Chapel), were added to the circuit. J. W. Paschall, C. H. Murry, M. Waugh, Dan Berry, W. E. Gillsepie, Ben Neiser, E. Prill, F. Sweet, B. Butt, A. Doughman, S. Gilliam, Thomas Richardson, J. Ross and W. R. Sterling attended the conference of the Arcola Circuit in 1879.

Additional classrooms were constructed on the south end of the building in 1919, and in 1926 a vestibule and cloakroom were added. In 1955 the land east and south of the building was cleared and restrooms, a kitchen and automatic heat were installed. Further remodeling was finished in1958 and in 1990.

Following is a list of ministers: 1870 - J. C. McLin, 1873 - A. C. Pattee, 1874 - S. Bacon, 1875 - J. S. McElwee, 1876 - N. Baker, 1878 - J. W. Paschall, 1879 - A G. McCarter, 1880 - H. D. Bridge, 1881 - B. Sawyer, 1882 - J. W. Singer, 1884 - R. W. Whitford, 1885- J. S. Beatty, 1886 - T. T. French, 1888 - R. H. Smith, 1889 - I. W. Kimberling, 1890 - C. M. Hollopeter, 1893 - G. Cockling, 1895- N. P. Barton, 1897 - W. A. Breist, 1899 - D. I. Hower, 1901 - E. M. Foster, 1904 - E. B. Parker, 1905 - J. C. Woodruff, 1906 - M. C. Pittinger, 1908 - C. G. Nelson, 1909 - P. H. Walter, 1911 - E. P. Johnson, 1914 - E. B. Wright, 1916 - Joseph Grimes, 1918 - F. A. Shipley, 1919 - D. A. J. Brown, 1921 - F. McClumphry, 1922 - A. F. Uphoff, 1924 - H. E. Forbes, 1926 - L. C. Wisner, 1928 – H. V. Cummins, 1929 - D. K. Finch, 1932 - F. J. Hutsinpiller, 1936 - C. W. Harrod, 1936 - U. S. A. Bridge, 1937 - C. D. Pyles, 1939 - C. B. Sweeny, 1944 - W. L. Skinner, 1949 - A. E. Burk, 1953 - C. I. Miller, 1956 - Ralph High, 1960 - Emory Reece, 1963 - Ernest Cobbs, 1967- George Manley, 1971 - Robert Schreffler, 1977 - Hugh Rohrer, 1982 - Cletus Hirschy, 1984 - Edwin Clark, 1986 - Harvey King, 1988 - John Cowan, 1996 - Linda S. Craig, 1997- Karen S. Ottjes, 1999 - Harold Klinker.

Members of Arcola Church in 1920s: Mr. Fred Long, Mr. & Mrs. James Lopshire, Mr. & Mrs. James Turner, Mr. & Mrs. William Sitton, Mr. & Mrs. Ed Pillers,

Arcola United Methodist Church

Sr., Mr. & Mrs. Ward Combs, Mrs. Pearl Hiler, Mrs. Cook, Mrs. Rapp and son Bill, Mr. & Mrs. George Sherman and sons Virgil, Kenneth & Russell, Mr. & Mrs. Pratt (Mr. Pratt was killed by a train along with John Hoffner ca. 1932), Troas Sitton, Mrs. Stouder (Drugstore), Mrs. Laney, Mr. & Mrs. Archie Nicholson, (Lester Brunner and George Brunner became ministers.)

Members of the church in 1930s: Dwight & Helen Byeerly (moved to Fort Wayne in 50s), Mr. and Mrs. Alfred Gross. Orchestra members in 1930s: Bill McVity (Director, W. Ed Pillers (Violin), Wilma Combs (Violin), Lois Combs, (Violin), Howard More (sax), Mary Cook (sax), Jack Long (trombone), Vick Hickman (cornet), Wayne Lopshire (cornet), Ralph Lopshire (cornet), Fred Long (drums)

Members of the church in 1940s: John & Pauline Swoverland and family, Ray and Edna Dafforn and family, Woodie and Elaine Noe and Family, Homer and Jean Schipper (came to Arcola temporarily and stayed 50 years plus), DeWitt and Beverly Alexander, Paul and Betty Brumbaugh (opened a grocery store), George and Geraldine Zeimmer (Geraldine was here from early 30s), Mr. & Mrs. James Turner (Bible on the communion table is in memory of their son Jamie)

In **1919** the office and a classroom were added. In **1926** the first narthex was added. In **1955** the basement was dug out by hand taking dirt out through the east side and added to the hill to make it not so steep. In the **1950s,** the low area south of the church was the town dump. This was cleaned up and ditch channels were made. Land was donated by Mrs. Linton if it was cleaned up. Richard Keinert brought two bulldozers and cleared the area. In the late **1960s** the inside of the church was remodeled, mostly done by Don Davis. Homer Ohlwine (Ohlwine Orchards) made the cross that is in the front of the church. Garnett Bryant painted the large picture of Christ at the door, that hangs over the door.

By **1980** attendance was 23-30. In **1990** the church was sided. $4,000 pledges came in and were enough to pad the pews and add carpeting down the center and on the stage. In **1997** air conditioning was installed. In **2001** parking space was increased with donation of land across the street, given by Ruth Sitton. A bathroom upstairs, two outside ramps, patio bricks and flowerpots were added; an enlarged narthex was completed, all with out borrowing ($28,000). In 2005 there is an active Youth Group, Methodist Mens Group, Methodist Womens Group, and a Robed Chancel Choir. Pastor Klinker also serves Lake Chapel United Methodist Church.

The following are attending in 2005: Beverly Alexander; Mark & Linda Alexander; Dan Andress; Vivian Andress; Don & Judy Ashbaugh; Melissa Ashbaugh; John Ashbaugh, Jill Landis, Emma Landis Ashbaugh, Avery Landis Ashbaugh, & Nicholas; Rebecca & Jennifer Bell; Alys Berlin, Dennis, Ron; Judy Bennett; Marjorie Brumbaugh; Paul and Betty Brumbaugh; Duane & Joann Burkley; Jim and Pam Burt; Thad & LuAnn Coverstone; Jerry, Rhonda & Dean Cearbaugh; Dustin Cearbaugh & Brianna; Edna Dafforn; Jason & Karen Dafforn; Helen Delancey; Danuel & Debra Dilts, Erica & Max; Monte & Becky Dull; Todd & Sharon Felkner & Morgan; Sam & Diane Fogwell, Connie & Noel; Max Foor; Stephen & Tonya Foor; Ruth Hackett; Jeff & Sharon Hoffman, Andrew, Elizabeth; Laura Hoffman, Crystal & Holly King; Lori Hamilton; Mark & May Hardy, Jesse, Luke, Casey; Paul & Pat Hardy; Francis (Bud) & Shirley Hunnicutt; Shane & Kim Kennedy, Nicholas, Andrew, Kristen; Charles & Elizabeth Kille & David & Martha; Harold (Rev.) and Joy Klinker (Pastor); Melonie & Braden Klinker; Tim & Amanda Klinker, Tim, Chelsey, Chase; David & Kathy Krueckeburg; Ralph & Carol Laramie; Betty Lopshire; Andrew & Lora Maggard, Hunter & Allan; Sharon Markle; Nancy McLaughlin; Jim & Rose Newton; Homer & Eleanor Ohlwine; Kyle & Shannon Palm & Kaydance; Elvan & Leona Pelz; Ruth Sitton; Brian & Kathryn Slabaugh, Jennefer, Benjamin; Charles & Marie Spicer, Ryan, Tyler; Flavel (Smitty) & Ora Smith; Ralph (Rev.) & Glendia Thornton; Dan & Sandy Trimmer & Jennifer; Nieta Van Englenhoven, Shannon & Jesse; Lindsey Ward; Tom & Shawn Ward, Rebecca, Ashley, Michael; Tracy & Erica Ward, Ahnika; Walter Jr. & Lolly Ward; Walter & Mary Ward; David & Beverly Wisebach; Randy Williams, Cindy Gerke & Justin Williams; Wilma Zeimmer; Nancy Zobrosky.

Ascension Lutheran Church

Ascension Lutheran Church, located at 8811 St. Joe Road, was organized in early 1977, originally meeting for worship in the facilities of Trinity Presbyterian Church. The first members of Ascension wrote their Constitution, arranged for an interim Pastor, Reverend Henry Eggold, and chose a name. Ascension was underway with the blessing of our Almighty God.

Late in 1977, the Congregation asked the Indiana District of the Lutheran Church-Missouri Synod to supply them with a pastor. Jointly the Mission Board of the District and Ascension called Rev. David V. Dubbelde as "Missionary At Large." He began his ministry at Ascension in January of 1978.

The year 1978 saw the congregation growing and making plans for the future. In November a charter service was held and 64 members affixed their names to that historic document. In December, a building committee began its work and early in 1979, a 42-acre building site was purchased.

Midway through 1980, Ascension called Pastor Dubbelde to serve as "Resident Pastor" and their call was accepted by him.

Construction of the church building began in October of 1980. This building was then dedicated in June 1981, four years to the day from the first worship service of Ascension Lutheran Church. As the years passed, Ascension continued to grow and soon found its self running out of space. In April of 1987, a Long Range Planning Committee was formed to study future needs. A determination to build additional facilities was made and a building committee was formed.

Ascension Lutheran Church in 1988.

In March of 1989 Pastor Dubbelde accepted a call to serve as the Executive Director of Mission Development for the Indiana District of Synod. In June 1989 Ascension extended a Divine Call to Rev. John C. Stube in Provo, Utah. Rev. Stube accepted the call and was installed as Pastor on August 20, 1989.

In March of 1990, contracts were awarded for construction of the building expansion, and the new facilities were dedicated to the service of our Lord on December 16, 1990. In 1999 ground was broken for another school expansion and in February 2000 four new classrooms and a gymnasium were dedicated to God's glory.

Since its founding, Ascension has been committed to the Christian Education of our children and adults. One of Ascension's long-range goals was the operation of a Christian Day School. This goal began to take shape in the fall of 1994 with the opening of our preschool. Then, in the fall of 1997, we expanded our school by adding Kindergarten through grade six. In 1998 we added grade 7 and in 1999 we added grade 8.

God in His mercy has been most gracious to this Congregation. Ascension now is home for more than 500 people. Here they find the Word of God shared faithfully and the Sacraments administered according to the institution of Christ.

All of us, members and friends of Ascension, give all the glory to God as we look ahead to the opportunities we have, to face a challenging future, and to tell everyone what He has done.

Present day Ascension Lutheran Church.

Beacon Heights Church of the Brethren

Beacon Heights Church 2005

Beacon Heights Church of the Brethren is part of a denomination known in its beginning as the German Baptist Brethren. This church of Anabaptist/Pietist origin was founded in Schwarzenau, Germany, where, in 1708, its first eight adult members were baptized in the Eder River by trine immersion. Because of ongoing persecution, by 1729 most of the group had fled Germany and settled in Germantown, Pennsylvania, seeking the freedom to practice their non-creedal religious beliefs among the Mennonites and Quakers. From there the Brethren spread across the United States flourishing quickly in those early days among the rural people of Pennsylvania, Virginia, Ohio, and Indiana. To this day the Brethren remain most concentrated in those areas, though churches eventually developed throughout the United States.

In 1952 the members of the Smith Street Church of the Brethren felt the need for another Church of the Brethren in the Fort Wayne area. After careful consideration and prayer, a location was selected in an undeveloped area northeast of the city (which is now the corner of Beacon and Kenwood Streets). In May Church Council meetings of that same year, the treasurer reported the purchase of a 5.25 acre tract of land and the name Beacon Heights Church of the Brethren was adopted. On September 7th, the first worship service was held in the Portage Room of the local YMCA. On July 1, 1953, the first pastor was called to serve the church. A special Council Meeting on August 4, 1954, authorized construction of the church facility, and the dedication of the educational unit was held on May 29, 1955.

Construction "Educational Unit" (fellowship hall) 1954

Beacon Heights held its first "Love Feast" on October 3, 1954. This unique worship service recalls the Last Supper that Jesus shared with his disciples. It includes a time of self-examination, feet-washing, a fellowship meal and sharing the bread and cup of communion. Other ordinances of the Church of the Brethren include believer's baptism (the first of which was held at Beacon Heights in November of 1955), anointing for healing, and the laying on of hands as an out-pouring of the Holy Spirit.

Known from the beginning for its strong emphasis on following Jesus' way of non-violence, Beacon Heights maintains the Church of the Brethren passion for peace and social justice at its heart. Creative, inspiring worship is an important component of congregational life and provides opportunity for members to express their faith and share their journey. Numerous community-building and educational programs (such as the mentor program which pairs each middle school student with a mature adult mentor, an active youth program including youth-led Bible studies, and Simple Suppers which provide a meal and program for all ages) contribute to a sense of 'family' among the members. Financial outreach to support ministries reaching beyond Beacon Heights is also a high priority. Other emphases include living simply, active participation in the community of faith, and volunteer service opportunities.

On October 8, 1961, the present sanctuary was dedicated with office additions to follow. Since that time, with effective pastoral and lay leadership, the congregation continues to serve vital ministries within and beyond the City of Fort Wayne. These include: a nationally accredited preschool housed in the church, participation in the Interfaith Hospitality Network for the homeless, and reaching out to refugees (serving as sponsors and friends to Bosnian families, and hosting exchange students from Afghanistan). Other ministries are: maintaining a food bank for the Associated Churches, providing space for community groups to meet (such as music programs, neighborhood associations, support groups, scout troops), relating to sister congregations of different races and cultures (both here in Fort Wayne and Nicaragua.), and being an open and welcoming congregation for all who share the love of God and who seek to follow Jesus' footsteps- peacefully, simply, together.

Bethel United Methodist Church
1843 -2004

Bethel United Methodist Church, May 6, 1995.

Fort Wayne, in 1832, was only a pioneer settlement when George Ashley and a companion, William Cartwell, came to Allen County, Indiana from Green County, New York. They wanted to investigate the many stories they had read and heard about Indiana's fertile farmland, with the view of settling. These two men traveled from New York to Toledo, Ohio by boat and came on to Fort Wayne by stagecoach.

On arriving in the area northwest of Fort Wayne, near the Village of Wallen in Washington Township, Ashley and Cartwell found themselves far from the settlement of Fort Wayne with darkness approaching. In trying to return to the Fort in the dark, they came upon a tepee with an Indian facing them with a gun. The Indian did not threaten them but put the gun aside for a peace pipe. After the two white men and the Indian each had three times of blowing three puffs of smoke upward in the sign of friendship, the Indian cooked a supper of baked squash and venison or "jerk" as the Indian called it. They slept in the Indian tepee and were taken to a trail the next morning by the Indian's Squaw, and went toward Fort Wayne.

In 1834, the men bought seven teams of horses in Toledo for the covered wagon journey back to Fort Wayne. The families that came here were George H. Ashley and his parents, Mr. and Mrs. George J. Ashley. The Ashley daughters and their husbands were Daniel and Harriet Opliger, Steven and Phoebe Griswold and Riley and Polly Griswold. With them were William Cartwell and his family. The families assisted one another in building log homes in the vicinity of Bethel and Till Roads.

Mr. Ashley organized a group in 1837 that met in each other's homes. In 1840 a more formal organization took place calling it a class of the Methodist denomination. The group consisted of George Ashley, Steven and Riley Griswold, Daniel Opliger, Uriah Fleming and their families.

In 1843 Mr. Ashley donated land for a chapel and cemetery. The Chapel was a small log building and was named Bethel Chapel.

Through the years the community grew. In 1870 the members built a frame building a mile south of the Chapel in the Village of Wallen. This was known as the Wallen Methodist Episcopal Church. Once again the membership outgrew the building. In 1919 a larger brick building was erected on the Wallen Road. The Trustees were L. C. Pratt, Ed Griswold, W. A. Smith, T. D. Swaim, Daniel Edward Opliger, Ben Sunderland, R. S. Renenecker, C. W. Badiac, S. Krouse and Elmer M. Cook. Most of the male members did the actual labor.

Bethel United Methodist Church, March 15, 1993.

During the 50s and 60s, our church became surrounded by suburbia and the congregation was changing from farm people to townspeople. Once again we were in need of a larger building.

Ground was broken November 1, 1959 at 8405 Lima Road. During construction, services were held in the Washington Township School. Three educational buildings were erected. Services were held in the Fellowship Hall beginning October 2, 1960.

We became the United Methodist Church in 1969 when the Methodist Church united with the Evangelical United Brethren.

In 1969, we broke ground for the Sanctuary. The cornerstone was laid September 14, 1969. May 24, 1970 was a day to remember. Service began in the Fellowship Hall and concluded in the new Sanctuary. The Consecration was held November 8, 1970. Those officiating were Bishop Reuben Mueller, Rev. R. Edwin Green and Rev. Harley Shady.

In 1983 we celebrated 140 years and voted to change the name from Wallen, back to the original name of Bethel – Bethel United Methodist Church.

A steeple was erected on the roof of the Sanctuary in 1990 in memory of Elmer M. and Carrie Opliger Cook by their children. A Gathering Room was added in 1992 to connect the Sanctuary and the Fellowship Hall.

In 1994 ground was broken for the new addition, two offices, a library and Sunday school rooms.

Bethel celebrated 160 years in 2003. We have 14 members that are direct decedents of the founders. They are Carol Bowser, Juanita Cook Arnold, Robert Arnold, James McCrea, Tim McCrea, Lisa McCrea Genos, Phyllis Cook Itt, Charles Itt 2d, Jeanne Itt Burt, Joshua Burt, Michael Burt, Marcia Markey, Dorothy, Tom and Jane Cook.

Bethel is located at 8405 Lima Road. Come and join us for worship and fellowship. God is good all the time!

Bethlehem Lutheran Church

On August 27, 1925, a portable chapel, procured from Concordia College by Zion and Concordia Lutheran Churches, was moved to the 3200 block of Alexander Avenue to serve as a Southeast Side Lutheran School. Beginning in January 1926, regular Sunday morning services in German and English were also held for Zion and Concordia families living in the area. In September 1926 a formal church was organized as Bethlehem Evangelical Lutheran Church, affiliated with Lutheran Church Missouri Synod. H.D. Mensing served as temporary pastor. There were 46 charter members with 42 children in the school.

In November 1926, the congregation resolved to purchase two acres in the far southeast side of Fort Wayne. The land in the 3700 block of South Anthony Boulevard cost $7,500. In 1929 the cornerstone laying for the new church and school was held with dedication in January of 1930. The cost was $46,000 and the building was used for church services on Sunday and day-school during the week. Three years later, in 1933 the congregation still owed $2,200. The Church Council called for a special offering to meet the debt. Even though this was during the depression, the members raised an amount in excess of that figure.

Because of further church growth and classroom needs, ground-breaking for a new church was held on October 9, 1939 and dedicated on August 24, 1940 at a total cost of $91,000. H.C. Houser of Milwaukee was the architect with Schinnerer and Truemper as contractors. It was designed in English Gothic Style with the Nave seating 600 people and the choir loft seating 85. Many members and groups donated the stained glass windows and the baptismal font.

During WWII, the church membership continued to grow. Over 100 members served in the armed forces with all returning safely to their homes and families after the war.

Due to the rapid growth of the school, the church broke ground for an addition to the building in August 1947. The addition included nine classrooms, an auditorium, a library, and office space. The existing school was refaced with Indiana limestone to match the church and addition. A new parsonage was built across the street at this time. Due to further growth, another addition of five new classrooms, a kitchen and cafeteria, and gymnasium was completed in 1955 by Grewe Contractors. By 1958 Day School enrollment peaked at 693 students, the largest elementary school in the Lutheran Church, Missouri Synod. The present church was completed when three bells were installed in the bell tower in 1965. They still continue to ring every evening at 6:00 P.M. and before church services.

Southeast Side Lutheran School in 1926.

By the 1970s church membership had grown to 2,500 souls, served by three pastors. From May 1970 through June 1993, Bethlehem School and Trinity Lutheran School on Decatur Road joined together in a consolidated school.

For over 75 years Bethlehem Lutheran Church has been blessed with the service of the following ordained Lutheran pastors: H.D. Mensing, M.E. Reinke, Arno Scholz, Henry Blanke, Herbert Mueller, Robert Meier, B.Dale Thomas, Richard Widmann, Walter Barth, Jeffrey Olsen, David Schlie, Gary Williams, Andrew Northrop, S.T. Williams, Thomas Eggold and Gregory Manning.

The church continues to serve its members and the community around it today in a new and varied way under the direction of Pastor Thomas Eggold. Programs at the church include neighborhood outreach such as a Food Bank, Say Yes (after school tutoring) and Prime Time (in cooperation with Youth for Christ). Ministries to the Vietnamese and Hispanic communities are actively conducted. Calls on church visitors are made weekly.

Programs serving both church members and the community include a Christian Counseling Service, a Vacation Bible School and a Young Adults Ministry. The church supports a Shepherding Program for on-going contact with all active members, a Stephen Ministry which provides individual encouragement and a Luke Ministry for those who are homebound. Outreach and service to all has become the goal of Bethlehem Church with emphasis on following our Savior's command, "Go and make disciples of all nations!"

Present Church 1955 to 2005.

Broadway Christian Church

The building housing Broadway Christian Church was erected in 1871 by the Methodist Church. Originally known as West Wayne Street Methodist Church, the structure was purchased by the Broadway Congregation in the fall of 1973. Pastor Robert Yawberg was frustrated when finances were not available to expand the North Highlands Church of Christ on Archer Avenue. Out of space, leaders prayed daily at 5:30 A.M. for an answer.

During that time, Mayor Ivan Lebamoff challenged a group of pastors in the city; he pleaded with them to look at the need in downtown Fort Wayne for leadership and influence. Churches and businesses were leaving the area. As he spoke, the Lord laid on the heart of Pastor Yawberg the empty church building at Broadway and Wayne. He drove there following the meeting to find the one hundred year old structure for sale. Entering the sanctuary, he beheld the same floor plan and arrangement they had planned to build in the suburbs.

The vision of preaching Christ in downtown Fort Wayne burned in Pastor Yawberg's heart. He issued a call for those who would follow to start a new congregation at the central city location. Three hundred believers responded to the call. Twenty-three years later, five services were being held at two locations and 1,500 people attended on a weekly basis. Racial and denominational barriers were overcome as hurting people came from across the city and beyond.

The church became known for her ministry to the poor and hungry, and they came often for loving, personal care. Utility bills were paid, clothing given and food made available – all in the name of Christ. Global missions became a priority as well, as many were sent to various parts of the world. Eventually people came to 910 Broadway from all parts of the city. Buildings on adjoining property were purchased and renovated to house the ever-growing congregation.

After twenty-three years leading and developing this ministry, Pastor Robert Yawberg asked to be released to serve pastors in the church-at-large. Broadway Christian Church continues to be an oasis of light and love to the city. Jason Baeuerle, who attended the church as a young adult, now serves as Senior Pastor.

Cathedral of the Immaculate Conception

The Cathedral of the Immaculate Conception is dedicated to the Blessed Virgin Mary, Mother of God, who, under the title of the Immaculate Conception, is also the patroness of the United States and the Diocese of Fort Wayne-South Bend.

From humble beginnings as a 35 by 65 ft. log structure called St. Augustine, the church evolved over the years to its present status as the focal point of Cathedral Square, located in downtown Fort Wayne.

It was not until the early 1800s that pioneer settlers of the Catholic faith were able to think about building a church and having a resident pastor. Father Stephen Badin, who performed the first Catholic marriage in Fort Wayne, helped local Catholics select the site, and in 1831 they purchased a large portion of the present square from Samuel and Eliza Hanna for $100. The first Catholic Church was built on the property, and Fr. Louis Mueller was named as the first permanent pastor.

Fr. Julian Benoit, a French-born priest who became rector in 1840, was most instrumental in the development of the Cathedral. Popular with local citizens and the Miami Indians in the area, he served missionary stations throughout northeastern Indiana and northwestern Ohio.

When Pope Pius IX established the Diocese of Fort Wayne in 1857, Fr. Benoit talked with many Catholics, as well as local Protestants, about building a permanent Cathedral to serve the Diocese. Fr. Benoit had already purchased the remaining property in the block-square area, so St. Augustine Church was moved to the east side of the square to make way for the new Cathedral.

Fr. Benoit and Thomas Lau were co-architects and overseers of the construction. The Cathedral cornerstone was placed on June 19, 1859, and the completed Cathedral of the Immaculate Conception was dedicated on December 8, 1860. The *Fort Wayne Weekly Sentinel* at that time called the Cathedral "one of the finest churches on the continent and possibly the grandest structure in the West." Named to the National Register of Historic Places in 1980, the church "is believed to be the oldest building in continuous use in Northeastern Indiana."

The present 15 Gothic stained-glass windows were crafted at the Royal Bavarian Art Institute in Munich, Germany, and are a tribute to Mary, the Mother of God. The Stations of the Cross made in Oberammergau, Germany, and the communion railing fabricated in Italy were also installed in the 1890s. The large mission crucifix was originally in St. Augustine Church. The altar stone, carried by the Catholic missionaries to this area before being placed in the Saint Augustine Church altar, was transferred to the Cathedral and has been in the permanent altar since 1859.

Underneath the main altar is the Crypt where the first four bishops—John Henry Luers, Joseph Dwenger, Joseph Rademacher, Joseph Alerding—and the first three rectors—Julian Benoit, Joseph Brammer and Patrick Roche—are buried. Another burial site believed to be on Cathedral Square is that of Miami Chief Jean Baptiste de Richardville.

In 1924 extensive modifications were begun by Msgr. Thomas Conroy, sometimes called "the Rebuilder of the Cathedral." The ornate wooden contour frames of the Stations, which harmonize with the stained glass windows, were introduced. Under his leadership the hand-carved sanctuary reredos in Belgian oak, also from Oberammergau, Germany, and later the Bishop's chair (1935) were added as well. The figures are done in "grotesque Gothic" and are set in Gothic turrets.

On September 22, 1982, the Diocese of Fort Wayne-South Bend celebrated the 125th Anniversary of its establishment. A historical marker was erected on Cathedral Square. In 1986, the Cathedral Parish celebrated its sesquicentennial (1836-1986) anniversary.

The Cathedral closed on Easter Sunday 1998 for major restoration/renovation to the interior. Work was done to preserve the grandeur of the Cathedral, while also assuring that the fitting celebration of the Eucharist remained the dynamic focus of Catholic faith. This beautiful edifice stands in the midst of our city as a place where generations have come to lift their hearts to God. The church was rededicated by Most Rev. John M. D'Arcy, Bishop of the Diocese of Fort Wayne-South Bend, on December 8, 1998 with diocesan priests, dignitaries, parishioners and friends from throughout the diocese attending.

The Cathedral of the Immaculate Conception is well into its second century of service to the People of God. This architectural masterpiece, a shrine to the spirit and sacrifices of pioneer priests, religious and lay people of northeast Indiana, continues to be known for its beauty and remains today a place where the worship of God is the focus of all activity.

Congregation Achduth Vesholom

1848 - Nirdlinger Home 1857 - First Temple

1876 - Second Temple 1917 - Third Temple

Our Present Home - Temple Achduth Vesholom

Congregation Achduth Vesholom's roots date to 1848, distinguishing it as the oldest Jewish congregation in Indiana. Initially established as a burial society, its first official act was to acquire the old burial ground adjoining what is now McCulloch Park for $200.

In keeping with Orthodox German tradition, men and women worshiped in separate parlors in private homes in the early part of the congregation's existence. During its first thirty years, the minutes of all meeting were kept in German. In 1859, Achduth Vesholom ("Unity and Peace" in Hebrew) moved to its first house of worship, a former German Methodist Church at Wayne and Harrison Streets. The dedication ceremony, attended by many Christians, was considered so impressive that it was repeated the following day.

The more progressive approach of the Reform Movement of Judaism began to make inroads in Jewish communities throughout the country during the 1860s. For example, by January 1866, men, women and children were allowed to sit together for worship. Eight years later, Achduth Vesholom, also known as the Temple, became a charter member of what is now called the Union for Reform Judaism.

In 1884, the congregation built a new Temple at the corner of Harrison and Wayne and purchased two acres of land at Lindenwood Cemetery. By 1891, prayers and sermons were no longer presented in German.

The third Temple at Wayne and Fairfield was dedicated over a three-day period beginning December 28, 1917. Rabbi Frederic Doppelt, who occupied the pulpit from 1940 to 1969, served the longest tenure and was the first rabbi emeritus in the congregation's history.

In 1956, Betty Stein became the first woman to serve on the Temple's board of directors under an equal rights amendment enabling "members' wives" to hold office and vote. She was later elected as the first woman president of the congregation in 1984.

The current Temple building at 5200 Old Mill Road, the congregation's fourth, was dedicated in 1961. Stained glass windows in the Sanctuary depict the epic story of the Jewish people, representing periods from biblical times to the present. A memorial sculpture by Fort Wayne artist Nancy McCroskey at the front of the building seeks to communicate the horror of Holocaust and the endurance of the Jewish people.

Rabbi Richard B. Safran joined the Temple in 1969 and took an active role in congregational and community affairs during his 26-year tenure. He became rabbi emeritus in 1995 when Rabbi Sandford R. Kopnick arrived. Rabbi Kopnick's focus on youth helped boost attendance of our young people at the Reform Movement's Goldman Union Camp Institute in Zionsville, Indiana, which is named after the late Myron S. Goldman, a former Temple president and generous supporter of the camp.

Achduth Vesholom celebrated its 150th anniversary in October 1998. In conjunction with this event, members made contributions to restore a Torah that had been rescued from destruction during the Holocaust. A master scribe came to Fort Wayne to demonstrate the intricate process of Torah writing in what Rabbi Kopnick described as one of the most extraordinary events in Temple history. The completed Torah brings together sections written in the mid-18th century with modern script.

Rabbi Jonathan R. Katz became the 19th rabbi in the summer of 2001, only the fourth spiritual leader in more than a half-century. In addition to his efforts to rejuvenate worship and make Jewish education more compelling, Rabbi Katz works actively in the community to foster greater interfaith understanding.

The congregation views itself as a "community" of members who support one another in periods of difficulty, share life's blessings at times of joy and work together to bring about tikkun olam, the betterment of the world around us.

Social action work by Temple members includes an ongoing Jewish-Catholic Dialogue group with St. Mary's Catholic Church, Mitzvah Day to assist an array of community organizations, a partnership with Wellspring Interfaith Social Services, and food drives to aid area food banks.

In July 2003, Achduth Vesholom, along with many of its neighbors, faced the threat of flooding from the St. Marys River. Temple members were joined by many non-Jewish friends in a successful sandbagging.

With nearly 250 families as members, Achduth Vesholom remains a thriving, vibrant congregation working to keep the Jewish spirit alive in Northeast Indiana and dedicated to caring for others around us.

East Liberty United Methodist Church

East Liberty United Methodist Church is located in the southeastern corner of Monroe Township, which in turn is the southeasternmost township in Allen County, Indiana. It took its name from the community of East Liberty, which was plotted in 1848.

The first church services held in Monroe Township were at the home of John Friedline, a prominent local farmer who had migrated from Carroll County, Ohio in 1838. In 1845 the small congregation used the services of a circuit-riding preacher from Van Wert, Ohio by the name of Reverend Exline. The early church was called Bethlehem Church of the United Brethren in Christ and had seven charter members, all men. The first full time minister for the congregation was the Reverend Seiberry. Early church services were held in the homes of various church members and often in a barn owned by Samuel Clem. As the population of East Liberty grew, the first church was built next to the subscription school, on the southeast corner of what is now known as State Highway 101 and the Barkley Road.

East Liberty Church in 1926

East Liberty United Methodist Church in 2005.

The East Liberty community boasted of having a grocery store, a post office, a tannery, two churches, a blacksmith shop, a brick kiln, the subscription school, a saloon and many homes. The church, although large for the times, was home to several denominations and was also used as a Sabbath School during the summer months, with an average attendance of 90 students. Sermons at the church were based on uncritical interpretations of the scriptures with realistic depictions of the glories of Heaven and the fiery torments of Hell. Many people were converted during revivals, amid shouting, singing and the spiritual agony of salvation. In the 1860s the Pennsylvania railroad crossed Highway 101 three miles north of the community of East Liberty, and in 1866, the town of Monroeville was incorporated at the intersection, spelling the eventual demise of the East Liberty community. The United Brethren Church stayed true to its mission, ministering to the spiritual needs of East Liberty even as the community declined.

In July 1872 a new church was built on the northwest corner of Barkley Road and State Highway 101, at its present location. The ground was part of the John Friedline farm, one of the original charter members of the church. Specifications for the new church building were very specific as to size and cost. The new church would be 34 feet wide, 46 feet long and 14 feet to the square, with plain cornices. It would have a seven-feet square by nine-feet tall belfry. The building would have four plain windows on each side with two entrance doors in front. The door to the left was for men only and the door to the right was for women only. Inside there would be two aisles and a pulpit with three rows of seating, with the outside pews running to the walls. The pews to the left were reserved for men only; pews to the right were for women only, with the middle pews for the older children. It was to be heated with two pot-bellied stoves, centrally located on each side of the building. Lamps would be hung between the windows for additional lighting. Construction cost for the new church was $460.00. Since the original construction, the church building has undergone several major renovations, culminating in the modern building of today.

During its early life, East Liberty Church played parent for the organization of other churches in the area. One was the Sugar Ridge Church (1900-1918), at the corner of old U.S. 30 (Lincoln Highway) and Simmers Road. Although the brick church building has been razed, its cemetery is still maintained on the north side of the highway. Others were the Baldwin Church (1915-1918), along the old Finley railroad line and the State Line Road, and the Grace Church in Monroeville (1905-1965). Though short-lived, they were a testament to the evangelizing efforts of the original founders and their followers of East Liberty Church.

Throughout the life of the Church the women of the congregation played a significant role in cleaning, maintaining and upgrading the Church's interior, earning money by providing meals at local farm auctions, hosting mush and milk suppers and chicken dinners. The women hand-knitted comforters, quilted blankets, made aprons, bonnets and "dust covers." These earnings provided the church with the additional dollars needed to purchase Bibles, carpets, chairs and church pews. They also visited the sick and served numerous mission projects every year.

Through the years the Church has had several affiliations. In 1946 the Church changed its name to East Liberty Evangelical United Brethren Church. In 1968 the Church merged with the Methodist Church and hence has been called the East Liberty United Methodist Church. Throughout its 160 years the Church has provide God's word and grace to the community.

Emmaus Lutheran Church

The rich history of Emmaus Lutheran Church and School began more than a century ago and represents over 100 years of service and outreach to the Fort Wayne community.

On January 1, 1900, the voting members of Emmanuel Lutheran Church agreed to organize a new congregation. The new church would be called Emmaus Evangelical Lutheran Church. The site for the church was 2322 Broadway, located on what was then the southern outskirts of Fort Wayne. Reverend Phillip Wambsganss was called to be the congregation's first pastor.

On April 28, 1901, the church, along with a new school, was dedicated to the service of God. It was a great day for the members of the young congregation. All sister congregations in Fort Wayne suspended their services that Sunday morning and special excursion trains from places as far as 100 miles away brought many Lutherans to rejoice with the people of Emmaus.

As the parish flourished, the congregation voted to build a modern parish hall, which was completed in 1911. The parish hall was the first building of its kind in local church circles and blazed the way for construction of similar buildings by other congregations.

During his tenure as pastor, Rev. Wambsganss was blessed with steady growth of the church and school. He was also one of the leading pioneers in the establishment of charitable organizations, including Lutheran Hospital.

In 1918, Rev. Wambsganss was succeeded by his son, Pastor Fred Wambsganss. Under his leadership, Emmaus continued to grow as southwest sections of Fort Wayne were quickly developing. In 1924, the congregation purchased land in Waynedale and developed a mission, which became Mount Calvary Lutheran Church, then located at 2416 Lower Huntington Road. Peace Lutheran Church, 4900 Fairfield Avenue, was organized in 1945 as another "daughter" congregation.

Outreach also came in the form of a religious radio program. In the late 1920s, Emmaus became the first local church to sponsor such a program, which featured solo music interspersed with music from the 12-bell set of chimes in the belfry. Placing a microphone outside one of the classrooms and opening the windows enabled the sounds of the chimes to be recorded.

Reverend Fred Wambsganss continued to support new ministries and serve the congregation until 1952, when Reverend Erwin Tepker was installed as only the third pastor in Emmaus' history. During his ministry, the church and school continued to flourish with God's blessings.

In 1963, Reverend Carl Schlutz was called as pastor of Emmaus. Outreach again played a role in the history of Emmaus as the church initiated and conducted outdoor church services at a drive-in-theater. This mission project thrived for nearly 20 years, until the drive-in-theater closed.

Emmaus' radio ministry eventually expanded into a full hour of programming heard on WFCV-1090 every Sunday morning. Today, it consists of a Bible study and discussion program called "Christian Perspective," followed by portions of Emmaus' worship service, called "30 Minutes with Jesus."

Pastor Schlutz also guided the congregation through a major building project, which involved a new edifice housing a modern gym for the school and several new rooms for Bible classes, meetings, choir rehearsals and social activities. For all of his efforts during his tenure, Pastor Schlutz was eventually honored by Emmaus congregation and given the title Pastor Emeritus.

In 1980, Reverend K. Michael Simminger became pastor and served the congregation for three years. Reverend Albert Keller, the current pastor of Emmaus, succeeded him. Pastor Soren Urberg serves the congregation as visitation pastor. Reverend Aaron Robins was welcomed as assistant to the pastor in 2004. Pastor Daniel Coffey was installed as an associate pastor in 2005 to help facilitate his full-time law enforcement chaplaincy.

Today, Emmaus serves its congregation through two locations. Church services, Bible study and Sunday school are offered each Sunday at both 2322 Broadway and 8626 Covington Road. The church's youth are very active through the Lutheran Youth Fellowship of Emmaus (LYFE). The 55 Club keeps senior members of Emmaus busy with trips, speakers and potlucks.

The Emmaus Ladies' Aid, organized shortly after the congregation was established, offers ongoing support to the congregation. A cheer committee makes over 200 sick and shut-in calls per year. Plus, the group holds a large annual bazaar and provides a multitude of other services to the community at large.

Emmaus Lutheran School

Emmaus Lutheran School has been a powerful influence for children since its inception in the early 1900s. A nationally accredited Lutheran school, Emmaus provides a program of academic excellence that has spanned generations. In 2000, Emmaus broke ground for a new campus, located at 8626 Covington Road. This facility was dedicated in September 2001.

Today, a dedicated staff of teachers continues the Emmaus legacy, providing a caring, quality, Christ-centered education to children from preschool through eighth grade.

Emmaus Lutheran Church

Emmaus Lutheran School

Emmanuel Evangelical Lutheran

Emmanuel Lutheran Church

Frederick Wilhelm Soest, a 24 year-old immigrant from Germany, arrived in Fort Wayne in 1836, and married Margarethe Griebel at St. Paul's Lutheran Church in 1840. The couple then purchased 40 acres along Wayne Trace, added to later, in Marion Township. There they built a log house, raised ten children, and were among the settlers ministered to by Rev. Friedrich Wyneken, who began German-speaking congregations in Allen and Adams counties. Their children established homes, operated businesses, and with the coming of a postal station, the Soest name was attached to the community.

Starting in 1841, worship services, baptisms, and weddings were conducted among the community's families, but it was not until 1845 that Rev. Friedrich Husmann became their full-time pastor. St. Paul Evangelical Lutheran Church of Marion Township was organized on December 25, 1845. A log church built near Thompson Road was dedicated on Christmas Day 1846, with an adjacent area used for a cemetery. The congregation joined the Lutheran Church-Missouri Synod in 1853.

The growing congregation built a larger church at the congregation's present site (9909 Wayne Trace) that also includes a cemetery. Local timber was cut and dried in nearby forests and a framed structure designed on more conventional lines was dedicated in December 1861.

A parsonage was erected in 1863. That year Rev. Husmann took a call to Ohio and was succeeded by Rev. Phillip Fleischmann in 1864. During his pastorate, the congregation resolved to amalgamate with the St. John congregation in Adams Township on Hartzel Road. The pastors up to that time taught the parish children during the week and a primary reason for unification was that a full-time teacher could then be called to educate both parishes' children. The two congregations elected to use the St. Paul church on Wayne Trace, but changed the name of the united congregation to Emmanuel. Prior to the merger, Rev. Fleischmann had moved to Kendallville and so Rev. Johann Bundenthal, St. John's pastor, became the pastor of Emmanuel until 1874. In 1872, a teacher, Mr. Nahrwold, arrived to take over the instruction of the children.

Rev. Carl Zschoche was the pastor from 1874 until he resigned due to ill health in 1907. During his tenure, a 1,000 pound bell was installed in the church steeple, a hand-pumped pipe organ was purchased for $700, and a new school building was built in 1901.

Rev. George Blievernecht was Emmanuel's pastor from 1907 to 1910, the first who was born in America. In 1908 Emmanuel's present brick sanctuary was constructed. Designed to seat 500 at a cost of $26,000, it was dedicated on February 28, 1909. The bell and organ were transferred to the new edifice. However, a fierce storm on June 13, 1957, struck the taller of its two steeples, which fell through the front end of the building and caved in the balcony, destroying the organ. The total cost for re-building with reduced steeples, almost fifty years later, was $55,000. A new organ cost $26,000.

Rev. Charles (Carl) Rodenbeck was Emmanuel's pastor from 1910 until his retirement in 1944. During his pastorate English began to replace German in the worship services. A new parsonage was built in 1912 and in the next years electricity and telephones came to all of the buildings, with indoor plumbing installed in 1943.

As the congregation celebrated its 100th anniversary, Rev. Walter Bowman became pastor in 1945 and served until 1949. He was followed by Rev. Otto Mueller from 1950 until 1973. During his ministry a new school was erected at a cost of $96,000 and dedicated in April 1955. Upon Pastor Mueller's retirement, Rev. David Thierfelder served Emmanuel from 1973 until 1976 and he was succeeded in 1977 by Rev. Albert Bierlein, who was Emmanuel's pastor in 2005. In 1990, a Christian Growth Center, which provided additional space for Sunday school classes, meeting, and fellowship gathering, was attached to the church building, costing about $700,000.

More than 40 dedicated teachers served in Emmanuel's parochial school through the years. In 1974, an arrangement with St. John Lutheran Church, 12912 Franke Road, provided for Emmanuel's children to attend its school, with Emmanuel's building still used for preschool. In the fall of 2005, the preschool and the first three grades of the school began to meet in Emmanuel's school building, with more classrooms, offices, and a gymnasium.

In its 160th year, Emmanuel congregation, numbering 646 members, continue to proclaim in the Soest community the Good News of Jesus Christ, the Savior of the world who is Emmanuel – "God with us." Its members gather to be strengthened in their faith and equipped to live their lives to God's glory and invite all to join them.

First Christian Church (Disciples of Christ)

Belief and Origin

The Christian Church (Disciples of Christ), a Protestant denomination rooted in the 19th Century United States, stands on the Bible alone as its doctrine. Freedom of belief, open Communion, oneness of the body of all Christians, and the ministry of all believers are emphasized. The Church practices baptism by immersion of adults and young people who profess their faith in Jesus Christ, Son of the Living God, as their Savior.

Missionaries were sent to Fort Wayne in 1846 and 1847 to preach these ideals, and a congregation of 50 members existed by 1847. However, a lasting congregation was not established in Fort Wayne until 1871 when Elder N. J. Aylsworth, former pastor of the Christian Church at Ligonier, was sent to Fort Wayne to preach. He held meetings in the Anderson Block at Broadway and Jefferson. He and William I. Miller organized this congregation on November 5th of that year. Meetings were held at Nestell's Block at the same intersection until a church building was dedicated on September 26, 1875 at the southeast corner of West Jefferson and Griffith (now Fairfield Avenue).

Church Name

Various names have been used for this congregation including Christian Chapel, West Jefferson Street Church of Christ, First Church of Christ West Jefferson Street, and First Christian Church (Disciples of Christ). The congregation has maintained ties with the Christian Church (Disciples of Christ) denomination.

Church on W. Jefferson Street in the 1940s.

Buildings

The first church building was 45 by 80 feet costing $10,000. The auditorium had ten stained glass windows and was furnished with plain seats and six oil chandeliers. The second structure, of brick and sandstone, was constructed at the same site in 1897. The original structure was retained as part of the design and was adapted to serve as space for a social room, chapel, vestibule, offices, and a furnace room. The building was 72 by 102 feet, had a tower 76 feet high, and a balcony. The interior was finished in oak and included stained glass windows and a fresco of Christ and his apostles. This structure was later demolished after another building campaign materialized in the 1940s. The current structure was built in 1952 on a full city block at Calhoun & Pettit. The architectural design is rich in Christian symbolism. The stained glass windows, rich in shades of red and blue, depict the Beatitudes from Christ's Sermon on the Mount.

Pastors

The following pastors have served First Christian Church: John Aylsworth (1871), Leewell Carpenter (c.1878), William Gleason (c. 1879), Thomas Mason (c.1880), William Aylsworth (c.1880), Gilbert Ireland (c.1883), George Slade (c.1885), M. L. Blaney (c.1888), George Sims (c.1889), Jacob Updike (c.1893), Perry Rice (1893), Edgar Allen (1900), Ray Miller (1906), Earl Todd (1908), O. E. Tomes (1913), Ira Parvin (1918), Ezra McKim (1923), Arthur Wilson (1929), Barton Johnson (1934), Samuel Burgess (1938), Robert Beck (1943), George Wascovich (1956), Franklin McGuire (1967), Harold Cline (1971), Richard Hamm (1982), Jerry Zehr (1991), and Neil Allen (1998)

Other Congregations

Some pastors of this church went on to serve new sister congregations in this city. Blaney pastored the Central Christian Church on Harrison Street which existed about 1891-1896. Updike was the first pastor of the West Creighton Avenue Church in 1896. E. Allen worked to build the East Creighton Avenue Church in 1904. This congregation was once known as Third Church of Christ but is now called Colony Heights Church of Christ. McKim was involved with Fourth Church at Curdes and Carew which lasted 1925 to 1935. Beck worked to establish the North Christian Church on Camden Drive in 1956. Another Central Christian Church, founded in 1929, is now North Highlands Church of Christ.

Current First Christian Church

Current Activity at First Christian

Two Sunday morning services are offered during the non-summer months: a traditional service in the chapel at 8:15 and a slightly more contemporary worship in the sanctuary at 10:45. The summer service is held in the sanctuary at 10:00. Bible study opportunities are available for all age groups.

Organ, piano, and choral music grace the worship services. In 2005, the church contracted with Peebles-Herzog Organ Company of Columbus, Ohio, to construct a $162,000 two-manual organ which will utilize pipework and equipment from First Christian's aged instrument and from a newer "homeless" organ in Ohio, all refurbished to new condition and supplemented with digital voices.

The church participates in the Associated Churches food bank program and houses A Baby's Closet which distributes baby items to needy families.

The church presents a Walk to Bethlehem each December. This community event features vignettes depicting events surrounding Christ's birth, a Bible-times market, and an impressive display of over 200 nativities from around the world.

As it approaches its 135th anniversary, First Christian Church continues to celebrate Christ's life and love for all.

First Church Of Christ, Scientist, Fort Wayne

In 1879, a little band of earnest seekers after Truth, members of evangelical churches and students of Mary Baker Eddy, known as "Christian Scientists," met to form a church without creeds. They voted—"To organize a church designed to commemorate the word and works of our Master, which should reinstate primitive Christianity and its lost element of healing" (from the Church Manual by Mary Baker Eddy). Also in the Manual, "the chief corner stone whereof is, that Christian Science, as taught and demonstrated by our Master, casts our error, heals the sick, and restores the lost Israel."

Mary Baker Eddy, the discoverer and founder of Christian Science, wrote SCIENCE AND HEALTH WITH KEY TO THE SCRIPTURES and it was published the first time in 1875. It is read along with the Bible during the church services. These two books are our dual pastors. These two books and the same services are read in branches throughout the world every Sunday.

In 1992, SCIENCE AND HEALTH was recognized by the Women's National Book Association as one of the 75 major books by women, whose words have changed the world. Mrs. Eddy was inducted into the National Women's Hall of Fame in 1995 -noting that she made "an indelible mark on religion, medicine and journalism."

Mrs. Eddy says in her book Prose Works, "All Science is a revelation. It's Principle is divine, not human, reaching higher then the stars of heaven." She also says, "I named it Christian, because it is compassionate, helpful and spiritual."

First Church of Christ, Scientist, Fort Wayne, first held services in homes starting in 1890, when Miss Ora Beatrice Shaver moved to this city. She and her sister, Mrs. Grace Shaver Weissenborn and the George Mudd family, from Springfield, Illinois, regularly met at their homes to read the Christian Science Bible lessons. The church was incorporated in March 1898 and services were then held at Kimball Hall and other locations around town including the Masonic Temple, and the Old Jewish Synagogue. In 1913, the McCulloch homestead at Ewing and Wayne was purchased and remodeled to include an auditorium, a Sunday school, a Reading Room and committee rooms. This property was dedicated in 1920.

In 1925, the Church purchased a lot on the southeast corner of Fairfield and Pierce Avenues in a quiet, residential section to build a new edifice. The Church property on Ewing Street was sold to the Chamber of Commerce in April 1926. Ground breaking for the new Church edifice at 2410 Fairfield Avenue was on March 8, 1927. The cornerstone was laid July 5, 1927 with a simple ceremony. Items placed in the cornerstone were the Bible, all of Mary Baker Eddy's books, Church by-laws, a history of the Church in Fort Wayne up to 1927, and a list of the Board of Directors, Building Committee, the first and second Readers, and all members of the Church. The building was completed and opened for services on September 9, 1928. The architect for the Church was Howard Cheney of Chicago; the general contractor was Rump, Kintz Co.; and plumbing, heating and wiring was by A. Hattersley.

This property was sold in 1994 as the members decided to build at a new location, a wooded lot at 4242 Buesching Drive. The architect for this new building was Sherbondy Association; the general contractor was Harold McComb and Son, Inc. Ground breaking was on December 2, 1997. The first services were held on October 4, 1998. A new Allen organ was donated by Edith Smith of Hicksville, Ohio in memory of her sister Kathleen Dougherty, who was organist at First Church of Christ, Scientist, Auburn, Indiana. A Centennial open house was held Sunday December 13, 1998 offering a tour of the building, a short program and an organ recital. The Church was dedicated at the Sunday morning service on March 12, 2000.

It was decided to maintain a Reading Room at a location separate from the church. The Reading Room occupied seven different locations from 1905 through 1968 when it was located at 207 West Wayne Street just one block from the Allen County Library and Grand Wayne Convention Center. It has remained there through 2005. It is a lending library as well as a place to purchase authorized Christian Science books, magazines, tapes, videos, the Christian Science Monitor which is an international daily newspaper, and a place to study The Bible, concordances and other research or reference books.

Church services are held Sundays and Wednesdays, and Sunday school meets at the same time as church and is for students up to the age of 20. Child care for the very young is provided for both services.

As Christian Scientists, we recognize the Leadership of Mary Baker Eddy in discovering and founding a church built on the healing work demonstrated so perfectly by Christ Jesus. Mrs. Eddy says in Science and Health with Key to the Scriptures on page 450, line 19; "The Christian Scientist has enlisted to lessen evil, disease, and death; and he will overcome them by understanding their nothingness and the allness of God, or good." Christian Scientists all over the United States, like here in Fort Wayne and in many foreign countries, continue in their healing work and at each Wednesday Evening Testimony Service share the healings they have experienced.

First Mennonite Church

First Mennonite Church had its beginnings in 1903 as The Fort Wayne Mennonite Mission. The work began as a joint mission outreach of the Indiana-Michigan Mennonite Conference and the Indiana-Michigan Amish Mennonite Conference. A layman, John Federspeil, is credited with the vision that led to the establishment of the Mission. Federspeil carried a heavy burden for the spiritual and physical welfare of the poor people of Fort Wayne. Finally, after 20 years of prayer and many contacts with church officials, the first service was held on July 19, 1903. The service was held in a rented room above Hartman's Dance Hall at 1921 Hanna Street. Other temporary locations included a storefront at 2237 Oxford Street and a building at 1436 Third Street. When it became apparent that available rental facilities were not adequate for a sustained ministry, a mission house was built at 1209 St. Mary's Avenue. The house, still standing next to the present church building, was built in 1909 for $5,500. It was made possible by a gift of $3,000 from Louise Snavely of Columbus Grove, Ohio.

Worship services and Sunday school classes were held on the first floor of the Mission House while the mission workers lived on the second floor. The mission staff consisted of the Mission Superintendent, his family, and college-age volunteers from area Mennonite churches. The first Superintendent was John G. Bressler. Ben B. King, the second Superintendent, served as pastor and administrator from 1905 to 1930, and is credited with establishing a more secure basis for the work. During the depression years, Mennonite churches in Ohio and Indiana donated many tons of food and clothing that were distributed to the needy in Fort Wayne. The church became an independent congregation in 1960 and changed its name to First Mennonite Church.

In the 1960s, the Boys Club of First Mennonite Church was recognized by the Fort Wayne religious community and by city officials for its innovative and effective youth program. Other significant community contributions over the years include providing substantial leadership and resources to establish both the Fort Wayne Rescue Mission and the Fort Wayne Youth for Christ. The church also maintains an active role in Allen County Jail ministry.

Distinctive tenants of faith include following the teaching and example of Jesus Christ in daily life rather than viewing them as impractical ideals, giving God allegiance that supersedes all other allegiances, baptism of believers, and living in peaceful relationship with all people rather than choosing wars and violence as solutions to conflict.

The current Pastor is Peter G. Janzen. Challenges facing First Mennonite include meeting the spiritual and physical needs of those left behind in a changing economy and maintaining an inner city ministry as the more affluent move to the suburban churches.

First Mennonite Church

FORT WAYNE PRIMITIVE BAPTIST CHURCH
"Growing In Grace"
Sunday 10:30 am
Pastor: Buddy Abernathy 417-7839

Fort Wayne Primitive Baptist Church was constituted in 1926. Prior to this time, a small group held meetings in different homes to worship God and sing songs of praise to His Holy name. The people in this group consisted of ten members of Wabash Primitive Baptist Church, located five miles east of Huntington on US 224, one member of Lebanon Primitive Baptist Church in Mount Summit, Indiana, and several friends in the area. Elders M. Sylveus and E. L. Kinter, both from Ohio, assisted during this time. On October 9, 1926, members from fourteen different Primitive Baptist Churches met in Fort Wayne to help constitute the church. The charter members of the church were Clarence Foland, Charles Plybon, Omer Summers, Catherine Foland, Lela Foland, Virgil Foland, Rose Mills, Rebecca Scott, Mary Skinner, Lizzie Summers, and Leota Whiteman. Elder C. W. Radcliff served as moderator of the meeting and Brother Jacob Saylors served as clerk. Brother Omer Summers was accepted as deacon and the church agreed to ordain Brother Charles Plybon to the office of deacon as well. Elder E. L. Kinter was chosen as pastor and Sister Lela Foland was chosen as church clerk. The church agreed to adopt the Articles of Faith and Rules of Decorum as written by Elder Walter Cash. For the first eleven years, the church held their meetings in the Northern Indiana Public Service Company building located at the intersection of Hale Avenue and Riedmiller Avenue. The first meeting was held in the present building on March 5th, 1938. It is located at 2006 Nuttman Avenue near the intersection of Brooklyn Avenue and Nuttman Avenue.

Two members have been ordained as Elders (preachers) since the church was constituted in 1926. They were Brother Clarence Foland in 1929 and Brother Manning Temples in 1955. The following Elders have served as pastors of the church: E. L. Kinter (1926-1927), Earl Dailey (1927-1932), Ed Allen (1932-1941), Clarence Foland (1932-1942 as assistant pastor), Adam Sarber (1941-1963), Ivan Hindal (1963-1968), Wayne Thacker (1968-1983), Lloyd Pitney (1983-1988), Alvin Bryant (1988-1991), Manasseh Gillam (1991-1996), Tommy Sarber (1996-1997), Doug Meeks (1997-2002), and Buddy Abernathy (2004-present).

The priority of Fort Wayne Primitive Baptist Church has been to worship God in spirit and in truth. The format of the worship service and the doctrines taught by the church, have not been changed since the church was constituted. The church practices congregational singing without instrumental accompaniment. The songs are not selected in advance. Members have the opportunity to select a hymn of their choice during the singing segment of the worship which lasts twenty to thirty minutes. The church believes this practice allows for sensitivity to the guidance of the Holy Spirit as the members select hymns that are upon their hearts at the time of worship. The church believes the scriptures of the Old and New Testament are the inspired and infallible word of God and contain everything we need to know in order to worship God and live a Christian life. Therefore, the pastor preaches directly from the Bible. He teaches the meaning of the scriptures and also relates the meaning to the circumstances of our life in the modern world. The following excerpt was taken from a pamphlet recently published by the church for the purpose of introducing people to the basic beliefs of the church: "At Fort Wayne Primitive Baptist Church, we believe that eternal salvation is entirely by the grace of God. While many proclaim that heaven is a reward given to those who meet the necessary requirements, we rejoice to know that Jesus Christ did everything necessary to secure our eternal destiny. We believe that God loved a great multitude of people in Christ before the world began. We believe that Jesus died on the cross to save His people from their sins. We believe the Holy Spirit imparts eternal life to every one that Jesus saved (This is often referred to as "the new birth" or "being born again"). We believe that nothing shall be able to separate us from the love of God which is in Christ Jesus our Lord. We believe Jesus is coming again to resurrect the dead and take His people home to live with him forever in eternal glory. We believe the church has two primary purposes: (1) To glorify God by declaring the gospel. The word "gospel" means "good news" or "glad tidings". It informs people of the perfect work of Jesus so that they may rest in His finished work instead of relying upon their own works for salvation. (2) To teach God's children how to honor their Heavenly Father. We believe this is accomplished by learning and obeying God's word. That's why our pastor strives to preach about grace and godly living."

Fort Wayne Primitive Baptist Church currently meets to worship at 10:30 a.m. each Sunday. Visitors are always welcome. For more information, contact Pastor Buddy Abernathy at (260) 417-7839 or BuddyAbenathy@juno.com.

Good Shepherd United Methodist Church

Good Shepherd United Methodist Church arose from what had been a wheat field at the southwest corner of Vance Avenue and Reed Road in 1964. The residential neighborhood was growing, but the nearest Methodist church was a few miles away. On August 25, 1964, the Methodists began doing something about that.

At an organizational meeting that day, several people were selected to start the congregation – Verna Bloom, worship chairman; Mel Arnold, finance chairman; Richard Horn, education chairman; Elmer Matthews, membership and visitation chairman; and Floyd E. Blake, pastor.

The first worship service was held November 8, 1964, at Brentwood Elementary School. At that first service, 114 people attended and $166.51 in offering was collected. The name "Good Shepherd Methodist" won a contest from among 35 entries. The congregation adopted "United Methodist" after the merger of the Methodist and Evangelical United Brethren churches nationwide in 1968.

The groundbreaking service was in May 1965. A Christmas Eve service was held in the sanctuary of the incomplete building that year which 120 people attended. The first service at a completed Good Shepherd building was February 6, 1966.

As time went on, the church facilities underwent a number of expansions as growth of the congregation necessitated a larger sanctuary, more classrooms and meeting rooms, and a bigger parking lot. Adding to the need for more space was the congregation's weekday preschool for 2-to-5 year olds, which began in 1975.

The church had nine Senior and ten Associate pastors in its first 40 years. Pastor Blake, of course, deserves credit as Good Shepherd's founding pastor. He and his wife, Marge, stayed until 1971.

Pastors at Good Shepherd Church

Senior Pastors: Floyd Blake (1964-1971), Robert Sievers (1971-1974), Joseph Penrod (1974-1978), Harold Oechsle (1978-1984), Michael Coyner (1984-1990), Ted Blosser (1990-2000), Cindy Reynolds (2000), Jacob Williams (2001), and Philip Emerson (2002-present). **Associate Pastors:** Larry Humbert (1967–1970), Ted Blosser (1975-1982), Jim Dance (1982-1985), Craig LaSuer (1985-1989), Evan Lash (1990-1992), Jack Scott (1992-1994), Kris McPherson (1994-2002), Donna Goings (1999-2005), Patrick Somers (2002-2005), Stacy Stackhouse (2005-present)

Present church at 4700 Vance Avenue.

Another notable minister was Dr. Michael Coyner. He served as senior pastor from 1984 to 1990. During his tenure, the church began a 9:45 a.m. Sunday service, the congregation's third. It already offered services at 8:30 and 11 a.m. The 9:45 a.m. service eventually became its most popular. Dr. Coyner's wife, Marsha, began the first handbell choir in 1987. By 2005, Good Shepherd had handbell choirs on beginner, intermediate, and experienced levels. The church also had vocal choirs for all ages, from preschoolers to adults. Dr. Coyner went on to become the bishop of North and South Dakota. In 2004, he was appointed bishop of Indiana.

The Rev. Ted Blosser served as associate pastor form 1975 to 1982 and as senior pastor from 1990 to 2000. Much of the church's expansion in membership and facilities came during his tenure as senior pastor. He and his wife, Lynn, shared their love of and talent for music with the congregation. Lynn Blosser directed Teen Rejoice, the youth choir, and led youth Bible classes. In all, Pastor Blosser served for 17 years, almost half of the church's history up to that time.

One of the last long-term projects begun under Pastor Blosser's leadership, meanwhile, started with the closure of Epworth United Methodist Church on Hessen Cassel Road in the spring of 2000. Good Shepherd took over the property and cleaned and refurbished it. It was renamed Open Arms Ministries for its stained-glass window showing Jesus welcoming people.

When the Rev. Philip Emerson became pastor of Good Shepherd in 2002, his vision for Good Shepherd was ABU – Attracting, Building, and Utilizing disciples for Jesus Christ. The congregation continued to be busy doing just that. As Good Shepherd celebrated its 40th anniversary in 2005, it had more then 1,300 members, with an average weekend worship attendance nearing 700. It had a Saturday night service and three Sunday morning services, plus Bible classes, choir rehearsals, youth programs, and other activities during the week, led by more than a dozen full-and part –time staff members and many volunteers.

As part of the congregation's anniversary celebrations in 2005, it dedicated a "Sending Wall," honoring the following members who have joined the ministry or mission fields: David S. Arnold, Rachel D. Bales-Case, Mark Bollwinkel, Donald Dexheimer, William Garver, Marilyn J. Gebert, Donna K. Goings, Richard Lyth, Randy S. McQueen, Jack L. Rhoades, Sr., Keith R. Schreffler, V. Robert Seewald, Thomas Watt, and Douglas A. Witt.

Open Arms Ministries also was thriving, under the leadership of Evangelist/Director Donovan Coley, who became a full-time employee in 2004, after Good Shepherd was given a $100,000, three-year grant from the North Indiana Conference of the United Methodist Church. Average attendance was more than 50 and Open Arms had services and Bible studies in both English and Spanish.

Change is inevitable at Good Shepherd and in life. The congregation, however, intends to continue to move forward, doing the work of Jesus Christ.

Grabill Missionary Church

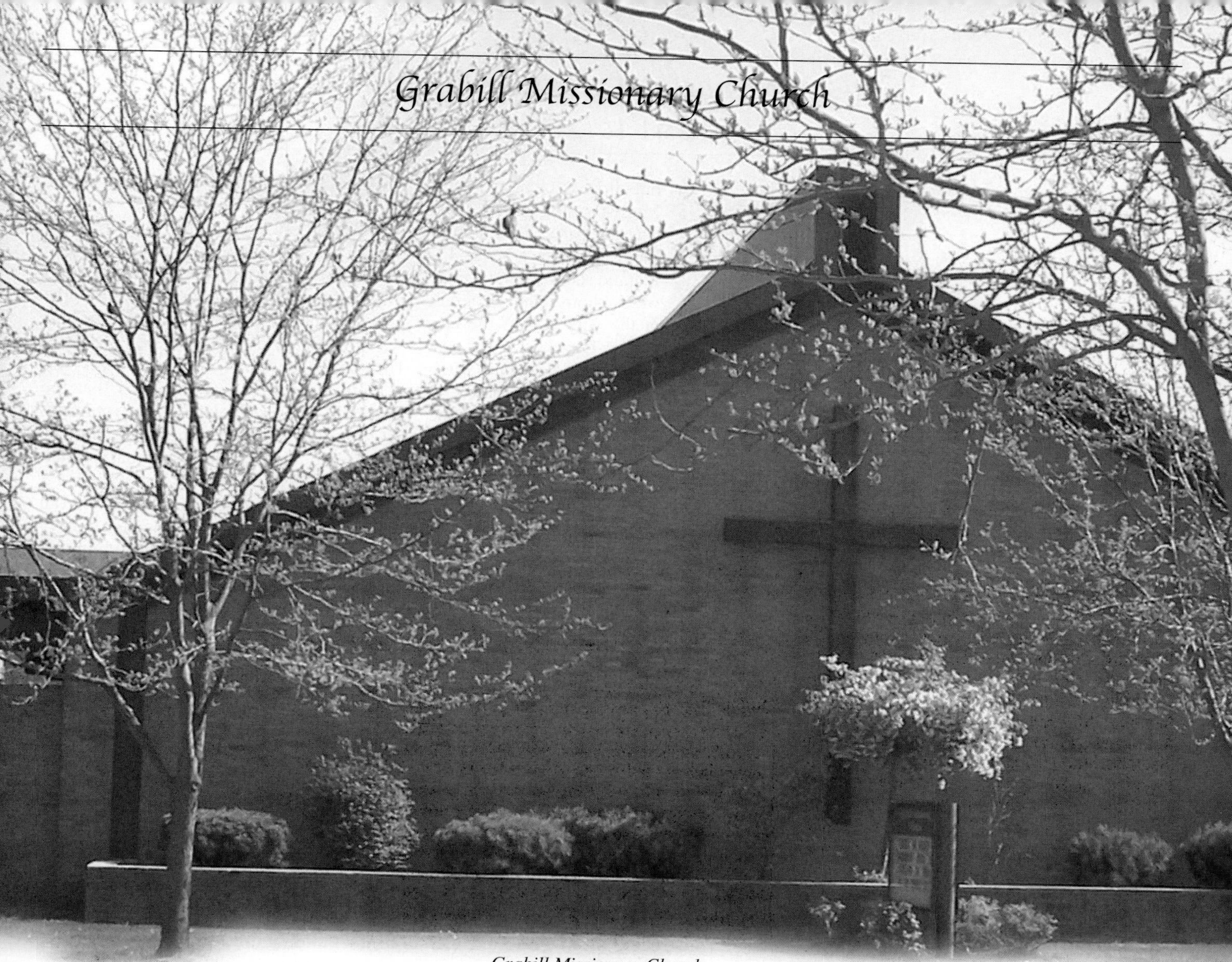

Grabill Missionary Church

The Grabill Missionary Church formally organized as a congregation and dedicated its first church building on November 3, 1901. There were thirty-seven charter members. The charter members all came from a Mennonite background. David and Henry Roth were the first pastors. Because of their zeal for foreign missions and their strong belief that the gospel should be taken to the ends of the earth, they joined the Missionary Church Association whose headquarters are still in Fort Wayne.

In the summer of 1901, work began on the first Grabill Missionary Church building on its present site. This was the year the Wabash Railroad had been built and a station erected called Grabill. Before that time the town was not on the map. The Grabill Missionary Church was one of the first buildings in Grabill. There were building programs in 1916, the 1940s, 1955, and our present facilities were built in 1985 and 2002. Attendance has grown steadily with three services on Sunday a.m. There is usually a combined attendance from 700-800 each Sunday.

Over the years many from this church have gone into the Christian ministry in this country and also into foreign countries all over the world.

Grace Evangelical Lutheran Church
1891 to 2004

As members of St. John Lutheran Church on Washington Boulevard moved south and east in Fort Wayne they found that it was difficult to get to church, and more importantly, very difficult to get their children to school. In December of 1890 twenty-two families asked the St. John's church council if a church and school could be started in the southeast area of town. At the congregational meeting on January 4, 1891, the congregation voted to release the families living in the area to be members of a daughter congregation, and permit Pastor Dannecker, pastor of St. John's, to serve them as well until the new church could get its own pastor. The St. John's congregation also bought property and provided $3,200.00 in cash for the new congregation.

The new congregation was organized on January 27, 1891, and four lots at Gay and Pontiac were purchased for $2,150.00. On September 14th the church was dedicated and the first pastor, Theodore Stillborn, was installed June 26, 1892. The dedication of the day school was held January 28, 1894. A parsonage was built in 1895 also.

This church building served the Grace congregation well until the present church was built in 1926-1927 at the corner of Anthony and Colerick Avenues. The former Grace Church building is still standing and remains a house of the Lord for the Missionary Baptist Church.

The church for many years had both English and German language services but chose to change to only English in the early 1920s. There began a discussion of building a new larger building and school at the corner of Anthony and Colerick at the very end of the city limits. The church was surrounded by farm land when it was built. The church on Anthony was built, but the depression began and the congregation had some difficulty paying for it. Some of the members came to the rescue by mortgaging their homes to help finance the church and the mission of Christ went on.

Pastor Frederick H. Holtineyer, a beloved pastor of Grace for 36 years, was installed as pastor in 1925. During his ministry all the buildings, the church, the school, the parsonage, and the educational addition were built.

When the church was built, it had the walls and glass for the windows and the benches from the old church. Over the years the stained glass windows, the wood paneling, the carpet and the organ were added.

The wood paneling and the altar are all constructed from imported German wood. The windows are stained and painted glass, dating from the 1930s and are priceless to replace. The organ is a Roderer tracker organ. A tracker organ has nothing electronic. Instead the mechanical action allows more subtlety of tone than does an electronic keyboard. The parts all came from Germany and were constructed in this country by Kurt Roderer, a well known organ builder. The organ was dedicated in 1979.

The school was an intricate part of the church life at Grace until it closed in 1958. At that time the congregation made a commitment to erect an educational unit to the church which included a gymnasium. This was completed in 1961 just before Pastor Holtmeyer retired.

Recently it was determined that the original slate roof needed to be replaced. At the same time the congregation decided to remodel the church sanctuary which was completed in 2004.

Over the years Grace Lutheran Church has been a part of the community and the neighborhood by providing not only a spiritual life but also an educational life for its children. At one point a lighted cross was placed on the top of the bell tower. This cross shone at night, providing comfort to the neighborhood as they went to sleep and providing a path for airplanes as they began their descent to the airport.

This cross was a symbol of Christ's light in the world shining on us for our salvation. The cross is no longer lit as the cost to fix it is prohibitive as well as difficult because of the height. However, Grace Lutheran Church is still a light or beacon to the neighborhood as it provides for the physical and spiritual needs of the families of the area. Grace rents a portion of the building to Lutheran Social Services for an early childhood day care center. A food bank is operated three mornings a week. The Community Outreach Center runs a clothing bank, an after school program and gives out household goods and furniture. As a people of God called by Him, Grace Lutheran Church's mission is to continue to share Christ's love in service to our church and our community.

Harvester Avenue Missionary Church

In the spring of 1929 Rev. John Rohrs and Rev. Sam Grabill agreed there was a need to build a church on the corner of Harvester and Fleetwood Avenues. Before the building could be built, Sunday school and Services were held in a house on Edsall Avenue. Tent Meetings were held through the summer; by fall the meetings were held in a nearby creamery. Rev. Rohrs walked the neighborhood encouraging people to come to the new church. He worked without a salary depending on the Lord to care for him and the family. The group grew.

•1930 Rev. Michael E. Ramseyer gave leadership. In the fall a little church, 24'X28', was dedicated and called The Missionary Chapel.

•1932 A larger church building was needed. The little church was turned around to face east and a new larger building was built which is now our chapel. Rev. Ramseyer served 17 years.

•1946 His son-in-law Rev. Carl and Mrs. Parlee began Sunset Gospel Hour and Gospel Melody Hour radio ministries. He later became Pastor of Harvester Church.

•1953 Rev. and Mrs. Oscar A. Eicher ministered at Harvester Church for 19 years. The church members multiplied.

•1956 & 1957 The present large sanctuary addition was connected to the front of the chapel and the present chapel. Rev. Eicher started a radio outreach program, The Tower of Strength, featuring the choir and sermons.

•1973 This year brought Rev. Robert Strubhar as Interim Pastor. Rev. and Mrs. Joseph Klopenstein assisted as Visitation Pastors. Rev. and Mrs. Reginald Alford also came in the summer of 1973. They added a Bicycle Ministry, a Bus Ministry, Puppet Ministries and more Children's Ministries as the congregation made a new commitment to serve the community.

•1974 Pastor Max Wanner came to serve as Christian Education and Director of Youth. Upon the Home Going of Rev. Klopfenstein, Rev. Wanner became the Pastor of Visitation in addition to Administrative Pastor. Having a degree in Music and being an accomplished organ player, he also became the Director of Music.

•1978 Dr. Wesley Gerig came to Harvester Church to fill the position of Interim Pastor when Rev. and Mrs. Alford left. He came first as an Interim Pastor but soon became Senior Pastor. His teaching of Greek Studies and his responsibilities at Taylor University increased. He resigned as pastor in 1989, after 11 years of strong emphasis on prayer and personal Bible study.

•1980 Pastor Max Wanner took a wife, Rachel, who had planned to be a missionary. She found a Mission Field in the Harvester Church area. We believe this to be of God's planning.

•1983 On March 27, 1983, Rev. Max Wanner was ordained.

•1989 On July 1, 1989, Rev. Max Wanner was entreated to take the position of Senior Pastor. He was a prayerful, compassionate pastor. He was a pastor to the neighborhood people by walking the area with a jolly invitation to attend services and learn of the Savior. They left in 2001 for a different kind of mission after 27 years at Harvester Church.

•1995 Rev. and Mrs. David Binkley joined the staff as a part-time Youth Director and Associate Pastor. He encouraged Bible Quizzing and youth activities to build leadership skills. We were glad to have him return to this neighborhood. His parents, Mr. and Mrs. Jim Binkley, raised their family of four sons as parishioners at Harvester Church.

•2001 On July 1, 2001, Rev. David Binkley became Senior Pastor. His goal was to improve the sound system and video systems to enhance the worship and praise services and to send tapes to our missionaries. A garage was built to protect our bus and vans from vandalism. He prayerfully asks of God what He would have us do to reach this area.

•2003 Staff members serving are: Director of Children's Ministries, Nyletta Hetrick; Music Director, Michael Mortensen; Youth Pastor, Richard Harris; and Secretary, Holly Pepple.

•2004 In September a Celebration, for 75 Years of serving, was held with music, former pastors, former members and dinner at Geoglein Banquet Hall. Praise the Lord!

•2005 This year brought us a new Youth Pastor, Shawn La Rue, and a new Secretary, Lori Wiederkehr.

•2006 Plans are being made to add a Community Outreach Center, which will include a gymnasium. Plans are to build on the lots west of the Sanctuary. **The future looks as bright as the promises of God.**

Indiana District Of The Lutheran Church-Missouri Synod
1145 South Barr Street, Fort Wayne

Lutheran immigrants from Germany organized St. Paul's Lutheran Church on Barr Street in Fort Wayne in 1837, with Rev. Jesse Hoover as their first pastor. He was succeeded by Rev. Friedrich Wyneken, who was instrumental in starting more German-speaking congregations in Allen and Adams counties.

Rev. Wilhelm Sihler became the next pastor of St. Paul's and with other Lutherans, mostly from mid-west states, had a primary role in the formation of the Lutheran Church-Missouri Synod. Three preliminary meetings, the last of which was held at St. Paul's in July 1846, led to the organization of the synod (which in Greek means "walking the road together") in Chicago on April 26, 1847, with 17 pastors and a few other representatives present. St. Paul's congregation was one of the original congregations that elected to join the new synod. Its original name was the German Evangelical-Lutheran Synod of Missouri, Ohio, and Other States, but was changed in 1947 to the Lutheran Church-Missouri Synod and now usually is simply called "The Missouri Synod."

The Synod initially established six conference districts, with headquarters at St. Louis, Chicago; Fort Wayne; Monroe, Michigan; Fairfield County, Ohio; and New York City. Rev. Sihler was its first vice-president and oversaw its eastern part. Rapid membership growth had the Synod in 1853 divide into four districts, starting in 1854, one of which was the Central District, comprising Ohio, West Virginia, Indiana, and northern Kentucky, with 34 congregations, still presided over by Rev. Sihler from Fort Wayne.

Clergy presidents of the Central District subsequent to Wm. Sihler (1854-60) were H. Schwan (1860-78); W. Stubnatzi (1878-80); J. Niemann (1880-1909); J. Wefel (1909-15); J. Schmidt (1919-20); J. Matthius (1920-27); W. Lichtsinn (1927-47); J. Meyer (1947-51); and Ottomar Krueger (1951-63). Each of them was a full-time pastor, who lived in the community where he served and who came to Fort Wayne for meetings. Offices for the supportive staff of the District were in homes on the southeast corner of Barr and Madison Streets, across from St. Paul's Church. In 1959, a new office building, now numbered 1145 South Barr Street, was erected at the site and renovated in 1997.

By 1962 the Central District consisted of 338 congregations with about 175,000 members. That year the Synod decided to divide it, starting in 1963, into two districts, the Ohio District and the Indiana District. The Indiana District, including areas of Kentucky immediately south of Indiana, numbered 197 congregations with about 106,000 members. The first Indiana District president was Rev. Edgar Rakow (1963-70), who served part-time from his pastorate in Evansville, Indiana. Rev. Elwood Zimmermann (1970-88) was then elected to the position full-time and resided in Fort Wayne, as did those who followed him. Subsequent presidents were Rev. Reuben Garber (1988-91) and Rev. Timothy Sims (1991-2003). Rev. Daniel May was elected in 2003. In 2005, the Indiana District numbered 239 congregations with about 115,000 members. 27 of the congregations were in Allen County and had a combined membership of about 21,700 members.

The Indiana District, as a part of the Lutheran Church-Missouri Synod, supports the larger work of the Synod, such as world missions and the education of church workers. Its congregations also support a full-time Indiana District staff that encourages and assists the Christian outreach and nurture of the District's congregations and other ministries. That staff in 2005 included executives Rev. David Dubbelde, for Congregational Outreach; Dr. David Ebeling, for Congregational Services; and Mr. Lawrence Jung, for Congregational Resources.

Most Missouri Synod congregations in Allen County for many years used the German language exclusively during worship. However, the sensitivities aroused by World War I against Germany led to English becoming the dominant language and by World War II German services were limited and soon after eliminated entirely. Though much of the membership was still of German descent, people of many other backgrounds became members. Also, in the last decades of the twentieth century, areas of Indiana experienced an influx of immigrants from the Orient, Africa, and Spanish-speaking countries. To proclaim the Gospel of Jesus Christ to those new arrivals in particular, the Indiana District intentionally staffed its Outreach Department with missionary-pastors, reared in those cultures, to achieve a new generation of international believers. A number of such congregations were formed in Allen County, some in conjunction with existing congregations. Both new and older congregations, in which all people are welcomed regardless of their race or ethnic background, thus have seen significant change in the church body from within. In 2005, the congregations continued to meet human need with compassion and the unchanging message of the Bible, just as it had already been spoken to the lives of those who first bore the name "Lutheran" in Allen County.

District Office Building
Indiana District of the Lutheran Church-Missouri Synod

Lake Chapel United Methodist Church

Lake Chapel Methodist Church 1925

Lake Chapel United Methodist Church 2005

Rev. Black of the Methodist Church held the first religious service in the home of William Grayless in 1834 in Lake Township. In January 1850, Eli Pierce granted a deed as a donation to the trustees: Wm. Grayless, Milton Waugh, Absolono Heir, Nathan Smith, Francis Sweet, Joseph Taylor, and Wm. Smith. This 15 ½ rod square piece of land is in the southeast corner of the NW quarter of Section 7, town 31, Range 11 for the purpose of a meeting house for the use of the Methodist Episcopal Church; also for burying ground under the control of Lake Chapel. The trustees paid fifty cents for receiving the acknowledgement of the deed.

Rev. Amby Johnson dedicated Lake Chapel on October 27, 1850 to the service of the Lord. T.F. Palmer was the first minister for the conference year 1849 and 1850. The Arcola Circuit was formed in April 1867 and Lake Chapel was one of several stations. The ministry was supported by "classes." Those named were: Arcola, Lake Chapel, Town House, Heifer, Johnson, Union, Hadley, and Red, White and Blue, Rhoades, Jefferson and Stirks School. This was cut down to four churches: Coesse, Lake Chapel, Arcola and Jefferson Chapel. In 1912, the four church circuit was split, of which Lake Chapel and Arcola still continue.

The original meeting house accommodated the congregation for 75 years. The building was placed on a basement foundation at its present location in 1925, during the ministry of Rev. E.P. Uphoff, and continued under the ministry of Rev. Hugh E. Forbes. The building was finished with durable stucco which is still in good condition.

The Ladies Aid was organized in 1905 with 13 members. They, along with the Women's Missionary Society, merged in 1940 into what was known as the Womens Society for Christian Service. Today, they are known as The United Methodist Women.

In 1957 the basement was refinished and an automatic gas furnace was installed. Restrooms were also installed. The sanctuary was refinished; new pews and chancel furniture were purchased, costing $11,212. Rev. Ralph High was minister during this big improvement. The M.Y.F. presented the church a bronze cross and candle holders for the altar. A candle lighter was given by Marcilla Andrew and first used at her wedding. They were replaced in 1978.

A church bus was purchased in 1963, to pick up residents at the Lake Everett area for church services. The bus drivers were Joe Mann or Rev. Ernest Cobbs. Memorial services have been held at the cemetery on the Sunday preceding Memorial Day, following Worship Service since Rev. George Manley started them on May 30, 1968.

The Methodists and Evangelical United Brethern Churches joined to become the United Methodist Church in 1968. Vacation Bible School was first conducted in 1947 by Rev. Lavern Skinner. Directors have included Bernice Andrew, for 14 years; Elizabeth Johnson for 17 years, and several different persons have taken that responsibility in recent years. The U.M.Y.F. participated in youth camps at Epworth Heights and Epworth Forest through the years 1944-present. It was usually this group that was in charge of Easter Sunrise Services and Christmas caroling.

A ranch style parsonage, with office, was built next to Lake Chapel Church in 1959. The land was donated by the Schoch family. Sporting events have been a part of Lake Chapel. The trophy case holds at least 11 trophies and some certificates. A very talented basketball team in the early 1950s received trophies in 1953 and 1954. Softball was the sport of interest in 1977 and 1978.

An expansion of the basement on the South side of the church added space for classrooms and a social room. Everyone worked to make it possible for 12 members to go to Henderson Settlement on a work mission trip in 1996. The church office was moved from the parsonage to the Arcola UMC in June 1996.

The UMW has continued monthly meetings and annual events: observance of Week of Prayer and Self-Denial; Prayer breakfast in March; Mother/Daughter Banquet in May; Auction and Salad Bar in October. The ladies have served sale dinners and funeral dinners. During the late 1930s and early 1940s the men would set up facilities to serve Chicken Noodle meals at Old Settler's Day in Columbia City. Our recent projects have been making and raffling quilts, one in 1999 and another in 2004. We continue to support local and foreign missions through the Fort Wayne District UMW.

Lake Chapel's Mission Statement reads: Our foundation is found in the Scriptures. Our goal is to help others in need and spread the Good News beyond these doors, presenting Christ's love and forgiveness to all.

Maple Grove Friends Meeting

In the seventeenth and eighteenth centuries, an influx of Quakers from England arrived in America searching for religious freedom without persecution. These Quakers stood for honesty, strong Christian values, and integrity. They became respected businessmen, landowners, and teachers.

Many, believing there is that of God in everyone, were strongly opposed to the growing practice of slavery in America. By the early nineteenth century, one small group of Quakers in North Carolina felt they could no longer bear to see black men all about them in chains and slavery. They moved to Indiana, settling in Huntington and Wabash Counties. With no established Quaker Meetings in the immediate area, they formed their own Meetings.

The group settling in Huntington County started Maple Grove Preparatory Meeting in Dallas Township, Huntington County, Indiana. This Meeting was sponsored by Whitewater Monthly Meeting in Richmond, Indiana. Those settling in Wabash County started Rush Creek Preparatory Meeting at Lincolnville. Rush Creek was sponsored by Fall Creek Monthly Meeting, Pendleton, Indiana. These Friends opposition to slavery remained strong as did their desire to do something about it. Prior to the Civil War, Maple Grove was actively involved in the Underground Railroad. In the 1840s and 1850s, Frederick Kindly operated a way station between Jonesboro and Manchester in Indiana.

It was recorded in the Minutes for Maple Grove that William McKimmy and a few Friends began meeting for worship "in the midst of the towering forest and perpetual shade (God's first temple)." Choosing a site, they built a 16 feet by 20 feet house of round log construction. In reference to their new meeting house they recorded, "In this primitive edifice, shut in from the hideous howling of hound and hunter, twice a week on first and fourth days (Sunday and Wednesday) these Friends bent low before their maker in solemn communication.

Rush Creek Meeting (Maple Grove) was started about 1840, becoming the first established church in Lincolnville. The original list of members of (Rush Creek) Maple Grove was recorded as follows: David Batty, Marmaduke Batty, Mrs. Rachel Batty, Jese Elliot, William Ferris, Benjamin Griffith, Aaron Haecock, Jesse Heacock, Mrs. Eliza Heacock, Amos Holloway, Israel Holloway, Jason Holloway, Jess Holloway, Job Holloway, John Holloway, Mrs. Edna Hollowell, David James, James K. James, Jesse H. James, Asa Kindly, Frederick Kindly, William McKimmy, Mrs. McKimmy, Mordecia Morris, Jesse Pinkering, Job Ridgeway, Jacob Sletler, Henry White, and the respective families.

In 1854, the four Meetings, Fall Creek, Maple Grove, Rush Creek and Whitewater, presented a joint concern to the Whitewater Quarterly Meeting requesting that Maple Grove Preparatory and Rush Creek Preparatory Meetings join Whitewater Quarterly Meeting jointly under the name of Maple Grove Monthly Meeting.

The first monthly meeting was held in November, 1854. This arrangement continued until 1914 when Maple Grove at Huntington was laid down. At this time, all assets were converted to the Maple Grove Cemetery Association. Rush Creek Meeting, which had been Maple Grove Monthly Meeting jointly with Maple Grove Meeting at Huntington, took the name Maple Grove. As Maple Grove, the meeting flourished in Lincolnville for many years.

Regular meetings for worship and for business were held in Lincolnville into the early twentieth century. Around 1920, the membership declined as the young people began leaving the crossroads town to seek career opportunities elsewhere. At this time, Maple Grove began meeting on an irregular basis until 1927.

In 1927, M. Sherman Pressler (grandson of Job Holloway) and his wife Edna moved Maple Grove to Fort Wayne. Having nearly died out in Lincolnville, the Presslers gave Maple Grove new life in Fort Wayne. Under the leadership of Sherman and Edna Pressler, Maple Grove in Fort Wayne had ups and downs averaging about thirty members. The last recorded clerk of Maple Grove was Julia Dunn, daughter of Sherman and Edna Pressler.

In Fort Wayne, members were active in promoting peace and nonviolence. During World War II, Sherman Pressler (clerk of Maple Grove for twenty-five years) was appointed to the Advisory Board for the five draft boards in the Fort Wayne area. He worked with local young men helping them to understand their option for alternative service. Sherman was a representative to the Friends World Committee in Oxford, England in 1952 (featured in a story in the Fort Wayne News Sentinel) and Waterford, Ireland in 1964.

From the 1960s to the 1990s, James Dunn of Maple Grove served on the Friends Committee on National Legislation using his background as an attorney to lobby for legislation supporting peace and non-violence.

Although Maple Grove is inactive as a Meeting due to declining membership, members are still actively doing God's work. Mr. Dunn continues to serve on the American Friends Council on Indian Affairs which works with six reservations across the United States working with Native Americans, preserving their heritage and improving their quality of life. *Written and submitted by Judith West, granddaughter of M. Sherman Pressler*

Maples United Methodist Church

The Maples United Methodist Church is located at the southwest corner of Church and Bird Streets in the Village of Maples on Franke Road, Jefferson Township, in Allen County, Indiana.

In 1871 land was donated for a church and a parsonage by Mr. and Mrs. Lewis Maples, Mr. and Mrs. Aehming Bird, and Mr. and Mrs. Jacob Bowser. The deed for the land states that any religious denomination may use the building, but it must be called a Methodist Church.

Six men volunteered to cut timber for the church building. Within six days, the timber was cut from Mooney's woods and was milled. The church was dedicated on August 16, 1871. The parsonage was completed ten years later in 1881.

Painting of Maples United Methodist Church by Georgia Guebard, a member of the church.

Mr. Mooney also donated the church's first pews. These were used until 1951 when new pews were installed. One original pew still remains in the church basement.

The building was finished and a new church began its life of testimony and witnessing to the community. One thing was lacking for this new church - the steeple held no bell. This void was soon to be filled. In 1891 a bell was purchased for $100 from a company in Cincinnati, Ohio. A team of Amish workers hung the bell from the steeple rafters. It was dedicated on Christmas Eve of that year. It rang every Sunday until 1990. Bell ringing was stopped at that time due to needed steeple repairs. A special fund has been established to raise money for repairing the steeple in the hopes that once again the bell will be able to be heard around the Maples community and throughout the surrounding countryside.

Throughout the years there have been repairs and additions to the original building. In July of 1907 new windows were installed. 1927 saw a big change with the introduction of electricity (from kerosene). A basement was dug in the 1940s. The extra space has been used for classrooms, a kitchen, and a fellowship hall. A furnace was also installed in the basement (which replaced the coal stove in the sanctuary). In the 1950s asbestos shingles were added and the steeple repaired. The parsonage was used until 1956 at which time it was tore down. Another major improvement came in 1967 - 1968 with the installation of a well, septic tank, and bathroom facilities, thus replacing the outhouse. Other major improvements were extensive tile work in 1984 to stop flooding in the basement; in 1987 a gas furnace replaced an oil furnace, followed by exterior and interior painting; and in 1991 new carpet was installed in the sanctuary. Continuing on into the late 1990s and the early 2000s, a new exterior sign, roofing, and gutter work; the installation of central air conditioning, automatic heating and cooling programming; and upgrades in the water heating and basement heating systems were other improvements to the original church structure.

Throughout the years the Methodist Church merged with other denominations. These mergers resulted in name changes. The changes have been reflected in the name of Maples' church as well. In 1871 the name was Maples Methodist Protestant. In 1939 it was known as Methodist Episcopal. When the Methodist and Brethren denominations merged, the name became Maples United Methodist Church.

The church has shared pastors with the United Methodist churches in Monroeville, New Haven, Harlan, Mount Taber and Milan Center throughout many of the years from 1871 until 1989. Since that time we have been assigned part-time ministers as a solo charge.

Church members have continued to give to the church during its ministry. The church began with donations of land, timber, and pews. In May 1972 an organ was donated in memory of John Nail, Sr. This generous donation was followed by another in 1981, when a piano was given in memory of Juliette and Gertrude Nail. When Maples was no longer on the circuit with another church, members and friends gave generously for the purchase of a copier. New hymnals were donated by Earl and Evelyn Cramer in 1990. Ann and Parnell Hisner clean the church each week. Gary and Debbie Spry, and Dan and Judy Burch, contribute time to the landscape surrounding the building. Each Sunday all who enter are cheerfully welcomed by Mary Ann Yoder.

And so the church continues. Members support various missions which include a former pastor's mission work in Brazil, Operation Classroom in Africa, Charis House, Monroeville Youth Center, Habitat for Humanity, and local food banks. Though the number of people who gather each Sunday may be small, the worship and service to God are great in spirit. (Sunday School is at 9:30 a.m. Church services are at 10:30 a.m.) After 134 years of service, the original church still stands. It is hoped that it lasts for many, many years to come.

Martini Lutheran Church
333E Moeller Road, New Haven

In 1848, area Lutheran Churches were few. Many attended St. Paul's Lutheran Church, Fort Wayne, because they could walk to services and school. A group of members lived east. Roads were full of ruts, so getting to church and school was difficult. Dr. William Sihler, pastor of St. Paul's, advised these members to start their own school.

Their priority was schooling, so they obtained a house owned by Fred Heine, and engaged Mr. Andrew Zagel to teach. He came from Germany to help in the mission field of the Middle West. The members later erected a school, on two acres purchased from Marvin Bowen. It was near the present MacMillen Park. Each member donated two logs. Mr. Zagel taught until 1853. He accepted a call to Indianapolis.

Pastor Sibler advised them to hire someone from the Fort Wayne Seminary to preach and teach. Frederick Koestering, an 1853 graduate, accepted the call. Martini Church was founded on November 13, 1853 by the following 23 members: H. Moeller, A. Brueck, H. Meier, W. Bradtmueller, L. Niemeyer, F. Heine, C. Piepenbrink, F. Kiel, T. Weisheit, Chr. Wiese, Chr. Neier, H. Bradtmueller, C. Bradtmueller, F. Wehrs, E. Bredemeyer, J. Gombert, Chr. Schroeder, Chr. Rebber, H. Lange, E. Witte, C. Hockemeier, F. Prange, and G. Schleenbecker.

The first officers were: F. Heine and F. Kiel (elders), and Adam Brueck and Christian Meyer (deacons), H. Moeller and Chr. Schroeder (trustees).

They had Pastor and teacher in young Frederick Koestering whom Pastor S. F. Stock, in historical records, calls a gifted, zealous, and faithful pastor and teacher. The building doubled for worship and school. Soon they needed a better location. At a meeting held March 19, 1854, they decided to erect a building, 32 feet by 22 feet, on Moeller Road just a few hundred feet east of Meyer Road. Again, each supplied two logs, one of each length. Frederick Boese erected the building for $41.00. A white frame church was erected in 1870. In 1885, a brick parsonage was added. In 1858, Pastor Koestering accepted a call elsewhere. Pastor J. George Streckfuss, of Trinity Lutheran Church on Decatur Road, served Trinity and Martini together. Installed on July 4, 1858, he served for two years. The third Pastor Martin Stephan, assistant at St. Paul's, was installed on April 22, 1860. He served and taught through the hardships of the Civil War. Still the congregation prospered. In August 1865 he accepted a call to New York. Pastor Zagel served the vacancy until S. Ferdinand Stock, from St. Louis Seminary, accepted Martini's call. Ordained and installed July 8, 1866, he taught school until 1875 when Theo. Kuechle, was called and taught until August 26, 1877. Rudolph Mueller remained Martini's teacher until 1909. He resigned due to ailing health. Mr. Wm. Widenhoefer taught until he was called to Ohio in 1918.

Martini Lutheran Church

On July 9, 1916 Pastor Stock celebrated 50 years. Because of poor health he resigned on July 6, 1919. The fifth Pastor, August Buuck, was installed September 7, 1919 and served until 1945. Also in 1919, Mr. Albert H. Meyer accepted a call to teach in Martini's school, now a one-room brick building. Mr. Meyer served from November 16, 1919 for thirty-two years. During this time, electricity and water were added. In July 1950 it was resolved to join sister congregations, Emanuel, New Haven, and St. Paul's, Gar Creek, to build Central Lutheran School in New Haven. April 1952, Mr. Meyer started at the new school.

In November of 1945, Pastor Buuck resigned due to age. The sixth Pastor, Otto Marschke, was installed on Sunday, November 4, 1945. Pastor Marschke held services in English and German until June 28, 1964 when he retired. Pastor Ronald Michel accepted as the seventh Pastor. He was installed on April 25, 1965 but resigned on December 31, 1966 due to illness. Rev. E.D. Busch served the vacancy. The eighth pastor, Pastor Donald Rauhut, was installed on May 21, 1967 and served until February 1971 when he was released to start Shepherd of the City Mission Church. Martini had grown and needed a new building. They decided it should be east of the present church, away from industry. Ground breaking was on August 21, 1966. Participating were Pastor Marschke; Otto Seddelmeyer, building chairman; Raymond Kinder, Kinder Co.; and a member from each group of the congregation. The cornerstone was laid on June 11, 1967 on eight acres bought from Stratton/Koehlinger with 560-ft. frontage on Moeller Road. The last worship service in the old church was October 29, 1967. The congregation worshiped there for 97 years. The new church was dedicated on November 5, 1967. In the morning dedication service Professor Breljie of Concordia Senior College preached. Rev. Rauhut, Rev. Michel, and Rev. Marschke assisted. The organist was Mrs. Gerald Bremer, who with her husband, taught at Central L.S., and were assigned to Martini.

Under Pastor Michel and Pastor Rauhut, the church grew rapidly. Vacation bible School was held in Meadowbrook School in 1965 and was attended by 105 students. In 1968, Vacation Bible School was held in Meadowbrook School with 196 students attending. Only 43 were from Martini. Communicant membership had grown at this time to 304, with baptized members at 467. Pastor Rauhut and Ludella Wiese started a Sunday school class for the mentally challenged, and there were between 10-15 attending. Most were later baptized and confirmed.

The ninth Pastor, Edwin B. Bishop, accepted a call October 10, 1971. In 1976, the tenth Anniversary of the new church, and in 1978, the 125th anniversary of Martini congregation were celebrated. He asked for a peaceful release on February 1, 1980. Pastor Daniel Reunig, Professor at Concordia Seminary, was vacancy pastor. The tenth Pastor, Herbert Gerken of Rockford, Illinois accepted Martini's call, was installed on April 5, 1981, and still serves Martini.

On November 3, 1985 Martini praised God as they burned the mortgage.

Pastor Gerken's 25 years of service were honored on October 13, 1991 with a Service, meal, and program.

From November 2003 through November 2004, Martini celebrated 150 years. Past teachers still active in the church are Mr. Fay Richert, retired Principal, organist; and Theodore Meyer, retired teacher, organist; and Barbara Johnson, teacher, and current organist. Three teachers, who currently serve the congregation and teach at Central Lutheran School, are Mr. Donald Wichman, Mrs. Deborah Schmidt, and Mrs. Janet Hayward. *Submitted by Patricia Augenstein, member since 1956*

Memorial Baptist Church
2900 North Anthony Boulevard, Fort Wayne

The Memorial Baptist Church came into being when in June 1944, steps were taken to organize a new church of the Baptist faith to serve the northeast section of Fort Wayne. (A significant note of historical context places this date within days of the massive World War II D-Day invasion of Normandy, France by the Allied Expeditionary Forces. The fact that the United States had at this time been involved in the war effort both at home and abroad for over two and one-half years would seem to have been an amazing moment in history to undertake the establishment of a new church.)

This new church on Fort Wayne's northeast side would be affiliated with the Indiana Baptist and American Baptist Churches (then known as the Northern Baptist Convention). Twenty family units consisting of some seventy-five individuals, led by Dr. T. J. Parsons the founding pastor, constituted the original founding members. After having held Sunday evening services for the first few weeks in the Forest Park Boulevard home of one of the first charter members, a store front building on the corner of Kentucky and Tennessee avenues was rented and made into a chapel. Throughout the next few months the members of a location committee used up much of their combined war-era gasoline ration coupons to make a thorough survey of locations before the site at Anthony Boulevard and Kenwood Avenue was purchased. The entire 2900 block facing North Anthony Boulevard was purchased for the then princely sum of $11,700. To record that this site cost was completely paid for in six months time shows the spirit of this original group of members. In April 1946, at a cost of $54,337, the church completed the basement portion of their building and relocated to their present location. This basement facility served for twelve years as their church home. For many years, passers by along Anthony Boulevard knew and referred to Memorial as being "the basement church". The Sanctuary was constructed in 1958 at a cost of $115,728. Within two years plans were being drawn and preparations underway for the addition of the Education wing of the building. This third building program, in just fifteen years, doubled the size of the facility. Built at a cost of $259,911, and dedicated in 1966, this addition completed the church edifice as it continues to exist today.

Memorial Baptist Church

During the ministries of A. J. Esperson, Donald W. Lane and M. Richard Mitchell, Memorial Baptist's quick and vigorous growth occurred during the 1950s and 1960s as her location placed her on the outer edge of Fort Wayne's rapid geographic expansion. At that time the Allen County War Memorial Coliseum, Northcrest Shopping Center and Glenbrook Mall were built and a Regional Fort Wayne Indiana-Purdue University Extension Campus was being established. The now congested traffic artery of Coliseum Boulevard was then just a two lane road surrounded on both sides by large tracts of undeveloped farm land. In the early 1960s, Memorial established one of the area's first State of Indiana accredited Weekday Nursery School programs. For many years this program continued through the enthusiastic and vigorous support of the community and neighborhood. In subsequent years, the city's center of expansion moved miles farther out northeast as well as to the southwest. Still Memorial Baptist, seasoned and matured with age, continues her Christian service and ministry of consecration and outreach.

Throughout the intervening years the church has been served by five subsequent pastors, the current being Rev. David A. Mitchell, since 1999. The church celebrated its Fiftieth Anniversary in 1994 having retired and ceremoniously "burned" all outstanding mortgages two years earlier in 1992. Memorial's Diamond (60th) Anniversary, achieved in 2004, represents the most recent milestone of significance in the church's history.

Memorial Baptist continues in her commitment to a balanced ministry of celebrating in worship ... caring for one another ... cultivating the fullest spiritual life possible ... communicating God's truth at every opportunity; believing that the gospel calls all Christians to a strong commitment to Christ and to active Christian service throughout both the community and the world.

Memorial Baptist Church may mean many different things to different people, yet, to any who know its membership, it must mean determination and dedication to the worship and service of God. Characteristic of its fellowship, Memorial Baptist continues to display both a cross and a faith big enough to symbolize and to proclaim the power of Almighty God to save the whole world!

Nine Mile United Methodist Church

The Indianapolis Trail was the first to be surveyed as a road in Pleasant Township. Following the Indianapolis Road nine miles southwest from the courthouse in Fort Wayne, where a blacksmith shop, a grocery store and post office were located, is the town of Nine Mile.

A church was organized January 3, 1853 at the home of John Miller by Rev. Casey with 16 charter members. One acre of ground was sold by Daniel Buskirk and wife Lucy Ann, for $10.00 to the trustees of the United Brethren Church. For a period of five years the meetings were held in the homes of various members. In 1859 they erected a log church just west of the present building in Section 7, Pleasant Township. Rev. P. Landon was then the pastor and dedicated the church.

In 1868 a frame building was erected, being named Liberty Chapel. It was served through the Ossian circuit until 1869 when it changed to the Zanesville circuit.

The first Christian Endeavor Society at Liberty was organized in 1904 by Alonzo Nicodemus (later Rev.) and Doctor King, a medical doctor.

A new foundation was made in 1906 to where the frame building was moved and turned east and west. An adjoining room was added to the south. Stained glass windows were added. The building was brick and concrete veneered and was dedicated.

Across the road a parsonage of brick veneer was built in 1927. This building cost $9,000 plus many donated hours by devoted members and was dedicated. The church was made the Nine Mile charge by the conference.

A man came through the community hunting work in 1928 and while working on the Daniel Buskirk farm it was discovered he was an artist. In Germany, his grandfather had sent him to art school. He agreed to paint a picture for the church and the result was a large picture of "Christ before Pilate" painted by Louis Nelson in 1931. An offering was received and given to him which totaled $37.00. The masterpiece still adorns the sanctuary and is worth the viewing.

In 1935 the hot air furnace was replaced with a steam heating plant. A new coal bin was added.

The Evangelical and United Brethren in Christ denominations joined hands to become the Evangelical United Brethren Church on November 17, 1946.

In 1948 the need for more Sunday school rooms became apparent. An army barracks from Baer Field was purchased and torn down by the men of the church. This was used to create an educational unit of five rooms, a nursery, and restrooms. The sanctuary was replastered, pews refinished, new carpet laid, and indirect lighting installed. The project was completed and dedicated April 16, 1950, at a cost of $20,000. During the year of 1954 the attic room was finished to be used as a classroom and named "The Upper Room".

"Christ before Pilate" painted by Louis Nelson in 1931

The main structure and belfry was refaced with limestone. Also a new entrance to the sanctuary and basement were added and dedicated on May 8, 1960.

In 1956 a new piano and electric organ were purchased.

More classrooms were created in the basement. The old southwest entrance was closed to make a nursery in 1964.

In June 1968, a Wurlitzer organ was purchased. Also the United Methodist Church was formed by the joining of the Evangelical United Brethren Church and the Methodist denomination.

In 1972 the sanctuary and foyer were improved. New pews with gold padded seats were placed in the sanctuary ($4,000). A half bath and laundry room were added to the parsonage in 1975 at a cost of $4,500. Other improvements have been made through the years.

April 2005, a handicap lift, installed at the old southwest entrance making all three levels accessible, was dedicated.

Nine Mile has produced seven ministers through the years and supported various home and foreign missionaries. At the present time in 2005 the church is supporting "The Wings of the Morning" mission in Africa.

Nine Mile United Methodist Church

North Christian Church (Disciples of Christ)

5201 Camden Drive, Fort Wayne

North Christian Church of Fort Wayne, Indiana had its first worship service and church school at the downtown YMCA on January 1, 1956 with the Reverend Robert T. Beck as pastor. One hundred people were present.

On Easter Sunday, April 12, 1959, the church moved into the first unit of a planned three unit facility on 4 1/2 acres in the Northcrest Addition, located in a growing north central area of Fort Wayne. The first unit of the facility included a fellowship hall, an office, a kitchen, several classrooms, and a maintenance area.

With the steady growth of the congregation and its programs, the educational unit of classrooms, chapel, storage units, and more was constructed in 1967, and the original unit was remodeled.

The sanctuary, the third unit, was built and occupied in 1974. The completed three units enclosed a beautiful courtyard which has been used for outdoor worship, weddings, and a place for reflection and prayer.

North Christian Church has always observed the Disciples traditions of open communion every Sunday, of baptism by immersion, and of working with others for Christian unity.

The church is an active participant of the Associated Churches of Fort Wayne and Allen County and houses one of its food banks on the premises. Congregational members have served on Associated Churches board of directors and participated in numerous ministry projects and ecumenical worship services.

North Christian is well known for its preschool and daycare ministry, now in its 32nd year. In the fall of 2002 a full-day Kindergarten was added to the program and is enjoying great academic success.

There is a very active Christian Women's Fellowship (CWF) at the church. Bible studies, Junior Worship, and a seniors group also give opportunities for spiritual growth and fellowship. The church has made its facilities available to various community groups including scouts, TOPS, an aerobics class and Northcrest Little League events.

Pastors serving North Christian have been: Robert T. Beck (1956-until his death in 1961); R. LaVerne Ervin (1962-1976); James Kendall (1978-1981); David McCracken (1981 -1988); and John L. Vickrey (1989-2004).

The Reverend Rolland G. Pfile is currently serving as Interim Senior Minister of the congregation. The congregation is in the process of examining its future ministry for the next decade.

Sunday worship is at 9:30 a.m. Saturday informal worship is at 6:00 p.m.

Dedication Day of 1st unit of North Christian Church in 1959.

North Christian Church Sanctuary, 2005.

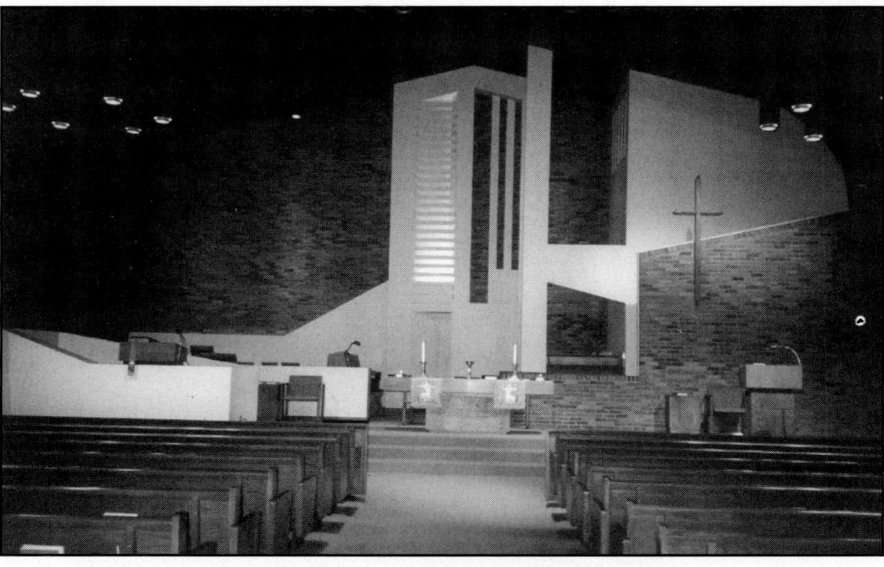

Inside the North Christian Church Sanctuary.

North Scipio United Methodist Church

According to available records, the North Scipio Church began as a result of meetings held in 1840 by the Rev. Benjamin Dorsey who was a local Methodist preacher. Mr. Dorsey was born in England in 1786 and came to this country in 1830. He was a wagon maker by trade who lived first in Ohio before settling in Scipio Township in Indiana. After moving to this area, he realized that it was important to have a church to honor God and for the purpose of spiritual reinforcement, social contact, and Christian fellowship. In 1841, the first log church was built on land in an angle between Campbell Road and the "Ridge Road" (which is known today as State Road 37). Sometime later, between 1860 and 1880, this log structure was replaced by a frame church on the same site.

North Scipio 1860 Church

The land where the church currently stands was given to the church by Mr. McClain McCurdy and his wife Sarah (Dorsey) McCurdy for "as long as worship services continue to be held." This generous contribution provided room for a larger brick structure dedicated in 1898, which is the front sanctuary part of the current church building. Almost 100 years later, on July 19, 1997, the church then purchased from the McCurdy Family 3.6 acres of land immediately to the south of the church.

Outside, the church building looked the same for many years, but many building improvements continued to take place through the years...in 1937 gas lights were replaced with electric lights. In 1952, (when North Scipio changed from the Spencerville Circuit to the Harlan Circuit) the chancel floor was raised one step and a new oil furnace replaced the unsafe coal furnace. In 1970, a restroom was added in the entry area and in 1974, new pews were installed. In 1999, central air conditioning was installed, and in 2000 a wheelchair accessible ramp to the front entrance was built. Then, as the congregation looked toward future ministry opportunities, a ground breaking ceremony was held on November 10, 2002 for a new church building addition. It includes a fellowship hall, large kitchen, classrooms, office, restrooms, and a wheelchair accessible covered carport entry. This building addition was dedicated on Sunday, October 5, 2003 with 200 people attending the worship service, the dedication ceremony, and a carry-in dinner.

Although the history of the North Scipio Church building is interesting and important, it is the building's purpose that is most important...for it was and continues to be a place where people gather for Christian worship, weddings, funerals, Bible studies, Vacation Bible School, Christmas programs, children and youth activities, and many other ministry and fellowship activities. There are so many important, interesting, and life-changing stories of individuals and groups. From 1840 to 2005, eighty ministers have served the church and countless people have volunteered their time and talents as leaders, teachers, musicians, caretakers, and community outreach volunteers. The church continues to be involved in activities and fund raising that benefit the community such as Harlan Days, Harlan Youth Center, Habitat for Humanity, Fort Wayne Rescue Mission, and Operation Classroom to name just a few. On July 30, 2000, the North Scipio United Methodist Church congregation celebrated the church's 160th anniversary of ministry in Allen County...and it continues to this day to be a place of light and hope not only on State Road 37, but most importantly on Life's highway. North Scipio United Methodist Church is truly a place "where good things are happening!"

North Scipio Current Church

Our Hope Lutheran Church & School
1826 Trinity Drive Huntertown

Welcome to Our Hope Lutheran Church in Huntertown, Indiana. The following is the history of how we began and how we have grown over the last 42 years.

Following a religious census in Huntertown and the surrounding areas by the Greater Fort Wayne Association of Lutheran Churches, Lutheran families of the area met and held their first worship service on November 10, 1963. With 65 people in attendance, the first worship service was conducted in the old Huntertown Library, now the Town Hall. Pastor Harold Ott of Trinity Lutheran Church in Fort Wayne presided over the service.

By the first Sunday in December, worship attendance had grown to 84, necessitating a search for a larger facility. On December 9, 1963 the congregation chose its name and accepted the Constitution, as suggested by Dr. William Birkener, Secretary of the Mission Board. An empty store building located one block north of the library was rented. The first service was held there on December 22, 1963.

Our Hope Lutheran Church was taken into membership of the Lutheran Church - Missouri Synod on June 16, 1964. Communicant membership was 51.

Rev. Philip Schroeder of the Concordia Lutheran High School faculty and Dr. Warren Rubel, professor at Concordia Senior College, conducted worship services until Vicar Thomas Hammond was appointed to serve during the summer of 1964. Then, following a call to the Board of Assignments of the Synod, Rev. Richard Gahl, of the graduating class of 1965 became the first full-time pastor. He was installed on August 1, 1965 and served as pastor until September 1970.

Our Hope then searched for land on which to build a church. 16 acres were purchased at 1826 Trinity Drive in Huntertown, Indiana. The cornerstone laying took place on September 15, 1968. Our Hope held its first worship service in its new building on December 8, 1968.

Various pastors have served Our Hope over the years. The Rev. Ed Folkening was installed in February 1971 and served until January 1978. Then in February 1979, Rev. Philip Schoenherr was installed as pastor and served until March 1988. From March 1988 until January 1995, Our Hope was under the leadership of Rev. Timothy Anderson.

By 1983, the membership had grown, demonstrating the need to add more space. In April 1986 a ground breaking ceremony took place and the dedication of the expanded facility followed in November 1986. The addition included a formal chancel extension of the worship area, pews, and carpeting, fellowship hall with dividers for extra classrooms, youth room expanded entrance, redecorated library/ lounge and restructured storage areas.

Following the departure of Rev. Anderson, the Rev. Philip Schamehorn was placed as vacancy pastor until August 1996 when he received a call by Our Hope to become their full time pastor. Rev. Schamehorn was installed on August 18, 1996. He was raised in the greater Detroit area and worked for Ford Motor Company before leaving to continue his education and become a pastor. He received his Master of Divinity degree and the PhD in Missiology degree from Concordia Theological Seminary in Fort Wayne. He lives in Fort Wayne with his wife Martha and their son Phil.

In the fall of 1998, Our Hope began a preschool program, showing the church's commitment to Christian Education. Preschool began with five children. Today, Our Hope Preschool has over 80 children enrolled. In 1999 a Parent's Day Out program was started for children ages 1-3. This program gives parents a chance to do errands while their child is in a caring and learning environment.

As the preschool grew, so did talk about starting an elementary school and the need for a larger building to house classrooms. In 2000 a committee was formed to investigate beginning a school and a building committee was formed to choose an architect. In 2001, a new 15,000 square foot school building was built at a cost of over $600,000. This addition includes a large Family Activity Center, school offices, six classrooms, computer lab, kitchen, and storage space. Our Hope Lutheran Church & School now offers a Christian Elementary Education for children through the fifth grade with an additional grade added each year. In 2003 enough funds were raised to purchase a large playground set for the children.

On March 6, 2005 a worship service was held in our Family Activity Center to dedicate our new Contemporary Worship Facility. With the help of a grant from the Lutheran Foundation, a collapsible stage, an automated screen, and sound system were purchased for use in our contemporary services. Now those who enjoy the contemporary service can do so much easier.

Our Hope has grown to over 330 communicant members with the blessings of the Holy Spirit and will continue to be strong in the work of the Lord and committed to the spreading of the Gospel.

Our Lady of Good Hope Catholic Church

In 1969, with the rapid growth of the northeast Fort Wayne area, Bishop Leo Pursley saw a need for a new parish between St. Charles and St. Vincent. Fr. William Hodde was appointed founding pastor and set about forming the new church. Albert and Mary Poinsatte gifted the Diocese about 10 acres of land on St. Joe Road for the church. Much of this area had once belonged to Miami Indian Chief Richardville, including what is now Riverbend Golf Course. On this property was a farmhouse built around 1860 that was at one time, the Poinsatte's home. The house was remodeled and Fr. Hodde moved in.

The name, Our Lady of Good Hope, was chosen for the church because the Poinsattes had a great devotion to Mary, the Mother of Jesus. They requested the parish be named for her. The new parish met for Sunday Masses in Bishop Dwenger High School cafeteria from October 1969 to August 1972. Weekday Masses and baptisms were celebrated in a small chapel above the rectory garage. Weddings and funerals took place at St. Charles and St.Vincent parishes.

Our Lady of Good Hope was formed with 295 families. The first Steering Committee members were Mr. and Mrs. Herb Mettler, Tom Butler, Bernard Centlivre, Paul Faylor, Stan Fisher Jr., Bob Moeller and Leroy McAbee. It took a year to complete the church building. The first Mass was celebrated on August 13, 1972. The church was formally dedicated by Bishop Pursley the following May. The building committee included Bernie Niezer, Stan Fisher Jr., Jack Paul, Bob Spice, Alan Fritz and James Kinder. Bob Feeley acted as chairman. Mr. Feeley also made the altars and other sanctuary furnishings.

Almost immediately, the parishioners realized that due to rapid growth more room was needed. They began planning for Phase II. By 1977, Fr. Hodde had overseen the fundraising necessary and the construction of expanded seating in the church, ten classrooms for religious education, offices, a library and an expanded recreation hall. After 12 years Fr. Hodde had done his task and the parish was well established. Bishop William McManus then appointed Fr. Hodde to St. Thomas Parish in Elkhart, Indiana.

When Fr. Lawrence Kramer was named the second pastor of Our Lady in July 1981, there were 700 member families. During the 16 years of Fr. Kramer's pastorate, the parish population grew to 1,100 families. He oversaw Phase III, the expansion of the education wing and the addition of day-care, pre-school and kindergarten programs. Although the parish does not have an elementary school, it does have an active religious education program for elementary age children and a Youth Ministry program for high school students.

Bishop John D'Arcy appointed Fr. Kramer to St. Joseph parish in Bluffton Indiana. The third pastor, Fr.David Voors, was named in June of 1997. He had previously served at St. Michael in Plymouth, Indiana.

In her thirty-fifth year, Our Lady of Good Hope, under the guidance of Fr. Voors, remains a faithful and caring community of the Catholic Church.

Peace Evangelical Lutheran Church And School
4900 Fairfield Avenue, Fort Wayne

Although Peace Lutheran Church was formally organized on January 27, 1946 and joined The Lutheran Church-Missouri Synod that summer, its origin began some twenty years before. Emmaus Lutheran Church on Broadway had operated a branch parochial school since 1923 at property on Lexington Street between Harrison and Webster Streets. Members of Emmaus who lived on the south side of Fort Wayne and had children in the branch school discussed during those years forming a daughter congregation nearer to where they lived. When the branch school was closed, proceeds from the property sale were designated for use by a new congregation, with the stipulation that it must be south of Pettit Avenue and started by the end of 1945.

In June 1945, the south-side families quickly planned. When builder John Worthman purchased a 100 acre farm southwest of Fairfield and Pettit avenues from Mrs. Nellie Wood, she first arranged to sell about three acres at the north-east point of the land, now known as the Woodhurst sub-division, to the forming congregation for only $100.

On November 25, 1945, 107 people gathered at the Sears Pavilion in Foster Park for worship. Subsequent services were conducted by retired Pastor W. C. Meinzen at the Jefferson Community Center, once at the corner of Jefferson and Ewing Streets, now the site of a McDonald's restaurant. Charter members of the congregation in 1946 included the families of Theodore Fuelling, Harry Grote, Edward Lebrecht, Herman Melcher, Edwin Moellering, Jacob Schaefer, Edward Schroeder, Lawrence Springer, Henry Volmerding, Albert Wehmeyer, and Lester Zollinger. The congregation numbered 104 baptized members.

On September 8, 1946 the Rev. Edgar H. Albers became the congregation's first full-time pastor. During his pastorate of nine years, a combined chapel and classroom building designed by Milwaukee architect Mr. Hugo Haeuser and with Fred H. Grote and Son as the general contractor, was built on the Fairfield site. A new parochial school of only the first four grades, with Mr. Carl Bloedel as teacher, began to use a room in the still uncompleted building in the fall of 1948. The chapel/school was then dedicated on June 12, 1949. That September the school began to offer eight grades with added teachers and had Mr. Theodore Beckler as its principal until 1958.

Pastor Albers accepted a pastorate in Southport, Indiana in 1955 and the Rev. Hartwig M. Schwehn became Peace's pastor on February 19, 1956. Greatly increased membership by 1960 called for the construction of a larger sanctuary. It was designed by Charles Stade and Associates of Parkview, Illinois, and was attached to the north end of the original building. General contractor C. Doenges and Son began work at the end of 1961; and the new church, with large areas of stained glass designed and fabricated at City Glass of Fort Wayne, was dedicated on March 17, 1963. On November 17, 1963, a 23 rank pipe organ manufactured by The Tellers Organ Company of Erie, PA was dedicated. Pastor Schwehn died of a heart attack on July 4, 1968. At the end of his twelve and a half years as pastor, the membership of the congregation numbered over 1,100 members.

The Rev. Luther G. Strasen was installed as the next pastor on November 17, 1968 and served for twenty-eight years. In September of 1968, Peace and Redeemer Lutheran Church on Rudisill Avenue began an arrangement that unified their resources and facilities to form Peace-Redeemer Lutheran School, with an enrollment of 235 students. Mount Calvary Lutheran Church in Waynedale joined the school in September 1973 and the name of the school was changed to Unity Lutheran School, with classes held in all three of the congregations' buildings. Redeemer Lutheran Church elected not to participate in the inter-parish school after the 1976-77 school year. Plans were advanced in 1981 to add a library and gymnasium to the south end of the Peace school building, but were abandoned that July when the Fort Wayne Community School announced the sale of its South Calhoun elementary school. Peace congregation purchased the campus so that all of the Unity School classes began meeting in the South Calhoun building in the fall of 1982. Subsequent principals of the parochial school were Messers Floyd Rogner (1958-1971), Wayne Clements (1971-1977), Raymond Rosenthal (1977-1979), Will Neumeyer (1979-1987), Richard Brune (1987-2001) and Mrs. Joyce Pixley (2001-2005).

After Pastor Strasen retired in 1996, Pastor James R. Teasdale became the pastor of the congregation on November 30, 1997. During his pastorate, a ministry to the growing Hispanic community was initiated and a vibrant youth ministry flourished. In 2005 the congregation continued to proclaim the Gospel of Jesus Christ. Its mission stated: "Peace Lutheran Church is here to serve the faithful and reach the lost through Word and Sacrament ministry."

Plymouth Congregational Church of Fort Wayne

On September 20, 1870, twenty-six persons--ten men and sixteen women--were received as charter members of Plymouth Congregational Church. Rev. John B. Fairbank was called as the first pastor on October 24, 1870, and in December the church held its first communion service under its own pastor.

Initially, services were conducted in the German Methodist Church building on the northeast corner of Washington and Fulton Streets. On September 3, 1871, the congregation dedicated its own building on the northwest corner of Washington and Fulton Streets. The church was illuminated with oil lamps and heated with a wood-burning furnace. Later, gas was used for lighting.

The 1890s were years of growth, and the second building was constructed in 1893 at the corner of Harrison and Jefferson streets. The young organization had barely entered upon its existence when a period of financial depression occurred. In common with other religious organizations, the church entered into almost every activity which would develop Christian patience and also bring in some money. There were home socials, sewing societies, church dinners, Japanese weddings, strawberry festivals, and excursions to Chicago and Rome City. The boys of the church even put in a garden behind the church building and sold the produce from the garden to do their share in contributing to church funds.

After reaching the capacity of the building at Jefferson and Harrison, the Cressler home on the corner of Berry and Fairfield was purchased in 1916, and the present limestone church was built. The cornerstone was set on August 26, 1923, and construction was completed in 1924.

Vincent Slater became director of music in 1948, and in 1951 an Aeolian-Skinner pipe organ was purchased from a church in New York City.

By 1955, when the congregation numbered more than 2000, the building was filled to overflowing. A remodeling program completed in May 1957 included an enlarged religious education building with a new youth center and a remodeled and redecorated sanctuary.

By congregational vote on November 29, 1960, Plymouth Church became a part of the United Church of Christ (UCC). The UCC is one of the most diverse Christian churches in the United States. Along with the sacraments of Baptism and Holy Communion, doing justice, seeking peace, and building community are central to the UCC's identity. UCC churches affirm that Christians can live together in communion without always agreeing with one another.

Plymouth Church has had outstanding pastors including Charles Folsom (1910-1933), Charles Houser (1933-1944), Elmer Voelkel (1945-1960), Lawrence Fairchild (1961-1973), Richard Stanger (1974-1988), Thomas Dicken (1989-1997), and currently John P. Gardner who was called in 1998. Ordained clergy who shared the ministerial leadership include Edward Ouellette, William Howenstein, Larry Loving, Leonard Ebel, Greig Ritchie, Nicholas Natelli, Paul Koons, Kenneth Childs, Howard Brown, Philip Schairbaum, Stephanie Weiner, David Young, Clare Walter, Dale Susan Edmonds, Jeane Spoor, and currently Ruth E. Phillips who was called in 2001.

Plymouth Church is exceptional in its commitment and dedication. The people of Plymouth are active participants in many community affairs as well as donors of many hours given to church projects. The congregation is among the first to try what is new and innovative. Rev. Stephanie Weiner (called in 1976) was the first woman pastor in Fort Wayne, and Rev. Dale Susan Edmonds (called in 1984) was the first African-American woman to serve what was then an all-white congregation. Carole Green in 1984 was elected as Plymouth's first woman moderator (presiding officer).

An article in The Journal Gazette (September 2, 1995) referring to the 125th anniversary of Plymouth Church stated, "Over the years, Plymouth has been known in Fort Wayne as both a patron of the arts and of social justice. The dual emphasis is reflected in two of its best known annual activities, the Boar's Head and Yule Log Festival ... and the Martin Luther King Jr. Memorial Service of Repentance and Reconciliation hosted by Plymouth under the sponsorship of Associated Churches of Fort Wayne and Allen County and the Interdenominational Ministerial Alliance."

The congregation voted to be identified as open and affirming in May 2001 and national recognition of that status was given at the UCC General Synod in July 2001.

Along with other significant property enhancements, the sanctuary was completely renovated in 2004, and a porte cochere was added to facilitate access to the building. The renovation also included replacement of the pipe organ with a custom-designed, state-of-the-art digital organ that is the largest in the state. Under the leadership of Robert Nance, organist and director of music, Plymouth continues to build on its tradition of exceptional musical programming.

Plymouth Church recognizes each individual as a child of God and believes all are called to be one reconciled body of Christ with many members. In its diversity, Plymouth Church finds strength and a way to understand the inclusiveness of God.

The church in 1871.

Porte Cochere added in 2004.

Redeemer Lutheran Church

Redeemer Lutheran Church was founded as the first English speaking Lutheran Church in Fort Wayne in 1892. At the time the predominant language of Lutheran Churches in Fort Wayne was German. Redeemer's members wanted to hold to the doctrinal heritage of their fathers, but be fully American in culture and language as well as welcome people who were not of German ancestry.

Eleven charter members (William Spiegel, Henry Ehle, R.C. Reinewald, Herman Kucher, Henry Salge, Charles Bente, William Kirchner, William Klingman, H. G. Steup, John Christlieb, and Thomas Baxter) formed Redeemer Lutheran Church. Services were held on Sunday evenings alternately at St. Paul's Lutheran Church and Emmanuel Lutheran Church until a building was purchased from Plymouth Congregational Church on Washington Boulevard and Fulton Street later that year. The church joined the English Lutheran Synod of Missouri, Ohio and other States, which then became the English District of the Lutheran Church–Missouri Synod in 1911.

The first pastor of Redeemer Lutheran Church, the Reverend C.F.W. Meyer, served Redeemer from 1893 to 1902. Then the Reverend Theodore Hahn accepted the call and served Redeemer as pastor from 1903 to 1910. In 1911, the Reverend J. R. Graebner became pastor of Redeemer, and it was during his ministry at Redeemer that plans for a new church building began. The plans began in 1920, with land at the corner of Rudisill Boulevard and Harrison Street purchased in 1922. A contract was signed with W. A. Sheets construction in 1923 to follow the plans for a new church building according to the architectural plans of Riebel Sons and Matheny of Columbus, Ohio. The cornerstone for this building was laid on July 1, 1923, and the building was finally dedicated on June 1, 1924. Rev. Graebner accepted another call in 1923, prior to the completion of the building, and the Reverend C. W. Baer became Redeemer's new pastor that same year overseeing the final touches to Redeemer's current sanctuary. In the dedication bulletin for the new building, a paragraph of appreciation was written for the building committee, comprised of the following members: C. E. Strasburg, Chairman; William Moeller; Charles Bleke; Harry Baals; H.G. Steup; Oscar Bender; Herman Rippe; Edward Spiegel; E.W. Hickman; William Eisenacher; Pastor C. W. Baer; Carl S. Steup; Charles Adams; Elmer Pierson; Charles Kierspe.

The original building of the Redeemer Lutheran Church.

The church was complete, and the ministry of Redeemer continued in its new location. On May 29, 1941 the congregation was grieved by the death of their pastor. Rev. Erwin Kurth became the new pastor in the same year. Rev. Kurth stayed until 1951, when he left and the Reverend Herbert Lindemann accepted the call to Redeemer. Rev. Lindemann was Redeemer's pastor for almost twenty-five years, when he accepted another call, and the Reverend Charles Evanson came to Redeemer in 1975. Rev. Evanson left when he accepted a call to be deployed to Lithuania to be a professor there after twenty-five years at Redeemer. When Rev. Evanson left in the year 2000, the Reverend Daniel Reuning, Kantor of Redeemer Lutheran Church, served as vacancy pastor until the Reverend David H. Petersen accepted the call to become the pastor of Redeemer Lutheran Church in September of 2000.

Redeemer's sanctuary itself has several interesting points. The three bells of Redeemer were made by St. Louis Bell Foundry and weigh 2780 pounds. The tones of FAC rang for the first time on April 20, 1924 on Easter Sunday, before the actual dedication of the building itself. These bells continue to sound in the bell tower today. The windows of Redeemer were created in the Von Gerichton Ecclesiastic Studios in Munich Bavaria, Germany, and Columbus, Ohio. The colors were burned/baked into the glass. The windows on the north side of the nave were given as memorials, and the windows on the south side were given in gratitude and appreciation. The big east window was given in memory of Mr. and Mrs. Gottlieb Brudi by Mr. and Mrs. Frank Sthair. This window "is a true copy of the famous picture, Jesus, the Good Shepherd." The first organ at Redeemer was built in 1923 by Hillgreen, Lane and Company and donated by the Ladies' Aid. This organ served the church well for 35 years when the current Schlicker organ was built in 1958. This organ was revoiced in 1991 by Noack, and the organ currently has 26 Registers, 32 Stops, 38 Ranks, and 2015 Pipes. The organ was rededicated on November 3, 1991, celebrated with an organ recital by David Fienen, a former music director of Redeemer.

Interior of Redeemer Lutheran Church

Over the years, Redeemer Lutheran Church has had many faithful pastors to administer God's Word and Sacrament and provided many people with a place of worship. The church provides liturgical worship and faithful teaching for the Spanish-speaking community, too. The building is used by various groups and many of Redeemer's neighbors join us for social events. It is also home to the Bach Collegium-Fort Wayne under the direction of Dr. Daniel Reuning.

Fort Wayne Rescue Mission Ministries

Rescue Ministry began in 1903 in Fort Wayne by area Christians who were concerned about the inner city's poor, hungry, homeless, and un-churched. The original Fort Wayne Rescue Home and Mission was located at 118 East Columbia Street, near where the City-County Building now stands. Incorporation occurred in 1908. The Mission moved to 343 E. Columbia Street in 1915.

In 1922, the ministry also became a social service agency when it joined eleven others in forming the Community Chest (now United Way of Allen County). During the early years the Mission provided housing, food and religious services for both local and transient homeless men, as well as many youth programs and Sunday School activities.

In 1964 the Mission expanded its housing and feeding ministries when it moved to 301 West Superior Street. The Mission's Women and Children's Division was added in 1985 with a 16-bed facility at 710 West Superior Street.

In 1990 the Mission opened a large multi-purpose room for classes and worship services, offices and an on-site thrift store at its headquarters building. In 1992 an anonymous donor gave the Mission a building on Lafayette and DeWald Streets, which was developed for use as a second thrift store to bring in revenue to fund the Mission, but also to provide clothing and furnishings to the Mission's residents and offer low cost goods to the city's poor.

Vowing not to charge for its services or accept government funding, in 1989 the Mission began to use direct mail to raise funds, increasing the services offered. An early beneficiary from the increased funding was the educational program. In 1993 a state-of-the-art computer Learning Center opened at 326 W. Superior to provide men and women with the opportunity for educational advancement, lost memory restoration, adult literacy and computer skills, and GED exam preparation.

With more reliable funding, the Mission in 1994 was able to begin hiring a professional ministry and management team to face the double edged challenge of a homeless population that had grown increasingly younger (thus making their rehabilitation a major goal) and who came to the Mission with more complex problems.

January, 1995, began the intensive, residential six month program that required the participants to pursue the program full-time to effectively deal with whatever issues had resulted in their homelessness. The end outcome was to produce graduates who would be able to be "fully functioning members of society," as well as develop their relationship to a loving God. Later, long term and transitional programs were added.

The Women and Children's Division's reputation as a caring and loving place caused the facility to be outgrown. In 1996, a building at 533 West Washington Boulevard was purchased and renovated to accommodate up to 42 women and children for both emergency housing and restoration programming. It was given the name Charis (meaning Grace) House.

In 1999, remodeling expanded the Rescue Mission's computer learning center, class rooms, office space and handicapped accessible rest rooms.

In March of 2001, the Rescue Mission facilities were expanded again to accommodate the influx of homeless men who found themselves on the street due to the economic recession, doubling its Emergency Program capacity to 42 beds and ten cots for those needing housing for up to 30 nights.

In 2001, the Mission incorporated Fort Wayne Rescue Mission Ministries Foundation as a nonprofit endowment to insure the long-term financial viability of the ministries. The Board of Trustees of community leaders began approving grants to the ministries from the income generated by the Foundation's investments.

Wanting to reflect the ever-broadening ministries to a variety of audiences, the name was changed in 2004 to Rescue Ministries, encompassing the ministries of The Rescue Mission, Charis House, Bargains Galore, and other initiatives the Lord may open in the future.

Rescue Ministries works collaboratively with other organizations that provide a variety of needed social and medical services to the homeless and indigent population of Allen and surrounding counties. The Christian-based ministries welcome people of all faiths as well as those with no religious background. Approximately 45% of the total staff were once residents at Charis House or the Rescue Mission and are now helping others change as they did.

Rescue Ministries has a bed capacity to serve 154 men, women and children per night. The Rescue Mission and Charis House serve hundreds of different residents annually, who typically fill over 35,000 bed nights. Approximately 140,000 free meals are served to those in the community who come for lunch and dinner seven days a week, and to those who stay as residents.

After one hundred years of service, Fort Wayne Rescue Ministries still exists "to provide, through the power of Jesus Christ, a home for the homeless, food for the hungry, and hope for their future."

Fort Wayne Rescue Mission

Sacred Heart Parish 1947-2005

The first Sacred Heart Church.

Sacred Heart Parish was founded in the near Southeast neighborhood in 1947. In the succeeding 58 years of ministry it has experienced many changes in its service to the people, lately because of a shift in demographics.

Archbishop John F. Noll appointed Rev. Fred Westendorf to oversee the founding needed to care for the rapidly expanding membership. Ralph Shirmeyer donated a six-plot of ground at the corner of Gaywood and Capitol Avenues. Father Thomas Durkin was made first Pastor of the church, a converted hospital barracks moved there from the then known Baer Field. The parish men reconditioned the building and first Mass was held at midnight Christmas of 1948. Due to a building boom and growth, ground was broken in 1949 for an eight classroom, modern school to care for 800 families' needs. By 1954, the school was expanded to 16 classrooms, a library, a central office and storage rooms. The basement was used as a chapel to accommodate the overflow crowd at the church. Rev. Lawrence Gollner was pastor at the time.

In 1963, the old church was burned to make way for the present church. Parishioner and architect, James J. McCarron designed the new 660-seat church. Rev. Andrew Mathieu was pastor and Bishop Leo Pursley dedicated the church in 1964.

Holy Cross Sisters initially staffed the school; later the Sisters of St. Joseph and Sisters of Providence were engaged.

Pastors who have served Sacred Heart Parish since this time include: Reverend John Gillig 1972-1979, Reverend Robert Hammond 1979-1980, Reverend Patrick Durkin 1980-1987, Reverend James Seculoff 1987-1992, Reverend Phillip Widmann 1992-1994, Reverend Glen Kohrman 1994-1998, Reverend Thomas Shoemaker 1998-2001, Reverend Polycarp Fernando 2001-2003, Reverend Emmanuel Chikezie, 2003-present.

With the founding of St. Henry's parish, the aging of homes over the years, former residents gradually moving out, the declining enrollment and fewer nuns to staff the school, plans were made to merge Sacred Heart School within St. Henry's school building, which was renamed Benoit Academy. The last school year at Sacred Heart was 1993-94. It was not without a few tears that students and parishioners gave up their school but the financial debt was too great a burden.

On May 6, 1990, with approval of the Bishop, the Tridentine Latin Mass was offered at Sacred Heart and continues on Sundays and Holy days. Many younger families and their children are drawn to the solemn liturgy, the Gregorian chant and polyphony music.

Since 1998 the parish of 167 families today share pastor, Rev. Emmanuel Chikezie, the Mass, devotional schedules and youth ministry with St. Henry's.

The parish has a St. Vincent de Paul Society and hosts the active South Side Catholic Seniors once a month. The former 16 classrooms offer space for a combined Sacred Heart and St. Henry Church office, Catholic Charities, Christ Child Society, Franciscan Center outreach program, diocesan Archives, two groups of AA, Golden Heart 4-H club and recently added is CCD in conjunction with the Spanish Mass offered by Father Emmanuel Saturday evenings.

In this brief history, we must remember that the Sacred Heart of Jesus has accomplished much more than is recorded here. He has used priests, sisters and laity to do His work among His people. It is our prayer that Sacred Heart Parish remains faithful to the Catholic Church and members continue their spiritual growth through prayer, good works, and service to others.

Sacred Heart Church built in 1963.

Saint Elizabeth Ann Seton Catholic Church

St. Elizabeth Ann Seton Catholic Church in Fort Wayne.

If one in four residents in Aboite Township in Allen County is a Catholic – as the population demographics suggest at the turn of the twenty-first century – it also suggests the need for an exciting, vibrant and burgeoning parish with a large parking lot. It may be true that Catholics flock in numbers to their Eucharist-centered Masses, however, serving their spiritual and social demands requires a myriad of activities.

For Saint Elizabeth Ann Seton Catholic Church, it began in the late 1970s when Aboite Township people began talking about the need for a parish. Until that time, Aboite was part of St. Joseph Catholic Church in Fort Wayne. Families, however, were also choosing Mass schedules at St. Patrick in Arcola, St. Joseph in Roanoke or Cathedral of the Immaculate Conception downtown. Before population expansion of the area, it all seemed to be a satisfactory arrangement. Beginning in the summer of 1984, parish priests began traveling to a St. Joseph mission in Aboite when permission was granted to begin a Mass in Haverhill School. The neighborhood faithful responded, gathering together each Sunday morning in a large semicircle around a makeshift altar in the elementary school's auditorium. A year later Religious Education classes began in the school and in parishioners' homes.

Rapid increases in population continued. At last, Aboite Township learned of the news that Bishop John M. D'Arcy had announced that Rev. Robert C. Schulte was to be the founding pastor of a new parish to be called St. Elizabeth Ann Seton Catholic Church. On January 3, 1988, the feast of the Epiphany, the first Mass of the new parish was celebrated at Haverhill School with 375 families forming the new community.

Soon building and development committees were organized and a fund raising drive netted over $800,000 in pledges for the construction of a new church. On August 6, 1989, groundbreaking ceremonies took place in a donated crop field on the northeast corner of Aboite Center and Homestead Roads. Bishop D'Arcy led the congregation in prayer, followed with a single shovel of dirt that kicked off a major construction effort. On Saturday evening, September 8, 1990, the first Mass was celebrated in a new church that was not totally completed. Religious Education classes also began that weekend. The complex included a church, daily Mass chapel, Eucharistic chapel, parish hall that could serve as classrooms, and a parish office all surrounding a large gathering area. By the late September dedication, one half of the $2.2 million construction costs had been paid from offertory income and a substantial donation.

An additional fourteen acres of land was purchased in March 1992, east of the church, to allow for future expansion. By December 1994 ground was broken for the new rectory, which was completed on August 4, 1995.

As St. Elizabeth continued to grow in membership, interior space became critical. A 1995 study led to a February 15, 1998, dedication by Bishop D'Arcy. Included were a new ten classroom catechetical center, a new parish office center, an atrium for the Catechesis of the Good Shepherd, a new nursery, a music room and a church basement expansion. Renovated too was the church building, increasing seating capacity from 800 to 1,000 and the daily Mass Chapel was created in the former office area.

In 1997, the St. Joseph School administration proposed the sponsorship of a joint school. Because of the increasing enrollment on the St. Joseph campus, expanded by a large percentage of St. Elizabeth students, it was suggested that the St. Elizabeth Religious Education classrooms be used during the school day by kindergarten, first and second grade students, while the upper grades would remain at St. Joseph School. Both Rev. Schulte and Rev. Larry Tippman, pastor of St. Joseph Church, gained Bishop D'Arcy's approval to establish a joint school beginning with the 1998-99 school year. Two busses were purchased to facilitate transportation between the two campuses. By the end of the 2000 school year, over 400 students were enrolled.

Today, the St. Elizabeth Ann Seton Church parishioner base of 1,950 families, enjoy a myriad of programs and opportunities on a daily basis. More than 900 students are currently enrolled in Religious Education, which uses all available meeting spaces. The parish continues to grow with a net gain of about one hundred families each year amid requests for more adult education, bible study offerings and family events. A study indicates that growth will continue and a building and campus expansion campaign is currently underway to raise over $7 million.

Truly answering a need for a Catholic presence in the booming Aboite Township, St. Elizabeth is a beautiful setting for worshipping our Lord, learning about Christ, and celebrating God's love. *Submitted by Tom Castaldi*

Saint Henry Catholic Church Fort Wayne, Indiana
Established 1956

Die Geschichte! History!! Elbert Hubbard said that "It is not deeds or acts that last; it is the written record of those deeds and acts." What a wise decision to have St. Henry Catholic Church, Fort Wayne, Indiana, be part and parcel of the Allen County History Book project! More interesting is the fact that the Parish, established in 1956, celebrated her Golden Jubilee in 2006. Fifty Years of Solid Catholic Faith!

The Parish began in the south-eastern part of Allen County with the six acres of land donated by parishioners, late Benjamin W. and Marie Hoevel. Benjamin's father, Henry, had dreamed of seeing a Catholic Church on this site for many years. It seems most appropriate, then, that Henry Hoevel's grandson, Robert, be the first pastor of the new parish, and that the church be named after St. Henry (973-1024), Duke of Bavaria and Emperor of the Holy Roman Empire. The aforementioned Father Robert J. Hoevel was appointed as its first pastor on June 8, 1956. The spot chosen for the church and school was at the intersection of Hessen Cassel and Paulding Roads. At that time the area was just beginning to grow. It was feeling the effects of the rapid expansion in the southeast of Fort Wayne that came immediately after World War II. The parish began with 278 families and 185 children who were then attending Catholic grade schools in the area. There was a committed building committee, members who included Roy Westrick, Henry Hoevel, Albert Zuber, Richard Doster, Frank Young, Frank Helmsing and Ferd Kuentzel. The groundbreaking was on April 13, 1957. Architect James J. McCarron designed the three-floor combination church/school building to be built of reinforced concrete with lift slab construction. It was the first building of this type of construction to be erected in Fort Wayne. Using the lift slab method, the concrete floors were poured on the ground, one on top of the other, and then lifted into place. The construction of St. Henry's church and school attracted a good deal of local media attention in 1957. On October 8 of that year, Bishop Leo A. Pursley dedicated the church. And father Robert Hoevel celebrated the first Mass in the new church on Christmas Eve 1957. There was also the construction of a rectory, and a Convent that stood just north of the rectory, which housed the Sisters of St. Agnes. Joan and Gene Mount, one of the most dedicated couples of the parish, live in the former, first seven-bedroom convent, which they once shared with their seven children. St. Henry School opened with an enrollment of 248 pupils in grades one through six. Sister Mary Joellen, C.S.A., was the first principal of the school. The School will later be called Benoit Academy. In fact, in its first five years, it had 599 children enrolled in the school (747 by 1964), and nearly 500 families registered. By 1982, there were 775 families.

St. Henry Catholic Church

Among the priests from the parish is Fr. Richard Hire. Meanwhile, the parish remains grateful for the pastoral ministry of these Pastors: Fr. Robert J. Hoevel, 1956-1968; Fr. James J. O'Connor, 1968 -1991; Fr. Kenneth J. Sarrazine 1991-1998; Fr. Thomas Shoemaker 1998-2001 (in residence priest, Fr. Vigny Bellerive); Fr. Polycarp Fernando 2001-2003 (in residence priest, Fr. Dan Chukwuleta); and Fr. Emmanuel Chikezie 2003-till date (in residence priest, Fr. Dan Chukwuleta).

However, the above seemingly rosy and beautiful picture would be sustained for quite sometime. With a vibrant manufacturing climate, many residents were drawn to the southeast side. There was the auto-manufacturing industry; the booming and famous South Town Mall, etc. All that would change with time and the effects of time, including what someone described as a result of "bad rap of the southeast side" by some of the city's core journals. Tempus fugit! The founding of St. Henry Parish and school, renamed after the French Missionary priest Monsignor Benoit to replace the former name St. Henry Catholic School, boosted enrollments. Much of this came from a nearby sister parish, Sacred Heart at Gaywood Drive, whose school was closed down in 1994. That was the very first handwriting on the wall of the neighborhood, as well as a foretaste of the things to come for St. Henry Parish and Benoit Academy! "More recently, the parish has reflected the dramatic changes that occur with the city's dwindling industrial base. With closing of International Harvester and other manufacturing firms, many moved from the area, thereby impacting the Church membership and school enrollments", Sharon Little of the Fort Wayne/South Bend diocesan newspaper, Today's Catholic, writes. Nonetheless, there are associations that still render services, like St. Vincent the Paul Society, South Side Seniors group and First Friday Association, inter alia. Parishioners often help at the Franciscan Center. No doubt, the area may once again witness revival as well as enjoy another era of boom and glory.

Clearly, any account of St. Henry Catholic Parish, will be incomplete without a mention of her German roots, especially of the Patron Saint, King Henry II, the Duke of Bavaria and Emperor of the Holy Roman Empire! Power corrupts, supposedly, but that didn't hold true for King Henry II. He got power and used it for good. He was a reformer, built churches and monasteries, and ruled wisely, tempering justice with mercy. He died at Gottingen in 1024, and was buried in the Cathedral at Bamberg. He is the patron saint of the childless, of Dukes, of the handicapped and those rejected by religious orders. He was canonized in 1146. Annual feast day is July 13. *Compiled by Fr. Emmanuel Chikezie, Pastor*

St. John the Baptist Fort Wayne, Indiana

On August 14, 1929, the Rev. S. Joachim Ryder was appointed the first pastor. Within the established boundaries of the parish he found two hundred and two families with one hundred and thirty-one children of school age. Both figures are four times as large today. A residence at 4610 South Wayne Avenue was bought to serve as a rectory. Located a block from the parish property it was occupied by Father Ryder on December 25, 1929. A combination church and school building on the corner of Fairfield Avenue and Pasadena Drive was begun on January 29, 1930 and dedicated on October 19 of the same year. Many will remember this period of widespread unemployment, of desperate economic depression. Interest rates were high and incomes were low, if not entirely lacking. Only the most self-sacrificing efforts of a zealous pastor and a loyal congregation enabled the parish to carry its financial burden in these early years.

In 1938 the Rev. Matthew J. Lange was assigned to help Father Ryder in his increasingly heavy work. In May of 1939 the lay board met with the pastor to consider plans for a new convent. Up to that time the Sisters of Providence, in charge of the school, had been living in two classrooms on the upper floor. It was agreed also at this meeting that a new rectory was needed. The convent was completed in 1940 but the rectory project was deferred for lack of funds to a more favorable time.

On Christmas eve, 1941, as the faithful were assembling for the Midnight Mass, word came from the hospital that Father Ryder, ill for some months, had died. This is the proper occasion to renew our tribute of praise and thanks to him for the substantial contribution which only

St. John The Baptist Church
4525 Arlington Avenue, Fort Wayne

the founder of a parish can make to its progress, not merely in terms of stone and steel, which must sometime pass away, but to the everlasting values of the spirit. Father Ryder was succeeded on February 4, 1942 by the present pastor.

It was plain at this time that the parish had one immediate objective-to pay off the debt. The hope of doing so seemed assured by all the factors involved. Few realized, however, that before the end of 1946 the parish would be entirely free of debt and a building fund underway. In 1949 the present rectory at 4525 Arlington Avenue was built, the convent was considerably enlarged and adjacent real estate was purchased and improved to provide playground and parking space. The total cost of these projects was all but written off by the end of 1951 when the necessity of drafting plans for the new church forced us back into the "red".

The next and last stage of building was begun on August 25, 1952 when ground was broken for the new church at Fairfield Avenue and Sherwood Terrace, the last remaining plot of ground available on the parish property. It was thought at first that only the basement would be finished and used as a church until the "old" church in the school building could be converted entirely into urgently needed class rooms. This plan was later given up as impractical and dangerous. During the summer of 1953 a spacious stairway was added to the rear of the school to insure greater safety and convenience for the teachers and pupils. On September 8, of the same year, the masonry work on the superstructure of the new church was started. The corner-stone was blessed on November 22, 1953. It was planned, of course, that immediately upon occupancy of the new church the "old" one which served the parish for a quarter of a century and to which many had become attached, would be converted into class rooms, so that the parish would have for the first time a school building devoted entirely to school purposes. The final chapter of this brief sketch brings us up to the dedication of the new church on June 24, 1955, Feast of our Glorious Patron. The story will need no further telling until another milestone shall have been reached and most of us who are now on the scene will be elsewhere-in this world or the next. *This historical sketch was originally written by Most Reverend Leo A. Pursley, D.D.*

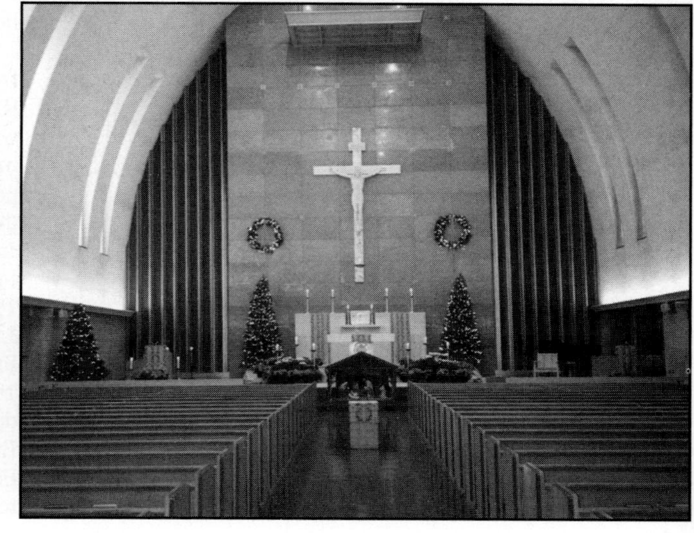

St. John Lutheran Cemetery

St. John Lutheran Church Cemetery

As was common amongst immigrants, especially Lutheran, who had been encouraged by Martin Luther to care for those of the household of faith, schools, cemeteries, and social organizations were established early, followed by various welfare, financial and health care institutions.

St. John congregation first purchased five acres for $900.00 on a site shared with a community cemetery known now as McCollough Park. As the area developed, neighbors were "uncomfortable" (probably due to grave robbers and some beliefs about the dead). Litigation motivated the congregation to purchase property further south, now known as Maple and Park Avenues. Six acres were purchased at the cost of $133.00 in September of 1864. The same event occurred again.

Therefore 40 acres of farmland was financially secured and dedicated in August of 1872. Graves were moved from Maple Avenue, a farmer/caretaker site was erected and in 1879 a guard house was built at the southwest corner for protection from grave robbers.

In 1913 the entrance was tiled, curbs and side roads were paved in 1991 and in 1995 asphalted. The latter was from bequests.

In 1950 two acres of land were given for a mission of the ALC (American Lutheran Church). This congregation joined the English Dist. LCMS in the 1980s.

Fences were installed on the south in 1966 and in front in 1974. The pole barn for equipment was built in 1969.

All founders except Michael Mueller are buried at the cemetery. There are burials of five persons identified as having been born in the 1790s.

During the 1990s, volunteers worked to revitalize the grounds, buildings and equipment including removal of dead and dangerous trees, and plantings of small interest gardens dedicated to past clergy who served more than 20 years (Dannecker, Kucher, Amelung, and Boerger).

September 2002 served as the dedication date for a statue to Jesus based on a sculpture by Thorwaldsen of Denmark similar to that on the altar of the church. This was a gift from the estate of Margaret Spiegel.

Members of all ELCA Congregations and/or members whose relatives are interred are welcome to purchase sites.

St. John Evangelical Lutheran Church (Flatrock)

12912 Franke Road, Monroeville

St. John Evangelical Lutheran Church and School (Flatrock) was founded on October 1, 1849 under the name "The German Evangelical Lutheran Congregation of Madison Township, Allen County". Pastor Frederick Wilhelm Husmann (b. 1807, Nordel, Hanover, Germany) was the founding Pastor. In 1845 Pastor Husmann was Called to serve as Pastor and teacher of St. Paul's Lutheran Church, Marion Township (now known as Emmanuel, Soest); Pastor Husmann also began to serve St. John Lutheran Church, Bingen and St. Peter Lutheran Church, Fuelling.

On Sunday, January 3, 1847, Pastor Husmann conducted the first worship service for what would become St. John, Flatrock. The service was held in the home of Jacob Frey in the German settlement of Madison Township. The home is about two miles east of the current location along Monroeville Road and was most recently known as the old Burkamp place. Those who gathered for worship were members of St. John, Bingen. Because of the distance and condition of roads to St. John, Bingen, the members of the German settlement requested the formation of a separate congregation. On September 10, 1849, Pastor Husmann held a meeting at the home of Juergen (George) Brouwer (sometimes spelled "Brauer") to discuss the matter. Those in attendance agreed to the formation of a separate congregation. On October 1, 1849 the congregation came into formal existence with 27 communicants (11 men, 14 women, one confirmed girl and one confirmed boy) and 35 children (19 boys and 16 girls), 62 souls in all. The new congregation immediately took steps to join the Evangelical Lutheran Synod of Missouri, Ohio, and other States (now known as The Lutheran Church-Missouri Synod). Pastor Husmann was Called as the pastor and was to preach every three to four weeks and teach school one day a week. Pastor Husmann continued to serve other congregations as well as serving as Secretary of the newly organized Missouri Synod. There was significant growth in these early years for by 1881 the congregation numbered 240 baptized souls.

St. John Lutheran Church (Flatrock), picture of the church, the school and the parsonage taken about 1889. This view is looking southwest from what is now Franke Road.

St. John Lutheran Church (Flatrock), picture of the church, the school, part of the parsonage, and part of the gymnasium as it appeared in 2005. This view is looking southwest from what is now Franke Road.

Founding members of the congregation are William Aumann, Juergen Brouwer, Henry Franke, Jacob Frey, Sr., Conrad Frey, Fred Hillman, Ludwig Hoffmeier, William Molthan, Philip Neff, Carl Wiebke, Jacob Marquard and William Kruse. Soon to join the new congregation were the families of Fred Grotrian, Fred Klenke, Robert Duenger, John Lenker, Christian Wiegmann, Fred Grotrian, Jr., Henry Wiebke and Martin Frey.

At its founding the families went on record to purchase ten acres for $30.00 from Carl Wiebke. Each family was to contribute $3.00 towards the purchase and any funds beyond the cost would go into a building fund. The congregation is still located on this original site. St. John was originally called Bielefeld because many members were from Bielefeld, Germany. Later it was referred to as Flatrock to relate to the geographical location of the Flatrock Clearing.

The first permanent church building was completed and dedicated to the service of the Triune God on Pentecost Sunday, May 15, 1853. The building also served as a parochial school classroom for about 25 years. The second church building (architect Michael J. Fackler) was dedicated in 1881. The third (and present) church building was dedicated in 1955.

The congregation's school has been in continuous operation from the founding of the congregation and currently serves over 160 students in Pre-K through 8th grade. The first separate school building was dedicated in 1883. On September 27, 1914 a new school building was dedicated. On September 10, 1967 the current school building was dedicated. The Gymnasium-Parish Hall was dedicated on October 30, 1977. A year-long celebration of the congregation's 150th Anniversary was held during 1999-2000. In the summer of 2005 the congregation began a remodeling and expansion program, Branching Out in Christ. This program will remodel the current school building, and add a new Parish Hall and new school related rooms.

As of December 31, 2004, St. John's membership consists of 522 Communicants and 656 Baptized souls.

St. Joseph - Hessen Cassel Church

11337 Old U.S. 27 South, Fort Wayne

St. Joseph Hessen Cassel – The 1857 Rectory is on the left side of the picture. In the center is the 1857 church, enlarged in 2001. On the right side of the picture is the activity center and school.

Early members came to Fort Wayne from the Hessen and Cassel areas of Germany around 1814. As early as 1833, familiar names in the parish such as Herber, Kleber, Minnich, Schmidt, Sorg and others, purchased land in Marion Township, eight miles southeast of Fort Wayne on the Piqua Trail near the St. Mary's River. In 1841, 29 charter members pledged to support a priest. Traveling missionaries such as Frs. Julian Benoit, Joseph Rudolp, Alphones Muncina, and Edward Faller celebrated Mass in the homes. Peter Schmidt donated the land on which a log church was erected in 1851. Officially designated a mission parish, the congregation was served by Frs. B. H. Schultes, Joseph Weutz, Julian Benoit, and Edward Faller. When Fr. John Force began ministry in 1857, the congregation began building a brick church, seating 250, which was named St. Joseph by Bishop John Luers. Progress on the building continued during the pastorate of Fr. L. Schneider (1858) and was completed under the guidance of Fr. Jacob Mayer, S. J. in 1863 at a cost of $5,000.

Frs. Martin Kink, John Wemhoff and William Woeste served the parish until 1872. Invited by Bishop Luers, eight Poor Handmaids of Jesus Christ came from Dernbach, Germany to Fort Wayne and began a school at Hessen Cassel (1868) and St. Joseph Hospital (1869). Fr. Joseph Nussbaum was appointed in 1873 and became the first resident pastor with the completion of the rectory begun in 1875. Fr. John Hueser arrived in 1877 and welcomed the Franciscan Sisters of the Sacred Heart (Joliet, Illinois) who staffed the school. In 1879, Fr. Hueser built a two-story brick school building to house the sisters and serve 100 students. Fr. John Mark was appointed in 1880, and during his pastorate, completed major renovations to the church in 1892. Fr. Maximilian Benzinger began his pastorate in 1897 and in 1925 constructed a new convent, separated from the school building. In 1927, Fr. Fridolin Hasler reported that during his tenure electricity was installed and the school was enlarged. Frs. Joachim Baker (1934-1939), Charles Seeberger (1939-1946) and Frederick Westendorf (1946-1947) served the congregation.

Fr. Lawrence Gollner began serving this growing parish in 1947. The existing recreation hall was built in 1948 to serve the social needs of the parish and, presently, the school cafeteria. Fr. Matthias Bodinger, who reported as pastor in 1956, began the construction of a new school to accommodate the growing enrollment of more than 190 students. Msgr. Robert Contant began his service as pastor in 1964. He purchased a new organ for the church (1980). The Msgr. Contant Activity Center was constructed for sports programs (1986). The Franciscan Sisters of the Sacred Heart ceased staffing the school in 1988. The school continued to prosper and three new classrooms were added in 1992. A soccer field and a baseball diamond were added in 1994. Upon his retirement in 1997, Fr. Robert Van Kempen was assigned as pastor and oversaw the enlargement of the 1857 church and its rededication in 2001. He was relieved by Fr. Edward Erpelding in 2002. He was ordained for the Diocese of Fort Wayne-South Bend in 1966, and served parishes in Fort Wayne, Huntington, and South Bend. Licensed in Indiana, he taught at Bishop Dwenger and served as principal of Huntington Catholic and Mishawaka Marian high schools. He was commissioned a Navy chaplain and served reserve and regular units of the Coast Guard, Marine Corps and Navy. Upon his retirement with the grade of Captain in 1996, he was assigned to St. Martin de Porres, Syracuse, Indiana until his appointment as pastor of St. Joseph with 390 households.

Saint Joseph United Methodist Church Ministries

Saint Joseph Ministries began in 1836 when a group of people meeting under a tree on the Saint Joseph River invited a circuit rider of the Methodist Episcopal Church to be their spiritual leader. Another person who often met in these early gatherings was a man named John Chapman, a missionary of the Swedenborgian faith, who was better known as Johnny Appleseed. Although he was never a member of the congregation, records show that when he died on March 11, 1847, his funeral was conducted by the Methodist circuit rider.

In 1863, the Saint Joseph Methodist Episcopal Church was formally chartered and the Rev. James M. Greer was appointed as its founding Pastor. In the Fall of 1863, the church's first wood-frame building was erected at the intersection of St. Joe and Papermill Roads where the Parker Cemetery is now located. With the growth of the congregation, a second building was erected of brick on the northeast side of the same intersection. The new building was constructed and dedicated on May 6, 1916. This church building contained a Tiffany stained-glass window of the Good Shepherd, whose main panel can still be seen in the church's current building.

In 1955, ninety-two years after its founding, the congregation now had a full-time pastor and 220 members. The congregation then decided to purchase 7 ½ acres on the northeast corner of the intersection of St. Joe Center and Reed Roads just one mile east of their founding location. A new brick building was erected and consecrated on February 2, 1958.

The 1960s saw much growth and change for the church. In 1960, Saint Joseph began its Weekday Children's School ministry with its preschool program. On December 8, 1963, the congregation celebrated its centennial by baptizing 48 persons and receiving 105 persons into membership. The church's membership grew to over 700. The present sanctuary and two classroom wings were built and then consecrated on October 15, 1967. In 1968 Saint Joseph joined with other Methodist and Evangelical United Brethren church congregations throughout this community and the world in recognizing its new United Methodist connection.

St. Joe Chapel erected in 1916 at the intersection of St. Joe and St. Joe Center Road for a total cost of $6,500.

Since then, Saint Joseph Ministries has continued to grow, change and expand to meet the needs of its congregation and community outreach. A pipe organ was installed in the sanctuary in 1977. Two more building additions of over 13,000 sq. ft. were added to the building in 1979 and in 1992 which included a narthex, office complex, additional class/meeting rooms and a worship center. Many ministry, outreach, and support programs have and continue to take place, which keep the church doors open daily from early morning until late at night. Additional worship services and worship styles have been added including the "HEbrews Joe Coffeehouse" worship that was added in 2004. The pastoral and ministry staff has increased in number as the church today has well over 1,500 members and constituents. Saint Joseph has had over sixty-seven clergy persons serve as senior and associate pastors throughout its history in addition to the many lay staff persons who have served in many ministry program areas.

In May of 2005, the church purchased 29 ½ acres just ¼ mile east of its current site on the south side of St. Joe Center Road. This new land or mission field will continue to allow Saint Joseph Ministries to expand its ministry/outreach opportunities and work to fulfill its mission statement ... "Hearing God's call, the congregation of Saint Joseph United Methodist Ministries commits itself to: be an authentic New Testament Church (Acts 2:42-27); reach the unchurched (Luke 5:27); and develop full mature disciples (1Timothy 6:11-14, 17-19). With this mission, we will fulfill God's will for us in this community and around the world."

Saint Joseph United Methodist

St. Louis Besancon Catholic Church

In the early 1840s French speaking immigrants made up the settlement in Jefferson Township and parts of Jackson and Adams Townships that was know as "New France." A great many of the settlers were from the diocese of Besancon in France. Reverend Besonies came regularly from Fort Wayne to say Mass at the log home of Joseph Dodane. In January 1851 Gideon Dickerson donated four acres and a small frame church was built under the patronage of St. Louis. C.F. Lomont and Joseph Dodane bore the bulk of the expense of the building. In 1870 the settlement became know only by "Besancon." The congregation at this time numbered 600 and Father Adam began construction of a new, larger and more substantial church. He found a unique way to collect funds for the building project. He asked the head of each family to raise a calf until the age of three years with proceeds going to the church. Father Adam branded each calf at the time of birth, and on a given date a public sale was advertised, and the buyers came from far and wide. The sale of these cattle netted over $3,000. The cornerstone was laid in 1871. It is interesting to note the new church was built around the little log cabin so the people could continue to attend Mass. When the new building was complete enough for Mass to be held there, the old church was dismantled and carried out in pieces. St. Louis looks today much as it did in 1871. A brick church, it was later covered by a process called "sham rocking" which gives the building a look of stone. Because the early parishioners thought beauty was important for their place of worship, many people donated extra funds for the leaded stained glass windows. St. Louis continues to watch over the small community. It has seen many changes: from the time the early trail in front of the church was once know as Ridge Road/ Sugar Ridge Road to Lincoln Highway and then U.S. Hwy 30 and now Old Lincoln Highway. Beautiful old trees, surround buildings consisting of the 2 ½ story Queen Anne rectory, built in 1893, and the St. Louis Academy built in 1915. The recreation hall was built in 1948 and the St. Louis Convent house was built in 1915. On all sides the rich farmland extends as far as you can see. The small picket fence, lovely gardens and pine trees give the feeling of a true rural hamlet.

St. Marks Evangelical Lutheran Church - Monroeville

First Evangelical Lutheran Church on the southeast corner of Elm and Mill Streets in Monroeville, Indiana, circa 1910 (after steeple was blown off in windstorm and never repaired). The church was erected in 1867 and razed in the early 1920s.

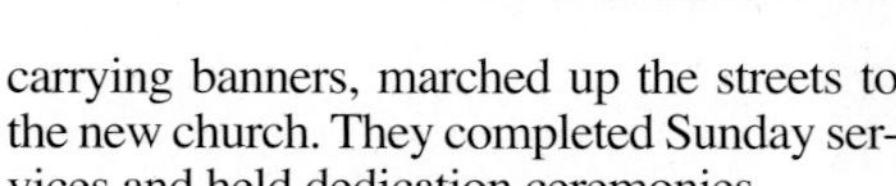

St. Marks Lutheran Church, Ohio and South Streets, Monroeville, Indiana, August 1993. The church was erected in 1913 and the Parish Hall in 1961.

When Monroeville, Indiana was founded in 1851 there were only a few people living in Monroe Township. As a result, circuit riders served Lutherans living in the area by holding worship services in their homes.

By 1864 these persons wanted to assemble in a regular church and they needed a place to hold Sunday services. They began meeting at the corner of South and Summit Streets in Monroeville in a wooden frame hall owned by Samuel Poole. They were known as the First Lutheran Society.

Alpheus Swift donated a lot in 1866 at the south edge of town. A wooden frame building was erected on the southeast corner of Elm and Mill Streets in 1867. Construction costs were $2,250. The congregation was called the Evangelical Lutheran Church.

This new church originally had a high steeple, but a few years later the steeple blew down in a wind storm and was never rebuilt. The parsonage was located across the street at 403 Elm Street.

In 1911 members realized their church was not large enough. They purchased land in 1912 closer to the center of Monroeville. By 1913 the congregation, now using the name of St. Marks Evangelical Lutheran Church, had erected a large brick building at the corner of South and Ohio Streets. Construction costs were $8,000. The bell from the old church was installed in the bell tower of the new church and is in use today.

On June 14, 1914 the congregation assembled for an opening service at the old church site. Members, singing hymns and carrying banners, marched up the streets to the new church. They completed Sunday services and held dedication ceremonies.

The main floor consisted of the sanctuary, tiny tots and adult Sunday School rooms. Colorful stained glass windows were installed in every wall. Youngsters used the basement for their Sunday School classes. That was where special events were held. There was a kitchen for preparing meals for socials and banquets. A modern furnace was installed in the utility area. Inside restrooms were located nearby.

The old church stood vacant for several years and in the early 1920s it was razed.

In 1918 a modern two story brick parsonage was constructed just east of the church. The old parsonage on Elm Street was sold.

Monroeville's most renowned resident and author was the Reverend Lloyd C. Douglas. He had lived in town during his boyhood years. In 1947, while living in California, he donated an electric organ to the church. It was dedicated in memory of his parents, the Reverend Alexander Jackson and Mrs. Sarah "Jennie" Douglas. The senior Douglas was pastor of this church three different times. After her husband died, Mrs. Douglas lived in Monroeville and attended St. Marks until she died in 1939. Whenever Lloyd visited his mother he attended this church also. Lloyd Douglas was famous for his many novels, some were made into movies. *The Robe* was the most well known. In his autobiography, *Time to Remember* he wrote about his early life in Monroeville and of his father being the pastor. Lloyd said that he always considered Monroeville to be "his home."

The main floor of the church was gutted in an extensive remodeling program in February, 1948. Only the beautiful stained glass windows were left untouched. Dedication of the remodeled sanctuary was on June 19, 1949. The social area in the basement was remodeled with a modern kitchen. An office and pastor's study were added.

In the late 1950s the Sunday School membership needed more classrooms, so plans were made to expand. The parsonage was sold in 1960 and moved from its location to become a private family home. A new brick parsonage was built at the corner of Oak and Summit Streets. A brick parish hall was erected in 1961 on the site of the parsonage and was connected to the church. Besides several classrooms there was a lounge with a kitchenette and more restrooms. Over the years the church's sanctuary and grounds have been enhanced by improvements.

For many years St. Marks Lutheran Church had shared a pastor with the Marquardt Lutheran Church located west of Monroeville in Madison Township. In 1964 each church ended this arrangement and had a pastor to serve its own congregation.

A nursery school program for three and four year olds started in September 1965. The school is still operating and is open to all children regardless of their church affiliation.

A food bank program began in the early 1980s and is operated from the basement. It currently serves many families who live in the community. The food bank is stocked from the Allen County Associated Church Food Bank, from donations of citizens and area churches.

St. Nicholas Orthodox Church

The fires of World War II were still burning furiously in their homeland when a group of committed Macedonians dedicated themselves to building a new Eastern Orthodox Church in Fort Wayne. The result was the founding of St. Nicholas Eastern Orthodox Church, now located at 3535 Crescent Avenue, adjacent to the IVY Tech campus.

In the spring of 1944, Mike Kozma, Nicholas Gouloff and Vasil K. Litchin were named to be trustees of a group to collect funds to establish a church for the Macedonian people in Fort Wayne. Some ninety families of Macedonian and Bulgarian descent contributed to the cause, and St. Nicholas Eastern Orthodox Church was incorporated on June 23, 1947.

Services were first held in the new temple at 3506 Warsaw Street, and for the next six years Divine Liturgy was served on alternating Sundays by Archimandrite Kyrill (Yonchev). The first Board of Trustees consisted of Vasil K. Litchin, Nicholas Gouloff, Mike Kozma, Argire Lebamoff, Dimitry Lebamoff, Argire Kiproff, Vasil Eshcoff, Thomas Lazoff, and Lazar Laycoff. According to these men, the purpose of St. Nicholas parish was to "preserve and propagate the Orthodox Christian Faith in its purity and fullness in accordance with the teachings of our Lord Jesus Christ, as it is transmitted to us by the Holy Apostles and the Fathers of the Church." During those first several years, the services were done in Slavonic, but have since been done in English.

A member of the Orthodox Church of America: Bulgarian Diocese, the church is dedicated to Saint Nicholas, the Wonderworker, Archbishop of Myra in Lycia, who is famed as a great saint pleasing unto God. He was born in the city of Patara in the region of Lycia (on the south coast of the Asia Minor peninsula), and was the only son of pious parents Theophanes and Nonna, who had vowed to dedicate him to God.

Despite his great gentleness of spirit and purity of heart, St. Nicholas was a zealous and ardent warrior of the Church of Christ. Fighting evil spirits, the saint made the rounds of the pagan temples and shrines in the city of Myra and its surroundings, shattering the idols and turning the temples to dust.

St. Nicholas is the patron of travelers, and church members pray to him for deliverance from floods, poverty, or any misfortunes. He has promised to help those who remember his parents, Theophanes and Nonna. St. Nicholas is commemorated on May 9th (the transfer of his relics) and on July 29th (his nativity).

In 1956, the parish trustees secured the services of an immigrant priest, a young man from Bulgaria, Fr. George Nedelkoff. Fr. Nedelkoff would serve the next 37 years at St Nicholas. As the first full-time rector, the task fell to Fr. Nedelkoff to seek out the sizeable Macedonian population in Fort Wayne, to encourage them to return to the Orthodox fold, and to remind them of the faith of their fathers. Under the pastorate of Fr. Nedelkoff, a Sunday school for children and adults, a Women's Guild and a number of other activities were begun, which are still active and viable.

Because for many years, it was the only Eastern Orthodox church in Fort Wayne, its parishioners hail from many backgrounds, including Syrian, Russian, Ukranian, Serbian, Romanian, German and English.

In about 1980, the parish felt itself outgrowing the building on Warsaw Street and began making plans and raising funds for a new temple to be located at 3535 Crescent Ave. This project included a large Fellowship Hall. The cornerstone of the building was laid on September 12, 1983, and the first Divine Liturgy was celebrated by His Grace Bishop Kyrill on November 1, 1983.

St. Nicholas Orthodox Church

In December of 1992, at the annual St. Nicholas Day banquet, Fr. Nedelkoff announced that he was going to retire. The next six months would prove to be a time of great testing for the parish, as members saw a different priest virtually every Sunday. Fr. Nedelkoff was truly missed during this period, a time whose difficulty was aggravated by the realization that Orthodox priests were in short supply.

In June 1993, Fr. Brooks (Thomas) Ledford was assigned as parish priest. During Fr. Brooks' pastorate a number of new ministries were launched, including a Charity & Benevolence Ministry, Outreach Ministry, a parish lending library, and a parish bookstore/gift shop. In March 1996, Deacon Michael Myers joined the church, where he continues to serve today. In August 2000, Fr. Ledford left for a different assignment, and His Eminence, Archbishop Kyrill assigned Fr. David Meinzen to be the new Rector.

St Nicholas parish, with gratitude to God in Christ, to the Fathers of the Holy Orthodox Church, and to the Macedonian fathers listed above, looks forward to carrying the Gospel of our Lord and Savior Jesus Christ into the twenty-first century.

St. Patrick's Parish

In 1889 Bishop Joseph Dwenger announced the forming of a new parish--St. Patrick's. Four lots were acquired at the corner of DeWald and Harrison Streets. The owner objected to selling the land for use as a church. Thus, Mr. George Gordon bought the lots and resold them to the parish! Two more lots were purchased so the parish would own the entire block.

Ground was broken in April 1890 and the cornerstone was set on May 20th. The beautiful Gothic-style church was completed in November 1891. It was the first parish in the diocese of Fort Wayne to receive the honor of being a consecrated church, meaning that the church was free of debt. A school directly behind the church on DeWald Street and a rectory on Harrison Street were built at the same time. Later that school would become a part of St. Catherine's Academy.

In 1907 a hand-carved Carrara marble communion railing was installed in the church in memory of Mr. and Mrs. George DeWald. In 1912 the wonderful marble altar was in place, a gift of Miss Elizabeth DeWald. A matching marble pulpit was added, donated by Mr. and Mrs. William Noll.

In 1901 St. Catherine's Academy was built. The name was chosen to honor Sister Mary Catherine McGrath, the first superior of St. Patrick's School. During its 37 years existence, more than 650 young ladies were educated "to earn a living as well as how to live a life." The Academy was closed in 1938 when Central Catholic High School was opened. The building was razed in 1959 after a disastrous fire.

In 1910 the Lyceum was completed. This building became a landmark for Catholic social and religious events in the community. There was a stage; meeting rooms; space for basketball, dodge-ball, bowling, and dances; plus a cafeteria. It remains in great use to this day.

The large brick school on Butler Street was completed in 1918. The old school on DeWald Street had become part of the Academy. The new school had seventeen rooms. The enrollment was 639 and the number of families in the parish had risen to 736. By 1934, there were 902 families in the parish.

In 1929 a new convent was built for the Sisters of Providence, who had staffed the schools since the beginning of the parish. Each Sister had her own room and there was a beautiful chapel on the second floor.

In 1946 two elegant marble side altars were installed in the church, designed to match the main altar. They were donated in memory of Henry and Mary Miller.

During the years following the Vatican Council, liturgical changes were made, including the installation of an altar facing the congregation and the scheduling of evening Masses. Ecumenical services were also held with other religious communities.

As the population in the city shifted, enrollment in the school declined. Also, many Sisters were retiring and the convent was put to other uses. In 1984 the Latin American Educational Center moved into the convent. Programs were designed for non-English speaking people, and also personal counseling was offered.

Due to declining enrollment (170), the school was closed in 1994. St. Patrick's combined with Sacred Heart and St. Henry's parishes in pooling their resources to open Benoit Academy in the St. Henry's facility. St. Patrick's convent was torn down and a memorial garden was installed, featuring an inspirational statue of Jesus, surrounded by children of many races.

As Bishop D'Arcy described in a 1989 letter: "St. Patrick's has been a parish that has reserved a special place for the immigrant and the stranger. At its very inception, it welcomed people from other nations. Many of them worked on the railroads for small wages and in difficult conditions to build a church and the schools that surround it."

In 2003 it was announced that the mostly Hispanic St. Paul's Parish would be merged with St. Patrick's. St. Paul's physical plant was deteriorating as their membership was increasing to approximately 900 families. At the same time, St. Patrick's membership had diminished to almost 600 families. The empty school at St. Patrick's would afford a great opportunity to house the large Religious Education Classes of the two combined parishes.

A great many adjustments and activities were involved and St. Patrick's moved forward with its Anglo, Hispanic and Vietnamese parishioners. Masses are offered in all three languages to accommodate the three-fold membership. The people of St. Patrick's have always embraced any and all people who come to its beautiful church and we will continue to do so.

Former pastors include: Rev. Thomas O'Leary 1889, Msgr. Joseph Delaney 1889-1935, Msgr. Lawrence Monahan 1935-1962, Rev. Edward Miller 1962-1971, Rev. Vernon Rosenthal 1971-1974, Rev. Robert Hammond 1974-1975, Rev. Raymond Balzer 1975-1981, Rev. Thomas Doriot 1981-1983, Rev. Richard Hire 1983-1991, Rev. James Koons 1991-1998, Rev. Glenn Kohrman 1998-2000, Rev. Jeffery Largent 2000-2003, and Rev. Angel Valdez 2003-2004. The present pastor, since 2004, is Msgr. William Lester. *Compiled from previous histories and composed by Jean Suelzer Streicher.*

"Where people are even more beautiful than our historic Church"

St. Paul's Evangelical Lutheran Church

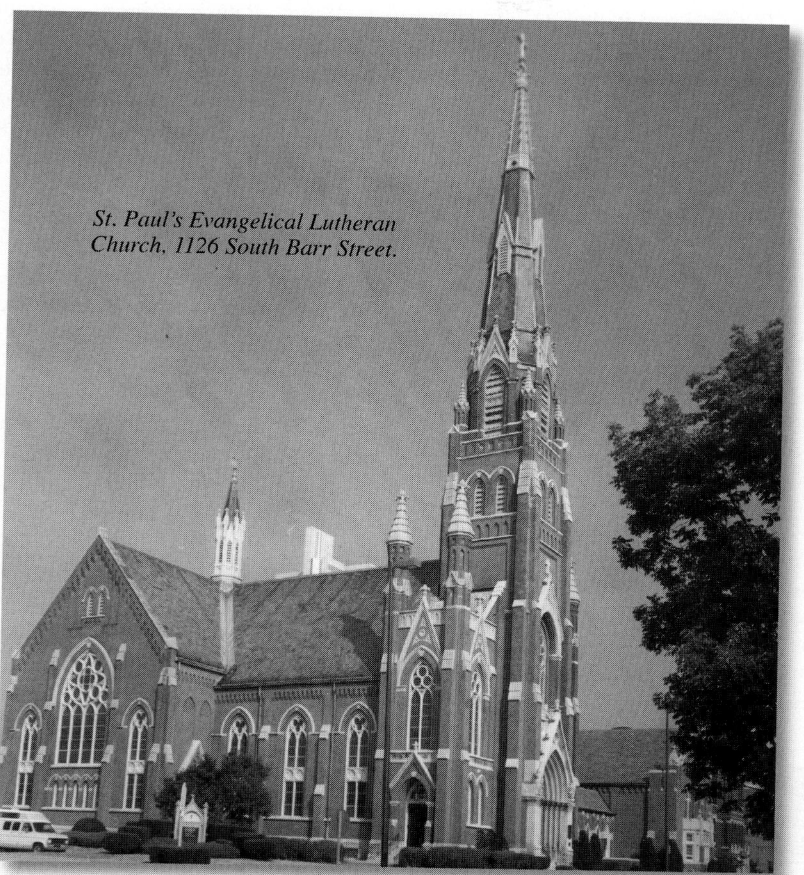

St. Paul's Evangelical Lutheran Church, 1126 South Barr Street.

St. Paul's Evangelical Lutheran Church, at the corner of Barr and Lewis Streets in Fort Wayne, was officially organized on October 14, 1837. The congregation traces its beginnings to Henry Rudisill, a Fort Wayne businessman, who wrote to Eastern periodicals advertising for a Lutheran pastor to come to Fort Wayne.

The Rev. Jesse Hoover responded to the call in 1836. Rev. Hoover organized the German Lutherans in the area in late summer of that year with services being held in the Court House. By January 1837, the first Holy Communion service was held. Sixty-three individuals received the Sacrament. Originally known as The First German Evangelical Lutheran Church, German was the language of choice in the service. Pastor Hoover was very aware of the need for education for the children. In August of 1837 he began teaching in the non-sectarian Fort Wayne Academy, also serving as principal. This was the origin of St. Paul's Lutheran School. At the first business meeting, Adam Wefel and Henry Trier were elected elders, and Conrad Nill and Henry Rudisill were elected deacons.

After the death of Jesse Hoover in May of 1838, Pastor Frederick Wyneken responded to the call for a pastor. Wyneken was not only the pastor of St. Paul's but he was also a missionary, organizing congregations as far East as the Ohio line and as far North as Frankenmuth, Michigan. The first church building (40 ft. x 24 ft.) was built in 1839. Pastor Wyneken, who was in Germany for health care for a throat ailment, enlisted pastors for the area, including Dr. William Sihler, who later succeeded Wyneken at St. Paul's.

Rev. Sihler was installed as pastor July 15, 1845. With tremendous growth of membership, a second church building (66 ft. x 44 ft.) was needed. The first building was moved to the back of the lot and the new structure faced Barr Street. This church building was enlarged in 1862. In 1845 Pastor Sihler continued the work started by Pastor Wyneken in training men for the ministry. Classrooms were added to the rear of the church building for this purpose. This was the beginning of Concordia Theological Seminary, established in 1846. The same year, the name of the church was changed to The German Evangelical St. Paul's Lutheran Church. The name St. Paul's Evangelical Lutheran Church was adopted in 1922. The congregation grew rapidly. St. Paul's School had an enrollment of 500 students, who were instructed by six teachers. The congregation resolved (September 1850) "henceforth the English language is to be taught in the school."

The Rev. Henry Sauer came to St. Paul's in 1875 as a second called pastor. Sihler and Sauer served together for ten years. At Sihler's death in October 1885, Henry Sauer became pastor. In January of 1887, the congregation resolved to build a new church. The present German Gothic church building was dedicated September 15, 1889. The old school building was razed and a new building was constructed across the street from the church. As the church grew, daughter congregations began to be established, giving St. Paul's the designation of "mother" Lutheran Church in the Fort Wayne area.

On December 3, 1903, the church was gutted by fire which had started in the basement, traveled underneath the building, and up the steeple. Flames were seen engulfing the steeple at five a.m. in the morning. All that remained were the four walls and the brick portion of the steeple. The congregation vowed to rebuild. Members came from near and far to help with the clean up of the area and construction began on the new structure using the fire scarred walls as the base. Today you can touch the burned timbers in the basement and see the fire scars on the walls of the steeple.

With Pastor's Sauer's death on May 6, 1896, St. Paul's sought a new senior pastor, and Pastor Jacob Miller accepted the call in the same year. The present school building was built in 1913. Two branch schools were organized, and the Luther Institute was established, during Rev. Jacob Miller's pastorate. Rev. Paul Miller was called to be his father's assistant in 1910. At this time English was established as the second pulpit language. At his father's death in 1933, Pastor Paul Miller became the sixth senior pastor of St. Paul's. Serving during the war years of the 1940s, Pastor Paul Miller saw daughter congregations being established as well as the refurbishing of the church building itself. He served until his retirement in 1950 at which time Pastor Edwin A. Nerger was called to the pastorate of St. Paul's.

Pastor Richard S. Radtke came to St. Paul's as Associate Pastor in February 1980 and was called as Senior Pastor in 1981. Under Pastor Radtke's leadership, both the church and school buildings are being updated. The congregation continues to be a leader in the Lutheran community.

Saint Peter's Catholic Church

The years following the American Civil War saw a great increase in the numbers of peoples moving from the central section of the city of Fort Wayne. One of the areas seeing the greatest influx was the immediate southeast area. By the early 1870s, it was evident that a new parish to serve the predominantly German-speaking peoples was needed. (In fact, this particular area was known as "Germantown.") In the summer of 1871, a group of Catholics assembled for just this purpose. The initial meeting, chaired by Peter Mettler, who for many years had shown great interest in just such a project, unanimously decided to approach Bishop Joseph Dwenger in order to receive the necessary Episcopal approval. The approval was immediate in coming and it was decided to name the new parish (the city's fourth, and the third basically German speaking parish) Saint Peter's. In making this choice, the new parish would be placed directly under the protection of the Prince of the Apostles and the first Pope, but also, would in an indirect manner, honor the man (Peter Mettler) who for so many years led the crusade to have this parish established.

Saint Peter's beginnings were humble. Land was purchased in what was known as the LaSalle Addition. On this property was originally built a combination brick two-story church and school. The first floor provided for four large classrooms, while the second floor served as the church which could easily accommodate 300 persons. The School Sisters of Notre Dame were brought in to staff the school.

The early years of Saint Peter's saw rapid growth. In 1892, work was begun on a new permanent church building. Plans for this structure were drawn by architect Peter Diedrich of Detroit, Michigan and the building contract was given to John Suelzer, parishioner. The new Saint Peter's Church was completed and dedicated on November 4, 1894. Gothic in style, it measures 190 feet by 80 feet and can seat approximately 1,100 people. The total cost including furnishing was $75,000.00!

In 1904, the first wing of a new, permanent school was begun on St. Martins Street. Eventually, the school was completed in 1914 and included additions on Hanna and DeWald Streets. Saint Peter's School continued to operate for exactly 100 years, closing its doors in 1972 due to declining enrollment.

In 1908, the present three beautifully illuminated altars were installed in the sanctuary of Saint Peter's Church. These three altars are wood-carved, with a profusion of Gothic style finials. In excess of 700 electric bulbs make for a spectacular appearance! The main scene on the high altar shows a relief of Christ handing the keys of heaven to St. Peter, based on the sixteenth chapter of St. Matthew's Gospel. These altars were designed by the Emil Hackner Company of LaCrosse, Wisconsin at a cost of $8,000.00. At this time too, the present Stations of the Cross as well as the Communion rail were installed.

Saint Peter's Parish continued to flourish throughout the first half of the twentieth century. However, beginning in the 1960s there began a dramatic change in parish demographics. For the first time in its history, the parish began to lose membership.

In the late 1980s this downward trend in membership subsided and new members were again being added. In 1991, Saint Peter's Church, School and Rectory were placed on the National Register of Historic Places. In observance of the 100th anniversary of the present church building, the entire church interior was cleaned and redecorated. In 1997, all forty-six stained glass windows were totally restored. In 1998, a rebuilt 1958 Aeolian-Skinner Opus 1337 Organ was installed in the loft. This organ has three-manuals containing 37 ranks and some 2,218 pipes. The entire cost of this almost ten year restoration project was in excess of one million dollars.

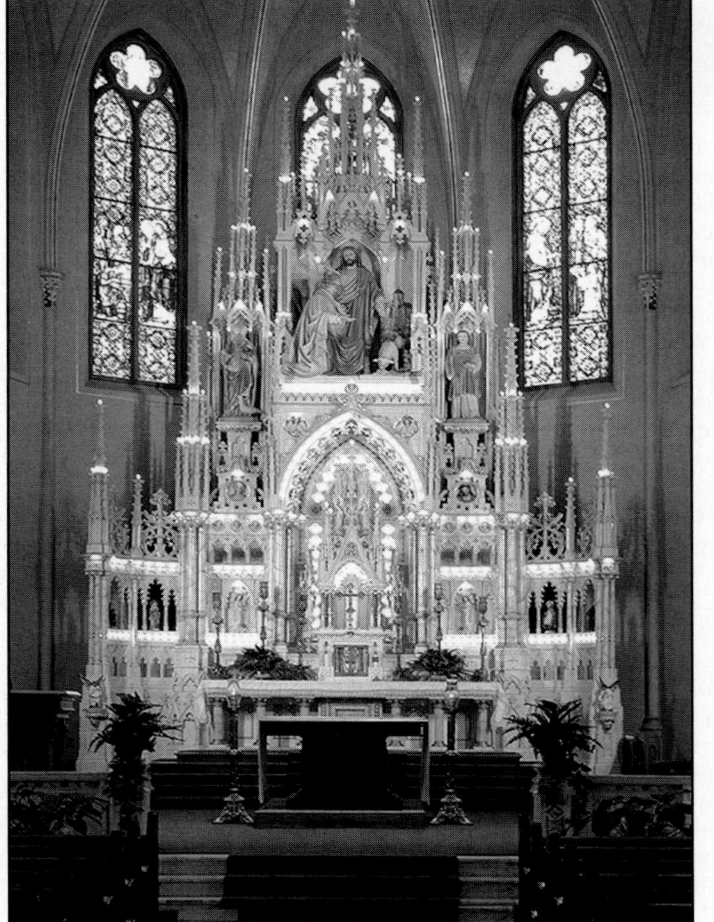

Main Altar, St. Peter Catholic Church, Fort Wayne, Indiana (January 2005, photo © by Gerard Kessens)

In 1997, in close cooperation with the city of Fort Wayne, Project Renew and nearby Zion Church, Saint Peter's entered into a partnership to help revitalize its neighborhood. Deteriorated housing and other structures were removed. New homes were built and others have been repaired and restored. Saint Peter's School building was sold and is currently being revamped to contain some forty plus apartments for seniors. In 2004, a new parish hall, primarily for social functions, was built and named the Saint Peter's Pavilion.

While times, faces, and landscapes change, Saint Peter's remains. The impact of Saint Peter's Parish to revitalize itself, should stand as an inspiration to others. The heritage of those early, pioneer parishioners remains. The age-old Catholic belief that nothing can be too beautiful for God's House can be seen in Saint Peter's Church – "the Splendor of the South Side since 1872" – "perhaps, the most beautiful Church in the Diocese, if not the entire Midwest."

St. Peter's Lutheran Church and School
St. Joseph Township, Allen County, Indiana

Church Building, 1870 to 1958.

St. Peter's Lutheran Church and School was founded in 1855 by Lutheran German immigrants who settled in the southeast corner of St. Joseph Township and the southwest corner of Milan Township. In June 1856 the church families constructed and dedicated a log cabin building on the northwest corner of Trier and Lahmeyer Roads that served as the church's first school and building for worship. The church became affiliated with the Lutheran Church Missouri Synod in 1856; St. Peter's is the oldest continuously existing congregation in St. Joseph Township, celebrating its 150th anniversary in 2005. In 1864 the church families found a need to build a second log school, located in Milan Township on the south side of Parent Road, just east of Koester Creek. Both log schools continued to serve the church until 1892.

In 1870 the congregation purchased three acres of land on the southwest corner of the intersection of East State Boulevard and Maysville Roads. There they constructed a wood frame church building 36 feet by 72 feet, and dedicated the building in June 1870. This was also the year the church's west cemetery first came into use. Prior to that, two smaller cemeteries existed -- one on the south side of Stellhorn Road about ½ mile east of Reed Road, and the other on the east side of Goeglein Road about 500 feet north of Trier Road. St. Peter's north cemetery on East State and Maysville Road began use in 1904.

In 1892 the congregation constructed two brick one-room school buildings, one located just west of the log school on Trier Road, and the other located on the south side of Stellhorn Road in Milan Township, just to the east of what is, in 2005, Interstate 469.That school building was demolished in about 1990 to make room for the interstate. The brick school on Trier Road, west of Lahmeyer, still exists in 2005 and is used as a personal residence. These one-room schools continued to be used until 1947, when the congregation constructed a four room school building on the southeast corner of East State Boulevard and Maysville Road.

In the 1920s and 30s, the congregation began the transition from the German language to English, although German worship services were occasionally held until the early 1960s.

The present church building at 7710 East State Boulevard was constructed in 1959, along with the gymnasium addition to the school building. In 1978 the congregation constructed an office and meeting room addition to the church building and a six classroom and cafeteria addition to the school building. In 2001 the congregation began a preschool program. In 2005 the elementary school includes grades kindergarten through eighth grade with 209 students. The preschool in 2005 has an enrollment of 56 students, ages 2 ½ to 5.

During its 150 year history, the congregation has been served by 13 pastors: Rev. Friedrich John, 1856-1859; Rev. Conrad Bode, 1860-1881; Rev. Moritz Michael, 1881-1899; Rev. P. Jensen, 1899-1903; Rev. Alfred Doerffler, 1903-1933; Rev. Henry Abram, 1933-1960; Rev. E. D. Busch, 1960-1986; Rev. Daniel May, 1974-1976; Rev. James Beyer, 1977-1984; Rev. Thomas Batsky, 1984-1993; Rev. Alan Parks, 1987-1998; Rev. Donald Nord, 1994 to the present; and Rev. Steven Ahlersmeyer, 2000 to the present.

Church Building, June 12, 2005.

St. Therese Catholic Church
2304 Lower Huntington Road, Fort Wayne

St. Therese Catholic Church

In 1946 Waynedale was a quiet little town southwest of Fort Wayne. Several Catholic families lived in the area and they longed for a church to call their own. They petitioned Bishop John F. Noll and he responded by appointing Rev. Herman Schoudel, a former Army chaplain, as their new pastor. The far-sighted Bishop had, in 1937, already purchased a plot of land in the Liberty Gardens addition of Waynedale for just that purpose.

On March 10, 1947, Fr. Schoudel met with local Catholics at the Wayne Township Fire House to form a Catholic Founders Club and plan for the new parish. The first Mass was held on April 13 that year in the Wayne Township School gymnasium. Parishioners set up a folding table for the altar and the pastor used his Army Mass kit for the sacred vessels. They sat on folding chairs, knelt on the floor and praised God with joyful hearts.

Since their own property was too wet, members held the first of their annual parish festivals at St. Aloysius Church in Yoder. Meanwhile, the pastor purchased a former Army air base chapel from Baer Field and parishioners prepared the land on Liberty Drive for its arrival, removing tree stumps with dynamite and draining the standing water. In January of 1948 the 87-ton building came lumbering across frozen fields and country roads on a flatbed truck with four dozen big, soft tires. An electric company crew walked ahead, dropping overhead wires so it could pass safely. The chapel was settled on a foundation built for it by eager hands and both the interior and exterior were refurbished appropriately.

Because Fr. Schoudel had celebrated his first Mass in Europe near Lisieux, France, the birthplace of St. Therese Martin, he chose her as the patroness of his new parish. He and his congregation joyfully celebrated the first Mass in their new spiritual home on March 7, 1948. The church was officially dedicated by Bishop Noll the following October 3, the original feast day of St. Therese that is now observed on October 1. The congregation numbered about fifty families.

On February 25, 1950, a fire gutted the church's interior. An Army barracks at Baer Field served as a substitute worship space until repairs could be made and it wasn't long before the church was occupied again. The congregation had grown to more than four times its original size and included many children whose parents wanted them to have a Catholic education. In 1955, the Sisters of St. Francis of Perpetual Adoration from Mishawaka agreed to staff a school, once it was built. In 1956, Fr. Albert Senn, OFM, became the first of nearly forty Franciscan friars who would serve the spiritual needs of the parish. A year later, construction began on a unique, semi-circular lift-slab building with twelve classrooms. Its unconventional design was teasingly dubbed "Fr. Albert's Folly" by some members. St. Therese School opened in the fall of 1958 and three sisters began teaching 201 children in grades 1-6.

On December 6, 1970, fire again damaged the church's interior. Parish women held the first annual Christmas Bazaar to raise funds for repairs. They scrubbed and scraped and soon had the basement ready to use for worship. Masses were held there and in some classrooms while the pastor and parish leaders consulted with the Fire Marshall and the insurance company. When the structure was deemed unsafe for large gatherings, parishioners decided to convert most of the new school's first floor into a worship space and use the old church as a parish hall. This second worship space was dedicated on October 17, 1971. The old church was razed in 1979 after a new parish hall/gymnasium opened that August.

Due to their declining numbers, the Franciscan Friars left St. Therese in June of 1994 and Diocesan priests once again staffed the Waynedale parish. In 1996, under the leadership of Rev. Michael Rossworm, the people of St. Therese began to work together to design and build a beautiful, 3.6 million dollar church. It was completed under the direction of Rev. Joseph Rulli who became pastor in the fall of 1999 and dedicated by Bishop John M. D'Arcy during the first Mass on Palm Sunday, April 10, 2003.

Today St. Therese is home to about 850 families--nearly 2,400 individuals. The school's fourteen teachers instruct 180 children in grades K-8. Along with the required subjects, students benefit from classes in Religion, Computers, Music, Art and Physical Education. The Religious Education program serves 75 public school students and a lively Youth Ministry program works with teens and young adults. St. Therese Church continues to be a solid anchor for the Waynedale community and a spiritual home for its parish family.

South Wayne Baptist Church

On Sunday, September 10, 1911, Jeanette Duryee Myers and Mary Palmer Graham were brought to the first worship of this church on this very spot, the corner of Indiana and Cottage Avenues. We came as infants, doubtless sleepy and inattentive, but were here; and ninety-two years later we are still here, devoted members of the South Wayne Baptist Church.

That 1911 service was not the real beginning of this church. In 1890 this neighborhood was known as South Wayne, an incorporated town for five years. Several of its residents were members of the First Baptist Church on Jefferson Street in downtown Fort Wayne. These families worked toward and obtained a Baptist Mission Sunday School in their own neighborhood. They met in the Town Hall at Lincoln and Indiana Avenues on Sunday mornings, and then went by horse-drawn streetcars or family carriages to the mother church for worship services and baptism.

This trek quickly became tiresome. With the blessing and assistance of the downtown church, plans for their own church were presented on September 5, 1911. By that time, two good Baptist residents of South Wayne had offered help: Judge Allen Zollars offered the land at the corner of Indiana and Cottage Avenues, and Mr. Augustus C. Beaver offered a frame chapel then on the banks of the St. Mary's River. His offer required us to move it to the corner lot offered by Judge Zollars. Somehow it was done, and we named it Beaver Chapel.

By the end of 1911, 86 individuals were named as charter members of the South Side Baptist Church. In 1915 its name was changed to the South Wayne Baptist Church in recognition of the town that had helped give it birth. In a similar move, the public school across the street was named for this early town. All this compounded the confusion for strangers even today as they expect both school and church to be on South Wayne Avenue. So much for memorializing history! We did it at risk of missing some potential Baptist members we would have been glad to have!

Our 86 charter members plus newcomers were a hardy bunch. As you look at their pictures hanging in our lobby, give them a bow. Of those charter members there were, as by custom then, only about 30 who were breadwinners; wives generally stayed at home caring for children. Evidence of the determination of this congregation is their action in less than two years to plan and build a large brick edifice to house a Sunday School, sanctuary, meeting rooms, dining room and kitchen, office, furnace room and restrooms. The cost was $11,000, with $10,000 borrowed – and paid off shortly after dedication in January 1913. How often do we take bold steps like these?

All churches experience periods of high enthusiasm and increase in membership. We have done so, but – like all others – have endured times of stress and loss such as national epidemics of disease like influenza and polio, the call up of young men (and women) for wartime duty, social and political unrest, economic down-times like the Great Depression of the 1930s – all these brought questions and doubt about the future for families, churches, businesses, and communities. We lived with and through all such trials, as did others. Today we recognize our need for that personal courage and commitment.

As we outgrew our 1913 building, we planned a new sanctuary (the one we still use!).

Once more we needed a loan – a big one. A donor granted it, with a string attached not of our choice; he required TWELVE of our members to sign an agreement to pay back the loan if our church defaulted on it. The church did not default, but twelve families lived in financial uncertainty for several years.

That sanctuary, still beautiful though occasionally showing its age, was dedicated in March 1926. We now serve two congregations with this sanctuary and an educational building erected in 1959. We worship as South Wayne Baptist and as Hispanics Iglesia Bautista Emanuel, sharing our facilities at different hours and occasional joint services.

Under the leadership of our pastor, Rev. Doyle R. Carpenter, we are currently trying to map out our future as a church. To do so, with the aid of the church council, we have accepted a Mission Statement appropriate, we think, for our congregation and the community we wish to serve. We believe this Mission Statement embodies the basic efforts needed and possible for us to assume:

We are a caring community of believers, Inviting persons from all walks of life to meet Jesus Christ and experience the new life the Spirit of God gives.

We are presently considering various series of steps to accept as our Vision of how best to implement this purpose.

Some of us, like Jeanette and I, are still here – but not because of long years of habit! We are here because this church offers encouragement, friendship, a deepening Christian faith, and opportunities to serve others.

Statewood Baptist Church
(June 1958-Present)

2208 North Coliseum Boulevard, Fort Wayne

In the summer of 1956, a group of Christians who called themselves "Missionary Baptists" were meeting in an abandoned store building at Gay and Creighton Streets in Fort Wayne, Indiana. By autumn most of them had withdrawn to form an independent Baptist Church elsewhere in the city. Among those remaining were two ministers, Henry Munderich and Kemuel Warstler.

In December, 1956, Perry Hollandsworth moved to Fort Wayne from Owensville, Missouri. Within a short time he found the remnant group now discouraged and considering the matter of disbanding. Hollandsworth's appearance seems to have given the group the necessary encouragement, because an enlistment program was begun which reached several children and revived the spirits of the mission leaders. Early in 1957, the movement became affiliated with the Southern Baptist Convention. Thus was born "Southern Baptist Mission" under the sponsorship of First Southern Baptist Church of Mishawaka, Indiana. Walter Adams was the first "official" pastor on February 16, 1958. Prior to this time Munderich, Warstler and Arl Varble had served as pastors. Under Adams' leadership the group sought, and attained, church status. On June 1, 1958, "Southern Baptist Mission" became "Maumee Valley Baptist Church." There were twenty charter members. On October 12, 1958, the church requested membership in the Northern Indiana Baptist Association, which was then affiliated with the Illinois Baptist State Convention.

In November 1958, a dwelling house was procured at 2123 Wells Street. In March 1960, Area Missionary H. J. Conger assumed many of the pastoral duties. A pastoral missionary, Galen Irby was called as pastor, May 8, 1960. Under Irby's guidance the church made one of it most significant moves in the summer of 1960 - the purchase of its present building site. By autumn of that year the church was quartered into two old buildings located at 2208 North Bueter Road (later changed to US Highway 30, By-Pass, North). Before the year's end the name was changed to "First Southern Baptist Church". During 1962, the first unit of four proposed buildings was constructed. In January 1963, the first meeting was conducted in the new building with a dedication service on the following May 26th.

On December 6, 1964, Irby resigned to assume duties as pastor of Beacon Baptist Mission which had recently been formed out of the membership of "First Southern" and was soon appointed area missionary for Northeastern Indiana Association. Earl Croxton was then called as Pastor, and a pattern set previously (a new name with each pastor) became a tradition, because on January 1, 1966 the name was changed for the third time to "Statewood Baptist Church". Not to be outdone were the "city fathers" who have since renamed the street as Coliseum Boulevard. On January 4, 1970, the lower floor of the new two-story structure was occupied by the departments ranging from birth through age eight.

December 1976 brought Ken Taylor as Pastor who ministered through July 1982. Fred Woodward was called as Pastor in January 1983 and served through August 1988 when he returned to seminary to further his biblical studies. That same year, James Moser began as pastor and the church grew and added a food bank ministry in 1992. It also began broadcasting morning worship services, "Rejoice," on the local channel 10 cable station. In 1997, the front porch was enclosed, a new steeple was placed on the roof, and interior renovations began. Pastor Jim retired in Jan 2000 and was followed by Greg Byman as Pastor until September 2002. Brother Don Hamm began as interim Pastor in January 2003 and in May 2003 began as Pastor. Pastor Don retired in March 2005. During his tenure the church grew and new members were baptized. An elevator was installed in the educational building and the upstairs recarpeted. Upon Pastor Don's retirement, Ron Hollandsworth felt God's calling to pastor the church until the church is able to find a permanent full time Pastor. Pastor Ron was licensed February 27 and called as pastor on March 9, 2005.

The future is in God's hands. It is the prayer of every member that God will continue to bless and to use the members of Statewood Baptist Church. (www.statewoodbaptistchurch.com)

Taylor United Methodist Church
10145 Maysville Road

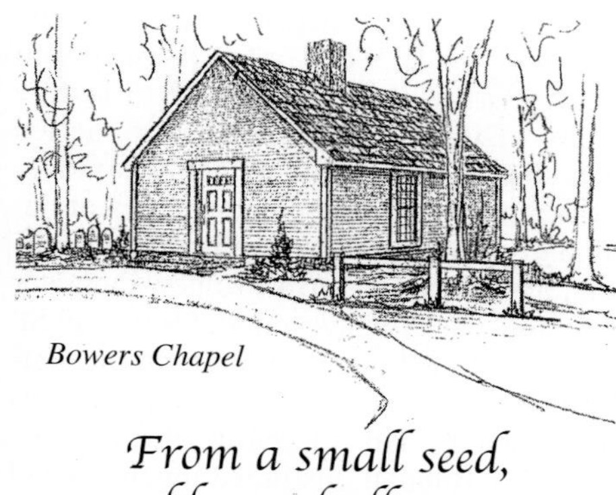
Bowers Chapel

From a small seed, a bloom shall grow.

A minister of the Methodist Episcopal Church, the Rev. Trew Pattee, came to St. Joseph Township in 1836, locating in Section 24. In the years following, he preached in schoolhouses, homes or wherever people would gather, and is credited with holding religious meetings not only in St. Joseph, but also in Milan and Springfield Townships. His preaching influenced a small "seed" of people who remained closely united. Their unity became the history of Taylor Chapel.

In 1851, David and Susannah Bowers emigrated from Ohio to Indiana along a trail in Section 24 known as Ridge Road (later to become Maysville Road/Indiana State Road 37). On August 14, 1855, Mr. Bowers deeded ½ acre of his land to the M.E. Church for building Bowers Chapel. Additional acreage was donated by David Colerick, and by the heirs of Mr. Bowers. The property, on the corner of Wheelock and State Road 37, became Bowers Cemetery and it continues this legacy today. In 1870, the Bowers Cemetery Association was organized. The president of it today is Gary Merriman.

It cannot be determined exactly where the little church known as Bowers Chapel was erected in the Bowers Cemetery, but some historical accounts state that it stood by the "old oak tree." Proof of the existence of Bowers Chapel is found in records from the North Indiana Conference of the M.E. Church stating that in 1865, donations for the Missionary Society were received from members of Bowers Chapel.

In 1891, the Rev. Charles Tinkham, appointed to the New Haven Circuit, became minister at a time when the congregation had outgrown little Bowers Chapel. On September 8, 1891, Arthur and Mary Vilas Taylor donated a half acre of land to the Bowers congregation. This land was about three-quarters of a mile northeast of Bowers Chapel along Maysville Road. After months of toil, a beautiful white and wood frame building was erected on a fieldstone and mortar foundation. It was heated by pot-bellied stoves and lighted by coal oil lamps. Dr. Reade, of the Fort Wayne College, dedicated it as Taylor Chapel Church on February 19, 1893.

Under the ministry of the Rev. John Stewart, remodeling occurred in 1920 with the addition of a coal furnace and lighting provided by a Delco System. Rural electricity became available in 1928 and a well was drilled in 1951.

As the congregation grew in size, land was needed for a parsonage and for parking. Bert and Perepa McNett deeded land for additional parking. Albert and Bertha Chausse (after his death, she married Henry Lantz) gave land on the south side of Maysville Road for erection of a parsonage (now the location of a Bob Evans Restaurant).

The "seed" continued to bloom, growing into our present day church, Taylor Chapel United Methodist Church (the E.U.B. and M.E. denominations combined into the United Methodist Church in 1968). Additional land was purchased from the Chausses for erecting our beautiful brick church. Ground breaking was held in 1963, with Rev. Richard Applegate officiating. The first service was held March 15, 1964 with Rev. Charles Rutherford as pastor.

As Taylor Chapel continued to reach out in Christian fellowship to the community, additional space was needed for Sunday school, the on-going daily preschool, the expanding music department, the vital youth program and of course, administrative offices. Reconfigured offices, a larger fellowship hall and kitchen, a second basement, and the educational wing were added in 1980. Additional remodeling was accomplished in 1995-96, but the congregation's true spirit of faith and effort occurred in 1998 when there was extensive damage to the sanctuary caused by a tornado. Church members and friends gave hours and hours of just plain "grub" work to renovate the sanctuary and narthex.

So, what became of the original church structures of Bowers Chapel and the little white frame Taylor Chapel?

It is believed that Dr. I. S. Null bought Bowers Chapel to incorporate into his office in New Haven. If you drive past the Chapel Ridge shopping area on Maysville Road, you also pass the original Taylor Chapel site. It was razed in 2001 to make room for the commercial businesses. Fortunately for our congregation, we can reminisce about the "old" churches as we review photos, drawings, and stories of our history. We continue to pray for the future of Taylor Chapel United Methodist Church and the surrounding community.

Our pastors are the Rev. William Farmer and the Rev. Diane Barrett. Other staff members are Kevin Klee, Jana Jay, Chris Stalman, Veronica Gatchell, Kathy Weinert, Jan Fife, Brenda Niccum and Tom Marcotte.

From that small "seed" of parishioners in 1865, to now in 2005, the Taylor Chapel United Methodist Church has continued to "bloom" in a corner of St. Joseph Township in northeast Allen County.

Taylor United Methodist Church, 2006.

Trinity Episcopal Church, Fort Wayne

Trinity Episcopal Church

The Episcopal Church in Fort Wayne can trace its beginnings to the Right Rev. Jackson Kemper, the Church's first Missionary Bishop, who visited for the first time in 1837 to preach and assess the feasibility of organizing a congregation. Two years passed before he could send a missionary. Under the leadership of Rev. Benjamin Hutchins, Christ Episcopal Church was organized on May 26, 1839, but it soon floundered. A local editor commented, "We are not yet old enough for a society of this kind. In other words, there are not people enough in this county who are constitutionally fitted to be Episcopalians."

In 1844, Peter Bailey, a New York entrepreneur and devout Episcopalian, organized lay readings in the courthouse. Kemper dispatched another missionary, Rev. Benjamin Halsted, who with a small group of members organized Trinity Episcopal Church. Though initially poor, the congregated eventually built a wood-frame chapel at the southeast corner of Berry and Harrison in 1848. A new priest, Rev. Joseph Large, who arrived the same year, brought the congregation much-needed stability.

The new church drew from a variety of local citizens, including Episcopalians from the East, British and Canadian immigrants, and newcomers to the faith, many of which were well educated. They found its sermons intellectual, its structure democratic, its liturgy appealing, and an atmosphere that was not overly political, disciplinary, or judgmental. It had also established a strong tradition of lay leadership, however, that could often be hard on its rectors.

In 1866, under Large's second rectorate, the congregation completed construction of a Gothic Revival edifice designed by Toledo architect Charles Crosby Miller. Located at Berry and Fulton, the new building featured split-faced Indiana sandstone and English-designed stained glass windows, making it one of the finest examples of its architectural style in the region.

In its new location Trinity joined the ranks of several congregations as a "society church," attracting for its membership many of the city's political, professional and business leadership. The remainder of the 19th century saw a succession of rectors – Colin Tate, William Webbe, and Alexander Seabrease - all of whom preached a social gospel message from the pulpit, advocating temperance, women's suffrage, missionary outreach, and social responsibility to the poor.

The turn of the 20th century brought new liturgical changes that made Trinity Church increasingly Anglo-Catholic in style. Edward W. Averill, Trinity's tenth rector and the first to be called "Father," improved the music and expanded both parish programming and the congregation's expectations of his own pastoral ministry. In 1924, his successor, Rev. Louis Rocca, borrowed money for refurbishing the church and redecorated it in an elaborate style, including an ornate rood screen. James McNeal Wheatley, perhaps the most Anglo-Catholic rector, helped to guide the parish successfully through a period of economic austerity during the Great Depression.

When the congregation split over Wheatley's forced departure in 1947, the Rev. George B. Wood, a brash, outspoken former army chaplain, arrived to restore unity. During his 21-year tenure, he led the construction of a new administrative-education building, invited a series of nationally renowned theologians as lecturers, and helped to form two new daughter missions, St. Alban's and St. Philip and St. James'. But Wood's authoritarian leadership style alienated as many members as it attracted. His successor, the Rev. C. Corydon Randall, instituted much-needed reforms that included an expansion of lay leadership through the formation of new vestry commissions. He also built up the church's endowments and spearheaded a major restoration of the edifice that included placement on the National Register of Historic Places. His successor, Frank H. Moss III, who arrived in 1990, continued the lay ministry foundation and brought the congregation renewed sense of unity. The Catechesis of the Good Shepherd program was established, offering children a unique interactive way to learn about the Bible, sacraments, and faith.

In 2001, Trinity called the Rev. Rebecca Ferrell Nickel as its first female rector and the first female pastor of a large downtown parish in Fort Wayne. Creative and energetic, she attracted new members and strengthened Trinity's commitment to diversity. However, her leadership led to new fissures within the congregation, some along generational lines, and her departure in 2004 left Trinity at a crossroads. Under interim rector Robert Askren, the congregation continues to celebrate the sacraments in its historic edifice. It retains its long-standing support for the West Central Neighborhood ministry and cherishes its tradition of musical excellence in Christian worship. It also is guided by its motto: "Ministry to all in Christ; all in ministry for Christ."

Blessing of Animals

Children's Atrium

Trinity Evangelical Lutheran Church

7819 Decatur Road, Fort Wayne

Lutheranism first took visible form on the Piqua Road, now known as the Decatur Road, about five miles south of the downtown district of Fort Wayne in the year 1846. Members of St. Paul's Evangelical Lutheran Church, Fort Wayne, organized a school in the above-mentioned area of Fort Wayne in the year 1846. The land on which the present church and school have been erected was purchased in the year 1847, at which time a log school house was built. In the year 1848 a teacher's residence, which later became the parsonage, was built on the Decatur Road.

In the year 1853 Trinity congregation was organized. The first constitution was submitted and subscribed to by thirty men. Divine services were conducted in the log school house.

On September 13, 1853, the cornerstone of a new frame church was laid, and the new frame church was dedicated on Pentecost Monday in the year 1854. This frame church served as the house of worship for the congregation until the year 1903.

Through Trinity's 151 years, it has been served by fourteen pastors: Pastor George F. Dietz 1854-56; Pastor John Streckfusz 1856-59; Pastor John A. Zagel 1860-83; Pastor Frederick W. Franke 1883-1913; Pastor John C. Bauer 1914-19; Pastor Karl F. Wyneken 1920-43; Pastor Norman C. Schumm 1943-46; Pastor Werner Schmidtke 1947-53; Pastor Louis J. Fuchs 1953-66; Pastor Roland Fritz 1967-78; Pastor David Jentsch 1978-86; Pastor Robert Eichmann 1987-93; Interim Pastor Donald Fischer 1993-94; and Pastor Gregory S. Cynova 1994-Present.

Records show that Trinity's school was served until its consolidation with Bethlehem Lutheran School by the following teachers: Mr. Ernst A. Eggers 1852-62; Mr. Peter Kestel 1863-65; from 1865 to 1921 the pastors of the congregation also taught school; Mr. Herman Teske 1921-28; Mr. Edwin L. Nicol 1928-66; Miss Elaine Nicol 1953-57; Mrs. Ellen Schnabel 1956-58, 1960-62; Miss June Kanning 1957-59; Mrs. Mary Schmidt 1958-60; Miss Thelma Weissmiller 1959-62; Miss Linda Borausky 1961-63; Miss Dorothy Fick 1962-63; Miss Lois Warnke 1963-64; Mrs. Helen Brown 1963-65; Miss Barbara Werfelmann 1974-64; Mrs. Raymond Sprehe 1965-consolidation; Mrs. Lois Reddemann 1965-68; Mr. Leonard Weber 1966-consolidation; Mrs. Warian Weber 1966-68; Mrs. Eileen Widmann 1968-69; and Miss Janet Hasselman 1968-69.

In 1884, a brick one room school building was erected, and in May of the year 1904 the present brick sanctuary was dedicated.

In 1914, Trinity's Ladies' Aid was organized with 30 women. The women would meet together in their homes for the day and would bring their preschool age children with them.

On June 11, 1926 the Church Council approved a resolution which allowed a monthly English worship service be held. As the congregation continued to grow, the attendance at the German services dwindled. In 1971, the four German services held each year were discontinued due to the difficulty in finding a German speaking pastor to lead them.

Trinity's Men's Club was organized in 1940 with 17 charter members.

In 1941 a Sunday school program was established at Trinity for its children and the first Children's Christmas Eve Service was conducted in English.

In 1942, separate English and German Lenten services were held and the first English translation of the Constitution of the congregation was approved.

A new school building was completed and then dedicated on April 19, 1953 replacing the 69 year old brick one room school.

In June 1957, Trinity's first Kindergarten class was established. By the end of July, 22 children had enrolled, so a limit of 25 was set. Enrollment for the 8 grades of our school had grown from 61 students in 1956 to 90 students in 1959. In 1970, Trinity consolidated its elementary school with Bethlehem on South Anthony. In April 1992, Trinity withdrew from the consolidation and established an Early Childhood program in its education building.

The Ladies Guild was organized on November 6, 1957. This group met in the evening to accommodate young women and mothers with small children.

Trinity congregation conducted its first Vacation Bible School, July 27 through August 7, 1964 – 76 children were enrolled – a total of 90 attended.

Trinity built the present parsonage in 1965 to replace its 117 year old parsonage.

Since 1994, Trinity has remained stable and at peace; multiple ongoing Bible studies have been established; an African Immigrant Mission, headquartered in its facility, has been established; and an expanding mission to the growing Hispanic population is involving many of its lay-people and pastor.

Trinity congregation continues to serve Fort Wayne's south side and seeks to bring Christ's message of salvation to its neighbors.

Christmas at Trinity Lutheran Church

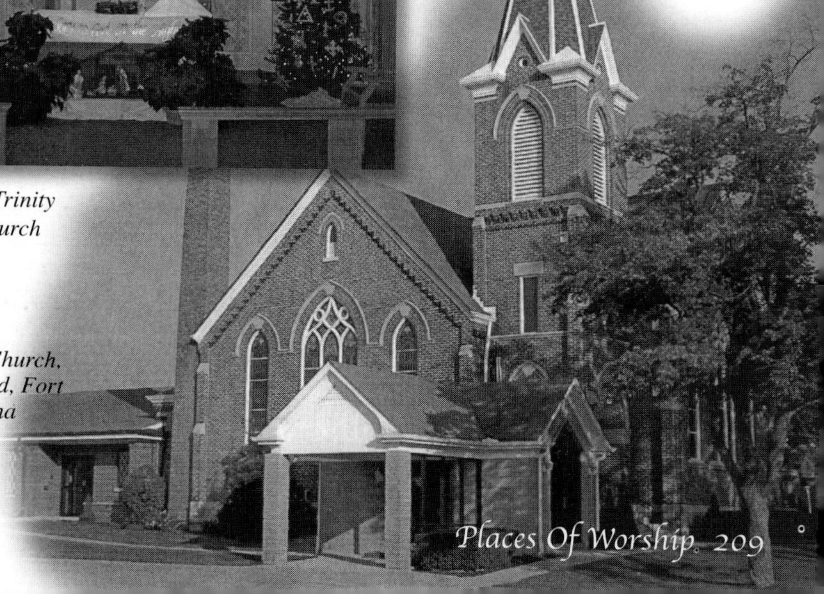

Trinity Lutheran Church, 7819 Decatur Road, Fort Wayne, Indiana

Trier Ridge Community Church, Inc.
(Formerly First Church of God)

Trier Ridge Community Church, Inc. at the corner of Hessen Cassel and Tillman Roads, Fort Wayne (March 2005)

First Church of God, Wildwood and Piqua Street, Fort Wayne

The history of Trier Ridge Community Church stretches back to January 1907 when members of some area Churches of God organized a Missionary Society in Fort Wayne. In September 1907 the Society petitioned the Indiana Eldership to send a minister to Fort Wayne to organize a church.

Vordermark's Hall at 624 South Calhoun Street was rented for Sunday morning services, with the first service held on November 24, 1907. On August 23, 1908 the First Church of God in Fort Wayne, Indiana was officially organized with 40 charter members.

On February 6, 1909 the church purchased the property known as Sunnyside Chapel (an old school house) located at 3201 South Lafayette Street. In August 1909 the annual Sunday school picnic was held in the park on Hanna Street, known as the first woods on Hanna Street (Weisser Park). In September 1909 the local church entertained the State Missionary convention.

Dr. Charles Manchester became pastor in October 1913; under his pastorate, a lot at the corner of Piqua and Wildwood Avenues was purchased for $2,000. Very little progress was made toward building during the 1914-1915 Eldership year because of opposition to building on such a small lot. In 1916 Wildwood Builders Association, developers of the subdivision, deeded another lot, just north of the one purchased, to the Eldership trustees. The cornerstone was laid in 1917 and dedication services were held in 1918. This landmark was also known as the church with the round dome. The congregation conducted services at this location until March 28, 1976.

Ladies formed the very active Dorcas Aid Society; through their efforts much money was raised for worthwhile causes or needs which arose in the church. In June 1954 a Women's Christian Service Council was formed.

The church celebrated its 50th anniversary on September 14, 1958. The property just north of the church was purchased in October 1958. The Piqua House, as it was named, was dedicated in December 1958.

In March 1975 the church purchased 4.6 acres of land located at the southeast corner of Hessen Cassel and Tillman Roads. April 4, 1976 First Church of God conducted Sunday school and worship services at Southwick Elementary School due to the construction of the new church. On May 16, 1976 it was decided the new church would be called Trier Ridge Community Church. The first service was held February 6, 1977, and the first council meeting was held February 7, 1977. A service of praise and celebration for Trier Ridge Community Church was held April 24, 1977. The new church had a sanctuary seating capacity of 200 with an overflow area for 60, ten classrooms, nursery, church office, pastor's study, kitchen, and fellowship hall to seat 125. The parking lot accommodates 80 cars.

March 15, 1986 a new parsonage was purchased in Trier Ridge subdivision at 7603 Ensign Court.

On August 28, 1988, the 80th Anniversary celebration of the First Church of God/Trier Ridge Community Church was held. In July 1993, a 20-year mortgage was paid off and a mortgage burning service was held October 3, 1993.

As advancements in video technology progressed, the church council voted to purchase a video projector. This provided a new concept in presenting the Word of God in song and scripture.

The covered main entrance to the church needed some structural changes and in March 1999 approval was given to have a larger brick faced entrance built to coordinate with the existing building. About the same time, we were given the privilege to apply for a neighborhood grant. An application was submitted requesting funding for playground equipment. The grant was approved and a playground area was established to benefit the church and neighborhood.

Over the years there were discussions and dreams about a building addition to the west end for classrooms, a larger activities area, and storage. Various plans were considered, and at the November 21, 1999 congregational meeting, approval was given to the church council to proceed with plans for a one-story west end addition. At a special congregational meeting on June 11, 2000, final approval was given to build the west end addition. Ground breaking was held September 17, 2000.

Construction started the middle of December 2000. God provided warm enough weather to get the building under roof so that construction could proceed during the winter months. It was with great joy and thankfulness that the new building addition was dedicated on October 7, 2001.

As the church looks ahead, the leadership faces many challenges and questions concerning the ministry God has for Trier Ridge Community Church, but we are confident of God's continued faithfulness and direction.

Trinity Evangelical Lutheran Church

During the early 1890s, members from St. Paul Lutheran Church saw a need for a Christian school in the northwest part of Fort Wayne. In 1893 they erected a two story brick building on the southwest corner of Oakland and Huffman Streets. The school was organized, and area families began sending their children to Trinity Lutheran School. It was a one-room school with Mr. A. Nehrenz as teacher. In 1895 Trinity Evangelical Lutheran Church was organized. The first members called the Rev. J. A. Bohn, Assistant Pastor at St. Paul, to serve as pastor.

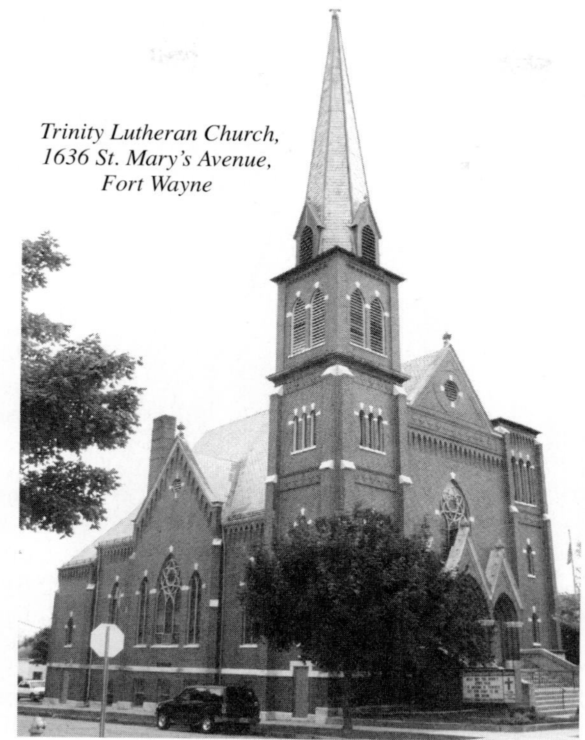

Trinity Lutheran Church, 1636 St. Mary's Avenue, Fort Wayne

The original building provided facilities for both education and worship. Eventually there were two classrooms on the first floor and a sanctuary on the second floor. It was a modern building at the time, but lacked conveniences commonly enjoyed today. The sanctuary's location on the second floor also provided a challenge to pallbearers during funerals.

Throughout the years, the school saw numerous improvements. The congregation installed city water in 1898. They also placed hitching posts on Oakland Street so those attending services or visiting the facility could tie up their horses. In 1911 men of the congregation dug out enough space to install bowling alleys.

The Bloomingdale area grew, and membership at Trinity Church and School increased accordingly. It soon became necessary to construct a new sanctuary. In 1916 the present church was completed and dedicated. With new facilities for worship, the upper floor of the original building became available for other uses. The "Unique Society" (quilters) and the Men's Club occupied the east room, and the west room was a classroom. Another area was used as a kitchen. Teams played basketball on the upper floor, but the ceiling was too low and plaster began to fall in the classrooms below.

In the early fifties, the old building was becoming obsolete. After several years of planning, members took steps to build a new school facing St. Mary's Avenue. Ground was broken during the summer of 1956, and construction began on the present school building. The dedication took place September 8, 1957, under the direction of Rev. C. W. Brueggemann. The school opened with 180 Kindergarten through eighth grade students. The old building was razed in 1957 to make room for more parking. During the next few years the congregation worked hard to complete the rooms on the first floor of the new school since they had not been finished at the time of construction.

In the mid-1950s, drive-in theaters were popular, and Trinity began to utilize the Lincolndale Theater as another venue to reach out to the neighborhood. Cars would drive in on Sunday morning with Mom, Dad, and the children sometimes in pajamas, perhaps even bringing the family pet. They placed the speaker on the window of the car to listen to the sermon. The pastor stood on the top of the refreshment stand, rain or shine, and delivered the sermon. This service continued until the Lincolndale was torn down in 1979. In 1979, this early morning service moved to the Foellinger Outdoor Theater. "Worship in the Park", as it is called, has been very popular with both Trinity members and visitors, and celebrated 25 years in 2004.

In 1966, many improvements were made to the church proper in preparation for the golden jubilee. The most significant was rebuilding the organ and moving it from the front of the church to the balcony. The organ continues to be a regular part of worship at Trinity.

During the seventies, the church acquired three houses on Oakland Street. In 1976 the parking area was extended to the rear portion of these properties, and a playground was erected for the children. Two adjacent St. Mary's Avenue houses were purchased and then demolished in 2004.

The congregation continues to upgrade the aging facility. An elevator was installed in 1998, giving handicapped and elderly people access to all levels of the building. Air conditioning was installed in 2002, making the building more comfortable on hot humid days. A classroom was converted to a modern office area in 2000, and various classrooms areas were air-conditioned in 2002. The church installed video equipment in 2000, with church services then televised on local cable television.

Due to the aging population of the congregation and families moving to the suburbs, the enrollment in grades one through eight steadily declined. In 2002, the focus of the church's ministry changed from day school to early childhood ministry. Child-care was added in 2001, with preschool and kindergarten classes continuing. The congregation also launched neighborhood ministry in 2004.

Since its beginning, Trinity Lutheran Church has been served by the following pastors: J. Bohn (1895-1902); Paul Stoeppelworth (1902-1914); G. W .F. Doege (1914-1928); Herbert Levihn (1928-1952); Harold Georg (1948-1950); Carl Brueggemann (1953-1958); Harold Ott (1958-1968); Theodore R. Taykowski (1969-1999); A. O. Kaltwasser (1973-1999), and David A. Easterday (1999-present).

Trinity United Methodist Church
609 Putnam Street Fort Wayne

In 1874 the North Indiana Conference met in Fort Wayne and determined the time had arrived when an expansion to Methodism should be undertaken in the Ninth Ward of the City. A local preacher, R. S. Reed, was sent to obtain a place for services. At the time, many school buildings had been outgrown, so some of these buildings, plus a lot at Third and Marion Streets, were purchased for the sum of $1,678.03. The buildings were moved to the lot, remodeled, and on September 12, 1875 the church was dedicated. Reverend D. M. Brown was named pastor of this North Ward M.E. Church. Fourteen members were received into full membership and 56 were received on probation. The average attendance was 38 and the pastor's salary was $300.00. The members decided to change the name of the church in 1876 and it became Third Street M.E. Church.

By 1884, with increased membership, the congregation outgrew the small worship building. Property at Cass and Fourth Streets became available in July of that year and the property was purchased from the First Presbyterian Church. The name of the church was changed again and at this time it became known as Trinity M.E. Church. This small church served the needs of the congregation until 1898 when an expansion program was undertaken. Sunday school rooms were added and the parsonage was improved.

By 1915, however, a movement was started for the building of a great, new church -- one that would amply serve the congregation and community for years to come. With a gift of $26,400, the trustees purchased a property for the church on the southwest corner of Short and Putnam Streets on October 16, 1919. Perry W. Fair was employed as architect and the cornerstone was laid and building started in 1921. The minister, Rev. M. C. Wright envisioned a great edifice, much larger than funds available could make possible. He inspired his congregation to sacrifice in money and in personal work on the project. An overseer was hired for the actual construction, and labor was hired only when made necessary by work requiring trained craftsmen. Men of the congregation poured cement in to the forms, poured the concrete steps to the basement, dug and placed the drains, laid shingles, pounded nails into timber, and laid all the hardwood floors. Women of the congregation truly said that their husbands spent so much time on the church building that they neglected family and home. Rev. Wright, donning work clothes, labored with them. Then, taking off on his bicycle, would persuade a company or individual to contribute materials or money for the church. There came to be a familiar expression in the community that "Rev. Wright carries the church on his bicycle." Women played a great part in the building movement also, and through the Ladies Aid Society worked actively in raising funds. They presented two of the beautiful stained glass windows that grace the church today. Despite the great contributions in labor and money, it was necessary to obtain a loan of $25,000 from Tri State Loan and Trust Company. By 1925 the church membership was 840.

Many improvements were made to the inside of the church throughout the 1940s and early '50s, but by 1955 the congregation again realized that additional space was necessary. An educational unit was needed. Under Rev. C. Elson's leadership a large addition was completed in 1959 providing a large gymnasium/fellowship hall and several new rooms for office, nursery, and Sunday school classes. By 1980 land had been acquired and parking lots were developed to accommodate the growing congregation.

Today Trinity is a beacon to the neighborhood through its many services and ministries. "Trinity Ministries" includes a Head Start program, Baby's Closet, Food Bank, Thrift Shop, and Evergreen Park. In addition many organizations use the facility for their meetings and support groups.

Trinity has met the spiritual needs of its members through the following ministers who faithfully served His church from 1875 through 2005: The Reverends D. M. Brown, 1875-77; W. D. Parr, 1878; H. C. Myer, 1879; J. M. Wolpert, 1879; G. D. Miller, 1880-82; J. R. Connehy, 1883-84; C. H. Murray, 1885; L. H. Merlin, 1886-87; J. C. Cook, 1888; N. D. Shackelford, 1889-90; W. R. Wones, 1891-92; J. B. Alleman, 1893; H. M. Johnson, 1894-95; E. F. Albertson, 1896-97; Sherman Powell, 1898-99; C. E. White, 1900-02; David Wells, 1903; George Cocking, 1904; J. K. Cecil, 1904-05; R. L. Seamons, 1906-07; W. P. Herron, 1908-09; T. M. Hill, 1910-15; Charles Shoemaker, 1916; Manfred C. Wright, 1917-23; L. G. Jacobs, 1923-26; Herman R. Carson, 1927-29; E. E. Trippeer, 1929-1935; Robert J. Bums, 1935-41; Daymon K. Finch, 1941-45; Charles C. Ford, 1945-52; D. Charles Elson, 1952-60; John M. Kirkpatrick, 1960-68; G. R. Brittenham, 1962-63; Daniel Stone, 1964-68; L. Hershel Dyer, 1967-69; Carl C. Bosse, 1968-71; Charles Alexander, 1969; James C. Stansell, 1970-75; Donald R. Abbey, 1971-75; Laurence I. Smith, 1975-80; Keith D. Davis, 1980-87; Jay A. Morris, 1987-92; Robert J. Dexter, 1992-2001; Justin Fisher, 2001-02; David Ballinger, 2003-.

Unitarian Universalism in Fort Wayne

Many Allen County citizens are not aware that two Unitarian ministers are on a frieze on the side of the county courthouse. William Ellery Channing and Theodore Parker are together on the southwest corner of the building. They reflect a long historical connection with the county. Universalist ministers preached regularly at the Allen County Courthouse in the 1840s when Fort Wayne was considered a wild and wicked place. During the 1850s and 1860s Universalist congregations met in Huntertown, New Haven and Sheldon (now Yoder). In Fort Wayne, the First Universalist Church was founded in 1875. At about the same time, Unitarians began to hold services in Fort Wayne. By the end of the 19th century, however, congregations of both faiths had disbanded.

The Unitarian Universalist Congregation of Fort Wayne traces its founding to 1937 when the American Unitarian Association canvassed Fort Wayne residents to see if there was sufficient interest to start a Unitarian congregation. Ministers from the region visited the city. On April 16, 1939, twenty-seven charter members formally organized the Unitarian Congregation of Fort Wayne. When the Unitarian and Universalist denominations merged in 1961, it took its current name.

The new church first met in the auditorium of the Fort Wayne Art School on Sunday evenings. In the fall of 1939, members gathered on Sunday mornings in the reception rooms of the Fairfield Manor apartments. The minister during those years was Universalist Rev. Robert Hoagland. In the early years of that decade he had studied in Europe, influencing his stand as a pacifist.

The second minister to the congregation was Rev. Aaron S. Gilmartin. He led a group which had finally purchased its own home, a house at 2929 Fairfield, directly across from Lutheran Hospital. Ministers during the 1950s were Rev. John Fordon and Rev. Hugo Leaming. The congregation's current home at 5310 Old Mill Road, designed by architect Ken Cole, was dedicated on January 29, 1960. Rev. Eugene Luening served the group in the early 60s.

Rev. Richard Langhinrichs came to the congregation in 1965 and served the parish (and the community) for 24 years until his retirement in 1989. Rev. Langhinrichs was active in the effort to desegregate Fort Wayne Community Schools, in protesting the war in Viet Nam, and in abortion counseling. He supported non-violence and the creation of the Center for Non-Violence in Fort Wayne. He spoke out against the John Birch Society. He was known for his stimulating sermons and, as part of his involvement in the Ohio Valley District of the Unitarian Universalist Association, helped to found new churches within the district.

Rev. Laurie Proctor became the congregation's first woman minister in 1991. Her interest in social justice issues involved her with interfaith boards, including the YWCA and the Clergy Action Panel on Youth and Violence. In addition to her community involvement, she led the movement for an expanded building for the congregation. The new addition, with rooms for religious education, meetings, choir rehearsals and office space, was dedicated in December 2000. Dr. Proctor retired in 2004 and has been named minister emeritus.

The current minister is Rev. Dr. Jay Abernathy Jr., who came to the congregation in August 2004. In addition to his interest in race relations, through his degree in architecture he has become knowledgeable in the field of church architecture. Before being installed as minister in Fort Wayne, he served churches in Canada, New England and the south. His special affiliations have been with Planned Parenthood, Mental Health Association, United Way, NAACP, Memorial Society, Equal Housing and other social and civil rights groups.

Members of the congregation have founded or led several community organizations, including SCAN (Stop Child Abuse Now), ACRES (a land trust to preserve natural areas in northeast Indiana), Cinema Center, Metropolitan Human Relations Commission, Aging and In Home Services (a nine-county advocacy group for senior citizens), Fox Island Alliance (a volunteer group supporting Fox Island County Park), Fort Wayne/Allen County League of Women Voters, Girl Scouts, Fort Wayne Women's Bureau, and Science Central.

Currently the congregation extends its support for civil rights to the gay, lesbian, bisexual and transgender communities. Church members read with second graders at South Wayne Elementary School each month and support a food bank and other activities at the school. The Bhajan Society, a Hindu group, meets and worships in the building. The Langhinrichs Gallery, in the center of the building, serves as a show place for community art work with ongoing exhibits open to the public.

We are proud of the results of practicing our liberal faith in the Fort Wayne community in the past and present, and look forward to a future of contributing more to community, church and one another.

Material collected by Edwin Powers, Michael T. Biesiada, and Peggy Seigel. History prepared by Carol Ver Wiebe, February 2005.

Unitarian Universalist Congregation
5310 Old Mill Road, Fort Wayne

Waynedale United Methodist Church
2501 Church Street Fort Wayne, Indiana 46809

More than 100 years ago a small chapel was built just south of what is now Waynedale on land donated by Charles Dalman. The chapel was used by several Protestant congregations. In 1903, some of the worshippers formed the Union Chapel Methodist Episcopal Church on the Fort Wayne Circuit. The eleven charter members were David Greider; Ellen and Lida Hoke; Cora, Nora, and John Prince; Hattie Krill; Edward and Maggie Koons; and Aaron and Alice Wells. The first pastor, Enoch Bunner, served five churches. The membership grew and Reverend Bunner served until 1908, followed by pastors E. B. Brown 1908-1909; L. V. Sims 1909-1910; David Corkwell 1910-1911; Joshua Jarvis, W. Z. Horbury 1911-1912; Alda R. Gillian 1912-1914; Charles Metts 1914-1915; and J. M. Stewart 1915-1919.

In 1919 this congregation and the Monson Chapel congregation separated from the Fort Wayne Circuit and formed the Waynedale Methodist Episcopal Church. The sixty-five members asked Abner S. Elzey, of Ossian, to become pastor. He served until 1926 without pay. The congregation met in the Waynedale Public School, then moved to a converted barn on Huntington Road. In 1924 they moved to an apartment house on Bluffton Road, the present location of Elzey Patterson Rodak Home for Funerals at 6810 Old Trail Road.

In 1925, the congregation started raising money to build a parsonage. Lynn Young was appointed the first ordained pastor. Abner Elzey donated a parcel of land large enough for the parsonage and a church at the corner of Church Street and Old Trail Road. The parsonage was built in 1926. Mr. Elzey dreamed of a church with a bell and a pipe organ that would become the landmark of the community. In 1926 the Allen County Farm (Orphan Home and County Infirmary at Brooklyn and Bluffton Road) was being sold. Andrew Rehm and Louis Wiegman (son-in-law) purchased one of the brick buildings as a gift to the church. The building had to be torn down and moved. Church members hauled bricks in horse drawn wagons, cleaned them, and broke ground for the new church in April 1927. Reverend Carl G. Adams was minister 1927-1932. The cornerstone was laid in August 1927 with the inscription Rev. C. G. Adams, pastor, and Board of Trustees: E. R. Harris, T. L. Hodgens, O. O. Parkison, L. A. Wiegman, J. S. Parkison, S. G. Beers, J. W. Phares. The building was dedicated on March 18, 1928. Sixteen members were taken in that day and membership grew to 183. Cost of the building was $32,222.63.

Union Chapel Methodist Episcopal Church Building (A. S. Elzey 1919-1926)

The depression in 1929 caused members to be unemployed or earn meager salaries, the pastor received no salary, and the mortgage could not be paid. Church suppers were served with donated food for ten cents. Church plays were staged. Some members mortgaged their homes to donate funds. Membership grew, with Reverend Adams taking in seventy people at one revival. J. M. Roger served as minister 1932-1934 and H. A. Kirk served in 1934. The church mortgage was held by the Hicks' Estate and foreclosure was threatened. Reverend Kirk requested financial help from the board of Home Missions and Church Extensions and received $8000.00. The mortgage was paid in 1934.

Membership grew to 345 in the next 10 years and to over 800 in 1951. Ministers during this time were Charles Jennings 1934-1939, F. A. Ruder 1939-1945, L. Earl Clayton 1945-1949, and P. B. Smith 1949-1959. In 1953, when the building was 25 years old, expansion was needed. Ground was broken for an educational unit for the 1200 members on January 29, 1956. Susannah Wesley Hall, furnished, cost $250,000.00, and was consecrated on February 21, 1957. The church organist for 30 years, Alma Rehm Wiegman Brydon, donated money toward a new organ to replace the 1950s electronic organ. It was dedicated as a memorial to her on October 9, 1966, shortly after her death. Ministers until the next expansion were Phill Stephens 1959-1963; C. Raymond Earle 1963-1966; Wilbur Yates, assistant, 1965-1966; Darrel Taggart and Rex Custer, assistant, 1967-1973; Dale Hoak, assistant, 1969-1973; Allan Byrne and Cletus Hirschy, assistant, 1973-1977.

A groundbreaking service for a new sanctuary was held on April 20, 1975 and on May 9, 1976 the congregation marched from the old sanctuary to the new. The cost of this addition was $700,000. In the 1990s the building was upgraded and a new organ was purchased. Ministers during this time were Harold Leininger 1977-1982; Lamar Imes, assistant, 1977-1981; Scott Carmer, assistant, 1981-1982; Nancy Nedwell, assistant, 1981-1983; Jack Thomas 1982-1987; Mike Reed, assistant, 1983-1986; James MacDonald, assistant, 1986-1992; John Dicken 1987-1994; Sandra Knepple, assistant, 1992-1994; Rick Pettys and Mike Smith, assistant, 1994-1998; Ken Jackson, assistant, 1996-2003; Mike Harris 1998-20-- ; and Becky Conelly, assistant, 2000-20--.

As its name changed to Waynedale Methodist and then to Waynedale United Methodist, the church has served its members, the Waynedale community, and others in Christian outreach. This ministry is its heritage.

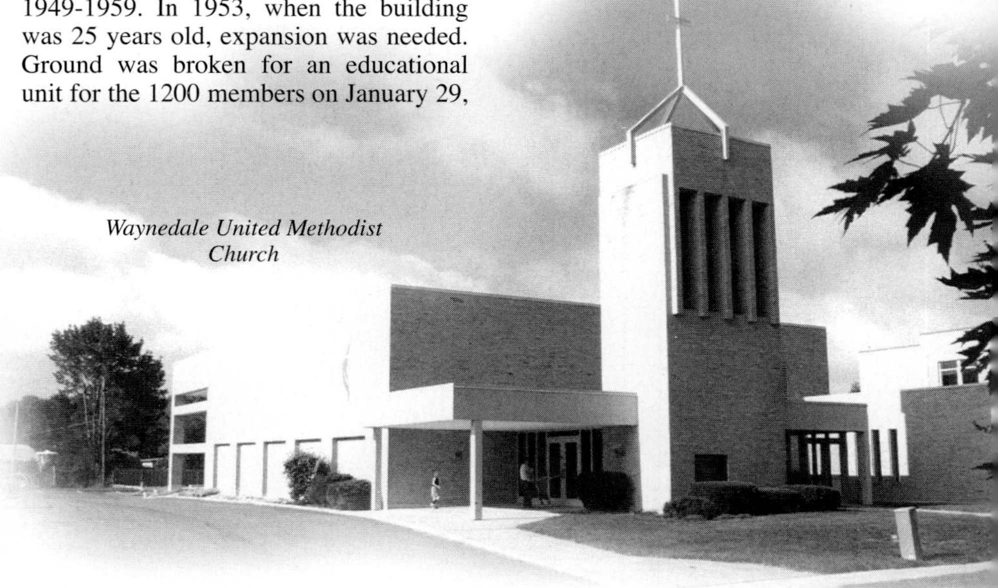

Waynedale United Methodist Church

Wesley Chapel United Methodist Church

Wesley Chapel United Methodist Church
13733 Wesley Chapel Road

In the early 1800s, the William Watterson Family came to Eel River Township in Allen County, Indiana. They came from Pennsylvania, leaving behind, parents, brothers, and sisters. The family of John McKee had also moved there to settle. Local families felt the need for a place of worship, so neighbors came and gathered together for religious services at the McKee home. John McKee was an ordained minister and later donated land for a chapel. He died before the original chapel was built on the land across the road from where it stands today. Samuel K. Watterson, son of William Watterson, was married to John McKee's daughter Ann Elizabeth, and ministered there in 1866 when it was dedicated on February 18th. The original building measured 40 by 60 feet and cost $2,500.00. In the year of 1880, they were included in a five-point circuit that included Huntertown, Wallen, Swan, and Cedar Creek. Then about 1890, Wesley Chapel was separated from Huntertown and placed on a circuit with Salem and Churubusco. In 1911 the circuit was again changed, and Wesley Chapel was put with Blue River and Charter Oak to form the Churubusco Circuit.

Although no bell was rung to invite people to the church, people came to Wesley Chapel by walking, buggies and wagons; and in the winter months by sleighs and sleds, even by horseback.

In the year 1900 and 1901 the church was remodeled, in as much as two isles were changed to one. A vestibule was built with a belfry and a bell - the carpenter work was done by Bridge Hollopeter. When this work was completed, the church was rededicated on February 17, 1901.

In 1915, the old pump organ was replaced by a piano. In 1927, the church was remodeled again, with a basement containing three rooms: kitchen, dining room and furnace room. And in 1937, the old plaster was torn off and replaced with interior stucco.

As Wesley Chapel Sunday School grew in numbers, the building became inadequate for classrooms. A Building committee was appointed in 1952 to make plans and decide how to enlarge the church. The remodeling included a balcony, four classrooms, a cloakroom, a public address system, electric pump, electric stove and cupboards in the kitchen. In 1955, a lighted bulletin board was installed in front of the church. A new roof and exterior painting completed the work. In 1956, Wesley Chapel was moved into the Fort Wayne District.

In 1963, the sanctuary was remodeled with new carpet and new furniture. The church bought 7.3 acres to the west in 1995 and built a pavilion for which they have found many uses.

Below are the name of ministers that have served since its first beginning in 1837: 1837 - John McKee, 1865 - D. P. Hartman, 1880 - S. K. Watterson, 1911 - L. J. Sheldon, 1927 - F. Young, 1935 - E. J. Hults, 1952 – C. Echelbarger, 1960 - J. Evan, 1963 - K. Tousley, 1965 - C. Hill, 1968 - G. Dilley, 1972 - H. Schram, 1974 - D. Shoemaker, 1976 - J. Rhine, 1977 - M. Bales, 1978 - J. O'Dell, 1986 - J. Thompson, 1987 - L. Smith.

Pastor Larry L. Smith grew up in Wesley Chapel. His parents Dorothy and Leo Smith, never missed a Sunday going to church. They were very active in church, farmed a muck farm, raised peppermint and distilled the oil. Across from the dwellings was their peppermint distillery on Shoaff Road. *This history was written by Max Waterson, grandson of Sam K. Watterson.*

Wesley Chapel, 2006

Westview Alliance Church

Belief

Westview Alliance Church is affiliated with the Christian and Missionary Alliance, an Evangelical Protestant denomination rooted in 1880s North America. Founded as an independent association for the promotion of missionary work, the Alliance developed into a denomination by the 1930s. The Church's beliefs are summed up in the "Four-Fold Gospel" model of Alliance founder Dr. A.B. Simpson: "Christ Our Saviour, Christ Our Sanctifier, Christ Our Healer, and Christ Our Coming King."

Origin

The Midwest District of the Christian and Missionary Alliance and twenty area families joined forces to purchase about 4.5 acres of land at 9804 Illinois Road in Aboite Township in 1974. The congregation began holding services at the Anthony Wayne School cafeteria in July 1975 and was officially organized with 42 charter members that September. Gary E. Russell was the first Pastor.

Merger

The Westview congregation made the important step of merging with its sister congregation, Fort Wayne Gospel Temple, in 1990. Gospel Temple had served Fort Wayne for decades but, by then, had a declining membership and an underutilized aging facility at 117 East Rudisill Boulevard. At the time, Westview's worship attendance was 75 and Gospel Temple's was 180. Westview's site and name were chosen for the combined congregation because Westview was an established church with an ample modern facility in a growing area. A governing board was formed with equal representation from each congregation and the first meeting as one congregation occurred September 30, 1990. Because Westview had been without a pastor, Rev. A. H. McNally of Gospel Temple was called to serve the merged congregation.

Gospel Temple Origin

Benjamin E. Rediger and his wife Edith founded the Fort Wayne Gospel Tabernacle as an inter-denominational evangelistic center in 1927. The first structure at 2329 Winter Street, purchased that same year, soon proved to be inadequate to meet the needs of the growing ministry. Rediger purchased lots at the northeast corner of Rudisill Boulevard and Clinton Streets and secured a mortgage for the construction of the new Gospel Temple. Even as the cornerstone was laid on September 7, 1930, Rediger felt the impact of the Great Depression. His faith guided him and the building project continued. When completed, the Fort Wayne Gospel Temple had a seating capacity of 3,030. The congregation's rapid growth was due, in part, to the weekly Gospel Hour broadcasts on WOWO radio which began in 1928. Over the years, additional broadcasts throughout the week were added. Other successful ministries included the Gospel Temple Bookshop established in 1938 and the Temple Timbers camp.

Temple Missionary Training School

Gospel Temple established the Temple Missionary Training School and housed it from 1942 until about 1951 when it closed. It offered post-secondary programs in pulpit ministry, Christian education, mission work, general Bible, music ministry, and secretarial work.

Buildings

Ground breaking for Westview's 4,200 sq. ft. building was held October 19, 1975 and construction was completed the following spring. An additional two acres were acquired in 1983 and a new 240-seat sanctuary and offices were dedicated in June 1984.

In anticipation of the 1990 merger, Gospel Temple sold their building on Rudisill Boulevard to Tippmann Properties for $220,000. The congregation removed their cornerstone and dedication marker on September 23, 1990, the day of their last service on Rudisill. Soon after, the Gospel Temple Bookshop was moved to the Parkwest Shopping Center and Gospel Temple was demolished. In the mid-1990s, the congregation sold the bookshop to Zondervan Publishing and used the proceeds to aid the building of the Westview Activity Center east of the existing church structure in 1997. The old Gospel Temple cornerstone was laid in this new wing which houses classrooms, a library, kitchen, and multi-purpose gymnasium.

Pastors

Pastors at the Gospel Temple have included: Benjamin Rediger (1927), C. E. Rediger (1932), E. Dewitt Johnson (1932), Bert Williams (1934), Paul Rader, Clifford Hollifield (1936), Lloyd Clark (1943), Ralph Neighbor (1943), Stewart Billings (1948), Herbert Pugmire (1957), Carl Bennett (1960), Paul Edwardson (1965), Paul Currie (1972), Nathan Penland (1976), Elwood Nielson (1980), Norman Nelson (1985), and Al McNally (1987).

Westview pastors have included: Gary Russell (1975), Thomas Barnts (1989), Al McNally (1990), John Teschan (1995), and Robert Petty (2005).

Current Activity at Westview

Sunday worship and Childrens Church are held at 10 a.m. with Sunday school for all ages at 9 a.m. Music and congregational singing are led by the Worship Team, vocalists accompanied by various instruments and percussion. Throughout the week, home groups, youth group meetings, activities for children, and adult prayer meetings provide opportunities for Christian growth. Westview offers Upward basketball and cheerleading as a ministry to area youth and participates in mission activities in Thailand, West Africa, the Netherlands, and Montana. Westview Alliance Church continues nearly 80 years of ministry in the Fort Wayne area by ministering the Gospel of Christ to the people in relevant and meaningful ways.

Westview Alliance Church, 9804 Illinois Road, Fort Wayne

Fort Wayne Gospel Temple, 117 East Rudisell Boulevard

Worship For Shut-Ins
Lutheran Ministries Media, Inc.

Since 1980, "Worship for Shut-Ins" has been broadcasting weekly worship services for those who are homebound, in nursing care facilities, or hospitalized. This 30 minute television program has been on WPTA-TV21 exclusively since inception.

The concept of the program actually was founded in the early 1970s by the Rev. Oswald Henry Bertram of Good Shepherd Lutheran Church in Toledo, Ohio. However, when Pastor Bertram died of cancer in 1979, the production and broadcast of the first "Worship for Shut-Ins" ceased.

Several Fort Wayne area pastors and church members, who knew that many of their own shut-ins had been served through this ministry, felt the need to revive such a program. Therefore, under the guidance of Mr. Raymond Huebschman, Minister of Christian Education at Holy Cross Lutheran Church in Fort Wayne, the program began its second life on October 5, 1980. The independent not-for-profit organization, called Lutheran Ministries Media, Inc., was formed to govern the ministry and produce 52 programs every year.

Since that date, every program has been filmed in the Lupke Memorial Chapel on the campus of Holy Cross. Wood carvings of a full length, life-size Christ (see picture) and a family group with a dove overhead, are from Germany and add a spiritual atmosphere for the televising.

The program's format stayed similar to the Toledo version, and presently, still resembles its early years which contain: Scripture readings, prayers, hymns by choirs, and a personalized message to the shut-ins by Lutheran pastors.

Financially, a grant was received by the Ranke Foundation of Fort Wayne which added impetus to seeing that the program would become a reality. The balance of the needed funds to purchase two broadcast quality cameras and control room equipment came from area Lutheran churches' congregational members.

Prior to the first telecast, the volunteers who would help Mr. Huebschman with the production were trained by WPTA-TV.

Today, there are three full time staff personnel and over 70 volunteers to assist them in this TV ministry. They are under the supervision of Mr. Kenneth M. Schilf, the Executive Director. When Mr. Huebschman left to become a professor at Concordia University, Seward, Nebraska, Mr. Schilf took his position. The position was part-time until October of 2003, when the Board of Directors of the corporation decided that a full time director was needed because of the growth of the ministry.

From camera operators, to sound technicians, to office assistants, closed captioning proof readers, couriers who distribute the programs weekly (the list is endless), Lutheran Ministries Media continues to produce worship services that are commercial free. The services are taped separate from weekend services. Pastors are generally taped on Tuesdays, while choirs, soloists and small groups are usually taped on Sunday afternoons. The host, who is the only one who appears weekly on the program, is taped on afternoons during the week. There is no congregation present because this is a one to one ministry focused on the shut-in needs.

Once all the segments are taped, the Program Director, Paul Melin, edits the program and sends it out to all the TV markets about 10 days in advance. "Worship for Shut-Ins" is also distributed to various nursing care facilities and hospitals in northeast Indiana on a weekly or monthly basis, depending on the need of the facility.

Lupke Memorial Chapel, a wood carving of Christ.

WPTA-TV is the flagship station to 15 other stations in 10 different states. Lutheran Ministries Media is a member of the National Religious Broadcasters, and adheres to their religious code of ethics based on the Bible. For more information about this unique ministry, contact us at 3225 Crescent Avenue; Fort Wayne, IN-46805. You can call 260-471-5683 or e-mail us at info@worshipforshutins.org. Our web site is: www.worshipforshutins.org. *Submitted by Kenneth M. Schilf*

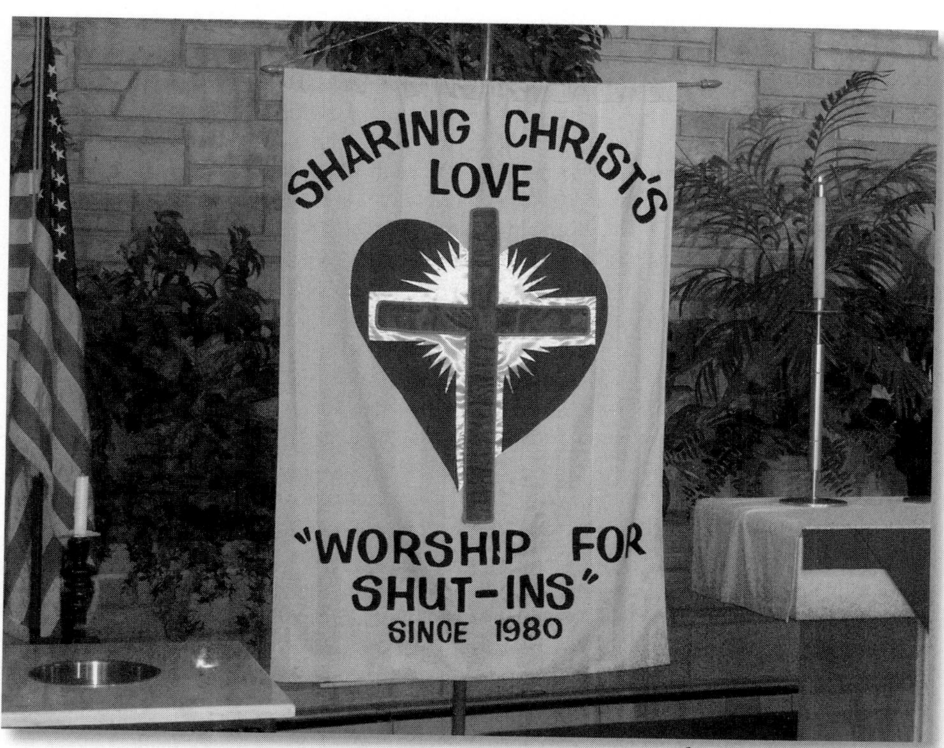

Zion Lutheran Church
2313 S. Hanna Street, Fort Wayne

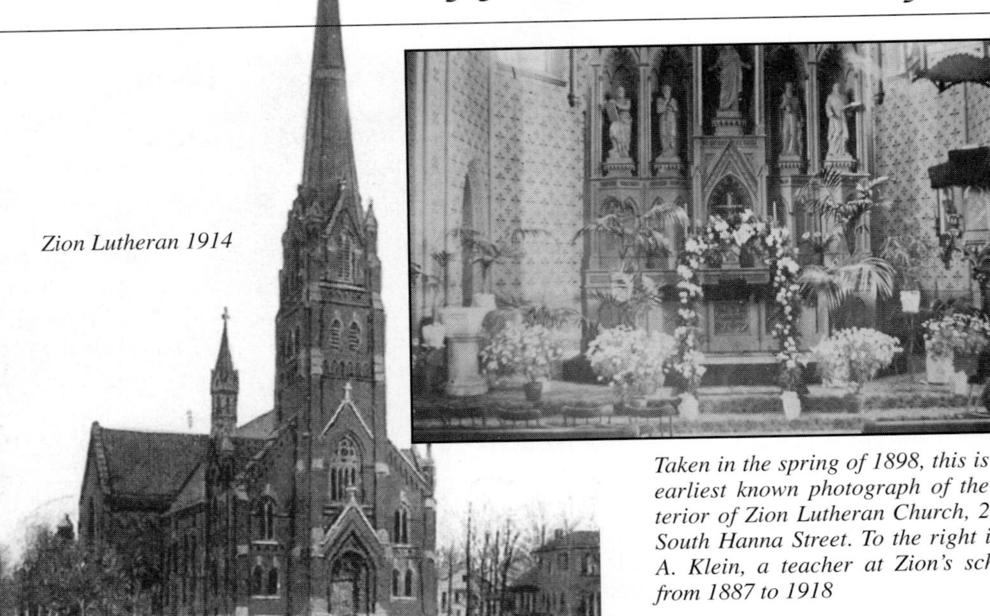
Zion Lutheran 1914

Taken in the spring of 1898, this is the earliest known photograph of the interior of Zion Lutheran Church, 2313 South Hanna Street. To the right is F. A. Klein, a teacher at Zion's school from 1887 to 1918

On February 18, 1883, eighty members of St. Paul's Lutheran Church in downtown Fort Wayne organized a new congregation in the fast-growing area south of the Pennsylvania Railroad tracks then known as "Frenchtown."

The church they founded – named after the heavenly city of God – has been ministering to the Hanna-Creighton neighborhood, and all of Fort Wayne, ever since.

With the help of a $3,300 gift from their mother congregation, the first members of Zion Lutheran Church bought land at 2313 South Hanna Street, and by September had erected a $4,500 brick building that served as both a church and school for more than eight years.

By 1889, Zion was home to 270 families and 260 students, creating a desperate need for worship space. To meet that need, the congregation raised $45,000 for a new sanctuary, which was dedicated on October 4, 1891, and is still in use today. The Gothic Revival structure, designed by noted Fort Wayne architects Wing and Mahurin, measures 124 feet by 80 feet and seats about 1,300 people.

Karl Seibel was the first principal of Zion School, and the largely German-American congregation called the Rev. Fred Dreyer as its first pastor, serving from 1883 to 1886. Zion's longest-serving senior pastor to date was the Rev. Paul Dannenfeldt, who led the congregation from 1927 to 1956.

Zion's early years were marked by rapid growth. The school building was expanded in 1904 at a cost of $8,000, and a large parish hall costing $135,000 was dedicated on October 11, 1923. By 1929, communicant membership had reached nearly 1,700.

Zion's beautiful sanctuary evolved over the years, too. A $2,150 redecoration in 1911 replaced many of the building's original Victorian decorations with more delicate flourishes and stencil work on the walls and ceiling. A far more extensive redecoration in 1940 cost $17,000 and included installation of new lights and interior stencil work modeled after European cathedrals. And in 1970, an $89,000 redecoration saw the sanctuary's interior brightened considerably by a color scheme dominated by tans and gold leaf.

In 1948, when Zion had nearly 2,000 members, it replaced the original organ with a $34,000 "peace organ" dedicated as a memorial to the members of Zion who served and died during World War II. An annex, including meeting rooms and offices for the pastors, was built in 1960 at a cost of $65,000, and in the late 1960s Zion's 1923 parish hall was remodeled into a modern school at a cost of $276,000. The original school was razed.

Despite all the changes to Zion's buildings, ministry and a commitment to serving Fort Wayne's central city has always been the congregation's priority. In 1928, Zion opened branch Sunday schools on Hanna and Oxford streets. And in 1961 Zion began Easter sunrise services at Reservoir Park that continued for years.

But as Fort Wayne changed, Zion changed, too – as illustrated by the congregation's decision to end regular German-language services on September 1, 1957.

As many of the Hanna-Creighton neighborhood's traditional residents died or moved, they were replaced by blacks and members of other ethnic groups. Although this posed numerous challenges for Zion – including a decrease in membership – the church embraced these changes as an opportunity, not a threat.

Zion was one of the first mainline churches in Fort Wayne to integrate, and in 1975 sponsored the city's first refugees from Vietnam. And, at a time when some congregations were fleeing the central city, Zion recommitted itself to the Hanna-Creighton neighborhood, selling land it had purchased at Hessen Cassel and Paulding roads and deciding instead to invest in the facilities that continue to serve the neighborhood and city today. Through it all, Zion continues to offer traditional liturgy and music, and doctrine faithful to Scripture and historic Lutheran practice.

Zion's commitment to the Hanna-Creighton neighborhood was seen again in 1997, when together with nearby St. Peter's Catholic Church it began a renewal program that has helped turn a once-blighted area into a nationally recognized model for urban renewal.

Funded in part by the Lutheran Foundation, the St. Peter's/Zion Project has built several new homes, and land once earmarked as an athletic field for Zion Academy is now a campus featuring a new Head Start center, Urban League headquarters, public bus transfer station and a branch library.

Zion contributed to the neighborhood renaissance as well, replacing its outdated 40-year-old annex with a new $2 million, handicapped-accessible office and parish hall building designed to be architecturally compatible with both the century-old church and the new buildings in the adjacent social-service campus.

Despite Zion's many past accomplishments and challenges, it continues to look ahead in faith, confident in God's eternal promises to those who believe in His Son.

Submitted by Kevin Leininger

Zion Lutheran Church (Bull Rapids) Woodburn Indiana

Over one hundred years ago, when the history of Zion Lutheran Church began, much of Maumee Township and surrounding area was still covered with virgin forest and swamp land.

The nearest Lutheran Church at the time was St. Paul, Gar Creek, but because of the primitive road conditions, which were almost impassable at times, these people of Lutheran stock found it difficult to attend services regularly. As a result, a desire awakened in the hearts of these Christians to have a church of their own. Henry Woebbeking, Sr., who with his family had moved here from Adams County, invited fellow Lutherans to his house or to a nearby public school, where he then conducted "Reading Services." At the same time, the group earnestly petitioned the Reverend A. Schupmann of Gar Creek to serve them occasionally on Sunday afternoons with the message of the Word and the administration of the Sacraments.

Under the guidance and leadership of the Reverend Schupmann, Zion Congregation was organized on March 25, 1888, at the home of Henry Lagemann and incorporated the following year. The Rev. A. Schupmann was requested to serve the congregation every three to four weeks and to perform such official acts as were necessary.

Soon after the organization of Zion Congregation, a five acre tract of land on the banks of the Maumee River at Bull Rapids was purchased from Mr. Andrew Little. A portion on the eastern end of this tract was set aside for a cemetery. During the first summer the members cut down trees in the woods of Petere Vonderau, trimmed the logs to size, smoothed them with a broadax, and erected a log building on their property, which served them as both church and school.

The Reverend William Heine was installed November 1, 1900. Under his able leadership plans for a new church progressed and materialized. The actual building operations did not get under way until the early part of 1902. The cornerstone was laid with appropriate ceremonies on June 1, 1902. With great joy and enthusiasm and in the spirit of unity they resolved to give of their time and substance to erect a brick church with large stained-glass windows to the honor and glory of God. This they accomplished at a cost of a little more than $6000. This house of God was one of the finer rural churches in Indiana at that time, of which they could justly be proud. It has served the congregation well unto the present time.

Faithfully serving Zion (Bull Rapids) has been the Reverends F. H. Eickhoff 1889-1892, William Meinzen 1893-1900, William Hine 1900-1905, William Georgi 1905-1925, Herman Reinking 1926-1943, Christian Schmidt 1944-1973, Harvey Hendrickson 1973-1977, Gary Galen 1978-1983, and David Triplett 1984-1999. Currently the Reverend Joseph M. Adams II, a graduate of Concordia Theological Seminary, Fort Wayne, is shepherding Zion. Pastor Adams' home congregation is Hope Lutheran Church, Adrian, Michigan.

Over the past century, God has certainly blessed the members and community of Zion Congregation. Through His guidance and protection, many people have come to know Jesus Christ as their Savior. With the continued blessings of God, we hope to see the following numbers grow. Current statistics for Zion Lutheran Church since its inception include: 886 people baptized, 772 people confirmed, 284 couples married, and 255 funerals conducted.

B'nai Jacob Conservative Synagogue

In 1894, a group of Russian Jewish immigrants formed an Orthodox synagogue named B'Israel (House of Israel). In 1912 another group (of Polish and Lithuanian background) formed a second Orthodox congregation named B'nai Jacob (House of Jacob). B'nai Jacob constructed their first synagogue at Wayne and Monroe Streets, of "modern architectural design". By 1928 the Congregation had grown, and the Hebrew Center was added to the building accommodating a religious school, a gymnasium and an auditorium.

B'nai Israel merged with B'nai Jacob in 1937, and became a Conservative congregation. With the outbreak of World War II, and the opening of Bear Field, the Synagogue became a refuge for soldiers who wanted spiritual guidance and good meals.

In 1955 a larger, modern synagogue was opened on Fairfield Avenue, including more classrooms, a social hall with stage, a small chapel and a beautiful sanctuary. The Sisterhood appreciated the large kitchen while preparing food for many and varied occasions.

On our Sabbath, Saturday morning, April 16, 1960, the Synagogue was defiled with swastikas. On that infamous day, the Christian ministers of Fort Wayne donned blue jeans and sweat shirts and tried to scrub off the spray painted red swastikas desecrating the outside brick walls. This remarkable show of brotherhood was picked up by the wire services and made the national news.

In 1997, the Congregation moved to its current location, 7227 Bittersweet Moors Drive. The building, situated in an attractive garden setting, is intimate and welcoming. B'nai Jacob, lead by Rabbi Mitchell Kornspan since 2004, remains an active, moderately sized, family oriented congregation.

In addition to serving the spiritual and community needs of members, the Synagogue regularly hosts members of other faiths. Guests are invited to attend services, learn about Judaism, and the common roots of Judeo-Christian observances.

Church of Divine Science, Incorporated

A building that once housed a bank at 1615 Wells Street in Fort Wayne has become known as "The Little Church with A Big Heart." The original pastor, the Reverend Bernice Brock, received her charter for the Spiritualist Church of Divine Science on May 19, 1945. The Reverends Bernice and Omer Brock continued to serve our church until 1985. At that time, the Reverend A. Jay Fisher became pastor and was assisted by the Reverend Edward Cummings until he relocated in 1998. On May 21, 1994, a new charter was established with the United Metaphysical Churches, and the name was changed to Church of Divine Science, Incorporated. The United Metaphysical Churches national headquarters is located in Roanoke, Virginia, and the Reverend Fisher is a trustee on the National Board. He continues to serve our church not only as pastor but also as musical and educational director.

The purpose of our church is to promote through our services, lessons, classes and daily living the Principles of Divine Metaphysics. Throughout the years, many people have received spiritual guidance and the keys necessary for their spiritual well-being. Our church has contributed to the community through its outreach programs that include seminars, workshops, classes and donations to local charities. For the last sixty years on Thursday evenings and Sunday mornings, our doors have been open to the public and continue to remain open for all those seeking spiritual understanding.

Present Church

Inside of Present Church

Grabill Evangelical Mennonite Church

Grabill EMC had its beginnings in a humble frame building located between Leo and Grabill. The original structure was built in 1874 and was used for worship for nearly forty years by a group of worshippers who had separated from the local Amish community around 1871. In 1912 the congregation built a brick church in the village of Grabill. The congregation still worships there although numerous additions and remodeling efforts have enlarged the structure. It currently includes an enlarged sanctuary, classrooms, a lovely kitchen and Fellowship Hall, a quilt room, plus offices for three pastors, along with secretarial offices.

Originally known as part of the Egly Amish denomination, in 1900 the denomination became Defenseless Mennonite. This was changed in 1948 to the Evangelical Mennonite Church (EMC) and in 2003 the denomination again changed its name to the Fellowship of Evangelical Churches (FEC).

The congregation has been served by numerous pastors over its 131 year history. One of the most interesting was Reverend Aaron Souder, who served from 1916-1919. During his short tenure, singing schools were established, a choir was formed, Sunday School was started, and the beginning of "helpfulness to others of the brotherhood who were unfortunate." This effort eventually resulted in the formation of the present day Brotherhood Mutual Insurance Company.

Following Reverend Souder's untimely death in 1919, the congregation was served by various pastors. The longest tenure was that of Reverend J. H. Sauder who served for 24 years. Reverend Sauder was the first pastor to have earned both a college and a seminary degree. Reverend Sauder, also a business owner, served the church without pay for his entire tenure. Reverend David Sauder, father of J. H. Sauder, was a denominational elder and assisted in numerous capacities over a period of more than 40 years.

The congregation is under the current leadership of senior pastor Jack Teeple. Present programs for this congregation of 200 include Adventure Club, an outreach program for children; a strong emphasis on missions; a vibrant youth program directed by Pastor Jonathan Hyde; plus an outreach program under the direction of Pastor Hal Lehman. Two secretaries support the work of the congregation. In early 2004 the congregation began two worship services. One

Grabill EMC Church

is patterned after a more traditional service while the contemporary service includes a Praise Band.

In 2000 the congregation purchased a 24 acre property between Leo and Grabill. Plans are being developed for the future construction of a new worship center. There the ministry of Grabill EMC will continue as the congregation seeks to serve the Lord both in Grabill and around the world.

The Lighthouse Free Methodist Church

An Unexpected Blessing

The local Free Methodist Church's move across the city to West Wallen Road in 2004 was preceded by a move across the street about 100 years earlier. At that time, the congregation had been worshiping in a one-story, wooden frame building at 1318 East Creighton Avenue. The property was desired by industrialist S. F. Bowser as a site on which to build a multistory office building for his gasoline pump company. It is believed that the Free Methodist congregation accepted an offer from him, a church member, to construct the brick church pictured. Its location would be across Holton Avenue from their existing building. On September 20, 1909, three members were elected to the church building committee to look after the construction. There was $10.65 in their treasury. In 1911 the congregation moved across to their new building, The Bowser Free Methodist Church. Today, at 2317 Holton Avenue, a new congregation worships there. The multistory office building of the Bowser Company is the main office of the Fort Wayne Police Department. *Submitted by Jack and Eleanor Guthrie, The Lighthouse Free Methodist Church Historians*

St. Michael Evangelical Lutheran Church

St. Michael Evangelical Lutheran Church was established in September of 1953 after fifty-four families, members of Redeemer Lutheran Church and living in the Time Comers area, felt that they needed a place of worship closer to home. The Mission Board of the English District of the Lutheran Church Missouri Synod then purchased a barracks building and a 26 ½ acre tract of land on Getz Road. The first worship service of St. Michael Evangelical Lutheran Church, led by Reverend Herbert Lindemann, was held in this building on February 7, 1954. In June of 1954 Rev. Bernard Hemmeter preached his first sermon as pastor of St. Michael. He held that position for 14 years until his retirement in 1968. By this time St. Michael had grown to 350 communicants and over 500 souls. Rev. Donald Meyers was installed as St. Michael's second pastor who served until January 1977. Then from January 1977 to April 1978, St. Michael experienced a pastoral vacancy. It was in April 1978 that Robert Bruckner commenced his call to lead God's people as pastor of St. Michael and is shepherding them still. With continued growth an associate pastor was called in 1986. The Rev. Wayne Berkesch served in this capacity until he accepted a call to Fremont, Indiana in 1994. The following summer, 1995, Rev. David Moore joined the congregation as associate pastor and remains so to this day.

Being dedicated to Christian education since its inception, St. Michael Lutheran Church supported St. Michael Lutheran School as the school began holding classes for kindergartners in 1954 with first grade the following year. By 1961 the number of children attending had increased to the point of needing a full kindergarten through eighth grade elementary school. The 1961-62 school year marked a new venture--an "inter-parish school." This was the beginning of Emmanuel-St. Michael Lutheran School at Union Street, as the two congregations came together in joint support of educating their children. In 1989 St. Michael added an education wing, allowing for the first class of Emmanuel-St. Michael to be located at the Getz Road site. In 2001 another education expansion took place and brought the kindergarten through second grades of Emmanuel-St. Michael to the Getz Road campus. In addition to the K-8 program supported by our congregation, we also support St. Michael Preschool, operating since 1974, adding to many children's educational experience here at St. Michael.

As St. Michael celebrated their 50 year anniversary in 2003, the words of Rev. Lindemann, spoken in February of 1954 are remembered: "A good beginning has been made, and we are confident that the new congregation will begin its history with every assurance of God's blessing upon it."

St. Michael Lutheran Church-LCMS, 2131 Getz Road, Fort Wayne

St. Patrick Catholic Church of Arcola

The history of St. Patrick's Parish began in 1845 when services for the early Catholic Settlers in the Arcola area were held at Victor Munier's home, and were celebrated by Rev. Julian Benoit and occasionally by other missionary priests.

Officially the parish was named St. Patrick of Arcola in 1862, and in 1866 regular Masses were begun in an old schoolhouse in the area. The small frame church building begun by Fr. Madden was completed by Fr. Van der Poel. He also erected a priest's residence, a two-story building of several rooms, adjoining the church building. The two structures were built on a lot of three acres. A cemetery was laid out one and a half miles from the church, and records state it was named Calvary Cemetery.

In 1880 the first school was built near the church building. At this time there were seventy-five registered families of Irish, German, or French origin or descent. In 1895 a small residence was erected for the three sisters from the Poor Handmaids of Jesus Christ, who were to take charge of the parochial school. They arrived in December of 1895. A new school was opened in January of 1896 with thirty-nine children registered. The corner stone of the present church building was laid on the first Sunday of October in 1898 and was dedicated on October 29, 1899. Records show that the building was erected at a cost of $10,934.

During Fr. Peter Schmitt's tenure, in 1903, our beautiful brick walkway in front of the church was put in by James and Mary Kaough to protect their daughter's wedding gown from getting dirty as she made her way inside the church.

In 1907, the present rectory was built. The present day school and convent buildings were built in 1935.

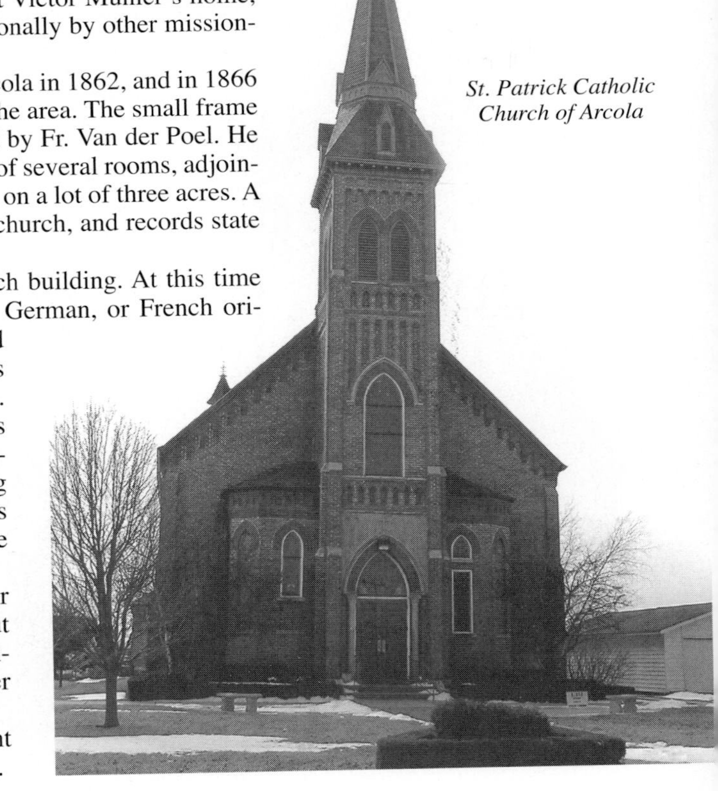

St. Patrick Catholic Church of Arcola

The United Methodist Church Of The Covenant

10001 Coldwater Road, Fort Wayne

Church of the Covenant held its first worship service at Lincoln Elementary School in Fort Wayne on March 16, 1980, with 350 persons present. The organizing pastor was the Reverend Michael Snyder. Dr. R. Sheldon Duecker was Superintendent of the Fort Wayne District of The United Methodist Church. During the mid-1960s, the Fort Wayne United Methodist Church Builders purchased 37 acres of land on Coldwater Road, just south of Dupont Road, as a future building site. Darrell E. Morlan was the President of Church Builders and Dr. Virgil V. Bjork was District Superintendent at that time. Charter Sunday was October 12, 1980 and 190 persons were received as Charter Members. Worship services and church school were held for three years in the gymnasium and classrooms of the Lincoln Elementary School as the congregation made plans for building at the Coldwater Road site. Groundbreaking for the first phase of the new church home was on November 21, 1982. The first service in the new building was held on October 2, 1983. The sanctuary was enlarged, and an educational wing, fellowship hall and offices were added to the original structure in 1992. A second educational wing for youth and children was added in 2005. Pastors serving Church of the Covenant have been Dr. Michael A. Snyder (1980-1984), Dr. Ronald F. Verlee (1984-1993), the Reverend Katharine W. Lehman (1993-1995), Dr. Derek C. Weber (1995-2001), and Dr. Steven Conner (2001-present). Associate pastors have been Eric Foley, Steve Elliott, and Larry Saunders. Rev. Harold Oechsle has also served the church part time. As of January 2005, United Methodist Church of the Covenant had 613 members. Three worship services are held each Sunday morning including "The Connection", a contemporary worship experience. Average worship attendance is 504 and average church school attendance is 114.

West Creighton Avenue Christian Church (Disciples of Christ)

West Creighton Avenue Christian Church (Disciples of Christ) of Fort Wayne was organized in April 1896. It originated from Sunday School meetings held at the South Wayne Hall beginning in 1892. The cornerstone was laid at the southeast corner of Creighton and Miner in June 1896 and the building was dedicated that November. Jacob Updike was the first pastor. An educational wing was added in 1925 and the sanctuary was completely renovated in 1953.

Worship attendance now averages about twenty-five and Susan Beamer of Wabash, Indiana serves as interim pastor.

West Creighton Avenue Christian Church, 845 West Creighton Avenue, Fort Wayne

Maplewood Mennonite Church

Maplewood Mennonite Church is located at 4129 Maplecrest Road. It was established by the Men's Fellowship of First Mennonite Church in Berne, Indiana in 1960. The first building was erected in 1962. As the congregation grew, a sanctuary and educational classrooms were added in 1974. The first pastor was Leonard Wiebe who served the congregation for fourteen years. It has a membership of 150 persons. The congregation is a member of Mennonite Church, USA.

Maplewood Mennonite Church

Northpoint Community Church

10513 Leo Road, Fort Wayne
northpointcc@comcast.net

Northpoint Community Church was started in 1993 as a church plant of Grabill Missionary Church with Greg Getz as the pastor. They first met in the basement of Coldwell Banker on Dupont Road but soon rented space and held their services in the Coldwater Crossing Theater. Northpoint's current facility was originally built sometime around 1976 by the Victory Life Praise Center and then was purchased by Berean Community Church around 1996. Northpoint purchased the property at 10513 Leo Road in November 2000 and after some remodeling moved in during January 2001. After two years of having interim pastors, the church hired Tom Swank as their pastor in June 2003.

Northpoint's rnission is to build God-honoring, reproducing, disciplines of Jesus. They have small groups and Bible Studies for men, women, and couples that meet on a regular basis. There is a youth group for junior and senior high kids that meets weekly and a children's ministry called Praiseland for children three years through sixth grade which meets on Sunday mornings. In the future Northpoint would like to develop missions projects and expand our outreach to the community.

Demolition of St. Mary's Catholic Church after the fire of 1993. (Photo by Shawna Robb Niblick)

Allen County Organizations

Quest Club, circa 1948.

Preserving Fort Wayne's rich heritage was roundly toasted at the inaugural banquet of the Fort Wayne Historical Society on February 12, 1921. The leaders of the city gathered at the Wolf and Dessauer Auditorium that evening proclaiming in a lovingly detailed program that "History is a Pageant, not a Philosophy." The language was different, but the purpose of the Society has always been centered on preserving our heritage and passing it onto future generations. We no longer speak of relics, but of artifacts, and while the wording of the mission statement has changed, the dedication to learning has remained constant.

A parade of dignitaries gave addresses, including Dr. Harlow Lindley of Earlham College, who spoke on "Popularizing History," the Rev. Matthew J. Walsh, President of Notre Dame, and Fort Wayne's own B.J. Griswold, who reported on the Society's organizing efforts. No doubt all of these addresses laid a vigorous intellectual and organizational framework for the Society to build and expand upon. Dr. Lindley and President Walsh went back to their ivory towers of learning, but Griswold and dozens of other members went on to serve the Society, taking inspiration from the city's proud past. The Society they built cared about their heritage and they wanted to pass it on.

The Daughters of the American Revolution, Mary Penrose Wayne Chapter was the first agency to give concrete or at least "artifact" reality to the ideals of historic preservation of Fort Wayne. In 1902, almost two decades before the Society was formed, the DAR's "Relic Room" in the courthouse exhibited some of the city's oldest and most important artifacts. Today, the Society is privileged to preserve and exhibit these artifacts. General Anthony Wayne's camp bed has exhibited it's mobility as it has followed the growth of the Society from the Courthouse, to the Swinney Homestead in 1924 and finally to the renovated 1893 City Hall Building in 1980, which later was renamed the History Center.

In 1986, the Society merged with Historic Fort Wayne in a rescue attempt to keep the fort open – a move that proved to be an unsuccessful enterprise. Other expansions include Barr Street Market and the 1827 Chief Richardville House in 1991. The Society has sponsored bus, boat, and hiking tours over the years, each exploring the rich heritage of the County and region.

A review of the organization would not be complete without mention of the many involvements and accomplishments of the Society during the bicentennial in 1976. In addition to written publications and various celebrations, the Society engaged Channel 15 to compile and broadcast a series of Bicentennial Minutes on the history of Fort Wayne. Today, visitors to the History Center can view the series at the push of a button in the museum's new interactive history room. This room features audiovisual kiosks as well as usifacts, artifacts, demonstration areas and a restored section of the Old City Hall building that overlooks Fort Wayne's current cityscape.

When public funding for school trips to the History Center was withdrawn, the Society's Board of Directors responded by creating the Heritage Education Fund, which has not only filled the funding gap, but also enabled the society to expand its educational activities, including tours of the Chief Richardville House and adding new educational programs to its repertoire.

The interior of the Thomas Swinney House c. 1928. The building housed the Allen County/Fort Wayne Historical Society from 1927-1980. (l. to r.) Frank Taylor, Mrs. Samuel Taylor and Colonel David Foster.

The Fort Wayne City Building December 7, 1899. The building was constructed in 1893. Currently the headquarters of the Allen County/Fort Wayne Historical Scoiety.

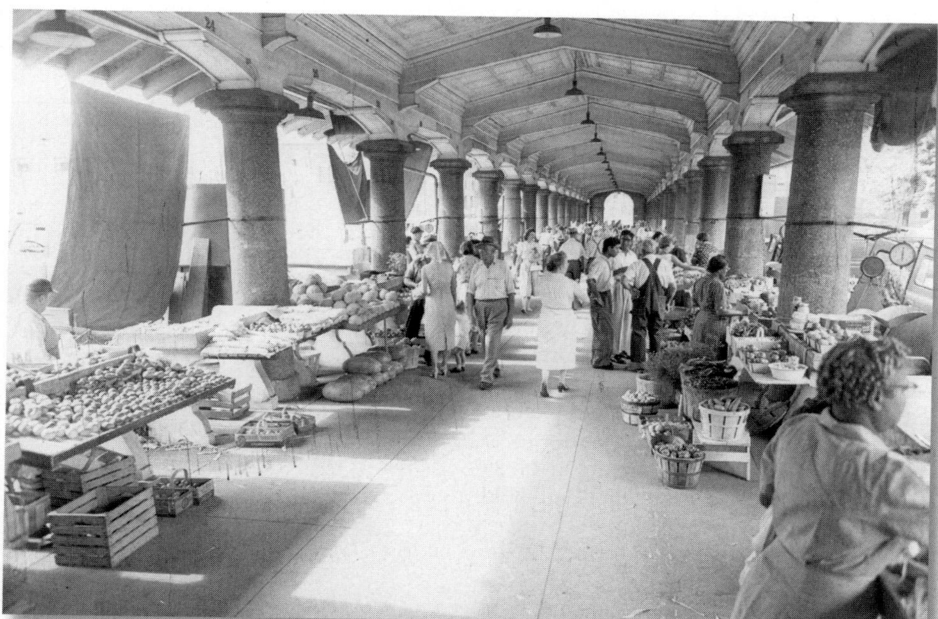

The Barr Street Market on August 2, 1957. The Barr Street Market pavilion was constructed in 1910 and razed in 1957. Samuel Hanna donated the land for the market in 1837.

The Miami Chief Richardville House. The house was constructed in 1827 and is the oldest structure in Northeastern Indiana. The exterior of the house was restored in 2003.

In 2002, the Society adopted nine themes that illustrate the substance of our region through the ages: location, a community of faith, a community of laws, a community of innovation, excellence in sports and education, a community of immigrants and the heritage of the Miami. These themes are demonstrated in the History Center as well as throughout the Society's educational programs and activities.

At the Chief Richardville House, the last two themes come together to tell the story of Miami Chief Richardville. This tale is not one of battles and gore, but of how a wise Chief worked to make peace for the benefit of all, a story that is timeless.

Perhaps the most important thread has been the ongoing tradition of stimulating lectures and publications. The lectures have brought fabled authors to tell of a wide range of historic topics, including Johnny Appleseed and the location of his four nurseries in Allen County. Publications have included the biannual *Old Fort News* history magazine and the first biography on Hugh McCulloch, Secretary of the Treasury for three presidents and a former Fort Wayne resident, entitled, *Hugh McCulloch: Father of Modern Banking*. Books by Society members such as Rev. George Mather, John Beatty and two-time Society President, the Honorable William C. Lee, have documented Fort Wayne as a city of churches as well as a city of faith. Partnerships with local organizations, such as the Allen County Genealogical Society, have resulted in publication of this *Allen County History Book*, the first comprehensive narrative history of Allen County in more than 87 years.

The beat of the pageant of history continues to accelerate and take unexpected forms. Since that inaugural dinner in 1921, there has been a singular dedication of purpose and goal, striving to advance the mission of the Society. The names and the words keep changing, but the Society continues to preserve and pass on the inspirations of its founders. At the Society's February, 2005 board meeting, a new mission statement was adopted stating the Society's goal, "to preserve, educate, and celebrate the diverse heritage of Fort Wayne and Allen County."

The future of the historic preservation in Fort Wayne rests, in part, on the three initiatives by the Society. The first is making Downtown Improvement District's concept of Heritage Square a reality. This effort would make the area around Berry and Barr Streets a destination point for experiencing our community's rich heritage, from the 1893 City Hall Building (now know as the History Center), to a revival of the 1837 Barr Street Market, to the ARCH and Indiana Landmarks restoration of the c. 1830s Alexander Rankin house and the 1880s McCulloch-Weatherhogg house.

The second goal is the national designation of the Maumee Valley as a National Heritage Corridor. Purdue University students have provided the vision, but it will take years of work to make it a reality.

The third initiative is purchasing or securing a buffer for the Chief Richardville house so that there is room for interpreting the unique heritage of the home and keep it shielded from anachronistic intrusions.

One of the first historians, Herodotus, advised to avoid making predictions within historical examinations. However, given the Society's goals and momentum, it is the sincere hope that in 100 years the Society will have succeeded in infusing a sense of pride of place that enables our community to move forward based upon the rich and diverse power of this place at the three rivers. The lectures in 1921 by Dr. Lindley and President Walsh on the importance of popularizing history happened long ago, but their importance is not forgotten. Their message lives on in the Society's collection of 22,000 artifacts, the Chief Richardville house, the Barr Street Market, and the History Center. These pieces of history enable young and old the opportunity to experience the full scope of our community's rich history for the benefit of present and future generations. *Submitted by Donn P. Werling, Executive Director and Todd Pelfrey, Education Director*

The Isaac Knapp Dental Society, a local dental organization, was formed by seven Fort Wayne dentists on January 20, 1891. The group was formed to provide social and educational exchanges among its members. They named the organization after Dr. Isaac Knapp because, "He was the first dentist to come to Fort Wayne and stay. He had the reputation of being a fine dentist, a gentleman, and a cultural leader." Dr. Knapp came to Fort Wayne in 1854 and was the only dentist here for many of his 29 years of practice.

The Fort Wayne District Dental Society was chartered in 1917 by the American Dental Association to include the nine counties of Adams, Allen, DeKalb, Jay, LaGrange, Noble, Steuben, Whitley, and Wells. The annual dues were set at $6.00 in 1922, as a combined fee to include membership in the local, state, and national sections of the American Dental Association (ADA).

The Fort Wayne District Dental Society and the Isaac Knapp Dental Coterie were consolidated into the Isaac Knapp District Dental Society (IKDDS) in the spring of 1928 by unanimous vote of each organization. Their treasuries were combined in April of that year (Huntington County also became part of IKDDS in October 1950).

The first formal meeting of the IKDDS was held May 10, 1928. As its first official act, members passed a formal resolution to take to the Indiana Dental Association annual meeting. It called for all components to join with the IDA in promoting and urging passage of legislation that would establish and maintain an adequate system of dental inspection and advice for the benefit of the children attending public schools. Throughout the coming years, IKDDS dentists would continue to speak out for measures to improve the dental health of the public.

The first official social event of IKDDS was a picnic and golf outing in June 1928. It was held at the Sylvan Lake cottage of Jay C. Link. Due to the prohibition era then in effect, the event was B.Y.O.B. (bring your own bottle). According to the 1928 memoirs of Dr. Harold C. Dimmich, an IKDDS member, the Great Depression was beginning and many dentists had to cash in scrap gold from extracted teeth to raise the $2.00 to $3.00 needed to go to the event. This was the beginning of an IKDDS annual golf outing that is still held in September each year.

A Ladies Auxiliary was formed by the wives of the IKDDS dentists in 1934. The group began as a social group, but soon changed their focus to educating school children on the importance of oral health and good dental hygiene. In the 1940s and 1950s, they joined with the area dentists and dental assistants to do volunteer dental exams in the elementary schools. The ladies presented educational talks, slide shows, and talking movies to all first and second grade students. This program was expanded to include high school students in 1943. Their dental health education programs would eventually be expanded to nursery schools and pre-natal clinics, as well.

The 1950s changed dentistry forever. The focus of dentistry changed from treatment of infection, tooth decay, and tooth extraction to patient education, tooth restoration, and the prevention of dental diseases. This was accomplished through many scientific changes in the way dentistry was practiced, as well as widespread educational and public health programs. A Children's Dental Health Day was first held locally in November 1950. By 1962, Fort Wayne Community Schools approved a formal dental health education program as part of the curriculum for their students in grades one through four. As a result, the students got 30 minutes of dental health per week for a ten-week period.

Also in the 1950s, widespread discussion was held throughout the area on the fluoridation of drinking water. The IKDDS dentists worked hard to endorse this program and Fort Wayne became the first Indiana city to fluoridate the community water supply. This process of adding tiny amounts of fluoride to the drinking water combined with the newly developed fluoridated toothpastes would eventually lead to a 75% reduction in tooth decay in the children of that and future generations.

Isaac Knapp
"He was the first dentist to come to Fort Wayne and stay. He had the reputation of being a fine dentist, a gentleman, and a cultural leader."

As the public became more aware of dental health issues, the demand for dental services increased. In an effort to increase the numbers of available dental personnel, the IKDDS dentists worked with Indiana University to establish local training programs at the Indiana University Purdue University Fort Wayne campus. The School of Dental Hygiene enrolled its first class of eight students in 1962, under the direction of Mrs. Gloria Huxoll, RDH, MS (who remained as director of the school until 1987). A new program was started to train dental assistants at the Fort Wayne campus in 1965. The course was the first of its kind in the state, being one academic year in length, and included over 1100 hours of lecture, laboratory, and clinical instruction. The first class of 16 women graduated in 1966. These programs have continued to provide well-trained dental hygienists and assistants to the area for over forty years.

The 1960s also saw a significant change in the way dental services were paid for by many Allen County residents. During the decade, many local businesses began offering their employees dental insurance coverage as an employment benefit. The labor unions often negotiated these benefit programs, which were funded by the employers and administered by an insurance company. The IKDDS devised a standardized claim form 1965 for dental insurance claims, which was eventually adopted by the IDA. Indiana became the first state to adopt a statewide claim form, the IKDDS form, which eventually became a model for all of the dental insurance forms used in the nation.

The Isaac Knapp Dental Education Foundation was incorporated in June 1987 when eight area dentists each donated $1,000.00. The Foundation was established to "expand and enhance" local programs in the interest of public health. A goal of soliciting the members of IKDDS and raising $100,000 by the IKDDS Centennial Year (1991) was established. The dentists' donations have far exceeded that goal and the Foundation has given money to fund many educational programs in Allen County. They have donated funding and many hours of services to the Matthew 25 Dental Clinic, a free clinic for low income citizens in downtown Fort Wayne. The local dentists and their wives, both personally and through the IKDDS Foundation, have contributed to establish a dental exhibit at the McMillen Center for Health Education which is utilized by many Allen County school systems for their health education programs. The Foundation also established a scholarship fund for students from northeast Indiana enrolled in programs leading to a degree in dentistry.

In the 21st Century, the IKDDS dentists joined with many dentists across the U.S. to participate in an annual "Give Kids a Smile" program sponsored by the ADA. This program, which involves needy children receiving free dental care at private dental offices, was held on a given Friday every February. IKDDS members, Dr. Catherine Periolat, the Indiana chairman of the Give Kids a Smile program, reported that hundreds of children benefited from thousands of hours of free dental work done across Indiana by participating dentists, dental hygienists, dental assistants, and dental labs.

In keeping with its mission statement, the Isaac Knapp District Dental Society has continued to encourage the improvement of the health of the public and to promote the art and science of dentistry in northeast Indiana. Many IKDDS members have served on local, state, and national offices and committees with 18 IKDDS dentists serving as president of the Indiana Dental Association by 2005.

Dr. Ralph Merkel, IKDDS archivist, summarized the changes in dentistry over the past century. He stated, "Before the 1950s, most people, including many dentists, felt that they would eventually lose their teeth. Then, through the use of fluorides, x-ray exams, and amalgam or composite restorations, many people saved their teeth. As the profession and the public became more aware of the benefits of oral health care, the entire picture began to change. Now, at the beginning of the 21st Century, the present children have a life expectancy near 100 years. They need to maintain their permanent dentition for 94 years. The use of sealants, lasers, routine orthodontia, and improved home care make that possible. They can maintain a beautiful smile for a lifetime, with excellent dental health and no restorations!! What a marvelous time to be involved in the dental profession!"

Isaac Knapp District Dental Society members who served as Indiana Dental Association president from 1976-2005. (l. to r.) Drs. R. Stetzel, J. Platt, G. Kaufman, J. Frey, L. Hagedorn, and D. Matthews.

The Fort Wayne Civic Theatre

In 1927 the Fort Wayne Community Theatre Guild was formed. That year the volunteer group produced two shows, one in a local high school and the second at a neighborhood church.

In 1928 another group, the Fort Wayne Civic Theatre Guild, comprised of many of the same people as the original group, began producing shows. They had no permanent home and mounted three to five shows each season. In 1931 this group of dedicated theatre volunteers changed their name to the Old Fort Players and continued to move from venue to venue. Then in 1933 the Players moved into the 800 seat Majestic Theatre in downtown Fort Wayne. The stage was so large (80' wide and 40' deep) that for a 1930s production of Ben Hur, live horses were used on a treadmill for the chariot race! The building was leased in the early years, then in 1940, a mortgage was drawn up and the building was purchased by the company.

Though classes in acting and other theatre arts had been offered to the public since 1933, the classes were formalized in 1940 and included instruction in scenic and lighting design, voice and diction, make up, and set construction as well as acting and pantomime. Also, the children's theatre grew from an audience of 900 in 1933 to over 10,000 in 1946. Then in 1940 tax-exempt status was awarded by the state and the company changed the name to the Fort Wayne Civic Theatre. The Anthony Awards were given out for the first time in 1953. Only four trophies were handed out that year. In 1955 the Women's Guild was formed. This branch of the organization is still active and vibrant.

A total of 231 productions were mounted in the beautiful Majestic Theatre until the city condemned the building and tore it down in 1957. So the organization moved, temporarily, into the Palace Theatre The plan was to move into the new Fine Arts Building, at that time still in the planning stages. But the Fine Arts Building never came to be and the Civic Theatre remained until 1969 at the Palace Theatre.

In 1966 the Youtheatre, as the children's theatre arm was called, hired their own director for the first time, beginning the process that would eventually make them an independent company. To this day the Youtheatre shares space with the Civic Theatre, but thrives as a separate theatre organization.

When the Palace could no longer support the Civic Theatre, the company

Majestic Theatre

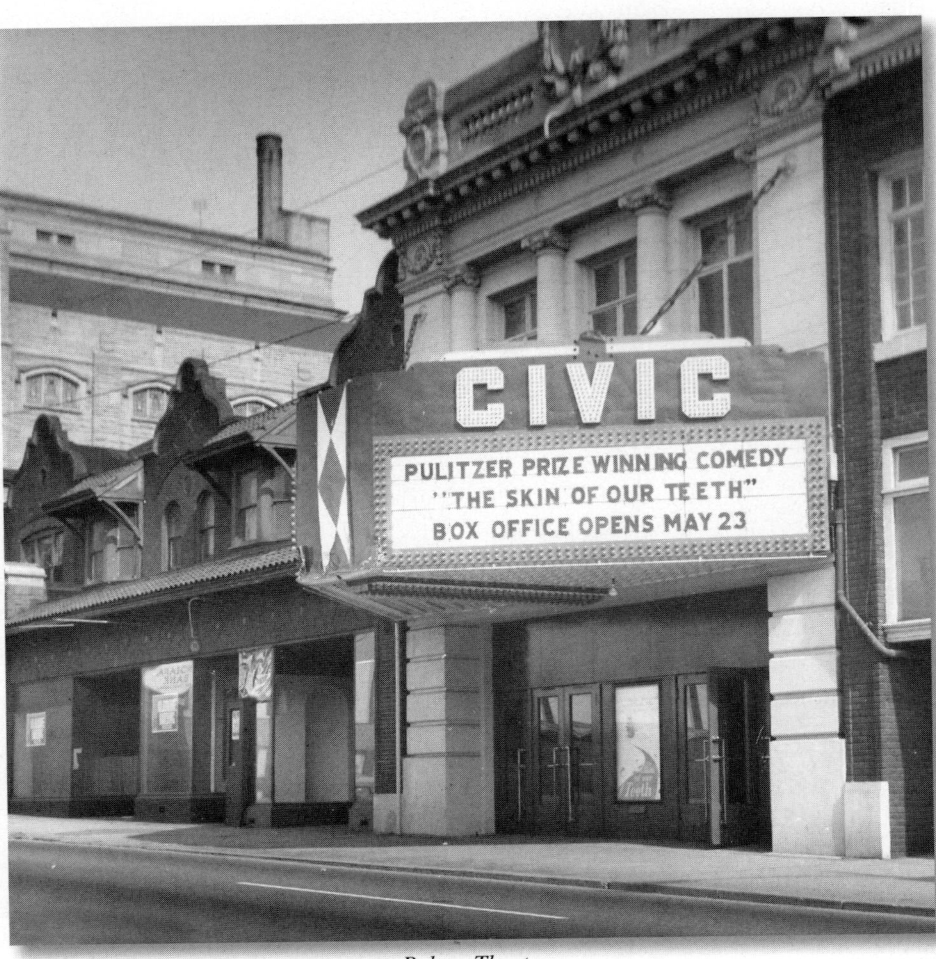

Palace Theatre

moved for three years into a building on Maiden Lane. The space had only about 150 seats and didn't serve the company well at all. By the end of the 1972 season, the Fine Arts Foundation (ancestor to Arts United) neared completion on the Performing Arts Center and the company prepared to make another move by giving Arts United $30,000 toward building of the center.

The Fort Wayne Civic Theatre moved into the brand new Performing Arts Center in 1973, designed by Louis Kahn and constructed after his death. The 1966 budget was $77,500 and by 2006 the budget was $807,670. The 2003-2004 Season marked the 75th Anniversary of the Fort Wayne Civic Theatre. By the middle of the 2005-2006 season the Civic Theatre had produced 600 productions; established an endowment of $45,318; was 1,555 members strong; and approved to conduct a feasibility study researching the possibility of developing a second stage. The current executive director, Phillip H. Colglazier, is number 27 in the long line of directors.

The Lifetime Achievement Award began in 1996-1997 recognizing the contributions of Mildred Cutchin. George H. Koegel was recognized in 1997-1998; in 1998-1999 Jayne Kelley; and in 1999-2000, Bill Wunderlin. Then in 2000-2001 the George H. Koegel Lifetime Achievement Award was established honoring George H. Koegel, as well as Robert D. Sandmaier, Scenic Designer/Artists.

The George H. Koegel Lifetime Achievement recognized the contributions of Harvey G. Cocks in 2001-2002, in 2002-2003 Jayne Kelley, and in 2003-2004 Joyce Van Ry. The Civic Theatre honored Arts United with a Special Recognition Anthony Award in celebration of their 50th Anniversary in 2004-2005.

George H. Koegel

Arts United Center

Fort Wayne Country Club

Old Clubhouse

At the turn of the century, golf was introduced to Fort Wayne. The earliest golf courses were developed on leased properties by a group known first as the Fort Wayne Golf Club and later as the Kekionga Golf Club.

Seventy five members officially formed Fort Wayne Country Club (FWCC) in 1908; purchased the original 88-acre portion of the 355 acres the club occupies today; and began a three-year building process. The Kekionga Golf Club merged with Fort Wayne Country Club in 1910. A family club from its inception, the Fort Wayne Country Club opened its doors in 1911. Facilities included the clubhouse complete with dining rooms, card rooms, music rooms, and locker rooms, a 9-hole golf course, and tennis courts, "... all blend into the scheme of beckoning attractiveness for the tired city businessman and his family".

David McIntosh, a Scottish expert, laid out the original nine holes of golf. Noted golf-course architect, William B. Langford, Chicago, was retained in 1916 to expand the golf course to 18 holes. Mr. Langford designed, planned, and personally supervised all construction work on eighteen new greens, thirty bunkers, and thirty-nine traps. "We have the foundation of a Standard Championship Course, 6,263 yards in length, second to none in the West." Installation of water on the fairways began as early as 1934. And in the mid-1980s, Arthur Hill was retained to develop a master plan for the course. Mr. Hill's plan guides continued course development yet today.

The original clubhouse was put to rest when the "new" clubhouse was opened in 1960. The beautiful southern colonial overlooking the 9th and 18th greens was expanded to the east in 1968, to the west in 1981, and again to the west in 1990 to the present 38,000 square feet. In addition to the Clubhouse, the FWCC property contains 15 additional buildings including the Tennis Center, Golf Shop, and Pool area. This historic property contains part of the original Fort Wayne portage, the Wabash-Eric canal, and the roadbed for the old Northern Indiana Traction Company, which is still visible across the number 6 fairway.

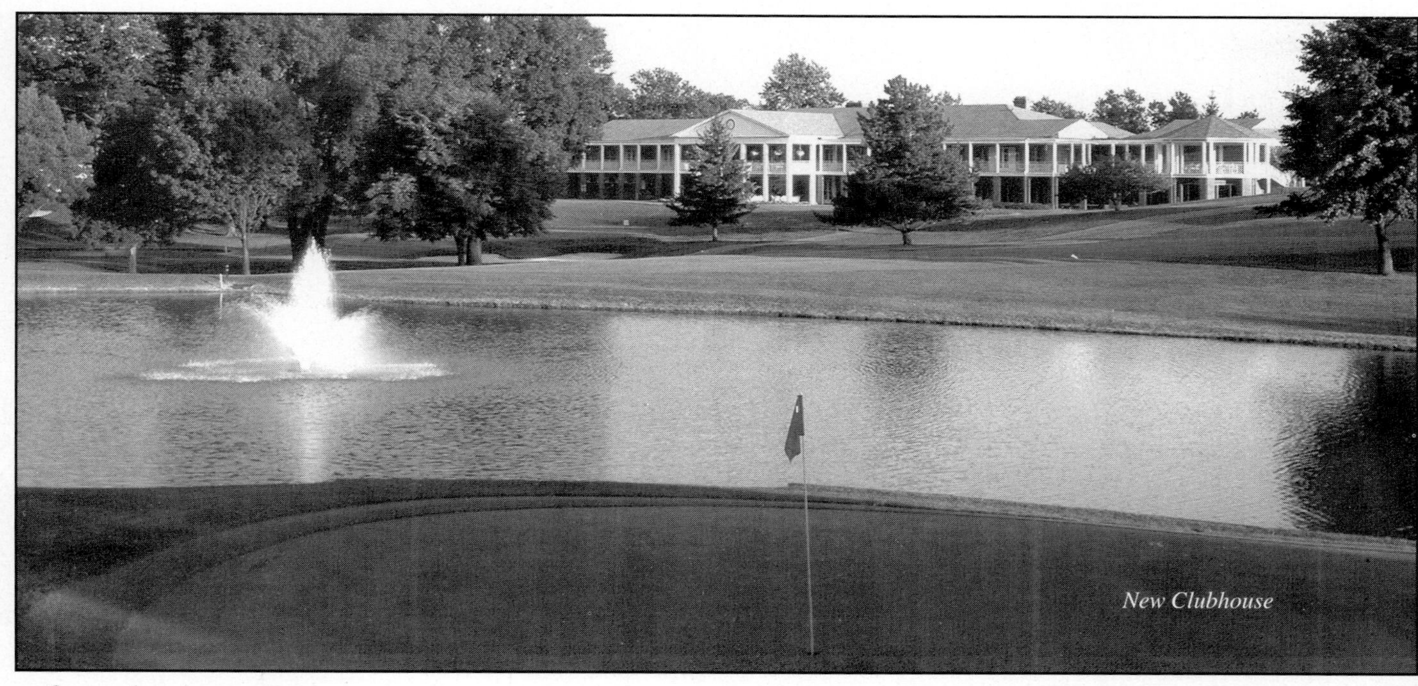
New Clubhouse

Over the years Fort Wayne Country Club has been an interesting participant in the game of golf. Gene Sarazen's "Thirty Years of Championship Golf," started here at Fort Wayne Country Club in 1920 when Sarazen, at age 18, was working as caddymaster and assistant to golf professional, Ramsey Hunter. Members encouraged and financially supported Sarazen to enter the National Open that season at Inverness in Toledo. Sarazen went on to win the U.S. Open in 1922 and in 1935 became the first golfer to ever win all four of the game's major events.

For many years, beginning in 1958, FWCC was the annual host for the Mad Anthony Hoosier Celebrity Golf Tournament. Our fairways and greens have accepted the shot-making of such professionals as Arnold Palmer, Jack Nicklaus, Gary Player, Ben Hogan, Sam Snead, Cathy Whitworth, Mickey Wright, Patty Berg and many others during this colorful era of Fort Wayne golf. Fort Wayne Country Club is also proud of its support of the Evans Scholarship Foundation. Since 1963 over 100 young adults have received college degrees through the caddie program and members support.

The Fort Wayne Country Club will celebrate its 100th birthday in 2008. It is this area's original premier country club and home to over 600 member families. Over the years the club and its members have hosted many of Fort Wayne's charitable gala events. As the club enters its second century, quality, tradition, family, and community continue to be the hallmarks of the Fort Wayne Country Club.

Old Dance Porch

The Lincoln Museum

The Lincoln Museum Lobby

In 1905 Robert Todd Lincoln authorized the use of Abraham Lincoln's image and sent a photograph of his father that was reproduced on the letterhead of the new business, Lincoln National Life Insurance Company. Arthur Hall, one of the founders of The Lincoln National Life Insurance Company and later its president, was a long-time admirer of the 16th President. By the late 1920s he felt that the company should repay the debt it owed Abraham Lincoln for the success it achieved by using his name.

Arthur Hall met Louis A. Warren, a Lincoln Scholar, at a meeting to discuss a Lincoln Memorial Highway that would run through Kentucky, Indiana and Illinois. After hearing Dr. Warren speak, Arthur Hall invited him to Fort Wayne to establish a Lincoln memorial project. Hall described the goal of this project, "No motive of commercialism or profit entered into our plans to assemble this wealth of Lincolniana – We seek merely to provide the means and the channel through which there may continue to flow an ever increasing volume of information concerning Lincoln, especially to the youth of our land, that they may be influenced to think and to live as Lincoln did –'with malice towards none and charity for all.'" Warren started work on February 12, 1928.

Lincoln's inkwell and pocket knife.

Hall and Warren created the Lincoln Historical Research Foundation. By 1932 the name was changed to the Lincoln National Life Foundation and its sole purpose was to operate a museum dedicated to perpetuating "an active interest in the life of Abraham Lincoln." The Museum developed the country's largest private collection of Lincolniana.

Lincoln National Life Insurance executives began acquiring Lincoln items prior to establishing the Museum. These items included the photograph received from Robert Todd Lincoln for use on the company's letterhead; the Pickett bronze bas-relief plaque used at the dedication of the first company-owned building on November 7, 1923; and a white rose bud from Lincoln's casket given to Arthur Hall by his mother in 1912. This company-executive collection included more than 1600 items and formed the basis of the new Museum's collection. Dr. Warren expanded it when he brought three more collections with him to Fort Wayne. Through his research he had obtained the Helm-Haycraft and the Hanks-Hitchcock collections. Assembled by John Helm, surveyor, and Samuel Haycraft, historian, this collection consists of documents and manuscripts from the communities where Lincoln's parents lived. The Hanks-Hitchcock collection includes over 1200 lists of Hanks families and hundreds of family records and letters. Amassed by Warren, the third collection is called the Warren collection. It encompasses thousands of Virginia, Kentucky, Indiana and Illinois records referencing the Lincolns and neighboring families.

As his first major acquisition after his arrival at Lincoln National Life Insurance Company, Warren purchased the Richard Thompson collection from his estate in 1928. Thompson had gathered over 2000 manuscripts—Lincoln letters, the correspondence of his contemporaries, etc. Thompson had been a friend of Lincoln's and a leading Indiana Whig.

The first permanent exhibition of materials from these collections was located on the fourth floor of the company's home office in Fort Wayne. Warren displayed documents and artifacts that illustrated the story of Abraham Lincoln. He also featured them through the publication of *Lincoln Lore* beginning in 1929. Warren intended *Lincoln Lore* to become a cumulative encyclopedia on Lincoln. A weekly newssheet for 27 years, *Lincoln Lore* expanded to four pages in 1956 when it became a monthly bulletin. Almost 40 years later the format was augmented again when the publication was issued quarterly in 1995. It is the longest continuously published periodical featuring Abraham Lincoln and in 2005 was named by the *Chicago Tribune* as one of the top 50 magazines in the U.S.

Warren wanted to purchase the library of Judge Daniel Fish of Minneapolis, one of the five largest collections of Lincoln books and documents in the nation. Judge Fish died in 1906, so to augment his collection Warren recommended the additional purchase of the Albert H. Griffith collection, which complemented the Fish collection because it added 20th century Lincoln material. On February 7, 1930, the executive committee of the Lincoln National Life Insurance Company voted to purchase both collections. Arthur Hall said, "When an individual collector dies, his collection may be sold at auction and scattered. A corporation does not die, and this collection is in permanent hands." Dr. Warren served as The Lincoln Museum's director until 1956.

The Museum's second director, Dr. R. Gerald McMurtry, significantly enlarged the collection. During his tenure, which began in July 1956, the Museum moved from the fourth floor to the first floor of Lincoln National Life Insurance's Harrison Street building, and the number of exhibits increased. Dr. McMurtry's acquisitions included the life mask of Lincoln's face and hands made in 1860 by Leonard Wells Volk. Dr. McMurtry is honored by the annual McMurtry Lecture, which brings a nationally known Lincoln authority to Fort Wayne to speak.

In 1972 McMurtry retired and historian Dr. Mark E. Neely, Jr. became The Lincoln Museum's third director. Like his predecessors, Neely made important additions to the collection including the Lincoln Family collection of photographs, purchased in 1986. Under Neely's guidance, the Museum moved to larger facilities in the company's Clinton Street building, and an exhibit of 60 displays depicting the life and career of Abraham Lincoln was added. The Museum's 50th anniversary was celebrated with the establishment of both this new permanent exhibit and the McMurtry Lecture, described above. In 1992, Neely won a Pulitzer Prize in history for his book, *Fate of Liberty, Abraham Lincoln and Civil Liberties* and he accepted a position at St. Louis University.

The next year, plans were made to expand the Museum's operation. To guide the expansion and relocation of the Museum to it present site at 200 East Berry Street, the company selected its first professional museum administrator, Joan L. Flinspach, who serves as President and CEO of the Museum today.

The new facility, The Lincoln Museum, opened to the public on October 1, 1995 expanding to nearly three times the size of the previous one. It has eleven state-of-the-art galleries with eighteen computerized or hands-on exhibits and three theaters. The project represented a multi-million dollar investment to make the legacy of Abraham Lincoln accessible into the twenty-first century.

An overview of the Museum's current collection includes approximately 18,000 volumes of books, over 5000 19th century photographs, numerous Lincoln artifacts, 300 Lincoln manuscripts, more than 6,000 19th century prints, broadsides and political cartoons and the Lincoln family's personal photographs. The Museum owns scores of artifacts – including the inkwell Lincoln used to sign the Emancipation Proclamation, and Lincoln's pocketknife, legal wallet and shawl. In 1998 with the retirement of Ian M. Rolland as CEO of Lincoln National Corporation, the Lincoln Financial Group Foundation, Inc. voted to purchase an extremely rare edition of the Emancipation Proclamation signed by Lincoln for the Museum. One of eight in the world, it is the only one on permanent exhibition. In 2005 to celebrate Lincoln National Corporation's 100th anniversary, the Foundation purchased one of 13 copies of the 13th Amendment to the Constitution signed by Abraham Lincoln, making The Lincoln Museum one of only five locations in the world owning both these documents which together ended slavery in the United States.

Lincoln's America

Sources

Ninety Years and Growing: The Story of Lincoln National by Michael Hawfield

Lincoln Lore # 1842, #1610

The Lutheran Foundation

In 1878 in Fort Wayne, Indiana, people from the northeast Indiana Lutheran Community came together with a realization for the future: That a physically and spiritually sound community will be a vibrant, prosperous and progressive community.

An original notice, in German, of the effort to build Lutheran Hospital in Fort Wayne.

That premise led to a mission of hope, one that would benefit their immediate neighbors and have an impact far beyond the reaches of the tri-state region.

To that end, these 19th-century visionaries began putting their dreams for the future into action: raising funds, purchasing land and property, developing a plan that at once was audacious, fiscally responsible and self-sufficient to the core. These plans were a reflection of the souls of the men and women implementing it.

Lutheran Hospital's dedication ceremony.

These men and women lived their beliefs, focusing on service to others beyond self, especially the compassionate care for others based on the basic human mission of love for their fellow man as exemplified by the life of Jesus Christ.

Poetically so, on Thanksgiving Day, November 24, 1904, the first fruits of their dreams became a reality with the dedication and formal opening of Lutheran Hospital, a 25-bed facility that was formerly the Judge Lindley M. Ninde homestead at the corner of Fairfield and Wildwood Avenues. Little did they realize that with the dedication of this dream that they were creating much more than a hospital. They were laying the foundation for a tradition of service to all that would last well over a century.

The Reverend Phillip Wambsganss

During the dedication ceremony on that late autumn day, the tone and definition for this mission was defined by The Reverend Phillip Wambsganss – then Pastor of Emmaus Lutheran Church – when he stated that all these efforts and the fruits of those labors were dedicated "to the service of suffering humanity and to the glory of God." Since then, the Reverend Wambsganss' words have been powerfully distilled into the Latin phrase *"Soli Deo Gloria"* — "To God Alone Be The Glory."

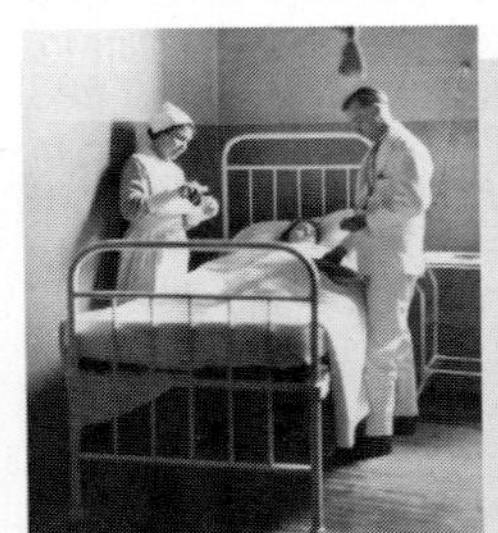

A patient receives treatment from a nurse and physician at Lutheran Hospitlal in 1926.

Thanks in part to the consecrated leadership of dedicated Lutherans, coupled with the rich blessing of our Lord, this modest 21-room, 25-bed hospital progressed to a facility which could care for more than 550 patients. As a result, Lutheran Hospital took its place at the forefront of healthcare in the state of Indiana.

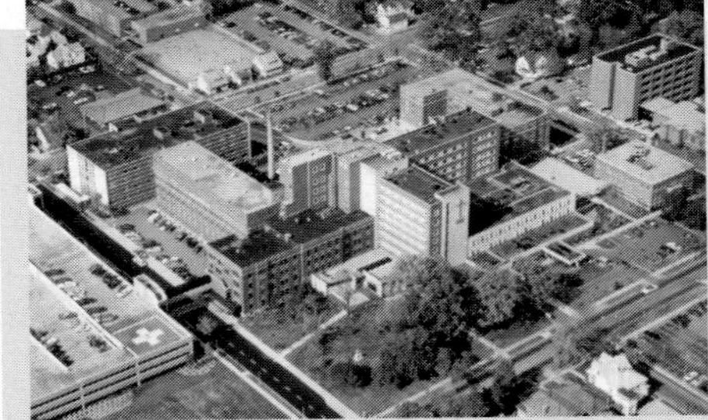

The Lutheran Hospital campus as seen in an aerial view in the 1970s, before its sale.

A Century Of Service Since 1904

The Lutheran Foundation

Educational initiatives and programs for all ages remain a high-priority for The Lutheran Foundation.

On July 31, 1995, Lutheran Hospital was sold and the dreams and visions of the original founders were reborn. After providing for the medical needs of individuals in northern Indiana for over 90 years, the mission of service to the community and compassion for all transcended the brick and mortar reality of a healthcare facility.

Following the sale of Lutheran Hospital, 34 Lutheran congregations — 24 of which were affiliated with the Lutheran Church-Missouri Synod and the remaining ten with the Evangelical Lutheran Church in America — established The Lutheran Foundation with the proceeds of the sale, approximately $140 million. This metamorphosis from hospital to community foundation was indeed a quantum shift in terms of identity, but remained true to the guiding tenet as defined by Reverend Wambsganss in 1904.

A cornerstone of The Lutheran Foundation's ethos is its commitment to the spiritual vitality of this region.

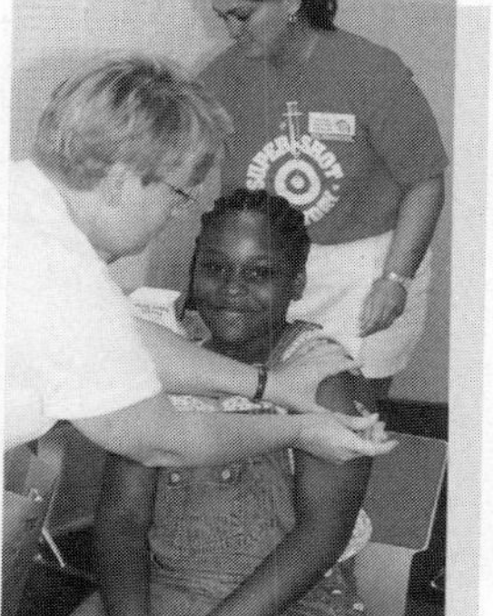

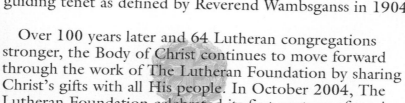

Community-wide healthcare programs are recipients of grants from The Lutheran Foundation.

Over 100 years later and 64 Lutheran congregations stronger, the Body of Christ continues to move forward through the work of The Lutheran Foundation by sharing Christ's gifts with all His people. In October 2004, The Lutheran Foundation celebrated its first century of service to the communities and people it serves. With leadership from the 18-member Board of Directors and input from its 431 Delegates, The Lutheran Foundation continues to fulfill its mission of "demonstrating the compassion of Christ by promoting, improving and enhancing the quality of life for individuals, families, congregations and communities."

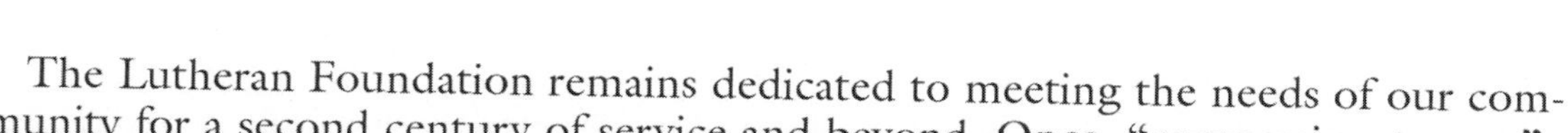

The Lutheran Foundation remains dedicated to meeting the needs of our community for a second century of service and beyond. Once, "compassionate care" for others meant treating physical illnesses. Today, The Lutheran Foundation's efforts cut across the community boundaries, ethnic, social and economic backgrounds. The Lutheran Foundation annually provides millions of dollars in grants to support educational initiatives, missions, spiritual outreach and healthcare programs that enrich the lives of thousands of citizens in our area. It is able to do so and remain flexible in its reach by combining sound, cutting-edge fiscal management of its core assets and developing additional sources of funding for the future while always remaining true to the core principle of its visionary founders —

The Lutheran Foundation's offices are housed in the Deumling Clinic building located at the site of the former Lutheran Hospital campus site.

"Soli Deo Gloria" — "To God Alone be The Glory."

Soli Deo Gloria

Old Fort Coin Club

Old Fort Coin Club Membership, 2006.

In 1956 coin collecting existed at a different level. It was possible to obtain an entire series from your pocket change. Barber dimes still could be found along side Mercury and Roosevelt dimes. Standing Liberty quarters could be found in circulation. There was a belief that those dateless Buffalo Nickels would be circulating fifty years in the future. People received half dollars in change. It was even possible to get an Indian Head penny from your daily purchases. A large percentage of the population collected coins. It was something that both adults and children could do. It was easy and rather inexpensive. Drug stores and Five & Dimes sold coin albums. It had become a familiar American past time.

Within the Fort Wayne area there was a loose relationship among coin collectors. Individuals knew individuals that knew individuals who then knew of others that were interested in the hobby. Coin shops had begun to open to service the growing interest. One such location was A.D. Noble on Lower Huntington Road in Fort Wayne. People would see others at these shops and a discussion about a coin club would ensue. The number of coin clubs was growing. Chicago had a coin club since 1919 and there was the American Numismatic Association, which had begun in 1890. The real leap for a local club came from Glen Shake of New Haven, Indiana. He placed a small notice in the newspaper asking all interested parties to meet at the YMCA. In October 1956 the first meeting of the Old Fort Coin Club was held. Those present included: Glen Shake, Harry McKown, David Rasor, Earl Fankhauser, William McNagny, John Rasor, and James Fairfield, Sr. The interest and enthusiasm was so high they formed the club that first night.

Meetings continued to be held on the second floor of the YMCA Building at 226 East Washington Boulevard in Fort Wayne until March of 1957. During this time a Constitution and By-laws were written and sent to the Attorney General of the state. A board was developed and club goals were outlined. By March 1957 the club had fifty-three members. It was decided at that time that all affiliates up to that point would be considered Charter Members.

Glen Shake, who had been so important in the creation of the club and its first President, by 1957 had been transferred to Arizona by his company. Claire H. Stukey became President in 1957. From April to June 1957 the club meetings were held at the Keenan Hotel at 1016 South Harrison Street in Fort Wayne. Then later that year it was moved to the Fort Wayne National Bank at 1825 McKinnie. This was the club's location from July 1957 to February 1959.

The club's newsletter, *The Old Fort Coin Chatter*, found its beginnings during this time frame. By March 1957 a card was being sent to the membership by the Club Secretary to remind them of the meetings. Later that became a one-sheet letter and finally it evolved into a newsletter. A.D. Noble completed the first issue of *The Old Fort Coin Chatter* on August 5, 1958. In various forms it has continued since then. In February 1963 the name was changed to just the *Chatter*.

It is not totally clear how the organization settled on the name Old Fort Coin Club. The membership did include individuals from the surrounding area and Ohio. It was felt that the name should not be specific to Fort Wayne. Early in the history of the club this issue was hotly debated. There was even a ballot and vote on the topic. Within the club there was a group that wanted the club to be called the Fort Wayne Coin Club, but the logic of the name Old Fort Coin Club won out.

The first annual coin show was held in 1958 at the National Guard Armory at 330 South Clinton Street in Fort Wayne. That continued for the next fifteen years. By 1973 the shows were moved to the Sheraton Motor Hotel, then the Ramada Inn from 1975 to 1979, and then on to Imperial House from 1980 to 1983. There were seven shows at the Grand Wayne Center from 1985 to 1991. One show was held at the Allen County Fair Grounds in 1992 before returning to the Ramada Inn from 1993 to 1995. In 1996 the club had returned to the Fair Grounds and has continued having shows at this location through 2005.

Meetings of the club were held at the Fruehauf Union Hall from April 1959 to February 1966. The largest membership occurred during this time frame. The club had over 200 members. They later met at the Lantern, Saint Andrews Catholic Church, and American Legion Post #82. From October 1974 to December 1986, meetings were held at the Shawnee Branch Library on Noll Avenue. In January 1987 the Coin Club meetings were moved to the Good Shepherd United Methodist Church on Vance Avenue and have been there ever since.

There is a format to the club meetings. At the beginning of the meeting general matters are discussed, both old and new business would be reviewed. News within the numismatic community, changes, and club activities would be covered. Club members would be able to present new items during a show and tell period. There is a coin quiz. The club then has an intermission where cookies and soft drinks are served. After the intermission there is an educational program. An outside lecturer or member of the club will discuss a numismatic topic. Then the club will have a coin auction. Guests will have an opportunity to introduce themselves and throughout the night there are drawings. There would be a membership drawing and a silver dollar drawing. This format has been consistent throughout the history of the club.

The organization has contributed in many ways to the area. Numismatic books have been purchased for the library and local schools. The group has done scores of coin appraisal in connection with other events. We have worked with Boy Scouts attempting to earn their merit badges in coin collecting. At various times coin displays have been created both at the Allen County Historical Society and at Swinney Park. The display at Swinney Park was stolen in January 1963. Numerous coins, broken bank notes, Fort Wayne Civil War Tokens, and Medals were lost. Coin donation of 1816 and displays were given to the Old Fort and its foundation. The Old Fort Coin Club has been given Proclamations by the City of Fort Wayne in April 1959, October 1981, and in October 2002. The club was issued a Proclamation by the Vice President of the United States in April 1967.

The Old Fort Coin Club is considered to be one of the oldest organizations in Allen County. It meets the second Thursday of every month, with a picnic in July and a Holiday dinner in December. There have been seventy-one different officers of the club and three times that number have served on the Board. The club has continued to be true to its original design. It represents a point of education, exchange, and fellowship. *Submitted by George Courtesis and Rodney Scott*

Old Fort Coin Club
50th Anniversary Coin, 2006.

Swinney Homestead operated by Settlers, Inc. at 1424 West Jefferson Boulevard in Fort Wayne.

The early settlers of the Fort Wayne area endowed us with a legacy of the knowledge and skills they practiced in their daily lives on the frontier. To perpetuate the historical significance of this legacy a group of skilled artisans headed by Phyllis Florea and Susie Livensparger met to explore the feasibility of sharing their knowledge and skills. They instituted various classes in both hand arts and domestic arts with the dual focus of historical data and hands-on activities. The initial meeting of these classes was held in 1971 at the Plymouth Congregational Church. As the series of classes became popular within the community, the areas of interest were expanded to include fireplace cookery, spinning, weaving, dyeing, needlework arts, reverse glass painting, rug hooking, rug braiding, basketry, corn husk crafts, wheat weaving, tin punch, soap, herbs, stenciling, all kinds of paper arts, quilting, and more.

Settlers is one of the founding sponsors of the Johnny Appleseed Festival, the most successful two-day festival in the state of Indiana. You can find the Settlers in the Pioneer village offering wonderful foods, demonstrations, a country store, and music. The festival celebrated 31 years of historical activities and entertainment in 2005.

An herb garden dedicated in 1976 developed under the direction of Wilma and Robert Rowe is located on the Swinney Homestead grounds. Herbs and flowers for culinary, medicinal, cosmetic, and home use are grown there. An herb sale is held every May along with a Membership Tea and a bake sale.

Music was an important part of the life of the early pioneers. The Settlers formed a music group, The Hearthstone Ensemble, in 1978 under the direction of Carol Kent and Lea Woodrum. The Ensemble entertains at Settler events, festivals, schools, and other community functions.

Settlers entered a long-term lease agreement with the Fort Wayne Parks Department for the use of the Swinney Homestead in 1979. The historic home built in 1844 by land developer and businessman, Thomas Swinney and his wife, Lucy Tabor, is on the National Register of Historic Places. Settlers found a new home along with the responsibility for its restoration and preservation. The 1894 Ulrich log house from Lancaster Township in Huntington County, Indiana, was purchased in 1976 and reconstructed in 1978 on the site of the Swinney family's log home in which they lived from 1826 until their new brick home was built.

Over the years, the Settlers have hosted the Tri-State Folk Music Society concerts, presented hands-on activities for the participants in the F.A.M.E. festival, volunteered many hours at the Old Fort when it was first opened, still help support the History Center through dual membership in both organizations, and continue to participate in the West Central Historic Home Tour. The Victorian Repast presented annually in early December in the beautifully decorated Homestead includes a wonderful Victorian-style dinner, presentations of Christmas traditions, music, and a Christmas Shop.

The Settler's Speakers Bureau provides many area schools and other organizations in the community with programs and demonstrations of early American hand arts, domestic arts, and music. A special series additionally is offered for home-schooled students.

Settlers, Inc. is a not-for-profit volunteer organization. The proceeds realized from its activities help maintain and restore Swinney Homestead, the log house, and the herb garden.

Settlers' Log House on the Swinney Homestead.

Settler's Inc. Hearthstone Ensemble

Hearthstone Ensemble

The Hearthstone Ensemble is the music organization of Settlers, Inc. and has been active since1978. Several Settlers gathered in 1976 to sing revolutionary period songs for the Fort Wayne Bicentennial Parade, but they did not continue as a group. In 1978 using some of those songs and singers, Carol Kent and Lea Woodrum with her lap dulcimer, formed the Hearthstone Ensemble, a musical group consisting of fifteen talented ladies. Their first performance was at the Settlers' membership tea in May 1978. Today traditional instruments such as the hammered dulcimer, the lap dulcimer, bowed psaltery, tin whistle, Irish harp, and the autoharp are played to accompany the singers.

Music was an important part of settler life. Music could provide relief from the hardships encountered on the frontier. There was music from the homeland, songs for work, worship, entertainment, and the songs that told of current events. The Hearthstone Ensemble has endeavored to preserve this music and share it with the community. And share it we have!! This year, 2005, will mark our 27th appearance at the Johnny Appleseed Festival. We have performed for many of the area festivals, schools, churches, libraries, clubs, Settler gatherings, Victorian Repasts, Membership Teas, and many more. Our travels have taken us to Dearborn, Michigan, northwest Ohio, west and northwest Indiana, south to Centerville, Indiana and many places in between.

Beverly Williams, Lea Woodrum, and Jeanne Bornefeld at the display garden at the Allen County Extension Office on July 12, 1999.

In order to share our music with the community the Hearthstone Ensemble has recorded two CDs. The Settler Songbag is a collection of some of our favorite folk songs from the Midwest and the Settler Christmas CD has traditional Christmas carols and folk songs that have been widely enjoyed.

Hearthstone members have come and gone in our 27 years of performing and we give many thanks to all who have unselfishly given of their time and talents. A special thanks goes to the core group who has devoted so many hours to the success of the Hearthstone Ensemble. We not only work hard together but we also have fun doing it!

Proceeds from the more than 650 paid performances have enable Hearthstone to purchase many items and artifacts for the Swinney Homestead and the adjacent log house.

Hearthstone Ensemble

Allen County Genealogical Society of Indiana

A group of Senior citizens who met regularly at the Senior Center were very interested in genealogy. Encouraged by their enthusiasm for family history, Mrs. Carol Barngrover Clark, Director of the Senior Citizens Center, and Mrs. Kay LaRue decided to organize a group of budding genealogists in 1976. They sought advice from Dorothy Lower who was then manager of the genealogy department of the Allen County Public Library. Word was spread asking that anyone interested in genealogy attend a meeting on the subject. The response was more than expected. Several meetings were held to form committees, write the organization's bylaws, and set up membership guidelines. Jean Blance was elected the first president in June 1976 and Kay LaRue was the recording secretary. Charter membership was available until December 1976 and 43 people joined this group. Membership was then opened to anyone of any age interested in genealogy.

A Society logo was designed. A quarterly publication called *Allen County LINES* would be printed for members and a copy placed in the library. The first issue was published in March 1977. A preview issue of February 9, 1977 listed a concern of the group that asked, "How long will we survive if we use this association for the sole purpose of pursuit of our own individual research?" Thirty years later, the Society, with input of the 1,327 members over the years, has proven extremely adequate at fulfilling the changing needs of its members.

The first genealogy fair was held at the Senior Citizens Center to help those who wanted to learn more about researching family history. The following year a Cemetery committee was formed to locate and read all the cemeteries in Allen County and publish that information for future generations. The seven volumes of cemetery books became a financial mainstay of the Society and continue to be best sellers. The cemetery project led to the publication of the Index to Known Burial Sites and Church Records Survey, both mainstays of Allen County research. Other sale items included an ACGSI logo pin, tee shirts, polo shirts, sweatshirts, tote bag, and pencils, all of which financially supported the Society's goals.

In 1978, the Society participated in the Three Rivers Festival for the first time by putting up a display where Society volunteers answered questions, promoted genealogy, and solicited new members. The Society continued to participate in the festival each year and added Germanfest and Johnny Appleseed Festival to their summer schedule of events.

Members have always been asked to contribute their family history charts to the Society for preservation. The result of this collection produced six volumes of the surname file index. Over 1,400 charts were microfilmed in 2004. The film is permanently stored in the genealogy department of the Allen County Public Library.

By 1981, Society members began volunteering their time and expertise in the library's genealogy department on a regular basis. The first gift in 1981 was self-serving. It was an electric pencil sharpener, which is still in use today. The Society continuously supports the Allen County Public Library Historical Genealogy Department through monetary gifts, totaling almost $25,000 and thousands of hours of volunteer's support.

Many more projects were developed and implemented over the years that have aided Allen County researchers tremendously. The First Families Project was conceived to identify early settlers in Allen County in conjunction with the Fort Wayne Bicentennial Celebration in 1994. This and the Homesteaders of Allen County are ongoing projects. The records of these families were microfilmed and presented to the Genealogy Department in 2004. An index provides researchers easy access.

Gathering original church and mortuary records for copying and placement in the library has been an active project for some time. In cooperation with the genealogy department, church records have been loaned to the Society for photocopying and binding at no expense to the church. One copy remains in the library's collection while another copy is returned to the participating church as a gift. The It's Not Trash It's Treasure campaign was instituted to gather albums, yearbooks, scrapbooks, diaries, family histories, etc., that might otherwise be thrown out and to preserve these items for posterity in the library. Society volunteers provide the labor for these projects.

Genealogy education has remained a priority with over fifty workshops presented over the years to almost 2,000 interested participants. The Society was ahead of its time when they sponsored a successful series of Teleconferences in 1996-1997.

The Society maintains the Allen County Gen Web Page and has its own website, both of which continue to grow. The website offers information, free lookups, and searchable databases. The Society's Computer Interest Group helps members with computer problems and questions. It encourages sharing of new ideas and presents programs that are relevant to computer genealogy.

The latest project was this publication, the Allen County History Book, published in conjunction with the Allen County-Fort Wayne Historical Society.

Allen County Genealogical Society of Indiana, Executive Officers and Committee Chairmen.

Allen County Democratic Party

Fort Wayne had actually been incorporated in 1829, but there was no mayor or city council. In these early years the best the municipal government could be called was a frontier collection of civic activists. There was a primitive Board of Trustees and they were elected annually. They oversaw the administrative needs of this fledgling community, but they met rarely and kept few records. Most of these community leaders were far more interested in their own business dealings or their own basic survival needs than elaborate civic projects. The Board of Trustees took little action to collect delinquent taxes or to construct any public buildings.

This all changed in 1840. Franklin Randall, a Fort Wayne attorney, was charged with developing a new Charter of Incorporation for the City of Fort Wayne. This had to be approved by the Indiana State Legislature. The community was experiencing growing pains and this new Charter was needed to address issues related to street improvement, property assessment, fire protection, police services, and especially bridges. It was at this point a political awareness occurred within the city of Fort Wayne and the surrounding area of Allen County. There was an understanding that there was a place for local government and the political apparatus that went along with it. Henry Rudisilll, Joseph Morgan, William Rockhill, Thomas Tigar, Henry Lotz, and others formed the Allen County Democratic Party.

What is unique about this situation was that this collection of civil activists and community leaders never considered themselves anything else but Democrats. This act occurred in a vacuum without any other competing political body present. Those individuals that moved west were generally Democrats. They saw themselves linked to the Jeffersonian principles of decentralization of government and agrarianism. There was a shared agreement on values, priorities, and productive effort that was common among western settlers. As a rule they stood against the elitism and "well ordered society" of the Federalists.

In 1842 a crisis developed among the local Democrats when the farmers of Allen County demanded a greater say within the Party. A meeting was held at the Kiser General Store. Judge James Borden was asked to draw up plans to reorganize the Party. A draft was submitted and accepted by both the Fort Wayne and Allen County elected officials.

Democratic President Franklin Roosevelt appearance in Fort Wayne on October 28, 1944, at the Pennsylvania Railroad Station. (Courtesy of Allen County Public Library)

All of the early mayors of Fort Wayne were Democrats. It was also an unpaid position and many had other responsibilities that conflicted with the job. Municipal offices were also in the hands of the Democrats; the few Whigs that did exist in the area were found within the business community. This continued up to and through the American Civil War. Even when considerable regional support for the new Republican Party developed after the Civil War, Fort Wayne remained a bastion of Democratic activities.

A new face appeared on party politics in the late Nineteenth Century. Fort Wayne and the surrounding area became like most cities in the north. It was a time of party bosses and patronage. An example can be made of William Hosey. He was the elected Democrat mayor of Fort Wayne four times. Each term was preceded by four years when he was out of office. Jobs, positions, appointments, and careers went through the hands of our elected officials. Hosey governed not only the affairs of the city but the economic lives of the citizens as well. While the patronage system has many dissenters, it was part of the times and the Democratic Party was seen as a bonding force within the community.

As Allen County and Fort Wayne changed so did the Democratic Party. While always seen as the party of the working class this reached a new height as our nation moved into the center of the Twentieth Century. Fort Wayne became a manufacturing hub. Factories and service industries brought an expanding population. Franklin Roosevelt and the New Deal allowed for a great voice from labor. Allied with labor, the Democratic Party continued to thrive and expand within Allen County.

As we move into the Twenty-First Century the Allen County Democratic Party remains active and energetic. Graham Richard, the Democratic mayor, will complete his current term in 2008. At that moment, and as we look back over the last fifty years of Fort Wayne history, there will have been five Democratic mayors and three from other parties. In 2005, the Allen County Democratic Party Chairperson is Kevin Knuth. He presides over a vast group of community outreach programs, Precinct Chairs, an Advisory Committee, and the Executive Committee. Subcommittees also exist to service the Precincts, the Party Platform, Candidate Recruitment and Training, the DAF, and Community Involvement. Separate positions exist for Media Relations, Correspondence, and the Executive Director. The Allen County Democratic Party has a long history in our area. Their ideals of economic and social justice appeared with the first settlers. Equally it must be said that those same views are just as valid and essential today.

Allen County Republican Party

During the first three decades of the twentieth century, the Allen County Democrat Party was very strong and controlled both City and County government. In the early 1930s, four young Republican attorneys, Harry Hogan, Dan Flanagan, Walter E. Helmke, and Lloyd Hartzler determined to create a vibrant new Republican Party for the City and County. Dan Flanagan, later a Judge of the Indiana Supreme Court, was elected County Chairman and Walter E. Helmke was appointed City Chairman. In 1934, they were successful in electing Harry W. Baals as Mayor of the City of Fort Wayne. Walter E. Helmke was appointed City Attorney and Lloyd Hartzler, the Assistant City Attorney. Harry Baals was re-elected in 1938 and 1942.

After almost four decades of Democrat rule in the County, the Republican Party took control of the County in 1938 with the election of the Circuit Court Judge, two of the three County Commissioners, the Sheriff, the Prosecuting Attorney, and the Congressman for the Fourth Congressional District. The new Congressman, George W. Gillie, was a veterinarian who served ten years in the U.S. Congress. He had previously served as Sheriff of Allen County.

The Chairmanship of the Allen County Republican Party changed hands in 1940 when Walter E. Helmke was elected County Chairman. He served in that capacity until 1950, when Lloyd Hartzler replaced him as County Chairman. Lloyd Hartzler served in that capacity until 1955 when he was appointed Judge of the newly created Superior Court No. 3 of Allen County. Thomas Gallmeyer was elected in 1955 and served in that capacity until 1962 when he became Indiana State Republican Chairman. Orvas E. Beers was elected in 1962 and served in that capacity until attorney Steven R. Shine was elected County Chairman in 1993.

Orvis Beers

Steve Shine

Except for one four year period between 1958 and 1962, when the Democrats took control of most of the County offices, Republicans have held almost all of the County offices since 1938. A Democrat, Henry Branning, was elected Mayor in 1947 but was defeated for re-election in 1951 by Harry Baals who died in office in May of 1954. He was succeeded by Robert E. Meyers, the City Controller, who served the remaining one year of Harry Baal's term and then was elected Mayor for four years in 1955 and served until 1959. A Democrat, Paul Mike Burns, was elected Mayor in 1959, but was defeated in his bid for re-election in 1963 by Republican Harold Zeis, a former Allen County Sheriff. Harold Zeis served two terms and was defeated in his bid for a third term in 1971 by Ivan Lebamoff, who served for four years and was defeated in his bid for re-election by Republican Robert Armstrong. Armstrong was defeated in his bid for re-election by Win Moses, who served two terms and was defeated in his bid for a third term by Paul Helmke in 1987. Paul Helmke served three terms, choosing not to run for re-election in 1999. He was succeeded by Democrat Graham A. Richard.

Allen County Parks

Around 12,000 years ago, all of Allen County was under ice. As the glaciers receded from the Fort Wayne area, they left behind rivers and terraces, rocks and sand. Once the glaciers had left, people arrived. They wandered through the area, settled into encampments, villages, and towns, to become our native people. When the Europeans arrived, they continued to shape the land even more. You can discover evidence of all of these events within our Allen County Parks.

After the Allen County Park Board formed in 1965, the search for the first Allen County Park settled on Fox Island. The area was recognized as a geological gem for its unique sand dunes formed after the receding glaciers. These sand dunes were created after a glacial lake broke past its shoreline to carve out a river. The dunes formed as sand blew up the Little River valley.

After the Little River was channelized, the sand dunes rising above surrounding the wetlands appeared as a wooded island amidst glades, ponds, and marshes. Fox Island was named when a fox den was discovered by the Yahne family, the tenant farmers who worked the land. Fox Island County Park has become an island of nature in a sea of developing Fort Wayne.

In 1971, the first 381 acres of land was purchased for Fox Island County Park. 220 of those acres were dedicated as state nature preserve. The park opened to the public in 1974, and Pat Bolman was hired by the parks board to be our first naturalist. Many of the people who worked to see Fox Island first named as a park, then developed into the haven it is today, make up the Fox Island Alliance. This amazing team of volunteers raised money to purchase two nature centers, educational materials, amazing exhibits, and more. Even more valuable is the time they have given towards educating our children and the entire community about the beauty of our natural heritage.

As of 2005, Fox Island County Park is our largest park with over 600 acres, and the most extensive facilities. Glacial influences exist in the form of now-forested wind blown sand dunes, large rocks brought by the glaciers from Canada, and large spans of wetlands. Archaeologists have found evidence of where native people hunted and passed through Fox Island on portage between rivers. If you look carefully, you'll be able to deduce which sections of the park were farm fields, and where the old Winchester Gun Club members shot at clay pigeons. And you don't have to look far to find people enjoying the beauty of Fox Island's wildlife and plant communities.

Our second largest county park was acquired in parcels, beginning in 1984. Metea County Park was named after Chief Metea of the Potawatomi Indians. One of the most well known Potawatomi of our area, his village was located near present-day Cedarville, close to the park. Located along Cedar Creek, in two parts, this beautiful park is roughly 250 acres, and contains the 120-acre Meno-aki State Dedicated Nature Preserve. This park was developed in part with State Rivergreenway funding, and the Federal Land and Water Conservation Fund. A new Nature Center was built in 2005. The Friends of Metea worked with the parks board to acquire the park land and the new facility. They have been working tirelessly since the 1980s to bring environmental education opportunities to the north side of the county.

Our third largest park, Payton County Park, is a lovely little park suited for an afternoon stroll through fields and woods. This property was willed to the county parks system by Orville Payton. His will states that the real estate must "be used solely as a public park for the benefit of the general public." Once a farm for onions and other vegetables, these nearly 40 acres of mixed forest, wetlands, and field can now be enjoyed by everyone. Willow Creek runs along the south border, and the farm pond that Payton himself dug remains a haven for aquatic critters.

Cook's Landing is our smallest county park, measuring just under five acres. This property was donated by then parks board member Cook Loughead. Located at the corner of Shoaff and Coldwater Roads, it provides access to Cedar Creek. A picnic shelter makes this the perfect place to either start or finish a day of canoeing, kayaking, or fishing.

Altogether, the county parks consist of nearly 900 acres of fields and forests, creeks and ponds, wetlands and hills. Here you can ramble over miles of trails, and traces of bygone days still remain for those who know where to look.

The Allen County Parks Mission: *To establish and manage a permanent park system incorporating conservation, education, outdoor values and nature preservation, and to provide recreational opportunities for the people of Allen County within this structure.*

The Fox Island Nature Center was opened in the spring of 1997.

Boys exploring Cedar Creek at Metea County Park. Cedar Creek also runs along Cook's Landing County Park.

Anthony Halberstadt Chapter Sons of the American Revolution

The Indiana SAR color guard marking the 225th anniversary of the Col. Augustin de LaBalme massacre in Whitley County, Indiana near Allen County, along the Eel River, on November 5, 2005. The area is one of only two Revolutionary War sites in Indiana. At this location on November 5, 1780, Col. Augustin de LaBalme and his men were defeated by Miami Indiana Chief Little Turtle and his braves as the native Americans retaliated for the surprise raid of Kekionga, now Fort Wayne. This event included SAR and DAR members, local dignitaries, members of the Miami Indiana nation, Boy Scouts and over 100 guests.

The Anthony Halberstadt Chapter Sons of the American Revolution was founded in Adams County. However, the Anthony Halberstadt Chapter has many members in Allen County as well. The Chapter was chartered in Decatur, Indiana in 1979. It was organized by James F. Halberstadt of Decatur.

After many months of study, travel, and research James Halberstadt became a member of the Indiana Sons of the American Revolution based on the record of his ancestor, Nathaniel Hazen.

Halberstadt then began the long and arduous task of organizing a local chapter.

Membership in the Sons of the American Revolution is limited to men 18 years or older who are citizens of good repute in the community and are lineal descendants of an ancestor who was at all times loyal to, and rendered active service in, the cause of American Independence. This service may have been as an officer, soldier, seaman, marine, militia man, or minuteman in the armed forces of the Continental Congress or any of the colonies or states, as signer of the Declaration of Independence, or as a member of the committee of Safety or Correspondence, or as a member of any Continental, Provincial, or Colonial Congress, or as a recognized patriot who performed actual service by overt act of resistance to the authority of Great Britain; provided, however, that no person advocating the overthrow of the government of the United States by the use of force shall be eligible for membership.

The primary purpose of the Sons of the American Revolution is to preserve the ideas and principles of those dedicated patriots who won Liberty for our country. Its purpose is not to worship the past, but rather to emphasize the principles of the past in order to illuminate the present and safeguard the future.

The charter members of the Anthony Halberstadt Chapter were James F. Halberstadt, Jr., Douglas Halberstadt, Max Halberstadt, James F. Halberstadt, Sr., Alonzo F. Halberstadt, Dick Heller, Jr., Jerome Yager, Luther Yager, Jay Jerome Yager, Don A. Melching, Melvin D. Werling, Lester Halberstadt, and Harvey Jones.

The chapter was named for Anthony Halberstadt who was born in Prussia. He was a Hessian who was conscripted by the British and turned and fought with the colonists for independence.

The Chapter has been active in sponsoring speech contests, essay contests, and Boy Scout programs in order to encourage research into our founding principles, so that our posterity will not forget them.

Although the chapter was chartered in Decatur, it has members in Fort Wayne, Bluffton, Columbia City, and Pierceton, Indiana, and four other states.

As of September 2005, the officers of the Chapter were President DouglasWellman, Sr., of Fort Wayne; Clark Brown of Fort Wayne, Secretary; Treasurer Scott Wellman of Warsaw; Historian and former president, charter member Don A. Melching; and Chaplain, charter member, and former president, Harvey Jones of Decatur. Still serving in the chapter are former chapter and state Indiana Sons of the American Revolution presidents Dr. Neal Pitts of Bluffton and Roger Barnhart of Churubusco. Also still active are former presidents Blaine Sowers of Fort Wayne, Tom Langley of Florida, and Ray Jewel of Auburn.

Arena Dinner Theatre

January, 1974: a theatre is born! Arena Dinner Theatre came into existence as a result of budget cuts in the Fort Wayne Parks Department. Formerly known as "Theatre Workshop," it was the only theatre in the city at that time to perform regularly in the "round" at the old Jefferson Center on the southwest corner of Jefferson and Fairfield. The theatre became the victim of an austerity program of a former city administration. Funding was eliminated and the theatre's future looked bleak.

Not willing to abandon the unique concept of the theatre which had been in operation since 1962, the board of the theatre (under the direction of Robert Behr, former artistic director of the Fort Wayne Civic Theatre) sought a new location and funding to continue operating as a separate not-for-profit entity. Board members David Barngrover, Larry Wardlaw, Kathy Belchner, Mike Thompson, Wayne Schaltenbrand, Michael Greene, and Ann Douglas approached then-director of the Greater Fort Wayne Chamber of Commerce, Don Petrocelli, about the prospect of opening a dinner theatre in the Anthony Wayne Ballroom of the Chamber of Commerce building. He was excited about the idea and a relationship was forged that would last for ten years. Meals were prepared in the Chamber's kitchen under head chef Margaret Grammer. Performances were in the round on a stage and lights had to be assembled and struck every weekend. After a change in direction and policy at the Chamber, Arena was once again in a position of seeking a new home.

For the next ten years it became known as a theatre on the move, performing at no less than eight other sites, including The Roadway Inn, Sunset Catering, Waynedale Conservation Club, Downtown Holiday Inn, Scottish Rite Shrine, The Crosier House, Allen County Fairgrounds, and the Fort Wayne Senior-Community Center (rehearsing at nearly as many sites) before finally finding a permanent home on Rockhill in the historic West Central Neighborhood. Thanks to grants from many arts-supportive foundations, philanthropic organizations, and private citizens, Arena was able to purchase and renovate the much-deteriorated Fort Wayne Art School Little Theatre built in the 1920s. The transformation of the building into an intimate (dining capacity of about 100) yet elegant dinner theatre space was astounding. Arena has been there for the past ten years and doesn't plan on moving again! The schedule of seven shows per year provides acting, directing, technical, management, and production opportunities for those in the region with theatrical interests, both experienced and novice. The selection of shows offers something for everyone and provides a pleasant, enjoyable, and entertaining evening! The 2005-2006 board of directors is Darrell Monroe, President; Fred Krauskopf, Vice President; Rhonda Andrews Woodruff, Secretary; David Thompson, Treasurer; David Frey, Kathi Lanksky, Becky Niccum, Kathy Pelter, Wayne Schaltenbrand (founding member), David Siples, and Stan Volz, board members.

Arts United (formerly the Fine Arts Foundation)

Arts United of Greater Fort Wayne is the third oldest United Arts Fund in the United States and the second largest arts council in Indiana. Originally established in 1955 as the Fort Wayne Fine Arts Foundation, with Sam Rea as the first president of the board, it served three member groups: the Fort Arts School and Museum, the Fort Wayne Civic Theatre, and the Fort Wayne Musical Society (later renamed the Fort Wayne Philharmonic). The original purpose of the organization was to provide funding, facilities, and awareness of the arts through an arts festival. By its 50th anniversary, in 2005, Arts United had evolved into a two million dollar umbrella organization for over seventy non-profit arts groups.

The Arts United Fund Drive has always been a major source of support for the arts in Northeast Indiana. Its modest beginnings reflect the spirit established during the inaugural fund drive when Arts United volunteers boarded buses and drove from neighborhood to neighborhood, going door to door to collect nickels, dimes and quarters for the arts. That first effort raised about $2,500. Arts United has continued, over the 50 years of its history, to be an effective fundraiser. The funds raised as part of the annual fund drive provide general operating support to ten well-established arts groups in the community, as well as grants to scores of other organizations.

After 33 years as the Fine Arts Foundation, the name was changed to Arts United of Greater Fort Wayne to reflect the expanded membership and the larger geographic area encompassed by Arts United. One goal of the organization from the late 1950s, in addition to raising operating funds, was to build a facility that would meet the needs of the member groups. Finding suitable housing for the city's arts groups has been important throughout the organization's history. Renowned architect Louis I. Kahn was selected in 1961 to design a proposed arts complex that would address the needs of area arts groups and the community. A capital fund drive in 1964 and two subsequent drives raised the money necessary to construct the Performing Arts Center as the first phase of the proposed arts complex. Construction of this building began in June 1970, with the dedication in October 1973. A 1980 capital drive raised money for the adjacent Museum of Art, which was dedicated in April, 1984. The Performing Arts Center was renamed the Arts United Center in the organization's 50th anniversary year of 2005, and is the main performing space for the Civic Theatre, Youtheatre, Ballet, and the Dance Collective, as well as the Spectrum and Unplugged Series of the Fort Wayne Philharmonic. The building also serves as a community resource, with all areas of it available to the public to rent.

In keeping with its commitment to capital needs, Arts United launched a major drive in 1986 to repair, renovate and maintain a number of arts structures in Fort Wayne. The Renaissance Campaign raised $7.1 million to insure the long-term stability of the arts community's homes. One project made possible by the initial expenditure of Renaissance funds was the renovation of the former Doubleday Building, a 1990 gift to Arts United from the Foellinger Foundation. Now known as the Hall Community Art Center, this building houses ARCH, Artlink, Cinema Center, and the Dance Collective. Arts United also owns the Fort Wayne Ballet building and the historic Canal House, home to their administrative offices.

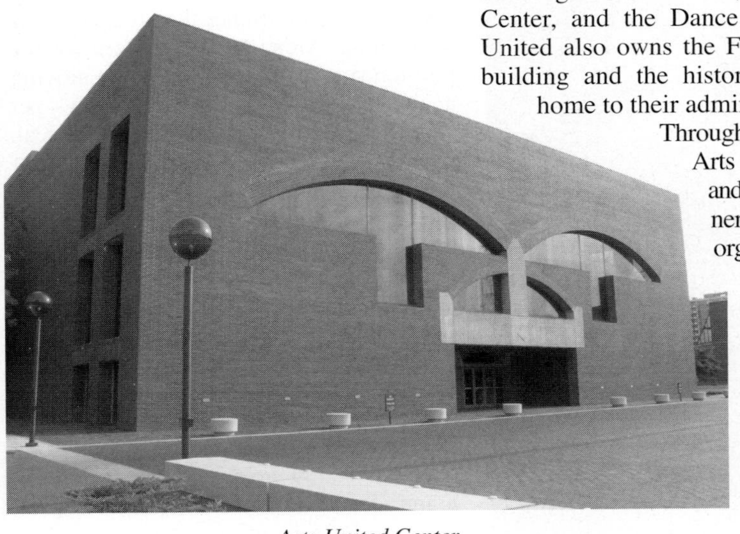

Arts United Center

Throughout its history, Arts United has formed and strengthened partnerships with other organizations to not only promote the arts but to also increase community outreach efforts designed to benefit youth, their families and the greater community. The CAP (Creative Alternative Programs) grant program, administered by Arts United and funded by the Lincoln Financial Group Foundation and the Foellinger Foundation, was established in 1995. CAP partners non-profit, youth serving organizations with real artists who develop art programs for at-risk youth in Allen County. CAP is based on the belief that hands-on arts experiences can be a stabilizing influence in the lives of youth placed at-risk, stimulating the development of personal responsibility, creativity, problem solving skills, judgment, values identification, intercultural tolerance and understanding, and job opportunities through education.

In 2000, Arts United became a Regional Partner of the Indiana Arts Commission. Through this public-private partnership, Arts United serves northeast Indiana in the areas of cultural planning, technical assistance, information and referral and grantmaking.

General awareness of the arts has always been a central part of Arts United's mission. The Fort Wayne Fine Arts Foundation held its first Fine Arts Festival at Franke Park in May of 1958. Margaret Ann Keegan chaired and organized this event and it was held annually until 1975. In the late 1980s, the Forte Festival was created to again serve as a community arts festival, and it was held until the early 1990s. Arts United continues to support the visibility of arts through festivals and community events. Independent arts festivals may apply to Arts United's Community Partnership Grants program for funding of events that address such issues as education, diversity and multiculturalism.

From its simple beginnings fifty years ago to its status now as a successful, nationally recognized united arts fund, Arts United has grown and evolved with the community. As it looks to the future, it remains committed to its original mission: providing for the community through support of the arts.

Audiences Unlimited, Inc.

Audiences Unlimited, Inc. was started thirty-three years ago by Lillian C. Embick as a result of her spending her early years in a local orphan's home and experiencing the joy and excitement of a community outing or a nice program brought in by a church, sorority, or other organization. After she was taken out of the orphan's home, she was given piano lessons and became quite accomplished at playing the piano. Her church youth group presented a Christmas program at the then-called Fort Wayne State Hospital and Training Center; the residents responded with much enthusiasm and asked her to return soon to play again for them.

Eventually, Lillian became a Red Cross volunteer and arranged sing-a-longs and other music programs for five different nursing homes. She noted the enthusiasm and pleasure the residents received and asked other friends and musicians to join her in this quest to bring more programs into these institutions.

Lillian knew that she would have to set up a non-profit organization in order to do fundraising to pay musicians. After much searching, she read about a New York-based organization called Hospital Audiences, Inc. that was written up in the *Parade* section of the *Journal Gazette* in June of 1972. It was agreed that Fort Wayne could be affiliated with New York's office after a trip to New York City and many telephone calls. The local group was started in 1972 with much assistance from the staff of the HAI office and called Hospital Audiences, Inc.

Lillian met with nursing home staff members and they all agreed that it would be a wonderful program. There were no activity directors at that time. There was not much to do in the nursing homes but rock the day away and these residents needed activities. Lillian moved into the Foellinger Center Building, home to the United Way of Allen County. AUI has grown from serving 2,000 residents in the first year, to serving 136,659 last year with approximately 7,726 wheelchair residents. Twenty-five nursing and retirement homes are now served on a regular basis. By writing numerous grants and doing a great deal of fundraising, approximately 250 programs and outings are planned and executed each month.

The mission is to enrich the quality of life for residents residing in health facilities, in residential care facilities, and in subsidized independent living quarters by providing cultural resources that refresh and inspire mind, body, and spirit. The name of the organization was changed to Audiences Unlimited, Inc. in 1978 and became autonomous severing the connection with the New York office. The program has written grants to the Lincoln Financial Group Foundation that has enabled it to bring the first Philharmonic ensembles into the nursing homes. Residents have thoroughly enjoyed this beautiful classical music that they hear so little of. Small music combos, bands, orchestras, dance groups, travelogs, pianists and organists, and soloists of all kinds regularly perform at the various facilities to present daily programs. Due to the fact that the residents are aging and cannot go out for community activities as they once did, twenty-two musicians regularly go room-to-room to sing, play, and briefly visit with the bedfast, and this activity has proven very successful. Even semi-comatose residents have responded to the music for the first time and have tried to sing, mouth the words, or keep time in some fashion, and begin to come back to reality. Free tickets or dress rehearsal privileges are offered the AUI program and 97,339 residents have enjoyed Philharmonic concerts, Civic Theatre plays, Arena Theatre plays, museum exhibits, organ concerts, movies, church programs, high school programs and numerous seasonal programs as the Festival of Wreathes at the Foellinger-Freimann Conservatory which are so much enjoyed by everyone. Vans and buses are chartered to take the residents to the community event if the facility doesn't have a van of its own, or supplementary lift-vans are provided by the AUI program for the wheelchair residents to get them out to these community outings which are so stimulating for them.

Lillian has served as a totally volunteer Executive Director and has won numerous local, state, and national awards for the work that has been done. She received the Sagamore of the Wabash recognition, presented by Representative Ben GiaQuinta at the 20th anniversary of AUI; this is the highest award presented by the governor of Indiana to a Hoosier. Other recognition included being a Senior Queen at the 1989 Indiana State Fair, Channel 15's "15 Who Care" awards, and three nominations by U.S. Congressman Mark Souder. These were the Congressional Johnny Appleseed Volunteerism Award in 1999, the Ageless Hero Community Involvement Award in 2000, and the MetLife Foundation Older Volunteers Enrich America which was a national award and she was flown to Washington, D.C. to receive it. These have been exciting awards, but the main impact was to expose the program to numerous other groups and people.

Lillian now has a part time paid assistant to help with the expanding program. Totally, over 2,216,377 residents have been served in numerous ways by the program in thirty-three years. A ten-member board oversees the operation and is now headed by Linda Buskirk, president. The hours aren't counted, but the joy generated by all the wonderful dedicated musicians as well as the many wonderful foundations, businesses, and individuals who have contributed to the great program is the reward.

"Tow-Path Singers" Beverly Williams and Jeanne Bornefled entertaining at a nursing home.

Cancer Services of Allen County

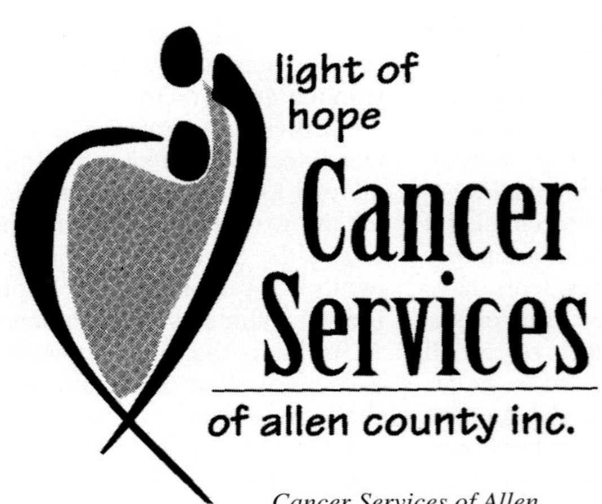

Cancer Services of Allen County old logo.

Cancer Services of Allen County new logo.

The mission of Cancer Services of Allen County, Inc. (CSAC) is to provide non-medial resources, education, and support to individuals diagnosed with cancer, to their families, and to the community.

Cancer Services of Allen County was organized in 1944 as the Allen County Cancer Society, Inc., through the efforts of Robert Punsky, the Women's Field Army, and the Fort Wayne Jaycees.

After reading an article about cancer in *Reader's Digest* in 1943, Bob Punsky wrote a letter with appreciation to the author. He was the only Hoosier who did and he received a letter in return asking him to organize the fight against cancer in Northeast Indiana. He accepted the challenge and his efforts resulted in what began as Allen County Cancer Society (ACCS).

ACCS was a local unit of the American Cancer Society at the beginning, based in New York. The agency became affiliated with the United Fund in 1953, which is now United Way of Allen County. The national headquarters of the American Cancer Society in New York ordered all local chapters to carry on a separate fund drive and to not participate in United Fund. Allen County Cancer Society, along with 100 chapters nationally and with the backing of the Fort Wayne Medical Society, decided to remain with United Fund. Thus the national charter was revoked and the two became separate agencies.

The agency was first located at 1021 West Wayne Street. ACCS moved to a newly purchased building at 2925 East State Boulevard in 1975. A building expansion drive was held during 1980 and thanks to the generosity of the community, a new warehouse was added to maintain equipment and supplies that are loaned or given to cancer patients of Allen County or to those who work in Allen County.

The agency acquired the property directly to the north of the State Boulevard building in 1990. This property at the corner of Santa Rosa and Lynn Avenue was extensively remodeled and renovated. It is now the Healing Arts Center for the agency. Most of the support groups meet in this building.

The name was changed to Cancer Services of Allen County, Inc. to celebrate the 50th anniversary of the agency in 1994. Through the years the agency has experienced highs and lows in its funding sources. Many service agencies have experienced these same financial problems. The agency had to slash its budget by one-fourth in 2000-2001. However, due to expert leadership from board officers, board members, and the dedicated staff, CSAC adjusted and there was minimal impact upon who were served.

In 2001 a "Client Advocate Program" was developed and was recognized by the Robert Wood Johnson Foundation as a national model for the care of those with cancer. With the support of that foundation as well as support from the English, Bonter, Mitchell Trust, the Saint Joseph Community Health, and the Lincoln Financial Group foundations, the agency is now able to offer this program to those diagnosed with cancer in Allen County.

The client advocate or "cancer guide" works with clients and families throughout diagnosis, treatment, recovery, and if needed, the end-stages of the disease. The client advocate reaches clients in the very early stages of diagnosis, frequently a time when the client and their family may be overwhelmed with feelings of anxiety, anger, and confusion about what comes next. The client advocate will assist clients in receiving non-medical needs. They aid in connecting clients with the correct support group, individual counseling, financial assistance, and transportation. The advocate is the link between the client and the resources they may need.

Supporting the activities of the client advocate component with CSAC is a well-organized volunteer network. There are thirty-eight sewing groups consisting of approximately 200 volunteers, who make fifteen to twenty thousand bed pads each year that are available to clients.

There are another 165 regular volunteers who provide transportation to clients and various other needs of the agency.

CSAC provides at no cost to the client, transportation, bed pads, durable medical equipment, nutritional drinks, wigs, turbans, and more.

Several support groups are organized through the agency: Us Too (prostate cancer), Woman with Color, Esophageal Group, Bereavement, and the Candlelighters, a group for children with cancer and their families. There are several other specialized groups.

Volunteers are recognized at a Christmas Breakfast each year.

An educational symposium for nurses, clients, and the general public is offered each year with varying themes. There is a minimal cost for attendance.

Staff and volunteers man the CSAC booths at the many health fairs held throughout the city and county. These are for educating the community on the prevention, detection, and treatment options of cancer.

In 2004, CSAC celebrated its 60th year of service to Allen County. A renovation and remodeling of the State Boulevard building was a part of that anniversary.

The agency looks forward to continued service meeting the needs of people with cancer.

CANI Fighting Poverty. Building Hope.

COMMUNITY ACTION OF NORTHEAST INDIANA

Community Action of Northeast Indiana (CANI) was born amid the hope and idealism of the 1960s War on Poverty during the administration of President Lyndon B. Johnson. CANI observed "Building Hope for 40 Years" in 2005.

CANI, a private, not-for-profit social service agency, administers several programs to help low-income people become self-sufficient. It also collaborates with the other agencies to broaden the scope of assistance the agency can give individuals and serve them more effectively. In addition, CANI advocates for low-income people and provides research on poverty to other organizations.

Like many non-profits, it receives some funding from state and federal governments. However, CANI increasingly relies on gifts from local individuals and foundations to continue and expand its work.

CANI's beginnings go back to an act of Congress. Congress passed the Economic Opportunity Act in 1964 and its purpose was to "...mobilize the human and financial resources of the nation, to combat poverty in the United States."

Under the leadership of United Way of Allen County, community leaders discussed forming a Community Action Agency. CANI was created as the Allen County Economic Opportunity Council (ACEOC) in April 1965. William G. Williams, a United Way staff member, became the ACEOC's first executive director. It's first programs that summer were Head Start and a youth employment project.

That summer, Head Start served 429 children at seven sites. The Youth Employment Program served 202 youth at 58 public or private non-profit agencies. After that, the East Wayne Street Center became the first full-year Head Start program in Indiana.

The ACEOC's fortunes ebbed and flowed as political and economic changes occurred nationwide over the next several years.

In the 1980s, the Regan administration abolished the Federal Community Services Administration, which had funded Community Action Agencies (CAAs). Money for CAAs was channeled instead to Community Services Block Grants. Those grants enabled the ACEOC to expand to five surrounding counties: DeKalb, LaGrange, Noble, Steuben, and Whitley. The ACEOC became CANI, Community Action for Northeast Indiana to reflect this change. Joseph H. Conrad became executive director in 1981, a position he still holds.

CANI has served as a kind of incubator for programs, helping them get started before spinning them off into separate organizations. For example:

•CANI helped start the Community Harvest Food Bank through distributing cheese and other commodities in the 1980s;

•CANI brought WIC (nutrition for Women, Infants, and Children) to Northeast Indiana;

•CANI began programs such as Legal Aid, Foster Grandparents, and Adult Basic Education;

•CANI accepted the responsibility for the struggling Court Appointed Special Advocate (CASA) program in 1988. CASA trains and supervises volunteers who serve juvenile courts as independent child advocates in abuse or neglect cases. CANI transferred the program to a new, not-for-profit under direct court supervision in 1997 after getting CASA more firmly established;

•CANI also was instrumental in creating more than a dozen neighborhood associations in Fort Wayne.

Today, CANI helps families by promoting self-sufficiency and healthy relationships. CANI's mission is to help people plan for and work toward the removal of causes and conditions of poverty.

"We're providing support to the neediest families in the community," explained Pam Brookshire director of program operations at CANI. "We work with families one-on-one, to guide them towards self-sufficiency and help keep them safe and secure."

CANI operates a Head Start program for about 800 preschoolers annually in Allen, Noble, and Whitley counties. CANI opened a new Head Start facility in Fort Wayne's Hanna-Creighton neighborhood in 2004.

About 10,000 households annually receive help with utility bills. CANI also performs energy audits on homes and hires contractors to make necessary repairs or equipment replacements.

In Allen County, CANI participates in the Community Alliance for Healthy Families, which helps prevent child abuse and neglect through direct intervention with families, often young parents who have been abused or neglected themselves.

CANI's childcare vouchers help low-income parent to get an education or keep a job. Families learn to use their strengths to work toward their goals in Family Development, such as better jobs, better housing, or better education.

CANI and other Allen County agencies have developed a case coordination system that reduces redundancy, coordinates service delivery to clients, and measures outcomes across agencies. A "No Wrong Door" system allows clients to apply at one agency and connect to services available at each agency. CANI's partners are Catholic Charities, First Call for Help, Lutheran Social Services, the Salvation Army, United Way, and the Wayne Township Trustee's Office.

But to do all of this, CANI needs the help and financial support of our community. Please consider supporting CANI today. To learn more about CANI, or to help fight poverty through a donation, visit CANI's website at www.canihelp.org or contact: CANI, P. O. Box 10570, Fort Wayne, IN 46854-0570, (260) 423-3546.

The Fort Wayne/Allen County Police Museum and Memorial

The idea for the museum started in 1975 with the beginning of the collecting of artifacts. Hundreds have been acquired, stored, and cataloged by Walter Font, curator, of the Historical Society. The Police Museum is located in the lower level (the old jail area) of the History Center at 302 East Berry Street.

The board of directors of the Historical Society gave approval on June 14, 1981, to raise the necessary funds for the renovation and remodeling of the area to be used for the exhibits. The board approved and established a "Fort Wayne Police Museum" on September 24, 1981. The Police Museum was dedicated on October 20, 1985 and opened to the public. The display was called "The Calaboose."

The police memorial was established November 25, 1988; it is located at 302 East Berry Street, just east of the History Center Building. The memorial consists of a section of iron fence from the original Allen County jail on Calhoun Street, three flagpoles, and a large concrete and granite monument.

Many thanks to the board of directors of the Allen County Historical Society and especially to Michael Hawfield who made the museum possible. A special thanks to all the individuals, companies, and associations who donated the funds and materials to make the museum and memorial a reality.

Fort Wayne Ballet, Inc.

Fort Wayne Ballet, Inc. was incorporated in 1956 as a non-profit organization. It was created because several local families believed the community of Fort Wayne could benefit from quality regional ballet instruction and productions, and would complement the already thriving arts community. Families and multiple community businesses/foundations have been instrumental in shaping the organization as it celebrates its fiftieth anniversary in the 2006-2007 Season.

In the early years, Fort Wayne Ballet benefited from the support of the Fine Arts Foundation and the Ballet Angels. These two organizations evolved into Arts United of Greater Fort Wayne and The Fort Wayne Ballet Guild. Both groups have been instrumental in supporting growth for Fort Wayne Ballet. Organizational leadership includes Artistic Directors John Neff, Colin Worth, Arnot Mader, James Franklin, Michael Tevlin, and Karen Gibbons-Brown. At times, interim directors Mary Kay Perkins, Robert Kelly, Radmilla Novosel, and Kennet Oberly have also led the organization.

Chelsea Teel and Juan Pablo Trujillo from the performance of Sleeping Beauty in 2002. Photo taken by John Escosa.

Through the years, Fort Wayne Ballet has placed its efforts in three main areas: education, productions, and outreach. The Academy of Fort Wayne Ballet was first known as The School of Fort Wayne Ballet, located on 1126 Broadway. In August of 1969, the organization moved to its present location at 324 Penn Avenue. Productions of ballet pieces began early on and include repertoire pieces as well as evening-length ballets. They have ranged from classical to contemporary, including cutting-edge choreography making dance relevant to the audiences. The first evening-length ballet performed by Fort Wayne Ballet was "Cinderella." A special tribute of this production is a part of the fiftieth celebration for the community to honor that event. Other notable productions include: "The Sleeping Beauty," "Giselle," "Swan Lake," "The Nutcracker," "Coppelia," and "Peter and the Wolf," as well as numerous other pieces set by artistic staff and guest choreographers. Outreach is vital to the growth of Fort Wayne Ballet as a means to produce the next generation of audience members, as well as spread the joy of ballet to new artists. A long-standing partnership exists with Weisser Park Arts Magnet School to expose their students to this art. Exploratory programs, free public presentations, lecture demonstrations, and a complimentary ticket program are other means to spread the joy this art form brings the community.

As Fort Wayne Ballet progresses into the 21st century, the organization hopes to strengthen its collaborations with arts groups, community organizations, and expand new international collaborations. The quality education which was always offered has expanded to include not just technique classes, but academic classes as well which address topics like terminology, career planning, and injury prevention. The nationally recognized Summer Intensive workshop hosts a national audition tour. As the Academy grows to strain the current space, additional satellite sites are in the works to increase the opportunity for the growing community to access quality dance education. Fort Wayne Ballet's hope for the future is to expand, improve, and grow artistically as this is important to the soul of our community. The mission of Fort Wayne Ballet, Inc. is to inspire and nurture an appreciation for the art of dance through educational excellence, artistic achievement, performance experiences and outreach activities in the community and beyond. Fort Wayne Ballet remains committed to the principle foundations which laid the foundation for the first fifty years of the organization.

Fort Wayne Children's Choir

Jocelyn Basse created the Children of Peace Choristers in 1973 to fulfill the need for an extra-curricular choral opportunity for area youth. Basse devoted many years of time and energy in her pursuit of artistic excellence. Under her leadership, the small school choir developed a reputation and soon, others from the community joined the group. They were known in the Fort Wayne community as the premiere children's choir in Northeast Indiana. After more than a decade of performing through the city and beyond, the growing choir was incorporated and renamed The Fort Wayne Children's Choir (FWCC).

First Fort Wayne Children's Choir

Following in her footsteps was a dedicated music educator who shared Basse's passion for instilling the love of music into children – Twila Miller Magsig. During Magsig's tenure with the FWCC, the group experienced new growth and traveled internationally for the first time. It was also during this time that the high school division of the FWCC, the Fort Wayne Youth Chorale, was formed. All of this occurred while operating the organization out of the basement of her home.

After ten years of unwavering dedication to the organization, Magsig passed the role of Artistic Director over to Fred Meads in 1999. Previous to this position, Meads spent several years as an accompanist and choir director with the FWCC. It was his spirited enthusiasm, both on stage and in the classroom that made Meads a perfect fit for this position. Meads continued the upward spiral of growth and artistic achievement set by his predecessors. In his seventh season as artistic director, the choir has expanded to represent over 300 singers from 88 schools throughout the community. The FWCC has produced two professionally recorded CD's, "Celebrate: Seasonal Carol" and "Everlasting Melodies," and has toured all over the world, including trips to the Central European Festival in Germany and France; the Youth Sing Festival in Toronto, Canada; and the Pacific Rim Children's Chorus Festival in Hawaii. The FWCC has performed with several local arts organizations including the Fort Wayne Philharmonic, the Fort Wayne Ballet, the Civic Theatre, and the Indiana Purdue Fort Wayne University Choir and Orchestra. The FWCC has also performed for local businesses including the Fort Wayne Wizards baseball team and the Fort Wayne Komets hockey team. The FWCC has collaborated with such guest artists and composers as Dennis DeYoung, former lead singer of STYX, Jean Berger, Rollo Dilworth, Ken Medema, and Nick Page.

In 1998, the role of Executive Director was added to the leadership of the FWCC. Working in tandem with the Artistic Director, the Executive Director focuses on the business and administrative aspects of the organization. Along with the Board of Directors, the Executive Director oversees the fiscal management of the FWCC. Elaine Skoog was hired as the first Executive Director in 1999. She was succeeded by Kim Hinzy in 2001 and by Katey Wilks Houston in 2004. Janet Treadway, Director of Operations, has contributed her energy and passion to the success of the organization since 1996.

The passion, leadership, and vision of everyone involved in the growth of the FWCC has paved the way for hundreds of future musicians, educators, and performances and has inspired the love of music in hundreds of children throughout the years. As the FWCC marks its 32nd anniversary milestone, its mission and vision still hold true today as they did in 1973. The mission of the Fort Wayne Children's Choir is to offer a choral music program which exemplifies artistic and educational excellence to children from all backgrounds. The FWCC endeavors to contribute to the community's cultural offerings by providing the opportunity to experience the unique beauty of professionally trained young voices.

Fort Wayne Children's Choir, 2005.

Over 50 Years of Welcoming the World to Fort Wayne

Dan O'Connell, CVB President

Fort Wayne Visitor's Center

The Fort Wayne/Allen County Convention and Visitors Bureau (CVB) is Fort Wayne's official destination marketing organization, responsible for marketing Fort Wayne and Allen County as a desirable destination for conventions, tourism activities and sports tournaments.

The CVB was founded in 1949 by a group of local citizens with a vision for Fort Wayne's potential as a regional destination for visitors and conventions.

The group started from scratch, designing maps, brochures and trip itineraries to promote local attractions, festivals, and meeting facilities. Helene Foellinger was one of many civic leaders who served on a volunteer CVB board, championing the idea of promoting tourism as a way to infuse more money into the local economy.

Their first effort to attract a large convention came in 1952, when the group helped bring the National Bowling Association Tournament to the brand new Memorial Coliseum. Special bowling lanes were brought in to accommodate the 5,000 competitors.

In 1965, the CVB took another large stride forward when they hired their first full-time executive director, Dean Phillips, who was instrumental in growing the CVB and Fort Wayne's tourism industry.

Phillips recalls, "The CVB was founded by enthusiastic people, but it was time to take it to the next level. We had two big problems: a very small budget at $9,800 a year, and we only had two aging hotels downtown (The Van Orman and The Keenan) and very few on the interstate. But we had a lot going for us too. Our biggest attraction was our history, like Johnny Appleseed and Chief Little Turtle, and the newly built Children's Zoo. Of course, even back then, Fort Wayne was well known for its outstanding restaurants.

"In order to jump start our efforts, a group of board members and volunteers determined that Fort Wayne needed a festival, so on a rainy Saturday morning in 1968 a few community volunteers with big dreams held the first committee meeting of the Three Rivers Festival. We asked for $500 from each of the town's five banks as seed money and went about building one of Fort Wayne's early tourist draws. The next year, we held the first Festival parade on the river. It was a huge success, even though a few of the events held on July 21 hurt for attendance because they were held at the same time that the first man walked on the moon!"

In 1980, the Fort Wayne's economy fell on hard times and since dues for not-for-profits were scarce, the CVB and several other community groups were relocated to the Chamber of Commerce in order for them to continue to promote Fort Wayne, but on a reduced scale.

In 1990, the CVB was reorganized as an independent organization once again, hiring Dan O'Connell as the new executive director. He helped secure additional funding from the Allen County War Memorial Coliseum, the Grand Wayne Center, and many local businesses, in order to better expand the city's tourism and convention promotion efforts.

In 1991, the CVB opened the Visitor Information Center at 1021 South Calhoun Street. It became the "front door" for the city and served as the CVB offices. The Visitors Center provides directions, guides, maps, and information to Fort Wayne's visitors, handling over 30,000 requests per year. In addition, they promote Fort Wayne over the Internet via www.visitfortwayne.com, which hosted over 200,000 unique visitors in 2004 alone.

Today, the CVB has eight full-time, professionally trained staff who sell Fort Wayne to attract conventions, trade shows, sports tournaments and families on short getaway trips. The CVB is the primary marketing organization for area museums, festivals, hotels, restaurants, sports venues and arts and cultural events, garnering the economic and social benefits of a prosperous tourism industry for our community. For example, in 2002, the CVB secured the largest convention in the city's history - the Gold Wing Road Riders Association - where over 15,000 visitors attended their annual "Wing Ding" in Fort Wayne. We were so successful that we were able to bring this group back again in the summer of 2005.

One of the CVB's more popular community events is "Be A Tourist In Your Own Hometown," where area families can enjoy 14 area attractions for free, and learn more about our vibrant tourism community. Over 15,000 people participate each year.

Convention and Visitors Bureau President Dan O'Connell adds, "The CVB is a total community effort. We're making Fort Wayne a better place to live and work, as well as visit."

And the economic impact of those visitors has grown substantially over the past 50 years too, thanks in part to those early visionary volunteers. Visitor spending puts more than $370 million annually into the local economy, helping to sustain more than 6,400 jobs.

Clearly, the Convention & Visitors Bureau has grown into an community-wide organization that lives up to it's mission, and slogan – "Welcoming the World to Fort Wayne!

Fort Wayne Dance Collective

26 years of Dance and Movement, and Still Growing

Five women met at a modern dance workshop in the summer of 1978 sponsored by the Fort Wayne Womens Bureau. Following the three-week workshop Cathy Craighead, Ranny Levy, Liz Monnier, Krista Schloss, and Lisa Tsetse decided to continue the momentum of creative expression by starting a non-profit modern dance organization. The Fort Wayne Dance Collective (FWDC) was born.

Incorporated in January 1979, FWDC began above Artlink, Inc. when it was located at 1126 Broadway in the West Central Neighborhood of Fort Wayne. It quickly opened the studios to other dancers, musicians, and poets focused on creating an organization to support alternative kinds of performance material and a school that would allow dance to be taught from the heart as well as from the book.

Guest artists from New York City, San Francisco, and elsewhere expanded the range of skills both technically and creatively through intensive summer workshops. The second floor studio supported the creation of a variety of dances that were performed in theatres, visual arts spaces, parks, and elementary school gymnasiums. FWDC started an outreach program to allow movement to be explored by a wide range of individuals including inner-city school students, the differently-abled, and seniors.

In 1985 FWDC was welcomed into the Indiana Arts Commission Artists-in-Education program that expanded the organization's abilities to teach on a statewide basis. FWDC continued educating the public about modern dance by sponsoring national and internationally known dance companies in 1989.

Since that time the organization has presented such cutting-edge companies as Pilobolus, Urban Bush Women, Katari Taiko, F'loom, Renie Harris Puremovement, Joe Goode Performance Group, Garth Fagan, and Trisha Brown Dance Company.

The Fort Wayne Dance Collective moved into a newly renovated arts space in 1991 owned and operated by Arts United of Greater Fort Wayne. The Hall Community Arts Center, located at 437 East Berry Street in downtown, also houses Cinema Center, Arch, and Artlink Artspace. FWDC became a funded member of Arts United in 1999.

Programming has expanded to include on-site classes, a four-member touring company, outreach programs, and the Three Rivers Jenbé Ensemble (TRJE). Classes and workshops continue to evolve and reflect the interests and needs of the community.

The Touring Company offers different programs for schools and social service agencies. The literacy-based program, "Dancing Through the Pages," brings books to life for elementary audiences. "A Village Beyond" celebrates Asian culture through Taiko drumming, T'ai Chi movement, and Haiku poetry.

The outreach program for youth began in 1995 and serves social service agencies with dance, drumming, puppetry, and poetry. The "Identity Bridge" program was chosen as a 2005 Coming Up Taller semifinalist by the President's Committee on the Arts and the Humanities and its partner agencies, the Institute of Museum and Library Services, National Endowment for the Arts, and National Endowment for the Humanities. This selection distinguishes Fort Wayne Dance Collective's "Identity Bridge" as "...one of the premier arts- and humanities-based programs in the country serving youth beyond the school hours."

Other outreach programs have been created for Bi-County Services (since 1992), Easter Seals ARC, Lutheran Homes, and Very Special Arts.

TRJE, a cultural outreach program of FWDC, serves the artistic needs of underserved youth by mentoring them in a non-coercive environment to build relationships that support positive self-esteem, respect for elders, an inquisitive mind, and a spirit of community service. Through teaching African traditional drumming, dance, and culture the TRJE program has received regional awards as well as national recognition from the National Endowment for the Arts.

FWDC has also received regional and national awards for arts programming which are produced and aired on the public access channel. FWDC continues to serve the Fort Wayne community and surrounding counties with a progressive art form usually only found in much larger cities. FWDC served 26,000 children, youth, and adults in the greater Fort Wayne community in 2005.

FWDC will host and produce the Indiana Dance Festival in 2006. It is the first of its kind for dancers from the region to gather, learn, perform, and share information about dance. TRJE will also be traveling to Africa in 2006 in order to offer students an opportunity to learn African drumming, dance, and culture first hand.

FWDC staff and board are excited about the future as it continues to offer cutting-edge opportunities to promote the importance and excellence of movement for the healthy minds and bodies of the community.

Fort Wayne Maennerchor/Damenchor

Founding Fathers of the Fort Wayne Männerchor/Damenchor 1869.

The first German male chorus, established by German immigrants, was organized in Fort Wayne under the name of the Fort Wayne Saengerbund on October 4, 1869. Since its origin the chorus has been dedicated to the preservation and promotion of their German heritage as expressed in choral music.

Eventually, there were eight singing societies in the city: the Saengerbund, Eintracht, Concordia, Teutonia, Germania, Frohsinn, Lieder Tafel, and the Maenner Gesangverein. In 1899 these eight choruses combined under the name of Concordia Gesangverein, which consolidated with the Saxonia Gesangverein in 1922. Four years later this consolidation became the Fort Wayne Maennerchor. A Ladies' Auxiliary was organized in 1938, but the ladies only began singing in 1974. In 1997 they became full members of the chorus and it became known as the Fort Wayne Maennerchor/Damenchor.

The chorus joined the North American Saengerbund in 1871. On September 5, 1897 it became one of the founding members of the Indiana District. In November 1974, they joined the Southern Ohio, Kentucky, and Indiana district, successor to the old Indiana District.

Originally rehearsals were held weekly at Strodel's Saloon at Columbia and Barr Streets. Activities were held at various locations until 1922, when the chorus moved to a new location at 1804½ West Main Street, where it remained for 79 years. On May 1, 2001 the Fort Wayne Maennerchor/Damenchor, along with the German Heritage Society, purchased a new home at 3355 Elmhurst Drive, known as "Park Edelweiss." The chorus uses the building for rehearsals, concerts, meetings, picnics, and other club activities. It is also available for a limited number of receptions and/or banquets.

Since 1936 the Fort Wayne Maennerchor/Damenchor has participated in district conferences involving approximately 350 singers, which are held each year in April or May. Every three years they are involved in the National Saengerfest, which has had as many as 4,000 participants.

On the occasion of its 100th anniversary the chorus received the "Zelter-Plakette," an award named after Carl Friedrich Zelter, the father of choral music in Germany. The German government awards it to choral groups all over the world on the occasion of the celebration of 100 years of continuous German choral singing.

Because of their enthusiasm for German heritage, members of the Maennerchor/ Damenchor sponsor a number of traditional German activities every year. In the early days they held monthly dances. Today, they continue their interest in the preservation of German heritage with a full schedule of annual activities, including:

Oktoberfest, which includes a traditional German meal, a concert, and lively dancing open to the public at Park Edelweiss.

The annual Weihnachtskonzert (Christmas Concert) at St. Peter's Catholic church in early December. This is a more formal activity of the chorus.

Fasching is the German form of Mardi Gras. The members of the Maennerchor/ Damenchor and their guests dress in costumes and enjoy an evening of "Gemütlichkeit" and merriment.

Schlachtfest was first held in 1929. Each spring members make the bratwurst that is served at the dinner, followed by a short concert by the chorus and music for dancing.

The chorus was one of the founding organizations of the Fort Wayne Germanfest in 1982, held each year for one week in June. The Maennerchor/Damenchor opens the festivities with a concert at Park Edelweiss, followed by "Heimatabend," an evening meal and dancing. Other events, including a Wiener Dog Race, a Lederhosen/Legs Contest, and a Children's Day, continue through the week. The highlight of Germanfest is the Beer Tent, which provides German food, drink, and entertainment for four days.

Stiftungsfest celebrates the anniversary of the founding of the chorus with a banquet at which members are recognized for their years of service to the organization. Members are recognized for belonging to the chorus for ten, twenty, or even fifty years or more. It is not unusual for chorus members to be third or fourth generation singers.

The most recent activity is the Christkindel Markt, sponsored in association with the German Heritage Society. First organized in 2002, the market now takes place in Headwaters Park over the Thanksgiving weekend. It is fashioned after similar markets that can be found in cities all over Germany in the weeks before Christmas. Vendors' tents offer all kinds of specialty products as well as food and drink.

Members have taken two Konzertreisen (concert trips) to Germany. They have sung in programs all over Germany, with stops both times in Gera, Fort Wayne's Sister City. Three times they have hosted choruses from Gera. They hosted the 55th District Saengerfest in May 2005, including a concert at the Scottish Rite Center with approximately 400 singers on stage.

Members of the Fort Wayne Maennerchor/Damenchor are proud to continue the tradition of German choral music in Fort Wayne.

The Fort Wayne Männerchor/Damenchor December 2004.

The Optimist Clubs of Fort Wayne

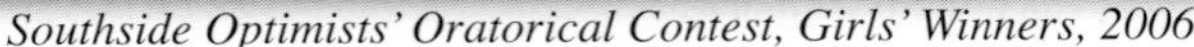

Southside Optimists' Oratorical Contest, Girls' Winners, 2006

Southside Optimists' Oratorical Contest, Boys' Winners, 2006

Citizens began forming voluntary organizations to address the needs of the communities in the early 1900s as industrialization and urbanization brought many new problems to society. Some groups took the name, "Optimist Club," to express their desire for a positive outlook in the face of problems. The impetus for a nationwide Optimist movement began when the Optimist Club of Indianapolis was formed in 1916 and attempted to start Optimist Clubs in many other cities. Optimist International was founded in 1919 and took as its official motto, "Friend of Youth" in 1972 to reflect commitment to services and programs designed toward the development of boys and girls in each community. Today, there are more than 3,200 autonomous Optimist Clubs, all a part of Optimist International, which share a common creed and mission.

The Fort Wayne, Indiana Optimist Club was founded on December 1, 1947 and continues to meet every Monday at noon in downtown Fort Wayne. Currently, the 30 members of this Club, known as the "Downtown Optimist Club," hold their lunch meetings at the Mitzpah Shrine. This club sponsored the Fort Wayne-South Side, Indiana Optimist Club which was chartered on January 17, 1956 and meets every Tuesday at 7:00 a.m. at the Atz's Ice Cream Shop on Tillman Road on the south side of the city. This Club has 40 members. The South Side Optimists, in turn, sponsored a club in Decatur, and later the Fort Wayne-North Side, Indiana Optimist Club was founded on September 1, 1989. Originally, this club met at Shoney's until 1997 when the restaurant closed. It now has 17 members and meets at Cosmos Restaurant on the U.S. 30 Coliseum Boulevard bypass on the northeast side of Fort Wayne every Wednesday at 7:00 a.m.

Mission Statement: Optimist International's mission is to foster an optimistic way of life, through a network of optimists dedicated to the full development of their potential in order to provide ever-expanding service to youth, the community, and the world. Optimist Clubs have been "Bringing out the Best in Kids" through positive service projects aimed at giving a helping hand to youth. Club members are known in the community for their upbeat attitude and their belief in young people. Through the many and varied activities for youth, Optimists aim to empower youth to be the best they can be, and thus make the world a better place to live.

Typical events for youth include Tri-Star Basketball Competition, assisting the Indiana State Police and sponsoring attendees at the Respect for Law Camp, and Youth in Government programs. Oratorical and essay contests sponsored by the local clubs not only provide growth and experiential opportunities for youth, but can result in scholarships for college education. The North Side Club finances youth trips to enriching programs such as the International Youth Conference, and the Downtown Fort Wayne Club provides art classes and support for "residences for youth." The South Side Club has sent participants to Girls' State, and also regularly sponsors a baseball team for girls. Each club also selects particular causes for youth annually, depending on the funds and volunteers available. For example, the South Side Club gives high priority to the Help Them Hear program that provides assistive devices for children with hearing impairments, and gives recognition to high school gymnasts, whereas the Downtown Fort Wayne Club contributes to the Yoder and Krider Youth Homes.

The clubs hold annual fundraisers such as food sales the Johnny Appleseed Festival or County Fair, and local chicken barbecue sales to the public in order to fund their programs. Any event or meeting sponsored by these Optimist Clubs is sure to be marked by their hearty optimism, good fun, laughter, and a pervasive exuberance to contribute to the community through our youth. Regular meetings generally last one hour and include an informative guest speaker. Meetings are open to the public; guests and new members are always welcome.

The Optimist Creed

Promise Yourself

To be so strong that nothing can disturb your peace of mind.

To talk health, happiness and prosperity to every person you meet.

To make all your friends feel that there is something in them.

To look at the sunny side of everything and make your optimism come true.

To think only of the best, to work only for the best, and to expect only the best.

To be just as enthusiastic about the success of others as you are about your own.

To forget the mistakes of the past and press on to the greater achievements of the future.

To wear a cheerful countenance at all times and give every living creature you meet a smile.

To give so much time to the improvement of yourself that you have not time to criticize others.

To be too large for worry, too noble for anger, too strong for fear, and too happy to permit the presence of trouble.

Fort Wayne Sister Cities International, Inc.

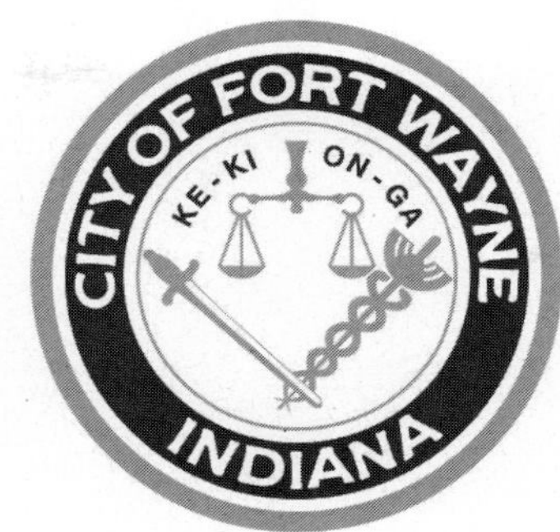

www.fortwaynesistercities.com

Fort Wayne Sister Cities International (FWSCI) was established in 1976 and formally organized in 1983 as a not-for-profit Indiana Corporation. The organization is dedicated to facilitating cultural understanding between the residents of Fort Wayne and the citizens of its Sister Cities. FWSCI has established Sister City relationship with Takaoka, Japan (1977); Plock, Poland (1989); and Gera, Germany (1991).

FWSCI is governed by 27 board members. The charter of the organization is maintained by the City of Fort Wayne. FWSCI is funded, in part, by an appropriation by the Common Council of the City of Fort Wayne. Additional funds are derived from membership dues and other fund raising events. Board meetings are televised on Access Fort Wayne City TV Channel 58. Cultural Connections, a quarterly newsletter, is mailed to over 500 persons; a Web site is also available.

FWSCI is affiliated with Sister Cities International (SCI), which is headquartered in Washington, D.C. SCI serves as the facilitator of Sister Cities programs throughout the U.S.A. SCI evolved from the People to People program founded in 1956 by former President Dwight D. Eisenhower to help foster peace and understanding one friendship at a time.

FWSCI is also affiliated with the Indiana Sister Cities organization. Approximately 30 Indiana cities have active Sister Cities programs.

FWSCI believes that international travel and exchange experiences for all young people have positive educational value. Two major programs are dedicated to meet these needs. The Koshimae International Exchange Program intially funded a citizen of Takaoka. Since 1990, the program has sponsored groups of five high school students and a teacher-chaperone from Fort Wayne and Takaoka to participate in exchanges each year. Students stay with local families, attend school classes and extra-curricular activities with host students, and enjoy learning about their Sister Cities. The Chapman Exchange Program was established by Howard and Betsy Chapman in September 2000. Administered by the Community Foundation of Greater Fort Wayne, the program provides financial assistance to exchange students, aged 14-21, traveling between Fort Wayne and any of the Sister Cities.

Takaoka, Japan

In 1975, Mayor Ivan Lebamoff appointed Howard Chapman, Evelyn Blitz, LaDonna Huntley, Gabriel DeLobbe, Donald Doxsee, Pat Parker, and Mary Ball Brant to explore a Sister City relationship as part of America's Bi-Centennial Celebration of 1976. In 1976, a delegation from Takaoka visited Fort Wayne to explore the proposed alliance and the Fort Wayne mayor, Robert Armstrong, presented a resolution to the Fort Wayne City Council to recognize the relationship. In 1977, Mayor Armstrong and a delegation of approximately 50 people went to Takaoka for the signing of the covenant.

Four Fort Wayne high schools have established Sister School relationships with four high schools in Takaoka. These include Bishop Luers (Fushiki); Elmhurst (Kogei); North Side (Koryo); and Snider (Takaoka Commercial).

Plock, Poland

Indiana University Purdue University Fort Wayne Visiting Professor Bronislaw Misztal suggested in 1989 that Plock become Fort Wayne's second Sister City. FWSCI contacted the White Eagle Lodge, an affiliate of the Polish National Alliance, to support this relationship. Polish Senator Andrezcj Celinski carried a statement of intent from FWSCI, signed by FWSCI Co-Presidents Gabriel DeLobbe and Mary Ball Brant, to Plock. Fort Wayne Mayor Paul Helmke and Plock Mayor Andre Dretkiewicz completed the official recognition in March 1990.

A Sister School relationship between Bishop Dwenger High School and Malachowianka Lyceum was established in 2004.

Gera, German

The alliance with Gera stemmed from the large population of citizens of German heritage in Fort Wayne. Judge Ken Scheibenberger and several other members of the German Heritage Society were instrumental in the development of the Sister City relationship between Gera and Fort Wayne. Following the fall of the Berlin Wall and the opening of former East German cities, visits from Fort Wayne were made to Gera, where interest in establishing a Sister City relationship was high. The German Heritage Society was asked to participate in and support this partnership. The formal agreement was signed in Gera in June 1992, by Fort Wayne Mayor Paul Helmke and Gera Mayor Michael Galley.

Sister school relationships have been established between Zabel Gymnasium and North Side High School; Goethe Gymnasium and Northrop High School; and Staatiches Regionales Forderzentrum and Blackhawk Middle School.

Sister City exchanges have brought three foreign cities and their countries to Fort Wayne and taken Fort Wayne citizens to them through numerous educational and cultural opportunities. As the mission of FWSCI states, this organization truly is "... promoting peace through mutual respect, understanding, and cooperation—one individual, one community at a time."

Fort Wayne Sport Club

Fort Wayne Sports Club, 2006

Early Years: 1927–1937

The Fort Wayne Sport Club was founded by soccer players who had come to the city from Germany. These young men, who played for the local industrial teams of General Electric, the Pennsylvania Railroad, and International Harvester, met on March 18, 1927, at the Männerchor (Men's Choir) Hall on Main Street, and organized the Club for "the Promotion of Soccer Football and German culture."

For four years the Club had no home of its own. It joined the National Soccer League, and played its home games at International Harvester or on the General Electric field on Taylor Street at Brooklyn Avenue. Games were usually played on Sunday afternoon, with a dinner and dance the evening before. Social activities were held at the Männerchor Hall, St. Peter's Church Hall, and the Kreis Stolzenau Hall.

The Sport Club purchased four and one-half acres of land in 1931 on Ardmore Avenue (then Hayden Road) and this has been its home ever since. The first clubhouse was built in 1931, and the Ladies Auxiliary formed that same year. Home brew, home-made wine, dances and card games were features of early entertainment. A dance hall, kitchen, rest rooms and caretaker's quarters were added and dedicated in 1934.

Critical Years: 1937–1950

The Club began several challenging years in 1937. Original team members were older and recruiting was difficult, since young men no longer came from Germany. During World War II, the soccer program ceased, membership dropped, and social activities were curtailed accordingly.

In 1947, soccer resumed. The Club recruited young men from the Lutheran Walther League, and experienced South American and Mexican players from Indiana Tech. These players, along with some old timers, comprised the initial post-war teams. For the first time, the Sport Club and its soccer team had taken on a true international flavor.

Golden Years: 1951–1977

The influx of new European and South American soccer talent in the 1950s helped boost membership and revitalize all phases of club activity. The Club joined the Ohio-Indiana Soccer League and soon became a powerhouse, winning championships in the 1954-55, 1956-57 and 1959-60 seasons. The team many consider the finest in Sport Club history enjoyed an undefeated season in 1962-63 and won five consecutive titles ending with the 1967-68 season. They also won the League Tournament in 1963, 1964, and 1967, as well as invitational tournament championships in Milwaukee, Chicago, Detroit, Toledo, Columbus, and Cincinnati.

The present, beautiful club home was completed in November 1967 and was paid off in less than two years – a permanent tribute to the talents and dedication of its members.

In 1969, a second team entered league competition, and Junior Soccer made its debut, teaching boys the fundamentals of the game. Although soccer dominated, bowling became an active club sport during winter months, while the social scene featured the annual Schützenfest, family suppers, dinner dances and even a mixed chorus, in 1974.

Growth Years: 1977–2005

The Sport Club, Fort Wayne Turners, and Männerchor began Fort Wayne's annual Germanfest in 1981 as a cooperative effort. Today, Club members continue to enjoy a varied social calendar including dances, holiday parties, and the annual Schützenfest.

Club soccer programs, for players of all ages and skill levels, have grown along with the rise of the sport in America. From a handful of teams in the 1970s and 1980s, hundreds of players, ages four to eighteen, now participate in the youth soccer recreational program. The competitive youth travel program, now boasting two dozen teams, has produced numerous state champions, as well as a 2005 U15 girls' national championship. Volunteer coaches in both highly-regarded programs emphasize skill development, sportsmanship, fair play, and a love of the game.

Adult soccer also flourishes on several fronts. The Club's First Team, including many current and former college players, continues to be the team to beat in this area of the state. Competing in the city's amateur league against players half their age, the Men's 30 and Over team has also been very successful, winning consecutive state championships in 1991, 1992, and 1993. In the early 1990s, recreational Over-30 and Co-Ed 6 vs. 6 programs were introduced to bring new adults to the game and keep the Club's old timers playing. A growing number of men and women ages 30 to 70 enjoy the friendly competition. Since 2001, fall has also featured a friendly, Men's 50-and-Over match with long-time rival, Edelweiss Club from Dayton, Ohio.

Play began in 2004 on two additional fields, the "Jim Kelley Fort Wayne Sport Club Youth Soccer Complex," built on land donated by and developed through the generosity and foresight of local businessman James E. Kelley. The Club's four professionally-groomed fields will offer a quality home to area soccer enthusiasts of all ages for years to come.

Fort Wayne Youtheatre

It was 1934 when Mrs. Chan Ray and Mrs. Lester Jacobs dreamed of a children's theatre for the youth of Fort Wayne. They approached Dr. Clive McAllister, president of the Old Fort Players (now the Civic Theatre) for his help in making their dream come true. He, in turn, presented the idea to his board of directors. Soon a new theatre was born for the children of Fort Wayne. It was given the name "Children's Theatre" and designated as a committee member of the adult theatre group. The date was October 19, 1934.

The new theatre's mission was: "To develop poise and better diction through creative dramatics, to give one play each year using children from the classes, to bring good theatre to awaken their enthusiasm for beauty in art and integrity in literature." The first class had 40 students. They paid a fee of $1.00 for eight classes. Mrs. Ray acted as registrar and Mrs. Charles House, Miss Mabel Fry, and Mrs. Hilary Kuhl were the teachers.

"The Steadfast Tin Soldier," Children's Theatre at the Majestic Theatre, May 18, 1935.

"Yankee Doodle," Fort Wayne Youtheatre, April 1999.

The first play was "The Steadfast Tin Soldier" with a cast of 75 children directed by Mrs. Kuhl. It opened May 18, 1935 at the Majestic Theatre, the home of the Old Fort Players (it was located in what is now the Renaissance Square parking lot). Tickets cost 10 cents for children and 25 cents for adults.

Class enrollment by 1936 was 44 but classes were held at the YMCA because the old theatre was too expensive to heat. This was the year that Mabel Fry (later Mrs. Maurice Holmes) not only taught drama but directed the plays and became the strongest influence in the success of the young theatre. She was to author many original plays through the years. The Holiday Show that year was "The Bird's Christmas Carol." Mrs. Ray recalled that they had to "dip" into one day's box office receipts to buy coal to heat the theatre. Sarah Shroyer, later Sarah Shroyer Smith, appeared as Mrs. Bird and began her 62 years as a volunteer. She was the group's treasurer for 24 of those years and twice its president. She bequeathed funds to the theatre at her death enabling the Youtheatre to offer the Sarah Shroyer Smith Scholarship to a high school graduate wishing to continue the study of the theatre in college (the Children's Theatre was renamed the Youtheatre during the 1963-1964 season).

After another class transfer to the Little Arts Theatre at the Fort Wayne Art School in 1938, permission was received to renovate two rooms in a loft at the Majestic Theatre. They became permanent classrooms at a cost of $28.95 for two gas heaters and $58.00 for paint.

The first season memberships were offered in 1941 at a cost of $1.10 for children and $1.65 for adults. This same year, Reid Erekson, the first salaried and permanent director, began a successful eight-year career. His wife, Evelyn, joined the teaching staff, with both deeply involved in the children's series of plays. Erekson brought David Fisher into the fold as technical director. This not only increased the quality of the Civic Theatre plays, but also enabled the production of "Mary Poppins" with its trap doors and flying equipment. The Children's Theatre received national notice when a photograph of this highly acclaimed show appeared on the cover of Theatre Arts Monthly, the country's leading stage publication.

Calamity struck in 1947 when the Fire Marshall declared the ancient Majestic unsafe for children. The group began a ten-year nomadic existence. North Side and South Side High Schools, the Masonic Temple, St. John Evangelical Church, and Harrison Hill School were a few of the theatre's temporary homes. David Fisher and Lois Peterson held forth as directors. The Civic Theatre finally pulled the group back into the fold when it set up shop in the former Palace Theatre. Jay Broad came on board as director and his wife, too, taught acting. The Palace felt the weight of the wrecking ball in 1969 and forced another move to the Elks building on Maiden Lane. There they withstood the ballroom's cramped size until 1973 when they eagerly moved into their current home at the new Performing Arts Center on Main Street (the theatre is owned by Arts United of Fort Wayne; the Civic and Youtheatre are funded members). The Youtheatre separated from the Civic Theatre in 1984 to become autonomous. It was an amicable separation after a 50-year association.

The success of the Youtheatre was achieved by thousands of children, 30 presidents, 45 set designers, and 25 directors without whom it would not have survived for 72 years. Harvey Cocks joined the Youtheatre as its first executive director in 1978 and continues to hold this position today. It remains the third oldest children's theatre in the country, behind Cleveland and San Diego; now presents four annual plays and 16 weeks of theatre classes; is deeply involved with schools and children's service organizations; and been recognized as one of the few children's theatres in the country presenting theatre for, by, and with children.

German Heritage Society

German immigrants played a large part in the history of Fort Wayne. They founded many industries, served as community leaders and government officials, and worked in the factories and businesses. After World War I, the German presence withered because of anti-German sentiment.

Jim Sack, Ken Scheibenberger, Dan Witucki, Dave Riethmiller, and Dave Moser determined in 1986 that this rich German heritage ought to be recognized and formed the German Heritage Society (GHS). The purpose of this not-for-profit organization is to preserve and promote Fort Wayne's German heritage. The group's first program was the organization of cultural events surrounding the annual Germanfest celebration.

Since then many other programs have been organized and supported by the GHS. Perhaps the most notable was formation of a Sister City relationship with Gera, Germany. Due to the tireless efforts of Jim Sack this relationship began in 1991 and a student exchange program was begun. Numerous Fort Wayne students have gone to Gera for study, while many students from Gera have spent a year in Fort Wayne studying. The GHS provides funds for those students. Additionally, there have been many visits from Gera officials to Fort Wayne as well as local officials traveling to Gera.

The GHS also supports a German Language scholarship program that awards college scholarships to students who wish to study German. Thousands of dollars have been used to benefit students.

We also co-sponsor an annual Christkindel Markt—a German Christmas Market that is a regular part of German culture. There is no better way to enjoy the Christmas season than by attending this event and learning about German Christmas traditions.

Many of our members were interviewed as part of Public Television Channel 39's local history program entitled, "Fort Wayne—A Most German Town."

We partnered with the Maennerchor/Damenchor in 2001 and purchased our home, called Park Edelweiss, located at 3225 Elmhurst Drive. This gave us a place to hold our monthly meetings as well as our fund-raising efforts. We are proud of our "Little Part of Germany."

Current officers of the GHS include President Ken Scheibenberger, Vice-President Jutta Hornbeck (a native German)), Treasurer Robert Anweiler, and Secretary Abby Scheibenberger.

German Heritage Society 2005

Headwaters Park

The Headwaters Flood Control and Park project is an environmentally sound addition to the Fort Wayne area, bringing several important goals together. Among these goals are flood mitigation, economic development, recreation, and outdoor education.

The first and most important aspect of the Headwaters project is to curb the flooding problem and the damage it causes to the citizens of Fort Wayne. The park's natural construction will actually aid in the free flowing of the Saint Mary's River. Because structures are no longer located in the thumb area of the park, they do not act as an impediment to the flowing of the floodwaters. Therefore, Headwaters Park should actually decrease some of the devastating effects caused by recent flooding. Because businesses will no longer be located in this flood- prone area, the damage to the city's economy will be much less severe after a flood is experienced. In 1985 the damage in the thumb alone was estimated to be $3.9 million – more than half the total damage estimated for the entire community. Flood damage to the area from the floods of 1978, 1982, and 1991 amounted to over $10 million.

Another goal of the project is to enhance the overall economic development efforts of the community. Headwaters has become home to such annual festivals as Germanfest, the Three Rivers Festival, and many others. The park provides use to thousands of people and has become a focal point for festivals and other events. Twelve festivals joined almost 20 other not-for-profit, business, and children's events in finding a home in the park in 2005.

A third important aspect of the park is to connect the downtown area with the Rivergreenway. Headwaters serves as an intermediary point along the Rivergreenway, which consists of a series of parks and trails along the rivers of Fort Wayne. Educational opportunities, especially for our area's young people, abound in the park. They can spend time learning about and identifying various kinds of trees, flowers, and native Indiana grasses near the Great Meadow, as fog misters shoot from the top of a 21st century pavilion and from around the parks. At the same time, they can learn about an environmentally conscious way of dealing with floodwaters. During festival season from May until October, young people can experience various kinds of languages, dance interpretations, craft design, and other applications of the arts. On hot summer days, they can refresh in the two large, interactive water fountains. Nearly 30,000 people have skated on the outdoor ice rink during the past two winter seasons.

Geoff Paddock, Executive Director of the Headwaters Park Alliance and Indiana Governor Frank O'Bannon cut the ribbon at the dedication of the Headwaters Park Flood Control Project.

Headwaters Park is bringing more people to downtown Fort Wayne. It attracts citizens to the city from all parts of northeast Indiana and northwest Ohio and serves as a welcome addition to the economic development efforts of the Fort Wayne area.

The architectural plan, as developed by Eric R. Kuhne and Associates and implemented by Grinsfelder Associates, took years to develop and perfect. The architects determined this plan would best serve the ultimate use of a park located in a flood plain. It was only after careful study and public input that this plan was adopted by the Headwaters Park Commission.

In the late 1990s, Headwaters Park became one of the largest public-private partnerships existing in Northern Indiana. Together, both the public and private sectors raised nearly $17 million to complete the downtown revitalization. Because of its broad appeal, support came from all areas of the community. The State of Indiana contributed $2 million, mostly through Build Indiana funds for land acquisition. Fort Wayne and Allen County governments contributed $5.2 million for land acquisition, environmental remediation, and business relocation costs. The Headwaters Park Commission raised just over $9.7 million from private sources and secured $850,000 of this as a partial maintenance and operating endowment. Over 2,000 citizens had their names engraved on walkway bricks. Others purchased park benches, lampposts, or one of over 600 trees added to the downtown landscape.

Headwaters Park was endorsed by the Izaac Walton League, business and labor groups, the Fort Wayne Chamber of Commerce, and the Convention and Visitor's Bureau. It is a lasting legacy to the city that saved itself from devastating flooding and was dedicated on October 22, 1999, the city's 205th birthday. Truly, this project has united our community and will serve it a century from now.

Headwaters Park Alliance in 2005: Eleanor H. Marine, President, Tim Borne, Jomare Bowers-Mizzell, Madelane Elston, Christoher Guerin, Andy Haddock, Molly McCray, Suzon Motz, Jan Paflas, Ian Rolland, Nancy Ruedesbusch, John Shoaff, David Steiner, Nancy Stewart, Judy Zehner, Shelley Yoder, and Mike Holley. *Submitted by Geoff Paddock, Executive Director, Headwaters Park Alliance.*

Aerial view of Headwaters Park at completion. (Courtesy of Stedman Studio)

Heartland Chamber Chorale

Heartland Chamber Chorale is the premier mixed voice choral ensemble in Fort Wayne and Northeast Indiana.

The Heartland Chamber Chorale (HCC) is a mixed-voice professional choral ensemble in metro Fort Wayne and Northeastern Indiana. HCC came to life in 1997 when a devoted group of singers and music lovers who had conceived, nurtured, and supported a group called Opus 18, hired Robert Nance as the group's music and executive director. The Board of Directors and Singers believed in Nance's proposed vision and organizational plan, committing their time and money to bring Northeastern Indiana a standard of musical talent and performance necessary for inspiration to all lovers of the choral art. Today, the HCC is known for quality performance, educational programs, and entrepreneurial spirit.

With a mission statement declaring, "A vibrant community is a singing community," the HCC has a four-part approach to its mission: to represent the best in choral music performance; to be a proactive resource for choral music education; to serve as an advocate for all Choral Arts; and bring hope and joy to the community by encouraging all citizens to bring song into their lives.

Believing that Northeast Indiana deserves the very best talent both local and world famous, Heartland Chamber Chorale has brought clinicians from San Francisco, Pittsburgh, Los Angeles, New York, Minneapolis, South Bend, Salt Lake City, and Chicago to coach student choirs, encourage church choirs, and direct the Chorale.

HCC's educational programs are designed to help choristers of all ages. Since 1997, over 250 such programs have been presented. The annual Church Music Clinic brings clinicians and church choirs from Northeastern Indiana together for a day of singing and praise designed to support the very organizations where many singers get their first taste of choral singing. In-school programs feature members of the Chorale, along with director Robert Nance and various HCC guest artists. Guest artists include Jerry Rubino, Robert Page, Albert McNeil, Craig Jessop, Alice Parker, Nancy Menk, Linda Tedford, Carver Cossey, and Vance George.

The HCC has many accolades to its credit, including: the HCC was selected to perform at the Indiana Choral Director's Association conference in 1999; Music Director Robert Nance directed the Mormon Tabernacle Choir in 2001; and the HCC was selected to perform at the American Choral Directors Central Division convention in Indianapolis in 2004. And in 2005, Audiences Unlimited recognized HCC efforts to bring the choral arts to underserved audiences.

Heartland commissions new music annually. Composers include Dan Gawthrop, Alice Parker, Adrian Mann, Robert Hobby, and William Hawley.

The leadership of the HCC has included Dana Leininger, Lynne Salomon, Otto Behrens, Kari Cynar, John Faylor, Janet McCauley, Margaret Boerger, Steve Ross, Ron Venderly, Doug Powers, Carol Jackson, John Escosa, Fred Haines, Mary Jo Meyer, William Schmitt, Geoffrey Kelsaw, Antoinette Lee, Libby Schleuter, Dennis Bowman, Judy Green, Kenneth Athon, Kevin Clancy, Paul Martin, Cathy Norton, Diane Behrens, Debra Faye Williams-Robbins, Mark Rupp, Jim Wooten, Dr. Judy Zacher, Betty Stein, Sara Davis, Dee Smith, Dina Patterson, Wendell Cree, Dr. Ronald Phillips, Randy Gilmore, Dr. Miles S. Edwards, Sherrill Colvin, Pam Kessie, Robert Kabisch, Patricia Edwards, JoAnn Grevenow, Sally Hinkle-Teegarden, and Deb Peterson. The organization is committed to maintaining a presence in downtown Fort Wayne because of its central location and great performing spaces. HCC has performed at First Wayne Street Unted Methodist Church, Plymouth Congregational Church, First Presbyterian Church, St. Patrick's Catholic Church, the Performing Arts Center, the Embassy Theater, and others.

Heartland Chamber Chorale brings together member supporters who love the art of choral singing and contribute time and money to insure a standard of excellence in choral music, encouraging children to work toward that standard. HCC believes that a singing community is a healthy, civically involved city and a city that will continue to attract young people and families to participate in the community. Singing is a life-long skill. Any age group benefits physically and mentally from singing for any age group. The Heartland Chamber Chorale provides excellence in the choral art, adding yet another legacy to the tradition of quality arts in Fort Wayne.

Homebound Meals, Inc.

Homebound Meals, Inc. has been delivering hot nutritional meals in the city of Fort Wayne since 1971. The mission of the program is to deliver the meals to clients who are unable to prepare their own meals due to age, illness, or disabilities. Martha McBride and the Fort Wayne Medical Alliance founded the Homebound Meals, Inc. program.

Martha McBride was the first program administrator. She has served 25 years as a dietician and nutritionist at Indiana University, University of Michigan, and the Red Cross. Following Martha McBride as the administrator was Judy Alatza who served 27 years. Judy Alatza had been a dietician for 25 years at Lutheran Hospital, I.U. Medical Center, and two hospitals in New Orleans. As of 2005, Judy Gregg has been administrator for seven years. Judy Gregg had been a Social Worker and Program Organizer for18 years.

Home-delivered meals originated in Great Britain in 1939 during The Blitz when many people lost their homes and had no place to prepare their meals. The Women's Volunteer Service for the Civil Defense delivered prepared meals to disadvantaged neighbors. These same women brought refreshments in canteens to servicemen during World War II. The canteens were affectionately called "Meals on Wheels." The home-delivered idea spread to Philadelphia, Pennsylvania in 1954.

In Fort Wayne, the first route by Homebound Meals, Inc. started on March 1, 1972, from Lutheran Hospital with four meals. Soon after, other routes were added. Fourteen routes had been established by 2005, with an average of 159 meals each day and 28,485 meals delivered a year. The dietary staffs of Lutheran, Parkview, and St. Joseph Hospitals, and the University Park Nursing Home prepare the meals. Volunteer drivers deliver meals Monday through Friday.

Homebound Meals, Inc. is a nonprofit organization. Clients pay a fee that covers the cost of their meals; however, subsidies are available to clients who are unable to pay the full cost of the meals. Homebound Meals, Inc. is the only service in Fort Wayne to provide a specialized diet to clients with medical needs, and to deliver to clients younger than 62 years. Many younger clients who have special medical problems fall through the cracks of other services provided in the community. Many clients with medical problems are homebound and do not have the ability to prepare hot nutritional meals. A well-balanced meal for these clients will lead to a healthier life. Because the driver may be the only person the client will see during the day, this people contact helps to improve the client's life.

The backbone of the program is the wonderful volunteer drivers who use their own car and gas to deliver the meals. The thousands of meals Homebound Meals, Inc. has delivered since 1971 would not have been delivered without these dedicated drivers who also deliver their own special diet of love, concern, and caring for the clients. The drivers check up on the client's well being. Over the years, the drivers have found clients in various medical emergencies such as broken hips or diabetic shock. A number of times the clients fell over the weekend and lay on the floor until Monday. The Homebound Meals, Inc. office was notified by the observant volunteer driver and help was sent. Thus the program has offered security to the clients, their family members, and caregivers.

The volunteer drivers for Homebound Meals, Inc. are a dedicated group. Most notable are the volunteers who have served more than 25 years with the program. They are Judy Alatza, Peggy Bergendahl, Katherine Blichert, Ann Marie Chamar, Sue Dahling, Fran and John Foster, Marion Haughey, Mary Hoffman, Maxine Leininger, Cardy McComas, Bettie Myers, Vivian Priddy, Opal Sauer, Darlene Stucky, Harry and Bonnie Wann, and Stephen Williams.

The Homebound Meals, Inc. board of directors and the staff are proud of the service that the program has offered the homebound population in the city of Fort Wayne. Thousands of meals have been served to people in need. Most clients receive their meals to allow them to remain in the homes where they have spent most of their lives.

Homebound Meals, Inc. has great pride in their volunteer drivers. The program has continued since 1971 because of the dedication of these wonderful people.

The Homebound Meals, Inc. office has been housed at the Trinity Episcopal Church at 611 West Berry Street since the beginning of the program.

Judy Alatza (left) works with Edith Mapps to set up routes for homebound meals in 1976.

Peg Meek (left) and Betty VanEvery delivering meals in 1998.

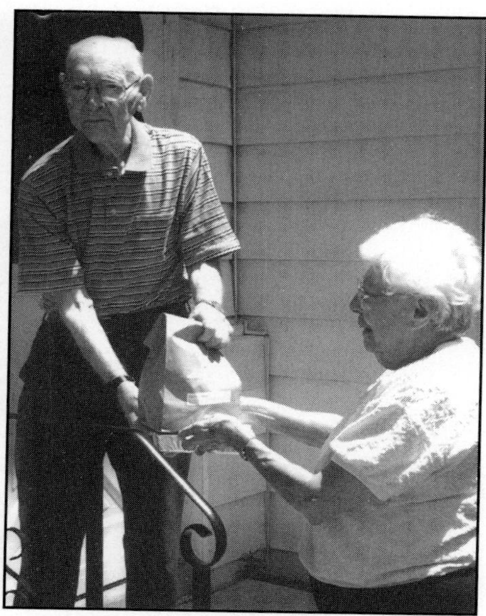

Betty Statz delivers meals to Kenneth Johnston in 2003.

Lutheran Health Services Society, Inc. (Formerly Lutheran Hospital Auxiliary, Inc.) 1904 - 2006

The Lutheran Health Services Society, Inc., began on October 7, 1904. Reverend Phillip Wambsganss (president of Lutheran Hospital and pastor of Emmaus Lutheran Church) called a meeting of thirty-nine Lutheran women to organize "The Hospital Aid Society" for the purpose of "rendering services to the hospital and its patients – and for promoting the health of the community." Reverend Wambsganss, recognized as the founder of Lutheran Hospital, outlined the objectives: to help by means of contributions and sewing for the hospital.

The first committee was the "Needle Work Guild" which began sewing sheets, pillowcases, and towels for the opening of Lutheran Hospital on Thanksgiving Day 1904.

To raise funds, the Hospital Aid Society charged a fifty-cent entrance fee for new members and twenty-five cents a month dues. Meetings were held twice a month and considered an obligation. Meetings were conducted and recorded in German. As the hospital grew, so did the need for nurses. The Lutheran Hospital Training School for Nurses opened in 1913.

The Needle Work Guild made nurses' uniforms and aprons. Annual apron sales were held. The Society provided a banquet for the nurses upon graduation. Each nurse received a scarf-pin as a gift. The Society raised funds by selling cookbooks, holding Bunco parties, needlework, suppers, bake sales, and bazaars. The hospital borrowed five hundred dollars to purchase patient beds. When the loan was repaid (at 6% interest) the Society furnished a patient room. They also purchased bedding, rugs, and chairs for the hospital.

By 1918 there was a recruitment effort for new members. The Society changed its name to The Ladies Society of Lutheran Hospital of Fort Wayne. Women from Trinity English Lutheran Church and St. John's Lutheran Church were invited to join. The Society changed its name to The Lutheran Hospital Auxiliary in 1958. The Auxiliary was called upon to broaden the scope of its support services. Society president, Elizabeth Lepper, and vice president, Lucy Lupke, brought the gift shop program to Lutheran Hospital in 1962. This would be the first of five gift shops over the next thirty-eight years (the organization raised many millions of dollars). Thelma Heine in 1962 was the buyer and later manager of each gift shop – a job she held until the last gift shop was closed in the spring of 2000. In addition, Mrs. Heine was chairwoman for all fund-raising projects until 2001. Elmer Petzold volunteered as business manager for many years. Myrtle McConnel volunteered as assistant gift shop manager for many years.

The Auxilians volunteered thousands of hours in the gift shops in the 1970s, held card parties, bake sales, boutiques, provided baby pictures for new mothers, and underwrote the purchase of televisions in patient's rooms and then collected the rental fees. The Auxilians underwrote the cost of the Atrium Gift Shoppe and the beautification of the main lobby, which were completed in 1982. The Second Time Around Shop was opened in 1983. It closed in 1986 due to competition in the neighborhood.

Over the years, the Auxiliary underwrote the purchase of medical equipment, instruments, monitors, and relocation costs for the Pediatric Units, Coronary Care Units, and Emergency Room – to name a few. The auxiliary pledged one million dollars for Children's Services in the new hospital on West Jefferson Boulevard. The final contribution was within sight when the sale of Lutheran Hospital was announced in 1995. The new owner was an investor-owned corporation, Quorum Health Group, Inc.

The Auxiliary changed its name to The Lutheran Health Services Society. It applied for and received a 501c(3) designation as a private, philanthropic organization. Since the balance of its pledge was no longer needed by the hospital, the Society invested the balance of the pledge. The interest is used for charitable giving.

The major fund-raiser for the Society is the Annual Festival of Wines which began in 1985. The beneficiary of the proceeds is now the Hospice Home on Homestead Road, Fort Wayne, Indiana. Proceeds are designated for patient care needs, among which was The Quiet Room. Additional fund-raising projects to benefit Hospice Home are the annual card parties, every penny counts, and the end of the year memorial for deceased Society members.

The corporate office for the society is located in the Lutheran Foundation Building on 3024 Fairfield Avenue, Fort Wayne, the former Duemling Clinic. Board of directors meetings are held in the Lutheran Foundation Building. The Lutheran Health Services Society's luncheon meetings are held at Lutheran Home/Concord Village on South Anthony Boulevard, Fort Wayne.

The Festival of Wines continues to be held at the Fort Wayne Country Club on Covington Road, as are the May luncheon meetings of the Society's membership. The Christmas luncheon meetings have also been held at the Fort Wayne Country Club.

Lutheran Hospital Auxiliary in the earlier years.

After the Christmas Luncheon in December of 2003.

Lutheran Social Services of Indiana

Lutheran Social Services building, 2005

The story of Lutheran Social Services of Indiana began just after the turn of the 20th Century. The Rev. Phillip Wambsganss, pastor of Emmaus Lutheran Church, Fort Wayne (a congregation of The Lutheran Church-Missouri Synod), initiated a local adoption program and family foster care service for homeless children. This happened in 1901 and marks the beginning of the Lutheran Children's Friend Society of Indiana and Ohio. To meet the counseling and financial needs of Lutheran families in Fort Wayne, in 1926 Lutherans established a second separate organization, Lutheran Social Service League (LSSL) and employed Miss Emmie Jensen as the first social worker.

Miss Jensen was succeeded by Marie Zucker in 1927. Under her direction as Executive Secretary, the Lutheran Social Service League served needy families in the community through the 1930s and 1940s when all volunteer agencies combined offices with the Department of Public Welfare on the second floor of the Hollywood Building.

The Lutheran Social Service League and the Lutheran Children's Friend Society merged in 1951 to form Lutheran Social Services, Inc. (LSSI). By 1958, Lutheran Social Services staff had grown to five including Miss Zucker and Lloyd O. Allen, Executive Secretary, with headquarters in Emmanuel Lutheran Church's former parsonage at 901 West Jefferson Boulevard, Fort Wayne. Miss Zucker remained as a social worker with the agency until 1965 when she retired.

On February 1, 1960, the Rev. Charles F. Tuschling, Jr. joined Lutheran Social Services as Executive Secretary and served the agency in that capacity until 1985 when he took on a new role as Director of Church Relations for the agency. He ended his tenure with the agency in 1986.

Lutheran Social Services reincorporated as an inter-Lutheran agency of all the Lutheran congregations in Allen County in 1961. A permanent office was constructed at 330 Madison Street, Fort Wayne in 1965 that continues to serve as administrative headquarters.

Rev. Keith D. Ingle became Executive Director of Lutheran Social Services in 1986, serving in that capacity until February of 1995. Also in 1986, Lutheran Social Services, Inc. assumed the programs of Lutheran Outreach, a ministry of Shepherd of the City Lutheran Church (Fort Wayne) and the congregation's pastor, Rev. Donald Rauhut. These services included a childcare center, friendship services for the developmentally disabled, and home care services for the elderly.

Lutheran Social Services, Inc. took the business name of Lutheran Social Services of Indiana (LSSI) in 1991. In February 1991 LSSI assumed management of the Child Care Center at Grace. Lutheran Social Services assumed the counseling and adoption services of the Lutheran Child and Family Services, Merrillville, Indiana in October of 1992 expanding the service area to all of northern Indiana. In 1993 a permanent office building was purchased and renovated at 1400 North Broad Street in Griffith, Indiana. The growing childcare center was moved to the lower level of Redeemer Lutheran Church, Fort Wayne in 1988 and in 1990 a building at 3316 South Calhoun Street, Fort Wayne was purchased and renovated to permanently house the center.

Stan Veit assumed the leadership role at LSSI as Executive Director on October 31, 1996.

Lutheran Social Services acquired property at 3326 South Calhoun Street to house five case management programs and 20 staff members in April of 1998.

LSSI services include: adoption (international, domestic, and step-parent); counseling (adults, families, children) provided in Griffith, Fort Wayne, Decatur, Columbia City, Kendallville, and Valparaiso; faith-based initiative (churches mentoring welfare-to-work families); Healthy Families (assessing new parents for the prevention of child abuse); teen parenting (in all Allen County public high schools and middle schools, and Anthis Career center); family preservation (reuniting addicted parents with children removed from the home by the court system); case management initiative (working with dysfunctional families); medical case management (working with dysfunctional families who also have medical problems); childcare center for low-income families (licensed for 48 children ages three to five); emergency assistance (advocacy, planning, and once-a-year financial help); Nursing Home Ombudsman (serves 67 nursing homes in nine northeast Indiana counties); disability outreach (connecting mentally disabled with church and providing a camp experience); and foster parent training for all of Lake County, Indiana.

Our mission: "Lutheran Social Services of Indiana is a social ministry organization guided and sustained by the love of Jesus Christ. We will serve those in need, particularly those with few options and opportunities."

God is calling us to the next chapter of our ministry. Lutheran Social Services of Indiana will continue to be dedicated to our founding principle of keeping Christ at the center of our services. Our core values of faith, integrity, stewardship, and service will be our guide.

Mad Anthonys, Inc.

Hit the links to benefit Fort Wayne

Committed to Excellence

The Mad Anthony Charity Classic for Children has annually hosted one of the nation's premier golf classics since 1958. In addition to raising funds for various youth-serving charities, the Mad Anthonys have provided golfing entertainment for the community and brought positive national recognition to Fort Wayne and Indiana.

Those who have competed on the links represent a veritable Who's Who in the sports and entertainment worlds. Participating golf legends have included Arnold Palmer, Jack Nicklaus, Marlene Bauer Hagge, Sam Snead, Kathy Whitworth, Ben Hogan, and Don January. Famous Hoosiers participants have included Hoagy Carmichael, Neil Armstrong, The Four Horsemen of Notre Dame, Chris Schenkel, Janie Fricke, and Shelly Long.

The Mad Anthonys today rotate the Charity Classic for Children among three sites – the Fort Wayne Country Club (where the event started), Orchard Ridge Country Club, and Sycamore Hills Golf Club. Now played with fivesomes, it is still a 'one best ball' event. Sports and entertainment celebrities as well as PGA and LPGA touring professionals serve as captains for the 42 to 45 teams.

Sunday evening prior to the tournament, the Mad Anthonys host the famed Red Coat dinner to honor one or more Hoosier Celebrities of the Year. Hoosiers by birth or association, each celebrity receives a red jacket as emblematic of the honor.

Challenged to make a Difference

During the early 1950s, the Fort Wayne Jaycees established a regular PGA tour – the Fort Wayne Open – with a $15,000 purse. A string of financial struggles followed. Unwilling to lose the PGA for Fort Wayne, Harold Van Orman, Jr., part owner of the Fort Wayne Komets, gathered with civic friends and businessmen in 1956 and created a Pro-Am to take place before the big Open.

Tournament committee members wore ribbons on their golf sleeves for identification and became known as the Sleevers. Playing in threesomes, there were 183 entrants. Support, however, was not forthcoming and the PGA moved to Indianapolis in 1957.

Sleever supporters reorganized and in 1958, the Mad Anthonys were born. The group met for the first time as an incorporated entity at the Hotel Van Orman. Officers elected were C. W. Anderson, president; Dan Ingebrand, vice president; John Cooper, secretary; and Arnold Lee, treasurer. Major discussion focused on a Celebrities Golf Tournament that would feature a "name" entertainer.

At the initial meeting, a board of 18 governors was named. Those named to three-year terms included C. W. Anderson, D. Ingebrand, J. Cooper, E. Dolsen, A. Lee, and C. Bennett. Those serving two-year terms included Harold Van Orman, Norman Thomas, Hal Schmidt, Otto Adams, Frank Dunigan, and Rodger Nelson. One-year terms included Gunnar Elliott, Sid Hutner, R. A. Bender, Gordon Banks, Bert Clauss, and Bob Centlivre.

The first Hoosier Celebrity (1958) named was Terry Brennan, the young Notre Dame coach trying to bring the Fighting Irish back into national football. Weeb Ewbank, who had just led the Baltimore Colts to the National Pro Championship, was the Celebrity in 1959. Tony Hulman, owner of the Indianapolis Speedway, was Hoosier Celebrity in 1960. That was the year Jack Nicklaus, a young amateur from Columbus, Ohio, competed. Seeing the Country Club layout for the first time, he shot a 66. Later that year, Nicklaus went on to win the National Amateur crown.

One of the special events hosted by the Mad Anthonys in 1960 featured Arnold Palmer and Gary Player. They teed off at the Fort Wayne Country Club for the first in a round-the-world series of 25 competitions for a $100,000 purse. It was an appropriate location for Palmer who had collected his first PGA winnings here – about $280.00 for finishing 25th at an Elks match in 1955. Another Mad Anthony special activity was sponsoring the Ben Hogan Tour for three years beginning in 1990. The PGA staff consistently noted that Fort Wayne had the best-organized event of the 33 sites on the circuit.

Care for the Community's Children

Over the past 18 years, the Mad Anthonys have generated $3.1 million for charity. Based on "dedication for enriching the lives of young people in the Fort Wayne community," the organization was the first annual recipient of Mayor Graham Richard's Youth Development Award (2003).

The Mad Anthonys are serious about helping kids in Fort Wayne! During the past ten years alone, the group has funded the following projects:

- Development of a handicap-accessible lake at Red Cedar Center;
- Purchase of 15 passenger vans for Boys' & Girls' Clubs and Boy Scouts;
- Construction of the three Mad Anthony par-3 teaching and learning golf courses at McMillen Park;
- Significant accessories to the Red Cedar Center lake (affectionately called the Mad Anthonys' Old Swimmin' Hole).

For year 2005, the organization focused on helping SCAN refurbish and expand its facilities and parking lot.

For nearly a half century, the Mad Anthonys have improved the quality of life for children and citizens in the Fort Wayne community, brought pride to the city and state, and provided a rousing good time for all participants.

Some of the original members at the Van Orman Hotel in 1960. (l. to r.) John Cooper, Bob Chappuis, Bob Morris, Jim Kelley, and Hal Schmidt.

Mary Penrose Wayne Chapter National Society Daughters of the American Revolution

The National Society Daughters of the American Revolution (NSDAR) is a non-profit, non-political worldwide service organization devoted to Historic Preservation, Education, and Patriotism. Membership is open to women 18 years of age or older who are able to prove their lineage to a Revolutionary War Patriot.

Mary Penrose Wayne Chapter NSDAR in Fort Wayne was organized on December 18, 1901; the charter was issued on January 20, 1902. The original sheepskin charter was framed in wood from the palisades of the old fort and hangs in the Allen County History Center.

The chapter name was chosen to honor the wife of General Anthony Wayne who was known as the Savior of the West and Founder of Fort Wayne. Mary Penrose was born in 1749 and married Anthony Wayne in Philadelphia in 1766. She remained at their homestead, "Waynesborough," in Chester County, Pennsylvania throughout the Revolutionary War and was endangered many times by the approach of British soldiers as she managed the farm and tannery. She died there in April 1793.

The chapter organizing regent was Frances Haberly Robertson, who served as chapter regent for two years. She led European tours and was a published writer and art critic who resided at 635 West Berry Street in Fort Wayne. She was associated with the planning and dedication of the 1902 Allen County Courthouse and the General Anthony Wayne statue.

In the early days of the chapter, Revolutionary War relics were collected from throughout the Fort Wayne community and displayed in a room in the courthouse. The relics included Anthony Wayne's camp bed, oil portraits, lock from the old fort, an armchair of Chief LaFontaine, and many Indiana, early pioneer, and Revolutionary War items. The collection grew to become a major gift to the Allen County Historical Society and was the nucleus for their collection. The artifacts are now housed in the Allen County History Center.

Mary Penrose Wayne Chapter also played a significant part in the formation of the now-famous genealogy collection of the Allen County Public Library by early donations of DAR lineage books and bequests of funds and genealogical materials. Chapter members compiled records of local cemeteries, early Allen County historical records, and donated published and unpublished materials. Today chapter members continue the partnership with the genealogy department of the library by volunteering assistance in genealogical research focusing on lineal descent from Revolutionary War patriots.

As early as 1905, the chapter began to place historical markers throughout the City of Fort Wayne to preserve the memory of local events and to mark locations of historical significance. The fourteen brass markers placed around the city are to recognize historical trails, the sites of the forts, Harmar's Defeat, Chief Richardville, and the Allen County Soldiers of the Revolution.

celebration luncheon in January 2002, attended by many guests and dignitaries. Artifacts were displayed and the luncheon was followed by new member installation, awards, and the announcement of special Sister-Chapter status with the España Chapter in Madrid, Spain. A time capsule was prepared and presented to the Allen County History Center. A Centennial Celebration Book was written documenting chapter history and member's Revolutionary War patriots. Copies were presented to the Allen County Public Library, the Indiana State Library in Indianapolis, and the NSDAR Archives and Library in Washington, D.C.

Today the chapter has nearly 190 members and plays a leadership role in the state. Committees that focus on DAR schools, student scholarships, conservation, American Indians, American history and good citizen student contests, as well as others, keep members active. Chapter genealogists assist those who are interested in membership. Chapter members also participate in local naturalization ceremonies, donating flags to new American citizens. Many meetings are held on Saturdays to accommodate working women. Members are linked together through the internet websites and E-mail. Social outings are enjoyed by members and they share volunteer activities.

Today the new DAR abides by the same focus on education, patriotism, and historical preservation and the motto of "God, Home and Country" while adapting to life in the new millennium.

Chapter Centennial Celebration, January 2002. 2001-2002 Officers (l. to r.) Regent Barbara Tracey, Vice Regent Donna Sharp, Chaplain Pat Heemstra, Recording Secretary Janeen Peters, Corresponding Secretary Jeanette Sterling, Registrar Martha Barnhart, Historian Phyllis Robb, and Librarian Rosalie Hamilton.

Over the more than one hundred-year history of the chapter, members have spent countless hours in various local volunteer efforts. During World War II, some members worked seven days a week at the Red Cross. Others made surgical dressings, worked at social centers and served as hostesses at Baer Field, prepared buddy bags for servicemen, prepared war service records and purchased war bonds. Volunteerism continues today with a focus on the veteran patients at the local Veterans Affairs Hospital, the library, and other local agencies.

Mary Penrose Wayne Chapter celebrated its centennial anniversary year beginning with a donation of microfiche records to the Allen County Library and History Center and ending with a special

Northeast Indiana Baseball Association
(Fort Wayne Oldtimer's Baseball Association)

What started out as a loose-knit group of mostly players and former players in 1946 became more organized in the early 1950s, revamped themselves in the early 1960s, and, following a six-year absence (1992-1997), resurfaced in 1998 to ultimately become today's Northeast Indiana Baseball Association.

Although little is known about the group during the period 1946-1960, it is known that they played an annual oldtimers game beginning in 1946 or 1947. These games were sponsored by the Fort Wayne Baseball Federation and played for the benefit of amateur baseball in Fort Wayne. Other than an occasional get-together to talk baseball, usually at a local bar, there was little formal activity until 1953.

On January 19, 1953 six members of the group including Edward "Red" Carrington and Elmer Wagner, president and secretary-treasurer of the Fort Wayne Baseball Federation, met in the Portage Room of the YMCA where they conducted an election of officers for their newly chartered branch of the National Hot Stove League of America. Elected were Bob Parker, President; Charles Wilt, Vice President; Red Carrington, Secretary; Jim Wagner, Treasurer; and a board of directors, most of whom were representatives of the new media.

While the Hot Stove League meetings were well attended early on, attendance started to dwindle toward the later part of the decade. Even the occasional showing of World Series films was not enough to stem the tide. With the membership and media both showing signs of losing interest, Carrington and Parker devised a new game plan.

This plan began to take shape in late 1960 or early 1961 beginning with a name change. Out went the Hot Stove League and in came the Fort Wayne Oldtimers Baseball Association (FWOBA). Told that an ambitious new program would soon be introduced, the media showed up in force at an FWOBA meeting on Monday, October 16, 1961.

At this meeting co-chairmen Red Carrington and Elmer Wagner announced the formation of the Fort Wayne Baseball Hall of Fame. Following the evenings' naming of the Hall's' first two inductees, Lou Holterman and James "Hub" Hart, Red told the gathering that a nine-person Hall of Fame committee would soon be named to oversee the selection process in future years.

By November 30, 1961, the naming of the committee had been completed. Among those named were Parker (chairman), Carrington, Elmer Wagner, four other local baseball "oldtimers," and two members of the media.

This group held its first meeting on January 19, 1962 in the Centlivre (Brewery) Hospitality Room where Holterman and Hart were presented with their HOF plaques, a certificate, and a permanent plaque that was to be displayed at a prominent Fort Wayne location, an awards tradition that continues to this day.

The Oldtimers began hosting four major events annually in 1961. These included a Kickoff Stag in January, the Hall of Fame Awards Banquet in April/May (held at the Chamber of Commerce and later at Lester's Party Room and Goeglein's Reserve), the Oldtimers Baseball Game in August, and the Fall Roundup Stag (local amateur awards) in October.

This all came to a halt by 1992 with the passing in recent years of several of the more active members. However, in 1998 the organization gained new life thanks principally to Bob Parker. The first order of business was to revive the annual Hall of Fame Awards banquet and begin anew the induction of those deserving Hall of Fame status. Three other awards were presented at these banquets over the years as well: the Elmer J. Wagner Memorial Award (1971-2002); the Bob Parker Memorial Award (1999-present); and the Colin Lister Award (2003-present). Starting in 1998, these banquets were held at the Knights of Columbus, Indiana Tech, American Heritage Village (Auburn), and more recently at the History Center in Fort Wayne.

An organizational goal virtually since its inception in 1961 was finally realized in December 2002 when the Dean Kruse Foundation's American Heritage Village stepped up to the plate and invited the organization to house its long-sought museum and Hall of Fame inside that complex. The organization's leaders began work on the project in January 2003 and it has since become a quite popular exhibit. It includes artifacts and collectibles from the late 19th century up to the present day. Little League, Federation League, Daisies, Semi-Pro, and Major League baseball among others, are all part of the exhibit. And all of this under the watchful eyes of the Hall of Famers (currently 159) whose pictures are located on a wall overlooking the exhibit.

In June 2003, the organization changed its name to the Northeast Indiana Baseball Association (NEIBA). In addition to its current activities, the museum and hall of fame and the annual Hall of Fame Awards Banquet, the NEIBA publishes a quarterly news publication, *Line Drives*, a copy each of which is permanently housed at the Allen County Public Library.

The Northeast Indiana Baseball Association: dedicated to the greatest game ever invented – Baseball!

Allen County Nurses Make History

Significant contributions to the nursing profession and health care by residents and professionals from Allen County, Indiana, are numerous. To mention them all is beyond the scope of this writing; however, two individuals deserve elaboration so as not to be forgotten. These include women from two different centuries: Eliza George, a nurse who served during the Civil War; and E. Gertrude Fournier, one of the founding members of the Indiana State Nurses Association in the early 1900s.

Eliza George was fifty-five years old when she left her home in Fort Wayne in 1863 to serve in the Indiana Sanitary Commission. This commission was formed in 1862 by then Governor Oliver P. Morton to provide supplies, transportation services, and nursing and medical care to Hoosier soldiers. As a nurse, Mrs. George cared for wounded soldiers in Tennessee, Georgia, and Mississippi. She aided in the establishment of field hospitals and ambulance services that transported soldiers from battlefields. Her work was often dangerous as she served behind battle lines. Although she was never wounded, the effects of the war eventually took her life. Once the war ended, she continued to nurse prisoners of war in Wilmington, North Carolina, but contracted typhoid fever. Due to age and the exertions of war, she was unable to fight the infection. Her body was escorted back to Fort Wayne, where the Indiana Sanitary Commission erected a monument in honor of her service.[1]

Another nurse from Allen County, E. Gertrude Fournier, was instrumental in establishing the Indiana State Nurses Association in 1903. That year, representing the state's first nursing alumnae association from Fort Wayne's Hope Hospital, Mrs. Fournier, superintendent of nurses at the hospital, was a delegate to the National Convention of the Nurses Associated Alumnae. Nursing leaders had called for the formation of state nurses' associations with the initial purpose of passing laws for the registration of nurses. At that time, many women were calling themselves "nurses." One leader wrote, "[T]he public are woefully ignorant in regard to the education and requirements of the modern trained nurse....But let any woman go into a community, adopt a nurse's uniform, and call herself a trained nurse, and her statement will be accepted without question by the majority of physicians and the public at large."[2] Indeed, no legal restrictions prevented any person from representing herself as a trained nursing graduate. State registration would establish fixed professional standards for nurses, impose order and uniformity to the profession, and protect the public.

Mrs. Fournier's efforts to improve nursing at this time took place during the Progressive Era, a broad-based reform movement that was influenced by the ills stemming from industrialization and urbanization. Accompanying reform was a growing emphasis on professionalization with its imposition of standards and the licensing of personnel. In 1897, a law had established the Indiana State Board of Medical Registration and Examination.[3] The lack of uniform standards in nursing led to nursing leaders' efforts to do the same.

Encouraged by the national organization's charge, Mrs. Fournier and the Hope Hospital Alumnae Association issued circulars to as many hospitals as could be located where training schools existed, inviting nurses to attend a meeting at Hope Hospital on September 3, 1903. They also sent notices to the American Journal of Nursing and to major newspapers across the state. When the moment arrived, Mrs. Fournier presented the national association's request. The motion to organize the state nurses association was "thoroughly discussed and finally carried." Afterward, the women adopted a constitution and by-laws.[4]

On November 27, 1903, nurses from seven different cities met once again in Fort Wayne to elect officers and form committees. The 65 attendees enrolled as charter members of the ISNA and elected Mrs. Fournier as the first president. After her installation, Mrs. Fournier addressed the group, "expressing her elation over the success of the organization and over the excellent prospects for the future."[5]

At the next meeting in February 1904, the association chose the motto, "Memor," Latin for "mindful." Nurses divided the state into thirteen districts and voted to have semi-annual meetings at alternating sites.[6] The local Fort Wayne newspaper reported the following address by Mrs. Fournier: "The time has come when our profession will be recognized by law, and we should regulate these coming laws, rather than the physicians."[7] The ISNA incorporated on March 4, 1904, with the purpose of advancing educational and literary standards of nurses and nursing, furthering efficient and scientific care of the sick, maintaining "the honor and character of the nursing profession," and furthering "cordial relations" among nurses in Indiana, other states, and countries.[8]

Through the efforts of women such as Eliza George and E. Gertrude Fournier, nursing became a legitimate field for women to enter. Indeed, Allen County was very instrumental in creating a new profession of nurses. Since its auspicious beginnings, the ISNA has grown to over 1,500 members. In October 2003, at its 100th Anniversary State Convention, appropriately celebrated in Fort Wayne, issues that impact the nursing profession and subsequently the health of Indiana citizens remained at the forefront of the association's agenda.

Endnotes

[1] Elizabeth Moreland Wishard, *William Henry Wishard, A Doctor of the Old School* (Indianapolis: Hollenbeck Press, 1920), 278; Peggy B. Seigel, "She Went to War: Indiana Women Nurses in the Civil War," *Indiana Magazine of History* 86 (1990): 1-27; and Frank Moore, *Women of the War* (Hartford, CT: National Publishing Co. 1866) 333-340.

[2] "The Editor," *AJN* 1, no. 2 (November 1900): 166.

[3] Clifton J. Phillips, *Indiana in Transition: The Emergence of an Industrial Commonwealth, 1880-1920* (Indianapolis: Indiana Historical Bureau and Indiana Historical Society, 1968), 473.

[4] Fournier;" and Maude W. McConnell to Miss June Gray, April 20 (no year), Box 12, folder 9, Indiana Historical Society (hereafter cited as IHS).

[5] 1903 ISNA Minutes, Box 2, folder 1, IHS. Quotation is in "Official Reports of Societies - Fort Wayne, Ind.," *AJN* 4, no. 4 (January 1904): 314.

[6] 1904 ISNA Minutes, IHS.

[7] Typed copy of newspaper article, "Indiana Nurses Will Demand Registration," sometime around February 22, 1904, Box 12, folder 9, IHS.

[8] Article I, "Articles of Incorporation," Box 10, folder 10, IHS.

Indianapolis was the site of the 1908 ISNA annual meeting. E. Gertrude Fournier, Fort Wayne, first ISNA president, is seated on the far left in the dark dress. (Photo courtesy of ISNA)

North Side High School Alumni Association

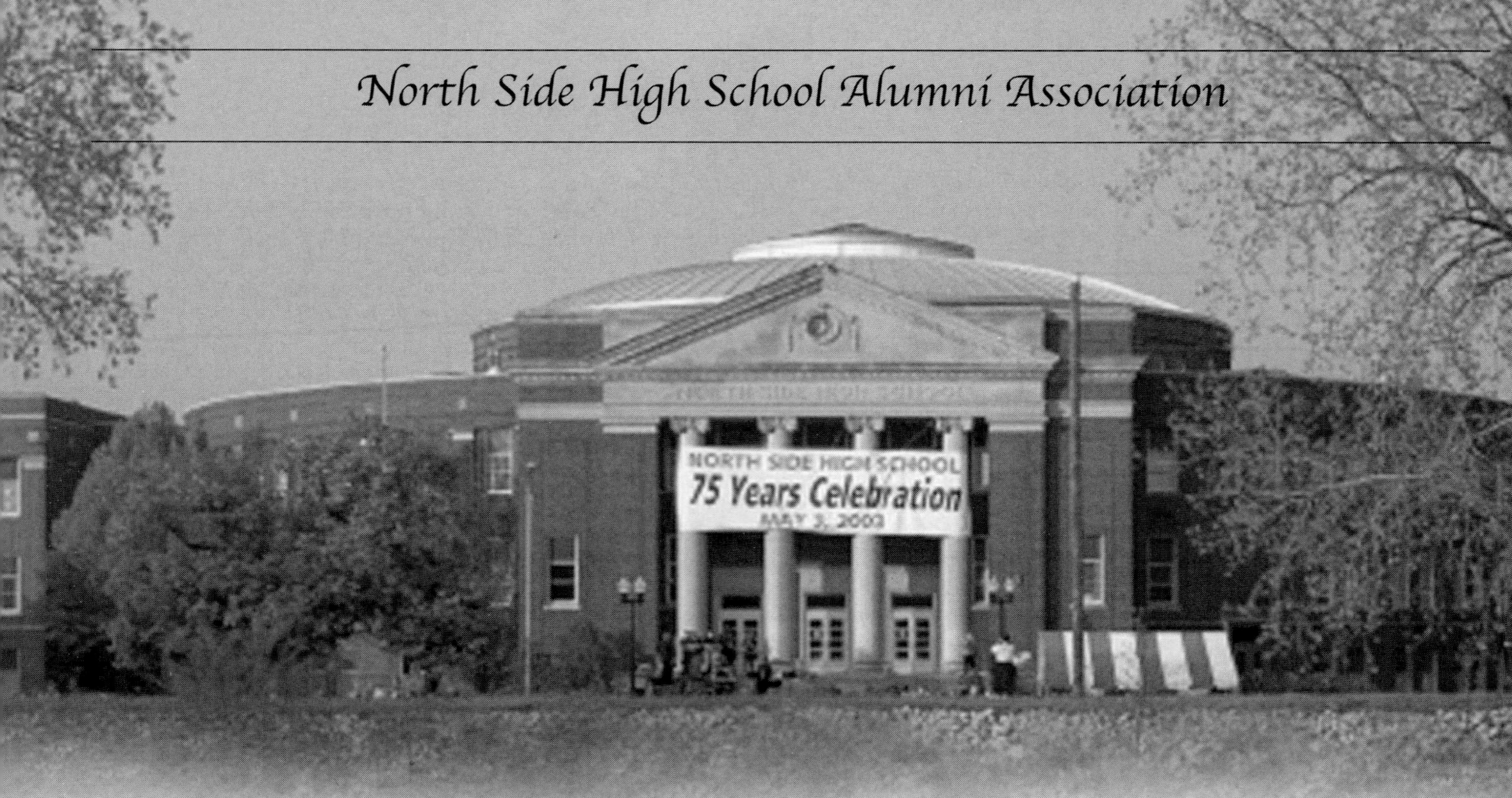

In the spring of 1986, North Side High School principal, Dan Howe, returned to Fort Wayne from a national education conference in Washington, D.C. with an exciting idea. He invited Federal Judge William Lee, North Side class of 1955, Mayor Paul Helmke, class of 1966, Barrett-McNagney attorney, Bob Walters, class of 1959, and retired educator, Patty Martone, class of 1949 to meet with him to learn about a project he considered a unique opportunity for North Side.

Howe proposed to his four guests the creation of a public high school alumni association. He had visited such an organization in inner city Washington and was impressed with the benefits brought to students and staff through the efforts of graduates. Howe convinced the four listeners that North Side should be the first public high school in the county to establish an alumni effort.

One graduate from each class (1928-1987) was invited to meet, to analyze the idea, and voice an opinion. A mission statement was drafted, goals and objectives were written, and the first officers and board of directors took office. Early in the association's existence, other public high schools throughout the area sought assistance and took form.

Judge Lee guided the group for the first two years with a board comprised of member representatives from six decades, drafting policy. Patty Martone wrote and introduced Totem Tales, a quarterly newsletter, and the Redskin Review, a twice-a-year magazine.

The creation and administration of student scholarships, support of staff development, student incentive programs, and the ongoing involvement of graduates with their high school are goals that have grown and developed in the nearly 20 years of the group's existence.

The awarding of scholarships, grants, and achievement awards continues to be the focus of the North Side High School Alumni Association. Ten $500.00 scholarships are awarded each year and four named scholarships (The Catherine Zwick-Lee Memorial, the David and Jan Bleeke, the Tom Garman, and the Holly Love Faulkner Memorial) assist graduates with future education. Over $124,000 has been awarded, and 181 students have received Alumni Association scholarships. Almost $107,000 in grants has been awarded to individual students, teachers, and for special programs at the school. Achievement awards totaling $2,500 are presented at the end of the year to those North Side High School students who have shown significant academic progress during the current school year.

Since 1988, the association has had its own office, executive secretary, and a membership of over 1,000 members. In addition, there are presently 110 Life Members of the NSHSAA. Each of these graduates have donated $1,000 to the Alumni Association, and all the interest earned from these monies has gone to support the annual North Side High School Alumni Scholarships. Dan Howe's dream caught hold, stimulated early pioneers and continues to grow, assist and inspire North Side High School.

Northside Neighborhood Association

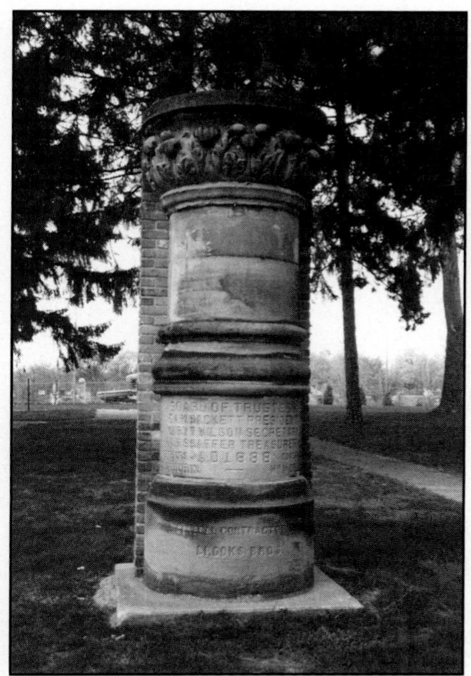

1888 State School Monument

The Northside Neighborhood Association (NNA) was formed in 1975 following the success of local neighbors in the rejection of siting a regional correction center at the old "State School" property north of State Boulevard, previously known as the "Indiana Home for the Feeble Minded," "Fort Wayne State School," and finally, "The State Hospital and Training Center." Use of the nearly 60-acre campus lying north of State Boulevard between Parnell Avenue and Kentucky Avenue was in question following removal of the State School operation and was in the process of being converted to other state uses beginning in 1970 with one possibility being a jail or penal institution.

The local neighbors saw an opportunity to express their opinion and promote the transformation of this large area into a community park. The site was dominated by a very large, historic, four-story brick 1900s administrative/hospital building with multiple other two-story brick cottage-type buildings scattered about the property, which also included a large power plant for the combined heating system and a gymnasium. There was also a ball field east of the center of the complex and a tall iron fence encircled the block. Ball games used to be played in the evenings and could be attended by some of the patients who lived at this complex which served mostly mentally handicapped and disabled children and young adults.

The replacement for the State School operation was a new, modern complex built north east of the Stellhorn Road and Hobson Road intersection. Now was the time (early 1970s) to decide the fate of this land with its collection of many very old, large buildings. A long battle ensued over the use of the property. The eventual winner was the residential community surrounding the complex and the property was turned into a beautiful park with ball fields, a swimming pool (added in 1980), tennis courts, and a community meeting building converted from one of the original brick buildings. The park was named North Side Park.

The twelve members of the original "Corrections Center Opponents" organized a committee with the help of City Councilman Don Schmidt on November 30, 1974. The members were the following: Katherine Hoffman, Diane Duly, Richard Regedanz (treasurer), Emily Jantz, David Schmidt, Robert Pio, Fane Hein, Robert Rommel, Jack Carter, Carol Lantz, Adolph Pence, and Robert Wire.

A newspaper article on January 11, 1975 stated, "Public's Wish Spurred Site Veto, Governor Says," and included a photo with Governor Bowen, Sheriff Charles Meeks, group representative Carol Lantz, and attorney Jack Lawson. After successfully stopping the siting of the corrections center at the State Street property, the North Side Opponents group put out a notice for a meeting on February 17, 1975 to be held at the Riverside School (Kentucky and Vance Avenues) for the purpose of forming a neighborhood association which became known as the Northside Neighborhood Association.

Police Athletic League

In 1957 an idea nurtured for a number of years by several police officers came to fruition. A youth-focused program for all of Allen County called the Police Athletic League (popularly termed PAL) was established.

This new idea linking police officers with young people who sought involvement in sports was patterned after a long-established New York City organization dating back to the 1930s. Numbers of PAL programs were founded throughout the country serving a diverse population of young participants.

In Fort Wayne and Allen County the mission was clear. The purpose was to connect area youngsters with local law enforcement officers in mutual athletic enjoyment. The objectives were to encourage good sportsmanship and provide fun, with winning a secondary goal. PAL has accepted both boys and girls regardless of race, religion, or economic status from the beginning. The inability to pay small insurance costs, photo charges, or incidental fees has never been a deterrent to participation.

The influence of police officers is important to the program. The officer is a mentor, and the adult-youth relationship is positive and preventive not corrective. For a youngster in need of discipline, it is a vehicle where someone who genuinely cares gives direction.

The local program began with boxing when a ring was built on the top floor of the Cooney Building on Calhoun Street across from the Cathedral of the Immaculate Conception. Several Golden Glove champions were trained by police officers Bill Dileo and Red Smith, men with broad experience in boxing and the coaching of the sport.

Early success in PAL boxing caught the attention of Fort Wayne businessman, L. W. Dailey. Interested in furthering the police department's effort to serve youngsters, Dailey donated a generous piece of land between West Main and West Washington Streets for the construction of a baseball playing area. Officers John Nelson, Carl Wilcoxson, and Jerry Neu extended the physical labor in 1950 to create Dailey Field. It is estimated more than 5,000 youngsters played on that field.

As the need for kids to have a "place to play" became apparent, many officers as well as a growing number of community volunteers began to discuss the possibility of a PAL Center. A committee with the help of Schenkel & Sons Construction Company broke ground in 1960 in northwest Fort Wayne on Olladale Drive for a building to house programs designed for youth involvement. Local workmen eager to contribute to young people came calling and furnished labor and every aspect of development. Off-duty officers, community volunteers, and representative firms, construction, electrical, heating, and the like, gave heart and hand to the project. When the building was completed, then-Chief Paul Clark said, "It is one of the most successful endeavors ever performed by area volunteers."

Mural painted by Sgt. Bill Atkinson on the PAL office wall in 1975.

By 1968, PAL's programs were many. Basketball was a very popular activity with 56 teams playing each week. Buses ran throughout the city bringing kids from every neighborhood to play at the PAL Center. Other1960-1970s offerings were boxing, weight lifting, volleyball, ice hockey (at the Memorial Coliseum), track and field as well as a mentoring service serving youngsters referred from the Juvenile Aid Bureau, Fort Wayne Police Department, and Superior Court.

The signature sport, Youth Football, was introduced in 1969. Following a conservative beginning with only four teams involved, by 1974 over 500 participants filled rosters of twelve teams. Early volunteers (some of whom still participate) were Tony Martone, Tom Rody, Jerry Moore, Jeron Biddle, Gary Fryback, Bill Dileo, Mike Nedeff, Dallas Ramsey, and Dick Renbarger.

It has taken a great deal of money, time, and effort to sustain PAL's extensive football program. The organizational skills, untiring dedication and selflessness of volunteer managers, coaches, and helpers have made the program envied throughout the state of Indiana.

The Police Athletic Association is governed by a Board of Directors and carries a volunteer staff of one hundred community men and women. One retired police officer is in charge of the center's operation. New programs are introduced each year. Some fail but most develop into fresh opportunities for participants. Cheerleading, self-defense, tennis, and Boy Scouting for the physically challenged are among recent additions to the traditional menu.

For forty-seven years boys and girls have found recreation, guidance, and positive adult role models through association with police officers and willing community helpers who are their "Pals." What began as a policemen's dream has become a strong reality. Allen County has been well served by a group of civil servants who cared about kids and decided to exercise that concern through action.

PTA Mothersingers, Southmoor Singers, and the Northern Notes

Northern Notes and Southmoor Singers in concert in the 1980s.

PTA Mothersingers

Parent Teachers Associations (PTA) formed and sponsored Mothersingers groups in the 1950s throughout the United States. These choirs were made up of mothers of school-age children who enjoyed singing and were willing to entertain at PTA functions. The individual school PTAs purchased the music used by the singers. The choirs would combine once a year to entertain at the statewide convention of their parent group. As the number of mothers with time to participate became fewer, the individual school choirs joined together to continue their activities. The singers from schools in the south half of the city formed the Southmoor singers in 1955. Their northern Fort Wayne counterparts formed the Northern Notes in 1959. The groups continued to entertain at PTA meetings and the PTA continued to fund their music purchases until the early 1970s. About that time the groups dropped the name Mothersingers.

Southmoor Singers

The Southmoor Singers were founded in February 1955 by Dorothy Spencer as a Mothersingers group. The first director was Jo Gerig and Mrs. Lloyd Miller was their first accompanist. Most of the members lived in the south part of Fort Wayne and their children attended school there. One of the highlights during the early years was singing at the Chicagoland Festival in 1960 at which the group received a first-place rating. Sara Collins became the chorus director in 1961. She led the group for many years. Helen Sherbondy was accompanist during that time. Joan Lininger began as accompanist in 1983 and became Director-Accompanist in 1996.

The Southmoor Singers do a dinner and show for family and friends once a year. They enjoy all-day bus trips to varying places of interest. Their social activities include a spring brunch with the Northern Notes, a holiday party, a summer picnic, and a monthly coffee-tea.

Northern Notes

Virginia Shambaugh, wife of Robert Shambaugh, Director of Music for Fort Wayne Community Schools, was the driving force behind the formation of the Northern Notes in late 1959. She gathered 14 singers who had children in the schools in the north half of the city and became the director and accompanist for the group. With their formal organization on January 18, 1960, they chose the name Northern Notes and began to accept singing dates. The first couple of years PTAs were their main audiences, but soon they began to branch out. They sang for church groups, service clubs, and other community organizations. Kay Brown, Lillian Embick, and Sara Collins were three of the charter members. Lillian became Executive Director of Audiences Unlimited; Sara, Director of Southmoor Singers; and Kay, Director of Northern Notes in 1966. She remained the energetic and demanding director for over 36 years. Betty Lou Lancia followed Kay as their lively director in 2002. The group has been blessed with many wonderful accompanists including Beverly Nordyke, Doris Watson, Joan Phillips, Florence Isaacs, Adrien Provenzano, Jean Roth, Deb Rendon, Linda Ballowe, and Karen Steiner. Their present talented pianist is Pauline Eversole.

The Northern Notes and the Southmoor Singers perform repertoires that consist of popular, sacred, patriotic, show, and novelty numbers with a membership of about 20 each. The members delight in the joyful experience of sharing music with others. Forest Park United Methodist Church has generously given Northern Notes a rehearsal space Tuesday mornings since 1964. The Southmoors also rehearse Tuesday mornings at Lincolnshire Church of the Brethren.

2006 Northern Notes (N) and Southmoor Singers (S) (l. to r.) Sitting: Judy Lennon (N), Director and Accompanist-Joan Lininger (S), Director-Betty Lou Lancia (N), Director Emeritus-Kay Brown (N), Louise Fultz (S), Marcia Clupper (N), Sue Saner (N) and Donna Spina (S). Standing: Ellen Merchant (N), Accompanist-Pauline Eversole (N), Rose Marie Atz (N), Kari Cynar (N), Tina Robinson (N), Irene Koehl (S), Susan Prowant (N), Jean Curtis (N), Helen Pancake (N), Vicki Beeks (S), Agnes Farnbaugh (N), Anne Colburn (S), Donna Winters (N), Sally Paters (N), Leah Tourkow (S), Mary Lemert (N), Carole Meikle (S), Dorothy Rioux (N), Lois Hess (S), Vera Uhlig (N), Maxine Yater (S), Gay Craghead (S), Judy Meyer (N), Sharon McKay (S), Leah Woodrum (N). Absent: Diane Shirey (S), Ditty Bourne (S), Bobbie Shaw (S), and Judy Wittikampe (N).

Ancient Accepted Scottish Rite Of Freemasonry
Northern Masonic Jurisdiction Fort Wayne, Indiana

The Scottish Rite came to the Fort Wayne area when it was chartered on September 19, 1888 as what is known geographically as the Valley of Fort Wayne. The Valley of Fort Wayne covers 18 counties surrounding Fort Wayne in Indiana. The Scottish Rite in Fort Wayne is part of an international Masonic organization and when a member joins will have bestowed on him the 32nd degree. The degrees received are lessons in life that are portrayed in drama vignettes demonstrating how a man should live his life. As a Masonic organization, the Scottish Rite, even though housed in what many refer to as a cathedral, is not a religious organization nor does it attempt to replace religion in any way. Also, even though the title of the organization has the word Scottish in it, the organization has no connection to Scotland. As the story goes, a man from Scotland while living in France came up with the idea of additional degrees for the Masons and thus started what is now known as the Scottish Rite.

The fraternity in Fort Wayne was first housed in the Masonic Lodge until they built their own building, dedicated in 1909, on the corner of Washington and Clinton, which is now a parking lot, currently next to the Masonic Temple and Wendy's restaurant. The building, known for its architecturally noted cake style architecture, housed the Fraternity for fifty years. When the Scottish Rite outgrew the building in the mid 1950s the fraternity purchased the Quimby Theater, built and formerly owned by the Shrine. (Shrine and Scottish Rite are both Masonic organizations, but are totally separate entities) The Scottish Rite has used the building on Berry Street since 1958 and added an addition on the west side in 1962.

The history of the current home of the Scottish Rite at 431 West Berry Street began in 1924, when construction began on the building, promising to provide Northeast Indiana with a much needed community meeting place to host speakers and theatrical productions as well as banquet facilities. The auditorium sat over 2,400 patrons, while the Banquet Hall could seat over 2,000. The auditorium was to be provided to the public for use, with the fraternity requiring it for only four or five days a year. The Chamber of Commerce had this to say about the construction of the Building; "For years, the people of Fort Wayne have felt keenly the necessity and urgent need of an auditorium in this city with sufficient capacity to accommodate conventions, where great statesmen and orators might speak to a worthwhile audience; where exhibitions of all kinds might be held - in general, a community house for gatherings of every conceivable kind. "

Well-known local architect and one of the original Scottish Rite founders, Guy Mahurin, was chosen as architect for the project, with Max Irmscher & Sons being the contractor. "To me, as the architect, the construction of the new auditorium and banquet hall is the creation of a structure of artistic designs that will serve as a community building for the civic interests of Fort Wayne and northern Indiana," he said.

Construction began in April 1924, with about two hundred workers involved. For the most part, local labor was used in the project. The excavation of the Ballroom took two steam shovels and six weeks to complete. More than 350,000 bricks were used in the construction and hundreds of barrels of cement mixed with gravel and water. The building was said to be the most "fire-proof' structure in the city at the time. Construction costs were over $1,000,000.

In 1937, during the depression, the Shrine lost the building into receivership (though they retained their current property located east of the Scottish Rite.) The city contemplated purchasing the Auditorium for municipal use, but in the end, Kaplan Realty bought it at a reported cost of only $52,500. The city continued to use it as a community center, housing the Fort Wayne Philharmonic and other civic events. The Shrine Circus even performed in the Auditorium until the Allen County War Memorial Coliseum was built in 1952.

In 1953, the Scottish Rite purchased the Auditorium and Ballroom from KMK Realty Co. In 1958, a large renovation (and the last major renovation prior to current efforts) was conducted, which included updating the Valencia Ballroom, kitchen, sound system, new auditorium curtains, installation of a Wurlitzer concert organ and painting the Horseshoe Lobby.

In the late 1990s, many Scottish Rite leaders decided to undertake another multi-million dollar renovation to update the ailing facility. In 1999, an event staff was formed to begin marketing the facility and focusing on NonMasonic events. To date, the 431 Foundation, formed to raise the funds and oversee the renovations, has collected over $2 million of the needed $3.1 million from not only members but also many patrons of the community and leading community foundations and trusts, to complete all of the renovation projects.

The Scottish Rite has had a rich history in Fort Wayne and the surrounding counties. As with many Masonic organizations, philanthropic efforts are a mainstay to the organization. The four major contributions include the funding of research grants for brain research specifically dealing with schizophrenia; funding for the museum in Lexington, Massachusetts for American Heritage; funding for academic scholarships annually and the latest effort of establishing a Learning Center for children having reading problems due to dyslexia. The Learning Center in Fort Wayne works with children in a one on one tutoring program at no cost to the student or parent.

To date, 6,000 men are members of the Scottish Rite. Members have come from all walks of life including several professional, business leaders, national, state and local politicians and mayors of the city. A couple of its more famous members included Dave Thomas, founder of Wendy's and Thomas R. Marshall, Vice-President of the United States during the Wilson era. The vice-president's flag, made especially for Marshall, still hangs in the Scottish Rite lounge today.

Science Central and City Light & Power's Generating Plant

1908 to 1975

In 1908, the city of Fort Wayne founded City Light & Power, and built a steampowered generating plant in Lawton Park, next to the city's water pumping station #1. The city began with two, 500-kW machines, then expanded power production through the years by adding generators ranging from 1500 kW to 4000kW. In the late 1920s, a major expansion began. A 7,500-kW generator replaced some of the older generators, and three new boilers replaced the four in operation at that time. A newer 15,000-kW generator (on display today) was added before expansion plans were completed in 1933.

The plant operated up until February 28, 1975, with a final arrangement of five boilers feeding two, 15,000-kW and one, 10,000-kW generator, serving about 33,000 Fort Wayne customers. Maximum demand was slightly less than 100 megawatts.

1929

The major power plant improvement, begun in 1929, eventually replaced all previous additions and expansions to the original 1908 power plant. This expansion coincided with the 1933 water-utility upgrade to river water when the Up-river Dam and Filtration Plant were built.

1969

The last attempt to upgrade the City Light power plant was in 1969 when a gas/oil-fired boiler was added to replace the1933 #3 boiler, and a gas/oil-fired 15,000-kW gas-turbine generator was installed on Fourth Street along the St. Mary's River and was located east of the two, steam-plant cooling-pond pump buildings. It last ran December 31, 1999 to January 1, 2000 for Y2K protection.

1975

The City Light power plant last produced electricity on February 28, 1975, and on the following day, the city utility was leased to I&M for 35 years.

1975 to 1991

The City Light power plant was vacant and sustained regular vandal damage.

1978 to 1989

Eureka Express supporters, lead by Greg Jacobs, formed the Solar Collective of Northeast Indiana in 1981.

1989

The Solar Collective of Northeast Indiana changes it's name to Science Central.

Science Central sponsored "Dinosaurs Alive" at the Fort Wayne Children's Zoo.

1991

The City of Fort Wayne transferred use of the power plant building to Science Central.

In November, I&M contracted with Martin Inc. to remove excess power plant equipment as part of the agreement between the city and I&M to remove the power plant from the lease agreement, and for the eventual city lease of the power plant building to Science Central.

1992

On July 9, Mayor Paul Helmke and I&M Fort Wayne Division Manager Ron Prater presented the power plant building key to Science Central at a news conference.

From July 11-19, the power plant was cleaned and scrubbed, displays were prepared and the building opened for tours by Science Central as an attraction during the Three Rivers Festival.

1993

Additional stabilization work was completed on the power plant building by I&M.

1995

On May 4, Science Central opened its doors as a science discovery center, 20 years and 9 months after the lease of the City Light & Power plant to I&M.

South Side High School Alumni Association and South Side High School Foundation

South Side High School, Fort Wayne's oldest institution of secondary education, opened in September of 1922. The first class graduated in 1923 and since then thousands of students have received diplomas from South Side. In January of 1990, principal Jack Weicker called a meeting of persons interested in forming an alumni association. Various informal alumni associations had existed at South Side as far back as the 1920s. These early alumni associations were primarily social in nature. It was Mr. Weicker's vision that this modern alumni association should have a formalized structure.

As a result of organizational meetings held in January and February of 1990, the South Side Alumni Association, Inc. was officially incorporated in April of 1990. The alumni association established a permanent office at South Side High School and publishes a newsletter called *Archer Arrows*. The membership of the association has remained constant at approximately fifteen hundred persons. The association has recognized the achievements of many outstanding graduates by periodically presenting Distinguished Alumni Awards.

The South Side High School Foundation was established by the alumni association in 1994 as a vehicle through which individuals could include South Side in their regular charitable giving or estate planning. The Foundation is an Indiana not-for-profit trust, which permits gifts to be fully tax deductible to the donor. Income derived from the trust investments is for the sole and exclusive benefit of South Side High School, its teachers, and students. Through the years, the alumni association and Foundation have contributed thousands of dollars to the programs of South Side High School and have presented educational scholarships to scores of South Side graduates.

South Side High School

United Way of Allen County

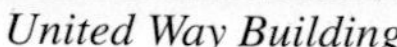

United Way Building

McCulloch-WeatherhoggHouse

Lincoln National Life Insurance Co. executive Arthur F. Hall, one of the founding members of what was to become United Way of Allen County, set out the philanthropic principle that has guided the region's attention to human service needs for more than 80 years.

"The entire community," he wrote in a 1926 newspaper article, "volunteers assumption of the burden of charity. Relief cannot be given spasmodically. Welfare organizations must be continuously supported and on a scale sufficient to meet the needs of a community that is growing as fast as Fort Wayne."

This strategy of a united effort to help people become self-sufficient led to the debut of the Council of Social Agencies in 1922. Since then, the group has changed names numerous times, often to address periods of specific need. It became the Fort Wayne Community Chest in 1925, Federated Relief Agencies Inc. in 1931 in the midst of the Depression, a member of the United War Chest in 1942, Allen County Community Chest and Social Planning Council in 1945, United Chest-Council of Allen County in 1956, United Community Services in 1963 and finally United Way of Allen County (UWAC) in 1972.

UWAC is now one of 1,350 United Ways nationwide. Although all are members of United Way of America, they are independent, separately incorporated and governed by a local board of directors.

In Allen County, UWAC's nonprofit campaigns to raise money for various programs have risen from $124,813 in the organization's first year to $6.4 million in 2004. The number of agency partners – human service organizations that benefit from UWAC's fundraising – has grown from 19 to 38. And its offices have changed locations several times, most recently moving from the historic United Way Building at 227 East Washington Boulevard to the historic McCulloch-Weatherhogg House at 334 East Berry Street.

More importantly, the organization has evolved to become more than merely a fundraiser. At its core is a mission to encourage collaborative planning and community human service action – to bring organizations, people and resources together to focus on critical issues.

United Way of Allen County is the lead organization for Success By 6, an effort to ensure the area's children are ready to enter school by the age of 6. UWAC was the first in Indiana to activate First Call For Help/2-1-1, an information and referral phone service that links people to various human services. And UWAC has been at the forefront of promoting all forms of diversity in the region, embarking on a Women's Initiative designed to energize women philanthropists.

UWAC has also developed public-project campaigns that strive to make Allen County a better place in which to live and work. Volunteer-driven Day of Caring and Youth Day of Caring continue to prosper, sending out teams of workers to fix homes, groom properties and lift spirits. In 2005, a record 13,000-plus people, most of them schoolchildren, participated in Youth Day of Caring. It was the largest event of its kind in the nation.

As it has for more than 80 years, UWAC relies on the board of directors, staff and thousands of volunteers to carry out its many missions, which recently came under the banner "Kids, Family, Community. That's What Matters."

Board members, staff and volunteers have included some of the brightest, most dedicated people in the community and have represented a diverse spectrum of interests, backgrounds and cultures.

The organization has been a trailblazer for equal opportunity. In 2002, Stephanie McCormick became United Way of Allen County's first woman chief executive officer. In 2004, Frances Ganaway became the organization's first black woman board president.

The Allen County organization has also been a collaborative regional planner. It is part of a collection of 13 United Ways called Northeast Indiana Consortium of United Ways/Funds that work together on various issues, including marketing.

Remarkably, some of the same human service agencies that came under the umbrella of the Council of Social Agencies in 1922 remain United Way of Allen County agency partners today. Among them: Fort Wayne Rescue Mission, Fort Wayne Jewish Federation and Salvation Army of Allen County.

Were he alive today, Arthur F. Hall would likely be gratified to see his vision still intact – one of a unified front in addressing the community needs that matter most.

His words in 1926 about Fort Wayne Community Chest are just as appropriate now as they were then: "No large community, with its complexities of modern city life, should try to conduct its welfare program without a central planning body of some kind. Putting all of the plans and budgets on the table is developing a habit of seeing the community's problems as a whole. This is leading to real teamwork and to a feeling that all are united in the master task of lessening the ills of poverty, sickness and a crowded life."

Unity Performing Arts Foundation (UPAF) was the result of an ingenious vision of Marshall White. Mr. White, a resident of Fort Wayne and former music director of True Love Baptist Church, began to pen the thoughts and ideas that would meet a need among young urban and suburban youth in the city in 1993. He saw that there was no platform for youth to learn, study, and perform mainstream music, which he later titled the soulful art forms. He wanted to give young people the chance to be exposed to something that had never been established before. Mr. White's vision consisted of starting a foundation that would allow youth to study and perform soulful styles of music (blues, hip-hop, gospel, R & B, jazz, and spirituals) through choral arrangements and dance. He also wanted to include creative writing, oratory, drama, and instrumental music programs. He had hopes of using the performing arts as a tool to make character building fun and appealing for youth.

The first official meeting was held on August 1, 1997, to present Mr. White's vision to a select group of artistically talented members of the community chosen by him. Many meetings took place up until1999, bringing more people to join in the organization of UPAF. Mrs. Cindy White, the wife of Mr. White, joined the circle of organizers on October 4, 1997, to help set organizational goals. A committee was formed in 1998 to begin conducting research, formulating ideas on class curriculums, audition sessions, fee structures, and many other aspects needed to build UPAF.

Mr. White was introduced to attorney David Boyer II in March of 2000 by attorney Payne Brown, who later registered the official papers for the organization. Mr. White, with the help of colleague Shirley Phifer-Smith, and Attorney Boyer sent the papers to the state to be filed. After receiving the official corporation papers for UPAF in May of 2000, Mr. White made the first executive step as founder of UPAF, by appointing Shirley Phifer-Smith as business assistant.

UPAF was well on its way to coming into existence, but the question of where rehearsals would be held for the youth choral program still remained. Mr. White and Mrs. Phifer-Smith met with the Chancellor of Indiana Purdue Fort Wayne (IPFW), Michael Wartell, on June 13, 2000, to present information about UPAF and request rehearsal space on the campus. IPAF was granted the needed space on trial, with hopes of becoming a long-term resident of IPFW. The thirty-two charter members voted on the name, "The Voices of Unity Youth Choir," on July 9, 2000, at the very first meeting of members of the youth choral program.

Officers were appointed soon after the first meeting of the Voices of Unity Youth Choir (VOU) to head the organization, in partnership with Mr. White. Mr. White, President/CEO and Music Director of VOU selected Shirley Phifer-Smith as Business Administrator/Vice President, Lucine Woodson as Administrative Assistant/Secretary, Dorothy Billingsley as Financial Secretary, and Patricia Johnson as Coordinator of Volunteers. These individuals would help in carrying out all administrative tasks for UPAF and VOU. UPAF's vision also includes launching other artistic programs in the future that would include an Adult Choral Program, Creative Writing Program, Oratory Program, Theatre Program, and an Instrumental Program that would include a soulful music youth orchestra.

In April of 2001 preparation began for the debut concert of VOU. The Voices of Unity Youth Choir was featured in their debut performance entitled, "Join the Caravan of Love," at Neff Hall at IPFW on June 16 and 17 of 2001. Mrs. And Mrs. Ian Rolland donated the first $2,000.00 to help UPAF get started. Other grants were given order to establish a payroll for UPAF staff members. The UPAF board of directors was officially established on June 11, 2001. The names of the board members were Marvin Eady, Jr., Pat Johnson, Renee Morrison, Janice Wagner, Nicole Brown, Shirley Phifer-Smith, Chuck Surack, Lucine Woodson, Fred Gilbert, Cindy Bolinger, Mac McAllister, Jim Markinton, and Dave Boyer II.

Marshall White

In years following the debut concert, UPAF produced many first-rate performances, trips, and fundraisers. The choirs' first vocal camp was held in October of 2001 at Camp Potawatomie, followed by VOU's first Annual Soulful Holiday Celebration on December 30, 2001, the first Living the Good Life Tour of the Lansing, Michigan school district in June of 2002, many other major performances, and countless other small performances throughout the community and surrounding areas; and a summer music program entitled, "Soulful Arts Awareness Program (SAAP)," in June of 2004, ending in August. UPAF goes down in history as being the first performing arts organization in the state of Indiana to provide youth with a platform for learning and performing the soulful art forms and simultaneously building character and empowering its youth to be successful and effective leaders for the future.

UNITY PERFORMING ARTS FOUNDATION, INC.

Building and Shaping Stars for the Future

P.O. Box 10394, Fort Wayne, IN 46852-0394
(260) 482-6899 • UPAF2000@aol.com

Visiting Nurse & Hospice Home

Over 100 years of caring traced back to our roots

Visiting Nurse & Hospice Home is a community-based, non-profit agency that has operated in the Fort Wayne area for over 100 years.

The roots of Visiting Nurse & Hospice Home can be traced to 1888 when the Ladies' Relief Union was formed to provide volunteer services in the home for the poor and the needy. Two years later, these volunteers established a visiting nurse committee based upon the works of Clara Barton.

In 1900, the program, now renamed the Visiting Nurse League, hired its first nurse, Josephine Shatzer, who made home visits to deliver health care and babies as necessary. For the next 23 years, she worked alone for pay of $10 per week.

In 1922, the League began to receive support from the Community Chest, the predecessor of today's United Way of Allen County. In 1935 nearly 60 percent of the agency's funding came from the Community Chest; that figure in 2005 is 1.5 percent.

The 1930s saw the League working in conjunction with the Allen County and Red Cross Nursing Services under shared supervision. The groups disbanded their relationship in 1942, reunited again for a time under the name "Public Health Nursing Service of Fort Wayne and Allen County," and then parted ways again. The League formally changed its name to the Visiting Nurse Service in 1954. The first "housekeeping aides," later known as home health aides, began visiting patients in 1958. In 1966, Visiting Nurse Service of Fort Wayne received the first home health Medicare provider number in the state of Indiana.

Competition from other agencies began to affect the Visiting Nurse Service as early as 1979. The first strategic planning for the Visiting Nurse Service occurred in 1982, when goals were set to increase referrals, visits and productivity, and to decrease visit costs.

In 1986, Parkview and Lutheran Hospitals merged their hospice programs with Visiting Nurse Service under the new agency Visiting Nurse Service and Hospice.

The next decade brought many changes including the dissolution of the Parkview-Lutheran-VNSH partnership in 1995. Visiting Nurse Service and Hospice reverted to being a freestanding, community-based agency without formal ties to either hospital.

Visiting Nurses, early 1900s.

Still, such was the demand for hospice services that the agency expanded into Adams, Wells and Huntington counties. In 1995, following a nearly three-year feasibility study, "Hospice Home of Northeast Indiana" opened on the eighth floor of the former Lutheran Hospital on Fairfield Avenue. Hospice Home (as it is now known) was devoted to patients who were unable to remain in their homes, and was the only in-patient facility dedicated solely to hospice care in the region, and one of only five in the entire state.

In 1998 Visiting Nurse Service and Hospice refocused its mission to exclusively provide end-of-life care. The board sold the traditional home health care program to St. Joseph Hospital and, at the same time, closed the private duty program. The agency retained its home health license to provide palliative care for patients facing life-threatening illnesses. These patients are pursuing curative treatment and are not enrolled in hospice care.

In 2001, a free-standing Hospice Home became a reality. A capital campaign raised $2 million to construct a new building on Homestead Road, where the VNHH offices and 11-bed Hospice Home are now located.

In the fall of 2004, Visiting Nurse & Hospice Home (as the agency was renamed in 2004) opened an office in Marion, Indiana. The staff in Marion cares for patients in Blackford, Delaware, Grant, Howard, Madison, Miami and Tipton counties. This is addition to the counties served by the Fort Wayne office: Adams, Allen, DeKalb, Huntington, Noble, Wabash, Wells and Whitley.

In 2005, Visiting Nurse & Hospice Home continues to provide hospice and palliative care in patients' residences (including nursing homes) or in its Hospice Home. The demand for hospice care in the Hospice Home and at home prompted the agency to conduct a capital campaign ($1.37 million) to add three additional patient rooms, a quiet room, a larger family room and work areas for the hospice team.

As the agency reflects on the more than 100 years of service to the Fort Wayne area, the dedicated, caring staff of Visiting Nurse & Hospice Home considers it a privilege to care for patients and families in the finals stages of life. The agency is guided by its mission: "People are important until the last moment of their lives. Visiting Nurse & Hospice Home provides compassionate medical care and emotional and spiritual support to those entering the last stages of their lives and to the loved ones who go on living."

YWCA of Northeast Indiana

YWCA Lunchroom

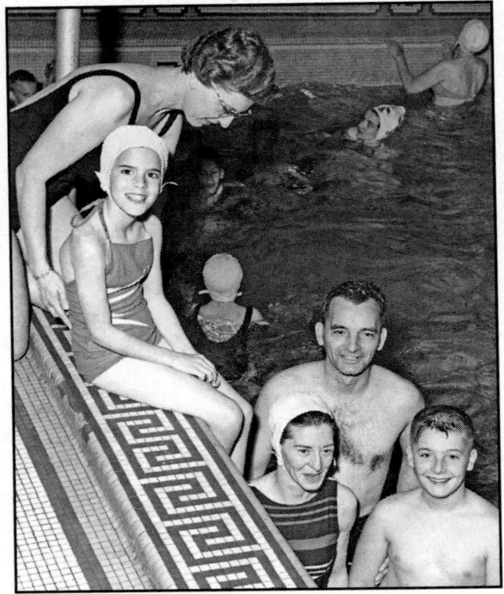

Members enjoying the YWCA pool.

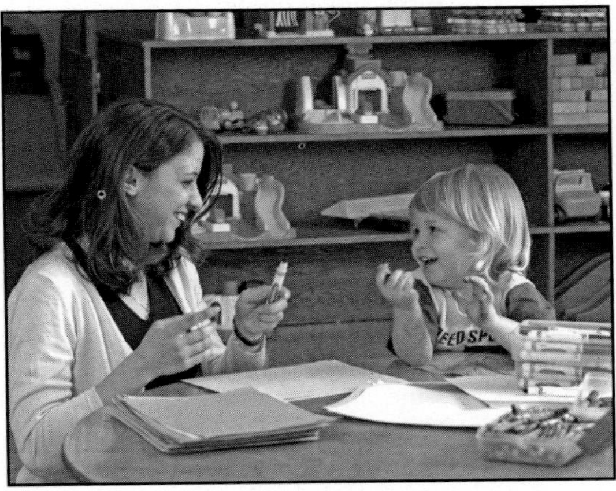

Fun with art at the YWCA.

The Young Women's Christian Association (YWCA) started in 1855 in London by Emma Roberts and Mrs. Arthur Kinnaird. It first began in the United States as the Ladies Christian Association in New York City and in 1859 Boston was the first association to use the name YWCA.

The YWCA's history in Fort Wayne goes back to 1894 and was founded by Agnes Hamilton, Minnie Moon, and Rena Nelson. The YWCA became an organization of "firsts." The early members started the first cafeteria in Fort Wayne for working women and served as a safe housing location for single women and sponsored programs for families. The YWCA also organized the first Community Forum with such famous speakers as W.E.B. DuBois, and suffragette Carrie Chapman Catt. Thousands of children and adults have learned to swim at the YWCA; the first public indoor swimming pool in Fort Wayne was built at the YWCA on West Wayne Street. In the 1960s, the Fort Wayne YWCA offered the first black history course as it prepared to support the adoption of the National YWCA's One Imperative: To thrust our collective power toward the elimination of racism wherever it exists and by any means necessary. In April 1976, in response to a 1975 YWCA study that named domestic violence as a major problem in the Fort Wayne community, the YWCA opened the doors of the first shelter for abused women in the state of Indiana.

When the Allen County Public Library purchased the YWCA building on Berry Street in 1978, the board of directors purchased the St. Vincent's Villa Orphanage, a 23-acre property on Wells Street owned by the Roman Catholic Archdiocese of Fort Wayne-South Bend. In doing so, the YWCA became the owner of the largest one-site YWCA in the United States. In 1981, development of new programming followed, along with an expansion of the facilities with the addition of a new pool and racquetball courts that were added to the health and fitness area.

A new domestic violence crisis shelter was built in 1986 to house women and children in danger. This shelter is the second largest in the state and at the time it opened it was the only shelter designed specifically for domestic violence victims. In the fall of 1988, the YWCA began offering shelter outreach services to domestic violence victims in the nine-county northeast Indiana service area. Advocates make personal contact and take resources to the participants in those counties.

The YWCA opened a transitional housing program in 1991 for women whose histories of abuse are barriers to their educational and employment potential and their children. It is the only transitional housing program in our nine-county area focusing on serving domestic violence victims.

The Fort Wayne YWCA celebrated its centennial in 1994. In that year all seven buildings on the YWCA campus were added to the National Registry of Historic Places. There was a major campus-wide renovation to the buildings in 1995.

In 2001 the national YWCA had an organizational shift from a "top down to bottom up" organization forming regional boards and a two-pronged mission was outlined. In 2002, Becky Hill, Fort Wayne YWCA Chief Executive Officer, and Rosetta Moses-Hill, community activist and former YWCA board president, presented the first "White Privilege/Black Baggage" presentation through a partnership between the YWCA and the United Way of Allen County. The presentation creates awareness about the existence of racism and prejudice and improves community dialogue through a point-counterpoint perspective. In 2004 the YWCA launched a new brand to reaffirm its mission of elimination of racism and economic empowerment of women.

The YWCA has always adapted to the changing issues and needs of women and their families, having done so for 111 years in northeast Indiana. The cafeteria for working women of a century ago was provided to keep women, newly emerging into the workplace, safe. Since the 1970s, safety and violence prevention for women and their families serve as the foundation of our domestic violence programs. Our priorities include the children who are caught in the middle because they have witnessed abuse between their caregivers, and without intervention, 80 per cent of them will become abusers or victims when they become adults. In 2003, we established the Lavon Kelley Children's Fund to augment and enhance services to children to meet their special needs through music therapy, art therapy, and anger management.

We believe hope for peace in our community and in our world begins with peace in our homes.

Arthur J. Blaising Community Center

The Arthur J. Blaising Community Center began as the Eastside Neighborhood Center, funded by the Fort Wayne Foundation and Neighbors, Inc. in 1966. Neighbors, Inc. identified the Riverhaven community as a community in need. Arthur J. Blaising, a resident of Riverhaven, was instrumental in the inception of the center. Nicholas A. Roembke was named director.

Mary Blaising was named the new director in 1970 and with the volunteer labor of the Navy Sea Bees the building was expanded. This allowed additional space for social and recreational programming. From1972 to 1975, the agency was able to acquire dollars from the Fort Wayne Foundation and others that made possible the purchase of land adjacent to the building, and the installation of a basketball court.

The Agency became a United Way of Allen County member agency in 1977, marking its potential for growth and sustainability as a community-serving entity. The agency took on the official title of "Arthur J. Blaising Social Services " in 1979.

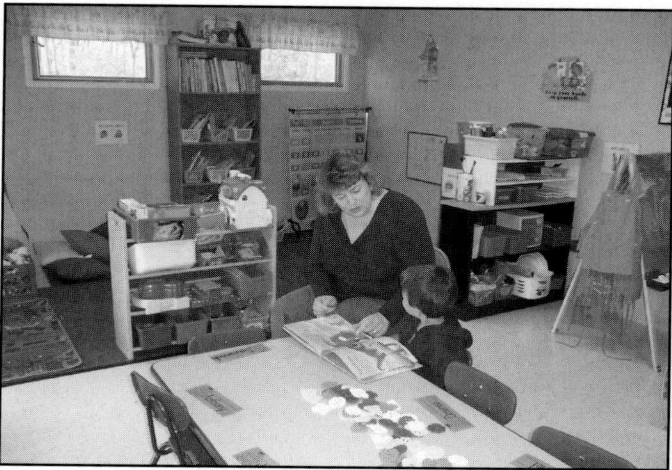

Sharon Wilson, Executive Director, and her son, Spencer, who attends Arthur J. Blaising Preschool which is marking its 40th year.

After a period of steady growth and community involvement in the forms of community dinners, youth sports, a GED program, etc., Youth Resources funded the installation of playground equipment, and New Haven United Methodist church donated capital for fencing around the playground in 1988.

Loaine Wilson was appointed the new Executive Director in 1990. A preschool program was started in 1991 as well as a valuable partnership with the New Haven-Adams Township Park Department. Sharon Wilson was appointed to the Executive Director position in 1997. Funding from the Foellinger Foundation for renovations to the building, and from the Fort Wayne Community Foundation for new computers and office equipment were acquired immediately.

In 1998 the agency adopted the official title, "Arthur J. Blaising Community Center, Inc." and has operated under that name providing community recreation, youth development, and social programs to East Allen county residents.

Besancon Historical Society

In 1992 a committee met to establish the Besancon Historical Society (BHS). Besancon is a small community located east of New Haven on old route 30, which is also called the Lincoln Highway. French, French Swiss, and German immigrants settled this area in the 1840s. The purpose of BHS is to promote historical and genealogical research, conserve historic sites, collect and preserve artifacts, and stimulate interest in history and genealogy

The society is located on the second floor of the parish office of St. Louis Besancon Church. The BHS archives consist of five rooms that are the office, the Lomont/Gladieux photo gallery, Isabey research library, Townsend library genealogy collections, and the Gladys Lomont room. The Lomont room honors the memory of Gladys by displaying pictures and objects that mark the years of her life. She was a part of the committee that established the historical society and put the church buildings on the National Register.

In November 1994 the first issue of the Besancon Chronicles was published. The Chronicles is published three times a year. The first officers of BHS were Mark Robbins, President; Jim Lomont, Treasurer; and Al Bowers, Secretary.

The BHS established the "Album in the Attic Project" as part of its archives in 1996. The project was headed by Father Thom Lombardi and Diana Voors. The purpose of the project was to collect photographs that documented the rich history of the settlers in eastern Allen County (mainly Jefferson, Jackson, Madison, and Monroe Townships) from the 1850s through the 1920s. The archives how has over 1,000 photos of people, towns, farms, transportation, and events.

The St. Louis Besancon district was placed on the National Register of Historic Places in 1996, and in 2000 the BHS presented a plaque commemorating this occasion. This plaque is located inside the church.

The families of the parish donated the stained glass windows in the church in 1871 when the present structure was built. The names on the lower part of the windows are Bertrand, Begue, Beugnot, Bowers, Chevillot, Cochoit, Cunin, Didier, Dodane, Dupeyron, Frene, Girard, Girardat, Gladieux, Havert, Huguenard, Joly, Kline, Loraine, Monnot, Pailloz, Pepe, Pernot, Rausis, Roy, Schmucker, Sebastian, Urbaine, and Voirol. A dedication of the restoration of the windows was held in 1996. The descendents of the original donors responded overwhelmingly with donations to this project.

Other prominent names that have been in the vicinity of Besancon are Bacon, Beauchot, Converset, Coonrod, Coulardot, Dager, Giant, Gromeaux, Jacquay, Lomont, Lothamer, Martin, Monnier, Rorick, Roussey, Sordelet, Ternet, Townsend, Venderly, and Yoquelet.

Canal Society of Indiana

CANAL SOCIETY of INDIANA
Celebrating
Indiana's Canal Era 1832-1874

The Canal Society of Indiana (CSI) was organized at the History Center in Fort Wayne on May 22, 1982 as a statewide not-for-profit corporation. Fort Wayne continues to be the state headquarters for this organization, which brings together persons who share a common interest in Indiana's canal heritage. The group helps focus attention on these early interstate waterways through a variety of publications and programs. Its aim is to provide interpretation of the era, to preserve canal bed and structural remains, and to support restoration of historic canal-related sites. Each year the Society conducts a spring and fall tour to expand its members' knowledge of Hoosier canals. The tour weekends feature speakers, videos, and music related to this colorful era and include a wide variety of related cultural activities such as home and building tours and craft demonstrations. Members of CSI receive a monthly copy of the news and journal, *The Hoosier Packet*, which includes articles on canal history, reprints of original documents, and reports about the technical aspects of canalling. It keeps members informed about canal-related events, tours and book availability, and shares the growing knowledge of the canal era.

Significant accomplishments of CSI include completing two videos on Indiana's canals via Indiana Heritage Research grants and placing several historical markers throughout the state. Members were instrumental in archeological work at the Gronauer lock and Huntington floodgate. CSI supports local canal groups in Indiana with funding and advice as they seek to build museums and save structures. It has led the way to a tremendous increase in canal heritage awareness. Trails are being built to follow old towpaths. Teachers and students take a new look at an era when horses pulled boats and Indiana developed its interstate canal transportation system to improve commerce.

Cedar Creek Wildlife Project, Inc.

Cedar Creek Wildlife Project, Inc. (CCWP), a not-for profit membership organization, was established in 1965 to foster preservation, stewardship, and appreciation of the Cedar Creek and its natural environment. Voting membership is limited to watershed property owners, and CCWP also maintains a non-voting support membership, with 150 members. Jane and Tom Dustin, together with many other active Cedar Creek watershed property owners and the Fort Wayne Chapter of the Izaak Walton League of America, were the original sponsors of CCWP. The organization remains headquartered in northern Allen County and is led in 2005 by long-time resident, Alan Diefenbach.

Cedar Creek valley property owners have worked diligently to defend and steward the Cedar Creek land, woods, and waters. The members support preservation tools that do not infringe on private property rights and yet create protection for the valley's scenic and natural qualities. CCWP has helped shape public policy by securing the designation of the entire stream in Allen County (approximately 14 miles) and one mile into DeKalb County as protected waters under the Indiana Natural, Scenic, and Recreational Rivers Act. The group has consistently opposed all public and private actions held incompatible with protection of the natural features of Cedar Creek and its associated ecosystem.

CCWP has for over forty years recognized the unique geology, history, and ecology of the Cedar Creek valley in Allen County. The organization has worked with The Nature Conservancy, Acres, Inc., the St. Joseph River Watershed Project, and many governmental agencies to protect Cedar Creek and the quality of its environment.

Cedar Creek state scenic river at flood stage looking downstream to Allen County from bridge at DeKalb County CR72 (County Line Road).

Curios Antique Club

Curios Antique Club was founded in February 1966. This club is governed by a constitution, by-laws, and the normal cast of officers and committees. Female membership consists of honorary members and twenty-five regular members with a waiting list of those wishing to join. Their purpose is to study antiques and promote an interest therein. Each member has an interest to contribute. With those interests and the programs presented at monthly meetings the range is from A to Z. Lessons are presented by members or outside speakers. Annual dues have remained nominal (less that the cost of one antique book). Meetings are held usually in members' homes the first Tuesday of each month, September through June. Several traditions held by the membership: drawing names for a Christmas gift exchange and purchasing something that person would desire; Christmas party; an annual day trip; and a June picnic.

(l. to r.) Seated: Sue Cserep, Margaret Mills, Lois Gooley, Gloria Laird, Barbara Wiesenberg. Standing front row: Donna Heckters, Rosemary Otto, Pat Sheets, Sue Arnold, Ruth Stoll, Zayda Coll, Darleen Butler. Back row: Phyllis Robb, Rosie Stech, Ruth Sprague, Janette Maidment, Christy Sittler, Sue Schlagenhauf, Sandy Mott, Sue Bonahoom, Nancy Wiening, Carol Roberts, Nancy Murphy. Absent: Mona Chambers, Helen Hemrick, Judi Andorfer, Maxine Coffman, Joan Dobbins. * Charter member*

The Embassy Theatre and Indiana Hotel

The Embassy Theatre, Indiana's largest historic theatre, opened its doors May 14,1928. It was built by the Fox Realty Company and originally named the Emboyd Theatre as a tribute to Emmaline Boyd Quimby, the mother of W. Clyde Quimby, the first lessee/manager of the theatre. The name was changed to the Embassy in 1952 when the Alliance Theatre chain purchased the Emboyd.

The Embassy impacted the entertainment scene in Fort Wayne from the beginning. With 3,000 seats, it was by far the largest and grandest of the city's theatres, bringing in the nation's top entertainers as well as first-run movies. In the mid-1960s, however, it began to lose its position as an entertainment venue and eventually closed.

When the building was threatened with demolition in the early 1970s, a small group of individuals headed by Robert Goldstine formed the Embassy Theatre Foundation, a not-for-profit organization with the goal of saving the theatre and hotel complex and operating it as a performing arts center. Many improvements in the 35 years since that time have been made including new heating/cooling equipment, a state-of-the-art expanded stage, improved seating, renovation of the pipe organ, and restoration of the Indiana Hotel lobby.

Today the theatre hosts the Fort Wayne Philharmonic Orchestra, Broadway touring companies, nationally known entertainers, organ performances, various music concerts, speakers, comedians, and a variety of local performers.

Early in the 20th century, community leaders understood the economic sense of building a large, opulent theatre. Their efforts made a statement about the value of performing arts to the Fort Wayne area. In return the community has continued to invest in the theatre. Today, through the generosity of the region's corporate and private citizens, the Embassy is able to offer world-class entertainment in a beautiful and efficient building that is truly a showplace of northeastern Indiana.

Fort Wayne Turners

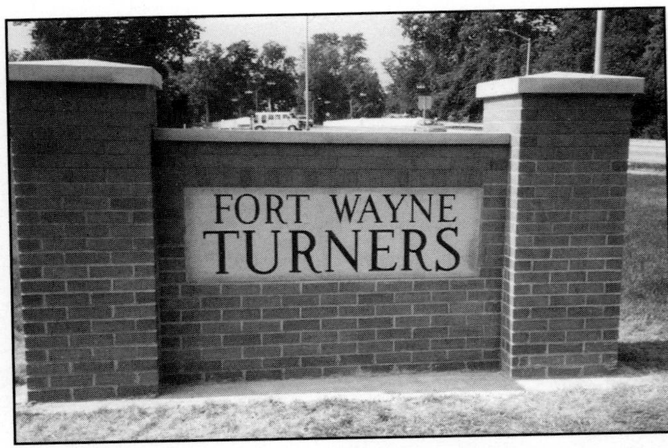

Fort Wayne Turn Verein was organized in March of 1865 and held its meetings in the old Randall Hotel on the Landing. It acquired the McCulloch Homestead at 616 West Superior Street in 1906 for their club. Ten acres of land and an old house at 3636 Parnell was purchased in 1950 and used as a "summer home" until they permanently moved in May of 1964. A gymnasium, two lighted softball diamonds, a children's playground, and two sand volleyball courts have been added since then.

In the late 1840s, during a period of political unrest in Germany, many left their homeland for the United States. They formed Turn Vereins similar to the ones they had belonged to back home. The word "turn" means exercise and "vereins" means club in German, hence exercise club, sport, or athletic club. The first American Turner club was organized in 1848 in Cincinnati and still exists.

Fort Wayne Turn Verein Vorwaerts changed its name to Fort Wayne Turners in 1941. Turners is part of a national organization of American Turners, a group to promote health, physical and cultural education. A major contribution to the City of Fort Wayne was the introduction of physical education into the public school system in 1901. Henry Meyers, an instructor at Turners became the public schools' Director of Physical Education in 1908, a position he held for 35 years.

Fort Wayne Turners is a family organization with activities for the children of all members that include gymnastic classes starting at two years of age. They compete on a local, district, and national level. The children are also instructed in softball, basketball, volleyball, bowling, and recently ice hockey has been added, and they compete in appropriate leagues. There are also softball leagues for women, men, and an over-55 division. Women have a sand volleyball league. Euchre is a favorite card game for a large group of members each month, along with a retiree's luncheon. There are classes for painting, quilting, and language.

The club participates in civic activities such as Germanfest, Johnny Appleseed Festival, and Three Rivers Festival. Fort Wayne Turners continues to promote our motto: "A Sound Mind in a Sound Body."

Fort Wayne Woman's Club

Fort Wayne Woman's Club was organized on March 10, 1925. The opening reception was held at the home of Mrs. John Bass (now the University of St. Francis). The object of the club was to form an organized center for the intellectual, aesthetic, and philanthropic development of its members and for the civic betterment of the community. Laura B. Moring was the founder and its first president.

The club occupies the third floor of the Chamber of Commerce building, 422 West Wayne Street. The women and the Chamber raised the monies for the construction of the building jointly. Therefore, it was agreed that the third floor would be specifically built for the Woman's Club. Mrs. Moring wrote that in the second year of existence the membership was 890 and the Club rented the Moose Auditorium for their headquarters until the club rooms were built and dedicated on March 9, 1928. Eventually the membership grew to 1,000, with a waiting list; it was one of the largest Federated Clubs in Indiana.

The Woman's Club has always been committed to the betterment of this community. It lent it's influence, labor, and money in the community's numerous war efforts during World War II, organized Christmas parties for underprivileged children, and has raised money to support many philanthropic projects in our community. In 1950, it's 25th anniversary, editorials in the *Journal Gazette* and *News Sentinel* paid tribute to the Woman's Club as one whose influence has reached every corner of the community, and recognized it as being a beacon of light during it's entire existence.

Famous personalities have lectured there over the years, such as Dr. Alice Hamilton, Carl Sandburg, and Paul Harvey, among others. There have been concerts, film presentations, and art exhibits.

Even though membership is much smaller today, the purpose of the organization remains the same.

Harold W. McMillen Center for Health Education

"Building Healthy Communities One Life at A Time"

The Harold W. McMillen Center for Health Education has been one of the crown jewels in Allen County since 1981. Over one million young people have experienced the excitement of hands-on interactive programs where learning is fun and the human body is portrayed as an amazing machine! This has made Allen County a healthier place to live because all of the youth are given the ability to make positive health choices when they receive this fact-based education.

The original idea came about in 1974 when a member of the Inter-Agency Drug Alcohol Council (IADAC) visited the Crown Health Education Center in Illinois. The leaders of IADAC were so impressed with the Crown Center and its programs, exhibits, props, audio-visuals, and the educators who combined health education with a dramatic flair, they decided Fort Wayne should have a center like it. With the help of Marv Fishman, the first project coordinator, the McMillen Foundation, Central Soya, and Jim and Lavon Kelley, the Center took shape and opened its doors in 1981.

Today, the Center has been the focal point for health education by providing 41 different programs in-house and outreach to 28 counties in Northeast Indiana and Northwest Ohio. The topics covered are in the categories of general health issues, drug and alcohol prevention, human sexuality, and anti-bullying. The human sexuality programs are taught on an abstinence (only)-until-marriage basis as being the healthiest physical and emotional choice. All the programs are created and taught by the professional teaching staff.

The future of the Center is based on being the voice of positive health choices for our future generations. Programs will also be expanded to cover the health issues of all segments of society. The McMillen Center for Health Education will continue to promote positive health choices by providing fact-based education which will build a healthier community one life at a time.

Kekionga Voyageurs

Pere Marquette in berets! July 1965

Heinz Wahl and nine others instigated the group on April 8, 1965. The group, organized for cruising streams in canoes and kayaks, became all-season with backpacking, camping, and cross-country skiing. In 1966 it was the first affiliate with the American Waterway Association. Annual $5.00 dues supported environmental groups. Membership peaked at 80, the median age of the remnant, which meets sporadically for lunch. Meeting minutes, outdoor survival tips, and trip records are in the Allen County Library.

Psi Iota Xi - Pi Chapter

Psi Iota Xi began in 1897 in Muncie, Indiana; grew throughout Indiana; and soon became a national philanthropic organization. The ninth chapter was installed in Fort Wayne on August 9, 1919 with eleven initiates: Gladys Becker, Martha Canaday, Gertrude Gross, Lorraine Gross, Victoria Gross, Meribah Ingham, Ethel Peterson, Velma Grossjean Rodger, Hilda Schwehn, Margaret Strieder, and Mary Zent.

The main recipients of monies nationally have been in the areas of speech and hearing, music, art, and literature. Pi has supported these areas as well as funding other needs in the community such as parks and recreation, and mental health. Preferred projects are long term, affect large numbers of people, and money is used for tangible items.

Psi Otes have donated thousands of dollars toward recreation in Fort Wayne: Psi Ote Park, Franke Park Nature Lodge, Children's Zoo, Historic Fort Wayne, Botanical Conservatory, Science Central, Headwaters Park, and the renovation of the barn at the former State Development Center, now known as Psi Ote Barn in Northside Park (recently renamed Bob Arnold Park.) Pi co-sponsored the Fort Wayne Charity Horse Show for 20 years and sponsored Tennis Classics. Pi received a Governor's Award and a State Award in the 1950s for recreational contributions.

The arts have been supported through donations to the Museum of Art, Ballet, Embassy Theatre, Philharmonic, and Civic Theatre. Many renowned speakers and plays were brought to Fort Wayne. Literature, music, and fine arts awards are given annually to Indiana Purdue Fort Wayne students.

Almost every organization serving children's and family needs has received funds or in-kind donations. The city was honored as Pi produced "Salute to the Stars" at the Embassy as a finale to the Bicentennial Celebration.

Pi members have happily waitressed, ushered, sponsored antique shows, made Hoosier baskets, held luncheons, published cookbooks, had garage sales, sold tickets and numerous items. The community has received nearly $1,000,000 from Pi.

Zeta Tau Alpha

Zeta Tau Alpha was founded in Virginia in 1898. The Fort Wayne Alumnae Chapter was organized in 1927, and chartered in 1934. The following were the 1927 members:

•Lillian Rolf (born February 11, 1907, died July 4, 2003), an Indiana University graduate, of West Rudisill Boulevard, was the first chapter president and a teacher at South Calhoun until 1971.

•Miriam Dinklage (born April 2, 1910, died March 1983), Indiana University, of South Wayne Avenue, was married to Theodore Benson and was a teacher and social worker.

•Elizabeth Little (born July 3, 1905, died February 2, 1991), Ohio University, of Indiana Avenue, was an English teacher at North Side High School until 1966, served on the National ZTA Philanthropic Committee, and was a midwife in Currin, Virginia for ZTA.

•Bernice Riebhart, Indiana University of Glencoe Avenue, was married to Robert Rumple.

•Helen Gerberding, University of Michigan, of Kensington Avenue, was married to Ivan Hitchcook.

There were fourteen members in 1934. There were 157 alumnae from 11 universities in 2004. They met monthly for social teas, card parties, picnics, and community service projects.

Notices were by e-mail during 2004-2005; meetings were informal and included community service projects such as the American Red Cross, Matthew 25 Health and Dental Clinic, and college scholarships. Since 1992, the Chapter has distributed educational materials, pink ribbons, and donated to breast cancer awareness.

They were awarded the National Gold Crown Award as outstanding Alumnae Chapter. They gave a statewide collegiate service award named after Anne Winnes Redmond (born about 1913), a Franklin College graduate, a member for 65 years, National Service Officer 50 years, and a teacher at South Side.

The 2005-2006 officers are Benita Sheets Steyer, president; Jessica Piwok Harris, vice president; Amy Rhoads Smith, treasurer; Erin Rode Adams, secretary; Susan Eckart Trent, historian; Sylvia Fleisher Stephens, calling; and Melissa McIntosh, service.

Zeta Tau Alpha Fort Wayne Alumnae Chapter. (l. to r.) Back:Erin Adams, Sara Esterline, Mary Winters, Marcella Ellenwood, Rene Weymouth, Jean Rotruck, Syl Stephens, Benita Steyer, and Joan Kelham. Front: Lynn Johnson, Susen Trent, and Gail Bradley.

The Barr Street Irregulars

The Barr Street Irregulars or BSI was formed in 1979 through the efforts of Freda Withers, a well-known history teacher and Historical Society board member. This group has through the years sponsored bus trips, served as docents for the History Center, raised money for museum projects such as the restoration of portraits, and volunteered countless hours to the annual Festival of Gingerbread.

One special project was the 1993 donation of $500.00 for the museum project of labeling. This labeling has a picture and description of the original use of each room when the History Center building was Fort Wayne's City Hall.

The name Barr Street Irregulars was chosen because Freda Withers was a devoted fan of Sherlock Homes and his Baker Street Irregulars. Because the History Center sits on the corner of Barr Street this name seemed to be appropriate.

This group continues to meet monthly to support the History Center, and provides refreshments for the Sunday Lecture Series.

Barr Street Irregulars

Early Childhood Alliance

Early Childhood Alliance is a nonprofit organization committed to building better futures for young children. Since our beginning as Westfield Neighborhood Center (1941) our services have expanded throughout northeast Indiana, to include quality, affordable child care in accredited centers, training and mentoring for early childhood professionals, a parent education program, and community partnerships advocating for young children and families. Incorporated–1953; renamed Neighbors (1963), Child Care of Allen County (1971), and Early Childhood Alliance (1997).

Early Childhood Alliance Building

Mary Penrose Wayne Dar Ball, 1925.

Mary Penrose Wayne DAR dedication of a bronze tablet on a granite boulder at the site of General Anthony Wayne's 1794 fort, located at the corner of Clay and Berry, 1934.

Allen County Memorials and Tributes

Standing beside the plaque given to the Allen County - Fort Wayne Historical Society on December 30, 1971, commemorating Samuel Hanna are (l. to r.) Roy Bates, Fred Reynolds and Harold Zeis. Samuel Hanna was known for spearheading the construction of the Wabash-Erie Canal, building Fort Wayne's first plank roads, and building the Pittsburgh-Fort Wayne-Chicago Railroad.

Memorial
James J. Hayes

James J. Hayes

DECEMBER 5, 1924, *THE FORT WAYNE NEWS SENTINEL*
REPORTED AS FOLLOWS

"JAMES J. HAYES SUCCUMBS TODAY

Was Former City Councilman and a Member of the City board of Safety

LIVED HERE 43 YEARS

James J. Hayes, aged 64, 1314 West Washington Boulevard, former city councilman and a member of the Fort Wayne Board of Safety for eight years, died at 3:04 o'clock this morning at the St. Joseph Hospital, death resulting from a complication of diseases. Mr. Hayes was born in Adrian, Michigan, and came here in 1881.

He served the Pennsylvania Railroad Company for 21 years as an engineer and upon retiring operated the Harmon Hotel for five years. He then built the New Hayes Hotel, which was opened January 1, 1906. Mr. Hayes retired from active business in 1918.

Mr. Hayes was active in politics for many years and served one term as city councilman, representing the Fourth ward, and was a member of the Board of Safety from 1906 to 1910 and from 1914 to 1918. He was chairman of the board during his first term.

He was a member of the Cathedral of the Immaculate Conception, was a past president of the Holy Name Society, a past county president of the Ancient Order of Hibernians, a member of the Knights of Columbus No. 451." *Submitted by Cornelius B. (Neil) Hayes*

Memorial
C. Byron Hayes

C. Byron Hayes

ON JULY 2, 1975, A MEMORIAL RESOLUTION OF THE ALLEN COUNTY BAR ASSOCIATION ON C. BYRON HAYES READ AS FOLLOWS:

"Mr. President, members of the Allen County Bar Association and friends,

A long period of service to the public in the legal affairs of the people has come to an end. We mourn the passing of C. Byron Hayes.

A native of Fort Wayne, he graduated from St. Joseph's College, Rensselear, Indiana in 1910, and received his law degree from the University of Notre Dame in 1913. During his many years in the practice of law, he was associated in different periods of time with the late Otto E. Grant, Sr., the late Otto Koenig and Fred D. Schoppman, and more recently, for the last 27 years of his life, with his son J. Byron Hayes.

Mr. Hayes was always interested and active in the affairs of the legal profession and held membership in the Indiana Bar Association, the American Bar Association, and the Allen County Bar Association of which he was a former president.

During his active life, he was active in the affairs of the Democratic Party and in governmental affairs. He served as the Allen County Prosecuting Attorney for two terms during the 1930's, and he also served as Associate City Attorney.

Mr. Hayes was active in religious affairs of the community, and in his own church. At the time of his death, he was a member of the Cathedral of the Immaculate Conception. He also served as a member of the Knights of Columbus, and was a past Master of the Fourth Degree.

During his earlier years, he was an avid golfer and was one of the organizers, as well as a charter and life member, of the Orchard Ridge Country Club.

In the practice of law, C. Byron Hayes was an aggressive advocate, and throughout all controversies remained a warm, human being with a fine sense of humor.

Mr. Hayes is survived by his son J. Byron Hayes and four grandchildren to whom he was devoted. To those survivors we extend our deepest sympathy as we share in their loss.

Mr. President, I move that the Allen County Bar Association give public expressions of the sorrow of its members upon the death of C. Byron Hayes;

That a copy of this Resolution be transmitted to his son and family;

That a copy of this Resolution be spread of Record in the permanent records of the Courts of Allen County, Indiana, to evidence the respect and affection of the members of the Association for its departed brother." *Submitted by Cornelius B. (Neil) Hayes*

Memorial
J. Byron Hayes

J. Byron Hayes

THE MEMORIAL COMMITTEE OF THE ALLEN COUNTY BAR ASSOCIATION SUBMITTED THE FOLLOWING MEMORIAL RESOLUTION TO BE SPREAD OF RECORD IN THE PERMANENT RECORD OF THE COURTS OF ALLEN COUNTY:

J. BYRON HAYES

October 22, 1920 - January 11, 1986

We meet today to honor our friend, J. Byron Hayes, whose fighting, Irish heart finally wore out on January 11, 1986, after an illness of many years.

Byron was the son of one lawyer, the father of another and himself a prominent member of our Bar for nearly forty years.

He was born in Fort Wayne on October 22, 1920. He attended Cathedral Grade School and went from there to Central Catholic High School where, as "Jughead Hayes", he was a fine and versatile athlete. After high school, he went to Notre Dame and received his A.B. in the fateful year 1942. He went into the Navy. He spent thirty-seven months on a destroyer in the South Pacific and attained the rank of Lieutenant. During this period he married Barbara Roth, whom he loved deeply until her death nearly two years ago.

After the war, he returned to Notre Dame where he received his L.L.B. in 1948. He served as an Assistant United States Attorney from 1950 to 1953, and he practiced for many years with his father, C. Byron Hayes.

He and Barbara had four children who were born in the early days of his law practice, Sheila, Linda, Neil and Mary Beth. He was always a devoted husband and father. He is remembered by his children for his kindness and sound advice, for his always being there and most important, for making each child feel special. No matter how busy his day, his feet were always under the dinner table in the evening.

Just as he cared for his family, so he cared for his clients, and for the whole human race.

Although he never articulated this, maybe not even to himself, he saw the practice of law as a means of helping others. He was a wise and patient counselor, and he was tireless in seeking to right injustices.

He served as Allen County Prosecutor from 1959 to 1963 and then, out of loyalty to his party, selflessly assumed a thankless job as County Chairman of a shattered party.

Throughout his life he was a devout Catholic. His was a warm and loving Catholicism, and he kept his faith until the day he died.

He was honored for his various activities by being named a Sagamore of the Wabash. In 1973, he was appointed to the Committee of Character And Fitness Of The Supreme Court, a position he held until he died.

He had a big heart, figuratively and literally. Physically, it was twice the normal size, figuratively, it was even larger. This courage stood him in good stead, because his later years were burdened with illness, his own and his wife's. He suffered a heart attack in 1981 and never recovered. In 1983, Barbara was diagnosed as having terminal cancer. He spent every possible moment with her until her death.

Despite these afflictions, he continued to face the world with courtesy and without complaint. He enjoyed his nine grandchildren, and he enjoyed lunches with his hunting and fishing companions from the old days. He enjoyed his time in the office with his clients.

To the end, he exemplified the good father, the good counselor and the good Christian.

It is appropriate to close with a passage from the Book of Isaiah: "He shall swallow up death in victory; and the Lord God will wipe away tears from off all faces."

It is moved that this Memorial Resolution be approved and adopted by the Association, with appropriate copies to the Court Records, and to his family. *Submitted by Cornelius B. (Neil) Hayes*

Memorial
Anthony Wayne

A ceremony in Hayden Park in 1920 to celebrate Anthony Wayne and to dedicate his statue.

Tribute

Margaret Ray Ringenberg

This speech presented by Margaret Ray Ringenberg shares her life story. We present it here as a tribute to her life.
Her family

Margaret Ray
1944

Here I am...83 years old. I look back at the decisions I had to make as a high school senior in Hoagland, Indiana. What was I going to do after graduation? I could be a teacher, a nurse, wait tables or get married, but I was fascinated with airplanes. I decided I would be an airline stewardess because "girls can't be pilots." Then I thought...what if something happened to the pilot? I thought I'd better take a few flying lessons.

And that is how it started. I took my first flying lesson in 1940 when I was 19 years old, and I loved it! I got my private license when I was 20 and soon after that I was invited to become a Women's Air Force Service Pilot, a WASP. As a WASP, I got my single and multi-engine commercial license and had the marvelous experience of flying all over the United States and serving my country in a time of war while doing it. After the WASPs were disbanded, I returned to Fort Wayne where I got my instructor's rating in March of 1945.

I married Morris Ringenberg, a banker from Grabill, in 1946, and we started our family. Life got busy, but I still managed to teach a few students. In 1957 I started flying the Powder Puff Derby each year. Suddenly I was FORTY years old...it seemed so OLD. Could I continue to fly? Brownies, Girl Scouting, and being high school band "Mom" soon filled my days, but I continued to squeeze in flying the Powder Puff Derby and the Air Race Classic plus doing some instructing and corporate flying. Before I knew it I became the grandmother of five awesome grandchildren and a school career day speaker.

Before I knew it I was SIXTY! Now it was getting trickier. It was harder to get insurance to be chief pilot for corporations because of my age. It was harder to crawl in and out of the cockpit!

As a pilot, I ventured out internationally for the first time in 1993 when I picked up a plane in Australia and brought it to the USA and then flew it in the 'Round the World Air Race.' I used my new international flying skills again in 2001 as a part of the Skytrekker team flying a race from London, England to Sydney, Australia.

I was featured in Tom Brokaw's book, *The Greatest Generation*, and wrote my own book, *Girl's Can't Be Pilots*. All of a sudden, people were wanting to hear my story. I was receiving invitations to speak.

I was thrilled when I was invited to address the Cadets at the Air Force Academy in Colorado Springs. They asked me if I would do a motivational speech. I told them I would be glad to, and we set the date. As soon as I hung up I said, "What's a motivational speech?" What I did must have been right. This Indiana grandmother received a beautiful standing ovation from the cadets.

In May of 2001 I flew the Illi-nines Air Derby with my grandson, and we won so now all five grandchildren have trophies with me. In June of that year my daughter, Marsha, and I flew the Air Race Classic and made the top ten. The following year the race ended at Kitty Hawk, and I placed second...not too bad for an 82 year old!

In 2002 I had a call from Johnson Space Center in Houston. NASA was asking me to speak to the ASTRONAUTS. Wow! Was I ever honored. They even arranged for me to fly the space shuttle simulator. My eighteen-year-old granddaughter, Jaala, went with me. I do think she was proud of her grandma. But when is it one is supposed to slow down?

I have now passed the big EIGHT O. Morris and I had been married for over 56 years when he died, so I am learning to live as a widow. I am a great-grandmother now and love babysitting. I still have the privilege of sharing my story with audiences several times a week, and am listed as a distinguished lecturer of NASA. (Funny, I don't feel distinguished!) Most of my flying is done on an airliner now. I am thrilled when I find a woman in the cockpit. When they find out I was a WASP, they are thrilled.

But I am not finished crawling in and out of the cockpit yet. I am still flying races every summer. I can hardly wait to see what the NEXT twenty years will bring!

Memorial
Morris J. Ringenberg
October 10, 1916 - October 1, 2003

On March 29, 2001 Morris J. Ringenberg gave this presentation at the Grabill Senior Citizens meeting. It summarizes his commitment to his country, family and community. We present it as a memorial to his life.

His Family

Serving in this community has been an extremely important part of my life. I want to share with you some of my memories. Perhaps it will bring back some memories of your own.

My parents went to North Dakota with a group of people who moved from Grabill to homestead. I was born in Brinsmade, North Dakota , in 1916. My father, Jonas, managed a lumber company during the week and preached on Sundays. Later when I was in grades one to four he was a full-time minister in Nebraska.

In 1925 my family moved back to Grabill where my father was pastor of the Grabill Missionary Church. I attended grades five through seven in a one-room school on the second floor of what was later Souders. My teachers were Ida Spencer and Abner Gerig.

From the eighth to the twelfth grade I attended Leo High School. My favorite activity was playing trumpet both in the town band and in the school band. I also loved singing in a quartet with Junior Bowen, Dale Beck and Jess Gerig. We took first place in the first barbershop singing contest in America. We sang on WOWO in Fort Wayne and got to travel to Chicago to sing on live radio there.

After graduation I worked for the Standard Oil Company delivering oil to area residents. In 1939 everyone was required to register for the draft. Numbers were drawn from a fish bowl in Washington, D.C. and read over national radio. My number was the first to be drawn. I went to boot camp at Camp Shelby, Mississippi. One day my commander came to me and said, "Morris, what have you done? A general is coming to the camp because of you." What the general brought was an invitation to play trumpet in the Army Band. We traveled all over the country playing both marches and big band music. It was much better than marching through the mud carrying a gun! I was in Hattiesburg, Mississippi, when a jeep came through town announcing that Pearl Harbor had been bombed, and all military personnel were to report to their units.

Morris J. Ringenberg
1943

From there I was sent to the South Pacific where my unit of the Army Corp of Engineering created airstrips on the island of New Caledonia. Every night we had to take cover from the attacks of "bed-check Charlie." I was on my way to Australia for officer's school when we were involved in the Battle of the Coral Sea. I was reassigned as an intelligence officer in Germany where I received a Purple Heart at the Battle of the Bulge. When the American troops met the Russian troops, I had my picture taken with General Eisenhower and General Patton.

After the war I returned to Grabill and prepared to start my job with Standard Oil again when I was offered an opportunity to start a bank. Several men in the community sent me to Bluffton for training where I learned every aspect of banking. Marcella Felger and I were the first two employees of the brand new Grabill Bank.

I married Margaret Ray who I had known from church when I attended First Missionary Church in Fort Wayne. She and my sister, Lois, were friends. Margaret and I did more at the bank than just dealing with money. We cleaned the building, shoveled the sidewalks, and fired the furnace.

I love serving the Lord and serving the community. I seemed to have two gifts to use: financial understanding and music. I started as chorister at Grabill Missionary Church as a youth. Later I was the adult song leader. I sang in the choir all my life and joined the Senior Saints when that group was started. I was treasurer of the church for many years and started the Missionary Church Investment Foundation.

Margaret and I were married in 1946 with my father as minister. We had a unique and interesting marriage because she was a pilot. I used to tell people, "I let her fly races, and she lets me play golf." We have a daughter, Marsha and a son, Michael. Now we have five grandchildren, and all of them are involved in music and ministry.

I finally retired from the bank in 2001 but it is my desire to never "retire" from serving people in whatever way I can.

Memorial
George and Marguerite App

George and Marguerite App

In the late 19th and early 20th century the App Shoe Store was thriving on Calhoun Street in the center of the "downtown" business district. Coming from Germany, the Apps were cobblers. One son, George App, married Elizabeth Brink in 1892. Three children were born of that union, the last a son named Lawrence George. When Lawrence was only three months old, his Father died. Elizabeth supported her family by being a seamstress and doing laundry for others. Those were the days of treadle sewing machines and scrub boards.

Upon the death of his father in 1898, little Lawrence became "George" and was so called thereafter at the request of his mother. It wasn't until "George" needed a copy of his birth certificate for security purposes during WWII (he was employed by General Electric) did he learn that his true name was Lawrence George. He continued to be George App until his death in 1978.

George married Marguerite Finan, a true Irish beauty, on May 31, 1921. Their son Bob, (Robert George) was born in 1924. After graduating Central Catholic High School, he went to Kalamazoo College. During WWII Bob was a B-17 bomber pilot and completed 35 missions over Europe. After the war he completed his studies and graduated Indiana University School of Medicine in 1951. He was a family physician practicing in Saginaw, Michigan until his death in 1993.

A daughter, Marilyn, was born in 1930. She, too, attended Central Catholic High School. In 1955, Marilyn was selected by the Junior Chamber of Commerce to be a member of an exchange program and served as a Community Ambassador. For six weeks she lived in Switzerland with a family. The *News-Sentinel* published the weekly reports she sent home describing her experiences.

In 1960 Marilyn married Ken Fahey. It was a good union. Marilyn with her German and Irish heritage combined with Ken's Irish and German background. Two daughters, Laura and Maureen, were born from that marriage. Fort Wayne has been home to members of the Finan and App families for more than 150 years. *Submitted by Marilyn Fahey.*

Tribute
Charles H. Buesching and The Lincoln Tower

The Lincoln Bank Tower

Charles H. Buesching

Charles and Lillian Buesching

Lincoln National Bank and Trust Company, at first named the German American Bank, was formed by Samuel Foster and Theodore Wentz on May 20, 1905.

Charles H. Buesching, age 16, laid the floor of the new Bank on Barr Street. His father, Frederick H. Buesching, was the contractor. While his brothers went to Purdue, Charles, who had migraine headaches, was put to work to learn carpentry and bricklaying and build himself up. One day, as he was laying the floor, Mr. Foster came in and asked him if he were planning on continuing in carpentry. With his usual genuine smile, Charles announced he wasn't sure. Where upon Mr. Foster offered him the job of messenger, at reduced pay, for the new Bank.

Charles was a native of Fort Wayne. He was born March 6, 1889, the son of Frederick H. and Johanna Hagerman Buesching. He attended St. Paul's Lutheran School and the Fort Wayne Public Schools, and then he took a course of study at the International Business College. During his early years, Charles learned the art of meeting and knowing people. One of the elements that made Charles valuable was his willingness and his aptness to cooperate in the building of the community and of customers who had the courage and skill to build their own companies. He often said he loaned money "on the character in the face." He was an active worker in the City's commercial as well as charitable movements and served as President of the Indiana State Bankers Association.

On the 16th day of June 1915, Charles was united in marriage with Lillian C. Busch, daughter of John and Elizabeth Busch of Fort Wayne. This began a partnership that was strengthening for both. Charles said that during the Depression, he would come home tired and care worn and Lillian would send him off in the morning whistling.

On November 19, 1923, they had a daughter, Joan Elizabeth who married William F. McNagny in 1949. Charles and Lillian adored their three grandchildren, and the love was returned.

The Lincoln Tower, designed by Walker & Weeks of Cleveland with the Strauss firm of Fort Wayne as local associate architect, was begun thirty days after the October 1929 stock market crash that ushered in the Great Depression of the 1930's. The Buesching Hagerman Construction Company, with Frederick "Buesching as senior partner, built the Tower.

"The year 1929 was important for the Bank, not only because of the stock market crash, but also because it was that year that the dynamic and powerful personality of Charles Buesching came into the presidency of the Bank. Having risen in the Bank from his first position as a teenage messenger, he was widely respected as a daring, yet responsible businessman. He was president for 29 years.

Charles convinced the Board to build the Tower, saying he would take full responsibility. They only agreed after taking an insurance policy on his life.

By then, the German American Bank had been renamed the Lincoln National Bank (1918). Ten years later, the Bank absorbed the Lincoln Trust Company and formed the Lincoln National Bank and Trust Company. It became one of the largest and most respected financial institutions in the country." Quote from Michael Hawfield "Magnificent Tower symbol of stability in Depression Era." *News Sentinel*, August 6, 1983.

Charles Buesching served the Lincoln Bank as CEO from 1958 until his death in 1962. He died of a heart attack at the end of a dinner in his honor for 55 years of service to the Bank. He died, as he lived, happily surrounded by family, Bank directors, employees and friends.

In the years following, men would stop his daughter on the street and, with tears in their eyes, would say: "Without your Dad, I would not be where I am today." *Submitted by Mrs. William F. (Joan B.) McNagny*

Tribute
Harvey G. Cocks

Harvey G. Cocks first felt the lure of show business when he, as a boy of 15, landed his first job "hawking midway concessions" for Paddy McMahon, a well-known circus owner on the East Coast. He always maintained that he "found himself" while learning the secrets of the Big Top.

Fire Chief Edward Loraine, Mayor Harold Zeis and Harvey Cocks receiving badge designating him as an "Honorary Fire Chief"

He was known as "that Cocks kid" in his hometown of Glen Clove, Long Island where he was born on August 23, 1904. His reputation had been acquired because of his bicycle exploits, antics in school and swimming and diving feats in his beloved Long Island Sound. One of his sisters said of him, "he was a character right out of a Mark Twain novel."

It was a local theatre owner, Harry Hedges, who became the strongest influence on his future life in show business. Hedges trained him as a 'gofer', stage-hand, usher and curtain-puller before exposing him to the ins and outs of film booking (silent pictures at the time) and live stage entertainment.

There was a brief three-year spell when he enlisted in the navy, with parental permission, and served aboard the battle cruiser Pueblo. During a leave he married his "sweetheart", Ray Drugan, from a New Jersey pottery manufacturing family. (A daughter, Jane, was born in 1923, and in 1925, a son, Harvey G., Jr.)

After his naval experience Hedges arranged his enrollment in a leading managerial training program conducted by Paramount-Publix Pictures at the former Paramount Theatre, on Times Square, in New York City. Practical training was received as one of the theatre's assistant managers.

The fledging manager was given the Fields Corner Theatre, in Boston, Massachusetts, as his first theatre. Next was the Allyn Theatre in Hartford, Connecticut, which was one of the company's major "presentation houses." It presented not only Paramount's major film product but featured live stage entertainment with many of the era's famous stars and orchestras plus national road companies of Broadway shows. He rubbed elbows with the likes of Jack Haley, Ted Lewis, Harry Richman, Bing Crosby, Paul Whiteman and Cab Calloway. Several became life-long friends.

It was 1929 when Paramount assigned him the task to seek the completion of the former Paramount Theatre and to create a gala opening in April of 1930. Then it was back to New England to the Paramount Theatre in New Haven, Connecticut and others that followed in Vermont, Pennsylvania, Ohio and Illinois. During this time he had gained the reputation as a premiere "trouble-shooter," saving many a theatre from oblivion during the dark days of the nation's depression. He was finally the reason that Paramount-Publix was forced to declare bankruptcy in 1933. The "trouble-shooter" services were snatched up by Warner Brothers Studio that allowed him to continue a successful career in Akron, Cleveland and Marion, Ohio.

In 1937 because of pleasant memories and the offer to become General Manager of the Quimby Theatres in Fort Wayne - the Emboyd, Place, Paramount and Jefferson - he returned to Fort Wayne. There was a short spell with R.K.O. Pictures in Syracuse, New York where he ran two theatres during 1939. He had, however, found himself homesick for Fort Wayne and what he referred to as "a great show town", so he came back in 1940 to pick up where he had left off.

He once stated that the next 31 years were his 'happiest". He added the Shrine Auditorium (now the Scottish Rite) and turned the small Capitol Theatre into the Little Cinema where the first foreign films were presented in Fort Wayne. During World War II he made sure that every major entertainer at the Palace Theatre also traveled to Baer Field to entertain the troops. He kept in close contact with the United States War Department to keep star-studded war bond tours booked into his "adopted hometown". Defying all warnings he presented the Pollock Brothers Circus on the Palace stage - elephant, tigers, trapeze artists and all.

Harvey G. Cocks at Palace Theatre Stage Door with entertainers from Pollock Brothers Circus.

In the early 1950s Quimby Enterprises dissolved their downtown theatre holdings and moved to Bluffton Road and the development of Quimby Village. It joined stores with the Clyde Theatre, the Stage Door Lounge and the Village Bowl as a bright entertainment center. The year was 1952. Helen Quimby, at her death, left the remainder of the business to her "loyal friend" who became President of Quimby Enterprises.

The colorful showman died of heart failure on March 23, 1971. The funeral home could barely handle the many local friends and celebrities from all over the country who had come to Fort Wayne to pay homage to one who many called the "the showman's showman". His funeral cortege was headed by the then Mayor Harold Zeis, Fire Chief Edward Loraine and a full police escort. Flags at the fire stations along the route to the Catholic Cemetery fluttered at half-mast in honor of the City's Third Honorary Fire Chief. The fifth grader from the small village on Long Island had truly "found himself."

Submitted by Harvey G. Cocks, Jr.

My Tribute To
Grandma Marie M. (Kelly) Disser

It's my bet that not another person on earth could say that he/she vacationed to Mackinaw Island and the Soo Locks in Michigan with their three maiden aunts, two widowed grandmothers, two sisters, and one set of parents, but I did just that in the summer of 1963! I have my Kodak Brownie camera photos that captured this rarity. This meant Dad was the ONLY male during this week's trip (a role which he would often find himself). The one major problem daily for our two-car caravan was finding "suitable roadside restrooms," while enjoying the spectacular sights in the Upper Peninsula with its cool temperatures. Although this was the most unique time spent with my Grandma D, three Kelly great aunts, Grandma Stella, my sisters and my parents, Marge and Bob Heiny, I have fond memories also of superb trips to Chicago's Pearson Hotel.

It was during the five years or so following Grandma's broken hip that seven of her local grandchildren (from the Ed Disser, Heiny and Welling families) took a weekly turn staying overnight with her for " nurse duty," i.e. "Just in Case of an Emergency," and walking to St. John's grade school or Bishop Luers from 4807 South Fairfield Avenue, where Grandma lived since 1952 in a new General Home. It was a great chance for each one's own "spoiling time" while sharing Gram's usual morning routines in what we perceived as preparing us a huge, healthy breakfast. A breakfast that consisted of juice, cereal with banana, a three-minute egg served in an egg cup with toast pieces, half a grapefruit or prunes, and coffee. I observed that Grandma daily put on her corset and a DRESS quite easily, but she struggled getting shoes onto her swollen ankles. She had me, "Promise to always take excellent care of your teeth since God gives you only one set," while soaking her dentures. Even today, I think of her words to me whenever I brush my teeth. Often, Grandma permitted me to brush her thick gray hair "while making her so gorgeous for Mike Sturm's birthday party" (obviously, MY first social event); plus we girls could play "Dress-up" with her girl's old gowns. Grandma ensured we used our table manners while playing Tea Party with dolls, so we could be treated later to Wolf & Dessauer's fancy Tea Room and speak to Santa Claus on television.

While most children fight over sitting in the car's front seat, we three girls squabbled more about who could walk

Marie M. (Kelly) Disser

alongside Grandma as escort to and from our car going to church, the grocery, a restaurant, etc. Grandma walked to daily Mass herself for many years because she never drove an auto, but she taught many a fidgety passenger to say The Rosary on long car trips.

Even before I was born, Grandma could easily enlist helpers for doing the household chores by saying "The Bishop is coming to dinner" or that "The Lord Lieutenant of Ireland might just drop by our house!" Also Gram's favorite Irish traditions, were playing her grand collection of music from Ireland on Hi-Fi records during the month prior to Saint Patrick's Day, relating the meaning of a shamrock while wearing her two large crystal shamrock broaches, and serving Irish Coffee to all visitors. Even the day before Marie passed away at Saint Joseph's Hospital she served Irish Coffee in her room to everyone.

And speaking of recipes, the few I have in her handwriting are some very special treasures in my cookbook. I remember best Grandma's Irish stew, snapping green beans, and baking apple crisp or those fantastic oatmeal cookies with me at her side. She often mentioned she missed having salt and fresh tomatoes or strawberries in her diet. She cautioned me to always clean my plate and appreciate all one's blessing from God. Grandma taught me to play Bridge at a young age, to plant geraniums each May around Mother's Day, and to send a birthday card as a remembrance of each person's special arrival on earth. Cherished toys from past years were kept in a hallway bottom drawer accessible for her many small grandchildren.

After Mass on holidays, the big family meals were spent visiting with so many or our immediate relatives that we rented the Keenan Hotel and later expanded into the Pancake House in New Haven to hold everyone, and where the fun lasted long in to the evenings.

Numerous snapshots of Grandma D show us grandchildren that she liked wearing a fashionable hat, but I remember more her beautiful chapel veils for Mass, which were of various colors and as gorgeous as her Rosaries. When the style for young girls' hemline got shorter in the late 1960's, Gram really grumbled about sewing mine, asking, "Why would any lady want to show off those ugly knee joints?' And speaking of "ladies," they were neither to chew gum nor wear slacks in public. I even have one photo of my mother, Marge, wearing a skirt while on a snow sled at Pokagon Park with her twin sisters and us three youngsters in snowsuits.

Grandma lived in her new apartment, an addition to my parent's family home at 1020 W. Petit Avenue, during the last few years of her life – truly special time for me even while away at college. For my Family Sociology class I remember making a poster presentation with a five-pointed star which had Grandma D circled in its middle because of her unique relationship within our nuclear family structure. She was mobile only in a wheelchair by then, but gave us each our centering focus and a daily impetus to venture outward individually into life's space.

As her last major undertaking, Grandma D gave freely of her considerable experience (eight weddings) toward the preparations for both my engagement party followed by all the pre-nuptial events during1970 for both myself and for Janet Disser Ward, her second grandchild to marry that August. Thus began the second generation's matrimonial unions from Grandma Disser's clan, and who are presently living scattered all across our United States.

Although I think my youngest sister is the lucky one, to be named after Marie Margaret, I thank God for the special privilege to know, to learn to watch, to respect, and to love my maternal grandmother. But more importantly, I am thankful for that unique and fantastic marital relationship of Marie M. Kelly with Edward J. Disser, which started this numerous, ongoing arrival of all their proud German/Irish descendants, my fun relatives! *Submitted by Ann Therese (Heiny) Long, #3 grandchild*

A Tribute
Tom and Jan Dustin,
Environmental Advocates

Tom and Jan lived in Allen County for 50 years. They served environmental issues not only in the County but also in Indiana and other states. Early in life they had formed a deep, lifelong commitment to the protection of earth's environments and the quality of life they sustain. They understood that long-term protection of clean and healthy environments underlies human health and economic stability, an understanding not yet respected by many with short-term interests. That understanding, together with their travelling, camping and backpacking experiences, fostered their environmental activities.

They educated themselves about environmental laws and formed networks in developing legislative and public understanding and support of environmental issues. They both worked willingly with officials and also against them, as their beliefs required. Tom was also an inveterate article and letter writer, on political as well as environmental issues and his articles were widely published. He corresponded often with Senators Stuart Udall, Paul Simon and Evan Bayh.

Both Tom and Jane were active members of the Izaak Walton League of America. It served as a base for their work. Tom served as President of the Indiana Division of the League and with it developed the support of many educators, scientist and activists. For many years he edited the *Hoosier Waltonian*. Jane's wide knowledge of laws and practices affecting environmental issues, especially those bearing on water quality, enabled her to become chairperson of the national League's Water Quality Committee.

Honored for their environmental work, both Tom and Jane received the League's highest recognition, the 54 Founders' Award, and more recently Jane received an IPALCO award. Among their favorite challenges and pleasures were confronting the Army Corp of Engineers and local surveyors and developers for their actions impairing the quality of streams and wetlands, and the practices of the Indiana Department of Environmental Management in granting permits.

Significant areas in Indiana in which Tom and Jan played key roles are:

• Formation with others in 1960 of Acres, Inc., the first land trust to be organized to protect natural areas solely in Indiana. It now holds some fifty areas comprising about 4200 acres, most open to the public;

• Establishment, with key local and legislative help, of Allen County's Fox Island Park, with its dedicated nature preserve and educational activities, widely used by school children and adults. Tom was President of the Park Board at the time and it was through his efforts that the Park was established in the face of severe opposition;

• Crucial public relations work in the creation of the Indiana Dunes National Lakeshore in the 1950's and 60's, by developing nationwide awareness of its importance as an ecological area of international significance.

• Passage of the Indiana Nature Preserves Act in 1967 (an important step for Acres Land Trust) under which the State now protects some 200 natural areas;

• Tom was a President of the Hoosier Environmental Council, a key organization serving environmental interests in Indiana;

• Jane's long efforts led to a significant improvement in Indiana's water quality standards;

• Passage of the Scenic Rivers Act to protect Indiana's natural streams, including their beloved Cedar Creek;

• Development of best management practices to counterbalance excessive stream clearing;

• Recognition of the significance of Big Walnut Creek in Putnam County and promoting its protection.

Outside Indiana they fought dams in Dinosaur National Monument and the Grand Canyon, supported protection of the Boundary Waters Canoe Area and sought to protect their most beloved areas of Wyoming's Red Desert, the areas around Steamboat Mountain and the Boar's Tusk, loveliest of desert lands.

At their comfortable home above Cedar Creek, where they raised three children, Jane was a gracious, thoughtful hostess. The Dustin's Christmas Eve parties were heartwarming – with Jane's delicious food, the Christmas tree rising to the high ceiling, festooned with lights and a myriad of decorations and surrounded by presents (many made by Tom over the years), and with the ritual reading by them and their many guests of "A Child's Christmas in Wales" by Dylan Thomas.

Perhaps the best tribute to Tom and Jane is the vocal appreciation of local and state government officials who recognized that Tom and Jane both put officials to the test of law and policy by devoting their knowledge, energies and commitment to important environmental issues. As one was quoted as saying, "They worked very had for what they believed in, and that's what they'll be remembered for. With people like Jane or Tom around, you'd better be doing it right."

Jane died in 2003, Tom in 2004. Committed to sound environmental values, intelligent, passionate, creative, unflinching in the fact of powerful opposing interests, they served environmental interests well for some fifty years. They left a legacy and inspiration for others to follow. *Submitted by James M. Barrett.*

Tom and Jan Dustin

The Dyer Family

A Lesson is Courage and Love

Bud Dyer, the son of William Pete Dyer, Sr., and Claudia Dyer, was born in 1936 in Toledo, Ohio. He had a brother, Pete Dyer, Jr., who now lives in Fostoria, Ohio, where the family later moved. Bud attended Fostoria High School and Toledo University. Pat, the only child of Dwight and Rosella Cahill, was born in Fostoria in 1939. Her family later moved to Lakewood, Ohio, where she graduated from John Marshall High School. She went on to Bowling Green State University where she received her Bachelor and Master degrees in Elementary Education.

Bud, Pat, and Jeneé Dyer

While Pat was attending Bowling Green, Bud and Pat met on a blind date. After Pat graduated, she taught in Fostoria, Ohio. They married on June 10, 1961, and moved to Forest, Ohio, where Bud ran a grocery store and Pat taught school. By 1963 they had moved to Napoleon, Ohio, where Bud ran a grocery store. While in Napoleon, they were blessed with the birth of their only child, Jeneé Lynn. In 1965 Bud became a food broker, and worked in this field until his retirement in 1997. In 1966 the family moved to Fort Wayne where Pat taught at Croninger, Harris, Lincoln, and Washington Center Elementary schools. In 1994 Pat received the Excellence in Education Award and was recognized for organizing the popular Young Authors Conference for Fort Wayne Community Schools.

Daughter, Jeneé, grew up in Fort Wayne, attending St. Joe Center and Northrop High School and Ball State University. In 1989 this family received the devastating news that Jeneé had been diagnosed with lymphocytic leukemia. She would go through chemotherapy and radiation treatments, and the cancer would go into remission. During these years she was a receptionist and volunteer at Cancer Services of Allen County, a member and deacon of Faith Baptist Church, and active in Big Brothers/Big Sisters of Allen County Inc., Camp Whatcha-Wanna-Do. She organized National Cancer Survivors Day locally. In 1992 she was matched with her Little Sister, Amanda, through the Big Brothers/Big Sisters program. Amanda was eight years old at the time, and they were to have several wonderful years during which time Amanda became an important part of Jeneé's life, and loved by Bud and Pat. In November of 1994 Jeneé was honored by the city of Fort Wayne as a "Hometown Hero" for her work with other cancer victims.

In January of 1995 the leukemia reoccurred, and she needed a bone marrow transplant. After a donor was found, she went to the University of Minnesota Bone Marrow Transplant Center, Minneapolis in March of 1995, for the procedure. She received her transplant and was in the hospital for 77 days before passing away on August 11, 1995.

During the six years of her illness, Jeneé went to a cancer camp in West Lafayette for adults, and was so impressed that she wanted to start one in Fort Wayne. As she was dying, Pat and Bud promised her they would keep up her dream of starting the camp. In 1996, after much hard work, Pat and Bud Dyer announced the birth of Camp Jeneé, an adult cancer survivors' weekend retreat based at the YMCA Camp Potawotami location near Kendallville. Camp Jeneé has taken the form of twice-annual long weekend retreats in the spring and fall. According to Pat, the highlight of the retreat was "the bonding that occurs in that one weekend, and the making of 20 plus friends that you never knew before." Registration fees are small, and no camper is turned away for lack of funds. In 1997 Pat and Bud received the Wayne TV 15 "Who Care" Golden Rule Award for their work in establishing Camp Jeneé.

In 1998 Bud and Pat were once again to receive heartbreaking news. Pat was diagnosed with ovarian cancer. She maintained a upbeat, positive attitude during the long years of often painful treatments. She continued to volunteer at Faith Baptist Church, Camp Jeneé and Camp Watcha-Wanna-Do, with one goal in mind, helping those in need. Her faith in God and loving spirit was an inspiration to all her many friends. Bud cared for her himself until near the end. She passed away Saturday, September 10, 2005 at her home. She has taken her beautiful smile to heaven and has been reunited with her daughter, Jeneé Lynn, and her parents. At her death, Bud established the Pat Dyer Memorial Fund to continue Camp Jeneé and to expand the program to help more of those in need. Bud remains active in fundraising efforts for leukemia and cancer patients. His work supports the Leukemia & Lymphoma Society, the National Cancer Society, Camp Jeneé, and Camp Whatcha-Wanna-Do.

In creating Camp Jeneé, these dear people, with inspiration from their beloved daughter and guardian angel, Jeneé, laid aside their own sorrow and replaced it with serenity, peace and love for not only cancer survivors, but also for each other, and the friends they met along the way. *Submitted by Dr. and Mrs. Robert F. Robb*

A Tribute to Helene Foellinger and the Foellinger Foundation

In 1935, as he was preparing to leave on a hunting trip, Fort Wayne Businessman Oscar G. Foellinger wrote a letter to his wife and two daughters. A successful newspaper publisher, friend of national politicians and leader in his hometown, Foellinger recognized that the people he loved didn't understand why he devoted so much of himself to business and civic affairs. It wasn't to get rich. "I have always looked upon it as merely the stamp of approval placed on my earnest efforts in attempting to serve my community," Foellinger wrote.

Unfortunately, he would die one year later, but his words inspired the women he left behind to keep alive his community spirit. Today that spirit survives as the Foellinger Foundation, which last year distributed nearly seven million in grants to Allen County nonprofits.

It was Oscar's grandfather who brought the Foellinger name to Fort Wayne. Arriving in 1836 from Germany, 18-year old Jacob Foellinger started a business and leapt into community involvement, getting elected to the city council and helping to start the public schools.

Jacob's son, Martin, passed the family's commercial and civic acumen to Oscar, who by the age of 32 had become a partner in the News Publishing Company, which owned the *News-Sentinel*. Two years later, he bought the newspaper.

As he built his business, Oscar also built community connections. He and his wife, Esther, played a role in developing some of the city's leading civic organizations and nonprofit community service agencies. In addition, he became active in local and national Republican Party politics.

The Foellingers had two daughters, Helene and Loretta. It was Helene, a 25 year-old editor at the *News-Sentinel* when Oscar died in 1936, who took over the family business, becoming in the process the nation's youngest newspaper publisher. Helene inherited more than a love for newspapers from her father; along with her sister, she also acquired his devotion to Fort Wayne. She and her sister and mother furthered the family's community activity, volunteering and giving generously.

When Loretta and her husband, Richard Teeple, were killed in a 1950 plane crash, Esther and Helene grew closer. They shared a home for a number of years, and enjoyed traveling together. It was during preparations for a European trip in 1958 that they created the Foellinger Foundation, hoping to ensure that their support of the community would continue even if something happened to them. When Esther passed away in 1969, she left the bulk of her estate to the Foundation, increasing its assets to six million by 1973.

The Martin and Christine Foellinger Family. Oscar Foellinger pictured back row center

Helene Foellinger in her office at the News-Sentinel.

Helene Foellinger (right) and her mother Esther Foellinger (left).

Helene served as the Foundations' board president from 1958 to 1987. After selling the newspaper in 1980, she spent the remaining seven years of her life in community service, earning the Indiana Individual Philanthropist of the Year award in 1985. When she died in 1987, her estate distributed seventy-four million to the Foundation.

When they created the Foellinger Foundation, Esther and Helene Foellinger sought not just to provide money to community organizations, but also to perpetuate the family's values and core principles of integrity, accountability, responsibility and results. They believed that nonprofit organizations can play a vital role by complementing – but not replacing – the government's efforts that address society's needs. Their belief that such organizations work best by channeling the commitment of many individual donors and volunteers had guided the Foundation's work as a grantmaking organization.

Today, the Foundation focuses 85 percent of its grants on organizations, programs and projects serving Allen County children and their families, especially those with the greatest economic need and least opportunity. In the area of early childhood development, the Foundation emphasizes education and school readiness, quality child care and child care worker training. In the area of youth development, it supports mentoring, out-of-school opportunities and youth worker training priorities, and in the area of family development, it puts family services and family resource centers, parent enrichment, family literacy and intergenerational opportunities at the top of the list.

The Foundation designates the remaining 15 percent of its grants for general community interests, allowing it to provide resources for programs that don't fall into its primary areas of focus but do improve the quality of life in Allen County. These include arts and cultural programs, as well as broader community enrichment.

Each day, organizations that receive Foellinger Foundation grants reach out to Allen County children and their families, continually striving to make lives better. In doing so, they're operating under the same premise that drove Oscar Foellinger to compose a letter to the women in his life some 70 years ago: a belief that it should be our highest aim to serve our community. *Submitted by Terry Stevens, Foellinger Foundation*

George C. Hood
1910-1992

George C. Hood

George C. Hood was born on July 4, 1910, in Paragould, Arkansas. He was a member of the Fort Wayne Fire Department from 1937 until 1964. From 1948 until 1956 he served as Chief of the Fire Prevention Bureau. George came to Fort Wayne when he was ten years of age. He graduated from South Side High School where he was captain of the varsity football team and earned All City and All State honors. He was also a member of the varsity basketball team and was sports editor and feature writer for the *South Side Times*.

In January of 1948 Democrat Mayor Henry Branning, Jr. appointed him Chief of the Fire Prevention Bureau. He was re-appointed by Republican Mayor Harry W. Baals effective January 1, 1952. During his tenure as Fire Prevention Chief, Fort Wayne was the only city in the country to receive three major awards in one year. These included best city rating, best radio coverage of fire prevention, and best industrial fire prevention program. George lectured on arson and fire prevention at Purdue University, the War Department, the State Fire Marshall's office, and at numerous fire schools.

Following his retirement from the fire department, George was chief of plant protection and security at the Winter Street General Electric Plant in Fort Wayne. *Submitted by G. Stanley Hood*

Memorial
Dr. Isaac Knapp,
Fort Wayne's First Dentist

Dr. Isaac Knapp
M.D., D.D.S.
1814-1883

Isaac Knapp was born on March 7, 1814 in Dummerston, Vermont. He received an M.D. degree from Columbia Medical College in New York, and practiced medicine in Pomeroy, Ohio for 10 years. Then, poor health forced him to change his profession. He apprenticed with a dentist, Dr. Wilson of North Bloomfield, New York for one year.

In the fall of 1854, Dr. Knapp came to Fort Wayne, then a city of about 13,000 people. He set up a dental office at the corner of Court and Main Streets. He practiced here for 29 years, and was the only dentist here for many of those years.

Dr. Knapp fervently believed that dentistry should be a profession separate from the practice of general medicine. He taught many "dental students" in his evening hours and worked to organize the existing dentists into study clubs, to exchange ideas and better their skills. Dr. Knapp was known to be a very intellectual and social man and an ardent abolitionist who worked tirelessly to eliminate slavery. In 1857, he was one of eight men who started the Allen County Republican Club.

In his later years, Dr. Knapp was associated in practice with his son, Dr. Will B. Knapp. Their practice consisted mainly of treating dental infections with tooth removal, performed with alcohol consumption as the only form of anesthesia available. For their wealthier patients, they also diagnosed and treated tooth decay by filling the cavities with gold restorations.

Following the Civil War, their office was located in the Keystone Building, at Calhoun and Columbia Street, the first building in the city to have running water and central heat. This era saw the introduction of dental amalgam as a restorative material for dental cavities. This combination of mercury and silver shavings was much less expensive than the gold fillings, and restorative dentistry became more available to the common citizens.

Dr. Knapp helped establish a statewide professional organization, the Indiana Dental Association, in 1858, and was chosen as its second president in 1860. He was also elected IDA president in 1866 and 1877. He was the vice-president of the national group, the American Dental Association, when he died on May 9, 1883. He is buried in Lindenwood Cemetery in Fort Wayne.

The Isaac Knapp Dental Coterie, a local dental organization, was formed by seven Fort Wayne dentists on January 20, 1891. The group was formed to provide social and educational exchanges among its members. They named the organization after Dr. Knapp because "he was the first dentist to come to Fort Wayne and stay. He had the reputation of being a fine dentist, a gentleman, and a cultural leader".

Dental operatory, circa 1880.

Judy K. (Potts) Koevets
November 30, 1948 - March 19, 2004

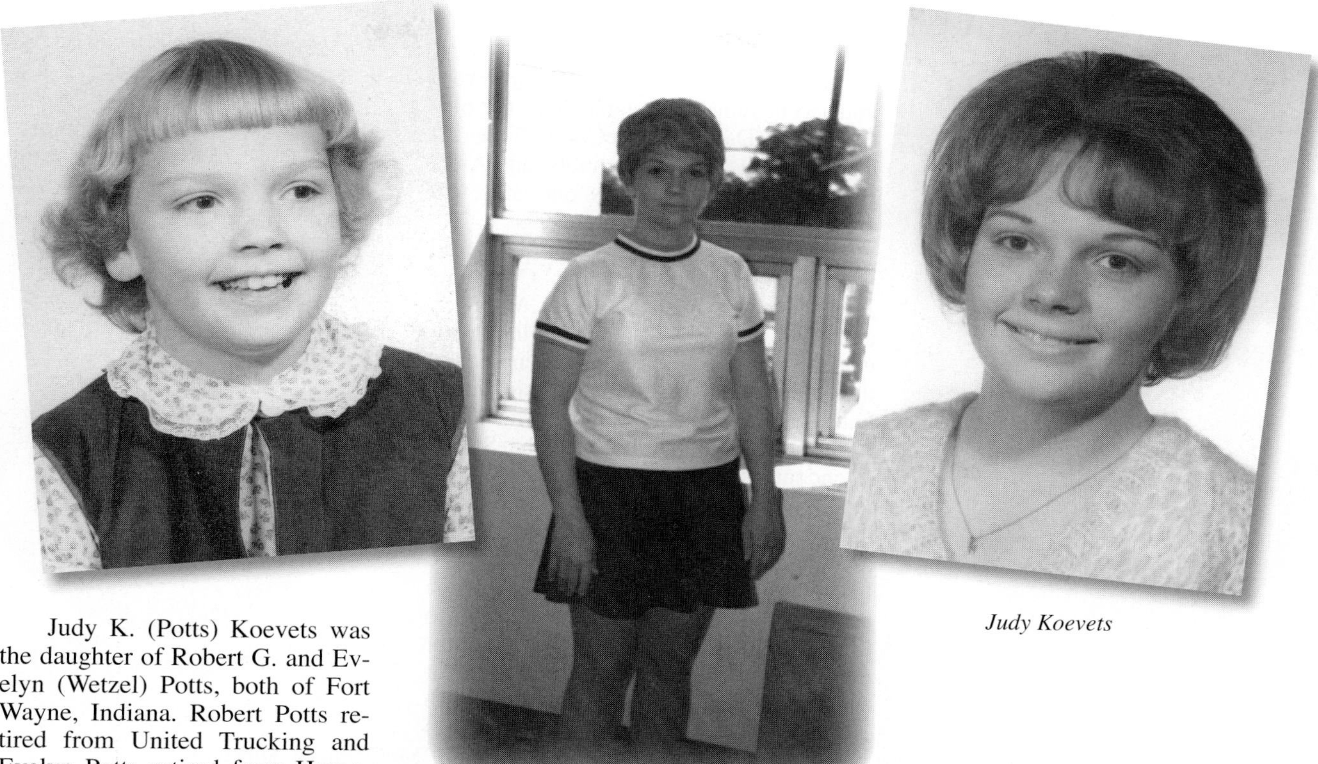

Judy Koevets

Judy K. (Potts) Koevets was the daughter of Robert G. and Evelyn (Wetzel) Potts, both of Fort Wayne, Indiana. Robert Potts retired from United Trucking and Evelyn Potts retired from Homestead High School.

Judy Potts attended Central High School, and married Steve B. Koevets February 5, 1966, at Bethany Presbyterian Church on West Main Street. They had three daughters, Cindy who married Chris Roberts, Candy who married Gary Brown and Stephanie who married Steven Weaver. They also had six grandchildren; Julia, Andy and Katie Roberts, Natalie and Nicole Brown and Haley Weaver.

Judy lived her entire life in Fort Wayne. She grew up around the Main Street area and had many fond memories of that time. She often talked about the Cremo, The Restaurant and Roux Drug Store, all on Main Street. She talked about Swinney Park and the Record Party at Debbie and Jodie's home, which also was on Main Street. This is the same area where she met our Dad, Steve Koevets.

My mother never met a stranger. We all miss her very much. Thanks for everything, Mom. I will see you again one day. *Submitted by Candy Brown.*

Julia Roberts, Natalie Brown, Judy Koevets

A Tribute to James and Madeleine McComb

James McComb

Madeleine McComb

James and Madeleine McComb were married in June 1925. James was the oldest son of David O. McComb, Superintendent of the County Schools, and Anna McComb. Madeleine was one of seven children of John and Rosa Burlage.

Both James and Madeleine worked for Horton Manufacturing Company. James was the Assistant Sales Manager, and Madeleine was Secretary to the President. It was after the birth of their second daughter in 1929 that the depression came with the bad times.

David O. McComb, still the Superintendent of County Schools, and Walter McComb, James' younger brother, had opened a funeral home in the family home at 1140 Lake Avenue. Walter was a licensed embalmer and in charge of this business. By 1932 people were unable to pay for funerals and the debts of the company had escalated. David O. McComb Sr. and Walter McComb asked James to leave Horton Company, and bring his business expertise to form a partnership with Walter known as D. O. McComb & Sons. James became the business manager of that partnership. He began with helping families choose affordable funerals matched with deferred payment plans. He started an advertising campaign with fans for every church and public building. James sought the County Pauper funerals. He offered free ambulance service. On Christmas day long-term hospital patients were conveyed home to be with family and back to the hospital in the same evening. He sponsored many civic events, offered free funeral home chair use to everyone. James had a free fireworks display on the Fourth of July in a vacant lot behind his home courtesy of D.O. McComb & Sons.

Madeleine helped by being active in community organizations. Like other women, she sewed, canned and even baked beautiful cakes for special gifts. Their three daughters, Betty, Pat, and Jeanne put up and took down folding chairs for funerals. Many time the girls led Catholic prayers for funerals.

By World War II, D.O. McComb & Sons was remodeled, out of debt, and well established in Fort Wayne. Unfortunately, James did not live to see the growth of this partnership. After three years of lung cancer, he died at the young age of fifty in 1952.

Madeleine, widowed at age fifty, needed to work. She applied her fine secretarial skills first at the Department of Speech and Hearing in the Fort Wayne Community Schools until age sixty-five. Then, she was immediately hired at the Library of Bishop Dwenger as secretary, where she worked until 1979. She often said with pride, "I chose to retire at age seventy six." Madeleine lived until age eighty happy with the love of her daughters six grandchildren and many dear friends.

James and Madeleine's modest home on Bayer Avenue was a warm haven, open to all neighbors, young people, and students in need of a place to live. They will be remembered as a generous couple who sincerely loved people. *Submitted by Patricia A. Wilson*

In Memory
Charles "Bud" Meeks

American Historian James Adams once wrote "The great use of life is to spend it on something that will outlast it." The truth of Adam's remarks was exemplified by the life and legacy of Allen County native Charles "Bud" Meeks . . .whose career of public service to his county, state, and nation spanned nearly half a century.

Born on January 31, 1937 to Roy and Esther (Bauermeister) Meeks, Bud graduated from Central High School in 1954, and promptly began serving his country by enlisting in the U.S. Navy. He married his high school sweetheart Marjorie (Crews) Meeks on December 12, 1955. Their son Brian was born in 1960 followed by two other children, David and Brenda, who were both lost at birth in 1965 and 1966 respectively.

Following his honorable discharge from the Navy in 1958, Bud worked briefly in private industry at ITT before joining the Allen County Sheriff's Department in January of 1961. In the 28 years that followed, Meeks served in a variety of divisions within the department, culminating with his election as Sheriff of Allen County by wide margins in both 1974 and 1978.

During his tenure with the Sheriff's Department, Meeks served as the county's first narcotics officer and took extensive training at specialized drug schools in New York and Washington, D.C. Bud became well known for developing and presenting drug education programs before local and area schools, colleges, and civic organizations. Because of these and other efforts, he was presented with the Outstanding Deputy Sheriff Award by both the Fort Wayne Jaycees in 1972 and the American Legion in 1973.

Realizing the importance of continuing education, Meeks graduated from the National Sheriff's Institute of the University of Southern California in 1974 and the FBI National Academy in Quantico, Virginia in 1978.

During his eight years as Sheriff, Meeks oversaw a variety of successful projects, including the building of a new jail in 1981 using state and federal funds, without increasing local property taxes. Meeks was also instrumental in establishing a new Communications Division, and laid the groundwork for the implementation of the 911 Emergency System in Allen County.

After serving the legal maximum of two terms as Sheriff, Bud was appointed Chief Deputy by incoming Sheriff Dan Figel, a post he held until his retirement from the department in 1989.

Charles "Bud" Meeks

Shortly after his retirement Meeks was appointed Executive Director of the 28,000 member National Sheriff's Association in Washington, D.C. where he served for eight years representing the nation's Sheriffs and other law enforcement officers. His varied duties included being called upon to testify before Congress, as well as lobby for more federal support of effective law enforcement at the national and local level.

The Meeks family returned to Allen County in 1997, where Bud was elected the following year as Indiana State Senator representing the 14th District, encompassing portions of Allen, Dekalb and Steuben Counties. During his time in the Statehouse, which included election to a second term in 2002, Meeks served on a variety of committees, including Chairman of the Public Safety Sub-Committee, as well as membership on the Public Policy Committee, Banking and Insurance Committee, and Corrections Committee. He was also known as a staunch advocate for increased state funding for higher education at both IPFW and Ivy Tech's Fort Wayne campus, where numerous programs and projects benefited from his support.

In addition to his career in law enforcement and polities, Meeks was also a well-liked member of the Indiana Air National Guard's 122nd Tactical Fighter Wing in Fort Wayne, where he served for 24 years before retiring in 1990 at the rank of Lt. Colonel. He was also co-owner of the Cedar Creek Golf Course from 1982 to 1999.

Charles "Bud" Meeks went to be with the Lord on March 22, 2004, leaving behind his loving wife of 48 years Marjorie, son Brian and daughter-in-law Renee and grandchildren Chad, Sarah and Roy Meeks. He will long be remembered as a devoted husband, father and grandfather, as well as a dedicated public servant to his county, state and nation. *Submitted by Marjorie Meeks.*

Charles "Bud" Meeks and family.

A Tribute
The Red Birds

50 YEARS TOGETHER: THE RED BIRDS REMEMBER is the title of the book written by Joe Taylor and his partner of those 50 years, Patty Corbett. The book takes you through each year as a diary of their achievements, their disappointments, and their heartaches. All the highs and the lows they experienced in their careers in country music.

The Red Birds (at first called Indiana Red Birds) were organized by Taylor in 1948 in response to a request by a lady locally to have him make a recording. Of the songs recorded that year was a tune he had written entitled "He's a Cowboy Auctioneer." The first song to use an auctioneer's chant, it was inspired following Joe's graduation from Decatur's Reppart School of Auctioneering and his love of western and country music. The cowboy legend Tex Ritter recorded the song in 1950 on Capitol Records.

Joe's wife, Pauline, had quite a talented younger sister, Patty; so at age 15, Patty became a member of the Red Birds. She became one of the first female square dance callers in the country.

In the 50s and 60s, the Red Birds broadcast live Saturday programs over WOWO and WGL, the latter for more than 17 years. Many of their guests went on to national stardom. For 16 years, the Red Birds opened shows at "Nashville of the North's" Buck Lake Ranch, Angola, Indiana, for hundreds of super stars, including Gene Autry, Rex Allen, Tex Ritter, Johnny Cash, Buddy Holly and the Crickets, Bill Haley and the Comets, Minnie Pearl, Roy Acuff, Kitty Wells, Roger Miller, Ernest Tubb, Red Foley, Everly Brothers, Jimmy Dean, Hank William, Jr., Pee Wee (The "Tennessee Waltz") King, Dolly Parton, Statler Brothers, George Jones, Mickey Rooney and the Lennon Sisters. The group traveled extensively, performing show and dance gigs not only in Northeastern Indiana but also many Midwest states. Taylor and Corbett wrote and recorded over 50 tunes for at least seven labels.

After more than 50 years in the county music scene, they retired the band New Year's Eve of 1998. During those 50 years, Taylor was recognized in numerous national country music publications. In 1988 he was honored with a plaque signed by Emmylou Harris of Nashville's Country Music Hall of Fame for his achievements and commitment to the industry. Taylor was one of just several Hoosiers among 1200 included in a 1995 book sold internationally entitled, *Definitive Country: the Ultimate Encyclopedia of Country Music and Its Performers.* Gov. Frank O'Bannon in 1997 named him a Sagamore of the Wabash recipient, the highest state award given a civilian. The Indiana State Legislature in 1999 presented him with a Resolution thanking him and his band for countless hours of happiness brought to their audiences. The Fort Wayne Historical Museum is the recipient of a multitude of items from their musical past to be preserved for future generations to view. *Submitted by Patricia Corbat.*

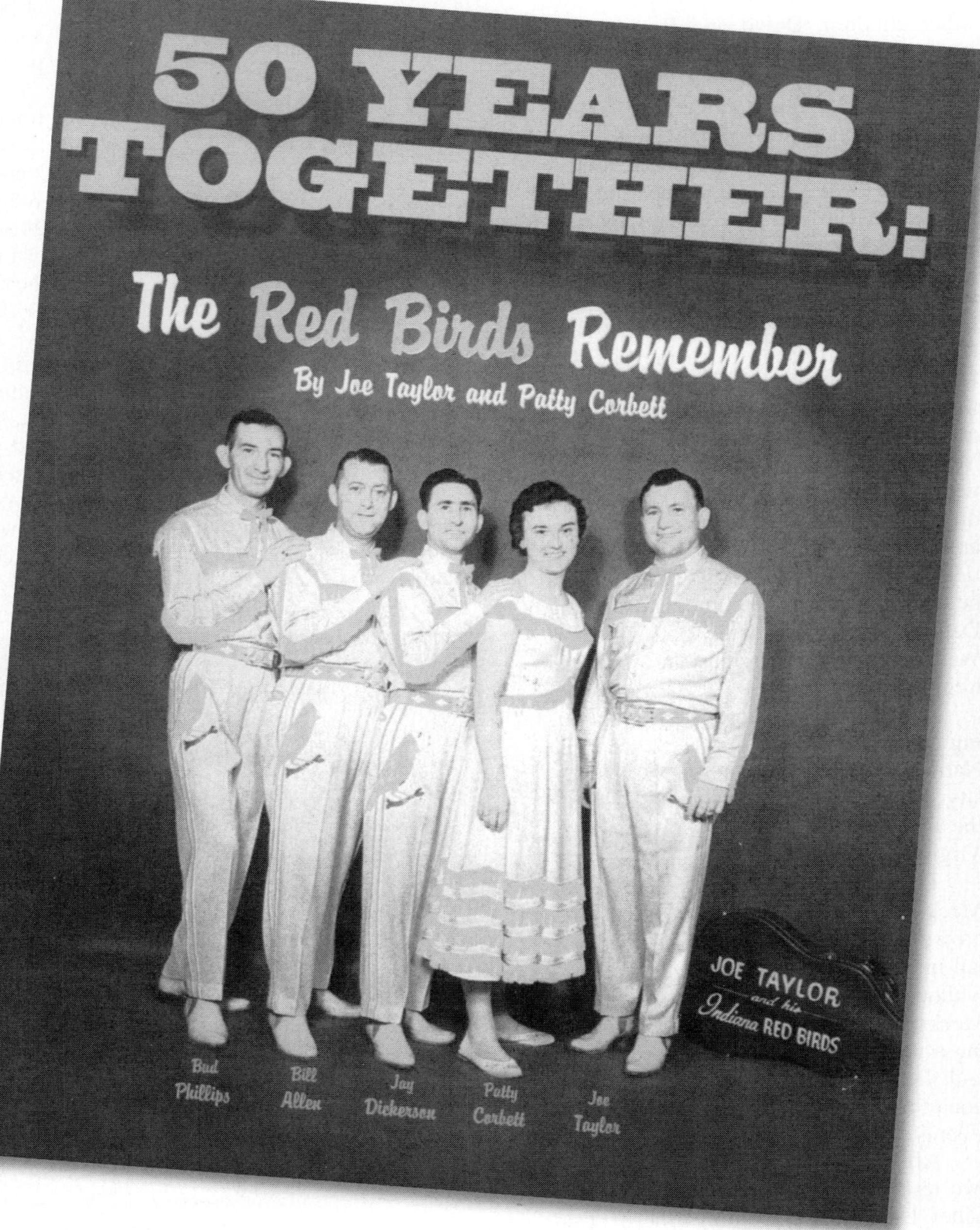

50 YEARS TOGETHER:
The Red Birds Remember
By Joe Taylor and Patty Corbett
JOE TAYLOR and his Indiana RED BIRDS
Bud Phillips
Bill Allen
Jay Dickerson
Patty Corbett
Joe Taylor

A Tribute to
Moss and Harris

(l. to r.) Mickey M. Miller and Martin P. Torborg, they joined the law firm in 1948 and 1935 respectively. Jeannette M. Frye was the secretary/receptionist for 35 years. Pictured in the background are two of the firm's original founders: Samuel Cleland (left) and Clyde Reed (center). John Eggeman (right), former circuit court judge of Allen County, was one of the earliest partners.

The law firm Moss & Harris dates back to 1926 when it was founded by Clyde Reed, Samuel Cleland and Abe Ackerman. After Judge John Eggeman joined the firm as a partner, it was for many years Reed, Cleland, Eggeman, and Torborg.

In the early years the emphasis was on trial work--both Cleland and Ackerman were prominent trial lawyers. Martin Torborg can remember doing little else when he joined the firm as an associate in 1935. "When I came into the firm I did almost nothing but prepare cases for trial, on both sides of the litigation," he said.

Ackerman and Cleland were also heavily involved in politics, the later once running for congress.

After Ackerman and Eggeman's deaths, Torborg becoming a partner in 1942 and Cleland's death in 1948, Reed and Torborg not only ended the firm's political activities, but also moved away from trial work.

Reed died in 1958. Four years later, Mickey Miller and Lindy Moss became partners in the firm, under the name Torborg, Miller & Moss.

William Harris and Michael Yates became partners, in 1967 and 1981 respectively. In 1989, the firm merged with Jerrald Crowell's practice, whose office was next door on the 18th floor of the Fort Wayne National Bank Building. Torborg and Miller having retired, the result was Moss, Crowell, Harris & Yates.

Current partners include Lindy G. Moss, William E. Harris, Kirby G. Moss and Parker L. Moss. They handle civil litigation, personal injury, trusts and estates, family law, commercial litigation, bankruptcy, real estate, insurance subrogation, collections, social security disability and business and corporate law. Other partners over the years have included Michael Yates, now State Senator David Long, and John Bohdan. Torborg and Crowell are now deceased and Mickey Miller is retired.

A characteristic of the firm is its community-mindedness, which dates back to the firm's founders. Reed served on the Fort Wayne Community Schools board for four years, Torborg for eight (including one year as president), and Moss for one. Torborg, Miller, Moss and Crowell all have served as president of the Allen County Bar Association. Moss is a past president of the Indiana University Law Alumni Association, Fort Wayne Rotary, Fort Wayne Quest Club, and Parkview Memorial Hospital. Harris served as president of public television station WFWA-TV, Fort Wayne Rotary, Child Care of Allen County, and the Association for Children with Learning Disabilities. Kirby Moss is a past chairman of the McMillen Center for Health Education and past treasurer of the Indiana University Alumni Club of Northeast Indiana and of the La Cabreah Community Association. He remains on the boards of the Indiana University Alumni Club of Northeast Indiana, the East Wayne Street Center and the Fort Wayne Urban League. Parker Moss is a former board member of the Ove Jorgensen YMCA and is very active as a consultant with Junior Achievement of Northeast Indiana.

Memories Of Margaret And Harold Sheehan

Margaret Ann (originally Mathilda) Gepfert Sheehan was born May 10, 1914. She was one of seven children of William Henry Gepfert (born February 23, 1877 and died December 7, 1922) and Edith (Ida) Charlotte Witte (born Mary 19, 1883 and died May 17, 1930). Margaret was the third generation of Gepferts in America. Her grandfather, Burnhardt (Barney) Goepfert and grandmother, Margaretha Weisenberger immigrated to the United States in the 1860s from Germany. Her mother's parents came to America from Germany and Prussia. Many of the Gepferts are buried at Lindenwood Cemetery in Fort Wayne, Indiana.

Margaret's brothers and sisters include: Edward Albert, Erma Marie, Charles Eberhardt, (all deceased) and William Frederick of Fort Wayne, Irene Augusta of Fayetteville, North Carolina and Edna Louise of Edgerton, Ohio.

Margaret and her brothers and sisters grew up in Fort Wayne. Due to the death of their parents (both to illness) when the children were young, all of them except Edward were taken to the Allen County Children's Home on Lima Road in Fort Wayne in April 1930. In a few months, Margaret left the Children's Home and eventually found an apartment in a home on Barthold Street. The owners of the home were Lester and Mable Rosswurm. Mable's brother, Harold, was living with them, and according to Joan Rosswurm Keever, daughter of Mable and Lester, this is how Harold and met Margaret.

Harold John Sheehan was born May 29, 1913. He was one of ten children and was the son of John Lawrence Sheehan (born May 14, 1869 and died February 12, 1934) and Bertha M. Poorman (born March 18, 1880 and died June 4, 1937). Harold was the fifth generation of Sheehan's in America. His great great grandfather was William Sheehan from Ireland. Many of the Sheehan's are buried at the Monroeville Cemetery in Monroeville, Indiana.

Harold's brothers and sisters included Mable, Irvin, Helen (who died at 2 years old), Richard, Rebecca, Russell, (Harold), Isabel, and Pete. All are deceased.

Harold at a young age farmed with his family and for neighbors in Monroeville, Indiana, and at age 16 went to work for the Nickle Plate Railroad. Later he worked at the US Rubber Company until the company moved out of Fort Wayne in 1958. He then went to work for the Dana Corporation in Auburn, Indiana as a millwright where he worked until age 64.

Harold and Margaret were married January 13, 1934 in Decatur, Indiana. Bruce was born April 28, 1937. Eventually, they moved to Sinclair Street where Dan was born December 11, 1942. Sandra was born July 23, 1946, and Rebecca was born September 11, 1947. When the girls were born, the family was living on Third Street. In 1950 Harold and Margaret purchased a home "in the country" with nine acres on Goshen Road (Highway 33).

Margaret and Harold Sheehan and Family.

Harold and Margaret loved to square and round dance, and when they were young would go out almost every Saturday night. In 1934 Harold bought a '34 Chevrolet and paid $600.00 for it according to "Aunt Irene" who lived with them at that time. It was all about family back in those days. Families gathered regularly to play cards (euchre and pinochle) eat meals and enjoy each other's company. Both Margaret and Harold lived through the Depression and World War II and would tell about the rations (War Ration Books) and shortages during the war. Harold and Margaret were both cigarette smokers (Camels) as were many people in those days.

Although Margaret and Harold did not finish high school, both of them were hard workers and provided a good living for the family. Margaret worked at several different places: GE on Winter Street, the Fort Wayne Tailoring Company, ARA Food Services, ITT, and at Fort Wayne National Bank. Margaret did not drive (although she did have a driver's license). Margaret was one of the founders of the Hamlyn Club (connected to the Purdue Extension) in 1952. It was a homemaker's club, and many women on Goshen Road were invited to join. Margaret made many long lasting friendships through this organization.

Harold and Margaret were baptized Lutherans and attended Trinity English Lutheran Church downtown Fort Wayne, St. John's Lutheran Church in Lake Township and St. Matthew's Lutheran Church on Goshen Road.

Most of Harold and Margaret's time in the 50s and 60s was spent remodeling the home on Goshen Road. It took many years, but the end result was a beautiful home with a manicured lawn containing several flower gardens and a large vegetable garden behind the barn. Harold and Margaret were loyal Democrats and daily read the *Fort Wayne Journal Gazette* from cover to cover. Both worked at Aunt Becky's (Rebecca Sheehan Youse) tavern in Elmira, Indiana during the middle 50s. Aunt Becky developed cancer and needed help on Saturday nights to bartend and wait tables. Young Sandy and Becky even went along and washed dishes and made salads.

Because vacations were seldom an option, since Harold would take the extra pay to help supplement the family income, but the family did get away for a week at Crooked Lake in 1958.

Sadly, Margaret at age 54 developed a blood clot and died July 15, 1968 at St. Joseph Hospital in Fort Wayne. Harold remarried in 1969 to Lavon Comment Geis. Harold died of long cancer and heart problems on February 28, 1977 at Parkview Hospital. Both Harold and Margaret are buried at the Monroeville Cemetery. *Submitted by Sandy Sheehan Getts.*

R. Nelson Snider
1898-1976

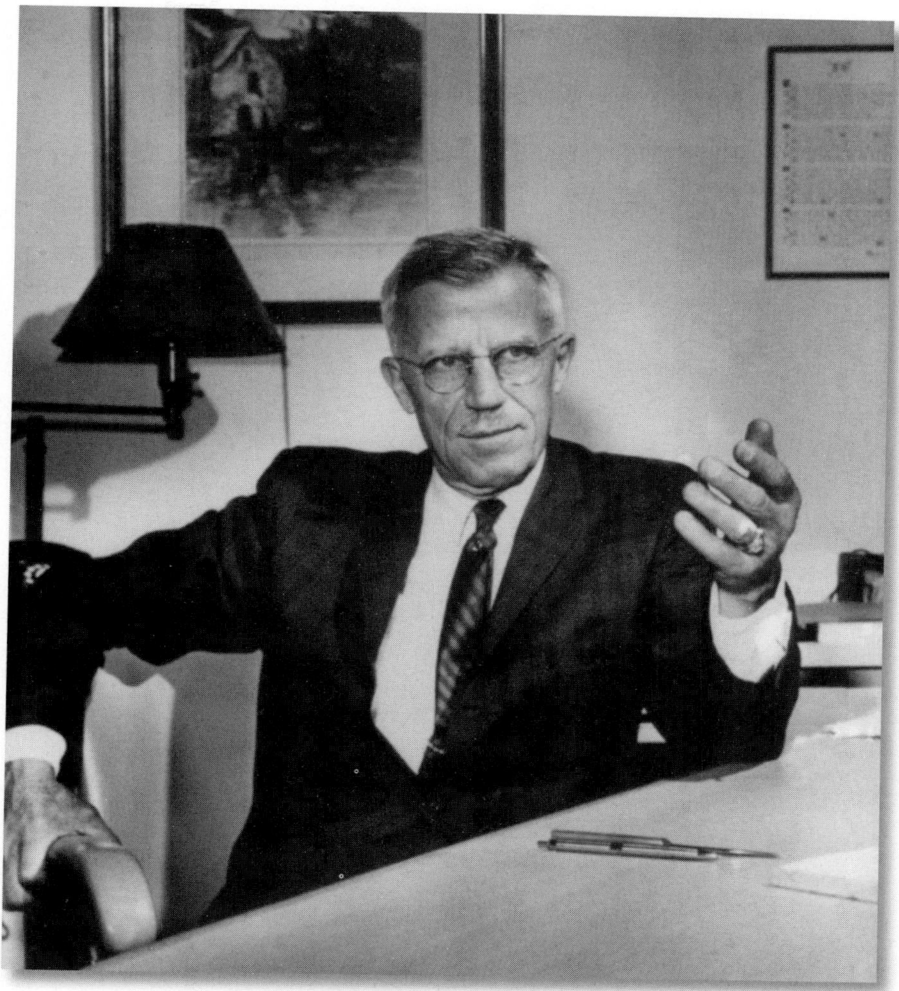

R. Nelson Snider

Roy Nelson Snider was born January 4, 1898, in the village of DeSoto, located in Delaware County, Indiana. In 1914, Mr. Snider graduated from DeSoto High School at the age of 16, being the youngest member of his graduating class. He then entered Indiana Normal School in Muncie (later Ball State University) for the twelve week course to obtain his teacher's license. He began teaching in a one-room schoolhouse in Delaware County when he was 17 years of age. His salary was two dollars and fifty cents per day, in addition, he served as janitor.

R. Nelson Snider received his bachelor's degree in 1922 and was elected president of the junior and senior classes as well as serving as captain of the Ball State basketball team. In 1922 Mr. Snider came to Fort Wayne and was the youngest principal in the school system. He served first at the old Jefferson School located at the corner of Jefferson and Fairfield and then at James H. Smart located on Pontiac Street.

In 1926, R. Nelson Snider, twenty-eight years of age, was named principal at South Side High School. He served in that capacity for thirty-seven years until his retirement in 1963. During this time more than 14,000 young people earned their South Side diplomas under his supervision. Mr. Snider received his masters degree from Columbia University in New York City and was awarded an honorary Doctor of Laws degree from Ball State University. During his long and outstanding career in education, Mr. Snider served on the executive committee of the prestigious North Central Association of Colleges and Secondary Schools. In addition, he was extremely active in civic affairs holding membership in the Quest Club and Fortnightly Club. He also served as president of the Rotary Club. Always in demand as a public speaker, he authored a presentation entitled "The Anatomy of Humor." This presentation, given first as a Quest Club paper in 1944, was repeated more than 700 times over the years, always to the delight of the audiences.

When Mr. Snider retired as South Side principal in 1963 he was honored by more than 5,000 former students and friends at a gala farewell party held at Memorial Coliseum. R. Nelson Snider High School in Fort Wayne was named in his honor. At the dedication of this school in 1963 Mr. Snider received a congratulatory telegram from then President of the United States, John F. Kennedy. On September 2, 1925, Mr. Snider was married to the former Reba Houck. Their marriage lasted more than fifty years until the death of R. Nelson Snider in 1976. Mr. and Mrs. Snider had no children. In an editorial appearing shortly after his death, the *News-Sentinel* stated "If the measure of our days rests on our influence on others, R. Nelson Snider casts a longer shadow than most." *Submitted by G. Stanley Hood.*

Jack Edward Weicker
1924-2001

Jack Edward Weicker

Jack Edward Weicker was born in Harlan, Indiana. He lived his early years in East Allen County, attending a one room country school, and graduating valedictorian of his Harlan High School class of 1942. In 1947 he received an A.B. Degree, Magna Cum Laude, from Indiana University. He received an M.A. Degree in history in 1950 and completed the course work for a Ph.D in 1951.

Active in education all of his life, he served as Teacher, College Counselor, and Assistant Principal at South Side High School until he became Principal in 1963. He retired as Principal in 1990.

He received the title of Principal Emeritus of South Side High School in 1996. He was appointed to two terms on the State Scholarship Commission by Governors Whitcomb and Bowen. He was a member as past president of the Fort Wayne Principal's Association, as well as a member of the National Association of Secondary School Principals and the Indiana Secondary School Administrators Association. He was also a proud member of Phi Beta Kappa, Phi Delta Kappa, and Phi Alpha Theta.

Jack co authored, *Indiana, The Hoosier State*, which was used as a school text by scores of Indiana children, and wrote many published articles.

Honors included Ball State University "Principal of the Year" Award, and Indiana Secondary School Administrator's "Outstanding Principal of the Year Award." Region 2. He also received the "Sagamore of the Wabash" Award from Governor Evan Bayh.

Active in the community, he was a member of First Christian Church (Disciples of Christ) of Fort Wayne, where he taught Sunday School and served as a church elder for many years. He was a member and past president of Fort Wayne Rotary Club, Quest Club, and Fortnightly Club.

He was married to his wife Janet Kathryn for 53 years. They had four children, John Henry, Kathryn Ann, Jane Elizabeth and Emily Jo.

In 2002 the Fort Wayne Community Schools and South Side High School honored the long time service and memory of Mr. Weicker, by officially naming the stadium located at the school, the "JACK E. WEICKER STADIUM." *Submitted by John H. Weicker.*

A Tribute to
Paul Eugene Brumbaugh

Paul Eugene Brumbaugh

Paul Eugene Brumbaugh was born in the bedroom of his parent's Noble County farmhouse. He attended Jefferson Township Elementary, a one-room school, through the eighth grade. At Albion High School he played basketball, ran track, and worked at the Kroger store, but he was primarily recognized for his voice, a powerful tenor.

After graduating he moved to Arcola in Allen County. He married his high school sweetheart, Betty Forker, and with his dad and brother, owned and operated Brumbaugh IGA. His gregarious and enthusiastic nature drew him quickly into the community. He was one of the original members of the Arcola Volunteer Fire Department, a charter member of the Arcola Lions Club, and sang in local productions and celebrations. In fact, he was given to singing spontaneously in almost any situation!

Passionate in serving others, he found a perfect fit with the philosophy of the Lions Clubs of America. He served the community through his local club, and has taken an active role in the larger organization. He was one of the youngest District Governors in Indiana, and was honored in 2004 with the prestigious Melvin Jones Award.

Following the sale of the family business in 1973, Paul answered other calls to public service. He served on the Allen County Fairgrounds Board since its inception. He helped organize and was a member of the Allen County Sewer District. Then in 1982, he ran for a seat on the Allen County Council, which he won and held for twenty years. As a councilman, he represented his constituents with honesty and common sense. His consistent intentions were to preserve the principles of representative government.

Paul is retired, living in Fort Wayne with Betty, his wife of 57 years. He remains and active member of the Arcola United Methodist Church, the Arcola Lions Club, and Sol D. Bayless Masonic Lodge. He sings in his church choir as well as the Scottish Rite Choir, and enjoys working with local youth each year in the "We the People" competition. *Submitted by Susan Pape.*

Memorial
Louis F. Crosby

Louis F. Crosby was born in Cleveland, Ohio on February 14, 1888. He moved to Fort Wayne, Indiana two years later when his father, who was a locomotive engineer on the Nickle Plate Railroad, was transferred to this city. He was the son of Elbert N. and Louisa M. Crosby. He had one brother, Charles N. Crosby.

Mr. Crosby attended the Fort Wayne Public Schools and received his A.B. and LLB degrees from the University of Michigan in 1913. While at Michigan, he was a member of Phi Kappa Sigma fraternity and the center on the Law College football team.

Mr. Crosby began his practice of law in Fort Wayne following his graduation from the University of Michigan and his admission to the Indiana bar. He joined Charles Neizer in 1914. From 1915 to 1922 he was a member of the law firm of Neizer, Crosby, and Murphy. Mr. Crosby served as deputy prosecuting attorney of Allen County from January 1918 until 1922 except for the time he was in the service in the U. S. Navy. He was honorably discharged from the Navy in 1919.

Elected prosecuting attorney in November 1920, he filled that office until January 1924. From 1926 to 1930 Mr. Crosby served as City Attorney in the administration of Mayor William C. Geake. In 1935 he was appointed City Controller of the city of Fort Wayne, a position he held until his death on October 13, 1943.

He was a 32nd degree Scottish Rite Mason, a member of the Fort Wayne Chamber of Commerce, Fort Wayne Post No. 47, American Legion, Allen County Republican Club, Fort Wayne Chapter, Citizens' Historical Society, and the Elk's Lodge, of which he was a past exalted ruler and past district deputy exalted ruler.

Mr. Crosby was married to Margaret Rippe on February 14, 1928. They had two children, Carolyn L. Crosby and Garet N. Crosby. *Submitted by Carolyn L. Crosby and Garet N. Crosby.*

Louis F. Crosby

Memorial
John R. Hartman

John R. Hartman (1904-1966) was born in Fort Wayne, Indiana, on October 4, 1904 to John Henry and Frances (Thurkettle) Hartman. He resided in the same house his entire life at 2238 N. Clinton Street, Fort Wayne.

On June 26, 1926, he married Mildred L. Reynolds, (1906-200_) daughter of Louis C. and Ida E. (Brown) Reynolds. To this union were born four children: June J., Phyllis A., John D., and Marilyn A. Hartman. After completing training as a journeyman plumber, Mr. Hartman founded North Side Plumbing & Heating in 1929 and operated the business until he entered politics in 1960. He son, John D. Hartman, succeeded him in the business.

Mr. Hartman was a graduate of Central High School and a member of Trinity Methodist Church. He was also a member of Maumee Lodge 725, F & A.M., Central Lions Club, and Allen County Republican Club. In addition he was a life member of the Allen County-Fort Wayne Historical Society and was a first aid instructor for the American Red Cross. Mr. Hartman was the first chairman of the Fort Wayne State School Volunteer Services and he served on the advisory committee of that organization. He was a former chairman of the Allen County Civil Defense Rescue Service and was a merit badge counselor for the Boy Scouts of America. He was a past president of the Fort Wayne Plumbers Association and a member of the Fort Wayne Foreman's Club.

Mr. Hartman was active in the Republican Party and was elected Allen County Commissioner in 1960. As a Commissioner he worked with the City and County Governments to formulate the plans and financing of the new City County Building. He also worked for the expansion of the All County Home. He was a member of the County Commissioners Association of Indiana. While serving his second term, and as president of the Board of County Commissioners, Mr. Hartman died of a heart attack on February 17, 1966. He was buried in Lindenwood Cemetery. *Submitted by Sharon Hartman.*

John R. Hartman

Memorial
Dr. Martin E. Leininger

Dr. Martin E. Leininger

Dr. Martin E. Leininger practiced dentistry for most of his 54 years at 304 East Wayne Street at Barr Street. West of the building was the Barr Street Market. From his second floor dental office you could see the produce trucks and farmers buggies lined up to their stalls.

Dr. Leininger graduated from Loyola University Dental School in 1910. He moved to Fort Wayne shortly after that. In 1964 in Indianapolis, he was honored by The Indiana Dental Association as the Indiana Dentist of the Year. He retired in 1966. *Submitted by Marcile Keck.*

The office of Dr. Martin E. Leininger at 304 East Wayne Street.

Allen County Schools

History of Fort Wayne & Allen County, Indiana

1700 2005

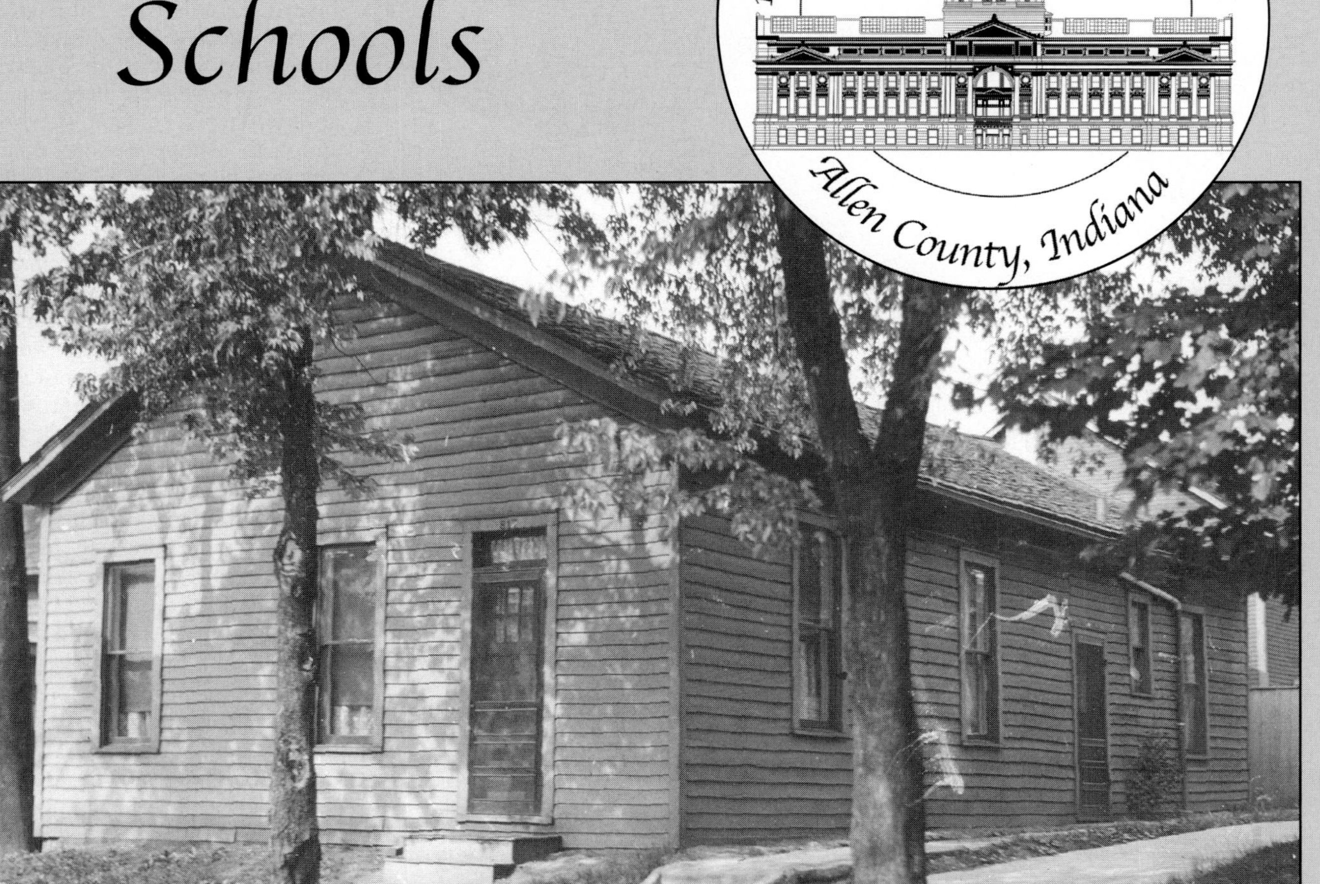

Fort Wayne's first public school building was built in 1838 by Alexander McJunkin on the east side of Lafayette between Berry and Wayne Streets. Initially a private subscription school, it reopened in 1853 as a public or "free" school. By the 1850s, the Clay School and the Jefferson School were built, which may have rendered this school unnecessary. It continued to stand into the twentieth century.

Bishop Dwenger High School

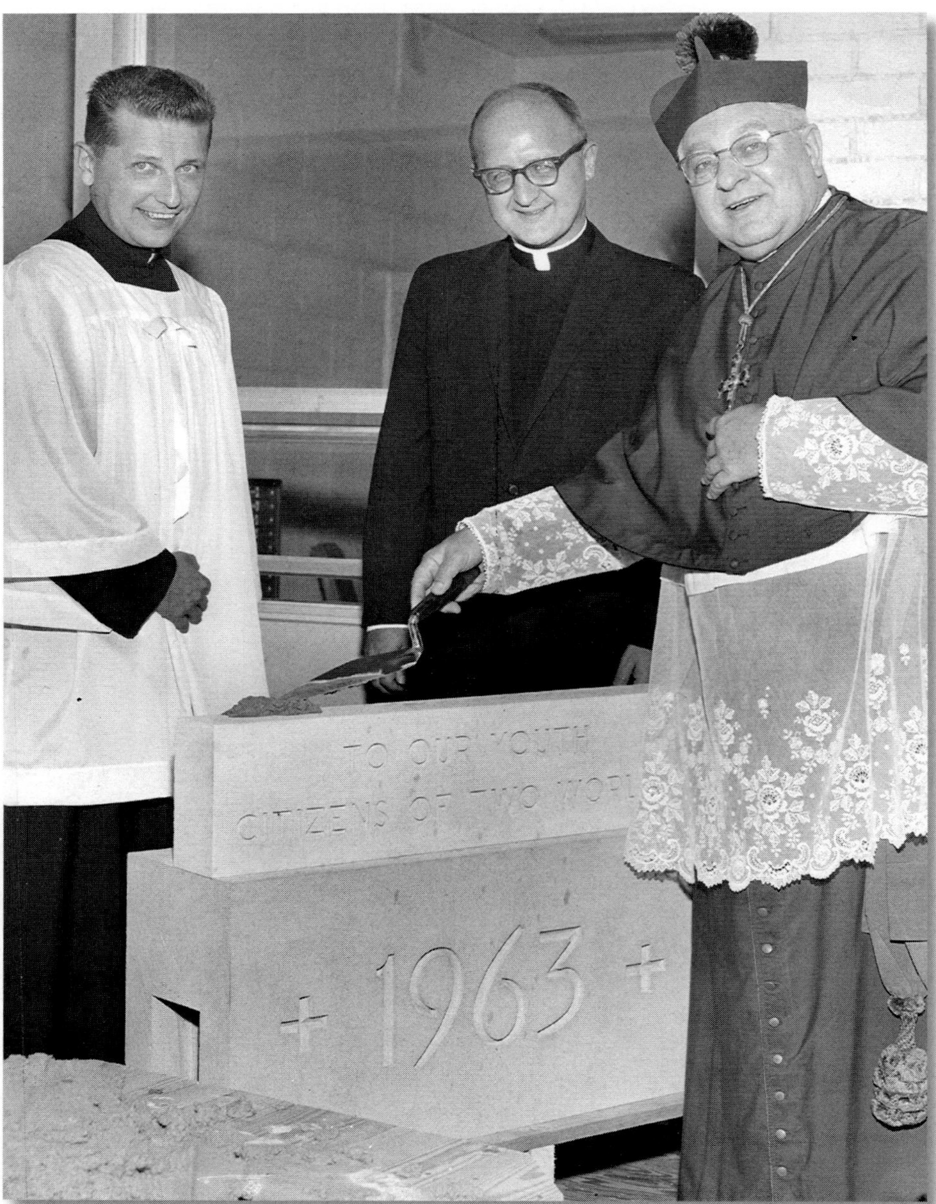

(l. to r.) Fr. Edward Krason (1st principal), Msgr. William Lester (Superintendent of Schools) and Bishop Leo A. Pursley prepare to lay the cornerstone for the newly constructed Bishop Dwenger High School.

Anticipating the growing educational needs of Fort Wayne Catholics, Bishop Leo A. Pursley, D.D., launched an effort to construct a series of secondary schools within the diocese. One of those schools became Bishop Dwenger High School, named after the second bishop of the Fort Wayne diocese.

Ground was broken for the structure on October 21, 1962. Named in honor of Bishop Joseph Dwenger, the school opened its doors to 210 freshmen in September, 1963.

On September 8, Bishop Pursley laid the cornerstone in a ceremony that attracted some 500 guests. The inscription reads: "To Our Youth.. .Citizens of Two Worlds." Bishop Leo Pursley explained the motto in his remarks at the formal dedication which took place on April 24, 1964. "Because they are citizens of this world we believe in educating them to live in this world. But because they are also citizens of another world we believe in educating them to also live in that world," he said. "The two objectives compliment and fulfill each other; they make it possible to educate the whole child... to recognize a student's identity as a child of God and an heir of heaven."

The school continued to grow over the next three years as each new grade was added. The enrollment reached 859 students in the school's fourth year of operation. The first concert was held on December 9, 1963. The school newspaper, *The Golden Trumpet*, made its debut on November 27 of that year. Michael Shields was elected to head the first student council. The initial memory book, *Golden Memories*, would eventually give way to the *Aureate*.

The first varsity athletic season began with football in 1965. Dwenger defeated the Lakeland Lakers 14-0 in the season opener. Dennis Kitt and Chuck Bayman scored TDs and Tim Zimmerman booted the extra points for the Saints. Unfortunately, it was their only victory of the season. Two years later, the Saints would go on to capture the city championship and thus began a storied history of Bishop Dwenger football that continues to this day.

Bishop Dwenger continued to grow and flourish and reached its peak enrollment of 1091 students during the 1976-77 school year. Enrollment would decline through the 1991-92 school year when it reached 687. Continued growth in northern Allen County would again push the enrollment upwards and it reached 1067 at the beginning of the 2004-05 school year.

In Dwenger's brief history, there have been only three principals, Fr. Edward Krason (1963-1979), John F. Gaughan (1979-1994), and J. Fred Tone (1994 - Present). As the first lay principal, Gaughan led Dwenger into a new era as they earned accreditation from the North Central Association of Colleges and Schools. Under the leadership of Fred Tone, Dwenger entered a period of renewed growth with increased enrollment and the school's first major expansion and renovation efforts since Dwenger was originally built in the early 1960s.

A $3.1 million effort created a new library-media center, cafeteria, auxiliary gym, weight room, and additional locker rooms. The original library was converted into classroom space and now houses three computer labs as well as a regular classroom.

Bishop Dwenger High School continues to adhere to the basic principles of educating students for both this world and the next. The school remains a family and embraces alumni, parents both past and present, students, faculty and staff. Each day, Bishop Dwenger students reach

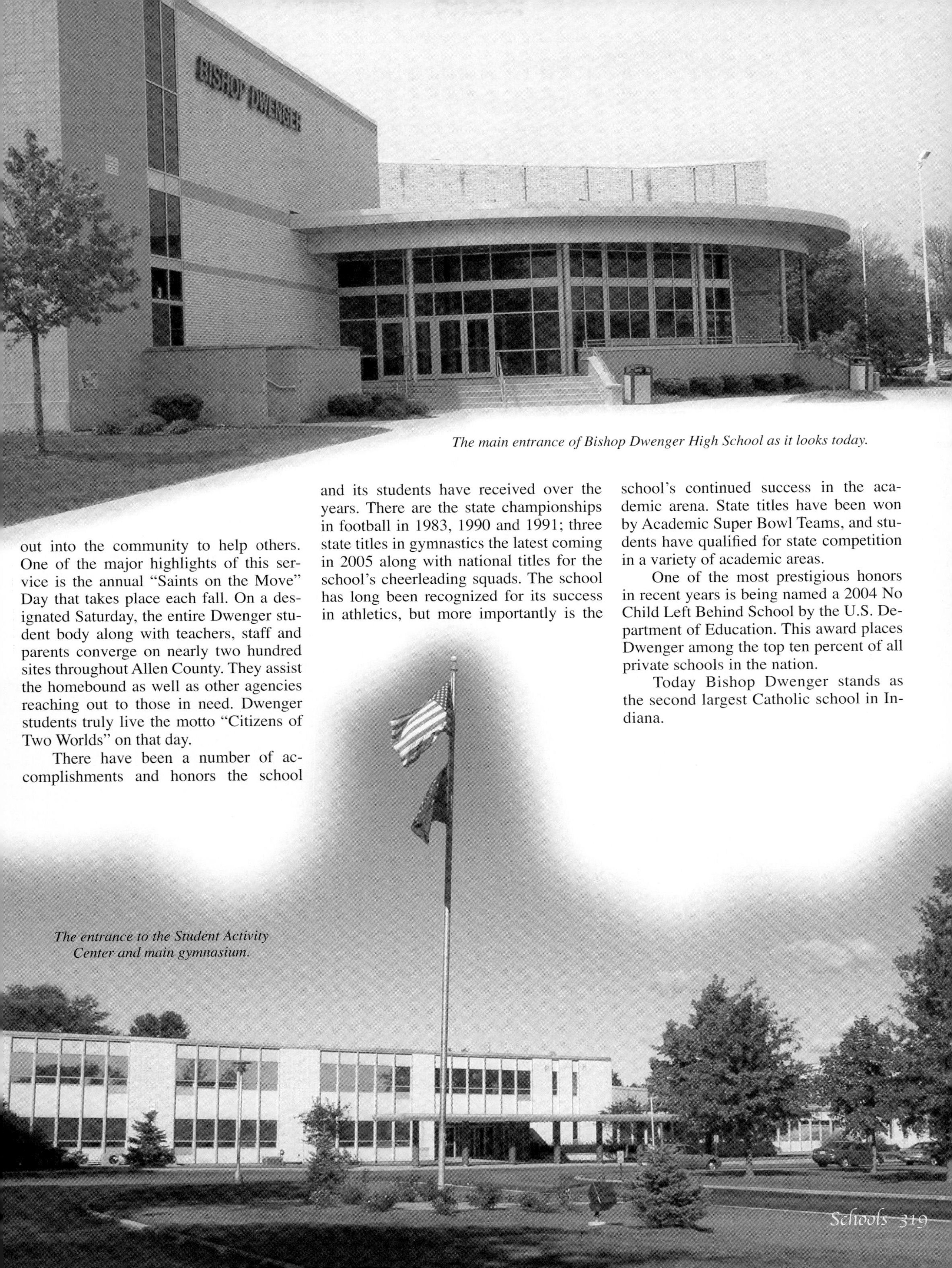

The main entrance of Bishop Dwenger High School as it looks today.

out into the community to help others. One of the major highlights of this service is the annual "Saints on the Move" Day that takes place each fall. On a designated Saturday, the entire Dwenger student body along with teachers, staff and parents converge on nearly two hundred sites throughout Allen County. They assist the homebound as well as other agencies reaching out to those in need. Dwenger students truly live the motto "Citizens of Two Worlds" on that day.

There have been a number of accomplishments and honors the school and its students have received over the years. There are the state championships in football in 1983, 1990 and 1991; three state titles in gymnastics the latest coming in 2005 along with national titles for the school's cheerleading squads. The school has long been recognized for its success in athletics, but more importantly is the school's continued success in the academic arena. State titles have been won by Academic Super Bowl Teams, and students have qualified for state competition in a variety of academic areas.

One of the most prestigious honors in recent years is being named a 2004 No Child Left Behind School by the U.S. Department of Education. This award places Dwenger among the top ten percent of all private schools in the nation.

Today Bishop Dwenger stands as the second largest Catholic school in Indiana.

The entrance to the Student Activity Center and main gymnasium.

Central Catholic High School

In 1846 Fr. Julian Benoit, pastor of St. Augustine Catholic Church, now known as the Cathedral, built a brick school and convent. He petitioned Mother Guerin, founder of the Sisters of Providence, to provide sisters to serve in the new school as teachers. She consented to send five sisters who traveled to Fort Wayne from southern Indiana by covered wagon. The school opened with 150 students. St. Mary's opened their school in 1853, five years after the parish had been established by German speaking Catholics.

So began the church schools which gave the children their education in religion and other basic subjects. In those years boys and girls were kept separate for classes. The schools did not go beyond eight grades. Catholic education progressed when St. Mary's instituted the first Commercial High School in 1896. Several other parishes followed with commercial courses.

As early as 1884 Bishop Joseph Dwenger began appealing to pastors to join together to erect a centrally located high school for boys. Bishop Herman Ahlerding was finally able to implement the plan and a central school was established on the first floor of Library Hall on the northeast corner of Lewis and Calhoun Streets. This building had been built as a parish hall and library for Cathedral parish. Central Catholic Boys High School was opened September 7, 1909. The principal and the teachers were all Brothers of the Holy Cross. Students were few in number in the beginning. St. Mary's, Cathedral, St. Paul's, St. Peter's and later St. Andrew's and Precious Blood Parishes continued their post eighth grade commercial courses. St. Catherine's Academy at St. Patrick's and St. Augustine's at Cathedral, both schools for girls, also continued to be well attended.

Bishop John Noll, a graduate of Cathedral Boys School, felt the same need for centralized quality education, but for both boys and girls. In the mid 1930s the bishop again went to the parish pastors for support for this concept. It would mean closing of the post eighth grade programs, but the support needed was forthcoming and the new Central Catholic High School was to become a reality. A. M. Strauss was engaged as the architect.

The 58,000 square foot school was built across from Cathedral Square on the southwest corner of Clinton and Lewis Streets. The school was built of fireproof materials that required very little maintenance. It was U-shaped with the open end toward Lewis Street containing an auditorium-gymnasium. It was 245 feet long with a Carara marble statue of Jesus, "The Christ of Lewis Street", in the center above the auditorium doors. A relief of the Blessed Virgin Mary was above the Clinton Street entrance. The building was 145 feet deep. The exterior was warm tan colored brick with Indiana limestone trim.

The inside of the building was not quite finished when the first students entered in September 1938. Initial enrollment was 1140 boys and girls. The school represented an investment of $500.00 per student and was totally free from indebtedness when completed. A modest tuition of $20.00 per student per year was asked. Formal dedication by Bishop Noll took place on January 8, 1939.

Faculty for the first year consisted of Brothers of the Holy Cross, three priests, Sisters of Providence and the School Sisters of Notre Dame from St. Mary's who continued to teach the commercial courses. Fr. Murphy served as the first Spiritual Director. Prayer marked the start of each school day, which began at 8:20 am and ended at 3:20 pm. Uniforms were required

Central Catholic High School

for girls. Many students walked to school, the rest rode city busses or were dropped off by their parents. Many brought brown bag lunches, most ate in the cafeteria and some went to lunch counters downtown. The first class to complete four years at Central Catholic graduated in June 1942.

Sports were always a source of pride and school spirit. In 1939 and 1940 the boys' basketball team, coached by John Levicki won the National Catholic championship. The football team of 1951, coached by Forest Anderson, won the Indiana State Football Championship. The football team played on the school's field on Dwenger Avenue. The practice field was at St. Vincent's Villa on Wells Street, which is now the site of the YWCA.

The school took their team's name, "The Fighting Irish", and the fight song, "Cheer, Cheer for Old CC High" from Notre Dame University. Official school colors were Purple and Gold. The yearbook continued to bear the name *Echo*, which was chosen in 1909 by the students of the first CCHS in 1909. The bi-weekly and sometime monthly newspaper was called *The Shamrock*. The students were involved in many religious, academic and service clubs mentored by the faculty. Fr. Edward Miller started the music department in 1940 and the school always had large numbers of students in band, orchestra and chorus. Joseph Woods was Music Director from 1946 through 1972. Julia Heighway taught the girl's physical education from the day the doors opened until they closed 36 years later. Msgr. Lester was the principal from 1951 through 1960 when the student population reached a peak of 1,781 students who represented 94% of the graduates of the Allen County Catholic grade schools. Some other of the longer serving principals and assistant principals were Sister Charlotte, Fr. Robert Hammond and Sister Maurene Therese. There was a unity of spirit because CC was the only Catholic high school in the county. The students came from many ethnic, cultural and economic backgrounds.

As the city grew, travel distances to school became longer and more students drove to school, parking became a problem. CCHS was totally surrounded by businesses, Fort Wayne Community School buildings and Cathedral Square. With population shifting away from the central city and the high school overcrowding, Bishop Leo Pursley saw the need to acquire larger pieces of property on which to build. The land for additional high schools was purchased on Paulding Road in south Fort Wayne and Washington Center Road on the north side. Two new schools were built and named after the first and second bishops of the diocese. Bishop Luers was opened in 1958 and Bishop Dwenger in 1963.

With the opening of the new schools the enrollment of CCHS began to decline. The number of students at CC in 1972 was 648 students. The increasing financial burden of three high schools could not be sustained.

Strategies had been suggested by parents, students and others on ways to keep the school open but to no avail. The decision was made in January 1972 by Bishop William McManus that the June graduating class would be the last.

Mayor Ivan Lebamoff gave the commencement address and with that, the last of the slightly over 10,000 students to graduate from Central Catholic were gone.

Those that passed through the school left with a solid foundation based on the four stone tablets incorporated into the front of the building representing Religion, Education, Morality and Patriotism.

The fortress of a building remained standing for another 12 years, serving as a site for CYO sports, a temporary home for Asian refugees, relief headquarters for the victims of the flood of 1982 and a home for the Latin American Education Center. Bishop McManus finally made the decision that the building must be taken down after spending $500,000.00 to keep it in operation between 1972 and 1984. The bishop opened the building for all graduates of CCHS to attend a going away party for the school in July 1984. It was torn down in November.

The site is now a parking lot that was badly needed by the Cathedral. Fittingly the statue of "The Christ of Lewis Street" remains in its original location.

IPFW

IPFW's Willis Family Bridge spans Crescent Avenue, connecting the main campus with Student Housing. The bridge, which is 246-feet long, was designed by architect Kurt Heidenreich of Engineering Resources Inc. in Fort Wayne. Just one other bridge in the United States (in Frankfort, Ill.) has a similar design.

Becoming a community cornerstone

IPFW exemplifies excellence for students, regio

Alfred W. Kettler: One of IPFW's founders.

Alfred W. Kettler was the Johnny Appleseed of his day: He had a vision, and he fulfilled it.

Kettler, a long-time Fort Wayne businessman and community leader, was the originator of an idea to create a new university in his beloved city. His inspiration planted the seed for what would become Indiana University–Purdue University Fort Wayne, the product of two internationally recognized Big Ten schools.

He saw two separate extension centers serving th region — Indiana University opening in 1917 and Purdue University opening in 1942 — and wondered why the liberal arts tradition of IU and the technical excellence of Purdue couldn't become a hybrid on one campus. His proposal was revolutionary, since two universities had never combined into a single institution anywhere in the United States.

In 1958, Kettler and other local leaders took the first step to help germinate the new campus. They established the Indiana-Purdue Foundation, which purchased 216 acres of farmland — complete with a dairy barn and silos — along the St. Joseph River. Local supporters — individuals and businesses in the Fort Wayne community who hoped to grow the new university into a world-class institution — contributed much of the funding to purchase the land. Kettler's idea became a reality in 1964, when the Education Building, later renamed Alfred W. Kettler Hall, opened its doors to 3,100 students.

Almost simultaneously with the campus opening, both IU and Purdue leadership announced goals to offer several programs at IPFW, including certificates and associate, bachelor's, and master's degree options. As the

Throughout the years

A brief look at IPFW's past, present, and future within the community.

1962 Breaking ground for the Education Building

1964 Dedication of the Education Building (now Kettler Hall)

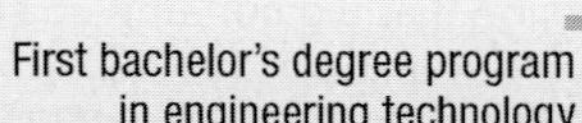

1965 First bachelor's degree program in engineering technology

1968 First degrees conferred

1970 Mastodon selected as mascot

Early 1970s Construction of Neff Hall and Walb Student Union

1972 Students and faculty relocate books to the newly constructed Helmke Library during the Book Walk

1974 Administrative unification of Indiana University at Fort Wayne and Purdue University at Fort Wayne under one chancellor, Donald Schwartz

Early 1980s Construction of Hilliard Gates Sports Center and dedication of Classroom-Medical Building

1986 First named professorship establishe (Jack W. Schrey Professorship)

1988 Indiana-Purdue Foundation acquires 152-acre William T. McKay property adjacent to the campus academic offerings branched out, so did enrollment. By 1970, the student population topped 6,000. Within a decade, nearly 10,000 students were taking classes. Today, IPFW offers more than 190 academic program options and serves nearly 12,000 full- and part-time students, and some 9,000 additional students pursue non-credit continuing education courses. The university offers more academic and extracurricular opportunities than any other higher education institution in northeast Indiana, which represents an 11-county service area.

The increase in the student body population has, in turn, fostered growth with the campus infrastructure. Today, 20 academic and athletics buildings grace the landscape. And more than 350 esteemed faculty members have worked to propagate the institution's vitality — both through continued excellence in teaching and research and toward securing grants and contracts, which represented $4.1 million during the 2004–05 fiscal year.

Since IPFW took root 40 years ago, it now boasts more than 40,000 alumni. These graduates nourish the workforce of hundreds of public, private, and not-for-profit entities in northeast Indiana. The university has become a premier contributor to the region's academic, cultural, and economic development.

Future IPFW harvests promise a variety of ongoing projects and collaborations. The campus, itself, will continue to blossom, with six major physical expansion projects during the next three years. Projects with themes as diverse as a hotel, park, and a pedestrian bridge spanning the St. Joseph River to an interconnected student services and library complex are planned. Additionally, the Center of Excellence in Systems Engineering is poised to become a national model for industry and university collaborations, ranging from the procurement of national defense contracts to becoming a leader in systems engineering education and research.

On the web
▼ Visit IPFW online at ***www.ipfw.edu***

Through present-day IPFW Chancellor Michael A. Wartell's vision and leadership, the university remains committed to excellence in teaching, research, and philanthropy, while at the same time, responding to the needs of the region at-large. It is a relationship that will continue to bear fruit well into the future.

Future

Construction of student services and library complex (pictured right), medical education building, hotel, park, a second pedestrian/bicycle bridge, and expanded student housing

2005

IPFW creates Mastodons on Parade, Fort Wayne's first community art project, to benefit United Way; Northeast Indiana Innovation Center opens; Construction of music building begins

2004

Dedication of bronze mastodon on campus; Student Housing opens; IPFW celebrates 40th anniversary

2003

Completion of the Willis Family Bridge; IPFW Warsaw Center opens; Discover IPFW campaign announced with a goal of raising $20 million

2002

The Chapman Professor of English established as IPFW's first endowed professorship; Fort Wayne Public Television Center opens on land leased from IPFW

Michael Stapleton

2001

Athletics program begins transition to Division I affiliation

2000

Nine Centers of Excellence recognized to pair the intellectual resources of the university with the concerns of businesses and service organizations in northeast Indiana

1990s

Construction of arts, science, and engineering and technology facilities

1993

Theatre arts building dedicated on April 16 and named for Ernest E. Williams, the late editor of *The News-Sentinel* from 1966 to 1982

1994

IPFW hosts and competes in the men's volleyball NCAA Final Four

Lloy Ball

1995

Omnibus Lecture Series initiated

1998

IPFW sponsors first all-campus Undergraduate Research and Creative Endeavor Symposium; The "Plex" opens on the McKay Farm to provide indoor soccer facilities

Lutheran Hospital School of Nursing

The Lutheran Hospital was organized in 1903 by the corporation known as the Lutheran Hospital Association of Fort Wayne. In the articles of corporation of the Lutheran Hospital, a school of nursing was provided for, and was conducted beginning with the opening of the institution. The first student was Miss Augusta Fisher who was admitted in late 1904. The first class of seven students was organized by July 1, 1905. Miss Minnie Walker, the school's first superintendent, served from 1904 to 1908. The students were housed in the attic of the original Lutheran Hospital, the Ninde homestead, in the 3000 block of South Fairfield Avenue. The Judge Ninde Homestead was converted to a 25-bed hospital and opened on Thanksgiving Day, November 24, 1904.

Caregiving was not the only task of these early nurses. The night nurse started at 4 a.m. emptying ashes and securing kindling for each floor of the hospital. Nurses a century ago, through at least 1950, often worked from 7 a.m. to 7 p.m. In addition to providing patient care, their duties included serving meal trays, washing dishes, laundering curtains, dusting rooms, and mopping the floors. Anna Lauman Driver, who graduated with the class of 1907, wrote this description for a history that was sealed in a time capsule for the cornerstone of the nurses residence built in 1948: "Although there were seven beds in the attic, it housed nine occupants who comprised the school and its faculty. The Superintendent and her assistant had beds of their own, but the other five beds served as a rotating service to accommodate five of the seven nurses who were on day duty. The two night nurses occupied the beds during the day. The problem of where to spend one's off duty hours was easily solved because there were no off duty hours. The first classroom was the operating room so of necessity the classes were held at night."

The Judge Allen Homestead, adjacent to the hospital, was purchased in 1913. It initially housed 35 students, and soon housed 85 students with the addition of two annexes in 1916 and 1918. The attic of the original hospital building was again occupied by students. Then, in 1934, an old building in the rear of the nurses home was remodeled to house 12 more students.

By 1929, the hospital had expanded to 190 beds and the nursing school enrolled 93 students. In 1934 all students admitted for training had to pay an entrance fee of $25.00 and had to pay for books and uniforms. The pay for a 20 hour shift was $5.00 or 25 cents per hour.The war emergency and the corresponding need for more nurses, meant additional space was needed. The Deaconess home was purchased in 1943 and named Victory Residence. It housed 12 more students.

Miss Atula Holtman, a member of the 1911 graduating class, became principle of the School of Nursing in 1919 and served until 1931. Miss Pauline Bischoff, who graduated in 1918, was appointed Assistant Director of Nurses and an instructor. In 1931 she was named Director of Nursing, a post she held until her retirement in July 1951. Miss Bischoff worked very hard to improve the education of the students. She instigated the six-day work week and reduced night duty to an eight hour shift. She increased the number of professional instructors on the teaching staff. During her tenure from 1931-1951, Miss Bischoff guided 654 girls through training at Lutheran Hospital School of Nursing.

The first Capping ceremony of Lutheran Hospital was held in June 1940. This ceremony was a solemn occasion held after a probationary period of six months, during which the students received the cap of their school, recited the Nightingale Pledge and heard an address by a minister. A reception for students and family at the Nurses residence followed the ceremony. For the first six months, the students wore a blue cotton under dress with a stiffly starched white apron. At capping, a bib was added to the uniform. White hose and white shoes completed the student attire.

In 1941 the Lutheran Hospital was accepted into the U.S. Cadet Nurse Corps program. Some 57 of the 123 students signed the pledge to become members of the Cadet Corps. That number jumped to 78 out of 121 by 1945. In 1948, one student admitted was a widow. Her husband was killed in Europe while serving in the Army.

In 1947, the life of a student nurse began at 6 a.m. with a warning from a rising bell. At 6:25 a.m., each student was required to be in Chapel, assembling in lines according to class. After chapel and breakfast in the cafeteria, she reported to her assigned floor for duty. The individual case method was used which made each student responsible for the care, treatment and medicines of the individual patient assigned to her. It was generally believed that this method improved the quality of nursing, eliminating mechanical care with the student taking more pride in the individual care of her patients six days a week. Students were on floor duty from 7 to 9 a.m. and 5 to 7 p.m. for "AM Care and PM Care." They attended classes during the middle of the day, and in the evening when Physicians were the instructors.

Nurse's residence on Fairfield Avenue.

Fiftieth anniversary reunion of the class of 1950, Lutheran Hospital School of Nursing.

The new student was automatically a member of the Student Nurse Association of the Lutheran Hospital School of Nursing. Each student had a voice in the organization through her elected class representative. A composite of representatives from each class and the Faculty Advisor, Class Sponsors and Social Director met monthly with administrative personnel of the school to discuss mutual problems and student activities.

Parties for special occasions were planned during the year. A monthly school newspaper titled *The Lamplighter* enjoyed a wide circulation among graduates, doctors and friends of the school. All graduates joined the Alumnae Association which was an organization of mutual benefit and pleasure and afforded an opportunity to advance the interests of the nursing profession. *The Bulletin* was published periodically listing changes in the school. A thumbnail sketch of each graduate was provided. The nurse received a well-rounded, clinical experience in the medical, surgical, pediatric, and obstetrical departments in surgery, pharmacy, diet kitchen and emergency room. The course of study covered three years after which the graduate must take an examination to receive her license to practice as a Registered Nurse. State Board Examinations were held in Indianapolis.

The Nursing School's growth was not without controversy. In 1948, an African-American woman applied to become a nursing student. While the hospital's Board of Directors approved of allowing the student to enroll, the hospital's medical staff objected. They were over ruled and she was allowed to stay. Miss Mable Martin graduated with the class of 1951.

Miss Blanche Purdy was the Operating Room Supervisor for many years and instructed the students in surgical technique. Students "scrubbed" for the operations and assisted the surgeons by passing instruments and sutures and holding retractors. Students were "ON CALL" for emergency surgical procedures and could have their sleep interrupted on occasion.

The students who worked the night shift served for five weeks and then were given a weekend off. Miss Dorcas Brown was the Night Shift Supervisor. She planned a picnic at Foster Park for the students when their tour of "Nights" was over. Students working the night shift were expected to get up and attend class during the day. Senior students in 1948 were allowed two overnights a month. No students were allowed to marry. An 11 p.m. curfew was enforced and a House Mother was on duty to see that everyone signed in and out of the residence.

During the 1950s, three women held the directorship of the school of nursing; Miss Myrtle Lewis, Miss Helen Succop, and Miss Marie Moehring.

In 1973, two Lutheran graduates were named to top management positions with the hospital. Dolores Stickan Gladieux class of 1959, was promoted to director of nursing education and Ethel Klopfenstein was named director of nursing services. The nursing program was 120 weeks in length with 40 weeks in each year and was approved by the Indiana State Board. By 1973, the hospital again expanded the nursing school facilities, purchasing the old Duemling clinic building and converting it to an educational center.

By 1975, the daily schedule of each student nurse, including the rising hour was determined by each student according to individual plans. Daily chapel attendance was no longer required. The students generally attended class and worked in clinical areas only on week days. Courses were designed to give the student the best background in preparation for the role of registered nurse. Assignments in the classical area were planned so that the students cared for the type of patient they were learning about in the classroom. Courses included experiences in medical-surgical nursing units, pediatrics, psychiatry, obstetrics, nursing management, and observation of the nurse in community health agencies. College credit for science courses was attained through attendance at Concordia Senior College. Dorm hours were much less restrictive, with seniors being free to come and go as they pleased. The students who attended in 1975 could choose not to live in the residence and may marry. Male students were readily accepted into the program. The first two came in 1973, one from Pennsylvania and one from Ohio. After men were admitted to the school, the name of the Alumnae Association was changed to Lutheran Hospital Nurses Alumni Association.

The pin of the School of Nursing was presented during graduation ceremonies. The insignia embraces and combines the Greek cross, rose, wreath, open book and the letters L.H.S.N. The cross, in red, is symbolic of unselfish service and love of one's fellowman, and is the emblem for relief of sick and wounded. The rose, in gold, signifies the goodness of God, and is indicative of Messianic promise and human love. The lotus wreath is representative of esteem, honor, and merit. The open book signifies the word of God. The letters L.H.S.N. denotes the Lutheran Hospital School of Nursing.

The school became the Lutheran College of Health Professions in the fall of 1987 and merged with the University of Saint Francis in May of 1998. The Lutheran Hospital moved to West Jefferson in 1992 and was purchased by Quorum Health in 1995. The proceeds from the sale endowed the Lutheran Foundation which is housed in the old Duemling Clinic located at the corner of Fairfield and Home avenues. The other buildings on Fairfield Avenue were demolished. The grounds have become a city park with the centerpiece being the statue of The Healing Christ which is held in high esteem by all of the graduates of Lutheran School of Nursing.

Lutheran graduates are now considered Alumni of the University of Saint Francis, and several classes have held reunions on the local campus.

Submitted by Kathryn Bowen Bloom graduate of the Class of 1950 L.H.S.N. Contributing writers: Bonnie Blackburn and Kathryn Bloom

St Joseph's Hospital School of Nursing
Fort Wayne

Right Rev. John Henry Luers, first Bishop of the newly formed Fort Wayne Diocese, saw a great need for care for the sick in the area. He purchased a sixty-nine room hotel on the corner of Main Street and Broadway, known as Rockhill House, which had fallen upon hard times. He petitioned the Poor Handmaids of Jesus Christ, a religious order of sisters in Germany, to come to run the institution. This community of nuns had been formed with the purpose of caring for the sick and needy and the education of children. The sisters answered his call and journeyed to their new home. Soon St. Joseph Hospital opened its doors as the first facility for the sick in Fort Wayne. The year was 1869.

In the beginning the hospital was staffed totally by the sisters. As the hospital grew, more nursing sisters were needed, so a private education program was started to train new sisters to care for the sick. In September 1918, near the end of WWI the decision was made to also admit young lay women to the training program. There were 19 accepted into the first combined class. By the following November the school had been accredited by the Indiana State Board of Nursing Education and Registration. On May 28, 1921 twelve young women who completed the three-year course were graduated and qualified to be Registered Nurses.

The candidates for St. Joseph's Hospital School of Nursing were required to be of good character and willing to practice their profession by faithfully meeting the needs of people. This was implied by the school motto, "Propter Humanitatem" which means "For the Sake of Humanity." This motto is on the school pin, which was awarded to each nurse during her graduation ceremony.

The school was first located in the hospital, but in 1929 a new building, dedicated solely to nursing was completed. It was located across the street from, the then, main entrance of the hospital at 735 West Berry Street. There were rooms for up to 120 nurses. There were also classrooms, nursing lab, library, offices, lounge, auditorium, kitchen, laundry facilities, sundeck and tennis court. Most of the rooms were doubles but there were a few singles and triples.

From the beginning of the program almost all students lived at the school during the three years it took to earn their diploma. After their Probationary Period, which lasted six months, the students could serve as nurses in the hospital. During this period they attended science and nursing classes and were referred to as "Probies."

St. Joseph Hospital School of Nursing

Evelyn Summers Martin
Cadet, 1944

Susan Berghoff Prowant
Student, 1954

Connie Kaminski Lehman
Student, 1964

Karen Giant Leffers
Student, 1974

Sciences were taught in collaboration with the local colleges. Students who successfully completed this period participated in a ceremony in which they were rewarded with their white nurse's cap, which was placed on their head by the director of the school. As a body, as they held a lighted candle, they solemnly recited the Florence Nightingale Pledge to uphold the principles of nursing.

They attended classes and worked in the hospital year round. The tuition for the three year course in the mid-1950s was $389.00.

As they progressed through their courses and their clinical experience, caring for patients under the supervision of their instructors, they were given more responsibility. Eventually they were assigned to all shifts and all specialty units. They were graduated with the knowledge of, and the hands-on experience in, Medical, Surgical, Psychiatric, Obstetric and Pediatric Nursing.

With our country's entry into WWII there was suddenly a greater demand for nurses. St. Joseph participated in the United States Cadet Nurse Program offered by the government, by which women who enrolled received tuition assistance in return for their commitment to serve in the military upon graduation if needed. The school added a spring enrollment in addition to the usual fall class, and the number of nurses graduating increased greatly during the time of our country's need. Many St. Joseph nurses volunteered to serve in the military.

As the education of nurses changed, mainly from pressure from professional nursing organizations, the emphasis was more on education and less on service in the hospital. This made the Diploma schools of nursing more expensive for the hospitals to maintain. The school did many things to provide an excellent education while conserving resources. They were the first school in the city to teach basic science by TV classes from the University of Minnesota in 1965.

In the late 1970s young women had many more career choices. Nursing became less popular leading to sagging enrollment and a nursing shortage. About that time the first male students were admitted. The school began to offer classes for part-time students including day or night classes in 1980. The faculty remained dedicated to education of nurses that included extensive clinical experience. With fewer students St. Joseph found it necessary to form an alliance with St. Francis College. Basic sciences were taught at St. Francis and nursing courses at St. Joseph. Students who graduated with a diploma from St. Joseph could continue at St. Francis and complete their degree in 12 months. Sadly, the decision was made by the administration of St. Joseph Hospital to close the school for financial reasons. The last class graduated in 1987. Student records were transferred to, the now, University of St Francis.

In the sixty-nine year history of St. Joseph's Hospital School of Nursing over 1500 well prepared, hands-on nurses were graduated and were welcomed as professionals in Fort Wayne, the Midwest and all over the country. *Submitted by Susan Berghoff Prowant.*

Bishop Luers High School

Mission statement: "You are the light of the world. . . your light must shine before others, that they may see your good deeds and glorify your heavenly Father." (Matthew 5:14-16) "The Mission of the Bishop Luers High School family is to create a Catholic educational community that instills in each student the qualities of faith, respect and responsibility necessary to reach his or her God-given potential spiritually, academically, and socially. This maturity nurtured by Catholic truths will enable each graduate to face the challenges in his or her own life while serving God and others in a changing society. We are the light of the world." This is not just the mission of Bishop Luers High School, it is also a way of life, and what makes Luers stand out from others. Our graduates are well prepared for college, and more importantly, well prepared to be leaders and stewards of the church and the community.

Bishop Luers High School is proud to be a stronghold, and a viable part of Fort Wayne, where students excel in academics, sports, and extra-curricular activities. The school was dedicated on May 3, 1959, by Bishop Leo Pursley. The school opened with a total of 150 students and held its first graduation ceremony on June 3, 1962, with 121 students receiving diplomas. Bishop Luers High School was dedicated during the centennial celebration for the Diocese, and thus named in honor of the first bishop. Bishop John Henry Luers served the Diocese from January 10, 1858, to June 29, 1871, when he died suddenly at age 52. Bishop Luers was born in Westphalia, Germany, and raised in Cincinnati, Ohio.

Bishop Luers High School was originally operated by the Franciscan Fathers of the St. John the Baptist Province in Cincinnati, Ohio. They had much support and help from the Sisters of St. Francis Province of Mishawaka, Indiana. Together the priests, brothers, sisters, and lay teachers contributed to making Luers what it is today. The Franciscans ruled the school under the direction of the Diocese until 1984, when Luers had its first lay principal, and several lay successors to follow. Fr. Edmund Moore was the first principal to serve at Bishop Luers High School; he served the school from 1959 to 1963.

Bishop Luers High School prides itself on several areas of excellence for its students. Academically, on the average over 93% of all graduates go on to a four-year college. The graduation rate is 98% for our seniors. Approximately 40% of our current students are children of former Luers students. Our graduates are offered approximately $1.3 million dollars in scholarship awards annually.

Our Luers alumni have made a significant impact on their local communities as doctors, lawyers, priests or religious, teachers, business owners, etc. Luers is accredited by the North Central Association Commission on Accreditation and School Improvement (NCA).

The Bishop Luers Knights pride themselves on having a top class athletic program. Sports offered include: baseball, basketball, bowling, cheerleading, cross country, football, golf, lacrosse, rifle team, soccer, swimming, tennis, track & field, volleyball and wrestling. Our "Knights" athletic programs have won many awards from the S.A.C. level, to sectionals, regional, semi-state, and state championships. Luers is proud to have won the following athletic awards: Boys Sports – S.A.C., 24; Sectional, 30; Regional, 14; Semi-State, 16; State, 8. Girls Sports – S.A.C., 22; Sectional, 46; Regional, 17; Semi-State, 12; State, 4.

Luers offers many other extra-curricular activities including an outstanding performing arts department. Luers is the host to the longest running show-choir invitational in the United States. The Minstrels (Luers show-choir) are known nationally. In 2003 the Minstrels hosted their 30th anniversary invitational. The show choir's many awards include Grand Champions, First Runners-up, Outstanding Show Band, Outstanding Tech Crew, and Outstanding Vocals. The Drama Department has three productions a year; a children's theater that performs at the feeder schools, and is involved with performances for Luers Knight, one of the most popular activities at the school. This Performing Arts Department involves over 30% of the student body in a given year.

Luers has multiple clubs and service opportunities for students. The Key Club has won the state level "Club of the Year" over 25 times, received international recognition, and our students have held several state level District Governor's and Lieutenant Governor's offices. Key Club consistently averages 100 members per year with most members performing 30 or more hours of community service each.

Bishop Luers High School always has been, and continues to be an outstanding institution where students come first. They grow and mature to be outstanding young men and women who are committed to Christ and ready for the world beyond our walls. There is a real sense of family at Luers. The Luers Spirit is alive and well. The sense of community continues long after graduation.

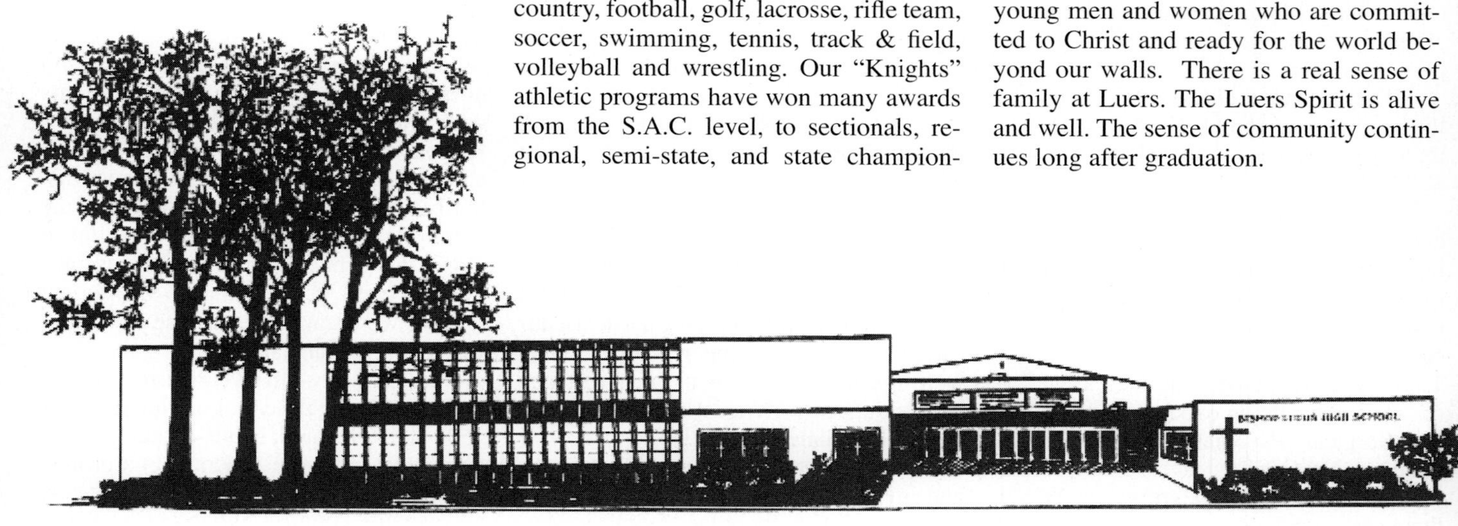

Central High School

Cental – Dear Central
Your sons and daughters were the white and blue,
White for honor pure, blue making heart endure,
And you have endured.

There have been many changes since your conception in 1904 when you moved from East Wayne Street to the corners of Barr and Lewis streets. Fort Wayne High and Manual Training School opened its doors with 480 pupils and 17 teachers. These numbers increased to 75 faculty members and over 2300 students thus requiring a bigger campus. To help alleviate this problem, South Side High School was built in 1922. At this time Fort Wayne High changed it's name, to what many of us have come to know and love – Central High School – home of the Tigers. The first enrollment at Central High School, in 1922, had 1200 students, but rapidly grew to over 2000 by 1927 which created a need for another high school, North Side.

A new building was created at Central about 1923, just west of the alley, to accommodate the shop work moved from the old Franklin School. The girls and boys gymnasiums were built in 1930, neither of which were large enough for inter-school games; and for this reason all home basketball games were played at North Side High School. In 1936 the woodworking shops moved across Clinton Street into the old Craig Building. The old shop building on the west and the Hamilton Homestead were razed, and a modern building was added housing the music department and the Lewis Activities Room. The music department provided for the development in choral and instrumental work enabling the musicians to give much requested concerts and programs throughout the community.

This building also included more classrooms and modern shops. Central was fortunate to have an oversized cafeteria (which is still revered by all today). We remember the caring and sparkling kitchen staff, and people still talk with passion about the marvelous food – especially their famous sloppy joes. It was a place where you could feel enthusiasm, eagerness, vitality, and warmth, which made it a perfect place to hold other activities such as carnivals, our fun-loving after game sock hops, and our grand and beautiful proms.

On the other side of the school was the fantastic Central library which spawned many great thinkers of our generation, and for those of you who should have spent more time there, it contained around 8000 volumes and all current publications and materials. But be careful. As we all know, it was necessary to follow the rules and regulations designated or you would have been asked to leave.

Central High School 1864-1971

Around the corner from the library were the Guidance and Counseling Departments which were beneficial to all students. At this time a night school began where adults could complete their high school diplomas or take classes to enhance their training and efficiency for work in the businesses or industries in the city. Also citizenship classes were held for those who wanted to learn to speak and write English to prepare to become citizens of the United States. This became a vital role after World War II for the many immigrants striving to become citizens.

Meanwhile throughout the State of Indiana a fervor for athletics reached a new level of popularity, competitiveness and talent. Central carried these ideals in its proud tradition in athletics. This was no more apparent than 1943, when Central won the Indiana High School Athletic Association Basketball Championship. The ball used in the tourney was auctioned off one afternoon in the boy's gym for $750,000 in victory bonds to the Lincoln National Bank, who then donated it back to Central, and it is now in a trophy case on the second floor of the 1904 Building. High School sports furnished an opportunity for morale building, leadership, and teamwork. Nothing being more evident than when Central won the Indiana State High School Track Meet in 1944 with only four boys, while the other schools had teams of 15 to 20 boys.

Central's publications, the *Spotlight* and the *Caldron*, the weekly newspaper and the school's annual yearbook, furnished many pupils with journalism and photography experience preparing them for careers in those fields. Our famous Art, Speech, and Drama Departments' performances and displays were some of the most outstanding in the state. We can also boast of a spacious and dignified auditorium which has since been renovated. Central, being Fort Wayne's first and only high school until 1922, means she can brag of a great many prominent men and women in business, industry, and the professions who graduated from Central. Neither will we ever forget the hundreds of men and women who served their country in the different military branches. Seventy-two who served in World War II never returned.

While graduates were the real products and measure of a school, there was another greater element, "the Spirit of Central," which lives on in her thousands of graduates and alumni that time and change cannot erase. After Central's closing in 1971, the building reopened as the Anthis Career Center where education still fills the building – carrying on a great Fort Wayne tradition.

Thanks to the Anthis Staff, the Central Tigers have been restored to the building and once again roam!!!

Written by Janice R. Gunder Arnold (Alumni 1952); Collaborator Eric J. Smith (Grandson); Edited by Nellie B. Maloley (Alumni 1944) Excerpts taken from an article written by Fred H. Croninger (Principal from 1921-1948 Central) entitled "Fifty Years is a Long Time" (reprinted from Golden Anniversary 1904-1954 program)

Central,
We will cherish thee down through the years,
And we will always love you,
Through smiles and tears,
Dear Central – our own!!!

Concordia Lutheran High School

Serving the Community Since 1935

Concordia Lutheran High School as it exists today is an ongoing example of the historical emphasis that the Lutheran church has placed on Christian education since its very beginnings.

The origins of Concordia Lutheran High School can be traced to the Luther Institute which began in 1916. Initially housed at St. Paul's Lutheran School in Fort Wayne, it offered a two-year post elementary school curriculum which focused primarily on business education.

Due to continued growth and increased demand, the Luther Institute moved into its own facilities in a building erected on the north side of St. Paul's Lutheran Church in 1924.

Increased educational expectations required a move to Hanser Hall on the campus of Concordia Junior College (the current location of Indiana Institute of Technology). In 1935, the program was combined with the pre-ministerial curriculum at the college and a four-year, co-educational high school; the Lutheran High School on the campus of Concordia College, was the result.

That same year, seven Lutheran congregations formed the Association that began the Lutheran High School. The original members were Bethlehem, Corcordia, Emmanuel, Emmaus, St. Paul's, St. Peter's and Zion Lutheran churches. In 2005 twenty congregations are owner/members of the high school association.

Continuing enrollment increases and the need for modern facilities resulted in the building of a new educational plant for Concordia Lutheran High School, which opened in 1952 on the corner of the college campus (Maumee & South Anthony). Escalating demand created by additional new students led to an expansion of the facility in 1957.

In 1963 with growing enrollment, the campus of Concordia Lutheran High School moved to its present location on North Anthony Boulevard at the corner of St. Joe River Drive. The current 43 acre campus includes the "Our Creator's Classroom" Environment Study Center and the Fred Zollner Athletic Complex.

A special feature of Concordia is the Army Junior ROTC program. It began in 1906 as part of the Concordia Junior College program, which included a high school component. Girls were admitted to the program in 1973. Concordia is one of 51 high school JROTCs in the State of Indiana.

The Concordia Educational Foundation was established in 1959 as a source for tuition assistance for Concordia scholars. With the endowment approaching seven million dollars in 2005, the Foundation has provided millions of dollars in support of Concordia students and programs.

Throughout its history, Concordia has offered an expansive co-curricular program, along with its quality core Christ-centered educational curriculum. In addition to its JROTC Program, Concordia has provided many additional opportunities for its students to participate and successfully compete with other schools in a wide variety of activities including athletics, music, drama, the arts and many similar programs.

Concordia Lutheran High School-Hanser Hall

Concordia Lutheran High School 1952

Concordia Lutheran High School 2005

Concordia Theological Seminary

Statue of Martin Luther created by Friederich Adolf Soetebier of Germany

Concordia Theological Seminary was founded as a result of the efforts of Dr. Johannes Konrad Wilhelm Loehe of Bavaria, Germany, Wilhelm Sihler, and Dr. Friedrich Conrad Dietrich Wyneken of Fort Wayne, Indiana. Dr. Wyneken recognized the need to minister to the thousands of German immigrants who had come to America in the mid-1800s and pleaded with his fellow Lutherans in Germany to send pastors or to finance their training.

Concordia Theological Seminary was established in Fort Wayne in 1846, one year before the Lutheran Church – Missouri Synod was organized, and has served the Synod ever since, training men for the office of the Holy Ministry. The seminary was moved to St. Louis, Missouri, in 1861 and then to Springfield, Illinois, in 1875 before returning to Fort Wayne in 1976.

During the absence of the seminary from Fort Wayne, The Lutheran Church – Missouri Synod maintained Concordia Junior College in Fort Wayne from 1861 to 1957 and established Concordia Senior College on this campus in 1957. In 1975 the Synod elected to move the Senior College program to Ann Arbor, Michigan, and to return the seminary to Fort Wayne. Thus Fort Wayne has the distinction of being the only city in the country that has never been without one of the Synod's ministerial schools.

The 191 acres on which the seminary now resides were originally an Indian reservation deeded to Pe-chewa, a Miami Indian chief who later became a Christian. In the early 1900s the land was purchased by the Charles Kramer family, who homesteaded it. The Kramer homestead was then acquired by the Synod, which built the campus between 1955 and 1957 to be the home of Concordia Senior College.

The campus was designed by Eero Saarinen whose design credits include the Gateway Arch in St. Louis, Missouri. Saarinen's plans for the campus follow the Scandinavian village design popular from 1300-1700 AD, where the chapel was front and center while still sheltering the courtyard from wind and other weather. According to Saarinen, the buildings were grouped in the village design so as to "provide a quiet, unified environment in which the students could find a complete, balanced life, and yet one which was related to the outside world." The Concordia Senior College campus was the first college campus in America to receive a First Honor Award from the American Institute of Architects.

Each dorm has 18 rooms and is designed to be a mini-village within a building. In order to get more than one floor under one set of walls and one roof, the "mezzanine" concept was used. The library and dining hall are the most prominent examples of this concept. At the time of design no provisions were made for the handicapped. In recent years handicapped access has been added including elevators, ramps, and parking facilities.

The diamond shaped bricks, patented as the "Concordia Bricks," run horizontally on the main campus buildings representing our relationship to one another in community. Kramer Chapel, however, presents the one exception as its bricks run vertically to symbolize God's relationship with us. Kramer Chapel rises far above all other campus building, and can be seen from any point on campus. The interior rises to a height of 97 feet, and due to choir loft renovations in 1997 the chapel seats 750. The chapel is noted for its fine acoustics, complementary to spoken, sung, and instrumental activities. The 54-rank Schlicker pipe organ was designed by Saarinen and organ designer Herman L. Schlicker and built by the Schlicker Organ Company of Buffalo, New York. Two thousand nine hundred and nine pipes, some of which rise to a height of 50 feet, are displayed on the west wall of the chapel.

At the entrance of the campus stands a statue of the young Martin Luther. The statue, created by Friederich Adolf Soetebier of Germany, stands over 12 feet high and weighs more than two tons. The finely modeled face is a combination of two pictures of Luther by Lucas Cranach the Elder. His hands are the sensitive hands of a scholar, molded from casts taken of Luther's hands after his death. Luther is firmly grasping the Bible to his heart, yet it is open for the world to see the Word of God.

Since its founding in 1846, Concordia Theological Seminary continues to be a community that believes, teaches, and confesses the saving power of baptismal water, proclaims the Gospel, and receives the gifts of the Lord's body and blood. It is through these means of grace that our community finds its life. By continually receiving the life-giving Gospel of Christ, we are empowered to live by faith as we prepare to serve the church and proclaim Christ to all the nations.

Concordia Theological Seminary

East Allen County Schools

First row: W. Gordon Jackson, Donald Johnson, and John Bollinger.
Second row: Thomas Kurtz, Charles H. Reynolds, Walter M. Oehler, Sr., and Chris Roemke.

East Allen County Schools has a rich heritage of community interest and involvement in its schools. Adams Township's first school opened in 1829. In 1853, citizens in Fort Wayne petitioned for free public schools and public schools started opening in the various townships of Allen County. Township schools, overseen by township trustees, proved public education to the extent that they could build and staff schools. Some township corporations consolidated to provide comprehensive high schools for their students. Eventually, Allen County had 15 school corporations: 10 township corporations, three (3)-consolidated corporations, New Haven Public Schools, and Fort Wayne Community Schools.

As some of the smaller township corporations struggled from a financial and curriculum perspective, the impracticality of running a district with less than 1,000 students was addressed by the State of Indiana. The School Corporation Reorganization Act of 1959 sought to equalize educational opportunities for students and create greater equity in tax rates. The Act set a reorganization target date of March 15, 1963.

The *Comprehensive Plan for the Reorganization of the School Corporations of Allen County, Indiana* analyzed 19 possible reconfigurations of the county. One of these plans, dubbed the "doughnut" plan, left Fort Wayne Community Schools and the New Haven – Adams Township Schools in place. The plan offered some equalization of assessed valuation, but created transportation issues. Support of any plan embroiled districts into fighting over sections of townships. The "doughnut" plan created the interest that prompted the formation of Northwest Allen County Schools. In the east side of the county, the ongoing battle between Fort Wayne Community Schools and New Haven Public Schools over Adams Township continued. Having grown from a predominantly agricultural area to a strong business and industrial center, the growing professional population looking for good schools and providing a lucrative tax base made Adams Township prime school district property. The southwest townships continued to resist affiliation with Fort Wayne Community Schools, eventually forming Southwest Allen County Schools.

After months of battles, on December 23, 1962, a petition signed by 12,093 of 15,851 registered voters residing within what would become the borders of East Allen County Schools was presented to the Allen County Committee for the Reorganization of School Corporations, certified through the Allen Circuit Court. The first meeting of the Board of Education of East Allen County Schools took place on June 16, 1964. The first board members appointed by townships and/or townships schools included (see photo):

•John Bollinger – Cedar Creek and Springfield Townships; elected as Treasurer

•W. Gordon Jackson – Jefferson, Jackson, and Monroe Townships

•Chris Roemke – Cedar Creek, Springfield, Scipio, Maumee, Milan, Adams, Jackson, Jefferson, Monroe, Madison and Marion Townships; elected as Vice-President

•Donald Johnson – New Haven Public Schools; elected as President

•Walter M. Oehler, Sr., – New Haven Public Schools

•Fred King – Madison-Marion Consolidated Schools; elected as Secretary and replaced by Charles H. Reynolds, April 5, 1995, with Mr. King's move out of Allen County

•Thomas Kurtz – Schipio Township, Maumee Milan Consolidated Schools.

The new board unanimously appointed Mr. Paul Harding as Superintendent of East Allen County Schools.

Today, East Allen County Schools serves 10,000+ students and is comprised of 11 elementary schools (Cedarville, Harlan, Highland Terrace, Hoagland, Leo, Meadowbrook, Monroeville, New Haven, Southwick, Village and Woodburn); two middle schools (New Haven and Prince Chapman Academy); three junior/senior high schools (Heritage, Leo and Woodlan); and two senior high schools (New Haven and Paul Harding).

To this day, a strong commitment to attendance area schools echoes the roots of local interest in traditions formed and reformed decades before. The School Board takes to heart their service to all East Allen County Schools taxpayers. Guided by the mission of "...students distinguished by achievement, knowledge, skills and character" East Allen County Schools' focus is on building meaningful relationship with students to help them learn, develop, and grow as individuals. Always a district with visions and faith, East Allen County Schools have been and continue to be an example of what works in Indiana and nationwide. EACS will continue to honor its past as it moves toward the future.

In the early 1980s an old idea was beginning to sweep the nation – home education. Allen County was no exception. We say "old idea" because schooling certainly took place locally at home in log cabins where there was no school for miles, if at all. Local historians have documented that in the late 1800s Fort Wayne's accomplished Hamilton sisters were schooled at home because their parents "disapproved of the standard public school curriculum." Edith became an internationally recognized expert in Greek civilization and culture. Alice became a medical doctor, worked at Jane Adams' Hull House in Chicago, and later taught at Harvard. And little sister Norah was an artist who worked with James McNeil Whistler in Paris and eventually taught at Hull House, also.

Skipping ahead about one hundred years, three couples from the Fort Wayne area, Ron and Sharon Hoot, David and Karen Pratte, and Mike and Jan Sasser, met in September 1983 to encourage each other in their decision to homeschool their children. At that meeting, they planned a picnic for October 1, 1983 in order to meet other like-mined parents. This led to the organization Fort Wayne Area Home Schools (FWAHS), and they formed the governing board.

At its inception, FWAHS consisted of thirty families that had an interest in homeschooling. Eighteen were from Allen County, three from DeKalb, Wells County had four families, Adams and Noble County each had two, and Huntington had one.

Of the thirty families, twenty actually homeschooled that year. Eight families with children ages five and under and one family with children of school age were seriously considering homeschooling, and one was researching it as a possibility. There were a grand total of six teenagers being homeschooled.

At that time, most of the families had a similar reason for homeschooling their children. Most were evangelical Christians who felt that the secular public schools either ignored or challenged their children's faith. They felt a Biblical call to teach their children in the context of their faith. Through the years, many parents have chosen to homeschool for many other reasons, but Christians are still prominent in the movement and particularly in FWAHS.

FWAHS began the newsletter *Homemade News* to spread information on curriculum and local resources; keep an eye on the legislature in case any anti-homeschooling legislation was introduced; provide information on field trips; and announce group activities such as roller skating parties and square dances.

A reenactment of the First Thanksgiving Feast November 1983 – FWAHS First "Official" Function

As the number of home schools grew in the area and support groups were formed to meet many different needs, FWAHS went from being the support group for six counties to being an umbrella organization with most of its influence in Allen County. It now holds regular orientation meetings, an annual Resource Expo, achievement testing, and high school commencement exercises. FWAHS also provides sponsorship for the Spelling Bee, the Geography Bee, and a Science Fair, all of which feed into the national contests. *Homemade News* now includes classified advertisements, a teen section, local resources and opportunities and a calendar of activities for the group-at-large and specific support groups.

In 1980, FWAHS added a telephone update service, the Info-Line, to get time-sensitive information out faster than *Homemade News* could. This has been replaced by email updates and a website.

For the pioneering homeschool families, it almost became a joke that one of two questions would predictable be asked: "Is that legal?" or "What about socialization?" Some state officials and lawyers felt that the U.S. Constitution and Indiana law provided for the option of homeschooling even from the early years. Local attendance officers were not usually so informed and early homeschoolers dreaded that knock on the door. Except for a couple cases of suspected educational neglect, all inquiries were satisfactorily resolved, and Indiana has become known as one of the best states for home education.

While homeschoolers never feared for their children's social skills, believing that a higher ratio of adult interaction was actually beneficial and that most children had siblings, neighbors, relatives, and church friends with which to interact, it has ironically almost become an issue again today, but not for the same reasons. Now, a homeschooler can be tempted to socialize too much. *Homemade News* is filled with opportunities for special classes and extracurricular activities.

As of fall 1990, over two hundred families subscribed to *Homemade News*, and subscriptions topped seven hundred by May 2005. Currently, Brent and Ambia Cooper, Brad and Shawn Gerber, Tim and Sandie Paden, Brian and Barb Powers, Jim and Denise Snyder and Todd and Lisa Willin serve the homeschooling community as the FWAHS Board of Directors. Today homeschoolders can be found at their basketball and volleyball games, ballroom dancing classes, homeschool choir practice, speech and debate meets, science co-ops. . . and, of yeah, around the kitchen table reading, writing and doing 'rithmetic'!

Fort Wayne Area Home Schools 2005 Graduating Class.

Fort Wayne Community Schools

Celebrating success...one student at a time

Fort Wayne Community Schools

Fort Wayne Community Schools is approaching its 150th year of providing high quality, comprehensive educational services to the citizens of this community. From its beginnings when the first superintendent was hired in 1856, through today, FWCS has provided generations of children with the skills they need to be successful.

FWCS is the second largest public school corporation in Indiana, boasting nearly 32,000 students in 53 schools and a regional career center. The district has flourished because it has embraced changes in the community, state and nation not as obstacles but as opportunities. For example, during World War II years, FWCS enlarged programs for training adults to fit the city's industrial needs while at the same time providing additional services to children by broadening health screenings and providing well-balanced hot lunches - very important during the days of rationing.

Today, FWCS is one of only a few districts in the nation committed to maintaining racial balance in each of its schools – making it one of the few places where children learn first-hand the rich lessons diversity teaches us. In fact, there are more than 73 native languages represented by its students.

The district's choice program gives parents the opportunity to select the school that is best suited for their student. Five magnet elementary schools and one middle school include focuses such as fine arts, math and science, and Montessori. They attract students from across the 146 square miles FWCS serves. Its nearly 300 buses cover 30,000 miles collectively every school day ensuring the choice program is available to all.

Indiana Institute of Technology (Indiana Tech)

Pierson Center, a residence hall dedicated in 2001.

Zollner Engineer Center, the engineering and science center, renovated and doubled in size, and rededicated in 2002.

Seitz Center - The historic administration building built in 1857 to house a Lutheran seminary is the oldest building in Fort Wayne still being used for its original purpose - education.

Abbott Center, a new administration center dedicated in 2001.

Campus of Indiana Tech, 1600 East Washington Boulevard. The college was founded in June of 1930 by John A. Kalbfleisch.

Northwest Allen County Shcools
Then And Now

Northwest Allen County Schools in its beginnings consisted of Eel River, Lake Township and Perry Township. These three townships have since changed to meet the growth during the 1990s in the area. Initially, each township had their own schools, but the Progressive Era of Education in the 1920s caused consolidation to occur. Huntertown School and Arcola School emerged as grades K-12 buildings. Then, in 1959, the General Assembly passed the School Reorganization Act which directed the small township schools found in rural areas to consolidate into larger schools. The result of the School Reorganization Act brought the consolidation of Arcola High School and Huntertown High School. With this consolidation and opening of Carroll High School in 1967, the students saw an increase in both curricular and extra-curricular offerings and opportunities.

When Northwest Allen County Schools (NACS) began in 1965, it was viewed mainly as a rural school corporation. Today, NACS is basically a suburban school corporation with some farming areas.

Due to the population increase in the NACS area, the NACS Superintendent and school board members have used the services of Gann-McKibben Demographics to look at the future growth. The results of the most recent study resulted in the construction of Cedar Canyon Elementary School (Gr. K-5) to open in the fall of 2006.

As the corporation has grown in student numbers, there are those things which have remained the same – the small community/family feeling in each school, staff interested in each student achieving their personal best, students finding success through academic and extra-curricular offerings, strong parent support and volunteerism, and community partnerships.

Schools in the Corporation
Total Enrollment Approximately 5,300 students

Carroll High School (Grades 10-12)
Carroll Freshman Campus (Grade 9)
Carroll Middle School (Grades 6-8)
Maple Creek Middle School (Grades 6-8)
Arcola Elementary School (Grades K-5)
Hickory Center Elementary School (Grades K-5)
Huntertown Elementary School (GradesK-5)
Oak View Elementary School (Grades K-2)
Perry Hill Elementary (Grades 3-5)

Arcola School

Huntertown School

Southwest Allen County Schools

The first school in Aboite Township was a log house donated by George and Rosamond Bullard in 1836 at what is now the southwest corner of U.S. 24 West and Aboite Center Roads, and Miss Livinia Pierce was hired as the first teacher. Bullard School, by 2005, has grown to include ten school buildings; a central office building; a fleet of 62 buses and a bus garage; two maintenance buildings; an 1893 brick one-room schoolhouse whose bell tower is the logo for the school district; 828 employees, 6,281 students; and a budget of $37,900,000.

By early 1890 Aboite had eight brick one-room schoolhouses, roughly two miles apart, as state laws stipulated, to cover the 35.4 square miles of the township. Students in the 1-8 grade schools went shanks mare (walked) to school until retired farmers put planks across wagons and "Rode" the students to school. In 1946 the Consolidation Act closed the one-room schools. The township then had to pay to transfer students to other school districts until Aboite School was built in 1954 on Homestead Road for grades 1-8, and High School students were transferred to Fort Wayne or Whitley County until Homestead High School was opened in 1970.

The township bought 155 acres of land in 1961 along Homestead and Aboite Center Roads for future expansion of the schools and for a 26-acre park. Lafayette Township joined Aboite in 1967 to form the Metropolitan School District of Southwest Allen.

Center School, the one-room brick schoolhouse at the intersection of Aboite Center and Homestead Road, built in 1893, was the fifth brick school in the township. It fell to ruin after 1946 and was bought in the 1960s and restored by the Aboite Township Community Association. Mrs. Linda Huge, a secondary history teacher, began teaching students from area schools in the early 1970s to pay for the upkeep of the building. The Southwest School district reclaimed the building in 1992 and moved it to the south side of the 10,000 block of Aboite Center Road between Summit Middle School and the YMCA. Mrs. Huge is still teaching history in the building as the Schoolmarm.

Center School 1893

Taylor University Fort Wayne

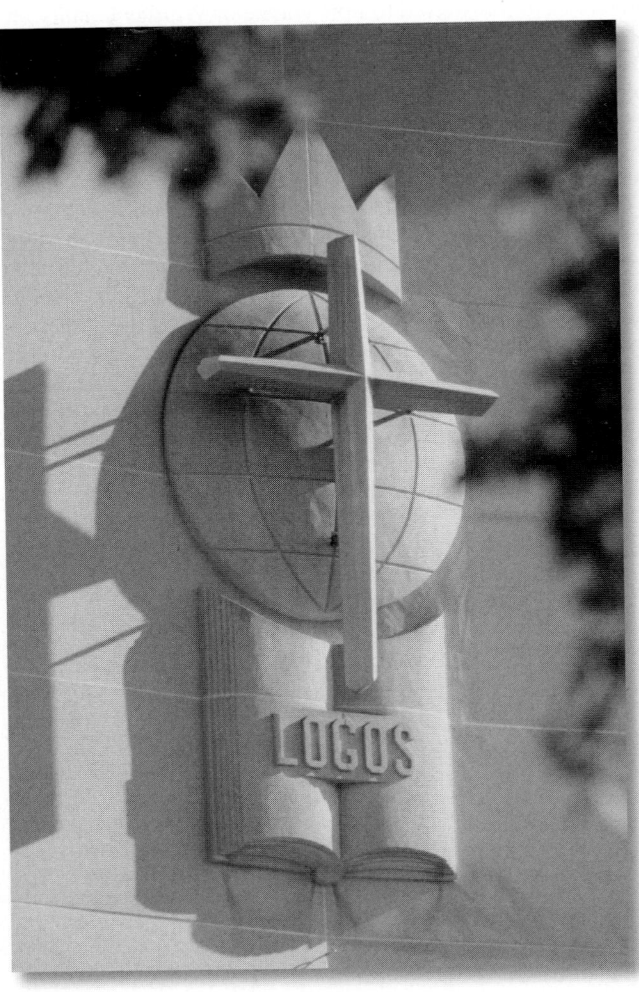

Forged in the fire of intense religious beliefs, Taylor University was destined to become one of the oldest evangelical Christian colleges in America. Conceptualized with the conviction that women as well as men should have an opportunity for higher education, Taylor University began as Fort Wayne Female College in Fort Wayne, Indiana, and then became Fort Wayne College.

Following the example of Oberlin College (which became the first coeducational college in America and the first to award college degrees to women in 1841); Fort Wayne College became coeducational in 1855. In 1890, the school merged with the Fort Wayne College of Medicine and changed its name to Taylor University in honor of Bishop William Taylor.

Perhaps the most influential student at Taylor University in Fort Wayne during the 19th century was Samuel Morris. Born Prince Kaboo, he miraculously escaped certain death during intertribal warfare in Liberia, Africa, was converted to Christ by Methodist missionaries, baptized under the name Samuel Morris, and eventually enrolled at Taylor University in 1891. His passion for God deeply impacted the campus and African American community. On May 12, 1893, Samuel Morris died after contracting a severe cold. Morris' burial at Lindenwood Cemetery, Fort Wayne, remains one of the most frequently visited graves. Inspired by his life, numerous students entered cross-cultural missions and proceeds from his life story helped save the University financially.

In 1893, because of resources provided by the natural gas boom in the central part of the state, Taylor University moved to Upland, Indiana.

Meanwhile, a vision and concern for a Bible Institute was in the mind and heart of Benjamin P. Lugibihl. He founded Bethany Bible Institute, in Bluffton, Ohio, November 1, 1895.

The institute closed in 1901 and was reopened in 1904 under Missionary Church Association direction; D. Y. Schultz, who had served at Bethany Bible Institute in Bluffton since 1896, became superintendent. The stability, growth and survival of the school in the early years can be attributed largely to him. He was involved more than any others in the architectural planning of the first building, which was later named Schultz Hall in his memory.

Shortly thereafter Lugibihl sold the Bluffton property and moved to Fort Wayne to assist in the establishment of the institute in its new location. The search concluded with the purchase of a four and one-half acre lot at South Wayne Avenue and Richardsville Road (currently Rudisill Boulevard); the school moved to its present location in Fort Wayne in 1904 and became know as Fort Wayne Bible Training School.

To the faith and vision of six men must be credited the founding of the Fort Wayne Bible Training School in 1904. They were Joseph E. Ramseyer (president, 1911-44), Daniel Y. Schultz, (superintendent, 1904-11) Benjamin P. Lugibihl, Henry Roth, David Roth and William Egle.

The name changed to Fort Wayne Bible Institute in 1931. Under Dr. Safara Witmer the institute granted four-year degrees (1945), 14 of the remaining 22 acres of the Wiebke Estate were purchased (1946), it became affiliated with Lutheran Hospital for nurses training and was approved by the state for teacher training. In 1950 the institution was renamed Fort Wayne Bible College. Three years later intercollegiate athletics began and in 1958 the remaining eight acres of the Wiebke Estate, along with the Wiebke Homestead were purchased, completing the south campus property. Ground was broken for the S. A. Lehman Memorial Library in 1959. Groundbreaking for S.A. Witmer Memorial Hall took place in 1969. The WBCL radio station was established in 1976 and the college was granted accreditation by North Central Association in 1985. For marketing purposes, the college was renamed Summit Christian College in 1989 and then in 1992, Summit Christian College asked Taylor University to take over the operations of the Fort Wayne Campus, allowing Taylor University to re-established its presence in Fort Wayne.

With this heritage, Taylor University entered the twentieth century. Taylor University's historian, Dr. William Ringenberg, noted, "The intellectual revolution at the turn-of-the-century cracked the spiritual foundations of major universities" in America by challenging the role of the Christian worldview. "This, coupled with the dehumanizing of education" and the unrest caused by "the inability of secular education to guide students in their quest for meaning" helped to further shape, strengthen, and define Taylor's Christian educational mission. Since 1846 Taylor has been faithful to the mission of training men and women for life-long learning to be ambassadors for Jesus Christ to our world in need.

Excerpts taken from "A Vine of God's Own Planting," Dr. Jared Gerig; "Taylor University, the First 150 Years," William C. Ringenberg, "Samuel Morris," Lindley Baldwin, and Taylor University's catalog.

University of Saint Francis - The Bass Mansion

The Bass Mansion is located on the campus of the University of Saint Francis, 2701 Spring Street, Fort Wayne.

Listed on the National Register of Historic Places, the Bass Mansion was the first building on the University of Saint Francis campus.

Originally known as "Brookside," the mansion was the home of industrialist John Henry Bass (1835-1922), a native of Salem, Kentucky, who came to Fort Wayne in 1852, entered the iron foundry business in 1859 and was soon the sole owner of the Bass Foundry and Machine Works, the nationally preeminent maker of castings used in the rail industry.

In 1889, Bass hired local architects to design a summer cottage for a 65-acre tract of land west of the city. When completed that same year, the $15,000 house was named "Brookside" because of the small creek that flowed across the property.

In 1892, Bass had the frame of the house encased in sandstone. He then decided to dam the creek to create Mirror Lake.

In February 1902, a boiler explosion in the basement ignited a fire that left only a portion of the masonry veneer standing. Bass narrowly avoided being crushed by falling stone while trying to save valuables from his library.

By the summer of 1903, the Bass Mansion had been completely rebuilt in stone, concrete and steel. Bass enjoyed his country estate until his death in 1922. His widow, Laura Bass, was prominent in local society until her death in 1935. In 1943, daughter Laura Grace Bass Leslie reluctantly decided to sell the property.

In 1944, the Sisters of Saint Francis of Perpetual Adoration purchased the Bass Mansion as a new home for their women's college. By September, their move from Lafayette, Indiana was complete, and classes began at the Bass Mansion for 62 young women and 14 sisters.

Over the next decade, the Bass Mansion housed the majority of the school. Eventually as the college constructed other buildings, the mansion became the library for the campus. In 2006, upon the completion of the Pope John Paul II Center Library, the Bass Mansion will be renovated to serve as offices and meeting rooms.

The original features of the building including marble fireplaces, murals, staircases, moldings, and lighting fixtures have been preserved. The public is invited to tour the building during library hours, and a booklet on the building's history with photographs is available.

Over the years, the Franciscan university that once was housed in a single building has grown to more than 2000 students and more than 20 buildings including four residence halls. The Bass Mansion is still at its heart.

University of Saint Francis Doermer Family Center of Health Science Education.

Canterbury School

It began in 1976 as a goal shared by a dedicated group of parents: to find or create an educational program that would better challenge their children.

Their first inquiries, beginning with the Episcopal Church and gaining momentum with the National Association of Independent Schools, led them to articulate a vision for a school that would inspire and motivate students while instilling Christian values and morals, cultivating an appreciation for the fine arts, developing foreign language skills and setting high standards for teaching and learning.

That vision was realized on September 8, 1977, when Canterbury School opened as a nondenominational, self-supported school with 89 students in Kindergarten through Grade Six. Though Trinity Episcopal Church provided space for Canterbury in its first three years, the founders chose to operate as an independent school to maintain greater flexibility in the curriculum and to encourage a wider range of families to participate.

Led by Headmaster Jim King, the school enrolled an increasing number of students each year. In 1980, Canterbury moved into an unoccupied Fort Wayne Community Schools building on Covington Road. Again, parents were the driving force, painting walls and scrubbing halls. As Canterbury grew, so did its reputation as a school offering rigorous academic programs.

It seemed only natural that those programs extend to college preparation. When Jonathan Hancock arrived as the fourth headmaster in 1983, he oversaw Canterbury's expansion to Grade 12. And in 1987, the year the first seniors graduated from Canterbury, the school grew yet again, opening a campus for grades nine through 12 on Smith Road. Programs for students as young as two were added that year, providing opportunities for children of every age to meet and embrace the educational challenges envisioned by those caring and dedicated parents who first served as an example of what can be achieved.

Canterbury School

Lafayette Central High School

Lafayette Central High School was constructed in the year 1921. Lunch pails became a thing of the past when a cafeteria was built in 1924. The school also graduated its first class in 1924 with two members receiving diplomas. Soon after 1940 portable classrooms were added to the main structure, giving the school a different appearance.

The Lafayette school band was organized in 1950. For three years mothers worked in the cafeteria without salary so band uniforms could be purchased. A chemistry lab was also supplied the same year. Additional classrooms and a new gymnasium were added to the school in 1954 and 1955.

The high school closed in 1963, having graduated 727 students. During 1969 the original structure and the portables were torn down to make room for the construction of additional classrooms and a new cafeteria. Lafayette Central then served the community as an elementary school with an enrollment of 335 students in the year 1976. In the fall of 1988 and 1989 a science lab, media center and art room were added and enrollment was 223 students. In June 2003, 197 Lafayette Central students bid a fond farewell as the school was closed.

The Lafayette Central school building is located in the center of Lafayette Township and is now the property of the Roanoke Baptist Church and serves them as a church, school, and academy. A new elementary school was built in Lafayette Township and opened in the fall of 2004 in the northern most part of the township.

Alumni from Lafayette Central High School gather each year for a reunion. In 2005 they decided to buy a display case for memorabilia of the school which will be housed in the new Lafayette Meadows Elementary school for all to see.

Lafayette Central High School as it looked 1923-1969 on Lafayette Center Road in Allen County.

Allen County Families

The Nick and Katie Bloom Family, 1980.
Seated, Nick, Bryan Gregory Baltzell, born March 16, 1980, and Katie. First row, l to r: Martha and Jeffrey. Back row, l to r: Gary Baltzell (husband of Janet), Linda, James, Karen, Robert, and Janet. Katie is the Co-Chair of the Allen County History Book Project.

John and Amy Beatty and daughter, Julia, 2006. John is editor of Volume I.

Lee family, 1997. Left corner: granddaughter Carly. L to R: Bill, Jan, Rich, Catherine, Mark, Katie (in arms), Judy. Judge Lee is the Co-Chair of the Allen County History Book Project.

Robb Family, Robert, Phyllis, Shawna, and Brian. Easter of 1971. Phyllis is the editor of Volume II.

DEBRA NELSON ADAIR

Debra (Nelson) Adair was born in Clinton, Indiana, Vermilion County, on July 13, 1954, to Charles E. Nelson and Shirley (Straw) Nelson. Charles was from Fort Wayne, in Allen County, and was stationed at the Air Force Base in Rockville, Indiana at the time. He was born in Fort Wayne on May 18, 1932, to Roy Sylvester Nelson and Mae (Frame) Nelson. The Nelson family moved to Fort Wayne in the 1920's. The Nelson family previously lived in Decatur, Indiana, and northern Ohio, and can be traced to a Charles Nelson listed on the 1791 Kentucky census. Debra's grandmother, Mae (Frame) Nelson, had family in Aboite Township in Allen County. They had followed the westward migration from New York through Ohio. They can be traced to Ireland and Scotland in the 1780's. Mae Nelson was a kind and gentle soul, and much beloved by her family.

Rosa, Douglass, Carol and Debra Adair, Thermal, California 2003.

Shirley was born in Clinton on July22, 1935, to Charles R. Straw and Ruth (Seldomridge) Straw. The Straw lineage can be traced from Southern Indiana to Virginia, where the name had been Stroh in the 1790's. The Seldomridge lineage is traced to Dayton, Ohio, back to Virginia, and then to Pennsylvania, where it was originally Zeltenreich.

Debra moved to Lafayette Indiana while her father Charles attended Purdue University. The family then moved to Fort Wayne. She attended various schools in the Fort Wayne area, graduating in the first graduating class from Homestead Jr/Sr High School in 1972. She attended Ball State University in Muncie for one year, majoring in Music. Events then led her to Southern California, where she worked as a volunteer for the United Farm Workers Union. She met and married her husband, Douglass G. Adair III, in the Coachella Valley. Debra went on to earn a Bachelor of Science in Nursing from California State University. She worked for many years as an obstetrical nurse, and then moved into Public Health Nursing. Her husband Douglass was born in Princeton, New Jersey on December 10, 1942, lived for many years in Williamsburg, Virginia, and then moved to Claremont, California in the 1950s.He earned degrees in History from Pomona College and Claremont Graduate School. He then joined the farm workers in the central valley of California in 1965, and worked as editor of the Union newspaper, "El Macriado". He worked for a number of years in various capacities with the United Farm Workers. He farmed in the Coachella Valley, growing organic dates. Debra and Douglass lived in Thermal, California, and had two daughters, Rosa K. Adair, born May 28, 1978, and Carol R. Adair, born January 26, 1980. Debra had two siblings, Steven A. Nelson, born December 5, 1959, in Fort Wayne, and Sharla J. (Nelson) Parrish, born February 27,1965, in Phoenix, Arizona, where the family resided for one year. They also graduated from Homestead High School. Steven lived in Las Vegas, and Sharla resided north of Fort Wayne in Ashley, Indiana.

Submitted by Debra Nelson Adair.

FRED ANDREW & VERNA MAY SHOECRAFT ADAMS

Dr. Verna May Shoecraft Adams, her husband Fred Andrew Adams, and infant daughter (Jacqueline) moved to Fort Wayne, Indiana from Toledo, Ohio in early Spring, 1947. After his World War II discharge from the army, Fred was offered a civil service job as mail carrier at the US Post Office in Fort Wayne. After retirement as Special Delivery Mail Carrier, he worked as an apartment complex manager and real estate broker. Verna began a career in the field of education.

Verna May Shoecraft was born July 1, 1928 in Toledo, Ohio and Fred Andrew Adams was born in Monktown, Texas, September 21, 1917. They had four children: Jacqueline Ogrietta Adams Redd, Fred Andrew Adams, Jr., Douglas Frederick Adams, and Cynthia Verna Adams McBride.

Verna's parents are John Henry Shoecraft, Jr., born in Marion, Indiana, on January 21, 1890, and Ogrietta Armena Lee Shoecraft, born in Mobile, Alabama, on July 14, 1902. John H. Shoecraft, Jr.'s parents were John Henry Shoecraft and Alice Grey Shoecraft. They had five children: Esther May Shoecraft Allen, Mabel Shoecraft Hall, Ernest Shoecraft, Gertrude Shoecraft and John H. Shoecraft, Jr. Ogrietta Armena Lee Shoecraft's parents were Charles Lee and Cecelia Thornton Lee. They had six children: Marietta Lee Russell, Moses Lee, Ogrietta Armena Lee Shoecraft, Bernistine Lee White, William Alphonse Lee, Charles Lee, Jr , and Marcella Lee Sayers.,

Fred's parents are Oscar Adams, born in Texas and Gertrude Mikel Adams, born in Texas. They had four children: Fred Andrew Adams, Josephine Adams Henderson, Paul Lawrence Dunbar Adams, and Arma Adams.

In 1961, Verna May Shoecraft Adams became an elementary public school teacher in the Fort Wayne school system. Throughout the years, she held other positions as Guidance Counselor for the Adult Basic Education Program, Elementary School Consultant Teacher, Elementary school principal, and Director of federally funded Title 1 Program. She retired in 1980 as Director of Supplemental Education Programs. She also served as a faculty member of St. Francis College as a part-time Lecturer-Instructor.

Submitted by Verna May Shoecraft Adams, Ed.D

MARCIA ADAMS

Marcia Adams, award winning food columnist, cookbook author and TV personality, moved to Fort Wayne in 1966 with her small son Gerard. She had been raised in Steuben County by her school teacher parents, Esther and Merle Grabill, both active community leaders. Attending Bowling Green State University, she was previously married to Armand Sicard, and lived in Butler, Indiana. That marriage ended in divorce.

Marcia Adams

Moving to Fort Wayne, she began a live daily half hour television show with WPTA in 1968. Covering everything from macaroni and cheese, to Mozart, to Martin Luther King, her show was popular from its very beginning.

She later remarried and became active in all the arts, among them her favorite, the Fort Wayne Museum of Art. She served on that board for eight years. When the Louis Kahn designed Performing Arts Center was built, she was co-chairperson for Community Giving.

Later, when the new Museum of Art was built, she was again chairperson of the Community Giving Division.

They moved to Warsaw in 1989. "I am a trailing spouse," she mournfully observed; however, she became active in that community as well, forming the Winona Lake Preservation Association. She sparked an ongoing interest in retaining the historical sites that were associated with the baseball evangelist, Billy Sunday. Winona Lake was the Sunday family's favorite tabernacle.

During the years in Winona Lake, she became a corporate art consultant, designing and developing art programs for large businesses around the state. In 1993 she was named to the Indiana Arts Commission.

Also while in Winona Lake, she began her food writing career, publishing her prize-winning and well-known, COOKING FROM QUILT COUNTRY, based on the lifestyle and food ways among Indiana Amish. This book was quickly followed by other highly acclaimed pieces of American food history; HEARTLAND COOKING, CHRISTMAS IN THE HEARTLAND, HEIRLOOM COOKING, FAVORITE RECIPES and NEW RECIPES FROM QUILT COUNTRY.

All of her books were made into public television series and were aired around the world on the Armed Forces Network. At this time she was named a "Sagamore of the Wabash."

Returning to Fort Wayne in 1999 and suffering from heart disease, she wrote two more books, MARCIA ADAMS: HEART TO HEART, and MARCIA ADAMS; HEART ANEW describing her wait for an available heart for transplant.. These books were made into a national prize-winning television documentary.

Having waited thirteen months for a new heart, she had a successful heart transplant in April of 2001. In 2004, she was selected by the Woman's Bureau as one of six women to receive the Hidden Heroines award.

Now living on a quiet lake in Fort Wayne, she continues to write, travels, gardens, and entertains. Currently she is writing a new book on gardening in the midwest. Its working title is BLOOM.

Submitted by Marcia Adams

JOHN & SUSAN (SCHMIT) ADANG FAMILY

Following their births in Seneca County, Ohio, and their growth to maturity, neighbors John Adang and Susan Schmit were married in 1883 in Alvadea, Ohio. Mary, William, and Catherine were born to the couple. The young family then moved to Indiana, and eventually settled on a farm in Jay County, Indiana. The family farm was on a rural Geneva, Indiana, mail delivery route. Here the younger children were born, Charles, Edward, Frank, Joseph, Emma, and Alfred.

As the family grew, the eldest child, Mary, moved to Fort Wayne to work in a private residence. She was soon followed by her sister Catherine, and brothers Charles, Edward, Joseph, and Alfred "Happy". All of these brothers became employees of the Nickel Plate Railroad in Fort Wayne. It was at the Nickel Plate Railroad that the pronunciation of the family name became A Dang. (In Jay County, and earlier in Seneca County, Ohio, it was Adding.) The paymaster calling the pay packets used the pronunciation A Dang. Edward Adang, who served in World War I, and worked in Ohio for several decades following his military service, was the only family member to retain the older version of the surname. Documentation of the earlier pronunciation of the name is found in the Landeck, Ohio, centennial book. A group photo identifies John Adang's brother as Frank Adding. Further verification of the original Adding pronunciation of the family name is given by the descendants of John's brother, Nicholas, who settled in Columbia City where the family was always known as Adding.

William Adang married Catherine Kinney and remained on the family farm in Jay County. Frank Adang died as a youth and is buried with his parents in the family plot at Saint Mary's Church, Geneva, Indiana. Emma married Joe Topp and moved to Delphos, Ohio. Alfred Adang was transferred to Ohio by the railroad, but returned to Indiana in his retirement.

Mary Adang married Joseph Reitz. Their children were Helen, married Willarad Moses, Herbert, married Mildred Westerman, Robert, married Kaye, and Rita, married Richard Cullen, deceased, and second, Granger Baron.

Catherine married Mr. Heidrich. Their children were Mary Lou (Smith), Richard "Brick", Mildred (Snyder), and Dorothy (Rice).

Charles married Josephine Topp. Their children were Jeanette, who died in childhood, Dorothy who married Robert Quinn, John who married Ann Bauermester, Leroy who married Letha Bainbridge, Frank, and Dale who married Janice Alvey.

Edward married Dorothy Duffy in Canton, Ohio. Their children, both born in Ohio, were Ann who married Jack Oxley, and Robert who married Joan Freiburger. After several decades in Columbus, Ohio, Edward Adang and family moved to Fort Wayne where he worked as state supervisor for the Catholic Order of Forester.

Joseph Adang married Matilda Boyce. Their children were Joan who married Carl Koch, and Mary Lou who married Kenneth Merz.

Most of the siblings and their children were Allen County residents from the second decade of the twentieth century onward. Descendants of Catherine, Joseph, Charles and Edward Adang, continue to reside in Allen County.

Submitted by Ann Oxley.

ADLER-LUTTMAN FAMILY

Oscar and Louise Adler owned Adler's Dairy Company. Oscar immigrated to Fort Wayne with his brother Alphonse and other family members from Lutz, Poland, although they spoke German and were of German descent. Louise emigrated from Ulm, Germany and they married, having three children, Gertrude, William and Helen. The Dairy existed into the 1930's. Oscar and Louise also owned a tavern and a meat market in later years. They have grandchildren and great grandchildren in the Fort Wayne area.

Adler's Dairy Company Milk Wagon in front of Lutheran Hospital in 1913.

Left, Martin Luttman and clerk, 1920s.

Martin Luttman owned a grocery store at 1220 East Pontiac Street in Fort Wayne, Indiana in the 1920's. Mart was the second husband of Edda (Smith) Robinson whose family was one of the first settlers of Hoagland, Indiana. She was the mother of Darce C. Robinson and Clarence B. Robinson. Darce and Olive Robinson had two children, Phyllis (Robinson) Adler and Keith Robinson (Rita). Clarence and his wife, Betty Robinson, had one child, Robert Robinson (Jodie).

These three grandchildren would go to the grocery store after it closed for the day to be with Grandpa Mart while he counted the day's earnings. Their presence made it safe because a robber would not rob a store if children were present.

Submitted by Janet Meyers.

AHLSCHWEDE FAMILY

It certainly never crossed his mind when George "Friedrich" Ahlschwede wrote his unpublished diary that this document would help his descendants become acquainted with one another two centuries later. "A History of The Ahlschwede Family" covers the time from 1808, when Friedrich was born in Ottenstein, Germany, to the 1860s in Adams Township, Allen County, Indiana.

Friedrich was the first-born of George Heinrich Conrad "Phillip" Ahlschwede (1785-1852) and Elizabeth Wilhelmina, nee Koch, (born circa 1783) who lived in Hajen on the Weser River. The first siblings to emigrate left March 11, 1846, and sailed with their families from Copenhagen to Buffalo, New York. Ludwig went directly to Wisconsin, and George and sister, Friedericke, to Marion Township. On December 14, 1847, Friedericke married Heinrich Lepper at St. Paul Lutheran Church, Soest.

On April 27, 1850, their brother Christian left his wife behind and immigrated to Indiana. Then after years of floods, crop failures, and a cholera epidemic, ten more family members emigrated via Copenhagen on September 4,1851: the parents, son Friedrich with his pregnant wife and their three children, as well as a son by his deceased first wife Mary, nee Winckelman; daughter Caroline; and Christian's wife Louise, nee Arneke. Twenty-eight days later, they debarked in New York and arrived in Allen County on October 31. Friedrich wrote that the first thing he and Christian did was to buy 80 acres of land (on Tillman Road). The brothers paid $350.00 and divided the land to give each one 40 acres. Friedericke and the Lepper family purchased 80 acres next to them and relocated to their land "in thick forest" in March 1852.

Tragedy soon struck the family. Friedrich wrote that when he went to visit George at his house, he found his brother sick. George died on September 14. "On the evening of September 15 father and I laid his corpse into the casket... we went home in seemingly good health. . .but father became sick. . . and the Lord called him home on the 17th. . . on the 15th the little daughter (Maria "Wilhelmina" Lepper) of my sister died. She was buried at the same time my brother was buried. . . on the 26th. . . on the way home (from Church) my wife became ill." Johanna Louise, nee Flugel, died two days later at age 29.

Friedrich remarried in 1853 and had five more children with his wife Anna Katherine, nee Grimm. Caroline married August Reiling circa 1854 and lived in Fort Wayne. In 1866, the last sibling, the widow Wilhelmina Ahlschwede Starke, and her five children left Hajen and settled in Huntington. She married Jacob Shenkel in 1876. After his death, the widow and son of George who had died in 1852 also moved to Huntington. Christian had five children and Friedericke had seven. Now, in 2005, names like Ahlschwede, Stark, Reiling, Steigmeyer, Wilkinson, Trier, Thiem, Meyer, Lepper, Jackemeyer, Krauskopf, and Kikuchi can be found in places like Indiana, Hawaii, Alaska, North Dakota, Wisconsin, Nebraska, Florida, Illinois, and throughout the United States.

Submitted by Delores Jackemeyer Kikuchi

BILLY GLENN & BERNICE MARILYN (PARKER) ALLEN FAMILY

Billy Glenn Allen was born September 25, 1926 in Buckeye Hollow, Moore County, Tennessee to William (Willie) David and Ida Lee (Woodard) Allen. He was the youngest of six children. Billy's father died when he was fourteen years old. He had to quit school in the eighth grade to help provide for the family. Billy met Bernice Marilyn Parker, born December 25, 1925 in Goosepond Community, Coffee County, Tennessee, in a shoe factory in Tullahoma, Tennessee. Bernice was the second of six children of Levi Orman and Inez Miriam (Leek) Parker. After returning from active duty in World War II, Billy married Bernice on December 20, 1946. They had two boys. Glenn Parker Allen, born March 15, 1948 in Tullahoma, is married to Rebecca Jo Gabe. He has two children: Rita Yvonne, born October 27, 1974 (from a previous marriage) and Alexandra Michelle born October 1992.

Glenn, Bernice, Wayne, Billly Allen, 1955

Wayne William Allen, born January 19, 1951 in Tullahoma, married Carolyn Louise Paxson on December 23, 1972 at Harvester Avenue Missionary Church in Fort Wayne. They have three children: Joshua Cole, born August 16, 1974 in Fort Wayne, Rachel Marie, born June 1, 1977 in Fort Wayne and Caleb Wayne, born June 30, 1987 in West Kalimantan, Indonesia.

Bill was unable to find work in Tennessee. Bernice's sister who was living in Fort Wayne encouraged them to join her there. In 1953, they moved to Fort Wayne. Bill found various jobs to pay the bills, keep food on the table and clothes on their backs. In 1955, the family started attending Harvester Avenue Missionary Church and the family later became members. Bill served as trustee and usher and Bernice served as a Sunday School teacher for many years and sang in the choir. In 1960 Bernice got a job at General Electric and a couple of years later Bill got a job at Eckrich Meat Packing. Life became a little easier. The boys, Glenn and Wayne, attended Adams Elementary School and later Central High School. Glenn graduated from Central in 1966. Wayne had to transfer to South Side, graduating in 1969. Both graduated from college. In December 1976, a job related injury started a downturn in Bernice's health. She lived to see and love only her first three grandchildren, passing away on August 29, 1984, at 58 years of age. She is buried in Covington Memorial Gardens. When Eckrich closed in Fort Wayne, Bill took an early retirement, but drove cars for the Indiana Auto Auction for nearly ten years before retiring again. Bill is still enjoying a little gardening, tinkering in the yard, his sons, grandchildren, and great-grandchildren. *Submitted by B. Allen*

CYRUS & ISAAC ALLEN FAMILY

Cyrus came to Fort Wayne in 1838, and Isaac came in 1846. Isaac was born December 10, 1787 in Cumberland, Maine. He married Elizabeth Coy, born April 11, 1812 in Androscoggin, Maine. Isaac died November 8, 1862 in Fort Wayne and Elizabeth died in Fort Wayne, May 3, 1891. They are buried in Lindenwood Cemetery. They had the following children: Sarah Ann born July 4, 1814 in Maine; Cyrus W. born February 7, 1817 in Paris Oxford, Maine; Cyrus (submitter's great grandfather); Samuel; John B. born December 14, 1818 in Maine; Abigail Lou; Judith Rodantha born 1825 in Greenville, Penobscot, Maine.

Cyrus Allen, who came to Fort Wayne in 1838, was a ship's carpenter in Maine, and when he came to Fort Wayne, he had a carpenter shop on the west side of Fulton Street, south of Wayne Street. Cyrus joined the Westminster Presbyterian Church in 1845. He served as 4th Ward alderman in 1855. He married Cynthia Matilda Ferris of Fort Wayne, whose father was Ezekial Farris, on November 22, 1855. She was born November 23,1813 in New York and died in Fort Wayne May 3, 1891 at Cyrus's home. She and Cyrus are buried in Lindenwood Cemetery. According to the Fort Wayne Directories, Cyrus lived on Fulton, Street; 165 West Wayne Street; 171 West Wayne; 324 West Washington; and 256 East Creighton Street.

His parents, Isaac and Elizabeth Allen, came from Greenville, Maine to Perrysburg, Ohio. In 1846 the family moved to Fort Wayne by way of the Wabash-Erie canal from Toledo, Ohio on a packet boat. Some of their children stayed in Ohio, but, in the census of 1850, John B. and Rodantha were listed in Fort Wayne.

Cyrus and Cynthia had six children: William C. born March 30, 1857; Jennie M. born 1859; Frank F. born 1862; George J. born 1864; Albert born 1867; and Ethan born September 2, 1871. Ethan was submitter's grandfather. He became a medical doctor and graduated in the Class of 1898 from Fort Wayne Medical College. He started his medical practice at the Indiana State Soldiers Home in West Lafayette where he met submitter's grandmother, Lenore Hord. They were married there March 12,1898. He was killed in an auto accident in Sheldon, Illinois January 19, 1912. They had two daughters, Helene Lenore born November 9, 1902, and Jessie Catherine born February 26, 1905.

Helene married Norel T. McLaughlin October 25, 1925 in Indianapolis, and they had two daughters, (Alice) Priscilla born March 2, 1929 and Catherine Suzanne born June 30, 1934. Submitter says, "My sister and I treasure the fact that we have two First Familes Certificates from The Allen County Genealogical Society of Indiana: one for Cyrus W. Allen and one for Ezekiel Mead Ferris."

Submitted by Priscilla McLaughlin Baumheckel

ALLEN, REID & BOUILLON FAMILIES

Isaac Allen was born in 1756 at Cape May, Massachusetts. He served in the Revolutionary War from 1777 through October 1780 and received a pension. He married Abigail Bradbury in 1782 and she bore 13 children. Isaac died in Minot, Maine, in 1854 at age 98. Abigail died in 1832 in Minot. Their son, Isaac, was born in 1787 in Minot, where he married Elizabeth Coy in 1812. In 1835 his family moved to Perrysburg, Ohio, via the Wabash-Erie Canal and in 1846 moved to Fort Wayne, Indiana. Their six children came with them and most lived in the Fort Wayne area. Isaac died in 1862 when he was run over by a truck. Elizabeth died in 1865. Both are buried in Lindenwood Cemetery.

The youngest Allen daughter, Rodantha Allen, was born in Greenville, Maine, in 1825. She married Adam Daniel Reid in 1854 in Fort Wayne. Adam Daniel was born in Richmond, Indiana, in 1826. In 1850, he walked to Fort Wayne and in 1852 he began the manufacture of steel plows at the corner of Water and Clinton, Lot 5, original plat. In 1854, he moved to Main Street west of Harrison, Lot 537, in Hanna's Addition. In 1857, he moved to southwest corner of Main and Maiden Lane, retiring in 1868 because of poor health. He died in 1900 and is buried in Lindenwood Cemetery. In 1911, his widow, Rodantha, moved to Los Angeles with two sons where she died in 1915, aged 90 and is buried. Adam and Rodantha had five children.

1870 Fort Wayne Directory advertisement for A.D. Reid & Co.

Arthur Allen Reid was born in 1861 in Fort Wayne. He worked at the Bass Foundry and retired in 1926. As a young lad he was one of many who swam in the aqueduct, and his name appears on the Aqueduct statue on Main Street along with his brother, Charles. Arthur married Wilhemina Schoppman in 1898, and they had three children. The only daughter, Edith May Reid, was born in 1900. She attended Clay School and later worked at the Edison Lamp Works assembling light bulbs. She married Lloyd Bouillon in 1923. He was an automobile mechanic and worked for Browers on Broadway for many years. He was a Mason in Home Lodge. They had two children; Lois who married James Gooley in 1949, and he died in 1979. They had three children, Christine, James and Matthew. Lois continues to live in Fort Wayne. Lloyd and Edith's son, Richard, was born in 1924, played football at Northside High School, graduated in 1942 and joined the Army Air Corps. He became a pilot and made the U.S. Air Force his career, retiring in 1970. He married Harriet Weber in 1953. She died in 1961 leaving five children; Andrea, Phillip, Jeffrey, Anne and Lee. Richard married Alice Culbert in 1962. The family returned to Fort Wayne when Richard retired. He died January 13, 2005, and is buried in Lindenwood. There are eight grandchildren; Jennifer, Brian, Michael, Ryan, Erin, Andrew, Noah and Colin to survive him.

Submitted by Alice (Culbert) Bouillon

WAYNE WILLIAM & CAROLYN LOUISE (PAXSON) ALLEN FAMILY

Wayne William Allen was born January 19, 1951 in Tullahoma, Tennessee, to Billy Glenn and Bernice Marilyn (Parker) Allen. He was the younger of the two boys. He moved with his family to Fort Wayne in 1953 after his father was unable to find work in Tennessee. Wayne and Carolyn Louise Paxson, born August 2, 1952 to Robert Devereaux and Dorothy Almira (Shaneyfelt) Paxson, met at Harvester Avenue Missionary Church while they.were very young, and later married on December 23, 1972 at Harvester Church.

Caleb, Wayne, Josh, Rachel, and Carolyn, Christmas 1989

Wayne graduated from South Side High School in 1969, got a full time job at General Electric and enrolled at IUPU (as it was then known). After Carolyn's graduation from North Side High School in 1970, they both enrolled at Fort Wayne Bible College. After a year Carolyn continued her studies at Lutheran Hospital School of Nursing, and midway through their college years they married. Carolyn received a diploma in nursing in 1974 and gave birth to their first son, Joshua Cole, two months later, August 16, 1974. (Josh married Lisa Jill Paul on August 5, 2000, in Fort Wayne.)

Carolyn worked at Lutheran Hospital until Wayne finished his degree in missions at Fort Wayne Bible College in June 1975. Following a mission internship, the birth of their daughter, Rachel Marie on June 1, 1977 (Rachel married Scott Stanley Amstutz on December 19, 1998 in Fort Wayne.) and fundraising, the family moved to West Kalimantan, Indonesia on December 31, 1977. Ten years later a second son, Caleb Wayne was born on June 30, 1987 in West Kalimantan, Indonesia.

Wayne completed two master degrees, one from Grace Theological Seminary in 1981 and one from Fuller Theological Seminary in 1991. In December 1990 the family moved back to Fort Wayne after 13 years in Indonesia. Wayne headed up the missions department at Summit Christian College (formerly FWBC) and Carolyn worked at Lutheran Homes, Inc. and Transitional Care Unit at St. Joseph Hospital. When Summit merged with Taylor University (1992) Wayne got the pink slip. He then enrolled at Concordia Theological Seminary and finished his Ph. D. in Intercultural Studies in May 1997, the same month Josh graduated from IPFW with a degree in Structural Engineering Technology. Josh, '92, and Rachel, '95, both graduated from South Side High School. While Josh and Rachel attended IPFW Wayne, Carolyn and Caleb moved to Kingston, Jamaica where Wayne chaired the missions department at The Caribbean Graduate School of Theology from June 1996-December 2002. In January 2003 Wayne became the Regional Director for Asia and the Middle East for World Partners, USA. Caleb will graduate from Keystone Schools, Inc. in Fort Wayne on May 27, 2005 as valedictorian. He has been accepted at Purdue and Rose Hulman Institute of Technology. He plans on entering the field of engineering.

Scott and Rachel have given us two grandchildren, Aleah Marie, born April 18, 2003 and Bruce Wayne, born January 23, 2005.

Submitted by Carolyn Allen

WILFORD G. ALLEN & MARGARET M. ANKENBRUCK FAMILY

Wilford G. Allen was born in Mobile, Alabama, on October 29, 1928, the son of Richard Hart Allen and Valena Peters Allen. When Wilford was five years old, his family moved to Pittsburgh, where Wilford distinguished himself as a member of the swim team, and the football team at Peabody High School.

In July 1949 he joined the U.S. Air Force and was a member of the first integrated Air Force basic training squadron at Lackland Air Force Base. After serving as a radio operator during the Korean War, Wilford returned home and played semi-pro football for the Pittsburgh Cubs for several years. The highlight of his semi-pro career came in November 1955, when he intercepted a pass thrown by Johnny Unitas, then quarterback of the Bloomfield Rams. (Unitas had been drafted that year by the Pittsburgh Steelers but was cut from the team, and the next year he began his Hall of Fame career with the Baltimore Colts.)

Margaret Ankenbruck, Wilford Allen and Preston Allen

Wilford operated a barbershop in Pittsburgh, and later worked in the Veterans Administration hospitals in Pittsburgh, and Martinsburg, West Virginia. In 1979 he moved to Fort Wayne where he met and married Fort Wayne native, Margaret M. Ankenbruck.

Margaret, born August 12, 1949, is the daughter of Thomas and Katherine (Allgeier) Ankenbruck. Margaret was a member of the first graduating class at Bishop Dwenger High School in 1967. She later earned a B.A. in political science from the University of Dayton, and a J.D. from the Indiana University School of Law in Bloomington, Indiana. When Margaret was hired in 1974 by the law division of Lincoln National Corporation, she was one of only three or four female attorneys practicing in Fort Wayne. In 1983 Margaret joined the editorial page staff of The News-Sentinel, where she wrote a bi-weekly column for many years. She is now an attorney for the Social Security Administration Office of Hearings and Appeals.

Margaret served as an at-large member of the Allen County Council from 2001 to 2004, and was active as a board member of many community organizations, including Northeast Indiana Public Radio, Girl Scouts of the Limberlost, and Fort Wayne Youtheatre. She also performed for many years as a member of the Fort Wayne Philharmonic Chorus, and in productions of the Civic Theatre, First Presbyterian Theatre, and Arena Dinner theatre. She won an Anthony Award for best ensemble performance in 1993 for her role in "Hans Christian Andersen."

Margaret and Wilford have one son, Preston W. Allen, born May 19, 1985.

Submitted by Margaret Ankenbruck.

DANIEL ALLGEIER

Stephen and Mary (Bashab) Allgeier had six children. Their names were Mary, Henry, Daniel, Peter, August and Mary Francis. Stephen had four children from a previous marriage, of which he was a widower. Their names were: Charles, Catherine, Frank J. and Matilda.

Daniel was born on June 28, 1859. He married Eva Lerch on October 11, 1910. Eva was born on March 4, 1893 to Henry and Sabina (Gebhart) Lerch. Daniel and Eva Allgeier had six children. Daniel died on February 22, 1929. Eva Allgeier died on December 28, 1967.

The six children of Daniel and Eva went their separate ways but always kept in touch.

Henry was born on July 11, 1911. He married June Catherine Martin in 1950. There were no children. Henry died on August 20, 1986. June Catherine lived at St. Anne's Home in Fort Wayne.

Mary S. was born around May 21, 1912 and died in infancy.

Andrew E. was born on May 7, 1913. He never married. Andrew stayed on the farm until 1971, He lived at Byron Health Center, where he stayed until his death on February 19, 1981.

Marion D. was born on May 7, 1916 and married Norbert Korty from Lafayette, Indiana, on November 25, 1943. They had 14 children. Marion died.on December 24, 1979 of breast cancer.

Daniel F. was born on April 2, 1918. He never married. He was involved in World War II in the Pacific before getting transferred to the air force in 1943. Daniel died in combat at the Battle of the Bulge in Germany on December 24, 1944. He later was buried in the Catholic Cemetery in August 1948.

Georgian J. was born on November 9, 1921. She went to New Haven High School and graduated in 1940. She married Howard Hoevel on November 20, 1948. They had three daughters - Madonna, Catherine and Diane Hoevel. Howard Hoevel had a heart attack and preceded Georgian in death in 1982.

Madonna M. Hoevel was born on September 1, 1949. She married Neil S. Reynolds on August 25, 1973. They have two children - Clint

Reynolds, who was born on June 21, 1977 and Amanda Reynolds, who was born on March 6, 1982. The Reynolds family lives in Hoagland. They own and operated the Northeast Indiana Grain Inspection.

Catherine A. Hoevel was born on September 13, 1952. She married James Lassen on June 2, 1973. They had two children by adoption from Columbia, South America: Christopher J. Lassen, born February 12, 1983 and Ana M. Lassen, born January 20, 1987. Catherine and James divorced on January 20, 2001.

Diane C. Hoevel was born on May 2,1956. She married Blane P. Ryan on May 31,1981. They had three children: Colette M., who was born on March 19, 1984; Eric P., who was born on May 10, 1988; and Leslie A., who was born on December 23, 1991. They lived in Monroeville.

Submitted by Cathy (Hoevel) Lassen

HENRY G. & MAGDALENE (FISHER) ALLGEIER FAMILY

Henry G. Allgeier Sr. (1857-1928), was born in Fort Wayne, Indiana, the son of Stephen and Mary (Baschab) Allgeier. Stephen Allgeier, born in 1818, had come to the United States in 1836, from Baden, Germany. Stephen's parents, who remained in Germany, were Lorenz and Salome Allgeier.

Henry Allgeier married Magdalene "Lena" Fisher on June 24, 1884. Lena was born in 1863, in Huntington, Indiana. Her parents, Jacob Fisher, a gardener, and Barbara (Moller) Fisher, had come to Indiana from Prussia in 1853, with the five children they had at that time, Nicholas, John, Michael, Marguerite, and Elizabeth.

Of Henry and Lena's 11 surviving children, seven entered the religious life: Msgr. J. Nicholas Allgeier (1886-1972) was ordained in 1911, and was pastor of St. Mary's Catholic Church in Fort Wayne from 1935 to 1963. Julius (1887-1972), a Christian Brother, was a high school teacher and athletic director in Philadelphia. Joseph (1889-1961), a Christian Brother, was a teacher in Pittsburgh. Albert (1891-1983), a Christian Brother, was bursar at LaSalle College in Philadelphia. Bernadette "Sister Bernadette" (1893-1990) was principal at St. Mary's Catholic School in Fort Wayne. Marie "Sister Gregory" (1897), deceased, and Hildegard "Sister De La-Salle" (1899), deceased, both taught at St. Peter's Catholic School. All three were members of the School Sisters of Notre Dame.

Henry and Lena's other children were: Charles (1883-1939), a child by a previous marriage; Henry G. Jr. (1895-1954), a cashier at Lincoln National Bank; Alphonse (1903-1964), an employee of Berghoff Brewery; and Agnes McCuen Pottit (1908), deceased, an Army nurse during World War II. Two other children died in infancy.

Henry G. Allgeier Sr. owned the Allgeier Manufacturing Company, which fabricated barrels for Berghoff Brewery at a factory located on Francis Street, near Lewis Street in Fort Wayne.

Submitted by David and Freda Ankenbruck.

HENRY G. & MARIE (HARTMAN) ALLGEIER FAMILY

Henry G. "Peach" Allgeier Jr. was born in Fort Wayne on March 7, 1895 and died August 23, 1954. He was one of 13 children of Henry George Allgeier and Magdalene "Lena" (Fisher) Allgeier. Peach, who earned his nickname by being such "a peach of a guy", graduated from the St. Mary's Commercial School and a business course. He was an early employee of the German American Bank, which became Lincoln National Bank. He used his banking skills as a member of the Army quartermaster corps during World War I. Later, he managed the south branch of Lincoln Bank until it was closed during the Great Depression. He then returned to the main branch as a cashier until his death, after 44 years of service.

Henry married Marie Ann Hartman on October 21, 1919. Marie, born June 5, 1895, died April 26, 1949. She was one of eight children of Jacob and Annie (Ankenbruck) Hartman. She graduated from St. Mary's Commercial School and worked as secretary to Bert Griswold during the period when he was compiling a history of Fort Wayne families. Henry and Marie had two daughters: Mary Ann, born June 24, 1921, who married Joseph Voors Jr., and Katherine Marie, born October 15, 1926, who married Thomas Ankenbruck.

Henry and Marie were charter members of St. Jude Catholic Church, established in 1929. Henry served as a trustee of the parish for two terms.

Submitted by Joseph and Mary Voors.

Henry G. Allgeier family.
Front row, Charles, Agnes, Henry G., Magdalene, J. Nicholas, Alphonse. Back row, Henry (Peach), Joseph, Marie, Julius, Bernadette, Albert, Hildegard.

Henry G. Allgeier II and Marie A. Hartman wedding, October 21, 1919.

ANTON & ANGELA (BERG) ALT

Anton (1848-1898) and Angela (Berg) Alt (1855-1933) arrived in New York from near Trier, Germany with six children on the Westerland, June 27, 1888. Anton is passenger #601 and Gertrude Berg, age 22, is #610, sister of Angela. Later, the sisters sent for their brother, Peter Berg.

Rose (1878-1956) married Orville L. Creasey. She raised her nephew John Maxwell after his mother's death.

Nicholas (1881-1950) married Edith Christina Broeking and had 12 children: Helen (1907-1913), Anthony J. (1908 Youngstown -1991) married in 1929, M. Juanita Hamilton. Edith (1910 Youngstown -1992 Detroit) married in 1934, George Taylor. William Vincent (1912-1997) married in 1934, Bernice Roser, (divorced). Marie "Mary" Rose (1914-1916). James (1915) married in 1939, Geraldine Firestine. **Gertrude (1918-1997) married in 1939, Robert Lauer. Madeline Helen (October 1919-November 1919). Genevieve (1921-1995 Cleveland) married in 1942, Robert Proehl. **Dorothy (1923) married in 1950, Paul E. Nicola. Richard Paul (1925) married in 1946, **Ruth Nichter. Joseph Anthony (March 1927-June 1927).

Jacob (1882-1961) married Florence Pairan and lived in Kendallville, Indiana.

Mercedes (1922) married Arthur Luttman and John Alt (1924-1943), who was killed in action on the Italian Front, November 8, during World War II.

Barbara (1884-1913) married John Maxwell and had one son, John F. Maxwell, Jr.

Mathias (1885-1954) married Loretta Lee. Their three daughters are Vera (1913-1974) married on Thanksgiving 1933, Norbert X. Klingenberger, **Luella "Lover"(1914-1988) married in 1939, Mallory Verner Clark, and **Loretta (1917-1975) married Don Collier in 1934.

John (1888-1944) married Anna Rochal and had three children: **Alberta Loretta (1913-1990) married in 1936, Frank Edward Oddou, Jr. **Cecilia "Tweet" (1919) married in 1940, Richard Dale Miller, Sr., and John "Pete" Francis (1921 - 2000 Lowell, Indiana) married in 1948, Patricia Laughlin. A World War II veteran, he is buried in Catholic Cemetery, Fort Wayne.

After arriving in Fort Wayne, three Alt sons were born. Peter J. (1890-1961) about 1930 married Erma Lee-Neumann. She was the sister of Loretta Lee above. She had two children Byron and Alyce.

William Adam (1891-1968) married in 1919, Anna E. Keller-Jenkins. She had two children, Albert and Virginia Jenkins. Arthur Joseph (Abt. 1920) married in 1941, Phyllis Ellen Sharb. Anna Elizabeth (1925-1925). Alline (1933 -1997) married several times, but buried under surname Alt. Richard M. (1935) married in 1960, Mary Steinkamp.

Anton J. (1894-1897)

Margaret DeYorka (1902-1995 Riverside, California) married Robert Tansey. She and her sister came from New York on an orphan train. Margaret was raised by Angela Alt. Mercedes went to live with the Wagner family.

Often the Alts would picnic at Foster Park. The brothers enjoyed baseball and horseshoes. Most of the family attended Saint Peter's and

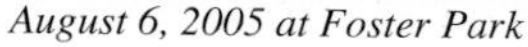

August 6, 2005 at Foster Park

Andorfer children and grandchildren, 2005

are buried in the Catholic Cemetery. As the granddaughters had their own families, they started **COUSIN CLUB to play cards monthly. Another club member was Mrs. Norman (Margaret) Miller from the Gertrude Berg-Herres side. They began an annual picnic, for everyone. Edith would have copies of the latest family history. This Family Reunion is over 50 years old. Mass is included as part of the weekend.

Submitted by Marilyn Klingenberger Horrell

WILSON & DELIA (BENNETT) ANDERSON FAMILY

Wilson D. Anderson was born in Fort Wayne in 1861, and died in 1916, at the age of 54. He married Delia Bennett who was born in 1864, in Palatine, Illinois, and died in 1956, at the age of 92. They were buried in Lindenwood Cemetery. Her parents were Grove Bennett and Hannah McKee. The couple lived in Chicago until their first child was born in 1901, and when moving to Fort Wayne, they made their home at 1316 McClellan Street. Wilson worked for the Eskay Dairy.

Back row, Wilson and Delia Anderson. Front row, Marian, Sarah and Elmina Anderson.

Wilson and Delia had three children: Marian (1901-1979) married Dwight W. Black in 1925, and they had four children, William, Robert, Barbara and Harold. Marian and Dwight are buried in Lindenwood Cemetery. Sarah (1903-1973) married Zoyral Elder in 1929, and they had six children, Imogene, Mageline, Wilson, Eugene, Edward, and Frederick. Sarah and Zoyral are buried in Covington Memorial Gardens. Elmina Adeline (1905-1978) married Garland A. Roby in 1923, and Adam L. Baker in 1939. Elmina and Adam are buried in Sweet Cemetery in Noble County. She had one child, Garland G. Roby.

Submitted by G. Dene Roby.

BYRON WILLIAM ANDORFER FAMILY

Byron William Andorfer was born in Fort Wayne, Indiana, on August 14, 1936, the son of Leonard John Andorfer (1907-1972) and Blanch Marie Mock (1905-1944).

His father, Leonard, was raised in Yoder, Indiana. Leonard's parents were Jacob Andorfer and Rose Lahmiller. In 1930 Leonard married Blanch Mock, a native of Hartford City, Indiana. She was the daughter of Tillman William Mock and Belle Maser. Leonard was a CPA and had an accounting firm in Fort Wayne. He and Blanch had five children including Byron William.

In 1958 Byron William Andorfer married Judith Louise Allgeier. Judith was the second of three children, and was born in Fort Wayne, Indiana, on March 22, 1939 to Robert F. Allgeier (1909-1974) and Catherine R. Murphy (1917-2004). Robert's parents were Nicholas Allgeier and Odellia Blaising. Robert owned Allgeier Meat Market on Taylor Street near Broadway, and also ran a catering business. Catherine's parents were Thomas Henry Murphy, who came to this country from Ireland as a child, and Louise Henriette Diecher. The Murphy's owned and operated Murphy's Bakery, located next to Allgeier Meat Market, and this is how Robert and Catherine met.

Byron William is a graduate of St. Joseph College in Rensselaer, Indiana. He is a CPA, and has had an accounting business in Fort Wayne since 1958. He enjoys playing poker and golf, and Judy enjoys porcelain painting. Byron William and Judith Andorfer have six children:

The oldest child, born in 1960, is Jeffery William. He married Rebecca Zekes, and they have three sons, Jason born 1983, Justin 1986, and Bradley 1987. They reside in Crown Point Indiana. Jeffery is a car salesman.

Nancy Louise married Michael Kovac, and they have two sons, Nicholas Michael born 1985, and Ryan William, in 1987. They reside in Alpharetta, Georgia. She is a loan officer at a bank, and he is a vice president and partner in Arby's Restaurants.

Anthony Robert married Marie Katherine Teders, and they have two daughters, Mary Catherine born 1988, and Kristiana Marie born 1992. They reside in Fort Wayne. Tony is the music director at St. Vincents Church, and Marie is the pianist at St. Charles Church.

Timothy John married Michele Betzynski, and they have two daughters, Rachel Elizabeth born 1993, and Molly Debbra, born 1995. They reside in Pampa, Texas. He is an engineer, and she is a teacher at St. Vincents Catholic School.

Catherine Marie married Kurt V. Rudolph. They reside in Indianapolis, Indiana. He is a CPA, and she is in management with an area company.

Amy Allgeier married Bryan Michael Pulliam, and they have three daughters and one son, Anna Kate born in 1995, Elaine Murphy in 1997, Grace Julianne in 1999, and son, Bryan Michael born in 2003. They reside in Covington, Georgia. Bryan is an attorney with his own firm and Amy is a teacher.

Submitted by Judi Andorfer

BETTY LORENE (CARRION) ANDREWS FAMILY

Betty Lorene Carrion was born at St. Joseph Hospital in Fort Wayne, Indiana on July 30, 1958 to Thelma Lorena Shoemaker and Isabel Carrion. She was the seventh of nine children, all born in Fort Wayne.

Thelma Lorena Shoemaker was born September 29, 1921 and grew up in Carlisle, Pennsylvania. Thelma's parents are Raymond Hikes Shoemaker, born September 22, 1897 in Shippensburg, Pennsylvania, and Lorena Matilda Davis, born June 3, 1895 in Carlisle, Pennsylvania. Isabel Carrion was born October 6, 1922 and grew up in Carlsbad, New Mexico. Isabel's parents were Jesus Carrion and Nicolosa Bustillos whose birthplaces were in Mexico. Thelma and Isabel were married on September 18, 1944 in Fort Wayne. Their nine children are David, Barbara, Beverly, Daniel, Dennis, Bonnie, Betty, Donald, and Brenda. Brenda lives now in California and Dan in Oklahoma. The rest are residents of Fort Wayne.

Betty Carrion attended St. Joseph grade school in Fort Wayne up to eighth grade. She then went to Portage Middle School for ninth grade and on to Elmhurst High School where she played volleyball, tennis, and ran track. Betty attended

The Betty Lorene (Carrion) Andrews Family

Martin App and Elizabeth Kramer wedding June 19, 1888.

Thomas J. and Katherine (Allgeier) Ankenbruck family. Front row, Margaret, Thomas J., Katherine Ankenbruck and Janet Piercy. Back row, Marie Davis, John, Steven and David Ankenbruck.

IPFW and graduated with an associate's degree in nursing. She married James (Jim) Stephan Andrews on May 7, 1983 at St. Joseph Catholic Church in Fort Wayne. They lived in Muncie, Indiana until the fall of 1988. Two daughters were born during this time. Susana Marie was born May 31, 1984 at Ball Memorial Hospital in Muncie. Kathryn (Katy) Ann was born September 21, 1986 in Yorktown, Indiana.

In the fall of 1988, the Andrews family moved to Pittsfield, Massachusetts where Jim grew up. Jim was born in Hartford, Connecticut on May 17, 1953 to Virgil Lord Andrews, Jr. and Jane Egan. Betty and Jim's son, David James, was born November 7, 1988 in Pittsfield, Massachusetts. Jeffrey (Jeff) Michael was born December 21, 1990, and Claire Lolita was born September 3, 1994. The children went to school at Sacred Heart Elementary School and St. Mark Middle School in Pittsfield.

In June 1998, Betty moved the family to Fort Wayne, Indiana. Betty began working at St. Anne's nursing home as a Registered Nurse. Then she got a job at Lutheran Hospital, but switched over to St. Joseph Hospital where she is currently working. The children attend St. Joseph - St. Elizabeth School and Bishop Luers High School. Jacob Christopher was born January 29, 1999 in Fort Wayne. Betty and Jim were divorced in January 2000. Susana graduated from Bishop Luers in 2002 and attends Ball State University. Katy graduated from Bishop Luers in 2004 and attends Dayton University. The Andrews family are members of St. Joseph Catholic Church. They enjoy walking around the Fort Wayne Zoo, listening to concerts at Foellinger Theatre, and attending the different events of the Three Rivers Festival and the Johnny Appleseed Festival.

Submitted by Susana Andrews

CARL & CECELIA (APP) ANKENBRUCK FAMILY

Carl B. Ankenbruck (1895-1963) was the only son of John A. Ankenbruck (1866-1950) and Margaret (Mausbaum) Ankenbruck. Carl had two sisters, Clara Ankenbruck (1893-1972) and Helen Fiedler (1900-1946). Carl was a carpenter, who began his career in his father's contracting business. Carl's grandfather, Bernard Ankenbruck, who came to the United States from Germany at age five, was a truck farmer who lived on nine acres in the area that is now McMillen Park.

Carl Ankenbruck married Cecelia Julia App on June 23, 1920. Cecelia (1898-1997) was the daughter of Martin App (1863-1951) and Elizabeth (Kramer) App (1864-1945). Carl and Cecelia had six children: Mary, born 1921, married Paul Trey, Thomas J., born 1923, married Katherine Allgeier, Rita, born 1925, married Ernie Miller, Catherine, born 1928, married Gene Foley, Charles, born 1930, married Beatrice Heck, and Elizabeth "Betsy", born 1935, married Richard Meyer. Carl and Cecelia had 28 grandchildren.

The App family traces its roots to Germany. Martin App's father, Mathias App (1830-1912), was a boot maker who came to the United States in 1852, from Ertingen, Riedling, Germany. Mathias App married Rosina Wagner in 1858, and later arrived in Fort Wayne and established App's Shoe Store in 1867. The store was located at 916 South Calhoun Street, and it flourished there until 1940. Great grandson, Thomas Ankenbruck, made shoe deliveries for the store on his bicycle as a teenager. Mathias' daughter, Anna App (1872-1959), lived her entire life in the family home. This property is part of the current site of the downtown Allen County Public Library building.

Cecelia's parents, Martin and Elizabeth App, had four other daughters: Rose (1890-1990), a homemaker; Marie (1892-1990), an accountant for App's Shoe Store; Agnes (1895-1987), who worked in the office of Wayne Knitting Mill; and Hilda (1900-1994), who married Hugh Hart and taught music in several Fort Wayne area schools.

Submitted by Jon and Shannon Ankenbruck.

THOMAS J. & KATHERINE (ALLGEIER) ANKENBRUCK FAMILY

Thomas John "Tom" Ankenbruck was born in Fort Wayne on March 2, 1923, the oldest son of Carl B. Ankenbruck and Cecelia (App) Ankenbruck. He graduated from Central Catholic High School in 1941, and served in the U.S. Army 88th Infantry Division from 1943 to 1946. Tom was a member of the medical battalion and an aide with the 88th signal company during the Italian campaign, where he earned four battle stars, and also served briefly in North Africa. After returning to Fort Wayne, Tom worked at International Harvester for a short time before beginning a long career with Prudential Life Insurance Company.

Tom had met Katherine Marie Allgeier before he went overseas to fight in World War II. He carried her picture for three years, and after he returned, they married on October 18, 1947. Katherine, born October 15, 1926, is the daughter of Henry G. Allgeier Jr. and Marie (Hartman) Allgeier. She graduated from Central Catholic High School in 1944, and received a two-year degree in 1946 from the Fort Wayne Art School, where she studied with Homer Davisson. Renowned artist, Jim McBride, was a fellow student. Katherine was a tea room model at the Wolf & Dessauer department store for three years before she and Tom started a family, and modeled in special fashion shows after that. Later, she was a secretary at Snider High School until retirement in 1992.

Katherine's parents were charter members of St. Jude's Catholic Church, and Tom and Katherine are dedicated members today. Tom has served the church as an usher, choir member and parish council member. Tom also was president of (then) St. Jude's Little League in the 1960s. The league's diamond was located on the ground where St. Jude's church now stands.

Both Tom and Katherine have deep roots in Allen County, with ancestors who settled here in the 1850s. And today, five of Tom and Katherine's six children still live in Fort Wayne. Margaret Marie, born 1949, an attorney with the Social Security Administration, is married to Wilford G. Allen and has a son, Preston Wilford; David Thomas, born 1951, an office products salesman, is married to Freda Turner; John Nicholas, born 1952, athletic director at Homestead High School, is married to Sharman Dale Harter and has sons, John Robert "J.R.", Nicholas Lee, and Thomas Andrew; Janet Kay, born 1955, a Fort Wayne Community Schools music teacher and a vocalist, is married to William Piercy and has children, Elizabeth Kay, Katherine Marie, and Steven Thomas; Marie Ann, born 1961, of Brighton, Michigan, an artist and clay modeler in the automobile industry, is married to James C. Davis and has children, Andrew Steven and Jillian Amanda; and Steven Joseph, born 1964, a media specialist at North Side High School, is married to Jana Lynn Goeglein and has children, Mary Ann, Jack Thomas, and Michael William.

Submitted by Thomas J. Ankenbruck.

PAUL & BETTY HARMON ARCHER FAMILY

Paul Walter Archer was born in Fort Wayne in 1926. His father, Guy Arthur, was born in Lake Township in 1882 and died in 1948. His Mother, Caroline Kallen, was born in Fort Wayne in 1892 and died in 1977. They were married on March 10, 1915 in St. John's Evangelical Lutheran Church. They had five children, all born in Fort Wayne. Carl was born in 1916 and later lived in Texas. Ruth was born in 1918, Arthur in 1921, Lula in 1923, and Paul was the youngest.

Paul married Betty Irene Harmon on June 6, 1947. Betty was born in Utica, Licking County, Ohio in 1929 to Jess and Elsie Harmon.

Paul and Betty Archer, married June 10, 1947.

Jess Harmon was born in Coopers, West Virginia. Elsie Irene Tracey was born in Fort Wayne in 1907. Elsie was one of 15 children and was a member of the Westfield Presbyterian Church. After knowing each other for only ten days, Betty's parents married in 1926. Jess and Elsie had six children. Richard was born in 1927 and married Lorraine Rose. They had three children. Dorothy was born in 1928. She married Wayne Redwanski and they had four children, including artist Patria Smith. Next came Betty in 1929. Kenneth was born in 1936 and had four children. Donald was born in 1941 and married Carol Osborne. They had one child. Kay was born in 1944 and lives in Georgia. She had seven children.

Paul and Betty Archer had five children, all born in Fort Wayne. Bill, born in 1949, served in the Vietnam War. He married Debi Thomas in 1970 while in Hawaii on leave. They have two children: Scott and Melissa. Sandra was born in 1951. She graduated from South Side High School, and married Gerald Roby in 1973. They have five children: Brian, Megan, Gretchen, Adam and Casey. Cindy was born in 1955 and married Jeffrey Clark in 1973. They have two children: Jeffrey and Jennifer. The Clarks live in Seminole, Florida. Karen was born in 1957. She married Joseph Sorg and has two children: Joseph and Levi. The boys are currently serving in the National Guard in Afghanistan. Melodie was born in 1966. She lives in Steuben County with longtime partner Tim Troxell.

Paul was working at Phelps Dodge when he joined the Navy. He was stationed in the Marshall Islands during World War II. When he came home he went back to work at Phelps Dodge as a shipping clerk. Paul retired in 1979 after 45 years of service. Betty was a model for a short time at the downtown Grand Leader store. She had several jobs throughout her life, but the longest was with General Electric. Betty died in 2001 after 53 years of marriage. Paul remembers having a home with no insulation and being cold all the time. When he was a child, rather than go to the grocery store, peddlers and farmers came along with chickens and other livestock, and you picked what you wanted to eat. Betty remembered the first time the family bought bread from the store (already sliced!) rather than making it at home.

Submitted by Paul Archer

ARCHIBALD

The Archibald family has lived in Fort Wayne for more than 120 years. The family originates with David Archibald, a probable native of Londonderry, Ireland, who as a youth was impressed into the British army and brought to America before 1768. He eventually gained his freedom and settled in Cumberland County, Pennsylvania, where, during the Revolutionary War, he served in the Fourth Battalion of Cumberland County Militia. Late in his life he moved to Montgomery County, Ohio, where he died in 1818. With his wife Sarah he had at least seven children: Nancy, Hannah, Christena, Robert, Jenny, Andrew, and David.

Abraham Archibald , Kenneth Archibald, Velma June Harrod Archibald

Andrew Archibald, son of David and Sarah, was born perhaps about 1777. He married Catherine Shields and lived variously in Allegheny, Beaver, and Union counties, Pennsylvania before his death after 1830. Their children were: James, David, Sarah, Hannah, John, Catherine, Robert, Andrew, and George Dixson.

Robert Archibald, the fourth son, was born on October 10, 1814 in Allegheny County. In his youth he moved with several brothers and cousins to Tippecanoe County, Indiana, where he married Caroline Fry, daughter of Abraham and Mary (Cox) Fry, on June 30, 1842. She was born on May 9, 1822 and died on January 21, 1871. They had eight children, including Walter Cox, Almon Worth, Mary Catherine, Abraham Fry, Frank Shields, Laura Ann, Charles Freemont, and Fanny Fatima. During the Civil War, Robert served as a Private in the Tenth Indiana Light Artillery. After the war he worked in a shoe factory in Lafayette. He died there on November 24, 1887.

Abraham Fry Archibald was born February 9, 1851 in Lafayette. Shortly after 1880 he moved to Fort Wayne, where he worked first as a railroad clerk before becoming a clerk for the U.S. Post Office. He married Edith Bowen, daughter of Daniel and Mary Eliza (Smith) Bowen, on December 18, 1886 in Fort Wayne. They were members of Plymouth Congregational Church and for many years resided at 305 West Pontiac Street. Abe died on July 10, 1939; Edith followed on February 7, 1939. They had three children: Evelyn, Raymond, and Robert Kenneth.

Robert Kenneth Archibald was born on May 15, 1894, and married Velma June Harrod on December 26, 1929. She was the daughter of Dr. Morse and Jennie (Lipes) Harrod of Fort Wayne. They had one child, Susan, born on August 24, 1932. For many years Kenneth worked for General Electric Company. He was a veteran of World War I. He died in Fort Wayne on November 6, 1970. June followed on March 21, 1981.

Susan Archibald worked as an agent for the Bureau of Indian Affairs. She later had a long career with the Fort Wayne News-Sentinel, serving for a time as its Food Editor. She married Jack Stone on October 10, 1964. Their only daughter, Amy June Stone, was born on November 21, 1967. Amy is presently the wife of John David Beatty of Fort Wayne.

Submitted by Susan A. Stone

JAMES ARMAN & FAMILY

James Arman is the son of Olga and George Arman who emigrated from the Macedonia Region of Northern Greece in the 1920's to Fort Wayne, Indiana. James was born at St. Joseph Hospital at Broadway and Main on May 30,1930. James has one sister, Vasilica Lovely, who is one year older than he.

James went to Hanna Elementary at Lafayette and Williams from 1936 to 1942, and then to James H. Smart Elementary on Pontiac Street from 1942 to 1944. He graduated from Central High School at Clinton and Douglas in 1948.

James first job was with the Pennsylvania Railroad at Baker Street to service passenger trains from 1948 to 1950. His second job was with the Capehart Farnsworth on Pontiac Street where he worked on an assembly line and in the storeroom from 1950 to 1951.

In November 1951, James joined the U.S. Navy and was sent to the Great Lakes Naval Training Station in Chicago, Illinois for boot camp. James was assigned to the battleship U.S.S. Wisconsin BB64. He left the training center by passenger train to San Francisco to get on a troop ship the U.S.S. Randall, which was headed for Yokosuka, Japan. He was assigned to the receiving station in Yokosuka until the U.S.S.

James Arman

Wisconsin came to port after receiving a shell hit from shore batteries in the Korean waters. James returned to the U.S. on the U.S.S. Wisconsin. The ship arrived at San Francisco and then sailed through the Panama Canal to Norfolk, Virginia. James was transferred to the heavy cruiser U.S.S. Pittsburg GA 72 and traveled the Mediterranean, then through the Suez Canal to Madras in India; Karachi in Pakistan and other ports in the Indian Ocean. The ship returned through the Suez Canal and to the Mediterranean to Naples in Italy; Cannes in France; Majorca in Spain; the Rock of Gibraltar, and then across the Atlantic Ocean to Norfolk, Virginia. James was discharged from the Navy in November 1953 and returned to work for the Pennsylvania Railroad as a teletype operator until 1956.

James joined the Fort Wayne Fire Department in June 1956 and served as a private at Fire Station No.5 on Broadway, FS No.1 on Main, and FS No.2 on Wallace. In 1964, under Mayor Harold Zeis, James was promoted to lieutenant at FS No.3 on West Washington. In 1965, he was promoted to captain of the C Shift at FS No.3 until 1972. When Ivan Lebamoff became mayor, James was assigned to FS No. 12 on South Anthony. James retired from the Fire Department in 1978.

Upon retiring from the Fire Department, James began working in the Maintenance Department at Indiana & Michigan Electric on Spy Run in 1978. James retired in 1993 following bypass heart surgery.

James is now enjoying life with his wife Zhivka and their family. His son, George Arman, is married to Anita Arman and has a son, Nicholas Arman, His daughter Diana (Arman) Campbell is married to Dell Campbell and they have two sons, Alex and Andrew Campbell.

Submitted by James Arman

ELIJAH ARNOLD

Elijah Arnold was born April 14, 1813, in Miami County, Ohio. In November 1835 he purchased land on the southeast bank of the Eel River in Eel River Township, Allen County, Indiana, from the Fort Wayne Federal Land Office. This farm consisted of 80 acres and remained in the possession of the Arnold family until 1978. Soon after settling in Allen County, he met and married Juliann Nickey. They had seven children: Eli was born in 1838, Hester (Porter) in 1840, Henry in 1845, Mary Ann in 1848, Albert in. 1853, William in 1860 and Charles in.1865.

The Arnolds were well known in the Eel River Township area and were often involved in local politics and other events. Elijah and Juliann endured a unique time in American history alongside a growing family. The area they lived in was largely wilderness in 1835, and much of their time was spent in clearing the land to make it productive. Disease also took its toll upon their family, taking Mary Ann in 1863. Although it is uncertain, diphtheria was likely the cause. However, the ultimate tragedy for the Arnolds occurred in September of 1869. Elijah and his wife Juliann died within four days of each other. She likely succumbed to tuberculosis, commonly known as consumption. Elijah died four days later, probably from pneumonia from standing in the cold rain at her funeral. They passed away at a fairly young age, he 53 and she 49. Henry, at the time in his early 20's, took on the primary responsibility of running the farm. Albert stayed at the farm while the younger brothers, William and Charles, became the wards of William Ross until 1873 when Jackson Valentine became their legal guardian. Hester and Eli had already married and moved away by this time.

Elijah & Juliann Arnold

In 1875, Henry married Catherine Mahan, born of Irish immigrants. They had four children: Henry Montgomery was born in 1876 (Lillia Ott), Mamie in 1880 (Elmer Cotten), Nelle in 1882 (Arthur Johnson), and Willard in 1885 (Daisy Dafforn). After the marriage of Henry Montgomery, Henry and Catherine moved to Fort Wayne where they bought property, and he dealt in real estate. Henry Montgomery operated the farm for his father from 1900 until his father's death in 1935 at which time he purchased the farm and operated it until his death in 1943. Henry Montgomey and Lillia (Ott) had six children: Henry Forrest was born in 1902 (Helen LaRue), George in 1904 (Lillian Hitzeman), Donald in 1906 (Lena Sible), Ralph in 1908, Catherine in 1911 (John Leech), and Kenneth in 1915 (Delores Stonestreet). Henry Montgomery was also involved in local politics and was trustee of Eel River Township for several years. After Henry Montgomery's death in 1943, his son Ralph, who resided on the farm with his mother, farmed it until his death in 1976.

Submitted by Eleanor E. Lydy

GEORGE HALE ASHLEY

George Hale Ashley was born June 1,1814, in Catskill, Greene County, New York, the son of John Hale Ashley born December 18, 1777, in New York and Elizabeth Johnson born May 27, 1761, in New Haven, Connecticut. John is listed in *First Families of Allen County, Indiana*.

In 1832 George came by boat to Toledo, Ohio, and then by stage to Fort Wayne to investigate the stories he had heard about Indiana's fertile farm land. He was a fearless man exploring the wild land around the fort on horseback and encountering Indians in his travels. He filed claims with the government for land, some of which included canal lands along the Maumee River in both Ohio and Indiana. It also included the former site of Anthony's old outpost of Fort Harrison, the Netga Indian Reservation, and later the town of New Harrison, a river trading post for rafts pushing their supplies from Toledo to Fort Wayne.

George married Esther Linzey on January 18, 1837, in Catskill, New York. Shortly thereafter the young couple began their journey to Indiana by wagon teams. They were accompanied by his parents, John and Elizabeth, and his five married sisters and their husbands, Polly and Riley Griswold, Phoebe and Stephen Griswold, Betsy and Edmund Bunnell, Harriet and Daniel Opliger, Clarissa and James Cash, and Rebecca who was unmarried. A brother, John Joseph, a baker, remained in New York.

George settled first in Washington Township where he reclaimed wild land for cultivation. Various families assisted each other in building log homes in the vicinity of Wallen. Here he donated land for the first log chapel, Bethel Meeting House, later to become Wallen Methodist Church.

In 1844, George moved to Maumee Township where he again cleared land for cultivation, building a home on the Maumee River near the Ohio-Indiana state line. During the building of the Wabash Erie Canal, their home served as a boarding house for canal workers. That home still stands and is owned by one of his descendants. Clearing the land, he shipped the lumber down river for sale to the government and during the Civil War for the manufacture of coffins. Active in politics he was originally a Whig, then a Republican. He was a trustee in Maumee Township.

In 1846 he moved to St. Joseph Township purchasing 160 acres. In 1863 he gave land at the corner of St. Joe and St. Joe Center Road and $500.00 for the construction of the St. Joseph Methodist Church. Some of his farm later became a part of Shoaff Park.

George and Esther had seven children, three dying in infancy. Elizabeth married James Greer a Methodist minister. Sarah married Nathan Doctor a farmer. George Linzey a farmer, mail carrier and Allen County Recorder, married Josephine Darling, Adessa Miller and Zella Culver. Theodore Hale, a farmer married Emma Thomas.

George died August 7, 1868, and was buried in Lindenwood Cemetery. Esther, who shared the hardships of pioneer life with him, died February 8, 1879, and was also buried in Lindenwood Cemetery.

Submitted by Naomi Jane Johnson

BACKS

The Backs family presence in the Fort Wayne area began when a recent Concordia Theological Seminary (Springfield, Illinois) graduate, Rev. Herman H. Backs received a divine call to start a church in south Fort Wayne (Waynedale), known as Waynedale Lutheran, now Mount Calvary Lutheran Church. Pastor Backs was 24 and single when he arrived in 1928. He canvassed the area for prospects and the Church was begun with four families serving as charter members. In 1928, Waynedale was a small unincorporated town just south of Fort Wayne consisting mainly of working class families. The area had no sewer and water and few sidewalks, and the streets were largely unpaved. It was not part of Fort Wayne, but was an unincorporated community. Pastor Backs, as he worked in Waynedale, saw the many needs of the area and was instrumental in encouraging the development of much-needed services to Waynedale such as fire protection and banking.

One year after coming to Mount Calvary, Pastor Backs married Edna Fetter from Napoleon, Ohio. He opened a Christian grade school, grades 1 through 8 and taught all eight grades in a one-room school behind the Church. Pastor Backs remained at Mount Calvary for the first 44 years as head Pastor and later as Pastor Emeritus until his death in 2000 for a total of 70 years at Mount Calvary. During this period, Mount Calvary grew from four families to a membership of over 1200.

Pastor and Mrs. Backs had two children. Their daughter, Marcile E. Backs, is a specialist with the Department of Health and Human Services, an agency of the U. S. Government. Their second child was a son, Vincent J. Backs, who lives in Fort Wayne and was one of the founding partners in the law firm of Beers Mallers Backs & Salin, LLP. Vincent received his law degree from Indiana University (Bloomington) in 1965 and has practiced law in Fort Wayne since then. He was the founder of Fort Wayne Federal Savings & Loan, now part of successor banking institutions. Mr. Backs is currently a member of the Advisory Board of Salin Bank & Trust Company. Mr. Backs was also involved in the formation of other enterprises, including Branstrator Aluminum Products, Truck Engineering Company, Ltd., LLC, Orange County Environmental, LLC (Orlando Florida Landfill) and Preferred Management, LLC (Newark/Columbus Ohio Landfill). Mr. Backs also sits on the Board of Directors of numerous other for profit companies, including Cole Hardwood, Inc. and Indiana Dimensions, Inc. Mr. Backs served as President of Mount Calvary Lutheran Church for over 30 years and served on the Board of Directors of Lutheran Social Services.

Vincent married Judith Brown in 1964. Judith was a graduate of the Indiana University School of Music, and she taught piano in Fort Wayne schools for many years. They have two sons, Jon, a real estate broker in Indianapolis and Fort Wayne, and Charles who graduated from Valparaiso Law School and is a partner in Beers Mallers Backs & Salin, LLP. Charles married Heather Green in 2004.

Submitted by Vincent Backs.

SAM BACON

On October 10, 1834, Samuel Bacon was born in Detroit, Michigan. Detroit was one of the many stops that his family made as they migrated west from Massachusetts. Sam's parents were Socrates and Anna (Earp) Bacon. Socrates was born in Charlton, Massachusetts on March 1, 1807 and Anna in England in 1805. They were married in Philadelphia on March 26, 1826.1 Socrates' ancestry can be traced to Puritan Michael Bacon who in 1640 moved from County Suffolk, England, settling in the Massachusetts Bay Colony.

In 1838 Socrates brought his family to Allen County, purchasing 100 acres of land east of New Haven on what is now the Fackler Road. It was a particularly harsh time to be entering Indiana, for the state was suffering the effects of a drought that lasted through Christmas of 1838. The rivers were so low that supplies could not be moved. The harvest that year was almost a total loss.

The Bacon children from left: Ephraim, Albert, Louis, Charles, Sam Jr., Arhur, Lucy, Annie, Mary and Ida May

In 1840, Socrates joined with his neighbors, and they organized Jefferson Township. His acreage was situated in Section 28 of this new division. Socrates built the "Bacon" schoolhouse on his farm so that his children, as well as the neighbors', might receive an education. In 1850, Socrates established Jefferson Township's first post office at his home. The *History of the Sam Bacon Family of Allen County Indiana* 1850 census listed Socrates and Anna with seven children and birthplaces: Charles, 19, Pennsylvania; Sam, 16, Michigan; Amanda, 13, Ohio; John, 9; Adeline, 6; Laura, 4; and Lucy, one month, all in Indiana. Their daughter Ann, 23, had married Earl Adams in 1846.

In the nearby community of Besancon, the family of Alexis and Marie (Rivard) Girardot (Gerardot) had settled in the early 1850s. Alexis was born in France on June 7, 1809. Marie was born in France about 1800. Their daughter Jane (Virginie) who was born in Ohio on August 3,1832, married the younger Sam Bacon on November 25, 1854. On February 20, 1855, their first child was born and he was named Charles. In June of 1857, William was born. In 1858, Sam took over Socrates' farm on Fackler Road when his father bought property in New Haven. There Socrates platted Bacon's Addition that lies along Green Street at the corner of Summit. Sam and Jane had another child, Louis, born February 16, 1858. John was born May 1, 1859. Both William and John died at the beginning of the Civil War.

During the war, Sam enlisted in the 91st Regiment of Indiana Volunteers in November 1864. Stationed in North Carolina, he was mustered out on August 31, 1865. In his absence, Jane had given birth to their first daughter, Mary, on August 1. Daughter Anne was born on July 6, 1869 and Lucy on September 12,1871. Unexpectedly, on August 16, 1872, Jane died. Sam's second wife was Josephine Didier. She was the daughter of Victor and Lucienne (Barbaret) Didier. They were also born in France: Victor on August 3, 1818 and Lucienne on October 31, 1824. Josephine was born in Ohio in 1855. Sam and Josephine were married by the Rev. A. Adams on July 14, 1873 at St. Louis Besancon Catholic Church. Their first son, Albert, was born October 30, 1873. Ephraim was born on June 25, 1875. On September 16, 1879, Edward was born and Arthur arrived on July 22, 1882. Their only daughter, Ida May, entered this world on June 16, 1884. On February 15, 1890, their youngest, Samuel J. Bacon was born.

Josephine died in May 1907. Sam lived to be 78 years old and died May 5, 1917. They were both buried in the family plot and their graves were later moved to the Odd Fellows Cemetery in New Haven, Indiana

See *The Ancestors of Socrates Bacon,* Warrick, LaDonna Gulley, Fort Wayne, 1982, Bert Griswold, *A Pictorial History of Fort Wayne Indiana;* Chicago: 1917, p. 340, Also see *The Descendants of Samuel Bacon of Allen County Indiana,* Biesiada & Overmyer, Fort Wayne, 1984.

Submitted by LaDonna J. Warrick

PASTOR C. W. BAER

Clarence William Baer was born in Cleveland, Ohio, December 11, 1879, the only child of William Baer and his wife, Matilda, nee Giel. At the age of three his father died after a long illness and he was befriended by Pastor Carl Zorn at Zion Lutheran Church. After his confirmation he entered Concordia College in Fort Wayne, Indiana. After graduation he entered Concordia Seminary in St. Louis and graduated in 1902. He became pastor of churches in Dillsboro, Cold Springs, and Tipton, Indiana, and Emmanuel Church, in Valparaiso, Indiana. When World War I broke out, Pastor Baer became a camp pastor when the government built barracks for soldiers and recruits where Valparaiso University stands today.

He was married June 22, 1905, to Miss Flora Haker of Cleveland, Ohio. They had two children, Flora Matilda, and William Carl Baer, both born in Tipton, Indiana. His devotion to his family was unusually strong. He loved sports, especially football, and he and his son attended many games together.

Pastor Baer accepted a call to Redeemer Lutheran Church in Fort Wayne, Indiana, and assumed his pastoral duties on May 27, 1923. The cornerstone of the new church was laid, and placed into the cornerstone were the Bible, Dr. Luther's Small Catechism, the Lutheran Witness, and an inscribed parchment with the names of the members of the building committee, the congregational officers, the charter members, the pastors who served the congregation since its inception, the architect and the builder, and a brief history of the congregation. The new church, which cost $110,000, was dedicated on June 1, 1924. Special gifts included a $10,000 pipe organ

Rev. C. William Baer.

William C. Baer

Rosemary and Glenn Baker

from the Ladies' Aid Society, and a number of art glass windows by individual members in memory of loved ones. Their names may be seen on the identifying bronze tables. The bells were the gift of four families whose names are found on the bronze tables in the entryway.

Under the dynamic leadership of Pastor Baer, the congregation prospered in its new location with membership more than doubling. The debt incurred while building the new church was systematically reduced even though the economic Depression of the 1930s made this accomplishment extremely difficult.

Those trying days undermined Pastor Baer's health and suddenly, after a week of heart attacks, he died on May 29, 1941. His untimely death stunned his congregation. In Lindenwood Cemetery stands a congregational monument, symbol of the loving esteem of those he had served faithfully and well. His congregation said of him, "he went about doing good".

Submitted by Linda F. Dearing.

WILLIAM C. & DOROTHY (LINDENBERG) BAER

William Carl Baer, son of C. William and Flora (Haker) Baer, was born in Tipton, Indiana, on November 20, 1908. Several years after William's birth the family moved to Valparaiso, Indiana. At age fifteen his parents moved to Fort Wayne where his father, C. W. Baer, accepted a call as Pastor of Redeemer Lutheran Church on Rudisill Boulevard.

He attended and was graduated from South Side High School. He matriculated to Northwestern University in Chicago intending to pursue a legal degree and play college football. After sustaining a career ending football injury he eventually transferred to Purdue University at West Lafayette, Indiana, becoming a mechanical engineer in 1934.

Bill worked for several architectural and engineering firms from the east coast to St. Paul, Minnesota, before settling in his home state and starting his own engineering business. Over the following years he was responsible for the design and engineering work on many schools, churches, restaurants, fire stations, and sub-divisions including much work for both the Amish community near Leo-Grabill, and the African-American community in Fort Wayne. He was an excellent surveyor and completed thousands of surveys for Indiana and Ohio residents.

At the age of eighty-seven Bill was still working on several projects at the time of his death on February 14, 1996. Preceding him in death was his first wife, Dorothy (Lindenberg), and his oldest daughter, Carole. His other children included Stephen William Baer and Linda Baer-Dearing, as well as his stepchildren, Diane Porter, and John Porter. His second wife, Mable Irene Baer, died in 2003.

He enjoyed teaching Sunday school at Redeemer Lutheran Church, working in Boy Scouts, sports, and his grandchildren. Everywhere he went Bill would always know someone. He was well liked and respected both professionally and personally.

Submitted by Sara L. Hoeppner.

HAROLD GLENN BAKER FAMILY

Glenn Baker was born in Ohio, and enlisted in the Air Corps in July 1941. While training in North Carolina with some Airmen from Lafayette, Indiana, Glenn saw a picture of a girl from Lafayette, Ellen Hudgens, and wrote her a "pen-pal" letter. That was the start of a four-year letter writing campaign, during which, in spite of the long distances, they managed to actually meet four times.

After Glenn returned from overseas in 1945 he and Ellen were married, and settled in Lafayette, Indiana. Ellen worked at ALCOA, while Glenn started to work for the General Telephone Company, living at 2120 Hawthorne Lane. In 1952, Glenn returned to duty in the Air Force Reserve and served for one year as a part of the Korean War call up. They became the parents of two sons, Michael, born in 1948, and David, born in 1953.

In 1959, along with GTE, the family moved to Fort Wayne, and built a house at 23 10 Bellevue Drive in Concordia Gardens. There, after a long illness, Ellen succumbed to cancer in September 1966 and is buried in Greenlawn Memorial Park in Fort Wayne.

In April 1968 Glenn remarried, to Rosemary Whetzel, a fellow worker at General Telephone. They became the parents of two girls, Christina Marie and Rebecca Sue. In 1976, they moved to 7218 West Dupont Road, where a house on four acres provided more living space. A large pole barn permitted setting up a wood working shop, and, as another of one of the countless hobbies, a wine- grape vineyard was planted, amounting to over 1000 vines.

While initially the grapes were a hobby, they developed into a part-time business. Many wine makers from the Fort Wayne area availed themselves of the supply of preferred French Hybrid wine grapes for their own wines.

In 1973 Glenn retired from General Telephone Company and devoted his time to being a clockmaker and a vinedresser. Rosemary retired at the same time.

By 1982, the mowing of the four acres, as well as the spring pruning and summer spraying of the grapes started to prove too laborious. In 2001, a decision was made to move from the tri-level house to a smaller single-floor dwelling. In March 2002 Glenn and Rosemary moved to 3922 Spurwood Circle, in Aboite Township. There in a single floor dwelling, a more leisurely lifestyle was enjoyed.

Son, Michael, was married in 1974 to Karen Gorman, and in 1975, they were parents of a daughter, Emily. He also retired from General Telephone Company.

David has a daughter, Courtney, and in September 2004 married Janet Nicol, of Fort Wayne.

Christina married David Bobay in 1995. He is a member of the Air Guard Reserve, and they are the parents of two boys, Alexander Matthew and Thomas James, living in Fort Wayne.

Rebecca, who is a kindergarten teacher, married Jeffrey Gongwer in 1996. They are the parents of Ian Jeffrey, and live in Huntertown.

Submitted by Glenn Baker

GARY LEWIS & JANET MARIE (BLOOM) BALTZELL

Janet Marie (Bloom) Baltzell was born October 12, 1953, in Fort Wayne, Allen County, Indiana. She is the daughter of Clarence Nicholas and Kathryn Ann (Bowen) Bloom, whose residence at the time of her birth was 2313 California Avenue. Her father is a native of Noble County, Indiana, and her mother was raised in LaGrange County. Her siblings are Karen Ann Bloom, of Chicago, Linda Jean Burrell, James Gregory, Robert Paul, and Martha Jane Conkling, all of Fort Wayne, and Jeffrey Thomas, of San Diego, California.

She attended Forest Park Elementary school for kindergarten, St. Jude Catholic School grades one through eight, and graduated from Bishop Dwenger High School. She is a graduate of Fort Wayne Community School's licensed practical nurse course, and has been employed at Lutheran Hospital for 30 years. In 2000, she returned to college with the goal of earning a registered nurse degree. She completed the required classes and graduated from the University of St. Francis in

December 2004. Her employment continues at Lutheran Hospital. She enjoys working in her flowerbeds during the summer months.

Janet married Gary Lewis Baltzell in Fort Wayne on April 28, 1979. He was born in Indianapolis, Indiana, October 6, 1953. His parents are Dr. Lewis Gayle Baltzell, who was born in Mendon, Ohio, and Anna Heady, who was born in Providence, Kentucky. They were married June 28, 1952, in Indianapolis, Indiana. Gary's sibling is Diana Kay, wife of Mark Alan Bennett and they have two daughters, Katie and Becky. Lewis is retired from chiropractic practice and resides in Indianapolis. Anna died February 23, 2004.

Cara, Gary, Janet, and Bryan Baltzell.

Gary attended Ben Davis High School and graduated from Ball State University in 1977. He was employed as a director by WISE TV, Channel 33, in Fort Wayne until the sale of the station to Granite Broadcasting. He coached the girl's soccer team at Elmhurst High School and was involved in "TRYSA" youth soccer. In 2000, he returned to college at Ivy Tech to help his wife with her algebra classes. He will graduate from IPFW in 2005 with a teaching certificate in communications and English.

Gary and Janet have a son, Bryan Gregory, born March 16, 1980 in Fort Wayne. He attended Southwest Allen County schools and graduated from Homestead High School in 1998. He graduated from Indiana University at Bloomington, Indiana, and is currently residing in Denver, Colorado. His favorite sport in high school was soccer. They also have a daughter, Cara Lynn, born October 20, 1982, in Fort Wayne. She attended Southwest Allen County schools and graduated from Homestead High School in 2001. Cara graduated from Indiana University at Bloomington in May 2005, with a degree in family therapy and plans to earn a Master's degree in her chosen field at the local campus of IPFW. She is currently employed at Pier One at Jefferson Point in Fort Wayne and resides at the family home on Aboite Center Road.

Submitted by Janet and Gary Baltzell.

EMMETT LOUIS BANDELIER

Emmett Louis Bandelier was born July 10, 1856 in Switzerland, and died February 25, 1954. He came to the United States from Switzerland in 1863 with his father. He married Mary Adams, and they had seven children.

Mary was the first woman in the United Methodist Church to have a ladies circle of women of the United Methodist Church who met in their homes. She was a direct descendent of John Adams and John Quincy Adams. She believed liquor was bad, and believed people should abstain from it. She died April 7, 1943. In her last years she lived with her daughter, Esther Yant. Emmett also lived with Esther until his death.

Mr. Bandelier had the advanced mind of a genius, and he had the first patent and invention of the four-wheel drive differential. He talked with Henry Ford about the invention, and, finally, with monies limited, he let the patent expire.

He was a well-known thresher of wheat and oats in the Adams and Jefferson Township areas around New Haven and extended communities. He drove his 1928 Plymouth until he was 97 years old. He had knowledge beyond his time, and was a man ahead of his era.

He had two farms, one on Edgerton Road in Jefferson Township, and another in Adams Township by the Maumee River on the corner of Hartzell Road and Parrott Road, New Haven.

In the family plot at Odd Fellows Cemetery off Hartzel Road are buried: Emmett, 97 years; Mary A. Bandelier, 73 years; Emery, 1 month; Kenneth, 16 years; daughter Esther Bandelier Yant, 87 years; and son-in-law Kenneth M. Yant, 71 years.

Submitted by Delores Bandelier.

CLAUDE FRANCIOS BARDEY

Claude Francios Bardey was born November 22, 1828, in France to Jean Baptist Bardey and Pierrette DeRay, and died February 2, 1902, in Fort Wayne, Indiana. He lived at various times in New York state, Toledo, Ohio, where he was a saloon keeper, and in Allen County where he was a farmer.

Claude's first wife was Rose Louise (Chavanne), the daughter of Maurice Chavanne and Maria Rosa (Talon), born 1846 in Upper-Rhine, France. Rose died by 1870. They had two children, Francis Joseph and Stephen. Francis Joseph was born May 18, 1865, Erie County, New York, and died September 3, 1868, in Toledo, Lucas County, Ohio. Their son, Stephan was born September 6, 1867, in Erie County, New York; he married Araminta Emenhiser in June 29, 1893, at Besancon, Allen County, Indiana. Araminta was born March 17, 1868, in Allen County, Indiana, to Joseph Emenhiser and Adaline Clark of Allen County, Indiana and was one of fifteen siblings. Stephan and Araminta had eight children, and lived in Buffalo, New York, all their lives after their marriage.

Claude Bardey's second marriage was to Felicia Dodane on July 7, 1870, at Besancon, Allen County, Indiana. Felicia was born February 23, 1850, in Starke County, Ohio, to Francis Joseph Dodane and Mary Justine Monnot, and is one of eleven siblings. Felicia died April 5, 1919, in Allen County, Indiana. Claude and Felicia had four children: Mary Catherine, Francios Claude, Josephine (Jennie) Eugenie, and Joseph Louis.

Mary Catherine Bardey was born April 1, 1871, in Ohio. On April 29, 1890, Mary married Louis August Voiral, son of Jules and Eleonora (Dupont) Voiral. They had thirteen children.

Francois Claude Bardey was born March 23, 1873, in Lucas County, Ohio. He was first married to Bertha Minnecker. They divorced, and he married Martha Ann Smith. No children were born to either union.

Josephine (Jennie) Eugenie Bardey was born February 11, 1880, in Allen County, Indiana. On

Claude and Felecia (Dodane) Bardey

November 5, 1901, he married Louise Maldeney, born in France, and to this union ten children where born.

Joseph Louis Bardey was born October 26, 1886, in Allen County, Indiana. On September 8, 1914, he married Clara C. Monnier. She was born September 3, 1895, to Edward William Monnier and Mary Louise Lawyer in Allen County, Indiana. She was one of fifteen siblings. Joseph and Clara had two children: Cecelia Agnes and Louis Joseph. Joseph Bardey and wife, Clara, divorced. Clara was remarried to Andrew Cochren, and no children were born to this union. Joseph then remarried twice, first to Marie Benton, and then to Deloris Blubaugh. There were no children to these two marriages.

Cecelia Agnes Bardey was born October 28, 1915, in Allen County, Indiana, and died 2003 in New Carlisle, Ohio. Cecelia's first marriage was to Joseph Benard Sanders, and to this union was born Phyllis Sanders. Cecelia's second marriage was to Frank Winicker, and no children were born to this union.

Louis Joseph Bardey was born September 30, 1917, in Allen County, Indiana, and died 2002 in New Carlisle, Ohio. Louis first married Lucille Marjorie Moser. Lucille was born in Adams County, Indiana, to Jesse Moser and Olga Wahli. To this union were born two children, Richard Louis Bardey and Patricia Agnes Bardey. Richard Bardey married Beverly (Hughes) of Allen County, Indiana. Beverly's parents were Robert Hughes and Genevieve (Beard). To this union were born four children, all in Allen County, Indiana. They were Connie, Annette, Nadine, and Michael Bardey. Connie first married Terrance Pyles, and to this union was born one child. She then married Chester Cadwell, and no children were born to this union. Annette married Jerry Wolfe, and they had twins. Nadine had one son and married Justin Erne. Michael was unmarried. Patricia Agnes (Bardey) Palmer, the second child of Louis Joseph Bardley and Lucille Marjorie Moser, had two children, Lorraine (Palmer) Mossbarger and William Palmer.

Submitted by Connie Cadwell.

VALENTINE BARGO/ BARRIGER FAMILY

Wanda Schultz was born in Muncie, Delaware County, Indiana. Her great-great-great grandparents, were Valentine Bargo and Molly Williams. Valentine was born in 1797 in Virginia, and died 1861 in Trimble County, Kentucky. In 1797 Valentine "Felty" Bargo served as a member of the Shelby County, Kentucky Volunteer Militia.

Clara Francis Barriger

Valentine married Molly Williams October 13, 1814 in Gallatin County, Kentucky. Molly's father's name was Simpson Williams. Molly was born about 1795 and died between 1815-1820 in Gallatin County, Kentucky. Valentine and Molly Bargo had one son, Madison Bargo, born in 1815, and died between 1860-1865 in Trimble County, Kentucky. The family named changed between 1850-1860 from Bargo to Barriger.

Madison Barriger married Rebecca Roseberry February 25, 1839 in Trimble County, Kentucky. Rebecca was born April 15, 1823, and died June 8, 1914 in Indiana. Madison and Rebecca had two sons, Francis M. and James M. James was born in 1843 and died before 1900 in Kentucky.

Francis "Soldier" M. Barriger, was born December 13, 1842 in Kentucky, and died March 11, 1910 in Indiana. Francis, called Frank, served as a member of Company H Indiana Calvary between August 27, 1861 and June 24, 1862. Frank married Catharine "Kate" Caley Gaylord December 18, 1893 in Indiana. Kate, the daughter of Charles Gaylord and Susan Morrison of Indiana, was born October 1878, and died June 11, 1913 in Indiana. Frank and Kate had seven children: Mary Ann, Frank McKinley, Howard Gardner, Lillian Dell, Verna Mae, James Rodgers, and Clara Francis, who was born March 4, 1910 in Indiana, and died January 26, 1990 in Tennessee.

Clara Francis married Robert Barnes, born 1905 in Michigan, and they became the parents of Dorothy Pearl Barriger, who was born October 21, 1926, and died January 15, 1970 in Indiana. Clara and Robert later had a son Gerald Hardamon, who was born January 28, 1929, and died July 2000 in Indiana, and a daughter Virginia T. Hardamon, who was born May 23, 1930 and died June 10, 1984. Clara later married Donald Haffner, who was born February 20, 1902 in Indiana, and died April 14, 1988 in Tennessee.

Dorothy Pearl Barriger married Robert "Bob" Irwin McCune March 18, 1948. Bob, born July 11, 1921, died September 2, 1994 in Indiana. Bob's parents were Gola McCune and Cordelia "Delia" Cranfill. Bob and Dorothy had three children, Wanda Joy, Linda Lou, and David Lee, all born in Indiana.

Wanda Joy married Lee LaVern Shultz June 1, 1968. Lee, was born July 22, 1944 in Indiana and died 1985 in Tyler, Texas. Lee's parents were Robert Shultz and Ruth Marie Lawrence. Lee and Wanda had three children; Michelle "Shellie" Lee; Jonathan "Jon" Brian, born in Indiana; and Mitchell "Mitch" Wade, born in Michigan.

Michelle Lee married Steven Wayne Mix, December 8, 1990. Steve's parents are Tom and Sherry Mix. Steve and Shellie have two children, Brittney Tacconi and Alex Wayne.

Jonathan Brian married Diana Lynn Honeick and they have two children, Jake Christopher and Olivia Ileen.

Mitchell Wade is engaged to Lisa Mauger and they will marry in September 2006.

Submitted by Wanda Shultz.

MARY FRANCES BARKSDALE

Mary Frances Barksdale was born April 5, 1934 in Richmond, Indiana, the fifth of seven daughters born. to Charles and Mary A. Woodson. She graduated from Richmond Senior High School and attended Earlham College. In 1953, she relocated to Fort Wayne, Indiana, following her marriage to Wayne Barksdale. They are the parents of three children: Wayne, Jr., Stacey, and Vickki. Because her husband was born in Fort Wayne, their permanent home became Fort Wayne, Indiana.

Mary was employed in the office at Fort Wayne Safety Cab Company from August 1953 until May 1964. June 1, 1964, just prior to implementation of Title VII of the Civil Rights Act, Mary was employed at International Harvester as a typist clerk. She was promoted to several clerical positions from August 1968 until 1974, when she was promoted to Employment Supervisor. She was the first black female in management at the Fort Wayne Plant of approximately 10,000 employees. Her responsibilities included the hiring of all factory and office personnel.

In 1977 she was promoted to Labor Relations Supervisor, serving as liaison between the company and the local UAW Union that covered salaried and technical employees. Promotions followed: Human Resources Manager at the Materials Manager Center, Compensation and Development Manager at the Engineering Technical Center, and Manager of Human Resources of the Reliability and Quality Organization during the years 1981 until her retirement in 1999.

As a busy wife, mother, and employee she became involved in volunteer and community activities. In 1970, Mary was one of two minority persons appointed to the Board of Directors of Parkview Memorial Hospital. Following the first three-year term, ending in 1973, she was invited to serve additional terms on this Board: 1974-77, 1985- and 1995-97. Responsible for paving the way for minorities to serve on this board was Ian Rolland. Providing support and encouragement during the years was Dr. R. B. Wilson. During Mary's tenure in her second term on the Board of Directors, she served one year as secretary of the board and one year as Vice Chairperson.

Mary Frances Barksdale

In 1973, Wayne and Mary relocated the family into the East Allen County School District with 5% minority enrollment. Their family was the second black family to move into Colonial Heritage, an addition of 100 homes. Most of the children in this addition attended St. Henry Catholic School, a block away, and Bishop Luers High School.

While the bus rides to Village Elementary and Village Woods Middle Schools presented some challenges for Wayne and Mary's children, the bus rides to Paul Harding were the ones that caused tears. Their children learned the harsh reality of being black. Mary was always proud of the way they handled themselves in order to attend this prestigious school district.

In 1979, Mary was invited to fill the unexpired term on the East Allen County School Board of Trustees of a trustee who moved out of the district. Mary's beginning service caused publicity as the first black to serve on this board and her ending proved more volatile. Because this was an elected board, Mary ran for election and was elected in 1980 and was re-elected in 1984 and 1988.

The school district began experiencing financial difficulty during her last term and school closings were proposed. She supported the closings and was targeted for defeat in the re-election in 1992. The people spoke and four of a seven-member board, who supported the closings, were defeated or did not run for re-election. *New York Post* columnist, Pulitzer Prize winner and author, David Maraniss followed this issue in East Allen County Schools. This story and Mary's involvement appeared on the front page of the *Washington Post*. A wonderful Superintendent of Schools resigned and was employed in another school district in Indiana.

Healthcare and education concerns covered many years of volunteer activity for Mary Barksdale. She was invited and served on the following volunteer boards: Committee of 24 1968- 1980; Board of Community Advisors for Indiana-Purdue University from l976-1989; Fort Wayne Urban League, 1979-1985; United Way of Allen County, 1983-1986; Leadership Fort Wayne, 1983-1991; Fort Wayne Museum of Art, 1991-1993; Foellinger Foundation Board of Directors, 1997- present; Midwest Alliance for Health Education, 1997-present; and Sheriff's Merit Board, 2000-present. She is listed in *Who's Who among African Americans* and *Who's Who among Americans in Education*.

Mary was a charter member of the national black service organization, The Links, Inc., from the charter in 1979 until she resigned in 1992. During her time in this organization, she chaired a pilot project in Fort Wayne for the Links, Inc. which was funded through the YMCA National Board. She presented the results of this three-year program, working with 50 abused young women to the regional convention of The Links, Inc. in Tulsa, Oklahoma. She chaired several committees and, during her membership, was elected and served two-year terms as secretary, vice- president, and president.

While she received a number of community awards for her volunteer activities, her goal has always to do what she could to make a difference for others.

Submitted by Mary Frances Barksdale

JAMES M. BARRETT

The Barrett family stems from the Ewing, Bond and Woodworth families.

The Ewings were Irish patriots forced from Ireland. Alexander was the first Ewing in Allen County. Alexander (b 1763, d 1827) married Charlotte Griffith (d 1843). They had three children, one of whom, Charles W. Ewing (d 1843), was Fort Wayne's best lawyer at the time. He married Abigale Bryant Woodworth in 1829. Her remote ancestor Walter Woodworth emigrated from England as a Pilgrim. Charles and Abigale had seven children, including Lavinia Anna Ewing (b 1835, d 1909).

Lavinia married Charles D. Bond (b 1831, d 1873), son of Stephen Brown Bond of New York and his wife Adelia Darrow. They had five children, Marian Anna Bond (b 1857, d 1935) being their only daughter who survived childhood. Charles was a prominent banker in F ort Wayne.

James M. Barrett, 1927

James M. Barrett (b 1852, d 5/1/1929) was the son of Benjamin and Elizabeth Barrett, emigrants from Ireland about 1832. They settled in Illinois. After graduating with honors from schools and the University of Michigan, he moved to Fort Wayne in 1876 to practice law. The Fort Wayne firm of Barrett & McNagny dates from that time. He married Marian Anna Bond in 1877. She was long active in the community. James was the leading member of the Fort Wayne bar, served in the Indiana Senate in late 1890's, sponsored the Barrett law, permitting property owners to finance improvements, and was Allen County Attorney during construction of the Courthouse, dedicating it to the citizens on September 23, 1902. He was a Trustee of Purdue University.

James and Marian had four children, the youngest being James M. Barrett, Jr. (b1895, d 5/6/1979). He also was a prominent corporate and tax lawyer in his father's firm from 1920. He negotiated with The Reconstruction Finance Corp. for the formation of Fort Wayne National Bank in 1933, and served it as a director and attorney until retirement in 1972. He was wounded in World War I and during World War II served as Allen County Civilian Defense Director.

On February 17, 1922 James, Jr. married Edna Heit Fee (b 1890, d 1981), widow of Herbert Fee, by whom she had a daughter, Joan Fee, whom James adopted. James and Edna had one child, James M. Barrett III, who practiced law with the firm, retiring in 1990. He served on the Fort Wayne National Bank board for 32 years. One of the organizers of Acres Land Trust in 1960, he served as its attorney for about thirty-five years, during which he drafted the Indiana Nature Preserves Act, under which the State now holds some 200 natural areas.

In 1953 he married Patricia Dunten, who was a member of the Fort Wayne Philharmonic and also one of the founders of radio station WBNI. They have two daughters, Florence Ann and Barbara, and a son, Robert Ewing. Ann married Jeffrey Hicks of New York. They have three daughters, Kelsey, Jennifer and Madison.

Submitted by James M. Barrett.

BARRONE/LUDE

Elmer Bino Barrone was born July 20, 1910 in Bergville, Minnesota to Amos Stewart and Ada Jane Barnhart Barrone. Amos (1869-1921), a native of Allen County, was born to Michael and Polly (Brown) Barrone, pioneers who settled in Monroe Township, Allen County, in the 1840s. After brief stays in Paulding County, Ohio and Calhoun County, Michigan, Amos and family homesteaded in Alvwood Township, Itasca County, Minnesota, starting in 1903, and moved to Oneida County, Wisconsin by 1920. After Elmer's mother died in 1926, he and his brothers Otha and Clyde Barrone went to California. By the 1930s, Otha, Elmer, and their two sisters, Bessie and Eliza Belle Barrone, were living in Fort Wayne. Eliza Belle had been adopted by Elizabeth Baulky in Fort Wayne and renamed Annabelle.

Edith & Elmer Barrone

Edith Amelia Lude (born 1921) came to Fort Wayne with her family about 1942. Her family included siblings John, Rosemary, James, Theodore, and Leonard Lude, grandmother Amelia Feisley Lude, and parents, Robert and Aldine Gerber Lude. They settled on Greenview Avenue, Rural Route 8. The Ludes had been farmers at Craigville, Indiana. The Lude family owned and operated an ice cream parlor, Frosty's, at 101 West Williams in the early 1950s. Robert Lude was an employee of Moellering Mills. Edith had been a restaurant cook at the Alpine Haus where Annabelle Barrone McCurdy was a waitress. Annabelle introduced Edith to her brother, Elmer. Edith and Elmer were married April 8, 1944 at Fort Wayne. They purchased their Greenview Avenue home from Edith's grandmother. This home was next door to the Robert Lude family home.

Elmer and Edith Barrone had three children, Daisy (born 1945), Dennis (born 1949) and Randall (1966-1968). Elmer was an employee of Bowser, Inc., and Systems Engineering and Sales Co. He died in 1977.

Daisy married Bobby Thompson, an Alabama native. Their first three children, Darrell, Cheryl, and Gregory, were born at Fort Wayne. Their fourth child, Jason, was born at Norfolk, Virginia. Daisy, Cheryl, and Jason now live in Fort Worth, Texas. Darrell and Gregory reside in California and Alabama respectively.

Dennis, a 1968 Elmhurst High School graduate, married Beverly Crothers, daughter of Harry and Edna Sutton Crothers, in 1970 at the West Creighton Avenue Christian Church. Beverly was a 1967 graduate of Central High School. Dennis is a 35-year employee of Fort Wayne Newspapers. Their children are twins Adam and Carla (born 1978) and Samuel (born 1985).

Adam, an IPFW graduate, married Mysti Schammert, a Hobart, Indiana, native, at First Christian Church in 2001. He, a former Fort Wayne Community Schools teacher, is employed by the Allen County Public Library Foundation. Their son, Caleb, was born in 2002 in Fort Wayne.

Carla, wife of Colleaf Andrews, is a certified nursing assistant who provide in-home care. She also does clerical work for the Lutheran Health Network. She and Colleaf were married in 2004 in Reno, Nevada. Carla's daughter, LeeAnna Washington, was born in 1996 in Fort Wayne.

Samuel is a computer science student at IPFW.

Submitted by Adam Barrone

CHRISTIAN & MARGARET (STRUCHEN) BARTH

Christian Barth II was born January 3, 1825, in Canton, Berne, Switzerland to Christian and Elizabeth (Hurny) Barth. He came to America in 1844, and married Margaret Struchen and lived in Tuscarawas County, Ohio. They had thirteen children, Oliver, C. Henry, David, John, Daniel, Benjamin, Eli, Lewis, Albert, Mary, Sophia, Rosanna, and Carrie. The family moved to Wyandot County, Ohio in 1858. Christian was a farmer and carpenter for over forty years. He died December 19, 1898.

Christian Barth's son, Oliver, was born in 1853. Oliver married Sara Ann Duley on March 13, 1877. They had nine children, Margaret, Mary, Charles, Minnie, Blanche, Cora, Fredrick, Ezra, and Christ Arthur. They lived near Upper Sandusky, Ohio. Oliver and his son, Charles, died August 8, 1898, from gases in their well. Eighteen months later, his wife and daughter, Blanche, died of typhoid fever. The younger children were sent to an orphanage in Allen County, Indiana.

Christian Barth II family, 1875; Front row, Lewis, Caroline, Margaret, Albert, Christian II, Mary, and Oliver. Back row, David, John, Eli, Daniel, and Henry.

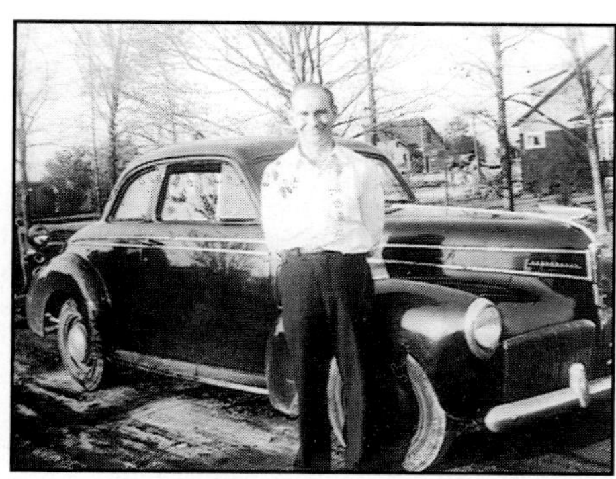

Robert Barth.

Oliver's son, Christ Arthur Barth, was born March 16, 1895, and married Beatrice Manier on November 1, 1917, in Arcola. Indiana. Her parents were Robert Manier and M. Catherine Kinder, and her four siblings were Bernadette, Madonna, Dorothy, and Leoba. Christ and Beatrice had five children, Robert, Rodney N., Imogene, Patricia, and June. He was a farmer and worked at Falstaff Brewery. Christ died March 30, 1988, in Ruskin, Florida.

Christ's son, Robert Barth, was born June 5, 1918, in Arcola, Indiana. He married Margaret Downend on March 20, 1937. Her parents were Bacil Downend and Ethel A. Waters, who had two other children, Virginia and Glenn. Robert was a machinist for Dana Corporation and ran a campground. He brought stray animals home, loved morel mushroom hunting, ice fishing, and deer hunting in Wyoming. Margaret loved gardening, and was a good cook. They had seven children, Roger, Sandra, Cynthia, Duane, Linda, Janet, and Anita. They have seventeen grandchildren and twenty-three great grandchildren. Robert died June 21, 1980, and Margaret died May 6, 1997.

Names associated with the family are Kinder, Manier, Christman, Leeuw, Kirkhoff, Ott, Kraus, Schaefer, Jones, Hurny, Struchen, Duley, Downend, Waters, and Arlic. Countries from where the families originated are France, England, Germany, and Switzerland.

Submitted by Sandra M. Smith.

MARGARET (DOWNEND) & ROBERT J. BARTH

Margaret (Downend) Barth was born July 14, 1919, to Ethel (Waters) and Bacil Downend in Allen County, Indiana. She was married to Robert J. Barth in Noble County, Indiana, on March 20, 1937. They moved to Whitley County where they developed and ran the Blue Lake campgrounds. They attended St. John Bosco and Ege Catholic Church. Robert loved to fish and hunt. Margaret enjoyed homemaking, gardening and her children. They moved back to Allen County. Robert worked at Dana Corporation as a machinist repairman and retired from there. They moved to Ruskin, Florida, for retirement. They then moved back to Kendallville, Indiana, where they stayed until their deaths. They are both buried at Ege Cemetery.

Margaret taught many values to her children by treating everyone with kindness and taking in sick animals. Her house was always filled with neighbors and friends. Her seven children are Roger Barth (Louise Fields) who was a supervisor at Kraft Foods and lives in Kimmel, Indiana. Sandra (Jim) Smith was a data entry operator and lives in Grabill. Cynthia (Bob) Allen works for the U.S. Postal Service and lives in Albion. Duane Barth (Linda McClure) was a bricklayer and worked for Slater Steel and lives in Columbia City. Linda (Paul) Smith is a homemaker and lives in Allen County. Janet (John) McIntosh worked at Raytheon Corporation and lives in Allen County. Anita Barth is deceased and is buried at Ege Cemetery. Margaret has 17 grandchildren and numerous great grandchildren.

Margaret's father was a very loving grandfather whose grandchildren loved to sit on his lap and listen to his pocket watch. Margaret's mother took care of her grandmother in later years after her sickness. She loved gardening and astrology. They used to go to Robinson Park when they were going together.

Bacil and Ethel (Waters) Downend.

Robert and Margaret (Downend) Barth.

Albert and Florence (Guiff) Waters family.

Margaret's grandfather, Albert Waters, was a schoolteacher at a one-room schoolhouse in Allen County. Her grandmother was Florence (Guiff) Waters.

John Claude Juif (John C. Guiff) came to Allen County in 1850, from France. He built buildings on Columbia Street. He resided on Dupont Road then moved to the Ege, Indiana, area where he made bricks for roads and one-room schoolhouses. He was married to Matilda (Brun) Guiff.

Elias Waters came from Pennsylvania and Ohio in 1834, to Allen County. He married Mary Clapper. Elias was a prosperous farmer and landowner, owning thousands of acres. He died when he was 65 years old and was buried on the Waters farm. His family originated from England.

James Downend came from England to Richland County, Ohio. He married Mary Shaw. His son, James, came to DeKalb County, Indiana. He married Elizabeth Nickerson. His son, John, married Lottie B. Roberts. They were farmers and worked on the railroad in Garrett.

Names associated with the family are Waters Guiff, Downend, Roberts, Coffinberry, Clapper Shaw, Nickerson, Cook, Pepe, Brun, Hawthorne Ervin, Cory, Grosjean, Petgieny, Coutirier, Gilki son, and Reingner.

Countries of origination are Scotland, England, France, and Germany. Migrations were from Rhode Island, Massachusetts, Maryland Pennsylvania, and Ohio then to Indiana.

Submitted by Janet McIntosh

DAVID WINFIELD BASH SR.

David Wayne Bash was born at 914 West Washington Street in Fort Wayne, Indiana, on September 3, 1910, but his family soon renamed him David Winfield Bash after a favorite uncle Winfield Scott Bash. A superior athlete in his youth, he was captain of the football team at Central High School, as well as captain of the basketball team. Deemed too light for football at his alma mater, Wabash College in Crawfordsville, Indiana, he played guard on the basketball team, where in his senior year he was captain of the team, as well as president of his fraternity, Kappa Sigma. In the early 1930s, he played basketball with the Fort Wayne Caseys. This team, sponsored by The Knights of Columbus, was formed in 1919 and a founding member in 1926 of the first nationwide pro- basketball league - the American Basketball Association. His pay in those depression years was five dollars and a steak dinner per game. In his adult years, he played on the basketball team at Trinity English Lutheran Church and enjoyed ice-skating on a family pond, which he had created and stocked with fish.

During school breaks, David worked on the family farm, first purchased by his grandfather, Solomon Bash, and for the family flour mill, Mayflower Mills, founded in 1889. (See the history of Mayflower Mills elsewhere in this book.) After college graduation in 1932, David started at Mayflower Mills as an assistant flour sales manager and worked there all his adult life, eventually serving as president and manager of the mill. He married Florence Louise Kendrick on April 6, 1935, in Gary, Indiana, and they raised four children in Fort Wayne: Judith Ann (Bash) Lee, Roberta Louise (Bash) Hall, David Winfield Bash Jr., and Charles Dayton Bash. A man of varied interests, David Sr. raised dogs that he showed at American Kennel Club meets around the country, enjoyed vegetable and flower gardening, and served as usher and Sunday School treasurer of his church.

David's parents were Harry Edward Bash of Fort Wayne, Indiana, and Lola French of Fremont, Steuben County, Indiana. Harry's principal business activity also was the Mayflower Mills, where he served as president.

In 1848, Harry's father, Solomon Bash, came to Indiana from Stark County, Ohio, where he obtained a farm near his brother, John Bash, who earlier had located from Ohio to Huntington County, Indiana. In 1852, Solomon returned to Ohio to marry his childhood sweetheart, Rebecca Ketterer, and they moved to Fort Wayne in 1854. Solomon and several of his sons - most notably Harry and Charles Sumner Bash - had a major impact on Fort Wayne. Solomon was an early dealer in grains and he used the Wabash and

Erie Canal system to facilitate the transport of the grain. Later Charles was a major, but largely unsuccessful, supporter of increased canal building in the area. Solomon entered into partnership with Stewart Eakin in 1856 to establish the company called "Bash and Eakin, Grain Dealers." In 1870, Solomon started another company called "S. Bash and Co.," a commission grain firm. Solomon became active in Fort Wayne affairs by serving on the City Council for the Fifth Ward and assisting in founding the Fort Wayne Board of Trade. During his tenure on the City Council, the city was distressed over the problem of a permanent water supply. This concern prompted a strong effort to purchase a feeder canal as a means of supplying water to the growing city. With D. L. Harding, Charles F. Pfeiffer, Christian Hetler, James E. Graham, and others, Solomon worked to establish a system of municipally owned waterworks.

David Winfield Bash

Solomon was one of the founders of the First National Bank of Fort Wayne, as well as the Westminster Presbyterian Church in Fort Wayne, where for many years he served as an elder until his death in 1912. He gave many thousands of dollars for the inauguration of the Westminster Church building project, and, with Frederick Antrup, was the financial mainstay during its establishment. Solomon began actively pursuing farming interests in 1872. Then, in the early 1880s, he retired from active participation in his business activities and divided these interests among his children. Harry consolidated ownership of the Mayflower Mills Corporation and became the head of it. Charles became manager of S. Bash & Co. Charles also was one of the founders of the Solomon Mining and Gas Company, and the first blaze from gas in Fort Wayne was lighted in his house at 1114 West Wayne Street in 1890. This was a gala affair at which hundreds gathered both in and out of the house to witness the lighting.

Submitted by David W. Bash

JONATHAN DALE BATDORFF

Jonathan Dale Batdorff was born April 17, 1967 in Coos Bay, Oregon to James and Alfreda (Pinther) Batdorff. Jonathan grew up in Coos Bay and graduated from Marshfield High School. Following graduation he enrolled in Oregon State University in Corvallis. In his sophomore year he transferred to Oregon Institute of Technology in Klamath Falls, Oregon and graduated from that institution in 1982 with a BS degree in

Jonathan Dale Batdorff

Mechanical Engineering. He worked for Morrison Knudsen Rail Corporation in Boise, Idaho between 1992 and 1994 designing parts for rail locomotives. Jon moved to Fort Wayne, Indiana in 1995 to accept a job with Navistar International Transportation Corportion. He currently works for Navistar designing truck parts. In addition Jon works on management teams composed of engineering, manufacturing, and vendor engineers on projects optimizing quality, cost and manufacturability.

Jon is an Indiana State Licensed Engineering Intern and a member of the Society of Automotive Engineers, in addition to being a Six Sigma Qualtec Certified Black Belt. His hobbies include: active participating in the Scottish Highland Games, photography, car racing, hiking, genealogy, and traveling. He enjoys working on family genealogy during the two to three months each year when his parents visit in Fort Wayne researching in the Allen County Public Library. The Batdorff family in America dates back to the early 1700's of which Jon is a 12th generation descendent. Jon is a member of the Missionary Fellowship Church and St. Judes Roman Catholic Church of Fort Wayne.

Submitted by James H. Batdorff.

GARLAND RIDGEWAY BAUCH

Garland Ridgeway Bauch was born on July 28,1882 in Fort Wayne, Indiana, the son of Ed and Lizzie Bauch. He had four brothers: Ed, Henry, Oscar, Grover, a stepbrother and stepsister, Albert and Anna Hartstine. His stepmother was Rosina Hartstine, and his stepfather was Valentine Berger.

Garland was a member of St. John Lutheran Church and attended it's school. On April 5,1896 Garland received confirmation at St. John.

On September 24, 1902 he married Myrtle Roebel. They had the following children: Ethel (January 27,1903 –April 6, 1903), Clifton M. (March 28, 1904-1968), Viola (September 7, 1906-1968), Delford M. (August 28,1908-April 1909), Evelyn L. (December 11, 1910), Robert W. (May 7, 1913), Clarence K. (December 9, 1916), Herbert W. (April 6, 1919-), and Lawrence G. (December 11, 1922).

Garland worked all his life at the Horton Manufacturing Company. Garland liked baseball, and Myrtle liked to cook. He died in 1940. His wife, Myrtle, married again to Henry Wedellen. He also passed away, and she was married again to Thomas Hall.

Myrtle Roebel died in 1959.

Submitted by David Bauch

JOHN & AMY BEATTY

John David Beatty is one of the compilers and editors of this volume. He was born in 1960 in Detroit, grew up in the northern suburb of Birmingham, Michigan, and was a son of David Jerome and Mary Katherine (Neal) Beatty. His father was President of Beatty Lumber Company, a wholesale lumber distributor founded in 1947 by the subject's grandfather, William Edgar Beatty. The Beatty family came from Ballycanew, County Wexford, Ireland, and was founded in America by the subject's third great grandfather, Dempster Beatty, in 1796.

John attended the local schools in Birmingham and matriculated at the University of Michigan, receiving a B.A. with High Honors in History in 1982 and an M.A. with Honors in History and Library Science in 1984. Having a deep interest in genealogical research since his youth, he came to Fort Wayne in 1984 to become a Reference Librarian in the Genealogy Department of the Allen County Public Library. Since that time he has also become its Bibliographer

John and Amy Beatty, Robert and Julia

and has played a significant role in developing its nationally renowned collection.

John married Amy June Stone on May 23, 1998. She was born in 1967 in Fort Wayne and was the daughter of Jack and Susan (Archibald) Stone. Through her mother she is descended from several early pioneer families in Allen County. She is a graduate of South Side High School aud is presently a student at Taylor University. She is a former Citizen's Advocate for the City of Fort Wayne in the Helmke administration and also worked as Director of Regional Services for Arts United. She has been a dealer of antiques with A Z Coins & Stamps, Inc. for 16 years. Receiving training from Leadership Fort Wayne, she has volunteered for and helped coordinate numerous local events, including the Fort Wayne Bicentennial, for which she was also employed as Special Events Coordinator, and the Allen County Courthouse Preservation Trust. Currently, she serves on the boards of ARCH, Friends of the Parks (chairing the Hat Luncheon fundraiser), and the Fort Wayne Antique Dealers Association, for which she is Treasurer.

John and Amy are members of Trinity Episcopal Church. John is a cradle Episcopalian, while Amy was raised in First Baptist Church before joining Trinity in 1997. John has served twice on its vestry and authored its sesquicentennial history in 1994. He is also the author of fifteen other books on local history and genealogy. Politically, John and Amy are Independents, generally voting Democratic in national elections and supporting both parties in local elections.

They have two children: Robert Archibald Ross, born in 2002, and Julia Susan Abra, born in 2004.

Submitted by John Beatty.

BRAD & LESLIE BEAUCHAMP

Brad Beauchamp was born in Fort Wayne, Indiana on July 16, 1963. His parents, Gerald Beauchamp, born April 20, 1941 in Fort Wayne, Indiana, and Sarah Shultz, born January 14, 1941 in Warren, Indiana, lived in Fort Wayne all of their married life. Brad has a sister, Jill Graber, born April 3, 1967 in Fort Wayne, Indiana who married David Graber born August 8, 1958 in Auburn, Indiana on November 7, 1998. The Graber's live in Auburn, Indiana with children, Nicolas, 5, Sydney, 3, and Alex, 1 month.

Leslie (Wood) Beauchamp was born in Wichita, Kansas on November 28, 1966. Her parents are David Wood, born September 21, 1937 in Fort Wayne, Indiana, and Pamela Roberts, born December 6, 1938 in London, England. David was in the U.S. Air Force, and after retiring and living in London for a few years, moved the family back to his hometown of Fort Wayne in 1977. Leslie has a brother, Keith Clyde "K.C." born February 16, 1959 in London, England, and two sisters, Michele "Micki" born January 17, 1963 in Wichita, Kansas, and Anna Matusik, born February 20, 1973 in Landstuhl, Germany who married James Matusik, born on March 17, 1970 in Southfield, Michigan, on August 22, 1998. All live in Fort Wayne. Leslie's family history includes the Smith's and Chambers' of Allen County history.

Brad and Leslie married on October 3, 1992 at Simpson United Methodist Church with a reception following at the Fort Wayne Women's Club. Brad graduated from Homestead High School in 1981 where he excelled in fine and performing arts. He furthered his artistic training at St. Francis College. Leslie graduated from New Haven High School in 1985 where she was involved in music, performing arts and was a

Brad & Leslie Beauchamp Family December 2003.

member of the Honor Society. Leslie obtained a B.S. degree in Interpersonal Communication and an Associates degree in Supervision from IPFW. Brad was the Youth and Adult Sports Program Director at the Central YMCA from 1985-1990, and then joined Sarah in the family transportation business, SJB Enterprises, where he is currently the President. Brad and his comedy partner Larry Bower perform regularly the Abbot and Costello classic Who's on First and were invited to perform for the grand opening of the Cincinnati Reds Baseball Museum and Hall of Fame in August of 2004 in front of baseball greats including Joe Nuxhall and Sparky Anderson. Brad served on Arena Theatre's Board as Vice President and President. Leslie worked for 11 years at Pier 1 Imports, and served as the Assistant to the Dean of Fine and Performing Arts at IPFW, and was also involved on the Board of Youtheatre. Both Brad and Leslie are heavily involved in the community's arts scene, volunteering in many capacities.

They have two beautiful daughters, Emma Jordan Beauchamp, born August 5, 1995, and Ava Blake Beauchamp, born May 18, 2002, both born in Fort Wayne. Emma is involved on the SWAC swim team and Ava enjoys her preschool's activities.

Submitted by Leslie Beauchamp.

ALVIN C. BECK FAMILY

Alvin Chance married Golda May Dunlap on January 9, 1934, in Allen County, Indiana. Alvin was born in Blue Creek Township (Paulding) Ohio, on January 2, 1885. Golda was born November 9, 1886 in Putnam County, Ohio. Alvin was a brick mason, and his work can be seen on the porch at the home where he lived at 807 Home Avenue in Fort Wayne. He did the brick on many homes along Lafayette Street.

He loved to fish and hunt and often went with his cousin, Dr. Claude Scheffer Beck, who was a heart surgeon at the University Hospitals of Cleveland. In 1947, Dr. Beck successfully defibrillated a 14-year-old boy whose heart when into fibrillation after an operation. Alvin also liked to make dandelion wine.

Golda was trained as a teacher at Ohio Normal College (now Ohio Northern) in Ada, Ohio. She taught at schools in Paulding County before marrying. She was also trained as a nurse and was an accomplished pianist.

Alvin and Golda had six children: Marvin, Mary Louise, Alvin C. Jr., Margaret, Robert, and Harold. Alvin died January 9, 1934, when his youngest son was only nine years old.

During World War II, Marvin became head of the family. He began his education at General Electric apprentice school, went to Purdue, and came back to work at G.E.

Mary Louise's husband, Donald Jenkins, joined the Army.

Alvin C. Jr. joined the Army Air Force and was commander of a B-29 bomber named "Fort Wayne" that flew from Tinian.

Margaret's husband, George Townsend, joined the Army Air Force and worked on planes on Guam and Saipan. Robert joined the Navy and was aboard the U.S.S. Pennsylvania.

Alvin and Golda Beck

Harold, Bob, Margaret, Alvin, Mary Louise, Marvin

Golda died February 9, 1956 in Fort Wayne at the home of her youngest son, Harold. Both Alvin and Golda are buried at Blue Creek Cemetery in Paulding County, Ohio.

Alvin's parents were Lewis Franklin and Susan (Baughman) Beck. Lewis was born November 23, 1846, in Columbiana County, Ohio, to Alvin and Enzie Beck. Susan was born December 8, 1849, to Simon and Rebecca Baughman in Hancock County, Ohio. They were married May 9, 1868, in Hancock County, Ohio. They came to Paulding County before 1870, and on February 23, 1877, Lewis bought 40 acres in Blue Creek Township in Paulding County, Ohio, for $400 and built a two-room log cabin with a loft. He

Lewis and Susan Beck at log cabin

Ed Dunlap family

farmed the land. They had ten children: Martha, Mary Jane, Anza, Eber, an infant (born and died 1880), Artinca, Lewis, Alvin, Richard, and Verna. Susan died September 23, 1922 in Blue Creek Township. After Susan died, the children would come and wash his dishes and clean for him. He would often be using the backs of the plates before they got there. He died September 14, 1928, in Wortsville, Ohio. Lewis and Susan are both buried in Blue Creek Cemetery in Paulding County, Ohio.

Golda's parents were William "Edward" and Tabitha "Jane" (Jenkins) Dunlap. Edward was born in Putnam County, Ohio, on September 12, 1863, to Lester Adam and Mary (young) Dunlap. Lester was in the Civil War in the 151 Ohio National Guard. He was assigned to guard and patrol duty in Maryland and in the District of Columbia. William married Tabitha in 1882 in Putnam County, Ohio. Jane was born October 4, 1862, in Union County, Ohio, to William and Lucinda Walker (Holycross) Jenkins. Jane only weighed two pounds when she was born. They kept her on the open oven door of a coal-burning stove to keep her warm. They had a farm in Paulding County, where they had six children: Golda, Edna, Harry, Forest, Glen, and Ralph. They sold their farm in Paulding County in 1897 and bought a farm in Ossian, Indiana, where they lived until 1931. They then moved to 1120 Nelson Street in Fort Wayne. Edward died January 13, 1932 at the University Hospital in Ann Arbor, Michigan. Jane died May 20, 1943, in Fort Wayne.

Submitted by Nancy Townsend

FREDRICK & MARGARET (JENNEWEIN) BECKER

Fredrick Becker, his wife Margaret (Jennewein) Becker, and their daughter, Sophia Becker arrived at the Port of New York on the packet ship, Ship St. Denis, August 5, 1848. Because they were not listed as "cabin passengers," they must have sailed in steerage. All three had been born in Saarbrucken, Germany: Fredrick on September 24, 1819; Margaret on August 28, 1819; and Sophia in 1848. Fredrick and Margaret were married there in 1847.

The Maumee River Basin by Charles Elihu Slocum stated that Fredrick and Margaret (Jennewein) Becker came to Fort Wayne "by way of the Great Lakes to Toledo, Ohio, and from that port they came by canal to Fort Wayne." B. J. Griswold in *The Pictorial History of Fort Wayne, Indiana* wrote, "Fredrick Becker, who arrived from Europe the preceding year, made a large number of wagons of the prairie schooner type for the Forty Niners who departed from Fort Wayne."

Fredrick and his brother, Christian Becker, applied for United States citizenship on July 27, 1850. In the Fort Wayne City Directory for 1858-1859, Fred is shown as a blacksmith, shop on the north side of Washington between Calhoun and Clinton; and Christian is a stone cutter on the north side of Berry between Van Buren and Jackson.

Fredrick and Margaret became the parents of six more children, Fredrick, born November 4, 1849; Wilhelmina, born August 25, 1852; Charles F., born August 10, 1854; Wilhelm, born February 18, 1856 and died six days later; Mary, born February 23, 1857; and Henry William, born February 21, 1859. Little Sophia, after surviving the ocean voyage from Germany, died of cholera on September 24, 1852.

The picture is of the Becker family home at 11 East Washington, next to Fred's blacksmith shop. The Becker house was often a haven for new arrivals to Fort Wayne. Fredrick would invite people from his home area in Germany to stay with his family until the immigrants could get settled in their own homes. One family stayed an entire year! The Becker house and blacksmith shop were later dismantled to make way for the Wolf and Dessauer Building.

Margaret (Jennewein) Becker kept a cow and supplied her neighbors with milk. By saving the earnings from her milk business, Margaret was able to buy a very special sofa which was upholstered in a red horsehair fabric. Her children, who enjoyed teasing their mother, lovingly named her new sofa, "The Red Cow." Although the fabric was changed two times, that name followed the sofa as it was handed down through the family.

Home of Fredrick and Margaret (Jennewein) Becker, 11 East Washington Blvd., Fort Wayne, Indiana

Of the five children of Fredrick and Margaret Becker, only one, Henry William, married; so, of course, the sofa eventually went to Henry's children who also treasured "The Red Cow." After gracing the Becker parlors in several homes, the sofa was donated by Kenneth Lawrence Lauer, a great-grandson of Margaret, to the Old Fort Settlers for use in their Swinney Homestead. This house is located at the west end of Washington Boulevard; straight down that street from Summit One, Fort Wayne's tallest building; and Summit One stands where Fredrick had his blacksmith shop and where "The Red Cow" enhanced Margaret's parlor.

Submitted by Mary Smith

HENRY WILLIAM & LAVINA CAROLINE (ENGLERT) BECKER

Henry William Becker, the son of Fredrick and Margaret (Jennewein) Becker, was born in Fort Wayne on February 21, 1859, and educated in St. Paul's Lutheran School. As a youth, he served a thorough apprenticeship in the stonecutter trade, became a certified stonecutter, and was a partner in Griebel, Wyckoff & Becker at 74 and 76 West Main.

During the Civil War, on September 23, 1863, Lavina Caroline Englert was born into the family of Frank and Theresa (Felter) Englert. She attended St. Paul's Catholic School, but, when she was only 13, her mother died. Her only brother had already married. She and her sisters were sent out to work as domestics and to live with the families for whom they worked. Lavina's position was at 90 West Main.

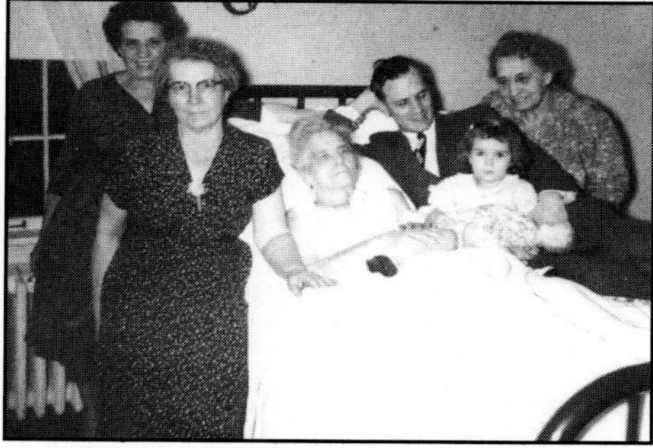

Left to right: Florence Elizabeth (Becker) Lauer, Mary Madaline Becker, Lavina Caroline (Englert) Becker, Kenneth Lawrence Lauer, Beth Ann Lauer, Mary Margaret Becker – February 27, 1955

Just before her 21st birthday, she and Henry eloped and were married in Sturgis, Michigan. They lived above the blacksmith shop of his parents and later had homes at 134 Francis and 1014 East Jefferson. After 20 years as a stonecutter, Henry became Wayne Township Assessor, then Secretary of the Board of Public Works from 1905 until his death on March 26, 1919.

The six children of Henry and Lavina were educated in St. Mary's Catholic School. On Sundays, the family walked to church. Lavina, with the three daughters and three sons, worshipped in St. Mary's Catholic Church; Henry continued to St. Paul's Lutheran Church. After the service there, he walked back to St. Mary's to meet his family, and they all walked home together.

The three girls also attended St. Mary's Commercial School and did office work. Madaline became the secretary-treasurer of the Bass Foundry and Machine Shop. After its closing, she managed the Bass estate and assisted with the sale of it to the Sisters of St. Francis for St. Francis College. M. Margaret Becker, after some stenographic positions, was the financial secretary of Fort Wayne Public Library from September 1926 until June 1956. Florence Elizabeth Becker married Paul Anthony Lauer and had six children.

Henry Joseph Becker, oldest of the three sons, married Leura J. Baker, had no children, and was superintendent of the electric company in Troy, Ohio. Roy David Becker married Faye Ashton Swartz, had one son named for himself, and was paymaster for Colonial Supply Company in Louisville, Kentucky. Henry and Roy fought with the American Expeditionary Forces in France during World War I and were there when their father died. Fredrick Michael Becker was superintendent of maintenance at Baer Field.

Records show that, besides the six children they reared, Lavina and Henry also lost a baby on April 26, 1885 and another on Christmas Day, 1892. At age 80, Lavina broke her arm. Deciding that she had only two weeks to live anyhow, she went to bed to rest up for heaven; and she was in bed for 19 years. From her bed, she ruled the family; or so she thought. The above picture shows her with family members gathered around. When she died at age 99 on November 5, 1962, she was survived by two sons, two daughters, seven grandchildren, and 15 great-grandchildren.

Submitted by Sandra Lauer

WILLIAM & SOPHIA (FUELLING) BECKER

The Becker family has well-established roots in Allen County, Indiana. It was on March 29,1884, that Friedrich August Wilhelm "William" Becker (1860-1923) and his brother, August E.C. Becker (1854-1939) arrived in New York from their homeland in Germany. Migrating to Indiana, William chose to set up residence, first in the township of Wayne, and later in Adams. Presumably, that is where he met Sophia Fuelling (1859-1953) of Adams County, the daughter of Frederick (1823-1869) and Lizetta (Mayland) Fuelling (1827-) whom he married on November 3, 1887 in Decatur. A staunch Republican, William was a bold supporter of the cause and even served a term as Adams Township Supervisor at one time. By 1888, William had signed a naturalization document in Allen County, thereby renouncing all allegiance to his birth country. For many years, William owned a large parcel of property on Seiler Road in New Haven and was widely respected as one of the most industrious and successful stock-growing farmers in the area.

William & Sophia (Fuelling) Becker on their wedding day, November 3, 1887, Decatur, Indiana

Theodore and Catherine "Kate" (Gable) Behrman, Indiana, 1942, Photo courtesy Elna (Becker) Szink

William's brother, August, settled in Fort Wayne, where he owned a grocery store on Fairfield Avenue. August was considered a wealthy man, having amassed a large fortune in the stock market. He was a longtime member of Emmaus Evangelical Lutheran Church in Fort Wayne and benefactor of the Becker Memorial Carillons for the bell tower in 1922. The gigantic marble obelisk at Concordia Lutheran Cemetery in Fort Wayne serves as the Becker family marker for August, three of his former wives, a son, Theodore H. Becker (1885-1935) and possibly another son, Louis Becker (1881-1883).

William and Sophia (Fuelling) Becker had one child, Arthur William "Art" Becker (1890-1966), who married Edith Catherine Behrman (1893-1980) on August 11, 1912 at Imanuel Lutheran Church (aka Soest Community Church) in Fort Wayne. Edith (Behrman) Becker (1893-1980) was the daughter of Theodore Wilhelm Friedrich "Ted" (1865-1960) and Catherine "Kate" (Gable) Behrman (1870-1960), who were both natives of Fort Wayne. Ted Behrman owned a large farm on Tillman Road in Fort Wayne, where he was a road supervisor for the county.

Arthur and Edith (Behrman) Becker on their wedding day, August 11, 1912, Emmanuel Lutheran Church (aka Soest Community Church) Wayne Trace, Fort Wayne Indiana

Edith and Arthur Becker (seated) and their children. L to R: Elna (Becker) Szink, Hilda (Becker) Gabet, Carl Becker, Wilma (Becker) Martin, Naomi (Becker) Hathaway

Ted and Kate married on October 27, 1892 in Fort Wayne and had two other children, Malinda "Linda" (Behrman) Heckman (1897-1955) and Willis Behrman (1902-1904).

Arthur and Edith (Behrman) Becker had seven children: Naomi (Becker) Hathaway (1913-), Wilma (Becker) Martin (1915-), Hilda (Becker) Gabet (1918-), Elmer Becker (1919-1944), Carl Becker (1920-1992), Ervin Becker (1924-1939) and Elna (Becker) Szink (1926-). Wilma, Hilda and Elna have been lifelong residents of New Haven, as was Carl, who was the owner of Carl's Tavern in downtown New Haven for many years. T/Sgt. Elmer Becker was a decorated WWII hero, having participated in the Normandy D-Day invasion in France. He was with the 741st Tank Batallion at the Battle of the Bulge in Belgium when he was killed in December 1944.

Many descendants of the William and Sophia (Fuelling) Becker family still reside in the New Haven/Fort Wayne area, including William "Bill" Becker (Owner, Pro Resources, Inc.), Dennis "Denny" Becker (Attorney at Law, Barnes & Thornburg LLP), Jeffrey "Jeff" Becker, Rebecca "Becky" Lynch, Linda Lewis, Tammy Bruns, Susan "Suzie" Dirrim (Owner, Party Time Balloons), Nancy Graham and Benjamin "Ben" Szink.

Written and submitted by Lisa Hathaway

BECKMAN & SORG

Johann Adam Sorg, 1775-1845, and Maria Elizabeth Bös and nine of their children left Germany and sailed for America on the ship "Favorite". They came from the German Principality of Hessen Cassel in the year 1834 and landed in New York City. They made their way overland to Fort Wayne, Indiana where they settled south of Fort Wayne with other German settlers in the community of Hessen Cassel.

Johann Melchior (John Michael) Sorg, 1809-1890, married Teresa Baver. They had seven children, one of which was Anton (Tony) David Sorg, 1849-1931. He settled on a farm on Flatrock Road. One day a photographer came and took his picture. It is in the Smithsonian Institute in Washington, DC as one of the first pioneer families who settled here. Anton David Sorg married Elizabeth Schmidt, 1863-1922, whose parents were Henry Schmidt and Catherine (Münch) Minnich.

John Michael's first wife died and he married Mary Anna Barbara Lauer, 1827-1906, and they had five children including a son, John Michael "Mike" Jr., 1862-1950. He also had a farm on Flatrock Road.

John Michael Jr., married Susan Bubb. Her father, Anthony Bubb, 1840-1908, owned Nine Mile Tavern, which still stands on U. S. 27 South. He was killed in 1908 when he stepped in front of the Interurban that ran past the tavern. Anthony Bubb's wife was Susanna Renninger. The Renningers came to this area around 1770.

Alma Sorg, 1899-1987, married Joseph Beckman, 1891-1968, whose family came in 1836 and established a farm on Flatrock Road.

Heinrich Wilhelm (Henry William) Beckman, 1805-1884, was from Osnabruck, Hanover, Germany. He married Bernhardina Caroline Freking, 1816-1870, from Prussia, Germany. They had seven children, one of which was Nicholas Beckman, 1851-1915. He married Margaret Hoffman. It was said that he killed the last bear that roamed this area.

Joseph Anthony Sorg, 1889-1968, married Louise Edith Hergenroether, 1893-1974, whose father was Henry Joseph Hergenroether, 1855-1930. Henry was a bricklayer and helped build the tower on the old St. Mary's Church. His wife was Katherine Rupple, 1861-1936. Henry's family came from Germany in 1854. His father was Mathias Hergenroether, 1822-1912, who married a widow, Mary Anna Kronoble-Mittendorf.

Walter Francis Beckman, 1921-1978, was the oldest of eight children. His wife, Kathleen, 1924, was the oldest of three. They were second half cousins on the Sorg side of the family. This is only a small branch of the large Sorg family. Most of the elder generation is buried in the St. Joseph Hessen Cassel Cemetery. Many of the family still live in the area on farms established in earlier times.

Submitted by Mary L. Beckman.

BEERMAN

Henry Beerman was born (Germany) February, 1853, and died July 20, 1922. Johanna Lucinda (Ruhle) Beerman was born (Frankford, Germany) January, 1850, died February 1, 1929. They married in September of 1874; both are buried in Lindenwood Cemetery, Fort Wayne.

Henry Beerman was born on a ship coming from Germany. When he was two years old he arrived in Fort Wayne coming through New York. Johanna Ruhle was born in Frankford, Germany. They met while working for the Bass Family on the Bass Road, located where St Francis College is presently. He was a blacksmith/horse trainer and Johanna was a governess/teacher. Johanna met the Bass Family at a fair in Frankford, Germany while they were vacationing. She agreed to tutor their children on the long ship ride home and thereafter. Johanna was seventeen at this time. Johanna's family was not happy about this; they had other plans for her and educated her accordingly: she could speak seven languages. Later they bought acreage and built a home on the Illinois road, they had a large truck farm and sold vegetables and flowers. They had five sons and three daughters.

Charles (Jon) Guy Beerman, August 27, 1883 to October31, 1931: He was the grandfather of Donnie Clark, submitter of this article. He had many talents. He was a blacksmith by trade; his shop was on Columbia Street on the Landing. Later this was the location of the Forge Tavern. He could play any instrument and loved to dance. However, when they rolled up the carpet (they took turns going to each others houses and rolled up the carpet so that they could dance on the wood floor) he usually had to playa fiddle or other instrument and call square dancing. Therefore, he seldom got the opportunity to dance. He was a natural engineer as well as a builder. He built several homes on the south side of Fort Wayne. When Mr. Miller (owner of Greenlawn cemeteries) vacationed in California and saw the cemeteries there, he had a dream that he shared with Jon. He told Jon how the cemeteries were laid out and asked Jon if he could construct one like the ones in California. Jon agreed and designed and constructed Greenlawn Cemetery. While at work the day he died, at 46 years of age, he was standing on the spot where he is buried. He told his sons and brother, Bill, "This is the most beautiful spot in the cemetery; this is where I want be buried."

Jon and his sons traveled to Greenlawn daily by horse and wagon to work with the horses and a slip scoop to build Greenlawn. (His nieces sometimes came with their dad, Bill, to watch). Jon's sons and brother, Bill, helped him; they even did all the landscaping. As this was during the depression, some of his payment was in cemetery lots. His son, William (Bill), came home from his first semester at college to help the family, and continued his father's job for two years after his father's unexpected death.

Beerman Horse Shoeing, 124 Columbia Street, 1905. L to R: William Beerman, Harry Beerman, Walter Beerman, Charles (Jon) Beerman. The man in center front is unknown.

The author remembers her uncle, Bill (son of Jon), saying the job he hated most was when they were having trouble with a funeral director in Fort Wayne. He was ordered to open all the caskets and check that the corpse was dressed appropriately and everything was ok before they were buried. After two years, a family member of Mr. Miller's replaced Bill because they wanted all family to work for Greenlawn.

Jon died on Halloween. The family had just had supper and his sons, Don and Paul (author's father and uncle), came into the room dressed for Halloween to go trick and treating when he collapsed. The death certificate said he died of consumption, which was really a massive heart attack. Both Don and Paul thought they caused the attack by scarring him to death with their costumes. Halloween was not a favorite time for either of them.

Jon had purchased a farm with a mortgage, his dream, shortly before his unexpected death. His widow, Ivy, devastated by his death and not being a businessperson, lost all the homes he had built to back taxes because her tenants could not pay the rent and she could not make the payments. She almost lost the farm until the sons split the acreage of the farm so that they could share in payment of the mortgage and the taxes. The farm survives by Poe and is family owned. Ivy was a wonderful wallpaperer and mid wife. She could do wonders and was sought by many. However, she was not paid for her services. During WWII she got her first paying job when General Electric hired women to replace the men going to war. She had to give up her position when the men returned from the war. She lived with her son, Donald, his wife Jean and their daughter, Donnie. Ivy taught Jean to wallpaper. They continued to wallpaper without pay; in the early 50s this was a lost art. Jon had married Ivy Kitty May Zuber, June 26,1907. They had five sons and one daughter. (Ivy) Kitty May was born December, 12,1885 and died August 19,1958. Both are buried in Greenlawn Cemetery, Fort Wayne.

Robert (Bob) Charles, April 16, 1908 - February, 1977 - was a bricklayer. Bob married Enid Stilwell and they had three children, Norman, Barbara and Marilyn. Norman and Marilyn live in Florida. Barbara, a pharmacist, married Robert Nichter, and they live by Poe. They have one son, Lauren. He married Naomi Cook, and they have four sons and live in the Poe area. Bob's second wife was Maxine Heckber (no children), buried at Williamsport, Poe.

Ralph (Rex) Victor, November 10, 1910 - 1984 - worked at General Electric for 40 years and was a horse trader. When the author was a young teenager she would go to horse auctions. He would tell her if she could ride it he would buy it. He married Margaret Wisman, and they had three sons and two daughters. Son Randy had one daughter, Beeper, and Mark had one son, Josh. Randy and Mark are deceased. Scott married Jane Strack they have two sons, Charles and Ralph, and one daughter, Estella. They live in Coldwater Michigan. Roxie had a son, Zack, and daughter, Josie. Dan Burch is their father. Zack is married and has a son; they live in Allen County. Josie is married and has two children. Kelly married David Mourey and had two daughters, Markie and Ivy (deceased), and a son, David. David and Markie Mourey live by Poe. Buried Greenlawn, Fort Wayne.

William (Bill) Henry, January 20, 1913 - May 11, 1996 - He worked for Greenlawn Cemetery for two years, then he went to work for the Pennsylvania Railroad as an engineer where he retired after 40 years. Bill played basketball for Southside and married his high school sweetheart, Jane Lorine Welsh. They moved to the family farm near Poe after they were married, and joined brother Don. Bill went to college for one semester playing basketball. However, he came home to take over his father's project at Greenlawn when his father died unexpectedly. Later Bill and Jane built a home on the 20 acres that they purchased of the family farm, to help save the farm. They built the house with help from his brothers. They tore down an old pop factory for the lumber and built their house with the material that they salvaged. The first year they lived in the garage while they were finishing the house. Bill was also the family barber. He had a barber chair that he purchased from his sister-in law Hannah Jones Beerman's uncle, in his basement. It was really something, and he cut all the family's hair. They had two sons who carried the love of basketball. Larry, a plant manager at Phillips Dodge, and Tom, a teacher, both played for Hoagland High School. Tom was on the team when Hoagland won the county tourney in 1958. He later was an alternate for the U.S. Olympic Volleyball Team. He taught Volleyball in Fort Wayne and at IU, Bloomington. Tom has two sons, Jon and Christopher, and one daughter, Shelly, all great volleyball players. Larry married Doris Grotrian and they had one son, Brad, married Marcia Albersmeyer, and two daughters, Jodi married Ryan Kennedy, and Vickie married Donald Rupp. Daughter, Jodi, was Miss Basketball and her team, Heritage High School Girls Basketball, won State in 1982. Bill is buried at Greenlawn, Fort Wayne.

Joan Louise, September 29, 1915 - October 8, 1991. She was named Johanna Lucinda after both grandmothers; when she was 18 she legally changed her name. She worked for Magnavox for two years and played on the Magnavox basketball team until General Electric recruited her. She was a great basketball player and GE wanted her on their team. Most companies had basketball teams, bowling teams and employee activities at this time. She worked for General Electric for 43 years before she retired. After a fire at the cottage at Blue Lake, her brothers rebuilt it, and she and her husband moved up there. She lived there for fifty years. Again, the family pooled together when their father died and saved this property. They were unable to save several houses that were sold for back taxes. Joan moved close to her brothers by Poe after she retired. She married Ervin France (who bowled for the GE team); they had no children. Buried Greenlawn, Fort Wayne.

Paul Harry, September 9, 1923 - July 21, 2004 - was the salesman in the family. He could sell snow to Eskimos. He is best known for selling sweepers for Kirby and Sears. After serving in WWII, he came home and married his high school sweetheart, Hannah Lois Jones, born in September of 1924. They had one son, Paul, who married Anne Marolff. Her grand parents were the founders of County Line Cheese. They live in Fort Wayne. He owns Beerman's Brass Rail tavern on Broadway, Fort Wayne. They had three daughters, Paulana, a realtor, auctioneer, no children; Paulette, a realtor, married to Jerry Rauner, two daughters, Jerrica and Lindsey, and live in Allen County; Patricia (Patty), a nurse, married Les Marks and they have one daughter, Ashley, and two sons, Garrett and Matthew. They live in Steuben County. Paul is buried at Williamsport, Poe, Indiana.

Donald Fredrick, March 28, 1920 - May 25, 1993 - The author's father was a farmer. He loved the land. He started out farming with horses and later farmed 500 acres with a one and later two bottom plow with a Bradley and later, Allis Chalmer tractor .He also worked for the State Highway Department. He moved to the family farm before the rest of the family when he was only a teenager, living and working the land with a team of horses and walking to school at Poe. Later Paul and his mother joined him, and Paul also went to school at Poe. He was a great ball player, both softball and basketball, where he played for Ossian High when they beat South Side in the semi-state tournament in 1939. He continued to pitch softball for years. The young players called him the old man. One team was Sheares Market in Poe. He loved kids and was always there for all the neighbor kids. They came to him with their problems, and he would talk to them or help fix their car. When they were complaining that they did not have a basketball net at the Poe school in 1950, he and Bill built one and put it up so the kids could play at recess.

Family farm, Winchester Road near Poe, Indiana

He married Katherine Jean Bowman (October 12, 1924 - June 17, 1990) in 1942 at Bethlehem Lutheran, and they had one daughter, Don Jeanine (Donnie). Both are buried at the Williamsport seminary in Poe. Don Jeanine was a Human Resources Manager at Seyfert Foods for 17 years and at Alpha Shirt for eight years. She married Douglas E.Clark they have four children. Sheila and first husband, Ronald Martin, had two children, Danielle and Alex. Sheila then married Jeff Bear who has four children, and they have six grandchildren. Kirt married Dixie Will, and they have two sons, Brent and Brian. Dawn married Doug Will, and they have two daughters, Malarie and Hannah. Heather married Scott Twomey, and they have two daughters, Regan and Campbell. The family all lives near Poe.

Other children of Henry and Johanna:

John (Edward) Beerman, March 27, 1875 - November 6, 1935, was a postman. He married Ella F.Comner, 1879 -1934, and they had four children, sons John and Henry, and daughters, Helen Finker and Mildred Bouicel.

Carrie Ricka, December 16, 1876 - February 16, 1877, (Infant)

Elizabeth (Rose), January of 1878 - July 4, 1918, married Robert Work, no children.

Harry Beerman, July 11, 1886 - February of 1981, was a legend of Joslyn Steel where he started to work as a teen and moved up to Superintendent. An interesting story is when he died they found a ledger that he kept where he wrote down all the expenses and where he purchased the material to build his house. He carted all material by horse and cart buggy. He built this house in 1913 for a total cost of supplies $1500. He build the house with the help of his brothers so there were no labor charges. This house is located at 3708 Bass Road near Leesburg. He married Ethel Merriman and had three daughters. La Vern married Rastic (RR) Powell; they had three sons and one daughter. Richard, Bob, married Judy, they had two daughters Pam and Deb and Steve and daughter name unknown. She had cerebral palsy. Evelyn Hile married Kenneth Hile and had two sons, Dan and William. Dan (December 24, 1930 - 1978) married Jean Reighter, and they had three children. Dan and Bill were adopted and raised by Harry and Ethel. Their natural father Kenneth Hile lite a cigarette by a car and it blew up and he burned to death in 1934. An interesting note is that on Dan's birth certificate it listed mother Evelyn Hile as mother and Harry Beerman as father even through he had a natural father. Evelyn's second husband was Virgil Billing, they had no children. Geraldine (Jerri), first husband's last name was Barnhart, second husband was C. E. Keller Klein; they had two sons. Ronald married Phyllis Helmke and had three children, Brian, Valeria and Bradley. The other son's name is unknown.

Walter Beerman, born in March of 1889, moved to Michigan where he was principal of a high school and later had a resort. He married Hilen Waris, mother of Dorothy. His second wife was Darlene Freeman; they had one daughter, Dorothy Himmelberger.

William Henry Fredrick Beerman, born September of 1880 - died 1970 (twins with Caroline). He had 28 acres on the Getz Road. He was a truck farmer, well know for his vegetables and flowers, especially gladiolas. He had a vegetable wagon pulled by horses that he drove to Fort Wayne daily. His route was around Main Street. He went to a restaurant on the corner of Main and Ewing daily. Later he upgraded to a truck that he used to deliver his vegetables. He often took his daughters with him on his route. He had the most beautiful white sand on his farm; this is where the author's parents went every year to get sand for her sand box. There is a housing division called Beerman Addition off Getz; this was land from his farm. Now there is a strip mall where his house was located. Uncle Bill built this home. He bought a house in Fort Wayne and tore it down and piece by piece carried the material to the new location on Getz Road and duplicated the home. It was a large two-story four-bedroom house. He built this home with the help of his brothers. William married Margaret Loretta (Rette) Vocter. Rette was born wealthy in Pennsylvania. At 17 years of age her parents sent her to Fort Wayne to live with her Aunt Annie (an old maid). They lived in the first house build on Getz Road. It was considered a mansion. William and Rette met at a dance. They had four daughters: Eleanor Cates kept the family together. She never missed sending a letter or card to all family even extended family for all holidays. She had no children and died at age 89. Katherine Avery (second husband, Gray) had two sons and one daughter. Son, Mark

Avery (deceased), married Aldena; they had three sons, Shane, Joshua and Ryan. Son, Kevin Avery. Daughter, Becki Mathieu, married Charles; their son was Joseph. Wilma Hag died at 46 years of age; she had one daughter, Patricia King. Margaret Minowich had three daughters. Connie married Sherrill Ferguson they live in Avilla, Indiana, and have two sons. Margo married Don Heck and they had three daughters. Margo died very young of an aneurysm. Daughters of Margo are Sherry Heck Will, who married Darren Will. Sherry is a sister-in law of Dawn Clark Will and Kirt Clark, Chris Heck and Melissa Heck. Nancy - Nancy also died very young.

Caroline (Carrie), twin with William, was born September of 1880, died in 1942 in Santa Monica, California. She married Eirlston O'Neal; they had no children.

Submited by Don Jeanine (Donnie) Beerman Clark

NORMAN G. BELL

Norman G. Bell was born in Monroeville, Indiana, on January 11, 1916, to Charles and Nellie Schlup Bell. He attended New Haven High School and graduated in 1934. In high school he was active in Boy Scouts and progressed from scout to leader to neighborhood commissioner and he served as a camp counselor for two summers.

Following high school Norm joined the Civilian Conservation Corp (CCC) and shipped to the San Bernardino Mountains in California. He returned in 1935, and went to the Blue Ridge Mountain area in Virginia, where he worked as a surveyor. In 1937, he returned home and joined his father building homes. When the war began in 1941, he joined the U.S. Government Civil Service and was assigned to the Army Air Corp as an aircraft mechanic.

Norman G. Bell, 1986.

In November 1941, Norman and Barbara Ann Larimore, daughter of Roland and Marie Pierre Larimore of Fort Wayne, were married. They had two children, Kathleen Marie and Gregory Allen (Catherine Huser Bell). Kathleen married Michael Skinner and they had Norm's only grandchild, Andrew Michael Skinner, in 1988. Unfortunately, Barbara died in January 1988, before their grandchild was born.

Following the war in 1945, Norman and associate, Robert Federspiel, founded Customcraft, Inc., designing and fabricating custom commercial cabinetry. Later the company's focus changed to industrial products used in trade show exhibits. Their customer base included most of the areas major companies. During that period Norman and his brother-in-law, John Larimore, co-designed and built the Inland Cat, one of the very first all fiberglass sailboats built. A large fleet of Inland Cats continues to be very active at Lake George.

Norman was very active in many service and trade organizations including the Jaycees, Optimist, Rotary, Fort Wayne Advertising Club, Indiana Manufacturing Association, and the Fort Wayne Builders Association. He was involved with the first sports and home shows locally and was instrumental in the efforts to have the Coliseum built and the Embassy Theater saved and restored.

In 1979, Customcraft, Inc. was sold and became what is now Icon, Inc. He remained with Icon as general manager until he retired in 1981. After retirement he became an avid wood turner, which has been a life-long interest. He belongs to the International Wood Collectors and the American Woodturners associations as well as local woodturning groups.

For the past 65 years Norman has spent as much time as possible at Lake George. In September 1988, he married Patricia Maxwell Alban. For the past 17 years Norm and Pat have spent their summers at Lake George where they remain very active with the Inland Cat Association and he has received various recognitions for his service and contributions in that community. Winters are spent at Siesta Key, Florida, where Norman has served many terms as president of the Condo Owners Association. There, too, his contributions have been publicly acknowledged. His days remain filled with wood turning projects, Inland Cat activities, and hosting the annual gathering at Lake George of his lifetime fellow friends and members of the Exhausted Roosters Club (former Jaycees).

Submitted by Norman G. Bell.

BRICE D. & MELISSA L. (BURKS) BENNETT

Brice Donald Bennett was born at Lutheran Hospital in Fort Wayne, Indiana, on June 10, 1985. He is the son of Stephen W. Bennett of Whitley County and Pollyanna Edwards Wymer of Allen County. Brice attended Lafayette Elementary School through grade two and was home schooled for the remainder of his school days. He graduated high school in May 2002, at age sixteen. Brice attended Taylor University Fort Wayne beginning in 2000 through a dual credit program for high school students. In May 2005, Brice graduated with a Bachelor's degree in pastoral ministries at the age of nineteen.

In June 2003, Brice accepted an associate pastor position at Decatur Missionary Church in Decatur, Indiana. It was there he met his future wife, Melissa L. Burks, the pastor's daughter.

Melissa Leigh (Burks) Bennett was born at Saint Francis Medical Center in Peoria, Illinois, on April 14, 1985. She is the daughter of Daryl Ray and Teresa Lynn (Quick) Burks, both natives of Mason County, Illinois. Melissa attended Peoria Christian School through the sixth grade, and then transferred to Midwest Central Middle School in Green Valley, Illinois. She attended Midwest Central High School in Manito, Illinois, through grade eleven. Melissa moved with her family to Decatur, Indiana, in 2002. She completed her schooling at Bellmont High School's ACCES program and graduated in December 2002. Melissa attended Illinois Central

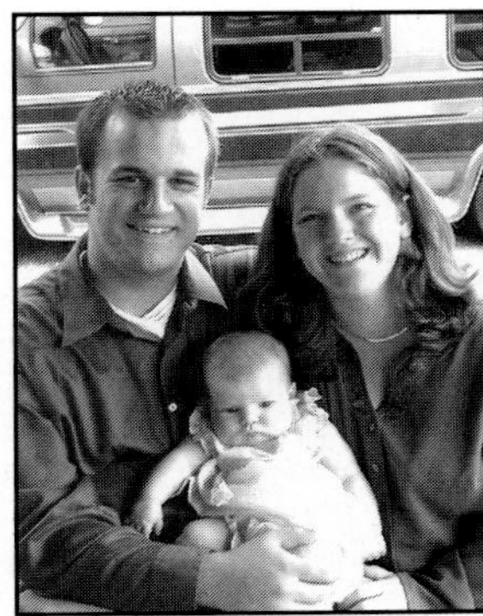

Brice, Maci, and Melissa Bennett

College in East Peoria, Illinois, for one semester before transferring to Taylor University Fort Wayne, where she studied elementary education until leaving school in 2003 to work at the Even Start Family Literacy Program in Decatur, Indiana.

Brice and Melissa were married on December 27, 2003, at Decatur Missionary Church. Brice worked there until February 2004, when he accepted a youth pastor position at Monroe United Brethren Church in Monroe, Indiana. Melissa worked as an administrative assistant at the Even Start Family Literacy Center in Decatur, Indiana, until April 2005, when she left the workforce to become a homemaker.

The Bennett's have one daughter, Maci Leigh Bennett, born at the Bluffton Regional Medical Center in Bluffton, Indiana, on May 9, 2005. Brice and Melissa moved their family from Decatur, Indiana, to Ossian, Indiana, in August 2005.

Submitted by Brice Bennett.

BROCK S. & RICHELLE (BEST) BENNETT FAMILY

Brock Stephen Bennett was born on May 14, 1983, at Lutheran Hospital in Fort Wayne. He is the son of Stephen Bennett and Pollyanna Wymer. He has a brother, Brice, who graduated from Taylor University Fort Wayne, in 2005, and a sister, Baili, who is a home-schooled junior who is also taking early entry classes at Taylor University.

Brock attended Lafayette Central Elementary School through fourth grade. From that point forward he was home-schooled and entered Huntington College at age 16. He graduated from there in 2003, with a Bachelor of Science degree in business economics and finance. During his junior high years he played football at Norwell. At high school age he played hockey in Fort Wayne at McMillan arena. A waiter at Davis Restaurant, he also worked summers for Doug's Lawn Service.

Richelle, Logan, and Brock Bennett.

He married Richelle Best on July 4, 2002, at the Markle Church of Christ with Mark Cleaveland officiating. Richelle, the daughter of Terry and Tracy (Davis) Best, was born on January 24, 1984, at Wells County Hospital in Bluffton, Indiana. A graduate of Huntington North High School, Richelle was on the junior high swim team advancing in her ninth and tenth year to the high school team. She worked at United Technologies as a co-op student her senior year as an assistant secretary and returned to that position in January 2003, for six months. Richelle has a sister, Kendra, who is a freshman at Ivy Tech University in Bloomington. She also has a brother, Derek, a junior at Huntington North High School where he is on the tennis team. Richelle's grandparents are Jim and Bea Davis, and Bevin and Virginia Best, all of Markle, Indiana.

Brock's grandparents are Kenny and Melba Edwards of Zanesville, Indiana, and Nila Bennett of Columbia City, Indiana. Brock and Richelle were very involved in the youth group at the Markle Church of Christ throughout junior high and high school. It was at this youth gathering that they met. Richelle's parents were youth leaders there for 20 years. They now attend Emmanuel Church in Roanoke, Indiana, where they lead the youth.

The Bennetts lived in Zanesville the first two years of their marriage. While there, a son, Logan Michael, was born on March 13, 2004, at Lutheran Hospital in Fort Wayne. He came home to a property where he was the eighth generation to dwell there. Logan has a very spirited personality. The family then moved to a house just south of Zanesville in Wells County where they now reside.

After graduation Brock was employed as a manager with Kroger in Fort Wayne and is now employed as a sales analyst with Wabash Alloys in Wabash, Indiana.

Submitted by Brock Bennett.

PATRICIA SUE JOHNSON BENNETT

Patricia Sue was the fourth child and third daughter of Robert Philip Johnson and Angela Sheehan Johnson. She was born June 17, 1957, at Decatur Memorial Hospital, Decatur, Indiana. At the time of Patty's birth, the family made their home in New Haven, Indiana. They lived in a large white house on the corner of Powers Street and Green Street. When she was two, the family made their final move to 2717 Plaza Drive, Fort Wayne, Indiana.

During her childhood there were many children in the neighborhood to play with and she went to school with friends at St. Hyacinth Catholic School. Upon completion of her elementary education, she attended South Side High School, graduating in 1975.

Upon graduating, she joined the army to enable her to continue her education. Feeling unsuited for the army, she obtained an honorable discharge and returned home. She obtained employment at Lincoln National Life Insurance Company and attended IPFW.

She then made the decision to transfer to the Bloomington campus of Indiana University and attend school full time, graduating in December 1980. At that time her brother, Gregory, decided to move to Texas and, due to a recession and lack of jobs, Patty went also. They found employment and rented an apartment in Arlington, Texas. Being so far from family and friends did not suit her and she eventually returned to Indianapolis.

Angela Bennett and Leo Bennett

In Indianapolis she met Loren Matthew Bennett. They were married in Reno, Nevada, on March 13, 1989. On November 1, 1990, their only child, Leo Matthew Bennett, was born. The family bought a home on Emerson Avenue in Indianapolis, Indiana. Patty worked at Mayflower Moving, then at American United Life Insurance Company as a computer programmer. Loren and Patty divorced, but along with Leo she continued to live in their home on Emerson Avenue for 25 years.

American United Life downsized, leaving Patricia unemployed. Seeking employment and a better education for Leo, she sold her home to her nephew, Scott Houser, and they moved to Worthington, Ohio, where they now live. Scott uses the house as a rental property.

Patty and Leo are descendents of the Johnsons, Schlemmers, Sheehans, and Geis families, pioneer settlers in the rural area of Monroe Township, Monroeville, Indiana.

Submitted by Patricia Sue Johnson Bennett

BENSCH & TRILLENBERG FAMILIES

War and Opportunity Send the Bensch and Trillenberg Families on the Move: the history, flight, reunion, and emigration of two families:

Once upon a time, in a tiny far away Germanic village of Brueckenort (renamed Gross Borek) by Rosenberg (now Borki Wielkie by Olesno in presently Poland) there lived a branch of the Bensch family. This village was part of Upper Silesia and had been seized and made part of Prussia in 1742 by Frederick II. A century later, in 1845, Great-grandpa Silvester Ambrosius Bensch was born there. Nearby a tiny village of Bensch-Muehle (Bensch Mill) carried the family name, and we can only speculate the mill was owned by a member of the family. Silvester became a gardener and married Marie Paprotny who bore their son, Johann Bensch, in 1884.

Just a few years earlier, in 1871, 39 independent Germanic states –including the region of the Bensch ancestors—were unified into the German Empire under King William I of Prussia, who became German emperor with a powerful military. Grandpa Johann Bensch married Marie Freier and had twelve children: Johann, Martha, Victor, Valentin, Marie, Felix, Wilhelm, Emilie, Adolf, Alexander, Bernhard and Serafin. Their vocations became: farmer, nun, carpenter, tailor, housewife, carpenter, storekeeper, housewife, storekeeper, tailor, organist, respectively. Papa Wilhelm Bensch was born 1914 still in Brueckenort during the World War I (1914-1918). Germany still had an Emperor William II who abdicated in 1918. The following year, 1919, Germany established the Weimar Republic.

Wilhelm married Frieda Melanie Burkhard, a homemaker, in 1939. Melanie had been born in Klein Bardau, a very small village by Leipzig. Her mother, Elsa Frieda Crell, was born in Machern by Leipzig and married to a Burhard. Wilhelm and Melanie married during World War II (1939-1945) and lived in Oranienburg by Berlin. Wilhelm fought in the War but sustained an injury to one eye, greatly impairing his vision. Melanie gave birth to three children: Horst Wilhelm, Monika and Horst Wolfgang Bensch, born in 1944 in Doehlen by Leipzig. (Doehlen later became part of the city of Markransteadt.) Melanie has lived, attended school and worked in Doehlen prior to her marriage. Part of the manor at which she worked in the kitchen and cared for animals is still standing today as evident on a picture supplied by Doehlen historian, Guenter Schmidt, in 2004. We can only speculate why Melanie returned to Doehlen to give birth to Wolfgang—possibly due to the bombardment of Berlin or a continued family presence in town.

After World II, Leipzig and surrounding areas were controlled by the Soviet Union, becoming part of East Germany. The aftermath of the war separated the Bensch family as well as the Burhard family. Wilhelm, Melanie and their two surviving children fled to West Germany with the help of the United States military after secretly transporting clothing and essentials to West Berlin by train—one trip at a time. Some of Wilhelm's brothers also fled to West Germany, while other siblings stayed behind. One of Melanie's brothers went to Switzerland, one brother and her mother stayed in East Germany.

The documented Trillenberg family history goes back to 1786 when Johann Michael Trillenberg was born in Kunnersdorf, now part of Shoepstal-Landkreis (township) Goerlitz, Regierungsbezirk (county) Liegnitz, Silesia (state), about four kilometers northwest of Goerlitz. The Trillenberg family resided in Kunnersdorf for three generations. Johann earned a living as gardener and shoemaker there. His son, Johann Friedrich, (born in 1823) earned his living there as a farmer and his son, Friedrich Gustav, (born in 1856) worked for the railroad. The next son, Otto Bruno, was born in 1892 in Machern by Leipzig. He also worked for the railroad and he married Ida Alma Crell, the sister of Elsa Frieda Crell, who had married in the Bensch family. They gave birth to Karl Fritz Trillenberg in Wurzen by Leipzig in 1922. His schooling, as electrician, was cut short one year due to World War II. He was retrained as an airplane electrician by the German military in Polenz, still close to home. Then he was transferred to German-occupied Trondheim in Norway. He learned Norwegian and became an interpreter. At the end of World War II, he became a prisoner of war and was interned by the English. Not wanting to return to his communist-occupied hometown, he worked for the English for awhile and eventually was

Bensch Family Members Estimated Year 1939

Doehlen, part of Markranstaedt 2004. The mansion (upper left) was originally surrounded by buildings forming a square. The small house on the lower left was Horst Wolfgang's birthplace, occupied by Melanie's brother Fritz Burkhard at one time.

Gross Borek Oberschlesien prior to 1939

Alma Ida Cress Trillenberg

Elsa Frieda Crell Burkhard

Alma Ida Crell Trillenberg and Otto Bruno Trillenberg

Jacky, Ingo, Vincent, and Tino Bensch.

Horst Wolfgang

Upper: Nicola Wirczakowski Marion Jaggi, Marco Jaggi, Oliver Wirczakowski, Beat Jaggi, Mary Trillenberg-Jaggi, Lorenz Jaggi. Lower: Karl Wirczakowski, Angelika Trillenberg-Bensch, Fritz Trillenberg, Gerda Trillenberg, Rafat Wirczakowski and Pascal Wirczakowski

released in Leck, bei Flensburg. His parents had stayed in East Germany. In Leck, Fritz met Gerda Erika Gross Wirczakowski.

Gerda had just given birth in a bunker on November 6, 1944, in Danzig (now Gdansk in Poland) during an air raid. In the winter of 1944, she fled the encroaching Russian army by freight train with baby Karl Heinz Paul and her family. Gerda's first husband had died in the war and her mother shortly thereafter, in 1945 in Magdeburg. She located her husband's parents in Bottropp, West Germany. Then she found her sister in Leck and moved up north. In Leck, Gerda gave birth to Angelika Christa Gitta Trillenberg in 1947 and to a second daughter, Mary Hannelore, in 1951. Eventually, Gerda and Fritz married and settled in Gerlafingen, Switzerland, where Fritz worked as an electrician at Von Roll, an iron factory, until his retirement. All three children went to school in Switzerland.

The Bensch and Trillenberg families were about to become united. In April 1965, Fritz took Angelika along for a family visit to Germany to see his cousin, Melanie Bensch and her family in Berkheim/Esslingen near Stuttgart, where they ultimately settled after fleeing East Germany. Melanie and Wilhelm's son, Wolfgang, just happened to be home on visit from the military. Angelika and Wolfgang began dating long distance at first and eventually married in Munich on November 17, 1966.

Horst Ingo Bensch was born in Munich on April 15, 1967. Angelika stayed home to take care of Ingo while Wolfgang launched an international career with North American Van Lines in Munich. By the time the Munich office closed, Wolfgang had become general manager and was transferred to the company's headquarters in Fort Wayne, Indiana, in the United Sates. They said good-bye to their families in Germany and Switzerland and packed up some of their furniture and their favorite German wines, which held up their shipment for months! In 1978, the "American Dream" became a reality for the Bensch family. They took out a mortgage for the ranch type house on Evergreen Lane in Allen County. Owning a house and land still feels like a dream to Angelika who stayed there after the Bensch marriage ended in divorce in 1990. Wolfgang moved to Australia where he remarried in 1992 before returning to Chicago, where he became an American citizen in 2003 and died in 2004. Angelika first worked at Standard Federal Bank on Main Street. After they transferred their servicing to Detroit, she started her career in 1992 at Waterfield Mortgage Company, Inc. and became an American citizen in 1993.

Horst Ingo Bensch went to Snider High School, received his college degree at Stanford University and was introduced to a fellow German, Jacqueline Jugenheimer, by an Indian "matchmaker" in graduate school at Indiana University. They married in 1994. Their sons, Vincent Bensch and Constantin Bensch, were born in 1998 and 2001 respectively. This newest Bensch generation lives in Madison, Wisconsin. Americans, but with continuing ties to their German roots.

Submitted by Angelique Bensch

PAULA CELESTE (HENRY) BENTLEY

Paula Celeste Henry was born in Jackson, Michigan on December 15, 1952, the third child of Jerome F. and Marganelle (Applegate) Henry. She is one of 17 children.

She attended St. Charles Borromeo and Most Precious Blood Catholic Schools in Fort Wayne, Indiana. Later she attended Central Catholic High School in Fort Wayne.

In 1970, Paula married James Allen Todoran, first son of Nicholas and Lois (Wood) Todoran. James attended St. Joseph School and graduated from Central Catholic High School in 1968. He was a patternmaker, working in Fort Wayne and Coldwater, Michigan. They have two sons, James Allen Jr., born in Fort Wayne in 1971 and Nicholas Jerome, born in Coldwater, Michigan in 1972.

James Sr. died suddenly in 1973. Paula remarried in 1975 to William Richard Bentley, the fourth child of Richard and Solina (Weigand) Bentley. William, born in 1949, attended Most Precious Blood Catholic grade school and is a 1968 graduate of Central Catholic High School in Fort Wayne. He is a veteran of the Vietnam War and has worked at General Electric, Lockheed Martin, and, currently, BEA Systems. Paula is a homemaker.

Bill and Paula have four children, Aaron Joseph, born in Fort Wayne in 1976, Matthew William, born in Fort Wayne in 1978, Sara Marie, born in Fort Wayne in 1983 and Melissa Celeste, born in Fort Wayne in 1991.

Submitted by Paula Bentley

DAVID LINCOLN BENTON

David Lincoln Benton was born July 11, 1866 in Savannah, Ohio to William Benton and Christina Berry Benton, both born in Scotland.

David graduated from Ohio Normal University, in Pharmacy, (now Ohio Northern University) and operated a drug store in Nebraska for several years. He located to Fort Wayne in 1898.

On June 28, 1900 he married Eva Lena Stover at the home of her parents, George and Mary Stover, 335 West Main Street. They had two children, Glenn Weldon Benton, born May 10, 1902 and Helen La Von Benton, born February 10, 1906. David Benton was a member of Sol D. Bayless Lodge No. 359, F&A.M., a thirty-second Degree Mason, and Cilso of K. of P. Lodge No. 101.

David Benton also belonged to the Genesia Tennis Club, which met from about 1900 until 1910 in Fort Wayne.

Eva Stover Benton was born October 16, 1878, in Ossian, Indiana. She lived in Fort Wayne most of her life.

Eva was a member of the Druggists Ladies Association and was a charter member of Bethany Presbyterian Church. She passed away at the age of 80 on December 1, 1958. Eva Stover Benton is buried in Lindenwood Cemetery.

David Lincoln Benton was a popular Pharmacist on West Main Street in Fort Wayne and was known as D. L. His home was on West Main Street across from his drug store. David Lincoln Benton passed away after a sickness of several months on January 17,1913 at the age of 46, and is buried in Lindenwood Cemetery.

Submitted by Marjean Schneider

D. L. Benton Drug Store on West Main Street, Fort Wayne, Indiana. D. L. Benton, is standing on the steps at the right, with his shopkeepers. ca. early 1900s

GLENN WELDON BENTON

Glenn Weldon Benton was born May 10, 1902 in Fort Wayne, Indiana to David Lincoln Benton and Eva Stover Benton. Glenn graduated from Fort Wayne High School in 1922. He attended Purdue University School of Pharmacy, Lafayette, Indiana and then graduated from Indianapolis College of Pharmacy in June 1930 with a Pharmaceutical Chemist degree. He became a Registered Pharmacist by the Indiana Board of Pharmacy in 1931.

In 1936 he met a lovely young lady who became the love of his life and they were married September 16, 1937 in Tillsonburg, Ontario, Canada. Grace McCurdy Benton was born in Dutton, Ontario, Canada, on November 23, 1915. She graduated from London Normal School in 1935 with a certificate to teach in the public schools. She taught in the Otter Valley School in Tillsonburg, Ontario until her marriage to Glenn. They located to Michigan where their first daughter, Marjean, was born and in 1941 Grace became a naturalized citizen. In 1943 the family moved to Fort Wayne. Glenn worked for several pharmacists until he started his own business in August 1945, which was located at 1302 S. Calhoun Street on the corner of Douglas. It first was called Benton's Pharmacy and later became known as Benton's Owl Store as he remained open until 2:00 a.m. He was the only pharmacist open that late. Grace enjoyed working in the drug store helping Glenn whenever she could and daughter Marjean enjoyed coming to the store after school to "help" her daddy. Glenn belonged to the Fort Wayne Pharmaceutical Association, South Wayne Baptist Church, Sol D. Bayless Lodge No. 359, F&AM, the Fort Wayne Consistory of the Scottish Rite and the Sheriffs Emergency Reserve. He was also a thirty-second degree Mason.

In 1947 a son, David, was born and in 1954 another daughter, Amy, was welcomed into the family. Soon after Amy arrived, Glenn became ill and was unable to work from May 1956 until his death at the age of 54, on September 4, 1956. Glenn's daughter, Marjean Benton, started Kindergarten at Harrison Hill, graduated, and then went on to South Side High School and graduated in 1957. Grace Benton sold the drug store and returned to Michigan with her children in the summer of 1957, to be near her sisters and brothers.

Marjean Benton is a retired secretary and a member of the Ezra Parker Chapter Daughters of the American Revolution. She lives in Michigan with her husband Charles Schneider. Amy Suzanne Benton resides in Michigan and works for the Birmingham School System. David McCurdy Benton has his own small businesses and resides in Flagstaff, Arizona. Glenn Weldon Benton is buried in Lindenwood Cemetery in the family plot.

Submitted by Marjean Schneider

BENZINGER FAMILY

In 1840, the first Benzinger, Frederick, came to Indiana in an ox cart across the Black Swamp and settled in what is now Marion Township, on Monroeville and Emmanuel Roads. There were no roads then, only Indian trails. He gave land for the Emmanuel Road which cut his farm in half. Frederick had to dig a new well because the old one was across the road. Later he sold land on the west to a neighbor. The land was all woods so they cleared the land, built a house that later burned and was rebuilt along with barns. Over the years, they planted fruit trees, berries, grapes, and raised geese, chickens, cows, horses and sheep. Once he and the neighbors rerouted a creek through the farm. Today the farm is still lived on by the Benzinger's sixth and seventh generations.

Glenn Benton dispensing medicine in his drug store. Ca. Early 1950s

Most of the early Benzinger's are buried at the Lutheran Church (Soest) Cemetery.

Submitted by Mrs. Elmer Benzinger

HUBERT BERGHOFF FAMILY

Between 1874 and 1883, four sons of Anton Berghoff and Elizabeth Boelhauve arrived in Fort Wayne, Indiana, and made it their home. They were born, raised and educated in Dortmund Westphalia Prussia. They were all employed immediately as clerks, bookkeepers and traveling agents. Soon they opened their own businesses.

Herman started a brewery in Fort Wayne and, later, a restaurant in Chicago. Henry was in several businesses, politics, law and banking. Hubert eventually joined his brothers in the Berghoff Brewery. Gustav owned the Rub No More Soap Company, Hoff Brau Brewery and Wayne Home Equipment.

Hubert Berghoff, born November 21, 1860, was 19 when he arrived. His two older brothers had already married. Henry had wed Theresa Mayer, and Herman, Walberga Mayer, both in St. Marys Catholic Church. Both were daughters of Lorenz Mayer and Maria Engesser, who had arrived in Fort Wayne in 1847 from Geisingen Baden Germany.

In 1882, in St. Marys, Hubert married the youngest Mayer daughter, Johanna, born December 19, 1858. He was a bookkeeper for AC Trentman Wholesale Grocery House at the time. They became parents of Hubert L., Herman Joseph Valentine, Henry E. and Elizabeth M. Aurentz.

Hubert joined his brothers in the brewery and managed the plant from the time brother, Herman, moved to Chicago in 1898 until 1908. He was later Secretary of Gustav's soap company. He passed away in 1926, the year Gustav sold the soap company. Johanna lived with daughter, Elizabeth, and died in 1934.

Hubert L., born August 14, 1884, died March 23, 1961, married Marie, daughter of Joseph Labbe. He was Secretary-Treasurer of the Allen County Abstract Co. They had no children.

Herman Joseph was born on Valentine's Day 1887, the year the Berghoff Brewery was established. He was named after his Uncle Herman. He attended St. Marys School and graduated from their Commercial High School as did all of his siblings. His Uncle Gustav employed him as a bookkeeper for the Rub No More Soap Company after graduation. He married Alice C., born April 13, 1889, daughter of Gregor Klug, a shoe merchant, and Elizabeth Alter. Herman J. V. and Alice became parents of seven boys and four girls that they raised at 1139 Oak Street. The children all attended St. Marys School and Church.

The eldest son, Anthony H., born April 29, 1912, died March 26, 1990, married Dorothy H, daughter of Amos Pence and Ethel McDermott. Gilbert J., born December 15, 1930, Nancy M. Kispert, born March 18, 1932, and George A., born July 13, 1939, are their children. Anthony was very bright and enjoyed electronics, aviation and photography.

Herman and Alice's second son, George, born November 18, 1913, died at four months of a heart defect.

Paul L, the third son, born February 24, 1915, was employed at the Berghoff Brewery. He married Ethel M., daughter of Albert Jauch, Secretary of Rub No More, and Mary Monahan. Their children are Susan Prowant, born December 23, 1936, Thomas A. born January 27, 1939, Michael J., born August 29, 1941, Paula J. Martin, born April 8, 1948, and Herman D., born January 26, 1955. Paul served in the Army during WWII in the Tank Corps in the Phillipines. Upon returning, he opened the Berghoff Inn Restaurant at 1125 Maumee Ave. He was elected Wayne Township Trustee in 1959 and later served as Deputy Trustee for eight years. He also owned and operated Berghoff Catering Service for over 20 years retiring at age 75. He gave many of his grandchildren, nieces and nephews their first job. He is noted for being a kind, generous and optimistic person.

Thomas J., born March 16, 1917, the fourth son, served in WWII in France, Belgium and the Battle of the Bulge. Upon his return, he married Mariana, daughter of Samuel Newell and Anna Swayze. Their children are Joseph H., born January 15, 1948, Martha A. Ottman, born December 20, 1949, Franklin J., born June 27, 1951, Margery L. Foster, born October 19, 1952, Richard P., born May 26, 1954, Raymond T., born September 17, 1955, died November 27, 1986, and Jean C. Sheets, born February 18, 1958. Thomas retired after a long career with Essex Wire.

The fifth son, Bernard J., born June 22, 1919, served in WWII in Australia and New Guinea. After the war he married Helen C., daughter of Ben Hoevel, an Adams Township farmer, and Marie Steib. Their children are James B., born October 1, 1948, Patricia A, Hayes, born August 26, 1949, Donna M Ballinger, born February 7, 1951, Dr. Robert H., born February 13, 1952, Mary A. Bundza, born May 18, 1953, John J., born February 1, 1955, Gregory B., born March 7, 1956 and Elizabeth A Gordon, born February 3, 1958. Bernard worked in sales for Moellering Supply. He is known for his dry sense of humor and for his hobby, carving small figures.

Herman J. V. Berghoff Family. Standing: Anthony, Paul, Thomas, Bernard, Gustave, and Robert. Seated: Alice Devine, Mary Cambre, Herman J. V., Alice Klug Berghoff, Carol Coffaro, and Helen Nix

Gustav H., born August 22, 1921, died May 5, 1989, son number six, served as an airplane mechanic in the Aleutian Islands during WWII. He married Josephine C., daughter of Edward Gfell and Hilda Rosswurm. Gustav worked for General Electric as did Jo before their marriage. They also farmed in Perry Township. Their son is Gustav H., Jr., born April 26, 1955.

Robert R., born February 19, 1923, the last son, served in the Navy. Following WWII he graduated from Purdue University and was employed by General Electric as an EE. He holds a related patent. He married Rose M., daughter of Arthur Miller and Gertrude Reffelt of Decatur, Indiana. Their children are Matthew F., born July 11, 1956, Mark E., born November 12, 1957, Michael R., born November 29, 1958, Ann M. Reisinger, born December 29, 1960, and Patrick J., born January 21, 1965. Rose passed away in 1993. Robert married Mary Jane Lauer Biggins in 1998.

When the Rub No More Soap Company was sold in 1926, Herman J. V. decided to go into the auto repair and maintenance business on the corner of Hanna and Jefferson. The business was called the Day N Nite Garage. The enterprise went well for a few years but by the early 30s the Great Depression was taking its toll and he had to close the doors. Luckily, Prohibition ended April 1933, so he went to work at the Berghoff Brewery as a timekeeper and checker.

After seven sons, Herman J.V. and Alice had a daughter named for her mother. Alice C., Jr., born November 25, 1924, died April 1, 2004. She thought she might enlist after graduation from Central Catholic High School, but her father strongly discouraged her. She took a job at International Harvester in the war effort instead. She met a man from New York who was stationed in Fort Wayne. He had served earlier in the Army Railroad Battalion in Iran. Alice married William T. Devine, son of W. T. Devine and Mary McCarthy of Watertown, New York, where the couple moved after the wedding. They became parents of William T., born May 20, 1946, Kathryn J. O'Connell, born June 21, 1947, Margaret A., born September 21, 1945, Daniel T., born January 29, 1953, Michael D., born September 28, 1957, John J., born November 6, 1960, and Alice C., born November 6, 1962. Bill continued to work for the railroad. Alice was a warm, loving, tolerant mom who treated everyone the same.

Daughter number two, Helen E., born November 30, 1926, graduated from Central Catholic High School and also took a job in the war effort at Inca Wire Phelps Dodge. She met Zeno Nix, son of Florence Nix and Theresa Genth, in high school. When he returned from the US Marines they were married at St. Marys. Their children are Barbara S. Roberts, born May 10, 1952, Steven J., born November 22, 1953, Phillip G., born July 6, 1955, Brother Samuel CFR, born November 11, 1957, Marilyn Nix, born June 10, 1958, Sarah A. Didier, born November 20, 1959, Gerald J., born September 15, 1952, and Mary H. Wertz, born April 17, 1965. Zeno retired after a career with General Telephone Company. Helen is the family's news center. She uses the computer to communicate with Herman and Alice's many descendents, and is a very involved mother and grandmother.

Berghoff Brothers, Gustave, Paul, Robert, Bernard, and Thomas

Richard Berghoff and Joan Berghoff Jehl

Mary and Henry E. Berghoff

Daughter number three, Mary Ann Cambre, born June 10, 1928, worked for the Park Department and General Electric after graduation from CCHS. She met Max A, son of Max A. and Carrie Daigle of Reserve, Louisiana, through Catholic Young Adults. They were married at St. Marys. Max is an EE and retired from General Electric, Fort Wayne. Their children are John B., born September 26, 1961, Louis P., born September 28, 1964, and Cecile M. Cambre, born October 12, 1969. Mary is active at church and enjoys her home and sewing.

The last daughter, Carol A., born March 15, 1930, graduated from St. Joseph Hospital School of Nursing. She worked for Dr. J. Baltes. Joseph, son of Francis Coffaro and Josephine Petorizzi of New York, graduated from Indiana Institute of Technology in Fort Wayne after he served in the Navy. They met and were married at St. Marys. Joe worked in five states over his career as an EE for Harris Corp. They are parents of Francis N., born July 31, 1955, Anthony H., born September 14, 1956, Mary Jo Coffaro, born May 31, 1958, Theresa S. Grunder, born January 6, 1960, Carol L. Schexnayder, born May 20, 1962, Joseph, Jr., born June 18, 1963 and Thomas J., born April 19, 1969. They retired to Rockledge, Florida. Carol also sews, keeps her family up on each other by computer and makes beautiful cards.

Five of Herman J. V. and Alice's sons served their country and all returned home unharmed. Herman passed away in his sleep unexpectedly at the early age of 62. Alice remained very active and sharp to the age of 88. She died at the home of her son Gustav on All Saints Day 1977.

Herman J.V.'s younger brother, Henry E., born October 16, 1889, died May 31, 1962, was named for his Uncle Henry C. Berghoff. He graduated from St. Joseph College Renssalaer and Marquette University in Business. He was associated with City Carriage Works before and after his service in the Army in WWI. He married Mary M., daughter of Timothy Corbett and Margaret Durkin of Decatur, Indiana. They made their home at 923 Forest Avenue and were charter members of St. Jude Church. He ran City Carriage Works for 35 years and finished his working career with Wayne Home Equipment. Mary was a lady with a sunny smile. She volunteered many years at St. Joseph Hospital.

Henry and Mary were the parents of a girl and a boy. Joan M., born May 1, 1922,was employed by Wayne Pump Company between graduation from CCHS and her marriage to Joseph H. Jehl, a classmate and son of Leo Jehl and Margaret Hoock. He served in the Navy from 1942 to 1946, and worked for the US Postal Service. He retired in1980 and passed away on Christmas Day 1989. Joan and Joe's children are Daniel J., born March 9, 1947, Ann M. Phillips Goggins, born July 18, 1949, died May 7, 2003, Mark H., born May 24, 1952, Kevin G., born May 16, 1956, and Edward J., born July 15, 1961, died January 22, 2005. Joan is a loving mother, a good friend and a big Cubs fan.

Henry E.'s son, Richard H., born February 20, 1924, served in the Army under General Patton in Europe after graduation from CCHS. He was employed as an underwriter at Lincoln National Life Insurance before and after his service until his retirement in 1983. After WWII Richard married Rita A., daughter of Alfred Zurbuch and Mary Eckrich. They are parents of David R., born February 9, 1951, Dennis J., born January 9, 1952, died June 19, 1983, Mary E. Berghoff Meyer, born October 5, 1953, Jane A. Nason, born June 25, 1958, Gerard J., born April 8, 1961 and Timothy P., born January 1, 1964. Richard and Rita spend their winters in Tucson, Arizona.

Hubert and Johanna's only daughter and forth child was Elizabeth M., born May 25, 1892, died June 4, 1979. She was well educated, having attended Sacred Heart Academy and Josephinum Academy in Chicago. At age 30, she married Raymond J, son of Simon Aurentz and Anna Monning. He was 38. He had studied and worked in New York City. He apprenticed in architecture. Upon his return to Fort Wayne he worked for S. F. Bowser and later was self-employed as an architect. Elizabeth and Ray had no children of their own but had many nieces and nephews to shower with love. They were always cheerful and hospitable. Ray was almost 100 years old when he passed away.

Hubert and Johanna had 12 grandchildren from two of their sons and 65 great grandchildren.

Submitted by Susan Berghoff Prowant

ANTONI & KATHRYN (DUJAK) BIESIADA FAMILY

Antoni Biesiada was born on January 17, 1850, in what was once Poland in the western province of Poznan'. Prussia had annexed the area in 1793. The Prussians were harsh occupiers and the Polish language was forbidden in public use, being replaced by German. Poznan' was renamed Posen. Antoni grew to know the harsh realities of Prussian domination. Although he attended school, his lessons were in German. In the month of his thirteenth birthday, a rebellion erupted in Posen and four Prussian army corps were moved into the area to quell the recalcitrants.

In his late teens, Antoni met Kathryn (Katarzyna) Dujak. She too, was a native Poznanian, born December 18, 1852. They were wed with all the pomp and festivities of a Polish wedding.

Kathryn (Dujak) and Antoni Biesiada at home on Morgan Road, 1903.

On July 19, 1870, France declared war on Prussia and Antoni was conscripted into the Prussian army. The Prussians quickly defeated the French and Antoni became part of the army of occupation. The French were forced to hand over reparations and the Prussians stayed until the sum was paid. In September of 1873, the French debt was remunerated. Not long after, Antoni returned to his beloved Kathryn.

Because of his performance as a soldier, Antoni was made supervisor over some of the Poles working in the potato fields and was given a horse. Using his position, Antoni became an outspoken critic of the injustices his people suffered at the hands of their oppressors. The job did earn Antoni enough money to secure a small home for his family. Their daughter Rose was born about 1874, and Mary entered the world on June 15, 1876. On December 18, 1880, Thomas was born and Frances was born in 1885. Kathryn gave birth to Margaret on July 15, 1887.

Early one morning in the spring of 1889, Antoni made the decision to leave Posen and drafted plans to travel to America. He packed up his family and headed north towards the Baltic seaports. They crossed the North Atlantic in a steamship and in mid April 1889, arrived at Detroit, Michigan. The 1889 and 1890 city directories listed the

Thomas Biesiada in front of his father's barn on Morgan Road.

Victoria Biesiada (Sr. Mary Genevieve), Russell Hoover, Antoni Biesiada and his grandson, Fr. Lawrence Seidel, 1932.

family at 135 St. Joseph Street. In 1891, Antoni found a job at a foundry in the city of Findlay, Ohio, and headed south with his family.

In the 1892-93 Findlay city directory, there appeared the listing: Biesiada, Anthony, iron-worker, residence: west side of Fargo Avenue, third house east of Orchard. On October 31, 1891, Antoni signed his first naturalization papers at the Hancock County Court House in Findlay. Antoni would become a citizen on September 2, 1893. On December 18, 1893, their daughter, Victoria, was born at Findlay.

To the west of Findlay, a railroad had been constructed. On December 31, 1894, the line was connected with its western terminus-the city of Fort Wayne, Indiana. On June 3, 1895, the first train left that town and the *Findlay, Fort Wayne and Western Railroad* began service between the two cities. The railroad opened up new territory in eastern Allen County, Indiana, and reports of the inexpensive farmland reached Antoni. Early one morning in the summer of 1895, Antoni and his son, Thomas, headed west along the dusty road that ran beside the freshly laid tracks. Antoni entered 60 acres on Morgan Road just south of the little settlement of Smith Mills west of Baldwin, Indiana, in Jackson Township. Antoni found work with the Smith family at the mill and he and Thomas built a small log cabin on their acreage.

The family soon joined them and construction of the homestead began. It was completed in the summer of 1902, and still stands on Morgan Road. In 1909, Antoni and Kathryn bought an 80-acre farm on Aboite Center Road and their son, Thomas, bought 40 acres across the road. In 1910, St. Hyacinth's Catholic Church was organized in Fort Wayne. The parish was Polish-Catholic and sometimes the family would ride into Fort Wayne for Mass. On Sunday, September 24, 1916, Antoni and Kathryn were leaving St. Hyacinth's in their horse and buggy to return to their farm. The buggy's harness came loose from its rigging and the horse kicked back and both Antoni and Kathryn were injured. Kathryn died that evening at St. Joseph's Hospital in Fort Wayne. Antoni would live to be 91 and died on January 31, 1941, at the St. Joseph Hospital nursing home. Antoni and Kathryn are buried in the mausoleum at the Catholic Cemetery in Fort Wayne.

Of Antoni and Kathryn's children, Rose Biesiada married John Leahey and they raised two boys at Lima, Ohio: John and Elmer. Mary wed Max Wendlikowski and settled in Findlay, Ohio. They had seven children: Amelia, John, Kathryn, Ann, Elizabeth, Margaret, and Leo. Thomas Biesiada stayed in Allen County and married Ella Bacon, the daughter of Charles and Theresa (Coonrod) Bacon. They had 12 children: Joseph, Pearl, Mearl, Edward, Jesse, Dorothy, Erma, Norman, Rosalind, Robert, Thomas, and Carl. Frances married Ira Miller of Allen County and they had five children: Melvin, Mae, Vera, Esther, and Francis. Margaret married Bernard Seidel of Detroit and they had two sons: Lawrence and Joseph. Victoria joined the Order of the Poor Handmaids of Jesus and became Sr. Mary Genevieve. She died at 98 in 1991, at Donaldson, Indiana.

Submitted by Michael T. Biesiada.

JOSEPH BIGGS FAMILY

Joseph Biggs was born in Hanover, New Hampshire, on September 18, 1926. His mother, Dora, was born in Lafayette, Indiana. She was one of 13 children of Ida and James Biggs of Oklahoma. Joseph had one sibling, a sister named Lenora. After his mother passed away in 1938, Joe and Lenora moved to Fort Wayne to live with their aunt and uncle, George and Lucy Wilson. They lived in the 300 block of East Douglas Street, less than half a block from Central High School, now the Anthis Career Center. Their Uncle George was a well-respected boxing coach for several outstanding Golden Glove boxers in the late 1930s and early 1940s.

Lenora attended Central High School. She married Sam Davis from North Carolina and they moved to West Newton, Massachusetts. They have three children: Jacqueline, Nicholas, and Stephanie.

Joe Biggs attended Harmar Junior High School and was a key member of the Harmar basketball team that won the city Junior High championship in 1942. He was also an outstanding athlete in track and field at Harmar. He entered Central High School in 1942 and graduated in 1946. In 1945 and 1946 he was the starting center on the Central "Tigers" basketball team. In 1946 the "Tigers" were the second best team in the state of Indiana, losing only to Anderson High School for the state championship. Joe was also outstanding in both the high jump and high hurdles.

Joseph Biggs received a full athletic scholarship to North Carolina A&T college in Greensboro, North Carolina. There he met and married Anniebelle Little, also a student at that school. After their marriage, they moved to West Newton, Massachusetts, and later to Stamford, Connecticut. They had one son, Joseph Biggs Jr., and three daughters; Jo-Ann, Cherie, and Michelle. In Connecticut he continued his sports activities as a member of the New York Renaissance Basketball Team. It was one of several Negro professional teams that organized and played in their own league during that time.

He began his work career as the director of the Youth Sports Program at the West Main Community Center in Stamford, Connecticut. After seventeen years as director of the Youth Center, he moved the family to Nanuet, New York. There he accepted the position as Commissioner on Human Rights. He finished his public service work career as the vice president of N.R.P. Urban Development Resources in Newark, New Jersey, a city housing agency .

Throughout his work years, Joe Biggs continued to participate in sports. He became an outstanding pitcher in fast pitch softball and won the Stamford Mayor's Trophy seven years consecutively. He pitched for Clancy's in Patterson, New Jersey, in 1948. This team was ranked 17th in the nation. They won the Patterson Invitational Championship, the Bud Lite Classic Tournament in Middletown , New York, and the New Jersey State Championship, along with several other awards. One of his fondest memories was pitching in a 21-inning game that his team won by a score of 1 to 0. After he retired from active competition, he became a part-time coach for girls softball at the high school level in Nanuet, New York. He received many letters of appreciation from parents and school staff for his teaching and encouragement of his young charges. Joe passed away in Fort Wayne, Indiana, on September 28, 2002, during one of his many return trips to the city of his youth, which he loved.

Submitted by Anniebelle Biggs, Maurice Fowler, and Guy A. Jones

BISSON - TIEMEY FAMILY

Martin Bisson was born in 1852 in Anstadt, Germany, (Alsace-Loraine) arrived in the U.S. in 1860 with his mother, Mary Bisson (later Eckrich-Boxberger), and was naturalized in 1869. He married Mary Schenkel. After her death he was married to Mary Elzey-McCague (Archbold) in 1890. Martin manufactured small potash, which he sold internationally. He purchased several tracts of land in the Fort Wayne area which he worked or rented to others, selling one portion to Gus Berghoff for the Rub-No-More soap factory. The homestead and potash factory were at the corner of Glasgow and Dwenger. He worked on the construction of the old (German) St. Mary's church. He and Mary had two daughters, Veronica in 1893 and Gladys in 1900.

Veronica married Earl Smith, a musician and songwriter, and Gladys married Donald J. Tiemey in 1920. Veronica's family included Alyce, Bertha, Wayne, Mary Jane, and Ruth. After her death in 1923, the children returned to the homestead until graduation and marriage. Gladys and Donald had three children: Nadyne (born 1921), Donald (born 1930), and Martin (born 1935).

Martin Bisson and his wife, Mary, died within a week of each other during the depression in the 1930's. Donald and Gladys Tiemey and their children moved to Dodge Avenue in Fort Wayne in 1939. Donald, who worked for the Wayne Pump Company, had been an outstanding athlete in basketball, bowling, and golf, winning several tournaments. Gladys became known as an excellent local painter/artist and also a contest winner, writing columns for Contest Magazine and conducting the local contest club. Gladys won the Pillsbury Bake-off, as well as the National Chicken Cooking Contest.

Nadyne married Ervin Recht in 1941 and had six children: Diane, Douglas, Jeannine, Mark, Cynthia, and Michael. Their son, Doug, died as a result of Agent Orange after the Vietnam War. Ervin died in 2001, followed by Nadyne in 2003. Mark had joined his mother, Nadyne, in her realty firm, Recht and Recht. Nadyne had become very active and well known in the realty field locally.

Donald Tiemey Jr. became an engineer and worked for Lockheed in the "skunkworks" division; developing the U-2; the Stealth Bomber, and other classified projects. A control panel which he designed is on exhibit in the Wright-Patterson museum.

Martin Tiemey, who had been valedictorian of his Central Catholic class, won a full scholarship to Notre Dame and graduated with honors in 1957 with a B.A. in Modern Languages. He also became a Fulbright Fellow, traveling to Chile to fulfill his fellowship, where he studied with Latin American authors, including Eduardo Barrios and Nobel Laureate Pablo Neruda. Martin had already performed in many musicals on stage in Fort Wayne and Indianapolis and in college. In Chile, he learned the classical guitar from Spanish expatriates from Franco's regime. Singing with a jazz band Portillo and on radio in Santiago, he won an award as the outstanding new entertainer there. After returning to the United States, he continued acting and singing in Chicago, New York, and Europe. After obtaining an M.A. in Spanish from Indiana University in 1960, he began his college teaching career at Indiana Purdue Fort Wayne University, and later in Colorado taught Spanish and also English for non-English speakers. At the same time, he worked five years for the Fort Wayne Community Schools, and later thirty-three years for the Diocese of Fort Wayne at Central Catholic and at Dwenger High School, teaching Spanish, English, World Literature, and directing plays. A writer of poetry ("Sawdust Dreams" and "Empty Dreams"), Martin also wrote songs, usually for musical presentations like "Sugar Water Sunday," on which he collaborated with Harvey Cocks of New York and Civic Theater fame. Martin spends retirement traveling and writing a new musical setting for "The Picture of Dorian Gray" called "Portrait".

Submitted by Martin Bisson Tiemey

REGINA MARIE (RYAN) & KERRY JOSEPH BLANCHETTE FAMILY

Regina Marie Ryan Blanchette was born at Parkview Hospital in Fort Wayne, Indiana on July 25, 1954. Regina was the daughter of Rose Marie Hart Ryan and James Richard Ryan. Regina can trace her family back to 1751 to Ertingen, Germany and her great great great great grandfather, Felix App. Regina's great great grandfather was Mathias App, who owned the App Shoe store on Calhoun Street for many years in the late 1800s. Regina's father James Richard Ryan was a Fort Wayne native. He was the son of Lelah Petgen Ryan and George Franklin Ryan.

Left to right, Travis D. Blanchette, Kerry Blanchette, Regina (Ryan) Blanchette, James Ryan, Chelsea Blanchette Silvers, Rose (Hart) Ryan, Scott R. Silvers, Jason E. Blanchette, Kalissa N. Blanchette, 2003.

Regina was the oldest of James and Rose Ryan's six children. She has two brothers, Timothy James Ryan of Fort Wayne, and Sean Hart Ryan of Cincinnati, Ohio. Regina also has three sisters, Rebecca Susan Ryan Laughlin, Kara Ann Ryan Slocum and Molly Kathleen Ryan Smethers all of Fort Wayne. Regina grew up on the south side of Fort Wayne, first living on Colerick Street, and then on South Anthony until adulthood. She attended Irwin Elementary School for Kindergarten and then St. Hyacinth Catholic Elementary School through 7th grade. In 8th grade she transferred to Weisser Park Junior High School. She graduated from South Side High School in 1972, a member of the school's 50th graduating class. Regina continued on to St. Francis College in Fort Wayne, where she pursued a degree in Liberal Arts as an Art Major.

It was at St. Francis College where Regina met Kerry Joseph Blanchette. Kerry was from Wolcott, Indiana, a small town of about 900 near Lafayette, Indiana. He was born at St. Elizabeth Hospital in Lafayette, Indiana, on August 18, 1953. Kerry was one of seven children of Rita Billings Blanchette and Everal Leo Blanchette. Rita and Everal trace their roots to the St. Anne, Illinois area and Everal can trace his roots to the French area of Canada through his mother Nelda Bissonnette. Kerry has one brother, Kenneth Blanchette of Wolcott, Indiana. Kerry has five sisters, Joyce Blanchette Beaver of Arizona, JoAnn Blanchette Kyburz of Wolcott, Janet Blanchette Murphy Prescott of Oregon, Kathleen Blanchette Ryan of Fort Wayne, Indiana, and Karen Blanchette Dennison White of Fort Wayne. Kathleen Blanchette Ryan is married to Regina Ryan Blanchette's brother, Timothy James Ryan. Kathleen and Timothy met through Regina and Kerry Blanchette.

Kerry Blanchette attended elementary school at Sacred Heart Catholic school in Remington, Indiana, and junior high school at Wolcott Junior High in Wolcott, Indiana. He attended high school in Lockport, Illinois at St. Charles Borremeo Catholic Seminary. Kerry's father, Everal, was the first cousin of Romeo Blanchette, the Bishop of the Roman Catholic Diocese of Joliet, Illinois at the time. Kerry decided after high school not to continue as a seminarian for the priesthood and instead continued his college education at St. Francis College in Fort Wayne. He graduated Cum Laude in 1994 with a Bachelor of Arts Degree with an English Major and Business minor.

Regina Ryan Blanchette met Kerry Blanchette in January 1974 at St. Francis College. They fell fast in love and were married on August 3, 1974 at St. Marys Catholic Church in Fort Wayne. Father Thomas O'Connor officiated. They have been married for over 30 years. Regina and Kerry had four children. Their oldest son, Jason Everal Blanchette, was born on October 13,1978. He graduated from North Side High School in 1997. He received an Associate Degree in HVAC from Ivy Tech in Fort Wayne and is continuing his education at IPFW to obtain a Bachelors Degree. He works at J.O. Mory and lives in Fort Wayne. Regina and Kerry's younger son is Travis Daniel Blanchette, born January 21, 1985. Travis attended Northrop High School and currently attends Ivy Tech and IPFW pursuing automotive and engineering degrees. Travis is employed with Don Ayres Automotive in Fort Wayne. Kerry and Regina's oldest daughter is Chelsea Camille Blanchette Silvers. Chelsea was born November 16,1982. She graduated from North Side High School in 2001. She currently attends IPFW pursuing an Elementary Education Degree. She is student teaching first grade at Washington Elementary School in downtown Fort Wayne and will graduate from IPFW in December of 2005. She has worked at La Petite Academy in Fort Wayne for several years. On August 9, 2003 she married Scott Richard Silvers of Fort Wayne. Regina and Kerry's youngest child is daughter Kalissa Nicole Blanchette, born November 16, 1987. Kalissa attends Northrop High School and will graduate in January of 2006. She plans to attend the University of St. Francis in Fort Wayne beginning in January, 2006 to pursue a degree in Nursing. She works at Dairy Queen in Fort Wayne.

Kerry Blanchette worked for North American Van Lines in Fort Wayne for 29 years. Regina Blanchette has worked for Scotts Foods in Fort Wayne for 14 years.

Submitted by Regina Blanchette.

CARL EMMETT BLAUVELT

Carl Emmett Blauvelt was born April 13, 1897, and died January 15, 1979. He was the son of Augusta L. Blauvelt and Mary Catherine Geiger, was born in Van Wert, Ohio, and married Irene G. Gebhard on June 15, 1921. They had five children, Dorothy, Richard, Marilyn, Rosie, and Ronald.

Carl retired from Phelps Dodge Company where he was a machinist. He previously worked for the Pennsylvania Railroad along with his five brothers and his father.

L to R: Carl with 43 years of service from 1913 to 1956, Earl with 30 years of service from 1918 to 1948, and Orley with 43 years service from 1911 to 1954. Orley started the Indiana Umpire Association.

Carl lived in Fort Wayne since 1906 and was a member of St. Patricks Catholic Church and its Holy Name Society. He was an army veteran of World War I.

Carl "Cocky" Blauvelt was inducted into the Fort Wayne Baseball Hall of Fame in 1976. Carl's career started at sixteen when he joined the Comets in 1913. In 1914, Carl jumped to Bluffton before he started his career with the Pennsylvania Railroad in 1915. He played with the Pennsy Leaguers before and after his army stint, and was with the Pennsy team on and off until 1923. In the five remaining years, he played with Lincoln Life, and Jess Walker's Berghoff team, then to the WPA Recreation, and then joined Superior Malt-Berghoff. His Lincoln Life team played Babe Ruth in an exhibition game. He also played semi-pro football for the Fort Wayne Cavaliers.

In 1928, Carl started umpiring and was an umpire for the next 28 years.

Carl and his two brothers, Earl and Orley, represented a combined total of 116 years playing and umpiring baseball in Fort Wayne. The total covered a span of 45 years.

Submitted by Robert Blauvelt

AUGUSTAN & MARY CATHERINE BLAUVELT FAMILY

The Blauvelt brothers, Earl, Orley, Carl, Herbert, and A.L., had railroading in their blood. The Pennsylvania railroad played a big part in the Blauvelt family of Fort Wayne and the Blauvelt family of Fort Wayne played a big part in the Pennsylvania railroad.

Their father, Augustan Blauvelt worked for the Pennsylvania railroad. Earl Blauvelt was formerly in the engine house at Fort Wayne and a foreman at a local plant. Orley Blauvelt was a stockman at the east car shop. Carl Blauvelt was at the waste reclamation plant at the east car shop. Herbert Blauvelt was a meat cutter for Peter Eckrich Company. A. L. Blauvelt was a freight conductor at Fort Wayne. Another son, Richard Blauvelt, was employed as a brakeman and was killed on the job in 1915.

Carl Blauvelt's two sons, Richard C. and Ronald, both worked on the Pennsylvania railroad. Richard was a fireman and engine man and Ronald was the crew dispatcher.

Submitted by Richard Blauvelt.

Pennsy Team

FREDERICK O. & THELMA A. (KNIPSTEIN) BLEDSOE FAMILY

Frederick O. Bledsoe "Fritz" was born August 1, 1917, in Terre Haute, Indiana. His father, Fred O. Bledsoe and mother, Maude Ethyl Goldman Bledsoe, moved their family of seven children, Josephine, Albert, Beulah, Frederick, Sherman, Lois, and Frank to San Francisco, California, in 1926. It took them 18 months and two Model Ts to make the trip. They moved to Phoenix, Arizona, in 1928. Josephine was the first to move to Fort Wayne. Fritz then promised his mother whenever she wanted to move back to Indiana and to Fort Wayne, he would bring her. One day in 1940, he came home from work and she had her bags packed and was ready to go. Everyone, except Sherman, lived in Fort Wayne after that. He stayed in Arizona.

Fritz married Thelma Adele Knipstein on September 27, 1941. Thelma, born June 8, 1922, was the daughter of Edwin and Viola (Miller) Knipstein who lived on Barthold Street in Fort Wayne. Her siblings were Eileen, Paul, Ralph, Edwin, and Fred.

Fritz and Thelma had four children, Charlotte, born November 27, 1942, Frederick O., born September 28, 1946, Ruth, born August 5, 1948, and Penny, born October 18, 1950. Soon after Charlotte was born, World War II broke out and Fritz joined the Air Force. He was sent to France and landed on Normandy Beach on "D" Day. Charlotte lives in Fort Wayne. She has two sons, Edward Booker and Rodney Sebring, who owns R & R Welding in Fort Wayne. Fred lives in Ossian with his wife Elisabeth. Fred has two daughters, Dawn Rose of Fort Wayne and Mary Kay Taylor of Florida. Ruth married William "Bill" E. Pulver on January 25, 1969, and had one son, James Daniel "J.D." born on May 31, 1970. They lived in Harlan for 20 years and in 1994, moved to Conway, Arkansas, for four and

Fred and Thelma Bledsoe's 50th wedding anniversary.

F.O. Bledsoe, Inc

a half years when Bill was transferred with Nucor Fastener. They then moved to the Crawfordsville, Indiana area after he again was transferred with Nucor. They moved back to Fort Wayne in 2004. Penny moved to Leander, Texas, in the 1980s and is still living there. She has three boys, Jeff, Jaison, and Jeremy, all of Leander, Texas.

Fritz worked for 25 years at Ottenweller & Sons Company on Superior Street. While there he helped build conveyors for Seyfert Potato Chips, helping to modernize the company. He then worked for Trans-Power on Wells Street for a few years before starting his own steel fabrication business, F.O. Bledsoe, Inc. Fritz was the owner-operator and Thelma was the office manager. He built the toboggan that was in Franke Park for a few years, helped build the Safari automated cars, built a conveyor for Perfection Bakery, built and installed machinery for Mayflower Mill, and did steel fabrication for various companies in Fort Wayne. The company was located just north of the Wood Youth Center on Wallywood Drive close to the children's zoo. Fritz retired in 1989.

Fritz was a member of the Scottish Rite, Mizpah Shrine, and Waynedale Masonic Lodge 739. Thelma was a member of the Waynedale Eastern Stars. Thelma was a hostage at the Bob Evans restaurant on February 14, 1998. It was a scary time for all. She survived that, however, she succumbed to cancer on June 29, 1998. Fritz followed her on August 2, 2000.

Submitted by William and Ruth Pulver.

DAVID ALTON & JANICE KAY (SHIDAKER) BLEEKE

David Alton Bleeke was born in Fort Wayne, Indiana on October 24, 1936. His parents were Alton Frederick Bleeke and Gertrude Emma (Scherer) Bleeke. He went to grade school (K-8) at Trinity Evangelical Lutheran School. He graduated from North Side High School in 1954. He was awarded membership in The National Honor Society. He started his college career at Purdue Center in Fort Wayne in chemical engineering.

Jan and David Bleeke.

At the end of his sophomore year, he transferred to Indiana University to pursue a course of study that would lead to dentistry. He graduated from Indiana University School of Dentistry in 1964. He received the International College of Dentists Award. After graduation he returned to Fort Wayne to set up his practice.

In 1962, he married Janice Kay Shidaker. They met in 1961 while Janice was working as a dental assistant for Dr. Edwin C. Errington. Janice was born on November 25, 1939, and was raised in Kewanna, Indiana. She graduated from Kewanna High School, and then went to Elkhart University for her degree in dental assisting. She moved to Fort Wayne in 1958.

During his dental career, Dr. Bleeke served on most of the committee's of Isaac Knapp District Dental Society. He was president of Isaac Knapp during 1976-1977. He was awarded fellowships in the Academy of General Dentistry, the American College of Dentists, and the International College of Dentists. He is past-president of the Northern Indiana Society of Occlusal Studies 1984-1985. He served on the Indiana State Board of Dental Examiners 1988 through 1994, and served as president 1992-1993. He is a Life Member of the American Dental Association. He is also a member of the Indiana Dental Association.

With regard to his community involvement, he has been a member of the Mad Anthonys since 1975, and served as president 1997-1999. He is currently involved with the fund raising arm of the Mad Anthonys. He has been a director of the Western Golf Association associated with the Evans Scholars Program since 1995. He has been a member of the Chamber of Commerce since 1964. He was a founding member of the North Side High School Alumni Association, and served as president 1992-1994. He is currently involved with fund raising for college scholarships for North Side High School students. He has been a member of the board of directors of the Fort Wayne-Allen County Historical Society since 1999.

Dr. Bleeke retired from practice in 2005, but continues to volunteer at Matthew 25 Dental Clinic, and the Neighborhood Health Clinics. His hobbies include golf, gardening, orchids, and photography.

Submitted by David A. Bleeke, DDS

BLESSINGS

In 1837, John and Mary Riehm Blessing sailed from Schlast Goeppingen, Germany with their eight children for a new country... AMERICA. They were very courageous to sail to this new land with only the stars of heaven to guide them. They were blown off course and it took them four months to cross the Atlantic. They landed in New York, purchased a covered wagon, horses, food and supplies, including an axe and saw to cut trails for the wagon to get them through the wilderness. They settled in Fort Wayne, population 500.

John died three weeks later and Mary had eight children to raise. The eldest child was fourteen years old and the youngest was two. She purchased forty acres of ground for $1.25 an acre where the Huguenard/Butler Road is now located.

Peter purchased a farm in Lake Township, and built a one room house of logs in which he, his wife and nine children lived. One of his nine children was Henry.

Henry John Blessing, born in 1857, married Catharine Elizabeth Henline in 1885 in Fort Wayne. Their farm was located in Washington Township, and this land remains in the Blessing family.

Lawrence Blessing, born in 1896, married Julia Mae Nelson, the pretty young school teacher who taught third grade at the old Lincoln School. They continued the farming tradition, raising three daughters, Margie, Dorothy and Carol Blessing.

Blessing Farm and Home. Henry Blessing, Catherine (Henline) Blessing, Clara, Lucinda Carl and Lawrence Blessing

Life on the farm was "A Family Affair". Mother joined Dad working in the fields shocking wheat, husking corn and each morning/evening milking nine cows. The three daughters were not exempt from chores. Gathering eggs, caring for the rabbits and pulling weeds in the garden were summer activities. Skipping rope, playing "jacks" and euchre with one trip to Trier's Park completed the summer. Needless to say, the daughters enjoyed getting back to school in September.

The highlight of the summer was when the "thrashing machine" arrived to separate the grains from the sheaths, leaving the sweet smelling straw. Neighbors came from nearby farms. Men came to thrash and the women to prepare the meals. Another highlight on the farm was "Butchering Day" in November. This would be meat for the year and another occasion for neighbors to lend a helping hand. Each neighbor left tired and satisfied, and with a package of meat. Lawrence was ninety-nine years old when he died in January, 1996. He saw many changes in the world from the horse drawn buggy to his first automobile, a 1917 Dodge. He purchased it in Detroit and drove back to Fort Wayne. No driver's licenses were required, so the salesman gave him minimal driving instructions. Until that time, he had only driven a team of horses.

He cherished his three daughters and was privileged to see five generations of his family flourish. The Blessing heritage continues in Allen County through his granddaughter, Marla Irving, who is presently Allen County Commissioner.

Allen County is the BLESSING past, present and future.

Submitted by Margie K. Smiley

PETER BLESSING FAMILY

On December 1, 1845 the ship Albany landed in New York Harbor. One of the immigrant families setting foot on American soil was Johann Georg Blessing, born August 5, 1794 died September 1849. With him was his wife Cordula (Maier) Blessing born February 3, 1798 died about 1863 and their eight children: Johann Georg born September 12, 1823 died June 6, 1899; Johann Peter born December 13, 1825 died August 29, 1898; Cordula (Mrs. Louis Hitzfield) born September 6, 1827 died January 15, 1908; Rosine (Mrs. Joseph Wasserman) born March 29, 1831 died unknown; Mary (Mrs. Jacob Fink) born October 31, 1834 died unknown; Catherine (Mrs. William Kase) born December. 21, 1836 died April 15, 1895; Friedrika (Mrs. Fredrick Felger, Sr.) born December 24, 1840 died March 31, 1875; Christoff born January 5, 1845 died about 1857. All were born in the state of Wurttemberg, Germany, in the village of Schlat, not far from the Swiss border.

After spending some time in the Buffalo, New York, area the parents and younger children arrived in Allen County and purchased a forty-acre farm in Washington Township. Peter, the subject of this writing, stayed in Buffalo, working for Abner Bryant, a nurseryman. By 1853, Peter had also moved to Allen County, as this is when he first purchased land in Lake Township. The farm is still owned by his descendants.

On July 12, 1855 in St. John German Evangelical Church, Fort Wayne, he married Catherine Dosch, daughter of Nicholas Dosch, also a German immigrant, living near Avilla, Indiana, in Noble County. To them were born eight children: Charles, John, Henry, Frederick, William, Otto,

Peter Blessing Family 1895 Front row: Frederick, Peter, Elizabeth, Catherine, and William. Back row: John, George, Mary, Henry, and Charles.

Mary (#1 Mrs. George Seeger, #2 Mrs. Michael Fick), and Elizabeth (Mrs. George Ohneck).

Peter was a most prosperous, ambitious, and respected man of his community. He owned 400 acres of land and was able to loan money to his friends and neighbors when they started their farming ventures. In addition to farming, Peter was a chainman for surveyors when laying out farms. Peter and Catherine were charter members and one of the founders of St. John's Lutheran Church, Lake Township.

As the result of a broken leg received by a runaway horse and wagon, Peter died August 29, 1889, and was laid to rest in Eel River Cemetery. His obituary states,"Mr. Blessing was one of the successful farmers of this section of the county and he had a host of friends both in the county and in Fort Wayne. His sad accident has been a matter of concern to numerous friends ever since it occurred and the announcement of his death will be received by them with sincere regret."

His wife died December 19, 1912, and is buried with her beloved husband and son Otto, who died at age 11 of scarlet fever. Many descendants of the Blessing name can be found in Allen County and surrounding areas. They carry the name Graft, Schaefer, Bercot, Fick, Felger, Fortmeyer, Ohneck to name of few, and, of course, Blessing.

Submitted by Ardean Ebert

JOHN GREGG & ROSALIE MARIE (KOESTER) BLOCHER FAMILY

John Gregg was born March 12, 1939, to John Louis Blocher Jr. and Ocie Dale (McCleery) Blocher in Bluffton, Indiana. Rosalie Marie was born March 10, 1938, to Paul William and Marie Kathryn (Goeglein) Koester in Fort Wayne, Indiana. John has a half-sister, Rosemary (Grogg) Billington. Rosalie has three sisters: Phyllis May Schumacher, Gloria Luella Buhr, and Marilyn Loraine Meyer.

John's great grandfather, John Blocher, was born November 14, 1846, in Wittenburg, Germany. He immigrated to America in 1862, and settled in Pittsburg. Other great grandfathers were Patrick Coyne, and Alexander McCleery, who was born October 5, 1846 in Bluffton. John's great grandmother, Louise Sieman, was born October 10, 1848, in Stratfritz, Germany, and came to America at age six. She died December 27, 1931, in Muncie, Indiana. Other great grandmothers were Mary, born in Glasgow, Scotland, and Rebeccah Anabelle Smith, who was born October 12, 1856, and died December 12, 1924.

John's grandfather, John Louis Blocher, was born February 11, 1870 in Pittsburg and had four brothers and two sisters. He died October 20, 1928. His other grandfather, Charles Samuel McCleery, was born March 28, 1880, in Warren, Indiana, and had five sisters. Charles died May 18, 1945.

John's grandmother, Katheren Mary Coyne, was born March 31, 1871, in Newport, County Mayo, Ireland. She married John Blocher on June 19, 1898, in Peoria, Illinois. Katheren had three brothers and two sisters. She died August 28, 1913, in West Baden, Indiana. His other grandmother, Martha Debbie Mounsey, was born April 2, 1884, in Liberty Center, Indiana. She married Charles McCleery on May 21, 1902. Martha had two sisters and one brother who died July 25, 1939.

Rosalie's great grandfather's were Christian Koester Sr., who was born in Germany on November 11, 1813, and died October 21, 1891, John F. Gerke, who was born in Germany, and John Goeglein, who was born June 1848, in Pomeroy, Ohio.

Rosalie's grandfather was Johann Christian Wilhelm Koester who was born December 30, 1851. He died December 2, 1947. Her other grandfather, Louis Adam Goeglein, was born September 18, 1878. Louis had five brothers and four sisters. He married Marie Meyers on May 5, 1904, and died March 28, 1964.

Grandmothers of Rosalie are Marie Meyers who was born February 24, 1882. She had three brothers and one sister. Marie died July 8, 1968. Maria Margaretha Catherine Gerke was born December 5, 1861, and married Christian Koester on April 29, 1880. She had two brothers and four sisters. Maria died August 3, 1950.

John and Rosalie Blocher have two sons and two daughters: John Louis III, who was born July 9, 1963 in Conway, South Carolina; Lisa Ann, born September 21, 1965, in Fort Wayne, married Billy Darmawan on July 12, 1987 and they have two children, Ian Luke, born May 23, 1992, and Sara Grace born February 26, 1996, in Fort Wayne, Indiana; Lana Sue was born June 25, 1969 in Fort Wayne and married Brian Lee Bienz on September 28, 1996. They have two children, James Kiro Bienz, born August 20, 2002, in Buffalo, New York and Erin Kaya Bienz, born August 23, 2004, in Marion, Indiana; Kevin David was born January 16, 1977, in Fort Wayne and he married Kathleen Marie Todd on June 21, 2003, in Des Moines. Iowa.

Submitted by John G. Blocher.

CLARENCE NICHOLAS & KATHRYN BOWEN BLOOM

Clarence Nicholas Bloom, was born August 14, 1926, in Swan Township, Noble County, Indiana. His parents were Margaret Oakes and Stephen Joseph Bloom who were first generation American citizens, their parents being born in Poland. Their Polish surnames are Dombek and Kwiatkowski. His siblings were Clement Howard, Mary Esther, Michael Benedict, Luella May and Donald Joseph. His grandfather, Michael Bloom came to the United States of America at age 36 through the port of Bremen, Germany arriving in New York on May 15, 1868. His Certificate of Naturalization is in the Noble County Clerk's office dated October 10, 1874. Michael married Mary Katherine Walt (Walaczek) 1863/1866 in the province of Poznan, Poland. Michael and Mary had nine children all born in America.

"Nick's" father, Stephen, was born March 23, 1884, in Noble County Indiana. He was a farmer. He married Margaret (Dombek) Oakes who was born March 13, 1893 in Swan Township, Noble County Indiana. She was one of twelve children born to John and Josephine Wesolek Oakes Bloom. Stephen Bloom and Margaret Oakes were married on November 23, 1920 at Immaculate Conception Catholic Church at Ege by Rev. I. Nicholas Allgeier.

"Nick" graduated from LaOtto grade school and Huntertown High school with the class of 1944. He worked at International Harvester before being drafted by the Army. He left December 26, 1944 for Indianapolis and was sent for basic training in Texas. He was going to be sent to Europe when the war ended. His unit was then sent across the continent by train and departed for the Philippine Islands. The war in Japan ended on his nineteenth birthday August 14, 1946. He joined the 108th Regiment of the 40th Division and was sent to Korea with the Army of Occupation. He was discharged on May 31, 1947 from Letterman General Hospital in San Francisco, California.

Katie and Nick Bloom, 1950

For three seasons after his discharge he played professional basketball with a barnstorming team sponsored by the House of David of Benton Harbor, Michigan.

He married Kathryn Ann Bowen who was born August 22, 1929 in Sturgis, St. Joseph County, Michigan. Her parents were J. T. and Marguerite Rowe Bowen of LaGrange, Indiana. Her brothers were Robert Lee of Georgia, Jack T. of LaGrange and Jean R. of California (all 3 deceased). Sisters are Mary Ellen Dalrymple of Elkhart and Janice E Hummel of LaGrange. All six Bowen children graduated from LaGrange High School. Kathryn attended Fort Wayne Lutheran Hospital School of Nursing 1947-1950. She worked at the LaGrange County Hospital until her marriage on September 8, 1951 in LaGrange.

The family belonged to St. Jude Catholic church for thirty years, and Nick and Katie became members of St. Charles church in 1984. She retired from Parkview Hospital in 1984. They have seven children: Karen Ann, Janet Marie, Linda Jean , James Gregory, Robert Paul, Martha Jane and Jeffrey Thomas.

Nick was a city letter carrier from 1950 to 1969 on Business Route Number 2. He was promoted to Route Examiner in 1969. He was promoted to Assistant Manager of Delivery and Collection for the Fort Wayne Sectional Center on August 21, 1972. He was named Manager in 1973. He retired December 27, 1981after 33 years of service. He was a life-long New York Yankee fan and followed the activities of the Lady Boiler Basketball team at Purdue University. Family genealogy was a hobby he enjoyed for many years. Nick died May 19, 2005 after losing his battle with Leukemia. He is buried in a crypt in the Mother Theodore Guerin Mausoleum at Catholic Cemetery.

"Katie" has been a member of Settlers, Inc. and Hearthstone Ensemble for 25 years. She is currently President of the Allen County Genealogical Society and Co-Chair of the History Book project. She serves on the Board of the History Center and on the Alumni Council at University of St. Francis representing Lutheran Hospital School of Nursing. She has been a member of Mary Penrose Wayne Chapter of the Daughters of the American Revolution for 25 years and has served in many offices including two terms as Regent. She served as Registrar for Indiana DAR 1990-1994. She has been President of the Parkview Ambassadors, an organization for Parkview Retirees, and publishes the quarterly newsletter. She was a Girl Scout leader and member of Limberlost Girl Scout Council for 35 years.

Submitted Kathryn A. Bloom

JAMES GREGORY BLOOM

Jim is the son of Clarence Nicholas and Kathryn Ann Bowen Bloom. He was born April 25, 1959, in Fort Wayne, Allen County, Indiana. His siblings are Karen Ann, Janet Marie Baltzell, Linda Jean Burrell, Robert Paul Bloom, Martha Jane Conkling, and Jeffrey Thomas Bloom. The family resided at 1857 Florida Drive and 1835 Florida for 25 years. He enjoyed going to Lakeside Rose gardens which was just two blocks away. He played Little League baseball and was a member of Boy Scouts.

James Gregory Bloom.

He attended Forest Park School for kindergarten, St. Jude Catholic School, Lakeside Middle School, and graduated from North Side High School. He is employed by Huth Tool and Machine Shop on Clinton Street where he operates a computerized lathe.

For a number of years he lived at Canterbury Green apartments where he enjoyed playing golf. He purchased a home in Glenwood Park where he now resides. His hobbies include golf, playing the guitar and Native American flute, bike hiking, and traveling.

Submitted by James G. Bloom.

JEFFREY THOMAS BLOOM

Jeff was born October 27, 1971 in Fort Wayne, Allen County, Indiana. His parents are Clarence Nicholas and Kathryn Ann Bowen Bloom who have been residents of Fort Wayne since their marriage in 1951 in LaGrange Indiana. He is the seventh child born to this family. His siblings are Karen Ann who lives in Chicago; Janet Marie Baltzell, wife of Gary; Linda Jean Burrell, wife of Robert C.; James Gregory; Robert Paul (wife Mary) and Martha Jane Conkling, wife of Andy.

Jeffrey and Nicola Bloom

He attended Forest Park Kindergarten, St. Jude Grade School, Lane Middle School and graduated from Snider High School. He played football at Lane and Snider and was involved in Little League and Boy Scouting. He attended Indiana University at Bloomington and graduated with a degree in general studies.

He is currently employed by The Oceanaire Seafood restaurant in San Diego, California. On July 16, 2005, he married Nicola Gabriele in Las Vegas, Nevada. Nicola is a graduate of Elmhurst High School and Indiana University. She was born January 3, 1978 in Fort Wayne and is employed by The Palm restaurant chain.

Submitted by Jeffrey Thomas Bloom

KAREN ANN BLOOM

Karen Ann Bloom was born August 1, 1952, in Fort Wayne, Indiana. Her parents are C. Nicholas and Kathryn Ann Bowen Bloom. The family lived at 2313 California Avenue until 1957, when they moved to 1857 Florida Drive. She attended Forest Park Elementary School for kindergarten, St. Jude grade school, Bishop Dwenger High School and graduated from North Side High School in 1970. She graduated from Ball State University earning a B.S. in social work in 1974. Karen earned her MSW degree from the University of Michigan in Ann Arbor in 1977, and was employed in the human services field as a social work administrator until 1984, when she moved to Chicago and began her career in executive search.

Karen formed a company with Barbara Gross in 1988, known as Bloom, Gross & Associates, Inc. and they specialized in the recruitment of marketing and communications professionals on a national basis. The two partners jointly ran the firm until Barbara's retirement in 1993. Karen took over as the principal of the company, and its sole owner. Over the years she has added associates who work in three practice areas: marketing and market research, advertising, and PR/corporate communications. Offices are located at 625 N. Michigan Avenue, Suite 200, Chicago, Illinois.

Widely quoted about her observations and experiences regarding employment trends and practices, Karen was a contributor to the book, *On Staffing: Advice and Perspectives from HR Leaders*, published in 2004, by John Wiley & Sons. Karen is a frequent speaker at graduate schools of business, professional organizations, and outplacement firms and has served on the board of directors for the Institute of Business & Professional Ethics at DePaul University. She sat on the board of directors for the Employment Management Association (EMA)-a professional emphasis group of the Society for Human Resource Management (SHRM) and the EMA Foundation as well as serving the EMA as area vice president and vice president at-large. In Chicago, Karen sits on the board of directors and served as vice president of programs for EMA Chicago. Karen was a member of the inaugural Workforce Staffing and Deployment Panel for SHRM. She was also one of the founding board members for the Eclipse Theatre Company, a well-established and critically acclaimed theater company in Chicago.

Karen Ann Bloom.

Karen has a second home in Santa Fe, New Mexico, and is passionate about hiking in the southwest. She enjoys travel and has been to numerous places in the United States as well as other countries including Mexico, Canada, Scotland, England, Ireland, France, Italy, Belgium, and the Netherlands. In her one trip to South America, she hiked the Inca Trail to Machu Picchu in Peru.

Submitted by Karen A. Bloom.

ROBERT PAUL & MARY ROSE DIFILIPPO BLOOM FAMILY

Robert Paul Bloom is the son of Clarence Nicholas and Kathryn Ann Bowen Bloom. He was born October 7, 1963 at Parkview Hospital in Fort Wayne Indiana. At the time of his birth, the family lived at 1857 Florida Drive near Lakeside Rose Gardens. His siblings are Karen Ann Bloom of Chicago, Janet Bloom Baltzell, Linda Jean Burrell, James Gregory Bloom, and Martha Jane Conkling, all of Fort Wayne, and Jeffrey Thomas Bloom of San Diego, California.

He attended Kindergarten at Forest Park School followed by eight grades at St. Jude Catholic grade school. He graduated from Bishop Dwenger High School in the class of 1982, and earned a BS in Biology from Purdue University in 1986. He married Mary Rose Difilippo on September 3, 1988 at St. Charles Catholic Church. She is the daughter of Donald T. and Frances Minnick Difilippo, and was born December 6, 1963 in Fort Wayne Indiana. She is the youngest of eight children in her family. Her siblings are Virginia, John, Joseph, Connie, Donald, Margaret Diehl and Rita Lightner. Her father worked for the Fort Wayne Police Department and Indiana Michigan Electric Company. He died June 26, 2001. Her brothers, John and Joe, are currently serving as Fort Wayne Police officers. Mary is employed part time at Sport's Den in Georgetown Shopping Center.

Robert Paul Bloom, wift Mary, son Alex, and daughter Andrea on vaction in Florida.

They have two children. Alexander Robert was born March 28, 1991 and Andrea Marie was born September 23, 1994, at Parkview Hospital in Fort Wayne Indiana. Alex attended St. Charles grade school where he participated in basketball, football and soccer. He excels academically and was on the Honor roll. He is a freshman at Bishop Dwenger High School. He enjoyed playing baseball with the St. Joe Central All Star Team that won the Central Division Regional Championship and advanced to the World Series playoffs at Taylor Michigan in August 2005. They played the team from the Netherlands in the consolation game, winning 7-3. Andrea attends St. Charles grade school. She is taking gymnastics classes and will be on the cheer leading squad at St. Charles for her grade level.

Bob began to work for Scott's Foods while still in high school, beginning as a carry-out. After college he continued to work for Scott's for 23 years. He was store director for the store in Auburn from 1991 to 2000. From 2000 to 2005 he was director of the store at West State Street in Fort Wayne He is currently employed by Executive Management Services, Inc. in the Fort Wayne office. His hobbies include golf, coaching sports, home improvement projects and reading U.S. History.

The family enjoys vacationing in Michigan during the summer and trips to Florida for Spring Break.

Submitted by Bob and Mary Bloom

BLUME FAMILY

On September 4, 1874, Martin and Margaret Heim Bloom bought a 155-acre parcel of land in the northwest corner of the Ann Hackley Reserve. In 1891 Andrew and May Black Blume bought the land from his father and mother and there farmed and raised six children: Celeste (Willie Waikart), Willie (Georgia Martin), John "Callie" (Ada), Ralph (Geraldine B.), Virgil (Etta Forker), and Rachel (Bruce Ruch).

Willie Blume married Georgia Martin and settled in St. Joseph Township. Georgia was left a widow when Willie died during the flu epidemic of 1918. Georgia went on to become the first woman elected to public office in Allen County, serving as county recorder from 1923 to 1926.

Smokehouse (over 100 years old and now used as a garden shed)

Virgil was born in 1894 and married Etta Forker. She was born to Gene and Mae Hockenbarger Forker and spent her early years in Noble County near Kendallville, Indiana. Virgil and Etta lived on the family farm in St. Joseph Township all of their married lives, except two years, 1933-34, when they worked for the State of Indiana on the Blackhawk Farm on State Street extended (now housing and the Georgetown shopping area). In addition to farming, Virgil sheared sheep. Small flocks, 60 head or less, were present on numerous farms in the early and middle 1900s. Virgil and Etta had three children: Ervin, Josephine, and Billy. All three graduated from the St. Joseph Township Grade School and North Side High School in Fort Wayne.

Ervin received his D.V.M. degree from Michigan State College, now MSU, in 1943. He then served in the Army Veterinary Corps. In 1946 he met and married Marjorie Evans, daughter of Josiah and Ethel Scott Evans, from Hamilton, Missouri. He returned to Indiana after WWII and set up in 1946 a private veterinary practice in Butler, Indiana, and Edgerton, Ohio. After selling his Butler practice, Ervin and Marjorie moved back to Fort Wayne to live on the family farm (original house and smokehouse are still standing). They live on a small plot of his great grandfather Blume's 160 acres. Ervin worked for the United States Department of Agriculture, Animal & Plant Health Inspection Service, Veterinarian Service, and the Indiana State Board of Animal Health for over 16 years. Their son, James, is an optometrist in Fort Wayne and his wife, Wanda, is a teacher for Fort Wayne Community Schools. They have a daughter, Erika, and a son, Michael.

James' sister, Rebecca, lives in Durango, Colorado, where she and her husband, Jon-Pierre Bleger, own and operate a French bakery. They have two sons and one daughter: Jerome, Adam, and Celene.

Ervin's sister, Josephine, and her husband, Russell "Pat" Anspach, are both deceased. Their son, Marty, and his wife, Judy, live in St. Joe, Indiana. Josephine and Pat's daughter, Joan, and her husband, Fred Gaff, live at Blue Lake near Churubusco.

Ervin's brother, Billy, and his wife, Louise, are both deceased. Billy graduated from MSU and was a manager of large Angus and Hereford herds in New York and Michigan. Their daughters are Cathy (Mark) Cook, who lives in Auburn, Indiana, and Pam ("Buzz") Crossman, who lives in Ada, Michigan.

Submitted by Dr. Ervin Blume

BOBAY FAMILY

The earliest records of the Bobay family are the result of information provided by Father Charles Banet, formerly a teacher at Saint Joseph's College, in Rensselaer, Indiana. He performed extensive research in the area of Belfort and Colmar, France, especially in the village of St. Germaine. While researching the Banet family, he also accumulated valuable data on the Bobay family, which originated in the same local area, and to which Father Banet had ties in America through marriages.

Germaine Bobay was born in St. Germaine, France, in 1807 and emigrated to the United States, leaving the port of LeHarve, France, on March 19, 1840, and landing in New York on May 6, 1840. His wife, the former Pauline Perry, as well as his two sons, Jean Baptiste and Philip, were born in France; while Jean August was born in 1843, and later, Josephine, Ferdinand, and Francis were all born in Indiana.

The Bobay family developed homestead property sometime after 1840 in northeastern Washington Township, Allen County, Indiana, south of what is now Dupont Road and just east of Interstate 69. According to B.J. Griswald's *Pictorial History of Fort Wayne*: "There they built a log cabin in which they lived through many years of toil and hardships. Their only route to the trading point at Fort Wayne being seven miles through woods so wild that it was necessary to mark the trees with an axe when making trips to blaze a trail for their safe return." That from a homestead in an area now occupied by hospitals and fast food restaurants.

Between 1849 and 1860 there was a severe cholera epidemic in the Fort Wayne, Indiana area. A large number of St. Vincent's Catholic Church's parishioners perished, including Germaine Bobay. He, along with the many others was buried in an unmarked common grave near the church.

The Bobays continued to acquire farmland holdings in adjacent areas until the 1900s, when the families began to join the migration from the rural areas to the more lucrative life in the industrial urban areas. Later, Bobays were involved in the development and growth of some of the more significant industries of Fort Wayne. Several of the Bobays were employed in the railroad-centered activities of the Pennsylvania Railroad Shops in Fort Wayne as car builders, painters, and machinists. Others were brewers with the Centlivre Brewing Company and mechanics with the Home Telephone and Telegraph Company.

Christina, David, Alexander, and Thomas Bobay

Today, descendants of the early Bobays continue the workingman tradition as machinists, automobile tire makers, electricians, jet-fuel specialists, and cabinetmakers. One of Germaine's descendants is in the Indiana Air National Guard, another works for a local building materials supplier, and another is an insurance firm office manager. Their children, the seventh Allen County generation, four sons and a daughter, continue to perpetuate the Bobay line.

Submitted by Christina Bobay

BOERGER FAMILY

The Boerger family originated in Hoste, a small village about five miles west of Lienen, Westphalia, Germany. The immigrant ancestor was Eberhardt Jacob Boerger, born May 12, 1788, the son of Herman Heinrich Boerger and Catharine Margaretha Kortepeter. On February 12, 1812, he married Anna Catharine Buller, the daughter of Herman Wilhelm Buller and Anna Margaretha Bierbaum. They had five sons and one daughter; one son Eberhardt died in Germany. Two sons, William and Rudolph, came to America before Jacob, reportedly in 1834 and 1836. Eberhardt Jacob and Anna Catharine arrived in New York on the ship Arkansas from Liverpool on September 5, 1837. Their daughter, Sophia, celebrated her thirteenth birthday on the ocean. Unfortunately, the mother, Anna Catharine Boerger, died in 1838 shortly after their arrival in Fort Wayne. She was buried in McCulloch Cemetery, as were two of the babies of her son William.

In 1848, Eberhardt Jacob, Rudolph, Jacob, Harmon, and William Boerger, bought from Samuel Hanna and Allen Hamilton, Lot 1, containing 42.7 acres, in the Richardville Reserve east of the St. Mary's River, which they later subdivided. The Abstract of Title to Lot 48 of Boerger's Addition to Fort Wayne details the history of this land.

Jacob Boerger died November 9, 1863, and is buried in the Boerger plot, Section D, Lot 4 in Lindenwood Cemetery. He has a tall, badly weathered, sandstone marker, the inscription in German script. There are at least twenty Boerger burials in this plot, mostly from the families of William and Rudolph.

Jacob's first son William, born February 14, 1813, in Hoste, married Elizabeth Spring, daughter of Christian Spring and Elizabeth Goetschmann of Canton Bern, Switzerland, on August 18, 1854, in St. John Reformed Church in 1868. They had eleven children. William was a contractor, specializing in house moving. He and his brother, Rudolph, were among the founders of Salem Reformed Church in 1868. Allied families by marriage are Hardung, Seelig, Oppliger, and Close.

The remaining living children of Jacob, all born in Hoste, were Rudolph, born November 12, 1814; Jacob born January 28, 1817; Harmon born March 9, 1819; and Sophia born August 28,1824.

Rudolph was married twice, the second time to Friedericka Suhre and they had eight children, however very few descendants. Their first son, Henry, committed suicide after the death of his wife and baby. Their sixth child, Gustave, married Kittie Burkas, and they had six children; four living to adulthood and marrying.

Jacob married Engel Fuelling in 1845 and eventually moved to Root Township, Adams County, where he was a farmer. They had nine children and many descendants.

Harmon died in August 1849 of cholera, leaving one son.

Sophia was married twice, first to Henry Trier, and then second to McIntire Seymour of Noble County. She was the beloved mother and stepmother of many children.

Submitted by Mary Hormann

ANDREW BOGLE & AMY FREYGANG-BOGLE FAMILY

Andrew Bogle was born in Toledo, Ohio, to John and Margaret Ann (Dietsch) Bogle. Andrew is the older of two children, he and his younger brother Rob. They traveled around a good deal growing up and finally settled in Fort Wayne for good in 1985.

Andrew Bogle family

After graduating from Snider High School, Andrew attended Indiana University in Bloomington in the Liberal Arts Program. He received an A.A.S. (with honors) in Mechanical Engineering from Purdue University and a B.S. (with honors) in Management from Tri-State University.

Amy (Freygang) was born at St. Joseph Hospital and is the youngest of ten children born to Richard and Martha Freygang of Fort Wayne. After graduating from Elmhurst High School, Amy attended Vincennes University and St. Francis College.

Andrew and Amy met while working at Wayne Combustion Systems.

They married in October 1998 at the Cathedral of the Immaculate Conception Chapel. Andrew is a sales engineer and Amy currently stays home with their children.

Andrew and Amy have four children; the first is Rachel Freygang, who was born February 14, 1996. She is in the third grade. Elly (Elizabeth) Bogle was born January 31, 2000. She is in preschool and preparing for kindergarten next year. Michael was born October 7, 2001. He is now an active three-year old boy. Mark Henry was born (one day after his Grandpa Freygang's birth date) on August 22, 2003.

Submitted by Andrew Bogle and Amy Freygang-Bogle

MICHAEL (MIKE) RICHARD BOHNKE, SARA (SALLY) ELAINE BOHNKE & DAUGHTER, LAURA DIANE BOHNKE

Michael and Sara met during their high school years. He attended Concordia High School, and she attended Dwenger High School. They both worked at Kern's Toyland on North Anthony Boulevard. They were married at Concordia High School in 1970. Michael graduated from Purdue University with degrees in biology and nursing. He has worked at St. Joseph Hospital for 28 years. Sara has worked in retail sales, and for the past six years has worked as a teacher's aide at St. John Lutheran Grade School (Flatrock), Madison Township near Monroeville. Their daughter, Laura graduated in 2005 from St. John (Flatrock). She was the fifth consecutive generation of the family educated there and continued her education at Concordia High School this fall.

The farm land Michael and Sara own near Maples, in Madison Township, has been owned by their family since the 1890s. It was first owned by Michael's great grandparents, Fred and Louise Grotrian. Their home still stands on the property. Louise came to the area as a babe-in-arms with her parents Fred and Louise Knipstein. Family tradition says that they came at least part of the way via the Wabash and Erie Canal. If that tradition is true, they would have been some of the last travelers to arrive in that manner. One of Fred and Louise Grotrian's children, Edna, was Michael's paternal grandmother. Edna was married to Lawrence (Joe) Bohnke.

Sara, Michael and Laura Bohnke, 2004

One of Lawrence Bohnke's ancestors, Johann Heinrich Franke, Jr. (also known as Heinrich Franke), Michael's great, great, great grandfather, was one of the earliest settlers in Madison Township. He and his family arrived from Germany in the late summer of 1845. In 1849, Heinrich was one of the charter members who established St. John Lutheran Church and School (Flatrock).

Michael's parents are both living. Michael has one brother, Patrick (deceased), and three sisters, Michele, Peggy, and Patricia. Michael's father, Richard Bohnke, worked for Rea Magnet Wire, and is still involved in farming. Michael's mother, Rhea West Bohnke, grew up in Colorado. Rhea, at age seventeen, was the teacher in a one-room school in Colorado. She moved to Indiana in 1947 to become the first woman teacher at

St. John (Flatrock), and her arrival doubled the faculty. She continued to teach for many years. Her ancestors helped to open the "American West" by serving in the military during the early Indian Wars just after the Civil War and as civil engineers building the C. B. & Q (later known as the Burlington Route) railroad across the Great Plains.

Both of Sara's parents are deceased. Sara has three brothers and one sister, Robert, Joseph, James, and Mary. Sara's father, Edwin Bugert, worked as a route salesman (milkman) for the Eskay dairy. Sara's mother, Marcella Nix Bugert, was a pediatric nurse at St. Joseph Hospital. Marcella's ancestors established Nix Settlement and St. Catharine's Roman Catholic Church in southeastern Whitley County, Indiana.

Submitted by Michael R. Bohnke

BOJRAB FAMILY

George David Bojrab and wife, Sadie Slymon, were born in Bloudan, Syria. They had eight children: Halla (Helen), David George, Moses M., Herbert John, Samuel, Assad, Abraham, and Mary, all born in Bloudan. In January of 1914 George died of yellow fever. Four of the sons, David, George, Moses M., and Herbert John were sent to the United States. Then Samuel Bojrab came to the United States in 1920. The story told by Herman Surber, Samuel Bojrab's son-in-law, was that the Bojrab family did not want their sons to go to war in Syria. Samuel told him: "It is the Syrian custom for the oldest sons to look after the younger sons."

They came by boat to Ellis Island. First they went to Bryan, Ohio, and then to Fort Wayne, Indiana. When Samuel arrived, he went to live with Moses M. until he found a place to live. Samuel Bojrab married Labebe (Libby) Slyby, also born in Bloudan, on April 20, 1920, at her father's home in Wilmington, Ohio. She came to the United States with her parents, Michael and Mary (Ferris) Slyby.

Not much is known about Halla (Helen), Assad, Abraham, or Mary. They stayed in Bloudan. Assad is said to have had three wives and a son by each wife.

David George Bojrab, the second born, came to the United States when he was very young. He married Sarah Abdullah when he was thirty-one years old. They had seven children: Sadie, Margaret, George David, Gladys, Peter Davis, Adele, and Isaac Paul. They all married and had families except for Adele who died in 1924 at age four. The ashes in a wood cook stove caught her dress on fire, and she was badly burned.

The Samuel Bojrab Family. Top, L to R: Mary, George W., Lucy. Bottom, L to R: Norman, Libby, Samuel

Moses M. Bojrab, the third born, married Mary (Hend) Khoury. They had five sons: Joseph, Imen, Fred, Charles Moses, and John. They also married and had families.

Herbert John, the fourth born, married Rahami (Ruth) Bojrab. They had three children: Albert, Rose, and John Herbert. Albert and John Herbert married and had families, but Rose never married. Herbert John Bojrab, lived to 101. He was born in 1882 and died in 1983.

Samuel Bojrab, the fifth child, married Labebe (Libby) Slyby. They had six children: Lucy, Norman, Roger, James, and George W. Lucy, Norman, Mary and George married and had families. Roger and James both died on the same day, June 28, 1927, of pneumonia. Roger was three years, seven months and 17 days old, and James was two years and 29 days old. Mary married but never had any children.

May God always bless this Bojrab family.

Submitted by Norman S. Bojrab, Jr.

BEDIA J. 'MIKE' BONAHOOM & LOUISE M. FARRAH FAMILY

Mike, son of Saleem and Sultana Bonahoom, was born in 1899 in Toledo, Ohio. He attended Hoagland Elementary School and Central High School. He enjoyed fishing and hunting and was a charter member of The Summit City Barbershop Chorus.

In 1929 he married Louise, (born 1910) daughter of Charles Farrah and Najeebe Etoll of Williams County, Ohio. They lived in Indianapolis for the first eight years where Mike was the Superintendent of Sears Roebuck and Co., then the biggest Sears store in the country.

In 1937, after the death of his uncle, Otto Bonahoom, owner of the Dairy Lunch restaurant, he moved to Fort Wayne to manage the restaurant. About 1946, he and his brothers, Isay and Fuad, divided the building at 128 West Main Street into two parts, a smaller restaurant owned by his brother, Fuad, called "Bonnie's Grill," and a cigar store and card room, called "Main Cigar Store," owned by him and his brother Isay.

Bedia 'Mike' Bonahoom and Louise Ferrah Bonahoom

About 1940, Mike's Aunt Anna Maloley bought a house and three acres of land on Brooklyn Avenue. She gave the house to Fuad, and built a double house which she gave to Isay and Mike, and a single house for herself, all right next door to each other. After Anna died, Mike's widowed sister, Selma Bonahoom, was given Anna's house for her and her two children Mike and Norm. The three brothers and the sister with their eleven children lived on Brooklyn Avenue for over twenty years, freely going in and out of one another's homes and enjoying a unique family community which bound all the cousins together as brothers and sisters. Before TV, the fathers and the children would gather around Aunt Selma's baby grand piano and sing songs which she played using sheet music from 1899 to 1950. Otto still knows the words to almost all of the songs of the era from pops, classical and musicals. All of the Bonahoom siblings attended St. Joseph's Catholic Church and School and Central Catholic High School.

Mike retired about 1960 and died in 1965 leaving Louise and three children, Otto M. Bonahoom, Mary Lou Zarick, and Tatla A. Dager. At his funeral, the funeral director at Mungovan and Sons asked Otto what his father had done because his was the largest funeral they ever served. He was particularly impressed by the fact that all the visitors seemed to be personal friends of Mike who were relating to each other of the many kindnesses they had received from him.

Louise, who is 94 as this is written, was born on a farm in Williams County, Ohio, received a grammar school education in a one room country school, attended Ravenscroft Beauty School about 1951, passed the state exam with the highest grade and was a beautician on Brooklyn Avenue for over 25 years. She has 17 grandchildren, 41 great grandchildren and one great great grandchild.

This article was written by Otto M. Bonahoom and submitted by Philip S. Bonahoom

ELIAS J. & ANGELINE M. BONAHOOM FAMILY

Angeline Bonahoom was the fourth of five children of Saleem (Sam) and Sultana (Mary Bonahoom. She was born in Fort Wayne, Indiana, January 21, 1910. Angeline never knew her father's parents because they never came to this country. She did know her mother's parents, whom she lived with for several years in their home on Wiebke and Lafayette streets.

Angeline attended Hoagland elementary school and Central High School.

Her mother loved music and encouraged her children to play some instrument. She especially loved the piano. Her family purchased a piano, and Angeline learned to play very well. She was taught by her sister Selma who herself never had a lesson. Music was a very important part of the Bonahoom family. All of her brothers and sister were very musically talented.

Angeline met and married Elias Joseph Bonahoom, who had the same last name, but who was from another Bonahoom family. He was the brother of Michael who was married to Angeline's sister, Selma. She met Elias while visiting her sister, Selma, in Chicago. After her marriage, she moved to Chicago where her husband worked as a truck driver. They had two children: a son John, who was born on July 18, 1931, and who died a few days after birth of an RH blood disorder, and a daughter, Stephanie, who was born on June 24, 1935. Angeline lived in Chicago, Illinois, until 1943. In that year Her sister Selma's husband, Michael, died of pneumonia. After Michael's death, Selma moved back to Fort Wayne with her two children. Angeline and her husband, Elias, and daughter, Stephanie,

Angeline M. Bonahoom and Elias J. Bonahoom

also moved back to Fort Wayne into a home on Calhoun Street, which was left to them by an aunt, Anna Maloley.

Angeline worked as a secretary for Michael Stephan, who was the owner of Stephan Candy and Tobacco. She held that job for several years. When the Stephan Candy and Tobacco business closed, she worked in the Wayne Township Assessors office for Walter Summers, who was the Wayne Township Assessor. Angeline was very active in Republican politics in Allen County. In addition to her love of music, Angeline loved working with ceramics and playing cards.

Angeline died on December 27, 1968 at the age of 58. She left one daughter, Stephanie Bonahoom Ewing, and her husband, Elias, and three grand children, Robert Timothy, Stephen Paul, and Jennifer Angel. Her husband, Elias, died on February 12, 1972, at the age of 74, and her daughter Stephanie died on July 15, 1986 at the age of 51.

This article was written by Angeline's nephew, Michael J. Bonahoom, and submitted by her nephew, Philip S. Bonahoom.

FUAD GEORGE BONAHOOM GARNET RICHARDSON BONAHOOM FAMILY

Fuad G. Bonahoom (Bonnie) was the fourth of five children born to Saleem and Sultana Bonahoom. Fuad's siblings are older brothers Isay and Mike, older sister Selma, and younger sister Angeline. Fuad, along with his family, spent his early years living with his mother's parents at 3404 Lafayette Street. Several years later, he moved with his family to a building at 1828 South Calhoun Street that his father bought to operate a fruit business and to house his family. Like his brothers and sisters, he attended Hoagland elementary school and Central High School.

Fuad's mother loved music and encouraged her children to play some instrument. Fuad played the piano, banjo, ukulele, and had a beautiful singing voice. He sang in a barbershop quartet for many years and enjoyed having his only son, Jim, sing with him in the quartet. Fuad and his brother, Mike, were also charter members of the Summit City Barbershop Chorus. Having inherited his grandfather, Nihmie's, love of hunting and fishing, he spent many hours at those activities also sharing the fun with his son, Jim. Fuad was a Ham Radio enthusiast (W9YQV), and loved riding one of his several motorcycles.

Fuad married Garnet Richardson, daughter of Alva Richardson and Elizabeth Mae Knapp, on December 31, 1926 in St. Patrick Catholic Church, Fort Wayne. Children of Fuad and Garnet are: Barbara June Bonahoom Davenport, James Bonahoom, Wanda Bonahoom Schrader, and Judith Ann Bonahoom Attar. Grandchildren of Fuad and Garnet are Kevan, Keith, Kim, Kerry, Kirk, Kent and Kelley Davenport, Kathy Davenport Novak, Kristin Davenport Delauney, Karen Davenport Robertson; Stephen and Kevin Bonahoom, Julie Bonahoom Kincaid, and Jamie Bonahoom; Rick Schrader, Lisa Schrader Deville, Lori Schrader Koval, and Renee Schrader Bender; Andy, Jeff and Scott Attar, Jody Attar Gee, and Jennifer Attar.

Like his brothers, Isay and Mike, Fuad worked many years in the Bonahoom family businesses, The Dairy Lunch Restaurant, although he worked for a while in the old Wayne Knitting Mills in the west end of Fort Wayne. Fuad operated his own business for a few years when he and his brothers partitioned the building housing the family business into two sections. He operated Bonnie's Grill at 126 West Main Street. Later Fuad became a deputy sheriff for 16 years. Being interested in politics, Fuad served as a Republican Precinct Committeeman for many years and as City Clerk for the City of Fort Wayne.

Faud G. Bonahoom and Garnet Richardson Bonahoom

Garnet, in addition to helping Fuad in his restaurant, was a housewife, raising her four children and providing a loving nurturing home for her family. Garnet was a very independent woman and she instilled a great sense of independence and self-reliance in all of her children and grandchildren.

Birth and death dates on above mentioned people: Fuad G. Bonahoom March 26, 1907-July 28, 1974; Isay Bonahoom March 3, 1898-October 11, 1949; Mike Bonahoom December 26, 1899-February 28, 1965; Selma Bonahoom June 26, 1904-January 31, 1999; Angeline Bonahoom January 21, 1910-December 27, 1968; Garnet Richardson December 24, 1906-May 1, 2003; James Bonahoom January 31, 1929-September 27, 1966.

This article submitted by Judith A. Bonahoom Altar and written by Philip S. Bonahoom Sr. on behalf of the children of Fuad and Garnet Bonahoom

ISAY C. BONAHOOM ADELLE ESSI BONAHOOM FAMILY

Isay Bonahoom was the oldest son of the oldest son and first of five children of Saleem and Sultana Bonahoom. He moved to Fort Wayne with his parents, a brother Mike, and a sister Selma, in 1906. Isay never knew his father's parents because they never came to this country. He did, however, know his mother's parents very well and lived with them for several years in their home at 3404 Lafayette Street along with his whole family which grew by one brother, Fuad, and one sister, Angeline.

Isay attended Hoagland elementary school and Central High school where he was active in sports. Isay enlisted in the Army in 1917 during the First World War but saw no overseas duty. He achieved the rank of Corporal before being honorably discharged in 1919.

Upon returning home Isay spent some years working on the Police force and then worked in the family business on West Main Street. After the death of his uncle, Otto Bonahoom, in 1937, Isay, along with his brothers, Mike and Fuad, took over the family business on west Main Street. In the late 40s, they partitioned the building on west main and ran two businesses. Isay, and Mike ran a card room and cigar store, "Main Cigar Store", until Isay's untimely death in 1949, at which time Mike became sole owner of the business. Isay took after his maternal grandfather, Nihmie, in his love of hunting and fishing. He would visit his cousin Dick Bonahoom, in Raton, New Mexico, and go Elk hunting. He also loved local lake fishing and deep-sea fishing. Isay liked attending business conventions around the country with his friend, Mike Stephan, and was an avid card player.

On January 15, 1936, he married Adelle Essi from Bryan, Ohio, one of nine children of Assid Essi and Minnie Etoll of Bryan, Ohio, both immigrants from Zahleh, Lebanon. As a young lady, Adelle worked in Toledo, Ohio, at the Inverness Country club where she also played an occasional round of golf and collected autographs of some celebrities who played there. After her marriage to Isay, she worked in the Bonahoom family restaurant, but mostly stayed home to raise her two children. A few years after the death of her husband, Adelle went to work running the new school cafeteria at St. Joseph's Catholic Church on Brooklyn Avenue until her retirement in the early 1970s. Living close to her children and grandchildren allowed Adelle to enjoy her retirement by spending much time with them until her death in 1991.

Isay C. Bonahoom and Adelle Essi Bonahoom

Children of Isay and Adelle are Philip S. Bonahoom Sr. and Luconda A. Bonahoom Nusbaum. Grandchildren are Philip S. Bonahoom Jr., Renee Lynn Bonahoom Sakri, Rachele Marie Bonahoom Fiddes, Scott Anthony Bonahoom and Luconda Susan Bonahoom.

Birth and death dates of those mentioned above: Isay Bonahoom, March 3, 1898-October 11, 1949; Mike Bonahoom December 26, 1899-February 28, 1965; Selma Bonahoom June 26, 1904-January 31, 1999, Fuad Bonahoom March 26, 1907-July 28, 1974, Angeline Bonahoom January 21, 1910-December 27, 1968; Adelle Essi March 29, 1903-October 8, 1991; Assid Essi 1885-June 6, 1920; Minnie Etoll, July 15, 1875-

July 27, 1938; Luconda A. Bonahoom Nusbaum July 24, 1939- August 8, 2001.

Submitted by grandson, Philip S. Bonahoom Jr.

MICHAEL J. BONAHOOM, ANNA MARIE MOHRE BONAHOOM FAMILY

Michael is the eldest of two children of Selma Bonahoom and Michael Bonahoom. His brother, Saleem Norman, was born two years after Michael. Michael and S. Norman were both born in Chicago, Illinois, where they lived until their father died, in 1943. The family then moved to Fort Wayne, Indiana. Michael attended St. Joseph Catholic Elementary School and Central Catholic High School. He graduated from high school in June 1949. He attended the University of Dayton and graduated in 1953 with a BS degree in Education.

On June 27, 1953, he married Anna Marie Mohre in Blakeslee, Ohio. They lived in Fort Wayne, Indiana until September 1953 when Michael took a teaching job in Cromwell, Indiana where he taught for one year. On May 7, 1954, their first child, Diane Marie, was born, and on June 6, 1954, Michael was drafted into the Army. On June 18, 1955, while Michael was serving in the army, their son, Michael Joseph III, was born in Montpelier, Ohio.

Michael J. Bonahoom and Anna Marie Mohr Bonahoom

Michael was discharged from the army on May 7, 1956. He and his family moved to Bloomington, Indiana, where Michael attended Indiana University, and earned a Masters Degree in Counseling and Guidance. While in Bloomington, their third child, Catherine Ann, was born on April 16, 1957.

In September 1957, Michael took a teaching job at New Haven High School as an English teacher. In 1959, he became a school counselor, and in 1961 he was appointed Assistant Principal. On June 3, 1959, their fourth child, Matthew John was born, and on May 9, 1962 their fifth and last child Regina Louise was born.

In January 1972, Michael was appointed Principal of the new Paul Harding High School. The School opened in September 1973. Michael served as Principal for fifteen years. In 1988, he left the Principal's job to take the position of Coordinator of State and Special Programs for the East Allen County Schools.

In June 1992, Michael retired from the East Allen County Schools, and in 1994, Anna Marie retired form the Fort Wayne Community Schools, where she worked as a Library aide for over twenty years. Both Michael and Anna Marie are avid bridge players. They are Life Masters and belong to the American Contract Bridge League and the Fort Wayne Duplicate Bridge Club. Michael is a certified bridge director and served many years as President of the Fort Wayne Duplicate Bridge Club. Together with Anna Marie, they run two bridge games a week.

Michael and Anna Marie are enjoying their retirement and spending time with their ten grandchildren: Anna Marie and Matthew Ensley who live in Fort Wayne; Heather and Katrina Bonahoom who live in Warsaw; Indiana; John and Michael Arnett who live in North Potomac, Maryland; Steven and Joseph Bonahoom, who live in Columbus, Ohio; and Phillip and Rachel Talarico, who live in New Haven, Indiana.

Submitted by Michael J. Bonahoom, Jr.

SELMA B. BONAHOOM MICHAEL J. BONAHOOM FAMILY

Selma Bonahoom was the third of five children of Saleem (Sam) and Sultana (Mary) Bonahoom. She was born in Toledo, Ohio, June 26, 1904. She moved to Fort Wayne, with her parents around 1906. Selma never knew her father's parents because they never came to this country. She did know her mother's parents, whom she lived with for several years in their home on Wiebke and Lafayette streets.

Selma attended Hoagland elementary school and Central High School. She had to leave high school at the end of her second year because of the death of her mother. Being the oldest girl in the family, she had to assume the responsibilities of taking care of the family. She had two older brothers, Isay and Bedia (Mike) and two younger siblings, Angeline and Fuad, as well as her father.

Selma's mother loved music and encouraged her children to play some instrument; she especially loved the piano. Her brother Mike purchased a piano for the family, and Selma learned to play very well (never having taken a lesson). Music was a very important part of the Bonahoom family. All of her brothers and her sister were very musically talented.

Selma met and married Michael Joseph Bonahoom, who had the same last name, but who was from another Bonahoom family. They were married on Selma's twenty-first birthday June 26, 1925. After her marriage, she moved to live in Chicago where her husband worked as a mail carrier. They had two children, Michael Joseph Jr. who was born on September 14, 1931, and Saleem Norman, who was born on December 30, 1933. Selma lived in Chicago, Illinois, until 1943 when her husband, Michael, died of pneumonia on May 18. After Michael's death, Selma moved back to Fort Wayne with her two children. Michael and Norman grew up in a home on Brooklyn Avenue which was left to her by her aunt, Anna Maloley. It was one of four adjacent homes, three of which belonged to Selma's brothers. Michael and Norman were reared in close proximity to their cousins, aunts and uncles, which provided for much love, affection and guidance.

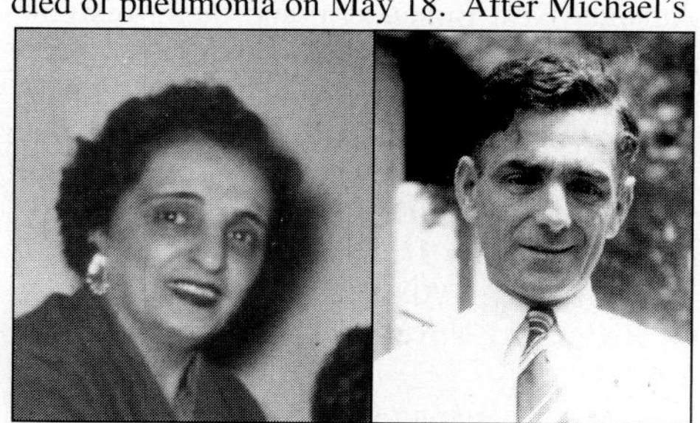

Selma B. Bonahoom and Michael J. Bonahoom, Sr.

She worked in the family restaurant, the Dairy Lunch, which was located on Main Street and was owned and operated by her, and her brothers and sister. When the restaurant closed in 1949, she took a job with Fishman's, a woman's clothing store in Fort Wayne. She worked for the Fishman brothers as one of their top salespersons until she retired in 1979. She also worked in the Fort Wayne City Clerks office for her brother, Fuad, who was City Clerk.

Selma died on January 31, 1999 at the age of 94. She left her two son's, Michael and S. Norman, nine grandchildren: Diane (Ensley), Michael III, Catherine (Arnett), Matthew, Regina (Talarico), Barbara (Rumsey), Gregory, Brian, and James, and fifteen great grandchildren.

Submitted by Bryan Bonahoom, grandson, and written by Michael J. Bonahoom

OTTO M. BONAHOOM FAMILY

Otto M.Bonahoom, son of Bedia J. "Mike" Bonahoom and Louise Ferrah, was born November 5, 1930 in Fort Wayne, Indiana. On July 30, 1955, he married Jane E. Nemoir (born November 9, 1933) of Milwaukee, Wisconsin, in Nurnberg, Germany, where he was stationed in the army. While there, they honeymooned in Garmisch and visited every major and minor city in West Germany, Paris, Amsterdam, London, Florence and Rome. They had six children: Elizabeth(Partee), Therese(Cera), Mark, Joseph, Mary Lou (Mettler) and Christine (Nix), and twelve grandchildren.

Otto graduated from Central Catholic High-School (1948) and received an A. B. (1952) and a J.D. (1954) from Marquette University. He was elected State Representative from Allen and Whitley Counties (1963-64), served as Allen County Probate Commissioner (1965-75), president of the Allen County Bar Association (1972), and the Indiana Bar Foundation (1992). He was a co-founder and first president of the Martin Luther King Montessori School and Vincent House Home for the Homeless and attorney for Matthew 25 for twenty years. A past president of the Quest Club, Otto was the host and producer of *The Elder Angle* , a weekly one hour, live talk show on WGL radio, and a monthly half hour show of the same name on WFWA TV.

All six of Jane and Otto's children graduated from Bishop Dwenger High School where Jane chaired "Saints Alive", it's most successful fund-raiser. For the St. Joseph Hospital Auxiliary, Jane chaired a fund-raiser never before attempted in Indiana. She led her committee in purchasing a lot in North Point Woods, approving house plans, signing a building contract and selling enough raffle tickets in 2 weeks to donate over $300,000 to the Children's Unit of St. Joseph's Hospital. Jane was a co-founder and a president of the Allen

Otto and Jane Bonahoom

County Lawyer's Auxiliary and a Board Member of the Indiana Lawyer's Auxiliary. Jane is also an extraordinary chef, preparing gourmet meals for her family and friends and also preparing eight-course Lebanese Dinners for charity auctions. Otto and Jane are avid theatregoers actively supporting First Presbyterian Theatre and the Civic theatre and attending the Shakespeare Festival (Stratford, Ontario) and the Shaw Festival (Niagara on the Lake, Ontario).

Elizabeth was a legal receptionist and is presently employed by Parkview Hospital's Food Service Division. Therese, Mark, Joseph and Christine all graduated from Marquette University. Therese is married, lives in Wauwatosa, Wisconsin, has five children, and is the Wauwatosa Substitute Teacher Coordinator. Mark is single, the business manager for Hospital Laundry Services, is a champion barbershop quartet singer and a low-handicap golfer. Joseph is married, has three sons, is an attorney, the attorney for the Fort Wayne City Council, and a licensed Sports Business Agent. MaryLou is married, has two children, graduated with honors from Purdue University, and has been employed as a pharmacist at Parkview Hospital since graduation. Christine is married, has two children, was Director of Communications for the Diocese of Fort Wayne-South Bend for 14 years and owns Christine's Cuisine- Lebanese Tradition.

Submitted by Joseph G. Bonahoom, son of Otto and Jane

PHILIP S. BONAHOOM, MARY S. STRAUB BONAHOOM & LUCONDA A BONAHOOM NUSBAUM, WELDON N. NUSBAUM FAMILIES

Luconda Bonahoom was the eldest of two children of Isay Bonahoom and Adelle Essi Bonahoom. Philip S. Bonahoom, her brother, came along a couple of years later. Philip and Luconda grew up in one of four adjacent homes on Brooklyn Avenue belonging to their father and their father's two brothers and one sister. Being reared in close proximity with their cousins, aunts and uncles, provided a unique opportunity for much additional love affection and guidance. They attended elementary school at St. Joseph's Catholic School and Central Catholic High School. Luconda and Philip both attended International Business College in downtown Fort Wayne, she for a secretarial degree, and he for an Associate BSC in Business Administration and Finance.

Luconda married Weldon N. Nusbaum of Harlan, Indiana, second of four children of Nicholas Nusbaum and Francis Ashton, and worked as an Executive Secretary in Fort Wayne until her death in 2001. She had no children. Luconda's big joy in her life was spoiling her nieces and nephews and those of her husband, Weldon, buying them clothes and gifts at Christmas and on their birthdays. She loved seeing the joy in their eyes upon receiving these gifts, as the gifts were always well chosen, unique and of fine quality.

Philip married Mary Susan Straub of Fort Wayne, third of five daughters of Anthony J. "Tony" Straub, an immigrant from Germany, and Rita G. Redmerski. Philip worked at Wolf & Dessauer Department Store, Allstate Insurance Co., Peoples Trust Bank and Lincoln National Bank, retiring from Wells Fargo Bank after a 28-year banking career. Philip was involved in local Republican politics as a Precinct Committeemen, Delegate to several Republican State Conventions, and two-time candidate for City Council at Large. Philip was very involved in community affairs, belonging to several service clubs and serving on the Embassy Theatre Foundation Board of Directors for seven years, three years as that organization's second President. Phil sang for many years with the award winning Summit City Barbershop Chorus and a quartet he organized, 'The Fourtinears'.

L to R: Philip S. Bonahoom and Mary S. Straub Bonahoom, Luconda A. Bonahoom Nusbaum and Weldon N. Nusbaum

Having now retired, Philip enjoys spending time with his five children and four grand children, working on his family's genealogy, playing golf and lively discussions with his friends. The children and grandchildren of Philip and Mary are Philip S. Jr., his wife Cindee Carper Bonahoom and his son Philip Scott Bonahoom; Renee Lynn Bonahoom Sakri, her husband Hunar Fiasal Sakri and their son Ary Hunar Sakri; Rachele Marie Bonahoom Fiddes, her husband Phillip Alan Fiddes and their two daughters, Kelsey Ann Fiddes and Ericka Marie Fiddes; Scott Anthony Bonahoom and his wife Amanda West Bonahoom; and their youngest child Luconda Susan Bonahoom.

Birth and death dates on persons mentioned above: Luconda Bonahoom July 24, 1939-August 8, 2001; Nicholas Nusbaum October 10, 1909-March 2, 1999; Francis Ashton January 30, 1909-January 21, 2003; Anthony J. "Tony" Straub June 1, 1908-November 3, 1990; Rita G. Redmerski November 14, 1917-August 3, 1995.

Submitted by Scott A. Bonahoom, son of Philip S. Sr.

SALEEM NORMAN BONAHOOM, PATRICIA A. MORAN BONAHOOM, & PATRICIA J. CENTLIVRE PIERCE BONAHOOM FAMILY

Norman was the youngest of the two sons of Selma and Michael Bonahoom. His brother Michael Jr. was two years older. Both were born in Chicago, Illinois, where they lived until 1943 when their father passed away. At that time Selma moved the family to Fort Wayne in order to be closer to her family. There were four houses next to each other on Brooklyn Avenue that were owned by the Bonahoom families, and they grew up very close to their aunts, uncles, and cousins.

Norman attended St. Joseph's elementary school and Central Catholic High School. He was very active in sports and had an academic scholarship to Central Catholic. One year after graduating from high school (1953) Norman joined the US Air Force for four years. While stationed at Lowery AFB in Denver, Colorado, he met Patricia Moran. She was an operating room nurse at one of the local hospitals. On August 31, 1957 they got married in Nashville, Illinois, a few days after Norman's discharge from the Air Force. Norman entered Purdue University in September of 1957 and received a Bachelors degree (1961) and Masters degree (1962) in Electrical Engineering. In March of 1961 Norm and Pat were blessed with their first child, Barbara Marie, while living in West Lafayette, Indiana.

In September of 1962 the family moved back to Fort Wayne where Norman went to work for ITT Industrial Laboratories. Also in September a son Gregory Norman was born. Norman worked for ITT for 11 years before changing to Magnavox, also located in Fort Wayne. During those 11 years Norman and Patricia were blessed with two more sons, Bryan Joseph (1965) and James David (1971).

In February 1981 Patricia died of colon cancer. Barbara and Gregory were in college and Bryan and James were still in High School and Grade School respectively. Patricia's death had a tremendous impact on the family, but they had lots of support from their extended family and many close friends. In June of 1981 Norman met Patricia J. Centlivre Pierce, a former high school classmate. She had lost her husband about two years earlier and had six children. They were married on December 26, 1981.

Norman's career progressed through engineering, management, and he was Vice president of Business Development when Magnavox was acquired by The Carlyle Group who later sold it to Hughes Electronics, and was later bought by The Raytheon Co. Most of his career was spent in the area of advancing the science of Air Traffic Control Automation. He retired from the Raytheon Co. in 1998 and continued working part time as a consultant for ITT Aerospace Communications Division. He took up woodworking and enjoyed building things for his 8 grandchildren and his 17 step grandchildren. He also enjoyed golf and spending time with his wife landscaping their new house.

Submitted by S. Norman Bonahoom

BONAHOOM FAMILY IMMIGRANTS

The Bonahoom families in Allen County started with the immigration of two separate Bonahoom families from Lebanon.

Saleem (Sam) Bonahoom*, the oldest of seven children born to Barakat Bonahoom and Mulaka Kassouff both of Zahle, Lebanon, was in his early 30s when he and several siblings immigrated from Zahleh, Lebanon to Chicago in the early 1880s.

Lauconda Rahal Bonahoom* was a woman in her early 40s when she immigrated to Fort Wayne from Zahleh, Lebanon in the late 1880s. She was a woman of tremendous courage and strong determination to succeed and she began life here as a peddler and sold her goods walking from house to house. She saved enough money doing this to send for her husband, Nihmie Bonahoom* and their three children to come to live here with her. All three of Lauconda's children married and lived in Fort Wayne. Tatla, (Anna)* married Mike Maloley* in Fort Wayne and Abdow, (Otto)* married Schifica, (Eva) Bonahoom* in Fort Wayne in 1905.

Her oldest daughter, Sultana, (Mary)* married Saleem Bonahoom in Chicago on February 12, 1893 and they moved to Toledo, Ohio. Saleem and Sultana moved to Fort Wayne from Toledo around 1906 with their three children Isay, Mike and Selma. Sultana had also lost one infant child, Jamil. Son Fuad and daughter Angeline were born in Fort Wayne. By that time Saleem's in-laws owned a large home at 3404 Lafayette Street and he moved his family in with them for a few years. He later bought a building at 1828 South Calhoun Street to which he relocated his family. He operated a fruit store on the first floor at this site and lived on the second floor for several years. The children of Saleem and Sultana attended school at Hoagland elementary and Central High School.

Saleem was self educated and well read. He enjoyed reading the bible and studying various religions. His family was Catholic. He followed world events and loved to discuss them with knowledgeable people like his good friend Judge Mungovan. Saleem was a leader among the Arabic speaking community in Allen County. He settled arguments and family disputes for his fellow countrymen. His wife, Sultana, on the other hand was a very quiet, stay at home mother who worked very hard keeping house and raising her children.

Although Saleem lost his business to a fire in the spring of 1920 Saleem's in-laws were very successful in business. They started in the 100 block of East Main Street in Fort Wayne with the "Busy Bee Candies and Fruits" store in the early 1900s and ended with "The Dairy Lunch" Restaurant at 126 West Main Street during the 30s and 40s. Saleem's sons worked with their mother's family in their businesses helping build the businesses and providing themselves with employment for many years.

Saleem (Sam) Bobahoom and Sultana (Mary) Bonahoom

Saleem (Sam) Bonahoom 1858-1932, Lauconda Rahal Bonahoom 1857-1925, Nihmie Bonahoom 1854-1928, Tatla, (Anna) 1879-1940, Mike Maloley 1880-1918, Abdow, (Otto) 1882-1937, Schifica, (Eva) Bonahoom 1887.

This article submitted and written by Philip S. Bonahoom Sr. on behalf of the Bonahoom Family.

CHARLES LEWIS & MARY ETTA (PARKS) BONHAM

Charles Lewis and Mary Etta (Parks) Bonham were born in Greene County, Indiana, and were married there on November 8, 1896. They settled in Fort Wayne in about 1914, bringing with them their five children and Mrs. Bonham's widowed mother.

Mr. Bonham, the son of David Peter and Sarah J. (Ault) Bonham, was born December 31, 1871. His mother died in 1875, and his father subsequently married Martha Hatfield. He had a brother (Henry) and three half-siblings (Arna, Robert, and Martin). His paternal grandparents were Martin and Elizabeth (Heller) Bonham. His great grandparents, David and Tacy (Phillips) Bonham, left Fauquier County, Virginia, in the early 19th century and spent a few years in Ohio, where six of their eleven children were born, before moving on to Greene County. It has been reported that the Bonhams are descended from Nicholas Bonham, whose wife Hannah Fuller was the daughter of a Mayflower passenger. Mr. Bonham's maternal grandparents probably were Charles and Mary Ault, who were in Greene County by 1860.

Mrs. Bonham, the only child of Martin Wayne and Mary Jane (Todd) Parks, was born November 9, 1876. Her paternal grandparents probably were Philip and Mary Parks, who were living in Greene County by 1860. The Todd family settled in Wells County, Indiana, in 1851, having come from Beaver County, Pennsylvania. Mrs. Bonham's maternal grandparents were John Wesley Todd, who served briefly with the 101st Indiana Volunteers during the Civil War, and Abigail Glass, whose family was in Wells County by 1850. Abigail died August 24,1859. John Wesley Todd's second wife was Angeline Biddle; they had several children, and they were living in Greene County by 1880.

Mr. and Mrs. Bonham's children were:

(Charles) Lloyd, born July 1, 1898, whose wife was Martha Kyle. He died September 30, 1964, and Martha died March 29, 1977, both in Fort Wayne. They had no children.

(Marie) Lucile, born October 22, 1906, whose husband was Robert Carr. She died December 13, 1994 in Florida, and Bob died November 6, 2003 in Fort Wayne. Their children are: Barbara and Michael.

Hazel Maxine, born December 29, 1908; she died October 13, 2001 in Florida. She did not marry.

Virginia Grace (Tiny), born February 12, 1912, whose husband was Robert Weihe. She died February 15, 1991, and he died December 12, 1986, both in Florida. Their children are: Mary, Charles, Nancy, and Susan.

Walter Wayne, born January 23, 1913, whose wife was Gertrude Paulson. He died March 8, 1992, and she died March 13, 1999, both in Fort Wayne. Their children are: Walter, Mark, Louis, Judith, Kathy, and Terry.

Mr. Bonham worked for the Pelltier Funeral Home, and Mrs. Bonham worked in the alterations department of the Hutner-Paris store. Daughters Lucile and Hazel graduated from Central High School and son Walter graduated from North Side High School.

Mr. Bonham died March 12, 1950 in Fort Wayne, and Mrs. Bonham died January 21, 1946 in Fort Wayne. Both are buried in Lindenwood Cemetery, Fort Wayne.

Submitted by Barbara L. Carr.

WALTER W., SR. & GERTRUDE BONHAM

Walter Wayne and Gertrude (Paulson) Bonham, long time residents of Allen County, Indiana, were married on January 25, 1936 in Fort Wayne.

Walter, the son of Charles Lewis and Mary Etta (Parks) Bonham, was born January 23, 1913, in Lafayette, Indiana, moving to Fort Wayne with his parents about 1915. His mother died January 21, 1946, and his father died March 12, 1950, both in Fort Wayne. His parents were originally from Greene County, Indiana. His paternal grandparents were David Peter and Sarah J. (Ault) Bonham. His great grandparents were Martin and Elizabeth (Heller) Bonham.

Mrs. Bonham, the daughter of Axel John and Mary Maude (Shull) Paulson, was born June 14, 1917, in Fort Wayne, Indiana. Her father was born July 5, 1882 in Harplinge Haverdohl, Sweden. Her mother was born June 2, 1886. They were married July 21, 1904 in Butler, Indiana, and settled in Fort Wayne by spring of 1905. Mrs. Bonham's paternal grandfather, William Henning Palsson, migrated from Sweden to America and Muskegon, Michigan in the spring of 1891, and her grandmother, Nellie Augusta (Peterson), arrived on Labor Day, 1892. Soon after arriving, they changed the spelling of their last name to Paulson.

Mr. And Mrs. Bonham's children are: Walter Wayne, Jr., born February 18, 1937, whose wife is Betsy Ann Kidde; their children are: Stephen, Barbara, Susan, and Christopher. They have seven grandchildren. Mark William, born October 5, 1940, whose wife is Carol Raftree; they have no children. Louis Alan, born June 14, 1944, whose wife is Sandra Kay Dean; their children are Kelly and Craig. They have one grandchild. Judith Joan, born May 13, 1948. Kathy Sue, born August 2, 1957, whose husband is Keith Calvin; they have no children. Terry Lee, born July 26, 1960.

Mr. And Mrs. Bonham graduated from North Side High School, he in 1931 and she in 1935. Mr. Bonham worked for Rea Magnet Wire Company, serving as their purchasing agent for many years, retiring in 1975. Mr. Bonham was well regarded as an athlete in high school, participating in basketball and football. Following high school he played with several amateur baseball teams advancing to national championships three times.

He was inducted into the Fort Wayne Baseball Hall of Fame in 1991. He also was well known in the Fort Wayne area as a basketball referee. Mrs. Bonham worked several years as a part-time employee of the Fort Wayne Park Board. Being fond of dancing, she was also a tap dancer with the group called the "Alley Kats".

Mr. Bonham died March 8, 1992 in Fort Wayne, and Mrs. Bonham died March 12, 1999 in Fort Wayne. Both are buried in Covington Memorial Garden, Fort Wayne.

Submitted by Walter W. Bonham, Jr.

WALDEMAR & HILDA BORCHELT

Hilda Koenemann Borchelt was born on Columbus Day 1900. Her great grandparents, Johann Heinrich Meyer and Anna Catherine Bischoff Meyer, came to America on June 20, 1845 from Hanover Germany. Hilda, daughter of Edward and Sophia Koenemann, was baptized, confirmed and married at St. John Lutheran Church, Bingen.

She married Waldemar H. Borchelt on June 11, 1922. His great grandfather was born in Sundurn, Germany, near Engter, and relocated in Washington County Illinois, about 1840. He was the firstborn son of John and Augusta Borchelt, who moved to Fort Wayne when he was twelve years old. He was confirmed at Emmaus Lutheran School and sang solos in church when he was in grade school. He graduated from International Business College and worked for Bendix from 1939-1942, then he took a job in South Bend, Indiana, traveling northern Indiana and Ohio and southern Michigan. He worked for the Gray Company as an automotive sales representative until 1960. At that time he took the best job he ever had as business manager for Zion Lutheran Church.

They purchased a home at 2431 South Hanna Street in 1938, and lived there until 1963 after all the children were on their own. Hilda was a very concientious homemaker and mother of eight children: Raymond married Beverly Delp and raised seven Concordia graduates. Eileen married Rev. Charles Felton and raised four children in California and South Bend Indiana. Lucille married Tom Downey and raised four children in Tennesee and Philidelphia. Donald was a Navy pilot and died in an airplane crash in 1955 in Norfolk Virginia. Wallace married Ruth Strasser and raised eleven Concordia Lutheran High graduates; after Ruth's death, he married Reta Scheele. Kenneth married Lois Manne and raised four children in Hobart Indiana. Martha married Don Bielke who played basketball for the Zolmer Pistons, and then coached college ball in California where they raised three children. Carolyn married Roger Macke and raised ten Concordia Lutheran High graduates in Hoagland Indiana.

Hilda sewed, canned perfect jars of fruit and jelly, kept a spotless house and even ironed the handkerchiefs. She also made delicious economical meals and the children all loved her many soups. She taught her children the fundamentals of keeping a home in good repair and they all helped with the cleaning, canning, and laundry.

The children were all baptized and confirmed in the Lutheran Church and graduated from Concordia Lutheran High School.

First Row, L to R: Amanda Borchelt Carter, Hilda Koeneman Borchelt, Alvere Koeneman Gresley, Waldemar Borchelt. Second Row, L to R: Edith Koeneman Hilgeman, Clara Hoeneman Grotrian, Unknown, Edna Borchlet, Otis Borchelt

Hilda enjoyed working with the ladies from Zion Lutheran Church on the altar guild and ladies aid societies. She was also active with the flower shows for the grade school children and enjoyed the flowers in her yards.

Hilda and Wally enjoyed fishing and spent summers atAtwood and Diamond Lakes. The children enjoyed helping with the farm work and large garden at Atwood Lake and the various water activities at Diamond Lake. In their later years Hilda and Wally relaxed in a trailer camp at Atwood Lake.

Waldemar died in 1994 from complications following knee surgery. Hilda, at age 79, moved to the Lutheran Home, and lived till 2001. She did enjoy her 100th birthday party at the Sears Pavilion, Foster Park with 180 relatives and friends.

Submitted by Carrie Macke

DR. THEODORE R. BORDERS, EARLY AFRICAN AMERICAN DOCTOR

An early African American doctor in Fort Wayne, Dr. Theodore R. Borders paved the way for others of his race to set up practice in the Summit City. Borders came to the Summit City in 1931 after graduating from Howard University in Washington D.C. and serving his internship at General Hospital in Kansas City, Missouri. For a short period of time he was the only black doctor in Fort Wayne.

He was born in Rome, Georgia to a family of professionals and raised in Fort Worth, Texas. His father's name was Theodore R. Borders, and his mother was a Cherokee Indian. After graduation, a colleague encouraged him to come to Fort Wayne, Indiana where he opened an office on the second floor of the Masonic Lodge Building on Lafayette Street. He later married, and he and his family lived in the back of his office.

Fort Wayne was a hard place for Borders to start a practice, but due to shortage of doctors after the start of World War II, his practice increased. Borders was embraced by his patients; however it was with much difficulty that local hospitals agreed to accept him. He was not permitted to serve on any boards at the hospital, although he could serve his own patients, once admitted. Borders was eventually included to serve on the board at Methodist Hospital, now Parkview Hospital, after the insistenc of several white doctors.

Borders was very active in th community and belonged to a numbe of organizations. He was a dedicate doctor and made house calls. He woul sit up all night with his patients if neces sary. Dr. Borders was a friend to all. H died at the age of 58 from a heart attac in August, 1960.

Beatrice Elaine Borders

Beatrice Borders of Omaha, Ne braska, was raised in California. He father and mother were Henry an Lillian Black. Her father was the fir postman in Omaha, Nebraska, and th president of the NAACP. She marrie Dr. Theodore Borders in 1940 and cam to Fort Wayne where she found a highl segregated community. People of colc could not sit downstairs in the theaters; they ha to sit in the balcony. But they relegated her to th front because she looked caucasian. As the wi of a prominent doctor, Mrs. Borders became beacon for inclusion of African American aware ness within the community. She sat on the boar of the American Red Cross and was the first pe son of color to join the Fort Wayne Philharmoni Choral Group and Women's Committee, wi which she performed for nearly 30 years.

Theodore and Beatrice Elaine Borders

Despite the Borders' acceptance amon whites, a real row was raised when the coupl attempted to integrate a white neighborhood o North Anthony Boulevard, which today is a sec tion of grand old homes owned by many Parkvie doctors. "In 1954, we built this house," she sai from her living room, "and the whole town wer into an uproar. The Chamber of Commerce had meeting with us to say we couldn't build here an they wouldn't let lenders give us the money. Th only reason we could build the house was becaus they didn't know how we got the money." Whe neighbors in the area caught wind of the Border plans, they turned up en masse at the house. Mr Borders said she told her upset neighbors, "Wh do you want, when a person is highly educate and pays taxes? What is it that you want?" sh said. "And, when my husband walked into th room and he's as white as they were, they didn know what to say. One man even said, "I'm sorr I came on this mission."

Mrs. Borders was outstanding in her churc service at Turner Chapel A.M.E. where she serve as president and director of the choir for man years. She also served as a Trustee of the churc receiving the honor of Emeritus.

Mrs. Border served the community in many ıpacities, being former treasurer of the NAACP, former secretary of the Women's Medical Aux-ıary, and served on the cabinet under Mayor arold Zeis. She was co-founder of the Metro uman Relation Commission. She served on e 1976 Fort Wayne Bicentennial Committee. ne was also a board member of the Fort Wayne rban League and, formerly, Phyllis Wheatley ocial Center. Mrs. Borders was honored with e Sagamore of the Wabash Award on April 21, 984, by Governor Orrr, presented by the House Representatives, General Assembly for 63 ears of service to NAACP. She remained active the African American community and beyond r many years. She died March 4, 1998 after an xtended illness.

The children of Beatrice and Theodore Bor-ers are Theodore R., Jr. and Arthur C. Theo-ore has no children. Arthur's daughter, Diane orders, is currently in nursing school. She has daughter, Aniha Borders.

Submitted by Theodore R. Borders, M.D.

LARRY STEPHEN & JEANNE MARIE (GEBHARDT) BORNEFELD FAMILY

Larry and Jeanne Bornefeld settled in Fort Vayne, Indiana from Jackson, Michigan in 998. Previously, they had lived in Lanham, laryland.

Larry was born January 1, 1943 in Evansville, ıdiana to Robert Gustav, a tool and die maker, nd Valeda Josephine (Nett) Bornefeld. Jeanne as born August 1, 1945 in Evansville, Indiana Edwin Orville and Marie Agnes (Greminger) ebhardt. The three children of Larry and Jeanne e: Todd Allen, born May 31, 1965 in Evansville, ndiana, married Rebecca Kynczkowski and sides in Canton, Michigan; Brian Christopher, orn October 2, 1967 in Washington, D.C., mar-ed first to Julie Perkins. Their children are: Dusty cott and Carson Todd. Brian married second to isa (Richardson) Pezon and resides in Jackson, lichigan. Larry and Jeanne's daughter, Jen-ifer Marie, born May 6, 1971, in Washington, .C., married Jody Wolf and resides in Jackson, lichigan. Their children are: Michael, Thomas, atherine, Matthew (deceased), and Adam. Larry an electrical engineer who received a B.S. EE om Evansville University and an M.S. EE from lichigan State University. Jeanne is a musician nd family historian.

Larry's great-grandfather, Gustav, immigrated ith his parents and siblings from Dhunn, Rhein-and, Germany in 1848. His parents, Johann Karl ornefeld and Johanna Schmitz, died 1851 and 849, respectively. Larry's father, Robert, is a son f Alfred Bornefeld, who is a son of Gustav and is wife Bertha Jurgensmeier, a daughter of Her-nan Jurgensmeier and Dorothea Goeke. When he ied, Herman was President of the Zion Lutheran hurch in Posey County, Indiana. Alfred Borne-eld was a businessman who hauled coal for the nines in Evansville. He was married to Elizabeth ritz, a daughter of Charles W. and Wilhelmina arolina (Dormeier) Britz. Charles was a son of acob and Augusta (Goerlitz) Britz, who owned nd operated a leather business on Main Street in vansville. Wilhelmina Carolina Dormeier was daughter of William Dormeier and Wilhelmina

Larry and Jeanne Bornefeld.

Carolina Vespermann who were born in Hanover, Germany in 1837 and 1838, respectively.

Gustav Bornefeld was a carpenter who hand carved the woodwork in the old State Hospital building in Evansville. Some of his work is displayed in the Evansville Museum.

Larry's mother, Valeda Josephine (Nett) Bornefeld was the daughter of Joseph John and Monica (Grabowski) Nett. Monica was a daughter of August and Rosalia (Kott) Grabowski from Buthen, Silesia. August worked for the L & N Railroad. John's parents, Martin and Julia (Daslalske) Nett, from north of Warsaw, West Prussia, Germany, owned the Sunnyside Coal Company in Evansville, Indiana.

Jeanne's father, Edwin Orville Gebhardt, was a tool and die engineer in Evansville, Indiana and at General Electric in Louisville, Kentucky. He was a son of Frank Sydney and Laura Elizabeth (Becker) Gebhardt. Frank, like his father, operated a grocery and bakery on West Virginia Street in Evansville. Frank's sister Flo was in Ziegfeld's Follies and brother, Conrad, was a gold prospector in California. Frank's father, Frederick J. Gebhardt, was married to Clara Wambach, the daughter of Conrad and Margaretha (Röse) Gebhardt. Frederick immigrated with his mother, Fredericka Niebling, born in Denzlingen, Baden Germany in 1837.

Marie Agnes Greminger was born April 4, 1920 in Windthorst, Texas to Nicholas George and Catherine Marie (Schenk) Greminger. Catherine was a daughter of John B. and Mary Bernadina (Humpert) Schenk. John B. was a son of Valentine Schenk of Hatzenbuehl, Baden, Germany and Gertrude Reinbold of Wingersheim, Elsass, France. Valentine was previously married to Maria Eva Himmelsbach, who died at St. Wendel, Indiana. Mary Bernadina was a daughter of Frank and Mary Ann (Schenk) Humpert. Frank was a son of Francis Ernest and Margaret (Plesser) Humpert of Stockum, Westfallen, Germany. Mary Ann Schenk was a daughter of Gaudens and Theodora (Ferber) Schenk born Allagen, Westfallen, Germany, 1789 and 1796, respectively.

Nicholas Greminger's parents were Joseph and Mary Ann (Eisenmann) Gremminger. Joseph's parents were John and Barbara (Guethle) Gremminger. Mary Ann's parents were Joseph and Sophia (Brischle) Eisenmann. The Gremminger family is from Rammersweier, Baden and the Eisenmann family is from Hoffweier, Baden.

The Joseph Greminger family left Ste. Genevieve, Missouri and settled in Windthorst, Texas, the last German Colony in the U.S. named for Baron von Windthorst as a Catholic refuge. German Catholic families (Schenk, Humpert, Weinzapfel) came from Vanderburgh and Posey Counties, Indiana to found the Windthorst Colony (1891) as did people from Ste. Genevieve, Missouri. Nicholas and Catherine (Schenk) Greminger owned a ranch there and raised greyhounds. After they moved to Evansville, Nicholas worked for the L & N Railroad and Swift Packing Company.

Laura Elizabeth (Becker) Gebhardt's parents were John and Caroline (Hufnagel) Becker of Posey County, Indiana. John Becker, a carpenter, was the oldest son of Wilhelm Georg and Elizabeth (McGray/McCray) Becker. Elizabeth McGray/McCray became the servant of Johannes and Katarina (Heinzerling) Becker (of Neumorschen on der Fulda, Hesse) when her parents, James and Mahala Jane (Hawkins) McGray/McCray, born 1820 and 1821 respectively, suddenly "died on or before 13 February 1863" in Posey County, Indiana. They were married in 1844 in Ohio County, Kentucky and removed in 1859 to Posey County, Indiana. James (Cherokee) was part of the "Removal" in 1834-35. Mahala's parents were Aaron W. and Elizabeth A. (Madox) Hawkins who lived in Anderson County, Tennessee prior to coming to the Yellow Banks (Owensboro), Kentucky in 1818. Elizabeth was Powhatan/Cherokee. Aaron, who served in the War of 1812, was a son of Matthew Hawkins, who served in the Fincastle Militia (Virginia) in 1774. He also signed the Watauga Petition in 1776, one of the earliest Declarations of Independence. Matthew's parents were Nathan and Ruth (Cole) Hawkins of Baltimore County, Maryland and Sullivan County, Tennessee. Nathan's estate settlement was 1781-1783. They left Baltimore County, Maryland 1768-69 for the North of Holston Settlements with their children: Aaron, Matthew, Joseph, Wilson, John, Nicholas, Nathan, Rebecca (married John Crocket), Mary Elizabeth, (married David Lewis), and, Ruth (married Jonathan Webb). Nathan Hawkins' great-grandfather, John Hawkins the Mariner, a Quaker, sailed into Anne Arundel County, Maryland in 1651 from New England.

Jeanne is a member of "First Families of Tennessee". More information about these families can be found in "Once a Hoosier" by Jeanne Bornefeld.

Submitted by Jeanne Bornefeld.

BOSEKER FAMILY

William Louis Boseker (1875-1939), born at Cowling, Illinois, came to Fort Wayne in 1893, and dropped the letter "c" from Bosecker. He studied in Beloit, Wisconsin, and returned to Fort Wayne and worked as a tool and die maker for General Electric for the remainder of his life. He always walked to work twice a day, including lunchtime, from his home on Swinney Avenue to the plant on Broadway, although he was one of the first to own an automobile in 1914. He was quiet, warm, and thoughtful. He was bilingual in German and English. He enjoyed tinkering in a small machine shop in his garage. He married Adeline Reinking and they had three sons: Herbert, Lawrence, and Arthur.

Herbert William (1905-1995) married Helen M. Mueller. He was kind, friendly, generous, and almost never became upset. As a teenager, he rode his bicycle from west central Fort Wayne down the Wayne Trace Road to visit his maternal grandparents at their farm just west of Decatur, Indiana. There he learned to read and write German, his grandparents' day-to-day language. He was a long-time knitter at Wayne Knitting Mills. He became a good craftsman, especially in carpentry, and excelled at darts. He had two sons: Edward and William. Edward Herbert (1936), University of Michigan BS, Indiana University MD, University of Minnesota, and Mayo Graduate School MS in Medicine, is an orthopedic surgeon. He married Yvonne Park and lives in Santa Ana, California, and Lake James, Fremont, Indiana. Edward has four daughters: Andrea Lynn (1965), Susan Annette (1967), Resa Nadine (1972), and Tanya Ira (1967). William Charles (1939) Indiana University BA, a retired government fuel procurer, resides in Visalia, California.

Seated: William Louis Boseker and Adeline Boseker with three sons l. to r. Herbert William Boseker, Lawrence Edwin Boseker, and Arthur Frederick Boseker (about 1928)

Lawrence Edwin (1907-1992) married Alice Trout. He was tall, had a deep voice, had an outgoing personality, was the life of a party, and a great storyteller. He worked at General Knitting until WW II, when he served in the Navy and was partly responsible for shooting down Japanese suicide planes. Later, he became a postman. He had two sons: Warren and David. Warren John (1936-1979), married Marilyn Kurtz, and later married Linda Sweitzer. He had three children: Lisa Ann (1958), Warren John (1959), and Chris (1970). David Carl (1939-1996) married Judy Frankenstein and had two children: Michael Allen (1960-2001) and Angela Lynn (1976).

Arthur Frederick (1910-2003) married Erna Kruse. He was very pleasant, intelligent, and industrious. He was a tool and die maker and co-founder of General Tool and Die. He served as president of Orchard Ridge Country Club, and was an excellent golfer until age 90. He had three children: Kenneth, Larry, and Sheila. Kenneth Allen (1941), Valparaiso University BA, a self-employed CPA in Kendallville (retired), married Janet Long and is now married to Donna Martin and lives near Waterloo, Indiana. He has four children: Deanna Jo (adopted) (1962), Todd Allen (1967), Julie Lynn (1971), and Chad Ryan (1977). Larry Arthur (1942), Valparaiso University BSME & BA, Columbia University MBA, married Jennie Rohrdan and lives in Fort Wayne. He owns Royal Industries in Auburn and has researched the Boseker history. Larry has one son, Thomas Rohrdan (1994). Sheila Ann (1947) lives in Illinois.

The ancestors of William Louis were: William George (or George Wilheim) Bosecker (1847-1914 Adams County and is buried in Concordia Cemetery, Fort Wayne) who married Sophie Nahrwold. Also, Johannes Bosecker (1816-1896 Veilsdorf, Germany, and is buried in Mt. Carmel, Illinois) who left Germany with his wife and one son, an older brother (Karl), and a cousin named Peter, and immigrated to America in 1846 via the port of New Orleans, settling in Cowling, Illinois. Johannes' paternal ancestors were farmers near Veilsdorf, Saxony, Germany, including the following: Johannes Heinrich Bosecker (1771-1846). Johann Michael Bosecker (1743-). Johann Bosecker (1720-). According to the wife of the present Lutheran minister at Veilsdorf, family members were recorded back to the 1200s, but church records prior to 1650 are lost because of a church fire.

Submitted by Edward H. Boseker

BOSLER FAMILY

Henry Bosler was born 1809 in Stark County, Ohio. He married Margaret Studebaker in 1831. She was born 1815 in Miami County, Ohio to John and Hannah Ulrey Studebaker. Margaret was a descendant of the Studebaker family known for the manufacturing of wagons, buggies and automobiles in South Bend, Indiana.

Henry and Margaret lived in Sidney, Shelby County, Ohio, and moved to Eel River Township, Allen County in 1836. They were original land owners of 80 acres in the west half of section 12. Henry was a farmer and the first blacksmith in the township.

Henry and Margaret Bosler were the parents of four children: George, Mary, John, and Elizabeth. Mary married Samuel Black: Elizabeth married Moses Brubaker, both families lived in Illinois. John married Lydia Studebaker and Amanda Smith. John lived in Salem, Oregon.

After Margaret Bosler died In 1844, Henry Bosler married his deceased brother George's widow, Esther Mooney Bosler, in 1847. Esther and Henry were the parents of five children, three living to maturity: Isaac, Sylvia, and Nancy. George and Esther Bosler's two daughters, Mary Louisa and Sarah Jane, were raised in this home. Henry Bosler died 1865 and Esther 1868.

George Bosler, son of Henry and Margaret, was born in Ohio in 1833. He married Phoebe Ann Williams in 1855. Phoebe was born in 1836 in New York, the daughter of Peter and Ann Tripp Williams. George died in Eel River Township in 1890, and Phoebe died in Whitley County in 1914. George and Phoebe were the parents of Eugene, Albertus Henry, Florence, Cassius Milo, Edgar Ray, and Fay Augusta. Albertus and Fay were the only ones to marry.

Fay Bosler married Daisy Geiger and had two daughters, Mary and Elda. During the time of the labor union organization in 1922, Fay was murdered in Fort Wayne. It was not known if the motive was revenge or robbery. The crime remains unsolved.

Albertus Bosler was born 1859 and married Sarah Jane Sloffer 1884. They were both born in Eel River Township. Sarah was born in 1863 to Aaron and Suzanna Miller Sloffer. They first lived in Marshall County, Indiana where Albertus sold Flint & Walling windmills. They moved back to Noble County in the late 1880s, and then to Eel River Township. In 1911 a cement block home was constructed, and the home still stands today (2005) on the North Allen County Line Road. They had thirteen children: Carey born in 1885 married Frank Andrews. Nellie, born in 188[illegible] married Elmer Pepple. Verna, born in 1888, married Edward Hatch. Sylvia, born in 1889 married Chester Pepple. Alice, born in 1891 married Jesse Bolinger. Zeno, born in1892 married Walter Spitler. Eva, born in 1893 married Arly Smith. Elva, born in 1895, married James Fulk. Erma born in1897 married Howard Rhoads. Gloyd born in 1898 married Florence Bolinger. Howard born in1899 married Edith Gump. Edna, born in 1901 married William Hiller. Horace, born in 1903 married Marie Sloffer. Carey, Zeno, Gloyd, Erma, and Edna moved west and raised their families in California. Gloyd was a lumberjack. Edna was a registered nurse having graduated from Lutheran Hospital in Fort Wayne. Howard, a physician, spent many years on the mission field in Africa. Horace taught school and was a principal in the Fort Wayne area. Verna taught school prior to her marriage; she wrote speeches for politicians and traveled to Washington, D.C. and Cuba. Eva worked at the Auburn Rubber Factory. Some of the girls didn't work outside the home, but were dedicated to the well being of their families. The family was very active in the Pleasant Hill Dunkard Church.

Elva Alberta Bosler married James Frederick Fulk on November 18, 1914. They lived on the Fulk homestead in Eel River Township. Elva raised chickens, milked cows, taught Sunday School, gardened, and helped in the fields, along with cooking and sewing for her family. She designed and sewed her wedding dress. Elva and James had six children, Jacob Lynn, Lenora Ellen (Geiger), John, Jay, Lee, Jacob Earl, and Ruth (Arehart).

Submitted by Ruth A. Arehart

Bosler Family. In front, Edna. First row, L to R: Verna, Gloyd, Albertus Henry Bosler, Horace, Sarah Jane Sloffer Bosler, Howard, Erma, Elva. Back row, L to R: Zeno, Alice, Nellie, Carey, Eva and Sylvia

ARTHUR & ELAINE BOURIE

The Bourie family moved to Fort Wayne in 1952 from Richmond, California where Arthur Dale was employed by the Western Pacific Railroad and where the three children, Jane Elaine, Richard Dale and Barbara Anne, were born. Elaine Roberts married Arthur Dale Bourie in Van Buren, Ohio on March 10, 1944, while he was on leave during World War II. Both had grown up in the area.

They built a house at 8510 South Anthony in Fort Wayne where the family lived for forty-four years. Arthur Dale died in May 1994 having worked his entire life for the railroad, namely, Nickel Plate, Norfolk & Western, and Norfolk & Southern, as both a passenger and freight conductor.

After the children began elementary school at Hillcrest, Elaine Bourie began a forty-four year career as a professional secretary retiring from Lutheran Hospital Administration in 1990.

In 2000, Elaine began a new life with Albert E. Schmid, Jr., and they continue to enjoy living in New Haven, Indiana, and Pinellas Park, Florida, each for six months of the year. They both enjoy good health while cruising, dancing, golfing and traveling each year.

Arthur and Elaine Bourie Family. Arthur and Elaine in back. In front, Richard Dale, Barbara Anne, and Jane Elaine

All three Bourie children graduated from Elmhurst High School. Both Jane and Barbara received their bachelor and masters degrees from St. Francis College in Fort Wayne. Richard has both bachelor and Doctor of Veterinary Medicine from Purdue University in West Lafayette, Indiana.

In 1970 Jane Elaine Bourie married a St. Francis classmate, Russell Noel Grose, a Viet Nam veteran. Both are teachers and have a son, Rustan Dale, who graduated from Valparaiso University with a degree in business, and Janna Elaine, who just received her teaching degree from Manchester College. Rustan (Rusty) continued to follow his grandfather as a conductor for the Norfolk & Southern Railroad.

In 1971 Richard Bourie married a high school classmate, Carolyn Irene Frech, a graduate of Ball State University. They reside in New Glarus, Wisconsin, where Carolyn is employed by the State of Wisconsin Highway Department and Richard is a supervisor of Veterinarians in Madison Wisconsin. They have three grown children, Scott Allen, Stephanie Renee, and Suzanne Marie. Scott currently is a professional accountant and is completing his graduate degree. Stephanie has a degree in Health and Physical Education and operates her own business as a massage therapist at a sports complex in Merrill, Wisconsin. Suzanne lacks one year of completing her bachelor's degree in nursing.

Barbara Anne Bourie is a teacher in the Fort Wayne Community School System and is married to Robert Ervin Babbitt. He is a Korean War veteran and Material Inventory control specialist at Super Value Corporation in Fort Wayne, Indiana. They have two sons, Michael Robert and Matthew Scott. Michael attended Purdue University and is a woodworking specialist living in Warsaw, Indiana. Matthew holds a teaching degree from Ball State University and completed his masters in Sports Psychology at Ball State.

Submitted by Elaine R. Bourie

WILLIAM A. & DELIA C. BOURNE FAMILY

William Allen Bourne was born June 15, 1952 in Phoenix, Arizona, eldest child of Bruce Richard and Mildred Jane Jorgensen Bourne, of Chicago and East Chicago respectively. Delia Louise Cothrun was born October 30, 1953 in Lexington, Kentucky, youngest daughter of Pope Montgomery and Delia Burbank Holt Cothrun. Both the Bournes and the Cothruns lived in various states during the 1950s to 1970s. William and Delia met at the University of Arkansas in Fayetteville, graduated in 1974 and 1975 respectively, and married there May 29, 1975.

The couple moved to Fort Wayne from Fayetteville after William earned a master's degree in business. They lived first at the Wildwood Place Apartments on Portage Boulevard, and were living there during the Blizzard of 1978. They recall a snowdrift that came almost up to the roof in front of their door, although they could get out through the back door. After several days, and suffering from cabin fever, they walked up to the Scott's grocery which was then at Park West Shopping Center.

In December 1979, they purchased their first house, at 1002 Northwood Boulevard on the city's northeast side. The house badly needed painting when they moved in and William spent most of the spring and summer scraping and painting. In 1988, the family moved outside the city limits to 3422 Walden Run in the Community of Walden. They lived there through much of the annexation debate, moving in 2003 to Bridgewater in Aboite Township.

William worked in several businesses during their years in Fort Wayne. He was an active volunteer for many years with Junior Achievement as an advisor, center manager, both in Fort Wayne and Columbia City, and as an instructor in all level of the schools in Fort Wayne and Whitley County, receiving the Golden Achievement Award in 1997. He was also a member of the Walden Neighborhood Board, serving as secretary and working on the committee that rewrote the covenants. During the 1990s, he attended Indiana University-Purdue University at Fort Wayne to obtain a certificate in accounting. Delia started working in the Allen County Public Library's Reference Department in 1977, moving to the Genealogy Department in 1983.

Their daughter, Catherine Elizabeth, was born at Parkview May 22, 1984. She attended St. Jude's Catholic School, then St. Charles, and graduated from Snider High in 2002. She started dance lessons at the Rose Aimie Dance Academy in 1988, moving on to Northeast School of Dance in 1989, continuing there until she graduated from high school, working in her teen years as a class assistant and attending several competitions. She was a founding member of the Snider High Panther Pride Dance Team in 2000, staying with the team through graduation and working as an assistant coach for the team for the 2002-2003 season. She attended Indiana University-Purdue University at Fort Wayne for one year before transferring to Ball State University where she is majoring in accounting.

Submitted by Delia Cothrun Bourne

WILLIAM BOWEN

William Bowen, a pioneer of Fort Wayne, was born on October 4, 1806 in Chenango County, New York, and was a son of Calvin and Charlotte (Watson) Bowen. He was a descendant of Richard Bowen, a 17th century settler of Rehoboth, Massachusetts. On November 17, 1828, William married Charlotte Lindsey Ellerson, daughter of Daniel Ellerson Jr. and Lepha Bliss (Kingsley) and a grandson of David Ellerson, a Revolutionary hero and sharpshooter with Morgan's Rifleman. Charlotte was born on May 6, 1810 in Schoharie County, New York, and died at Fort Wayne on August 1, 1847. They had: David Ellerson, born August 29, 1829; Daniel W., born October 9, 1831; Rosina, born February 5, 1833; John Leroy, born August 29, 1839; and Rosetta America, born March 5, 1844.

Daniel Bowen

William moved with his family and parents to Monroe County, Michigan in 1836 and later to Plymouth, Indiana. Soon after this date he moved to Fort Wayne and opened a saddle shop on Columbia Street. After Charlotte's death he married in 1848 Loretta Cooper, who was born September 19, 1822. They had: George Rainsford, born June 10, 1850; William, born June 7, 1853; Julia Louretta, born March 8, 1856; and Clara, born April 13, 1857. William died on October 16, 1869; Loretta on March 30, 1880.

Daniel W. Bowen, son of William and Charlotte, was born in Broome County, New York and came to Fort Wayne with his parents in his youth. While attending college at South Hanover, Indiana, he married Mary Eliza Smith on November 14, 1854. She was born on November 12, 1832

Back: Mary Smith Bowen. Baby Evelyn Archibald, and center l to r: Julia Ransom Smith and Edith Bowen Archibald

at Salem, Indiana, the daughter of William and Julia Ann (Ransom) Smith and granddaughter of Israel Ransom, a Revolutionary soldier. Daniel practiced law for some time but gave up the practice during the Civil War to become a sutler. Later he returned to work as an attorney and also worked as a traveling agent. He belonged to both First Presbyterian and First Christian churches. The children of John and Mary were: Clara, born 1857, wife of L. R. Stout; Edward, born 1858, died young; Ada, born 1859, wife of J. C. Barnett; Edith, born March 3, 1863; and Lillie, born 1865, wife of John Wagner.

Edith Bowen, daughter of Daniel and Mary, married Abraham Fry Archibald on December 18, 1886. They had three children: Evelyn, Raymond, and Robert Kenneth. Edith was a member of Plymouth Congregational Church and died in Fort Wayne on February 7, 1939.

Submitted by John Beatty

BOWSER FAMILY

Henry J. Bowser, Sr., was born May 29, 1787 in Pennsylvania, and died January 10, 1870 in Perry Township, Allen County. He married Lenah, the daughter of Daniel Sprinkle and Christina Myers. They had seven children, John H., George W., Henry J., Lucinda, Theodore, Samuel, and William. In 1836, three of Henry's sons married daughters of Frederick and Elizabeth (Lindsay) Kariger, also from Pennsylvania.

The Children of Henry and Lenah:

John H. (1812 Pennsylvania -1879 Fort Wayne) married Eliza Keiger on July 14, 1836 in Perry Township. They had nine children. Among them was Sylvanus Freelove Bowser, born August 8, 1854, in Perry Township, and died October 3, 1938, in Fort Wayne. S.F. Bowser invented the Bowser gasoline pump.

GeorgeW. (1817 Pennsylvania -1888) married Margaret Kariger (1819-1913) on December 6, 1836, in Perry Township and had twelve children.

Henry J., Jr. was born 1820 in Pennsylvania and died July 26, 1888. He married Mary Kariger on June 17, 1836 in Allen County. She was born June 30, 1816 in Pennsylvania and died March 22, 1879. They had eleven children: Isaiah (1837); Adelia (1840); Elmira (1842); Lucinda (1843-1912 in Fort Wayne) married Solomon Duly; Alonzo (1844); Henry (1846); Wesley (1848); Theodore (1852); Frank and Francilla (about 1854); and Mary (1858). Henry J. Bowser, Sr., married, second, Catherine Williams. Their six children were: Maria, Lucy, Martha, Lewis (1838-1912), Levi born 1840 and Emma (1857-1895).

Samuel was born in Pennsylvania (1823-1891).

William was born 1824 in Ohio.

Theodore and Celia Bowser Family:Theo (1852-1927) married on Celia A. Gloyd (1856-1916) on October 7, 1875. She was also of Perry Township, daughter of George and Magdalene Gloyd, one of eight children. Theo and Celia had three sons, Raymond, Ivan, and Homer. Ivan C. (1880-1941) married Estella Archer. Homer G. (1889-1969) married Bessie Shoaff.

Raymond Ulysses Bowser was born September 17, 1878 in Perry Township, and died April of 1953 in Fort Wayne. At eighteen, he entered

Raymond Ulysses Bowser, 1878-1953

the Bowser factory, where he learned a trade as a mechanic and machinist. October 25, 1899 in Fort Wayne, he married Ethel Brockerman (1878 -1952). In 1900, they migrated just north to a farm in Dekalb. They had four children, Roy Ivan, Cleo Celia, Gale Theodore, and Ada Ethel. Roy Ivan Bowser was born October 2, 1902 in Spencerville and died March 29, 1988 in Butler. He married Catharine Kinsey (1903-1993). Cleo Celia (1905 -1995) married James Reed. Their daughter is Adair Alice Reed Schultz (1935). Gale Theodore (1908 -1989) married Janice Wade. Their sons are James (1931-1978) and Jerry (1932). Ada Ethel (1910 –) died 1994 in Highland, Indiana.) married Charles Whitacre. Their children are Ada "Yvonne" and Dorvin H. Whitacre. She then married Henry Sutter.

Roy Ivan Bowser lived in Saint Joe, Indiana, and had three children, the sixth generation of this family: April Dawn (1927-1987), Jo Anne (1934) and Jack Stewart Bowser, born February 11, 1931. Jack attended Culver Military Academy and served in the Navy. He married Sharon Smith, daughter of David Smith (Huntington) and Margaret Jane Skelton, on August 20, 1955. They celebrated their 50th anniversary. They and daughter, Catherine Jane (1960), live in Fort Wayne. Their son, Kim Stewart Bowser (1956), lives near Indianapolis.

Submitted by Jack and Sharon Bowser

ALFRED J. & BETTY J. (DEAM) BOWSER FAMILY

Alfred J. Bowser was born on September 13, 1935 in Fort Wayne, Indiana. Alfred's ancestor, Heinrich J. Bousser, emigrated from Switzerland about 1733. The second generation, after coming to America, changed the spelling from Bousser to Bowser. Alfred's great grandfather, Henry J. Bowser, moved from Pennsylvania to Allen County, Indiana and married Mary Keiger on June 17, 1836. Henry J. and Mary had eleven children: Malinda, Isaiah, Adelia, Almira, Frank, Alonzo, Henry J., Wesley, Theodore, Francilla and Mary Bowser. Henry J. Bowser owned a 120 acre farm in northern Allen County, Indiana. Frank Bowser married Anna Otto and they had seven children, Chester, Irene, Alberta, Ralph 0., Homer, Marie and Bessie Bowser.

Alfred J. & Betty J. (Deam) Bowser

Ralph O. Bowser was born July 11, 1889 in Warrensburg, Missouri and married Alice Havert June 24, 1913 in Fort Wayne. Ralph was a passenger conductor on the Pennsylvania Railroad most of his life. Alice was born April 6, 1893 in the Havert homestead east of Fort Wayne. Her parents were Theodore and Alice (Kelly) Havert. Ralph and Alice had seven children; Genevieve Bowser married Charles Fritz; Janet Bowser married Edward Fritz; Alice Bowser married Amos Bloomfield; Ralph E.Bowser married Jean Meads; Gerald Bowser died at the age of ten from diphtheria; Patricia Bowser married John Bloomfield; and, Alfred Bowser married Betty J. Deam.

After serving three years in the Army as a non-commissioned officer in charge of the Signal Corp, Radar Repair School, Alfred married Betty J. Deam on February 15, 1958. Betty's parents are Marcella (McKown) Deam and the late Ralph V. Deam who were married on September 16, 1933 in Fort Wayne, Indiana. Ralph was born August 5, 1912 in Fort Wayne, Indiana and Marcella was born August 23, 1914 in Madison, Wisconsin. Ralph was a machinist at Wayne Pump most of his life. Betty has three siblings, Bonnie Ruhl, currently from Winimac, Indiana, Linda Knittle and Marjorie Edwards, both from Decatur, Indiana. Alfred and Betty have three children. Thomas was born February 10, 1959 and married Ellen Carter on August 6, 1994. They have four children; Adam Bowser, Alicia Carter, Lauren Carter and Shauna Bowser. Thomas graduated from Indiana University with a degree in Commercial Art and is self employed. Anthony Bowser married Barbara Miserendino May 11, 1991 and they have four children; Aaron Bowser, Blake Bowser, Corin Bowser and Derek Bowser. Anthony Bowser graduated from Indiana University with Bachelors in Accounting and he is a CPA employed at Medical Protective in Fort Wayne. Theresa Bowser was born January 5, 1962 and she has a Bachelors in Anthropology from Indiana University, Masters in Archaeology from The Ohio State University and a Masters in Educational Administration from the University of Dayton. She is presently an Assistant Principal of Bishop Ready High School in Columbus, Ohio. Alfred has a Bachelor from Indiana Institute of Technology in electrical engineering and is retired from the North American Philips Corporation. Betty retired from Fort Wayne Community Schools.

Submitted by Alfred J. Bowser

WAYNE E. BOYD & LINDA L. JONES BOYD FAMILY

Wayne E. Boyd was born on March 11, 1940, in New Castle, Indiana. For the first eighteen years of his life he lived in Hagerstown, Indiana. His father, Ralph Boyd, was plant manager of the Hagerstown Perfect Circle plant. Margaret Foulke Boyd, his mother, worked as a telephone operator, beautician, and retired from the office of Perfect Circle/Dana. Wayne vividly recalls sharing grand times with all four grandparents and at least six great-grandparents.

Linda L. Jones was born on May 13, 1940, in Chicago, Illinois, to Earl D. Jones and Florence M. Sirrine Jones. Linda's only sibling, Dian M. Jones Devlin, was born on October 6, 1936. Earl's position with Libby, McNeill, and Libby dictated a number of family moves. During Linda's first four years of school, she attended five grade schools. Linda completed grade school in Chicago and then graduated from Nappanee High School in Nappanee, Indiana.

Upon completion of a degree in Engineering, Drawing, and Design from Tri-State University in Angola, Indiana, Wayne was hired by Mutschler Brothers in Nappanee, Indiana. Wayne and Linda met at work and were married in the Nappanee Methodist Church on May 5, 1961. They moved to Fort Wayne, Indiana, where Wayne was employed by the Wayne Pump Company.

1967 was a year of life-changing events for the Boyds. Christine Ann was born in April and in May they started their first company, Panco, Inc. Victoria Lynn was born in August 1968, joyfully completing their family. During the girls pre-school years, Wayne and Linda were foster parents for newborn babies through Lutheran Social Services.

In April 1969, the Boyds departed for their first major road trip. Their destination was Fort Myers Beach, Florida. Upon their return to Indiana, they purchased a cottage on Adams Lake. The cottage evolved through five remodeling projects and served the family for over thirty years.

Christine and Victoria attended Huntertown Grade School and Canterbury School, with both graduating from Carroll High School. Christine attended Purdue and completed her business degree from Indiana University in Fort Wayne. Victoria holds bachelor and master degrees in education from Saint Francis College, Fort Wayne.

Victoria married Michael G. Devine in June 1991. Their son, Alec Boyd Devine, was born in July 1996, and the family lives in Fort Wayne. Christine was married in 1994 and her son, Keaton Alexander Boyd, was born in October 1996. Christine and Keaton live in Jacksonville, Florida.

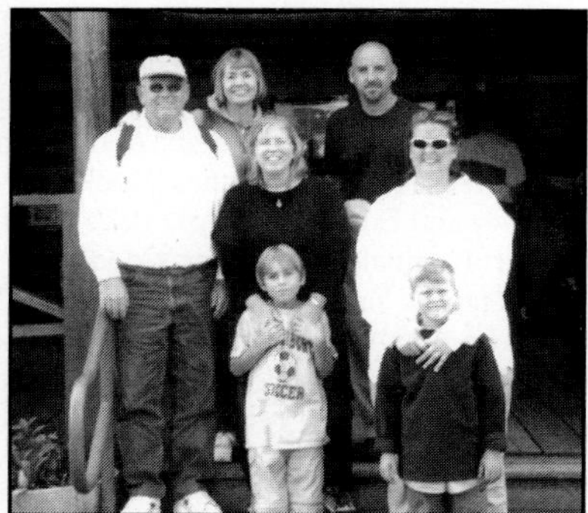

Front row: Alec Devine and Keaton Boyd. Middle row: Victoria Devine and Christine Boyd. Back row: Wayne and Linda Boyd, Michael Devine.

The family years found Wayne traveling a great deal, busily meeting the changing demands of a growing company. Linda completed a bachelor's degree from Indiana University in 1983. During this time she also served as a scout leader, Sunday school teacher, and served on the boards of Lutheran Social Services and the Y.W.C.A. Wayne retired in 1989 and the Boyds now divide their time between Sanibel, Florida, and Fort Wayne, Indiana.

Submitted by Wayne and Linda Boyd

DANIEL WADE BOYLAN & NANCY KATHERINE HAFFNER FAMILY

Daniel Wade Boylan and Nancy Katherine Haffner met while working on their Master's Degrees at Ball State University. Both were teachers and, when they married, decided to have a large family. They also decided to take foster children and had some seventy come in and out of their home in the next seven years. The family eventually had their own eight children: Andrew Wade (Carole Calland), Katherine Annette (Steven Fuelling), Sarah Elizabeth (G. Christopher Mattes), Nicholas Benedict (Susan Hunter), Daniel Haffner (Heather Hoffman), Adam Richard, Aaron Martin, and Theodore Kim. They also have had 20 grandchildren.

Daniel, born June 9, 1927, is the son of Francis Wade Boylan and Antoinette Hageman. Francis (called Wade) was born in Altoona, Pennsylvania, where his father, James, a brakeman on a train, was killed when Wade was only eleven days old. James' father, Joseph, was born in County Tyrone in Northern Ireland and had come to Pennsylvania to work on the railroad. Wade and his mother moved to Fort Wayne with other family members while he was in elementary school. Daniel has one brother, Ned Jerome Boylan. Antoinette was born in Fort Wayne, daughter of John Hageman and Amelia Schrage. John, a builder and contractor, built Saint Andrew's and Precious Blood Catholic, and also St. Paul's Methodist Churches, as well as Anthony Wayne and Lafayette Center Schools. John Hageman's father, Joseph, was born in Munster, Germany. While in his teens, Joseph went to the docks to see a friend off who was going to the United States. Joseph decided to stow away and came to this country then. His family never knew what became of him. Joseph married Caroline Volkerding, and they developed a successful truck farm at Gar Creek.

Nancy, born September 25,1932, is the daughter of Eugene Haffner and Katherine Neuhaus. Eugene's grandfather, Christian Haffner, was born in Marbach, Germany. He was a baker and brought this trade with him when he came to Allen County. His bakery, The Haffner Star Bakery, became one of the largest bakeries in Fort Wayne in the early 1900s. His son and grandson followed Christian in the bakery business. Eugene's parents were George Haffner and Helen Catherine Noll. Her father, Benedict Noll, a pharmacist, invented and patented the popular cough medicine Pinex which was sold nationally and in Canada. Nancy's maternal grandparents, George Neuhaus and Florence Poinsett, had nine children. Katherine was the oldest. George's father, Reinhard, came from Germany in 1854 when he was only a few weeks old. He married Frances Wiesmer in 1879. He had a shoemaking business. Florence's parents were John Stockton Poinsett, Jr. and Dora Scarlett.

Nancy is a member of the National Society of The Daughters of the American Revolution (DAR) through the lineage of two ancestors: Solomon Rockhill of Burlington, New Jersey, and

Daniel Wade Boylan and Nancy Katherine Haffner Boylan

Newman Scarlett of Tewksbury, Massachusetts. These two 5th great-grandfathers of Nancy were Revolutionary War Patriots. Newman Scarlett's home was just north of Boston, and when Paul Revere rode through his village on April 19, 1775, Newman grabbed his rifle and headed for Lexington and Concord with the other local farmers. Newman, the school teacher and town clerk in Tewksbury, was the father of seventeen children, thirteen of whom grew to adulthood and married.

Nancy's siblings are Marilyn Joan Smethers, John Michael Haffner, and Sister M. Katherine Haffner O.S.F.

Submitted by Nancy K. Boylan

FREDRICK & LOUISE (WIESE) BRADTMUELLER

Fredrick Bradtmueller (1865-1916) married Louise Wiese (1863-1941) on April 16, 1885 in Martini Lutheran church. Both were first generation Americans.

Fredrick Bradtmueller's ancestors came from Meinsen Prussia and were as follows:

Johann Heinrich Bradtmueller (dates unknown). He married Anna Elenora Meier in 1749 in Prussia.

Johann Bradtmueller (1755-1837), who married Engel Wilhann (1759-1807) in Meinsen, Prussia.

Heinrich Carl Bradtmueller (1784-1855) was born in Meinsen, Prussia and died in Allen County. He married Christena Tagmeyer (1794-1880) in 1816 in Prussia. They had five children.

Wilhelm Bradtmueller (1822-1895) was born in Meinsen Prussia and died in Allen County. He married Louise Kellermeier (1822-1900) in 1845 in Allen County. They had seven children.

Fredrick and Louise Bradtmueller family, c. 1901. Seated, L to R: Anna, Adolph, Louise, Fredrick, Bertha. Back Row, L to R: Fredrick, William and Theodore (Theodore and Bertha were twins)

Family Reunion, c. 1933, at the Bradtmueller farm on Sieler Road. Children: L to R: Julia Doctor, Helen Bradtmueller, Bernice Bradtmueller, Leona Bradtmueller, Doris Doctor, Selma Doctor, Marcella Bradtmueller, Otto Bradtmueller, Ailene Bradtmueller, Clarence Bradtmueller, Louise Bradtmueller holding baby Bradtmueller and Vesta Doctor, Rudolf Braun, Aaron Doctor, Weldon Bradtmueller, Herman Bradtmueller, Alvin Bradtmueller, Clint Doctor, Norbert Bradtmueller, Lawrance Bradtmueller, Arthur Bradtmueller, Elmer Theye and Elmer Bradtmueller. Adults, L to R: William Bradtmueller, Adolph Bradtmueller, Bertha Braun, Anna Doctor, Lena Bradtmueller, Elna Bradtmueller, Fredinand Bradtmueller, Lydia Braun, Flora Bradtmueller, Miss Theye, Della Bradtmueller, Wilma Theye, Carl Bradtmueller, Oscar Doctor, Viola Bradtmueller holding Norma Bradtmueller, Edwin Bradtmueller, Frieda Bradtmueller holding Lois Bradtmueller, George Braun, Martha Braun, Loreta Bradtmueller, Fredrick Bradtmueller Jr., Theodore Bradtmueller and Clara Bradtmueller.

He purchased land on the Sieler road in Adams Township in 1843. The land was part of what was known as the Erie Canal farm.

Louise's ancestors came from Wietersheim Preus Minden, Germany and were as follows:

Carl Christian Wiese (1789-1915) married Louise Sophie Moeller in 1811.

Christian Heinrich Wiese (1829-1915) married Anna Elisabeth Weisheit in 1852 at St. Paul's Lutheran Church in Fort Wayne. He arrived in the U.S. in 1844. Christian donated land and helped to organize Martini Lutheran Church on Moeller Road. They raised a family of ten children.

Fredrick and Louise had nine children: 1) William married Lena Berning. They had twelve children. 2) Bertha married George Braun. They had three children. Bertha and Theodore were twins. 3) Theodore married Clara Bobay. They had twelve children. 4) Fredrick married Frieda Theye. They had one child, and she had three children. 5) Martha died as a child. 6) Anna married Oscar Doctor. They had six children. 7) Adolph married Viola Nuoffer. They had three children. 8) Herman died as a child. 9) Ferdinand married Flora Oetting. They had one child.

Frederick and Louise purchased the land from his father, Wilhelm, and they lived and raised their family on the farm. Louise and her children ran the farm after Frederick's death, and she lived there until she died. Theodore and Clara purchased the farm from Louise in 1939, and they lived there until they both died. Ted and Clara had their own electrical plant long before others had electricity. They had many dairy cows and bottled milk to sell. They had square dances in the barn for celebrations, reunions and parties. Music was provided by relatives, neighbors and friends, and son, Ed, did the calling. Their son, Elmer, and then son, Gilbert, lived on and farmed the land. Gilbert is retired, and he built a home on the property. Presently he helps son, Gary, farm the land. Gary lives in the farm house.

Submitted by JoAnn M. Pullen

BRAMES-ALLGEIER

Henry C. Brames was born September 8, 1868 and died October 6,1960 at the age of 92. Mary F. Allgeier was born July 13, 1871 and died April 13, 1955 at the age of 83. They met and were married February 11, 1896 in St. Mary's Catholic Church, Fort Wayne. They bought and moved to a farm near Monroeville on the southeast corner of Sampson and Hoffman Roads that same year.

Over the years, they bought more ground while farming with a team of horses. They had cows, pigs, chickens, a big garden and a large apple orchard. Henry would load a wagon with apples and leave early in the morning by horse-drawn cart to go to Fort Wayne and sell the apples. It would be late at night when he would return home.

Their children were: Paul, Luke, David, Clement, Benedict and finally a girl, Laura A. Paul married Marie (Minnich) and built across the intersection from his parents homestead. Clem married Mary (Ternet) and moved to rural New Haven to farm. David married Constance (Schmitz) and lived in Fort Wayne. Ben married Luella (Pranger) and lived in Fort Wayne. Luke stayed at home to farm for his parents. He bought most of the farm after his parents death. He lived there until 2 1/2 years before his death. Now his granddaughter and family live there and continue to farm this homestead. Laura left for the convent of the Sisters of St. Francis right after eighth grade. She was a teacher in Arlington, Illinois, area most of her teaching years. She was a very kind, quiet woman, very knowledgeable and an excellent teacher. She tutored many years after full-time teaching was too much for her. She loved to go fishing with brother, Dave, at his Lake Jimmerson cottage, and always visited as many family as possible on her trips back to Fort Wayne. She would always have special stories she told with much enthusiasm and little gifts for the children and family alike. She was a blessing to this family in many ways, but to the entire world as she touched so many lives with that small country warmth found in northeastern Indiana, so easily lost in a busy city life today.

Front Row, L to R: Sister Lauraline, O.S.F., Henry Brames, Mary (Allgeier) Brames. Back row, L to R: Ben, Clem, Paul, Luke, and David Brames

Submitted by Jean Bacon

NORBERT & LINDA (MARBACH) BRENNEKE FAMILY

August Brenneke (1856-1953), the grandfather of Norbert Brenneke, came to Allen County from Eddesse, Germany in 1884. He married Sophia Fuesse (1854-1925), born in Germany. August was a charter member of Zion Lutheran Church, Woodburn, organized in 1888, and was a member of its building committee. Sophia was the first president of its Ladies Aid. August served as township trustee 1908-1915, during which time Woodburn's brick grade and high school was built. He also served as president of Woodburn Bank from 1917-1951. He was an active member of the Republican Party for 60 years. August and Sophia were the parents of three sons, Herman and Henry (twins) and William. August lived to be 97 years of age, spending his last few years in a wheel-chair entertaining his great-grandchildren.

Diedrick Rekeweg (1852-1926), Norbert's maternal grandfather, was born in Germany and came to the United States in 1871. Elizabeth (Louisa) Korte (1857-1928), also born in Germany, came to the United States in 1873. They were married in 1880 in Allen County. They owned a farm in Milan Township and had ten children: Louisa (Brenneke), William, Caroline (Brenneke), Frederick, Carl, Emma (Brenneke), Anna (Brenneke), Dorthea, Arthur, and Dora (Roemke). Note that three daughters of Diedrick and Elizabeth married the three sons of August and Sophia Brenneke. One daughter married Henry Brenneke and upon his death, married Karl Brenneke.

William Brenneke (1890-1943) and Anna Rekeweg (1893-1922) were both born in Allen County. They were married on October 23, 1913 in Zion Lutheran Church, Woodburn. William helped manage his father's farm until he bought it. Anna died in 1922 of rheumatic fever, leaving three young children for William to care for. In 1927, William married Ida Maehlman, who brought her daughter, Pauline, to the marriage. William and Anna were the parents of three children, Norbert (1915-1990), Esther (Hockemeyer) (1917-1984) and Edna (Werling) (1920-2004).

Norbert Brenneke lived near Woodburn and owned the family farm. Linda Marbach (1918-1991) was born in Adams County, Indiana. Norbert and Linda were married on a cold January 19, 1941. Linda's parents gave them a bedroom suite and one cow as a wedding gift. That was the beginning of a large dairy farm that is still in operation today and is owned by their son, Bruce. Linda was an expert quilter and gave her grandchildren quilts. Norbert and Linda were the parents of six children: Lloyd (1943), Roger (1945), Irene (1948), Phyllis (1951), Bruce (1955) and Mark (1962). Lloyd married Sharon Gallmeyer, lives in Hoagland and has three children and five grandchildren. Roger married Ruth Rosenberry, lives in Antwerp, Ohio and has four children and six grandchildren. Irene married Steve Benschneider, lives in Payne, Ohio and has three children

Norbert Brenneke's grandparents and father, early 1900s

and two grandchildren. Phyllis married Richard Helmke, lives in Addison, Illinois and has two children. Bruce married Elizabeth (Ruth) Patterson, lives in Woodburn, has nine children/stepchildren and one grandchild. Mark married Tami Figert, lives in Woodburn, and has three children. The family continues to grow!

Submitted by Phyllis Helmke

BRODERICK FAMILY

John Broderick was born in Ireland about 1804. He came to Indiana and purchased forty acres in Jefferson Township on October 13, 1835. He married Ellen Mehan September 23,1840 in the Cathedral in Fort Wayne, Indiana. Ellen was born about 1823 in the Parish of Ballyhooly, County Cork, Ireland. The couple had ten children, Mary, James, Ellen, John, Thomas, Michael, Bridget, William, Edward and Daniel. Ellen died September 26, 1863 at age 40. She is buried in the Catholic Cemetery in Fort Wayne. John remained on the farm for a short time after her death before moving to New Haven. He died before June 1873.

Mary Broderick married Thomas Ryan January 20, 1862 in Allen County, Indiana. After her father died, Mary became the guardian of her three youngest brothers, raising Daniel to adulthood. Mary had ten children, six living to be adults.

James Broderick worked in a stave factory in New Haven, Indiana. He went to Michigan City, Indiana to join the Civil War serving in the 16th Battalion, Indiana Light Artillery. A severally wounded leg would cause him to limp the rest of his life. Returning home, he again worked in the stave factory. He married Lydia Dickerson September 22, 1868 in Trinity Episcopal Church in Fort Wayne. They had two sons. James died 1908 in Mount Clemens, Michigan.

Ellen Broderick came to Fort Wayne to work as a seamstress. She married James Quinlan July 15, 1879. Two children were born in Fort Wayne. They moved to Payne, Ohio where two more children were born. The youngest son, Thomas, became a priest. Ellen died 1921 and is buried in the Catholic Cemetery in Payne, Ohio.

Thomas Broderick worked in several stave factories eventually owning one in Auburn, Indiana. Here he married Della Parish in 1878. They had three children but only one survived. Tom lost his business and continuously moved around the country. He died in 1906 in Louisiana, and his body was returned to Auburn for burial in the Catholic Cemetery.

Michael Broderick never married. His later years were spent at the County Farm where he died in 1935. He is buried near his mother.

Bridget Broderick worked as a seamstress with her sister, Ellen. She married Michael Shea June 22, 1875 in Fort Wayne. They had eight children, none of whom married. Her son Michael became a priest, and he said the funeral masses for a brother and two sisters.

William Broderick married twice. His only child died at age 11. William became a wanderer working as a laborer. He died in 1930 and is buried in Portland, Indiana.

Edward Broderick married Phoebe Kemler in 1885 at Paulding, Ohio. One of their three children lived to adulthood. They moved to Bryan, Ohio. Edward died in 1918 and is buried there.

Daniel Broderick married Theresa Ehinger in 1885. He worked on the railroad and moved to Huntington, Indiana. They had two sons. Daniel died in 1930 at age 71. He is buried in Mount Calvary Cemetery.

Submitted by Jane Schurr

HENRY C. BROOKS FAMILY

Henry C. Brooks was the contractor who built the original buildings for the Fort Wayne State School on State Boulevard. He married Charlotte Nestel, who was a sister to Charles and Eliza Nestel, Fort Wayne's midgets, and lived next door to Miner School on Dewald Street. They had two daughters, Etta and Olive.

Etta Brooks married Willard Smith and they had two sons, Brooks and Carl.

The Brooks family had a horse and buggy for transportation. Anthony was the horse's name and on Sunday afternoons the family would go for a ride to see how the State School project was progressing. Charlotte Brooks also took Anthony when she went downtown to go shopping. She tied the horse to a hitching post. A woman walked by with a flowered hat and the horse ate the flowers off her hat so Charlotte bought the woman a new hat.

In the early 1920's, Miner School needed more room for a playground. They bought Charlotte's home and the Smith home on Dewald Street. Charlotte's home was moved a block and a half to Fox Avenue. The moving company put large steel dollies under the house, set up a big winch in the middle of Dewald Street, tied it to the large Maple trees along the street and with a huge rope and a team of horses, pulled the house out and down the street.

The Smith family moved right across the alley to Creighton Avenue. Their old house was used as a school for handicapped children for a few years before it was torn down. Carl Smith went to kindergarten there, in his old house.

Henry C. Brooks also built the original St. Mary's Catholic Church and other buildings in the area.

Originally there were no other houses between the Brooks' home and Broadway. Etta Smith often would tell about watching, on a Saturday night, old Indian Godefroi, staggering home to the reservation, where Waynedale is now.

When Willard Smith was young, he was a stable boy for Dr. Miles F. Porter, Sr. Gene Stratton Porter's father at Geneva, Indiana was a brother. The Porters, at Geneva, had a horse for Dr. Porter. Willard ice-skated on the St. Mary's River down to Decatur, Indiana, and hitched a ride to Geneva. The next day, he rode the horse back to Fort Wayne.

Submitted by Carl Smith

ALFRED BROTHERS JR. & SANDRA J. WOOTEN FAMILY HISTORY

Alfred S. Brothers Jr. was born on December 14, 1942 in Boston, Massachusetts to Alfred S. Brothers Sr. and Edith Irene Yates. They lived in Roxbury, Massachusetts while Al and his sister Donna grew up. They later moved to Mattapan, Massachusetts after both children left home and were on their own. Donna is married to William Jones and they reside in Chicago, Illinois with their daughter Monica.

Al met his wife to be, Sandra J. Wooten, in 1959 while attending a back to school party in Boston. They were married on August 24, 1968 in Newton, Massachusetts, Sandra's hometown. Al graduated from Boston Latin School, the oldest public high school in the country in 1960. He attended Boston University College of Engineering and received a B.S. degree in Aeronautical Engineering and a commission as a second Lieutenant in the U.S. Air Force in 1964. Al also received a M.A. degree in Public Administration from Golden Gate University, a M.P.M. Degree in Personnel Management from Central Michigan University and a Ph.D. in Business Administration from Century University. He served in the Air Force from 1964 until 1986 with service as a pilot, engineer and AFROTC unit commander. He joined Magnavox in 1986, and moved to Fort Wayne. He has worked there 19 years. The company is now part of the Raytheon Company. Sandra graduated from Newton High School in 1965 and then attended Children's Hospital School of Nursing in Boston, graduating in August 1968 as a R. N. She received her B.A. in Social Psychology from Park College in 1983.

The Alfred Brothers Family

Al's family, the Brothers, are originally from Annapolis Royal, Nova Scotia, Canada. The progenitor, Sam Brothers, emigrated there in 1783 from New York City after the American revolutionaries won New York. His grandfather, Lewis Owen Brothers, immigrated to the United States in 1912 from Canada. His mother's family moved to Boston from Washington, DC in 1923. Al and his wife, Sandi, have lived in North Dakota, Florida, Utah, New Hampshire, Ohio and New York while Al was in the service. Al served in the Vietnam conflict from 1972 to 1974 and was stationed in Thailand, Okinawa, and Guam while flying B-52 and B-57 aircraft.

Al has been very involved in the community serving with the following organizations: Chair-Science Central, TV 39, African African-American Historical Society, and North Indiana United Methodist Trustees; President - Anthony Wayne Area Council, BSA; secretary of the Fort Wayne Learning Center; Scoutmaster to Scout World Jamborees in Chile 1998 and Thailand 2002; and member of the Anthony Wayne Rotary, Quest Club, and the Fort Wayne Urban League.

Sandi's family lived in Newton, Massachusetts while growing up. She has two sisters, Cheryl, who lives in Vermont and Chris, who lives in Massachusetts, and a brother David who lives in California. Her parents' families were from North Carolina (mother Eleanor Perry) and West Virginia (father Dover Wooten).

Sandi worked as a Real Estate sales person and broker with Graber Realtors, which later became Roth, Wehrly, Graber Coldwell Banker. She also worked with a Fort Wayne Reading Readiness program and then became a quilt consultant and instructor opening her own quilt shop, a Quilt of Many Colors, in 2005.

Sandi's community involvement includes the Girl Scouts of Limberlost Council, the United Way of Allen County, the YWCA, WFWA TV-39, Leo United Methodist Church, the Leo Cedarville Chamber of Commerce and the Fort Wayne Urban League.

Sandi and Al are parents of Alfred S. Brothers III, born in Minot, North Dakota on July 15, 1969 and Barbara Ann Brothers born in Minot, North Dakota on July 18, 1970 while Al was stationed at Minot AFB in B-52 aircraft. Al III and Barbara attended schools in New Hampshire, Ohio, New York, and Fort Wayne, Indiana. Both graduated from Concordia High School in 1987 and 1988 respectively. Al III graduated from Indiana Weslyan University in 2003 and currently manages the tire replacement and repair shop for Ryder Truck Company in Fort Wayne. He is the proud father of Ebony Jane Brothers who was born December 10, 1998. Her mother is Janna Broxtan Brothers. Barbara graduated from Boston University College of Communications in 1992 and currently operates an after school academy for the Benjamin Banneker Charter School in Cambridge Massachusetts.

Submitted by Alfred S. Brothers, Jr.

ALFRED & PEARL BROWN

Alfred Theodore Brown was born in 1876 in Whitley County, Indiana, and died 1961 in Fort Wayne, Indiana. His occupation was as a finish Carpenter. He married Lauretta Pearl Beard in 1902. She was the daughter of William Harvey Beard and Elizabeth Ruth Scott. Lauretta was born 1883 in Whitley County, Indiana. She died in 1964 in Fort Wayne, Indiana. They had two children, Marvin (1904-1986), and Martha, (1906-1975).

Marvin Brown and his wife, Gervea Adeline Davenport, were married in 1930 in Fort Wayne, Indiana. Both died in Dearborn, Michigan. They had three children: Marvin the III, Cecila Ann who married Benjamin Robinson, and Tamela Lee.

Martha Brown was married to Robert Eli Ritter in 1932, and they had two children: Martha, who married Bill Bolles, and Norman. Martha was remarried to Arthur Harris (1922-1994). Martha and Art died in Fort Wayne, Indiana.

Submitted by Beverly Bardey

Alfred and Pearl Brown

CLARK C. BROWN FAMILY

Clark C. Brown was born June 21, 1968 in Fort Wayne, Indiana to Charles and Carolyn Brown, his other siblings being Kimberly (1954), Michael (1958), and Chris (1970).

Clark's great-great-great grandfather, William Brown, was a soldier in the Revolutionary War. He served in the Pennsylvania Militia from April 1778 to August 1778 and helped construct Fort Roberdeau. In 1805, the family moved to Walnut Township, Pickaway County, Ohio. In 1813 William's son, Elisha, served as a volunteer to chase the British Army out of Ohio. Approximately 1829, Elisha moved to Hancock County, Ohio, near the present day village of Vanlue. William eventually moved to Hancock County after his wife, Ruth Lane Brown, passed away. Both veterans are buried outside the village limits in Lee Cemetery.

Elisha's youngest son, William Lane Brown, was responsible for bringing the family to Fort Wayne in 1924. William L. Brown was looking for work and found it in the ice houses providing blocks of ice for the new invention called the ice box. The particular building where he cut ice was on Delaware Avenue. William L. Brown's children, Jesse, Pauline, Wanda, Sylvia, William Clark, Glendola, Ray, Paul and Wilbur Lane Brown grew up in Fort Wayne. William Clark Brown married Viola McCoy on January 21, 1931 and had four children, William Lane, Charles (Jimmy), Sandy and Joyce.

Viola's family already had deep roots in Fort Wayne. Her great-grandparents were George Washington McCoy and Martha Oakley McCoy. George McCoy owned the land that is currently the Catholic Cemetery on Lake Avenue until 1873, when he sold it to Bishop Dwenger. Martha Oakley McCoy's brother was Chauncey B. Oakley who became Mayor of Fort Wayne from 1894 to 1896. Mayor Oakley served only two years because the previous mayor had a heart attack while in the middle of his term.

Clark C. Brown married Charity Molargik on March 11, 1995 at Faith Baptist Church and has one daughter, Sierra. Charity is the daughter of Phil and Penny Molargik, whose family biography is included under Phillip S. Molargik. Charity

Sierra Brown, Clark, Charity, Easter 2005

graduated from Woodlan High School in Woodburn, Indiana, in 1988 and met Clark while they were both employed at Ponderosa Steakhouse on East State Blvd. in September of 1986.

Clark is employed by IIT Industries as a Senior Troubleshooter and is also currently a member of IUE/CW A Local 999. He is also a member of the Anthony Halberstaadt Chapter of the Sons of the American Revolution with his national number being 149565 and state number 3486. In his spare time you can find him at the Allen County Public Library researching genealogy or volunteering in the Television Services Area where he won a Philo Farnsworth award for video production in October 2004.

Sierra was born and grew up in the Northside Neighborhood Area at 541 Charlotte Avenue. Northside Park is where she learned to ride a bicycle and throw a frisbee.

Submitted by Clark C. Brown

GARY DALE & CANDACE LEE (KOEVETS) BROWN FAMILY

Gary Dale Brown was born January 8, 1970, in Fort Wayne, Indiana. His grandparents were Bruce and Esther Brown of Fort Wayne. Bruce retired from General Electric and Esther was a homemaker. They had three children who included Gary's father, Robert L. Brown. Gary's parents were Robert L. Brown and Sherrie J. (Elder) Wall. Robert L. Brown retired from Slater Steel and Sherrie was a homemaker. Sherrie J. (Elder) Wall was the daughter of Marvin and Elsie Elder of Middletown, Indiana. She was one of five children. Marvin retired from Delco-Remy and Elsie was a homemaker.

Gary and Candace (Koevets) Brown, and daughters Nicole and Natalie

Gary had two sisters, Linda Brown (Brian) and Karen Sommers (Tim). Gary graduated from Northrop High School in 1988. He spent many years at Pyromation located in Fort Wayne.

His wife, Candace L. (Koevets) Brown, was also born in Fort Wayne on January 23, 1969, and she also graduated from Northrop High School in 1987. She spent many years working for Verizon. Her parents were Steve B. and Judy K. (Potts) Koevets, also of Fort Wayne. Her father was the son of Frank J. and Della M. Koevets of Marion, Indiana. They had two children, Steve and one sister. Candy's father retired from Verizon and her mother was a homemaker. Her mother, Judy K. (Potts) Koevets was the daughter of Robert G. and Evelyn M. Potts, both of Fort Wayne. They had two children, Judy, and one brother. Judy's father retired from United Trucking, and her mother retired from Homestead High School.

Gary and Candace were married April 24, 1993 and moved to Huntertown, Indiana, in 2003. They had two daughters, Natalie M. Brown, born march 29, 1998, and Nicole L. Brown born March 7, 2001.

Submitted by Candace Brown

KEITH ALLEN & GERALDINE HUGHES BROWN FAMILY

Keith Allen Brown was born April 27, 1933, in Fort Wayne, Indiana. His great-great grandparents, David and Sarah Catherine Brown, came from Tupulehocken, Berks County, Pennsylvania, to Miami County, Ohio, in the early 1850s. David was a weaver of tapestries, and was killed in a horse accident 1857. Catherine brought their five sons, Solomon, Jonathan L., Jacob M., David F., and Philip M. to Wells County, Indiana, in 1862.

Brown Family 50th Anniversary dinner at Triangle Park Restaurant, Fort Wayne, Indiana, August 17, 2004. L to R: Keith, Brian, Lari, Bruce, Gerri, Derek and Colin

Keith's great-grandparents, David Franklin and Sarah Elizabeth Werking Brown, had three children, John H., George F. and Jennie C. They farmed in Wells County. His grandparents were George F. and Bertha O. Allen Brown. She was the daughter of Hamon and Laura A. Brickley Allen, Markle, Indiana. George F. and Bertha had three children, Laverne Koch, Bruce Allen and Edward R. George was a machinist at Kunkle Valve.

Bruce Allen, who was a welder at General Electric, married Esther R. Rosen, daughter of August and Mollie Gemmer Rosen, Andrews, Indiana. They had three sons, Keith Allen, Larry G., and Robert Lee, all making their homes in Fort Wayne, Indiana.

Keith went to Adams School and Central High School, graduating in 1951. He joined tbe U. S. Marine Corp in 1953, and served aboard cruisers USS Helena and Toledo, of the 7th Fleet, during the Korean War. He married Geraldine Faye Hughes, of Orcutt, California in 1954, She is the daughter of Glenn and Evelyn B. Brooks Hughes, and was born July 15, 1935, in Santa Maria, California. Keith, Gerri and their young son, Bruce Allen II, born June 2,1955, in Santa Maria, California, returned to Fort Wayne after his discharge in 1956. A second son, Brian Keith, was born January 11, 1958. Keith worked at Kimble Garage before going to International Harvester Engineering as a mechanic in Road Test, retiring after 32 year in 1989.

Bruce Allen married Lori Rachel Cheesman in 1991, and they are the parents of two sons, Colin Allen and Derek James. She is the daughter of James and Sharon Campbell Cheesman, Rochester, Indiana. Bruce is a wood patternmaker at Standard Pattern.

Brian has remained single. He works for Grabill Cabinet Company and also is a freelance writer/photographer/Indy car historian.

As a family, the Browns have always had an interest in the restoration/preservation of Duesenberg automobiles and Indy race cars. A 1933 Model J Duesenberg Derham convertible sedan has been part of the Brown family for these past 42 years, the three Indy cars for ten. Brian won the 1972 Fort Wayne Soap Box Derby. Bruce supervised the Derby Barn (Franke Park) building of cars in the mid 1970s and served on the board of directors.

Submitted by Geraldine Hughes Brown

BRUCK FAMILY

The history of the Bruck Family in Fort Wayne is really Joseph Arnold Bruck's story. As a young boy he arrived in Fort Wayne in the back seat of a Studebaker convertible driven by his half brother who recently returned from WWI. Highway 24 was still a dirt road and the side curtains did little to keep the dust from filtering into the passenger compartment of the new car. The family moved to Fort Wayne so that Joseph's father, Nicholas Bruck, could join his brothers in the hotel business. Joseph Arnold Bruck was ten years old and hated to leave the excitement of the circus town, Peru, Indiana. His mother, Laura, was relieved to be away from a town that was prone to flooding and where circus animals frequently got loose to roam the streets.

The Bruck boys had arrived a few years earlier and were owners of three hotels in the area, the Wayne Hotel and the Centlivere Hotel in Fort Wayne, as well as the Kelly House in Kendallville. The year was 1918; railroad travel was King and the hotel business was good. Nicholas Bruck eventually became manager of the Centlivere Hotel that was located across from the Penn Central train station on Baker Street. Joseph Arnold frequently made spending money by being a bellhop during summer vacation from St. Peters Catholic grade school.

For a few years things were good, but by the time Joseph Arnold reached high school age

Arnold A. Bruck, salesman

the depression hit. Salesmen quit traveling and the hotel business went into a sharp decline. By this time the family had settled into a home on the south end of town at 320 Esmond Street. To help make house payments, Joseph Arnold took on a paper route and any job he could get, but the family eventually lost everything.

It was at South Side High School in the class of 1932, that Joseph Arnold met another student who would later play a pivotal roll in his life. This friend was John Slick II.

Out of high school, Joseph Arnold Bruck had several part time jobs, firing the boilers at St. Joseph Hospital and driving a wrecker for Goudy's Tire Service, until by chance he applied at Slick's Laundry. It was then his high school friend, John Slick II, talked to his father and got him the job. The country was still in the grips of the depression, and a steady job meant a lot to a young family. For the next thirty years Joseph Arnold would work for the Slicks. Even during the war years, the Slicks declared him essential to their business and exempted him from the draft. During these years this article's submitter, son, Roger, was born, along with three brothers and one sister who have yet to write our own story.

Submitted by Roger Bruck

PAUL EUGENE & BETTY JEAN (FORKER) BRUMBAUGH

Paul Eugene and Betty Jean (Forker) Brumbaugh were married December 16, 1948, and moved to Arcola, in western Allen County, where they lived for the next fifty-six years.

Paul, born April 6, 1928 in Noble County, was the son of Melvin and Velma (Strouse). He had four brothers: Arnold (1921-1991), Rodger (1924-1927), Galen (1933-2004) and William (1941-).

Betty, also from Noble County, was the only daughter of Oliver and Faye (Hoffman) Forker. She had three brothers: Kenneth (1919-2000), Paul (1925-1945), and her twin brother Bill. Paul and Betty graduated from Albion High School in the class of 1946. After high school, Betty earned an associate degree in accounting at International Business College.

Paul became a partner with his father and oldest brother in the Brumbaugh Grocery and Locker. Paul was the head meatcutter, a trade he had learned while working at Kroger in Albion during high school. Paul and Betty lived in an apartment above the grocery for the next sixteen years with their two daughters, Susan (1950) and Sharon (1954). In 1965, they moved into a house close to the Arcola School, where they remained until 2002.

The family grocery was sold in 1973, and Paul began selling insurance. Betty worked for Higgins and Swift Attorneys and John Christman Accounting Service. In 1984 Paul and Betty started a small bookkeeping business together. Two years earlier, in1982, Paul had been elected to the Allen County Council and continued serving in that position until 2002. During 2003, they sold their Arcola home, moved to Fort Wayne, and retired from their business.

Daughter Sharon and her husband, Jeff Hoffman, are the operators of Chick-fil-A Restaurant at Jefferson Pointe. From 1978 until 2002 they worked together in Christian Music Ministries, traveling with their two children, Andrew and Elizabeth, and Robin Howard. Andrew is student at North Side High School where he is active in the show choir, jazz band and marching band. Elizabeth will begin ninth grade in the fall of 2005 where she will be in show choir and orchestra. Sharon also teaches voice and piano in their home.

Susan, a teacher with Fort Wayne Community Schools, married Robert Warner and had a son, Robert J. Warner (wife, Jamie, and daughters, Ashtyn and Morgan) now living near Atlanta, Georgia. She later married Robert L. Pape. He had three sons: Robert E. Pape (children Leslie, Lindsay, and Roberta), Michael J. Pape (wife, Tanya, and children, Amber, Brittany, and Ethan), John D. Pape (wife, Joy, children, Brandon Sowder, Erica Sowder, and twins Nicole and Logan) who all live in northeast Fort Wayne. Together, they had two children: Jeffery A. Pape who, with his wife YuNah, owns a home in Whitley County and Jennifer M. Pape, the youngest, who works and lives in Fort Wayne.

Submitted by Susan Pape

FRED ALLEN BRUNSON & THE FORT WAYNE FRUIT COMPANY

This is not just a family history but also the history of the Fort Wayne Fruit Company. Fred A. Brunson was the great, great grandson of Aden Brunson who was born in New York sometime between 1770 and 1780. His ancestors came from England in 1630.

The Brunson family left New York in 1833 for Indiana. Their journey was by the way of the Ohio River to Cincinnati and then to Dearborn County, Indiana from which he came overland by ox team. Aden settled in Allen County in 1833 and rented a farm in Wayne Township, where he lived until 1836. He then purchased 132 acres in Marion Township off the Marion Center Road now named Brunson Road. Pioneer life was rugged but he worked hard and as they said of him, "he hewed a fine farm". He and his wife had four children, Nathan, Reuben who died at ten, Mary Ann, and Eliza Jane.

Nathan stayed on the farm after Aden's death, becoming the owner of the farm. Nathan enjoyed the life into which he was born. He worked hard, cleared the lands, and turned them into productive fields of wheat and Indian maize. His early rearing had been like the other young men of the community, much labor and perseverance. His religious life centered around a little church near his home. His schooling consisted of a few months each winter. That is

Paul and Betty Brumbaugh

where he met Hannah Halliday, who was two years younger. He was taken with her and one evening in October, he gathered the courage to ask for her hand in marriage. Engagements were short then, so that same evening, arrangements were made for their marriage, in two weeks if he could arrange for a minister. Early the next morning, young Nathan set out on horseback for a little settlement on the bank of the Great Miami. It was a long and tiresome ride but his excitement kept him going. He was lucky to find the minister at home and very pleased to find that he could marry the couple at the desired time. At last, the day arrived and the couple was married.

Here the story varies. In one version Homer Halliday, professor of music at Manchester College and descendant of the Halliday's, wrote for the Brethren Church saying that during the ceremony, as the Reverend was giving the benediction, a loud knocking reverberated through the room and a quaint figure with a large pack entered. Sensing the solemnity of the occasion, he quickly opened his pack, withdrew a large red apple and offered it to Hannah and Nathan with these words, "plant the seed from this fruit, and in your old age, your children and grandchildren will enjoy the fruit. Silver and gold I do not have," said the traveler, "but what I have, I want to give." Another version offered down through the family for ages, was the visitor and Nathan were friends. Nathan had at times shared his home with this traveler named Johnny Chapman, better known as "Johnny Appleseed". To repay him for his kindness, Nathan was given a wedding present of a few apple seedlings and some seeds. Nathan eventually raised an orchard from the gift, and was able to pass it on to his eldest son, Nathan Allen.

Regardless of which story is correct, Nathan and Hannah had the beginnings of an apple orchard. They also produced a family of four, Nathan Allen, known as Allen, Eliza Jane, Drusilla, and Thompson. Allen had one son, Fred, and one daughter, Elizabeth. He was a graduate of the Old Methodist College, taught school for a number of years, and later took employment with the Fort Wayne Street Car Company where he worked for twenty-five years and never had an accident. His father, Nathan, and his son Fred Allen, started the Fort Wayne Fruit Company.

Fred married Margaret McNaughton and they moved to Oregon to start fruit orchards. They shipped fruit back to Fort Wayne until 1917 when Fred was killed in a tragic accident. Fred was only thirty-eight. Fred and Margaret had one child, a daughter, Dorothy Allene. She was born on October 13, 1911, and was only six when Fred died. Margaret and her daughter accompanied the coffin back to Fort Wayne. The only family they had was here. Margaret came from a family of thirteen children. Her parents came from Scotland. Margaret later married Herb Steiner of Fort Wayne but she died at forty-two of pneumonia, leaving the teen-aged Dorothy an orphan. Fred's daughter married Cecil Carl Schubert in 1930. Cecil was the bandleader on WOWO and also worked at Lincoln Bank as an accountant until the Depression forced the bank to close. They packed up baby daughter, Patricia, and moved to Toledo, Ohio, to find work. Cecil later became manager of the Western Auto Store in Fort Wayne. They had four children, Patricia Louise (Augenstein), Larry Carl, Lynne Allene (Colyer), and Julie Kay (Lefforge). Dorothy died in 1986 of a brain tumor. Cecil died in 1990. All four children survive. Patricia lives in New Haven, Larry in Illinois, Lynne in Indianapolis, and Julie in Bluffton, Indiana.

Submitted by Patricia Augenstein.

OZRO LEE (O.L.) BRYANT

Ozro Lee Bryant was born July 15, 1882 near Swayzee, Indiana. His parents were William Bryant and Olive Ladd. Ozro married Laura Effie Echelbarger, born July 2, 1881. Her parents were Jarret Echelbarger and Sarah Covalt. Ozro and Laura had four children: Myrl, Frances, Vernon, and Gaynell, and twelve grandchildren. Ozro and his family moved to Allen County in 1912 from Howard County, Indiana. He purchased an eighty acre farm on the Thiele Road and the Allen-Wells County Line Road.

Mr. Bryant was a very progressive farmer. He stayed in close contact with Purdue University Agriculture Department who encouraged him to use new advancements and methods of farming. He tested new seeds for them and planted a test plot of soybeans. Soybeans previously had been used only to make hay to feed cattle. The neighbors laughed at him and said there was no future in soybeans. Ozro started to experiment with hybrid corn. He had to pay his neighbors to keep their corn so many rods away so it would not pollinate his hybrid corn. He won the title of Corn King of Indiana from 1928-1933 after entering a contest sponsored by Lincoln National Life Insurance Company. The contest required farmers to produce the most corn per acre on five acres. He then started a successful seed business selling corn, wheat, and soybeans.

Ozro died at the age of 81 on November 2, 1963, after using a combine to pick corn the day before. His son Vernon and grandson Ross Bryant are the only descendants to follow farming as a profession.

Daughter Myrl married George Fryback. Their children are Lois and Dale.

Lois married Osborne Parker and they had Sarah and Mark. Sarah married Todd Linder, and their children are Rachel and Sean. Mark married Marlee Holdren and their children are Megan and Mariah. Dale married Joan Burns and their children are Laura and Wayne. Laura married Dr. Joseph Schnecker.

Daughter Frances married Clarence Robrock and their children are Roselyn, Arlene, and Blaine. Arlene married Carl Hack and their child Jana married Reo Parrett Their children are Tucker, Cassidy, and Jericho. Blaine married Joyce Auer and their children are Valerie and Eileen. Valerie married Paul Collins and their children are Michael and Margaret. Dr. Eileen Robrock

Ozro Lee (O.L.) Bryant

married Kevin Raywood and their children are twins Aubrey and Cameron.

Son Vernon married Geneva Greek and their children are Lee, Guilia, Ross, and Deanna. Lee married Phyllis Schnepp and their child Dewayne (deceased) married Cindy Rodrique. Their children are Erin and David. Guilia married Hugh Maxwell and their children are Sherri, Douglas and Barry. Dr. Sherri married Lt Col. Thomas Duquette. Douglas married Charlotte Burman and their children are Robert, Michael and William. Ross married Betty Stevenson and their children are Brenda and Bonnie. Brenda married Joseph Blazer and their children are Brittany and Kent. Bonnie married Scott Smith. Deanna married Robert Patten and their children are Troy and Tracy. Troy married Wendy Shirley and their children are Eric and Cassie. Troy then married Angie Tukei. Tracy married Tonia Moore, and their children are McKinzie, Sullivan and step-daughter Haleigh.

Daughter Gaynell married Wendell Martin Shady and their children are Lynn, Marcella, and Neal. Lynn married Donna McCague, and they had a child, Gregory. Marcella married Charles Neal Bordner and their children are Mark, Stephen (Steve), and Laura. Mark married Michelle Zedick. Steve married Kelly Baldwin and their children are Stephen and Andrew. Laura married Jeffrey Adams.

Submitted by Gaynell Shady

ERNST WILLIAM GEORGE BULTEMEIER

Ernst William George Bultemeier, son of Christian Bultemeier and Louise Huser, was born October 5, 1884, in Friedheim, Adams County, Indiana, and died March 19, 1963, in Fort Wayne. Ernst married Wilhelmina "Minnie" Schaaf, daughter of Peter Schaaf and Magdalena Rottmueller, on June 12, 1910, in her parent's home in rural Allen County. Minnie was born October 7, 1884, Allen County, Indiana and died January 5, 1975, in Fort Wayne. They lived in Auburn, DeKalb County, Indiana, for ten years, where Ernst was a blacksmith and worked for the Auburn car industry. Their children, Velma, Hilda, Wilbert, and Herbert were born in Auburn. About 1920, Ernst and Minnie moved their family to Fort Wayne so their children would be able to attend St. Paul's Lutheran School. Ernst gained employment at General Electric, where he worked until his retirement in 1948. Their other children, Robert and Marcella, were born in Fort Wayne.

The families of Ernst and Minnie's children:

Velma Bultemeier was born April 10, 1911, in Auburn, Indiana, and married Gustav Kruse, son of Wilhelm and Minna Kruse, on July 28, 1934, in St. Paul's Lutheran Church, Fort Wayne. Gustav was born November 10, 1907, in Halle, Germany, and died February 28, 1992, in Fort Wayne. They had three children, Marlene, Karen, and David.

Hilda Bultemeier was born June 1, 1913, in Auburn, Indiana, and died February 5, 1985, in Independence, Missouri. She married Louis Sher on April 19, 1936, in Redeemer Lutheran Church, Fort Wayne. Louis was born July 28, 1897, in Philadelphia, Pennsylvania, and died December 17, 1974, in Independence, Missouri. They had one child, Harry.

Wilbert C. Bultemeier was born January 26, 1916, in Auburn, Indiana, and died October 19, 1954, in Fort Wayne. Wilbert married Beatrice Meyer, daughter of Arnold Meyer and Bertha Machts, on June 29, 1940, in Zion Lutheran Church, Fort Wayne. Beatrice was born March 9, 1920, in Fort Wayne and died November 22, 1987, in Fort Wayne. They had four children, Paul, Ron, Ruth, and Linda.

Herbert Bultemeier was born August 7, 1918, in Auburn, Indiana, and married Gwyneth Harrett, daughter of William Harrett and Sara Evans, on September 21, 1947, in Trinity Lutheran Church, Sidman, Pennsylvania. Gwyneth was born October 13, 1924, in Glynneath, Wales. They had two children, Mark and Craig.

Bultemeier family, 1951

Robert Bultemeier was born March 1, 1921, in Fort Wayne and died July 17, 1988, in Fort Wayne. Robert married Suzanne Crumrine, daughter of Lawrence Crumrine, on June 10, 1950, in Bethlehem Lutheran Church, Fort Wayne. Suzanne was born May 13, 1917, in Fort Wayne. They had two children, Cynthia and Jeffrey.

Marcella Bultemeier was born September 4, 1923, in Fort Wayne and married Joe Stephenson, son of Joe Stephenson and Lela Brosher, on August 18, 1945, in Redeemer Lutheran Church, Fort Wayne. Joe was born November 17, 1916, in Fort Wayne and died January 16, 2005, in Fort Wayne. They had four children, Gregory, Douglas, Bradley, and Kevin.

Submitted by Ruth Adams

PAUL CARL & FRIEDA (KOENEMAN) BULTEMEIER FAMILY

Paul Carl Bultemeier was born March 5, 1908, in Preble, Indiana, to Adolph and Minnie (Stoppenhagen) Bultemeier.

Paul's great-great-great-grandparents, Heinrich and Sophie (Kaiser) Bultemeier, were married on September 29, 1815, in Windheim, Germany. In 1831, after Heinrich died, Sophie with her two sons, Ernest and Conrad Bultemeier, came to the United States. Sophie met her future husband, Ludwig Kaaze, on the ship. They settled in Preble, Indiana.

Paul's great-great-grandfather, Ernest Bultemeier, married Marie Witte on October 3, 1845. They had eight children, including Paul's grandfather, William. Ernest was one of the founders of Zion Lutheran (Friedheim) Church.

William Bultemeier and Sophie Blomenberg were married February 3, 1876. They had eight children including Paul's father, Adolph.

Adolph Bultemeier married Minnie Stoppenhagen on January 6, 1907. They lived on a farm in Preble, Indiana. They had five children: Paul, Gerhard, and Clarence are deceased and Elmer and Eldora (Fuelling) are still living in the Preble area. In 1925, Adolph helped to form a corporation of farmers to string wire for the first electricity in Preble.

Paul Bultemeier was raised on the farm and attended Zion Lutheran (Friedheim) Church and its school. He and Frieda Koeneman were married on April 20, 1930.

Frieda (Koeneman) Bultemeier was born on August 29, 1911, to Louis and Nettie (Herman) Koeneman. They had four children (all deceased): Frieda (Paul), August (Esther Bieberich), Edwin (Helen Dicke), and Arthur.

Louis Koeneman's great-grandparents came from Windheim, Germany, and settled in Adam County Indiana. His parents were August and Sophia (Selking) Koeneman and they purchased a 100-acre farm on Franke Road by Hoagland, Indiana. Louis and Nettie Koeneman were the second generation to live on this farm, and they raised Belgium show horses. Their son and his wife, August and Esther Koeneman, were the third generation to own the farm.

Nettie (Herman) Koeneman was born on August 29, 1890, to Jacob and Barbara (Waldschmidt) Herman. Her parents came to the United States from Kulmbach, Germany, in 1881. They settled on a 40-acre farm near Monroeville, Indiana. They had seven children including Nettie. The two oldest were born in Germany. Their oldest son, Jacob, his wife, Louise, and their daughter, Melve, were killed in a train accident on July 9, 1918, at Maples, Indiana.

Paul and Frieda (Koeneman) Bultemeier had seven children: Edna (Virgil) Buelow, Wilbert (who died four days after birth), Eileen (Loren) Tribby, Carol Eberly, Duane (Mary Ann Weirath Schwaben), Michael (Sharman Fliger), and Kenneth (Carolyn Weesner).

In 1942, they moved to New Haven, Indiana, and built their home on Canal Street. All the children spent their younger years at that home and continued living in Allen County, except Eileen, who lives in Centerville, Ohio. Paul Bultemeier retired from Fruehauf Trailer Company after 35 years as an electrician. Frieda Bultemeier would do laundry and ironing for people to help support the family.

Paul and Frieda Bultemeier were married 43 years when Frieda passed away on December 27, 1973. Paul died on July 11, 1987.

In 2004 Eileen and Loren Tribby's grandson, Matthew Rich, (Paul and Frieda Bultemeier s great-grandson) had a dream to replace trees being cut down for land development. As a community project, Matthew organized the planting of 1,200 hardwood trees at the Frank Liske Park in Concord, North Carolina, with help from his mother, Melody, and his brother, David. Matthew brought local and state government officials together along with business leaders and area students to complete this project.

Submitted by Eileen Tribby and Carol Eberly

August of 1980. Juanity and Bob, Lorene and Lloyd, Becky and Gary, Judy and Dean, Shirley and Paul

Judy, Jennifer and Dean Bunn

CLARENCE & DOROTHY (GRAHAM) BUNN

Clarence Harmon Bunn was born January 25, 1907, to Jefferson L. Bunn and Minnie C. Genth, then living at 2431 Thompson Avenue, Fort Wayne, Indiana. Clarence lived in many different places in the Fort Wayne and surrounding area during his childhood. Though he was only able to attend school through the 8th grade he went on to become the successful owner of C. H. Bunn Trucking. On June 28, 1927 Clarence and Dorothy Marian Graham eloped to Huntington County Indiana. Clarence later told the story that he gave his birth date as 1906 on the marriage license application in order to be age twenty-one.

Clarence and Dorothy Bunn

Dorothy was born September 18, 1908, to James F. Graham and Mary F. Cunnison. She spent her pre-marriage years at her family's home on the west side of Hayden Road (now Ardmore Avenue) at the intersection of Sandpoint Road. In 1925 she graduated from South Side High School where she was on the indoor baseball squad.

Five of Clarence and Dorothy's seven children reached adulthood, Robert Louis (1927-2000), Lorene Mae, James Clarence (1932-1941), Dean Edward (1933-1998), Paul Eugene, Ronald Clark (1938-1938), and Gary Wayne. From their home at 2604 Oliver Avenue, four of them went to Central High School in Fort Wayne. By the time Gary was in high school the family home and truck garage was on Mason Drive, in the Elmhurst High School area.

Clarence worked as a mechanic at the DeWald Service Station before operating "Bunn's General Service Station", a Shell Station, at the northeast corner of Lafayette and Wayne in partnership with Harry Schram. Losing the tip of a finger ended his mechanic days. He then purchased a 1942 red single axle Ford dump truck and thus began his dump truck business that kept expanding until he retired and sold it to Chuck Graves in 1969. In the mid 1940s his trucks, from an alley garage near East Washington and Clay, worked on the upgrading of the Baer Field Airport. The early 1950s brought work on the Indiana Toll Road. When the construction on Interstate 69 began in the early sixties Clarence started a company called Central Mix. It was the first company to haul wet concrete to the Interstate. His trucks regularly hauled asphalt for Wayne Asphalt and Construction Company. All the boys worked for their father and all continued in the road construction business after Clarence retired.

Dorothy had her hands full as bookkeeper for the trucking company and making a home for her family through many seasonal moves as Clarence's business took them to different locales as far away as Camden, Arkansas (1947). There Dean and Paul lowered themselves via rope down a steep embankment to the railroad tracks to put pennies on the tracks and tried, with minimum success, to hop on the trains. Many winters found them in Florida.

Robert married Juanita Cox and they had five sons, Mike, John, Steve, Greg and Robert (1960-2005). Lorene married Lloyd Gump and they had four children, Cindy, James (1950-1951), William and Rebecca. Dean married, first, Pat Miller, and they had Mark, Robin and Charles. Dean then married Judy Obear and they had Joseph (1971-1971) and Jennifer. Paul married Shirley McKay and they had Dennis, Bonnie, Bart and Kelly. Gary married Rebecca and they had Beth, Amy, Molly and Heidi.

Dorothy died on February 25, 1975. Clarence died on November 8, 1977. They are buried in Prairie Grove Cemetery, along with six generations of Dorothy's family.

Submitted by Judy Bunn

DEAN EDWARD & JUDITH ANNE (OBEAR) BUNN

Dean was born December 23, 1933 to Clarence H. Bunn and Dorothy M. Graham. He spent his youth in the Fort Wayne area attending Huntertown School, James Smart School and graduating from Central High School in 1952. Summers were sometimes spent in various parts of Indiana and other states as his father's business, C. H. Bunn Trucking Company traveled to job sites. One summer found them staying at Ridinger Lake where Dean and his younger brother, Paul, drove Dad's pickup truck into the lake to wash it; and took Mom on a ride in the front of a row boat and let the front of the boat hang suspended over a small dam. Dean and Paul's sense of humor stayed with them throughout their lives. Dean owned dump trucks, leasing them to his father's company and later to other companies. For a time he had his own company and hired other drivers and trucks.

On February 11, 1955 Dean eloped with Patricia Miller to Angola, Indiana. They made their home in Fort Wayne on the same block of Mason Drive as Dad and Mom and the families of brothers Bob and Paul.

Dean and Pat had three children, Mark Alan, Robin Joan and Charles Edward. All three have birthdays on the 23rd day of the month, the same as their father. Mark has a son KC Alan (Alecia Waymire) and three grandsons, Waylon, Wesley and William who live in Oklahoma. Mark first lived in Florida, but currently lives in South Carolina. Robin has three children, Amanda, Erica and Michael and lives in North Carolina with husband E. Todd Kissel. Amanda has a son Christopher L. Yarbrough. Chuck and Joyce Kleber Bunn have two children Jodie and Bryan and make Fort Wayne their home. Dean and Pat divorced in 1970 and Pat moved to Florida.

Judy was born in 1937 to George W. Obear and Margaret F. Fry and raised in Delphi, Indiana. She attended Delphi School, grades one through twelve, all in the same building, graduating in 1955. Then it was on to DePauw University for four years, following in the footsteps of her father, uncle, sister and cousins. After college she married Fred Augspurger and lived in Germany for fourteen months and then Indianapolis for several years before moving, in 1964, to Fred's hometown, Fort Wayne. They divorced in 1970.

Dean and Judy were married in Fort Wayne and had two children, Joseph Dean (1971-1971) and Jennifer Joanne. Jennifer married Chad Hogle. After their divorce, a job took her to San Francisco where she makes her home.

Dean loved to play the piano and organ. His father, Clarence, taught him different chords on the piano that he had learned from his father,

Charles, Pat, Mark, Dean and Robin Bunn

Jefferson. Dean took it from there, never reading a note of music, playing the piano and organ entirely by ear. Dean died December 3, 1998, after a long struggle with emphysema.

Judy worked for Fort Wayne National Bank and retired from National City Bank as Assistant Vice President and Trust Officer.

Submitted by Jennifer Bunn

JEFFERSON LEWIS & MINNIE CATHERN (GENTH) BUNN

Jefferson was one of three children born to Harmon and Amanda Lavina (Wallace) Bunn in Putnam County, Ohio, on March 26, 1878. Harmon (1854-1908) and Amanda (1853-1914) came to Allen County around 1879 and settled on a farm in Pleasant Township near Nine Mile. Harmon was the twelfth of fourteen children born to James (1812-1880) and Rosanna (1810-1868) (Bushong) Bunn. Harmon's paternal grandparents were Peter Bunn (1748-1828) of Berks County, Pennsylvania, and Ross County, Ohio, and Mary Lewis (1769-1851) of Virginia. Peter Bunn's father Nicholas (1721-1777) and grandfather, Peter Bon/Bun (1675-1745) resided in Montgomery County, Pennsylvania. This last Peter emigrated from Haarlen, The Netherlands. Harmon's maternal grandparents were George and Lydia (Rush) Bushong. Harmon's maternal great-grandparents were Virginians, John Bushong and Janet Sumners.

Jefferson and Minnie (Genth) Bunn

Minnie was born on April 22, 1880 in Lafayette Township, the first of four children to Eli and Anna "Annie" E. (Layman) Genth. Minnie's paternal grandfather, Adam Genth (1816-1878) immigrated from Wertenburg, Germany, to Stark County, Ohio, where he married Katharina Roller (1815-1897). They then settled on a farm in Lafayette Township. Anna Layman (1859-1930) was the daughter of John Layman (1832-1915) and Mary Lininger (1840-1908) of Huntington County, Indiana.

Jeff and Minnie were married on June 23, 1904, and had ten children: Russell Lewis (Margaret Heiney, Ruby Oyer), Clarence Harmon (Dorothy Graham), Merle Leroy (Viola Oyer), Opal Catherine (Randall Houser, John DeWitt), Minnie May (1914-1922), Ralph Jefferson (Lorranine Blanchard, Margaret Curry), Edward Eugene (Dawn Faust, Helen Hillegass), Anna Helen (Joseph Christlieb, Fred Davis), James Junior (Katherine Arnold, Genevieve Barrand, Mary Hornett Wirick), and Donald Earl (M. Christine Hallmark).

Anna (Layman) and Eli Genth

Jeff was a carpenter by trade and musician at heart. He built many four square houses in the Fort Wayne area. During the twenties and thirties he had a swing and square dance band, playing the violin and calling the square dances. The dances in the Pennsylvania Employees' Club Room at Jefferson and Harrison Streets were a family affair. Minnie made and sold sandwiches, Opal and Anna took tickets and checked coats. There Opal met Randall, a band member who played a variety of instruments. Merle, Clarence and Jim provided chords on the piano. Jim continued playing the piano, entertaining family and friends playing entirely by ear. Jeff's violin remains in the family with his great-granddaughter, Becky Gump Prater. Jeff and Minnie spent the last years of their lives in Garrett, Indiana.

Russell (1905-1996) owned the Huntertown Auto Sales from 1934 to 1957. He retired to his Emily, Minnesota, resort in the summer and Fort Lauderdale, Florida, in the winter. He was in the Army from 1942 to 1945. Russ and Ruby (1913-1996) took nephew Gene Bunn to raise has their own.

Clarence (1907-1977) and Dorothy (1908-1975) had seven children, five survived to adulthood. Clarence was the owner of C. H. Bunn Trucking Co.

Merle (1908-1958) and Viola (1910-1980) had four children, Velma, Gene, Dale and Keith. After Merle died, Vi married Harve Neuenschwander. Garrett, Indiana, was their home.

Opal (1910-2002) and Randall (1905-1957) had three children, Randall, Maxine and Jack (1946-1949). The Huntertown area was their residence.

Ralph (1915-1991) and Lorraine (1922-1957) had Barbara. Ralph and Margaret had Dale and Ralph. They made their home in Churubusco, Indiana.

Ed (1917-1998) and Helen (1925-1992) had seven children, Tom, David, Ken, Jo Ann, Wayne, Monica and Ed. Garrett, Indiana was home to them.

Ralph, Anna, Clarence, Russ, Ed, Opal, Jim, Don

Anna helped raise Fred's children, Dulane and Donell. Anna retired from Kraft Foods after 24 years. Fred (1923-1997) retired from International Harvester after 34 years. They arrived in Fort Lauderdale, Florida, on January 6, 1975. There, after a few years of leisure, they went back to work. Anna retired after 13 years from Marrow's Nut House and Fred retired after 18 years as a golf cart mechanic. They had many hobbies and interests. Anna enjoyed bowling, bingo, cards, ceramics, and Las Vegas. Fred enjoyed golf and cards, but his main interest was helping people.

Jim (1923-1997) and Katie (1925-1992) had three children, Jerry (1943-1943), Carolyn Marie and Richard. Jim and Genevieve (1924-1991) had James and Rhonda.

Don (1926-2002) and Chris had seven children, Donnie (killed in Vietnam), Dennis, Larry, Linda, Randy (1957-1957), Jeff and Kathy. They made Fort Wayne their home.

Jeff and Minnie spent the last years of their lives in Garrett, Indiana. They are buried in the Huntertown Cemetery, Huntertown, Indiana.

Submitted by Mark Bunn

BURNS (BYRNE), LONERGAN, WERONETZKI FAMILIES

James Burns was baptized July 3, 1835, in St. Patrick's Catholic Church, Rathvilly, County Carlow, Ireland. His parents were Mick Byrne and Bridget Neill of Rathmore, Ireland. It is believed that James traveled to America at a very young age with Patrick Burns. The latter is believed to have been about 20 years of age at the time and was either an older brother or other relative of James. Information available from the 1893 obituary of Patrick indicates that they landed in New Orleans, traveled north and then followed the canal route, settling first in Lima, Ohio, and then to Fort Wayne, Indiana. During this journey, James married Mary Lonergan, one of four daughters of John Lonergan and Bridget White in Ohio. Patrick and his wife, Ellen, were married in Xenia, Ohio, in 1861 and eventually both families settled in Fort Wayne. Patrick became a well-known and highly respected citizen. He was one of the pioneer settlers in Fort Wayne and contributed his share to the material prosperity of the community.

James worked at the Pennsylvania Railroad shops as a toolmaker for 40 years. He was a proud member of the Ancient Order of Hibernians and St. Patrick's Catholic Church. James and Mary had five children all born in Indiana: Mary (John Zuber), Julia (William Schafer), Edward (Anna Weronetzki), James, and John. The last child, John, met with a tragic death at age two, when he drowned in a ditch while playing at their home on Bass Street. One month prior, his mother had died at age 30. After this double tragedy, James Burns married Ellen Kennelly and they eventually had three children: Michael (Helen Dodane), Collette (Joe Jolley), and Margarette (George Ardewin). Michael was elected Seventh Ward district councilman in Fort Wayne and held the office from 1922 to 1935. Some 25 years later, his son, Paul "Mike" Burns, was elected mayor of Fort Wayne from 1960 to 1964.

Anna Veronica Weronetzki, the future bride of Edward Burns, the son of James Burns and Mary Lonergan, arrived in the United States on April 21, 1882, at the age of three traveling with

James Burns (1900)

Sisters, Mary (Lonergan) Burns and Johanna Lonergan (1870)

her parents, Joseph and Amelia Weronetzki, from Hamburg, Germany, along with a younger sister, Minnie (Henry Dirig). Upon settling in Fort Wayne, two more daughters were born, Mary (Lloyd Slater, Martin Fiegel) and Louise (Frank Vevia). Joseph Weronetzki worked for the Bass Foundry until his death in 1890. His widow, Amelia, married again to Charles Rastenberg and that marriage produced three more children: William, Selma (Robert Sims, Art Gordon), and Amanda (Melvin Sims).

The marriage of Anna Veronica Weronetzki to Edward Burns in 1898 produced ten children:

Amelia and Joseph Weronetzki and daughter, Anna (Burns) (1882)

Robert (Kate Fulk), Harry (Edna Wynn), Evelyn (Anthony Holocher), Blanche (Elmer Amstutz), Violet (George Gillardo), Alice (John Wendling), Grace (Marshall Bobay), Ruth (Gregor Klug), Jeanette (died at age three), and Geraldine (Robert Lytle). Edward was affectionately called "Pop" by his children and grandchildren. He spent most of his working years at Fort Wayne Dairy Equipment on Winter Street as a mold maker. He took pleasure in cultivating his grape arbors to make his own wine. Anna was known for her German cooking and especially her homemade sauerkraut, which she made in a ten-gallon crock. Their home became a gathering place for any and all occasions. Most of Anna and Edward's married children lived in surrounding houses next to their parents, which caused that area to become known as "Burnsville". An unfortunate fall caused Edward to die unexpectedly in 1942 whereas Anna lived to be 80 years old. Both Edward and Anna are buried in the Catholic Cemetery in Fort Wayne, Indiana

Submitted by Sharon Windling

ROBERT CLYDE & LINDA JEAN BLOOM BURRELL FAMILY

Linda Jean Bloom was born September 14, 1956 at Parkview Hospital in Fort Wayne, Indiana. She is the daughter of Clarence Nicholas and Kathryn Ann Bowen Bloom. She was born while the family lived at 2313 California Avenue. When she was two years old, they moved to 1857 Florida Drive. She attended Forest Park kindergarten, St. Jude grade school, Lakeside Middle School, and graduated from North Side High School in 1974. Upon graduating, she enrolled in the Parkview School of Radiologic Technology and Indiana University, DOTS. She worked at Parkview as a radiologic technologist in the special procedure area after graduation. She left Parkview to work for Fort Wayne Radiology in one of their private offices and eventually became the office manager of the Breast Diagnostic Center.

Her siblings are Karen Bloom of Chicago, Janet Baltzell, James and Robert Bloom and Martha Conkling all of Fort Wayne and Jeff Bloom of San Diego, California.

Linda married Robert Clyde Burrell on November 13, 1982, at St. Jude Catholic Church. He is the son of Thomas Charles and Marguerite Watt Burrell and was born January 17, 1956, in Fort Wayne. As a child, he acquired the nickname "Gus." He attended South Wayne Grade School, Harrison Hill and graduated from South Side in 1974. When Gus was a young boy, his parents purchased land at Big Long Lake in LaGrange County. His father built a cottage there and the family, to this day, enjoys time at the lake. Gus attended Indiana University, Fort Wayne and is President of Group Insurance Services whose company is headquartered at 3609 Lake Avenue. He has been in the insurance business since 1977. Gus has sisters Elizabeth Burrell Weitz, Laurel Donner and a brother Matt.

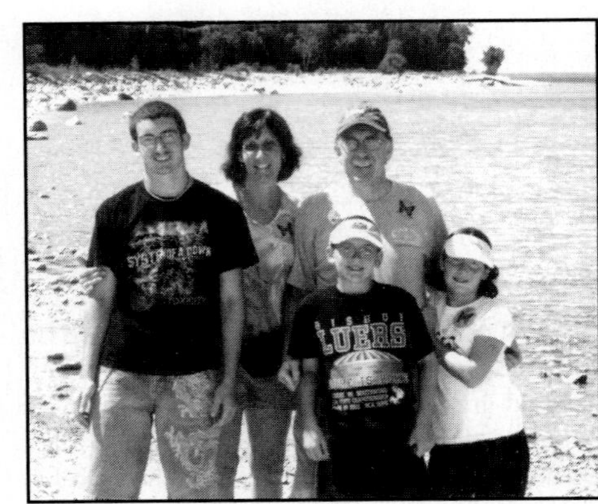

The Burrell Family

They have three children: Zachary Robert born December 5, 1987, Natalie Rose born November 16, 1992 and Nicholas Charles born December 23, 1994. The family belongs to St. John the Baptist Catholic Church. Zachary is a senior at Bishop Luers High School where he is captain of the cross country and track teams. He has been named to the High Honor Roll every year. He is active in Key Club, National Honor Society, Academic Super Bowl, World Culture Club, and FBLA. The highlight of his 2005 summer was a trip to Spain with a group from Bishop Luers. He has attained the rank of Eagle Scout with his project being the remodeling of the Girl Scout Room at St. John's. Natalie is in the seventh grade at St. John's. She plays CYO basketball and Foster Park Little League softball. Natalie loves horses and catching butterflies. Nicholas is in the fifth grade at Saint John's and plays baseball for the Foster Park Little League. This year he is a lineman on the football team.

In 2004, the Burrells purchased a lake home on Big Long Lake not far from Gus's family cottage. Over the last two summers, the two younger children have enjoyed lake life and have made friends with all of the human and animal neighbors.

Submitted by Robert C. and Linda Burrell

ANDREW BURRY

Andrew Burry

In 1873 Andrew Burry was born in Untervillier, Switzerland, and grew up in the farming village of Souboz, where he attended a two-room schoolhouse. At age eleven, with five siblings and his mother, he immigrated to the United States to join his eldest brother and father, who had established a farm for the family in Berne, Indiana. Andrew, who spoke French and German, mastered English and could quote *Caesar's Gallic Wars* in Latin when he was in his nineties. A proud new American, he gave himself the middle name George in honor of George Washington.

After studying at Oberlin College, where he also taught French classes, he moved to Fort Wayne and bought a bookbindery in partnership with Joel Welty in 1896. On a trip to California, he met Ida Adela Lister (1881-1962) from Glidden, Iowa. She had left school to care for her mother, who was going blind. After her mother's death, she, two brothers and a sister homesteaded in Stratton, Colorado, where she was the postmistress. Her brother Len introduced them, and they were married January 6,1909. They had two children, Ralph Lister (1910-1987) and Alice Louise (1916).

With his wife, Kathryn Gerlach, and children, Lynn Wolff and Dennis, Ralph moved to Los Gatos, California, in 1950 and resided in that area for the rest of his life. Alice, who married attorney John Edward Hoffman (1915-1997) in 1941, continues to live in Fort Wayne as does her son, John Andrew, who owns the Hoffman Collection in Covington Plaza. Her daughters Lissa (Alice Lister) Petersen and Laurie Ann Budash reside in California, and her daughter Susan Elizabeth Rehrer, in Michigan.

In 1897 the Fort Wayne Book Bindery took an unexpected detour when R.T. McDonald, who ran the city's electric company, hired Andrew to build handmade filing boxes for him. They impressed Louis Fox, who ran a candy and baking business. He commissioned large numbers of boxes as did the hosiery plant (later Wayne Knitting Mills). So in 1898 Joel Welty and Andrew founded the Wayne Paper Box and Printing Corporation, which prospered until, in 1955, it merged with Container Corporation of America, which was eventually bought by Exxon-Mobil. Andrew was elected treasurer in 1904, president in 1934, and Chair of the Board/CEO in 1941. He retired in 1955 at age 82.

Over the years he held many diverse leadership posts. In 1908 he co-founded the Fort Wayne Rescue Mission. He was president of Hope Hospital Association and the Methodist Hospital Board and served as a board member of Lincoln National Bank. He was president of the National Federation of Paper Box Manufacturers, Rotary Club, YMCA, Associated Churches, and the Board of Trustees of Plymouth Congregational Church. He earned the Boy Scouts' Silver Beaver award and became a 33rd degree Mason.

After retirement he remained active in the community, took daily walks, and lived a healthy life with a sharp mind until he died January 22, 1975, ten days before his 102nd birthday.

Submitted by Alice Louise Burry Hoffman.

THE ROY ALAN BUSKIRK FAMILY

Roy and Karen Buskirk

Roy Alan Buskirk was born June 25, 1944, in Allen County, Indiana, to Ruhl D. and Lois Clarene (Coverdale-Ploughe) Buskirk. Ruhl and Lois lived on the family farm in Section 7, Pleasant Township, with their five children: Claris C., Amy L., Arlene M., Marvin D. and Roy A. Claris married Kedric Eversole of Wells County, Amy married Stanley Zent of Huntington County, Arlene married Bruce L. Lenich of Lebanon County, Pennsylvania, and Marvin married Anna Mae Schlaudroff of Allen County.

Roy married Becky Ann (Platt) Switzer on November 29, 1969. The marriage ended in divorce in 1992. They had three children: Michael Alan, Michelle Ann and Matthew Troy. On January 6, 1995, Roy married Karen J. (Creager-Charleswood) Teegardin. Karen had two children, Shannon Rena and Shawn Owen.

Roy graduated from Lafayette Center High School in 1962 where he lettered in cross county track, volleyball, baseball and basketball. He also played on the ping pong team in the 1961 Allen County Athletic Conference Tournament. In the 1961 ACAC Conference Basketball Tournament, Lafayette Center trailed Bishop Luers by 19 points starting the fourth quarter. After two overtimes, the game went to sudden death with Lafayette Center making the first basket and winning the game. It is believed that this was the last sudden death game in Indiana basketball. Roy was selected to the 1962 ACAC Conference All Star Basketball Team. Roy attended Fort Wayne International Business College, while working for City Service Oil Company and Jet Air Freight, until entering the U. S. Army in August of 1965. Roy served in the 82nd Airborne Military Police assigned to Criminal Investigations Division (CID) until September 1966, when he volunteered for service in Vietnam. While in Vietnam, he was attached to the 89th Military Police Group. In August 1967, he received an honorary discharge from the Army, obtaining a rank of sergeant. Upon returning home, he immediately re-enrolled at International Business College, and obtained an Associate Degree in Business Administration and Finance in March 1968. In 1968, Roy and his brother, Marvin, formed a farming partnership, which continued for five years. While farming with his brother, Roy also worked for the National Farmers Organization as a Regional Supervisor, covering the northern half of Indiana and the southern six counties in Michigan. In 1972, after obtaining his real estate license, Roy left farming and started his real estate career with Nick Stayanoff, Auctioneer and Realtor. In 1982, Roy was employed by Sturges, Griffin and Trent Commercial Real Estate, working in their appraising division for twelve years. In 1994, Roy started his own real estate firm, specializing in locating commercial sites, appraising and right-of-way buying for roads, sewer and water. In January 2003, Roy was elected by the Republican Party Caucus to an at-large position on the Allen County Council. In the 2004 county election, Roy was re-elected to a four year term, which he currently serves.

In 1967, Karen graduated from Ashley High School and in 1969 graduated from the Fort Wayne Beauty College. She currently drives a school bus for special needs children. The Buskirk family settled in Section 7 of Pleasant Township in 1850, coming from the Sandusky, Ohio, area. Roy and Karen currently live on part of the farm and their son, Matthew and his wife, Jill, own part of the original farm. Matthew is the eighth generation of Buskirks owning property in Section 7. Direct-line surnames from Allen County include Coverdale, Branstrator and Fogwell. The Buskirks are proud of their family heritage in Allen County and hope to be able to contribute back to the county and its people.

Submitted by Roy A. Buskirk

BUSSE FAMILY TREE

Karl Busse was born May 17, 1841, in Hargenstadt in Hanover, Germany, and married Wilhelmina (Minnie) Reiter on September 17, 1871. Minnie was born January 11, 1851, in Minden in Hanover, Germany.

Karl Busse had three brothers living in Germany, Henry, Dietrick, and William, and two sisters, Minnie (Busse) Boeler, and Sophia (Busse) Hilgemeier. William and his wife, Christina (Dickmeyer) Busse came to America in 1892 and lived here in Fort Wayne. Both died in the house they built on New Haven Avenue.

When Karl Busse came to America in 1862, he was 20 years old. He was a carpenter by trade and helped build The Martini Lutheran Church on the Moeller Road; he put the cross on the steeple of the church. The church still stands.

They had the following children: Wilhelm Busse married Caroline Marhenke (date unknown); Louise Busse married Henry Weber, October 13, 1895; Sophie Busse died at birth; Dietrick Busse died at 11 years old; Karl (Charlie) Busse married Christina Dickie April 30, 1905; Henry Busse married Mary Siemumd October 14,1902; Herman Busse died at 11 months old; Christian Busse married Louise Brockmeyer (date unknown); Herman Busse married Lela Bowman April 15, 1914; Minnie Busse married Fred Wietfeldt May 7, 1908; August Busse married Louise Hannefeldt July 24, 1912. Carl Busse died July 14, 1907 and Minnie died May 1, 1901.

Karl (Charlie) and Christina Busse's family: Christina Busse, Hilda Busse Peters, Arthur Busse, Frieda Busse Linker, and Karl (Charlie) Busse

Charlie and Christina first lived in Fort Wayne and later bought the Busse home place on the Parent Road near New Haven. They had three children:

Frieda married Edgar Linker October 3, 1936, and they had two sons: Roger; and James married Connie Rushart July 22, 1967.

Hilda married Robert Peters June 21, 1934, and they had three children: Ronald married Mary Brager August 10, 1957; Kenneth married Billie Brooks June 7, 1958; and Jane married Jack Helton June 26, 1970.

Arthur married Velma Peters November 24, 1934 and they had three children: Carl married Ruth Buuck November 27, 1957; Marilyn married Gilbert Bradtmueller July 4, 1958; and Janice married Otto Bradtmueller Jr. February 14, 1959.

Karl (Charlie) died December 13, 1957. Christina remained on the farm where her daughter, Frieda Linker, and family lived with her until her death in March 22, 1966 when the farm was then sold.

Submitted by Janice Busse Brandtmueller

BUTLER FAMILY & THE CATHOLIC CEMETERY 1893-1965

In 1889, Thomas P. Butler came from Ballyragget, County Kilkenny, Ireland. He had been the chief gardener to Lord Ashbrook. He worked at Winona Lake, Indiana, before coming to Fort Wayne in 1891 to work at St. Patrick's Catholic Church. Thomas married Flora Oles in 1891 in Columbia City, Indiana. In 1893, he was appointed Superintendent of the Fort Wayne Catholic Cemetery. They had nine children, of which only four survived past infancy and one of them, James C. Butler, Sr., followed in Thomas' footsteps. Thomas and James cared for and protected the treasures of the cemetery for seventy-three years. Often they had to pay the laborers when times were hard and money was scarce.

Original Entrance, Catholic Cemetery

Thomas Butler was a charter member of the Northern Indiana Association of Cemetery Superintendents and Officials and was one of its past presidents. He, at one time, held a membership in the American Association of Cemetery Superintendents.

The Butlers lived in both of the cemetery houses, one built in 1874 and the other in 1915. There was a greenhouse adjacent to the home and they grew the flowers that were planted in 900 vases for the gravesites. The original home and greenhouse were torn down in 1915 and the new home and greenhouse was built on the same location.

That same year, the mausoleum was built which is a block away from the homesite. It is one of a kind and the oldest in the United States. The architect was Charles Weatherhogg. The marble altar was torn out after the Butlers moved from the cemetery and before anyone else realized its uniqueness and value. A smaller altar was made from parts of the original altar.

Thomas Butler died and was laid out in the newer house. James C. Butler, Sr. died in the same room where his father had been laid out. Bishop Pursley officiated over James' funeral and Bishop Crowley wrote about his life. Bishop D'Arcy had a plaque placed in the Cathedral Museum to also honor James. This plaque was donated by Steven Butler, Sr., son of James, Sr., and is a copy of the life story written by Bishop Crowley. James C. Butler, Sr. is the first layman to be honored in the Cathedral Museum.

Thomas and Flora's oldest son John worked at the cemetery along with his two sons, Patrick and Joe. Another son, Thomas, worked at the cemetery through his high school years. He left the cemetery to pursue another career and died at the age of 26.

Original marble alter at the Catholic Cemetery Mausoleum, built 1915 torn out sometime after 1966

Original greenhouse at the Catholic Cemetery built in 1903. Thomas P. Butler and his wife, Flora, picture prior to 1915.

William A. Butler, another son of Thomas, spent fifty years working along with him and James, at the cemetery. William's sons, Richard, William, Robert and Donald, a son-in-law, Hank McNeal, and grandsons, Bob McNeal and Denny Butler also worked there.

James was named Assistant Superintendent in 1933. He set up the books and took care of them beginning at the age of 17. He became Superintendent in 1954 and remained there until his death in 1965. He is the only one who ever held both Assistant Superintendent and Superintendent. James C. Butler, Sr. was a 1931 graduate of Central Catholic High School. He married Verdona Feichter on October 13, 1932. They had three children, James C., Jr., Sally (who became Sister Donna) and Steven M., Sr. Both James, Jr. and Steven, Sr. worked at the cemetery until the death of James, Sr. James, Jr. worked another month handling funerals and the payroll until a replacement could be found.

In 1955, James C. Butler, Sr. was the Second Vice President of the Indiana Association of Cemetery Officials. He was elected President in 1957. In 1963, he was the Welcome Chairman of Indiana Association of Cemetery Officials.

The new chapel is built on the site of the two former homes and is named in honor of Blessed Mother Theodore Guerin, founder of the Sisters of Providence to which Sister Donna Butler belongs. So, in essence, the Butler home is still there...Just in a different form.

In 2004 and 2005, James Butler, Jr. returned to the Catholic Cemetery to care for the two large urns at the Breen Memorial Altar in the main circle. The last time he had cared for the urns was in 1952 at age 18. It signifies that the Butler family has cared and still cares for the cemetery for a period spanning the last three centuries.

Submitted by James C. Butler, Jr., Joyce A. Butler, Sister Donna Butler, Steven M. Butler, Sr., and Rebecca K. Butler. James, Jr. is the Butler family and Catholic Cemetery historian.

ALBERT HEINRICH BUUCK

Albert Heinrich Buuck (1878-1943) married June 2, 1901, Clara Hildebrandt in Fort Wayne. They had four children: Lorena, Walter, Gertrude, and Helen.

First home at Catholic Cemetery (built 1874), greenhouse and barn, c.1907. L to R: Thomas P. Butler, unknown, Flora, William and John

L to R: Flora Oles Butler, James C. Butler, Sr., and father, Thomas P. Butler, c. 1928

Butler family, September 20, 1987, Last Thanksgiving at the cemetery before the house was torn down

Second home at Catholic Cemetery, 1915-1987

Verdona P. Butler (1914-1953), wife of James C. Butler, Sr. c. 1949

L to R: Steve, Becky, Sister Donna, Joyce, and Jim Butler

James C. Butler, Sr., 5th Superintendent of the Catholic Cemetery, Fort Wayne, Indiana

L to R: James Sr., Verdona, and James Jr. Butler

L to R: Sally A. Butler and her father, James C. Butler, Sr., on Sally's high school graduation from St. Mary of the Woods College, June 1958

James C. Butler, Sr.'s office, built in 1941 and still standing

Donna Butler, Sisters of Providence, holding the plaque with the story of her father, James Butler Sr.'s life, by Bishop Crowley. Steven Butler Sr., had the plaque made for the Cathedral Museum

Donna Butler, Sisters of Providence, 1965

William A. Butler, and wife Linda married 50 years. William, son of Thomas P. and Flora, worked 50 years at the cemetery

James C. Butler, Sr., James Jr., Verdona P., 1937, Washington, D.C.

Albert was the son of Dietrich Conrad Buuck (1834-1906) and Marie Werfelman (1839-1927). Dietrich had thirteen children and settled in Fort Wayne after 1890. His father, Karl Frederick (12 children) and Uncle Ernst Buuck, Jr. (9 children) came to this country from Windheim, Germany, in 1836. They settled at Friedheim in Adams County, just outside of Decatur.

Albert was a businessman starting out as a sales clerk in his father's business known as D. Buuck and Co. The store at 119 East Lewis carried groceries, flour, and feed. In 1909, Albert started his own business known as Al Buuck and Co: Wholesale Tobacco and was located at 1022 South Barr Street. By 1922 he was president/manager of Wayne Tobacco Company at 119 East Washington with his daughter Lorena as stenographer. At the last, he was president of Wayne Cigar Company located at 113 East Columbia. In 1927, he got out of the tobacco business.

Shortly after that, he purchased the property at the northwest comer of West Wayne Street and Fulton. It was turned into a rooming house known as the University Club for young men enrolled in college. Most of the boarders attended Indiana Tech, which was then located at 219 East Washington. There were enough rooms to accommodate ten to twelve men. When the house-was full the family stayed in an apartment in the carriage house on Fulton. This building is now an art gallery.

Clara was born in 1880, the daughter of Fred (1848-1917) and Minnie Hildebrand. She had two brothers, Charles and Otto. Until her death in January 1940, Clara did all of the cooking, laundry, and cleaning for the University Club. Albert continued operating the house until his death in December 1943.

It was in this house that Helen (1918-1987) met her future husband, Ed Connell (1916-1978). During his stay at the house, he occupied much of the third floor. It was there that he perfected his magic act with Helen being his assistant. They, along with other magicians in

Clara and Albert Buuck wedding photo.

the area, would put on shows for various occasions. He left Indiana Tech to join the Air Force at the start of World War II. Ed later retired as a colonel. After his death, Helen moved to Indianapolis to be with her sons, Barry and Richard. She died there.

Gertrude (1908-June 1978) was a stenographer for many years for the Pennsylvania Railroad, now Conrail. She married Elmer Mohrhardt (1903-1950). They had no children.

Walter (1905-1956) followed in his father's footsteps by becoming a salesman, first for Peter Eckrich and Sons, and later for Parrot Packing Co. He married Ruth Center (1895-1949), a Dictaphone operator for S.F. Bowser Company for 35 years. They had one child Marjorie Buuck-Davis (1932).

Lorena (1903 to Nov. 1978) married Fred Speckman (1895-1958). They had two children, Albert (1923-1977) and Betty Speckman-Twist.

Submitted by Marge Buuck Davis

HELEN LOUISE COOK BYERLY

Mrs. Helen Louise Cook Byerly was very much a part of the Lake Township, Arcola, Indiana, history, and she still is. She was 100 years old August 1, 2004. She was born in Arcola in 1904 in a house on the northeast corner of Main Street. The house is no longer there, having been torn down quite a few years ago.

Helen Louise Cook Byerly

Helen was born to Arthur P. Cook (age 38), and Mary Ella Shaffer (age 25), both born in Lake Township, Arcola, seven years after their marriage on May 15, 1897. In the Allen County records it says they had three children.

Helen attended Arcola Grade School, then Central High School in Fort Wayne. Arcola didn't have high school until 1922 when the new school was built. Helen then went to college at Manchester College and Indiana University. She was a first grade teacher at Arcola beginning with the 1926-1927 year.

She met Dwight (Pete) Paul Byerly, from Adams County, Indiana. He was born October 20, 1903, to Jessie Byerly and Armitta Early Byerly in Adams County. Pete Byerly was the coach of boys and girls basketball at Arcola from 1927 to 1931. In 1931 he was Helen O. Vaughn Miller's coach; Helen is 91 years old and still lives in Arcola. Pete was a very fine coach of the Arcola Greyhounds.

Dwight and Helen married July 30, 1932, at Helen's church, the Arcola Methodist, and they were married for 59 years.

Helen was a first grade teacher at Arcola for 43 years, from 1926 until 1969 when she retired. She lived in Arcola until 1954 when she moved to Fort Wayne. Dwight was a teacher in Fort Wayne.

Arcola became just a grade school in 1968. After that, all the children from Arcola Grade School went to Carroll High School, which serves the Arcola and Huntertown area.

Helen is now 100 years old and lives at Westlake, Ohio. May God bless her.

Submitted by Kenny Kurtz

DEMETRIO CACCAMO & JOSEPHINE AMUSO FAMILY

Demetrio Caccamo was born on February 11, 1890, in Calabria Italy. Josephine Amuso was born on August 15, 1892, also in Calabria, Italy. They met and were married in 1911. Demetrio moved to Chicago, and in 1920, Josephine and their daughter, Grace, joined him. Demetrio worked at various jobs, and Josephine took care of their growing family. Dominic (Doc) was born in 1921, Carmella (Carm) in 1922, Joseph (Joe) in 1923, Michael in 1924 (died at 9 months), and Micheline in 1925. The family then moved to Fort Wayne in 1926, where Demetrio worked at Fort Wayne Tailoring. In 1927 Demetrio and Josephine had another son, Frank. Their family continued to grow with John (Johnny) in 1929, Stella in 1930 (died in childhood), Rosemary in 1931 and Margaret (Marge) in 1933.

Their first child, Grace (now deceased), married Guido Pilot (now deceased), and they had a son named James. They lived in Texas for awhile where Guido farmed orange groves, but they returned to Fort Wayne and opened a restaurant, The Venice, with Grace's brother, Doc, and his wife, Yolanda.

Doc (now deceased) married Yolanda (Londi) Gigli, and they had three children: Ronald, Kathy and Donna. Upon retiring, Doc and Londi moved to Angola and opened another restaurant on Lake James.

Carm married Dante Sartori, and they had five daughters: Rita, Donna, Cynthia, Patricia and Lisa. Carm and Dante moved numerous times with Dante's construction job but eventually settled in Kokomo, Indiana.

Joe married Jean Newswander (now deceased) and their children were Joseph, Jerry, Judy, Janice, Joannie and Johnny (died at age 13). Joe and Jean remained in Fort Wayne, where Joe worked at Wayne Candies.

Micheline (now deceased) married Charles (Chuck) Montagna, and they had Deborah, Frank Jr. (now deceased) and Linda. They moved to New Jersey, where Chuck worked for Lionel.

Frank (now deceased) married Elvira Richardson, and they had no children. Frank worked at Harvester.

Demetrio Caccamo and Josephine Amuso Family, 1928. Top Row, L to R: Detetrio, Josephine, Grace. Front Row, L to R: Carmella, Micheline, Frank, Joseph, Dominic

Johnny married Jeannette Redman and they had Karen, Michael, Kevin and Debra. Johnnny worked at Zollner Piston.

Rosemary (now deceased) married Donald (Don) Kaylor (now deceased), and they had Steven, Linda, Mark, Michael and David. Don worked for a warehouse distribution center and also a bakery.

Marge (now deceased) married Jerry Elward (now deceased) and they had Cynthia, Suzette, Therese, David and Michael (stillborn). Jerry worked at Bowmar and then Dana.

Demetrio and Josephine's heritage continues to grow with great grandchildren and great, great grandchildren, who, for the most part, either live in Fort Wayne or nearby cities.

Submitted by Rita Turflinger

CALLAHAN/MORAN FAMILIES

Callahan and Moran ancestry dates back to the great Ireland potato famine. 1846-1847. Submitter's mother's family, Moran, begins with Peter J. Moran (1819-1880), in Multifarm, County of Westmeath, Ireland, who arrived in the United States 1835, settling in Frederick County, Maryland, where he was employed as a leather tanner. Here he married in 1846 Rachel Nuesbaum, whose father, John, was a plantation owner, possibly with slaves. John, born 1747, had 21 children by three wives, and died August 14, 1827, leaving a widow (who must have died 1850s) and bequeathing Rachel $800, which she, in turn gave to her husband, Peter, for starting the Moran Ice Company in Fort Wayne.

Family lore says that Peter immediately sent for his parents to come to America, resulting in his parents, Patrick (1791-1852) and Mary (1794-1836) Moran, coming directly to Fort Wayne in 1835 by way of canal boat (per Aunt Babe), where the canal was being extended from Fort Wayne past Lagro. Both parents were born in Westmeath County and are buried in Fort Wayne. Disease was rampant on crowded canal boats; it is possible that her life was shortened due to the canal experience.

Rachel and Peter moved from Maryland to Cincinnati and then to Fort Wayne, where they purchased land on East Wayne Street in 1849. Peter J. initially began selling ice from a wheelbarrow, but being very industrious, he soon had an ice storage facility and several horses and delivery wagons. Early on, he also had a contract with the government to pick up mail from arriving canal boats, later from trains, and then delivering each pickup promptly to the post office (trains started going through about 1855).

May 10, 1883 Wedding Portraits James T. Callahan and Margaret A. Dolan (Parents of Frank Callahan)

1922 Lawrence Heiny and Stella Loos Heiny Family, 2510 Hoagland Avenue, Fort Wayne

59th Wedding Anniversary of James T. Callahan and Margaret Dolan-Callahan, May 1942, Fort Wayne, Indiana, taken in front of Louis Fox Niezer Home, North Washington Road

June 2004 picture of nine children of Nick and Dorothy Heiny (including spouses) on Ohio River Cruise on "Mississippi Queen" steamboat. Occasion: Nick's 90th birthday.

When Peter J. died, his son Peter Aloysius (1855-1907) took over the ice business, later joined by sons, Peter J. (1882-1922) and Bernard (1883-1934). At Peter A.'s death, sons Peter and Bernard ran the business—until their untimely deaths.

At this point in time, submitter's father, Frank J. Callahan (1885-1973), enters the picture; he had married her mother, Mary Margaret Moran, sister of Peter and Bernard, on June 15, 1909. Frank bought the ice business from the three surviving widows, namely Grandmother Mary Baker-Moran (1859-1939). Peter's widow, Henrietta Schrage-Moran (died 1963), and Bernard's widow, Fern Carey-Moran. The business prospered until after World War II, for although artificial refrigeration was expanded in the 1920s, it was not available in the 1940s when all manufacturing switched to armament making for World War II. People had refrigerators available again, after the War era, and ice sales declined, with Moran Ice closing its doors June 10, 1967.

Mary Margaret Moran-Callahan and Frank Callahan, 1946

Family-wise, other children of Peter J. and Rachel were Mary (1847-1848), Margaret (Albert) Dittoe (1849-1934), William (1851-1892), Marie (1853-1858), James (1857-1882), and Jacob (not listed in Bible). Grandfather Peter A. Moran (1855-1907), had married Mary Baker (1859-1939) on May 24, 1881. Their children, in addition to Peter A., Bernard and Mary, were Gertrude (1887-1887), Alphonsus (1888-1889), Celeste (1890-1901), Thomas (1892-1898) and Amelia (Joseph) Emanuel (1896-1987) (Aunt Babe), who lived in the family home at 617 East Wayne Street, a Federal-style house, until death.

For Callahan ancestors, John C. Callahan (b.c.1833), emigrated from County Clare, Ireland, about 1847 and married Mary Reynolds (1839-1909), also from County Clare, in Susquehanna, Pennsylvania, in 1857, where they had eight children, the oldest of whom was James Thomas Callahan (1858-1942), who married Margaret Dolan (1858-1944) May 10, 1883, in Garrett, Indiana. Other children of John and Mary were John (1860), Joseph (c. 1862), Edward (1864), Mary (1867) (aka Sister Feliciitas Ryan), Thomas (1869), and Elizabeth (1871). Margaret Dolan came to Indiana from Yonkers, New York, with her parents, Thomas Dolan (c. 1821-1904) and Bedelia Moran (1833-1909) (a different family). Thomas sported a long flowing white beard. He and his wife Bedelia lived some 30 years in Garrett, burial in Catholic Cemetery there.

Francis (Frank) J. Callahan, was the second oldest of James and Margaret. Oldest child was Winifred Callahan-Gaehr (1884-1966), who married late in life to David Gaehr, Cleveland, and served overseas with the American Red Cross, World War I. Copies of some World War I letters are on file at Fort Wayne Library and the Women's Service Memorial in Washington, DC. Frank attended Holy Cross College, Worcester, Massachusetts. A very charismatic person, he was an avid Notre Dame football fan, attending all home games and some distant games. An honorary Fire Chief, his name is inscribed on a memorial plaque at Fire Station No. 1, Fort Wayne. Next child was Stephen (1890-1926), with a law degree from Valparaiso University, serving as prosecuting attorney in Fort Wayne, but died prematurely from a burst appendix (no antibiotics). He had spearheaded fund raising for the now defunct Catholic Community Center. Youngest child of James and Margaret, Robert D. (1899-1987), served as an engineer with Western Electric, Chicago.

Most Callahan men in Susquehanna worked for railroads, now criss-crossing the country. James T. first worked as a telegraph operator in New York, eventually reaching position of chief train dispatcher with the Nickel Plate, Fort Wayne. His retirement after 40 years was marked by an elegant banquet here in 1928.

Children of Frank and Mary are Mary (Bernard) Dohn (1910), Rosemary (Louis) Niezer (1911-1995), James (1913-1948), Catherine (1915-1922), Dorothy (Nicholas) Heiny (1917-), Virginia (Cornelius) Sterling (1919-), Bernard 1921-1921), Margaret (Richard) Higginbotham (1922-), Helen (Thomas) Shank (1924-), and Patricia (1927-1945).

Submitted by Dorothy M. Heiny

HOMER EARNEST CAMPBELL

Homer Earnest Campbell (1882-1966) was a most interesting person. Born in Albion, Indiana, he established the H.E. Campbell Body Building and Practical Painting business in 1898. In 1910, he purchased a lot at 2921 Broadway and erected a shop at the rear of the property. Inside the main door was a large wood plank elevator which was hand operated with a large rope, gears and counterweights. It was originally used to raise carriages and wagons to the paint shop on the second floor. Besides carriage building and painting, he also rebuilt and refinished pianos. His auto body repair shop was one of the first in Fort Wayne.

In 1915 he built his residence at the front of the same lot on Broadway. In the late 1920s he built horse vans for J.C. Hutzell's Ovelmo Stables. He built, painted and hand lettered in gold leaf many horse drawn delivery vehicles. Fisher Truck chassis were received and bodies built to the owner's needs. Some companies included Taylor Produce Company, The Hoover Suction Sweeper Company, Becky's Best Milk Company and Wayne Tobacco Company.

He also built truck bodies for Home Telephone, General Telephone, City Light and Northern Indiana Public Service Company. He hand painted many names and logos on trucks for Butler Paper; many dairies including Allen, Eskay, Central, Sunshine and Tonne; Broadway Bakery, Somers Bakery, Huser-Paul Cigar Company, National Mill Supply, Mossman-Yarnelle, Perfection Biscuit Company, Fort Wayne Lumber, Rhoads-Morgan Paint Company and Troy Laundry.

In 1937 he married Mary Marjorie Moore. In the following years, they had three sons, Allan J., Donald E., and Russell E. The writer has fond memories of growing up and working with his three cousins who are still his close friends today.

Also in 1937, Homer designed a gun sight for shotguns or rifles and had it patented. Before and after WWII, Campbell's Dispatch Gun Sights were manufactured and installed at the shop on Broadway.

Homer Earnest Campbell

In 1953 Homer devised a plan to raise the roof on his house about six feet to create an upstairs apartment. By using a series of screw jacks around the perimeter and many extra hands (including my Dad), he doubled the size of his house.

In the early 1950s he designed Slick's Big Fat Wash Woman and painted it on all of their trucks. During the 1950s he also repainted many colored telephones for General Telephone, and every December was spent painting Christmas trees in dark green, blues, white, red, pink, gold and silver. They were sold at Scott's Grocery and Bolyards Service Center.

In the late 1950s, Homer designed and obtained a patent for a new style mechanism for Lazy Susans. He manufactured and sold the hardware to Grabill Cabinet Company for installation in their custom built cabinets.

A favorite memory of the author: "Shortly before I graduated from high school in 1963, I was attempting to repaint my Dad's Oldsmobile after two years of smashing its fenders. When my uncle checked on my progress and saw an impending disaster, he took over the spray gun and covered up all my mistakes. He made a difficult job look easy, even at the age of 81." Thank You Uncle Homer! Your Nephew, Paul W. Leipold

Submitted by Paul W. Leipold

HENRY & CAROLINE (BUNN) CANNADY

The Cannadys were one of the first pioneer families of Allen County. They were from free-born black families that migrated to the Northwest Territory from the U.S. Southeast region.

James Cannady married Elizabeth Scott on February 20, 1808, in Sussex County, Virginia. Their son, Henry, was born in Virginia in 1818. As a youngster, Henry moved to Wayne Township, Allen County, Indiana. In 1842, Henry and five other black men, including his brother, James Jr., were summoned into local court to give accounting for failing to post a $500 bond. By Indiana law all blacks entering the state to settle after 1831 had to pay a bond to assure against indemnity. If the charge was proven, the offender could be hired out for six months by the overseer of poor relief. The Cannadys hired legal counsel, won their case, and thereby were not required to post any bonds. Apparently, Cannadys had resided in Allen County since the 1820s.

In 1823, Caroline was born to Jeremiah and Sophia Bunn, in Virginia. Both parents, who were natives of Virginia, moved their young family to Stark County, Ohio, in 1829. By 1850, Caroline had married Henry Cannady and the couple had five children: Augustus (8), Emily (6), Olive (4), Eliza (2), and William Walter (1). The family resided on the southwest corner of Hanna and Lewis Streets in Fort Wayne. Henry was running his own prosperous plastering business. In 1849, Henry, a community leader, with other board trustees, bought at public auction land for Fort Wayne's first A.M.E. church. It was later known as Turner Chapel A.M.E., the oldest black church in the area. Because an Indiana law required spousal signatures to appear on legal documents, the trustee's wives also signed the county deed. Only Caroline's signature, however, was made with a mark; Caroline could neither read nor write.

By 1862, Caroline had three more children, her namesake; Caroline, Hattie, nicknamed "Carrie," and Charles. During that same year her oldest son, Augustus, married Mary Grojean at his material grandmother's home in Cass County, Michigan. Augustus and his new bride made their home in Fort Wayne.

In 1869, the Cannadys moved to Porter Township, Cass County, Michigan. There their last child, a daughter named Minnie, was born. Henry, who owned real estate valued at $4,000 with personal property worth $500, was farming, while Caroline kept the house and cared for their children. By 1872, the couple owned 73 ½ acres of land. Young Walter had followed his father's path into the plastering business. On June 3, 1882, Henry died from pneumonia.

Seven years later, Caroline married a gentleman farmer, Isaac Stewart. By 1900, she was widowed again and living with her son-in-law and daughter, Allen and Emily Brown, in Allegan County, Michigan. In the autumn of that year, she died and is laid to rest next to Henry in Calvin County Cemetery.

Submitted by Marsha Smiley

DOLORES ELIZABETH BROWN-GREENE-CANSLER

Delores Elizabeth Brown was the second child born to Seno E. Brown Sr. and Della Mae (Warfield) Brown. She was born on September 7, 1927, the middle of three children. At birth she was small and rather quiet, but grew to be a very opinionated, outspoken, and spiritual person. At age three her father died and she, her mother, brother, and sister lived with her Grandmother Warfield until they were grown.

She grew up in Fort Wayne, Indiana, and attended Hanna and Harmar grade schools. She graduated from Central High School in 1945. She attended Fort Wayne Bible School for two years and also took classes at IPFW. She studied Biblical studies, but also Black Culture and Women's studies. During her formative years, Dolores helped her grandmother throughout the neighborhood doing midwife chores for the new mothers of babies in the community, as well as becoming the babysitter for those and other children in the neighborhood. Grandmother Warfield was the daughter of a Baptist preacher, and she had a very deep understanding of the Holy Bible and daily she taught her family "to live for Christ in all that we say and do." Dolores became a loving and caring person because of this early training. This was the beginning of Dolores' spiritual journey. She is a deep abiding Christian who knows and walks with Christ.

During her younger life there were only a few black families in Fort Wayne. The Brown family knew every black family in their area over on Brackenridge, Eliza, and Hayden streets and in the Rolling Mill area, which was off of Taylor Street near the Joslyn steel plant. Black families also lived on Metlia Street and Taylor Street at that time. Jobs available were farming and steel millwork for men; housemaids, restaurant, and clerking jobs for women. Segregation and discrimination was subtle in the north and the Browns learned a lot from their new neighbors from the south about the problems of segregation and discrimination they had faced. Until the "great migration," blacks shared some of the same public facilities as whites because there were so few blacks in Fort Wayne. When the great migration from the south came to Fort Wayne in the '40s and '50s, the Harvester factory opened some jobs for black men and homes for blacks became available on Douglas Avenue and Lewis Street. As the black population grew blacks began moving to other central areas of the city.

As a young person Delores was active at the Wheatly Social Center located in the 400 block of East Douglas Avenue. It was the place that assisted families to get services that were needed. It was a place where the black children could have clubs, games, and an inside area for skating. It was where adults held their social events and celebrations such as skating parties, dances, and stage shows. The center held annual Easter parades, style (fashion) shows, minstrel shows, and Halloween parties. Delores remembers that it was a caring community. She remembers that people like Mr. Unthanks, John Ridley, T. E. Lewis, Ms. Emma Alsup, R. T. Shaw, John Miles, Danny Jones, E. W. Warfield, Francis Warfield, John and Charlie Warfield, Oliver Lee, Sam Stewart, Art Williams, the Porters, the Bryants, the Rhoades, and the Wilcliffs were some, but not all of the early families. They were strong Christian families and they attended one of the black community's two churches, Turner Chapel A.M.E. or Mount Olive Baptist Church.

Delores Greene Cansler

Delores often shares with others what God has done for her all of her life, what it means to serve Jesus, and how he has cared for her and her family. She has worked as an activist/professional for over 50 years. She started out as an outreach person in the neighborhood. She has been a member of Union Baptist Church (formerly Mount Olive Baptist Church) all her life, where she has been on many committees and served as a Sunday school teacher. Dolores has volunteered for numerous causes, beginning with the United Church Women (now Church Women United) in 1941, where she served as president for four years and is still an active member. During the 1960s she recalls that the civil rights movement was underway and they met to integrate jobs, housing, and public accommodations.

Dolores held jobs with the United Way of Allen County, the Fort Wayne Metropolitan Human Relations Committee, and later she was hired as Director of the Inter-Religion Action Council, a social action program in the 1970s. With her knowledge of the people and the community, she was very successful in this program. She was able to get over 500 volunteers from local churches and synagogues, paired with ADC families. The learning process and the caring concern were some of the greatest educational tools Fort Wayne had witnessed. "It was a great experience on both sides," she recalls. Other jobs, such as YWCA Adult Staff Family Program Director, working with the Red Cross, and a case manager for Aging and In-Home Services of Allen County, where she worked forty hours a week until retiring in 2002, made her a great influence throughout the community.

Other volunteer work included Head Start Community representative, YWCA board member, Cub Scout den mother, Brownie Senior Scout and Troop leader, East Central Neighborhood Association, and Project Renew. Delores Cansler's commitment is and has been measured by her involvement in what the issue is and how the masses will be affected. She was married with three children so it was not easy. But she attended these events while taking her children with her in order to stay abreast of things that were going on. She was able to schedule lunches, evenings, vacations, and personal days to do those things which have enhanced her life, making her life fulfilling for herself as well as for those persons lives she helped to change for the better. She accomplished her lifelong goal of sharing and helping others with the lessons life has taught her.

Submitted by Delores Cansler

CHARLES FRANKLIN CARBAUGH & ADELINE GENTH

On February 22, 1900, in Allen County, Charles Franklin Carbaugh and Adeline Genth became man and wife. Called Frank, he had been born October 9, 1870 in Shawnee Township, Cherokee County, Kansas, the second son of William Henry and Elizabeth (Johnson) Carbaugh. In 1875, William and Elizabeth brought their three sons back to Allen County, and Frank grew up on a farm in Lafayette Township. Adeline's parents, also Allen County farmers, were John Peter and Anna Maria (Krumma) Genth.

Frank and Adeline farmed on Brindle Road near Yoder. Frank also drove for the Fort Wayne Transit Company. He actually started with horse-drawn cars, then electric street cars, then trolley coaches, and finally buses. In fact, he was pictured in the newspaper preparing for the last run of streetcars in 1947. Frank and Adeline missed celebrating their 60th wedding anniversary because of her death on September 15, 1959. Frank, at age 92, died of injuries sustained while he was burning a tree stump on his farm. Both he and Adeline are buried in Maple Lawn Cemetery at Nine Mile with their three babies, Arthur William (1901), Selma Vandora (1908), and Larry (1911).

Their older daughter, Gertrude Marie, born September 11, 1903, became Mrs. Russell Welbaum and can be traced in an article about James Phillip and Wilma Carolyn (Welbaum) Nierman. The younger daughter of Frank and Adeline, Lula Berneda, born April 12, 1906, married Frank William Dobbins on February 6, 1926 in Zanesville, Allen County. Their farm was located on Branstrator Road; and their only child, Helen Maxine Dobbins, was born December 17, 1927.

Adeline and Charles Carbaugh

Helen attended Lafayette Central School and there met William Hollis Gregory. He had been born July 24, 1924 to John Meddie and Betty (Dobbs) Gregory in Coopersville, Kentucky. Orphaned at age eight, he lived with his Grandma Dobbs in Kentucky. Then he came to Allen County, lived with Edwin and Rose Dalman on Ferguson Road, and went to Lafayette Central School. During World War II, Bill was in the 656th Tank Destroyer Battalion in the European Theater. The unit served for a while under General George S. Patton and also saved the Lipizzan horses in Czechoslovakia. Meanwhile Helen was a bookkeeper for Lincoln National Bank and Trust Company in Fort Wayne. Then, after the war, Bill and Helen were married on May 15, 1948 in the Evangelical United Brethren Church at Nine Mile.

Bill and Helen's only child, Sharon Kay Gregory, was born May 21, 1951 in Fort Wayne. Twenty years later, she married Morris Edward Ford on December 23. Their children are Samuel Jess Ford and Heather Jo Ford. Heather married Nicholas Zirkle, June 20, 1998; and they have Jason James and Shelby Faith. Samuel married Stephanie Stouter, December 6, 2002. Their little girl is Alissa Gabriella.

Submitted by Sharon Ford

WILLIAM HENRY & ELIZABETH (JOHNSON) CARBAUGH

The ninth child of James and Rebecca (Baxter) Johnson was Elizabeth. Born in Columbiana County, Ohio on April 1, 1839, she came with her family to Allen County in the 1850s and lived with them on a farm at the corner of the south Allen County Line and Coverdale Roads. Elizabeth married William Henry Carbaugh on March 19, 1867, after his return from the Civil War.

They moved to Shawnee Township, Cherokee County, Kansas, where their three sons were born. Then the entire family returned to Allen County. William worked as a laborer, then rented a farm, eventually purchased 40 acres in Lafayette Township, and became a successful farmer.

The first son, Oliver Calvin Carbaugh, born December 14, 1868, married Charlotte Frances Keller on December 24, 1891. This couple had no children, and Oliver died September 2, 1933.

Charles Franklin Carbaugh was born October 9, 1870 and married Adaline Genth on February 22, 1900. Their children were Arthur William Carbaugh, Gertrude Marie Carbaugh, Lula Berneda Carbaugh, Selma Vandora Carbaugh, and Larry Carbaugh. Only Gertrude Marie and Lula Berneda, who appear elsewhere in *Allen County History Book*, lived to adulthood, married, and had descendants.

The third son, Alonzo Wilson Carbaugh, was born October 25, 1871. He married Zillah May Bradbury on June 1, 1893. Their six children were Clarence Franklin Carbaugh, Edna Mae Carbaugh, Mildred M. Carbaugh, Ralph Edward Carbaugh, Glenn Bradbury Carbaugh, and Harold Emerson Carbaugh.

For more information about the Carbaughs, see *Johnson Tree: Branch 9* in the Genealogy Department of Allen County Public Library.

Submitted by Helen Maxine (Dobbins) Gregory

JOSEPH & DONNA CARON FAMILY

Donna A. Dowell Caron, born at Fort Wayne's old Lutheran Hospital in 1944, was the only child of Floyd L. and Melzene F. Dowell. Donna was educated in Fort Wayne Community Schools, graduating from North Side High School in 1962. She began her college education at Purdue University and later graduated from the University of St. Francis (St. Francis College then), completing degrees in Elementary Education (BS -1967/MS-1970).

Elizabeth (Johnson) Carbaugh

In June 1966 Donna married Joseph I. Caron (born 1939), who was originally from Lewiston, Maine. He came to Fort Wayne to attend Indiana Institute of Technology after serving in the U.S. Navy. While attending IIT, Joseph Caron was a member of Theta Xi Fraternity. Before completing the engineering program at IIT, he took a position with Falstaff Brewing Corporation and was later employed at Gridcraft Corporation in Huntertown, Indiana.

The Caron's were married June 11, 1966, at St. Jude Catholic Church in Fort Wayne. After their marriage Donna was an elementary teacher for Fort Wayne Community Schools until they started their family. She returned to work in 1979 with FWCS, first as a part-time aide, then a secretary, and eventually full time as a specialist in the Human Resources Department, where she worked until her retirement from FWCS in 2004.

The Caron's two daughters, Nicole A. Caron Allred (born 1968) and Jennifer I. Caron Murphy (born 1973), have always been Fort Wayne residents. They now each have families of their own and have given the Carons five grandchildren.

Over the years the Carons have been members of Our Lady of Good Hope Catholic Church. Previously, Donna had been active in the St. Joe Central Elementary School PTA when their daughters were students there and also the American Association of University Women and Theta Theta Chapter of Psi Iota Xi Sorority.

In the fall of 2001 Joseph Caron developed lung cancer and after undergoing extensive treatment, he passed away in October 2002.

After being employed by FWCS for nearly 25 years, Donna retired in January 2004 and later that same year took a part-time position with the Northeast Indiana Innovation Center.

The Dowell and Caron families have been residents of Fort Wayne for a combined total of over 70 years and were always proud to call it their home and wouldn't have considered living anywhere else!

Submitted by Donna A. Dowell Caron

BOB & LUCILE (BONHAM) CARR

Neither Robert Forest (Bob) Carr nor (Marie) Lucile (Bonham) Carr was born in Allen County, but they met and married here. They lived here for a number of years, and their children were born here. Bob was born September 25, 1909 near Willshire, Van Wert County, Ohio. His parents were Samuel Dolson Carr and Jessie Harriet (Smalley) Carr. Bob's paternal grandparents were David and Sarah Ellen (Sapp) Carr. His maternal grandparents were Francis Marion and Sarah Clementine (Purdy) Smalley. The Carr, Smalley, Sapp, and Purdy families were in Ohio early in the 19th century, and they were farmers in Mercer County, Ohio, by 1870. Bob grew up in Mercer County with his six siblings, Dewey, Marie, Kenneth, David, Mary, and Sarah. He graduated from Rockford High School.

Lucile was born October 22, 1906, in Jasonville, Greene County, Indiana. Her parents were Charles Lewis and Mary Etta (Parks) Bonham. Lucile's paternal grandparents were David and Sarah (Ault) Bonham, and her maternal grandparents were Martin Wayne and Mary Jane (Todd) Parks. The Bonham, Parks, Ault, and Todd families were in Indiana by the middle of the 19th century. Mr. Bonham had moved his family to West Lafayette, Indiana, by 1910. By 1920 the family was living in Fort Wayne, where Mr. Bonham worked for the Peltier Funeral Home. Lucile's siblings were Lloyd, Hazel, Grace, and Walter. She graduated from Fort Wayne Central High School.

Bob worked for General Electric in Fort Wayne and Lucile was a legal secretary with the Fort Wayne firm, Hartzell & Todd. They met at a dance; Bob pointed her out to a friend saying that was the girl he was going to marry. They were married May 18, 1935, in the Congregational Church in Fort Wayne and lived in Fort Wayne until 1946 when they moved to Adams County, Indiana. Lucile stopped working when her daughter was born, and Bob left General Electric a few years after they moved to a farm near Decatur. Lucile was a receptionist/bookkeeper for doctors in Decatur in the 1950s while Bob farmed. In retirement they spent summers at their cottage on Sylvan Lake and winters in Florida. Eventually, they lived in Florida year round.

Bob and Lucile had two children: Barbara Lee (Bobbie), who was born September 3, 1938, and Michael Richard, who was born July 13, 1943. Bobbie and Mike both graduated from Monmouth High School and Indiana University. Bobbie, who has not married, had a 33-year career with the federal government. She lives in McLean, Virginia. Mike spent 36 years with Aetna Life Insurance Company. He is retired and lives in Minneapolis, Minnesota, with his wife Ann (Engebretson), born April 17, 1948 in Minneapolis. They have two children: Alex, born January 18, 1979, who lives in Minneapolis, and Caroline, born May 6, 1982, who lives in New York City.

Lucile died in Florida on December 13, 1994 and Bob died in Fort Wayne on November 6 2003. Both are buried in Willshire Cemetery.

Submitted by Barbara L. Carr

CARREL FAMILY

On October 24, 1853, David Louis Carrel (1817-1898), his wife, Catherine Louise Carrel (1819-1882), and their three children (David Louis, age 9, Aimee Alfred, age 7 Angelique Louise, age 6, and Cecile Lina Bertha, age 5 months) left their home in Lamboing, Bern, Switzerland, and sailed from LeHarve, France, aboard the ship *Manchester*

They arrived at the port of New York on November 1, 1853.

The family came directly to St. Joseph Township, Allen County, Indiana, where David purchased land on November 4,1853. He acquired a forty-acre tract of farmland for $400. He later sold that parcel and purchased other land further to the east.

David, although still a farmer, purchased three lots in the first McCulloch Addition in Fort Wayne. He also purchased property at 142 Maumee Street in Fort Wayne.

Catherine Louise died in 1882 of dropsy and paralysis. By 1888, David Louis had sold the last of his farmland and in 1894 he married Mrs. Mary Evard. He died in 1898 as the result of a hernia. He was said to have been widely known and respected.

Carolyn Ann Meek Long (1931-2004)

Aimee Alfred Carrel (1840-1892) was the only adult son of David and Louise Carrel. When he married Mary Bertha Bueche on February 19, 1870, he already had eighty acres of farmland in St. Joseph Township.

Alfred was a land speculator who bought and sold more than 370 acres and several farms between 1865 and his death in 1892.

Alfred and Bertha had nine children: Louis A. (1871-1889), Edward Henry "Uncle Ed" (1872-1950), Sophia Bertha (1874-1906), Mary Louise (1874-1951), a fifth child was stillborn, Lucie born in May 1880 died shortly after birth, Emile A. (1881-1908), Alfred A. (1882-1883), and Charles William (1884-1928).

Bertha moved her family from place to place until 1902 when she purchased a home at 1232 Wefel Street for $1150. She was a quiet, hard working, and not openly demonstrative. She was remembered as a very loving grandmother.

In 1906, Alfred and Bertha Carrel's son, Charles, married Emma Ida Miller. They had three children: Charles William Jr. (1906-1959), Wealtha Louise (1910-1998), and Delores Maxine (1923-). In 1915, they built a home at 1235 Sherman Street for the sum of $4000.

In the summer of 1919, Charles spent several months at the Standard Steel Car Company in Hammond, Indiana. The company's 4,500 employees were on strike and there were a thousand troops from all over the state at the plant, assigned by Governor James P. Goodrich for riot control.

Charles worked for the M. J. Blitz Cigar Store. He also sold general insurance, just as a new upstart company was coming onto the scene, The Lincoln National Life Insurance Company. Charles bought a vast amount of stock in the new company.

Emma Carrel had no skills to support herself when her husband died in 1928 leaving her with three children at home, but she did have the stock Charles Carrel had bought.

Wealtha Louise married Clifford Ray Meek in 1930. They had three children: Carolyn Ann (1931-2004), Frank Ray (1933-2003), and Ray Charles (1944-).

Charles William Jr. married Ruth O. Meyer in 1931. They had five children: Robert Louis (1933-), Richard Allen (1935-), Donald Clark (1937-), James Merritt (1940-1942), and Sharon Ruth (1944-).

Delores Maxine married Theodore Lauterberg in 1942 Their children are as follows: Susan Carol (1943-), Martha Jean (1946-), John Michael (1948-1957), Steven John (1957-), Mary Lynn (1960-), and Thomas Kim (1960-1984).

As these families continue to grow and have families of their own, they will help build the future. They will carry the Carrel family history with them into the future, each generation adding its own distinct part to a rich and abundant family legacy.

Submitted by Catherine A. Simonds

WILLIAM CARROLL 1801-1862

William Carroll was born c. 1801 in Connaught Province, Ireland. He immigrated to Canada around 1813. William worked at a 'distillery' (probably a tavern) in Canada and about 1840 he married Hannah Cochran (born circa 1820 in Canada) and they moved to Allen County, Indiana along with her brother, John. William was naturalized an American citizen on October 10, 1840. His earliest Allen County land record is dated June 15, 1839 in Perry Township.

William and Hannah had five children, all born in Indiana: Mary born 1841; Jane born 1844; Charles born 1844; Hannah born 1847; and Catharine born 1849. Hannah Cochran Carroll died in 1849 of unknown cause. There are no records of her death or burial.

The 1850 Allen County census lists Catharine, Charles, Hannah, Jane, Mary, Sarah and William (Farmer: 2500 acres). This census also lists Michael (Farmer: 500 acres) and Catharine Carroll with their children Jane, Ellen, Elizabeth and Thomas; plus James (Farmer: 400 acres) and Elizabeth Carroll and their daughter, Elizabeth.

"Michael Carroll, an old settler of Perry township, died Wednesday, aged sixty-five (*Fort Wayne Weekly Sentinel*, January 8, 1879)." Michael was born circa 1806 in Ireland and immigrated to Allen County in 1840. He married Catherine in Ireland. She was born circa 1812. They had five daughters and one son.

James married Elizabeth Shaw in Allen County on March 2, 1848. Both were born in Ireland; James circa 1817 and Elizabeth around 1832. They had six daughters and one son.

William married Sarah Greer on June 17, 1849. He was about 48; Sarah was 17. The Greers were another Catholic immigrant family in Pleasant Township. Sarah was born April 19, 1832, in Pittsburgh, the daughter of Thomas Greer (1794-1859) and Sarah Turner (1803-1870). William and Sarah had six children: Elizabeth born 1850; William born 1852; John born 1856; Rosanna born 1858; Dominic born 1860; and Sarah Helene, born June 15, 1862. William died on April 21, 1862. Sarah was left with 11 children and 150 acres.

William's land was divided among his heirs in March 1863. Sarah deeded her land to Daniel Kelly on October 27, 1863 and married him on November 9.

William and Sarah's son, John (born 1856), is the only one of these 11 children to spend his life in Allen County, dying in Fort Wayne on September 11, 1899. John married Catherine Relihan at the Cathedral in Fort Wayne in August 1879. Catherine immigrated from County Kerry, Ireland, on the ship *Sandusky* from Tralee to New York, arriving on August 24, 1857. She was a "domestic" and he was a "porter" at the Aveline Hotel. John went to work for the Wabash Railroad around 1891 and was known as an "engine tamer." He broke in the new engines and tested engines that had been overhauled.

They had six children. Their oldest child, Joseph, married and had one son, Kenneth. Kenneth never married. Only their daughter Genevieve married and had children.

Catherine Relihan Carroll (1848-1934), Mary Ellen Carroll (1882-1965), William Carroll (1884-1938), Genevieve Carroll Bartholomy (1893-1918), and Marjorie Sheffield Carroll (1884-1969). Photo taken at 401 West Williams Street, Fort Wayne around 1912.

Genevieve was baptized, married and buried from St. Patrick's Church in Fort Wayne. She married Louis J. Bartholomy (1893-1971) on November 24, 1914. She was born November 23, 1893 and died from the 'flu' on November 12, 1918. Their two children were Dorothy Carroll (1916-1995) and Wayne Lee (born December 31, 1917). Carroll married Robert Donald Mettler and had six children. Wayne married Patricia Guillaume and had seven children.

This branch of the Carroll family is a Certified First Family of Allen County. It is believed Carroll Road was named for them and consequently, Carroll High School. However, there are no descendants of this family with the surname of Carroll in Allen County.

Submitted by Meg Mettler

FRANCIS ANTOINE & EUGENIA (MANIER) CASSO FAMILY

Francis Antoine "Frank" Casso was born in Marsicovetere, Italy, on September 21, 1841, and immigrated to the United States in 1864. His passport lists his occupation as a traveling musician. Frank was one of the first Italians to settle in Fort Wayne. On February 20, 1871, Frank married Eugenia Manier, the daughter of Hippolite and Margaret (Poirson) Manier, in the Cathedral of the Immaculate Conception. They were devout Catholics and became active members of St. Peter's Catholic Church.

They had eight children: Rose Angela (1872-1936), who married Jules Emile Cochoit; Joseph Antonio (1873-1883), who drowned in the Maumee River at the foot of Hanna Street; Angelo Frank (1877-1939), who married Anna Rahe and then Lulu Lawrence; Francis Hypolite (1880-1952); Almeda Theresa (1889-1964), who married John J. Johnson; Elmer Joseph (1891-1891), who died at the age of five months; Leo Victor (1892-1970), who married Eva V. Albert; and Emmet Rayamond (1895-1949), who married Opal Van Matre. Frank and Eugenia's son, Frank, was injured from a fall from a cart when he was a young man and developed blindness and palsy due to nerve damage. His memory stopped after the injury, but he was a talented harmonica player and could play any tune he ever heard.

Frank and Eugenia had six grandchildren born to Rose and Jules Cochoit: Stella J., Joseph J., Charlotte H., Marie G., Lucille J., and Jules Emil; and one grandson, Leo R., born to Leo and Eva Casso.

Francis Antoine Casso with harp, circa 1900.

The Fort Wayne city directories state that from 1875-1876 Frank was a bottler of Cincinnati Lager Beer (Frank Casso's Bottled Beer) at 88 E. Columbia and that he had a billiard room at 67 E. Main. In 1877, Frank is listed, along with Frank Hake, as 'Beer Bottlers and Saloon' (Casso and Hake's Bottled Beer) and having the billiard hall. In addition to being a saloon proprietor, in 1878 Frank was well known for his musical ability and often furnished music for balls and parties. 1879-1880 lists Frank as a 'confectioner' at 116 Calhoun and as having a saloon at 36 Barr. 1882-1887 lists Frank's saloons at 264 Calhoun, 241 Calhoun, and 267 E. Wayne. His residence addresses were 36 Barr, 17 Baker, 41 Baker, and 42 Lasselle. In 1888, Frank and Frank J. Delagrange were proprietors of the Oriental Sample Room (bar and saloon) at 303 Lafayette. Frank and James Conley were known at that time as the Royal String Band. 1889 lists Frank as a musician, with Frank Delagrange continuing the saloon. From 1890-1896, Frank was in the 'fruits' retail business at 156 Calhoun and was known for playing the harp, along with his son, Angelo, who played the violin. 1899 lists Casso and Sons as musicians (music teachers) at 236 Calhoun.

Frank and Eugenia were married for 48 years, until her death on August 7, 1919. Frank died on July 28, 1923, due to injuries suffered in an automobile accident on March 4, 1923.

Submitted by Leo R. Casso.

CASTALDI FAMILY

In 1957, Linda Jackson, a senior at Ward Township High School in Randolph County, listened to WOWO radio station in Fort Wayne. Tuning in at the same time, Logansport High senior, Tom Castaldi was enjoying the same popular music selections by teenagers of the 1950s. Later in 1962, Linda, having graduated Ball State and employed as a fifth grade teacher at Mary McClellan Elementary in Indianapolis, met Tom by chance at a social gathering at his alma mater in Bloomington. A relationship developed and, on June 8, 1963, they were married at St. Joseph's Catholic Church in Logansport. Linda continued at McClellan and Tom began working at American Fletcher National Bank in Indianapolis. On May 28, 1964, Angel Kay was born at the IU Medical Center, during the midst of an Indy 500 weekend.

When an opportunity for Tom to work for Essex Wire Corporation came, the family moved from Indianapolis to Logansport. Linda became a fifth grade teacher at Daniel Webster Elementary School. It was in Logansport that Tom Jr., was born on August 24, 1966. Shortly thereafter, a transfer sent Tom Sr., and the family to a new home in Allen County. Elizabeth Ann was born at St. Joseph Hospital on December 23, 1967. During 1970, a move to Jones & Taylor Advertising Agency transferred the family to South Bend. There the second half of the Castaldi children entered the world. Cathleen Lee and Christine Marie were born January 18, 1971, in St. Joseph's Hospital. Regina Maria was born on October 20, 1975, at South Bend's Memorial Hospital.

Two years later, an invitation to return to work with Essex meant that the family returned to Fort Wayne in 1977. Here the youngsters attended the South West Allen County school system, graduating from Homestead High School. Linda continued using her teaching skills, accepting a position at Aldersgate Nursery School, where she worked with hundreds of young children from 1981 through her retirement in 1999. Tom retired from Essex in 1998 as vice president of public relations and government liaison; shortly thereafter took a position as executive director of the Electrical Insulation Conference, and in 2002 was appointed Allen County Historian.

Castaldi family gathered together in 2005 Thanksgiving Day.

Angela and Tom Jr., both studied engineering at Purdue University graduating with BS degrees in 1987 and 1990 respectively and Angela received a masters from Purdue in 1989. Elizabeth completed studies in interior design from IU Bloomington in 1990. Cathleen graduated from Ball State, along with her twin Christine, in 1995; both had attended IPFW before heading to Muncie. Christine gained a second degree in art education from Bowling Green State University. Regina completed a BS degree in elementary education at IU Bloomington in 1999 and continued pursuing a graduate degree.

In 1989, Angela married Minnesota resident Curt Weitnauer and have three sons, Cletis Clayton, Marcus Thomas and Cameron Curtis. Tom Jr. married Karen Darby of Beaver Creek, Ohio, and are the parents of Thomas III, Darby Jackson and Dominick Logan. Elizabeth is married to Fort Wayne-native John Seculoff and they have two children, Catherine Elizabeth and Jacob Thomas. Cathleen married Wells County-born Carl Lampton and they have two sons, Carl Castaldi and Joey Castaldi Lampton. Christine married Brent Royster and teaches art at Muncie South. Regina teaches in Bloomington, Indiana.

Before the Castaldi children left home to begin their own lives in the world, it was common on a winter's morning to find them together listening for school closings…on WOWO.

Submitted by Tom Castaldi.

ERVIN DWIGHT & EILEEN MARY (OBERLEY) CASTLEMAN FAMILY

Ervin Dwight Castleman was born February 4, 1916 in Jackson Township, Allen County, Indiana, to David Dwight and Louisa Mary (Smith) Castleman. Ervin had four siblings – Herman, Theresa, Helen, and Walter. Eileen was born June 27, 1918, in Jefferson Township, Allen County, Indiana, to Arthur and Amelia (Mourey) Oberley. Eileen had five siblings – Esther, her twin Edith, Robert, Arnold, and Wilbur.

Ervin graduated from St. Joseph School, Monroeville, Indiana, for his primary education and attended Monroeville High School for one year. ileen graduated from St. Louis Academy, Besancon, Indiana, for her primary education and did not attend high school.

Ervin and Eileen were married on January 19, 1939, in St. Louis Church, Besancon, Indiana. They had nine children – Mary Ann, James, Edwin, Joseph, Carol, David, Kenneth, John, and Ronald. Mary Ann passed away a few hours after her birth. James married Marilyn Sorg in 1963. Edwin married Edna Biddle in 1964. Joe married Jane Kennerk in 1967. Carol married Edward Lubomirski in 1972. David married Carol Haiflich in 1972 and have since divorced. Kenneth married Jean VanHorn in 1974. John is unmarried. Ronald married Patricia O'Shaughnessey in 1975. Ervin and

Eileen have thirty-one grand children, and forty-four great-grandchildren.

Ervin was a self-employed farmer for his entire life, farming as many as 360 acres in Southeast Allen County. He also worked as a bus driver for Jackson Township/East Allen County Schools for twenty-one years. Eileen worked as a full-time homemaker for their eight surviving children. Ervin passed away in May 2000.

Ervin and Eileen (Oberley) Castleman

The Castleman family arrived in southeast Allen County in 1835 when David's ancestors, Henry and Rachel, settled in the center of Jefferson Township, Allen County, Indiana. They were the parents of eleven girls and two boys. It is believed there were two sets of girl twins included in their children. Henry and Rachel moved to Monroe Township, Allen County, Indiana in 1847.

The Oberley family arrived in southeast Allen County in when Christian Oberley, born in 1835 in Baden, Germany, married Mary Bernadette Weaver Shumac on January 17, 1857, in Jefferson Township, Allen County, Indiana. Christian was in the 12th U.S. Regiment Infantry Co. B out of Indianapolis during the Civil War. Christian and Mary were the parents of two girls and two boys.

The majority of Ervin's and Eileen's children and grandchildren still live in the area.

Submitted by Heather Castleman

HENRY CASTLEMAN FAMILY

Henry Castleman was born in 1790 in Virginia. He married Rachel Saltzman. They lived in Jefferson Township. They were the parents of 11 girls and two boys including two sets of girl twins. Henry opened the first tavern on the new Van Wert Road and named it "The Castleman Inn." In 1847, Henry and Rachel moved to Monroe Township where he died in 1852.

Henry and Rachel had a son named Henry born in 1834 in Richland County, Ohio. He married Mary Louisa Webster on February 13, 1860 in Allen County. Rachel died in 1860 and Henry died in 1914 in Allen County.

Henry and Rachel were the parents of Walter S., Henry Allen, Sarah Louisa, and David Dwight (Dwight) Castleman. Our family history begins with David Dwight born October 19, 1875. He married Cora E. Giant on May 29, 1894, but Cora died August 20, 1897. Dwight married Louisa Mary Smith (Lucy) October 21, 1903. She was born April 12, 1883, and died October 6, 1962. Dwight died May 23, 1960. Both are buried in the Catholic Cemetery in Monroeville, Indiana.

Dwight and Lucy were the parents of Herman William, Theresa Mary, Helen Sophia, Walter Jay, and Ervin Dwight Castleman. Ervin (Boob) Dwight was born February 4, 1916, in Allen County. He married Eileen Mary Oberley January 19, 1939. Eileen was born June 27, 1918. Ervin died May 30, 2000, and is buried in the St. Louis Besancon Cemetery in Allen County.

Ervin and Eileen are the parents of nine children. Mary Ann was born December 11, 1940, and died December 12, 1940. Mary Ann is buried in the Smith-Castleman plot in the Catholic Cemetery in Monroeville, Indiana. Their other children are James Louis, Edwin Joseph, Joseph Ervin, Carol Ann, David Allen, Kenneth Arthur, John Jay, and Ronald Lee.

Ervin was a farmer and a school bus driver. He served on the Board of Directors of his local cooperative. Ervin and his family were members of the St. Rose Catholic Church in Monroeville, Indiana, until his retirement. At that time they became members of St. Louis Besancon Catholic Church. In his younger days, Ervin enjoyed hunting, trapping, and fishing.

In 1963, after the death of both of his parents, Ervin and Eileen purchased 120 acres of farm ground and the house that they lived in from his parents' estate sale. In 1972, Ervin retired from farming and they moved to a smaller house on the Lincoln Highway. They enjoyed several years of retirement fishing, traveling, and visiting with friends and relatives.

Ervin was a great storyteller of the "Old Days." He loved his family and loved to have them all visit as often as possible. On Mother's Day 2000, Ervin fell and broke his leg and shoulder. He never recovered from this accident and died on May 30, 2000. He is remembered by many people both young and old.

At her present age of 87, Eileen is still living in their retirement home on Lincoln Highway. She enjoys making baby quilts for all of her great-grandchildren. Ervin and Eileen's family has 106 living members at the present time and two more great-grandchildren will be added in 2005. She has three sets of twin boy grandsons and one set of twin girl great-granddaughters.

Submitted by Edna Castleman

CHARLES LOUIS CENTLIVRE (1827-1894)

He was a native from Lutran, France, the son of Louis Centlivre (1803-1877) and Marie Jeanne Lemmelet, and was bom September 23, 1827. He immigrated to the United States in 1850 with a background in farming and cooperage. He spent a short time with relatives in New Orleans before settling in Louisville, Canton, Ohio, where he met and married his wife, Marie Anne Houmaire. They relocated to northeastern Iowa for seven years where he established his first French Brewery under the tutelage of Christian Magnus, a German emigrant, and second generation brewmiester.

In 1861, Charles L. Centlivre brought his family to Fort Wayne and constructed the French Brewery on the north end of Spy Run Avenue. The business grew rapidly from the production of five hundred barrels of brew the first year to well over one hundred thousand per year with the addition of a malting plant, artificial refrigeration, bottling plant, all of which contributed to the quality and productivity.

A Chicago based brewmiester, Peter Nussbaum, joined the firm in the 1870s and contributed greatly to the diversity of brews as the old labels attest. Nussbaum remained with the brewery for thirty-seven years. In 1887 the C. L. Centlivre Street Railway Company, a horse-drawn carline was constructed north of the brewery, and in 1888, he expanded it from Spy Run to Calhoun streets, enabling the townspeople to travel to the Centlivre Park for family outings. 1889 was the year of devastation with a horrific fire that destroyed most of the brewery. Within a year Charles' brewery was rebuilt, larger and capable of even greater productivity.

Charles L. Centlivre, 1827-1894

Charles L. Centlivre was known as a man with a vision. He gave much and expected loyalty and hard work from his employees, which eamed him the title of "the gentlemanly brewer." From the building of an almost primitive brewery in 1861 until his death in 1894, one sees the progress and success that he experienced. Of all of the accolades written, the highest compliments that truly expresses the quality of this man were: He was honest, compassionate, generous, and always a gentleman. His funeral procession from home to the Cathedral was said to have been the longest the city had ever seen; five miles of mourners in their horse drawn carriages

Submitted by Patricia Bonahoom

LOUIS ALPHONSE CENTLIVRE

Louis Alphonse Centlivre was born in Dubuque, Iowa, on September 27, 1857. He was the son of Charles L. Centlivre (1827-1894) and Marie Anne Houmaire (1829-1886), both French emigrants from the neighboring villages of Lutran and Phaffan. Charles and Marie first met in Louisville, Ohio, where they were married on September 26, 1854, at St. Louis Catholic Church. They settled in Dubuque, Iowa, where they began their family and Charles started his first brewery.

Amelia Frances (1855-1935) was the first born, followed by Louis Alphonse (1857-1942) and Joseph (born and died in infancy). The family relocated to Winneshiek County, Iowa, where their son Charles F. (1861-1926) was born. In

1861 Louis' father, Charles, chose Fort Wayne to be the family's final home and there built the French Brewery, later renamed the C. L. Centlivre Brewery, and finally the Centlivre Brewery. Another son, Francis P., was born in 1862 and died in 1864. Joseph, born in 1864, died at the age of 18 from typhoid.

Charles' brewery expanded over the years and he became known as "The Gentlemanly Brewer" in the city. His son, Louis, received only eight years of formal education at the Cathedral Boys School and then entered his father's business at age thirteen. He was the third generation of Centlivre brewers. (His grandfather, Louis, came from France in 1853 and joined the establishment.) He worked by his father's side and learned every aspect of the art of brewing, the skill of barrel making, preservation of the brew, advertising, bookkeeping, accounts receivable, collections, delivery, canal and railway shipping, public relations, ordering supplies, sales, tending the horses, and repairing wagons. It was said that by the time he was twenty years old he could have run the business single-handedly.

Louis entertained with the grace of a king and was much sought after socially. He was an impeccable dresser, worked hard and played hard. Generosity and optimism were synonymous with his name. At the age of twenty-six, he built his prized possession, the steamboat *Amelia*, named after his sister. It could accommodate thirty-five passengers and was used principally for excursions up the scenic St. Joe River, from the brewery to Robison Park and back. Eventually he added more boats, and then catamarans that could be towed behind the boats that seated forty more people. Townspeople often chartered the boats for summer outings and naturally their voyage always ended at Centlivre Park for a cool taste of brew along with singing, dancing, and band concerts. Many of his boats were destroyed in 1889 when a raging fire destroyed most of the brewery.

Louis was at the helm after the fire and most instrumental in rebuilding and adding many improvements to the facility. He was not only a brewer, but was involved in politics and the French Benevolent Society. He was an equestrian and owned thoroughbred horses, which were nationally known. He established the L. A. Centlivre Manufacturing Co. (gas engines and pumps) and served on Indiana Governor Claud Matthews' staff from 1893-1896. He was an Allen county councilman from 1906-1912 and a few years later he became a deputy sheriff. He drilled to supply water to the Orphan's Home and in 1919 brought the first traveling circus to Centlivre Park that so delighted many for years. Louis also built a streetcar line connecting areas in the St. Joe River - Spy Run area. He was president of the brewery for over forty years.

Louis was married August 19, 1896, to an Irish lass from Chicago, Maud Cleary (1873-1938). She was the daughter of Colonel Patrick Cleary (1826-1896) and Margaret Touhey Cleary (1839-1923). Four children blessed their union: Marie Houmaire (1898-1967); Louis Alphonse "Buzz" (1900-1943); Charles Louis (born and died 1906); and Margaret Angela "Angele" (1908-1993).

Louis Alphonse Centlivre was devoted to his family, his business, and the city of Fort Wayne. He was Catholic and attended daily mass. He died on February 15, 1942. A portion of his obituary reads: "In his lifetime, he counted his friends by the hundreds, acquaintances by the thousands. With them, the lively spirit of a shrewd but kindly man, who left a definite helpful and constructive imprint on the city of Fort Wayne, will live on, beloved in memory as he was long so dearly loved on this level of mortal existence."

Submitted by Patricia Bonahoom

CHAMBERLIN & MCKEAN FAMILY

James Edward Chamberlin was born December 9, 1927 in Mishawaka, Indiana, at St Joseph Hospital to J. James Chamberlin and Katharine C Clauss Chamberlin. He married Carole Sue McKean in Fort Wayne, Indiana, on October 9, 1948 at St Paul's Catholic Church. He died December. 3, 1972, in Argos, Indiana, where he and Carole had moved from Fort Wayne in 1970, with their seven children. He had purchased a small restaurant, Chamberlin's Harvey's Cafe. He had worked for his uncles at the Hobby House Restaurants for nearly 22 years in Fort Wayne before the purchase of his own place and the subsequent move to Argos, Indiana.

Carole Sue McKean was born August 10, 1929 in Fort Wayne, Indiana at St. Joseph Hospital to Henry Francis McKean and Maree Estelle Getz. The McKeans and Getzs were both pioneer families of Allen County. She was baptized at St. Patrick's Parish, where her mother's family had all been baptized, also.

James and Carole had seven children: James E. Jr. born November 5, 1949; Christine Maree born August 8, 1952; Rebecca Ann born December 12, 1953; David Henry born October l0, 1955; Thomas Gerard born March 3, 1957; John Paul born January 30, 1959; Matthew Anthony born July 7, 1962. They were each born in St. Joseph Hospital at Fort Wayne, Indiana; all but John and Matthew were baptized at St. Patrick's Church. They were baptized at St. Vincent's Church.

James and Carole both graduated from Central Catholic High School. Carole went to St. Joseph Nursing School for one year. Their children, James and Christine graduated from Bishop Dwenger High School. Rebecca attended there for two years before their move out of town. Rebecca, David, Tom, John and Matt graduated from Argos High School. Before the family moved to Argos, they lived on a small farm on Cedar Canyon Road off of Hwy. 27. It was called Cemetery Road at the time they purchased their family home.

The family farmhouse that the children basically grew up in had been the "Old Habig Farm," which was the original homestead for the area (they were told). The home was built in 1865. When the family moved there in 1957, the road was not paved and there were no housing additions as there are now. The Holmes family lived on a cattle and sheep farm next door. The children took a bus into St. Vincent's by way of Huntertown. The family loved the little farmette, where vegetables, beef, sheep, pigs, goats and chickens were raised It was a good life!

Today, four of the sixteen grandchildren now live in the area, where perhaps life will be starting all over again for the future Chamberlins.

Carole's mother, who was of Getz/Perriguay lineage was a pioneer family. The original family farm was off of Hwy.14, where she was born. The Getz Road was named for the Henry and Charles Getz farms located there.

The Getzs came from Baden, Germany, to Salem, Ohio, to Fort Wayne. The Perriqueys and Vougiers came from Alsace Lorraine, France, to Allen County. William McKean came by Canal from Pennsylvania in 1855 to Allen County.

Submitted by
Carole McKean Chamberlin Meredith

REID G. CHAPMAN

Reid Chapman is reading the newspaper - not with his eyes, but with his ears. Because of limited vision caused by macular degeneration, he listens on a special radio to *The Journal Gazette* and *The News-Sentinel* read by volunteers of the Northeast Indiana Radio Reading Service, which provides the sight-impaired with a window on the world. Whatever sight limitation Reid has, he more than makes up for with a clear vision of his life to this point.

Reid Gillis Chapman was born July 27, 1920, in Indianapolis to Arthur R. and Esther (Gillis) Chapman. Reid and his four siblings - Janet, Ann, Marian and Bob - grew up at 5649 College Avenue, where they played, studied and pursued their dreams.

The seed for Reid's career in broadcasting was probably planted in the late 1920s when he visited his cousin in Norwood, Ohio. Reid's uncle bought his son a crystal set, a precursor to the modern radio. The boys hooked up the antenna to the bed springs and by using earphones and twisting something called a "cat whisker," they were able to pick up WLW in Cincinnati, one of the nation's early radio stations. In grade school, Reid was allowed to go around the classrooms promoting paper and cookie sales using a make-believe microphone, made from a broomstick and tin can with holes, while imitating the radio announcers with whom he was infatuated. He also took part in activities that allowed him to recite something on stage or be part of a singing group. At home in his bedroom, he recreated baseball games from his press-box window over the backyard. In elementary school, Reid did have his first date with Madelyn Pugh, who went on to become one of the head writers of "I Love Lucy" (they walked to a movie). Reid graduated from Broad Ripple High School in 1938 and attended Butler University from 1938 to 1940.

In 1942, two events inspired Reid to enlist in the Navy: receiving his draft notice, and seeing the highly patriotic, Academy Award-winning film "Mrs. Miniver." After a brief stay at Great Lakes Naval Training Station, he was sent home with an honorable discharge.

Reid married Janet Passwater, whom he met in the church choir, on October 30, 1942, following a six-month courtship. Janet was born in Noblesville on December 31, 1919, to Howard and Martha (Woodburn) Passwater. Janet told her cousin, who knew the manager of WISH Radio in Indianapolis, about Reid's desire to get into broadcasting. He got an audition, but was told he needed more experience. Then in 1943, he got his first radio job at WAOV in Vincennes through a friend of his father, a CPA. Besides being a fellow Rotarian, the friend was also the station's manager. One of the "highlights" of Reid's career at WAOV was covering the Vincennes flood from a motorboat on the Wabash River, which reached almost to the tops of telephone poles. After seven months at WAOV, Reid received a letter from the program manager at WISH saying that there was an opening as music librarian, thus beginning a 12-year stay for Reid in Indianapolis.

Besides being music librarian during the day, Reid played records for 30 minutes at night at no extra pay. Between the records he read commercials for the sponsor, Chuckles candy, told little jokes or two-liners, and then chuckled. As a result, he became known as "Chuckles" Chapman. Tipping the scales at 120, he described himself on air as a "250-pound ton of fun." He also did station breaks on Saturday afternoons during the broadcast of the Metropolitan Opera. Reid's career at WISH progressed to host of "Breakfast with Chuckles" from the Circle in downtown Indianapolis, complete with the "Goofy Hat Contest" for the ladies, to "Chuckles Open House" in studio, as well as on location (peddling peat moss and other sponsors' products) and on WISH-TV. During his years in Indianapolis, Reid was also program and promotion director for radio and announcer for TV.

In 1956, Reid was transferred to Fort Wayne to manage WANE Radio. In 1958, he also became vice president and general manager of WANE-TV. The radio station was sold in the mid-'60s and Reid continued running the TV station until his semi-retirement in 1984. One of the many highlights of his long career in Fort Wayne was hosting "Meet the Manager," during which Reid answered viewers' questions in an off-the-cuff manner somewhat reminiscent of "Chuckles." In describing the show, one of his children kiddingly said he reads a question, gets sidetracked on something else and never answers the question. Under Reid, the station's news department became an innovative leader in investigative reporting and the first to do editorials.

In 1963, during the aftermath of President John F. Kennedy's assassination, Reid, as president of the Indiana Broadcasters Association, found himself counseling small radio stations across the state who were not affiliated with a network and who called him wondering how they should handle the tragedy. "Cancel all regular programming, all commercials, and get out everything you can find in your [music] library in the way of appropriate music and play it until this whole period of mourning is over," he advised them. Later that year, Reid received a call from Governor Matt Welsh. The governor had heard from another broadcaster that a new hit record, "Louie, Louie" by The Kingsmen, might be too suggestive for air play. Welsh, realizing he was treading on dangerous ground on a matter relating to censorship, called Reid to see if he, as IBA president, could alert stations throughout the state about a song that should possibly be taken off the air. Supposedly there were two sets of lyrics - one more explicit than the other - but this was never proven. Reid bought the record, played it for his children and told them about his concern. They laughed and said, "Oh, Dad, there's nothing wrong with that song." Needless to say, "Louie Louie" was never taken off the air in Indiana because no one could really make out what it said. Years later, as a TV station executive, Reid had an opportunity to preview a new show CBS was allowing affiliates to see on closed circuit before it premiered on the air because of sensitive material. Like "Louie, Louie," it was also controversial. And like "Louie, Louie," it became a classic. The show was "All in the Family."

L to R: Reid Chapman, Mark Chapman, James Chapman, Rosalie Hanefeld, Martha Shull, Mark Adamcik, Arthur (Churck" Chapman

Reid and Janet had five children. Arthur (nicknamed Chuck, after "Chuckles"), born in 1944, married Linda Truesdale; they have two children, Paul and Kimberly. Martha, born in 1946, married Linwood Shull; they have three children - Sara, Aimee and Elizabeth. Mark, born in 1951, married Janet Gipperich; they have five children - Kathryn, Joseph, Michael, John and Peter. Rosalie, born in 1953, married Gene Hanefeld; they have three children - Andrew, Janet and Jordan. James, born in 1960, married Peggy McCarty; they have a son, Joel. Reid's nephew, Mark Adamcik, joined the family in 1969 following the death of his mother Marian, Reid's sister. On July 2, 1976, Reid's wife Janet passed away at age 56 from complications of lupus. Besides his 14 grandchildren, Reid has five great-grandchildren - Katelynne, McKenna, Jensen, Gillian and Spencer - with another boy due in May 2005.

In the mid-'70s, Reid saw a magazine ad and, through Janet's encouragement, discovered a new talent of oil painting, a hobby he pursues to this day, even with his macular degeneration. His work adorns the homes of his children and grandchildren.

After his retirement from WANE-TV, Reid continued his broadcasting career as acting manager of WBWB-FM in Bloomington in 1988 and as sales consultant at WCBK-FM in Martinsville from 1989 to 1991, both during his residency in Nashville. In 1991, he decided he wanted to be closer to his children and moved back "home" to live with his daughter Rosie and her family in New Haven. When the Northeast Indiana Radio Reading Service found itself in a fight for survival, Reid answered the call, serving as executive director from 1991 to 1994.

In 1981, as president of the national and Indiana chapters of Broadcast Pioneers, Reid recommended that the state chapter establish a Hall of Fame to recognize Hoosier broadcasters who have made significant contributions to the industry. That same year, Reid and other national broadcasters were invited to the White House to present a lifetime membership in Broadcast Pioneers to President Ronald Reagan. Reid made the actual presentation and shook Reagan's hand. Years later, the Indiana Broadcast pioneers were looking for a place to house the Hall of Fame and received an invitation from the Indiana State Museum in Indianapolis, where the exhibit now stands.

Reid was also president and Silver Medal Award recipient of the Fort Wayne Advertising Club, charter member and past president of the Fort Wayne Press Club, past chairman and roastmaster of the Press Club Gridiron and was president or director of several other organizations. At WANE-TV he encouraged department heads to become members of civic groups because he felt it was their responsibility to become involved in the community. In Fort Wayne, he is currently a member of the Downtown Rotary Club and Quest Club and an elder at First Presbyterian Church, where he has been a member for 40 years. Because of his eyesight, Reid's family gets him to the meetings, the doctor, and, of course, the church on time.

Two additional honors Reid is particularly proud of are receiving the Sagamore of the Wabash, the highest award bestowed by the governor of Indiana for service to the state, presented by Gov. Evan Bayh and the Thirty-third Honorary Degree, the highest honor of Scottish Rite Freemasonry.

Reid survived a bout with colon cancer and three open-heart surgeries, the latter two multiple-bypasses. He credits his surgeons, a strong faith in God and the loving care of his wife and family for pulling him through. As this biography was written, the vision in Reid's left eye has improved following cataract surgeries and new glasses. Despite his macular degeneration, he enjoys an active lifestyle including the companionship of Bette Harris.

As Reid listens to the Radio Reading Service, he thinks of all the people in his life who have given him help, guidance and encouragement to pursue his goals and dreams and overcome his limitations and those who have provided health care to prolong his life; his school teachers; his wife and family; his employers; his doctors; his art instructors; NEIRRS volunteer readers. He is blessed. Reid's view of the people and events that have shaped his life is not unlike that of Woodrow Call, a character in Reid's favorite miniseries, "Lonesome Dove." A reporter interviewing Call tells him, "They say you're a man of vision." And so is Reid.

Submitted by Arthur R. Chapman

PRINCE & ROSA (DANSBY) CHAPMAN FAMILY

Prince was born on May 1, 1934, in Marion, Alabama, to Earl and Beatrice Chapman who where southern sharecroppers. Their children were Bessie, Earlean, Prince, Cora, Beatrice, Edward, Mary, Joyce and Aubresye. Just eight short years later the family moved to Fort Wayne, Indiana, in 1942, along with six of their nine children.

Prince's first marriage was to Miss Eva Davis in 1958, while he was still in the U.S Military. To this union one child, Anthony, was born in 1959. Shortly afterward, Eva Davis Chapman passed away.

Prince married Rosa Dansby on July 31, 1960, in Uniontown, Alabama. Rosa was born February 19, 1942 to Earlean Jimmerson and Joe Dansby of Uniontown, Alabama, and graduated from Perry County High School. Rosa pursued a trade in cosmetology. After getting married to Prince at the age of 18, Rosa worked this trade for 30 years as an independent owner, and operator. Rosa has five sisters and two brothers who live in various cities throughout the country. To this date, her mother still resides in her hometown, in the south. Her father passed away the same year as did her husband Prince.

Born to the union of Prince Chapman and Rosa Dansby Chapman are four wonderful children, Anthony, Bryan, Eric and Sandra Chapman. During the first thirty years, Rosa and Prince trained and reared up these four beautiful children, who produced ten wonderful grandchildren. Rosa has given tireless years to reaching others through ministry. Prince and Rosa were married 38 years.

Prince graduated from Central High School in Fort Wayne, Indiana. By age 16, Prince became a mechanic by trade. At the age of 18 a young Prince Chapman gained employment with the International Harvester Company. Mr. Chapman went on to do his military duties, and after serving his country, he returned to Fort Wayne, to resume his employment with the International Harvester Company, where he served for 30 years as a Mechanical Engineer.

Mr. Prince Chapman retired in 1985. He found enjoyment in retirement as he continued his business as an auto mechanic which he had operated for 40 years. Prince coached and mentored young athletes in sports, by encouraging hard work and a team effort, to achieve their goals, knowing these skills would foster a better life for each individual, but also instilling a foundation for a successful adult life.

Prince and Rosa dedicated their life to this mission work of helping along our younger generation. Yet, an untimely, and unfortunate senseless act by a twelve year old boy ended in Prince Chapman's brutal murder just a few steps away from his place of business. Prince Chapman's life ended on November 30, 1998.

After the death of Mr. Prince Chapman, in 2002, an 18 million dollar school was constructed and dedicated in his name: "THE PRINCE CHAPMAN ACADEMY MIDDLE SCHOOL." It is the first school named after an African American male from the City of Fort Wayne.

Rosa Chapman, now at the age of 63, continues to touch the lives of the citizens of this city and our country. She serves as Director/Founder of a non-profit organization called Friends of Bethany founded, among others, by her late husband Prince. FOB is a Christian organization with programs to mentor and come along the side of young parents and their children to help in developing stronger families. Rosa is an active ordained minister of the gospel. She is currently involved in several local outreaches of faith, and to this date, is serving in full time ministry. Many years of ministry has reached hundreds of families, and have impacted countless lives in our community.

Prince and Rosa's children went on from high school to continue their higher education. Anthony is presently a Mechanical Engineer in Temple, Texas. Bryan is Vice President of Esource Systems and Integration Co., Indianapolis, Indiana. Eric is Founder/President of Esource Systems and Integration Co. in Charlotte, North Carolina. Sandra is an Investigative Reporter for WTHR Channel 13, TV station in Indianapolis, Indiana. Anthony is married to Regina Crawford with two children, one son and a daughter. Bryan married Sharon Moody, they have two sons. Eric is also married to Jacquelyn Cooper, with one son and two daughters. Sandra became the wife of Randall Taylor, and to that union two sons and one daughter were born.

Prince Chapman and his family will live on forever, doing the work and the will of God, in this city and country.

Submitted by the family of Prince and Rosa Chapman.

Prince Chapman.

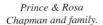

Prince & Rosa Chapman and family.

DONALD V. CHARAIS & LEILA D. THIEL FAMILY

Donald V. Charais was born December 6, 1922 in Renesslaer, Indiana, to Cyprian A. Charais and Evelyn W. Michael. Don was the middle of three children. Charlotte K., wife of John I. Bird, was the oldest and Juanita M., wife of Raymond G. Roth, being the youngest. Don's maternal great grandfather emigrated from Ireland in 1853 and settled in Jasper County, Indiana. His father's ancestors emigrated from France around 1834 to Canada, and then to America in 1863, and settled in and around Kentland and Fowler, Indiana. Don grew up on the farm around Monticello, Indiana, and graduated from Roosevelt High School in Monticello in 1940.

Don married Leila D. Thiel June 15, 1944 in Reynolds, Indiana. Leila was born December 21, 1922 in Edgerton, Ohio, to Albert G. Thiel and Margorie F. Warner from Hicksville, Ohio. She was the oldest of four children. Following in order are Letha M., wife of David E. Pressler, Deloy M. Thiel, husband of Shirley Arend, and Kenneth L. Thiel, husband of Barbara Kennedy. A beautician after graduating from Beauty School, Leila soon became busy raising eight children, the first arriving while Don was at war. Lee was a kind, gentle yet strong woman admired by everyone. She was active in her church and also found time to garden, sew, crochet, and quilt. Leila's paternal great grandfather emigrated from Luxembourg to America in 1847 and settled in Williams County, Ohio. Leila's great grandmother married Arthur Farnsworth, a cousin of Philo T. Farnsworth.

Don joined the Navy on February 6, 1943. He served as a radioman and tailgunner on PBMs in the Asiatic-Pacific Area Campaign were he received the Bronze Star, Navy Wings (5 stars), Air Medal (2 stars), Distinguished Flying Cross (2 stars), American Campaign (4 stars), World War II Medal, Philippine Independence Medal, Combat Service Medal, and Aircrew Insignia. He was honorably discharged October 8, 1945.

L to R: Christopher Charais, Dawn, Irene, Donald Charais, Leila Thiel Charais, Barbara Phillip, Anita, Teresa, Cecile

After Don moved to Fort Wayne, he was employed by Wayne Pump, by Bowmar Instruments as production control manager, as president of New Century of Fort Wayne, with D & M of Muncie and C& S of Toledo. He also was salesman for CTD, and office manager for Advanced Laser. Don was an avid sports fan, both watching and participating in many sporting activities especially bowling and golfing. He won the Men's City Bowling Championship four times and was inducted into the Fort Wayne Men's Bowling Hall of Fame in 1994. He was League Secretary for the Senior Men's Golf Association. He also sang in the St. Patrick's Catholic Church Choir for 35 years.

Don and Leila are the parents of eight children: Phillip L. Charais, husband of Cynthia S. Waldrop; Dawn C., wife of Steven M. Wamement; Anita L., wife of Terry McCutcheon; Irene D., wife of Michael R. Harris; Barbara L. Charais; Teresa A. Charais; Cecile E. Charais; and Christopher D. Charais, husband of Laura B. Krengel. They have 20 grandchildren and 17 great-grandchildren.

Submitted by Donald and Leila Charais

ROBERT C. & GERALD F. CHRISTEN FAMILIES

Robert and Gerald are the sons of Albert A. Christen, who was a co-founder of Lewis and Christen Office Supplies. Albert worked there until his death in 1965.

Robert C. Christen founded Robert C. Christen Accounting firm in 1966, and worked there until his retirement in 1996. He was born in Fort Wayne on May 9, 1936. He is a graduate of Central Catholic High School, Fort Wayne, and St. Joseph College, Rensselaer, Indiana. He was married to Laura Conklin, daughter of Linnie and Ernest Conklin of Sturgis, Michigan, on September 12, 1959. They have three children: Michael, Kathleen (Keller), and David. Michael lives in Indianapolis and has three children: Ryan, Drake, and Riley. Kathleen lives in Fort Wayne and has one daughter, Linnie. David lives in Fort Wayne and has three children: Spencer, Sidney, and Cameron.

Gerald F. Christen founded Christen Janitorial Supplies, Inc. in 1979 and operated the company until he sold it in 2003 and retired. He was born in Fort Wayne, Indiana, June 17, 1937, and is a graduate of Central Catholic High School. He was married November 9, 1962, to Loretta Walters, daughter of Florence and Kenneth Walters of Francesville, Indiana. They have three children. Maria (Sciole), Linda (O'Brien), and Stephen. Maria lives in Fort Wayne and has two children: Theresa and Julia. Linda lives in Sarasota, Florida, and has three children: Kelsey, Connor, and Courtney. Stephen lives in Fort Wayne with his wife, Joetta.

Robert and Gerald's grandfather was Henry Christen, who married Marie Suelzer in 1906. Their great grandfather was John Suelzer, Sr. He was born near Cologne, Germany, and came to the United States in 1881. After spending a short time in the southern and western states, he located in Fort Wayne, becoming one of the outstanding building contractors in northern Indiana. He was a contractor for St. Patrick's, St. Paul's, and St. Peter's Catholic Churches in Fort Wayne. Among the city's industrial plants, he erected the Berghoff brewery plant, the addition to the Old National Bank building, and the Pennsylvania and Spy Run powerhouses. He organized the Fort Wayne Builders' Supply Company, acting as its president until his retirement in 1922.

Submitted by Loretta Christen

ELI F. CHRISTLIEB FAMILY

Eli F. Christlieb married Dianthe J. Fike, and they had one known son, William Franklin Christlieb, who was born September 7, 1875, in Ohio, and died November 17, 1954, in Noble County, Indiana.

William Franklin married Florence Edna Burke on August 12, 1900, in LaOtto, Noble County, Indiana. Florence was the daughter of Delbert Burke and Mary Leiter. She was born October 22, 1882, near LaOtto, Noble County, Indiana, and died March 27, 1970 at the age of 87 in the Garrett Community Hospital, DeKalb County, Indiana.

William and Florence were a very loving, caring, hard working, and God fearing family. William was a powerful and very big man standing six feet, two inches tall. He had a mustache and was very good looking, well mannered, and prone to laugh, rather than fight. Florence was a very small lady, very beautiful, with big loving eyes, and naturally curly hair.

William and Florence had eight children. Blanche Marie was born March 21, 1901, in Allen County, Indiana. She married William H. Klinger in 1916, and they had nine children. Blanche died July 25, 1936, in childbirth. Violet Lavelle was born June 5, 1903 in Allen County, Indiana. She married Otis Van Wagner, and they had two children. Violet died December 25, 1995. Ruth May was born August 1, 1905, in Noble County, Indiana. She married Howard Fike December 20, 1921, and they had five children. Ruth died December 20, 1987. Thaddeus Raymond "Ray" was born April 6, 1908, in Noble County, Indiana, and married Mildred K. Damman November 27, 1937, in LaOtto, Noble County, Indiana. They had one son. Ray died June 21, 1971. Mary Dianthe was born July 18, 1912, in Noble County, Indiana, and married Robert Iddings. They had eight children. Howard Richardson was born May 26, 1915, and died May 26, 1915, in Noble County, Indiana. Leona Lois was born February 18, 1918, in Auburn, DeKalb County, Indiana, and married Bruce Friend March 24, 1938. They had two daughters. Joseph Eli was born March 26 in DeKalb County, Indiana, and he married Anna Bunn on January 25, 1942. They had no children. Joe died April 9, 1954, in Kendallville, Noble County, Indiana, in a single car accident.

L to R: Ruth, Florence, Ana, William, and Ray Christlieb

Submitted by Chris Fike

RALPH E. CHURCH FAMILY

The history of the Ralph E. Church family in Fort Wayne began at General Electric Company on Broadway in the early 1950s. Ralph E. Church was born in Wichita, Kansas, June 6, 1931, and attended Kansas State in Manhatten, Kansas. After graduating in 1953 with a degree in electrical engineering, Ralph went to work for GE in Erie, Pennsylvania, but within six months transferred to Fort Wayne as a test engineer.

Judith Snyder Keirn was a single mother from Whitley County; she was working for GE in Building 19. Ralph and Judy encountered each other in the plant cafeteria and managed to find mutual friends to introduce them. When Ralph's career was interrupted by the draft, they decided to get married. The wedding took place on February 18, 1956, at the home of Murray and Monica McLean in Columbia City, Indiana. Ralph and Judy spent their first year of marriage in Las Cruces, New Mexico. Ralph was stationed at nearby White Sands Proving Grounds.

After completing his military service in 1957, Ralph returned to GE to continue his career. In 1964 Ralph and Judy purchased a home in the Anthony Wayne Village neighborhood. Their sons attended East Allen County Schools. Don Nicholas "Nick" Keirn graduated from New Haven High School in 1970. Cory Rex Church graduated from Paul Harding High School in 1978. Daniel Kent Church graduated from Paul Harding High School in 1979. All three sons were born at Lutheran Hospital on Fairfield Avenue.

Ralph and Judy Church became members of First Christian Church at 4800 South Calhoun Street in 1958, and remained active through the years. All three sons were baptized at First Christian Church. Boy Scout Troop 306 and the Village Little League Baseball program also played important roles in the lives of the Church family.

Dan Church graduated from Indiana University at Bloomington, Indiana, in 1983, with a B.A. degree. Dan resides in Fort Wayne and is a partner in TDR Screen Graphics, Inc. located on Highview Drive in Fort Wayne.

Cory Church graduated from Ball State University in Muncie, Indiana, in 1982, with a B.S.

Ralph E. Church family

Front row, L to R: Paul, Edna, Charles, Eugene. Back row, L to R: William, Loraine, Edna, Wilbur, Page, Susan, Rita, James

degree in marketing. After living in Albuquerque, New Mexico, for 20 years, Cory moved to Las Vegas, Nevada, where he works for the Clark County Schools.

Nick Keirn attended IPFW and received a degree in psychology from Purdue University. At the time of his death in 1991, he was married to Angela E. Quinn of Fort Wayne and had two children, Pauline E. Quinn and Jacob N. Keirn. During Nick's career as a social worker, he worked for the Allen County Department of Public Welfare.

Judy started working part time for Fort Wayne National Bank in 1986. At the time of her retirement in January 1999, Fort Wayne National Bank had become National City Bank.

Ralph retired from GE in 1995 after 42 years as a design engineer. Ralph died June 8, 1999, and is buried in Lindenwood Cemetery.

Submitted by Judy Church

CHARLES J. P. CHURCHWARD FAMILY

Charles Churchward was born in Drogheda, Ireland, on May 17, 1892, while his father was serving with the British Coast Guard. His parents were Charles G. H. Churchward and Susan Stapleton of Cornwall, England.

The sound of the anvil fascinated him as a youngster and, at the appropriate age, he chose to be apprenticed to a master blacksmith. During the five-year commitment he virtually became a member of the smith's family. Upon completion, he decided to pursue his trade in Canada. He arrived in Portland, Maine, on May 29, 1913, and boarded a train for Toronto, Canada. There was an Englishman known to him already at work in Toronto, and he saw that Charles got settled.

He was not in Toronto long when he got a call from his brother-in-law, William Rodda, also a blacksmith who owned a shop in Poe, Indiana. Rodda had purchased a promising shop in Ossian and called upon Charles to take over his shop in Poe.

It was in Poe that Charles met Edna J. Herber, born December 12, 1897, daughter of John Herber and Louise Kallmeyer. The Herber family was one of the pioneer families in Marion Township, having come from Germany in 1834. Charles and Edna were married January 20, 1915, at St. Joseph Catholic Church, Hessen Cassel, Indiana. In 1933 they moved to Waynedale and Charles opened a blacksmith shop near the comer of Old Trail and Lower Huntington Roads. In 1941 he moved the shop west on Lower Huntington Road to the corner of Bradberry.

Charles claimed several firsts in the blacksmith business in this area. He believed he was the first blacksmith to put a gas welding outfit in his shop. He bought the first smith welding torch that Mossman Yarnelle sold. He designed and made the first attachment for corn planters to keep the fertilizer from dropping directly on the seed and burning it when it sprouted. He also said he built a rotary mower two years before they appeared on the market. He built the first tank truck to haul extra water to fires for the Waynedale Fire Department.

He was also involved with other Waynedale residents in the formation of the Waynedale Park. He was a long time member of the Waynedale Lions Club.

Edna died on April 25, 1972, and Charles died on August 28, 1975. Both are buried at Prairie Grove Cemetery in Waynedale.

They were the parents of eleven children:

1. Wilbur Charles (April 27, 1915 - November 15, 1957) married Martha Richardson on August 23, 1936. They have three children: David, Charles and Susan. On May 14, 1946, he married Mildred B. Rayman. They have three children: Michael, Daniel and Joanne.

2. John Page (February 13, 1917 - August 15, 2005) married Iva L. Seeman on September 24, 1938. They have two sons: John and Steven.

3. James Stanley (October 13, 1918 - September 27, 1987) married Dorothy Miller on January 8, 1944. They have two children: Victor and Linda.

4. Rita B. (April 29, 1920) married John H. Kendrick on October 1, 1939. They have nine children: Cecilia Ann, John Max, Elizabeth B., James D., William S., Mary C., Paul A., Gary T., and Edward P.

5. Eugene Ivo (March 22, 1922) married Anna F. Ayres on November 15, 1947. They have two daughters: Jean Ann and Sharon May.

6. William Warren (September 28, 1923) married Virginia Akey on June 30, 1945. They have two children: Crystal Ann and Robert Eugene.

7. Edna May (April 9, 1925 - May 16, 2005) married William S. Pennycoff on October 13, 1951. They have one son: Robert Owen. On November 13, 1976, she married Thomas Edward Imel.

8. Susan Louise (June 27, 1927) married Matthew Vorich on July 1, 1947. They have three daughters: Virginia Loraine, Barbara Jo and Karen.

9. Cecilia Helena (March 1927 - January 14, 1935)

10. Verba Loraine (April 20, 1935) married Lee Travis July 7, 1953. They have three sons: Mark, Richard and Daniel. On April 19, 1969, she married John Hoss.

11. Paul Anthony (September 21, 1937) married Jan Hefflinger on June 10, 1960. They have three children: Risa Lea, Bart Matthew and Holly Jo. On August 28, 1993, he married Carolyn Cline.

Submitted by John and Linda Churchward

DOUGLAS (DOUG) CLARK FAMILY 1940-2005

Douglas (Doug) Clark is the oldest of four sons of Robert and Marjorie (Cole) Clark. Don Jeanine (Donnie) Beerman is the only child of Donald and Katherine Jean (Bowman) Beerman. Douglas and Don Jeanine were married February 14, 1959, Simpson Methodist Church, Fort Wayne.

Douglas (Doug) was born and raised in Fort Wayne and attended Harmar Grade School, Central High School, and graduated from Hoagland High School. Don Jeanine (Donnie) was born in Fort Wayne and raised in Marion Township near Poe.

Donnie attended first grade in a two-room school at Poe, where there was outside toilets. They only used one room as they only had one teacher for all eight grades. Music, art, and sometimes dancing were taught in the other room once a week by a traveling teacher. When Madison and Marion Townships consolidated and the school at Poe closed, she attended Hoagland Grade and High School.

Doug's family moved to the Poe area in 1956, where they attended Poe United Methodist Church. Doug and Donnie began dating in 1957 during Methodist Church Camp at Lake Webster. They have four children.

Daughter, Sheila Martin Bear, married Jeffery Bear, son of Lura and Kevin Bear from Wells County in 1992; they live near Poe. Combined they have six children. Danielle Martin and Alex Martin (father Ron Martin) are Sheila's. Jeremy (Marcia), Jessica (Mark McAllister), Marissa, and Brittany Bear are Jeff's children. Jeremy and Marcia have three children; Jacob, Joshua, and Miaah, and live in Churubusco. Jessica and Mark have two daughters, Remy and Georgia, and a son, Wade, and live in Indianapolis. Sheila was a computer operator at Lincoln Life for twenty years, and she is currently a travel agent for Allen

Travel. Jeff is a certified electrician and works for Havel Brothers.

Son, Kirt Douglas Clark, married Dixie Will, daughter of Donald and Doris Will, in June 1984, and they have two sons, Brent Donald and Brian Douglas. They live near Poe. Kirt was a medic in the Navy, a printer for 20 years, and an electrician. Dixie is a gemologist and works for Will Jewelry.

Daughter, Dawn, married Douglas Will, son of Donald and Doris Will, in June 1985, and they have two daughters, Malarie and Hannah. They live near Poe. Doug is a gemologist and appraiser for Will Jewelry. Dawn worked in sales at Madison Cabinets, Hoagland, and currently at Will Jewelry.

Daughter, Heather, married Scott Twomey, son of Ronald and Helen Twomey, of Roanoke, Indiana, in May 1996.They have two daughters, Regan and Campbell. They live near the County Line Road west of Fort Wayne. Scott is Marketing Manager at Biomet in Warsaw Indiana. Heather is a CPA and teaches accounting at Manchester College in North Manchester, Indiana.

Clark Family, Front: Dawn, Sheila
Back: Kirt, Donnie, Doug, Heather

Doug was a tree surgeon for Fort Wayne Parks Department, Supervisor at Joslyn Steel, and also worked construction for Irmscher where he worked on the General Motors building from start to finish. He retired from the labor union and started D&D Cleaning. Donnie built chassis for Magnavox, and motors for General Electric, while attending IPFW before she became involved in human resources. She was Personnel Manager for Seyfert Foods for 17 years, and, since 1997, Human Resources Manager for Alpha Shirt Company.

Submitted by Sheila Bear

CLAYTON FAMILY

John and Elly Clayton and their adult children settled in Allen County, Indiana, in the mid-1840s, after leaving Richland County, Ohio, where they were pioneers. John, son of William and Elizabeth Clayton, was born in Virginia about 1769. Elly was born about 1779 in northwestern Maryland. Once in Allen County, John Clayton purchased land in Cedar Creek Township and engaged in general farming with the help of his adult sons. He died there on June 9, 1847, and is buried in Old Leo Cemetery. According to a family Bible, Elly Clayton died May 9, 1856, but her place of death is unknown. She may have accompanied two of her daughters and their families to Iowa; she is not listed among those buried in Old Leo Cemetery.

John Clayton died leaving a will naming his surviving adult children. Samuel Clayton (1798 – 1879) and Thomas Clayton (1803 – 1852) were both born in Virginia. Neither lived in Allen County. The remainder of the Clayton children, all born in Richland County, Ohio, migrated to Allen County about 1845. Elizabeth Clayton (1807 - 1894) married Frederick Roop, Jr. They were living in Allen County with their children at the time of the 1850 Census. William Clayton was unmarried and living in Allen County with his widowed mother in 1850. Ann Clayton married John Osborn of DeKalb County in 1850. Ruth Clayton married Eli Gitchell and they resided in Cedar Creek Township with their children at the time of the 1850 and 1860 Census. Ruth died prior to the 1870 Census, but her husband was still residing in Cedar Creek Township at that time. Mary Caroline Clayton (1814 - 1900) married Andrew John Hursh in 1836. They are enumerated with their children in Allen County in 1850. Henry Clayton married Sarah Essig in 1851 in DeKalb County; after her death, he married Emily Showers in Allen County and was found there with his wife and two children in 1860. He subsequently married Lavina [--?--] and is listed in 1870, but his whereabouts thereafter are unknown. Jane Clayton accompanied her parents to Allen County and was a single woman living with Elly Clayton in Cedar Creek Township in 1850. Daniel Clayton (1824 - 1902) was widowed for the first time when his wife, Mary Craig Clayton, died in December 1846 in Cedar Creek Township. He married again to Miraba DePew, daughter of Issac DePew and Margaret Williams, in Allen County in 1849 and was widowed again in 1852, following the death of the couple's infant daughter. Shortly thereafter, Daniel Clayton, Mary Caroline Clayton Hursh, and Elizabeth Clayton Roop and their families migrated to Iowa, where Daniel remarried. His third union lasted forty-seven years. Mary Caroline Hursh and Elizabeth and Frederick Roop's families remained in Iowa until their deaths, but Daniel and his third wife, Cyrene Moore, followed the Oregon trail with Cyrene's parents William Moore and Priscilla Ayers to southeastern Washington.

Daniel ad Cyrene Moore Clayton, c. 1860s

Submitted by Meri Arnett-Kremian, great-great granddaughter of Daniel & Cyrene Moore Clayton

SAMUEL C. CLELAND FAMILY

Samuel Clayton Cleland was born August 6, 1892, to John S. Cleland and Julia Busz Cleland on a farm in Noble County. Four Busz sisters married four Cleland brothers and had forty double cousins.

John was elected sheriff of Noble County in 1910, moved the family to Albion, where he was caretaker of the jail. Julia prepared meals for the prisoners, preached temperance, and read to them from the Bible.

Samuel had a sister Dorthea Beitrice born in October,1903.

In 1910, Samuel graduated from Albion High School and then enrolled in Tri State College in Angola, later returning to teach in the Noble County Schools.

In 1915, he entered Indiana University, where his studies were interrupted when he entered the military services in World War I. He was commissioned a Second Lieutenant. In 1918, while serving in France in the Battle of the Argonne, Samuel was severly wounded, spending 14 months in army hospitals recuperating from his injuries.

After returning home, he married Bertha Marie Hart on January 1, 1920, in Albion. She was the daughter of William Henry Hart of Brimfield and Anna Gerber Hart of Ligonier. Henry Hart owned the grocery store in Albion. During the war years, Bertha, a violinist, studied music at Oberlin College, and later taught at a rural school near Ames, Iowa.

Samuel Clayton Cleland

Samuel and Bertha moved to Bloomington so he could to resume studies at Indiana University Law School. Bertha played violin in the orchestra for the silent movies to help the family purse. He became a member of the Ciof- Scholastic Legal Fraternity, and was awarded his LL.B and LL.M degrees.

After moving to Fort Wayne, Samuel began practice in the firm of the late Judge John W. Eggeman and remained a member until his own death. He had an extensive trial practice, was Allen County Attorney from 1930-33, was active in Democratic politics and served as party chairman for several years.

In 1942 Samuel was Democratic nominee for Congress from this district. He was a member of the Indiana and American Bar Associations, the American Legion, Veterans of Foreign Wars, Disabled Veterans, Order of the Purple Heart, the Scottish Rite, The Optimist Club, and was a member of Plymouth Congregational Church. Samuel was a grand orator, giving political and patrotic speeches for the common cause. When the Fort Wayne

Philharmonic (in which Bertha played the violin for 30 years) reorganized in 1942 with Han Schweiger as director, Mr. Cleland served as their attorney.

Samuel and Bertha raised two children. John Hart was born December 5, 1922. He married Lucy Cooper of Russiaville and they had two children, Samuel C. Cleland, born in1950 and William V. born 1952.

Their daughter, Mary Elizabeth, born August 25, 1925, was married on November 4, 1950 to Donald G. Young, born August 2 1926. He was the son of Edward W. Young and Loraine Gross Young, who also had a daughter, Marilyn born April 27, 1922. The Donald Youngs had three daughters, Barbara Ann born September 26, 1952, Patricia Louise, born January 8, 1956, and Janet Susan born January 13, 1958. There are seven grandchildren, Ana, Douglas and Luke, children of Barbara and Stockton Wulsin; Brian and Joseph, children of Patricia and James Vail; Haley and Andrea, children of Janet and James Richter. Samuel Clayton Cleland died on January 2, 1948, at the age of 56.

The Cleland family, then called Kneland, traced to the 13th Century, were among the Vikings who overran Northern Europe. During the following 100 years, the Clelands migrated to Ireland, giving a lineage called Scots-Irish.

Submitted by Mary Cleland Young

CASPER C. CLUTTER

Casper Clayton Clutter, born October 28, 1833, Licking County, Ohio, died March 16, 1880, Fort Wayne, Indiana. His parents were Jonathon Parsons Clutter, born December 25, 1794, Harper's Ferry, Virginia, died June 11, 1889, Waterloo, Indiana, and Jane Ryan Carrell/Corroll, born June 8, 1802, Allegheny County, Pennsylvania, died August, 1875, Waterloo, Indiana. Casper and Phebe Ann Kimball/Kimble, born January 31, 1836, Sussex County, New Jersey, died June 20, 1900, were married August 13, 1854 in Columbus, Ohio. They moved to Allen County in 1864. They are buried in the Old Huntertown Cemetery with one daughter and one son and his wife. Casper and Phebe had five children:

William Moses Clutter, born March 7, 1855, Columbus, Ohio, married March 20, 1884, in Allen County, Indiana, to Clara M. Sordelet, died November 7, 1932.

Lillian Rebecca Clutter, born January 25, 1857, Ottawa Township, Putnam County, Ohio, married July 15, 1879, Allen County, to Homer F. Hoagland.

Mary Frances Clutter, born January 1860, Ottawa Township, Putnam County, Ohio, married August 5, 1880, Allen County to Leo John Parrish.

Luella A. Clutter was born February 11, 1869, Allen County, Indiana.

Thomas Jay Clutter was born May 7, 1877, Huntertown, Indiana.

From 1874-1878 Casper was a local itinerant Methodist Minister in northern Indiana and western Ohio. It was during this period that Thomas Jay Clutter, was born. Sadly, his father died in 1880 of consumption (tuberculosis) so Thomas was raised by his older brother, William, and his wife, Clara M. Sordelet, born October 13, 1861, DeKalb County, Indiana, died May 24, 1936, Allen County, Indiana, who helped raise seven children, but never had any children of their own. William Moses Clutter was an Allen County bailiff in 1930. Phebe "Anna" Clutter remarried Harvey Ross on March 30, 1895, in Allen County.

Thomas Jay Clutter lived with his widowed mother and siblings in Fort Wayne on Harrison Street in mid 1890s while a "student." He served in the 1898 Spanish American War and then trained to become a physician at the University of Michigan Medical School (1900-1902) and Rush Medical College in Chicago. Thomas met Bessie Leona Bybee, born April 17, 1883, Mentone, Indiana, married April 11, 1905, Kosciusko County, died November 30, 1929, Rochester, Indiana, at John Racine's Saloon and Boarding House where William M. Clutter had been a saloonkeeper as noted in the 1880 census. Thomas and Bessie moved to Atwood, Indiana, where their only child, William Clayton Clutter, was born September 14, 1907. Moving to Mentone, Indiana, in 1911, Dr. Clutter practiced medicine until the 1940s. On December 24, 1950, he died in Mentone, Indiana, of prostate cancer. However, William Clayton Clutter had married Alma LaVerne Felix, born February 16 1911, Lorain, Ohio, in 1932 in Kendallville, Indiana. They had five children:

Casper and Phoebe Clutter.

Judith Jeannine Clutter, born July 1, 1935, Warsaw, married Larry Lee Tracy, March 1956, Petoskey, Michigan, died March 28, 1975, North Webster, Indiana.

John Jay Clutter, born February 23, 1937, Warsaw, Indiana, married Delores Rae Burkett.

Thomas Jay Clutter, born October 7, 1940, Warsaw, married Judith Hammond, June 1968, North Webster, Indiana.

Joyce Ellen Clutter, born July 25, 1947, Warsaw, Indiana, married Donald Logan, 1968, California.

William Hollis Clutter, born October 7, 1950, Warsaw, Kosciusko County, Indiana.

While the family did not reside in Allen County for many years, some descendents did return even though they did not know their ancestors had once lived in Allen County: David Allen Tracy, born January 9, 1957, El Paso, Texas, and his wife Kathy Jo Hayes, born November 29, 1960, Fort Wayne, lived in Fort Wayne from 1977, to present; Michelle Rae Clutter Brandt born April 4, 1966, and her two daughters, Hope Elise Brandt, born September 27, 1995, and Holly Rae Brandt born March 7, 1998, from 1988.

Submitted by Dyanne Marie Tracy.

LOWELL S. COATS FAMILY

Lowell S. Coats (born in Warren County, Indiana, August 2, 1918, died in Allen county, Indiana, April 2, 1993) came to Allen County in 1953 with his wife, Virginia (Keeney) (born in Hendricks County, Indiana, October 6, 1919), and son, James Nelson (born in Wabash County, Indiana, June 3, 1949), from North Manchester, Indiana, to teach at New Haven Junior-Senior High School. That same summer son David Lowell was born (August 1, 1953). Lowell's and Virginia's undergraduate degrees were from Central Normal College in Danville, Indiana, with graduate degrees from the University of Michigan and The Eastman School of Music, respectively.

Lowell's teaching career began in White County, Indiana, but was interrupted by a four-year stint in the U.S. Army during World War II, including the Battle of the Bulge. After the war, and prior to coming to Allen County, his teaching assignments were in Monticello and North Manchester, Indiana, schools. Virginia's teaching experience prior to Allen County included schools in Jamestown, Frankfort, Lagro and North Manchester, Indiana.

After four years with the New Haven schools, Lowell moved to South Side High School in Fort Wayne where he taught English and, on occasion, Latin for nine years. The next ten years were spent as Fort Wayne Community Schools' English Consultant for the junior and senior high schools, two years later retiring from Wayne High School. During his teaching years, he was active in the National Council of Teachers of English and served one term as president of the Indiana Council of Teachers of English. Virginia taught music at Anthony Wayne Elementary School (Wayne Township), Kekionga Junior High School (Fort Wayne Community Schools) and Sunnymede Elementary School (East Allen County Schools). During these years, the family was active in the New Haven Methodist Church where Lowell held offices and Virginia directed the Junior Choir.

Both Nelson and David graduated from New Haven High School (1967 and 1971). Nelson continued his education at Ball State University (Class of 1972). After teaching high school English in Tipton, Indiana, Nelson returned to Fort Wayne where he became affiliated with, and later a shareholder of, the CPA firm of Dulin, Ward & DeWald, Inc. Nelson received his Certified Public Accountant's license in 1979. Nelson has served on several community boards, including United Way of Allen County, Leadership Fort Wayne, Park Center and Citilink, among others. He has also been active in the Fort Wayne Area Community Band (French Horn) since 1980. Nelson married Mary Neuendorf Aldrich (7/30/85), a graduate of Indiana University (Class of 1969). Mary taught physical education, coached and was Assistant Athletic Director for the Fort Wayne Community Schools before retiring from Northrop High School in 2002, after thirty-three years in the school system.

David graduated from Indiana University in 1976 with a degree in business. After graduation, David worked in sales in Minneapolis and Chicago before moving in 1986 to Southern California, Orange County, where he continues to work as a sales and marketing manager, currently for Kosakura & Associates. David married Cindy Kay Gratz (12/30/89), a graduate of the University of Southern California (Class of 1981) with a bachelors degree in business. Cindy has also worked in sales and is currently employed at K&V Management as an accountant and tax preparer. David and Cindy are the parents of Alexander David Coats (b. Orange County, California, April 25, 1991). The family is active in the Red Hill Lutheran Church, Tustin, California, where David sings in the choir and occasionally plays cello.

Virginia, retired, continues to live in Allen County. She is, or has been, active in the Indiana-Purdue Community Orchestra, the Allen County Retired Educators Association and the Fort Wayne Women's Club. Virginia is a member of the First Presbyterian Church and sings in its choir.

Submitted by J. Nelson Coats

COCHOIT FAMILY

The Cochoit family first settled in Allen County in 1854 when Joseph Cochoit emigrated from France. He was born November 3, 1826 in Orleans, Loiret, France. Joseph and his brother, Etienne, arrived in the United States on April 21, 1854 through the Port of New York on the ship *Howard*. Joseph made his Declaration of Intent on October 2, 1854, in Allen County. On October 21, 1858, in the Cathedral of the Immaculate Conception, he married Hortense Julia (Rondot) Julliard, the daughter of Claude F. and Marie Jeanne (Pataillot) Rondot, early French settlers of Perry Township. Hortense was born in France in 1826 and came to Allen County in 1850. She married Francois Julliard October 14, 1852; Francois died November 20, 1856, leaving her with two daughters.

By 1868 Joseph and Hortense had moved to Section 20 in Jefferson Township where they owned 70 acres. They lived in the family home on Ridge Road until their deaths in 1901 and 1902. In addition to Hortense's daughters, Justine and Marie Philomene, who married Paul E. Miller and then William Harkenrider, Joseph and Hortense had four children: Jules Emile (1859-1936) who married Rose Angela Casso (1872-1936) on May 2, 1892; Francis Joseph "Frank" (1861-1931) who married Clara Freiburger (1879-1958) on February 17, 1906; Julie Frances (1864-before 1917) who married William O. France (1864-1946) on February 27, 1889; and Mary Sophia (1866-1893) who married John Baptist Zuber (1867-1940) on January 7, 1891.

Joseph and Hortense became part of the St. Louis Church community and Joseph is listed in the parish books on the 1868 roster. The parish books show that he rented pew # 1 for the years 1870-1871. Joseph Cochoit's name is found on one of the stained-glass windows of the St. Louis Church in Besancon. Hortense died May 11, 1901, and Joseph died eleven months later on April 10, 1902. They are buried in the old St. Louis Catholic Cemetery.

Submitted by Leanne Casso-Beeching

JULES EMIL & EDITH MATILDA (SORG) COCHOIT

Jules Emil Cochoit was born January 23, 1912, in Fort Wayne, Allen County, Indiana, and baptized in the Cathedral of the Immaculate Conception. He graduated from Central Catholic High in 1930. On December 30, 1939 he married Edith Matilda Sorg, the daughter of John Michael and Mary Margaret (McLaughlin) Sorg. They had two children, Jules Emil, III, and Angela Rose.

While living in Fort Wayne, Jules was employed by General Electric and Edith was employed by General Hosiery. In 1947 they moved west and settled in Pomona, California. Jules was an active member of St. Joseph Catholic Church where he was a Fourth Degree member of the Knights of Columbus. Jules joined the Brotherhood of Painters and Allied Trades Union (Local Union 979) where he was the Financial Secretary for 26 years.

After his retirement in 1977, Jules and Edith enjoyed spending time with their children and grandchildren. Edith died in November of 1982 and Jules died five months later in April of 1983.

Their son, Jules Emil, III, married Kathleen Ann Eaton in l964, and Patricia Ruth Schmidt in 1983. He graduated from UCLA and then joined the U.S. Air Force. He later went to work for the Xerox Corporation until his recent retirement. He has two children, Joseph E. who married Marilyn Howard, and Julie M. who married Alvin "Neil" Chambers, and four grandsons.

December 30, 1939.
Edith Matilda (Sorg) and Jules Emil Cochoit

Angela Rose graduated from Mt. San Antonio College and married Raymond Eugene Shoults. She has two children, Richard D. who married Katherine M. Olson, and Corrine L. who married David O. Cotton, and two stepchildren, Randy D. and Rena A. Angela and Raymond have ten grandchildren, and two great-grandsons.

Jules' father was Jules Emile, the first of Joseph and Hortense Julia (Rondot) (Julliard) Cochoit's four children. He was born July 26, 1859, in Academie, Allen County, Indiana. On May 2, 1892 he married Rose Angela Casso in the St. Louis Catholic Church in Besancon. Rose was the daughter of Frank and Eugenia (Manier) Casso. Jules resided in Jefferson Township most of his life and was an employee of the Pennsylvania Railroad for 43 years. Rose died on May 19, 1936, and Jules died two months later on July 13, 1936. They are buried in the Catholic Cemetery in Fort Wayne.

Jules and Rose had six children. Stella J. (1892-1977) who married Alvin C. Hartman and had two sons, Jules (1917-1938) and Richard A. (1923-1994); Joseph J. (1894-1972) who had one daughter, Pauline Rosella, who was born in 1914; Charlotte H. (1895-1939) who married Lester Klingman and then Parl L. Fry; Marie G. (1897-1975) who married Frank Pommert and then Grant S. Cooper and had one son, Paul J. Pommert (1918-1956); Lucille J. (born in 1902) who married James L. Hamilton and had four sons: James, John, Joseph, and Francis Patrick "Charles"; and Jules Emil (1912-1983) who is the subject of this biography.

Submitted by Jules Emil Cochoit, III

COLE-BAZETOUX FAMILY

Edward Herbert Cole was born in 1924 in Cleveland, at home, of German, English, Scot, Welsh, and Irish ancestors, some veterans of the War of Independence and Civil War. He was a son of Herbert Hugh Cole, WWI veteran, (son of Homer Franklin Cole and Elizabeth Helen Pore) and of Manola Mason Vero, army nurse, (daughter of Edward Vero and Roberta Eloise Harshaw).

Edward attended Trenton, New Jersey, public schools and dropped out of high school to work for Postal Telegraph-Cable Co. After enlisting in World War II, Edward was called to duty with the Signal Corps in 1943, and served with Company B, 3110th Signal Service Battalion, in England, France, and Germany. At discharge, Technician 4th Grade, he wore the European Theater of Operations ribbon with two bronze stars, Good Conduct Medal, Victory Medal, Occupation ribbon, American Theater ribbon, Marksman Medal and insignia indicating the Battalion's receipt of the Meritorious Service Unit Plaque.

In 1946, while still a soldier in Paris, he married Gabrielle Helene Marguerite Bazetoux, of a 400 year old Correze, France, family. She was the daughter of Eugenie Marie Rougerie and Leonard Auguste Bazetoux. Marriage ceremonies were conducted by the mayor of the 15th Arrondissement, and later at St. George's English Church. Occupying Berlin as soldier and civilian, he worked there for a year for the War Department, becoming Assistant to the Officer in Charge, Berlin Signal Center. Mrs. Cole joined him there.

He received his Associate in Arts degree in 1959 from Jersey City Junior College. He was valedictorian. Edward graduated in 1963 *summa cum laude* from Rugers University College, earning a Bachelor of Science in Management, first in a class of 308 with a perfect 1.0 grade. He was awarded two scholarship keys and was president of the Honor Society.

Edward and Gabrielle's son, Eric Alain Cole, went to Fort Wayne's Indiana Institute of Technology. Eric married Mayflower descendant Cheryl Ann Mertens, daughter of Willis George Mertens and Ida Alice Hedges. Before their divorce, they had a child, Michelle Marguerite, who married James Mauricio Dominguez (son of John R. Dominguez and Ophelia Mauricio). They had a son, Jesse Cole Dominguez, and later divorced.

After graduation from Doane College, Crete, Nebraska, Edward and Gabrielle Cole's daughter,

Carol Linda Cole, married Thomas Richard Prest (son of Dr. James Richard Prest and Elizabeth Ann Evans). They had sons Edouard Kirkpatrick and James Gabriel.

Edward became (1968) coach of the Jersey City YWCA swimming team. Mrs. Cole was a Y Board member and program chairman. Edward was awarded $500 for the Best Tutorial Paper at the 1974 Chicago National Engineering Conference. His paper, presented and published, was entitled *Domestic Teletypewriter Exchange and Related Services*. He represented Western Union on the Board of Directors of the Railway Systems Suppliers, Inc., and was elected in 1976 as their chairman and president.

He retired in 1983 from the Western Union Telegraph Company, Upper Saddle River, New Jersey, after 39 years, rising from messenger to Assistant Vice President. In 1958 he was assigned sales responsibility for the newly begun U.S. Telex business and became WD's sales/marketing person most closely identified with Telex and with development of Telex computer services.

Edward and Gabrielle Cole

As an adult, he resided at Trenton, New Jersey; Berlin (Germany); Westville; Vineland; Sewell, Jersey City; Bayonne and Allendale, New Jersey, and Fort Wayne. He was the family genealogist, preparing and distributing separate works on Gaut, Boyd, Cole, and Harshaw families. The Allen County Public Library has added those efforts and an autobiography to their collection. He loved tennis, playing thrice weekly at 80. At the Wildwood Racquet Club he organized and ran doubles and singles groups, took a weekly lesson, and played on the USTA tour.

These were his best results:

- (1985) Finalist 55s Singles Fort Wayne City Championship;
- (1988) Champion 55s Doubles French Lick;
- Northern Indiana USTA Ranking: #1 65s Doubles; #4 65s Singles;
- (1989) Western Division USTA Ranking: #6 Singles 65s;
- (1990) Champion 65s Doubles Wildwood USTA Super Seniors;
- Champion 65s Singles FW City Championship;
- (1991) Champion 65s Singles FW Senior Olympics;
- Champion 60s Doubles FW Senior Olympics.

Edward was a self-taught italic calligrapher and a prosperous amateur financial guru versed in statistical analysis, who enjoyed mathematics and taught himself computer programming. He spoke French well, enough Italian to get about, and a little Spanish. He traveled with his wife to much of North America, Northern Africa, the Middle East, Russia, Central America, China, and all of Europe, Italy and France being frequent destinations. A bit of a memory expert, he could recite the capitals of the fifty states alphabetically and could name all of the presidents, the year of their elections, and the date and reason for their deaths if occurring in office.

Edward had a quick temper and acerbate wit, was uncommonly punctual and parsimonious. From his days at junior college, he was a man of highest integrity, which he translated as fidelity, honesty, punctuality, and honoring commitments. He was just under six feet tall, slender, good looking despite his broken nose. He liked dancing, reading spy stories, working on a computer, and playing pool. He enjoyed classical music, particularly opera, Puccini and Verdi being favorites. His favorite painting, by Raffaello Sanzio, was *Madonna dela Seggiola,* Galleria Pitti, Florence.

He lived by four guiding principles:

The longest journey begins with but a single step. (Lao-tzu)

I cried because I had no shoes until I saw a man who had no feet. (The Gulistan of Sa'di by Sa'di)

Man must be persuaded to excel; man must be given reason to believe he can excel. (Edward Herbert Cole)

The culmination of healthy self-development is integrity. (Erik H. Erikson)

Submitted by Edward H. Cole.

WARREN G. & VALORIE A. (HOLLIS) COLGLAZIER FAMILY

Warren Gene Colglazier was born June 29, 1929 in Richmond, Indiana, to Chester Sturgeon, nickname Pard, (born March 13, 1903, died April 25, 1981) and Mildred (Davis) Colglazier (born May 30, 1901, died April 2, 1982). A son, Phil Davis (born April 23, 1927, died January 30, 1937), died of pneumonia. At the age nine, Warren's family, including brothers, William Lee (born May 27, 1930) and Donald Edward (born May 6, 1935), moved to Salem, Indiana, where his father went into farming. A son, Stanley Walter (born August 29, 1940), was born in Salem, Indiana, to the family.

During his school years Warren's interests were basketball, track, cross country, baseball and band. He graduated from Salem High School in 1947. He worked on his parent's farm, Voyles Clothing Store and the Salem Creamery before entering the U.S. Air Force during the Korean War. He was shipped to Lackenheath R.A.F. B. in England. The last year of service was spent at Limestone A.F. B., Maine. With an honorable discharge in 1954, he enrolled at Ball State Teachers College (Ball State University) in education. He played baseball for four seasons at B.S.T.C. In college he met Valorie A. Hollis Gentry who was majoring in elementary education. They were married at College Avenue Methodist Church in Muncie, Indiana, on October 5, 1956. Valorie completed her Bachelor Degree in 1957 and Warren completed his in 1959.

Valorie Ann Hollis was born June 30, 1933, in Muncie, Indiana, to Samuel Allen Hollis (born May 15, 1907, died April 20, 1998) and Veda Helen (Nelson) Hollis (born November 30, 1906, died October 20, 1998). Valorie's father, a pharmacist, and her mother, a teacher, moved to Hartford City, Indiana, to help with and later own the family grocery business. Later, her father was the Blackford County Hospital pharmacist for several years. Two more daughters, Carol Lee (born May 15, 1938) and Helen Kay (born October 31, 1945) were born to family in Hartford City, Indiana.

Bottom row: Warren Gene and Valorie Ann. Middle: Karen Michelle and Ann Adele. Back: Renee Lorraine, Stephen Allen and Phillip Hollis

Valorie taught elementary school in New Castle, Anderson, and Muncie, Indiana. Warren worked for N. G. Gilbert Corporation (Electrical Contractor) in Liberia, Africa, as an office manager. Returning from Africa, he taught one year a Muncie Central High School before working for K.J. Brown brokerage for two years and one year for Waddell and Reed Investments.

Warren and Valorie completed their Masters Degrees in Education in 1966 and the family moved to Fort Wayne, Indiana, in August of that year. Their five children grew up in this city attending Glenwood Elementary, Lane Middle School, and Snider High School. They resided in the Old Glenwood Addition. Karen Michelle (born January 13, 1954, San Diego, California) lives in St. Louis, Missouri, with husband, Raymond F. Beaver (born May 5, 1959). They have three children and four grandchildren. Stephen Allen (born January 19, 1955, Hartford City, Indiana) lives in Ann Arbor, Michigan, with wife, Christine Jane McCamont (born April 21, 1951). Reneé Lorraine (born June 6, 1957, Muncie, Indiana) lives in Whitley County, Indiana, with husband, George Vernon Lord (born August 15, 1957), and their two children. Ann Adele (born September 5, 1958 in Muncie, Indiana) lives in Fort Wayne, Indiana, with husband, Richard Alan Dolsen Sr. (born June 9, 1954). They have three children and four grandchildren. Phillip Hollis (born September 4, 1959 in Muncie, Indiana) lives in Fort Wayne, Indiana. He became the Executive Director of the Fort Wayne Civic Theatre in 2000.

Warren taught for the Fort Wayne Training Center until 1974 when he and the program was transferred to the Fort Wayne Community School system. He taught at Kekionga Middle School and Elmhurst High School until retirement in 1987 with 25 1/2 years of service. Valorie taught in Fort Wayne Community Schools at Shambaugh, Lincoln, Weisser Park-Whitney Young elementary schools, until retirement in 1994 with the total of 36 years in her teaching career.

This Colglazier family has been established in Fort Wayne for forty years. Warren coached girls softball with Fort Wayne Turners Athletic Club, Rehm Insurance, and Pape Paint girls softball teams. Earlier Valorie was active in Tri Kappa Sorority. She is still an active member of Delta Kappa Gamma and is involved in Study Connection with Fort Wayne Community Schools. Both are active members of Good Shepherd United Methodist Church on 4700 Vance Avenue. Valorie had the opportunity of designing several windows for the church.

Submitted by Warren Colglazier

STEPHEN FOSTER COLLIER FAMILY

The Stephen Foster Collier family moved from Anderson, Madison County, Indiana, to Allen County in the spring of 1965. The family consisted of husband Stephen, who was born in Noblesville, Indiana, on June 8, 1941, and his bride Marlene L. (Stottlemyer), who was born in Anderson, Indiana, on April 10, 1945. Their parents were Russell Lovine Collier and Ruth Alberta Collingwood and Lilburn Stottlemyer and Lenna Ethel Hoppes, respectively.

Steve and Marlene were married at the Whetstone United Church of Christ in Anderson on June 20, 1965. Steve was a new graduate of Ball State University with a degree in accounting and came to Fort Wayne to work for the Magnavox Corporation. The company was later bought by Raytheon Electronics. He continued working there until his retirement in 2003. Marlene continued her education at St. Francis University and graduated with a degree in medical technology. She worked for several years, first for Lutheran Hospital, then Parkview Hospital, in Fort Wayne.

In 1971 they had their first child, LeAnn Michele, born on January 1. On July 16,1994, she married Timothy Richard Pancake, of Auburn, Indiana. They currently reside in the city of Fort Wayne and have three children: Elizabeth Grace, born Sept 29, 1998, William Graham, born Sept 30, 2001, and Theodore Collier, born December 30, 2004. LeAnn works as a physical therapist at Parkview Hospital. Tim owns and manages Cornerstone Landscape Group.

On February 5,1974, a son was born, whom they named Jason Philip. He graduated from Purdue University in 1997. He worked for the state of Arkansas as a forester and currently works for the U.S. Forest Service in San Bernardino, California.

In 1969 Steve and Marlene purchased five acres at 1123 Pion Road in Perry Township, for the price of $1,000 and acre. They still reside there, pursuing their lifelong hobby of trail riding their pleasure horses.

Submitted by Stephen and Marlene Collier

CLIFTON W. & ALMA J. (HICKS) COLLINS

Clifton Wheeler Collins was born on March 13,1914, in Faunsdale, Hale County, Alabama, to Henry and Lucile Page Collins, one of three children. His father was a coal miner, carpenter, and minister. His mother was a homemaker.

Clifton attended Parker High School where he completed the eleventh grade. He accepted his calling to preach the word and began his ministerial studies in 1931. While attending a Baptist convention in November 1934, Clifton met a lovely young woman named Alma Jean Hicks. She was born in Crenshaw County, Alabama, to Thomas and Nicey Parmer Hicks on April 1, 1916. When Clifton approached Alma, he took her hand and his first words to her were, "One day you are going to be my wife." Alma didn't take to his polished looks right away, but in time, he charmed his way into her heart. After an extended courtship, Clifton Collins and Alma Hicks were married in Birmingham, Alabama, on January 22, 1936. They were blessed with five children: Clifton, Henrietta, Robert, Harry, and Beverly.

Clifton W. and Alma H. Collins

In April 1944, Clifton traveled to Alliance, Ohio, for the funeral of his maternal grandmother, Della Page Hart. While attending the service Clifton met two of his cousins from the Page family who found employment with the International Harvester Company in Fort Wayne, Indiana. They propositioned him with an employment opportunity. After contemplating for several months, Clifton contacted his cousins, Moses and Ned Moore, and headed to Fort Wayne arriving in Allen County on October 15, 1944. The International Harvester Company hired him the next day. Alma and the children came to join Clifton after he secured a home on the west side of town. After they settled in the city, the Collins family joined the Seventh Day Adventist Church on Hanna Street.

Clifton and Alma Collins lived in contentment surrounded by their family and friends, including Alicia Vasquez and her family, who lived next to Mr. and Mrs. Collins for several decades. Clifton retired from International Harvester Company in 1982, after thirty-seven years. Alma retired from American Linen the same year after thirty years of dedicated service.

Clifton lived to reach his seventies. On September 18, 1989, at Three Rivers Nursing Home, he passed away at seventy-five years of age. He was interred at Covington Memorial Cemetery.

Alma Collins is thriving with vitality as she approaches her ninetieth birthday.

She has a sharp mind and has educated her grandchildren about the struggles she and grandfather endured to survive the Depression and the Civil Rights Era. The Collins heritage traces to Kent County, England, to John Collins I, born in 1569. Nelly Collins was the former slave of an English Collins descendant from Caroline County, Virginia. She was born in May 1792, and may have lived to reach 108 years of age. Nelly had children with John Collins, a bachelor, of Marengo County, Alabama, a descendant of John Collins I, and one of the wealthiest plantation owners of the south. We are descendants of John and Nelly Collins.

Submitted by Michael L. Robertson

ANDREW TODD & MARTHA JANE BLOOM CONKLING FAMILY

Martha Jane Bloom was born September 5, 1969, at Parkview Hospital in Fort Wayne, Indiana. She is the daughter of Clarence Nicholas and Kathryn Ann Bowen Bloom. When Martha was born, the family lived at 1857 Florida Drive near Lakeside Park. Her father worked for the U.S. Postal Service and her mother was a nurse at Parkview. Her siblings are Karen Ann of Chicago, Janet Baltzell, Linda Burrell, James Gregory and Robert Paul all of Fort Wayne and Jeffrey Thomas of San Diego, California.

Martha attended Forest Park Elementary, St. Jude's Grade School and graduated in 1987 from Snider High School. She obtained a B.S. degree from Purdue University's School of Pharmacy in 1992 and works as a Pharmacist for Walmart. She married Andrew Todd Conkling on July 11, 1992. Andy is the son of Glenn and Peggy Conkling and was born February 23, 1969. He attended Haley Elementary, Blackhawk Middle School and graduated from Snider in 1987. He spent four years in the U.S. Navy stationed in Okinawa, Japan and Keflavik, Iceland. After his military service, he obtained a B.S. degree in Construction Management from Purdue University's School of Technology in 1996. Andy is part-owner in Farmington Homes and Newcastle Concrete.

Martha and Andrew Conkling on their wedding day

Emily and Claire Conkling

Andy and Martha have two daughters: Emily Nicole was born January 30, 1996, in Lafayette, Indiana, and Claire Danielle was born May 8, 2001, in Fort Wayne. Emily attends Perry Hill Elementary where she is a fourth grade student. Claire is a student at Pine Hills Kiddie Garden. Both girls take dance lessons at Tiffany & Co. Studio of Dance. The family enjoys trips to the Fort Wayne Children's Zoo. They also like to spend time hiking at Metea Park and summer weekends at Lake James.

Submitted by Martha and Andy Conkling

COOMER FAMILY

The Coomer family came from England (Welch) in the early 1700s. Brief history tells us they lived for a short time in the state of Rhode Island. Through the years a family, of which we are descendants, lived in Newfane County, New York, east of Niagara Falls. The Jim Coomer family, while traveling there about 1974, found roads named Coomer Road and Old Coomer Road. They also located an abandoned railroad depot named Coomer Station.

It was in Newfane County that Jonathan Coomer, father of Albert Coomer, lived until Albert was 14 years of age. They moved from Newfane County to Delaware County, Ohio, and then to the Payne, Ohio, area about 1857. Albert Coomer married Mary Keltner on February 22, 1843. There were nine children born to this union. Their eldest, Daniel Webster Coomer, lived on the farm near Payne, Ohio, where his father had started his pioneer life.

Daniel Webster Coomer's oldest son, Jonathan, brother of Samuel, lived to be 100 years old and retired as a brick mason in the Detroit, Michigan, area.

Samuel Allen Coomer was the youngest son, born September 22, 1868, near Payne, Ohio. October 23, 1888 he married Elizabeth Lehman. To this union three sons were born, Albert, Samuel Peter, and John, who died at infancy.

Elizabeth passed away on May 4, 1896. Samuel married Della May Allison September 25, 1897. To this union two children were born, Virgil, April 1, 1906, and Celia who died in infancy.

Samuel farmed his entire lifetime, starting in the Payne, Ohio, area and then moving to a farm southeast of Woodburn in section 26 and 27 of Maumee Township in 1912. At this time this farm was known as the Spangler farm. Sam also had the reputation of being a good judge of horses. He bought horses from farmers in the area and shipped them to Buffalo and New York, New York, for uses on the fire departments, milk wagons, and other uses. Grandson Jim heard many stories of how Samuel would ride one horse and lead several at a time and put them on a railroad car in Van Wert, Ohio. Sam passed away on January 9, 1941; his wife Della died April 23, 1971. They are buried in the Lehman Cemetery west of Payne, Ohio.

Sam's son, Virgil Coomer, began farming with his father on the Spangler farm in Maumee Township. Sam retired in 1937, and Virgil rented the same Spangler farm until moving one mile west in 1951. He also farmed other land in the area, as well as producing and selling Indiana Certified Seed.

Virgil married Esther Cartwright October 25, 1931. There were three children born of this marriage, James (Jim, 1932), Marianne (1935) and Janice (1941). Marianne married Hugh Stevenson and lives in Phoenix, Arizona, and Janice married Manfred (Doug) Ort and lives east of New Haven, Indiana. Jim married Marilyn Becker on January 19, 1952. Six children were born to this union: Gerry who died in infancy, Carol Rebecca married Greg Garrison, Ruth Ellen married Mark Pease (deceased), Rex Ellis married Kelly Shull, Michael Lee married Marie Cenko, and Peggy Sue married Brian Meyer.

Jim farmed with Virgil until Virgil retired in 1971. Virgil died December 13, 1991, and Esther died May 4, 2003. Both are buried at Lehman Cemetery in Payne, Ohio.

Jim expanded the farming and also raised and sold seed to farmers. Jim and Marilyn incorporated Coomer Seeds in 1979 and expanded the seed business to much greater volume. Jim retired in 1997 and rented the land to Rex; he quit the seed business a few years later.

Rex and Kelly now live in and own the home farm of Rex's parents in section 34, Maumee Township. They have two sons, Justin and Jacob, who attend Woodland High School. Rex now farms the Spangler farm that was sold to Jack Carpenter in the 1960s and since is owned by Bob Basting and Betty Miller, daughter of Jack Carpenter. This makes the fourth generation of Coomers (although not consecutively) to farm this land.

Over the course of these generations, they have seen horses pulling two row planters to tractors pulling 16 row planters. Corn was being picked by hand that is now being harvested by combines and tractors with auto steer.

Submitted by Kelly A. Coomer

PETER COONRAD

Peter Coonrad was born March 13, 1836, in Orandaga, New York. He came to Indiana in 1857. He entered the Civil War in 1865. He died in Ennis, Texas, in August 13, 1915. He married Mary Christina Huth, born October 22, 1841, in Richland County, Ohio. She died in Ennis, Texas, in March 1926 at the age of 85. They came to New Haven, Indiana, and were married November 28, 1861, in St. John's Catholic Church in New Haven. They lived on the Minnich Road near the Paulding Road, southeast of New Haven. They had seven children, Henry, Erwin, Clara, Theresa, Martha, Emma, and Rosa. They moved to Ennis, Texas, and settled on a farm in 1884. Mary Christina moved to 802 South Dallas Street, Ennis, Texas, where she died at the age of 85.

Written in 1981 by Marcella Pranger Weller, Rose's daughter.

Submitted by Patricia Jensen, Pana, Illinois

CORBAT BROTHERS ROBERT & JAMES

Quoting from the book entitled *The Maumee River Basin* in the Allen County Public Library, "the Corbat Brothers, Alphonse and Frank, were numbered among the representative farmers of Allen County, their landed estate being a large and well-improved one, ranking among the best in this favored section of the state."

The Corbat Brothers
(Left to right) Robert and James

Alphonse was born in Canton Berne, Switzerland ,in 1854 and Frank in Huntington County in 1859. They were sons of Vandelin and Rose Corbat who immigrated to America in 1857 making Indiana their destination. In 1868, the family moved from Huntington County to Aboite Township in Allen County where Alphonse built the present homestead on Bass Road in 1885. Frank remained a bachelor while Alphonse married Elizabeth Manier in 1876 and they produced ten children: Celia, Frank, Joseph, Rose, Julian, Florence, Albert, James, Mary and Robert, all now deceased. According to the above named book, they were communicants of St. Patrick's Catholic Church in Arcola.

The photo shows two of the ten children, James and Robert, in their World War I Army uniforms. James had three daughters: Margaret Winicker, who pre-deceased him, and still living are Pauline Taylor and Patricia Corbat. Robert had two children. Both still living are Robert, Jr., and Barbara Keiser. Many Corbat descendents, grandchildren, great-grandchildren and great-great grandchildren, are residents of Allen County. The Bass Road farm where Robert Jr. still lives was recognized circa 1980 by the Indiana Historical Bureau and Indiana Department of Commerce with the award, Hoosier Homestead Farm, given when the land has been in the same family for 100 or more years.

Submitted by Patricia Corbat

CORNEILLE FAMILY

Robert Michael Curts was born on May 15, 1959, at Madigan Army Hospital in Tacoma, Washington. He graduated from Elmhurst High School in Fort Wayne, Indiana, and Indiana University in Bloomington, Indiana, and now teaches health and science at Greenwood High School in Greenwood, Indiana.

His sister, Connie Lynn Curts Carter Cramblit, was born March 5, 1961, at the Luthern Hospital in Fort Wayne, Indiana. She graduated from Elmhurst High School and is currently employed by Kroger Company in Columbus, Ohio. She has two children by her first marriage and two from her second marriage.

Robert and Connie are the children of Robert Eugene Curts, born February 10, 1936, in Mt. Carmel, Illinois, and Arlene Dodane Curts, born March 28, 1936, in Fort Wayne, Indiana. Robert E. served in the army with the 35th Artillery, 2nd Howzier Battalion. He was employed by Tokheim Corporation, and Arlene worked for Essex Wire and United Technologies.

Robert M. and Connie L.'s great great grandfather, John Baptiste Corneille, born on August 18, 1837, in France, was an early pioneer in Fort

Wayne. After 60 days at sea, he arrived in the United States from France in 1843 at the age of five, along with his parents Claude S. F. Corneille and Rosalie Moinet Corneille, and siblings. Landing in New York, they made their way to Toledo, Ohio, and embarked for Fort Wayne on the Wabash and Erie Canal. Land was purchased in St. Joseph Township and cleared for farming.

John B. Corneille married Rosalie Mattey on May 8, 1863. Rosalie was born on March 6, 1845; her family, like John's, was also French. From this union 13 children were born, but only one son and seven daughters lived to adulthood. Their son, Charles, served with Battery E, Rainbow Division in World War I, and is buried in Arlington National Cemetery in Washington D.C.

John Baptiste and Rosalie Corneille

John was an associate with the dry goods establishments of Abbot and Company and Root & Company. In later years he devoted his time to notary work and French correspondence. He was also a volunteer with the Alert Hook & Ladder Company firefighters. He died April 22, 1917 outliving his wife by six years. Both John and Rosalie are buried at the Catholic Cemetery on Lake Avenue in Fort Wayne.

On August 29, 1882, John and Rosalie Corneille's daughter, Alma Lydia, was born. She married Charles Dodane on August 14, 1906. Charles Dodane came from a French family who had settled around Besancon, Indiana. Charles worked for Penn Company and Dudlo. He passed away on June 11, 1937. His widow surpassed him by 30 years, passing away on April 7, 1967. They are also buried at the Catholic Cemetery on Lake Avenue in Fort Wayne.

Charles and Alma Dodane's second child, Norbert Francis, born on March 1, 1908, married Imogene L. Brooks on April 28, 1932, in Indianapolis, Indiana. Imogene was born on March 10, 1908, in Carterville, Missouri. Norbert worked for Wayne Pump in Fort Wayne until his death in June 26, 1951. He is buried at the Catholic Cemetery on Lake Avenue. His widow then married Charles Hubert. She passed away on March 27, 1972, and is buried outside of Payne, Ohio, at Blue Creek Cemetery. Norbert and Imogene are survived by their only child Arlene Dodane Curts.

Submitted by Robert M. Curts

PAUL O. COTTRELL & RUTH (MCKEEMAN) COTTRELL FAMILY

Paul was born in Antwerp, Ohio, on May 30, 1905, the only child of Noah and Myrtle (Lutz) Cottrell.

Abandoned by his father, he was raised by his mother and grandmother, Martha (Ely) Lutz, in the small town of Woodburn, Indiana. He once said "the whole town had their eyes on me and helped me grow up."

After completing grade school, he went to work in a number of occupations but seemed to find selling products his greatest interest. He found that grocery stores were his choice and joined the Great Atlantic and Pacific (A&P) Tea Company as the manager of a small store in Fort Wayne. He realized that he needed to continue his education to succeed further and attended the International Business College in Fort Wayne studying business and accounting courses. Following this, his company sent him to its business office in Toledo, Ohio, for more advanced training in their industry. He was promoted to district supervisor of multiple stores in this area. He ultimately opened the first "supermarket" in the area and later was in charge of seven of these large stores that replaced the small local stores in Indiana and Ohio.

After twenty years with the A&P, he retired and opened his own grocery store at Lake George, Indiana. This was a successful business. He also became a licensed business realtor, and returned to Fort Wayne to establish a firm. He pursued this field for the last twenty years of his life.

He was a 32nd degree Mason, and an avid hunter and fisherman.

He died February 9, 1995 and is buried in the Lindenwood Cemetery.

Ruth Cottrell was born April 18, 1907 in Fort Wayne, Indiana. She was the daughter of Robert Benjamin McKeeman, M.D. and Susie May (Hocker) McKeeman.

She was raised in Fort Wayne and was one of the early graduates of South Side High School. She lived in this city for most of her life. She married Paul Cottrell on February 24, 1927. A quiet and retiring lady, she was a dedicated wife to her husband and a caring mother to her only child, Robert F. Cottrell, M.D. who was born on April 14, 1929. Her life was enriched by her interests in five grandchildren and multiple great-grandchildren.

She died February 17, 1994 and was buried in the Lindenwood Cemetery.

Submitted by Robert F. Cottrell, M.D.

COURTESIS FAMILY CHRIST GEORGE COURTESIS RUTH ALEANE SLONIKER

Christ George Courtesis was born December 22, 1896, in Neohori, Greece. A short time after serving a few years in the Greek Army, Christ applied for a visa to the United States on December 27, 1920. Christ paid $100 dollars in gold for the trip to America. That was equal to fourteen Greek drachmas, and left him with forty United States dollars in his pocket. December 31, 1920, was boarding day for the second-cabin passengers on the S.S. *Megali Hellas*. Its home port was Andros, an island east of Athens. With Master L. Hazapis at the helm the ship departed the harbor of Piraeus, which is the seaport for Athens. It arrived in New York harbor on January 20, 1921. Originally Christ's last name was Kourtesis, with a K, but as he moved through immigration the K

Christ Courtesis and Ruth Sloniker, c. 1927-1928

became a C. It was never corrected and from that point forward he became Courtesis.

Needing more money for his trip to Fort Wayne, Indiana, Christ found work at a hot dog stand on the Coney Island boardwalk. Later, in 1921, he completed his trip to Indiana to join Charles Lambrakis and James Heliotes. They both were long time family friends, and they worked at the Columbia Candy Kitchen at 1008 and 1314 South Calhoun Street. Christ found work in the restaurant and confectionary trade as a dishwasher, waiter, and proprietor.

He patronized the Summit City Cafeteria at 118 East Wayne Street, and there Christ noticed an attractive young woman working the serving line. He would stand behind a large column and peer at Ruth Sloniker. In time a relationship grew. Christ was naturalized on June 29, 1928, and he married Ruth on November 19, 1928.

Ruth was born on March 5, 1911. She came to Fort Wayne in late 1924 with her parents, Joseph and Anna Sloniker, from Lawrence County, Illinois. Christ and Ruth had three children. Christina Jeanie (Husting) was born April 30, 1931; Patricia Ann (Holley) was born March 1, 1934; and George Christ Courtesis was born December 21, 1935.

By 1930, Christ co-owned with John Manitaras the Rainbow Ice Cream Company at 1902 South Calhoun Street. His partner died in 1944. The Rainbow was a full service ice cream shop with wonderful furnishings of the time. There were marble counters, mirror backdrops, wire backed chairs, bent cane chairs, and marble top tables with wire legs. They tried curb service on Calhoun Street, however the customers liked the glassware and silver trays. They drove off with them, thus ending the curb service. Another ill-fated venture was insulated boxes with shoulder straps. They would send boys out to canvas the area with various frozen confectioneries. Most never returned, and the police found the boxes along the riverbanks. They produced twelve delicious ice cream flavors. They had caramel apples, peanut brittle, fountain drinks and other candies, all made on the premises. The Rainbow survived both the Depression and World War II.

Christ sold his interest in the Rainbow and in 1946 started the Dixie Ice Cream Company. A new building was constructed at 3808 South Calhoun Street. It served the same needs as the Rainbow and had a 1940s interior. It was a good learning experience for all the children. Over time each worked in the store with their father.

Christ operated the Dixie until March 1962 when he retired.

Working some pleasure into his busy schedule, Christ was a member of the Holy Trinity Greek Orthodox Church, the Red Man Lodge, Maumee Lodge 725 F&AM, Scottish Rite, and the Mizpah Temple. In his youth he played the Greek bouzouki, which is a pear-shaped instrument resembling a guitar. When he could, he enjoyed traveling with the family. Ruth was always busy being a housewife and mother. She also helped in the store. She played the piano for the family. In later years she did babysitting with Fort Wayne Babysitting Service. She attended Trinity Episcopal Church.

Christ died on April 7, 1964. Ruth died on January 18, 1995. Ruth and Christ, through hard work and long hours, had great accomplishments in a short time and the family is very proud of them.

Submitted by George C. Courtesis

DALLAS CRISMORE FAMILY

In the summer of 1930 (Depression days) the Dallas Crismores moved to Allen County, Nine Miles (it was nine miles to the Allen County Court House), also called Five Points (five roads met at the same point) located on the old route of Indianapolis Road. Nine Mile was then the location of Mt. Zion Lutheran Church, the United Brethren Church, and a set of buildings bought and remodeled by Clyde Newhard, a Nine Mile farmer, for a grocery store that also sold gas. It was a house connected by a breezeway, with the downstairs room devoted to selling ice cream, candy, and snacks. Nine Mile had been without a grocery store for several years, so Clyde asked Dallas Crismore and his wife, Flossie, to manage the grocery store, an ice house, and the food shop in the house. Dallas (born April 23, 1886 near Uniondale, Wells County; died September 8, 1958) had degrees from business schools in Valparaiso and Bluffton. Flossie Wickliffe Crismore (born February 12, 1888 in Zanesville, Wells County; died March 3, 1972) was a good cook who made salads and sandwiches for the food shop that she managed. Dallas had been employed at the Jim Waid general store in Uniondale but had been laid off by Jim due to the impact of the Depression. So, Dallas needed a job, and Clyde needed managers.

Of course, their adopted nine year old son, Edward Noel, went along. Ed had been living in the old Allen County Children's Home (with two brothers and a sister) on Bluffton Road by the St. Mary's River. When adopted, Ed was 17 months old. He was born on July 14, 1921, in Fort Wayne. His mother was Helen Giant from Fort Wayne (born December 23, 1897, died September 4, 1921) who had tuberculosis and died from it at Irene Byron Sanitarium. His father, Williard Christlieb was born in Avilla, DeKalb County (born June 23, 1880), married Helen in 1916, worked in Fort Wayne, moved to Detroit and died in 1952. So, Earl Howard Christlieb became Edward Noel Crismore in 1922. Although he lived in Pleasant Township, Ed went to grade four in Lafayette township at Lafayette School because there was bus service there from his home. But the township transfer costs were too much for his parents, so he attended the Putt School in Nine Mile for fifth grade, getting a ride from the Rice neighbors. Ed loved the one room grade 1-8 school experience at Putt.

Dallas also had a twice a week huckster route near Nine Mile, traveling about five or six miles in each direction in his customized Ford Model A truck. The truck had groceries on each side of the truck bed with fold down doors and room between the grocery shelves for chicken coops with live chickens or egg crates, since his customers often bartered for groceries. Ed learned to drive the huckster truck when he was nine years old. Dallas taught him. Ed loved driving the truck when school was not in session. Ed also drove the truck, his dad sitting next to him, to Fort Wayne for grocery store supplies, to candy wholesalers Clark Fruit, Bursley, L. C. Mercantile Companies, and to sell the chickens and eggs after going to City Scales for weighing them. Some of the money received was used for fun that day: a beer for each of them at a tavern near Transfer Corners, a noon meal at a second floor cafeteria nearby, and a movie at the Emboyd, Rialto or Family Theater. In those days, a nine-year old could drive a truck and drink a beer!

Dallas also started, managed, and often fed, a hungry Nine Mile baseball team, the Rangers, with Ed as the mascot. This team played against teams from Fort Wayne, Waynedale, and area town teams. Nine Mile area families appreciated the grocery store, gas pumps, ice, churches, and baseball team, the Newhards, Barsock, Gent, Fogwell, Welbaum, Rice, Smith, Coverdale, Minnich, Branstrator and other families. The Crismores moved back to Uniondale in spring 1932 so that Dallas could open his own grocery store. Good bye Allen County!

Submitted by Avon Crismore

CROTHERS

Harry Dalton Crothers (1916-1983) and Edna Opal Sutton Crothers (1916-1993), natives of York Township, Noble County, came to Fort Wayne from Huntington County with their daughters, Carol and June in the early 1940s. They made their home on Stophlet Street. Their children Arthur, William, Beverly, and John were born in Fort Wayne. Harry repaired appliances for Schulers and later operated Crothers Appliance Service.

Carol Joan Crothers (born 1939) married James Collett in 1957. Their children are Sandra Caldwell of Fort Wayne, Catherine Newcomer, of rural Butler, Indiana, and James Collett of Toledo. Carol later married Barry Brunson and Eugene Fisher. She operates Fisher Tax Service in Fort Wayne.

June, John, Carol, & Arthur Crothers Billy & Beverly Crothers

June Elaine Crothers (born 1940), wife of Roy Vogel, resides in Yardley, Pennsylvania. She is chief financial officer and controller of the Princeton (New Jersey) Packet newspaper group. Their children are Clayton Vogel and Venetia Johnson. June had son Victor Murray from an earlier marriage. They all reside out-of-state.

Arthur Edward Crothers (born 1943) married Sharon Harrington in 1963. Their children are Arthur Edward Crothers, II, of rural Spencerville, and Sharee Christopher of Fort Wayne. Their father later married Vada Lucille Morrison. He died in 1996 in Auburn, Indiana.

William H. Crothers (born 1944), known as Billy, was stricken with a severe case of polio at the age of 8. His paralysis kept him confined to an iron lung much of the time. His iron lung was provided by the March of Dimes. He enjoyed visits from television stars including Gene Autry, Roy Rogers, Dale Evans, and Barnabus Collins. Even more important to Billy were visits from his buddies at the Fort Wayne Fire Department. Firefighters at the Washington Street station visited often, serviced his iron lung, and came with generators to operate the iron lung whenever a power outage occurred. Billy's grade school teacher, Mrs. Dennis Parquet, came to the house to tutor him, and the Visiting Nurse Service provided him medical care. He was taught at home all through high school and graduated from Central High School with honors. When the family overlooked graduation announcements, the Fire Department raised a ladder in front of their Stophlet Street home and used a bullhorn to announce it to the entire neighborhood. In 1968, at age 24, the firefighters took Billy to St. Joseph Hospital, and operated the hand pump on the iron lung all the way to the operating room. Not long after, Chief Talarico and the firefighters donned their dress uniforms and carried Billy once again, this time free of his iron lung, to his grave at Lindenwood Cemetery.

Beverly Kay Crothers (born 1949) married Dennis Barrone in 1970. The Barrone family information can be found elsewhere in this book.

John Richard Crothers (born 1952) married Linda Grothouse in 1978. John is employed by BAE Systems of Fort Wayne. Their daughter, Dawn (born 1981) is a graduate of Indiana University and is doing masters work in international studies at UCLA.

Submitted by Beverly Barrone

DESCENDANTS OF SAMUEL CUTSHALL

Samuel Cutshall, born in 1789 in Maryland, came to Allen County, Indiana, in1837 with a Federal Land Grant for one hundred eighty acres north of Fort Wayne. He was accompanied by his wife, Mary Darner, and nine of their children; the first four were born in Maryland, the rest in Ohio except the tenth, Thomas, who was born in Indiana. They settled in Wallen, Indiana, and are buried there.

Their children were Elizabeth, who married David Keever in Maryland. They had a farm in Fort Wayne area and are buried in Parker Cemetery, Fort Wayne. Eli, who married Dorcas Price and went to Iowa. Catherine Ann, who married John Arnold in 1837. Samuel, who married Rachael Klinger; he had his own farm and

Cutshall family, beginning top row, left: Edith, Eva, Frank, Amelia, W. Sherman, Theodore, Angeline, William Harden, Elizabeth. September 1915

was an elder at Trinity English Lutheran Church 1846-1849. Marie, who married Lewellen Price. George Whitney, who married Nancy Toltson and moved out west. Martha Ann, who married William Golden in 1853. Joseph, who married Elizabeth Shultz. William Harden, who married Angeline Meyers. And Thomas, who married Marietta Klinger.

William Harden Cutshall was born in Dayton, Ohio, his wife in Germany. He and Angeline lived on the farm until they moved to Fort Wayne, had a family of ten; eight survived to adulthood. Mary and Frederick died young and are buried in the Wallen Cemetery. Eva married Harvey Baughman. She was widowed early and was a school teacher at Hanna, Clay and Hoagland schools in Fort Wayne. Elizabeth married twice: Charles Collins and then Charles Todd. Amelia married John Druhot; they had two daughters and one son. William Sherman married Harriet Myers and was Fort Wayne's war mayor from 1917 to 1920. Theodore Myer married Fredricka Honeck October 30, 1895; he was a streetcar motorman for 43 years in Fort Wayne. Edith married Montgomery Beaver who owned the Fort Wayne Lumber Company. Frank Henry married Blanche Coombs, then Daisy Dean; Frank was a banker and businessman in Fort Wayne.

Theodore and Fredricka Cutshall had four boys. Ralph died young. Chester Sherman was a Purdue University professor; he married Hattie Flaig November 8, 1920; they lived in West Lafayette with two children, Theodore Wayne and Nancy Carolyn. Norman was an accountant who married Bessie Ronk and lived in Detroit. They had three children, an infant, Lloyd and Norman, Jr. Stanley married Ethel Horrock; he was in business and lived in Cleveland first, then Detroit, and finally Kalamazoo, Michigan. They had two children, Louise and Robert.

Submitted by Mrs. Theodore W. Cutshall

DAGER & LESH FAMILIES

Two early settler families of Jefferson Township, Allen County, Indiana, were joined together in 1903 with the marriage of Peter Dager III and Minnie Alice Lesh.

The Dager family came from Bavaria (Germany) and the original family surname was believed to be Deger or Degen. Johan Peter Dager, Sr., his wife Catharina, and children Johan Peter Jr., Johan George, and Anna Barbara came to America in 1836. A fourth child, Margaret, was born shortly after their arrival. The family spent a few years in Richland County, Ohio. Catharina died not long after Margaret's birth, and Peter, Sr. remarried in 1842 to Magdalena Bassinger. Three more children arrived while the family was in Ohio: Frederick, Regina, and Elizabeth. The Dager family made their way to Indiana, settling in Jefferson Township east of Besancon, where Peter, Sr. purchased a 40-acre farm from Thomas DeKay in April of 1850. In addition to farming, Peter, Sr. was also a carpenter. Peter and Magdalena had one more child, John, who was born in 1850.

Peter Dager, Sr., died tragically in March of 1875. He was headed home from Fort Wayne with a wagonload of supplies and was traveling on the towpath of the Erie Canal, east of New Haven. Peter's wagon tipped over and fell on top of him, trapping him in the mud at the water's edge, where he suffocated. His death was a front-page news item in the *Fort Wayne Daily News.*

Peter, Jr. was married to Anna Maria Petzold and had two daughters, Anna Margarit and Emily. Following Anna Maria's death in 1870, Peter married Mary Weaver Oberley, a young widow with four children: Frank, Rosa, Alex, and Louisa. Mary's first husband, Christian, was killed while serving with the army in Wyoming after the Civil War. Peter, Jr. and Mary went on to add six children to their combined family: John, George, Elizabeth, Peter III, Joseph, and Mary Mollie.

Anna Barbara Dager was briefly married to a gentleman named Moore and had a son, David Henry Moore. She then married Jacob Smail of Madison Township.

Frederick Dager married Carlista Daniels and had a family of eight: Ella Elizabeth, Mary Ellen, Frederick Jr., Henry, Charles, Lafayette, William, and a child who died in infancy. They spent many years in Van Wert County, Ohio, but some of the children came back to Indiana and settled in Jackson and Monroe townships, near Monroeville.

Regina "Roxie" Dager married August Merrillat and had five children: John, Louis, George, Ellen Elizabeth, and Emily. The Merrillat family farm was located east of Zulu, Indiana.

Elizabeth Dager married August Fluttrow and had seven children; John, Louis, William, Sarah, Elizabeth, Clarence, and Mary Ellen. After Elizabeth's death about 1891, August remarried to Jennie Leininger. He was killed in the March 1920 tornados, one of which destroyed the settlement of Townley, Indiana, in Jackson Township.

The other children of Peter Dager, Sr. - George, Margaret, and John - appear to have died in childhood or in their teen years.

Isaac Newton Lesh and his wife, Sarah (Revert), came to Jefferson Township from Stark County, Ohio, in 1864, following Sarah's younger brothers who came to Indiana about 1860. Their children were Lucinda, Emanuel, Alice, Levi (died in early childhood), and Emmett. The Lesh family roots were in Germany but they had been in America well before the Revolutionary War; Isaac's grandfather, Heinrich Loesch, resided in Montgomery County, Pennsylvania in the 1760s. Isaac purchased two tracts of land west of Zulu, Indiana, from the Platt family. In addition to farming, Isaac was an accomplished carpenter and cabinetmaker, having learned woodworking skills in his father's sawmill in Stark County. When Isaac died in 1915, his obituary made note of his reputation for producing sturdy, well-built furniture.

Lucinda Lesh was married to David Bowers of Jefferson Township, following the death of his first wife. They had seven children: Alfreda, William, Henry ("Harry"), John, Arthur, Glenola, and Frances. Harry Bowers was the publisher and editor of the *New Haven Herald* newspaper in the early part of the 1900s, and William served two terms as an Indiana state senator in the 1920s.

Emanuel Lesh married Eve Ann Neal, and his sister, Alice, married Eve Ann's brother, Caleb Neal. In addition to farming and carpentry work, Emanuel ran a general store and also served as postmaster in Zulu in the 1880s. Emanuel and Eve Ann had five children: Albert, Minnie Alice, Clarence, Grover, and William. Alice and Caleb had a daughter, Pearl; two other children, Lloyd and Ruth, died in early childhood.

Emmett Lesh was married first to Everetta Brittingham and had a son, Leonard, and then married Florence Squires and had a daughter, Esther.

Peter Dager III and Minnie Alice Lesh had a family of nine children, some of whom are still living as of 2005. Many descendants of the Dager and Lesh families still live in eastern Allen County today.

Submitted by Diane Dager

WILLIAM THOMPSON DAILEY 1802 - 1877

William Thompson Dailey was born in 1802 in Bedford County, Pennsylvania, the last of five children born to Edward Dailey and Eleanor Davidson. Many, if not all, of his ancestors were Ulster-Scots. His maternal grandfather, Samuel Davidson, was a well-to-do community leader in Bedford and the surrounding area. William was surely named after one of his maternal great-grandfathers, William Thompson, who served as an officer during the Revolutionary War. The spelling of the family name in public records occurs as both "Daily" and "Dailey."

William learned farming while growing up on his family's farm in Bedford County in south-central Pennsylvania. He may also have apprenticed to be a tanner since his grandfather owned a local tannery. By the 1820 census, Eleanor Dailey had moved her family to Fairfield County in east-central Ohio. On October 7, 1824 at age 21, William married Sarah McCormick in Perry County, Ohio, a county adjacent to Fairfield County. Sarah was the daughter of Hugh McCormick and Martha Martin. She was also a second cousin of Cyrus McCormick who developed the modern combine.

Around 1828, William moved his wife west to Seneca County, Ohio, where he received a land grant for 80 acres in Clinton Township, south of the town of Tiffin. He cleared the land and began farming. An early Seneca County history also indicates that "the first tannery [in Tiffin] was located where the gas plant stands and was owned by Wm. Dailey." In 1838, William served in the First Company of the Ohio militia.

William and Sarah's ten children were all born in Seneca County between 1828 and 1845. Two died young in 1844.

In August 1848, William joined several other families from Seneca County and relocated his family to 160 acres in Cedar Creek Township in Allen County, Indiana. Moving to Indiana must have been a daunting task. When he arrived, the land was "wholly wooded" and needed to be cleared before any farming could begin. Within his new community, William was a highly respected citizen known for his "sterling integrity and unflinching honesty." In addition to farming, he served as a township trustee. William died on a Sunday, January 13, 1877, at age 74. His wife Sarah had preceded him on September 3, 1875. The couple is buried in the Old Leo Cemetery in Leo, Indiana.

The eight children who grew to adulthood were Ellen (Deaver), Martha (McCormick), Marie (Manning), Samuel, John, William M., Edward, and Clarissa (Deaver). Samuel Dailey, the oldest son, remained on the family farm and took care of his parents in their old age. The three remaining sons, John, William M., and Edward, all struck out for Colorado around 1859 seeking gold. John, who had apprenticed as a printer in Fort Wayne, joined the gold rush, but made his fortune as cofounder of the *Rocky Mountain News*.

Submitted by Dale Dailey

DARBY FAMILY

The first of the Darby family to come to Allen County, Indiana, was Christian Darby, his wife, Dina Jane Golden Darby, and their six children. They were here by the 1850 census. Christian Darby was born in Pennsylvania on July 4, 1783. Dina Jane Golden, his wife, was born October 28, 1783, in Pennsylvania. Christian died December 29, 1852, and is buried in the Hatfield Cemetery next to his wife who died December 1, 1852.

Their children were Joseph Darby, born in Pennsylvania on August 28, 1815. He died September 6, 1852, and is buried in the Hatfield Cemetery. Joseph never married.

William Darby, born January 14, 1817, in Pennsylvania, was married September 12, 1847, in Allen County, Indiana, to Ann Jones, who was born March 10, 1828, in Welshpool, Montgomeryshire, North Wales, to John and Mary Humphreys Jones. William Darby died February 28, 1858, and is buried in the Hatfield Cemetery with his wife, Ann, who died February 13, 1904.

Catherine Darby, born 1819 in Pennsylvania, was married November 17, 1843, in Westmoreland County, Pennsylvania, to James Laughlin who was born in 1820 in Pennsylvania.

John Doe Darby, christened October 13, 1822, in Mt. Pleasant Township, Westmoreland County, Pennsylvania, was married December 20, 1847, in Westmoreland County, Pennsylvania, to Elizabeth Stairs, who was born about 1821 in Pennsylvania.

Henry Darby, born about 1825 in Pennsylvania, was married October 2, 1851, in Allen County, Indiana, to Lydia M. Baird/Beard born about 1832 in New York.

Rebecca Darby, born about 1834 in Ohio, married Jacob Overly.

The children of William (Christian Darby's second child) and Ann Jones Darby were George H. Darby, born January 6, 1848, in Allen County, Indiana. He ran the family farm for his mother in Lake Township, Allen County, Indiana. George never married. He died December 27, 1927, and is buried in the Hatfield Cemetery, although the stone could not be found.

Mary Ann Darby, born August 5, 1850, in Allen County, Indiana, was married August 13, 1874, in Roanoke, Allen County, Indiana, to John Edward Payson Irwin, who was born August 14, 1851, in Ohio. John died September 25, 1917, in Allen County, Indiana. Mary Ann died September 26, 1928. They had five children: Charles, Cora, Clara, William, and Dora.

Ann Jones Darby and Children. Standing: Jane Darby Korten, Sarah E. Darby Cole, Christina C. Darby Prill. Seated: George H. Darby, (Mother) Ann Jones Darby, Mary Ann Darby Irwin

Sarah Elizabeth Darby, born March 22, 1852, in Allen County, Indiana, was married December 25, 1869, in Allen County, to James K. R. Coles who was born March 30, 1845, in Fort Wayne. James died July 11, 1915, in Warrenton, Oregon. Sarah (Sadie) died November 11, 1934, in Astoria, Oregon. They are buried at the Masonic Cemetery, McMinnville, Oregon. They had five children: Elizabeth, Lottie, Clara Belle, Annie, and Martin Spencer Coles. James and Sarah lived in Allen County, Indiana, and Petoskey, Michigan, before moving to Oregon.

William Darby, Jr., was born July 13, 1854, in Allen County. He married Delia Ann Larrimore on June 28, 1876, in Allen County (Book 12 page 81). Adehelia was born April 1855 or 1859 in Indiana and died May 4, 1883, in Greenville, Michigan. She is buried in the Eel River Cemetery, Allen County. They had two children: Clarence Darby and Ada May Darby. Ada was a ward of her uncle, George Darby. She disappeared in 1906 at the age of 26. William Darby then was married on December 5, 1899, in Allen County, (Book 23 page 551) to Catherine Wright, born March 22, 1874, in Ohio. They had six children: Charley, Dorothy who married Hyde, Clyde, Jenny who married Closson, Elnora Loretta who married Burgess, and Marion Donnabell who married Brigner. Catherine Wright Darby died May 25, 1922, in Greenville, Michigan, and William died December 26, 1934. Both are buried at Baldwin Lake, Greenville, Michigan.

Jane Darby was born February 1856 in Allen County. She was married for a short time to a man by the name of Corten or Kortin. The marriage was annulled. Jane lived in Greenville, Michigan, with her brother, William, after his wife died. Jane died February 12, 1934, in Greenville.

Christina Catherine Darby was born January 12 or 18, 1858, in Lake Township, Allen County. She was born a little over a month before her father died. On March 18, 1880, in Allen County, Christina (Teeny) gave birth to Jesse Wilbert Darby. He was not mentioned in the 1880 census or in the 1900 census. In the 1900 census, when Teeny was asked how many children she has had, she said 'only one' and that would have been her daughter by her then husband. Jesse's father is unknown. Christina was married December 3, 1885, in Allen County (Book 16 page 447) to Benjamin Franklin Prill. He was previously married to Claricia Ann Davis on May 1, 1873, in Allen County (Book 9 page 218). Ben and Claricia had divorced. Christina and Benjamin Prill had Elsie Harriet Prill on February 10, 1890, in Allen County. Elsie married George Washington Smith, who was born July 25, 1887, in Harlan, Allen County, Indiana, on September 10, 1908. Elsie died October 29, 1973 in Warrenton, Oregon. George died September 27, 1962, in Astoria, Oregon. They had two children. Leslie George Smith was born November 20, 1910, in Fort Wayne, and died February 14, 1990, in Astoria, Oregon. Leslie never married. Camilla Kathryn Smith was born July 26, 1916, in Fort Wayne, Indiana. She married Arnold Ole Lyngsted and then Arthur Stuart. Camilla died August 12, 2000, in Astoria, Oregon. She and Arnold had two sons. Benjamin Franklin Prill died February 23, 1917, in Fort Wayne, Indiana, and is buried in the Eel River Cemetery. Christina C. Darby Prill died August 24, 1935, in Warrenton, Oregon, and is buried in Warrenton Ocean View Cemetery.

Jesse Wilbert Darby, was the son of Christina C. Darby and an unknown father. Jesse was interested in the railroad from the time he was very young. He became a telegrapher, which took him to Davis Station, Starke County, Indiana, in 1900. There he met and married Edna Pearl Davis on May 22, 1901. She was born October 26, 1883, in Starke County, Indiana. The railroad took them to LaPorte County, Indiana, and St. Joseph County, Indiana, where Jesse retired from the railroad station at Mishawaka, Indiana, where he had been from 1927 to 1948. J. W. Darby died March 26, 1959, in Mishawaka, St. Joseph County, Indiana. Edna Pearl Davis Darby died July 8, 1971, at age 88. She was the daughter of James Monroe and Sarah Elizabeth Kelley Davis. Jesse and Pearl are buried in the Chapel Hill Cemetery in St Joseph County, Indiana.

The children of Jesse and E. Pearl Davis Darby are Hazel Fern Darby who was born March 31, 1903, in Hannah, Starke County, Indiana. She married Ed Johnson and they divorced. Then she married Russell Hill and they also divorced. There were no children of those marriages. Fern died December 1, 1986, in Mishawaka, Indiana, and is buried at the Chapel Hill Cemetery.

Clyde Leon Darby, born March 17, 1905, in Hamlet, Starke County, Indiana, was married on September 11, 1937, in St. Joseph County, Indiana, to Rose Alice Miller, who was born March

11, 1918, in Perry County, Indiana. Rose Alice (Zal) died July 24, 1975, in Evansville, Indiana. On August 8, 1981, Clyde married Viola Magnuson Hurst in Michigan City, Indiana. Clyde died in Michigan City, Indiana, on April 14, 1986. He had no children. Clyde was an engineer with the New York Central Railroad until he retired.

Glenn LaVern Darby, born August 15, 1908, in Knox, Starke County, Indiana, was married to Lucyle Lung. They divorced. On February 10, 1933, in St. Joseph County, Indiana, he married Lorraine Marie Wood, born February 21, 1913, in Watsonville, Santa Cruz County, California. They divorced in about 1946 and Glenn remarried Lucyle, who had married and divorced also. She was then Lucyle West. Glenn and Lucyle again divorced and Glenn and Lorraine remarried in 1948 and stayed married the rest of their lives. Glenn and Lucyle had no children. Glenn died April 16, 1990, in Mishawaka, St. Joseph County, Indiana. Lorraine died January 1, 1992, in Mishawaka, Indiana. Both were cremated and buried in the Adamsville Cemetery, Adamsville, Michigan. They had three children: Jack La Vern, Donald Robert, and Peggy Arlene Darby.

Alma Mae Darby, born November 9, 1910, in Rolling Prairie, LaPorte County, Indiana, was married December 24, 1926, to Robert C. Bickel. They divorced October 1935. One child died young and is buried in the Fairview Cemetery, Mishawaka, Indiana. Alma then married William Rosco Rittenhouse on January 4, 1936. William was born February 3, 1905, in Columbia City, Indiana. He died June 10, 1989, in Mishawaka, Indiana. They had one son, William Eugene Rittenhouse, born July 8, 1940, and died November 17, 1954, in Mishawaka, Indiana. William Rosco and William (Genie) Eugene are buried in the Fairview Cemetery, Mishawaka, near William Rosco's parents. Alma is living at this writing in 2005.

Rose Donnabelle Darby, born November 4, 1916, in Chesterton, Indiana, was married to Frank Zavor, born November 8, 1916, in Mishawaka, Indiana. They had three children: Franklin Kaye, Donna Lee, and Zelda Mae. Frankie died October 25, 1992. They were divorced. Donnabelle then married Angelo Messana, who was born May 30, 1919, in Mishawaka, Indiana. They married on February 19, 1955, in Mishawaka, Indiana. Angie had three children by a previous marriage and he and Donnabelle had three together: Rose Ann, Angelo Ross, and Diane Annette Messana, all born in South Bend, Indiana. Ross died October 13, 1986, in a motorcycle accident and Angelo died March 15, 1995, at a VA Hospital in Marion, Indiana. Donnabelle is living at this writing in 2005.

Submitted by Peggy A. Darby Martin

Taken at the Catholic Community Center before a style show performance sponsored by Local No. 116 United Garment Workers are chorus director Mrs. Ruth Thompson; Mrs. Lelah Evens at the piano. President, Mrs. Virgie Alvords; Treasurer, Mrs. Nettie Bouillion: Publicity chairman, Mrs. Jennie Allen; and Business manager, Mrs. Cora Ruth David (front row far right).

CORA RUTH HILDRED DAVID

Cora Ruth Hildred was born on March 14, 1890, in Montreal, Canada. She was one of six children born to Charles Robert Hildred (born August 1, 1864) of Dewsbury, England. After her birth and the death of her mother, Annie Speight of England, Charles Robert remarried and moved to the states through Maine, settling in the Boston, Massachusetts area. After the death of Cora Ruth's husband, she moved her children to Geneva, Indiana, where her sixth child was born. In 1925, looking for work to raise her six children, she came to Fort Wayne. Employed by Pollak Brothers as a seamstress, Cora Ruth Hildred David sang in the Waynetette Chorus.

July 4, 1957. Left to right: Lillian Fousnought, Herbert Pollard, Isabella Dornsief, Jess Reed, Emiley Wiedman, Florence Dey.

Baby Dolls, third grade class at Adams School, New Haven Avenue, 1944. Third from left is Myrtie "Ruth" Fousnought Wiegmann, granddaughter of Cora Ruth and daughter of Lillian Fousnought. Fourth from left is Phyllis Koble.

The children of Cora Ruth Hildred David all married and raised their families in Fort Wayne. Only two survive. Lillian (Fousnought) had one daughter; Herbert Pollard had two children; Isabella (Dornsief) had five children; Jess Reed, is living in Phoenix, Arizona, and had one son; Emiley (Wiedman) had five children; Florence (Dey), living in Fort Wayne, had six children.

Submitted by Ruth Wiegmann

ELLSWORTH DAVIS FAMILY

Ellsworth Davis, the son of Josiah Davis and Elizabeth Fry, was born February 11, 1878, in Wells County, Indiana. Ellsworth's grandfather Elias Davis migrated to Wells County in 1840 from the Hocking/Athens County Ohio area. Ellsworth married Olive Leona Johnson on January 13, 1898, in Wells County. Olive was the daughter of David Johnson and Mary Belle Russell.

Around 1908 Ellsworth moved his family from Wells County to Allen County and settled in Fort Wayne. From 1908 to at least 1917 Ellsworth was a fireman for the Pennsylvania Railroad Company. From 1918 until his death in 1932, Ellsworth worked for the General Electric Company.

Ellsworth and Olive had seven children, Harold Russell born in 1900, Reta Myrl born in 1901, Ruth Mildred born in 1903, Homer Johnson born in 1905, Hugh Kenneth born in 1908, Ruby Mae born in 1910 and Robert E. born in 1913. In 1912 Hugh Kenneth was playing with some other boys outside their home on Pontiac Street, and he was run over by a streetcar and died. This was a huge trauma for the family. In 1913 the Davis' filed for divorce. On October 10, 1917, Ellsworth remarried. He married Louise Sefton, daughter of Andrew Barninger and Mary Pfleegor; this was a second marriage for both of them.

Ellsworth and Olive Davis

Child 1: Harold Russell Davis married first Audrey Icel Yelton, and second Erma Olmspacher. Harold and Audrey had four children, Wendell Eugene, Mary Maxine, Mayme Leona and Jack Wayne. Harold and Erma are buried in Sturgis, Michigan. Audrey is buried in Covington Memorial Gardens, Fort Wayne.

Child 2: Reta Myrl Davis married first Dale Burnett, second Earl Dyer, and third Harry Faylor. Reta and Dale had one child, Kathleen Mae "Kate". Reta and Earl had one child, Shirley Louise. Reta is buried in Covington Memorial Gardens, Fort Wayne. Dale is buried in Lindenwood Cemetery, Fort Wayne.

Child 3: Ruth Mildred Davis married first Aaron Houtz, and second Mark Heaston. Ruth and Aaron had one child, Dorothy Katherine. Ruth and Aaron are buried in Greenlawn Cemetery, Fort Wayne.

Child 4: Homer Johnson Davis was married once then married Itha Ellen Harrington, and third Dorothy Lee King. Homer's first wife was the daughter of an Oklahoma oilman. On their honeymoon they went ice-skating; they fell through the ice and caught pneumonia. She died and he did not. Homer and Dorothy had seven children; Dolly Lee, Everett Franklin, Lee Allen (died at 3 days of age), Patsy Ann "Pat", Beverly Jean, Debbie Kay and Kathleen Mae "Kathy". Homer and Dorothy are buried in Fairview Cemetery, Bluffton. Itha is buried in Lindenwood Cemetery, Fort Wayne. Homer retired from General Electric in 1967.

H. J. Davis Family

Child 6: Ruby Mae Davis married first Mode Cranor, second Clifton Howell, and third Hubert Woodmansee. Ruby and Mode had two children, Keith and Robert. Ruby and Mode are buried in Converse Cemetery, Converse.

Child 7: Robert E. Davis married at least three times, first Wanda Ulmer, second Elsie Schoeff, and third Evelyn. Robert and Wanda had one child, Sharon Marlene. Robert and Elsie had one child, Judy Ann. Robert was cremated and buried at sea. Elsie is buried in Huntington and Wanda is buried at I.O.O.F. Cemetery, Montpelier.

Submitted by Kathy Davis

DAWKINS FAMILY

The Dawkins family came from County Kent, England in 1840, arriving on the ship Toronto on October 3 and landing in New Jersey. They settled in Allen County the following year. The parents were William Dawkins and Mary Ann Young, who were born and married in East Kent, England in 1819. All but one of their children was born in England before they made the great journey to America to find new opportunities for their family. The parents and their children came not long after the Fort Wayne area was settled, and helped to carve a civilized and prosperous county out of the wilderness. The family made an indelible impression upon the area and the minds of their fellow citizens. Unfortunately, not long after their resettlement in Allen County, the father died. Mary soon after, married Eben Burgess.

William and Mary Dawkins had five boys: William, James, Henry, John and Benjamin. William, James and Henry served honorably in the Civil War. All of the sons and many of their descendants were also members of the International Order of the Odd Fellows (IOOF). William was married to Sarah Ann Clear. James was married to Harriet Rogers, a daughter of early Allen County settler, Jabez Rogers. Henry was married to Kittie Moss and after her death, to Sarah Gottshalk. John was married to Wilmina Martin, Amanda Johnson and Rachel Miller. Benjamin died young. William and Mary had six daughters: Sarah, Jane, Ellen, Emily, Mary and Susannah. Sarah was the wife of John Hough, Jr., a lawyer and distinguished citizen of Fort Wayne. Jane was the wife of Theodore Conklin, and died much too young. Ellen never married, but was a member of the Jesse Lynch Williams household for many years. Emily never married and died early as well. Mary stayed in England and was the wife of Thomas Ralph. Susannah, born in Indiana, was married to Ira Bryant. There may have also been some infants that died in England. Although their descendants are not as numerous as some families, there are many of us who pay homage to the Dawkins family for their courage, determination and hard work which brought them from their home in England to America, their new home.

Submitted by Matthew L Mapes

JIM & NAN DELANEY FAMILY

The Jim and Nan Delaney family (from 1964) is made up from the families of Delaney, Thomas, Donahue, and McLaughlin. This present generation adds the names Fowler, Randall, Richard, Hudson, Anderson, Christie, and Pflueger to the mix. The Delaney surname arrived in Fort Wayne in the early 1930s when Jim's father, Ed Delaney (1906 -'97) came to work for his uncle, Bob Deel, who married Ed's aunt and twin of his father, Columbkill Patrick (CP) Delaney. CP and his sister Margaret Deel were one of three sets of twins and two single births born to Andrew and Ellen Delaney of Delphi, Indiana. Andrew's father, Colum Delaney, was the first Delaney to come to Indiana from Ireland in 1850. He married Margaret Ricketts, also from Ireland. CP's wife was Susan (Martin) and she and CP had three children: Martin, Edward (Ed), and Mary.

Ed Delaney came to Fort Wayne from Logansport, Indiana, in 1930 to work for contractor, Deel/Dailey, installing electric underground power cables from the newly expanded City Light Power Plant in Lawton Park to the new Filtration plant located where the St. Mary's and St. Joseph's rivers combine to form the Maumee. Two 13,800 volt, paper insulated, lead covered cables were installed underground in ducts and manholes from the power plant to Fourth Street, across the Spy Run Creek, and down Spy Run Avenue to the filtration plant's Three Rivers Substation. These cables supplied reliable pumping and treatment power until the mid 1990s.

In 1936 Ed was hired by City Light and Power (CL&P) when uncle, Bob Deel, became the Superintendent of Light Construction. With a steady job and good pay, Ed proposed to Alice Thomas (1908 - '89), and they married on Thanksgiving day, 1938. Alice was the youngest of four children born to Richard Melvin and Minnie Thomas from Grass Creek, Indiana where "Mel" owned the local "Thomas Hardware" and was the area's John Deere dealer. Grass Creek was very small but had a grain elevator, railroad station, post office and local grade and high school. Alice taught at the elementary school and had many nieces and nephews in her classes.

Alice was raised Evangelical United Brethren and Ed was Irish Catholic - an interesting match. Alice moved to Fort Wayne in 1939, after finishing the school year in Grass Creek. Ed and Alice rented first, but soon bought a home at 1515 Crescent Avenue one-half block north of the Crescent Avenue EUB church. Alice continued her teaching at Sunday School and later at one of the first pre-schools that was started at the church at Crescent and Tennessee. Ed and Alice had three sons: Tomas Edward, James Andrew, and Michael Eugene who attended St. Jude grade school and Central Catholic High School and went to college at St. Joseph's College in Rensselaer, Indiana.

Jim and Nan Delaney Family, December 2004

Ed began work at CL&P as a lineman but soon moved to underground at a time when many CL&P facilities were being put below ground. The new power plant expansion (higher pressure turbines; 7500kW, #1 and 15000kW, #2 and three modern 1933 boilers) continued with underground installation of main feeder circuits from the power plant to substations. Cables were installed to Lafayette Substation (north of Reservoir Park) in addition to the Three Rivers Substation cables and were some of the first 13,800 volt cables installed in the area.

In 1938 CL&P started a major underground effort to eliminate the many overhead lines serving the city's main retail downtown shopping district. Three 4000 volt primary circuits of paper-insulated, lead-covered, cables were installed from Three Rivers Substation, under the St. Mary's River, to the downtown to supply power to a large secondary network grid. This network had 20 underground submersible transformer vaults connected to one secondary grid of heavy copper cables through special "protector" switches and provided the most reliable service available. This network operated until 1991 when the last transformation was upgraded by I&M.

Ed's son Jim married Nan Donahue on April 1, 1964 following their graduations from St. Joseph's College and St. Joseph's School of Nursing. Nan also attended St. Jude and Central Catholic High School. Her father, Patrick Donahue, was an attorney, worked for I&M, and was a city Councilman-at-Large. Nan's mother Geraldine, was a McLaughlin and the youngest of ten children (seven girls and three boys). Both Pat and Jerry grew up in Fort Wayne.

Patrick was youngest of five children born to Patrick and Estella Donahue. His father was a railroad engineer, retired in 1933 from the Nickle Plate Railroad at 70 years of age. Pat went to Notre Dame ('27), played freshman football under Knute Rockne at the time of the four horsemen, and then to Georgetown Law school ('29). Pat served with the IRS in the Alcohol unit as an "revenuer" during prohibition. He received a Navy commission in 1943 serving in WWII in intelligence. He met Henry Ford at the Ford Museum while researching photo collections for the planned invasion of Japan. He was in Iwo Jima following the island invasion. Pat helped start the Naval Reserve in Fort Wayne. In the 60s Pat was a Councilman-at-Large while working at I&M where he retired in 1970 from the right-of-way department securing transmission line R/W.

Jim and Nan's marriage brought together two interesting Irish families, the fathers working for the two electric utilities. Jim called it a mixed marriage. When dating, Jim and Nan used to shock their friends telling them they wanted ten children. Before all the counting was done in 1986, they did have their ten children. In order with spouses they are: Kathleen (and Dean Fowler), Patrick (and Liz Randall), Susan, Jennifer (and Greg Richard), Christine (and Danny Hudson), Daniel (and Amy Anderson), John (and Sarah Christie), Colleen (and Adam Pflueger), Matthew and Shannon (the only cesarean).

Jim's first job, from 1963 to 1967, was at Central Catholic High School where he taught math, physical science and drafting, and coached wrestling, football and track. He then went to work for CL&P and then I&M for a total of 36 years. Nan was an RN at St. Joseph's Hospital for the first few years, and, in later years, as the children grew up, went back to work as an RN to help with college tuition while helping with school nurse duties at the grade and high schools.

Jim and Nan first lived in a two-bedroom home on West Wayne until buying a larger home on Parnell in 1970. There they continued to raise the growing family, sending them to their own St. Jude grade school, and enjoying the newly developed North Side Park. Fort Wayne is still home to the Delaney's and their children - all ten children still live and work in Fort Wayne and live within a five mile radius of home. The family gets together weekly with brunch every Sunday after mass. The grandchild count now stands at 21 with two on the way in 2005: Nathan, Nicholas and Jenna Fowler; Corey, Carter, Riley and Molley Delaney; Kelsey, MacKenzie, Hayley and Delaney Richard; Andrew, James, and David Hudson; Emmett, Aileen and (?) Delaney; Shane and Eric Delaney; and Emma, Lucille, Ethan and (?) Pflueger.

Submitted by James A. Delaney

TIMOTHY JOSEPH & CONNIE SUE (WARE) DENIHAN FAMILY

Timothy was born April 18, 1954 in Dayton, Montgomery County, Ohio. His maternal great-great great grandparents, Mathias Hiram and Sarah W. (Peters) Baker, were married in Hamilton County, Ohio by Rev. I. Palmerton on November 20, 1828. Mathias bought land in Shelby County, Ohio, in December 1828 in the "Land Between the Miami's". He died there sometime before 1860. Sarah died January 8, 1880 in Miami County, Ohio. They had seven known children (Nancy, Ephraim, Henry L., Sarah E., Mary Ann, Colman Peter, and Andrew), Ephraim being Timothy's great-great grandfather.

Ephraim Baker was born September 5, 1837 in Shelby County, Washington Township, Ohio, and was married to Amizetta Cain on November 23, 1862 in Shelby County, Ohio. They both died in Shelby County, Ohio - Ephraim on April 24, 1908 and Amizetta on February 1, 1896. He was a farmer and lived his entire life in Shelby County, Ohio. They had eight known children (Jeanette "June" Ann, Flora Almeda, Albert Maynard, James Leo, William Franklin, George Milton, Ida Alma, and Mark Alonzo), George Milton being Timothy's great grandfather.

George Milton Baker was born February 11, 1875 in Shelby County, Washington Township, Ohio and was married three times. He had two children by his first wife (Marian Adell Filler-married August 18, 1901). She was born January 3, 1880, in Bedford County, Pennsylvania and died August 24, 1917 in Shelby County, Ohio. He married her sister on February 15, 1919, Anna E. Filler (born May 29, 1873 in Bedford County, Pennsylvania, and died June 26, 1930 in Miami County, Ohio). He married his third wife on October 14, 1931, Cozella Roberts (born April 14, 1882 in Miami County, Ohio, and died January 31, 1964 in Hamilton County, Ohio). George died July 6, 1958 in Miami County, Ohio. He worked for the Miami County Highway Department. His children were William Ephraim and Alfred LeRoy.

L to R: William J., Katherine, and Timothy J. Denihan

Timothy's grandfather, William Ephraim, was born November 13, 1904 in Shelby County, Ohio and married Mary Lucille Roberts May 29, 1929. They had two children, Marian Diane and Patricia Anne. William worked for Burrough's Adding Machine Company, then Armco Steel. When he retired they moved to Estero, Florida. William died March 5, 1984 and Mary died October 11, 1988.

Timothy's mother, Marian Diane, was born on March 5,1930 in Dayton, Montgomery County, Ohio, and married Carl Joseph Denihan October 14, 1950 in Butler County, Hamilton, Ohio. They lived in Vandalia, Ohio, after their marriage and moved to Fort Wayne, Allen County, Indiana, in 1961, then to Whitley County, Indiana, in 1966. Carl's parents were Edward Francis and Edna Leota (Elliott) Denihan. Carl's ancestors were Patrick and Rose (Morgan) Denihan, Stephen and Johannah (Carroll) Denihan, Joseph Monroe and Anna Elizabeth (Fosnight) Elliott, Richard and Catherine (Abbott) Elliott, and Absalom and Sarah L. (Carter) Fosnight. Carl was the owner of Denihan Homes in Columbia City, Indiana. He died October 24, 1973 in Whitley County, Thorncreek Township, Indiana. Diane and Carl had three children, Timothy Joseph, Marianne, and Patrick William, all born in Dayton, Montgomery County, Ohio.

Timothy was married twice. He had two children by his first wife (Lora Lee Christman-married June 7, 1975 in Whitley County, Indiana). They are William Joseph and Kathtrine. His second marriage was to Connie Sue Ware Overholser on February 2, 2002. Connie's parents are Orren Albert and Deloris May (Geeting) Ware and are referenced in this book. They live in Whitley County, Indiana.

Timothy has been in the construction business all his life, starting out with his father at Denihan Homes, Inc. in Columbia City, Indiana. He then moved to Cincinnati, Ohio, and Grapevine, Texas, before returning to Columbia City. Connie has been in the insurance business all her life and was a partner at Insurance & Risk Management in Fort Wayne, Indiana.

Submitted by Tim and Connie Denihan

WALTER CHARLES DENNEY

Walter, a.k.a. "Walt," is the owner of Walt Denney Trucking and lives with his wife Patricia in Fort Wayne, Indiana. They have been blessed with three children. Carolyn graduated from Elmhurst High School and received a bachelor degree in music education from Indiana Purdue Fort Wayne. Carolyn married Arlan Blackburn and they now reside in Phoenix, Arizona.

After graduating from Elmhurst High School, Charles joined the Army National Guard. Charles married Heather Schurring and their children are Austin, Leah, Brenna and McKenna.

Following graduation from Elmhurst High School, Mary attended the Columbus School of Art. Mary married Richard O'Claire and their children are Caleb and Nathan.

Denney Lineage is as follows:

Walter C. Denney was born in Allen County, Indiana, and married Patricia C. East, born in Washington County, Virginia.

Roscoe Denney (1892-1983) was born in Indiana, married first, Stella Mutton. Second marriage was to Frieda (Kuntz) Smith.

Elva Denney (1872-1909) was born in Indiana and married Emmaline Hanauer

Rolandus Denney (1848-1917) was born in Virginia and married Elizabeth J. Bell

Walter Denney (1820-1883) is said to have been born in Ireland and married Mary Owens.

Submitted by Walter C. Denney

DENNIS, WRIGHT, BRANSTRATOR FAMILIES

Farmers tilling in the wilderness helped the young city to grow and prosper. In the early 1800s several Dennis and Wright families came to Lafayette Township in southwest Allen County and established homesteads. Brothers Nathaniel and Ananias Wright began farming around 1850. Both were born in Ohio, Ananias in 1826 and Nathaniel in 1830. They found wives and married in Allen County. Nathaniel and Maria Hayes married on June 23, 1853 and had ten children. Ananias and Sara Elizabeth Mills married December 4, 1870 and had eight children.

Several Dennis families came early. Jacob Dennis brought his young wife, Nancy Hickman, in 1843. They had twelve children. In 1853, David Dennis came with his wife, Elizabeth, and small son in a horse drawn wagon and basic tools to start a homestead. He bought a "forty" of uncleared land, grubbed out a clearing for a small log cabin as many of the settlers did, and began his farm. Christopher Dennis as well as

John Dennis are other men who made their homes here in the wilderness.

April 15, 1876, John Dennis, the son of David, married 19-year-old Aminda "Minnie" Wright. Lydia Aminda Wright, was born March 30, 1857, the second child of Nathaniel and Maria. John was a young engineer operating a boiler at Emory's Sawmill in Lafayette Township. He was killed there when the boiler exploded on February 18, 1878. Minnie was eight months pregnant and had a two-year-old son, Francis Marion. A month later, she gave birth to a daughter, Pearl. Several years later, Minnie married Amos Branstrator and had two more children but was soon widowed again.

Lydia Aminda "Minnie" and Amos Branstrator, c. 1890.

Supporting herself by housekeeping, Minnie became a matron at the Old Folks Home that was located on the banks of the St. Mary's River and Bluffton Road on the south side of Fort Wayne. She died in 1931 at age 74. A great lover of reading, an antique bookcase filled with her books is a treasured remembrance of her.

Francis Dennis was an excellent carpenter. He built a small home on Lower Huntington Road in Waynedale that still stood until last year (2004). His daughter, Lois, and five of her cousins were born in this house. Francis married twice, had five children and died February 27, 1940 at 64 years of age.

In those early years, families were of necessity large and close knit. Many of the children preferred city life and became the backbone of the city workforce instead of farming. These servants of the community became nurses, teachers, carpenters, iron- workers, mechanics, roofers, and factory workers. A little removed from their farm roots, they are a class that labors long and faithfully contributing their abilities for the betterment of the community. Many retain a love of farming with small vegetable gardens in the city and flowers nurtured around their homes.

Submitted by Lois Finkhousen.

ANDREW JACKSON DEVINNEY

Six generations of the DeVinney family have, at various times, lived in Allen County beginning with Andrew Jackson Devinney (the capital "V" came later). He was born in Preble County, Ohio, on August 7, 1829, and was raised in an orphanage, his parents listed as "unknown" on all official records. The earliest of those is dated January 31, 1848, when Andrew enlisted in the Mexican War—Co. G, 2nd Regiment, US Infantry and fought at Vera Cruz under Captain Westfall.

On October 26, 1852, Andrew married Nancy Jane Wolf (October 26, 1836-March 24, 1930) in Dayton. A daughter Rachel Frances was born November 20, 1853. The couple divorced shortly thereafter.

Andrew moved to Decatur, Indiana, where, on January 20, 1858, he married Catherine Ewing of Peterson, Indiana.

A son William was born about 1860. He married Mary Reynolds in Decatur on April 8, 1880. They had two children before they divorced. William moved east, apparently to Pennsylvania where he died, but no family records exist to indicate when or where.

A second son Elmer was born September 27, 1862. He later moved to Lima, Ohio, where he worked as a plumber. Elmer married Lavinna Johnson in May 1898, but the couple eventually divorced without children. He died January 21, 1919.

Devinney Family about 1890: Front Row Andrew Jackson Devinney, Marion Dee and Sarah Jane (Zediker). Back Row: Aaron, Flora (Sudduth), William and Bertha

On December 14, 1863, Andrew enlisted in the Civil War and learned the blacksmith trade while serving in Company C, 11th Regiment Indiana Cavalry, 126 Indiana Volunteers. He mustered out September 19, 1865.

The following July, another son Aaron was born. On November 20, 1888, Aaron married Flora Jenetta Sudduth in Decatur. They had no children. Flora died in 1927; Aaron in 1929.

Following Aaron's birth, Andrew moved his family to Monroeville, Allen County, Indiana, where he worked for F.M. Deel, a blacksmith and wagon maker. There, Catherine died about 1869.

In nearby Madison Township, Sarah Jane Zediker was living with her sister's family, Margaret and Andrew Largent. Sara Jane (born September 14, 1843, in Ohio, daughter of Mary and Daniel Zediker) married Andrew Jackson Devinney in January of 1871 or 1873.

Their daughter Bertha was born in Monroeville, September 25, 1873. Bertha lived at times in Lima, Ohio, and Chicago, Illinois, before settling in Fort Wayne where she worked for Slick's Laundry and the Methodist Hospital. She died November 30, 1962, and is buried in the Catholic Cemetery.

By 1877, Andrew and Sarah Jane had moved to Pleasant Mills, Adams County, Indiana, where Andrew had his own blacksmith shop. A son Marion Dee (always known as "Dee," and was the one who capitalized the "V" in DeVinney) was born on May 5, 1877. The family eventually settled in Decatur where Andrew died on August 11, 1911.

Thereafter, Sarah Jane lived with her son Dee and his family, including a grandson Robert who remembers that she smoked a pipe and the embers often burned holes in her apron. Sarah died in Fort Wayne on January 21, 1930, and is buried in Mount Tabor Cemetery at Pleasant Mills.

Submitted by Mimi Bommelje

JAMES ANDRE DEVINNEY

James ("Jim") Andre DeVinney, son of Robert A. DeVinney and Mary M. Roche, was born in Chicago on January 6, 1942, but grew up in Fort Wayne, Indiana. He attended St. Peter Catholic School and graduated from Central Catholic High School in 1960.

As a teenager, Jim had three passions: 1) Gilbert and Sullivan—he wanted to get on the TV quiz show, *The $64,000 Question* as an expert but the show was cancelled before he learned all their operas; 2) Chess—he was city park champion for several years; 3) Marionettes—he gave many performances in Fort Wayne with his parents helping behind the scenes.

After high school, Jim attended Indiana University Extension on Barr Street, St. Francis College, and graduated from The Pennsylvania State University in 1971 with a BA degree in Liberal Arts.

On June 17, 1961, Jim married Nancy Helen Rosswurm (b. September 22, 1941), daughter of Glenn J. Rosswurm and Lucille M. Krick of New Haven. Their first two children were born in Fort Wayne: Michele Renee, December 11, 1961, and Mary Frances ("Mimi"), May 23, 1964. They had two more children: Tara Marie (born at Bellefonte, Pennsylvania, on November 18, 1968) and Robert Glenn (born at Rochester, New York on April 21, 1971). Jim and Nancy were divorced in 1976. He married Mary Virginia Flynn of Rochester on June 28, 1986; they were divorced in Barnstable, Massachusetts, in 2004.

James A. DeVinney while filming a PBS documentary, June, 1999.

Jim began a long television career in Fort Wayne, working at WPTA-TV (1960-1963) and WANE-TV (1963-1966). In 1966, he joined WPSX-TV, Penn State's educational television station and soon became its executive producer for performing arts programming. In 1971 he went to WXXI-TV in Rochester, New York, where he produced his first PBS programs including a jazz series *At the Top,* featuring performances by such artists as Count Basie, Woody Herman, and Dave Brubeck.

In 1971 he moved to Pittsburgh, Pennsylvania where he produced the PBS series *Previn and the Pittsburgh* featuring Andre Previn conducting the Pittsburgh Symphony Orchestra. After that he produced the dramatic series *Once Upon a Classic,* hosted by the late Bill Bixby, for which he received six Emmy nominations, winning once for a production of the Charles Dickens classic *A Tale of Two Cities* (Outstanding Children's Entertainment Series, 1980-81).

After moving to Boston, Massachusetts in 1986, he earned three more Emmys in documentary writing for his work on *Eyes on the Prize* and *American Experience: The Kennedys*. His program "Bridge to Freedom," part of the *Eyes on the Prize* series, was nominated for an Academy Award (Best Documentary Feature, 1987).

During his career, Jim has written for many celebrities, including Sam Waterston, Michelle Pfeiffer, Peter Gallagher, Judith Light and William F. Buckley.

For ten years, DeVinney taught writing for television at Boston University. In 2003, DeVinney moved back to Fort Wayne where he works as a writer and independent filmmaker. He teaches scriptwriting at Indiana-Purdue Fort Wayne, enjoys playing softball, and spends an inordinate amount of time working on his family's genealogy.

Submitted by James A. DeVinney

MARION (JAMES) DEE DEVINNEY

Marion Dee DeVinney, son of Andrew Jackson Devinney and Sarah Jane Zediker, was born May 5, 1877 in Pleasant Mills, Indiana. Known as "Dee," he grew up in Decatur where he played baseball and worked as a paperhanger.

On October 26, 1900, Dee married Rose Harding (April 20, 1885 - August 27, 1923) of Peru, Indiana. A son Barton Eugene was born July 11, 1901. On October 7, 1922, Bart married Lula Chapman (April 21, 1904 - March 7, 1998) in Fort Wayne where Bart worked as a brakeman for the Pennsylvania Railroad. The couple had a daughter Jeane Annette (February 28, 1923 - July 1, 1995). After their divorce, Bart married three more times, including a marriage (July 31, 1946 at Chicago, Illinois) to Mary E. Holzem. They moved to Minneapolis, Minnesota where three sons were born: Robert Eugene - September 30, 1947 (died in Vietnam December 7, 1969), Richard James - June 12, 1949, and Ronald Lee - April 24, 1952. Bart died in Minnesota on December 16, 1991.

Dee continued to play baseball for teams in Decatur, Muncie and Dallas, Texas. His career ended in 1908 when he broke an ankle sliding into second base.

DeVinney Family 1934: Marion Dee DeVinney, Margaret (Holly) DeVinney, Robert Andrew DeVinney, Sarah Jane DeVinney

His marriage to Rose was a stormy one, with several separations followed by brief reconciliations. Finally Dee and Rose were divorced in May 1910 at Lima, Ohio.

While hanging wallpaper at a hotel called The Lima House, Dee met a chambermaid Margaret ("Maggie") Holly. According to family records, Maggie was born in Ireland on October 7, 1882 (Irish records give the birth date as December 15) at Tullahinell, County Kerry near the mouth of the River Shannon. She immigrated to the United States on board the *S. S. Oceanic,* arriving in America on June 6, 1906.

Dee subsequently joined the Catholic Church, taking the baptismal name James (although he continued to be called Dee) and married Maggie at Cincinnati, Ohio, on July 26, 1911. A son Robert Andrew was born in Lima on December 28, 1914. A daughter Sarah Jane (she went by Jane) was born in Decatur, Indiana on May 19, 1920.

After moving to Fort Wayne, the couple helped several members of Maggie's Irish family immigrate to this country. Their small house on John Street was home for their two children, Dee's widowed mother Sarah Jane, Barton and Lula, plus several nieces and a nephew from County Kerry. Some descendents claim that people slept four to a bed but Robert says that's not true!

The family soon moved to Chicago but in the early 1940s returned to Fort Wayne where Dee died on December 12, 1951. Maggie died September 21, 1963. They are buried in the Catholic Cemetery.

Their daughter Jane married John E. Gill (August 27, 1917 - December 23, 2001) in Chicago on August 9, 1941. A daughter Barbara Jean, born August 19, 1942, lives today with her husband Martin J. Hnetynka in Huntsville, Alabama. They have two daughters Vicki Ann and Wendy Marie.

Jane died in San Antonio, Texas on December 29, 1997.

Submitted by Tara DeVinney Torrance

MICHELE RENEE DEVINNEY

Michele Renee DeVinney was born to James Andre and Nancy Helen (Rosswurm) DeVinney on December 11, 1961 at Lutheran Hospital in Fort Wayne, Indiana. Her early years were spent surrounded by a large family of parents, grandparents, aunts, uncles, cousins, and, eventually, a sister, Mary Frances (Mimi) DeVinney, born in 1964. She has strong memories of walks around the St. Joseph River with her father, weekends with her Aunt Linda Rosswurm babysitting, and family gatherings that allowed her to perform for the elders.

When the family moved to State College, Pennsylvania in 1966, she was bereft, missing her family in Indiana. She found great comfort, though, in the beautiful surroundings of Penn State University, where her father worked and attended college. She and her sister would often accompany him to the campus, and they particularly enjoyed visiting the Nittany Lion monument. The most significant event during her years in State College, however, was the arrival in 1968 of sister Tara Marie DeVinney, whose unspeakable cuteness was to be one of the few

DeVinney Family: Robert G. DeVinney, Michele R. DeVinney, Mimi (DeVinney) Bommelje, Tara (DeVinney) Torrance

things Michele and Mimi were to agree upon for many years.

About the time she had settled into Pennsylvania, the DeVinney family moved again in 1971, this time to Henrietta, New York, a small town outside of Rochester. Soon after, the DeVinney sisters were joined by their final sibling, a much-hoped-for brother, Robert Glenn DeVinney. Michele often helped care for her younger siblings, especially after the divorce of her parents in 1975. She also spent a lot of time with her studies, graduating from Charles H. Roth High School in Henrietta with a double major in math and music in 1979.

Upon graduation Michele chose to return to Fort Wayne to study Radio-TV-Film at Indiana University-Purdue University Fort Wayne rather than attending a school in the State University of New York system as most of her friends did. The biggest draw was the family she had left behind some thirteen years earlier, particularly her paternal grandparents, Robert and Mary DeVinney. As children, Michele and her siblings spent summer vacations in Fort Wayne, watching silent movies on their grandfather's trusty projector and going to Murphy's department store downtown with their grandmother. Michele was certain that living with her grandparents during her college years would provide more of the same riches, and she was happily correct.

Michele was married to Brian Stoner of Portland, Indiana, from 1983 until 2001, and together they had three children: Alexander Robert DeVinney-Stoner in 1984, Jameson Andre DeVinney-Stoner in 1986, and Andrea Caitlin DeVinney-Stoner in 1989. After spending many years as a stay-at-home mother and freelance writer with *WhatzUp,* Michele returned to IPFW in 1998 as a student (receiving her Master's Degree in Liberal Studies in 2001) and, in 1999, as staff, becoming assistant to the dean of Arts and Sciences in 2002. Sons Alex and Jamie graduated from North Side (in 2002 and 2005, respectively) and attend IPFW. Daughter Andrea will graduate from North Side in 2008.

Submitted by Michele R. DeVinney

ROBERT ANDREW DEVINNEY

Robert Andrew DeVinney (born December 28, 1914 at Lima, Ohio), son of Marion (James) Dee DeVinney and Margaret Holly, grew up in Lima, Ohio, Decatur, Indiana, and Fort Wayne. He attended St. Peter Catholic School and went on to Central Catholic High School where, as a freshman, he won an oratory contest for his interpretation of Sparticus' speech to the Gladiators. By the following year, his family had moved to Chicago where Robert soon developed a passion for magic. He began accumulating tricks purchased from local magic stores and made many of them himself. He witnessed performances by some of the great magicians of the 20th Century, from Thurston to David Copperfield.

On April 3, 1937, Robert went on a date arranged by his sister. Mary Roche, born October 16, 1920, was a Mercy High School classmate of Jane DeVinney and the daughter of Charles Kelly Roche (September 13, 1885 - April 3, 1964) and Mary Agnes Moore (June 10, 1885 - April 14, 1962). They were married at Holy Cross Catholic Church in Chicago on June 29, 1940. A son James Andre was born on January 6, 1942.

In February 1944, Robert was drafted into the United States Army and sent to Fort Leonard Wood, Missouri, for basic training. By October he was at Camp Shelby, Mississippi, where he became a member of the 526th Engineer Light Pontoon Co.

Mary (Roche) and Robert A. DeVinney on their wedding day. June 29, 1940

On February 10, 1945, Robert's unit was on board the troop ship *SS Gibbons,* under tight security, as it left from New York City en route to France. Their goal was to build a bridge across the Rhine River, regarded as Germany's last natural line of defense. The anticipated battle would be difficult with a high rate of casualties. But on March 7, the 9th Armored Division captured a bridge at Remagen that gave the Allies a much-needed foothold on the east bank of the Rhine, thereby nullifying the mission of the 526th. With a sense of relief, PFC DeVinney was soon on his way home, returning safely to his wife and son.

After serving in the U.S. Army during World War II, the DeVinneys settled in Fort Wayne where they have lived ever since.

Robert worked as a house painter until he retired in 1980. During his years painting homes and businesses in Fort Wayne, he became interested in the histories of the people who lived and worked at those places. With Mary's assistance, Robert researched and wrote about many local houses and buildings. He frequently wrote descriptions that accompanied neighborhood tours sponsored by ARCH Historical Preservation and was often interviewed by local reporters writing on the history of Fort Wayne. From 1995 to 2001, he wrote a regular column for the North Side Newsletter, describing the history of buildings and houses in that neighborhood.

To this day, Robert and Mary continue to live in the city they have called home for more than sixty years.

Submitted by Robert A. DeVinney

DEY SISTERS

The Dey sisters were all born in Fort Wayne, Allen County, Indiana. How their parents Fred Dey and Florence M. (Reed) Dey ended up in Allen County was due to many interesting journeys.

Sharon R. Dey was born 1940. She married David V. Smith (Sr.) on June 7, 1958. She has worked at St. Joseph Hospital for 32 years. Retirement will come in 2005. Sharon and Dave have four children, three sons and one daughter. They also have many grandchildren and great grandchildren. Sharon is widowed and still lives in Fort Wayne.

Fay M. Dey was born 1941. She married first James Hans and had a daughter and a son. She married second Phillip Kleber and became step mom to his four children. The Hans/Kleber family has nine grandchildren and more to come. Currently retired, Fay helped start a medical transportation company several years ago.

Peggy L. Dey was born 1943. She married first W. Philip Lykins and had two daughters. Peggy married second Donald Bowers and that union brought together their children, grandchildren and great grandchildren. Peggy retired from Central Soya after 34 years. She resides in Fort Wayne, Allen County.

Linda K. Dey was born 1948. She has been married since 1966 to John Stoffer. They have two sons and one granddaughter. Linda has worked at Lincoln Life Insurance Co. for 30 years. She and her family still live in Fort Wayne.

E. Joan(n) Dey was born 1949. She has one son and two granddaughters. She has worked in the eyecare field for many years, currently at Cunningham Optical One. She also resides in Fort Wayne.

All of the Dey sisters attended Franklin School and North Side High School. Many of their children and grandchildren also attended or attend NSHS. The sisters are close and do many fun things together. The Three Rivers Festival parade and Fourth of July fireworks are some of their family activities. They also visit the "old City Hall" Fort Wayne History Center and Allen County Courthouse.

The Fort Wayne Children's Zoo has always been a fun place to get their families together. A Smith/Dey brick is placed in the zoo near the Rain Forest. A brick for their mother Florence has been placed in Headwaters Park. The Dey sisters enjoy talking about and showing their families the special "growing up" places in Fort Wayne. When they were young, Trier/Swinney Park was the place that their family spent time together riding on the roller coaster, merry-go-round, and bumper cars. Hamilton Park was where they played during the summer and went sledding down the hills in the winter. They went to the Wells Theater on Saturdays to watch movies, news reels, and cartoons. Sometimes, they got to go again on Sundays and there would be new movies to see. It only cost a quarter for the movie and Slowpoke sucker or movie and popcorn. The sisters would baby sit for fifty cents an hour so they could have money to go to the movies. As they got older, they loved to roller skate at the Roller Dome. In the winter, ice skating on the ponds at Franke Park and Reservoir Park was fun. Allen county has been a good home for these sisters and their families.

Dey Family

More Deys:

The sisters have a brother, Fred. He lives in Illinois with wife Marge. Fred has three children by a previous marriage. Fred and Marge visit Fort Wayne as often as possible.

Richard Dey is a cousin. He grew up in Fort Wayne, met his late wife Ellen in Fort Wayne and then moved to Warsaw. His daughter was born in Germany and now lives in New York near the area where some of the Dey ancestors lived. Richard helps cousins Sharon and Peggy with their family research. The three of them travel to New York, New Jersey, Ohio and Michigan. Their travels will take them to Maine and Canada in 2005.

The Journeys:

The first Dey to come to America was Laurens Duyts. He arrived in New Amsterdam (New York) on the ship "The Fire of Troy" in 1639. He had come from Denmark and Holland. Laurens is buried in New Jersey. The Duyts/Dye/Dey descendants, Hans, James Hans, James, Capt John (American Revolution battle of Monmouth, New Jersey). William and their family lived in New York, New Jersey and Ohio. John Ely Dey and Sarah Moutt Dey lived in Lebanon, Ohio and bought land all over Ohio. In, 1855, their son Samuel C. Dey settled on some of that land near Defiance. Ohio. He married Mary Elizabeth Bowdle and had six children. Their son Wade met Elizabeth Zeschke in Defiance, married and had four children. Their son Elson C. Dey met Leota Fay Sauvain in Paulding County. Ohio. Leota's grandparents Augustus and Mary Ann Sauvain were natives of Switzerland. They sailed from Havre, France to New York in 1852 on the "Bark Hahnemann" with three children. They traveled from New York to Allen County, Indiana. While in Indiana they had four more children, moved to Ohio, and then settled in Kansas. Their son Lewis Sauvain, who had been born in Fort Wayne, Allen County, returned to Ohio and married Emma R Coughlin. Emma's parents Dennis Coughlin and Sarah Jane Evans Coughlin had come from Ireland and settled in Paulding County, Ohio. Lewis and Emma had several children. Their daughter Leota married Elson C. Dey (mentioned above). They had one daughter and two sons. Elson, Fay and children moved to Fort Wayne, Allen County. Indiana where Elson worked for International Harvester until he retired in 1960. Their children were: Evelyn F. Dey (Oaks), DeWayne E. Dey, and Fred Dey. Evelyn graduated from South Side High School. DeWayne and Fred graduated from Central High School.

Both of the brothers served in the National Guard.

While the Deys and Sauvains were getting settled, a family named Hildred had come from England to Canada. Eventually, they settled in Massachusetts. Their daughter Cora Ruth Hildred married a WWI soldier Jesse H. Reed who was from Dayton, Ohio. His ancestors were Reed, Alexander, Black. and Dynes. Jesse and Cora had three children: Isabella born in Massachusetts, Florence M born in Connecticut, and Jesse H. Reed. Jr. born in Indiana. Cora's other children were Emily, Lillian, and Herbert. Jesse Sr. worked for the railroad, was blinded in an accident and moved to the Soldier's Home in Dayton, Ohio. Cora moved the children to Fort Wayne, Allen County.

Two of the children from the Dey and Reed families (Fred Dey and Florence Reed) met, fell in love, and were married. They had six children, five daughters (Dey Sisters) and one son.

The journeys from Denmark, Switzerland, England, Ireland, and Germany brought the Dey/Sauvain and Reed/Hildred families together in America. That's how the Dey sisters began their lives in Fort Wayne, Allen County, Indiana and they continue to live in the area today.

Submitted by Sharon Dey Smith

LOWELL DICKES FAMILY

Lowell Roger Dickes was born December 4, 1932 in Allen County to Carl Byram born September 3, 1910 died October 12, 1969 and Donna Elizabeth Myers born May 10, 1910 died March 7, 1998. His brother, Philip Warren was born May 18, 1931; he married Charlene Mae Smith born June 2, 1931, daughter of Raymond and Grace Johnson Smith on December 23, 1950.

Lowell was married on January 1, 1954 to Wanda Jean Knafel born May 31, 1935, the daughter of Paul Rowland Knafel born October 9, 1910 died July 27, 1999 and DeElda Elmira Gaff born August 19, 1912.

Dickes Family, L to R: Lowell, Debra Jean, Wanda, Roger Duane, Darryl Alan, and David Warren

Of their union were born four children: Debra Jean, born September 29, 1954. Roger Duane, born April 2, 1956, who married Susan Elaine Dickey born January 27, 1956 on August 9, 1975; they have two children, Melody Sue, born September 23, 1977 and Carl Duane born September 27, 1979.

Darryl Alan, born August 24, 1957 married Doris Jean Belcher born July 15, 1961 on May 12, 1979. They had three daughters, Stacey Elizabeth born February 23, 1980, Stephanie Christine born March 25, 1982, and Samantha Danielle born July 6, 1984. Their marriage was dissolved on August 21, 1991; Darryl subsequently married Laura Lynn Monnier born August 7, 1965. They have one daughter, Victoria Lynn born October 23, 1994.

David Warren was born December 31, 1959; he married Teresa Katherine Wright born February 17, 1958 on December 23, 1983. They have two children, Megan Alisa born July 6, 1984 and Warren Lowell born July 14, 1986. This union was dissolved on May 28, 1997 and David then married Mary Susan Kilby on February 14,2004.

Lowell graduated from Eel River-Perry High School, was a member of the Huntertown United Methodist Church, the Masonic Lodge, and Scottish Rite. During his lifetime, he helped farm with his father, worked at the Huntertown Elevator, had a milk route for Allen County Co-op and worked at Dana Corporation in Fort Wayne. He died in a traffic accident in Steuben County on November 18, 1967 and is buried in the Huntertown Cemetery.

His wife, Wanda, then married Donald Lewis Genth, born (August 14, 1927 died October 28, 1994, from cancer); he is buried in the Huntertown cemetery. They spent their married lives in the same house on Shoaff Road, near Huntertown, that Lowell and Wanda had built.

Wanda then married Richard Joseph Maroney born on December 19, 1937.

The John Philip Dickes family emigrated from the Rhine Valley in Germany. In fear of their male children being taken into the German army, John and Maria Magdalena Steitz Dickes decided to sail to America. They sold everything in preparation of the trip and suddenly John took sick and died on a Tuesday, was buried on Friday and on the next Monday, a pregnant, and very courageous, Maria and her ten children set sail, arriving in America in March 1852 after a very arduous trip. Their last son, Philip, was born in Buffalo, New York.

Submitted by Wanda Maroney

JACOB DIFFENDARFER

Jacob Diffendarfer, his wife, Barbara (Kirsch/Kinsch), and family came to Indiana about 1830. He was born about 1796 in Pennsylvania and died in Allen County, Indiana, February 8, 1871. The couple married November 11, 1819 at Trinity Lutheran Church in Lancaster, Pennsylvania. They are buried at Eel River Baptist Church cemetery, at the church he helped build and where he was a trustee. Jacob purchased, first in 1834, many tracts of land in Eel River and Lake Townships in Allen County. Their children were Emanuel, Henry, Beautus, John, Susannah, Barbara, Jacob, Samuel, Marean, Lisa Ann, and two stillborn.

Emanuel Diffendarfer born October 26, 1822, died December 4, 1863 during the Civil War at Bowling Green, Kentucky. His wife was Eliza (Gray), 1829-1917, and their children were Augusta, Mary, Angeline, Sarah, Homer Samuel Spencer, James Madison, and Hutoka Jane.

Homer Diffendarfer, born June 9, 1854, died February 3, 1929 at the homestead in Noble County, Indiana north of Churubusco. He married Sarah Martin McCoy November 16, 1875 in Noble County. Their children were Eliza Ann,

Homer and Sarah (McCoy) Diffendarfer.

Letitia, Emanuel, Bertha Ellen, Jessie, Maggie, Isaac, Clara, John Lawrence, Edna (who's son still lives on the homestead), her twin Eddie, Bessie, Zellie, an infant, Eva, and Lura.

Eliza Ann Diffendarfer, born July 25, 1876 at the homestead in Noble County married Edward Eugene Keller, son of John Calvin and Mary (Story) Keller on March 3, 1898 at Avilla, Indiana. Edward, born August 26, 1876, died August 4, 1907. Both are buried at Gray cemetery near the home place. Their children were Raleigh H., Glen Eugene, Ralph and William (died at birth). After Edward died, Eliza married her sister Ellen's widower and together they raised their two families. Many times over the years they had grandchildren and great grandchildren living or staying with them. The cousins, many from farms of the original homestead, spent their younger years basking in the love of Grandmother Eliza. There were wonderful family reunions and they attended Green Center Methodist Church that was surrounded by family farms.

Raleigh H. Keller, born June 30, 1898, married Evie Kathryn Miller on November 7, 1918 at Albion, Indiana. Evie was born October 27, 1898 in Noble County, Indiana to Andrew Paul and Cora (Harrold) Miller. Cora was the daughter of Moses and Hannah (Tschupp) Harrold. Raleigh died April 24, 1933 and Evie died January 7, 1996. They are buried at Eel River Cemetery. They had four children: La Velda Catherine who married Dale McCoy and had William Roger, Jenna Mae, Dorothy Arlene, and Hermione McCoy; Isaac D. Keller married Mary June Kaiser and had Sandra Jean; Isaac married Berneta Lentz after Mary June died; Pauline Evelyn, who married Arthur Troyer, had Michael Lynn (deceased), Philip Allan, Don Leslie, and Paula Jo (deceased).

Lucille "Lucy" Keller is the fourth child of Raleigh and Evie Keller. She was born August 18, 1932 in Huntertown, Indiana. Lucy lived

Back row- l to r Barb Green, Don Peters, Jason Peters, Lonnie Peters, David Green. Front row- l to r Lisa Peters, Lester Green, Lucy Green, Kelsey Peters.

in Churubusco until moving with her mother and brother to Fort Wayne. She married Lester H. Green, son of Othel L. and Nellie Marie (Valentine) Green, on March 12, 1954 at Forest Park Methodist Church in Fort Wayne, Indiana. Lester "Buss" Green was born January 19, 1930 in Sidney, Shelby County, Ohio. They have two children. David H. Green, their son, was born November 14, 1955 in Fort Wayne. David married Barbara Elaine Jeffers on June 26, 1982 at the Bible Baptist Church in Fort Wayne. Their daughter, Lonnie Sue Green, was born November 25, 1958 in Fort Wayne. She married Donald Claude Peters, son of Edward and Kathryn (Smith) Peters, May 1, 1982 at First Presbyterian Church in Fort Wayne, Indiana. Lonnie and Don have three children: Jason Tyler born May 4, 1984 in Fort Wayne, Lisa Marie born October 29, 1987 in Marshalltown, Iowa, and Kelsey Lynne born March 28, 1990 at Fort Dodge, Iowa. Lonnie, Don and family live in Missouri.

Submitted by Lucille "Lucy" Green

FAMILY OF MARIE M. (KELLY)DISSER & EDWARD JOHN DISSER

These two Allen County residents hailed from a strong Catholic, Irish, and/or German ancestry which shaped the early commercial and parochial landmarks of their hometown, Fort Wayne, Indiana. Edward John Disser (b .May 4, 1886; d. December 11, 1938), a financier and member of St. Mary's Church, was educated at that parish grade school and the secondary commercial school. Marie Margaret Kelly (b. May 15, 1892; d. March 18, 1971), whose parents were charter members of The Most Precious Blood Catholic Church, attended this grade school for seven years, and then graduated in 1908 after three years at Saint Augustine Girls' Academy as the Salutatorian. This couple's large wedding ceremony was held November 15, 1916, at Precious Blood Parish and mentioned in great detail within *The Journal Gazette*. Marie Kelly's family home still stands at 704 West Third Street at Barthold "in Bloomingdale," as she always described it; likewise, this was the birthplace of her own father plus all his eight children!

Marie's mother was formerly Ellen Ryan (b. 1866 in Rushville, Indiana; d.1940), the daughter of Marie (Downey) Ryan and James Ryan, a contractor (b. June 15, 1837; d .January18, 1902), both from the same county in Ireland. Marie's father was Robert Emmet Kelly (b.October 27, 1864; d. October 26, 1938), the only son of Thomas F. Kelly (b.1831 in County Roscommon, Ireland; d.1893), who was a canal boat captain on the Wabash & Erie Canal, and Margaret (Clark) Kelly (b. November 6, 1842 in Toledo, Ohio; d.1912), where they married and moved to Fort Wayne in 1858. Marie's dad originally worked as a messenger boy and then became an engineer at age 21 on the Fort Wayne, Cincinnati & Louisville Railroad until injured in an accident; he served as Secretary of Brotherhood of Electrical Engineers (1908-1938), as well as the Treasurer of Ancient Order of Hibernians of Indiana (1912-15). As a Democrat, Robert Kelly was elected Allen County's Recorder (1908-1912) during Mayor Hosey's administration, and appointed to the City Board of Public Works (1914-1918, two years as Chairman). He then established a commercial electrical installation business named Dix-Kelly Electric Company with his partner Frank J. Dix, which operated locally for over fifty years, and supplied the lighting for The Lincoln Tower, Emboyd Theatre (now Embassy), several churches, and Fort Wayne Newspaper Building on Main Street, just to name a few. In addition to serving four years as Secretary of City Light & Power, Robert Kelly's other civic memberships included Knights of Columbus, Elks Lodge and the Aquatic Club. Married on May 16, 1888, in Rushville's Catholic Church, Robert and Ellen Kelly also celebrated their Fiftieth Wedding Anniversary with a Mass, and just five months prior to his death. The newspaper's Society Page describing those 1938 events listed as the attendees all twenty grandchildren with their seven children: Thomas J. Kelly, a district manager for NIPSCO (b. 1889; d.1951), Mrs. Edward J. Disser, Robert J. Kelly, a Deputy State Fire Marshall (b. 1899; d.1980), Laurence W. Kelly of Omaha, Nebraska (b.1901; d.1959), and Misses Josephine A., B. Ann, and Kathryn G. Kelly (who died in 1980, 1967, 1988 respectively). Marie's single sisters always shared the holiday festivities, vacations, and other joyful occasions at Disser's home in their cherished role of Aunts, later as "The Great Aunts!"

Caption: Family of Edward and Marie Disser seated with twins, Nancy and Suzanne Marie. Top row: Ed, Mary Ellen, Marge and Bob. Middle Row: Genevieve, Sally and Josephine, 1938.

Edward John (Ed) was the second son of Joseph P. Disser, an orphan from Germany (d. 1934), who worked as a foreman on the Pennsylvania Railroad after arriving here, and his wife Elizabeth Yobst (d. September, 1931), who married in Fort Wayne and lived on S. Hanna Street. Ed and his two siblings were baptized at Saint Mary's Church as John Winston, the eldest, and their sister Margaret (b. June 25, 1884; d .March l0, 1952), who never married and was called Aunt Miggy. His brother John W. married the former Katherine Smith, nicknamed Kit, and their two children were known as (John) Winston (d. February 25, 1945) and (Katherine) Kappy Disser when they lived on Oakdale Drive here.

Ed Disser was first employed like his dad at the Pennsylvania Railroad, but then joined the law firm of Judge Vesey in 1910. He worked as the Managing Secretary of the First Joint Stock Land Bank until 1932, as well as the Secretary of the Fort Wayne Investment Co. and the Secretary/Treasurer of Lake Everett Stock Farm Company. Following the sparse Depression Era, Ed became the VP/Manager of General Refunding Corp., as well as the financial advisor for this Diocese and Bishop John F. Noll during the building campaigns for Saint Joseph Hospital and Central Catholic High School. His many other civic organizations included the Rotary Club, Democratic Party, Knights of Columbus, Isaac Walton League, Hundred Percent Club, Elks Club, and the Fort Wayne Real Estate Board.

Before her marriage Marie Kelly was employed as Deputy County Recorder from 1908-1916, but spent her remaining years as one busy homemaker who enjoyed a good game of Bridge with her sisters or friends, Saturday evening poker games, and relaxing vacations at the lake! Since their family residence was at 2525 S. Webster Street, Saint Patrick's Church Parish School, and Central Catholic High were responsible for the sacrament receptions and education for all nine of the Disser children - namely Edward Joseph (b. July 2, 1917, prematurely at under 4 lbs), Robert Kelly (b. July 18, 1920, making up for his brother at over 10 lbs; d. October 6, 1995), Mary Ellen D. Russell (b. August 19, 1921), Margaret Ann D. Heiny (b. September 23, 1923), Genevieve Elizabeth D. Welling (b. December l0, 1926; d. July 11, 1990), Sara Therese D. Weigand (b. March, 1930), Josephine Catherine D. Barger (b. October 9, 1931) and formerly Sister Edward Joseph, C.S.C. (August 15, 1956), Anne Marie (Nancy) D. Hatton-Hollerbach and Suzanne Marie D. Libbing (b. April 2, 1934). The twins' arrival was a surprise duality even for their doctor!

When a couple young German girls, the first one named Johanna, then Anna Eisenman, arrived to assist Marie with her family, Ed practiced his German language each morning relating their chores, but their German cooking talents and spoiling the babies translated terrifically and were "wünderbar". Marie's youngest girls were merely four years old when she was unfortunately widowed by Ed's sudden heart attack at age 52. A senior at the University of Notre Dame, son Edward was just six months away from Commencement, but he returned home to his family, of course, never completing that degree. Going to work at early ages, all Marie's children had to learn some hard life lessons, but they could follow her own especially staunch example of fortitude, faith, and trust in God; with the assistance of their family unity, each likewise became strong and undaunted along life's pathways, even when tested once again by a fire within their home (1943), and also during the World War II years.

Marie and Ed Disser's children: Ed, Josephine, Nancy, Sue, Sally. Front: Marge, Genevieve, Mary Ellen and Bob, 1987

Marie (Kelly) Disser with Linda, Mimi and Marge Disser Heiny, 1957.

"Now, for the rest of the story. . ." all these nine Disser children married some truly fantastic spouses, the majority also from Fort Wayne, and who eventually presented "Mother D" with a total of forty-seven living grandchildren, all of whom are still blessed by Our Lord with good health today! Some forty of these cousins have lived in Fort Wayne at various times, the only exceptions being those seven Hattons who come to "Disserville" just to party!

There are numerous stories left untold here, but which made it into the local newspapers -- from Bob's Purple Heart, to anonymous scholarships, to spelling awards, to cooking with Betty Crocker, to the twins' big April Fool's joke, and even to four grandchildren pulling taffy with Grandma Disser in her kitchen (1960)! Anyone of our relatives here will gladly chat about these happenings (or even our cute younger generations), equally and without hesitation, because our family pride knows no time limits! Just as our Family Reunion 1994 and the Reunion 2000's memory booklets stated "God so loved us that he gave us life in the Disser family. Let us reunite in Love, Peace, and Prayer." All the heirs who attended those two weekends (around 150) luckily reaped the many wonderful efforts of some industrious aunts and cousins, plus enjoyed super fun times at creating current memories, as will surely happen again one day soon.

Submitted by Ann Heiny Long

CLINTON AND HELEN (MOHR) DOCTOR

Clinton Doctor was the second child born to Oscar and Anna Doctor. Clinton married Helen Mohr on August 23, 1947. They had five children.

The first child was Allan Clinton Doctor. He married Marilyn Oetting (January 3, 1948 to September 17, 1997) at Trinity Suburban Lutheran Church in Fort Wayne on October 15, 1966. Allan made his living in the sheet metal trade where he served as foreman and union president. Marilyn was a real estate broker until the time of her passing at age 49 from breast cancer. They had two children, Brent and Christine. Allan's second marriage was to Carol Ann (Busche) Hosier on April 18, 1975, at Trinity Evangelical Lutheran Church in Fort Wayne. Carol worked as a bookkeeper. She had two children, Cindy and Kathy.

The second child was Sharon Ann Doctor. She married Alan Clark Thompson on October 14, 1967 at Trinity Suburban Lutheran Church in Fort Wayne. Sharon was a homemaker and library and Girl Scout volunteer. Alan served in the Air Force. He was a software engineer in DBA. They had two children, Tonya and Dean.

The third child was Charlene Kay Doctor. She married Donald Robert Ferrell on January 31, 1970 at Trinity Suburban Lutheran Church in Fort Wayne. Charlene is a schoolteacher. She earned her Bachelor of Science in Education at Indiana University in 1992. She earned her masters degree in education at Indiana Wesleyan in 2001. Don served in the Indiana Air National Guard for eleven years. He makes his living in construction. They had five children, Christopher, Victoria, Camilla, Laura, and D. Nathan.

Helen and Clinton Doctor

The fourth child was Karen Dianne Doctor. She married twice. The first marriage was to Johnnie (John) Ray Herman on September 24, 1977 at Waynedale United Methodist Church. They divorced December 5, 1991. They had two children, Alicia and David. The second marriage was to Robert Dale Koons on May 16, 1998 at St. Peter's Lutheran Church in Fort Wayne. Karen earned her Bachelor of Science degree in education through Indiana University in May 1996.

The fifth child was Arlene Reanata Doctor. She married twice. The first marriage was to Michael Hartsough. They had one child, Samantha. Her second marriage was to Randy Patrick O'Keefe on August 15, 1999. Arlene earned a B.A. in psychological sciences through Purdue University. Randy served in the Army Reserve. He earned a B.S. in mechanical engineering through Rose Hulman. Randy has been involved with electrical power plants for twenty years. They had one child, Diana.

Allan Doctor, the first child listed above, and his son, Brent Doctor, purchased the farmland located at 7418 Flatrock Road, Hoagland, Indiana, on September 23, 2002. Allan and Brent became the fifth Doctor and sixth current owners of the Doctor family farmland. The fifth Doctor and current owner of the family farmhouse located at 7418 Flatrock Road, Hoagland, is Brent Doctor. He purchased the family house on May 23, 2003. Brent married Susan Paprstein on October 22, 1994 at Messiah Lutheran Church in Fort Wayne. Brent makes his living as a registered architect. Susan is a graphic designer. They have three children, Alexandra, Julia, and Henry.

Submitted by Helen Doctor

GEORGE DOCTOR & ALISABETH (GRIEBEL) DOCTOR

George Doctor came to live in Allen County, Indiana with his parents Heinrich and Christina Doctor in 1834 at the age of ten. Alizabeth Griebel came to live in Allen County, Indiana with her parents in 1834 at the age of three. It is uncertain if the Doctor and Griebel families knew each other in Germany. It is known that the two families sailed on the same ship the, "Virginia," and arrived in the United States at the same time. Both families settled in Marion Township, Allen County, Indiana. George Doctor and Alisabeth Griebel were married at Emmanuel Lutheran Church, Soest, on June 10, 1852. They purchased a farm that was located on Wayne Trace in Allen County, south of the Emmanuel Lutheran Church. They had eleven children.

The first child was Wilhelm Doctor (October 4, 1853-August 5, 1854). He died at ten months of age and was buried at Emmanuel Lutheran Church Cemetery, Soest.

The second child was Louis Doctor (April 25, 1855-November 14, 1941). He married Julia Agnes Soest (December 20, 1863-August 16, 1936) on May 27, 1886 at Emmanuel Lutheran Church, Soest. They had seven children. Louis's father, George Doctor, purchased the farm located at 7418 Flatrock Road, Hoagland, from the Emmens family on October 5, 1872. This farm became Louis and Julia's on November 1, 1887. When the 100-acre farm on Flatrock Road was purchased, there was a log barn, and only one acre of land had been cleared. So that Louis could farm, he cleared all but 22 acres of trees. Louis was the second Doctor to own the farm and the first Doctor to live on it. George remained at his farm located on Wayne Trace Road.

George Doctor and Alisabeth Griebel-Doctor

The third child was Frederick Phillip Doctor (1856- death between 1920 and 1930). He married Anna Caroline Fackler (1874- death after 1953) on September 16, 1897 in Allen County, Indiana. They moved to Denver, Colorado sometime after 1920. They had three children.

The fourth child was George Doctor (1861-March 27, 1947). He married Lulu E. Copp (1868-Novembr 22, 1926) on April 21, 1889 in Allen County, Indiana. They had no children. George made his living as a blacksmith who worked out of Fort Wayne and Decatur, Indiana.

The fifth child was Charles (Carl) Heinrich Conrad Doctor (September 21, 1863- ?). He married L. Wilhelmina (Minnie) Fackler (?-May 17, 1953) on June 23, 1901 in Allen County, Indiana. They had two children.

The sixth child was Mathias William Doctor (January 1, 1865-November 31, 1930). He married Wilhelmine E. (Minnie) Lepper (1866-December 16, 1941) on September 21, 1890 in Allen County, Indiana. They had three children. Mathias died of pneumonia at the age of 65.

The seventh child was William Doctor (1867-April 12, 1931). He married Sophia Moyer (1872-February 18, 1951) on August 28, 1897 at Zion Lutheran Church. They had four children. William made his living as a carpenter.

The eighth child was Leuiza (Maggie) Margaret Catherine Doctor (September 2, 1869- April 18, 1905). She married Tobias Johannes (John) Fackler (June 29, 1871-February 8, 1950) on October 29, 1896 in Allen County, Indiana. They had six children.

The ninth child was Mary Catherine Doctor (November 9, 1871-March 22, 1930). She married Jacob F. Schmidt (1865-November 16, 1941) on May 11, 1902 at Emmanuel Lutheran Church, Soest. They had eight children.

The tenth child was Katherine Leuiza Doctor (January 5, 1874-March 2, 1961). She married Heinrich A. (Henry) Schmidt (1866-1938) on November 9, 1902 at Emmanuel Lutheran Church, Soest.

The eleventh child was Martin Heinrich Wilhelm Doctor (January 5, 1874-March 2, 1961). He married Maria (Mary) Anabelle Christina Schlaudroff (February 24, 1884-October 5, 1948) on October 29, 1903 at Emmanuel Lutheran Church, Soest. He lived on the Wayne Trace farm after his father George died.

Submitted by Charlene Ferrell

HEIMICH DOCTOR & CHRISTINA ELIZABETH WIESNER DOCTOR

Heimich Doctor was the child of Johannes Doctor and Anna Margartha Wagner Doctor, both of Konigsberg, Hessen, Germany. Johannes was born in 1745 and Anna was born in 1745. They were married on April 7, 1768 in Germany. Anna died on January 26, 1785 at age 40. Heimich Doctor was born December 27, 1781 in Konigsberg, Hessen, Germany, and he died July 18, 1868 at age 87 in Allen County, Indiana. He was buried at Soest Cemetery. Christina, Heimich's wife, was born December 26, 1791 in Konigsberg, Hessen, Germany and. died June 24, 1865 at age 74 in Allen County Indiana. She also was buried at Soest Cemetery.

Heinrich and Christina Doctor both came to America with their five children on the ship named "Virginia", which ported at Baltimore, Maryland onSeptmber 2, 1834. They purchased farmland in October 1840 on Wayne Trace Road in Allen County and made their living farming. Heinrich and Christina went to St. Pauls Lutheran, the log church on Thompson Road. They were charter members of Soest Lutheran Church on Wayne Trace Road, which later became Soest Emmanuel Lutheran Church. Heimich was buried at Soest Cemetery.

The name was spelled "Dokter" on the ships passenger list and was spelled "Docter" on the tombstones of Heinrich and Christina. His son and daughter-in-law, George and Elizabeth also show the spelling of "Docter" on their tombstones. The following generations were then spelled "Doctor".

The names of Heimich and Christina's five children are as follows: First child was Charles S. L. Doctor, Born December 30, 1817, Married Louisa Coleman at Soest Emmanuel Lutheran Church on April 9, 1843. He died May 10, 1857 at age 40 and was buried at Soest Cemetery. They had eight children together.

Second child was Ludwig Theodore Doctor, Born December 4, 1819, Died September 3, 1849 at age 29 and was buried at Soest Cemetery. Ludwig did not marry and had no children.

Third child was Margartha Doctor born April 27, 1821, Married Mathias Bradenstein at Soest Emmanuel Lutheran Church on March 17, 1842. Died May 20, 1884 at age 63 and was buried at Soest Cemetery. They had two children.

Fourth child was George Doctor, born February 14, 1823, died December 26, 1901 at age 78 and was buried at Soest Cemetery. He married twice. His first wife was Louisa Bachelier, born July 5, 1832. She died of complications of childbirth on October 13, 1851 at age 19 and was buried at Soest Cemetery. They were married at Soest Emmanuel Lutheran Church on December 5, 1850. They had one child, named Heinrich George Doctor, born October 9, 1851, died on August 7, 1852 and was buried at Soest Cemetery. His second wife was Alisabeth (Elizabeth) Griebel, born April 14, 1831, died July 17, 1904 at age 73 and was buried at Soest Cemetery. She died from a fractured skull after jumping from a run away horse and buggy at the Doctor farm near Hoagland, Indiana. George Doctor and Elizabeth Griebel were married at Soest Emmanuel Lutheran Church on June 10, 1852. They had eleven children together, who were all baptized at Soest Emmanuel Lutheran Church. George Doctor helped all of his children who were interested in farming to purchase farms.

Fifth child was Catherine Doctor, born in 1825, died in 1901. She married John Phillip Coleman at Soest Emmanuel Lutheran Church on June 3, 1847. Catherine and her husband John moved to Crawford County, Wisconsin. She was buried in Wisconsin upon her death in 1901 at age 76. They had seven children together.

Submitted by Karen Koons

LOUIS DOCTOR & JULIA AGNES (SOEST) DOCTOR

Louis Doctor (April 28, 1855-November 14, 1941) was the son of George and Alisabeth (Elizabeth Griebel) Doctor. He married Julia Agnes Soest (December 20, 1863-August 16, 1936) on May, 27, 1886, at Emmanuel Lutheran Church, Soest. Julia was the daughter of Frederick Soest. Louis was the second Doctor to own the farm at 7418 Flatrock Road, Hoagland, Indiana. They had seven children.

The first child was Frederick Christian Doctor (May 17, 1887-September 10, 1964). He married Emma A. Ropa (March 9, 1882-January 24, 1975) on June 8, 1911, in Allen County, Indiana. He became a Lutheran minister and served the Lord and church mainly in Wyoming and Nebraska. He and his wife passed away in Nebraska. They had six children.

The second child was Anna M. Doctor (April 18, 1889-December 25, 1914). She was engaged to be married to a Schmidt. Anna died during surgery at St. Joseph Hospital in Fort Wayne, Indiana. She had been ill for several weeks, and it has been said that her appendix burst. She was 25 years, eight months, and seven days of age at her passing.

The third child was Karl Heinrich Oscar Doctor (August 10, 1891-April 10, 1966). He married Anna Louise Bradtmueller (April 30, 1896-May 1, 1933) on October 6, 1918, at Emmanuel Lutheran Church, Soest. She died of pneumonia one day after her 37th birthday. Oscar purchased the family farm on November 14, 1941 and was the third Doctor to own the farm at 7418 Flatrock Road, Hoagland, Indiana. They had six children.

Louis Doctor and Julia Agnes Soest Doctor

Louis Doctor Family, L to R: Oscar, Louis, Lewis, Frederick, Anna, Julia, and Clara in front

The fourth child was Clara Lydia Marie Doctor (November 5, 1893-October 25, 1972). She married Casper Adam Martin Griebel (July 6, 1885-December 13, 1971) on March 30, 1917, at Soest Emmanuel Lutheran Church. Martin was a bank president, insurance company president, farmer, and Marion Township trustee. They had six children.

The fifth child was Lewis Mathias Doctor (February 16, 1896-April 15, 1982). He married Frances Elizabeth Frohnepful (February 15, 1893-December 20, 1955) on February 17, 1920, in Allen County, Indiana. They moved to Glendale, California. Lewis worked in the knitting mill and owned a chair caning business. They had two children.

The sixth child was Wilhelm Louis Curt Doctor (August 6, 1899-October 26, 1899). He was less than two months of age at his passing.

The seventh child was Milton Heinrich Martin Doctor (January 19, 1906-June 26, 1986). He married Vesta Marie Helsby (August 24, 1911-August 31, 1997) in California. Milton moved to Glendale, California, as a young man, and this is where he made his home. He worked at the knitting mill. They had two children.

Submitted by Arlene O'Keefe

OSCAR & ANNA (BRADTMUELLER) DOCTOR

Oscar Doctor, the third child of Louis and Julia Doctor, and his wife Anna (Bradtmueller) Doctor had six children.

The first child was Aaron Frederick Doctor (March 7, 1920-March 1, 2001). He married Mildred Rose Sponseller (January 2, 1924-March 3, 1982) on September 17, 1949 at Emmanuel Lutheran Church, Soest. He served in the Army during WWII, farmed, and was employed at the International Harvester in Fort Wayne. They had five children.

The second child was Clinton Lewis Theodore Doctor. He married Helen Marcile Mohr on August 23, 1947. Clinton purchased the farm at 7418 Flatrock Road, Hoagland, Indiana, on December 14, 1963, and was the fourth Doctor to own the family farm. He was an employee of Allen County before farming. In addition to farming he was employed by a sheet metal company. Clinton earned his private pilot license through Baer Field. Helen was employed by the Kresge Corporation for 26 years and was part of their management team for 15 years. Clinton and Helen were presented with the Hoosier Homestead Award on October 23, 1984. They had five children.

Karl Heinrich Oscar Doctor and Anna Bradtmueller-Doctor

The third child was Selma Bertha Doctor (February 8, 1924-July 29, 1998). She married Roy Rudolph Hans on August 10, 1946, at Emmaus Lutheran Church. Roy was a graduate of the General Electric apprentice school of drafting. He served in the Navy during WWII. Selma retired from General Electric after 34 years. They had four children.

The fourth child was Doris Viola Doctor. She married William Gustave Rathert (June 26, 1926-December 19, 1999) on June 29, 1946 at Emmanuel Lutheran Church, Soest. William made his living at Fruhaugf Corporation. They had four children.

The fifth child was Julia Edna Doctor. She married Garland Gerald Roby (July 19, 1924-December 26, 1965) on August 10, 1946, at Emmaus Lutheran Church. Garland was a graduate of General Electric Apprentice School of Drafting. He served the Air Force during WWII. At age 41, he drowned in the St. Joe River during a scouting event. They had five children. Julia married Edmund Schulz on January 23, 1970, at Gethsemane Lutheran Church, Fort Wayne. He was a graduate of the school of engineering at Purdue University. He was employed with I&M Electric Company, and he had one daughter.

The sixth child was Vesta Della Doctor (January 28, 1931-April 7, 2000). She married Wayne Arthur Lee (April 24, 1927-June 27, 1987) on April 28, 1948, at Emmanuel Lutheran Church, Soest. Wayne made his living as a truck driver for Hoagy's. They had six children.

Submitted by Brent Doctor

DODANE FAMILY

Arlene Lee Dodane was born in Fort Wayne, Indiana on March 28, 1936, and married Robert Eugene Curts, who was born in Mt. Carmel, Illinois on February 10, 1936. The ceremony was performed at St. Mary's Catholic Church. Two children were born of this union; Robert Michael Curts born May 15, 1959 at Madigan Army Hospital in Tacoma, Washington, and Connie Lynn Curts Carter Cramblit born March 5, 1961 at Lutheran Hospital in Fort Wayne, Indiana.

To follow the Dodane ancestory one has to go back to France in the1830s. France was a turbulence of unrest at this time. Between the 1830 revolution and the apprehension of the revolution to come in 1848, many families fled to the United States. One such family was the Dodanes.

The Dodane family came from the village of Morteau near Besancon, France, a few kilometers from the Swiss border. In 1838 Constantine Dodane, wife Genereuse Marie Favret Dodane, and their children boarded the ship Xylon at Le Havre, France and arrived in New York in June, 1838, a journey taking over two months. Constantine was 61 years old at the time. They made their way to Louisville, Ohio, in Starke County where Constantine remained until his death in 1856.

Frank Joseph and Mary Artemis Monnot Dodane

Constantine's son, Joseph Marcellin Dodane, born in France in 1813, married Caroline Pequignot in Starke County on June 8, 1846. They left Starke County soon after and settled east of New Haven, Indiana, where, along with other French families, they named the area Little Besancon. Farming was the main occupation of the community.

Visiting missionary priests would say mass in the homes of the settlers. Joseph's log cabin was one of the first homes used for this purpose. His name is on the sanctuary window of the present St. Louis Besancon Catholic Church.

Caroline died in 1867 giving birth to their eighth child, who also died soon after. Joseph was left to raise their seven children. He never remarried.

Frank Dodane, their oldest son, was born in 1853. He married Mary Artemis Monnot on July 1, 1875. Mary's French family had also settled in Besancon, Indiana. They continued the family tradition of farming. Of this union eight children were born. Frank died in 1913, and his widow died in 1927 after being hit by a car. Both Frank and Mary are buried in the cemetery next to the St. Louis Besancon Catholic Church.

Charles J., son of Frank and Mary Dodane, was born February 11, 1882. He married Alma Lydia Corneille on August 14, 1906. Her family of French ancestors orginially settled in the St. Vincent area in Fort Wayne. Charles and Alma's children were Hilda, Norbert, Elmer (Al), LaVonne, Howard, Mary, Edith and Joseph (who died soon after birth). Charles left the farm and moved to Fort Wayne. He worked at Penn Company and Dudlo, and died in 1937. His widow died 30 years later in 1967. They are buried in the Catholic Cemetery on Lake Avenue in Fort Wayne.

Their son Norbert was born in 1908 and married Imogene L. Brooks on April 28, 1932, in Indianapolis, Indiana. The French line was broken as Imogene was Scottish and English. They had one child, Arlene L. Dodane Curts. Norbert was employed at Wayne Pump until his death at the age of 42 in 1951. He is buried at the Catholic Cemetery on Lake Avenue in Fort Wayne. His widow then married Charles Hubert. She passed away in 1972, and is buried outside of Payne, Ohio at Blue Creek Cemetery.

Submitted by Arlene Curts

FRANCOIS JOSEPH & JOSEPH MARCELLIN DODANE

Joseph Marcellin Dodane (1815-1875) was the first of his family to come from France to America, having sailed from Havre on the *Sully* and arriving in New York 10 April 1837. His father, Felix Constantine (1877-?) and Constantine's wife, Marie Genereuse Favret, arrived in New York aboard the *Xylon* in June 1838. With them were six more of their children: Francois Joseph (1814-1892), Marie Cesarie (1817-1895), Rosalie (1820-?), Marie Eleonore (1821-?), Jean Baptiste (1825-1887) and Eugene (1829-?). As many of Constantine's descendants were farmers, it is suspected that he was also. They settled in Stark County, Ohio. While it appears that the younger children stayed in Ohio, the two oldest sons moved on to Allen County.

Francois Joseph Dodane married Justine Monnot in Louisville, Ohio. They were the parents of Felicite (1850-?), Amadeus (1852-1935), Louise (1854-?), Marie Eulalia (1856-1916), Catherine (1858-1939), Pierre Francis (1860-1940), Marie Eugenie (Jane) (1862-1916), Stephanie Frances (1865-1882), Elizabeth (1867-1955), Emma (1871-1962), and Louis (1873-1879).

Pierre Francis was born in Ohio, but later moved to Allen County where he married Mary Sarah Girardot (1869-1953) in 1886 at St. Louis Besancon Catholic Church. They were the parents of nine children: Isabella (1887-1978), Alma (1888-1949), Bertha (1890-1970), Helene (1892-1973), Lillian (1893-?), William (1896-1981),

Golden Wedding Anniversary of Mr. and Mrs. Peter Francis Dodane.

Zoa Marie (1897-1986), Henrietta (1900-1989), and LaVonne (1906-1973).

Isabella Dodane was born in Besancon and married Albert Smith (1881-1958). They had four children, Mary Angeline (1909-1976), Leroy (1911-1994), Zoa Marie (1913-2004), and Charles.

Leroy Smith was born in Texas and married Mary Alice Parrot (1912-2003). They had one daughter, Barbara Rose, who was born in Fort Wayne.

After coming to America, Joseph Marcellin Dodane lived for a time near Canton, Ohio, where he married Caroline Pequignot (1826-1867) in 1846. Before 1850 they moved to eastern Allen County where they acquired a farm and built a log cabin. Their children, all born in Allen County, were Francis Joseph (1853-1913), Mary Rose (1855-1908), Philomene (1856-1927), Edward (1858-1913), Charles (1860-1933), Rose (1862-1936), Caroline (1864-1901), and Francois Louis (July-Sep.1867). Joseph's wife died in July 1867, and Joseph died in 1875.

Rose Dodane was born in New Haven, and married Jean Baptiste Langard. They had three children: Lillian (1883-1960), Joseph (1885-1955), and Rosella (1888-1955).

Lillian Victoria Langard was born in Fort Wayne, and married Joseph Walter Parrot in 1905. They had six children, John (1906-1965), Frank (1908-1973), Catherine Josephine (1910-1965), Mary Alice (1912-2003), Richard (1916-1997), and Joseph Walter, Jr. (1920-1994).

Joseph Parrot, Jr., married Patricia Pease, and they had five children, all born in Fort Wayne: Sharon Rose, John, Joseph Edward (1949-2003), James, and Jerome.

Joseph Marcellin Dodane and his family were among the early French settlers in the Besancon area, and when the missionary priests came to say Mass for the families, his log cabin was one of the homes used before the construction of St. Louis Church. In recognition of his support of the church, his name is to be found on the left hand sanctuary window.

Submitted by Barbara Smith Landgren.

MARY (SHEEHAN) DODANE

Mary Sheehan was born April 11, 1910, and she died on February 12, 1946. She was only thirty-five years old and cancer was the cause. She was the seventh child and fourth daughter of John L. and Bertha (Poorman) Sheehan. She was born in Jackson Township along U.S. 30 and received her schooling from the Stevenson School and one year of high school at Monroeville. Mary worked at the Dudlow Wire Co. on Wall Street and also the General Electric in Fort Wayne as did her future husband, Merlin Dodane. He was also a native of Jackson Township, born in 1910. They were married in 1931 and always lived in Fort Wayne, Indiana. Of this union were born two sons, Gordon born April 18, 1934, married Barbara Lauer; Lawrence born December 19, 1937, married Judith Weingartner. Merlin remarried to have help caring for his young sons. Her name was Rose Barl, a spinster. In July of 1952 Merlin died unexpectedly of a cerebral hemorrhage. Both are buried in St. Louis Besanson Cemetery (new section).

Submitted by Judy Dodane

WALTER DODGE

Fort Wayne natives fondly remember the signs of such notable companies as Seyferts Potato Chips, Joe Goldstein & Sons, Burlsey & Company, Borden's Ice Cream, Maiers Menswear, Acme Bar, Key Hotel, Key Lanes, Azars Big Boy, Fortmeyers, Rogers Markets, Rice Oldsmobile, Burdsal-Haffner Paint Co., Scott's Grocery, and Gouloff's Paramount Grille. What many don't know is the man responsible for all those signs, Walter Dodge.

Born three years after the turn of the 20th century in Bluffton, Ohio, Walter was one of eight children. Family life was irreparably severed at the tender age of eight when his mother died and the siblings were divided among various family and church members. Forced to be self-reliant and courageous, and armed with an eighth-grade education, spirited and adventurous Walter Dodge was eager to set his own course. He worked in Detroit, Chicago and San Francisco, returning home at 21 when his childhood sweetheart, Iva Marie Stager, informed him she had another suitor.

Walter and Marie married in 1924, and Walter began his career as a sign maker in Lima, Ohio. In 1925 he had an offer to work for an Indiana company, G & H Sign, and Walter and his new bride moved to Fort Wayne. Neon signage was new to the area, and Walter seized the opportunity to further develop his talent. He worked on the eight-foot neon roof sign for Tri State Bank, later known as Fort Wayne National Bank, signage for multiple John Deer Implement Company locations, the Indiana Hotel marquee, and the original Emboyd (now known as the Embassy) Theatre sign.

During the Depression, G & H filed for bankruptcy, and Walter lost his job. That became the impetus to start his own sign company, Dodge Displays. Moving his family and business to a house at the corner of Oxford and Wiebke Streets, he expanded the garage into a shop where he would design and build signs, bend neon and handletter trucks, and his business sign, Dodge Displays, became a recognizable landmark.

Walter and Marie raised three children, Joan, Winifred and Richard. Dick worked along side his father from a very early age and later utilized his own talent and training to head his company, Dodge & Associates, one of Fort Wayne's prominent advertising agencies during the late 1960s to mid 1980s.

Walter Dodge worked many years beyond retirement age in his original shop, and he lost his wife of 57 years to cancer in 1981. In 2004, a three-piece neon sign, "Seasons Greetings," designed and crafted by Walter Dodge circa 1950 and traditionally hung in the shop window during the holiday season for several decades, was donated to the Embassy Theatre to honor Walter Dodge. It was given by his children: Joan (Dodge) Sterling, Winifred (Dodge) Schelper, Richard Dodge; grandchildren: Steven Sterling, Deborah (Sterling) Pierce, Sandra Sterling, Dawn (Dodge) Nolan, Andrew Dodge; and great-grandchildren: Blythe Nolan, Evan Nolan, and Ian Sterling.

Submitted by Dick Dodge

CONRAD DIETRICK ERNST DOEHRMANN FAMILY

Conrad Dietrick Ernst Doehrmann was the patriarch of the Doehrmann family who came from Germany. Born on February 18, 1817 in Windheim, Minden, Prussia, he left in late June of 1836 from the port of Bremen on the ship Sophia arriving in New York on August 8, 1836. He remained in New York for one year and then settled in Preble Township in 1839. He purchased 80 acres of farm ground, 20 of which he sold to Zion Lutheran Church (Freidheim). On April 15, 1842, Conrad married Sophia Wilhelmina Zwick. Sophia was born February 2, 1822 to Gerhard Henry Zwick and Sophia Dorothy Elizabeth Schroeder in Buchholz, Westfalen, Prussia. She was baptized at Petershagen Evangelical Lutheran Church in Buchholz, Westfalen.

Doehrmann Tire Service. Walter W. Doehrmann (left), Douglas B. Doehrmann (right). Circa 1980

Conrad and Sophia had eight children, one of whom was Ernst Friederich Wilhelm (William) born December 27, 1850 and died December 17, 1927. He moved to Fort Wayne around 1866. Listed in the Fort Wayne City Directory 1879/1880, William Doehrmann was a border at 208 Madison Street. He was co-owner of the Doehrmann & Hitzeman grocery at 56 Barr Street. The other owner was George Hitzeman. The business at the time of his death was at 622-24 Barr Street. At that time sons Fred and Martin were involved in the grocery with him. William married Sophia Schroeder on October 21, 1880. Both William and Sophia were raised in the German farming community in Preble Township, Adams County, Indiana. Both of their families were pioneers and had a connection to Zion Lutheran Church in Adams County. In 1900 the family lived in Fort Wayne at 339 Washington Street and in the 1920s lived at 1015 East Washington Street. They were members of St. Paul's Lutheran Church. William was a member of the city board of works during the administration of Mayor H.C. Berghoff and served 16 years on the Fort Wayne City Council representing the eighth ward, as well as being the president of the Retail Grocers Association. At the time of his death he was the organization's treasurer.

William and Sophia had six children, the second of whom was Frederick Henry born January 31, 1884. Frederick married Frieda A. Trier on her twenty-first birthday, June 16, 1908. They had four children, Leona, Valette, Walter and Lloyd. Walter William Doehrmann was born January 23, 1915 and died July 2, 1992. He married Genevieve Ethel Dunlap on September 5, 1937. Walter worked as a supervisor at General Electric during the war. In 1947 he opened the Doehrmann Tire Service, a Mobile gas station, at 601 East State Boulevard, Doehrmann Tire Service was one of the first businesses in town to sell freshly cut Christmas trees beginning the day after Thanksgiving. Doug, Walt's eldest son was born February 12, 1939. He helped to run the business and took over the management of the business upon Walter's retirement. Doug married Jane Ann Guhl on April 23, 1960. Many members of the Doehrmann family live in and around Fort Wayne today.

Submitted by Jennifer Wiehe

WALTER ANTHONY & COLLEEN MALOY DOERFLEIN FAMILY

Walter Anthony Doerflein was born May 23, 1916, in his family's home in Cedar Grove in Franklin County, Indiana, the son of Charles Edward Doerflein and Mathilda Rose Wuestefeld. Charles and Mathilda were grandchildren of German immigrants. His family attended Holy Guardian Angels Catholic Church in Cedar Grove, where Walter also attended school as a child. He graduated from Brookville High School in 1934. He finished his higher education at Indiana University in Bloomington, Indiana, earning a B.A. in 1938. He was head basketball and baseball coach at St. Mary's Catholic High School in Anderson and Washington-Clay High School, South Bend. He served in the Navy during World War II. In 1946, he started his own business in Fort Wayne, Walter A. Doerflein Insurance & Financial Services, Inc. By the early 1950s, his first marriage to Josephine Hartman had ended in divorce. During this time, he continued to build his business, first located on Wells Street above the Freeman Jewelry store, then at 463 East Pontiac Street.

Walter and Colleen Maloy Doerflein, about 1959

Charles and Marie (Taylor) Maloy, 1925

In 1955, he met Colleen Perth Maloy when she applied for a secretarial job with his business. They married in Fort Wayne on July 2, 1959. Colleen was born in Monroeville, Indiana, on June 1, 1930, the daughter of Charles William Maloy and Edna Marie Taylor. Colleen graduated from Monroeville High School as the Salutatorian in 1948. In the 1950s, she worked for Magnavox in Fort Wayne and sang with the Magnavox Choir. After she and Walter married, they had three daughters: Stephanie, Jennifer, and Kimberly.

Walter and Colleen eventually relocated their business to 1201 East State Street, where Colleen eventually worked with him. Together, they traveled the world while attending many insurance business conventions.

Colleen's father, Charles William Maloy, was born in Monroeville, Indiana, on March 8, 1899, the son of Thomas Murphy Maloy and Margaret Ellen "Ella" Vizard. In 1917, Charles began working for the Pennsylvania Railroad Company, first as a trackman, then as a brakeman, then as a conductor. Charles' father, Thomas Murphy Maloy, was born June 13, 1862, in Ohio, the son of Charles Maloy and Margaret Murphy, immigrants from Ireland. By 1900, Thomas had arrived in Allen County, Indiana, and was working as a saloon keeper in Monroeville.

Colleen's mother, Edna Marie Taylor, was born in Monroeville, Indiana, on March 1, 1902, the daughter of Charles R. Taylor and Daisy Mae Null. Charles was born in Auglaize County, Ohio, and Daisy Mae was a native of Allen County, Indiana. Marie graduated from Monroeville High School in 1921. After graduation, she went to work for S.F. Bowser'in Fort Wayne. Marie and her sister, Maude, rode the interurban from Monroeville to work in Fort Wayne. Charles and Marie met at a wedding reception in Monroeville. They were married on December 22, 1925, in Hoagland, Indiana, and had two children: Gayle and Colleen, in later years, Marie worked at W & D's in Fort Wayne and then at the Irene Byron Health Center.

Submitted by Colleen Doerflein

DORAN FAMILY

Jerry Doran was a self-made successful businessman in Allen County, well-known and well-liked. He owned and operated several businesses, including grocery stores, used and new car lots, and salvage yards, the most notable being Jerry Doran Auto Parts on Brooklyn Avenue, a fixture in the city for many years. When he retired he became active in the Kiwanis and was elected state governor in 1992.

Originally from Peru, Indiana, he met his wife, Dorothy Jean Briggs, at a dance in her hometown of Logansport where they were married in 1940. They then moved to Fort Wayne where their first son, Terry, was born in 1941. He was followed by three more sons: Jan, Rick and Chris.

In late December 1962, at age 42, Dorothy Jean ended her life by swallowing sleeping pills. Terry was about to graduate from Indiana University, Jan was a teen-ager, Rick was nine, and Chris was four months old. In the summer of 2000 Rick, 47, "followed in his mother's tortured footsteps" (*Journal Gazette*) and shot and killed himself, and his wife, Dale. Rick was a talented singer/songwriter/novelist who was reduced to working as a computer programmer to pay the bills.

In between suicides Chris managed to grow up and moved as far away from Allen County as he could get, to Australia, where he is an award-winning author and a teacher at the University of Newcastle. Jan, a poet and teacher, also escaped, to Traverse City, Michigan. Terry, bless his heart, still lives in Allen County. In 2004 he survived a five bypass open heart surgery. He gives all the credit to the skilled medical personnel who worked so hard to save his life, but adds "Don't hold it against them. They meant well."

He somehow managed to produce documentaries on life in the area, ran the Loft, an open space for artistic expression, published a book and wrote editorials railing against the city for being named after a genocidal maniac. He also started the *Fort Wayne Folk School*, which is credited with being the inspiration for the creation of the women's movement in the city, and *Theater for Ideas*, a community discussion program that helped to found the cable access television system that is enjoyed by so many. "For the most part," he says, "the people who have benefited have never forgiven me."

The boys grew up in the preachings of the Lutheran Church here in the City of Churches. All but Jan graduated from Concordia Lutheran High School, and all became disillusioned when they learned that the founder, Martin Luther, advocated rounding up Jewish human beings and locking them in a barn and setting it on fire.

Jerry Doran died of cancer in late July 1999, two months before the birth of his only grand child and almost exactly one year before his son Rick made his exit.

Submitted by Terry Doran

THOMAS DORSEY

Scipio Township, Allen County was the settlement of many Dorseys.

Benjamin Dorsey was born in June 1786 in Elloughton, Yorkshire, England. He was a wagon maker by trade and became a preacher of the Methodist Episcopal faith. Benjamin came to

America in 1830; his family the following year, first settling in Milan, Erie County, Ohio. They moved to Scipio Township, Allen County, Indiana, in 1842. He was the first Methodist preacher in Scipio Township, where he preached in a log church near where the present United Methodist Church now stands on State Road #37 ("Ridge Road") in Scipio Township. He died in Scipio Township, September 7, 1865.

Benjamin Dorsey married Jane Jefferson (1791 - December 23, 1844). They had ten children who were all born in England: William, George, Sarah Ann, Robert, John, Thomas, Mary Ann, Christopher and twin brother, and Jonathan. Benjamin's sons, George and Robert, came to Scipio Township, March 16, 1838 when this part of Indiana was yet a forest inhabited by Indians, bears and wolves. After the death of Jane, Benjamin, Mary Ann, John and Thomas came to Scipio Township.

Thomas and Polly Whaley Dorsey

Thomas Dorsey, (September 5, 1824 - April 11, 1885), married Polly M. Whaley (August 26, 1831 - March 1, 1904) on August 26, 1849. They had three children: Sarah Ann, Allen (July 7, 1878 - November 21, 1944), and Phoebe E. (June 11, 1861 - July 31, 1939). Thomas and Polly Dorsey settled on land along Allen Road, Scipio Township, Allen County. The original family homestead, where Thomas and Polly lived, is where Phoebe, her daughter Donnie, and her daughter Doris were all born. Although the house is no longer there, that location is the present site of Doris' daughter, Sue Bryson's, home.

Phoebe E. married Ira Nelson (February 2, 1864 - August 26, 1921) on August 18, 1886. They had seven children, five of whom died shortly after childbirth. The two remaining children were Ralph Verge and Donnie Dessie (March 23, 1900 - October 2, 1941).

Donnie D. married Clair L. Warstler (November 20, 1893 - September 19, 1961) on May 10, 1920. They had four children: Kemuel George (February 23, 1921 - January 24, 1992), Gera Estes (July 30, 1922 - January 15, 2002), Doris Ruth, December 20, 1924, and Violet Esther who died shortly after birth. Clair was honorably discharged from the army in WWI. With Clair shell-shocked from the war and the Great Depression, these were difficult times for the family.

The U.S. Navy Seabees, a construction battalion in WWII, gave Kemuel and Gera a lifelong purpose in construction work. They helped build many roads and bridges in the tri-state area. Along with their great-great-grandfather Benjamin Dorsey, they were missionaries. Kemuel started many Southern Baptist churches in the Fort Wayne and surrounding areas.

Doris' Christian faith has been important in raising her family as well. One daughter, Shannon, married Earl J. Bercot, who became a pastor. The missionary heritage has continued in the Dorsey family since they started an Independent Baptist Church in Saint Ignace, Michigan, in 1992. Doris married Delta Paul Inlow (October 10, 1920), on April 3, 1943. Doris and D. Paul purchased the rest of the farmland from her brothers in 1946. They moved into an existing home that had been built by Doris' great Uncle Allen and great Aunt Daisy Dorsey. Both the home and original barn has parts of native wood - some of the barn beams are hand-hewed and have pegs to help support the structure. The barn was built in 1903, and plans for the house were made in August of 1904. They are still successful in farming the homestead land today.

They have raised a family of six children: Gary A. Inlow (June 25, 1944), Sue I. Bryson (May 27, 1947), Sharon R. Inlow-Rose (May 2, 1952), Shannon J. Bercot (September 26, 1955), Shawn E. Nichols (April 2, 1959), and Sharman A. Knapp (August 31, 1960). They have ten grandchildren and four great-grandchildren. One great-grandchild, Shaelyn M. Iyer, was born exactly 100 years after her great-great-grandmother Donnie Dessie Nelson!

Submitted by Sharon Inlow-Rose

DOTY FAMILY

Doty road off State Road 37 in east Allen County was named after Solomon Doty. Solomon was the eighth generation descendent of Edward Doty who came over on the Mayflower, which landed at Plymouth Rock in December 1620. What has come down in American tradition, as the "First Thanksgiving" was actually a harvest festival. In the spring of 1621, the colonists planted their first crops in abandoned fields. While they had limited success with wheat and barley, their corn crop proved very successful, thanks to Squanto [Tisquantum] who taught them how to plant corn, using fish as fertilizer. In October of 1621, the Pilgrims celebrated their first harvest with feasting and games, as was the custom in England, as well as prayer. The celebration served to boost the morale of the 50 remaining colonists and also to impress their allies.

Edward came over as an indentured servant and signed the Mayflower Compact, the first document that set laws for the new land of America. Edward was one of only 52 people to survive the first, harsh winter that the pilgrims endured. He went on to marry Faithe Clark and have nine children. Records of the time indicate that Edward was involved in the last sword duel held in Plymouth. Luckily for his descendents, he survived that duel. He died in Plymouth in 1655 at the age of 55. Some of his children went on to New Jersey and ultimately from those lines would settle in Allen County, Indiana. It was six generations later that the Doty line moved to Milan Township in Allen County. Joseph and Rachel Doty had nine children that included Solomon Doty. When he was older, Solomon purchased his homestead from the money that he saved from teaching school.

Front, Estella Jane Doty; Row 2, Solomon and Sarah Doty; Row 3, Emma Jerusha Doty; Row 4, Philip Henry Doty and Joseph Elmer Doty.

With family members scattered in and around northeast Indiana and western Ohio, the family decided to have its first family reunion, which was held in 1924. Records from the third reunion indicate that 105 people attended and the fourth reunion had 150 attendees. Only a few reunions were cancelled due to the various wars of the twentieth century. Many families, including Marshall and Pat (Doty) Kellermeier, volunteered their homes and several reunions were held in the parks of Fort Wayne. Out of all the reunions two families were almost always there, Robert and Bertha Stauffer, and Forest and Edna Smith from Ohio, made the trip and always had a kind word and smile for everyone.

The newest member of the Doty line and thirteenth generation Mayflower descendent, and seventh generation Allen County resident is Gabrielle Rose Mix. Gabrielle was born March 16, 2005 to Brad and Nicole (Jensen) Mix.

Many thanks go out to Philip C. Doty, current family historian, and the late Philip H. Doty and Harriet (Mae) Daniels for their many years of family history gathering and preservation.

Submitted by Nancy Doty Mix.

HUBERT OSCAR & NORA ELLEN (GOYINGS) DOUD

Harvey M. Doud and Mary Belle Jones had two sons: Hubert Oscar Doud, born September 30, 1900, and Delbert Edward Doud, born September 2, 1902. Mary Belle died July 15, 1907, of gastric tuberculosis, in Peru County, Indiana. Harvey married Eva Kissinger, a schoolteacher, to help raise his sons. Hubert graduated from The Watch Making School in Butler, Indiana. He went to Fort Wayne, Indiana, looking for a job to use his new skill. A position opened at the General Electric Company in the Meter Division. He noticed a lovely lady across from him, Nora E. Goyings. She was born February 21, 1904 in Cecil, Ohio. Her father, Jesse Albert Goyings, and mother, Lillian May Burke, were married March 18, 1900. Six siblings were born.

Nora was raised on farms in Ohio and Michigan until her father, Jesse, died December 1, 1921. Nora came to Fort Wayne, Indiana, to General Electric to work. Now they were both at GE in Fort Wayne, Indiana.

Delbert returned from Missouri and said "there are no watchmakers in Missouri and Hubert could make a fortune." So Hubert and Nora married March 1, 1923, and went to Desloge, Missouri, and set up a shop. It was a poor town and nobody had any watches! Hubert fixed clocks and made rings and other art objects until they decided to return to Fort Wayne, Indiana, for better prospects. A daughter, Barbara Ellen, born June 3, 1925, and a son, Merlin Hubert,

Indiana Senators and Nora E. Doud, age 87, at Spring Briefing

born November 3, 1926, were born in Desloge, Missouri.

Hubert bought the Art Watch Company on Court Street across from the Allen County Court House. There he built a following for his shop, he joined The Junior Chamber of Commerce and they voted him The Businessman Most Likely to Succeed in Fort Wayne in 1930.

Hubert and Nora bought a home at 1406 Third Street. He built a brick garage, planted an asparagus patch and a huge arbor for four kinds of grapes. He also put in a sunken fishpond, which the children loved. Two more children were born: a son, Norman Douglas, born November 24, 1928, and a daughter, Gloria Annette, born December 1, 1930. Hubert developed a lifestyle that did not include the family and left the home and family except for occasional visits. He continued owning the Art Watch Company. He died January 11, 1965. He is buried in Greenlawn Cemetery, Fort Wayne, Indiana.

Nora fended for the family as well as she could by farming and selling produce from the two lots on Third Street. It was a very sparse life for all on Third Street. Nora retuned to work at GE and traveled to nineteen countries on vacations. She belonged to the Republican Inner Circle and attended a Spring Briefing Meeting, in Washington, D.C. honoring President George H. W. Bush. She did not tell anyone that she was going until she returned! She lived at the Third Street home for 69 years. She died September 12, 1997, and is buried in Lindenwood Cemetery.

Barbara married three times, Harold R. Johnson, Robert S. Richard, and Edward C. Belote, and has seven wonderful children. Merlin enlisted in the U.S. Navy. He married Bertha Stark. They had one son Royce Edmond. He married two more times. Norman and Barbara married and had one daughter DeElla Sue. His second wife is Jacquelyn Boggs. Gloria married James Schory and had two daughters, Kathryn Sue and Nancy Annette and son, Daniel Lee Schory. James Schory died August 10, 1998. Gloria died May 23, 2004. They are buried in the Catholic Cemetery.

See the rest of the story of Barbara Ellen (Doud) Johnson-Richard-Belote in another part of this book.

Submitted by Barbara E. Belote

MERLIN HUBERT DOUD

Merlin Hubert Doud was born in Desloge, Missouri, on November 3, 1926. His parents were Hubert O. Doud and Nora Ellen Goyings. He grew up in Fort Wayne, Indiana, during World War II. He quit high school and joined the U.S. Navy at age 17. He studied to be a signalman and learned the International Morse Code, Semaphore Code and others. He was assigned a ship, an L.S.T. and went through the Panama Canal and headed to the South Pacific to battle Japan.

Merlin's job was a signalman up on the bridge with the captain, sending and receiving messages using a blinker light utilizing International Morse Code. When in a convoy of many ships, his job was to watch the flagship and interpret maneuvering instructions so all would turn or move at the same time, avoiding ship-hitting-ship at sea. During the battle of Okinawa, he was in a small boat with the Marines and their equipment, making their invasion. Merlin was their signalman; since he did not get killed, he returned to the ship and joined a gun crew shooting down Kamikaze [suicidal] planes. After the war was won, he returned to the United States. A few islands and places he was at were Manila [Philippines], Guam, Lete, Formosa [Taiwan], Tsingtoa [China].

Merlin and Louise Doud

After Merlin returned to Fort Wayne, he studied to become a machinist and tool and die maker. He also did watch repair with his dad, Hubert O. Doud, owner of The Art Watch Company in Fort Wayne, Indiana.

After one failed marriage and gaining a son, Royce E. Doud, he remarried and they all moved to California in 1952. He got work at Convair Aircraft Company building guidance systems for intercontinental ballistic missiles. The Cold War with Russia was starting. In 1957, after his second failed marriage, he took his son Royce and moved north to Sacramento, California, for cleaner air and a new start. Merlin got a machinist and tool-making job at Aero Jet, building rocket engines for NASA, U.S. Air Force, etc. They built ICBMs and the O.M.S. engines for the Space Shuttle. Engines of many kinds for various purposes were built for going to the moon and back, and for most space flights and defense of the country. He was doing watch repair on the side.

In 1958, Merlin met the love of his life on a dance floor. Louise and Merlin were taking ballroom dance lessons. She was a wonderful, talented, and caring teacher of emotionally disturbed or handicapped people. A recent widow, she started her own private school. Merlin helped her. After ten years of dating, they were married in 1968. He sold his trailer home, watch repair tools, and moved to her home. Louise ran her school, called Sierra Schools. She had four teachers on the payroll with her. She worked until she was 76 years old. Merlin worked at Aero Jet building rocket engines. At age 80, Louise showed signs of early Alzheimer's disease. In 1989 at age 62, Merlin quit work to care for her at home. After many difficult years, Louise died on January 13, 2000, at age 92. Merlin sold out and returned to Fort Wayne, Indiana, to rub his sore spots and see what the good Lord had in store for him next. On July 14, 2003, he received his Central High School Diploma at age 76. Merlin is volunteering with the R.S.V.P. organization and tinkers in a small shop he has in his garage. He is a Trustee in the Harvester Missionary Church. The future looks as bright as the promises of God.

Submitted by Merlin H. Doud

DOUGHERTY FAMILY

Mildred L. and Lyle G. Dougherty celebrated their sixtieth wedding anniversary March 6, 1986. They had three children: Neal Berlean, born/died March 1931. Sharon Cozette born August 23, 1932. Thomas Alan born February 9, 1936. The 1930s were harsh, uncertain times. They survived illnesses, near death episodes, and economic disaster. They lived through and accepted tunnel-vision, social conditions of the times. They had little money and lots of love.

Lyle George Aloysius was born November 11, 1905 in Tocsin, Indiana, to Thomas William Dougherty and Bertha Beard. He was one of four children who lived and one older brother who died young. Lyle was empathetic and generous. He was pragmatic and planned for the future. Lyle was instrumental in completing the road around Lake Gage in Steuben County in the late 1940s. And in the early 1950s, as the elected Business Agent for General Electric's Local 901, he designed and promoted the larger Union Hall built at 1427 Broadway north of 1635 Broadway General Electric.

T.W. was over six feet tall, adventuresome and an entrepreneur. Bertha was a petite, gentle, intelligent English and Music Teacher. She later taught her own children those skills. Bertha also gave her children a strong sense of family ties. In 1889, when T.W. was eighteen years old, his father was awarded a Government Land Grant in Michigan's Upper Peninsula. The two of them traveled from Villa North, to Trinary. They logged the forestland and plotted a town they named "Dougherty." Later the name was changed to Trinary. T.W. was called "Tommy Will" by his father and often called "Big Tom" by his friends. Bertha was teaching there. T.W. and Bertha were married in Trinary, Michigan, on April 6, 1897.

Before prohibition was passed, T.W. owned several different taverns in the Wells and Allen County area. Around the turn of the Twentieth Century he owned the tavern at the southeast comer of Harrison and Columbia Streets. Lyle worked in his father's saloons when he was very young. At twelve or fourteen years of age, Lyle went on the Apprentice Program with General Electric. But Lyle quit school and rode the rails (hopped on freight trains) to Florida when he was seventeen years old. In the 1920s, T.W. and Bertha purchased the Jacob Bower home built in 1846 in Fort Wayne's Bloomingdale. It is now the C. M. Sloan and Sons Funeral Home at 1327 Wells Street. T.W. and Bertha invested in the **John F. Class Mineral Fume Health System** franchise. It was among the first alternative health systems in the United States. Mr. John F. Class originated the Health System somewhere in the southwestern United States. In the 1930s and early 1940s, President Franklin D. Roosevelt would make famous a similar alternative health practice when he vacationed at a Mineral Hot Springs in the Southeast. The Mineral Vapo Bath was respected for the relief it offered to those suffering with debilitating diseases. Clients came regularly from great distances to take a Fume Bath. The Mineral Bathhouse (as it was referred to) was mysterious to those that didn't understand what a Mineral Fumes Health System offered. Bertha's and T.W.'s grandchildren later learned from people living in the Bloomingdale neighborhood that some unenlightened neighbors rumored it to be a house of ill repute. Seventy years later, these incorrect rumors have evolved into an urban legend.

Mildred Dougherty, 1926 Lyle Dougherty, 1934

T. W. was born in Villa North, Indiana, to Francis (Frank) and Melvina Jane (Shady). Frank was a Union soldier in the Civil War before he married. T. W. was the only son and had six older sisters. Villa North was seven miles north of Bluffton at that time and the large Dougherty home was considered among the most modern with the newest conveniences. It contained an upstairs bathroom complete with indoor plumbing and a bathtub. Frank was the first child born in the United States to Christopher O. Dougherty and Jane Daly. In the 1830s, Frank's parents came to the United States with Christopher's cousin on a ship from Donegal or Meath counties near Dublin, Ireland. Jane and Christopher lost their first baby on the trip to America. Frank was the first born here. Christopher chose to Americanize his Irish name and spelled it Dougherty with a soft "dough" pronunciation while his cousin spelled it Daugherty with the Celtic "dock" pronunciation. Both families settled in Wells County. Christopher's parents were James Doherty and Sophia Keegan. Christopher's paternal grandparents were Christ Doherty and Mary Stevens.

Christopher's maternal grandparents were Patrick (and wife unknown) Keegan. The Doherty/Daugherty Clan was one of the largest clans in Ireland. Jane's parents were Francis Daly and Margaret Lovely. Jane's paternal grandmother's maiden name was Nugent. Her maternal grandmother's maiden name was Plunket.

Melvina Jane's family came from Fairfield County, Ohio. Her parents were Lewis Shady and Rachel Mills. Lewis Shady's parents were William and Susan (Grim) from Pennsylvania.

T.W. got his stature from his grandfather, Lewis Shady, and his dark hair and blue eyes from his father. Frank had an Irish complexion, dark hair and blue eyes. Lyle had his father's blue eyes.

At one time there was a Dougherty Reunion but it was discontinued in the 1930s.

Bertha Beard was born in South Bend, Indiana, to George Beard and Clara Spohn. George was an Architectural Engineer; he designed and built bridges. Ultimately he moved West leaving his much younger wife, Clara, and two small daughters. Clara remarried I. Darr, a medical doctor. "Doc" Darr raised the young girls and sent them to college to become teachers. Clara studied medicine and became a chiropractor. George Beard's parents were Magdalin and John Baert (Burt) of Germany. Clara's parents were David Spohn and Sarah Roof. David's grandfather, Jonathan Spohn, fought in the American Revolutionary War. David was a Union soldier and died in the battle of Chickamauga, Tennessee. His mother couldn't write to him because she couldn't read or write. His young widow, Sarah, died a year after his death of a broken heart. Sarah's parents, Margaret and Daniel Roof came from Germany in the 1840s. They were proprietors of an icehouse in South Bend and raised their granddaughter, Clara, after her parents' deaths.

Mildred Lola Barrow was born November 18, 1906 east of New Haven, Allen County, Indiana, to Irma and Allen Barrow. She had three younger siblings. When she was fifteen years old she moved to Fort Wayne and roomed with Mrs. Trier. Mrs. Trier was a widow and the owner of Trier's Amusement Park adjacent to the Swinney Homestead and Swinney Park. Mildred later roomed with her father's only sister on John Street in Fort Wayne. "Millie" worked first at Coney Byres Cigar Factory and later at Perfection Biscuit Company. She lived frugally and sent money home for her family. Millie was instructed by her mother on how to be a housemaid. It was an honorable profession for women of the time. Mildred's mother was a respected midwife and caregiver. But it was decided that Mildred could earn more money by working in Fort Wayne. Mildred was high energy. She enjoyed dancing. She and a (New Haven) neighbor boy won multiple dance contests held at the Trier's Dance Hall. She also enjoyed classical music, art, and was a consummate storyteller. Mildred described how she and Lyle met and courted. She described the drama of the 1912 Lakeside flood. She told of taking coffee and sandwiches to the soldiers leaving at the train station during the 1917 World War. She portrayed how ill she was with influenza during the pandemic epidemic in 1919. And she enjoyed telling how she and Lyle saw one another for the first time as children but never met; i.e., as recreation, Lyle and some other young, city boys would roam the old Lincoln Highway in a horse-drawn hay wagon. Young Millie regarded the wagon of noisy city boys from a hidden perch in her favorite apple tree as it went by her home.

Mildred grew up on her grandfather Barrow's homestead along the Wabash-Erie Canal. Mildred's father, Allen John Barrow, had a twin brother. Allen farmed the homestead and maintained his blacksmith shop but his interests were in science and history. He built a wireless radio and his family was among the first in the area to own a radio and entertain guests with it. Allen's father, Henry Castleman Barrow was one of the founders of the IOOF Cemetery in New Haven. In 1812, Henry's father, Richard, was in his late 20's or early 30's. He came from England and courted the fifteen year old Catherine Castleman. She was a housemaid and caregiver to the neighbor's children. He married her. Richard died of consumption (TB) and left a young widow and small children. Allen's mother Samantha Biggs had naturally curly, long, red hair. Mildred enjoyed combing her grandmother Samantha's hair. Mildred had Samantha's green eyes. Samantha's parents were Joseph Richard Biggs and Margaret George. Samatha was proud of her Scottish heritage.

Mildred and Lyle Dougherty, 1927, First Anniversary

Mildred's mother, Irma Inez Rothgeb, was born in Garcreek, Indiana. Irma's younger sister married Allen's twin brother. Irma's four children and her sister's one daughter grew up as siblings. Irma's father, Eli Rothgeb, had a twin brother. Eli was among the founders of the IOOF Cemetery in New Haven. The Rothgeb family and the Barrow family each held an annual reunion in the summer for many years. One was in June and the other was in August. To a small child it seemed as if hundreds of people were there and many sets of twins at each family's reunion. Sadly somewhere around the 1950s both of the family's reunions were discontinued.

Eli's father Ezekias, and his mother Melinda Skives were from Galloplois, Ohio. Ezekias' parents were Michael Rothgeb and Mary Doudle. Michael's parents were Barbara Bear and George Rothgeb. Michael's paternal grandfather was John Jacob Rothgeb (possibly Roadgate at one time). John Jacob married three times and outlived all three wives with a total of eighteen children. He was probably German and possibly lived in France. It's said that John Jacob's father worked five years in Egypt to get his wife out of bondage so he could marry her.

Irma's mother, Genevra Lowrey, was strikingly attractive. Genevra's parents were Abram Lowrey and Juliette Adams. Juliette left Massachusetts to travel down the Wabash Erie Canal with her new, young husband in the 1840s. Juliette's parents were Dr. Jesse and Laura (Edmunds) Adams. Her maternal grandparents were Eliphelet Edmunds and Delia Wilson. Her paternal grandfather was a minister and a brother of President Adams. The family was heart sick to see Juliette leave her affluent life style to travel into the unknown, wild new country knowing they probably would never see her again.

This information was collected through verbal and written correspondence with older relations. There's pleasure in discovering unknown relatives. There are injustices of the past that were accepted as normal. But our ancestors were just people the same as we are. Lyle as his mother before him, stressed family is first. Mildred never tired of telling stories about her "famous" forefathers. Lyle and Mildred grew up in an appalling time when children weren't protected by child labor laws. However, it's important to remember the pleasant times.

Submitted by Sharon C. Sabastion

FLOYD L. DOWELL

Floyd L. Dowell (born 1911) and Melzene F. Beachler Dowell (born 1907) were from Columbia City, Indiana, and moved to Fort Wayne after their marriage on April 12, 1936. Both came from large families that would probably be considered "poor" today. Floyd Dowell graduated from Columbia City High School; Melzene (Beachler) Dowell did not complete high school, as she was needed at home to help care for younger sisters and brothers. She later moved to Fort Wayne and was employed as a seamstress at the Fort Wayne Tailoring Company. Prior to their marriage, Floyd Dowell completed the apprenticeship program at General Electric to prepare to be a toolmaker. He was the first one from his class to complete any type of higher education beyond high school. After completing this apprenticeship, he became a toolmaker at General Electric and was employed there for nearly forty years. He was the sole support of the family. Melzene was a homemaker and never worked outside the home after their marriage.

Over the years they both became active members of the Masonic Lodge and Eastern Star in Fort Wayne. They were also members of Crescent Avenue United Methodist Church (known as Evangelical United Brethren at that time).

Floyd Dowell, being a strong believer in the importance of an education, had always saved and planned for his children to attend college. Their only child, Donna A. Dowell Caron, was born in 1944. Her story is included in this book. A son was stillborn in 1942 on the same date as Donna's birth. Donna was educated in Fort Wayne Community Schools at Rudisill Elementary, Forest Park Middle, and North Side High School, graduating in 1962. As her parents had hoped, she went on to college first at Purdue University in West Lafayette Indiana, and then transferred to St. Francis College (now the University of St. Francis), where she graduated with a B.S. degree in elementary education in 1967. Donna married Joseph I. Caron in 1966 and completed a M.S. degree in elementary education at St. Francis in 1970.

Floyd and Melzene Dowell were killed in an auto accident on December 17, 1969, at Lagro, Indiana, while traveling to visit Melzene s sister in Peru, Indiana. She always hoped to live long enough to see a grandchild and her wish was granted, when the Caron's had their first child, a daughter, Nicole, in 1968. The Dowell's did not live long enough, though, to really enjoy this granddaughter and to see a second daughter, Jennifer, born to the Carons in 1973.

The Dowell and Caron families have been residents of Fort Wayne for a combined total of over 70 years and have always been proud to call it their home and wouldn't have considered living anywhere else!

Submitted by Jennifer Murphy

CHARLES L. & ELOISE (BEERY) DOWNEY FAMILY

Charles L. and Eloise (Beery) Downey came to Allen County, Indiana, from Bluffton, Indiana, in 1948. They bought property at South Anthony and Decatur Roads and opened "Downey's Market." It was previously called "John's Place." Downey's Market even had their own trading stamps. They lived in the house next to the market with their sons, Charles and Richard. After giving up the market, Charles worked for Inland Oils Company in Waynedale. In retirement,

Walter Downey store

Downey trading stamps

Downey Market

Beery Barbershop Quartet

he kept bees, sold honey, and made beeswax candles. He was a past president of Northeastern Indiana Beekeepers Association. They also were involved with the Nut Growers Association. Charles was born November 22, 1911, in Francisco, Gibson County, Indiana, and Eloise was born August 11, 1908, in Westfield, Hamilton County, Indiana. They were married July 24, 1938, in Knightstown, Henry County, Indiana. Charles died February 3, 1985, and Eloise died October 20, 2000.

Charles' parents were Walter Festus and Carrie Ann (Lowery) Downey. They lived in Francisco, Indiana. Walter had a restaurant and pool hall in Francisco. Carrie was a seamstress and sewed children's clothing. They had four sons, Raymond, Everett, Charles and Jack. Walter was born April 7, 1872, in Francisco and lived all his life in Gibson County. Carrie was born December 31, 1880, in Oakland City, also Gibson County. They married July 3, 1905. Walter died June 16, 1939, and Carrie died March 4, 1947, in Indianapolis.

Eloise was a "birthright" Quaker. Her parents were Clarence and Grace (Brittain) Beery, who lived in Westfield, Indiana. They had three children, Eloise, Edwin Douglas and Doris. They belonged to the Westfield Monthly Meeting. Clarence worked a farm with his brother Homer. Their mother, Maggie Beery owned the farm. Clarence and his family lived in a small house on the farm. The house had a wood cooking range in the kitchen and a pot-bellied wood or coal stove in the main room. They slept in cold bedrooms on straw tick beds and used kerosene lamps. Clarence sang in a quartet and traveled widely in the area to sing. Eloise remembered a tornado at their farm and her father struggling to hold the door shut against the wind. Fortunately their house wasn't damaged, and no one was hurt. A field of corn in shocks was blown away and a horse that was in a barn was carried away and dropped in a nearby creek, dead.

Clarence was born October 19, 1883, in Hamilton County, Indiana. Grace was born March 12, 1886, also in Hamilton County. They were married July 24, 1907, in Hamilton County. Clarence died April. 2, 1930, and Grace died May 20, 1946, in Bluffton, Indiana, at her daughter's house.

Submitted by Richard A. Downey

ROBERT E. & SUZANNE JOYCE DUNLAP FAMILY

Robert Eugene Dunlap was born January 27, 1946, in Van Wert, Ohio to Charles Kohn and Donavieve Ruth (Bebout) Dunlap. Robert had six siblings, Roger, Phyllis, Nancy, Ruth, Charles, Jr. and Jerry. Robert married Suzanne Joyce Henschen on May 23, 1970 in Fort Wayne, Indiana. Suzanne was born October 25, 1946 to Edith Beatrice (Kinerk) and Chalmer Vernon Henschen in Fort Wayne, Indiana. She was the fourth child of Chalmer and Beatrice with brothers, Lynn, Noel, and Jay Henschen.

Robert graduated from Crestview High School, Convoy, Ohio in 1964. After graduation from high school he went to work for General Electric in Fort Wayne. Robert worked thirty-six years for General Electric before retiring in. 2000. He-also served four years (1966-1970) in the United States Air Force and spent eighteen months of his tour in Viet Nam. After retirement, Robert became employed with Von Maur as a part-time employee.

Suzanne graduated from Elmhurst High School, Fort Wayne in 1965. She went to work for Lincoln National Life Insurance Company where she stayed until 1992 when the Employee Benefit Division of Lincoln National Life was sold. She presently is working for Pro-Claim Plus, Fort Wayne, Indiana. Suzanne has been in the Insurance Industry as a claims benefit analyst for forty years.

Robert and Suzanne have three daughters. Cherie Renee was born June 1, 1975; Michelle Suzanne was born February 8, 1977; and Jennifer Nichole was born November 1, 1978. All three were born at Lutheran Hospital, Fort Wayne, Indiana. Cherie married Randall Hackworth from South Whitley on September 23, 2000. They have a daughter, Mallory Olivia, born July 25, 2004. Cherie, Randy and Mallory live in Brownsburg, Indiana.

Submitted by Suzanne Dunlap

DUNTEN (DUNTON) FAMILY

Horace Friend Dunten and his uncle, Thomas Dunten, were early pioneers who arrived in Allen County in 1833 from Jefferson County, New York. After finding suitable land, they returned with their families (including Ephraim H. Dunten, a veteran of the War of 1812), to settle in Perry Township.

The Dunten family arrived in America from England about 1647, and first lived in Massachussetts. It was in Sturbridge, Massachussetts where Ephraim's father (Thomas) and grandfather (Ebenezer) enlisted in the Revolutionary War. Ephraim was born in Sturbridge in 1779. The Dunten's moved to Vermont for a short time and then to upstate New York (Jefferson County) around 1800. Ephraim's father, Thomas, died in 1832 and, the following year, much of the family migrated to Allen County, Perry Township, Indiana to what is now called Huntertown.

Horace worked on the construction of the Wabash and Erie Canal through the area, buying farmland with his earnings. Horace erected the first hewn-log house (Perry Township) in 1834. The first religious meeting was held at the house of Horace F. Dunten in 1834. In 1837 Horace married Almena Timmerman, daughter of Henry Timmerman and Anna (Broughton) Timmerman who also migrated

Row 1, L to R: Horace Friend Dunten, Father (1813-1904), Alexander B. Dunten (1845-1930), Granville S. Dunten (1837-1909). Row 2, L to R: Milton B. Dunten (1843-1926, Henry C. Dunten (1852-1926), Charles J. Dunten (1859-1934)

from Jefferson County, New York to Allen County in 1834, and later settled in Swan, Noble County, Indiana. Horace and Almena had nine boys and one girl. Their children were Granville Sherwood, Manville Newton, Orville Alonzo, Milton Boyd, Alexander Burd, Winfield Scott, Friend B., Henry Clay, Mary Helen (Gump), and Charles Johnson Dunten. Five sons served in the union army during the Civil War.

In 1850, in the company with his brother George Dunten, James Ballou, and others from Allen County, Horace Dunten started overland to the gold fields of California on March 20, and arrived at Placerville (then called "Hangtown") on August 4. They remained about a year mining gold. The return trip was made by water to Colon, across the Isthmus of Panama by ox-teams to the city of Panama, then by water to Kingston, Jamaica, and on to New York, making the final lap of the homeward journey by rai1. Horace died in December, 1904 at age 91 in Huntertown, and his obituary stated "He insisted upon being carried to the polls that he might cast what he realized would be his last vote" because of failing health in November 1904.

Horace's son, Orville, died in 1871 at age 28 from an accidental gunshot. Sons Manville and Henry remained in Allen County with many descendents still residing there today. One of Manville's granddaughters, Freedonna Dunten Smith (her mother's maiden name was Hunter), was a resident of Huntertown from her birth in 1899 until her death in 2001, a life that spanned parts of three centuries. Several of Horace and Almena's children homesteaded west to Nebraska and beyond. Granville moved to Illinois, Charles to California, and Friend was last known to be in Colorado. Alexander, Winfield, Milton, and Mary moved to Nebraska.

Milton married Eliza Rhodes-Badiac in 1870 in Allen County before homesteading to Nebraska later that year. They had five children. The oldest, Horace Frank, drowned at age ten. The other four were Carrie Almena (Mawe), Effie M. (Jones), Jay F. (WWI veteran), and Mildred Adeline Dunten. Milton and Eliza moved to Omaha around 1895. Mildred Dunton married Samuel Whitten, son of Irish immigrants, in 1910 and they lived in Omaha until they died in the 1960s. Sam and Mildred had four daughters, Helen (Ralston James), Jean (Edward Morris), Dorothy (Robert Meyer), and Ruth (David Meese and Gerald Boswell).

Dorothy joined the Women's Marine Corps during World War II, and met and married Robert Meyer in San Francisco, California in 1945, a Marine from Cincinnati, Ohio. After the war in 1946, they drove across the country in a 1929 Model A Ford with fellow Marines and friends that would remain so for over sixty years, Leroy and Jonnie Martens. Robert and Dorothy have made their home in Cincinnati, Ohio since 1946. They have five children, Robert, Linda (Laub), Dennis, Michael, and Thomas, twelve grandchildren, and three great-grandchildren. Son Michael Meyer has returned to Allen County on occasion to research and reacquaint with his Dunten relatives. He and his wife Janice (Earhart) Meyer reside in Cincinnati, Ohio with children Beth, Daniel, and Nicole Meyer.

Submitted by Michael J. Meyer

DONALD & LYDIA MCCOMB DUNTEN

Donald and Lydia McComb Dunten lived their lives in or near Huntertown, Indiana, Perr Township, Allen County.

Donald's ancestors, Robert and Samuel Dunten, came to the United States in 1647 and established residences in the Jefferson County Watertown, New York, area. It is believed that Thomas, Ephraim, Horace, and Ephraim Jr Dunten came to the Huntertown area to work a abolitionists.

Donald (April 21, 1894 - March 24, 1981 was born to Elmer Lewis Dunten and Zella Izor Hunter, along with his brothers, Elmer and Jean and sisters, Bernice, Bertha Slatter, Glen Shrock and Freedonna Smith. He served in World War as an ambulance driver.

It is interesting to note that Huntertown was originally called Somerville, but the name was changed when Zella's uncle, William Todd Hunter, gave land to the Grand Rapids Railroad for a station.

Lydia's ancestors, Robert and Margaret Mc Comb, came from Ireland in 1830. James, their son, was raised by the Newbroughs as their own son when his mother became ill. The Newbroughs bought land on Auburn Road where they, and James and his wife, Margaret, built houses.

Lydia (June 17, 1899 - April 6, 1986) was born to Morton Theophilus McComb and Ro setta Bush along with her brothers, Verne, Lynn and Glen, and sister, Elsie Jones. She graduated from the Fort Wayne Normal School and began teaching at Hanna School and later at Rudisil School.

Donald was discharged from the army in 1919 and began working at the Irene Byron Sanitarium. He and Lydia were married in January 1923 and in 1924 began building their home in Huntertown where they would live the rest of their lives.

Donald and Lydia McComb Dunten (photo taken in 1973)

Donald enjoyed playing in local bands--the Mizpah Shrine band and the American Legion Post 47 band. He was liked by many and was often called upon to come fix this or mend that Lydia enjoyed activities at the Huntertown Methodist Church and often volunteered at Parkview Hospital. They spent their retirement years in Florida during the winter months.

Their children are Kathryn Schwartz, Patricia Barrett, and Stanley Dunten.

Submitted by Barbara Barrett

THOMAS & JOANNA HOWARD DUNTEN FAMILY

Thomas Dunten (1779-1832) was born in Massachusetts. He married Joanna Howard Blair (1748-1826) in 1773 in Massachusetts. She was born in Nova Scotia, Canada. They had eight children. Thomas and his father, Ebenezer, spelled Dunten or Dunton, both served in the Revolutionary War from Sturbridge, Massachusetts. Thomas moved his family to Jefferson County, New York where his third son, Ephriam Howard Dunten, fought at Sacketts Harbor, New York, during the War of 1812. Ephriam married Abigail Ann Ball (1785-1863) in 1806. After his father Thomas' death, he and his wife moved to Perry Township, Allen County, Indiana in August of 1833. Their four grown children, all of whom where born in Jefferson County, New York, moved with them. Their youngest child, Horace Friend Dunten, (1813-1904) was 21 years of age when he came to Indiana. He married Almena Timmerman (1816-1890) in 1837, in Swan Township, Noble County, Indiana. They lived in Huntertown were all eleven of their children were born. Five of their sons served as soldiers in the union army during the Civil War: Granville Sherwood, Orville Alonzo, Milton Boyd, Alexander Burd, and Winfield Scott. Their second son, Manville Newton Dunten, (1839-1912) married Martha Ann Lewis (1843-1877) in Huntertown in 1861. Manville lived in Huntertown until his death. His wife was born in Indiana. They had five children all of who lived and died in Huntertown: Lila U., Elmer Lewis, Cora Alice and Bertha May. Bertha died around the age of six. Manville married his second wife, Mary J. Beardsley, in 1881. Manville's brother, Milton Boyd, spelled his last name Dunton. Elmer Lewis Dunten, Manville and Martha's second child, married Zella Izora Hunter (1864-1938) in 1883. She was born in Allen County and her parents were Sidney and Mary Geraldine DeLong Hunter. Her grandparents were William Todd and Jane Ranney Buckingham Hunter. William T. Hunter settled in Perry Township in 1837 and later established a hotel and a tavern. Huntertown was named after him. Zella and Elmer had eight children all born in Huntertown. They lived in the house that Manville, Elmer's father, built. A daughter, Bernice Louise (1885-1981), served as a nurse in France during World War I as did a son, Donald Lewis (1894-1981). Their other children were Bertha Beryl (1888-1983), Glenn (1891-1979), Eugene Lewis (1892-?), Elmer Hunter (1896-1971), and Jean Milton (1905-?). Elmer and Zella lived in the house that Manville, Elmer's dad, built. A younger daughter, Freedonna (1899-2001), married Almon Smith (1902-1984) in 1924, and they also lived in the same house. Almon Smith had a twin brother, Alvin, and their parents were Samuel and Ida Bear Smith in Allen County. Freedonna and Almon had two children, Lewis Fred and Mardell Myrth, who were born in Allen County. Lewis married Lavern Ellen McBride, daughter of Charlotte and Grover McBride. They had three children born in Allen County and are all living in Huntertown. Mardell married James W. Messmann. They have four children who live in Fort Wayne and Huntertown area.

A photo of Horace, Alexander, Granville, Milton, Henry, and Charles Dunten can be found in the Dunten (Dunton) Family History on the opposite page.

Submitted by Cheryl Smith.

Jesse Lee Dutton and Mary Celestia with their four children, Kenneth, Carl, Lucille and Josephine.

JESSE LEE DUTTON FAMILY

Jesse Lee Dutton (1875-1937) was born in Clark Township, Ohio, to John B. and Nancy Dutton. He was orphaned in his early teens and came to live with a married brother, John, and his wife, Addie, in Williamstown, Ohio. He began admiring Mary Celestia Evans (1882-1974) and even remarked to a friend, "That's the girl I'm going to marry" and he did on January 9, 1901. She was the daughter of Benjamin David Evans, a horse and buggy doctor, and Mary Cramer Evans.

Jesse and his bride moved to Dunkirk, Ohio, where he and a cousin opened a barber shop. They were parents of four children: Kenneth, Carl, Lucille, and Josephine. A huge fire in Dunkirk burned their house and several blocks of that small town in 1913. In the fall the family moved to 2021 Nelson Street, Fort Wayne, Indiana. The four children attended Minor School on Dewald and Broadway.

Jesse and his cousin opened a barber shop on Calhoun Street near the Baker Street Pennsylvania Railroad Station. The shop was open till 8 p.m. on Saturday nights, and Mary Celestia and daughters would walk to meet Jesse. They would walk home past the Eskay Dairy Ice Cream Parlor and sometimes (but not always) stop for a treat.

Lucille Dutton Snyder and Josephine Dutton Biedenweg at a 2003 family gathering with Lucille's descendents, Barbara and Richard Hill, Charles and Ruth Snyder, Betsy and Jay VanMarkwyk, Tim and Barbara Hill, and their two children, Griffin Timothy, and Emily Elizabeth.

The four children of Jesse Lee and Mary Celestia Dutton--Kenneth, Carl, Lucille, and Josephine.

Kenneth practiced optometry in Kokomo, Indiana. Carl was a geology professor at Madison, Wisconsin , and a consultant for the U.S. Geological Survey.

Lucille, (1907-2004), graduated from South Side High School in 1926 and soon after married Irvin Leroy Snyder (1905-1954), a graduate of Central High School. Irvin was a payroll-timekeeper for International Harvester. Lucille was a homemaker, and retired from Sears on Rudisill Boulevard as the "candy lady". They had two children, Charles Richard and Barbara Ann.

Charles (1930) worked at Lincoln Life, retiring at age 55. His wife is Ruth (Carey). Barbara (1933) is an RN, and a Professor Emeritus from IPFW. She is married to Dr Richard E. Hill (1930), who is also a Professor Emeritus from IPFW. They have two married, children, Betsy (1963) Van Markwyk, and Tim (1960). Tim and Barbara J. (Simonson) have two children, Griffin (1997) and Emily (2001).

Josephine, born January 16, 1911, graduated from South Side High School and also Ball State Teachers College. After a few years of teaching, Josephine married Clarence A. Biedenweg, a graduate of Michigan University, and moved to Calumet, Michigan where he pursued his teaching career. They moved back to Fort Wayne when he was offered a contract to teach at Franklin School. After three years he became an administrator with Fort Wayne Community Schools. Josephine taught at Merle J. Abbett School for several years before accepting a mentoring position within Fort Wayne Community Schools. Josephine and Clarence retired after 34 and 40 years respectively. Josephine still lives in Fort Wayne, enjoys reading and playing the piano. She is happily the author of this family history.

Jesse, Mary Celestia, Lucille, Irvin, and Clarence are all buried in Lindenwood Cemetery.

Submitted by Josephine Biedenweg

EAGER

The Eager family's history in Scipio Township begins with Thomas Eager, a Civil War veteran who brought his family to the township from Delaware County, Ohio, in 1885. He had been a teamster for the Union forces and was nearly lost in a blizzard when walking beside the wagon to stay warm. He began to stumble, but was able to grip the end gate of the wagon and was dragged back to camp by the team, where his comrades pried his fingers from the wagon and revived him. After his discharge, Thomas married Rachel Hardin in 1865 and they set up farming and reared a family. Their children were Major, George, Lester, Amy, and Grover. They settled on a farm in South Scipio, where their children were raised.

Lester Harlan, known as Harley or Buck, married Laura Burrier in 1899. Laura was descended from Adam Burrier, one of the founding pioneers of the township, through his son, Philip. To this marriage were born three sons, Forest, Leland, and Clarence, of whom only Leland, called Lee, survived past infancy. Buck was a farmer, mechanic, and a steam engine man for the local threshing ring. It was said of him that the only thing more satisfying than a day's work in the field was if the tractor would break down and he could tear it apart to work on it. Buck died in 1932 at age 56. Laura lived until1960. Lee courted Myrtle Mae Cole (born December 20, 1902) of Newville, Indiana. They were married January 30, 1921, which was Lee's 19th birthday and they resided in the family homestead that had been built by Adam Burrier on Scipio Road. The children of Lee and Mae were Lawrence Dale, Helen, and Georgia. Lee was a farmer his whole life and had a great love of fishing. Lee passed away April 16, 1982. Mae left this life November 4, 1999.

Dale was born December 30, 1923. He was educated at Center Scipio School and Harlan High School, graduating in 1941. He enlisted in the Army Air Force, where he became a radio operator, serving in Burma and India, supporting the China airlifts. Upon his return to the States at the end of WW II, he married Betty Hill of Harlan on February 10, 1946, and resumed the life of farming. Their children are Steven, Donna, and Brian. Dale passed away August 4, 2004. Steve married Kathleen Plumb in 1978 and they reside in Scipio Township. Donna married Paul Fordham of Springfield Township in 1971. Their children are Pamela, Karen, and Brad. Brian married Barbara Daily of Leo in 1979 and their children are Rebecca, Benjamin, and Brent, who are the seventh generation to live in the original homestead.

Helen was born February 11, 1928, and was educated at Center and South Scipio Schools and graduated from Harlan High School, class of 1945. She married George Arthur Harter of Springfield Township, November 9, 1946. George was also a Harlan graduate and after his military service received his engineering degrees from Purdue. George's career was predominantly with TRW Corporation in California, where he was involved with satellite development. George and Helen's children are Sue and George, Jr.

Georgia was born December 24, 1932, and was educated at Center and South Scipio Schools and graduated from Harlan High School, class of 1949. Her first marriage was to John Powell, also of Scipio. Their children are Cathy, Lee, and Holly. Her second marriage was to Robert Zimmerman of Leo, who was an electronics engineer for International Harvester Company, and they were blessed with a daughter, Joy.

Submitted by Brian Eager

DONALD P. ECKRICH

From his obituary, February 18, 1997, Journal Gazette, Fort Wayne, Indiana

Donald P. Eckrich, who went from skinning cellulose casings off wieners to presiding over the family meat company's most rapid expansion, died Monday. He was the son of Clement and Beatrice Eckrich, born in Kalamazoo, Michigan, June 6, 1924.

Mr. Eckrich, 72, became president of Peter Eckrich & Sons, Inc. in 1969. He was the last family member to head the company founded by his grandfather on Wallace Stgreet in 1894. Peter Eckrich & Sons incorporated in 1925 and was capitalized with $50,000. It moved its headquarters from Fort Wayne to Kalamazoo, Michigan, in 1930 (returning to Fort Wayne in 1939), and Mr. Eckrich's father moved with it.

Donald Eckrich began his career in the sausage department at 14. He held plant, sales and buying positions on his way up to promotion as manager of the Kalamazoo processing plant in 1958. He was named corporate general operations manager in 1962, director of operations in 1965, and executive vice president a year later.

The company, which went public in 1969, enjoyed a strong increase in volume, market share and profits during the early 1970s, having transformed itself from a family-owned business with a small market into a major Midwestern processed-meat company. By the time Beatrice Foods Co. purchased it in 1972, Peter Eckrich & Sons had sales of $250 million. Mr. Eckrich joined the Beatrice board. In 1979, he was named president and chief operating officer of Beatrice, then one of the largest companies in the United States.

Donald P. Eckrich

He retired from Beatrice in 1982 and was serving on several boards, including that of Central Soya Co., which named him president and chief executive in 1985. Mr. Eckrich retired from Central Soya in 1988 after the company was sold.

In 1990, Mr. Eckrich was inducted into the Greater Fort Wayne Business Hall of Fame.

Among the other boards Mr. Eckrich served on were those of Lincoln Financial Corp., the American Meat Institute, Knappen Milling Co., the Junior Achievement Foundation and General Telephone Co. of Indiana Inc. His other activities included serving as president of the St. Joseph's Medical Center board and as president of the Fort Wayne Redevelopment Commission.

A World War II veteran, Mr. Eckrich received a Purple Heart after being wounded, captured and held as a prisoner of war in Germany. Pfc. Eckrich was with an infantry division in France when he was reported missing in action on November 22, 1944. His family, in Kalamazoo, feared he was dead. On March 5, 1945, the postman delivered an unstamped letter written Christmas Eve in which the family first learned he had been wounded by shrapnel in his hand and side, the Kalamazoo Gazettte reported. He was liberated by the Russians. He returned to the United States during the summer and resumed his studies at the University of Michigan.

Youth was among Mr. Eckrich's strongest commitments. With Junior Achievement of Northern Indiana, he was particularly involved in the management structure and fundraising.

Surviving Mr. Eckrich are his wife, Barbara J.; three sons, George of Austin, Texas, Joseph of Kalamazoo and James of Fort Wayne; five daughters, Emily Wright of Olympia Fields, Illinois, Ellen Heiny of Fort Wayne, Eleanor Bannigan of Kalamazoo, and Louise Ostrow and Diane Pai, both of Colorado Springs, Colorado.

Submitted by Barbara Eckrich

PETER ECKRICH

Peter Eckrich was born January 21, 1874, in Waldsee, Germany. He came to America in 1881 at age 16. He settled in Fort Wayne, where he married Dina Hilker on January 17, 1888, at St. Mary's Catholic Church.

Peter and Dina had fourteen children. One boy died at birth and Edna died at 2 ½ months. The remaining children were: John, Clement, Henry, Herman, Joseph, Mary (Zurbuch), Bernadette (Mueller), Loretta (Fritz), Helen (Baker), Florence (Herber), Martha (Schenkel) and Dorothy (Rissing).

Peter and Dina started the Eckrich meat business in their home at Lewis and Francis. During the early years, their family grew; a child was born every two years. Each child was expected to do their chores in the market, dressing chickens, delivering meat, telephone orders and keeping books. They instilled the lifelong work ethic that helped the company grow and prosper.

Quality has been the rule of operation for Eckrich since the company was founded before the turn of the century—quality of product, quality of service and quality in all aspects of business.

"Quality is that invisible ingredient distilled from pride of workmanship and measured out and added, bit by bit, by every individual who feels a personal responsibility for producing a superior product." Peter Eckrich

At Eckrich, quality was more than a word—it was the standard.

In 1902, Peter Eckrich opened a second meat market, and in 1907, Eckrich started to sell his product at wholesale. In 1911, Eckrich purchased the building and property at the second meat

Peter Eckrich

market site and converted it into a plant-market. In 1925, Peter Eckrich incorporated his company, forming Peter Eckrich and Sons, and started expanding in earnest. Starting with one branch sales office in South Bend, Indiana, at the time of incorporation, the company established 37 branches in 17 states over the next 55 years. In 1926, Peter Eckrich and Sons purchased a second plant in Kalamazoo, Michigan. New plants and additions followed in rapid succession. In time, the floor area of Eckrich plants and branch offices totaled more than 150,000 square feet, or more than three acres. In 1932, after 37 years in the retail business, Peter Eckrich and Sons closed its last retail store.

Peter and Dina celebrated their 50th wedding anniversary on January 9, 1938. Peter died March 30, 1942, in Coral Gables, Florida, but Peter Eckrich and Sons continued to prosper.

In 1972, Eckrich became a wholly owned subsidiary and separate operating division of Beatrice Foods Company, Chicago. In 1986, Beatrice merged Swift and Company and Peter Eckrich and Sons, creating Swift-Eckrich.

Submitted by Margaret Eckrich

EDLAVITCH & STEIN

Baruch M. Edlavitch, M.D., a graduate of Johns Hopkins, came to Fort Wayne in 1912 from Ames, Iowa, where he had been teaching pathology at Iowa State University. His move was in response to a recruiting effort by a group of local physicians whom he joined in practice. After opening his office, he went back to his hometown, Baltimore, Maryland, married his fiancée, Rena Salomon, and moved her to Fort Wayne. They arrived just in time for the flood of 1913. She was one of the crew who went around in rowboats handing food to people trapped in their water-besieged homes.

In 1917 Dr. Edlavitch went to Fort Benjamin Harrison as a 2nd lieutenant and served during World War I as a transport surgeon, ferrying troops across the Atlantic. At the end of the war, he returned to Fort Wayne and his family, his wife and two children, Samuel and Betty. Samuel eventually left Fort Wayne, but Betty married Curtis Stein and they established their home here. After Curt's Army service in World War II and the death of his father, he took over the fledgling family business, Stein Advertising, a specialty-advertising firm. They, too, had two children, John and Rena; all have made their homes here and have been very active in the community and their house of worship. John entered the family advertising specialty business, building it into an award-winning concern, and Rena is a successful Realtor and manager of a real estate firm. Now another generation is active in the family business and community, Wendy Stein, the younger of John's two daughters.

The family's activities have been many and varied. Among them: Dr. Edlavitch served the local draft board during World War II. Curt Stein was the first house chairman of the new Summit Club. Betty is an educator and newspaper columnist and serves on the Allen County Alcoholic Beverage Commission. John served on the PTC board and was its chairman. Rena was a co-founder of the Rape Crisis Center. Wendy is president of the Junior League of Fort Wayne. Her husband, Mike Kelly, is on the board of Cinema Center.

Submitted by Betty E. Stein

DOUGLAS EDWARDS

Douglas Edwards was born in Wells County on May 25, 1956. He was the first born of Kenny and Melba Edwards. He spent most of his growing up years in Markle. His parents moved there in 1957. As a baby, he lived just out the back door of his grandparent's farm house one-half mile south of Zanesville. His mother and father had purchased a nineteen foot Palace mobile home from his Uncle Maurice McBride for $300. He was perfectly satisfied living right next to Grandpa Don McBride who spent many hours taking him to the barn to see the cows and having him help feed the chickens. He also enjoyed the good food Grandma Mary made for him almost every day. Mom and Dad had to spoil this by moving to a larger place in Markle when he was getting close to two years old. That place was so much roomier that he noticed everything and broke lots of his Mom's special knickknacks. Another move took his family a few blocks north where they purchased in 1959 a three bedroom all electric brand new home in Skyline Addition for only $14,500. Grandpa Don was against it. He said, "You'll never be able to pay for it." After all, the house traded for the down payment only cost $2,500!

Grandpa Don didn't mind a bit when Doug's mom and dad decided to move back home to Zanesville into the house where Grandpa was born and had grown up. By then Doug was 17. He had spent all his school years at Norwell and Mom and Dad were moving across the county line into Allen County. Not being able to bear the thought of his last year being spent anywhere else; tuition was paid in the fall--ninety-one dollars a month until graduation. Of course, he couldn't bear the thought of not seeing his wife-to-be, Tammy Green, every day.

In late 1974, Doug purchased a 1969, 60 foot Vindale Mobile Home and placed it on the lot in Zanesville where his Great-great-great grandfather lived in 1866. He and his wife, Tammy, moved in March 1975 and lived there until 1977 when they moved to Bluffton. Doug and Tammy were the parents of two sons. Shane (born in 1977) is now a math teacher/baseball coach at Oak Hill High School. He is married to Nicole Green and they have a daughter Mia. Skip (born in 1982) and his wife, Rosemary Aschilman, moved from Zanesville, Allen County, to Scottsdale, Arizona, where he teaches at The Little Gym.

Doug Edwards, wife Tammy, sons Shane and Skip

Doug and Tammy lived in Bluffton until 1983. They then bought a home near Uniondale where Doug spent the rest of his life. His biggest thrill was seeing his boys grow up in the Norwell School system that he loved.

He never wanted to be cooped up so he went into business for himself doing business as Doug's Lawn Service. He coached many boys for many years in Bluffton's Little League. He loved baseball, basketball and football. In 1994, out of the blue, Doug was diagnosed with cancer. It was in his cheek and then a tumor appeared at the top of his lung below his shoulder. In September 1996, he passed away at home. A diabetic since age five, he, nor his family, never dreamed that cancer would take his life.

A memorial stone was placed in the park in Bluffton where he was a beloved coach. It sets right in the center field under the American Flag that is raised at each game. There is also a coach's award given each year to an outstanding coach in his honor.

Doug's wife Tammy remarried. Her husband, Leon Berning, was a coaching friend of Doug. They reside just south of Uniondale. To learn more about Doug and his family refer to the Wells County Family History 1992 and the Kenneth and Melba Edwards article in this publication.

Submitted by Melba Edwards

JAMES MCBRIDE & JENNY (HINE) EDWARDS

James McBride Edwards was born at the Wells County Hospital on June 5, 1970. He was the fifth child of Kenneth and Melba Edwards who at that time lived in Skyline Addition on the north edge of Markle. Jimmy, as he was called growing up, was named for his great-grandfather, James L. McBride, who was a doctor in Zanesville from 1892 until his death in 1941. At Jimmy's birth, his parents had no idea that in the spring of 1973 they would be moving to Zanesville into the very house where J.L. practiced medicine.

Jimmy was five years younger than any other sibling so he got lots of attention from his siblings. Older brother, Doug, took him everywhere. He was very artistic and loved to match fabrics for upholstering when his mother went shopping. As she sewed, he sat on the edge of the table and watched. To this day he has an eye for decorating. Jimmy attended Lafayette Central, Woodside, and graduated from Homestead High School. He entered Huntington College in the fall and graduated from there in 1992 with a degree in business management. In the fall of 1992, he moved to Muncie to get his master's degree from Ball State. Jim received his masters from Ball State in 1993.

While a student at Huntington, he met his future wife, Jenny Hine, on spring break in Florida. Jenny was still in high school. She then enrolled at Ball State University where she received an associate's degree in liberal arts. She went on the following year to Ivy Tech in Indianapolis where she received an associate's degree in surgical technology.

Jim and Jenny were married in 1995. The marriage took place in Franklin, Indiana, just south of

Indianapolis. Jenny was a native of Franklin and the Edwards still make their home there.

Jim and Jenny started out their married life by buying an old house in the historic district of Franklin. It needed lots of work, so many members of the Edwards family rented a motel room and headed for Franklin for a weekend. They tore into the house, leaving Jimmy with minor repairs and painting to do.

After a few years, a friend wanted to sell Jimmy his home out west on Route 144, so they moved out of town. Hoping to build a new house soon, they still reside on 144.

James Edwards Family:
Cole, Jenny, Jim, Quinn, and Kade

At graduation, Jim went job hunting. He worked for a year for Toyota in Columbus, Indiana. He then was hired by Hovair, a Seattle Company. Leaving them for a few months, he was urged by the owner to come back to work for him as CEO of the company. Jim complied with the offer and turned the company around in a year. He is now part owner and CEO of Hovair. They make material handling equipment for the assembly lines at Fort Motor, GM, and other automakers. The equipment hovers on air, thus the name of the company. Jim's other business is ENZA which he partners with a friend from South Africa. This business sells modular racking systems and shelving. The Hovair business started in England, moved to Seattle, and then Jim instigated the move to Detroit and then later to Franklin, Indiana. Another Allen County Homestead graduate that brought a business home to Indiana.

Jenny is a surgical nurse part time at Southside OBGYN on the south edge of Indianapolis. The Edwards have three sons: Cole Douglas (1997), Kade Alexander (1999), and Quinn McBride (2003).

Jim was a member of the Huntington College golf team, and he loves golfing to this day. Both Cole and Kade have clubs and spend weekends golfing with their dad and his friends. Jim likes decorating, racing, basketball, and cars. He loves spending time with his wife and boys and often stops off in Zanesville and Fort Wayne to spend time with his family and his school time friends.

Submitted by Melba Edwards

JEREMIAH MARTIN EDWARDS

Jeremiah Martin Edwards was born on April 18, 1977. He is the youngest son of Kenneth and Melba Edwards of Zanesville (Allen County). He was just five minutes younger than his twin brother, Jonathan. Only one baby was expected, so he was a real surprise. A name had to be selected in a hurry. It really needed to go with Jonathan, so Jeremiah's grandparents Don and Mary (Martin) McBride selected Jeremiah Martin. Martin being the maiden name of Grandma Mary and having a history way back in Allen County as settlers near Monroeville.

Jeremiah was brought home from the Wells Community Hospital to Zanesville when he was five days old. The bill for Mom and two babies was $999 and Dr. Gingerick charged $300 for the delivery. Jeremiah had a great time growing up in a big house that had been in his family since 1858. He had two older brothers and three older sisters to take care of him. He also always had Jonathan.

The twins attended Lafayette Central through the fifth grade and then they spent sixth, seventh and eighth grades at St. Peter's Lutheran in Huntington. There they made many friends. They entered high school at Homestead as freshmen and then graduated from there in 1995.

Jeremiah was an outdoor guy working for his brother Doug in the lawn service. He just wasn't interested in college. In 1996, his brother Doug died of cancer and his boys took over the business. Later in 1999, they sold the business to Jeremiah, and he still runs it now doing mowing for customers all over the area.

In August 1994, Jeremiah spied a cute little thing at the Huntington County 4-H Fair. He struck up a conversation with her and wrote her number down on a $10 bill that he still carries to this day. The family was leaving for a ten day trip to the east coast the next morning. He was miserable on vacation as he was anxious to get home and dial that number. It was love at first sight, and he and Brandy Fishbaugh were married in March 1997. Their first home was a little house that Jeremiah remodeled three times in Uniondale. They then moved to a farm house on 1000N just south of Zanesville. Two years later, the old Settlemeyer farm house with two enormous barns came up for sale. They moved east one mile and that is where they make their home today. The Edwards have three children: Elijah Issac (2000), Emma Gracelynn (2002), and Noah Riley (2005).

Jeremiah does lawn and landscaping and helps his sisters in remodeling houses they buy. He likes to make trips to Detroit to see his brother. They hardly go a day without talking to each other.

Emma, Jeremiah, Elijah, Brandy,
Noah Edwards and their dog Sweetie

Brandy is a stay-at-home mom who keeps busy with the bookwork for the business.

Growing up in a historic house was kind of neat, but Jeremiah was allowed to redo his bedroom upstairs with all Larry Bird memorabilia. Jonathan's room was a Michael Jordan room. Every year the Lafayette Central third graders came for a tour. Years after Jeremiah moved out, siblings of former third graders would ask right away if they could see the "Larry Bird" room!

This year, 2005, Jeremiah is into "Git-R-Done." He loves remodeling, decorating, painting, working on cars, looking at photo ad car books, and race tracks. He loves red neck jokes but most of all he loves family and talking!!!

Zanesville is an area where twins are prevalent and always has been. They say it is in the water!

To learn more about Jeremiah and his family refer to the Wells County Family History Book 1992 and the Kenneth and Melba Edwards article in this publication.

Submitted by Melba Edwards

JONATHAN MICHAEL EDWARDS

Jonathan Michael Edwards was born at Wells Community Hospital on Monday evening April 18, 1977, just five minutes before his twin brother, Jeremiah Martin Edwards. Jonathan was expected but Jeremiah was a surprise to all.

Jonathan is the sixth child of Kenneth and Melba Edwards. He returned home from the hospital to his parent's home in the town of Zanesville. His home sets on the Allen County side of town. It is the same house that his great-great-grandfather Jonathan Michael bought in 1855. It is the same house where his great-grandmother Almissa was born and the same house where she married Dr. J. L. McBride in 1892. It is the same house where Dr. J. L. delivered his firstborn son, Jonathan's grandfather, Donald McBride in 1894, and the same house that Jonathan's parents moved into in the spring of 1973.

What fun it was to grow up with two older brothers and three older sisters that just spoiled you rotten. The girls had prayed for twins all along because they knew one baby would just not go around. There would be so many fights to hold one!!

On April Fool's Day the girls called all the relatives and told them that their mom had twin boys. April Fool! On April 18, when the call was made no one believed them!

Jonathan had a big house and yard to roam in, and he never had to look for a playmate as Jeremiah was always there and also he had Shane, his nephew, who was born just three months after him. Three babies! What a time our family had.

Jonathan entered kindergarten at Lafayette Central, the same school that his Grandmother

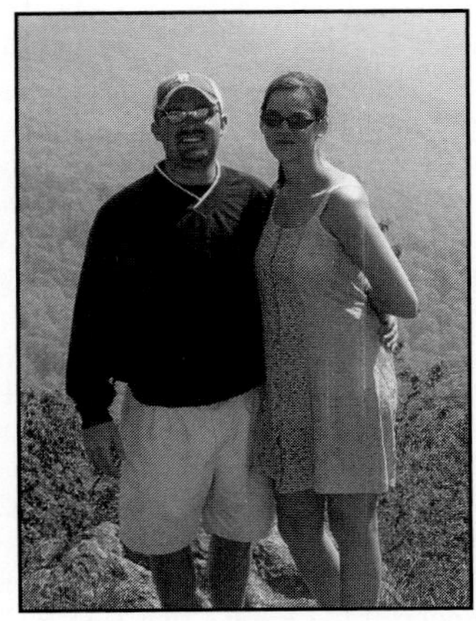

Jonathan Edwards and Sarah Bonsky

Edwards and his father had graduated from. He was a good student, and as he grew he passed on from Lafayette to St. Peter's Lutheran in Huntington where he went to the sixth through eighth grades. He entered Homestead High School his freshman year and graduated from there in 1995.

For two years he attended Huntington College (now Huntington University). Wanting a business career, he transferred to Indiana University Kelly's School of Business in Indianapolis. Graduating with a B.S. Degree in Business Administration he moved back home in the summer of 1999. He had been employed as a waiter at Richard's Restaurant in Huntington and Bob Evans at Coventry in Fort Wayne. He also worked for his brother, Doug, in Doug's Lawn Service. The decision was made to go back to school in August to get his master's degree. One month into schooling Jonathan's brother, Jim, called and wanted him to take a job as salesman for his company. Jonathan moved to Detroit to take the job. He is still with the company, Hovair Automotive as their Midwest Regional Manager. He lives in Oxford, Michigan, on the northwest side of Detroit.

Jonathan at this writing is single, but he is engaged to Sarah Bonsky who is a nanny studying to be an art teacher. If they get married in 2005, he will be married 150 years from the year that his namesake Jonathan Michael married his beloved Sarah. Jonathan's Sarah passed away in 1864, and they were so much in love that he promised her on her death bed that he would never marry another. He kept his promise until his death in 1913.

Jonathan loves big city life, nice cars, exotic foods, and all the new technology. He, however, hasn't forgotten his friends from Zanesville and school, and he stops in often on his way to the company's home office in Franklin just south of Indianapolis.

Being on the golf team at Huntington College, he shares the love of golf with his brother Jim and Jim's small sons who adore him. In fact, all the nieces and nephews love their Uncle "Jonny."

When he was only ten years old he decided to be a soloist, and he has been hired to sing at several weddings. He will sing at his mother and father's 50th anniversary celebration in 2005 as they renew their vows. Jonathan is a friend to all, a great kidder, a loving son, brother, and uncle. He will surely become a great husband and father.

Submitted by Melba Edwards

KENNETH & MELBA EDWARDS FAMILY

Kenny and Melba Edwards live in Zanesville on the South County Line at the southern most part of Allen County. The home where they live was purchased by Melba's great grandfather, Jonathan Michael, a native of Sultz, Germany. He came to America in 1834 at the age of two. In 1854 he traveled from Clear Spring, Maryland to take a shoemaking job in Fort Wayne. He had to pass through Zanesville on his journey and decided that he would like to live there. The home where the Edwards live was purchased by Jonathan in 1858, and it has remained in the family ever since. At the time Jonathan purchased the home it was the Zanesville House Hotel. Later, out back he established a tanning business, and made shoes in a room inside the hotel. In 1892, his daughter, Almissa, married a young doctor named J. L. McBride. His office was also in the hotel. The hotel closed in 1900, and J. L. continued with his medical practice until his death in 1941. The house was sold to a great granddaughter, Mary Lou Burkhart, and her husband Kenneth, in 1963 at the death of Almissa. They lived in the house for ten years and sold it to the Edwards in 1973.

The Edwards have seven children. Their eldest son, Doug passed way in 1996 at the age of forty. He was a cancer victim. His wife, Tammy, lives in Uniondale, and she is now married to a friend of Doug's, Leon Berning. Doug and Tammy had two son's, and they are both teachers. Shane married Nicole Green, and they have a daughter, Mia. Skip married Rosemary Aschilman, and they live in Zanesville.

A daughter, Robin Phillips, is a graduate of Huntington University. She owns and operates Davis Restaurant in Markle Indiana and is engaged to Tom Lloyd.

Daughter, Pollyanna, and her husband, Fred Wymer, live just south of Zaneville. She has three children by her first husband. Brock Bennett is married to Richelle Best and they have a son, Logan. Brice Bennett is married to Melissa Burk; they are expecting a child in May of 2005. Baili Bennett is a home school junior who attends Taylor University part time. Fred has a son, Matt Wymer, and a daughter, Lisa Wymer.

Daughter Jenny and her husband, J.P. Miller, live in Columbia, Missouri, and they are parents of nine children, all at home. They are; Andrew 19, Abigaill seven, Amy 15, Anna 13, Aarika 11, Avery nine, Amber seven, Ashley four, and Addy one. Jenny home school's her children. J.P. owns and operates Animal Solutions and Alpha Net, a radon testing company.

Son, Jim, lives with his wife, Jenny, and their sons Cole seven, Kade five, and Quinn one, just south of Indianapolis in Franklin. Jim has a company there called Hovair, and another company, ENZA. Jim is a graduate of Huntington College and Ball State University.

The Edwards last two children are twin boys. Jonathan lives in Oxford, Michigan where he is a salesman to Ford Motor Company for Jim's business. He is 28 and single. He attended Huntington College and graduated from Indiana University's Kelly School of Business. Jeremiah, his twin, lives just south of Zanesville. He purchased his brother, Doug's, Lawn Service after his death and has been running it ever since. He and his wife, Brandy Fishbaugh, have three children; Elijah five, Emma three, and Noah, a newborn.

The family loves just about every activity; music, theater, antiques, history, baseball, basketball, travel, cars, and, of course, shopping. They are involved in church, Lions Club and all community affairs. Kenny, a tool, die and mold maker, is employed at JB Tool in Fort Wayne. Melba, a mother, wife, and homemaker has kept busy sewing, upholstering and volunteering. In 1976 she initiated the writing of the Zanesville, Indiana, history book, and, for the past 18 years, she has been writing a news column for the Huntington County Tab and the Bluffton News Banner. In 1991 she was one of just a few people who worked to get the town incorporated so grants could be obtained to help pay for a state mandated sewer system. She became the first clerk treasurer of the new town of Zanesville, even though Zanesville had existed since 1848. She served in that capacity for three years, passing the job on after the sewer system was completed.

Kenneth and Melba Edwards

The Edwards were married on September 2, 1955 at the Zanesville Church of God just across the street from where they now live. The family is preparing for a 50th wedding anniversary at Bear Creek Farms for the weekend.

For more family history refer to; Zanesville, Indiana History 1976, J.L. McBride, Biographical Memoirs of Wells County 1903, David Martin Sr., Griswold's 1917 Pictorial History of Fort Wayne, Samuel Clem and Jonathan Michael, History of Allen County 1880, and Jonathan Michael (page 798), Jonas Cline (page 285), Clems (page 327 and 444) in the Biographical and Historical Record of Adams and Wells County, 1887, and all the Michael grandfathers - Sulz am neckar German History 1984, Wells County, Indiana, Family History 1992.

Submitted by Melba McBride Edwards

MILES S. EDWARDS, PH.D.

ASSISTANT PRINCIPAL WASHINGTON ELEMENTARY SCHOOL

Miles S. Edwards, Ph.D. was born in Fort Wayne, Indiana. He attended school K through 12th grade with Fort Wayne Community Schools (FWCS). He is a graduate of Fort Wayne's South Side High School. Three generations of his family on his mother's side have graduated from South Side, starting with his mother, class of 1933. Dr. Edwards owns a home on the street that his maternal great-grandfather, Nathaniel Blanks moved to in 1895, at 462 Helen St. (Dalman).

Miles Edwards' parents were Wanda Leona Woods and William Howard Edwards. His siblings are William, Jr., Marilyn, Nathaniel, and Elaine.

His mother, Wanda Leona Woods, was the daughter of Ross Woods and Louise Blanks. Her siblings were Ross, Jr., Florence Rowena, Roger Henry, and Chester. Louise Blanks was the daughter of Nathanial and Cornelia Hopson Jamison Blanks. Cornelia had been married previously, and she had a son, Henry Jamison, who was born in Mississippi.

In the past Miles Edwards has served on many boards in the city: The History Center, Cinema Center, The Martin Luther King Montessori School Board, and others too numerous to mention. He is a member of several Educational Honor Societies and holds life memberships to the Alpha Phi Alpha Fraternity, Inc., The National Alliance of Black School Educators and the NAACP. He is a graduate of Leadership Fort Wayne, class of 1996 and served as first Vice President.

Dr. Edwards now serves on Boards of the following organizations:

• The Heartland Chamber Chorale, Inc., 2001 to present; currently the president.

• Indiana Black Expo, Inc. - Fort Wayne Chapter, 1982 to present.

•The African/African-American Historical Society, (AAAHS) Inc., 1998 to present. He is one of the founding members of the AAAHS.

Dr. Edwards has had the distinction of having been named to "Who's Who Among African Americans" several times. He has also been named to "Who's Who Among Educators in America." He has been named to "Who's Who in the World." Dr. Edwards was also named to the U.S. Jaycees, "Outstanding Young Men of America."

Dr. Edwards received his B.S. degree from Ball State University in 1973. He received the Master of Science in Education from Indiana University in 1978. He was awarded the Doctor of Philosophy Degree from the University of Akron in 1994.

He has written for educational publications and newspapers. The title of his Dissertation was "A Comparative Analysis of Teachers' Backgrounds As A Factor In Their Perceptions And Attitudes Of Cultural Diversity In Two Urban School Districts."

He retired in 1999 as the Assistant Principal of Washington Elementary School of the Fort Wayne Community Schools after 23.5 years with that district. He is most proud of starting the Multi-cultural Program for FWCS in 1990.

Submitted by Miles S. Edwards, Ph.D.

SAM & BETTY (KRINN) EICHHORN

Sam and Betty Eichhorn were married on June 19, 1940. Sam was born in Clarksville, Texas, where his parents Charles and Harriet Eichhorn lived at the time. The date was December 26, 1912, making Sam the eldest gentleman in Zanesville in 2005. Sam's parents moved to Indiana in 1918, settling in Rockcreek Township, Wells County for two years and then moving to Uniondale in Union Township where Sam grew up. He graduated from East Union Center in 1930. Sam's brothers were twins, Don and Von, and Charles Jr.; and sisters, Aline Denney and Hazel Todd. Two siblings died young.

At the Bluffton Street Fair in 1936, Sam met Betty Krinn and they went to Liberty Center's prom together. Betty was a little upset her senior year at Liberty Center because her speech teacher kept wanting her to make speeches every day. Little known to her, she was the valedictorian, and when graduation came she had to make an impromptu speech on the spot. Betty was born May 14, 1919, in Wells County, where she lived most of her life, to George and Jessie Krinn. She was one of eight children. Her parents moved for just a few years to Kansas where her father worked in the salt mines, but they soon returned to Wells County. Her grandfather, Daniel Krinn, was a Civil War Veteran who moved from Ohio to Indiana between 1870 and 1875. Betty went to Bly School in Liberty Township and graduated from Liberty Center in 1936. Love blossomed for the Sam and Betty and on June 19, 1940, they were secretly married in Covington, Kentucky. The cost $2. On October 4, 1940, they made their marriage public, and a reception was held at the Eichhorn parents in Uniondale.

Sam and Betty Eichhorn

Before the Eichhorns were married, Sam and his brother, Von, ran a filling station in Uniondale. Von went on to be state senator from 1930 to 1958. When Von lived on the Allen County side of Zanesville, a small daughter died. He bought a plot for her in Hoverstock Cemetery. If you were to seek public office, you had to be a land owner. Von could not qualify until those wanting him to run found out that a cemetery plot is considered real estate. He went on to be elected and served Indiana for 28 years.

Sam and Betty moved to Waynedale for a time where Sam ran another filling station. He later worked for the Frank Welch Company doing screens for billboards. He says they had 6000 colors to use. The company later sold to 3M and after 38 years Sam retired in 1981 at the age of 69. In September 1990, the Eichhorns moved back to Allen County. They purchased Sam's sister Aline Denny's home. The Eichhorns have three children:

Darrel, the oldest, is a teacher and lives in Valparaiso. His children are: Melinda, Kevin, and Allison.

Son, Terrell, works for Franklin Electric and lives with his parents in Zanesville.

Daughter, Carol Mincoff, lives in Fort Wayne where she is employed at Ash Brokerage. Carol has a stepson, Brandon.

The Eichhorns have been married 65 years. Sam currently (August 2005) drives the seven miles to Markle each day to stay the day with his wife, Betty, who is a resident at Markle Health Care.

Submitted by Melba Edwards

LEWIS GLENDALE ELLINGHAM

About a century has passed since Lewis Glendale Ellingham came to Fort Wayne from Wells County with his new family. His father, Charles came to Wells County as a child in the 1830s, with his father, William Ellingham, and step-mother, his father's second wife, Hannah Scotton, from villages now a part of Coventry, in England. Hannah's father, John Scotton, too, came from the same area, and it seems certain that both men knew each other in Coventry. Both were shoemakers there. They pioneered farms in Rock Creek Township in Wells County, the Scottons occupying land adjacent to the Ellinghams. Both grew to substantial families today spread over America.

Lewis Ellingham, known by his initials 'L. G.', youngest of nine children, had early in his life settled on a newspaper career, and began learning the trade hands-on in its mechanical and editorial aspects by buying a series of small newspapers, by 1903 owning The Daily Democrat in Decatur, Indiana. His political ambitions paralleled his journalistic aspirations. He was elected and served from 1910 to 1914 as Indiana's Secretary of State. By 1916 he had purchased The Fort Wayne Journal Gazette, and remained its publisher until 1934. The remaining five years of his life were spent as Acting Postmaster of Fort Wayne, while his only son, Miller Ellingham, retained connection with the newspaper, by the 1950s becoming The Journal Gazette's executive vice-president. Miller Ellingham died in Florida in 1968.

Louis Glendale Ellingham

When L. G. Ellingham came to Fort Wayne, before the first World War, his small family consisted of his wife, Margaret Ellen 'Nell' Miller, his oldest child, Winifred, and his son, Miller. Nell Miller was the daughter of Colonel Marin B. Miller and his wife Sarah Jane Aker, early families of Randolph County, Indiana, and was their only child who lived to adulthood.

Colonel Miller had led his regiment in the Civil War, and was a lawyer in Winchester. The Millers are from Puritan settlers who crossed to Massachusetts Bay Colony in 1630; the Akers a German family who came to America from Alsace in the 18th century.

Winifred Ellingham married a World War I infantry captain, James Ewing Bond (Sr), whose family was long established in Allen County life. Their only son, James Ewing Bond (Jr) today lives in Elkhart, Indiana, with his wife, the former Rosemary Kryder. They have two children, Carolyn and Richard Ewing Bond, and three grandchildren, Elliott, Andrew and Madeline Bond.

Miller Ellingham was twice married, and by his first wife, Margery Hyman, had three children. Two of these three, Michael and Margaret, are dead; a third, Charles Lewis, Margaret's twin, lives in San Francisco. Margaret married in Italy; her two children live in Milan.

The Ellinghams and related families have all been studied (genealogy websites find them). In addition, Fort Wayne - Allen County Library's Genealogy Department contains multi-volume works by Lewis Ellingham on the Ellinghams and Millers (*Two Coventry Shoemakers Become Indi-*

ana Farmers & The Ancestries of David Miller and Clarissa Moore of Torringford, Connecticut).

Submitted by Lewis Ellingham

ELLIS FAMILY

Mabel Harper Ellis was the daughter of Richard and Sattana Hill Harper of Brighton, Alabama. Arthur Ellis was the son of Charsley and Amaziah Ellis of Tuscaloosa, Alabama. Mabel Harper married Arthur Ellis in Crown Point, Indiana August 1926. They had four daughters: Etta Mae (born October 25, 1918), Margaret Dorothy (born September 17, 1920) in Brighton, Alabama. Pallas Ruth (born June 10, 1927) in Gary, Indiana and Geneva (born June 4, 1932) in Fort Wayne, Indiana.

The family moved to Fort Wayne in 1927 and lived on Eliza Street. Arthur Ellis was a founding member of St. John's C.M.E. Church and was faithful in his attendance and support of the church. Mabel Ellis was a member of McKee Church of God.

Arthur Ellis died on September 28, 1965 and Mabel Ellis died on April 24, 1974.

Etta Mae Ellis married Albert George Jennings, on October 1, 1935 in Fort Wayne, Indiana. Albert G. Jennings was the son of John and Mittie Jennings, born August 10, 1912 in Lexington, Georgia. Etta and Al were faithful members of Union Baptist Church. To this union, two children were born, a daughter, Anita Louise, born on May 16, 1945, and a son, Albert Ellis Jennings born November 18, 1957. Albert G. Jennings died on Jan. 6, 1991 and Etta Jennings died on December 30, 1999.

Anita Louise married John Preston Dortch, Jr. on July 3, 1971 at Union Baptist Church in Fort Wayne, Indiana. To this union, two daughters were born, Andrea Jonelle, September 1, 1974 and Nichole Jennings on June 23, 1977. Andrea Jonelle Dortch married Marlan Henry on April 11, 2004 in Ocho Rios, Jamaica. They reside in Pembroke Pines, Florida. Nichole resides in Nashville, Tennessee.

Albert Ellis Jennings married Carla Sherell Hunter on August 21, 1982 at Shiloh Baptist Church in Fort Wayne. To this union, four children were born: Adrienne Jameal (June 6, 1985), Albert Gabriel II (May 22, 1992), Jasmine Marie (February 27, 1994) and Annika Joy (July 17, 1997). Albert E. Jennings has a daughter, Janeille Lanae, who was born June 27, 1981.

Submitted by Anita L. Dortch

LEONARD & MARIE ELLIS FAMILY

Leonard Paul Ellis, son of Samuel E. and Jenny G. (Neidic) Ellis and Frances Marie Koehnlein, daughter of John M. and Nellie B. (Kuffie) Koehnlein met at the one-room School in Huntertown, Indiana in 1916, when both were in the seventh grade. Both families had recently moved to that area, the Ellises from Waterloo, Indiana, and the Koehnleins from the Fort Wayne area.

Marie's Grandfather, Adam, had emigrated from Bavaria, Germany in 1864 and was a butcher by trade. He married Kathryn Mutzfaldt in the late 1860s. Her father, John Michael, was employed by the Fort Wayne Transit, and was a motorman on the Main Street Line, later the Robison Park Line, and later still, the Taylor Street Line. He met his wife-to-be, Nellie B. Kuffie, as she rode to and from work as a secretary at the Fred Eckert's Meat Packing Plant on West Main Street.

Leonard's grandfather, William Daggert, married to Mary Topper, was from Hicksville, Ohio, and came to Waterloo/Butler area and bought a farm. His father, Sutherland, it is thought, was from Roxbury, Vermont. Leonard's father, Samuel Elsworth, was married to Jenny Grace Neidic (1900) and lived on a farm at the edge of Huntertown on State Road # 3.

After Leonard completed the eighth grade, the Koehnleins' moved southwest of Fort Wayne to Aboite Township. Leonard continued to keep in contact with Marie, and on April 27, 1922 they were married at the Huntertown Methodist Church. The Koehnleins gave them a plot of ground next to their home on Ellison Road, and Leonard built a bungalow-style home.

Leonard was self-employed and owned a truck. He would pick up milk from the area farmers in the early morning hours and deliver to Eskay Dairy for processing. His afternoons were spent delivering meat for the Peter Eckrich Butcher Shop. As sales for the butcher shop increased, Leonard added additional trucks, and sold his milk route. He worked full time for Peter Eckrich. The meat business continued to prosper, and in 1939, Peter Eckrich purchased the fleet of trucks from Leonard. He continued on with that firm for another ten years.

Leonard and Marie Ellis Family. Front, L to R: Richard, Gloria, Marie, Leonard, Roselyn. Back L to R: Robert, Arlie, James, William, Donald, John and Leonard Jr.

The family grew down through the years and made several moves. The first home on Ellison Road was always "home" to them, so they purchased it and remodeled, adding a second story and enclosing the porches. The family of eight boys, (Robert, Donald, John, Richard, William, James, Leonard, Jr. and Arlie) lived there for several years. In 1939 a new home was built next to their original home. The new home was designed for the large family. On the third floor it had eight built-in bunks with closets, a lavatory, drinking fountain, bookcase, study or game table and a clothes chute. The finished basement contained kitchen and dining area, laundry, storage room for home canned fruit and vegetables, and a shower.

Two girls, Roselyn and Gloria, joined the family of boys in 1940 and 1943 respectively.

The boys worked at area farms during their early years as Aboite Township was then a farming community. Nearby were the Spring Grove, Bash, Ridge Brook and Floyd Dennis Farms. Later, Robert was employed at a Fleet Wing Service Center, servicing major truck lines with petroleum products. He then purchased and managed the center. Donald chose a local bakery, worked there for five years and, in 1945, opened his own "bakeshop" in the car-and-a-half garage at the home place. (See Ellison Bakery, Inc. - A Family Affair) John was employed at Peter Eckrich for several years maintaining their fleet of trucks. Richard, after graduation, bought a panel truck and delivered bakery products for his brother's bake shop. William has always been affiliated with the bakery business. James worked at a local drive-in restaurant in the kitchen for a few years. Leonard, Jr. and Arlie, being the youngest of the boys, other than working on local farms, have always been associated with the family business. The girls have held various positions in the bakery business. Donald's "venture" prospered down through the years, making several moves and changes. By 1949, the entire Ellis family became involved in one aspect or another of the bakery business, and, in 2004, the third and fourth generations are in the management positions.

Submitted by James A. Ellis

ENGLE FAMILY

Johannes Engle was born in Stark County, Ohio, in 1815. He was the son of Michael and Sarah (Edgington) Engle and grandson of John Edgington who served in the Revolutionary War as a private in Captain James Munn's Company Second Battalion, Washington, Pennsylvania, Militia. Margaret (Keifer) Engle was born in Elsas, Germany, in 1820 and came to America in 1826 and settled in Stark County, Ohio.

On February 16, 1841, John and Margaret married and the couple moved to Fort Wayne, Indiana, and purchased farm property in 1843. The central portion of Fort Wayne was forestland and was infested with various wild animals. Margaret told of how fires had to be built around the farm to protect the livestock from the wild animals. The homestead was where the Kekionga Junior High School now stands. When the school was being built, gold coins, arrowheads, and other artifacts were found on the property. Engle Road was named after John and Margaret. In 1872 Engle farmland was acquired for the St. John Cemetery. Margaret was a charter member of St. John's Lutheran Church. Margaret could relate the history of the city and was often consulted as an authority.

John and Margaret had eight children: John (Civil War private, Indiana Company C Forty-fourth Regiment), Anna, Sarah, William, Mary, Adeline, George, and Alex. Their son, George, resided on Engle Road and married Louise Luxenberger in 1874. Louise came from Buffalo, New York, by way of the Erie Canal. They had seven children: Margaret, John, Catherine, Mureah, Savannah, Charles L., and Arthur.

Charles L. Engle married Marie Holzhauer in 1909. In 1919, Charles and Marie purchased a home at the intersection of Bluffton and Sandpoint Roads for $1800. The interurban tracks bordered their property, and Pizza King now stands on the property. Charles L. Engle worked at General Electric 43 years and retired from there. In 1907, Marie Holzhauer worked where light bulbs were made on Clinton and Brackenridge Streets. Their four children (Elaine, Helen, Charles, and Arnold) graduated from South Side and Elmhurst High Schools and were active in sports.

George and Louise (Luxenberger) Engle with children and grandchildren, Charles and Marie (Holzhauer), Elaine (Engle) Parquet

Light bulbs were being made on Clinton and Brackenridge Streets in 1907. Marie Holzhauer is second from large center post. She is wearing a dark dress.

Elaine Engle taught grades three and four at Anthony Wayne and Waynedale Schools from 1937-1941, coached the Anthony Wayne Girls Basketball team, taught homebound students, and retired from the Fort Wayne State Hospital. She married Dennis Parquet in 1941. Their son, Robert (1942), married Janice Geiger in 1972. Their children are Suzanne, David, and Steven. Dennis, Robert, and Suzanne Parquet began their careers at Dana Corporation on West State Street.

Helen Engle married Harry Hull in 1958. He died in 1966. She then married Arlo Sheets in 1969. She spoiled her nieces and nephews with gifts and cards from her world travels. Each Christmas and Easter they could count on a special religious ceramic created by her. She retired from General Electric with 44 years service.

Charles A. Engle was a Staff Sergeant in World War II and was in the first wave of men drafted in 1940. As a reservist he was in the first group to go to Korea, served in a MASH Unit, and received a Purple Heart. He was a chiropractor with an office on Broadway. He married Ruth Dailey in 1943 and they had a son, Charles James.

Rev. Dr. C. James (Engle) Cress married Candace Ann Bastress in 1972 and they have two daughters, Cassandra and Colette. Charles A. Engle later married Myrtle Neeley in 1952 and they had two children. Michael and Sally. Michael Engle, D.O., married Karen Williams in 1989. They have three children: Joshua, Jacob, and Emily. Sally Engle is the fifth generation Engles living in Allen County. She is a registered nurse and served in the Air National Guard for 21 and a half years, serving in the 1991 Gulf War, England, and Korea. Mike and Sally attended Kekionga Junior High School, the site of the original Engle homestead.

Arnold Engle served in the Navy during WW II as a Machinist Mate Third Class. He married Mary Yentes in 1943 and lived on Getz Road in Fort Wayne. He was a toolmaker at General Electric Company and was transferred in 1952 to the new GE factory in Linton, Indiana, as a tool room foreman. Later he became a manufacturing engineer and retired from GE after 42 years of service. Mary and Arnold had five daughters. Karen, an RN, married Ralph Wallem in 1966 and had two children, Mark and Katherine. Katherine was a lawyer in Senator Lugar's Washington, DC office. She died at age 32. Pamela, a dental hygienist, married William Guyton in 1973 and they had a daughter, Johanna, a teacher. Catherine died in infancy. Debra, a teacher, married Michael Poole in 1975. They have two sons, Cade and Douglas. Cade served four and a half years in the Navy on the Vincennes, an Aegis Class Cruiser, during the second Gulf War. Janice married James Stahl and they had one son, Jeffery. Janice then married Donald Hines in 2003.

The descendants of Johannes and Margaret Engle's son, George, include a doctor, lawyer, corporate manager, dental hygienist, engineer, business owner, minister, postmistress, nurses, teachers, and all branches of the military, with religious affiliations in the Presbyterian, Lutheran, and United Church of Christ faiths.

Submitted by Robert C. Parquet

ALBERT HOWARD & LILLIAN JEAN ROGERS ERICSON FAMILY

Lillian Jean Rogers was born November 29, 1917 at Wellington, Illinois. Her parents were William R. Rogers and Lulu Sutherland Umberger who were both natives of Wytheville, Virginia. She has a brother, George Milton Rogers, who was born October 27, 1913 in Wellington. He is currently residing at his farm home on Hathaway Road.

"Jean" lived with her family in Wellington until 1937. She has had an interest in music all her life. She began lessons at age six and played for the church in Wellington. After she graduated from high school, her parents moved to LaOtto, Indiana. They lived on a farm and were members of the Lutheran church. Jean continued her study of the piano and played for her church while the family lived at LaOtto.

She clerked in the Enos Young grocery store for three years. In 1941, she moved to Chicago and found work at the Eversharp Pen and Pencil company. It was there she met Albert Howard Ericson who was born in Chicago on February 1, 1919. They were married June 16, 1945. In 1952 Jean quit her job at Eversharp.

A son, Howard William was born in 1953, and a daughter, Karen Louise, in 1954. In 1960 the family moved to Fort Wayne when Al took a job as Mobile Auditor for the Air Force and the Navy. Jean obtained her license to teach and taught piano lessons for ten years until her sight failed.

Albert died March 14, 1993.

Lillian Jean and Albert Ericson

One of Jean's hobbies is genealogy. She has a collection of scrapbooks about her families. She became a member of the Mary Penrose Wayne Chapter of the Daughters of the American Revolution in 1994 through proven lineal descent from James Crockett, Ensign of Virginia; William Patterson, Private of Virginia; and John Montgomery, Patriotic Service of Virginia. Jean plays the piano at the DAR meetings for the singing of the National Anthem and has played background music on several occasions since becoming a member.

She enjoys knitting even though she is legally blind. She has donated caps, mittens and scarves to several agencies. Jean Joly, Director of the Retired Senior Volunteer Program, took some to Russia when she visited that country. A niece took some to children of the military in Czechoslovakia. They have been given to needy children in China, to children in DAR schools, to students at Fort Wayne schools, to Faith Lutheran Church where Jean is a member, and to the YWCA Women's Shelter. Jean's family helps her with selecting colors since she cannot distinguish the different colors of the yarn. Jean is a member of the League for the Blind and Workers for the Blind and Disabled.

Howard William is married and lives in Fort Wayne with his family. Karen married Vincent Maloney of Buffalo, New York on July 9, 1994. They live in Fort Wayne with their daughter, Dana.

Submitted by Kathryn Bloom on behalf of the Ericson family

FREDERICK L. & JOAN L. (SUTTON) ERICKSON

Frederick (Fred) Logan and Joan Louise Erickson came to Fort Wayne from Evansville, Indiana in 1960 when Fred accepted a mechanical engineering position at Magnavox. Fred worked for Magnavox and Philips for over 30 years. Fred and Joan were high school sweethearts and were married on December 29, 1954 in Boonville, Indiana. They enjoyed golf, dancing (their favorite dance was the swing), traveling and going out to eat with friends on Friday nights. Fred and Joan were married for 49 years when Fred passed away June 23, 2004.

Fred was born in Forsyth, Montana October 6, 1932 to Lolan M. (Clark) and Frederick E. Erickson. Fred was raised by his mother, Lolan. She served as Warrick County Clerk in the 1950s. She was also a Daughter of the American Revolution (DAR). Her national DAR number was 369815. Lolan's father, Logan Clark's ancestry goes back to Captain Henry Gonterman who was born in 1745 in Germany and died in Bullitt County, Kentucky.

Fred worked at an airport at the age of thirteen. Part of his pay was free flight instruction in a tandem Aeronca Champion. He was able to put an airplane into a spin and recover from it when he was fourteen. Before serving in the Air Force, Fred and his brother-in-law, Shirley West, rebuilt a tandem L-2 observation plane and flew it off Shirley's farm in Chandler, Indiana.

Fred loved engines and mechanical devices from a very young age. He tinkered with U-Control airplane engines and loved to work on his motorcycle engine. He loved motorcycles and loved to drive them wide open. He constantly took his motorcycle engines apart to fix them and put them back together. All his high school buddies would take their bikes to Fred when they had trouble with them. They said, "Fred can get any engine started". When Fred was in his mid-thirties, he brought home a 1949 British AJS motorcycle that was just a bunch of parts in a basket. He restored the AJS like new and provided lots of fun rides on that vintage motorcycle.

Fred received his BSME from Purdue University. The majority of his life was involved in some way with the U.S. Military. He was in the ROTC in college and after graduation he served in the U.S. Air Force as a navigator of a KC-97 Stratotanker re-fueling aircraft. He navigated those big planes over the artic circle by using a sexton and the stars. His crew was part of the Strategic Air Command (SAC). They would fly 12-14 hour missions to refuel B-47 and B-52 bombers. During most of his career at Magnavox he helped design and test all types of sonabuoys that are still used to help protect our country's naval vessels. Fred also worked for Magnavox's parent company Philips and was a co-inventor of a camless engine that used computer controlled valve actuators.

Fred's hobby was inventing new internal combustion engines. This led to the creation of a new company that he operated while still working as an engineer at Magnavox. Fred was the founder and President of Engine Research Associates, Inc. and Erickson Motors, LLC which developed prototype engines to be used for military generators, unmanned aerial vehicles and various commercial applications. Fred was the inventor of the Migrating Combustion Chamber (MCC) Engine and several fluid mechanisms. He received U.S. patents on his inventions in 1971, 1978, 1982, 1984, 1994 and 1997. The MCC Engine was the first practical full expansion internal combustion engine. This unique engine's exhaust was so quiet it did not need a muffler. Fred's company won several Small Business Innovative Research (SBIR) contracts to develop the MCC Engine for special military applications.

Fred and Joan Erickson.

The MCC Engine was also manufactured for several years for the Model Airplane market. Prototype MCC Engines were produced for string trimmers, lawnmowers and generators. He also invented a fluid meter mechanism which was successfully tested by Tokheim by running over one million gallons of gasoline through it.

Late in his life, Fred became interested in digital photography and electric radio control helicopters and spent a lot of time with those hobbies. He really enjoyed taking pictures of his family and grandchildren. He took some great pictures.

Joan was born to Charles R. and Jewell (Fuquay) Sutton in Boonville, Indiana June 7, 1935. Charles Sutton was one-quarter Native American. His great grandmother was a Native America, but her tribe was not known. Joan was an honor student and graduated from Chandler High School. She worked at Old National Bank as a bookkeeper. Joan married Fred during his senior year at Purdue and she worked at a Life Insurance company in Lafayette, Indiana. Joan stayed at home to raise their three children until her youngest child started grade school. During this time she did volunteer work at the schools and also served on the school board for Brentwood Elementary School. She was active in the PTA and worked at the election polls as an inspector. Joan enjoyed participating in bowling leagues, golf leagues, bridge club and gourmet club. She was an accomplished seamstress and sewed coats, dresses and other clothing for herself and her daughter.

In 1967 Joan went back to college and received her B.S. and M.S. in elementary education from Indiana University. Joan taught and substituted in Fort Wayne Community Schools for almost 20 years. She especially enjoyed her assignments teaching special education students. Joan retired in 2003 from teaching. Joan enjoyed doing tole painting and woodcrafts and sold her crafts at many craft shows including the Grabill Fair for seven years. Joan also enjoyed scrap booking, stamping and gardening.

Fred and Joan's children include Frederick (Rick) Lynn, Jeffery Logan and Rhonda Lynette. Rick Erickson married Cheryl (Cheri) Renee Herndon and had four children: Lindsey, Jennifer, Frederick (Derick) and Andrew. Rick and Cheri's daughter Lindsey Erickson married Todd Zepke and had three children: Lydia, Liam and Kiera. Jeff Erickson married LuAnn May and had two children: Megan and Chelsea. Rhonda Erickson married Daniel Godfrey and had three children: Amanda, Daniel and Shaina.

Submitted by Jeff Erickson

MARY & HERMAN EWIGLEBEN

Herman Ewigleben was born JuJy 8, 1852 in Behringen, Germany and emigrated to this country in 1874 . Mary Loennies was born in Suelze, Schwerin, Germany March 4, 1868 and came over in 1887, a venturesome soul who made the journey alone. She had one brother, Karl, who then came and lived in Chicago. Herman had two brothers who came earlier and settled in the Hobart-Portage Indiana area..

Herman and Mary married in Defiance, Ohio, on December 29, 1890. A daughter, Gertrude, was born in 1893. They soon went to Chicago and here was born a son, Walter, in 1895. The family then moved to Hobart, Indiana, and another son, Harry Peter, was born in 1897. By 1900 they made their final move to the Summit city and sons Martin and Albert were born in 1900 and 1903.

Gertrude married Fort Wayne native Frank Gowen in 1912, and they had a son, William Henry, in 1913; the child lived but eight months. Gertrude later married Henry Claymiller; this couple had a daughter, Helen. Helen died in 1925 of tuberculosis, and the young parents had no more children. But Gertrude was a loving Aunt to her nieces and nephews. Gertrude died in 1963 and is buried in old Concordia Cemetery.

Harry, Martin, Gertrude and Walter Ewigleben

Walter served with the U.S. Army, participating in several battles on the Western Front including Chateau Thierry and Argonne Forest. He married Gladys Nickerson in 1926, and they spent their early married life in South Bend where a son, Walter Jr., was born in 1927. They made a final move to Columbia City where a daughter, Luann, was born in 1936. Walter worked many years at Daniel Brothers, and, with Gladys, owned a small grocery store that was attached to their house. Walter died in 1965 and is buried in Greenhill Cemetery in Columbia City.

Harry married Vesta Caldwell and spent all of his working years at the Fort Wayne Dairy Equipment Co. He and Vesta raised three daughters, Dorothy born in 1926, Betty in 1930 and Denelda Jean, completing the family in 1932. All of Harry's daughters were educated in the public school system, all graduating form South Side High School. Harry died in 1975 and is resting in Lindenwood Cemetery.

Martin's first wife, Anna Malnowski, died in childbirth, and he later married Muriel. Martin was a toolmaker by trade and was owner-operator of Advance Machine Works.

Albert lived his life in Lansing Michigan, and was a lifelong auto worker in the Oldsmobile Division. He married Frieda Marie Ruger and they had two children, Robert, born in 1928, and Nancy Ann, born in 1941.

Herman was a laborer all his life, for many years a driver for a brewing company. Also working as a plumber and a teamster, he labored hard for his wife and children. He was the typical close-mouthed, stern German Papa. Mary was the matriarch of the family and raised a loving and loyal family. Herman and Mary have but four related families still living in Fort Wayne. Their many descendants can be found in Columbia City and Valparaiso in Indiana, and in Arizona, Florida, Michigan, Illinois and Ohio. Herman died in 1918 while his son was serving in WWI in France. Mary died of complications of diabetes in 1923, succumbing to a disease that was passed on to each of her children. Herman and Mary are resting side by side in old Concordia Cemetery in Fort Wayne.

Submitted by Betty Nuttle

EXNER FAMILY

Robert Rudolph Exner was born March 28, 1858 near Krumhuebel, Germany now called Karpacz, Poland. His father's name was Ernest Exner, mother's name unknown. He lived in a small village in the mountains near Breslau, Germany now Wroclaw, Poland situated on both sides of the Oder River in Lower Silesia, Prussia. Krumhuebel was a great place for wood carving which Robert learned as a boy. Throughout his lifetime he decorated nearly everything he made of wood with a little woodcarving. Robert's uncles and cousins lived in nearby Exner Valley. He went to school for a few years but was orphaned while very young and was forced to make his own living.

Back, L to R: Albert, Otto, Herman and Ernest. Front, L to R: Elsie, Robert, Richard Augusta, Della and Emma

At age 23, he decided to come to America. After earning and saving as much as he could, he agreed to work in the boiler room in the bottom of the ship shoveling coal into the boilers to help pay his passage. Robert sailed from Bremen, Germany to New York in the fall of 1881 with the Liebig family on the steamship "Rhine". He was sent to Wanatah, Indiana and got work on a farm owned by Mr. Boese where he worked for a year, then went to work for the Albany (Nonan) Railroad as a section hand.

In 1882 he met a young lady at church who recently arrived from Germany. She didn't speak English so they enjoyed talking to each other in German. Her name was Augusta Wilhelmina Rekow. Augusta was born in Posen, Germany now Posen, Poland, near the Reisen Mountains on October 11, 1859. Her parents were Daniel and Wilhelmina and siblings August, William, Emile, and Ernestine. Augusta's mother died when she was one and a half years old and an aunt reluctantly agreed to care for her. When she was seven years old, her father met a tragic death and she was sent from one home to another to people with large families. An aunt in America, who remembered her, sent for her because she knew Augusta would have a chance for a happy life and better opportunities in America. Augusta received enough money from her aunt to pay for the trip.

In the spring of 1882, Augusta, 22, took the train to Posen, Germany with two cousins, William Albert Boettcher and Ernest Rekow and their families. From Posen they traveled to Berlin and then to Hamburg where they boarded the steamship "Westphalia". The party arrived in America 18 days later, and Augusta went directly to Wanatah, Indiana where her aunt, Caroline Utroska, lived.

Augusta began attending the local Lutheran Church and was introduced to Robert Exner, a young man who arrived in America a few months before her. They had much to talk about and became good friends and enjoyed special dates. They started talking about marriage. After a short romance, Reverend Julius Gruenert married them November 23, 1883 at the Salem Reformed Church in Wanatah.

They lived in Wanatah for about six years where three children joined the family. Ernest was born August 7, 1884, Elsa April 16, 1886, and Emma April 8, 1888. The family moved to Fort Wayne in the spring of 1889 and lived on a little farm for about a year, but that didn't work out. Herman was born May 29, 1890 while they lived on the farm.

The family moved to a house on New Haven Avenue. Robert, small in stature but very strong, went to work for the Wabash Railroad as a section hand for a year before going to work for the Pennsylvania Railroad. He worked on the coal docks about a year, then in the car repair shops as a blacksmith's helper. Later he was promoted to head blacksmith, a job he kept for about 40 years. A son Otto was born March 7, 1894 while they lived on New Haven Avenue. Then they moved to Edsall Street where Albert arrived July 16, 1896 and Edward on May 23, 1899. Edward only lived four months. Next came daughter Della on July 11, 1901 and Richard arrived February 2, 1907. The family lived on Edsall Street until 1924.

Their son, Ernest, helped Robert build a new home at 1717 Lumbard Street. They moved there in 1924 with Richard, the only child still at home. Robert continued working until he became fatally ill with cancer. He died at home August 6, 1931 at age 73 and was buried in the Odd Fellows Cemetery on Hartzell Road in New Haven, Indiana.

Augusta remained in the Lumbard Street home and in her later years was cared for by her widowed daughter, Elsa (Elsie) Beamer. Augusta died at home January 11, 1946 at age 86. She was buried beside her husband, Robert.

The first Exner reunion in 1925 was held at Fred Linker's farm and was held there for many years thereafter.

Submitted by Roger W. Linker

AMON FARMER FAMILY

Amon Farmer, son of Andrew and Catharine (Bennett) Farmer, was born about December 24, 1842 in Allen County, Indiana and died June 20, 1910 in Anthony, Harper County, Kansas, where he is buried in Forest Park Cemetery. During the Civil War he enlisted from Hellers Corners in Allen County and served as a Private and Corporal in Company E., 88 Indiana Volunteer Infantry. Amon was wounded in battle on Utoy Creek near Atlanta, Georgia on August 7, 1864, and later received a disability pension. He was discharged June 7, 1865 and returned to Allen County. Amon married first on October 19, 1865, Sarah "Sadie" Steepleton. She died September 8, 1869 and was buried in Eel River Cemetery. It is unknown whether Amon and Sarah had children. In 1870 he was working in a sawmill in Allen County and was apparently single with no children.. He married second, August 7, 1871, to Fransetta Hyatt, (daughter of William Hyatt?) Amon and Fransetta moved west with their first two children to the prairies of Kansas and by 1880 were located in Anthony, Harper County, a southernmost county bordering Oklahoma. Amon, however, was in southwest Kansas in the summer of 1886, when he filed for a pension increase at Meade Center in Meade County. (Perhaps he was there to work the wheat harvest.) In Harper County he farmed in Berlin Township.

Amon and Fransetta (Hyatt) Farmer Family, Anthony Kansas, 1890s

Known children of Amon Farmer and Fransetta Hyatt: Rufus Omer Farmer, born ca. May 1872, Allen County, Indiana; married September14, 1897, Harper County, Kansas, to Eliza (Susan Eliza?) Mock. Lorina May Farmer, born ca. June 1875, Allen County, Indiana; married August 28, 1901, Harper County, Kansas, to Elmer F. Bonhert.

Mary Luella "Minnie", born ca. October 1881 (Harper?) County, Kansas; married November 24, 1898, Harper County, Kansas, to George M. Huffman. Orvis M. "Orvie" Farmer, born ca. July 1882, Harper County, Kansas. Otto Earl Farmer, born ca. February 1885, Harper County, Kansas. Adda Maud Farmer, born ca. August 1890, Harper County, Kansas.

Submitted by Becky (Farmer) Harris

ANDREW FARMER FAMILY

Andrew Farmer's first known connection with Allen County was when he, "of Miami County, Ohio," received a U.S. land patent for forty acres in Eel River Township on February 10, 1835. He had been married on October 20, 1832 in Miami County, Ohio to Catharine Bennett, who was born in Pennsylvania. With his parents, William and Jane (Wyatt) Farmer, Andrew had arrived in Miami County about 1819 from Franklin County, Virginia, where he was born July 20, 1812. By June 1836 Andrew and Catharine Farmer were residents of Allen County, Indiana.

Andrew and Catharine joined the local Methodists and were listed in James Johnston's Pastor's Pocket Records as members of "Thompson's Class of Allen Circuit" in 1856-1857. Catharine died June 5, 1863 and was buried in Eel River Cemetery. Andrew remarried June 24, 1864 Nancy (Hiatt/Hyatt?) Hollopeter. By 1880 Andrew and Nancy had relocated to Columbia City, Whitley County, where he was a grocer. Andrew died there September 30, 1897 at age eighty-five. He was buried beside his first wife, Catharine Bennett, in Eel River Cemetery. The following events took place in Allen County, Indiana unless otherwise noted.

Known children of Andrew Farmer and Catharine Bennett:

Rosanna Farmer, born ca.1833, (Miami County, Ohio?); married on June 19, 1851, Gideon Kinzy. Rosanna and Gideon may have had a son, John, born ca.1853. Rosanna may have died, because Gideon Kinzy later married her sister, Sarah Ann Farmer, (see below.)

Andrew Farmer, 1812-1897

Margaret Jane Farmer, born July 17, 1839; died January 24, 1908; married first on September 26, 1858, John Maxwell; married second on December 21, 1867, Thomas J. Timmerson. See Margaret Jane Farmer-Maxwell-Timmerson Family.

Sarah Ann Farmer, born ca.1840; died after January 12, 1920; married on January 29, 1860, Gideon Kinzy.

Amon Farmer, born ca. December 24, 1842; died June 20, 1910, Harper County, Kansas; married first on October 19, 1865, Sarah Steepleton; married second on August 17, 1871, Francetta Hyatt. See Amon Farmer Family.

Martha?/Mathew? Farmer, b. ca. 1844?

John W. Farmer, born ca. June 22, 1848; died June 1921, Noble County, Indiana; married, second(?), Sara Ann Harp. See John W. Farmer Family.

George Washington Farmer, born June 20, 1851; died January 11, 1947, Alden, Rice County, Kansas; married September 8, 1872, Martha Ann Hutsel. See George Washington Farmer Family.

Naomi Farmer, born ca.1854, and Olive Farmer (?) born ca.1859.)

Known children of Andrew Farmer and Nancy (Hiatt/Hyatt?) Hollopeter:

Rosa Farmer, born April 11, 1865; died 1946, (Whitley County?); married April 25, (1880?), Whitley County, William A. "Allie" Patterson.

Nora Jane Farmer, born ca.1869, (Whitley County?); married March 6, 1887, Whitley County, Arthur Beck.

Daisy A. Farmer, born ca.1872, (Whitley County?)

Submitted by Kurt Hulse

GEORGE WASHINGTON FARMER FAMILY

George Washington Farmer, son of Andrew and Catharine (Bennett) Farmer, was born June 20, 1851 in Eel River Township. On September 19, 1872 he married Martha Ann Hutsel of Wesley Chapel, the daughter of George M. and Mary M. (Rock) Hutsel. Martha predeceased George, and died November 11, 1933 while they lived in Sterling, Rice County Kansas. A few years later George moved to Alden, also in Rice County, and made his home with his son, Andrew Mitchell Farmer, where he died January 11, 1947 at age ninety-five. Both George and Martha are buried in the Alden-Valley Cemetery.

They made the move to the dry and treeless Kansas plains in November 1883, traveling the last leg of the journey on the Santa Fe railroad that had opened the area to settlement only a decade earlier. They were not the only Allen County people to migrate there; others included the Ross and Fair families. On the trip George rode in the baggage car with the furniture and livestock. They settled in Raymond Township in Rice County, where Martha's stepfather was getting a 160-acre homestead. The nearby town of Raymond was one of the robust end-of-the-cattle-trail shipping points of the 1800s, and enjoyed a reputation to match. George and Martha Farmer, however, remained steadfast Methodists all their lives, and probably attended the rural Wesleyan Methodist Church a mile away from their home, or the Methodist Episcopal Church in Raymond.

After retiring from farming, they moved to the thriving little city of Sterling. There George spent his time as custodian of the large Methodist Church. Their children spread to other locales and had varied careers, but kept in touch with the relatives back in Allen County.

Children of George Washington Farmer and Martha Ann Hutsel born in Allen County, Indiana:

Maud Farmer, born July 25, 1873; died August 25, 1873.

Andrew Mitchell Farmer, born December 16, 1784; died June 27, 1955, Sterling, Rice County, Kansas; married, first, on January 8, 1905, in Shawnee, Pottowatomie County, Oklahoma, Mary Sylvia Warcup; divorced; married second, on November 9, 1927, in Newton, Harvey County, Kansas, Jessie May (Mosier) Farmer, widow of Andrew's younger brother, Lawrence Boyd Farmer, (see below.) Andrew became a successful farmer and cattleman in the Raymond and Alden area.

George and Martha (Hutsel) Farmer, Mary, and Richard Wayne, Raymond Kansas, ca. 1908

Fred Dwight Farmer, born June 6, 1877; died February 24, 1949, Helena, Lewis and Clark County, Montana, where he had prospected for gold and traveled with wheat threshing crews. He never married.

Bessie Olive Farmer, born January 3, 1880; married on September 24, 1903, Samuel Lipp; died in childbirth, rural Raymond, July 17, 1904.

Mary Helen Farmer, born June 15, 1883; died January 16, 1942, Fayetteville, Washington County, Arkansas; married ca.1918, (Independence, Montgomery County, Kansas?), Edward J. Mout. Mary was a nurse in Arkansas City, Kansas until her marriage, after which she and "E. J." Mout operated a dairy farm in Fayetteville.

Children of George Washington Farmer and Martha Hutsel born in Raymond Township, Rice County, Kansas:

Lawrence Boyd Farmer, born April 17, 1886; died June 24, 1919, Douthat, Oklahoma; married July 2, 1912, Joplin, Jasper County, Missouri, Jessie May Mosier. "Boyd" worked the lead and zinc mines in northwest Oklahoma and southwest Missouri.

Richard Wayne Farmer, born April 7, 1901; died September 19, 1965, Tucson, Pima County, Arizona; married, first in Rice County, Kansas, Lucille Hollowell; divorced; married second, on January 31, 1936, in Cherokee, Alfalfa County, Oklahoma, Leola Mae (Beutler) Harder; no children.

Submitted by Doris Farmer Hulse

JOHN W. FARMER FAMILY

John W. Farmer, son of Andrew and Catharine (Bennett) Farmer, was born in Allen County, Indiana ca. June 22, 1848. He grew up in Eel River Township, but it was in neighboring Whitley County that he married Sarah Ann Harp on November 17, 1872. She was born in October 1854. In 1880 John and Sarah, with their young family, were living in Churubusco, Whitley County. John was working as a teamster. By 1900 they lived in Swan Township of Noble County, Indiana where John died in June 1921. He was buried in Eel River Cemetery back in Allen County. Sometime after her husband's death, Sarah Ann moved into LaOtto where she made her home with their son, Albert, "Bert" Farmer.

She died there September 2, 1937 and was also buried in Eel River Cemetery.

Known children of John W. Farmer and Sarah Ann Harp:

Charles Farmer, born ca.1874, (Whitley County?)

Elinor J. Farmer, born ca.1876, (Whitley County?)

Myrtle I. Farmer, born ca. 1878, (Whitley County?)

Andrew Oliver Farmer, born May 22, 1880; died ca. July 2, 1954, Noble County; married December 21, 1906, Noble County, Lida Ann LaFevor, daughter of Samuel LaFevor and Cora Ross. Lida Ann was born June 18, 1888.

William E. Farmer, born March 5, 1882, (Whitley County?); married first on November 13, 1905, Noble County, Catherine (Wolf) Weaver, daughter of Benville Wolf and Lillie Perkins. Catherine was born March 7, 1885. Catherine may have died, because William E. Farmer later married Mina "Minnie" E. Richards on April 5, 1911, also in Noble County. Mina was the daughter of George W. Richards and Sarah A. Huff. Mina had been born July 6, 1879.

George Albert "Bert" Farmer, born ca. June 1885, (Whitley County?); died after 1930; never married?

Ocie C. Farmer, born ca. October 1886, (Whitley County?); (married ca. 1906, George H. Brodt?)

Lester E. Farmer, born ca. August 1890, (Whitley County?); died May 10, 1903, Noble County.

Submitted by John W. Farmer

MARGARET JANE FARMER-MAXWELL-JIMMERSON FAMILY

Margaret Jane Farmer, daughter of Andrew and Catharine (Bennett) Farmer, was born July 17, 1839, in Eel River Township. She died January 24, 1908 and was buried in Lindenwood Cemetery in Fort Wayne. Margaret Jane married first, on September 26, 1858, John Maxwell. John had been born in 1839, also in Allen County. He farmed for a short time before enlisting to fight in the Civil War. He died on August 30, 1863 while serving in Company E, 88 Indiana Volunteer Infantry. Margaret was left a widow with two small children. She married, second on December 21, 1867, Thomas J. Jimmerson and had another child. Jimmerson apparently left his family, and is thought to have died by 1870. The following events took place in Allen County.

Children of Margaret Jane Farmer and John Maxwell:

William Maxwell, born on September 9, 1859; (married ca.1893, Daisy ____?)

Sarah Anna "Anna" Maxwell, born on May 2, 1861; died May 18, 1935; married December 13, 1877, David Wiley Watterson. He was born June 15, 1857 and died January 31, 1835. See Sweet-Watterson Family.

Children of Margaret Jane Farmer and Thomas J. Jimmerson:

Lena May Jimmerson, born ca. August 1868; (married ca.1884, Walter S. Shoaff?) [Margaret Jimmerson, a widow age 61 is living in their household in St. Joseph Township in 1900 and is identified as Walter's mother-in-law.]

Submitted by Stephanie Borntreger

BALTZAR & MARY LOUISE (SCHAAB) FEDERSPIEL JR. FAMILY

Baltzar Federspiel Sr. was born in 1815 in Alsace-Lorraine, France, an area between Germany and France. Control of the area changed through the centuries, depending on who won the last war. In 1815 it was under the control of France, so Baltzar is listed as being born in France. He came to America when he was 15 and stayed in New York until he was 21. Little is known about his wife and children, other than their son, Baltzar, Jr., who was born in Wisconsin in 1842. The family moved to the village of New Haven and Baltzar, Sr., opened a blacksmith shop.

Baltzar, Jr., succeeded his father in the blacksmith shop. On November 19, 1874, in Saint John's Catholic Church, New Haven, he married Mary Louise Schaab, who was born in Ohio in 1855. They had seven children: Cecelia, John, William, Raymond, Leo, Clair, and Eugene. Baltzar, Jr. died in 1915 when, while picking cherries at his home in New Haven, he fell ten feet to the ground. It was the opinion of the attending physician and the coroner, E. H. Kruis that his death was due to a stroke rather than the fall. Mary Louise died in 1936 and they are buried side-by-side in Saint John's Catholic Cemetery in New Haven.

William H. Federspiel, son of Baltzar and Mary Louise, was born in New Haven in 1881. He followed in his father's footsteps as a young man and became a blacksmith. He and his brothers, John and Eugene, took over the business after their father died in 1915. On October 27, 1904, in Saint John's Catholic Church, Will married Leoma L. Thompson, daughter of George W. and Mary Jane (Morrow) Thompson of New Haven. They had four children: Ronald, who died at birth in 1905; Donald, born in 1908; Mary C., born in 1911; and Helena, born in 1915.

Will was a very successful man. He had no formal education, but was a self-taught farmer and banker and he was successful at both ventures. He left the blacksmith business in 1923 to operate his own truck farm until 1948. He was on the board of directors of the old Peoples State Bank from 1916, when it was founded, until it merged with Lincoln National Bank and Trust Company. He served as vice president from 1921 to 1941, when he became the president of the bank until the merger.

Leoma developed nephritis after the birth of her third child. For six months she suffered greatly with this disease, for which there was no cure at the time. Leoma died on September 29, 1915. During Leoma's illness, to help care for the home and children, Will hired a housekeeper by the name of Frieda Wellman, who stayed until Leoma's death. At that time, Mary Jane Thompson, Leoma's mother, moved in and cared for Donald and Mary. Helena was taken to Baltzar and Mary Louise Federspiel's home and was cared for by them. Mary Jane Thompson filled a huge void in the children's lives and they remembered her affectionately all their lives. She helped Will care for them until he married the young woman he had hired as a housekeeper earlier, Frieda Wellman. Will and Frieda had five children: Lucille, Marjorie, Eleanor, Deloris, and James.

William Federspiel died on June 27, 1963, and is buried in Saint John's Catholic Cemetery in New Haven, with his two wives on either side of him. Frieda died on November 18, 1986.

Submitted by Carolyn Holbrook.

IGNATIUS & ANNA MARIA (HIBLER/HUBLER) FELTER

Ignatius and Anna Maria (Hibler/Hubler) Felter came to Allen County from Alsace, France. They left Havre de Grace, France on March 3, 1838 on the ship Emerald and arrived in New York City on April 25, 1838. With them were their children, Theresa, Mary M., Louisa M., and Ignatius John. Tradition and the 1880 Census have John born on the ocean. In 1841 in Fort Wayne, the last baby, Alexander, died the day of his birth. On December 31, 1842, Ignatius declared his intention to become a citizen of the United States and of the State of Indiana and to "renounce forever all allegiance and fidelity to every Foreign Prince, Potentate, State, or Sovereignty whatsoever and particularly to Lewis Phillippe, King of the French of whom I am now a subject." His citizenship was granted on June 19, 1847. Ignatius died February 8, 1851, and he is buried in the Catholic Cemetery.

Felter Sisters and Brother John, circa 1875

Careful examination of his tombstone leads to an interesting story. Beneath the dates of birth and death, the following translated from German says, "Here I am and wait for you. Don't give up, and pray for me." At the bottom, also translated from German, "And for our son, Johan Felter." Obviously, the widow and her surviving children ordered this tribute to son John. As a teenager he had been apprenticed to Peltier, the undertaker. Hating the work, John ran away and was never heard from. Consequently, Ignatius died thinking that John was dead. However, about 25 years later, John suddenly came to visit his sisters and mother. All those years, he had been living in Denver, and then in Vinta County, Wyoming. *Vinta County, Its Place in History* contributes the following: "Another man named John Felter, who had made South Pass a stopping place after an unfortunate financial experience in Denver, came to Evanston about the samee time as Anthony. He took up land across the river and sold milk... He was sexton of the cemetery, and before the purchase of a hearse in the town, the cart from which milk was peddled in the morning hours often bore in the afternoon a casket to its final resting place. He died in 1920. The story is told that he gave directions that his body should be placed beside that of his wife in a vault he had built several years before in the Catholic cemetery, and that the side of the vault should be closed and sealed, never to be reopened. Why he who had laid so many to rest in Mother Earth should object to having his own body interred, is a matter of fruitless speculation."

Because the 1840 Census of Allen County includes "Ignatz Felden (Other spellings-Felder)", descendants of Ignatius are eligible for the Society of Indiana Pioneers, and Kenneth Lawrence Lauer, a great-great-grandson, has honored Ignatius by becoming a member.

Submitted by Nancy Jenkins

FERGUSON FAMILY

Moses Ferguson married Elizabeth Kennels in Columbiana County, Ohio, April 29, 1824. Their son, James, born in Ohio, married on October 21, 1855, in Mahoning County to Dorothy Altman, daughter of John Altman and first wife, Sally Meese.

These families were in Huntington County, Indiana, by 1850. In the census, James is listed as a Blacksmith in Bippis. Children born to James and Dorothy were Emily, Peridora, Mahula, Charles, Walter, Elmer, James and John. John was the submitter's great-grandfather who was married July 24, 1879 in Kosciusko County to Margaret Gall, daughter of Jacob Gall of Silver Lake. John and Margaret were the parents of four daughters born in Kosciusko County; Dora Pearl, Clara, Kathryn and Ida.

By 1900 James and Dorothy and John and Margaret, along with others, moved to Fort Wayne, living on Holden Avenue. The Ferguson boys worked on the railroad except John, who had a store. The girls worked as seamstresses at Fort Wayne tailoring shops. Ida's uncles worked with Willard Watson, and he was introduced to Ida. Ida and Willard were married in Fort Wayne, September 2, 1903. Willard was the son of Aaron and Tabitha (Howey) Watson of DeKalb County. The Howeys were pioneers in Allen and DeKalb Counties. Refer to *Allen County Pioneers, William Howey*, by Patricia Watson Dyson.

Willard and Ida built a home near Route 427 and the railroad tracks at Auburn, and Willard worked as a grinder at the Auburn Automobile Company. Life was good, and Willard and Ida had two boys, Elroy (submitter's father) and Irvin, and two girls, Nellie and Annabelle. Elroy related that his dad walked to work and one day came home with a great big watermelon in a shiny red wagon. His mother made delicious cherry pies from the picked cherries in their yard. He remembers his grandpa, Aaron, and his dad pouring black coffee over their shoes to shine them.

The flu took its toll in 1918. Ida died two weeks after Annabelle was born, July 5, 1918. The following year Willard died in Garrett Hospital in October, 1919. He had a car and toured the doctor around visiting the sick during the flu epidemic. He was exposed to the flu and also had emery dust in his lungs from the grinders at work.

James, Dorothy, John and Margaret Ferguson are buried in Lindenwood Cemetery, Fort Wayne. Ida, Willard, Aaron and Tabitha Watson are buried in Woodlawn Cemetery in Auburn.

Willard Watson, Ida and Tony Lindeman, Kate and John Barnhart, Arthur Blombach Front Row: Dora P. Elroy, Nellie and Irvin Watson, John and Margaret (Gall) Ferguson, 2 children (uk), Clara and Otto Blombach, girl (uk) Picture about 1913

Elroy was adopted by Bill and Goldie Zerns. He later took the Watson name back according to Well County courts. Elroy married Vera Bender, Wells County, December 8, 1934. Elroy's death was on August 13, 1995, and Vera's death was February 1, 2004. Both are buried at Fairview Cemetery, Bluffton, Indiana. The submitter was the only child. She married Robert Dyson of Wabash County and had one son and four daughters, six grandchildren and three great-granddaughters.

Robert and Patricia Dyson resided in Allen County from 1955 to 1970.

Submitted by Patricia Dyson

MICHAEL FICK

This story is about how the house shown in the picture became the home of Michael Fick.

Somewhere around the middle of the nineteenth century, Adam Seeger and his wife, Christina; came to America and settled on their farm in Lake Township in Allen County. To them was born one son, George, in 1857. George married Mary Blessing, the daughter of Peter Blessing, another early Lake Township settler.

To the couple four children were born, including twins, Charles and Henry, and Emma and Martha. Adam Seeger died at the age of 67. Six weeks later his son, George, died at the age of 33. Left behind was Grandmother Seeger with her daughter-in-law, Mary and Mary's four small children.

At this time, Michael Fick was already living in America, arriving from Germany in 1880. He came to Ellis Island, dug potatoes for 30 days straight in Pennsylvania, and then immigrated west till he came to Indiana where he found a large settlement of German people. He then was able to find work on a farm south of Fort Wayne.

The deaths of both her husband and son left Grandma Seeger in dire need of someone to help work the farm. She soon found out about Michael Fick and persuaded him to come and farm the land. Michael became her farmhand, but soon became attached to the Seeger family.

In 1892, he married Mary Seeger, George's young widow. Michael soon became like a second father to Mary's children. During the next ten years, three more children were born to Michael and Mary. Those three you see in the picture. Mary left Michael a widower with three children (the older children had already left home) when she died at 49 in the year, 1909. Grandmother Christina Seeger agreed to give Michael Fick the farm if he promised to take keep her the rest of her life, which he did.

The house pictured was probably built in the 1860s, replacing the previous log cabin.

Michael died in 1934, leaving the farm to his son, Paul (seen in the picture). Paul was forced to tear down this house after it fell into disrepair. He built a new, similar-type house in its place in 1937. During the building of the new house, Paul and his family lived in the old kitchen, which was turned and moved to the side and sat over a cellar. This structure still stands today. Paul Fick died in 1966, leaving the farm to his son, Carl. Carl retired in 1989 and turned the farm over to his son, Ronald. He, his wife, Elizabeth, and daughter, Maleah, now live on the farm.

Submitted by Elizabeth Fick, as told to her by her father-in-law, Carl Fick (Michael Fick's grandson). Picture was given to Elizabeth by the late Flora Fick (Carl Fick's mother).

Michael Fick, and children, Paul, Louis, and Bertha

WAYNE FIKE FAMILY

Wayne Merle Fike was a home birth at Toledo Pike, Allen Township, Noble County, Indiana. His great-great-great grandparents, Samuel and Catherine Fike, were both from Pennsylvania and migrated to Ohio, where Elias was born in 1826. Then, before 1850, the family migrated to Michigan. In the 1850 Federal Census of Sherman Township, St. Joseph County, Michigan, Catherine, age 63, is found living with Jacob, age 30; Elias, age 23; Charles, age 8; and Sarah, age 5.

Elias Fike married Louise Sprague in St. Joseph County, Michigan, on October 16, 1851. Louise was born in Michigan. Elias and Louise had three sons: William Riley was born April 9, 1856, in Michigan, and died April 19, 1906, in DeKalb County, Indiana; Charles Henry was born May 13, 1858, in Michigan, and died December 15, 1926, in Indiana; and Jefferson was born in 1861 in Michigan and died in 1936 in Indiana.

William Riley Fike married Ella Estelle Sowers on November 22, 1883, in Noble County, Indiana. Ella was born September 23, 1865, in Noble County, Indiana, and died December 21, 1962, in Butler, DeKalb County, Indiana. Ella is the daughter of Phillip Sowers and Amanda Harriet Yeakey. William and Ella had five sons: Raymond, Warren William, Harry, Howard (who was born April 9, 1895, and died August 10, 1974 in Allen County, Indiana), and Arthur Sr. William was a great judge of good horse flesh and always had fine horse on the farm.

Howard Fike married Ruth May Christlieb on December 20, 1921. Ruth was born August 1, 1905, in Noble County, Indiana, and died December 20, 1987, in Fort Wayne, Allen County, Indiana. Ruth was the daughter of William Christlieb and Florence Burke. Howard and Ruth became the parents of five children: Annabel M., Dorothy Ella, Glen LeRoy, Beulah Irene, and Wayne Merle. At the time of Howard's death he was working for the Desoto School System as a janitor. Howard was much loved by the staff and students and there are stories of Howard taking time out of his busy schedule to talk with them, play a quick game, or comfort them when they were hurt. Howard left many pleasant memories behind.

Wayne Merle Fike married Orphia Ann Stayer on June 30, 1956, in Auburn, Noble County, Indiana. Ann was born May 31, 1938, in Angola, Steuben County, Indiana and died June 11, 2001, in Fort Wayne, Allen County, Indiana. Ann's parents were James Stayer and Velma Smith. Wayne and Ann have six children: Christopher Allen, Cheryl Ann, Larry Wayne, Cynthia Kay, Catherine May, and Carla Jo. Times were hard for this family, knowing the heartbreak of an untimely death of son, Larry Wayne, July 6, 1962, at the age of nearly 27 months. They also experienced many happy family times and vacations. Wayne held many jobs and sometimes worked two jobs at a time to care for his large family. In time, Wayne was able to go to work for Dana Corporation from where he retired in 2000.

Submitted by Wayne Fike

Wayne Fike family
Front row: Howard, Wayne, Beulah, Ruth
Back row: Dorothy, Glen, Annabel

FILLMAN FAMILY

Andrew Fillman was born March 29, 1868, in Sweden to Andreas Nilson and Elsa Christianson Fillman. Andrew came to America in 1882 at age 14, settled in Illinois and married Paulina Marie Hallburg on December 24, 1892. They lived in Wynet, Illinois on a farm where three children were born: Fred, on December 10, 1893; Elise on September 21, 1897; and Howard on October 6, 1902. They moved to a farm northwest of Princeton, Illinois where two daughters were born: Florence, January 5, 1905, who lived ten months, dying November 5, 1905, and Rosa on March 9, 1907. Paulina died of pneumonia after childbirth on March 13, 1907. Rosa was raised by Andrew's neice, Esther Sanderhome, in Illinois.

Andrew remarried on December 16, 1909, to Anna Erikson. On March 1, 1911, Andrew left Illinois with his wife Anna, sons Fred and Howard, and daughter Elise, and moved to a farm in Ohio. In August 1913, Andrew moved his family to Allen County, Indiana from Ohio and purchased a farm northeast of Grabill, Indiana, on Cuba and Springfield Center roads. A brick school, then known as the Egypt Grade School, was on the corner of their farm. There Howard finished his elementary school years. Andrew and his sons enjoyed farming. Andrew was proud of his cattle. They were members at the St. Mark's Lutheran church in Harlan, Indiana, now Holy Trinity. Elise had a heart ailment and.died April 11, 1918, at home. Andrew stayed on the farm until he retired in January 1937, and went back to Illinois to live near his daughter Rosa. He died 21 years later on August 27, 1958.

Fred married Cozy Overhosler on September 3, 1936, in the Overhosler home northwest of Harlan, Indiana. They never had children. They lived on three farms, the last being at Georgetown on Highway 37, east of Harlan. They farmed and raised livestock until they became disabled. They were in the Fountain Manor home in Hicksville, Ohio where Cozy died May 17, 1978. Fred died in Hicksville Hospital on February 22, 1982. They are buried in Scipo Cemetery.

L to R: Howard, Marie, Rosa, Ruth, Fred and Cozy Fillman. August, 1958

Howard married Edith Marie Amstutz on April 20, 1930, at the home of the bride's parents, David and Jennie (Haifley) Amstutz on Spencerville Road, two and a half miles north of Harlan, Indiana. Howard and Marie lived in ten different homes, all in Allen County except for three and a half years of their married life. Their daughter, Ruth Marie was born November 17, 1934, in Fort Wayne. She graduated from Leo High School in 1953. Their last farm was north of Leo on Schlatter Road, just off of Highway 1. Ruth married Edward Wilder on November 26, 1959 at St. Vincent's Church on the edge of Fort Wayne. They resided in Adams County, Indiana and had four daughters, Roxanne, Rozann, Ronda, and Rolisa. Howard died in Fort Wayne on September 12, 1986. Edith died in New Haven on January 4, 1996. They are buried in Leo Cemetery.

Submitted by Ruth Wilder

IVESTER ABRAHAM LINCOLN FISHER & EMMALINE MYERS

One month before Abraham Lincoln was nominated for president of the United States, Ivester was given the middle name Abraham Lincoln. Ivester, born April 4, 1860, Lafayette Twp., Allen County, Indiana, was son of Samuel Fisher and Hannah Bowman. Ivester died November 21, 1828, Roanoke, Huntington County, Indiana.

Samuel Fisher came to Allen County about 1853 from Columbiana County, Ohio, He came with Henry and Harriet Jane (Armstrong) Bowman and was their hired hand. On July 4, 1859, Samuel and Hannah, the daughter of Henry and Harriet Bowman, slipped away from a picnic in Fort Wayne and were married at the court house. For history of Samuel Fisher and Henry Bowman see: *Pictorial History of Fort Wayne, 1917, Grisswold, V.11*

Emmaline Myers, born September 16, 1858, Clear Creek Township, Huntington County, Indiana, was the daughter of John David Myers, born September 13, 1815, Maryland, and Esther Thomas, born January 16, 1819, Starke County, Ohio. John and Esther were married in Ohio and moved to Huntington County about 1853. Emmaline died January 18, 1924, Fort Wayne.

Ivester and Emmaline were married January 21, 1886, Huntington County, Indiana. Ivester farmed and Emmaline wove rugs. Their children were:

(1) William Wade Oliver Myers/Fisher, born December 21, 1879, d. November 19, 1906, married Sarah Fairchild.

(2) Irma, born May 12, 1887, died February 25, 1913, married first, Jesse M. Forrest,

Samuel, Ivy, Irma, and Helen

second, Henry Hartman. She had the following children: Helen Forrest (Johnson), Eldon Hartman, Evelyn Hartman (Blanchard, Anderson)

(3) Edna Ione, born July 4, 1888, died April 17, 1974, married Donald DeWitt; they had the following children: Audra, Francil, Ruth

(4) Esther Ann, born January 4, 1890, died about 1902

(5) Eva, born December 10, 1891, died May 8, 1962, married Lloyd Griffith; they adopted a daughter, Erma Jean.

(6) Elda, born December 10, 1891, died December 25, 1941, married Nancy Schell. Their children were: Harley, Maxine (Heth). Elda and Nancy were divorced and he married an Isabelle

(7) Linnie Alverta, born January 10, 1894, died October 9, 1972, married Walter Rindchen. Their children were: Wilhelmina (Szydlowski), Doris (Fuelling), Vivian (Beckman), Luana (Boedeker)

(8) Marion, born July 28, 1895, died July 29, 1982, married Hazel Smith. Their children: Leota (Haverstick), Zola (Kusick). His second marriage was to Della Brandstrator. Their child, Garland Spencer Fisher died an infant. His third marriage was to Dorothy Swarts.

(9) John Samuel, born October 9, 1896, died April 29, 1939, married Mabel Lombard. No children.

(10) Florence Bertha, born January 24, 1898, died January 31, 1965, married Henry Peters. Their children: Dorothy (Johnson, Schinbeckler), Catherine (Parkins)

After the death of Jesse Forrest in 1907 and Irma (Fisher) Forrest in 1913, Ivester and Emmaline raised their granddaughter, Helen Forrest. Helen was born March 9, 1907, died November 26, 1994. She married James L. Johnson, March 13, 1924 in Fort Wayne. They lived in Yoder, Pleasant Township, Allen County, Indiana. Their children are: Gilford, Walter, Marjorie (Kientz), Harold, Bruce, and Dennis.

Submitted by Walter Johnson

FISHMAN FAMILY

David Baer Fishman (known as DB) was born in 1880 in Odessa, Russia, emigrating to the U.S. when he was 19, the first of nine siblings who eventually settled in New York, Indiana and California. DB came from Ellis Island to Indiana by train, where a cousin showed him how to sell clothes from a pushcart, in small Indiana towns, traveling by horse and buggy.

In his travels, DB met Rosa Spector, who was born in the U.S.; they married in 1905 in Lafayette, Indiana, where he opened *The Fashion,* one of the first women's specialty stores in the state, and where their children were born: Ethel, Marvin and Stanley.

In 1921, DB moved the family to Fort Wayne, where he opened *Fishman's,* a store known for exclusive women's fashions, next to W&D on Calhoun Street. DB merged his two stores in 1925 to form a group of twelve specialty stores in the East, Midwest and South. He moved his family to New York so he could manage the group. In 1935 DB returned to Fort Wayne with son Marvin and later with son Stanley (both of whom graduated from the Wharton Business School) to operate his two stores.

Following military service in World War II, the sons assumed the stores' management, and DB and Rosa retired to California where daughter Ethel lived. She graduated from South Side High and Goucher College, married Dr. Milton Firestone (who started his medical practice in 1932 in Fort Wayne) and had daughter Sue, who married Lee Miller and lives in California with their four children: Janet, David, Laurie and Matthew.

Marvin married Betty Grae Lunger in 1949. Daughter Katherine graduated from Carroll High, Kenyon College and Indiana University, married Nick Eastridge, and now lives in Princeton New Jersey with sons John and David. Daughter Marguerite went to Carroll High School, Ohio State and Mills College, and resides in Redwood City, California.

Stanley married Mary Agnes Houlihan in 1947, and had two sons and two daughters: Stan D. who attended South Side High and Bucknell University, married Elizabeth White, and has a daughter Jamie, a son JJ, and all live in Florida. Jeff graduated from Elmhurst High and Carnegie Mellon University, married Marie Zerwas, and lives in Salt Lake City with sons, David and Jacob. Daughter Nancy went to Elmhurst High, Colorado College and Indiana University, and lives in Portland, Oregan; daughter Carol Rose attended Elmhurst High and Stephens College, married Jim Levy and lives in Fort Wayne with children, Jena and Joel.

In 1965 a second *Fishman's* store opened in Glenbrook Square. When the downtown store was demolished to make room for Summit Square in 1974, *Fishman's* moved across the street to the former Walgreen building. Stan D, who worked in retailing at Bullocks Los Angeles and Van Law's in Illinois, returned to Fort Wayne in 1977 to assist in buying and managing duties due to Marvin's retirement. Another branch was opened at Georgetown Square. All three stores were dissolved in the 80s when small stores were on the wane, and national ownerships were taking over retailing.

In 1961, Rosa was the victim of a tragic accident in California. DB returned to Fort Wayne where he died in 1963. Their daughter Ethel died 1997 in California, Marvin, here in 2001.

Stanley is retired and lives with Mary in Fort Wayne, as does daughter Carol with Jim Levy. The other grandchildren of Rosa and DB pursue a variety of careers in the East. West, and South.

Submitted by Stan Fishman

The Fishman Family

FITCH FAMILY HISTORY

Warren John Fitch was born April 15, 1929, in Allen County, Indiana, to Otis and Esther (Doll) Fitch who lived on a farm on the Allen-DeKalb Co. line, containing land in both counties. May 13, 1950 he married Betty Brown, born May 18, 1930, daughter of Guy and Mary (Klinker) Brown. Both the Brown and Klinker families were residents of Monroe Township, Allen County, Indiana. Warren and Betty have four children: Cathy Wies, wife of Rick Wies (Huntertown) now living in Montana. They have two sons, Kyle and Jason Wies. Carol Lockwood, wife of Tim Lockwood (Fort Wayne) now living at Churubusco. They have three children, Daniel, Jared and Lisa. John A. Fitch married Amy Cantu (Huntertown) and they have four children, Judy, Jennifer, Jeremy and David. Larry M. Fitch married Mary Belekanic (Elyria, Ohio) and they have three children, Kelly, Timothy, Katie. Two of the grandchildren are married: Judy to Gabe LaGrange and they have a son, Luke; Lisa to Brandon Bland and she has three children, Chase, Kyle, and Isaiah.

Warren and Betty lived in Avilla for about ten years where he owned Fitch Electric, selling and repairing television and appliances. After a two year stay at LaOtto they moved to Perry Township to build their own home. Warren worked at Magnavox in Fort Wayne for more than twenty years. Betty worked at the Singer Company and JoAnn Fabrics in Fort Wayne. The children all graduated from Carroll High School. Warren passed away on April 25, 2000.

John Fitch and Rosa Belle Hollopeter, Wedding - 1898

Warren had two sisters, Elsie, deceased, and Maxine. Maxine is still living in Florida. She married Richard Ober, deceased, of Garrett and they have four children, Gerry, Susan, Sharon and Teresa. Elsie married Robert Fulk, had three children, Karen, Keith, Kevin. Both boys as well as the parents are deceased.

Warren's family line dates back to Nathaniel Fitch, a very early settler in Perry Township. Nathaniel Fitch and Sarah DeLong (married 1840) had fifteen children. Nathaniel's second son, Mathias married Frances Vandolah in 1867, and they had a son John who married Belle Hollopeter in 1898. John and Belle lived on their farm on the Allen-DeKalb County line. They had three children, Grace, Maurice and Otis. Otis was Warren's father. Grace married Charles Caple and had John and Leann. Maurice married Lois Byerley and had Bryce and Noel. Nathaniel and his descendants have been in Allen County since 1837. He was born in Pennsylvania but his descendants can be traced back to Connecticut to Puritan days and to England before that. Sarah DeLong came from Miami County, Ohio. Frances Vandolah's parents came from Greene County, Ohio, and her father was in the business of building mills. The Hollopeters are a well-known family in Cedar Creek township. Otis Fitch married Esther Doll whose ancestors were the Shillings and Dolls from DeKalb County, Indiana, and emigrated from Stark County, Ohio.

Otis Fitch (1904-1976) worked more than forty years for General Electric as an electrician. His father, John Fitch, (1872-1947) was a farmer and township assessor along with his wife, Belle. John's father Mathias (1843-1923) was a farmer, and ran the sawmill started by his father, Nathaniel, which was in operation until after the turn of the century on Fitch Road in northern Allen County.

Submitted by Betty L. Fitch

FITZGERALD FAMILY

EARLY ALLEN COUNTY SETTLERS FROM IRELAND TO ST. LAWRENCE COUNTY, NEW YORK, TO ALLEN COUNTY, INDIANA

This story starts in Johnstown Parish, Meath County, Ireland; has sojourns in Waddington, Madrid Township, St. Lawrence County, New York, and continues to this day in Fort Wayne, Indiana.

St. Lawrence County officials actively encouraged immigration to the up-state New York area. To this end, several acts were passed to permit aliens to own property. To qualify for this right, the alien must have initiated the process of becoming a naturalized citizen. One of the most significant acts of this process was to denounce allegiance to any and all countries and governments. *Waddington - A Look at Our Past* documents happenings in St. Lawrence County. A bulletin "Lands for Sale on the River St. Lawrence" (page 16) dated December 28, 1819, is evidence of this effort to encourage immigrants. The location, attributes and price of land are some of the details in the bulletin. To establish the legitimacy of these details, there is a "Copy of a Certificate" that included the names of then-current St. Lawrence County alien residents. These residents were from Ireland, Scotland and England.

Among these immigrant residents was William Fitzgerald Jun. from Meath County, Ireland. This was the same William Fitzgerald Sr. who came to Allen County, Indiana in the early 1840s. We will return to him on several occasions later.

The above solicitation was successful because ultimately an area developed in Madrid Township known as the "Irish Settlement" (page 48). In the "Lands for Sale" bulletin it is noted that there were Episcopalian and Presbyterian churches in the area at that time. In the above referenced book, it is noted (page 49) that a group of Catholic men including William Fitzgerald sought incorporation at the county seat in Canton, New York, in 1829. This resulted in a document called the "First Catholic Congregation in the Town of Madrid."

In the St. Lawrence County, New York Alien Book A8, William Fitzgerald appears on page 10. His age was 43 when his "Report of Declaration" was entered March 10, 1829; his arrival date was 1819. This made him eligible to own land (page 50) and (page 185). William Fitzgerald ultimately became a land owner when he purchased one parcel of land from Chas. Sears, January 31, 1832, (page 725) and two other parcels, July 8, 1834, and December 27, 1839, from Joshua Waddington (page 725). William Fitzgerald Jun. (alien in 1819) had a son named William (born in 1814). William (born 1814) was named William Jr. in a land purchase, December 27, 1839, (page 725) from Thos. L. Ogden. The original William Fitzgerald Jun. will subsequently be referred to as William Sr. in the rest of this account.

At local Potsdam, St. Lawrence County, resident named Horace Allen (page 258) was a lawyer from Williston, Vermont. He was active in local civic and political affairs. He had acquired significant land holdings in St. Lawrence County where deed records indicate he purchased more than 37 parcels from 1841 through 1854. We know from Allen County, Indiana, deed records that Horace Allen had acquired at least 4,800 acres in 20 parcels. One such land entry appears in the "Tract Book" page 89, Auditor's Office.

During a period from March 1, 1844, through January 13, 1845, Horace Allen sold Allen County, Indiana, land to Timothy Bacon, John Hagan, David Hoyt, Michael Berry (Barry), William Fitzgerald Sr. and Jr., Andrew Tiernan (Turner) and David Judson. These same individuals sold land in St. Lawrence County, New York, to Horace Allen during a period from October 20, 1843, through September 24, 1845.

No information has been uncovered that explains what caused the re-location of these eight families. It is possible that with additional research the names of Philander D. Randall, Sylvanus Burnham, and James M. Burnham could be added to the above list of families. They are listed as grantees from Horace Allen in *Index of Deeds, Allen County, Indiana*.

It might be reasoned that this 600-700 mile re-location was an achievement at that time, but as we continue to follow William Fitzgerald Jr., we find a hardy family willing to go beyond farming. We have newspaper accounts of William Fitzgerald Jr.'s son, William, (born 1844) having participated in the 1864 gold rush in Montana. He drove an ox team from Fort Wayne to Virginia City, Montana. He remained there for three years. He was credited with building the first shanty in Diamond City, Colorado, in 1867 and giving the city its name. Later on William Fitzgerald Jr.'s son, William (born 1844), and his son, Charles, as well as William Jr.'s sons Henry and Francis and Henry's son, Frank, participated in the Alaskan gold rush. Henry and Frank were there at least three years. William (born 1844) had been in Alaska at least three times.

There are still descendents of William Jr. in Fort Wayne in 2005. They are Michael Fitzgerald through William Jr.'s son Francis, and also Mary Jane Dickmeyer, Junetta Henry and Constance Wells through William Jr.'s son Henry. Through these individuals there are at least two more generations of William Jr. descendents in the Fort Wayne area.

Submitted by R. L. Wells

GEORGE FITZGERALD

He is the eldest son of George and Elsie. He has two brothers William and Joseph, two sisters Mary Beggs and Annette Jette who is deceased. His grandfather was also named George; both his father and grandfather were born, married and died in Kansas City, Missouri. His great grandfather Michael came from Ireland, as did his great-grandmother. She also was a Fitzgerald and she had had several brothers and sisters; a sister Catherine married John Fitzgerald and a brother Frank who married Julia Fitzgerald. Catherine and John lived in Chicago, Illinois. Mary had another sister, Hannora, who married Tom Lacy and they lived in Elmira with Michael and Mary in 1865; they also moved to Kansas City. The Lacys had a daughter Elizabeth, who married Michael Fitzgerald who was born in Ireland and they lived in Omaha, Nebraska, in the early 1900s. Michael and Mary lived in Dubuque, Iowa, in the 1860s then they lived in Elmira, New York, and then moved to Kansas City in 1868.

George's mother was born in Germany and came to the United States in 1924.

George was born in Kansas City, Missouri in 1933. He attended Saint Joseph's Seminary in Kirkwood, Missouri, in 1945-1946 and then he attended Rockhurst High School in Kansas City and graduated in 1950. He joined the Air Force in 1952 and was discharged in 1956. He went to Parks AFB, California for basic training, Keesler AFB, Mississippi for basic electronics and ECM Technician School and spent the remaining time at Biggs AFB, Texas. He attended the University of Missouri where he received a BSEE in February 1960. He went back to graduate school at the University of Missouri 1960-1961. He worked for several companies as an Electrical Engineer in Kansas City, Wichita, Kansas, New Orleans, Louisiana, and St. Louis, Missouri. He moved to Fort Wayne, Indiana in 1976 as an Engineer with ITT Corporation. He never married and has developed an interest in sports and genealogy. George is a volunteer at the Allen County Library in the Genealogy Department and is also a member of the Allen County Genealogical Society.

He is also a world traveler and has attended 12 Olympic games and other sporting events. He retired in 1995 and has spent most of his time playing golf, volunteering and traveling. He is also a collector of Fort Wayne and Olympic memorabilia. George developed an interest in Hugh McCulloch, who lived in Fort Wayne from 1833 to 1865, and compiled Hugh's genealogy. When he found that two of Hugh's cousins married Fairfields, he also did the Fort Wayne Fairfields' genealogy.

He is a member of the Fort Wayne Elks Club and is an avid golfer playing between 120 and 150 rounds a year. On May 19, 2005, George played 72 holes of golf to celebrate his 72nd birthday.

Submitted by George Fitzgerald

MICHAEL & JEAN (JOHNSON) FITZGERALD FAMILY

Michael Martin Fitzgerald was born August 26, 1940, in Fort Wayne, Indiana, to Jess and Waneta Dennie Fitzgerald. Waneta was the daughter of Frank Dennie (1874-1946) and Edith J. Weist

(1878-1954). Jess and Waneta's family included four sons: John, William, Patrick, and Michael.

Mike's great-great-great grandparents, William and Alice Anthony Fitzgerald, came to America in 1819 from County Meath, Ireland, and settled in Madrid, St. Lawrence County, New York. In 1844, the Fitzgerald family traded their land in St. Lawrence County, New York, for land in Allen County, Indiana, owned by Horace Allen, the original landowner of a large part of Allen County. They came to Allen County via the Erie Canal, loaded their household goods on boats and, by that means, were taken up the St. Joseph River to their destination in Cedar Creek Township near Leo, Indiana.

William and Mary Ann Hagan Fitzgerald Family in1885

William and Alice Fitzgerald's family included one daughter, Ann, and three sons, John, William, and Peter. Ann (1809-1852) and her husband, Walter Drew (1800-1871), lived in Cedar Creek Township on the corner of Page and Witmer Roads. Walter and Ann had seven children: Jane, Michael, Bridget, William, Mary Ann, Stephen, and Alice. Many long-time Allen County families have resulted from the marriages in this family — the Muldoons, Codys, and Herberts.

John (1810-1857) and Mary Leonard Fitzgerald (1811-1897) lived on the Springfield Center Road in Cedar Creek Township. Mary was born in Clunis, County Monaghan, Ireland, and came to America in 1833. John and Mary had six children. William (1839-1920) was a pioneer schoolmaster in Milan and Springfield Townships. He left for the Australian gold fields and was there for thirty-three years, then moved to St. Joe, Montana, but returned to live his last twenty years back in Allen County, Indiana. Ellen was married to Michael Tancey, Jane to Thomas O'Brien, Mary to John O'Connor, John to Flora Brown and they moved to Houston, Texas, and Hugh moved to Diamond City, Utah. After John's death in 1857, Mary married Andrew Tieman in 1860.

Peter Fitzgerald (1825-1885) married Ellen Guilford Dills (1834-1908) on April 17, 1865, and lived in Leo, Indiana. Ellen was born in Massachusetts and came with her parents to Allen County at the age of ten. Some of the Guilfords are buried in the Viberg Chapel Cemetery north of Leo. Peter and Ellen had three children: William, Newman, and Lillian. Ellen had three children with her first husband, Charles Dills: Lucy, Lema, and Charles E. Dills.

Mike's great-great-grandparents, William (1812-1888), and Mary Ann Hagan Fitzgerald, (1820-1888), and their eight children (Margaret, Alice, William, Henry, Frank, Elizabeth, Michael, and Mary Jane) lived on the Ricker Road in Milan Township. William and Mary Ann are buried in the small Catholic Cemetery in Leo, Indiana, along with three infants that died shortly after their birth.

Margaret (1840-1900) married John Motherwell (1841-1910) in 1862. John was captain of an Erie Canal boat. They lived on Orchard Street in Fort Wayne, Indiana, with their eleven children

Alice (1841-1923) married Thomas Tieman in 1867 at the Cathedral of the Immaculate Conception in Fort Wayne. Thomas (1843-1918), the son of Andrew and Margaret Craven Tieman, and Alice had nine children. In 1898 they ran a dairy on the New Haven Road, later moving to Fort Wayne.

William (1844-1917) married Mary Rebecca Harber (1840-1905) and lived in St. Joseph Township, Allen County. They had two sons, Edward (1875-1897) and Charles Albert (1877-1957). William was a very successful farmer and also a gold miner. In 1864 he drove an oxen team from Fort Wayne to Virginia City, Montana, at the time of the opening of the large gold fields in that district. In one location he made an exceptionally good strike. It was there that Diamond City was founded, which place he named. In 1898 he went to the Klondike gold fields in Alaska, along with his son, Charles, and his brothers, Henry and Frank. Charles (1877-1957) married Tillie Grash (1874-1937) in 1901. Charlie and Tillie lived on the Leo Road next to Robinson Park and had two sons, William and George. William (1901-1992) married Anna Dannells in 1924 and they had one daughter, June. William's second marriage was to Mary Bobay, daughter of Andrew and Susan Gill Bobay. In 1947 they moved to Fairbanks, Alaska. William and Mary had seven children. George (1904-1981) married Atha Kanauer in 1931 at St. Vincent de Paul Church, Fort Wayne, Indiana. They had two children, Carl and Sally. Sally married Maurice Schrader, son of Maurice Schrader and Anna Binder, in 1952.

Henry (1848-1930) married Sarah Andrews (1848-1922) on May 9, 1871, in the Catholic Church in Leo and resided in Fort Wayne, Indiana. They had five children: Mary, Franklin, John, and two infants that died shortly after birth. Mary Elizabeth married Emanuel Zehendner and John married Myrtle Bellinger. Henry's family residence was on St. Mary' s Avenue.

Elizabeth (1856-1919) married Maurice Weikart (1860-1942), son of William and Sarah Lawhead Weikart, on Oct. 27, 1885, at the Cathedral of the Immaculate Conception, Fort Wayne, Indiana. They had six children: William, Harvey, Earl, Mabel, Sarah, and Helen. Maurice was a well-known salesman for Freiburger & Co.

Michael (1859-1929) married Frances Jenkins (1862-1898) on December 30, 1879. Three of their five children died during infancy and are buried in the Catholic Cemetery in Leo, Indiana. Michael and Frances moved to South Haven, Michigan, in 1897 and she died in 1898. Michael moved to Kalamazoo, Michigan, with their two remaining children.

Mary Jane (1862-1892) married Henry Bickel (1861-1953) on May 26, 1885. Henry was the son of Henry and Mary Benjeot Bickel. Mary Jane and Henry had two children, Joseph and Elizabeth. Mary Jane died when she was thirty and is buried in the Catholic Cemetery at Leo, near her parents.

Mike's great-grandparents, Frank (1851-1914) and Mary Hazelett Fitzgerald (1853-1930), were married in 1873 and lived on Orchard Street in Fort Wayne, Indiana. In 1898 Frank went to the Klondike, mining for gold. Mary remained in Fort Wayne with their three children, Alice, Margaret, and William. Alice was married to John Woulfe, Margaret to Anthony Luley, and William to Mary Catherine Cunningham, of Dunfee, Indiana. William worked on the railroad, as did Mary Catherine's father, Michael Cunningham. Michael Cunningham (1839-1912) was born in Ireland and came to this country in 1862. He first located in New York, married Mary Lyons in Brooklyn, New York, in 1863, and in 1872 came to Allen County.

William, Mike's grandfather (1874-1914), and Mary Catherine Cunningham Fitzgerald (1881-1958), had three sons: Jess William, (1906-1985), and twins, Robert J. (died six weeks after his birth) and John Michael (1909-1968). Jess and John (Jake) both served in the Army during WWII. After the war they owned produce/grocery stores in Fort Wayne, Indiana.

Mike, the son of Jess and Waneta Fitzgerald, and Jean were married in 1959. Jean is the daughter of Lloyd V. Johnson (1914-1972) and Bernice A. Oberley Johnson (1916-1988) of Monroeville, Indiana. Mike and Jean have two children, Kim and Kirk. Kim married Andy Vandermotten, son of Roderick and Mary McHugh Vandermotten, in 1989. They have three children, Kyle and twins, Kelsey and Kaley. Kirk married Susan Elizabeth Ellison, daughter of William and Mary Lauer Ellison in 1995 and they have two children, Parker Lloyd and Natalie Marie.

Mike, along with most of his family, John, Bill and Ruth, Pat and Wanda, and Jean were employed at the International Harvester Company in Fort Wayne. After the plant closed in 1983, Mike started his own wholesale produce business, following in his father's footsteps. Ten years later he went to work for J. P. Foodservice as a buyer and remained there until he retired, both from J. P. Foodservice and from International Truck & Engine. Jean was employed at Tokheim Corp. and ITT Aerospace/Communications.

Submitted by Jean Fitzgerald

FOGLE FAMILY

Martin Jacob Fogle was born June 20, 1881, in Sarahsville, Ohio. Elsie Gertrude Clore was born July 25, 1881, near Hartford City, Indiana. They were married on April 7, 1901. After residing in Paulding County, Ohio, for a number of years, they moved to Allen County, Indiana, in 1939. They were accompanied by their three youngest sons, Forest, Kenith, and Roy. Their eldest son, Merlin, was married to Inez

Klinger and they resided in Defiance County, Ohio. A fourth son, Raymond, was married to Clara Hershberger and they joined in the move. These two families moved into homes on Spencerville Road just north of Antwerp Road in Harlan. A sixth son, Ralph, had died earlier. A previous relationship with the Reichelderfer family in the 1930s played a role in this move. The approximate 180 acres along the west side of Spencerville Road had been part of the early Reichelderfer holdings and extended north from Antwerp Road. Also a part of this farm in 1939 was a few acres which became the Harlan Park in the late 1940s. This tract was fenced for livestock at the time and served as summer pasture for the Fogle's young dairy animals.

The Fogle families operated typical diversified grain and livestock farms. Much of the livestock operation and housing was less than one city block north of the Harlan Elementary and High Schools. Two large barns and associated smaller structures, including a feed grinding facility, were present. Dairy cattle, swine, sheep, poultry, and rabbits were raised within sight and smell of those institutions of learning.

Both horsepower and tractor power were used on this farm. The last team of horses left the Fogle farm in the mid-1940s, purchased by an Amish neighbor. Rapid mechanization was adopted on this farm and a majority of it was John Deere green. A relationship with Mr. Oliver Repp, township trustee, led to the farming of several hundred acres of his land east of Harlan by the Fogles.

Raymond and Clara reared two children, Charles and Floyd, in their Harlan home.

Roy Sirvane Fogle married Mildred Lucille Haase in 1941. They had two children, Joe and Elsie, and this farm family consisted of nine members up to the death of Mr. Clore in the farmhouse, surrounded by his family in 1950, at the age of 94. Forest and Kenith did not marry. Also during 1941, Kenith left Harlan to serve in the United States Air Force, returning to the farm at the end of his tour. The household often included assorted aunts, cousins, and others for varying periods.

In the late 1950s, both Roy and Mildred worked as custodians at the new Harlan Elementary, and Roy and Forest were school bus drivers for many years. Roy also worked for the EACS Corporation as building/maintenance supervisor. Mildred still lives in the farm home in Harlan, baking cookies in the winter and mowing grass in the summer.

Submitted by J. W. Fogle

THOMAS FOLLIS FAMILY

In 1900, Thomas Jefferson Follis and wife Matilda Jane Timmons lived on West Main Street across from the new courthouse dedicated September 23, 1902, where Thomas was a construction worker. Their pioneer families came from southeast Indiana and southwest Ohio, starting early churches and cemeteries in the Dayton, Ohio, area after coming from Virginia through Kentucky around 1800.

Third great-grandfather, Thomas Fallis, purchased land in Frederick County, Virginia around the time young George Washington began his surveyor career in 1748 at Winchester. Thomas Fallis came in 1731 from Quaker New Jersey a few miles from Philadelphia, the largest city in the Colonies where young Ben Franklin set up his printing shop. Third great-grandfather Henry Landis' stone home, built in 1750 Ringoes, New Jersey, the oldest home in Hunterdon County, was used by Lafayette to recuperate from Valley Forge during the Revolutionary War.

Matilda's great-grandfather, John Timmons, a Revolutionary War veteran born in 1757 in Virginia settled in early 1800s southern Ohio. Her Foreman ancestors from England were our earliest family arriving around 1645 in Long Island, New York.

Thomas and Matilda Timmons Follis

Matilda's Kelker ancestors came from Switzerland in 1745 to Pennsylvania.

Uncles Anthony and Samuel Kelker were railroad engineers. Grandfather David Kelker ran boarding houses in Fort Wayne in 1869 as the rails were laid from Pittsburgh, Pennsylvania, through Ohio into Indiana. Anthony unloaded and drove the first engine off a canal boat in Delphos, Ohio, and into Fort Wayne, where he was living by 1858. Anthony set early railroad speed records, was a popular figure in early newspapers, and on the city councilman in 1894. Anthony met President McKinley on May 29, 1901 in Fort Wayne on a train engineered by brother Samuel. He helped organize the early parks department. Civil War veteran, Samuel, organized G.A.R. meetings, annual Memorial Day parades with thousands of spectators, and promoted veteran statues in local parks.

Thomas Follis, born January 24, 1856, in Wabash County, Indiana, had a son, Arthur, with first wife Cynthia Huddleston, born November 14, 1879 in Wabash County. Thomas married Matilda Timmons on November 16, 1882 in Delphos, Ohio. Matilda was born there on July 10, 1866. Thomas and Matilda's children born in Delphos were Lewis, December 30, 1885; William, February 11, 1888; Milo, June 20, 1890; Viola, October 20, 1892; Ethel, October 11, 1894; and Nellie, August 5, 1896. Their last two children, Helen, October 27, 1899, and Chester, July 6, 1902, were born in Fort Wayne. Chester, Helen's husband, John Heiny, and Nellie's husband, Paul Reinkensmeier, ran local grocery stores.

Son Milo's wife, Elizabeth Schnieder, was born September 17, 1890 in Massillon, Stark County, Ohio. Elizabeth's family arrived in Philadelphia, Pennsylvania, on May 16, 1881, from Alsace, Germany. Married May 7, 1912, in Fort Wayne, their children were Carl, Paul, Ralph, Helen, Frank, Louis, James and Jack. Elizabeth died November 12, 1932, and Milo died April 7, 1944. Sons, Paul of Columbus, Ohio, and Ralph of Fort Wayne, survive, with at least 23 grandchildren and 49 great-grandchildren.

Submitted by Milo's great-grandson Stanley J. Follis

MAURICE L. FOWLER FAMILY

Julie Mason Dixie and William Dixie moved to Fort Wayne, Indiana, from Alabama in 1916.

William was a sharecropper near Selma, Alabama, and moved to Fort Wayne for a better life. William and Julie had seven children when they migrated to Fort Wayne. The daughters were Virginia and Eliza. Eliza was born in 1907. The sons were William, Joseph, Timothy, Curtis, and Thomas. William worked for the railroad at the "Roundhouse." Julie worked as a domestic helper and as a cook. At one time she was a cook at the Wilson "Chicken Shack" in the "Rolling Mill"section of Fort Wayne. Julie died in 1944 and William died in 1949. All of their sons and daughters are deceased.

Eliza was born in 1907, and she was nine when the family moved to Fort Wayne. She attended the Harmar, McCulloch, and Clay schools. She dropped out of school to work. She worked at the Keenan Hotel as a maid and at the Palace Theater as an usher. While working at the Palace Theater, she met Fred Fowler. Fred had moved to Fort Wayne from Washington, D.C. Fred was born in Lynchburg, Virginia, in 1901. His father, Samuel, was a brick mason. Samuel died in 1971. His mother's name was Nanny. He had one sister, Bessie.

Fred and Eliza were married in 1923. They had four children: Ulysses, born in 1923; Maurice, born in 1930; Mildred, born in 1933; and Karen born in 1951. In addition, Fred had a son, Ellsworth, born in 1920. Ellsworth lived in New York City with his mother except for a short period in the mid 1930s when he lived in Fort Wayne with Fred and Eliza and his half siblings, Ulysses, Maurice, and Mildred. Fred and Eliza lived most of their married life in the 300 and 400 blocks of East Douglas Street, except for a few months in 1940-41 when they briefly lived in the 400 block of Wallace Street. In 1984, Eliza moved to Sherrill Drive.

Fred worked at the Wolf and Dessaur Department Store for several years cleaning and custom dying shoes. In the late 1930s he opened his own business located with The Pawlisch Shoe Repair Shop on Jefferson Street next to the old Jefferson Theatre. The Pawlisch Shop and Fred later relocated to Calhoun Street between Douglas and Lewis Streets. When World War II opened racial hiring practices in local industries, Eliza joined the war effort and went to work for The General Electric Company (GE). She worked for GE for 28 years. She became a Union Steward. One of her most memorable events was speaking to Ronald Reagan when he visited the Fort Wayne GE operation. Mr. Reagan was the host of the GE television program at the time. Fred and Eliza were married for over 50 years. Fred died in 1973 at the age of 72. Eliza died in 2002 at the age of 95.

Ellsworth Fowler was born in 1920, and he lived in New York City his entire life except for a short period in the 1930s when he lived in Fort Wayne with Eliza and his siblings: Ulysses, Maurice, and Mildred. Ellsworth had five sons, Freddie, Ronnie, James, Vernon, and Maurice and three daughters, Delores, Carolyn, and Frieda. He enlisted in the U. S. Navy in World War II, and he served his tour of duty at the Great Lakes

Training Station near Chicago. Ellsworth was a jewelry designer and craftsman. He died in 1992. Frieda Fowler holds a Ph.D. and is currently on the faculty of Illinois University in Urbana, Illinois.

Ulysses Fowler was born in 1923 in Fort Wayne. He had five children. He had one son, Ronald, (who died at the age of two), and one daughter, Sheila (deceased), with his first wife Maddie Thorpe (deceased). He had three daughters, Kay, Toni, and Cheryl with his second wife Lillian (Midge) Durrah (deceased). His third wife Evelyne (divorced) and his fourth wife, Laselle Issacs Fowler, live in New York City. He graduated from Harmar Junior High School and attended Central High School. At the beginning of World War II he joined the Merchant Marine Service. He sailed some of the most dangerous sea supply routes, transporting war equipment to Russia and to U.S. troops in Europe and Africa. He returned to Fort Wayne after the war and worked for GE. Responding to the call of the sea he moved his family to New York City and returned to his calling as a merchant seaman. He retired and lived in New York City for several years and then returned to live in Fort Wayne until his death in 1994.

Mildred Fowler Harris was born in Fort Wayne in 1933. She attended Hanna Grade School for one semester of the second grade and graduated from Harmar School. She attended Central High School. She was married to Jerome Harris (divorced), Robert Leonard (divorced), and Don Ricketts (divorced). She had three daughters, Laurice Harris, Kathy Bowen, and Carol Dates. Mildred worked at the Magnavox Company until she became disabled and became a stay-at-home mother. Laurice is a teacher in Los Angeles, California; Kathy and Carol reside in Fort Wayne.

Karen Fowler Williams was born in 1951 in Fort Wayne. Karen was a premature birth, weighing only 2 1/2 pounds, and remained in the Methodist Hospital located on Lewis Street for several weeks before she could be brought home. Karen graduated from Harmar Elementary and Central Junior and Senior High School. She was a majorette and active in drama at Central. She earned an Associate Degree from Purdue University and a Bachelors Degree from Indiana Wesleyan University. Karen has two sons, Shawn and Christopher. Karen was the Director of the Indiana Civil Rights Commission from 1981 to 1989 under Governor Orr. She also held the position of Governor Orr's Executive Assistant for Minority Affairs. She returned to Fort Wayne to take the position of Director of Human Resources at Lincoln National Life Insurance Company. Karen was also very active in protecting civil rights in Fort Wayne on a volunteer basis. She performed in one of the lead roles in a Fort Wayne production of "A Raisin in the Sun" at the Fort Wayne Civic Theater. In 2003, Karen was promoted to the position of Vice President of Employee Relations and Diversity at Lincoln Financial Group. Karen relocated from Fort Wayne to Philadelphia, Pennsylvania, where she currently resides.

Maurice Fowler was born in Fort Wayne in 1930. Except for one semester in 1940-41 at the Hanna school, he attended Harmar School from where he graduated in 1944. At Harmar he played on the dodge ball, basketball, softball, and track teams. In the seventh and eighth grades he won blue ribbons for the 75 and 100 yard dashes, the 75 yard hurdles, the high jump, and the 110 X 4 relay in city track meets. He entered Central High School in 1944 and graduated in 1948. At Central he earned varsity letters in basketball, football, and track. He served as president of the Student Council in his junior and senior years. He was elected vice president of his junior class. He was president of the History Club in his senior year, and a member of the Speech Club. He was selected to the National Honor Society in his senior year. Upon graduation he was selected for a "Kilbourne Charitable Educational and Religious Fund Scholarship". In 1947, Maurice was elected as Lieutenant Governor at the American Legion "Hoosier Boys State". He was one of 312 people to receive the 1947 certificate of recognition by *Opportunity Journal of Negro Life*, the official publication of the National Urban League. In 1948 he was a junior delegate to the NAACP National Convention. He was president and a member of the "Peerless Boys Club" at the Phyllis Wheatly Center on Douglas Street.

Maurice L. Fowler

In 1948, Maurice enrolled at West Virginia State College near Charleston, West Virginia. He was a member of the junior varsity basketball team. In 1949 he transferred to Albion College in Albion, Michigan. At Albion he was a member of the varsity football, basketball, and track teams. In his senior year he was selected to Omicron Delta Kappa, a national honorary fraternity. He graduated from Albion in 1952 and was drafted into the U. S. Army in 1952. He took basic training at Fort Bliss, Texas, and attended Officer Candidates School at Fort Benning, Georgia. He was commissioned as a second lieutenant in the Army in September 1953. He was stationed at Fort Knox, Kentucky, from September 1953 to March 1955 when he was released from active duty. He served in the Army Reserves from 1955 to 1965, reaching the rank of captain.

He returned to Fort Wayne in 1955 and worked briefly at International Harvester and Capehart Farnsworth. In 1956 he was hired by the U.S. Air Force's Air Material Command, located at Wright Patterson Air Force Base, in Dayton, Ohio, as a General Schedule level 5 Procurement Technician. He was Buyer/Contract Negotiator for the B-70 IX bomber. He was named to the Wright Patterson interdepartmental basketball league "All Star" team three years. He was a member of the Wright Patterson Base basketball team in 1958.

In 1960 he transferred from the Air Material Command to the Electronic System Division located at Hanscom Air Force Base in Bedford, Massachusetts. He was promoted through the ranks to the Senior Executive Service in 1976. His position was that of Assistant Deputy for Contracting at the Electronic Systems Division. While at the Electronic System Division, he had a key role in planning for the development and procurement of many major command and control, communication, surveillance, and intelligence systems for the Continental Air Defense during the Cold War. Some of these systems are the Airborne Warning and Control System (AWACS), Airborne Ground Surveillance Radar (Joint Stars), Over the Horizon Radar (OTH), Ballistic Missile Early Warning System Upgrade" (BMEWS), and North Warning. Systems, such as Command and Control Systems for Saudi Arabia (Peace Shield) and for Thailand, were also developed and procured for foreign countries. His awards and recognitions include (1) A 1983 award from the Boston Federal Executive Board, New England Minority Business Opportunity Committee, for excellence in minority business development. The Electronic System Divisions contract awards to minority business increased from $170,000 in 1976 when he became Deputy of Procurement to $51,900,000 in 1983; (2) Selected for Presidential Meritorious Executive Rank Award in 1986; (3) Selected for Air Force Performance Award in 1987; (4) Selected for Presidential Distinguished Executive Rank Award in 1988; and (5) Selected for Department of Defense Distinguished Civilian Service Award in 1990. He is co-author of a book titled *Air Force Trivia*. Shortly after moving to Massachusetts in 1960 he was involved in a housing discrimination suit. The Massachusetts Supreme Court made a landmark decision in his favor in 1962.

Submitted by Maurice L. Fowler

CHARLES LESTER FRANK & MARY CATHERINE REMMERT FAMILY

Charles Lester Frank was born February 23,1890, to George Adam Frank and Catherine Mary Bequette. Charles Lester had six siblings: Bernadette Mary, John George, Henrietta Frank Simonis, Constant Bequette, Lawrence Leroy and Thelma Theresa. Charles Lester worked for Bursley & Company, a wholesale food distributor in Fort Wayne. He went from assembling orders and loading horse-drawn wagons to general manager of the company's Lima, Ohio, branch. Charles Lester was instrumental in the birth and growth of the Lima branch, which helped Bursley & Company expand its distribution area into Ohio. He retired from Bursley & Company in 1956, after 49 years. His career was interrupted when the United States entered World War I in May of 1917. He spent more than two years in France and Germany under General Pershing and participated in the Meusse-Argonne Offensive. He married Mary Catherine Remmert on June 1, 1921. They had two sons, George Edward and John Lester.

Mary Catherine Remmert, born January 8, 1889, was the daughter of John Remmert and Nellie G. Flannigan, who came to Fort Wayne about 1890 from the Cincinnati area. Mary Catherine

Charles L. Frank, 1920

had three siblings; Edward T., Helen Remmert Landis, and Elizabeth Remmert Thornton.

George Edward Frank, born April 4, 1922, in Fort Wayne, spent many years in the building business as a salesman and architect. Both George Edward and his brother John Lester were veterans of World War II. George Edward married Rita Rose Bensman of Lima, Ohio, and they had one daughter, Cecelia Frank Bryan. His second marriage to Rita Catherine Birkmeyer of Lima, Ohio, produced four daughters; Judith Frank Doan, Rose Frank Shaw, Maureen Frank Davis, and Pamela Frank Getz. Rita Birkmeyer Frank earned her nursing degree from St. Rita's Hospital in Lima. She worked as an RN for Parkview and St. Joseph Hospitals. She also worked for Dr. Harry W. Salon for 18 years.

John Lester Frank, born December 21, 1923, worked as a special agent for the IRS. He wed Patricia Ann Drussell on May 5, 1951. Patricia worked as a secretary for International Harvester. They had three children, Geoffrey Edward, Charles Raymond, and Catherine Frank Schroer.

Charles Lester Frank's father, George Adam Frank was born January 7,1857, in New Orleans to Adam and Margaretta Frank. Adam and Margaretta came to the Fort Wayne area with their family about 1864. George Adam Frank had four siblings; John T., Alberta Frank Mack, Josephine Frank Heldman, and Magdalena Frank Ogier. George Adam married Catherine M. Bequette on October 23, 1884, and worked for the Pennsylvania Railroad for 39 years. Catherine Mary Bequette was born October 18, 1862, in Fort Wayne to John Baptiste Bequette and Elizabeth Baker. Catherine Mary had seven siblings; Jacob, John A., Henry G., George F., Mary E., Elizabeth C., and Theresa H.

John Baptiste Bequette was born January 13, 1824, in Detroit. He came to Fort Wayne at the age of two with his parents, John Baptiste Becquette and Teresa Buret. John Baptiste (the son) worked as a brick mason. He had five siblings: Harriet, Francis, Julian, Philomena, and Teresa. His wife, Elizabeth Baker, was born November 18, 1832 in Hesse Darmstat, Germany, to Georg Baker and Katharina Borschinger. Elizabeth had seven siblings: John, Magdalena, Jacob, Conrad, Catherine, Henry and Kilian. Georg Baker, his wife Katharina Borschinger, and their children arrived in Fort Wayne in 1838 from Hesse Darmstadt, Germany. Georg Baker and his sons opened the first sawmill, wagon-making shop and plow-making shop in this area.

John Baptiste Becquette (the father), was born August 15, 1786 in Detroit. He was a silversmith by trade. Located on Columbia Street near Clinton, he employed about thirty French workmen who made beads, jewelry and other items that were of interest to the Miami Indians of this area. He was known as "Father Becquette".

Submitted by Judith A. Doan

FRANKE, DASELER, KELTSCH & NIEMEYER

KREUZUNG – THE INTERSECTION

In the 1840s, German migration had started and the end destination was the midwest United States. The recent platting of Indiana land for sale, good transportation via the Erie Canal and inexpensive farm ground similar to Germany made Indiana an attractive location for dissatisfied Germans. Fort Wayne was the intersection of four German families to the U.S. nearly 150 years ago.

Heinrich Franke and Heinrich Daseler were farmers who immigrated with their families in the summer of 1845 on the ship *Copernicus* from Breman to New York. (See, *The Scheumanns Come to America*). In Germany, their farms were about three miles apart. Lahde and Ilse in the state of Westfalia. (See, *Who Upset the Tar Bucket?* by Roger Franke.) Heinrich Franke settled in Madison Township, corner of Hoagland and Franke Roads. Heinrich Daseler bought 40 acres in St. Joe Township, at the corner of St. Joe Center and Reed Roads. These two families probably knew each other in Germany and definitely knew each other on the two month voyage to America.

Keltsch Family (Circa 1941) Seated: Ida Voelkening Kelstch, Ruth Keltsch, Carl Keltsch Standing: Maurice Keltsch, Mildred Keltsch Franke, Donald Keltsch

Franke Reunion (Circa 2003) Front Row: Ray Franke, Kay Franke Seated: Sally Franke, Helen Reynolds, Charles Reynolds Standing: Ralph Franke, Roger Franke, Robert Franke, Mildred Franke, Pat Franke

Ernest Niemeyer and Family (Circa 1980) Seated: Louis Niemeyer, Caroline Bruggeman Niemeyer, John Henry Niemeyer, and William Niemeyer Standing: Ernest F. Niemeyer, Henry C. Niemeyer, Mary Niemeyer Honeick, Emilia Niemeyer Hattendorf

Franke Family Reunion (Circa 2004) Back Row: Corky Franke, Luke Franke, Roger Franke, German visitor Christian Kanne, Martin Franke, Clint Reynolds, Neil Reynolds, Madonna Reynolds Porch Roof: Angie Yager, Angie's friend, Kara Yeager, Amy Franke, Marsden Giolas, Buzz Yeager Porch: Joe Franke, Mackenzie Franke, Steve Franke, Jordan Franke, Devon Franke, Kay Franke, Ray Franke, Tammi Franke Giolas Seated: Chris Franke Hudson, Sally Franke, Ralph Franke, Terry Hudson 4x4: Ron Daseler, Aaron Daseler, Colin Daseler Seated: Kari Franke Parker, Patricia Franke, May Franke, Reggie Parker, Max Franke, Arthur Franke, Brad Parker, Charles Reynolds, Helen Reynolds, Bob Franke, Mildred Franke In Grass: Christine Franke, Elly Franke, Maggie Franke, Haus Franke

Daseler Family (Circa 2004) Front Row: Alex Kem, Laura Daseler Kem, Bryan Kem, Cheryl Franke Daseler, Allison Daseler, Maggie Daseler, Ben Daseler, Patrick Kem, Linda Daseler Gjesvold Back Row: Dian Roe, Tom Daseler, Ron Daseler, Aaron Daseler, Tim Daseler, Colin Daseler

The intersection of families was lost until 1972 when Cheryl Franke and Ron Daseler were married—and family histories had been researched and compared.

The other two German families' intersections are Keltsch and Niemeyer. Cheryl's mother Mildred was a Keltsch and Ron's mother was a Niemeyer. The Niemeyers came over in 1836 from Duedinghausen and the Keltschs came from Hamburg in 1875.

One common connection they shared when immigrating and yet today is Lutheranism. Portions of the Frankes, Daselers, Niemeyers, and Keltschs belong to Lutheran congregations in and near Fort Wayne. Some of the Frankes were charter members at St. Johns Flatrock. Niemeyers and Daselers were early members at St. Paul and Keltschs at Trinity Lutheran, Fort Wayne. Today, members of these four families have been in nearly every Lutheran congregation in Fort Wayne.

Even though many family members live farther apart, there is still the opportunity for more intersections to be made among those still in Fort Wayne.

Submitted by Ron Daseler

DERWARD D. FRANKE

Derward D. Franke was born, December 14, 1929, in Fort Wayne, Indiana. He is the only son of Lester W. and Ella (Ramm) Franke of Fort Wayne. On Christmas morning 1957, Lester died at the age of 64. Ella died in January 1991 at the age of 95. On August 30, 1952, Derward married Lorna J. Mertens. The site of the marriage was Trinity Evangelical Lutheran Church in Fort Wayne, Indiana. Lorna was born May 24, 1930, the oldest daughter of Ernest and Emilie (Schmidt) Mertens of Fort Wayne. She was a 1948 graduate of North Side High School. Lorna worked at the Lincoln Life for ten years before becoming a full-time homemaker and caretaker of her aged mother. Lorna has one sister, Dorothy, who married Wayne Springer and they reside in Fort Wayne. Derward and Lorna have resided in Fort Wayne their entire life. They had no children.

Derward and Lorna Fanke

Derward attended L. C. Ward School for six grades; J. H. Smart School for grades seven and eight, and graduated from Central High School in 1948. He worked for General Electric of Fort Wayne starting in 1949. He entered the G.E. Apprentice School in 1951. In 1950, Derward enlisted in the 122nd AC&W Squadron of the Indiana Air National Guard unit based at Baer Field. The squadron reported to active duty on November 1, 1951, and was assigned to Alexandria AFB, Louisiana.

Upon his release from active duty in June 1953, he resumed his apprentice training and graduated in 1956. He worked as a tool designer with General Electric for a total of 24 years. The economy interrupted his G. E. service two times. His other employment was eight years with the Magnavox Company of Fort Wayne. He also worked three and one half years with the Littler Die Cast Company of Albany, Indiana, and ten years with C & A Tool of Churubusco, Indiana. He retired after ten years from C & A in August 1996.

After retirement, Derward taught two years at IVY Tech College. Derward is a lifetime member of the Lutheran Church. His membership included Grace Lutheran (ALC) the place of his confirmation, Zion Lutheran (LCMS), Trinity Lutheran (LCMS). Beautiful Savior Lutheran (WELS), and Emmaus Lutheran (LCMS). In these congregations he held several offices that included treasurer, elder, and president. In his youth Derward was active in sports. He played basketball for church and G.E. interdepartmental teams and later became an above average bowler in several leagues.

Submitted by Derward Franke

WILLIAM FRANKE

(1841-1926)

As the *Copernicus* inched its way westward across the Atlantic during the summer of 1845, a relatively minor incident occurred on board that created a lasting impression in the mind of one of its passengers. It was a pleasant day and some of the 176 German emigrants took advantage of the fresh air and sunshine to spend a little time away from their cramped quarters in steerage and moved onto the open deck of the three-mast ship to relax. Among those who made the transition to more comfortable surroundings were Johann Heinrich Franke, his wife Marie Sophie, nee Berg, and their two young sons, ages three and a half and one and a half. The elder of the two boys, Friedrich Wilhelm, who came to be known later in life in Allen County as F. William is the subject of this article and the instigator of the incident which follows.

F. William Franke home about 1893-94, one and a half mile east of Hoagland on the Hoagland Road. L-R: William Franke (son), Caroline Franke (Holle) twins, Herman Franke in mother Caroline's arms, Charles Franke pulling wagon, F. William (father), Mary Franke (Busick), Lizzie Franke (Busick), Minnie Franke (Bohnke), Fred Franke, Ferdinand Hockemeyer (nephew of Caroline) hired man.

William's parents selected a suitable spot to relax and began to settle in. Younger brother Frederick needed closer supervision and was kept near at hand while William was given a little more latitude to roam. His papa admonished him not to get into trouble and added the not-so-subtle warning that the sailors would throw him overboard if he misbehaved. William had heard this warning before, but gave it little thought as he meandered away from the vicinity and attention of his parents. There were so many things on the deck of a ship to look at, to touch, and to manipulate. He spied a tar bucket sitting at the side and the thought took hold to give it a closer examination. As he neared the bucket, he noted that it was in dire need of rearrangement. Like a fussy housewife rearranging the decor of a room, he set about to make the proper adjustments: a little movement to the right, then to the back, and just a little twist to position it's best side forward. Oops! The bucket tipped over and the tar began to ooze out over the deck.

William quickly realized that he was in deep trouble, but fortunately his deed remained as yet undiscovered. What to do? The prospect of being thrown overboard by the sailors began to loom large in his imagination. So he searched out a nearby cavity accessible only to a little boy, and tucked himself into it and waited. It wasn't long until a passing sailor discovered the deed and let out a cry of dismay that quickly turned to anger. He uprighted the now mostly empty tar bucket and continued his outcry. Other sailors rushed to his aid. Their tempers flared, giving rise to words: nasty words, profane words, words that threatened eternal condemnation upon the doer of the deed.

F. William Franke Home, about 1893-94. L to R. William Franke (son) and Caroline Franke (Holle) twins, Herman Franke in mother Caroline's arms, Charles Franke pulling wagon, F. William (father), Mary Franke (Busick), Lizzie Franke (Busick), Minnie Franke (Bohnke), Fred Franke, Ferdinand Hockemeyer (nephew of Caroline) hired man.

William's papa also raced to the scene. He stood there momentarily frozen as he surveyed the damage and considered its likely cause. But the perpetrator had vanished. A search was launched, which soon resulted in locating the boy's hiding place. He was ordered to come out. No compliance. He was asked to come out. No compliance. Requests soon deteriorated into coaxing. The boy remained firm in his resolve. In the end, only when convinced that the plan to throw him overboard had been abandoned, did the boy emerge from his hiding place.

When the *Copernicus* arrived at New York on July 31, the boy's mental wound from the verbal thrashing had for the most part healed. The trip had been exhausting; up the Weser River to Bremen and fifty-seven days on the ocean. Several more weeks of travel yet lay before them, mostly by way of water and canal, from New York to Toledo and finally to the Fort Wayne area. Added to all of this was the delicate physical condition of Marie Sophie, pregnant with her third child and destined to give birth to William's native born American sister in October.

But the arduous journey from New York to Allen County was eased somewhat by pleasant

Hermand Ferdinand Martin Franke, born June 3, 1892 and Iva Martha Lisetta Bucher, born June 3, 1895.

company. At least a few on board the *Copernicus* traveled with them, for they too were headed to Allen and Adams Counties. Most of the ship's passengers came from small farm villages in the area of Minden on the Weser River. They spoke the same dialect of German, called "Plattdeutsch" or Low German. They knew the same folk songs, the same popular songs, and some the same church hymns. They supported each other in their determination to make a go of it in a foreign country.

Within two weeks of their arrival in August of 1845, the Franke family had acquired 40 acres of mostly wooded land in section 20 of Madison Township for the sum of $95. Their first accommodation was a typical pioneer log house. It proved to be sturdy enough to be standing yet in the 1960s. It was located near the southern end of a road that stretches today from Highway 30 in the north to Hoagland Road in the south, a distance of about seven miles. Because of the farm's end-of-the-road location, the road today bears the name of Franke Road.

In the course of time little William became big brother William. He and his younger brother, Frederick, were born on German soil in the village of Quetzen on Farm 21 and were baptized in the nearby evangelical Lutheran church at Lahde. The remainder of William's siblings were born on American soil. Shortly after their arrival in Madison Township, the two brothers were able to hold a baby sister in their arms, but Wilhelmine Christina survived only until the age of five. Then came Mary, Henry C., Elise, Charles, August, and finally in 1857, Herman. Some of these have current descendants in Allen County and vicinity.

It was in Madison Township in the late 1840s and into the 1850s that William gained a formal religious training and the rudiments of a formal education, most likely taught by the circuit-riding pastor, Fred W. Husmann, at a location nearby that later became known as Flatrock. At a confirmation ceremony in 1856, William officially became a member of the congregation of St. John Lutheran Church. In his later teens he learned the carpentry trade, an occupation that he pursued for a number of years before turning to farming. As his world widened to include non-ethnic Germans, he acquired English, the predominant language of his adopted country and the language that would serve him well in his later pursuits in public life.

In the 1870s, William developed an interest in a young lady who lived across the road. Her name was Caroline Meyer. She and her siblings were children of Christian and Wilhelmine (Oetting) Meyer. The relationship blossomed and in 1873 they were married. This union produced a second generation of German-Americans. The first three children (Minnie, Mary, and Fred) were born in a log house just southeast of the original homestead.

Shortly after his father, Henry, passed away in 1879, William moved his wife, Caroline, and their three children to the adjoining farm east on Hoagland Road and into another log house. At that location they had six more children. They were Lizzie, twins Carrie and Willy, Charlie, and the writer's father, Herman. A final child Lucinda, born in 1894, did not survive infancy.

In the late 1880s, William's interests turned to politics. He served two terms as Madison Township trustee starting in 1889. During his tenure in that office a number of one-room brick schoolhouses were constructed in the township, but only one remains standing yet with his name on the commemorative stone. He continued to farm, but now that a passion for politics had been ignited, his interest in farming diminished, leaving much of the work in the hands of his sons, Herman and Charlie. He ran for Allen County commissioner on the Democratic ticket in 1906, but the joy of victory in November of that year was tempered by the death of his mother, Mary, several months earlier in August. He began his second term as commissioner in 1911. One project during this term was the completion of the Tennessee Avenue Bridge in 1912, on which his name appears.

If not for son Herman (born 1892), the surname Franke would have ceased to exist among the numerous descendants of F. William and Caroline. Herman's three brothers produced no sons to continue the family name. Herman married Iva Bucher in 1914, but unlike his father and grandfather who each had nine children, Herman and Iva had only five, one girl and four boys. From the time of their wedding they lived with Caroline and F. William on the home farm on Hoagland Road until their deaths in 1923 and 1926.

The home farm today is the residence of Neil Reynolds and his family. Neil is a great-grandson of F. William and Caroline and a grandson of Herman and Iva through Helen and Charles Reynolds.

Herman and Iva's sons, Robert and Ralph, moved to Fort Wayne, and Ray and Roger left Allen County in adulthood. Several of the sons produced a fourth generation of Frankes who maintain their family surname: Bruce, Dean, Stanley, Steve, Tammi, Martin, and Courtney. Fifth generation descendants with the name Franke currently include, Jennifer, Megan, Joseph, Mackenzie, Jordon, Devin, Arthur, Maggie, Hans, Max, Elly, and Luke. In addition to the name Franke, the following surnames at present appear among the descendants of Herman and Iva: Reynolds, Daseler, Borchelt, Hudson, Yager, Giolas, and Parker.

Looking into the mischievous eyes of the writer's grandson, three-year-old Luke Franke, one is carried back to that time long ago on board the *Copernicus* and to someone who upset the tar bucket.

Submitted by Roger Franke.

F. WILLIAM FRANKE

Dorothy Wiegmann's father, William Hockemeyer, died in March 1923. On the day of his funeral, Herman Franke, brother of F. William Franke, watched the funeral procession go to the Flat Rock Lutheran Church. Herman, not feeling well, decided not to attend the funeral. Herman passed away less than an hour later. The viewing for Herman took place at the old Franke homestead. His funeral was held on Saturday and he was buried in Flatrock Cemetery. On Sunday morning, F. William Franke's wife, Caroline, was ill with pneumonia and lived only three days, dying the following Wednesday. She was 73 years old. All eight children of F. William and Caroline were at her bedside.

Herman, being the youngest surviving child of F. William and Caroline, brought his wife, Iva, and stayed in his parents home to help on the farm. His father was more interested in politics and carpentry than in farming so Herman worked the farm. Herman had two children, Helen and Robert. Iva was now the only woman on the farm and was even busier than before her mother-in-law's death. She didn't mind the farm work and her favorite work was the garden. One day while Iva was milking the cows in the barn and the children were playing nearby, Robert fell into the horse tank full of water. F. William found him and fished him out in time to prevent drowning.

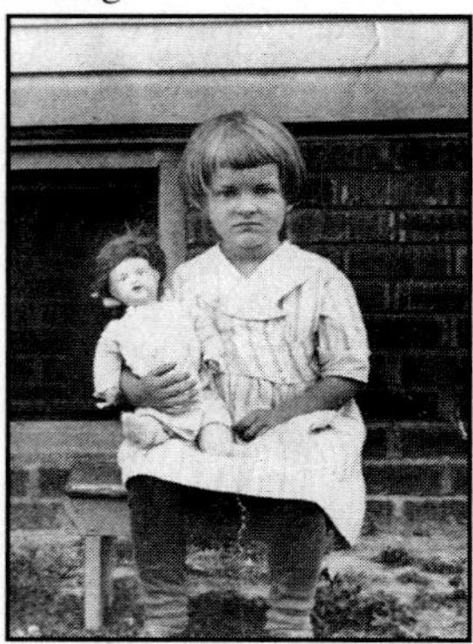

Helen Franke Reynolds.

Helen and Robert had never known any other life than that of living with their parents and grandparents. Helen became a special favorite of F. William and she followed him all over the farm. F. William often helped Iva with the big garden. He also planted many fruit trees all around the home. Helen loved the apple, cherry, plum, peach, pear, and mulberry trees. In the fall there were grapes of several varieties on the arbors. Helen often had to be scrubbed after she tried to hull black walnuts. She loved to play in the old log house right in front of the frame house where she lived.

Helen's grandfather, being a carpenter, had built the house they lived in and added several additions from time to time. They now had a very large kitchen, a back porch, a basement for keeping things cool, and even a pantry. Helen admired her grandfather's handiwork as she looked at the brown plaster walls, the cream colored ceilings, and the shiny, varnished wainscoting.

Weekends were busy and fun. Herman's seven brothers and sisters with their families often came to visit. That meant the week's baking of fresh bread and coffeecake went quickly.

In the fall of 1925, F. William fell off the porch and broke his hip and was bedfast. Helen read the daily newspaper to him every day when she came home from school. He especially loved to have her read the continued stories. On March 14, 1926, at age 85, F. William passed away just three years to the day after the passing of his wife, Caroline.

Submitted by Mrs. Charles (Helen Franke) Reynolds

HENRY C. FRANKE

Henry C. Franke was born on the Franke farm in Allen County, Madison Township, Indiana, on June 3, 1848. Baptized Carl Heinrich at St. John's Lutheran Church, Bingen, in Adams County, Indiana. He Americanized his name to Henry Carl. In 1873, Henry purchased property in Fort Wayne on the southeast corner of East Washington Boulevard and Walter Street, where he lived until his death. He became a prominent member of St. Paul's Lutheran Church and the B.U.V. German Society. Henry married twice. He married his first spouse, Friederika Grotrian, in July 1874 at St. John's Lutheran Church (Flatrock) on Franke Road. She and her family had recently immigrated from Ottenstein, Germany. They settled in the crossroad village of Maples on Franke Road. After only four years of marriage, Friedericka died in March of 1878 at the age of 26. They produced one child, Henry F., who died in 1917 a year before his father. In January 1879, Henry married Marie Scheimann in Emmanuel Lutheran Church, Fort Wayne. Marie's family immigrated to America on the same ship as Henry's family. Marie was born, February 28, 1858. She was some ten years younger than Henry. Their marriage produced ten children (all deceased): Marie, Ernst, Leonore, Adele, Edna, Walter, Elmer, Lester, Lorene, and Alvan.

Henry C. Franke

Henry was a carpenter by trade, but also was very active in Fort Wayne politics. City Marshal Dietrich Meyer appointed Henry as deputy in 1886. Because of some public scandal in the Mayor and Marshal offices during their term, the party nominated Henry and the voters elected him as City Marshall in 1889. He served as marshal through 1894. He later served a number of years as city street superintendent under Mayor Scherer and then retired from politics in 1905. The highlight of his career was during the electric railway strike of 1893 when he had to make a speech to calm down a rowdy crowd. One September day, in 1917, while returning from a job, Henry suffered a stroke. He was riding in a street car and the conductor thought at first Henry was drunk. Henry was bedridden for nine months with terrible pain before he died in May 1918.

Johann Heinrich and Maria (Berg) Franke, Henry's parents, emigrated from Bremen, Germany, in August 1845, on the ship *Copernicus*. Two children, Friedrich Wilhelm and Heinrich Friedrich accompanied them. The family settled on land purchased on the Franke Road near Hoagland Road where they cleared the land and built a log cabin. Some of the remains of the cabin stood until the early '70s. They were charter members of St. John's Lutheran Church (Flatrock) on the Franke Road. Johann was born June 5, 1811, in Quetzen in Westphalia, Germany. Maria was born in Quetzen on October 3, 1815. They married at the Lutheran church in Lahde. Johann died December 24, 1879. Maria died August 16, 1906. Johann and Maria produced seven more children: Christina, Sophie, Henry C., Johanna, Karl Conrad (Charles), August, and Heinrich Hermann.

Submitted by Walter Michels

HERMAN FRANKE FAMILY

Herman F. Franke (1892-1967) was one of nine children born to Friedrich William Franke (1841-1923) and Karoline Meier (1850-1920). Herman's siblings were Wilhelmina "Minnie" (1874-1949), Marie "Mary" (1876-1879), Friedrich "Fred"(1877-1948), Elise "Lizzie" (1881-1961), twins Wilhelm "Willie" (1883-1946) and Anna "Carrie" (1883-1965), Karl "Charlie" (1889-1954), and Lucinda (1894-1895).

Friedrich William, know as F. William was the son of Johann Heinrich Franke (1811-1879) and Marie Sophie Berg (1816-1906), married in Lahde, Germany. Both Johann and Marie were residents of Quetzen, a village close to Minden in Westfalen, Germany. The story of Johann, Marie, and their two sons, Friedrich Wilhelm and Heinrich Friedrich's arrival in America and the subsequent settlement and growth of the family is detailed in the family genealogy, *Who Upset the Tar Bucket?* written by Johann's great grandson, Roger Franke, youngest son of Herman Franke. F. William's family settled on a farm on Hoagland Road in Madison Township, Allen County, Indiana.

When Herman Franke married Iva Bucher (1895-1984) on Christmas Eve, 1914, they remained on the home farm and lived and farmed with F. William and Karoline. The family grew to three generations with the addition of Herman and Iva's children, Helen Louise (1915-), Robert (1919-), Ralph (1925-2005), Ray (1934-), and Roger (1940-). Today, this farm is owned by F. William's great grandson, Neil Reynolds (1952-), the youngest son of Herman's daughter, Helen, who married Charles Reynolds.

Herman's wife, Iva Bucher, was one of ten children born to Christian Bucher (1854-1935) and Louisa Knapp (1859-1956): William (1879-1961), Sophie (1877-?), Christian (1880-1966), Ella (1880-?), Christena (1883-1884), Henry (1885-1978), Anna (1890-1971), Albert (1892-1923), Iva (1895-1984), and Harvey (1896-1957).

The Franke family in America was politically active from the beginning. F. William was elected Madison Township Trustee in 1888 and 1892, and later elected Allen County Commissioner in 1906 and 1909. Herman followed in his father's political footsteps, being elected to Madison Township Trustee in 1935. Herman and Iva were life long members of St. John Lutheran Church, Flatrock (Monroeville, Indiana) and are buried in the church cemetery there.

Submitted by Mrs. Charles Reynolds

JAY WESLEY FRANKLIN

Jay Wesley Franklin was born in Portland, Jay County, Indiana, on January 11, 1941, the youngest of six children of Frederick Christian and Lulu Esther Grile Franklin. His family had been residents of Jay County since the 1850s.

Jay attended school in Portland, and it was in first grade at the General Shanks Grade School that he first met his future wife, Phyllis Kay Strock. Phyllis was born in Portland, July 5, 1941, the oldest of the three daughters of Merle Raymond and Geraldine Mae Shauver Strock. Geraldine's family had been residents of Jay County before the counties formation in 1832. Merle's family came to Portland in the early 1900s.

Merle's job with the United Telephone Company took Phyllis's family to Starke County, Indiana, in 1949. When they returned to Portland in the summer of 1954 she began high school at Portland. Jay and Phyllis began dating in September of 1955 after going on a Girl Scout hayride together. They continued to date throughout high school, becoming engaged with plans to wait for marriage until Phyllis completed her education at Ball Memorial Hospital School of Nursing, Muncie, Indiana. Jay and Phyllis were married on June 6, 1962, in Portland. Phyllis graduated on August 31, 1962. She then worked at the Jay County Hospital, and Jay worked at the Drop Forge and Sheller Globe in Portland.

During the time they lived in Portland, their two sons were born: Bradley Scott, March 22, 1963, and Brian Jay, April 26, 1965. In late 1969, Jay accepted a job with Syncro Corporation, Hicksville, Ohio. The Franklin's moved to Hicksville, Ohio, and six months later to a farm know as the Hall Farm, located just east of the 101/37 intersection on Highway 37 in Indiana. The boys attended school at Harlan Elementary, where Phyllis was a school nurse. They then attended junior and senior high school at Woodlan. Brad graduating in 1981 and Brian in 1983.

During the middle 1970s Jay became the business manager of the IVY Tech College, Fort Wayne campus, and continued there until his poor health caused him to stop work. During his time there, the campus was enlarged and the new college was built on Coliseum Boulevard. Phyllis became employed at Parkveiw Hospital in Fort Wayne, June 1977, working there for 28 years.

Brad graduated from Purdue, Fort Wayne, with a degree in Structural Engineering. He then married his high school sweetheart, Jill Elaine Franklin, daughter of Eugene and Verna Koeneman Ehle. Brad is part owner of a concrete construction company. They have four children. Megan Elaine, Chelsea Renae, Austin Bradley, and Morgan Allison. Their busy life includes sports, school, and attendance at St. Peters Lutheran Church. They currently reside near Woodburn.

Brian married Christina M. Minich, daughter of Roger Minich and Katherine Smith. Brian is stepfather of Jesse and Jamie Minich. He and his wife, Tina, have four boys, Cody Jay, Cory Joseph, Joshua Raymond, and Jacob Earl. Brian is a diesel mechanic having graduated from North West Tech in Lima, Ohio. Brian and family live at Fulton, Indiana.

On September 30, 1991, Jay was the recipient of a heart transplant, the 86th done at Lutheran Hospital in Fort Wayne. Jay has spent many hours volunteering for The Organ Donor Alliance, being their top volunteer for several years, sharing information about the benefits of organ donation.

Phyllis is retired and enjoying the pursuits of genealogy, crafting, reading, writing, friends and family. Phyllis and Jay currently live in New Haven, Indiana

Submitted by Phyllis Franklin

ALLEN & SANDRA (HOFFMEIER) FRANZ

Allen and Sandra Hoffmeier Franz are the parents of Audra, Austin, Shauna, and Laura. Allen's parents were Erwin and Rosella (Zelt) Franz. Sandra is the daughter of William and Adelia (Bradtmueller) Hoffmeier.

Allen's Franz ancestors who settled in Allen County were Christian Franz, born August 15, 1849, in Root Township, Adams County, Indiana, and died May 20, 1933, and his wife Maria (Bucher), born May 14, 1852, in Fairfield County, Ohio, and died April 14, 1891, in Madison Township. Both are buried in St. Peter Fuelling Lutheran Cemetery, Root Township, Adams County. Their son, Albert Franz, was the father of Erwin Franz.

Rosella (Zelt) Franz's parents were Arthur Zelt, son of Theodore, and Della Lepper, daughter of Adolph. Adolph Lepper, son of George, was married to Wilhelmina Keohlinger, daughter of Phillip. Theodore Zelt was the son of Jacob, and Theodore's wife was Wilhelmina Rebber, daughter of Friedrich.

Jacob Zelt was born January 22, 1837, Jackson Township, Hamilton County, Indiana, and died November 25, 1927, Fort Wayne. His wife, Sophia (Gallmeier), was born December 3, 1841, in Rosenhagen, Westfalen, Germany, and died July 17, 1929, Adams Township. He and Sophia are buried in Martini Lutheran Cemetery, Adams Township. Sophia's father, Christian Gallmeier, was born April 11, 1805, in Joessen, Westfaen, Germany, died December 3, 1887, Adams Township, and is buried in Martini Lutheran. His wife Louise (Huxoll), was born December 6, 1808, in Rosenhagen, Westfalen, Germany, died September 14, 1874, in Adams Township. They are buried in Martini Lutheran.

Theodore Zelt, son of Jacob, was born August 11, 1863, Jackson Township, Hamilton County, Indiana, and died July 15, 1948, Adams Township. He is buried in Martini Lutheran Cemetery. His wife was Wilhelmina Rebber.

Wilhelmina's grandfather, Heinrich Rebber, was born 1791 in Hunteburg, Hannover, Germany, and died November 3, 1871, in Adams Township, and her grandmother was Dorothea (Greve), born August 19, 1795, in Bohmte, Hannover, Germany, and died July 3, 1851, Adams Township. Both are buried in Martini Lutheran Cemetery. Their son, Friedrich Rebber, was born October 15, 1828, Bohmte, Hannover, Germany, and died August 28, 1898, Adams Township; his wife was Sophia (Bradtmueller), born April 8, 1833 in Meinsen, Schaumburg-Lippe, Germany, and died July 29,1878, in Adams Township. Both are buried at Martini Lutheran. Sophia's father was Karl Bradtmueller, born January 8, 1786, in Meinsen, Schaumburg-Lippe, Germany, and died August 21, 1855, Adams Township, and mother was Christina (Tegtmeier), born December 3, 1794 in Meinsen, Schaumburg-Lippe, Germany, and died December 7, 1880, Adams Township. Both are buried in Martini Lutheran.

Rosella (Zelt) Franz's mother was Della Lepper. Della's great-grandparents were Heinrich Lepper, born February 14, 1788, in Koenigsberg, Hessen-Darmstadt, Germany, died April 16, 1857, in Marion Township, and buried in St. Johannes Lutheran Cemetery, Marion Township, and Louisa (Schlaudraff), born August 27, 1786, in Koenigsberg, Hessen-Darmstadt, Germany, died September 9, 1851, in Marion Township, and buried at St. Paul Lutheran Cemetery, Marion Township. Their son, George Lepper, was born February 14, 1817, in Koenigsberg, Hessen Darmstadt, Germany, and died October 7, 1890, in Marion Township, buried Odd Fellows Cemetery, New Haven. His wife was Juliana (Griebel), born August 22, 1824, in Koenigsberg, Hessen-Darmstadt, Germany, died July 2, 1903, in Marion Township, and buried Emmanuel Lutheran Soest Cemetery, Marion Township. Juliana Griebel's mother, Katharina (Wagner), was born September 3, 1794, in Rossbach, Hessen-Darmstadt, Germany, died January 26, 1880, in Marion Township, and is buried in Emmanuel Lutheran Soest Cemetery.

Rosella (Zelt) Franz's Koehlinger line begins with Heinrich Koehlinger, born April 28, 1804, in Blasbach, Rheinland, Germany, and died July 31, 1868, in Adams Township, buried at St. Johannes Lutheran. His wife, Christina (Weber), was born Janaury 12, 1806, in Oberbiel, Rheinland, Germany, died April 29, 1896, in Adams Township. She is buried at Emmanuel Lutheran, Soest. Their son, Philipp Koehlinger, was born November 27, 1830, in Blasbach, Rheinland, Germany, died March 6, 1904, in Fort Wayne, and is buried at Concordia Lutheran Cemetery, Fort Wayne. His wife, Bridget (Sliman), was born November 10, 1831, in Ireland, died May 9, 1864, in Jackson Township, and is buried at St. Louis Besancon Catholic Cemetery, Jefferson Township.

Submitted by Allen L. Franz

HENRY & MARTHA JANE FRECH

Henry Frech was born Heinrich Frech on October 8, 1843, at Ilfield, Besighem, Wurtemburg, the son of Heinrich and Christina (Axter) Frech. Heinrich and Christina Frech came to Allen County, Indiana, in 1853, bringing four of their six children: Jacob Frederich, Heinrich, Johann Gottlieb, and Christian Elizabeth. Soon after settling on an eighty-acre farm in the northwest quarter of section twenty-two, Aboite Township, both Heinriches changed their names to Henry, and Johann became John.

On July 8, 1862, the younger Henry Frech enlisted at Fort Wayne, Indiana, in Company B, 12th Indiana Infantry of the Union Army. He was injured at Missionary Ridge; taken captive at Richmond, Kentucky; and paroled on field. Henry was discharged at Washington, D. C., on June 8, 1865. Henry was an active member of the Grand Army of the Republic at Bass Post 40. He took part in Decoration Day (now Memorial Day) parades as long as his health allowed. Henry Frech married Martha Jane "Jenny" Bierly on November 4, 1870. Jenny was born January 11, 1844, at Pickaway County, Ohio, the daughter of David and Anna (Bowser) Bierly. Jenny died

Henry Frech

on June 13, 1915, and Henry died on August 21, 1926, both in Allen County, Indiana. They are buried at Bullard (Oak Grove) Cemetery, Aboite Township, Allen County, Indiana.

After returning to Allen County after the war Henry was in the ice business for a time and then settled on eighty acres in Aboite Township. He cleared the land and first built a log cabin. Later he added another forty acres and over the years built a large barn, a number of out buildings and a large brick house at what is now 9405 Aboite Center Road. The buildings have been torn down and Haverhill housing development is built on the Frech farm.

Henry Frech was a member of the Lutheran church and the Republican Party. Henry and Jenny Frech were the parents of seven children: Minnie Mae Frech (1871-1879); Frank Frech (1873-1935) who married Louise Dornte; Anna D. Frech (1875-1950) who married John A. Clark; Charles A. Frech (1877-1941) who married Norah Kendall; Ida A. Frech (1879-1964) who married Ulysses Grant Simons; Jessie M. Frech (1881-1977) who married Henry William McMaken; and Florence P. Frech (1886-1945) who married Charles F. Gerding.

Henry and Jenny retired from the farm in 1912 and moved to 754 Superior Street, Fort Wayne, where they lived out their remaining years. Their son, Charles, took over the farm. Later Frank's son, Henry O. Frech, purchased the farm. He was the last of the Frech descendants to live in the brick house.

Submitted by Linda E. Hollenbaugh

HENRY FRECH, JR.

"Grandpa" Frech, as he was called, was born in the Kingdom of Wuertttemberg, Bavaria, Germany, on October 8, 1943, one of six children born to Henry and Christina (Exner) Frech, Sr. They emigrated to the United States in 1853 and settled in Aboite Township in 1854, purchasing 80 acres of timbered land, clearing it and building a little log cabin as the family home. Henry, Jr. assisted in the turning of this land into a productive farm.

On July 8, 1862, at the age of 18, Henry, Jr. enlisted as a Private in Company B, Twelfth Indiana Infantry, to participate in the Civil War. Some of the campaigns were Vicksburg, Missionary Ridge, and Atlanta, with Sherman's march to the sea. During his enlistment, he was in every Southern state except Texas and Florida and marched more than six thousand miles. After the final surrender he took part in the Grand

Review in Washington, D.C. He was discharged on June 8, 1865.

"Grandpa" married Martha Jane Birely on October 4, 1870. They had seven children: Minnie, Frank, Anna, Charles, Ida, Jessie, and Florence. He was engaged in the ice business prior to purchasing 80 acres of unimproved land in Aboite Township. Henry, Jr. constructed a primitive log house and cleared and improved the farm to which he later added 40 acres. He resided there until 1912, when he moved to Fort Wayne. He died August 21, 1926.

"Grandpa's" daughter, Jessie, married Henry W. (Billy) McMaken on April 4, 1901. They had six children: Henry, Ruth, Herbert, Margaret, Wilma, and Edith. The couple first set up residence on Miller Road, later purchasing a farm in Aboite Township adjacent to the original Frech homestead. After living in the original residence for some years, they built a larger home on the property. This McMaken home, although extensively remodeled, still stands. The home of Grandpa and Grandma McMaken was the site of many happy family gatherings through the years. During their marriage, Jessie sold eggs and butter to customers in Fort Wayne. During the flood of 1913, she, along with the older children, crossed the flood swollen St. Mary's River on a footbridge in order that her customers would have their eggs and butter. Jessie maintained a closeness with her siblings over the years — visiting from Huntington County to northern Allen County as well as in Fort Wayne. Following a long residence on Aboite Center Road, the couple moved to Roanoke, where they resided until their deaths. Henry W. died in 1962 and Jessie died in 1977 at the age of 96.

For many years the "Frech" Reunion was held in "Grandpa's" honor on the Sunday in October closest to his birthday, with family members of each branch in attendance. Now "Grandpa" Frech's "McMaken" great-grandchildren hold a "Cousin" reunion in his honor annually on the first Saturday of October, an event which is planned to continue as long as possible.

Submitted by Adelia Jackson, Great-granddaughter

JOHN FREISTROFFER FAMILY

Simon and Elizabeth Engel Freistroffer immigrated in the 1840s, and were married in Franklin County, Ohio, December 27, 1853. Their first two children, Henry and John, were born in Ohio. John was born November 30, 1856. Simon and Elizabeth moved to Adams Township in Allen County around 1858. Their last six children, Simon, Maria Theresa, Leopold, Clara, Anna, and Jacob, were all born in Allen County.

John Freistroffer married Gertrude Hake October 3, 1883, in St. Joseph Catholic Church, Hessen Cassel. Gertrude was the youngest daughter of John and Gertrude Neireitter Hake. Her father settled in Allen County in 1834. Gertrude was born in July 1862. At the time of their marriage John Freistroffer was 26 years old and Gertrude Hake was 21.

John and Gertrude lived on a 56-acre farm in Section 4 of Marion Township, Allen County, that John purchased around 1882.

Mary Rose, their first child, was born July 2, 1884. She died in Seattle, Washington, August 19, 1912. Clara Gertrude, born July 23, 1886, married Richard Wade June 29, 1911, and moved to Calgary, Alberta, Canada. Aloysius, born March 2, 1889, died in Davenport, Iowa, November 16, 1907. Hildegard was born June 25, 1891. At the age of 15, Hildegard went to Mokena, Illinois, to become a Sister of St. Francis of the Sacred Heart. She took the name Sister Mary Virgilia. Sister Virgilia spent most of her years as a nun in the Avilla, Indiana, region. She died July 10, 1989, at the age of 98. She had been a sister for 83 years. Dorothy, born February 2, 1894, married Clem Getty August 27, 1912. They had 11 daughters and one son. Dorothy died October 16, 1992.

The family moved to Summit Street in Fort Wayne in 1895 or 1896. John still owned his farm, but worked at a local bakery taking care of the horses and making deliveries. He sold the farm around 1900.

Seated: Robert; Gertrude (mother); Germaine; John (father); Paul (Pete) Standing: Dorothy; Sister Virgilia (Hildegard); Marie; Clara. Pictures on wall: Aloysius; Mary Rose

Marie, born June 8, 1896, married Ralph Heminger October 4, 1921. They had seven children, four girls and three boys. Marie died February 22, 1968. Robert, born in April 1899, served in the army during World War I as a private in the Field Artillery. Robert drowned in Lake James June 3, 1922.

Paul John Freistroffer was born June 9, 1902. He married Marie Dieckman September 15, 1925. Marie was born September 9, 1901. They had four children: Jeanne, born May 5, 1927; Dorothy, born August 22, 1929; Nancy, born July 4, 1933; and John Paul, born March 29, 1941. Paul, also known as "Pete", worked for over 25 years as a knitter at Wayne Knitting Mills until the mill moved to Tennessee. He then worked as a custodian at South Wayne Elementary School. Marie died January 14, 1966, and Pete died July 24, 1992, at the age of 90.

Germaine, born November 30, 1905, married Erhard Zoch September 21, 1931. They had five children, four boys and one girl. Germaine died September 25, 1989.

Submitted by Nancy C. Murphy

RICHARD & MARTHA FREYGANG FAMILY

Richard Freygang was born in Fort Wayne on August 21, 1925, to Carl and Clementine (Minich) Freygang. Richard is the oldest of six children, the rest of whom are Pauline, Howard, Kenny, Roy, and Doris.

Freygang family at Kay & Dave's wedding in California

Martha was born on December 27, 1929, in Chicago, Illinois, to Wayne and Laura (Howard) Herrick and reared in Farmer City, Illinois. Martha was one of four children. Her siblings are Robert, Donald, and Julia.

Richard joined the Navy right out of Central Catholic High School and served during World War II for two and one-half years. Martha studied nursing after graduating from Moore Township High School and became a registered nurse. Later she graduated from Defiance College with a Bachelor of Science degree.

Richard and Martha met at a dance in Chicago, Illinois, where Martha was attending St. Joe Nursing School and Richard was attending DePaul University. They married in October 1952 in Farmer City, Illinois, and made their home in Fort Wayne. Richard retired from General Electric after 42 years of service. Martha worked as a registered nurse in various locations throughout the city.

Richard and Martha have ten children who attended and graduated from St. Therese grade school and Elmhurst High School. Their first child, Ayn married Robert Adams. They have two children (Eli, Hannah) and reside in Arkansas. Pat married Larry Samuels and they have three children (Raina, Scott, Riley) and live in Florida. Kay and her husband Dave Odland have five children (Lisa, Dasha, Katia, Alexi, Sophia) and live in Minnesota. Mary married Ron James and they have two children (Nate, Luke) and live in Huntertown. Richard and Martha's fifth child, Mike, married Kim (Floyd) from Huntington. They have five children (Kelley, Katie, Ben, Sarah, David) and live in Fort Wayne. Jim married Diane (Holloway) and they have three children (Joe, Jenny, Jessica) and reside in Roanoke. Bill is married to Lisa, who is from China. They recently resided in Saipan. The eighth Freygang born to Richard and Martha is Ed, who lives in Colorado and is an avid runner. Laurie married Alan Whisler and they have four children (Hollie, Josh, Austin, Adam) and reside in Fort Wayne. Amy is married to Andrew Bogle and they have four children (Rachel, Elly, Michael, Mark Henry) and live in Fort Wayne.

This will be the eighteenth year the Freygangs have had an annual get-together. The get-togethers have been in Tennessee, North Carolina, South Carolina, Illinois, Kentucky, Arkansas, Florida, Maryland, Georgia, and Michigan. The vacation is for a week and was started so everyone could see each other at least once a year.

Submitted by Richard and Martha Freygang

HARRY ALBERT FRITZ & TREVA DALE (LIECHTY)

Harry Albert Fritz, born September 28, 1902, died June 10, 1977, married Treva Dale (Liechty) on February 28, 1924. She was born February 28, 1906, and died December 31, 1955. Harry's second marriage was to Juanita Repine (Ott) on August 5, 1962. Harry and Treva had six children: Richard Harry Fritz, born November 24, 1924; Florence Jean (Simon, Smith), born October 24, 1926, died May 29, 2002; Dolores May (Kuehnert), February 2, 1929; Betty Lucille (Dunten), January 1, 1931; Alvin Wayne Fritz, August 19, 1934; and Kenneth Paul Fritz, July 28, 1937. They all live in Allen County.

Harry and Treva lived on the Fritz homestead, 10028 Fritz Road. Harry was a school bus driver for Washington Township school for 21 years, worked at Joslyn Steel Mill, and farmed. Treva was a homemaker. They had a housekeeper as she was ill often. She went to Mayo Clinic for treatment, and died at the age of forty nine.

Harry's father was Henry Fritz, born June 7, 1864, died May 13, 1930. Henry married Katherine Lamle, 1861-1934. He came from Stuttgart, Germany, on a ship. There were three families named Fritz on the ship, none related.

Submitted by Judy Ott

RICHARD HARRY FRITZ & ALICE LUCILLE (SMITH)

Richard was born November 24, 1924, the son of Harry Albert Fritz and Treva Dale (Liechty). Alice Lucille Smith was born September 5, 1925, the daughter of Alvin Frank Smith and Blanche Irene (Johnston). They were married February 5, 1944. Richard went to work for Huntertown Grain and Lumber Company after high school, one year driving truck, 22 years running the mill. He then drove a Standard Oil truck for 19 years. He farmed all his life.

Richard and Alice rented a house at 10511 Bethel Road for $20 a month. In 1946 they built a house on Dupont Road in Washington Township. Richard mowed Dupont Road with a team of horses, and grass grew in the middle of the road. His dad got one dollar a mile for mowing; they would see only one or two cars.

In 1963 they bought the John Geller farm in Eel River Township at 11327 Bethel Road. Northwest Allen County Schools bought 40 acres at the corner of Hand and Bethel for Carroll High School. In 1994 Northwest Allen County Schools bought 96 acres, the house and buildings. Grandson, Russell Ott, bought the house and moved it to 14110 Hand Road. Richard and Alice had 13 acres left, and built a new home which they moved into on December, 1995, at 4004 Baird Road.

Their children were James Wayne, born August 4, 1944; Jean Ann, born June 6, 1945, died in 1945; Judy Ann, May 17, 1946; Joseph Richard, May 20, 1947.

James married Helen Jean (LaFlur) on June 3, 1976. Their children James Wayne, Jr., born April 16, 1969; Jeremy Wade, October 17, 1971; Johnathon William, October 19, 1976; and Jason Warren, March 24, 1978. James Jr. married Cheryl (Hamburg) on August 14, 1995. Their children are Izak Wayne, born October 30, 1997; Ian James, August 18, 2001. Jeremy married Brooke Ellen (Johnston) August 12, 1995. Their children, Madysen Paige, born August 30, 1997; McCoy Wade, January 24, 2002; Maguire Mann, April 8, 2003. Jonathan William married Janelle Lynn (Jensen) on August 5, 2000. Jason married Katherine Lynn (Jenson) on June 23, 2000. Their son, Samuel James, was born October 23, 2002.

Judy married Darwin Russell Ott on October 3, 1964. Their children: Russell Alan, born September 16, 1965, and Kristina Kay, July 22, 1969. Russell Allen married Christine Renee (Herendeen) on April 20, 1991. Their children: Elizabeth Christine, born May 9, 1994; Benjamin Russell, May 10, 1995; Luke Alan, August 27, 1997; Matthew Hunter, December 2, 1999. Kristina Kay married Brent Kevin Beverly on April 11, 1992. Their children: Kevin Allen, born December 2, 1991; Morgan Dean, July 17, 1994.

Joseph married Lana Lynn (Rich) on June 10, 1969. Their children: Tamyra LyJo, born September 9, 1969; Timothy Joseph, June 15, 1974; Tiffany Ann, January 29, 1977; and Troy Joshua, February 17, 1982. Tamyra LyJo married Chester Robert Zeidler on December 8, 1990. Their children: Rochester Robert, born February 1, 2000; Lillian Jo, December 22, 2003. Timothy Joseph married Michelle Lynn (Hagen) on October 18, 1997. Their son, Jackson Timothy, was born June 19, 1974. Tiffany Ann married Mark King on August 24, 2002. Daughter, Kylee Lee Ann King, was born July16, 1999. Tiffany Ann was remarried to Justin Fergerson on December 28, 2003. Troy Joshua married Nicki Dity, daughter Dezirae Nickole, on September 16, 2001.

Richard and Alice fry fish for community organizations and churches, and they were 4-H Leaders for 30 years. He was on the County Extension Board for nine years, and Northwest School Board twelve years. He was Honorary Chapter Farmer from Carroll High School F.F.A., and received a Master Farm Conservation Award 2003.

He is chairman of Allen County Farm Bureau. They are Chairman and Women's Leader of Washington Township Farm Bureau. Richard and Alice are members of St. John's Lutheran Church, Lake Township where they were Sunday School teachers and held many offices in the Church. They camp and fish at Crooked Lake, Angola, Indiana.

Submitted by Richard and Alice Fritz

Back row standing: Ruth Brouwer Scott, Carl Scott, John Kno[x], Russell Noll, Charles Brouwer, Walter Bolyard, W. Herma[n] Gresley, Irene Brouwer Gresley Third row sitting: Elsie F[ry] Giant, Grace Fry Knox, Inez Fry Noll, Lena Heckler Fry, Doll[ie] Fry Brouwer, Cristina (Tena)Fry Bolyard Second row kneelin[g] Juanita Bolyard, Devetta Bolyard Gick, Thelma Knox, Ma[ry] Knox, Ray Giant, Russell Brouwer First row sitting: Lest[er] (Buddy) Gick, Johanna Knox (in Buddy's lap), Doyle Scott, Luan[n] Brames, Rosemary Noll, Bonnie Scott

FRY FAMILY

Mary Magelena Heckler married Lewis Fry December 25, 1889. He was the son of Phillip and Emily J. Fry. They had five daughters and lived on a farm west of Monroeville. Unfortunately, Lewis died at a young age and left Mary (Lena) with the girls to raise.

The oldest daughter, Dollie, married Charles Brouwer. They ran the grocery and general store at rural Boston for many years. Charlie delivered ice for iceboxes around the area. They had a daughter, Irene, who married Herman Gresley. When their daughter, Ann was four years old, sadly, Irene died of cancer. Dollie and Charlie's son, Russel, married Mary Morningstar. They ha[d] a daughter, Wanda, and a son, Douglas.

Inez married Russell Noll and lived in For[t] Wayne. Their first adopted daughter, Nedra, die[d] as a baby. They then adopted Rosemary wh[o] married Bill Duff. They had daughters Tammy, Lisa, Indie and son, Greg.

Christina (Tena) married Walter Bolyard. H[e] ran the drainage tile mill west of Monroevill[e] for many years. They had daughters DeVett[a] and Juanita. DeVetta married Lester Gick wh[o] was killed in World War II leaving her an[d] their son, Gene. DeVetta later married Georg[e] Rothegeb. They had sons, Dean, Gale, Neal and Mark. Juanita married Mike Clay and had [a] son, Louis, and daughter, Christine. A baby gir[l] died at birth.

Twin girls, Elsie and Grace rounded ou[t] the family. Grace married John Knox. They ra[n] the restaurant, gas station and sleeping cabin[s] on the very busy US 30 west of 101 for man[y] years. The log cabin house they lived in is stil[l] there. They raised daughters, Mary, Thelma an[d] Johanna. Mary married Harold McBride, Thelm[a] married Jim Borcherdine and Johanna marrie[d] Von Hoffacker.

Elsie married Hershel Giant, the son o[f] Jacob Giant and Elizabeth Gerardot. Elsie an[d] Hershel had a son Ray. When Ray was five year[s] old, the family saw the infamous 1920 cyclon[e] coming at them. They attempted to get Jacob'[s] storm cellar, but didn't make it. They put Ra[y] into the ditch, Elsie next and Hershel coverin[g] both, holding onto the fence and post. Hersche[l] died a few days later from the extensive injuries. Elsie, who was 25 years old, was badly hurt. Even after many surgeries, she lived with [a] stiff arm and died at age 48 from injuries to he[r] kidneys. Ray had minor injuries. The families helped out, but their life was difficult. Elsie ran [a] cream station in Monroeville until it closed. Ray was a very talented boy. He taught himself how to play the guitar and piano by ear. By age 17, he was playing in a local band. Later, he formed his own band and was well known throughout northern Indiana and Ohio. Elsie had a daughter later in life. LuAnn was only eight years old when Elsie died. She and Ray lived with family until Ray married Pauline Kohlenberg. They had met at work in the Lugenbill Wire Die factory. They married February 27, 1946, and daughter Mary Catherine was born in December. Their only child brought them much happiness. Mary Catherine married Stephen Federspiel. They were both nurses at Fort Wayne VA Hospital before moving to Long Beach, California.

LuAnn married Robert Kennerk, son of Frank and Genevieve (Gladieux), August 18, 1956. Their daughter, Karen married John Bauman, son of Edward and Joan (Martin) Bauman. Daughter, Kathleen (Kathy), married Wayne Rorick, son of John and Gertrude (Sarrazine) Rorick.

By now, many grandchildren and great-grandchildren have blessed the entire Fry-Heckler family.

Submitted by LuAnn Kennerk

WADE ELDON & DOROTHY JANE (NUSBAUM) FRY FAMILY

Wade was born August 19, 1935 in Maples. His great-grandfather, Philip, born in 1842, was a native of Madison Township where he bought and sold livestock. He trained with the Indiana Militia during the Civil War, but was never called to active duty. His wife, Emily J. Bowls, born in 1847, came to America from England. To this union was born nine children, Louis (Lena Heckler), James (Lucy Filling), Jesse (Sadie), Fred (Laverta), Edward DeFord (Louise Viola Gerardot) (Wade's grandparents), Bert, Rhoda (Charlie Welsch), Clara (Albert Flynn), Florence (Mr. Bauckman).

Wade and Dorothy Fry

Wade's grandfather, Edward, retired from Essex. They had two children, Harvey Albert (Mary Ellen Ellis) (Wade's parents), and Viola Louise (Carl Diltz, Gene Stewart). Harvey, born December 25, 1903, retired from Pennsylvania Railroad and lived 100 years, 7 months, 2 days. In 1917 at the age of 14, he attended the raising of the flag ceremony at Four Presidents Corners, Jackson, Jefferson, Momoe, Madison. Harvey and Mary celebrated 71 years of marriage.

After serving in the United States Army (1954-1956), Wade and Dorothy (born April 28, 1935), married on December 1,1956.

Dorothy graduated from Parkview Methodist School of Nursing. Her parents, L. Howard and Mary Jane (Adams) were married January 28, 1928, and had six children. Frances (Harry Sheefel Jr.), Phyllis (Blaine Kimes), Richard (Deloris Keller, Donna Prather), Dorothy, Ralph (Phyllis Baker), Ronald (Gureta Edwards). Dorothy's mother was one of six daughters born to Raleigh and Elnora Pearl (Shaffer), married November 5, 1903: Vera (Alpha Blake), Lula (Carlus Miller), Erma (Darwin Richards), Mary, Ruth (Earl Lake), Edith (Lester May).

Raleigh was a farmer; he and Elnora celebrated 57 years of marriage. Raleigh's father, Gabriel Richard, came here in 1865 from Bethlehem, Pennsylvania. He was born in Yadkin County, North Carolina, April 24, 1833. At the age of thirty, he enlisted in the thirty-third North Carolina regiment of the Confederate Army. It was six months in service before being captured and held in prison for six months in Washington. When released, he was marked and ordered to never cross the Mason/Dixon Line again. Not being permitted to return to his native state, he was directed Westward by way of Pennsylvania and Ohio, arriving in Madison Township in 1865. He married Mary Ellen Chapman in 1871, descendant of Edward Chapman, same family as John (Johnny Appleseed) Chapman. She was born in Mercer County, Pennsylvania, in 1849. They moved to Madison Township in 1860. They were farmers. To this union ten children were born, infant daughter, Ida (WM Johnson), Alfred (Ola Eagy), Raleigh (Elnora Shaffer), Mary (Johnson May), Lucy (Louis McBride), James Madison (Clara Wagner), John (Mable Marquet), Chancey (Lorena Grey), Allen (Frances Draper).

Wade and Dorothy's family includes two daughters, Desiree (Scott Rayl), Cincinnati, Ohio, Nanette (James Alkire II), Dallas, Texas, five grandchildren and three great-grandchildren. Wade retired from Navistar, now International Truck, and Dorothy from Parkview Hospital.

Submitted by Wade E. Fry

FULK FAMILY

Jacob Fulk (1818-1894), son of Daniel and Sarah (Souder) Fulk, married Margaret Richey (1820-1882), daughter of John and Magdalena (Fawley) Ritchie (1799-1860). Jacob's great-grandfather was Matthew Fulk who married an Indian woman from the Shenandoah Valley. Jacob and Margaret were born at Fulk's Run, Rockingham County, Virginia, and came to Noble County, Indiana, in late 1850. In 1861, they bought forty acres of land in Section 6, Eel River Township, Allen County, Indiana. They had seven children: Daniel (1844); John (1845); George (1850); Sarah (1856); Adam (1860); Margaret (1862); and Jacob A. (January 25, 1865).

Jacob A. Fulk married Nora Frances Johnson on January 1, 1887. Nora was born March 7, 1869, the daughter of William Riley and Ellen (Madden) Johnson. Jacob also farmed the land in Eel River Township. They had one child, James F. Fulk (1891-1968). Jacob died April 1, 1937, and Nora died October 5, 1963.

James F. Fulk married Elva Alberta Bosler on November 18, 1914. Elva was the daughter of Albertus Henry and Sarah Jane (Sloffer) Bosler. James was the third generation to farm the land in Eel River Township. James worked on the WPA during the construction of State Road 205, which was built by hand with long handled shovels and wheelbarrows. Because James had an old flatbed truck, he did not have to shovel, he drove the truck to haul dirt. James helped build the power lines at Ari. Every week in the late 1930s and

Jacob A., James F. and Nora Fulk

early 1940s, James, Elva and their children raised, dressed and supplied broiler chickens to St. Joseph Hospital. In the early 1930s, the airmail planes flying from South Bend to Fort Wayne used barn lights as a landmark guide, one of which was on the Fulk barn.

James and Elva were the parents of seven children: Jacob Lynn (March 3, 1916-April 16, 1916). Lenora Ellen (1918) married Franklin Geiger in 1941. She was a teacher at Huntertown for the years 1938-1941. Her teaching contract was for $100 a month. She and Franklin had three children: Joan, Janice and John.

John Joseph (1919-1975) married Phyllis McCoy in 1941. They resided on a farm about a mile from the original homestead in Swan Township.

Jay Franklin (1921-1999) married Ilene Freeman in 1941. They resided in Huntertown and had two children, Dean and Sherry. Dean and his mother graduated from Huntertown and Sherry graduated from Carroll High School. Jay worked at the Allen County War Memorial Coliseum and Ilene was very active with Allen County 4-H.

Alton Lee (1926-2003) married Nevah Gaff in 1946. They had four children: Rose Ann, William, James and Joseph. After their home was destroyed by Hurricane Andrew in Florida, they returned to Allen County and resided on part of the original Fulk homestead until their deaths.

Jacob Earl (1931) married Joyce Platt in 1955. Jacob E. is the fourth generation Fulk to live on and farm the land in Eel River Township. They had five children: Michael, David, Jeanette, Daniel and Teresa. Their children graduated from Carroll High School as well as several grandchildren. Jacob served in the Army 1952-1954.

Ruth Ann (1935) married Phillip Arehart in 1953. Ruth attended Huntertown School. They had seven children: Renee, Jonathan, Jeffrey, Carol Ann, Jayne, Pamela and Christina.

Submitted by Joyce Fulk

DAVID M. FULLER

Albert McBride lived in Iowa, Illinois, Ohio, and finally Madison Township, Allen County, Indiana. He was David M. Fuller's maternal grandfather. David was never to know this grandfather, as Albert, in trying to restrain his horse, was kicked and badly injured. He died May 20, 1912, at St. Joseph Hospital, Fort Wayne, Indiana.

Albert McBride was born December 3, 1883, in Sac County, Iowa, to Jacob McBride and Phoebe Green. It is not known why this child was born in Iowa as other children in the family were born in Piatt County, Illinois.

Albert was married to Clara Bell Clay September 30, 1905. She was the daughter of Francis Clay and Sarah Allen of Mercer County, Ohio. Before Albert's death, he fathered six children and lost two of them due to illness. The remaining children were Willard (1906), Wilford (1907), Francis (1908), and Marcelle (1911).

Albert s widow, Clara, married Alfred Green of Fort Wayne, Indiana, on May 15, 1915. They had two sons: Alfred Dwayne (1919) and Charles LaVerne (1921).

Marcelle McBride was married December 1, 1928, to Willard Fuller of Wells County, Indiana. They had nine children before the marriage ended in divorce. The children were Garnet (Lantz), David, James (deceased), Larry, George (deceased), Hurb, Jeanne, Bonnie (Pace), and Patricia (Davidson).

David Fuller grew up on a farm near Uniondale, Indiana. He graduated from Rock Creek High School in Wells County, Indiana. He had his private pilot license when he was seventeen. He served in the U.S. Army during the Korean War as a paratrooper with the 82nd Airborne Division.

In 1955, David married Frances J. Knobeloch of Gas City, Indiana. They made their home in Fort Wayne, Indiana. They are the parents of three sons: Stephen, Stuart, and Jeffrey. They also have eight grandchildren.

Phelps Dodge Magnet Wire employed David for 38 years. He obtained his glider pilot license and liked to read, camp, hike, canoe, and target shoot.

The great-grandparents of Frances, Heinrich and Katherine Knobeloch of Germany, settled in Perry County, Indiana, in the 1850s. Frances parents, Jesse and Ellen Knobeloch, came to Grant County, Indiana, in the early 1930s.

In 1952, Frances graduated from Mississinewa High School in Grant County, Indiana. She then came to Fort Wayne to study at International Business College, and made Fort Wayne her home after that. She volunteered at elementary schools for 25 years, tutoring first graders in reading. She was the first woman to serve as president of the Springwood Neighborhood Association. She has done much work on the genealogies of her family and David's family, has served on PTA boards, North Christian Church's board, as well as a member of its church choir and bell choir, and for ten years was an Area Captain for area TOPS chapters.

The most important thing David and Frances accomplished was to encourage and help finance their sons college educations.

Submitted by Frances J. Fuller

DIEDRICH FRIEDRICH GALLMEYER

Three Gallmeyer siblings came to Allen County from Bierde 31, Lahde, near Hannover, Germany. Conrad Friedrich (1838-1910) came before 1864 and settled in Milan Township. He married Christina Maria Louisa Bradtmuller in 1864 in Martini Lutheran Church. The couple had twelve children: Friedrich Dietrich, Wilhelmina Christina Louise, Wilhelmina Christina Sophia, Hanna Sophia Louisa, Christina Louise Sophia, Emilie Lisette, Friedrich Diedrich, Heinrich Ferdinand, Carl Johanna Friedrich, Emma Louise, Emma Wilhelmine, and Christine Katherine. The first four children were baptized at Martini; the next four at Emmanuel Lutheran Church, New Haven, and the last four at St. Paul Lutheran Church, Gar Creek. The parents are buried in Emmanuel Cemetery.

Diedrich Gallmeyer Family – Front: Ernest, Ferdinand, Herman, Gustav. Seated: Christina nee Luehrs, Diedrich holding Carl. Standing: William, Sophia, Henry, Diedrich, Jr.

Johanna "Hanne" Marie Christine Gallmeyer (1841-1906) and her brother Diedrich Friedrich Wilhelm (1844-1909) immigrated in 1870 on the ship Rhein via Bremen to New York. They, too, settled in Milan Township. On June 8 of the next year, Hanne married the widower Friedrich Conrad Christian Gallmeier, her third cousin, in Zion Lutheran Church, Friedheim. They are buried in that cemetery. Their common great great grandparents were Johann Friedrich Gallmeyer (1728-1811) and Anna Margareta Ilsabe, nee Vahlsing (1737-1788) of Windheim, Germany. Hanne and Friedrich's six children were Friedrich C., Christine Wilhelmine, August, Auguste Wilhelmine, an unnamed infant, and Rosine Christine.

Diedrich and Christine Wilhelmine Luehrs (1852-1901) married on October 3, 1872, at Emmanuel Lutheran Church, New Haven, and then became members of St. Paul Lutheran Church, Gar Creek, after its establishment. Both are buried in Emmanuel Cemetery. Heinrich Friedrich (1873-1928) was their eldest child. After marrying Berta Spadholtz (1876-1957, from Jewell, Ohio), Henry bought a farm on Seiler Road, where two daughters were born. The elder daughter, Edna (1910-1996), married Emil Jackemeyer (1905-1954) and had three children: Elwood (born 1938), Loren (born 1940), and Delores (born 1943). Amelia (1915-1978) married Paul Wesling (1906-1955) and had two daughters, Carolyn (born 1947) and Ellen (born 1948).

In 2005, Elwood Jackemeyer lives in Estero, Florida; Loren in Angola, Indiana; and Delores Kikuchi in Koloa, Kauai, Hawaii. Carolyn Wesling lives in Eagan, Minnesota; and Ellen Wesling Holstein resides in Morgantown, Indiana. The next two generations' surnames are Harkenrider, Konow, Guy, Jackemeyer, Fulbright, Palenapa, Samonte, Kaska, and Motooka.

Diedrich and Christine Luehr's remaining 11 children were Friedrich Heinrich; Sophie Hanna (married Carl Wiese, lived in Denver, Colorado); Carl Wilhelm (married Mary Bremer, lived in Phoenix, Arizona); Conrad Friedrich (married Ida Van Buren, lived in Stanwood, Iowa); Caroline; Ernst (married Maria Lahmeyer, lived in Fort Wayne); Ferdinand (married Sophie Lehrman, lived in Auburn, Washington); Hermann (married Elizabeth Kettler, lived in Iowa); August (married Emma, lived in Gar Creek); Carl; and Friedrich Carl (married Bertha Gottshalk, lived in Iowa).

Submitted by Amy Fulbright

JOSEPH CONRAD GALLMEYER

APRIL 14, 1927 – DECEMBER 23, 2003

Joseph C. Gallmeyer was born in Fort Wayne and spent most of his adult life in Indiana. He attended Fort Wayne South Side School and eventually graduated from Central High School in 1946. While in high school he met the vivacious Alice Denner. He knew immediately that she was the girl that he would marry, and they shared life's experiences for 56 years. Joe and Alice raised three wonderful children, Debbie, Diane, and Mark, who all live and work in Fort Wayne.

After high school, Joe began his business career working for Indiana Bearings. With a strong aptitude for sales and an extraordinary people skills, Joe worked diligently to learn the power transmission business top to bottom. He was exceptionally gifted when it came to helping manufacturing companies solve complex problems with complicated gears, belts, and associated parts. This mechanical aptitude, combined with his keen ability to select and manage the very best and brightest people, secured his place as a successful Fort Wayne businessman.

Joseph C. Gallmeyer, December 22, 1994 "Happy Times"

When a opportunity to become a part owner and start a local power transmission business presented itself, he did not hesitate to join the venture and start Trans Power Incorporated. The company headquarters was located at 3025 North Wells Street and initially employed 15 people. As time passed, and the business grew, Joe successfully bought out his business partner and became the primary owner of Trans Power Incorporated. Trans Power's reputation for quality service and competitive pricing served the company well and it grew quickly. Eventually, the company was expanded to seven branches in Indiana and Ohio, employing 92 people with annual sales in excess of $11 million dollars. Mr. Gallmeyer sold the company in 1980 to Kaman Incorporated. Kaman continues to manage facilities with a continuing presence in Fort Wayne.

After selling the company Joe traveled between Fort Wayne and the eastern shore of Florida where, over the years, he and his wife Alice owned several properties. The Gallmeyers also enjoyed traveling extensively to locations around the world. Away from business, Joe always placed family first. He loved a good, home cooked meal with family and friends. He especially enjoyed spending time with his three children, six grandchildren, and one great grandchild.

He was a founding member of Faith Lutheran Church.

Joe Gallmeyer's life and career in business demonstrates the rewards of hard work, honesty, diligence and a true compassion for his family and his community. His is a self-made success story. He touched the lives of so many and definitely contributed a great deal to the Fort Wayne area. Many lives were enriched through personal and professional association with Joe Gallmeyer.

Submitted Alice L. Gallmeyer

RAYMOND & BERTHA B. GARRETT FAMILY

Raymond Garrett was born on August 7, 1922, the son of Charley W. and Louella M. Priest Garrett. They lived in Penn Township, Jay County. Raymond taught math at Elmhurst High School for 30 years, retiring in 1987. He taught one year at Pennville and nine years at Union Center in Wells County before Elmhurst.

Bertha Brittingham was born on March 24, 1926, the daughter of Robert and Anna Hunt Brittingham, in Washington Township, Gibson County. Bertha taught at LaFontaine, Lancaster in Huntington County, Lancaster and Rock Creek in Wells County, and both Ivy Tech and IUPU.

Raymond and Bertha graduated from Ball State in 1947. They were married at the First Methodist Church in Tell City on October 25, 1947. They lived in LaFontaine, then Huntington, then north of Bluffton in Wells County, before moving to Ferguson Road in Allen County on August 7, 1962.

Their son, Paul B. Garrett, was born at Wells County Hospital August 5, 1952. He attended Lancaster School through fourth grade, then Pleasant Center School, Kekionga Junior High, and graduated from Elmhurst High School in 1970. He graduated from Purdue with both a Bachelor and Masters degree in mathematics in 1973. After his Ph.D. from Princeton University, he taught at Yale and Stanford. Since 1982, he has been a professor of mathematics at the University of Minnesota in Minneapolis. His wife, Carol M. Brunzell, is a registered dietitian. Their daughter, Olivia C. Brunzell-Garrett, was born November 13, 1992.

Back row: Paul, Nate, David, Karen, Joe, Joey Middle row: Carl, Olivia, Junko, Elaine, Natalie, Matt. Front row: Raymond and Bertha Garrett (2002).

Second son, Joseph B. Garrett (Joe) was born on May 2, 1954, in Wells County. He scored the first run for the Wayne High School baseball team (its first year). He and Steve Underwood won the first sectional title (doubles tennis) for Wayne. He played tenor sax in the Elmhurst Jazz Band, prior to the opening of Wayne High School. Joe graduated from Wayne in 1972 and from Purdue in 1976. Since 1976, Joe has been with City Securities Corporation in South Bend. His wife, Elaine A. (Penner) Garrett, is a kindergarten teacher. Their children are Natalie, born March 5, 1980; Joseph, born April 29, 1982; and Matthew, born October 11, 1984.

Third son, David B. Garrett, was born May 6, 1959, in Wells County. He graduated from Wayne High School in 1976. In 1979 he received a Bachelors degree in music from Ball State. His Masters degree was from the University of Texas in San Antonio, and, in 1998, he received the Doctor of Musical Arts at the University of Texas in Houston. David has been a cellist in the symphonies of Grand Rapids, New Orleans, Shreveport, San Antonio, and Houston. Since 2000, he has been in the Los Angeles Philharmonic.

David has been a cello instructor on the faculties of Trinity University, University of Texas at San Antonio, and presently is at California State University at Long Beach. Nathaniel, born March 23, 1983, is David's son from his marriage to Debra A. Thomas. David's present wife is Junko Uno Garrett, from Tokyo. She is a concert pianist and teacher of piano.

Daughter, Karen Ann Garrett, was born February 21, 1964, at Wells County Hospital. She graduated from Wayne High School in 1981. In 1985 she graduated from Purdue with a B.S. in International Agronomy. At Colorado State she completed a Masters degree in both Plant Pathology and in Statistics. She received her Ph.D. in Botany and Plant Pathology at Oregon State. She has just been granted tenure on the faculty at Kansas State University (2005).

Her husband is Peter Garfinkel, a social worker and photographer.

Submitted by Bertha B. Garrett

DAVID C & PHILAMON LEE (MALY) GASTINEAU FAMILY

Dr. David C (no period) Gastineau was born on June 24, 1924, in Indianapolis, the son of Dr. Frank and Ethel (Hughes) Gastineau. His father was a professor of dermatology at the Indiana University School of Medicine.

David graduated from Shortridge High School in Indianapolis in 1942 and then attended the University of Michigan. He entered the Indiana University School of Medicine and fulfilled his internship and residency at Robert Long Hospital in Indianapolis, specializing in radiology. Upon graduation, he joined the staff of the Indiana University School of Medicine and was an associate professor of radiology until 1957. He also joined the Indiana National Guard and retired after twenty years as a lieutenant colonel.

Philamon Maly was born on January 22, 1927, in Norwood, Ohio, the daughter of Ralph Joseph and Blanche Low (Dickins) Maly. She attended Clifton High School in Cincinnati and then took her senior year at Shortridge High School in Indianapolis, graduating in 1944. She enrolled at Butler University, Indianapolis, for two years and then took medical stenography courses at Indiana Business College in Indianapolis for another year. In 1947 she began working at Robert Long Hospital as a medical stenographer and there met David Gastineau. They were married on December 17, 1949.

In 1957, Drs. Jack Loudermilk, Richard Datzman, James Lorman, and Harold Griffith, invited Dr. Gastineau to join their group in Fort Wayne. Together they started Fort Wayne Radiology. He was recognized by his medical peers as being a pioneer in radiation therapy at Parkview Memorial Hospital, Fort Wayne.

David and Philamon purchased a home in Fort Wayne at 8203 Westridge Road in the Waterswolde Addition. Just before leaving Indianapolis, David and Philamon Gastineau adopted Pamela Sue, who was born on May 12, 1957. They then adopted twin boys, Michael David and Cary Dickins, who were born on May 15, 1959. Bruce Thomas was born to Philamon on May 3, 1961.

Pamela Sue lives in Florida, was married to Don Hlvaka, and has three children, David, Hunter, and Avery. Michael is married to Catherine Strasen. They live in Fort Wayne and have four children, Mitchell, Claire, Philip, and Connor. Cary, who was married to Cynthia Potts, died on January 3, 1982, of cancer. Their daughter, Kari Sue, has two children, Karissa and Gabrielle. Bruce is married to Nola Issacson. They live on Marco Island, Florida, and have three children, Lauren, Dalton, and Morgan.

In 1984, David Gastineau underwent coronary by-pass surgery and a few days later suffered a stroke. While it affected his speech and movement of his limbs on his left side, he remained mentally sharp and physically active. His condition called for a warmer climate; so he and Philamon moved to a home they purchased in 1978 on Marco Island, Florida.

David was a 33rd degree Mason in Fort Wayne and, while in Florida, continued his Masonic associations, his keen interest in just about everything, and volunteering with Habitat for Humanity. He and Philamon took 25 cruises after his retirement and before his death at home on January 16, 1995. He is buried in Greenlawn Cemetery in Fort Wayne.

Philamon lives in the home on Marco Island. She has belonged to the Daughters of the Nile for 28 years, is a past Queen, and regularly attends its functions. She enjoys sewing and cross-stitch and continues to take cruises with her friends.

Submitted by Philamon Gastineau

KATE & MIKE GAVIN FAMILY

Kate (Mary Kathryn) was born January 1936, in Niles, Michigan. Kate's mother was Naomi Ruth Hiatt (teacher) (October 1908-October 1967), one of eleven children of Luther and Nora (Schultz) Hiatt of Green Township, Jay County. Kate's father, Orvel Glenn Glassburn, (Radar) (October 1907 – October 1943) was the eldest of nine of the George Glassburn family of Geneva. Kate and her sister, Jane, grew up in Portland. Kate graduated from Portland High School in 1954 and Ball State Teachers College in 1957

Kate and Mike Gavin Family, 1973
John, Brad, Bruce, Mike, Kate, Kara

(BS) and 1959 (MA). She taught kindergarten in Muncie while finishing her masters in Science and married Michael Eugene (Mike) Gavin (November 1954) from Portland. Mike was the son of Frank Garrett and Ethel (Bisel) Gavin. He has one sister, Patricia.

Mike and Kate moved to Fort Wayne in 1959 where Kate taught at South Wayne School and Mike went to Indiana Tech, graduating as an Electronics Engineer in 1960. They moved to Michigan where Mike worked at Sparton Electronics in Jackson. They had two sons, Bradley Scott (November 1960) and Bruce Allan (February 1962) who were born at Foote Hospital. The family moved to Fort Wayne in 1962, where Mike worked at Magnavox. John Mark (December 1963) and Kara Ruth (March 1966) were born at Lutheran Hospital.

Brad started at Croninger School when it opened in 1967. Kate taught kindergarten there until Haley opened in 1970 and Park State East families were moved to Haley. Kate taught at Haley 18 years. The children graduated from Snider High School in 1978, 1979, 1981, and 1984.

Mike and Kate divorced in 1978, and Mike moved to California.

The boys graduated from Purdue University—Brad in Chemical Engineering, Bruce in Electrical Engineering and John in Coastal Engineering. Kara graduated with an education degree from IPFW.

Brad worked for IDEM in Indianapolis for nine years then went to Vermont Law School in South Royalton, Vermont, and obtained an Environmental Attorney degree. He is working for Indiana again as General Counsel for SEMA. He has two girls, Tegan and Hallie.

Bruce married Susan Erwin of Fort Wayne. Susan is the daughter of Dick and Barbara Erwin. Bruce worked in California while Sue finished her medical degree at Indiana University and in Phoenix where she went for residency. Sue started her medical practice in Kentucky. Ethan, Colleen and Rachael came along and Bruce stayed home with the children.

John went to Honduras with the Peace Corps where he met Chian Carmichael from Phoenix. After his return, he spent a year with the International Rescue Committee in Sudan, later going to Khartoum to handle aid programs for the State Department. He and Chian married and moved to Washington, DC. John works with Third World Countries through an engineering firm. Chian is a counselor for FAA.

Kara taught at Ben Geyer in Fort Wayne, then moved to Key West and taught there. She met and married Steve Zeamer who is an Architect-Builder. They moved to Virginia and now have two little boys, Gavin and Alex.

Kate taught with Fort Wayne Community Schools for 25 years. She married Bill Ferguson (November 1918) of Chicago in 1984. Bill's daughter, Linda (Steve) Schroeder of Fort Wayne introduced them. Kate has spent many years volunteering in the community with Fox Island Alliance, Science Central, Settlers and the Master Gardener Program.

Submitted by Kate Gavin Ferguson

CHARLES GAYLORD

Michelle Lee Shultz married Steven Wayne Mix, December 8, 1990.

Steve's parents are Tom and Sherry Mix. Steve and Shellie have two children, Brittney Tacconi and Alex Wayne. Shellie's great-great-great-great grandparents were Charles Gaylord Sr., born about 1823 in Massachusetts, and died between 1888 and 1891 in Clark County, Indiana. Charles married Amanda Melinda Gamble, daughter of Richard Gamble and Rachel. Rachel was born about 1835 in Kentucky. They had three known sons: Charles Jr., born about 1853 and died about 1897, George, and William. Charles Sr. had been in shipbuilding in Massachusetts before migrating east, becoming a farmer in Indiana.

Charles Jr. and Susan Morrison Gaylord

Charles Jr. married Susan Mary Morrison July 25, 1872, in Clark County, Indiana. Susan was born May 4, 1853, and died May 9, 1916, in Little Cyprus, Marshall County, Kentucky. They had ten children together, all born in Indiana: Melvina, Maggie May, Catherine Caley born October 1877, Susan, Emma, Charley, Fannie, William, Cash, and Ellen.

Catharine "Kate" Caley Gaylord married Francis "Frank" M. Barriger on December 18, 1893, in Indiana. Frank, the son of Madison Barriger and Rebecca Roseberry, was born December 13, 1842, in Kentucky, and died March 11, 1910, in Indiana. Frank and Kate had seven children; Mary Ann, Frank McKinley, Howard Gardner, Lillian Dell, Verna Mae, James Rodgers, and Clara Francis, who born March 4, 1910, in Indiana, and died January 26, 1990, in Tennessee. Kate was a young widow and she later had a daughter, Elizabeth Aleen, born January 1913 who died at the age of seven months on September 6, 1913, in Madison, Jefferson County, Indiana. Frank, Kate, and Elizabeth are all buried at Springdale Cemetery in Madison, Jefferson County, Indiana.

Clara Francis Barriger met Robert Barnes, born 1905 in Michigan, and they become the parents of Dorothy Pearl Barriger, who was born October 21, 1926, and died January 15, 1970, in Dunkirk. Clara also had a son, Gerald Hardamon, who was born January 28, 1929, and died July 20, 2000, in Indiana. He is buried in Tennessee with his daughter, Virginia T. Hardamon, who was born May 23, 1930, and died June 10, 1984, in Indiana. Clara married Donald Haffner, who was born February 20, 1902, in Indiana, and died April 14, 1988, in Tennessee.

Dorothy Pearl Barriger married Robert "Bob" Irwin McCune on March 18, 1948. Bob was born July 11, 1921, and died September 2, 1994, in Dunkirk. Bob's parents were Gola McCune and Cordelia "Delia" Cranfill. They had three children: Wanda Joy, Linda Lou, and David Lee, all born in Indiana. Bob worked and retired from Armstrong Cork Company, Dunkirk, Jay County, Indiana.

Wanda Joy McCune married Lee LaVern Shultz on June 1, 1968. Lee was born July 22, 1944, in Indiana and died in 1985 in Tyler, Texas. Lee's parents were Robert Shultz and Ruth Marie Lawrence. Lee and Wanda Shultz had three children: Michelle "Shellie" Lee; Jonathan "Jon" Brian, born in Indiana; and Mitchell "Mitch" Wade, born in Michigan.

Jonathan Brian Shultz met Diana Lynn Honeick and they have two children, Jake Christopher and Olivia Ileen.

Submitted by Michelle Shultz

GEAR FAMILY HISTORY

George R. Gear was born January 17, 1903, in Lagrange, Illinois. Helen J. McKinney Gear was born July 20, 1904, in Kirklin, Indiana. They were married June 20, 1933, in Kirklin, Indiana. They had two children, Mary Pat Gear Nelson and George John Gear. Both children graduated from South Side High School.

George and Helen Gear,
25th Wedding Anniversary, 1958.

They lived in Frankfort, Indiana, where Mary Pat was born, and South Bend, where George John was born, before being transferred to Fort Wayne by International Harvester Company in 1945.

George was Branch Manager of the Truck Sales Division for Harvester. Both George and Helen were active in community affairs. George was a member and past president of the Rotary Club, a member of the Chamber of Commerce, chairing the Agricultural Committee and member of the Executive Club.

Helen was a member of the Fort Wayne Women's Club and Vice-President of the Fort Wayne Children's Day Care Association.

Submitted by Mary Pat Gear Nelson

THOMAS & MARY JANE MCGUIRE GEIGER FAMILY

Thomas and Mary Jane McGuire Geiger were first time land owners in Allen County. The Geigers migrated from Licking County, Ohio, and on October 15, 1836, Thomas Geiger purchased 40 acres in the northwest quarter of Section 19 in Eel River Township. While living there Thomas cleared two miles of the Goshen Road and assisted in digging the first grave in the Eel River Cemetery for the burial of a lone traveler. Thomas was the son of Anthony and Mary Kirk Geiger. Mary Jane was the daughter of John and Ann O'Brian McGuire. In 1838 Thomas (1814-1886) and his wife, Mary Jane McGuire (1814-1879), moved to Green Township, Noble County where they raised their children: Harvey (1836-1898) married Jennie Moore, second marriage was Wretha McCreary; Mary (1838-1915) married David VanHouten, second marriage was Enos Reed; George (1841 -1923) married Rebecca Russell, second marriage was Alice Roberson; Ann (1843-1904) married Ransom Workman; John (1846-1860) married Nancy Simmons, second marriage was Hetty Hayes; Joseph (1850-1851); William E. (1852-1930) married Margaret Summers; Alfred B. (1855-1915) married Sadie Shambaugh; Clara J. (1859-1936) married Horace McDuffee; and Catherine "Irene" (1862-1941) married James Harter.

Harvey and George enlisted in Allen County and served in the Civil War. George married Rebecca Russell (1839-1913) August 12, 1862, in Albion, Indiana. The following children were born to this union: Katurah (1864-1942) married William Hosler; Laverna (1866-1866); Dora (1871) married Clement Krider; Alfred Marion "Manie" (1874-1966) married Lettie McGuire; and Herschel (1881-1958) married Leona Eberly (1886-1954) June 27, 1906.

Herschel had farmed some and worked on the railroad. They moved to Avilla where he ran a garage and jitney service to Fort Wayne. They lived in Fort Wayne for a short time where Herschel worked for Bowsers. In 1917 Leona bought her sister's share of the farm, and they moved back to Noble County. Herschel became a crane operator and helped to construct the former Speedway Race Track. Herschel and Leona had the following children: Earl (1907-1962) married Mary Harter; twins, Ormar and Owen (1909-1909); Franklin (1914-); Everett (1916-1995) an electrician for General Electric; Thomas (1922-) married Betty Kuglin, second marriage was Bernadette Korte; and William (1926-1996) married Esther Miller Marschand. Everett and Thomas served in World War II.

Franklin married Lenora Ellen Fulk (1918-) February 27, 1941, and three children were born to this union: Joan married Hanson Young; Janice married Robert Engle Parquet, a graduate of South Side High School; and John married Janis Coon Henderson, a graduate of Huntertown. Lenora was born and raised in Eel River Township, and is a descendant of Henry Bosler and Jacob Fulk who were early settlers in Eel River Township. She taught her first year at Huntertown and taught for an additional thirty-one years in Noble and Whitley Schools. She graduated from Manchester College and Indiana University. Joan and Hanson have two sons; Carey, and Lamar married Joyce Hoover, and two grandsons, Sam and Max. Janice and Bob have three children; Suzanne, David married Jackie Brouwer, and Steven, and two grandchildren, Morgan and William. John and Janis have three sons; Matthew married Melissa Fenker, Andrew, and Nicholas married Andrea Martin. Andrew and Nicholas are serving in the Air Force. Hanson Young taught science for thirty-five years in Fort Wayne Community Schools, and Bob Parquet taught for a time at Carroll High School.

Rebecca Russell, George Geiger's wife, came to Fort Wayne with her parents when she was nine years old. Her father, James (1809-1892), followed teaming and hauling merchandise and other commodities from Pittsburgh to the Lakes. He and his wife, Mary Ulrich (1812-1892) lived in Ohio a number of years, then moved to Fort Wayne in 1849. While living in Fort Wayne, James built two miles of the Goshen Road, commencing about 80 rods southeast of what is known as Spy Run. He prepared the grade, hauled the planks and placed them ready for travel. In payment for this service he received a deed to 160 acres of land in Section 22, Green Township, Noble County, located at the intersection of county roads 400S and 300E. They moved there in the spring of 1855.

Allen County has been home to many members of this family and has provided job and educational opportunities. The family continues to depend on Fort Wayne for its goods and services.

Submitted by Lenora Ellen Fulk Geiger

ALOYSIUS GEIS FAMILY

Aloysius Geis was born December 24, 1880, in Franklin County, Highland Township, St. Peter, Indiana. He was the son of George Adam and Margaret (Young) Geis. Margaret was the second wife of George. His first wife, Anna Marie Roell, died July 9, 1869. He had three brothers, one sister and seven half brothers and sisters.

When he was four years old, his father was killed in an accident. As his mother could not care for such a large family alone, some of the children were raised by friends and neighbors in the close knit community. Aloysius went to live with the Wilhelm family.

Aloysius Geis

When Aloysius was a young man he worked as a farm hand traveling with the seasons and availability of work.

He traveled to the Neoga/Siegel, Illinois, area husking corn and doing other farm labor. Here he met his wife (Francis) Elizabeth Mittendorf. They were married May 28, 1907.

An uncle of Elizabeth was a realtor and land owner with acreage near Monroeville, Indiana. He asked Aloysius to farm 160 acres for him. Thus the Geis family, including children, Alberta, Joseph and Bernard, moved to Allen County, Monroe Township in 1913. They moved into their first home on the Barkley Road. Three more children, Robert, Leland and Rita were born to the couple.

The family traveled by train and brought farm animals on a separate train. It was in the midst of the 1913 flood, and they could not unload the animals for several days.

In the spring of 1919, Aloysius purchased a farm on State Road 101. He raised sugar beets, corn, wheat, oats and had many milk cows. There were chickens for eggs and eating. He had a large orchard and vegetable garden. He lived on this farm until his death.

Aloysius, known by Ollie, was an excellent farmer. While other farmers were losing their land during the Depression, he prospered. He worked very hard and overcame many difficulties in his life—his father's death early in his life, his nomad life style, and economic hardships.

Elizabeth died in 1927 from complications of childbirth. The infant also died. Aloysius never remarried and raised his children by himself, along with his oldest daughter, Alberta, and his unmarried sister, Barbara. In 1929, Alberta married Irvin Sheehan and started her own family. Barbara's health was failing, the children were getting older, and Ollie kept his family together himself.

War was looming and Robert and Leland were of draft age. This was a worry, but a bigger heartache came into his life. In the summer of 1941, his youngest son, Leland, drowned in a boating accident at Lake James, Indiana, along with three friends from Monroeville. The tragedy devastated Ollie.

He developed stomach cancer, and after several years of suffering, died at the home of his son, Bernard, on February 19, 1949. He, Elizabeth, infant daughter, Robert, Leland, Rita Geis Herndon, Alberta and her husband, Irvin Sheehan, are buried in the Catholic Cemetery, Monroeville, Indiana.

Submitted by Sherry Kill

JOSEPH GEIS & KATHERINE (FLAHERTY) GEIS

Joseph George Geis, son of Aloysius and Elizabeth (Mittendorf) Geis, was born in Siegel, Illinois, on October 19, 1909. The Geis family moved to a farm south of Monroeville, Indiana in 1913. Joseph was the second oldest of six children. Alberta (Geis) Sheehan and Rita (Geis) Smitley Herndon were sisters of Joseph and his brothers were Bernard, Robert, and Leland. Elizabeth died from childbirth in 1927, the baby dying also.

Joseph was educated at St. Joseph School and at a small business school on Summit Street in Monroeville. Joe owned a truck and was hired to haul sugar beets, wooden barrels, and at one time hauled a priest's belongings from one parish to another.

Joe met his wife, Katherine Agnes Flaherty, at a party on the Ditlinger farm east of Monroeville. Katherine was born in Penfield, Illinois to

Bernard John and Julia (Early) Flaherty on July 19, 1915. The Flaherty family moved to Ohio in the 1920's. Katherine had three sisters, Mary B. Schaadt, Anna Cooper, Theresa Anderson, and one brother, John who died at birth. The family farm was located in Van Wert County west of Middlepoint, Ohio. Katherine was educated at the Ridge Township School. Joe and Katherine were married on January 24, 1934 in St. Mary's Church in Van Wert, Ohio.

Joe and Katherine lived above a pool hall in Monroeville, Indiana, where Joe and Irvin Sheehan were co-owners. As time went on the partnership was dissolved and the hall sold. Joe and Katherine rented farms in the Monroeville and New Haven area. The family belonged to St. Rose Catholic Church in Monroeville, Indiana. Their daughter, Sheilah Joyce, was born on December 18, 1936. Sandra Elaine was born fifteen months later on March 11, 1938. (Sandra passed away on June 7, 1997.) Tommy Joe was born on April 4, 1944, and passed away at the age of eight from a ruptured appendix. His death was a terrible loss to the family. Daughter Sheryl Kay was born on February 25, 1951. The youngest child, Randy, was born March 2, 1955.

Joe and Katherine bought a farm, with cash, in 1948, in Jackson Township. Katherine helped Joe milk the cows and farm. They worked very hard to make their dairy and grain farm prosperous and beautiful. In 1956, the dairy cows were sold. Joe bought sheep and sold the wool until the mid 1960s. Joe was on the board of directors at the elevator in Edgerton, Indiana. In the 1970s through the 1980s, Joe was farming up to 1,000 acres along with his son and son-in-law.

Katherine passed away on November 2, 1996, at age 81 from heart failure. Joe lived with Sherry and Jerome Kill before passing away July 20, 2001 at age 91 from a stroke. The Geis couple is buried at St. Rose Catholic Cemetery beside their son, Tommy Joe.

Submitted by Sheryl K. Kill

DAVID GENSHEIMER - DESCENDANT OF AUGUST & LAURA WILLIG

David Wayne Gensheimer was born on August 24, 1958 in Fort Wayne, Indiana. He is the oldest child of Maurine (Hartman) and Robert Gensheimer. He graduated from Bishop Luers High School in 1976, earned a degree in Horticulture from Purdue University in 1980, and a degree in Accounting from IPFW in 1992. He is employed by the State of Indiana activating EBT (food stamps). His hobbies are reading biographies and history books, watching White Sox baseball games, playing volleyball, and working out at the gym. He challenges himself by running 5K races.

His great-great grandfather was August (Gus) Willig. He was born on April 12, 1862 in Durmenach, France. He married Katrenia Sophia Dirig there on June 27, 1885. They spoke "Elation," a mixture of French and German. Sophia Dirig was born on May 23, 1864 in Basal, Switzerland.

August and his wife, Sophia, their young daughter, Anna, and Sophia's parents and brother and sisters came over on the same ship. There were ten Dirigs listed on the ship's manifest.

Grandma and Grandpa Willig

They purchased their tickets for the ship at Basal, Switzerland. The family left the port of Le Havre on July 2, 1888, on the steam ship *La Gascogne* of the Red Star Line. After arriving at New York on July 30, 1888, the family settled in Fort Wayne, Indiana. Sophia was pregnant at that time with their first son, August. He was born about three months after arriving in the United States. August and Sophia eventually had eleven children. They were Anne, born September 6, 1886, August (David Gensheimer's great-grandfather), born October 9, 1888, Joseph Bernard, born October 15, 1889, Margaret, born July 8, 1891, Alexander, born October 29, 1892, Carl, born October 1893, Bernard, born November 19, 1895, Anthony, born May 16, 1898, John, born February 3, 1900, Leonard, born August 10, 1902, and Marie, born January 4, 1906,

August and Sophia and seven of their children took a voyage back to the old county and returned, entering at Ellis Island, on December 15, 1909, from South Hampton, England.

August made his Declaration of Intention on September 28, 1920, in Fort Wayne, Indiana. He was employed as a brick contractor in 1900. He was a furnace tender in 1906. He was a sewer builder in 1909. He was a general contractor in 1916. August died at the age of 62 of kidney failure. He and his wife are buried in the Catholic Cemetery in Fort Wayne.

August's oldest son, also named August, also worked with his hands. He would collect field stone from farmer's fields for building. He built beautiful homes, lake cottages, and alters out of these stones. One alter that he built is in the old cemetery at St. Vincent's Catholic Church, and another was crafted at St. Vincent's Villa, (Children's Orphanage) on Wells Street. This impressive alter had a 17 ton Italian imported marble statue of the Blessed Mother on it. August dedicated this alter in memory of his parents, Sophia and August Willig.

Submitted by David Gensheimer

JEANIE GENSHEIMER - DESCENDED FROM FELIX ROUSSEY

Her legal name is Janine Beverly Gensheimer. Her middle name is also her mother's middle name. She was originally supposed to be named Beverly Ann, but since she was the firstborn, her family thought she should be named Maurine, after her father, Maurice. When she was born, her mother called her Jeanie, and she didn't know her legal name was Janine until she entered kindergarten. her mother thought she should begin using Janine at that time and told everyone to call her Janine. Everyone, except her mother did call her Janine; she still called her Jeanie. She refused to answer for awhile, but eventually got used to the name. By the time she left college, she went back to Jeanie.

Jeanie is interested in many things, gymnastics, martial arts, and most things physical. In the summer of 2004 she participated in her first triathlon. She also took sailboarding lessons.

Her academic career began at St. Henry's grade school. She is the product of twelve years of parochial education. Her bachelor's degree is in Psychology and Early Childhood Education from Ball State University. She received a Master's Degree in Marital and Family Therapy from Butler University in 1996.

For most of her life, Jeanie have worked with children – first as a volunteer at the YMCA in Fort Wayne teaching gymnastics and trampoline. In 1986 she moved to Indianapolis and taught kindergarten for a year and then was the Director for Girls Incorporated (non-traditional after school and summer programs) for sixteen years where she helped girls become strong, smart, and bold. During that time, she began studying karate and earned a black belt in karate. In 1994 she started her own mobile gymnastics and karate program (Rapunzel's Gymnastics and Little Dragon's Karate.) Her gymnastics business' name comes from her defining feature, which is her very long blonde hair. Although, to most of the preschools where she teaches she is simply known as Miss Gymnastics.

Jeanie & Maurine Gensheimer

Jeanie the great-great granddaughter of Felix Roussey and Elizabeth Coonrad. Felix was born April 15, 1838, in France and immigrated in 1847. Elizabeth Coonrad was born February 11, 1846, in Syracuse, New York. She and her family made their way from New York to Fort Wayne via the Erie Canal when she was eleven years old. Felix and Elizabeth married on October 17, 1865, in New Haven, Indiana. They had nine children: Joseph, Peter, John, Amos, Mary, Edward, William, Leo, and Laura. Felix served in the 88th Division of the Indiana Infantry during the Civil War. Felix died January 9, 1895, and Elizabeth died June 16, 1916. They are buried in St. John's Cemetery, New Haven. Laura, Jeanie's great-grandmother, married August Willig on November 24, 1910, in St. Mary's Catholic Church. August Willig sold Seiberling Tires at Willig Tire Service located at 208 West Main Street, Fort Wayne. Laura's brother, Leo Roussey, worked for August. Laura and August Willig had seven children: Leona, Virginia, Iona, Eleanor, Ivon, Audrey, and Leslie.

Submitted by Jeanie Gensheimer

MAURINE HARTMAN GENSHEIMER

DAUGHTER OF IONA WILLIG & MAURICE HARTMAN

Maurine Gensheimer was born April 15, 1938 in Fort Wayne, Indiana, on Good Friday. Her parents, Iona Willig and Maurice Hartman, were born in Fort Wayne in 1913 and 1914, respectively. They met at Rome City, Sylvan Lake, where they lived across the lake from each other. They were married on June 25, 1936 at Precious Blood Church in Fort Wayne. They both loved to swim. Maurine is the oldest of four children and loved school. Her Dad had blue eyes, curly black hair and a husky or chubby build. Her Mom thought he was the handsomest man she had ever seen. Maurice was athletic as a young man. He won medals for diving. He liked to fish and swim. It was natural for him being at a lake so much. When he and Iona got married he got a job on the Nickel Plate railroad—first as a fireman stoking up the engine with fuel. Later, he became an engineer driving the train from Fort Wayne to Chicago. He was friendly and liked to socialize with friends, playing cards and swapping railroad stories.

Maurine relates her memories: "I remember a lot of foods he liked and taught me to eat. When I was a child, maybe 10 or 11 years old, I remember trying pickled pigs feet, head cheese, tongue, heart, brains, limburger cheese, hasenpfeffer rabbit, and barbecued ribs he brought home from Kips Tavern on Broadway. They were the best ribs ever. When it was payday he would yell "IT'S PAYDAY" and throw all of his two weeks pay in cash on the kitchen table for us to see. I got sixty cents for the two weeks allowance but in 1948 it was pretty much. He called me "Reenie" or "Beenie." I remember he loved bean soup and always ate it with vinegar in it. To this day I cannot eat it without vinegar. He was proud that I got good grades in school. When he was in the hospital from heart trouble I took him bean soup. As he neared death he worried about my Mom when she left to go to the store or somewhere. He would watch out the window for her. In a lot of ways he was very sensitive though he could be brusque. He died of a heart attack in his sleep at age 71, January 4, 1986."

Maurine and Robert Gensheimer

Maurine's favorite T.V. program is "Jeopardy." She married husband Bob Gensheimer in 1957. They have five children: David, Debra, Laurie, Janine and Patrick. They camped a lot when the children were growing up and have traveled to 49 of the 50 states. Bob and Maurine race walked for about 15 years and also did running races. After their children were older she worked for a market research company for 20 years. She is am now doing volunteer work at a pro life center and at an elementary school. She likes to keep busy and is hoping to continue to enjoy good health.

Submitted by Maurine Hartman Gensheimer

GERARDOT - PEQUIGNOT

Alexis Gerardot, born in 1811, was the first-born child of Xavier and Marie Gerardot. The potato blight forced his and nearly forty other Gerardot families to leave their land just north of Besancon, France, and board a ship for America. Their destination was Pennsylvania where they were promised free land. The clan settled in Lewiston, Pennsylvania, until word reached them that land in Ohio was more fertile for farming. Sending two scouts to Stark County, Ohio, it was not long before confirmation came that indeed the land in Ohio was promising. The families relocated to Stark County. It was here that Alexis and his new wife, Mary Rivard, began a family of their own with nine children, John, Virginia, Julia, Alexis, Anthony, Louis, Joseph, Adeline and Edward. In the late 1840s the families relocated for the final time to eastern Allen County, Indiana.

Maurice Gerardot.

Lillian Gerardot, eastern Allen County

Knowing that black oak, beech, sycamore, walnut, ash and sugar maple trees generally meant good black, loamy soil, the families purchased 1,600 acres bounded by what are now Ternet, Maples, Tillman and Franke Roads in eastern Allen County. Hard manual labor from sunup to sundown, cutting large trees with a cross cut saw, using dynamite to clean away the stumps, the group worked together to clear the land for farming.

The seventh child of Alexis and Marie, Joseph Lafayette Gerardot worked along side generations of his family as they not only cleared the land but also worked to establish the Catholic community and parish of St. Louis Besancon. Within the community, Joseph met and married Mary Rose (1845); they filled their home at the corner of Tillman and Gerardot Roads with thirteen children, James, Francis, Lucy, Mary,

Frank Pequignot

Barclay Girls

Virginia, Maurice, Rosa, Joseph, Mariam, Henry, Leandrum, Sherman and John.

The third son of Joseph and Mary (Rose) Gerardot, Maurice married Ellen Ryan. This would be one of three marriages between the Ryan and Gerardot families. The Ryans' ancestors left County Tipperary, Ireland, for the same reason the Gerardots left France many years before.

Maurice and Ellen called their farm on Gerardot Road "White Diamond Farms" saying it was their intention to leave their family a jewel. They brought into this world six sons and one daughter, Lillian. Lillian met Amuel Barclay as he worked to clear the ditches in eastern Allen County. The Barclays would raise their children on the same jewel of a farm. In contrast, the Barclays had seven daughters and one son, Donna, Dorothy, Neil, Betty, Carol, Judy, Gloria and Monica.

Betty married her high school sweetheart, Michael Pequignot, in 1958. The Pequignots raised their children in the Hoagland area and owned and operated the Hayloft Reception Hall. Their children: Julie, Jan, Jill, Jodi and Michael continue to live in the communities of Besancon and Hoagland in eastern Allen County.

Submitted by Julie Nolan

JOSEPH & LAURA (PATON) GERARDOT

Laura Edith Paton was born February 2, 1883, in St. Clair County, Michigan. She married Vernon Pray, a master electrician in Detroit, and had two sons, Gordon Edward, and Jack Alphonso. For years, Laura was the head of millinery at Hudson's Department Store. After her husband died in the 1918 influenza epidemic, Laura turned her home into a boarding house where she prepared breakfast and supper, packed lunches, and did the laundry and general housekeeping for nine men.

A friend of Laura's from childhood, Addie Gerardot, introduced Laura to her brother-in-law, Joseph, who was born in Allen County in 1885.

Joseph and Laura Gerardot with granddaughter in 1942.

Joe and Laura married in Detroit in 1925 and then moved with her two sons to Joe's farm west of Monroeville. For a while, they lived on North Clinton Street in Fort Wayne before moving into Monroeville itself.

In the mid-1940s, the Gerardots visited Laura's brother, Robert, who owned a large avocado farm in southern California. One Christmas, Robert sent a dozen avocados to each of his five sisters. No one knew what to do with them, so they threw them out.

Laura died in Fort Wayne on June 8, 1964, at age 81. Joe later married Alpha Kennedy of Monroeville. He died in Payne, Ohio, on Thanksgiving Day 1975, at age 90. Joe and Laura are buried with her oldest son in New Haven's I.O.O.F. Cemetery.

Submitted by Helen Pray.

LEONARD & ALETA GERARDOT FAMILY

Leonard Sylvester Gerardot and Aleta Rose Singer were united in marriage on February 5, 1946, in San Diego, California, while Leonard was serving in the Navy during WW II.

Leonard was born September 19, 1922, the son of Charles and Ellen (Cayot) Gerardot. His father was a farmer and his mother was a homemaker. Leonard graduated from Woodburn High School in 1940 and enlisted in the Navy on November 19, 1942. He served as a metal smith aboard the USS *Balduck* and received an honorable discharge February 21, 1946.

Aleta was born October 31, 1929, to Ernest and Mary M. (Murchland) Singer and graduated from Monroeville High School in 1945. Her father received a law degree and worked in time study at International Harvester Company. Her mother was a homemaker and also an accomplished baker. She had a booth at Barr Street Market in Fort Wayne and was well known for her baked goods.

Aleta and Leonard have eleven children: Jeanne Marie Gerardot Mears Koch (born November 7, 1946) graduated from Monroeville High School in 1965 and received her teaching degree from Saint Francis College. She married Earl E. Mears on July 7, 1967, and they have two children, Jennifer (Jeff) Haughey and Jason (Jennifer Kurtz) Mears. Earl died August 4, 1987. She then married Ron Koch on August 8, 1992. They reside in Harlan and she works as a coding specialist at Parkview.

Nora Louise Gerardot Orr (born October 30, 1947 and died October 24, 2001) graduated from Monroeville High School in 1966 and then earned a nursing degree. She married Victor Orr and they had two children: Vincent Heath and Noruise Christine. She worked at the VA Hospital prior to her death.

Lois Ann Gerardot Ternet (born June 24, 1951) graduated from Heritage High School in 1969 and received a MHT degree from Purdue (IPFW). She married Neil A. Ternet on August 6, 1971. They have two children: Amy Lyn (Jon) Sorrell and Nicholas Alan (Jennifer Klima) Ternet. Lois is editor of *The Monroeville News*.

Joyce Lynn Gerardot Harshbarger Pommer Seward (born April 10, 1954) graduated from Heritage High School in 1972. She married Brian Harshbarger and they have three children: Sara (Jason) McCarty, Aaron, and Kyle. They divorced and she married Steve Seward. She works at Lincoln Life as a manager and resides in Fort Wayne.

Aleta and Leonard Gerardot

Jill Beth Gerardot Johnson (born July 3, 1957) graduated from Heritage High School in 1975 and served four years in the United States Army (Band). She married James Paul Johnson on January 16, 1978. They have three children: Jonathon, Jakob, and Jina. They divorced and the family lives in Columbia, South Carolina, where she works in the school guidance department.

Mary Ellen Gerardot (born October 25, 1958) graduated from Heritage High School in 1977 and continued her education at Ivy Tech State College. She has three daughters: Melissa, Nichole, and Heather.

Ernest Eugene Gerardot (born January 9, 1962) graduated from Heritage High School in 1980 and received a B.S in fine arts (1984) from Ball State University. He married Kim David on July 5, 1986, but is now divorced. He resides in Carmel, Indiana, and is a free-lance graphic designer.

Jane Gayle Gerardot Ward (born July 17, 1963) graduated from Heritage High School in 1981. She married David Ward in May 2000 and has a son, Nathan. Jane is employed in customer service (Lowe's) and the family resides in Kendallville.

Lisa Kay Augustyniak (born July 28, 1967) graduated from Heritage High School in 1985. She married Peter Augustyniak on January 9, 1991, and is now divorced. She has three sons, Wyatt and Noah Augustyniak, and Brayden Sefranck. She now resides in Montgomery, Illinois, and works as an administrative assistant.

Mark Christopher Gerardot (born October 11, 1968) graduated from Heritage High School in 1987 and received an art degree from Saint Francis College. He married Jennair on October 23, 1993, and they reside in Carmel. Mark is self-employed as a graphic artist.

Barry Allan Gerardot (born September 9, 1970) graduated from Heritage High School in 1989. He attended IPFW and graduated from the Connecticut School of Broadcasting. He is employed as an on-air personality for K-105 FM radio. He married Jana Arnold on June 9, 2001, and they have one son, Carter.

Leonard is now retired from B. F. Goodrich, where he worked in the machine shop. Leonard and Aleta now reside in Fort Wayne.

Submitted by Leonard and Aleta Gerardot

JESSE J. GERIG FAMILY

Jesse J. Gerig was the fifth child of Benjamin and Lydia (Klopfenstein) Gerig. He had four brothers and three sisters. Jesse married Hulda Stucky, daughter of Mr. and Mrs. Henry Stucky of Adams County, Indiana. Jesse and Hulda had three sons: Robert, Jess, and Paul. Robert died at birth.

Eventually Jesse and Hulda bought the farm formerly owned by his parents. The soil was good and somewhat sandy. They grew a variety of grain and raised livestock. In addition to farming, Jesse was a United States postal employee, sometimes as a rural carrier, until he retired after twenty years of service. Jesse also served as Cedar Creek Township Trustee for nearly two terms. He started and managed the Grabill Branch of the Allen County License Bureau. The business was located in the basement of the Grabill Bank.

Jesse and Hulda Gerig

Hulda enjoyed cooking, canning, reading, sewing, and crocheting. Jesse always liked gardening. His hobbies were reading and fishing.

In 1935, Jesse took his family nearly 500 miles North to Bright Lake, Ontario, Canada, for a week of fishing. The roads were gravel and so sandy that at times only one car could pass for fear of getting stuck in sand. They also had to ferry across the Straits of Mackinaw and Sault Saint Marie. Jesse and Hulda enjoyed the Canadian area so much that they bought a lot on the lake. In 1948, they built a cottage on the lot. The extended Gerig families still travel to this Canadian cottage for peaceful, relaxing vacations.

When Jesse retired from farming, he and Hulda moved to Leo. They spent their summers at their cottage on Bright Lake and winters in the milder climate of Leo. They made many friends in Canada and were able to live out their devotions to Christ and His church both at home in Leo and in Canada.

They celebrated 65 years of married life together before Hulda preceded Jesse in death. Hulda passed in 1981 and Jesse in 1985.

Submitted by Christine J. Gerig

JESS J. GERIG FAMILY

Jess Gerig is the oldest son of Jesse and Hulda (Stucky) Gerig. Jess was born on August 15, 1918.

Jess graduated from Leo High School in 1936. He then served in the army during World War II. He took his basic training in Mississippi, where he met and married Iva Hodges on May 1, 1943. Iva remained in the States and found work as a nurse, while Jess served overseas in the Signal Core for 22 months. Upon returning to the States, Jess and Iva returned to Indiana to help with the family farm. Iva worked for Dr. Emmy. Besides working on the farm, Jess drove school bus and later worked at Zollner Piston Corporation of Fort Wayne. He retired from Zollner in 1984.

Jess and Iva Gerig family

Jess and Iva had two children. Barbara, the oldest, was born August 29, 1946. She was musically gifted and shared her talents while attending Leo High School. She had just completed her Bachelor of Arts degree from Taylor University and was enjoying teaching at Village Woods when she was tragically killed in an automobile/train accident on February 14, 1969.

Michael, their son, was born April 11, 1950. He graduated from Leo High School and received an Associate Degree in Marketing from Indiana University, Fort Wayne. He is employed by KSU (formerly Zollner Piston). He married Theresa Smale from Bedford, Indiana. She teaches elementary school in the DeKalb Eastern School system. They have two sons, Chad and Ryan. Both boys were active in sports and graduated from Leo High School. Chad received his teaching degree from Indiana University and currently is teaching in the DeKalb Central School system. Ryan is finishing his degree at Indiana University. Chad married Stacey Bender of St. Louis, Missouri, in December 2003. She also is an elementary teacher in the DeKalb Central School system.

Jess and Iva celebrated 60 years of marriage on May 1, 2003. Jess died in July 2003. All members of the Jess Gerig family are believers and followers of Christ. They trust God with their daily walks of life and pray that He will guide their ways.

Submitted by Theresa Gerig

JOHN GERIG FAMILY

Abner Gerig's great-grandfather, John Gerig, was born in 1806 and died in 1859 in Alsace-Lorraine. He had eight children. Joseph, the third child was born in 1833. He was a weaver by trade and made all of the clothes for his family. Daniel, the father of Abner Gerig, was one of Joseph's 12 children.

The family came to America somewhere around 1888 when Daniel Gerig was 14 years old. They landed in New York after a journey by sea that lasted for 40 days. Soon after they landed, someone stole all their luggage. Interestingly enough, the very fellow who had stolen the luggage helped them hunt for it. Eventually they found the luggage.

Abner Gerig and his brother Rev. Chris Gerig

They came to this country for a couple of reasons. In Alsace-Lorraine, they only had small plots of land to support their families. Another reason was that they were being conscripted to serve in the army, something they had strong convictions against. Joseph Gerig was an Amish bishop, but later became a Mennonite, leaving the Amish religion.

After landing in New York and finding their luggage, they sailed across Lake Erie and came down the Wabash and Erie Canal through Ohio and Indiana. The boat was pulled by two mules all the way to Fort Wayne, Indiana. From there they walked all the way to Cedar Creek Township, where another Gerig had married a Steiner. They stayed around there.

Daniel Gerig married Mary Sauder in 1898. They built a log house on a tract of land just north of what is now Grabill. About 1900, the old Wabash Railroad built a track to Toledo from Fort Wayne. It cut into Daniel's farmland. In the early 1900s, he built a house off the Roth Road where Abner Gerig was born.

Daniel Gerig and Mary, his wife, had three children. Chris, the oldest, was born in 1899. He was a pharmacist in a drugstore in Grabill, owned by Mr. Greenbaugh and Daniel Gerig. Chris felt God's call to become a minister and left the pharmacy profession to attend the Fort Wayne Bible Training School. He pastored in Missionary Churches for many years.

Flossie, born in 1904, worked at the Grabill drugstore until Mr. Greenbaugh sold the store. She then became a bookkeeper at the Grabill Grain Company until she married Harold Welty in 1944.

Abner Gerig, born in 1907, attended Marion College, where he received his teaching certificate. He taught for two years in a country school, which is now Cedarville, another school in Amish territory on Page Road, and the last two years in Grabill.

After leaving teaching in 1930, he went into the hardware business in Grabill. A few months later he married Annabelle Smith. To them were born four children: Dwain, who was born in 1932 and died in 1946; Grace Arlene, Charlotte, and Lowena. Annabelle died in 1968. Abner then married Janneth Schrock in 1969.

In 2005, Abner Gerig was 97 years old and living at The Cedars in assisted living.

Submitted by Abner Gerig

PAUL R. GERIG FAMILY

Paul Gerig is the youngest son of Jesse and Hulda (Stucky) Gerig, He was born November 8, 1925.

During World War II, the army classification system placed Paul's older brother Jess on active duty, while Paul, being the youngest son, took on the responsibility of helping with his father's farm.

In 1949, Paul married Christine Steiner, daughter of the Reverend and Mrs. Armin Steiner. Her father was the pastor of the Grabill Missionary Church at the time.

Paul continued to farm and for eight years drove school bus for East Allen County Schools until 1963. At that time he joined the work force at the Zollner Corporation. Paul retired from Zollner in 1991.

Paul and Christine have two sons, Mark and James (Jim). Both sons worked for Abner Gerig at Grabill Hardware when they were fifteen and sixteen years old. Both boys graduated from Leo High School.

Mark Gerig, Paul and Christine's oldest son, graduated from IPFW. He then went on to further his education at Trinity College in Deerfield, Illinois, and Toledo University, where he received his Doctorate in Psychology. Mark married Michelle Keim, daughter of Merrill and Carolyn Keim, in 1980. They have two children, Brandon and Lauren. Mark teaches at Bethel College in Mishawaka, Indiana.

Jim, Paul and Christine's youngest son, is still employed at Grabill Hardware. He was part owner for about ten years. Jim has been an active member of the Grabill Chamber of Commerce and for some time served as its vice-president. He also served on the Grabill Promotion Committee. This committee has been and still is very busy. They have been quite successful in promoting the Grabill area. Jim married Jill Rodecker, daughter of Kenneth and Gwen Rodecker. They have two daughters, Brook and Paige.

All the members of the Paul Gerig family are followers of Christ and are active in their churches. We pray that they will remain faithful to that calling.

Submitted by Christine J. Gerig

Paul Gerig Family

WILLIAM GERNHARDT

William Gernhardt immigrated to the United States from Bebra, Germany, arriving in Fulton County, Ohio, July 4, 1881. He married Mary Rupp of Wauseon, Ohio.

He was one of our earliest settlers having moved to Woodburn in November 1894 with his wife and three children, Ella, Lucinda, and Jess. Later Barbara was born. He bought 80 acres of land lying south of what is now Main Street, Woodburn. Their first place of residence was in a frame house that was located near the Wabash Railroad on the ground now owned by the Woodburn Equity Exchange on the west side of Union Street, now Bull Rapids Road.

The original plat of Woodburn was filed in 1865. Otto Knoblaugh owned the property from the railroad south to Main Street, which lay on both sides of Union Street. On April 13, 1895, Mr. Knoblaugh divided this property into 23 lots. Then in May 1895 William Gernhardt filed a corrected town plat and completed the block to a new East-West street called "Stenger Street". This plat gave the town a new name, Shirley City, and additional 23 lots.

There being no churches in Woodburn at this time, William was instrumental in helping form the Evangelical Mennonite Church and donated the one acre of land where the present Mennonite Church is located on Becker Road, once named Gernhardt Road. It was estimated the church building cost approximately $1,000.

After a number of years living a pioneer life among the trees, stumps, and mud, all the Fulton County settlers, except William Gernhardt, sold out and returned to their native community just when the land value was rising. He owned a hardware store and for twenty years and from 1898 to 1918 he was Justice of the Peace. He helped promote the formation of the Woodburn High School. His son, Jess, was in the first graduating class. William died in 1942.

Submitted by Loretta Lawson McCann

CHARLES WILLIAM GETZ III FAMILY

Charles William Getz III was born in St. Joseph's hospital in Fort Wayne on March 8, 1924, second son of Raymond Lewis Getz and Marie Cleary Getz.(See *The Getz Family in Allen County* and *The Raymond Lewis and Marie Cleary Getz Family*). The family called him "Billy," "Willy," or "Bill" because Grandpa Getz was called "Charlie." Bill had an older brother, Raymond Joseph Getz, Jr. (1918-1965). Bill graduated from St. Jude's Grade School in 1938, attended one year at Central Catholic High School, and graduated from Morgan Park Military Academy in Chicago in May 1942. That same month he enlisted as an Army Aviation Cadet and was commissioned a 2nd Lieutenant pilot on July 28, 1943. He flew combat in Europe with the 8th Air Force during World War II, flying B-24 bombers and P-51 fighters. In 1946, Bill married JoLynn Green (1923-1974) of Salt Lake City, second oldest of six daughters of Leo (1899-1967) and Leah Elliott (1901-1978) Green. Their son, Charles William Getz IV was born in 1948 at Tachikawa Air Base, Japan, where Bill and Jo were stationed. Their daughter, Jerilyn, was born in1952 in Albuquerque, New Mexico.

L to R: Charles William Getz III, Charles William Getz IV, JoLynn Green Getz, and Jerilyn Getz

L to R: Vicki D'Amico Getz, Charles William Getz III, and Linda Getz Murphy

A career Air Force officer, Bill participated in the H-Bomb Program and was one of the first military officers in the nation's ballistic missiles and space programs. He retired from the Air Force as a Lieutenant Colonel in 1962. Subsequently, he worked for Lockheed Missiles and Space Company, was Assistant Controller of the Atomic Energy Commission, Vice President of Chilton Corporation and later VISA International, and held other industry and government positions. He is a publisher and author. BA degree from the University of New Mexico (1952); Masters in Industrial Management, University of Pittsburgh (1955); Doctorate in Business Administration, George Washington University (1970). JoLynn Getz was active in many military-related social programs, full-time mother and strong supporter of her husband. She died from heart complications in 1974. Charles IV graduated from UCLA (1969) and USC Law School (1973) and has been a Deputy Attorney General in California since graduation. Son Charles is married to Margaret Leung (1953-) Getz, and lives in San Carlos, California. Daughter Jerilyn graduated from the San Francisco Academy of Art in 1978. She is married to Karl Glaser (1949-), a Chemist. Jerilyn has a son, Trevor Lortie (1989-) from a previous marriage. Jerilyn is an artist and art teacher. They reside in Longmont, Colorado. In 1976 Bill married Vittorina (Vicki) D'Amico (1937 -), a native of San Francisco, the youngest of three daughters of Sebastiano (1910-1984) and Lena Gentile (1913-1994) D'Amico, and mother of nine-year old Linda (1965 -) from a previous marriage. Linda changed her surname to "Getz" upon reaching 18 years of age. She graduated from the University of Arizona, Geology major. Linda is married to Brian Murphy (1961-), a native of New Jersey. They have two children: Grant (1995-), and Morgan (1996-). They live in Burlingame, California. Bill and Vicki Getz have lived in Hillsborough, California, since 1976.

Submitted by Bill Getz

RAYMOND LEWIS GETZ & MARIE CLEARY GETZ FAMILY

Raymond Lewis Getz (1899-1976) was the third eldest child of Charles W. Getz II (1858-1942) and Mary Theresa Perriguey Getz (1862-1953). (See *The Getz Family in Allen County*). Ray had six sisters, one brother, and two foster sisters, all born and raised in Fort Wayne. Ray's early life was on the farm located on what is now Getz Road. Ray's father was a farmer and joint operator with his brother Henry (1856-1932) of a brickyard, which was located in the area of the present intersection of the Illinois and Getz Roads.

Ray attended the old Central Catholic High School, torn down in the early 1940s. At the age of 15 (1904), Ray worked as a messenger in the German-American National Bank located on the corner of Calhoun and Berry. In the 1920s the bank became the Lincoln National Bank & Trust Company. Ray and Henry Getz were original investors in the new bank. Ray was an Assistant Cashier, then worked in the Trust Department beginning in 1925, and later with Central Securities.

In 1937 he joined Leonard Fertig and Company, an investment house located on the corner of Court and Berry, the old bus terminal. In 1940, he and several friends formed the Fort Wayne Securities Company, which was located on Clinton Street.

Raymond Lewis Getz, Sr.

Ray married Marie Berhilda Cleary (1900-1968) September 1915. Marie was the daughter of Dennis Cleary (1874-1945) and Anna Ehinger Cleary (1879-1921). Dennis emigrated from County Cork, Ireland, in 1895 when he was 21 years old, and worked for the Pennsylvania Railroad.

Raymond Joseph Getz, Jr., Marie Cleary Getz, and Charles William Getz III

Marie and Ray's first son, Raymond Joseph Getz, Jr. (1918-1965) was born at St. Joseph's hospital as was their second son, Charles William Getz III (1924 -). Ray Getz and his family lived in a series of homes on Spy Run Avenue, Northwood Boulevard, Dodge Avenue, Columbia Avenue, finally purchasing a home at 1031 Kensington Boulevard in 1935.

Raymond Joseph, Jr., graduated from Central Catholic High School in 1935 and Indiana Medical School in 1942 and immediately reported for duty as a First Lieutenant, Medical Officer in the United States Army. He was with Patton's 3rd Army in Europe in World War II.

Son, Charles William III, graduated from Morgan Park Military Academy (high school) in May 1942 and became an Aviation Cadet in the Army Air Corps the same month and was a combat pilot in Europe in World War II.

Ray Sr. and Marie Getz were divorced in 1940. Marie moved to Los Angeles to be near her only sibling, Sylvia Cleary Willett, who was married to Irving Willett, M.D., a veteran of both World Wars. During World War II, Marie Getz worked for Douglas Aircraft Company. Marie Getz died in 1968, and is buried in Westwood, California. Raymond Lewis Getz continued his business until 1954 when he retired to Denver, Colorado, to live with his eldest son, Raymond Jr. and his family. Ray Lewis Getz died in 1976 and is buried in Denver. He was preceded in death by his son, Raymond Joseph, Jr. Charles William III lives in northern California. (June 2005).

Submitted by Charles W. Getz III

GEVERS FAMILY

A GEVERSVILLE LOVE STORY

Martin (Mart) Gevers entered seventh grade in the one-room school at Emmanuel Lutheran Church (Soest) conscious of the curious stares a new student generates. He was unaware, however, that an impressionable little first-grade girl thought this blond, blue-eyed new kid was 'the most handsome MAN' she'd ever seen.

Mart was the youngest of William and Anna (Meyer) Gevers' eleven children. William Gevers was born March 10, 1876, and died February 7, 1964. Anna Meyer was born December 23, 1879, and died November 21, 1921. They were married October 16, 1902.

Mart was born December 24, 1918, on a farm at Gar Creek, near New Haven. Anna died when Mart was a toddler, so his grandparents came to help.

The family moved into town when William took a job in a Fort Wayne factory. They lived across the street from their Hockemeyer relatives. Caroline Gevers (d. 1930), Bill's sister, had married Herman Hockemeyer (d. 1929).

Mart and his cousin Flo Hockemeyer sometimes seemed interchangeable in the two households, especially at mealtime when a favorite dish or a most-disliked food was being served. The two would check their mothers' menus and go to eat at the house with the most appetizing choice.

After a few years, the Gevers returned to Gar Creek until they finally settled in the area near Emmanuel.

The parochial school only had seven grades so Mart walked to the Gorham public school for eighth grade. High school attendance was not required then, if there was no public secondary school in the township. Mart helped his family with farming, milk collection and other farm chores until war seemed imminent, when he joined the Marines.

Meanwhile, Berniece Lepper, that impressionable first grader, had been growing up on a neighboring Marion township farm. Born September 18, 1925, she lived with her brother Raymond, parents Lawrence and Irma (Grotrian) Lepper and grandparents Charles and Louise (Buuck) Lepper in the original log house built on the homestead.

Mart was in boot camp at San Diego when Pearl Harbor was attacked. He was among the first to be shipped to the south Pacific, where he was shot in the head. His family received a telegram advising them that Mart was "missing in action and presumed dead."

Berniece Lepper and Martin Gevers wedding

Mart was paralyzed for many months, and was hospitalized in New Zealand and San Francisco before he was allowed to return home. Despite his desire to complete his tour of duty, he was presented with a Purple Heart and discharged. He came back to Indiana to finish recuperating, and to put a new life together as a permanently disabled veteran.

One summer evening, he and his brother Ed went to Hoagland to see an outdoor movie. They were early enough to enjoy a soda at the drugstore, and watch the crowd gather. They both recognized Berniece, the pretty brown-eyed farmer's daughter they knew from church. Mart nudged Ed and said, "See that good-looking brunette? I'm going to get to know her a lot better!"

Berniece married her handsome hero and Mart was united with the love of his life on September 22, 1945, at Emmanuel. Mart's interchangeable cousin Flo and her sisters sang at the wedding, which was followed by a barn dance reception.

They lived at four Allen County addresses during more than 55 years of marriage, each home referred to fondly by their family as 'Geversville.'

Mart and Berniece had three daughters: Marcia; Connie who married Robert D. Frye; and Lois who married Ronald Howe. Connie has two children, Robert J. and Kristine Frye. Lois has three, Sarah, Emily and Andrew Howe.

Berniece died August 4, 2001, and Mart died March 26, 2005. They left a legacy of love for God, family, friends and country, and a wealth of memories to be treasured for generations.

Submitted by Marcia Gevers

CARLTON MANFORD & CHARLOTTE LOUISE (SMITH) GIANT FAMILY

Carlton Manford Giant was born on September 21, 1914 in Monroeville, Indiana, the eldest of six children, to Joseph A. Giant and Chloe I. Myers. His five siblings were Randolph Howard (b. January 13, 1916; wife Pauline), Maybelle Marie Wilkinson (b. January 15, 1918; husband Tom), and Mary Marcella Sorg (b. March 26, 1922; husband Tom), Joseph John "Jake"(b. November 2, 1924; wife Monica) and James Louis (b. March 31, 1931; wife Beverly). He grew up in the Monroeville area where he attended District School #9, Jefferson Township Elementary and graduated from Monroeville High School in 1931 at the age of 16. He went on to Ball State University receiving his teaching certificate, and later earned his bachelor's degree at St. Francis College. His association with the Allen County School System spanned over 45 years with 10 years in teaching and 35 years as Attendance Officer. He started teaching as a fifth and sixth grade teacher in a one-room school in Jackson Township. Over the next 10 years he was principal, coach and taught fifth thru eight grades in Jackson Township. As Attendance Officer, Carlton was instrumental in Amish children attending public high schools and starting the Social Workers program in the East Allen County Schools. He also initiated coordination of the schools, the county courts and the county school social workers program. During his years with the Allen County school system he held the positions of president of the Allen County Teacher Association, president of the Northeast Indiana Attendance Officers Association as well as a member of State Attendance Officer Advisory Committee, Fort Wayne-Allen County Child Study Commission, Juvenile Justice Task Force and the SCAN Organization. He retired from East Allen County Schools in 1980.

Carlton also sold casualty and life insurance for 30 years and managed his 100+ acre farm located in the Monroeville area. He was a member of the St. Louis Besancon Catholic Church and remained active in parish activities. He became the first president of the Besancon Parish Council, the first president of the CYO, a member of the St. Louis Historical Society presiding as president and treasurer and co-chaired the St. Louis Church committee to restore the church's stained glass windows in 1994. He was a member of the St. Vincent de Paul Society, Harvest House, the Knights of Columbus and the Retired Teachers Association. He served on the Board of Directors of the Big Brothers & Big Sisters Organization in Fort Wayne, a Director at the Johnny Appleseed School and coached Little League Baseball in Monroeville for 10 years.

Carlton married Charlotte Louise Smith on May 25, 1940, in the St. Rose de Lima Catholic Church in Monroeville. Charlotte was the youngest of eleven children born to Charles John (b. September 17, 1860) and Louise Mary (Gfell) (b. August 20, 1875) Smith on October 24, 1917. Siblings were Laura (b. June 28,1893; Sisters of Providence), Cecelia (b. October 16, 1894; Sisters of Providence), Pernetta Linder (b. May 23, 1896; husband William), Esther (b. December 30, 1897; Sisters of Providence), Ralph (b. August

30, 1899), Bernard (b. November 19, 1901; wife Leona), Irma McArdle (b. November 16, 1903; husband James), Harold (b. August 30, 1908; wife Madelyn), Imelda Doetschman (b. February 10, 1911; husband Robert), Noelle Wise (b. December 25, 1914; husband Russell). Charlotte grew up on her father's farm outside of Monroeville. She attended St. Rose Academy Grade School. After grade school she completed a two-year commercial course for business trades and then attended Monroeville High School the final two years graduating in 1935. Following high school she worked for General Electric in Fort Wayne until her marriage to Carlton. Charlotte was also a member of St. Louis Besancon Catholic Church and remained active in all parish activities.

Carlton Manford and Charlotte Louise (Smith) Giant

Together they raised seven children: Nancy Lou Canull (b. January 5, 1942, teacher/counselor, Indianapolis), Jacqueline Ann Mann (b. June 14,1944, interior designer; Toledo, Ohio), Jeannine Kay Phillips (b. June 15, 1948, nursing; Fort Wayne; husband Marvin), Stanley Charles (b. June 7 1951, engineer; Seattle, Washington; wife Marcia), Gregory Allen (b. December 2, 1954; pharmacist, Chicago, Illinois), Beth Marie Kline (b. January 25,1957, homemaker, Monroeville; husband Paul) and Michelle Sue Thomas (b. September 27,1959, homemaker, Fort Wayne; husband John). Descendants of Carlton and Charlotte now include 17 grandchildren and six step-grandchildren, eight great grandchildren and 10 step great grandchildren.

Carlton's' great-great-great grandparents, Jean Pierre and Anastansia Sellier Geant, came to America from Rougemont, Department of Haute Rhine in 1840 with seven other families. They were accompanied by their children, the eldest of them being Jean Pierre Geant Jr. who was born on January 1, 1805, in Rougemont, France. He married Marguerie Dupont (b. December 13, 1807) in 1829. They had five children. Their eldest son, Jacques, was born in France on June 5, 1830. Jacques (Carlton's great grandfather) is listed in the 1868 "registre" of St. Louis de Besancon Catholic Church, Allen County. He was married to Catherine Monnier on May 6, 1852 and they had three children. Their eldest son, Joseph Jacob Giant was born October 2, 1856 in Allen County. He married Mary Louise Evard (b. September 15, 1856) on December 5,1878 in St. Louis de Besancon Catholic Church. Together they had 12 children. The ninth child was a son by the name of Joseph Alfred Giant (Carlton's father) who was born on December 18, 1892. He grew up in the Monroeville area. He married Chloe Ione Myers (b. November 6, 1893) also from Monroeville on October 22, 1913. Carlton's father was a farmer in Jefferson Township and held the position of township trustee.

Charlotte's grandfather, Anton Smith (Schmidt) (b. October 30, 1816) came to this country along with his parents at the age of 19. They traveled from Bavaria, Germany, and settled in a German settlement outside of Sandusky, Ohio. Her grandmother, Anna Maria (Courtade), (b. June 1, 1825) came to this country with her parents at the age of 13, about the same time from Alsace Lorraine, France and eventually settled in Erie County, Ohio. They were married on February 2, 1845. Anton was a logger and a stonecutter in the Sandusky area. They had twelve children. Their eleventh child, Charles John Smith (Charlotte's father), was born on September 17, 1860. Charles grew up on his parents' farm. As a young man he was in the U.S. Merchant Marine operating on the Great Lakes. In 1890 he moved to Monroeville where he, along with his brother William and Gustave Gfell bought timberland in an area of Jackson Township referred to as the "North Woods" also known as the "Black Swamp." They established the Smith Brothers and Gfell Saw Mill in 1891. A community by the name of Smiths' Mill existed during the mill's operation which finally closed down in 1908. After the sawmill was closed, Charles engaged in farming on a number of the properties which he had cleared for his lumber mill. He married Louise Mary Gfell on August 31, 1892 at St. Rose de Lima Catholic Church in Monroeville. They remained in the Monroeville area where they raised their 11 children.

Submitted by Stanley Giant

PAUL GIESEKING FAMILY

Paul Diederick Gieseking was born on August 18, 1965, in Fort Wayne. He was the second of four children of his parents, Philip Lee (1937-) and Kathryn Louise (1937-) Gieseking. He has two sisters and one brother: Nancy Kay (Brittingham), born January 16, 1964, and living in Canton, Ohio; Cynthia Anne (Golemon), born May 3, 1968, and living in Bastrop, Texas; and Steven Charles, born July 16, 1969, of Fort Wayne, Indiana.

Paul went to North Side High School and was a 1988 graduate of Purdue University. He married Margaret Ann Lessie in May 1993. Both he and his wife were employed as pharmaceutical sales representatives although for different companies. They have two children, Caitlin Elizabeth, born April 8, 1995 and Samantha Nicole, born May 25, 1997.

Paul retired from the pharmaceutical company in 2004. He now manages several rental properties and the Indian Lakes Campground at Messick Lake northeast of Wolcottville, which he purchased in 2000.

Submitted by Paul Gieseking

Paul Gieseking Family

PHILIP GIESEKING FAMILY

Philip Lee Gieseking was born on August 9 1937, in Fort Wayne. His great-great-grandfather Diederich Wilhelm Gieseking, was born August 3, 1817, in the village of Quetzen, Westphalia Prussia. After serving two years in the Prussian army, Diederich sailed May 5, 1841, on the *Alwena* landing in New York July 10, 1841, and came to Fort Wayne.

Diederich married Miss Mary Gocke (died November 10, 1876), a Catholic born in Germany. They agreed that girls would be Catholic and boys Lutheran. They had three sons, William F. (1843-1928); Frederick William (1845-1911) and John Diederich (1848-1922). Diederich first purchased 80 acres of land paying $4 per acre in Section 12, Lake Township in Allen County then after a brief time, he purchased more land until he aggregated 910 acres. In 1866, he purchased a farm in Washington Township of 252 acres.

Philip Gieseking Family

In the spring of 1873, Diederich journeyed back to his native land. Paying a visit to his old home near Minden, he continued on to behold the wonders of the "World's Fair" at Vienna. He toured many cities through the kingdoms of Germany, Austria and then to Berlin across Prussia to return home by way of London and Liverpool. In 1876, he visited the Centennial Exhibition at Philadelphia.

Diederich Wilhelm Gieseking died October 19, 1900, and his funeral was officiated by Dr Wagenhals of Trinity English Lutheran Church where he had been a member for many years. He planned his own funeral in every detail and was buried at Lindenwood. His home, still standing north of Fort Wayne, is pictured in *The History of Allen County 1880*, published by Kingman Brothers, Chicago.

His three sons continued as farmers and businessmen. William F. and Frederick William continued to be active in the Trinity English Lutheran Church.

John Diederick married Carolyn Larimore and had two sons and two daughters. The family burial site is at Eel River Cemetery on the Carroll Road. One daughter, Bertha, died as an infant. The other children were Oral Wilmont (1880-1963); Floyd William (1887-1962); and Golda F. (Sovine) (1882-1947).

Oral was the grandfather of Philip Gieseking. Oral married Myrtle Aldora Hyndman (1880-1955) and remained in farming. Oral had four children: Lawrence Jay (1903-1982); Clarence Ray (1908-1993); Hilda (1909-1982); and Agnes Mae (1911-2005). He became successful in farming. He enjoyed playing the violin and the mouth harp, entertaining all when the family gathered on Sunday. He had a hired hand, Otis, to manage the farm so that for many years he and Myrtle wintered in Palmetto, Florida. Even after Myrtle died, he went to Florida every winter until his health failed in 1963.

Lawrence Jay married Bertha Sophia Bakke (1903-2003) of Minnesota, from north of Isle. Bertha had an identical twin, Ingeborg, (1903-2005) who lived in Grand Rapids, Minnesota. Bertha and Ingeborg's parents immigrated from Norway and homesteaded in Minnesota. Lawrence and Bertha had two children: Philip Lee (1937-) and Janet Marie (1941-).

Janet taught school in Minneapolis, married Peter Grottodden, and had three children: Julie, Lisa and John. With their children married, Janet and Peter are enjoying their retirement.

Philip, a 1959 graduate of Purdue University, worked at Magnavox from 1959 until he retired in 1992. He married Kathryn Louise Eloph September 9, 1961. The ceremony was officiated by Dr. Paul H. Krauss at Trinity English Lutheran Church, where they are still members. They are both 1955 graduates of Central High School. In 1975, Philip opened Phil's Hobby Shop which he currently owns. His hobby is flying radio controlled airplanes. He also enjoys wind surfing and sailing. They have four children: Nancy Kay (Brittingham), born January 16, 1964, and living in Canton, Ohio; Paul Diederick, born August 18, 1965, and living at Whitmer Lake, Wolcottville, Indiana; Cynthia Anne (Golemon), born May 3, 1968, and living in Bastrop, Texas; and Steven Charles, born July 16, 1969, of Fort Wayne. Philip and Kathryn now have eleven grandchildren.

Submitted by Philip Gieseking

STEVE GIESEKING FAMILY

Steven Charles Gieseking was born on July 16, 1969, in Fort Wayne. He was the fourth of four children for his parents, Philip Lee (1937-) and Kathryn Louise (1937-) Gieseking. He has two sisters and one brother: Nancy Kay (Brittingham) born January 1964, and living in Canton, Ohio; Paul Diederick born August 18, 1966, and living at Whitmer Lake, Wolcottville, Indiana; and Cynthia Anne (Golemon) born May 3, 1968, and living in Bastrop, Texas.

Steven Gieseking Family

Steven graduated from North Side High School in 1988. He married Wendy Louise Dawson in October 1994. They have two children, Bradley Charles, born May 20, 1999 and Deven Matthew, born September 18, 2002. They are expecting a third child in December 2005.

Steven joined the family business, Phil's Hobby Shop, in 1996. With creative ideas, he managed the Defiance store bringing in new business and growth. With Defiance doing well, now managed by Chris Bercaw, Steven was able to turn his attention to helping more at the Lake Avenue store. He developed the company web site which has become an important part of the company sales. He also sells many items through EBay listings. Steven has also purchased several rental properties.

Submitted by Steve Gieseking

GOERIZ & SWEET FAMILIES

Adolphus Gustavus Goeriz was born December 2, 1812, in Stuttgart, Wurttemberg, Germany. According to his son, Charles Goeriz, while immigrating to America in the 1840s, Adolphus was shipwrecked on Lake Erie, going to Buffalo, and floated in on a leather trunk, which Charles kept in his attic for many years. Adolphus received a medical degree in Germany and opened a practice in Putnam County, Ohio, before 1849.

On April 7, 1852, he married Tenna Brower in Brunnersburg, Defiance County, Ohio. They lived in various counties in Indiana; their six children were born in Elkhart, Steuben, and DeKalb counties from 1853 to 1863. They were divorced in April 1868. The children of the first marriage, some of whom were raised by their father and stepmother, were Frederick Adolphus, who died in Darby, Ravalli County, Montana; Louis Thomas, who is buried in Bryan, Ohio; Mary Helen, who married John Allison Neill and is buried in Fountain Grove Cemetery in Bryan, Ohio; Laura Emilie, who married Peter Rosenfelder and lived and died in Cleveland, Ohio; Steven Douglas, who died at age one; and Gustavus Daniel, who died in Eugene, Oregon.

After locating in Fort Wayne, Dr. Goeriz's office was at 80 Columbia Street, and at one time he advertised himself as a water doctor . He married Anna Mary Wilson on September 9, 1868, in Fort Wayne at the Berry Street Methodist Episcopal Chapel. Anna was the daughter of William C. Wilson, born 1812, in Westmoreland County, Pennsylvania, of Irish heritage, and Elizabeth Ann Cole, of Ohio. William and Elizabeth were most likely married in Steubenville, Jefferson County, Ohio.

There were three children of the marriage of Adolphus Goeriz and Anna Mary Wilson. Adolphus and Anna are buried in Lindenwood Cemetery, Section D, lot 109. All three of their children were born and remained in Fort Wayne.

Fanny Wilson Goeriz was born July 15, 1869, and married George Bernard McCormick, the son of Thomas McCormick and Sarah Ann Morris of Virginia. Fanny and George had ten children, three of whom died as babies. The family story goes that Fanny was Catholic but that when one of the babies was dying, the priest would not come. After that the children were raised in another faith.

The second child was Anna Georgia May, born November 8,1871. She married Charles Myers, and died in 1907 of tuberculosis, a disease that plagued many of the Wilsons.

The third child was Charles Ferdinand, born January 7, 1873. He married Grace Mary Sweet on December 12, 1900, in Fort Wayne. Grace was the daughter of Warren Joseph Sweet and Cassandra Alvira Brunson. Related families are Ashley, Bohne, Gaskill, Halladay, and Levi Harrod, whose brother founded Harrodsburg, Kentucky.

Submitted by Phyllis Goeriz Robinson

LEONARD M. GOLDSTEIN

It all started in the spring of 1945. Leonard Goldstein was working as a classification analyst at the U.S. Air Base in Columbus, Ohio. Rikki was preparing for her final exams to complete her sophomore year at Ohio State University.

One morning, in the mail coming to Leonard's desk was an announcement that the State Department was taking applications for Vice Consul positions. On a whim, perhaps out of boredom, he filled in the forms and sent them on to Washington. (He had returned from the air base in Trinidad only a few months earlier and wasn't eager to go overseas again).

Surprisingly, he received an invitation for an interview along with train tickets, hotel, and food vouchers. What fun — a free trip to Washington! The interview was with Dean Acheson, at that time an under-secretary, and even more surprising, Leonard received a letter of appointment a short time later.

Now one has to back up a bit. During Leonard's undergraduate years at Ohio State, 1938-1942, the country was still in a depression period where jobs were hard to find. He learned that the father of his fraternity brother, Bill Platka, had an export business in Fort Wayne and thinking ahead, he majored in International Trade. So with the war coming to a close, Germany was done and a decision about the State Department job needed, he phoned Bill who was already working with his father, and asked his advice. Obviously, Leonard was hoping that Bill would say turn the State Department job down and come to work with us. He didn't. Instead Bill said he thought it would be great experience for Leonard.

So Leonard then called Rikki, who was at home in Sioux City enjoying her summer break. He told her that he would accept the job if she would marry him. She agreed and they began to make plans. The time was now July and Leonard was scheduled for job training in Washington in early August. They would be married in mid September, he would be assigned overseas, and Rikki would join him later.

Leonard resigned his Columbus job, took the Milwaukee train to Sioux City to meet the family and be entertained. His return to Columbus was to coincide with instructions and documents to get him to Washington. They were not there. When he called to find out what had happened, he was told that through a clerical error, his papers had been misplaced and he would need to wait for the September training class!

Obviously, he was distressed. He had quit his job, and his funds were low. Their wedding plans were fouled up and to top it off, Leonard really wasn't enthusiastic about going overseas again! Knowing how he felt, a very good friend suggested that he call Bill Platka again. Leonard reminded him that he had called a month ago and Bill had advised him to take the offer. Notwithstanding, his friend urged Leonard to call again. He did, and this time Bill asked him to come in and talk.

The conversation resulted in a job offer with Platka Export, which Leonard accepted on VJ Day, 1945. He later learned that the day of his second call, Bill's desk was inundated with correspondence from European businessmen who were eager to get back in trade after a six-year hiatus.

Rikki and Leonard were married in October 1945, and have lived in Fort Wayne for nearly 60 years. But, considering how their lives were changed, as well as everyone they have touched — all because of some unknown's clerical error — it almost makes one a fatalist!

Submitted by Leonard M. Goldstein

GONGWER FAMILY

William Grayless, ancestor of the present day Gongwer family, came to Allen County, Indiana, in 1834. He, along with George Slagle, settled in Section 5 of Lake Township. The house of William Grayless was opened for the first religious service held in the township in 1834, under the ministrations of Reverend Black of the Methodist Church. Meetings were held at this house for a number of years. William Grayless continued to live in Lake Township until his death in 1855, when he was buried in the Lake Chapel Cemetery in Lake Township, Allen County, Indiana.

His son, Charles, who was born in 1818 in Ohio, continued to reside in Lake Township, where he was married to Rebecca Jane Turner and later Nancy Sweet, until 1910, when he died and was buried in the Lake Chapel Cemetery. Their son, Oliver, was born in Allen County in 1844. By 1860, he had moved to Union Township, Whitley County, where he was a successful farmer. During the Civil War, he was a member of the 88th Indiana Volunteers in Whitley County.

Peter and Ollie Gongwer Family: Peter and Ollie on the left, with Franklin Sr. perched on top the wheel

His daughter, Ollie, was born in Whitley County on April 15, 1874, and married Peter Vincent Gongwer in the Lutheran Church at Coesse, Whitley County, on October 23, 1895. Their family of six children was all born in Whitley County, Indiana.

The youngest, Franklin David Sr., was born on December 11, 1903. During his lifetime, he was married four times: to Eunice Forbes in 1926, to Elizabeth Ripple in 1932, to Marcelle Hoerner in 1939 and, finally, to Lillian Ponsett in 1985. He worked as a mechanic. He died in Fort Wayne on November 2, 1986, and is buried in the Highland Park Cemetery in Allen County, Indiana.

Franklin developed a farm on the west side of Coldwater Road, just north of Dupont Road. It featured a huge double barn, the site of many social gatherings and celebrations. In 1954, the farm was subdivided and became the Mardego Hills subdivision.

He and Marcelle had one son, Franklin David Gongwer Jr., born March 16, 1944. Franklin Jr. married Nancy Ann Partee on May 1, 1965, in Fort Wayne, Indiana. They were the parents of three children: Lisa Marie, born December 16, 1965; Keith David, born May 15, 1968; and Jeffrey Paul, born October 22, 1970, all in Fort Wayne, Indiana.

Lisa Marie Gongwer married Rick Isenbarger on September 16, 1986, and they have two children, Taylor, born in 1994, and Kendall, born in 1997. Lisa is a partner in the accounting firm of Haines, Isenbarger, and Skiba.

Keith David Gongwer married Noelle Robbins on December 23,1990; they have two children, Elise Diane, born in 1990, and Paul David, born in 1993. Keith is employed by the Shambaugh Company installing fire-prevention systems.

Jeffrey Paul married Rebecca Sue Baker on June 29, 1996, and they have one son, Ian Jeffrey, born May 8, 2002. Jeffery is self-employed and maintains car wash equipment.

Submitted by Rebecca Gongwer

LOUIS AND MARIE GOODRICH

Louis L. Goodrich, the third son of Earl and Alpha (Miller) Goodrich, was born July 19, 1937, in Wewoka, Oklahoma. Lou lived in Oklahoma until he was six when the family moved to Fontana, California, for four years before moving back to Oklahoma. He graduated from Beggs High School in 1955 and Oklahoma A & M in 1957. He worked as an electronic technician until 1964 with Boeing Aircraft Company in Wichita, Kansas, and Federal Electric in Paramus, New Jersey. During this time he spent six months in the Philippines and two years in Taiwan.

On August 10, 1963, he married Marie A. Boyce who was born August 22, 1936, in Tecumseh, Michigan. Marie was the oldest daughter of Wilbur and Elizabeth (Kidman) Boyce. Marie graduated from Tecumseh High School in 1954, and Alma College in 1958 with a degree in elementary education. She taught sixth grade in St. Clair Shores, Michigan, until she and Lou were married.

While Lou attended Eastern Michigan University where he got a degree in business management, Marie taught school in Livonia, Michigan. They moved to Muskegon in 1967 when Lou started working for General Telephone, and Marie taught fifth and sixth grades in Muskegon Public Schools until 1972 when their daughter, Linda, was born on June 27. Two years later Louis II was born on May 9, 1974. Both of them were born in Grand Haven. While they were in the Muskegon area, Lou and Marie lived in Grand Haven until 1975 when they moved to Fruitport.

In 1984 Lou was transferred to Fort Wayne with General Telephone/GTE and they moved to the north side of Fort Wayne in Perry Township. Lou continued to work for GTE until he retired in 1996. Marie developed an interest in family history, doing research professionally as well as teaching genealogy classes. She has been active in the Allen County Genealogical Society of Indiana. Both Lou and Marie are members of the United Methodist Church of the Covenant. Both Linda and Louie graduated from Carroll High School. Linda graduated from Indiana State University in 1994 and Louie from Rose-Hulman in 1996.

On June 15, 1996, Louie married Robin Richmond, daughter of Scott and Linda (Huff) Richmond. Robin was born October 8, 1974. She graduated as a registered nurse from Indiana State University. They lived in Colorado where Louie worked in computer science and Robin as a nurse until 2001. In 2001 they moved to the north side of Fort Wayne where they live with their children Alec, born June 25,2001, and Ella, born March 19, 2005.

Linda married Brian Beitzel in Madison, Wisconsin, on March 30,2002. Brian was born on September 27, 1970, to David and Enid (Speidel) Beitzel. Linda worked for InterVarsity Christian Fellowship. Brian finished work on his doctorate in educational psychology from the University of Wisconsin. In 2004 they moved to Otego, New York, where Brian now teaches at the nearby State University of New York in Oneonta.

Submitted by Marie Goodrich

GORMAN FAMILY

Dennis Gorman was born in Ireland about 1810, and immigrated to the United States prior to 1860. He bought land and settled in Section 29, Lake Township, Allen County, Indiana. He and his wife, Bridget, raised two sons: Thomas, born in 1848 in Ireland, and Dennis, born about 1857 in Boston, Massachusetts.

Thomas and his wife Mary (Sullivan) later purchased additional land in Section 30, which increased their holdings to 120 acres. They were the parents of eight children, all of them born in Lake Township. Times must have been hard, because several of the children died at an early age: Mary, at 21 days; Timothy, at one month; Bernadette, one year; Julia, two years; and Catherine, who died at 15.

Thomas died in 1897 and is buried in the Catholic Cemetery in Lake Township. The 1910 Census shows his wife and children (Bridget, Dennis, Thomas Jr., William, as well as Catherine) all living in Lake Township. Most of the early Gormans are buried in St. Patrick's Catholic Cemetery in Lake Township.

The Gorman family was very active in the activities of St. Patrick's Catholic Church in Arcola. All of the children attended St. Patrick's School through the early 1900s. The first St. Patrick's School was built in the 1880s and Dennis Gorman was one of the early teachers. This school was used until 1950, when it was replaced. A picture of all eight grades of the two-room Arcola School about 1910 includes teacher, "Ella" (Bridget Ellen) Gorman, daughter of Thomas Gorman.

St. Patrick's Catholic Cemetery on Bass Road

While most of the Gormans were farmers, Thomas Gorman Jr. was employed as a railroad telegrapher. According to a family story, while at work and about to suffer a heart attack, he managed to set the railroad signals against an oncoming train, and thereby averted a disaster. Another son of Thomas, William P., was also employed as a railroad telegrapher.

William's son, Edward Joseph Gorman, attended Central Catholic High School in Fort Wayne and was a basketball player on Central Catholic's national championship team in 1939. He graduated from Indiana University in 1943, after which he was employed by Essex Wire Company. He then enlisted in the U.S. Army in December 1943, and was wounded in action on February 2, 1945, during the "Battle of the Bulge." He returned to the United States and resided in Bryan, Ohio. Edward's brother, Thomas, was a captain in the Air Corps, and another, Robert, was a corporal, also in the Air Corps.

Edward's daughter, Karen, graduated from Indiana University in 1972 and is married to Michael Baker, who graduated from Indiana Technical College on June 12, 1971. Michael retired from The General Telephone Company in 1999, and lives in St. Charles, Missouri. They have a daughter, Emily, who is a lawyer in St. Louis, Missouri, and is married to Matt Crossman. He is employed as an assistant editor at *Sporting News*.

Submitted by Karen Baker

JOSEPH A. GRABILL (1866-1959)

Joseph A. Grabill, oldest of seven, was born January 14, 1866, in a log cabin on a 60 acre farm between Grabill and Harlan. At age 18 he re-roofed his parents' house. His father, Joseph Krahenbuhl (1826-1909), and mother, Magdalena Gerig (1837-1913), were born in the Alsace region of France and immigrated in the 1850s via the Great Lakes to Allen County. His parents were members of an Amish community in France that illegally refused universal military conscription, could not own land, and fled to America to escape persecution.

Joseph A. Grabill, 50 years old, 1916

Magdalena's father, John Gerig, was a prominent Amish bishop. From the 1860s to the 1890s the originally homogenous Amish community in northeast Allen County split into such factions as the Old Order Amish, Defenseless Mennonite Church, and Missionary Church. Joseph served as trustee of the Grabill Missionary Church for fifty years as well as general construction manager in 1916 of the brick, neo-Gothic predecessor to the current structure.

Young Joseph went to elementary school for four years, his only formal education, in then Maysville (now Harlan). He told the teacher his name, Krahenbuhl (meaning Mother Crow Hill), in Swiss-German and she, not knowing Swiss-German, wrote down "Grabill."

Outliving his wives, he married Emma Sauder in 1890. A daughter was Lillian (Roth). In 1897, he married Catherine Nofsinger. Children were Priscilla (Ramseyer), Wilma (Sauder), and Clifford. He married Verena Wiederkehr in 1919.

In 1899, Joseph bought a brick house built in 1882 (now Grabill's oldest house) and its farm. On January 1, 1902, the Wabash Railroad completed a line going through the northeast corner of Joseph's farm and put up a depot named West Maysville. Local people resisted this name and put "Grabill" on the depot. In February 1902, Joseph recorded the original plat of the town with 23 lots.

He became Grabill's first postmaster and was the first to own an automobile, a Model T Ford. He helped start the elementary school, Grabill Bank, and Grabill Grain Company, serving on their boards for many years. Other early businesses included a lumberyard, department store, hotel, saloon, drugstore, harness shop, and print shop. A volunteer fire department, dentist, doctor, and telephone and electrical service all came to this new town by the time the Grabill Barn was erected in 1917 (now the Town Hall).

Joseph lined the streets with sugar maples from the woods at the southwest corner of his farm and donated the area next to the woods as the first Grabill Park. In his '70s he built a retirement bungalow where the Grabill Museum stands today. In 1945, the family of his son, Clifford, moved into his 1882 house, a property owned today by the family of Nayda Grabill Miller, Joseph's great-granddaughter.

Joseph A. Grabill helped dream a town community into existence, dying at 93 on August 2, 1959, a few yards away from the house he bought in 1899. Other Josephs in his lineage includes his grandfather, father, grandson (university professor), and great-great grandson, Alexander Joseph Grabill, born in 2000.

Submitted by Joe Grabill

EARL A. & FLORENCE (FRETZ) GRAHAM FAMILY

Earl A. Graham was born January 13, 1884, in Tingley, Iowa, to William Andrew and Orpha Rush Graham. The family moved to nearby Eagleville, Missouri, where Earl spent his formative years. In 1902, he moved to Los Angeles, California, where he began his career as a barber. He married Florence Fretz, a beauty operator, July 3, 1906, in Los Angeles. Florence was born December 3, 1886, in Auburn, Indiana. They moved to Auburn in late 1906 or early 1907. In 1912, as a member of Journeymen Barber's Union Local 649, Earl helped organize the first Local 649 St. Valentine's Day annual ball and reception at the old Armory Hall. The couple had eight children: Raymond Rollin, Ruth Virginia, Helen Elizabeth, John Earl, William Samuel, Robert Ervin, James Edward, and Fairy Angeline. They divorced December 17, 1928.

In the early 1930s Florence married barber, Cecil George "Cap" Getz, and the two moved to Fort Wayne. Following Mr. Getz's death in 1957, Florence moved back to Auburn to care for her elderly sister who died in 1962. Florence remained in Auburn until her death December 4, 1964.

Earl moved to Fort Wayne about 1936 where he barbered at four known locations: 630 South Barr, 113 East Main, 231 East Main, and 624 South Barr Streets. He and companion Grace Bowers lived together as common law husband and wife until his passing July 18, 1964. Earl and Florence are buried in Woodlawn Cemetery in Auburn.

Raymond "Bud" was a barber in Auburn, Indiana, about 1928-1933. He married Florence Snow June 7, 1928, in Montpelier, Ohio. They had three children, one of whom lived to adulthood. Florence died in September, 1933. Bud went to work at a furniture factory in Bryan, Ohio, about 1934. He married Helen Rosendaul May 5, 1934, a union that produced three children. The family moved to Albion, Indiana, about 1940 and to Fort Wayne in 1943 where Bud worked as a salesman, grocery store owner and for the City, among others. He died April 4, 1984, and is buried in Covington Memorial Gardens.

Ruth Virginia married Howard Dean June 2, 1928. They had two children while still living in Auburn. They later moved to Hamilton Lake where they lived for many years. Ruth Virginia now resides in a nursing home in Angola, Indiana.

Helen married John Bloom Sr. October 30, 1930, in Garrett, Indiana, They had eight children. They lived in Auburn and Garrett before moving to Fort Wayne (1940-1943). Helen died June 13, 1980, and is buried in the Catholic Cemetery.

John was in the carpet and flooring business. He married Ardith Mauer in March 1937, in Fort Wayne. They had three children. The couple moved to Dayton, Ohio (1938-1940) and to Florida (1977-1978). John died June 30, 1989. He was cremated.

William was a bartender by trade. He married June Crowl (about 1935-1938) in Fort Wayne. They had one son. William served in the Navy in World War II aboard the submarine "Fish" which was depth charged in Tokyo Bay. The family settled in LaJolla, California, where William died October 9, 1966.

Seated left to right: Florence Fretz Graham, Earl A. Graham. Standing left to right: Ruth Virginia, William Samuel, James Edward, Raymond Rollin, John Earl, Helen Elizabeth

Robert was a machinist. He married Izetta Mendel about 1937-1939 in Fort Wayne. The couple had four children. They moved to San Diego, California, (1946-1947) where Robert died April 22, 1967.

James worked as a salesman, truck driver and taxi driver. He served in the Army during World War II on Guadalcanal. He married Ruth Brissy March 8, 1945, in South Bend, Indiana (divorced); Hazel Noe January 27, 1949, in Lafayette, Indiana, a union that produced five children (divorced); and Mildred Madden January 27, 1962, in Auburn, Indiana. Jim lived most of his life in Fort Wayne and died there December 20, 1997. He is buried in Forest Home Cemetery, Hicksville, Ohio.

Fairy married Jimmy Rossi December 2, 1938, in Fort Wayne. They had one child. The couple divorced May 2, 1940. Fairy married Lawrence Johnson in 1941 in Fort Wayne, a union that produced two children. She died February 12, 1945, and is buried in Lindenwood Cemetery.

Submitted by Don F. Graham, son of Raymond Rollin Graham

DON F. & MARGERY M. (RYAN) GRAHAM FAMILY

Don Franklin Graham was born March 8, 1938, in Bryan, Williams County, Ohio. His parents were Raymond Rollin "Bud" Graham and Helen Hope Rosendaul. His siblings are Jerry DeWitt, a half-brother and son of Raymond from a previous marriage, Raymond Dennis, and Carol Jan Bennett.

Raymond R. Graham, Don's father, was born November 1, 1907, in Auburn, DeKalb County, Indiana. He was the oldest of eight children born to Earl A. Graham and Florence Fretz. "Bud" was a jack-of-all-trades having worked for Ohio Art Company, Delta Products, the WPA, and the Hollabird Corporation while living in Bryan, Ohio, the Hollabird Corporation while living in Albion, Indiana, and for Fruehauf Trailer, Allen County Foods, B & H Superette as grocery store owner, American Coal & Supply Thrift Center, Tri-State Plumbing, City of Fort Wayne, and Associated Tires while living in Fort Wayne, Indiana. He married Helen Rosendaul on May 5, 1934, at midnight in the Methodist parsonage in Edgerton, Ohio. Helen was born March 29, 1913, in Bryan, Ohio, the daughter of Burt Franklin and Catherine Bernice (Connin) Rosendaul. She had an older half-brother, a son of Catherine Bernice.

Don attended Minor, St. John's Lutheran, Emmanuel Lutheran, Washington and Adams grade schools in Fort Wayne. He graduated from Central High School in 1956, and Indiana-Purdue University in Fort Wayne in 1987, with an associate's degree in general studies. As a teenager he worked several jobs including Scott's Recreation, A & W Root Beer Drive-In, Eavey's Super Market, and Hire's Bottling Company before going to work full-time at Lincoln National Life Insurance Company in 1956. He also worked for Parrot Packing Company, International Harvester, the City of Fort Wayne as a police officer, and CNA, a Columbus, Ohio, based personnel and labor relations consulting firm. Don formed his own personnel and labor relations consulting business, DFG Enterprises, in 1986. In recent years he has been reducing his client base in preparation for retirement in 2007.

Don played basketball, ran track, and was a pitcher for his seventh and eighth grade baseball team while at Adams School. He also played basketball in a local Junior Industrial League during the early 1950s. During the 1960s he bowled on a team sponsored by his employer, Parrot Packing Company that won the league championship. He won the award for the most improved bowler in the league that year. Don is a history buff and avid collector of local, national, but mainly sports memorabilia and artifacts. He was a die-hard Brooklyn Dodgers fan and as a youngster named his first dog, you guessed it, Dodger. He is currently secretary of the Northeast Indiana Baseball Association, which houses a Museum and Hall of Fame in the American Heritage Village complex near Auburn, Indiana, and he is the editor of that organization's quarterly news publication, *Line Drives*. He has gained recognition as a local sports historian and has set up several local historical sports exhibits in recent years at the Allen County Public Library in downtown Fort Wayne. Don also volunteers at the library. He has also written local historical sports articles for a project sponsored by the Fort Wayne Sports Corporation and starting in 2006, has been doing the same for the Fort Wayne *News-Sentinel* on a periodic basis. He also enjoys family genealogy with his wife.

Margery and Don Graham.

Don married Margery Marie Ryan on July 27, 1957. She was born May 8, 1939, in Fort Wayne, Indiana, to Byron Patrick and Stella E. (Becraft) Ryan. Her siblings are James P. Ryan and Jane E. Schurr. Don and Margery had two children, Bryan Christopher, and Kerry Douglas who died as an infant.

Marge attended St. Andrew's School and graduated from Central Catholic High School in 1957. Her career includes 14 years with Waldenbooks in several managerial positions. As regional manager her responsibilities included 125 retail stores in the Midwest. After leaving the retail business, she began genealogy research turning a hobby into an occupation. She has been a professional researcher for over 20 years, a genealogy instructor for workshops and Elderhostel classes, and has worked several summers as a reference assistant in the genealogy department of the Allen County Public Library where she also volunteers. She is very active in the local genealogy society having served in almost every capacity including four years as president and currently serves as vice-president. Marge is a member of the Daughters of the American Revolution, Mary Penrose Wayne Chapter. Her hobbies include decorating, quilting, gardening, and bird watching.

Submitted by Jerry Graham.

JAMES FORD & MARY FRANCES (CUNNISON) GRAHAM

James Graham, the fifth child of Jacob Graham and Elizabeth Jane Ford, was born February 28, 1868 in Richmond, Indiana. Jacob Graham (1835-1910) was born in Wayne County, Indiana to David Graham (1811-1889) and Rachel Minerva Sands (1810-1881). David and Rachel were married in Green County, Tennessee, on October 13, 1830. By 1834 they were in Wayne County, Indiana, and by 1844 they had made Preble County, Ohio, their home. David was the son of Charles Graham (1766-1838) and Elizabeth C. McCallum (1770-1841). Charles and Elizabeth moved to Vermilion County, Illinois, around 1836. Rachel's parents were Jacob Sands (1776-1849) and Ann Brown (1780-1855). They also migrated from Tennessee to Wayne County Indiana.

James Ford Graham

Mary Cunnison was born February 25, 1868, in Allen County Indiana to Robert W. Cunnison (1836-1876) and Matilda Beck (1838-1917). Mary's siblings were Charles L. (1860-1930), George P. (1862), Edith (1864-1876), Clara Bell (1865-1943) and Fielding (1870).

Robert's parents were Robert Cunnison (1800-1843) and Margaret Ramsey (1799-1891) who came from Kirkmichel, Perthshire, Scotland, to Allen County in 1833. Robert and Margaret had another son, James. He married Mary Rebecca Dalman. Margaret's second husband was John Whetten. Matilda's parents were William and Susan (Simpson) Beck.

Margaret Ramsey Cunnison Whetten

Jacob and Elizabeth Graham had eight children. Margaret M. (1858-1939) married Emory Smith Druley (1852-1932). Annie B. (1860-1896) married John W. Lloyd. Oliver Grant (1864-1946) never married. Charles Allen (1866-1929) never married. James Ford. Edna Maude (1870-1943) married Elga William Smith. William Roy (1873-1953) married Catherine Oma Branstrator (1879-1950). Vera Veranica (1878-1950) married John Beard and Charles Hillman. They brought seven of them to Allen County around 1887 settling on land on Lower Huntington Road.

James bought land on the west side of Hayden Road (now Ardmore Ave) at the intersection of Sandpoint Road. There he and Mary raised six children.

L to R: Dick, Mary and Alice Graham. The next two persons are unknown. Then Matilda Cunnison, Dorothy and Madeline Graham

Annie Laurie (1892-1965) married Clifford E. Wells. They did not have any children. Alice M. (1896-1931) never married. Madeline Rae (1898-1929) married George E. Roller and they had Mary, George and Dorothy. Donald Russell (1900-1967) married Virginia Sterlin. Before divorcing they had Marjorie, Joan, Patsy and Robert. Richard Fielding (1906-1955) never married. The youngest child was Dorothy Marian (1908-1975). She married Clarence Harmon Bunn, son of Jefferson Lewis and Minnie Cathern Genth Bunn.

James was a successful market farmer and owner of a gravel pit on Elmhurst Drive. He was fifty-five years old when he drown in his gravel pit while swimming with his seventeen-year-old son, Richard. All of James' family is buried in the Prairie Grove Cemetery, Fort Wayne, Indiana.

Submited by Robin Bunn Kissel

GRANDOS FAMILY HISTORY

Doris (Parker) Grandos was born December 13, 1930, in Fort Wayne's Lutheran Hospital. Her parents, Ethel and Elmer Parker, took her home to 2716 Buena Vista Drive where she lived for the next twenty-six years. The school she first attended was in a temporary wooden building with a pot bellied stove for heat. After Slocum School, she attended Forest Park and then North Side High School. Doris received a degree in Elementary Education from Indiana University. She returned to Fort Wayne and taught at James Smart School on Pontiac Street for seven years. She married Norman Grandos on December 21, 1957, and by 1959 she was expecting their first child and gave up her teaching career. Doris later worked as a historic interpreter at the Old Fort reconstruction. She has given many talks on Fort Wayne history and continues to give spinning demonstrations in the public schools.

Norman Grandos was born in Chicago of Norwegian immigrants who met on the ship from Norway. His father was a carpenter and his mother a dressmaker. Norm came to Fort Wayne to work as an Electrical Engineer for Magnavox. He worked for Motorola previous to coming to Fort Wayne. He was a graduate of the University of Illinois and had served in the Marine Corps as an airplane mechanic.

Norm and Doris have five children who spent most of their childhood at 2828 Whitegate Drive, the Grandos home for over 30 years. All the children attended Frances Slocum Elementary, Lakeside Junior High and North Side High School. All graduated from Indiana University except for Susan who has a degree from Purdue. None of the Grandos children stayed in Indiana. A desire to live out West lured three of the girls away while job opportunities near Chicago appealed to the others.

James (February 17, 1959) works as a CFO near Chicago. He married Deb Lorimor in 1993. They have two children, Allison and Mark, and reside in Lindenhurst, Illinois, where they can often be found exploring the Chain of Lakes by boat.

Susan (June 9, 1960) moved to Washington State where she met her husband Steve Maggio. The Maggios have two sons, Logan and Jesse. Sue shows Siberian Huskies and currently owns three champions.

The Grandos Family, 1972.

Jane (September 21, 1963) met her husband, Jerome Boundy of Birmingham, England, while working as a corporate recruiter in Boston, Massachusetts. The Boundy twins, Samuel and Hannah, were born in Barrington, Illinois. The family moved to London, England, in 2005.

Patricia (July 8, 1967) moved to Spokane, Washington, where she met her husband Jeff Howard. They have two children, Benjamin Howard and Alihna Grandos. Alihna was born in Pohnpei, Micronesia, where the family lived while Patty taught English as a Second Language at the College of Micronesia.

Elizabeth (Betsy) (October 26, 1970) has mainly lived in the Denver, Colorado, since leaving Indiana. Betsy works in the wholesale mortgage industry, when not indulging her passion for training and showing horses in Three-Day Events.

Submitted by Patty Grandos.

FRANK JAMES, LAURIE ANNE, & VICTORIA ROSE GRAY FAMILY

Frank and Laurie Gray are both attorneys and were married on February 14, 2001, in their Aboite Township home. Frank James Gray

was born in Chicago, Illinois, on July 3, 1941, to Frank Willard Gray, Jr. (October 11, 1914 - January 22, 2003) and Ellen Rose Krahn (July 25, 1911 - December 18, 1991). He graduated from Calumet High School in Chicago in 1959 and earned his B.A. in History in 1963 and his J.D. in 1966, both from Valparaiso University, Valparaiso, Indiana. Frank enlisted in the Army in 1967 and was awarded the Combat Infantryman's Badge, Bronze Star (with two oak leaf clusters), the Army Commendation Medal for Valor, an Air Medal, and the Vietnam Cross of Gallantry for his combat tour in Vietnam before being honorably discharged in 1969.

Frank moved to Fort Wayne in 1969 to practice law at Bloom & Bloom. Frank was an Assistant United States Attorney from 1974 - 1977, has an AV rating (highest) with Martindale-Hubbell, is a Fellow in the American College of Trial Lawyers, and past president of the American Inns of Court, Benjamin Harrison Chapter. Frank represents business clients and litigates personal injury, criminal, intellectual property, and probate matters. Frank has served Canterbury School as a volunteer soccer coach for over two decades and also on the Board of Trustees.

Frank has two children from his first marriage to Joyce D. Pelz of Washburn, Illinois. Allison Hope Gray (November 15, 1970) resides in Durham, North Carolina, with her husband, John Rayner Spencer. Lincoln Fredrich Gray (September 28, 1973) resides in Arden, North Carolina, with his wife, Elizabeth Sutphin Gray and their daughter, Georgia Elizabeth Gray (September 7, 2003).

Laurie Anne Virgil was born in Auburn, Indiana, on October 21, 1963 to Victor Reed Virgil (November 11, 1939) and Peggy Louise Suter (June 2, 1941). Laurie graduated from Triton High School, Bourbon, Indiana, in 1982 and received her B.A. in Spanish Secondary Education with a minor in English Education from Goshen College, Goshen, Indiana, in 1986. After teaching and coaching at Whitko High School, South Whitley, Indiana, for four years, Laurie was admitted to Indiana University School of Law, Bloomington. In 1990, Laurie married Devinder K.G. Singh, a citizen of Malaysia who attended Indiana Institute of Technology and St. Francis College.

Laurie moved to Fort Wayne and began practicing law under the name Laurie A. Singh in 1993. After seven years in private practice, Laurie joined the Allen County Prosecuting Attorney's Office focusing on felony sex crimes and the Child Advocacy Center. Laurie parented full time from September 2001 to November 2003, when she returned to work at the Prosecutor's Office part-time. Laurie is also an aspiring author and the creator of Socratic Parenting, LLC.

On September 12, 2001, while the rest of the country was in shock following the terrorist attacks of 9-11, Laurie went into labor. She and Frank labored together for two days before Victoria Rose Gray was delivered directly into her father's hands at Lutheran Hospital in Fort Wayne, Indiana, on September 14, 2001.

Submitted by Frank and Laurie Gray

WESLEY EDWARD & GERALDINE ANN (LEFFERS) GRAY FAMILY

The Gray family has had a rich history in the United States since coming to the New World prior to the Revolutionary War. John Gray (died 1814) and his son, Matthew (1747-1836), were among the first settlers in the northern territories of Kentucky in the mid to late 1700s. Side by side with Daniel Boone, they helped organize the Kentucky wilderness into the Territories of Bourbon and Mason (which later became counties). Matthew's son, Alexander (1776-1854), and grandson, Wilkinson (1802-1882), moved to Wayne County, Indiana, in 1816, and then on to Randolph County, Indiana, in 1835. They finally settled near Losantville, Indiana. "The settlers in this region had peculiarly severe hardships in the early time. Some of them were very poor and all of them were greatly "Put to it" to make their way." (*Randolph County History Book*). Wilkinson and his son, Hiram (1826-1892), while continuing the family tradition of farming, were both involved in the social organizations of the Masons and the I.O.O.F. in which they each held high offices.

David Gray (1853-1942), son of Hiram, moved to Mooreland where he, with his six children, sold chickens and eggs from his canvas covered flatbed truck, affectionately known to the townsfolk as the "Chicken Six." One of David's six children, Harlan Colby Gray (1882-1948), moved with his wife, Elsie May (Cochran), to Indianapolis and then to Fort Wayne, where they finally put down roots.

Harlan led an exciting life racing motorcycles and greyhounds. While employed by the circus, he could be found performing many daring acts such as hanging by his teeth from a tight rope or strapping himself to an untethered, basketless hot air balloon that would launch him into the air and from which he would then release himself from the parachute back to the ground. Harlan's later days were spent as a brakeman on the Nickel Plate Railroad, while Elsie May was a homemaker and raised their four children.

Wesley Edward Gray ("Ed"), the youngest of the four children, was born on June 8, 1932, at Lutheran Hospital on Fairfield Avenue. The family resided at 629 Fifth Street. Ed's siblings include Pauline Brunson (1911-1982), Raymond (1913-1930), and Betty Lotter (1925-1995). Ed attended Bloomingdale Elementary, Franklin Junior High, and graduated in 1950 from North Side High School. While in high school, he was the school photographer and worked at Howard's Camera and Gift Shop. Upon graduating, he joined the Air Force and attended Air Police School at Tyndall Field in Panama City, Florida. During his tour, he was stationed at Lakenheath Air Force Base in England and traveled to Germany and France. In his free time he began taking flying lessons. The first plane he learned to fly was a Tiger Moth. In 1952, he married Christine Carey. Their son, Shaughn Edward Gray, was born on March 28, 1954, in Mountain Home, Idaho. After four years of service they returned to Fort Wayne, where Ed continued to take flying lessons at Smith Field. He earned his private pilot's license in 1955. Ed worked at Enterprise Glass Company and later was employed by Magnavox. Ed and Christine were divorced in 1955.

In 1959, Ed Gray joined the Catholic Young Adults Club and met Geraldine Ann Leffers. Geraldine was born on July 24, 1936, at Saint Joseph Hospital. Her parents were Joseph A. Leffers (September 19, 1894 -July 22, 1963) and Beatrice (Davis) Leffers (January 1, 1895 - April 17, 1982).

Joseph Leffers' parents, John and Margaret, came to America in 1880 and 1877, respectively. Margaret, of the titled German Von Der Leeuw family, was sent to America in 1877 by her father in an attempt to separate her from her beau, John Leffers. The ploy failed, as John deserted from Prussia's mammoth war machine and stowed away in the hold of a ship. John joined his beloved Margaret in 1880. They soon married, August 30, 1881, and produced ten children; Joseph was the seventh.

Wesley and Geraldine Gray

Joseph worked at Horton Washing Machine Company on Osage Street and following his retirement, he was a self-employed painter. His wife, Beatrice Davis, who was born in Staffordshire, England, remained a homemaker and raised eight girls during the Depression years. The family resided at 1915 Ellen Avenue. Geraldine was the youngest of the eight daughters. Her siblings are Dorothy Till (September 12, 1920 - 2003), Eileen Roach (August 2, 1922), Marjorie Houser (December 26, 1924 - January 13, 1980), Evelyn (Dammeier) McAbee (February 28, 1926), Helen Bauer (February 9, 1927), Mildred Hursh (August 13, 1930), and Mary Lou Bodeker (April 6, 1934). Geraldine attended Most Precious Blood Catholic School and graduated from Central Catholic High School in 1954. After graduating, she worked at Wayne Knitting Mill and Dana Corporation.

Ed Gray and Geraldine were married on October 14, 1961, at Queen of Angels Catholic Church. They resided at 1915 1/2 Ellen Avenue for six years until they moved to 1509 Archer Avenue in 1967. They had five children, all born in Fort Wayne: Mark Alan Gray (September 30, 1962), Shelly Renae Gray (March 5, 1965 - August 28, 1968), Matthew Wayne Gray (January 10, 1967), Scott Joseph Gray (May 15, 1968), and Troy David Gray (November 4, 1975).

Professionally, Ed became a printer pressman and retired from Craftsman Lithograph on Maumee Avenue in 1994. Over the years he also held various part-time jobs, including taxi driver, newspaper delivery driver, and custodian. Geraldine dedicated her life to being a full-time mom and homemaker. She also ran a successful in-home daycare.

Ed and Geraldine were happily married for 31 years until Geraldine's death on October 23, 1992. During their life together they enjoyed spending time with their children and grandchildren and would often take family camping trips to Chain O'Lakes State Park and Cedar Point Amusement Park.

Submitted by Wesley Gray

AMIEL GREEN

Amiel Nicholas Green was born June 23, 1884, at Broadlands, Illinois, in Champaign County. He was the son of immigrant parents. Carl F. Green first came to America in 1872 from the German State of Schleswig Holstein, Germany, and the village of Sieseby. In 1878 Carl returned to Germany, where he persuaded Louise Bruhn to be his bride.

Amiel's formative years were spent with his siblings — Edward, William, Theodore, Elmer, and Laura on the family farm. As the result of a childish dare between Amiel and his brother, Ted, a portion of his index finger was chopped off by an ax. He received such education as was deemed necessary in those times.

On December 25, 1907, in Homer, Illinois, he married Lulu Mae Nichols. Their first home was a farm in Elkhart County, Indiana, near Millersburg. There on February 18,1909, their first child, Florence Mae (Mrs. Harry J. Blessing), was born. A short time later the family moved to Kosciusko County, where three children were born: Charles F. born June 19,1910, died April 28, 1985; Chester R. born July 8, 1911, died January 26, 2004; and Ruth N. (Mrs. Lawrence Cox) now living in Lake Township.

Lula and Amiel Green married on December 25, 1907

Foreseeing better farming opportunities in Noble County, the family moved near Ligonier. Amiel always credited the Jewish community for backing him in his farming ventures by means of their bank loans. From Ligonier, the family moved north of Churubusco in Noble County. There their last child, Howard, was born August 3, 1915. He died October 24, 1994.

In 1918 the family moved to Allen County, Eel River Township, on what is known as the Schelling farm, not far from Wesley Chapel Church, of which they were members and loyal supporters. Their gift to the building fund was buying the lights in the sanctuary. They were members of the Farm Bureau. Lulu was a member of the Ladies Aid, as well as the Indiana Extension Homemakers organization. This directed their children to the 4-H program, with which they were associated for many years. Florence received the high honor of representing the county at National 4-H Club Congress in 1926 and Howard (Jim) was for 38 years a 4-H leader in Eel River Township.

Amiel and Lulu were good parents endeavoring to teach their children the Golden Rule and make their lives pleasant. Amiel was known to carve toy animals for his children's pleasure. They were also amused by his ability to blow smoke rings. For a Halloween party, Lulu has been known to roll up the living room rug, decorate the room with corn shocks, pumpkins, etc. and allow their children and neighboring guests to bob for apples in a wash tub. Such was the norm in a simpler life.

Amiel Green and his family were much respected in their community. Stories of the parents' unselfish generosity and assistance to their neighbors, both monetarily and otherwise, are still told. Years later Amiel and his wife retired and moved to Churubusco. He died on April 13, 1960, and on February 16, 1972, Lulu joined him. Both are buried in Eel River Cemetery.

Submitted by Karna Ley

STEPHEN P. GRIEBEL FAMILY

Stephen P. Griebel was born October 14, 1964, in the State of New York, in the village of Gowanda, near Buffalo. Stephen is the direct descendant (great-great-great grandson) of a pioneer (Wilhelm Griebel), who settled in Allen County (Marion Township), Indiana, in 1839. Stephen is a member of both the First Families of Allen County, Indiana, and The Society of Indiana Pioneers. He is married to Deborah Ann (Runkel), and they have a daughter, Olivia. Stephen is an attorney, his diploma coming from R. Nelson Snider High School, his B.A. in History from Indiana University, Bloomington, and his J.D from the University of Michigan Law School

Griebel Coat of Arms

in Ann Arbor. He practices with Van Gilder & Trzynka, P.C. in Fort Wayne.

Stephen's father, the late Reverend William Walter Louis Griebel, served as an ordained Lutheran minister in LaPorte, Indiana, Circleville, Pennsylvania, Gowanda, New York, Freeport, Illinois, and Fort Wayne; while in Circleville, Pennsylvania, Pastor Griebel founded Calvary Lutheran Church in Murrysville, Pennsylvania. Pastor Griebel was married for over 44 years to the late Virginia Delores (Hoffman), herself a descendent of an early Allen County settler, Henry (Henrich) Doctor; they had six children, of whom Stephen is the youngest. Stephen's sister, Mary, died in an auto accident at the age of eight.

Martin A. Griebel, Stephen's paternal grandfather, was a farmer and also a Marion Township trustee for two terms from 1926-1930 and 1930-1934; his wife, Clara, was Trustee from 1934-1938. (Dick Griebel, Stephen's uncle, served as Trustee from 1959-1966 and also from 1971-1982). Martin was one of the organizers of the First State Bank of Hoagland (later Lincoln National Bank and eventually Wells Fargo Bank), serving as its president. He was also president of the German Mutual Fire Insurance Company for twenty years.

Stephen's great-grandfather is William (Wilhelm) Griebel, who was born in Allen County in 1854. Stephen's great-great grandfather, (Johann) George Griebel, was born in the village of Konigsberg bei Giessen, in the grand Duchy of Hesse-Darmstadt, Germany, in 1830, as was Stephen's great-great-great grandfather, William (Wilhelm) Georg Griebel, who was born in 1803. William and his son George left Bremen, Germany, on July 10, 1834, and arrived in Baltimore, Maryland, on September 3, 1834; they initially settled in Allentown, Pennsylvania, before settling on a farm in southeast Allen County in 1839. The eldest Griebel was naturalized on July 8, 1843.

A cousin to Stephen's great-grandfather, also named William Griebel (born in 1847, on October 14, as is Stephen), served in the Civil War as a Commander of Bass-Lawton Post #40, G.A.R, and was a member of Company G, 152nd Indiana Infantry from Fort Wayne.

The southeast Allen County land on which the eldest Griebels settled has been designated an Indiana Hoosier Homestead, as it has remained uninterrupted with Griebels since 1839. It currently belongs to Stephen's first cousin, Jim Griebel, with his wife Jill and their children.

Submitted by Stephen P. Griebel

CRAWFORD GRISWOLD

Crawford Griswold was born July 27, 1842, in Chatham, Columbia County, New York. He was the grandson of Jabez and Ann Spencer Griswold, early settlers from Connecticut, and a son of Norman Francis and Deborah Richmond Griswold.

In 1862 he enlisted in the 1st regiment, New York Mounted Rifles, was promoted to sergeant, and served until the end of the Civil War. After his discharge, he clerked in his father's store until he obtained a job with the Pennsylvania Railroad. He moved to Lima, Ohio, where on March 9, 1871, he married Louisa Kesler, daughter of Samuel and Louisa Frazier Kesler of nearby Middlepoint. In 1875 he was appointed foreman of the central division bridge gang and the family moved to Fort Wayne. He died on October 7, 1913. Graves of the family are in Lindenwood Cemetery.

Retaining a keen interest in the Civil War, Crawford corresponded with many of his former compatriots, wrote newspaper articles on their experiences, and was a Commander of Lawton - Wayne Post, G.A.R. He was a 32nd degree Mason, a charter member of the Railroad YMCA, and a member of Simpson Methodist Church. Louisa Griswold's community activities included ice cream socials and chicken dinners to raise money for the building of Simpson church. She died before its completion, and is memorialized by the stained glass window behind the choir. Her death was September 9, 1910.

Three of their children left descendants: Lena B. Davis (Mrs. Robert Bums Davis). Ethel L. Ellis (Mrs. Ernest Ellis), and Grace Deborah (Mrs. Harry Wheeler Johnson).

Submitted by Mrs. Virgil W. Lawson

ABNER GROSS FAMILY

Abner Gross was born into a farming family headed by Jacob and Lidda Gross on August 21, 1838, in Gallia County, Ohio.

Abner married Nancy Roush on October 8, 1860, and together they had eight children: John, Lydia, Curtis, Rose, Morris, Mary, Ella, and William.

Front Row: William, Abner, Nancy (Roush), Ella (Rife). Back Row: John, Lydia (Lock), Curtis, Rose (Steerhoff), Morris, Mary (Boggs)

On November 2, 1861, Abner enlisted in the Union Army where he served with Infantry Company E in the Fifty-sixth Regiment, Ohio Volunteer Army.

The Gross family homestead was established in Allen County, Indiana, July 13, 1867, with the purchase of Lake Township property. Eventually, the family relocated to Whitley County where they continued farming.

On March 24, 1911, Abner Gross died and was later buried in Eel River Cemetery.

Submitted by Timothy B. Gross, Great-great-grandson

GROTRIAN/GRODRIAN FAMILY

Charles Frederick Grotrian (1807-1863) and Wilhelmine Friederike Henriette Herrell Grotrian emigrated from Ottenstein, Germany, with their six children. Upon arrival at the port of New York on June 22, 1854, Charles Frederick resumed his shoemaker's trade and anglicized the children's names to Fred, Charles, August William, Wilhelmina, William, and Frederick. In 1856, Charles Frederick purchased land for a farm in Madison Township in Allen County, where the family lived for generations. They

The William Frederick Grodrian Family. Back: Elmer, Ralph, Ethel, Herbert, Alvin, Walter. Front: William, Russell, Nancy, taken about 1912 on their farm.

were members of the German Lutheran Church. There are many descendants of this family who continue to live in the county and there is still a Grotrian Road east of Fort Wayne. A line of the family identified with the Grotrian-Steinweg Piano Company in Germany adopted the surname Grotrian-Steinweg.

August William Grotrian (1841-1907), third child of Charles Frederick and Wilhelmine Grotrian, married his first wife, Mary Maples (1847-1866), in Indiana and after she died, he married Rachel Mooney (1849-1932). Rachel was born to early settlers in Allen County. She bore him ten children: William Frederick, Lewis August, Mary Amanda, Clara Belle, Charles Munson, Edward Albert, August Christian, George Washington, John Walter, and Clarence Wilford. August William changed the family surname to Grodrian about 1870 to make it sound less German. The family belonged to the Methodist Protestant Church. August William Grodrian was a truant officer in 1902. Rachel Grodrian took in needy people during the depression in the 1930s.

William Frederick Grodrian (1869-1938), oldest child of August William and Rachel Grodrian, was born in Allen County. William's oldest son, Herbert, went back to using Grotrian and his son, Delmer, and his children also use the Grotrian spelling. William married Nancy Ann McCarty Johnson (1869-1915), who was born in Jefferson County, Indiana. He worked on his farm and was a carpenter. Their 11 children were born near Fort Wayne in Madison Township, went to school in Maples and helped on the farm. The children were Marion (1875-1875), Ora (1896-1896), Herbert, Ralph, Ethel, Walter (1901-1929, died of tuberculosis), Elmer, Alvin, Russell, Glenn (1911-1911) and Matilda (1912-1912). After Nancy Grodrian died, William married Lena Guttermuth.

Herbert Grotrian (1897-1941) married Bertha Frederick (1897-1987), owned the Grotrian Sign Company, and was electrocuted while making a neon sign. They had one son Delmer, who learned the trade and kept up the business after his father died. In 1950 Delmer then went to work for General Electric and in 1967 he began working for Pepsi. He is now retired. Delmer was married briefly to Eileen. He later married Elisabeth, who was born in Germany. Delmer and Elisabeth have three sons, Paul, Ronald and Gary. Paul Grotrian retired from Texas Instruments, is married to Barbara and they have two children. Ronald Grotrian, a Vice President at L.H. Industries, is married to Sandra and they have two children. Gary Grotrian owns Kirchheim Water Gardening and is married to Shirley.

Ralph Grodrian (1898-1967) married Eleanor Smith (1898-1966). They moved to St. Louis, where Ralph worked on the railroad. Later, they returned to Allen County where they had a chicken farm. Their daughter, Doris (1920-1974), married Anton Hummel and had five children.

Ethel Grodrian (1900-1927) married Alfred F. Van Horn, who worked at International Harvester. Their children are Alfred "Bill", Robert, Howard and Betty. When Ethel died of scarlet fever, people had to look through the window to see the casket because the house was quarantined.

Elmer Grodrian (1904-1992) married Ruth Johnson and worked for the Electric Company. They had two daughters, Betty and Nancy. Betty married Tommy Shanyfelt and had two children. Nancy (1934-1997) married Merle Nicholas and had three children. After Merle died, Nancy married Kenneth Hallmark and they moved to Alabama.

Alvin Grodrian (1904-1980) moved to Inglewood, California, in the mid-1920s and was an Executive for the Boy Scouts of America for many years. Alvin's first wife Goldie Marshall died shortly after they were married. He then married Lucy (1906-1993), who was born in England, and they had two daughters, Janice and Sharon.

Russell Grodrian (1907-1974) delivered blocks of ice with a horse-drawn cart as a teenager. He moved to Inglewood, California, in 1929 and became a mechanic and service station owner. He married Margaret (1913-1998), who was born in Canada. Their children are Jean and Carol (twins), Glenn, and Nancy, and they all live in California.

Submitted by Delmer Grotrian and Carol Grodrian Satterthwaite

AUGUST GUMBERT FAMILY

August Gumbert was born in Hesse, Germany, in the village of Konigsberg on January 23, 1828. His father, Ludwig, was a farmer. His mother's name is unknown. There were at least three children in this family, with August being the youngest. One of his older brothers was John G. who came to the United States in 1848 and settled in the New Haven area where he became a prominent farmer and one of the founders of the original Martini Lutheran Church in that area.

August married Margaretha Meyer in Konigsberg in 1849, and four children, Heinrich, Carl, George and Phillip were born prior to their departure to the U.S.A. in 1858. They arrived in New York on September 6, 1858. Their eventual destination was to join brother, John.

They finally settled in what became known as the Soest area of East Allen County where he farmed and helped organize the St. Johannes Lutheran Church in 1857. This church merged with St. Paul's of Marion Township in 1871 to form Emmanuel of Soest.

In 1860, Wilhelm was born and in 1861, their sixth child, John, was born. Prior to John's birth in 1861, tragedy entered their lives. Both George, age eight, and Phillip, age four, died, probably from infectious disease. Their deaths were followed by the death of Wilhelm, age two, in 1862 and, the father, August, age 36, died in 1864 as a result of a farm accident. All are buried in St Johannes Cemetery located just west of the present day Emmanuel Lutheran Church on Wayne Trace. This left the widow, Margaretha and the three remaining children. The eldest, Heinrich took over the farm when he was 15. With help from August's older brother, John, and friends they were able to continue life on the farm until 1878 when Heinrich married. Charles married earlier, so this left Margaretha and the youngest son to manage the farm. Unable to handle this task, they moved in with Charles and his wife Elizabeth (Ellett). Margaretha never remarried after the death of August, living with Charles until her death in 1894. She, Charles and Elizabeth are all buried at the Emmanuel Soest Cemetery.

Submitted by Jack Gumbert, M.D.

JACK L. GUMBERT, MD

Jack Lee Gumbert was born in Fort Wayne on July 14, 1934, the oldest son of Martin Fredrick Gumbert and Beulah (McClain) Gumbert. He had three younger brothers, Jerry Max, born 1936, died 2004, Daniel Lamoyne, born1938, and Gene Allen born1941.

Jack graduated from Adams Grade School in 1948 and Central High School in 1953. While at Central he played football, basketball and track. During the 1953 basketball season he broke the city scoring record previously held by Johnny Bright. He was named to many all star teams and was awarded a basketball scholarship at Kansas State University. He was also named to the National Honor Society in high school and won the Foley academic scholarship for his academic achievements. His classmates voted him as the best boy citizen of the class of 1953. After a year at Kansas State he transferred to the University of Cincinnati where he again played basketball, finishing his career by scoring 15 points in his team's loss to St. Bonaventure at Madison Square Garden in the National Invitation Tournament. While at undergraduate school he studied premedicine and in 1957 was admitted to the Medical School class of 1961 at Cincinnati.

Jack Gumbert Family. Back, L to R: Brad, Grant, Jack Jr. Front, L to R: Lori, Dr. Jack, Lois, Joe

On June 15, 1957 he married Lois I. Scheimann at Emmanuel Lutheran Church in Fort Wayne. In 1961 he received his Doctor of Medicine degree from Cincinnati University then went back to Indianapolis, Indiana, for residency in General Surgery which was completed in 1966. Two years were then spent in the U.S.Army where he served as surgeon at Fort Rucker Army Hospital at Fort Rucker, Alabama. While there he also became a flight surgeon. His last nine months in the Army was in Vietnam where he was flight surgeon with the 45th helicopter unit and also surgeon with the 24th evacuation hospital.

Prior to leaving for Vietnam, he and Lois had three children, Jack Jr., born in 1959, Lori, born in 1961, and Brad born in 1964. While in Vietnam, Grant was born in 1968. After returning to Fort Wayne in 1968, he started his practice in General Surgery. In 1969 he became a Diplomat of the American Board of Surgery and in 1971 a fellow of the American College of Surgeons. Their last child Joseph was born in 1973.

During his career in surgery he served on the Board of Directors of the Indiana College of Surgeons, Parkview Hospital, Allen County Board of Health and Physicians Health Plan (PHP) of Northern Indiana. He was also president of the medical staff of Parkview Hospital, PHP, and Pine Valley Country Club. In 1978 he was elected to the Indiana Basketball Hall of Fame as a member of the 25th Silver Anniversary All-State High School Team. He retired from surgery in 1998 as a founding member of the Indiana Surgical Specialists Group. Since then he has been a medical missionary to the Dominican Republic.

He is an active member of Praise Lutheran Church and enjoys golf, fishing, genealogy, growing dahlias and being with his family.

Jack and Lois still live in Pine Valley where they have been since 1970.

Submitted by Lois Gumbert

JOHN GUMBERT

John Gumbert was born in December 24, 1861, in Adams Township, the youngest son of August Gumbert and Margaretha (Meyer) Gumbert. His early life was marred by the death of his father (see history of August). His education was limited because he spent much of his early life helping run the family farm.

John Gumbert family in the early 1920s. Back L to R: Martha, Albert, Mary, Martin, Christina, Emelie. Front L to R: John, Susanne, Elizabeth

He married Elizabeth Peppler at St. Johannes Lutheran Church on November 21, 1886. He and his wife continued farming until 1914 when they moved into Fort Wayne where John became a laborer at the Concordia Lutheran Cemetery on Maumee Avenue. By this time they had seven children. Mary was the eldest, born in 1888, and had married William H. Peters in 1906. The rest of the children moved into the city with John and Elizabeth in 1914. By this time the family consisted of Christina, born in 1889, Al born in 1891, Emelie, born in 1893, Martha, born in 1900, Martin Fredrick, born in 1902, and Susanne, born in 1905. Another child Johannes, was born in 1895 but died shortly after birth. In 1920, John was named superintendent of Concordia Cemetery, a position he held until his death in 1942. His wife Elizabeth preceded him in death in 1933. Both are buried in the cemetery he faithfully served for almost 30 years.

At the time of John's death, all his children had married, and they in turn had children, with the exception of Susanne. His obituary states he had 38 grandchildren and 16 great grandchildren.

Submitted by Jack Gumbert, M.D.

FORREST RAY (PETE) GUMP

Forrest Ray (Pete) Gump was born on June 12, 1900. The son of George Calvin Gump and Icey Maudy Gump, he was born in the Gump farmhouse on Gump Road between Coldwater Road and Old Auburn Road. He was a lifetime farmer and a very good one. In those days a small farmer had to be good in order to make a good living.

In 1922 he married Vonnell (Peg) Heffelfinger. They had three boys and one girl. Two boys and the girl died when they were infants. One son, Marlow, survived and had five children and nine grandchildren. Pete enjoyed children and loved talking to and teasing them. Pete would have enjoyed his grandchildren if he had lived longer. He died at the age of 63. One of his grandsons was named Peter, and Peter named his son, George, in honor of his great-grandfather.

One of Pete's side jobs was driving a school bus, which he did for thirty some years. He enjoyed doing this and several years he drove the players' bus for the Huntertown basketball team.

When he had some spare time, he loved playing cards with some of his friends at the Huntertown Grain Elevator. In the winter he worked for Dick McComb and at lunchtime they enjoyed playing cards. Pete always said, "Someday Fort Wayne will meet Huntertown." I think we are there.

Pete would sure have been happy if he were here when the Forrest Gump movie came out. The best part was that it was a very good movie. When I'm asked my name and people ask are you related to Forrest Gump, I say, Yes, he's my dad! Of course no one believes me. I just tell them to drive out the Cedar Canyon Road to the cemetery and they can see his name on a tombstone.

He was an avid member of the Masonic Lodge. He enjoyed his short time on earth and everyone was his friend.

Submitted by Marlow Gump

RUDOLPH HENRY & CATHERINE (HOLLY) HAHN FAMILY

Rudolph was born June 28, 1906 in Fort Wayne. His father, Henry was born in the 1880s on John Street in Fort Wayne. Henry worked at the Bass Foundry and later at General Electric. In 1905 he married Rosa Hoffmann, who was born near Hessen Cassel in rural Allen County. In addition to Rudolph, they had three other children: Frank, Elizabeth (who married John Junk) and Clarence, who died in childhood.

Rudolph married Catherine Holly on June 28, 1930. Catherine was born January 9, 1906, in Asdee, County Kerry, Ireland. She came to Fort Wayne as a young woman and was given a place to live with her aunt and uncle, Margaret (Holly) and James D. DeVinney. The DeVinneys lived a block away from the Hahn family on John Street. This is how Rudolph and Catherine met. They purchased a home at 3226 Winter Street in Fort Wayne, where they lived for the remainder of their married life. Rudolph worked for City Utilities and retired from International Harvester. Catherine was a homemaker and worked at Lutheran Hospital before her marriage. Catherine died on October 28, 1979, and Rudolph on July 10, 1984.

Their children are Mary Catherine Hahn, Ann Eileen (Gerald) Mullins, Bertha Jane (Francis) Brohman, Anthony Wayne (Kathleen Dwyer) Hahn, Joseph Dominic (Jean Bruns) Hahn. and Virginia Marie Hahn.

Mary Catherine earned her B.S. Degree in Science and Mathematics from Saint Francis College (later named University of Saint Francis) in Fort Wayne, and her M.S. in Mathematics from Purdue University. She has retired from teaching after 31 years.

Rudolph and Catherine Hahn Family in 1970. L to R: Mary Catherine, Bertha (Beth), Anthony, Catherine, Rudolph, Joseph, Virginia, Ann Eileen

Ann Eileen earned her R.N. from St. Joseph's Hospital School of Nursing, Fort Wayne. She worked at St. Joseph's while she and her husband, Jerry, raised seven children: Theresa (David) Bradtmiller, Erin (Ignacio) Rivera, Nicholas (Janet Slater) Mullins, Johanna Mullins, Timothy (Mary McDonald) Mullins, Catherine (Bruce) Whitman, and Margaret (Marian) Barrigan.

Bertha "Beth" earned her R.N. from Saint Elizabeth's School of Nursing in Lafayette, Indiana, and returned to Fort Wayne to work at St. Joseph's Hospital. She and her husband, Francis "Vince" had six children: Patrick Brohman, Julia Brohman, Katrina Brohman, Suzanne (Pete) Kowalchuk, Stephen Brohman, and Michael Brohman. Due to a job change, the Brohman family moved to Colorado Springs, Colorado, in 1981.

Anthony Wayne received his B.A. degree from Indiana University and M.S. in Education from St. Francis College. He taught in Fort Wayne for the Fort Wayne Catholic Diocese and, after marrying and moving to Valparaiso, Indiana, in the Valparaiso Catholic School System. Later he went to work at Bethlehem Steel as a computer programmer. He and Kathleen are the parents of three children: Nathan Hahn, Noah Hahn, and Sarah Hahn.

Joseph studied computer science at Indiana-Purdue Fort Wayne and worked at Tokheim and then Magnavox, which eventually became Raytheon where he currently works. Joseph and Jean have two sons: Christopher (Melissa Wiegand) Hahn and Jason (Eileen Barnes) Hahn.

Virginia studied at Indiana, Purdue Fort Wayne. She worked at Hutner's Paris, Lincoln National Life Insurance, and Saint Hyacinth-Saint Andrew's parishes in Fort Wayne. She is currently engaged in home health care.

Rudolph and Catherine's family now includes 22 great-grandchildren and two great-great grandchildren.

Submitted by Mary Catherine Hahn

ADOLPH HALLER

Adolph Haller was born in Reinach, Switzerland, on May 21, 1865. According to the naturalization records of Allen County, he arrived in New York on January 28, 1883. He was 18 years old.

Prior to Adolph arriving in the United States, the records show that the following Hallers, also natives of Switzerland, arrived in the United States and settled in Fort Wayne. We believe they were all related as brothers or cousins. Samuel Haller arrived on March 1, 1869; Gottlieb on October 20, 1872; William on September 5, 1881; Adolph on January 28, 1883; and another Samuel on October 1, 1891.

Adolph came to Fort Wayne and went to work for Gottlieb Haller in a meat market at 366 Calhoun Street. He also worked for Weil Brothers and Company and resided at 34 Elm Street. On September 30, 1886, at the age of 21, he appeared in Allen Circuit Court and applied for naturalization. He then waited nineteen years before becoming a citizen, which was granted in Allen Circuit Court on October 11, 1905.

Mr. and Mrs. Adolph Haller

Adolph was married to Minna A. Wehnert on September 30, 1886, in St John's Reformed Church by Rev. C. Schaaf. They lived at 1224 Elm Street and became the parents of eight children: Elizabeth Wilhelmena, January 25, 1887; Bertha S., May 8, 1888; Carl Adolph, February 18, 1890; John F., February 16, 1892; Frieda Loretta, November 10, 1893; Walter Frederick, January 18, 1896; Frank William, November 28, 1897; and Arthur Adolph, May 17, 1907. Bertha died at six years of age from Brights disease and John at age two of scarlet fever. Except for Elizabeth and Carl, the other children made Fort Wayne their home.

In 1893 Adolph started working as a butcher for J. W. Suelzer. He worked for this company until 1898 when he opened his own meat market at 228 West Main. In 1904 he moved his market to 940 West Main, and in 1912 his son, Walter, joined him in the business and it remained open until 1943.

Adolph and Minna were members of Salem Evangelical & Reformed Church. They celebrated their 50th wedding anniversary on September 30, 1936. Adolph was treasurer of the Fort Wayne Maennerchor. On June 11, 1941, Adolph died of a heart attack. Minna died on July 11, 1942, after being hit by a taxi while crossing the street in the 1200 block of West Main Street. They are buried in Lindenwood Cemetery.

Submitted by Mary Jane Haller

RICHARD HAMILTON

Richard Lee Hamilton, a native of Fort Wayne, currently residing in Indianapolis, is the son of the late Frank Frederick Hamilton and rural New Haven native, the late Hilda Gay (Koehlinger) Hamilton. The subject resided in Fort Wayne as an adult, and spent part of his childhood years in New Haven before moving to rural Roanoke, where his parents operated the Hamilton Motel for many years.

Rich, as the subject is commonly known, is a descendant of the Brudi and Koehlinger families - two of Allen County s oldest German Lutheran pioneering families.

Heinrich Koehlinger's children

The roots of the Brudi family go back to Dettingen, Wuerttemberg where Daniel and Ursula Barbara (Durr) Brudi's son John George Brudi, was born on April 24, 1794. John George resided in Dettingen and was married twice. He had five children with his first wife, Ursula Barbara (Notz) Brudi. Two of those children, Maria Barbara (Mrs. Christian Buob) and John George immigrated to the USA. In 1826, a year after the death of his first wife, John George married Altdorf, Wuerttemberg native Anna Barbara Handle. John, George and Anna Barbara resided in Dettingen and, later, in Yebenhausen, Wuerttemburg. Nine children were born to the second union: Johannes, Joseph Karl, Gottlieb, Christian F., Joseph, Maria, Johanna, and Wilhelm. John George emigrated from Germany alone, crossing through America in 1845 in search of a new home for his family. In 1846 Anna Barbara and many of the Brudi's children immigrated to the USA. During their journey across the ocean the youngest child, Wilhelm, died. After settling in rural Jefferson Township in 1846 the Brudis became farmers.

In addition to their farming careers, John George's sons and sons-in-law were enterprising men, operating a flour mill and a shingle and tile business in New Haven, among other pursuits. Following in their footsteps, although now in semi-retirement, the subject, the great-grandson of John George Brudi's younger daughter, Johanna (Brudi) Koehlinger, often peruses the internet, using E-Bay auction sites to search for, and generate business.

Rich's Koehlinger ancestors trace their roots to Heinrich Koehlinger, a native of rural Blasbach, Prussia. Today, Blasbach is considered a northeastern suburb of the city of Wetzlar, in the Hessen region of Germany. Heinrich was a farmer and the father of nine children.

The subject, the great-great-grandson of Heinrich Koehlinger, is a descendant of Heinrich's son, John Henry Koehlinger. John Henry, a veteran of the Union army, was employed as a cooper in New Haven and a farmer in Adams Township. John Henry's 100 acre farm, now a part of the town of New Haven, extended north from Moeller Road, with 20 acres lying on the west side of Green Road, and 80 acres on the east side of Green Road, extending north to about Berwick Lane. The farm was passed down through the family to John Henry's son Fred C. Koehlinger, a founder and President of the old Peoples State Bank, and then to Fred's son Russell Koehlinger, who developed the land into housing.

Submitted by Tom Frohnapfel

GEORGE WASHINGTON & REBECCA ELIZABETH (CAINE) HAND

George W. Hand was born September 26, 1819 to Sarah Hand-Erickson in Greene County, Ohio. In 1838 at 17 years of age he came to Eel River Township with his mother Sarah, grandmother Phebe Hand, his uncle John Hand, and aunt Mary Polly Hand Vandolah. Rebecca's sister, Emaline, married James Tucker on November 27, 1837. They came to Eel River Township and lived close to the Hand farm. Rebecca Caine came to stay with Emaline and became acquainted with George W., thus leading to marriage. On February 3, 1842 George married Rebecca Elizabeth Caine. Rebecca was born June 24, 1824 in Green County, Ohio to Abner (February 13, 1797) and Betsy Caine (June 26, 1894).

During the pioneer days George was a successful trapper and deer hunter. He was strong in character and became prominent in business, social and political circles. He was a recognized Democratic leader presiding over many political gatherings. He served as Township Assessor, Chairman of the County Democratic Central Committee and Jury Commissioner. He was a candidate for Sheriff but was defeated by Isaac Campbell by one vote. He also was a carpenter and built several homes in

George Washington Hand

the Huntertown area including the large home and barn on the Hand Homestead. He was a member of the Huntertown Lodge of Masons. His funeral services were held at the Huntertown Methodist Church on Friday August 7, 1901 at 11:00 a.m.; the Rev. McCall officiated. He is buried in the old section of the Huntertown Cemetery.

George and Rebecca's children were: Josephus (February 3, 1843 to February 10, 1843) 7 days old; Lucetta (March 24, 1844 to 1909), married Robert Dolin, December 1878 married Henry Golden; William Erickson (December 28, 1845 to February 22, 1916), married Arminda Essex; Sara Elizabeth (May 6, 1848 to October 4, 1849) 1 1/2 years old; Mary Jane (July 27, 1850 to 1928), married Jefferson Sickler. George died in 1901, and Rebecca died in 1894.

Submitted by Carroll Hand

JESSE VALENTINE & MARY AMELIA (ROY) HAND

Jesse was born August 19, 1888 in Allen County, Indiana to William Erikson Hand and Arminda Mae (Essex) Hand. As a young man Jesse played sandlot baseball with the area team. He was a hard-working and successful farmer, first helping his father, William Erickson Hand, on the 320 acre homestead (which included the nine-room house and barn that was built by grandfather George W. Hand). Later Jesse bought his own farm in Huntington County.

Jesse V. and Mary A. (Roy) Hand with children Ruth, William and Kenny

In 1910 he married Mary Amelia Roy, daughter of Frank and Elizabeth Zimmerman Roy. Mary was born July 7, 1887 in Royville, Indiana, Allen County (corner of Coldwater road and Union Chapel Road). Her mother, Elizabeth, was of German birth and came to America as a teenager on one of her father's ships. Her money was stolen while on the ship so the ship's captain took her under his wing until she met up with her uncle in America.

Jesse and Mary moved to LaOtto, Indiana, after retiring from farming. In their retirement they enjoyed gardening which included various flowers, plants and 100 rosebushes. Mary died August 6, 1960 and Jesse died June 23, 1969. They are buried in the Huntertown Cemetery.

Jesse and Mary's children are: Helen died in infancy (December 10, 1910); William Joseph (October 21, 1911 to November 5, 1989), married Marie Warsler; Kenneth Earl (March 31, 1914 to January 22, 2003), married Lalia Kimmel; Ruth Irene (December 22, 1916 to October 16, 1998), married Russell Waters; Betty Mae (May 22, 1924 -), married James Britt.

Submitted by Bill Hand

WILLIAM HAND & PHEBE (JENNINGS) HAND

William and Phebe were born on the eastern seaboard, and they had ten children. William was born in 1760 in Essex County, New Jersey and died December 16, 1819 in Sugar Creek Township, Green County, Ohio. Phebe Jennings was born 1761 in New Jersey and died January 14, 1845 in Allen County. They married June 3, 1786 in Westfield, Essex County, New Jersey. The census of 1790 has them living in Elizabeth, New Jersey. Around 1816 they migrated to Green County, Ohio. There they lived in a double log house on a small farm in Sugarcreek Township. One evening Joseph Vandolah showed up at the door and asked to stay overnight. He was dressed in a buckskin hunting shirt, homespun pantaloons, coonskin cap and barefooted. He was carrying $200 in silver dollars in a stocking leg to purchase the quarter section of land opposite where the Hands lived. Daughter Mary "Polly" found Joseph to be attractive, and they became engaged on the spot. They married around 1805 and built a log cabin on the land that Joseph had purchased.

When William died in 1819, Phebe and some of the children continued to live on the farm. Their daughter Sarah, born November 25, 1799 in Frederick County, Maryland, gave birth to son, George Washington Hand on September 26, 1819. His father was a soldier but never married Sarah. On December 2, 1824 Sarah married William Erickson. In 1838, Phebe came to Eel River Township with her son, John, and daughter, Mary "Polly" with her son, James Vandolah (Joseph died in 1818 in Greene County, Ohio), and daughter, Sarah, with her son George Washington Hand. They had all bought ajoining land from the government. This land was in the Cedar Creek area, the DeKalb area and the Eel River Township area. James Vandolah built several water powered grist mills to grind flour, corn meal and other animal feeds. Phebe died January 14, 1845 in Allen County, Indiana, and is buried in the old section of the Huntertown Cemetery.

William and Phebe's children: Mary Polly (1788-about 1850), married Joseph Vandolah around 1805; Sarah (November 25, 1799-September 27, 1865), married William Erickson on December 2, 1824; James (1792- ?), married Ann ?; Benjamin (1790-August 1, 1841), married Sarah Sackett on April 10, 1816; Samuel (June 17, 1805-June 12, 1858), married Mary ? around 1830; John (1803-1837), married Sarah Jane Johnson on June 16, 1831; Phebe (1800-?), married Matthew Erickson on June 5, 1826; Betsy (1794- ?) in New Jersey; Martha (1796- ?) in New Jersey; Serepta (1807-?) in Ohio.

Submitted by Marsha Myers

WILLIAM ERICKSON, ARMINDA MAE (ESSEX) HAND (1845-1916), & ARMINDA MAE ESSEX (1859-1948)

William E. Hand was born in Allen County, Indiana on December 28, 1845 to George W. Hand, born September 26, 1819 in Greene County, Ohio, and Rebecca E. Cain, born June 24, 1824 in Greene County, Ohio. George and Rebecca married February 3, 1842 and moved to Eel River Township in Allen County, Indiana. William grew up working on the family farm. On February 14, 1882 he was married to Arminda Mae Essex in Allen County, Indiana.

Arminda was born January 30, 1859 in Henry County, Ohio to Sarah Eleanor Wagoner Rennecker and David Orlando Essex. Her mother, Sarah, born in Stark County, Ohio in 1825 to Peter Wagoner and Nancy Renick, was of German ancestry. Sarah married John Rennecker in 1843. They had four daughters, Mary Jane, Lydia, Ella and Isabelle. A son died in infancy. John Rennecker was struck by a falling tree while cutting timber and died a year later. Sarah later married David Orlando Essex and they had two children: Arminda Mae, born January 30, 1859 and Jesse Valentine, born in September of 1860. They moved to Adams County, Indiana, near Decatur and Monroe. David Essex enlisted in the Union Army, fought in the Civil War and was killed. About 1872 Sarah married Stephen Whicker and moved to Eel River Township, Allen County, Indiana to a farm on Carroll Road. Jesse V. Essex stayed in Adams County. Arminda attended the old Methodist College in Fort Wayne, Indiana, and obtained a teacher's license. She taught school in Eel River Township schools.

William Essex Hand family: L to R, standing, George, Jesse, Zelpha, Gladys Hand Rhinehold. Sitting, Sara Hand Sage, Alice Hand Agar, William, Father William Hand, Mother Arminda Essex Hand, Luella Hand Hursh

On February 14, 1882 Arminda and William Erickson Hand were married. They lived on the Hand Homestead that was built by George W. Hand and together George and William owned and farmed land in sections 24, 25, and 26 in Eel River Township. William died in 1916, and Arminda in 1948.

William and Arminda's children were: George Washington (December 11, 1882-January 12, 1964), married Ella Tessen; Luella Mae (May 11, 1884-October 23, 1978), married Walter Hursh; Jesse Valentine (August 19, 1888-June 23, 1969), married Mary Roy; Sarah Elizabeth (July 21, 1890-August 2, 1960), married Herbert Sage; Zelpha Marie (February 15, 1893-March 29, 1979); Gladys Viola (January 9, 1898- 1988), married Curtis Rinehold; William Essex (November 8, 1904- ?), married Geneva Danford;

Alice Lucille (July 30, 1902-September 5, 1981), married John Agger.

Submitted by Larry Hand

WILLIAM JOSEPH & ESTELLA MARIE (WARSLER) HAND

William Hand was born October 21, 1911 in Allen County, Indiana, to Jesse Valentine Hand and Mary Amelia (Roy) Hand. As a young child he was called Willie, and as he became older, he was known as Bill. While growing up, he enjoyed playing baseball, and he worked on the family farm.

William and Marie (Warsler) Hand

On January 3, 1935 he and E. Marie Warsler were wed. Marie was born July 10, 1918 in DeKalb County, Indiana, to Curtis Edward Warsler and Anna C. (Armstrong) Warsler. As a young girl, Marie sang duet in church with her sister, Juanita, and played piano. Bill farmed in Huntington County for 18 years with his father, Jesse Valentine Hand. In 1955 he purchased his own 200 acre farm on the corner of Carroll and Bethel Roads. He raised grain and livestock while working for the Dana Corp. in Churubusco. Marie was a homemaker who raised and canned her own fruits and vegetables, baked her own pies and breads, and sewed many of her children's clothes. She was organized and ran a tight ship with each child having their own specific duties. The home was always clean and tidy and the children well groomed when going to school or on outings.

Bill retired from Dana and farming in 1972. He and Marie moved to Ossian, Indiana, and lived there for ten years. Bill died November 5, 1989. Marie then moved back to Huntertown. She died Friday, June 11, 2004 at 5:45 p.m. They are buried in the Huntertown Cemetery.

William and Marie's children are: Carroll Lee (1935), married Shirley Jean Scott; Larry Edward (1937), married Joyce Louise Freeman; DeMarise Jean (1938), married Lynn Paul Martin; Barbara Kay (1940), married Larry Lee Deetz, deceased, married Ray Kissner; Billy Dale (1942), married Sandra Jean Grossman; Jesse Max (1945), married Jacqueline Sue Cartwright; Shirley Fay (1949), married James VanDewark; Marsha Sue (1951), married Richard Craig Myers.

Submitted by Barb Kissner

DON & CHARLOTTE HANLEY

Donald Wayne Hanley was born April 16, 1959 in Rensselaer, Indiana. Don's parents were Leon Clyde "Bud" Hanley and Linda Louise Hickman who were married on December 24, 1955. Bud died on October 9, 2000 and Linda died March 18, 2004. They are both buried in Fair Oaks Cemetery, Fair Oaks, Indiana. Don has a younger brother, Dale Alan Hanley who lives in Fort Wayne, Indiana. Dale has two children, Dale Alan, Jr., born February 8, 1990 and Austin Michael, born July 15, 1992.

Don married Charlotte June Macrae on December 21, 1985. He owns Hanley Builders Construction Company. Charlotte is a registered nurse. They have the following children: Andrea Sue born December 30, 1993, Jessica Ann born November 26, 1996, Eric Alan born November 17, 1997, died November 17, 1997, and Adam Scott born March 26, 2002.

Bud's parents were Clyde Alan Hanley, born September 24, 1908, and Luella S. Brocker, born June 25, 1915. They were married December 31, 1931. Clyde died October 20, 1981. Luella died September 6, 1989. Both are buried in the Fair Oaks Cemetery, Fair Oaks, Indiana.

Linda Hanley's parents were Herschel Hickman and Mildred Louise Kennedy. They were married April 18, 1935. Herschel was born February 18, 1908 and died April 16, 1992. He is buried in South Bend, Indiana. Mildred was born January 28, 1913. Mildred died early in life after having surgery on December 16, 1950. She is buried in Rensselaer, Indiana.

Charlotte June Macrae was born July 22, 1963 in Camden, Maine. Charlotte's parents are Donald Swan Macrae and Beverly Irene Shutt. Don and Beverly were married October 3, 1961 in Camden, Maine. Don was born August 11, 1920 in Providence, Rhode Island. He died November 24, 2000 and is buried in Covington Memorial Gardens in Fort Wayne, Indiana. Don served in the Army in World War II. Charlotte had a younger sister, Ruth Helene Macrae. She was born December 31, 1965. Ruth died December 31, 1965 and is buried at Duck Trap, Maine.

Don Macrae's parents were Alexander Macrae and Helen June McCormick. They were married October 1, 1919. Alexander was born in April 1879. He died January 21, 1924 and is buried in Swan Point Cemetery, Providence, Rhode Island. Alexander served in the Army in World War I. Helen was born June 8, 1888 in Providence, Rhode Island. She died June 16, 1960 and is buried in Duck Trap, Maine. Don Macrae was an only child.

Beverly Irene Macrae's parents were Edward Michael Shutt and Charlotte Alice Woodcock. They were married February 18, 1930. Edward was born on October 1, 1903 in Woodburn, Indiana. He died August 24, 1992. Charlotte Woodcock was born June 10, 1911 in Garrett, Indiana. She died April 25, 1992 in an auto accident in Garrett, Indiana. Both are buried in Cedar Creek Cemetery, DeKalb County, Indiana.

Submitted by Don Hanley.

THOMAS H. & MARY AGNES (ANDORFER) HARBER

Thomas H. Harber, the son of Jacob Harber and Elenora Minnich, was born November 17, 1898. He married Mary Agnes Andorfer on June 26, 1923 at St. Aloysius Church near Yoder(formerly Sheldon) Indiana. She was born March 12, 1900 to Jacob Andorfer and Rosa Lehmiller. They lived their entire lives in Pleasant Township, Allen County, Indiana and attended St. Aloysius grade school. Thomas grew up on the Harber Homestead on the west side of Bluffton Road, halfway between the Hamilton and Pleasant Center Roads. In his adult life, he farmed the 192 acre homestead. They had twelve children: Jacob, Alberta (Giese), Kenneth, Earl (Fr. Earl), Richard,Norbert, Jeanette (Garey), Carl, Dale, Juanita (Mattes), Rita and Mary (Bruskotter). Thomas died March 18, 1973: Mary Agnes died March 17, 1978.

The Harber farm on Bluffton Road has been in the family for 148 years and it was recently granted the Hoosier Homestead Award, for being in the same family for over 100 years. It is still owned by several children of Thomas and Mary Agnes Harber. The home was originally a two-story log house, now covered over with modern siding. It was likely one of the earliest houses in Pleasant Township and is still occupied by a family member. One of the lower rooms was used for Catholic services for a period of time.

The first Harbers to come to America were Thomas' great grandparents, Johann Heinrich Herber (German spelling) and his wife, Anna Maria Krack, and their five children: Martin, Martha, Nicholas, Johann, and Gerhardt. On May 8, 1834, they began their voyage from Bremen, Germany aboard the ship, Brig Favourite, and arrived in New York on June 18,1834.

They came to Allen County, Indiana, along with Johann Heinrich's brother, Johann Gerhardt Herber, and purchased land in July 1834 to clear for farming. Johann Heinrich Herber (also known as Henry Harber)was born in Germany on February 25,1790 and died May 31,1867. Anna Maria was born in Germany on December 8, 1796 and died October 3, 1877. They were married circa 1818 and are buried in St. Aloysius Church Cemetery.

Thomas H. and Mary Agnes (Andorfer) Harber, July 2, 1966

Thomas Harber's grandfather, Johann Herber/John Harber was born in Germany on September 25, 1827. On September 3, 1861 he married Maria (Mayer) Krouse, the mother of Harmon and Cosmas Krouse. Maria was born July 22, 1828.They had four children: Jacob, Casper, Adam and Daniel. Johann died October 31, 1879 and Maria died February 23, 1897.

Jacob Harber, Thomas Harber's father, was born in Allen County, Indiana on June 20, 1862 and lived his entire life in Pleasant Township. On February 3, 1891, he married Elenora Minnich. Elenora was born in Hoagland, Indiana on May

29,1871. At one time, Jacob owned and operated the grain elevator in Yoder, Indiana.

They had nine children: Veronica (Freiburger), Ferdinand, Clarence, Andrew, Thomas, Mary (Landstoffer), Myrtle(Sr. Celeste), and twins, Aloysius and Mildred. Ferdinand and Andrew died in childhood. Jacob died September 19, 1923 and Elenora died May 1, 1932. They are buried in St. Aloysius Cemetery.

Submitted by Richard and Marian Harber

FLOYD RUFUS HARDY FAMILY

Floyd Hardy was born on December 23, 1918 in Watauga County North Carolina. He was the son of Hubert Hardy and Daisey (Brown) Hardy. He grew up in Boone, North Carolina where he attended school. His mother was a matron at Applachian State Teachers College.

He married Josie Ethel Stanbery, daughter of Arthur O. Stanbery and Bertie (Coffey) Stanbery on May 9, 1936 at Mountain City, Tennessee. Floyd worked at Applachian State Teachers College in Boone, North Carolina. Floyd and Josie both worked at W.P.A. in Boone in 1939-1941. They moved to Elizabethton, Tennessee in 1942 and Floyd worked at a factory in Kingsport, Tennessee doing war work. The family moved to St. Petersburg, Florida in 1943, and there he helped build the Tampa airport. Then in May of 1944 he was called into the army. He was inducted on June 19, 1944 in Boone, N.C. He was a cannoneer, served as assistant tank driver and bow gunner. He served with the 7th and 3rd Armies in combat and saw action in France, Germany and Holland. He was discharged in November 1945. After his discharge from the army he worked for the Tennessee Valley Authority in 1947-1950. After working for Tennessee Valley Authority he came to Fort Wayne, Indiana in January of 1951 because of job opportunities. He worked at General Electric six years and then Zollner Pistons for twenty-four years until his retirement in December of 1980. Floyd died July 7, 1995 and is buried in I.O.O.F. cemetery in New Haven, Indiana. Josie worked for General Electric five years and Montgomery Ward nine years. Floyd and Josie had three daughters, Joy Bernice, Carolyn Louise and Frances Lynne.

Joy Bernice:

Joy was born January 7, 1938 in Boone, North Carolina. She attended Happy Valley School in Elizabethton, Tennessee. The family moved to Fort Wayne, Indiana where she attended Harmar grade school and graduated from Central High School in 1956. She also attended International Business College. Joy married Robert Ames, son of Theodore and Mable Ames of Ohio City, Ohio on September 7, 1957. They had two sons and a daughter: Kevin Lynn born October 9, 1958. Timothy Scott born July 7, 1960, and Tammy Jo born August 21, 1963.

Kevin attended East Allen County schools and graduated from New Haven High School in 1978 and attended Ivy Tech. He graduated from Wesley College with a Bachelor of Business degree. He married Sue Ann Bonney on December 30, 1978 in Fort Wayne, Indiana. They have a son and two daughters: Heather Bonney born November 24, 1982, Jeremy Matthew born June 7, 1984, and Sarah Elizabeth born January 13, 1990. All were born in Fort Wayne, Indiana. Kevin moved to Indianapolis, Indiana where he now resides.

Timothy attended East Allen County Schools and graduated from New Haven High School in 1979. Tim married Eileen Harrington on May 10,1985 in Fort Wayne, Indiana. They were divorced in December 2002. They had four sons. Tim resides in New Haven, Indiana. Chad Donald Harrington was born December 17, 1982. Tim adopted Chad in 1985. Theodore Robert born October 28, 1985. Joshua Scott born November 7, 1986. Michael Joseph born December 29, 1995. Tim and Eileen adopted Michael. He was her great nephew. They were all born in Fort Wayne, Indiana.

Tammy attended East Allen County Schools and graduated from New Haven High School in 1982. She went to Ivy Tech and graduated in 1987 with a bachelor of Science degree. She married Mark Andrew Downing April 13, 1985 in Harlan, Indiana. She lives in Grabill, Indiana now. She has twins, a daughter and a son: Erin Elizabeth and Miles Andrew born August 24, 1989.

L-R: Carolyn Pletcher, David Pletcher, Josie and Floyd Hardy, Jo Ames and Robert Ames, Lynn and Wm. Doctor

Carolyn Louise:

Carolyn was born on August 2, 1939 in Boone, North Carolina. Carolyn attended Happy Valley School in Elizabethton, Tennessee and when her family moved to Indiana she attended Harmar Grade School and Central High School graduating in 1957. Carolyn married David Leroy Pletcher on August 10, 1957. He was the son of Walter Jacob and Florence (Fink) Pletcher of Syrcuse, Indiana. They had four children: Donald Leroy born December 29, 1959 at Fort Rucker, Alabama, Robin Annette born January 6, 1962 in South Bend, Indiana, Vicki Kay born April 22, 1964 in Dayton, Ohio, and Rhonda Lynn born March 12. 1971 in Wabash, Indiana.

Donald attended Fort Wayne Community schools and Elmhurst High School. He married Darleen (Dovey), (Luley) on April 27, 1984. They had one daughter, Jamie Lee born May 9, 1982. He also had two stepchildren, Jennifer Luley and Jason Luley. He has lived in the Syracuse Indiana area most of his adult life and works at Marque, Inc., builders of medical vans.

Robin attended Fort Wayne Community schools and graduated from Elmhurst High School in 1980. She married Timothy Robert Foote, son of Robert and Suzanne Foote on June 19, 1982. They had two sons: Spencer David born May 7, 1994, and Timothy Logan born April 19, 1999. Robin was employed at Parkview Hospital until she became a full-time mom. She now home-schools her two boys.

Vicki attended Fort Wayne Community Schools and graduated from Elmhurst High School in 1982. She married Jeffery David Saine on June 11, 1983. He is the son of Phillip Gene and Marilyn (Krick) Saine. Jeff and Vicki have two children, a son and a daughter: Benjamin David born October 3, 1985, and Rachel Joy born July 27, 1989. In 1998 Vicki and her family moved to Maple Grove, Minnesota. Vicki is an avid cake decorator and is assistant head cook at Rice Lake Elementary school in Maple Grove.

Rhonda attended Fort Wayne Community Schools and graduated from Elmhurst High School in 1990. She was a foster daughter of David and Carolyn until she was three years old when they adopted her. Her biological name was Reahard. Her mother's name was Marsha Reahard and her father was Timothy Michael Owens whom she never met. She married Scott Brian Ellenberger on May 17, 1991. He is the son of Glenn and Cindy (Geradot) Ellenberger. They had three children, two sons and a daughter: Austin Michael born September 4, 1990. Dalton Brian born January 30, 1992, and Halie Nicole born September 30, 1993. Rhonda died on May 31, 2000 while awaiting a liver transplant. She is buried in Prairie Grove Cemetery in Waynedale, Indiana.

Frances Lynn:

Frances Lynne was born on June 28, 1947 in Elizabethton, Tennessee at the Franklin Clinic. She was the first baby born in the new hospital. Lynne was three years old when the family moved to Fort Wayne. She attended Fort Wayne Community Schools and graduated from Leo High School in 1965. She married Joe Brecount in May 1965 and had two sons: Joel Alan born August 1, 1966, and Steven Floyd born August 16, 1970. The marriage to Joe ended in 1976 and on December 31,1980 she married William Doctor, son of William and Lillian Doctor. They had one daughter, Megan Leigh born May 10, 1982. Lynne has worked in various business organizations all her life.

Joel attended Fort Wayne Community Schools and graduated from Northside High School in 1984. He enlisted in the Air National Guard after high school. He graduated from Concordia College in Fort Wayne, Indiana in 1996. He is currently employed by Temper Tru. He married Tia Marie Kramer in November 1990. They have two children, a son and a daughter: Lesiene Marie born May 14, 1991, and Hogan born April 13, 1995.

Steven attended Fort Wayne Community Schools and graduated from Northside High School in 1988. He went into the Navy. After he came home he trained to become an ironworker. He married Briann Borders on October 28, 2001. They have two sons and a daughter: Savanah Marie (Till) born September 3, 1993, Chance Bailey born August 23, 1996, and Corbin Forge born March 23, 2001.

Megan attended Fort Wayne Community Schools and graduated from Northside High School in 2000 and graduated from Ball State University in 2004 with a degree in Exercise Science and Wellness specializing in fitness for older adults.

Submitted by Carolyn Pletcher

BETTY JACOBY HARRIS

This biography is about how a young girl from a small town in Missouri got to a city like Fort Wayne, Indiana.

Her grandparents years ago moved from Indiana and Ohio to a small town in Missouri called Holden. Abraham Lincoln Nowell was a farmer with eight children, one of whom was Betty's mother (Elsie) born in 1902. William Jacoby was a railroader with three boys, one of whom was her father (Rolla), born in 1890. Rolla and Elsie married when Rolla returned from WWI, after serving in France. He got a job as railroad foreman for Missouri Pacific. They moved to Centerview, Missouri, where they started a family, first a girl born in 1922, named Marguerite, and two years later in 1924, a girl named Betty.

The mother, Elsie, died in 1933 leaving the two little girls, eight and ten years old. Rolla became mother and father, but Marguerite, being the oldest, took on Betty as her responsibility. Both graduated from high school at Centerview, Missouri. Marguerite went on to college at Warrensburg, Missouri.

Rolla transferred his job to another small town, Smithton, Missouri. Betty got a job at Smithton Creamery. Marguerite left college during WWII and started working at Sedalia, Missouri, Army Air Base packing parachutes.

In the spring of 1943 Baer Field in Fort Wayne, Indiana, put a call to air fields for experienced parachute packers. Marguerite Jacoby and four friends volunteered to come to Fort Wayne. Betty wanted to come along, so it was settled; they would leave in July of that year.

As it turned out, the four friends left without the sisters because, on the day they were to leave, their father, Rolla Jacoby (railroader) was killed by a train at work. Two weeks later the sisters arrived in Fort Wayne, a big city to them.

Marguerite and friends started at Baer Field packing parachutes, and Betty started at Baer Field shipping and receiving. Betty was alone a lot because they were on nights and she on days. The sisters had an apartment on Creighton, and their friends had rented a house.

Four of the group married Ohio boys; two of them were soldiers from Baer Field.

Marguerite's soldier was Fred Fishbaugh. They were married at Baer Field Chapel in 1945 and made their home in Fort Wayne. Fred drove trucks for Borgman Trucking for several years and raised their family of two boys, both graduating from North Side High School. David and Larry were both in the service during Vietnam. Larry died in 1983 leaving two children, Megan and Ryan. Ryan still lives in Allen County.

Betty met and married Ohio man Carroll Harris from Antwerp, Ohio after he had already served in WWII. He had been in the Pacific and was out on medical discharge. They also met at Baer Field where he went to work after the Army. They were married in Third Presbyterian Church on Harrison Street in Fort Wayne, which later burned down. They bought a home on Sprunger Avenue in 1944 and started a family. Their first born was Jerry A. Harris in 1945, then daughter Mary Ann in 1948. Both were born in the Old Methodist Hospital which is no longer there. The family moved from Sprunger in 1954 to New Haven, Indiana and started a business, Custom Carpet Service. Another son, Rolla L. Harris was born in 1962 in the new Parkview hospital. Jerry and Mary Ann graduated from New Haven High School.

Carroll and Betty kept the business for twenty years before selling and moving to Blue Lake at Churubusco, Indiana, where Rolla graduated. It is where Betty still lives after losing Carroll in 2000, and her sister, Marguerite, in January of same year. Son Jerry owns a business in Fort Wayne called *"Waves"* and still lives in the area. Mary Ann died of leukemia in 1983 leaving two sons who now live in Michigan. Rolla works for a large building company and still lives close.

They never regretted leaving Missouri for Fort Wayne, a great place, and it has been good for the two sisters from Missouri.

Submitted by Betty Jacoby Harris

CHARLES WILLIAM HARRIS

On May 18, 1930 Charles William Harris was born in Bloomington, Indiana and lived close to Bean Blossom Creek in the tiny village of Dolan, northeast of Bloomington. His early school years were full of changes as the family moved from town to town as Raymond Harris pursued his civil engineering career. His mother, Lucile Harris, guided sons, Richard, Charles and Willard to handle new schools and new surroundings. The family settled in the 1940s at Eagle Lake, near Edwardsburg, Michigan. His father, Raymond Harris commuted to his job in Chicago spending weekends with his family. In 1940 Douglas was born, completing the family of four boys

Charles Harris family, August 1969, Pittsburgh, Pennsylvania

In Chicago, on January 1, 1933, Bette (birth name Betty) Marie Larson was born into the family of Carl Werner and Walborg (known as Valborg) Marie (Gentzell) Larson. She was welcomed by older brothers, Carl Edwin and Robert Alvin. The first eleven years of Bette's life were spent in the pleasant town of Oak Lawn (a suburb of Chicago) enjoying the safe and secure environment of that community. In August of 1944 the Larson family moved to a 50 acre farm on the outskirts of Edwardsburg, Michigan. Bette remembers the first days at the Edwardsburg Consolidated School. It was there that she first laid eyes on Chuck Harris! They were married nine years later - August 29, 1953 in South Bend, Indiana at Gloria Dei Lutheran Church.

Prior to their marriage, Chuck served four years in the U.S. Navy, serving as flight photographer on the carrier U.S.S. Saigon. Chuck and Bette Harris began their married life in Ann Arbor, Michigan where Chuck was attending the University of Michigan in the School of Architecture and Design. He was aided by the G.I. Bill, Bette's job at Argus Cameras and his part-time job in the X-Ray Department of the University Hospital. Their two children were born in Ann Arbor: Cynthia Beth Harris on November 3, 1954 and Gregory Stephen Harris on June 17, 1956.

Chuck graduated from the University of Michigan in January of 1956 (going to summer school to complete early) and received a Fine Arts Degree with a Major in Industrial Design and a Minor in Ceramics and Political Science. His first job was with Chrysler Corporation as a Stylist. They bought their first house in September of 1956 in a new community, Herrinton Hills, on the east side of Pontiac, Michigan. In 1963 the family moved to Pittsburgh, Pennsylvania. Chuck was an Account Executive with Gardner Displays, working with major corporations developing their companies' exhibits for trade shows. A major account at this time was National Cash Register's "House of Good Taste" at the New York World Fair. He left Gardner Displays for a marketing position with U. S. Steel. This was an exciting time designing and developing new steel products, including developing designs for furnishings at the Contemporary Resort at the new Disney World in Florida.

In August of 1969, Chuck began his career at International Harvester in Fort Wayne. Chuck and Bette were delighted to return to the Midwest and especially to Fort Wayne. Chuck loved his position as Assistant Design Manager and then as Design Manager. He also was happy to pursue his lifelong interest in aviation by learning to fly a sailplane. His father, Raymond Harris, built a glider in the early 20s in Dolan, Indiana. Chuck eventually built his own glider, and that plane can be seen at the EAA (Experimental Aviation Association) Museum in Oshkosh, Wisconsin.

His interest in his profession and his avocation were evident in his involvement in both the IDSA (Industrial Design Society of America) and SSA (Soaring Society of America). Favorite weekends were spent with friends of the Bryan Soaring Club - at both Bryan and Montpelier, Ohio. Soaring competition, even when not completing the task (landing out) was a good experience, especially when his "crew" would arrive in his beloved International Harvester Scout to rescue him from a farm field.

Chuck Harris was to know only two of his four grandchildren. Christopher, born January 19, 1987 and whom he adored, gave Chuck two and a half years of love. Anna Lynn, born on May 7, 1989 was held in his arms when she was two months and again at five months. It was Anna Lynn who woke the family with cries of hunger and alerted all of Chuck's family to the final moments of his life. Cynthia Beth Harris married Timothy Patrick O'Brien; their children are Christopher Lars Harris O'Brien, January 19, 1987; and Elizabeth Harris O'Brien, September 20, 1992. Gregory Stephen Harris married Judith Lynn Huett; their children are Anna Lynn Huett Harris, May 7, 1989; and Jakob William Harris, April 8, 1992.

Charles William Harris - A man of keen intellect, artistic talents, athletic ability and a great sense of humor. He had an intense interest in aviaton, in history, in politics, in travel and in people. He affected all who knew him in a most positive way. A truly remarkable man!

Submitted by Bette Harris

JOHN V. HARRIS FAMILY

John V. Harris was born on October 22, 1824 in Shropshire, England, to John and Elizabeth Harris. John and Elizabeth moved to Carryall Township (Antwerp), Ohio, in 1830. John V. married Mary Wilkins on August 30, 1844. Their son James was born on December 20, 1850.

John V. was a Civil War veteran who was killed on September 16, 1864.

James married Esther Collins on December 31, 1873. Their son Fordyce W. Harris was born on November 5, 1891 in Antwerp, Ohio. James died on January 18,1923, and is buried in Antwerp.

Fordyce married Gladys Eager on December 10, 1910. They moved to Allen County where Fordyce served as Deputy Sheriff for many years. Much of their lives were spent in Harlan, Indiana, as well as South Harrison Street in Fort Wayne. Their son Richard R. Harris (Bus) was born on July 11, 1916. Fordyce passed away in 1976 and is buried in North Scipio Cemetery east of Harlan on SR 37.

Richard (Bus) married his high school sweetheart Gayle Spindler on March 14, 1937. They were life long residents of Harlan, Indiana. Their son Richard R. Harris, Jr. (Dick) born on October 4, 1939. Bus died on March 27, 1997, and is buried in Harlan.

Fordyce, Richard Sr., Richard Jr., Richard III taken in Franke Park, July 1967

Richard (Dick) married Eunice Kay Bachman of Hopedale, Illinois, on September 26, 1964. They gave birth to Richard R. Harris, III, (Rick) on August 31, 1965. He married Robin Rae Boyd of Danville, Indiana, on August 30, 1986. They gave birth to Richard R. Harris, IV, (Ross) on November 1, 1989.

At the time of this publishing, Rick and Robin lived in Leo, Indiana. Their son Ross was a freshman at Leo High School.

Rick owns Harris Water Conditioning in Grabill, IN.

By Rick Harris
Ancestor information provided by Donald D. Harris

ALBERT & CHLOE HARRISON

In 2004 a new housing development was initiated on what had been a family farm in Aboite Township. The addition covers 70 acres of an 80.33 acre farm that last belonged to sisters, Joan Crowell and Nancy deAngelis-Kraft. The addition is called "Harrison Fields".

Albert and Chloe (Robinette) Harrison on the porch in front of their home, 1932. Current address is 1319W County Line S.

In 1837 John E. Hill and his wife, Eliza Jane, obtained this land as part of a 120.66 acre land grant provided by an 1820 Act of Congress, an Act making further provision for the sale of Public Lands. President Martin Van Buren endorsed the Hills' right to the property in a document dated August 1, 1837, and signed by him. In 1848, Mr. Hill sold 80.33 acres of his holdings to John Harper and his wife, Eliza, for the sum of $400.00.

Forty-one years later, in 1889, Albert D. Harrison and his wife, Chloe, purchased the 80.33 acre farm for $3,300.00. Here, Albert and Chloe remained for the remainder of their lives, raising five sons and one daughter: Charles, the oldest, then William Roy, Lyda, Howard Dale, Benjamin and Raymond (Tom).

In 1939 Benjamin and his wife, Helen, purchased the farm from the other heirs. It was their home until 1990 when it became the property of their two daughters.

Submitted by Joan Crowell

HARROD FAMILY

The Harrod family has had a distinguished history in Allen County for 150 years. Levi Harrod, a Revolutionary soldier, was born in Greene County, Pennsylvania on January 22, 1750 and settled in Knox County, Ohio, where he died on October 2, 1825. Among the children he had with his wife Rachel Mills was William Harrod, born in Greene County on August 13, 1785 and died on September 17, 1863 in Knox County. William married Rhoda Pipes, daughter of Joseph Pipes. She was born on June 23, 1790 and died May 27, 1876 in Knox County, Ohio.

Among their children was Morgan Harrod, who was born on July 25, 1826 in Knox County. In 1844, he moved to Allen County, Indiana, where he married Belinda Beam on March 5, 1852. The daughter of Cornelius and Elizabeth (Martin) Beam, she was born on November 16, 1832 in Knox County. They had the following children: Theron Royal, born October 3, 1852; Marion, born November 4, 1855; Charity, born September 6, 1857; Clay, born January 11, 1859; Mills, born September 15, 1860; John, born January 4, 1863; Sherman, born April 30, 1864; Morse, born April 4, 1866; Clark, born November 10, 1867; Delila E., born March 21, 1869, and Dessie, born September 2, 1875. Morgan Harrod was an assessor and later trustee of Marion Township, a Methodist, and a successful businessman. He died on August 24, 1908. Belinda died on December 29, 1916 in Fort Wayne.

Dr. Morse Harrod was one of Fort Wayne's leading citizens in the early 20th century. A general practitioner, he was on the staff of St. Joseph Hospital and served a few years as coroner. He married Jennie Lipes, and they had three children, Camilla, Wayne Allen, and June. In 1905, Morse built a large brick house at the corner of Washington and Hanna streets. His office was in the house with a separate entry. His hobby was remodeling the house, partly because some of his patients paid in trade. He tried every new heating system. With property extending to the alley, he added rental units – a double-house on Hanna and an apartment over the two-car garage. He remodeled his home to include a second floor apartment and another in the basement. Jennie died from injuries received in an interurban accident. Later, Morse married Bertha Ludwig, who had been a telephone operator. Morse died on May 15, 1941.

Rhoda Pipes Harrod

Morgan Harrod

Camilla married Sidney Karn. They had two daughters, Jean and Alice. Sid and his uncle were partners in a meat market in Chicago. Returning to Fort Wayne, Sid managed the meat department at the Grand Leader. After he died, Camilla had a News-Sentinel rural delivery route. Later she was a saleswoman at Wolf & Dessauer and the Boston Store. Jean married Ray E. Sanderson and helped him start O'Brien & Sanderson Insurance with partner Bob O'Brien. They had two sons, Ray Morse "Morrie," who became a partner in the insurance company, and Jack, now an arson investigator. Alice married Paul Merkert Jr., a Purdue engineer who sold Diesel engines for heavy equipment. He had a large Midwest territory for General Motors, and they lived in Detroit, then in Milwaukee. They had one son, Paul Thomas.

Morse Harrod

June Harrod Archibald

Sid and Camilla Karn

Wayne Harrod went to Colorado School of Mines and Metallurgy. He was in the army in France during World War I and a civil engineer building ships in California during World War II. He married Anna Loughlin, They lived in the Los Angeles area, where he was a civil engineer on many civic buildings. They had one son, Wayne Allen Jr., an accountant.

June lived two years with Jennie's sister, Lydia DeVilbiss, while studying to be a kindergarten teacher. She taught in Fort Wayne for several years. She married Robert Kenneth Archibald, son of long-time family friends and neighbors, A. F. and Edith Bowen Archibald. He had worked on the Panama Canal. After a few months in the Army during World War II, he was a distributor for Wayne Pump Co. in New York City and Albany.

Susan Stone

June and Kenny married in 1929 and had one daughter, Susan, She was a sales correspondent for S. F. Bowser Co., then for General Electric. She was a substitute teacher for a few years and a part-time driver for her father when he made house calls. She continued her father's work with First Baptist Church; she was superintendent of the Junior Department of Sunday school for sixteen years.

Susan graduated from Franklin College, taught briefly, including one year at Escola Americana de Campinas in Brazil, then did social work. She married Jack Stone and had one daughter, Amy June. She spent many years as a feature writer and food editor of the News-Sentinel. She continued her mother's work at First Baptist in the choir and on the Mission Board.

Amy married John Beatty, a genealogy librarian. They have two children, Robert and Julia. Amy is a part-time antique dealer.

Submitted by Susan Stone

HARTER

The Harter family history in Springfield Township began with William H. Harter (1833-1916), a fourth generation descendent of Andreas Harter who immigrated from Wuerttemberg, Germany to Lancaster County, Pennsylvania in 1750. William was born on a farm in Stark County, Ohio, and at the age of 21 took up the machinist's trade with Cooper, Bass, & Company in Fort Wayne. There he met Lorinda Hall, who was the only daughter of Isaac and Margarett Hall. Isaac had settled in the unbroken wilderness of Indiana (20 miles northeast of Fort Wayne) in 1836, on a quarter section of land purchased through a federal land grant signed by President Martin Van Buren. Isaac had established a post office at his residence, and the location at the corner of State Road 37 and Scipio Road became known as "Hall's Corners."

William and Lorinda Harter were married on August 11, 1859, in her parent's home at Hall's Corners. In 1870, they acquired the old Hall homestead where William eventually built the largest and best bank barn in Allen County. He often said that he could drive a team and wagon in one door, turn around in the barn without stopping, and drive out the same doorway. The barn had 93 windows, and was a landmark in northeast Indiana until torn down in 1982. William was first elected trustee of Springfield Township in the year 1866, serving a total of 13 years. He was also president of the Hicksville, Ohio Fair Association for many years. William and Lorinda had five children between 1861 and 1871, including Theodore Arthur Liston Harter, who became the next owner of the original Hall homestead.

Arthur Harter (1862-1929) was a farmer and lived his entire life on the farm at Hall's Corners, first with his parents and then after his marriage with his wife, Ella Shutt Harter. Arthur and Ella had two children, Estella Gertrude Harter and George William (Bill) Harter, who became the next owner of the original Hall homestead.

Like his father, Bill Harter (1893-1981) also was a farmer and lived his entire life on what was now known as the Harter Farm. Bill served in the navy during World War I and later attended Indiana University. In addition to farming, he taught for 42 years in the Springfield Township elementary schools. At the age of 32, Bill met and married Ella Sabina Wood, an elementary school teacher from Cleveland, Ohio. Bill and Ella had four children, George Arthur, Nellie Elizabeth, William Wood (Bill) and Stella May. All four children graduated from Harlan High School and all later graduated with degrees from Purdue University. Two of the children found local spouses; George marrying Helen Eager, a close neighbor and high school sweetheart; Nellie marrying Kenneth Bandelier from New Haven. After college, three of the children settled in the Los Angeles area of California, Nellie and her family moving to Dillon, Montana.

William and Lorinda Harter Circa 1890

Every generation of the Hall/Harter family attended the North Scipio Methodist Church, located at State Road 37, a short distance east of the farm. The adjoining Scipio Cemetery contains burial stones for five generations.

Submitted by George A. Harter

JACOB & ANNIE (ANKENBRUCK) HARTMAN FAMILY

Jacob Hartman (1862-1938), was born in Fort Wayne, the son of Joseph Hartman (1838-1899) and Caroline (Hoffman) Hartman (died 1915). Jacob owned a grocery store on Harmer Street, and later founded the Hartman Insurance Agency, a brokerage for life, property and casualty insurance. He was active in local Democratic politics with Mayor William Hosey, and served two terms on the Fort Wayne City Council – 1906-1910 and 1930-1935.

Annie (Ankenbruck) and Jacob Hartman

Jacob married Annie Ankenbruck on October 18, 1883. Annie (1862-1941) was the daughter of Bernard Ankenbruck and Katherine (Timmi) Ankenbruck. Jacob and Annie had eight surviving children: Augusta (born 1885), married Joseph Hake; Andrew (born 1888), married Edith Auer; Jack (born 1890), who designed the lighted "GE" sign visible in downtown Fort Wayne; Marie Ann (born 1895), married to Henry G. Allgeier, Jr.; Elsie (born 1899), married to George Queen; Leo (born 1906), married to Connie Morgan; William (born 1907), married to Agnes Getz; and Irma (born 1908), a musician and businesswoman. Upon Jacob's death, Irma Hartman took over her father's insurance agency, becoming the first female insurance agent in Fort Wayne. She taught at the European School of Music and played first violin in the Fort Wayne Philharmonic in the 1930s and 1940s under the baton of Gaston Bailey, Hans Schwieger and Igor Buketoff.

Submitted by Janet and Bill Piercy

JOHN D. & SHARON L. (KLOPFENSTEIN) HARTMAN FAMILY

John David Hartman, son of John R. and Mildred (Reynolds) Hartman, was born May 13, 1936 in Fort Wayne, Indiana. He graduated from North Side High School in 1955 and from Ranken Technical Institute in St. Louis, Missouri. He joined the U.S. Marine Corps in 1958 and took his basic training at Parris Island, South Carolina. In September 1960, he was married to Sharon Louise Klopfenstein in St. Luke's Lutheran Church. To this union was born Kimberly Marie, December 9, 1961; Debra Lynn, May 22, 1963; Timothy Thaine, September 30, 1967; John David, Jr., September 25, 1968; and Tara Leigh, July 5, 1981. John D. joined his family's plumbing business, North Side Plumbing & Heating Co., Inc. in 1958 and successfully operated the business until his semi-retirement in 2005 at which time his son, John Jr. succeeded him. The Hartman family, including grandparents and great-grandparents, have been long time members of Trinity United Methodist Church, Fort Wayne. John D.'s paternal great-great-grandparents, Valentine and Apollonia (Zink) immigrated from Hesse, Germany to Fort Wayne in 1853. They had eight children, including John Henry Hartman who married Frances I. Thurkettle. Thus began the succession of John Russel Hartman, John David Hartman, and John David Hartman, Jr. Other paternal family names include Biggam and Van Husen.

John D.'s maternal family names include Jesse Brown and Susanna Roudebush, Albert and Louis Reynolds, Miller, Bottenberg, Studebaker, Townsend, and VanHorn. These families were from the Monroeville/New Haven area. D. W. Miller donated the land for the I.O.O.F. cemetery in New Haven. John D.'s great-great-grandmother, Jane Driver Reynolds, was the first white female child to be born in a cave within the borders of Fort Wayne in 1812. Runners had met the family to announce that there were Indian attacks and they should wait until proceeding to the Fort.

Sharon Klopfenstein Hartman, daughter of Kenneth and Ilo (Akey) Klopfenstein was born May 29, 1941, in Fort Wayne. She is a graduate of South Side High School. Her paternal great-great-grandparents, Michael and Lydia (Sauder) Klopfenstein, emigrated to Ohio and Indiana from Belfort, France in 1840 and settled in the Leo/Grabill area. Her great-grandparents were David and Magdelana (Lantz) Klopfenstein, and grandparents were Howard and Anna (Prange) Klopfenstein. Other family names include Amstutz, Shrock, Rupp, and Riemenschneider.

John and Sharon Hartman family

Sharon's maternal family lines included the surnames of Akey, Lochner, Comiskey, Lucas, and Gregg. Research has also traced the family back to 1603 and to Wyandanch, Chief of the Montauk Indians of Long Island, New York. Wyandanch's daughter, Catoneras, married Cornelius Van Tassel of Sleepy Hollow, New York. Their great-great-grandson, Zachariah P. DeWitt and wife, Elizabeth, moved to Oxford, Ohio, in 1805 where their log home stands today. As a historic home it is managed by the Oxford Museum Association and Miami University, and tours of the home and grounds are open to the public.

The majority of the Hartman/Klopfenstein immediate ancestors were born, raised, and buried in Allen County. They were successful farmers, businessmen and entrepreneurs. The line continues with Kimberly Hartman's marriage to John E. Boulton, with children Kelsey, John P., and Samuel J. Boulton; and Debra Hartman's marriage to Matthew Foreman, with children Elizabeth and Jackson Foreman.

Submitted by Sharon Hartman

PHILIP JAMES HARTMAN,

GREAT-GREAT-GRANDSON OF HERMAN HARTMAN

Philip James Hartman was born August 17, 1940 at St. Joseph Hospital in Fort Wayne, Indiana. He was baptized at St. Mary's Catholic Church, and received his First Communion and Confirmation at St. Jude Catholic Church. He graduated from St. Jude Catholic grade school in June 1954, where he played on the football team in fifth, sixth, seventh and eighth grades. Phil continued playing football at Central Catholic High School on the Varsity Team his sophomore, junior and senior years, and he was selected First Team All-City both his junior and senior year.

Phil is the son of Richard Paul Justin and Vera Louise (Adams) Hartman. He is the grandson of Joseph Clement and Frances Catherine (Schmitt) Hartman, great-grandson of John Hubert (Hobby) and Louisa (Aubrey) Hartman, and great-great grandson of Herman and Anna Maria (Richter) Hartman.

Phil is the proud father of five daughters, Linda Sue Hartman, born August 6, 1960; Marybeth Hartman, born October 12, 1961; Karen Ann (Hartman) Weller, born January 16, 1963; Julie Ann (Hartman) Chmielewski, born September 5, 1965; Dianne Lynn (Hartman) Mullens, born February 16, 1969; and the proud grandfather of four grandsons and four granddaughters.

After graduation from Central Catholic High School, he worked for General Telephone Company as a lineman and cable splicer, 1958-1967. On September 1, 1967, he bought the Pickwick Tavern, 2701 John Street, the southeast corner of Pontiac and John Streets. January 1, 1970, he bought Jim's Rib Room, 1723 East Wayne Street, northwest corner of Wayne and Anthony. Phil's father, Richard Paul Justin Hartman, recommended that Phil call his bar Hartman's Place, continuing in the Hartman family tradition. On May 1, 1976, Phil bought Merle's Tavern at Lake Wawasee and continued in that business until May 1, 1978. In 1979, he bought the River Tavern, 1201 West Main Street, southwest corner of Main and Cherry Streets, which he owned through 1989. From 1982 through 1985, he owned the Olde Inn, 2908 Wayne Trace and from 1992 through 1994 he owned The Pantry, 1202 Wells Street, northwest corner of Wells and Fourth street. In 1990, he opened Hartman's Bar, 1201 Wells street, northeast corner of Wells and Fourth Streets, and again named and dedicated his bar in memory of his father, Richard Paul Justin Hartman, who passed away on January 15, 1990. Over the years Phil was also proud that many former patrons of his father's bar, Hartman's Brew Haven, 701 East Jefferson, northeast corner of Jefferson and Hanna, another generation of Hartmans in the bar and tavern business patronized his bars. Phil is proud of the fact that after purchasing many of these bars that were unprofitable businesses at the time, and he made them into prosperous bar businesses.

Phil is also proud that he is the fifth generation of the Hartman family in the bar/tavern business!

Submitted by Philip Hartman

PHYLLIS ANN HARTMAN

Phyllis Ann Hartman was born on September 18, 1925 in Fort Wayne, Indiana. She was the youngest of four children of Clement and Frances (Schmitt) Hartman. Phyllis attended grade school at St. John the Baptist and graduated from Central Catholic High School in 1943. Phyllis married Herman Klug on June 8, 1946 at St. John the Baptist Catholic Church. Herman Klug was born on March 17, 1920 in Fort Wayne, Indiana. Herman graduated from Central High School in 1938.

Phyllis and Herman had four children: Daniel, Stanley, Julia, and Laura. Phyllis and Herman currently reside in Waynedale, Indiana and also have a cottage on Sylvan Lake, near Rome City, Indiana. The cottage has been in the family for over 104 years! Herman and Phyllis enjoy catch-

Hartman's Brewery Saloon Grocery 1853-1900's

Frances (Schmitt) Hartman at top of steps with baby Hubert "Boot" Hartman and friends at Frisco Cottage in 1909.

Louisa (Aubrey) Hartman, second from left, wife of John Hubert Hartman and his sisters.

ing fish at the lake. The cottage was built in 1901 by Phyllis' grandfather, John Hubert (Hobby) Hartman so that the family could get out of the city where the air was healthier. This attempt for healthier living didn't help his daughter Eva who died of tuberculosis at the age of 25. The cottage was named "Frisco Cottage". The inspiration for this name apparently came from Hobby's three sisters who moved from Fort Wayne to live in San Francisco and the surrounding area.

John Hubert's sister, Theresa Hartman, married William Peters at St. Mary's Church in Fort Wayne, Indiana and moved out to San Francisco before their first child, Flora was born in May 1877. They also had more children there named; Harry, Francis, Willie, and Theresa. Some of the occupations that William Peters had were dry good merchant, saloonkeeper, and vineyardist. Another sister, Anna Hartman moved out to California and married Charles Kuhn in Mendocino, California on September 27, 1892. They had two girls named Flora and Teresa. One of Charles Kuhn's occupations was an oilier for street railroad. Hobby's third sister, Regina followed her two sisters out there to enjoy the glorious climate in California. Regina married Charles Wall and had two boys named Charles and Herbert. Charles Wall worked as an insurance agent.

Hobby's fourth sister Frances was also born in Fort Wayne, but she didn't stay here either. She left Fort Wayne at the age of sixteen to become a Roman Catholic Nun. She first went to a convent in Milwaukee, Wisconsin on August 5, 1886 and eventually became Sister Mary Nicholina of the order of Notre Dame. She traveled the United States teaching school in Green Bay, Wisconsin, St. Louis, Missouri, Teutopolis, Illinois, Detroit, Michigan, Madison Lake, Minnesota, West Spokane, Washington, and Mankato, Wisconsin. She died at the Mankato Motherhouse on May 8, 1935.

Submitted by Phyllis Klug

LARRY & RUTH CRAIG HASTE FAMILY

Larry Dean Haste was born December 23, 1949, in Bedford, Indiana, to Walter Lee and Christeen (Bastin) Haste. The Haste family lived in Mitchell, Indiana, until Larry was about six at which time his father went into the ministry and they moved to Morristown, Tennessee. The family also lived in Yale and Texhoma, Oklahoma, where Larry graduated from high school in 1968.

In 1966 Larry met Norma Ruth Craig, daughter of Benjamin Paul and Mary Alice (Huff) Craig. Ruth was born January 16, 1949, in Anadarko, Oklahoma. Ruth also lived in Atoka and Walters, Oklahoma, graduating from Walters High School in 1967. They were married at Northside Church of God, Friday, June 13, 1969, in Houston, Texas, where they were attending college at Gulf Coast Bible College.

Larry was drafted and served with the United States Army (1971-72). His basic training was at Fort Polk, Louisiana. He served in Viet Nam with the 1st Cavalry Division in Co C 1st Bn 5th Cav, S&T Co 1st CSSB, and Co A 229th Avn Bn. Larry returned to college, graduating in 1977 from Cameron University in Lawton, Oklahoma. He accepted a teacher/coach position at Seiling Oklahoma Public School where he taught Oklahoma History, Civics, and Driver Education, and was head basketball and assistant football coach from 1977 to 1980, head baseball coach 1977-1979, and head girls' tennis coach in 1980. Larry resigned his position in 1980 to work for Panhandle Eastern Pipeline Company. Since leaving Seiling in 1981, Larry and his family have lived in North Newton and Emporia, Kansas, Fort Wayne and Noblesville, Indiana. In 1992, Larry's job was abolished in Kansas, so the family relocated in Fort Wayne. Larry is a Senior Safety Rep. for the Midwest Division of Panhandle Energy.

Ruth worked at Cameron University in financial aids, as secretary at Presbyterian Manors of MidAmerica, DISRS in Dewey County Oklahoma, Seiling Elementary School, and Emporia Church of the Nazarene. She was self-employed as a family history researcher while in Fort Wayne.

Larry and Ruth have three children:

Vicki Jean, born December 21, 1970 in Delhi, Louisiana, married Richard Milner July 26, 1990. They have three children: Chelsea Rene, born March 8, 1991, Dylan Dee, born June 26, 1993 both born in Emporia, Kansas, and Alyssa Darlene, born January 22, 2001 in Eldorado. They live in Eldorado, Kansas.

Freeman Bradley, born October 9, 1972 in Conroe, Texas, married Susan Thomas June 1, 1991, and was divorced in January 1999. They have one son, Devan Tyler, born April 9, 1997 in Overland Park, Kansas. Freeman married Kari (Carson) Fink November 9, 2000. Freeman's family lives in Parkville, Missouri.

Benjamin Paul, born May 8, 1977 in Lawton, Oklahoma, married Faith McCormick December 28, 1996. Their children are Charity Marie, born October 20, 1995, Kyle Matthew, born December 21, 1996, and Hope Elizabeth, born July 2, 1999. All three children were born in Fort Wayne, Indiana. They currently live in Monroeville, Indiana.

Submitted by N. Ruth Craig Haste

DR. ANTON PAUL & ELIZABETH (DECKER) HATTENDORF FAMILY

Dr. Anton Paul Hattendorf (born August 23, 1903; died February 10, 1986) and Elizabeth Edna Decker (born November 8, 1905; died May 11, 1997) were married August 6, 1932. Dr. Hattendorf was known as Paul or Tony.

His father, Anton Heinrich Friedrich Hattendorf (born December 27, 1875; died March 7, 1957) arrived in Fort Wayne in 1890 from Germany. Paul's mother, whose father emigrated from Germany, was Emma Marie Meyer (born July 29, 1874; died June 10, 1932). Anton (Tony) and Emma were residents of Fort Wayne where Mr. Hattendorf was a grocer and involved with the German language newspaper. Their six children born between 1900 and 1907 are all deceased. They were Helen (m. Robert J. Bangert); twins, Carl (m. Hulda) and Henry (Hank) (m. Rosella); Anton Paul; Elsie (m. Ralph J. Didier); and Herbert (m. Lillian).

Anton Paul and Elizabeth Decker Hattendorf Family (1941). Elizabeth, Janice, Joan, Jane and Paul

Elizabeth (Lib) Decker's parents were Carl William and Emma Ethel (Misner) Decker from Lawrenceburg, Indiana, in Dearborn County.

Paul was a life long member of Zion Evangelical Lutheran Church and attended Zion's school. He became a tool and die maker before attending Indiana University and IU Medical School. He graduated in 1931 and interned at St. Vincent's Hospital in Indianapolis where he met Lib, who was a patient of his. She was a teacher and IU alumna. They settled in Fort Wayne in 1932 when Paul established his General Practice above Howard Wefel's Drug Store at the corner of Hanna and Pontiac Streets.

At the onset of WWII Paul enlisted in the Army Medical Corps and served in the North African campaign. After his discharge, he took a residence in Gastroenterology/Proctology and returned to Fort Wayne to practice until his retirement in the late 1970s. Active in Republican politics, he was elected Allen County Coroner and served that office before and after WWII.

Among his many community activities were Fort Wayne-Allen County Health Commissioner, President of the Board of Directors of the Allen County War Memorial Coliseum, President of the Fort Wayne Medical Society and Red Cross Civil Defense Board member.

Lib and Paul had three daughters: Jane, Joan, and Janice, all of whom remained in Fort Wayne.

Jane (1934-) married James Peterson (Pete) Scudder, M.D. Their children are James P., Jr. (Peter) (m. Laura Helmkamp of Fort Wayne); Paul (m. Cynthia Fountain of Bedford, Indiana); Sara (Sallie) (m. John R. Corbat of Fort Wayne); Susan (m. David K. McCracken of Fort Wayne); and Sandra (m. Peter W. Cates of Bloomington, Indiana) Both IU graduates, Dr. Scudder practiced Urology and Occupational Medicine in Fort Wayne until his death November 15, 2004; Jane was a teacher. She later became a Registered Nurse receiving her degree from Purdue University.

Joan (1937-) married Harold Varketta of Fort Wayne. Their children are Kara (m. Dennis Mertz of Fort Wayne) and Keith. Joan, an IU graduate, taught in the Fort Wayne Community Schools. Harold held an optometry degree from IU; he was a teacher at the State Developmental Center.

Janice (1939-1998) received a Juris Doctor degree from IU School of Law and was an attorney at Lincoln National Life Insurance Company.

Submitted by Jane H. Scudder

THOMAS & EDITH (ROEHLING) HAYDEN

Thomas Edward Hayden was born on November 9, 1907, in Warsaw, Indiana.

His father was Eugene Edward Hayden, born in Whitley County, Indiana (near Collamer) on December 18, 1884. Eugene would serve as one of the youngest non-commissioned officers in the Spanish-American War (1898). In the First World War, he was wounded in France and returned a decorated soldier. His mother was Nelta (Nettie) Schannep who was born on January 7, 1867, in Whitley County. She was a daughter of David and Mary (Moore) Schannep. David was born in Green County, Ohio, on March 13, 1828; Mary in Madison County, Indiana, in 1831. David Schannep was the son of Joseph and Susannah (Frost) Schannep. Joseph was born in Pennsylvania in 1799 and came to Whitley County in 1846. He died in an accident felling trees on April 30, 1848. Eugene's mother, Nettie died on August 3, 1885.

Eugene's father, Arthur, who was born April 2, 1865, purportedly in Fort Wayne, was adopted into the Hayden family. Arthur's adoptive parents were Charles W. and Anna (Hoover) Hayden. After his mother's death, Eugene was raised by his grandparents, Charles and Anna. Charles' father, David Fletcher Hayden, migrated to Whitley County in 1836 from Hayden, Ohio. Charles was born on August 12, 1837, in Richland Township.

Thomas Hayden's mother was Mamie Marie Jenkins who was born on August 19, 1883, in Warsaw, Indiana. Mamie's parents were Albert and Margaret (Shannon) Jenkins. Margaret's parents were John and Mary Shannon. Mamie Jenkins and Eugene Hayden were married on August 5, 1902. They would have six children: Ruth, Robert, Thomas, George, Eva and Donald.

Eugene and Mamie divorced and she moved to Mansfield, Ohio, with her daughter Ruth. Mamie died in Mansfield on November 24, 1935.

Eugene met Wilma Luree Carlin, who was born on October 7, 1899, in North Manchester, Indiana. They married in Fort Wayne on December 22, 1921, and had three children: Eugene Edward, Donna Rose and Betty Jane. Eugene died of a heart attack on February 16, 1942, in Texarkana, Arkansas, where he had taken a job as a foreman in the construction of a defense plant. Wilma moved to Florida with her daughters and died in New Port Richey on November 2, 1988.

Edith and Thomas Hayden on their wedding day, September 29, 1927

Thomas Hayden spent most of his early years in Kosciusko County. He moved to Fort Wayne in his late teens where he met Edista (Edith) Roehling. Edith was born in Fort Wayne on June 5, 1906. Her parents were Frank and Lillian (Fegan) Roehling. Frank was born on May 13, 1877 in Fort Wayne. His parents, John and Theresa (Becker) Roehling, came from Prussia in the 1860s. John was born on December 27, 1838 and Theresa in May of 1838. Lillian Roehling was born on November 25, 1881 in Cleveland, Ohio. Her parents were Joseph and Catherine (Steppard) Fegan.

Tom and Edith were married at Precious Blood Catholic Church in Fort Wayne on September 29, 1927. On November 13, 1928, they had a daughter and named her Lillian Marie (Joy). On February 10, 1930, Louis Catherine was born and on September 30, 1935, Thomas Eugene (Jr.) arrived. Edith's youngest child was stillborn on July 20, 1948; he was named Robert Joseph.

In 1928, Thomas started to work at the General Electric Company in Fort Wayne. In the late 1940s, he was an active union member at Local 901. He campaigned to evict the Communist led United Electrical, Radio and Machine Workers (UE), which represented the union membership at GE. In 1949, the CIO expelled the UE. Later that year, the International Union of Electrical, Radio and Machine Workers (IUE) was chartered and a contract was negotiated with GE in 1950. In 1953, Tom was elected president of Local 901. He would serve until 1956 and again from 1962-1964. He successfully led the contract negotiations with GE in 1955 when there were over 10, 000 employees in Fort Wayne.

In 1952, Tom and Edith purchased property on Gilead Lake in Branch County, Michigan. There they built a home to which they retired in 1968. Tom was in failing health and on June 18, 1973, he died in their home on Gilead Lake. Edith died at St. Joseph's Hospital in Fort Wayne on December 6, 1980.

Tom and Edith's daughter, Joy, married Thomas Biesiada and they had eight children: Michael, Edward (deceased), Lois, Joyanne, Thomas, Joseph (deceased), David and Lawrence. Lois Hayden married James Mills and they had four children: Patrick, Daniel, Laura and Edith (twins). Thomas Jr. married Carol Taylor and they had five children: Thomas, Timothy, Nancy, Andrew and Jon.

Submitted by Thomas E. Hayden, Jr.

Photo with Ronald Reagan at GE 1953c

HEATH FAMILY

The Heath family were among the first families to settle in Allen County and the Fort Wayne area. The William Heath family arrived in Roxbury (now Boston) Massachusetts in September of 1632 departing the ship *Lyon*. The Heaths were Puritans escaping religious persecution in England. They came from the hamlet of Nazeing, County Essex, England, a few miles north of London. The Heaths were landowners and farmers. Four generations later, General William Heath led the colonial militia against the British at the first battle of the Revolutionary War at Lexington and Concord. His exploits are set out in various history books, including Hallahan's *The Day the American Revolution Began*. The Heath family migrated to Connecticut, upstate New York, Ohio and finally arrived in Allen County when John Heath settled in northeast Allen County in 1834. John Heath was born in Otis, Berkshire County, Massachusetts in 1799. The descendants of John Heath remain in Allen County and through the generations served as farmers, carpenters, public servants, a violin-maker, a Judge and a scientist, among other things. John Heath's son, Stephen, had a particularly challenging but inspiring life. When his parents and aunt and uncle died (before he reached his fifteenth birthday) he lived with his cousins, the Milliman family. His older brother, a soldier during the Civil War, was captured and died at the Andersonville Confederate Prison. Despite these travails, according to his obituary in the May 14, 1935 issue of the Fort Wayne *Jour-*

Dan Heath Family

Heckler Family

nal-Gazette he was "well known" and elected to serve as Allen County's first County Assessor in 1896 and "was the first Assessor in the present courthouse building." Stephen had six children, among them Orren (who would become a nationally renowned violin maker) and J. William (who served several terms as St. Joe Township Assessor). J. William Heath had eight children, two of whom survive today—Ann Wroggeman and Edward Heath. J. William Heath's son, Willard (a long-time Allen County farmer who died in 1979), was the father of Judge Daniel G. Heath, who was narrowly defeated in a Special Election for Congress in 1989, and now serves as a Judge of the Allen Superior Court in the same courthouse in which Stephen was a first occupant as Assessor. Judge Heath's identical twin brother, Lt. Col. David Heath, Ph.D. serves as a scientist for the Army at the USAMRID at Fort Detrick, Maryland. David Heath's research led to a cure for the bubonic plague which will help ensure the safety of our troops and help against the outbreak of the plague throughout the world. Willard Heath's oldest son, John Heath, is a Deputy Sheriff while youngest son Scott Heath boards fine horses. Judge Dan Heath's wife, Patricia, is a teacher, son Andrew attends law school, son Ryan Heath graduated with an economics degree from Columbia University and daughter Sarah attends Indiana University, majoring in Education. Heath descendants continue to live in Allen County serving as nurses, photographers, educators and businessmen.

Submitted by Daniel Heath

HECKLER - FRY FAMILY

Elizabeth Schmidt, daughter of Peter S. Schmidt and his wife, Elizabeth Wenrick Schmidt, was born in Hessen Darmstadt, Germany on November 23, 1836. At the age of four, she and parents left Germany and arrived at Baltimore, Maryland in June of 1840. They traveled to Pennsylvania then to Allen County, Indiana, on September 29, 1844. John Thomas Heckler, son of John Thomas Heckler and his wife, Barbara Bauch, was born in Illingen, Wurttemberg, Germany on July 20, 1820. He left Germany March 5, 1840, at the age of 20. He came to New York, to New Ark, Ohio, and then to Allen County, Indiana in December of 1844.

Young John Thomas Heckler and Elizabeth Schmidt, at the age of 16, were married September 9, 1852. They both immigrated in the same year. To this marriage, twelve children were born. One daughter, Margaret died at age eight. The other children were: John Heckler of Madison township; Daniel of Jefferson Township; Chris of Madison Township; Addie of Monroe Township; Mary Lopshire of Harlan, Indiana; Christena Fry of Monroeville, Indiana; Louisa O'Brien of Fort Wayne; Lena Fry of Monroeville, Miernie Henry of Fort Wayne; Hanna O'Brien of Bucyrus, Ohio; Emma Nicolson of Fort Wayne.

John died on November 9, 1883 at 63 years of age. This was the same age his father died in Germany on October 30, 1786. Young John's mother, Barbra died at the age of 93. When Elizabeth died on May 4, 1927, she was 90. By that time there were 62 grandchildren, 97 great-grandchildren, and one great, great-grandchild. Elizabeth is buried at Flatrock Lutheran Cemetery near Hoagland, Indiana. She outlived John by 44 years.

Submitted by Karen Bauman

BARNEY & MARY (HOLLEPETER) HEFFELFINGER FAMILY

Artemus Ward Beecher Barney Heffelfinger was born January 17, 1873, died on December 23, 1945, in Dunedin, Florida. He married Mary Euletha Hollopeter on September 25, 1895. Mary Hollopeter was born on June 13, 1877, and died on August 26, 1949, in Allen County, Indiana. They are buried in Cedar Chapel Cemetery, Garrett, Indiana. In this family there were born nine children, two sons and seven daughters.

1. Frances (Marie) was born on May 29, 1897. She married Harold Walters and had three daughters, Harriet Emily, March 9, 1917, Bonnie Beth, February 14, 1919, and Phyllis Marcia, August 18, 1922. Marie divorced and married Conrad Tucker on October 2, 1936. In this union, there were no children.

2. Iva Irene Heffelfinger was born on January 12, 1899. She married Stanley Potter on April 13, 1935. She was a schoolteacher in Garrett, Huntertown, and Churubusco, Indiana. There were no children.

3. Vonell Heffelfinger was born on October 3, 1900. She married Forrest Gump on October 12, 1924. In this family there were born four children, three sons and one daughter. Marlow Gump was born on January 30, 1924. Gloria Maxine was born on September 27, 1927, and died as a small baby. Two boys also died at birth.

4. Laura Inez Heffelfinger was born on July 24, 1903. She married Merl J. Amstutz on April 10, 1924. In this family there three children. Janice Fay, November 10, 1925, Gerald Merle was born on September 25, 1927, and Nancy (Diane), born on August 31, 1931.

5. Herman Taft Heffelfinger was born on December 15, 1908. He married Helen Stohlmann on November 23, 1932. In this family were born two children, Richard Lionel, born on February 14, 1934, and Shirley Ann, born on March 9, 1935.

6. Ruth Geraldine Heffelfinger was born on July 29, 1911. She married George Lucas on June 27, 1932. In this family were born two daughters, Barbara June, July 29, 1933, and Georgia Ann born December 23, 1939.

7. Keith Miles Heffelfinger was born on September 19, 1916. He married Ruth Elizabeth Hess on August 10, 1940. To this union there were born four children. David Errol was born on May 29, 1941, Mary Genevieve was born on April 7, 1943, Mark was born on January 13, 1946, and Keith J. was born on February 1, 1948.

8. Mary Kathryn Heffelfinger was born on June 17, 1913. (Katie) married George Fogel on September 30, 1939. There were no children of this union.

9. Betty Rebecca Heffelfinger was born on October 13, 1918. She married Harvey L. Bell on July 22, 1939. In this family there were three children. Barney Edward was born on July 22, 1939, Patricia was born on May 4, 1942, and Iva was born on March 6, 1945.

Barney and Mary Heffelfinger

Barney Heffelfinger was the son of Martin Heffelfinger and Rebecca Spratt. Martin was the son of Captain John Kirby Heffelfinger who came with his three brothers to Eel River Township in the spring of 1848. The original family came from Hafelfinger, Switzerland in 1723.

Rebecca was the daughter of Dr. Spratt from Leo, Indiana. He came to this country in 1813, through New Orleans, when he was 13 years old, and apprenticed himself out to a doctor to learn the practice of medicine. He later practiced medicine in Leo, Indiana, Allen County.

Barney raised produce crops for market. He had the only irrigation operation in the area. He lived on a farm south of Garrett, Indiana, and sold it just before the depression to a gravel company. The addition is now called Holliday Lakes. He built a home on Lima Road just north of Huntertown and sold produce in his roadside market. He was known for his wonderful melons. He later retired to Dunedin, Florida, during the winter and in the summer at Wall Lake, Orland, Indiana.

Submitted by Shirley Underwood

MARTIN & REBECCA HEFFELFINGER

Martin Heffelfinger was born on March 24, 1836, and died March 24, 1903. Martin is buried in the Cedar Chapel Cemetery in Garrett, Indiana. Martin was married four times. His daughter by his first marriage was Louella, and she married John Keeler. Her mother died of childbirth in Tennessee. He had one daughter, Melvina, by his second marriage to Elizabeth. Elizabeth died on November 10, 1871 at 21 years of age. Melvina married Ed Fisher. His third marriage ended in divorce. He married Rebecca Sprat in his fourth marriage and had seven children, one daughter and six boys.

Standing: Alf, Florence, and Charles; Sitting: Martin and Rebecca; Sitting on the porch: Ed, George, and Barney

Martin and Rebecca's children were: Artimus Ward Barney (January 17, 1873-December 23, 1945) (m. Mary Hollopeter September 25, 1895); George (August 15, 1875-August 1, 1952) (m. Eva, divorced); Ed (November 15, 1882-1953) (m. Carman Whitney June 10, 1910); Alpha (September 8, 1886- ?) (m. Emma E.); Florence (1888-1956; Charles (1877-1958) (m. Amanda Thompson (1884-1936)

Rebecca Spratt, Martin's wife, was born on October 17, 1850, and died on January 4, 1916. She is also buried in the Cedar Chapel Cemetery with Martin.

Martin's father was Captain John Kirby Heffelfinger who was born on March 14, 1799, and died February 8, 1858. John Kirby was the son of Phillip Heffelfinger who was from Cumberland County, Pennsylvania. Captain John Kirby Heffelfinger came to Eel River Township from Cumberland County with his three brothers in the spring of 1848. His wife was Elizabeth Moler, who was born on January 3, 1803, and died on January 25, 1868.

There were six children born to them: Jeremiah (August 15, 1832-1906) (m. Margaret Leticia) Slagle (1860); Martin (March 24, 1836-March 4, 1903) (m. Rebecca Spratt); Samuel (birth, death and marriage dates unknown); Jacob (June 2, 1843-January 1, 1932) (m. Beth Ann Harter); Sarah Jane (1830-1907) (m. Samuel Diffendarfer); Elizabeth (1840-1904) (m. Dr. Woodward and m. Dave Derbyshire).

Rebecca's father, Dr. Spratt, came to this country in 1813 when he was 13 years old. He landed in New Orleans, Louisiana, and was English. He apprenticed himself out to a doctor to learn the practice of medicine. He practiced medicine in Leo, Indiana, Allen County. His pestle, mortar, and dental tools remain family heirlooms.

Submitted by Shirley Underwood

FRIEDRICH HEGERFELD FAMILY

The Hegerfeld families of Allen County originated in Nordrhein-Westphalia, Germany, in the town of Sundern, having resided in that area since the 1600s.

Wilhelm Carl Friedrich Hegerfeld (March 17, 1830-April 9, 1907) and Anna Maria Louise Boenker (March 20, 1829-September 2, 1911) of Sundern had the following children: Henrietta, Christian, Wilhelm, Charles "Carl", Friedrich Wilhelm Gottlieb, Louis, and Friedrich Gottlieb Ludwig.

Friedrich Wilhelm Gottlieb Hegerfeld was born September 21, 1855, in Sundern. He was the third oldest of seven children of Wilhelm Carl and Anna Maria. He immigrated to Allen County on May 8, 1882, with his brother William, aboard the ship S.S. Baltimore, from the Port of Bremen. They told of the ship hitting a whale during their long voyage. The ship's manifest listed these men as "farmers" with intent to become inhabitants of Iowa. Their journey was apparently shortened or the manifest was in error as they stayed in Allen County.

Louis immigrated on April 11, 1886, aboard the ship "Herman." Christian and Carl came earlier. Christian worked as the City Weighmaster and owned a grocery store on Broadway for 21 years.

Henrietta and Friedrich Ludwig remained in Germany. It is believed Henrietta disappeared during World War II.

The Friedrich Hegerfeld Family

Friedrich was baptized October 7, 1855, and confirmed April 10, 1870, in Levern. On October 27, 1884, he appeared before John Hale, Adams County Circuit Court Clerk and petitioned for naturalization. He became a U.S. Citizen October 9, 1890. Friedrich married Wilhelmina Louise Melcher of Adams County, January 28, 1886, at St. Peter Lutheran Church, Adams County. She was born September 22, 1858, the daughter of Friedrich and Louise (Hegerfeld) Melcher. He bought 80 acres of land on August 13, 1890, in the northwest quarter, Section 28, Township 29 on Hoagland Road. This was one-half of the acreage James McFadden received by land grant from President Martin VanBuren on November 2, 1837. Friedrich died July 18, 1915, and Wilhelmina died March 29, 1949. Both are interred at St. John Lutheran (Flat Rock) Cemetery, Madison Township.

Their five sons, Frederick (May 9, 1887-August 6, 1979), William (August 27, 1889-April 17, 1979), Henry (July 6, 1891-August 11, 1960), Herman (December 28, 1893-October 9, 1965) and Martin (June 28, 1898-September 1, 1991) grew up on the family farm and resided in the area throughout their lives. Herman worked and resided on the family farm. He married Anna Caroline Hockemeyer February 23, 1919. Anna was the daughter of Herman and Louise (Bohnke) Hockemeyer. She was born March 20, 1894 and died August 26, 1991. They raised livestock, grain, hay and Anna was known for raising chickens.

Their six children attended grade school at St. John Lutheran (Flat Rock) and graduated from Hoagland High School. Herman and Anna's children are: Luella, Dorothy, Robert, Bernice, Arnold and Marceil.

Luella married Oscar Lepper, both are deceased. Dorothy married Gerhard Werling. Robert married Helene Werling. Bernice married Harvey Caston (deceased). Marceil married Alfred Baatz.

Arnold (Peanut), the youngest son, took over the farming operation after Herman's death. The farm was sold in 1995 to Robert Scott. Arnold still resides on the northwest portion of the family farm where he built a log home. These children were the last generation to live in the "Hegerfeld Farmhouse." The house in Madison Township on Hoagland Road stands today, but is unoccupied.

Many Hegerfeld descendants still reside in Germany and the Allen County area today.

Submitted by Bernice Caston

HEINY FAMILY

Clemens Heini, 30, of Baden, Germany, married Barbara Richet, 31, of France and honeymooned on the ship "Europe," arriving in New York May 1836. Great-grandson, Nicholas Heiny, has their oil wedding portraits. Clemens was a cabinet maker, and Nick is the current owner of a cherry dresser and night stand made about 1840 for their New York home, 280 West 32nd Street, Manhattan. Earlier on, Nick's fifth great-grandfather, Jacob Heyni, was married in Baden on January 19, 1686.

Granddaughter, Grace Gruber-Zickgraf, who lived to 101, told Nick that her mother, Elizabeth Heiny, and the other children were taken shortly after birth across the street to be baptized at the Catholic Church.

With his eyesight deteriorating, he sold the family home May 1, 1859, (for $3,000), upon the advice of his physician. (A later owner sold the house in 1905 to the Pennsylvania RR for $21,000. They shipped their furniture by canal and they themselves traveled by train to Fort Wayne, after first stopping for a farewell visit with cousins in Elizabeth, New Jersey. After arriving here in 1859, they promptly bought 80 acres for $4,000 at the southwest corner of Illinois and Hadley roads.

With help of neighbors, Clemens felled trees to build a house, pump house and barn, after which all enjoyed a barn-raising dance.

Nicholas L. Heiny (1914-)

Clemens's widow sold out following his death in 1871. Clemens's death came after he had enjoyed semi-retirement raising and selling produce. An interesting note: Clemens died in his wagon enroute from the Barr Street Market, with the horse continuing on to his home.

Clemens's son, Nicholas Heiny (1842-1915), raised his family of fourteen children at 418 East Wayne Street, five children by first wife, Mary Schele, and nine by second wife, Margaret Weisbrod. Margaret had cared for his children during Mary's illness and death. Nicholas was employed as sales manager for A.C. Trentman, a well known wholesale grocer. A hand-me-down account notes that Nicholas became acquainted with August Berghoff, an apprentice at Trentman's, to whom he loaned $500 to start the Rub-No-More Soap Company later sold to Proctor and Gamble. Proceeds from this sale, it is believed, helped start Berghoff Brewery, which later became Falstaff Brewing.

Another son of Clemens, Erhardt, who married Catherine Crimmins, owned a retail grocery in Fort Wayne, but early on moved to Chattanooga, Tennessee, where he raised a family of eight children. (In this era, there were many neighborhood grocery stores because people shopped frequently as there was no refrigeration except ice to preserve foods. Clemens's daughter, Catherine, died in New York at age twelve. His other daughter, Elizabeth, who attended St. Augustine Academy in Fort Wayne, married Joseph Gruber, together raising eight children. Their son, Andrew Gruber, published the Lima (Ohio) *Daily News* for many years. Another son was Dr. Charles Gruber, a well-known veterinarian in Fort Wayne.

In his semi-retirement years, Nicholas, son of Clemens, opened a grocery in 1898 at 1241 Wells Street, Fort Wayne, with his son Lawrence. Later, Lawrence expanded to 1418 Calhoun Street, from which he moved in 1925 to 435 West Creighton Avenue. Son, Nicholas (1914 -), joined the business in 1945, being further joined with his brothers Joseph and Robert upon their return from WWII military service. Robert left about 1954 and Joe and Nick sold the business in 1981. After a devastating 1983 fire, the new owners closed the business. History of this grocery is in a booklet at the Allen County Public Library, "Heiny's Market - 85 Years in Fort Wayne."

John Heiny, brother of Lawrence, bought the Wells Street store in 1919 and continued the business until his retirement in 1970.

Othmar Heiny, another brother, became Trust Officer for Old-First National Bank in Fort Wayne, and held that position until his untimely death in 1932.

The author of this account, Nicholas Heiny, age 90, lives in active retirement as a family genealogist and community volunteer, as does his wife Dorothy Callahan-Heiny, a former book and society editor of the *New-Sentinel*. Nick and Dorothy have nine children, 23 grandchildren and two great-grandchildren.

Submitted by Nicholas L. Heiny

HELMKE FAMILY

The Helmke family first came to Fort Wayne after Edward Helmke, born 1842, immigrated to the United States from Germany in 1857. Edward had a grocery in the 100 block of West Main Street (later sold to Main Auto). He also owned the three-story "Helmke Block" at South Calhoun and Douglas (later purchased by Lincoln Life).

Edward, who died in 1916, had four sons including Herman, born 1867, who became a cobbler. Herman and his wife, Mary Engle, born in Germany, had three children, including Walter Edward Helmke, born 1901.

Walter E. Helmke attended Fort Wayne High School and received both an under grad and law degree from Indiana University. After marrying Wilma Wehrenberg, he was elected Allen County Prosecutor in 1928. Walter E. served as City Attorney for Mayor Harry Baals from 1935 until 1948. He was the Allen County Republican Chair for most of the 1940s. He served on the Indiana University Board of Trustees in the mid-1950s and helped start the local Indiana-Purdue Foundation and the Indiana-Purdue Fort Wayne campus. Walter E. had three children, including Walter Paul Helmke, born 1927.

L to R: Walter P. Helmke, Walter E. Helmke, Paul Helmke, October 1973

Walter P. Helmke attended St. Paul's Lutheran Grade School, North Side High School, Indiana University, and Valparaiso Law School and then returned to Fort Wayne to join his father's law firm. He was elected Prosecutor in 1962 and re-elected in 1966. He was elected State Senator in 1970 and was the Republican nominee for U. S. Congress in 1974. Walter P. has been active with a number of civic organizations, including president of the Chamber of Commerce, Parkview Hospital and Allen County Bar Association. Walter P. and his wife, Rowene Crabill, have three children: Walter Paul Helmke, Jr. born 1948; Mark C. Helmke, a former reporter for the *Fort Wayne News Sentinel*, presently on the staff of the United States Senate Foreign Relations Committee, born 1951; and Marsha Helmke Shirk, born 1954, now living in Oriental, North Carolina.

Paul Helmke continued the family's tradition of civic involvement in Fort Wayne. After being educated at St. Paul's Lutheran Grade School, North Side High School, Indiana University, and Yale University, Paul returned to Fort Wayne to practice law with his father and grandfather. He served as an Assistant Allen County Attorney from 1974 till his election as Mayor of Fort Wayne in 1987. Paul served for twelve years, being re-elected in 1991 and 1995. Paul received national and statewide recognition as President of the United States Conference of Mayors, President of the Indiana Association of Cities and Towns and as the Republican nominee for United States Senate in 1998. Paul and his wife, the former Deborah Andrews, a kindergarten teacher, have two children, Laura, born in 1977, and Kathryn, born in 1981. Laura now works for the Environmental Protection Agency in Washington, D.C., and Kathryn has been a reporter for the Naples Daily News in Florida.

Throughout their 150 years in the Fort Wayne area, the Helmke family has contributed much to the civic, political, and legal life in the community.

Submitted by Paul Helmke

GEORGE HENKENIUS & REGINA HAKE FAMILY

Franz Henkenius and his bride, Fernadine (Grashot) arrived in New Orleans June 13, 1853. The promise of rich farmland and plenty of work led the industrious young couple to leave their homeland of Westfalen, Prussia and travel the long distance to Fort Wayne.

Franz Henkenius was employed by Trentman Sons and worked there for 23 years until his death October 3, 1877. He left behind his wife and six children. George, Peter, Clem, Tina (Keller), August, and Frank. Fernadine passed away January 19,1901.

Frank Hake and his wife Christine (Backhauls) arrived in Baltimore from Westphalia June 3, 1866. They also had six children: Mary (Dennis), Nettie (Thone), Christina (Limbert), Regina (Henkenius), Helena (Bieker-Noll), and Frank Jr. Frank owned F. Hake Bottling Works on Wells Street. An 1894 influenza epidemic took Frank

Hake Family: Nettie, Regina, Mary, Christina (Tina), Frank Jr., Frank, Christina, Lena (Helena)

Henkenius Family, Ruth, holding her son, Mike; Jean; Emma (Mother) Carolyn, Emma, Leo, Charles, Tom, Charlene, and Glen, 1950

Henkenius children, Ruth, Mary, Caroline, 1923

1889. Hake Bottling company, Wells Street. George Henkenius in center, Frank Hake on crutches

on December 12 and Frank Jr. on December 25. Christina passed away October 2, 1900.

The Hakes and Henkenius families had been friends for years. When George and Regina wed September 21, 1882, both families were pleased. George and Regina had seven children: Frances (May 12, 1884), Joseph (December 17, 1886), Charles (December 16, 1889), John (February 1, 1891), Albert (July 17, 1893), Clarence (June 18, 1896), and Leo Daniel (January 18, 1899).

George retired from the Pennsylvania Railroad in 1927. During a 1927 *News-Sentinel* interview, George recalled early days in the "Fort." He was a member of the Aqueduct Club, remembered two German theaters on Wells Street, and hunting in what is now Sinclair Street. He also noted that winter was much milder than during his childhood. When he was young, snow was deep enough for sleigh rides on Thanksgiving. George died April 15, 1931.

Charles Henkenius married Emma Forsythe of Paris, Michigan on January 30, 1918. They had ten children: Ruth (Teagarden), Mary (Hessert), Carolyn, (Sister of the Precious Blood Order) Rita, Jean (Crowl), Leo (Francele Piepenbrink), Tom (Lois Lang), Emma (Seelig), Charlene (Freiburger), and Glen (Jean Kable). Emma, trained as a nurse, was well able to handle the Henkenius brood. The family home on Sinclair Avenue held many precious memories for the children. Charles and his brothers played musical instruments and they would get together for singing and dancing. Charlie played the guitar and harmonica for the family's favorite "You Are My Sunshine." Ruth remembers her great-uncle Pete was famous for his chocolates. He worked for Aurantz located on Main and Broadway. Pete, an avid fisherman, patented the "Henkenius-Kane Spinner" designed to "catch more fish than any other device ever invented."

Large families were a dynamic part of Fort Wayne's growth, and family life was quite different in the 1930s. Ruth remembers all the babies being born at home. She recalled one night when her Grandfather George was laying in state in one room while Emma was being born in another. In 1927 the household was quarantined due to black diphtheria. Rita passed away suddenly and Jean and Caroline became ill. Nobody was allowed to enter or leave the house for a month.

Leo Henkenius was listed as MIA November 28, 1950 during the Korean War. Mary Henkenius Hessert died in childbirth in 1943. Emma Henkenius passed away December of 1951. Charles died August 1969, and Jean Henkenius Crowl passed away December 2003. They leave behind a large circle of friends and family who remember and love them dearly.

Submitted by Julie Magsamen

HENNINGER-ORMSBY

Keith Allan Henninger was born May 18, 1942 in Fort Wayne, Indiana to William Eugene (1905-1970) and Mary Marguerite Ardern Grayless Henninger (1906-1995). William and Mary lived their married lives entirely in Fort Wayne, living on Dayton Street for 21 years. Keith's siblings were an older sister and brother, Bonnie Jean, born January 19, 1933 and Robert Eugene, born April 16, 1936. Bonnie was married to William Davis, now deceased, and resides in Elkhart, Indiana. Robert married Sue Plasket, now deceased, and lives in Fort Wayne.

Nancy Lou Ormsby Henninger was born in Fort Wayne June 24, 1942, the third daughter of Argus L. (1894-1967) and Edna Chloe (1914-2003) Mann Ormsby. Nancy's siblings were Catherine Elizabeth (Betty), born in 1935 and Judith Elaine Ormsby born in 1941. Catherine Elizabeth Williams resides in New Haven with Kenneth. Robert Erwin Richter and Judith Elaine reside in Albion, Indiana.

Keith and Nancy were high school sweethearts and married July 27, 1963 at St. John Evangelical Lutheran Church in Fort Wayne. Keith and Nancy both graduated from South Side High School in Fort Wayne with the class of 1960. After their marriage, they lived in Muncie, Indiana for 14 years. In Muncie, Keith was employed by Transpower and Nancy by Clevepak. In 1984, Keith and Nancy moved back to Fort Wayne and continue to reside in Glenwood Park subdivision. Keith is employed at L & L Fittings since 1991, and Nancy retired in 2004 after 20 years with National Servall in the accounting department. Keith and Nancy both enjoy collecting antiques and going to auctions. Keith also likes to fish and Nancy likes to bowl. Keith was also a avid hunter, traveling west to hunt mule, deer and antelope and locally hunted rabbit.

L to R: First row, Madison Henninger, Garret Sommers. Second row, Carmen Henninger, Stacy Hare, Joseph Hare. Third row, Brian Henninger, Shelby Hare. Fourth row, Keith and Nancy Henninger

Two children were born to this marriage. Brian Keith was born July 29, 1966 in Muncie, Indiana where he graduated from Delta High School in 1984. He now resides in the Warsaw, Indiana area and is married to Carmen Castleman Sommers. They were married May 17, 1997 at Trinity United Methodist Church in Fort Wayne. She brought into the family her son, Garret Loyd, from an earlier marriage. Madison Lee, their daughter, was born November 4, 1997 in Fort Wayne. Brian is employed at Precision Technology of Warsaw, managing the engineering department.

Stacy Diane was born June 8, 1968 in Muncie and graduated from Homestead High School, Fort Wayne in 1986. She married Joseph Scott Hare on May 28, 1994 in Fort Wayne at Trinity United Methodist Church. Joe and Stacy still reside in Fort Wayne and are the parents of Shelby Alexandria, born November 5, 1994. Joe is employed at American Wire Rope and Sling and Stacy is employed at Panoramic since 1987.

Submitted by Keith Henninger

HENRY FAMILY

The Henry family can be traced to the early 1700s. An extended history of the Henry family can be found at Allen County Public Library Genealogy Department under the name of Charles Banet. He was the submitter's first cousin on his father's side. He has developed an extensive history of the Henry family tree.

The Henrys, known as the Henrichs before the name was "Americanized" in the early 20th Century, came from a town in Germany called Steinfeld, Pflaz, and Kapsweyer/KR, Bergzabern, and Niederotterbach, Bergzabern. We still have relatives living in that area.

Jacob Henrich was born in 1784 in Steinfield, Platz. He married Margaret Franck in 1810. She was born in 1789 in Steinfeld, Kreiss Bergfzabern, Rheinland Pflatz. Jacob's father was George Henrich and his mother was Margaret Ott. His wife's father was Joseph Franck and her mother's maiden name was Margaret Dillman. Jacob and Margaret had 12 children. Both Jacob and Margaret died and were buried in the Canton, Ohio Catholic Cemetery. When they came to America is unknown, however, they were still in Germany in 1834.

The wedding of Charles Martin Henry and Irene Degitz in 1923. From left to right: Catherine Henry, Charles Henry, Irene Degitz and Arthur Degitz.

The family of Charles Martin and Irene (Degitz) Henry in 1951. Front row from left to right: Irene and Charles Sr. Back row: Charles Jr., Jerome, Carol, Eugene (Hank) and Morton.

Their first son, Joseph Henrich, was born in 1810 at Stinfeld, Kreis Bergzabern, Rheinland, Pflaz. He married Elizabeth Schneider in 1835 in Philadelphia, Pennsylvania. She was born in Alsace, France in 1817. Joseph died and was buried in Canton in 1891; Elizabeth died in 1916 and was also buried in Canton.

The couple had 11 children, one of whom was Charles Matthias Henrich, born in Canton on October 26, 1859, after the family had moved to Ohio from Pennsylvania. Charles was a boot maker and had made boots for President William McKinley, who was from that area. It is said that the assassinated president was buried wearing boots made by Charles Henrich.

In 1893, Charles married Ida Louise Schuster. She was the daughter of John and Elizabeth (Kreischer) Schuster. John Schuster was born in the Rheinland area of Germany in 1836. In 1854 he married Elizabeth Kreischer in Canton, Ohio. She was born in the Rheinland area in 1834. John Schuster died in 1898 in Canton, and his wife died in 1916 in Fort Wayne. Both are buried in Canton.

Charles and Ida moved to Fort Wayne from Massillion, Ohio along with Charles' two brothers in the early 1900s. He opened his shoe shop on Broadway across from the firehouse near Hendrix Street. Charles and his brothers changed their name from Henrich to Henry when they left Ohio and came to Fort Wayne. We still have relatives in Massillion, however, with the name of Henrich. Tommy Henrich was an outfielder for the New York Yankees. His nickname was "old reliable."

Charles and Ida Henry had four children: Marie, Joseph, Charles Martin and Catherine.

Charles Martin Henry was born in Canton in 1896. "Charlie" served in France during World War I and, after returning to the states, earned a journeyman's card in electrical contracting.

Charlie Henry married Irene Degitz in 1923. Irene was born in Fort Wayne in 1902. She was the daughter of Carl (Charles) and Theresa (Riegel) Degitz. Charles Degitz was born in September of 1873 in Fort Wayne. He owned a grocery store on Spring Street (the present-day Green Frog Inn, which, coincidentally, is owned by his grandson Tom's wife, Cindy) and a saloon on Wells Street. Charles Degitz married Theresa Riegel in July 1896. Theresa Riegel was born in Avilla, Indiana in 1873. Charles died in Fort Wayne in 1932; Theresa died in 1956. Both are buried in the Catholic Cemetery.

In the early 1930s, Charlie and Irene Henry founded the Henry Electric Co., which still thrives today. The company is owned and operated by Charlie's grandson, Charles III. Charlie and Irene had five children: Charles Jr., Jerome, Eugene (Hank), Carol, and Morton. He died in Fort Wayne in 1955 and is buried in the Catholic Cemetery. Irene died in 1992 and is buried at Charlie's side.

Charles Jr. took over the reigns of Henry Electric Co. after Charles Sr. died. He married Barbara Beekman. They had five children. Jerome became a prominent social worker and political activist. He ran unsuccessfully for several elective offices and served two terms on the local school board. He married Marganelle Ruth Applegate. They had 17 children. Eugene became an electrician. He initially worked for his father and later moved to Florida to practice his trade. He married Peggy Westbrook. They had no children. Carol became a nurse and worked at Fort Wayne's St. Josep Hospital for many years. She married Gera Venderley. They had seven children. Morto also joined the electrical trade and followed h brother Eugene to Florida. He married Mary Fu len. They had no children. Mary died in 1998 ar is buried in the Fort Wayne Catholic Cemeter Mort later married Dee Buckland in 2000.

Submitted by Jerome F. Henry, S

The children of Joseph Henrich (Henry) at the time of his death in 1891. Front row from left to right: Elizabeth (Shoob), Maley (Fielding), Catherine (Bast) and Margaret (Halter). Back row: John, Charles Matthias, Jacob and August.

HENRY HOMESTEAD

In April 22, 1722, George Heinrich was bo in Pfalz, Germany. He migrated to Pennsylvan and changed his last name to Henry. One of h children was George whose son was Abrahan David Henry was born to Abraham. David ma ried Mary Beckley and migrated to Ohio an then walked to Indiana to buy a farm for eac of his five sons.

Son Samuel B. Henry's farm was at Sectic 15*. Samuel married Desdomona J. Robiso They had one son, William David, born Februa 21, 1873; he married Nora Jane Earl, Septemb 10, 1896. A first born died at birth, then Florenc Pearl, Samuel, Mable, and Herman were bo into the family. They bought twenty acres with house one half mile west on Winters Road, Se tion 10**. Later, twenty acres was purchase directly across the road, also with an existin home, to be replaced with a new home.

William and Nora Jane Henry, 1940

Florence married Edward Buskirk, they ha nine children and moved to California. Florenc died May 4, 1940.

Pearl married Russell Harding, they had tw children and lived in Fort Wayne. Pearl die October 15, 1942.

Samuel E. married Camilla Mahnensmit October 20, 1923. After the death of his grand parents, they moved to the farm* in 1919. Tw children, Lynn and Anna Belle were born in tha home. In 1934 they moved to the Smith Road an spent most of their remaining years there. Rev Lynn (Melba) Henry lives in Franklin, Indiana and has three sons. Anna Belle (Robert) Knap lives in Fort Wayne and has two daughters.

Mable married Russell Umber and later di vorced. After the passing of her Father Octobe 30, 1941, she lived with her Mother at Sectio 10** until her death, March 30, 1948. She the moved to Fort Wayne; Mable passed away October 10, 1992.

Herman married Grace Tom April 25, 193 and lived at the Section 15 farm. Two childre Paul and Marilyn (Judy) were born in that home Herman farmed Section 10** and 15* until retirement. After their Mother's death, March 20 1948 Herman and Grace bought Section 10** and Samuel and Camilla bought Section 15*. Herman and Grace lived in the homestead until their deaths, Herman July 15, 1979 and Grace December 6, 1999.

Paul (Carol) Henry built a home in 1992 on four acres land purchased across the road from Grace. They are parents of Brenda Terhune, Kenton Henry, and Rhonda Enterline who purchased four acres and the Henry Homestead in 2000. Marilyn (Larry) Smith live in rural Ossian in Allen County and are parents of Jodi Jump and Janell Petre. The Henry homestead has been in the family for nearly one hundred years. The swing still hangs in the same place and has held many family members as well as friends.

* Section 15 farm at Thiele and Winters Roads, Pleasant Township, Allen County

** Section 10 farm on Winters Road, Pleasant Township, Allen County

Submitted by Anna Belle Henry Knapp and Marilyn Henry Smith

ANTHONY M. HENRY

Anthony Martin Henry was born in Jackson, Michigan October 22, 1953 along with fraternal twin brother, Timothy Andrew. Tony was the fifth child born to Jerome F. and Marganelle (Applegate) Henry. He is one of 17 children.

His early primary years of school were at St. Charles Borromeo and Most Precious Blood Catholic grade schools. He also attended Central Catholic High School and, after a stint in the United States Marine Corp Reserves, graduated from North Side High School in 1973. His twin brother Tim continued in the Marine Corp and served in Vietnam. He died on January 25, 1977, at the age of 23, due to complications of post traumatic stress. Timothy never recovered emotionally from an accident while on ship.

In 1978 Tony joined the Franciscan order of Religion and entered college at Saint Louis University in Saint Louis, where he earned a BA in Philosophy and Fine Arts in 1985. He entered graduate studies in the fall of 1985 and earned a Masters in Education in 1988 at The Catholic University of America in Washington, D.C.

Tony left the Franciscan Order of Convents at the expiration of simple vows in 1986. He taught high school in Washington, D.C., and performed chaplaincy work as a layman directing regionally a pastoral care program for a long term health care facility. He returned to Fort Wayne in 1995 to assist a brother in the beverage business. In 1997, Tony purchased Deer Park Lodge, a pub adjacent to the University of St. Francis in Fort Wayne. In addition, he directed a Religious Education program for Saint Patrick's, Fort Wayne, from 1995 to 2003. He was hired as pastoral associate for Saint Andrews in 2002 until its closing in 2003. Tony continues to work pastorally for the Church as pastoral associate of St. Mary's and St. Peter's on a part-time basis. He cantors at St. Patrick's for special liturgies.

In April 2001, Tony married Susan Barbieri, a Catholic school teacher. She has two children: Daniel and Elizabeth. Daniel attends DePauw University and Elizabeth attends Bishop Luer's High School.

Tony enjoys being married, politics, classical music, nature, a good cigar, and imported beer or two and working with people.

Submitted by Anthony M. Henry

JEROME FRANCIS SR. & MARGANELLE RUTH (APPLEGATE) HENRY

Jerome Henry was born in Fort Wayne on January 19, 1926. He was the second son of Charles Martin Henry, Sr. and Irene (Degitz). He was one of five children —Charles, Jerome, Eugene, Carol, and Morton.

The Henry family always lived in the Bloomingdale area, first at 1703 Courtland Street and later at 602 West State Blvd. His father, Charles M. Henry, owned Henry Electric Company, and his mother, Irene, was the office manager and bookkeeper. The business was operated out of the family home.

Jerome, or Jerry, attended The Most Precious Blood Catholic Grade School and Central Catholic High School. He played football and was senior class president, graduating in 1944. He entered the United States Navy in June of that year and became a Radio Operator. Jerry was discharged in June 1946, and returned home to work with his dad in the electrical business. Before long, however, he decided to go back to school. He attended St. Joseph College in Rensalear, Indiana, Indiana Institute of Technology (Fort Wayne), and graduated from Indiana University (Bloomington and Fort Wayne).

Marganelle Applegate was the second child of five born to Emery and Genevieve (Compton) Applegate. Her parents came from Yorktown and Daleville, Indiana. Her father was a long time, well respected newspaper man, having worked early in his profession as a reporter, and later as an editorial writer and columnist for the *News-Sentinel*. Genevieve was a homemaker who was also interested in community theater, performing in a number of local productions.

Marganelle, or Margie, was born in Yorktown, Indiana. on May 31, 1929. She had three brothers, Cameron (Camille), Michael and William, and a sister Marney. Her family moved from Yorktown to Fort Wayne when she was four years old. Margie attended public grade schools and graduated from Central Catholic High School in 1947. An interest in art and fabrics, beginning when she was a young child, has continued through her life.

Jerry and Margie were married on August 20, 1949 at Saint Jude Catholic Church. The two then set out on what Margie would fondly refer to as "their great adventure."

Ten months after their honeymoon, Jerry Junior was born. The young family was living on the campus at Indiana University in Bloomington while Jerry was finishing up his undergraduate degree in Psychology. In 1951, Thomas was born. By this time the growing family was living in Indianapolis while Jerry pursued a graduate degree in Social Work.

By the next year, Margie was pregnant with Paula and the family moved to Jackson, Michigan, where Jerry began his career in social work at the Jackson Family and Children Agency. The following year, Jerry and Margie had their first set of twins, Timothy and Anthony. Then came Andrea in 1954. The couple had six children in less than five years of marriage.

In 1955, Jerry accepted a position at the neuro-psychiatric clinic at the University of Michigan at Ann Arbor. He was making a name for himself in the social work field while Margie was tending to her small gaggle of children, which grew by one that year with the addition of Denise.

Word of Jerry's innovative work in Ann Arbor traveled back to Fort Wayne and in 1956 the superintendent of the State School, now known as the State Development Center, offered Jerry a position. The state couldn't pay much, but offered free housing, which for the Henrys, was a big plus. So the family moved back to Fort Wayne and into a big farmhouse on the State School grounds on Saint Joe Road, near the present day IPFW campus. The farmhouse was old and rickety, but it was big and had plenty of acreage for the kids to play. And though poor as church mice, as Jerry would say, the family was healthy and happy and growing. The Henrys lived on Saint Joe Road from 1956 through 1964 and during this time Erik was born, followed by the second set of twins, Matthew and Martin. A year later, almost to the day, the third set of twins, Kurt and Karl,

The Jerome F. Sr. and Marganelle R. Henry family in 1978. Pictured from left to right are, front row, Denise, Sonya, Paula, Jessica, Lisa and Andrea. Back row: Martin, Karl, Matt, Tony, Tom, Margie, Jerry Sr., Jerry Jr., Erik, Kurt, Louie and Chris. Inset: Tim (deseased, 1977)

were born. Sonya came the following year and Louis (Louie the 14th) a year later. After 12 years of marriage, Jerry and Margie had 14 children, five of whom were in cloth diapers.

In 1964 the state began building the Indiana University-Purdue University extension on the grounds of the old homestead so, sadly, the family had to move. For a brief time the Henrys lived in a home they had purchased on West Fifth Street, which is where Christopher was born. With 14 children and a newborn, the West Fifth Street home proved too small, and the next year they bought a large home at the corner of Howell and Rumsey streets.

By 1966 Jerry had made quite an impact in the field of social work by implementing several innovative programs at the State School. Impressed with his work, then-Gov. Roger Brannigan asked Jerry to apply some of his new ideas as Superintendent of the Indiana Reformatory in Pendleton. Jerry accepted the position, sold the big home, and the family of 15 moved to the prison grounds.

Pendleton provided plenty of space for to play, including a tennis court, a swimming pool, membership at the country club, and more. In 1967, the family, along with the entire prison population, celebrated the birth of Lisa Michelle, number 16. The family's experience at Pendleton was great, but short lived. Jerry's programs proved too controversial, and after two and one-half years he was asked to resign. It was a sad time for Jerry and Margie. Ironically, many of Jerry's controversial programs are today a common practice in the criminal justice system.

Upon hearing about Jerry's impending resignation from the Reformatory, Monsignor John Reed of Catholic Charities in Fort Wayne asked him to consider a position as director of Catholic Social Services. Jerry accepted and the family moved back to the Summit City, taking residence once again at the home they still owned on West Fifth Street.

A fire and lack of room at the Fifth Street home made it necessary for the family to find another place to live. So in 1970, Jerry bought the old Kover Homestead at the corner of Howell and Runnion streets. The home was beautiful with its huge cobblestone porches and spacious yard. Most importantly, the house was large enough to accommodate the family 15 still living at home.

The early '70s also saw the arrival of Henry grandchildren, which, with a family their size, was expected. What Jerry and Margie didn't anticipate, however, was an addition to their immediate family. Much to everyone's surprise and delight was the birth of Jessica Joy in 1973.

The joy of the 1970s made a tragic turn with the death of Timothy. While on a tour of duty in Vietnam, Tim was seriously injured in an accident on board a ship in Okinawa. Despite years of treatment, Tim never fully recovered from his injuries and its related afflictions and he died in early 1977 at the age of 23. Tim's accident and subsequent death devastated the family, but they pulled together and their love for each other grew even stronger.

About this time Jerry became active in local politics and entered several races for elective office. His races became a family affair. Margie designed the brochures, her brother Mike Applegate printed them, and the kids would walk from precinct to precinct handing them out. He usually won impressive victories in the Democratic primaries, but was never able to win in the general election.

Throughout the late 1970s and the '80s, the older children were moving out of the nest almost as quickly as they entered it. Jerry continued making news professionally and politically while Margie began to concentrate on her art. In the mid 1980s, at the urging of Jerry and others, Margie introduced a series of greeting cards which were met with modest success. She also mastered other artistic techniques including oil painting, clay sculptures, scrafitto and paper collage.

In 1991 Jerry Henry retired. After making a major impact on the delivery of social services in Fort Wayne, he and Margie were recognized for their achievements with a big retirement party. Everyone figured they would enjoy their retirement by taking it easy. But Jerry and Margie had other plans. Margie began designing and creating liturgical vestments, religious banners and fabric art. Jerry ran for – and won – a seat on the Fort Wayne Community School Board of Trustees.

Today Jerry and Margie can often be seen sitting on the large porch swing of their beloved homestead on Howell Street, reminiscing about, one can be sure, their great adventure.

Submitted by Jerome F. Henry, Sr.

JEROME F. HENRY, JR.

Jerome F. Henry, Jr. was born on June 24, 1950 in Bloomington, Indiana. He was the first child of Jerome Francis and Marganelle Ruth (Applegate) Henry. He is one of 17 children. He attended primary school at both the Most Precious Blood and St. Charles Borromeo Catholic schools.

Jerry graduated from Central Catholic High School in 1968. On November 28, 1970 he married Rebecca Joan Keefer, the second oldest child of Ed and Virginia (Colone) Keefer.

Jerry was self-employed as a teenager and owns several steel-related companies and commercial properties in northeast Indiana. Jerry and Becky reside in Fort Wayne, Indiana. They have five children, Molly Camille Henry-Malloy (June 15, 1974); Peter Vincent (August 29, 1975); Joseph Edward (May 31, 1977); Phillip Lawrence (October 19, 1979); Maria Teresa Henry (January 11, 1988).

Submitted by Jerome F. Henry, Jr.

JESSICA JOY HENRY

Jessica Joy Henry was born in Fort Wayne, Indiana on August 16, 1973. She is the seventeenth child of Jerome and Marganelle Henry. She attended Most Precious Blood School until the eighth grade and graduated from North Side High School in 1991. She received her Bachelor of Arts degree from St. Joseph's College in Rensselaer, Indiana in May of 1995 where she majored in communications/theatre art.

After college, she lived in the United Kingdom and was employed by Citibank London. Upon her return to the states, she worked for such employers as the University of St. Francis (Fort Wayne), St. Patrick's Catholic Church, the City of Fort Wayne's Mayor's office, Paragon Steel, and, currently, Midwest Pipe & Steel.

She greatly enjoys volunteering and helping others. She also loves animals, most especially her many cats and dogs. She currently resides in the Nebraska neighborhood near downtown Fort Wayne.

Submitted by Jessica J. Henry

MATTHEW ROBERT & ANN MARIE (FAIR) HENRY

Matthew Robert Henry was born in Fort Wayne, Indiana on September 1, 1958. He is the ninth child born to Jerome F. Henry, Sr. and Marganelle (Applegate). He is one of 17 children — Jerome, Jr., Paula, Anthony and Timothy (twins), Andrea, Denise, Erik, Matthew and Martin (twins), Kurt and Karl (twins), Sonya, Louis, Christopher, Lisa and Jessica — and one of three sets of twins.

During Matt's formative years, the Henry family lived at the corner of Howell and Runnion streets, in the area of Fort Wayne known as "Hungry Hill." His father was a well-respected social worker and political activist; his mother, in addition to running a household of 17 children, was an admired artist.

Matt and his siblings were the third generation of Henrys to attend The Most Precious Blood Catholic Grade School. Matt graduated in 1977 from North Side High School, where he was active in student government and served as Student Council president. He went on to earn a Bachelor of Science degree in Communications in 1984 from Purdue University at Fort Wayne.

The Matt and Ann Henry family in 1999. Pictured left to right are: Ann, Adam, Matt, Emilie, Reid, Caitlin and Olivia.

Ann Marie Fair was born in Fort Wayne on July 30, 1960. She is the third and last child born to Richard A. and Sylvie (Sult) Fair. Her parents were born and raised in Fort Wayne. Her father was a well-known and respected pharmaceutical representative, retiring in 1997. He died in 2005 and is entombed at the Catholic Cemetery in Fort Wayne. Ann's mother raised her children and later began a career as an independent interior decorator. She retired in 2000.

Ann, who also goes as Anne, has two brothers: Gregory A. and Kevin K. Fair. She attended St. Jude Catholic Grade School and graduated in 1978 from R. Nelson Snider High School, where she was active in theater.

Matt and Anne were married on July 17, 1982 at St. Jude Catholic Church. On November 16 of that same year their first son, Adam Matthew, was born. Matt was going to college at the time and working for the Indiana Department of Corrections. He also was working as a part-time staff writer for the Fort Wayne *Journal-Gazette*. Anne stayed home with the baby.

Shortly after graduation from Purdue, Matt accepted a position at St. Joseph's Hospital in downtown Fort Wayne. On September 2, 1985, the very day Matt began employment at St. Joe, Emilie Celeste was born.

In 1986, Matt ran as a Democrat for a seat on the Allen County Council, but was defeated.

The following year Caitlin Elizabeth was born on July 30, 1987. Coincidentally, she shares the same birthday as her mother and her grandmother, Sylvie.

In September 1988, Matt left St. Joe Hospital and founded Patterson Riegel Advertising, named after his maternal great-grandparents. The company specializes in full-service advertising for many well-known companies throughout the Fort Wayne area.

On January 14, 1992, Olivia Ann was born, followed by the birth of Reid Francis on April 24, 1996.

While Anne stays busy at home raising the children, Matt is active serving on several local boards including the Allen County Park Board, the Allen County/Fort Wayne Historical Society Board; the Fort Wayne Catholic Cemetery Board, the Fort Wayne Youtheatre Board; the Fort Wayne Community School Scholarship Board; and many others. He also teaches religious education at St. Jude Catholic School.

In 1998 the family moved to the Chandler's Landing subdivision in northeast Allen County, where they live today.

Submitted by Matt Henry

CHALMER VERNON & EDITH BEATRICE HENSCHEN FAMILY

Chalmer, born February 22, 1906, grew up in Adams and Wells counties where his grandparents, Jacob and Mary (Spangler) Henschen, were barn builders/farmers and Absolom and Alice (Somers) Ginter were farmers. Chalmer's parents, Charles William and Elta Clyde (Ginter) Henschen were farmers. Chalmer graduated from Kirkland High School where he played on the basketball team, then he attended one year at Ball State University. He worked on the pipeline that summer. Once he discovered that he could earn more money at a factory in Fort Wayne, Chalmer moved to Waynedale in 1928 taking a job first at Dudlo Wire Company, then at Inca Division of Phelps-Dodge.

In 1932, Chalmer met Edith Beatrice ("Bea") Kinerk on a Waynedale Methodist Church picnic. Bea was born on the family farm on Ferguson Road on January 15, 1910 where her parents, Martin Monroe and Edith Lucinda (Bovine) Kinerk were farmers/insurance agent. Bea graduated from Fort Wayne Central High School then worked at Frank's Dry Goods Department store. Her grandparents were: William R. and Malinda (Beck) Kinerk, and David and Emma Ella (Smith) Bovine, all of Allen County. Chalmer and Bea eloped to Frankfort, Illinois on June 24, 1933. In 1935 they had their first of four children and Bea became a stay at-home mom. All four children grew up in Waynedale attending Waynedale Elementary and Elmhurst High School.

Lynn Duane has been with Branstrator Family of Businesses for over fifty years; Noel Vernon worked for Trainer's Service Center and has been a mechanic (with two years service in the Army) for over 40 years; Jay Eldon graduated from Purdue as a pharmacist and worked 38 years for Parkview Hospital; and Suzanne Joyce (Mrs. Robert Dunlap) has worked as an insurance claims analyst for over 40 years at Lincoln Life and ProClaim.

The Chalmer Vernon and Edith Beatrice Henschen family, January, 1947.

Bea lived until August 22, 1990 and Chalmer retired from C. L. Schust Roofing and Sheet Metal Company in 1972; he lived until February 7, 2002. Chalmer and Bea resided at 7710 Bluffton Road from 1935 to 1959 then moved to a new home at 1930 Ferguson Road. They were long-time members of Waynedale Methodist Church. Chalmer's enjoyment was gardening, Pistons and IU Basketball, and visiting with family and friends. Bea's enjoyment was similar to Chalmer's, plus she really enjoyed cooking, canning, and sewing. They were proud of their four children and eleven grandchildren and fifteen great-grandchildren. Chalmer and Bea are both interred at Prairie Grove Cemetery in Waynedale.

Submitted by Jay E. Henschen

JAY ELDON & SANDRA SUE HENSCHEN FAMILY

Jay, born November 24, 1942, in Allen County, grew up in Waynedale at 7710 Bluffton Road. His parents were Chalmer Vernon and Edith Beatrice (Kinerk) Henschen. His dad was a factory worker and mom was a full-time homemaker. His grandparents were Charles William and Elta Clyde (Ginter) Henschen, farmers in Wells County; and Martin Monroe and Edith Lucinda (Bovine) Kinerk who were farmers on Ferguson Road in Allen County.

Jay attended Waynedale Methodist Church, Waynedale Elementary School, and Elmhurst High School graduating in 1961. He went on to Purdue University graduating January 1967, with a B.S. in Pharmacy. From age 12 to 15, he delivered the *News Sentinel*, from 16 to 18 worked part-time at Waynedale Pharmacy, and summers during college years worked at Eckrich Cold Meats Plant.

While attending Purdue, Jay was introduced to Sandra Sue Johnson by a friend. Sandra had also grown up in Allen County on Sutton Drive. She was born October 15, 1943, in Whitley County, Indiana. She attended St. Michael Lutheran Church, Anthony Wayne Grade School, and Elmhurst High School graduating in 1962. Sandy continued at Parkview Methodist School of Nursing graduating in 1965. After graduation, Sandy took a nursing position at Passavant Hospital in Chicago. Then on June 11, 1966, Jay and Sandy were married at St. Michael Lutheran Church on Getz Road in Fort Wayne. That summer Sandy worked for Parkview Hospital while Jay did his pharmacy apprenticeship. Jay had one last semester that fall at Purdue where he worked part-time at the Chemistry Library and Sandy worked part-time at the University Hospital.

That fall, Purdue had an excellent football team which won the right to go to the Rose Bowl for the first time, Jay and Sandy were there when Purdue won.

Sandy's parents were William David and Mary Margaret (Wherry) Johnson. Her dad was a steel worker at Joslyn Steel Company, and her mom was a homemaker and key punch operator. Her grandparents were James David and Rose (Whitaker) Johnson; and Orville Sylvester and Mary Alice (Barkley) Wherry.

After graduation, Jay accepted a pharmacist position at Parkview Hospital. Sandy worked there also as an RN until their first child was born. The year 1968 was significant for this family as they bought a new home at 1223 Pion Road in northern Allen County, bought a bright red 1968 Dodge Charger, and their first child was born...Liesl Marie was born October 2, 1968; Lawrence Wayne was born August 18, 1970; and Alan Jay was born August 31, 1971 all at Parkview Hospital in Fort Wayne.

From 1975 to 1990 Sandy worked part-time as office nurse for Dr. John Hamer. The family attended Robinson Chapel United Methodist Church, the kids attended and graduated from Perry Hill Grade School and Carroll High School. Liesl played tennis, Larry played football, and Alan played soccer and football as varsity sports. Liesl went on to get a degree in Chemical Engineering from Purdue then worked for Abbott Labs for five years. She became the wife of William Richard Shen. Liesl met William at Purdue. They married October 1993. William, also an engineer, worked at Baxter Labs north of Chicago. They had two boys and one girl (Henry, John and Arden).

Larry attended two years at IPFW University studying accounting, then on June 15, 1991, a tragic swimming accident took his life.

Alan joined the Air Force in 1990 and trained to become an F-15 crew chief. That December he married his high school sweetheart, Lisa Marie Hoover. They were stationed in Okinawa for two years. They had two boys (Dillon and Andrew). After the Air Force, Alan became a licensed journeyman in heating and air conditioning. His first marriage dissolved, and in June 2004, he

Jay Eldon and Sandra Sue Henschen Family

married Lea Marie. They moved to Somerset, Kentucky, where Lea worked as a nurse, and Alan in heating and air. Lea's children were also in Somerset: daughter, Sondra; and son, Chris, and wife, Christina, with new baby Dillon Anthony Carnes. This made Alan and Lea quite young grandparents. Meanwhile, Jay's wife Sandy developed breast cancer and it eventually took her life April 10, 1997. Both Sandy and Son, Larry, are interred at Highland Park Cemetery on Wallen Road.

Jay remarried on January 6, 2001 to Joan Kathleen (Cole) Fernandez. They met at a Focus On The Family seminar at Colorado Springs. Joan was originally from northwest Indiana, then Green Bay, Wisconsin. She worked as a retail service-representative and retired after three years at Anchor Room Book Store here in Fort Wayne. Jay worked until 2005 retiring from Parkview Health System after 38 years.

Submitted by Jay Henschen

HENSINGER, MUHN & FORD FAMILY

There is no History, only fictions of various degrees of plausibility. Voltaire.

Families are the product of generations. My mother's forbears, Johannes and Sabine (Mueller) Hensinger lived in Germany, and Johann Jacob Hensinger, the third of their six children, was the first generation in America, settling in east central Pennsylvania in 1753. The fourth generation Hensinger was Harrison, who traveled with the Kistler family to Seneca County, Ohio, where on April 4, 1850 he married Mary Ann Kistler. Harrison's wife stayed in Ohio while he and his younger brother, Owen, traveled that spring across the Black Swamp to Dutch Ridge in northern Perry Township, Allen County, to clear some land and built a cabin where the couple raised a family of five; the fourth became my grandmother, Rosie Ann Ellen Hensinger.

In the meantime, Ann Barbara (Kirchner) and Johann Wilhelm Muhn and two sons (three more children later) left Baden about 1845, and came to Dutch Ridge about 1858, where their second son Michael raised a family of eight; the third became my grandfather, John Martin Muhn, born 1868. Working in the woods as a preteen teamster's helper, he became an expert teamster. The day before the March 13, 1888 marriage of Rosie Ann and John, the notorious tornado of 1888 ripped through Dutch Ridge. According to Grandpa, it pulled a pump (probably driven by a windmill) and forty feet of pipe from the ground and carried it to the Ohio line. In 1900 he moved his family to DeKalb County, continued logging, plowed gardens and dug most of the basements in Auburn.

Geneva Myrtle Muhn was the fourth of five children. Geneva didn't care for housework, preferring to work in the fields with her father until she was sixteen. Then Grandma said it was time to learn housework. Being a headstrong young lady, she found a sales job at Little's Jewelry Store in Auburn.

George Ford had moved into London, England, with his ten children. His four sons traded with the Far East, and in one storm lost all four four-masted ships off the coast of South Africa. Suddenly impoverished, they apprenticed as printers. With only his bag of tools, each learned to build his own printing press, cut type and then do the printing. The second son, Edward Augustus, came to America in 1879, set up business in the seaport town of Haverhill, Massachusetts, with his son, Henry Wetton Ford, who courted and married a local milliner, Leola Imogene Whitten. This couple had two sons, Charles Lester and Arthur Whitten Ford.

About Christmas time, 1914, Arthur Ford visited his Uncle Louis Whitten in Auburn, shopped extensively at Little's Jewelry Store, and in June married the clerk, Geneva. They lived in and around Auburn, Indiana, had two girls, Leola Ellen and Barbara Jane, and a son, Henry Wetton Ford. After discharge from the Army Air Corps, WWII, Henry lived in Allen County, an electronic design engineer and a Quality Assurance engineer at Farnsworth and Magnavox until retirement.

Submitted by Henry W. Ford

The Muhn Family. *From left to right: Roland Muhn Junior (1922), Marjorie Ann Richey (1920), David Henderson Richey (1924), John Roland Muhn (1891), Perry Arthur Muhn (1920), Henry Wetton Ford (1924), Dessa Lavina (Muhn) Kingsbury (1888), Catherine Ann (Dye) Muhn (1902), Thomas Martin Muhn (1927), Barbara Jane Ford (1921, Charles Edward Kingsbury (1888), Rosie Ann Ellen (Hensinger) Muhn (1868), Clarence Clifton "Tib" Muhn (1893), Geneva Myrtle (Muhn) Ford (1898), John Martin Muhn (1868), Leola Ellen Ford (1917), John Henry Muhn (1918), Arthur Whitten Ford (1895), Naomi Lavon (Muhn) Richey (1900), Henderson Moore Richey (1894), Louella (Moon) Richey (1859)*

HERBER FAMILY

Anna Marie Herber, born September 17, 1905, was the youngest child of Anton and Martha (Schmidt) Herber. The Herber farm was located at Monroeville and Marion Center Roads and was the playground for Ambrose, Blanche, Robert and Elizabeth. The family didn't have electricity until Roosevelt was in office. Marie's brother had a radio that ran on batteries and they remember listening to Opera.

The Herber children attended St. Joseph Hessen Cassel School, where religion class was presented in German. Marie's sister Blanche, didn't know any English until she started school. Following elementary school, Marie and Elizabeth attended St. Augustine's Girls Academy in Fort Wayne at Jefferson and Calhoun Streets. Marie had to get from her home to St. Joseph's and then catch the interurban to downtown. In the winter months she lived full time at the school, where she worked for her room and board. Her sister Elizabeth, was the first girl in Marion Township to graduate from high school and after graduation she joined the convent. She lives at St. Mary of the Woods and is 101 years old.

Cousin Amuel Herber took Marie with him to a CYO dance at St. Louis Besancon where her future would begin with a dance. Earl told Marie she was a good dancer and she replied that it was because he was a good partner. Earl visited the Herber home each Sunday following that dance to court Marie. One day they were talking about brides. Earl asked if she was going to be his bride some day. Marie knew then they would be married. On June 21, 1941, Earl Bowers and Marie became life partners at St. Joseph Hessen Cassel.

Blanche organized the neighborhood ladies to help with the reception for 150 guests. The barn was cleaned out for the dance. The floor was rough and uneven, but everyone had a good time. It rained every Saturday that month except the day Marie and Earl married. It was a hot day, "good for drinking beer." The couple moved into Earl's grandparents' home on Moore Road, near the State Line, where Marie lives now. The farm has been in the Bowers family over 100 years. Nine children filled the farmhouse. Michael arrived in 1942, Bill in 1943, Tom and Nancy in 1944, Marcia and Noreen in 1945, John in 1946, Jerome in 1947 and Brenda in 1949.

The kids played outdoors, explored the many farm buildings, milked cows and brought in coal and wood. During summer they collected mussels and catfish from the creek for Aunt Blanche to cook. Earl kept order at the table by shaking his knife handle. Each member had an assigned seat with Earl in the center of one side. The youngest daughter, Brenda, sat beside him where he didn't see the many faces she made to get the others laughing as he tried to bring order. Marie and Earl raised their children with a Catholic education.

Grandmother of 23 and great grandmother to 12, Marie will turn 100 in September.

Submitted by Julie (Pequignot) Nolan

HERMAN & WACASEY FAMILIES

Steven Park Herman was born in Fort Wayne, Indiana. Steve is the son of Gervase Park and Mary Ann (Prendergast) Herman. He married Karen Jean Clifford June 7, 1975 at St. Vincent's Catholic Church, Fort Wayne, Indiana. Karen was born in Cincinnati, Ohio, to George Lawrence and Helen Ruth (Brower) Clifford. Steve and Karen went to high school at Bishop Dwenger, Fort Wayne, Indiana. He is employed as a conductor by the Norfolk Southern Railroad. Steve also volunteers as a fireman for the Grabill VFD and is a board member for Cedar Creek Township. Karen is a homemaker and enjoys crafts. To this marriage were born three children.

Samuel Park Herman was born in Fort Wayne, Indiana, and is a graduate of Leo High School. Sam is also a member of the Grabill VFD and works for Dutch Made Inc. as a cabinetmaker.

Patrick Scott Herman was born in Fort Wayne. Patrick is a graduate of Leo High School and Northwestern University in Lima, Ohio. He is a member of the Grabill Volunteer Fire Department and currently works for Dutch Made Inc. as a cabinetmaker. Pat was married October 14, 2000 to Krista Lynn Tuscan, daughter of Joel Thomas and Diane Joyce (Coon) Tuscan, in Harlan at the United Methodist Church. They have one child at this writing, Michael Park, born in Fort Wayne, Indiana. Krista is a graduate of Woodlan High School. She graduated from IPFW in 1999 and works for Grabill Bank.

Jennifer Ann Herman was born Fort Wayne, Indiana. She was married April 13, 2002 at the Allen County Courthouse to Kenneth Randell (Randy) Wacasey who was born in Fort Wayne, Indiana, son of Kenneth Richard and Monika Veronica (Froelich) Wacasey. Both are graduates of Leo High School. Jennifer and Randy have two children, Kaeda Rose and Ava Elizabeth, both born in Fort Wayne Indiana. Randy married Jennifer Ann Herman April 13, 2002. Randy is a graduate of Leo High School. He is also a graduate of ITT College in Electrical Engineering and currently works for Inotek in Garrett, Indiana. Jennifer is a graduate of Leo High School and Indiana Business College in Health claims.

Gervase Park Herman Jr., (Gus), was born October 18, 1929 in Fremont, Ohio. Gus was the son of Gervase Protase and Sylvia Frances (Mulligan) Herman. Gus married Mary Ann Prendergast June 26, 1954 in Fort Wayne, Indiana.

Mary Ann is the daughter of Giles Anthony and Mildred Pauline (Fisher) Prendergast. She was born in Aurora, Illinois, and moved to Fort Wayne in 1950 from New York when her father came to Fort Wayne to manage the Grand Leader Department Store. Mary went into business on the Landing in Fort Wayne, owning an antique store. Later she worked at Carl's tavern with Gus.

Gus was a graduate of Central Catholic High School. He served in the U.S. Army as a military policeman during the Korean War and was a member of the Fort Wayne Police Department holding the rank of patrolman and later Detective Sergeant from 1953 until 1973. Gus and Mary were partners with Bob and Rita Landstoffer in Carl's Tavern in New Haven for 29 years.

To this marriage were born five children. Steven Park, Sandra Pauline, Judith Frances, Cynthia Jean and Theresa Ann. All the children were born in Fort Wayne, Indiana.

Gus passed away on June 16, 1992 in Fort Wayne, Indiana after a long illness and is buried in the Catholic Cemetery in Fort Wayne.

Submitted by Steve Herman

CLAUDE TAFT & MABEL MALISSA (HUFFMAN) HEROLD FAMILY

Claude and Mabel met when their roommates introduced them in Fort Wayne, Indiana. Claude Taft Herold was living at 729 Columbia Avenue in Fort Wayne. He was attending Anthony Wayne Business College. He worked at Conrad Tire Service as an assistant bookkeeper and Goodyear as a clerk. Claude was born March 8, 1909, in Switz City, Indiana. He was the only child of Roscoe and Olive Herold. Claude's parents sent

Claude T. Herold and Mabel (Hoffman) Herold Second Year Wedding Anniversary, June 1934. Pale Green Wedding Dress

him to Fort Wayne for an education in business to help them with their Elwood Tire Sales store in Elwood, Indiana.

Mabel Malissa Huffman was living at 901 Columbia Avenue and working at Magnavox. Her parents were Verne and Elfa Huffman residing in Fort Wayne. When Mabel was asked to meet Claude Herold by her roommate, Mabel said, "Claude Herold Who?" She thought Herold was his second name. Dating during the Depression was a challenge. They walked or took the trolley to the movies and shared a bag of popcorn. Lakeside Park was nearby and a beautiful place to court a girl. They married June 23, 1932, at Mabel's church, Concordia Evangelical Lutheran Church at the corner of Alliger and Anthony Boulevard. They lived at 1040 Lake Avenue after the wedding. They moved to Elwood, Indiana, before their daughter, Marian Alice, was born December 11, 1934.

Mabel Malissa was born in Roanoke, Indiana, on March 24, 1909. Mabel moved to Fort Wayne with her family in 1926 from Roanoke, Indiana, when she was 17 years old. In Roanoke, she had been promoted several grades as a result of reading and studying her older sisters' primers from school. She was third in a family of nine children. Her father didn't want her to finish high school, and she went to work at Murphy's Dime Store. Her boss learned of her dream and allowed her to leave early to attend classes at Central High School so she could earn enough credits to graduate. She was very proud of her diploma and didn't tell her father until she was 41 years old.

Claude and Mabel divorced in 1941 in Kokomo, Indiana. Claude retired from Goodyear in Indianapolis and remarried February 14, 1973, to Geraldine Edwards in Plainfield, Indiana. He passed away January 26, 1983, and is buried by his parents in Switz City, Indiana.

Mabel remarried John William Curry in 1948 while living in Parkersburg, West Virginia. They had two children, Hal C. Curry born in 1949 and Melinda J. Curry born in 1950. They were divorced in 1950. Mabel moved with her three children to Fort Wayne and began working at General Electric. "Bill" Curry passed away January 1951 in Athens, Ohio, and is buried by his parents in Athens. Mabel retired from General Electric in 1971. She died in Garrett, Indiana, on November 12, 1996, and is buried by her parents in Lindenwood Cemetery, Fort Wayne, Indiana.

Mabel's children are still living as of this date. Marian Herold Klinger lives in Garrett, Indiana. Hal Curry lives in Texas. Melinda Curry Peppler lives in Fort Wayne.

Peter and Elizabeth (Helfrich) Herold immigrated to the United States in 1828. They were originally from Reichenbach, Germany, an area then known as "Hesse-Darmstadt." It is a little town in the Odenwald about a 40 minute drive southeast of Frankfurt. They traveled through Pennsylvania and settled in Carrollton, Ohio. Their son, Dr. Henry Herold, moved to Indiana in 1868.

The Huffmans immigrated from Germany. They arrived in Virginia and lived in Ashland, Ashland County, Ohio, before William Huffman moved to Huntington County, Indiana in 1845.

Submitted by Lois Bullard

DON HERTIG FAMILY

Don and Marquita Hertig of Springfield Township, Harlan, Indiana, were Harlan High School sweethearts who married in 1957 in the old Harlan United Methodist Church. Don is the son of Charles and Geraldine Hertig of Harlan. (Charles died in 2000.) Don was born in Fort Wayne in 1937 and has one sister, Shirley (Spindler), and two brothers, David and Steve, all of whom live in the Harlan area.

Marquita (Richmond) was born in Sherwood, Ohio to Darrell and Lucille (Mettert) Richmond of Harlan. (Darrell died in 1995.) Marquita has one brother, Rex, of Harlan.

Don and Marquita have two children, Richard (Rick) and Kimberly, and five grandsons. Rick married Cathleen (DeWaelsch) in 1979 and they have three sons, Nathan, Adam and Andrew. All live in the Harlan area. Kim married Kirk Davis in 1989 and they live in Leo, Indiana with their two sons, Kody and Carter.

Don and Marquita are members of the Harlan United Methodist Church. Marquita is the Church

Don Hertig Family, 1990. Front seated: Andy, Adam, Nate Hertig; Darrel and Lucille Richmond; Charlie Hertig. Standing: Marquita and Don Hertig; Kim (Hertig) Davis, Kirk Davis; Geraldine Hertig; Rick and Cathy (DeWaelsch) Hertig

Historian and enjoys keeping a history of the church as well as of the town of Harlan. She is also a member of the Harlan Business Association, helping with the goal of continually improving the town. Don is a member of the Harlan Masonic Lodge and Fort Wayne Shrine Club.

Don graduated from Ball State Teachers College in 1963, and Marquita graduated from

Indiana University in 1995. Don was a teacher in the Fort Wayne School system for several years after graduation but recently retired from the insurance business after 30 years as an agent and manager. His job took them away from Harlan in 1980, and they were moved to several Indiana towns before they were able to finally move back "home" to Harlan in 2000. Marquita has been a real estate agent for many years and recently sold the old 1855 Maysville Graded School and Odd Fellows Lodge Building (which they saved and restored) at 17525 State Road 37 in Harlan where she owned and operated Mardon Real Estate.

Nature continues to be one of their favorite hobbies and planting trees and flowers and maintaining their twelve acres which includes a pond, woods, covered bridge, log cabin and hundreds of pines and hardwoods keeps them very busy. This year (2005) finds them still enjoy traveling, attending grandsons' ballgames, and helping with community events.

Submitted by Marquita Hertig

GEORGE M. HESS FAMILY

In 1936, George M. Hess was looking for a farm to rent. His cousin, Ervin Hess, ran a bread route. One of his stops was at Barney Heffelfinger's farm near Huntertown. Barney owned two farms, and one was for rent.

George grabbed the opportunity and went to see Barney. Ervin had already told Barney that George was a good farmer. The only drawback was that George had ten children. Barney replied, "That's no problem, I have nine!"

So George loaded up his family and earthly goods and left the Avilla area where he and his wife Lenore lived all their lives to a small 80 acre farm north of Huntertown. When they moved, their ten children were ranging in age from the eldest Genevieve, 17, to the youngest, George Jr., 1-1/2 years of age.

Times were getting better after the Great Depression, but money was still scarce. The whole family would weed onions for Louie Ruderman, except George and George, Jr. George and family, besides farming, did a lot of truck farming to sell at the farmer's market in Fort Wayne along with eggs and poultry.

There were free movies in LaOtto on Tuesday nights and in Huntertown on Friday nights, which George and his family enjoyed a great deal.

In the fall, Lenore and the older children again worked at Ruderman's onion farm, topping onions with sheep shears and putting them in crates. What did the children do with their wages? They laid aside enough money for school books, a little spending money, and a dollar or two for Christmas gifts.

Hess Family: First Row: Lois. Second Row: Hubert, Lenore (Mother), holding George, George (Father), and Merlin. Last row: Richard, Ruth, Merton, Jenny, Illene and Howard

With the small farm, truck farming, and working elsewhere when something was available, George and his family made an honest living where they all enjoyed the country life.

Monday through Saturday were days of work and little play for the family, but Sunday was a day of rest. They all went to church and then came home to a big family dinner with an afternoon or softball game in the cow pasture.

George farmed all those years with horses and the boys kept begging for something more modern, so one day George came chugging up the road with his first tractor, a McCormick Deering 1020.

George and his boys could raise hogs to two hundred pounds in less time than anyone in the neighborhood.

Barney Heffelfinger decided to sell the farm, so George bought it for $9,000, raising hogs with Merton's help those few years.

George and Lenore had six boys and four girls. From the oldest on down: Genevieve, Ruth, Richard, Eileen, Merton, Hubert, Howard, Merlyn, Lois, and George, Jr. George's daughter Ruth dated and married Barney Heffelfinger's son, Keith.

The family attended a Lutheran church in Avilla. Half of the family remained in the Allen County area their whole lives, with Howard, Merlyn, and George Jr. still living on the home farm ground.

Descendants of George and Lenore are 46 grandchildren, 138 great-grandchildren, and 31 great-great-grandchildren.

Submitted by George L. Hess

RICHARD M. HESS

Richard Morton Hess was born February 23, 1925, in Lutheran Hospital in Fort Wayne, Indiana. Doctor A. L. Schneider was the attending doctor. His mother is Edna Boegli, born 1894 died 1981. She is the daughter of Katharina Amstutz and Peter Boegli. His father is Elmer Eugene Hess, born 1897 died 1996, the son of Emma Siemon and George Franklin Hess.

His brothers and sisters are as follows. Gretchen Hess Friend, born April17, 1917, and died May 12,1989, in Warren, Ohio. Eugene E. Hess born January 11,1918, married Jean Burgoyne and is living in Oklahoma. Pauline Hess born February 3, 1920, married Lee Tawes and lives in Florida. Corliss B. Hess born October 18, 1923, married Betty Squires and lives in Fort Wayne. Marilyn born August 24, 1926, married Darrell Gerig and lives in Monroe, Indiana.

Richard married Phyllis Irene Lafferty on December 9, 1951, at the First United Methodist Church in Warren, Ohio. Phyllis was born in Harrisburg, Pennsylvania, on July 17, 1928. Her parents are Nellie Hancock and G. Howard Lafferty of Warren, Ohio. She has one brother, Donald E. Lafferty of Strongsville, Ohio.

Richard graduated from Central High School in 1943 and was drafted into the Army that same year. He received his Paratroopers Boots and Wings on New Years Eve 1944. He served in the Pacific theater: New Guinea, the Philippines, Leyte, and Dutch East Indies. He received the Purple Heart after his jump on Corregidor. He was a member of the 503rd Infantry Paratroop Unit. He also received the Bronze Star Medal, Combat Infantry Badge, the United States Presidential Unit Citation, Philippine Presidential Unit Citation, American Campaign Medal, World War II Victory Medal, Asiatic Pacific Theater Campaign Medal with two Bronze Stars and one Arrowhead, Philippine Liberation Ribbon, and a Good Conduct Medal.

Upon his return to Fort Wayne, Richard enrolled at Indiana Technical Institute. He received a Bachelor of Science Degree in mechanical engineering in 1948. Richard left Fort Wayne and found a job in Warren, Ohio, with Packard Electric Division of General Motors as a senior engineer. He worked there 38 years, retiring in 1987.

On June 27, 2001, the Packard Museum Association welcomed Richard into the Packard Electric Excellence Hall of Fame, Delphi Automotive Systems. "In recognition of outstanding achievements, which contributed to our success."

Richard and Phyllis have three children. Kenneth married Connie Irish; they have one daughter, Amber, and live in California. Jeffrey married Patricia Berry; they have two sons, Kyle and Christopher, and live in Texas. Linda married Mitchell Nelson; they have two children, Logan and Lucy, and live in California.

George F. Hess, grandfather of Richard M. Hess, was born January 1, 1872, in Fort Wayne, the son of Varolina Werner of Delphos, Ohio, and Jacob Philip Hess. Emma Siemon, his wife, was born November 30, 1872, in Fort Wayne, the daughter of Paul and Anna Margaret Kohlbacker Siemon. George F. Hess was general superintendent of motive power Wabash Railroad, located in Decatur, Illinois.

Jacob Philip Hess, 1841 - 1921, immigrated as a young man on the ship "Favorita" on August 14, 1864, from Pfullingen, Wurtemberg, Germany, to New York. He worked as a machinist. He retired from the Pennsylvania Railroad after 47 years. He married Varolina in Fort Wayne November 27, 1870. They raised a daughter, Bertha, born February 12, 1879, died August 22, 1916, and four sons: George F.; William J., born October 31,1873, married Mary Cairns; Philip E., born October 6, 1876, married Mary Vesta Wilson; and Edmund W., born July 1, 1883, married Zephora Jett. The family home was on East Creighton Street.

Submitted by Richard and Phyllis Hess

JOHN & JANE (IDDINGS) HIGGINS FAMILY

On June 16, 1973, John Owen Higgins and Jane Iddings were married at St. Joseph Catholic Church in Garrett, Indiana. John earned a mathematics undergraduate degree from Purdue and masters degree in systems management from the University of Southern California. He served as an active duty officer in the United States Air Force. The couple lived in California, Okinawa, Japan, and Virginia before settling in Fort Wayne in 1979. John retired as a Lt. Colonel from the Indiana Air National Guard at Fort Wayne. John worked at both ITT Aerospace/Optical Division for 25 years as a senior project engineer, and

L. to R. John, Jane, and Patrick Higgins

with General Dynamics Command Systems here in Fort Wayne.

John can trace his family history on his mother's side to 1620 in Rappahannock County, Virginia. These ancestors were originally from Upper Slaughter, Gloucester, England. On his father's Higgins side John's relatives lived in Sligo County, Ireland, before settling in Canada and finally Chicago, Illinois. John was born in 1942 in South Bend, the son of Harold and Marceille (Murley) Higgins. John's only sister, Anne Marie, is a Fort Wayne Community schoolteacher.

Jane (Iddings) Higgins can trace her ancestors to the 1066 Domesday Book in England. The Iddings came to America in 1697\98 with William Penn and eventually moved to Ohio and later Indiana. One of the most famous Iddings relatives was Anthony Wayne, Revolutionary War general and namesake of the city of Fort Wayne. Anthony Wayne's mother was Elizabeth Iddings Wayne. Anthony was born on January 1, 1745, in Waynesboro, Pennsylvania. Jane is also descended from the Rowan, Scott, and Milleman families.

On Jane's mother's side her ancestors were from Scotland and England. The Milleman family, Jane's paternal grandmother, was originally from the Alsace-Lorraine region of Europe.

Jane graduated from Ball State University with a degree in secondary education. She was the first of six children born to Warren and Mary Katherine (Rowan) Iddings in Sturgis, Michigan in 1947.

A son, Patrick Samuel Higgins, was born in 1984 and graduated from Bishop Dwenger High School in 2003. Patrick is currently a student at Purdue University in West Lafayette.

Submitted by John Higgins

HARRY H. HILGEMANN

Judge Harry H. Hilgemann's "notable professional career included Allen County Circuit Court judge, defense counsel, and prosecuting attorney. An unusually capable lawyer who contended uncompromisingly for what he thought was right, he nevertheless carried with him into the courts a gentility of manner that will always be remembered. On the bench he evidenced an admirable judicial temperament, combined with a remarkably comprehensive knowledge of the law and its application. He was indeed one of Fort Wayne's most revered, responsible and valuable citizens" *(Fort Wayne News Sentinel* editorial, June 26, 1957).

Family history and education

Harry Hilgemann was born in Fort Wayne, August 19, 1881. His grandparents, Henry Eberhard Hilgemann and Frederika Hilgemann, emigrated to the US from Lienen, Germany, in 1848 or 1850. His father, Henry Frederick Hilgemann (1851-1904) married Lisette Bueker (1852-1920) who came to Fort Wayne in 1870 from Tek1enberg, Lengerich, Germany. In 1884, Harry's parents opened the Hilgemann Grocery and Meat Market at 121 West Jefferson Street. (As a high school student, Harry hitched up their horse and buggy early in the morning to pick up the grocery's meat from the slaughter house. Because times were hard, customers bought the cheaper cuts first, often leaving the family with porterhouse steaks!) Harry graduated from Fort Wayne High School in 1900, then worked his way through the University of Michigan (Ann Arbor) law school as a hotel waiter and night clerk, graduating with an LLD degree in 1903.

In 1909, he married Minnie E. Horn (1884 - 1977), his legal secretary, who had attended Valparaiso University (1901-1903) and taught in the Madden and Arcola Schools (1903 - 1905). Their daughter, Vera Mae (Hilgemann Hathaway) Dulin, was born May 12, 1919. Grandchildren are Carol Ann (Hathaway Dulin) Roberts (1943), Dianne (Dulin) Craft (1949), and Gary Stephen Dulin (1954).

Law career

After graduating from the University of Michigan, Harry returned to Fort Wayne where he continued studying and practicing law. He was appointed Deputy Allen County Prosecutor (1908-1912) and Allen County Prosecutor (1912 to 1916), positions in which he obtained important legislation at both state and national levels. He successfully prosecuted the "milk cases" which, when carried to the Supreme Court, resulted in the compulsory bottling of milk [originally customers came out to the street where milk was ladled into their containers from pails in a horse-drawn milk wagon]. He launched a successful campaign against habit-forming drugs, and his work with the Indiana narcotics law led to a requirement of compulsory prescriptions for many narcotics. He succeeded in breaking up local operations of the famous nationwide "arson trust," winning a test case which resulted in the Federal government formulating and enacting a clearer law *(Fort Wayne Journal Gazette,* June 25, 1957).

As Circuit Court judge, he not only rigidly enforced but also improved "the laws relating to wife-desertion and child-neglect" that he knew were grossly inadequate *(Biographical Sketches of Fort Wayne and Allen County,* page 291, date unknown). The *Fort Wayne News Sentinel* editorial of June 26, 1957, summarized: " . . . he was not merely content to prosecute, or hand down judgments in criminal cases, but he also exemplified a profound sense of responsibility therein, in pressing for reforms that would help obviate the human misery associated with them." This "profound sense of responsibility" is strongly affirmed in the Allen County Bar Association's memorials to Harry H. Hilgemann (June 26, 1957). For example: "The judge was a great jurist and attorney, an outstanding member of the bench and bar, one of the great men of our community.. brilliant.. When he was city attorney, I marveled at his keen intellect and grasp of the law in handling the many knotty situations that arose" (Arthur Fruechtenicht). "As judge, he was able to . . . without fear or prejudice and with that fine mind of his, hear the evidence. . . and always come down with a decision that combined justice and charity" (C. Byron Hayes).

Judge Harry H. Hilgemann

He was nominated and ran for the Democratic nomination for Congress in 1916 and 1918, both times narrowly defeated. His congressional campaign ads ran in both English and German language newspapers. He served as Allen County Attorney (1933-1936), Judge of the Allen County Circuit Court (1936-1943), and Fort Wayne City Attorney (1949-1952). He practiced law with Townsend, Thomas and Hilgemann and later with Hilgemann, Congdon and Kaag in the Standard (Elektron) Building (built by Genny Electric at 215 East Berry Street).

Civic initiatives

Hilgemann's activities extended far beyond the realm of political fields to such organizations as the Izaak Walton League of America to which he gave his vision and inspiration. As president of the local chapter, he played leadership roles both locally and nationally in the early movement for conservation, better sportsmanship, and prevention of soil erosion and stream pollution. "Judge Hilgemann was a leader before the conservation movement became popular.. .. The first great activity of the [Fort Wayne] chapter under his leadership was a mass meeting attended by more than 1500 citizens to discuss the Upper Mississippi Wildlife Refuge Bill. . . . Judge Hilgemann then played a key role in getting this bill passed in the US Senate. His initiatives also led to establishing the first municipal fish hatchery (1924), plans for a state park for Northeastern Indiana, and pollution abatement in the St. Mary's River" (Izaak Walton League, *"In Memoriam,"* June 1957).

A scholar of both history and issues of justice, Harry Hilgemann translated several books from German into English and wrote two books, *When Justice Smiles*, and *Little Turtle, Gentleman* (about the great Miami leader). He served on the Board of Governors of the Allen County Historical Society, was first president and first governor of the Fort Wayne Moose Lodge, a Scottish Rite Mason, and an active member of the YMCA, Council of Boy Scouts, and the Allen County and Indiana Bar Associations.

T*he Fort Wayne Journal Gazette* editorial of June 26, 1957, described him thus: "Judge Harry H. Hilgemann of the Allen Circuit Court. . . possessed rare gifts of mind, heart, and character which endeared him to everyone who knew him. His learning was wide and deep, his memory sharp and retentive. He knew the history of his community, of his nation, and the world.

He was equally at home with books and with people. There was never a more considerate man or one who had more genuine humility. He could be and he was a fighting, fearless prosecuting attorney, but he was just as careful not to prosecute an innocent man. . . . Whether upon the bench or at the bar, he was the friend and advisor of young lawyers. . . He was always in popular demand as a public speaker [as a "Minute Man" during WW II, he would give, "at a minute's notice," a rousing speech to raise money for war bonds]. . . So this tolerant, learned man with the insatiable curiosity about everything, lived to age 75 years and never lost his interests. Now as his friends mourn his passing, they consider what was the secret of the unusual esteem in which he was held. We would like to offer the explanation that perhaps early in life he learned that kindness is one of the greatest virtues that any human being can possess. And that he followed that knowledge like a guiding star."

Submitted by Carol Roberts

GEORGE FREEMAN HILL

George Freeman Hill was born on March 22, 1799 in Biddeford, Maine, son of Elisha Hill and Charlotte (Freeman). Through his father he descended from Peter Hill, who came to Saco in 1633. Through his mother he descended from William Brewster of Mayflower fame, and Gov. Thomas Dudley of Massachusetts.

On January 8, 1832, George married Abra Hayes, daughter of John and Sarah Alden (King) Hayes of Saco. She was born on May 31, 1804. Her mother was a cousin of the Federalist statesman Rufus King. George King Hill their son was born on January 23, 1833 in Saco. The Hills moved to Fort Wayne in 1835 in the company of Abra's cousins Asa, Oliver, and Charles Fairfield, but Abra died within a year.

George King Hill and Margaret Watson (Edgar) Hill

George married (2) Jane Hultz on March 5, 1844 but had no children. In 1846, he ran unsuccessfully for county sheriff on the Whig ticket. He became a brick mason and was one of the founding members of the Working Men's Institute Library, the first circulating library in the city. After living a number of years at the southeast comer of Washington and Fairfield, he moved to Noble County, where he farmed for a time before returning to Fort Wayne. He died in February 1875.

George King Hill followed the masonry trade of his father, working for contractor David Silver and on his own. On November 21, 1860, he married Margaret Watson Edgar after eloping to St. Joseph County, Michigan. She was a former schoolteacher, born in 1830 in Clark County, Ohio, the daughter of Andrew and Margaret (Kirkpatrick) Edgar. At the age of four she moved with her parents to Van Buren Township, Kosciusko County, Indiana, and came to Fort Wayne in the late 1850s to work as a dressmaker. George and Margaret had four children: Edgar Freeman, born September 1, 1861; Mary Abra Ella, August 1, 1863; William Andrew, August 26, 1865; and Georgia Margaret, February 22, 1867. The first three were baptized in First Presbyterian Church, which Margaret joined in 1862.

George was killed on a falling scaffold on October 19, 1867 while painting a building at the corner of Main and Harrison. A newspaper praised him as "a highly esteemed citizen and an industrious and intelligent mechanic." His death brought hardship to his widow, who was left nearly destitute. For a time in 1871 the family moved to Goshen, where Margaret taught at the Pike Street School, but they returned to Fort Wayne. An unscrupulous guardian swindled the children out of their rightful inheritance left them by their grandfather. Then on December 1, 1879, Margaret died of pneumonia.

After living for a time with Oliver Fairfield's family, Mary married William Warren Beatty in 1882 in Kosciusko County. They had a large family of nine children, including Georgia, Ethel, Florence, Marie, Jessie, Edgar, Herbert, Mary, and Abra. She later moved to Chicago, but died on August 20, 1947 in Livonia, Michigan. Of her siblings, the eldest, Edgar, moved to Glen Ellyn, Illinois, was twice married, and died in 1937. William never married and died in Chicago. Georgia married Wylie Bonine, but died from pregnancy complications in 1893.

Submitted by David J. Beatty

GARY L. & JENNIFER DOERFLEIN HINES FAMILY

Gary L. Hines was born October 5, 1953, in Fort Wayne, Indiana, the son of Harold R. Hines, Jr., and A. Joan Baxter. Harold Jr. was also born in Fort Wayne, the son of Harold R. Hines, Sr., and Ellen A. Lyons.

Harold Sr. and Ellen came to Fort Wayne in 1925 from Niles, Michigan, and later moved to Cedarville. Harold Sr. was an auto mechanic and owner operator of Leo Body Shop in Leo, Indiana.

Harold Jr. was a World War II Navy veteran and an employee of ITT in Fort Wayne for 39 years. He married Joan Baxter July 20, 1952, in Fort Wayne. Joan was born in Fort Wayne, the daughter of Gaylord N. Baxter and M. Bernice Chambers. Gaylord and Bernice grew up in Van Wert County, Ohio, and came to Fort Wayne

Gary and Jennifer Hines, Noah, John and Sarah

A. Joan Baxter and Harold R. Hines, Jr., July 20, 1952, First Methodist Church, Fort Wayne

in 1926. Gaylord was a furnace salesman for Rybolt and Lennox furnace companies, Bernice an employee of Lutheran Hospital, Fort Wayne. Joan was a bookkeeper for Fort Wayne National Bank, Lincoln National Bank, and Visiting Nurse Service in Fort Wayne.

Gary was valedictorian of the first Wayne High School graduating class in 1972 and earned B.A. and M.S. degrees from Ball State University, an M.A. from the University of Arizona, and a B.S. from Indiana University-Purdue University in Fort Wayne (IPFW). Since 1985 he has worked for Magnavox/Raytheon in Fort Wayne as a software engineer. Gary met Jennifer at the IPFW campus while taking a German language class. Their courtship years included weekly dinners at the downtown Wendy's restaurant followed by a few hours of family history research at the Allen County Public Library. They were married on May 18, 1991, at Taylor Chapel United Methodist Church in Fort Wayne.

Jennifer Robin Doerflein was born March 4, 1964, in Fort Wayne, Indiana, the daughter of Walter Anthony Doerflein and Colleen Perth Maloy. Walter came to Fort Wayne in the 1940s from Franklin County, Indiana, starting his own business, Walter A. Doerflein Insurance & Financial Services, Inc. Colleen was born in Monroeville, Indiana, and worked at Magnavox before marrying Walter in Fort Wayne on July 2, 1959.

Jennifer graduated from Snider High School in 1982. She then studied history and journalism at Indiana University in Bloomington, Indiana, earning a B.A. while pursuing her musical interests in groups such as the Marching Hundred, basketball pep band, and concert band. After working as a travel agent, she became a librarian at the Allen County Public Library in Fort Wayne, earning her M.L.S. from Indiana University in 1994. Jennifer is a fifth generation Allen County resident. Her family lines date back to 1839 in Allen County. Her ancestral surnames include: Maloy, Taylor, Vizard, Null, Ratledge, and Hutson.

Gary and Jennifer have three children: Sarah Colleen Hines, Noah Baxter Hines, and John Maloy Hines.

Submitted by Gary and Jennifer Hines

JOHN CHRISTIAN HINTON 1855-1926

John Christian Hinton (1855-1916) was born in Fort Wayne. He was the son and grandson of

John C. Hinton (1855-1916). Children in dad's car.

early settlers of the area. His parents were Samuel Hinton (1815-1892) and Joanna Schmidt (1823-1900). His parents and grandparents had migrated to Fort Wayne in 1833.

John's first known employment was as a conductor of the Pennsylvania Railroad. However, following in the footsteps of his family, in the 1880s, he opened a restaurant called The Boston Restaurant or just plain Hinton's. It was located at 1516 Calhoun Street. The restaurant was one of the first in the city that wasn't located inside of a hotel or inn.

In 1889, John married Anna Josephine Welten (1868-1938), a resident of the city. She was the daughter of John and Christina Welten. They lived in a home at 220 West Butler, which they had built in 1866.

After they were married, Anna became involved in the running of the restaurant. John and Anna had an apartment above the restaurant and there were also rooms for women who worked in the kitchen and a nurse girl for the children. In the restaurant itself there was a room in front with a long counter and a formal dining room to the back. A baker came in each day at four a.m. to make fresh pies and other baked goods. There were chickens raised and butchered on the premises. Anna would take a horse and wagon to the Eckert Packing Company on Main Street. and bring back a side of beef with specialty meats thrown in for good measure. It prospered and became a popular eating place for those in town and those using the railroad.

Upon John's death in 1926 Anna took over the business and ran it until 1930 when she sold it. She became the first woman member of the Fort Wayne Chamber of Commerce during that time. After the sale of the restaurant, Anna lived with her sister Caroline and her daughter Evelyn in the old family home on Butler Street. John was a member of the Ben Hurs and Knights of Pythias Lodges and the couple belonged to the First Presbyterian Church.

The couple had five children:

Verma Cemelia (1890-1969) married to Christian H. W. Lueeke (1890-1973) who was the son of President Luecke of Concordia College. They had four children.

Walter Harry Hinton (1891-1968) married to Alta Parker. They were divorced and he later married Nellie Taylor. He had four children.

Chester John (1893-1963) married to Sarah Elizabeth Marshall who was from Texas They had three children.

Lucille Alberta (1894-1978) married to Paul McKinley Axline. They eloped, which was unheard of then! They had three children and lived near Lansing Michigan.

Evelyn Irene (1899-1994). She was unmarried.

The grandchildren of the couple heard many stories about ''the restaurant". One of these took place on a Sunday evening. A sister of Anna's was working alone in the front of the restaurant when a black man came in, asked to be served and she complied. Shortly thereafter, they were visited by robed members of the KKK who threatened her and burned a cross on the street outside.

The Hintons are buried in the family plot in Lindenwood.

Submitted by Connie LaBrash

SAMUEL HINTON - 1815-1892

Samuel Hinton (1815-1892)was born in Pooghkeepsie, New York and accompanied his parents, Thomas and Mary, to Fort Wayne in 1833. They came by raft via Lake Erie and the Maumee River. Samuel was the oldest of six children but little is known about the others. Edmund, a bachelor, farmed near Arcola. Two other sons went to California during the Gold Rush and were never heard from again.

Samuel Hinton 1806-1892

Samuel's father, Thomas, was born around 1790 in New York and was a sailmaker by trade. In Allen county, he acquired considerable acreage in what was known as the Bloomingdale area. Samuel helped farm part of the land but Thomas and his family were better known as the proprietors of "The Bullshead Inn" located near what would be the north end of Wells Street today. This was one of the first hotels or wayside inns in the area and a very popular stopping place. Thomas sold all of his property about a month before he died.

Samuel at first worked on the family farm and business but later branched out on his own going into the grocery business and the manufacture of soap and candies. He became more and more involved in other trades as the years went by.

He married Johanna Smith (Schmidet?) (1823-1900) on February 20, 1842. They were the parents of nine children:

John Christian (1855-1916) married to Anna J. Welten (1865-1938) who became a restaurateur They had five children.

Samuel died of typhus as a child.

Cornelia (1843-1900) married to Christian Boseker (1841-1900) who was a local contractor i.e. Old City Hall, now Fort Wayne Historical Society. They had four children.

Sarah (1846) married Wilima Henderson.

William (1850) was killed working on the railroad.

Catherine (1854) married Warren Carpenter and had one son.

Harriet married Charles Scott of Joliet, Illinois.

Alice never married.

Lauren (d. 1940) married to John Cline and later Fellman Kring and had two children.

The couple were members of the Berry Street Methodist Church located at Berry and Harrison. Samuel was very involved in political affairs, belonging first to the Whig and later Republican parties but never ran for office himself. In their later years, they lived with their son, John, although Samuel still owned a farm in Croesse, Whitley County. He is buried in Lindenwood Cemetery.

There are some descendants of these children still living in the Fort Wayne area with names such as Blue, Bolyard, Hinton, Jones and LaBrash.

Submitted by Connie LaBrash

RICHARD LEE & BEVERLY ANN (DEWITT) HIRSCH FAMILY

Richard (Dick) Hirsch was born September 19, 1931, at Woodburn, Indiana. His parents were Herman Carl and Emilie (Hankel) Hirsch. They were married at St. Paul Lutheran Church (Gar Creek), New Haven, Indiana, on November 29, 1923. After living in Fort Wayne briefly, they moved north of Woodburn on State Road 101, then later to Schaffer Road, Woodburn. They had two other children who have also resided north of Woodburn, Virgil Herman born December 30, 1925, (deceased) and Berdine Kathryn (Hirsch) Kammeyer born January 23, 1929. Herman and Emilie were farmers and raised turkeys for many years on the farm at Woodburn. In 1951 they moved east of New Haven on U.S.24. There they built a turkey hatchery and along with Virgil and Richard, formed Hirsch Turkey Farm and Hatchery, Inc.

L to R. Beverly and Richard Richard Hirsch and daughters Holly, Connie, Jackie, and Vicki

Richard was drafted into the Armed Forces in July 1952, and served in Korea, being honorably discharged in April 1954. Richard married Beverly Ann (DeWitt) Hirsch on August 6, 1955, at Huntertown, Indiana. Beverly was born August 12, 1936, in Allen County to Abraham and

Margaret (Freeman) DeWitt. Abe and Margaret were married February 8, 1934, and lived several years in Allen County, but purchased and moved to Abe's grandfather Leiter's homestead west of LaOtto in Noble County in 1948. They also had one son, Dwight DeWitt, who was born on January 14, 1935, and he still resides on the Leiter homestead.

When Richard and Beverly married, they resided in Woodburn one year, then moved east of New Haven on U.S.24 until 1962 when they purchased the "Tillie Schaefer Farm" on Notestine Road north of Woodburn. They have four daughters: Connie Ann born October 27, 1956, married James W. Thompson, Jr. April 24, 1976; Vicki Lynn born September 21, 1958, married Mitchel H. Thompson November 26, 1977; Jacquelyn Lee born May 23, 1961, married Bradley J. Kees April 23, 1983; and Holly Sue born December 15, 1965, married Todd Fisher April 21, 1990.

Richard farmed and operated the turkey hatchery, and in November 1961 began working at B.F. Goodrich at Woodburn, Indiana. After moving to the farm, he raised turkeys and continued at the factory for 32 years, retiring in 1993.

Beverly is a musician and played in several dance bands for many wedding receptions and parties in the tri-state area. She was a square dance caller and played the accordion. She taught piano and accordion lessons at the Music Center of Fort Wayne, then later in their home. She's always been active in their church, accompanying choirs, directing choirs, and playing the organ or piano for services. Beverly worked as bookkeeper at Grabill Grain, Inc. and still works part-time at Midwest Tile and Concrete at Woodburn.

Upon retiring, Dick and Bev moved to Ball Lake in 1994 for six years, and now reside in northeast Fort Wayne. Richard passed away May 20, 2005. Bev's time is spent enjoying her children and nine grandchildren and their activities, playing golf and bridge, traveling, and participating in church activities at St. Peter's Lutheran Church, Fort Wayne.

Submitted by Beverly Hirsch

BRIAN & RHONDA (JACQUAY) HOCKEMEYER FAMILY

Brian and Rhonda have roots in Allen County on both sides of their family. Brian's descendants came from Germany on both sides of his family while Rhonda's descendants came from Germany on her mother's side and from France on her father's side of the family. Brian was born February 7, 1966 to David E. and Janice M.L. (Nicol) Hockemeyer at Parkview Hospital in Fort Wayne. His grandparents are Lawrence (1918-1988) and Velma (Ehlerding) Hockemeyer of Madison Township and Robert (1904-1996) and Edna (1907-1984) (Gruenbaum) Nicol of Marysville, Ohio. Brian has two younger brothers, Jonathan Lane Hockemeyer (1968-1997) and David Jason Hockemeyer.

Rhonda was born October 28, 1965 to Thomas A. and Helen L. (Fox) Jacquay at Parkview Hospital in Fort Wayne. Her grandparents are Alban (1912-1991) and Helen (1916-2000) (Mourey) Jacquay of Monroeville and Andrew (1899-1973) and Bernice (1912-1980) (Kleber) Fox of Fort Wayne. Rhonda has five younger siblings, Theodore Allen Jacquay, Jane Ann Knight, Amy Sue Collins, Anita Helen Keppel, and Andrew Thomas Jacquay.

Front, Emily, middle L to R, Katelyn, Rhonda, Rear, Brian Hockemeyer.

Brian and Rhonda were married May 14, 1988 at St. John Lutheran Church (Flatrock), Monroeville, and lived on Barkley Road in rural Hoagland for seven years. They have two daughters, Katelyn Marie, born January 16, 1992 and Emily Nicole, born May 7, 1994, each at Parkview Hospital in Fort Wayne. Brian, Rhonda, and their daughters currently live in Madison Township on the Hockemeyer family farm established June 23, 1899. Brian follows Friederich, Charles, Lawrence, and David as the fifth generation Hockemeyer to live and work on that 80-acre farm. The Hockemeyers are members at St. John Lutheran Church (Flatrock) and their daughters attend St. John Lutheran School where grades pre-K through eight is taught. Brian and Rhonda are both 1984 graduates of Heritage High School, rural Monroeville. Brian earned a bachelor's degree in Mechanical Engineering from Purdue University, Fort Wayne in 1992 and worked during a portion of his college years at Zollner Pistons and Poly Hi Solidur. He currently is a partner with his father and brother at Peridot, Inc. in Hoagland providing engineering prototyping services for a variety of industries since 1997. Rhonda is a 1985 graduate of Hixson's School of Floral Design, Lakewood, Ohio and of Ivy Tech, Fort Wayne with an associate's degree in early childhood education. She currently is a 16-year employee of Aetna Insurance and a floral designer at Forever Friends Floral in New Haven.

The Hockemeyers are avid sports fans and enjoy attending their daughter's volleyball, basketball, soccer, and softball games. Brian coaches basketball and softball while Rhonda assists with volleyball and in a variety of ways for the other sports. The family especially enjoys the excitement of a season of college football games at Purdue University and traveling to their bowl games during the holidays. They also enjoy traveling to national parks, hiking, fishing, and being involved in 4H.

Submitted by Brian Hockemeyer.

DAVID E. & JANICE M. HOCKEMEYER FAMILY

David E. and Janice M. Hockemeyer reside at 15730 Fackler Road, near Hoagland, Indiana. They built their present home in 1973 in a woods on the north edge of their family farm purchased from David's parents, Lawrence and Velma Hockemeyer. Lawrence resided there his entire life, 1917 to 1988, when he died suddenly from a heart attack. Velma survives and resides in the Golden Years Homestead in Fort Wayne.

Dave was born on his family's farm in 1941. Dave was baptized, confirmed and attended St. John Lutheran (Flatrock) Christian day school through eighth grade. He graduated from Hoagland High School in 1959. He worked at Eckrich Meats in Fort Wayne while attending Purdue University. In 1960 he was hired at International Harvester as a machinist. After 38 years he retired from International engineering in 1998.

Jan was born in a rural farming community in Marysville, Ohio, to Robert and Edna Gruenbaum Nicol. She attended Christian day school at St. John's Lutheran, Marysville, Ohio; she was baptized and confirmed there as well. She graduated from Chuckery-Darby High School. Her desire to become a nurse led her to college at Lutheran Hospital School of Nursing, Fort Wayne. Upon graduation, she attended Ohio State University and worked at Riverside Hospital in Columbus.

Dave and Jan met on a blind date while in college in 1960. They married June 9, 1963, and purchased their first home in Woodburn, Indiana. In 1964 Dave and Jan started a business, Hockemeyer Trucking and Excavating. The business grew and existed for ten years in addition to their fulltime jobs. Jan worked with Visiting Nurse Service. In 1966 their first son, Brian Lynn. was born on February 7. Jan choose part-time employment, one day a week at Parkview Hospital. Their second son, Jonathan Lane, was born on August 14, 1968.

In 1973 Dave and Jan purchased the family farm, and they constructed their present home. On January 2, 1974, their third son, David Jason, was born. All three sons graduated from Purdue University in Engineering.

In 1976 Dave and Jan bought acreage at 12120 Flatrock Road which they continue to farm along with the farm on Fackler Road.

From 1977 to 1989 Jan was employed as the school nurse at Monroeville/Woodburn Elementary Schools in East Allen County Schools. In 1989 Jan was hired as the Occupational Health Nurse at ITT Industries and remains there to the present.

Dave served on the East Allen County School Board from 1978 to 1990.

Son, Jonathan Lane, employed by General Mills, in Albuquerque, New Mexico, was stricken suddenly on January 13, 1997 with a massive brain tumor which, following surgery, took his life on January 20, 1997. He is survived by wife, Holly and son, Jonathan David in Lincoln, Nebraska. After

David E. Hockemeyer family

Dave's retirement from Navistar (IH), he and Jan along with sons, Brian and David Jason, started their own engineering, prototyping business: Peridot Inc. Rapid Prototyping. The business began in the Wayne Haven Industrial Park, Fort Wayne, 1997. In 2003 they purchased a larger facility in Hoagland Industrial Park and remain there today.

Submitted by David E. Hockemeyer

DAVID J. & KELLIE HOCKEMEYER FAMILY

David Jason and Kellie Lou Hockemeyer reside at 12120 Flatrock Road, near Hoagland, Indiana. They built their present home in 2004 in a woods on a family farm on land purchased from David's parents, David E. and Janice Hockemeyer. David E. and Janice purchased the farm in 1986 from the Charles Molthan estate, and they continue to farm it today.

David Jason, Kellie Lou, and Micah Lane Hockemeyer

David was born January 2, 1974. David was baptized, confirmed, and attended St. John Lutheran (Flatrock) day school. He graduated from Heritage High School in 1992. He graduated from Purdue University - West Lafayette in 1996 with a B.S. in Mechanical Engineering where he lived at the Beta Sigma Psi Lutheran Fraternity. In 1996 he was hired by Poly Hi Solidur, a polymer manufacturer, as an application development engineer. In November 1997 David, along with brother Brian and father David E., founded Peridot Incorporated; a prototyping and engineering company located in Hoagland, Indiana. He continues to work at Peridot today as the company continues to grow using emerging technologies.

Kellie was born in Hammond, Indiana on June 17, 1971, to Edward and Kathleen (Burkhart) Coy. In 1982 Kellie and her family moved to the Fort Wayne area where she attended Shambaugh Elementary School. She graduated from Bishop Dwenger High School in 1989 and graduated from Purdue University in 2000 with a B.S. in Psychology. From 1998 to present she has held various marketing positions, and since 2001 has been employed by Star Financial Bank as the Web Designer and Developer.

David and Kellie met on a blind date in 1996. In April 1998, Kellie was surprised at a Fort Wayne Wizards baseball game with a marriage proposal that was announced and displayed on the scoreboard. Kellie was confirmed at St. John Lutheran (Flatrock) in 1998, and they married on May 29, 1999 at St. John. They purchased their first home in New Haven, Indiana. In 2002 their first child, a daughter, Micah Lane was born March 31, on Easter. They are looking forward to their second child who is to be born in December of 2005.

Kellie and David are active members of St. John Lutheran (Flatrock) church and school, participating on various committees and volunteer roles. David also enjoys singing with a choral group and is a committee person for the local chapter of Ducks Unlimited, a wetlands conservation organization. In their free time, Kellie enjoys arts and crafts and clay sculpting, and David enjoys hunting, sports, and the great outdoors. Micah is an active girl who is a good helper and an aspiring gymnast. The family is a loyal supporter of their alma mater, Purdue University.

Kellie has one younger brother, Matthew Coy, who resides in Chicago, Illinois. David has two older brothers, Brian Lynn and Jonathan Lane. Jonathan Lane, while living in Albuquerque, New Mexico, was stricken in 1997 with a brain tumor and following surgery it took his life on January 20, 1997. The Hockemeyer family engineering business, Peridot Inc., is named in Jonathan Lane's honor using his birthstone as the company name.

Submitted by David J. Hockemeyer

CHRISTOPHER D. HOEPPNER

Christopher D. Hoeppner is the grandson of Richard Paul Justin Hartman, great-grandson of Joseph Clement Hartman, great-great grandson of John Hubert (Hobby) Hartman, and great-great-great grandson of Herman Hartman.

Christopher D. Hoeppner was born December 21, 1970, at Saint Joseph's Hospital in Fort Wayne, Indiana. He graduated from Holy Cross Lutheran School as Salutatorian of his class in June 1985. He graduated from Concordia Lutheran High School in June 1989. He lettered his freshman, sophomore, junior and senior years in baseball. He was selected to the 1st Team, All-Sac Baseball, his sophmore, junior and senior year, and was also selected to the All-Area Baseball Team. In Chris's senior year, he helped Concordia High School advance to the Final Four in the state in baseball. He also lettered on the basketball team his sophmore, junior and senior years, was an unanimous selection by the coaches to the 1st Team, All-Sac. He helped lead his team to the Sweet-Sixteen in the state advancing to the Notre Dame Convocation Center, South Bend, Indiana, the very first year the semi-state was played there.

He graduated with a Bachelor's degree in Business Management and Sports Management from Anderson University, Anderson, Indiana in 1993. Chris was a two-time NAJA All-American outfielder for Anderson University in 1991-1992. His senior year he was a NCAA Division III, 1st team All-American as an outfielder in 1993. He was selected to the 1st Team, All Region Baseball Team for the year 1993 presented by the American Baseball Coaches Association and Converse. He was also a three-time INAC Player of the Year for 1991, 1992, and 1993 seasons, where he helped lead Anderson University to the 1993 Division III College Baseball World Series.

Chris married Kara Lynn Kloer on July 25, 2000. They have three children, Emalyn Nicole, Olivia Christine and Coleson David. They are expecting their fourth child February 2006. Chris and Kara own and operate the Legends Sports Bar, 4104 North Clinton Street, Fort Wayne, Indiana. Chris is the sixth generation of the Hartman family in the tavern business. Chris owns Hoepp's Collectibles, a sports card Internet business for over five years and has been an EBAY Power Seller ever since.

Chris, Kara, Coleson, Olivia, and Emalyn Hoeppner

Herman Hartman established the first Brewery, in Fort Wayne, Indiana, at 128 East Washington Street which later became 414 East Washington, south side of the street between Lafayette and Clay. John Hubert (Hobby) Hartman, Chris' great-great grandfather, opened a saloon at 126 East Washington in 1878. In 1877, he opened and operated a grocery at 231 East Jefferson, now 701 East Jefferson, northeast corner of Hanna and Jefferson. After Prohibition, Chris' great-grandfather, Joseph Clement Hartman, opened a tavern at this location, and after Clem's death on November 29, 1935, Richard continued in the bar business establishing "Hartman's Brew Haven" which he operated through 1959, when he was sworn in as Allen County Recorder on January 1, 1959. This property remained in the Hartman family into the late 1960s.

Chris's mother, Patricia Louise (Hartman) Hoeppner, started in the tavern business at the Gay Street Tavern, 2035 Gay Street, northeast corner of Gay and Buchanan Streets, in 1966 and 1967. This liquor license was transferred to 1601 South Harri-

J. H. Hartman's Grocery, 231 East Jefferson, 1877

Hartman's Brew Haven, 701 East Jefferson Boulevard, 1937

Hartman's, 701 East Jefferson, 1920

son in 1968, the southeast corner of Harrison and Grand Streets, which became "The Club Cabaret" In 1971. she opened "Mister D's Night Club," 1508 South Calhoun Street, at the southwest comer of Calhoun and Baker Streets. In 1973, she opened Denny's V.I.P. Lounge, 2701 West Jefferson, becoming the fifth generation in the Hartman family in the saloon, bar, tavern, night club business. She also sold a liquor license in the 1970s to Red Lobster. Inc. of Gainesville, Florida, who still operates the Red Lobster Restaurant on 4825 Coldwater Road.

Submitted by Christopher D. Hoeppner

PATRICIA LOUISE (HARTMAN) HOEPPNER, GREAT, GREAT GRANDDAUGHTER OF HERMAN HARTMAN

Patricia Louise (Hartman) Hoeppner was born June 5, 1944 at Saint Joseph's Hospital in Fort Wayne, Indiana. She graduated from St. Jude Catholic Grade School in June, 1958 and Central Catholic High School in June, 1962. She is the daughter of Richard Paul Justin and Vera Louise (Adams) Hartman. Patricia is the grand daughter of Joseph Clement and Frances Catherine (Schmitt) Hartman, great-granddaughter of John Hubert (Hobby) and Louisa (Aubrey) Hartman, and great-great granddaughter of Herman and Anna Maria (Richter) Hartman.

She is the mother of Sherri Lynne (Hoeppner) Recht, born February 25, 1963, Stephen Scott Hoeppner, born March 30, 1964, and Christopher D. Hoeppner, born December 21, 1970. Patricia's father, Richard Hartman, was a prominent Hartman family businessman who owned and operated the Hartman's Brew Haven, 701 East Jefferson, located on the northeast corner of Hanna and Jefferson, from 1935 through 1959. This property was purchased by the Hartman family in 1877. J. H. Hartman opened and operated a grocery at this location from 1877 through 1892. Richard Hartman sold Hartman's Brew Haven when he was elected and served as Allen County Recorder from 1959 through 1962. Patricia's great-grandfather, J H. Hartman Grocer, roots began at 126 East Washington Street in 1875. He opened another grocery store at 231 East Jefferson, the northeast corner of Hanna and Jefferson in 1877. In 1878 he opened a saloon at the East Washington Street location. The saloon is where the 412 Club is now. He owned a grocery and saloon at 1921 South Hanna from 1893 through 1921. Patricia's grandfather, Clement, took over his father's grocery business and other Hartman business interests.

This is the story of Patricia's grandfather John Hubert (Hobby) Hartman who was the first born and only son of Herman Hartman. Hobby followed in his father's footsteps by being a prominent businessman, in the Hartman tradition. The family grocery became J. H. Hartman and Son Groceries. This is demonstrated by his obituary in the *Fort Wayne Daily News* dated January 23, 1917.

J. H. HARTMAN PASSES AWAY

RETIRED GROCER DIES SUDDENLY EARLY THIS MORNING.

Heart Trouble Causes Death-Had Conducted Grocery Here For Many Years.

John H. Hartman, a retired grocer and one of Fort Wayne's best known most progressive business men died suddenly this morning at the family home, 1913 Hanna street, death being due to an attack of heart trouble. He had been in comparatively good health and his death came very unexpectedly. Mr. Hartman was 61 years old and had resided in Fort Wayne his entire life. Mr. Hartman arose at 4 o'clock this morning, soon after complaining to members of the family of pains about the heart. Dr. J. E. Bickel was hurriedly summoned, but before he could arrive, Mr. Hartman had breathed his last.

Coroner J. E. McArdle was called and he substantiated Dr. Bickel's deduction that death was due to an acute attack of heart trouble. While Mr. Hartman had suffered a period of illness about a year ago, and had been confined to his home for sometime, he had improved greatly during the past six months and was apparently enjoying excellent health recently. His death, therefore, come as a distinct shock to his many friends who knew that he had been steadily improving in

1921 South Hanna, J.H. Hartman & Son Groceries

Hartman Grocery, Hanna Street

health lately. He had been very actively engaged during the past half year in personally conducting his various business obligations. Mr. Hartman was born in this city April 15, 1855, and had resided here ever since. He received his education in the parochial schools of St. Mary's Catholic Church, and when a young man began his career in the grocery business. He was for many years engaged in the grocery business at 1921 Hanna Street. He also operated a grocery at 412 East Washington Boulevard for a number of years. He retired several years ago and has since been engaged in supervising his many other business interests. He was a prominent figure in business circles of Fort Wayne, and enjoyed a large acquaintanceship throughout the city. He was a member of St. Peter's Catholic Church and of the Holy Name society. He was also a member of the order of Catholic Knights of America. Survivors include his wife, Louisa (Aubrey) Hartman, a son, Clemence Hartman, who resides at home; an adopted son, the Rev. John F. Delagrange, of Dunnington, Indiana; and three sister, Mrs. W. C. Peters, of San Francisco; Mrs. Anna Kuhn, of Cloverdale, California.; and Sister Nicolina, of Madison Lake, Wisconsin. Two grandchildren also survive; Hubert Clement and Maurice Wilfred Hartman.

J.H. Hartman also had a daughter named Eva (Hartman) Delagrange who died of tuberculosis at the age of 28 on January 29, 1906.

Submitted by Patricia Hoeppner

CLEMENT HOEVEL

Henry and Lizzie (Meyer) Hoevel married on October 30, 1877. Clement Hovel was one of ten children. He was born in Allen County August 1, 1888, and was a veteran of World War I. He married Erma Welling on April 20, 1920. Erma (Welling) Hoevel was born on July 4, 1894. They had two children - Howard and Donald Hoevel.

Howard A. Hoevel was born on February 12, 1923. He married Georgian J. Allgeier on November 20, 1948 at St. Andrew Catholic Church. They had three daughters - Madonna, Catherine and Diane Hoevel. Howard died on March I, 1982 of a heart attack and is buried in the Catholic Cemetery.

Madonna M. Reynolds was born on September 1, 1949. She married Neil S. Reynolds on August 25, 1973. They had two children -Clint Reynolds, who was born on June 21, 1977 and Amanda Reynolds, who was born on March 6, 1982. The Reynolds family lived in Hoagland. They owned and operated the Northeast Indiana Grain Inspection.

Catherine A. Lassen was born on September 13, 1952. She married James Lassen on June 2, 1973. They had two children by adoption from Columbia, South America - Christopher J. Lassen, February 12, 1983 and Ana M. Lassen, January 20, 1987. They divorced on January 20, 2001.

Diane C. Ryan was born on May 2, 1956. She married Blane P. Ryan on May 31, 1981. They had three children whose names were - Colette M., who was born on March 19, 1984; Eric P., who was born on May 10, 1988; and Leslie A., who was born on December 23, 1991. They lived in Monroeville.

Donald Hoevel was born on April 12, 1926. He married Marie H. Smith on September 13, 1947. They had one son, Dennis. Marie Hoevel died on January 30, 1955. Dennis Hoevel was born on July 6, 1950. He married Ellen Bauman on April 23, 1976. They had one daughter, Audra, who was born on September 26,1981.

Georgian J. and Howard A. Hoevel

Don then married Beatrice Minnich, who was born on February 2, 1929 in Bryant in Jay County, Indiana, on June 10, 1961. They had three children - Robert, Judith, and Mary. Don and Bea later divorced on August 2, 1985. Don died on October 5, 1985. Robert E. Hoevel was born on March 22, 1962 and lived in Kailua, Hawaii, where he married Tracy Ann (Chalfant), who was born on May 3, 1965, on December 29, 2003. They had one daughter, Sydney Claire, on December 26, 2002. Judith A. Hoevel was born on May 18, 1963 and married Mark Kulwik, who was born on October 23, 1961, on September 10, 1988. They had three children - Brian, who was born on October 26, 1992; Christopher, who was born on September 20, 1995 and Amy, who was born on July 28, 1997. Mary Hoevel was born on February 28, 1966 and she joined the Sisters of Notre Dame. She became Sister Mary Lizette when she took her final vows on July 24, 1994.

Submitted by Georgian (Allgeier) Hoevel

ADAM HOFFMAN FAMILY

The Hoffman family members are reported to have come to Fort Wayne in the early 1800s. One of the original Hoffmans was married to a young lady whose surname was Reinhart. She was believed to have been the first Caucasian girl to be born in the original Fort Wayne.

From the original Hoffman family, Adam Hoffman was born in 1862. Adam married a Miss Mettler and they had a son named Norman. Unfortunately, as was not uncommon in those days, Adam's wife died at a young age. Adam then married Louisa Braun (d. circa 1905) and together they had two daughters, Annetta (1898-1984) and Marie (1897-1949). Louisa died while her two daughters were quite young. Her sister, Katherine Braun (1869-1960), who never married, moved in with the family and became a surrogate mother to Annetta and Marie and then later a surrogate grandmother to Marie's children. Aunt Kitty, as she was known, was a buyer at Wolf & Dessauer department store and had an avocation as an artist. She painted beautiful landscapes, including scenes of the Lakeside Park area near the family

Annetta Hoffman a/k/a Sister Giovanni, S.S.N.D. (Circa 1915)

home on Alabama Avenue. In 1937 Adam Hoffman was struck and killed by a car while he was crossing Maumee Avenue.

Annetta joined the Catholic order of nuns in Milwaukee, Wisconsin, known as the School Sisters of Notre Dame. She took the name Sister Giovanni. Marie married Albert Poinsatte and they had two sons, James (b.1921) and Charles (b.1925).

James Poinsatte graduated from the University of Notre Dame in 1942 and then immediately enlisted in the US Army. He served in the 551st Artillery Battalion, attached to the First Army in World War II, and saw combat in the allied invasion of Normandy. When the war ended James stayed in Europe, studying at the University of Paris and teaching in Germany for a short period of time. Upon returning to the United States, he met Maxine Lapp. The two were married in 1947 at Precious Blood Catholic Church and moved to Chicago while James attended the University of Chicago. Later, they moved back to Fort Wayne and James worked as a businessman in the automotive industry for a number of years. James, a student of linguistics, speaks five languages. Maxine was quite an energetic woman raising 12 children in their home on the northeast section Fort Wayne. The family attended St. Jude's Catholic Church and School as well as Central Catholic and Bishop Dwenger High Schools. Maxine also studied languages including early computer programming languages in the 1970s. Later in life, Maxine joined her husband in the automotive industry as a financial comptroller.

Marie and Albert's second son, Charles Poinsatte, also attend the University of Notre Dame and then later served in the Korean War. Upon returning to Notre Dame, Charles met Anne Marie Harle, who was born and raised in Paris, France. They were married in the old log chapel on the campus of Notre Dame in 1957. Both Charles and Anne Marie obtained their doctorates at the University of Notre Dame and served as professors at St. Mary's College and Indiana University. They have three children and currently reside in South Bend, Indiana.

Submitted by Anne Poinsatte Wall

JOHN HOFFMAN & EMMA JACKEMEYER FAMILY HISTORY

John Hoffman (1865-1941) and Emma Jackemeyer (1880-1942) were married June 23, 1901. They raised their family of eight children: Esther, Edwin, Olga, Velma, Linda, Nicholas, John, and Arthur, on a farm along the Monroeville Road in Allen County, Indiana. The family attended St. John Lutheran Church (Flatrock), and the couple was buried at the IOOF Cemetery in New Haven.

Left to right: Seated Emma Jackemeyer and John Hoffman. Back row: Christ Jackemeyer (brother to Emma) and his wife Caroline Muntz. The next two in the wedding party are unidentified

John Hoffman was the son of Nicholas J. Hoffman (1832-1905) and Elizabeth Marquardt (1820-1904). Nicholas J. Hoffman was born in Bavaria, Germany and Elizabeth Marquardt was born in Gadernheim, Starkenberg, Hessen, Germany. They were married January 18, 1864 and were buried at the Marquardt Lutheran Church Cemetery in Madison Township.

Elizabeth Marquardt was the daughter of Johann Jakob Marquardt (1808-1852) and Anna Hoffenbarger or Kaffenbarger (1807-1888). They were buried in the St. John Lutheran (Flatrock) Cemetery.

Emma Jackemeyer was the daughter of Conrad Jackemeyer (1825-1909) and Catharina Schlemmer (1834-1903) and was raised on a farm along the Seiler Road near New Haven. Conrad and Catharina were married at St. Paul's Lutheran Church in 1854 and were buried at the Emmanuel Lutheran Church (New Haven) Cemetery on Edgerton Road. Conrad Jackemeyer was born in Windheim, Germany to Johann Fredrick Wilhelm Jackemeyer (1801-1858) and Marie Sophia Elisabeth Hoeltcke (1795-1836). Both of Conrad's parents were also born in Windheim, Germany.

Catharina Schlemmer was born in Stark, Ohio to Jean Pierre Schlemmer (1795-1860) and Catharina Sali (1795-1839?). Jean Pierre was born in Alsace Lorraine, Germany and Catharina Sali was born in Melsheim, Germany.

Velma worked at the General Electric in Fort Wayne during the 1930s before marrying Andrew Werling III January 1, 1936. They made their home on a farm just north of Tocsin, Indiana, and they were the parents of four children: Ervin, Amos, Virginia, and Calvin.

Ervin Werling graduated from Ossian High School in 1955 and went to work at the International Harvester in Fort Wayne before retiring in 1987. He married Beverly Fuelling in 1965 at St. Peter Lutheran Church north of Decatur. Ervin and Beverly made their home on a farm near Ossian, and they were the parents of two children: Randall and Julie.

Submitted by Ervin Werling

WILLIAM & ADELIA (BRADTMUELLER) HOFFMEIER

William Hoffmeier's parents were William and Ema (Heinig) Hoffmeier. The father, William, was the son of Wilhelm and Anna (Thiele) Hoffmeier. Wilhelm was the son of Conrad Hoffmeier. Anna (Thiele) was the daughter of Friedrich Thiel. Ema (Heinig) was the daughter of Robert.

Adelia Bradtmueller Hoffmeier's parents were Theodore Hoffmeier, son of Friedrich, and Clara (Bobay), daughter of Joseph and Anna (Baatz) Bobay. Friedrich Bradtmueller's father was Wilhelm. Joseph Bobay's father was John.

William and Adelia's children are Jeffrey, Sandra Franz, Terry, and Alice Anderson.

William's ancestors who settled in Allen County were:

Conrad Hoffmeier, born July 31, 1812 Windheim, Westfalen, Germany, died October 20, 1863, St. Joseph Township, buried St. Peter Goeglein Lutheran Cemetery, St. Joseph Township; his wife was Caroline (Buesching), born April 15, 1822, Jenhorst, Hannover, Germany, died October 23, 1904, in Lake Township, buried Suburban Bethlehem Lutheran Cemetery, Washington Township.

Friedrich Thiele, born March 7, 1827, in Bierde, Westfalen, Germany, and died June 4, 1914, in Washington Township. His wife, Wilhelmina (Koldewey), was born September 6, 1833, in Haustedt, Hannover, Germany, and died February 9, 1910, in Washington Township. Both are buried in Suburban Bethlehem Lutheran Cemetery.

Amalie (Zuelchner) Heinig was born July 16, 1840, in Sachsen, Germany, and died May 25, 1923, in Fort Wayne. She is buried in Lindenwood Cemetery, Fort Wayne. Her son, Robert Heinig, was born April 5, 1876, in Sachsen, Germany, and died November 26, 1921, in Fort Wayne. His wife, Flora (Pester), was born February 20, 1878, in Hartmannsdorf, Sachsen, Germany, died October 23, 1930, in Washington Township. Both are buried Lindenwood. Flora's father, Edward Pester, was born January 30, 1857, in Hartmannsdorf, Sachsen, Germany, and died August 26, 1934, in Fort Wayne. His wife Louisa, (Rauner), was born December 5, 1857 in Hartmannsdorf, Sachsen, Germany, and died December 18, 1928 Fort Wayne. Both are buried in Lindenwood.

Adelia's ancestors who settled in Allen County were:

Karl Bradtmueller, born January 18, 1786, in Meinsen, Schaumburg Lippe, Germany, and died August 21, 1855, in Adams Township. His wife was Christina (Tegtmeier), born December 13,

1794, in Meinsen, Schaumburg-Lippe, Germany, and died December 7, 1880, in Adams Township. Both are buried in Martini Lutheran Cemetery. Their son, Wilhelm Bradtmueller, was born January 11, 1822, in Meinsen Schaumburg-Lippe, Germany, and died April 3, 1895, in Fort Wayne. His wife was Louise (Kellermeier), was born February 6, 1822, in Frille, Westfalen, Germany, and died December 7, 1900, in Fort Wayne. Both are buried in Concordia Lutheran Cemetery.

Christian Wiese was born March 9, 1829, in Wietersheim, Westfalen, Germany, and died May 11, 1915, in Adams Township. His wife, Anna (Weisheit), was born December 18, 1832, in Erksdorf, Hessen-Darmstadt, Germany, and died June 26, 1880, in Adams Township. Both are buried in Martini Lutheran Cemetery. Her father, Peter Weisheit, was born December 21, 1797, in Erksdorf, Hessen Darmstadt, Germany, and died April 16, 1877, in Adams Township. He is buried in Martini Lutheran Cemetery.

Germain Bobay was born February 24, 1807, in St. Germain, Haut-Rhin, France, and died in the1850s in Washington Township. His wife, Pauline (Perrez), was born April 29, 1806, Offemont, Haut-Rhin, France, and died in the 1860s in Washington Township. Both are buried in St. Vincent Catholic Church Cemetery. Their son John Bobay, was born October 23, 1834, in Offemont, Haut-Rhin, France, and died December 4, 1910, in St. Joseph Township. His wife, Julie (Sarrazin), was born September 4, 1841, in France, and died June 21, 1892, in St. Joseph Township. Both are buried at St. Michael Catholic Cemetery.

Anna (Baatz) Bobay was born January 5, 1876, in Beerwalde, Sachsen, Germany, and died July 25, 1940, in Fort Wayne, and is buried at St. Peter Goeglein Lutheran. Her father, Herman Baatz, was born January 21, 1843, at Crossen, Sachsen, Germany, and died September 27, 1915, in St. Joseph Township. His wife, Emilie (Poch), was born July 25, 1848, in Neumilkau, Sachsen, Germany, and died March 17, 1917, in St. Joseph Township. Both are buried at St. Peter Goeglein Lutheran.

Submitted by William Hoffmeier

HOLLMANN FAMILY

Johann Friedrich Hollmann, born June 18, 1810, in Osnabruck, Hanover, Germany, emigrated from Bremen April 10, 1834, and arrived in New York May 26,1834. He journeyed to Pennsylvania where he resided for one year. In 1835 Mr. Hollmann traveled by river to Fort Wayne. On December 15 he filed a claim on 65.2 acres of land on the St. Mary's River in Marion Township, Allen County, Indiana. Another tract of 50.26 acres was later added. This farm is still in existence and is located at South Anthony Extended and Ferguson Road.

In May 1836 Johann Hollmann returned to Fort Wayne with his future bride, Maria Engel Kolkmeier. They were married on May 11, 1836. They became the parents of six sons. The sons, Friedrich, Heinrich, William, Frank, Edward, and John were born between 1835 and 1847. Mr. Hollmann died January 27, 1847, from influenza and was buried in McCulloch Park on Broadway. Mr. Hollmann was one of the original landowners of Allen County, Indiana. He and his wife were one of the founding families of St. Paul's Lutheran Church in Fort Wayne.

Hollmann Brothers 1865 (sons of Johann and Maria Hollmann): l. to r. Friedrich, Heinrich, William, Frank, Edward, John

Friedrich married Mary Nierman. He owned a sawmill in Washington Township.

Heinrich moved to Oklahoma.

William married Susanna Von Der Au and farmed in both Milan and St. Joseph Townships.

Frank married Sophia Trier, daughter of Conrad Trier, and farmed in Marion Township.

Edward married Sophia Cramer and farmed in St. Joseph Township.

John married Marie Grieser and moved to Whitley County, Indiana, where he farmed.

Frank and Sophia (Trier) Hollmann had eight children: William, Johann, Friedrich, Frank, Paul, Emilie, Martha, and Marie. William married Louisa Sophia Kohlmeier on July 28, 1892, in Fort Wayne. Their three children were Olga, Arnold, and Luella. Arnold Hollmann was born November 4, 1893. He married Alma Marie Bobay on May 5, 1918. Their children were Marcella, Earl, Ralph, Donald, Geraldine, Dallas, Dorthy, Eileen, Joan, William, and Larry. Alma Bobay was the great-granddaughter of Germain and Pauline (Perrey) Bobay who immigrated to Fort Wayne from St. Germain, Canton of Fontaine, France, in 1840. The Bobays were among the founding families of St. Vincent's Catholic Church.

Arnold Hollmann was an electrician and worked as maintenance foreman at Bowser Pump Company when he died January 25, 1948. Earlier in his career, Mr. Hollmann was superintendent for the Indiana Service Company. He was in charge of installing the first high-tension electrical lines in Fort Wayne and building electrical substations around town. He also supervised the coal plant on Superior Street where coal was burned to produce gas. Mr. Hollmann worked at Trier's Amusement Park where he was in charge of building the roller coaster.

Arnold Hollmann's maternal great-grandfather was Christian Kohlmeier, who emigrated from Westphalia, Germany, in 1840. His grandparents were Christian and Wilhelmina (Krueckeberg) Kohlmeier.

Dorthy Hollmann, the seventh child of Arnold and Alma (Bobay) Hollmann, was born September 19,1931, and graduated from South Side High School in 1949. She was employed for ten years by Lincoln Life Insurance as a supervisor in the accounting department and later was an office manager for Rogers Market. Dorthy married Douglas George Rockne Knuth on December 27, 1958. Douglas was born in Brown County, Wisconsin, August 4, 1931. He graduated from the University of Wisconsin. He came to Fort Wayne to work for Lincoln Life Insurance and retired in 1996 as an Underwriting Assistant Vice-President. Dorthy and Douglas have three children, Denise, Mark, and Erica.

Other names in the Hollmann lineage include Cordier, Linker, Perrey, Sarazen, and Schroeder.

Submitted by Dorothy Knuth

ISREAL HOLLOPETER

Isreal Hollopeter was born on August 30, 1840, and died February 25, 1916 in Huntertown, Indiana. Jemima Hanna Stevick was born on April 7, 1849, and died August 29, 1933 in Huntertown, Indiana. They were married June 15, 1916 in Leo, Indiana, Allen County, Indiana, after he returned from service throughout the Civil War as a private in the 11th Indiana Infantry. They lived in Eel River Township, Allen County, Indiana. Both are buried in the Huntertown Cemetery on Cedar Canyon Road, in Perry Township, Allen County, Indiana. To this family were born eleven children, eight boys and three girls:

1) Cora May, born May 4, 1866

2) Elmer Jacob, born on February 3, 1869, married Mina Hollopeter, June 12, 1895, died March 15, 1909, Leo, Indiana. Mina Hollopeter died January 14, 1945, in Leo, Indiana. They had one daughter, Eva May, born May 10, 1899. She married Joe Newhouser December 29, 1915. Joe was born May 29, 1897. In this family were one son and two daughters.

3) Hiram Elbridge, born September 30, 1870, married Minnie Vancise, August 30, 1904. He died February 15, 1935. Minnie was born January 29, 1875. In this family were three children, Hazel, born June 19, 1905; Ralph, born May 23, 1907; and Robert Lee, born May 6, 1912

4) Charles Wilson, was born on April 28, 1873, and died October 24, 1895. He married

Hollopeter Family. First Row, L to R: Albert, Herschel, Arthur. Second Row: Cora (partial picure), Zend, Jemima (mother), Isreal (father), Alfred. Third Row: Elmer, Anna Luellen, Hiram, Charles, Mary

Ema Altice Paulus on October 6, 1895. Emma was born in Columbia City, Indiana on March 15, 1877, and died on October 24, 1932. In this family were eleven children: Florence Audry, born at Churubusco, Indiana, March 15, 1896; Opel Adril, born at Huntertown, Indiana, December 8, 1897; Gladys Bell, born at Churubusco, Indiana, March 5, 1899, died October 1, 1899; Dorothy May, born in La Otto, Indiana, May 10, 1900, died May 12, 1900; Simon Albert, born at Collins, Indiana, February 25, 1903; Isreal Paulis, born at Arcola, Indiana, October 21, 1908; Emma Rosetta, born at Churubusco, Indiana, April 6, 1911; Virginia Garlendine, born at Churubusco, Indiana, July 26, 1913; Hanna Jemima, born at Jerome, Idaho, March 6, 1916; James Eldon, born at Jerome, Idaho, November 29, 1918. Charles married his second wife, Lela Armstrong, March 22, 1935.

5) Anna Luellen Hollopeter, born June 18, 1875, married John Sherman Heffelfinger on January 24, 1892. In this family there were six children: Pearl May, born July 8, 1892; Isreal Franklin, born May 19, 1895; Ada Vietta, born August 23, 1897; Evadna Orminda, born September 12, 1899; Lucille Bernice, born September 6, 1901; Alice Margaret, born October 16, 1910; and adopted son Waldo Heffelfinger, born October 15, 1917.

6) Mary Euletha Hollopeter, born June 13, 1877, married A.W. Barney Heffelfinger, September 25, 1895. A.W. Barney was born June 17, 1873. In this family were born nine children, seven daughters and two sons: Francis Marie, born May 29, 1897; Iva Irene, born January 12, 1897; Vonell, born October 3, 1900; Laura Inez, born July 24, 1903; Herman Taft, born December 15, 1908 (twin died at birth, Howard Taft); Mary Katherine, born June 17, 1913; Keith Miles, born September 19, 1916; Betty Rebecca, born October 13, 1918.

7) Alfred Monroe Hollopeter, born September 2, 1879, married Corda Bell Kaiser, December 23, 1939. They had no children.

8) Arthur Lee Hollopeter, born September 26, 1883, married Ida May Hippenhamer, September 22, 1910. Ida May was born October 27, 1891, in Allen County, Indiana. There was one daughter, Marjorie Marie, born 1911. She married Elmer Jackson March 1932.

9) Albert Eugene Hollopeter, born September 26, 1885, married Sylvia Freeman, November 11, 1906. Sylvania was born August 4, 1886, and died August 28, 1943. In this family were born ten children, six sons and four daughters: Agnes Marjorie, May 7, 1907; Ronald Eugene, July 23, 1909; Earl Freeman, April 9, 1912; Eleanor Catherine, April 4, 1914; Everett Otis, June 13, 1916; Frank Elwood, July 18, 1918; Maurice Albert, November 7, 1920; Martha Ellen, April 27, 1923; Hazel Elizabeth, September 14, 1924.

10) Herschel Ambrose Hollopeter, born April 5, 1889, married Emma Louise Tilden December 14, 1912, in Huntertown, Indiana. Emma Louise was born December 23, 1892. In this family was born one daughter, Mary J., April 9, 1914.

11) Zend Aventus Hollopeter, born August 9, 1881, married Florence Nevada Myers, February 17, 1907, at Albion, Noble County, Indiana. Florence Nevada was born November 7, 1887. In this family were born nine children, five sons and four daughters: Juanita, born December 13, 1907; Elmer August 13, 1909, died at age of eight days August 21, 1909; Russell Elmer, born May 9, 1911; Madge Marcella, November 17, 1915; Mary Winifred, born November 25, 1917; Kenneth Warren, born May 25, 1922; Margaret Hattebell, May 20, 1920, died July 8, 1921; Herman Eugene, born December 16, 1925; and Gene, born 1933, died the same day.

Submitted by Shirley Underwood

MATTHIAS HOLLOPETER

Matthias Hollopeter was born in 1728, probably in Germany. By 1754 he had arrived in the U.S. and bought one hundred acres in York County, Pennsylvania. He married Barbara Rusz (Roose) and died in York County in 1799. They were members of a Lutheran church. Andrew, their son, was born in 1777 in York County. He married Phebe Blatchford, whose twin sister Margaret married Andrew's brother, Abe. Phebe and Margaret were excommunicated from their Quaker church when they married the Hollopeter brothers. Andrew and Phebe moved to Wayne County, Ohio, in 1824, with their children, including Abraham (born in 1800), and joined a Methodist church there, only twenty-two years after Methodism was first established in the U.S. An unusually large number of their descendants have been ministers and local leaders in Methodist and Wesleyan churches.

Mathias and Mary Hollopeter and children: James Milton, Bertram, Mable, Lester, and Franklin

Andrew, a carpenter, moved his family to Seneca County, Ohio, about 1834. Abraham had married Lydia Myers in 1819 in York County before the move to Ohio. They owned eighty acres of land in Wayne County before moving to Holmes County and then to Seneca County.

After his father died there, Abraham moved to Allen County, Indiana, sometime after 1842, and bought 120 acres. Besides farming, he also worked as a carpenter, cabinetmaker, and township trustee.

Their son, Matthias, was born in Wayne County in 1833 and moved with his parents to Allen County, Indiana, where he grew up cutting timber and burning brush on a pioneer farm. He received a common school education and became a teacher at age 21. He married Susan Hanan and later Mary Stevick Hollopeter, who died in 1933. After teaching for several years, he worked as a carpenter and was a Justice of the Peace. Lester Hollopeter (1883-1966) was the son of Matthias and Mary. He married Alice Badiac, born in 1883. Their children, Charles, Parintha, Virginia, Lois, Margery, May, and Dorothy, were all born in Fort Wayne. After his wife's death, Lester lived with his daughter, May, and her family on a farm in Noble County, Indiana. Charles (1911-1972), first married Adeline Bellar, and later married Bernita Phillips. They adopted a daughter, Mary Kay. Parintha married Clifford Shuler and had three children: Barbara Gallespie McComb, Gene, and Paul. Virginia (1914-1994) married Paul Moss. Lois married Willard (Red) Buelow and had two sons, Gary and John. Margery married Eugene "Hap" Noll and had two daughters, Suzanne and Linda. May (1920-1973) married Richard Troyer and had four children: David, George, James, and Rebecca. David and George pastor Wesleyan churches, as does Rebecca's husband. Dorothy (1922-) married Herman Davis and had six children: Robert, Donald, Lucinda, Charles, Carol, and Margaret.

Primary source: *The Hollopeter Family Record* by Eva Hollopeter Ridenour and Wanda Hollopeter Burris

Submitted by James and Beverly Troyer

JEREMIAH HOLLY

Jeremiah Holly was born to Michael and Johanna (O'Connor) Holly, January 1, 1907, at Asdee, County Kerry, Ireland. He came to Fort Wayne in September 1929. He died July 30, 1991. He married Loretta Borchers (daughter of Henry and Francis (Hilgeford) Borchers of Fort Laramie, Ohio, on June 2, 1934. Loretta was born June 20, 1908, and died October 15, 2001. Together, they had eight children.

Patricia A. was born March 30, 1935. She entered the convent of the Franciscan Sisters of the Poor in 1952. She died February 25, 1997.

Michael H. was born May 3, 1936, in Fort Wayne, Indiana. He married Sarah Jane (Sally) Giles on September 1, 1962. They had four sons: Mark D., Timothy E., Patrick M., and Vincent W. Michael and Sarah live in Fort Wayne.

Dennis L. was born October 11, 1937. He is a priest with the Glenmary Home Missionaries. He is currently in Lafayette, Tennessee.

Mary J. was born March 7, 1940. She married Jim Kindler of Fort Wayne. They had three children: Daniel, Cynthia, and Erick. She later married James Shultz and they had one son, John. James Shultz died April 2, 2003. Mary lives in Indianapolis, Indiana.

Sheila J. was born September 28, 1941. She married David Freiburger of Fort Wayne. They had nine children: Lisa, Laura, Linda, Jane, Jeff, Sarah, Susan, Sandy, and Andrew. David died May 3, 2002. Sheila lives in Carmel, Indiana.

Kathleen F. was born July 5, 1943. She married James Rey of Fort Wayne. They had four children: Kelly, Amy, Christopher, and Heidi. She later married Ed Stark of Cincinnati, Ohio. They had one daughter, Holly. Kay and Ed live in Naperville, Illinois.

Daniel J. was born January 18, 1945. He married Charlene Rolf of Fort Wayne. They had three children: Matthew, Erin, and Kate. Daniel and Charlene live in Fort Wayne.

Margaret R. was born February 1, 1946. She married Ike Hullinger of Bunker Hill, Indiana. They were childless. Margaret died April 17, 1997.

Jeremiah and Loretta have 82 direct descendants as of this publication. This includes eight children, 24 grandchildren, and 50 great-grandchildren. Jeremiah retired from International Harvester, and Loretta retired from Lutheran Hospital.

Submitted by Michael H. Holly

WILLIAM P. HOLMES FAMILY

William P. Holmes arrived in Allen County sometime before 1844. He was born on June 2, 1823, in Lucerne County, Pennsylvania. He worked his way here from Pennsylvania, leaving his parents behind. His parents, William and Rocksinie Blood Holmes, were both born in England and settled in Pennsylvania sometime before 1823. William helped build the Pennsylvania Railroad into Fort Wayne and left the employment of the railroad in 1855.

William married Anne Eliza Driver on August 8, 1844, in New Haven, Indiana. In 1846 the first of their eight children, Wyman, was born. At the age of 17 Wyman enlisted in the Indiana 131st Regiment, 13th Calvary; Company G. He was killed in the tragic Sultana riverboat explosion on April 16, 1865, dying from burns.

William and Anna's first four children, Wyman-1846; Ann-1848; Lenona-1850; and Willard-1852, were all born in Madison Township, Allen County, Indiana. Then, between 1852 and 1855, the family moved to Davenport, Iowa, where their last four children were born: Erie-1855; Julia-1858; Exter-1867; and Flora-1862.

Left to right: Jennie Arter Holmes and Germaine Ruth Holmes

On June 19, 1862, William enlisted in the Civil War and served as a Private in Company G of the 18th Iowa Infantry, under the command of General John A. Logan. He mustered out of the service on July 20, 1865, in Little Rock, Arkansas, receiving his final discharge in Davenport, Iowa, in August 1865. His company took part in some of the heaviest engagements of the war west of the Mississippi River.

Shortly after leaving the Army, William moved his family back to Indiana and settled on a farm north of Maples, Indiana. The 1870 census shows William, Willard, and Exter working in a stove factory. During William's active years he was a member of Sion S. Bass Post No. 40, G.A.R. He was also an honorary member of Wayne Circle, Ladies of the G.A.R.

William lived until 1924, just shy of his 101st birthday. He died May 25 in Fort Wayne at the home of his daughter, Mrs. Erie Seibert, on West Taylor Street. He was a member of the New Haven Methodist Church. He is buried in New Haven IOOF Cemetery, Section A Plot 138.

His wife, Anna Eliza Driver, was born February 1, 1824, in Defiance, Ohio. She died August 3, 1897, at the age of 73. She is buried next to her husband.

William and Anna's seventh child, Exter D. Holmes, was born June 23, 1857, in Davenport, Iowa. He married Mary Jane Ladig of Maples, Indiana, on September 23, 1880. He was 23 years old and she was 17 years old. Both of their families owned farms two miles north of Maples. The Jefferson Township map shows Exter as a property owner in 1907.

They had six children: Otis Hirshil in 1883; Frederick Allen-1886; Minnie Olive-1892; Mildred G.-1897; Grace-1889; and Marguate R. (Deetta)-1907. Exter was well known throughout Jefferson Township and Allen County, and was an industrious farmer. At the age of 51 he developed stomach cancer, and on January 16, 1909, he died, leaving his wife and their youngest child, Deetta, with the farm. By the time Exter died, most all of his children had married and left the farm.

Otis Hirshil Holmes was born July 27, 1883, on either his father's farm or his grandfather's (Nicholas Ladig) farm. He married Jennie L. Arter May 26, 1903, in Fort Wayne, Indiana. Otis was a railroad worker for the Nickel Plate Railroad. He met Jennie in Old Fort, Ohio, where her mother, Rachel Blodgett/Arter, ran a boarding house. Jennie helped her mother cook for the railroad boarders, which were most of their customers.

Otis and Jennie lived on his parents' farm for approximately ten years. Their first child, Germaine Ruth, was born there on February 28, 1904. After his father died, Otis moved his family to Fort Wayne into a house at 2507 Lillie Street. This is where their second child was born on October 20,1913, and she was named Hortense Camille. Germaine died in 1977 and Hortense died in 2001. They each married twice but neither had children.

In 1924 Otis and Jennie's third child, Richard Arter, was born on Ramsey Street in Fort Wayne. Richard married Frances Nellie Small in 1951. Frances was from Chicago, Illinois. They raised their three children, Flaim Camille-1952, Colby Jay-1954, and Cindy Lee-1958, in Fort Wayne.

Frances died in 1984. Richard remarried in 1986 to Anna Rambo Morgan. Flaim married William Cupp, Jr. in 1980 and they have two children, Casey Lee and Brittany Ann. Colby married Jeannie Ridlen and they have one child, Kimberly. Cindy married Jake Fine of Chicago, Illinois, and they have three children: Jessica, Callie, and Willy. All but Cindy's family live in Fort Wayne.

Submitted by Flaim Cupp of Angola

WILLIAM D. HOLTERMAN FAMILY

William D. Holterman was a native of the state of Missouri. A graduate of Woodville Teachers College in 1891, he taught for several years at Grace Lutheran school in Fort Wayne. He lived in the area for seventy years and was a charter member of Concordia Lutheran Church. He was the son of Peter Holterman, a Lutheran Minister from Germany. He married Caroline B. and they had two children, Louis and Emily.

Caroline died November 8, 1945 and is buried at Concordia Cemetery.

She and William raised an exotic breed of chickens and shipped them all over the world. Caroline would shoot rats if they bothered her flock. George Gillie, who was a Veterinarian and Congressman, developed a formula for chicken feed and William sold it to the public at a good profit. He built the castle-like structure on the left side of the Lincoln Highway going to New Haven. There was a six- or eight-sided red and white two-story barn where the chicken feed was mixed and bagged to sell.

L to R: Front row: Caroline B. Holterman and Mrs. Rippe (neighbor). Back Row: Emily Kleeberg. Walter Kleeberg, William B. Holterman, Colleen Kleeberg, Louis Holterman and Hazel Holterman

There was a little red and white playhouse on the property. Also on the property was a large three car garage with an upstairs where William had his insurance office. On the dining room wall was a picture about eighteen inches wide and seven inches tall. It was a panoramic view of the whole property with Louis and Emily on horseback under a curved wrought iron arch labeled "Holder's Roost".

Their daughter, Emily, married Walter Kleeberg and had a log cabin built up close to the Castle. When her father remarried in his eighties, Emily became upset and moved the cabin across the creek. Emily and Walter had no children, but did raise a niece of Walter's whose name was Colleen Kleeberg. Colleen graduated from the Lutheran Hospital School of Nursing in the class of 1949. She married a man named Rowlett and lives in Texas.

William and Caroline's son, Louis, married Florence who died of Tuberculosis. They enclosed the side porch at their home with screens where they cared for her. After her death , Louis married Hazel and they had a son and a daughter. Louis owned a bar on Pontiac Street for many years. He and Walter Kleeberg, his brother-in-law, played on one of the first "Old Timer" Baseball teams.

William D. Holterman's obituary appeared in the News Sentinel on July 30, 1960. He died at Lutheran Hospital at the age of 87. Reverend Osmar Lehenbauer officiated at the funeral with burial at Concordia Cemetery. He was survived by his wife, Lillian, a son, Lou, and a daughter, Mrs. Walter Kleeberg of Fort Wayne; three stepchildren, Gerald Sheiman, Mrs. Romine and Raymond Swift, all of South Bend; a brother, Emil, of Fort Wayne and two sisters, Mrs. Otto Kubitz, Madison, Wisconsin, and Mrs. Bertha Rietdorf, Oshkosh, Wisconsin.

Submitted by Catherine E. Parkins, great-niece of William D. Holterman

GEORGE CHRISTOPHER & KATHLEEN VIRGINIA (BITNER) HOOD FAMILY

George Christopher Hood was born in Paragould, Arkansas, on July 4, 1910, and died in Fort Wayne, Indiana, on April 13, 1992. Kathleen Virginia Bitner Hood was born in Fort Wayne, Indiana, on May 27, 1913, and is still living.

George Christopher Hood was the only child born to Chris Hood and Minnie Lutencia Butler Hood. Chris Hood, the child of George Hood and Margaret Rankin Hood, was born February 13, 1881, in Carmi, White County, Illinois, and died March 17, 1911, in Carmi, White County, Illinois. Minnie Lutencia Butler Hood, the child of Deloss N. Butler and Florence Ward Butler, was born in Van Wert County, Ohio, on October 12, 1890. Chris Hood and Minnie Lutencia Butler, also known as Tennie Butler, were married February 5, 1909, in Paragould, Greene County, Arkansas.

The Hood Family in 1943
Left to right: Kathleen Hood, G. Stanley Hood, James C. Hood and George C. Hood

Tennie Butler Hood, mother of George Christopher Hood and widow of Chris Hood, was later known as Marie L. Hood and then Marie L. Payton following her marriage to J. William Payton, which occurred in Fort Wayne, Indiana, in 1926. She was a continuous resident of Fort Wayne until her death on August 13, 1963. Marie L. Payton (Tennie Hood) was very active in work for the blind. She organized the Sunshine Motor Corps to transport blind people and was very active in the annual white cane drive. For many years she operated the Little Indiana Tourist Home, located at 2029 Maumee Avenue at the corner of Wabash Avenue, in the City of Fort Wayne. George Christopher Hood came to Fort Wayne with his widowed mother in approximately 1920.

Kathleen Virginia Bitner Hood was one of seven children born to Charles Leroy Bitner and Helena Clara Guettner Bitner. Charles Leroy, known as Roy, was born in Fort Wayne on June 28, 1884, and died in Fort Wayne on December 26, 1963. He was the son of John R. Bitner and Emma Helfrich Bitner. Helena was born on December 26, 1885, in Vincennes, Indiana, the child of Herman Wilhem Guettner and Emilee Schriber Guettner. She died in Fort Wayne on June 14, 1967. When Helena was two years old, her mother died and she moved with her father to Fort Wayne. Helena and Charles Leroy were married in January of 1907 in Fort Wayne. They met when they were both employees of Freiburger Glove Factory. Charles Leroy Bitner was employed for many years at Wayne Oil Burner Factory in Fort Wayne. Later he was the elevator operator at the old Methodist Hospital located on Lewis Street in Fort Wayne. When Parkview Hospital opened in 1953, he operated the elevator at that facility until automated elevators were installed.

The Bitner family has a long history in Allen County, Indiana. Andrew Jackson Bitner, paternal great grandfather of Kathleen Virginia Bitner Hood, was born in Centre County, Pennsylvania, on December 18, 1816, and died in Fort Wayne on November 7, 1887. Andrew Bitner married Eliza Nave, who was born in Franklin County, Pennsylvania, on July 8, 1827, and died in Fort Wayne on February 29, 1892. The marriage took place on June 8, 1846, in Holmes County, Ohio. John R. Bitner, child of Andrew and Eliza and paternal grandfather of Kathleen Virginia Bitner Hood, was born in Galion, Ohio, on November 23, 1850.

In 1856, the Andrew J. Bitner family moved to Roanoke, Huntington County, Indiana, where they resided until the autumn of 1863 when they moved briefly back to Holmes County, Ohio. In 1864, the Bitner family moved back to Indiana and made their home on Bluffton Road, twelve miles south of Fort Wayne. They moved into the city of Fort Wayne in May of 1865.

John R. Bitner married Emma Helfrich, a native of Crestline, Ohio, on November 7, 1877. John R. Bitner went to work for the Pennsylvania Railroad in 1869 and worked there more than fifty years. He had one of the longest perfect attendance records in company history and eventually became a master mechanic in the Pennsylvania Railroad repair shops located in Fort Wayne. John R. Bitner died on January 1, 1923, in Fort Wayne and Emma Helfrich Bitner died on April 15, 1938, in Fort Wayne.

On September 28, 1935, George Christopher Hood and Kathleen Virginia Bitner were married at Trinity English Lutheran Church in Fort Wayne. George was a graduate of South Side High School where he had earned all city and all state honors in football and was captain of the team. Kathleen graduated from Central High School and in 1930 was named "Fort Wayne's most beautiful red head" in a contest held at the Emboyd Theater. George was employed for twenty-seven years by the Fort Wayne Fire Department and served eight years as chief of the Fire Prevention Bureau. Following his retirement from the fire department, he served as chief of plant protection and security for the Winter Street General Electric plant in Fort Wayne. Kathleen was a homemaker and in addition worked at Wayne Knitting Mills. For thirty years she was a legal secretary in Fort Wayne.

Two children were born to George Christopher Hood and Kathleen Virginia Bitner Hood. George Stanley Hood was born on April 23, 1938, and James Charles Hood was born on June 8, 1941. Both Stan and Jim graduated from South Side High School in Fort Wayne. Stan is a graduate of the Indiana University School of Law and has been a practicing attorney in Fort Wayne for the past forty years. He is married to the former Ruth Ann Reinhard and is the father of two children, Christopher Hood and Cynthia Hood, both of whom reside in Dallas, Texas. Jim served in the United States Army and was employed by Rogers Market, International Harvester, and Lutheran Hospital. He is married to the former Lucy Ford and is the father of two children, Douglas Hood and Ryan Hood, both of whom reside in Fort Wayne.

Submitted by G. Stanley Hood

ROBERT LAWRENCE HOPE & DOLORES JOANNE KOEHL FAMILY

Robert (Bob) Lawrence Hope was born April 3, 1923, in Pierceton, Indiana, the son of Otho Alfred Hope (1880-1953) and Cora Cecelia Tracy (1883-1974). The family farm was located on Route 13, two miles north of Sidney, in Kosciusko County, Indiana.

The Hope family heritage in the United States has been traced back to William Kane Hope, Robert's great-grandfather, who was born in 1814 in Virginia. Primarily of English descent, the Hope family tree includes English, Scotch-Irish, French and German heritage.

Robert was the youngest of five children. His siblings are Rosemond Annabell (1908-1995), married Raymond Travis; Paul Otho Tracy (1911-1977), married Velma Nellie Hagel; Lorraine Claire Cecelia (born 1914), married Laurence R. Walsh, divorced and married Karl I. Heinzelman; Cora Maxine Agnes (b. 1917), married Harold L. Henry, divorced and married Claude Tibbs; divorced and married Elmer Wilhite.

Shortly after Bob was born, his mother contracted what was diagnosed to be tuberculosis and was not expected to live. Concerned neighbors and friends wanted to adopt Bob, but the family refused. Cora recovered and later lived until the age of 91 years.

Bob was baptized and a member of St. Francis Xavier Catholic Church, Pierceton, Indiana, and attended public school, graduating from Pierceton High School in 1941. Over the objections of his parents, Bob left the family farm and moved to Fort Wayne, Indiana. He took a job at the Pennsylvania Railroad firing engines by stoking them with coal. Bob's tenure at the railroad was brief. The country was entering World War II. Had he stayed on the farm, Bob could have received a deferment. But he wanted to serve his country, and was drafted into the Army on January 23, 1943. Bob served in the 1303 Army Corp of Engineers. His unit was one of the later groups to enter the Battle of the Bulge, seeing action in Normandy, Northern France, Rhineland, Central Europe and the Ardennes Region of France. Their job was to rebuild the bridges the enemy had destroyed as the Allied forces advanced. Bob supervised the construction and repair of buildings, drainage systems, airport waterworks, culverts, etc. He interpreted blueprints and so forth.

Marriage of Robert L. and Dolores Hope, May 18, 1946. L to R: Madonna Vance, Margaret Vance, Irene Mueller, Patricia Walsh (flower girl), Dolores (Koehl) Hope, Robert L. Hope, Thomas Koehl, Herbert Koehl, "Red" Busz

Two Bob Hopes, left, comedian Bob Hope, right, Robert L. Hope, Las Vegas, February of 1952

Like many WWII veterans, Bob did not speak much about his experiences in the war. He did recall one event when a bridge he was working on came under attack. An enemy plane was approaching and about to bomb the bridge. The soldiers with Bob scrambled to clear the bridge, but instead, Bob swung himself under the bridge out of the machine gun fire. He said later that he somehow knew the bomb would miss the bridge. Bob was hit by shrapnel and knocked off the bridge into the Rhine River. His buddies rescued him from the river, but thought he was dead. For a few moments, he could not communicate to tell them he was alive. Suddenly, he began to cough up the water he had taken in, and came around. Bob could have received a Purple Heart for his wounds, but never submitted the request. Ironically, many of the soldiers who had cleared the bridge died when the bomb missed its target.

Bob's unit was on a ship in the harbor of the Philippines in July 1945, ready to enter the Pacific arena when the war ended. He was honorably discharged from the Army on October 19, 1945. He achieved the rank of Sergeant, receiving the European Theatre Award (EAME, five bronze stars), and the Philippine Liberation ribbon (1 bronze star) and the Good Conduct Ribbon.

After the war, Bob returned home to the farm. Shortly after coming home, he began to date Dolores Joanne Koehl (born in 1926), whom he had met prior to the war. After a brief engagement, the couple was married May 18, 1946, at the Cathedral of the Immaculate Conception, in Fort Wayne.

Dolores was the daughter of Franz (Frank) Adam Koehl (1892-1967) and Alma Loretta Brown (1890-1968) of Fort Wayne, Indiana. Dolores' father was a monument engraver and owner of Jacob Koehl & Sons. Born in Fort Wayne, she attended school in Rome City, Indiana, and Cathedral Elementary School, Fort Wayne, Indiana. Her family were members of the Cathedral of the Immaculate Conception Catholic Church. Dolores graduated from Central Catholic High School in 1944. Dolores' siblings include Noreen Frances (1915-1980), Herbert Eugene (1917-1919), Marceille Marie (1921-1928), and Thomas Vincent (born 1928). As a young woman, Dolores took one year of nurses' training at St. Joseph Hospital, before leaving for other occupations prior to her marriage to Bob. A loving mother and homemaker, she later would work at Magnavox in the government contracts division and retire after over 25 years as an engineering aid.

Bob and Dolores lived on the Hope family farm for six months before moving to Fort Wayne, where they would eventually raise their children. Bob returned to the Pennsylvania Railroad, becoming an electrician as the railroads moved from steam locomotion to electric engines. During his 33 years with the railroad, he was considered a top electrician, and also worked as a foreman. Before his retirement, the Pennsylvania Railroad would merge with the New York Central to become the Penn-Central Railroad, and later Conrail.

Bob served in the Air National Guard at Baer Field Air Base in Fort Wayne for two years. He was activated during the Korean conflict on February 1, 1951, through September 12, 1952, and worked as an aircraft mechanic with the 163rd Fighter Interceptor Squad.

Bob and Dolores raised five children: Stephen Gregory (born 1948), married to Nancy Elaine Gase; Robert Patrick (1951-1966); Karen Ann (born 1956); Joseph Edward (born 1957), married to Marchelle Devon Wreford; and John Francis (born 1959), married to Jennifer Elizabeth Rohyans. They moved to St. Joseph Township on the northeast side of Fort Wayne in 1958.

The family was active at St. Charles Borromeo Catholic Church, where most of the children attended elementary school and Bob was involved with Boy Scout Troop 307, serving as the first scoutmaster when the troop was established in 1959. His years in the Army as Drill Instructor filtered down to his work with the Boy Scouts. Bob's troop knew and performed the "Close Order Drill," a series of maneuvers performed on parade by soldiers and marching bands. He used his Army training to teach discipline and other skills to the young boys, always following the Scout motto "Be Prepared." He made the scouting experience fun, with one memorable squirt-gun battle ending with 30 squirt gunned armed scouts attacking the scoutmaster!

Bob was a member of the Civil Defense Police for many years during the late 1950s through the 1960s. As a CD policeman, Bob would direct traffic for city events, including the annual July 4th Fireworks which were then held at McMillen Park. The Civil Defense Police also assisted the city and county officers during the tense Civil Rights marches of the 1960s.

The family enjoyed the many times their "famous" names brought them attention. They were often asked if they were related to comedian and film star "Bob" Hope (and his wife, Dolores). The two "Bobs" were photographed together when Robert L. was still in military service. While a true relationship has yet to be documented, Robert L. was fond of referring to the comedian as his "Thirty-Second Cousin, Twice Removed."

Tragically, the Hopes' son Robert Patrick (Bobby) was killed by a drunk driver at 15 years of age in an early morning accident while delivering newspapers as a carrier for the *Fort Wayne Journal-Gazette* on August 30, 1966. Their beloved son was laid to rest in Catholic Cemetery, Fort Wayne, Indiana on September 2, 1966.

The four remaining children have produced ten grandchildren (including adopted and step-grandchildren) and nine great-grandchildren. Robert L. Hope died just after his 67th birthday, on April 7, 1990. He is interred next to his son in Catholic Cemetery, Fort Wayne, Indiana.

Submitted by Karen Hope

ROBERT ALAN HOULIHAN & SANDRA ANN GLASS FAMILY

Robert Alan Houlihan was born on April 17, 1938 in Ansonia, Connecticut, to Robert John and Meda Alice (Hull) Houlihan. Robert married Sandra Ann Glass on November 3, 1962. Two children were born to Robert and Sandra, a son Mahlon Lucius on May 28, 1964, and a daughter Rachel Louise on December 23, 1969.

Sandra was born on February 19, 1939, to George Enos Glass and Mary Ellen Somers. Sandra was first married to Jean Howard Marquardt on September 1, 1956 and to them was born a

Robert and Sandra (Glass) Houlihan

son, Scott Wesley Marquardt on February 13, 1959. They divorced.

Sandra is an avid genealogist with strong ties to both Allen and Wells counties. Her father was the son of Enos Adolphos Glass and Edna Ella Eckhart. He served as Prosecuting Attorney in Wells County for four years before practicing law in Fort Wayne. George died of a heart attack at age 44 and is buried in the Fairview Cemetery, Bluffton. Her mother was secretary to Dr. M. A. Davidoff and died of lung cancer at age 49. She is buried in the Poe Cemetery, Poe, Indiana. Mary Ellen was the daughter of Harley Holmes Somers and Etna Grace Trenary. Through diligent research she has traced her ancestry to her great-great grandfather Richard Trenary and discovered a cousin with the same passion for family history, Tom Trenary Barker of Traverse City, Michigan. The two collaborated to publish "The Richard Trenary Family Tree" in 1979. This spiral bound recording of the family's members known to date was published and made available at a Trenary reunion held that same year. The work didn't stop, however, and by 2004 the data had exploded into a full-fledged, bound and hard-covered book of nearly four hundred pages containing not only birth, marriage and death dates, but hundreds of family photos, transcriptions of diaries, photocopies of significant documents and much more. Copies of the book were presented to the Wells County and Allen County libraries for their archives.

Concurrently, Robert and Sandra were active in many other areas and also raising a family. Robert worked in several segments of the insurance industry before hiring in at Brotherhood Mutual Insurance Company where he eventually became Vice-President of Underwriting before retiring in 2003. Robert's work with the Fire and Arson Squad Team (FAST) came naturally and his broad knowledge of insurance added to the organization's effectiveness.

Robert's political ambitions were not as aggressive as Sandra's and he was content to serve as Pleasant Township Precinct Committeeman for many years. Sandra, however, sought and was elected to the Allen County Council in 1978 and then again in 1985 where she served until 2002. In 1991 she became the first woman to be elected President of the Council. She also taught piano and organ lessons for many years.

Now retired, they live in a restored farmhouse in Wells County on land purchased by an ancestor in 1840. They remain active in church, enjoy traveling and spending time with their children and grandchildren.

Submitted by Mahlon Houlihan

SALLY ANN HOULIHAN

Sally was born August 1, 1932, at St. Joseph Hospital in Fort Wayne. She was the fourth child of Margaret Alice Palmer and Joseph Emmett Houlihan. She was baptized at St. Patrick's and resided at 441 West Williams. She was preceded by siblings Margaret Alice, James Joseph, Mary Agnes, and followed by Margaret Ellen "Peggy".

A consummate student, she started grade school at St. Patrick's then transferred to St. John the Baptist after WW II. She graduated from Central Catholic High School in 1950 then completed her R.N. at St. Joseph Hospital in 1953.

She took a break in her studies to marry Carl A. Wall, the son of one of her patients, Herbert C. Wall, on September 25, 1954, at St. John's. Her children are Gregory Conrad, Lisa Ellen, David Joseph, and Jennifer Ann. During her child-rearing years she was a member of the Junior League and was active in the Cursillo movement.

Sally Ann Houlihan

She received her B.S. in Psychology from Indiana University in 1971 and her Masters in Social Work from the same University in 1981.

She has used her knowledge to direct the Methadone Clinic started in Fort Wayne in 1971 for the Vietnam veterans. She also worked at the Mental Health and Park Centers in Fort Wayne. After working several years at the Caylor-Nickel Clinic in Bluffton, she is currently working for J. Dunn & Associates in Fort Wayne as a clinical therapist.

Celestia Crow was the only one of Sally's grandparents to be born in Fort Wayne. Her birthday is June 5, 1862. Her father, Jonathan, was a pioneer farmer who came to the Fort Wayne area in 1845 to clear the land which became his home. Celestia married Albert David Palmer of Junction City, Ohio, on October 25, 1881, in Yoder. Albert was one of twelve children and was a charter member of St. Patrick's. His parents, David and Jane, moved to Fort Wayne in 1864.

Sally's other grandparents, John Joseph Houlihan of Springfield, Massachusetts, and Ellen Anne Lynch of Vincennes, Indiana, were married on October 20, 1888, in Fort Wayne. John worked for the Wabash Railroad for 35 years.

Sally's father, Joseph Emmett Houlihan, was born May 5, 1882, in Fort Wayne where he spent his entire life. He attended grade school at St. Patrick's and then attended the Old Brother School for Boys on Calhoun and Lewis. He worked for 32 years at the Wayne Pump Company and retired as a foreman. He died at his home on 304 Maple Grove Avenue on August 19, 1953.

Joseph married Alice Margaret Palmer on October 25, 1917, in Fort Wayne. Margaret was born February 6, 1885, in Fort Wayne. She also attended St. Patrick's school, and then attended St. Catherine's Academy on DeWald and Butler. She died one month after the birth of her fifth child on February 7, 1936, from complications related to the birth.

Submitted by Lisa Ellen Wall

KATHLEEN MARIE JOHNSON HOUSER ANKENBRUCK FAMILY

Kathleen Marie Johnson, (Kathy) first child of Robert Philip and Mary Angela Sheehan Johnson, was born April 1, 1951, in Fort Wayne, Indiana. The family moved to Crown Point, Indiana, then to Decatur, Monroeville, and New Haven, finally making their permanent home in Fort Wayne, Indiana.

Kathy attended St. Hyacinth Catholic School and graduated from Central Catholic High School in 1969. After graduation she worked at Lincoln National Life Insurance Company.

She met Lynn Eugene Houser at Mr. Wiggs Department Store and on May 6, 1972, they were married at St. Jude's Catholic Church. They had three sons: Scott Eugene (September 27, 1973), Bradley Robert (June 18, 1976), and Andrew Lynn (November 11, 1977). They made their home on Ivy League Drive later building a home in the Hillsboro addition.

Lynn worked for Conrail and was gone from home during the week. Kathy attended IPFW and obtained her Pre-School Certification. She began the Pre-School program at St. Jude's Catholic School in 1983. The program was very successful.

Kathy and Lynn were divorced in March 1987. With her boys she moved to Dover Drive in Fort Wayne. She continued teaching at St. Jude's and working part time at Hall's Restaurant.

She met Ronald Ankenbruck, the father of five grown children, at Pilgrimage, a singles support group at St. Jude's. Five years later, July 9, 1999, they were married at St. Jude's Catholic Church. Ron is self-employed in the rental property business.

Being self-employed, Ron was able to spend winters in Florida. After teaching at St. Jude's for 17 years, Kathy took early retirement in 2001 to be a full-time homemaker. Ron and Kathy divide their time between homes at Lake James near Angola, Indiana; Clearwater, Florida; and Fort Wayne, Indiana.

Kathy, Scott, Bradley, and Andrew (November 1989)

Scott, Bradley, and Andrew graduated from St. Jude's Elementary School and Bishop Dwenger High School in Fort Wayne, Indiana. Scott and Andrew graduated from Indiana University in Bloomington, Indiana.

After graduation, Scott taught biology and coached football at Roncolli High School. Presently he teaches and coaches at Franklin Central High School, Indianapolis. He married Karen Sue Schnell on May 15, 2002, at St. Jude Catholic Church in Indianapolis, Indiana, where they now live with their daughter, Lucy, born April 13, 2003.

Bradley attended Indiana State University for one year before enlisting in the U.S. Coast Guard. He is now an electrician for Conrail and makes his home in Auburn, Indiana. He has one daughter, Samantha Lynn, born August 6, 1998.

Submitted by Kathleen Ankenbruck

KENNETH EUGENE & CAROLYN FRY HOUSER FAMILY

Kenneth Eugene Houser was born October 24, 1928, in Maples, Allen County, Indiana. His parents were Ray Elmer and Myrtle Virginia Croy Houser. When he was seven years old his family moved to Payne, Ohio, where he attended elementary and high school. During high school he worked at International Harvester and after school worked at Essex Wire. He retired from B. F. Goodrich in 1999.

He married Carolyn Ann Fry on October 7, 1950, in Payne, Ohio. The family has resided in Allen County since 1950. Carolyn graduated from Payne High School and Lutheran Hospital School of Nursing, class of 1950. She was employed at Lutheran Hospital for eight years and retired from Parkview Hospital after 30 years of service. They have four sons: Lynn Eugene, Mark Edward, Brian David and Gregory Todd.

Lynn graduated from Snider High School in the Class of 1970. He married Kathleen Marie Johnson and they had three sons: Scott, Bradley and Andrew. They later divorced. Lynn is currently Director of Program Construction with CSX Railroad. He and his wife, Robin, live in Jacksonville, Florida. Scott and Andy both graduated from Indiana University. Scott is married to Karen Schnell Houser who is employed by Eli Lilly. They reside in Indianapolis where Scott is a freshman Biology Teacher at Franklin Central High School. He also coaches football. They have a daughter, Lucy Catherine. Andy married Amy Bartling. They live in Chicago where he attends law school at John Marshall Law School. He is employed with the law firm of Merlo, Kanofsky, Brinkmeier and Gregg LTD. Amy is employed at Careerbuilder.com. Brad spent four years in the Coast Guard and is now a road electrician with CSX Railroad. He lives in Auburn. He has a daughter Samantha.

Mark Edward died at age 15 of a congenital heart defect. He is buried at Concordia Gardens Cemetery.

Brian and Gregory graduated from Northrop High School in 1976 and 1983, respectively.

Brian married Tamara Syndram Houser. They live in Fort Wayne and have two children. Nicholas graduated from Northrop and will attend Indiana University in Bloomington in the fall of 2005. Stephanie is a junior at Northrop. Brian is a track foreman for Atlas Railroad and Tammy works at Brotherhood Mutual Life Insurance Company.

Greg is Manager of Radiology at Parkview North. He is married to Dawn Solari Houser who is employed at Design Collaborative. They live in Fort Wayne with their two children Taylor eight and Brian six.

Submitted by Carolyn Houser.

HOWARD-BELL FAMILY HISTORY

Arthur Howard, son of Captain William Howard of Huron County, Ohio, and gr-gr-gr-gr grandson of Roger Williams, founder of Providence, Rhode Island, was born April 28, 1804, in New York. He married Lydia Ann Draper on December 3, 1848, in Huron County, Ohio. They settled in Allen County, Monroe Township, about 1867 or 1868. They had at least three children, William Perry, Austin and Minerva Adalade.

Arthur Howard

William Perry, Annie, Leonard, Ada and Goldie Howard 1908

Another resident of Monroeville was a John H. Bender, his wife, Mary E., and their adopted daughter Annie. John H. Bender died May 24, 1878, and is buried in the Masonic Cemetery in Monroeville.

By 1880 Arthur and his son, Austin, were farming 40 and 80 acre plats east of Monroeville between Hoagland Road and Rider Road, bordered by Lortie Road. William Perry farmed 40 acres west of town. Austin married Mary Ellen Wade, October 1, 1878.

Their neighbor was the widowed Mary E. Bender and her new husband, Nathaniel Scott, and their 14 year old adopted daughter, Annie.

William Perry, born April 1, 1850 in Huron County, Ohio, married Anna Elizabeth J. Bender on November 24, 1881, in Allen County. Nathaniel Scott, witnessed the marriage..

Arthur died May 28, 1892, at the residence of his son, William Perry Howard, who resided west of town. Arthur was the oldest resident of Monroe Township at the time of his death. Lydia died November 5, 1888. They are both buried in the Monroeville Memorial Cemetery.

After Arthur died, William Perry left for Daviess County, Indiana, and Austin ended up in Dayton, Ohio.

Minerva Adalade and husband, Hamilton Bell, stayed in Monroeville with children Charles, Lillie, James and Van Howard Bell. Minerva Adalade Bell inherited Arthur's 40 acres. Their son, Van Howard Bell, who married Martha Ehling, then inherited the same 40 acres. It was finally sold to Lois Klinker after Van's death in 1969 after almost 100 years as "Howard" farmland.

William Perry and Annie had seven children. Mamie, Goldie, and Ada, and three other children, were all born in Allen County. Their youngest, Leonard, was born January 30, 1900, in Davies County, Indiana.

The Howard and Bell children attended the Schlemmer School, and Arthur Howard was once school director of District 8.

Three of William Perry and Annie's children are buried in the Monroeville Cemetery with their grandparents, Arthur and Lydia. The story goes that all three children died at the same time from illness that swept Allen County in the late 1880s.

After the loss of their children and his parents, William Perry and Anna left Monroeville, settling in Odon, Daviess County, Indiana, at Bunkum in 1897. William Perry died January 27, 1924. Annie died January 2, 1940. They are both buried with daughter Mamie at Walnut Hill Cemetery in Odon, Indiana.

Leonard, the only surviving male Howard, worried that the "Howard" name would end with him.

As of August 2005, he and wife Alma Smith (married March 31, 1923) now have 106 descendents.

Submitted by J. Faye Howard-Fitzgerald

VERNON HAYDEN DIXIE HOWELL & THURSTON ANTOINE HOWELL FAMILY

Vernon Millicent Hayden was born December 28, 1914, in Laurel, Mississippi, the third child of Rev. Charles Douglas Hayden and Bessie Harris Hayden. The other children born to that union were Jettie, Alvon, Charles and Harrison (deceased). Bessie died in childbirth with her fifth child and Rev. C. D. Hayden was remarried to Maude McLeod in 1918. There were five sons born to that union: Fred, John (deceased) William, Walter and Andrew. Jettie and Maude were educators and Rev. Hayden was an A.M.E. pastor. His last pastorate was Hopewell A.M.E. Church, Birmingham, Alabama. He and his wife are deceased. Vernon, William, Walter and Charles moved to Fort Wayne. Vernon was a nanny for her uncle, Rev. Gerald Hayden's family as well as a domestic worker. She married Charles Monroe Dixie on July 14, 1936, and on April 17, 1937, a daughter Veronica was born. Charles worked at the Harvester and was a part time boxer. He died in 1939. Charles' parents were John Dixie and Martha Fields Dixie and they had nine other children: Leona, Ernestine, Bill, Martha, Chris, Johnny, Sam, Clarence and Elizabeth (all deceased). Vernon remarried Thurston Antoine Howell, a fine carpenter and General Electric factory worker. That union produced Laurence, Kevin and Quay Howell. Laurence (Tony) resides in Wayne, New Jersey, with his wife, Rosemary and he has a son, Marc, by his previous wife, Mary. Kevin is in education in Fort Wayne. Quay and her husband Vernon live in Columbus, Ohio, and they both work for the government. Their daughter, Charnon, is a college graduate of Marquette University and their son, Matthew attends Ohio University.

Vernon Hayden Dixie Howell and Thurston Antoine Howell

Thurston Howell was born to John and Emma, Arkansas, May 27, 1908. He had five sisters and three brothers all deceased. Thurston and his brother Thurman were businessmen and their brother Harry was in the insurance business. Thurman had the first Black-owned hotel in Fort Wayne located on the corner of Weisser Park and Wallace Street. Thurston with Vernon had the finest restaurant, social center for teens and young people called "Howell's Barn". This fun place was on Wallace Street from 1949 until 1959. Howell's Barn reunions are still being held every two or three years. Vanessa, one of Thurston's sisters, had two daughters, Bertha May and Dorothy Jean. Harry and Zella Howell (deceased) had two daughters, Mary and Cleosia. Vernon Howell decided to go to college after her children had finished college. She worked for the State of Indiana doing music therapy for mentally challenged children and then she graduated Magna Cum Laude in 1979 from Indiana Institute of Technology at age 64 with a BS degree in Recreational Management. She worked for the Lincoln National Corporation as Resident Coordinator providing home ownership in rebuilt urban communities. Vernon Howell died on December 14, 2002, in Columbus, Ohio, and Thurston Howell died October 19, 1991, in Fort Wayne. Veronica lives in Cincinnati, Ohio, and is an educator. She was married to the late Dr. Royal Jordan in 1959 and had three sons: Royal, Kurt and Scott. Royal married Velma Hicks and had Royal and Donte. Kurt has a degree in heating and air conditioning and works for the filtration plant; Scott is in retail management. A second marriage to Samuel Gillespie in 1966 produced Pamela, Trent, David and April. Pamela lives in Dayton with her husband Jeff Baugham and their five children: Jonathan, David, Benjamin, Andrew and Anna. Trent attended Ohio University and works in retail in Fort Wayne. David lives in Cincinnati, working at the post office and is a videographer. April is a graduate of the University of Cincinnati and is an Account Manager in Chicago.

Submitted by Veronica Gillespie

WILLIAM HOWEY

William Howey was in Westmoreland County, Pennsylvania, with a land warrant in 1769. In 1798, his will revealed his wife, Catherina, was requested that she not remarry until the children were raised. Their children were Peggy, John, Jean, Mary, Caterina, William, Matty, George W., James and Thomas.

Their son William married Elizabeth Corvin. They lived in Richland County, Ohio, before moving to Allen County, Indiana, where William died in 1858. His will names two sons, William and George, and a son-in-law, Obed Andrews. Elizabeth lived out her life with her children.

William Howey III was married in Ashland County, Ohio, to Mary Jane Reed and their children were James R., William Corvin, John K., Mary E., Tabitha, Sarah and Isabell. The family moved to Allen and DeKalb Counties, Indiana, sometime after 1852.

Tabitha married Aaron Watson in Allen County in 1871. Three children were born to this marriage: Willard, Mary Jane and Artie May. Willard married Dora Pearl Ferguson in Allen County. He worked on the railroad in Fort Wayne and Dora Pearl was a seamstress in a Fort Wayne shop. In the 1900s Tabitha and Aaron, and Dora and Willard built new homes in Auburn, Indiana. Aaron worked as a laborer and Tabitha worked as a housekeeper for Spencerville area people attending Spencerville Methodist Church.

Willard worked as a grinder for the Auburn Automotive Company in Auburn. He and Dora had four children: Elroy, Irvin, Nellie and Annabelle. The flu epidemic took its toll on the family and Willard and Dora Pearl died in 1918. Irvin was adopted by Claude Hilkert, Nellie was adopted by "Joke" Johnson of Bluffton, Indiana, and Annabelle was adopted by Harry Boon of Fort Wayne.

Elroy was adopted by William Zerns and when he was of legal age, Elroy went to court in Wells County and had his Watson surname restored. Elroy and Irvin lived with their grandma Tabitha until her death in 1922. Both boys worked on farms and for the Auburn Automotive Company until about 1930 when Elroy went to Wells County where he met his wife, Vera Bender. They continued to live and farm in Wells County. They had one daughter, Patricia.

Dyson family: Robert, Patricia, David; Lorinda Gregory, DeAnn, Dawn, and Lois Brandenburg.

Patricia Watson married Robert Dyson of Wabash County in 1954. Five children were born to this union: David, Lois, Lorinda, DeAnn and Dawn. All were born while living in Allen County except Dawn. David and Lois are married with children and grandchildren. Lorinda married and has two daughters residing in California. DeAnn lives at home in Albion, Indiana. Dawn lives in Los Angeles, California.

The Dyson family lived in Allen County from 1955 through 1970. Patricia is very active in Allen County genealogy as well as several other genealogy and historical societies.

Submitted by David Dyson

FREDERICK & ANNA KATHERINE (LAUER) HUBER

John Frederick Huber, one of the five children of George John and Caroline (Kalbacher) Huber, was born February 16, 1862, in Fort Wayne; and Anna Katherine Lauer, daughter of Paul A. and Barbara (Seibels) Lauer, was born in February 1863, also in Fort Wayne. These two married on June 4, 1889; their only child, Paul Anthony, was born February 20, 1890. They were divorced December 19, 1892.

After working as a finisher for N. G. Olds & Sons, John Frederick Huber became a fireman. He served as hose man and tiller man and then became captain of No. 8 Engine House on the east side of Fairfield Avenue between DeWald and Creighton. In the 1893 picture seen here, he is the tallest fireman, and is in the middle of the back row.

When John died, January 26, 1923, among the survivors mentioned in his obituary, his son and three grandchildren were not included. Interment was in the Huber lot in the Catholic Cemetery with his mother, siblings, and Huber relatives. In 1881, his father had been buried in Saint John's Lutheran Cemetery but was moved to Lindenwood Cemetery on October 11, 1919, to rest with other family members.

Obviously, John's parents were of different faiths. His mother, Caroline Magdalene (Kalbacher) Huber was born March 16, 1834, at Rangeadingen, near Hechingen, Province of Hohenzollern, Prussia. In 1853, she came from Prussia with her parents, Marx and Ursula (Dieringer) Kalbacher. They embarked from Havre, arrived at the Port of New York on October 27, 1853, and settled in Delphos, Ohio. In 1854 at age 43, the mother died. In the same year, Caroline and George Huber were married. In 1855 Marx and the entire family moved to Fort Wayne. On October 14, 1856, he applied for naturalization. Marx Kalbacher lived into his 78th year and died in 1886.

According to her 1905 obituary, Caroline Magdalene (Kalbacher) Huber "was one of the founders of Saint Mary's Catholic Church and worshipped in the first edifice, the pioneer building erected in the fifties; in the second, which was destroyed by an explosion in 1886; and, in the third, the present beautiful structure." (In 1993, the third church was struck by lightning and destroyed by one of Fort Wayne's worst fires.) This dear pioneer woman was "survived by Captain

Fort Wayne Fire Department 1893 at East Berry and Court Street

Idell and Otto Huebner (wedding photo 1929)

Verne A. Huffman and Elfa E. (Carter) Huffman 1935

John Huber of the city fire department; Anton J. Huber, George Huber, Mrs. Carrie Burlage, and Miss Katie Huber. Another daughter died in infancy."

Very little is known about George John Huber, except that he was from Wurttemberg, was a butcher, had the above family, and died when only 50 years old.

Submitted by Sue Ellen (Lauer) Giles

OTTO & IDELL HUEBNER FAMILY

Otto Karl Huebner was born on his parents' farm on August 7, 1899, near Briceton, Ohio. His parents were William and Johanna (Zielke) Huebner who had each immigrated to America in 1892 from Pomerania, Germany.

Beatrice Idell Noyer was born in Monroeville, Indiana, on October 7, 1905. Her parents were Clyde and Mary (Marquardt) Noyer. Idell's mother died from influenza a few months after her birth, and she was raised by her Uncle Charles and Aunt Hattie (Noyer) Taylor on their dairy farm located on the outskirts of Monroeville.

Otto and Idell met while both worked in Fort Wayne at General Electric. They were married on January 15, 1929, at Saint John's Lutheran Church in Briceton, Ohio. The newlyweds moved to Idell' s family farm in Monroeville, and Otto took over the Taylor Dairy. Throughout the 1930s, Otto ran the dairy under the name of the Huebner Dairy in Monroeville. During the 1940s, the Huebner Dairy ceased as an independent dairy. Otto, along with many other rural dairy farmers in Allen County, became a supplier for Allen Dairy.

Since the family farm was located next to the Pennsylvania Railroad, the farm was a common stop for many hobos traveling during the years of the depression. A free plate of food awaited any that knocked at the door. Otto learned that a telephone pole along the railroad near their home was marked with some sort of a 'dinner' symbol that, to hobos, meant a free home cooked meal was available at the next farm.

During World War II, Otto was a civil defense blackout officer. His job was to survey the skies around his farm and the surrounding area to make sure all area farms and homes observed the mandatory blackout, and the skies were free of any surprise attacks from the Japanese or the German.

Otto and Idell were active members of Saint Mark's Lutheran Church in Monroeville. The church and its many activities were a central part of their family life. They had four children: Burton, Berneta (Sherck), Burrell, and Bonell (Kopke). Burton is retired as co-owner of the Monroeville Box & Pallet Company, Berneta works in Indianapolis with literacy programs, Burrell died as a young man while serving his country in Vietnam, and Bonell is a retired speech teacher.

The older grandchildren remember many enjoyable times out on the Huebner farm. They especially recall bike rides with grandpa, and grandma's good cooking. Otto and ldell's grandchildren are Jayne Staight, John Huebner, Joel Huebner, Kevin Shoppell, Scott Shoppell, Brad Shoppell, Robyn Rabatin, and Janelle Schilling. Their great grandchildren are Amanda Staight, Chelsea Staight, Alisha Huebner, Chantelle Huebner, Luke Huebner, Joshua Huebner, Katherine Shoppell, Tyler Shoppell, Emily Shoppell, Ashley Reinholtz, Matthew Shoppell, and Marc Shoppell. Their great great grandchild is Mackenzie Reinholtz.

Submitted by John Huebner

VERNE A. HUFFMAN & ELFA E. (CARTER) HUFFMAN FAMILY

Verne and Elfa Huffman moved to Fort Wayne in 1926 to be close to Elfa's doctor and Lutheran Hospital. Elfa was experiencing problems in her pregnancy with her tenth child. Her previous nine children were born at home in Roanoke. This child, the first to be born in a hospital, was named Elizabeth L.(Betty). She only lived one week. The Koontz-Lynch Funeral Home records have April 4, 1926, as her death date. She is buried in IOOF Cemetery in Roanoke.

Verne, Elfa, and their nine children lived at 1350 Park Avenue until they bought a home at 547 West Wildwood Avenue. This home was across from the emergency entrance to Lutheran Hospital. They rented rooms to nurses working at Lutheran Hospital for $4 a week after most of their children left home. Elfa lived there until her death May 30, 1943, at the age of 60.

Verne Abram Huffman was born in Roanoke, Indiana, on January 1, 1882. His parents were Abram Cuppy and Aurora B. (Comstock) Huffman. Abram C. Huffman was a commissioner of Jackson Township, Huntington County, in 1904. Verne was a farmer, horticulturist, photographer, carpenter, and entrepreneur. In 1903 Verne traveled to St. Louis, Missouri, to learn photography. He farmed the family's Chestnut Hill Farm for many years.

In the late 1920s Verne developed the Chestnut Hill Golf Links and managed it until after he moved to Fort Wayne. R. Nelson Snider was a frequent player. The older children gave golf lessons.

After moving to Fort Wayne, Verne held jobs at Packard Piano and as a florist for Clarence Comincavish. Verne opened three photography studios named Huffman Studios. One was in Elwood, Indiana, another in Mishawaka, Indiana, and one in Fort Wayne at 627 South Calhoun Street. After his wife, Elfa, passed away, Verne bought five acres on Fillmore Avenue and raised gladioluses, which he sold at Fort Wayne's Barr Street Market. He hybridized varieties himself. He lived with his daughter, Ruth, and her husband, Dr. John W. Kannel, until his death October 24, 1959, at the age of 77.

Elfa E. Carter was born in Hillsboro, Fountain County, Indiana. Elfa was a member of the Christian Church. She met Verne A. Huffman in Roanoke, Indiana. Her parents, Hiram and Emiline America "Minnie" Carter, owned a general store in Roanoke, and Elfa was a milliner. When she and Verne married on July 15, 1905, Elfa had an eighteen-inch waistline. She would invite her children into her bedroom and they were in awe of the beauty and fragrances of her room.

Verne and Alfa had five boys and four girls. LaVerna Abigail was born July 11, 1906, and died December 24, 1982. Ruth Elizabeth was born December 13, 1907, and died July 29, 1975. Mabel Malissa was born March 24, 1909, and died November 12, 1996. Doyle Carter was born November 14, 1911, and died December 24, 1987. Byron Abram was born January 29, 1914,

Front: Mildred Finrow, Mabel Herold, Ruth Huffman, LaVerna Craig Back: Byron Huffman, Woodward Huffman, Bayless Huffman, Albert Huffman, Doyle Huffman

and died November 6, 1964. Woodrow Owen was born November 15, 1916, and died January 22, 1991. Thomas Albert was born June 25, 1918, and died December 4, 1998. Bayless Vern was born April 16, 1920, and died November 23, 1975. Elfa Mildred was born October 4, 1921, and is still living in Fort Wayne.

Submitted by Marian A. Klinger

ANDERSON CURTIS HUGHES & WILLIE MILBURN HUGHES FAMILIES

Anderson Curtis Hughes was born June 9, 1882, in Menifee County, Kentucky. He married Lizzie Jane Brown in Morehead, Rowan County, Kentucky. He was the son of Christopher Columbus and Emily Gibbs Hughes. Lizzie was the daughter of Green Berry and Mary Etta Sorrell Brown. Curt founded the Korea Church of God in Korea, Kentucky, and, after moving to Fort Wayne, he founded the Third Street Church of God. Curt, as he was known, and Lizzie Hughes had eleven children. The first child, Clarence, was born April 25 1905, and married Ethel Spencer. The second child, James Wesley, was stillborn on August 17, 1906. Noah was born October 25, 1907, and married Alta Spencer (sister to Ethel). The fourth child was Willie Milburn (Bill), born October 12, 1909, who married Frankie Lee Caskey. Child five was Emily Etta, born December 7, 1911, who married Curt Hunter. The sixth child was Artie May, born April 14, 1913 who married Frances Snell, then Robert Jackson, and later Ambrose Roten. The seventh child was Victor Green, born January 20, 1916, who married Annabelle White. Child eight was Lexie Jane, born September 29, who married Russell Wheaton and then Morris Eubank. The ninth child, Bruce, was born and died July 9, 1922. Child ten, Mary Magdalene, was born September 4, 1923, in Big Woods, Menifee County, Kentucky, married Cloyd Jerome Counterman, The eleventh child, Bennie Mitchell, was born April 13, 1925 in Denniston, Menifee County, married June Marjorie Peters.

Lizzie Jane Brown Hughes died March 20, 1957, in Middletown, Butler County, Ohio. Anderson Curtis died on March 27, 1966, in Fort Wayne. Both are buried in Lindenwood Cemetery, Fort Wayne, Indiana.

WILLIE MILBURN HUGHES FAMILY

Willie Milburn Hughes, known as Bill, was born October 12, 1909, in Korea, Menifee County, Kentucky, to Anderson Curtis and Lizzie Jane Brown Hughes. The family moved to northern Indiana in about 1930, and there he met Frankie Lee Caskey. She was born September 13, 1912, in Yocum, Morgan County, to Kelly and Mary Catherine (Katie) Oakley Caskey. Bill and Frankie were married in 1931 in LaGrange County, Indiana.

In 1940, they moved their family to Fort Wayne where Bill had a job lined up at Tokheim Tank & Oil Corp. These were depression years, so he felt very fortunate to get a factory job. Three daughters were born to their marriage. Helen Louetta Hughes was born on February 25, 1933. She married Myron L. (Mike) Martin. Second daughter Betty Marie Hughes, born July 4, 1935, married Thomas William (Bill) McKinney, and Shirley May Hughes, born September 13, 1937, married Gaylord Miller.

Bill worked at Tokheim, both on the line and as a lead man, retiring July 31, 1972. Frankie did not work outside the home until 1949, when she worked for Halls and later as manager of Miller's Ice Cream store, across from South Side High School. Bill's hobbies were going fishing and hunting.

Frankie died suddenly of a massive heart attack on November 12, 1978. Bill's death occurred June 2, 1994. They are both buried in Lindenwood Cemetery, Fort Wayne, Indiana, in the Praying Hands section.

Submitted by Betty McKinney

Front: Shirley May Hughes, Frankie Oakley Caskey Hughes. Row 2: Betty Marie Hughes, Bill Hughes. Back: Helen Louetta Hughes. Approximately 1948

HUGUENARD & HARBER FAMILY

When Clement August Huguenard and Irene Mary Harber married on October 4, 1927, at St. Paul's Catholic Church, they joined some of Allen County's earliest French and German settlers into a common line. Clem's grandfather, Pierre Claude, brought his family from Courchaton, Haute Saone, France, in 1850 on the ship *Seine*. Two of Irene's great-grandfathers, Johann Heinrich Herber and John Stier, arrived from Marbom, Hessen Cassel, Germany, on the same ship, *Bark Favorite*, in 1834. Her great-grandfather, Franz Munch, came in 1838 aboard the *Burgundy*.

Clem and Irene moved into their own home at 918 Kinsmoor, in St. Patrick's parish, where all four of their children were born. Clem worked continuously at General Electric Company as a machinist until he retired in 1952. He died in 1963; she in 1978.

L to R: Irene Harber Huguenard, Eleanor Ann Huguenard (Wheeler), Herbert Maurice Huguenard, Kenneth Francis Huguenard, Clement August Huguenard (about 1935 or 1936)

Herbert, their oldest child, graduated from St. Patrick's in 1942 with a perfect attendance record. He played basketball for Central Catholic High School, and after graduation in 1945, worked for many years at Lincoln National Bank, before retiring from City National Bank of Auburn, Indiana, in 1990. He married Colleen Donahue. They had four children. Claudia lives in New Haven, Gary in Atlanta, Michelle in Fort Myers, Florida, and Jeanna in Indianapolis.

Kenneth and Eleanor (and later, Ron) transferred to St. Joseph grade school when the family moved west to a new home they built on North Bend Drive in 1941.

Ken also played basketball at Central Catholic High School and was a class officer. He worked for a year at Joslyn Steel Mill before going to Cincinnati, Ohio, and Xavier University in 1949. He served two years in the U.S. Army during the Korean Conflict. He then moved to Indianapolis to work at Eli Lilly Company, where he met and married Virginia Hagens. All their married life has been spent in that city and their three children (John, Jane, and Andrew) continue to live there.

Eleanor followed Ken by one year in graduating from Central Catholic High School in 1949. She was a scholarship student at St. Mary-of-the-Woods College, class of 1953, and received a graduate degree from Kansas State College in 1954. At the University of Illinois she met her husband, Kevin Wheeler, a Chicago native. Five children were born to them in Champaign, Illinois. A job change brought them to the Chicago area in 1969. Sons Owen, Hugh, Paul, and Neil all live in the region, while the youngest, daughter Kathleen, lives near Detroit, Michigan.

Ronald finished grade school at St. Jude in 1951, and graduated from Central Catholic High School in 1955. He earned a degree from the School of Optometry, Indiana University in 1962, and practiced on the northeast side of Fort Wayne until retirement in 2000. He married Mary Evelyn Moran and had four daughters. Three of his daughters are still Hoosiers—Beth and Karen live in rural Auburn, and Susan lives on the Ohio River. Anne is in San Diego, California. Later Ron married Cheryl Klenzak.

Though the family has scattered somewhat, they keep in touch with annual reunions.

Submitted by Eleanor H. Wheeler

DALE WILLARD & LOIS JEANETTE (ROBERSON) HULL

Dale was born May 9, 1933, in Whitley County, Indiana. His great great grand-parents Adam and Elizabeth (Hevener) Hull homesteaded west to Fort Wayne, Indiana, from Shelby County, Ohio, in 1830. Their first home was in Pendleton County, West Virginina. They purchased land in the Eel River Township in 1831. When they arrived in the township, their first task was to construct a toll bridge over the Eel River. Adam was also appointed postmaster and elected justice of the peace. They had nine children who included Dale's great grandfather Rufus, his wife was Altha Taylor. Altha's parents were Abram and Roxie (Lane) Taylor.

They had twelve children who included Dale's grandfather Abram Taylor whose wife was Mary Agnes (Briggs) Hull.

Mary's parents were Andrew and Sarah (Moore) Briggs. They had seven children who included Dale's father Joseph Briggs whose wife was Flora (Doonan) Hull. Their children were Eloise (Leo) Souder, Mary (Woodrow) Craig, Marie Hull, Howard (Bessie) Hull, Marjorie Hull, Helen (Charles) Krider, Richard Hull, Gale (Agnes) Hull and Dale, the youngest child.

Dale's mother's parents were William and Mary (Rhodes) Doonan. They were blessed with two sets of twins, Mary, Marie and Gale, Dale. They were all born on May 9, but were nineteen years apart.

Dale and Lois displaying the hearse at Stoner's Trace, Noble County, September, 1997.

Dale and Gale's early life was spent inside the family cook stove which substituted for an incubator. Their weight at birth was barely three pounds each. Dale graduated from Churubusco High School in 1951 and went to work for International Harvester (1951-1988). Dale and Lois were married December 27, 1952, in Eel River Township. They resided in Churubusco, Indiana, until the summer of 1968. They moved to a farm in Eel River Township in the fall of 1968. Dale's favorite hobby was restoring and driving antique automobiles. Dale passed away after a brief illness on May 26, 2004.

His wife Lois Jeanette Roberson Hull was born in Eel River Township on January 14, 1935. Her great great grandparents, Augustus Wych and Elizabeth Jane (Iliff) Roberson settled in Eel River Township in the 1850's arriving from Greene County, Ohio. Augustus' occupations were undertaker, carpentry, and farming. They had several children, however only one survived to adulthood. Lois's great grandfather was David Anderson and his wife was Hannah (Koogler) Roberson. Hannah's parents were Samuel and Sarah (Illif) Koogler of Greene County, Ohio. They had five children who included Lois's grandfather Leslie W; his wife was Hortense (Burton) Roberson. Hortense's parents were Levi and Hannah (Tully) Burton. They had one son, Ralph Lawrence whose wife was Madeline (Rosenogle) Roberson. Their son was Lois's father. Madeline's parents were Charles and Pearl (Clingerman) Rosenogle. Besides Lois they had the following children: Bruce (deceased), and twins Sharon Roberson and Karen Roberson. Lois graduated from Huntertown High School in 1953 and retired from the Dana Corporation (1968-1997). Her most prized possession is the original horse drawn funeral hearse her great great grandfather Augustus purchased used in the 1860's for three hundred pounds of gold. Dale and Lois's four children includes Randall Allen (deceased) and wife Rebecca (Warstler) Hull, Bradley Lee and wife Deborah (Hallgren) Hull, Zondra Lou Hull and Gregory Joe Hull. Their six grandchildren include Randall and Becky's daughters Chelsea Hull and Caitlin Hull. Bradley and Deborah's daughters Anne Hull Dunfee and husband Kyle, Heather Hull, Emily Hull, and son Adam Hull.

Submitted by Gregory J. Hull

HUNT FAMILY

The first Hunt family ancestor to immigrate to America from England was Ralph Hunt in 1652. From Long Island, the family went to New Jersey, later to North Carolina, and by 1818 was in Wayne County, Indiana. In 1851 Franklin Hunt was in northern Indiana, homesteading on the land granted his father, Smith James Hunt, in 1836, for service in the militia. Smith James Hunt's mother-in-law was Hannah Boone, a first cousin of frontiersman Daniel Boone.

Franklin Hunt married Martha Jane Long in 1853. His grandson, Leigh Lavon Hunt, was born on the family farm in Etna Township, Whitley County on June 28, 1899, to Franklin (Ben) Hunt, Jr. and Eva Alta Scott Hunt, daughter of Civil War veteran Henry Clay Scott and Sarah Jones Scott. Leigh had one brother, Homer H. Hunt (1891-1972), who married Iva Ames. The family was of Scottish, Irish and English descent, affiliated with the Presbyterian Church and traditionally Republican.

Leigh L. Hunt, 1960

Leigh Hunt attended the Etna School and Columbia City High School, and went on to Indiana University. In 1918 he served briefly in the Officers' Training and Corps until WW I ended. After his undergraduate work, he began the study of law in Bloomington. On August 25, 1921 he married fellow student Mary Ruth VanNatta of Otterbein, Indiana. She was born on June 23, 1901, to Aaron Earl and Lizzie Chenoweth VanNatta who were themselves children of the earliest settlers in Tippecanoe Country in central Indiana.

Leigh taught school in Whitley County and was principal of Churubusco High School in Allen County in 1923-1925, while he continued his law study in the summers. He was admitted to the Indiana Bar in 1922, and began his full-time career in the practice of law in 1925 with the Fort Wayne firm Barrett, Barrett, Peters and McNagny. He left that firm in 1949 to establish his own partnership with George Mountz of Auburn, then with a number of other partners. The firm became known as Hunt and Suedhoff in 1958, and in subsequent years involved several prominent attorneys in the area, including Thomas Longfellow, Carl Suedhoff, Jr., William Borrer, Lee Eilbacher, Robert Kabisch and William C. Lee. This firm dealt with such clients as General Electric, Firestone Tire and Rubber, Standard Oil of Indiana, Baltimore and Ohio and several other railroads, Sears Roebuck and many well known insurance companies. Hunt's own expertise lay in workman's compensation litigation, for which he was widely known. He appeared before the Indiana Court of Appeals, the Supreme Court of Indiana, the Federal Seventh Circuit Court of Appeals and the United States Supreme Court.

Leigh and Ruth Hunt moved to Fort Wayne from Churubusco in 1925. They lived on West Main Street, Packard and Indiana Avenues. In 1933 they moved to the northern part of the city and reared their children on Kensington Boulevard. They had three daughters: Mary Patricia (1924) became the wife of Byron Clinton Jackson, an Army Air Corps veteran of WW II and a lifelong educator with Fort Wayne schools; Priscilla Jane (1928), a senior at Bryn Mawr when she was killed in an auto accident in 1949; and Ellen VanNatta (1932) who married William Lee Wilks. Wilks practiced law with his father-in-law for ten years before the family moved to Pennsylvania.

The Jacksons gave Leigh and Ruth two grandsons and a granddaughter. The Wilks had three daughters and son David, the only grandchild to follow Leigh's profession, who now practices law in Delaware. The other grandchildren are involved in educational and artistic pursuits and the ministry. Many of the couple's descendants still reside in Allen County: daughter Patricia Jackson, granddaughter Jennifer Thompson, great-grandchildren Emily McCord and Leigh Kuleff, and great-great-grandson Brady McCord, Jr.

Leigh Hunt loved to read history, to garden and to fish. It gave him great satisfaction to buy back the ancestral farm in Whitley County, and he spent much time there. He especially enjoyed trial law, which he pursued until his death on February 25, 1975. Ruth Hunt died on January 5, 1981.

The law firm founded by Leigh L. Hunt in 1949 is still a prominent one in Allen County, and is known today as Hunt Suedhoff Kalamaros.

Submitted by Patricia Jackson

JAMES BOYD & LILLIAN THEODOSIA (MCKEEMAN) HUNTER FAMILY

James Boyd Hunter was born June 18, 1900 in Chicago, Illinois. Just four months prior to his birth, his father, James Boyd Hunter, suffered a cerebral hemorrhage while riding a Michigan Central train and died at St. Luke's Hospital. Eva Nellie (Holden) Hunter now had four small children to raise: Jim, and Flora Jane, age seven; Frederick, age four; and Hamilton Wellington, age three. Eva Nellie soon moved her family to Valparaiso, Indiana, and began selling encyclopedias. When Jim was just four years old, his brother Fred died from a ruptured appendix.

Jim was sent with brother Ham to Howe Military School and, when he was ten years old, his mother remarried and moved to Fort Wayne, Indiana. Jim went to high school at Fort Wayne

James and Lillian Hunter

(Central) High School where he met Lillian Theodosia (Doad) McKeeman. Jim worked as a clerk at the Wayne Stamp Company in 1916. In 1917 he was a messenger for the U.S. Weather Bureau. Jim enlisted in the U.S. Navy in World War I, and went to optician school in Detroit, Michigan. In 1922 he was working as a wholesale optician in Fort Wayne. The next year Jim took a job as grocer in Mishawaka, Indiana.

On November 1, 1925 Jim married his high school sweetheart, Doad McKeeman, born July 11, 1901, and daughter of Dr. and Mrs. Robert B. McKeeman. The marriage took place at Third Presbyterian Church in Fort Wayne. In 1926 Jim was employed as a switchman at the Home Telephone Company. Donald James was born December 19, 1926, and, in 1927, the family moved to 2522 Maple Place. Maurice Edward was born October 25, 1930, and Joseph Richard was born November 26, 1931. In 1933 Jim's mother died. She lived across the street from the family on Maple Place. In 1936 all three boys were severely ill with scarlet fever. Little Joseph Richard died from complications on February 21, 1936.

The family was active at Third Presbyterian Church with many of the McKeeman relatives. On June 8, 1943, Jane Anne was born. Jim continued his work for Home Telephone and Telegraph. He was an Elder at the church. The family moved to 314 North Cornell Circle. Jim died October 31, 1954, after a brief hospitalization at St. Joseph Hospital in Fort Wayne. He is buried at Lindenwood Cemetery.

Donald married Geraldine Widney in Fort Wayne September 3, 1950. Edward married Melva Doxtater in Van Wert, Ohio, June 19, 1955. Jane married Daniel Hodgson in Fort Wayne August 8,1964.

Doad married DeWitt Clinton Jones on July-6, 1967, and moved to Tucson, Arizona, where she lived near her daughter. Doad and De joined Beautiful Savior Lutheran Church as charter members February 5, 1978. Jane's husband, Daniel Hodgson, was pastor of this church for 28 years.

Doad died June 6, 1988, leaving 11 grandchildren and several great-grandchildren. She is buried in Tucson, Arizona, at Evergreen Cemetery. Memorials plaques to James Boyd, Lillian Theodosia and DeWitt Jones have been placed in the Memorial Garden at Beautiful Savior Lutheran Church in Tucson, Arizona.

Submitted by Edward Hunter

RALPH & HELEN (HAUEISEN) HUSS FAMILY

Still sharp at 101 years, Fort Wayne native, Helen Haueisen Huss, lives at the Marquette Manor in Indianapolis. For her first 85 years, she was a Fort Wayne resident.

Helen's grandparents, Jacob and Elizabeth Haueisen, came to Allen County, Indiana, from Muensingen, Wirtenberg, Germany, in 1881, with sons Louis and Jacob. They immigrated through the Port of New York and established the family farm in Eel River Township.

Son Louis (born 1877) was a stonecutter by trade, worked at Menefee Foundry, and later became a foreman at Minford. A member of Trinity English Lutheran Church, he married Minnie Ohse in 1898, and had six children. Helen was born on February 7, 1904. George (born1899) and Allen (born 1911) never married. Cecilia (born 1902) married Howard Tyler. Edna (born 1915) married J. J. LaMar. Little Carrie (born 1900) died at age two.

Helen married high school sweetheart Ralph Huss on June 20, 1926, at Trinity. Ralph became a supervisor at Lincoln National Life Insurance Company.

Ralph's great-grandfather, Abraham Huss, came to Indiana from Pennsylvania during the mid-1800s. He married Jane Bodell and farmed in Wells County. Their son Elisha O. Huss was born in 1843 and fought in the Civil War as a Private in Company F of the 88th Indiana Infantry mustered in Fort Wayne. After the war, Elisha was a carpenter and farmer in Allen County. He married Margaret Parkinson and had three sons: Frank, Ernest, and John. Elisha and Margaret are buried at Lindenwood Cemetery.

John Huss (born 1884) became a railroad conductor and married Sylvia Chaney in 1902. Ralph was born Sept. 1, 1903. His sister, Vesta, in 1905.

Ralph and Helen Huss had two children, Ned (born 1933) and Sylvia (born 1935). Both graduated from South Side High School and Indiana University.

Ned married Judie Wire, also of Fort Wayne. They had Steven and Michael and moved to Connecticut where Ned worked as an accountant for AT & T. After retiring, Ned and Judie relocated to Indianapolis where Judie works for Tucker Realty. In his retirement, Ned has owned an art and framing gallery and now enjoys a volunteer career as a docent at the renowned Eidelgeorge Museum.

Sylvia Huss received a master's degree from St. Francis University and was Canterbury School's lower school administrator until 1988. She married Jerald Andrew in 1957 and had children Joseph, John, Barbara, and David. On July 4, 1976, Sylvia married Lincoln Life executive Jay Hanselmann. They moved to Indianapolis in 1988, where she is Director of Learning Services at Park Tudor School.

Submitted by Caroline Andrew

SYLVIA HUSS & FAMILY

Sylvia (Huss) Hanselmann is the epicenter of a family that spreads across the country yet maintains its Fort Wayne and Allen County roots.

Born in 1935 to Ralph and Helen (Haueisen) Huss, Sylvia graduated from South Side High School and became her family's first female to go to college. Sylvia earned a degree in education from Indiana University, Bloomington, in 1953. After teaching in Gary, she married Jerald Andrew and supported him through medical school and a brief tour of duty as an Army MASH unit, during which time Sylvia and her toddler sons Joe (born 1960) and John (born 1961) moved to Germany where Jerald was stationed. After the army, the family returned to Fort Wayne. Barbara was born in 1965, David, in 1969. Joe, John, and Barbara all graduated from Wayne High School; David, from Canterbury School.

Sylvia married Lincoln Life executive Jay Hanselmann on July 4, 1976, and was a lower school administrator at the Canterbury School until 1988, when she and Jay relocated to Indianapolis. Sylvia is the Director of Learning Services at Park Tudor School.

Joe, a graduate of Yale University and Yale Law School, is the former head of the Indiana Democratic Party and former chairman of the Democratic National Committee. He married attorney Anne Slaughter. They have two children, Meredith (born 1993) and William (born 1995).

John graduated from the University of Chicago. John married Robyn Gunderson, a clinical psychologist. They have Benjamin (born 1997) and Jeremy (born 1999) and live in Northfield, Minnesota. John works for Computer Associates.

Barbara earned her undergraduate degree from Vassar and a Ph.D. in Philosophy from SUNY-Stonybrook. Barbara and her spouse, Bruce Milem, have lived throughout the country, including Montana and Oregon. They now reside in Central Valley, New York, with son Luke (born 2004). They are both philosophy professors.

In 1993, David married fellow Fort Wayne-native Caroline Paulison at Trinity English Lutheran Church, where they were both confirmed nearly a decade earlier. David and Caroline have resided in Chicago's North Shore suburbs since graduating from Northwestern University. David is a project management executive. Caroline, also a Wayne graduate, received her M.B.A. from Loyola University Chicago and is a freelance writer and marketing consultant. They have three children: Katharine (born 1997), Samuel (born 1999), and Peter (born 2000). Katharine was christened at Trinity English Lutheran Church nearly 100 years after her great-grandmother, Helen Huss.

Submitted by Sylvia Hanselmann.

DENNIS JAMES HUTCHINGS

Master Sergeant Dennis James Hutchings, the son of Charles Stephen Hutchings, Jr. and Mary Ruth Kauzor, was born January 30, 1947, in Los Angeles, California. His father was born in Milwaukee, Wisconsin, on August 11, 1909, and his mother was born on March 28, 1918, in Pittsburgh, Pennsylvania. They became the parents of nine children.

In 1946, Charles Stephen Hutchings, Jr., a veteran of WW II, co-founded GI Trucking Company in Los Angeles, California. Today, GI Trucking is super-regional with 58 terminals serving 13 western states, including Hawaii and Alaska. When the children were grown, Mary Ruth became an accomplished businesswoman. After Charles' death in 1973, she married Milton Young.

Dennis' paternal ancestors came from Scotland and England in the 1630s and were instrumental in the founding of East- and South-Hampton, Long Island, New York, and New Haven, Connecticut. His great-great grandparents were pioneer families in Cleveland, Ohio, and Milwaukee, Wisconsin. Dennis' maternal ancestors were natives of Germany and immigrated to the United States in the mid-19th century. Mary Ruth's father, John Everest Kauzor, and his brother, Anthony, were architects of national repute, designing over 50 Catholic churches and government buildings. One example of their outstanding designs is Our Mother of Good Counsel Church in Los Angeles, where Dennis' parents were married and Dennis was baptized.

Dennis James Hutchings

Dennis entered the United States Air Force on March 23, 1967, and retired on March 31, 1987. His first six years were spent as a medical corpsman and the remaining years were spent in hyperbaric medicine. Dennis was stationed at Castle AFB, Merced, California; Fairchild AFB, Spokane, Washington; School of Aerospace Medicine, Brooks AFB, San Antonio, Texas; and the Armed Forces Institute of Pathology, Washington, D.C. He continued in hyperbaric medicine upon retirement and assisted in the establishment of Hyperbaric Medicine Specialties at the UCSD Medical Center, San Diego, California; Hermann Hospital, Houston, Texas; and finally, St. Joseph Medical Center, Fort. Wayne, Indiana. In October 1996, in a career change, Dennis established the ABBA House, a Catholic/Christian resource center in Fort Wayne and has made Fort Wayne his home.

Dennis married Suzanne Elizabeth Wells, an orthodontist assistant, in her hometown of Bakersfield (Kern County), California. They were married at Our Lady of Perpetual Help Catholic Church on July 1, 1967. Dennis and Susan have twin daughters, Michelle Marie and Melissa Ann, born on April 1, 1969, at Castle AFB Hospital, Merced, California. Dennis and Susan divorced in 1975. Dennis then married Jeneal Afton Miskin in 1976 at the Brooks AFB Chapel. Their son, Scott Anthony, was born at Wilford Hall Medical Center, Lackland AFB, San Antonio, Texas, on November 23, 1977. This union dissolved in May 1981.

Dennis is an avid parishioner of St. Jude Catholic Church since December 1990 and has attended daily mass since 1995. He also attends Sacred Heart Catholic Church and sings in the Regina Coeli Latin Mass Choir. His hobbies include SCUBA diving, storm chasing, and genealogy.

Submitted by Dennis Hutchings

SCOTT ANTHONY HUTCHINGS FAMILY

Scott Anthony Hutchings was born November 23, 1977, at Wilford Hall Medical Center, Lackland Air Force Base, San Antonio, Texas. His father, Dennis James Hutchings, was born January 30, 1947, in Los Angeles, California. In 1967, Dennis entered the United States Air Force for a 20-year career in hyperbaric medicine. He spent an additional six years in this specialty after his retirement. Scott's mother, Jeneal Afton Miskin, was born October 24, 1957, Fort Lewis Army Reservation, Washington. Scott's parents married in San Antonio, Texas, on March 7, 1976, while both were in the Air Force, later divorcing in 1981. Jeneal worked in supply for four years before leaving the Air Force.

Scott's paternal ancestors came from Scotland and England in the 1630s and were instrumental in the founding of New Haven, Connecticut, and the Hamptons in New York. In 1776, two paternal ancestors fought in the Revolutionary War from the state of Connecticut and are listed in the DAR Patriot Index. During the Civil War, two of his great-great grandfathers were soldiers in the Civil War—one confederate, one rebel.

Scott and his father traveled extensively and lived in San Antonio, Texas; Washington D.C.; San Diego, California; and Houston, Texas, before coming to Fort Wayne in December 1990. Scott attended Lakeside Middle School and North Side High School where he met his wife, Delaney Renee Taylor. Her mother is Patricia Robin Taylor of Fort Wayne, Indiana. Robin works in a factory for Paramount Tube Company. Her father is Oscar Ray Smith of Ohio and he operates a lawn care business. Delaney was born October 12, 1977, at Lutheran Hospital, Fort Wayne, Indiana. Scott and Delaney were married on September 11, 2001, at the courthouse in Fort Wayne.

In O ctober 1996, Scott and Delaney assisted Scott's father in establishing the ABBA House, a Catholic/Christian resource center, on North Anthony Boulevard. Leaving the ABBA House, Scott pursued a career with the ironworkers joining the Iron Workers Union Local 147. While receiving his apprenticeship training, Scott helped in the construction of a multitude of schools and other significant structures in and around Fort Wayne and San Antonio. He received Journeyman Certification in Fort Wayne in December 2003.

Scott, holding Jasmine; Dominic, Dennis; and Delaney holding Calista

Delaney has spent some time in California and San Antonio and enjoys many aspects of art, including painting, sculpting, and drawing. She is currently working as a waitress at one of Fort Wayne's oldest restaurant establishments, Hall's Prime Rib, on East State Boulevard. Scott and Delaney have three children, all born in Fort Wayne. They are Dominic Charles, born May 5, 1997, at St. Joseph Medical Center; Calista Allesandra, born September 20, 2001, at Parkview Hospital; and Jasmine Rose, born September 18, 2002, at Lutheran Hospital. Dominic is entering the third grade at Forest Park Elementary School and is enjoying taking karate lessons with his father. Scott is looking forward to entering Indiana Purdue University in the fall of 2005 and seeking a degree in science.

Submitted by Scott Hutchings

HUTSELL FAMILY

Debra Kay Hutsell was born March 15, 1959, at Fort Wayne, Allen County, Indiana, to Marvin D. and Alta C. (Thrasher) Hutsell. Debra had a brother, Dean, born October 28, 1961, at Fort Wayne, Indiana, who married Debra M. Luttman on June 8, 1991, at Fort Wayne, Indiana.

Debra K. graduated from Purdue in 1983 with a B.S. degree in Agriculture Communications and from Indiana University in 1990 with a M.S. degree in Secondary Education. Dean, a 1984 graduate from Ivy Tech with an associates degree in Electrical Engineering, is currently working at Verizon.

Marvin D. Hutsell was the son of Edgar B. Sr. and Minnie F. (Winklepleck). He was born December 24, 1935, at Fort Wayne, Allen County, Indiana. He married Alta Catherine Thrasher June 21, 1958, at Pendleton, Madison County, Indiana. Marvin died February 28, 1992 at Fort Wayne. He is buried at the Eel River Cemetery in northwest Allen County. Alta Thrasher was born April 24, 1938, at Warsaw, Kosciusko County, Indiana, to Harold M. and Edna C. (Rasor) Thrasher. Alta had two older brothers, Fredrick M. (1928-1991) and Norman E. (1932-).

Edgar B. Sr. and Minnie F. (Winklepleck) Hutsell, parents of Marvin, moved to Allen County shortly after their marriage. They had four sons, all born in Fort Wayne: Donald L. (1928-2001), Edgar B. Jr. (1925-2005), Harold L. (1930-1964) and Marvin D. (1935-1992). Edgar Sr., a blackout captain during World War II, was a wire drawer for Rea-Magnet Wire. He was the son of Lewis A. and Sarah E. E. (Folk) Hutsell. He was born August 12, 1902, in Comanche County, Oklahoma. He married Minnie F. Winklepleck April 20, 1924 in Owen County, Indiana, and moved to Allen County, Indiana. Minnie F. Winklepleck was born January 2, 1906, in Owen County to John W. and Theodosha M. (Slaughter-Ennis) Winklepleck. Minnie had one sister, Beulah B. (1908-1983) and five half siblings, Daniel R. (1889-1918), Bruce (1886-1964), Carl N. (1891-1965), Ira E. (1887-1921), and Sylvia P. (1883-1929). Edgar B. died October 7, 1981, at Naples, Collier County, Florida, and Minnie F. died August 9, 1974, at Fort Wayne. They are buried at the Eel River Cemetery in northwest Allen County.

Lewis A. and Sarah E., parents of Edgar B., had Edgar while homesteading in Oklahoma about 1901. Lewis and Sarah moved back to Indiana by 1905, and had ten children: John D. (1897-1966), Thomas G. (1899-1960), Edgar B. (1902-1981), Sarah C. (1905-1952), Joseph

L. (1908-1975), Sharp F. (1910-1990), Elizabeth (1913-1913), Martha F. (1914-1988), Margaret E. (1919-1977) and Eugene D. (1923-1974). Lewis died August 28, 1937, at Churubusco, Indiana, and Sarah (Folk) died May 14, 1959, at Fort Wayne, Allen County, Indiana. They are buried at the Eel River Cemetery in northwest Allen County.

Submitted by Debra Hutsell

JOHN HYDMAN FAMILY

John Hydman, a native of Londonderry County, Ireland, was born in 1809 and emigrated to America in 1835.

With very little of this world's wealth, he stowed away on a ship bound for America and after the ship was out to sea, he appeared and worked his passage over. The ship was wrecked in crossing; it took four or five months to cross.

With less than fifty cents in his pocket on arrival, he worked at odd jobs until he arrived in Fort Wayne, Indiana. Here, he worked on the canal for a time, then started in the blacksmith trade, at which he worked for several years.

In 1844, he entered forty acres in Allen County, and afterwards traded this for eighty acres in Eel River Township, where he lived the remainder of his life.

He lived a bachelor until early in the forties, when he was married to Lucy Jackson. There were seven children born to this union, four boys and three daughters: Joseph, born August 11, 1843, died June 12, 1916, was married to Lucy Louise Craig; Samuel, born August 23, 1845, died December 16, 1907, was married to Mary M. Gloyd; Nelson, born September 24, 1848, died November 11, 1912, was married to Mary Melcina Pumphrey; Mercy Jane, born October 25, 1849, died January 8, 1892, was married to Andrew Knox; Nancy A., born October 28, 1853, died July 6, 1910, was married to Issac S. Plants; Rachel, born October 20, 1859, died November 2, 1938, was married to William A. Moore; George B., born July 18, 1861, died November 13, 1935, was married to Ella Bear.

John and Lucy Jackson Hydman were members of the Baptist Church in Eel River Township. He was always friendly toward schools, churches and all laudable enterprises and was a leading citizen.

Due to tenacity and hard work, at the time of his death, April 20, 1874, (from pneumonia) he owned 855 acres of land in Eel River Township and 155 acres in Illinois. He and Lucy were able to give each of their children a farm in Allen County, or the equivalent thereof.

The Hyndman family flourished and multiplied; all were destined to take part in the development of Allen and surrounding counties.

Submitted by Wanda J. Maroney

SAMUEL V. & MARY E. IMLER FAMILY

The Samuel V. and Mary E. (Betty) Imler family had its beginnings when the couple married in St. Peter's Catholic Church on April 10, 1942.

Samuel (born September 13, 1915; died December 13, 1981) was the only child of Ora E. and Anna B. Surfus (born September 1, 1884; died March 6, 1967). O.E. was himself an only child with roots probably in the Noblesville, Indiana, area and surely earlier in Pennsylvania Dutch country. Anna was one of three children of the earliest families of northern Indiana/Allen-DeKalb Counties: herself, a sister Frances E. (born November 13, 1882; died November 28, 1970) who never married, and a brother Harry born August 27, 1988, died February of 1968, whom with his wife Mary D. (1895-1921) had a son, Joseph, who never married. The trio's father Samuel (born about 1851) was one of 14 children born to the farmer John Surfus (born October 7, 1812; died March 31, 1891) and Ellen DeLong (born 1816; died February 20, 1897). John's obituary in the Auburn *Courier* of April 9, 1891 begins, "John Surfus, one of the best known of the early settlers of the region..." and ends, "Thus passed from earth another of those pioneers to whom northern Indiana owes so much."

Betty (born November 20, 1917) was the eldest of five daughters—herself, Rosemary Bonner, Ruth Ann DeWald, (Mary) Louise Lowe, and Julianne Hipskind—born to John Suelzer (born March 30, 1894; died September 8, 1958) and Marie T. Berghoff (born September 10, 1891; died July 5, 1984). Both this John, president of The Fort Wayne Builders Supply, and his father, John, were prominent local builders, e.g., St. Peter's and St. Patrick's Catholic Churches. The elder John and his wife emigrated from Bergisch Gladbach near Cologne. Marie's father, Gustav, came from Dortmund and was a local businessman, e.g., Berghoff Brewery, Lincoln Life Insurance, and Rub-No-More soap acquired by Proctor & Gamble.

Samuel and Betty had seven children: (1) John (born May 12, 1946) married Joan Smiley and had one daughter Megan. (Joan was the grandchild of Lester B. Smiley who ran two popular local pharmacies/soda fountains bearing that family name.) (2) Anne Marie (born May 11, 1948) married Michael Blombach and had six children: Aimee (married Jeffrey Bierbaum—Elizabeth, Allison), Molly (married Ryan Shock—Elaine), Kathryn Anne (married Zachary Brough), Sarah, Timothy, and Joseph. (3) Kathryn Ann (born January 18, 1950) was single and taught many years at Bishop Luers High School (4) Margaret (born January 9, 1952) married Steven Krouse and had six children: Brian, Peter, Andrew, Luke, Sally, and Julie. (5) Mary Elizabeth (born April 9, 1953) became a nun of The Franciscan Sisters of the Sacred Heart. (6) Julia Ann (born December 19, 1955) married Christopher Doyal. (7) Joan (born October 6, 1958) married James Grass and had two children: Alex and Samuel.

Submitted by John Imler

CONRAD JACKEMEYER SR.

The Jackemeyer name traces back to the 1600s in Germany when Catharine Ilsabe Jackemeyer, presumably a widow, married Hans Hitzemann, who took her surname. Catharine was one of six children of Jasper Sehling and Ilse Gerling.

Two centuries later, on April 15, 1850, brothers Carl Conrad (June 7, 1825 - December 22, 1909) and Heinrich Dietrich "Fred" (June 16, 1834 - September 29, 1869) left their ancestral home at Windheim 73 and emigrated from Bremen on the ship *Out of Prussia*. After arriving in New York, the two men made their way to Fort Wayne and immediately joined St. Paul's Lutheran Church on July 10, 1850. Conrad married Catharina Schlemmer (April 13, 1835 -October 1, 1903) of Monroeville in St. Paul's four years later on August 11, 1854. The couple homesteaded an 80-acre farm on Seiler Road in Adams Township where they lived out their lives. On November 7, 1858, Conrad became one of 13 men to sign the original constitution to found Emanuel Lutheran Church, New Haven.

Front l to r: Louise, Catharine, Conrad Sr., Sophie. Back: Emma, Lizetta, Henry, Katie, Conrad Jr., Emma, Christian

The couple's 13 children were all born at home. George, Johanna Marie, Johanna Sophia, and Fredrick died young and are buried beside their parents in Emanuel Cemetery. Sophia (married Johann Hummel); Louisa, Johanna Sophia's twin (William Niemeyer); Lizetta (Leonard Roeder); Katie (Philip Hummel); Henry (Johanna Brudi); Conrad, Jr. (Wilhelmina Lepper); Anna (Henry Faust); Emma (Johann Hoffmann); and Christian (Caroline Muntz) all were baptized and schooled at Emanuel.

After marrying, Sophia, Lizetta, and Katie moved to the Bremen area where many of their descendants still reside. Having moved to Essington, Pennsylvania, the last of Anna's family died in 1952. Louisa lived on Tillman Road in Adams Township and Emma on a farm three miles west of Monroeville.

Conrad Sr. bought three 80-acre farms; he left one to each of his sons. Henry received land on the southwest corner of the intersection of Seiler and Minnich Roads, and Conrad Jr. on the southeast corner of Minnich and Paulding Roads. Conrad Jr. chose to leave the property in farmland and lived with his Lepper in-laws on Tillman Road. Christian inherited the original homestead, eventually passing it on to his son, Paul (Margaret Werling).

After Paul's death on February 7, 2004, Christian's descendants decided to sell the property. When word spread that an auction was being planned, phone calls, e-mails, and letters from family around the country were exchanged and travel reservations made. Relatives from Hawaii, Florida, Georgia, Ohio, Michigan, and Indiana gathered on August 14, 2004, to share memories at the auction and at the first modern All-Jackemeyer Reunion. Without the communication made possible by the internet, few of the relatives would have gotten to know one another - let alone discover that the others even existed. In a sense, the tie that bound the Jackemeyers together was the original homestead. Now, the tie that binds them is the Internet, with connections from Hawaii to Connecticut, from Alaska to Florida, from Texas and California to Michigan, and numerous states in between.

Submitted by Jody Harkenrider

LEMUEL JACQUAY, PIONEER

Lemuel Jacquay was born near Canton, Ohio, June 12, 1843. At about the age of ten years, he came with his parents to Akron, thence to Cleveland via canal boat, thence to Toledo via Lake Erie and from Toledo to Fort Wayne via canal. Cleveland at that time was but a small village and Toledo a small unloading port. Fort Wayne, when Mr. Jacquay arrived, consisted of but several houses, a grocery store and shoemaker shop. The present Calhoun Street was but a forest, the now Columbia Street being the main thoroughfare. From Fort Wayne he went with his parents to Newville where his mother died when he was about eleven years of age. From there with his father he came to Jefferson Township where he remained until his eighteenth year. His education was obtained in a public school in Jefferson Township. When eighteen years of age, he came to New Haven which at that time consisted of about a half dozen families. New Haven is where Mr. Jacquay would live and serve the community for sixty-six years.

Mr. Jacquay was a contractor and builder by trade and besides the many buildings he constructed in New Haven and surrounding country, he built St. John's Catholic Church and Emanuel Lutheran Church of this place, and the Catholic church at Delaware Bend, Ohio. For many years he was a member of the New Haven town board.

On October 31, 1866, Lemuel was married to Mary J. Welling in the church which is now known as St. John's Hall. Mary J., the daughter of Ignatius and Maria Welling, was born in Germany, August 29, 1847. She came to the United States at the age of six years with her parents and settled in Fort Wayne. Mrs. Lemuel Jacquay was a zealous member of St. John's Catholic Church and of the St. Mary's Sodality for nearly sixty years. The poor and sick were always remembered and it was her custom that no beggar ever left her door hungry. She was a pioneer of New Haven, a faithful wife, and a loving mother. She passed away on January 3, 1924. To this union were born eleven children, five of whom survived; Henry and John of Fort Wayne, Louis of Detroit, Margaret Belling of Los Angeles, California, and Clara Albert of New Haven. They had fourteen grandchildren and nine great grandchildren.

Mr. Jacquay was always very active and worked until the last two years of his life. He passed away on March 15, 1927. In his passing, New Haven lost a pioneer citizen who spent most of his life in making the nucleus of the present thriving town of New Haven. The man is gone but his labors will serve as a monument to his memory in the town that was so much of his making. He was buried in the New Haven Catholic cemetery. Lemuel Jacquay had two brothers, August and Louis Jacquay, of Jefferson Township, who survived him.

Submitted by Gloria Drouillard

RONALD & MARYANN JAMES FAMILY

Ronald "Ron" Eugene James was born in Frankfort, Indiana, the third child of Earl A. James, Jr., of Grant county, and Peggy Z. (Amy) James, of Harrison County, on August 17, 1954. A 1972 graduate of Columbia City High School, he studied at St. Joseph's College in Rensselaer before graduating from Indiana University, Bloomington (BA '76; JD '79). Coming to Fort Wayne as a law clerk for the Allen Superior Court, he went into civil practice and became a founding partner of the law firm of Benson, Pantello, Morris, James & Logan in 1983. He had a civil trial practice, accepting principally plaintiff's causes as well as elder law clients, for over 25 years. He became the Executive Director of the Wabash River Heritage Corridor Commission in 2004 after serving as the Allen County representative from his appointment in 1997. In his non-business time he pursued a variety of environmental and social interests such as tutoring middle school students as a Study Connection tutor (1989 –), public education as a Fort Wayne Zoo docent (1984-), creation of greenbelt strips with the Little River Wetlands Project, (including President 1996 - 1997), environment protection with the Izaak Walton League (including time as the Fort Wayne Chapter's President (1998 – 2005) and on the board of directors of the Cedar Creek Wildlife Project, and grassroots organizations like the Rudisill-Plaza Neighborhood Association (President, 1985).

Ronald and MaryAnn James Family

Ron met MaryAnn Freygang in 1981, and they were married on August 7, 1982. MaryAnn was born in Fort Wayne on March 1, 1957, the fourth daughter of Richard Freygang, of Allen County and Martha (Herrick) Freygang, of DeWitt county, Illinois. A 1975 graduate of Elmhurst High School, MaryAnn initially went into nursing (LPN) and then turned to business with a secretarial degree from Indiana Business College. Working for a period as a medical-paralegal for Sowers & Benson (a law firm which disbanded in 1983), this interest lead her to an Associate Degree in Personnel (I.U.) and a Bachelor's Degree in Administration (P.U.) before obtaining her M.B.A. (Purdue, Fort Wayne) in 1999. Going on to pick-up her teaching credentials from St. Francis University, she taught high school business classes until becoming an Adjunct Professor at I.P.F.W. (Personal Communication 2004 -) and Brown-Macke College (Business 2003 -).

Ron and MaryAnn were gifted with two children, Nathaniel "Nate" Earl James, born October 27, 1987, and Zachary Luke "Luke" James, born April 15, 1995. Both boys attended St. Vincent School, with Nate going on to study at Carroll High School in Huntertown. These children are actively engaged in piano training (regular ribbon winners in the Arts Festival at Taylor University) as well as soccer.

The family moved from Fort Wayne to 22 acres in northern Allen County in 1988, converting the acreage from agricultural, wooded pasture and row crop production, to environmental, wetland and woods. In 1992, they built the county's first fully earth-sheltered home, with a layout of their own design.

Submitted by Ronald E. James

JAXTHEIMER FAMILY

In 1862, Leonard W. Jaxtheimer (1836-1912) left his home in Bremen, Germany. His father, William, a tailor and cobbler, provided each of his six sons with enough money to get to America. Russia was attacking Germany again and he, "did not want his sons to die as fodder for the Czar's army."

In London, Leonard married Bertha Hume (1837-1913). Bertha's father was a lawyer and member of the House of Commons. Leonard and Bertha came to Fort Wayne in 1865 and established the Jaxtheimer Tailoring Company where Lincoln Tower stands today. In 1871 they became U.S. citizens. Their children were Alexander (1865-1924), and Henrietta (1873-1931). The family attended St. Paul's Lutheran and then Trinity English Lutheran Church.

Henrietta was active socially and in her fifties she married Nathanial Beadell, a Fort Wayne newspaper's photographer. On their honeymoon they traveled to England to meet Henrietta's maternal relatives. Nate took many panoramic photographs that have survived the years. Nate and Henrietta were tragically killed in 1931 when their car stalled at a railroad crossing. Nate's brother co-founded Lincoln National Life Insurance Company.

Alexander married Katherine Mouser (1866-1929). Young Alex learned tailoring then went on to establish the PURAQ Water Company. PURAQ provided large bottles of water to offices and factories from extremely deep wells. The bottles sat in metal rockers and dispensed amounts of water into paper cups. PURAQ had a dozen delivery trucks during World War II when the electric water cooler caused the company's shutdown. Alex led the Fort Wayne Merchant's Association and served on the County Council. He was a member of the Big Wheel Bicycle Club and on the YMCA board of directors.

Alex and Katherine had two sons, Ronald (1906-1985) and Ralph (1903-1976). Ralph owned and operated PURAQ until it's demise during World War II. In his youth he swam competitively for the Fort Wayne YMCA. He once swam against the great Johnny Weissmuller in New York and won. He taught swimming at the YMCA and Camp Potowatomi. At age 33, Ralph married Margie Black (1900-1978). They sang for over 20 years in the Trinity English Lutheran

Church choir. They had two sons, Thomas (1939-1943) and William R. (1934-1999).

Ronald left the water business and attended Tri State University. He was a civil engineer and worked for the U.S. Government. He retired in Chicago and married at age 60.

In 1957 William married his high school sweetheart, Kay Casper (1937-). Bill was a purchaser at Magnavox for 40 years retiring in 1989. He was a 25-year member of the Mizpah Shrine Chanters. Bill and Kay moved to Adams Lake in 1983. Their sons, Scott W. (1958-) and Thomas A. (1961-) reside in Fort Wayne. Scott married Laura Gremaux in 1983. Their children, Jessica, Jacob and Jillian, live at home. Scott worked in finance. Tom married Jennifer Irvin in 1984. They have two daughters, Kelsey and Taylor. Tom works as a DJ using the professional name Jack Hammer. They are all active at Crosspointe Community Church in music and children's ministries.

Submitted by Jenny Jaxtheimer.

TIMOTHY EUGENE JEFFERIES

Timothy Eugene Jefferies, born May 18, 1951, in Fort Wayne, received his elementary education in the graded schools of Allen County and Fort Wayne including the Lincoln School built in 1912, South Side High School and Ivy Tech. He is an Independent Evangelical Christian and attends the Carroll Road Christian Church. Timothy enjoys an average of two hours of prayer before beginning each day. Reading has been a favorite habit since he was nine years old after reading western novels for children. He also enjoys genealogy, history, and movies.

Timothy is employed at Advance Machine Works as a programmer set-up man on Milling Machine Centers and is occasionally called upon to be a tool and die maker. He has been in the machining trade most of thirty-six years. In the past, he has been a foreman. He is a sixth generation machinist beginning with Thomas R. Saffen who came to Fort Wayne in 1861 and was foreman and journeyman machinist for Bass Foundry and Machine Works.

Timothy is the son of Eugene Paul and Charlotte Eileen (born Heck) Jefferies. Both were born in Fort Wayne. They have six children of whom Timothy is the eldest. The others are Colleen Rochelle, Nancy Jean, Renee Elaine, Matthew Everett and Paul William.

At age eighteen, Timothy started the machinist trade as his father's helper at Triumph Corporation in Tempe, Arizona. They set up and made carbide-cutting tools for Swiss Automatics and Eugene was also a cam-maker. Eugene was a self-supporting missionary to the Native Americans. He and Mrs. Jefferies, together with Ernie Burk, pioneered the Salt River Community Church on Ernie's land. Ernie is of the Pima tribe.

Timothy married Phoebe Smith of the Maricopa tribe in 1971. The Pima Maricopa tribes share the Salt River reservation. Tim and Phoebe lived in the Lehi province of Salt River reservation. They have a daughter, Heather April. They were divorced at the tribal court May 1973. Heather married Paul Anthony Williams and has three sons, Angelo Little Rain, Paul Anthony, and Sage Morning Sun. Timothy has remained a bachelor for nearly thirty-two years.

In 1681, Robert Jefferies, an ancestor of this family arrived in America from Pewsey, Wiltshire, England. He was born in 1656 and married Jane Chandler circa 1692. She arrived in America 1687 from England with her family. Her father, George, died on the ship from smallpox. Robert and Jane owned 900 acres of land along the Brandywine River near West Chester, Pennsylvania. A bridge crossing the Brandywine is named Jefferies Bridge.

Their grandson Joseph was appointed a member of the York County, Pennsylvania Committee of Observation to the Continental Congress December 16, 1774. He later joined the York County Militia and Associates to fight in the Revolutionary War and by April 5, 1778, was promoted to Colonel and Commanding Officer. In December 1778, Joseph was appointed Wagon Master General for York County. He was responsible for procuring wagons and horses to transport the men and equipment of British General Burgoyne's defeated army from Susquehanna to Charlottesville, Virginia.

Joseph's son, John, served as a Captain. He started as a drummer boy and filled in for his father who was away in Lancaster, Pennsylvania, voting for two Generals. John fought at Germantown, Brandywine, and other battles. He hauled freight between Philadelphia and Pittsburgh and made liquor for a living. He had twenty-three children. His son, Thomas, was an architect and builder and served on city counsels of Lancaster, Pennsylvania. Thomas' son, John Landis Jefferies, was Captain in the 110th Pennsylvania of the Union Army during the Civil War to preserve the Union and free the slaves. Even though he was shot in two battles he lived until 1901. His brother, Captain Robert McClure Jefferies, while leading his company into battle before Petersburg, was shot through the head by a rebel sharpshooter before Petersburg. John Landis Jefferies' son, William Thomas Jefferies, born July 18, 1853, in Philadelphia, Pennsylvania, arrived in Fort Wayne in 1877 from Cincinnati, Ohio. He married Flora Samantha Bitner on December 8, 1878. He served three terms as City Clerk of Fort Wayne.

Timothy Eugene Jefferies, 2003.

Timothy's mother's grandparents, Abraham and Allie (born Campbell) Heck and family arrived in Fort Wayne in 1918 from Delphi, Carroll County, Indiana. Their eldest son, Granville Everett Heck, and Timothy's grandfather arrived about the same time. He was temporarily living in Peru, Indiana, and later sent for his wife, Birdie May (born Granel) Heck and children, Donald, Verna Belle, and Francis William "Bill".

This family's ancestor, Andrew Heck, arrived in Lancaster, Pennsylvania, from Germany aboard the *Ketly*, a two-masted sailing vessel in October 1752. He married Barbara Bender in 1762. He served as a private in the American Revolution. Lancaster, Pennsylvania, is called the heart of Pennsylvania Dutch Country. Many of the branches of the Hecks and Jefferies are from Lancaster. The term Dutch is a mispronunciation of the German word "Deutsch". Deutsch means German. This Heck family always refers to themselves as a Pennsylvania Dutch family.

Submitted by Timothy Jefferies

LEO & ELIZABETH (HOOCK) JEHL, SR.

The family of Leo John Jehl, Sr. and Elizabeth Therese (Hoock) Jehl has contributed much to the growth and enrichment of Fort Wayne. Leo was the son of immigrants, Eugene Jehl from Alsace Lorraine, France, and Maria Katharine Lennert, of Hessen - Darmstadt, Germany. Elizabeth's parents were Nicholas Hoock, from Baden, Germany, and Elizabeth Laier, also a German émigré.

June 10, 1919, was the wedding date of Leo John Jehl and Elizabeth Hoock. This very special ceremony at St. Peter's Catholic Church was simply another step in the continuing of a love relationship that had begun before World War I and would continue in this life for more than 65 years and the next life forever. These were two special persons who produced a fine family of nine: Paul Richard, Joseph, Jerome, Mary, Dolores, Leo Thomas and Elizabeth. What was the ancestral background of these two individuals that they shared with the church and civic community their family and began an ancestral line that would be known for loyalty and fidelity to church, family friends and work - and would always strive for love and peace in all their relationships, particularly to their own families.

At the beginning of their marriage, Leo and Elizabeth (Mom and Dad) made their home with Elizabeth's mother at 2526 Warsaw Street while Leo rented his home at 425 LaSalle Street. The original renters were Henry and Mary Berghoff who had a daughter Joan while living there. In years to come, Joan and Leo's son, Joe, would meet and marry.

Elizabeth and Leo had a family of nine - six boys and three girls between the years of 1920 and 1931. The two oldest boys, Paul (May 6, 1920) and Richard (May 16, 1921), were born on Warsaw Street. The next son, Joseph (August 24,1922 and the oldest girl, Mary (August 17, 1925) were born at St. Joseph's Hospital, and the rest of the children: Jerome (December 19, 1923), Dolores (November 26, 1926), Leo (February 26, 1928) Thomas (March 13, 1930) and Elizabeth (November 5, 1931), were all born at 425 LaSalle Street. In later years when Leo was asked how it happened that two were born at the hospital - and both in August, he thought possibly he had had enough money ahead at that time for hospitalization.

Leo, a WWI veteran, worked on the police force and also was a master mechanic on the Pennsylvania Railroad. He spent time in and out of the Marion Veteran's Hospital, beginning in the early 1930s, and Elizabeth had to work especially hard with all the children to keep providing for the family. Family life centered around their

The Jehl Brothers, developers of Georgetown Square, at the grand opening of their Lake Forest Apartments, 6700 Maysville Road. Left to right: Paul, Tom and Leo Jr., Summer 1968

Leo John Sr. and Elizabeth Jehl (center) at their 50th anniversary, June 10, 1969, flanked by their children, from left to right: Tom, Paul, Dick, Liz, Leo Jr., Joe, Mary, Jerry, and Dolores.

LaSalle Street neighborhood, St. Peter's Church and school, and Central Catholic High School, where the nine children attended school. Elizabeth instilled in her children a strong work ethic: "What you do - you do to the best of your ability." The family heeded that advice.

Leo, Sr. died October 14, 1979 and Elizabeth died February 27, 1980.

The four oldest boys served during WWII; a flag hung in the LaSalle Street window with four stars. Paul and Dick served in the Army, with Paul receiving two Purple Hearts and the Bronze Star. Dick received a Purple Heart. Joe served in the Navy and Jerry in the Coast Guard, both receiving Good Conduct Medals. Tom served in the Air Force in Germany during the Cold War. All nine children have contributed much to their Fort Wayne home with strong marriages, careers and vocations.

Paul married Irene Kleber on June 27, 1942, and had one child. Paul was well-liked by his co-workers at Joslyn Steel and later worked in the real estate and development business. They lived on Moeller Road in New Haven.

Richard married Kay Ruffner Carnahan on October 27, 1951, and had four children. Dick worked as a Post Office supervisor downtown and in retirement at the Lincoln National Bank. They lived many years in the Lakeside neighborhood.

Joseph married Joan Berghoff on February 9, 1946, and had five children. He held supervisory and administrative positions at the Post Office, from where he retired. Their brick home near St. Charles has been the scene of many family and neighborhood events.

Jerry married Jeanne Kochs on November 26, 1946 and had two children. They lived in Ohio for 15 years as Jerry worked in the plastics industry. His family returned to Fort Wayne in 1970, and he and Jeanne operated Professional Search Employment Agency, Welcome Services, and Follow Charlie Car Wash in Georgetown, where many Jehl family members worked. They lived in Lake Forest.

Mary married Joseph Doust on June 1, 1946 and had ten children. She raised the children and sent them to St. Peter's and St. Patrick's Catholic schools. Joseph was a court administrator and received much recognition from the city of Fort Wayne.

Dolores Marie Jehl entered the religious order of School Sisters of Notre Dame in Milwaukee. She was a teacher in Wisconsin and Michigan. Sr. Dolores returned to Fort Wayne in 1974, at the family's request, where she had the exceptional privilege of caring for a very special lady- "Mom Jehl." Dolores' special care for her mother allowed the family to share in Elizabeth and Leo's 65th anniversary on June 10, 1979. Dolores also had opportunities to teach at Bishop Dwenger and IPFW in Fort Wayne, as well as minister at Parkview Hospital and St. Peter's Church.

Leo Jr., known to many as Clem, married Ruth Sanders on July 10, 1948, and had five children. He taught and coached at his alma mater, Central Catholic High School. He then became involved in real estate, building, and development in Fort Wayne. They lived in the St. Charles area and also in Fremont.

Thomas married Margaret Bougher on June 27, 1954, in Killarney, Ireland, and had six children. He started in home sales and then ventured into land development, building, and property ownership, mostly in northeast Fort Wayne. The children attended St. Jude Catholic Church. Their home, which was originally built by Margaret's parents, was only a block away from the school and church.

Elizabeth, the youngest, married Harvey Stump on August 26, 1950, and had three children. Married at St. Peter's, they soon moved to Lafayette, Indiana. Liz and Harvey took jobs at Hughes Aircraft and later Harvey started two electronics companies. The family spent most of their time in California where Liz became a well-known artist.

Paul, Leo Jr. and Tom teamed up as brothers and partners to build the Lake Forest and Georgetown Apartments, a total of 381 units, in the late 1960s and early 1970s. They were partners in Georgetown Square Shopping Center, a northeast Fort Wayne landmark. Other well-known developments by the Jehl Brothers include: Camelot, Park State East, Kingston Park, Executive Park, Presidential Village, and Lake Forest - a Parade of Homes site.

Jehl Park, located adjacent to Lake Forest, is a Fort Wayne city park made possible by the Jehl Brothers. Memorial Stadium, the baseball arena at the Coliseum, was spearheaded by Tom Jehl and donations from Tom and Leo and their families. In appreciation for many years of support to the Georgetown Little League since its beginnings, the Major League diamond is called "Tom Jehl Field". Because of Tom's support of the University of St. Francis' football program, the football facility is named the Tom Jehl Football Complex. Tom also began and continues to fund the Lifetime Sports Academy (a project of the Fort Wayne Parks and the Fort Wayne Sports Corporation) where children are taught golf, tennis, and swimming during the summer at McMillen Park.

Leo and Elizabeth had 36 grandchildren and many great grandchildren, most of whom also remain in the Fort Wayne area and contribute to their Community.

Submitted by Steve Jehl

BARBARA ELLEN (DOUD) JOHNSON-RICHARD-BELOTE

Barbara Ellen Doud was born in Desloge, Missouri, June 3, 1925, to Hubert O. Doud and Nora E. (Goyings) Doud. She married early in life and bore seven wonderful children. She finished high school by getting her G.E.D. in 1964, as she wanted to work as an aide in the Special Education Class of the Fort Wayne school system. She needed more education, so she enrolled in the Indiana University Extension in Fort Wayne. She graduated with a degree in Secretarial Science. However, she discovered she did not want to be a secretary for the rest of her life. The Superior Iron and Metal Company employed her. At the same time, she helped to manage the Pontiac Restaurant with her husband, Edward. She then worked for the home office of the Brotherhood Mutual Insurance Company as a supervisor of the print shop, mail department, and supply department. She retired after 23 years of service.

She was missions chairman for 29 years at Harvester Missionary Church, where she was saved in 1955. Her life was changed; it was the best decision she ever made. She is happy with her children, grandchildren and great grandchildren. She volunteers at the Embassy and Civic Theatres and for RSVP events and is a clerk at the polls during elections. She also uses her artistic abilities by decorating the church sanctuary and helping with church events. Genealogy is her hobby and she has written a book about her mother's family. It is in the Library of Congress, titled *Goings-Goyings and Allied Families*. The search for the children's fathers' history is a current project. She has traced her father's line to Elihu Doud, a private in the American Revolution in Massachusetts, thereby becoming eligible to be a member of the D.A.R.

After the children left home, she looked for a smaller home and found a lot close to Franke Park and the Lord made it available. She had a home built to her liking. She applied for certification by The Natural Wild Life Federation to declare it a Backyard Wildlife Habitat. She has traveled to 12 different countries to see this amazing world the Lord has created and she has been able to visit.

Harold Robert Johnson was her first husband. Three children were born to them, two sons, Robert Armond, March 6, 1942, and Ronald Edward, September 22, 1943; and one daughter, Cheryl Ann, December 24, 1944.

Robert Armond has two sons, Michael Wade, May 2, 1961 and Robert Allen, September 8, 1962 with first wife Barbara L. Zartman. His second wife is Linda Marshall; no children. Michael Wade has two daughters; Andrea Lee, March 22, 1981 with first wife, Donna Zolteck, and Sarah Marie, October 7, 1994, with second wife, Beth Salge. "Rob" has not married.

Front row: Darlene, Cheryl, Joyce, Bob left center: mother Barbara. Back row: Nyletta, Ron, Alan.

Ronald Edward Johnson married Linda Lee Heath and they have two children, a daughter, Julie Lynette, June 25, 1975, who has a daughter Jacinda Darrien-Dora Bouce, August 19, 1998, and a son, Legend Apollo Mains September 17, 2002. Rev. Ronald and Linda have a son, Brian Wade, May 17, 1978 who married Joanna Napier July 31, 2004.

Cheryl Ann married Paul Edward Hines and they have two children. Their son, Jeff Andrew, January 10, 1972, who married Natalie Lynn Hrinko and they have a son, Devin Xavier, January 7, 1998, and daughter, Natasha Alexis, October 14, 2002. Cheryl and Paul also have a daughter, Rebecca Lynn, who married Michael Eugene Howell. They have two sons, Michael Eugene Howell Jr., February 12, 1993, and Vinson Eugene, October 19, 1996.

Robert Starr Richard was Barbara Ellen's second husband. Three children were born to them; Darlene, Alan and Joyce. Darlene Sue, January 3, 1947, married Almon Ford and they have one daughter, Sarah Renee, April 16, 1974. She married Scott Allen Amick and they have two daughters, Sophie Ellen, September 19, 2000 and Sydni Grace, October 30, 2002.

Alan Starr Richard married Diana Kay Biddle. They have six children, three daughters and three sons: Jamie Lynn, September 22, 1979, married Richard Lynn Gilson and they have two sons, Joseph David, August 15, 2000, and Callum Nathaniel, January 28, 2003; Emily Marie, November 10, 1984; Christy Renee, February 20, 1987, who has a son, Marcos Domicio Richard, November 12, 2002; Michael Andrew, March 5, 1983; David Aaron, July 24, 1981; and Daniel Alan, October 18, 1988.

Joyce Ellen Richard married Edward Lee Kolberg and they have two daughters: Elizabeth Ann, September 20, 1982, who married Larry Schaffer and they have one son, Bryce Samuel, October 13, 2001; and Tracy Nicole, September 20, 1987.

Edward Coli Belote was Barbara Ellen's third husband. One daughter was born to them. Nyletta Faye, July 31, 1956. She married Jerry Andrew Hetrick and they have two children, a son Andrew Evan, July 29, 1985, and a daughter, Amy Ellen, May 4, 1983.

They are all educated, working, and attending to the care of their families and their churches. God is good.

Submitted by Nyletta Hetrick

BENJAMIN FRANKLIN JOHNSON FAMILY

Benjamin Franklin Johnson was born on December 29, 1806, in Berkshire, Franklin County, Vermont, son of James H. and Abigail Johnson. He moved with his parents to Middlebury Township, Knox County, Ohio, in 1814. James H. Johnson, 1781-1856, was a farmer and a justice of the peace. He and his wife Abigail, 1788-1869, are buried near their home in Waterford-Levering Cemetery, Knox County, Ohio. James Johnson served in the War of 1812 in the Vermont Militia.

B. F. Johnson married Lydia Zolman on September 3, 1829, in Knox County, Ohio. Lydia was the daughter of John and Catherine (Passey) Zolman. Lydia was born July 12, 1811, in Fredrick County, Maryland. John Zolman lived from 1785 to 1857 and Catherine from 1789-1862. They are buried in the Berlin Cemetery, Knox County, Ohio.

B.F. Johnson and Lydia bought 118 acres of land in Section 7 of Eel River Township, Allen County, Indiana, on October 20, 1856. B.F. died December 7, 1857 and Lydia died February 4, 1886. They are buried in the Eel River Cemetery.

Their children were as follows: Orville Johnson, 1830, married Betsy Zolman; James Johnson 1831- 1909, married, Hannah Oaks; Nathan Artemus Johnson, 1833-1909, married Mary Gump; William Riley Johnson, 1835-1895, married Ellen Madden; Elizabeth Johnson, 1837-1900, married Benjamin Harter; George Johnson, 1839-1913; Catherine Johnson, 1842-1915; Mary A. Johnson, 1845-1909, married Festus Crabill; Benjamin Franklin Johnson, 1848-1909, married Lucy Falkenburg and Nancy Crone; Almina Johnson, 1855-1930, married Cyrus Shelton.

William Riley Johnson married Ellen Madden on February 7, 1861. Ellen was born in 1840 and died July 11, 1877. Their children were: Thomas, 1863-1930, married Margaret Piggot; Mary, 1864 -1948, married William Goodfellow; Eliza Elizabeth, 1865 -1947, married John Schenher; Albert, 1867-1895, never married; Nora Frances, 1869-1963, married Jacob Fulk; Ellen Johanna, 1871-1951, married John C Fulk; Theresa Nancy, 1872-1835, married Samuel Wagner; John Joseph, 1876-1961, married Ollie McBride and Almeda Casso.

William and Ellen Johnson owned 40 acres of land in Section 5 of Eel River Township. They were farmers. There was a huckleberry marsh on their land. Ellen died young and is buried in the Catholic Cemetery at Ege, Indiana,

Their fifth child, Nora Frances Johnson, was born March 7, 1869. She married Jacob Fulk on January 1, 1887. Jacob was born January 25, 1865 in Swan Township, Noble County, Indiana. Jacob died April 1, 1937. Nora lived until October 5, 1963. Their only child, James Fredrick Fulk was born October 24, 1891.

Submitted by Mrs. Franklin Geiger

BENJAMIN LEVI JOHNSON & OLLIE ELIZABETH SCHLEMMER FAMILY

Benjamin Levi Johnson, 1889-1965, was born in Tully Township, Van Wert County, Ohio. He was the son of Leander and Elizabeth Harden Johnson. In 1913, Ben married Ollie Elizabeth Schlemmer and lived in Monroe Township, Allen County, Indiana, the remainder of his life.

Ollie was born in 1891 to Philip and Caroline Britzius Schlemmer. Ollie's great grandparents, Peter and Katherine Sali Schlemmer, emigrated from Germany in 1828, first settling in Carroll County, Ohio, and then in 1835 they came to Allen County, Indiana. They raised their eight children, Peter, George, Philip, Jacob, Christian, Sophia, John, and Catherine, on their farm in Monroe Township. Katherine's death was the first in Monroe Township. She was buried in the Schlemmer Cemetery on the corner of the Hoagland and Lortie Roads. In 1841, Peter cast the deciding vote in the first election in Monroe Township. Thirteen men voted and Peter's vote was challenged. He drove his horse and buggy home and returned with proof of his right to vote and the tie was broken.

Benjamin L. Johnson and Ollie Schlemmer family. Lloyd, Forest, and Robert

Ollie's grandparents, Philip and Catherine Scaer, also had eight children: Christina, Elizabeth, Martha, George, Philip, Katherine, Charles, and Walter. Their son Philip married Caroline Britzius on October 10, 1878, in Monroe Township. Philip and Caroline had six children: George, Zetta, Jacob, Esther, Ollie, and Carl. Zetta, Jacob, and Ollie remained in Allen County, Indiana. George moved to LaGrange, Indiana, Carl raised his family near Ligionier, Indiana, and Esther lived in Bucyrus, Ohio.

Ben and Ollie Johnson lived on the Rider Road, southeast of Monroeville, Indiana. Ben was a farmer most of his life, worked for the Highway Department several years, and later became the County Highway Superintendent for Allen County. He loved politics and was quite active in local government. They had three sons: Lloyd 1914-1972; Forest 1916-1999; and Robert 1924-1975. The three sons formed a group that played for many dances during the late thirties. Lloyd and Forest remained in Monroe Township with their families and Robert moved to Fort Wayne, Indiana.

Lloyd married Bernice Oberley, daughter of Edward and Lucille Gladieux Oberley, in 1939, and had seven children: Richard, Jean, David, Gary, Jack, Michael, and Louis. Lloyd worked for

General Electric Company in Fort Wayne, Indiana, for many years as a tool and die maker. Lloyd and Bernice built their home north of Monroeville.

Forest married Hilda Jacquay, daughter of Clarence and Clara Coonrod Jacquay, in 1937. They also had seven children: James, Mary, Donald, John, Robert, Joan, and Carol. Forest and Hilda lived on the Rider Road, across the road from Ben and Ollie. Forest worked all his life at International Harvester Company in Fort Wayne, Indiana.

Robert married Mary Angela Sheehan, daughter of Irvin and Alberta Geis Sheehan, in 1950. Bob and Angela lived most of their lives in Fort Wayne with their eight children: Kathleen, Philip, Deborah, Patricia, Gregory, Douglas, Bennett, and Rodney. Bob went to Tri State College in Angola, Indiana, was a pilot in WWII, and was very successful in business and real estate in the Fort Wayne area.

Submitted by Kim Vandermotten

BENNETT LYNN JOHNSON

Bennett Lynn Johnson was born on February 23, 1963, in Adams County, Decatur, Indiana. He was the son of Robert P. and Mary Angela Sheehan Johnson. His family made their home at 2717 Plaza Drive, Fort Wayne, Indiana. There were six siblings: Kathleen Marie, Philip Robert, Deborah Ann, Patricia Sue, Gregory Allen, and Douglas Edward.

Bennett Johnson

His education began at Sacred Heart Catholic School and continued at Ben Geyer Junior High. When Bennett was to enter high school, the family moved and he attended North Side High School. He struggled with meeting new friends and a new school situation and dropped out of high school. He did obtain his GED certificate at a later date.

In November 1981, Bennett married Stephanie York at the Allen County, Indiana, courthouse. They had one daughter, Sarah Lynn. He joined the Coast Guard and Stephanie took their small daughter and moved to North Carolina to be close to her parents while Bennett was in basic training. After basic training, the small family moved to Seattle, Washington, where he was stationed. His next assignment was to Washington, DC. At that time Bennett and Stephanie divorced and she returned with their daughter to North Carolina.

When his enlistment was up, Bennett returned to Fort Wayne and started working at ITT and he met Shelly Chavez from Auburn, Indiana. They were married at St. Jude Catholic Church on June 9, 1990, in Fort Wayne, Indiana. The couple made their home in Auburn, Indiana. Bennett started his own real estate company, and they built a home across from the golf course on State Road 427. They had one son, Quinton, and Sarah (Bennett's daughter) came to live with them. Ultimately, Bennett and Shelly obtained a divorce. Bennett dissolved his real estate business and moved to the Orlando, Florida, area.

Sarah lives with her daughter in North Manchester, Indiana, and attends North Manchester College. Quinton lives with his mother in Auburn, Indiana.

Submitted by Jeannie Melinder

DOUGLAS EDWARD JOHNSON FAMILY

Douglas Edward Johnson was born on February 16,1961. His parents were Robert P. and Mary Angela Sheehan Johnson. He was born at Adams County Memorial Hospital, Decatur, Indiana. Douglas spent his childhood in the activities common for the times. There were many children in the neighborhood and they spent hours at McMillen Park participating in Little League, swimming, and hockey. His interest in hockey is still alive today and he plays on an adult hockey team.

Douglas Edward Johnson family

His elementary education was obtained at Sacred Heart Catholic School and he graduated from South Side High School. After high school he attended Indiana University, Bloomington, Indiana, for two years. However, Social Security benefits for full-time, dependent students over 18, of deceased parents, were eliminated; therefore, he put his education on hold and decided to join the army. He took his basic training at Fort Nix, New Jersey, and was stationed at Fort Bragg, North Carolina. At the outbreak of the Granada War he was scheduled to ship out, but as the war was short-lived he did not have to go. He served in Korea and was honorably discharged upon his return. Upon his discharge he returned to Fort Wayne and found employment with Avco Financial. Again, a change took him to Fort Wayne Metals.

In the meantime, he met his future wife, Lisa Ann Gonzalez, who was born on November 11, 1964. They were married at St. Peter's Catholic Church on October 22, 1988. Their first home was an apartment on Lake Avenue. They then moved to the Concord Hills Addition on Rothman Road. After Lisa became pregnant with twins, Jacob and Jessica (December 29, 1993), they sold this home and moved in with her parents for the help they could provide. After living with her parents several years they purchased a house in the Highland Park area across from Hamilton Park. Amanda (March 14, 1995) and Maci (August 19, 1998) were born there.

Making another life decision, Douglas decided to obtain his college diploma and returned to school. While working full time, raising a family, going to school part time, and studying, he obtained a degree in accounting from St. Francis College, Fort Wayne, Indiana. After graduating from St. Francis, he sought employment with Arrow Electronics where he sold electronic components to O.E.M. customers in northern Indiana until he went to work for C.E. Electronics in Bryan Ohio, where, at the present time, he is the materials manager.

Lisa studied for a degree in nursing, and worked part-time at St. Anne Nursing Home while raising four children. She has a nursing degree from St. Francis University and works for Northeast Orthopedics.

Doug and Lisa purchased a home west of Fort Wayne, off Homestead Road on Sheffield Way, where they are now living. They are descendants of the Johnson, Schlemmer, Sheehan, and Geis families of Monroe Township.

Submitted by Douglas E. Johnson

ELBE C. JOHNSON

Elbe C. Johnson was born on February 24, 1868, in Union Township, Wells County, and the oldest of six children of Emmitt and Emma Catherine Smetzer Johnson. Between the 1870 and 1880 censuses, the family moved to Sheldon in Allen County and, in 1880, Elbe was twelve years old and attending school. The family then moved to Fort Wayne. Elbe appears in the Fort Wayne City and Allen County Directories between 1885 and 1900 as a carriage trimmer for E. C. Smith and a painter for Peters Box and Lumber Company and then Fleming Manufacturing Company.

On September 27, 1890, he married Sarah Catherine Fulton of Laketon, Wabash County, Indiana. Two children were born to this union: Gertrude Ercil, March 19, 1891, and Admiral Dewey, November 5, 1898. The son lived only six months. He had been named for the famous admiral because, during the Spanish American War, Elbe had served in Company G 157th Regiment Indiana Volunteer Infantry, familiarly known as the Studebaker Tigers.

Soon after his return, a new home was built on the northeast comer of West Main Street in Laketon, one block south of the (then) United

Front row: Andrew, Barbara, Margaret, and Matthew Knecht.Middle: Carey, Mary Ellen, Richard, William, Marjorie, Alex, Luke, Jeanne, and Sam Knecht. Back: Jay, Mark, John Knecht, Catherine and Peter Van Houten

Brethren in Christ Church. Elbe worked as an interior decorator most of his life. In his later years his hobby was designing and piecing quilts. During his last few years, he lived with his daughter Gertrude in Mentone and in the Veterans' Home in Lafayette. On May 17, 1953, he died in the Veterans' Hospital in Fort Wayne and is buried in the family plot in Laketon Cemetery.

Gertrude completed eight years at the Laketon Public School. She became an accomplished seamstress, as her mother Kate was, and learned other needlecrafts, particularly crocheting. In 1908, the Reverend Silas Milton Hill was assigned to the Laketon United Brethren Church and moved into the parsonage with his wife Cora, one son Ellis, and three daughters: Cloe, Mildred, and Lois. The following year, Cora Hill became seriously ill and the young unattached Gertrude was called in to help out with the two younger children, Mildred and Lois. Cora died in 1909. In October 1910, Rev. Hill and Gertrude were married. Having been born on April 3, 1871, he was 39, twenty years older than Gertrude. Their pastoral assignments were in Butler, Colburn, Atwood, and Bourbon, where their daughter, Marjorie Ellen, the only grandchild of Elbe and Kate Johnson, was born, March 1, 1921. From 1933 to 1936, Silas and Gertrude served the Nine Mile United Methodist Church in Allen County.

Gertrude was a faithful and effective pastor's wife. She often played the piano for services and was a gracious hostess in the parsonage. She enjoyed needlework, especially crocheting. After Silas' death in 1949, she remained in Mentone where they had retired. She married Ellis Hill in 1956, and they often spent their winters in Arizona. She died in the Kosciusko County Hospital, November 5, 1984, and is buried in the family plot in the Laketon Cemetery.

Marjorie Hill married John Knecht on May 30, 1943. Their children are Catherine (VanHouten), Mark, Luke, and Matthew. The Knechts served as missionaries in China and two pastorates in Indiana. Later, John was president of United Seminary in Dayton, Ohio, for twenty years. While their children were in college, Marjorie taught at Dunbar High School. They now live at Peabody Retirement Community in North Manchester, Indiana.

Submitted by Mr. and Mrs. John R. Knecht

EMMITT ENOS & EMMA CATHERINE (SMETZER) JOHNSON

On Christmas in 1847, Emmitt Enos Johnson was born in Columbiana County, Ohio. He, with his parents, Noah and Sarah (Thomas) Johnson, later moved to Wells County, Indiana. (Articles about them appear in *Biographical Memoirs of Wells County, Indiana* and in *Wells County, Indiana Family History 1837-1992).* On a farm there, Emmitt grew up with two brothers and five sisters; and they were only one mile away from their paternal grandparents, James and Rebecca (Baxter) Johnson. At the age of 21, Emmitt married Emma Catherine Smetzer in Allen County. Although they lived on the Wells County farm for awhile, they moved to the Village of Sheldon in Allen County and then to Fort Wayne. Emmitt worked for the Chicago and Erie Railroad.

Emmitt Enos Johnson ca. 1915

This couple had six children: Elbe C. Johnson, who married Sarah Catherine Fulton, was a painter and decorator in Fort Wayne and Laketon, Indiana. He also fought with the Studebaker Tigers in the Spanish-American War. Elbe and Sarah had a daughter, Gertrude Ercil (Johnson) Hill and a baby son, Admiral Dewey Johnson, who lived for only six months. Their only grandchild was Marjorie Ellen (Hill) Knecht.

Izora Johnson became the wife of Charles Taylor Trevey and the mother of Sylva Clayton, Ralph Emerson, Gail, Mary Catherine, and an unnamed baby. Izora was an excellent homemaker, a good wife and mother, and a professional seamstress. Her very sudden and unexpected death on February 28, 1908, created ripples of problems that affected the next two generations.

Melvin Abraham Johnson was a freight solicitor for railroads. In later life, he moved from Fort Wayne to Los Angeles, California, where he owned an apartment building. He never married. His younger sister, Lenora (Della) Johnson, worked at Fort Wayne Knitting Mills for many years and then moved to Los Angeles to live with Melvin. Della, always loving, was the glue that held the family together, and she did everything she could to help each of her siblings, their children, and their grandchildren.

Perry Joseph Johnson first married Minnie Louise Meyers; and, after their divorce, he and Savannah Michael were wed. He worked at General Electric Company for 35 years. Perry and Minnie's only child, Emmitt Frederick Johnson, was a brand new baby when during the 1913 flood, he and others of the Johnson family were evacuated by row boat from the second story of his grandparents' home at the corner of Boon and Cherry Streets.

In April 1900, Ray, the sixth child, fell off his bicycle in front of a street car at the intersection of Broadway and Berry Streets in Fort Wayne and was killed. He was only 13 years old.

At that time, Emma Catherine was already extremely ill with heart disease. She had been born in Wooster, Wayne County, Ohio, on May 16, 1851. Her father was John Smetzer. Her mother has not been proven. In 1850, John, with his son, Abraham, was living with George and Catherine Fortney in Wooster. By 1860, John was gone, but Abraham remained with the Fortneys; and they had moved to Huntington, Indiana. It was in Huntington that Emmitt and Emma Catherine met. They may have been introduced by a Smetzer co-worker of Emmitt on the railroad.

Emma Catherine, or Kate as she was called, died July 28, 1905, in Fort Wayne. Emmitt survived until February 3, 1921. His death occurred in Laketon, Wabash County, Indiana. Both are buried in Lindenwood Cemetery with Melvin, Della and Ray. Izora, her husband, and two of their children are buried in an adjoining plot.

Emmitt Enos Johnson built a dolly cradle for Izora. Five generations of little girls have played with it: first Izora, then Mary Catherine (Trevey) Piatt, Mary Joan (Piatt) Lauer, Beth Ann and Linda Sue Lauer, and now Emmitt's great-great-great granddaughter, Audrey Charun Lauer.

Submitted by Beth A. Lauer

EMMITT F. & BONNIE M. (ANGELL) JOHNSON

Allen County has many memorable citizens but mostly it's comprised of ordinary people like Emmitt and Bonnie Johnson. Emmitt Frederick Johnson was born February 27, 1913, in Fort Wayne, the son of Minnie Louise Meyers and Perry Joseph Johnson. As an infant, he was rescued by rowboat during the great flood. Bonnie Celene Mary Angell was born in Fort Wayne on Palm Sunday, March 29, 1914, the daughter of Martha Sophia Wagner and Peter Angell, a recent immigrant from Norway.

Emmitt and Bonnie's childhoods had some remarkable similarities – only children, single mothers with multiple marriages and divorces, and no first cousins.

Emmitt was raised in Fort Wayne and Chicago, where he excelled at drafting at Senn High School and for fun sneaked into Wrigley Field to watch the Cubs play baseball. Bonnie graduated from Central High School, and although she had dreamed of going to nursing school, that wasn't to happen.

They met at a dance hall in Fort Wayne. By way of introduction, Bonnie irreverently flipped Emmitt's tie, quite atypical for the "petite and shy" Bonnie. On September 29, 1934, they began a successful marriage that spanned 48 years.

Laid off from his first job at a utility company, Emmitt went on to have a prosperous career at International Harvester, becoming Assistant Plant Manager. Since the production of half-tracks during World War II was critical to our country's defense, Emmitt was deferred from military service.

Emmitt F. & Bonnie M. Johnson with daughter Sherrill Ann, July, 1943.

Emmitt worked at "The Harvester" until his retirement in 1973 and counted among his accomplishments the successful construction of the Scout line. He was a 32nd Degree Mason, a Shriner, and enjoyed bowling and golf. He especially cherished being at his Coldwater Lake (Michigan) cottage.

Bonnie was a homemaker until the early 50s, when she ventured out to clerk at Fort Wayne's largest department store, Wolf and Dessauer. Soon after, she landed a patronage job as cashier at the Bureau of Motor Vehicles. She loved both the job and the people. When the administration changed and employees were ousted, she became the office assistant at her church, Trinity Episcopal. Bonnie was active in the Eastern Star and socialized with her high school friends in "Chatta Gabba Club."

Post retirement, Emmitt and Bonnie enjoyed two memorable trips to England and Mexico. They wintered in Florida and had just purchased a condominium in Englewood when Emmitt was diagnosed with cancer. He passed away in Venice, Florida, April 18, 1982. After his death, Bonnie returned to Fort Wayne, volunteering at the church office, until declining health necessitated relocating near her daughter. After a valiant battle with Alzheimer's, she passed away in St. Charles, Illinois, August 23, 2004. Bonnie and Emmitt are buried in Greenlawn Memorial Park.

These two "only children" had only one child, Sherrill Ann, born May 26, 1943. They were blessed with two grandchildren, whom they adored: Kimberly Ann Lloyd, born March 8, 1965, (just weeks before the Palm Sunday tornado destroyed their cottage) and John Thomas (J.T.) Lloyd, born July 19, 1969, as man walked on the moon.

Submitted by Beth A. Lauer

GREGORY ALLEN JOHNSON FAMILY

Although Gregory Allen Johnson was born to Robert P. and Mary Angela (Sheehan) Johnson on April 26, 1959 in Adams County, Indiana, his family resided in Fort Wayne, Allen County, Indiana. At the time of his birth there were four other children at home: Kathleen (1951), Philip (1952), Deborah (1954), and Patricia (1957). Three more sons would join the family: Douglas (February 16, 1961), Bennett (February 23, 1963), and Rodney (1967). The family residence was on Plaza Drive, Fort Wayne.

Greg thrived as a child and, when school age, he attended St. Hyacinth's until the fifth grade, when the school closed. He then attended Sacred Heart Catholic School, Ben Geyer Junior High School, and graduated in 1978 from South Side High School. While growing up, McMillen Park was close to his home and there he played Little League baseball, was on the swim, diving and water polo teams, and played hockey on an outdoor rink in the winter. He started on the varsity football team in high school. He also worked part time at the Standard Oil Station on North Anthony Boulevard.

After graduation, Greg worked at Rea Magnet Wire, but knew that was not what he wanted to do forever. Several of his friends were moving to Texas and he decided to join them. His sister, Patricia, had just graduated from Indiana University in Bloomington and they left for Texas shortly after the beginning of 1981. They settled in Arlington, Texas.

Gregory Allen Johnson family

Greg met Joann Marie Vanderbosch, who was born March 26, 1960, while a senior in high school. After Greg moved to Texas, Joann enrolled at Ball State University. Upon her graduation, Greg came home from Texas and they were married at Sacred Heart Catholic Church on September 4, 1982. After a honeymoon on South Padre Island, the newlyweds returned to Arlington, Texas, where they reside today along with their two children, Dana Rose (November 13, 1987) and Kyle Robert (March 22, 1981).

For 23 years Greg worked for Graybar Electronics and in December 2003 he took early retirement. Becoming restless, he decided to pursue a job opportunity with JD Martin Company. Joann has been employed at Merck Pharmaceuticals in Dallas, Texas, for 14 years as an assistant to the regional manager.

Dana is a junior at Lamar High School in Arlington, Texas. She played volleyball, but decided to concentrate her athletic abilities on her favorite sport, basketball. She is a starter on the varsity team. Kyle is in eighth grade at Schakelford Middle School and plays basketball, football, and baseball.

Greg is an avid golfer and a fan of the Dallas Cowboys football team, Texas Rangers baseball team, and the biggest fan of Dana and Kyle.

He is a descendent of the Johnson, Schlemmer, Sheehan, and Geis families from the rural area of Monroeville, Indiana.

Submitted by Gregory Allen Johnson

ISAAC & ELIZABETH JOHNSON

Isaac Abraham Johnson, born May 2, 1864, Jefferson Township, Wells County, Indiana, died February 16, 1936 in Richmond, Indiana, was a logger and farmer in Pleasant Township, Allen County, Indiana. He was the grandson of James and Rebecca (Baxter) Johnson, both of whom were born in Pennsylvania, moved to Columbiana County, Ohio and then settled in Pleasant Township, Allen County, Indiana in 1853. Isaac's father, Jacob, married Elizabeth (Biddle) and settled in Jefferson Township, Wells County. Elizabeth Biddle was the daughter of John and Susannah (Bevington) Biddle of Jefferson Township, Wells County, Indiana. Isaac married Elizabeth C. Smith, March 31, 1887, in Allen County, Indiana. Elizabeth C. (Smith) Johnson was born March 1, 1868 in Pleasant Township and died December 11, 1919 in Pleasant Township. She was the daughter of Finley and Almira (Clark) Smith. Finley was the son of Jacob and Elizabeth (First) Smith, early settlers of Pleasant Township. Jacob and Elizabeth (First) Smith were married in Wayne County, Ohio. Almira was the daughter of Orson and Isabell (Miller) Clark. Orson was born in Genessee County, New York and married Isabell in Wayne County, Ohio. Orson's land patent in Wells County, Indiana was dated December 14, 1849.

Life was not easy for Isaac and Elizabeth. Their first child, Wesley, died when only 16 days old and Curtis, the second child, died at the age of six months. Isaac suffered from asthma and Elizabeth contracted influenza during the great epidemic of 1918. She never recovered and died in 1919. Their house burned around 1909. Isaac and the older sons rebuilt it while Elizabeth and the younger children stayed with various relatives in the area. Isaac and Elizabeth had the following children, all born in Pleasant Township, Allen County, Indiana:

James Johnson, Isaac Johnson and Gilford Johnson

(1) Welsey, born May 1, 1888, died May 16, 1888.

(2) Curtis, born October 15, 1889, died June 15, 1890.

(3) Susie Eva, born June 3, 1891, died February 7, 1961. She was married to Alexander Peake on November 25, 1923. Susie had the following children: Charles Johnson and Mary Elizabeth Peake (Mobley).

(4) Alfred Hardesty, born December 13, 1894, died February 2, 1990. Alfred married Edith Counsellor. Their children were: Robert, Dorothy (Patten), Mary (Dowty), Carl, Raymond, Merle, Norma (Snyder) and Arlon.

(5) Ralph Jacob, born February 20, 1897, died October 27, 1981. He married Tolless Leonard. Their children were: Earl, Paul and Leona (Mahnensmith).

(6) Almira Elizabeth, born May 2, 1900, died June 15, 1998. She married Benjamin Taylor. Their children were: Dale, Wayne, Donald, and Annabelle (Notestine).

(7) James Lynn, born 18 March 1903, died November 26, 1994, married Helen Forrest. Their children were: Gilford, Walter, Marjorie (Kientz), Harold, Bruce, and Dennis.

(8) Wilmetta Marie, born November 9, 1914, died December 13, 1981, married Harold Messick. Their children were: Joan (Coulson, Grate) and Evelyn (Runyon).

More information can be found in the book *Johnson Tree: Branch 6, Jacob Johnson and Elizabeth Biddle*. This book is located in the Allen County Public Library.

Submitted by Dennis Johnson

JAMES AND REBECCA (BAXTER) JOHNSON

In Allen County at the southeast comer of Coverdale and South County Line Roads, there is a beautiful home. An onlooker might never guess that within the two-story portion is the log house built by James and Rebecca (Baxter) Johnson. They purchased the 188-plus acre farm on April 22, 1854, for $1,500. James and his older sons had to clear the land, fell the trees, and cut the logs. Their hand-hewn tree trunks supporting the structure can still be seen from the basement.

Born in Allegheny County, Pennsylvania, on January 18, 1802, James was the grandson of Peter Johnson and Mary Phillips, and the son of Solomon Johnson and Fannie Warne. Fannie was the daughter of Joseph Warne and Dorcas Miller. Joseph fought in the American Revolution as a private in Lieutenant Colonel Theophilus Phillips' Fifth Battalion, County of Westmoreland, Pennsylvania.

Johnson home - log house within

Rebecca was the daughter of James and Altha Mariah (Legg) Baxter of Washington County, Pennsylvania. James and Rebecca married on June 23, 1825, in that county and their first two children, Noah and Frances, were born there. Isabella and Harriet, their next children, may have been born in Pennsylvania or in Ohio. Isaac R., Jacob, Harvey, Abraham, Elizabeth, Lewis, Josiah, Martha, Altha Ann, and John Jackman were born in Columbiana County, Ohio.

When the family moved to Allen County, the children ranged in age from 28 to six. James was 52, and Rebecca was 49. Sadly, only five years later, James died. Rebecca lived until 1891. Abraham had died as an infant in Ohio and John Jackman died in 1864. All of the remaining twelve married and had children, grandchildren, and so forth. Starting in 1984, some descendants of these Johnsons have met each July at the Johnson Roots Conference to study their Johnson family history and to share stories that have been handed down through the generations. *Johnson Roots*, published annually since 1990, features articles about Johnson ancestors, copies of documents, pictures, and vital statistics.

One goal of the conference has been the recording of Johnson genealogy. So far, books about the descendants of Noah, Harriet, Jacob, Elizabeth, Lewis, and Altha Ann have been published and donated to the Allen County Public Library. They are entitled *Johnson Tree: Branch 1, Johnson Tree: Branch 4*, and so forth. James and Rebecca (Baxter) Johnson are buried in Uniontown Cemetery, which is only two miles from their farm.

Submitted by Lavona (Johnson) Turpchinoff

JOHN WILMER JOHNSON

It is fitting that John Wilmer Johnson is included in the biographical section of a history book, as genealogy was a hobby he began when he was just 17. Johnny is best known for his involvement in sports, especially tennis. He is one of the members of the local Tennis Hall of Fame and is known for having a scholarship and a sportsmanship trophy named in his honor. He also officiated basketball, baseball and football games, working football games until he was 75. He completed 39 consecutive years as a football official and never missed an assignment.

Johnny's great-great-grandmother was Sarah Cook Johnson, an intrepid Quaker who, in widowhood, brought her five children from the Isle of Wight County, Virginia, to Henry County, Indiana in 1833. Sarah was born in 1788 and married Laban Johnson in 1809 when she was about 21 years old. Laban died in 1827 so "Sarah made ready to move to Indiana where there was fertile land and opportunity." Friends and neighbors joined her for the long trek by horse and wagon over the Wilderness Road. After their arrival, they settled on adjoining farms near New Castle and continued to honor their Quaker faith. The nickname for the road where the Johnson clan resided side-by-side was "Stringtown," but it was best known as the Richsquare community.

Johnny's great grandfather, the son of Laban and Sarah, was Joel Johnson, who married Elizabeth Davis in 1837. One of their sons was John Johnson, born in 1847. He married Elizabeth Black in 1875 and two children were born to their union. They were Lulu Mae, who was born in 1882, and Myrton Lewis Johnson, Johnny's father, who was born on January 4, 1876.

Myrton Johnson, after his graduation from the Richsquare Academy, entered Earlham College in Richmond, Indiana from where he graduated in 1897. During his college days he played football and basketball. He began teaching school and also farmed his and his father's land. Myrton married Emma "Bessie" Leo Jefferis on June 28, 1905. Bessie was one of Myrton's pupils when he was teaching at the Richsquare Academy. His and Bessie's home was a popular place for the young people of the community. A special attraction was the tennis court, on which his sons became expert players. Myrton had learned to play tennis at Earlham and, after graduation, he built a tennis court in the side yard. A favorite remark made by the Johnson family was that on some days "it was too wet to plow, but not too wet for tennis." Another favorite family game was croquet.

Myrton was active in the Friends meeting and was the presiding elder for several years. Always interested in young people, he led a drive for funds to purchase an organ for the meeting; much to their joy, but with considerable misgiving by some of the older members. He was active in the Henry County chapter of the Farm Bureau and was a charter member.

Myrton and Bessie had four children. Johnny was the firstborn, on July 3, 1906. He was named John Wilmer and was always called "Wilmer" by family and friends. However, while at Earlham, he wanted to enroll in a dance class and used the name "John" so that his parents would not find out about the class when the class list would appear in the local paper.

Johnny had two brothers, Orville and Ralph, and one sister, Janet Roberts. Orville and Johnny Wilmer competed with each other in local tennis tournaments, but they preferred to play doubles together. All of the siblings graduated from Earlham College and the three brothers played on the Earlham tennis team. Orville coached tennis there for many years and has been inducted in their Tennis Hall of Fame. Janet and her husband Kirk play regularly in Palo Alto, California.

After graduation from Earlham and with additional hours from State, Johnny taught history and coached high school athletics for nine years. On August 30, 1931, he married Thelma Boyd who was one of his students at New Lisbon High School. He was also rooming at her grandparent's home. They had two children, Marilyn Johnson Rousseau (Edwin), born in 1933, and Dr. John Myrton Johnson, born in 1941. Dr. John pursued a career in teaching at the university level and has spent most of his life at Arizona State University.

Johnny Johnson

Johnny and Thelma had six grandchildren who are: Mark Rousseau, Renee Rousseau, Denise Rousseau VanderHagen, and Suzanne Rousseau Hausfeld; also Kailey Johnson and Kyle Johnson, children of Dr. John Myrton and Dr. Kathleen Ferraro.

Great grandchildren are Michelle, Brett, and Ryan, children of Mark and Lynne Carter Rousseau. Other great grandchildren are Josh, Joe, and Andrew Kearby, children of Renee Rousseau and David Kearby; Lauren, Mitchell, Lynnel, and Mya VanderHagen, children of Denise and Mark VanderHagen; Anthony, Allison, and Amy Hausfeld, children of Suzanne and Mike Hausfeld. Great-great-grandchildren are Anikah and Aubrey Kearby, children of Josh and Brenda Breidenstein Kearby.

Dr. John played tennis at North Side High School and at Indiana University. Marilyn and Ed's children made the most of their legacy with the daughters winning athletic letters in tennis at Snider High School and Mark winning tournaments in the Fort Wayne Park's summer programs. Renee was a member of the Ball State women's tennis team.

In 1938, Johnny decided to enter the business world and worked for the Goodyear Tire and Rubber Company in New Castle, Peru, and Fort Wayne. He was hired by the Wolf & Dessauer Department Store to start up an auto accessory store in 1945. After a fire at the store, he sold major appliances for L. S. Ayres. He retired when he was 72. Thelma worked for Nobbson's, a ladies' clothing store, as a bookkeeper and for Fort Wayne National Bank as a teller.

Johnny continued playing tennis throughout his life and even played at Swinney park under tough conditions. He and his friends were known to shovel snow from the courts when necessary. During his long career, Johnny played in 43 city singles tournaments, playing his last one at age 88. In 1985, Johnny, age 79, and his partner Jean Smith, age 69, won the gold medal in the Men's Doubles tournament of the White River Park State Games, competing in the 65-and-older division. In 1993, Johnny was an award recipient for the Sports Corporation. He was one of the initial appointments to the Fort Wayne Tennis Commission in 1948. He was a 32nd degree Mason and, while a member of the Downtown Kiwanis Club, he was awarded a pin for his 50 years of perfect attendance. He was a member of the Forest Park United Methodist Church.

He died on November 2, 1995, of multiple myeloma at age 89. He will be remembered as an ambassador for tennis because of his friendly appeal and sportsmanlike conduct. It would be unlike Johnny to beat anyone 6-0, or to walk off the court without a few kind remarks about his opponent's game.

Johnny lived life to the fullest and took pleasure in life itself. For example, he took Thelma outside to see the full moon every month for 63 years and he went down the big water slide at Diamond Jim's when he was 85 years old. He maintained contact with college friends and relatives with great passion. He had an endearing relationship with all of his close family members. At his passing, the most often mentioned characteristic of Johnny's was that he was a true gentleman.

Submitted by Renee Rousseau

KENNETH (KEN) EUGENE & CHARLOTTE ELEANORE (CUPP) JOHNSON FAMILY

Ken Johnson was born on June 30, 1938 in Fort Wayne, Indiana at home. Ken graduated from Hamilton High School in Steuben County, Indiana. In 1956, he joined the Air National Guard and went to electronics school. Ken was employed at Farnsworth Electronics in Fort Wayne from 1957 until 1960 and then by the Indiana State Police from 1960 until 1985, when he retired. He received his associate degree in business administration from the University of St. Francis in Fort Wayne. He then worked for the U.S. Air Force as an intelligence analyst assigned to the Drug Enforcement Agency and then to the Allen County Drug Task Force until retirement from the U.S. Military in 1998, with a total of 34 years in the Air National Guard. Ken then worked for the Allen County Sheriff Department until final retirement in 2004.

On April 24, 1960, Ken and Charlotte Eleanore (Cupp) were married. Charlotte was born in Bluffton on January 2, 1939, and graduated from Rockcreek High School in Wells County. Charlotte was a homemaker, but later, after the children were raised, she worked at the VA Hospital in Fort Wayne. Since then, and until the present time, she works for the Allen County Sheriff Department.

Ken and Charlotte's children are Terry Lee, born July 1, 1961; Keith Allen, born October 31, 1962; Chris Alan, born January 18, 1967; Brian Eugene, born April 19, 1969; and Brenda Sue, born July 10, 1970.

Ken has two brothers, Cecil Merle Johnson and Rex Lou Johnson. Ken's father is Robert Eugene Johnson and his mother is Grace Ethyl (Marquardt). Robert's parents were Alfred and Edith (Counseller) Johnson. Alfred's parents were Isaac and Elizabeth (Smith) Johnson. Isaac's parents were Jacob and Elizabeth C. (Biddle) Johnson. Jacob's parents were James and Rebecca (Baxter) Johnson. James' parents were Solomon and Francis (Warne) Johnson. Francis's father served in the American Revolution. Solomon's parents were Peter and Polly (Phillips) Johnson, who came to America about 1710 from Scotland or Wales and settled in Allegheny County, Pennsylvania.

The Kenneth Johnson Family

Charlotte Johnson's parents were Harry Dana Guy Cupp and Eileen Laura (Dustman). Dana's parents were Otto Luther and Amy (Lewellan) Cupp. Dana had twelve brothers and sisters. Charlotte's mother's parents were Earl Alfred Dustman and Esther Charlotte (Miller) from Fort Wayne. Charlotte has two sisters, Mona Diane Rice and Barbara Joan Lehrman. A brother, Thomas Edward died at seven months. Otto Cupp's parents were William and Anna Maria (Weimer) Cupp. They had seven children and came to Markle, Indiana, from Perry County, Ohio, in 1865. William's parents were John D. and Elizabeth (Simon) Cupp. John was later married to Margaret E. Hayes. John's parents were Valentine and Mary (Fahl) Cupp and Valentine's parents were Marcus and Margretta (Adams) Cupp. Valentine was born in Montgomery County, Pennsylvania. Marcus' father was Johann Jacob Cupp Jr. from Mufringen, Wuerttenburg, Germany. He arrived in America September 15, 1749 on the ship *Edinburgh* (Breitbard). Johann Jacob's parents were Johann Jacob Kapp and Anne Marta Henna. Johann Kapp Sr. was born in 1684.

Submitted by Kenneth & Charlotte Johnson

LAWRENCE JOHNSON FAMILY

Lawrence K., Marilyn (Drommer), Cory and Heather Johnson moved to Fort Wayne, January 1971, from Holden, Massachusetts. All four were born in Sioux City, Iowa. Larry was General Manager, Paul Revere Insurance. In 1981, Larry joined Fort Wayne National Bank in Private Banking. The children completed twelve years of public school in Fort Wayne, and both

The Lawrence Johnson Family, 1988

went on to graduate from Indiana University. Heather completed her Masters' Degree at Iowa University. Cory used his Journalism and English degree and became a writer. He formed Creative-Media, a production company. Cory moved to Denver, Colorado and met Lorie who had a daughter, Tessa. They married and had a son, Tanner. Heather married Gregory Bleeke from Decatur, Indiana. They settled in Fort Wayne and have a daughter, Sarah, and son, Sam. Marilyn went into sales of industrial printed products and retired in 1995; Larry retired from National City Bank in 2002. He became VP, Executive and Professional Services, at Salin Bank and Trust in 2003. Larry retained ownership of a large farm in South Dakota; Marilyn retained ownership of a smaller farm in Iowa. They also owned property in Naples, Florida where the family vacationed in winter months.

Submitted by Marilyn Johnson

JOHNSON/PATTERSON FAMILY

Jerry J. Johnson was born in 1876 near Faunsdale, Alabama. He spent his early years as a teacher in a church-based elementary school. In 1892, he and Hattie Ravizee were joined together in matrimony. To this union, two girls, one of whom was the author's mother, Lena, and two boys were born. She would marry Archie E. Patterson who was from Uniontown, Alabama in 1919 and five children were born to this union.

While life was less than ideal, Jerry Johnson had no immediate thoughts about leaving Faunsdale until the "incident". His only brother David, who was younger, was deliberately run down by a white man in a horse and wagon. It would be over a year before David recovered; however, he would be permanently disabled. Through this ordeal, Jerry began to sense that there would be more trouble. He made a decision to leave the teaching job, which he dearly loved, and took a job with the Pennsylvania Railroad that allowed him to travel all across the country and look for a place to relocate his family. Based upon his travels, he came across Fort Wayne and was told about the Westfield area where blacks were permitted to purchase land and build their own home. After viewing the site, he told the family that he thought Fort Wayne would be a better place to live, and encouraged them to move there, which they did in 1916.

After moving to Fort Wayne, the family got involved with their neighbors in Westfield and became active in the African Methodist Church. Jerry Johnson became one of the founding members of the Allen County Colored Republican

Club. After the Pennsylvania Railroad went bankrupt, because of his political involvement, Jerry would be able to get a job with the city street department from which he retired after 30 years. He was a familiar sight in the neighborhood because he walked to work everyday. He also became a precinct committee man for the Westfield area and remained a political activist for the rest of his life.

There was a Steel Plant in Westfield where many of the African-American settlers who lived in the neighborhood found jobs. The author's father, Archie Patterson, was among those men. However, he only worked there for about two years before he landed another job with Sears Auto Repair Center which enabled him to hone his auto mechanic repair skills. It was unheard of for a black man to find such a job in those days. But because of his fair skin, it was unknown to them that he was a man of color. Archie was the president and one of the founders of the Westfield Neighborhood Association. Part of his role was to serve as "chief cook" and "bottle washer" for the neighborhood. His barbecue and his barbecue sauce gained legendary status. To this day his daughter still gets calls around the 4th of July asking for recipes for his barbecue sauce. After Archie was no longer able to serve in this capacity, his son, Francis, took over the role as the "chief cook" and "bottle washer." He made some improvements in the sauce. Later it was bottled exclusively and sold at Didier Brothers Meat Market.

Archie's wife, Lena, graduated from Payne Theological Seminary in Alabama. She could not find employment as a teacher in Indiana in those days because of the color of her skin. She and her son, Archie Jr., worked part time for Micheaux Funeral Home. Later she found a permanent job as an elevator operator for the Grand Leader's (Stillman's Department Store). Promoted to Elevator Starter, she maintained this position until she retired. She was active in Sunday school as a teacher and superintendent for over 50 years. She served several terms as secretary of the local NAACP.

Their older son, Archie, graduated from the Indiana School of Mortuary Science in Indianapolis. He practiced for several years in Gary, Indiana but later decided to switch to the insurance business. Archie is the father of Kellee who became the first black Miss Indiana, while a student at Indiana University (Bloomington) in 1971.

Charles, the third son, was a graduate of Antioch College and Western Reserve University. He pursued post graduate work at U.C. (Berkeley). He was the first African-American to be awarded a fellowship by the Institute of Current World Affairs which allowed him to study at Cambridge University and later teach and study at Ibadan University in Nigeria. Of all the children, he had the most diverse career: serving as the Deputy Director of the Peace Corps for Africa, the first black major airline executive, and CEO of the Oakland Convention Center. Among his many volunteer activities he served as Chairman of the Board of the San Francisco Foundation for a number of years. Wounded and recuperating black soldiers from the European Theater were assigned to a base in South Carolina. At first black soldiers were given a bus to transport them wherever they had to go. This arrangement did not last very long. Black soldiers were told they would have to share the bus with white soldiers. As the black soldiers boarded the bus, they were told to move to the rear. They refused, and when ordered out at gunpoint, they turned the bus over. Although a war hero, Charles was now faced with the possibility of being court martialed and dishonorably discharged. It was through the intervention of Congressman E. Ross Adair that he was honorably discharged.

The youngest son, Francis, decided on a career with the steel industry and, under the auspice of Joslyn Stainless Steel Mill, he became the first African-American foreman. He remained there until his untimely death in 1991. Francis was both active in his community, church and lodge.

Throughout their life span the family continued to be involved in church and community affairs and served in many different leadership roles. It was clear to daughter, Jacqueline, at an early age that she would follow a similar path. She retired in 1993 after 32 years of service at the local, regional and national Urban League.

Submitted by Jacqueline J. Patterson

PHILIP ROBERT JOHNSON FAMILY

Philip Robert Johnson was the first son of Robert P. and Mary Angela Johnson. He was born August 3, 1952, at Memorial Hospital, Decatur, Indiana. After moving several times prior to his entering elementary school, his parents purchased a home at 2727 Plaza Drive, in Fort Wayne, Indiana. He lived there until 1975 when he married and purchased his first home at 4719 Karen Avenue, in Fort Wayne.

Philip attended Saint Hyacinth's Elementary School. For two years he attended Central Catholic High School and then graduated from South Side High School in 1970. He started working for the railroad industry in 1971 and worked for Penn Central Railroad and Conrail for 22 years.

He married Jayne Ellen Froebe on May 5, 1975. They had one daughter, Katie Ann, born May 11, 1981. Their marriage ended in 1983. He then purchased a home on Linker Road in rural Columbia City, Indiana.

In 1985 he met Janine Ellen Baermann and on August 29, 1987, they were married in Churubusco, Indiana. They had a son, Eric Robert, born May 23, 1989. The marriage ended in divorce in 1997.

Philip Robert Johnson

Philip invested in real estate throughout the state of Indiana and bought property in Brown County, Indiana. In 1999 he met Denise Lewis in Vincennes, Indiana, and they make their home at the Brown County property they purchased together.

Philip's interests include auto racing, ice hockey, real estate, and politics. He has attended the Daytona 500 annually for 35 years. Philip and Denise enjoy traveling, with Las Vegas and Florida among their favorite destinations.

Katie Ann, Philip's daughter, has lived with Josh Vanderbousch for five years and they have purchased a home on King Street in Garrett, Indiana. They have two sons, Jalen Joshua born November 20, 2001, and Kameron David born June 18, 2003. Katie attends IPFW studying art. She is employed at Kitchen Supply in Fort Wayne, Indiana.

Eric Robert is a freshman at Columbia City High School. He lives with his mother and stepfather in the same home since birth on Linker Road. Eric is active in basketball, track, his church youth group, and enjoys playing guitar.

Submitted by Philip Robert Johnson

ROBERT PHILIP JOHNSON & MARY ANGELA SHEEHAN FAMILY

Robert Philip Johnson (Bob) was the fourth child of Ben and Ollie Schlemmer Johnson. He was born February 19, 1924, near Monroeville, Indiana. As a child he attended Monroeville Elementary and High School. After graduation, as World War II was at its height, he joined the Army Air Corps and served in the South Pacific as a pilot. He graduated from Tri-State University, Angola, with a degree in aeronautical engineering.

In 1949 he met Mary Angela Sheehan (goes by Angela) at a dance and they were married July 1, 1950, at St. Rose Catholic Church, Monroeville. They had eight children: Kathleen Marie (1951), Philip Robert (1952), Deborah Ann (July 11, 1954), Patricia Sue (June 17, 1957), Gregory Allen (April 26, 1959), Douglas Edward (February 16, 1961), Bennett Lynn (February 23, 1963), and Rodney Lee (April 22, 1967). They lived on Plaza Drive in the south part of Fort Wayne.

Bob and Angela Johnson

Bob had a creative mind and used his engineering degree to good advantage. He invented an electric pencil sharpener and secured a patent for it. He also started his own plastic seal company, United Products Company. After seeing it on the road to success, he sold it to an Ohio company. He then went into the real estate business and established Johnson Real Estate, which he owned at the time of his death. He loved family vacations and camping through the United States. At one point he owned his own airplane. He loved being around the lakes and water sports. Being competitive, he liked winning at cards and all other games. Bob developed a brain tumor in 1974 and died May 27, 1975. He is buried in IOOF Cemetery, Monroeville, Indiana.

Angela was the first child of Irvin and Alberta Sheehan. She was born October 18, 1929, in Fort Wayne Indiana. She spent her formative years in the Monroeville area. Her first year of school was spent in a one-room schoolhouse on Tillman Road. Moving into Monroeville with her family, she attended St. Joseph Catholic School. After another move, she attended St. Louis Catholic Elementary School. She then graduated from Hoagland High School in 1947.

During the war years Angela worked at Magnavox in the summer, and after graduation she was employed by International Harvester. After her marriage she spent the early years raising her family. Later she worked at Art Iron, United Products and, after Bob's death, at Lincoln National Life for 18 years. She also worked part time at Kohl's Department store for eight years.

At the time of Bob's death seven children were still home. Kathleen had married. The youngest, Rodney, was eight. Within the year, Philip had married, Deborah moved into her own apartment, and Patricia joined the Army. In 1979 Angela sold the house on Plaza Drive and, along with the four sons remaining at home, moved across from Parkview Hospital on State Street where she lived over 20 years. She then moved to the Georgetown area, where she still lives. She is an active member of St. Jude Catholic Church.

Submitted by Mary Angela Sheehan Johnson

RODNEY LEE JOHNSON

Rodney Lee was the eighth and last child born to Robert P. and Mary Angela Sheehan Johnson. He was born at Adams County Memorial Hospital, Decatur, Indiana, on April 22, 1967. At that time the family home was at 2717 Plaza Drive, Fort Wayne, Indiana. His father died in 1975. In 1979 his mother, along with the four sons remaining at home, moved to a house across from Parkview Hospital on State Street.

Rodney started school at Sacred Heart Catholic School, and then went to Junior High at Lakeside Middle School. He graduated from North Side High School. In high school he played varsity football and was on the hockey team.

Rodney Lee Johnson

After graduation he started working at Kinney Shoe Company in Glenbrook Mall, and then transferred to their store in the Northcrest Shopping Center. When that store closed, he was assigned to the Georgetown store, where he was manager. A transfer took him to Toledo, Ohio. At that time he met Shawn Marie Destatte from Temperance, Michigan, who was an assistant manager at the Gap Store. They were married at St. Jude Catholic Church in Fort Wayne, Indiana, on March 23, 1991.

At the outbreak of Desert Storm, he enlisted in the Air Force. He took his basic training at Lockland Air Force Base in Texas. The war was over before basic training was completed. His first assignment was Chanute Air Force Base in Rantoul, Illinois. He was then stationed at Wright Patterson Base, Dayton, Ohio. While in the service, Rodney and Shawn had two daughters, Emily Marie (November 29, 1991) and Amy Catherine (April 23, 1993).

Upon leaving the service, the family returned to Fort Wayne, Indiana, and moved in with his mother. They lived with her nine months and then bought a home near her at 2427 Leroy Avenue, where they still live. Rodney obtained employment at Dana Corporation in Syracuse, Indiana, and Shawn continued to work at the Gap in Glenbrook Square until their third child, Erin Leanne (October 4, 1996) was born. She then stayed home to take care of her growing family. They had two more children, Mary Kate (June 22, 1999) and Robert Philip (August 3, 2000). The children are in elementary and pre-school and attend St. Jude Catholic School.

When Dana closed their Syracuse plant, Rodney worked for Advance-Trex and started a part-time lawn service. Shawn obtained employment at Vera Bradley Corporation.

This family's roots date to the early settlers of Monroe Township, Allen County, Indiana, - the Johnson, Schlemmer, Sheehan, and Geis families.

Submitted by Shawn Johnson

LUTHER HAMLIN JOHNSTON & FANNIE M (BINKLEY)

Luther Hamlin Johnston was born June 16, 1866 and died June 5, 1943. Fannie M. Binkley was born January 12, 1872, and died November 3, 1958. Luther's parents were Wesley Johnston, born in 1842 and died in 1928, and Martha (McKee) born 1843 and died in 1886. Fannie's parents were Levi Binkley, born 1847, died 1930, and Mary A. (Kreiger) born 1847, died 1910.

They had seventeen children: Edgar Levi, April 5, 1895 - June 13, 1963; Lewis McKinley, April 25, 1896 - October 10, 1958; Martha Faye (McComb), August 30, 1897 - November 19, 1996; James Hamlin, 1898 - 1997; Cleo May (McComb), October 16, 1900 - April 18, 1997; Lois Josphine (McColley), May 30, 1902 - October 2, 1998; Luther Kenneth, August 18, 1903 - May 12, 1983; Grace Ilene (Smith), May 30, 1906 - October 22, 2003; Blanche Irene (Smith), May 30, 1906 - May 9,1999; Perry Clifford, June 12, 1908 - July 16, 1987; Florence Geneva (Kruse), February 12, 1910 - November 2, 1990; Helen Virginna (Henry), September 3, 1914; Ellen Majorie (Bligh), September 3, 1914; Robert Gerald, June 9, 1917 - March 29, 1999.

Three children died: Floyd Cecil, born in1899, died November 25, 1899; Mary, December 28, 1905 to March 29, 1906; Bazel, March 17, 1912, died in 1913.

Submitted by Russell Ott

GUY A. JONES

According to old family records, Guy A. Jones' paternal great-great-grandfather, Johnny Jones, and his family migrated from around Guilford County, North Carolina, in the mid 1840s. They, along with several other free African American families, made the trip and settled in northeastern Indiana.

Guy was born in Fort Wayne, Indiana, on November 16, 1926, in a then rural section of the city. At that time it was referred to as the "Rolling Mill"; it is now known as "Westfield". It had been called the Rolling Mill because it was the early site of Jocelyn steel mill. He had two sisters, Elizabeth Katherine Jones, born September 20, 1925, and Darlene Jones, born December 11, 1931. Their parents were Guy William Jones and Virgin Marie Peak Jones.

Virgin Marie Peak's father, Moses Mack Peak, was born in Logansport, Indiana, in 1884. Her mother was Corriene Duncan, born in Kentucky. Guy Williams' father is unknown, but his maternal great-grandfather was Isiah Jones, born in North Carolina and the son of above mentioned Johnny Jones. His mother was Goldie Jones Stewart of Marion, Indiana.

Darlene married Robert Hatcher and they had four children: Lititia Cheray, Daryl Lynn, Robert Hatcher Jr., who changed his name to Kamari O. Mbwelera, and Kimberly Sue Hatcher. Their father Robert, hired by the Fort Wayne Police Department in the mid 1950s, was the first African American motorcycle police officer in Fort Wayne. Darlene graduated from Central High School. While there she became the first African American female to become a member of the Central High School Drum Corp. She retired from Magnavox Corporation in 1987.

Elizabeth moved to Chicago and worked at the famed Michael Reese Hospital. Later, after serving in the military, she moved to Washington and was employed by the Civil Service Commission, from which she retired.

Guy started school in 1931 at Justin Study Elementary in Westfield, but before completing the first grade the family moved into the central city, onto Hayden Street near the old Gay Street Bridge.

Their father, Guy William Jones, suffered from a recurring illness, which required frequent and long periods of hospitalization. As a result, he returned to the homestead in Marion, Indiana, and came under the care of his mother, Goldie Jones Stewart. He died in 1953. Virgin Marie and the children remained in Fort Wayne and ultimately moved to 718 Hugh Street. The children continued their education at Harmar Elementary School. In 1935 Virgin contracted tuberculosis and was sent to the Irene Byron Sanitarium on Lima Road, the hospital utilized for the many tuberculosis patients of the 1930s. The children were sent to the Allen County Children's Home, also on Lima Road, just a short distance from the sanitarium. The mother succumbed while the children were still at the Allen County Children's Home. Some years later they were sent to different foster homes.

Guy went to join the Huggins family. Eliza Huggins was a kind and loving woman and Guy was enrolled at James H. Smart Elementary School. While there, he played on both the softball and basketball teams. In 1941 he graduated from James Smart and enrolled at Central High School. Mr. Huggins died in 1942 and Guy was returned to the children's home.

He later found a home with the Romilda Elizabeth Jones Cunegin family and was able to return to Central High School. Although Romilda Cunegin's maiden name was Jones, and she and Virgin Jones were close friends, there is no evidence to establish a familial relationship. Romilda had three sons and one daughter of her own: Clifford the oldest, Michael the same age as Guy, Paul, and Ester. In addition, the family included "Grandmother," who was the mother of Romilda's late husband, and Charles Lee Cammack, her nephew. "Grandmother" was a tiny woman with long silky gray hair who had an infectious smile that made one feel happy at any time.

Charles Lee Cammack was full of vitality and was a kind and inquisitive eleven-year-old boy. He grew up, married Sarah Jackson, and had four sons. One of his sons became a vice president at Lincoln National Life Insurance Company in Fort Wayne. After Charles retired from International Harvester, he and his son established Cammack and Sons, a well-known electronic security business operating throughout Indiana. His sons were outstanding track athletes in both high school and college.

Michael Cunegin and Guy, about the same age, became very close and considered themselves as brothers. Michael served in the United States Coast Guard, raised a family, and ultimately retired from B.F. Goodrich Corporation. One of his sons became a well-respected Republican and was active at the state level.

Paul Cunegin went on to earn a Ph.D. in psychology from Boston University and became one of the few native Fort Wayne persons of either race to acquire a Ph.D. in the early 1970s.

As a member of this family, Guy developed his philosophy on life and enjoyed his final high school years. In his last two years at Central he was the starting left halfback on the football team. He helped lead his team to city runner up in 1944 and the city championship in1945. He was selected to the All-city team and received honorable mention for All-state football team. His teammates elected him team captain and he received the coveted gold captain's stripe. He was also a member of the track team as a high jumper and hurdler.

Upon graduation in June 1946 , Guy joined the U. S. Navy and took basic training at the United States Training Center in Bainbridge, Maryland. At Bainbridge he earned the starting spot on the Bainbridge Commodores football team. Following the football season he joined the basketball team as a first string guard.

As the only African American on either team, he was often subjected to racial slurs and mistreatment at college games. Bainbridge played both colleges and other military teams in Maryland, Virginia, and North Carolina. During bus return trips to the base, none of the restaurants at which they stopped would serve the team sit-down service. This, despite everyone being dressed in full uniform and accompanied by a U.S. States military officer. On one occasion they did receive service, but Guy and the escorting officer were taken to the back and upstairs to a tiny room barely large enough to accommodate the two of them. At one game Guy was asked and required to leave the basketball court before the game started, " because no colored boys had ever played on this court." This happened in the state of Maryland, before the start of a college game. Although he had often had racial epithets yelled at him at events when participating for Central High School in Indiana, he had never suffered the indignity he felt as a military man in the above mentioned states.

In February 1947 he was assigned as a seaman to the USS *Littlerock*, a light cruiser docked at Brooklyn Navy Yard. He immediately became a member of the ship s basketball team and competed around New York prior to departing overseas. In addition to playing against the aircraft carrier team of USS *Midway*, he played in both Italy and Greece, representing the USS *Littlerock*.

Mr. and Mrs. Guy A. Jones

After military service, he enrolled in West Virginia State College and became a member of the freshman basketball team. There he met and became friends with Earl Lloyd, who later became the first African American to play and to coach in the National Basketball Association. Many years later Earl was inducted into the NBA Hall of Fame.

West Virginia State College had an undefeated season and won the CIAA Championship. The following year, on recommendation of his high school coach, Guy received a football scholarship to Drake University in Des Moines, Iowa. He played on the freshman football team, but after the first semester transferred out and later joined a professional basketball touring team similar to the Harlem Globetrotters. It was a team organized and operated by one of the original Globetrotters and was named the Harlem Aces. He played on the team in the Canadian cities of Ottawa, Montreal, Sherbrooke, Shawinigan, Trois-Rivers, and Quebec. They performed in cities along the U.S. east coast, and as far west as Pine Bluff, Arkansas, and as far southwest as Houston Texas. Guy left the team as they were preparing to tour Mexico.

In a final flourish to his basketball days he was given a tryout for the Washington Capitols, forerunners to the NBA. After that tryout he returned to college to finish his education at Howard University in Washington, D.C .

In June 1951 Guy traveled to Boston, Massachusetts, and married Audrey Lorraine Reese, whom he had met while a student at West Virginia State College in 1948. She was born in Darlington, South Carolina, and raised in New York and Massachusetts. Her father, Lawrence Reese, and her mother, Juanita Johnson Reese, were born in Darlington and had been childhood sweethearts.

Audrey's paternal grandfather was also named Lawrence Reese, but he hailed from Marlboro County in South Carolina. He became a well-respected builder after he moved to Darlington, South Carolina, in 1885 . He built some 14 antebellum style houses on West Broad Street in Darlington, which became locally known as Reeses Row. They are all listed in the National Registry of Historic Places. He is listed in *African American Architects, A Biographical Dictionary 1865-1945*. He taught his son, Lawrence Reese, the trade and he became a well-respected master carpenter in Boston, Massachussetts. Audrey's mother, Juanita Johnson Reese, was a schoolteacher in Darlington.

Audrey followed in her mother's footsteps. She was awarded a fellowship and earned a masters' degree in education. She became a staff development teacher and retired from the District of Columbia school system. Guy and Audrey had one son, Guy Lawrence, who attended Howard University for a short period and was proficient in playing four musical instruments. He was a member of the well-known Howard University Marching Band. He died in 1987. In 1953 Guy received a bachelors degree with a major in business from Howard University. As a student he became the vice president of the Business Club and was elected president of Alph Phi Omega chapter at Howard. He and his wife have resided in Washington, D.C. over 50 years.

Guy A. Jones' work history includes employment with Mutual of Omaha, the federal government, Howard University Small Business Guidance and Development Center, and Northwest Settlement House where he served as the executive director and completed his full-time work career. His volunteer and community work has included chairmanship of Neighborhood Planning Council Number 7, chairmanship of Youth Committee of Lamond Riggs Civic Association, volunteer work with local Boy Scouts, director of Project Men, deputy foreman of a federal grand jury in Washington D.C., a member of Washington D.C. Mayor's Committee on Drug Abuse, and national president of Frontiers International Inc.

Submitted by Guy A. Jones

IVO CARL & GERALDINE KESSLER JONES

Geraldine Kessler was born in Auburn, Indiana, on December 14, 1920 and moved to Whitley County as a child. She graduated from Churubusco High School in 1939, and moved to Fort Wayne in 1940. Ivo Carl Jones was born September 6, 1919 in Whitley County. He

Ivo and Geraldine Kessler Jones

entered the U.S. Army on January 26, 1942, serving as a radio technician and repairman. Ivo and Geraldine were married in Columbia City on June 7, 1944 while he was still in the service. After Ivo was discharged on January 13, 1946, they lived with Gerry's older sister on Scott Avenue until they were able to move into their own home.

Ivo's older brother, Virgil, and his wife, Marie, had bought a home on Eastway Drive in Wild Rose Addition in December 1944. Virgil and Ivo were the first generation to leave the family farm in Whitley County to move to Fort Wayne in search of employment. Gerry and Ivo bought their first home on East Rudisill Boulevard in Wild Rose Addition, three blocks from Virgil and Marie's house. Soon after remodeling their first home, Gerry and Ivo bought the house next door. Because of his carpentry skills, Ivo not only completed extensive renovations to the new house but helped his brother remodel his home as well. Back then, Wild Rose Addition was about a mile outside the city limits. Each home had a well or cistern and a septic tank. To save on the cost of well repairs, several men in the neighborhood bought a "well rig" so they could help each other do their own well repairs.

Gerry and Ivo's three children were born while they lived on East Rudisill. They are: Larry Wayne Jones, born November 8, 1948; Barbara Jones Sommer, born January 10, 1953; and Kathleen Jones Myers, born April 13, 1956. Because they lived in the same neighborhood, they spent a lot of time with their three cousins, Virgil and Marie's daughters.

Ivo was employed as a carpenter with Shirmeyer Homes for several years before going into business for himself. His brother, Virgil, died unexpectedly of a heart attack on May 14, 1958. In 1960, Ivo build their new home in Northcrest Woods. He lived there until his unexpected death from a heart attack on February 18, 1981. His widow, Gerry, continued to live in that home until her death on May 5, 1997. Her youngest daughter, Kathy, lived in a number of places around the country after graduating from Northrop High School. Kathy came home to care for her mother during her final illness. She continued to live in the home that her father built until after her daughter, Laura's, graduation from Northrop High School in 2003. She now works as a nurse in San Diego, California. Her brother, Larry, and his sister, Barbara, live in Illinois. All six cousins who grew up in Wild Rose Addition have moved away from the Fort Wayne area.

Submitted by Sue Lewis

JOHN JONES FAMILY

John Jones was born August 8, 1795, in England or Wales. He was the son of Benjamin and Sarah (Cadwallader) Jones. John Jones married Mary Humphreys who was born October 20, 1795, in England or Wales. Mary was the daughter of Edward and Ann (Evans) Humphreys. John and Mary Jones came to America about 1841 and settled for a time in Tarrytown, New York. They had followed their son, Benjamin, to this country. After a couple of years they all came to Allen County, Indiana, and settled in Lake Township. Mary Humphreys Jones died August 18, 1855, and is buried in the Hatfield Cemetery. John Jones died April 10, 1876, and is also buried in the Hatfield Cemetery. The following are the four children of John and Mary Jones.

Benjamin Jones, born about 1820 in Montgomeryshire, North Wales. Benjamin married May 18, 1872, in Allen County, Indiana, (Book 8 page 549) to Sarah C. Carroll, who was born June 18, 1844, in Zanesville, Ohio. They adopted a girl, Mary Ann or Alice, born in 1875 and died November 16, 1893. Benjamin died May 29, 1895, in Allen County, Indiana. Sarah died in 1906 in Allen County, Indiana, and both are buried in the Hatfield Cemetery.

Mary Jones, born October 30, 1825, in Welshpool, Montgomeryshire, North Wales, married Albert Garrison who was born about 1820 in Tarrytown, New York. Mary died about 1886 in Fort Wayne, Allen County, Indiana, and Albert died in 1889 in Fort Wayne, Allen County, Indiana. Both are buried in Lindenwood Cemetery, Fort Wayne. Mary and Albert's children were: Mary Elizabeth Garrison, born in 1844 in Tarrytown, New York. She died October 7, 1920, in Fort Wayne, Indiana; John H. Garrison, born in 1846 married Janet Hislop, who was born in 1845 in Edinburgh, Scotland. John died in 1921 and Janet died in 1929; and Charles Albert Garrison, no information.

Ann Jones, born March 10, 1828, in Welshpool, Montgomeryshire, North Wales, married September 12, 1847, in Allen County, Indiana, to William Darby. Their information is in this book under the section with the Darby Family of Allen County, Indiana.

John Jones, Jr., born November 17, 1835, in Montgomeryshire, North Wales. John was in the Civil War. He married November 1, 1866, in Allen County, Indiana, (Book 6 page 438) to Ada Taylor, who was born in 1847 in Ohio. John, Jr. died January 29, 1914, in Fort Wayne. Ada died prior to October 1912. Both are buried in Lindenwood Cemetery, Fort Wayne, Indiana. They had seven children: Oliver S. Jones, Eva J. Jones, John Lincoln Jones, Benjamin F. Jones, Mary E. Jones, Charles E. Jones, and Ada T. Jones.

Sources: 1850, 1860, 1870, 1880, and 1900 census Allen County, Indiana; Will of John Jones, Jr. 1912 proved April 6, 1914; *Pictorial History of Fort Wayne, Indiana* by B. J. Griswold 1917; *Allen County, Indiana Marriage Record Books*; *WPA Index to Death Records, Allen County 1896-1920*; *Valley of the Upper Maumee River* by Robertson 1889; *Index to Allen County, Indiana, Marriages*; and *Allen County, Indiana, Deed Book #66* pages 169-170.

Submitted by Shelley Darby

JAMES "JIM" JOYNER,

"A MAN ON THE MOVE"

James Joyner was born in Farmsville, North Carolina, to Bert and Pearl Joyner. Bert was a farmer. James was drafted in the United States Army in 1942 from New York City, New York. Upon completion of basic training, he was assigned to Baer Field in Fort Wayne, Indiana. He served the military from September 1942 until January 12, 1946 at Baer Field as Mess Sergeant.

At the time of his honorable discharge from the service, his rank was Staff Sergeant. Joyner remained in Fort Wayne after the military. He began civilian life at the 113 Club, as Chef/Cook, and subsequently married Antwerp, Ohio native, Mary Louise Thomas on June 16, 1945. Their children are Dianne Louise Hairston, James Richard, John Thomas, Deborah Lynn, Donald Bert, Michael Allen and Eric Joseph Joyner. James served as Deputy Sheriff under Mayor Zeis from 1948-1955.

James Joyner, last person on the right of the first row, taken at Baer Field

Not content to work for someone else, Joyner was soon ready to venture out on his own. In 1948, he opened the Hollywood Bar and Grill at 1333 South Lafayette Street. The establishment featured different solo and group entertainers weekly and broadcast the shows live on radio.

In 1956, he opened a drive-in ice cream and sandwich shop at 1328 South Lafayette Street. In 1962, Joyner opened the Hollywood Restaurant at 1116 Maumee Avenue. It was at this location that he specialized in BBQ ribs, shrimp, chicken, and frog legs. He also had a restaurant at 1027 Maumee Street, which primarily served carry out meals. He opened the 1030 Club, located at 1030 Maumee. A fire forced the closing of that location which resulted in the opening of the Hollywood Ballroom in 1963, just a block away.

It was at this location that Joyner, inspired by his own love of music, again began bringing live name entertainment to the community. Included were the likes of Ellington, Count Basie, Ike & Tina Turner, the Ohio Players, Fats Domino, and others. It was a time that many local residents recall with great fondness.

Sadly, failing health caused the closing of Joyner's business. After becoming successful in business he never forgot his humble upbringing as a poor child in the south. He shared his success with many disadvantaged people in Fort Wayne.

Jim Joyner will always be remembered for his leadership, entrepreneurial ideas and the interest he took in the community. He did his best to make Fort Wayne a better and more enjoyable place to live.

Submitted by Deborah Lynn

KAADE & KEEN FAMILIES

Descendants have a huge responsibility. Not only must they understand themselves well enough to live, work, and give to their present-day world, but they must also understand and learn from their past in order to help build a community's future. Parents, grandparents, great-grandparents and great-great grandparents make the job much easier. When a family's history is recorded, preserved and communicated with pictures, news articles, jewelry, fashion, music, letters, achievements, awards, testimonials, stories, and oral recollections of many family celebrations, one's direction in life is so much easier to choose.

Robert Louis Kaade and Velma Pauline Keen were two Fort Wayne natives whose family histories and beliefs challenged their desire to marry in 1940. Velma graduated high school from Saint Catherine's Academy in 1932 and went right to work at NIPSCO where she met Robert in the Sales Department. Robert (Bob) was a North Side honor student and cheerleader, received a scholarship to attend DePauw University, graduated magna cum laude in 1935, and eventually worked his way up to Division Manager of NIPSCO in the early 1950s. Besides their love and natural attraction to one another, they shared another bond, which would eventually be passed on to their three children, their grandchildren, and now their great-grandchildren.

Bob was a natural born performer and leader. Velma was a classical pianist. At Saint Catherine's the nuns nurtured Velma's God-given musical talents. But the one bond they did not share was a common faith. In Fort Wayne in the 1940s it was not easy for a young woman to marry outside of her faith. Velma's decision to marry Bob outside of the Catholic Church was a subject of much discussion, family frustration; and yet the beauty of the story's ending is one of complete cooperation if one accepts the existing ecumenical spirit of 2005 in the Fort Wayne and Allen County communities.

Velma's parents' achievements speak for themselves. Mild-mannered, humble, quiet Ruth Doyle Keen from rural roots, mother of Velma, James, and Virginia, supported her husband's many creative sparks. He was a ventriloquist. His sidekick Johnny is still in the family. One of Chester's grandchildren has preserved the dummy's character, appearance and name, and all of Ruth and Chester's grandchildren expect to see him regularly at family gatherings.

Chester Keen has been recognized many times as Fort Wayne's "radio pioneer." Chester became interested enough in radio in 1919 to start his own radio station, WCWK and be the first to successfully transmit a signal. (Example: He broadcast the Cathedral's Midnight Mass at an early date - this detail could be verified through Cathedral records.) In the same way, the Internet and the World Wide Web continue to stir and ignite the imaginations of many creators,

Chester's faith, integrity, and indomitable spirit propelled him into a world of technical communications. To think that his simple design and 100 watt radio station, located on the second floor of an auto supply store at 1729 South Lafayette, would grow into the powerful Westinghouse Broadcasting Company, was a dream that his three children and their descendants lived to see. Chester even took the time to tell about his ideas, developing plans, and his feelings of loss during the Depression in his diary called *Homeward Bound*, another family treasure. While Chester witnessed the positives of radio and television in shows like *The Lone Ranger* (1933) and *Kukla, Fran, and Ollie* (1947), he also predicted broadcasting's power. One quote from his diary documents Chester's foresight because his prediction did come true. *When I started this station, radio was still in the red, but I enjoyed the brutal punishment, as I could see some day it would be a wonderful medium to raise Hell with, and radio will be the means of causing more trouble to the people than anything that God ever created. (diary entries were recorded 1919-1929)*

(Complete timeline of history of Fort Wayne radio can be accessed at www.wowo.com.)

In 1990, the Allen County Board of Commissioners named a street after Chester Keen, not just for his work in radio, but also because he was a cofounder of the Home Loan Savings, President of the Indiana Home Owners Association, and Chairman of the Ward Peace Council. Keen Place is in the Windmill Ridge subdivision of Allen County.

Robert's parents' achievements also speak for themselves. Herman Frederick Kaade was born in 1889 to father Ferdinand and mother Wilhelmina Stellhorn, both of whom had emigrated from Germany around 1880. He was one of seven children. Some of Ferdinand and Wilhelmina's descendants still live in and around Fort Wayne. Very proud of his German Lutheran background, Herman Frederick Kaade was a leader. He married Cecilia Gick and, after Robert's birth in 1913, they had Donald and Bonsilene; all children were born and raised in Fort Wayne.

With his wife's support, Herman founded, directed and operated a thriving lumber business in the 40s and 50s, Standard Lumber Company. As a stockholder in his own company and the Grabill Bank, he also gave generously of his time to the community. The Jewish community valued his musicianship as a cantor at the Temple. The larger Fort Wayne community honored him for his work spent leading the Plan Commission from 1947-1957. Upon his death in 1957, Herman was recognized for "unselfish duty, and unfailing loyalty to the Plan Commission" in a special proclamation to the city of Fort Wayne. Mr. Kaade also served on the Allen County Library Board. In fact, one of his seven grandchildren preserved a special book he received at the Allen County Library by recording and adapting some songs from *The Children's Music Box*, copyright 1945 by Paul Francis Webster and Frank E. Churchill. Herman and Cecilia Gick Kaade's grandchildren grew up singing these songs, and to this day, their great and great-great grandchildren are fond of two or three of the songs.

All the descendants of the Keens and the Kaades have much to be proud of. This family history is one of originality, risk-taking, leadership, community service, faith, and using God-given talent for the good of others. More importantly, like their parents and ancestors, they have opportunities every day to preserve and pass on their family's high standards to help build a better world.

Brief Keen, Kaade Genealogy

Chester W. and Ruth (Doyle) Keen were the parents of Velma Pauline (Keen) Kaade, James Keen, and Virginia (Keen) Murnane. Herman Frederick and Cecilia (Gick) Kaade were the parents of Robert Louis Kaade, Donald Kaade and Bonsilene (Kaade) Thompson.

Bob and Velma (Keen) Kaade are the parents of Sondra "Sunny" (Kaade) Miller of San Diego, Connie (Kaade) Anderson of Frisco, Colorado and Thomas Fredrick Kaade of South Bend.

Sunny and her husband, Bob Miller, are the parents of six children: Cheryl (Miller) Killingsworth who has four children and lives in Valencia, California; Christopher Miller who has one child and lives in San Diego; Kimberly (Miller) Dibble who has two children and lives in San Diego); Kevin Miller who lives in Honolulu, Bradley Miller who has one child and lives in San Diego; and Ryan Miller who lives in Honolulu.

Connie and Bruce Anderson have two children, Lindsay C. Anderson who has one child and lives in Chicago, and Haven Anderson who lives in Indianapolis.

Tom and Jan (Osborne) Kaade are the parents of Matthew Kaade of South Bend. They have these children from other marriages: Karah (Kaade) Palmer of Fort Wayne who has two children; Kimberly (Kaade) Hicks of Indianapolis who has one child; and Christopher Osborne Kaade, adopted, who has one child.

Submitted by Connie Kaade Anderson second daughter to Bob and Velma Kaade

**Please see page 760 for Kaade/Keen family photos*

JOHN KAISER & AUGUSTA (GALLMEYER) KAISER

John Kaiser and Augusta Gallmeyer were married Thanksgiving Day, November 26, 1908 at Zion Lutheran Church (Friedheim) in Adams County. They made their home along the Yoder Road in Allen County.

John Kaiser was the son of Ernest Kaiser and Amanda Miller. His mother, Amanda, was the daughter of John and Mary Miller of Washington Township, Whitley County. Amanda had one brother, John, and one sister, Mary. Mary was married to William Kaiser, a brother to Ernest.

John Kaiser had one brother, Frank, who served as his best man. Frank married Frieda Hockemeyer and was employed at National Mill as a salesman. The couple lived on Tacoma Avenue in Fort Wayne and were members of

Wedding photograph of John Kaiser and Augusta Gallmeyer

Emmaus Lutheran Church. Frank and Frieda had one daughter, Judie. Amanda Miller Kaiser was living with her son, Frank, when she passed away in 1940.

Augusta (Gallmeyer) Kaiser was the daughter of Friederich and Johanna Gallmeyer. Friederich was born in the U.S. (1842-1925) to immigrant parents from Germany, Conrad Gallmeier and Christine Kreft. Johanna (1842-1906) came to this country in 1870 from Germany with her brother Diedrich on the ship *Rhein*. Friederich and Johanna were members of Zion Lutheran Church (Friedheim) and raised their family on a farm along the Adams-Wells County line. Augusta had two brothers, Friederich and August.

Amanda Miller Kaiser with grandchildren, Clarence and Lillian Kaiser

John and Augusta Kaiser raised three children: Clarence, Lillian, and Raymond. The family were members of St. John Lutheran Church (Bingen) in Adams County. Lillian would later in life reminisce about taking the interurban that ran from Fort Wayne to Decatur to school and once playing Martha Washington in the school pageant. Lillian attended grades one through seven at St. John's parochial school and spent her eighth grade year at the public school in Poe.

Clarence Kaiser (1910-1940) married Lucille Busche. He worked at John Dahner Construction as a watchman and lived on Broadway in Fort Wayne. Clarence died from pneumonia. There were no children.

Lillian Kaiser (1912-1999) married Gustav Fuelling (1905-1965). Gustav played the violin as a member of "The Hoosier Eagles," performing at area barn dances. They raised their family in Adams County north of Decatur on a farm and were members of St. Peter Lutheran Church. Their two children were Wilmer and Beverly.

Beverly Fuelling graduated from Monmouth High School as class valedictorian and graduated from International Business College. She worked at General Electric in Fort Wayne before marrying Ervin Werling in 1965. They had two children, Randall and Julie, and two grandchildren, Ryan and Cecily Werling.

Raymond Kaiser, born in 1917, never married. He graduated from Lafayette Central High School and worked at Marrietta Construction Company in Waynedale. He passed away in 1975 from lung cancer.

John Kaiser died from throat cancer in 1941. His wife, Augusta, passed away in 1970 while living with her son, Raymond, in Waynedale. At that time she attended Mount Calvary Lutheran Church, which was near her home. She is buried with her two sons and husband at St. John's Lutheran Church (Bingen) Cemetery.

Submitted by Julie Werling

PETER & JOHANNA KATHERINE MANSDORFER KALLEN FAMILY

George Jacob Mansdorfer sailed from Havre, France, on the ship *Eastern Queen* with two of his sisters, Catharine and Julianna. They arrived in New York on May 10, 1852. George married Hannah Questera on August 7, 1854 in Reading, Pennsylvania. Their daughter, Johanna Katherine, was born June 25, 1855.

In 1860 he left his wife Hannah and came to Allen County with Johanna. Obtaining a divorce in Bluffton, Indiana, he then married Lisetta Kline on March 10, 1865. George and Lisetta had nine children: George Jacob Jr., Henry Phillip, Ernest Henry, Anna Dorothy, Caroline Mary, Charles, Kate Mary, Lewis, and Emma. Lisetta Kline

Johanna Katherine Mansdorfer Kallen and Peter Kallen.

Mansdorfer died July 29, 1881, after her dress caught fire from their cook stove. George Jacob Mansdorfer Sr. died September 16, 1894.

On March 10, 1874 Johanna Katherine Mansdorfer married Peter Kallen in Fort Wayne. Peter was born July 2, 1848. He worked as a Sawyer for J. C. Peters Company, a sawmill. Later he owned a grocery store where most of their children worked. The grocery was on Richardson, the same street where they lived. Peter was also an inventor and had two patents for a chum. The seven Kallen children were Katherine Elizabeth, Matilda Johanna, Louise Sophia, Sophia Katherine, Charles Peter, Caroline Marie, and Ruth Anna Marie.

Katherine Elizabeth Kallen was born March 15, 1875, in Woodburn. Kate married Franklin John Archer November 4, 1903. They had one child, Katherine Louise. After Frank died in 1934, Kate married Henry Lenz.

Matilda Johanna Kallen, born November 3, 1877, married Albert Russell Howard and moved to Norwalk, Ohio. They had two children: Chloe Ruth and Albert Peter.

Louise Sophia Kallen was born March 30, 1878, and married Elmer E. Miller of Wells County, Indiana, July 16, 1899. They lived in Arcola.

Sophia Katherine Kallen, born October 12, 1879, married Christian Theodore Kiefer on October 30, 1901. They had two children: Louise Marie and Hilda Marie Kiefer.

Charles Peter Kallen, born December 19, 1883, was employed at Wayne Knitting Mill. He married Louise Margaret Savio on August 19,

Caroline Kallen Archer, Charles Peter Kallen, Ruth Anna Marie Kallen Wiseley. Seated: Johanna Katherine Mansdorfer Kallen.

1913. They had three children together: Marie Kallen, Helen Kallen, and Ralph Kallen. Both Charles and two-year-old Ralph died of influenza, just fifteen minutes apart, on December 15, 1918.

Caroline Marie Kallen was born March 1, 1892. On March 10, 1915 Carrie married Arthur "Guy" Archer, the brother of Frank Archer and Carrie's sister Kate's husband. They had five children: Carl Arthur, Ruth L., Arthur Kallen, Lula Agnes, and Paul Walter Archer.

Ruth Anna Marie Kallen was born December 18, 1893. She married Waiter Alfred Wiseley of New Haven, Indiana April 15, 1915. Walter worked as a waiter and later as a butcher at Kroger. Ruth was employed at her father's store and at the Wayne Knitting Mill. During World War II she worked at General Electric. Walt and Ruth had four children: Charles Walter, LaDonna Marie, Allen Henry, and Walter Emil "Dude" Wiseley. Peter and Johanna Kallen and all of their children were married at St. John Evangelical Lutheran Church.

Submitted by Kathleen S. Zion

SCOTT & OPAL BANNING KAMPHUES

Scott W. Kamphues was born to Lawrence and Hazel Kamphues on November 18, 1923. He attended McCulloch and Adam's elementary school and graduated from Central High School in 1942. He entered the Navy in November 1942, and served in WWII and on a power ship. After the war he went to work at General Electric and then went to work for Guy Lawrence's packing house. From there he went to work at the Post Office and retired from there in 1983.

While working at General Electric he met and fell in love with Opal Banning from North Webster who was also working at GE. They were married on April 19, 1947, in Simpson United Methodist Church. They were the parents of Marilyn in 1948, who died when about three weeks old, of liver complications. On February 27, 1952, Candy Carolyn was born to them. In 1953 they had their first son, Ricky, who was born with spina bifida. He died after only living a week.

Opal Banning Kamphues was born to Alva and Lena Banning of North Webster on August 10, 1923. She attended North Webster School and then moved to Fort Wayne where she went to work for GE.

Scott's great-grandfather, Joseph Kamphues, immigrated to the U.S. in 1824 from Germany. His

Scott and Opal Kamphues

great-grandmother Mary Anna Goas Kamphues also immigrated to the U.S. from Germany in 1824. Joseph died around 1860 in Dayton Ohio. Mary Ann died in 1907 and is buried in the Catholic Cemetery in Fort Wayne. They were married in September of 1844 in Cincinnati, Ohio.

Scott's grandfather Henry Kamphues, son of Joseph, moved from Dayton to Fort Wayne, Indiana with his mother, Mary Anna, in 1873. Henry married Mary Hugenard in St. Paul's German Catholic Church in the 1890s. Mary died in 1905, before her mother-in-law Mary Anna. Henry Kamphues died in 1928 and is also buried in Catholic Cemetery in Fort Wayne. Lawrence Kamphues, Scott's father, died in 1964.

Scott enjoyed playing golf, hunting, and shooting. He was also a life member of the National Rifle Association.

Opal enjoyed crocheting, cooking, and baking. Primarily, she enjoyed doing things for others. She helped take care of her father-in-law when it was needed.

The Kamphues family made their home on the north east side of Fort Wayne near Parkview Hospital. They resided there into 2005.

Submitted by Scott Kamphues

RUTH LOUISE KANNING

Ruth was born September 27, 1930 in Fort Wayne, Indiana. Ruth's parents were Louis Henry Dietrich Kanning born October 14, 1893 - August 17, 1990, and Dorothea Anna Charlotte (Vonderau) Kanning born February 23, 1893 - died April 9, 1972.

Ruth's paternal grandparents were Henry Kanning, Sr. born May 7, 1848 - died August 18, 1921, and Caroline (Dicke) Kanning born February 8, 1858 - died April 1, 1936. Henry and Caroline Kanning lived on a farm on the Tillman Road, Adams Township, Allen County.

Her maternal grandparents were Herman Vonderau born February 11, 1855 - died November 3, 1941, and Katherine (Griebel)Vonderau born March 13, 1856 - died March 27, 1943. Herman and Katherine lived on a farm on the Parent Road, St. Joe Township, Allen County where her parents, Louis and Dorothea (Dora) were married May 21, 1922, by the Pastor of St. Peter's Lutheran Church (Goeglein).

Her father, Louis, was employed as a letter carrier in Fort Wayne, Indiana from 1920 - 1953. Her mother, Dora, was a homemaker, and Ruth was the only child. She remained single. She graduated from Concordia Lutheran High School June 3, 1948, and began working at the Lincoln National Bank & Trust Co. June 7, 1948. She was employed until January of 1982.

Ruth resides in Fort Wayne, Indiana.

Submitted by Ruth Kanning

ROBERT EMMETT & SHIRLEY KOPP KEARNEY FAMILY

Robert Emmett Kearney was born November 11, 1920, in Pittsburgh, Pennsylvania, the son of Leo Emmett and Margaret Martin Kearney. Leo was born in Medina, New York, and served in the Navy in WWI. Margaret was a registered nurse and was born in Nanticoke, Pennsylvania.

R.E. Kearney family

Leo brought his family to Fort Wayne during the Depression and found work at the Royal Typewriter Company. Leo and Margaret are buried in Medina, New York.

Bob graduated in 1939 from Central Catholic High School in the first graduating class. He was co-editor of the yearbook and an honor student. He was employed at the Allen County Public Library, driving the bookmobile. He attended classes at Indiana University Extension. He enlisted in the Navy in 1941 and was sent to Pensacola, Florida, for boot camp. He was selected for the Officer Candidate V-12 Program and was sent to Milligan College in Tennessee, which had been taken over by the Navy to train naval officers during the war. He was sent to Harvard Business School for Midshipman Officer's Class and then was sent overseas to Guam and the Pacific theatre. He served as an ensign and lieutenant first class in the Supply Corps. His class at Harvard held their 60th reunion September 29, 2005. While he was stationed on Guam, he wrote to Notre Dame, inquiring about attending that university after his discharge. He was accepted and in 1948 he graduated cum laude from Notre Dame with a BS in Commerce. He returned to Fort Wayne and worked for Peter Eckrich Company and for Phelps Dodge as an accountant.

On October 8, 1949, he married Shirley Kopp, who was born July 5, 1921, in Kent, Ohio. Her parents were Lucy Shelter and Frank J. Kopp. Shirley attended St. Mary of the Woods College, earning a BS in nutrition. She completed an internship at Good Samaritan Hospital in Cincinnati, Ohio, and became a registered dietitian in 1944. She was on staff at Johns Hopkins Hospital and taught in its School of Nursing for two years. She returned to Fort Wayne and worked for the American Red Cross in the Regional Blood Bank before her marriage. They have three sons: Kevin Robert, born July 2, 1950; Timothy Robert, born November 15, 1951; and Sean Robert, born May 6, 1957. They graduated from St. Jude's Elementary School, Bishop Dwenger High School and the University of Notre Dame. Kevin has a BS, MS and, through a Fellowship at Yale, he earned a PhD in Chemistry. He is married and has seven children. Timothy earned a BS in electrical engineering at Notre Dame and a Masters at Purdue. He is married and has four children. Sean has a BS in Biology from Notre Dame and is married with one son.

Shirley retired from the VA Hospital, where she was employed as a dietitian for seventeen years. Bob died April 15, 2000, and is buried at Catholic Cemetery. Shirley continues to reside in her home in Glenwood Park.

Submitted by Timothy R. Kearney

KEEFE (O'KEEFE) FAMILY

Dennis Keefe was born in 1805 in County Cork, Ireland. He came to America as a young man and lived in the state of Maryland. His wife's name was Margaret Curtain, also born in Ireland. With their daughter, Bridget, born in 1835 in Maryland, they soon migrated to Indiana. Eventually he purchased or homesteaded 160 acres of farmland in Allen County in Jefferson Township, section 10, just east of New Haven, Indiana. Subsequently, five more children were born; Dennis (1837), Edward (1840), John (1847), Daniel (1849) and Margaret (1854). In the 1870 census, his wife, Margaret, had apparently died and his second wife, Lucinda, is listed as age 51.

In Griswold's book *The History of Ft. Wayne*, it states that Dennis Keefe was a prominent early citizen of Jefferson Township and a staunch supporter for the growth of the township.

His oldest son, Dennis Jr., died April 2, 1864, while serving in the Union Army of the Ohio, 2nd Div., 30th Reg., Co. D at Louisville, Kentucky. His youngest daughter, Margaret (Stutz), died in 1878. His oldest daughter, Bridget (Webster), died in 1884. The remaining children, Edward, John and Daniel are mentioned in his will in 1885.

Dennis Keefe, Sr. died on September 15, 1885. The church burial records list him as a veteran. His second wife, Lucinda, died in 1901.

Edward Keefe circa 1910

They are buried in St. John's Catholic Cemetery, New Haven, Indiana, along with some of their children and grandchildren. There is no record where Margaret, first wife of Dennis, is buried.

Edward Keefe was born September 23, 1840, and was the third of six children born to Dennis and Margaret Keefe. He received his early education in the old Whitney School House in Jefferson Township, a farmer's landmark. He enjoyed telling the story of how he was treed by wolves on the way home from school and was rescued by his father and brother. He worked on his father's farm as a young man. He married Mary Jane Stoneman in 1869. She was born in Pennsylvania in 1845. They had three children: Edward C, born October 12, 1872; Alice Mary, born 1874; and Zoe, born in 1876. He served two terms as the town marshal of New Haven, Indiana, starting in 1879.

The *Fort Wayne Daily Gazette* reported that on May 21, 1879, the New Haven Stave Factory team ran away and collided with a wagon, seriously injuring a man, woman and child. The accident occurred in front of the home of Marshal Edward Keefe of New Haven. His wife was suffering at the time with palpitations of the heart and the scare occasioned her death, which took place later that evening.

Edward never remarried. He inherited half of his father's farm in 1885 and worked until he retired to a home at 2210 Maumee Avenue in Fort Wayne, which he shared with his daughter, Alice Mary. He enjoyed the fiddle and often played at square dances. He died on February 26, 1914, and his obituary indicated he was one of the best known farmers in Jefferson Township. He is buried with his wife and daughter Alice, close to his father's plot in St. John's Catholic Cemetery in New Haven.

Submitted by Thomas O'Keefe

KEINTZ FAMILY

Conrad Keinz married Sophia Schweigert April 9, 1826, in Buerstadt, Starkenburg, Hesse Darmstadt, Germany. Eight children were born there with four dying as infants. The four surviving children were Cecelia, Valentine, Elizabeth and John. The parents and the three younger children boarded the *Eastern Queen* at the port of Le Harve and arrived in New York on June 28, 1854. Their oldest daughter, Cecelia, married Charles Gebhard in 1853 in Buerstadt and immediately left on the ship *Advance* for New York, before her parents. Soon both families were reunited in Fort Wayne, settling in Wayne Township.

Sophia Keinz was widowed shortly after her arrival in America. To support herself, she purchased forty acres from her son-in-law, Charles Gebhard, in 1857. Her son Valentine was 20 years old and son John was 13 years old, both able to work a farm. Sophia remained on the farm many years. When she was taken ill, she was living with Valentine, whose home was on Bluffton Road. Sophia died there on August 29, 1878. She was buried in the Catholic Cemetery. After her death, the surname spelling of Keintz was adopted.

Cecelia and Charles Gebhard had seven children: Sophia, Valentine, Catherine, John, Charles, Jacob, and Edward. Jacob died at age three, while the other children reached adulthood, married and had families. Cecelia died May 16, 1894, and is buried near her mother.

Valentine Keintz became a citizen in 1860. He married Mary Anna Noll on November 3, 1863, in Fort Wayne. Mary Anna was born in the same town as her husband. Their six children were Elizabeth, Celia, Theresa, John, Valentine, and Mary. Having been a farmer all his life, Valentine made a prosperous living operating a market garden for over fifty years. For twenty-four years he served as deputy township assessor for Wayne Township, outside of the city of Fort Wayne. He served on jury duty, was interested in politics and was an active Democrat. Valentine died October 7, 1904, at age 67. A year before his death, his daughter, Theresa, Mrs. Andrew Jellison, was killed in a movie theater explosion in Chicago. She is buried in the Catholic Cemetery in Fort Wayne. Theresa had two sons, Lewis and John.

Elizabeth Keintz married John Wessel on November 12, 1855, in Chicago, Illinois. They lived for a short time in Detroit, Michigan, but soon settled in Fort Wayne. They had two surviving children, John and Sophia. The Wessel's enjoyed traveling extensively throughout the United States and Europe, returning many times to Germany for visits with family and friends. Elizabeth and her husband died two days apart on January 26 and 28, 1918. Their children preceded them in death.

John Keintz married Regina Kelleker in 1866. They had six children, all died as infants. John became a Fort Wayne city policeman on June 12, 1872, serving until 1877. He then operated a saloon on Lafayette Street, followed by railroad employment. His death occurred in 1894 when he was 49 years old.

Submitted by Stan Hench

ANDREW JOHN, JR. & KATHERINE ELIZABETH (BATES) KELLERMAN FAMILY

Andrew John Kellerman, Jr. and Katherine Elizabeth (Bates) Kellerman came to Fort Wayne to live not long after their marriage on August 24, 1931. Andy and Kit were wed in Middlebury, Indiana. Andy was born in Cincinnati, Ohio, on October 26, 1908, and Kit was born in Goshen, Indiana, on February 18, 1914.

Kit's brother in Fort Wayne thought that he could get Andy a job at Fort Wayne Tailoring Company on Brackenridge Street. Kit and Andy moved to Fort Wayne to stay with Kit's brother and his wife at their home on Wabash Avenue. The company needed only a female employee, so Kit started work sewing belt loops on men's pants. After a month Andy got a job there as a presser, and Kit quit.

Andy and Kit got their first apartment in a home on Barr Street across from Central High School. Later moves were to an apartment on Douglas Street, a duplex on Horace Street, houses on Wilson Drive, 2621 Indiana Avenue, and 1921 Taylor Street. In November 1934, they purchased their first home in the unincorporated town of Waynedale; the address was Route 4, Fort Wayne, later being 2409 Church Street. They soon had the $1,800 purchase price paid. Carol Ann was born on February 5, 1936.

Andrew, Katherine, Sandra and Carol Kellerman, 1950

Andy started raising show rabbits, building model railroad cars and engines to scale (1/4 inch scale - O gauge), which were sold throughout the country, and stamp collecting. Another daughter, Sandra Lee, was born on August 3, 1939.

Later, necessary lettering on the trains led to the purchase of a printing press to make decals. Kellerman Printing Company came from this start. Andy left Wayne Tailoring Company and was employed by Home Telephone Company. In late 1943 he was drafted at age 35, with daughters four and seven years old. He entered the Navy and spent a year in the U.S. After a brief leave home, he left on Christmas Eve 1944, sent to the Philippines. Kit worked some at the corner grocery (Gillespie's), did sewing, and took in ironing. At war's end, Andy came home and returned to work at Home Telephone Company as a switchman. Kit worked with him in the print shop. Carol and Sandy helped. The long hours put Carol and Sandy through Ball State Teachers' College.

Carol married Fred Buttell in 1961 and Sandra married Marion (Jack) Wirth in 1965. Grandchildren were born: Linda Jo Buttell (1962), Nancy Lee Buttell (1963), and Jennifer Lee Wirth (1971).

Kit and Andy sold their home and shop and bought a home at 1303 West Ludwig Road in 1969. Andy retired from what is now Verizon Telephone in October 1973. On Christmas Day 1976, Sandy, Jack, and Jenny Wirth were killed in a crash of their plane.

In 1987 Nancy married Blane Bade and Linda married John Walls. Great-grandchildren were born: Amanda Elizabeth Bade (1989), Nicholas Andrew Bade (1992), and Sarah Ann Bade (1994).

Andrew Kellerman died on February 20, 1995, and is buried in Greenlawn Memorial Park. Katherine Kellerman is 91.

Submitted by Dr. Carol A. Buttell

FLORENCE LOUISE KENDRICK

Florence Louise Kendrick, a descendant of William Brewster the Elder on the *Mayflower*, was born in Gary, Indiana, on February 26, 1911, but lived some of her childhood and all of her adult life in Fort Wayne, Indiana. She attended South Side High School, went to college at DePauw University, Greencastle, Indiana, for one year, and then transferred to Stephens Junior College, Columbia, Missouri, from which she graduated. She enrolled in a nurse-training program in Chicago, but health problems caused her to leave before graduation. In Fort Wayne, during her high school years, she met David Winfield Bash. Shortly after she left the nursing program, Florence and David married on April 6, 1935, in Gary, Indiana, and raised their four children in Fort Wayne: Judith Ann (Bash) Lee, Roberta Louise (Bash) Hall, David Winfield Bash Jr., and Charles Dayton Bash.

Florence was active in Trinity English Lutheran Church where she was a member of the church's Trinity Circle and she supported the youth program by sponsoring progressive dinners at her home, as well as other activities. Florence also served the Fort Wayne community through her involvement with Pi Chapter of the Psi Iota Xi

Florence Louise Kendrick

Society, a public service organization. She held several offices in the society, including vice-president, and for several years was in charge of ticket sales for their theater series, a major fundraiser for the society. Always heavily focused on home and family, Florence enjoyed rose gardening and was an excellent seamstress.

Florence's parents were Charles Edgar Kendrick and Ethel Katherine Jenness. Charles, after finishing his education in architecture in Chicago, moved to Fort Wayne in 1893, where his brother, Frank Butler Kendrick, was already an established architect and was moving into the construction business. About this time the rest of Charles' family (father, mother, two sisters, and three other brothers) also came to Fort Wayne. From then until about 1930 - when Charles moved back to Gary for the last time - Charles as architect, brother Frank as a construction contractor, and brother Harry Dechard Kendrick, a secretary of the Local No.2 Bricklayers, Masons, and Plasterers Union, had a strong influence on the construction activities and building trades in Fort Wayne and Allen County.

Charles was the architect of many structures in Fort Wayne. For example, Lakeside School on Rivermet Street and South Wayne School on Indiana Street in the late 1890s, plus St. Patrick's Roman Catholic Church on West Washington Street and St. Joseph Hospital on Main Street. Charles' father, William G. Kendrick, (who earlier in his life had had a fascinating career as a sea captain on round-the-world whaling expeditions and as a Union officer in the Civil War) and Charles' other brothers worked as masons and architects at times in the Allen County area.

Charles' wife Ethel was a schoolteacher before their marriage. In the late 1890s, she taught at the Bloomingdale and the Jefferson Schools in Fort Wayne. Ethel's parents were Charles Henry Jenness and Mary Jennie Alderman. The Jennesses lived in Ohio (where Ethel was born) and Kansas for short periods, but they spent a major part of their adult lives living in Allen County, Indiana, where Charles was a farmer and salesman. Mary's parents, William Alderman and Mary Swann, were early farmers in Allen County, arriving in 1852. They were known at that time for their innovative farming methods.

Submitted by David W. Bash

KENNERK-GLADIEUX FAMILY

Frank Kennerk can trace the family heritage back four generations to Askeatin County, Limerick, Ireland, in the early 1800s. His parents, John and Anna (Racht) Kennerk, owned a farm on US 14 east of New Haven across from the Casade Depot. Their children, Paul, Cornelius, Clarence, Bertha, Gertrude, Hildred, and Frank were raised there. Hildred's twin, Mildred, died at birth.

Kennerk Family, left to right. Front row:Geraldine (Kennerk) Mulligan, Genevieve (Gladieux) Kennerk. Back row: Bob, Frank, and Donald Kennerk

Several families settled around Besancon on US 30 east of New Haven. One family was Louis J. and Amelia C. (Coulardot) Gladieux, whose ancestors came from France. They had four daughters, Lela, Nora, and twins Bernedette and Genevieve. Frank had met Genevieve at their parish church, St. Louis Besancon. After serving in WWI in the Army, he came home to his beloved Genevieve. They were married in St. Louis Besancon Catholic Church on May 9, 1923. When they came out of church, there was four inches of snow on the buggy seat.

Frank and Genevieve were deeply devout Catholics whose church and family were very important to them. They were said to be a "cute couple" as they were both short in stature. They loved dancing, especially square dancing. Barn dances were popular in those days; people would clean out the barn, hire local musicians, and invite family and friends for a good time. Their life on the Snyder Road farm was like most other farmers. They used a team of horses to work the fields and raised cows, chickens, and sheep.

Frank and Genevieve had three children: Geraldine, Donald and Robert, but also lost three babies a few days after their births. The children attended St. Louis School (Academy, now) at Besancon and then went on to Central Catholic High School in Fort Wayne.

During WWII, Frank worked at Magnavox. They bought and moved to a larger farm near Monroeville. Unfortunately, Frank died suddenly at the age of 56 from kidney disease, after only four days of illness. Genevieve lived twenty some years longer.

During the Korean War, Donald farmed and Robert served in the Navy. Geraldine married John Mulligan and settled near Bryan, Ohio, to farm. They had four children; Connie, John Jr., Edward, and Patrick. Donald married Margie Giant and stayed on, farming the family farm on McArdle road at Monroeville. They also had four children; Daniel, Sally, Thomas, and Ned. Robert (Bob) married LuAnn Brames and lived on Franke Road in rural New Haven. Bob worked at ITT in Fort Wayne and Franklin Electric in Bluffton in the electronic field. They had two daughters, Karen and Kathleen.

Many of the grandchildren attended St. Louis Academy. Don's family went to Heritage High School and Bob's attended Bishop Luers High School. Bob and LuAnn's family are still members of St. Louis Besancon Catholic Church.

Unfortunately, early death continued in the family. Geraldine's husband Johnny died of a heart attack in his early 60s; Bob died at 56 and Don at 62. The families have remained strong and continue to raise the great-grandchildren with a strong faith and they continue to share many enjoyable fun-filled times together.

Submitted by Kathy Rorick

KETTLER FAMILY

Conrad Wilhelm Kettler was a boat captain born January 31, 1822. Elise Sophie Maria Rehorst Kettler (born January 31, 1821), his wife who was eight months pregnant, and their son, Wilhelm John Pietr Kettler (born December 22, 1850), immigrated to the United States from Leese, Germany. They settled in Fort Wayne in March 1853. Their daughter, Maria Carol, was born on April 21, 1853. Conrad bought the canal boat "William Edsall" from Heinrich Kammeier of Allen County for $180 on February 11, 1854. Their son, Conrad Frederick, was born on March 16, 1855. Conrad Wilhelm operated the canal boat for only two years, until his untimely death of Land's Disease on March 8, 1856. Elise, who was a member of the German Reformed Church and spoke both German and English, raised their three children alone, taking in laundry to support her family.

L.to R. Bob Jesse, John Ryan, IU President, Al Kettler, Art Hansen, PU President -- IUPU groundbreaking

Conrad Frederick Kettler grew up at 611 Jefferson Street, Fort Wayne. He was a member of Second Presbyterian Church and was a mail carrier. On May 16, 1889, he married Caroline Catherine Heth, one of the eight children of Jacob and Anna Katherine Adams Heth, who lived at 206 Lafayette Street. Conrad Frederick was promoted to superintendent of mails, and Caroline was a clerk for W. J. Bond. Conrad Frederick and Caroline had three children: Alfred William born October 4, 1892; Helen Marie born August 18, 1895; and Howard C. born December 31, 1899 who died at seven months old.

In 1911 Alfred William Kettler graduated from Fort Wayne High School, where he became re-acquainted with Margery Esther Pickard when she switched from the February to the September division. Al graduated from Purdue University with a bachelor's degree in civil engineering in 1915. In December 1915, he joined Indiana Engineering and Construction Company and later became its president. After delaying their 1917 wedding plans due to WWI, Al and Marge were married on August 27, 1918. Al made three attempts to join the service during WWI, but was turned down all three times because of a bad heart (rather ironic as he lived to be 92).

Al served as a trustee of Purdue University and on the board of directors of the Fort Wayne Park Board, Fort Wayne National Bank, the Fort Wayne Foundation, and the Indiana-Purdue Fort Wayne Foundation, and was an elder at First Presbyterian Church. In 1967 he received a Distinguished Alumni award from Purdue University, and in 1971 he was awarded an honorary Doctorate of Laws degree from Purdue.

Alfred is credited with conceiving the idea of a joint Indiana University/ Purdue University campus in Fort Wayne. One day in the 1950s, as he was walking by the nearby buildings that housed the totally separate Fort Wayne extensions of Indiana and Purdue Universities, he asked himself how many of their functions were duplicated. The thought stuck with him; so he gathered together other supporters of both Indiana and Purdue and shared his vision of joining the extensions. On November 8, 1964, the first building at the joint IPFW campus, the Alfred W. Kettler Hall, named in his honor, was dedicated.

Submitted by Carol Kettler

JONATHAN KIMBLE FAMILY

Mary Ann Smith, daughter of James and Susannah Smith, married Jonathan Kimble on October 20, 1853. They first had a son who was named James, presumably after James Smith. Later they had a daughter named Susannah who apparently died as an infant in 1863. On April 1, 1863 Mary Ann died also. Both Mary Ann and Susannah Kimble are buried in the Nine Mile Indiana Cemetery in the Smith Plot. Of the first twelve burials in this cemetery, seven of them were from this Smith family.

Submitted by Janet Smith

KINERK / KENNERK

Mary Ann Sibley was married to John Kinerk and lived at Asketon County, Limerick, Ireland. John had a son by a previous marriage, also named John, who, being engaged to a wealthy girl, needed to meet her dowry. John deeded his property to that son, leaving his second wife and five children with very little.

Mary Ann's eldest child, Edward Kinerk, born 1800 and died November 23,1870, was a "croppy boy" - part of a revolutionary gang, wanted by English police, with a price on his head. After being cornered in a house, Ed escaped by a ruse. He snapped his thumb nail against a brass candlestick, making a sound like a pistol cocking. Thus he gained a split second and escaped through a back window from the house where he was cornered. Rushing down to River Shannon, he was smuggled aboard a ship loading for Canada. Friendly Irish sailors nailed him in a barrel and loaded him as cargo. After three days he was let out and worked his passage. His possessions were just what he stood in. He made his way to New York where Irish workers were being hired to dig the Erie Canal.

Keeping contact with his mother, Ed by extraordinary thrift, gathered means so she could bring herself and the four younger children, two sons and two daughters, to America. On July 15, 1829 they left the ship and then found Ed. The daughters married and Mary Ann and her three sons came west about 1833, working on the construction of the Wabash-Erie Canal. Near

Kennerk - Kinerk Reunion, St. Mays Park, Fort Wayne, 1920

Wabash, Indiana, they each bought a quarter section of land along the canal. Wabash County separated from Allen County and, on the first day of court, the three brothers filed for citizenship. All could write their names, adding to credence that among the offences charged against Ed was that he was a "hedge-row teacher," a criminal act punishable by death for teaching an Irish child to read. Many only made an "X." Family tradition is that Ed was always a great reader.

A foreman on the canal, Edward Kinerk met and married Celina Dalman in Fort Wayne. She was born in England, daughter of John Dalman and Hannah Burcher, was brought to America at age ten with her parents and siblings. Industry and thrift gained the Dalman family several properties and a respected place in Pleasant Township.

Celina Kinerk went along on the canal, cooking for the men Ed hired, from 50 to 100. Open fires, limited help and supplies, along with weather, made Celina's first childbirth perilous. The birth of baby John, plus Indiana's financial situation, convinced Ed to take Celina and the baby back to Allen County to be near the Dalmans. Ed sold land along the canal to his brothers who stayed in Wabash County.

Ed's Mother, Mary Ann, died and is believed buried in Lagro, Indiana, in St. Patrick's Catholic Cemetery, in an unmarked grave.

Ed bought land in newly formed Pleasant Township. He cleared the land and built a hand-hewn log cabin. There Timothy was born, the first white child born in Pleasant Township. Brookwood golf course is now located there. Ed and Celina's house, and only one other, were located between Ossian and Fort Wayne. Ed logged trees and hauled them for ties on the new railroads, the canal having failed. Such farming as was done depended on Celina and children, who came along regularly. At least three babies died in infancy, eight survived.

John Kinerk, the eldest, lost an eye but was able to sell grain, testing its quality by smell. John married Margaret O'Shaughnessey and they had twelve children, three dying in infancy. Daughters, Cele and Margaret, helped to raise the others. There being no work in Fort Wayne, several went to work in Chicago on the railroad where two died accidental deaths.

Blanche Kinerk, another of John's daughters, married a McCormick and had two girls, Mary and Blanche. Blanche, the children's mother, died of flu in 1920. Her mother, who was caring for her, also died. They are buried in the same grave in Catholic Cemetery, Fort Wayne. Mary and Blanche were cared for by their aunts, Cele and Margaret, who remained spinsters. They had all their own siblings to raise, plus their two nieces, and neither wanted any more children! The aunts became devoted care-givers and feared McCormick would re-marry and take the girls. However, McCormick died from a railroad accident, so the girls had a happy home with the aunts. Mary became Sister Mary Cele McCormick of the Sisters of Providence. Blanche McCormick graduated, worked at General Electric, and became engaged to Bob Becker. They were to be married on a Saturday but Aunt Cele died on the previous Thursday of heart failure. Wanting to delay the wedding, but, after counsel from Father Couroy, Blanche married Bob Becker in the Sister's Chapel at St. Augustine's Convent. The funeral was held in the Cathedral as planned the same day.

The women born Kennerk/Kinerk (the different spelling of the name resulted from phonetic spelling on legal documents) and those women the Kennerk/Kinerk men married, were valiant souls. There was Mary Ann, braving a terrible Atlantic crossing, nearly shipwrecked, shepherding her family to meet Edward, to her death in Indiana. Then Celina, immigrant at ten married at 16, mother at 17, living in primitive conditions with a difficult husband and having babies regularly. These women survived back-breaking work, heat, cold, disease, mosquitoes, lack of sanitation and medical care, danger to selves and family, all making them truly heroic. Celina found an Indian on her porch and dispatched him promptly. Another relative, Nora Wickens, chased a runaway bull away from her two children with a mop. Big families were the norm and often babies were lost in infancy. One family lost two sets of twins. Even so, many lived to great age, notably Grace Koons Melching who died at 104 years. Heart and kidney disease, diabetes, flu, pneumonia, accidents were listed causes of death.

The characteristics which served Ed to defy the English police, stow-away, and supervise 100 men on the canal did not make him a kind and loving father and husband. Not recognizing changing times, the independence of his wife and children, and feeling himself a failure, he moved out. Deeding the home place to Celina, he thought she had her share and wrote her out of his will. Separated but never divorced, Celina sued to break his will, won and was awarded her widow's third of his estate. Give Ed credit for determination. He was law-abiding (in America), patriotic, voted, paid taxes, hard working and a good neighbor. He and his two brothers are buried at Largo, in St. Patrick's Cemetery. Celina is buried Prairie Grove Cemetery.

Ed and Celina Kinerk's son, William Richard (b. 1837), at age 17, volunteered for duty in the Union Army. He served the final one and one-half years of the Civil War with distinction in the 104th Infantry of Indiana. President Lincoln's body was brought through Fort Wayne on the way to its burial in Illinois. William Richard was chosen to stand in honor guard as mourners paid tribute to the fallen president. William was a faithful member of Grand Army of Republic (GAR) all his life. He became a successful farmer and served in public office. Kinerk road in Pleasant Township is named in tribute to him. Any old soldier, regardless of his condition, was welcomed at William Richard's home.

Timothy (born August 31, 1834) had no interest in slavery or the Civil War. He joined a wagon train going to the gold fields in Montana. He drove oxen through country where no teams and wagons had previously gone. Jim Bridger and Bozeman, famous trail guides, each guided the train at some times. It was three years of hardships and danger, but he did find gold. Coming home, Tim bought a farm and built a big brick house and barn. Tim Kinerk married Mary Hourigan and raised eight children. Timothy often told of events in "the diggings," even that he knew Mark Twain, saying about Twain that he was "dodging the draft like the rest of us." In great sorrow he mourned the death of his dear wife, Mary, and he spoke of her fine qualities and the hot biscuits she baked the morning after their wedding.

Many teachers adorn the roster of our families, from Norah in her one-room, eight grades school, to Martha Kelsey Shouldis, president of Mercy College. The inspiration and love of learning that shines in the successful farmers, business and industry, professional women and men can be traced to dedicated teachers. Truly they were King Harry's Makers. Tim's son, Harry became a prominent lawyer as did his son Hugh. These men, long remembered for their integrity, knowledge and skill in their profession, are buried at St. Aloysius Cemetery, Yoder.

A picture of a family reunion taken about 1920 tells graphically how these descendants of Ed and Celina have prospered over 100 years. Compare their successes to the friendless, impoverished stow-a-way, Ed Kinerk, to whom the Kinerk/Kennerks trace our ancestry.

The many members, men and women, who served this country in the armed forces as sailors, soldiers and nurses, rate stars and stripes on our flag. The spirit of adventure of Edward can be credited to the many descendants located far and wide from Allen County, notably Father Daniel Kennerk who served faithfully as a Holy Cross missionary to Bangladesh. He died in 2001, greatly mourned by Christians and non-Christians alike.

Taken from the unpublished family papers of Norah Wickens Kennerk – born 1876, died in1969.

Submitted by Gloria Kennerk Lamper

JAMES PARKER KING FAMILY

James Parker King, the son of James King, was born January 8, 1827, in Ohio or Kentucky. He married Emily Jane Bosley on December 13, 1872 in Bracken County, Kentucky. Emily is the daughter of Edward and Nancy Jane Curtis. Together they had eight known children, all born in Kentucky. December 17, 1915 they moved to Allen County, Indiana, from Brown County, Ohio. James died on February 15, 1916. James and Emily are both buried in Lindenwood Cemetery. James Parker King was a Civil War veteran.

William Nicholas King, Sr., Family, 1938

Children of James and Emily are:Lloyd Robert born in 1873, Juelyn born about 1874, Lewis Henry born in 1875, Mary Ellen born in 1876, William Nicholas born in 1880, Luther Hurell born in 1885, and twins; John T. and Otis Peter born in 1889.

Lloyd Robert King married twice; first to Clarinda "Clara" and second to Nanny. He remained in Brown County, Ohio, and is buried in Feesburg. Lloyd and Clarinda had one known child, Edith.

Lewis Henry King married a cousin, Mertie May King. He died in Allen County, Indiana, and is buried in Lindenwood Cemetery. Mertie May is buried in Georgetown, Ohio. Lewis and Mertie had six children. Anna Lee, Huey, Noah, Earl, Zola and Everett.

Mary Ellen King married twice; her first husband's last name was Herron, and her second husband was Hiram Atril Harrington. They are both buried in Lindenwood Cemetery. Mary Ellen and Mr. Herron had one child, Emma Elizabeth. Mary Ellen and Hiram had eight children: Ida May, Itha Ellen "Ike", John Christian Otis, Jessie Parker, Hubert Jasper "Pat", Julia Ann, William Henry, and Elmer Earl.

James Parker King

William Nicholas King married three times; his first wife was Sophia Elizabeth Lynd, second wife Mary Ann Donovan, and third wife Bessie Blevins. William and Sophia married about 1903 and had three children: Virgie Virginia, Minnie Ada and Raymond E. William and Mary Ann married in 1916 and they had one child, Herbert Wayne. William and Bessie married in 1924 and they had nine children and a set of twins who died at birth: Dorothy Lee, Thelma Jean, Maime, William Junior, Jennie Mae, Betty Jane, Helen Ilene, Cora Ellen and Ella Marie. William is buried in Lindenwood Cemetery and Bessie is buried in Prairie Grove Cemetery. Bessie has been found on documents as Bessie M. Bevins. In 1916 William worked as a railroader. In 1924 William worked as a boilermaker; in 1955 he retired from Central Foundry Company. The two oldest girls and two youngest girls were born in Kentucky. Herbert was born in Fort Wayne; the other children were all born in Ohio.

Luther Hurell King married twice, first to Anna Mae Lynd (sister to Sophia Lynd) and second to Alice. Luther and Anna had three children, Manuel Levi, Gordon Harley and Viola Mabel. Luther is buried in Mason County, Kentucky.

John T. King married twice, first to Annabelle Donovan and second to Nova Hoffman. John and Annabelle had two children, Bessie Mae and John Jr. John and Nova had three children, Floyd Robert, William Edward and Clifford "Corky". John is buried in Lindenwood Cemetery.

Otis Peter King married twice, first wife unknown, and second to Edith Adair. Otis and Edith had two children, a daughter and Curtis Otis. Otis died and was buried in Detroit, Michigan.

Submitted by K. M. Davis

KINTZ FAMILY

Louis T. Kintz, son of (William) Edward and Rosella (Peters) Kintz, was born on May 11, 1877, in Adams County, Indiana. On May 1, 1901 he married M. Gertrude Wertzberger, who was born September 18, 1875 to Anthony and Elizabeth (Hutker) Wertzberger, also of Adams County, Indiana. He brought his new bride to his farm on the south east side of Fort Wayne. From his dairy he drove a milk wagon to sell milk.

Louis and Gertrude had eleven children. Marie, born May 11, 1902, married Peter Pitzen. Lawrence, born June 21, 1903, married Irene Freehill. Dorothea born April 6, 1905, married Cletus Bacon. Irene, born March 28, 1906, married Joseph Pranger. Aquanita (Nettie), born February 3, 1908, married Clarence Gnau. Hilda, born November 18, 1909, died of diphtheria at age nine. Agnes, born October 10, 1911, entered the convent in Mishawaka, Indiana, and took the name Sister M. Alphonsilla, OSF. Vincent, born April 8, 1913, married Bernice Gnau. V. Rose, born June 21, 1915, married Richard Banet. Ruth, born February 24, 1917, married Richard Poiry. Joseph, born October 12, 1920, married Katherine Trentadue.

Around 1919, Fort Wayne businessmen, who were interested in buying properties near the railroad, approached Louis. The International Harvester was looking for land to build a factory. The farm, which sold in 1920 for $25,000, is now the site of the well known International Harvester Tower, at the corner of Coliseum Boulevard and Pontiac Street.

The family moved just east of St. Andrew's Catholic Church, of which he was a charter member. There, on New Haven Avenue, Louis owned a grocery store and the family lived upstairs. As his children grew older, Louis purchased homes in the neighborhood, planning to have them settle nearby when they married. Marie and Peter Pitzen, and Dorothy and Cletus Bacon lived and raised their families there.

During the Depression, rather than turn away hungry friends and neighbors, Louis allowed them to buy groceries on credit. Unfortunately, when they were unable to pay back what they owed, the Kintz family lost several of the houses, as well as the store. The family moved across the

Kintz Grocery, taken in 1924 on New Haven Avenue, east of St. Andrew's Catholic Church. L to R: Louis Kintz, owner, Dorothea (Kintz) Bacon, Mr. Lewis, a salesman, Frank (Butch) Carteaux, meat cutter

street to the largest house, where they lived until his death in 1936. Gertrude went to daily Mass, and lived to see many of her grandchildren attend St. Andrew's School. So many in fact, that almost all the students called her "Grandma Kintz". When she died in 1954 there were 55 grandchildren, who now have descendants numbering well over 500. Many still reside in the Fort Wayne area, but others are scattered around the world, as far away as Siberia. A grandson, Paul S. Pitzen, is a priest, residing in Australia.

As for the Kintz Grocery, the building lost in the Depression has held many businesses, and is currently a satellite of the St. Mary's Soup Kitchen, where hungry neighbors are fed, free of charge. The family tradition continues.

Submitted by Clara M. Sarrazine

GEORGE PAUL, JR. & VIRGINIA (PRATT) KIRBY FAMILY

The lake. What lake? Natives of Allen County are familiar with the phrase: The family is going to the lake on vacation or for the weekend. Non-natives ask: Where is 'the lake' everyone talks about? The lake could be any one of northeast Indiana's many glacier-formed lakes where families go to enjoy fishing, swimming, and relaxing.

For the family of George Paul, Jr. and Virginia (Pratt) Kirby, spending the family vacation at the lake was a special time together. Making the vacation extra special for their children, George Paul II and Linda Jean, was that Virginia's parents, Fred C. and Grace (Todd) Pratt, joined them. These lake vacations were family traditions. And, as years passed, they also became a time for family reunions.

The Kirbys and the Pratts both have origins in the United Kingdom and Germany. Their families came to the United States in the 1840s and made their way across New York, Pennsylvania, and Ohio before settling in Allen County, Indiana.

George Paul Kirby, Jr. was born October 27, 1912, in Toledo, Ohio, to George P. and Eva (Felt) Kirby. The family moved to Fort Wayne, Indiana, at the onset of the Great Depression in search of opportunities for employment for George, Sr. Virginia was born in Fort Wayne on September 14, 1914. George Paul, Jr. met Virginia Pratt at South Side High School, where they both graduated in 1932. The scarcity of jobs in 1932 led George, Jr. to join the government's Civilian Conservation Corps program, where he worked until he joined the United States Navy in 1934. Most of his Navy duty was spent in the Pacific on the U.S.S. *Dobbin*, where he learned his trade as a welder and mechanic. When he was discharged in 1938 he took Civil Service work at the Naval Yard in Philadelphia, Pennsylvania, where he worked through the end of World War II. Virginia was employed at G. C. Murphy and International Harvester during the time George served in the Navy.

George and Virginia were married in The First Baptist Church on Fairfield Avenue in Fort Wayne on December 30, 1939. Their wedding dinner was held at the former Keenan Hotel. At the end of World War II George and Virginia's rented duplex in Philadelphia was sold. George's work at the Naval Yard was finished. Returning servicemen were given first priority for housing and employment in Philadelphia.

Unable to find either, they returned to their families in Fort Wayne in 1947 where George found work as a welder with Fruehauf. He also joined the Indiana Air National Guard stationed at Baer Field where he served until the end of the Korean War. They took up residence in the New Haven area. George retired from Mobile Aerial Towers and Virginia retired from Western Auto Warehouse and H. S. Schroeder Company. George died February 3, 1992. Virginia died September 14, 1997. They are buried in the Todd family plot in Lindenwood Cemetery in Fort Wayne.

L. to R. Ryan Paul Kirby and Michael Anthony Kirby, Linda Jean Kirby, George Paul Kirby II, Sandra Kirby

George and Virginia's children are: Linda Jean Kirby, was born in Upper Darby, Pennsylvania, on January 7, 1943, and George P. Kirby II, was born in Fort Wayne, Indiana, on March 30, 1949. Linda graduated from New Haven High School in 1961 and George in 1967. Linda graduated from the University of Missouri-St. Louis and lives in Fort Wayne. George Paul II graduated from Ivy Tech. He served as a medic with the United States Army in Vietnam 1969-1971. He was married to Sandra Police, also from New Haven, on June 25, 1989. They live in New Haven and have two children: Ryan Paul, born September 24, 1992, and Michael Anthony, born July 29, 1996. George, Sandra, Ryan and Michael continue the family tradition of having a place at the lake.

Submitted by Linda K. Kirby

ALVIN "JONSEY" & IRENE (MUDRACK) KLEBER FAMILY

Alvin Joseph Kleber was born in a farmhouse near Hessen Cassel, Indiana, on March 25, 1920, to William (1889-1957) and Barbara Sorg (1890-1941) Kleber. As a boy he was always outside playing in the dirt and received the nickname "Jonsey" after a local trash man by that name. Jonsey grew up on the family farm and graduated from St. Joseph Catholic Grade School at Hessen Cassel. On April 6, 1942, he was inducted into the U.S. Army for World War II. He served two years as an instructor at the Field Artillery School in Fort Sill, Oklahoma, then fought in Europe with the 763rd Field Artillery Battalion, 23rd Corps as a staff sergeant. After Germany's defeat, Jonsey was part of the military occupation forces in Berlin, where he witnessed Hilter's bunker and death site. He was honorably discharged on March 26, 1946, and returned to work for Mays Construction Co.

Alvin and Irene Kleber wedding, 1948.

On July 24, 1948, Jonsey married Irene Mudrack at St. Andrew's Catholic Church in Fort Wayne. They resided their entire lives at 1328 Michigan Avenue and attended St. Joseph Catholic Church on Hale Avenue. When the Korean War began in 1950, Jonsey was called back into service with the 38th Infantry. On February 13, 1951, he was shot through the leg and captured by the Red Chinese during the Battle of Hoengsong, but managed to escape and make it back to the American lines after spending three days in severe cold with no provisions. Jonsey recuperated in Japan from severe frostbite and his gunshot wound, for which he received a Purple Heart and Bronze Star. Thereupon, he worked as an automobile mechanic at Allen County Motors from 1951 until his retirement in 1985. On March 3, 1992 Jonsey died from prostate cancer and on March 5, was buried in the Catholic Cemetery. Jonsey enjoyed working on cars, drinking beer, gardening, playing euchre, and square dancing. He had an easy-going, humorous personality and liked to joke around with people.

Irene Mary Mudrack was born June 28, 1927 in Fort Wayne, Indiana, to Andrew (1904-1983) and Louise Trabel (1901-1982) Mudrack. She received her education at St. Andrew's Grade School and Central Catholic High School, graduating in 1945. After her marriage in 1948, Irene resigned as a secretary for General Electric and worked as a dedicated mother and homemaker for the rest of her life. Irene died on April 16, 2003 after battling breast cancer for 19 years, and was buried next to Jonsey on April 22, 2003. Irene enjoyed traveling, talking with people, and visiting relatives. She was a loving, outgoing, strong-willed person and very interested in family history.

The seven children of Jonsey and Irene Kleber are Carl (1950), husband of Margaret

Minnick (1951), Gerald (1951), husband of Pamela Milewski (1952); Jeanne (1953), wife of Mervyn Porter (1950); Marilyn (1956), wife of Edwin Burgess (1953); Karen (1957); Kenneth (1961) husband of Linda Felger (1960); and Gary (1963).

Submitted by Seb Kleber

WILLIAM "BEELER" & BARBARA (SORG) KLEBER FAMILY

William Frederick Kleber was born in a farmhouse at Hessen Cassel, Indiana, on July 12, 1889 to Christoph (1849-1928) and Mary Hake (1852-1940) Kleber. He descended from Sebastian Klüber (1812-1879), who came to Allen County in 1840 from Eckardroth, Hessen-Cassel, Germany. Sebastian settled on a farm adjacent to St. Joseph Catholic Church at Hessen Cassel, Indiana, and was a founding member. The Klüber surname was eventually americanized to Kleber.

As a boy, William made primitive wooden wheels for the field wagons and received the nickname "Beeler" after a local wagon wheel-maker by that name. Beeler grew up farming and developed a love for horses. He was well known for his skill in handling and training horses. On September 12, 1911, Beeler married Barbara Sorg at the Hessen Cassel church, and they raised a large family on a tenant farm off the Decatur Road one-fourth mile south of the church, where K&N Carpet is currently located. On January 3, 1937, their farm house burned down completely due to a chimney fire and they lost all their possessions. A new house was built, which had electricity and running water.

William and Barbara (Sorg) Kleber, married September 12, 1911, Hessen Cassel, Indiana

Beeler was well-known in the area for his many outrageous pranks, teasing people, and trying to scare children. One favorite prank was threatening to cut off the ears of the local school children with his pocket knife. Since he frequently bobtailed many of the cats and dogs in the area, the children were often scared by his threats. One nephew said he is still afraid to walk his dog past Beeler's grave. Beeler enjoyed gardening, drinking home brew, chewing tobacco, playing euchre, wearing all types of hats, and joking around with people. Although ornery at times, Beeler was basically a fun-loving, kind-hearted person. On November 2, 1957, Beeler died from prostate cancer and was buried in the Catholic Church cemetery at Hessen Cassel. He had a horseshoe from his favorite horse "Doc" placed on his tombstone.

Barbara Josephine Sorg was born May 31, 1890 at Hessen Cassel, Indiana, to Charles (1859-1942) and Mary Fox (1867-1929) Sorg. She was a descendant of Johann Melchior Sorg (1809-1890), who also came to Allen County from Eckardroth, Germany, in 1834. Both Beeler and Barb were raised speaking German, but only did so when they didn't want their children to understand their conversation. Barbara lived the hard life of a typical farm wife while raising nine children without the modern conveniences of electricity or indoor plumbing. She was a sweet, kind, strongly religious woman and devoted mother and wife. Barb died on November 30, 1941, from high blood pressure.

The nine children of Beeler and Barb Kleber are: Bernice (1912-1980), wife of Andrew Fox; Berneda (1913-2003), wife of Beverly Vinson; Vera (1915-), wife of James Vinson; Cornelius (1916-2004), husband of Joan Hoevel; Luella (1918-), wife of Robert Offerle; Alvin (1920-1992), husband of Irene Mudrack; Ralph (1924-1976), husband of Dorothy Huey; Willard (1927-1984), husband of Mary Kintz; and Ervin (1932-), husband of Dolores Schall.

Submitted by Carl J. Kleber

KLINGENBERGER

Franz Andreas Klingenberger married Anna Maria Hofacherin in 1799. Both were born, married, and died in Germany. The child of Franz and Anna was Christof, born in Germany in 1806. *Christ of Klingenberger* came to America on the two-masted bark named *Favorite* in 1832. He married Margaret Barras. He died on September 25, 1871 in Fort Wayne Indiana. Christof and Margaret had six children born in Marion Township: John Xavier Sr. (1843-1921), Christof (1848), Joseph (1850), Christina (1857), Amandes (1857), and George (1864).

John Xavier Klingenberger, Sr., married Matilda Lauer (1845-1924) on May 20, 1865. They had five children: John Xavier Jr. (1867-1919), Justin (1869-1938), George Bernard (1871-1914 Ohio), Xavier "Seff" Francis (1875-1950), and Martha (1883-1939).

John Xavier Klingenberger Jr. married Mary Eising (1872-1914) on May 28, 1895 in Fort Wayne, Indiana They had six children: Matilda (1896-1975), John "Jack" Anthony (1898-1950), Rosella (1901), Julian George (1902-1984), Mary (1906-1906), and Norbert Xavier (1908-1974).

Julian George Klingenberger (1902-1984) married Lucille Clarice Sarrazen (1907-1950) on June 9, 1934 in Fort Wayne, Indiana. They had two children, Carol Lou and James Julian.

Carol Lou Klingenberger (1935) married William James Platter on June 29, 1957. They had ten children: William Edward (1959), Julia Lynne (1960), Daniel Joseph (1962), Jeannine Claire (1964), Jennette Carol (1965), Jennifier Elizebeth (1969), Michael (1973), Joyceann Marie (1975), Christopher George (1978), and Stephen Patrick (1979).

James Klingenberger on his pontoon, the Favorite

James Julian Klingenberger (1940) of Fort Wayne, Indiana, married Linda Kay Stevens (1944) on January 9, 1965 in Napoleon, Ohio. They had four children: Karen Kay (1967), Thomas James (1968) David Michael (1970), and Kevin Andrew (1973).

James was born the same month and day that Christof Klingenberger died, one hundred and thirty four years later. James can be found on his pontoon boat. The pontoon has been named the *Favorite------*of course.

Submitted by James J. Klingenberger

NORMAN KLINGER FAMILY

Norman was born August 11, 1926 to William and Blanch (Christlieb) Klinger, in Noble County. He was the fifth of nine children.

Norman was a farmer and Blanch was a homemaker. His father, William, was born on December 8, 1889, and died September 6, 1974. His mother, Blanch, was born March 3, 1901, and died July 25, 1936. She died giving birth to the last child at the age of 36.

William and Blanch Klinger's other children are as follows:

1. Florence Edna born August 31, 1917, died February 17, 1937
2. Walter William born March 10, 1919, died August 30, 1997
3. Jesse Howard born October 25, 1920, died January 5, 2004
4. Ellen Elane born October 1, 1922, died 1984
5. Thoe Nadaline born October 8, 1924
6. Barbara Faith born August 10, 1932
7. Delphus Earl born January 18, 1934
8. Joanne Irene born July 17, 1936

Norman was drafted into the Army during World War II on November 20, 1944, at the age of eighteen. He learned to drive heavy equipment and saw duty in Japan. He was honorably discharged on October 26, 1946. He worked for Omni Source for over forty years and retired from here in 1984.

Norm married Gladys (Royal) Klinger on July12, 1964, in Fort Wayne, Indiana. Gladys worked at Rogers Meat Department and Fort Wayne Community Schools until her retirement in 1980.

Norman and Gladys have six children

1. Ginger Sue born July 30, 1947
2. James William born February 25, 1948
3. Debbie Joe
4. Norman T. born October 6, 1957
5. Tammy Joe born April 27, 1959
6. Lisa Loraine born June 7, 1966

Most of the children still live in Indiana. James William lives in New Haven and works for Phelp Dodge. Norman and his wife Ronda live in Auburn. Norm and Ronda married on April 28, 1995. Norm works at Tower Automotive in Kendalville. Lisa and her husband, Delbert Springer, live in Fort Wayne. They have been married sixteen years and have one child, Nathaniel Matthew. Delbert works at Autoliv and Lisa works at Nietert Insurance.

By Lisa Springer

RALPH LEWIS WILLIAM & CAROLYN SUE (GARRISON) KLINKER FAMILY

Ralph Lewis William Klinker was born December 25, 1938, on a farm in Allen County near Monroeville, Indiana, to Ralph Ward and Lena Louise (Strunkenburg) Klinker. On May 22, 1959, Ralph L. W. Klinker married Carolyn Sue, daughter of Robert and Alma (Young) Garrison. Ralph and Carolyn have six children. Tamara and her husband, Christopher Spieth, are now living in the rural area near Monroeville, Indiana. They have four children, Joshua, Gabriel, Benjamin, and Rachel. Kenneth married Karen Schieber (Clearwater, Florida). They have one daughter, Amie, and now live in Dunedin, Florida. Janet is living in Clearwater, Florida. Mark married Cheryl Renniger (New Haven) and they have four children, Austin, Jordan, Alyssa and Jenna. They live in Fort Wayne. Matthew married Sandra Salway (Monroeville) and they have four children, Ryan, Christian, Derek and Hannah. They live in rural Monroeville. Anthony lives in Monroeville.

Ralph Lewis Klinker has three sisters, Louise, Lucille, and Betty. Louise married August Kaiser (deceased) of Monroeville. They have two children, Steven and Jane. Lucille married Larry Elliott (Antwerp, Ohio). They have four children, Brent, Debra, Dean, and Amy. Betty married Stanley Gorrell (deceased) of Garrett. They have three children, Gregory, Julie, and Gary. Ralph L. W. has one brother, Harold. He married Joy Farnsworth (Monroeville) and they have five children, Harold Joe, Regina, Timothy, Melonie, and April.

Carolyn Sue (Garrison) Klinker has five siblings. Beverly (deceased) married Richard Blair (deceased). Marilyn married Charles Kelso and they live in Canton, Michigan. Robert Lee lives in Las Vegas, Nevada. Vivian married Richard Hutson and they live in Indianapolis, Indiana. Jacquelyn married Ronald Springer and they live in Yoder, Indiana.

Ralph Lewis worked in several factories before retiring from there. Ralph graduated from Taylor University, Fort Wayne. Ralph then went into the ministry with the United Methodist Church. Carolyn worked for several years at Monroeville Elementary School in the cafeteria.

Lewis Henry and Hattie Margaret (Miller) Klinker, Ralph Lewis Klinker's grandparents, were married on January 8, 1896 and they had eleven children who were all raised on the farm. Several generations were farmers. Children of Lewis and Hattie were: Harry, Sadie, Raymond, Homer Pearl, Ralph Ward, Mary Ernest, Irene, Maxine, and Helen. They moved from Palmyra, Indiana and settled on a farm in Allen County located near Monroeville, Indiana.

The father of Lewis Klinker was Ernst Heinrich "Henry" Wilhelm Klinker, who was born in Westfalen, Germany on March 27, 1836. His wife was Mary Frances Lamping and they had twelve children. They were Anna Marie, Sophia, Lena, Lewis, William, Flora, Lucy, Katharena, Cora Stella, Benjamin, and Bertie.

The father of Hattie was Rudolph Henry Miller, who was born in Lengrich, Germany on October 14, 1833. His wife, Amanda Jane Simpson, and he had fourteen children. They were George Marion, Marinda, William, Alva, Flora, Goldie, Sylvia, Stella, George Washington, Anna, Hattie, Lyman, Noble, and Magdalena,

Both families came over from Germany in the 1860s. They both farmed and they each bought a farm close to each other in Indiana and that was when these families first met.

Submitted by Ralph L. Klinker

WILLIAM KLOMP

(1853-1937)

Born in East Prussia, his parents Johann and Elisabeth (Schultz) Klump, with four brothers lived in the Detroit area. He arrived here from Toledo, a widower with two children, William Jr. (1873) and Mary "Mae" Klomp-Frewin-Frank (1878). In 1893, William Jr. married Barbara Rodman at Fort Wayne. They had two children: William III (1894-1981) and Lillian (1901). They all lived in Chicago and were railroaders.

William III married Mary E. Nilsen and had two children, Bill and Marie.

Lillian married Pascal Perry (no children). They were a vaudeville sharpshooting team. Perry was a double and shooter in movies for Ken Maynard, the cowboy star in the late 1920-30s. Perry also played the "Bad Guy" in westerns. They lived in North Hollywood.

On January 24, 1889, William married Sophia Schmidt (1866-1940), the daughter of Frederick Jacob and Katherine (Wurms) Schmidt, both from Germany. They had nine children and operated a tavern near the Sears Pavilion. Sophie's first two children died. They are buried on the Schmidt-Klomp plot at Saint John's Lutheran Cemetery on Engle Road.

In the early 1930s, William and Sophie lived at 1314 Scott Avenue. He worked as a real estate agent and a salesman for the Packard Piano Company. He was fluent in six languages. Many Sundays after church, their grown family would gather on Scott Avenue. Sometimes the cousins would walk several blocks to the bridge on Hale Street and watch the outboard motorboats race on the Saint Mary's River.

Clara Klomp (1892-1967) lived at home. As a teenager, she had learned the millinery trade at 708 Calhoun, the Rurode's Dry Goods Company. Later, she and Miss Julia Alice Rossington started the Jule-Clare Hat Shop. It was located in the front of the Rossington family's home at 1133 South Clinton. Now torn down, it stood across from the rectory on Cathedral Square. Christmas Eve dinner on Scott Avenue was formal. The live tree was in the front parlor with the sliding doors closed, to keep it cool. On tables around the rooms, Aunt Clara placed a set of miniature Christmas shops, houses and people, ice-skating on a mirror. Her Christmas presents were a new hat for every lady, including her five nieces. Later, she moved to Fulton Street and held Christmas Eve there.

Edward Klomp (1895-1955) was in the navy during World War II. He married Janet Schultz in 1919. Both he and his daughter worked at G.E. They are buried at Lindenwood Cemetery. Their daughter: Mary Jane Klomp Horrell Kappel (1920-1997)

Esther Klomp (1902-1977) married Frederick "Emerson" Griffiths in 1925.After World War I, Emerson came from Kalida, Ohio to Fort Wayne to live with an aunt. Immediately, he got a job with Wayne Knitting Mills. After 1948, the mills twice transferred Emerson to Humbolt, Tennessee. They are buried in Ohio. Their daughters: Nancy Griffiths Speckman (see below), Bobette Griffiths Shaw and Jaymee Griffiths Seidel Colvin.

Clarence Carl Klomp (1905-1980) married Ruth Levine. His sister Mary introduced this couple in Chicago. They married in 1929. Their daughter: Marilyn Klomp Brockner. Clarence married second widow: Agnes Bell-Kougel with three children.

Front row seated, Evelyn Dennis Griffiths, Pauline Schmidt Krohn, Mary Jane Klomp, Sophia Schmidt Klomp holding Nancy Griffiths, Rocelia Geyer Dennis. Middle row: Mary Schmidt Bohne, Esther Klomp Griffiths, Willis Dennis, Helene Schmidt Carver. Back row: William Klomp, Dorothy Griffiths, John Griffiths, Jeanette Dennis, Emerson Griffiths, Janet Schultz Klomp, Edward Klomp, Clara Klomp, George Griffiths.

Times have changed, and milliner shops have disappeared but the family still enjoys the Christmas season together. William and Sophie's nine great-grandchildren now have nine children of their own.

Nancy May Griffiths married on January 11, 1947, Albert Fred Speckman (1923-1977), the son of Fred and Lorena (Buuck) Speckman. Al served in World War II and is buried at Covington Memorial Gardens. After his death, Nancy worked at the Saint Francis College library.

Submitted by Nancy Speckman.

KLOPFENSTEINS

John (Jean) Klopfenstein, Jr., born in 1813 in Florimont, Belfort, France, was one of the first Klopfensteins to immigrate to the New World. In 1831, he landed in New York and later moved to Stark County, Ohio, where he married and had seven children. In 1853, he moved to Allen

The Joseph Klopfenstein family in front of the house he built – now known as the Joseph Grabill home (next to the downtown area in Grabill—south side of the State Street)

County, Indiana, settling his family on a farm near Leo. Land had to be purchased, timber cut, a home built, and land cleared so crops could be planted. Other families also came, coming by way of hose and wagon and the Wabash and Erie Canal. On December 18, 1853, John Klopfenstein, Jr., purchased 80 acres of land for $400 in northeast Allen County from Isaac and Charlotte Ashley. Isaac and his brother, Simon, had paid $200 for 80 acres in 1844; the deed was issued and signed by President Martin VanBuren. In 1872, John purchased an additional 40 acres from Joseph Miller for $900 and, in 1873, an additional adjoining ten acres from Peter Fritzgerald for $300.

In 1862, John's oldest son, Joseph, purchased 80 acres from his father and mother for $800. Joseph was a farmer, owned a cider mill, and seemed to be the local casket maker. He built a large two-story brick home on his property in 1882 to house his family of twelve. In 1894, at the age of 55 years, Joseph was kicked by a farm animal, which resulted in his death. (Both John Jr., and Joseph are buried in the Yaggy Cemetery on Page Road near Grabill.) In 1900, the farm was divided and sold to David N. Klopfenstein, Joseph's second son, and to Joseph A. Grabill. Joseph A. Grabill purchased the house and the land south of the road (now State Street) and David N. Klopfenstein bought the land north of the road that included the cider mill.

Shortly after the purchase, both men started selling lots from their property and a community began to develop. In 1901, when the Wabash Railroad came through the area, a station was needed to service the growing town. It was built on land purchased from Joseph A. Grabill. The little community then became known as Grabill.

On March 27, 1902, a hand written deed, David N. and Caroline Klopfenstein donated a parcel of land to "The Trustees of the Mennonite Mission," now known as the Grabill Missionary Church located on State Street.

The Klopfensteins settled in Allen County and Adams County of Indiana and in parts of Illinois and Iowa when some families moved further west.

Resource:

•*Klopfenstein Family Record* by John Henry Klopfenstein

•Mary Lou Clegg, genealogist

•Deeds recorded in the Allen County Courthouse and owned by Grabill Missionary Church

•*Community Progress Newspaper*, dated September 7, 1934

Submitted by Carolyn Klopfenstein Johnson, Granddaughter of David N. Klopfenstein

RALPH KLOPFENSTEIN FAMILY

Ralph Klopfenstein was the son of David and Mattie Klopfenstein. David was the youngest son of Michael Klopfenstein.

The Ralph Klopfenstein family. Front row: Foster, Calvin and Beverly. Back row: parents, Edith and Ralph

Ralph and his wife, Edith, had two sons and one daughter.

Their first son, Foster, served in the U.S. Air Force during World War II. He married Willodean Ehrsman. Foster worked at Grabill Hardware for 18 years then bought Trinity in New Haven. Foster and Willodean had one daughter, Sandra (Jones) and two sons, David and Phillip. Foster died in February of 2002.

Ralph and Edith's other son, Calvin, served in the U.S. Army during the Korean War. Calvin married Marilyn (Ringenberg). They had three sons, Ron, Reggie and Rod. C. L. Klopfenstein Builders was started by Calvin, and now his son Ron is continuing the business. Ron married Lorene Lloyd. Reggie married Kay Grabill.

Ralph and Edith's daughter, Beverly, married Richard Schantz. They had two children, Dr. Brad Schantz and Renee (Shirley). Richard Schantz worked for Mutual Security as Vice President of Claims.

All of Ralph and Edith's children and their families have been followers of Christ and faithful in their local churches. They have served God and their country.

Submitted by Mrs. Beverly (Klopfenstein) Schantz, written by Christine J. Gerig

KLOTZ FAMILIES

Herman Klotz, born in Weilheim, Hohenzolleren, Germany (near Stuttgart), July 5, 1838, immigrated in 1881 to Fort Wayne. He came with his wife Barbara Wanamaker born July 3, 1849 in the nearby town of Rangendingen and their four children: Daniel, Elisabeth (married Joseph Forche), Maria (married Rufus P. Ormiston), and Eugene. Herman's parents were Joseph Kloz and Maria Anna Beck. Barbara's parents were Johann George Wannenmacher and Elisabeth Kalbacher. To conform to the restructuring of the German language a 't' was added in the early 1800s changing the name to Klotz.

Herman joined his brother, Daniel Klotz. Daniel is the ancestor of the Klotz families residing here presently who settled in Fort Wayne in 1863. Daniel established himself as a manufacturer and merchant owning a grocery store at Calhoun Street near Williams Street. Daniel resided at 308 East DeWald Street. He was born July 21, 1845 in Weilheim and married Anna Bauman, daughter of John and Sophia Bauman of Fort Wayne. They had nine children: Frank, Joseph, Clement, Anthony, Sylvester, Minnie, Agnes (Mrs. George T. Miller), Katharine, Edith, and Lenora (married Clarence Freiburger). Anna Klotz died January 2, 1929. Daniel Klotz died March 18, 1913. Both are buried at St. Peter's Catholic Cemetery

Herman was a car builder for the Pennsylvania Railroad. He worked long hours, and could not find the time to dig the cellar his wife desired. Shovel in hand, Barbara dug her own cellar at 700 South Calhoun Street. Born in Fort Wayne, Ed, and George Forrest were the last-born children of Herman and Barbara. After Herman's death on February 17, 1900, Barbara married Adam Thulen on September 11, 1902. Barbara Klotz (she reverted to her first married name) died March 24, 1936. Both Herman and Barbara are buried at St. Peter's Catholic Cemetery.

George Klotz, who married Dessa Velsetta Miller Somers of Tocsin June 1, 1916 in Jackson, Michigan, resided at 1350 Home Avenue. He was employed by the Western Gas Company making gas tanks until WWII when he went to Baltimore, Maryland, to make harbor tugs for the war effort. George and Dessa retired to Indian Rocks, Florida, and died there. Son George joined them in Indian Rocks and raised his family there. They were the parents of George, Ned, Bruce and Marianna (m. Frank Clark). Dessa's children from Francis Somers were: Erma (married Murray Crandall), Merville, and Maurese (married Harold Miller). The only male descendants of Herman are through his son George F., and they reside in Peru, New Castle, Indianapolis, and Tampa, Florida.

Submitted by Jane Smithenry Klotz

HERMAN KLUG

Julia Klug was born on April 17, 1959 in Fort Wayne, Indiana. She is the daughter of Phyllis Ann (Hartman) and Herman Patrick Klug. Julia attended grade school at St. John the Baptist and graduated from Bishop Luers High School on May 29, 1977. Julia went to college at the University of Dayton and earned a degree in Communication Arts/Public Relations in 1981. Since then, Julia has worked in a variety of marketing positions for Lincoln Property Company, The Walt Disney Company and Dow Jones and Company. In 1997, Julia started her own Internet Marketing consulting business, specializing in the promotion of Web sites for nonprofit organizations. On October 10, 1992 Julia married James Zauner in Orlando, Florida. James has worked with Dow Jones and Company since 1983. Currently he holds the position of Director of Circulation

Frank and Anna Feipel in front of Feipel Grocery Company, 618 Madison Street.

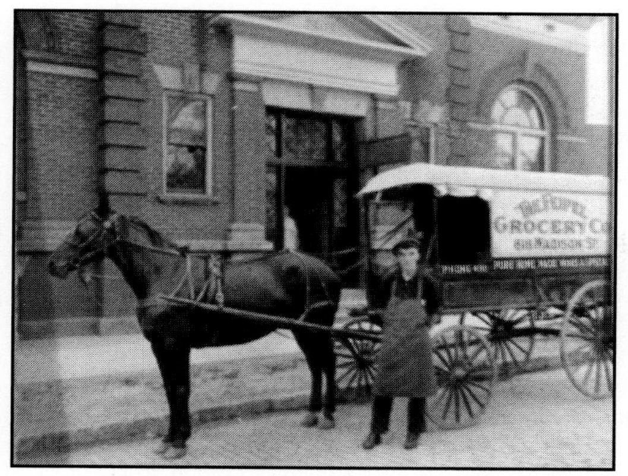

Abie Glabin, wagon driver for Feipel Grocery, pictured in front of Home Telephone Company's south side exchange on the southeast corner of Calhoun Street and Masterson Avenue, about 1910.

Business Operations. Julia and James have two children, Anna Virginia, born November, 1996, and Robert, born May, 1999. Julia and her family live in central New Jersey.

Julia's father, Herman Klug was born on March 17, 1920 in Fort Wayne, Indiana. He was the youngest of the four children of John and Virginia (Feipel) Klug who owned a grocery store at 618 Madison Street, next to their home at 614 Madison Street. This grocery was started by Virginia's parent's Frank and Anna (Schuermann) Feipel. In 1913, the same year that John Klug married Virgina Feipel, the Feipel Grocery Company formed a new corporation with members being Frank Feipel, Victor Feipel, Virginia Feipel and John Klug. The capital stock for this company was $10,000. Frank was a generous person. He would take two bit cigars from his store and would hand them out on the streetcars. He would also take change out of the cash register drawer and pass the coins out to kids on the street. Frank Feipel emigrated from Luxembourg, France in 1878 and became a naturalized citizen in 1913. The Feipel family remaining in the old county continued to own a large vineyard and made wine called Feipel-Star. Herman's parents used the family recipe to make wine here and sold it in their grocery. One of the places that this wine could be found was at Epcot Center at Disney World in Florida.

Herman Klug graduated from Central High School in 1938. Herman married Phyllis Hartman on June 8, 1946 at St. John the Baptist Catholic Church in Fort Wayne. Phyllis and Herman have four children; Daniel Clement, (Vida), Stanley Patrick (1955-1987), Julia Kathryn (James) Zauner, and Laura Jeanne (Jon) Pfeffer. They have six grandchildren: Amanda (Klug) (Justino) Jimenez, Jason (Jenny) Klug, Maia Pfeffer, Aron Pfeffer, Anna Zauner, and Bobby Zauner and three great-grandchildren: Jelicia Jimenez, Nikolas Jimenez and Brandon Klug.

Submitted by Julia Zauner.

PAUL KNAFEL FAMILY

Paul Rowland Knafel was born October 29, 1910 in Noble County and died July 27, 1999 in Allen County; he is buried in Eel River Cemetery. He was the oldest of five children born to Gustave Knafel born 1891 died in 1958 and May Pauline Rowland born December 19, 1887 died November 21, 1974. His four siblings were Elmer, Evelyn Marie, Emily Annah, and Lenora Pauline Knafel. Gustave is buried at Merriam Christian Chapel, while May is buried at West Side Cemetery in Goshen, Indiana.

On April 24, 1930, he was married to DeElda Elmira Gaffborn born August 19, 1912, the daughter of George Hayes born February 11, 1877 died October 9, 1949 and Florence Alverda Hyndman born November 7, 1882 died June 21, 1966; both are buried in Eel River Cemetery.

Of this union were born three daughters: Betty Joan born January 10, 1931, Wanda Jean born May 31, 1935, and Sandra Jenn born December 9, 1937. They also raised Senora Sue Cain born July 14, 1948, the daughter of Paul's sister, Evelyn, who had passed away.

Paul and DeElda moved several times during their married lives in Noble and Allen counties. They eventually settled on a small farm east of Churubusco in Allen County in 1946.

Paul worked at several places including General Electric in Fort Wayne and hauling bulk milk into County Line Cheese Company. He retired from Harlan's Hardware in LaOtto as a serviceman for gas furnaces. The couple were members of St. John's Lutheran Church on O'Day Road.

The Knafel's enjoyed their retirement years visiting with their daughters and many friends; they spent their winters in Alamo, Texas. They were very active in Western Square Dance groups and traveled extensively going to square dances.

William and Emilie Knoefel, grandparents of Paul, came to America from Germany and settled in Cleveland, Ohio. They had eight children, some having been born in Germany and the remainder born in America; they came to this country under the name of Knoefel, later changing it to Knafel. William died in Cleveland. Sometime later Emilie came to Indiana and settled in Noble County where she married a man by the name of Ennen. She passed away in 1940 and is buried in the Merriam Christian Chapel cemetery.

Submitted by Wanda Maroney

**Due to publisher error, please see page 760 for photo of Paul Knafel Family*

CHRISTIAN KNIPSTEIN & FREIDA (POEHLER) & WILBUR M. KNIPSTEIN & MAXINE E. (HEINE) FAMILIES

The original purchase of a 40-acre land tract that would eventually become the Poehler Homestead was made on March 14, 1842, and appears in certificate No. 3879 in the Federal Land office in Fort Wayne. This followed the 1820 Land Grant Acts of Congress under President James Monroe.

Christopher and Catherina Pfeifer sold the land to Harman Seddelmeyer, who married Maria Stellhorn. Harman was killed during construction of St. Paul's Lutheran Church on Barr Street in 1847.

Charles Poehler migrated to the area from Huntington and married Harman's widow, Maria, on June 10, 1847. They acquired 300 acres of land, eventually divided among their three sons, Christian, Charles and John.

Christian married Sophia Fruechtenicht about 1880. They had four sons and four daughters: Adolph, Fred, Emilie, Martin, Emma, Clara, Frieda and Arthur. The Poehler home place consisted of 140 acres at the southern end of Hanna Street bordered, in part, by the St. Mary's River.

It was then customary to put a son on 80 acres of land, so Christian purchased an additional 80 acres for son Fred, and 70 acres for son Martin. He built new homes and barns on those farms between 1901 and 1927. Sons Adolph and Arthur lived on the original 140 acres.

The youngest daughter, Frieda, married Christian Knipstein in 1919. Christian immigrated to the United States from Levern, Germany, in 1913. He traveled on the George Washington and passed through Ellis Island on his way to Indiana, where his uncle had a farm near Hoagland.

He and Frieda purchased her brother Fred's 80 acres in 1944 and lived on that farm located at 8602 S. Anthony Boulevard. Christian and Frieda had three sons: Alvin, Walter, and Wilbur. Freida died in 1961 and Christian died in 1980. Both are buried in the cemetery of Trinity Lutheran Church on Decatur Road, south of Fort Wayne.

Their youngest son, Wilbur, was born January 16, 1933. He married Maxine Heine on June 2, 1956, and purchased the farm from his father in 1962. Wilbur worked at International Harvester

L.to R. Front: Arthur Poehler, Sophia Poehler, Christian Poehler, Frieda Poehler Back: Emelie Poehler, Adolph Poehler, Clara Poehler, Fred Poehler, Emma Poehler, Martin Poehler

as an apprentice and later in various management positions until 1991. During this time, he continued to farm and raise Holstein dairy cattle, selling milk to Allen Dairy and later, Prairie Farms.

In 1976 he and Maxine purchased the adjoining Poehler homestead and continue to farm to this day. They have four daughters: Karen, married to Timothy Krupski; Luann, married to Dan Vachon; Janell married to William Vaughan; and Susan, married to Timothy Imler - and 13 grandchildren. Wilbur and Maxine are lifelong members of the Lutheran Church-Missouri Synod, belonging to Trinity Lutheran Church on Decatur Road until transferring to Mount Calvary in Waynedale in 1991. There Wilbur chaired two major building campaigns to erect a new sanctuary, preschool, and Family Life Center on Reservation Drive.

The photo shows the Christian Poehler family in front of their home on the Hanna Street Farm circa 1930.

Submitted by Wilbur Knipstein

DONALD HENRY & LINDA ANN (RAHDERT) KNOPF FAMILY

Donald was born October 20, 1936 in Belknap Township, Presque Isle County, Michigan on the Knopf Homestead, established 1873 by his great-grandparents, Charles and Pauline [Goltz] Knopf. They originally lived in Detroit, Michigan after arriving in America in 1869. Charles and Pauline had seven children who including Don's grandfather, Hermann and his wife Wilhelmine Algenstedt Knopf.

Wilhelmine's parents were Henry and Bertha [Horn] Armstadt who homesteaded land in neighboring Moltke Township, Presque Isle County, Michigan. Their children [all deceased] were Fredrick, Adeline Rosteck Grebe, Augusta Sommer, and Arthur and Don's father, Henry Emil Knopf.

Donald's mother was Helma Margaret Legner, and her parents were Albert and Johanna Wetzel Legner. Besides Donald, they had the following children: Eldon, the present owner of the Knopf Homestead; Elwood; and Karen Liedtke.

Donald and Linda Knopf

Donald's first introduction to Allen County was in 1951 when he enrolled in the Concordia Prep School on Maumee Avenue (that became Concordia Senior College in 1957 on Leo Road) majoring in Classical Languages and Theology. While attending Concordia Prep School he met his wife, Linda Ann Rahdert. She later enrolled at Concordia University in River Forest, Illinois majoring in Elementary Education. They were married following their June graduation July 25, 1959 in Linda's home church, St. Paul Evangelical Lutheran Church, on Barr Street. They earned their Master of Education degrees from St. Francis University.

Linda Ann Rahdert Knopf, was born in Fort Wayne on July 25, 1937, the daughter of Wilmer and Rosalind Rust Rahdert. Linda's brother, Dr. Richard Rahdert, was the Medical Director of the Wabash Valley Mental Health Hospital in West Lafayette, Indiana. Her father, Wilmer was born February 20, 1905 in Washington Township. Wilmer was a farmer in Perry Township on the Lima Road. Rosalind was born October 3, 1913 in Buckley [Iroquois County], Illinois, daughter of Fredrick and Martha Luhrsen Rust. She worked at Pollack Bros. and Lincoln Life Insurance Co. Wilmer's parents were Christian Rahdert and Elise Kramer whose farm was on the southwest corner of Coldwater Road and Coliseum Boulevard. Elise's parents were Charles and Sophie Rose Kramer whose farm was on the Leo Road.

Donald and Linda began their professional life as Lutheran elementary teachers in Evergreen Lutheran School in Detroit, Michigan, from 1959-1960. In 1960 they returned permanently to Allen County when Donald became the principal/teacher at the Emmanuel Lutheran School [Soest] from 1960 - 1969, and from 1969 - 1998 as elementary teacher at Hoagland and Harlan. Linda taught twenty-eight years at her home church school, St. Paul Lutheran, on Barr Street, and four years at Central Lutheran School in New Haven. Their family includes son, Timothy Tadd Knopf and daughter Alison Anne Knopf.

Submited by Donald Knopf

FRANZ "FRANK" ADAM & ALMA LORETTA (BROWN) KOEHL FAMILY

Franz "Frank" Adam Koehl was born November 28, 1892, in Fort Wayne, Indiana, the son of Jacob Koehl and Gertrude Theresia Kummerant, natives of OberRoden, Germany, who had immigrated to the United States. Jacob Koehl established the Fort Wayne monument business, Jacob Koehl & Sons. The monument business touched many parts of Fort Wayne, including work done at St. Peter Catholic Church (communion rail) and the Cathedral of the Immaculate Conception (communion rail). Jacob Koehl & Sons also prepared and installed in May of 1916 the monument to Johnny Appleseed which is located in East Sweeney Park between the Old Sweeney Homestead and the current tennis courts.

Frank was the youngest of five children: Gertrude (married Hubert Sallot), Louis M. (married Emma), Jacob M. (married Theresa, later married brother's wife, Emma), Andrew (married Blanche). The family resided in their home on Dewald Street. Frank was baptized and attended church and school at St. Peter Catholic Church in Fort Wayne.

Frank married Alma Loretta Brown on January 8, 1914, at the Cathedral of the Immaculate Conception in Fort Wayne. Loretta was one of fourteen children, the daughter of Aaron Brown (b. appx. 1850, d. appx. 1904) and Mary Melinda Kromenaker (b. 1863, d. 1963) and lived in New Haven, Indiana. She attended St. John the Baptist Catholic Church and school, graduating from the eighth grade on June 20, 1905. Loretta's siblings included: Albert

Frank and Loretta (Brown) Koehl

(died at age thirteen), Rose (married Albert Offner), Clarence (married Nellie, second wife), Bertha (died at birth), Francis (married Frances Dodane), Ethel (married George Nichter), Lorena (married John Giere), Agnes (married Charles Griffith), Louis (married Mary), Alfred (married Irma Woenker), Marie (married Albert Hamrick), Raymond (died at age five), and Herman (married Louise Bottenhorn).

Loretta worked at Wayne Knitting Mills as a young woman. Upon her marriage, she became a homemaker and mother. She returned to the labor force during WW II, working at Magnavox. She later worked at Peerless Cleaners. She was a seamstress and worked at a local bridal shop, as well as out of her own home. She made many wedding dresses, some of which have been recorded in photos.

Soon after marrying, the couple moved to Decatur, Illinois, where Frank worked for the New York Central in the yards as a welder. He left the railroad during a strike, when he refused to cross the picket lines and was fired. They returned to Fort Wayne, where Frank worked as a Prudential Insurance salesman.

Frank and Loretta had five children: Noreen Frances, born November 17, 1915 (married several times); Herbert Eugene, born February 18, 1917 (married Irene Agatha Becker); Marceille Marie, born December 8, 1921(d. 1928); Dolores Joanne, born April 18, 1926 (married Robert Lawrence Hope); Thomas Vincent, born June 15, 1928 (married Patricia Ann Newman, d. 1995; married Joan Garns Butler).

Daughter Marceille developed appendicitis in 1928. An incorrect diagnosis and treatment caused the appendix to rupture. She died from peritonitis as a result of the ruptured appendix. Nearly overnight, Frank's hair changed from black to white, which it remained for the rest of his life.

During the Great Depression, Frank lost his job and the family home on California Avenue, forcing them to move to Rome City, Indiana, where they lived from December 1931 through December 1937. During the Depression years, he worked for the WPA (Works Project Association). Loretta helped feed the family with her talent for fishing, catching blue gill, perch and catfish from nearby Sylvan Lake. The entire family assisted Loretta in baking bread, rolls and cakes, which they sold. The children would help prepare the dough, working late into the evening. Then Frank and Loretta would rise in the early morning to bake the goods, which Frank delivered to customers.

Daughter Dolores was severely burned on June 15, 1933, when she was seven years old. Kerosene, which had been ignited to burn it away, accidentally splashed onto Dolores, causing serious burns across her chest and arms, about one third of her body.

On July 10, 1933, Frank broke his neck falling out of a cherry tree while picking cherries. He was driven home by his son, Herb, who was just 16 years old and who had never driven a car. Frank was later taken to the hospital by ambulance. At first, the hospital (McCray Memorial, in Kendallville) did not treat him, thinking he was not going to live. However, about three days, later they put him in traction for his broken neck. He spent a week in the hospital. He came home from the hospital just as his daughter Dolores was going in for surgery for her burns.

Frank Koehl, Lincoln National Life Building, engraving 1962 man of the year award winner

The family returned to Fort Wayne in 1937, buying a home on Lake Avenue (where Dolores Koehl and Robert Hope later held their wedding reception). After returning to Fort Wayne, Frank began working with his brother, Jacob M. Koehl, in the family monument business, Jacob Koehl & Sons, on Calhoun Street (originally on Williams Street), doing engraving on granite stones for use in cemeteries. He took over the business when his brother Jacob died. The business was in great distress, but Frank was able to repay all the debts and turn the business around.

Frank's skill as a monument engraver was well known. He was invited by Gutson Borglum, sculptor and designer of the Mount Rushmore National Memorial, to join the team of stone cutters carving the faces of George Washington, Thomas Jefferson, Theodore Roosevelt and Abraham Lincoln into the granite of Mount Rushmore in the Black Hills of South Dakota. But since the work was volunteer labor, Frank had to decline the offer in order to continue to support his family.

In the mid-1950s, after many years of owning a business, Frank decided to sell the building. He began working for other monument makers, at one point working for three different monument makers (Becker, Huntington, Indiana; Birkmeyer & Sons, Fort Wayne; and Tony Schaab, Fort Wayne) as well as his own business. Frank was chosen to engrave the *Man of the Year* award winner's name on the lobby wall of the Lincoln National Life Building in 1961, 1962 and 1963.

A number of the stones he engraved are located in Catholic Cemetery, Fort Wayne, and in other cemeteries in the Fort Wayne area and throughout the northern part of Indiana. His work can be recognized by the depth of the engraving. During his lifetime, he engraved most of the stones for his family and his own gravesites (except his grandson, Bob). His son-in-law, Robert L. Hope, often helped him set the stones at the gravesites. Some have been recorded with photos.

Frank and Loretta spent their semi-retirement and retirement years at their lake cottage on Dallas Lake, near Wolcottville, Indiana in Noble County where Loretta continued her hobby of fishing. Their five children produced 36 grandchildren and 105 great-grandchildren, most residing in Allen County. Frank died in 1967, and Loretta died in 1968. Both are interred in Catholic Cemetery, Fort Wayne.

Submitted by Dolores J. Hope

EDWARD & SOPHIA KOENEMANN

This home (see picture) is located at 11009 East English Street, Hoagland, Indiana, (named for Pliny Hoagland, the director of the Grand Rapids and Indiana Railroad). When purchased by Edward Koenemann with 20 acres, it was one story and had no indoor plumbing. His grandfather, Frederich Koenemann, came from Quetzen 42, Lahde, Mendin, Prussia, and settled in Adams County where he married Sophia Allefeld on April 21,1842. Edward first worked with Centliver Corp. In 1910, Mr. Bash sold his seed business to Edward, which he developed into a large farm implement and grain store called "New Idea Farm Equipment". On its second floor was the only hall to rent in the Hoagland area.

On June 19,1895, Edward Koenemann married Sophia Meyer whose family lived at 9525 Muldoon Road, Fort Wayne, Indiana. Sophia's grandparents, Johann and Anna (Bischoff) Meyer, were married in Achim, Germany, the autumn of 1828. They arrived at Ellis Island on June 20, 1845. They traveled via the Hudson River to Albany, New York, through the Erie Canal to Toledo, Ohio, and the Wabash Erie Canal to Fort Wayne, Indiana. This brick home on Muldoon Road (built in 1878) is still standing. It was built on 40 acres purchased for three dollars an acre. Although Sophia was born prior to this house being built, her younger five siblings were born here.

Home of Edward and Sophia Koenemann in Hoagland, Indiana

Ed and Sophia were blessed with seven children: Erwin, Edith Hilgeman, Hilda Borchelt, Clara Grotrian, Clarence, Paul, and Elvera Gresley. The children were all baptized and confirmed at St. John Lutheran Church, Bingen, Indiana. They had a hand cranked Victrola, a large wood burning stove for cooking, a coal furnace in the basement, a barn for two horses and a cow, with an adjoining chicken house. There were ten plum trees, four cherry trees, and six apple trees, one acre of land for pasture and another large strip for corn, tomatoes, and other vegetables. Their transportation at that time was with their horse 'Pete," pulling either their wagon or sleigh.

While growing up the children attended dances at the Hoagland Hayloft, church baseball games, Walther League activities, or took an electric train to a park in Rome City. They enjoyed playing cards at home and going on hayrides during which they sang their favorite songs. When movies became available they were projected on the side of a building at dusk in the summertime and they all gathered to enjoy them.

Submitted by Eileen Felton

WILHELM & OLGA B. (HIEBER) KOHLENBERG

Wilhelm (Bill) Kohlenberg and his wife Olga B. (Hieber) lived on a farm at the corner of Paulding and Green roads of rural New Haven. Bill was the son of Wilhelm Kohlenberg and Sophia Bradtmiller. Olga's parents were Samuel Hieber and Sophia Bleeke. The farm had been owned by Bill's uncle Coonrod and wife Johanna Kohlenberg. Bill's only sibling was a brother Ernest. He and his wife Elsie lived one-half mile west on Paulding Road on the Kohlenberg farm. Olga's parents lived one-and-a-half mile west on Paulding Road.

Kohlenberg Family L. to R. Olga S. Kohlenberg, Olga B. (Hieber) Kohlenberg, Pauline E. (Kohlenberg) Giant, Wilhelm (Bill) Kohlenberg

Bill and Olga were always happy to have company. They farmed with a team of horses, milked cows, raised chickens, ducks, and sheep. Their garden and fruit trees provided many jars of food for the cold winters. Bill worked as a carpenter for many years. They had two daughters, Olga S. and Pauline E. Pauline married Ray Giant and had a daughter Mary Catherine. Mary Catherine was a sweet and happy child who brought much happiness to them. Olga S. never left home. Olga lived to be 86 and Bill to 95 before being called home to the Lord, the shepherd of their lives. They and daughter Olga S. are buried in the Emmanuel Lutheran Cemetery, rural New Haven.

Submitted by Mary C. Federspiel

ROBERT KOHRMAN FAMILY

Bob, born November 21, 1906, died October 6, 1985. Velma, born August 26, 1908, died September 9, 1985. Both were born and resided all their lives in Fort Wayne. They had three sons:

Kohrman Family.

James (Jim) Robert, Ronald (Ron) William, and Stephen (Steve) Francis. Bob graduated from St. Paul's Catholic School in 1921 and graduated from Indiana Technology College in 1934 with a BSEE degree. He retired from General Color Card, later Caldwell General Corporation, in 1971 after 25 years of service.

Jim, born November 11, 1937, married Janet Lou Hardgrove, on October 14, 1961 in Carrolton, Ohio. They resided in Fort Wayne until 1966 where two children were born, Malissa Elaine, August 17, 1963 and Craig Robert, November 20, 1964, who wed Jeanne Seurer August 22, 1992. They have three children: Nicole, born February 25, 1997, Marissa, born August 11, 1998 and Jonathon, born May 6, 2001.

Jim and Janet moved to Detroit, Michigan in June 1966 where three children were born, David James, January 6, 1966; Jeffrey Lewis, September 23, 1967, who wed Jennifer Strom June 6, 1993 and have two children: Madeline, born September 28, 1998, and Tollef, born April 9, 2002; Celia Dion, born October 10, 1970.

In June 1973 the entire family moved to Burnsville, Minnesota where Janet died in November 1999. Jim then married Carol A. Romary Bonar, May 1, 2001. All of his children except Celia reside in the Minneapolis area. Celia currently resides in Decatur, Georgia.

Ron, born January 19, 1940, wed Gloria Ann Endicott, born June 12, 1942 in Coldwater, Michigan on November 9, 1963. They reside in Fort Wayne. Gayle Ann was born in Terre Haute on August 16, 1964, wed Robert Carlson June 15, 1991. Children: Ryan, born October 12, 1993; Bradley, born June 8, 1995; William, born January 4, 1999; and Nicholas, born May 1, 2002. All reside in Carmel. Deborah Ann, was born in Muncie January 25, 1966, wed Vince Morken 1986, divorced 1994. Children: John, born April 22, 1987, Amanda, born August 21, 1990 wed David Crites on October 31, 2001. All family members reside in Fort Wayne.

Two children were born in Fort Wayne. Mary Lynn, born January 12, 1967 wed Brian Kinniry June 19, 1993. Children: Morgan, born August 18, 1995; Kelsey, born January 18, 1997; Lauren, born February 27, 1999; and Collin, born January 27, 2001. All reside in Fort Wayne. Jeannette Lynn, born October 24, 1968, wed Jameson Waters September 2, 1989. Children: Austin, born November 24, 1990; Chelsea, born October 5, 1992; and Luke, born August 24, 1994. All reside in Fort Wayne.

Steve Kohrman, born March 14, 1950 in Fort Wayne, moved to Mobile, Alabama in January 1974. He married Deborah Ann Lewis August 14, 1976. When they married Debbie had a son, William Jackson Hoppe (Billy), from a previous marriage. The trio moved to Tallahassee, Florida August 1977 and returned to Mobile in June 1979. Three children were born in Mobile, Alabama. Robert Scott, April 14, 1981; Jessica Lynn, November 18, 1983; Stephanie Michelle, June 9, 1988. The family resides in Mobile, Alabama.

Submitted by Steve Kohrman.

KOOMLER, LEHNEKE

Highlights of an article in the *News-Sentinel* October 6, 1942:

Mr. Ralph Johnson, chairman of the salvage committee, entered into a contract with Allen Koomler and Everett Lehneke who were pardoners in the Allen County waste material firm to remove metal for the war effort.

Two heavy old safes were donated, one by the Fort Wayne Dental Depot and the other by the owners of the Standard building.

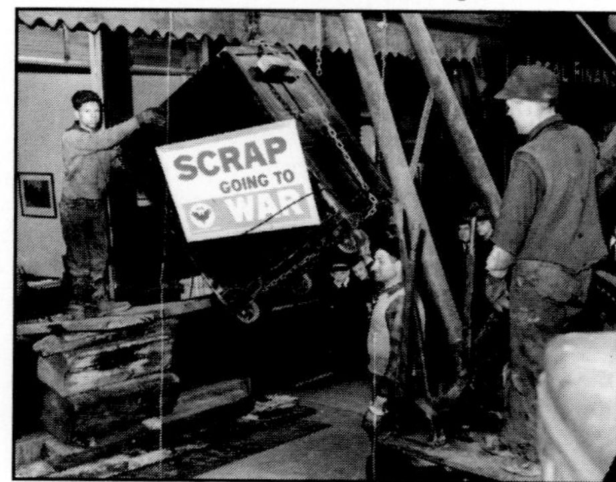

R to L: Allen Koomler, Everett Lehneke, and Vernon Koomler

The Newspaper Scrap Metal Drive opened September 28 and closed October 17, 1942. Donations of 1,700 pounds of steel from an old hand press, boilers, elevators, and an 850-pound automobile engine were collected. Schools had scrap days. The WPA collected 80 tons of salvage. Two families donated four iron fences on West Wayne Street; another lady gave a pair of fire tongs that were 102 years old. Typewriters, golf clubs, over 9,000 keys in addition to large amounts of other scrap were collected by school pupils.

The Fort Wayne Athletic Association donated its outdoor area on North Clinton Street for use as a scrap collection depot.

Submitted by Marilyn McFadden

LUCY AGNES SHELLER KOPP

Lucy Agnes Sheller Kopp was born June 27, 1901 in North Manchester, Indiana. She was the daughter of John and Mary Elizabeth Waltemade Sheller. John and his two brothers owned the Sheller Hotel in North Manchester, Indiana. That building is still in use today.

Lucy graduated from the Huntington County, Indiana, schools and was employed by the Our Sunday Visitor Publishing Company as a secretary. She sold copies of the Catholic paper after mass on Sundays. She became well acquainted with Fr. John Francis Noll who was the priest at St. Mary's parish. She also worked at Penfield Jewelry store as clerk and book-keeper.

She was visiting in Kent, Ohio, and met Frank J. Kopp who had graduated from the School of Engineering at St. Bonaventure in Olean, New York. They were married in

Lucy Kopp

Kent, Ohio, and, after the birth of their daughter, Shirley on July 5, 1921, they traveled to Huntington, Indiana, so Fr. Noll could baptize their daughter.

The family moved to Fort Wayne in 1924, where Frank was employed by the General Electric Company. Lucy attended classes at Indiana Extension and was skilled in short hand, typing, and accounting. She was employed as a law clerk and secretary for the firm of Eggeman, Reed and Cleland for seventeen years. Lucy then became office manager for Putnam and Green Road Construction Company where she advanced to vice president of the company. She was well-versed in tax law and prepared tax returns for individuals and corporations until her death on April 17, 1976. She always made her home with her daughter's family in Fort Wayne. She is buried in the Sheller family plot in the Catholic Cemetery in Huntington, Indiana.

Shirley graduated eighth grade from Cathedral School and from Central Catholic High School in the Class of 1939. She earned a BS in nutrition from St. Mary of the Woods College. After serving an internship in Cincinnati, Ohio, in 1944, she became a registered dietitian. She married Robert Emmett Kearney on October 8, 1949, at St Jude Catholic Church. They have three sons.

Submitted by Shirley Kearney

THE FLORIAN & ALVINA (ESSIG) KORTE FAMILY

Florian Christian Korte was born February 20, 1895 in Fort Wayne, Indiana. His grandparents, Conrad and Marie Mohlenbrock Korte, arrived at New York Harbor on October 26, 1854 on the ship Celle with their children, Conrad Jr. age three, and one year old Frederich, from the village of Dohren in Windheim, Germany.

Conrad Sr. became a farmer in St. Joseph Township, Allen County, Indiana, and attended St. Peter's Lutheran Church. He married Louisa Myers; they had two children Clara and Emma.

Florian and Alvina (Essig) Korte

Conrad and Marie's son, Frederich Korte, became a teamster and married Louis Gehle, the daughter of Fred Gehle and Lizette Prange. They had five children: Fred, Florian, Edwin and Karl (twins) and Waldemar. Karl and Waldemar died in infancy; Edwin died at age 19. Fred Jr. married Amelia Horman and had one child, Mildred. Fred eventually founded the Korte Paper Co. He died in 1968.

Florian Korte served in the army during WWI in France and then began his 48-year career with General Electric. He married Alvina Essig on May 18, 1940. Alvina arrived at Ellis Island on December 16, 1910 on the ship the Pennsylvania with her mother, Marie Josephine Essig, and four-month-old brother, Gottlieb Jr. Alvina's father had already located in Boston on May 21, 1910. He arrived at Ellis Island on the SS George Washington and settled with his brother-in-law Sylvester Homan in anticipation of the arrival of his family from the small village of Flacht, Leonberg, Wurtemberg, Germany.

Alvina's father, Gottlieb Essig, Sr., became a farmer in Huntington, Indiana. Alvina left school at a young age and became a cook for the Caswell family of Huntington, and for a while, her brother Gottlieb was a chauffeur for the same family. This offered Alvina the opportunity to travel with the Caswells to their homes in Chicago and Wallen Lake.

When Florian Korte and Alvina were married on May 18, 1940 she was 33 years old and he was 45 years old. They had three children, Ronald, Ruth and Robert. Ronald and Robert both served in the U.S. Army. Ronald began his career at General Electric in 1962 and retired after 39 years. He married Ila Bohlander on May 18 1986. Robert served in Vietnam and worked at General Electric for 12 years. He married Sharon Ort. They had one son, Christopher. Robert later became the Chief of Police in Albion, Indiana, retiring on April 1, 2005. Ruth married Peter Paulison and had two children, Caroline and Jonathan. Caroline married David Andrew on November 6, 1993. They have three children: Katharine, Samuel, and Peter, and live in Skokie, Illinois. Jonathan married Theresa Koehl, on August 14,1998. They live in Fort Wayne, Indiana.

Submitted by Ronald G. Korte

EDWARD & ERNA (ROEMKE) KRAMER FAMILY

Edward and Erna (Roemke) Kramer lived their entire lives in Allen County. Ed was employed at General Electric and at Concordia Senior College. Ed and Erna Kramer lived at 9337 Brooks Road, Fort Wayne, Indiana. Their three sons were Charles Edward, Max and Wade. Charles Edward, who was born July 19, 1951 in Fort Wayne, Indiana, married Patricia Ann Mueller on June 25, 1977, in Napoleon, Ohio. Patricia was born March 16, 1950, to Ludwig (Lewis) and Dorothy Sudholtz Mueller in Napoleon, Ohio. Max married Ann Marie Krohn on May 4, 1974, at Concordia Seminary in Kramer Chapel at Fort Wayne, Indiana. Ann grew up in rural Woodburn, Indiana. Wade married Susan Sutter on July 14, 1994, in Richtersville, Switzerland. Susan was raised in Switzerland.

Charles and Pat attended school at Concordia College, Seward, Nebraska. Charles received a Master of Education from Mankato State University, Mankato, Minnesota. In 2002, Charles graduated from Concordia Theological Seminary, Fort Wayne, Indiana. He is currently a pastor at St. Paul Lutheran Church, Napoleon, Ohio. Pat received her Master of Education from Defiance College, Defiance, Ohio. She is currently a Lutheran schoolteacher at St. Paul Lutheran School, Napoleon, Ohio. They have three children: Karl (Jessica) Kramer in Fort Wayne, Indiana; Kurtis Kramer of Delta, Ohio; and Sarah Kramer who is a student at Bowling Green State University, Ohio.

Max graduated from Purdue University with a degree in engineering. He has had life long employment at John Deere in Moline, Illinois. Max received his Master of Business Administration degree from the University of Iowa. Ann is the manager of Hallmark Card stores in Bettendorf, Iowa and Moline, Illinois. Their children are Brian and Jennifer.

Wade received his undergraduate degree from Valparaiso University, Valparaiso, Indiana. He received a master degree in hospital administration from the University of Michigan, Ann Arbor, Michigan. Kaiser Permanente in Baltimore, Maryland currently employs him. Wade and Susan have one son, Robert Sven Kramer.

Edward Kramer, Charles, Max, and Wade's father, was the oldest son of Henry and Anna (Salomon) Kramer. Her parents came from Germany and settled on the Dupont Road homestead in 1871. Additional children in Edward's family were Louise, Dorothy and Arnold. Anna and Henry and their families were farmers.

Erna (Roemke) Kramer's parents were John and Sophie (Kammeyer) Roemke. Their home was located on State Road 101 and Antwerp Road in rural Harlan, Indiana. Sophie Kammeyer came to America with her parents on the ship "Spree." They arrived in Sandy Hook, New York on June 20, 1895. Sophie was three years old when her family immigrated to America from Germany. Her siblings were: Ferdinand "Ernest," Louise, Wilhelm, Frederick, and Walter.

John Roemke's father arrived in New York on the ship "Kronpriz F. Wilhelm" on May 1, 1882. John's brothers and sisters were Karl, Wilhelmina "Minnie," Louise, Emma, Wilhelm "Bill," Meta, Friederich, Ida, Christian, Ernest, and Heinrich "Henry."

John and Sophie Roemke and their families were farmers. In addition to Erna, John and Sophie's children were Edwin, Nora, Herbert, Laura, Frieda and Alfred.

Submitted by Charles Kramer

MAROLYN JANE (HARTMAN) KRAUSS

Marolyn Jane (Hartman) Krauss was born January 5, 1951, at St. Joseph Hospital in Fort Wayne, Indiana. She is a 1965 graduate of St. Jude Catholic Grade School, a 1969 graduate of Bishop Dwenger High School (the third graduating class). and a 1973 graduate of Indiana University, Fort Wayne. Over the years, she has accumulated thirty-six graduate hours in elementary education. She is the daughter of Richard Paul Justin Hartman and Vera Louise (Adams) Hartman. Marolyn is the granddaughter of Joseph Clement and Frances Catherine (Schmitt) Hartman, the great granddaughter of John Hubert and Louisa (Aubrey) Hartman, the great-great granddaughter of Herman and Anna Maria (Richter) Hartman.

She married Leon Wayne Krauss on July 21, 1973. In July 1973, she moved to Bermuda with her new husband and taught elementary school there for four years. For the past eighteen years, she has been teaching third grade in the Penn-Harris-Madison School Corporation in Granger, Indiana. She is the mother of Kelby Chadwick Richard Krauss, born in Bermuda on September 30, 1976, (a 1999 Indiana University graduate), and Nicholas Wayne Krauss born December 13, 1979, (a 2003 Indiana University graduate).

Marolyn's father, Richard Paul Justin Hartman, was elected and served as Allen County Recorder from 1959 thru 1962. She and her twin sister, Carolyn Jean (Hartman) Schory, have many fond memories of campaigning for their father. They walked the parade routes and sat in the back of a convertible waving American flags,

Richard Paul Justin Hartman, Allen County Recorder, Swearing-in Ceremony, January 1, 1959

Carolyn Hartman Schory, Marolyn Hartman Krauss, Tommy Hartman, Patty Hartman Hoeppner, Richard Hartman, U.S. Senator Vance Hartke, Vera Hartman

dressed as cheerleaders, wearing the cheerleading black velvet beanies with white yarn balls, that their sister, Patricia Louise (Hartman) Hoeppner wore as a St Jude Catholic Grade School cheerleader. Marolyn attended her father's swearing-in ceremony, on January 1, 1959, in the rotunda of the Allen County Court House and has toured the Allen County Court House on many occasions.

Submitted by Marolyn Krauss

JOHN KRILL & DESCENDENTS

John Krill was born November 30, 1821, in Berks County, Pennsylvania. He was of German and Dutch ancestry, but his parents are unknown at this writing (2005). He was a miller by trade, continuing this vocation before coming to Indiana in 1850. He then became a farmer. For sixteen years he lived in Wells County near the town of Murray. During those years he met Sophia Henline, born May 18, 1825 in Stark County, Ohio, whose family moved to Wells County from Ohio in 1848. They were married April 22, 1852. Sophia's parents are not known. John and Sophia had four boys, William Henry, born January 22, 1853; David John, born November 7, 1856; James W., born May 28, 1858, who died in 1878 of unknown causes; and Samuel F., born August 20, 1862.

In 1866, John and his family came to Allen County and purchased land in Wayne Township, paying $6,500 for 140 acres. He traded part of this land to the county for its infirmary's use as a poor farm. Three years later, the county purchased new land two and one half miles nearer to Fort Wayne and made this the poor farm. (This new land later became Indian Village.) At this time, John secured possession of his original land, adding 42 more acres. This gave the farm a total of 182 acres. Today (2005), the property lines of this land would be the following: Starting at the intersection of Bluffton and Maplewood Roads, head south along Bluffton Road for one-half mile and stop just north of Lincoln Way Court. Turn east and head one-half mile, crossing Airport Expressway and the northern tip of Fort Wayne Regency Mobile Home Park, stopping at its property line. Turn north and head one-fourth mile, again crossing Airport Expressway, and stopping at a point in line with Reservation Drive. Turn east and head about one-fourth mile, again crossing Airport Expressway, stopping at the Richardville Reservation line. Turn north-northwest and head along the Richardville Reservation line for about three-eighths mile, while again crossing Airport Expressway, stopping at a point in line with Maplewood Road. Turn west and head about five-eighths mile to the starting point at Bluffton Road. In 2005, this area contains a southern part of Avalon Addition, including the swimming pool; American Legion Post 241, Miami Middle School, Mount Calvary Lutheran Church, the northern tip of Fort Wayne Regency Mobile Home Park, Waynewood Inn, Ash Brokerage, Waynedale Mobile Home Park, and parts of Airport Expressway.

In politics, John Krill was originally a Whig and later became a Republican. However, he never sought office and was not active in public affairs.

When they became of age, sons William and David helped their father work and manage the home farm. Son Samuel married Sarah J. (maiden name unknown) and became a successful farmer near Decatur in Adams County. It's unknown when and where Sarah was born, if she and Samuel had any children, or when they died.

Upon John Krill's death on January 23, 1889, sons William and David each received 63 and a half acres on the southern part of the farm. Their mother, Sophia, retained the other 55 acres which ran across the northern part of the farm and dog-legged along the Richardville Reservation line. Sophia's land was worked and managed by the two sons, but was sold a couple of years later. Sophia Krill died January 23, 1910, exactly 21 years after her husband, at Hope Hospital in Fort Wayne. (Hope Hospital later became St. Joseph Hospital.)

At the time of his father's death, it is documented that William Krill was unmarried and childless. There's no further information at this writing in 2005 as to whether William was ever married or had any children. William Henry Krill died October 30, 1918, and his 63 and a half acres of land were acquired by his brother, David.

David John Krill married Hettie Maria Greider, a childhood acquaintance, December 20, 1888. Hettie was born in Pleasant Township June 24, 1863. She was the ninth of 12 children born to David and Susannah Greider. David and Hettie Krill were members of the Methodist Episcopal Church. They attended The Union Chapel located at the southeast corner of Bluffton and Dunkelberg Roads.

David Greider also owned land which butted up to the southeast corner of the John Krill farm in Wayne Township. Most of the Greider land is currently, in 2005, owned by Gus Gerke.

Although horses were still the main power source in farming, David, like his father John, used progressive methods and machinery. David devoted his attention to diversified agriculture and raising excellent grade livestock.

In politics, David was a Republican. Although he never allowed his name to be considered in connection with public office, he was held in high popular esteem by his neighboring fellow farmers.

David and Hettie Krill had three boys: Charles Marion, born November 14, 1889; Frank O., born December 4, 1891; and Albert Ransler, born June 11, 1893. Growing up, the boys helped their father and their Uncle William work the two adjoining farms which totaled 127 acres.

Not liking farm life, Frank left home around age 20. He traveled around pursuing various occupations. Occasionally he would check back in at the farm for a while. Around the time of World War I, Frank played semi-pro football. Later, he was a semi-pro boxer. During Prohibition, Frank spent time in Chicago and Detroit. He claimed he was acquainted with the infamous criminals of those cities. His drinking and hard lifestyle eventually caught up with him. At age 45, Frank O. Krill died of pneumonia on April 3, 1937, in St. Joseph's Hospital in Fort Wayne. It is unknown if he ever married or had children. While Frank traveled, his brothers, Charles and Albert, continued to help work the two farms.

Charles Marion Krill married Laura Caroline Gebhardt, the daughter of David and Sophia Gebhardt, December 25, 1910. She had two brothers, George and Fred. Unlike the Krill men who stood an athletic six feet and taller, the Gebhardt men stood a stocky five feet, nine inches, and shorter. Laura, George, and Fred were first cousins to Charles Frederick Gebhardt, known on the silver screen as cowboy star Buck Jones.

Soon after Charles' marriage, it was decided more room was needed. David, Hettie, and his brother, Albert, moved into a house on the south end of the farm. In 2005, this house still stands in the 8400 block of Bluffton Road, next to the north side of Waynewood Inn. Charles took over living in the original home of the farm where his father and uncles grew up and where Charles, his brothers, and all of Charles' children were born.

Original house at 7675 Bluffton Road, 1898, David J. Krill and sons, Charles, Frank, and Albert on porch

David J. and Hettie M. Krill, 1898

1898, Charles M. (standing), Frank O. (on chair), Albert R. (on ottoman)

Original house, 1950, porch and summer kitchen added, Bluffton Road in front

L to R: Frank O. and Charles M. Krill, 1913

Albert R. Krill, WWI uniform, 1917

2003 arial photo of Wayne Township section 34, solid black lines are property lines of original 182 acre farm. Dotted line, northern property line of David Krill's 127 acres and Charles Krill's 49 acres. Circle is original Krill house at 7675 Bluffton Road. Square is second house at 8400 Bluffton Road.

Charles M and Laura C. Krill, California vacation, 1953

Maurice L. and Bonnie A. Krill, 1988

Donald M. and Yvonne M. Krill, 1999

In 2005, the house still stands at 7675 Bluffton Road just south of the American Legion Post 241.

Charles and Laura Krill had 11 children: David Charles, born November 25, 1912; Mabel Hettie, born January 10, 1914; John Edward, born July 14, 1917; Paul Albert, born September 29, 1919; Maurice Leroy, born January 3, 1921; Robert Lloyd, born February 27, 1923; Edna May, born June 28, 1925; Henry William, born April 26, 1927; Betty Jean, born November 11, 1929; Mary Lou, born December 21, 1931; and Florence Ellen, born May 25, 1934.

When the United States entered World War I, Albert, age 24 and single, enlisted. Since he wasn't yet 30, he figured he would be drafted anyway. Charles, age 27, married with three children, and the main work force of the family farm, didn't enlist, nor was he drafted.

David J. Krill had his land resurveyed around 1925 and found his farm contained 130 acres instead of 127. He had the land divided into four fairly equal sections, each containing around 32 and one half acres with about 530 feet of frontage along Bluffton Road.

After falling down his cellar stairs and breaking his hip a week earlier, David John Krill died January 29, 1929 at Methodist Hospital. After his death, brothers Charles and Albert, along with Charles' wife and children, continued to farm the 130 acres. However, the land was still considered owned by Hettie. A couple of years later, the south 32 acres were sold, leaving 98 acres divided into three equal sections.

Hettie Maria Krill died at home January 1, 1934. Her sons were then granted rights to her 8 acres of land. Charles received the northern section containing the original farm house, barns, and buildings. Frank received the middle section, which was bare farmland. Albert received the southern section containing the house he and his parents moved into plus two out buildings. When Frank died in 1937, his land was divided equally between the surviving brothers, giving each 49 acres.

Around 1930, Albert married Tess Shull, who had a son, Donald. The couple never had children together, nor did Albert adopt Donald. Albert and Tess divorced about five years later. Albert neither remarried nor had any children. Around 1932, he became a fireman, and later, an engineer for the Nickel-Plate Railroad. When he had time off, Albert would help his brother, Charles, farm the land. After 20 years with the railroad, Albert retired about 1952. He then sold his house and land and moved into an apartment in Fort Wayne.

During The Great Depression of the 1930s, Charles, needing an occupation in addition to farming to get by, became a construction worker. During that time, he laid many brick streets in Fort Wayne, dug and laid brick cisterns for houses, and dug and put in many miles of waterline and field tile in Waynedale. With great stamina and 21 inch biceps, Charles was called "The Human Backhoe" by his co-workers.

In 1950, Charles' wife, Laura, learned that she had contracted diabetes. In spite of that, Charles and Laura were able to take a trip to California. They enjoyed their time there from December, 1952 through March, 1953. When she could no longer manage the farm home due to diabetic complications, Charles built a new home in Waynedale. They moved into it in spring, 1954. In 2005, the house still stands at 2909 Waynewood Drive. Laura enjoyed the new home for awhile. After a lengthy struggle with diabetes and its complications, Laura Caroline Krill died of congestive heart failure August 18, 1954 at Lutheran Hospital. Shortly thereafter, Charles sold the last portion of the original 182 acre Krill Farm. In 1965, Charles' brother, Albert, moved in with him. In the spring of 1968, Charles decided it was time to move again. He sold his house and moved in with his son, Maurice, about a mile south of the original homestead. Albert moved in with his niece, Edna Proctor, in Fort Wayne. Charles Marion Krill died December 15, 1968, at Lutheran Hospital. Three months later, March 3, 1969, Albert Ransler Krill died at his niece's home.

The rest of this biographical sketch will deal with the children of Charles and Laura: 1) David, 2) Mabel, 3) John, 4) Paul, 5) Maurice, 6) Robert, 7) Edna, 8) Henry, 9) Betty, 10) Mary, and 11) Florence, and the progeny of those children. The birthdates of these children were given earlier in this sketch. All of the following information is as of the year 2005.

A lot of the information on 1) David Charles Krill was not available in time to put into this sketch. We do know David married Louella Lieberenz around 1932. They were divorced years later. He worked construction, operating heavy equipment. At age 62, David Charles Krill died on his birthday November 25, 1974. David and Louella had five children, Phyllis Jean, who died at age one and one half on July 2, 1936, after choking on a wood screw; Charles David, known as "Butch," married more than once, divorced, widowed, and fathered several children; Jack, who married and divorced Amy, and together they have two daughters, Tamara Sue and Shannon; Tom, who married Pat, and they have three children, Jodie, Daniel, and Dennis; and Frank, who married Sonny.

2) Mabel Hettie Krill married Ervin George Werling, known as "Jack," on June 16, 1932. They were divorced in 1953. Mabel and Jack had a daughter, Chalon Elaine, born February 23, 1933. Ervin died in 1966. Mabel Hettie Werling died February 21, 1999. Chalon married Billy Leo Reinhardt July 19, 1954, and settled in North Carolina. They divorced in 1980. Chalon and Billy have two sons, Michael Allen, born June 21, 1958, living in Florida, and Mitchell Alan, born November 3, 1963, living in North Carolina.

3) John Edward Krill, known as "Eddie," was 13 and a half when he was hit and killed by a car February 16, 1931. The fatal accident was witnessed by Eddie's ten-year-old brother, Maurice, in front of their home on Bluffton Road.

4) Paul Albert Krill, who was never married nor had any children, lived most of his life in Marion, Indiana. He died June 21, 2000.

5) Maurice Leroy Krill was known as "Maurie," but was called "Morris" by his father, Charles. As well as helping to work the family farm, Maurice followed his father into the construction occupation. He continued to do both until he was drafted October 27, 1942, during World War II. Maurice became an Army tank driver with the rank of sergeant. He was also responsible for the repair, maintenance, and operation of the tank in combat. Maurice and his three crewmen were in Troop E of the 89th Calvary Reconnaissance Squad of General Patton's 9th Armored Division and saw action in The Battle of the Bulge. Their job was to drive their tank deep into the Germans' front line and radio back information. Maurice was wounded March 2, 1942, and was sent to Walter Reed Hospital in Washington, D.C. to recuperate. After being discharged from the Army October 6, 1945, Maurice went to work for Magnavox in Fort Wayne, building speakers. Not caring for factory work and missing the outdoors, he quit Magnavox and went back to working in construction.

Maurice married Bonnie Augusta Hart February 28, 1942. They had five children, Judith Ann, born prematurely September 23, 1942, and died the same day; Karen Jeanne, born November 26, 1943, living in Fort Wayne; Marilyn Sue, born prematurely November 8, 1945, and died the next day; Diana June, born prematurely December 3, 1946, living in Fort Wayne; and Donald Maurice, born March 9, 1955, living near Hoagland, Indiana.

While working construction, Maurice built and moved into a new house in 1950. Over the next 30 years, he added a garage and two additions to the house. This house is located on Dunkelberg Road about a mile south of the original Krill homestead. Bonnie still lives in that home.

Maurice was a concrete project foreman for John Dehner Inc., a construction company he worked for before being drafted. After 22 years of continuous service, he retired from that company in March of 1986. Maurice and his crew paved some of the city sidewalks, city streets, and surrounding housing developments' streets that are walked and driven on by residents of Allen County every day. Maurice's son-in-law, Robert McIntosh, worked with Maurice's crew 1969 through 1970. Maurice's son, Donald, worked with the crew from the summer of 1973 till Maurice retired. He spent his retirement restoring old cars and, during winter, enjoying his place in Florida.

Maurice Leroy Krill died October 8, 1991.

Maurice and Bonnie's daughter, Karen, married Robert Dennis Long October 4, 1962. They divorced February 28, 1989. Karen and Robert, born June 14, 1941, have four sons, Robert Allen, born May 21, 1963, living in Fort Wayne; Randall Edward, born January 15, 1966, living near Chicago; Andrew Maurice, born April 4, 1968, living in Fort Wayne; and Brian David, born August 10, 1986, living in Fort Wayne. Of the four sons, Randall is the only one married. He married Chicago resident Betty Jo Baker February 11, 2002. Betty, born May 19, 1967, already had two children, Linda Faye, born July 15, 1988; and Justin Anthony, born August 28, 1994.

Maurice and Bonnie's daughter, Diana, married Robert Earl McIntosh December 5, 1969. Diana and Robert, born November 17, 1943, have two children, Jill Kristine, born April 9, 1970, living in Oceanside, California; and Glen Christopher, born October 7, 1971, living in Aurora, Colorado. Glen married Traci Lynn Weiss April 24, 1993. They divorced September 11, 1998. Glen and Traci, born April 17, 1972, have two children, Arielle Lynn Weiss, born September 28, 1991; and Preston Christopher, born February 1, 1996. These children reside with their mother in Wisconsin. Glen married Julie Ann Brown October 4, 1998. Julie, born March 8, 1971, already had a son, Austin Reid Brown, born September 13, 1996, whom Glen adopted. Together, Glen and Julie have a daughter, Katherine Grace, born July 24, 2002.

Maurice and Bonnie's son, Donald, married Yvonne Marie Calahan March 22, 1980. Donald and Yvonne, born November 6, 1955, have three sons, David Maurice, born March 20, 1984, living in San Antonio, Texas while serving in the Air Force; Derek Donald, born September 6, 1986, living near Hoagland; and Charles Aaron, born April 25, 1989, living near Hoagland.

6) Robert Lloyd Krill married Stella Ramage April 14, 1951. Stella, born February 16, 1921, already had a son, Robert Ramage, born January 15, 1944. Robert and Stella had a son together, John Charles, born September 29, 1952. Robert Lloyd Krill died April 16, 1994. Stella Krill died December 17, 1995.

Robert Ramage married Karen Anne Florent July 30, 1966. They are living in Illinois and have two sons, Michael Richard and Christopher John.

John Krill married Sharron Lynn Perry July 23, 1976. They are living in Fort Wayne. John and Sharron, born September 16, 1947, have three children, Jason Paul, born July 7, 1974; Stacy Lynn, born January 29, 1978; and Amanda Nicole, born June 1, 1988. Jason married Shannon Marie Oates April 24, 1999. They are living in Michigan. Jason and Shannon, born January 3,

1975, have two daughters, Brianna Marie, born February 14, 2001; and Desirae Elizabeth, born February 20, 2002.

7) Edna May Krill was athletic and played softball for various teams. She played very briefly with the Fort Wayne Daisies before injuring her knee. She now lives in Columbia City. Edna married Richard Earl Proctor March 11, 1943. Edna and Richard, born March 28, 1919, had four children: Richard Earl, Jr., born October 9, 1944, living at Tri Lakes; Ronald Lee, born March 23, 1948, living in Fort Wayne; Pamela Sue, born April 6, 1949, living in Columbia City; and Candela Jean, born March 21, 1950, living near Fort Wayne. Richard Earl Proctor, Sr. died June 1, 1989.

Richard Earl Proctor, Jr. married Ruth Ann Osterholt June 19, 1967. They divorced December 19, 1986. Richard, Jr. and Ruth, born July 13, 1946, have two children, Tanja Susan, born July 11, 1968; and Bradley Alan, born October 8, 1975. Tanja married Gregory Stephen Jones September 29, 1990. Tanja and Gregory, born April 26, 1962 have three children, Alexander Phillip, born January 27, 1992; Bethany Richelle, born May 12, 1994; and Chloe Renee, born August 17, 1996. Bradley has a daughter, Graisen Reid, born October 4, 1996.

Ronald Proctor married Marilyn Jane Cowell August 1, 1970. Ronald and Marilyn, born February 7, 1948, have two daughters, Marci Lynn, born August 1, 1972; and Erin Leigh, born January 3, 1976. Marci married Aaron Michael Stier September 20, 1997. Aaron, born January 15, 1971, already had twin sons, Patrick Lee and Preston Scott, born October 23, 1991. Together, Marci and Aaron have two daughters, Carson McKenzie, born June 6, 2000, and Caleigh Marie, born October 24, 2002. On August 9, 2003, Erin married Chris Burgess, born November, 1971.

Pamela Proctor married Ronald Eugene Ney August 27, 1988. Pamela and Ronald, born June 18, 1943, have no children.

Candela Proctor married Mark Alexander Confer November 1, 1975. Candela and Mark, born September 19, 1956, have two sons, Joseph David, born January 4, 1979, and Samuel Louis, born September 23, 1981.

8) Henry William Krill was stationed in Hawaii while serving in the Navy from 1946 till 1950. Henry was married to and divorced from Marg Lamb in the 1960s. Henry never fathered any children. He retired from NIPSCO in the 1980s. He liked playing golf in his spare time. His friends on the golf course called him "Hammerin' Hank" because of his long tee shot. Henry William Krill died October 13, 1994.

9) Betty Jean Krill married Everett Roland Resler May 12, 1951. Betty and Everett, born December 25, 1930, had three children, Cynda Lou, born February 7, 1953, living in Fort Wayne; Debra Jean, born May 24, 1954, living in Wells County; and Rick E., born August 1, 1957, living next-door to his mother in Ossian. Betty and Everett owned and operated a restaurant in downtown Ossian from the early-mid 1960s till the mid 1970s. Everett Resler died February 18, 1998.

Cynda Resler married John LaMar Bunting September 17, 1982. Cynda and John, born May 21, 1958, had three children: Sara Marie, born May 25, 1983, who died March 18, 1984; and twin sons, Mitchell Robert and Michael LaMar, born January 20, 1988, who died the same day.

Debra Resler married Jackie Joe Springer October 7, 1983. Debra and Jackie, born July 23, 1952, have two children, Eric Roland, born December 2, 1985, and Kristen Renee, born January 27, 1993.

Rick Resler married Deborah Sue May on July 10, 1982. Rick and Deborah, born December 22, 1961, had two children, Chad Allen, born December 2, 1981, who died June 2, 2001; and Angela Marie, born July 19, 1986.

10) Mary Lou Krill was the tenth child of Charles and Laura Krill. Since Laura's brother, George Gebhardt, and his wife, Effie May, couldn't have children, it was decided that they would adopt Mary after her first birthday when she was weaned. After that, she was known as Mary Lou Gebhardt. She married Leonard John Deininger November 25, 1961. Mary Lou and Leonard, born June 30, 1925, had a daughter, Sandra Jo, born October 24, 1964. May Lou Deininger died October 21, 1998. Sandra has a son, Seth Phillip, born May 13, 2004.

11) Florence Ellen Krill married Joe Trohanowsky September 9, 1951. They divorced in 1972. Florence and Joe moved to California July, 1952, where Florence is still living. Florence and Joe, born December 17, 1928, have four children, Mary Ellen, born April 12, 1952; Michael Lee, born March 4, 1955; Jo Ann, born December 22, 1958; and Robert Joseph, born April 22, 1964. On May 12, 1974, Florence married John McAnn Roesinger, born January 8, 1928.

Mary Ellen was married to and divorced from George Rudisell. They have two children, Angela and Paul.

Jo Ann is married to Eric Peterson. She has a son, Chris Mason.

Submitted by Don Krill

DON KROCKER

Don Krocker is a lifetime resident of Fort Wayne except a few years when young.

His father, Steven, moved here from Detroit where he was a policeman and also worked for the railroad. He married Rita Gick. They were both German. Don still remembers some German words, and one German song. But English was nearly always spoken in the home. Steven was a World War I veteran.

Don Krocker's siblings are half-brothers Howard Dietrick, George (Duke) Krocker, brother Charles Luhman, sisters Shirleen Miser and the late Beverly Hohocker.

They were raised in south Fort Wayne.

There was a gas station a few blocks away. The owner would hit golf balls across the street into a field, and he paid the children for all the golf balls they found and returned to him. Then they bought candy at the station.

Behind the station was a ravine filled with junk. Don and some friends hunted for metal, glass, and aluminum for the World War II effort. They also collected milkweed pods and sold those for the war effort.

There was a large metal bridge (possibly Bluffton Street Bridge) over the St. Marys River. Don and others would climb up on the high bridge and check out the bird nests. They fished below the bridge (the bridge is no longer there).

Don Krocker

They went to the Tillman Gravel Pit (which later became the Tillman Dump) and fished and swam there.

In 1942, Don's father bought a small grocery and meat market on Curdes Avenue. They moved to that area.

Don and his friends rode bikes to the Municipal Beach below the dam. There was a diving platform, and the steel poles from the platform are still there today. There were also concession stands.

In the 1940s Krocker and his friends bought hot dogs with onions 12 for $1 at Coney Island. They would go to the Palace, Capital, or Family Theatre and stink up the theatre with the onions. Try that today!

In the 1950s Krocker went to the South Anthony or High Banks racetrack to watch his brother, Duke Krocker, a well-known race driver, race.

Krocker bought his home in 1961. There were seven new homes in that addition with dirt roads. He has seen bare farm land there, six miles outside the city limit, fill with housing additions and businesses. Now the city limits has moved beyond that area by miles.

Don and the late Mildred (Wickliffe) Krocker were married in 1959. Their children are Brian, Brad, Brent, and Amy. There are ten grandchildren, one more on the way, also one great-grandchild. Mildred passed away in 1994. In 1997 he married Darlene Martindale. Her children are Wm., Jr. and Shelly Martindale. There are three grandchildren and one great-grandchild.

The Krockers enjoy fishing, gardening, Nascar, and birdwatching. Don is a member of Concordia Lutheran Church, and Darlene is a member of Northeast Christian Church. Don retired from General Electric wire mill as a foreman in 1990 after forty years.

Submitted by Darlene Krocker

KRUMWIEDE FAMILY

The Krumwiede family made its appearance in Allen County, Indiana in 1956, with the arrival of George A. H. Krumwiede, his wife Etta Theesfeld Krumwiede and their five children: Loretta Lourine, Allen Louis, Barbara Louise, James Henry and Gregory George. In 1958, their sixth child, Keith Carl, was born and is the only native of Allen County in the family.

George August Henry Krumwiede was born October 12, 1911 in Artesia Township, Iroquois County, Illinois to Henry Charles and Frederika Karolina "Minna" Sprehe Krumwiede. He attended St. John's Lutheran School (The German

Seated: George A. H. Krumwiede, Etta (Theesfeld) Krumwiede, Keith Carl Krumwiede. Standing: Loretta Krumwiede Jacob Barlow; Allen Louis Krumwiede; Barbara Krumwiede Nord; James Henry Krumwiede; Gregory George Krumwiede. Circa 1969

Lutheran School) through eighth grade, was confirmed at St. John's Lutheran Church, Buckley, Illinois, and hired out as a farm hand. He occasionally worked in other occupations, such as a laborer in area canning companies.

Etta Theesfeld was born August 16, 1920 in Chatsworth, Livingston County, Illinois to Lübbe (Louis) Janssen and Vallie "Lorraine" Vaughn Theesfeld. The family eventually settled in Crescent Township, Iroquois County, Illinois. Etta was confirmed at Immanuel Lutheran Church at Idaville in Iroquois County. She graduated from Onarga High School, Onarga, Illinois, and from Gallagher Business School, Kankakee, Illinois.

George and Etta were married January 1, 1940 at St. John's Lutheran Church, Buckley. After 1942, the family settled into The Rupert Place, a group of farms in Iroquois County, northeast of Buckley, which was being farmed by members of the Krumwiede family as tenant farmers, and continued to be farmed by members of the family for four generations.

Loretta Lourine was born May 28, 1942 in Watseka, Iroquois County, Illinois; Allen Louis was born November 10, 1943 in Watseka; Barbara Louise was born June 22, 1946 in Paxton, Ford County, Illinois; James Henry was born May 26, 1950 in Watseka; Gregory George was born May 28, 1953 in Watseka; and Keith Carl was born July 2, 1958 in Fort Wayne.

Loretta married Edwin Henry Jacob and William Nathan Barlow Jr.; Allen married Gloria Jean Roose; Barbara married Rev. Donald Dale Nord; James married Linda Kay Bultemeier; Gregory married Anne Elizabeth Donoghue; and Keith married Lisa Lee Vinson and Laurie Ann Lee.

In Fort Wayne, George worked first for Roy McNett Construction and then for Lincoln Manufacturing. Following retirement from full-time employment, he worked at the YMCA in a maintenance position.

Etta continued as homemaker and business manager while the family farmed. She returned to employment as an executive secretary about 1957 at Farnsworth's plant on Knitters Avenue (now Growth Avenue), her office being directly across the street from their home. She worked for Farnsworth and its successors, for the City of Fort Wayne as secretary to Chief of Police Kenneth Buckmaster, at Indiana-Purdue University Fort Wayne and for Magnavox Corporation, which transferred her to Knoxville, Tennessee, where she continued another ten years before retirement.

Etta Theesfeld Krumwiede died December 11, 1999, in Fort Wayne, aged 79, of pneumonia. George A.H. Krumwiede died June 9, 2002, aged 90, of congestive heart failure. They were survived by their six children; 20 grandchildren; and 11 great-grandchildren.

Submitted by Loretta Krumwiede Barlow

KURTZ FAMILY

John Kurtz was born in Stuttgart, Germany, on July 23, 1826. He married Barbara Stokes in 1847 and immigrated to America in 1849 on a sailing ship that took six weeks to make the voyage. They carried all of their worldly possession in two wooden chests. With them was their son, John Frederick. They landed in Havre-de-Grace, Maryland. They soon left Maryland and settled in Lancaster County, Pennsylvania, and later moved to Ashland County, Ohio. In 1872, the family again moved, this time to Allen County, Indiana, where they settled on a farm of 112 acres in Milan Township near Harlan. There is where their life as farmers continued.

John Kurtz
(July 23, 1826 - April 11, 1913)

Barbara A. Kurtz
(September 26, 1826 - February 15, 1911)

The union of John and Barbara produced ten children. They were John (married Mary Swift), Martha (married Stuart Milliman), Louisa (married Townsend Ward), Eliza (died in early childhood), Mary (died in infancy), Nancy (married M. James Milliman), Catherine (married John Bickhart), Henry (married Anna Ringwalt), William (died in infancy), and Arthur (never married).

John and Mary Swift's marriage bought into the world five children: Clarence (died in infancy), Eva (married Clint Kinsey), Carrie (married Calvin Stauffer), Agnes (married Jesse Macbeth), Amy (married William Spindler), and Gaylord (married Kathryn Zimmerman and Lena Brown). These unions produced forty- two grandchildren for John and Mary.

Martha and Stuart Milliman's marriage produced three children: Blanche (married David Spindler), Carrie (never married), and John (married Gertrude Schumann). Those marriages created five children.

James and Nancy Milliman bore two children: William (died at age five of typhoid) and Maude (married Thomas Blume). Thomas and Maude produced three children.

John and Catherine Bickhart had three children: Bertha (never married), Grace (never married), and John (married Maybelle Welch).

Townsend and Louisa Ward's union brought into this world two children: John (married Nell Stuart) and Estella (married George Hughes).

Henry and Anna Ringwalt produced two children: Ralph (married Erlena Yerks) and Florence (never married). Ralph and Erlena had eight children.

1909, John and Barbara sold a portion of their farm to their son, Henry, and in 1912 Henry and his wife, Anna (Ringwalt), purchased the remaining acres from Henry's brothers and sisters. Henry and Anna continued to grow the family farm. In 1917, Henry and Anna built a large brick house, having removed an old frame house that was present when the farm was originally acquired. This house still stands on Indiana State Road 37, approximately two miles west of Harlan.

As Henry retired from farming, he sold the acreage to his son, Ralph. Ralph and his sons continued the farming business until Ralph's retirement in 1958. The farm was then sold to three of Ralph and Erlena's sons: John, Thomas, and George. The three brothers have continued to own the farm, with George's son, Ralph, presently actively engaged in the operation of the farm. Of Ralph and Erlena's eight children, seven are still living. They are Marjorie (Keith) Klopfenstein, Catherine (J. Gladwyn) Klopfenstein, Doris (Gerold) DeLong, John (married MaryLou Oswalt) Kurtz, Thomas (married Dorothy Eager) Kurtz, Helen (Robert) Lantz, and George (married June Keller) Kurtz. Their oldest son, Robert, (married Bessie Applegate) is now deceased. The children of Ralph and Erlena produced twenty-six children.

Submitted by Thomas Kurtz

JOHN HAROLD LABRASH

1932-2001

John Harold LaBrash was born in Fort Wayne in 1932. He was the oldest son of Harold and Voleta LaBrash. His younger brother, James, died at the age of 42. John started school at Ward Elementary. In 1941, his parents built a home on West Fleming and he transferred to Harrison Hill. From there he went to South Side. In high school he was a good student and excelled on the track team. He ran both cross country in the fall and the half mile in track. For a while he held the state record in the half mile. Indiana University gave him an athletic scholarship and he ran there also. He graduated in 1954 with a BS in accounting. Upon graduation he served his two years in the Air Force in Tennessee.

John's wife, Cornelia Luecke (Connie), was born in Fort Wayne in 1932. Her parents

Wedding reception at Howard Johnstons. Connie, John, Carolyn (Matron of Honor), James LaBrash, best man and brother of groom.

were Christian and Verma Hinton Luecke. Their families had a long history in Allen County, the Hintons having come to the area in 1833 before the Wabash-Erie Canal was here. The Lueckes moved here in 1903 when her grandfather became president of Concordia College. Connie started school in Kokomo where her parents lived for a short time. Upon their return to Fort Wayne, she attended St. Paul's Lutheran School and then Concordia High School. From there she went to Valparaiso University where she received a BA in social work in 1954.

The couple was married in 1955 at St. Paul's Lutheran Church. They lived in Murfreesboro, Tennessee until John left the Air Force. In 1957 they purchased a home in Aboite Township. John joined his father's business, LaBrash Distributing Co. They were the local jobbers for Seyfert Foods, along with other products. In 1960 they were bought out by Seyferts and John continued working for them. When Borden's purchased Seyferts, he stayed with them until he retired. In 1969 Connie went back to school and received her teaching certification and masters degree in education from Indiana University. She taught for twenty-five years in Southwest Allen County Schools. During this time she became social studies coordinator at Woodside Middle School.

In 1957, the LaBrashes joined Trinity English Lutheran Church and were involved in various groups at the church. As a salesman, John became acquainted with many people in the area and was known for his friendliness and outgoing personality. John was a twenty-five year member of the Glacier Ridge Lion's Club, Scottish Rite and Shrine, where he was the Stage Director, and also worked on the Circus. After his death he was recognized as a 50 Year "I-Man" by Indiana University. He was one of IU's biggest sports fans.

Before teaching, Connie belonged to various groups such as Valparaiso Alumni, TTT Society, a Home Ec Club, a church circle and she was a Girl Scout Leader. After retirement she became very active in AAUW, where she was an officer and served on the board for ten years. She belongs to several interest groups with the association. She also belongs to Southwest Circle of her church and is involved in the Monday Morning Bible Study Group.

John and Connie had five children, all of whom attended Aboite Grade School and Homestead High School.

David (1955) - Graduate of Indiana University. Now President of Clarendon Hills Bank in Clarendon Hills, Illinois. He is married to Melissa Panko and a father of three daughters Hilary, Kelly and Alyssa.

Barbara (1956) -Graduate of Indiana University. A scientist with Roche Diagnostics. Lives in Fishers, Indiana. Married to William Wiler and has one son, Jordan.

James (1959) - Graduate of Purdue University. He is Plant Manager for Graham Packaging in Salt Lake City.

Daniel (1960) - Graduate of Indiana University. He is with the Pasha Group in International Moving. He married Rebecca Van Meter and they reside in Champaign, Illinois

William (1962) - Graduate ot Indiana University. He is the Baking Consultant for Hobart Systems. He married Jewell Gatken and they have two sons, Philip and Nicholas. They live in Fort Wayne.

John died on Memorial Day in 2001 and is buried in Lindenwood Cemetery. Connie still resides in Aboite Township.

Submitted by Connie LaBrash

LACKEY FAMILY

John Lackey of Ireland migrated to the United States and settled in Pennsylvania. There he met and married Sarah Taylor who was born in Pennsylvania.

Their son, John Alexander Lackey, was born January 4, 1824 in Pennsylvania and died March 7, 1901 at Butler, Indiana. He married Rachael A. York on June 30, 1853, in Tuscarawas, Ohio. She died in DeKalb County November 20, 1915. They had nine children, and lived in Wilmington Township. John A. was a farmer all his life.

1) The first born was Elizabeth A. in 1853 in Ohio.

2) Alzoynus was born in Ross County, Ohio. He married Martha Westover, and they had two daughters, Bertha and Maud.

3) Next came Eugene C. who married Lucinda Parker, and they had Lawrence and Dolly.

4 and 5) Next came the twins, Melvin Wilmont and William Madison, born January 3, 1860. The twins moved to Fort Wayne, and, at one time, both worked for the Pennsylvania Railroad. Melvin became the wreck master, and Madison worked in the car barns. The twins never lived more than a thirty minute walk from each other. They were identical both in looks and mannerisms. Melvin married Emma Kepler, and their children were Ruth M., who married Alexander Kincade, York R. who married Beatrice Burredtt (he was a surveyor). William Madison's family story follows the other children of John and Rachael.

6) The next child was Julia who married Lucius Collins, and their children were Hazel and Mabel.

7) Homer A. Lackey was born in 1856 and married twice, first to Ina R. Parker, and then to Nina I. Parker. His children were Homer, Helen B. and Jeanette.

8) Ella was born in 1858 and married Henry Hatch; they had one son, Henry.

9) George A. married Rhena and ran a grocery store in Swan, Indiana.

Family of twin, William Madison:

William Madison married Mary Lucinda Zuber. He worked for the Pennsylvania Railroad until 1922, and quit after the strike. He then worked for Fort Wayne Building and Supply Lumber Company. His wife was a seamstress all her life, and suffered from arthritis. He belonged to the Odd Fellows Lodge, and she to the Rebecca's. They had five children; Rachel died as an infant.

L to R: William Madison "Mad" Lackey, Melvin Wilmont "Mel" Lackey, at 70 years of age, and still had jet black hair

1) The second born was Glaydace who married Fredrick C. Grewe, Jr.; he made cigars. Her second marriage was to Martin Cunningham who sold beauty supplies. She owned and operated a beauty shop for a time.

2) Next was a son Gordon who resided in Indianapolis for 44 years. He was associated with A. D. Schwab. He was a pioneer pilot and owned and operated Sky Harbor Airport in Indianapolis for twenty years. He was a member and past president ofthe Indiana Hanger of Quiet Birdmen. He had one daughter, Marjorie.

3) Next came Velma who married Prentice L. Wearly of Huntington in 1920. They had two children, John William and Doris Jean. John married Mary Jo Krick of Decatur, Indiana. They had three children. Anne L. resides in Roanoke, Indiana, and is a dental hygienist. David W. is a dentist in Denver, Colorado married to Maryann Muhlke. They have three sons, Christen W. married to Catina Gibbs, Thomas M., and Joshua D. Jill was married to Steve Sipe and they have three daughters, Andrea, Devon, and Haley. Doris Jean married Glenn B. Hille, and they have four daughters. Marcia is a dietician at Lutheran hospital. Nadine married twice, first to Victor Conrady, and they had Nicholaus and Drew. The second marriage was to Arthur Putt, and they had Scott. Anita was married twice. First she married Robert Richmond, and they had two daughters, Jonell and Allison. The second marriage was to David Steinbacher, and they had John D. and Megan. The last daughter, Colleen, married Michael Neiderholtmeyer and they have five children, Amy, Adam, Amanda, Alexander, and Anna Lese.

4) Bernice married Ralph William Paulsen, and they had three sons, Robert E. R., Ralph W. R., and Richard A. Robert had two adopted children, Ralph William had two sons and six daughters, and Richard had one son.

Submitted by John W. Wearly

CLAUDE & CATHERINE LADIG

Claude Allen Ladig was born June 21, 1882 in Jefferson Township, Allen County, Indiana to parents Nicholas P. Ladig (1860-1928) and Sarah M. Rowbotham (1857-1937). He attended St.

Claude and Catherine Ladig, 1927

John's Catholic Church in New Haven alongside his eight siblings: James Roy (1879-1963), Peter I. (1884-1965), Sarah (1886-1934), Mary (1888-1976), Bertha (1891-1978), Clarence (1893-1945), Norbert (1896-1969), and Grace (1903-1989). Claude's father, Nicholas, engaged in farming. He was the son of Peter Ladig (born in France 1825, died in 1877) and Mary Kline (born at sea 1835, died in 1909), and the grandson of two early Jefferson Township settlers, Jacob Ladig (born in France 1796, died 1873) and Frederick Kline (born in France in 1800, died 1876). Claude's mother, Sarah, was the daughter of John Rowbotham and Rebecca Small (born in Maine in 1840, died in Indiana 1911).

Catherine (Katie) Anna Herman, born March 6, 1880 in Germany, immigrated to the United States with her parents, Jacob Herman (1849-1921) and Barbara Waldschmidt (1849-1896), and older brother, Jacob Jr. (1878-1918). They arrived at the port of New York on April, 18, 1881, and settled in Madison Township, Allen County, Indiana, where Jacob was a farmer. Their family increased with the births of Henry (1884-1964), John (1887-1948), Nettie (1890-1983), and Mary (1892-1969). In 1896 Catherine, at the age of 16, became caregiver to her younger siblings after the death of their mother. The Herman family were members of Saint John Lutheran Church Flatrock, Madison Township; and on April 28, 1904, it was the site where Claude Ladig and Catherine Herman were united in marriage.

Through hard work and determination, they purchased and farmed over 150 acres in Jefferson township near Minnich and Paulding Roads. Life was good, and they were blessed with eight children: Louis Nicholas (1905-1962), married Helen Kryder; Anna Mary (1907-1998), married 1) John Bennett, and 2) Ira Stults; Emma Lucille (1908-1992), married Howard Dawkins, Sr.; John Jacob (1912-1999), married Catherine Louraine; Charles Frank (1918-1968), married Marjorie Trim; Hazel Margaret (1920-2001), married Norbert Werling; Florence Mildred (1922-1966); and Blanch Betty (1925-1926).

After the Depression, Claude and Catherine's farmland was sold, and they moved to 1340 Canal Street in New Haven. Claude was employed at the American Fork and Hoe, and later as a switchman for the Wabash Railroad. In retirement, he enjoyed whittling and selling tool handles, was an avid euchre player, and had a good sense of humor. Catherine, who spoke with a German accent her entire life, stayed busy with cooking, canning, flower gardens, and the sewing circle at the New Haven Methodist Church where she and Claude were members.

Catherine died unexpectedly on October 7, 1955; and Claude passed away on October 14, 1967 after a long illness. They are buried in the New Haven IOOF Cemetery. Faith, home, and family were utmost to Claude and Catherine, and they have truly passed on a rich heritage to all their descendents.

Submitted by Patricia (Ladig) Prascsak

JOHN DAVID LAIRD

John David (Dave) Laird was born on June 14, 1936. He was the only son of Robert Wayne Laird (June 3, 1909 - December 26, 1991) and Cartha Gertrude Barnes (April 2, 1911 - December 19, 2003). Cartha was the daughter of Harley Clifford Barnes (August 24, 1884 - August 20, 1934) and Maude Gertrude Miller (June 3, 1887 - September 29, 1975). Dave's parents and these grandparents are buried in the Circle Hill Cemetery in Angola, Indiana. Robert Laird was the son of Dr. Ora Irving Laird (an optometrist) and Theo Rogers.

Dave Laird has two sisters, Janice Roberta (Green), born June 21, 1939, and Jeanne Elizabeth (Butts) born September 18, 1946. All three siblings graduated from Angola High School. Dave came to Fort Wayne in 1957 to attend International Business College. While attending college Dave was employed by and lived at the Klaehn Funeral Home, 420 West Wayne Street. This was during the time funeral homes served the community by making ambulance runs.

Gloria Jean Laird and John David Laird

While attending International Business College, Dave met Gloria Jean Hack (born December 2, 1939) from Wabash County, Chester Township. Gloria's parents are Glen Andrew Hack (April 10, 1897 - August 24, 1988) and Susie Mae Ryan (May 7, 1910 - February 19, 1988); they are buried in Beech Grove Cemetery, Huntington County, Clear Creek Township. Back then a farmer could raise a family by farming only 80 acres. Gloria has two sisters: Patsy Ann (Bechtold) born February 16, 1934, and Glenda Joy (Jobe) born October 6, 1949. Gloria worked for Liechty Optometrists on South Calhoun Street, while attending International Business College. Dave and Gloria were married August 1, 1959, in North Manchester, Indiana.

Dave started working for International Harvester Company early in 1959. That spring he was drafted into the army and reported for the next two years to the Adjutant General's Corp, Fort Knox, Kentucky. Gloria worked at the Fort Knox National Bank during this time. To complete his military obligation, Dave completed two more years in the army reserves and two years in the inactive reserves.

In 1961 they returned to Fort Wayne. They have two daughters: Loraine Michelle (Gibson Farnham) born on October 1, 1961, at Lutheran Hospital, and Cynthia Ann born on January 11, 1963, at Parkview Memorial Hospital. They both graduated from Snider High School.

When the local International Harvester Company closed, Dave had completed 25 years employment with them. He went on to work for Diamond Jim's Amusement Park, Hockemeyer Miller Funeral Home, and the War Memorial Coliseum for 15 years. Gloria worked for Salem United Church of Christ, Greater Fort Wayne Chamber of Commerce, and Fort Wayne National Bank/National City Bank. They both have various interests, as well as being avid antique buffs, and over the years have accumulated numerous collections. Dave is a self-taught taxidermist and enjoys making carved fish decoys.

They are blessed with four grandchildren: David James Gibson (January 24, 1982), Lauren Nichole Farnham (October 11, 1988), Daniel Robert Farnham (January 26, 1991), and Samuel David James Laird (December 16, 1999).

Submitted by Gloria Jean Laird

GENE CARROLL LAKER

On June 7, 1958, Gene Carroll Laker and Marcia Leigh (Jones) Laker were married in Racine, Wisconsin, where the Joneses are a one hundred-year resident family. Two days later, on June 9, Gene and Marcia moved to Fort Wayne, Indiana, where they have lived since that time, with the exception of two years when he was commissioned a captain in the U. S. Air Force and stationed at K. I. Sawyer Air Force Base in Gwinn, Michigan.

Gene Laker was born Gene Loercher in Danville, Illinois, on March 9, 1932. In 1954 he graduated from DePauw University in Greencastle, Indiana. He graduated from the Northwestern University Medical School in Chicago, Illinois, in 1958 and interned at Lutheran Hospital in Fort Wayne. In 1961 he founded the Waynedale Family Physicians and retired in 1999.

Marcia Laker graduated from the James Ward Thorne School of Nursing at Northwestern University. A registered nurse, she worked at Passavant Hospital in Chicago and, following her marriage, in pediatric nursing at Lutheran Hospital, Fort Wayne. She also has a master's degree in education from Indiana University.

Gene and Marcia had four children. Jaison Laker was born in Marquette, Michigan, on October 25, 1959. Carey Laker Bryson was born on September 1, 1961, at Lutheran Hospital in Fort Wayne, as was Craig Laker, born August 1, 1964, and Gene Carroll Laker, Jr., was born February 2, 1973. Gene Laker, Jr., died as a newborn, on February 2, 1973.

Jaison Laker is an ITT Tech graduate in electronic engineering and robotics. He works at Undersea Sensors and lives in Fort Wayne.

Carey Laker, an Indiana University graduate, married Joseph Morken on September 1, 1990. During their marriage two sons were born: Adrian Morken in Chicago, Illinois, on July 27, 1992, and William Morken in Rockford, Illinois, on November 18, 1994. Carey Laker Morken married David Bryson on September 1, 2001. Carey and David Bryson now live in Roanoke, Indiana.

Craig Laker is an Indiana University graduate with master s degrees in criminal justice and public affairs. He currently is a professor at Tri-State University in Angola, Indiana. On September 11, 1993, he married Suzanne (Lax) Laker; also an Indiana University graduate. The couple live at Crooked Lake with their three children, (twins) Alexandria and Elizabeth Laker, born in Fort Wayne on July 1, 1999, and Emma Laker, born in Fort Wayne on October 12, 2001.

Dr. Richard Laker, Gene's brother, a graduate of DePauw University and the Washington School of Medicine in St. Louis, Missouri, joined the Waynedale Family Physicians in 1962, following his internship at Lutheran Hospital. He retired in 1998. He was born on August 19, 1935, in Danville, Illinois, Gene and Richard Laker are sons of George and Edna Loercher.

Edna Loercher now lives at The Lutheran Home, having moved to Fort Wayne following the death of her husband in 1979.

On June 14, 1958, Richard Laker married Helen (Toni) Pigott in Homewood, Illinois. She is a DePauw University graduate. The couple now lives in Palm Desert, California, and in Fort Wayne.

Richard and Toni have three children. Joan Laker Scott lives in Richardson, Texas, with her husband, Steve Scott, and their four children: Joseph, Courtney, John, and Kelly. Michael and his wife, Susan, live in Houston, Texas, and have two daughters, Michelle and Kimberly. Susan Laker lives in Carmel, Indiana.

Submitted by Marcia Laker

CLAUDE JOSEPH LANGARD

Claude Joseph Langard, born in December 1830 in Gouhenans, France, was one of two sons of Etienne Langard and Antoinette Brepson. His brother, Claude Francois, remained in France, but Joseph left, sailing on the *Connecticut* and arriving at New York from Le Havre in October 1850. Joseph lived in Buffalo, New York, for a short time before moving to Arcola, Indiana, where he operated a farm. Sometime after his marriage to Victorine Manier at the Cathedral in Fort Wayne in 1856, Joseph moved to Fort Wayne.

Victorine, the seventh of nine children of Hippolite Manier and Marguerite Poirson, was born in Arcola in 1839. Joseph operated a saloon in Fort Wayne as early as 1870. He later owned a wholesale liquor company and boarding house. In the early 1880s Joseph and his sons owned a grocery store adjacent to the saloon. Many new French immigrants lived for a time at his boarding house, and the Allen County Lafayette Legion of the *Societe Franco Americain* held its meetings in Langard Hall, above the Langard saloon on Columbia Street between Clinton and Barr, which today is in the area of Freiman Square.

Joseph was a prominent figure in Democratic Party politics in the city, serving as a township trustee for a time, and more importantly, as a leader among French families of Allen County.

Joseph and Victorine had eight children born in Allen County: Francis (1857-1861), Jean Baptiste (1859-1902), married Rose Dodane; Joseph Louis (1861-1880); Marie Adele (1862-1923), married Frank Joly; Hippolite (1865-1876); Clarice Angeline (1870-1950), married George Parrot; Malinda Cecilia (1873-1941), married Joseph Foust; and Louis Claude (1876-1967), married Rallie Kline.

Jean Baptiste and Rose Dodane Langard

Joseph died after a five week illness in 1892. Victorine died in 1913. Both are buried in Catholic Cemetery.

John Baptist Langard, the second son, lived on Joseph's farm for a while, and then moved to Fort Wayne, where he later worked with his brother, Joseph, as a barkeeper in the Langard saloon. In 1881, John and his father opened their grocery store. John continued to operate the grocery store and saloon until his death. Like his father, John was influential in the Democratic Party and a leader of the city's French people. John married Rose Dodane in St. Louis Besancon Church. Rose, a daughter of Joseph Marcellin Dodane and Caroline Pequignot, was born near Monroeville in 1862. John and Rose had three children: Lillian (1883-1960), Joseph (1885-1955), and Rosella (1888-1955). John died in 1902, while Rose lived until 1936. They are buried in Catholic Cemetery.

Lillian married Joseph Parrot in 1905, and they were the parents of six children: John (1906-1965), Frank (1908-1973), Catherine (1910-1965), Mary Alice (1912-2003), Richard (1916-1997), and Joseph, Jr.. (1920-1994).

Joseph Parrot, Jr., married Patricia Pease in December 1945, and they were the parents of one daughter and four sons. At present, there are four grandchildren and one great grandchild.

Joseph Langard's youngest son, Louis, was the last remaining Langard when he died in 1967. Although the Langard name has died out in Allen County, Joseph's descendants still in Allen County bear family names of Parrot, Brenizer, and Zych.

Submitted by Sharon Parrot Subjak

LATZ FAMILY

It was in 1915 that G. Irving Latz came to Fort Wayne to start in business in the ladies ready-to-wear garment field. He was born in Baltimore, Maryland on July 31, 1888. He attended public schools up until he was thirteen, at which time his career began as an errand boy at H. B. Clafin Company, New York. (The other kids called him "Fatty" and that was reason enough for leaving school never to return.) His work experience led him to later management of departments in Frank Dry Goods in Fort Wayne. Following that in 1920, Mr. Latz along with several associates purchased Wolf & Dessauer (W&D). He became its Secretary and General Manager, positions he held throughout his years at W&D.

In personal life Mr. Latz married Carrie Stiefel in June of 1916. Three children came of this marriage – Jane Carolyn, G. Irving 2nd and William Smith Latz. The family became members of Congregation Achduth Vesholom in Fort Wayne, the oldest Jewish Congregation in Indiana.

Wolf & Dessauer and the Latz family interests became synonymous to the public. The ideals of "the store" while new to its local customers took hold and provided four competitors in the retail field. The customer was given full credit for returned goods, regardless of the condition of the merchandise. The customer was always right. Not only was the customer right, but over time this policy built a confidence that few stores had ever deserved up until then. There seemed to be no community cause that lacked the support of the store in reaching their goals. Store advertising often guided the publics' views on the national issues of the day. And the store grew in volume and customer confidence by the way W&D conducted business.

Latz was truly one of the original volunteers, and he took this a step further. When WWII came, W&D immediately sold War Bonds as a daily offering. W&D was a leader in various community causes.

Latz gave a talk at the Fort Wayne Chamber of Commerce suggesting that the local charitable agencies form one organization. The outcome was the Community Chest, which later evolved into what is now the United Way of Allen County.

The spirit of the Latz family, in a large sense, came from the continuing practices and character of G. Irving Latz. His background was certainly humble at best but his personal goals attracted many people to respect the store as it grew. His goal was to build a store that would be a credit to the community it served. He died in 1947 and is buried in Lindenwood Cemetery.

The family resided in two homes in Fort Wayne, which were both built by Latz:

1916 – 1936 1238 West Wayne Street

1936 – 1948 RFD 6, (now 11836) Covington Road.

The family stopped living on Covington Road in 1948 when WWII had three Latzes in service (father, Major; son, Lieutenant; and other son, Staff Sergeant).

Submitted by Jan Latz

RODNEY & JEANIE (CLINE) LANTZ

Nonna Jean (Jeanie) Cline was born September 9, 1949 in Jay County, Indiana, the daughter of Marion and Tabitha (Teeter) Cline. Marion, a native of Champaign County, Ohio, was the youngest child of John and Anna (Romine)Cline. Tabitha, a native of Adams County, Indiana, is the oldest daughter of John and Lucy (Decker) Teeter. Jeanie grew up in Jay County and graduated from Portland High School in 1967. She came to Fort Wayne in 1967. She was employed by Waterfield Mortgage in the Data Processing and Servicing Departments until 1973. She then went to Fort Wayne National Bank where she worked in the Data Processing Administration Department until 1977 at which time she left to become a

Rod and Jeanie Lantz Wedding, September 10, 1977

full time homemaker. She returned to the work force in 1987 and, since that time, has been employed by Misner & Associates as an Administrative Assistant. She married Rodney Lantz at the Avalon Missionary Church in Waynedale on September 10, 1977.

Rod, a native of Adams County, is the son of Earl and Pauline (Archbold) Lantz. Earl, a native of Adams County, was the son of Rev. Ezra and Veronica (Schlotzhauer) Lantz. Pauline, a native of Wells County, was the daughter of Alonzo and Stella (Conklin) Archbold. Rod grew up in Berne and graduated in 1963 from Berne High School. He worked for Giffords IGA and, after graduation, he worked at CTS of Berne. In 1965 he joined the Indiana Air National Guard based at Baer Field. In 1968 he became a full time Aircraft Technician where he was a Crew Chief with the 122nd Tactical Fighter Wing. He retired in 1998 with over 30 years of service.

Jeanie was an active 4-H leader in Allen County for several years and is a member of the Mary Penrose Wayne Chapter of the DAR. Rod is a member of the Berne, Indiana American Legion Post 468.

Submitted by Jeanie Lantz

KENNETH LAWRENCE & MARY JOAN (PIATT) LAUER

Kenneth Lawrence Lauer, fifth of the six children of Paul Anthony and Florence Elizabeth (Becker) Lauer, was born February 27, 1926, in the family home at 3310 Harrison Street, Fort Wayne, Indiana. His siblings were Margaret Ann, Richard Paul, Mary Alice, Phyllis Mae, and Lawrence James. Life was good: there was even the pony, Donna. Then, when Ken was only six, his father left and there was a divorce between his parents. From then on, "Aunt Tudie" (Mary Madaline Becker) and "Aunt Marge" (Mary Margaret Becker) helped Ken's mother rear the family.

Meanwhile, on February 20, 1928, Mary Joan Piatt was born to John Thomas and Mary Catherine (Trevey) Piatt in Saint Joseph Hospital, Fort Wayne. They lived with the baby's paternal grandparents at 2121 Broadway until she was almost two years old. Then her parents purchased a small apartment house at 3714 Shady Court. John Thomas Piatt, Jr. joined the family at the end of 1931.

Ken attended Saint Peter's Catholic School and Saint John the Baptist Catholic School; Joan went to South Wayne School and to Harrison Hill

L to R Austin Charun Lauer, Braden Charun Lauer, Audrey Charun Lauer; Linda Sue Lauer, Mary Joan (Piatt) Lauer, Philip Gregory Lauer, Kenneth Lawrence Lauer, Joletta Charun Lauer, Beth Ann Lauer

for junior high; and they both graduated from South Side High School when R. Nelson Snider was principal there. Those were the World War II years, and Ken served in the Merchant Marine. Joan, now called "Jo," became a teller at Fort Wayne National Bank and took evening classes at Indiana University Extension and later at Saint Francis College.

When Ken finished sailing, they began dating and were married January 27, 1951. By then he was completing his last semester at Butler University. They moved to Greeley, Colorado, for his graduate school at the University of Northern Colorado. Beth Ann Lauer was born there on June 28, 1952. Then Ken took a teaching postion in Lovington, New Mexico. After two years, they decided, "there's no place like home" and moved back to Fort Wayne. Linda Sue Lauer was born into the family on June 19, 1957, and Philip Gregory Lauer arrived on September 6, 1964. The family home is located at 4223 Tacoma Avenue. Jo's mother lived there with them for 32 years.

Ken was a tenured English professor at Indiana Institute of Technology. During a summertime job at Allen County Public Library, he was persuaded to get a masters in library science at Western Michigan University. He helped develop the genealogy collection for Allen County Public Library, opened the Wayneda1e Branch, the Hessen Cassel Branch, and the Shawnee Branch. He managed the latter until retirement in 1993. Since then, he has enjoyed working part-time at Do It Best Hardware. Jo retired in 2003 as Director of Music at Saint Therese Catholic Church.

All three of their children graduated from Saint John the Baptist Catholic School and Bishop Luers High School before choosing different colleges for their higher educations. Beth is Transitions Director for Fort Wayne State Developmental Center; Linda is Release Manager of Information Technology for Waterfield Mortgage Company; and Greg is Chief Financial Officer of Bond Safeguard Company and Lexon Insurance Company in Louisville, Kentucky. On June 23,1990, he married Joletta Elizabeth Charun, who was Senior Legal Counsel for Lincoln National Life Insurance Company. Their children are Austin Charun Lauer, born March 1,1992; Braden Charun Lauer, born February 12,1996; and Audrey Charun Lauer, born January 17, 2001.

Submitted by Kenneth and Mary Joan (Piatt) Lauer

PAUL & BARBARA (SEIBELS) LAUER

Paul Lauer came to the United States and to Fort Wayne from Koer Heisig, Germany, in the 1850s. Barbara Seibels embarked from Bremen on the Ship Albert and arrived at Port Baltimore on August 10, 1854, with her further destination Indiana. They were married in Fort Wayne on October 16, 1855, and both their home and their businesses were located on the southwest corner of Barr at Jefferson Streets. Paul was a brick mason, and the family had a saloon and a barbershop.

This couple had the following children: John, November 23, 1856, to November 15, 1922; Elizabeth, May 27, 1861, to May 7, 1944; Anna Katherine, February 1863 to August 31, 1916; Christine, December 3, 1865, to July 19, 1922; and Henry Paul, June 12, 1869, to August 12, 1925. When Paul Lauer died, November 7, 1874, he willed all his property both personal and real of every kind and description to his beloved wife, Barbara. She and her four living children were included in German Families in Allen County, Indiana 1918, a World War I book enumerating the German residents. Barbara died April 15, 1923. Her obituary described her as "one of Fort Wayne's oldest pioneer residents" and said that she was a charter member of Saint Mary's Catholic Church, and the Altar and Rosary societies."

Of the children of Paul and Barbara (Seibels) Lauer, John, Elizabeth, and Christine never married. Anna Katherine and her husband, John Frederick Huber, had only one child, Paul Anthony Lauer. Her family always said, "Anna Katherine took her baby and moved back to her parents' home." So they lived with Paul and Barbara Lauer, John Lauer, Elizabeth Lauer, and Christine Lauer.

Paul Anthony, although born a Huber, assumed Lauer as his surname and used it throughout his school days. However, when he wanted to marry, he had to petition the Allen Circuit Court in its September term of 1911 to change his name from Paul Anthony Huber to Paul Anthony Lauer. He explained that, when his mother secured a divorce from his father, the court awarded the custody of him "to his mother, with whom he had continued to live from that time until the present." Further, he desired "to bear and to be known by his mother's maiden name and that borne by the members of the family on his mother's side." To this end, Notice of Application for Change of Name had to be published "for three consecutive weeks in a weekly newspaper of general circulation, published in Allen County, Indiana." Paul had that done in the *Monroeville Weekly Breeze* on October 19 and 26 and November 2, 1911. His petition was granted on February 5, 1912.

Henry Paul Lauer, the youngest child of Paul and Barbara Lauer, married Mary Elizabeth Junk and had five children: Thelma Lauer married Hugo (Bill) J. Wilkins; Lillian Lauer died when only 14; Paul A. Lauer married Mary Gordon; Clarence Matthew Lauer married Edna Marie Hebert; and Mary Agnes Lauer married Jerome R. Miller.

Submitted by Charles William Lauer

PAUL ANTHONY & FLORENCE ELIZABETH (BECKER) LAUER

On May 28, 1912, in Saint Mary s Catholic Church, Paul Anthony Lauer, son of John Frederick and Anna Katherine (Lauer) Huber, married Florence Elizabeth Becker, daughter of Henry William and Lavina Caroline (Englert) Becker. At that time, Paul Anthony worked as billing clerk for Bowsers. In the first half of the 1920s, he was a bookkeeper, accountant, and auditor for Pennell's Auto Company. Then, with the $32,000 he made from the sale of the "Lauer Corner" at Jefferson and Barr Streets to the Catholic Community Center, he started Lauer Auto Company, a Ford dealership, at 2315 Calhoun. After only two years in the auto business, he bought Wilson Drycleaners in the Rialto Building at the corner of Calhoun and Pontiac. Also, he was one of the founders of WHBJ Radio, the forerunner of WGL.

Paul Anthony Lauer circa 1930

Paul and Florence were the parents of six children: Margaret Ann, Richard Paul, Mary Alice, Phyllis Mae, Kenneth Lawrence, and Lawrence James. On January 20, 1933, when the last child was not quite two-and-a-half, a divorce from Paul A. Lauer was granted to Florence E. Lauer.

With the help of her sisters, Mary Madaline Becker and Mary Margaret Becker, Florence reared all six children. They all attended Catholic grade school and five went to South Side High School. Margaret Ann graduated as a nurse from Michael Reese Hospital in Chicago. Richard Paul served as a staff sergeant in the 71st division of the United States Army in World War II, was a salesman for H. J. Heinz Company, and had his own milk distributing business. Mary Alice took a commercial course at Saint Peter's. Phyllis Mae was a photo fashion model for Wolf & Dessauer and a stewardess on Chicago and Southern Airlines. Kenneth Lawrence served in the Merchant Marine, was a professor of English at Indiana Institute of Technology, and was branch librarian at the Shawnee Branch of the Allen County Public Library. Lawrence James served in Korea during that war, sold for New York Dental Supply, and managed Par-Tee Pump Company.

Margaret Ann Lauer, 1914-1965, married James Philip Sherlock; Richard Paul Lauer, 1917-1987, married Clotilda Eileen Prince; Mary Alice Lauer, 1918-1991, married Phillip Alfred Burns; Phyllis Mae Lauer, 1923, married Robert Ferris Traylor; Kenneth Lawrence Lauer, 1926, married Mary Joan Piatt; and Lawrence James Lauer, 1930, married Nancy Ellen Moran. After the divorce, Paul Anthony Lauer was not a part of his children's lives. He missed all these marriages.

Paul Anthony Lauer married a second time to Myrtle (Bohde) Warman. When he died on December 20, 1955, his obituary stated, "He is survived by his wife, Myrtle; a daughter, Mrs. Morris Puryear, Fort Wayne, and one grandchild." An old saying applies here; "like father, like son." The obituary of Paul's father, John Frederick Huber, did not acknowledge his son and there is no mention in Paul's obituary of his six children from his marriage with Florence Elizabeth Becker. Although 12 of his 20 grandchildren had been born, he died without knowing any of them.

The grandchildren are Helen Mina Sherlock and Mary Elizabeth Sherlock; Sandra Marie Lauer, Sylvia Ann Lauer, Sue Ellen Lauer, Richard Michael Lauer, and Michael Thomas Lauer; Phillip Wayne Burns and Robert J. Rosenthal; Mark Becker Traylor, Anthony Ferris Traylor, Catherine Raymond Traylor, and Louise Marie Traylor; Beth Ann Lauer, Linda Sue Lauer, and Philip Gregory Lauer; Charles William Lauer, Cynthia Lee Lauer, Daniel Lawrence Lauer, and Thomas Lauer.

There were only 24 bloodline great grandchildren. Sylvia Ann (Lauer) Mitsch has two daughters: Angela Louise (Mitsch) Winn and Amy Michelle (Mitsch) Carolan. Richard Michael and Judith Annette (Crotcher) Lauer's first baby, Nicole Marie, lived only one day; their other daughter is Sara Elizabeth Lauer. Michael Thomas and Charlotte Elizabeth (King) Lauer had Sylvia Lynn (Lauer) Lane and Ian Michael Lauer. Phillip Wayne Burns' daughter is Christine Mary Burns. Robert J. Rosenthal had Ty Rosenthal, Stacey (Rosenthal) Watson, and Shelley (Rosenthal). Mark Becker and Leslie Jean (Karrip) had Philip George Traylor, Max Edward Traylor, Tess Darah Traylor, and Joseph Fredrik Traylor. The children of Anthony Ferris and Yvonne Marie Quinanola (Eleazar) Traylor are Jacob Eleazar Traylor, Maelin Traylor, and Lydia Irene Traylor. Lawrence Gerald and Catherine Raymond (Traylor) Gregory had Seth Ariyan Gregory, Adria Corrine Gregory, and Elizabeth Traylor Gregory. Philip Gregory and Joletta Elizabeth (Charun) Lauer had Austin Charun Lauer, Braden Charun Lauer, and Audrey Charun Lauer. Daniel Lawrence and Tanya Lynn (Landin) Lauer had Eric Daniel Lauer and Alexa Rae Lauer.

The fifth generation has a good start with Chloe Dean Winn, Quinn Thomas Carolan, Riley Kathleen Carolan, Jaden Alexander Lane, Cameron Ray Monroe, and Ayden Laran Cosby.

Submitted by Phillip Gregory Lauer

EARL LEROY LAYMAN & HILDA BERKES LAYMAN

Earl Leroy Layman was born December 23, 1907, on a farm near Avilla in Noble County, Indiana. His parents were Ernest Edward Mathias Layman and Lalah Mae Forker Layman. Earl's ancestor, Joseph Lehmann, emigrated from Baden-Wurttemburg, Germany, in 1751 and settled in Berks County, Pennsylvania. His son, Henry, served in the Revolutionary War, and a later descendant, Earl's grandfather, William W., served in the 142nd Indiana Infantry in the Civil War. His mother's family descends from the Dingman/Weeks families who settled in Allen County, Indiana, in the early 1800s.

Earl was the oldest of three children; his sisters were Mary Josephine Layman Axel and Ethel

Wedding of Earl and Hilda Layman, June 11, 1931

Ellen Layman Lash. Following graduation from Avilla High School in 1926, he moved to Fort Wayne to attend International Business College and worked at the Gibson House Restaurant on South Calhoun Street to help pay the expenses. Following college graduation, he worked briefly for the Dudlo Company and then in June 1929, he was hired by the U.S. Postal Service as a city letter carrier and, in 1942, became the carrier of Rural Route 10, which covered the southeastern area from South Anthony to Maples Road. In 1959, he transferred to Route 4, which extended south from Waynedale on various roads to Poe. He retired from the Postal Service in October 1969, after which he was employed by Lincoln Bank, retiring from there in 1975.

Hilda Ida Amelia Berkes was his high school sweetheart. During the years he was going to school and working in Fort Wayne, he would ride the Interurban, which ran by the Berkes farm, to visit her on weekends. They were married June 11, 1931, in Immanuel Lutheran Church in Avilla, a marriage that lasted 71 years. Hilda was born October 28, 1909. Her parents, William Michael and Laura Amelia Weimer Berkes, owned a farm between Avilla and Kendallvillle, where Hilda and her two brothers, Walter Henry Berkes and Norman Christian Berkes, were raised.

In 1935, they bought a home at the intersection of Getz Road and old U.S. 24 (now South Bend Drive), near the housing area called Country Club Gardens. This area was still largely undeveloped and, because of this, they were able to obtain acreage around their home for a large garden and an apple and pear orchard.

Hilda's grandfather, Peter Barkes, emigrated from Darmstadt, Germany, and her grandmother, Mary Ann Behler from Switzerland in the 1850s. Both settled in Wayne County, Ohio, where they met and married in 1862, moving to Noble County, Indiana, shortly afterward.

Earl and Hilda, members of Emmanuel Lutheran Church, Fort Wayne, were active in church activities, gardening, and traveling. Earl died June 24, 2002, at the age of 94. Hilda is now a resident of a local nursing home. Their children, Beverly Joann Layman Williams (Stanley A. Williams) and Robert Earl Layman (Vicki Kanost), reside in Allen County, Indiana.

Submitted by B. J. Williams

JOHN L. LAYMON (JR.)

John L. Laymon was born May 7, 1917, in Frankfort, Indiana. He was six years old when he arrived in Fort Wayne, Allen County, Indiana,

John L. Laymon, Jr. (60 years old in 1977)

with his parents at the home of his grandfather, Jacob Sprunger, on Pontiac Street. Jacob and Rachel Sprunger were the parents of John's mother, Estella Mable (Sprunger) Laymon, who was the wife of John L. Laymon, Sr.

John Jr. attended first grade at James Smart School, the second grade at Hamilton School on Pontiac Street, the third and fourth grades at Bloomingdale School, the fifth, sixth, seventh, and eighth grades at Hoagland School in Fort Wayne. He graduated from Central High School as a member of the National Honor Society and the Four-Year Honor Roll.

John is the sixth John Laymon, numbering from Rev. John Layman and Jane (Goodpasture) Layman. Rev. John Layman was born in approximately 1756 and lived until 1834. He and his family, the Goodpasture family, and a third family, left Shelby County, Kentucky, during an Indian uprising and went to a fort called Cincinnati. A few years later the Laymans moved to Indiana and bought land from Indians at one dollar per acre near Bloomington, Indiana. They said their parents came from Pennsylvania. They dressed similar to Old Order Mennonites or German Baptists. They may have come from Switzerland in the early 1700s. The name Layman was changed to Laymon to retain the German sound of the letter A.

John Jr. was with General Electric Company of Fort Wayne for 28 years as an industrial engineer, assistant superintendent, materials manager, and shop operations manager. John Jr. retired at age 80 as vice president of manufacturing, plant manager, and consultant for twenty years at Rexair Incorporated. They made electric motors and the Rainbow Vacuum Cleaner. Previously John Jr. had also worked for Hobart Manufacturing and Kitchen-Aid for eight and one-half years as corporate manager of manufacturing engineering. He was two and one half years, during World War Two, in the army in Papua New Guinea, Australia, Dutch New Guinea, and the Philippines until the war ended.

John Jr. was married 62 years to Ruth Viola (Keller) Laymon. She was born July 22, 1917. Ruth died in 2002 at 82 years old. John Jr. lived, at age 87, in Beijing, China, three months in 2004. He has over the years traveled in many countries of Europe, Asia, Africa, South and Central America, Australia, the Philippines, Canada, and the U.S.A. He and his family have lived near Waynedale, Allen County, in two locations for a total of seventeen years.

John Jr. and Ruth Laymon have three children, all were born in Fort Wayne: Anita Ruth Laymon, January 22, 1943; Susan Jane Laymon Jones, June 6, 1949; and Thomas John Laymon, December 30, 1953. Anita and Susan obtained degrees from Fort Wayne Bible College, which is now Taylor University. They then obtained master degrees in education. Rev. Thomas John is an ordained minister with a seminary master's degree and with completed studies required for a doctorate.

Anita has had several positions in education, Susan teaches in public school, and Tom is Executive Director of a city mission. All of the family has been active in the First Missionary Church in Fort Wayne whenever work did not take them out of Fort Wayne.

Anita married Jayson Lamos, born July 19, 1944. Anita and Jayson have a daughter, Valerie, born October 22, 1968. Valerie and her husband, Edward Labo, born August 16, 1967, have two sons: Logan and Carson. Susan married Robert Paul Jones, born August 18, 1949. Susan and Robert have two sons: Matthew and Jonathan. Thomas married Janice Mae Breithaupt, born May 4, 1955.

Submitted by John L. Laymon, Jr.

ARGIRE VASIL LEBAMOFF

Argire Vasil Lebamoff was born in 1892 in Visheni, part ofthe Kostur district of Macedonia, which today is Aegean Macedonia, or northern Greece. His parents were Maria Stumboff and Vasil George Lebamoff ofVisheni. Vasil was one of three children of George Dimitri Lebamoff.

In 1903 tragedy struck many Macedonians, including the Lebamoff family. On the August 2 feast day of St. Ilia, Macedonian peasant insurgents in several towns and villages began battling the Turks in what became known as the Ilinden Insurrection. Argire's grandfather George and mother, Maria, were at the village water fountain, located on their property. Across the street their neighbor Tipo Tsuleff (whose granddaughter would marry Argire's son, George, some fifty years later) was meeting with other revolutionaries in his house, their rifles placed against a window. When Turkish soldiers passing through town stopped to drink at the fountain, they noticed the glare from the rifles in Tipo's house and immediately began firing at both rebels and villagers. Several Macedonians were killed, including Tipo, as well as Argire's grandfather George and mother, Baba Maria, who died in his arms. He was eleven years old at the time.

Argire and Helen (Elena) Lebamoff

At the time of the insurrection, his brother, Thomas, was with the Internal Macedonian Revolutionary Organization rebels near Istanbul fighting Turkish soldiers. He was arrested for bombing an Istanbul bank and sentenced to prison. When he was released in 1904, Argire, age twelve, ran up the trail in spite of the danger of wolves and bears, to met Tom as he came down Vicho Planina Mountain. Thomas emigrated to America in 1905. Argire continued to live with relatives and various neighbors until 1907, when, at the age of fifteen, he traveled to Kastoria, where a Jewish merchant loaned him money to buy transit to the United States. He came third class on the French liner *Lorraine,* with a Turkish passport and name, Sultani Argeris; the ship arrived at Ellis Island on April 28, 1907. Tom met him and they worked for six months at an ice-cream plant in Steelton, Pennsylvania to earn their train fare to Fort Wayne.

Immigrants came to Fort Wayne because of its industry; they didn't need much education or to know the language well to do manual labor. Argire found work at the Bass Foundry. He lived with an elderly German woman. In exchange for low rent he did household chores, and did the grocery shopping at the store on the corner of Hanna and Hayden. Argire and Tom became friends with the owner, Mendel Frank, and Argire did chores for him as well. After a few years, Mr. Frank sold them his business. Even though Tom had a wife and three children and Argire was a bachelor, they split the profits equally. Eventually they decided to separate and begin their own businesses. Tom opened a grocery at Weisser Park and Pontiac Street. Argire bought property at 3230 Piqua Avenue (now South Clinton) and built Liberty Grocery.

Argire Lebamoff at the Liberty Grocery

Argire then returned to his homeland to meet and marry Elena (Helen) Kachandonov from Blatsa. His mother's Stumboff family lived in Blatsa, so this is probably how the marriage was arranged. Elena had to be smuggled out of Blatsa to the Bulgarian border, where Argire was waiting. They married in Plovdiv, honeymooned in Bulgaria, and sailed for the United States. They lived upstairs in the Liberty Grocery building. Their four children were born there, Maria Ann in 1925, George in 1927, Ivan in 1932, and Klement in 1939. Liberty Grocery expanded to include fresh produce, and eventually carried liquor in a building next door.

The brothers, Tom and Argire, helped establish a national organization of Macedonian immigrants in the United States and Canada, The Macedonian Patriotic Organization (MPO). Members in the United States and Canada supported an independent, united Macedonia. They held conventions and published a weekly newspaper, the *Macedonian Tribune*. The organization soon had 7,000 members.

Argire's son, George, fondly remembers Sundays when he would sit on his father's lap and learn songs about Bulgaria. Macedonian families were proud and worked hard; they believed welfare was shameful. It was a struggle, but they would write home once or twice a year inviting relatives or neighbors to come to America. The first Macedonians here made it easier for those who followed.

Argire died in 1970, and wife, Helen (Elena) in 1984.

Submitted by George Lebamoff

GEORGE LEBAMOFF FAMILY

George Argire Lebamoff was born in 1927 in Fort Wayne, Indiana, the son of Argire and Elena (Helen) Kachandonov Lebamoff. They were immigrants from Macedonia who ran Liberty Grocery store at 3230 Piqua Avenue (now South Clinton). His siblings were Maria, born 1925; Ivan Argire, born 1932; and Klement Argire, born 1939. From his early childhood George worked at the grocery store. He attended South Side High School and worked at the store in all his spare time to help his family during the war when help was scarce.

After high school graduation he attended IU extension locally for two years, transferred to IU Bloomington, then transferred again to Huntington College where he graduated with a degree in business administration. He was drafted in the army in 1951, and after basic training was stationed in Austria for most of his time before being discharged in 1953.

George married Rosemary Tsiguloff, daughter of George A. and Linka Tsiguloff and granddaughter of the guerrilla leader Tipo Tsuleff killed in the Ilinden Insurrection in 1903 in Vishеni, Macedonia, along with George Lebamoff's grandmother and great grandfather. George Tsiguloff operated the Royal Lunch Tavern and Restaurant on Main Street, and they lived on Rudisill. In addition to Rosie, born 1935, they had a son Chris, born 1932 in Macedonia, and Tommy, born 1940. Tipo Tsuleff's widow, Baba Despa, emigrated in 1935 and lived with the family.

Rosie and George married February 20, 1955. They lived with his parents for six months, then moved into the apartment above the Liberty Grocery Store. He purchased the liquor inventory, rented the building (next to the grocery) from his father, and went into business for himself, with Rosie helping at the store. In November 1955 their first daughter, Deborah, was born. Son Andrew was born in 1961, John in 1962, and Tom in 1965. In 1962 they moved to 1438 Ardis. They lived there for thirty-six years, remodeling and enlarging it several times.

In 1958 George opened his second liquor store, Variety Liquors on US 27. He soon expanded the business to include four more stores - on East State, Lafayette, Bluffton Road, and North Anthony. In 1964 he opened the Glenbrook store and changed the name of the business to Cap and Cork. Between 1975 and 1989, he opened stores in Georgetown, on Coldwater, at Broadway and Times Comers, and on Lima Road. Over the years some locations were sold, and others added. He turned over management to family members and retired in 1995.

At eighteen he joined the Macedonian Patriotic Organization which his father and Uncle Tom had helped establish. He has been active in this organization all his life, including serving as president of the local chapter and national treasurer. His brother, Ivan, served as national president. George has traveled to Macedonia many times, and worked with officials in Washington, D. C., for years on behalf of Macedonian freedom. In 2003 he was awarded a medal for distinguished service to the Macedonian people.

During the 1950s and 1960s George was active in the Democratic party and participated in the presidential campaign of John F. Kennedy. He and Rosie attended the Kennedy inauguration, the parade, and the parties hosted by Indiana Senators Vance Hartke and Birch Bayh. Brother Ivan ran and was elected mayor of Fort Wayne in 1970 on the Democratic ticket. Eventually George changed parties and became a Republican. In 1981 he and Rosie attended the Reagan inaugural.

Daughter Debbie married Joe Doust in 1979. Their children are Kara, Joshua, and Joseph. Andy married Deborah Lewandowski in 1989 and their children are Olivia, Natalie, and Nolan. Tommy married Aleria Kaplanis in 1986 and they live in Chicago. Their children are Chloe, Ciara, Clair and Whitney. Johnny is single and living in Scottsdale, Arizona.

George has written an interesting history of his family, *An American Macedonian,* and a copy is in the collection of the Allen County Public Library, Historical Genealogy Department.

Submitted by George Lebamoff

George Lebamoff Family

DANIEL LEDERMAN

Daniel Lederman was born January 28, 1864 in Wayne County, Ohio. He met Catherine (Katie) Neuhouser in Allen County, Indiana, and they married on January 25, 1894 in the St. Joseph River Mennonite Church. He moved from Wayne County, Ohio and established a farm home just west of Grabill, Indiana.

Catherine (Katie) Neuhouser's genealogy traces to the same time frame and location in Europe. Catherine's Grandfather, Peter Neuhouser, was born in Essert, France, a suburb of Belfort, France and about 40 miles west of Basel, Switzerland. He had one son Christian Neuhouser, born September 4, 1832 in Essert, France. Sometime between 1852 and 1882 Christian immigrated to the States and came to Allen County. He married Anna Schwartz on January 25, 1894 in the St. Joseph River Mennonite Church. They had 13 children with Catherine "Katie" Neuhouser being the third youngest. She was born January 25, 1894.

Daniel Lederman and Catherine (Katie) Neuhouser established a farm home just west of Grabill, Indiana. On this farm home they created a family of 14 children. Eleven of these children lived into adulthood. Pa, Daniel Lederman, died at home on the farm May 20, 1943. Ma, Catherine (Katie) Lederman died at her oldest daughter Emmy's home on May 21, 1982. Both are buried in the Yaggie Cemetery just south of Grabill and about a mile from the homestead.

Listed below are Daniel Lederman and Catherine (Katie) Neuhouser's children.

Emma Lederman was born November 22, 1894, at the farm home. Emma met and married Noah Stucky on March 27,1918 in the Leo Mennonite Church, Leo, Indiana. They ran a farm in Spencerville, Indiana, and later moved into Leo. Emma and Noah had no children. Emma died May 21, 1982 at home of a heart attack.

Harvey Lederman was born March 6, 1896 at home. Harvey had a rough life and died of Red Cholera 10 months 27 days after birth, on February 03, 1897.

Noah Lederman was born on September 28, 1897 at home. Noah lived 13 years and 11 months. He died from falling from a Hickory tree on August 31, 1911.

Amos Lederman was born on August 25, 1899 at home. Amos met and married Lillian Liechty on February 28, 1924. They were married at her parents home in Allen County. Amos was a farmer and helping hand, and did construction work. They farmed in Spencerville, Indiana, and

Daniel and Katie Ledernan, family gathering in Wauseon, Ohio, March 16, 1942

then moved to and lived in Leo. Amos and Lillie had three children; Kathryn Anna born April 12, 1925; Loveda May born May 18, 1926, and Leland Cornell born June 17, 1929. Amos died at age 55 on December 10, 1954 after 22 months of illness caused by a heart ailment.

Esther Lederman was born April 28, 1901 at home. Esther met and married Ervin Vern Beck on May 4, 1921 in Allen County. After they married, they lived in Harlan, Indiana, for awhile and then they moved to Ridgeville Township, Henry County, Ohio, where they lived on a farm. Esther and Ervin Beck had five children: Helen Marie born September 9, 1921; Vincent Stanley born January 14, 1923; Kathryn Elizabeth born July 21, 1926; Imogene born October 26, 1932; Ervin Beck Jr. born September 9, 1937. Esther died on or near the farm on January 6, 1904.

Amanda Lederman was born on January 16, 1903 at home. Amanda lived at home until she met Walter Rupp of Archbold, Ohio. They were married on January 1, 1925 in Fort Wayne, Allen County. After they were married they lived/farmed near Archbold, Ohio, then near Spencerville, Indiana. Walter then bought a farm near Quincy Michigan. Amanda lost Walter in April 1971 from a tractor accident. Amanda and Walter had seven children: Robert Daniel born October 29, 1925; Harold Gene born October 22, 1927; Walter Junior born September 22, 1930; James Edgar born April 30, 1936, died January 20, 1937; Larry Lee born May 17, 1938; Lynn Spencer born October 5, 1939; and Karen Ann born March 8, 1945. She continued to live on the farm until health problems in 1994 and then lived with her son, Larry, in York County, Lake Wylie, South Carolina, until her death on July 26, 1997.

Alpheus Lederman was born on November 30, 1904 at home. Alpheus met and married Edith Adella Amstutz of Stryker, Ohio, on June 14, 1927. They lived and worked all of their married life in Leo/Cedarville. Alpheus was a carpenter and builder and built or worked on many of the churches in the area. He had an accident in which he fell from a roof and broke his back. From that time on he was confined to a wheelchair. Alpheus and Edith had three children: Donnabell June born June 1, 1928; Maredith May born May 18, 1931; and Richard Allen born August 19, 1932. Alpheus died on August 4, 1978 from long term complications and congestion.

David Lederman was born on August 19, 1906 at home. David met Ruby Ruth Haarer and was married on December 15, 1930 at the home of her parents in Shipshewana, Indiana. They moved and established their home near Mendon, Michigan. David and Ruby had three children of their own plus an adopted a set of twins and one foster child: Betty Carolyn born October 6, 1931; Mirriam Marie born February 28,1940; Paul Edger born November 15, 1942; Bob Leon and William Lynn, adopted twins born May 13, 1956; Tom Allen Persons (foster child) born June 10, 1965. David died on his farm outside Mendon in a freak gun accident on April 17, 1996.

Elmer Lederman was born on February 26,1908 at home. He met and married Edna Marie Yoder on December 24, 1935 at the home of Jonas Yoder of Grabill in a double ceremony with his younger brother Glenn. Elmer was a lifetime farmer and had a farm just north of Leo, Indiana. Elmer and Edna had two children: Donald born June 4, 1940; Sheila Marie born January 6, 1947. She died of cancer March 30,1986. Elmer died at his son's home on his farm from lingering health problems.

Elsie Lederman was born on December 21, 1909 at home. Elsie was born premature and lived only 28 hours. She died December 22, 1909 at home.

Paul Lederman was born on April 6, 1911 at home. Paul met and married Catheryn Short on December 9, 1943. They lived in Leo for many years and Paul was the janitor for Leo High School. Paul and Catheryn had three boys: Roger born September 14, 1944; Darrell born February 5, 1947; Arnold Dean born January 7, 1952. After their three boys graduated, they followed the boys to Florida and established their homes there. Paul died in Florida on February 19, 1981.

Glenn Lederman was born on April 1, 1913 at home. He met and married Florence Violet Yoder on December 24, 1935 in a double ceremony with his brother Elmer. Elmer and Glenn were brothers and Edna and Florence were first cousins, thus the double wedding. They were married at the farm home of Florence's parents, Jonas and Rose Yoder. Glen took up farming with his father-in-law on a farm north of Grabill. After farming for 28 years, Glenn and Jonas traded the farm for the elevator, The Grabill Grain & Milling Co. in Grabill, in 1953. They both bought homes and moved into Grabill. The two of them ran the mill until Jonas Yoder died, and then Glenn ran it until 1968 when he sold the business. Glenn and Florence could not have children so they adopted two children: Llewellyn Niles born January 11, 1946; and Glennice Gail born July 22, 1948. On November 1, 1972, Florence died from complications with cancer. In 1980 Glenn started dating Mildred Klopfenstein, a cousin to Florence. They were married on August 1, 1981 at Simpson United Methodist Church, Fort Wayne, Indiana. Glenn Lederman died December 18, 1999 from congestive heart failure.

Edger Lederman was born June 10, 1915, at home. When he was 24, he met Vera Stuckey and they were married on June 18, 1939. Like Glenn, Edger lived his whole life in and around Grabill and Leo. Edger was a carpenter and worked at Delegrange Homes where he retired. Edger and Vera had three children: Diane Marie born March 6, 1944; Linda Lou born May 1, 1947; and Kent Eugene born January 21, 1956. Edger died on May 12, 1993 at his home in Leo of congestive heart failure.

Evelyn Lederman, was born on October 31 1918, at home. In her 20th year a dashing gentleman from Stryker, Ohio started calling. Evelyn and Raymond Schmucker were married on February 12, 1934, at the Leo Mennonite Church in Leo. Evelyn and Raymond have three children: Jeanine born January 21, 1942; Kendra born August 7, 1946; and Kelly born December 12, 1960. Evelyn is the only remaining sibling of this family still living as of March 2005.

Submitted by Lew Lederman

GLENN LEDERMAN & FLORENCE YODER FAMILY

Glenn Lederman was born April 1, 1913 at the Lederman farmstead home just west of Grabill, Allen County, Indiana. He met and married Florence Violet Yoder on December 24, 1935 in a double ceremony with his brother Elmer. Elmer and Glenn were brothers and Edna and Florence Yoder were first cousins, thus the double wedding. They were married at the farm home of Florence's parents Jonas and Rose Yoder. Jonas Yoder's (1885-1955) genealogy lineage traces to Western Germany near the border with Switzerland east of Basel in or near the Emmental Valley. Rosa (Klopfenstein) Yoder's 1885-1977 genealogy traces to an area near Belford, France.

Glenn Lederman (1913-1999) and Florence Yoder (1914-1972) took up farming with his father-in-law on a farm north of Grabill. After farming for 28 years, Glenn and Jonas traded the farm for the Elevator, The Grabill Grain & Milling Co. in Grabill in 1953. They both bought homes and moved into Grabill. Glenn and Florence bought the George King property in the center of Grabill. Glenn Lederman and Jonas Yoder ran the mill until 1968 when the business was sold. Glenn and Florence could not have children so they adopted two children: Llewellyn Niles Lederman born January 11 1946; and Glennice Gail Lederman born on July 22, 1948. On November 2, 1972, Florence died from complications with cancer. After years of mourning, Glenn started dating Mildred Klopfenstein, a cousin to Florence. They were married on August 1, 1981 at Simpson United Methodist Church, Fort Wayne, Indiana. Glenn Lederman died December 18, 1999 of congestive heart failure at the Cedars retirement home in Leo.

Listed below are Glenn Lederman and Florence Yoder's children and descendants.

Llewellyn Niles Lederman, was born January 11, 1946 and adopted 14 months later. He met Judith Plata from Bogota, Colombia, South America in Akron, Pennsylvania and they married on August 9, 1970 in the Evangelical Mennonite Church in Bogota, Colombia. Llewellyn and Judith had one daughter: Babette Lilian Lederman born on May 9, 1971. She met and married Robert Gierke on August 25, 2001 in Fort Wayne, Indiana. Rob and Babette have one daughter: Sara Alexandra Gierke, born October 10, 2004 and they are expecting their second child in February 2006.

Glennice Gail Lederman was born July 22, 1948 and then adopted. She met and married Gary Stauffer on June 7, 1969. Glennice and Gary Stauffer have two children: Mark Allen Stauffer born March 24, 1970 and Cindy Kay Stauffer born June 10, 1973. Mark Stauffer has two children: Josh Stephen Stauffer born June 13, 1997 and Cassidy Diane Stauffer born November 24, 1999. Cindy Stauffer met and married Matthew Lehn September 2, 1995. Cindy and Matt Lehn have two children: Noah Matthew Lehn born June 27, 2000, and Jacob Ryan Lehn born April 23, 2002.

Submitted by Lew Lederman

PETER LEDERMAN FAMILY

Daniel Lederman's parents and grandparents lived in the Emmental Valley, near the small town of Langnau which is southwest of Basel, Switzerland. Peter Lederman, born in 1794, and his wife Anna Schrag, born in 1797, Daniel's grandparents, along with their family of seven children, left their birth place area of Langnau, Switzerland and went to the port in Havre, France. They left Havre, France and immigrated to Ellis Island, New York, New York on the ship "Gallia" arriving on April 21, 1851. The Swiss/German spelling of their name Lederman means leather worker.

At the time of immigration the children of Peter Lederman and Anna Schrag were as follows: Twins, Johannes (John) Lederman, and Peter Lederman, born March 10, 1823 and age 28, Catherine Anna Lederman, born 1830 and age 21, Marie Lederman, born 1833 and age 18, Jacob Lederman, born 1836 and age 15, Barbara Lederman, born 1838 and age 13, Judith Lederman, born in 1843 and age 8. When they arrived at Ellis Island, the family was split into two lines. As they were processed and asked their names the two people recording the names in the different lines spelled their names differently. After going through processing at Ellis Island, Father Peter and Mother Anna, twin son Peter, daughter's Marie, Barbara, and Judith still had the Lederman name. But the other siblings; twin son John, Catherine Anna, and Jacob now had their name spelled Leatherman.

Peter Lederman and Anna (Schrag) Lederman

Twin son - Peter Lederman
Twin son - Johnannes (John) Leatherman
Daughter - Marie Lederman
Daughter - Catherine Anna Leatherman
Daughter - Barbara Lederman
Son - Jacob Leatherman
Daughter - Judith Lederman

As a side note attraction; on the same voyage and vessel there was a young lady named Anna Moser, born in 1831 and age 20. Twin son Johannes (John Lederman) Leatherman and Anna Moser developed a romance that started on the ship and they were later married after settling in Wayne County, Ohio. They had five children: Jacob, Jonas, Jeff, John, and Lydia.

Father, Peter Lederman died August 30, 1877 in Orrville, Wayne County, Ohio. He had owned a farm in Sugar Creek Township, Wayne County, Ohio.

Twin son Peter Lederman met and married Kathryn (Katie) Moser from Illinois. They had two children; Sarah Lederman, born November 1, 1862, and *Daniel Lederman, born January 28, 1864. Sarah was born in Wayne County Ohio. She later met and married Jacob J. Yoder and they moved to and settled in Davis County, in southern Indiana.

Submitted by Lew Lederman

BERT LEE & EDITH SWANSON LEE FAMILY

Bert Lee (Bernt Livgaard) was born on March 21, 1869 in South Livgaard, Hof Solor, Norway. He came to America at age 18. His sister Anna had preceded him to America. Eventually his other siblings, Olia, Agnette, Otto and Kaja and his widowed mother, Olianna, followed. The Livgaard family all settled in Muskegon, Michigan because Olianna had a brother who lived there who was a successful contractor and a sheriff in Muskegon County. The family name of Livgaard was derived from an area in Norway where the father, Ole had lived. Shortly after his arrival in Muskegon, Bert changed his name to Lee and his brother, Otto, did likewise.

The Livgaards were very entrpreneurial and started many businesses in the years immediately after their arrival. They settled in an ethnic neighborhood in Muskegon called "Pinchtown" and by the early 1890s had created a small shopping area of adjoining store fronts which included a dry goods store, a hardware store, a grocery store, and a meat market. The grocery store was known as "Bert Lee and Company." Bert became disenchanted with the grocery business because, according to his son Russell, he couldn' t bring himself to be aggressive enough about collecting unpaid bills. He became a teamster and became affiliated with the Rolling Mill in Muskegon and moved to Fort Wayne in 1906 when that business moved to Fort Wayne.

Edith Swanson Lee was born in Muskegon, Michigan on May 19, 1877, the daughter of Charles/Carl Swanson/Svenssen, born in Vase Parish, Sweden on November 4, 1850 and Amanda Olson born July 18, 1860 in Jevnaker, Oppland, Norway.

Bert and Edith reportedly met when Bert was living at a Scandinavian boarding house where Edith was employed. They were married in Muskegon, Michigan, the exact date unknown.

Bert and Edith had seven children that lived to adulthood: Olive Ida, born January 18, 1897; Arthur, born December 10, 1901; Margaret, born July 22, 1904; Alice, born May 30, 1906; Robert E., born November 6, 1908; Russell, born June 29, 1910; and Eleanora, born July 3, 1912, whose descendants can be found at the end of this document.

In 1906, the family moved to Fort Wayne and Bert pursued his occupation as a teamster with the Rolling Mill. When the family first moved to Fort Wayne, they lived in the Rolling Mill District but by 1910 they built a house at 1115 High Street in the heart of the Bloomingdale neighborhood. Even though the family was not particularly affluent, they owned one of the early automobiles in Fort Wayne, a Haynes Touring car, the model year apparently pre-dating 1910. This was due to the fact that Bert was acquainted through his employment with William Rockhill from whom he purchased the automobile. They took many Sunday rides in it. They also went on at least one camping trip all the way to Pennsylvania. Another favorite pastime was all day Sunday excursions to the countryside for picnics, frequently to Devil's Hollow. Bert was an avid reader and read constantly. His son, Russel, said that his most vivid memory of his father was his father sitting at the dining room table reading. He read all of the works of Shakespeare.

In 1928, Robert and Russell went to California to try life there, but after one year they were homesick and returned to Fort Wayne just in time for the Great Depression.

Edith died on July 7, 1930. Soon thereafter, Bert retired after completing the hauling of all of the steel for the Lincoln Tower. Bert lived out his retirement years with various of his children. He lived with his son, Robert, and his family, at the High Street residence. He then lived for many years with his daughter Olive and her husband, Ed Federspiel, at the Federspiel's farm on the McNabb Road between Leo and Spencerville until 1955. In 1955, he lived with his son, Russell, for a few months and then with his daughter Alice in Omak, Washington where he died on June 3, 1955. He was always treated with greatest respect and affection by his children.

Descendants of Bert and Edith Swanson Lee, to the third generation

Olive Ida Lee

Olive Ida Lee (January 18, 1897-June 8, 1950) married Ed Franklin Federspiel (1889-1955) on January 31, 1923, and they had five children: Dick, Edythe Alice, Bert, Ellen Marie, and Doris Leanna.

Dick Federspiel (November 27, 1923-November 30, 1923) died as an infant.

Edythe Alice Federspiel (born January 5, 1926) married Gerald Laverne Eager (born August 29, 1918) on April 17, 1949. They had three children: John Phillip, born March 20, 1951; Gerald Mark, born January of 1953; and Bonnie Elizabeth, born September 20, 1956.

Bert Federspiel (March 12, 1927-May 23, 1990) married Maxine Ruth Poisel (born January 5, 1929) on September 24, 1949. They had two children: Michael Robert, born April 7, 1957; and Denise Renee, born April 21, 1962.

Ellen Marie Federspiel (born March 27, 1929) married David Dudley Dean, Jr. (August 5, 1926-January 23, 1982) on June 29, 1957. They had three children: Carleton Lee, born January 1960; Mark Norman, born July 20, 1961; and Teresa Marie, born August 31, 1963.

Doris Leanna Federspiel (born May 15, 1930) married Edward Frederick Garber (born December 20, 1928) on July 26, 1959. They had two children: Curtis Allen, born June 30, 1960; and Catherine Phoebe, born August 3, 1962.

Arthur Lee

Arthur Lee (December 10, 1901-July 3, 1967) married Luella Anna Louise Stellhorn (born November 6, 1906) on September 12, 1931. They had two children, Mildred Joan and Arthur Wayne.

Mildred Joan Lee (born September 1, 1932) married David Earl Gearhart (born April 18, 1933) on September 6, 1952. They had two children: Leanne Kay, born September 19, 1956, and Alisa Maureen, born September 2, 1959.

Arthur Wayne Lee (born August 11, 1937) married Jeanine Mary Treft (born July 24, 1939) on May 11, 1957. They had three children, Carey Wayne, born April 10, 1958; Ronald Alan, born November 11, 1961; and Sarah Ann, born December 30, 1962.

Margaret Lee

Margaret Lee (July 22, 1904-July 15, 1985) married Archie Garrett Clowers (b. May 6, 1904) on December 12, 1932. They had one child.

Francis Marion Clowers (born November 6, 1934) married Bertie Joyce (born July 29, 1933) on December 28, 1959. They had four children: Vanessa Faye, born July 20, 1962; Gordon, born March 30, 1966; Kenneth Lee, born February 8, 1967; and Valerie, born July 2, 1969.

Alice Lee

Alice Lee (born May 30, 1906) married Paul Aron Dolgner (March 1, 1887-June 21, 1952) on July 29, 1939. They had one child, Kenneth Lorne Dolgner. Kenneth (born June 2, 1941), married Stella Delores Sparks (born April 1, 1941) on March 11, 1961. Kenneth and Stella had three children: Monica Ann, born June 16, 1962; Molly, born August 3, 1976; and Paul Lorne, born August 2, 1981.

Alice married George Edwin Kirby on September 7, 1957. Alice adopted Paul's son, Timothy David Kirby (born June 4, 1953) whose mother had died in childbirth.

Robert Lee

Robert Lee (November 6, 1908-August 23, 1973) married Fern M. Wright (March 4, 1906- March 2, 1968) on February 8, 1928. They had two children, Robert E., Jr., and Jack E.

Robert E. Lee, Jr., (November 1, 1928-July 10, 1974) married Marilyn R. Schoff (born October 31, 1930) on August 27, 1949. They had seven children: Katherine Ann, born October 18, 1950; Charles Allen, born April 12, 1952; Marie Alice, born May 27, 1955 and died March 3, 1971; Carolyn Ann, born February 1, 1959; Ronald Earl, born December 2, 1960; Timothy David, born February 12, 1962; and Michael, born June 21, 1964.

Jack E. Lee (born January 11, 1930) married Jean Spohn (born February 3, 1931)

The Bert Lee Family c. late 1920s. Front row from left to right: Alice, Eleanora, Edith, Bert; Back row from left to right: Margaret, Russell, Olive, Arthur, and Robert.

Bert Lee takes the neighbors for an all day picnic in the country in 1920.

Five of the Lee children standing in front of the family's Haynes Touring Car c. 1911. Left to right: Robert, Alice, Margaret, Arthur, Olive, and baby Russell.

Bert Lee with his son Arthur hauling a load of steel at the Rolling Mill in Fort Wayne.

Some of the Lee family at the Bass farm with Art Smith's airplane c. 1915. From left to right: Edith, Russell, Robert, and Eleanora.

on June 8, 1952. They had three daughters: Debora Jan, born April 26, 1954; Teresa Jo, born September 20, 1956; and Patricia Jean, born December 30, 1958.

<u>Russell Lee</u>

Russell Lee (June 29, 1910-January 8, 1989) married Catherine Louise Zwick (July 29, 1912- August 15, 1941) on May 29, 1935. They had one child, William Charles. Russell married, second, Alma Remenschneider (September 4, 1915-August 8, 1982) on May 9, 1942. They had one son, Walter Edward. They later divorced. Russell married, third, Martha Jane Arnold (September 6, 1915-July 27, 1995) on July 31, 1948.

William Charles Lee (born February 2, 1938) married Judith Bash (born June 2, 1937) on September 15, 1959. They had three children: Catherine Louise, born November 18, 1960; Mark Robert, born August 18, 1962; and Richard Russell, born May 31, 1971.

Walter Edward Lee was born November 29, 1944, and died February 11, 2004.

<u>Eleanora Lee</u>

Eleanora Lee (July 3, 1912-November 23, 1992) married Gilbert Alva Walker (born October 12, 1911) on September 20, 1930. They had two sons, Larry Lee and David Dean.

Larry Lee Walker (born July 11, 1932) married Rebecca Elizabeth Brown (born March 19, 1934) on June 9, 1957. They had five children: David Lee, born June 9, 1959; Daniel William, born November 17, 1960; Craig Allen, born February 20, 1964; Linda Gay, born December 30, 1968; Melissa Elizabeth, born January 27, 1973.

David Dean Walker (born October 4, 1937) married Lois Jane Brown (born September 17, 1937) on January 21, 1954. They are now divorced. They had three children: Susan Ann, born August 6, 1954; Barry Kevin, born February 14, 1959; Christopher Kent, born December 30, 1960.

Submitted by William C. Lee

CHRISTOPHER JOHN LEEPER & CYNTHIA LYNN (KING) LEEPER

Christopher was born on May 19, 1962, in Fort Wayne, Indiana. His parents, John P. Leeper and Velma K. (Whittenbarger) Leeper, were born and raised in Fort Wayne. Christopher has two sisters, Tina and Tracy, and one brother, Cory, who is vice president and co-owner of Leeper's Lawn Service, Incorporated.

Cynthia was born on June 10, 1960 in Fort Wayne, Indiana. Her parents, Roger N. King and Judith E. (Meyer) King (now Shugart), were born and raised in Fort Wayne. Cynthia has one brother, Todd, who is married and lives in the Columbia City area.

Christopher and Cynthia were married on October 18, 1986. They have two children, Tyler Dalton and Hilary Lynn. Tyler was born on July 24, 1990, and Hilary was born on April 4, 1992.

Christopher attended Elmhurst High School, the University of Massachusetts, and St. Francis University. Cynthia attended Concordia High School and IPFW , where she graduated with a degree in psychology. Christopher started Leeper's Lawn Service, Incorporated in 1984 and is still the current president and owner. Cynthia, after graduating, spent time in California and Fort Wayne working in law offices. She also worked for many years for her stepfather, Dr. Robert Shugart (deceased on March 30, 1996), at Fairfield Orthopedics as a physician's assistant. Cynthia is now office manager for Leeper's Lawn Service, Incorporated.

Cynthia, Hilary, Chris, and Tyler

Currently, Christopher enjoys golf, horseback riding, spending time with his family, and traveling. Cynthia enjoys animals of all types, especially dogs and horses. She currently tends to five horses, two dogs and four cats. She loves horseback riding and spending time with her family. Tyler currently enjoys guns and marksmanship, Taekwondo, and football. Hilar y enjoys animals of all types, movies, helping others, and spending time with her friends.

Recently, the Leeper family added several horse facilities to their property on Lower Huntington Road, including a stall barn and riding arena. At the same time, a shooting range for Tyler was added so he could practice his marksmanship. The Leepers have been involved in various charity functions and enjoy giving back to the community as much as possible.

Submitted by Chris and Cynthia Leeper

CORY & MARIA LEEPER FAMILY

Cory Phillip Leeper, the son of John and Velma Leeper, was born on September 19, 1969, at Lutheran Hospital on Fairfield Avenue in Fort Wayne, Indiana. Cory graduated from Wayne High School in 1988 and went on to attend college at IPFW and the University of Saint Francis.

Andrew Leeper, Cory Leeper, Maria Leeper, Grant Leeper

Cory currently is the vice president for the family business, Leeper's Lawn Service, Inc., which was started in 1984.

Maria Lynn Leeper (Watercutter), the daughter of Roger and Ella Mae Watercutter, was born on December 21, 1977, in Bethlehem, Pennsylvania. Maria graduated from Bishop Dwenger High School in 1996 and went on to attend Indiana University for two years.

Cory and Maria were married on November 6, 1999, at St. Vincent de Paul Catholic Church on Auburn Road in Fort Wayne, Indiana. Their first child, Andrew John Leeper, was born on June 11, 2003, at Dupont Hospital in Fort Wayne, Indiana. Their second child, Grant Michael Leeper, was born on September 28, 2004, at Dupont Hospital in Fort Wayne, Indiana.

Submitted by Cory Leeper

JOHN & AGNES MARGARET (BAUER) LEHMAN(N)

The parents of John Lehman(n) were Frederick Lehmann, Sr., born May 5, 1828, and his wife, Katerina Lehmann, born May 5, 1834, both in Baden, Germany. Their five children had much in common. All immigrated to Fort Wayne separately in the early 1880s; were members of the several German Lutheran churches; learned English well (although family scrapbooks indicated they read local German newspapers into the early 1900s); and all married young within the German community. In fact, two Lehmann brothers each married Bauer sisters. Their sons, and the husbands of their two daughters, all started working at the Bass Foundry, some continuing there until retiring, as did Frederick, Sr. who was the last to arrive in Fort Wayne in 1884. He died in 1901, his wife died in 1914, and both are buried in Lindenwood Cemetery.

The Frederick Lehmann, Sr. children and their spouses all lived to their 70s or mid 80s which was beyond the life expectancy for that time. The siblings of John Lehman were Frederick Lehmann, Jr. (1855-1935), married Christine Bauer, and their children were Fred, Lillian, Clara, and Bertha; Katherine Lehmann (1857-1930), married Oscar Kayser, and their children were Ella, Edna, Albert, and Hedwig; Charles Lehmann (1866-1940), married Henrietta Kahlenbeck, and their children were Salome, Elsie, Adele, Olive, Karl, and Harry; and Emma Caroline Lehmann (1874-1958), married William Wolfgang Kaestel, and they had no children.

John Lehman(n), born April 17,1863, in Karlsruhe, Baden, Germany, arrived in Fort Wayne in 1881 at age 18. His future wife, Agnes Margaret Bauer, born January 18, 1866, in Wurtemmburg, Germany, and orphaned in 1879, arrived in Fort Wayne in 1880 at age 14 with her brother, John Jacob, 16, and sisters Christine, 22, (above), Anna Marie, 25, and Susan Katherine, 29. John and Agnes were married January 3, 1886.

John Lehmann started at the Bass Foundry as a laborer, then helper, and finally as a molder. After 1887, he became a brewer at the Centlivre Brewery for the next 15 years. During this period newspapers frequently reported his activities in the brewers union. In February 1900, the *Sentinel* noted "John Lehmann, the well-known brewer, succeeded in getting an agreement between the boss brewers and their employees in Lafayette, Indiana, in which the men would be required to work only nine hours but would be paid for ten hours' labor." In 1895 he was elected president of the local union. He was the union's delegate to annual conventions in St. Louis, Chicago, and Cleveland. He was also active in the Concordia Lodge of the I.O.O.F, and a trustee in the Fort Wayne Saengerbund.

John and Agnes had resided in Centlivre Park and then at 26 Randolph Street, just south of State Street off Spy Run Avenue, where three of their children attended nearby Rudisill School. In 1902, they moved to St. Joseph Township. They purchased three acres in Section 33 where Meyer Road (later Maplecrest) ended at the Hicksville State Road (later East State Street extended), which property was adjacent to the present Georgetown Square. Here they ran a saloon and grocery (stocked with the "Little Elf" brands of the local Bursley wholesaler) and sold block ice from their large icehouse. A wide sign above the entrance porch of the store read "The Other Place" apparently acknowledging references made by a competitor several miles further to the east. By 1906, they added more acres on both sides of the road. The 1910 census shows that Agnes had a truck farm (for produce likely sold at the Barr Street Market),

In 1911, the Lehmans had a large brick home built on the north side of the road. (The story was that a contractor friend named Buesching offered to build them a new home "since his workers were not very busy." When it was finished, John asked, "How much do I owe you?") Later, a smokehouse and a double garage for a sleigh were added. He also for a time farmed part of the adjacent 200 acres owned by prominent bridge contractor, Henry W. Tapp (where the Buckingham Addition is now located).

Prohibition in 1919 effectively ended any saloon business at the store, which was moved to the corner across East State extended when it was widened and paved. Gas pumps were added for increased auto traffic. In 1922, John was elected to a four-year term as assessor of St. Joseph Township. By the 1990s, none of buildings or farm remained. Haley School (1969) occupies most of the land on the south side of State Street and businesses or residences the north side.

John and Agnes Margaret Lehman 1886

John Lehmann died December 16, 1932, and his wife, Agnes "Maggie" died January 21, 1941. They are buried in Lindenwood Cemetery, Fort Wayne. Their children and spouses, all deceased, were as follows:

1. Alma C. (1890-1961), married (1913) Wesford L. "Bill" Morris, who retired from Tokheim Corporation as a sales supervisor; one son, John W., married Lois Baker (three children -- Susan C., Katherine L., and John M.).

2. Lucia E. (1893-1980), married (1915) August G. Lepper, who retired from the Fort Wayne Police Department after 22 years; three children -- Margaret C., married Carl J. Miller; Ruth L., married Donald A. Distel -- one child, Sandra; and a son, Louis J., married Alberta Boehme (four children -- Luanna, Donna, Diana, and John).

3. Lydia G. (1895-1973), retired from Magnavox, married (1934) Lester W. Heine, self-employed in auto repair sales; one daughter, Carrol L., married Franklin Fuelling (two sons, Mark A. and Michael L.).

4. Frederick (1897-1898) died at age four months.

5. John A. "Jack" (1899-1980), the retired owner of Lehman's Standard Station at the corner of State and Wells, married first (1931) Irene D. Witt, who died in 1943; two daughters -- Barbara (married William L. Zongker) -- one daughter, Krista; and Judith A. (married Richard K. Young) -- two sons, Todd and Christopher. In 1945, John A. married again, Irene's sister, Ann D. Witt, (1912-2001) who retired as secretary at North Side High School. Their daughter, Marcia K., married Henry G. Fallek and then married Barry L. Cox.

6. Margaret B. (1903-1982), married (1924) Ferd E. Paul, a knitter first with the Wayne Knitting Mill, and then Thieme Hosiery in Los Angeles, from which both retired. Their only son died at birth in 1925.

Submitted by Carrol L. Fuelling

LEPPER FAMILY

Lawrence Lepper was the only child of Charles Lepper (1865-1949) and Louise Buuck (1869-1951). He was born June 24, 1898 in the original log house on land purchased by his German immigrant family.

The forty-acre farm in Marion township was about a mile from the Hoffman Road railway crossing. Lawrence could hear the whistles and even the clatter of the trains moving on the rails. He imagined what it would be like to ride the rails, and often thoughts about passengers, workmen and freight dominated his dreams.

Occasionally he got to see the mail exchange. He watched a railroad man grab the leather pouch from a long pole near the track while someone from the local postal station at Soest retrieved the incoming mailbag thrown from the train.

One exciting day in 1906, some men met a train at the crossing. Lawrence and his pa hauled the big altar for the new Emmanuel Lutheran (Soest) church building in the horse-drawn wagon.

Lawrence attended the one-room parochial school at Emmanuel where he received instruction entirely in German through the third grade. After that English was adopted, except for religious confirmation classes which continued in German.

Lawrence Lepper

Lawrence's best friend was his cousin, Gary Buuck. The boys spent time together whenever they could, that is, whenever the two families visited each other, for they did not live in the same neighborhood. As they approached adulthood, they talked and shared dreams of the future. Gary confided that he meant to work for the railroad and urged his cousin to come along so they could seek adventure and fortune together.

Lawrence was tempted, but he chose to remain on the farm. He loved the land, the crops and the animals that grew there. Trees were like personal friends and referred to individual ones as 'he' or she.'

Gary did have a very successful career with the railroad. He married, had a family and lived in Fort Wayne.

Lawrence married a pretty young woman, Irma Grotrian on November 26, 1922. He brought his bride to the homestead and they had two children there, Raymond (1924-2000) and Berniece (1925-2001).

Lawrence did not amass a worldly fortune, but he did value his heritage. He was a good steward of his land, so that he had a legacy to pass on to his descendants. He died February 24, 1975.

Irma continued on the farm and was presented with a Hoosier Homestead award. She was born September 17, 1903 and died October 26, 1992. His youngest grandson, Lee Lepper, now lives on a portion of the land, with evidence of the Leppers' history and their ties to that land proudly displayed.

Gary and Lawrence maintained a lifelong friendship even though their lives were vastly different. Eventually their children and grandchildren lost touch, but ironically, Jeremy Buuck and Robert J. Frye, great-grandsons of Gary and Lawrence, discovered their shared genealogy as high school friends at Concordia and college roommates at Purdue.

Submitted by Connie Frye and Lois Howe

JOSEPH & EDNA (PRICE) LEVINE

Joseph Levine was born in Modlodechno, Belarus on July 20,1907. He was the son of Zalman and Sylvia (Brown) Levine. In 1916, he left Modlodechno with his mother, two brothers and a sister. They traveled across Russia and Siberia in boxcars, then to Manchuria, Korea and Japan; arriving at Angel Island, near San Francisco in February 1917. They took a train to New Haven, Connecticut, where four older brothers, another sister and his father had settled.

Joe graduated from Hillhouse High School in 1926 and Franklin & Marshall College in 1930. Trained in social work, he became a parole officer, and was appointed Executive Case Supervisor of the New York State Division of Parole.

On December 23, 1934 he married Edna Price of Staten Island, New York. Born November 2, 1909, she was the daughter of Samuel and Pauline (Cooper) Price. The Price family had been in New York since 1848.

In business during World War II, Joe spent a year in Germany from 1945 to 1946 aiding and resettling Jewish Holocaust survivors.

The Levine family moved to Fort Wayne in September of 1947. Joe was Executive Director of the Fort Wayne Jewish Federation until 1972. He then founded and directed the Indiana Jewish Historical Society until 1992.

Edna passed away in March 1986. He later remarried to Rae Wolf. Joe died August of 1996. His passing was noted in both newspapers as "the conscience of the Jewish community." His presence impacted the entire city by reason of his many civic and philanthropic activities. Governor Evan Bayh named him a Sagamore of the Wabash. Rae Levine died a few years after Joe.

Joseph and Edna Levine

Joe and Edna had two children: Stanley born May 10, 1938 and Lois born October 14, 1942, both in Staten Island. They each graduated from South Side High School and Indiana University. Stanley graduated from Indiana University Law School in 1963, and practiced law in Fort Wayne until January, 1999, when he was appointed Judge of Allen Superior Court by Governor Frank O'Bannon. He is married to Jennifer (Moorman) Levine, R.N., M.A. They each have two children from previous marriages: Michael and Alan Levine, Jason Maurer and Kirsten Bouchard. Lois was a teacher in Illinois, and is married to Charles L. Edwards, a prominent attorney in Chicago, where they reside. They have two children, Laura Perkins and Karen Crelman. Both Levine children have been active in community affairs. Lois was an officer of the Brandeis University National Women's Committee. Stanley was a legal officer in the Indiana Air National Guard, President of the Allen County Bar Association, Legal Advisor to City Council, and is on the Board of Directors of Saint Joseph Hospital.

Edna Levine was a loving wife and mother, and a warm and kind active member of the Jewish community. Joseph Levine's impact as a Jewish historian and community leader in Fort Wayne was outstanding. His great-grandsons, Alec Joseph Bouchard and Benjamin Joseph Levine, are named for him.

Submitted by Stanley Levine

LEWIS & O'BRIAN FAMILIES

The John and Sara Lewis family is one of the oldest in the country. They came over from England on the Hercules in 1635, landing at New London, Connecticut.

Sylvester Lewis was born in Lewis Center, Ohio. He was a captain in the Indiana 7th Cavalry in the Civil War. He married Mary J. Redding on June 15, 1868. They had four children including Robert Curtis. Sylvester died November 20, 1890 and is buried in the Civil War section at Lindenwood. Mary died July 7, 1920, also buried in Lindenwood.

Robert Curtis was born May 1, 1877. He married Helene Caroline Voelker; they had three boys: Ernest, Robert, and Edwin. Helene died January 29, 1952 and is buried in Lindenwood. Curt died in January of 1967 and is buried in Lindenwood Cemetery.

Fiftieth Anniversary, Josephine and Ernest Lewis, October 1976. Front row, seated: Mary Helen O'Brian, Josephine Lewis, Ernest Lewis, Ginnie Lewis. Second row: John O'Brian, David Lewis, Molly O'Brian, Debra Lewis, Noel Lewis. Third row: Teri Lewis, Tim O'Brian, Kathy O'Brian, Kevin O'Brian, Lynne Lewis, Pat O'Brian, Mary Beth Lewis.

Helena and Curtis Lewis, Edwin, Robert, and Ernest

Ernest August was the first child of Robert Curtis and Helene. He married Anna Josephine Beiermann on October 30, 1924. They had two children: Mary Helen and Noel David. Ernie was purchasing agent of Wayne Knitting Mills until he retired in 1965. He was on the Board of Lutheran Hospital. He died April 15, 1980 of colon cancer; Anna died August 15, 1980 of heart disease. They are buried in Catholic Cemetery.

Noel David Lewis married Virginia Lee Reed of Rochester, Indiana. They settled in Blackford County where he was first a music and band teacher, and later, assistant prinipal of Blackford County High School. They had five children: Lynne Anne, Mary Elizabeth, Terese Marie, and twins David Noel and Debra Lee.

Mary Helen married John Francis O'Brian. John Francis (Jack) was born in Loogootee, Indiana on April 29, 1927, the second of five children of Myron F. and Monica Catherine (Strange) O'Brian. He graduated from Campion High School, Prairie du Chien, Wisconsin, was drafted into the army in August 1945, and discharged in March of 1947. He received a BS in 1951 from I.U. Bloomington and an MD from I.U. Medical School. He interned at St. Joseph Hospital, Fort Wayne.

Mary Helen Lewis was born at St. Joseph Hospital, Fort Wayne, on October 12, 1928. She graduated from Central Catholic High School and received a Bachelor's degree in Music Education from St. Mary of the Woods College in Terre Haute, Indiana. She taught instrumental music in the Catholic elementary schools.

They were married at the Cathedral of the Immaculate Conception on April 23, 1955. Jack started in Family Practice and later developed a subspecialty of Allergy and Environmental Medicine. He retired in 1993 after 38 years of medical practice. Mary Helen also taught third grade at St. Joseph's School in Fort Wayne as well as private music instructions. They had five children: Kevin Michael, Timothy Sean, Kathleen Marie (Dennis Christoff), Patrick Lewis, and Molly Anne (John Adams); four grandchildren: Meaghan Molly and John Padraic Adams, and Emma Kathleen Chun Feng and Hailey Ai Ni Christoff.

Mary Helen was a docent at The History Center for years. She and Jack started and chaired the Gingerbread Festival for two years. They also have been very active in Civil War history. They are now enjoying their retirement and their grandchildren.

Mary Helen is an eleventh generation descendant of John and Sarah Lewis who landed in New Haven, Connecticut in 1635.

Submitted by John F. O'Brian, M.D.

ROBERT C. & VELMA S. LEWIS

Robert C. Lewis was born on February 3, 1906, to Curtis R. Lewis, a native of Allen County, and Helena C. (Voelker) Lewis, an immigrant from Germany. Robert's grandfather, Sylvester Lewis, was a cavalry officer during the Civil War. Bob had two brothers, Ernest and Edwin.

Bob attended Concordia Lutheran Grade School; however, a hearing loss and economic reasons ended his schooling. At Concordia, Bob met and began a life long commitment to Velma S. Dudenhofer, his future wife. Velma was born in Fort Wayne on May 21, 1906. She was the first child of George and Maria (Zelt) Dudenhofer; both born and reared in Allen County. George operated Dudenhofer Grocery. The Lewis, Dudenhofer, and Zelt families have a long and continued presence in Allen County, immigrating in the 1830s.

Velma was one of the first graduates of Luther Institute, predecessor of Concordia Lutheran High School. Upon graduation and until marriage Velma worked at Allen County Abstract. Bob and Velma courted at church activities. They began their 60-year marriage October 15, 1929. Their union produced three children: Thomas C. Lewis, born August 31, 1931; Cynthia R. (Mrs. Richard Havel), born August 31, 1937; and Stephen E. Lewis, born February 6, 1944.

Bob had a long career in the office supply industry, starting at O'Rielly Office Supply. Although hearing impaired, Bob was a successful salesman, who, along with others, founded Lewis & Christen Office Supply in 1955. He retired from there as president in 1973.

Bob was an active and avid sports person. He played baseball, basketball, and golf. He always had time to go fishing with his friend, Red, his father Curtis, and his own sons. He supported Concordia High School athletics and was a loyal fan until he died in 1992. Bob never lost his enthusiasm for his work, faith, friends, and family. Bob's greatest love, however, was Velma. He never let his friends, children, and even strangers forget this fact.

Velma was a homemaker, who was fiercely loyal and supportive of Bob. When Bob was 47 years old, he mortgaged everything he and Velma owned to found Lewis & Christen; Velma never questioned it. She raised her children with sensitivity and care, never letting them forget that all people have value and that people with other points of view should be tolerated and respected. Her adroit mind was exemplified in her poetry and diaries. She loved anything of beauty, be it of music, nature, taste, or feel.

Bob and Velma stressed education, integrity, industry, loyalty, and faith to their children. All of their children attended Lutheran grade school and Concordia High School. Tom graduated from Valparaiso University in 1956 and Steve in 1966 and 1969 with a Jurist Doctor degree.

Both Bob and Velma continued their life as active participants of the Lutheran community. They were active members of Concordia Lutheran Church, charter members of Holy Cross Lutheran Church, and active at the Lake James Lutheran Chapel. By their life and their example they were truly representative members of the Allen County community and heritage.

Submitted by Stephen E. Lewis

LILLIE & GILLIE FAMILIES

James Lillie, born March 16, 1834, in Greenlaw, Berwickshire, Scotland was the youngest child of John and Elizabeth Parker (Hume) Lillie. James came to the Fort Wayne area (Ossian, Indiana) in 1851, at the age of 17, to join his eldest brother, John Lillie, who was beginning a large lime mining business, southwest of Fort Wayne. James labored to become a carpenter. In November 1859 he married Julia Ann Melissa Fink, daughter of Charles and Elizabeth (Pennewell) Fink, a prominent undertaker whose business was at 37 Maiden Lane in Fort Wayne.

Sometime in the 1850s James began a business as "James Lillie & Co.", Manufacturers of White Lime and dealers in Cement, Plaster, Sewer Pipe, etc., which was located at 1 North Calhoun. This would have been on the St. Mary's River. It was a successful business for about 26 years in Fort Wayne. Their home, at the time, was called the "Lillie Farm", now Franke Park. They later purchased two large lumber mills in Talbot and Escanaba, Michigan and completed a contract with the State of Indiana to build the State prison at Michigan City. James held many building contracts in Kankakee, Illinois during the 1870s, and in 1878 he moved his family to that city, where he had contracted with the State of Illinois to build the second largest sanitarium hospital in the U.S., the "Eastern lllinois Hospital for the Insane", a complex of 30 buildings, housing 2100 patients. The hospital is still in use in 2005.

By the early 1860s, all but one of John and James Lillie's seven brothers and sisters had come to the U.S. and settled in the Ossian and Huntington area of Indiana, that one being Jane Lillie, wife of George Gillie, who remained in Scotland.

In June of 1882, Mr. Lillie's nephew, James Gillie, joined them in Kankakee along with his wife, Janet (Taylor) Gillie and their first born son, George W. Gillie. James Gillie, born January 5, 1851, son of George and Jane (Lillie) Gillie, was also from Greenlaw, Berwickshire, Scotland. Mr Gillie worked for his uncle on the hospital for one year before moving onto the Lillie Farm in Fort Wayne.

In 1892, James's brother, John Gillie, born May 4, 1852, came with his family to Fort Wayne through Guelph, Ontario, Canada where they had lived about eight years. John and his wife Janet (Douglas), and their then family of eight children, initially located on the "Evans Farm" in St. Joseph Township, and equipped himself in the dairy business. This home was called Poinsette Place, on Goshen Road, about where McDonald's Restaurant is located. Eventually, James Gillie and his family moved from the Lillie Farm to the Bass Farm, called "Blackhawk Farm", and his brother John's family took over the Lillie farm.

By the turn of the century, James and John were then in the dairy business in a much bigger way and, together, they operated the "Greenlaw Dairy" in Fort Wayne. James and John Gillie were the only children of nine brothers and sisters who reached adulthood, to come to the U.S.

James and Janet (Taylor) Gillie raised a family of ten children in Fort Wayne, seven of which reached adulthood.

See picture: George W. (Grace Menon), Peter Taylor (Elizabeth Fyffe), Janetta C., Jane L., John Alexander (Marye Cadieux), Margaret Mable (Joseph Pearson), Agnes Florence (Arthur W. Boerger), James Jr., Harold Taylor (Cecelia Caton), and James Stewart (Helen Stolte).

After James Gillie's death in 1911, his wife Janet's sister, Mrs. Agnes (Taylor) Collie, who had been widowed in Scotland, immigrated to Fort Wayne to live with Janet. Agnes brought with her two of her four children, Grace and Allen Collie.

John and Janet (Douglas) Gillie raised a family of 15 children, 13 of which reached adulthood. See picture: George (Bertha Dedolph), Jessie Hunter (James R. VanEvery), James (Carrie Wor-

John and Janet (Douglas) Gillie's children. Picture taken in the year of mother, Janet's death, 1915. Robert Alexander (Ek) 1890-1968; John Lillie (Jack) 1888-1958; James 1883-1965; Elizabeth Hume Dacey 1889-1977; William Thomas 1897-1972; Jessie Hunter VanEvery 1881-1946; David 1901-1979; Isabelle Oswald 1895-1989; Margaret Bever 1894-1979; Andrew Douglas 1887-1944; Ralph 1903-1990; George (Doan) 1879-1963; Jane Lillie Sanborn 1885-1955.

James and Janet (Taylor) Gillie's children and mother Janet: Harold Taylor (Pat) 1896-1969; John Alexander (Jack) 1889-1957; Peter Taylor 1882-1944; Stewart Ainslee 1900-1983; Agnes Florence 1893-1962; Janet 1856-1940; Margaret Mable 1891-1984; Dr. George W. (Doc) gillie 1880-1963

man), Jane Lillie (Edward F. Sanborn), Andrew Douglas (Elsie Collie), John (Floyd Martin), Elizabeth Hume (Edward J. Dancey), Robert Alexander (Mona Dolan), Margaret (Frank J. Bever), Isabelle (William M. Oswald), William Thomas (Velma Oman), Mark, Helen, David (Ireta Cutler), and Ralph (Ila Mae Culver).

George W. Gillie, born August 15, 1880, Berwickshire, Scotland, the eldest son of James Gillie, graduated from Ohio State with a doctorate in Veterinary Science, VS '07. He married Grace Nanette Merion on June 24, 1908. Grace was also a graduate of Ohio State, BA '08, the daughter of Charles S. and Emma (Kienzle) Merion. For six years after graduation Dr. Gillie was in charge of meat and milk inspection for the city of Fort Wayne. His veterinary medical practice, which he began in 1915 in Allen County, was interrupted a year later when he was named assistant state veterinarian, again when he served four two year terms (1916, 1921, 1928, and 1934) as Sheriff of Allen County, and in 1938 when he began a ten year service as U.S. Congressman from the Indiana 4th District. He was a ranking member on the Agriculture Committee and was widely known for his effort to eliminate Hoof & Mouth disease in livestock. Dr. Gillie served on the board of the Fort Wayne - Allen County Historical Museum for a number of years. He was awarded the highest honor given by the American Veterinary Association, the AMVA Award, in 1953. He was a 50 year Kiwanis member and held the oldest membership in Plymouth Congregational Church, 69 years. His papers were left to the Fort Wayne Historical Society after his death on July 3, 1963. He then resided at 628 Oakdale Drive, Fort Wayne. Interestingly, in 1911, the remains of Chief Little Turtle, 1751-1812, of the Miami Indians, were found on the Lawton Place property where Dr. Gillie was building a house. The house has since been razed and a shrine placed there to Little Turtle. The grave was positively identified by the sword found in it that had been given to him by General George Washington.

Submitted by Robert and Margaret Gillie

LINKER FAMILY

Englehardt Linker left the port of Bremen, Germany on May 15, 1832 and arrived at the port of New York on July 13, 1832. The family migrated to Fort Wayne and lived in the Fort for approximately four years. Death records of Englehardt's daughter indicated that she was born in the Fort in February 1834. Englehardt applied for citizenship in December 1836 and became a citizen June 17, 1840. Englehardt and Anna Elizabeth Weisheit Linker were one of the fifty founding families of the St. Paul's Lutheran Church in Fort Wayne, Indiana in 1837.

Englehardt and Anna Elizabeth had five children as follows:

Elizabeth Linker was born February 22, 1836 and married Frederick Eckart September 5, 1852. Elizabeth died February 14, 1920 and Frederick died August 7, 1894.

Alice Linker.

Johann Heinrich (Henry) Linker was born April 24, 1840 and married Caroline Yergens December 23, 1865. Henry died March 8, 1923 and Caroline died October 11, 1922; they are buried in Martini Lutheran Cemetery.

Catherine Linker was born March 5, 1842 and married August Dammeyer February 27, 1870. Catherine died April 10, 1916 and is buried in Lindenwood Cemetery.

Henry Englehardt Linker was born November 3, 1843 and married Christine Snearly on February 7, 1869.

Anna married twice after Englehardt died on June 27, 1845. She married Frederick Weir on May 5, 1850 and on October 1, 1865 she married John P. Hedges. Anna Elizabeth Weisheit died on July 24, 1874.

The farm that Englehardt homesteaded southeast of Fort Wayne was willed to his son Johann Heinrich (Henry) who then willed the farm to his son, Fred Linker. Fred married Emma Exner July 28, 1907, and all their children were born on that farm. They had thirteen children, six sons and seven daughters: Pauline Linker was born October 28, 1907 and married Elmer Lepper June 10, 1928; Edgar Linker was born January 17, 1909 and married Frieda Busse October 3, 1936; Estella Linker was born March 5, 1911 and married Mart Brueck September 26, 1931; Earl Linker was born July 28, 1912 and married Ida Scherer October 29, 1938; Vern Linker was born April 20, 1914 and married Dorothy Ehlerding October 5, 1940; Leonard Linker was born October 23, 1915 and married Luella Nahrwold October 1, 1938; Robert Linker was born October 10, 1917 and married Edith Sroufe May 18, 1946; Irma Linker was born July 26, 1919 and married Arthur Bearman June 22, 1941; Donald Linker was born March 12, 1921 and married Ann Nern January 27, 1946; Evelyn Linker was born May 5, 1922 and married Raymond Lepper September 28, 1946; Vera Linker was born November 2, 1924 and married Jerry Rohrbach April 30, 1944. A pair of twin girls died at birth, all other eleven children were raised on that farm.

Back row, L to R: Edgar, Earl, Vern, Leonard, Robert, Donald. Front row, L to R: Vera, Fred, Pauline, Irma, Estella, Emma, Evelyn

Fred Linker died August 17, 1944 and Emma Linker died May 12, 1961.

Submitted by James Linker

ROGER W. LINKER

Roger W. Linker was born on December 16, 1938 in Fort Wayne, Indiana to Edgar and Frieda Busse Linker. He was brought home from the hospital on Christmas Day were he was placed under the Christmas Tree. He resided in Fort Wayne until July of 1945 when they moved to Waynedale. He attended Mt. Calvary Lutheran Church and School where he was confirmed in April 1952. He then attended Concordia Lutheran High School until graduation in June 1956. His maternal grandfather had passed away in December 1957, so the family moved on the farm with his grandmother until she passed away in March

Roger W. Linker

1966. He attended one year at Concordia Lutheran College after which he worked for an appliance wholesale firm until February 1958. He then began employment at Fort Wayne National Bank where he worked for the next 40 years. When National City bought out Fort Wayne National Bank, he retired into a life of volunteer work and genealogy research. He served on the board of the West Central Neighborhood Ministry and the Allen County Council on Aging, and publishes a family newsletter titled the *Link-er*. He served as President of the Allen County Genealogical Society of Indiana for three years.

He was also involved in assisting in the Church History section of this publication.

His brother James R. Linker was born into their family on February 24, 1947 and attended Mt. Calvary School also until 1958 when they moved to the Busse farm northeast of New Haven. He was confirmed from St. Peters Lutheran School and graduated from Woodlan High School where he met Connie Rushart whom he married July 22, 1967. They had two children: Julie who married Craig Sowers and they had two children, Cortlyn and Connor; and Jason who married Tina Schnebelt.

Submitted by Jason Linker

LIPES FAMILY

Several branches of the Lipes family have lived in Marion Township for over 150 years. The family originated with Moses Lipes or Leib of Botetourt County, Virginia, who was born in 1774 and married Rebecca ( ). Their children included Joseph, Christopher, Samuel, Barbara, Catherine, John, and Daniel. Christopher Lipes, the second son, was born in Botetourt County on April 4, 1799. On March 26, 1820, he married Susanna Dill, daughter of Henry Dill. She was born on February 21, 1798. They had: Andrew, Mary Ann, Joel, David Dill, Rebecca, Jacob, George, and Julia Ann. The family settled in Marion Township before 1838, where Christopher was a founder of Bethel Baptist Church, organized in his home. Christopher died on February 16, 1858; Susanna on November 8, 1856.

Jennie (Lipes) and Morse Harrod.

David and Mary Lipes.

David Dill Lipes was born September 28, 1826 in Botetourt County. He married Mary Jane Summers on October 21, 1847. She was born on April 26, 1832 in Shenandoah County, Virginia, daughter of Joshua and Lytha (Judd) Summers, who were also early settlers of Marion Township. David was a farmer, carpenter, and cabinet-maker. Their children were: Lydia Alvina, born February 3, 1850; Sarah Ette, born November 19, 1852; Sidney Frances, born July 4, 1855; Mary Alice, born January 23, 1858; John C., born September 30, 1860; Emma, born November 9, 1861; Ulissus Grant, born September 19, 1864; Eva Ann, born January 31, 1867; and Jennie Lorinda, born August 30, 1869. Of these, Sarah, Mary and John died young. David died on July 6, 1896. Mary Jane died on February 1, 1917.

Jennie Lorinda Lipes married Dr. Morse Harrod on May 31, 1888. A prominent Fort Wayne physician, he was born on April 4, 1866, the son of Morgan and Belinda (Beam) Harrod. They had three children: Camilla, Wayne, and Velma June. Jennie died on October 23, 1925. She and Morse were members of First Baptist Church.

Submitted by John Beatty.

JAMES G. & OLLIE JOHNSON LOGAN

James Guilford Logan's parents, James Smith Logan and his wife Mary McWhorter Logan, migrated from Ohio and located along the Wabash River in Wells County, one mile west of Murray, Indiana. A few years later they made the move to Allen County, where they purchased a farm one mile west of Sheldon (now Yoder). James Smith and Mary were the parents of four children: Calvin, Martha, Frank, and James G. Logan. James G. Logan was born, raised, and died on the farm his parents purchased west of Yoder.

James G. (January 28, 1867 - August 27, 1944) married Ollie Jane Johnson (November 30, 1874 - October 17, 1950) daughter of Lewis Johnson (December 27, 1840 - July 22, 1905) and Nancy Farrell (May 7, 1843 - 1914). The marriage of James G. and Ollie took place on April 23, 1892, at the home of the bride's parents, who lived in Lafayette Township. Their first child was born December 2, 1892, and died the same day. Another baby was stillborn on January 30, 1894. Then seven more children were born: Goldia Marie (April 13, 1895 - November 30, 1980), married Frank Rushart and James Morrow; Clifford Clayton (September 3, 1897 - April 6, 1906); Edna Blanch (May 10, 1899 - July 28, 1932), married Charles Genth; Carrie Lewis (May 1, 1901 - September 10, 1902); Lucille Hazel (May 9, 1903 - August 11, 1996), married Galen R. Smith; Flossie May (June 27, 1906 - December 16, 2000), married Ernest Putt; Chalmer Adam (May 13, 1908 - March 2, 1998) married Florence Klenke and Stella Palmer Taubitz.

Lucille Hazel (Logan) and Galen Smith started their married life on November 26, 1919, and together they had four children: Wayne A. (December 24, 1920), married Rosemary Covert and Claudine Kummer. Wayne and Rosemary had three daughters: Pam, Jean, and Lynne. Alma P. (September 1, 1923), married Robert Swank, and one daughter, Joyce, was born to them; Nona I. (March 15, 1930), married Richard Neuenschwander, and one son, Larry, was born to them; Nancy A. (September 11, 1941), married Stanley Davis and Donald Harkness. Nancy and Stanley had four children: Galen, Deborah, Priscilla, and Kevin.

James and Ollie Logan

Galen and Lucille Smith lived in Allen County until the spring of 1938 when the ground they lived on was purchased for the construction of Baer Field Airport. From there they moved to Wells County and then to Burr Oak, Michigan.

Submitted by Joyce Bauermeister

LOMBARD FAMILY

Joseph L. Lombard was born June 29, 1923 in Fort Wayne, Indiana, to Joseph Louis Lombard and Esther Lewis Lombard. Joe served in the Aviation Engineers in W.W. II in the Pacific Theatre. He was employed by the Pennsylvania R.R., Penn Central and Conrail R.R. for 42 years until retirement in 1984.

Joseph L. Lombard was married to Dorothy A. Danklefsen in Portland, Indiana, November 13, 1948. Joseph L. Lombard graduated from Beaverdam Ohio High School in 1941. Dorothy A Lombard graduated from Paulding Ohio High School in 1941. They have three children; Max S. Lombard (1949) married to Jean Deasley and their children Jacob Andrew and Joseph Scott; Joseph L.Lombard (1953) married to Babs Tatum and their children Lindy Tatum and Joseph Tate; Laura Lombard Himmelhaver (1958) married to Kevin Himmelhaver and their children Samuel Joseph and Ann Christine.

The Lombard Family

Joseph Louis Lombard, father (1899) worked for the Pennsylvania R.R. and was killed at the age of thirty on duty at Upper Sandusky, Ohio. Married in 1919 to Esther Lewis and the parents of two sons Joseph L. and Bus, deceased. Louis F. Lombard, grandfather (1864) worked as a career on the Pennsylvania R.R. and married Anna A. Draker from which five children were born; Irene Lombard Pettit, Azalea Lombard DeVillbiss, Nadine Lombard Worman, Joseph L. Lombard and John Draker Lombard.

Joseph L. Lombard, great-grandfather' (1837) was born in Hartford, Connecticut. After the Civil War, he married Emma Fowler of Oswego, Illinois, and moved to Fort Wayne, Indiana. He was a soldier in the Civil War and served as a Hospital Steward in Memphis Tenn. and a member of the Grand Army of the Republic. After moving to Fort Wayne, Indiana, in 1869, he was one of the early mail carriers in the city. He later was in the insurance and real estate business.

They had four children; Louis Lombard, Edith Lombard, Mary Lombard Kyler and Josie Lombard.

The last three generations of the Lombard family have worked for the Pennsylvania Railroad.

Submitted by Dorothy Lombard

JUSTIN PETER & EMMA MAGDALENE LOTHAMER LOMONT FAMILY

Justin was born in a log house in Jefferson Township July 23, 1876. Emma was born in Jackson Township, near the Ohio state line, on January 8, 1885. Justin was the fifth child in a family of seven boys and three girls born to Alphonse Lomont, who was born in Dept. of Doubs, France (1845 - 1926) and Victoria Gladieux Lomont, born in Stark County, Ohio (1848 - 1901).

Emma was the youngest in a family of seven boys and three girls born to Joseph Francis Lothamer (1834 - 1909) and Eliza Snyder Lothamer (1845 - 1919). Joseph was born in Guewenheim, Alsace, France. Eliza was born in Johnson Township, Champaign County, Ohio.

Justin and Emma were married on November 23, 1904 at St. Louis Catholic Church, Besancon, Indiana by the Reverend John Francis Noll. They purchased and farmed forty acres across the road from St. Louis Church. They lived in a small house for a short time while a two story cement block house was being built. Four children were born there: Cletus Eugene (1905 1993), Esther Agnes (March 16, 1907 – March 22, 1907), Joseph Alphonse (1909 - 1995), and Ursula Marcella (Sockrider) (1911 - 1999).

They sold that farm in 1912 and moved to Trumbull County, Ohio where Edna Eulalia (Reuille) was born (1913 - 1996). Seasons were short and crops were poor, so they sold that farm and purchased one at Route 2, Delphos, Ohio. Catherine Alice (Ristau) was born there in 1915. Both moves, with all their possessions, including livestock, were via railroad.

Their next and final move, March 1917, was back to Indiana to the farm where Justin was born. They purchased the 100 acre farm in 1918. This move was made with horses and wagons. A good neighbor, Glen Fry, helped drive one of the wagons in a snow storm.

Four more children were born in the two story brick farm house which was built in 1881 by Alphonse and Victoria Lomont when Justin was five years old. The children are: Mary Elizabeth (Brinker) (1921 - 2005), Robert Herman (1923 - 1976), Monica Ruth (Giant/Knecht) 1924; and Carolyn Louise (Hill) 1932. February 10, 1939, a cyclone leveled the barn, several other buildings, and twisted the rest except for the house. All of the horses, except one, and all of the cows were killed. The buildings were quickly rebuilt or renovated.

The house and farm remain in the Lomont family. The Hoosier Homestead Award was presented to them in 1983 recognizing a farm owned by the same family for a century or longer. Claude Francis Lomont, Justin's grandfather, purchased the land December 10, 1863. All but two of Justin and Emma's children remained in Allen County. Only one, Joseph Alphonse, pursued a career in agriculture. Emma died November 19, 1957. Justin lived at home until his death October 30, 1964 following an auto accident. Both are interred in the St. Louis Church, Besancon, cemetery.

Submitted by Monica Knecht

Emma Magdalene Lothamer Lomont and Justin Peter Lomont, November 23, 1904

REV. JESSE I. LOTHAMER

Jesse Irvin Lothamer (1885-1968) was the son of Joseph and Eliza (Snyder) Lothammer and the twin of Emma Lothamer Lomont. They were the youngest in a family of seven boys and three girls, all of whom were born on the family homestead located on Paulding Road, which property is now owned by the gas company.

Eliza, Jesse's mother, had raised her family as Lutheran, though they had been baptized Catholic. When Emma began dating Justin Lomont, she took instructions to prepare for first communion in the Catholic Church. Her twin, Jesse, went along with her, the result being that he also became active in the church. Subsequently, in 1906, at age 21, Jesse decided to study for the priesthood and was sent to the Sulpician Seminary of St. Charles College in Catonsville, Maryland. He graduated from St. Charles in 1911 and then went to Mount St. Mary's, the major seminary, in Cincinnati. He was the first of the Lothamer family to receive a college education.

He was ordained on June 15, 1917, by Bishop Alerding and celebrated his first mass at St. Louis, Besancon, (Allen County, Indiana) on June 17, 1917. He was not only the first priest to be ordained from the Besancon church but also the first of seven descendants of his grandparents, Theobald and Maria Magdalena (Gamber) Lothammer, who would eventually be ordained as well. The others were: Rev. Aubrey Tennant (a descendant of Anthony Lothammer), deceased, of Alberta, Canada; Rev. Daniel Peil, deceased; and his brother, Rev. William Peil, of Fort Wayne, Indiana, (descendants of Theresa Lothammer Brady); Rev. James W. Lothamer, S.S., of Lansing, Michigan (a descendant of Joseph Lothammer); Rev. Robert Sprott, O.F.M.; and Rev. Dennis A. Schaab, C.PP.S. of Kansas City, Kansas (descendants of Theresa Lothammer Brady).

Father Jesse Lothamer pictured with his two sisters, (l) Sarah Sade Lechler and (r) Emma Lomont, his twin

"Father Jesse", as he was called by many, served at St. Peter and Paul, Huntington, from 1917-1920, and then at the Cathedral in Fort Wayne from 1920-1922. He was pastor simultaneously of St. Paul, Columbia City, and Sacred Heart, Warsaw, from 1922-1935, and then of Sacred Heart alone from 1935-1937. His longest pastorate was at St. Aloysius, Yoder, from 1937-1951. In his later years he was pastor at St. Mary, Avilla, from 1951-1957, St. Mary, Bristol, from 1957-1959, and finally St. Francis Xavier, Pierceton, in 1959. In retirement he lived in both Fort Wayne and Avilla.

Father Jesse was an extremely popular and well-known figure in his Lothamer family, keeping close contacts with siblings, cousins, and many nieces and nephews in Indiana, Ohio, and Michigan. His frequent visits to family homes, his love for cards, family parties, and his great wit, made him a welcome figure.

In addition to his family, Father Jesse had a large number of lay friends. The ready welcome and frequent dinner invitations that many Protestants gave to him was a cause of surprise to more conservative Catholics. His annual Labor Day festivals at Yoder drew large crowds of Catholics and non-Catholics alike. As a priest, Father Jesse was a strong promoter of sports teams for Catholic youth, a good catechism teacher, and an avid reader. An ardent Republican - unusual for a priest in those days - he was a staunch opponent of Roosevelt and even went on the campaign trail for the Republican candidate for governor of Indiana in the 1940s.

Father Jesse Lothamer is buried in the Besancon cemetery, next to his parents. Among the Lothamer family, many "Father Jesse" stories continue to be told with great delight and affection.

Submitted by Monica Lomont Knecht

JOSEPH LOTHAMMER & ELIZA SNYDER

Joseph Lothammer (1834-1909) was the son of Theobald, Sr. and Maria Magdalena (Gamber) Lothammer. Born in Guewenheim, Alsace, he came to the U.S. in 1854 with his parents and seven siblings: Theobald Baldy (1832-1887) of Allen County, who married Mary M. Huth (1845-1913); Anthony (1836-1883) of Erie County, Ohio, who married Rosa Lack (1840-1919); Maria Magdalena (1838-1899) of Erie County, Ohio, who married Heinrich Stautzenberger (1830-1899); Theresa (1841-1916) of Payne County, Ohio, who married Peter Brady (1831-1905); Ignatius (1845-1928) of Kent County, Michigan, who married Mary "Katherine" Rosswurm (1862-1929); Maurice (1848-1921) of DeKalb County, Indiana, who married Barbara "Annie" Gillen (1856-1919); and Agatha "Nancy" (1852-1938) of Paulding County, Ohio, who married Francis

Joseph Lothammer of Jackson Township and Eliza Snyder of Benton Township on their wedding day, October 30, 1862.

Quince (1849-1880) and John Perl (1830-1904). Two other siblings, Joseph Gamber (1829-1829) and Catherine (1842-1843), died in Alsace.

The Lothammer family settled in Paulding County, Ohio, on the State Line Road, in late 1856, with brothers Baldy and Joseph moving to the Indiana side of the road shortly thereafter. In 1862, Joseph married Eliza Snyder (1845-1919), the daughter of Isaac Snyder, Sr. and Eliza Bodey, and the fourth of seventeen children from Isaac. The Snyders, originally from the Shenandoah Valley in Virginia, had come to Ohio in 1825 and to Paulding County in 1856.

Eliza was from a strong Lutheran family; her brother John, being pastor at the Payne Lutheran Church. And though the children were baptized Catholic, they were raised in Eliza's Lutheran faith. In later life, with her daughter, Emma, marrying into the Catholic Lomont family and son, Jesse, being ordained a Catholic priest, the family was religiously mixed. Eliza herself eventually became a Catholic.

Joseph and Eliza were the parents of ten children: Joseph (1863-1938) of Allen County, who married Elisabeth Auer (ca. 1863-?) and Lillie May Miller (1873-1942); Andrew (1866-1937) of Midland County, Michigan, who married Laura Mae Finney (1876-1963); Sarah Sophia (1869-1951) of Allen County, who married James A. Lechler (1873-1951); John (1871-1944) of Allen County, who married Ella May Adams (1875-1957) and Emma Ammons (1875-1948); Eliza Ann (1873-1886) of Allen County; Lester Lewis (1875-1909), of Allen County, who married Daisy L. Ruble (1880-1960); Charles "Oliver" (1878-1957) of Branch County, Michigan, who married Teresa Susan Westrick (1884-1955); Albert (1881-1953) of Detroit, Michigan, who married Bessie Edith Stradley Coling (1885-1911) and Adeline Sabine (1889-1974); Emma Magdalene (1885-1957) of Allen County, who married Justin Peter Lomont (1876-1964); and Rev. Jesse I. (1885-1968) of Allen County.

Joseph Lothamer (as the name came to be spelled) died in 1909. He was a long-time sufferer from rheumatism and paralysis "as a result of Bright's disease." Eliza, residing with her daughter, Emma Lomont, lived to see her son, Jesse, ordained a priest in 1917. Remembering her childhood days, granddaughter Clarice Lothamer Linder recalled "taking long walks with Grandma Eliza, where she would smoke her pipe and make me promise not to tell anyone." Clarice also noted that "Father Jesse got all of his mannerisms from his mother." For those who knew Father Jesse, Clarice's comment suggests that Eliza, the mother, had an energy and adventurous spirit that made her a well-loved family figure. Both Joseph and Eliza are buried in the St. Louis Cemetery at Besancon. A complete history of the Lothamer and Snyder families can be found in Lothammer-Lothamer, by Rev. James W. Lothamer, volume three.

Submitted by Rev. James W. Lothamer, a great grandson

NANCY LOUISE LOTHAMER

The mid-twentieth century found the economy of the United States recovering from the depression, WW II, and the Korean War. After many years of moving, the Irvin and Alberta (Geis) Sheehan family purchased a farm on the Grotrian Road along the Pennsylvania Railroad in Madison Township, Allen County, Indiana. Irvin's farming, milking, and working at International Harvester made life easier for Nancy (March 19, 1945) than for her older siblings, Angela, Eugene, William Neal, and Carl.

Living on a farm was lonely for Nancy. She filled her days helping with gardening, food preservation, and housekeeping and enjoyed staying with her sister, Angela, who was married with small children, and her cousin, Peggy. She received her primary education at St. Louis Catholic School, New Haven, and graduated from Hoagland High School.

In September 1962, Nancy had a blind date with Neil Lothamer from Monroeville. The Bluffton Street Fair was the start of a relationship that included marriage at St. Rose Catholic Church in Monroeville, Indiana (June, 27,1964), three children, living in Antwerp, Ohio, and then the marriage dissolving in 1978. Of this union were born: Nathan Ross (November 10, 1964), Renee Marie (October 22, 1965), and Kurtis Wayne (November 19, 1966).

Nathan married Vicki Harman, May 21, 1984, and they have one son, Neil Robert. They live at Tri-Lakes near Columbia City, Indiana. Renee married Todd Rasey on October 4, 1985, and had one daughter, Elizabeth Jean Rasey. They were divorced and she married a second time to Scott E. Moore on August, 21,1993. They live in Fort Wayne with their son, James Robert, and her daughter, Elizabeth. Kurtis was married to Teri McNabb on March 1, 1997, and they had a daughter, MacKenzie Allison, and a son, Boston Parker. The marriage ended, but Kurtis and the children still live in Fort Wayne.

Nancy and Neil Lothamer spent their married years in the Antwerp, Ohio, area. Neil worked at International Harvester, Fort Wayne, and Nancy had the privilege of being a homemaker, which she enjoyed. Baking, cooking, and preserving fruits and vegetables grown locally gave her great pleasure and satisfaction. She had time to be a Brownie and Girl Scout leader plus a den mother and an assistant to Neil when he was Cub Scout and Boy Scout master. The children were involved in band, choir concerts, drama, musicals, basketball, and baseball. Nancy attended all and supported them. She also was a member of the VFW Auxiliary, loved to bowl, camp, dance, and play cards.

L-R: Nathan, Nancy, Kurtis, and Renee Lothamer

After the divorce she remained in Antwerp until all of the children graduated from high school. She then moved to Fort Wayne. Her first job was with Eagle Pitcher Plastic, Grabill, Indiana (1978-1988). She then retired from Pyromation, Fort Wayne, in 2000. She is a member of St. Elizabeth Ann Seton Catholic Church. Because of poor health, Nancy is retired and lives with her son, Kurtis, in Fort Wayne.

Submitted by Nancy Louise Lothamer

THEOBALD "BALDY" & MARY M. (HUTH) LOTHAMMER

The Lothammer family of Allen County came from Guewenheim in Alsace (France). Tracing their origins to the early 1600s, to the village of Aspach-le-Bas near Guewenheim, the Alsatian Lothammers are most likely descended from the Lotthammer family of Pforzheim, Germany. Since the early 1900s, the family has spelled the name as "Lothamer."

The Alsatian Lothammers came to the U.S. at two different times. Brothers, Andrew and Peter Lothammer, along with their wives and children, came in 1833 and settled in Canton, Ohio. Theobald Lothammer (1808-1891), a distant cousin to Andrew and Peter, and his wife Maria Magdalena Gamber (1806-1887), came to the U.S. in 1854, along with eight of their ten children. Two had previously died in Alsace.

The family sailed from Le Havre, France, and arrived in New York on June 18, 1854. At the time of immigration, Theobald and Maria Magdalena were in their late forties, while their children ranged in ages from twenty-two to two. The Lothammers settled first in Jackson Township, in Crawford County, Ohio. In late 1856, they moved to Benton Township in Paulding County, settling right on the state line. They were the first German-speaking Catholic family in Benton Township.

Within a couple of years, two of their sons, Baldy (our subject) and Joseph, moved to the Indiana side of the State Line road, where each of them would eventually own their own farms. The farms bordered State Line and Paulding Roads.

In Crawford County, the Lothammers had met the Huth and Strickfaden families. Baldy's future wife, Mary Magdalena (1845-1913), was the daughter of Ervine Huth and Helena Strickfaden. Both the Huths and the Lothammers moved to the western edge of the Black Swamp around the same time, with the Huths, however, settling in Allen County. In 1864, Mary M. Huth gave birth to a daughter, Martha Ann (1864-1952), the father being Baltasar Federspiel. In 1866, Baldy Lothammer married Mary M. Huth

Theobald Lothammer, Sr. and his wife, Maria Magdalena Gamber, the parents of Theobald Baldy Lothammer

at St. John's Church, New Haven. Martha Ann, Mary's daughter, was always counted among the Lothammer children, though her legal name seems to have remained Federspiel. In 1883 Martha married Warren Bowers (1859-1906).

Baldy (1832-1887) and Mary M. were parents to nine additional children: Henry Theobald (1867-1910), who married Ellen Converset (1868-1947) in 1897; Mary Frances (1868-1937), who married Frank Ruble (1869-1958) in 1892; Morris Joseph (1870-1873); Christena Agnes (1872-1948), who married Michael A. Mayers (1872-1915) in 1897; William Franklin "Frank" (1873-1960), who married Grace M. Thompson (1882-1970) in 1900; Mary M. (1876-1878); Ella Clara (1879-1958), who married William Eugene Roussey (1873-1952) in 1902; Ervine Lawrence (1881-1934), who married Agnes Bertha Roy (1891-1954) in 1910; and Clarence Sylvester (1883-1897).

In 1886, Baldy was bit by a snake while working in the fields and died one year later. Mary M. lived for another 26 years, becoming the revered matriarch of a very large extended family. Though living in Allen County, the couple were faithful members of St. John's Catholic Church in Payne. A complete history of the Baldy Lothamer family can be found in Lothammer-Lothamer, by Rev. James W. Lothamer, volume two.

Submitted by James Lothamer, great grandson

CHRISTIAN HERMAN WILLIAM LUECKE 1890-1973

Christian Luecke was born in Troy, Illinois, where his father was pastor of the Lutheran church. His parents were Martin L. E. Luecke and Gesina Mansholdt Luecke. He was the middle child of nine, only two of whom were girls. When not quite two years old, his father accepted a call to Trinity Lutheran Church in Springfield. He graduated from Trinity school and at the age of 13, was enrolled in Concordia College, Fort Wayne (high school and junior college then). By that time his father was president of the institution and the family had moved to Fort Wayne. He graduated in 1909 and went on to Concordia Seminary, St. Louis, where he graduated in 1913. He served his vicarage years in Petoskey, Michigan, where he also taught in the school.

Upon graduation he accepted a call to Grace Lutheran Church in Portland, Oregon, which he served for two years. It was a congregation which had many problems, and becoming discouraged with the pastorate, he resigned in 1915. After this he taught school for awhile, and then worked for Pacific Bell. In 1917 he joined the Army Signal Corp, received a commission and was stationed at Kelly Field, San Antonio, Texas. He later was transferred to the War Department in Washington, D. C. until the end of the war.

Chris married Verma Hinton in 1918. She was with him in Washington and after the war they returned to Fort Wayne. Chris found employment with the Rub-No-More Company, which was the maker of Ivory Brand Soap. He was manager of bulk goods. Proctor and Gamble was interested in Ivory Soap and purchased the company from Berghoffs, so Chris was without a job. He went into the "Coffee Roasterie" as a partner with his brother-in-law, Chester Hinton. In 1937 Chris left the company and went to Washington for training with the newly created Social Security Administration. He first opened the office in Kokomo, Indiana and in 1960 came to Fort Wayne as manager of the office here. He held that position until he retired in 1960 at the age of 72.

Verma and Christian Luecke

Verma and Chris were very interested in classical music. Verma was secretary of the Community Concert Association for many years, and Chris was a member of the board. He was a member of the steering committee which organized the Fort Wayne Philharmonic Orchestra. Verma served as ticket chairman. Their youngest child remembers with pleasure attending all the concerts and the delight of going backstage at intermission to meet the guest artists. She also remembers that when Marian Anderson was appearing, no Fort Wayne hotels would permit her to stay with them. So James Fleming, publisher of the *Journal-Gazette*, had her as a guest in his home.

The Luecke's were members of St. Paul's Lutheran Church. Chris served as chairman of the congregation several times, and was on the board of directors for the Central District of the Lutheran Church-Missouri Synod. He was also a board member of Lutheran Social Services, Valparaiso Association, American Legion Post 97, Social Planning Council, was on a group which organized the Allen County League for the Blind, and various other social organizations.

The couple had four children:

Christian John (1919) married Mary Jo Newman of Kokomo. They had two sons. After her death, he married Mary Carter. Chris served in the Air Force from World War II through the Vietnam War. They live in Air Force Retirement Village, Riverside California.

Dorothy Adelaide (1921-1992). Married Richard Mygrant who was killed in France in World War II. She then married Robert Rohde of Grosse Pt. Michigan. They had three children.

Josephine Anne (1923 -) married Byron Ferguson of Valparaiso Indiana. They have no children and still reside in Valparaiso where Byron was a chemistry professor and Josephine retired from the Department of Education's office in Chicago. She is a Sagamore of the Wabash.

Cornelia Mary (1932) married John LaBrash of Fort Wayne. He was in the wholesale food business, and she a teacher in Southwest Allen County Schools. They had five children, one of whom, William, resides in Fort Wayne with his wife Jewell Gafken and their two sons.

Verma and Christian are buried in Lindenwood Cemetery.

Submitted by Connie LaBrash

MARTIN LOUIS ERNEST LUECKE 1859-1926

Martin Louis Ernest Luecke (1859 - 1926) came to Fort Wayne in 1903 to become president (director) of Concordia College. His father, Christian, had come to the US from Ruher, Hanover, Germany in 1828. His mother, Emile Van Henning had also come in 1828 from Berlin. Martin's father was principal of St. John's Lutheran School in Chicago which is where Martin was confirmed. At the age of thirteen his father brought him to Fort Wayne Concordia to begin the education necessary to become a pastor. From there he went to Concordia Seminary in St. Louis from which he graduated in 1881.

His first call was to Bethalto, Illinois where he served from 1881-1884. From there he went to the church in Troy and was there from 1884-1892. In 1892 he received a call to the church in Springfield which he served until he came to Fort Wayne. At each location he helped form new congregations in the small towns near them. In Springfield he started the first church to serve the Negro population. While in Springfield he discovered a great need for a new hospital as the only one was operated by the Catholic Church, and he and his parishioners were not permitted to be at the bedside of dying patients. As a result, he went to local doctors and influential men and was able to see the formation of the Lutheran Hospital.

Martin Luecke, 1859-1926

When he arrived at Concordia he found the school in financial straits and the student body rather undisciplined. These were the first two challenges he met and solved. While at Concordia he saw to the construction of the gymnasium, dining hall, a dormitory, heating plant, some professors housing plus the renovation of existing buildings. Besides serving as director he also taught New Testament Greek, Sacred History and Religion. The college is no longer in existence having been replaced by Concordia Seminary; however one thing he brought to it, the ROTC, is still in Fort Wayne at Concordia Lutheran High School. He and his eldest son, also named Martin, along with Pastor Wambsganss, were involved in the founding of Irene Byron Sanatorium. With the help of his wife, he formed the Martha Society of which she served as president.

During his life he was the author of several books, a history of the civil war, one on the life of Christ and outlines of the Old and New Testaments. An article on his life was also included in *Who's Who in America*.

In June 1882 he married Gesina Mansholdt of Bethalto, Illinois. The couple had nine children:

Martin 1883-1948, became a prominent attorney in Fort Wayne. He married Emma Foehlinger and they were the parents of one daughter.

Paul 1884-1951, became the organist and principal of the school for Trinity Church. He married Selma Scheifer. They had five children, one of whom, Harold, was the pastor of the church in New Haven for many years.

Emil 1886-1966, became a pastor and professor at Concordia Bronxville, New York. He married Emma Gallmeier. Their son James was an editorial page editor for the *JournalGazette* for many years.

Martha 1889-1921, married William Suhr. They had one child and Martha died in childbirth.

Christian 1890-1973, became a pastor but resigned. He was the manager of the Social Security office in Fort Wayne for many years. He married Verma Hinton. They had four children, one of whom still resides in the city.

Elise 1893-1956, married Dr. Walter Herrling, professor at Concordia. They adopted two daughters.

John became an executive for Standard Oil in New Orleans. He married Etta Schumacher, and after her death, Lydia Gerstner. They had no children.

Walter 1900-1970, became a pastor serving at various locations. The last twenty-five years were spent at St. John's Nottingham in Cleveland. He married Emma Trier. They had no children.

Wilber 1905-1965, was a pastor and also a professor at Concordia, Bronxville. He married Louise Rippe. They had three children.

Martin and Gesina are buried in the old Concordia Cemetery.

Submitted by Connie LaBrash

WALENTY LYZNIK

Walenty Lyznik was born February 10,1887 in Busk, Austria. He married Anastazya Miskiewicz on February 14, 1914 in Detroit, Michigan. She was born January 4, 1893 in Lwow, Ukraine. They lived in Detroit and Warren, Michigan. Walenty died February 26, 1970, and Anastazya died January 8, 1984.

Children were Eugenia, Casma, Anna, and Wanda.

Eugenia Lyznik was born September 14, 1914 in Detroit, Michigan. She married Joseph Rudy on May 19, 1940 in Detroit. She died July 28, 1983 in Warren, Michigan. Their children were Robert, born September 29, 1944 in Warren, Michigan, and Richard born December 3, 1946 in Warren, Michigan. On May 27, 1970, Robert married Myrna Baugh, born December 4, 1942. They were divorced in 1971. He then married Diane C. Dancy of Detroit on June 28, 1974. Their have a daughter, Katelyn, born May 3, 1988, St. Petersburgh, Russia, came to the U.S. June 1, 1995. Eugenia and Joseph's son, Richard, was born December 3, 1946 in Warren, Michigan. He married Elaine Soderstrom on June 20, 1970. She was born October 6, 1948 in Highland Park, Michigan, and was the daughter of Carl Soderstrom and Rose Ravi. Their children are Andrea Rudy, born January 1, 1972, Rochester, Michigan, and Aaron Rudy, born May 16, 1974, in Rochester, Michigan. Andrea married Edward Dewey on August 19, 1995 in Novi, Michigan and their children are: Logan Matthew, born June 11, 1999; Alexia Gabrelle, born August 16, 2001; and Andrienna Hope born June 19, 2004. Aaron Rudy married Julie Soboda, born January 8, 1980 in Michigan.

Mr. and Mrs. Walenty Lyznik, February 14, 1914

Casma Lyznik was born November 18, 1916 in Hamramck, Michigan. She first married Ignatius Widawski on May 28, 1938 in Detroit. Their son, Wayne Walter Widawski, was born June 9, 1942 in Hamtrajck, Michigan. He resided in Florida and died August 1, 2002. She then married Jose M. Argot on April 10, 1965 and they divorced in 1967.

Anne Lyznik was born February 8, 1920, and was married first to John Roman. Anna Lyznik was married a second time on May 8, 1987 in Fort Wayne, Indiana to John Manahan Siemer, born September 17, 1922 in Mt. Healthy, Ohio. Her children with John Roman are Alan John Roman, born September 27, 1946 in Highland Park, Michigan; Annette Louise Roman born November 27, 1948 in Highland Park Michigan; and Jeannette Lee Roman, born July 24, 1962, Fort Wayne, Indiana. Alan married Linda Overturf on June 21, 1969, in Ottumwa, Iowa. She was the daughter of Ralph Overturf and Bettye Dunn and was born April 24, 1947 in Ottumwa. Their children are: Amy Lynn Roman, born May 24, 1973, Rochester, Michigan; Michelle Lee Roman, born June 14, 1974, Rochester, Michigan. Annette married Garry Moorman on May 2, 1971 in Fort Wayne, Indiana. He was the son of Robert Moorman and Donna Lauber, and was born May 22, 1948 in Celina, Ohio. Jeanette Lee Roman married Mark Howell on September 17, 1988 in Fort Wayne, Indiana. Mark is the son of William Howell and Coleen Lehman, and was born March 18, 1964 in Decatur, Indiana. They divorced. Their children are: Miranda Lynn Howell, born October 27, 1991 in Fort Wayne, Indiana, and Amanda Lynn Howell, born March 15, 1994, in Fort Wayne, Indiana.

Wanda Lyznik was born April 25, 1923 in Detroit, Michigan. On August 15, 1943 in Detroit, Michigan, she married Henry Kielbowicz. Their children are: Glenn born June 12, 1948 in Detroit, Michigan; and Craig, born October 12, 1951, Highland Park, Michigan. Glen Kielbowicz married Patricia Lynn Tarrell on July 24, 1976 in Pontiac, Michigan. She was born October 7, 1952 in Pontiac, Michigan. They had a daughter, Holly Anastasia, born January 15, 1981 at Beaumont Hospital, Royal Oak, Michigan. Craig Kielbowicz married Pamela Lynn Frisbie on August 26, 1978, in Grosse Pointe, Michigan. Their children are Kelly Joyce, born September 17, 1980, in Detroit and Joel Craig, born April 20, 1983 in Detroit. Kelly Joyce married Ryan Vincent Rosse on June 5, 2004 in Grosse Pointe, Michigan.

Submitted by Ann Roman Siemer

LOUIS & MILDRED MABEE FAMILY

Louis Edward Mabee was born October 11, 1923 in Seidel, Illinois to Howard Mabee and Hazel Shuman. He married Mildred Ethel Sheets July 18, 1946 in Fort Wayne, Allen County, Indiana. She was born to Arthur Kenneth Sheets and Ocie Mildred Hallock, July 17, 1928, in Werner, Dunn County, North Dakota. She moved to Allen County, Indiana from North Dakota with her parents and brothers Lester and Donald March 25, 1937.

Louis served the Navy as a MOMM 1st Class in the South Pacific during World War II. He worked for Essex Wire as a Diesel Mechanic and retired October 1988. Mildred graduated from Elmhurst High School in 1946. She worked in payroll for Brotherhood Mutual Insurance and retired November 1990.

Mildred and Louis Mabee, December 2004

The children of Louis and Mildred Mabee are: Daniel Lee Mabee, born August 30, 1948, Fort Wayne, Indiana; Kenneth Edward Mabee, born October 14, 1954, Fort Wayne, Indiana; James Eugene Mabee, born January 15, 1957, Fort Wayne, Indiana; and Duane Jay Mabee, born February 4, 1960, Fort Wayne, Indiana.

Daniel Mabee married Barbara Jean Reed Caughlin December 31, 1991. She was born to Joseph and Rose Reed November 23, 1948,

Fort Wayne, Indiana. They have a home in St. Petersburg, Florida.

Kenneth Mabee married Patricia Annette LeFeaver December 15, 1973 in Fort Wayne, Indiana, daughter of Robert LeFeaver and Lillian Ladd. She was born July 30, 1954 in Fort Wayne, Indiana. The children of Kenneth and Patricia Mabee are: Jonathon Edward Mabee; Tammy Lynn Mabee; Keith Robert Mabee; and Kristin Nicole Mabee. They have a home in Aboite Township, Allen County, Indiana.

Duane Mabee married Karla Jean Traxler June 8, 1985. She was born to Delores Haines and Lyle Traxler September 14, 1960, Montpelier, Williams County, Ohio. The children of Duane and Karla are: Sarah Elizabeth Mabee; and Lydia Rachaell Mabee. Duane graduated from Fort Wayne Bible College May 1983, and is a minister at a Christian Missionary Alliance Church in Chattanooga, Tennessee, where they make their home.

Louie and Mildred Mabee are members of Avalon Missionary Church. In 1947, they moved into a home built by her parents on Ansley Drive, Allen County near the properties once owned by Mildred's parents Kenneth and Ocie Sheets.

Submitted by Louis and Mildred Mabee

DENNIS MADDEN & MARY JOURDAN

Dennis Madden (December 25, 1818 - January 25, 1906) emigrated from Ireland in 1850 and came to settle in Allen County where he married his wife Mary Jourdan (March 2, 1838-March 23, 1909). Dennis and Mary were married on February 10, 1861 in the Cathedral of Immaculate Conception, Fort Wayne, Indiana.

Dennis served in the Civil War in the One Hundred and Forty-Second Regiment Infantry. He was a Private and served his term in Nashville, Tennessee. His army papers describe him as being 52 years of age, 5 ft. 9 1/2 inches tall, fair complexion, black hair and blue eyes. It is also said that he was a lawyer in his native country.

Dennis and Mary lived on small piece of land consisting of a house and several acres in Wallen, Indiana, where he made his living selling produce. Dennis was very active in all of the soldier organizations. When they would have a celebration he would be there. He was an ardent Republican and a political power in the little town of Wallen. In his death announcement he was listed at the "Mayor of Wallen". Both Mary and Dennis are buried at the Hatfield cemetery on the Washington Center Road.

Mary Jourdan Madden. Ben, Joseph, Mary Agness, Edward on Mary's lap

Dennis and Mary had six children. Sarah married Able Hare and moved to the Chicago area. Sarah (September 22, 1864 - October 23, 1896) died giving birth to their first born child Vida. Benjamin Madden was born September 26, 1884, Joseph Maden was born October 26, 1877, Edward Madden was born July 26, 1884, Eliza Madden (Elizabetha) December 3, 1886 and Mary Agnes born May 1880. Edward lost his right arm at the age of 22 in a tile mill accident. He was adjusting a machine when his coat sleeve got caught in the machinery and crushed his arm. He was taken to the doctor's office the next morning and then to St. Joseph Hospital where his arm was amputated. But that didn't stop him. He moved to California and married Edith Parker. Their dogs were their only babies; every summer they would drive from California to Indiana in their car that had a standard transmission, with their dogs by their side. Eliza (Elizabetha) married Edward Swank and moved to Pleasant Township.

Submitted by Jodi Harwood

THOMAS & MARY (MEEHAN) MADDEN FAMILY

Thomas Madden was born 1813 in the Parish of Nicker, County Limerick, Ireland. He emigrated from Liverpool, England, on May 20, 1837, and arrived in New York on July 4, 1837. He applied for citizenship December 23, 1839, in Fort Wayne, Allen County, Indiana.

Mary Meehan was born in 1819 in Parish of Ballyhooly, County Cork, Ireland. She and Thomas Madden were married March 4, 1840, in the Cathedral of the Immaculate Conception in Fort Wayne, Indiana. They were the parents of eleven children; Ellen (1841-1877) married William Riley Johnson. Ellen taught school prior to marriage; Honora (1842-1843); Mary E. (1844-1910) married William Wilkinson; John (1846-1916) married Mary Doyle. John was a carpenter in Fort Wayne; Catherine (1848-1861); Nicholas (1850-1904) married Mary (Hopkin) Kilfoy. Nicholas was a watchman on the railroad in Fort Wayne, Indiana; Johannah (1852-1874) married James Maloney; Thomas (1854); James (1856) married Jane (Hull) Johnson. He was a hardware merchant in Hutchinson, Kansas; William K. (1858-1918) married Ella A. Kennedy. He farmed in Eel River Township; Michael "Patrick" (1862-1901) married Mary Collins. Patrick was a policeman in Fort Wayne, Indiana.

Thomas and Mary Madden bought land in Eel River Township, Allen County, Indiana; 40 acres in section 7 on November 1, 1856, from Joseph Duglay and another 40 acres in section 5, in 1862, from P. T. Lomax. They were farmers and lived, raised their family, and died on the home place on the Madden Road. They were members of the Immaculate Conception Church, Ege, Indiana, and are buried in the church cemetery.

Submitted by Jonathan L. Arehart.

JOHN WILLIAM MALCOLM

John William Malcolm was born July 11, 1837 in Hamilton County, Ontario to John and Eliza (Wright) Malcolm. John spent his childhood in Hamilton and learned a trade of carpenter by 1858. On April 16, 1859, he married Emily Sarah Hitchcock in St. George the Martyr Church in Toronto, Ontario. Emily Sarah was born in Suffolk, England. On November 9, 1859, John William emigrated from Toronto, Ontario to Fort Wayne, Indiana by way of Port Huron, Michigan. His first address was a rooming house on West Washington Street in Fort Wayne. His wife and firstborn son, James Worthington, arrived from Ontario sometime later; the family lived on Baker Street in Fort Wayne before moving to Huntertown about 1870. John was a brick mason and a carpenter and built their house on Edgerton Street in Huntertown. He also built Huntertown's first brick school house in 1890. His career included the position as Superintendent of the Universalist Church in Huntertown.

John W. and Emily Malcolm had a family of ten children: James W., Elizabeth Jennie, Frederick William, Maud, Adeline, Ellen, Robert, Mary Ellen and Horace. John W. Malcolm died on October 31, 1904, and his wife Emily Malcolm, died August 16, 1896; they are both in the old Section of Perry Township Cemetery

James Worthington Malcolm Family

James Worthington Malcolm was born February 5, 1860, in Toronto, Ontario and moved to Allen County with his family as a boy. James W. married Emma Elizabeth Preston on December 12, 1885, in Huntertown, Allen County, Indiana. They had four children: Ethel Preston, Morley Milner, Euna Jane and James Ewing.

James W. was a carpenter and a farmer. He had a farm of approximately 180 acres on Lima Road about one mile north of Huntertown. His granddaughter remembers him making a toy

Malcolm Family (about 1888) First row: John W. Malcolm, Emily Hitchcock Malcolm, Robert Malcolm, Emma Preston Malcolm, James W. Malcolm, Ethel Malcolm. Back row: Ellen Malcolm, Frederick W. Malcolm, Elizabeth Jane Malcolm, Adeline Wheelock Malcolm.

Malcolm Reunion, 1929. First Row:Esther Kiermaier, Janet Malcolm, Shirley Stonecipher, Robert Kiermaier, Maurice, John and Donald Malcolm, Harold Hoon and Jack Malcolm. Second Row: Joan Jackson (Elizabeth' sister-in-law), Martin and Adeline Emrich, Elizabeth (Malcolm), Jackson, James W. Malcolm, Lenora (Slater) Malcom, Edna Pulver and Robert Malcolm (baby). Third Row: Ida (Lantz) Malcolm, Arlene (Malcolm) Crummit, Ewing, Horace and Ethel Malcolm, Jenny (Smith) Malcolm, Marjorie Malcolm. Back Row: Lena (Ireland) Kiermaier, Grace (Jackson) Hoon, Estella (Emrich) Stonecipher, Russell and Ralph Malcolm, Forrest Crummit, Morley and Jean Malcolm.

musical instrument out of cornstalk and rosin. He was a lifelong member of the Huntertown Methodist Church. He died on December 2, 1951. His wife, Emma, died on February 10, 1914. They are both buried in the Old Section of Perry Township Cemetery.

Morley Milner Malcolm Family

Morley Malcolm was the second oldest of four children born to James Worthington Malcolm and Emma Elizabeth Preston. He was born on August 23, 1889 in Perry Township. He was educated in a one room school located one quarter mile south of the home farm.

On October 15, 1913, Morley married Edna Catherine Pulver at the Trinity M. E. Church Parsonage in Fort Wayne. Edna was born on October 20, 1892. She was the second of three children born to Franklin R. and Mary M. (Kell) Pulver at their home farm on Coldwater Road in Perry Township. After their marriage, Morley and Edna lived across the road from the home farm on Lima Road. The following nine children were born to them:

Marjorie R. (1914) married Lester Pool

Mary Elizabeth (1916) died at birth

Donald J. (1917) married Hillis Knafel and P. Rita Leather

John H. (1919) married Phyllis Sible and Marietta Ratherty

Kenneth R. (1921) died at birth

Maurice E. (1923) married Alberta Veazey

Jean I. (1927) married Donald Pontius

Robert M. (1929) married Beverly Gillen

Jackie L. (1931) died at age three.

They had sixteen grandchildren and nineteen great grandchildren. Morley Malcolm died on October 31, 1965; his wife Edna died on December 7, 1987. They are both buried in the New Section of Perry Township Cemetery.

Submitted by Jean I. Malcolm Pontius, (daughter of Morley Malcolm)

Morley M. Malcolm and Edna Catherine Pulver, married October 15, 1913.

The Malcolm Children, 1932. Donald, John H., and Maurice; Marjorie, Jackie, Robert and Jean.

MALLERS & SPIROU FAMILIES

Panayiotis Malleris set foot on Ellis Island, New York in 1911. He was 16 years old. The oldest son in a family of 12 children born to Georgious and Maria Malleris, Panayiotis was sent by his parents to America to find a job and make enough money to live on and send home to help his large family, which was struggling in the Peloponnesian village of Kerasitsa, outside of Tripolis, Greece.

Upon arriving at Ellis Island, Panayiotis, like most immigrants at that time, was encouraged to Americanize his name. From that moment, his name was Peter Mallers, and everyone knew him as "Pete". Pete traveled to Chicago to live with relatives, who owned a grocery business. Like most immigrants, he found America to be challenging, but exciting and full of opportunity.

A number of years later, Pete's brother, Odyseus, who became known as Charlie, emigrated from Greece and joined Pete. The young men had dreams of owning their own business, and they set out to find something to their liking.

Their first exposure to the movie theater business was in Springfield, Ohio with their uncle, Phil Chakares, owner of Chakares Theatres. After a brief stint owning a restaurant in Dayton, Ohio, they entered the theater business as owners in Lima, Ohio, with their cousin, George Mallers.

By this time, Pete had married Eleni Daskalakis, the daughter of a Greek Orthodox priest who had been sent by the church in 1914 to start an Orthodox parish in Lowell, Massachusetts. Pete and Eleni (Helen) were married in Indianapolis in 1925. While in Lima, two children were born to Pete and Helen, Mary in 1926 and George in 1928.

In 1928, Pete and Helen and their children moved to Fort Wayne, where Pete purchased the Riley Theatre. He and Charlie purchased a theater in Bluffton, Indiana, and they later brought in their cousin, George. Eventually, George's brother, Nick, emigrated from Greece, and the two sets of Mallers brothers opened The Lake Theatre in Warsaw.

Through their hard work, keen business sense and good luck (the movie theater business was one of the few that survived the depression), the Mallers Brother Theatres chain grew to include 20 theaters, including four outdoor drive-in theaters, which were some of the first drive-in theaters in Indiana. Many years later, after selling most of the theaters, the four owners took separate ownership of the remaining businesses in Bluffton (Charlie), Warsaw (Nick), Portland (George) and Fort Wayne (Pete).

In Fort Wayne, Pete and Helen resided with their family at 624 East Rudisill Boulevard, a large brick house at the southwest corner of Rudisill and Hanna, where Mary and George spent their formative years, attending Ward Elementary School and Weisser Park Junior High School. Mary graduated from South Side High School and went on to McMurray College and Columbia University. George graduated from Culver Military academy and went on to Indiana University and Valparaiso University Law School.

In 1950, George married Rubie Loomis, born in Washington D.C. to Greek immigrant parents, who were from the same small village near Sparta, Greece, as George's mother, Helen. After graduating from law school, George and Rubie moved to Fort Wayne, where George began his law partnership with Orvas Beers and E. Ross Adair.

While Mary was teaching speech and hearing therapy in New York, she met native New Yorker, Arthur Spirou, recently returned from the U.S. Navy after serving in the Pacific. Mary and Art married in 1952.

With the aid and encouragement of their fathers, George and his cousin, Bill Mallers, Charlie's son, and Roger Scherer, Pete Mallers' longtime friend and business associate, purchased the Holiday Theater in Park Forest, Illinois in 1953. Art and Mary moved to Park Forest so Art could assist in managing that operation. This began Art's long career in the movie theater business in partnership with Mary's brother, George, who had maintained involvement in the theater business while attending college and law school. Then, in 1964, George, Bill and Art built and opened the Holiday Theater at Northcrest Shopping Center. George and Art eventually acquired Bill's interest, and the two of them continued what would be a thirty-year partnership that grew to include Holiday 1, Holiday 2, Holiday 6, Georgetown, Quimby, Hillcrest and Coventry 8 Theaters in Fort Wayne, as well as theaters in Muncie and Lansing, Michigan, Georgetown Bowl and Village Bowl bowling centers and

Peter's, The Phoenician and Stage Door restaurants. The restaurants were sold in the 1980s, the theaters were sold to Regal Cinemas in 1993, and the bowling centers were sold in 2001.

During his legal career, George represented a wide variety of businesses, primarily as a business lawyer, and served as Allen County attorney from 1964-1972. He also served on and chaired the Allen County Sheriff's Merit Board and the Allen County Board of Health for many years. From 1955 until his death in 1994, George maintained a full time law practice and was an involved owner of the various businesses in partnership with Art.

Besides being an owner, Art was general manager and in charge of the daily operations of all of the business ventures of Mallers & Spirou Enterprises, Inc. He also served on the Allen County Plan Commission for 25 years and chaired it for 10 years. Art was active in his Masonic Lodge for many years, including as a Grand Master, and both Art and George served on the parish council of their church, Holy Trinity Greek Orthodox Church.

George and Rubie had four children – Peter (Fort Wayne- wife, Christine McAlister and two children); William (Indianapolis- wife, Vicki and four children); Elaine (Allendale, New Jersey - husband Gregory and two children).

Art and Mary had three children – Victoria (El Paso, Texas - husband, Keith and two children); George (Morgantown, West Virginia - wife, Eleni and two children); Elaine (Fairfax, Virginia - husband, Michael and three children).

Submitted by Peter G. Mallers

DANIEL JAMES MALLOY & NANETTE ELLEN (FLAHERTY) MALLOY FAMILY

Daniel James Malloy was born on July 2, 1961in Cedar Rapids, Iowa to the late Gerald and Dolores Malloy. He lived in Cedar Rapids with his parents and ten siblings up until the time he went to college at Iowa Wesleyan. That is where he met Nanette Ellen (Flaherty) Malloy. Nanette was the oldest of three girls. She was born in Hawkeye, Iowa on September 17, 1960 to Patrick and Marta Flaherty. She lived in Hawkeye, Iowa, Danville, Illinois, Morton, Illinois, and Monmoth, Illinois. They were married shortly after college.

They immediately moved to Indianapolis, Indiana where Daniel had a job at a local hospital. It was in Indianapolis that they started their family. Their first child was Abaigeal Ellen Malloy. Soon after came along Jacob Patrick Malloy. They lived there until Daniel accepted a different position in Elkhart, Indiana at a local hospital there. This was also where they had their third child Hannah Dolores Malloy.

They then made their way to Fort Wayne in 1989 because Daniel once again had a job transfer. In Fort Wayne they had a fourth and final child. His name was Matthew John Malloy. While living in Fort Wayne the children attended a local Catholic grade school and high school. They were members of St. Elizabeth Ann Seton Parish and participated regularly in their church community

Even though it meant that they had to take frequent trips to Cedar Rapids, Iowa to visit Daniel's family and to Peoria, Illinois to visit Nanette's family, they really loved living in Fort Wayne. They went to the Fort Wayne Zoo every summer and were frequent patrons at the local libraries.

Submitted by Abaigeal E. Malloy

HIPPOLITE & MARGARET (POIRSON) MANIER FAMILY

Hippolite Manier was born in Bourg of Foug, Meurthe-et-Moselle, Lorraine, France on July 14, 1809. He and his future wife, Margaret Poirson (1816-1886), born in the same Bourg, both immigrated to the United States in 1832. On June 25, 1833, they were married at St. Louis Catholic Church in Buffalo, New York.

The young couple then took passage to Toledo, Ohio, and from there walked to Fort Wayne, Indiana. The exact date of their arrival in Allen County is unknown, but records for the family at the Cathedral of the Immaculate Conception began in 1835. All eight of their children were born in Indiana, the last seven in Allen County. Francis Joseph (1834-1897), Victor Hubert (1837-?), Victorine Felicite (1839-1913), Frances (1841-1931), Mary Catherine (1845-1904), Adelaide (1847-1905), Margaret (1847 died before 1860), and Eugenie (1852-1919).

Hippolite Manier.

Francis "Frank" married Eileen Doyle and they were the parents of four children: Frank Hippolite (1862-1876), Joseph Peter (1864-1933), Mary (1866-1933), and Frances (born 1868).

Victor married Josephine Girard and they had one child, Philip (born 1860).

Victorine married Claude Joseph Langard and had eight children: Francois Joseph (1857-1861), Jean Baptiste (1859-1902), Joseph Louis (1861-1880), Marie Adele (1862-1923), Hippolite (1865-1876), Clarice Angeline (1870-1950), Malinda Cecelia (1873-1941), and Louis Claude (1876-1967).

Frances married Jules Reiniche, and they had seven children: Mary (born 1864), Julian (born 1867), Francis (born 1869), Joseph (born 1872), August (born 1874), Louise (born 1876), and Frances (born 1877). After Jules' death, she married Frank J. Delagrange, with whom she had two more children: one born in 1881 and Edward (1883-1966).

Mary Catherine married William Rudolph Reffelt and they were the parents of Margaret (1864-1865), William Rudolph III (1866-1913), Charles (1867-1953), Flora Angeline (1871-1949), Bertha (1874-1875), Mary (1875-1938), Harry (1878-1960), Louise (1882-1966), Charlotte (1886-1975), and Gertrude (1889-1929).

Adelaide married Jean Joseph Perrey and they were the parents of nine children: Frank Joseph (1866-1940), Edward Frank (1868-1934), Emma Mary Ann (1870-1957), Flora Frances (1873-1944), Joseph Victor (1876-1894), Julian John (1878-1971), Hippolyte Anthony (1881-1958), Felix Eugene (1885-1947), and Clementine Angeline (1887-1963).

Eugenie married Francis Antoine Casso and they had eight children: Rose Angela (1872-1936), Joseph (1873-1883), Angelo (1877-1939), Frank (1880-1952), Almeda (1889-1964), Elmer Joseph (born and died 1891), Leo (1892-1970), and Emmet Rayamond (1895-1949).

Hippolite worked for Chief Richardville and spent several years in service on the canal and other public improvements. On March 20, 1843, Hippolite made his declaration of intent to become a United States citizen. Later, Hippolite pursued farming for several years in Lake Township. In 1856, he and Margaret moved to Fort Wayne and, by 1858, Hippolite operated a grocery store in Fort Wayne, which was expanded by 1861 to include a liquor store and a boarding house. He operated these enterprises until his death on January 26, 1870. Margaret continued the business several years, and later with her son-in-law, Frank Casso. Margaret died on April 12, 1886.

Submitted by John C. Parrot.

JACOB MARQUARDT FAMILY

In 1920, Edith Koehlinger was nine years old, but she recalls standing on the porch of her family's temporary house watching as a tornado threatened to demolish their home. After the storm, the family went back to their farm to find the barns flattened, but the horses were not injured.

The Earl Marquardt family was living in Monroeville because their farmhouse burned in January due to a faulty chimney. The family lost everything but the clothes they were wearing, their player piano, a carom board and some dishes. At that time the family lived on a portion of the 320 acres that Edith's grandfather, Jacob Marquardt and his wife, Susanna Pyle, had cleared. Her grandfather was born in 1844 on the farm across the road from where her family lived. Jacob Marquardt's father, Johann Jacob, came to America from Germany at a young age and settled in Madison Township in the 1830s. Edith's grandfather, Jacob, was one of 12 children who helped reclaim the land for the family farm.

Edith remembers her grandfather Jacob as a tall man with a long beard. She recalls that her grandparents started the Marquardt Church which still serves a congregation today in the southeast corner of Allen County. The story was that someone criticized a bright colored cape her grandmother wore to church so they started their own church. To them, such minor gossip was inappropriate. Lloyd Douglas, a Lutheran minister and author of well-known books; among them *The Robe* and *Magnificent Obsession*, preached one of his first sermons in The Marquardt Church. In his book, *A Time to Remember*, Douglas describes his experience as a

Jacob and Susanna Marquardt Family c. 1909

humbling one when a young mother's baby cried louder than he could preach. She went to the front of the church and took a glass of water from the pulpit. Ole Jake Marquardt exploded in laughter as did everyone else.

Edith recalls another interesting story about her grandfather. During the 1890s the Packard Organ Company in Fort Wayne was commissioned to make an organ for Queen Victoria of England. The company manufactured only three of these special organs with logs cut from the family farm. Edith's father, Earl, helped cut the wood and deliver it to Fort Wayne. One organ was shipped to Queen Victoria, one was given to Edith's grandparents for furnishing the wood, and the third was purchased by the Myers Family and is still in the area. In 1947 the Marquardt home burned and with it their Packard Organ. Later the family learned that the organ made for Queen Victoria in celebration of her 60th year of reign, was also destroyed by fire.

In addition to Edith's grandfather being one of the first land owners in Madison Township, he was also a Civil War Veteran. He and his wife, Susanna, are buried in the Marquardt Cemetery on Hoffman Road. "I'm so glad the farm we lived on is still in the family," says Edith. "My youngest brother, James, lived there until his death in 2003. His son, Mace Marquardt, carries on our family traditions. He has three sons so the Marquardt family farm will remain intact for years to come."

Edith Koehlinger, a young 93, still lives close to the family farm, loves flower gardening, reading, and is collecting genealogical information to add to the Marquardt Family History.

Submitted by Linda Stephenson

E. LESLIE MARQUART

E. Leslie Marquart, son of Joseph King Lafayette Marquart and Mabel Snider, was born October 21, 1905. He was a descendant of two pioneer families that lived in southeast Allen County, Indiana. These ancestors came from Ohio, Pennsylvania and Virginia. His paternal great-grandparents were Jonathan and Catherine Bashore Marquart. His maternal great-grandparents were George and Elizabeth Platt Snider. He was born and lived his boyhood years in Madison Township, Allen County, Indiana. His first-born siblings were twins: Martha and Asa who were stillborn in 1902. His other siblings were Linford, Catherine, and Isaac Benjamin.

His father, Joseph, who was a mail carrier, was the founder of the Four Presidents Corner memorial, which commemorated the place in Allen County where four townships named for Presidents Jackson, Jefferson, Madison, and Monroe merged to a common boundary. Joseph lived nearby and he thought this corner was too important not to be remembered somehow.

Sadly, he never lived to see the dedication ceremony as he was killed in a tragic accident while delivering mail. A train struck him at the Ellison Crossing during a severe storm near the family home located on Dawson Road in Madison Township.

In 1918 Mabel and her children moved into Monroeville, Indiana and Leslie was employed by Seth and Gurney Painter of the Painter Brothers furniture and funeral parlor. He graduated in 1924 from Monroeville High School and entered the Royster-Askins College of Mortuary Science in Indianapolis, Indiana. He graduated in 1928 and worked as an embalmer for the Painters.

E. Leslie Marquart and Alta Ruppert Marquart

In 1928 he married Alta Ruppert, born June 1, 1908 and a daughter of Oscar and Mary Rebecca Billman Ruppert of Antwerp, Ohio. She was a descendant of prominent families of Ohio, Pennsylvania and Maryland such as the Billman, Bordens, Dorseys and Wyatts. To this marriage were born three children, E. Leslie Marquart Jr., who died the day after his birth in 1930, a daughter was born in 1932, and a son in 1941.

In 1932 the Painter Brothers purchased the J. B. Niezer home in town and converted it into a funeral home. Leslie moved his family to this house where they lived for the next 16 years and he was the manager of the firm. In the late 1930s Leslie entered into partnership with the Painter Brothers who also offered an ambulance service to the community. The business was known as the Painter-Marquart Funeral Home.

The Painter Brothers retired in the mid 1940s and Gurney's son, Joseph, joined the business. Joseph and Leslie entered into a partnership and the firm became the Marquart-Painter Funeral Home. The Painter Brothers sold the Niezer house so Leslie purchased a house in 1948 one block away and converted it into a funeral home.

In the early 1950s Joseph left the partnership. Leslie and Alta, who worked with him, were the sole owners and operators of what was now the Marquart Funeral Home and ambulance service.

He was active all his life in community organizations. He belonged to several Funeral Directors Associations. He was a member of the I.O.O.F., Redmen and Masonic Lodges. He belonged to the Monroeville Lions Club and the Chamber of Commerce.

He held offices in the Monroeville School P.T.A. He and his family were members of St. Marks Evangelical Lutheran Church in town, and he was church treasurer and served on the Church Council.

He was employed for ten years at the Monroeville Post Office and later worked at the First Citizens State Bank in town, which later became a branch of the Fort Wayne National Bank. He served for many years on the Advisors Board of Directors for the bank.

He was a trustee of the I.O.O.F. cemetery and a member of the Board of Directors. He was a volunteer fire fighter for ten years and served as fire chief.

As a young lad, Leslie discovered he had a talent for painting and he became an accomplished artist. He had a paint store in Monroeville and painted many buildings in the area. Years later Leslie was noted for his oil paintings of landscapes and scenes in the Monroeville area. He gave chalk talks as entertainment for town parties and organizations. At one time his character sketches of many town citizens were displayed in a local restaurant.

One of his noted oil paintings was called "Mother of Sorrows", his idea of the grief of the Mother of Christ at the foot of the cross during the crucifixion. His most famous painting was a portrait of Sarah Douglas, wife of Reverend A. J. Douglas, pastor of the Evangelical Lutheran Church years ago. She was a neighbor of the Marquart family. The Douglas's were parents of Monroeville's most famous author and citizen, Reverend Lloyd C. Douglas, who lived in town during his youth. Reverend Douglas wrote many novels and some were made into movies, such as *The Robe*. Reverend Douglas wrote his autobiography, *Time To Remember*. He reminisced about his parents, his early life in town and mentioned Leslie in this book.

Leslie developed his own line of hand lotion in his early years as a funeral director. A few years before he retired he sold his recipe to the Dodge Laboratories and this hand lotion is still being produced today.

By 1975, he no longer operated his ambulance service, which had been started 60 years before. The town had organized an E.M.S. station with certified technicians. In 1977 he retired after his wife died, and he sold his home and business. He had lived in that house for 29 years and been in the funeral business for 57 years.

Because of his service to the community, he was honored in 1982 by being the Grand Marshall of the annual parade which is held during Monroeville Harvest Festival Days. He was always working for the betterment of the community. He died April 19, 1983 and was survived by his daughter, son-in-law, five grandchildren, two brothers and one sister.

Submitted by Rosemary Dager

ISAAC MARQUART

Isaac Imes Marquart was born June 23, 1837, one of a set of triplets, to Jonathan and Catherine Bashore Marquart, a pioneer family. Isaac's ancestor was an immigrant, Nicholas Marquart, who was born in 1735 in what was then a part of Germany, the Alsace region. He settled in Martinsburg, Berkeley County, which was then located in Virginia. This part later became West Virginia.

Catherine Bashore, daughter of Frederick and Mary Elizabeth Keister, was born in Lancaster County, Pennsylvania January 31, 1804. She was the great-great-great-granddaughter of Albert Bashaar who was born about 1610 in the Palatinate region of Germany. The descendants of Albertus lived in Schweiperingern near Stuttgart.

By 1710, descendants of Albertus migrated to New York and on to Pennsylvania. Later the families made their way to Ohio. Catherine and Jonathan married in Fairfield County, Ohio in 1819. Their children were Frederick, Gertrude, Catherine, Clarissa, John, and George, the triplets: Abraham, Isaac and Jacob, J. Samuel, Marquis, and Jonathan Jr. Abraham, John and Jonathan Jr. died as young adults. The triplets were born in Perry County, Ohio but the other siblings all said they were born in Fairfield County, Ohio. This is where the family lived.

Evidence has shown that Jonathan, Catherine and children were in Allen County, Indiana by 1838. In 1857 the family was living in Madison Township on the southwest corner of Maples and Dawson Roads.

On June 28, 1866 Isaac married Martha Ann Clear, born June 11, 1840. She was the daughter of Henry and Sarah Simonton Clear. Sarah's father was John, an immigrant from Antrim, Ireland. Sarah's mother was Elizabeth Conrad. Prior to marrying Isaac, Martha Ann had been married to Isaac's brother, John Marquart. A daughter, Elizabeth, was born in 1859 and died in infancy. A son, Winfield Scott, was born in 1860, four months after John died in 1859.

Isaac joined the U.S. Army in 1861 as a private and was in Company D, 30th Regiment of the Indiana Infantry Volunteers. He fought in several battles during the Civil War, one of which was the Battle of Shiloh. He was discharged in 1864.

Six and a half years after John Marquart died and the Civil War was over, Martha Ann Clear Marquart married John's brother, Isaac. To this marriage were born Lucy Emma, Isaac Hurd, Catherine, Ira, David, Joseph King Lafayette, and Oliver Perry Morton Marquart. His nephew, Winfield Scott, by Martha's first marriage now became another son.

Winfield Scott married Elizabeth Boner and they had seven daughters. A son died in infancy. Emma Lucy married Nicholas Giant and they had two children. Isaac Hurd married Mary Giant and after her death he married Gertrude Bauserman. To this marriage was born one daughter. David married Cora Snider and they had seven living children. Two died in infancy. Joseph K. L. married Mabel Snider, who was a cousin to Cora Snider, and they had four living children. A set of twins was stillborn. Oliver P. M. married Bessie Knepper and they had three sons.

Isaac was known as one of the great hunters, not only in the area, but also in Maine, Wisconsin, and other hunting states. He was a superior marksman.

Isaac Imes Marquart

He was a member of the German Baptist Church in 1870 and served as deacon.

He and Martha owned a farm across the road from his parents on the southeast corner of Maples and Dawson Roads where he lived until his death on April 8, 1913. His wife died January 26, 1926. When Isaac died, family members found a pencil drawing for his tombstone hidden under his desk drawer. While serving in the Civil War he saw many gravestones that inspired him to design his own monument. Local monument people were contacted but this unique design could not be carved in this area. A quarry was located in New Hampshire that could engrave this ornate design. This design covers the entire front of this huge tombstone, which is an exact replica of his drawing. His gun was sent there so it could be exactly reproduced. It is carved on the base. Isaac and Martha Marquart are buried in front of this monument in Memorial Cemetery, formerly known as the I.O.O.F. Cemetery in Monroeville, Indiana.

Submitted by Gail Matthews

CHARLES JOSEPH HENRI MARTIN & JEANNE FRANCOIS MEUNIER

Charles Martin was born October 1, 1802 at 6 p.m. in Belvoir (Doubs), 50 miles east of Paris, France to Jean Nicolas Martin, a wooden shoe maker, and Jeanne Claude (Bouhelier) Martin. Charles was a soldier under Napoleon and later joined his father Jean in the wooden shoemaking profession located in Olerval dept. of Doubs, France.

On July 27, 1826 at the age of 24 he married 22 year old Jeanne Francois Meunier. She was born April 10, 1801 in Sourans, France to Marc and Therese Maizny. They were farmers living in the State of L'isle dept. of Doubs, France. Because Jeanne didn't know how to write, she was unable to sign her Marriage Document. They lived on a small farm in L'isle Seur Doubs, France with six children.

They sold the farm and immigrated to America with the children on an old sailing vessel. After the 24 day journey, they landed in New York on April 22, 1843. They traveled on to Canton, Ohio, by the way of the Hudson River and the Erie Canal. They lived in Louisville, Ohio (Starke County) for a year where daughter Marie Claire was born. Then they made their way to Fort Wayne, Indiana, by the way of the Wabash and Erie Canal, arriving in April 10, 1844. Charles bought an 80 acre farm in Perry Township, Allen County, Indiana, and paid $3 an acre. Their daughter Christine was born at this time.

On February 26, 1861 Charles was driving home from Fort Wayne in his horse drawn wagon along with his wife, a priest and another lady. As they crossed the St. Mary's River on the New Spy Run Avenue bridge, the wheels struck the edge of the bridge, which was higher than the approach, and the sudden shock broke one of the tugs. The horses were unable to hold the wagon on the steep and narrow approach, and the wagon ran off into the river. All escaped except for Charles whose body was not found until five weeks later. On Saturday, March 2, 1861 his son, Auguste Martin, posted a $50 reward in the Fort Wayne News Sentinel for the recovery of his body. Charles was described as being 60 years old, 6 ft. tall, hair and complexion sandy and bald on the top of his head. The right foot was bent inwards from the ankle being broken. He had on two heavy grey coats, black pants and high boots. He had $5 to $6 and some notes with him in a large pocketbook.

His wife, Jeanne "Francis" Martin, died February 22, 1892 at her home in Perry Township. They are both buried in the old St.Vincent de Paul Academie Catholic Cemetery, Fort Wayne, Indiana.

Charles and Jeanne's children were: August Joseph (1830-August 25, 1905), married on April 5, 1853 to Josephine Rassat; Constantin (1832-?), went to Nebraska and married Lucy Panyard; Elisabeth (1834-June 20, 1908), married on May 9, 1856 to Felix Roy; Delphin Francois (February 3, 1838-March 24, 1925), married on April 20, 1864 to Catherine Krugler; Marie (1839-1860); Eugenie (1841-January 26, 1926), married on February 3, 1863 to Pierre Bobay; Marie Claire (December,1843-September 29, 1919), married on March 9, 1861 to Louis Seraphin LaCroix; Christine (June 10, 1847-July 16, 1913), married May 5, 1891 to Francois Lordier.

Submitted by Emily Payonk

COSIE CORNELIUS MARTIN

Cosie Cornelius Martin, 1894-1968, born in Morgan County, Indiana, was the son of Paris Martin and Julia Ann Payton. Bessie Ruth Prather, 1896-1958, born in Illinois, was the daughter of Lewis William Prather and Rose Mabel Lemon, who moved from Illinois to Monroe County, Indiana between 1895 and 1898.

Cosie and Bessie Martin

Cosie and Bessie Martin Family

Zanesville Creamery

Both Cosie and Bessie spent their childhoods in Monroe County, Indiana, eloped via the Monon Railroad to Clark County, Indiana, and married on September 25, 1912. In 1918, they moved to Allen County, Indiana with son, Kenneth, 1915-2002, and daughter, Fay Maxine, 1918-1920. This was a big adjustment; it was said that at first they planned to move back to Monroe County when the birds began to sing, but stayed in Allen County.

They lived for a short time in Aboite, where Cosie worked for his father, Paris Martin, who leased the Bash Farm on the Upper Huntington Road. He also rode the interurban to Fort Wayne where he worked for the Fertilizer Plant. After his employment at the Fertilizer Plant, Cosie, Bessie and Kenneth moved to 3027 Maumee Avenue, Fort Wayne, Indiana, as shown in the Fort Wayne and Allen County Directory in 1921.

The 1922, the family moved to Zanesville, Wells County, Indiana, where Cosie worked for Keplinger Creamery and Dairy as a driver of the milk and butter truck to Fort Wayne. After the Keplinger Creamery and Dairy closed, the farmers in the area wanted a creamery, and they convinced Cosie to start one, which he did with very little financing. Being 1929, Depression time, the adventure required long hours and hard work, but the creamery business was successful. During this time Cosie purchased the Miller Buggy Shop building and rebuilt it into a home for the family.

The Zanesville Creamery was located in the Allen County part of Zanesville. Cosie bought the house north of the Zanesville Creamery and the family moved to Allen County in 1936. Bessie was, in all sense of the words, wife, mother, and grandmother.

In 1947, Cosie bought the Arthur Merriman farm, at the edge of Zanesville in Wells County. In 1948, he sold the creamery business to Sherman White in Fort Wayne, and farmed until 1966. After the death of Bessie, Cosie married Catherine Jones May on December 17, 1960; after her death, he married Flossie Freeman on June 12, 1965. He moved back to Monroe County, Indiana, where he died in 1968.

Children of Cosie and Bessie were Violet Evelyn, Kenneth Delmore, Fay Maxine, Pauline Loretta, Rose Imogene, Ruby Louise, Herbert Eugene, Ronald Lee, Shirley Ann, and Larry Dean.

The small town of Zanesville was an excellent place for the Martins to live. The family benefited from the shopping, entertainment, employment and library facilities in Wells County and Allen County. They attended the United Brethern Church in Christ, and all the children received high school diplomas either at Union Center School or Lafayette Central School. Early medical needs were aided by Dr. McBride, and later by Dr. Davidoff, Ossian.

Submitted by Ronald Martin

DELPHIN FRANCOIS & CATHERINE (KRUGLER) MARTIN

Delphin "Delphis" was born February 3, 1838 in L'isle Sur Doubs, France, 50 miles east of Paris, to Charles Joseph Henri Martin and Jeanne Francios (Meunier) Martin. His father, Charles, had been a soldier in Napoleon's Army and was a wooden shoe maker. Charles sold his small farm and, along with Jeanne and the six children, they immigrated to America on an old sailing vessel. Before departing from Havre France, 4 1/2 year old Delphin became separated from the family and almost missed the boat. When his Father took him to a store to buy a hat, instead of standing by the door to wait as was told, he misunderstood him to say that he should go back to the boarding house where they had been staying. When Delphin was finally located, the ship had already departed but was signaled to stop a half mile off shore. He was put in a small boat and rowed to the ship, uniting again with his family. The voyage took 24 days. At some point along the way an enormous whale was spotted in the path of the ship but the "monster" swam on.

The ship landed in New York on April 22, 1843. The family traveled on to Canton, Ohio by the way of the Hudson River and Erie Canal. They lived in Louisville, Ohio (Starke County) for a year then arrived in Fort Wayne, Indiana on April 10, 1844 by the way of the Wabash and Erie Canal, landing at the site of the City Mills. While the family were unloading their personal effects, 6 1/2 year old Delphin started out for a walk south on Clinton Street then east on Columbia Street. He became frightened when he spotted nine Indians and a squaw adorned with paint and feathers and scantily clothed, a sight he had never seen before. He made a hasty retreat back to his family.

Delphin was raised on the 80 acre farm that his Father purchased when arriving in Perry Township, Allen County. As a young man, he worked at a store in Fort Wayne for eleven months, but returned to the country, purchasing

Delphin Francois Martin with grandchildren Gerry, George, Delphis, and Ralph on lap, and Harry

10 acres of land. His father then gave him 40 additional acres of land adjoining, all in timber, totaling a farm of 50 acres on which he built a one room log cabin. This farm was located at the northeast corner of Auburn and Dupont Roads.

Delphin and Catherine Krugler were married April 26, 1864 at St. Vincent de Paul Academie Catholic Church by Father Benoit. Catherine was born 1844/45 in Rhineland, Germany (Prussia) to Nicholas Krugler and mother unknown. On March 3, 1868 the couple sold the farm and moved to the 150 acre farm on the Auburn Road ten miles north of Fort Wayne. In 1878 they built a large bank barn and a home which was, at that time, one of the finest between Fort Wayne and Auburn. Delphin eventually acquired 400 acres of land and owned six city properties. He was a Democrat, his first vote given to Stephen Douglas.

Delphin died March 24, 1925 and Catherine died January 30, 1915. They are both buried in the old St. Vincent de Paul Academe Catholic Cemetery, Fort Wayne, Indiana.

Delphin and Catherine's children, all born in Perry Township, were: Joseph Charles (February 6, 1865-1939), married on August 15, 1899 to Laura Ann Gorman Emilie (1867-May 8, 1880); William Henry (December 17, 1869-1957) married on February 24, 1900 to Clara Wertman Gerald (August 12, 1871-April 10, 1890); George Charles (December 28, 1873-May 5, 1942), married on June 5, 1900 to Elizabeth A. Hosler; Alice Matilda (November 21, 1875-1895).

Submitted by Johnathan Martin

GEORGE CHARLES & ELIZABETH A. (HOSLER) MARTIN

George Charles Martin was born December 28, 1873 in Perry Township, Allen County, to Delphin Francois Martin and Catherine (Kugler) Martin. He was raised on a farm on the Auburn Road ten miles north of Fort Wayne. George and Elizabeth Hosler were married June 5, 1900 at St. Vincent de Paul Academie Catholic Church. Elizabeth was born 1879 to John Hosler and mother unknown. George was a Perry Township Trustee and oversaw the construction of the new addition and gym of the Huntertown High School. George farmed 80 acres, raised livestock and set up plots of land for the poor people from Fort Wayne to come out and plant their own gardens. His son, George "Sam," was honored as School Teacher of the Year by the State of Indiana and went on to become Principal of Monroeville High School for 40 years.

The marriage of George Charles Martin and Elizabeth Hosler Martin on June 5, 1900

Gerry Lynn Paul Martin and Louise (Young) Martin

The marriage of Lynn Paul Martin and DeMarise Jean (Hand) Martin, September 12, 1959.

George died at the age of 68 on Thursday, May 5, 1942 at his home. The recitation of the Rosary was held at the residence on Friday at 8 p.m. by the Holy Name Society. Funeral services were held on Saturday May 8, 1942 at 9:30 a.m. at the residence and at 10 a.m. at St. Vincent de Paul Academie Catholic Church with the Rev. Edward Miller officiating. He is buried in the old St. Vincent de Paul Cemetery.

Elizabeth died at the age of 63 on Tuesday, June 22, 1942 at St. Joseph Hospital following an extended illness. The Rosary Society met at the residence on Wednesday at 8 p.m. for the recitation of the Rosary. Funeral services were held Thursday, June 24, 1942 at 9:30 a.m. at the residence and 10 a.m. at St. Vincent de Paul Academie Catholic Church with the Rev. Edward Miller officiating. Burial is next to her husband in the old St. Vincent de Paul Cemetery.

George and Elizabeth's children born in Perry Township were: Aldine Elizabeth (May 4, 1901-?), married on October 31, 1942 to William Sobraski; Maria Elizabeth (June 12, 1902-1978), married Oscar Bobay; Juanita Magdalene (September 30, 1902-June 27, 1922); Delphin "Delphis" John (January 20, 1908-July 2, 1977), married on September 29, 1931 to Martha Sloffer; Henry "Harry" William (December 17, 1909-?), married to Eileen Freck; Gerry Lynn Paul (September 15, 1911-May 20, 1969), married on June 25, 1935 to Louise Margaret Young; George "Sam" Glen (August 14, 1914-March 15, 1975), married Lois Beck; Ralph (October 13, 1917-May 1, 1986), married December 5, 1942 to Theo Merriman.

Submitted by Tom Martin

GERRY LYNN PAUL MARTIN & LOUISE MARGARET (YOUNG) MARTIN

Gerry was born September 15, 1911 to George Charles Martin and Elizabeth (Hosler) Martin. He was raised on a farm on Auburn Road ten miles north of Fort Wayne, Indiana. He attended Huntertown High School and was a good basketball player. He was the agent for the Standard Oil Company in Huntertown and for 35 years; he delivered gasoline and fuel oil to the homeowners and farmers in the area. He also owned the Standard Oil Gas Station in Huntertown. He married Louise Margaret Young on Tuesday at 9 a.m., June 24, 1935, at St. Vincent de Paul Academie Catholic Church with the Rev. Fallon performing the ceremony.

Louise Margaret Young was born June 18, 1913 to William and Winifred (Keirn) Young. She lived in Fort Wayne, Indiana as a girl, and attended Northside High School for two years. She moved with her family to a small farm on the Shoaff Road in Huntertown and completed her junior and senior years at Huntertown High School where she was a Yell Leader. After graduation she was employed as a stenographer for the Westerlin & Campbell Co. and later assisted Gerry in running the Standard Oil gas station. In her later years she worked for the Treasury Department at the City County Building.

Gerry and Louise raised three boys and were active in the boys' athletics, 4-H programs and the PTA. They were members of several card clubs with other couples in the area and were very active in the Huntertown community.

Gerry died May 20, 1969 at their Lake of the Woods lake cottage. Funeral services were held Friday, May 23, 1969 at 10 a.m. at St. Vincent de Paul Catholic Church with Rev. Lawrence Fettig officiating. Burial is in Highland Park Cemetery in Fort Wayne, Indiana. Louise died July 5, 1995 at her home in Fort Wayne. Funeral Services were held at St. Vincent Catholic Church with the Rev. John Kuzmich officiating. Burial is next to her husband at Highland Park Cemetery.

Gerry and Louise's children, all born in Fort Wayne, Indiana, are: Lynn Paul (born November 24, 1937), married DeMarise Hand; Gay (born December 10, 1942), married Roslyn Wisenberger; Tony Allen (born July 31, 1948), married Diane Schaab.

Submitted by Lynn Martin

LYNN PAUL & DEMARISE JEAN (HAND) MARTIN

Lynn Paul Martin was born November 24, 1937 to Gerry Martin and Louise (Young) Martin in Fort Wayne, Indiana. He grew up in Huntertown, Indiana, and attended Huntertown School. There he participated in basketball and track and played the clarinet in the band. He was President of his senior class. He was the Huntertown newspaper boy for two years and raised and showed hogs in 4-H.

Lynn and DeMarise were married September 12, 1959 at St. Vincent Catholic Church with the Rev. Lawrence Fettig officiating. DeMarise Jean Hand was born November 29, 1938 to William Hand and Marie (Warsler) Hand in Huntington County, Indiana. During her junior year in high school, she moved with her family to a 200 acre farm on the Carroll Road. She attended Huntertown High School where she played the saxophone in the band. She went on to graduate from the Warners Beauty School and was employed by Grandleader Department Store and Hutners Department Store. Lynn received his Doctorate of Veterinary Medicine from Purdue University and worked in several veterinary clinics. In June of 1969 he opened his own veterinary clinic, The Fort Wayne Pet Hospital, where he continues to practice to this day with his son, Dr. Marcus Martin, and his daughter, Kathy Payonk, as his assistant. Lynn and DeMarise have been active with the St. Vincent Boy Scouts and the Perry Boosters 4-H Club with their children and their grandchildren.

Lynn and DeMarise's children are Kathy Lynn, Thomas Lee, Johnathan Mark, and Marcus William.

Kathy Lynn (August 29, 1960), married Robert A. Payonk. Their children are Emily Kristine (December 27, 1986), Andrew Joseph (June 23, 1988), and Aaron Robert (October 8, 1992).

Thomas Lee (February 5, 1962), married Melissa Syndram. Their children are Keighlea Rose (May 2, 1991), Kyle Thomas (March 29, 1993), and Kendra Lee (April 12, 1997).

Johnathan Mark (April 19, 1968), married Kristie Tom. Their children are Allison Taylor (November 8, 1996), and Samuel David (June 9, 2000).

Marcus William (October 17, 1975), married Heather Hess. They have one child, Elliana Grace (July 17, 2003).

Submitted by DeMarise Martin

PARIS MARTIN

Paris Martin, 1866-1946, was born in Monroe County, Indiana and his wife, Julia Ann Payton, 1867-1935, was born in Indiana. They were married in December 1, 1886, in Morgan County, Indiana. Their children were born while living in Morgan and Monroe Counties.

Family stories relate that Paris came to Allen County prior to 1918, to investigate an advertisement he read in a farm journal for a tenant to lease acreage. After investigating the situation, he returned to declare to his wife, Julia Ann and family, "The dirt is as black as

Paris and Julia Martin

coal dust, and we are moving to Allen County." The land in Monroe County was very hilly and difficult to farm, thus his enthusiasm for the flat ground and black dirt of Allen County.

Paris leased and farmed 600 acres with horses, known as the Bash Farm, owned by Harry Bash, owner of the Mayflower Mills on the Landing, and later on Leesburg Road in Fort Wayne. The farm lies south of the U.S. 24 west of Fort Wayne near Redding Drive.

Julia was not pleased to be moving and leaving her friends and family. But she adapted to the move... when one of the cattle died on the farm she took her grandson, Kenneth, age five, with her and skinned the animal and sold the hide for $7.

The children still living at home moved with them: Alvin, Alta, Emma, Elsie, and Arthur. Belvia, a daughter married to Clyde Adams, and three children, moved to Allen County. Cosie, a son, married to Bessie Prather Martin, son, Kenneth, and daughter, Fay Maxine, moved to Allen County. Another son, Hugh and wife, Jesse Garringer, and children remained in Monroe County until about 1942 when they moved to Allen County.

An interesting story about Paris Martin family's move to Allen County follows:

One of the school bus drivers in Monroe County took the school bus bed off the truck and made a bed on the chassis; loaded five rooms of furniture and one old cow and started about 3:00 p.m., arriving about 3 a.m. in Fort Wayne. It was a blustery day in March or early April. With no cab or windshield, they nearly froze, stopping once in awhile and taking a walk just to warm up. They had placed the kitchen table on top of the other furniture in the truck, with the legs up. On the way, they ran under a bridge and knocked all the legs off the table. Reminds one of the Beverly Hillbillies.

Paris and Julia remained on the Bash farm for at least five years. They did return to Monroe County for a time as they were listed in the 1930 Monroe County census. After returning to Allen County, they lived on Lower Huntington Road in Waynedale. When Julia died in 1935, they were living in Wells County, Indiana. After 1935, Paris built two houses in Waynedale and was living in Allen County when he died in 1946.

Submitted by Shirley Martin Husband

ROSCOE L. MARTIN

Roscoe L. Martin was born March 18, 1913, in Townley, Indiana, in the county of Allen. He was the tenth of twelve children born to William, and Mahala (Disler) Martin, grandson of David Martin (Griswold's 1917 *Pictorial History of Fort Wayne*). Roscoe's father, William, was employed as a streetcar motorman in Fort Wayne, and also was a dredge operator for the Wabash Erie Canal. He was also engaged in farming. It was on the family farm that Roscoe was born during the 1913 flood that inundated the city of Fort Wayne and surrounding areas. The Martin farm home was completely surrounded by water, and in order for Doctor Menser to get to the home for delivery, it was necessary for him to use a boat for transportation. Upon arriving, he climbed through a window carrying his medical bag. The siblings were then transported to the barn until the "baby" arrived. Townley was a small community situated at the intersections of Highway 101 and Old 30.

At the age of seven, Roscoe and his family moved to a farm in Zanesville, Indiana. Roscoe was enrolled in the one room Dutch School where he studied under the guidance of Miss McIntosh. Roscoe transferred to Lafayette Central in sixth grade. There he studied Orthography, Reading, Writing, Arithmetic, Geography, English Grammar, Physiology, U.S. History, Agriculture, Domestic Science, and Music.

Roscoe L. Martin

He played forward on Lafayette's basketball team and remembers fondly the after game trips the teams made by school bus to visit Fort Wayne's famous Coney Island weiner stand. He also played the lead in the senior class production of "The Romance Hunters".

After high school Roscoe moved to Fort Wayne. At 18, he got a job working for Anthony Wayne Parking Garage. He vividly remembers having the experience of parking the car of none other than the infamous John Dilinger. Being an inquisitive and somewhat daring teenager, he rallied a few buddies to investigate. What they found gave them pause and the urge for a hasty retreat. Tucked in a leather compartment, secured with numerous snaps, was a cache of machine guns!

In November of 1933 he met Dorothy Heidemeich. He courted Dorothy in a 1929 Ford Roadster with a rumble seat. They married in July 1935, at St. Mary's Church, Fort Wayne. Odd jobs were the order of the day during the Great Depression, and Roscoe had three. He trapped furs and sold them, carried hod for a plasterer, and continued on at the Parking Garage. A daughter, Judith, was born December 1936.

In January of 1941 Roscoe hired in at General Electric Company. A second daughter, Linn, was born in April of that year.

Roscoe's hobbies are gardening, landscaping, golf, and fishing, which he enjoyed every weekend at the family cottage at Waldron Lake. He retired from the G.E. as Leading Operator with 35 years service. During retirement the Martins spent every winter in Fort Myers, Florida.

The Martins have been married 70 years, have 12 grandchildren, 24 great grand children, and one great great grand child. They live in their own apartment at New Haven Retirement Community.

Roscoe's family sees his legacy as one of private servitude to his fellow man. Along with his wife, they spent their years quietly attending to the elderly, the ill, and the needy in whatever capacity presented itself.

Submitted by Judith Reddin

MARTONE FAMILY

In 1910, a sixteen year old sailed from the port of Naples leaving his small village of Capodrise behind and carrying limited possessions and a smattering of English words to the "New World". His name was Antonio Martone and his destination was the city of Fort Wayne, Indiana.

After ten years laboring on the Pennsylvania Railroad, buying a modest home and saving a dowry to send back to Italy, Antonio welcomed sixteen year old Geovannia Raucci. She had left their common village in April of 1920 and sailed on the U. S. Taormina to Ellis Island arriving in June. She carried her spaghetti bowl wrapped in an alter cloth and spoke one or two English words.

The young couple courted for one year spending chaperoned Sunday afternoons in a relative's parlor. They married in 1921 at St. Mary's church in Fort Wayne having successfully completed the supervised courtship.

Three children were born to Tony and Jenny Martone. Mary was born in 1922, Madelaine in 1923 and Anthony Jr. (Tony) in 1932. The girls are deceased.

The family settled in the center city on Brandriff Street near Saint Patrick's school and church. They were surrounded by Italian neighbors so that the postage stamp sized yards, small white porches, green gardens and laden grape ar-

Sixteen year old Geovannia (Jennie) Raucci arrives at Ellis Island, New York.

bors were reminiscent of the "old country". They baked their own bread, grew their own vegetables and roses. They played bocci games in the cinder alley ways of the neighborhood.

The two Martone daughters married Italian brothers from Chicago. Rick and Frank Lobrillo had Fort Wayne relatives and had met the Martone sisters while visiting.

Limited English was spoken in the Martone home. The food prepared was pasta dishes with rich sauce, home baked bread, fresh vegetables and home grown fruit. Jennie baked delicious desserts and wine was the family's traditional beverage.

Everyone from the original family is gone except for young Tony who is retired from Verizon and was a well known athlete when he played quarterback for Central Catholic High School's 1950-1951 football championship team.

The rich heritage of this immigrant family has added a colorful thread to the tapestry that is Fort Wayne in Allen County.

Submitted by Patty and Tony Martone

TONY & PATTY (PAYNE) MARTONE

Tony Martone, son of Italian immigrant parents who arrived in Allen County in the early 1900s, and Patty Payne, the daughter of parents with Kentucky and Hoosier roots, were married in 1954 in Queen of Angels Catholic Church.

Both Martones were born in Fort Wayne and were graduated from local high schools, she from North Side and he from Central Catholic. Tony attended Ball State University where he lettered in football. Patty Martone earned degrees in education from Butler, Saint Francis and Ball State Universities.

Tony Martone retired from Verizon (General Telephone Company) in 1990 after 38 years of service in the telephone industry but his leisure time is dedicated to community service. He is president of the Verizon Retiree Club, a director of the Police Athletic League (PAL), serves as a Eucharistic Minister in his church and during the city's Millennium Celebration appeared as the mascot of the festivities.

Patty Martone retired from Fort Wayne Community Schools in 1986 as Assistant Superintendent. She was an English teacher, Dean of Students, and Central Office Director of Federal Programs and Community Services. She, too, gives her time to the community through numerous board memberships, project leadership roles

Tony and Patty Martone share retirement years with community projects.

Martone grandsons gather for a holiday photo.

and public speaking engagements. She chaired the city's Bicentennial cabinet and was a chairperson of the Millennium Celebration.

The Martones have two sons. Michael Martone is a full professor of Creative Writing at the University of Alabama in Tuscaloosa and Tim Martone is a fourth grade teacher at Brentwood Elementary School in Fort Wayne. Michael is the author/editor of numerous short story collections and Tim has spent over ten years as a high school football coaching assistant. He is presently a member of the Concordia High School gridiron staff.

Two daughters-in-law, Michael's wife Theresa and Tim's wife Amy (both teachers) as well as three grandsons, teenagers Sam and Ben, and eleven year old Nick complete the family.

The Martones have celebrated 50 years of marriage, all spent in Allen County. They travel, entertain friends and neighbors with annual July 4 and Christmas open houses and serve the community giving a myriad of volunteer hours. This is a couple, Allen County born and reared, who have chosen to "stay home" and give their time, talent and enthusiasm to this place.

Submitted by Timothy Martone

GEORGE MATHER FAMILY

The Rev. Dr. George Ross Mather was called to Fort Wayne in 1971 as Senior Pastor of First Presbyterian Church. He came from Trenton, New Jersey where he was born on June 1, 1930. He attended Trenton schools and was graduated from Princeton University and Princeton Theological Seminary. He was an Assistant Pastor of Abington Presbyterian Church near Philadelphia where he met and married Doris Anderson. He then became Senior Pastor of Ewing Presbyterian Church in Trenton, New Jersey for 13 fruitful years from 1958-1971 as the Church grew from 600 to 1200 members. He supervised many Seminary Interns and was a leader in Ecumenical relations.

During his pastorate at First Presbyterian Church in Fort Wayne, he started a Korean Language Congregation; hired a Minister of Drama; founded the Samaritan Training Program for Lay Pastoral Ministry and developed extensive educational, spiritual and supportive ministries. He was involved with Presbytery and Synod Committees. George co-founded "Clergy United for Action" and was involved in many ecumenical activities. He was chair of the Bicentennial Religious Heritage Committee in 1984 and wrote many of the Heritage Trail markers. He was a president and coordinator of Quest Club, president of the Board of Directors and the Foundation of the Allen County, Fort Wayne Public Library, member of the board of the Philharmonic, and the History Center where he started and chaired the Lecture Series. He was involved in many Ecumenical events.

George was pastor of Third Presbyterian Church from 1986 to 1995 when it joined Calvary Church to become Calvary Third Presbyterian Church. During this time he researched and wrote *Frontier Faith: The Story of the Pioneer Congregations of Fort Wayne, Indiana 1820-1860* in 1992. He also wrote *The Best of Fort Wayne Volumes I and II* in 2000 and 2001. He died on September 30, 2004.

George and Doris Mather

Wife, Doris A. Mather, has a BA from Beaver College (Arcadia University), an MA from Ball State and studied at Princeton Theological Seminary from 1969-1971. She was a consultant to Lancaster Theological Seminary for Professional Development for Clergy, and Clergy Wives' Retreats. She worked as a counselor at the West Central Neighborhood Ministry and at the Samaritan Counseling Center and was a Chaplain at St. Joseph Medical Center for 15 years. She is now an active Elder of First Presbyterian and Manager of the Chapel Bookstore.

Son, Geoffrey, was graduated from North Side High School and DePauw University. He worked for Lincoln National in Chicago before moving to Albuquerque where he lives with his wife Ellen, and Elizabeth, five, and Luke, two. He is an Elder in the First Presbyterian Church there and is the CEO of PHDX and President of the Board of Directors of Ghost Ranch National Conference Center.

Daughter, Catherine Mather-Grimes was graduated from North Side High School and Manchester College where she majored in sociology. She lives in Fort Wayne with her husband Dwight, and Emma, seven, and Ethan, five. She is a Deacon at First Presbyterian Church and active in the PTA. She is the Manager for Adult Residential Services at Park Center.

Submitted by Doris A. Mather

MATHEWS

Jacob and Fanny Smith Mathews had five young sons when Jacob died in Huron Ohio in 1836. Fanny was left to raise five boys ages two to nine, so she married Joseph Strickler on February 28, 1836 shortly after the death of her husband.

About 1848 the family moved from Ohio on west to Allen County. At least four of the boys can be found in the 1860 census in Eel River Township along with their mother Fanny Strickler. Fanny however changes her name back to Mathews in the census in 1870, and is buried in the Fairview Cemetery with son Samuel and his family. She is listed as Fanny, wife of Jacob Mathews.

William (1824) was not found in the census with the family and may have stayed in Ohio.

Samuel (1826-1905) married Elvira Rice on September 27, 1846 in Huron, Ohio. Together they had eleven children born to this union: Russell (1847-1848), Alfred (1849-1890), Fanny (1851) Greenwell, Mary (1853) Kniss, Samuel (1855), Commodore (1857-1934), Ellen (1859) Houser, Dexter (1862-1863), John (1864), Bertha (1867) Shaffstall and Lenora (1871) Maurer. Many of Samuel and Elvira's children stayed in the Eel River area. Sons Alfred, Samuel and Commodore as well as daughters Ellen, Fanny, Mary and Lenora farmed and raised families close to their parents. Bertha lived in Steuben County.

Henry (1827-1899) married Sarah Bailey on September 25, 1849 in Allen County. They would have twelve children born in this marriage: Theodore(1852), Joseph (1853-1936), Lucetha (1855) Hammers, Fannie (1856-1941) Carr, Henry (1858), William (1860-1879), Albert (1862-1942), Wilber (1868), Ada (1871), Rosa lee (1874) and Ida (1877) Atkinson. Henry and Sarah farmed in the Eel River area for about thirty years before selling their farm and moving with their family to Red Cloud Nebraska. Son Joseph would return and marry Mary Jane Pillars, daughter of John S. Pillars. They later moved back to Nebraska. Later they resided in Topeka, Kansas. Henry was killed when hit by a train, and both he and Sarah are buried in the Red Cloud Cemetery.

Joseph (1831) the fourth son of Jacob and Fanny was in the 1860 census in Eel River. It is not known where he went from there. He may have stayed in a neighboring county or moved on to another state.

Jacob Jackson (1834), the youngest son of Jacob and Fanny, married Eliza Pike on June 6, 1864. They would settle in Noble County and have three children: Homer (1867) married Dora Stough in 1890, Jennie (1869) married Homer Repine in 1887, and Edith (1875) married Edgar Pugsley in 1892.

Submitted by Marcia Penner

JOHN FELIX & MARIE ELIZABETH (SCHMITZ) MAUCH FAMILY

In June of 1943, John and Marie (Schmitz) Mauch moved their three children Donald, Carol and Gerald from Chicago to Fort Wayne where John had accepted a position as part owner and manager of the Alumag Company, an anodizing shop that did a great deal of work for the government. Both John and Marie had been born of German ancestry and married in 1930. The family bought a home on the north side of the city at 1011 Northwood Boulevard. In August of that year another child, Marlene, was born and in 1946 a fifth child, John, joined the family.

After the end of World War II John became part owner and manager of the newly established Fort Wayne Anodizing Corporation on Wayne Trace. He sold the business and retired in 1975.

Don, the oldest, graduated from Indiana University in 1954. He married his wife, Florence, upon discharge from the Army. He retired in 1996 from Fort Wayne National Bank, as Senior Vice-President, Manager of Commercial Loans. He and his wife, Florence, had four sons: Greg, who is a high school teacher and soccer coach, and his wife, Vesta, have two children, Christopher and Nakao; Paul, an Interstate Transportation Planner, and his wife, Kelly, have two sons, Ben and Andy; Tom, an Event Coordinator, and his wife, Kay, live in West Lafayette with their three children, Jason, and twins Kyle and Kellie; and Bill, who is an Employee Benefits Consultant, lives in Loveland, Ohio with his wife and three children, Christy, Joey and Brian.

John Felix and Marie (Schmitz) Mauch

Carol graduated from Saint Francis College in 1957 and received a Master's Degree from the Illinois Institute of Technology, Institute of Design. She spent 31 years as an art educator in Germany with the Department of Defense Dependents Schools. She taught high school art before she became Coordinator of the Art Program for the school system. After retiring in 1995 and returning to Fort Wayne, she spent seven years as Regional Director of the Scholastic Art Awards Program and holds a part-time position as Education Director for Artlink Gallery. She is an active member of the Fort Wayne Männerchor/Damenchor.

After graduating from St. Joseph College in Rensallear, Indiana Gerald became a Certified Public Accountant. He established his own accounting firm in Zionsville, Indiana. He and his wife, Barbara, have four children: Laura, Steven, Susan and Tim. Laura, who has her own bookkeeping business, and her husband, Kevin, have one son, Matthew. Steven is a Retail Manager for a sporting goods store and Susan works with member services for the YWCA. She and Steve both live in Indianapolis. Tim, who lives in Holland, Michigan, is a plant manager for a food products company. Gerald retired in 2004 and is active in community theater in the Indianapolis area.

Marlene married Tom Slater in 1965 and has three sons. The oldest, Mark, constructs golf courses, including Cherry Hill Golf Course in Fort Wayne. He and his wife, Melissa, have two sons, Mitchell and Shane. David, who lives in West Chester, Ohio, is a project manager/systems analyst. Matthew lives in Los Angeles and works for the Los Angeles Dodgers. He and his wife, Thomasine, have three children: Brandon and twins, Madison and Jacob. After Tom passed away Marlene married Dale Scherman, Finance Officer for the Fort Wayne Community Schools. Marlene worked 20 years for Fort Wayne Community Schools including 15 years as the school secretary at Holland Elementary School.

John Felix Jr. married Connie Hamman. He is the director of Mercy Siena Retirement Community in Dayton, Ohio, and lives in Lebanon, Ohio. They have three children. Jennifer is a physical therapist in Indianapolis. Aaron, who is a line manager for a printing company, and his wife, Julie, have two boys, Tyler and Tanner. They live in Mitchell, South Dakota. Vanessa, a nurse, and her husband, Scott, live in Westfield, Indiana and have two children, Olivia and Alex.

The next generation of Mauch's began on January 27, 2005 when Greg's son, Christopher and his wife, Erin, became the parents of a son, Coleman Harris.

Submitted by Carol A. Mauch

ORANGE WADE MAXFIELD FAMILY

Orange Wade (O.W.) Maxfield was born November 14, 1921 to James and Lillian (Yoder) Maxfield who had five other children. James operated a garage in Leo, Indiana for 34 years. John was born on May 21, 1913, Carl was born on February 8, 1915, Georgianna was born on January 11, 1918, Kenneth was born on October 26, 1924, and Mary Lou was born on April 22, 1927. All were born at home on the bank of the St. Joseph River in Leo, Indiana, which is the background for the family.

A small six foot dam was constructed on the river which the county called the little St. Joseph River by John Manning, Sr. on January 29, 1839. This was to give water power to an undershot wheel, which would operate a flour mill. This was then taken over by Thomas Hamilton on February 18, 1848. After several other families purchased the property through the years, it was sold to Orange Maxfield on March 22, 1873.

Orange was married to Martha Dever and they had seven children: Allie (1869), Ella (1876), William (1878), Daisy (1881), Adie (1883), Gearldine (1888), and James (1892). William Maxfield married Alta. He had a meat market in Leo and later a small tavern. They had two children named Edith and Nellie. Edith married Herman Conrad and they had two children named Pat and Marilyn. Nellie married Virgil Binder and they had no children. Allie Maxfield married Charles Dailey, who was a farmer. They had five children named George, Pete, June, Marge, and May. Ella Maxfield married John J. Garrett. They had an automotive parts store in Anderson, Indiana. They had three boys named Dallas, Dewey, and John, Jr. Daisy Maxfield married Clyde Kryder, who was a farmer. They had three children named Paul, Nidia, and Maxine. Gearldine Maxfield married Arthur Bleekman, who was a farmer. They had six children named May Fern, Gearldine, Max, Kate, Art Jr., and Jack. Adie Maxfield married Arlie Fredrick, who was a farmer. They had three children named Ross, Robert, and Gearldine. The river and the dam was always the recreation in the depression

days of the 1930s. O.W. Maxfield has the cement plaque, which shows the rebuilding of the dam by the Works Project Act (WPA) in 1933. The dam is now under water from the backup of the Cedarville Reservoir.

Orange W. Maxfield married Helen J. Klopfenstein on April 8, 1944 at Maxwell Field Air Force Base in Montgomery, Alabama. After training in the Air Corps, O.W. graduated as a Fighter Pilot in the 3rd Air Force, flying P-51s. Four children were born, Jyl Annette (February 3, 1946), James Allan (May 26, 1949), Julie Christine (December 20, 1956), and Jayne Leslie (October 22, 1958).

Jyl Maxfield married Kenneth Norr on June 15, 1968. Ken operates a Lawn and Garden Service in Fort Wayne. They have two girls named Jodi (September 12, 1974), and Jacque (February 15, 1978). Jodi married Glenn Claycomb on December 19, 1992. They have two children Kearstin (April 18, 1995), and Hunter (May 17, 1999). Jacque married Brian Jansing on October 4, 2003. James Maxfield married Judy Kitzmiller on September 10, 1977. He operates the family business, Scherer and Maxfield, Inc., in Leo. They have three children all grown, but none of them are married, Joe (April 8, 1979), Jason (April 4, 1981), and Sally (April 7, 1984). Julie Maxfield married Tom Gearhart on April 21, 1984. Julie is an Independent Branch Leader for the Longaberger Company and Tom is an insurance agent for Northwestern Mutual. They have one daughter, Kara (September 4, 1986). Jayne Maxfield married Michael Heller on August 6, 1977. Jayne teaches pre-school at Grabill Missionary Church, and Michael works for Hahn Systems in Fort Wayne. They have two children, Jayla (May 6, 1980), and Jordan (July 10, 1983). Neither is married.

John Maxfield was married to Dottie Alexander after six years in the Army Heavy Artillery in Africa, then Italy, and then to Germany. He worked and then owned Vim Sporting Goods store in Fort Wayne. They adopted two boys, John Jr., and Terry. Carl Maxfield married Florence Griswold and worked at G.E. and then moved to Fort Lauderdale, Florida and was in construction work. They had one child named Sandy. Georgianna was married to Charles Richards who went down flying a B25 in New Guinea. She was then a supervisor at La Rabida Sanitarium in Chicago. Kenneth Maxfield served three years in the Army and then returned and graduated from DePaul College in 1950. Kenneth returned to Fort Wayne and was President and CEO of North American Van Lines. He married Jean Sandfur in 1949 and they had two children named Kenneth, Jr., and Laura Susan. Jean passed away in 1993. He then married Bev Wehrenberg in 1995. Mary Lou was married to Robert Lauer and now lives in Tucson, Arizona. They had five girls named Rebecca, Lanetta, Jackie, Stacy, and Kris.

Submitted by O.W. Maxfield

DAN MCCAIN FAMILY

When Dan's career with the USDA Soil Conservation Service (SCS) took him to Allen County in 1969, it began an eighteen-year exciting endeavor. He was twenty-eight years old and ready for a challenge! His agency assigned him to become the District Conservationist with an office in New Haven. He brought his wife at that time, Ginger, and daughter, Nicki, who was two-years old. He lived in Allen County until 1990.

Dan was introduced to the countywide natural and cultural resources during an exploratory tour led by Frank Kirschner, a SCS soil scientist and Glenn Poe, retired SCS district conservationist.

Dan's recollections working with the staunch eastern township German Lutheran farming families was as most industrious with drainage and farm development. Their "planning and hard work" was remnant of the late 1800s. The Germans kept communities tight together as did the French Catholics in their neighborhoods.

Today's agricultural communities are commingled and working together between these former rural ethnic neighborhoods. Big barns and farmsteads yielded to the "overtopping" pace of urban / suburban development. An astounding change has come over Allen County since 1969—Maysville Road at Georgetown was still one of gravel.

Soil conservation work helps with outdoor education for elementary school children. Dan remembers annually thousands of students coming to Carl Salomon's farm along Indiana 3 north of the Interstate. Also, in his beginning years, he worked with farmers in the beautiful rolling countryside of the northern townships near Huntertown, Cedarville and Harlan. Fields were smaller and livestock were more prevalent than in the flatter parts of the county. Farming was marginal, but then came the 1970s national agricultural policy from the Nixon/Butz era — "farm border to border and feed the world." Changes came quickly to the landscape. It was harsh on natural resources and traditional family farming ethic.

Dan McCain

Landowners found their land values had risen overnight, and they could reap bigger benefits from their land if they would clear their pastures and woodlots with "sodbuster" tactics. They made more extensive crop fields by eliminating the former fencerow barriers of pastures, woodlots and idle areas and incorporating these acres into intensive production. Results were astounding and environmentally disastrous at times.

Erosion on these combined landscapes accelerated. There were fewer acres of grass and trees to filter the runoff and shade the hillsides. Need for soil conservation practices increased but application did not keep pace until later in the 1980s. Fort Wayne's drinking water supply, the St. Joe River, was in peril. Mayor Win Moses took affirmative action by created linkage between the City of Fort Wayne and the Soil Conservation District.

In nineteen years as USDA/SCS District Conservationist in Allen County there were many land treatment innovations. The coalition with the Allen Soil & Water Conservation District and addition of professional staff proved effective. Several significant federal and state grants allowed for innovative water quality projects and advances in no till farming techniques. All thanks to a great community with great leaders and a "can do" attitude.

Submitted by Dan McCain

DAVID ARNOLD & BARBARA LOUISE (SHORT) MCCANTS

David McCants was born June 2, 1937, in Dinwiddie County, Virginia. His parents were George Morris and Alma Louise (Skinner) McCants. Barbara was born May 20, 1939, in Petersburg, Virginia. Her parents were Dabney Eppes and Virginia Falconer Electra (Pegram) Short. David graduated from the University of Richmond (BA 1958) and Northwestern University (MA 1959, PhD 1964). Barbara attended Mary Washington College and graduated from the Medical College of Virginia (BSMT 1960). They married September 17, 1960. Barbara and David are the parents of three children: David Mark (born February 2, 1965), who is married to Siti Zuraihan (daughter Myra Mariana) and resides in Irvine, California; Ellen Ashley (born March 11, 1968), who is married to Joseph DeLynn Selking (sons Evan Reinhard, Collin David, and Dylan Joseph, and daughter Olivia Grace) and resides in Decatur, Indiana; and Matthew Reid (born December 21, 1969), who is married to Shari Marie Hartman (son Reid Morris and daughter Taylor Faye) and resides in Des Moines, Iowa.

Barbara and David McCants

Barbara and David moved to Fort Wayne in 1968 when David joined the faculty of Indiana University-Purdue University Fort Wayne as Associate Professor of Communication after filling teaching appointments at Amherst College (1962-65) and the University of Kentucky (1965-68). In 1970, he was named Chair of the Department of Communication, in 1981 Professor of Communication, in 1988 Associate Vice Chancellor for Academic Affairs, and in 2002 Emeritus Professor of Communication Purdue University. Barbara was employed as a medical technologist at Passavant Memorial Hospital, Chicago, Illinois (1960-1962), Cooley Dickinson Hospital, Northhampton, Massachusetts (1962-1964), and Lutheran Hospital, Fort Wayne, Indiana (1977-2001).

David is a Patrick Henry scholar. Among his publications is *Patrick Henry, The Orator* (Greenwood Press, 1990). He was active in the National Communication Association, president of the Religious Speech Communication Association, and president of the Indiana Speech Association. Locally, he was a member of the board of directors and president of the Fort Wayne Civic Theatre, a member of the board of trustees and treasurer of Northeastern Indiana Public Radio, and an elder and deacon of First Presbyterian Church.

Submitted by David A. McCants

THOMAS E. MCCARTHY II FAMILY

Thomas E. McCarthy II was born September 8, 1907 in Crestline, Ohio. He was the son of Thomas E. McCarthy and Dora Mae Murray. He had one sister, Kathryn (Earl Waters). His great grandfather, John McCarthy, left County Kerry, Ireland in 1849, bringing his family with him. Upon arriving in New York, the family quickly moved to Crestline, Crawford County, Ohio. All of the family took jobs working for the railroad.

Thomas II's father, Thomas I and his family, moved to Fort Wayne in 1910. Working for the railroad brought the family here. Thomas II attended St. Patrick's Grade School and graduated from Central Catholic High School in 1925. He then attended Purdue University. While in college, he worked for the Pennsylvania Railroad as a dining car attendant. In 1933, he married his long time girlfriend, Marcella Kirkhoff. Marcella was the eldest daughter of Louis Kirkhoff and Elizabeth Hilker, long time residents of Fort Wayne. Marcella had two sisters, Helen (William Royal) and Dorothy (Paul Hess).

Thomas was the manager of Richmond Brothers Clothiers and then in 1940 he became the men's wear buyer for Wolf and Dessauer. In 1950 Thomas, Robert Meyer and Gilbert Meyers opened Meyers and McCarthy Men's Wear at 128 West Wayne Street. Thomas was a member of St. Peter's Catholic Church, the Knights of Columbus and the Optimist Club in Fort Wayne.

Thomas II and Marcella had three children, Thomas III and Ellen (Norman Wall). A younger daughter, Mary Ann died shortly after birth.

Thomas III married Joan Grant in Sacramento, California in 1960. They have one son Thomas IV. Ellen married Norman D. Wall in 1959 in Fort Wayne and they have three children, Kathleen (Kevin Slane), Kimberly (Brad Boyd), and Kevin (Lisa Choate).

Submitted by Ellen Wall

CHARLIE MCCARTNEY

Charlie McCartney is an example of a true Cedar Creek Township "pioneer" family member. His father, Louis McCartney was born on the farm at 13307 Schwartz Road and lived to the age of 91. His father, grandfather, and great grandfather are all buried at the old Leo Memorial Cemetery. Charlie, the youngest of five children, was born in 1915 at the Hosler Road home that his father bought in 1895. Charlie lived in this same home until his health forced him to move to the Cedars in 1996.

Charlie takes great pride in his heritage and delights in recalling the "early days." In 1910, the Wayne Street Elementary School served as both elementary and high school. Two rooms downstairs were grades one through four in one room and in the other room grades five through eight; and the high school rooms were upstairs. Leo School had electricity in 1921 when he was in the second grade. However, it was not until 1937 that electricity was available to their rural Hosler Road farm.

Charlie McCartney, age 90, Cedars resident in Leo-Cedarville, Indiana.

Charlie walked to school as a youngster; however, he recalls the black "school hacks" that were pulled by horses that would bring children from Hurshtown and Grabill to Leo. Later, there was a black Model T school bus. The children would enter from the back of the bus and sit on each side of the center aisle.

His first experience with radio was a Leo School class project where the boys built their own crystal set. They could listen to Fort Wayne radio station, WOWO, but had to use earphones. He vividly recalls that in 1931, the high school had only one football, but there was a good basketball team! Charlie graduated from Leo High School in 1933, with 16 in his graduating class.

Charlie believes the two things that made the biggest impact in early Cedar Creek Township were electricity and paved roads. The townships were six miles square and the roads were mud and stone. The people would petition for road improvements, and eventually his Hosler Road farm was connected to Leo by a paved road. In 1937 he bought his first tractor, a Farmall F12, from Eli Warner in Leo. Charlie never married. He farmed, worked as an electrician, and, as the youngest son, cared for his father, who was blind.

Submitted by Lou Ann Gerdau.

RALPH & DORA MCCLAIN FAMILY

Marked above all by contributions in education, religion, and the arts, the Ralph and Dora McClain family's presence in Allen County began in 1943 when Ralph assumed a teaching position at Hoagland School. Ralph Edward McClain (born Berne, Indiana, April 4, 1912 to Mary Kratzer and Paul Harris McClain), who had previously taught at Berne and Ridgeville, Indiana, and his wife Dora Emma Nagel (born Berne, Indiana, June 16, 1912 to Mathilde Lehman and Emil Nagel, Sr.) rented a house at 2430 Pleasant Avenue and settled in Fort Wayne with their preschool children, George Douglas (born in Berne, September 24, 1938) and Margaret Jane (born in Ridgeville, February 17, 1942). The family later owned homes at 5620 Arbor Avenue and 4827 DeSoto Drive.

Ralph (Indiana University B.A. 1934, M.A. 1938) taught mathematics at South Side High School 1944-54, during which time he helped organize the local unit of the American Federation of Teachers and was often involved in salary negotiations. Thereafter he was principal at Merle J. Abbett , South Wayne, James H. Smart, Chester T. Lane, and John S. Irwin Schools.

Dora McClain (Bluffton College), was a homemaker and then, after her children were grown, worked as a record room and school librarian for the Fort Wayne and Allen County Library for seventeen years. Reflecting a lifelong passion for classical music, she regularly attended the Community Concerts series and the Fort Wayne Philharmonic. She made hundreds of trips to Berne to care for her aging parents.

The McClains rendered considerable volunteer service. Ralph gave leadership in the Exchange Club, various professional organizations, and golf and bowling leagues.

The McClains: Ralph, George, Dora, Jane, ca. 1947

Church activities, first at Forest Park and then at Simpson United Methodist were important in the family's life. Dora served as Sunday school teacher, youth advisor, and choir member. Ralph was Sunday school superintendent, youth advisor, board member, and treasurer, as well as promoter of senior activities. After their retirement in 1979, Dora and Ralph volunteered for two and a half years as teacher and librarian at McCurdy School in Española, New Mexico, a Methodist mission institution. Ralph died in 1993; Dora lives at Cameron Woods in Angola, Indiana.

Daughter Jane attended Waynedale and Hillcrest Schools, graduated from Elmhurst High School in 1960, and attended Indiana University. She married George John Gear (born 1943) of

Fort Wayne at Simpson Methodist Church in the first wedding service conducted by her newly ordained brother George. Jane is an artist creating original works and handicrafts in a variety of media, including watercolor, paper mache, mosaic, and textiles. She has been employed at Fabric Works in Fort Wayne for fifteen years. She and her husband, a sales executive, have lived in Fort Wayne; Coldwater; Michigan; San Mateo and Pollack Pines, California; and Naperville, Illinois; and now reside on Lake James in northeastern Indiana. Their children are Jeff, Ted (married to Christine Wickham, with daughters Samantha, Kailey, and Emma) and Jay (married to Alison Bandaria).

George attended Forest Park, Hillcrest, Harrison Hill Schools and graduated from South Side High School in 1956 as salutatorian, Yale University (B.A. 1960), Union Theological Seminary (M. Div. 1964), and New York Theological Seminary (D.Min. 1995). He also attended the University of Basel, Switzerland, as a Rotary Foundation Fellow sponsored by the Fort Wayne Rotary Club. A United Methodist clergyman, he served twenty-five years as national executive of the Methodist Federation for Social Action and currently teaches at New York Theological Seminary. With his wife, the Rev. Tilda Norberg (born 1941), he lives on Staten Island, New York City. Their children are Noah and Shana (with spouse Daniel Bodah and their son Silas).

Submitted by George and Dora McClain

FOREST JACKSON MCCOMB & CLARA BELLE GUMP

Forest McComb was born October 2, 1896, to John McComb and Amelia Jackson at a farm on Coldwater Road eight-mile north of Fort Wayne. Perry Hill School is now located there. He had three brothers, Hubert, Arthur, Ford, and a sister, Bertha.

Clara was born February 10, 1910, to George Calvin Gump and Icey Moudy, on a farm located three-fourths mile east of Coldwater Road (that house is now on the Historic Register). She had four brothers, Russell, Forest, George, and Walter, and two sisters, Martha and Eva.

Forest and Clara McComb

For his first eight years of school, Forest attended a one-room school at Royville near Coldwater and Union Chapel Roads. After that he went to Fort Wayne Central High School for one year. He became an avid reader and later studied writing by correspondence courses. He had several stories published in well-known magazines, but he is best known for his nostalgic articles in the E Section of the Sunday Fort Wayne *Journal Gazette*. They were favorites among local folk.

Clara also attended a one-room school on the corner of Coldwater and Gump Roads for eight years. She received many awards in mathematics, spelling, and writing. Later she took courses in bookkeeping and became an excellent bookkeeper for McComb Home Builders. She was known as one of the best cooks in the area, especially for her apple dumplings and her oyster dressing. She tightly guarded the secret of her dressing recipe for fear someone else would make it.

Forest McComb and Clara Gump were married January 1, 1919. They farmed for awhile and later moved to the city of Fort Wayne. This union produced six sons: Richard, Harold, Keith, Bruce, Jack, and Monty, who died at birth.

Richard and Keith served in World War II and Jack served in the Korean Conflict. Harold stayed home and worked as a tool and die maker. Bruce was still in school and helped run the farm. The family had strong ties and all survived the Great Depression years and WW II.

In 1943, Forest and Clara bought a farm one and a half-mile northwest of Huntertown on McComb Road and there they lived the remainder of their lives.

After WW II Richard started the McComb Construction Company; and one by one, the brothers joined the company, along with Forest. After a few years, an agreement was made to break into five construction companies to save overhead. On large jobs they would combine and work together.

Forest was a lifetime baseball fan and coached his boys in the sport. Due to his instruction some of his sons are now in the Fort Wayne Baseball Hall of Fame at the Kruse Museum in Auburn, Indiana. When the family gets together, they talk construction, baseball, euchre, or politics, but they all agree that the thing he taught them most was honesty and integrity.

Clara was killed in an automobile accident March 31, 1973, at the corner of Coldwater and Gump Roads. Forest died of natural courses on August 11, 1978.

Submitted by Keith McComb, a proud son

HAROLD LEROY MCCOMB

Harold McComb was directly related to General Stonewall Jackson through his great grandfather, Phanuel Jackson. He was the second of five sons born to Forest and Clara McComb on June 7, 1921. The sons were Richard, Harold, Keith, Bruce, and Jack.

Growing up on a farm during the Depression and hard times taught Harold to be a good firewood cutter. Necessity made him a good mechanic, working on farm machinery and the family car. Harold and his brothers attended Huntertown grade school and he graduated from North Side High School in Fort Wayne in 1939. As a teenager he became a very good baseball pitcher and threw several no-hit games in Federation Ball.

At North Side he met (Aileen) Dotty Bertram. They were married on February 3, 1940. They had six children in the following order; Terry, Alan, Tom, Dean, Karen, and Sheri.

Harold and Dotty McComb (1985)

Natural mechanical ability landed Harold a job with Swanson Machine Company on South Calhoun Street, as a set-up man. This factory produced parts vital to the effort of World War II. Having learned the construction business from his uncle, Art McComb, he started his own construction business building homes in 1951. His ability to fix things allowed him to invent tools used in his own business, though he never patented them. These included the first set of lightweight basement forms ever used in Fort Wayne. Until then it took two men to lift one form into place; one man could set these new forms.

Harold poured many concrete streets for new subdivisions. At that time you could buy a machine for about $100,000 that would level the concrete. He invented a self-propelled machine by which you could form up and pour 150 feet of street every day. This machine cost about $2,000. It was the talk of the industry. Others made special trips to his jobs to watch it work. This company still thrives today doing all types of construction, including commercial.

One of Harold's hobbies was building model airplanes with gasoline engines. He would spend months building them, fly them a few times, then hang them from the ceiling in his home. The basement housed his elaborate model train exhibit. A generous and loving family man, he enjoyed taking his children fishing and to major league baseball games. He also enjoyed watching them play in local leagues.

In this day and age, most children either move to other states or go into a different business from their family. All six of his children and five of his grandchildren are in the construction business in the area - a testament to family love. To date there are 14 grandchildren and 19 great grandchildren. He died March 7, 1996, leaving a legacy of kindness, compassion, and great skill.

Submitted by Terry L. McComb

KEITH L. MCCOMB

Keith McComb was born August 13, 1923, on a farm where Perry Hill School now stands. His parents were Forest J. McComb and Clara Belle Gump. He had five brothers, Richard, Harold, Bruce, Jack, and Monty, who died at birth.

He graduated from North Side High School in 1942. As an avid baseball fan, he played for the G.E. Club and Rudisill Service. In a handpicked team for an exhibition game, he was catcher for pitcher, Ned Garver, against a professional black team from Indianapolis.

Keith L. McComb

Drafted into the Army Air Corp in January 1943, he was trained as a mechanic and later re-trained in photoreconnaissance under Elliot Roosevelt. As a member of the Ninth Air Force, assigned to General Patton, his job was to install cameras and film in P-51 Mustang fighter planes and develop pictures. He served in England, France, and Germany.

On February 14, 1946, Keith McComb married Lucille Elaine Reynolds. They had three daughters: Theresa Kay (December 4, 1946), Janet Ann (September 22, 1949), and Peggy Jean (March 29, 1952). They were also foster parents to more than 50 children.

As president of the Huntertown Lions Club and father of three girls, he was instrumental in getting the Lions ball program changed from all-boys to co-ed. He continued coaching and sponsoring a team in the Fort Wayne Women's League, for which he was honored as the best sportsmanship coach in the league - an honor not normally given to a man.

After having worked several years as a carpenter for his brother, he formed McComb Home Builders (1955-1989). Most of his work was done in Allen County and the surrounding area. Many carpenters are still building in the area that trained under him.

His wife, Elaine, died of cancer on March 19, 1989. Keith married Geneva (Jenny) Hodge on June 30, 1990.

Keith is a 50-year Mason and served as commander of VFW Post 11314 for six years. In order to pass on the history of World War II, he shows slides at local schools of the pictures he took while in service. He also encourages the youth to make the best of their school years; as he credits North Side High School for the excellent training he received in mechanics, drafting, and shop.

In an effort to come up with new entertainment for the county fair and local festivals, in 2000 he gave birth to Rupley's Dixon Lawnmower Square Dancers. This consisted of dancers riding lawnmowers while performing patterned dances. It was such a novelty at local fairs that it eventually was shown on national television.

He has eight grandchildren and eleven great-grandchildren with more to come. His motto has always been, Do a person a good job at a fair price and you will never be out of work. He is a man of high integrity and unyielding patriotism.

Submitted by Geneva McComb

RICHARD STANLEY MCCOMB

Richard McComb was born August 24, 1919, on a farm where Perry Hill School is now located. He was the first of six boys born to Forest J. McComb and Clara Belle Gump. His brothers were Harold L., Keith L., Bruce L., Jackson C., and Monty McComb. He attended the Huntertown School five years. He also attended the Rome City School three years and one year at South Side High School in Fort Wayne.

He was a natural baseball player. When in the seventh grade in Rome City, he was asked to play shortstop on the high school team. They won the county tournament and the other coaches complained about Rome City playing a younger kid on the high school team. They were overruled and the victory stood. He was drafted into the Navy in 1944. He was put on their best ball team to entertain the troops, up and down the East Coast. Later he sponsored his own baseball team and had a lot of success managing and playing. He was inducted into the Fort Wayne Baseball Hall of Fame located in the World War II Victory Museum at Auburn.

In August 1940, Richard married Ruth Buehrer. They had three children, Joseph, David, and Kathy. After being discharged from the Navy in 1946, he put the construction skills he had learned at the General Electric Company and in the Navy to work in his own construction company. He was a very successful contractor and worked at it the rest of his life. He passed away on January 6, 1998. His wife, Ruth, and their two sons are still managing the McComb Construction Company.

Richard served on the board of the Allen County Fairgrounds and worked very closely with others to oversee the construction of the buildings there. Having an eye for a good deal, he helped get the most for the money. He was very proud of the fairgrounds and never missed the county fair. Growing up during the Depression, he thought hard work was more important than going for more education. Everyone says that his theory worked for him.

Submitted by Keith McComb

CHARLES EDWARD & ALBERTA VICTORIA (PRIDDY) MCCONNELL FAMILY

Charles and Alberta McConnell moved to Fort Wayne in 1983 from Lima, Ohio, where they had lived for nine years following their marriage on August 15, 1975, in Van Wert, Ohio. In Lima, Charles worked for Teledyne Ohio Steel and Alberta worked for Vistron Corporation-Chemical Division of Standard Oil Refinery.

Charles was born on February 15, 1952, to Glenn Robert and Fannie (Thompson) McConnell in Warsaw, Kosciusko County, Indiana. He was the eldest of five children. Charles lived with his family in Warsaw and Goshen, Indiana, and Jackson and Bremen, Ohio. Glenn worked for NIPSCO and for the uranium enrichment plant in Piketon, Ohio, then for General Mills. Fannie was employed as a healthcare worker for over 25 years.

The McConnell ancestors were farmers in Monroe Township, Kosciusko County. Glenn's parents were Myron and Bessie (Snellenberger) McConnell. Fannie's parents were Silas and Eunice (Wellman) Thompson, who resided in Louisa and Ashland, Kentucky. The ancestors of these families were railroad workers and farmers. Surnames of these two families included Tibbitts, Wertenberger, Funk, Hill, Bradley, and Wellman.

Alberta was born on December 31, 1952, in Fort Wayne, Indiana, to Josef and Ruth (Thompson) Priddy, who resided in Van Wert, Ohio. Josef worked for the Van Wert County engineer's office, then for the state highway department. Ruth taught elementary school for 32 years.

Josef's parents were Thomas Kirtland and Olive Ann (Beck) Priddy. The Priddy ancestors included a Revolutionary War patriot who received land in northwest Ohio as a benefit of his service. The Priddy family ancestor's occupations included farmers, contractors, construction workers, a lawyer, and seamstresses.

Charles and Alberta McConnell and sons.

Ruth Priddy's parents were Alfred Elsworth and Bessie (Adams) Thompson, who farmed in Jackson Township, Van Wert County, Ohio. Surnames of these two families included Rogers, Bowersock, Butler, Cox, Huffman, Price, and Sunderland.

Charles and Alberta have two children. Jeremy Ross McConnell was born June 24, 1984, in Allen County. He graduated from Elmhurst High School and currently attends IPFW. Jeremy has worked at Hall's Original Drive-in for four years, most recently as a line cook. Jethro Clark McConnell, born June 9, 1989, attends South Side High School. He is involved in a rock band outside of school and participates as a percussionist in the jazz band at school. He is employed at Catablu.

The family has lived in the beautiful neighborhood of Indian Village since 1984, a lovely place to raise a family, walk dogs, and visit with neighbors. They are members of Waynedale United Methodist Church. Charles graduated from the University of Cincinnati in 1975, with a B.S. in electrical engineering. He is employed by Foamex LLP as a project engineer. Alberta attended Bowling Green State University and graduated from International Business College in 1975. She enjoys working as a substitute school assistant and clerical worker for Fort Wayne Community Schools.

Submitted by Alberta V. McConnell.

STEPHEN & DAWN CORTNER MCCORD

Dawn Cortner-McCord was born August 25, 1970, in Union City, Indiana, to Delbert and Beverly Cortner. Beverly, a retired police dispatcher and city worker, currently lives in Winchester. Her parents are Gilbert and Mary Juanita (Bankson) Roberson and both worked in law enforcement. Delbert, a retired glass worker, remarried and lives with Mary Cortner in Kendallville. His parents were Marvin and Grace (Baldwin) Cortner. Dawn's siblings include Debbie Seidl of Anchorage, Alaska; David Cortner of Eaton, Ohio; and Dee Cortner of New Paris, Ohio.

Stephen Michael McCord was born December 20, 1970, in Winchester, Indiana, to Dick and Stephanie McCord. Stephanie (remarried) and Lauren Otis live in Fort Wayne, where she is the Human Resources director of Byron Health Center and Lauren is a chief mechanic in the Indiana Air National Guard. Stephanie's parents are Harold (served in Panama and South America during WW II in the Army Air Force) and Barbara (Shires) McCoy. Dick (remarried) and Betty McCord reside in Winchester. He has been a chief design engineer at Hobart, Borg-Warner, and Muncie Transmissions. His parents are Raymond and Ada (Burton) McCord. Steve has one sibling, Christen Staggs, a married sister living in South Bend.

Both Dawn and Steve have long family lines in the Randolph County, Indiana, and Darke County, Ohio area. While Stephen spent parts of his childhood in Ithaca, New York, and Troy, Ohio, Dawn was raised totally in Winchester. Both of them attended and graduated together from Winchester Community High School in 1989. Dawn received a BS in Education from Ball State, while Steve received a BA in History and Political Science from IU in 1993. Dawn has also earned a masters degree in Education from IPFW.

Stephen and Dawn McCord with daughters, Zara and Eliza

The couple moved to Fort Wayne in 1995. They were married March 29, 1996, at Main Street Christian Church in Winchester.

Dawn has been employed at schools in Indianapolis and Carmel before her current position as a special education teacher at Woodburn Elementary School, where she teaches grades K-6. Steve has worked as an intern in Congress, and at the Indiana State Library and Indiana Historical Society before beginning work for the Allen County Public Library. He has worked various positions and is currently a librarian at the Waynedale Branch Library.

Steve and Dawn have two children. Zara Marguerite was born December 15, 2000. She enjoys flying her grandpa's airplane, art, and dance. She will attend Whitney Young Elementary School this fall. Eliza Madeline was born August 22, 2003. She enjoys life very much. Both of these redheads are true joys to their parents and family. Before children, there were dogs; to date four miniature dachshunds have been an important part of the household.

The family enjoys traveling, biking, gardening, and antiquing. They reside in historic Southwood Park, where they are involved in association activities. Dawn has been a teachers' union representative. Steve is a board member of the IU Alumni Band. Both of them have been members of the Fort Wayne Community Band and have been actively involved in various Democratic political campaigns. The family attends Broadway Christian Church.

Submitted by Stephen McCord

EZRIAH (EZRA) JOSEPH MCCORMICK

Ezriah (Ezra) Joseph McCormick was born November 5, 1861, in Jefferson Township, Allen County, Indiana, to Patrick Joseph and Nancy "Ann" (Cox) McCormick. Ezra had one brother and two sisters. His sister, Mary McCormick, was born July 2, 1853, Ross County, Ohio, and died August 5, 1932, Highland County, Ohio. She married George Washington Storts, Jr., on April 7, 1873, in Chillicothe, Ross County, Ohio. He was the son of George Storts and Sarah Forsythe. He was born April 15, 1851, in Buckskin Township, Ross County, Ohio, and died May 13, 1933, in New Petersburg, Highland County, Ohio.

Ezra s brother, Thomas E. McCormick, was born May 1, 1856, Ross County, Ohio, and died March 28 1930, in Fort Wayne, Indiana. He never married. He was buried in Fort Wayne, Indiana. His sister, Rebecca B. McCormick, was born about 1859, Jefferson Township, Allen County, Indiana. Ezra also had a stepsister named Elizabeth "Lizzy" Cox, who was born June 15, 1845, in Ross County, Ohio. Lizzy's father was Moses Cox, of Ross County, Ohio. Lizzy never married. She died on May 1, 1921, in Jefferson Township, and is buried at the Odd Fellows Cemetery, New Haven, Indiana.

In a letter by Ezra's daughter, Ida (McCormick) Stanger, to her niece, Louise (Miller) Ladd, dated May 15, 1992, she wrote about Elizabeth Cox, "but when Aunt Lizzie came she always brought bananas and oranges and one time she brought grapefruit. Really, when Aunt Lizzie and Uncle Tom came it was sure a happy time."

Ezra's daughter, Elizabeth Ellen (McCormick) Tatman, recounts that when Ezra was a young man he went "out west" (how far is unknown). He talked to an old Indian woman and she told his future. She said that he would marry a woman who would give him a drink in a cup with two handles. When he returned to Indiana he joined the thrashers and went to work on the Bacon farm. After dinner there was no cup at the pump. After a lot of encouragement, Ezra went to the house and asked Mary Bacon for a cup for the well. Dinner was just over and all the dishes were dirty. She said, Just a minute and I'll find something, and she gave him a sugar bowl.

Ezriah (Ezra) married Mary Louise Bacon on May 1, 1883, at St. Louis Catholic Church, Besancon, Indiana. Ezra and Mary purchased a farm south of his parents' property in Section 36 of Jefferson Township. The land was situated on the Ternet Road near Tillman Road. Mary was the daughter of Samuel Bacon and Jane Girardot. They were married 65 years. Mary was born on August 1, 1865, in Jefferson Township, Allen County, Indiana, and died August 15, 1965.

Probate records show that Ezra's father, Patrick McCormick, Jr., on September 19, 1863, brought 80 acres of farm land in Jefferson Township, Allen County, Indiana, at 4 1/2 N.E. 1/4 Section 36 (Book 93, page 533), for $500 from Harry Lockwood of Litchfield, Connecticut. Ezra McCormick then bought 30 acres from his father, Patrick, December 6, 1889, for $400. In 1906 Ezra and Mary owned 80 acres (Book 116, page 175).

Ezra and Mary Bacon McCormick

Ezriah (Ezra) retired from farming in 1923, and he and Mary moved to 1430 Grant Avenue, Fort Wayne, Indiana. They still went "out to the "farm"; his son, Charlie McCormick, and his family lived there. Ezra liked to butcher and make apple butter. In the 1950s, a woman who lived on Grant Avenue mentioned that she still remembered taking her children out to the farm to make apple butter. At least up until the 1940s, the family still had reunions in Giant's woods. Son, Paul McCormick, who lived in New Jersey, came once and took movie pictures. These pictures were enjoyed by many through the years. Ezra liked to drink his beer warm and chew tobacco. When daughter, Lucy, and her husband, Charlie Tittle, came for a visit, she would send poems or a song, or such, so the grandkids could learn and participate in a little home entertainment. The biggest highlight was to get to dress-up in the "Ferdinand the Bull" costume (two pieces and two people - head and rump) and run at "the little kids". On those occasions Ezra would do us all the honor of performing an "Irish Jig" (we are never too far from our roots).

In 1948 Ezra was afflicted with cancer of the mouth. He was 86 years old and also was taking care of Mary, who had fallen and broken her hip. He died November 30, 1948, in Fort Wayne, Indiana, following his 87th birthday. Ezriah (Ezra) and Mary McCormick are buried together in the Odd Fellows Cemetery, New Haven, Indiana.

The children of Ezriah (Ezra) and Mary (Bacon) McCormick are:

Mary Louise McCormick, born November 27, 1883, Jefferson Township, Allen County, Indiana, and died May 10, 1921, Jefferson

Township, Allen County, Indiana. She married David Fredrick Miller on October 21, 1902, in St. Louis Catholic Church, Besancon, Indiana. He was born on September 16, 1878, in Allen County, Indiana, and died May 19, 1953, in Allen County, Indiana.

John Louise McCormick, born July 28, 1885, Jefferson Township, Allen County, Indiana, and died December 8, 1907, as the result of a train accident in Ohio. He is buried at St. Louis Catholic Cemetery, Besancon, Indiana.

Samuel Peter McCormick, born February 7, 1888, Jefferson Township, Allen County, Indiana, and died December 20, 1963, Fort Wayne, Indiana. He married Myrtle Hoover, July 27, 1920, in Fort Wayne, Indiana. She was the daughter of Henry and Phoebe Hoover. She was born on June 26, 1900, in Fort Wayne, Indiana, and died May 7, 1983, in Fort Wayne, Indiana.

Rose Ann McCormick, born April 5,1890, Jefferson Township, Allen County, Indiana, and died October 14, 1904, Jefferson Township, Allen County, Indiana.

Lucy Marie McCormick, born March 7, 1893, Jefferson Township, Allen County, Indiana, and died March 28, 1962, in Tucson, Arizona. She married Henry F. Mouldney, November 10, 1909, in Allen County, Indiana. He was born in 1885, Jefferson Township, Allen County, Indiana, and died April 25, 1950, in Fort Wayne, Indiana. She then married Charles Tittle, July 4, 1940. He was born in 1900 in Defiance, Ohio, and died February 25, 1981, in Tucson, Arizona.

Elizabeth Ellen McCormick, born December 3, 1895, Jefferson Township, Allen Country, Indiana, died December 15, 1988, in Fort Wayne, Indiana. She married William Elsworth Tatman, May 14, 1912, in Besancon Catholic Church, Allen County, Indiana. William, son of Charles and Hannah (Bellis) Tatman was born February 20, 1891, at Baldwin, Jackson Township, Allen County, Indiana, died July 31, 1971, Fort Wayne, Indiana. William and Elizabeth (McCormick) Tatman are buried at the Odd Fellows Cemetery, New Haven, Indiana.

Adline Marie McCormick, born February 1, 1898, in Jefferson Township, Allen County, Indiana, died July 18, 1952, Fort Wayne, Indiana. Adline is buried at Odd Fellows Cemetery, New Haven, Indiana. She was married to Phillip E Bellis, son of James and Mary "Ann" (Malott) Bellis, November 10, 1915, Fort Wayne, Indiana. Phillip E. Bellis was born February 24, 1887, in Dixon, Ohio, and died March 14, 1966, in Fort Wayne, Indiana. He was buried in the Odd Fellows Cemetery, New Haven, Indiana. She then married Jerry Mowery, who was born in Bluffton, Indiana.

Paul Ezra McCormick, born July 31, 1900, Jefferson Township, Allen County, Indiana, died October 29, 1968, in Trenton, Mercer County, New Jersey. He married Mabel Suydam Mains on March 30, 1921, in Elkton, Maryland. She was the daughter of Sylvester and Laura Berens Mains. She was born January 10, 1904, in Trenton, New Jersey, and died August 7, 1986, in Yardville, New Jersey. Paul McCormick, as was his wish, was cremated, and his ashes were returned to Indiana.

Ida Ruth McCormick, born September 1, 1901, Jefferson Township, Allen County, Indiana, died April 6, 2001. She married Roy Andrew Stanger. He was born February 16, 1901, in Antwerp, Ohio, and died February 22, 1956, in Tucson, Arizona. Roy and Ida Stanger are buried in Greenlawn Cemetery, Perryville, Ashland County, Ohio. They lived most of their life in Ashland County, Ohio, except for 12 years in Tucson, Arizona.

Charles William McCormick, born May 2,1904, Jefferson Township, Allen County, Indiana, died December 17, 1979, in Lordsburg, New Mexico. He married Helen Lucille Bubb, November 19, 1925, in Fort Wayne, Indiana. She was born July 5, 1905, in New Haven, Indiana, and died April 23, 1982, in Silver City, New Mexico. Parents of Helen Bubb are George and Wallburgie "Burgie" (Huth) Bubb. Charles and Helen McCormick are buried in Ajo, Arizona.

Submitted by Liela Heck

PATRICK JOSEPH MCCORMICK, JR.

Patrick Joseph McCormick, Jr., was born in Ireland, possibly County Cork, March 17, 1822, to Patrick and Mary (Duffy) McCormick. Patrick had one brother and two sisters. Thomas was born July 1823; date of death unknown. Margaret, born July 1, 1826; died August 15, 1900. She married Barney McCloskie in Ross County, Ohio. She is buried in St. Francis Xavier Cemetery, Ross County, Ohio. Catherine McCormick, born about 1828, married John Haney and moved to Illinois. No further information on her.

Patrick arrived in the U. S. in the 1840s from the Irish potato famine. He came to Ross County, Ohio, and, on October 24, 1852, married Nancy Ann Cox. She was the daughter of John Cox, born in 1798 in Kentucky, and Elizabeth Fisher born in 1799 in Ohio. Nancy Ann (called Ann in the census), was born in 1824 in Ross County, Ohio, and died about 1879. Patrick applied for naturalization, November 11, 1854, in Ross County, Ohio.

In 1860, Patrick moved his family to Jefferson Township, Allen County, Indiana, where he purchased eighty acres in Section 36 on the Ternet Road. The area later was called Tillmans after the family that had a bar and general store there.

Nancy Cox McCormick had a daughter from her first marriage named Elizabeth "Lizzy". She was born June 15, 1845, in Ross County, Ohio. Lizzy's father was Moses Cox of Ross County, Ohio. Lizzy never married. She died May 1, 1921, in Jefferson Township and is buried at the Odd Fellows Cemetery, New Haven, Indiana.

Patrick Joseph McCormick, Jr.
(picture taken from a tin type)

The children of Patrick and Nancy "Ann" (Duffy) McCormick are:

Mary McCormick, born July 2,1853, Ross County, Ohio, and died August 5, 1932, Highland County, Ohio. She married George Washington Storts, Jr., on April 7, 1873, in Chillicothe, Ross County, Ohio. He was the son of George Storts and Sarah Forsythe. He was born April 15, 1851, in Buckskin Township, Ross County, Ohio, and died May 13 1933, in New Petersburg Highland, Ohio.

Thomas E. McCormick, born May 1, 1856, Ross County, Ohio, and died March 28, 1930, Fort Wayne, Indiana. He never married, and was buried in Fort Wayne, Indiana.

Rebecca B. McCormick, born about 1859, Jefferson Township, Allen County, Indiana.

Ezriah Joseph McCormick, born November 5, 1861, Jefferson Township, Allen County, Indiana, and died November 30, 1948, in Fort Wayne, Indiana. He married Mary Louise Bacon, May 1, 1883, at St. Louis Catholic Church, Besancon, Indiana. She was the daughter of Samuel Bacon and Jane Girardot. Mary was born August 1, 1865, in Jefferson Township, Allen County, Indiana, and died August 15, 1965. Ezriah and Mary McCormick are buried together in the Odd Fellows Cemetery, New Haven, Indiana. Ezriah (Ezra) retired from farming in 1923, and moved to 1430 Grant Ave, Fort Wayne, Indiana.

Ellen McCormick, born 1863, Jefferson Township, Allen County. Indiana, and died December 1882, Jefferson Township, Allen County, Indiana. She is buried in the St. Louis Catholic Cemetery, Besancon, Allen County, Indiana.

Margaret Ann "Maggie" McCormick, born February 5, 1866, in Jefferson Township, Allen County, Indiana, and died November 1952 in San Francisco, California. She married George William Frietzsche, November 29, 1883, in Allen County, Indiana; he was the son of John and Margaret (Betts) Frietzsche. George Frietzsche was born May 14,1855, in Noblesville, Indiana, and date of death unknown.

Peter McCormick, born 1869, Jefferson Township, Allen County, Indiana, and date of death unknown.

Submitted by Paul McCormick

THOMAS AUGUST MCCORMICK

DESCENDANT OF PATRICK AND MARY (DUFFY) McCORMICK IN AMERICA

Thomas August McCormick was born July 1823, in Ireland and died in Indiana, place unknown. He married Elizabeth M. Martin about 1850, in Indiana. She was born October 27, 1822, in Ohio, the daughter of Andrew and Elizabeth (Owen) Martin. Elizabeth died April 28, 1896, and is buried in Saint Louis Catholic Church Cemetery, Besancon, Allen County, Indiana.

Thomas August Mc Cormick left Liverpool July 25, 1848, and arrived in New York August 25, 1848. He applied for naturalization April 4, 1853, in Fort Wayne, Allen County, Indiana. Thomas and Elizabeth Mc Cormick farmed and raised their family in section 23, Jefferson Township, Allen County, Indiana.

Children of Thomas and Elizabeth (Martin) Mc Cormick are:

Richard McCormick was born 1852, Jefferson Township, Allen County, Indiana, and died July 17, 1909, Roanoke, Indiana. He married Elizabeth, unknown, June 11, 1875. He owned property in Jefferson Township, Allen County, Indiana in 1888.

James McCormick was born 1853, in Jefferson Township, Allen County, Indiana, married Emma E., unknown, born 1860, Allen County, Indiana.

Elizabeth McCormick was born 1857, Jefferson Township, Allen County, married January 13, 1874, to John Ladig.

Catharine McCormick was born 1859, Jefferson Township, Allen County, Indiana, married September 1, 1879, to Sylvester Gray.

Joseph Michael McCormick was born April 4, 1863, Jefferson Township, Allen County, Indiana, died December 23, 1931, Fort Wayne, Indiana and is buried in the Catholic Cemetery, Fort Wayne, Indiana. He married Cora Mary Agnes Wilkins, June 29, 1884, daughter of David and Rebecca Daxtes Wilkins. Cora died April 27, 1899, and is buried in Saint Louis Catholic Cemetery, Besancon, Indiana.

Submitted by Thomas Brady

JOHN MCCUNE

Jonathan Brian Shultz was born January 24, 1975, in Allen County, Indiana. His eighth great grandfather was John McCune I, born in 1705 in Ireland. John's first wife is unknown. They had three known sons, John II, born in 1730; James, born in 1740; and Robert, born in 1732. John landed on Cape Henlopen, Delaware, between 1733 and 1738, and then went to Cumberland County, Pennsylvania. John I's second wife was Agnes LaMond-Hinkson.

Robert McCune, born in 1732, died in 1778 in Pennsylvania. Robert married Isabella Brady, daughter of Hugh Brady and Hannah McCormick, in 1759. Their children were John McCune III, Robert II, a daughter, Hugh, Isabella, and Samuel.

John McCune III, born in 1761, married Nancy Mathers in 1786. Their children were Robert McCune III, Margaret, Gavin, Samuel, Rosannah, Hugh, John M., Joseph, and Mary Ann Lacey.

Samuel McCune, born in 1793 in Cumberland County, Pennsylvania, married Margaret Dinsmore, daughter of John and Catherine Dinsmore, on January 27, 1814, in Nicholas County, Kentucky. Their children were John S., Perry, William, Catherine, Mary S., Elizabeth, Jane, and Elvira.

William McCune, born in 1819 in Highland County, Ohio, married Nancy Coon, daughter of John and Mary Coon, on September 21, 1843, in Delaware County, Indiana. Their children were John S., Mary Jane, William Jasper, Henry Newton, James Owen, and Perry Preston.

Henry Newton McCune, born August 25, 1869, in Hancock County, Indiana, married Agnes Idella Huggins on July 8, 1882, in Delaware County, Indiana. He died April 26, 1943. Agnes, daughter of John Huggins and Martha Mumford, was born July 18, 1863, in Miami County, Ohio. She died January 5, 1937, in Madison County, Indiana. Their children were Gola, Richard Ora, Dora Desilva, Rosa Etta, Ollie Virgil, Elzie L., and Arlie.

Gola McCune, born April 2, 1883, in Delaware County, Indiana, married Cordelia Cranfill on December 24, 1904. He died November 18, 1960. Cordelia, born November 9, 1879, died November 18, 1960. They both died in Jay County, Indiana. Her parents were William Cranfill and Louvenia Springer. Gola and Cordelia's children were Floyd Dewey, Frances Evelyn, Mary Lucile, Howard Newton, James Albert, and Robert Irwin.

Robert Irwin McCune, born July 11, 1921, in Randolph County, Indiana, married Dorothy Pearl Barriger March 18, 1948, in Randolph County, Indiana. Dorothy, daughter of Clara Barringer and Robert Barnes, was born October 21, 1926, in Jefferson County, Indiana, and died January 16, 1970. Robert died September 2, 1994. Their children were Wanda Joy, Linda Lou, and David Lee, all born in Indiana.

Wanda Joy McCune married Lee LaVern Shultz on June 1, 1968. Lee, son of Robert Shultz and Ruth Marie Lawrence, was born July 22, 1944, in Indiana, and died in 1985 in Tyler, Texas. They had three children, Michelle Lee, Jonathan Brian, and Mitchell Wade.

Michelle Lee Schultz married Steven Wayne Mix and their children are Brittney, Tacconi, and Alex Wayne.

Jonathan Brian Shultz met Diana Lynn Honeick. Their children are Jake Christopher and Olivia Ileen.

Submitted by Jonathan Shultz

ALFRED LEE MCDANIEL, JR. & MARIAN ALICE (HEROLD) MCDANIEL

Alfred "Al" McDaniel moved to Fort Wayne from Toledo, Ohio, in 1952 to live with his mother, Ruth Kathryn (Koella) Fenimore, and step-father, Robert "Bob" Fenimore. Ruth and Bob were managers of the Belmont Dime Store on Broadway Avenue. They lived at 4201 Holton Avenue. Ruth's father was Theodore Koella, first-chair violinist with the Pontiac Philharmonic Orchestra in Pontiac, Michigan. Al was born in Toledo on June 2, 1936. Al worked at the O-So Grape Bottling Company. Al's father, Alfred Lee McDaniel, Sr., and his sister, Patricia (McDaniel) Reinier, remained in Toledo.

Marian Alice Herold lived with her mother, Mable (Huffman) Curry, brother Hal C. Curry, and sister Melinda Jo Curry. Their address was 4129 Holton Avenue. Marian was born December 11, 1934, in Elwood, Indiana. She was the daughter of Claude Herold and Mable Huffman. She moved to Fort Wayne in July 1950. Marian graduated from South Side High School. Al McDaniel and Marian were married October 16, 1953. They divorced on October 22, 1965. They had five children, all born at Fort Wayne's Lutheran Hospital.

Lois Adele (McDaniel) Bullard was born November 4, 1953. Lois graduated from American School in Chicago and Four Winds Beauty College in Fort Wayne. She earned her LPN degree from Ivy Tech State College. She is pursuing her RN degree at Ivy Tech. Lois uses her artistic abilities to decorate her home. Her eye for design and color is impeccable. She has been teased for wearing diamond earrings while grouting tile. Lois lives with her husband, Douglas Bullard, in Fort Wayne. She works for The Towne House Retirement Community.

Alfred Lee McDaniel III was born February 3, 1958, and lives in New Haven. Alfred is an accomplished guitar player with an inherent ability. He bowls, plays golf, and rides his motorcycle. He has 29 years of service with Essex Wire, Fort Wayne.

Kathryn "Kathy" "KD" Marie McDaniel was born July 11, 1959. She graduated from South Side High School and Four Winds Beauty College. Kathy and Lois attended Four Winds together. Kathy works for Hair, Etc. on DuPont Road and resides in Fort Wayne. She is a mem-

L to R: Robert, Lucille, Delia, Evelyn, James, Floyd, Gola, and Howard McCune

L to R: Patrick McDaniel, Kathy McDaniel, Marian (Herold) Klinger, Lois (McDaniel) Bullard, Alfred McDaniel III, and Steve McDaniel (Christmas 2003)

ber of the Fort Wayne Ski Club and travels the United States and Europe to ski. Kathy has one daughter, Rachelle Kay Elsner, born October 13, 1977, and two grandchildren, Andrew (five) and Jessica (two). Rachelle's father is Michael Ehle. Rachelle is married to Phil Elsner. Phil works at Paramount Tube and they have a karaoke business called "Out There" and live in Fort Wayne.

Steven "Mac" Claude McDaniel was born August 28, 1960. He graduated from South Side High School. Steven was married to Kelly Gentry and they had two sons. Kenneth John McDaniel was born September 12, 1988 but only lived about 12 hours. He is buried in Babyland in Lindenwood Cemetery. Their second son is Derik Andrew McDaniel born October 9, 1989. He lives in Spencerville. Steven and Kelly are divorced. Steven lives in Waynedale and is an engineer for National Tube-Form Co., Inc. He belongs to the Southwest Conservation Club. Steven and Derik play drums, bass guitar and harmonica in the garage.

Patrick "Pat" Gene McDaniel was born on September 18, 1963. Pat strives to improve efficiency and has inventions that help in the home. He plays the guitar and goes fishing. Pat has three children. Shane Alan was born June 7, 1990. Raeann Lyen Sarrazine was born December 27, 1993. Mekynzi Kayelan Rice was born February 11, 1999. Pat works at No Sag in Kendallville, Indiana, and lives in Fort Wayne.

Al McDaniel was re-married to Ginger Kalusa in 1969. Ginger died in 2002. They had two children, Robin and Lee. Al is retired from the trucking industry and lives in LaGrange County.

Marian married Delphus Klinger on February 14, 1984. She is a member of the Daughters of The American Revolution since December 7, 1973. She belongs to The Mary Penrose Wayne Chapter of DAR and GE Elex Club. Delphus and Marian retired January 1, 1993, from General Electric Aircraft in Fort Wayne with 27 years of service. They are members of General Electric Quarter Century Club. They reside in Altona, Indiana.

Submitted by Patrick McDaniel

DONNELLY P. MCDONALD FAMILY

Donnelly Patrick McDonald (1890-1961) married Larene I. Travers (1893-1956) in 1921. Like his father, Patrick Joseph McDonald, he was a graduate of Notre Dame University and President of Peoples Trust and Savings Company, "The Bank under the Clock". His mother was Gertrude "Bonnie" Donnelly, and he had three brothers: Harry P. (1886-1929) never married; Kenneith V. B. (1888-1956) who married Irma Henderson in 1924, one child Mary Ruth (1927-2001); and William C. F. (1894-1964), the youngest brother who never married. They had four children: Donnelly P. Jr., Mary Larene Patricia (Pat), Josephine Ellen Emily (Joellen), and Francis Travers (Trav).

Donnelly P. McDonald Jr. (1922-1989) married Mary Anne Keenan in 1962. They had two adopted children, Nora Larene and Mary Carol (Mickey). He was an infantry captain, seeing action in the South Pacific during World War II, and was awarded the Bronze Star. A Notre Dame graduate, he served in the state legislature and as President and CEO of Peoples Trust Bank. He was instrumental, along with American Electric Power (I & M) officials, in the construction of 'One Summit Square,' presently the tallest building in downtown Fort Wayne.

Donnelly P. McDonald family 1947

Mary Larene Patricia (Pat) McDonald married George Clement Keller III in 1947. They had seven children: George Patrick, Mary Larene, Sarah Margaret, Peter Michael, John David, Mark Clement, and Anne Elizabeth. A graduate of St. Teresa of Winona, Minnesota, Pat moved with George and family to Wawatosa, Wisconsin.

Josephine Ellen Emily (Joellen) McDonald (1928-1970) married Herman Ankenbruck in 1951. They moved to Ann Arbor, Michigan. They had six children: Ellen Francis, Ruth Larene, James Matthew, Terese Ann, Erin Margaret, and Kathryn Sue. They divorced in 1968. Joellen was a graduate of St. Teresa, a bridge "Life Master," and one of the first lady stockbrokers in Michigan.

Francis Travers (Trav) McDonald, was the fourth and youngest child. He married Alicia Messing of Annette, Alaska, in 1956. She was originally from Philadelphia, Pennsylvania. They had five children: Cecile Maureen (1957-1962), Sheila Larene, Patrick Henry, Mary Travers, and Kathleen Sue. He served in the Coast Guard Air Sea Rescue during the Korean conflict. He retired in 1988 as Vice President at Summit Bank.

The Peoples Trust and Savings Company clock

Two sets of twins and red hair have surfaced among a group of twenty-eight great grandchildren. Life continues! Whatever happened to The Peoples Trust & Savings Company? There was a name change to Peoples Trust Bank, then a merger with the Indiana Bank in 1983 to become Summit Bank, then a merger with Anthony Wayne Bank in 1987. Next, in 1992, it merged with National Bank of Detroit, then merged in 1995 with First National Bank of Chicago, next Bank One, and is now merged with J. P. Morgan/Chase as of July 4, 2004. It is one of the largest banks in the country. Don't ask about the 'clock'!

Submitted by Travers McDonald

ELIJAH (FLUTE) MCDONALD

Elijah (Flute) McDonald was born in Texarkana, Arkansas. He moved to Fort Wayne with his mother, Eliza Palmer, in 1921. He was a graduate of Central High School. Shortly after high school, he married Bertha McClendon. The couple had seven children: Bobby McDonald, deceased; Peggy Odom, deceased; Jessie Parker, deceased; and Ernest McDonald, deceased. Other children of that union include Marlene McDonald, Elizabeth Brown and Sharon McDonald.

While raising seven children, the couple owned and operated The Huddle Bar-B-Que (for almost 30 years), famous for it's unique and delicious sauce, The Taste Freeze Ice Cream Parlor, and the Playboy Recreation, all located in the thirteen hundred block of Lafayette Street, better known as" The Avenue". He never closed The Huddle on Sundays or holidays. He said there may be some people who had no family or home and they may need a warm smile, a cup of coffee or just get in out of the cold. Mr. McDonald had established a city wide and out of state customer base to whom he delivered on a weekly basis for his restaurant. This included individuals as well as businesses. He also had another weekly delivery service. He delivered faithfully *The Jet* (15 cents), *The Ebony* (35 cents), *The Pittsburgh Courier* and *The Chicago Defender* for years, come rain, sleet, snow or sunshine. His customers were city wide. He owned several housing units which were always occupied by excellent tenants. He also worked at The International Harvester for 27 years until his health started to fail.

He was a member and first black sponsor of The Good Times Bowling League which received numerous first place trophies. The league was the first black league to use The Scott Bowling Alley which was located in downtown Fort Wayne on Calhoun Street. He was inducted into The Bowlers Hall Of Fame.

Mr. McDonald loved God and never forgot his Mother's teachings about God and to serve Him faithfully. He was never too busy to serve God. He joined The Union Baptist Church when it was still on Brackenridge Street. He was a faithful member of the church and a member of its male chorus. He loved to sing and use his baritone voice. He remained faithful to God, his family, customers and friends until his passing in 1975. He was always willing, ready and able to lend a helping hand especially to the less fortunate.

Submitted by Sharon McDonald

MCDOUGALL-ROUSH FAMILY

John and Rachel Hall McDougall left Fort Edward, Washington County. New York, in 1836-37 to join the pioneers moving west. They had seven children: Alexander, Thomas, Jane, John, Susan, Henry, and William. They settled in Mansfield, Ohio, for five years. Three more children were born in Mansfield: George, Robert, and Theodore. In 1842, they moved the family to Fort Wayne, Jefferson Township, Allen County, Indiana.

According to family stories, in the spring of 1843 the land was too wet to farm. John, his sons, and neighbors worked together digging ditches to drain the land. Unfortunately, mosquitoes that carried yellow fever came in great swarms. John's oldest son, Alexander, died of yellow fever in June 1843. The next year, in October 1844, John also died of yellow fever. This left Rachel, who was expecting another child, to carry on as best as she could. That child, Lucinda, was born later in 1844 in Wells County. The farm was put up for auction in July 1845, and their son, Thomas, made arrangements with the county to pay off the debt.

Soon after, the older children married. Thomas married Lavina Doyle on May 22, 1845; Sarah Jane married Philetus Clark on December 18, 1845; and Susan married James Martin on June 6, 1850.

With the onset of the Civil War, Henry, William, George, and Theodore enlisted in the Northern Army. Theodore was a drummer. Henry, William, and George stayed in the army after the war and served in the western Indian Wars. Also, after that war, three more children married: Robert to Sarah Bumpus on July 19, 1866; Lucinda to Peter Kaylor on March 23, 1871, and finally, Theodore, who had come home to live with his McDougall-Roush Family mother, married Martha Jane Roush on November 6,1869, in Wells County. Martha came to Allen County to live with Theodore and his mother.

Both the McDougalls and the Roush families had immigrated to the colonies around 1740. The McDougalls came from the Isle of Islay, Argyleshire, Scotland, and the Roush family from the Palatine area of Germany. The McDougalls settled in New York State and the Roushs in the Shenandoah Valley in Virginia. Both families supported the Revolutionary War cause and had soldiers in service.

When the Roush family joined the pioneers moving west, they came down the Ohio River on flat boats. Some family members settled in Ohio. The Philip Roush-Sarah Brenneman family came to Wells County, Indiana, around 1835. Their granddaughter, Martha Jane, the oldest child of their son, St. Clair, married Theodore McDougall on November 6, 1869, and joined Theodore and his mother on a farm in Allen County. Theodore and Martha had ten children, all born on this farm. The children's names were: Lester Martin, Mary Cecelia, Electa Jane, Foster Robert, Nettie Georgiana, Edna Bell, Harvey Davis, Henry Balis, Bert St. Clair, and Cleona Myrtle. They all lived, and married between 1895 and 1916. They married the following spouses: Lester married Neoma Allen; Mary married Joseph Soelinger; Electa married Rufus Hawk; Foster married Alice Toup; Nettie married Phillip Bouillon; Edna married Edward Halter; Harvey married Maud (McCormick) Johnson; Henry married Mary Ort; Bert married Ethel Harding; and Cleona married Grover Guillaume.

Theodore and Martha McDougall family 1891. L to R front row: Harvey, Cleona, Bert. Second row: Mary Cecilia, Father Theodore, Mother Martha, Edna, Henry. Third row: Electa, Lester, Foster, Nettie.

On October 10, 1876, Theodore's mother, Rachel, died. She was buried in the IOOF Cemetery in New Haven, Indiana. Theodore was an early member of the New Haven IOOF. He also was a member of the Bass-Lawton Post #40 G.A.R.

In 1891, Theodore and Martha moved the family to a farm on Schwartz Road in Allen County. They both were early members of the Taylor Chapel Methodist Church. The little white frame church stood in the corner of the Harding farm on Maysville Road. It was the scene of many McDougall weddings and funerals. A number of years ago, the congregation built a new church across the road.

Theodore's son, Bert, married Ethel Harding and farmed the Harding farm for many years. That farm is now part of the Chapel Ridge Shopping Complex.

Theodore's daughter, Cleona, married Grover Guillaume, and they stayed home to farm the McDougall farm. They raised three children there, and purchased the farm in 1919.

Theodore died on the farm on January 23, 1930. Martha died at the home of her daughter, Electa Jane Hawk, on August 20, 1941. The McDougall-Guillaume farm is the land upon which the Promise Lutheran Church was built on the Schwartz Road. Theodore and Martha Jane had ten children, 35 grandchildren, and 54 great grandchildren.

When the children married or left home, a tradition was started. Everyone was to come celebrate Theodore's birthday on July 4. While a fourth of July birthday party is no longer held, 2005 will mark the 108th McDougall family reunion!

Submitted by Lois Ann Bouillon Gooley Granddaughter of Nettie Georgiana McDougall and Phillip Bouillon, Daughter of Edith Reid and Lloyd Bouillon

NANCY HARTMAN STUART MCELWAIN FAMILY

Nancy (Hartman) McElwain was born to Maurice and Iona (Willig) Hartman, life-long Fort Wayne residents. They were sweethearts at Central Catholic High School and at their parents' cottages, in Rome City. Maurice became a Nickel Plate railroad engineer and Iona the perfect wife, and then mother of Maurine, Nancy, Maurice D. (Mickey) and Terry.

Nancy remembers a wonderful childhood, climbing trees, riding bikes and going to movies with her sweet sister, Maurine. Nancy attended St. Joseph and Sacred Heart Catholic grade schools and was toying with the idea of becoming a nun. The Lord had a different plan for her. After Central Catholic High School, she went to Purdue in West Lafayette. Her ideas began to change. She wanted to travel or maybe become an airline stewardess. Something wonderful happened at Purdue's Newman Club. Nancy met the love of her life, Stuart McElwain. They married in 1962, left dear old Fort Wayne, and were off to travel! Nancy happily became an Air Force officer's wife and mom for the next twenty years.

Stuart was born to Robert and Norma McElwain and grew up in Edwardsville, Illinois. Robert was an accountant for Union Electric in St. Louis. Stuart's mother, Norma, was a part time substitute teacher. Stuart and his younger brother, Bob, remember eating Grandma Stuart's wonderful pies, riding their bikes and going to Edwardsville High.

The Air Force life was a good! Stuart liked his job as aircraft maintenance officer. Nancy enjoyed being the traditional 1960s supporting Air Force Wife. She really enjoyed being a mother, baking cookies and going to the parks. Kathleen and Kelly were born two months early and only eight months apart, possibly a world record!

Stuart and Nancy McElwain

Their first four years were in Alexandria, Louisiana (England AFB) before Stuart went to Viet Nam. It was different living in the South in the 1960s and being a "Yankee", but all adapted well. The McElwain family lived in New York, Maine, Alabama, North Dakota, and, finally Castle AFB, Merced, California, in 1974. After 20 years, Air Force, Major Stuart McElwain retired in 1981. Stuart became Merced County's purchasing agent for another 20 years.

In Merced, Kathleen and Kelly were growing up, and going to high school and college. Nancy got her BA and Masters degree from Cal State University, in Education. Nancy truly enjoyed teaching English, reading and Developmental education classes for the next 26 Years at Merced College.

Retired, Stu and Nancy just returned from Italy and will be coming to Fort Wayne in the fall of 2005. Stu enjoys golfing and Barbershop harmonizing. Both love square dancing.

Kathleen McElwain has been enjoying teaching second grade for 13 years. She is delighted with her Merced home and garden. Kathleen is finishing her doctorate degree in Education.

Youngest daughter, Kelly, with husband Kevin Pound and their four children, live in Nampa, Idaho on a five acre ranch with eight horses. Kelly likes her work as a deputy sheriff correctional officer. Kyle is 17, Kerry 16, Kacey 12, and Kody 10.

The Hartman, McElwain family has been truly blessed! Nancy is proud to have been raised as a Hoosier in Fort Wayne.

Submitted by Stu and Nancy McElwain

SUSAN (MORRIS) MCGEE

Susan Christine Morris was born May 1, 1946 in Fort Wayne, the daughter of John Wesford and Lois (Baker) Morris. She first was a pupil at the original three room Riverside Elementary School, attended Forest Park school for a transition year and was among the first students to attend the new Lakeside Junior High. She was a student at North Side High while Johnny's Hamburger and Malt Shop was still in operation next door. While at North Side, she won several art awards, chief among them being the Suedhoff-Schiele Trophy.

Susan then became one of the first students to attend the newly opened Fort Wayne campus of IUPU where she majored in English and was active in the "PIT" (Purdue-Indiana Theater) group. While working part time at Lincoln National Life, she answered a newspaper ad to interview for United Air Lines, and after training in Chicago, was domiciled in New York as a flight attendant. During a nationwide airline strike, she returned to Chicago where she married Bertram E. Kisselburg, Jr. Barely a year later, he was killed in an automobile accident and Susan returned to Fort Wayne. During a visit with a friend to Fort Knox, Kentucky, she met her second husband. After leaving Fort Knox, they moved to Michigan where her two sons were born: Ryan P. McGee (nee Anderson, 1971) and Colin C. McGee (nee Anderson, 1972). After a divorce in 1977, Susan and her children moved to Sarasota, Florida where she planned to devote her energies in pursuit of an art career. It was here that she met and married Ronald R. McGee, Lt. Col. (U.S. Army, Retired) in 1982.

Since that time, Susan's paintings have appeared in numerous national art publications including the Watercolor Page of *American Artist Magazine*, a feature article in *Watercolor Magazine*, and appearances in *International Art Magazine*, *Southwest Art Magazine* and the old *U.S. Art Magazine* among others. Her work was selected for inclusion in such books as *Splash 3: 105 of America's Best Contemporary Watercolorists and Arts From The Parks - 74 Artists Celebrate North America's National Parks*. She has had one or more paintings chosen in eight separate years for inclusion in the Top 100 group in the National Arts For the Parks annual touring exhibition headquartered in Jackson Hole, Wyoming. In the year 2000, she earned the Silver Medallion as the national Region III winner. She has also received top awards in such shows as the American Artist Magazine Golden Anniversary exhibition in New York, the Art Quest '88 National Touring Exhibition and the Knickerbocker Artists Annual in New York City. Other important national exhibitions have included the annual shows of the National Watercolor Society, The Chautauqua National (New York), the Salmagundi Club Non-Member (New York City), the Catherine Lorillard Wolfe National (New York City), the American Realism Exhibition and numerous showings and awards in the annuals of the Southern and Midwest Watercolor Societies as well as the Florida, Montana and many local watercolor society exhibitions. She has been honored with several one and two artist shows nationally and is an elected member of the National League of American Pen Women and the Petticoat Painters, the oldest women's painting group in the state of Florida.

For over twelve years, Susan has been researching and compiling an illustrated history and genealogy of her Taggart family who were pioneer settlers in Jackson, Lawrence, Bartholomew and Brown counties, Indiana. This book includes many associated families and is currently in the publication process. She has long been a member and frequent officer in the National Society, Daughters of the American Revolution and is a member of the National Society of Colonial Dames of the 17th Century, the Society of Indiana Pioneers and the Indiana Historical Society. She is a part time resident of both Sarasota, Florida and Flathead County, Montana. She returns to Fort Wayne whenever possible to visit her father at the family home.

Submitted by Susan C. Morris McGee

DONALD HARRY COOK MCKEEMAN, M.D. & EULA RUDDELL FAMILY

Donald H.C. McKeeman was born in Fort Wayne, Indiana on January 12, 1904 to Robert B. McKeeman, M.D. and Susie May Hocker McKeeman. Don's siblings were Leland Stanford, Lillian Theodosia and Ruth B. McKeeman. Don attended Minor School and Fort Wayne High School. In 1922 he went to Indiana University and graduated in 1926, after which he attended Indiana School of Medicine, where he met student nurse, Eula Ruddell, from Sullivan, Indiana. On June 11,1929 they married in Sullivan. Eula was the daughter of George Ira Ruddell, grocer in Sullivan and Mary Ann Donnelly Ruddell who was born in England.

Don was graduated from medical school in 1931 and was licensed to practice medicine in Allen County, Indiana on August 3, 1931. Marilyn was born on January 30, 1932.

Don's father died March 4,1937 in Fort Wayne. Charlotte Sue was born in 1938 when the family was living at 633 West Wayne Street. The family later moved to 1615 Ardmore Avenue. In 1943 Don served with the U.S. Army Medical Corps as a surgeon, in France (Normandy invasion), Belgium (Battle of the Bulge) and Aachen, Germany. He was discharged in 1945. He returned to Fort Wayne and resumed his medical practice until he retired. He was on the staff of St. Joseph's Hospital. Don's Mother died on May 7, 1962. Charlotte Sue died in May 1973, unmarried. Eula died on May 8, 1985, and Don died two months later, July 4, 1985. They are buried in Lindenwood Cemetery. Their daughter Marilyn married Richard Farquhar in 1954 and divorced in 1988, and she has lived in Santa Fe, New Mexico for 41 years.

Submitted by Marilyn Farquhar.

LELAND STANFORD MCKEEMAN, M.D. & GRACE (KEENAN) MCKEEMAN FAMILY

Leland Stanford "Stan" McKeeman was born November 28, 1898 in Monroe, Adams County, Indiana to Robert B. McKeeman, M.D. and Susie May Hocker. In 1900 the family moved to Fort Wayne, Indiana where Dr. McKeeman set up his practice at 79 Broadway. Stan was baptized at Third Presbyterian Church on December 1, 1901. Stan's siblings were Lillian Theodosia, Donald Harry Cook, and Ruth Beatrice. In 1903 the family lived at 2103 South Broadway. They were active in Third Presbyterian Church, and in 1910 Stan became a communicant. The family moved to 2020 Broadway and the children attended Minor School. Stan attended high school at Fort Wayne (Central) High School. He was on the baseball and bowling teams. In 1914 Stan was the president of his senior class. He was in Pi Gamma Fraternity and appeared as the lead opposite Helen Scott in the Senior play, "All a Mistake." On June 15, 1917 Stan graduated from Fort Wayne High School.

Stan entered Indiana University at Bloomington, Indiana. In 1918 he enlisted in the United States Navy and was stationed at Boulder, Colorado. On December 23, 1918 he was honorably discharged. In 1922 Stan graduated with an A.B. degree from Indiana University. In 1924 he graduated from Indiana University Medical School with an M.D. degree. He did his internship at Indianapolis General Hospital. On July 1, 1925 Stan applied to practice medicine in Allen County, Indiana.

Stan married Mary Grace Keenan at the Cathedral on December 27, 1926. "Grace" was the daughter of the owner of the Keenan Hotel, Hugh Keenan and Mary Moffett Keenan, both formerly of Scranton, Pennsylvania. The couple had a son named Leland Stanford. The family belonged to St. Joseph's Catholic Church. Stan was a member of the American Legion Post 47, the Fort Wayne Country Club, Indiana University Alumni Club, and the Chamber of Commerce. In 1930 Stan became the Allen County coroner. Grace Joan and Mary Ellen were born. On March 4, 1937 Stan's father died. Stan occupied his father's office at 347 West Berry, continuing his practice for 36 years. He as on the staff at St. Joseph's Hospital.

Stan was a member of the Allen County Medical Society, the American Medical Association, the Industrial Medical Association, and the Central States Society of Industrial Medicine and Surgery. He enjoyed pike and bass fishing. The family lived on Covington Road.

From 1941 to 1947 Stan was the examining physician for the Selective Service. From 1951 to 1955 he was a member of the Selective Service Board of Appeals. He was the President of the staff at St. Joseph's Hospital.

On May 7, 1962 Stan's mother died. Stan's death followed on October 7, 1962. He was stricken with a heart attack at his home at 7701 Covington Road.

Grace lived in Fort Wayne until her death on January 22, 1990. The couple is buried at the Catholic Cemetery.

Submitted by Mary Ellen (Mrs. Edward) Rice

ROBERT BENJAMIN MCKEEMAN

Robert Benjamin McKeeman was the twelfth child of David Charles McKeeman and Margaret Ann McConahey. David and Margaret immigrated to America in 1851 from Bally o'Glaugh by Mosside and Deffrick in County Antrim, Ireland. Robert was born on February 27, 1874 in Hoagland, Madison Township, Allen County, Indiana. His mother was 45 and his father 53 when Robert was born. David lived only for two years after the birth of Robert. The young lad lived on the family farm near Hoagland and attended public school.

Robert loved academic studies and attended Taylor University in Upland, Indiana and the Indiana State Normal School in Marion, Indiana. He taught school in his native county from 1892 to 1894. In 1894 he enrolled in the Fort Wayne Medical College, graduating in 1897. There were 16 students in his medical class.

Robert established a practice in Monroe in Adams County, Indiana. In Monroe he met Susie May Hocker, born May 13, 1880, the daughter of Joseph Hocker, the local druggist, and Jesteen Sunier. The marriage was on October 5, 1897 at the home of Ed and Maggie Coffee in Decatur, Indiana. The couple resided in Monroe in a cottage behind Susie's father's drugstore.

Robert and Susie McKeeman

The first child, Leland Stanford McKeeman, was born on November 28, 1898. Robert and Susie moved to Fort Wayne, Indiana in 1900 where Dr. McKeeman hung out his first shingle at 1608 Calhoun Street. Lillian Theodosia was born on July 11, 1901. The family lived on Creighton Avenue near Fox for a short time but soon moved to Broadway near the railroad. Their next home was at 2020 Broadway, and Dr. McKeeman operated his office out of the home.

On January 12, 1904 a second son was born, Donald Harry Cook McKeeman. The family attended the Third Presbyterian Church at the corner of Creighton and DeWald Streets along with many of the other families of the McKeeman clan. On April 13, 1902 Dr. McKeeman became an elder in the church and all of the children were baptized there. Ruth Beatrice was born on April 18, 1907.

Dr. McKeeman was a member of the Scottish Rite, a 32nd degree Mason, and a Republican. He belonged to the American Medical Association, the Indiana State Medical Society, the Fort Wayne Academy of Medicine and he was the vice-president of the Fort Wayne Medical Society.

The children attended Minor School and the Fort Wayne High School. The family spent the summers at Clear Lake. In 1921 a new house was built at 721 Packard Avenue. At that time Dr. McKeeman moved his office into the Wayne Pharmacy Building at the corner of Berry and Ewing.

Robert conducted the practice of medicine until a few days before his death from influenza on March 4, 1937 at age 63 years and 5 days. Funeral services were conducted at the family residence by Rev. William N. Vincent of the Third Presbyterian Church with only the family and members of the Fort Wayne Medical Society attending. Burial was at Lindenwood Cemetery with pallbearers: Dr. Herbert N. Senseny, Dr. Lynn W. Elston, Dr. E.M. VanBuskirk, Dr. Philip S. Titus, Dr. Edward H. Schlegel and Dr. M.B. Catlett.

Minutes of the Fort Wayne Medical Society:

Whereas, Dr. R.B. McKeeman was an honored and respected member of the Fort Wayne Medical Society, a man noted for his honesty, integrity and fair dealings with his patients, his colleagues and people at large, and,

Whereas, Dr. R.B. McKeeman typified the ideal family physician who has played such a great role in the development of our American domestic and social life, and,

Whereas, Dr. R.B. McKeeman in his devotion to his patents spared no effort or sacrifice on his part, and,

Whereas, Dr. R.B. McKeeman always displayed the keenest interest in the progress of medicine, and,

Whereas, Dr. R.B. McKeeman was an outstanding member and vice-president of the Fort Wayne Medical Society,

Be It Resolved, That the Fort Wayne Medical Society record its most profound sorrow at the irreparable loss it has sustained, that it express its deepest sympathy to the bereaved family, that these resolutions be spread upon the minutes of the society, and that a copy thereof be forwarded to the bereaved widow.

Robert's brothers William, David and Alex, and a sister, Nancy, and his four children survived him. Susie May lived until May 7, 1962. She was buried alongside Robert at Lindenwood Cemetery.

Submitted by Jane Hunter Hodgson

WILLIAM F. & JOAN B. MCNAGNY FAMILV

William F. McNagny was born in Fort Wayne, Indiana on January 21, 1922. His great grandfather, Alexander Steele McNagny, was born in Pennsylvania in 1815 and came to Whitley County, Indiana in the 1830s. His grandfather, William F. McNagny, was born April 19, 1850 in Larwill, Indiana. He became one of the state's leading trial lawyers. He also served in Congress and was a law partner of Vice President Tom Marshall in Columbia City, Indiana. He and his wife, Elizabeth Wunderlich, had two sons - Judge Rob McNagny of Columbia City and Phil McClellan McNagny of Fort Wayne, also an outstanding trial lawyer in the state. He was born in 1886 and served in the State Legislature and rose to the rank of Major in World War I.

William And Joan B. McNagny in the garden at "Crestwood", Fort Wayne, Indiana

In 1920, Phil McNagny married Lucy McIntosh Cole, born September 14, 1900, in Marietta, Georgia. They moved to Fort Wayne after the death of his father, August 24, 1923. They had four children, William F., Phil, Jr., Bayard, and Lucy Ellison.

William F. attended Culver Military Academy on the Alumni Scholarship and graduated first in his class as had his father. He attended Swarthmore College, leaving at age 19 to serve three years in the Army during World War II with the rank of First Lieutenant. He graduated

William F. McNagny Family: L to R, back row: Eric and Lindsay Potthast, Charles and Deborah McNagny, Sally and Robert McNagny-Green, Joyce and Michael Critelli, Mike Critelli. Front row: Ryan McNagny, Joan McNagny, Courtney Green, Lachlan Green, Wm. McNagny, Nathan Green, Kaherine Critelli, James Critelli

from Indiana School of Law, first in his class and Order of the Coif, and joined his father's law firm Barrett, Barrett & McNagny, in 1947.

In 1949, in Fort Wayne, Indiana, he married Joan Elizabeth Buesching (born November 19, 1923), daughter of long-time President of The Lincoln National Bank and Trust Company, Charles H. Buesching (born March 6, 1889 in Fort Wayne) and Lillian Charlotte Busch (born November 25, 1989). Joan's grandfather, Frederick H. Buesching, came to Fort Wayne from Heddesdorf, Germany at age 20 in 1883. He started a construction company, and on April 30, 1885 married Johanna Hagerman, born in Liebenau, Germany. They had 12 children. As his company grew, Johanna invited her 14 year old brother, William Hagerman, to come from Germany and live with and work for her husband. The Buesching-Hagerman Construction Company built the Lincoln Bank Tower in 1929. It was the tallest building in Indiana for many years. Joan's grandfather on her mother's side, was born in 1838 in Hesse Darmstadt, Germany and her grandmother, Elizabeth Lange, was born in 1846 in Buckebury, Schaumburg Lippe. They eloped and sailed to New York City in 1866 going on to Fort Wayne, Indiana. They had nine children. John was a cabinet maker carving, among others, the altar and interior of Emanuel Lutheran Church in Fort Wayne.

Joan was educated in the Fort Wayne Public Schools. She graduated from Swarthmore College, Cum Laude and member of Mortar Board. Before her marriage, she was Book Editor of the *Annals of the American Academy of Political Social Science* in Philadelphia.

Bill and Joan rejoice in their family and have traveled extensively with them. They have three children. Charles William is an attorney in Fort Wayne, who graduated from Culver Military Academy, Harvard College and Indiana University School of Law and has a Masters Degree in Tax from Georgetown University. He has served on several community boards and is presently President of the Fort Wayne Park Board. He is married to Deborah Tesch, an RN. Joyce McNagny-Critelli, an attorney in Darien, Connecticut, graduated from Emma Willard and Swarthmore College and is married to Michael J. Critelli, CEO of Pitney Bowes. Dr. Sally McNagny-Green, an Internist and Vice President of The Medical Foundation in Boston graduated from the International School in Geneva, Stanford University (Phi Beta Kappa) and the Harvard Medical School. She is married to Dr. Robert C. Green, Professor of Neurology, Genetics and Epidemiology at Boston University. They live in Wellesley, Massachusetts. There are seven grandchildren -Michael, James and Katherine Critelli, Nathan, Courtney and Lachlan Green, Ryan William McNagny and two step-grandchildren - Eric and Lindsay Potthast.

From 1947 until his retirement as Senior Partner of Barrett & McNagny in 1993, Bill was active in the trial practice. He is a member of the Local, State and American Bar Associations and is a Fellow of the Indiana and American Bar Foundations. He is also a Fellow of the American College of Trial Lawyers and a member of the International Academy of Trial Lawyers. He is a Diplomat of the Indiana Defense Lawyers and a member of the Indiana Law Academy of Alumni Fellows. He served as Chairman and Director of the State Board of Law Examiners for five years.

He was General Counsel for The Lincoln National Bank and Trust Company and served for 35 years on its Board of Directors. He also served for many years as a Director and Secretary of Devils Hollows Corp. He was also Chairman and Director of the Advisory Board of American Trust and Management Company.

He has served on numerous community boards - as President of the Fort Wayne Art Institute and the Urban League, as a member of the Allen County Public Library Foundation, the Fort Wayne Historical Society, the Fort Wayne Community Foundation, the Historical Landmark Foundation, the Fort Wayne Fine Arts Foundation, the Civic Theatre, and a Trustee of the Y.W.C.A. He served as President and one of the founding Directors of the Wawasee Area Conservancy Foundation. He served on the Governing Board of Indiana Purdue Fort Wayne from 1975 to 1993. He was awarded the Broyles Medal by the Indiana Alumni Association. He is a 33rd Degree Mason, a member of the DeMoley Legion of Honor, a member of the David Parrish Post of the American Legion, the Quest Club, a Kentucky Colonel, and a member of the St. Andrews Society of Philadelphia.

Joan works in the field of education, including service on the Indiana State Board of Education, a member of The Governor's Commission on Youth Employment, and The Governor's Task Force on Citizenship Education. She was a member of the Adult Literacy Coalition and the Indiana Curriculum Advisory. She was a delegate to the White House Conferences on the Family and facilitator for the Governor's White House Conference on Children and Youth. She spent six weeks in Leningrad as guest of the Soviet Department of Education and three weeks in China with education leaders. Her main dedication was to Ivy Tech State College whose Board she joined in 1972. She served as a Trustee and as President until going on its Foundation, where she continues in 2004.

She was a Board member and President of the Indiana Public Broadcasting Society and also served on the Board of Fort Wayne Public Broadcasting. She was President of the Indiana Lawyers Auxiliary and also as President of the American Bar Auxiliary of the American Bar Association. The Indiana Bar chose her for the Lady Sarah Blackstone Award, and the Junior League, of which she was President, presented her with the Volunteer of the Year Award. She has been awarded three Sagamore of the Wabash awards by Indiana Governors.

Both Bill and Joan are members of the First Presbyterian Church. Their club memberships include The Summit Club, the Fort Wayne Country Club, The Union League Club of Chicago, the Indianapolis Columbia Club, and the Country Club of Naples.

The McNagnys make their home in Fort Wayne, Indiana, and at their vacation homes at Lake Wawasee and in Naples, Florida.

Submitted by Joan B. McNagny

MCNETT FAMILY

Bert McNett was born June 20, 1890. Parepa Hope Walker was born January 10, 1894. Both were born in Steuben County, Indiana. They met at a county fair and married New Year's Day, January 1, 1912. They had their first child, John Walker, on November 20, 1912. Then on January 28, 1914, George Sylvester was born. Three years later, on October 2, 1917, Lou Rose was born. A year later, on December 20, 1918, Roy Lynn was born.

About 1920, the family moved from their Steuben County Hampshire Hog Farm to a house on Calhoun Street in Fort Wayne. On May 4, 1923, a snowy day, Richard Joseph was born. Then on December 10, 1924, Lawrence Scott was born. About that same year the family moved to 1203 Cresent Avenue.

In the meantime Bert had attended International Business College to learn some business skills toward becoming a real estate salesman. His next move was to join the City and Suburban Real Estate firm. They sold many lots for building in the Indian Village area. While dealing in real estate, Bert listed the old Taylor farm of 110 acres northeast of Fort Wayne. Bert and Parepa liked the farm with woods, creeks and large fields so much they moved their family there in 1930. It was a good place to raise a large family.

The three older children, Walker, George and Lou Rose, attended North Side High School. Roy attended Leo High while Richard and Lawrence

Bert, Parepa, John, George, Rose, Roy, Richard, and Lawrence McNett, 1939.

went to New Haven High School. About the time of World War II, the young men joined the various military services.

For about twenty-five years, Bert and Parepa with some help from their children worked the fields and truck garden areas of the farm. Bert's favorite livestock were purebred Hampshire Hogs, Short Horn cattle, and Border and Scotch Collie dogs. In the late 1950s, Bert and Parepa held an auction sale and sold their farm. They moved into semi-retirement at cottage #68 at Lake Gage. Bert continued to sell real estate in the lake area.

The McNett children all married. John Walker married Lois Burden, a beauty contest winner. George married Florence Bahde, Bert's real estate office secretary. Lou Rose married a local farmer, Ralph Guillaume. Roy married Lois Cameron, a beauty shop owner. Richard married Gloria Lutz and Lawrence married Mildred Claussen of Rensselar, Indiana.

Now in place of the Old Taylor Farm lie the new Meijer Store, Menard Store, and the Chapel Ridge Shopping Center. Above the front door of the Taylor farmhouse was the inscription "Chandler Post Office". Now all gone.

Submitted by Richard J. McNett.

MCNULTY - KEGELMANN FAMILY

The first family members to arrive in America were John and Ellen Owens from Ireland. According to Indiana land records they purchased forty acres in Lake Township, Allen County, for $55.00 in 1839. Their home was a log cabin. Indians visited it occasionally, trading wild game for flour or sugar. The 1850 census states they had four children: Ellen, born August 5, 1842, Michale (sic), Margaret and Jeremiah. Ellen became a servant in Fort Wayne and lived at 144 East Main.

William McNulty, born July 11, 1840, in Ireland, lived through the potato famine and arrived in Oswego, New York on July 18, 1863, according to his naturalization record which is dated October 9, 1866. City Directories list him as a shoemaker as does his advertisement in the state Gazetteers of the late 1800s. William boarded at 86 East Main, not far from Ellen's address. They were married in the Cathedral on November 24, 1868.

Ellen died eleven years later at the age of 36. She left four children, the youngest of whom died less than a year later. The eldest child was John Charles, born in 1870. The 1880 census lists John as twelve and his two younger brothers, Charles and William as five and three.

The McNulty - Kegelmann family began with the marriage of John Charles McNulty (1870-1941) to Catherine Anna Kegelmann (1873-1963) at St. Mary's Catholic Church on February 23, 1892. John was 22 and Kate was 19. They moved to Omaha in 1893. Accompanying their brother and sister-in-law were John's two brothers, Charles, 18 and William, 16. They had already been a part of John's family. By 1897 John was listed in the Omaha city directory as the owner of a saloon, the Emerald, with his brother Charles listed as bartender. Their father, William McNulty Sr. had died in 1894 at the age of 54. He had lived through a famine and may have lost family members to starvation. In Indiana he never talked to his family about life in Ireland.

The Kegelmann half of this family began with emigration of Julius to Fort Wayne, arriving on Christmas Day in 1871. Julius was born on June 5, 1841 in Bayern, an alternative name for Bavaria. His immigration paper says he was born in Germany. His future wife, Anna Lembach, followed him and they were married on May 20, 1872. These two Catholics probably could not speak English as their wedding is recorded at St. John's Lutheran Church and other events in their life took place in Catholic churches.

Their first child was Catherine Anna Kegelmann, (born September 10, 1873). Katie, as she was known, was just a child with a younger brother when her mother died. Her father, Julius, then sent to Germany for Anna's sister to come and help with the children and they married soon after. The step-mother's name was Lena, but she asked people to call her Caroline.

John Charles McNulty and Catherine Anna Kegelmann Witnesses: Mr. Peter and Mrs. Emma Rothe

Julius had obtained land on the old Fort Wayne Street, now Wayne Street, near the corner of Anthony Boulevard, Walton Avenue at the time. The family home was on the South side of Wayne and he established a mattress factory across the street. Just as William did, Julius advertised his business in the state gazetteer. The Wabash and Erie Canal was just north of the factory and the materials used in the factory were delivered by canal. In later years Kate could remember sitting along the canal to watch the traffic. In 1898 Julius' son, Charles, aged 22, was injured in an accident at the factory. A machine part flew off and across the room hitting Charles in the head. The local paper referred to it as a "terrible havoc". He died later that day.

A few years later, on March 12, 1902, another tragedy was documented in the local papers. A fire had struck the factory just after delivery of new goods. All was lost. Julius died on March 23. His will listed the family property including the pots and pans. All was left to his wife, and she must have had to sell everything to pay for the mattress goods just delivered. She spent the rest of her life living with one or another of the children. The eldest child, Katie, had five step-sisters, Anna Myers, Elizabeth Phleiderer, Minnie Schramm, (whose husband purchased the mattress factory land and opened a garage) Mary Klingburger (sic) and Theresa Traxler, born between 1881 and 1893.

When Julius died, the eldest daughter, now Catherine McNulty of Omaha, returned to Fort Wayne by train with the children. She claimed she walked the whole distance as the baby, another Catherine, later known as Tuts, cried all the way. John sold what they had in Omaha and soon followed her to Fort Wayne. They bought a house on Lombard Street near the railroad tracks and John was soon walking along the tracks each day to reach General Electric on Anthony Boulevard. He became a molder and remained at G .E. until he retired. After they had built a cottage at Snow Lake he borrowed a G .E. truck to move furniture to the lake. Since he never drove, his friend, Roy Brown, drove the truck. Eleen reported on the trip to a niece writing "Mom, Tuts, Elmer, Jack (Tuts first son), and I came in the model T and we had 7 flat tires. When we got the 7th Elmer Bobay swore and said "I'll be dammed if I'll fix another tire". Tuts held the flashlight and Mom fixed the tire. We went for months before having another flat tire."

The grandchildren have since decided John and Kate could afford to build a cottage because John had a still in the basement. While he was working with the still Kate was in the kitchen scorching sugar to hide the smell. When Sheriff Steigerwald raided the house he really messed up the pantry but didn't find whiskey as it was hidden in the piano. Their grandchildren have many fond memories of visiting that cottage. A favorite happened once when the Grandparents took five of the grandchildren with them. Included were Rita, Jim and Tom Bobay and Patty and Jeanne McNulty. They were all in their Sunday best when they went to Angola for Mass. On the way home they started talking about getting out in the rowboat. As soon as Grandma eased the car up to a tree, they were out and running - yelling "Last one in is a monkey" - down the two sets of stairs to the pier, followed by a quick jump into the boat. Tom, the youngest, was last and he landed in the water wearing his best shoes, trousers, shirt and tie!

Kate and John's children were Sister Theodota (1893-mid 1980s), who taught school. John (1894-1971 in Mexico), Catherine (Tuts) (1898-1975), William (1900-1977), Bernard (1902-1992), and Eleen (1916-). John and his first wife, Frances, moved to Mexico where he opened a pop bottling business in his 60s. He had given up his first business, an automobile mechanic service when he entered the war effort at Wayne Company. When Frances died he married a native of Mexico, Regina. They had four children, some of whom live in Chicago. William moved to Milwaukee, married Catherine McConnell (in Kalamazoo, Michigan), and worked for a hosiery company. They owned McNulty's Bar in Milwaukee and had three children. William later returned to Fort Wayne and entered the real estate business. Catherine (Tuts) married Elmer Bobay and they had seven children. Bernard (while a traveling salesman) married Regina Reynolds of Ogden, Utah in Brigham City, Utah. They had three children, one born in Utah, and two after they moved to Fort Wayne around 1926. He was employed by International Harvester in the Engineering Department where he helped organize the union and was its first president. Eleen married Roger Pierson and they had one daughter. After

Roger died Eleen married Edward Hittner and they settled in Alamo, Texas.

The family stories related here came from Eleen and her mother Kate. Since the death of the first Ellen, wife of William, deaths have been reported in the Fort Wayne papers, which can be accessed at the Allen County Public Library as can the story of the tragedies at the mattress factory.

Submitted by Mary Jeanne McNulty Leffers

RICHARD C. MENGE

Richard C. Menge was born August 28, 1935 to Walter Otto Menge and Elsie Belle Cramer Menge in Ann Arbor, Michigan. Walter had been born in Buffalo, New York, to Jacob Menge and Elizabeth Hammelmann Menge. Richard, his sister, Joan Lou Menge, born April 2, 1931, and his mother and father moved to Fort Wayne in 1937. Walter, who had been a professor at the University of Michigan, took a job as an actuary for Lincoln National Life Insurance Company.

Richard (Dick) graduated from North Side High School in 1953, where he was Student Council President, and continued his education at the University of Michigan, graduating in 1957 with a B.S. in Psychology. The next two years were spent in the Army in Milwaukee, Wisconsin. Upon discharge as a First Lieutenant, Dick returned to the U of M, where he earned an MBA in 1961.

Richard C. Menge, 1980

Dick began his employment as a management trainee with Indiana Michigan Electric Company. He was first assigned as the Personnel Manager at the Tanner's Creek plant in Lawrenceburg, Indiana. Richard was then transferred as Personnel Manager of the Fort Wayne Division. and eventually became President of Indiana Michigan Electric Company. He retired in December, 1995.

Dick was a tireless volunteer for Trinity English Lutheran Church, Big Brothers/Big Sisters, Chamber of Commerce, Rotary, YMCA and many other organizations. He loved sports of all kinds, but especially enjoyed playing golf.

On July 1, 1961, Dick and Mary Carolyn Poe were married. Mary was born in Lima, Ohio, to Glenn William Poe and Winifred Anderson Poe on August 31, 1938. Her family included a sister, Virginia Ann Poe (Couch), and a brother, Alan Anderson Poe. They moved to Fort Wayne in 1945 when Glenn was transferred by the Soil Conservation Department. Mary was also a North Side High School graduate; she then graduated from Michigan State University. In 1986 she earned a Nursing Degree from IPFW, and worked at Neighborhood Health Clinics in Matemal and Child Health.

Dick and Mary had three children. David Cramer, born January 5, 1964, in Lawrenceburg, Indiana; Peter Richard, born August 18, 1965, in Fort Wayne; and Karen Ellen, born December 3, 1968, in Fort Wayne, Indiana. David graduated from Indiana University with a BA and Indiana Wesleyan with an MBA. He works as a bond trader for AEGON Insurance in Cedar Rapids. Iowa. Peter attended the University of Michigan, earning a PhD in nuclear engineering; he works at Bicron Labs near Chagrin Falls, Ohio. Karen graduated from Indiana University with a BA in Economics and from Purdue with a Masters in Business. She lives in West Lafayette, Indiana.

David and his wife, Pat Sprunger of New Haven, have a daughter, Marissa Elizabeth Cramer Menge, born March 18, 1995. Peter and his wife, Cynthia McGrae of Flint, Michigan, have a son, Madox Carver McGrae Menge, born February 2, 1998. Karen and her husband, Glenn Logan Jordan of England, Arkansas, have three children, Glenn Addison born June 4, 2000, Caroline Eliza born April 26, 2002, and Logan Palmer born June 16, 2004. Glenn Logan is Associate Dean of the Krannert Business School at Purdue.

Richard Cramer Menge died November 28, 1996 in Hong Kong, following a vacation.

Submitted by Mary M. Scrogham

WALTER O. MENGE

Walter was born in Buffalo, New York, on September 11, 1904. His parents were Jacob Henry August Menge and Fredricke Caroline Elizabeth Hammelmann Menge. Shortly after Walter's birth the family moved to Detroit, Michigan, where Jacob worked as a woodcarver. Walter had an older brother, Carlton Paul Henry Menge, and a younger brother, Milton Arthur Menge. All three sons graduated from the University of Michigan in actuarial science and went on to work for insurance companies.

On October 19, 1927, Walter and Elsie Belle Cramer were married. Elsie and her family were from West Branch, Michigan. They met at the Maccabees Insurance Company where Walter was doing some actuarial consulting and Elsie was working as a secretary. After graduating from the University of Michigan with a doctorate in Actuarial Science, Walter taught in that department for several years. During that time, he wrote a textbook, *The Mathematics of Life Insurance*, which is still in use today.

Walter and Elsie moved to Fort Wayne in 1937 where Walter took a position with the Lincoln National Life Insurance Company. He began as an actuary and eventually became President. He retired as Chairman of the Board in 1968. During his years in Fort Wayne, Walter was active in Trinity English Lutheran Church and economic development of the community.

Elsie died December 19, 1989, following a stroke. Walter died July 12, 2000, of pneumonia following surgery for a broken hip. Both are buried in Lindenwood Cemetery in Fort Wayne.

The Menges had two children, Joan Lou, born on April 2, 1931, and Richard Cramer born August 28, 1935; both were born in Ann Arbor, Michigan.

Walter O. Menge

Joan married Mark Allen Foreman on August 30, 1952. Mark was from Decatur, Indiana; they had three children, Paul Michael Foreman, Stephen Mark Foreman, and Walter Daniel Foreman. The Foreman family moved to Columbia, Missouri, in the early 1960s. Mark graduated from Purdue University in 1953 with a degree in Agriculture; Joan graduated from Stephens Women's College. Mark sold insurance for Lincoln Life and retired from his own agency in Columbia, Missouri.

Richard marrried Mary Carolyn Poe on July 1, 1961. Mary was born on August 31, 1938, in Lima, Ohio, to Glenn William and Winifred Anderson Poe. Her family moved to Fort Wayne in 1945. Richard graduated from the University of Michigan in 1961 with an MBA. He began his employment as a management trainee with Indiana Michigan Electric Company. He retired as President of I&M in December, 1995. Mary graduated in 1960 with a BA degree from Michigan State University. Dick and Mary had three children, David Cramer, Peter Richard, and Karen Ellen.

Walter and Elsie had five great-grandchildren, Marissa Menge, born to David Menge and Patricia Sprunger Menge, Madox McGrae Menge, born to Peter Menge and Cynthia McGrae, and Addison, Caroline and Palmer Jordan, born to Karen Menge Jordan and Glenn Logan Jordan. Son, Richard (Dick), died on November 28, 1996, in Hong Kong, following a vacation in China.

Submitted by Karen E. Jordan

JAMES LAWRENCE & ETHEL MAE (STEUP) MEURER

On September 25, 1912, James and his twin sister, Helen, were born to Margaret Amelia (Griffin) and Phillip Henry Meurer at home, 1904 Hillside Avenue. Jim was thought to be stillborn, but a neighbor wrapped him in towels and put him in a low-heat oven. The homemade incubator worked, and he survived even though he had double pneumonia and a broken shoulder. Several years later, Jim and Helen would cross the State Street Bridge towing a small wagon to his newspaper route along Spy Run and North Clinton.

After attending Lakeside Elementary and Cathedral Grade School, Jim became a messenger for Lincoln Life Insurance Company. In their late teens, Jim and two friends, Arnold and Gerhardt Bertram, drove a Model T Ford with

Jim and Ethel Meurer by the St. Joe River in 1941 with their Oldsmobile.

celluloid curtains to Mount Rushmore and back. As a young man, Jim participated in civil defense exercises at a tower along the St. Joe River; the tower later was used for training fire fighters.

Jim married on June 12, 1937. His wife, the former Ethel Mae Steup, was born May 10, 1910, to Harriet C. (Haight) and Louis H. Steup. Ethel attended Elmhurst Grade School and Fort Wayne Central High. She received a B.S. in Home Economics from Purdue University in 1932, and worked for several years at Allied Mills. The couple had one son, Philip Louis, born in 1949.

Jim enlisted in the U.S. Army in 1942, completing basic training in Golden, Colorado. He served in the 65th Military Police in North Africa; Marseilles and Lyon, France; and Corsica. A fellow M.P. with whom he became close friends was actor Douglas Fairbanks, Jr.

After the war, Jim worked in Lincoln Life's addressograph department. By the time he retired, after 42 years, he was the head of the computer department. Jim died on October 13, 1971 at age 59 and is buried in Lindenwood Cemetery.

In 1978, Ethel moved to Beaverton, Oregon, to be closer to her son, his wife Linda Lou (Whitacre, of Fort Wayne), and their two sons, James Lee and Gregory Robert. Ethel currently lives near her family in Bend, Oregon.

Submitted by Phil and Linda Meurer.

MARY MARGARET MEURER

Born at home, 1904 Hillside Avenue, on June 1, 1911, Mary was the first child of Phillip Henry and Margaret Amelia (Griffin) Meurer. Her only siblings, twins Helen Louise and James Lawrence, were born 15 months later.

As adults, children in the neighborhood reminisced about sledding down the steep hill that bordered the Hillside property. Some children would stop cars as other youngsters flew down the hill, across the street, and onto McDougal Avenue. Once, a young boy got off course, headed straight for the Meurer's house, then slid down the coal shute and over the coal pile into the basement! The sled cut his ear, causing him—almost rightfully—to think he was dying.

Mary attended Lakeside Elementary and Cathedral Grade School before graduating from St. Augustine's Academy "on Friday the 13th, 1930," as she often pointed out. As news of the bank failures leaked out later that year, Mary and her siblings lost all of their savings, $275 each.

Mary worked at both the Pioneer and Furnace Ice Cream plants and at Wayne Knitting Mill. Later, she was a statistical clerk for the Magnavox Corporation and in Lincoln National Corporation's Agency-Marketing Department. As a young woman, she traveled with friends to Kentucky; made several trips to Washington, DC; and went solo by train to visit her godparents in Montana. She also enjoyed taking lessons at Trier's Dancing School, spending weekends with family at Lake James, and riding the interurban to Russell's Point, Ohio, where she would spend weekends at Indian Lake.

While employed at Lincoln National, Mary began a lifelong habit of volunteer work visiting patients in hospitals and nursing homes. In 1973, she received the company's first Community Service Award. After 17 years, she retired, always looking forward to the annual retirement luncheon. She also was active in AARP and at the Perpetual Chapel of St. Jude's Catholic Church.

Many people know Mary Meurer for her lifelong volunteer work

Upon selling her car, she became a frequent user of the local bus system. Her photographs at bus stops were in the Fort Wayne newspaper from time to time. Her daily bus rides declined after a mini-stroke in 2003. An overnight stay during that medical episode marked her second hospital admission ever ... after having her tonsils out in 1930.

Over the years, Mary lived on Columbia Avenue and on Hazelwood. In 1996, she moved into an independent-living apartment at the St. Anne Home & Retirement Community. At age 93, she was recognized for volunteering in St. Anne's physical therapy center. Because she helped to move residents between their rooms and the center, the staff dubbed her their "Golden Retriever."

Submitted by Sharon Muir

PHILLIP HENRY & MARGARET AMELIA (GRIFFIN) MEURER

Phillip Henry Meurer was born in Mannheim, Germany, on June 8, 1871. He immigrated to the U.S. with his mother, Margareta, and sister, Emma, on the *S.S. Noorland*, arriving at the Castle Garden immigration center in New York City on May 24, 1884 or 1885. Margareta bought a house in Fort Wayne at 1808 Hillside Avenue (the postal service later changed the house number to 1904).

Henry became a naturalized citizen in Allen County on June 27, 1921. He worked first for the Wolfe Bedding and Mattress Company, then trained pupils in upholstery and mattress making at what was then called the Indiana School for the Feeble Minded on State Boulevard. There, he met his future wife, Margaret Amelia Griffin, who was the head cook. Maggie, born on November 2, 1876 at the family farm near Ogden, was a descendant of first-generation immigrants from County Cork, Ireland.

Henry and Margaret Meurer's 1910 wedding photo.

Henry and Maggie married on June 22, 1910, lived with his mother on Hillside, and had three children, Mary Margaret and twins, James Lawrence and Helen Louise. During World War I, Henry drilled with other civilians on Delaware Avenue one evening each week. Their neighbors to the south, William and Martha Brummer, eventually moved to California becoming butler and maid, first to the Marx Brothers and later for W. C. Fields.

After marriage, Henry became a gardener with the Park Board helping to develop Reservoir Park, the Rose Gardens at Lakeside Park, and the Japanese Gardens in West Swinney Park; he also supervised the greenhouses at Lawton Park. When he retired in 1947, he was supervisor of Franklin Meade's world flower collection in Foster Park. Henry also was a private gardener for the Victor Millers (Kensington Boulevard) and at the Meade home, Iris Crest (State at St. Joseph Boulevard). Henry hybridized irises for Mr. Meade, who shipped the bulbs all over the world.

Henry created a large garden around his Hillside Avenue home. It had tulip, locust, chestnut, and willow trees; lilac bushes; a rose garden, and a rock garden. The back yard boasted a rabbit hutch, a chicken coop, and every common vegetable. Cherry, crab apple, pear, peach, and plum trees stood near a grape arbor along with seven varieties of berry bushes. During World War II, authorities forced Henry to cut down his Japanese peach tree because of its name.

Maggie's good cooking skills drew hobos to Hillside Avenue. Hobos would leave signs on the alley fence to help their companions find a good meal. Once or twice a week, a hobo would show up at the back door. Maggie would have a small task for him to do so he could earn his meal. She then would fix the food on good plates and flatware, and their guest would sit on the back porch dining on the same food as the family ate. Maggie, age 74, died on July 13, 1951. Henry, age 87, died on January 7, 1958. They are buried in Lindenwood Cemetery.

Submitted by Raymond R. Griffin.

CARL HEINRICH "ARNOLD" MEYER

Carl Heinrich "Arnold" Meyer, son of Ferdinand Meyer and Isabelle Schumm, was born March 29, 1884, in Friedheim, Adams County, Indiana and died May 29, 1952, in Fort Wayne, Allen County, Indiana. Arnold married Bertha Dora Machts, daughter of Karl Machts and Margaretha Hagerer, on November 12, 1913, in Fort Wayne, Indiana. Bertha was born January 22, 1885, in Racine, Racine County, Wisconsin and died January 15, 1949 in Fort Wayne, Indiana. Arnold and Bertha resided in Fort Wayne all of their married life and attended Zion Lutheran Church. Bertha was a homemaker and Arnold worked for Western Gas Construction Company. Born to them were three children, Berthold, Audrey and Beatrice.

L to R: Arnold, Beatrice, Bertha, Audrey and Berthold Meyer, 1938

Berthold Paul Louis Meyer was born September 13, 1914, in Fort Wayne, Allen County, Indiana and died November 1, 1995, in Torrance, Los Angeles County, California. Berthold married Ruth Helen Passwater Stanley, daughter of John Passwater and Amanda Lloyd, on October 14, 1939. Ruth was born October 23, 1906, in Willshire, Van Wert County, Ohio and died February 17, 1996, in Torrance, Los Angeles County, California. They had one child, Ruth Marie Stanley.

Audrey Margaret Matilda Meyer was born May 7, 1917, in Fort Wayne, Allen County, Indiana and died February 3, 2004, in Richmond Heights, Cuyahoga County, Ohio. Audrey married Albert John Martic, son of Albert and Mary Martic on October 14, 1939, in St. Marks Church, Covington, Kenton County, Kentucky. Albert was born January 31, 1909, in Cleveland, Cuyahoga County, Ohio and died May 1, 1981, in Euclid, Cuyahoga County, Ohio. They had two children, Judith Ann and Thomas Brian.

Beatrice Lillian Lydia Meyer was born March 9, 1920, in Fort Wayne, Allen County, Indiana and died November 22, 1987, in Fort Wayne. Beatrice married Wilbert Christian Bultemeier, son of Ernst W.G. Bultemeier and Wilhelmina Schaaf on June 29, 1940, in Zion Lutheran Church, Fort Wayne, Indiana. Wilbert was born January 26, 1916 in Auburn, Dekalb County, Indiana and died October 19, 1954, in Fort Wayne, Indiana. They had four children, Paul Robert, Ronald Allan, Ruth Ann, and Linda Kay.

Beatrice's second marriage was to James Curtis Kettering, son of Nathaniel Curtis Kettering and Marie Louise Hartman, on February 14, 1970, in St. Luke's Lutheran Church, Fort Wayne, Indiana. James was born May 30, 1914, in Fort Wayne, Indiana and died November 26, 1993, in Fort Wayne, Indiana.

Submitted by Linda Krumwiede

HERBERT C. MEYER FAMILY

Herbert Carl was born on December 2, 1921 on the Milan Township family farm east of New Haven, first born son of Adolph H. and Margaret A. (Grime) Meyer. This makes Herbert the fifth generation American since the family first arrived in 1845 from Bremen, Germany and also the fourth generation to continuously own the family farm. Hebert's brother, Elvin F., a 1945 New Haven High School Bulldog basketball star, his wife Francis (both deceased) and son Terry also lived in Allen County.

Herbert graduated in 1940 from New Haven High School and went to work for General Electric. During the early years of World War II, Herbert attended and graduated from the General Electric Apprentice School as a Tool and Die Maker. While working at General Electric he met his future wife, Marilyn R. Nagel, and they were married May 18, 1945 in Camp Wolters, Texas, while Herbert was serving in the U.S. Army. After an honorable discharge in 1946, the couple returned to Fort Wayne where Herbert returned to work at General Electric, attended Purdue University and various G.E. sponsored educational programs. Herbert worked at General Electric for 44 years as a toolmaker and later in Industrial Engineering and Computer Systems.

Family of Herbert C. and Marilyn R. Meyer, 50th Wedding Anniversary, May 1995

After marriage, Marilyn, daughter of Fort Wayne residents Fred and Helen (Prange) Nagel and sister to Virginia, Carl, James. Donald and Herbert became a full-time housewife, garage sale aficionado and raised four highly diverse children, Steven, Jeanine, Brenda and Beth. The family lived in Fort Wayne's northeast side where the children attended Concordia Lutheran grade school and high school and Marilyn became the chauffeur and worked with the school/church activities. The four children are pursuing their chosen careers. Steven is a retired medical oncologist living in Saint Augustine, Florida with his wife Charlotte (Houk). They spend time fishing and spoiling their two grandchildren, Nathan and Charlea, by their children, Shawn and Sarah. Shawn is married to Julie Underwood and is a pilot for ATA Airlines, ferrying American troops to the Middle East. Sarah is married to Wesley Sims and they both work at the Jacksonville, Florida Zoo, she in marketing and he as a zoologist. Jeanine (Jedi Jean) is a Fine Art digital artist by day and a goat herder by night. Brenda is a Critical Care nurse and also teaches nursing at a local university. Beth is married to James G. Oas and they have a daughter, Kelley. Beth was a pharmaceutical representative and now is a teaching assistant. They live in Southern California where James manages a Pactiv plastic plant.

In his retirement Herbert remains active in church activities, flying, volunteering at Parkview Hospital, extensive genealogy research and maintaining the family farm. The Meyer's humble roots began in 1845 with an ocean voyage to the Port of New Orleans on the ship "Bark Diana" by Herbert's great, great grandparents, Heinrich and Margaret A. (Weigman), along with their six children. They traveled up the Mississippi to the Ohio River to Cincinnati, then took the canal system to Fort Wayne. They settled in the Goeglein Settlement in St. Joseph Township and were founding members of Saint Peter's Lutheran Church in 1855. In 1854 Herbert's great grandfather Johann married Sophia Luhman and they had five children. In 1875 Johann purchased land in Milan Township that now is the Meyer farm. All four generations prior to Herbert including his father Adolph were farmers in Allen County in either St. Joseph or Milan Township. Herbert's grandparents were Henry W. and Anna Maria Roehrs who were married October 9, 1884 and had five children.

Presently the Meyer farm is maintained by Herbert and the Harold Burchardt family, old friends and neighboring farmers. The Meyer family farm tradition continues.

Submitted by Herbert C. Meyer

TED EUGENE & MALINDA JANE MEYER FAMILY

Ted Eugene Meyer was born November 23, 1948 in Fort Wayne, Indiana to Hilbert and Erna (Arps) Meyer. Hilbert and Erna had four children, Frederick (Fritz) Herman, Ted Eugene, Dan H. and Martha Ann. Fritz is married to Linda Mozdan, Dan is married to Mary Hadley, and Martha to Eric White.

Ted graduated from Woodlan High School and the General Electric Company machinist toolmaker apprentice program. Ted was married to Malinda Jane Bonewitz on July 23, 1978. Malinda was born March 3, 1954 in Huntington, Indiana to Donald and Maribel (Phebus) Bonewitz. Don and Maribel had three children, Dennis Paul, Steven Dean, and Malinda Jane.

The Meyer Family July, 2000.

Dennis is married to Cathy Reed and Steve is married to Karen Fishbaugh. Malinda graduated from Huntington North High School and received her Associate Degree from Indiana University Division of General and Technical Studies in Fort Wayne.

Malinda and Ted have two children, Scott Michael born February 23, 1982 and Craig Eugene born October 30, 1984. Scott and Craig both graduated from Woodlan High School. They both are attending Indiana-Purdue University Fort Wayne. Scott is studying mechanical engineering and Craig is studying architectural technology.

Submitted by Ted E. Meyer

JAMES KELYNACK MICHELL FAMILY

James (Jim) Kelynack Michell was born to John Trewartha Michell and Nellie Kelynack July 7, 1887 in Tolcare, Newlyn (West), Cornwall, England. He married Elizabeth (Bess) Bone Jeffery in 1908 in Wesley Rock Chapel, Heamor, Madron, Cornwall, England. Bess was born to Joseph Jeffery and Mary Ann Oats on November 24, 1891, Street in Nowan, Newlyn (West), Cornwall, England. They had a son, James Stanley (Stan) Michell who was born in Newlyn (West) in 1909.

Jim decided to go to Akron, Ohio as many other Cornish families had done, arriving at Ellis Island, New York City on July 28, 1909. He worked at the Goodyear Rubber Company, a bakery, and at the International Harvester Company in Akron. He returned to Cornwall and brought his wife and son to Akron on January 12, 1911.

James Kelynack Michell Family Photo Back row left to right: James Stanley Michell, Donald Jeffery Michell. Middle row: James Kelynack Michell, Elizabeth Bone Jeffery Michell. Front row: William Kelynack Michell. Photo taken cira 1930, Patterson-Fletcher, Fort Wayne, Indiana

In 1912, Jim transferred to the International Harvester location in Chatham, Ontario, Canada. However, his wife didn't like the climate and returned to Cornwall. In 1915, Jim returned to Akron, and again worked for International Harvester. His wife and son again joined him arriving at Ellis Island on December 16, 1914. Jim and Bess had another son in 1920, Donald Jeffery (Jeff) Michell. Citizenship came on May 21, 1921 with the Common Pleas Court of Summit County, Ohio granting naturalization. Jim continued his job with International Harvester, performing various accounting duties.

As this company location grew, larger facilities were necessary. Although Jim tried to negotiate with the city of Akron on incentives for the company to remain, that was not be, and International Harvester built a plant in Fort Wayne, Indiana. And, in 1924, Jim was to become the plant's assistant auditor, a post he held until his retirement on July 31, 1947.

Jim and Bess had another son, William (Bill) Kelynack Michell, who was born in 1925. The family resided on North Anthony Boulevard, Cresent Avenue, and California Avenue in the Forest Park Neighborhood area of Fort Wayne. They were members of the Forest Park Methodist Church. All three sons, Stan, Jeff, and Bill, graduated from Central High School. Also, they worked at the International Harvester Plant, with Jeff and Bill retiring there with over thirty year's service. Stan pursued other career interests, most notably with Shell Oil as a salesperson and, for a short time, operator of the Lakeside Shell Service Station at Lake and Anthony.

Jeff and Bill enlisted in the Marine Corps during the Second World War and both served their country in the South Pacific.

All three sons married women in Fort Wayne, Stan to Cecile Marrow in 1941, Jeff to Mae Ruth Vanselow in 1944, and Bill to Gertrude Rohland in 1947. Stan had three children, two sons and a daughter. Jeff had four, two sons and two daughters. Bill also had four, two sons and two daughters. Bess Michell died in 1957, Jim Michell in 1971, Stan Michell in 1999, and Jeff in 2003.

Submitted by William C. Michell

DANIEL MILLER

Daniel Miller was one of the early settlers of Churubusco, Indiana. In December 1835, Daniel Miller purchased 160 acres in Section 25, and the second section from the south along the Allen County Line Road. He was 38 years old and his wife, Margaret Ann (Wolf) Miller, was 20 years old. Both were born in Pennsylvania. They lived in Ross County, Ohio, before coming to Smith Township, Whitley County, Indiana. Their first child was born in 1838.

In August and December of 1836 David and Sally Wolf, the father and mother of Margaret Ann Wolf Miller, came to the area and purchased the south section of 13 where Churubusco is now located. David Wolf, age 43, and his wife, Sally, age 45, were also born in Pennsylvania. David gave his residence on the deed as Allen County. In the 1840 census they had a son under 20, two daughters under 15, and one daughter under the age of 10. David and Sally are buried in Eel River Cemetery, right along the McDuffy Road. The tombstones are barely legible now.

Daniel and Margaret and were parents of twelve children, nine sons and three daughters: (1) William Alexander Miller married Sarah Ann Harter, (2) David V. Miller married Mary L. Trumbull, (3) Daniel Ebenezer Miller married Abbigail Tyler, (4) Sarah E. Miller married Charles C. Rapp, (5) George W. Miller died at 4 years and 3 months, (6) John B. Miller died at 24 years, 9 months, and 29 days, (7) James W. Miller married Mary E. Trumbull, (8) Henry A. Miller married Clementine Urbine, (9) Sampson Jacob Miller married Francis H., (10) Christena

Five generations of Millers: Helen Orphia Vaughn Miller, Gloria Joyce Miller Bojrab, Michael Wayne Bojrab, Kiana Sheena Bojrab Martin, and Blake Riley Martin

Jane Miller (Jennie Rockhill) married James W. Rockhill, (11) Mariah E. Miller married Robert A. Dolin, and (12) Josiah M. Miller died at age 7 years, 9 months, and 23 days. They are all buried in the Eel River Cemetery in Allen County, Indiana, except for Sampson J. Miller and family. He is buried in the Albion Cemetery in Albion, Indiana.

Third son, Daniel Ebenezer Miller, lived in a small house on Mulberry Street in Churubusco, Indiana, for many years. He was a first gunner on a cannon in the Civil War. He lost his hearing from the roar of the cannons. After the war he came back and married Abbigail Tyler. They had four children: Neoma Miller Tucker, Della Miller Patterson, Ollie Miller Madden, and one son, Martin Casby Miller.

Martin Casby Miller married Florence Rapp and they lived in Arcola, Indiana. Martin (alias Danny Miller) had four sons: Harry (Tootie) Miller, Wayne Woodruff Miller, Richard Miller, and Deloss Merle Miller. Harry and Deloss had no children.

Wayne Woodruff Miller married Helen Orphia Vaughn and they had three daughters: Gloria Joyce Miller, Marlene Marie Miller, and Judith Lynne Miller.

Gloria J. married George W. Bojrab, and they have three children: Michael Wayne Bojrab, Jodi Lynne Bojrab, and Timothy George Bojrab. Michael married Sherry Grim. They have two children: Kiana Sheena Bojrab and Micah Landon Bojrab. Kiana married Brian C. Martin and they have a son, Blake Riley Martin. Blake is the eighth generation of the Miller side and the ninth generation on the Wolf side.

Marlene Marie Miller married Lawrence John Miller of Oquawka, Illinois. They have two children: Lisa Marie and Alan Wayne Miller. Lawrence (Larry) died on July 7, 2002. Lisa Marie Stoikovic lives near Burlington, Iowa. She has three daughters: Kourtney Marie, Ashley Rachelle, and Rana Kathryn. Kourtney has a daughter, Taran Marie. Alan Wayne married Kristena Tharp and they have a son, Brody Lawrence Miller.

Judith Lynne Miller married Roger Alan Dafforn. They have two sons: Devin Alan and Darren Wayne Dafforn. Darren married Donna Schlotterback. They have a son, Drew Frances Dafforn, who was born September 9, 2004.

Richard Miller married Helen Sinnigan Miller. They had one son, Daniel Bernard Miller. He died in a silo accident on January 5, 1960. He was married to Linda Sheppard. She gave birth to a son named Anthony Bernard Miller after Danny died. Anthony (Tony) married Molly and they have a daughter and a son.

Helen Sinnigan Miller was 93 years young March 31, 2005. Since 1836, years have passed. May God bless each and everyone, and may there be many more generations of Millers and Wolfs.

Submitted by Gloria J. Miller Bojrab

HENRY MILLER

Henry Miller I, was born in Germany in 1761 and died in DeKalb County, Indiana in 1837. He, his wife, and their son fled Germany to avoid military service. He went to Holland and kept a store. At the time Napoleon overran Holland, he lost his wife and property. He married Ann Elizabeth Sheets and they, along with Henry's son, Henry Miller II, born 1802, immigrated to the United States in 1805. They first settled in Lehigh County, Pennsylvania, where Elizabeth, Jacob, Joseph, Benjamin, and Michael were born.

Henry Miller II married Mary Welsh in Pennsylvania, and had three children as follows: Abraham, 1822-1907, married Phoeba Erickson; Elizabeth, 1826-1904, married Lyman Holbrook; Andrew, 1828-1893, married Margaret Crabill.

The Miller families moved to Marion County, Ohio, in 1827. Henry II's wife died and he married Mary Snyder on June 23, 1833. Mary was born December 21, 1803, in Perry County, Pennsylvania. Her parents were George and Suzanna Peters Snyder. Henry and Mary Miller were the parents of the following children: Suzanna, 1835-1878, married Aaron Sloffer; Samuel, 1836; Rebecca, 1837-1923, married William Sloffer; Mary Jane, 1839-1898, married Daniel Rhodes; Sarah, 1839-1859; Magdalene, 1841-1862.

The Miller families moved to Butler Township, DeKalb County, Indiana, in 1836. They were among the first settlers in that township. They were farmers, and, in 1843, they bought land in section 1 in Eel River Township, Allen County.

Mary Miller died January 5, 1871, and Henry died September 29, 1872. They are buried in Swan Cemetery, Noble County, Indiana.

Suzanna and Rebecca Miller married brothers, Aaron and William Sloffer. They lived side by side on the North Allen County Road in section 1. Both couples lay near each other at the Swan Cemetery, Noble County, Indiana.

Submitted by Jayne Arehart.

JACOB S. MILLER

This is a brief account of the Jacob S. Miller and Isaac Miller family from a history of the Miller Family Reunions. The minutes from 1911 to 1988 are in a booklet that mentions "the next big one" in 1990. It's not known if it ever happened. The book ended with the 88th reunion. It was determined that this was the second year of which they were having a reunion every three years. The *Jacob S. Miller Reunion Book* may be found in the Allen County Public Library.

William Miller and Elizabeth Swoveland, parents of Jacob, were married in 1833 and had three children, Jacob, Andrew and Rebecca. The children came to the United States but their parents did not. William was a hatter by trade who made silk hats.

Jacob S. Miller, a blacksmith, and Anna Dewalt, both from Pennsylvania, moved with their parents to Poe, Allen County, Indiana. They married in 1833. Their children were Elizabeth, William, Henry, Samuel, Isaac, Rebecca, Mary, Carolyn, Charles, Andrew, and Harriett. Jacob died in 1865 and Anna in 1884.

Jacob's fifth child, Isaac, married Catherine Hoelle in 1865. Isaac was in the Civil War in Company F, 88th Regiment, Indiana Volunteer Infantry, commanded by Captain LeFever. He entered service August 7, 1862. While fighting in the Battle of Perryville, Kentucky on October 8, 1862, Isaac was struck by a musket ball from the enemy's line. He lost the use of his right arm below the elbow. Isaac Miller was a grocer with a store at Calhoun and Dewald Streets. Their house was next door on Calhoun. They had three children: Mary Ann, Clara Ida, and Laura Jane. Clara was struck by lightening and killed at the age of nineteen. Isaac died in Fort Wayne, Indiana in 1923, as did Catherine in 1920.

Mary Ann married Henry M. Miller, born in Gachlingen, Switzerland in 1885. They had seven children: Lauretta May, Clara Ida, Ralph, Maurice, Howard, Esther, and Carl. Henry was known for his gift of penmanship as he was hired to professionally use his talent. He did business out of a paint and wallpaper store at Calhoun and Tabor Streets.

Lauretta May married Karl C. Baltzell from Convoy, Ohio in 1912 and they were the parents of Elizabeth Miller Baltzell. Karl was a politician and builder of aircraft and boats.

Clara Ida married Milo J. Egly of Berne, Indiana in 1913 and they were the parents of Dorothy Jane and John Miller Egly.

Maurice Miller married Katherine Krouse in 1936 and they were the parents of Susan Marie, Michael, and Sarah Ann.

Ralph married Beatrice Miller; Howard married Maude Meese; Esther married Clifton Ross; Carl married Anna Stevens. They had no children.

Elizabeth Miller Baltzell married Franklin H. Ruby in 1941 and had two children: Karol Elizabeth Ann and Janet Elaine. Franklin died in 1970 and Elizabeth "Betty" still writes and publishes books on genealogy.

Submitted by Karol E. A. Ruby

JENNIFER (EDWARDS) MILLER

Jennifer Louise Edwards was born May 28, 1965, in Wells County. At the time of her birth, her parents, Kenneth and Melba Edwards, lived in the Skyline Addition on the north edge of Markle, Indiana.

Attending kindergarten, first and second grades at Rockcreek School, she made the transition to Lafayette Central Elementary when her parents moved to Zanesville, Allen County, in the spring of 1973. She attended Woodside Middle School and entered Homestead High School. As a freshman, she made the decision to work a little harder and graduate in three years. She wanted nothing to do with college as her dream was to be a wife and mother. The principal and guidance counselor tried to change her mind. Graduating in 1982, she had many credits and very good grades.

The Millers at Give Kids The World – Orlando. Anna's Make-A-Wish vacation 2004. On chairs: Abigail and Andrew. From left to right: J.P., Arrika, Ashley, Amber, Anna, Avery, Jenny holding Addy, and Amy.

Already having a full time job, she met her future husband as she was waitressing at Richard's Restaurant in Huntington. She married J.P. Miller on August 20, 1983. J.P. attended Huntington College for two years and in 1986, the couple moved to Toledo, Ohio, to help start a church there. On July 30, 1986, their son Andrew was born. In April 1987, they moved to Columbia, Missouri, again with the church. They live there at the present time. J.P. has a pest and animal control business there.

Jenny has certainly fulfilled her dream. She is now the mother of nine. She homeschools the younger ones, and as they reach high school age, they begin to take some classes at the local high school. Andrew is a freshman at Missouri State University in 2005. Abigail (1988), Amy (1990), Anna (1992), Aarika (1993), Avery (1995), Amber (1997), Ashley (2001) and Addy (2003) complete the family of nine children.

In 1994, two and one-half year old Anna was diagnosed with neuroblastoma, a deadly cancer. It was then that Jenny became a full time nurse to her ailing daughter. The four small siblings had to spend four months going back and forth to Indiana so Mom and Dad could be at the hospital. Anna's cancer was stage four. She had a two percent chance of surviving. Calls were made to medical sites all over the country. The whole family searched the internet. Through the Indiana Lions liaison at Riley Hospital, the family was to learn of a stem cell transplant using your own stem cells. Anna was the 21st one to have this procedure and it worked. With the care of the staff at Riley, especially Dr. Timmerman, and with her mother at her side, she was released in about six weeks to go home so all the family could be together again. A little over three years old at that time, she had to go through full body radiation and many chemo treatments. She lived a fairly uneventful but cautious life until the fall of 2003 when she developed what seemed to be an allergy, and her breathing was not quite right. As months went on, she was placed on oxygen. Fibroids of the lungs had developed, possibly the aftermath of the radiation at three. She was placed on the transplant list in late January 2004. The call came on April 5, 2004, the day that President Bush threw out the first baseball to open the season at the St. Louis ball field, just blocks from the Children's Hospital. Anna's lungs were on their way! The airspace was closed, but the helicopter was allowed to make the delivery. Anna is now getting along fine with no rejection. She just now has to take insulin because her medicine induces diabetes. Diabetes treatments are not new to Jenny as three of her children and J.P. are diabetic. She just takes it in stride.

The Millers are involved in church activities, and the kids always need a ride somewhere. They always enjoy visiting their grandparents and other family members that still remain in and near Zanesville.

To learn more about Anna's cure and her messages from God as a child, refer to Rebekah Montgomery's book entitled *Ordinary Miracles,* a collection of true stories of an extraordinary God who works in our everyday life.

Jenny never fails to praise God and all those who prayed for their family through these times of hardship. To learn more about Jenny and J.P. refer to the *Wells County Family History 1992* and the Kenneth and Melba Edwards article in this publication.

Submitted by Melba Edwards

MICKEY MILLER & JEANNE SEIDEL MILLER FAMILY

Mickey Miller was born May 19, 1920 on a farm outside Morgantown, Indiana to Ward W. and Olo Renner Miller.

After service in North Africa and Italy in World War II and being awarded the Silver Star for exceptionally meritorious conduct in action, he attended Indiana University School of Law in Bloomington. Here he met another law student, Jeanne Seidel. Jeanne was born October 4, 1925 in Fort Wayne, Indiana to Carl F. and Adah Gumpper Seidel. Mickey and Jeanne were married in 1947 and were both admitted to the Indiana Bar in 1948.

Thereafter Mickey Miller practiced law in Fort Wayne. He served as Commander of the Thomas Lau Suedoff Post 9500, Veterans of Foreign Wars, President of the Allen County Bar Association, President of Lutheran Social Services and Charter President of the Anthony Wayne Rotary Club. Jeanne Seidel Miller practiced law in New Haven. She served as President of the East Allen County School Board, a Trustee of Indiana University, and President of the Indiana State Bar Association.

Mickey and Jeanne have three children.

Ward William Miller was born March 27, 1949 in Fort Wayne. He is a graduate of Culver Military Academy, Dartmouth College, and Indiana University School of Law. He is an attorney, practicing in Fort Wayne. He is married to Mary McDonald.

Carl Michael Miller was born December 13, 1950 in Fort Wayne. He is a graduate of Culver Military Academy, Indiana University, and Indiana University School of Law. He is an attorney, practicing in New Haven. He is married to Marianne Blue. They have three children: Katie Miller Pierce, born December 11, 1978; Joseph Frederick Miller, born August 21, 1980; and Elizabeth Helen Miller, born November 9, 1986.

Marjorie Ann Miller was born January 19, 1954 in Fort Wayne. She died June 12, 2001. She was a graduate of Culver Academy for Girls,

Seated: Jeanne S. Miller, Mickey M. Miller Standing: Carl Miller, Marjorie Miller, Ward Miller

Indiana University, and University of Denver Law School. She was an attorney, practicing in Mesa County, Colorado She was married to Robert Hutchins with whom she had three children: Claire Seidel Hutchins, born November 23, 1993: Alexander Powell Hutchins, born September 26, 1995; and Rachel Miller Hutchins, born May 7, 1999.

Submitted by Jeanne S. Miller

NICHOLAS ALAN MILLER & KATHLEEN ANN THOMPSON

Stephan Schnurr was born August 3, 1837, in Baden, Germany. He came to America aboard the Admiral arriving in New York on December 21, 1859. During the Civil War, he entered the 107th Regiment Ohio Volunteer Infantry on August 22, 1862, serving as a drummer. After mustering out, he journeyed west to Fort Wayne, Indiana. On January 14, 1869, he married Mary Elizabeth Krummnelbein, born January 28, 1848 in Fort Wayne, Indiana, to Adam and Mary Link Krummnelbein. Stephan was a member of St. Mary's Church and a member of the Sangerbund, a German singing group. He worked at Ehrhart Heiny Grocers and various saloons in the city. Stephan and Mary Elizabeth were the parents of Anna, Agatha, Franziska, and John Napomesan Schnurr.

On June 5, 1901, John married Eva Theresa Landgraf, born May 18, 1878, in Fort Wayne. Eva's parents are John Landgraf and Elizabeth Lerch. John and Eva had eight children, Louis Anthony, Frances Joseph, Collette Amelia, Elizabeth Christina, Mary Catherine, Florence Clare, Herman Joseph, and John Robert. The family lived in various residences in the parishes of St. Peter's and St. Patrick's. John supported the family as a painter and wallpaper hanger.

Collette, born on August 27, 1906, was employed at Wayne Knitting Mills before marrying Neil Jerome Thompson on August 18, 1936. Neil was born on March 3,1908. He was a well-known organist at St. Patrick's Catholic Church for over 25 years. Neil was the fifth child of William Willard Thompson and Martha Josephine Kuntz. His siblings were Edith Marie, Erin Agnes, Kenneth Edward, and Helen Rosella. William's parents were Jeremiah Thompson and Susan Weeks. Both lived and died in Allen County. Their other children were Joseph, Frank, Henrietta, John, Marguret and Anna. Martha's parents were Peter Kuntz born in France and Elizabeth Emerich from Germany. Martha's siblings were Henrich, Samuel, and Barbara. Neil and Collette were the parents of William John, Kathleen Ann, Joseph Robert, and Edward James. All attended St. Patrick's School and graduated from Central Catholic High School. Kathleen, born September 6, 1941, married Nicholas Alan Miller on May 5, 1962, at St. Patrick's. Nicholas was born on August 26, 1941, in Marion, Indiana, to Daniel Miller Miller and Loretta Louise Alvey. He moved to Fort Wayne, graduated from South Side High School, and received degrees at Purdue University and Indiana University. He was a draftsman at Franklin Electric and, a mechanical engineer at Dana Corporation and International Harvester before beginning Miller Consulting where both he and Kathleen worked until retirement. To Nicholas and Kathleen were born Scott Christopher, Teri Christine, Timothy Alan, and Christy Michelle. They lived in Fort Wayne before moving to Auburn, Indiana, in 1973.

The Nicholas and Kathleen Miller Family, 2003.

Scott, who married Linda Kleber on August 8, 1992, and Teri, who married Christopher Baron on June 13, 1987, live in Allen County. Scott is the father of Taylor Scott Miller whose mother is Staci Thomason. Zelda Rae, John Michael, and Iris Luella are the children of Scott and Linda. Scott is the owner of a contracting business, Miller Built. Linda teaches piano at St. John the Baptist Catholic School and art at the Fort Wayne Art Museum. Zachary Sebastian, Nicole Christine, and Lexi Ann are the children of Teri and Chris. Teri is an ultrasound technician with Fort Wayne Ob/Gyn Consultants, and Christopher is vice-president and general manager of Micromatic in Berne, Indiana. Timothy moved to Portland, Oregon, and is a tax consultant and owner of Affiliated Tax Pros. Christy married Matthew Gary Kuziensky on October 30, 1999, in Indianapolis, Indiana, and moved to Portland, Oregon, in November 1999. They are the parents of Simon Miller Kuziensky, born on March 26, 2003. Christy is a marketing consultant, and Matthew is an environmental biologist with Jones and Stokes Associates.

Submitted by Kathleen A. Miller

STANLEY W. MILLER FAMILY

Stanley Wayne Allen Miller was born February 14, 1931 at St. Joseph Hospital in Fort Wayne to George Christian Miller and Stella Louise (Krueckeberg) Miller. He had two older brothers, George Jr. and K. James. Stanley's grandfather, Christian Miller, started C. Miller & Sons Roof-

Wedding day of Joanne Burgett and Stanley Miller, October 24, 1953

ing & Sheet Metal and his grandfather, August Krueckeberg, was a Fort Wayne Police Officer. Christian Miller came to America as a young lad by himself with only the clothes on his back and the family Bible. The Miller family settled in Huntington County but soon moved to Fort Wayne and established a successful roofing and sheet metal business that still serves the tri-state area today.

The Miller's were devout Lutherans and attended St. Paul's Lutheran Church on Barr Street, later transferring their membership to Emmanuel Lutheran Church on West Jefferson. Stanley attended Emmaus and Emmanuel grade schools and Concordia Lutheran High School, then on the corner of Maumee and Anthony, where he played football and track. After graduating in 1948, he worked full time for the family business as a roofer. He is very proud of the fact that he ran a major roofing job in Jeffersonville, Indiana at the age of nineteen. During the winter months he had a part-time job as a pinsetter at the American Legion Post 47, then on West Jefferson Street. It was there that he met and fell in love at first sight with Joanne Burgett, from Tuscola, Illinois, who was working in Fort Wayne for Dr. McNulty as a dental assistant. Stan and Joanne were married October 24, 1953 in Tuscola but came back to Fort Wayne to have a big reception at the Lunz Barn. A week later they were off to Florida where Stan was to serve in the Marine Corp. When his stint was up they returned to Fort Wayne and Stan began working in the family business, C. Miller & Sons.

In 1954 their first child, Catherine Louise was born, followed by Scott Allen in 1955, Bradley Wayne in 1959 and Phillip Christian in 1963. Catherine married Frederick Peterson and their children are Anna, Alexander and Molly. Fred is part of CMS Roofing. Scott and partner, Manuel Cruz, own and operate Then & Now Antiques in Angola, Indiana. Bradley married Angela (Keeley) and they have four children, Joshua, Jessica, Jordan and Jennifer. Bradley, too, is part of CMS Roofing as is Phillip who is married to Patricia (Rinehart). They have two daughters, Victoria and Kristine.

In 1980, the family business known as C. Miller & Sons Roofing & Sheet Metal, split to form two companies with Stan's brother, Jim, keeping C. Miller & Sons Sheet Metal and Stan forming CMS Roofing Inc. with his three sons and son-in-law. Today the business is strong and thriving and the family is very proud of Stanley's devotion to his family and the family business.

Submitted by Stanley W. Miller

VICTOR MILLER FAMILY

Victor Miller was born February 2, 1918 in New Haven, Indiana. He worked as a carpenter for Graber Homes before his death, March 25, 1998. His parents were David Miller, born November 2, 1886 and Lucy Delagrange, born December 6, 1892. Victor married Rosa Ann Delagrange, August 13, 1939. She was born May 10, 1922 in Grabill, Indiana as where her parents, Henry Delagrange, born March 30, 1888, and Catherine Graber, born May 1, 1895. Rosa was a homemaker and baked pies at Yoder's Restaurant in Hicksville, Ohio for ten years.

Victor and Rosa lived with his father for nine years after getting married to care for Victor's brothers and sisters because his mom died at a young age. They then purchased a 120-acre farm with farmhouse on Lochner Road, Spencerville, Indiana, in March 1947, for $12,000 where they lived the rest of their lives.

Victor and Rosa's children were: Elmer Miller born October 16, 1940, married Martha Miller, born March 12, 1942 in New Haven, Indiana. Elmer was self-employed, Elmar Plumbing and Heating, and Martha was a rental agent. They had two children: Wilmer Lee and Larry Dewayne.

Victor and Rosa Miller

Lavern Miller was born April 12, 1943 and died July 23, 1977. He married Barbara Graber, born September 11, 1944 in Grabill, Indiana. Lavern worked for Grabill Cabinets. They had three children: Mary Mae, Stephen and Naomi. Barbara remarried David Nolt, born March 29, 1937. Together they own the Nolt Family Dinner Haus in Grabill. They had one child: Joanna.

Laveda Miller was born August 15, 1945. She married Russell Ford Lilly, born April 27, 1940, died May 24, 2001 in Hicksvlle, Ohio. Laveda was a self-employed drywaller, and he was a carpenter. They had two children: Vicky Ray and Yvonne Marie.

Mervin Miller was born March 10, 1947. His wife was Rosalie Steury, born January 18, 1948 in Hamilton, Indiana. He was a self-employed drywaller, and she was a homemaker and cleaned houses for people. They had seven children: Merv Allen, Nathan James, twins David Lee and Darren Lynn, Andrea Rose, Adam Victor, and Grace Ann.

Marvin Miller was born December 25, 1948. He married Vickie Lynn Jones, born January 26, 1956 in Antwerp, Ohio. He was self-employed at Marv's Drywall and Insulation. They had four children, Jeremy Joe, Jason James, Jared John and Janelle Jean. Marvin had another child with Phyllis Shepherd, Angela Marie Phillips.

Catherine Irene Miller was born July 2, 1952. Her first husband was Jerry Morhart and they had one child, Cherry Lynn. Her second husband was Terry Hart, born April 4, 1947 in Hicksville, Ohio. Catherine worked at Yoder's Restaurant, and Terry was employed by Dietrich Industries until it closed in 2004. He's now employed by Con-Agra in Archbold, Ohio. They had two children, Cassandra Renee and Cynthia Marlene.

Reuben Miller was born May 20, 1955. He married Linda Kay Myers, born January 13, 1953 in Huntertown, Indiana. He was self-employed in construction, and she was a homemaker. They had five children, Rhoda Kay, Michelle Dawn, Ranetta Gail, Joshua Reuben and Renee Marlene.

Rose Marie Miller was born December 26, 1957. She married Randal Dean Davis, born November 21, 1956 in Decatur, Indiana. They later lived with Rosa after Victor died in 1998. Rose was a secretary at Medical and Dental Business Bureau. Randal was employed by Bunge a.k.a. Central Soya.

Verna Joy Miller was born March 19, 1960. Her first child with Dirk Ross was James Victor Miller. She married Douglas Ralph Phillips, born July 22, 1952 in Leo-Cedarville, Indiana. Verna was self-employed with an Amish hauling business. Douglas worked for Pella Windows in Fort Wayne, Indiana. They had five children, Jessyca Rose, Caleb Robert, Zachary Douglas, Nicholas Evan and Kaitlyn Ruth.

Submitted by V. Miller

MILLS FAMILY

George W. Mills, a prominent farmer of Lafayette Township, was born in Coshocton County, Ohio, on March 15, 1828. His father, James Mills, a native of New Jersey, left there at the age of nineteen and came to Ohio. He was married in Taylorville (Philo), Ohio, to Eliza Wright, and they moved to Coshocton. They had nine children, eight sons and one daughter, of whom eight survived childhood. They are as follows: George W; Robert B. of Oregon; Warren L. of Kansas; Daniel B. of Illinois; William B. of Illinois; John C. of Illinois; James Garvin of Dakota; and Eliza R., wife of Josiah Bays of Missouri. James Mills died in Morgan County, Ohio, in March 1844 and the mother died in Ossian, Indiana, at the age of 67, in 1873.

George W. Mills came to Indiana in 1848, after his father's death, and brought with him his mother and the children, who depended upon him until arriving of age. He settled in Lafayette Township and built a cabin where the Coverdale School House now stands. He entered forty acres of his present farm in 1849, the deed being signed by Zachary Taylor. He added to his farm until now it contained 104 acres of good land.

He was married in 1848 to Margaret, daughter of John and Elizabeth (Ryan) Hill. They had eleven children, eight of whom survived childhood: Robert; John; Elizabeth; Joseph C.; Matilda; Ella; Grant and Jane. Mr. Mills was elected Justice of the Peace in the spring of 1880 and served four years, filling the office very creditably. In politics he is a republican. He is a member of the Christian Church and has been active in church affairs for several years. He was a member of the 137th Indiana Volunteer Infantry, Company D, which went into active service in 1864. Mr. Mills is a man of honesty and integrity and is well respected by his neighbors and fellow citizens. He is a member of McGinnis Post, No. 167, G. A. R. of Roanoke, Indiana. *History of the Valley of the Upper Maumee, 1889.*

Picture taken c. 1898-1900. George Wright Mills, 1828-1908, and Margaret (Hill) Mills, 1826-1907

Robert Borders, first child of George W. and Margaret (Hill) Mills, was born near Roanoke, Indiana, on May 3, 1851. He was married on June 7, 1883, to Amelia Koons who resided at R#3, Roanoke, Indiana (at Aboite). His occupation was that of farmer and grocer, having operated a store at Aboite for several years. His death occurred of a complication of diseases on August 22, 1926, at the age of 75 years, burial at I.O.O.F. Cemetery at Roanoke, Indiana. To the above union were born four sons and one daughter as follows: Roy Allen Mills, George Arthur Mills, Elzie Richard Mills; Edith May Mills; Perry Robert Mills.

Arthur Mills, second child of Robert Borders Mills and Amelia (Koons) Mills, was born at Waynedale, Indiana, on October 8, 1885. He is a farmer on R#3, Roanoke, Indiana, near Aboite. He survived to 1980, aged 95. He married Grace Charlotte Blee (1894-1985) in 1917, and to this union were born two sons and two daughters: Thomas Arthur Mills; Kathryn Virginia Mills; Margaret Joan Mills; Donald Richard Mills. *Margaret Betts, a Pioneer of the 18th Century and Her Descendents by Minnie E. Fryback, 1933*

Thomas Arthur Mills was born in Fort Wayne, Indiana, on February 16, 1918. Thomas is a decorated (Purple Heart and Air Medal) WWII veteran and also served 25 years as an officer in the U. S. Air Force. He and his wife, Phyllis Ann (Hattersley) Mills were married in 1946. Phyllis was from a prominent Fort Wayne plumbing family, A. Hattersley & Sons, Inc., who came to Fort Wayne in the 1840s. Phyllis and Tom Mills raised five children in the U. S. Air Force, and in their home in Lafayette Township. To the union were born: Barbara Helen (Mills) Martin; Ted Harrison Mills; James Robert Mills; Amy Lou (Mills) Keefer; Patrick Thomas Mills.

Submitted by Barbara (Mills) Martin

GERALD & KATHRYN (GLASPER) MINNICK FAMILY

Gerald Alyosius Minnick was born in Hoagland, Indiana on April 4, 1922 to Albert (1892-1979) and Catherine Gebhard (1890-1928) Minnick. He is a descendant of Nikolaus Münch (1837-1906), who came to Allen County from Lampertheim, Germany, in 1838 as an infant with his parents, Franz (1795-1877) and Elisabetha Albrecht (1798-1855) Münch. The Franz Münch family settled on a farm in Madison Township near Hoagland and were charter members of St. Joseph Catholic Church at Hessen Cassel. They established the Minnich Road between Hoagland and New Haven. The various descendants Americanized the Münch surname to Muench, Minnick, Minnich, Minich, etc. The old Münch log house, called "Paradise", still stands at the Minnich and Monroeville Roads.

Gerald "Jerry" attended St. Peter's Catholic Grade School and graduated from Central Catholic High School in 1940. He served in Europe during WWII with the 609th Ordnance Battalion of the 3rd Army. On July 31, 1948, he married Kathryn Elizabeth Glasper at Precious Blood Catholic Church in Fort Wayne. Jerry worked building trucks at International Harvester and retired in 1982 after 41 years of service. He remains a loyal and active member of UAW local 57. Jerry is a jovial, easy-going man who is well liked by everyone. He never swears, but uses many unique phrases to show displeasure, such as "son-of-a-murphy-in-a-breeze." Jerry enjoys good food, gardening, Chicago Cubs baseball, Indiana University basketball, and attending sporting events of his children and grandchildren.

Gerald and Kathryn (Glasper) Minnick wedding, July 31, 1948.

Kathryn was born on December 8, 1929, in Detroit, Michigan, to Robert (1900-1984) and Josephine Stein (1900-1979) Glasper. Her father originated from Leith, Scotland, and served in the Gordon Highlanders 53rd Battalion during WWI. Her mother was a descendant of the Johann Martin Stein (1796-1865) family that settled in Mercer County, Ohio from Lauterecken, Bavaria, Germany, in 1836. Kathryn received her education at Precious Blood Grade School and Central Catholic High School, graduating in 1947. She was a dedicated mother and homemaker while raising her family. Then she worked as the science department secretary for St. Francis College, until retiring in 1992. Kathryn is a warm, loving, deeply religious person, who especially enjoys family events, church activities, and helping others.

The four children of Gerald and Kathryn Minnick are: Mary Catherine (1949), wife of Bradley Glass (1945); Margaret Ann (1951), wife of Carl Kleber (1950); Michael Gerald (1952), husband of Sandra Harris (1951); and Maureen Therese (1959), wife of William Yankowiak (1958).

Submitted by Maureen Yankowiak.

SCOTT & ALBERTA MITCHELL / GLADYS O. MITCHELL WILSON

Scott Van Meter Mitchell and Alberta Fletcher met at Kentucky State College in Frankfort, Kentucky. Both were from high-achieving families just a few years removed from slavery. Alberta's grandfather, George Cooper, who married America Pigg, owned over 600 acres of land in Powell County, Kentucky, at the time of his death in 1910. In 1895, the Cooper's daughter, Alice, while a student at Berea College, left to marry Charles Fletcher. Charles, the son of Firman and Mary (Allen) Fletcher, was reared on the family farm, which was inherited from his grandparents, Joseph and Katie Fletcher. Joseph and Katie lived to be centenarians and were married for sixty-seven years. Alice and Charles' first child, Alberta, was born in 1898 in West Bend, Kentucky. Scott Mitchell was born in 1896 to Josephine (Scott) and James Mitchell in Clintonville, Kentucky, blue-grass/horse racing country. Scott grew up on the farm of Brutus Clay, (a relative to the renowned Henry Clay). These Clays, who are referred to as "the unconventional Clays" within their family folklore, financed Scott's college education. He graduated magna cum laude.

1915, Alberta Fletcher Mitchell

1920, Scott VanMeter Mitchell, Graduation Day, Kentucky State College

College sweethearts Scott and Alberta were married on July 14, 1920 in West Bend. Scott went on to a teaching career, eventually becoming the principal of Oliver High School in Winchester, Kentucky, during 'the Great Depression.' While there, he led several of his school's basketball teams to Blue Grass Championships. In 1940, moving his family to Indiana, he made a career change, establishing his own general contracting company. He built homes for some of the most prominent members of Richmond's black community. He also owned a farm outside Richmond. Retiring in the 1950s, he sold his farm and relocated to Fort Wayne, where he found his spiritual heart's desire when he discovered the Baha'i Faith.

When the Mitchells both went blind, their granddaughter, Marsha Washington, came to live with them. In 1970, Alberta and Scott Mitchell celebrated their 50th wedding anniversary. Their

1958, Scott Mitchell built his retirement home on Lillie Street

2003 Poetry Recital, Gladys Wilson

1993, At home on Windjammer Court. Lacia and Tahirih Washington-Gorman

children are Scott Mitchell Jr., O. Coffield Mitchell, A. Josephine O'dell, Gladys Wilson, and Janet [Beauford] Williams. The Mitchells are laid to rest in Allen County, Indiana.

One of the Mitchell's daughters, Gladys, moved to Fort Wayne, too. Born in 1931, in West Bend, she has been married twice, and is the mother of seven: the twins, Marc and Marsha Washington (Smiley), Donald Jr., Paul, Rodney, Kim (Basnight), and Cheryl Wilson. After 33.1 years of service, Gladys retired as a tester in 1993 from the Magnavox Company. A textile artist, her quilts have been on public display, most recently at the Lincoln Museum. She has written three books of poetry. A well known area genealogist, she has published several pictorial histories on branches of her family tree.

Since retirement, Gladys has devoted herself to caring for her special needs daughter, Cheryl, who works in a sheltered workshop. Gladys is a founding member of the African/African-American Historical Society of Northeast Indiana. She continues to make quilts and research her family history. She has recently discovered in Paulding, Ohio, the final resting place of her great-great grandparents, Jarret and Mulhudda Ecton, in the Blue Lake cemetery.

Submitted by Gladys Wilson

JUDGE ALFRED W. MOELLERING

MOELLERINGS, SCHAEFERS, DREYERS AND SALOMONS

Judge Moellering's ancestors all came from villages in Westphalia, Prussia. His great-great-grandparents were August and Dorothea (Reckeweg) Moellering who lived in Heimsen. Their five children sailed to the United States before 1850. Alfred's great grandparents, Charles (emigrated from Heimsen in 1845) and his second wife, Mary (Ehlert) Moellering had seven children. Alfred's grandparents were Charles F. and his first wife, Anna (Schaefer) Moellering. Anna was the daughter of Wilhelm and Christina (Meyer) Schaefer (both emigrating 1845: Wilhelm from Hartum, Christina from Frille). They had four children. After Anna's death, Charles F. married Mary (Reber) Tielker and fathered two more children.

Alfred's parents were William C. and Hilda (Dreyer) Moellering. Hilda's parents were William and Louise (Salomon) Dreyer. William emigrated from Dielingen in 1872 and Louise, from Quetzen, at age ten with her parents, Anton and Christine (Gieseking) Salomon in 1871. William C. and Hilda Moellering were the parents of two sons. Paul C. (born February 5, 1920), married (August 27, 1949) Evelyn Hormann, daughter of Edwin F. and Martha (Wesling) Hormann. Paul and Evelyn are the parents of three children, Thomas, Michael and Michelle. The second son, Alfred W. (born December 13, 1926 in Fort Wayne, Indiana), on June 22, 1958, married Carol Lee Wortman, born February 4, 1932 to Dale and Wileta (Emery) Wortman of Van Wert County, Ohio. Alfred and Carol are the parents of two children: Caroline Wortman Moellering, married to Michael Gallagher (they have two children, Fiona and Fintan); and David Wortman Moellering married to Linda Paschen (Obergfell).

Judge Alfred W. Moellering

Alfred, a life-long resident of Fort Wayne, baptized and confirmed at St. Paul's Evangelical Lutheran Church, attended its elementary school. He's a 1945 graduate of South Side High School, was drafted into the U.S. Army immediately and was discharged November 1946. While working at General Electric, he enrolled at Indiana University Extension Center in 1947, became active in the Democratic Party and was the Democratic nominee for State Representative of Allen County in 1948. In 1949 he enrolled at I.U. Bloomington and was very involved in campus politics and student activities. He received his B.S. (Bus) degree in 1951 and his law degree in June 1953.

He practiced law in Fort Wayne, remained active in local Democratic politics and was the1955 Democratic nominee for mayor of Fort Wayne. He was President of the Festival Music Theater, served on the Ballet and Fort Wayne Philharmonic boards and was parliamentarian for the Women's International Bowling Congress for several years. In 1962 Alfred was appointed U.S. Attorney for the Northern District of Indiana by President Kennedy, was admitted to practice before the U. S. Supreme Court and, in 1966, was reappointed by President Johnson until 1970. He was then selected by the Democratic Party to run for Judge of Allen Superior Court, was elected, took office January 1971 and served until his retirement in December 1991.

Awards he received were Kentucky Colonel in 1971 and Sagamore of the Wabash in 1991.

Submitted by Carol Moellering

PHILLIP S. MOLARGIK FAMILY

Phillip S. Molargik has been a resident of Harlan, Indiana, in Northeast Allen County, for approximately 30 years. His parents, Anthony and Lois Molargik moved to Allen County from Noble County about 1940.

The surname Molargik is unique in its spelling because it is derived from Poland as Mularczyk. There are many different variants of spelling, although this unique variation is common to one ancestor, Casmir Mularczyk (Molargik), who immigrated to the United States about 1873.

The Phillip s. Molargik Family, 1975. Front Row, L to R: Lisa, Anthony, Lois, Charity. Back Row, L to R: Phil, Penny, Tammy

Phil married Penelope Jones on April 28, 1961 in Fort Wayne, Indiana. Penelope's parents were Ralph and Flora Jones. Flora was a granddaughter of Reverend Simon F. Stock, the pastor of Martini Lutheran Church in Adams Township, the biography that can be found in the book, *Valley of the Upper Maumee,* page 475. To this union were three daughters. Tammy (Jeff) Luker, Lisa (David) Korte and Charity (Clark) Brown.

Tammy has three children, Sean, Lindsay, and Ean. As of this writing, Lindsay has a son, Deven Hickman.

Lisa has two children, Chad and Taylor. The Korte family can be traced to the late 19th century Fort Wayne from the book, *Valley of the Upper Maumee,* page 241, through the name Fred Korte.

Charity and Clark have one daughter, Sierra. This specific Brown family came to Fort Wayne from Van Wert, Ohio in 1924. Further referencing can be found in a book written by Frederick Dale White.

Phil retired from Fruehauf Trucking after 30 years of service. In his spare time you can find him in his garage repairing automobiles or planning fishing trips to Lake Erie. Penelope retired from Dutch Made Cabinets and enjoys cooking and knitting quilts for her grandchildren, or for other people who may be in need.

Submitted by Penelope Molargik

ELIZABETH J. MONNIER

Artistic Director and Founding Member of the Fort Wayne Dance Collective

Elizabeth (Liz) Monnier was born October 30, 1953 in Fort Wayne. The Monnier family lived on a little farm they fondly called "Shady Lane" at the corner of Smith and Engle Roads from 1951-1959. Liz was the youngest of four children of Robert G. and Arveda (Mazelin) Monnier both originally from rural Adams County. Robert was the foster son of Chrystal and Samuel Everett Rice of Monroe, Indiana and the biological son of John Henry and Della Monnier. Arveda was the daughter of Mary (Schwartz) and David Mazelin. Liz's older siblings are Rebecca (Heinold), and Dan and David Monnier.

Liz Monnier, 1984.
Photo by John Hornberger

The Monnier's moved to Logansport, Indiana in 1959 and then to Columbus, Indiana in 1965 where Liz graduated from Columbus High School in 1971. She graduated from Indiana University in 1975 and was a founding member of the Windfall Dancers in Bloomington, Indiana. She returned to Fort Wayne in 1977 and was a founding member of the Fort Wayne Dance Collective (FWDC) in 1979 becoming its Artistic Director in 1985. She continues to study movement, dance and theatre forms with a number of national/international artists throughout the country. In 1991 and 1993 she was awarded Fellowships from Arts United and in 1993 she served as a Fort Wayne representative for a Sister City delegation in Plock, Poland. In 2003 Liz was awarded the Margaret Ann Keegan Award from Arts United for her on-going curriculum development of movement programs for physically and mentally challenged individuals specifically at Bi-County Services in Bluffton, Indiana. Since FWDCÕs founding, she has taught on-site and outreach classes as well as choreographed for FWDCÕs productions and Touring Company. In 2004 Liz Monnier was instrumental in beginning a dance minor program at Indiana Tech. During 2002-2003 she served on the Dance Standards Committee for the Indiana Department of Education. In 2003 she was awarded a Gene Wyall Award for her excellence in producing video programs for public access television.

Submitted by Liz Monnier

JOHN W. "JACK" & LOIS M. (BAKER) MORRIS FAMILY

John Wesford Morris is a grandson of John and Agnes Lehman (see associated story) who immigrated from Germany to Fort Wayne 1880-81. Their eldest daughter, Alma Catherine (1890-1962) married Wesford L. Morris of Tuscola, Illinois (1889-1975) in 1913. His parents, W.H.C. Morris of Lima, Ohio, and Marmian Taggart of Tuscola, Illinois, both had direct ancestors who fought in the American Revolution. The Taggarts were in the Scot-Irish migration through North Carolina, Tennessee, Kentucky, settling in Indiana before statehood in 1816 in what is now Brown County. A genealogy of Taggart and related families has been compiled for publication in 2005 by Susan Morris McGee.

In 1918, Alma and W. L. Morris moved to Kentucky where he was employed as district sales manager for Goodyear Tire and Rubber Company. Their son, John W., was born in Paducah in 1919. After residing in Lexington, the family returned in 1927 to Fort Wayne permanently.

John W. "Jack" Morris attended Forest Park school and graduated from North Side High, lettering in track. He served on all six 1937 Class Reunion Committees. In 1941, he graduated with a degee in economics from Northwestern University where he was a member of Sigma Alpha Epsilon, the Student Governing Board and Senior Class Commission. Later he attended American Aircraft Institute, Illinois Institute of Technology, Ohio State University, and Akron University, while a supervisor in airframe manufacturing at Pullman Aircraft in Chicago; Curtiss-Wright, Columbus; Firestone Aircraft and Goodyear Aircraft in Akron, Ohio.

At Goodyear, John met Lois Marie Baker, born 1924 in Altoona, Pennsylvania. Her parents, Susan (Sheehan) and Jesse Baker, moved to Pittsburgh where Lois won an Art Scholarship to Carnegie-Mellon University. Lois and John were married in 1945 in Akron and, at end of WW II, decided to live in Fort Wayne where their three children were born: Susan Christine, Katherine Leslie, and John Michael. All went to North Side High; Susan then to IU, Katie and John M. to Carnegie-Mellon, Pittsburgh.

Lois served as President of the Jaycee Wives in 1951 at its peak membership of 100. She was also President of the North Side High School PTA, and a member of the Fort Wayne Art League Evening Group, and the DAR. She also taught Saturday morning classes at Fort Wayne Art School for many years.

Lois and John became interested in genealogy at the Allen County Library. Vacations included visiting bookshops to find county histories, and this led to their mutually enjoyable hobby of collecting books on Americana, art and illustration. Lois also shared a love of British mysteries with her daughter Susan. After working part-time in the book department at Wolf and Dessauer and at Old Fort Books owned by Bill Rockhill, he suggested she start her own shop to fill a void left by Rudy Mueller retiring and closing his Modern Bookshop after many years. So in 1970, Lois opened the Forest Park Fine Used and Out-of-Print Book Shop in a building originally occupied by the Gerkin Grocery at 1412 Delaware Avenue, Fort Wayne across from Forest Park Elementary. Here she specialized in selected books in collectible condition and a nation-wide books search service among other dealers. Upon her retirement in 1997, it was one of the oldest of this type in Indiana.

John and Lois Morris

Lois Morris died March 26, 1999. Their son John Michael, who had been an editor of *Where Magazine* in Washington, D.C. and Assistant to the Dean of Fine Arts at IPFW, Fort Wayne, died April 1, 1999. Their daughter, Katherine L. (widow of John Tribby), had her own jewelry design business in Boise, Idaho where she also taught drawing classes, including at Boise State University. She died April 3, 2003, leaving two children, Jesse and Faith.

John W. Morris, in 1946, entered the life insurance business with The Equitable Society. 1951 to 1960, he was Northern Indiana health insurance field supervisor for the Hoosier Casualty Company of Indianapolis. During this time he and his father, W. L. Morris, who had just retired as a sales manager for Tokheim, formed the Insurancenter, a health insurance agency; and also the Morris Agency, which upon his father's retirement, was joined with and sold to the Waterfield, Colby & Wahl Agency (later the Strasser Agency.)

John was an Eagle Scout member of BSA Troop #11 at Miner School; the YMCA Camp Committee for 17 years; the Society of Indiana Pioneers; active in the Jaycees' start of first Home Show, Sports Show, and petition drive for the War Memorial Coliseum. He was President of the Fort Wayne Health Insurance Association and the Indiana state association. He was also President of Allen County Republican Club and on the state Goldwater-For-President committee. He helped start the local Book Collectors Club; the first book sale for the Friends of the Library; and the Portage Club (predicted to fail for lack of any purpose except commaraderie, but met for lunch in the YMCA Portage Room every Friday for almost 20 years). He retired from the group and health insurance business in 2005. He is still is a member of the Exhausted Roosters, a last-mans club formed by 70 ex-Jaycee officers, meeting every Thursday since 1957. He is currently completing a cartoon book *Tomb It May Concern* (by "Regus

Patoff") and an update of his bibliographical price guide, *Americana-in-Series* for bookdealers and collectors.

Submitted by John W. Morris

ANDREW & LOUISE (TRABEL) MUDRACK FAMILY

Andrew Richard Mudrack was born on June 9, 1904 at Brookside, Colorado, to Paul G. (1866-1921) and Mary Pecolar (1870-1938) Mudrack. Paul Mudrack came to America in 1883 from Lúcky, Slovakia and married Mary Pecolar in July 1889 in Hazleton, Pennsylvania. He worked first as a coal miner in Luzerne County, Pennsylvania and then in Fremont County, Colorado. Paul died from black lung disease on April 8, 1921 in Canon City, Colorado.

As a boy, Andrew also worked in the coalmines until he was almost killed in a mining accident. After his father died, Andrew, his mother, and younger siblings relocated to Fort Wayne, Indiana in July of 1921 to live with his older brothers. On October 5, 1926, Andrew married Louise Trabel at St. Joseph Catholic Church, Hessen Cassel, Indiana. They made a disparate couple with Louise at 4 feet 10 inches tall and Andrew over 6 feet in stature. Louise's grandfather, George Hartman, participated as the Mass server for the wedding. Andrew helped in building South Side High School, and then worked shortly as a security guard for the Wabash Railroad until he was shot at. Thereupon he drove trucks for Walton Coal Company, Archer Trucking, and Security Carthage. On one delivery to a warehouse in Chicago, he came face-to-face with the notorious gangster, Al Capone. In 1942 he began working for Zollner Corporation until his retirement in 1967. On August 20, 1983, Andrew died from a stroke and was buried in the Catholic Cemetery. He enjoyed gardening, raising flowers, drinking Coke, and smoking unfiltered Camel cigarettes. Andrew was a kind, witty, highly respected, very religious person who was affectionately called "Poppie" by his grandchildren.

Andrew and Louise Mudrack's wedding 1926.

Louise Catherine Trabel was born October 18, 1901 at Pesotum, Illinois, to Christian (1871-1952) and Mary Ann Hartman (1882-1957) Trabel. She was a descendant of Jacob Trabel (1840-1921), who came to Dearborn County, Indiana with his father, Nikolaus, from Lorraine Province, France, in 1847, and Johann Joseph Hartmann (1822-1882), who settled in adjacent Franklin County, Indiana in 1845 from Schimborn, Bavaria, Germany. Louise's parents moved from Illinois to a farm in Adams Township, Allen County, Indiana in 1909. Louise attended grade school at St. Joseph Catholic Church, Hessen Cassel, but had to quit to care for her younger siblings when her mother went blind. She also helped her father, who had a crippled leg, with the farming. He called her his "Johnny Boy". After 55 years of marriage, Louise died on May 7, 1982 from diabetes. She was a very bubbly, kind, religious woman who laughed easily. Louise was the perfect grandmother who always had a bowlful of candy on her table for the grandchildren.

The eight children of Andrew and Louise Mudrack are: Irene (1927-2003), wife of Alvin Kleber; Helen Mae (1929-1996), wife of Paul Ford; Richard (1930-1963), husband of Jacqueline Fey; Ralph (1931), husband of Sandra Garrison; Alice (1933-1946); Dorothy (1934-2003), wife of Ronald Redmond; Virginia (1936-1997), wife of Donald Gering; and Thomas (1937), husband of Ruth Cope.

Submitted by Jeanne Porter

JOHN RAULAND (ROLLIE) MUHN

John Rauland (Rome) Muhn, born June 24, 1891 in the Dutch Ridge area of Perry Township, Allen County, Indiana, was the third of five children of Rose Ann Ellen (Hensinger) who arrived here via covered wagon from Pennsylvania and Seneca County, Ohio, and John Martin Muhn, son of German immigrants. He was preceded in death on September 6, 1985 at age 94 by his three wives, Jennie Joy (Platner), Martha (Mountz, Williams) and Catherine Ann (Dye). He had three sons with Joy: John Henry, 1918; Perry Arthur, 1920; and Roland Muhn, Jr., 1922. With his fellow man, Rollie was a great tease.

When 14, he apprenticed as a carpenter, working "8 hours in the morning for God and 8 hours in the afternoon for man" seven days a week for 25 cents per day. He was apprenticed, along with Mack, an orphan boy from St. Vincent's Villa. Mack cried because he received no Christmas presents. They vowed that when they could, they would furnish presents for Villa orphans. Mack died in World War I; in 1926 Rollie began an annual tradition until the villa closed in 1970. Every Christmas Rollie and his friends donated gifts and treats for each orphan, as each listed in a letter to Santa. Rollie delivered the gifts in his velvet Santa Claus suit. He was one of ten 1984 Grandparents of the Year selected by the National Council for the Observance of Grandparents Day.

John Rauland (Rollie) Muhn, as Santa

Rollie was a contractor, responsible for many stucco homes and buildings in Auburn. When Mr. Cord insisted on installing windows flat in the roof of the Auburn Manufacturing plant to furnish light for the workers, Rome refused, but stood the windows upright with short slanted roof section backing to form a sawtooth roof, which became standard construction. When the county courthouse in Auburn burned, it was replaced by a fireproof structure of stone and metal; the judge asked Rollie to finish the courtroom interior, defining seat and bench locations and heights. Rome measured it, had the pieces cut in his factory, and that is the only flammable part of the courthouse.

Rollie's Philosophy, at 90: LOVE was the greatest gift of all. Love only one God and do unto your neighbor like you would have him do unto you. Give your love free to the people you live with and they too will love God. If you feel like crying, cry; it heals the heart.

Rollie recalled working one day in Allen County and heard someone call his name. There was no one around. He listened quietly. The voice said, "Tell your mother Ellen if she doesn't come to Fort Wayne before September to see her sister, Mary, it will be too late to talk to her." That's all he heard. He told his mother. She laughed, thought he was nuts, didn't go. In September mother got a call that told her of Mary's death. His autobiography, *MY LIFE'S STORY*, typed in 1981 by his niece, Barbara Ford, has many similar incidents and stories of life in those days.

Submitted by nephew, Henry W. Ford

DAN MUNSON FAMILY

Daniel David Munson 3rd was born August 30, 1932 to Daniel Munson, Jr. of Nebraska City, Nebraska and Mary M. Pukrop of South Bend, Indiana, and raised in Angola, Indiana. He graduated high school in Angola, and attended the University of Notre Dame in South Bend, Indiana, where he earned a B.S. in Physics. He attended on a Navy Scholarship and after commissioning as an Ensign, was sent to San Diego, California, where he was assigned to the U.S.S. Fort Marion, LSD-22.

He met his wife, Joyce Barlow, in San Diego while she was attending San Diego State College. She is the daughter of Frank Barlow and Gladys Gilmore Rochester of Salinas, California. She was born June 8, 1932 in Salinas. They were married in a Catholic church in San Diego on July 30, 1955. They have five children and six grandchildren.

After release from the Navy, they moved to Fort Wayne where he worked for ITT Aerospace Industries for ten years and as Supervisor of the Failure Analysis Lab for the Magnavox Electronic Systems Company for twenty six years until retirement in 1992. His wife, Joyce (Jo) worked for Peoples Trust Bank and its various mergers in the printing department before retiring in 1994 after 17 years.

Daniel David the 4th was born on May 18, 1956 at the Coronado Naval Air Station in California while Daniel was still in the Navy. He attended Notre Dame University on a Navy scholarship but did not serve in the Navy. He is a chef and club

L to R: Daniel David Munson 3rd, Joyce Barlow Munson, Daniel David Munson 4th, Michael Patrick Munson, Sandra Anne Munson Rath, Richard Joseph Munson, Thomas Edward Munson, 1998

manager working variously at Sycamore Hills Golf Club in Fort Wayne, Willow Bend Golf Club in Van Wert, Ohio, Stonehenge Golf Club in Warsaw, Indiana, and at Crystal Tree Golf Club in Orland Park, Illinois. He is no longer married.

Michael Patrick was born July 7, 1958 in Fort Wayne, as were their other three children. He is a Master Plumber in Gaithersburg, Maryland, has his own business and is married to Lucrecia Moreno of Lima, Peru. They have two adopted children, Jake and Rachelle.

Sandra Anne was born July 4, 1959. She was a Corpsman in the Navy for 22 years. She is married to John Rath of Hamlin, New York. John was also in the Navy and now works as a civilian contractor for the U.S. government. She continues to pursue her nursing as a Doctor's assistant in Gulfport, Mississippi. They have one son, Brandon.

Richard Joseph was born August 1, 1960. He also works as a civilian working for the Navy in Denver, Colorado, since his retirement after 20 years in the Navy. He is not married.

Thomas Edward was born December 25, 1961. He attended Indiana University studying Journalism. He works for a food vending company in Fort Wayne. He has three sons by his ex-wife Constance Furos: Thomas, Jr., Justin, and Nicholas.

Dan and Jo like to travel and do so at every opportunity.

Submitted by Joyce (Jo) Munson

ROBERT ROSS MURPHY & ROSA CHRISTINA (GUIFF) FAMILY

Immigrant, Robert S. Murphy, Sr., arrived in America about 1799. Robert was born in County Down, Ireland about 1776 of Scots-Irish heritage. Robert married Anna Jackson about 1802 in Washington County, Pennsylvania, and had seven children. Robert, Anna and their children settled in the Cincinnati, Ohio area for a time in the early 1800s before settling on a farm along the Maumee River in Paulding County, Ohio about 1828. Their oldest son, John Jackson Murphy (1803-1877), who was the father of Amos Peter Murphy, remained in the Cincinnati area in College Corner, Ohio, where he was a blacksmith for 25 years. About 1850 John Jackson Murphy and his second wife, Elizabeth, removed to DeKalb County. They are buried in Scipio Cemetery, Allen County.

Robert Ross Murphy was born August 14, 1863 in DeKalb County, Indiana, to Amos Peter Murphy (1840-1917) and Olive F. Chandler (1841-1878). Robert married Mary Irving (1863-1898) and had Edith (1888-1952), Ethel (1891-1976) and Ruth (1896-1957).

Rosa Guiff and Robert were married February 19, 1901 in Fort Wayne. Five children were born of this union on the family farm in Springfield Township: Roy Raymond (1907-2004); Harold Dewitt (1909-2000); John Lewis (1913-1998); Olive Emily (1916-); and Ernest 'David' (1923-2004). Robert was killed in an automobile accident August 4, 1939. Robert and Rosa were buried at Harlan Memorial Cemetery.

In July, 1921, Robert Murphy was one of the four new members added to the Board of School Trustees when the Fort Wayne Library extended its services throughout Allen County. Robert served on the library board for many years and was instrumental in the opening of the county libraries in Harlan and Monroeville. From his personal diary, Robert was still active on the library board as late as the November 13,1929 meeting in Fort Wayne.

Of French descent, Rosa Guiff was born September 8, 1880 in Whitley County, Indiana, and died February 24, 1969 in Fort Wayne. Rosa was a daughter of Lester George Guiff (1856-1899) and Emily Pepe (1858-1938). Lester's father was John C. Guiff (1826-1910) who arrived in New Orleans from Harve, France in 1847. John applied for Naturalization in Allen County in 1852 and farmed in Perry and Eel River Townships. Emily Pepe was a daughter of Louis Pepe (1830-1908) and Mary Petregney (1830-1913). Louis, age three, arrived in New York on the "Normandie" in 1834 with his parents, Joseph and Anna (Couturier) Pepe and siblings. Joseph and son, Louis, farmed in Washington Township. These families are buried in Sacred Heart Cemetery in Auburn, Indiana. Louis recorded family births, deaths, and marriages along with an accounting of purchases made. There is a copy of this interesting data at the Allen County Library.

The Chandler lineage (Olive F., wife of Amos Peter Murphy) goes back to the 1600s in Plymouth Colony, Massachusetts. Olive's parents were Freeman Chandler (c.1801-1869) and Esther Austin (c.1798 -1871). Freeman was born in Androscoggin County, Minot, Maine and farmed in Pickaway County, Ohio, and Henry County, Iowa, before purchasing a farm in Springfield Township prior to 1860. Esther was born in Oxford County, Buckfield, Maine.

1942, Allen County, Indiana. L to R: Karen Ann Murphy, held by father, Harold Murphy; Dorothy Ewing Murphy, Roy Murphy, Judith Murphy, held by mother, Margaret Husted Murphy; Marilyn Witmer, held by father, Merle Witmer; Olive Murphy Witmer; Mary DeLong Murphy; Sandra Murphy, held by father, John L. Murphy; Rosa C. Guiff Murphy. Three children in front, Linda L. Murphy, H. Kent Murphy, and Larry Murphy.

1942, Front, L to R: Rosa (Griff), and Olive Emily. Back L to R: Ernest "David", Roy R., John L., Harold D.

On September 15, 1934, Roy Raymond Murphy married Margaret Emily Husted (1912-2000) and had Larry, Linda, Judith and Jane. Roy and Margaret were buried at Scipio Cemetery.

Harold DeWitt Murphy and Dorothy Daisy Ewing (1913-1994) were married in Harlan on August 8, 1931. They are buried at IOOF Cemetery, New Haven. Their children were Kent, Karen, Thomas and Donald.

John Lewis Murphy and Mary Ellen DeLong (1916-) were wed on September 11, 1937. John was buried at Scipio Cemetery. Children were Sandra, John and Nancy.

On December 24, 1938, Olive Emily Murphy and Merle Edwin Witmer (1907-1994) were wed in Allen County. Merle was buried at Leo Memorial Cemetery. Children were Marilyn and Robert.

Ernest 'David' Murphy married Marilyn Holzworth on October 11, 1946 and had Paul. As his second wife, David married Ruth Griggs March 15, 1969 and had Clifford.

Submitted by Karen Avery

GEORGE MYERS

George Myers was born in Germany on April 28, 1834 to Anthony Myers and Anna Schnider. His year of immigration to the United States is not known, but it is assumed he came here at a

Rosa McBennett Myers (center) with her daughter, Catherine Myers Sonntag, to her right, Catherine's daughter Mary Sonntag Fessler, and Mary's daughter. To the left of Rosa is her son, George P. Myers, his son, Joseph George Myers, and his son, George Henry Myers. Sheboygan, Wisconsin, c. 1910

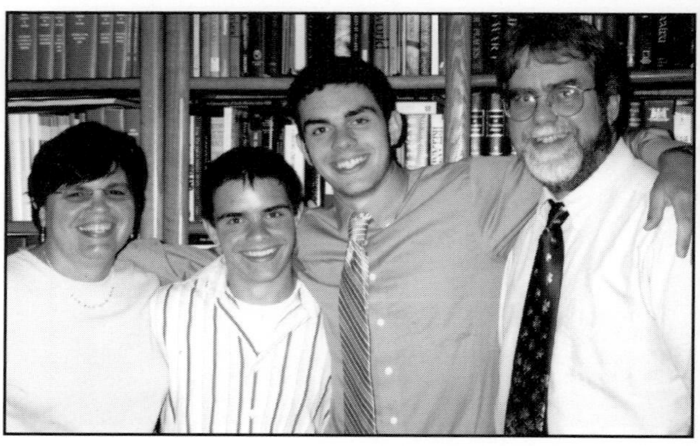

Linda, Brian, Matt and Steve Myers, 2005

young age and could speak English well before meeting his bride-to-be, Rosa McBennett, who had come to the U.S. on April 21, 1857. Rosa was born January 12, 1834 in Dunfelemy, County Monaghan, Ireland, the daughter of Francis McBennett and Catherine Bridget Lennon .

George and Rosa were married in St. Louis, Missouri on November 15, 1859 at Sts. Mary and Joseph church. George worked as a carpenter for the railroad in St. Louis at the time. Around 1863, in the middle of the Civil War, George and Rosa moved to Fort Wayne, Indiana with their two small children, George P. Myers and Catherine Ann Myers, who were born in St. Louis in 1860 and 1862. George worked as a carpenter in the railroad yard and later worked for the Pittsburgh, Fort Wayne & Chicago Railroad in their carpenter shops. The family lived at 66 Wilt Street in Fort Wayne, very close to the Wabash Railroad shops and tracks. They attended St. Paul's Catholic Church, where their other seven children were baptized: Francis Anthony "Frank" Myers (born October 14, 1864); Edward Eugene Myers (born October 11, 1866); Henry "John" Myers (born October 16, 1868); Mary Agnes Myers (born August 20, 1870); Rosanna Sophia Myers (born July 17, 1873); Owen Charles Myers (born June 17, 1875) and one child, whose name is unknown and died at a young age sometime around the move from St. Louis to Fort Wayne.

Henry married Louisa A. Whitman and died in Fort Wayne in 1910. Frank married Elizabeth Lyons and died in Chicago in 1895. Catherine married Louis Sonntag and moved to Sheboygan, Wisconsin. George P. married Catherine A. "Kate" Voors, the daughter of John G. Voors, Sr. and Elizabeth Rekers, and followed his sister to Sheboygan in January of 1886.

George Myers was a successful Fort Wayne business entrepreneur. After working in the railroad shops as a carpenter/builder for many years, he established a business by 1870 with George J. Jacoby and Sebastian Wiegand. They were "Dealers in Rough and Dressed Lumber and Manufacturers of sash, doors, blinds, etc. at the corner of Virginia and Murray." This partnership was short-lived and George set out on his own just three years later and by 1875 had set up his own lumber shop "Lumber, Lath and Shingles" located at southeast Broadway, north of the Pacific, Fort Wayne and Chicago Railroad, as well as a general contractor company with Harmon Rump at 100 Union.

For reasons unknown, George and Rosa were divorced in 1889 and Rosa moved to Sheboygan, Wisconsin with her youngest children, Rose and Owen, as well as Mary Agnes, who married Charles Meyer in Sheboygan in 1893. Rose later married John Bauer and lived in Evansville, Indiana. Owen moved back to Fort Wayne, married Anna R. Lauer, and lived in Fort Wayne for many years, then in Wapakoneta, Ohio, just over the state line.

After George and Rosa's divorce, George moved to Chicago, perhaps to assist in the building of the Pullman railroad cars there. He is believed to have died there in 1894 of small pox.

Rosa lived with her daughter Catharine Sonntag in Sheboygan, Wisconsin and died there in 1916. She is buried in the Calvary (Old North Side Cemetery) in Sheboygan, Wisconsin.

Submitted by Virginia A. "Gin" Myers Shaw

STEVE & LINDA MYERS FAMILY

Steven William Myers was born in Detroit, Michigan in 1954 to William Bernard Myers and Delores Elaine White. The oldest of three boys and a girl, he graduated from the University of Michigan, earning a B.A. with high distinction in anthropology in 1976, and an M.L.S., with a specialization in archival administration, in 1979. Linda Marie Dainty was born in Detroit, Michigan in 1956 to Kenneth Charles Dainty and Yvonne Alice Evans. The oldest of five girls and one boy, she also graduated from the University of Michigan, earning a B.A. with high honors in psychology in 1978, and an M.S.W. in 1980. Steve and Linda met in Ann Arbor at the Newman Center, where they were both active in the Catholic student organization, and were married on October 8, 1983 in a Catholic ceremony held at the Edgewood United Church in East Lansing, Michigan. They resided in downtown Lansing, Michigan for a time, Linda working as a social worker in a foster care program and Steve as director of the Center on Nonviolence and Disarmament, a small nonprofit research center he had founded in 1982.

Intent on starting a family, they moved on February 22, 1986 to Fort Wayne, Indiana, where Steve began work two days later as a reference librarian in the renowned Historical Genealogy Department at the Allen County Public Library. Two years later he became the department's assistant manager, in which capacity he continues. Steve lectures widely on genealogical topics including Irish research, his specialty, and was co-leader of the National Genealogical Society's research trips to Dublin and Belfast in 2001. He edited and republished Sir Richard Musgrave's *Memoirs of the Irish Rebellion of 1798* under the banner of Round Tower Books, his part time publishing and book selling business. He has served on the boards of several national genealogical organizations, and received the Federation of Genealogical Societies' Distinguished Service Award in 1991.

Linda stayed at home as a full time mom after their move to Fort Wayne, and found parenting to be the most rewarding and challenging job. She loved their beautiful, yet affordable old house and the wonderful city parks and library system that she frequented with their young sons. She returned to her social work profession part time in April, 1993, working first as a therapist for the Charter Beacon Intensive Outpatient Program (1993-94), then as a caseworker and casework supervisor for Big Brothers/Big Sisters of Northeast Indiana (1994-96), and later as an inpatient social worker at Parkview Behavioral Health (1996-98). Linda then split time between Bishop Luers High School and St. Jude Catholic School as a school social worker (1998-2000), before becoming a full time counselor at St. Jude's (2000), which position she enjoys most of all.

Steve and Linda have been active members of Beacon Heights Church of the Brethren in Fort Wayne since 1986, and moved north to eastern Perry Township in November, 1996 for the quality school system and a larger yard in which the boys could play. They have two sons, both born at home with the assistance of a lay midwife. Both boys attended the Beacon Heights Pre-School and Bunche Elementary, a Montessori magnet school. Matthew Steven Myers was born in 1986, graduated from Carroll High School in 2005, and now attends the University of North Carolina at Chapel Hill. Brian Patrick Myers was born in 1989, and is a junior at Carroll High School. Both boys played varsity high school soccer, while Steve took up the sport at the age of 40 and continues playing year round with friends at the Fort Wayne Sport Club. Steve has enjoyed researching the family history as a hobby since 1973, and is planning his seventh research trip to Ireland, his favorite place. Linda enjoys reading, crocheting, and listening to books on tape. They both enjoy walking, traveling to national parks and playing euchre, pinochle and board games with family and friends.

Submitted by Steve Myers

WARRELL MYRICK

Warrell Myrick, the oldest son of the late Mr. and Mrs. James Myrick, was born in Little Rock, Arkansas, October 29, 1911. His parents moved to Fort Wayne, Indiana, in 1912. His mother and father departed this life during World War I, both on the same day, during the influenze epidemic, and left three young children, Warrell, Clifton and Frances. Warrell and Clifton were adopted by Mr. and Mrs. Israel Graham of 1919 West Fourth Street, Fort Wayne, who preceded him in death. Warrell grew up in Faunsdale, Alabama, in a Christian home, with Mrs. Graham's father, Willis Ravizee, a deacon of First Baptist Church in Faunsdale. Warrell was converted at an early age and joined the First Baptist Church there.

He and his wife, Margaret L. Patterson, were puppy lovers in grade school. In 1935 they were united in holy matrimony in Chicago, Illinois. In 1936 they moved to Fort Wayne and joined Turner Chapel A.M.E. Church where he served until his death. He was a Senior Steward and a class leader of Class Number 11.

Warrell retired in 1976 from May Stone and Sand Company. He was a 33° Mason, belonged to St. Mary's Lodge #14 F&AM, FortWayne Consistory #66, Saudi Temple #50, and was Past Patron Emeritus of Rhoda K. Jones Chapter O-C-S-#54, Hametic Lodge. He also was a member of the Retired Men's Club of McCulloch Center, the N.A.AC.P., and was a board member of the Fort Wayne Rescue Mission.

He was baptized in the River Jordan in 1981 by Rev. Ernest Angley. He departed this life Wednesday, February 3, 1988, at, 7:30 p.m. in the Veterans' Administration Hospital, Fort Wayne.

He leaves to cherish his passing: devoted wife, Margaret L; a daughter, Maria L. Davis; a grandson, Warrell Booher and a granddaughter, Wendy Booher, of Fort Wayne; a sister, Francis R. Davis, of Fort Wayne; two brothers, Dr. James Graham, of Fort Wayne, and Wayne Graham, of Toledo, Ohio; two brothers-in-law, Fred Patterson and Peter Davis, of Fort Wayne; two Godchildren, Dorothy Mitchell and Inez Collins, of Fort Wayne; and a host of nieces, nephews, many other relatives and close friends. *From the Obituary of Warrell Myrick*

Submitted by Margaret Myrick

AUGUSTUS R. & CATHERINE STRACK NAGY FAMILY

Augustus "Gus" Nagy was born in Ashland, West Virginia on August 28, 1925. He was a first generation American born to Hungarian immigrants, Michael and Mary Seles Nagy. Gus played drum in the Gary High School Band. He was drafted into the United States Army during WW II and graduated from high school post-war. He served in the U.S. 20th Armored Division in Germany that liberated the concentration camp in Dakow.

After the war Gus studied mechanics/engineering in Chicago. Standing as Best Man in his brother's wedding, Gus met Catherine Strack, the Maid-of-Honor, and so began their life together. Catherine, daughter of Charles L. and Priscilla Strack, was born October 9,1928 in Allen County. She is a Miami Indian and descended from Tacumwah, Jean Baptiste Richardville, and LaBlonde Richardville. She studied at the St. Louis Institute of Music and taught piano. Gus and Catherine were married on May 20, 1950.

Gus hand-built their first home near Coesse, Indiana. As their family grew they moved to a farm near Arcola. Their family include children: Laura, Mary, Catherine, Matthew, Julia and Christopher. They are blessed with thirteen grandchildren and three great-grand children. They celebrated their 50th wedding anniversary May 2000.

Submitted by Laura Nagy

AUGUST NAHRWOLD FAMILY

See Donna Nahrwold Voldering family page 733.

FREDERICK C. NAHRWOLD - LOUIS H. NAHRWOLD FAMILY

He was just 14 years old as he emigrated from Bremen, Germany, a native of Prussia, to New York, when Frederick C. Nahrwold stepped onto U.S. soil on September 3, 1857. Frederick accompanied his two older brothers in their quest of a new life in America. At that time in Germany, work was scarce and conscription into the Kaiser's army was mandatory, hence many young men fled to America.

On his journey here, he had worked in the coal mines of Pennsylvania and the Wabash and Erie Canal. Wm. Flemary, clerk of Allen Circuit Court, naturalized Frederick at 25 years old on October 5, 1868 in Allen County, Indiana. On March 28, 1870 he bought the farm at the current location of 10625 Paulding Road, New Haven, for $2000 from F. and M. Wohnker. Frederick repaired wagon wheels in Fort Wayne as a wheelwright. His woodworking tools remain in the family to this day.

The original house and barn, built in 1834 with hand-hewn timbers, still stand, as does the granary built in 1872. Between 1905-1910, three additional rooms were added to the house.

Frederick (1843-1904) married Elizabeth Niemeyer (1846-1915), and had five children: Louis H., 1870-1928, (married Haty Messman, 1881-1914); Frederick E., 1872-1917 (married Minnie Koch); Christian C., 1874-1952 (married

Louis and Haty Nahrwold marriage photo, November 25, 1903

Elizabeth Buuck); Henry 1877-1947 (married Pauline Bradtmiller); Maria, 1879-1953 (married Wm. Keller who built the first Woodburn firetruck on a Model T chassis); and Louise (married Ernst Pruesse, who owned the 6 Mile Tavern on Wayne Trace).

Elizabeth Niemeyer's family was raised on a farm that the present day International Harvester grounds occupy.

To Louis and Hedwig (Haty), whose wedding picture is shown, were born: Clarence, 1905-1977 (married Helen Ross); Elmer H., 1910-1979 (married Bertha Schmidt); and Esther, 1913-1990 (married Clayton Edenfield). Haty had tuberculosis and spent her remaining days in a tent pitched in front of the house. She died from contracting pneumonia after the tent flap blew open in a rainstorm and she became cold and wet. Esther stayed with Uncle Christian much of the time while the boys and Louie cared for Haty and farmed. When Louis died at 58 years, he was buried in the same cemetery as his parents, Martini Lutheran Cemetery in New Haven.

Clarence, at 22 years old, was left, along with his brother and sister, to manage the farm. Elmer bought Clarence a house and four acres near Bethlehem Lutheran Church in Fort Wayne as his share of the farm. After 12 years, when WWII broke out and farming became profitable, he paid Esther her share and continued farming until he died in 1979.

When Elmer's first boys were born during the depression years, he had no money to pay Dr. G. A. Smith. One day the doctor saw him and asked when he was going to pay on his bill. Elmer replied that farming was just not profitable at that time. The doctor asked how much he had in his pocket, to which he replied $5. Dr Smith asked him for the $5, and told him his bill was paid in full. To Elmer and Bertha Schmidt Nahrwold were born Fred C., 1932-2001 (who married Norma Werling and was a printer in Fort Wayne as well as farmed in Ossian, Indiana); James born in 1934 (who served in Korea as an Air Force mechanic and later worked for city of New Haven, and currently farms at the home place); Elmer Jr., 1936 - 2001 (married Mary Lou Schrader and worked at International Harvester); Larry born in 1949 (who continues to farm at the home place), and Donald, 1949-1975, who died early from diabetes complications. He is interred with his parents in Emanuel Lutheran Cemetery outside of New Haven, Indiana.

Direct descendants of Louis Nahrwold who continue to reside in Allen County besides James and Larry include: Corine Nahrwold born in 1947 (daughter of Clarence); Dr. David born in 1954 (married Elaine Lund), veterinarian in Woodburn, son of Fred, and their son Seth born in 1986; Joel Nahrwold born in1968 (married Stephanie Dowdy), son of Elmer Jr., who works at Edy's Ice Cream, and their daughter Mallory born in1998 and son Jake born in 2003; sister Melanie Nahrwold born in 1986 with daughter Madison born in1998, and son Logan born in 2003; Danielle Edenfield, married Chad Inman, born in 1974 (granddaughter of Esther) and son Grant born 1996; and sister Cori Edenfield born in 1978. Their father, Dan Edenfield 1949-1998, married Tonne Batdorf, (son of Esther) died in the line of duty as an Allen County police officer.

Submitted by David F. Nahrwold DVM

NAHRWOLD FAMILY

Henry (Ernst Heinrich) Nahrwold immigrated to Fort Wayne from Rosenhagen, Kingdom of Prussia, in the early 1870s. He married Mary Poeppel, daughter of Johann and Christine (Kleine) Poeppel on March 17, 1872. Their first child Friedrich was born in Fort Wayne. In 1874 they moved to land on Parent Road, which Mary inherited and had children Wilhelmine, Sophie, Mary, Henry, Ernst, John Louis, Caroline, Christian, Lizzie and Anna. Henry died from cancer in 1893 leaving Mary to continue farming and raising her children and a granddaughter Emma.

In 1900, while clearing trees, one fell on John's right foot. By the time the doctor arrived, gangrene had set in, and the leg had to be amputated above the knee. Because of this accident, although he wasn't the youngest son, John was allowed to buy the farm. John married Anna Hartmann on November 16, 1913, at St. Paul's Lutheran Church, Gar Creek. They had seven children: stillborn twins, Gerhardt, John Henry, Leona, Pauline and Ruth. Since the farm was considered the "home place", John's brothers and sisters and their families were frequent visitors. John enjoyed farming and spent many hours tending the various crops and animals. Only after he turned 80 did he quit driving tractors. Anna was a devout Christian woman who was a charter member of St. Peter's Lutheran Church Ladies' Aid.

John H. married Helen C. Griebel on September 8, 1943, at St. Peter's. Their children are Brenda, Rhonda, Carol and John Michael. Leona married Otto Rinaker April 15, 1944. They have a daughter Lois Ann. Pauline married Herman Baatz on July 29, 1962, and has a son Herman Frederick II. Ruth married Elvin Baatz on April 30, 1949. Their children are Edward and Carolyn.

John was a farmer his entire life. He expanded the dairy operation, added a silo and many farm buildings to the "home place" and remodeled the house. In 1974, John and Helen hosted the Nahrwold centennial and invited relatives, friends and neighbors to celebrate the farm being in the family for 100 years. John had a profound interest in steam engines and built a half-scale Port Huron engine in 1954. He restored other engines as well as his father's 1924 Rio touring car. John was a founder and director of the Maumee Valley Steam and Gas Engine Association.

After John's death, Helen and John M. continued farming, making John M. the fourth generation of the family in farming. John, his wife Deborah and their children, Abigail, Kati, John Zachary, Jacob, Timothy, and Owen still live on the farm. Brenda and Roger Schuller have Mark, Jonathan and Elisabeth, who is married to Beau Rogers. Jonathan and his wife Dawn have Jonathan David (J.D.), Olivia and Sophie. Rhonda and Roger DeVaux have sons Randall (Randy) and Ryan. Randy and his wife Angela have Madison and Meghan. In retirement, Helen remains active in St. Peter's Ladies Aid, in the church's seniors group, and with the Federation of Lutheran Women. Carol is a librarian at the Allen County Public Library.

Submitted by Carol Nahrwold.

ANDREA MARIE (HENRY) NAVARRO

Andrea Marie Henry was born on November 17, 1954 in Jackson, Michigan. She is the sixth child born to Jerome F. and Marganelle (Applegate) Henry. She is one of 17 children.

She attended St. Charles Borromeo and Most Precious Blood Catholic grade schools and Central Catholic High School, Fort Wayne. Andrea was very athletic as a child. She was competitive in swimming, track and softball. She played for the Queens softball team at Packard Park, Fort Wayne. She also attended H&R Block tax preparation school.

In 1971 Andrea married Ramon DeLeon Navarro, son of Jesus and Helen Navarro. Andrea and Ramon have five sons, Ramon Jr. born in 1972, Christopher born in 1973, Patrick born in 1978, Paul born in 1981 and Joseph born in 1980. All were born in Fort Wayne. Paul died in a tragic car accident in 2001.

Andrea works at Midwest Pipe & Steel Company, owned by her brother, Jerry Jr., in Fort Wayne.

Submitted by Andrea Navarro

CALEB J. NEAL

Caleb J. Neal, born in 1859, was 78 years old when he died February 1, 1937. He worked as a cabinetmaker at the Packard Piano factory in Fort Wayne, Indiana until they closed their doors. He married Alice Rebecca Lesh on January 1, 1888. She was 93 when she died at the Lutheran hospital of pneumonia. Caleb and Alice are buried in I.O.O.F. Cemetery at New Haven, Indiana. They had three children, one boy and two girls. The boy and one girl died in childhood. The other daughter, Pearl, lived until she was 85. Pearl married Guy Addison McNeal and they had five children, Dale, Violet, Glen, Jack and Paul.

Guy McNeal worked and retired from the railroad. He loved to hunt, work in the garden, go fishing, and enjoyed life. He was handy and could fix anything. Pearl, an excellent homemaker, enjoyed canning vegetables and sewing. An accomplished seamstress, she made clothes for her daughter. Guy was 66 years old when he died on June 19, 1953. Pearl died of congestive heart failure twenty-two years later on April 17, 1975, at the age of 85.

The four McNeal brothers all served in World War II. Dale was stationed in Alaska helping build the Alaskan Highway. He died at age 85, on May 15, 2003. Glen served in Panama, returned home to marry and have two children, Greg and Linda. Jack served in Germany, married and has two sons and grandchildren. He was a steelworker and worked on the Allen County War Memorial Coliseum laying the steel framework. Paul served in the Navy, married and had two stepchildren. He died August 25, 1997.

Violet McNeal was the only daughter in the family. She worked at the General Electric Company as a coil winder during the war. The coils were used in motors. On June 15, 1941, she married Joseph M. Adam. Joseph also served in the war in Germany. They had two sons, Timothy and Terry. The boys married and Violet has three granddaughters, three step-grandchildren and six great grandchildren.

Submitted by Violet H. Adam

CHARLES E. NELSON FAMILY

Charles Edward Nelson was born on May 18, 1932 in Fort Wayne (Allen County) Indiana to Roy Sylvestor Nelson and Jeanette Mae (Frame) Nelson.

Roy Nelson moved to Allen County (Fort Wayne) Indiana in 1922 with his parents (Charles Frederick and Alice (Jones) Nelson and his three brothers and one sister. They came from Sloan (presently part of Imboden), Arkansas where his father managed a stone quarry. This Nelson family had lived in Adams County, Indiana for several generations. Roy Nelson was employed by the International Harvester Corp. until his death in 1947.

Charles and Mary Nelson

Jeanette Mae Frame was born in Fort Wayne, Indiana in 1900. Her parents were Edward Ingram Frame and Gertrude Pooler. She lived in Fort Wayne and attended local grammar schools and the "old" Fort Wayne High School graduating in 1918. It is of interest that the "old" high scbool celebrated it's 50 year anniversary in 1916 according to her yearbooks. She attended the Fort Wayne Art School and taught school in Michigan City, Indiana for several years. She resided in Fort Wayne for most of her 97 years. The ancestors of her mother, Gertrude Pooler, came to Allen County working on the construction of the Wabash and Erie Canal. Her father, Edward I. Frame, was born in 1872 on his father's farm, located on Homestead Road in Aboite Township, Allen

County, Indiana. Edward's father, Ingram Frame, came to Allen County in the 1860s.

Charles (Chuck) lived in Fort Wayne most of his life, attending local grammar schools and attending South Side High School, graduating in 1950. He served in the United States Air Force during the Korean War from 1950 to 1954.

After receiving an honorable discharge, he enrolled in Purdue University receiving a Bachelor of Science degree in Electrical Engineering. Charles has been employed in Fort Wayne at various times at both ITT and Magnavox. His Magnavox career included time spent in both Consumer and Government/Industrial Electronics, retiring in 1993.

Charles married Shirley Jane Straw in 1953, and they were divorced in 1977. Three children survive this union. They are Debra Kay, Steven Allan, and Sharla Jane Nelson. Debra is married to Douglas Adair, and they have two daughters, Rosa Katherine and Carol Rebecca. They all live Southern California. Steven lives in Las Vegas, Nevada. Sharla is married to Jeffery Parrish, and they reside in Dekalb County, Indiana.

Charles married Mary Pat Montes (Gear) in 1979, and they currently (2005) reside in Allen County Indiana.

Submitted by Charles E. Nelson

RUSSELL MEARKLE NEUMAN & DR. PAULA ANNE YOUNG NEUMAN FAMILY

Russell (Russ) Mearkle Neuman was born December 16, 1955 in Philadelphia, Pennsylvania to William (Bill) Lawrence Neuman (born April 8, 1924) and Elizabeth (Betty) Ruth Mearkle Neuman (born October 10, 1921). Bill's parents were Otto Neuman, born in Shenandoah, Pennsylvania, and Emma Hasher Neuman, born in Germany. Betty's parents were Percy Calvin Mearkle and Elizabeth Fresch Mearkle. Russ's parents were both born in Philadelphia and were married in Drexil Hill, Pennsylvania on June 12, 1948. The Neumans moved to Bluffton, Indiana in 1964 for Bill's work with Franklin Electric. They have four sons: Dr. W. Lawrence (Larry) (married Diane Mertins) currently of Madison, Wisconsin; Robert J. (Bob) currently of Detroit, Michigan; Russ; and Keith A. (married Ricki Sparrow) (four children) currently of Lenexa, Kansas.

Russ graduated from Norwell High School in 1973 and earned an Associate Degree in Computer Science from Purdue University (IPFW) in 1978. He has worked for over 25 years as a Computer Programmer for Lincoln National Corporation and for IBM Corporation since 1998. Russ is a Master Mason, member and officer of Wayne Lodge #25 and an officer for the Job's Daughters Bethel # 8 Council.

Dr. Paula Anne Young Neuman was born on September 15, 1960 in Tiffin, Ohio to Paul Everett Young and Mary Virginia Brocious Young. Paul was born June 5, 1914 in Athens County, Ohio to William Henry Young (born April 30, 1889; died October 15, 1958) and Elma Rebecca McKee Young (born August 10, 1891; died October 26, 1993). Mary was born in Ringtown, Pennsylvania on March 4, 1923 to William Roy Brocious (born July 30, 1891; died August 14, 1972) and Edith Mae Hasker Brocious (born March 21, 1904; died May 29, 1975). The Youngs met after Paul's service in WWII and were married in Dayton, Ohio on October 15, 1945. After living in Medina and Coshocton, Ohio, they moved to Tiffin, Ohio in 1952 for Paul's job with the U.S. Department of Agriculture (Soil Conservation Service.) Paula has three brothers, John P. Brocious of Spring Hill, Florida (wife Ruth, deceased June 2004), a retired Chief of Police (four children); David A. Young (married Brenda Wertz) of Tiffin, Ohio, a Vietnam War Veteran and retired police officer (two children); and Rodney O. Young (married Melinda Berry) of Tiffin, Ohio, a Vietnam War Veteran and Production Worker (two children).

Paula graduated from Tiffin Columbian High School (Ohio) in 1978, then earned a Bachelor of Science degree in Psychology from Heidelberg College in 1982, a Masters of Arts degree in Political Science/Public Administration from Bowling Green State University in 1987, a Master of Arts degree in Adult Education from Ball State University in 1996, and a Doctor of Education (Ed D.) degree from Nova Southeastern University in 2000. She is currently working toward a Doctor of Clinical Psychology (Psy D) degree from the Adler School of Professional Psychology. Paula is the President and Senior Research Consultant at Education and Development Consultants, Inc., Fort Wayne. Paula came to Fort Wayne in 1994 after a job transfer. Paula and her daughter, Samantha, are the co-founders of The Center for Children of Divorce and Broken Relationships in Fort Wayne, Indiana.

Paula and Russ were married on August 19, 2000 in Fort Wayne, Indiana. Their family includes: Paula's two grown daughters: Nichole Adele Cook Abbott (born December 31, 1977) (married Barry Abbott on September 16, 2000), New London, Wisconsin, and Jessica Theresa Cook (born September 7, 1979), Chicago, Illinois; and at home, Samantha Rebekah Chapman (born August 26, 1990) and Mary Elizabeth (Mimi) Neuman (born December 18, 2000) who was named after both of her grandmothers.

Submitted by Dr. Paula Neuman

JIM & ROSE (SHELDON) NEWTON

Jim and Rose Sheldon Newton, reside on Covington Road in Fort Wayne. They came to Fort Wayne in January 1971. Jim was a dispatcher for North American Van Lines, serving as Senior Dispatch Planner, Area Manager, Director of National Operations and Convention Director, retiring in 1993. He owns PakMail Franchises in Fort Wayne and Perrysburg, Ohio. Jim was born in Miami, Oklahoma. He has served as church treasurer and Sunday School Teacher in three churches and Arcola Methodist Men's group.

Rose, born in Telluride, Colorado, lived in Columbus, Kansas and Miami, Oklahoma. In Oklahoma Jim and Rose were Presidents in the Jaycee organization. Rose sang in and was President and assistant director of Southmoor Mother Singers of Fort Wayne several years. They are charter members of the Associated Churches Festival Choir of Peace and Understanding. The Festival Choir took a gift of English hand bells to Caputh bei Potsdam in Germany. The bells rang at Germany unification ceremonies. Jim was treasurer and concert tour director and Rose worked passports. The choir toured Europe four times and the U.S.A. They sing in the Celebration Singers ministering in area nursing homes. Rose has served as Minister of Music in five churches: Alaska, Oklahoma, and three in Fort Wayne. She is currently serving the Arcola, Indiana United Methodist Church.

Rose served as President of the Sheldon Family Association from 1985-1997. She is currently their genealogist and quarterly editor, working on a new series of lineage books for the Association. Rose is a member of Allen County Genealogical Society of Indiana and served as their editor. Rose has given genealogy talks for societies in Oklahoma, Missouri, Kansas, Vermont, and Ohio, and assists as needed in Allen County Genealogical Society.

Jim and Rose Newton.

Jim and Rose have two sons, James Michael Newton, born in Alaska when Jim was in the finance division of the U.S. Army. Mike served 11 years in the U.S. Navy Nuclear Submarines. His sub was used in the movie *The Hunt For Red October* while he was in the engine room. He is currently managing PakMail stores in Fort Wayne and Perrysburg, Ohio and has a son, Ian Sheldon Newton. He is the web master for the Beer Can Collectors Club of Fort Wayne.

Son John Andrew Newton, born in Missouri, is a rock singer with his own company, Dark Horizon Records, shipping orders all over the world. He sings with several bands, currently booked in Europe and Las Vegas. Andy has a son Zachariah James Newton and a stepdaughter, Danielle Nicole Kiracoffe. Andy often does comedy entertainment at the Munchie Emporium on Broadway.

Rose traces her ancestry from New England to England. She is a descendant of Isaac Sheldon of Windsor, Connecticut and member of Founders of the Descendants of Ancient Windsor. She is an American cousin of Lady Diana Spencer of England and also distantly, a cousin of Jesse James!

Rose has traced Jim's ancestry through Oklahoma, Missouri, and Tennessee to Spotsylvania, Virginia, looking for the connection to the county in Ireland.

Submitted by Rose Newton.

RAYMUND & SHAWNA NIBLICK FAMILY

Raymund Mark Niblick was born May 19, 1966 in Allen County. His parents are Roger and Madonna Niblick of Fort Wayne. Ray has 14 brothers and sisters: Sister Tina (Lael) Niblick of Bluefield's, Nicaragua; Mike (Vivian) Niblick of Cape Coral, Florida; Leo (Karen) Niblick of Fort Wayne; Pat Niblick of Mississippi; Paul (Wendy) of Maine; Guy Niblick of Bluffton; Herb

Max, Robb, and Ray Niblick. Seated, Shawna and Leila

(Cyndi) Niblick of Fort Wayne; Matthew Niblick, deceased; Jim Niblick of Fort Wayne; Mary (Allan) Frecker of Hoagland; Karl (Vicki) of Fort Wayne; Tom (Julie) Niblick of Fort Wayne; John (Joyce) of Cape Coral, Florida and Theresa (Karl) Keesling of Huntington, Indiana.

Shawna Kari (Robb) Niblick was born August 29, 1967 in Allen County. Her parents are Robert and Phyllis Robb of Fort Wayne. Shawna has one brother, Brian (Patti) Robb of Fort Wayne.

Ray went to St. Henry's grade school, Paul Harding High School, International Business College, and then enlisted in the United States Navy. He has an Associates Degree in Accounting from International Business College. He was in the Navy for six years as a Fire Control Technician Balistic Missile while serving on a Nuclear Submarine. After the Navy, he went to work for North American Van Lines for ten years. He is presently employed by Sheriff of Allen County as a Confinement Officer at the Allen County Jail. He enjoys Sci Fi, computers and reading.

Shawna went to St. Vincent's grade school, Bishop Dwenger High School, and Indiana-Purdue University at Fort Wayne. She has a Bachelor's of General Studies from IPFW. She has been in the banking field for 13 years and presently employed at Lake City Bank. She enjoys basket weaving, counted cross stitch and reading.

They were married on October 2, 1993 at Cathedral of the Immaculate Conception in Fort Wayne, Indiana. They have three children, Robb Matthew Niblick born in 1998, Maxwell Allen Niblick born in 2000 and Leila Shea Niblick born March of 2005. The family lives in Pine Valley subdivision.

Submitted by Shawna Niblick

RICHARD LOWELL NICHOLS

Fort Wayne native Dick Nichols, born March 12, 1926, is the first son and the second of four children born to the late Charles Lowell Nichols and the late Audrey (Stickley) Nichols. Dick's siblings include Phyllis Jeanne (Nichols) Runkle, Marilyn (Nichols) Leakey, and Dan F. Nichols.

Although his father was a native of Camden, Michigan, Dick is a lifelong Fort Wayne resident. A member of the Lutheran church, the subject married Rosemary Liechty on October 18, 1952. Rosemary was born in Berne, Indiana on March 17, 1931. She is the youngest of eight children born to the late Jacob L. Liechty and the late Susanna D. (Schwartz) Liechty.

Dick's hobbies include singing (he was a tenor soloist and member of various choirs for many years). Rosemary's hobbies include cross stitch, knitting, and computer work. Though now retired, Dick's working life was marked by several different careers. He was the owner and operator of a Fort Wayne eatery located in the heart of downtown Fort Wayne from 1952 to 1963.

Happily married for over 53 years, Dick and Rosemary are the parents of two sons, Richard Lowell Nichols, II, and Charles Lowell Nichols. Older son Rick, an Electrical Engineer and graduate of the University of Texas, lives in Austin, Texas. Younger son Chuck, a chemical engineer, graduated from Rose-Hulman and resides in Terre Haute, Indiana. Four grandchildren and a great-grandson round out the subject's family.

Dick's grandparents, Fort Wayne native Frederick C. Stickley and rural New Haven native Clara (Koehlinger) Stickley, were first-generation Americans of German heritage. From 1917-18 through 1939 the Stickleys operated a bicycle store on Broadway in Fort Wayne. Fred Stickley's parents, Jacob Stickley and Rosina (Stimlar) Stickley, were born in Germany. Jacob immigrated to America in about 1865. Rose immigrated in about 1870. Clara Koehlinger's parents, John Henry Koehlinger, a native of Blasbach, Prussia, and Johanna (Brudi) Koehlinger, a native of Wuerttemberg, arrived in America in 1849 and 1846, respectively.

John Henry Koehlinger was the son of Heinrich Koehlinger, and Christina (Weber) Koehlinger. The Koehlingers were blessed with nine children. In 1848 a son, Philipp, immigrated to America, settling in Alien County. The following year Heinrich and the rest of his family sailed aboard the Edwina, from Rotterdam, Holland, to New York, arriving on July 8, 1849. Departing New York, they journeyed directly to Fort Wayne, traveling by ox team. The reunited Koehlinger family carved out an 80 acre farm located along Maples Road. Today, Highway 469 runs just east of the old homestead. In an interesting twist of fate, Rosemary and her siblings, Milton and Ann Liechty, all married great-great-grandchildren of Heinrich and Christina Koehlinger.

Johanna Brudi was the daughter of John George Brudi and Anna Barbara (Handle) Brudi. Prior to emigrating from Le Havre, the Brudis made their home in Dettingen and Yebenhausen, Wuerttemberg. In 1845 the father journeyed to America, settling in Allen County. The wife and children, including Johanna, immigrated the following year, arriving in New York in November 1846; thence departing directly for Fort Wayne. The Brudis settled east of New Haven in rural Jefferson Township, Allen County.

Submitted by Rosemary Nichols

JAMES PHILLIP & WILMA CAROLYN (WELBAUM) NIERMAN

Both James Phillip Nierman and Wilma Carolyn Welbaum have deep roots in Allen County. Jim's maternal grandparents were Joe and Cora (Middaugh) Weaver. Their daughter, Ruth Weaver, and Kenneth (Bud) Nierman married in 1921 and lived in Fort Wayne until 1938. Then they built a home in Nine Mile; and, in 1962, they built a new home next door to the first. As a machinist, Bud worked on engines of the Nickel Plate Railroad at the New Haven Roundhouse. Ruth was employed by Dudlo Manufacturing Company and later by Kresge Warehouse. This couple had two sons, Wendell Kenneth Nierman and Jim. Wendell's three wives were Marceil Genth, Norma Shively, and Lavelle Sarpe. His children by Norma are Wendell Kenneth, Jr., Catherine (Nierman) Bennett, and Barbara (Nierman) Mueller. His step-children are Rick, Larry, and Alice Sarpe, Teresa (Sarpe) Coratti, and April (Sarpe) Watson.

Wilma's lineage traces back to James and Rebecca (Baxter) Johnson who came to Allen County in the 1850s and to their daughter, Elizabeth, who married William Henry Carbaugh. The middle son of this union, Charles Franklin Carbaugh, married Adaline Genth on February 22, 1900. Then, on November 24, 1923 in Zanesville, their daughter, Gertrude Marie Carbaugh married Russell Welbaum, a son of Marshall M. and Louisa J. (Hyser) Welbaum, and a grandson of David and Rebecca (Ewert) Welbaum.. Gertrude Marie was one of their five children; and all five are included in the article about William Henry and Elizabeth (Johnson) Carbaugh.

Left to right in the back row are Jessica Brooke (Simon), James Stitcher, John Austin Stuart, Jr., Joshua James Nierman, Randall James Simon Jr., Alexander Phillip Simon, Randall James Simon Sr., Mary Elizabeth McKenna; Kerry Lynn-Nierman. In the front row are Jamie Lynn Nierman, Jill Renae (Nierman) Hayes, Wilma and Jim, Cheryl Jean (Nierman) Simon, and Mallory Leigh Nierman.

Between December of 1924 and November of 1941, Russell and Marie also had five children. Arnold Wayne Welbaum married Anna Mae Sorrell, April 19, 1946 in Washington, D.C. Eldon Welbaum and Mary Kelly were married in Nine Mile United Methodist Church, Allen County, August 21, 1948. Married in the same church were Louella May Welbaum and Therman Mannix on May 5, 1951, and Wilma and Jim on August 7, 1954. Baby Larry L. Welbaum died shortly after birth and is buried with his parents in the church cemetery.

These four couples produced 18 grandchildren. Cassandra May, Melody Lee, Benjamin Wayne, and Christopher Russell are the children of Arnold and Anna Welbaum. James, Daniel, Bryan, and Roger, are the four sons of Eldon and Mary Welbaum. The seven children of Therman and Louella Mannix are Larry Alan, Lyle Dean, Lynn Thomas, Theda May, Tona, Timothy Dwayne, and Tara Diann. Jim and Wilma have Kerry, Cheryl, and Jill.

Jim served for 33 1/2 years as Power House Engineer at International Harvester Company, Fort Wayne Works. Wilma was employed by Zollner Corporation and Waynedale Bakery. After retirement, they moved to Indian Harbor Beach, Florida in 1995 and, following the 2004 hurricane season, moved inland.

The above picture was taken aboard a cruise ship as the family celebrated the 50th wedding anniversary of Jim and Wilma.

Submitted by Wilma C. Nierman

BENNETT NOEL & PATRICIA (OWENS) NOEL FAMILY

Bennett Noel was born March 6, 1932 in Butler Township, DeKalb County, Indiana, to Oscar Noel and Mary (Hixson) Noel. He was their only child. He was born on the farm which was started in 1873 by Phillip Noel and Mary (Stoner) Noel who were Bennett's great-grandparents. Bennett's great-great-grandfather, John Noel (1816-1858) and his wife, Elizabeth (Ensley) Noel (1816-1902) came from Seneca County, Ohio and settled in Butler Township, DeKalb County in 1839. His grandparents were John Noel (1869-1943) and Nora (Helmuth) Noel (1877-1947) and they lived on the farm started by Phillip Noel.

Bennett's maternal grandparents were Forrest A. Hixson (1877-1952) and Amanda (Houser) Hixson (1880-1961). They lived on a farm (known as Hixson's Gravel Pit) in Butler Township, DeKalb County which was founded by the maternal great-grandparents of Forrest, James Reynolds (1795-1879) and Mary (McClellan) Reynolds (1796-1881). Forrest's father, Bennett Hixson, was 14 when he came from Wayne County, Ohio around 1856 with his mother, Mary (Reynolds) Hixson (1818-1900) and his grandparents, the Reynolds.

Bennett and Patricia Owens were married on August 29, 1952 in the Presbyterian Church in Auburn, Indiana. They lived in Auburn until July of 1953 when they moved to Allen County just west of Fort Wayne International Airport. In September of 1954 they moved to Waynedale which later became a part of Fort Wayne, Indiana.

Patricia was born on March 18, 1932 to Fern W. Owens and Ellen (Springer) Owens in Garrett, Indiana. Her father was a conductor for fifty years on The Baltimore and Ohio Railroad. She had one brother, Jack Owens, and four sisters, Kathryn Manon, Maxine Feagler, Margaret (Peg) Sockrider and Jayne Kobiela. All are deceased. Her paternal grandparents were Grant Owens (1865-1926) and Ora (Hoffman) Owens (1868-1939); her maternal grandparents were Ralph Springer (1867-1934) and Theresa (Crist) Springer (1869-1953). Patricia is a descendant of Richard Warren who came over on the Mayflower from England. Patricia's paternal great-grandparents, John Owens (1827-1899) and Mary Jane (Culbertson) Owens (1837-1872) came from Eastern Ohio. Her maternal great grandparents, Phillip Crist and Rosa (?) Crist, came from Germany and Switzerland respectively.

Bennett was a member of the Indiana Air National Guard for 37 years and was a chief master sergeant when he retired in 1987. During those years he was called to active duty for the Korean War, and for the Berlin Wall call up in 1961. He was stationed near Metz, France during 1961-1962. Patricia worked for The Lincoln National Life Insurance Company for 30 years, retiring in 1998.

Bennett and Patricia have two children, Michael who was born January 24, 1954 and Janice, born February 3, 1955. Michael married Nancy (Butcher) Noel and they had three children, Joshua (killed in an automobile accident at age 21), Brandon and Erica who are twins. Brandon married Beth Cook in 2003 and they have a son, Clayton. Erica married Samuel Overbay in 2005. Michael's second marriage was to Lois (Gray Williams) Noel in 1994. Lois has five children, Kelly, Erin, Roxie, Kyle and Chelsea and six grandchildren. Janice married Donald Miller in 1978, and they have two children, Corey and Stacey. Stacey married Jason Householder in 2004; Jason has a daughter. Donald has two children from a previous marriage, Paul and Chad, and also has two grandchildren.

Submitted by Bennett A. Noel

SAMUEL DOY & NORMA JEANNE (TETLOW) NOVICK FAMILY

Samuel Doy Novick (Sam) was born May 5, 1925 in Adams County, Decatur, Indiana, to Samuel Joseph Novick and Louise Rose Bogner Novick. His birth in Decatur was strictly an accident as Louise was visiting her parents when she went into labor. Sam J. and Louise R. Novick were residents of Fort Wayne, Allen County.

Samuel J. Novick was the son of Stephen Novick, who came from Posen, Prussia, and Sophia Bobay Novick. Stephen first lived in North Dakota before moving to Fort Wayne. He was an electrician and opened his own business.

Sam D. Novick was an only child. He married Norma Jeanne Tetlow on April 23, 1955 at St. Josephs Catholic Church, on the comer of Brooklyn and Hale, by Fr. Stanley Manoski. Norma was born on November 12, 1932 in Fort Wayne, Indiana. She was the daughter of Frank Ashton Tetlow and Goldie Mae Shoemaker Tetlow who resided in Fort Wayne. Frank was born on October 25, 1900 on the family farm in Charlton County, Keytesville, Missouri. He came to Fort Wayne in 1917 to live with an uncle he had never met, after having a disagreement with his older brother. Goldie was born and raised in Allen County. Norma had one brother, James Ashton Tetlow. He was married to Barbara Ellen Tribolet, also of Fort Wayne. Both are deceased. They had a son, Michael Ashton Tetlow, and a daughter, Jeanne Ellen Tetlow. Neither live in Allen County.

Sam D. and Norma both graduated from North Side High School, he, in 1943; she, in 1951. Sam D. worked as a "carry-out" at Kroger while in school. After school, he enlisted in the U.S. Coast Guard. After discharge, he was employed by the City Utilities. He spent the next 30 years working in the Construction Department, the Service Department, and the Sub-Station Department. In 1975, the Power Department of the City Utilities was leased to Indiana Michigan Power Company, and, at some point, it became American Electric Power. He retired from AEP in 1987. After graduation, Norma went to work for the FBI in the Indianapolis Field Office for a year. She returned to Fort Wayne because her dad had a heart attack.

Sam J. and Louise Novick moved to Aboite Township in 1949. Sam D. and Norma Novick moved to Aboite Township in 1958.

Sam D. enjoyed working with wood and playing golf. Norma enjoys reading, needlework, sewing, scrapbooking and golf. But, at the top of the list for both, was, and is, spending time with family. They had two children: a daughter, Jo Ellen (Jodi) married to Robert A. Korte; and, a son, Stephen John Novick married to Lori Ann Graf. Jodi and Bob also reside in Aboite Township. Jodi is employed by Lowe's. Bob is employed by Raytheon. They have a son, Timothy Ashton, and two daughters, Kelli Jeanne and Maureen Lynn. Tim works at UPS and goes to school at IPFW. Kelli will graduate in the spring of 2005 from Ball State University with a Bachelors degree in Elementary Education and Special Education, with an endorsement in Hearing Impairment. Maureen is pursuing a career in Radiography. Steve and Lori were married May 3, 1986. They currently reside in Markleville, Hancock County, Indiana, with their three children: Stephen Jordan (Jord), Rachael Louise, and Samuel (Sammy) Jacob. Jord is a Junior at Eastern Hancock High School, and Rachael is a Freshman. Sammy is in the fourth grade at Eastern Hancock Elementary. Steve is employed by Graybar Electric as a Sales Representative, and Lori has a Masters Degree in Clinical Psychology, but is currently a stay at home mom.

Submitted by Norma J. Novick

JOHN NUTTLE

John Nuttle was born on November 8, 1803 to William and Lydia (Johnson) Nuttle. John was the second of six children and the second son. He married Sarah Delzell in Monroeville, Ohio before 1828. She was born in Edinburgh, Scotland. Nothing else is known about her background. A William Delzell does appear in the 1820 Ohio census.

Seven children were born to the union of John and Sarah: Robert D., James W., William J., Ami D., Sarah, and Margaret Elizabeth. John died on November 12, 1852 in Fort Wayne at the age of 49. Sarah died on February 4, 1865. They are buried in the Bowers Cemetery in Fort Wayne, lot 95C.

In Apri1 1820, John had applied for land through the Fort Wayne Land Office. He came to the area with his wife around 1833. The grant was awarded on June 22, 1835 for 80 acres in Milan Township. He paid one hundred dollars for the land. Records show that John Nuttle of New York was the earliest settler to fix a home site in Milan Township.

The Robert Nuttle Family, August 1892. Mrs. Lucinda Eby Nuttle, age 54, surrounded by her daughters. Back, Fyanna age 24, Mary age 31, and Dora age 22. Front: Maggie, age 19, Mom, Sophrona, age 16

John's will was dated November 10, 1852 in Allen County, Indiana. Robert Nuttle, his eldest son was named executor. John's land totaled 240 acres at his death. Each son received 40 acres. His wife was given the use of the plantation for her natural life and then the land would be divided. The two daughters each received a good bed, a cookstove, a table, a set of chairs, dishes, linens, various other furniture, and a cow.

Robert Nuttle was born on April 15, 1828 in New York to John and Sarah (Delzell) Nuttle. He was the oldest of six children. On August 17, 1856 he married Lucinda Eby in Allen County, Indiana. She was born on July 4, 1838 in Lancaster, Pennsylvania to Daniel and Anna (Schrantz) Eby. Lucinda was one of fourteen children, and she had a twin brother, Rufus. Robert and Lucinda had seven children; Mary Jane, William Franklin, Cora Eby, Fyanna Warnner, Dora Eby, Maggie Ammillia, and Sophrona Allice. William died at the age of one and Cora died at age three. Robert Nuttle died on May 26, 1883 in Allen County. He was 55 years old. Lucinda died on September 26, 1906 in Steuben County, Indiana. They, along with the two children, are buried in Jamestown Cemetery, west of Fremont Indiana.

Robert had inherited 40 acres of land in Allen County from his father. He and Lucinda sold the land to his brother, Ami, for four hundred dollars. The transaction was made in August of 1865.

Although Lucinda was widowed in middle life, she never remarried and raised her daughters without complaint. She was a member of the Methodist Church and faithfully participated in church activities. Her will was found in the Steuben County Will Records. She bequeathed everything to her daughter Dora. Dora, in turn, was to give fifty dollars to each of her sisters. Mary Jane married Leroy Crandall. Dora married Milton Phillips.

Maggie married John Wesley Chrysler, Jr. Sophrona married Amos Walter and then Charles Lewis Shattenberger. Fyanna never married. All of the daughters lived out their lives in Steuben County in the Fremont area. They are all buried in the Fremont area cemeteries.

Submitted by Lori Crandall

EDWARD C. & LUCY (GLADIEUX) OBERLEY

Edward Oberley, 1891-1972, was born in Jefferson Township, Allen County, Indiana, to Frank and Eugenia Voirol Oberley. He had four brothers, Arthur, Elmer, Alton and Russell. Ed's grandparents, Christian and Mary Weaver Oberley, were married in Allen County on January 17, 1857. Christian was born in Mittersaltz, France in 1838. His family emigrated from Germany, first residing in Stark County, Ohio, and then moved to Allen County, Indiana, in the early 1850s. Christian and Mary had three children, Frank, Rosa and Alexander.

During the Civil War, Christian enlisted in the Union Army, Co. B, 12th Regiment, Indiana Infantry on July 20, 1862. He served three years in the 12th Regiment, then shortly after his return home, he enlisted again, this time to Co. D, 18th Regiment, Indiana Infantry and was sent to Fort Philip Kearney in Dakota Territory. While on duty cutting timber for the post, he was killed by Indians at Peno Creek, on October 6, 1866. He was buried in the post cemetery.

Edward C. and Lucy (Gladieux) Oberley

A few years later, 1872, Mary married Peter Dager and remained in Allen County, Indiana.

Ed married Lucy Gladieux at St. Louis Catholic Church, Besancon, Allen County, Indiana on June 9, 1914. Lucy (1894-1972) was the daughter of Celestine and Virginia Havert Gladieux of Jefferson Township, Allen County, Indiana. Lucy's grandparents, Jean Pierre (Peter), (1812-1890) and Rosalie Rosset Gladieux, (1815-1905), departed from Alsace Lorraine, France on August 5, 1844 and arrived at the port in New York on the ship, Emerald, on September 17, 1844 along with two of their children, Francois, (1837-1916), and Josephine, (1841-1919). Peter and Rosalie had two more children, Celestine (1845-1914) and Victoria (1846-1905), while living in Stark County, Ohio. The Gladieux family moved to Jefferson Township, Allen County, Indiana in the early 1850s. Francis later became the sheriff of Allen County and Celestine was the township trustee of Jefferson Township, Allen County.

Before Ed and Lucy's marriage, Ed had been a catcher for the Zulu Grays, a well-known baseball team in that era. Ed worked for the Highway Department for many years. Later in life, Ed and Lucy ran a Standard Oil station located in Zulu, Indiana, which included a small restaurant. Every day during the week the same customers would stop for lunch: the milkman, mailman, bus drivers, delivery drivers, etc. The place had to be marked somehow, because every hobo would stop for a free lunch. They knew they were welcome. Every Wednesday evening in the summer time they would have free shows in the large empty lot next to the restaurant. A large outdoor screen was positioned at one end of the lot and the projector was placed in a car, along with speakers, at the other end. Everyone brought blankets and folding chairs to sit on. This all changed with the invention of television.

Ed and Lucy had three daughters, Bernice (1916-1988), Celeste (1918-1988) and Audrey (1920-1991).

Bernice married Lloyd V. Johnson, (1914-1958), son of Benjamin L. and Ollie E. Schlemmer Johnson, in 1939 at St. Louis Catholic Church, Besancon. They had seven children: Richard, Jean, David, Gary, Jack, Michael, and Louis.

Celeste married Alfred Thomas, (1915-1962), son of Floyd and Rozella Yarrington Thomas, in 1938, also at St. Louis Church, Besancon, Indiana. Celeste, "Toots" and Al had nine children: Robert, Sharon, Stephen, Carol, Susan, Donald, Kathy, Rita and Gerald.

Audrey never married, remained at home with her parents, and was employed by and retired from the General Electric Company on Broadway Street, Fort Wayne, Indiana.

Submitted by Kirk Fitzgerald

ODDOU FAMILY

The Oddou family has its roots in France. In the mid- 1800s Stephen Oddou and Constance DeLaGrange settled in Fort Wayne near what is now Saint Vincent's Church. Their son Peter and his wife Mary had six children who grew up and remained in Fort Wayne.

Frank Edward Oddou, Senior, was born on March 2, 1884 in Fort Wayne. He married Evangeline Steenman of Holland on August 23, 1905. Frank was a cabinetmaker who became ill and was unable to care for his family which included his children, Frank Junior and daughter, Virginia. Son Maurice had died in infancy.

Due to their financial situation Frank Junior left school after the sixth grade to support the family. Frank delivered groceries, cleaned buildings and did assorted odd jobs to earn money in order to care for his mother and sister. Evangeline earned money by sewing for others until her health failed and she died in 1932 when Frank was 18 years old.

Frank Junior served in the CCCs (Civilian Conservation Corps) in Idaho and in the Indiana National Guard. On November 26, 1936, he married Alberta Alt at St. Peter's Church in Fort Wayne. He worked as a milk delivery driver until becoming employed by the Nickel Plate Railroad as a Brakeman. Alberta worked as a switchboard operator at the Peoples Trust Bank. They were blessed with five children: Leanne (David) Mensing, Mary Elizabeth (James) Jacobs, Frank III (Dolores Grim), Rochelle (Robert) Schlup, and Christine (Larry) Lee and 15 grandchildren.

Frank Junior died on April 11, 1972, and Alberta died on October 15, 1990.

Three generations of this family lived near and were educated at Precious Blood Catholic School.

Frank and Alberta were outstanding examples of what parents should be. Family always came first. They were always supportive of their children and involved in their education and other activities. They formed the first PTA (Parent Teachers' Association) and organized the first school carnival at Precious Blood. Both of these activities continue today. Alberta was honored by the Limberlost Girl Scout Council for 25 years of service as a Girl Scout leader. They successfully passed the torch of involvement and volunteerism on to their five children.

As of this writing, Leanne is a retired Fort Wayne Community Schools administrator, whose husband, David, an electrical engineer with Magnavox, died on June 8, 2004. Son Keith and his wife Brenda (Theobold) reside in Columbus, Ohio. Daughter Lynn and husband Kevin Adamson reside in Fort Wayne, and have two children.

Left to Right: Leanne, Christine, Beth, Rochelle, Frank (Skip), August 12, 1997

Mary Elizabeth and husband Jim, who retired from the U.S. Government, live in Mount Airy, Maryland, near their three daughters, Jill (Jay) Carswell, Diana (Walter) Okada, Sally (Julian) Reading and their four grandchildren and one great-grandchild.

Frank III, manager of a chemical company, and wife Dolores have three children, Tracy (Mark) Erdosy, Heather (Ryan) Singleton, and Frank Matthew (Kim Scherer) , and four grandchildren.

Rochelle and Robert Schlup have four children, Kimberly (Tim) Magers, James, Jacqueline (Brett) Becker, Andrea (Kirk) Harmon, and nine grandchildren.

Christine and Larry reside in Montpelier, Ohio, and have three children, Joshua (Susan Damschroder), Christopher, and Katelyn.

The Oddou family continues to grow.

Submitted by Leanne Mensing

JOSEPH ODDOU

Joseph Oddou owned a grocery store, and in it he sold "Staple and Fancy Groceries." The Leader Grocery, located at 212 East Columbia Street, was one storefront wide and had a potbellied stove.

Joseph came to Fort Wayne as a very young boy from Stark County, Ohio. He was the second of six children born to Stephen (Etienne) and Constance de la Grange Oddou. Both of his parents emigrated from France in 1841. Stephen was a wagonmaker by trade.

On May 7,1872, Joseph Oddou married Adele Pepe at Saint Vincent Catholic Church. Adele's parents were also French immigrants. During the French Revolution, her great-grandfather was beheaded by Robespierre for aiding priests. Joseph and Adele were the parents of eight children. Frank, Louis, Cecelia, Henry, Constance, Estella, Grace, and George were all born in Fort Wayne. At one time, the family lived above the grocery store. Constance Olympia Stephana Mary Agnes Oddou, the submitter's grandmother, was born in July of 1879 and lived to the age of 83.

The Leader Grocery

Joseph and Adele Oddou were "pioneer" members of the Cathedral of the Immaculate Conception. In later years, as residents of South Harrison Street, they were members of Saint Patrick's parish. Joseph passed away in 1929 at the age of 79. Adele passed away in 1936 at the age of 86. They left 14 grandchildren.

Many members of the Oddou family are buried in Saint Vincent's cemetery, north of the old church, which has become a very popular "Haunted House" each Halloween. That might be another story!

Submitted by Carl Klenke, great-grandson of Joseph and Adele Oddou

EDWARD CLAUDE & MARY THERESA (THIEL) O'KEEFE FAMILY

Edward Claude O'Keefe was born October 12, 1872, the eldest of three children born to Edward and Mary Jane Keefe. He was raised on his father's farm, but farming was not for him. He worked on the Nickel Plate and Norfolk and Western Railroads, but spent most of his working life with the Pennsylvania Railroad, from which he would retire. Mary Theresa Thiel, his future wife, was born November 24, 1878, on a farm near Edgerton, Ohio. Her parents were Nicholas Thiel, Jr., born in 1855 in Ohio, and Sarah (Mack) Thiel, born in 1856 in New Haven, Indiana. At age 16, Mary and her 14-year-old sister, Louise, traveled to New Haven, Indiana, to live with her aunt, Rose Harmen, on the Landin Road near New Haven, Indiana. The two sisters were very close.

Edward C. and Mary (Thiel) O'Keefe wedding day January 31, 1900.

Ed and Mary met at a church dance and later were married at St. John's Catholic Church in New Haven, Indiana, on January 31, 1900. They purchased five acres on old U.S. 30 East and raised three sons, Eugene, Raymond and Albert. When the first child, Eugene, was to be baptized, the priest convinced them to add the "O" onto Keefe since that was the correct Irish spelling.

Mary died at age 51 on March 16, 1929, after a prolonged illness and is buried at St. John's Catholic Cemetery in New Haven, Indiana, as is her sister, Louise, and Louise's husband, Louis N. Snyder. Edward continued to work for the Pennsylvania Railroad and eventually retired. Since he loved the warm weather, he moved to St. Petersburg, Florida, and while there met and married his future wife, Caroline. He died on November 5, 1963, having lived to be 91 years old. He and Caroline are buried at Memorial Park Cemetery at 49th and 54th avenues in St. Petersburg, Florida.

Seated Mary C. (Federspiel), top right, Albert L. O'Keefe, wedding day, January 10, 1933.

Albert L. O'Keefe was born September 12, 1911, in Fort Wayne, Indiana. He was the third son of Edward and Mary O'Keefe. His primary education was at St. Andrew's Catholic grade school, followed by two years of high school at St. Augustine's Academy. Upon leaving high school, he followed in his brothers' footsteps, Gene and Ray, who were apprentices at General Electric and hired in at International Harvester in their apprentice department. The Depression suspended that program, but he remained, working in the factory for 13 years. He then joined the Fort Wayne Police Department and served honorably and advanced to the rank of lieutenant before his retirement in 1964. Following his retirement, he continued to work, first with the Wayne Township Assessor's Office and then D.O. McComb Funeral Home.

Mary C. Federspiel, Albert's future wife, was the second child born to William H. and Leoma L. (Thompson) Federspiel on February 10, 1911, in New Haven, Indiana. She attended St. John's grade school in New Haven, Indiana, and graduated from high school there in 1929. During her youth, she had three years of piano training and played in several recitals. She met Albert in the fall of 1930 and they were married on January 10, 1933, at St. John's Catholic Church in New Haven, Indiana.

Albert and Mary had six children: Patricia (Ronald Jordan); Donald (Jean Denman); Gerald (Rosaline Wyss); Colleen (Rudolph De Vito); Thomas (Sharon Wendling); and Carolyn (Michael Holbrook). Their son, Donald, died unexpectedly in 1993.

Al and Mary lived their entire married life in Fort Wayne. Mary died on May 13, 1979. In 1981, Albert married Margaret Danehy. Albert died August 16, 1988, and is buried next to Mary in the Catholic Cemetery in Fort Wayne. Margaret died in August of 1993 and is buried next to her first husband in the Catholic Cemetery in Fort Wayne, Indiana. Besides their six children, Albert and Mary were blessed with 21 grandchildren and several great-grandchildren.

Submitted by Patricia A. Jordan

O'KEEFE & WENDLING FAMILY

Thomas L. O'Keefe was born July 15, 1940 to Albert O'Keefe and Mary Federspiel in Fort Wayne, Indiana, one of six children. Albert was a city policeman and Mary was a homemaker. His siblings included, Patricia, Donald, Gerald, Colleen and Carolyn. He attended Precious Blood Catholic Grade School and Central Catholic High School. He entered the United States Marine Corps shortly thereafter and was stationed at Camp Pendleton in California. Part of that enlistment included one and a half years in Okinawa. After returning home in 1961, he worked for Rea Magnet Wire and then returned to California where he pursued a machinist apprenticeship. In 1965, he became employed at International Harvester. In July of 1970, he married Sharon Wendling of Fort Wayne.

Sharon Wendling O'Keefe was born January 22, 1942 to John Wendling and Alice Burns. She was the third of five children. Her siblings included John, Thomas, Marilyn and Bill. She attended St. Andrews Catholic School and Central Catholic High School. Upon graduation, she worked for Allstate Insurance Company and later as a secretary to the claims attorney of O'Rourke, Andrews and Maroney Insurance Company in Fort Wayne. During this time, she enjoyed traveling, especially to Europe, which she toured with a friend.

Because of International's plant closing in Fort Wayne, Indiana, Thomas relocated to the Springfield, Ohio, area in 1987 to maintain his employment with International Harvester. His family followed in 1990. International Harvester has since become known as Navistar. While living in Xenia, Ohio, just east of Dayton, Ohio, a tornado came within three blocks of their home, devastating much of the city.

After moving to Ohio with her husband, Sharon became employed with Miami Valley Hospital in Dayton, Ohio until she retired in 2002 at which time she and Tom located back to Fort Wayne. In retirement, Tom enjoys golfing, reading and his grandchildren.

Their children are Edward Thomas and Joseph Patrick. Edward Thomas attended St. John's Catholic Grade School in New Haven, Snider High School in Fort Wayne, Indiana, and Notre Dame University in South Bend, Indiana. He and his wife, Sherry Langendorf, a graduate of Northern Illinois University, now reside in Waukegan, Illinois, where Edward is employed at Abbott Laboratories. Second son, Joseph Patrick, was born and attended St. John's Catholic Grade School in New Haven, Indiana. After his parents moved to Xenia, Ohio, he attended Archbishop Carroll High School in Dayton, Ohio, where he played varsity football for three years and graduated from Sinclair Community College in Dayton. He and his wife, Pamela Henry, and their two sons, Patrick and Henry, now reside in Fort Wayne. Joseph is a machinist with Millcreek Power Tool.

Submitted by Joseph O'Keefe

Back row, L to R: Thomas and Sharon. Middle row, sons Edward and Joseph. Front row, Sherry, Patrick, Henry and Pam

ARGUS LUSTER & EDNA CHLOE (MANN) ORMSBY FAMILY

Argus Luster Ormsby was born in Wells County, Indiana on February 18, 1894, to Alonzo Eugene (1866-1916) and Mary Elizabeth Archbold Ormsby (1865-1948). His siblings were Ralph Augustus (1889-1969), Vilas Bryce (1896-1975), Everett Dale (1899-1966), and an infant sister, Chloe, born in 1900. His paternal grandparents were Oliver Ashton Ormsby (1842-1909) and Jane Fisher Ormsby (1841-1924). His maternal grandparents were William G. (1839-1913) and Elmira Ruby Archbold (1846-1871).

The Ormsby family goes back to Ireland with Thomas, born 1753, who married Elizabeth Rutledge. His son, who immigrated to America, was George (1774-1871). George Ormsby married Sarah McClellan and finally settled in Mahoning County, Ohio, after his arrival in Baltimore, Maryland. George's son was Alexander (1800-1876) and his wife was Nancy Wolfcale (1801-1877) and the parents of Oliver Ashton Ormsby. Alexander and many of the Ormsby people from Ohio traveled to Wells County, Indiana in 1852.

Argus and Edna Ormsby, 1943.

Argus Ormsby was schooled in Wells County, Indiana and came to Fort Wayne in 1918. He worked at the Weber Hotel as a waiter. That is where he met Edna Chloe Mann, who came to Fort Wayne in 1934, two years after her graduation from New Madison High School in Darke County, Ohio in 1932. She was born December 8, 1914, the fifth child of William Harvey and Sarah Catherine Wise Mann, and raised in Darke County, Ohio. She was one of twelve children: Gerald Kenneth, Wilbur Hubert, Eva Ellen, Elsie Pearl, Esther Ruth, Everett Elmo, Helen Maxine, Thelma Aileen and Velma Irene (twins), Norma Jean, and Rodney Dean. Edna's paternal grandparents were Stephen Elisha (1855-1937) and Mary Ellen Clevenger Mann (1858-1947). Her maternal grandparents were Daniel Cyrus (1863-1934) and Eva Minerva Sonday Wise (1865-1925).

Argus (Gus) was employed 17 years as a machinist for General Electric, retiring March 1, 1959. He ran for the office of city clerk in 1960 on the Democratic ticket, losing by a very small margin of votes. This was his first and last endeavor running for a public office. He was very active in the Masonic Southgate Lodge, achieving the 32nd degree through the Scottish Rite. Edna was employed 42 years for Troy Towel Supply in the office, retiring in 1985. To them were born three girls: Catherine Elizabeth, Judith Elaine, and Nancy Lou. They lived in Cedarville and then moved into Fort Wayne in late 1941. Gus and Edna were avid bowlers and golfers and traveled to different parts of the country competing in tournaments. They were members of St. John Evangelical Lutheran Church on West Washington Street since 1952.

Argus died November 27, 1967, in Fort Wayne and is buried in Prospect Cemetery in Ossian, Wells County, Indiana. This is where his father, grandfather, and great-grandfather are buried. Argus' family worshipped at the church, Prospect United Methodist.

Edna died May 20, 2003, in Fort Wayne and is also buried in Prospect Cemetery. She was active in her church and its ladies groups. She continued to bowl until two years before her death.

Catherine Elizabeth (Betty) Williams and Kenneth are living in New Haven, Indiana. Betty is the mother of seven children (six living), thirteen grandchildren, and two great-grandchildren. Judith Elaine, married Robert Erwin Richter and is living in Albion, Indiana, the parents of three children and seven grandchildren, six living. Nancy Lou married Keith Henninger and is living in Fort Wayne, Indiana, the parents of two children and two grandchildren, and one step grandson.

Submitted by Kevin Richter

THOMAS & EMELINE OVERLY

Thomas Overly was the son of Martin and Polly (Welch) Overly. Thomas was born in 1809. Thomas's wife's name was Emeline. The children born of this couple were Thomas, Issac, Denimus, and George. Thomas and his family appear in the 1850 Indiana Federal Census. This family is living on the property owned by James and Susannah Smith. (See James Smith). By the 1860 Federal census, the Overly family was in Pleasant Township in Allen County. Thomas died between the 1860 and 1870 census because the widow Emeline Overly and her family have moved to Wayne Township, Allen County for the 1870 Census. By the 1880 Federal Census, most of this Overly family has moved to Michigan and now resides in Walker Township, Kent County, Michigan with their children and their families.

Thomas Overly was a founding member of the United Brethren Evangelical Church in Nine Mile, Indiana in 1853. The church is presently known as Nine Mile United Methodist Church. Interesting details emerge about Thomas Overly, his brother-in-law, James Smith and other founding members in a historical overview written for the church's 100th anniversary which reads as follows: "THE HISTORY OF THE NINE MILE EVANGELICAL U. B. CHURCH This church was organized at the home of John Miller by Rev. Casey with 16 charter members. Daniel and wife Lucy Ann Buskirk sold One acre of ground for $10.00 to the trustees of the United Brethren Church, who were Gabriel Miller, Benjamin C. Davis, James Smith, Thomas Overly and Charles Miller, on January 3, 1853. For a period of five years, the meetings were held at the homes of the various members, but in 1859, they erected a log church on the present grounds in section 7, Pleasant township."

Submitted by Janet Smith

OXLEY FAMILY

Raymond R. and Irene L. Oxley, both Ohio natives, were married at Toledo, Ohio in 1922. They adopted Victor James Reaster (natural parents: James Reaster married Maria Malaska) from the Miami County Orphanage. The legal adoption in February of 1926 changed their son's name to Jack Raymond Oxley. In 1926, shortly after the adoption, the young family moved to Fort Wayne. Raymond Oxley was an employee of Typewriter Inspection Company. He was to become owner of two typewriter and office supply stores, Oxley Typewriter and O & W Company, both located on Lafayette Street at the current sites of Freiman Square and Bank One.

Jack R. Oxley attended and graduated from North Side High School in 1942. He enlisted in the USNR in 1942. Trained as a medic by the Merchant Marine service, he enlisted in the US Army and served on the Hospital Ship Maetsuycker in the South Pacific for the duration of WW II. (See website Jackoxley.com for WW II diaries etc.) He was discharged from the U.S. Army January 4, 1946. He joined his father in the office machine business for two decades. He later was a Magnavox employee.

Children of Jack and Ann Oxley

L to R, Back row: Kevin Oxley, Jeffrey Oxley, Jamie Oxley, Daniel Oxley. Middle row: Valerie Fouch, Amy Oxley, Sister Julie Marie Oxley, Joseph Oxley. Front row: Kathleen Wiggins, Maureen Gaff, Christeen Rhodes.

Jack R. Oxley married Ann V. Adang, daughter of Edward and Dorothy Adang of Fort Wayne, on August 10, 1946. Their children are: Kathleen (married Major Don Wiggins USMC), Maureen (married Alan Gaff), Joseph (married Maryann Minnich), Jeffrey (married Diane McCormick, divorced, married F. Jane Storer, divorced), Christeen (married Larry Rhodes), Daniel (married Mary Perryman of Marion, Indiana, later divorced), Juliannne (Sister Julie Marie O.S.F.), Jamie (married Sally Zahm), Kevin, (married Debby Wurm of Monroeville), Valerie (married Michael Fouch of Indianapolis), and Amy Oxley.

Three of the Oxley siblings served in the military...all enlisted: Kathleen Oxley Wiggins, USMC, Joseph R. Oxley USN, and Daniel E. Oxley USNR. .

Ann V. Oxley (B.A., MPA IU) was Research Director of Taxpayers Research Association, first manager of WFWA PBS affiliate, and national marketing director for Service Corps of Retired Executives.

Kathleen and Donald Wiggins (Orange, California) are the parents of Marc Wiggins and Keavin Wiggins also of Orange. Kathleen is retired from the electronics industry, and Major Wiggins from the U.S.M.C. Marc Wiggins is a staff member of the Orange Park and Beach Department. Keavin Wiggins is an entrepreneur.

Maureen and Alan Gaff are parents of Doctor Donald Gaff (married April Connolly) and Jeffrey (married Elaine Ridgeway-Young). Donald and April are the parents of Henry and Claudia Gaff and currently reside in Michigan. Maureen is Supervisor of Historical Genealogy Department Research as well as the Superintendent of the PERSI program of the Allen County Public Library Genealogical Department ACPL. Alan Gaff is a recognized historian with six published works to his credit.

Joseph (BS IIT) and Maryanne Oxley, RN, Fort Wayne, are the parents of Mary Helen (married Benjamin Ealing DVM), who is completing Veterinarian School at Purdue, Patrick Oxley, a senior at Purdue University, Lafayette, and Kathleen Oxley, a freshman at Ball State, Muncie. Joseph Oxley is an engineer with Delphi, and Maryanne Oxley R.N. is associated with FWO.

Jeffrey Oxley has lived and worked in the Fort Wayne area as a licensed electrician most of his adult life, and is now in retail sales with Home Depot.

Christeen Rhodes (BS in Education, IU) is the widow of Larry Rhodes who died December 27, 2003. Their children are Grant Rhodes and Kristen Rhodes, a senior at the University of California, San Diego. The family home is Camarillo, California.

Daniel Oxley was killed September, 2000 in an accident in Windsor, Ontario. He had no children. He is buried at the Military Cemetery in Marion, Indiana.

Julianne Oxley - Sister Julie Marie - is a professed member of the Franciscan Order and a graduate of Saint Francis College. She is stationed at the University of Saint Francis in Fort Wayne.

Jamie Oxley married Sally Zahm February 14, 1987, at Saint Jude's Church, Fort Wayne.

Kevin and Debbie Oxley are the parents of Andrew "Drew" Oxley, Sean Oxley, and Benjamin Oxley. The family lives in Avon Lakes, Ohio. Kevin (Notre Dame B.S.) is with the Wheels division of Alcoa International.

Valerie (BS Ed Saint Francis, MS Ball State) and Michael Fouch (BS Rose Hulman) and their family live outside of Indianapolis in Brownsburg, Indiana. The pair are the parents of Kayla, Reid, Michael, and Benjamin Fouch. Kayla and Benjamin Fouch attend Brownsburg High School. Michael and Benjamin Fouch attend Saint Malachy's School. Michael Fouch owns his own programming company. Valerie Fouch, prior to her marriage, taught for several years at Saint Jude, Fort Wayne.

Amy Oxley MS, NCC, LMHC, graduated from Saint Francis with a BS in Education. Amy also holds an MLS from the University of South Carolina, and an MS from Indiana University, Purdue University, Indianapolis. She is currently an employee of Volunteers of America in Indianapolis, Indiana.

Submitted by Ann V. Oxley

PADDOCK FAMILY

The Paddock family came to Allen County in 1956. Lawrence Gray Paddock, a native of Portland, and Kathleen Fryback Paddock, a native of Decatur, moved to Fort Wayne from Huntington with their two sons, Stephen Gray Paddock and Dee Geoffrey Paddock.

L. Gray Paddock, born 1920, was a graduate of DePauw University and worked as a pharmaceutical salesman and later expanded his career into real estate and insurance. He was active in Toastmasters, the Boy Scouts, and other community programs. He was the son of Lawrence and Virginia Paddock of Portland and passed away in 1991. He and Kathleen were active in the First Presbyterian Church in Fort Wayne.

Kathleen Fryback Paddock, born 1922, was a graduate of Huntington College with a master's degree from Ball State University. She taught in the Huntington and Allen County Public Schools and at Indiana University/Purdue University at Fort Wayne for forty years, retiring in 1988. Kathleen was a past president of Tri Kappa Sorority and the Allen County Mental Health Association, and was active with Arts United and the Fort Wayne Philharmonic Orchestra in the 1960s and 1970s. She was the daughter of Dee F. and Ireta Beavers Fryback of Decatur and married L. Gray Paddock in 1945. The Fryback and Paddock families have lived in Indiana since statehood. In 2002, Kathleen married Carl S. Offerle of Fort Wayne. They live in Fort Wayne and Boca Raton, Florida, where she remains active in real estate.

L to R: Geoff Paddock, Steve Paddock, Kathleen Paddock Offerle, Carl Offerle at Steve's wedding, March 30, 2002

Stephen Paddock, born 1951, graduated from Snider High School in Fort Wayne and from Florida Atlantic University in Boca Raton. He is married to Barbara Ann Haycook, born 1963 and formerly of Paterson, New Jersey. They have two children, Bridget Kathleen Paddock, born 2003 and Stephen Gray Paddock, II, born 2004. They live in Boca Raton, Florida, where Steve is the president of Prime Time Entertainment Company. Barbara is a flight attendant for South West Airlines. For the past 25 years, Steve has worked as a musician and produced many musical entertainment programs in South Florida. He also appeared on Miami Vice in the 1980s and in radio commercials.

Geoff Paddock, born 1955, is a graduate of Snider High School and also graduated from Indiana University, with a master's degree in public administration. He served with distinction in the administrations of Governor Evan Bayh and Congresswoman Jill Long and was a candidate for the Indiana Senate in 1992. From 1993 to the present, Geoff has been the director of the Headwaters Park Flood Control Project in downtown Fort Wayne. This project has revitalized a once blighted area of the city and provides flood control, economic development, and recreational opportunities for Fort Wayne. A festival center and outdoor ice skating rink bring in over 500,000 people downtown each year. He published a book, *Headwaters Park Fort Wayne's Lasting Legacy* in 2002.

Bridget Kathleen Paddock, age 2, and Stephen Gray Paddock, age 1.

In 2002, Geoff was elected to the Board of Trustees of the Fort Wayne Community Schools, where he currently serves as vice president. He was appointed to a transportation advisory committee by Governor Evan Bayh and Governor Frank O'Bannon, where he has worked to revitalize passenger rail service for Fort Wayne. He currently serves on the Board of Directors of Science Central and formerly served on the Board of the Allen County History Center. Geoff is an active community person who also supports the Lincoln Museum, the Fort Wayne Museum of Art, many other not for profit organizations and the First Presbyterian Church in Fort Wayne. He has served as an associate professor, teaching political science at Indiana/Purdue University in Fort Wayne and Junior Achievement in the public schools. Geoff has also written numerous newspaper and magazine articles and has been featured in *Traces of Indiana* and *Midwestern History*. He currently lives at 3744 South Washington Road, Fort Wayne.

Submitted by Geoff Paddock

PALMER FAMILY

The patriarch of the Palmer Family in Allen County, Indiana, was David Palmer. He was born on September 1, 1828, on a farm in Potter Township, Centre County, Pennsylvania, to John Palmer and his wife, Mary Spotts. His grandparents were Floyd and Barbara (Wolf) Palmer and David and Hannah Spatz. His great-grandfather, Solomon Palmer, originated from New York and served the cause of the Revolutionary War as a private in the Cumberland County (Pennsylvania) Militia.

In 1843 (when David was 15 years old) his family journeyed in a Conestoga wagon to Jackson Township, Perry County, Ohio, where his father worked as a farmer, cooper, and justice of the peace. David Palmer was the fourth oldest in the family of eleven children.

After falling in love with a young Irish lass from a nearby farm, David Palmer married Jane Ring, daughter of Mathew and Mary McMullen Ring, on April 25, 1851, at St. Patrick's Catholic Church near Junction City, Perry County, Ohio. They farmed during their thirteen years in Perry County, within which time six of their twelve children were born: John, James, William, Ira, Albert, and Mary.

During this time, David and his father-in-law, Mathew Ring, began to invest in land in Pleasant Township, Allen County, Indiana. In 1864, David and Jane Palmer left Perry County, Ohio, and moved to their farm in Pleasant Township, Allen County, Indiana (near Sheldon/Yoder). They had six additional children over the next 12 years: Anna, Joseph, Charles, Solomon, Amanda, and Louis.

David and Jane (Ring) Palmer -- tintype circa 1870

When their faming days were over, David and Jane Palmer moved to Fort Wayne and lived with their children. David died on October 10, 1896, at the age of 68 years, and Jane died on November 27, 1899, at the age of 69. They are buried in the Catholic Cemetery in Fort Wayne, Indiana.

The following descendants of David and Jane Palmer have distinguished themselves in a variety of occupations.

John Palmer, a city policeman, had nine children (Vincent, John, Andrew, Irene, Rose, Leo, Arthur, Clem, and Emmett).

William Palmer, a blacksmith at the Bass Foundry, had nine children (Augustin, Alberta, Martha, Hanorah, Lawrence, Henry, John Bernard, George, and Albert).

Albert Palmer, a dry-wall contractor, had eleven children (Flora, Mary, Loretta, Elizabeth, Helen, Albert, Walter, Margaret, Genevieve, James, and Eugene).

James, a carpenter, had two children (Agnes and Louis).

Ira had three children (Edward, Mary, and Francis).

Charles, a building contractor, had two children (Mary and Chauncey).

Joseph, a building contractor, had five children (Rose, Florence, Joseph, Clair, and Rose Anna).

Anna married William Harkenrider and had six children (Emmett, Cora, Irene, Ira, Iva, and Charlotte).

Amanda married Edward Parisot, and had six children (Clarence, Maurice, Helen, Loretta, Edward, and Royal).

The story of the Palmer family continues to be written by many descendants who live in Allen County and throughout the United States.

Submitted by Thomas E. Palmer

JAMES PETER & PATRICIA ROSEMARY (SWENDA) PAPAGIANNIS FAMILY

James Peter Papagiannis was born on February 15, 1951, in Metamorphosis, Greece. He is the son of Peter Theodore and Stephanie (Zissis) Papagiannis. Peter immigrated to the United States on August 4, 1951. Stephanie and James joined him in Fort Wayne on February 22, 1952 after he got a job at Holsum Bakery.

Patricia Rosemary Swenda was born on December 2, 1953, at St. Joseph Hospital in Fort Wayne. She is the daughter of Joseph J. Swenda and Mary Maude (Strack) Swenda. Joseph was born in Jeansville, Pennsylvania, and moved to Fort Wayne in 1949 after he married Mary, who was the sister of one of his army buddies. Patricia is a descendant of Chief Little Turtle of the Miami Tribe, which was native to the Fort Wayne area.

Papagiannis Family: Top: Patti and Jim; Middle Row: Andy and Jimmy; Bottom Row: Katie and Jodi March 2003

James and Patricia – or Jim and Patti—were married on October 12, 1975. Both graduated from Indiana-Purdue Fort Wayne—Jim in 1974 and Patti in 1975. Jim earned an Electrical Engineering Technology degree but went to work in his father's restaurant, Gateview Inn. The couple bought a 71 acre farm in northwest Allen County the summer before they were married. Jim and Patti set to work building a small starter house with their own hands and moved onto "Lost Creek Farm" just two weeks before their son, James Peter, Jr., was born on November 14, 1976. The farm was named "Lost Creek" because the survey shows three creeks running through the property, when there are really only two. On March 31, 1982, their family grew with the birth of their daughter, Katharine Alexandra. They were blessed again on June 28, 1984, with the birth of their son, Andrew Theodore. The family was growing, and in the summer of 1985, the size of the farm grew when they purchased an adjoining 44 acres.

Jim and Patti always had a dream to build a "real" house and, in 1991, they put this dream into motion. Jim bought a sawmill from the Wood-Mizer Company in Indianapolis. Jim and Patti cut down oak trees from Patti's parents' woods and hauled the logs home. They milled the logs into boards, had the boards dried, and set to work. They hired contractors for the cement work, bricklaying, framing, and drywall, but did almost everything else themselves. It took them 13 years to completely finish the house and the 6000 square foot home, with all the hand-made oak trim, wood floors, and cabinets, was truly a labor of love.

New owners took over the Gateview Inn on December 31, 1994. Jim looked for a way to utilize his degree and was lucky enough to be hired at International Harvester in Fort Wayne. He is currently a facilities engineer with International. Patti was a stay-at-home mom and helped at the restaurant on weekends. She started substitute teaching for Northwest Allen County Schools in October 1990, and works primarily at Carroll High School.

On July 17, 1999, James Peter, Jr. married Jodi Lynn Perry, a girl he had known from Huntertown Elementary School through Carroll High School, but never dated until three years after he graduated. He has a business degree from Indiana-Purdue Fort Wayne and works at Flagstar Bank. Katharine Alexandra must have been influenced by the homebuilding project, because she has a degree in Construction Engineering Technology from Indiana-Purdue. She works for an architecture and design firm, Design Collaborative, in Fort Wayne. Andrew Theodore excelled in sports at Carroll High School and is continuing his education and his football career at the University of St. Francis in Fort Wayne.

Submitted by James P. Papagiannis

PETER THEODORE & STEPHANIE P. (ZISSIS) PAPAGIANNIS FAMILY

Peter Papagiannis was born in Metamorphosis, Greece, on October 10, 1920, while his mother was picking corn. She wrapped him in her apron and took him home. His father died when he was just two. Life in the village was hard; Peter grew up farming and herding sheep. Stephanie's life was a little easier in Vissenia, Greece, where was born on July 25, 1925. Her father, Gregory Zissis, had been to America. He and his brother, Mike Kozma, owned Kozma Brothers Grocery on Brackenridge Street in Fort Wayne.

Both Peter and Stephanie suffered through the miseries and hunger of the Depression, Civil War in Greece, and World War II. When Peter came home after serving in the Greek Army, he asked Stephanie to marry him. On October 9, 1949, they were married and began to work toward coming to America and a better life.

Greg, Stephanie, Jim, Peter, and Liz Papagiannis celebrating 20 years in business at the Gateview Inn. November, 1985

They contacted Stephanie's Uncle Mike in Fort Wayne and asked him to sponsor them to come to America. With the help of Vasil Litchin and Vasil Eschoff, Mike Kozma arranged for Peter to come to America. Peter and Stephanie's first child, James Peter, was born on February 15, 1951. It was with a heavy heart that Peter left his wife and infant son, but he knew that he was going in search of a better life for his family.

He arrived at Ellis Island on August 4, 1951, and took the train to Fort Wayne. With the help of Mike Kozma, he got a job immediately as a furrier at Greenblatt's. He was laid off after Christmas and soon got a job at Holsum Bakery. He was earning more at this job and, by February 22, 1952, his wife and baby were able to join him in this land of opportunity. They lived with a cousin on Gay Street until they could buy a home of their own on Weisser Park Avenue. Their family was blessed with two more children, Elizabeth on August 3, 1953, and Gregory on November 12, 1958.

It was a struggle to learn the English language and American customs, but they worked hard and, in 1957, became American citizens. Peter was eager to attain more in this adopted country that he loved so much, so, on August 9, 1959, he became part owner of Pontiac Rib Bar. Business was good and in 1962 he bought out his partner. Peter loved the work, his customers, and the success he was enjoying. Soon he looked for land to build a new tavern and, on November 29, 1965, Gateview Inn opened on Goshen Road. From the beginning his wife was there next to him, working to make the business a success. His son, Jim, only 14 years old, washed dishes every weekend and after college went into business with his father. They soon purchased a home on Harris Road to be closer to work. After almost thirty years of serving their beloved customers, it was time for Peter and Stephanie to retire and, on December 31, 1994, The Gateview Inn was sold.

Peter and Stephanie loved to travel. Over the years they have been to Greece and Turkey. They took a trip around the world, visiting exotic locations such as Bangkok, Singapore and Tehran. They have enjoyed many three-month stays in Australia to visit relatives and many trips throughout the United States. Peter dreamed, as a sixth grader, of someday seeing the Amazon River and he was able to accomplish that. They are also famous for their flowers and huge gardens, and they cherish the time they spend with their children and five grandchildren. Not too bad for someone who was born in a corn field!

Submitted by Peter T. Papagiannis

ELMER E. PARKER FAMILY

The Parker family came to Fort Wayne from Utica, New York. Elmer E. Parker had accepted a sales position with Van Arman Manufacturing Company. He brought his wife Margaret (Maggie) and their three children, Elmer, Lucille, and Leroy to the Summit City about 1904. In 1912, they bought a home at 439 West Williams Street. They lived there for many years, later moving to 812 West Branning.

In 1925, Elmer was on a routine business trip to the west. He had written a letter to Maggie from Kansas City, Missouri, saying that he loved her and wished he could find someone to do the laundry so that she wouldn't have to work so hard. Two days later, as he was crossing the railroad tracks, he walked in front of a train. He was on his way to a business appointment in Tulsa, Oklahoma. Headlines in the *Tulsa Tribune* of January 24, 1925, read "Katy Train Crushes Man at Crossing." Elmer had become hard of hearing and evidently never heard the train. In a letter to the family, school superintendent L.C. Ward wrote, "He leaves a legacy better than gold, the memory of a good man."

Young Elmer went to Indiana University, graduating in 1920 with a degree in economics and finance. He worked for Bowser Company and then he joined the Wayne Hardware Company, where he spent most of his working years. When he retired, he had become President and General Manager of the company. Elmer married schoolteacher Ethel Haimbaugh, who was from Fulton County, Indiana, on August 24, 1927. They had one surviving child, Doris. Elmer was a Deacon and Chairman of the Board of Trustees at Plymouth Congregational Church; president of the Crippled Children's Society, Potentate of Mizpah Temple and was a 33 degreed Mason. A charter member of the Fort Wayne Children's Zoo, he also was active with the YMCA, Kiwanis Club and The Salvation Army.

Lucille went to teachers college and received her master's degree in education from Butler University. She never married and for the rest of her life she taught school as an able and well-loved kindergarten teacher at Franklin and Franke Park Schools. Long after the children left her care, she followed the achievements of "her boys and girls," as she affectionately called her kindergartners. One former student would visit her on the last day of school each year. That pupil became the Assistant Superintendent of Fort Wayne Community Schools, Patty Martone.

Leroy didn't seek advanced education, but chose to marry his sweetheart Helen Wilson of Roachdale, Indiana. They had two daughters, Barbara Lucille, born in 1927, and Nancy Faye, born in 1931. Barbara died at age 26, leaving two sons, Walter and Bruce Borneman. Nancy married Bill Erb and had three children, Bill Jr., Janice, and Cathy. Nancy later married Bill Bland and had another son, Bill (Bucky) Bland. Leroy retired from Wayne Hardware Company, having worked in the builder's hardware for many years.

Submitted by Jane Boundy

MACLYN PARKER FAMILY

The Parker family came to Fort Wayne in 1957 from San Francisco after Maclyn T. Parker completed service in the U.S. Navy.

Maclyn (Mac) Parker was born in New Castle, Indiana, in 1929. His father was Crawford Parker, who served as Indiana Secretary of State and then as Lt. Governor from 1956-1960 and was the Republican nominee for Governor in 1960, losing in a very close race.

Patricia (Pat) Parker was born in Sandusky, Ohio, in 1929 and subsequently lived in Chicago Heights, Illinois, where her father, Earle F. Opie, was president of Weber-Costello Company, a manufacturer of maps, globes, and school supplies.

Both Mac Parker and Pat Parker graduated from DePauw University. Pat attended the University of Stockholm, Sweden, for one year, and Mac attended the University of London for

The Parker Family enjoying one of their favorite sports...skiing. 1987

one year. Mac received his law degree from the University of Michigan.

After moving to Fort Wayne, Mac Parker joined the firm of Campbell, Livingston, Dildine and Haynie in the practice of law. He formed his own firm in 1967, and this firm was later merged with another firm, which then formed the Fort Wayne office of Baker & Daniels, one of Indiana's largest law firms.

The Parkers have three daughters. The oldest, Pamela, graduated from Indiana University and is presently a CPA in Portland, Oregon, where she resides with her husband, Rodney Johnson, and their two children. Carole graduated from Vanderbilt University and she and her husband, Dan Reicher, presently live in Vermont with their three children. Kristi graduated from Colorado College and the Kennedy School of Harvard University. She and her husband, Frank Celico, and their two children currently live in Dillon, Colorado.

Pat Parker has been very involved in the Fort Wayne community, including serving as President of the Junior League, President of Fort Wayne Community Foundation, and was a founder and long-time board member of the McMillen Center for Health Education, and a Trustee of the Boys and Girls Club.

During his Navy service, Mac Parker served as a lieutenant in Navy Air aboard carriers in the South Pacific. Upon coming to Fort Wayne, he has also been involved in the community. He twice served as Chairman of the Greater Fort Wayne Chamber of Commerce, served for many years on the Indiana State Economic Development Council, was President of the Memorial Coliseum Board of Trustees, and President of Fort Wayne Sports Corporation, among many other organizations. In 2003, he was awarded an honorary Doctor of Laws by Purdue University for his community service. He also received a Sagamore of the Wabash from Governor Frank O'Bannon in 1997. Mac Parker was also instrumental in starting a professional basketball team in Fort Wayne, the Fort Wayne Fury. This was a successful attraction in the area for a great number of years, providing entertainment to many families.

Having previously resided in Chicago and on the west coast, the Parkers chose a Midwestern medium-sized city to live in because of its many advantages. Fort Wayne has always offered a number of cultural advantages and the proximity to Chicago, Cleveland, and Indianapolis enhance these choices. The Parkers are proud to be members of the Fort Wayne community.

Submitted by Maclyn T. Parker

JOSEPH PARKS

OBITUARY

Joseph Parks, son of John and Mary A. (Geiger) Parks was born near Jacktown, Licking County, Ohio on January 15, 1831, departed this life in Eel River township, Allen County Ind., September 11, 1918: aged 87 years, 7 months and 26 days.

At the age of four years he moved with his widowed mother in a party of thirty- five, leaving Jacktown, Ohio September 9, 1935 in pursuit of a new home in what was then known as the "New Country." He was the last survivor of this party of those early emigrants. They located then on what is now the known as the Joseph Harter farm on the Lincoln Highway a short distance south of Churubusco. Therefore his early life was spent clearing the vast forests of their timber into broad fields for use by future generations.

He was united in marriage to Elizabeth Rhodes on August 4, 1853. She departed this life January 22, 1870, in Newton County, Missouri. They resided in Allen county, Indiana, for about 11 years after their marriage and then moved near Monroe Wisconsin, in 1864 and purchased a farm, living there about one year. At the close of the Civil War they moved near Carthage, Jasper county, Missouri, residing there for four years and again returning to Allen county, Indiana, where he has been a continuous resident.

Granddad Joseph Parks- front row, last on the right end with the full beard.

There was born to this union the following named children: Jennette McCullough, John Parks, Laura Jane Parks, Arreta Schrage, Dora Tenney, William Lewis and James Beecher Parks, all surviving him excepting John and Laura Parks.

By the death of Elizabeth (Rhodes) Parks it left him with the care of seven young motherless children ranging in ages from sixteen years to five months. Thereby requiring a great deal of responsibility and care of this father, until he united in marriage to Mary J. (Brown) Johnston on March 7, 1872, who was a widow with two small children. She departed this life December 15, 1916.

To this union was born the following named children: Elizabeth Ann, deceased, Eva Johnson and Charles Marion Parks. There are also surviving three half brothers namely William, Jacob and George W. Maxwell and 24 grand children, 13 great grandchildren and one great great grandchild, besides a large number of relatives and friends left to mourn their loss.

About 1891 he accepted Christ as his Savior under the leadership of Rev. Smith, and affiliated himself with the United Brethren Church Mt. Zion, where he remained a faithful member until this organization was abandoned, afterwards transferring his membership to the Wesley Chapel M. E. Church, where he remained a constant and faithful member until death.

Funeral services were held at Eel River, Friday at 2:30 by Rev. A. F. McCloe assisted by the Wesley Chapel choir.

Submitted by Katie (Parks) Reader

PARROTT FAMILY

The Parrot origin is Audincourt, Doubs, France. Jean Pierre Parrot departed France on March 15, 1850 [Declaration of Intent for Naturalization arrived New York on April 4, 1850 from Le Havre on the ship Elizabeth Danison].

John Peter Parrot was born in Audincourt, France, September 18, 1828, removing to USA at age 21. Coming to Fort Wayne a few years later, he married Miss Josephine Viron on November 4, 1860 in Fort Wayne. The Parrots lived at 1129 Oak Street and had eight children, six sons, two daughters.

Mr. Parrot served in Civil War as Private, Company G, 350th Regiment, Indiana Volunteer Infantry. He enlisted January 23, 1865 at Kendallville, Indiana, and was honorably discharged at Victoria, Texas, September 30, 1865. He was 5'5" tall, dark complexioned, hazel eyes, black hair and a wagon maker. He signed his pension paper with an X. His 1890 pension application said "he is now suffering with Rheumatism".

An original French letter was found amid Parrot family papers in Massillon, Ohio, about 1938 written by Peter to his brother, Louis. The letter transcribed to English, says "We have left Huntsville, Alabama March 25 to come here, the eastern part of Tennessee. There is almost 300 miles to Huntsville, I cannot tell you how long we will remain here. All the country that I saw around here are mountainous. I saw great montains. I saw some 700 ft. high and saw one 1500 ft. high. There is some forts on the summit."

An obituary in the Fort Wayne Journal November 17, 1902 said, "Mrs. Josephine Parrot, wife of J. Peter Parrot, who has resided in Allen Co. for more than half century died Sunday, November 16, 1902, at 7:30 p.m. at home of son, George Parrot, 317 East Jefferson Street, after five days illness, death was due to pneumonia."

Mr. Parrot died July 1, 1907. Burial was at Fort Wayne Lindenwood Cemetery, Main Street, Section Q, Lot AG, #23

John Peter Parrot's Children:

1.) Louis A. Parrot was born February 1, 1862, and married (1) Matilda Kline, July 6, 1886, and (2) Emma J. Griffith, June 30, 1909 after Matilda's death. Louis lived at 20 Francis Street, died June 8, 1938, and is buried in Catholic Cemetery, Lake Avenue, in Fort Wayne.

2.) Francis Joseph Parrot was born June 11, 1986, and married (1) Kunigunda Neidhart-Mutz, September 18, 1883, and (2) Catherine Theresa Angst, November 27, 1987, after Kunigunda's death. He died June 5, 1932 and is buried in Catholic Cemetery. Frank started the Parrot Meat Packing Company in Fort Wayne.

3.) Mary Catherine Parrot was born July 26, 1866, and married Louis Joseph Parnin on June 19, 1900; she died in Alhambra, California on February 3, 1947.

4.) Julia Josephine Parrot was born December 24, 1868, and married Charles Willard Geiger on February 25, 1892; she died in Chicago on January 30, 1953.

5.) George Joseph Parrot was born July 26, 1871, and married Clarice Angeline Langard on September 23, 1895. George was a gifted portrait photographer who won many awards. He died November 9, 1915 and is buried in Catholic Cemetery.

6.) Edward J. Parrott was born October 19, 1873 and mysteriously left Fort Wayne when a young man. No one knew what happened to him until his death in Dayton, Ohio, March 17, 1958 when someone in Ohio sent an obituary.

7.) John Peter Parrott was born March 20, 1876, and married Inez E. Dolan in 1896. He died in Flint, Michigan on September 15, 1962. He worked for Buick Motor Div., Crankshaft Department. He is buried in Gracelawn Cemetery, Flint, Michigan.

8.) Anthony Joseph Parrot was born January 14, 1880 and died oung on July 14, 1880.

Submitted by Donald Parrott

FRANCIS JOSEPH & KUNIGUNDA (NEIDHART) PARROT

Francis Joseph Parrot (1863-1932) was born in Fort Wayne, the second son of John Peter Parrot, who emigrated from France in 1850. He attended Cathedral Catholic School and later worked as a servant for a local doctor. In 1880, Frank began working as a butcher for the Charlie Kuhn meat company. Purchasing the shop around 1890, Frank went into business for himself: "Dealer in Fresh, Salt, and Smoked Meats, Poultry, Butter, Eggs, etc." Moving to Main Street in 1893, Frank operated a retail market and a slaughtering house.

Francis Joseph Parrot and Kunigunda Neidhart, 1890's.

Frank married Kunigunda Neidhart (1865-1895) at St. Mary's Catholic Church in September 1883. They had four children: Joseph (1884-1968), Ursula Bernadette (1885-1886), Edward (1887-1947), and Charles (1892-1965). After Kunigunda's death, Frank married Catherine Angst (1876-1936), the daughter of Leonard Angst and Theresa Neidhart. Frank and Catherine had one son, Lawrence (1899-1976).

The Parrot meat business outgrew the shop on Main Street, so a larger packing plant was built between Fort Wayne and New Haven. In May 1923, the Parrot Packing Company was incorporated by Frank, his sons Joseph, Edward and Charles, with John Weilling and Walter Hood. Frank owned the retail market and directed the packing plant until his death on June 5, 1932.

Joseph Parrot (1884-1968) was born in Fort Wayne. He attended St. Mary's Catholic School, and began working as a clerk in his father's meat market when he was 13. In June 1905, Joseph married Lillian Langard (1883-1960), daughter of John Langard and Rose Dodane, at the Cathedral. They had six children: John (1906-1965), Catherine (1910-1965), Frank (1908-1973), Mary Alice (1912-2003), Richard (1916-1997), and Joseph, Jr. (1920-1994).

When the Parrot Packing Company was incorporated, Joseph remained as manager of the meat market, and then became president of the Parrot Packing Company after the death of his father. He remained as president of the company until the time of his death, but had sold the market to his son John in 1938. Joseph was a member of the Knights of Columbus, the Chamber of Commerce, and a charter member of St. Jude Catholic Parish.

Joseph Parrot, Jr. (1920-1994) was born in Fort Wayne. He attended Cathedral Catholic School, but graduated from St. Jude's Catholic School before going to Central Catholic High School, graduating in 1938. When the United States entered World War II, he was working at his brother's market, but was soon drafted. Serving in the army from July 1942 until November 1945, he was a meat and dairy hygienist, but most often served in various hospitals in charge of rationing. Stationed in Italy, North Africa, and France, he was made a Tech 4th grade in 1944.

Shortly after completion of his service, Joseph married Patricia Pease (1922-2003), the daughter of Curtis Pease and Anna Masanz, on December 27, 1945, at St. John's Catholic Church in Fort Wayne. They had five children: Sharon, John, Joseph Edward (1949-2003), James, and Jerome.

Richard and Joseph entered the partnership with John in the Parrot Market in July 1955. They continued to operate the market until John's death in 1965. After the business was sold, Joseph later served as executive secretary of the Parrot Packing Company.

Submitted by James Parrot.

GEORGE JOSEPH & CLARICE ANGELINE (LAUGARD) PARROT FAMILY

A gifted portrait photographer, George Joseph Parrot, was born July 26, 1871 in Fort Wayne, the fifth child of Jean Pierre Parrot and Marcelline Josephine Viron. John Peter emigrated from France in 1850 at age 21. Josephine traveled from France with her family in July of 1845. On September 23, 1895, George married Clarice Angeline Langard, daughter of Claude Joseph Langard and Victorine Felicite Manier. Joe Langard, born December 31, 1830 in Gouhenans, France, the son of Etienne Langard and Antoinette Brepson, arrived in New York on October 24, 1850 at age 19. Coming to Indiana, he purchased a farm near Arcola, but soon relocated to Fort Wayne where he ran a saloon. "The Societe Franco-Americain" held its meetings above the Langard bar.

Clara's mother, Victoria, was born April 14, 1839 in Arcola, the seventh of nine children of Hippolite Manier and Margueritte Poirson, one of Fort Wayne's founding families. Shortly after their first child, John (Myron), as born on April 25, 1896, George and Clara moved to Warsaw, Indiana, where their second child, Leland, was born on June 16, 1897. George moved his photography studio back to Fort Wayne where two more children were born, George, April 21, 1907 and Louise Claire, April 25, 1906. Baby George tragically died of whooping cough on April 13, 1908. George Parrot built the family's Fort Wayne house at 2019 Crescent Avenue, where members of the family resided until it was sold in the 1990s. On November 6, 1916, George, suffering from depression, drowned in the river.

George Parrot

Neither Lee nor Lois ever married, but remained at home, caring for their mother until her death on September 10, 1950. Lee was an officer in the Parrot Packing Plant. He died in Fort Wayne on October 31, 1992. Lois taught at the Franklin school in Fort Wayne. In 1996 she relocated to Seattle, Washington, where she died on April 23, 2003.

Myron John (MJ) attended Fort Wayne Catholic schools, and was at Notre Dame when his father became ill and required his presence at home. Myron soon joined the British army in Canada, and later when the US entered WWI, transferred to the US Army. He remained in France for several years after the Armistice, returning to New York on February 21, 1921. After living in Provincetown for a while, he became a New York City, newspaperman and married Lucille Kahn of Sedalia, Missouri, the daughter of Sylvain and Florence Loebenstein. Myron and Lucille had a son, Sylvain Jean, born December 7, 1927. Tragically, Lucille died February 5, 1929 while carrying their second child.

Growing up with his grandmother in Fort Wayne, Sylvain Jean changed his name to Steven and married Priscilla Jean Stiller, daughter of Walter and Frances Cecelia Hoffman. They moved to New York where he had an advertising business. Steven died from a stroke on January 31, 1995, leaving four daughters, and seven grandchildren.

In 1936 Myron married Florence Evers and had a daughter Lucille. In 1966 Myron and Florence joined their daughter in California where they later died, Myron on November 26, 1975 and Florence on February 1, 1982, leaving five grandchildren and eight great grandchildren.

Submitted by Lucille Lois Parrot Lynch

PAUL & MARILYN (POUMADE) PARSONS FAMILY

Paul Henry Parsons was born June 11, 1931, in Fort Wayne, Indiana, to Elmer and Viola Parsons. He was the first of two siblings; Shelvy Jean followed his birth six years later. Shelvy lives in Bloomington, Indiana, with her husband, Norman Lee Horn.

Paul's family moved to White Fish Lake, Michigan. There he met and fell in love with Marilyn Freda Poumade, born May 12, 1931. She was one of five daughters of Earl Glen and Ena Poumade. Paul and Marilyn were married on November, 25, 1950. One week after their marriage they moved back to Fort Wayne, Indiana, and made it their home.

In 1950, Paul was hired at International Harvester and worked there for 31 years. His reputation was that of an honest, fair man and inherited the nickname of "Hop" from those who worked with him.

On March 19, 1952, Marilyn gave birth to Brenda Lou (Parsons) Burks. Brenda and her 19 year old son, Jeremy Ray, live in Fort Wayne, Indiana.

A year later, on July 17, 1953, Kip Allen Parsons was born. Kip and his wife, Connie, live in Fort Wayne, Indiana. Kip has a son, Travis Lee, born May 13, 1994.

On April 7, 1956 the third child arrived, Cheryl Lynn (Parsons) Lowe. Cheryl lives in Fort Wayne, Indiana, with her daughter, Jessica Joanne, born December 15, 1983.

Paul Parsons, June 2002

The fourth child arrived on January 10, 1958, and was named Steven Paul Parsons. Steven currently resides in Columbia, Tennessee. He has three children; Michael Steven, Amy Jo and Jennifer Ann, all residing in Columbia, Tennessee. Michael has a daughter, Jaylynn Michelle; Amy has a daughter, Autum Paige; and Jennifer has a son, Caleb Paul.

Paul and Marilyn's fifth child was born, June 12, 1962, and was named Randall Lee Parsons. Randall currently lives in Cincinnati, Ohio with his daughters Caryn Lynn and Rebekah Lee, ages eleven and six, respectively.

Paul loved to fish and camp. He enjoyed American history and took his family to many historical locations. He also loved to square dance and was well known in the square dance circuit.

He was an excellent story teller and anyone who met Paul Parsons can remember one of his tales. It was difficult to tell where truth and fiction met, but every story was told passionately and with a message.

Paul also collected trains. He was a member of the Train Collectors Association. Paul donated his time and trains at Christmas for the display at the Fort Wayne Children's Zoo.

After retiring from International Harvester on May 28, 1982, he started driving a school bus for Northwest Allen County Schools. He drove a "special needs" bus for several years and then began driving a regular full size school bus. Paul was recognized by the "red ball cap" he constantly wore.

Paul Henry Parsons passed away on September 19, 2002. He is remembered by many and held dear in the hearts of all who knew him.

Submitted by Marilyn Parsons

CHARLES EMERSON & RUTH JEANETTE (GUMPPER) PASK FAMILY

Charles (Charlie) Pask was born in Bryan, Ohio, September 30, 1886, to George Washington Pask and Kezia (Boyce) Pask. Ruth Jeanette Gumpper was born in Fort Wayne, Indiana, on March 28, 1894, to Charles Howard Gumpper and Emma Lena (Neireiter) Gumpper. As a young man, Charlie Pask was one of the founders of the Friars Club; was its first president and served a second term. He became friends with Knute Rockne, who was head coach of Notre Dame University, and who the Friars hired to play with the Friars semi-pro football team. The original Friars Club essentially ended with the start of World War I in 1917. Charlie went to war, returned to Fort Wayne, met Ruth Gumpper in 1921 and married in 1922. Ruth was a lovely, popular young lady who had gone to Washington, D.C. to work for the Federal Government during the War. She had been a fine vocalist in Fort Wayne society, singing for social functions, church services, weddings, and some stage shows.

In September 1923, Charlie and Ruth had a son named Charles Emerson Pask, Jr., born in Fort Wayne. Four years later, (having moved to South Bend, Indiana, to work for Studebaker Finance Corporation) they conceived a daughter, Joan Louise Pask, born in September 1927. The family lived across the street from the Knute Rockne family and a strong friendship formed. When Knute was killed in a plane crash over Kansas in 1931, the Pask children paid their respects to Knute by waiting in a very long line on their street to view his body as it "lay in state," so to speak. Joan was three and a half years old,

August 1939: Chuck age 53; Ruth age 44; Chuck, Jr. age 16, Joan age 12. Last picture of all of us. Five months later Dad died at age 53

so perhaps she could be among the very few, if any, people still alive, who witnessed that solemn occasion.

The Pask family moved to Cleveland Heights, Ohio, in 1934 after Charlie left Studebaker. His health slowly failed and he died in January 1940, at age 53. Son, Chuck, followed in his dad's footsteps by attending Purdue University until he enlisted in the U.S. Army Air Corps, and became a P-38 fighter pilot. He was killed in action on March 12, 1945, at age 22 and is buried in the U.S. National Cemetery at St. Avold, France. Mother Ruth lived a long life of 95 and a half years, passing in 1990. Both Ruth and Charlie rest in peace in Lindenwood Cemetery in Fort Wayne. Daughter Joan Pask graduated from Purdue University, married her Purdue sweetheart, Dwane Gail Mikelson (from South Bend, Indiana), and together they have two sons, Jeffrey Charles Mikelson and Scott Thomas Mikelson, and one daughter, Ann Ruth Mikelson Luchsinger. Joan is the last surviving member of the Pask-Gumpper family.

Submitted by Joan Pask Mikelson

PAULEY FAMILY

1838-1980

The year was 1838. The history of the Pauley family begins in Ireland when Thomas Joseph Pauley, the son of a tradesman John Pawley, was born in the small town of Coolmoohan, County Cork. When the Gorto Mor or Great Hunger of the potato famine struck Ireland in 1845, the Pawley family was somewhat protected by John's skill and trade. Thomas was only seven years old when he witnessed the mass starvation of thousands of people who were dependent upon the farmland for food. Thomas was there when the famine was followed by the epidemics of typhus, cholera, and scurvy, which took many of his friends and some of his own family. When Gorto Mor passed in 1851, Ireland was not the same. Over one million people died during the Gorto Mor and another two million fled to other countries. The national crisis caused by the Gorto Mor fired the political and religious unrest between Ireland and England. Nevertheless, Thomas and his family survived the Gorto Mor and they were counted among the fortunate.

Thomas grew up to become a blacksmith like his father. He married Mary Elizabeth Fox in 1861 and together, they had ten children, of which seven lived to adulthood. As a young man in Ireland, Thomas enjoyed a relaxation of some of the two hundred year old Penal Laws that limited the Irish Catholics' ability to vote, acquire land, own property including a horse, make wills, amass wealth, attend school, or to practice their Irish culture. The relaxation of the Penal Laws allowed Thomas to hold a position of a tradesman, acquire a small piece of property, and allowed his oldest sons to attended school learning to read and write.

The year was 1878. Thomas Pauley survived many great hardships, but the political circumstances in Ireland caused Thomas to emigrate with his family to America. The Penal Law allowed only for the oldest son to inherit land or property from the father, if the son converted to the Anglican Church. In this case, what little property Thomas owned would be lost or his four

St. Patricks Church

younger sons would have to find their fortunes in other countries. On the national level in 1879, the political news reported of a potential Irish rebellion as the leader of the Irish Home Rule Party gathered strength in Parliament. Rebellion meant hunger or loss of life; Thomas did not want to live through another Gorto Mor.

In the United States, James Fox, Thomas' brother-in-law, had been living in Fort Wayne for nearly 30 years. James immigrated to America in 1850. James kept the Pauleys informed of the changes and growth in America through the letters he sent home to Ireland. He wrote about the end of the War Between the States, the growth of businesses, new inventions, industry, strong family ties, religious and political freedom! Freedom and Opportunity are the things that brought many families to America long before the Gorto Mor.

Thomas was over 40 years old when he emigrated from Ireland alone. The 1880 U.S. Census showed Thomas living in Fort Wayne with his brother-in-law James Fox. James, a successful coal dealer, had a home on McClellan Street with his wife Ellen and his nine children. In 1881, two of Thomas' sons, John and Thomas Edwin, arrived in Fort Wayne. The following year, Thomas' wife Mary arrived with their five other children, Edward, Eugene, James, Mary, and Johanna.

The Pauley family settled in Fort Wayne, and Thomas was blacksmith at the Pennsylvania Company for nineteen years. He and Mary proudly owned a home on West Williams Street. Thomas and his five sons were founding members of St. Patrick's Catholic Church, and they were active in many of the Church societies. Thomas achieved in America what he could not have gained in Ireland. After a long life of struggle, Thomas died in 1899 at the age of 61 of stomach cancer. Mary died ten years later in 1909. Thomas and Mary are together at Catholic Cemetery.

All seven of Thomas and Mary's children lived on in Fort Wayne.

James Fox marker

Pauley marker at Catholic Cemetery

John followed his father from Ireland to Fort Wayne in 1881 at the age of 18 years. He married Ella Awilda Davis on June 21, 1887. They had two children, Maurice and Helen. Between the years 1890 to 1918, John was often mentioned in the Fort Wayne newspapers as a popular hotel clerk and unofficial ambassador of Fort Wayne's hotel industry. John, 'whose genial countenance beamed from behind the desk of the popular hostelry', was known for his generous hospitality and good humor. He was prepared to delight travelers with a smoke from his private stock of cigars or "don his diamonds" for important heads of state and delegations. John began his career as night clerk for a number of Fort Wayne's finest hotels including the Robinson, Brunswick, Rich Hotel, Anthony Hotel, Randall Hotel, and New Aveline. John's greatest sorrow was being on duty the night the New Aveline House Hotel burned down in 1908. John managed the Colonial Hotel on Lake Manitou in Rochester, Indiana from 1915 to his death in 1926. John is resting at Catholic Cemetery. After John's death, his wife, Ella, lived with her son-in-law and daughter, William and Helen Wolf of Elkhart Indiana until her death in 1951.

Thomas Edwin arrived in Fort Wayne with his brother, John, in 1881 at the age of 16 years. A few years later, the newspapers reported that Thomas Edwin moved to Toledo to work for the railroad ticket line. It was in Toledo he met and married Elizabeth Whiter. Thomas Edwin and Elizabeth visited the Pauley Family in Fort Wayne, but most of his life was spent in Toledo. Thomas Edwin and Elizabeth had three sons: Thomas Maurice, Howard, and George.

Olds marker

Nine months before Thomas Edwin died of pneumonia/tuberculosis, Elizabeth moved her sons back to Fort Wayne to live with the Pauley family. Thomas Edwin died under doctor's care in Toledo, on July 26,1917. He rests at Catholic Cemetery.

Edward and Eugene Pauley emigrated from Ireland with their mother in 1882. They were inseparable brothers in life and death. Edward and Eugene were active members in the community serving as business sponsors of a number of athletic teams such as the Five Star Baseball Team. They were active members of the Holy Name Society, the Knights of Columbus, and Ancient Order of Hibernians. Edward owned an infamous tavern on Grand Street called the "Pauley's Bunch". He married Mary Elizabeth Mullins in 1890, and they owned a home on Dawson Street. They had no children. Mary Elizabeth died in 1909 after a long struggle with Bright's disease. In 1911, Edward remarried to Margaret McDonald Cushing at the Cathedral in Fort Wayne. They lived on West Williams Street. His marriage to Margaret blessed Edward with a stepson named Arch Cassell, but they had no children of their own. Edward died suddenly on March 9, 1928 of heart disease.

His brother, Eugene, was a successful electrician and owned Eugene Pauley's Electrical on South Calhoun Street. He married Myrtle B. Doering in 1906. They had no children. Eugene was well known for his quality residential and commercial electrical contracting work. Eugene died suddenly three weeks after his brother Edward on March 28, 1928. They are all resting at Catholic Cemetery.

James was eleven years old when he came to live in Fort Wayne. At the age of 29, he became a boilermaker for the Pennsylvania Railroad Company and served there for 35 years. His life was a typical example ofthe hardships that many tradesmen experienced in the new industrial era. From the period 1900 to 1905, the newspapers reported James lost an eye, burned his hands by electricity or stream, injured his knees, lost several fingers, and his left thumb was reattached after being severed by stream-powered shears. James married Amelia J. Kreckmann in 1911. They owned a home on West Masterson Avenue. James and Amelia had two children: Thomas Edward and Eileen. In 1914, the newspapers reported that James visited the taverns all too often to the distress of his wife. It was only after Amelia sued James for divorce that James changed his ways. In 1915, Amelia withdrew her petition for divorce and he was unnoticed by the newspapers until his death in 1934. He rests at Catholic Cemetery. After James died, Amelia lived with her son until her death in 1980. She rests with her family at Lindenwood Cemetery.

Mary was the oldest daughter of Thomas and Mary Pauley. She was just six years old when she came with her mother to Fort Wayne. Miss Mary was a dressmaker and never married. She traveled extensively with her business partner, Rose Simons, to fashion and design shows in New York and Chicago. They operated the popular dress shop of Simon & Pauley on Schmitz in Fort Wayne. Miss Mary died in 1961 leaving a small estate to her sister Johanna. Miss Mary rests with her family at Catholic Cemetery.

Johanna, the youngest child of Thomas and Mary Pauley, was about four years old when she came to Fort Wayne with her mother. She had little memory of Ireland because Fort Wayne was her home for nearly 90 years. As a young woman, she worked at the Wayne Dry Goods Store on Calhoun Street. She retired her career as a sales clerk when she married Egbert "Bert" Olds in 1904. To accommodate his career, she traveled to St. Louis to marry so that Bert could continue his work on an electrical installation at the World's Fair Grounds. Like all the Olds family, Bert was very active in the community, but he traveled extensively for the construction units of Electric Light Works, Fort Wayne Electric, and General Electric. Bert and Johanna made their home on South Webster Street, and they had two children: Charlotte and Almyra. She had a long successful career as a wife, mother, and grandmother before she died in 1971. Bert and Johanna are resting with his family at Lindenwood Cemetery.

The history of the Pauley Family began in Ireland, moved to Fort Wayne, and spread successfully throughout the United States. Their history is similar to many families who emigrated to the United States due to religious, political, or financial distresses in their homelands. Thomas Pauley was drawn to Fort Wayne, Allen County by the promise of opportunity and he was blessed in coming. It is with thanks to Thomas Joseph Pauley and the People of Fort Wayne that we dedicate *The Pauley Family History 1836-1980* to the Allen County History Book.

Submitted by Colleen Pauley

PETER TRIER & RUTH ANN (KORTE) PAULISON FAMILY

Peter Trier Paulison was born on August 14, 1938, to Arthur and Virginia (Trier) Paulison, both of whom were descendants of pioneer families. Arthur Paulison was the sixth great-grandson of Cornelius Pauelson. He was the skipper of the ship the *Freedenberg* and arrived in New Amsterdam on November 2, 1640. Johannes Pawelson was the grandson of Cornelius and settled in Somerset, New Jersey. His son John married Sophia Barber. John was a soldier in the Revolutionary war. He died on February 2, 1822. His son, Issac Paulison, married Elizabeth Van Camp and moved west in 1832, settling in Adams County, Indiana. Their son Jacob was the father of Samuel, who married Rachel Merryman. They were the parents of Arthur and Walter Paulison and moved to Fort Wayne, Indiana. Samuel worked on the railroad. He and Rachel died within days of each other during the flu epidemic of 1917. Walter and Arthur both attended Northwestern University, Walter staying to become the sports information director. Arthur began his newspaper career in Fort Wayne. He married Virginia Trier and became the president of Enterprise Glass Company, and later the president of Lindenwood Cemetery. Arthur also had a second Revolutionary War ancestor on his mother's side, Thomas W. Archbold, who fought in the battle of Brandywine and married Mary Kent. He died on March 17, 1837 and is buried in Decatur, Indiana.

Virginia Trier was the great-granddaughter of Conrad Trier, who was born August 6, 1811, to Henry Trier and Catherine Schroder in Ercksdorf, Germany. Conrad immigrated to the United States on the ship the *Allegheny* and arrived in the port of Philadelphia on July 5, 1832. It was there that he began his long journey to Fort Wayne, Indiana, in search of land. He finally purchased land in 1835 after working on the Wabash Erie Canal and was one of the original landowners in Allen County, Indiana, in Adams Township. He was naturalized in Fort Wayne on December 26, 1836. He married Catharine Trier on January 1, 1837. They built their home and raised twelve children, one of which was Peter Trier, the maternal great-grandfather of Peter Paulison.

Peter Trier married Amelia Kellermeier on December 21, 1871, and they had two children, Henry Trier and Emilie Trier. Emilie Trier married Valentine Goeglein on June 21 1899; they had one child, Harold who was born February 15, 1902. Emilie died May 19, 1903. Henry Trier married Anna Geridwyn Davies on June 27, 1906. Anna was born in London, England, the daughter of Jonathan and Celia Davies. They were the parents of Virginia Trier Paulison, and the great-grandparents of Peter Trier Paulison. Peter Trier Paulison attended Culver military academy, North Side High School, and Butler University. He was in the commercial glass business in Fort Wayne for 40 years, an avid Northwestern University fan and Chicago Cub fan. He married Ruth Ann Korte of Fort Wayne in 1964 and they had two children. Caroline married David Andrew and has three children, Katharine, Samuel, and Peter. They live in Skokie, Illinois. Jonathan married Theresa Koehl. They live in Fort Wayne.

Peter Trier Paulison died on October 26, 2002.

Submitted by Ruth A. Paulison

ROBERT DEVEREAUX & DOROTHY (SHANEYFELT) PAXSON FAMILY

Robert (Bob) Devereaux Paxson was born January 17, 1921, in Kingston, Pennsylvania to William Benjamin and Edna (Devereaux) Paxson. He was the youngest of five children. He was a Boy Scout for many years. Bob graduated from Bucknell University in 1943 with a degree in Mechanical Engineering. That degree landed him a job with General Electric. He worked in West Lynn, Massachusetts, for three months, transferred to Erie, Pennsylvania for six months, then transferred to the Fort Wayne, Indiana plant, arriving on February 22, 1944.

While working in Fort Wayne, he met Dorothy Almira Shaneyfelt. Dorothy was the second of eight children of Shirley (George) Elrey and Beatrice Vernon (Barto) Shaneyfelt. They mar-

Carolyn, Bob, Dorothy, Lois Paxson, 1955

ried on July 26, 1947, at Harvester Avenue Missionary Church in Fort Wayne.

Even though his degree was in mechanical engineering, his job assignments were often electrical. Bob went back to school to get his Masters in Education, graduating from Ball State in 1953. He worked at a small school in Pleasant Township, Adams County, for three years, at Hanna Elementary School in Fort Wayne for four years, Washington Township Elementary School in Allen County for four years and Jefferson Township in Adams County. His final assignment was at JE Ober School in Garrett, Indiana, for the remainder of his 39 years of teaching. Bob enjoyed singing in the choir, playing his trumpet, bird watching and was treasurer at Harvester for 17 years.

Dorothy continued working at GE until their first child was born. They had two girls. Carolyn Louise Paxson was born August 2, 1952, in Fort Wayne and married Wayne William Allen on December 23, 1972, at Harvester Avenue Missionary Church. Carolyn and Wayne have three children: Joshua Cole, born August 16, 1974, in Fort Wayne; Rachel Marie, born June 1, 1977, in Fort Wayne, and Caleb Wayne, born June 30, 1987, in West Kalimantan, Indonesia.

Bob and Dorothy's second daughter, Lois Marie Paxson, was born April 1, 1954, in Fort Wayne and married Rollin Lloyd Jump on June 1, 1974, at Harvester Avenue Missionary Church. They have lived in Warsaw, Indiana, and helped start, and continue to serve in, the Christ Covenant Church. Rollin is also a supervisor at Dalton Foundry. Lois and Rollin adopted two newborns: Jonathan Michael, born August 14, 1983, and Jennifer Lynn, born October 28, 1985.

Dorothy taught Sunday School in the nursery/primary department at Harvester for many years. She faithfully visited her grandmother, Melissa Jane (Hart) Barto Miller in the nursing home in her later years, and then her father during his last years. She enjoyed lending a helping hand to those in need. She lived to see and love only her first two grandchildren. She was diagnosed with ovarian cancer the fall of 1980. She passed away about three years later, on July 11, 1983, and is entombed at Covington Memorial Gardens. Bob lived in their home until 2001. He now enjoys his Heritage Park assisted living apartment.

Submitted by R. Paxson

PAYNE FAMILY

In a "holler" tucked between the hills of Meade County, Kentucky, Annie Bryant Payne, a single parent whose husband had left to find work for the family, delivered the first of four children. James Charles Payne was born on a cold January morning in 1911 into a stark existence with minimal heat, sparse household furnishings and too little food for nourishment.

While the man of the "house in the holler" went from town to town seeking permanent employment, Annie Payne survived through the kindness of a few neighbors and far flung relatives who came by.

Lawrence Payne came and went and each time he left, another child was conceived and delivered. James Charles was joined by sister, Mary and brothers Arthur (Pooch) and Marcellus.

The children rode a mule to the Catholic Church in preparation for their first Holy Com-

Jim Payne donates his World War II scrapbooks to the Allen County-Fort Wayne Historical Society.

munion, to Miss Bonnie in the one room school at Louse Corner and created their own toys, games and childhood diversions.

In 1918 the young family left the holler, moved north to Indianapolis and settled in with relatives in that large city. Eventually the restless father moved the family once again. This move was to Fort Wayne where they found living space on Clinton Street across from the rectory of the Cathedral of the Immaculate Conception.

The two older boys enrolled in Cathedral School and began to serve daily mass. They also sold newspapers on the corner of Wayne and Harrison Streets. It was on that corner that they saw their younger brother run down and killed by a motorist unfamiliar with the city's first traffic light on its installation day.

Jim Payne never left Fort Wayne. He attended the Brother's High School on Cathedral Square, married Blanche Norton in 1929, and fathered two children, Patty Payne Martone in 1931 and Wayne Payne in 1941.

Although Jim Payne never had a formal education, he was well read, extremely verbal and quite industrious. He worked for City Utilities over 40 years and after retirement, found wonderful experiences as a "Carry Out Man" at Rogers Market on West State Boulevard. Jim Payne died in 1995 and his wife Blanche in 1991; however both children, educators with PhD's in Education, survive. Patty Martone, retired trom Fort Wayne Community Schools, resides in Fort Wayne. Wayne Payne, a retired professor from Ball State University, resides in Muncie, Indiana.

Jim Payne was a respected resident of northwest Fort Wayne. His infectious personality, incredible storytelling skill and devotion to his family and community live on.

Submitted by Michael Martone

ROBERT & KATHY (MARTIN) PAYONK

Kathy Lynn Martin was born August 29, 1960 in Fort Wayne, Indiana, to Lynn and DeMarise (Hand) Martin. She attended St. Vincent Grade School and Bishop Dwenger High School. She graduated from Purdue University, Fort Wayne, as a registered nurse and worked at Parkview Hospital.

Kathy and Robert Payonk were married December 17, 1983, at St. Vincent Catholic Church, with Rev. Miller officiating. Robert "Bob" Andrew Payonk was born in Chicago, Illinois, and is the son

The Payonk Family (left to right): Emily, Kathy (Martin), Andrew, Aaron and Robert

of Andrew and Lorraine (Wisniewski) Payonk. He moved to Fort Wayne in 1978 with his parents. He graduated from Purdue University, Fort Wayne, with a bachelor's degree in mechanical engineering, and from St. Francis College with a master of business administration in management degree. He has held engineering positions at General Electric, ITT Industries and the National Atmospheric and Space Administration (NASA). Currently he is mission assurance representative with the U. S. Missile Defense Agency (MDA). Since 1996 Kathy has worked as a Veterinary assistant for her father, Dr. Lynn Martin.

Robert and Kathy's children, born in Fort Wayne, Indiana, are: Emily Kristine (December 27, 1986); Andrew Joseph (June 23, 1988); and Aaron Robert (October 8, 1992).

Submitted by Kathy Payonk

WILFRED CURTIS PEASE & ANNA ELIZABETH MASANZ

W. Curtis Pease was born in Brockport, New York in 1895 to Edward Pease and Mary Curtis. He went with his family to Toledo and eventually to Defiance, Ohio, where he worked for a time as a clerk in his father's shoe store. After graduation from Defiance College, Curtis became an accountant. In 1916 Curtis married Anna Masanz, born in 1895 in Defiance, Ohio, a daughter of John Masanz and Barbara Pinker. Soon after their marriage, Curtis and Anna moved to Dayton, where, during World War I, Curtis did accounting work as a civilian at Wright-Patterson Air Force Base.

In 1918, Curtis and Anna and their son, Robert (1917-1989), moved to Fort Wayne. Dorothy, twins Patricia (1922-2003) and Maxine (1922-1988), Raymund, and John were all born in Fort Wayne. During his years in Fort Wayne, Curtis operated his own accounting firm, later to become Pease, Pease, and Pease when Robert and Raymund joined their father. Curtis died in 1956, and Anna died in 1957. Both are buried in the Catholic Cemetery, Fort Wayne.

Robert Pease married Marjorie Glass (1913-1974) in May 1941, and they had six children: Cynthia, Michael (1948-1993), Angela, twins Paula and Lisa, and Robert, Jr.

Dorothy Pease married Lawrence Tholen in April 1942, and they were the parents of three boys: David, Steven (1946-1999), and Ronald.

Patricia Pease was born shortly before midnight on September 10, 1922, while her twin sister Maxine was born shortly after midnight on the eleventh, their brother Robert's fifth birthday. Both did modeling for Wolf & Dessauer Department Store while attending Central Catholic High School. After graduation, Patricia worked

Wilfred Curtis Pease and Anna Elizabeth Masanz, 1932.

as a secretary in her father's accounting office. Maxine became a nurse.

On December 27, 1945, Patricia married Joseph W. Parrot, Jr., and they were the parents of five children: Sharon, John, Joseph Edward (1949-2003), James, and Jerome.

Maxine Pease married Roy Grimmer, Jr. in November 1946, and they had three children: Richard, Edward, and Nancy.

Raymund Pease married Joanne Huntine in April 1946, and they had eight children: Gregory, Alana Elaine (b.d. 1949), Andrea, Sylvia, Tamara, Jeffrey, Melinda (1958-1988), and Bradley.

John Pease married Barbara Chin (1938-1995) in July 1959, and they were the parents of six children: Michele, Raymund, Maria, Robert, Marta, and Randolph.

Sharon Parrot married Joseph S. Subjak, Jr., on November 29, 1969, and they are the parents of four children: Mary Patricia, married to Drew Michels, Monica, married to Nate Nickerson, Anna, married to Paul Newbury, and Thomas Subjak. Monica and Nate are the parents of Claire Marie Nickerson.

Submitted by Jerome J. Parrot

JEAN JOSEPH PERREY

Jean Joseph Perrey was born July 31, 1840 at Valonne, Doubs, France, a son of Antoine J. Perrey and Mary Josette Corty. He went by "Joseph." This biography is of his family and the family of his son, Edward F. Perrey.

Antoine and Mary Perrey and their eight surviving children departed from LaHavre aboard the "Bark Waltham" and arrived in New York on September 3, 1853. Their children were: Francois Ugene (born June 7, 1825 - died January 20, 1826); Marie Cesarie (born October 20, 1826 - died January 31, 1895); Marie Genevieve (born June 3, 1828 - died December 20, 1907) husband, Felix Duciot; Rose Genereuse (born August 30, 1829 - died May 26, 1898) husband, Claude F. Converset; Marie Rosalie (born April 23, 1831 - died June 18, 1911) husband, Claude S. Fevirer; Claude Joseph X. (born June 24, 1832 - died April 8, 1840); Francois Victor (born June 16, 1834 - died December 3, 1897) wife, Mary Ann Rush; Marie Victorine (born February 2, 1836 - died June 16, 1897) husband, P.X. Francis Boiteux; Jean Joseph (born July 30, 1840 - died April 8, 1890) wife, Adelaide M. Manier; M. Josephe Philomene (born July 29, 1842 - died September 6, 1867) husband, Claude S. Fevirer.

The family first settled in Louisville, Stark County, Ohio. Antoine only lived a short time and died in 1854. Their son, F. Victor, moved to Randolph County, Pennsylvania. The other siblings all came to Allen County, Indiana, after the 1860 Census.

Joseph married Adelaide M. Manier in Fort Wayne on September 5, 1865, and they had nine children: Frank Joseph (born March 29, 1866 - died October 7, 1940) wife, Veronika Wirsche; Edward F. (see below); Emma Mary (born September 21, 1870 - died January 26, 1957) husband Anthony T. Jordan; Flora Frances (born June 5, 1874 - died July 5, 1944); Joseph Victor (born August 26, 1876 - died February 7, 1894); Julian John (born October 29, 1878 - died June 20, 1971) wife, Rose M. Whitney; Hippolyte A. (born January 21, 1881 - died December 20, 1958) wife, Louise S. Bahde; Felix Eugene (born July 5, 1885 - died June 26, 1947) wife, Ada M. Brown; Clementine Angeline (born December 31, 1918 - died June 9, 1963) husband, Ezmark Bolt.

Joseph was a carpenter who was kown as a master stair builder. Family tradition relates that while he was home with a cold, his boss came and got him to consult on a current stair job. His trip that day resulted in his coming down with pneumonia and dying April 8, 1890.

Joseph and Adelaide's second son, Edward F. Perrey, born June 28, 1868, married Mary E. Diebold on June 23, 1896, and he died February 26, 1934. They had five children:

1) Alfred Joseph (born April 4, 1897 - died February 4, 1942) wife, M.Magdalen Mungovan. They had a daughter, Joan Marita, born September 19, 1926, who married Otto Bradmueller on November 16, 1949.

Jean Joseph Perrey

2) Reynold Henry (born November 9, 1898 - died March 13, 1962) wife, Irene J. Flaherty. They had four children: John Edward, born August 12, 1924 who married Helen L. Horstmeyer on April 30, 1949; Marjorie Ellen, born August 1, 1926, who married Robert F. Troutman on January 22, 1949; Donald Henry, born October 18, 1928, who married Caroline B. Newkirk on June 14, 1958 (he died September 5, 1996); Rita Irene, born September 21, 1933, who married Charles J. Lehner on June 15, 1957.

3) Helen Veronica (born June 8,1901 - died May 8, 1982) husband, H. Oscar Alter. They had two boys: Robert Edward, born October 2, 1928, who married Dolores L. Goneau on May 24, 1952 (he died July 3, 1978); and Thomas Oscar, born July 12, 1932, who married Carolyn R. Piepenbrink on June 19, 1954.

4) Rosella Agnes (born October 27, 1904 - died July 15, 1988) husband, Herman A. Erlenbaugh. They had two boys: Gerald Herman, born August 7, 1930, who married Mary Alice Cox on February 14, 1953; and James Perrey, born May 1, 1941, who married Mary Josephine Chesterson on February 3, 1962.

5) Alice Mary C. (born December 15, 1907 - died May 19, 2003) husband, Otto H. Lehman.

Edward was a prominent photographer and his multitude of photos of commercial groups, church, school and family portraits are in every facet of Fort Wayne life. Edward's early biography and picture is in Bert Griswold's *Builders of Greater Fort Wayne*.

Submitted by John E. Perrey

FREDERICK & SOPHIA (ALTEKRUSE) PETERS

It was mid-July 1866, when two German brothers, Frederick and Ernst Peters, left Lienen of Westphalia, which at that time was part of Prussia, to embark on a journey to America. They walked to Breman, and then took a small boat downriver to the port of Bremerhaven where they met the large steamship, the Bark Union. After a number of delays, the ship finally pulled anchor on July 24, traveling first through the English Channel and finally getting into the North Sea on August 3. The journey across the ocean was evidently very difficult because of lack of wind, or too strong a head wind, fog, and, because the length of the trip, sparse food supplies. However, the ship finally docked in Baltimore on September 27, 1866, carrying a total of 246 aliens to new lives in America.

Frederick Peters settled in Fort Wayne and became a naturalized citizen on September 7, 1868, at the age of 25. He had joined the St. John's Reformed Church and there he met Sophia Altekruse, who was born in Fort Wayne, the daughter of former German immigrants. They were married in St. John's Church on June 20, 1872. They would become the parents of five children: Matilda (Tillie), born 1876; John H., born 1877; Caroline S., born 1880; Henry J., born 1877; and Otto, born 1890. Frederick Peters probably worked at a local factory, providing a decent living for his family. They lived a devout and frugal life, speaking German at home and at church services. After the children were grown and had their own families, they often gathered at the parents' home for Sunday dinners. These were preceded and ended by lengthy prayers (according to one restless grandchild) recited in German. Another grandchild remembers that

Front Row: Frederick, Callie, Sophia. Back Row: John, Henry, Otto and Tillie

they were allowed to have either jam or butter to spread on bread, but never both.

Some copies of letters between America and Germany survived. In March 1880, Mr. F. H. Peters received a letter from the minister in Lienen, thanking him for sending money back home to two sisters, one widowed and one in need, to help with their living expenses. The minister also included an update on the family situations and news from the village. Then, in February 1923, he received a letter from a niece thanking him for sending a donation to help build a community center. After adding news from the family, she asked for a little money for her family, if he could see fit to spare it! Evidently, they thought the uncle who had gone to America had done quite well.

All of Frederick and Sophia's children lived in Fort Wayne and raised their own families. Tillie married Daniel Auer and they had two children, Edward and Lillian. John married Anna Klebe and they had five children: David, William, Paul, Kathleen and Sandra. Caroline (Callie) remained single. Henry married Caroline (Carrie) Moeller and they had four children: Dorothy, Elnor, Florence, and Robert H. Otto married Bertha Mennewisch and they had five children; James, Richard, Frederick, Kathryn, and Gertrude, who died in infancy. Many of the family descendants still live in Fort Wayne, but, as with many families, some have moved to other areas.

Submitted by Linda S. Seney

DAVID REED PETERSON FAMILY

David Reed Peterson became a resident of Fort Wayne on June 12, 1964. On June 5, 1960 he received a Bachelor of Science in Electrical Engineering (BSEE) from the University of Wisconsin in Madison and accepted a position as a Junior Electrical Engineer with the Magnavox Company. In subsequent years, with the support of Magnavox, he completed a Master of Science in Electrical Engineering (MSEE) in August 1967 and Doctor of Philosophy (Ph.D.) in May 1976, both from Purdue University.

Dr. Peterson was born May 7, 1942 in La Crosse, Wisconsin to Reed and Beverly (Schnell) Peterson. He graduated from La Crosse Central High School June 5, 1960. He attended La Crosse State College for one year and then transferred to the University of Wisconsin in the fall of 1961. On November 9, 1968 he married Janet Elaine Crosbie at Bethlehem Lutheran Church in Fort Wayne. Their offspring are Lisa Renee Peterson, born February 21, 1971, Brian David Peterson, born March 22, 1973, Scott Matthew Peterson, born February 18, 1976 and Sarah Lynn Peterson, born May 25, 1978. All four children attended Croninger Elementary School, Blackhawk Middle (Jr. High) School and R. Nelson Snider High School in Fort Wayne. The children graduated in the Snider classes of 1989, 1991, 1994, and 1996, respectively.

Dr. Peterson participated in the Tactical Communications Conference held in Fort Wayne in 1986, 1988, 1990, 1992, 1994, and 1996. He was the Papers Chairman in 1988, Technical Chairman in 1990, Vice Chair in 1992, and Conference Chair in 1994. The Armed Forces Communication-Electronics Association and the Institute of Electrical and Electronics Engineers were conference sponsors.

He attended the Program Management Course of the Defense Systems Management College at Fort Belvoir, Virginia from July to December 1983. He achieved 40 years with the Raytheon Company, the successor of Magnavox, Philips and Hughes.

Janet and David were divorced on June 10, 1998. DivorceCare at Saint Joseph United Methodist Church, and Beginning Experience changed his life. Participation in follow-on classes and the BE Presenting Team resulted in personal growth and openness. The DivorceCare group decided to move on and started a singles' group called Single Journey. Dave met Julia Davis in early 1999; they were best friends for over nine months. Finally realizing that they could be more than "just friends", they married April 28, 2001 in Van Wert County, Ohio. Julia is a native of Fort Wayne, born Julia May Berkheiser.

Lisa married Jason Scott McIntyre October 6, 2001 in Chicago, Illinois. They subsequently moved to Chandler, Arizona, where Kaitlyn Dorothy was born to them October 31, 2004.

Brian married Jennifer Louise Wille June 5, 1999 in Milwaukee, Wisconsin. They lived in Mohamet, Illinois until Jennifer completed her Ph.D. in Communications from the University of Illinois, at which time they moved to Menomonee Falls, Wisconsin, where Nicholas Brian was born June 13, 2004.

Scott married Kelly Rene Davenport June 30, 2001 in Charlestown, Indiana.

Sarah resides in Fort Wayne.

Submitted by David R. Peterson

FERDINAND & MARIE (MARY) LOUISE (PIERMAN) PFIERRMANN FAMILY

Ferdinand (1846-1922) landed in New York in 1863, along with his father Zackariah Pfierrmann (1816-1898), mother Christina (1810-1878), sister Elizabeth (1851-1898) from Bavaria, a state of Germany. They settled in what is now Springfield Township, at 16133 Spencerville Road, north of what is now Harlan, formerly Maysville.

They were farmers. Ferdinand received his naturalization papers August 25, 1868, in the County of Allen in Indiana. Ferdinand also had two other sisters; Kathryn, who married Frank Rahe and Christina, who married a Wellman. Ferdinand married Marie (Mary) Louise Pierman (1869-1952) August 7, 1899. Mary was the daughter of Andrew Pierman (1836-1905) and Frederickda (Gueth) Pierman (1842-1924); Andrew, with his parents, George Jacob Pierman and Katharina (Weymouth) Pierman, arrived from Baden Germany, in New Orleans in 1853.

Note the different spelling of Pfierrmann. Somewhere over the years one of the "r's" and one of the "n's" were dropped from Pfierrmann. The "f" was sounded in Germany and not in America. Mary's maiden name was always spelled Pierman.

Ferdinand and Mary had four children: Ernest Henry (1900-1972), Clara Louise (1901-1997), Clarence Andrew (1907-1929), and Floyd Isiah (1913-living). Ernest married Bessie Higgins in August 1922, and they had one son, Wilbur, born in November 1925. He married Wilma Krebbs. They had one son, Jack.

Clara married Zenno Ura Brandom (1904-1962) on May 25, 1933. Zenno was the only child of Edwin Dickisen Brandom (1878-1952) and Effie Mae Smith (1881-1949). Clara and Zenno had two daughters: Carol Louise (May 22, 1939) and Doris Mae (May 12, 1944). Carol married Thomas Wayne Harris on November 15, 1957. They had three sons: Thomas Robert (May 24, 1957), Timothy Jay (April 6, 1960), and Tyler Lee (September 15, 1970).

Ferdinand and Marie Louise (Mary) (Pierman) Pfierrmann August 7, 1899

Clarence died at a young age of an infection that set in after a tonsil operation. He never married.

Floyd Isiah married Rebecka Lawrence on October 6, 1940. They had four daughters: Sharon Ann (September 18, 1941), Sandra Sue (March 15, 1944), Linda Lou (October 6, 1946), and Joyce Yvonne (August 19, 1948).

Sharon married Maurice (Jim) Bashore. Sharon had Teresa Robin (October 30, 1963) and son, Stacey Alan (March 21, 1967). Sandra married John Heitz on December 19, 1964. They had three children: Angela Marie (August 3, 1970), Andrew Josh (November 15, 1975) and Matthew Todd (December 21, 1977). Linda Lou never married. Joyce married John Crain on September 6, 1969. They had two children: Dawn Yvonne (February 18, 1973) and Joshua Isaiah (September 14, 1982).

Clara and her father Ferdinand would take extra produce from their farm by horse and wagon to relatives and to the Barr Street Market in Fort Wayne, at least a 12 to 16 hour trip.

Having grandparents and great-grandparents that came directly from Germany and passed through Ellis Island and New Orleans always fascinated the Pfierrmann/Pierman descendants. They all spent many, many nights and weekends with their Grandmother Clara. One grandson, often said, "It's like talking to a living encyclopedia of the century. She lived through so many decades of progress and change."

It was probably the most changing time of the century. Clara lived through the horse to car era, two world wars, the great depression, and so many more life-changing events.

Submitted by Doris Allen

CONSTANCE ROBERTS PHILLIPS - ROSALIND ROBERTS - EMIL INDRECC-AUGUST DIDION FAMILY

August Joseph Didion, born August 27, 1877, Portland, Indiana, was a decorator-contractor and a farmer for many years. He died November 13, 1957 of a heart attack following an earlier stroke. August married Ida May Fought November 7, 1900, born March 26, 1884, died August 27, 1969 of cancer of the liver. They had five children: Florence Elizabeth Rose, December 14, 1901 - deceased; Anna Theresa, September 26, 1903; Leo Edward, March 30, 1905 - deceased; Olivia Clara Christina, September 1, 1908 - deceased; and Irene Magdalen Ann, July 20, 1912.

Florence married Emil Andrew Indrecc May 20, 1918. Emil, born October 15, 1888, Samobor, Yugoslavia, was thirteenth of fourteen children. He immigrated to the United States from Leipsic, Germany on the vessel Mossie, working as a steam fireman; he was naturalized on February 7, 1941 in Fort Wayne, Indiana. Emil died November 5, 1959. They had six children: Barbara May Euphemia, December 14, 1918; Rosalind Anna, December 28, 1919 - deceased; Mary Elizabeth, April 21, 1921 - deceased; Bernard Emil, September 16, 1922 - deceased; Thomas Leo, December 20, 1923 - deceased; Emil Andrew Thomas, June 13, 1932.

Rosalind Indrecc married Raymond Loffi. They had one child, Richard Raymond. Rosalind later married Kenneth Grant Roberts on February 29, 1937. Kenneth was born June 26, 1916 in Redkey, Indiana, died August 9, 1999 in St. Augustine, Florida, of heart failure and finally of lung cancer following an earlier quadruple bypass. Kenneth was a semi-truck driver for Transport. Rosalind, born in Fort Wayne, Indiana, died of lung cancer on February 15, 1985 after history of Ideopathic Thrombosis Purpura. They had seven children: Richard Raymond (adopted son of Kenneth), born June 5, 1938, Fort Wayne, died July 26, 1985; Edwin DeWayne, born October 4, 1940, Pendalton, Indiana; Kenneth Ronald, born May 10, 1945, Fort Wayne; Florence Theresa, born April 17, 1948, Fort Wayne; Daniel, born September 24,1950, died at birth; Sandra Roseann, born January 13, 1953, Tucson, Arizona; Ronald Lee (twin), born February 22, 1954, Fort Wayne; Constance Susan (twin), born February 22, 1954, Fort Wayne.

The Roberts Family: Top row, L -R: Terrie, Kenny, Dick, Ed. Middle row: Connie, Sandy, Ronnie. Bottom row: Parents, Rose & Ken.

Constance earned a bachelor's degree in Sociology, worked 30 years with 21 of those years at Charter Beacon Psychiatric Hospital with behavioral children. Constance married Louis Isadore Roy, born April 29, 1951 on July 3, 1974. They had one child, Carrie Elizabeth Roy, born February 10, 1978. Constance later married Douglas Allen Dammeier in 1981. They had one child, Dustin Douglas Dammeier, born October 15, 1981. Constance later married John Gregory Phillips on December 23, 1993. John, a self employed and co-owner of Kanning and Phillips Masonry, was born May 28, 1968 in Dallas, Texas. They had one child, Logan John Phillips, born November 19, 1994. They had four grandchildren. Born of Carrie (Roy) and Travis Cox: Jaiden Alizabeth, August 25, 2000. Jacob Allen, January 23, 2002. Joseph Allen, March 12, 2004. Born of Dustin and Jenna (Davis) Dammeier: Jacee Madelyn, October 30, 2004.

Submitted by Constance Roberts Phillips

ROBIN (EDWARDS) PHILLIPS

Robin Edwards was born in Wells County on August 17, 1958. Her parents, Kenny and Melba (McBride) Edwards lived in Markle at the time. Robin, a Homestead High School, Huntington University graduate, moved to Zanesville, Allen County, in 1973. She had begun her career in the restaurant business at the age of twelve working at the Gateway Inn in Markle. Graduating from college in 1979, Robin was hired by Don Strong as manager of Richards Restaurant in Huntington. In that position for sixteen years, she then went to work for two years for McMahon Engineers during the construction of Zanesville's sewer system. In the process of planning a new restaurant in Zanesville, word came to her of the availability of

Robin Edwards Phillips and Tom Lloyd

Davis Restaurant in Markle. In March 1996, she purchased Davis Restaurant and scrapped the plans for Zanesville. Three weeks of hard work in renovation and cleaning, with the help of the entire family, she was ready to open. She remains there today.

Living in Zanesville for many years, she now lives just one and one-half miles south of town where she fills her large house and pole barn with antiques and collectibles. She loves auctions and buying, fixing up, and selling houses.

Robin married Mike Phillips in 1980. After several years of marriage they parted friends. She now has a fiancé, Tom Lloyd. Tom grew up in Wren, Ohio, and is an employee of Thunderbird in Decatur. He shares her hobbies.

Robin has no children of her own, but she loves to spoil all her nieces and nephews and all the little ones that frequent the restaurant. More about Robin can be found in the *Wells County Family History 1992*. Also refer to the Kenneth and Melba Edwards article in this publication.

Submitted by Robin Phillips

JOHN THOMAS & MARY CATHERINE (TREVEY) PIATT

John Thomas Piatt was born November 7, 1893, in Bellaire, Belmont County, Ohio, and was the son of Martin Thomas and Irene Ellen (Angus) Piatt. Because Martin's work as a puddler in steel mills forced the family to move frequently, school attendance was problematic for Tom, as he was called. He started in Washington County, Pennsylvania, in a one-room school house and then moved from school to school as his father moved from job to job. When the family settled in Fort Wayne, Tom tried following in his father's footsteps as an ironworker for Fort Wayne Rolling Mills, but a serious accident convinced him to seek a different career, and he became a barber. He served briefly with the National Guard during World War I. After that, he graduated from the National College of Chiropractic and established his office at 2121 Broadway.

John Thomas and Mary Catherine (Trevey) Piatt 1921

Mary Catherine Trevey, the daughter of Charles Taylor and Izora (Johnson) Trevey, was born November 29, 1899, in Fort Wayne. Only eight years old when her mother died, Mary was sent to live with an uncle and aunt, Elbe C. and Sarah Catherine (Fulton) Johnson, in Laketon, Indiana. Then her father arranged for little Mary Catherine and himself to live with Aaron Albert and Emma (Trevey) Moses, and Mary attended the old Franklin School. When Charles remarried in 1910, Mary was switched to Miner School through grade six and went to Hoagland School for junior high. Getting through high school was a monumental task for her. She had to earn the money for her books. For clothing, she remodeled whatever her aunts and neighbors handed down to her. During what should have been her sophomore year, she had to stay out of school to help take care of her father who had contracted tuberculosis. Nevertheless, she returned to school the following year and graduated from Central High's Commercial Course. This education enabled her to do stenographic work at General Electric Company.

Tom and Mary were married September 26, 1927, in Wheeling, West Virginia. In 1930, they purchased the Shady Court Apartments and operated it for more than thirty years. They were the parents of Mary Joan Piatt, born 1928; John Thomas Piatt, Jr. born 1931; and Charles Ralph Piatt, who lived only eight hours in 1934. John Thomas Piatt died July 14, 1959, and Mary Catherine (Trevey) Piatt died May 14, 1992.

Submitted by John T. Piatt

JOHN THOMAS, JR. & PATTY LOU (BURNAU) PIATT

John Thomas Piatt, Jr., son of John Thomas, Sr. and Mary Catherine (Trevey) Piatt, was born on December 30, 1931, in Fort Wayne, Indiana. Nurse Winters at Lutheran Hospital called this baby "Skippy" after a newly created cartoon character. The nickname has stuck, and to this day, people still say, "There's no Skip in the phone book." When he was being registered for kindergarten, a given name had to be selected. John Thomas or Charles Ray were the choices. In that Skippy had been taken to school by John Thomas, Sr., the decision was obvious.

Patty Lou Burnau, the only child of Ford Deloss and Bertha Clara Nancy (McClintock) Burnau, was born October 4, 1933, in Fort Wayne, Indiana. When she was two, the family moved to Markle, and Patty was a first grade student there. Later, the Burnaus returned to Fort Wayne. Patty attended second and third grades at Justin Study School, fourth through sixth in Hamilton School, and seventh and eighth in James Smart School.

Both Skip and Patty attended and graduated from South Side High School. Later, when Skip was in the United States Air Force and home on leave, they were married on October 27, 1951, in West Creighton Avenue Christian Church. While he was stationed with the 777th Air Force Squadron in Requa, California, they lived in Crescent City, California, and at The Trees of Mystery in Klamath, California, where Patty was employed as gift shop operations manager, and Skip was a parking lot attendant and the voice of Paul Bunyan.

By July 11, 1954, when Thomas Patrick Piatt was born, Skip was out of the Air Force, and he and Patty had returned to Fort Wayne. Their daughter, Cheryl Lynn Piatt, was born June 23, 1955, and their second son, Michael Philip Piatt, arrived July 5, 1956, all in Fort Wayne, Indiana.

Skip was a salesman for Hunker & Dixon, manufacturers agents out of Indianapolis, before he started Piatt Sales, Inc. Later, he owned Man-U-Tech, Inc., an engraving company in Fort Wayne. He sold that business and moved back to Crescent City for four and a half years. There he operated a real estate office and taught business in the College of the Redwoods, while Mike attended college at the University of California in Eureka, California. They returned to Fort Wayne, Indiana, to help Patty's dad, Ford Deloss, because of his wife, Bertha's illness, and they started Electronic Engraving. The name indicated that it was a computer-controlled engraving business, which was operated totally by Skip and Patty until their retirement.

Piatt Family

Thomas Patrick Piatt married Cheryl Lynn Demo on July 21, 1973, in Fort Wayne. They own and operate Design Tech., which is an office designing firm that does floor plans and interior designs. Their children are Jeremy Thomas Piatt, born January 30, 1980, in Crescent City, California, and Barbara Kathryn Piatt, born August 31, 1983, in Fort Wayne. Barbara married Joseph Pleal Watts on August 18, 2003, also in Fort Wayne.

Cheryl Lynn Piatt and Randall Bruce Bringham were married May 31, 1974. Their first son, Timothy Randall Brigham, born December 16, 1977, married Michelle Marie Sellers on August 8, 1998, in Lafayette, Indiana. They have two little girls: Michaela Marie Bringham, born May 4, 2003, and Megan Kate Brigham, born November 23, 2004, both in Lafayette. Cheryl had two more sons: Mathew Ryan Brigham, born January 15, 1981, in Crescent City, California, and John Robert Brigham, born April 30, 1985, in Dothan, Alabama. Cheryl and Randy divorced. Cherie, Matt, and Robbie live together in Lafayette, Indiana.

Michael Philip Piatt has his own firm, Michael P. Piatt, CPA, Inc., an accounting firm in Fort Wayne, Indiana.

Submitted by John T. Piatt

MARTIN THOMAS & IRENE ELLEN (ANGUS) PIATT

In 1921, their new home at 2121 Broadway in Fort Wayne was purchased by Martin Thomas and Irene Ellen (Angus) Piatt. What an achievement this was for these two! He had grown up along a "holler" in the hills of West Virginia, and her life began in rural Monroe County, Ohio.

Martin, the thirteenth of fourteen children of Andrew Jackson and Margaret Ann (Winters) Piatt, was born October 15, 1867, near Letart, West Virginia. Because his parents had given some land for a school, Martin was educated there. Then he went to Wheeling and became a puddler in a steel factory.

Martin Thomas and Irene Ellen (Angus) Piatt circa 1890

Irene Ellen, always called "Ida," had just passed her sixth birthday on January 24, 1879, when her mother, Jemima Jane (Farmer) Angus, died. Her father, James Angus, placed each of the children in the home of a relative. Little Ida was sent to Wheeling to live with her aunt, Sophia (Farmer) Hosey, and her husband, John. He was quite cruel to Ida. So, on May 22, 1889, at age 16, she married Martin.

After Wheeling, they lived in various locations: Bellaire and Martins Ferry, Ohio; Washington County, Pennsylvania; Muncie, Indiana; and Fort Wayne. They had to move wherever a steel mill needed a puddler, and Martin's final job was with the Fort Wayne Rolling Mills. Meanwhile, Ida attended The National College of Chiropractic and became a chiropractor. She converted the kitchen of 2121 Broadway into her office and the dining room into a waiting room. Besides giving adjustments, she also did some faith healing and sold home remedies made by the C.P. Medicine Company. In 1928, she was tried in circuit court, and the jury found her not guilty of practicing medicine without a license. She continued taking care of people until her death on January 21, 1948. Martin had died on October 18, 1941.

This couple had two children: John Thomas Piatt and Abigail Edna (Piatt) Courdevey Carpenter. Their grandchildren were Mary Joan (Piatt) Lauer, John Thomas Piatt, Jr., Irene Genive (Courdevey) Benanti, and Alden Bruce Carpenter.

Submitted by Michael Philip Piatt

PICKARD FAMILY

Thomas Reed Pickard was born in Cornwall, England, in 1829. He immigrated to the United States, arriving in Fort Wayne (from Ohio) in 1854. He married Catherine Ann Stryker (born 1829), who had moved to Fort Wayne from Somerset County, New Jersey, in 1839. Catherine was a member of the missionary society of First Presbyterian Church. Thomas Reed was the general superintendent of the Bass Foundry. The Pickards had four sons: Peter Edgar, born November 23, 1857; Thomas Dexter; Harry Reed; and Artemas Ward.

Peter Edgar Pickard moved from Mt. Vernon, Ohio, to Fort Wayne as an infant. He attended Clay School and graduated from Fort Wayne High School in 1875. In 1889, he married Floy Russel Fowler, daughter of George Storr Fowler and Louise Esther Updegraff (daughter of Joseph and Hadassah McCullough Updegraff). Peter manufactured stoves at T. R. Pickard and Sons and sold furniture, stoves, and chinaware at Pickard Brothers, which later became Pickard House Furnishings Company, located at 112 and 114 East Columbia Street. Peter served on the Board of Deacons of First Presbyterian Church. Peter and Floy had three daughters: Louise Catherine, born May 2, 1890; Margery Esther, born February 28, 1893; and Florence Fowler, born October 2, 1896.

Margery Esther Pickard graduated as class valedictorian from Fort Wayne High School in 1911. She attended Wellesley College and the University of Michigan. She married Alfred William Kettler on August 27, 1918. Through her acquaintance with Maude James, Marge be-

1886 or 1887 newspaper photo of Pickard Sons Stove Foundry

came concerned about the lack of a place for the children of the Belmont section of Fort Wayne to play. So, in 1947, Al and Marge donated six acres of land to the city for a park that is named Kettler Park in Marge's honor.

Al and Marge had two children, Alfred William, Jr., born October 4, 1919; and Edgar Frederick, born February 10, 1923. Bill, a 1941 graduate of Purdue University, served as an artillery officer in the 28th Infantry Division of the U.S. Army during World War II. He joined his father in business at Indiana Construction Company and later purchased Wayne Metal Products in Markle, Indiana. He married Janet Shrock (August 30, 1920) of Decatur, Indiana, on June 25, 1954, and they had one child, Andrew William, born March 24, 1960.

Ed, a 1948 graduate of Indiana University, served as a bombardier/radar officer in the Army Air Corps during World War II. Ed married Mary Katherine Burgman (June 12, 1923), a 1947 graduate of Indiana University of Logansport and LaPorte, Indiana, on June 19, 1948. Ed became President of Fort Wayne Storage Company. Ed and Mary Kay had three children: Margery Linnea (May 3, 1949); Carol Ann (June 1, 1950); and Gregory Alan (March 21, 1953).

Linnea married Gary Edward Brunk (November 2, 1943) on April 6, 1974, and had two children, Merrilee Karyl (December 11, 1976) and Paul Edgar (May 3, 1980). Carol, a 1972 graduate of Indiana University, became an administrator with the Fort Wayne Community School system. Carol had one daughter, Andrea Linnea (June 3, 1976). Greg had two children, Kathryn Marie (February 25, 1984) and Bradley Alan (June 16, 1986). Andrew married Susan Yung (November 9, 1960) on August 23, 1986.

Merrilee Brunk married John David Ayers (June 21, 1978) on December 22, 2001.

Submitted by Linnea Brunk

PIEPER, KULL, FORTMEYER, RUNGE FAMILY

Following the death of her husband in Lindorf, Germany, Clara Fortmeyer sailed to the United States with her daughter and seven sons in 1887. Clara's brothers, Ernst and Friedrich Pieper, and her sister Maria (Mrs. Henry) Moellering had been living in Indiana since the mid-1850s, so after landing in New York, Clara and her family continued west. Two sons went to Chicago, and the rest of her children settled in Fort Wayne.

Daughter Mary (later Mrs. Cyrus Bender) moved in with her uncle Fred Pieper on Brackenridge Street, while Clara's sons quickly acquired farmland in Allen County and took up their accustomed occupations as farmers.

The Fortmeyers joined Saint John's Evangelical Lutheran Church on Washington Street, and it was likely there that Clara's eldest son, Henry Fortmeyer, met Maria Kull. Maria was the older of two surviving daughters of Fred Kull. In 1887, she lived with her mother, Dora, and sister, Louisa (later Mrs. Arno Schoenherr) on Saint Mary's Avenue in Bloomingdale, her father having died six years earlier. Fred Kull, born in Wurttemberg Germany in 1843, came to Fort Wayne in the 1850s and worked at Henry Wagner's drugstore on the corner of Main and Calhoun. In 1861, he'd joined the 74th Indiana Volunteer Infantry at Fort Wayne. After training at Camp Allen on West Main Street the troops left to fight for the Union, marching first south through Kentucky and Tennessee, then east with Sherman to Atlanta, and finally north to Richmond.

When the war ended in 1865, Fred proceeded to New York where he met the newly-arrived Cordes family: Ernst, Maria and their three daughters, Maria (Mrs. Wilhelm) Mundt, Dorothea, and Christina (later Mrs. Christian Westphal). Fred married Dorothea in Ulster County in 1868 and took up residence with the rest of her family in Brooklyn, New York. After Ernst Cordes died, the family relocated to Fort Wayne. In the 1870 census, mother Maria, the three sisters and their families (the Mundts, the Kulls, and the Westphals) all lived within a block of one another at Saint Mary's and Third Street in Bloomingdale.

Maria Kull was born to Fred and Dora in 1875 after their first two children had both succumbed to diphtheria in February of 1874. Maria grew up with her younger sister and numerous cousins in Bloomingdale, and after marrying Henry Fortmeyer in 1892, she moved to the country. On their farm at Washington Center and Goshen Roads, Henry and Maria raised four children: Fred, Paul, Henrietta, and Helen. After a childhood on the farm, Fred and Paul both moved back to within a block of the Saint Mary's Avenue home, and became city firefighters. Henrietta and her husband also moved back to Bloomingdale.

Herman and Helen Runge, 1925

Henry and Maria's youngest, Helen, born in 1906, lived her whole life on the family farm in Washington Township. She married Herman Runge, a recent immigrant from Gamsen-Gifhorn, in 1925, and she became the mother of eight before her untimely death from illness in 1940.

Submitted by SuzAnne Runge

PILLERS FAMILY

The Pillers are another family with deep ties to Allen County, Indiana. William Pillar (1790-1865) and Mary Baxter (1790-1859) of Washington County, Pennsylvania, followed the road west to Adams County, Indiana. Most of their eight children married and had families in Adams County, but one son, James S. Pillars, married Susannah Edwards (1819-1844) on May 23, 1839, in Allen County. After Susannah's death, James married Mary Jane Lingafelter, daughter of William Lingafelter and Elizabeth Roop of Allen County, Indiana, and granddaughter of Fredrick Roop and Elizabeth Abbott of Huntingdon County, Pennsylvania. James and Mary Jane had five children: Martha Pillars (1847-1904) married Milton Sheen (1843-1905) and had seven children; Elizabeth Pillars married Abraham Beaty on August 18, 1867 in Allen County and had four children; James P. Pillars married Sarah Ann Butler and had eight children; William Pillars married Harriet Gustin and had at least two children; and Mary Jane Pillars (1858-1947) married Joseph Mathews (1852-1936) on September 11, 1877 in DeKalb County and had three children.

John E. and Henrietta Pillers

James Pillars and Susannah Edwards' only son, John Edward Pillers, was born on June 23, 1841. The marriage of John Edward Pillers to Henrietta Backus on September 24, 1868, in Allen County, united two pioneer families.

Rachel (Roop) Zimmerman, youngest daughter of Fredrick Roop and Elizabeth Abbott and widow of Andrew Zimmerman, married Walley Backus on April 16, 1846, in Van Wert County, Ohio. Rachel and Walley had two children: Frederick Backus who died in 1863 in Bremer County, Iowa, without issue and Henrietta Backus (1848-1910) who married John Edward Pillers (1841-1917). John and Henrietta had seven children born in Allen County. They were Wallace Edward Pillers (1870-1947) who married Mamie Miller, then Rose D. Archer; Lee Hamilton Pillers (1874-

1963) married Pearl M. Densel; Olga Blanche Pillers (1877-1952) married Smith Calvin Nelson; Thomas Pillers (1879-1970) married Edith Pence; Susie Etta Pillers (1884-1949) married William R. Alleger, and two children who died in infancy. The obituary for John E. Pillers in the Fort Wayne *Journal-Gazette* states that John was the first white child born in Monroe Township.

Many of the families mentioned have descendants who still live and work in Allen County today. Fredrick Roop and Elizabeth Abbott's children, grandchildren and great-grandchildren were like most families, they migrated in groups, cared for both the aged and the young who needed homes, settled the land and reared their children while earning a living on the farm, or as carpenters, shoe makers, teachers or laborers. Most were hard working, industrious men and women who wanted a better way of life for their children and were not afraid to make the sacrifices necessary to achieve their goals. Most served their country with honor when called upon to defend the liberties that some unknown immigrant ancestor treasured enough to leave the Old World to start life anew in America. The current descendants are grateful for their ancestors' contributions to settling our great country!

Submitted by Margie Roop Pearce

PIO (PAILLOZ)

The Pailloz family came to Allen County, Indiana in or about 1850. The original French spelling was shortened to Pio as early as 1860. The family was from Bournois, Doubs, France. The immigrant ancestor, Jean Baptiste Pailloz, was born May 23, 1800. His headstone, however, reads July 20, 1802. Jean's parents were Jean Pierre Pailloz and Claude Francoise Vernier. On January 7, 1832 Jean Baptiste married Marie Josephine Roussey in Bournois. Marie was born in Bournois on February 14, 1804 to Claude Joseph Roussey and Jeanne Claude Vernier.

Jean and Marie Pailloz, along with their infant son Joseph Justin Pailloz (born July 20, 1833) and other family members (one believed to be Marie's widowed mother), departed France from the port of LeHavre on April 25, 1834. Their ship was the *Pierre Corneille*. They arrived in New York City on June 16, 1834. At this time Marie was expecting Francis Xavier (Frank), who was born November 15, 1834 in New York. The family eventually included two more sons: John William born October 2, 1843 and Frank Alexander (Alec) born on January 7, 1846. John William and Alec were born in Oswego County, New York.

Jean was a farmer, and in September 1840 Jean purchased land in Palermo, Oswego County, New York. In the fall of 1849, Jean and Marie sold this land. The next land purchase was recorded in Allen County, Indiana on September 30, 1850 in Washington Township. By 1854 the family settled in the community of Besancon in Jefferson Township. Jean died September 16, 1868. Marie died on November 10, 1872. Both are buried in the old section of St. Louis Besancon Cemetery in Jefferson Township. The Pailloz family were members of the St. Louis Besancon parish. The far southwest leaded glass window was donated when the present church was built in 1871. The names on the window are Marie Pailloz, Justine Pailloz, William Pailloz, and Alexandre Pailloz.

Justin married Pierrette Melitene Isabey on March 4, 1854. They had nine children. Melitene died on August 4, 1872 and on August 4, 1876 Justin married Catherine Sordelet. Shortly thereafter, Justin and Catherine and some of Justin's children moved to Kansas. Justin died on October 22, 1894 in Kansas.

Frank married Mary Ann Schuler on May 31, 1855 in Decatur, Indiana. They had five children. Frank died on January 15, 1916, and Mary Ann died on November 20, 1888. Both are buried in St. Joseph Cemetery in Decatur, Indiana.

William married Caroline Schwegel on January 11, 1866 in Fort Wayne, Indiana. He became a harness maker. In 1875 the family moved to Dayton, Ohio where they remained about a year. About 1877, the family moved to Milwaukee, Wisconsin. William remained in Wisconsin until his death on March 12, 1913.

The youngest son, Alec, married Mary Barbier on March 12, 1867 in Paulding County, Ohio. She was the daughter of Jacob Barbier and Marie Duprey. They had ten children. They were William Justin, Joseph Julian, Lenora Jane, Mary Ellen, Frank Alexander, Charles Edward, John Wesley, Henry Alfred, Frederick Jacob, and Emma Henrietta. Alec died on August 19, 1928 and Mary died on December 22, 1910. Both are buried at the Wiltsie Cemetery northeast of Payne, Ohio.

Joseph Julian married Cordelia Johnston on March 7, 1894 in Paulding County, Ohio. Their children were William Julian, Lester Irvin, Donald Lee, Clarence, and Harold Edward.

William married Myrtle Skinner on December 1, 1909 and had three children: Cecile, Carlyle, and Robert. Carlyle (Bud) married Genevieve Jones on October 6, 1935 and had Barbara and Carolyn Sue. Bud bought his first meat market in 1940 and at one time maintained three stores in Fort Wayne, Indiana.

Barbara married Donald Gorney on August 16, 1958. Their children are Terri, Donald, and Mark. Carolyn married Travis Walker May 3, 1962. Their children are Kim, Sean, and Wendy. Carolyn married Jerome (Tony) Kratzman and had one child, Kristy.

Submitted by Barbara Gorney

PION

On June 8, 1805 in Beveuge, France, Francois Pion (born 1784) and Jeanne-Claude Dumoulin (born 1790) were married. They had twelve children: Francoise (July 23, 1805) was the first born, Josephine Julie (December 3, 1807), Francois Joseph (February18, 1809), Charles Hubert (October 15, 1810), Josephine (April 26, 1812), Barbe (October 10, 1813), Marie Francoise (June 9, 1815), Claude Francois (March 19, 1817), Jeanne Baptiste (April 29, 1819), Claude Louis (March 4, 1821), Claude Marie (March 1, 1823), and Claude Alix (November 7, 1824) followed last.

Claude Francois Pion was the only known one from the family, who came to America. Claude married Anne Marguerite Pequinot (born February 23, 1819) in 1850 in France. On March 9, 1851, Claude Francis and Anne Margurerite Pion sailed from Le Harve, France, to America, taking with them their infant daughter Marie-

Frank Florentine Pion Family- Frank Floentine Pion, Arthur Gene, Lena Mae, Brenda Lou, Mary Louise Maria. Front Row: Mary Jane, Christine Rose, Frank Byron, Fred Curtis, Phillip Foster.

Josephine Selina (born September 30, 1850) in Gouhenans. During the voyage Anne died and was buried at sea.Claude was upset as he wanted her to be buried in America.

Claude and Marie arrived December 4, 1851, in New York, and settled in Huntertown near Fort Wayne, Indiana. Claude, a farmer and a member of the St. Vincent Catholic Church, became a U.S. citizen on October 6, 1855. In 1854 he married Justine Liallet, and their children were Florentine Frank Pion (born 1852), Emille John (born1854), and Louis Joseph (born January 12, 1858).

For an unknown reason, Marie Josephine Selina changed her name to Mary Elizabeth, and, on February 14, 1866, in Fort Wayne, Indiana, married James Hiram McAfee. He was born October 7, 1841, in Ashland County, Ohio. Sometime between 1870 and 1878, James Hiram, as wagon master, led a wagon train from Ohio to Kansas. They settled for a while in Cherry Vale and then moved to Grafton, north of Sedan, Kansas.

Florentine Frank Pion married Lucretia Lue Null on Oct 28, 1890; they settled down on the family farm and had 14 children. The oldest was Delphis Henry, followed by two infants who died shortly after birth, then Ervin Wesley, Ella Georgia Cecila, Thomas E. (worked in a circus), Francis Ernest who died when he was eight months old, Rosa Jennie, Josphine, Susie, Mary, and Frankie Florentine (writer's father). A son, Peter A.was next. He died at 1 1/2 year old and was buried in a Catholic graveyard, but the body had to be moved because he was not baptised at that time; this action caused Lucretia to quit the Catholic Church. The last child was Elizebeth Pion. Florentine F. Pion, 75, one of the oldest residents of Perry Township, died suddenly at his home on the Auburn Road one Sunday morning at four o'clock. He had been in good health apparently and Saturday was about his farm as usual. He became ill during the night from a heart attack and expired after a short time.

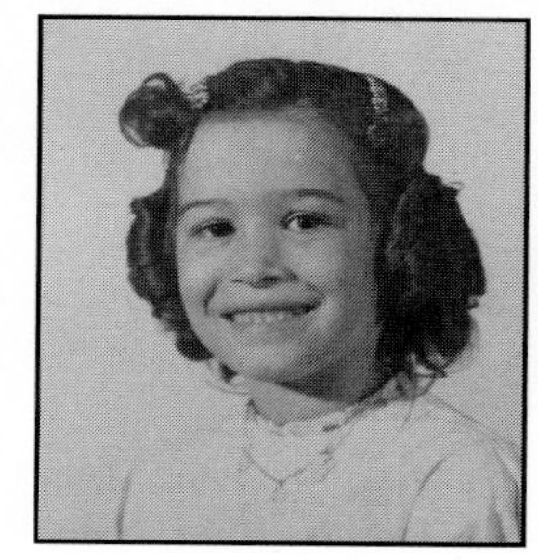

Lena Mae Pion

Florentine Frank lived his entire life in Perry Township, and died only a short distance from where he had lived for many years.

Frankie Florentine took over the family farm after his parents passed away. Frank married Mary Louise Marks (born April 1, 1921) and had nine children. Mary Louise is a decendant of Chief Little Turtle; that is another story. The oldest child was Arthur Gene (born July 27, 1941, died July 2, 1998), then Lena Mae (the author), Brenda Lou, Mary Jane, Christine Rose, Frank Byron and Fred Curtis (faternal twins), Phillip Foster, and Jacqueline Jo Pion. At the present, all are married and have children and grandchildren. Christine Rose Addis has the family farm. Jacqueline Jo owns five acres of the family farm and lives there with her family, Brenda has an acre, and Lena Mae has an acre.The old farmstead is still in the Pion family. It was know as the Cherry Tree Lane farm when Claude F. Pion planted cherry trees along the old lane.

Submitted by Lena Mae Slauf

DR. D. LEON & EMILY (PERSON) PIPPIN

Donald Leon Pippin was born January 30, 1934, in Oran, Missouri, to John Byrd and Ruth Mae (Moore) Pippin. He was the eighth of ten children, two of whom died in infancy. The family moved to Nashville, Michigan, in 1946 and there he graduated from high school. He received a B. A. in Christian Education from The King's College, New Castle, Delaware, in 1955.

Emily Lucille Person, the third of four children, was born May 6, 1934, in Wyoming, Minnesota, to Russell Vernon and Emily Rose (Zbytovsky) Person. The family moved from Wyoming to Center City, Minnesota, then to Benson, Nebraska, to Vienna, Virginia, and finally to Washington, D.C., where Emily graduated from Calvin Coolidge High School. She attended The American University one year and The King's College 1954-1958.

Leon and Emily were married September 10, 1955, in Washington, D.C. Their oldest child, Jeanne Marie, is married to Lt. Col. Daniel K. Hicks and they have four children: Daniel Kevin, Benjamin Loy, Michelle Erin (Hicks) Rodriguez, and Beth Emily. Their second child, Donald Leon II, is married to Norma Jean (Burnette) and they have three children: Joshua Caleb, Jonathan Graham, and Erin Christine. Their third child, Gregory Jon, lives in Colorado Springs, Colorado, and is an investment broker with Edward Jones Investments. Their fourth child, Brett Alan, was married to Angela Maria Giaimo and they have one son, Michael Jonathon.

Pippin Family

Leon and Emily are both teachers and have taught in the Fort Wayne area since their family moved here from Newton, Massachusetts, in the fall of 1966. Leon received an M.A. from Boston State University, a M.Ed. from Ball State University, and a Ph.D. from Bob Jones University in Greenville, South Carolina. He has taught English, speech, creative writing, journalism, literature, and drama on the high school and university level.

Emily received a B.S. in Music Education from The King's College, and a M.Ed. from St. Francis University, Fort Wayne. She has taught choir, band, art, keyboarding, Spanish, and Bible on the elementary and high school level.

As a team, Leon and Emily have mounted many plays and musicals and have directed, done stage construction, lighting plots, costuming, and choreography. Their Fort Wayne area community projects include Civic Theatre, Wabash Community Theater, Keystone Schools, Christ Child Festival, Festival of Trees, Bicentennial Celebration of the Signing of the Declaration of Independence, 60 Years of Celebration of Victory at the World War II Museum in Auburn. They also have participated in many church productions, including the Living Christmas Tree at Blackhawk Baptist Church for more than 18 years. Their being involved in projects and activities has been guided by the Scriptural admonition: "Whatever you do, do all to the glory of God."

Emily and Leon love family, music, theater, and writing. Emily has co-authored two Pippin family genealogy books and is currently writing the family history of her maternal and paternal lines. Leon has written poetry, monologues, skits, and plays. He is writing Scripture-based haiku, with accompanying devotional thoughts, and plans to publish in the near future. They have always been active in their church and freely state that, above all, their love for the Lord is their greatest joy.

Submitted by Emily L. Pippin

GLENN WILLIAM & WINIFRED (ANDERSON) POE FAMILY

Glenn William Poe was born in Hardin County, Ohio, on December 26, 1906. His parents were Marquis L. and Mary Emma Able Poe. Marquis was born on December 30, 1865, and died on June 20, 1945. Mary was born on October 28, 1873, and died on March 10, 1958.

Glenn was the youngest of three children. His sisters were Helen Elizabeth Poe Cayton, born May 26, 1902, and Margaret Poe McCarley (Walter), born November 25, 1903. Helen died January 29, 1968 and Margaret died November 20, 2004.

Glenn grew up on a farm near Roundhead, Ohio. He attended Ohio Northern for two years, and then transferred to Ohio State University. He received his BS in agriculture from Ohio State University. He taught agriculture in several high schools in Ohio.

Glenn and Winifred Poe

In the 1930s, he directed a Civilian Conservation Corps camp. He was then employed by the U.S. Department of Agriculture as a soil Conservationist. He was active at Forest Park Methodist Church and was a founding director of ACRES, Inc.

Glenn Poe and Winifred Anderson were married on July 2, 1936. Winifred was born March 16, 1904, in Lima, Ohio, to Frank and Bertha Gano Boyer Anderson. Frank was born on November 28, 1872, and Bertha was born April 2, 1875. Winifred's sister, Martha Lucile Anderson, was born September 20, 1901 and died June 11, 1919. Her brother, Kenneth, was born October 3, 1907.

Winifred grew up on a farm near Lima, Ohio. She graduated from Heidelberg College with a BA degree. She then attended Columbia University in the summers and earned a master in education. She taught high school English, Latin, and French in several Ohio schools.

Glenn and Winifred had three children: Mary Carolyn, born August 31, 1938; Virginia Ann, born October 6, 1939; and Alan Anderson, born July 24, 1941. The family moved to Fort Wayne in 1945 when Glenn was transferred to become the soil conservationist for Allen County. They lived in the Lakeside area until 1960. Glenn retired in that year and they moved to Crawford Road.

Winifred taught English and Latin at North Side High School, Kekionga Middle School, and Snider High School. She retired in 1966. She, too, was active in Forest Park Methodist Church and the Cedar Creek Women's Club.

Mary Carolyn Poe and her husband, Richard C. Menge, had three children; David C. Menge (Pat Sprunger), Peter R. Menge (Cynthia McGrae), and Karen E. Menge (Glenn Logan Jordan).

Virginia Ann Poe (Ray Couch) had four children: Terri Stokes Troia (Pat); Krista Stokes Caglar (Tunc); Matthew Stokes (Theresa Fuller); and Amy Stokes Henderson (Jeremy).

Alan Anderson Poe had three children: Andrew Alan Poe, Margaret Poe Amos (Neil), and Sarah Poe Hollingsworth (John).

Glenn W. Poe died on January 6, 1975; his wife, Winifred, died on September 15, 1997. They are both buried in Lindenwood Cemetery.

Submitted by Alan A. Poe

JACOB POINSATTE FAMILY

Jacob Poinsatte (born in 1852, died on December 8, 1926) at age 18 left his home in Alsace in the 1880s bound for adventure in the new world. Jacob was a barrel maker by trade and had a job waiting for him at a brewery in Defiance, Ohio. While Jacob was on the ship coming to the United States from Europe, he met a girl named Magdalena Dirig (1868-1959). Miss Dirig, who was also emigrating from Alsace, was on her way to a place called Fort Wayne. Young Jacob, desiring to be close to Miss Dirig, was able to make his way to Fort Wayne after a short stint in Defiance. He secured a position at the Berghoff Brewery. Jacob and Magdalena were married on September 15, 1888, at St. Mary's Catholic Church. Some time later Jacob opened a saloon on Maumee Ave at Division Street. (It was not the wild western saloon variety but rather what today would be know as a neighbor bar or local tavern.)

The Poinsatte family lived in the Fort Wayne east end which was a German speaking section of the city. Despite Jacob's French name, Jacob and Magdalena did not speak French. Most Alsatians in those days where culturally German and spoke that language. The family consisted of one daughter, Eugenia "Jane" (1888-1969), and sons Henry, Eugene (died circa 1924), Leo, Albert (1897-1973), William and Aloysius "A. Lyle".

Jacob Poinsatte, 1925, owner of one of the first automobiles in Fort Wayne

As time went on, Jacob became fascinated with the new invention of the automobile and purchased one of the first automobiles in Fort Wayne. The family's continued interest in the automobile lead three of the Poinsatte boys, Henry (wife: Georgie), William (wife: Hilda Schafer) and Albert (wife: Marie Hoffman), to open an automobile dealership, Poinsatte Auto Sales, in 1916. The other sons were ambitious as well. Eugene, although he died at an early age, was doing a thriving business as a tinsmith. Leo (wife: Irene) followed loosely in his father's foot steps by opening a beer and liquor distributorship, Columbia Liquors. Lyle (wife: Fay) was in the fur business as the owner of Poinsette Furs (note the use of the French spelling; perhaps considered a more elegant name for a fancy fur shop). The only daughter, Jane married a man named Harry Josef from Ludington, Michigan. They resided in Michigan for a number of years, but later were drawn to Fort Wayne.

Jacob died on December 8, 1926 and Magdalena passed away in 1959. One of their grandsons, James Poinsatte (son of Albert) with his wife Maxine Lapp-Poinsatte, continues, at the time of this writing, to reside in Fort Wayne. Grandson Steve Poinsatte was a resident of Fort Wayne until he passed away circa 2003. Other grandchildren live in Florida (Bill Poinsatte, Audrey Poinsatte-O'Connor), Indianapolis (Donald Poinsette), and South Bend (Charles Poinsatte).

Submitted by James Poinsatte

FRIEDRICH & ANNA BARBARA (ZEHENDNER) POPP FAMILY

Ever wonder about the origin of the slightly unusual name borne by the two-mile-long Popp Road in the northeast of Allen County?

It was in the year 1845 that eighteen-year-old Friedrich Popp — reputedly dismayed at the prospect of the universal military training facing all Kingdom of Bavaria male youth of his time — departed his small farming village of Markers-reuth and crossed the Atlantic to start a new life near future in-laws already settled in rural Allen County.

After a decade, he brought his then twenty-year-old home-village fiancée, Anna Barbara Zehendner, to join him in the New World. Her brothers, Jakob and Georg, opted for a further long journey onward to realize their eventual fortunes as merchants during the California Gold Rush. The new husband and wife began together a half-century life of farming and of founding the line of Popps which has descended from the land along the road that now bears their name.

To a certain extent, the history of the Popp family in Allen County during the nineteenth and twentieth centuries is concerned with its land as well as its people. Friedrich and Barbara's first eight children, including three who died in infancy, were born in a log cabin on the newly-purchased first eighty acres of the couple's farmstead. A four-bedroom house was later built, and the three youngest children were born there. In subsequent years, the oldest child, William, left the farm and went to California for life as a carpenter and cabinetmaker near his Zehendner uncles and cousins. Two sons, Henry and Jacob, stayed on the family farm; the two daughters, Mary and Christina, remained unmarried and lived together most of their lives in Fort Wayne. Son, George, left the farm and went into business in Lewiston, Idaho. Sons Harmon and Emanuel started a business college and co-founded Protective Electrical Supply Company, respectively, in Fort Wayne.

Shortly after the youngest son moved into Fort Wayne, mother Barbara died in 1899. Friedrich, the father, returned to his homeland (by now named Germany) in 1900, hoping, as the story goes, to hear the larks sing once more. Also, it is said, he was disappointed that the German language was no longer spoken on the Allen County farm. He extended his European visit in order to help his younger brother and host to build a new barn on their boyhood farmstead; but, unfortunately, he died there in 1901 before he was able to return to the United States. Following their father's death and burial abroad, sons Jacob and Henry carried onward at the family farm along and near the Popp Road and, for a number of years, emphasized use of the land as a dairy enterprise.

In 1936, the forty acres which had been left to Henry by his father were purchased by Friedrich's youngest son, Emanuel Popp. At the 1961 death of Jacob, the two-generation, 106-year history of the main property as a working farm came to its end. Thirty-three acres passed to Jacob's younger son, Arthur, and the original eighty acres were sold to a residential developer by the recent widow, Leila, with the stipulation that she be allowed to live out her days there. This she did in the house where, especially at threshing time, she had welcomed all her relatives, where she had nursed abandoned lambs in the kitchen, and where she had kept the old spinning wheel and a hoop skirt in the attic.

Emmanuel M. Popp

The forty acres purchased by E. M. Popp were utilized as a family retreat for over a half-century. In a large clearing, a cottage, garage, and pavilion for picnics and square-dancing were built just before and after World War II and were enjoyed by four generations of Popp descendants. An extensive garden and many beehives were lovingly tended; birthday parties and even a wedding were celebrated on this "patch" of land. But in the several decades following the deaths of E. M., and, later, of his widow Katherine — and, also, as a result of the departures from the region of many of subsequent generations — the forty acres fell into disuse, neglect, and vandalism. The rescue of this sole remaining parcel of the Popp farm came in the 1980s and 90s as third and fourth generation members of the family installed a caretaker/tenant, restored the clearing and its features to their earlier well-kept state, and established a shallow-water wildlife area and other nature-study efforts on the land.

With most members of the once-extensive family having died or moved away from the Allen County scene and with suburban development continuing to press from all sides, matriarch Jeannette Popp Kent accumulated others' interests in the surviving forty acres, donated the entire property to Acres Land Trust in 1994, and thus established the memorial to her father, which is now known as the Emanuel M. Popp Nature Preserve.

Submitted by Michael Popp

DAVID H. PORTER, II, M.D.

In 1977, David H. Porter, II, M.D. moved to Fort Wayne with his family to establish a pediatric practice. His was not just any pediatric practice, his was an inner-city practice where he treated many of the county's underserved and endangered children. He resided in Allen County until 1990 when he moved to Indianapolis.

Dr. Porter was a champion in the fight against child abuse, taking on cases that many doctors preferred to avoid. When a suspected abuse case did not have a doctor, he was contacted by social welfare workers and he never refused a case. He

David H. Porter, II, M.D.

spent many long hours testifying in court in abuse cases. In serving this way, he was a child advocate both for the community and for families. He said that families were relieved and not alienated, that there was finally someone to help them.

Dr. Porter was an original member of the Allen County child protection team and was an advocate for the Court Appointed Special Advocate program. In addition, he taught doctors, social workers, and nurses about child abuse prevention, detection, and treatment.

His role model for medicine was his grandfather, who was a rural physician in Decatur County, Indiana where Dr. Porter was raised. He became the country doctor in an urban neighborhood where he charged his patients on a sliding scale. If they couldn't pay, he managed anyway. In 1989, Dr. Porter was named the first Citizen of the Year by The *Journal Gazette*.

Submitted by Marjorie Porter

HIRAM PORTER

Hiram Porter came to Fort Wayne, Allen County, Indiana, in 1833 with his parents, John and Sarah (Null) Porter. They located on a farm on St. Joe Road, where the brick house is still in use.

Hiram taught school for sixteen terms, from 1847-1861. The log schoolhouse contained long benches around the sides and a big fireplace. Hiram got up before daylight to get to school and have the fire started on wintry days. Schools operated seven hours a day during November, December, January and February leaving ample time for him to farm. Thirty to forty pupils attended school, but they were never graded. The first books were the New Testament and a speller. His salary was $20.00 a month. This was considered good wages at the time, when potatoes were 15 cents a bushel, eggs were five cents a dozen, and coffee was ten cents a pound.

Hiram watched the growth of Fort Wayne from the days when it clustered about John's Grist Mill, where the water works plant now stands. In 1856, he saw the first brick house built in the city on Columbia Street near Calhoun Street. It belonged to the Alter family. Hiram knew the history of the canal, as his father, John helped build it. Hiram worked on the construction of the Wabash Railroad between Fort Wayne and Huntington. He toiled with a shovel and spade and worked five to six miles every day until he missed a step when alighting from a wagon and strained his leg. With the use of a cane, he was still able to walk one to two miles. Hiram had a glass eye in the right socket but his left eye

Hiram Porter Family, 1890. Standing: Charles, Malissa Jane, J. Sylvester, Hiram L., Oliver. Sitting: Mary Viola, Hiram (father), Hester (mother), Henry and Bethena

was unimpaired. This defect kept him from the Army in 1861.

He watched the growth of Allen County when trees covered all the land. He saw St. Joe Road blazed by markings on the sides of trees by his house. Before the Civil War, the woods about Fort Wayne were filled with herds of twenty or thirty deer that would scamper away through the thick forest as he trod to school in the late 1850s. Indians were constantly hanging about the place wanting to swap valuables. Hiram knew John Chapman, "Johnny Appleseed", who stayed at his home several times. He helped Johnny plant trees on Coldwater Road, near Appleseed Nursery. When Johnny died, Hiram and others purchased a coffin for him and attended the burial, although no minister was present at his grave.

Hiram was born in Scioto County, Ohio, November 11, 1828, and died, January 3, 1921, age 93. He is buried in Parker Cemetery. Hiram and Hester (Arnold), married February 26, 1857. Their children were: John Elijah, Melissa Jane, Henry Allen, Sarah Elizabeth, William Louis, James Sylvester, Bethena, Oliver F., Hiram L., Charles Walter and Mary Viola.

Submitted by Dessie M. Carboni

OLIVER POTTER FAMILY

Oliver Potter (1797-185_), the son of Pardon Potter and Rhoda Carver, purchased 440 acres of land in Eel River Township in 1836. Oliver was a descendant of both Robert Potter (d. 1655) of Warwick, Rhode Island, and Roger Williams (1604-1683), the founder of Rhode Island, who resided in Providence. On his mother's side, he was descended from eight Mayflower passengers. Oliver Potter married Clarissa Barnes (1800-187_). Their children were: James, Vernum, Galutia (1823-1873), Stephen, Columbus, Charles, Louisa Helen, and Caroline. Prior to settling in Eel River Township, Oliver and Clarissa Potter had lived in Butler Township, Wayne County, New York.

Oliver and Clarissa Potter built a very fine two-story, six-bay, frame Greek Revival style house on their Indiana farm. This house was later known as 7473 North County Line Road, Eel River Township, Allen County, Indiana.

In 1839, Samuel W. Coon (1780-1865), a widower and descendant of John Mac Coon (1630-1705) of Westerly, Rhode Island, left Orangeville Township, Wyoming County, New York, and followed his son, Amos Freeman Coon, to Indiana. The children of Samuel coon and Phebe Freeman (1788-1825), a Mayflower descendant, were: Francis, Anna, William, Amos Freeman, Preserved Brownell, Elisha, Phebe (1821-1888) and two babies who died in infancy. The 200 acres of land, which Amos had purchased in Eel River Township in 1836, abutted land owned by Oliver Potter.

On March 9, 1851, Galutia Potter married his sixth cousin and fellow Mayflower descendant, Phebe Coon. They settled on a farm west of Oliver Potter's residence on North County Line Road. Galutia and Phebe's children were: Anna E. (1851-1861); Charles Jesse (1854-1900); Newton Galutia (1860-1899); and Peter (1864-1866). Although raised as an Orthodox Quaker, Phebe Potter became a committed member of the Church of God. All of the members of this family are buried in Eel River Cemetery, as is Samuel W. Coon, who was listed as a member of Galutia Potter's household on the 1860 U.S. Census.

Oliver and Clarissa Barnes Potter's home at 7473 N. County Line Road, Eel River Township, Allen County, Indiana

Phebe Potter was a prolific letter writer. All of her letters, written after 1871, bear the return address of the Village of Potter's Station. In 1871, Galutia Potter deeded a right-of-way to the Detroit Ell River and Illinois Railroad Company. Family legend states that Galutia insisted that a railroad station be located on Potter land and be named "Potter's Station." Galutia Potter's estate inventory, dated April 4, 1874, states that he had sold, but not yet conveyed, four building lots in the Village of Potter's Station before his death. Galutia Potter still retained title to seven other lots in the village. In 1876, Potter's Station was listed as having a United States Post Office. Both the 1874 and 1893 plat maps of Noble County show the Village of Potter's Station straddling the Allen/Noble County boundary line. The village is now called Ari. Family oral tradition also says that Galutia's sons, Newton and Charles, operated a sawmill near the now abandoned railroad right-of-way. Charles Potter's son, Arthur, also kept a grocery store in Ari. The Potter sawmill, store and Oliver Potter's grand Greek Revival style house have since been razed.

Newton Galutia Potter married Maria Louise Young (Rillie) (1862-1911), daughter of Johann Jung, ("John Young") a Civil War veteran, and

Mary Elizabeth Grimm of Swan Township, Noble County, Indiana. Both John Young and his wife were of Pennsylvania Dutch descent. The children of Newton Galutia and Maria Potter were: Verna Potter Peckham, Newton Elroy Potter, and Fred Leslie Potter (1894-1985).

After Maria Potter's death, her children sold their farm in Ari and moved to Reno, Nevada, where all three married into pioneer Nevada families. After working on a government survey team, Fred managed a dry-goods store in Elko, Nevada, and later in Visalia, California. He married Florence Mildred Sutherland (1895-1993), the daughter of John Henry Sutherland and Mary Florence Luke. Fred and Mildred had one son, William Leslie Potter (1918-1997). William was an electrical engineer employed by the General Electric Company. On September 6, 1942, he married Olive Dundas, daughter of William John Dundas and Anna Helena Pilling of Rensselear County, New York. William Leslie Potter settled in Glen Mills, Pennsylvania. Like Oliver and Galutia, William designed and built his own residence and lived in it until his death. Like his father and eldest daughter, Leslie Barbara Potter, William returned to visit the Potter farmsteads and his cousins in Eel River and Swan Townships from time to time.

Submitted by Leslie Barbara Potter

REX MILES POTTERF

Rex Miles Potterf was born March 20, 1894 in Lewisville, Henry County, Indiana to Avanel Martin and Phoebe (Miles) Potterf. Early in life Rex was enamored with learning in general and education in particular. When he was eighteen years of age he began his teaching career in New Lisbon and was a principal and superintendent of schools in north central Indiana before coming to Fort Wayne in 1924. Rex taught history, economics and government at Central High School before becoming head librarian of the Allen County Public Library on January 2, 1935, a position he held for twenty-four years until his retirement in January of 1960. At his retirement and in recognization of his service to the Fort Wayne community he was named librarian emeritus.

Rex received an A.B. degree from Indiana University, an A.M. degree in political science from Indiana University, an A.M. degree in educational administration from Columbia University, and a B.S. degree in library science from the University of Illinois. In addition, Rex had done graduate work at the University of Wisconsin.

Rex was active in community affairs being a member of the Quest Club, past president of the Allen County Fort Wayne Historical Society, active member of the First Presbyterian Church and member of Kiwanis. Mr. Potterf authored numerous pamphlets on facets of American history, especially Indiana history.

Through the efforts of Mr. Potterf, the reputation of the Allen County Public Library began and continues to be recognized as one of our nation's top public libraries.

Mr. Potterf was married to the former Gladys Adelaide Barr. To that union one daugher, Helen C. Potterf, was born. Gladys died December 18, 1968 and Rex died April 4, 1978.

Submitted by James H. Batdorff

BEATRICE POWELL-GAULDEN

Beatrice Powell-Gaulden was born to Charlie and Rena Jones Powell in Choudrant, Louisiana, Ouachita Parish. Beatrice was the youngest born to this union: born July 29, 1907, died December 10,1981. Her siblings were: Girty, born November 22,1891, died January of 1897; Mallie L., born January 24,1894, died October of 1947; Willie L. Powell-Garner-Jackson, born July 14,1895, died March 30,1989; Flordia Powell-Younger, born March 3,1897, died in August of 1980; Linnie Powell-Jackson, born March 3, 1900, died in1941; John H. born March 27,1902, died in February of 1971. All are buried in Fort Wayne, Indiana, except Girty and Linnie. Her brothers, Mallie and John, came here in 1923 to work for the International Harvester. Her sisters were here also.

Beatrice Powell married Andrew Gaulden Jr. in Grambling, Louisiana, on May 30,1925. To this union five children were born, all in Grambling, Lincoln Parish.

Harold L. Gaulden was born on February 20, 1927. He married Maude Eva Smith, and their sons are Gregory, Gaylord and Gilbert Gaulden. During the war he was a member of the Tuskegee' Airmen. He spoke to area children about his experience while serving in the Air Force in Alabama.

Back L to R: Howard and Harold
Front L to R: Charles and Alma Josephine

Andrew Gaulden, III, was born in 1928 and died December 2, 1934.

Howard Gaulden was born December 15, 1930. He married twice, to Cecelia Jones and to Judy Ellenwood. His sons are Anthony Belcher and Eric Roman. Howard was a truck driver and a Jazz Musician. He played guitar in Fort Wayne and surrounding areas with Bob Green and other musicians. He also went to Washington, D.C., by invitation of Mayor Paul Helmke, to play for a political event.

Alma Josephine Gaulden was born November 6, 1932. Alma Josephine came to Fort Wayne in 1943. She married three times; her husbands were Raymond Mudd, William Storey Jr. and Franklin Chandler. Her children are Alma Gwendolyn Mudd-Earley, Vivian Marie Storey-Chandler-Daniels (adopted by Chandler), and Teresa Chandler-Lane-Green. Alma Josephine Chandler worked and retired from Magnavox Manufacturing.

Charles P. Gaulden was born August 16, 1934. He married Corine Keys, who was the mother of his children: Stephanie Gaulden-Simpson, Anthony Gaulden, and Beverly Gaulden- Brown. He then married twice more, first to Vivian Carr, then to Dorothea (last name not known). Charles worked for International Harvester and Joslyn Steel Mill.

Beatrice and son, Howard, came to Fort Wayne in 1946, Charles came in 1947, and Harold in 1948. Howard, Alma Josephine, and Charles attended school in Fort Wayne, Indiana.

Submitted by Alma Josephine Chandler

MALLIE LORAIN & MARY O. (CLAYTON) POWELL, SR. FAMILY

Mallie Lorain Powell and Mary O. Clayton were married in Fort Wayne in 1932. Mallie was born in Louisiana in 1894 to Charlie and Rena (Jones) Powell. Following his army service in World War I and honorable discharge in 1919, Mallie attended Tuskegee Institute and later returned to Louisiana to help his father get fair prices for crops at market. When Mallie insisted on accurate weighing, Charlie Powell was told that "daylight had better not" catch his uppity son in the county. Mallie immediately fled, ending up in West Virginia, and eventually moving to Ohio. He found employment at International Harvester and transferred to the plant in Fort Wayne in the mid-1920s.

The Powell Family, Back Row: Mallie, Sr. Mary Front Row Lois, Amy and Mallie, Jr. at Trier's Park ca. 1938

Ossa B. Clayton was born in 1912 in Mississippi, the third child of Dan and Mollie (Pittman) Clayton. They later had twin sons and also another child, who died at childbirth along with Mollie in 1915. Appealing to his mother for help, Dan moved his family to Brazil, Indiana. Teachers frequently mispronounced/misspelled his daughter's name. When she was ten, she asked to use her grandmother's name. Approval was given at once and from then on Ossa B. was known as Mary O. Clayton.

Graduating from Brazil High School in 1931, Mary worked for a physician in Terre Haute. In August, Dr. Lewis moved his practice to Fort

Wayne, taking along his young assistant. Mary became acquainted with an older patient, Mrs. Sally Dotson, and a friendship developed that lasted until both of the Dotsons died in the 1950s. Mr. John Dotson had a friend named Mallie Powell, who, when he met Mary, began courting her. Within a few months, Mary and Mallie were married in the home of the Dotsons and moved into the room that Mallie rented nearby on Division Street.

When their first child, Mallie, Jr., was born on June 20, 1933, they moved into a neighboring rental house. After their second child, Lois, was born on August 10, 1934, the family bought the house at 919 Eliza Street, where they lived until 1968. Their third child, Amy, was born on November 4, 1936, the day after Mary's 24th birthday.

Mary became a charter member of the Lillian Jones Brown Culture Club, was involved in the PTA at Harmar School, and was active in local politics. Mallie was very involved with his large extended family and the F&AM Lodge, where he rose to the 32nd degree.

During World War II, life for the Powells changed in many ways. Mary canned fruits and vegetables, as most commodities were rationed, Mallie had a Victory Garden, and the children churned raw milk, which Mallie had purchased from co-workers.

In 1946, Mallie became ill and was eventually admitted to the Veteran's Hospital in Indianapolis. On October 3, 1947, Mallie Powell died from complications of having ingested unsafe air at work.

Mallie had preferred that his wife not work and Mary had complied. The Social Security benefits for her children, ages 14, 13, and 10 were inadequate to support them. Therefore, she took jobs doing the only work readily available for black females—the domestic trade. In 1951, Mary obtained a position as a nursing assistant at the newly built VA Hospital, where she worked until retiring in 1976.

Mallie and Mary highly valued education, and their many sacrifices were rewarded by their children's achievements. Lois and Amy graduated from South Side High School and Mallie from Central High School. Lois graduated with honors from Indiana University and later earned a PhD from the University of Minnesota. Amy graduated with honors from Purdue University and earned a masters degree from Ball State University *magna cum laude*. Mallie, Jr. became the first non-degree employee to complete the management training program at International Harvester. He died in 1999 in Fort Wayne. A retired clinical psychologist and university professor, Lois lives in Maryland. Retiring as a university administrator in 1998, Amy returned to live in Fort Wayne, where Mary continues to live.

Submitted by Amy E. Powell

EDWIN L. & CYNTHIA FINCH POWERS

Ed and Cynthia, with their children Daniel and Marian, moved to Allen County in 1971 after Ed's discharge from the United States Air Force. Cynthia, a registered medical technologist, was hired by Dr. Walter Griest to work at Lutheran Hospital Laboratory. Ed started as a draftsman

Ed & Cynthia Powers on Ed's 65th Birthday.

at Corning Glass Works in Bluffton and later became a computer programmer.

Ed had long dreamed of building his own house, and soon began the project on a wooded lot on Yoder Road, near Zanesville. The cedar-sided house is built like a pole barn, with clerestory windows furnishing some passive solar heat. The mature oak trees, shrubs, and wildflowers were left in order to attract wildlife, especially birds. The family moved in as President Nixon was resigning, in 1974, and the children were enrolled in Southwest Allen Schools.

Ed was born October 18, 1937, in Portland, Indiana, the son of Harold Joseph Powers and Dorothy Kessler Powers. He was in the last class (1955) to graduate from Jefferson High School in Randolph County. Then he graduated from Purdue University in Engineering Sciences and was commissioned in the U. S. Air Force. He served in Texas, Washington, D. C., Japan, Thailand, and New York.

Cynthia was born March 10, 1939 in Waterville, Maine, of Hoosier parents. Her father was Sharon Lea Finch, and mother Mary Malinda Rennoe Finch. For many years they operated a country general store at Collett, in Jay County, and taught school in Jay and Randolph Counties. Mr. Finch was a volunteer weather observer for 20 years. Both were Phi Beta Kappa graduates of DePauw University, class of 1927. Cynthia graduated Phi Beta Kappa from Oberlin College in 1958, majoring in zoology. She then had a year of training in medical laboratory technology at Cleveland Metropolitan General Hospital.

Ed and Cynthia met when both were 4-H members in Pike Twp., Jay County. They were married September 20, 1959 at First Presbyterian Church, Portland, Indiana.

Their son Daniel Edwin Powers was born July 14, 1960 at Lafayette, Indiana. He graduated from Homestead High School and from the Oberlin Conservatory of Music, and is now a composer and violist with the Terre Haute and Columbus Symphony Orchestras. He is married to Martha Krasnican, a pianist at Indiana State University.

Their daughter Marian Lea Powers, born February 5, 1963 at Fort Belvoir, Virginia, graduated from Homestead High School and from Northland College in Ashland, Wisconsin, majoring in Outdoor Education. She has worked several years at the Fort Wayne Children's Zoo, including a stint as tiger keeper, and now does special projects. She and David Messmann are parents of twins, Forest and Marina Powers-Messmann, born May 13, 1997, to the delight of their grandparents.

Cynthia retired in 2002 after 31 years at Lutheran Hospital, and Ed in 1997 from Harden Industries (formerly VH Electronics.) They are active members of the Unitarian Universalist Congregation, the Stockbridge Audubon Society, the Canal Society of Indiana and the Fox Island Alliance.

Submitted by Cynthia Powers

LOUIS W. PRANGE 1893-1970

Louis W. Prange was one of Fort Wayne's loveable citizens who was known by many.

He graduated from the eighth grade and then went to work at Zimmerman's Drug Store on the corner of Lewis and Lafayette Streets. He joined the Army in WWI and his name is inscribed on the war memorial monument in Indianapolis. Though he did not attend high school, he went to Tri State College in Angola and graduated from the school of pharmacy. He then bought the Hutzell Drug Store on the corner of Main and Mechanic Streets, Fort Wayne.

Louie Prange

When the store opened most things were sold in bulk and had to be weighed and bagged. These included herbs, spices, perfumes in vials, and potato chips. The store had a marble soda fountain, ceramic tile floor, and tin patterned ceiling. There were antique tables and wire chairs which people used when they ate their ice cream. Louis had quarantine signs that were put on the front of houses to warn about diseases, such as diphtheria, epidemic influenza, measles, chicken pox, whooping cough, and spinal meningitis. He had prescriptions from the 1800s that were from different stores, most having just a two number address and phone number. Some had printed labels on them that said, "German spoken at this store."

Remodeling was done just before WWII, with a new soda fountain and booths in place of the chairs and tables. Pieces of the marble fountain were saved and made into end tables and a coffee table that his daughter is still using. During WWII he put a large bulletin board in the window that had the names of the neighborhood fellows that had joined the service. Letters, pictures, medals, money, captured flags and other items from them were displayed.

The 1943 flood rose to the top step from the basement, with several feet of water in the street. The Memorial Day Parade always came out Main Street on the way to Lindenwood Cemetery, passing the drugstore. Store hours in the beginning were from 8 a.m. until 10 p.m., seven days a week. Ice cream specials were painted on the front window in white, and some ice cream was hand packed. The store had a postal sub station and collected railroad workers union dues. There was a robbery one night just before closing, but no one was hurt and not much was taken, as the robber was scared off.

As the neighborhood druggist, Louis Prange was more than a pharmacist and store owner; he removed objects from people's eyes and splinters from fingers, was a psychologist, recommended lotions, and helped with baby problems.

As a member of the National Association of Retail Druggists he went to many national conventions all over the country. They helped him to keep current with products and methods.

After he retired and sold the store, he helped other area pharmacists when they wanted to take some days off or for a vacation. He did this for 20 years. He was jovial, soft spoken and everyone's friend.

A picture of the store in the 1930s was in the paper, and the first newspaper article was printed in 1947. A second article appeared in the 1990s. After that last newspaper article his daughter heard from long ago customers, some senior citizens and one man who knew the store when he was seven in the middle of WWII. She also received photos of some of the neighborhood kids with the druggist that bought the store from "Louie Prange."

Submitted by Patricia Prange Cunningham Schwartz

DONALD EUGENE PRANGER

Donald Eugene Pranger was born in 1927, in Fort Wayne, Indiana, the first son, and second of 17 children of Joseph and Irene (Kintz) Pranger. His father, Joseph, was a bookkeeper, but he lost their home during the Great Depression. The family lived in rented homes before living with Don's Grandfather and Grandmother Pranger. His Grandfather and Grandmother Kintz lived above their grocery store next to St Andrews Church until it was lost in the Depression. The families were close and devoutly Catholic. Money was tight, but their lives were rich. His mother, Irene, played the violin. There was always a piano in the house. His father, Joseph, took Don and other boys from Saint Andrews on Boy Scout camping trips outside the city. Don joined his grandfather Pranger, who worked for the railroad, on trips to Cleveland and Chicago. As the depression ended, Joseph worked for the WPA, and bought a home near the railroad. Don cleaned classrooms to pay his high school tuition, worked at a grocery after school to help support the family, and swept floors at a tavern to buy his first bicycle. He went to Central Catholic High for the day, and at 3 p.m., went across the alley to the vocational program at the Central High School, the public school, where he learned carpentry and patternmaking. At 16, he left school to work in a foundry, and then a bakery before becoming a patternmaker apprentice for Allen Patternworks. They made patterns for military parts, and did work for Zollner Pistons, General Electric and International Harvester. Don was drafted into the army at age 18, but WWII ended before Don was shipped overseas. There he was a carpenter and X-ray technician in a hospital in Germany, and bought his first camera. He returned to the Allen Patternworks where he was continued to help support his family, and bought his first car. Don met Joann Siebenaler at a Catholic Youth Organization picnic, and married her in 1952. He was an active in the Legion of Mary and Knights of Columbus. In 1967, he moved his growing family to Illinois, and worked as a patternmaker in the plastics industry. He and Joann had 14 children: Susan, Pamela, Gregory, Ron, Sharon, John, Joseph, Laurie, Christine, Matthew, Tim, Mary, Sally and Debra. Don continued his hobbies of carpentry and photography. In 1981, the family moved to Michigan, where Don worked in the Detroit automotive industry. Today, Don and Joann enjoy their retirement and their 14 grandchildren. Don builds ship models and is scanning a lifetime of photographs to share with his extended family.

Submitted by Susan Pranger

HERMAN PRANGER

Herman Pranger was born on February 11, 1838 in Saxon, Germany. He came directly to Fort Wayne, Indiana at the age of 21. He lived with his sister, Mrs. Kohrman, on East Washington Street. He met and married Elizabeth Jostworth at St. Mary's Catholic Church on the southeast corner of Lafayette and Jefferson Streets, on June 23, 1863. She was born February 26, 1844 in Fort Wayne. She attended St. Mary's School, Fort Wayne.

After they were married they bought and settled on a farm in Allen County, Adams Township, Northeast corner of Green and Paulding Road, which was a couple miles south of New Haven. They lived in two cabins, lived in one and slept in the other. He and Elizabeth lived on the farm until 1910, then they moved to 1015 University Street, Fort Wayne. They belonged to St. Johns Catholic Church while living near New Haven and the children attended St. Johns Catholic School. They celebrated their 50th Wedding Anniversary on June 23, 1913 at St. Mary's Catholic Church in Fort Wayne at 9:00 a.m. to the hour.

They died in January 1918 one week apart. They were both sick at the same time. They would bundle Marcella up and put her in a box on the sled and pull her over to see them. Grandma was sick in one room and Grandpa the other. Grandma asked to see Grandpa, they brought him in and Grandma said, "I am going to go now, but I'll come back and get you." Grandpa said "And I will come too." They died in Jan 1918 one week apart. They are buried in the Catholic Cemetery in Fort Wayne, Indiana.

Written by Marcella Pranger Weller, their granddaughter, in January 1981
Submitted by Patricia Jensen

JOSEPH W. PRANGER

Joseph W. Pranger, the son of John and Rosa Coonrad Pranger, was born May 11 in Dallas, Texas. His birth records show that he was born May 10, 1904 in Ennis, Texas so he must have two births recorded somewhere. He lived with his family there until he was fourteen years old. He then moved to Allen Country, where he lived with his family. He attended St. Peter's Catholic School, where he graduated with a degree in bookkeeping. He met Irene Kintz, the daughter of Louis and Gertrude Wertzberger Kintz. At this time, he worked at the Rose Jewelry in Fort

Joseph W. Pranger Family

Wayne, when he was in high school. He developed picture there. He designed and made a ring for Irene, but her parents would not allow her to have it since she was too young. He worked for the Pennsylvania Railroad, BASS, WPA, helped pave bricks for New Haven Avenue, one brick at a time, sold used cars for Buick and managed three stores for the railroad.

He married Irene C. Kintz in St. Andrew's Catholic Church on May 19, 1925. From this marriage came seventeen children. They are Delores (husband Richard Pemberton), Donald (wife Joann Siebenaler); Bernice (husband Clarence Harrison); Robert (wife Joan Huguenard); Stella (Joyce) (husband John Venaglia), Rita (husband Richard Bauer); John (wife Elner Bentz); Ruth (Rita) married to Chuck Sebaugh; Helen (husband Leo Buescher); James (wife Nancy Weiss); Thomas; Patricia (married James Jensen); Gloria, who died at birth; Richard married to Jennifer Buchanan; Michael married to Rita Moser, who died, then he married Joyce Oberley; Paul; and Judith married to George Ward. Four of these children, Delores, Bernice, Rita and James are deceased.

With all of these children, his life was full and busy and very difficult at times. He and his family attended St. Peter's Catholic Church and School; later they were members of St. Andrew's Catholic Church and school. He worked at Bowser Pump before Tokheim. He also raised Doberman Pinscher dogs that he sold to ranchers in South America, and sold Fuller Brush products. He was active in church, the Boy Scouts, was an artist and a great photographer, and was a member of the Knights of Columbus. He lived in Fort Wayne most of his adult life, until he moved to Grabill in 1956. When he retired, he enjoyed life in the country with his wife, Irene, until she died in 1969. In retirement, he built doghouses, raised pigeons and sold Fuller Brush products. He married Marge Cost in April 22, 1972

When he died on November 2, 1978, he had 67 grandchildren. He is buried in Scipio Cemetery, Indiana.

Submitted by Patricia A. Jensen

JACK ALPHONSO & HELEN LOUISE (MEURER) PRAY

Jack Alphonso was born in Detroit, Michigan, on September 21, 1912 to Vernon and Laura (Paton) Pray. His only sibling, Gordon Edward, was eight years older. After his father died in the

Helen and Jack Pray bring their first daughter home to their Tyler Street home in 1942.

1918 influenza epidemic, Laura married Joseph Gerardot and moved her family to the Gerardot farm west of Monroeville. Jack graduated from Madison Township High School (Hoagland) in 1929. Earlier that year, the five boys in the senior class miraculously won a major basketball tournament.

Jack was a representative for Remington Typewriter, graduated from the International Business College, and became a bookkeeper at Berghoff's Brewery and International Harvester. Four days after Jack's birth, Helen Louise and her twin brother, James Lawrence, were born to Phillip Henry and Margaret Amelia (Griffin) Meurer on the dining room table at home at 1904 Hillside Avenue. Twins were so rare in those days that complete strangers came to the house and asked to see the infants. About six months later, the St. Joseph River flooded, coming to within 10 feet of their front porch. Helen, her father, and her brother all survived after contracting influenza in the 1918 epidemic.

When a neighbor, Robert Majors, bought the first car in the neighborhood, he took the kids for a ride to New Haven; they thought they had been around the world. Helen babysat throughout the area and helped her brother deliver newspapers on a route across the St. Joe River. She also enjoyed going to the Colonial Theater where she paid five cents each week to see silent cliffhanger movies.

After attending Lakeside Elementary and the Cathedral Grade School, Helen completed a commercial program at St. Augustine Academy in 1930. She continued to enjoy movies during the Great Depression, which then cost 25 cents. One dish in a table service was given away by the theater each week. Eventually, she accumulated a full set for her mother. Helen worked at the Wayne Knitting Mill making nylon hose for Montgomery Ward and for the famous Bell Sharmeer line, which was sold in only the finest department stores.

Jack and Helen met at Trier's Dancing School and were married on April 15, 1927. They paid $3,000 for their first house at 709 Tyler before selling it only two years later for $7,000. While Helen was in Lutheran Hospital giving birth to their first daughter, Mary Sharon, her roommate was Mrs. Clouss, owner of the Hobby House. One of Mrs. Clouss's employees, Dave Thomas, visited them, several years before founding the Wendy's franchise in Columbus, Ohio.

The Prays left Fort Wayne in 1945 when Jack became a minister for the Community of Christ Church. They went on to live in Michigan, Ontario, Alabama, and Kansas before Jack died in 1960 at age 47. He is buried at Mound Grove Cemetery, Independence, Missouri. Helen lived in Independence for 30 years before moving in 1996 to Duluth, Georgia. There, she currently lives with daughter Jackie Ellen, son-in-law James Wolk, and her only grandchild, Benjamin Lawrence.

Submitted by Sharon Muir.

M. SHERMAN & EDNA LORA (HASTY) PRESSLER FAMILY

Michael Sherman Pressler was born July 18, 1894, in Lincolnville, Wabash County, Indiana, to Quaker parents. His mother, Jane (Jennie) Holloway (1859-1939), was the daughter of Job Holloway (1832-1921) and Louisa Rebecca Copeland (1831-1923). His father, John Abraham Lincoln (Link) Pressler (1866-1960), son of Michael Pressler (1834-1904) and Mary Catherine Brane (1840-1927), was born in a log cabin and lived to see the beginning of the space program.

Sherman was captain of the Lincolnville High School basketball team. Graduating in 1912, he obtained a teaching certificate and a job at Lincolnville School.

When Indiana began requiring a degree and teacher's license, Sherman earned a bachelors degree at Muncie Normal Institute (Ball State University). He went on to earn a Masters in Education at Indiana University and then studied for a Doctorate in Nuclear Physics at Case Institute of Technology in Cleveland, Ohio.

On August 19, 1917, Sherman married Edna Lora Hasty (1895-1973), the daughter of Arthur Swain Hasty and Rosetta Nancy (Rose) Young, the daughter of Mary Ellen Wiley and Lewis H. Young, in a Quaker ceremony attended by thirteen people in the Hasty's Muncie home.

Before moving to Fort Wayne, Sherman was the principal of Center and Daleville Schools in Delaware County and taught physics and chemistry at Hartford City.

In 1927, Sherman accepted a job with Fort Wayne Community Schools as a science instructor. Sherman, Edna, and children, Julia Alice (1921-) and Philip James (1923-1999), moved to Fort Wayne.

Two more children were born to the Presslers: Marilyn Sue, (1928-1999) and Robert Lex (1935-). Sherman supplemented his teacher's salary working nights in a factory and weekends in a shoe store. When the Depression came, he quit the factory and shoe store so others could have jobs.

During the 1930s, Sherman taught seventh and eighth graders at Washington School. Bud Meese of Fort Wayne remembers, "When I first saw Mr. Pressler, I thought I had the meanest teacher in the world, but he turned out to be the best teacher I ever had."

From 1940-1960, Sherman taught physics at North Side High School. Robert Weikel, who returned to school after serving in World War II, remembers "[Sherman] could keep a study hall in line with just a look, but he had a sense of humor." Shocking "old maid" teachers at North Side, Robert dated Sherman's daughter Sue. They were married April 16, 1949, in Fort Wayne.

Sherman's daughter Julia had married Attorney James Dunn from Union City, Indiana, in Fort Wayne on June 16, 1946.

M. Sherman and Edna Pressler 1917

In 1947, Sherman and Edna bought a 180 acre farm at the northeast corner of Coldwater and Cook Roads. In the 1950s, two lots on Cook Road were sold to daughter, Sue, and friends of the Weikels. In 1960, Sherman's daughter, Julia, purchased the second property.

Julia taught for Fort Wayne Community Schools from 1960-1983. Her husband, James Dunn, practiced law in Fort Wayne until the 1980s.

During his career, Sherman was president of the Fort Wayne Teacher's Association five years and chairman of the Joint Salary Committee of Fort Wayne Teacher's Association and Fort Wayne Teacher's Council twelve years. After retiring in 1960, he substituted in Fort Wayne Community Schools until his death October 24, 1967.

Submitted by Judith West

ELAINE EDWARDS PRUITT

Elaine Edwards Pruitt was born in Fort Wayne, Indiana. Her parents were Wanda Leona Woods and William Howard Edwards. Her siblings are Miles S., William, Jr., Marilyn, and Nathaniel. She graduated from South Side High School.

She descends from Nathanial and Cornelia Hopson Jamison Blanks who moved into a home on Helen St. (Dalman) in 1895.

Elaine was the first African American from Fort Wayne to be accepted, graduate and teach from Indiana University School of Dental Hygiene. She was also the first to pass the National Board Examination. She worked for Dr. Bernard Stuart and Dr. Wagoner as a Dental Hygienist. She taught in the School of Dentistry at IPFW and taught bacteriology at Ivy Tech for seven years.

Elaine is presently employed by the Allen County Board of Health as a health inspector. She is an Environmental Health Special Education Coordinator and a Commissioned Police Officer, and has worked in this capacity for over 25 years. Among her many duties are the inspections of grocery stores and restaurants for health hazards and contaminations.

She has two children, Tomohn Pruitt, and Tracy E. Pruitt, and a grandson, Tomohn Pruitt, II.

Submitted by Elaine Edwards Pruitt

HARRY & DESSIE (STABLER) PURVIS FAMILY

Harry Ellsworth Purvis, Sr. and Dessie Catherine Stabler were both born in Payne, Ohio. Harry Purvis and his family later moved to Deshler, Ohio. Harry and Dessie married and in 1913, moved to New Haven, Indiana, to open the Purvis Drug Store at the corner of Broadway and Main Streets. Ten years later, in 1924, Harry and Dessie built and moved to the location of 514 Broadway. They continued to operate the store, where prescriptions were filled, besides operating a food counter and a popular soda fountain. Wallpaper was also an important product sold in the store.

During these early years, Harry and Dessie raised four children: Harry Jr., Kathleen, Charles, and Daniel. All three of their sons eventually became pharmacists.

In December 1937, Harry Sr. became ill and died in early 1938 of a ruptured appendix, as penicillin and sulfa drugs were not available at that time.

Dessie continued to operate the drug store with the help of other pharmacists in the area until Harry Jr. graduated from pharmacy college. After World War II, Charles and Dan graduated from pharmacy college and also helped to continue the drug store in New Haven. Charles passed away in 1970 and, after Harry Jr. retired, Daniel continued to operate the original drug store and also opened three other stores in the New Haven and Fort Wayne area.

Submitted by Dan Purvis

ANGIE QUINN & STEVE NAGY

Angie Quinn and Steven J. Nagy were married March 20, 1999 at St. John the Baptist Catholic Church in Fort Wayne. Steven J. Nagy works as a teller at Public Service Credit Union. He is Treasurer of the Board of Directors of the Friends of the Parks of Allen County, and coaches youth soccer at Fort Wayne Sport Club.

Steve Nagy was born March 21, 1964 in Fort Wayne, to Steve T. Nagy and Seigrid (Tagtmeyer) Nagy. Steve Sr.'s parents, Joseph Blasko and Maria (Molnar) Blasko fled Hungary in 1956, and arrived in Fort Wayne through the Catholic Charities Resettlement program in 1960. Steve's mother, Seigrid Tagtmeyer was born to Fort Wayne natives Leonard and Helen Tagtmeyer. Steve has a sister, Christine, born September 30, 1965, who married Ramasotho Mokgadi. They have three children, Thabo, Kagiso, and Mogalli. They reside in Philadelphia.

Angie Quinn is Executive Director of ARCH, Inc., the Historic Preservation organization serving Allen County. She is Secretary of the Board of the Three Rivers Natural Food Co-op, on the Fort Wayne Historic Preservation Review Board, and is a founding board member of the Friends of the Parks of Allen County. She is a member of Quest Club and the Antiquarian Club. Her first husband, D. Nicholas Keirn was born in Laud, Whitley County, in 1952. They were married at the Universalist-Unitarian Meeting House, Fort Wayne, May 24, 1986. Nick died in 1991. Angie and Nick have two children, Pauline E. Quinn, born January 10, 1990 and Jacob N. Keirn, born December 23, 1991.

Quinn-Nagy Family

Angie was born February 25, 1964 to Fort Wayners Robert W. Quinn, Jr. and Rita J. (Wehrle) Quinn. Robert W. Quinn, Jr.'s parents were Robert W. Quinn and Dorothy E. (Adang) Quinn and Rita's parents were Paul A. Wehrle and Frances V. (Holthouse) Wehrle, all of Fort Wayne. Angie has five siblings: Gregory R. Quinn married Susan Bennett. They reside in Elm Grove, Wisconsin, and have twins, Cameron and Mackenzie. Jeffrey M. Quinn married Carmen Cortez. They reside in Park Forest, Illinois. Their children are Ellen, Connor, and Liam. Daniel C. Quinn married Kei Matsui. They reside in Fort Wayne and have three children: Rita, Sara, and Hana. Dan holds a Ph.D. in Classical Guitar, and teaches at colleges in the Fort Wayne area. Kei Matsui Quinn teaches at the Indianapolis Japanese Day School. Katharine A. Quinn married Paul Newburg. She has three children from a previous marriage: Danielle, Jessica and Emma. Katie and Paul reside in Fort Wayne. Katie is currently Secretary of the Fort Wayne Paralegal Association, and works for Benson, Pantello, Morris, James and Logan. Paul is employed by East Allen County School Corporation, as a middle school teacher, and as coach of the Leo High School Golf teams. Elizabeth J. Quinn (Betsy) married John Yankoviak. They have a daughter, Mary. Betsy works as Naturalist at Lindenwood Nature Preserve. John works for Roots Camp and Ski Haus. They serve as caretakers at the Izaac Walton League Conservation Club in rural Allen County.

Submitted by Angie Quinn.

WILLIAM & MARGARET QUINN

William Quinn was born November 29, 1843 on Prince Edward Island, Canada, to John Quinn and Margaret Connelly. He moved to Lafayette, Indiana before 1870. On October 25, 1876 he married Margaret Elizabeth Hannig, the daughter of Richard Hannig and Sara Connell, at St. Mary's Church in Lafayette. They farmed in Honey Creek Township, White County until about 1905 when they moved to Fort Wayne.

Their children were: John William Quinn married Frankey Marie Halverson February 16, 1905 in Fort Wayne. She was the daughter of Charles Halverson of Kankakee, Illinois, and Martha Ellen Coffinberry of Newton County, Indiana. They had five sons. Thomas Orville Quinn married Irene Hines (June 26, 1926) and lived in Fort Wayne. Joseph Bernard Quinn married Esther Mittemeyer, and lived in Fort Wayne. Robert William married Dorothy Adang (October 6, 1938), and had three children: Robert William Jr., James, and Deborah. Charles "Chick" Quinn married Ruth McAfee (1945), and lived in Fort Wayne. John Wilson Quinn was born in 1915 and died in 1919. "Leroy" Edward Quinn married Mary Louise, and lived in Fort Wayne.

Thomas J. Quinn married Loretta Swager November 11, 1905 in Fort Wayne. They lived in Fort Wayne.

Sara C. Quinn (Sadie) married Lark Hodge June 11, 1913 in Fort Wayne. They lived in Fort Wayne.

Margaret Quinn married Orley Obberwitte November 22, 1910 in Fort Wayne. They lived in Fort Wayne.

Charles Quinn married Anna Fenker June 18, 1914 in Fort Wayne. They lived in Fort Wayne.

Martin Quinn.

Theresa Quinn married Joseph Koorsen June 12, 1917 in Fort Wayne. They lived in Fort Wayne.

Submitted by Katie Quinn-Newberg.

LEO & DOROTHY (COLEMAN) RADEMAKER FAMILY

Held together by the strong bonds of love and duct tape, the Rademaker family fondly remembers their ancestry, revels in present-day gatherings, and harbors a bright hope for future generations.

Leo (Lee) Rademaker, Jr. was born June 17, 1924 in Louisville, Kentucky. His parents, Leo Sr., and Cecelia (Birkel) Rademaker were born in Louisville and also died there. Leo Sr.'s parents were born in Dubois County, Indiana, but died in Louisville. Cecilia's father, Louis Birkel, was born in Tell City, Indiana, and her mother, Anna (Mathes) Birkel, was born in Louisville; they both died in Louisville. All of Lee's great-grandparents were born in Germany, but arrived in the United States in their twenties.

Lee received his Bachelor of Electrical Engineering degree in 1945 from the University of Louisville. He spent most of his career as an engineer for the General Electric Co. (GE) in various locations. In Schenectady, New York, he met his future wife Dorothy (Dot) (Coleman) Rademaker.

Dot was born August 9, 1927 in Boston, Massachusetts. Her parents, Thomas Coleman and Margaret (Youngclaus) Coleman, were born in Boston and also died there. Thomas's father, David, was born in County Waterford, Ireland, while Thomas's mother, Francis (Walsh) Coleman, was born in Massachusetts. Margaret's father, Albert Youngclaus, and her mother, Abigail (Hohman) Youngclaus, were both born in Boston. All of Dot's grandparents died in Boston. Dot's Youngclaus ancestors originally came from Germany.

Dot received her Bachelor of Arts in Mathematics degree from Emmanuel College in Boston in 1948. She was then employed by GE as an Engineering Assistant in Schenectady. There, she and Lee became engaged and they were married on June 17, 1950 in Boston. As part of their honeymoon, Lee and Dot moved to Fort Wayne, where Lee had recently been transferred by GE.

Lee was a Senior Product Engineer when he retired from GE. Including some years of part-time consulting, he was employed by GE for 52 years. In 1994, he was honored as "Citizen Engineer of the Year" for northeast Indiana. During his life, he was active as a Scout Leader, Science Central Volunteer, and in various capacities at St. Joseph Catholic Church and church-related education work. Dot retired as Church Secretary at St. John Bosco in Churubusco. She was active in

Leo and Dorothy Rademaker, June 2003

Girl Scouting and at St. Joseph Catholic Church. Lee and Dot had three children.

Margaret (Peggy) was born June 7, 1951 and received her Bachelor of Science in 1973 from Indiana University, and is a part-time Medical Technologist at Lutheran Hospital. In 1974, she married Patrick Blose of Greencastle, Indiana, who received his Bachelor of Arts in 1973 from Indiana University. He received his Master of Science in Education from University of St. Francis in 1978, and has worked in the Fort Wayne Community School system for over 30 years. They have three children: Annette, Catherine, and David.

Edward was born September 30, 1953, graduated from Purdue University's School of Veterinary Medicine in 1977 and is owner of Allen Veterinary Clinic in Fort Wayne. In 1980, he married Elizabeth Ward of Fort Wayne, and they have three children: James, Lee, and Sara.

Carol was born April 2, 1959, received her Bachelor of Arts from Notre Dame in 1981 and her Master of Business Administration from David Lipscomb University in 2003. In 1983, she married Joseph Wieck of Nashville, Tennessee. He graduated from Notre Dame in 1981 and from the University of Tennessee School of Medicine in 1985, and now has an orthopedic practice. They live in Nashville, Tennessee, with their three children, Kevin, Martin, and Matthew.

The grandchildren of Lee and Dot are just beginning their adventures in the world. Annette received her Bachelor of Arts in Biology in 2000 from Depauw University and her Associate Degree in Nursing in 2003 and currently works as an Operating Room Nurse at Riley Hospital in Indianapolis, Indiana. Catherine received her Bachelor of Arts in Biology in 2002 from Hanover College and her Master of Arts in English in 2004. She works as an editor for Cadmus Professional Communications in Baltimore, Maryland. David is attending Ivy Tech in Fort Wayne and hopes to graduate with a degree in Business Management in 2007. James received a Bachelor of Science in Biology from Purdue University in 2004. He is currently earning his Doctorate of Veterinary Medicine from Purdue University and hopes to graduate in 2008 and join his father's practice in Fort Wayne. Lee will graduate with a Bachelor of Recreational Resource Management in 2005 from the University of Montana. Sara is attending Auburn University and plans to graduate in 2007 with a degree in Fisheries and Aquaculture. Kevin, Martin, and Matthew Wieck all attend the prestigious Montgomery Bell Academy in Nashville. Kevin will graduate in 2005; Martin will graduate in 2006; Matt will graduate in 2009. All three plan to attend college and conquer the world with their respective talents.

Submitted by Leo Rademaker

DEBORAH & JOHNSON RADFORD FAMILY

Deborah Ann was the second daughter and third child of Robert Philip Johnson and Mary Angela Johnson. She was born July 11, 1954, at Decatur Memorial Hospital in Decatur, Indiana. She was eager to be born and her parents, along with Grandma Sheehan for support, barely made it to the hospital.

At the time of her birth the family was living in a large brick house next to the grain elevator in Monroeville, Indiana. They purchased a home in Decatur, Indiana, as father Robert was working at Central Soya Company. The family made several more moves before making their permanent home in Fort Wayne, Indiana, at 2717 Plaza Drive, where they lived 20 years.

Debbie attended St. Hyacinth Catholic School. She was in the last class that graduated from Central Catholic High School in 1972. After graduation she was employed by Central Soya Company. She worked there until her first son was born in 1978.

She married Joseph Mac Radford at Lakeside Park on August 20, 1977. Joe had two daughters from a previous marriage, Joy and Teresa. They were living with their mother, but eventually came to make there home with Debbie and Joe. They made their first home on Devonshire Drive in Fort Wayne.

Debbie and Joe's first child, Nicholas Joseph, was born on November 22,1978. Three years later, Angela Nicole joined the family on May 6,1981. She was born with cerebral palsy. On July, 30, 1984, Rebecca Suzanne was born and on December 28, 1987, Zackery Charles, their last child, was born.

Joe made his living driving trucks for Consolidated Freightways. CF closed all its terminals in August 2002 and he took an early retirement. Debbie did baby sitting in her home so she could be with her family when the children were small. In 1989, they moved to a new home at 6123 Seabree Lane, where they still reside.

After the children were in school, Debbie went to work for Orkin Pest Control. As the children got older and entered high school, she started working third shift at the US Post Office Remote Encoding Center doing data entry. She is currently on loan to the Hazelwood Post Office.

Family always came first with Debbie. She shifted her working hours to be with her children when they were home. She went to all their sports events and school activities. She was a cheerleading coach and active at St. Charles Catholic School. She does volunteer work at Bishop Dwenger High School from which all her children have or will have graduated.

In high school, Nick was a wrestler and played on the football team for two years. Upon graduating he joined the US Navy. He was assigned to a Submarine, by request. He has been based in Georgia, Connecticut and now Hawaii. His enlistment will be up in 2007 and he will rejoin the civilian population.

Angie has endured many surgeries on her legs and eyes. She was born with cerebral palsy and cataracts. After high school she enrolled at IPFW and is currently going to Ivy Tech. She traveled to Sweden with a Christian Group from school and has gone to Florida with a friend.

Becky has been active in school activities, including cheerleading, Show Choir, and the bowling team. She is attending Ball State University, in Muncie, Indiana, and is a sophomore.

Zack is a junior at Bishop Dwenger High school. He has participated in the marching band, and is on the bowling team. He is employed part time at Do It Best Hardware on North Anthony Boulevard.

Ancestors include Johnson, Schlemmer, Sheehan and Geis families from the rural Monroeville, Indiana area.

Submitted by Deborah Ann Radford

RAMP

Who are our ancestors, where did they come from, when did they arrive in America? Why did they settle here? It takes lots of research to uncover the answers.

Jacob Ramp came to America in October 1753 from Wuerttemberg, Germany, settling in Cumberland Township, Berks Count, Pennsylvania. He owned a sawmill in Newville, Pennsylvania. His three sons fought with George Washington in the First Battalion in 1758. Great Grandfather, Phillip Ramp III, came west to Columbia City in December, 1850. He and his brother owned a sawmill on North Elm Street in Columbia City. His home is still standing at the corner of Elm and Joy Streets in Columbia City. The family was also into carriage building and horse training.

My grandfather, Edward Ramp, married Elizabeth Helbig in November, 1890. They moved to Fort Wayne around 1909. Their union produced ten children.

My father, Harold Ramp, was born September, 1911 and married Helen Schoenle in August, 1936. He worked for the Wayne Knitting Mills until the mill left town in the late 1950s. He then worked as Van Equipment Manager for North American Van Lines until his death in November, 1972. Helen worked as a cashier in the cafeterias at both Magnavox and International Harvester until her retirement in 1986.

They had three children, Suzanne, William and Stephen. Sue and Steve currently reside in Fort Wayne. Steve and his wife, Jane, worked at Lincoln National Life Insurance Company and are now affiliated with IBM. They have two daughters, Jennifer, a senior at Indiana University, Bloomington, Indiana, studying business, and Melissa, a senior at Snider High School. Bill resides in Jacksonville, Florida. He has two sons,

Christopher and Darin, who each have a son. Sue is retired from General Tire Company, Fort Wayne, with forty years of service in the office.

Submitted by Suzanne Ramp.

RAMP FAMILY

GRANDPA EDWARD, FATHER WALTER, & SON ROBERT

Walter Ramp was born July 12, 1896 and married Cora Biggs on December 25, 1917. Cora was born August 24, 1897. They had four children: Robert, born January 19, 1921; Betty born March 1, 1922; Kenneth born October 20, 1930; and Doris born December 13, 1933. Grandpa, Edward Ramp, with a team of horses, pulled logs from the woods on wagon and sleds. Using drag lines and horses he managed to scoop out basement and cellars. He sold ice from the neighborhood ice house and was janitor at church. He also had a good sense of humor and was well liked by all. Grandma, Lizzie Ramp, was a very hard worker who took in washing and ironing. Son Robert was always glad to go to her house for those butterscotch pies. She helped grandpa clean church. In Robert's early days spent at Grandpa and Grandma's house, Grandpa took Robert to the local amusement park many times, on picnics and to see the fireworks on Fourth of July. The house on Boone Street held many memories.

Robert went to the Nebraska School for awhile. During this time he also visited his Uncle Charles in Roanoke. On his farm Robert remembers playing in the hay barn, doing chores, feeding chickens, gathering the eggs, watching milking the cows, and riding the hay wagon to town. He also went on fishing trips with grandpa; that was fun.

Robert also went to Grandpa and Grandma Biggs in Columbia City, Indiana. Grandpa was a nurseryman; he grew veggies and had fruit trees. He loved to get those gingerbread cookies grandma baked in a wood burning stove.

Soon Robert's folks moved and rented a house on Spy Run Avenue, corner of Lawton Place. He spent many days at Lawton Park with his friends, and went to the Rudisill School for a short time. In 1933 his folks took him and Kenneth, who was three years old, to the World Fair in Chicago.

While living on Dodge Street (1930) Robert went to Forest Park School. He has lots of good memories, such as playing hide and seek with the dog (collie shepherd). He also liked to roller skate on California Avenue. It was very smooth skating. He had lots of good times playing with the kids in the neighborhood.

After Dad lost this home during the depression (1931), they moved to Shore Drive. While living on Shore Drive, Robert finished Forest Park and on to North Side High School where he made lots of friends; he especially remembers the "Camp Boys," Bernard and Richard. Robert carried the morning paper, *Journal Gazette*, all through his high school days. After school he worked at a local café (Candlelight) on State Street. At this time his mother worked at Messerschmidt Grocery Store, and later he started to work there as delivery boy.

Robert left home, being drafted into the army in September, 1942. He left behind his older sister, Betty and sister, Doris. Soon his sister Betty married Robert Coombs, who was in the army, stationed at Fort Riley, Kansas. Betty joined him to work at the Union Pacific Railroad.

Robert's folks bought a house on St. Marys Avenue in 1945 after he returned from the war. In 1946 Robert was living in Angola attending Tri State College, after which he moved back to St. Marys in Fort Wayne, where, in 1954, Kenneth, Dad and Robert built a garage. Robert was dating his wife-to-be. He worked at North American Van Lines beginning in 1950, and also got a job for his uncle, Harold Ramp. In 1957, Robert married Jane, who was working at Magnavox as telephone operator. They soon bought a house on Charlotte. Their basement was the center of lots of activities, for it was cozy on cold winter days. Jane had a good place to do her sewing, laundry, ironing, and Robert had a nice work bench to repair things.

Soon the family came along. First son, James D. was born in 1958, and in 1959 David M. came along. What happy days they had sledding in winter and picnicking in the backyard in the summer. All this time Robert was working at North American Van Lines as Assistant Superintendent of Maintenance, maintaining a fleet of trailers needing repairs and repainting. This job covered ten years. In 1961 he left this company and moved to Florida. He is now retired and living in sunny Tampa, Florida. He is glad for his upbringing in Fort Wayne where he learned lots of responsibility in those early days.

Submitted by Robert J. Ramp

LAMBERT & THERESA RAUNER FAMILY

Lambert (Leonarde) and Theresa Rauner emigrated from France. Their only daughter, Mary J., was born August 7, 1856, in New York. In 1858, the Rauners moved to Pleasant Township in Allen County, Indiana and bought 40 acres of ground, on which he farmed, for the amount of $700.

Mary J. married George Sorg, born in 1848, on November 4, 1873. They lived in Pleasant Township, raising a family.

George Rauner was born on February 1, 1860, in Allen County and married Anna Sorg on April 28, 1884. George passed away December 29, 1912, in Richmond, Indiana.

Joseph Rauner's birth in 1867 completed the family. On December 1, 1888, he married Mary C. Bollinger, who was born in 1861. Joseph died on January 16, 1894, in Allen County and his wife passed away November 7, 1898, leaving two sons, Lambert and Clement, as orphans.

Lambert and Theresa Rauer are buried in the St. Aloysius Catholic Church cemetery on State Road 1, south of Fort Wayne.

Submitted by Megan Harvey and Lila Rauner

MAURICE NICHOLAS & ANNA URSULA (JAURIS) RAUSIS FAMILY

Maurice Nicholas Rausis left Switzerland with his wife, Anna Ursula Jauris, and four children, Maurice, Alexandria, Louise, and Nicholas. They left from the port of Le Harve, France on the ship, *Baltimore*, August 30, 1849 and arrived in New York September 20, 1849. The family traveled to Stark County, Ohio, and settled in the French community in Nimishillen Township.

Maurice and Anna had only one child born in America, Mary Sarah, born in Stark County, Ohio. A number of the French families from Stark County were moving to another French settlement in Allen County, Indiana. Maurice and family also made the move, purchasing 80 acres in section 19 of Jefferson Township in 1856, where they remained the rest of their lives. After settling there, Maurice became a naturalized citizen in 1860.

The records of St. Louis Catholic Church contain many entries of Maurice and Anna as godparents and marriage witnesses. As members of St. Louis parish, they rented pew number 46. Maurice made a contribution for a beautiful blue and gold stained glass window that bears his name on the east side of the church.

Maurice died August 26, 1888, and is buried in the old cemetery of St. Louis Church. Anna wrote her will November 27, 1888, three months after her husband's death. She died the next day and is buried next to her husband. Their children were: Maurice (Morris) Felix, born March 22, 1842; Mary Alexandria, born June 22,1843; Mary Louise, born July 4, 1845; and Francis Nicholas born July 1849, all in Switzerland. Mary Sarah was born March 13, 1853, in Ohio.

Maurice F. Rausis married first Elizabeth A. Snyder August 11, 1865, in Allen County, Indiana. He died July 6, 1933, age 91, at Monroeville, Indiana. Elizabeth died November 17, 1901. They are buried in the I.O.O.F. cemetery at New Haven, Indiana. They had eleven children. Maurice married his second wife, Elizabeth Chapman, on June 16, 1903 in Fort Wayne, Indiana. Maurice (Morris) served in the Civil War, enlisting August 10, 1862, in Company D, 88th regiment, Indiana Volunteer Infantry. He obtained a pension from the State of Indiana and was a member of the William H. Link Post #301 GAR of Monroeville, Indiana.

Mary Alexandria Rausis married Francis Auguste "Frank" Savieo on March 28, 1861. After having nine children, Mary died March 22, 1884 at age 40. She is buried in St. Louis Catholic Church Cemetery.

Mary Louise Rausis married Joseph Gerardot August 23, 1866, at St. Louis Catholic Church. Louise had 14 children but names of only 12 have been found. She died August 3, 1911 and is buried in St. Louis Catholic Church Cemetery.

Francis "Frank" Nicholas Rausis married Lenora Monnier on September 5, 1874, in Allen County, Indiana. He died July 1, 1902, and is buried in St. Louis Catholic Church Cemetery. They had nine children.

Mary Sarah Rausis married Edward Gerardot on December 21, 1871. Sarah died on February 28, 1873, shortly after the birth of her child. She is buried in St. Louis Catholic Church Cemetery.

Submitted by Joyce Crowl

ALBERT B. RAY FAMILY

Albert Breton Ray was the fourth son and seventh child of Andrew and Mary Ann (McElhaney) Ray. He was born September 30, 1894, in Adams County, Indiana, near Salem. As a young man, he worked on the farm and in his father's general store in Willshire, Ohio. In 1913 he married Sarah Shalatti Ford "Lottie," and they moved to Fort Wayne, where he worked in the quality

Albert and Lottie Ray with Violet, Margaret Jane, and Mary, 1943.

control department at General Electric. They attended First Missionary Church.

Albert and Lottie had three daughters: Violet Elizabeth (1913-1984), Mary Fay (1914), and Margaret Jane (1921). In 1928 they purchased a small farm on the Flatrock Road near Hoagland and Albert became a gentleman farmer while continuing to work at General Electric. They also purchased their first car. The Rays hosted many events for their church family: hayrides, potlucks, making homemade ice cream, and "butchering" watermelons. There was plenty of food on the farm and the Great Depression was not an issue.

On June 1, 1940, Mary married Dean Thompson (1914). Margaret Jane, who had graduated from high school, got a job at General Electric with her father and started taking flying lessons. She got her flying license in 1942 and in 1943 was called to become a Women's Air Force Service Pilot (WASP). Margaret was able to attend Violet's wedding to Walter Davis on September 18, 1943, when she came home between training at Sweetwater, Texas, and her first posting in Wilmington, Delaware.

With the girls gone from home, Albert and Lottie found the farm too much to handle, so they moved back into Fort Wayne. When the WASP program was disbanded in December 1944, Margaret returned to a house in town.

Violet's husband, Walter Davis, and Mary's husband, Dean Thompson, joined to form the Adroit Company in 1941. In 1946 Margaret married a Grabill banker, Morris Ringenberg (1916 - 2003).

Walter and Violet Davis had two sons: Brian Ray (1948) and Charles Robert (1954-1979). Dean and Mary Thompson had a daughter: Janet Sue (1949). Morris and Margaret had Marsha Jane (1947) and Michael J. (1953).

After retiring in 1949, Albert and Lottie moved to Largo, Florida.

Submitted by Mary Thompson

CLEO JEANETTE REAM

Cleo Jeanette Ream was born November 26, 1911, the fifth of seven children. The parents, Claude and Bessie Shoaff Shaffer, lived to the respective ages of 99 and 103. The Shaffer family lived on Antoinette Street in Fort Wayne, and Cleo attended James Smart School, formerly located at the corner of Pontiac and Smith Streets. In 1927, when she was just 16, her father bought a farm located off Tonkel Road. The road was not paved, there were no utilities, they had an outhouse, pumped water, bathed in a galvanized tub and used kerosene. She learned quickly about farming and farm animals. What a change for a young girl who had been used to the conveniences of the city, had attended South Side High School, and just learned to drive a car on Rudisill Boulevard in Fort Wayne.

Cleo met Morris Ream while riding the school bus to Leo High School, and their first date was to a Sunday school class party. Morris had a carriage and horse they used for picnics and fun. Morris graduated in 1928 from Leo High School, Cleo in 1929. There were eight students in her graduating class. Rev. Burke married the Reams August 7, 1930, in the Harlan Parsonage. She fondly remembers they "had a belling" the evening of their wedding. According to Cleo, a belling is a group of friends that ring bells outside the bedroom window on your wedding night to annoy and tease.

The Reams bought their 80-acre family farm on St. Joe Road in 1936 for $5800, which included the house and barn. Cleo saw life as ordinary: she has attended Robinson Chapel Methodist Church on Tonkel Road for 70 years, had two children, Carol and Jerry, worked hard caring for animals, farming and canning and freezing from their large gardens. Morris worked for the ASCS offices for 30 years in addition to farming. After selling his cows, he drove a school bus for East Allen County School System for 13 years. He would say, "My cows are quieter and more obedient." Cleo also worked for EACS in the cafeteria. Morris died in 1994, and Cleo resides at the Cedars in Leo-Cedarville.

Submitted by Cleo Ream

MORRIS REAM FAMILY

Members of the Ream family have been homeowners in Allen County for over 150 years. Morris Ream's parents, Reams and Tonkels, were from northern Allen County, and his wife's parents, Shaffer and Spragues, were from rural Monroeville. They were all farmers who lived to be elderly.

Morris and Cleo (Shaffer) Ream graduated from Leo High School. After their marriage in 1930, they lived on several farms in Allen County, the latest near Cedarville, where they spent 56 years together. Morris and Cleo were employed by East Allen County Schools, as bus driver and cafeteria help. They had two children, Carol and Jerry, both of whom graduated from Leo High School, in 1950 and 1965 respectively.

Except for the time spent in the Air Force, Jerry has lived in Allen County with his wife, Diana (Henry) Ream, also of Allen County. Jerry was employed by Tokheim, and Diana is an elementary teacher with Fort Wayne Community Schools. Their two children, Tom and Amy, graduated from Leo High School but have moved elsewhere.

Carol Ream married Donald Warner of DeKalb County in May, 1953, and they moved to Fort Wayne. They had two children, David and Cathy, who graduated from Northrop High School, both of whom moved on also. Donald retired from Dana Corporation in 1988, after 36 years. Carol has been an active Parkview Hospital volunteer for 48 years, observing many changes in the health care field

They all are Christians, worshipping in United Methodist churches. Two of the Ream grandchildren became United Methodist pastors. They all have depended on their faith to get them through some difficult times. They have been blessed with love, good health, friends, relatives, and stability. Who could ask for more?

Submitted by Carol Warner

MILDRED REDIGER FAMILY

Family records begin in Bern, Switzerland with the birth of Johannes Reutiger c. 1669. His marriage to Barbara Jaggi produced a son, Sebastian c. 1720. Sebastian Reidiger modified the spelling of the family name and left the Reformed Church to become an Anabaptist due to his admiration for the faith of the Amish Mennonite farm family that employed him. Anna Letterer became his wife and bore (1773) Jakob Rediger who married Jokobina Gingerich and lived on Ottenweirhof, a large estate in Baden, Germany. The family name took on its present form with Jakob. In 1797 their son, Benjamin Rediger, was born. He later married Barbara Ehresman who bore Johannes Rediger (1828) in Lemach, Baden, Germany. Benjamin, fleeing Prussian military persecution, brought his family to Tazewell County, Illinois, where he died in 1848. Benjamin Rediger, was born to Johannes and Anna Birky Rediger in Woodford County in 1857. He married Lena Rich in Gridley, Illinois at the Salem Defenseless Mennonite Church. They moved to the Sterling, Kansas area where submitter's grandfather, Jacob Rediger, was born in 1890.

Ralph and Mildred Clifton

Lilly and Jacob Rediger

In 1904, at the age of fourteen, Jacob came with his family to the Woodburn, Allen County, Indiana area. Records reflect that Jacob, like his father, was a kind and gentle man who loved God. He married Lilly Gerig in 1913 and bore three children: Wilmer, Mildred and Harold. They were members of the Defenseless Mennonite Church and lived in Harlan where Jacob worked as a blacksmith. After Lilly died at the tender age of 38, Jake, married Emma Grabill, moved to a farm on Klopfenstein Road, Grabill and began attending Grabill Missionary Church (a congregation formed from the Mennonite Church). They had a son, Don, in addition to her sons Max and Paul. Jake worked hard as a carpenter and farmer during those depression years. Mom said grandpa would forego food at the dinner table so his children could have more to eat.

Mildred Marie Rediger, married Ralph Eugene Clifton in 1947. Ralph, a farm boy from Wren, Ohio, came to Fort Wayne to work as a truck driver after serving four years in World War II (Pacific). His father, Benjamin Harrison Clifton, was of English descent, his mother, Jenny Culbertson, of Scottish. They were United Brethren. Great grandpa Culbertson served as a UB Bishop with Milton Wright, father of the Wright brothers.

Mutual friends introduced Mildred and Ralph who rode the streetcars and dined at Coney Island on Main Street. Mildred worked at the Knitting Mills. Their first home was an upstairs apartment on State Street, Grabill. Ralph became the second CEO of Grabill Bank in 1965 and has lived in Grabill over fifty years. She worked part-time to enable the family to take vacations together. She sold Avon, worked at Grabill's Crosby Boat Factory and drove school bus, but her first love was always being a wife and mother. She inherited the kind and gentle spirit of her father and grandfathers. She died in 1999 and was preceded by her brother, Harold, the only other sibling to remain in Grabill. Our families remain close.

Brent Leon Clifton was born in 1951 and Vicki Lynn Clifton, in 1955. She graduated from Leo High School as Brent did, and became a supervisor at Lincoln Bank before marrying Edward Michael Bregenzer. She has two children who attend Leo, Andrew Michael and Cassandra Nicole Bregenzer. Brent studied at Fort Wayne Bible College and IPFW. He serves as the third CEO of Grabill Bank, a bank grandpa Rediger helped start in 1946. He met his wife, Vicki Rae Miller playing in a band her brother and Brent formed in the 60s. They attend Grabill Missionary and have three married children: Christopher (Mindy), a music minister in Florida, Joshua (Angela), a writer in Chicago and Justin (Christine), a filmmaker in Los Angeles. First grandchild Elijah James Clifton, born in 2003, lived briefly near Grabill before moving to Los Angeles. The eleventh generation in our Swiss Mennonite heritage, Elijah already radiates the Rediger spirit. Faith, family and community remain as important to us today and they have for the previous four centuries.

Submitted by Brent Clifton

W.M. REIFF FAMILY

Worley Morris Reiff was born in Wells County, Indiana, in 1889. He grew up there on the family farm and left to attend Purdue University in 1907. While attending Purdue, he was the pitching ace for Purdue's baseball team. In 1909 he was invited to spring training in Florida by the Detroit Tigers. After two weeks of training he received a letter from his family asking him to come home, because they felt that "ballplayers were all bums!" He complied with the request and returned to his studies at Purdue. He graduated in 1909 with a degree in Pharmaceutical Chemistry.

After graduation, he came to Fort Wayne, seeking work as a pharmacist. He was hired by Meyer Drug and worked at its store at Columbia and Calhoun Street as general manager. He married Grace Dufor in 1911. They resided in a house at Crescent and Tennessee Avenue, where their first child, Glenn Henry, was born in 1912. In the spring of 1913, the young family escaped the Great Flood by rowboat. They moved to a house on Rockhill Street, where their second child, Lyle Eugene, was born in 1915. A third son, Robert was born in 1918 and passed away in 1919 during the great flu epidemic.

In 1928, Worley purchased the Brandt Drug Store at Broadway and Lavina. By then the family had moved to the Lafayette Esplanade. Glenn graduated from South Side High School in 1930 and Gene in 1933. After a few years' hiatus to save up money, they both attended Purdue. Glenn graduated in 1938 from the School of Pharmacy and Gene graduated in 1940, also in Pharmacy.

Glenn married Margaret Anne Skillen of Royal Center, Indiana in 1938 and went to work with his father in the store on Broadway. Upon graduation, Gene bought the Miller Pharmacy at Fairfield and Dewald Street in 1940. The Reiff Pharmacy on Broadway was fondly remembered for many years by the many G.E. employees who ate lunch there during World War II. The Pharmacy on Fairfield Avenue was remembered for its excellent soda fountain.

Worley Reiff retired in the late 1950s and Glenn moved the pharmacy to Lafayette and McKinney Street in 1960. In 1968, the two stores were consolidated. Gene Reiff went to work for Hooks Drugs in LaGrange and moved to Lake George. Glenn Reiff operated the pharmacy on Fairfield Street until his retirement in 1978. He passed away in 1989.

The Reiff family maintains a presence in Allen County. Glenn's daughter, Jane Wilks, is Executive Director of Leadership Fort Wayne. His son, John Reiff, is retired and residing in Fort Wayne. John's son, Brian Reiff, continues the Reiff legacy at Purdue, and Jane's daughter, Kate Houston, is executive director of the Fort Wayne Children's Choir.

Submitted by J. T. Reiff

MICHAEL J. REILLY

Michael J. Reilly was born on September 20, 1877 in Fort Wayne, Indiana, and died on May 12, 1959 in Fort Wayne. In the early part of his life, he worked on the family farm located on the Illinois Road west of the city. On February 7, 1900, at the age of 23, he joined the Pennsylvania Railroad as a fireman. It was Fort Wayne's largest employer at that time. On November 22, 1904, he married Agnes Angela Junk at St. Peter's Catholic Church in Fort Wayne. That union was blessed with three children, two daughters and a son: Gertrude Bridget, born September 3, 1905, married on June 21, 1928 to Henry Edward Wyss in St. Patrick's Church, Fort Wayne, died July 20, 1961 at St. Joseph Hospital, Fort Wayne; Catherine Agnes, born June 1, 1907 in Fort Wayne, and died November 27, 1929 in Fort Wayne; and Michael Parnell Reilly, born October 10, 1920, and died October 2, 1924 in Fort Wayne.

Michael's father was James A. Reilly, born March 10, 1843 in Erris, County Mayo, Ireland, died May 16, 1921, in Fort Wayne. His mother was Brigid Ann Grady, born December 3, 1841, Clear Island, County Mayo, Ireland, died May 21, 1904, Fort Wayne. After Brigid's death, James married Ella Welsh on March 1, 1905. She was born September 12, 1854, and died July 20, 1939. She is buried in Catholic Cemetery, Section C 27, the same section as James. James and Brigid's other children were: Anna M., born 1870 in New Jersey and died June 22, 1945, in Chicago, spouse, Frank Belo; Mary Mitilda born November 25, 1872 in Fort Wayne, and died December 9, 1967; James A. Jr., born in 1874 in Fort Wayne, and died August 30, 1940; Catherine C., born September 15, 1897 in Fort Wayne, died February 8, 1906, spouse Carl E. Barnett; Margaret H., born December 12, 1881 in Fort Wayne, spouse Valentine Junk.

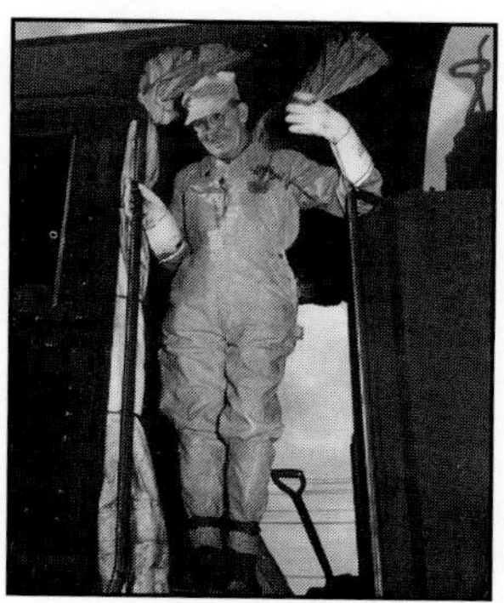

Michael J. Reilly

His wife, Agnes Junk Reilly was born September 2, 1878 in Trier, Germany, and died January 15, 1952 in Fort Wayne. Her parents were Nicholas Junk and Gertrude Weber. Gertrude was born in 1840 in Trier Germany and died 1918 in Fort Wayne. Nicholas and Gertrude's other children were Peter, Joseph, Matthew, and Jacob, and two sisters who married first a Lauer, and second a Brown.

In 1907, Michael Reilly was promoted to freight engineer and held that position for 18 years. In 1925, he as promoted to passenger engineer. At the time of his retirement, he was the engineer for the Rainbow Limited (Fort Wayne to Chicago) with total service of over 44 years. He retired at age 67, two years past the normal retirement age, due to a shortage of engineers caused by WWII. When requested, he willingly agreed to continue to work as long as he was needed.

At that time, railroads served as the primary method of transportation for military personnel.

Like most people, his life was not without tragedy and sadness. In 1924, his only son, Michael, age four, was killed in an auto accident. Five years later his youngest daughter, Catherine, age 22, died from complications of a disease that today would be considered curable.

Michael Reilly was an avid baseball fan and always believed that some day the Chicago White Sox would win the World Series. Politically, he was a very partisan Democrat and a very loyal American. Of Irish heritage, he was a member of the Hibernians and always celebrated St. Patrick's Day with fellow Irishmen at his favorite meeting place, the Match Box Tavern on East Pontiac

Street. His attire for that day included green shoestrings, shamrocks and white spats. Other memberships included St. Patrick's Catholic Church, Eagles and the Knights of Columbus.

Submitted by Robert Wyss, grandson

JOHN L. & MAIRE (KILEY) REUSS FAMILY

John L. Reuss was born on August 27, 1897, and died in October, 1967. He was the son of Emilie Centlivre and John B. Reuss. He was president of the former Centlivre Brewing Corporation, founded in Fort Wayne in 1862 by his grandfather, Charles L. Centlivre. Later, he was vice-president of Old Crown Brewery, before retiring in February, 1964.

John L. Reuss

John L. graduated from Central Catholic High School and the University of Notre Dame. He achieved much in his 71 years, including treasurer and a director of Baldwin-Montrose Chemical Company. He had been treasurer, general manager and president of the former Centlivre Brewery Corporation. He was also manager of the Kokomo Lithograph Company, the Ajax Brewing Company in Indianapolis, the toy division of Kingston Products Corporation, Kokomo, and sales manager of the Kokomo Stamped Metal Company. John was also treasurer and a director of the Brewers' Association of America and a director of the Deister Concentrator Company. He also served in World War I.

He was married to Maire Kiley and had one lovely daughter, Rosemary Reuss, who produced with her husband, Richard Scheele, ten children: William Scheele; John Scheele; Mary Scheele (Russell); Sara Scheele; Pat Scheele (Crawford); Tom Scheele; Nora Scheele (Sunderland); and Matthew Scheele.

Submitted by Patricia Crawford

DWIGHT M. REYNOLDS FAMILY

Dwight Moody Reynolds (nicknamed "Doogie") was born January 8, 1891 to Lewis Reynolds (July 13, 1869-February 25, 1914) and Anna Scott (July 15, 1870-August 28, 1891). Mother, Anna died when Dwight was about seven months old, so he was raised by his maternal grandparents, Leonidas Barnabas ("LB") Scott (May 24,1842-May 8, 1903) and Sarah Houk Scott (July 3, 1848-November 23,1924). After Anna's death, Lewis remarried to Edith Brown and had several more children. Lewis' father, Albert (December 2, 1837-April 23, 1923), operated canal boats between Toledo and Fort Wayne. Family tradition reports that Reynolds Street in Fort Wayne was named for Albert. Albert's parents were William Reynolds (June 19,1812-March 6, 1897) and Jane Driver (October 23, 1812-April 13, 1895). William was one of the earliest settlers in Madison Township, Allen County, while Jane was born in a cave near Upper Sandusky, Ohio during an Indian attack. Jane came to the fort at Fort Wayne with parents John and Elizabeth Driver as one of the earliest children to inhabit Fort Wayne. William's father, Ephraim Reynolds, was a soldier killed in the War of 1812. Dwight's grandfather, Albert and great-grandfather, William both served in the Union Army during the Civil War.

Dwight married Lulu Ruhl (June 3, 1893-February 14, 1922) March 18, 1911 and had three sons. Dwight was a lifelong farmer in Hoagland, Madison Township, Indiana. His oldest son, Howard Reynolds (October 26,1911-July 15, 1974), was a WWII Pacific War veteran, married Golda Sites, became a vice president for Commonwealth Insurance Company, and had a son, John and daughter, Susan, six grandchildren and two great grandchildren. Second son, Charles Harold Reynolds (June 3,1913-), married Helen Louise Franke (April 8, 1915-) on May 2, 1936, and was a farmer all his life. He served eight years as Madison Township Trustee and six years on the Board of Trustees of East Allen County Schools from 1964-1970. Charles and Helen had three sons. The oldest son, Robert Charles (February 22, 1943-), is an East Allen County teacher and the father of son, Robert Charles, Jr. (February 4,1978-) who is married to Mindy Funk (June 14, 1977-) and is the father of Austin Charles (September 1, 2004-), Charles' first great-grandchild. Robert's daughters, Jill Marie (September 3, 1980-) and Valerie Anne (February 9, 1987) are students. Charles and Helen's second son, David (March 24, 1948-June 29, 1953) died of leukemia. The third son, Neil Sylvan Reynolds (September 18, 1952-), is a federally licensed grain inspector and owner of Northeast Indiana Grain Inspection, married to Madonna Marie Hoevel (September 1, 1949-), and father of Clint Gregory (June 21,1977-) and Amanda Catherine (March 6, 1982), both students. Neil served on the East Allen County Schools Board of Trustees from 1990 to present. Dwight's third son, Glenn (October 25, 1918-) married Lorine Kline and had five children, Gene, Dale, Kenn, Joyce, and Kay. They have many grandchildren.

After Dwight's wife, Lulu's death of amoebic dysentery, he married four more times, the last to Nellie Clayton with whom he had a daughter Deanna Reynolds Smith (August 31, 1942-). Deanna had three children, Mark, Mike, and Lisa. She has several grandchildren. Dwight died October 28, 1979 and is buried with wives, Lulu Ruhl, Elexy Clayton, and Nellie Clayton in Antioch Community Cemetery, Hoagland, Indiana.

Submitted by Neil Reynolds

JOHN RAYMOND & RUTH NEEDHAM RHINEHART FAMILY

John was born September 29, 1916 in Monmouth, Illinois of Hedley and Minnie Loraine Bennett. He and his brothers, Lorence and Robert, were reared on their farm right across the road from Uncle Charlie's, where Hedley was born. John's patron family member Jacob Rhinehart, born about 1740 and from Germany, lived in Ulster County, New York, and married Maria Decker. Jacob's great-grandson David W. moved to Warren County, Illinois where he married Mariah Bruyn and reared eight children: William, Nathaniel B., Lefevre, Hedley, John, Cornelia, Laura, and Charles J. Most of John's family were farmers. His birth family raised corn, cows, chickens, pigs, a beautiful rose garden, and loved music.

John was graduated from the University of Illinois at Champaign with an Agricultural Masters and came to Allen County to work at Allied Mills. He started Calf-teria Sales on Polk Street and had patented a weaning valve for calves, as well as manufacturing a lambsaver nipple, which is also used for cleft palette children. When the company moved to Spencerville, then called Rhinehart Manufacturing, it had expanded to about 50 farm items. John worked everyday until a few days before entering Parkview Hospital and dying of congestive heart failure in 1999. He greatly enjoyed his family, inventing, First Presbyterian Church, Junior Chamber of Commerce, Toastmasters, music, and golf. His mother told him to find a young woman who could teach and play the piano, and he did! He and Ruth L. Needham met at a church event and married January 11, 1946.

John and Ruth Rhinehart's 50th Together

Ruth, born March 19, 1920, moved from Kendallvile to Fort Wayne with her parents, Basil Everd Needham and Inez E. Rimmel, at seven. Basil and Inez had been born in Noble County of Walter and Julia Dye Needham and Louis and Alpharetta Rimmel. Basil and Inez retained their farms of birth their entire lives. Ruth was an I.U. Bloomington graduate in Music and taught school. She and John lived on Indiana Avenue for about fifty years. Ruth's brother, Dan Needham, wife, Jane Wilcox, and their three children lived in Fort Wayne: Thomas Dean married Jane, Mark Wilcox married Dr. Anne Bueter, and Nancy Jane married Dino Sarpa.

Ruth helped John start their business at home on Edgewater, and they reared four children: Julie, Steven, Philip, and Lori. Ruth has always been very family and community oriented and belongs to Tri Kappa, Chi Omega, Art Appreciation Antiquarians, is a First Presbyterian deacon, and plays the piano for Canterbury School and Kingston Alzheimer's Unit as a volunteer. She also enjoys bridge, exercises with her personal trainer, and paints a mean turquise tree! When Ruth precipitates many gatherings at Kasota Lodge, their Clear Lake cottage, there are currently 27 of them who gather – since 1965!

All born in Allen County: Julie Ruth Rhinehart Waterfield, born March 21, 1947 is a retired teacher, volunteer, and mother of three: Richard Rhinehart Waterfield, born March 31,1971, of Newport Beach, California; John Randall Waterfield, born May 10,1973, of New York's Battery Park, New York; and Jill Loraine Waterfield, born

October 30, 1976, of San Francisco, California. Richard and Randy are in finance together and Jill is an art therapist. Steven Needham Rhinehart, a Fort Wayne oncologist, born April 26,1949, married Annemarie Hietberg of Indianapolis, and has three children: Alison Marie DeCastro (Donny) of Myrtle Beach, S.C., newscaster; Jonathan Ashley married Caty of Fort Wayne and has two children and Taylor (fourth generation Rhineharts); Michael Steven, Purdue University student. Philip Raymond Rhinehart, born June 10, 1950, married Kathleen Gray of Fort Wayne, and is President and Owner of Rhinehart Development and Rhinehart Finishing. They have four children: Elizabeth Rorick (Nick) of Iowa City, Iowa; David Raymond, Indiana Wesleyan student; Kimberly Gray, Xavier University student; and Andrew Lawrence, Concordia College in Chicago student. Susan Loraine Rhinehart Watkins (Robert N.) owns and manages Black Creek Crossing Quarter Horse Farm in Steuben County (Hamilton) and has four boys: John Robert, Indiana-Purdue Fort Wayne student; Peter William, Ball State student; Daniel Edward, American Academy of Drama Los Angeles student; and Theodore Ross, Angola High School student.

Other known surnames associated with this family are Jansen, Grimm, Baldridge, Walker, Hanna, Alleman, Kilgore, Brickly, White, Kringe, Strong, Robinson, Victor, Gildersleeve, Masincupp, Killough, Kennard, Terwilliger, Upright, Rittenhouse, Goodjoin, McWhorter, Cook, Hill, Berberick, Reitsma, Woodka, Traub, Areilise, Steffens, Kimball, Newton, Kann, Inhofe, Schoomnaker, and Petheridge.

Submitted by Julie Rhinehart Waterfield

BEVERLY RICHARDSON

Beverly Richardson was born in Tell City, Indiana on December 17, 1950, and moved to Fort Wayne in March 1979. She is the daughter of Herschel Clifford Richardson, DDS, and Ellen Elizabeth Baynes Richardson, both deceased.

She took a secretarial job with a small sales and publishing company. She took a second job at the Acme Bar on East State in June of 1979, working there part-time for 18 years. In 1986, she began a job as a secretary at the American Red Cross Blood Services on California Road. She spent 11½ years at the Red Cross in various positions, the last as a blood donor recruiter. She left the Red Cross to take a position with the Fort Wayne Philharmonic, as executive assistant to the President, in 1997. It allowed her to meet many of the guest artists who performed with the orchestra: Itzhak Perlman, Joshua Bell, Gil Shaham, K.D. Lang, Johnny Mathis, and many others. While working for the orchestra, she began working for a professor who had retired from the Eastman School of Music. At the time of this writing, she was assisting him in the preparation of the first complete English translation of the life-long correspondence between composers Johannes Brahms and Clara Schumann.

Beverly was working for the orchestra at the time of the attacks on September 11, 2001, which precipitated an additional crisis for the orchestra. Opening Night for the 2001-2002 season was scheduled for Saturday night, September 15, four days after the attacks, and the guest artist lived in Manhattan. The scheme to get the artist to Fort Wayne involved a former Fort Wayne resident and orchestra staffer who now lived in Stroudsburg, Pennsylvania about 90 minutes from New York. The artist would hire a taxi to take him from Manhattan to Wayne, New Jersey on Thursday afternoon, where he would meet a stranger whose wife used to work for the Philharmonic. That stranger would drive him to Stroudsburg. Beverly left Fort Wayne at 4 p.m. on Thursday, September 13, arriving in Stroudsburg about 3:30 in the morning after driving all night in rain. She slept a few hours then met the artist at 9 a.m. Friday morning. The two arrived in Fort Wayne at 7:45 p.m. Friday night. Beverly, having driven approximately 1300 miles in 27 hours, went home to sleep until noon the next day. The artist performed, as scheduled, for Opening Night.

Beverly changed jobs again in December 2004, working as a copy editor and proofreader for DRG in Berne, Indiana, while continuing to live in Fort Wayne.

A birdwatcher since the early 1990s, Beverly's interest in the hobby led to involvement in Soarin' Hawk Raptor Rehabilitation. Her activities began with helping at a couple of fundraising events and progressed to membership on the Board of Directors. She served two terms as Vice President and became President of the organization in 2005. She also edited the group's newsletter.

Submitted by Beverly Richardson.

WILLIAM & FAITH (CLARK) RICHARDSON

Bill and Faith (Clark) Richardson were married on June 30, 1940, at the First Methodist Church on Wayne Street in Fort Wayne. The ceremony was just supposed to be family, but something was going on downstairs and a bunch of people came up to watch. Faith about passed out, but Bill just thought they were supposed to be there. Bill bought a brand new suit for the occasion and Faith wore a long pink dress with a wedding coat over it. She purchased it in Fort Wayne for $12.50.

Wedding Picture,
William and Faith Lee Richardson, June 30, 1940

Bill and Faith started their Zanesville, Indiana, life when they purchased the John Smuts Grocery. That building now houses Customized Power Equipment and Zanesvile Antiques. The purchase was a business venture between Bill and his brother-in-law, Tom Bomar, on February 18, 1946. All went well, but the store was too small, so Tom sold his share to Bill and he named it Richardson's Grocery.

It was the first day of the new year of 1947 and housing was not to be had in Zanesville, so the family of four had to move into the back rooms of the store. They later moved to the house out back and, on July 4, 1955 (the hottest July 4th on record) they moved across the street to their new house.

William Lee Richardson (Bill) was born June 12, 1916, near Paris, Tennessee. He grew up in that rural community, graduated from high school and attended one year of college at Martin, Tennessee. At 19, he joined his brother-in-law, Lee Hill, driving a produce truck from Florida to Fort Wayne. In 1936, he moved to Fort Wayne where he met his future wife, Faith Clark. Faith was born June 5, 1920, in Dekalb County. At six months old, she moved to Fort Wayne where she grew up. In 1936 she met Bill.

Bill and Faith had two daughters; Katherine in 1942, and Marcia in 1944. Katherine attended East Union Center and International Business College, graduating from both with honors. She now lives and works in Fort Wayne. Marcia graduated from Lancaster High School and Huntington College. She taught two years, and, in June 1970, married John Wilson. They live near Minneapolis, Minnesota, and have one daughter, Christy, born in 1981.

Bill and Faith spent 25 years in the original store. Then, in 1970, they moved across the street when they purchased the Gaskill Grocery on the Allen County side. It was a larger building and they consolidated the stock.

In 1981 they sold the store and retired from the business. Faith has made many award winning quilts since her retirement, and Bill likes to spend time with friends at various restaurants, getting the news of the day and talking old times. He always gets home in time for the TV show, Judge Judy!! The Richardsons have always been a great asset to Zanesville. It's people like them that make little towns thrive!

Submitted by: Melba Edwards

ERWIN & ELEANOR (BULTEMEYER) RICHTER FAMILY

Erwin Ehregott Wilhelm Richter was born August 10, 1908, and raised in Wittenberg, Perry County, Missouri. He was the son of Joseph Wilhelm (born June 7, 1883) and Bertha Hulda Emilie (Vogel) Richter (born May 6, 1866). She was the daughter of William and Emma Hoehne Vogel from New Wells, Missouri.

The Richter family first came to Perry County in 1839, when Erwin's great grandparents, Johann Christian and Johanne Sophia Richter, came to America, so they might enjoy religious, political, and economic freedom. They sailed from Bremerhaven, Germany, on November 18, 1838, on the ship *Olbers*. They arrived in New Orleans on January 31, 1839 and in Perry County on April 26, 1839.

Johanne Sophia died shortly after arriving in America and Johann Christian Richter married Johanna Christiana Theilig. They had four children, including Ehregott Johann, born April 4, 1841.

Ehregott Richter married Elizabeth K Hartung on April 7, 1863. Elizabeth was born on June 16, 1844, the daughter of Michael and Sara Stephen Hartung from Cape Girardeau, Missouri. Ehregott and Elizabeth had ten children, all raised in Perry County. Their youngest was Joseph, Erwin's father.

Joseph Richter died November 13, 1921, in Perry County, so Bertha and her four boys came to Fort Wayne with Otto B. Lueders, a widower she had known from Perry County. Otto worked on the railroad in Fort Wayne. Their marriage in Fort Wayne was to take place on January 1, 1929, but a snowstorm prevented that, so they were married on January 2.

Erwin Richter had three younger brothers, Arnold Joseph, Enno Herbert and Melvin Adolph. The family had a strong Christian background in the Lutheran Church-Missouri Synod. Erwin's childhood church and school was St. Paul's Lutheran in Wittenberg, Missouri. He went to work at the General Electric Company. There he met Eleanor Ann Bultemeyer, daughter of Edward and Caroline (Wischmeyer) Bultemeyer. Eleanor was born in Adams County, Indiana, on January 12, 1909. She and her siblings, Corena, William, and Hilda were also Lutherans, belonging to St. John Lutheran Church at Bingen in Adams County.

Erwin and Eleanor Richter were married in Adams County on October 7, 1933. They started their married life in Fort Wayne, living on Paulding Road. Eventually, they lived on DeWald Street and belonged to Emmaus Lutheran Church.

After the birth of their first child, Robert Erwin, Eleanor became a full time mother. Robert was born July 28, 1938; his brother, Lynn David, was born August 13, 1941; and twin sisters, Jo Ann and Sue Ann, were born on December 29, 1945. The children were all schooled and confirmed at Emmaus Lutheran School. Lynn and the girls are still residents in Fort Wayne and Robert lives in Albion, Noble County, Indiana.

After Erwin Richter's retirement, he and Eleanor moved to Jackson, Cape Girardeau County, Missouri. They lived there until failing health forced them to move back to Fort Wayne. Erwin died December 18, 1993 and Eleanor died just seven weeks later on February 7, 1994. They are both buried in Lindenwood Cemetery, Fort Wayne.

Submitted by Karen Johnson

ROBERT ERWIN & JUDITH ELAINE (ORMSBY) RICHTER FAMILY

Robert (Bob) Erwin Richter was born July 28, 1938, in Fort Wayne, Allen County, Indiana to Erwin Wilhelm and Eleanor Ann (Bultemeyer) Richter. Bob has one brother, Lynn David, who has a son, Lynn David, Jr. Bob also has twin sisters, Jo Ann and Sue Ann.

Jo Ann married Michael John Sienk and they are the parents of three children: Mindy Sue Sienk Fleischer, Michael John Jr. and Matthew Allen. They have one grandchild.

Sue Ann married Stanley Joseph Stronczek. They also have three children: Douglas Edward, Amy Denise and Pamela Marie Stronczek Fitzsimmons. They have four grandchildren.

Judith (Judy) Elaine Ormsby was born January 10, 1941, to Argus Luster and Edna Chloe (Mann) Ormsby. Judy has two sisters: Catherine Elizabeth (Betty) Williams and Nancy Lou Henninger.

Bob attended elementary and middle school at Emmaus Lutheran School and then attended Central High School. After that, he was in the army reserve and served six months active duty and eight years reserve, receiving an honorable discharge. His interests are woodworking and art. He made a marble-topped table in high school, securing the marble from the steps of the old high school. He also made a pair of end tables; these items are still being used in his home today.

Judy was educated at Justin Study, South Wayne, and Harrison Hill schools, and graduated from South Side High School in 1959. Her interest is in history, and today she is an avid genealogist. Her family attended St. John Evangelical Lutheran Church where she was baptized in 1953, confirmed in 1955, and married.

Bob and Judy met through mutual friends while in high school and dated for two years, before being married at St. John's on August 22, 1959. Bob and Judy have three children: Karen Lynette Richter Johnson, born February 28, 1960; Kelly Renee Richter, born July 3, 1962; and Kevin Lee Richter, born June 26, 1963. They also have seven grandchildren. Zachary David Richter was born July 27, 1983, in Fort Wayne to Karen and died August 26, 1983 in Indianapolis, Indiana. Karen is married to David Gerard Johnson and lives in Churubusco, Indiana. They have two children: Cody David Johnson, born August 1, 1988; and Cassandra Lea Johnson, born February 8, 1996. Ashley Lynette Richter was born to Kelly on February 21, 1984, and they live in Albion, Indiana.

Kevin is married to Ruth Ann (Fike) Richter and they have three children: Katrina Ann Richter, born May 22, 1994; Spencer Lee Richter, born August 10, 1995; and Rachel Elaine Richter, born March 17, 1997.

Bob retired from C. F. Comma (formerly Dana-Weatherhead) as a forklift driver and Judy retired from Autojectors, Inc. as an electrical technician. Both retired in 2003. They are active members at St. John Lutheran Church in Kendallville, where all of the family worships together. Judy is a member of the Daughters of the American Revolution as a descendant of Thomas Archbold. Bob and Judy are still pursuing their genealogy research and both are volunteers at the Gene Stratton-Porter State Historic Site at Rome City.

God has richly blessed this family and they are very thankful and faithful to God, knowing that He will be at their sides through the rest of life's journey.

Robert Richter family, November 2004. Front: Karen, Cassandra, Judy, Rachel, Ruth Ann, Spencer. Middle: David, Robert, Kelly, Katrina. Back: Cody, Ashley, Kevin

(See related stories of Erwin Richter, Argus Ormsby, Catherine Williams, and Keith and Nancy Henninger)

Submitted by Robert and Judy Richter

RIDER FAMILY

WILLIAM & PAUL

William S. Rider was born December 16, 1898 near Scott, Ohio to Daniel S. Rider and Clara Schumaker Rider. After his schooling through the eighth grade, he began working with his father in his grocery store and working with the Huckster wagon that they would run out through the country around Scott. While working there he met Mable L. Cave, also from Scott, After a courtship of a short time they were married, and a couple of years later had a son, Paul W. Rider, January 22, 1920.

In 1924 William (Bill) and family moved from Ohio to Fort Wayne, Indiana to take a job with Hoosier Stores, a grocery at the corner of Pontiac and Gay Streets. It was a small grocery and was a few years later taken over by the Kroger Chain. He worked with them for twenty years, and in 1944 they decided to close their smaller stores and go into the super market operation. Bill was the manager of a Kroger at the corner of Hanna and Oxford when this all took place. They decided to close this store, and Bill decided to go into the business on his own.

Paul attended James H. Smart Elementary School. He attended South Side High School and graduated in 1938. He continued his education at International Business College. After college he worked in the sales department of S. F. Bowser Company, which made gasoline pumps.

In March 1942 he entered the Armed Forces and completed Basic Training at Fort Sill, Oklahoma. It was then on to The First Cavalry Division at Fort Bliss, Texas, where he was assigned to the 82nd Field Artillery Battalion, which was a horse mounted unit. July 4, 1943 the Division was sent to a staging area located at Camp Strathpine, near Brisbane, Australia. In February the Division was alerted and sent to the Admiralty Islands. October 1944 the unit was sent to the Phillipine Islands for the first battle at Leyte Island. January 1945 the unit was sent to Linguyan Gulf at Luzon Island. From this area he was assigned to a unit that was to make a dash to Manila to free 3700 Internees at the Santo Tomas University. The internees had been held under unsanitary conditions and starvation diets. He returned to the states and was discharged October 19, 1945.

Paul joined his father, William (Bill) in 1945 in the grocery business called Riders Market at the corner of Oxford and Hanna Streets. In 1959 the Rider Market was moved to the 6500 block of St. Joe Road. On September 30, 1971 Paul W. and his dad Bill ended their grocery careers.

October 19,1946 Paul W. and Dorotha Ross Newby were married. They had two children, Joyce Ann Newby Rider and Connie Sue Rider. Paul and Dorotha were married 51 years at her death in 1998. On February 18, 2000 he was joined in marriage to Patricia F. Wessels Ness from Cromwell, Indiana, who was born in Allen County on July1, 1931 to John Joseph and Anna Jane Wessels.

Paul has been affiliated with the Masonic order, Christ United and St. Joseph United Methodist Church, and St. Joseph Township Lions Club since November 1964. In 1970 the Lions club name was changed to Fort Wayne Shoaff Park Lions Club. He has been active as a Lion in many offices. He met his second wife while on a Lion/Vosh Eyeglass Mission. They have returned three times to work in Comayagua, Honduras representing their Club. Both are presently active in Operation Kidsight, screening the eyes of preschool children, and the Operation Friendship, hosting Lions from many countries in their home. Patricia is a standing member of Our Lady of Good Hope Catholic Church. She has seven children living in Noble and Whitley County.

Submitted by Patricia Rider

RIDLEY

EVERYDAY PEOPLE

DOING SPECIAL THINGS

The photograph of the Ridley family was taken in approximately 1892 in a wooded grove within Indiana. As shown on the photo itself, the photographer/artist was J.E. McLain. According to my deceased great aunt Tillie, this was a Christian retreat or evangelist prayer camp that was often attended and directed by the family. The individuals in the picture (right to left in the back row) are as follows: An unnamed white friend, Mrs. Lewis Artis, Daniel Ridley (my great grandfather), "Preacher" (a friend), Serlena Ridley (my great grandmother), Jimianna Ridley Bradshaw (my great aunt), Rev. Lewis Artis, Nellie Ridley (my great-great aunt & wife of great-great uncle William Ridley), blind Tommy Harrison (friend of the family). In the center row (left to right) are: Matilda Ridley Jones Durham (my great aunt Tillie), Anthony B. Ridley (my grandfather "grandpa Tony"). In the front/ bottom row (left to right) are the family pets: Zip (dog), Ketty (the cat in aunt Tillie's arms), Billy (goat), and Carlo (dog). A similar gathering in Ankey's Grove near Auburn, Indiana was documented in a 1907 Fort Wayne Sentinel news article.

The oral story states that three brothers, Daniel, John, and William Ridley, arrived in the Allen County area in 1866, coming from Nashville, Tennessee after John mustered out from military duty following the civil war. Uncle John Ridley arrived in Fort Wayne between 1870 and 1873. Submitter's great-grandfather Daniel Ridley and great-grandmother, Serlena Samuels Ridley joined John in 1881. The third brother, Reverend William Ridley, and his wife, Nellie Hanson Ridley, established residence shortly thereafter. Uncle William was the first minister of the Negro Baptist Church in Fort Wayne, which was established in May of 1890. Services were held at the W.C.T.U. hall on Harrison Street. Records indicate that the family spent a lot of time nurturing the growth of the Negro Baptist Church (now known as the Union Baptist Church) and the African Methodist Church (now known as Turner Chapel A.M.E. Church). Both Uncle John and great-grandpa Dan served as trustees at Turner Chapel where Aunt Tillie (Matilda Ridley Jones Durham) was baptized in 1883 in the old frame building, and, at age 14, directed the youth choir of the A.M.E. church. Daniel, Serlena and Aunt Jimianna Ridley Bradshaw (wife of Dr. Samuel Bradshaw) in particular, were committed servants and ardent workers towards the erection of Turner Chapel's new building, which was completed in 1917 at Francis and Wayne Streets (now the East Wayne Street Center).

Daniel was a hard working self employed whitewasher, as well as a barber by trade. Dan also had two other daughters, LeAnna Ridley Brown and Harriett Ridley, not shown in the photo. Serlena was born into slavery in April 3, 1850 in Nashville, Tennessee. She was later educated at Fisk University. Serlena used her training to educate and serve within the church.

Grandpa Tony (Anthony B. Ridley) was born in Fort Wayne on June 6, 1889. He was reared and educated in Fort Wayne. Tony worked in his father's trade as well as various other labor areas. He married Roberta F. Dean in Marion, Indiana, on November 13, 1912. They became the parents of Charlene Ridley Wise, Richard J. Ridley Sr. (submitter's father and one of the city's first African American mail carriers) Sarah L. Ridley, and Mildred V. Ridley Wallace.

This ancestry was the beginning of 135 years of Ridleys forging their way for everyday survival in Fort Wayne, Indiana. The family has continued to maintain commitments to church, education, civic duties and community involvement. Challenges to hold this African American family together have not evaded us, yet the underlying strength from the love of family has prevailed. Seven generations of Ridleys, have now inhabited Fort Wayne, Indiana. This is a glimpse of Fort Wayne Ridleys associated with Union Baptist Church, Turner Chapel A.M.E. Church, Redeemer Lutheran Church, Fort Wayne Community Schools, F.W. Police Dept., F.W. Fire Dept. (Richard J. Ridley, Jr.-the city's first African American appointed to the fire department), nursing, early childhood education, real estate, ministry, floor service, barbers, library services, and remarkable homemakers.

Roberta F. Ridley is a fourth generation family member, daughter of Richard J. Ridley Sr. and Oddie Essex Ridley. The union of Richard Sr. and Oddie reared eight other children: Juanita V. Ridley Wasson (Las Vegas, NV.), Richard J. Ridley Jr., Erma J. Essex Hogan, M. Laverne Ridley Hill (deceased), Lillian A. Ridley, Cynthia J. Ridley, Danielle D. Ridley, and James Irvin Ridley, Sr.

Submitted by Roberta Ridley

1892. Ridley Family. See the first paragraph of narrative for names of people and animals.

RICHARD J. RIDLEY, JR.

FORT WAYNE AND ALLEN COUNTY'S FIRST AFRICAN AMERICAN FIREFIGHTER

Richard J. Ridley, Jr. born in Fort Wayne November 8, 1937 is a third generation descendant of a Mississippi/Tennessee slave, who arrived in the city in 1880. Richard was the first African American to be appointed to the city's fire department. He must have had some sort of predetermined path of "first" events in his life, because he certainly has been on the frontline of "firsts" in this city. His story has been told in bits and pieces over the years, but always missing his inner feelings of the experience, that made history. He was a first grandson, first born son, first African American to play on the local "Pony League" baseball team in 1951, and more.This narrative will share a little more of his experience and the legacy.

At nine years old Richard was the only African American in attendance at Bethlehem Lutheran School, the only problem he recalls was a conflict he had with a Caucasian boy who transferred in from Florida. The boy was jealous because Richard was a better athlete, so he would pick and call names, until finally they fought. Richard won and the school put a stop to picking. Richard went on to attend Concordia Lutheran High School, where he was the first African American to attend four full years and graduate in 1956. Financially unable to attend college, Richard decided to join the U.S. Army. He served with the Army Airborne 101st Infantry Division until May of 1959. Military benefits allowed him to attend the International Business College in Fort Wayne, where he received his Computer Programming Certificate (again, the only minority in a class of 23). Ranking seventh in his class, he still was unable to secure employment in his field of training. Other classmates in the bottom of his class with no more experience and less understanding of the job received employment placement.

In the summer of 1961, he was approached by Corrine Brooks (with the Democratic Party)

Richard J. Ridley, Jr.

about working with the fire department. There were concerns about African American employment with the city. Since Richard had recently left the military, he did not find testing for firefighting to be difficult, and he was ready. There were a number of news articles written over the summer months that followed the testing, and in October of 1961 Richard made Allen County history.

Did he not know that he was making history?

"I was getting a job, a steady income. I had been struggling and all I wanted was to take care of my family. Had I known that I was making history, I would have taken notes along the way. My concerns were not racial. It was about survival. I have always believed that you treat a person the way you want to be treated and eventually they will respect you."

Richard entered his position with the fire department facing a lot of resentment and hostility, but he handled it like a man.

"I would consider the source, but if they put their hands on me, I stood my ground. I was not allowed to sleep in the engine houses overnight, and I was not allowed to fight fires. Two years later when Marvin Eady was hired on, we were able to do a rotation on the watchman position. We shared a special roll-a-way bed, because the other firefighters did not want to sleep in a bed that a black fireman had slept in. After about two years of that mess Fred Alban (a fellow firefighter) put an end to the bed problem, stating, "If he is good enough to be a fireman then, he's good enough to sleep behind."

"I was working in fire prevention until I fought my first fire, which was the Wolf & Dessauer Department Store fire downtown at Calhoun and Washington, in February of 1962. Fighting the fire was what I trained for and after jumping out of airplanes, then doing not much of anything; I was ready to fight that fire."

From 1961 through 1975 Richard and Marvin Eady were the only African Americans employed on the department in the county. He was a rookie for one year, became a first class firefighter, studied and achieved rank as a Master Firefighter. Then in 1974 Richard was promoted to Captain and appointed to Affirmative Action Officer and later chosen as Equal Employment Officer. His final promotion was that of District Chief. He worked hard and studied to advance and acceptance came over a period of time. In retrospect, "I have wondered if acceptance was a cover for rejection."

He is accredited with developing the Fort Wayne Firefighters Physical Fitness Program and a blueprint of that program is still maintained today. Richard was also a treasurer of the "Indiana Fire Instructors Association".

Richard retired in 1985.

The year of his retirement the Fort Wayne Fire Department had in its employ 28 African American men, three African American women, seven Hispanic men, and six men of other races. Currently they employ 27 African American men, four African American women, six Hispanic men, no Hispanic women, two Asian men, and 16 Caucasian women, in a total of 349 firefighters.

The legacy:

Richard credits his father for the drive behind his progress; "I was prepared for life by my father Richard J. Ridley, Sr. and ultimately able to handle the responsibilities of life."

His courage, self respect, and his concern for humanity provided opportunity for many who followed in his footsteps. Among those who have threaded this path are: James I. Ridley, Sr. (brother), Anthony J. Ridley (son), Richard J. Ridley, III (son), Marcus L. Ridley (nephew), Genori L. Hogan (nephew), and Kyle J. Hill (nephew). Richard beams at the list of family members that followed and other noble firefighters of Fort Wayne; but he is extremely proud of his younger brother James. James is the current president of the Fort Wayne Professional Firefighters Union Local 124, serving in his fourth consecutive term. Richard feels that James truly represents his fellow man and that's where he feels the most pride. "I wish I could have done as much."

Richard J. Ridley, Jr. is the son of Richard J. Ridley Sr. and Estella Collins; his stepmother is Oddie Essex Ridley. His siblings are: Juanita Ridley Wasson (Las Vegas, Nevada), Erma J. Essex Hogan, M. Laverne Ridley Hill (deceased), Roberta F. Ridley, Lillian A. Ridley, Cynthia J. Ridley, Danielle D. Ridley, James Irvin Ridley Sr. He is the father of Anthony J. Ridley, Richard J. Ridley III, Theresa M. Ridley Yarborough, Nicholas P. Ridley, and Randall C. Ridley. Richard also been blessed with grandchildren and great grandchildren to carry the torch.

Whether Mr. Ridley was accepted or rejected, he a beacon for the Ridley Family; and he definitely was and is a respected trail blazing African American MAN and FIREFIGHTER.

Submitted by Roberta F. Ridley (sister)

WILLIAM WALTER (DOC) RINEHART

William Walter "Doc" Rinehart was born December 22, 1897, the son of William and Theresa Rinehart. Doc's father was a blacksmith, and his shop was on the corner of Taylor and Broadway in Fort Wayne. When he was a young boy he helped in the shop and when he reached the age of about seventeen, he went to work with his father in the business learning the trade first hand. Doc met Florence Ann Scott, and they were married August 29, 1921.

Ready to go out on his own, in 1927 Doc put up his blacksmith sign over the door of a small black barn in Yoder, Indiana. When one entered the shop, the strong smell of horses would meet you. There would be hundreds of new and old horseshoes scattered over the tables and floor. Over the years the business changed from working with big workhorses to small saddle horses and ponies. Doc was proud of the fact that he was never kicked by a horse and could shoe all four feet of a horse in an hour if the horse behaved. He once said, "You need a strong back and a weak mind to do this job." Doc did a good job; he would guarantee if the horse's shoe didn't stay on, he would put another one on free. Very seldom did he have to replace a shoe.

William Walter (Doc) Rinehart's Blacksmith Shop in Yoder, Indiana.

In the back of the shop, against the wall on some shelves, one could find displays of other items that he made. There were candleholders made of horse shoes, some hooks used for gun racks, shoe scrappers, knives, hoes, and other useful gadgets. He also did welding and repair work, but shoeing was the main thing. Doc got his nickname because he could doctor up anything.

Doc Rinehart and Florence lived in Yoder all of their married life. To this union there were five children born: Elwood Dale (Evelyn) born June 8, 1923; Betty Jean (Daily) Sizemore born January 31, 1925; Donna Mae (Charles) Johnson born April 29, 1928; Carol Ann (Paul) Henry born April 19, 1936; and Norma Lou (Terry) Gronau, born April 14, 1938, with a second marriage to Bob Hughes.

Florence died July 17, 1962, and Doc married Mildred Baumgardner on June 10, 1967. When Doc retired, he and Mildred would spend their winters in Florida. Doc died November 17, 1990; he and Florence are buried in Covington Memorial Gardens, Fort Wayne, Indiana. Mildred died April 12, 1985, and is buried with her first husband in Oaklawn Cemetery in Ossian, Indiana.

Submitted by Donna M. Johnson

JONAS A. RINGENBERG FAMILY

On February 26, 1894, Jonas A. Ringenberg (1894-1993) was born to Peter (1867-1950) and Anna Mary Gerig Ringenberg (1868-1944) on a farm south of Harlan, Indiana. Jonas' grandfather, Peter (1839-1925), and his father, Peter (1867-1950) had come to America from Leissigen, Bern Canton, Switzerland, in 1871, when little Peter was just three years old. First they settled in the Orville-Massilon area of Ohio, but moved to Indiana in 1886.

Jonas was one of eight children. His parents were charter members of the Grabill Missionary Church in Grabill, Indiana. The family eventually moved to Leo, Indiana, where in 1913, Jonas graduated with the first class to graduate from Leo High School. He earned his teaching certificate from Indiana University and taught from 1913-1914 at the Thomas Grade School, a one-room school between Leo and Cedarville.

In 1914 the family, along with six other families from the Leo area, moved to North Dakota to homestead. While there, Jonas married Ada Ellen Witmer (1896-1957) on July 8, 1915. To this union were born Morris, Norman, Jesse, Lois, Faythe, and Ruth.

Jonas served as pastor in several churches in North Dakota. In 1925 he was asked to return to Indiana to pastor the Grabill Missionary Church. In 1935 the family moved to Ohio to pastor the Missionary Church in Archbold. Jonas wrote several books and served as editor of The Missionary Worker. He also served as president of the Missionary Church Association, interim president of Fort Wayne Bible Institute, a missionary in Kingston, Jamaica, and pastor of several churches. Fort Wayne Bible College awarded him an honorary Doctor of Divinity Degree in 1980.

Morris Ringenberg, Jaala Wright, J. A. Ringenberg, and Marsha Wright -- four generations 1986

In 1958 Jonas married Edna Pape (1907-1984), a former schoolteacher and missionary to Africa. He continued to write, preach, and minister to people well into his 90s.

Upon his death, on October 26, 1993, he was just four months short of his one-hundredth birthday. His funeral service was held at the Grabill Missionary Church, his home church where he had been pastor for ten years.

Submitted by Lois Laymon

MORRIS J. RINGENBERG FAMILY

On October 10, 1916, Morris J. Ringenberg was born in Brinsmade, North Dakota, to Jonas A. Ringenberg (1894-1993) and Ada Ellen Witmer (1896-1957), the first of six children. Six families from Grabill, Indiana, had moved to North Dakota to homestead. Morris lived his first nine years in North Dakota and Nebraska.

In 1925 the family moved back to Grabill where his father served as pastor of the Grabill Missionary Church. Morris attended grades five through seven in a one-room school above a store in Grabill. During grades eight through twelve at Leo High School, he played trumpet in the school band and sang in a men's quartet that became so popular they sang for radio programs and won a national contest. He was active at Grabill Missionary Church as a soloist and youth chorister. After graduation from high school, he delivered fuel in the Grabill area for the Standard Oil Company.

In 1939 his number was called by the selective service, and he reported for boot camp at Camp Shelby, Mississippi. While there, he was recruited to play in the army band. After the bombing of Pearl Harbor, he was stationed in the South Pacific on New Caledonia, was in the battle of the Coral Sea, and was in the Battle of the Bulge as an intelligence officer, where he earned a purple heart. After the war he returned to Grabill, where he started his life-long career with Grabill Bank.

Morris J. Ringenberg family: Michael, Marsha, Margaret, and Morris

Margaret Jane Ray was born in Fort Wayne to Albert Breton Ray (1894) and Sarah Shalatti Ford ("Lottie") on June 17, 1921. The Ray family lived in Fort Wayne until 1928, when they moved to a farm near Hoagland. After graduation Margaret worked at General Electric in Fort Wayne. She earned her private pilot rating in 1942 and was called to be a Women's Air Force Service pilot in 1943. In 1944 she returned to Fort Wayne.

Morris and Margaret met at First Missionary Church and were married on October 19, 1946. They lived in Grabill, where they were active in Grabill Missionary Church - Morris as song leader, treasurer, and choir member, and Margaret started a nursery. They had two children, Marsha Jane (1947) and Michael J. (1953).

Upon Marsha's graduation from Fort Wayne Bible College in 1970, she became a music teacher for Fort Wayne Community Schools and directed the choir at Grabill Missionary Church. In 1972 she married Stephen Harlan Wright (1948). In 1975 Marsha accepted a staff position at Grabill Missionary Church where she continues as Pastor of Worship Ministries. Stephen and Marsha have five children: Jonathan (1975), Joseph (1977), Joshua (1979), Jairus (1980), and Jaala (1983).

In 1993, Marsha started a senior adult choir called Senior Saints. Morris sang in this choir with his quartet friend from high school, Jess Gerig, whom he had sung next to for over 60 years. Morris' final concert with the Senior Saints was just three days before his passing on October 1, 2003.

Submitted by Margaret Ringenberg

BRIAN & PATTI ROBB

Brian D. Robb is the son of Robert and Phyllis Robb of Fort Wayne. His sister is Shawna (Ray) Niblick. Both have family histories in this section. Brian was raised in Fort Wayne and attended Huntertown School and Carroll High School. He married first, Misti Goller, of Fort Wayne and had two daughters, Randi (born 1989), and Candice (born 1990). Misti had a daughter, Mandi, born 1987. Brian then married Patricia Ann Hess Pinkerton of Huntington. She was previously married to Mark E. Pinkerton, and they had two sons, Adam K. Pinkerton (born 1985), and Cory J. Pinkerton (born 1988) of Huntington.

Brian & Patti Robb

Patti's father was Robert Hess, born in Richlands, Virginia. When he was about thirteen years old, his father died in a mining accident. His mother died in childbirth when his sister, Francis was born. She survived and was last known to live in Virginia Beach. Robert moved to Indiana around 1948. Patti's mother was Della "Maude" Hess of Richlands, Virginia. Maude first married James Williams and their children were Connie and Dianna (deceased 1993). She came to Indiana in 1950 and married Robert; their children were Robert (now in Alexandria, Indiana), Ricki (Greenville, Ohio), Micki (Berne, Indiana), Kay (died 1960), and Patricia. The family moved to Huntington in 1969. Both Maude and Robert are deceased.

Brian and Patti are both employed by Belmont Liquors. They are excellent cooks. Brian's home-made rolls are much anticipated at holiday dinners, as are Patti's southern dishes. Brian enjoys collecting and reading comics and gardening, and Patti enjoys flower arranging, gardening, and oil painting. They live on St. Mary's Avenue with their kitties, and their children visit often.

Submitted by Brian and Patti Robb

ROBERT F. ROBB FAMILY

Robert Francis (Bob) Robb, son of Frank and Marguerite Robb, was born in Toledo, Ohio. Frank Robb was the grandson of James and Catherine, Irish immigrants from Armagh, who settled in the Mitchell, Ontario, Canada area around 1840. Frank's father, Anthony, moved to Toledo around the turn of that century. Marguerite was the daughter of John C.T. and Margaret Gerard of Decatur, Indiana. He was a German immigrant, and she was second generation German. The family moved to Toledo around 1920.

Bob has two brothers, John of Aladdin, Wyoming, and Paul, a Jesuit priest living at Loyola University, Chicago, Illinois. His father was employed by Sinclair Oil Company. In the 1930s the family moved to Vincennes, Indiana, where the boys have many pleasant childhood memories. During their high school years, the family moved to Fort Wayne where Bob graduated from Central Catholic High School.

After high school he attended International Business College until the outbreak of the Korean War when he enlisted in the Navy. He spent two and one-half years of that enlistment on a destroyer escort, the Naifeh, DE352, with the Pacific Fleet, making three tours to Korea. He left the Navy with the rank of Personnelman 2nd Class. Bob and Phyllis attend many of the DESA reunions.

After leaving the Navy he attended Indiana University as an undergraduate, and then the School of Optometry where he graduated in 1960. He opened his own practice in the north

Bob and Phyllis Robb

part of Fort Wayne where he practiced for forty years. He held a number of offices in his professional organizations including President of the Northeast Society, and Trustee of the Indiana Optometric Association.

In 1965 he married Phyllis Musgrave of Findlay, Ohio, the daughter of Francis H. and Martha (Trout) Musgrave. Phyllis moved to Fort Wayne after high school to attend International Business College, and later graduated from St. Mary of the Woods College. She worked in management positions for a number of nonprofits including the National Multiple Sclerosis Society, Park Center, and Fort Wayne Medical Society. Phyllis is the editor of Volume II, this publication.

Phyllis' family settled in Hancock County, Ohio, in the 1830s; her genealogy research has found many of her lines in the colonies prior to the American Revolution. Her father's side was mostly English and Irish, and her mother's side was mostly German. She is a member of the Daughters of the American Revolution. Phyllis had two sisters and a brother. Sharon died at the age of twenty-one in Findlay; Sandra lives in Tucson, Arizona, and Dallas, who lived in Independence, Missouri, is deceased.

Their children are Shawna (Ray) Niblick, and Brian (Patti) Robb, both of Fort Wayne, five grandchildren, and three step-grandchildren, and one great-grandchild.

Bob and Phyllis owned property at Ball Lake in Steuben County near Hamilton for many years. In 1996 they donated part of their land to Acres Land Trust to create Robb Hidden Canyon Nature Preserve which has a State of Indiana nature preserve designation.

Submitted by Phyllis Robb

ROBERSON (ROBINSON) FAMILY

Littleberry "Gentleman" Robinson was born about 1715 at Brunswick, Virginia. He married Susannah Rottenberry (born September of 1719) in September of 1739 at Sussex County, Virginia. She died in 1767, and he died about 1792. Littleberry "Gentleman" Robinson was a Captain in the Revolutionary War. Littleberry and Susannah's son was James Robinson, born in 1740 at Brunswick County, Virginia, and married to Winnifred Fox (born about 1743) on February 27, 1781 at Brunswick County, Virginia. He died in 1801, she died September 13, 1823. James was also a Captain in the Revolutionary War.

James and Winnifred's son was Danus (or Darius) Robinson. He was born about 1785 at Greensville County, Virginia. He and Sarah "Sally" Jeffries (born between 1780 and1790) had a common law marriage. She was the daughter of Andrew Jeffries and Mary Dole. Darius was in the War of 1812. He died in August of 1838 at Greensville County, Virginia.

Ben and Roy Roberson with their mother, Marveta Gayle (White, Roberson) Brindle

Darius and Sally's son, Augustus Jeffries, was born in 1818 at Greensville County, Virginia. In 1843, Augustus petitioned the Greene County, Ohio, court to change his name to Augustus Wych Robinson. The petition was filed on May 8, 1843 and recorded May 29, 1843. He married Elizabeth Jane Iliff, (born 1822), on January 28, 1847, at Greene County, Ohio. Augustus died in 1887 at Allen County, Indiana. Elizabeth died in 1892 at Eel River, Allen County, Indiana. They appeared on Allen County, Indiana, census in 1850. In the time period between the 1850 and 1860 census, this family's name, for unknown reasons, became Roberson.

Augustus and Elizabeth's son, David A. Roberson, Sr. was born March 14, 1854 in Allen County, Indiana. He married Hannah E. Koogler or Kugler, born June 15, 1854, in Greene County, Ohio, on May 30, 1878. Hannah died March 31, 1930, at Eel River Township, Allen County, Indiana. David died July 12, 1941, at Eel River Township.

David, Sr. and Hannah's son, David Anderson Roberson, Jr., was born September 30, 1885, at Eel River Township, Allen County, Indiana, and married Hannah Emily Coffelt, (born April 22, 1883 in Van Wert, Ohio) on December 22, 1908 near Dayton, Ohio. Hannah E. died June 3, 1956, and David Jr. died August 9, 1970, both at Eel River Township.

David, Jr. and Hannah Emily's son, Jesse H. Roberson, was born January 11, 1914, at Churubusco, Allen County, Indiana. Jesse served in WW II. He married Martha E. Teague, (born April 3, 1926, at Paynes, near Bimble, Knox County, Kentucky), on September 7, 1943 at Churubusco. Martha died February 1, 2003 at Churubusco. Jesse is a retired farmer.

Back row, L to R: Jennifer Robin (Shaw) Roberson and Roy Roberson. Front row, L to R: Austin, Caleigh, and Brooke

Ben and Roy, and Roy's wife, Jennifer, with their grandfather, Jesse Roberson, at his 90th birthday party, January 11, 2004

Jesse and Martha's son, Leslie D. Roberson, was born October 23, 1947, at Wolf Lake, Indiana. He served in the USAF. He married Marveta Gayle White, (born September 20, 1951, Vici, Dewey County, Oklahoma), on January 7, 1970 at Wichita Falls, Wichita County, Texas. Leslie and Marveta Gayle had two sons, Roy D. Roberson, born April 5, 1972, and Ben J. Roberson, born September 3, 1974, both in Fort Wayne, Indiana. Roy served in the US Navy, and Ben served in the USAF. Roy married Jennifer Robin Shaw, (born December 23, 1973) on May 18, 1994 at Virginia Beach, Norfolk, Virginia. Roy and Jennifer's children, born in Fort Wayne, Indiana, are Brooke K. Roberson, born February 19, 1992, Austin P. D. Roberson, born September 3, 1993, and Caleigh Brynn Roberson, born March 30, 2000. Ben married Anastasia "Stacie" Marie Wagner (born October 12, 1982) on May 21, 2005 at Lookout Mountain Park, Golden, Colorado. Ben and Stacie have a daughter, Rozilynn Grace, born November 11, 2005, in Wheat Ridge, Jefferson County, Colorado.

Submitted by Marveta Gayle Brindle

CAROLYN EASTES ROBERTS FAMILY

Chester Raymond Eastes was born September 1901 in Markle, Indiana. He married Hazel Bell Shaffer who was born in Ohio County in 1920. They moved to Roanoke, Indiana, and, on July 18, 1920, William Burr Eastes was born. While they lived in Roanoke, Charles Robert, Chester Raymond Jr., and Rosa Juanita Ann also were born. They moved to Allen County where Rebecca Sue (deceased) and David Lee were born.

The submitter's father, William Burr Eastes, married Letha Irene Shepherd who was born in Saskatchewan, Canada on July 26, 1922. The marriage took place on November 1, 1941. William adopted Letha's daughter, Dorothy Louise, who was born October 15, 1938. Their daughter, Carolyn Irene, was born December 24, 1942 followed by William Charles on March 18, 1946 and Norma Jean on August 20, 1948.

On April 7, 1962, Carolyn married Edwin De Wayne Roberts who was born October 4, 1940 in Pendleton, Indiana. He is the son of Kenneth G. and Rose Ann Indrecc Roberts. Their daughter,

Tanya Sue, born 1962, graduated from Indiana University with a degree in Medical records. She married Henry David Freon on November 27, 1982. He was born September 24, 1962, and does Community Living Management. They have a daughter, Amber Nicole, born February 26, 1983. She graduated from Indiana University with a degree in Mathematics. She married Vincent Konwinski on August 13, 2005. Vincent has a degree in Architecture from Indiana University. A second daughter, Ashley Ann was born March 12, 1986 and attends Indiana University. Andrea Sue was born August 23, 1989 and attends Snider High School. Their son, Darren De Wayne died as an infant on October 24, 1968. Katina Susan was born December 5, 1972 and graduated with a Masters in Occupational Therapy from University of Indianapolis. She is self employed and works with children from infancy to three years of age. She married Mark Petroff on July 5, 1998. He was born May 15, 1973 and is a graduate of Indiana University with a BA in Comparative Literature. He earned a second degree at Indiana Wesleyan in Information Systems.

Carolyn graduated from Purdue School of Nursing as a Registered Nurse and worked 26 years at Parkview Hospital. Ed worked 40 years at Allen Dairy (now Prairie Dairy) as a driver. They share the year between St. Augustine, Florida, where they are energized by their beach home and Allen county which is "HOME" for them during the summer and holiday seasons.

Submitted by Carolyn and Ed Roberts

AMASA S. ROBINSON FAMILY

In 1836 Jonathan Robinson, a native of Ohio, moved into Indiana and settled in Madison Township. He and his wife, Sarah, transformed the wilderness into a successful farm and lived there until their deaths. One of ten children born to Jonathan and Sarah was Edith Koehlinger's grandfather, Amasa S. Robinson, born on January 7, 1849. Amasa attended the high school nearest to his home and, when 16 years old, went to work as a teacher in the local schools. He spent several years in that profession teaching in many of the one room schoolhouses in the area.

In 1881 he married Lillie Peckham and in 1900 they began the ice cream business in Monroeville. Edith remembers that in the winter blocks of ice were cut from the pond behind the Robinson home and stored in a block building. The pond was also open to skaters in the winter months. The ice house is gone, but the original ice cream factory is still standing.

Amasa was active in local politics and served Monroe Township for 11 years as the Assessor and five years as the Trustee. In 1915 he was appointed to the office of Postmaster in Monroeville. While he was Trustee, a large stone with his name and the year he was Trustee was made a part of the District No.1 Schoolhouse, called the Stephenson Schoolhouse. Edith's daughter, Linda, married the nephew of Homer Stephenson whose farm was home to the one room schoolhouse built in 1896. The Homer Stephensons gave the stone to Jack and Linda since Amasa was Linda's great grandfather. It is now in a garden they refer to as Robinson Park.

Seven children were born to Amasa and Lillie, one being Edith's mother, Ada, who married J. Earl Marquardt. Edith's aunt, Cara Robinson, became a school teacher and her uncles, Ralph and Harry Robinson, opened the first Harley Davidson Motorcycle business in Monroeville. In 1914 a cycle was sold to a local resident. Today that cycle is being restored by a relative of the original owner. Harry Robinson followed in his father's footsteps by going on to manage the Pioneer Ice Cream Factory in Fort Wayne. Ralph Robinson went on to serve the postal system as a railway clerk.

In later years Amasa and Lillie moved to a home on Monroe Street in Monroeville next to Lloyd Douglas' Mother. Lloyd Douglas was the well-known author and minister who once lived in the area. Edith remembers enjoying her visits with Mrs. Douglas because she had many interesting stories to tell. Lloyd Douglas had a toilet installed in his mother's house, but she promptly had it removed because she didn't think she needed it.

Edith's grandmother, Lillie, lived to be 96 years of age. Her great grandmother, Rebecca Peckham, lived to be 99, her Aunt Cara lived to be 99, and Edith will be 94 on her next birthday. She is still active and is an important part of her daughter and son-in-law's business, Cozme International.

Submitted by Linda Stephenson about the family of Edith Koehlinger

Amasa Robinson Family c. 1908, Schoolhouse stone, 2005

ELIJAH ROBINSON

Immigrant from Massachusetts, Progenitor of a ROBINSON Family in Allen County: Fort Wayne and Eel River and Lake Townships

Elijah Robinson was a lineal descendent of William Robinson of Dorchester, Massachusetts, who immigrated to America from St. Dunstans, Canterbury, England in 1637 after marrying Margaret Beech at age 21. Elijah Robinson was born September 16, 1807 in Holyoke, Massachusetts, and immigrated from Whateley, Massachusett, in 1835 or 1836 to Allen County, Indiana. Elijah Robinson's migration course took the following route, as described by Jay Lamont Robinson, family genealogist: "He came Erie Canal to Buffalo and Stage Coach the rest of the way, taking four weeks to make the trip." For most making this trek, the goal was fresh land in the "Ohio Country," first to be opened up after the Revolutionary War.

In 1836 he received a letter from his mother back east which starts off as follows:

"Whateley July 30, 1836 Dear Son

We received your letter dated Ohio. and your letter July 27 bearing date Indiana July 11. I have looked at it once and again it seems almost impossible that you are at such a vast distance from us, and that we can almost know what you are about; or that my letter will ever reach you in your lonely situation and be perused by one that is Eight hundred miles from me, yet I hope it will and find you enjoying good health and a contented mind I was very sorry you had such hard luck as to be detained by the break in the canal; we were all sorry you had not waited another week. I thought much of you and I should been glad to had you here but it could not be . . ." She brings him up-to-date on the affairs of all family members; informs him on how the crops in Massachusetts are doing; and indicates the high cost of farm labor: $1.25/1.50 per day, or $25 per month. Then, she gives him advice on choosing a marriage partner: *"You say you are not married yet. I hope you never will be; unless you can be actuated by better motives than George Fairfield was, that married Lydia Brown of Conway. Perhaps you recollect when they were married, it was in April. He has quit some time ago. Before they were married he owned* [up] *to her that he was in debt five hundred Dollars. She unbeknown to him deeded all her property to her Mother. Some one was kind enough to let him into the secret and it made a real fuss. I tell you he has gone off and it is doubtful whether he ever returns. It was her property he was after, not her person. My son if ever you settle, I advise you to let property bear no sway. Select one that will smooth the rough path which you in your Journey of life will have to pass through, none are without disappointments and trials. If we have a companion we want one that will participate in our sorrows as well as our joys and be a help meet in time of trouble. I have too good an opinion of you to think you would away by every foolish fancy: get one of good judgement, understanding, prudent and industrious and you will half forget you was in the wilderness. . . .*" She finishes her part of the letter by saying: "*I fear you will be tired of reading my long letter. The Thought has occurred since I commenced writing that this may be my last letter, but I conclude you have the same sun to shine on you there as here and the same God to guide and protect you and may he prosper all your undertakings.*

This from your Mother Elijah Robinson Nancy Wait"

Following the Mother's portion of the letter, his three step-sisters each write a few lines, commenting on his un-married state, and asking for samples of his "gooseberries, Plumbs, &C." Comments from the person who re-copied the letter in longhand, Miss Nellie Robinson, granddaughter of the recipient, who lived at 168 (later 1014) Huffman Boulevard with her father, Elijah Jr., her mother, Della (Jones) Robinson, and three sisters:

"This finished the above letter. Said letter was written on one sheet of paper 13 inches by 16 inches and is written with ink and is very visible and easy to read and is a completely beautiful

hand writing although some excuse their writing. The paper is folded in the center and written on three sides and the fourth was preserved for the address of sender and the one to receive it. The letter was folded to resemble an envelope although they used no envelopes in those days. There were no postage stamps but instead the Government sealed the letters with a government seal. My father (no. 2) (Elijah Robinson, Jr.) *said the cost of sending a letter from Mass. to Elijah Robinson (no. 1)* [Elijah Robinson Sr.] *of Allen County Indiana was 25 cts and money was a very big task to obtain in the early days of this U. S. This letter was carried by stagecoach. The address as it appears:"*

West Whately Mafs 25 August 3 Ages Mr. Elijah Robinson, Ft. Wayne, Allen County, Indiana

No copies of letters from Elijah Robinson Sr. back to Massachusetts have yet been located.

In the book *History of the Upper Mmmee Valley*, Vol. I, by Col. Robert S. Robertson and published by Brant & Fuller in 1889, Elijah Robinson was mentioned on page 302 as an early teacher in Eel River Township. Perhaps he taught first in order to make money to buy farmland, or perhaps he did them together, one in summer, one in winter.

On March 7, 1838 he did finally marry, to Sarah Chase, daughter of Stephen Chase and Hannah Leonard. In the book *The Richmond Family* by Joshua Bailey Richmond, 1897, Hannah Leonard is listed as a child of Mollie Richmond and Nehemiah Leonard of Williamsburg and Savoy, Massachusetts, and the inscription opposite Hannah's name says "married and went West." The person she had married was Stephen Chase (1784-1839). Stephen and Hannah (Leonard) Chase went west from Massachusetts into New York State, where Sarah Chase was born in Rochester, Monroe County, New York. The family then traveled to Livonia Township, Wayne County, Michigan. In 1832 the Chases, along with their [New York?] friends the John Hathaway Family, homesteaded adjacent parcels of land near each other in Eel River Township, Allen County. In the book of maps *Original Land Entries of Allen County, Indiana* c.1981 by Stuart Harter, Stephen Chase and John Hathaway are shown as initial buyers of land next to each other in Sections 22, 27, and 36, Eel River Township. In Section 22, Stephen Chase owned the E 1/2 of the SW 1/4 (80 acres). Immediately north of that piece of land was 40 acres owned by a John Chapman, purchased 1838. John Chapman became known as "Johnny Appleseed." Later, the Chapman property was owned by members of the Robinson family before passing into the hands of the current owners. (See page 6 of the *Journal Gazette* for May 21, 1996). It was after the Chases and Hathaways settled in Eel River Township that Elijah Robinson Sr. met Sarah Chase, and they were married here in Allen County on March 7, 1838.

Elijah and Sarah Robinson founded a family of nine children, including:

Nancy Robinson, born on August 29, 1838; died January 20, 1907; she married Ira Wainwright on October 13, 1860; they moved to Newago County, Michigan, and raised a large family.

Hannah Robinson was born August 29, 1840, and died 0ctober 6, 1853.

George Robinson was born September 25, 1842 and died April 6, 1916; he married Eliza Wicker in Fort Wayne on April 20, 1866. They remained in Eel River Township.

William Henry Robinson was born November 3, 1844, and died January 20, 1908. He married Alice Louise Pratt; they remained in Allen County and raised a large family. Many of his descendents are living in Fort Wayne today (2005).

Stephen Robinson was born September 10, 1847, and died February 7, 1880. He married Rose Ann Comer on March 24, 1872. They had two children. Stephen died in 1880, at about age 33, prior to his mother's decease.

Alonzo Robinson was born May 26, 1850, and died September 28, 1885. He was blinded, perhaps in a farm accident.

Levi Chase Robinson was born June 9, 1853, and died January 20, 1898. He married Isabelle Disler on June 10, 1883. They had a farm in Lake Township near Lake Everett. Levi Chase, named after his mother's brother, died in 1898, and the farm had to be sold. Isabelle administered the estate and then moved to a farm in Helmer, Indiana. The four children who went with her were: Jay LaMont Robinson, born in 1885, who became a telegrapher for the railroad and a Station Master in Wayland and Plainwell, Michigan, and a genealogist, using F. I. A. G.; Clarence Levi Robinson, born in 1886, a teacher, Clerk of Courts, Methodist Minister, and insurance agent. With wife Agnes (Minich) Robinson, he raised five children in Lagrange County: Maynard, Helen, Marjorie, Katherine, Vera Belle. Ethel Blanche Robinson, born in 1888, married Daniel Brumbaugh of LaGrange. Elam Edwin Robinson, born 1890, a telegrapher for the railroad in San Jose, California, married Zu1a Hatley, and they had a son, Raymond E. After removing to LaGrange County, the widow, Isabelle Robinson, married James Woodworth, and two additional children were born: Ruby Belle (Woodworth) Morrison, and Harry T. Woodworth. Ruby's daughter, Jean (Morrison) Hart and family live in Sturgis, Michigan, today.

James Nelson Robinson was born December 21, 1855; he was married first to Rosella Dice, and then to Emma (Haverstick) Parks. He had eight children. In December of 1919, when his half-brother Scott died, Nelson was living in Eel River Township.

Elijah Robinson, Jr., was born June 26, l859, and died June 30, 1929; he married on March 3, 188l to Della Jones. Elijah, Jr., was a "commercial traveler" for a feed company. He bought a house in Fort Wayne before 1891 at 168 (later l014) Huffman Street where three generations of his family lived and died, including his mother, Sarah. He and wife Della (Jones) Robinson had four daughters live to adulthood. The first three married and moved out of state. The fourth never married, and was known as Miss Nellie Robinson. She kept the family records, on which this piece is partially based. She was last owner of the house at 1014 Huffman.

After Elijah, Sr., died on October 4, 1859, Sara married Solomon Housholder. They had one son, Francis Scott Housholder, born January 8, 1863, and died December 10, 1919. He married, first, Anna Fosnaught, and second, Luella Stryker Malachi. After Solomon was gone, Sarah took back the name Robinson, and Scott followed suit. Scott was a foreman at the Chevron Refinery in Lima, Ohio.

When Elijah, Sr., died, his obituary in *Dawson's Fort Wayne Weekly Times* of October 12, 1859 stated: DlED-At his residence in Eel River Twp., Allen Co., Ind. on the 4th inst., of Flux, Mr. Elijah Robinson, in the 53rd year of his age. He left a wife and 8 children. *He was an old settler in that place.* [emp.added]

When Sarah died, her obituary appeared in the *Fort Wayne Sentinel* of Tuesday, January 13, 1891: [in part] THE FINAL REWARD - Mrs. Sarah Robinson called Home in Her Old age-The Deaths - *The deceased was beloved for her noble character and kind disposition, and her demise will recall many of her good deeds in a long and eventful life.*

Submitted by James A. Robinson

RAYMOND ROBINSON

Raymond Earl Robinson (birth certificate Charles Raymond) was born on what he was told was a cold day, March 15, 1914 on a farm between Churubusco and Huntertown. His parents were Marie Louise (Feuerstack of Jackson, Tennessee) and Charles William Robinson (born August 7,1883). He was the son of William Henry Robinson (born November 3, 1844, died January 23, 1908), Allen County, son of Elijah Robinson (born September 16 1807, died March 7, 1838) of Holyoke, Massachusetts. The Robinson's family farm was on Johnson Road in northwest Allen County until it was sold during the depression.

Ray's Plane

Raymond went to grade school at Green Center School, and then Huntertown High school, where he graduated in 1933. The story he often told when he grew up was about when he broke his arm when he was 12 years old. He was living with Uncle Wes, riding Carl Roberson's horse and fell, breaking his left arm. He had to eventually be taken to Lutheran Hospital and have the arm rebroken and treated for gangrene.

After graduating high school in the middle of the depression, he did what many did, joining the Federal government's works programs, the Civilian Conservation Corps, at Fort Knox Kentucky. He worked then in Jasper, Indiana building bridges and roads in park lands. It was about 1935, it is said, that he rejoined father Charles, driving to Florida in an old Model T. He was living out of the car, near Punta Gorda, fishing off the pier.

In 1937, at the age of 23, Ray moved back to Fort Wayne getting a job at Baer Field Airport (now called Smith Field). He lived in a room on a farm on Solomon Road. His jobs at the airport included driving a Caterpillar tractor, mowing grass, shoveling coal and fueling planes. He eventually worked his way up to become a radio range operator and Control Tower Operator. He married Elizabeth Ginther (born February 24, 1923) who lived on Lima Road near Ludwig, on February 24, 1940.

On March 1941 he was accepted as a Junior Airway Traffic Controller at the Chicago Center. Then he was transferred to Birmingham Alabama, then Savannah Georgia Control Tower. Shortly after that, it was back to Birmingham as Chief Controller.

Another transfer happened in April 1943 to West Palm Beach Tower in Florida where he was Chief Controller. Ray explained that the many promotions was the governments way of opening the many now Federally run airports that were being taken over from the cities as part of the war effort. Raymond was promoted to Atlanta Regional Office as Regional Traffic Control Inspector. In April 1947, Ray requested to be transferred to the newly commissioned Fort Wayne Tower at Baer Field south of town. He remained Chief until he retired due to health concerns in 1973.

Raymond and Elizabeth had ten children: Rose, David, Diane, Gary, Steve, Bruce, Carol, Dennis, Patricia and Janet. Raymond died on June 20, 1996.

Submitted by Dennis Robinson

HAROLD ROBISON FAMILY

In 1865, John R. and Sarah N. (Kerr) Robison moved their family from Crawford County, Ohio to Adams County, Indiana. It was there on June 17, 1872 that their son Orrin Melville Robison was born.

On October 29, 1899, Orrin Robison married Daisy Mae Teeter, daughter of John Fremont and Martha Ann (Baker) Teeter. Daisy was born on May 28, 1881 in Adams County. After residing there a few years, Orrin and Daisy Robison moved to Monroeville in 1909.

Orrin and Daisy had three children: Geraldine Marcella was born on April 10, 1905 in Decatur; Harold Deloss was born on October 15, 1910 in Monroeville; and Mildred Marcile was born on August 31, 1914 in Monroeville. Geraldine married Dewey Wayne Roth on January 24, 1927; they had a son, Robert, and a daughter, Sharon; Marcile married Doyle Lhamon Gilbert on February 17, 1940; they had a daughter, Myra Kay; and the subject of this sketch, Harold Deloss Robison, was married on May 28, 1932 to Edythe Elaine Smith, daughter of Frederick Laurin and Ethel Mae (Corbin) Smith.

Harold and Elaine Robison both graduated from Monroeville High School, he in 1928 and she in 1931. After their marriage in 1932, they lived in various rented houses in Monroeville and Fort Wayne. Elaine kept an immaculate house wherever they lived, and Harold took what odd jobs were available during the Depression, primarily house painting. In 1943, they finally bought their one and only home at 106 Short Street in Monroeville. Here they raised their five ornery kids and made a comfortable home for fifty years.

After World War II, Harold became interested in the printing business and launched the Monroeville News in June of 1947, publishing and editing the news every week until economic pressures forced him to sell the paper in 1962. Throughout this period and beyond, however, he also operated the Robison Printing Company, a successful business and a fixture in Monroeville until ill health forced its closure in 1991.

Harold and Elaine welcomed their first child, Harold Stanley, into their home on January 14, 1933. He was followed by Gary Alan on April 29, 1936, Max Frederick on March 28, 1938, Mary Luanne on April 5, 1939, and Thomas Corbin on June 15, 1948.

Harold Stanley Robison married Shirley Lou Lake of New Haven on July 31, 1951. They had four children; Phillip Stanley, Geoffrey Lynn, Craig Alan, and Julie Ann. Gary Alan Robison married Jean Kathleen Hatfield on June 22, 1963. They had four daughters; Kathleen Kay, Carolyn Sue, Karen Marie, and Amy Lynn. Max Frederick Robison married Sandra Sue Schlatter on September 23, 1961. They had two children; Timothy Alan and Jill Diane. Mary Luanne Robison married Maurice Jerome Hoffman on April 4, 1959. They had four children; Kimberly Ann, Scott Eugene, Stephen Thomas, and Michael Jerome. Thomas Corbin Robison married Carol Jean Bowman on August 3, 1974. They had two daughters, Amanda Marie and Mary Melissa.

Submitted by Tom Robinson

DANIEL A. ROBY FAMILY

Daniel A. Roby, born in Anderson, Indiana, on August 16, 1941, was one of two sons born to Virgil A. and Frances E. (Pouch) Roby. His older brother, Richard A. Roby, was born September 27, 1938, and lives with his wife, Mary Kay, in Anderson, Indiana. They have four sons: Brett, Brad (Bud), Barry, and Blake.

Daniel, Virgil, and Richard Roby

Daniel (Dan/Danny) Roby attended elementary school in Chesterfield, Indiana, and graduated from Anderson High School in 1959. He then graduated with honors from Indiana University in 1963 and from Indiana University School of Law in 1966, thereby becoming Chesterfield's first college graduate. He was admitted to practice on September 21, 1966, and taught Business Law at Indiana University in Bloomington for three semesters before moving with his wife Carolyn (Kerrie) to Fort Wayne in August of 1967 to take a position with a Fort Wayne law firm. He continued to teach Business Law part-time at IPFW for several years.

Dan and Kerrie, the daughter of Max and Ruth (Singleton) Eaton of Anderson, were married on June 14, 1964, and have one adopted daughter, Kerilynn, born in Fort Wayne on March 17, 1972.

Kerilynn (Keri) married Darren Minns on November 4, 1995, and they have one son, Connor Justin Minns, born April 11, 1996. Keri graduated from Carroll High School and from Indiana Wesleyan University. She works for a law firm and Darren is a UPS driver in Fort Wayne.

Following the dissolution of his marriage to Carolyn in 1996, Dan married the former Kathy Petrucelli of Huntington on December 4, 1998, and they continue to live and work in Fort Wayne, where Kathy is an aesthetician at her business called Skin Solutions.

Dan practiced law with the firm of Wyss, McCain, Mochamer, Roby, Ryan and Myers until 1983, when his partner, Thomas L. Ryan, became Circuit Court Judge of Allen County. At that same time, Dan joined G. Stanley Hood and formed Roby & Hood Law Firm, the first firm in Fort Wayne with practice limited to personal injury claims. They were later joined in business by Thomas A. Manges to form Roby Hood & Manges Law Firm.

Dan was active in the American Heart Association and served as its local President and also the Chairman of its Indiana Board of Directors. He was the moderator of Faith Baptist Church and served as lay minister to its Towne House Retirement Center. He was also actively involved in the Indiana Trial Lawyers Association (ITLA) and in teaching many seminars for ITLA and ICLEF. He was awarded ITLA's Trial Lawyer of the Year Award in 1986, served as its President in 1993, and was the recipient of its Lifetime Achievement Award in 2004. He is listed in *Best Lawyers in America* and *Who's Who in American Law.* He and his firm are listed in the *Bar Register of Preeminent Lawyers*. He was instrumental in drafting Indiana's mediation rules and has served as mediator in hundreds of civil disputes.

Dan possesses the family Bible of Joseph Matthias Pouch, born December 17, 1857. This Bible traces Dan's maternal lineage back to John Cake, born March 1, 1789, in County Johnson, Dorsetshire, England, and whose wife, Mary Elizabeth, was born May 16, 1785, in St. Peters Port Island of Guernsey.

Submitted by Daniel A. Roby

GERALD & SANDRA ARCHER ROBY FAMILY

Both Gerald Roby and Sandra Archer were born in Allen County in 1951. They met in 1969 and were married at Gethsemane Lutheran Church in Fort Wayne in 1973. Gerald is a graduate of North Side High School, where he played the violin in the orchestra, and Ivy Tech. He worked in the roofing industry for 25 years, but currently works for Young's Greenhouse and Flower Shop. Sandra graduated from South Side High School in 1969. She began working at the new G. C. Murphy variety store in Southtown Mall before it opened. She also worked at the Belmont Store in Washington Square before it closed. She now works for the Allen County Public Library.

Gerald Roby family 1998 clockwise: Gerald, Brian, Gretchen, Megan, Adam, Casey, and Sandy

Gerald and Sandra are in the process of raising five children: Brian, a Northrop High School graduate, married Trisha Ternet in 2003; Megan, a Valparaiso University graduate of 2002, married Scott Gurney in 2004; Gretchen graduated from Northrop in 2005 and went on to Valparaiso; Adam is currently a sophomore at Northrop; and Casey is a fifth grader at Shambaugh Elementary School.

Gerald was born to Garland Gerald and Julia Doctor Roby. Garland and Julia were married, simultaneously with her sister Selma Doctor, and her groom, Roy Hans, in 1946 at Emmaus Lutheran Church in Fort Wayne. Julia worked at Wayne Knitting Mills for a short while after her marriage and then raised five children: Linda Lee, Garland Dene, Gerald Lynn, John Frances, and JoAnn Marie. Garland graduated from Central High School. He then served in the Air Force during WW II. He became a draftsman at General Electric. Garland later died while chaperoning a Boy Scout outing. His mother was born at the family farm in Marion Township, Allen County, Indiana. The farm is a Hoosier Homestead Farm.

Sandra was born to Paul Walter and Betty Irene Harmon Archer. They were married in 1947 at Westfield Presbyterian Church in Fort Wayne. They had five children: William Guy, Sandra Lee, Cindy Jo, Karen Sue, and Melodie Ann. Betty, a native of Licking County, Ohio, was one of seven children. She moved to Fort Wayne in 1933 when she was four years old. She worked at Magnavox and General Electric. Paul was born in 1926 in Fort Wayne. He was in the Navy during WW II and served in the Marshall Islands. When he came home, he resumed work as a shipping clerk at Phelps Dodge Inca Division.

There have been many changes in Allen County, but Gerald and Sandy remember when there were fireworks held at McMillan Park; the Three Rivers Festival had a raft race, free rock concerts, a children's parade, and a bed race; there was a farm on Washington Center Road where the Wal-Mart now stands; and Washington Center Road was only two lanes wide. They also recall Peoples Trust Bank, Indiana Bank, Anthony Wayne Bank, and Eavey's Supermarket. Sandra remembers having the first color TV on her block. Gerald remembers when computers used punch cards.

Submitted by Sandra Roby

CHARLES KELLY & MARY AGNES ROCHE FAMILY

Charles Kelly Roche was born September 13, 1885, in Hampshire, Kane County, Illinois, the twelfth of fourteen children.

His father, William Roche, son of Martin Roche and Margaret Rice, was born in County Wexford, Ireland in March of 1834. Following Martin's death, William immigrated to the United States in 1853 and, for a time, worked at a cotton mill in Augusta, Maine (a trade he had learned in Ireland). In 1854, he moved to Illinois where he found work on various farms in the Hampshire area.

On July 10, 1864, William married Julia Kelley (March 17, 1848 - August 2, 1938). The fourth of six children, her parents were John Kelley and Bridget Doheny who, shortly before Julia was born, had immigrated to America from County Tipperary, Ireland, at the height of The Great Famine.

In 1882, William acquired his father-in-law's farm and his last four sons were born there, including Charles. William retired from farming around 1913 and moved to Elgin, Illinois. He died December 19, 1919. By that time, Charles had moved to Chicago and lived for a while with his sister and her husband, Mary (Mame) and Edgar Gray.

Charles had a friend who fixed him up on a blind date so they could go to a Knights of Columbus dance. The young lady who accompanied Charles that evening was Mary Agnes Moore, born June 10, 1885. They were married on October 22, 1919, in St. Dominic Catholic Church, at Chicago, Illinois. She was the daughter of Joseph Moore (1853 - May 10, 1891) and Mary O'Donnell (March 1860 - May 12, 1909). They were each born in Ireland, but met in Chicago, where they married on June 10, 1883. In the eight years that they were married, ending with Joseph's death, they had seven children, but only two survived infancy. One son, James P. (April, 1890 - June 28, 1891) died less than two months after his father's death.

Charles and Agnes had one child, a daughter Mary Roche, who was born October 16, 1920. She attended elementary school at St. Sylvester and St. Carthage, and graduated from Mercy High School. Among her classmates (besides Al Capone's daughter), was best friend Jane DeVinney, who arranged a date for her with Jane's brother, Robert. Mary and Robert were married on June 29, 1940. A son, James Andre, was born on January 6, 1942.

Charles Kelly Roche and Mary Agnes(Moore) Roche August, 1939

The family moved to Fort Wayne the following April, where Robert and Mary have lived ever since, except while Robert was serving in World War II, when Mary and James went back to Chicago to live with her parents.

Following his retirement from Shippers Dispatch, Charles and Agnes moved to Fort Wayne in 1957. Agnes died on April 14, 1962; Charles on April 3, 1964. They are buried in Catholic Cemetery.

Submitted by Robert G. DeVinney

THEODORE G. RODENBECK FAMILY

Back in the early fifties, Coldwater Road, known as Highway 27, was a two lane country road. It boasted old family farms, fenced-in sheep, goats, and old barns and houses.

In 1917, Martin Rodenbeck was born to Theodore and Amanda Rodenbeck in a farmhouse on the road. In August of 1953, Martin took a wife, Bernice, and moved into the farmhouse, remodeled to accommodate two family units; Martin and his wife, and Marie, Martin's sister, and their father, who moved to an upstairs apartment.

A century before this, in 1853, 80 acres of the farmland where Martin grew up was purchased by Conrad C. Rodenbeck from the Hamiltons. Conrad came to America as a lad in his mother's arms on a ship from Germany. He is buried in a little cemetery down the road, north of Washington Center Road that was saved when I69 was constructed. This cemetery was once part of a piece of land that boasted a house and a small country school, owned by St. Paul's Lutheran Church, on Barr Street. Many former St. Paul's members are buried in that cemetery.

In 1865, Conrad Rodenbeck purchased an adjoining 80 acres from Charles and Mary Bleke for $2,500. In 1890, 40 acres of this tract was purchased by his son, Fred C. and his wife, Mary Rodenbeck for $2,300. In April of 1918 Fred C. and Mary Rodenbeck sold acreage to Theodore Rodenbeck, their son, for $1500. This was the farmland on which Martin was raised. On this land was a two story farm house and several barns. Theodore and his family milked cows, raised chickens and pigs, planted corn, wheat, oats, and a vegetable garden. Martin, Marie and their parents worked the farm and sold eggs and milk. A younger brother, Edgar, was killed in Luzon on January 19, 1944, in World War II. Theodore's wife, Amanda died April 3, 1945. A funeral service was held for her at St. Paul's downtown on April 7, 1945, with a memorial service following for Edgar. He is buried in the National Army Cemetery, Luzon, Philippines.

Martin, Marie and their father, Theodore, continued to live in the farmhouse that had been remodeled and modernized through the years. It was last remodeled when Martin was married. Five children were born to Martin and his wife, Bernice, while in that farmhouse, which had only two bedrooms downstairs. It was time to make different arrangements. A tri-level house was built in the field south of the farm house and in early 1960, the family moved in. By 1965, another child was added to the family.

Coldwater Road farmhouse, 1903, with family of Frederick C. Rodenbeck and Mary (Rahdert) in front, and children Fred, Ida, Theodore and Martha in back.

Coldwater Road farm barn, built in 1901 by Henry Muessing, with family, Fred, Theodore, Martha, Ida and parents, Mary and Fred C. Rodenbeck. Horses and buggy used to bring family to church in town.

The scene along Coldwater Road had changed through the years. The road had been widened when I69 was built. There was a gas station at the corner of Washington Center and Coldwater Road. Stucky Brothers built a store next door. Tara Apartments grew up in the south edge of the farm. Across the road a house was moved in, saved from the construction of I69. Businesses started to appear across the road. There was Koehlingers a restaurant, and a church. When sister Marie died in 1985, a decision had to be made. The property had increased in value, and to buy the sister's interest was not an option, so the farm was sold. It was developed and became Coldwater Crossing.

Submitted by Bernice Rodenbeck

JOHN ROEBEL (1863-1933)

John Roebel was a native of Buffalo, New York. He was the son of Gustave and Katherine Huber or Hoover Roebel. The family of Gustave is listed in the 1850 New York census. They moved to Fort Wayne, Indiana, and were the parents of nine children. Katharine lived from 1820-1885.Gustave lived from 1818 –1888.

John's brothers and sisters were Christina, Caroline, Christain, Henry, Anna, William, Fred, and Mary or May.

Some documents list Gustave as George or Augustive Roebel. Sometimes the family name has been spelled Rabel. Gustave reportedly had a second marriage to Anna Maria Savalaid.

John Roebel married Catharine Chaemming or Corpeming. She was born in November 1849 and died in 1926. John was a shoe cobbler, and was reported to be the best in town in his day. His place of business for the year 1887 was listed as 80 Fairfield Avenue. His home was listed as 3 Brooklyn Ave. Their children were Minnie, John, Georgian, George Washington Roebel, Elizabeth Emils, Edward, and Arthur Roebel. His grandson Lawrence Bauch stated that "Grandfather John Roebel owned most of the land between what is now Covington Road and Whitmore Street alongside Brooklyn Avenue in Fort Wayne, Indiana."

John and Catharine Roebel's daughter, Myrtle Roebel, married Garland Bauch. In the early 1920s Garland had the new family home built by the Fort Wayne Lumber Company at 2801 Westveiw. This home intersected with Whitmore Street and was in the same block that John Roebel lived which was listed as 2014 Whitmore.

George Frederick Rabel and his wife, Rickie, lived also at 2014 Whitmore.

John and Catharine Roebel are buried at St. John Lutheran Cemetery

Submitted by David W. Bauch

THEODORE & GERTRUDE (WEINMAN) ROESENER FAMILY

Theodore Roesener was born in 1893 and served in World War I in France and Belgium from 1918 to1919. His parents came from Holtzen, Germany. After returning home to Fort Wayne, he married Gertrude Weinman in 1920. She was born in 1892 in Rockford, Ohio. Her father came from Alsace Lorraine and her mother from Germany. She was employed in the office at General Electric Company. A real estate tax bill was found, dated 1921, for their home: $15.75 each installment.

Theodore worked at the General Hosiery Company for over 40 years, and during the Depression, bought his three daughters a baby grand piano, and later a trumpet for his son. The girls studied classical piano.

Madelyne Roesener married Marvin Fritz of Fort Wayne, and taught music and directed a church choir in Rockford, Illinois, where her husband retired as a Lutheran pastor.

Lois Roesener working in the grape arbor, 2002

Lois Roesener worked at Kuhne Abstract Company and the Allen County Recorder's office, and later Lincoln Life. She followed light classical and improvisation, and played for the United Way under Ian Rolland and for group singing. She accompanied the children at Emmaus Lutheran Sunday School for 30 years, and was an Avon representative for 33 years.

Milton married Miriam Leimer, a former school teacher. He is a retired industrial and commercial painting contractor, and volunteers for Lutheran Social Service. In his youth, he played the trumpet in the school band and for Easter sunrise service at Emmaus Church.

Joan, who resides with her husband Robert Bergt in St. Louis, has served as church organist and is a professional accompanist for orchestras and choruses, including St. Louis symphony, and "Bach at the Sem," which her husband conducts. For five years Robert Bergt taught music and conducted an orchestra in Tokyo. They understood that, "Your talent is God's gift to you. What you do with that talent is your gift to God."

In the 1930s and 40s the Roeseners joined the spectacular crowds at Foster Park for the fireworks in July and ice skated at the reservoir in the winter. Of special interest and love to the family, which now includes ten grandchildren and sixteen great grandchildren, has been the grape arbor built in the early 1900s. There were some red, some white and blue concord grapes planted. The pruning was done in March and they ripened around Labor Day. Besides eating them, jelly, grape cordial and juice were made. In the first part of October, wine was prepared for storage until Thanksgiving, when the family enjoyed the taste of new wine.

In 1975 a *News Sentinel* photographer, Argil Shock, was in the area and asked permission to take a picture of the arbor. The caption read: "The shadows and patterns of a grape arbor in Fort Wayne bring back memories of bygone days... remember how cool they used to be?"

Submitted by Lois Roesener

GEORGE ROGERS

George Rogers was born October 27, 1913, in Wellington, Illinois to William R. Rogers and Lula Sutherland. He had one sister, Jean, two half sisters and one half brother. He graduated from high school in Wellington. He spent a year at Illinois State University until his brother, A. W. Umberger, bought a 340 acre farm south of LaOtto, and asked him to help farm it. He dropped out of college, invested in the farm and worked it for the next seven years. George met Daphne Appleman on a blind date and they were married in 1940. They had two daughters, Peggy, now deceased, (Richard Laesch) and Barbara (Randy Bellinger). They have four grandchildren.

In 1943, George purchased 160 acres on Hathaway Road. Three years later, he bought another 160 acres which lie south and directly across the road. He and Daphne lived in the smaller of the two homes on the original property, while tenants occupied the larger house. In the late 1960s, he undertook the remodeling and modernization of the bigger house and in 1970, he and Daphne moved in.

Besides regular farming, George has gone into specialty products. After taxing courses at Purdue University and Michigan State, he went into the sod business for eight years. He sold to local landscaping companies. "It was awfully hard work, and you didn't have a minute for yourself", he stated. He also produced carrots for the Campbell Soup Company and broccoli for Birdseye.

In 1963, as captain of the Fort Wayne Shrine Horse Patrol, George arranged the rail transportation of the group's 32 palomino horses to Pasadena, California, where they and their riders pranced in the Rose Bowl Parade.

Daphne was a teacher at Huntertown School so it was no surprise that she and George were both interested in the education of young people. Daphne passed away in September 1990. When Northwest Allen County Schools was looking for land to build a new middle school, George thought it fitting to have it built across the road from his original farm. Carroll Middle School stands there today with a small wooded park on the corner of Bethel and Hathaway Roads in honor of Daphne Rogers.

George is director emeritus at the Farmers and Merchants Bank in LaOtto. In the past he has served as chairman of the board and was instrumental in buying the Allen County Bank building in Huntertown as a branch bank. Recently the bank expanded with a branch in Churubusco.

He served as the grand marshal for the first Willow Creek Festival in Huntertown and once for the Allen County Fairground. George also purchased 4-H champion livestock for the bank. An avid Democrat, he thinks Harry Truman was the best president he remembers. When asked why, he says "Because he was his own man and not swayed by outside interests or party."

Submitted by Jenny McComb

CLAUDE FRANCOIS & MARIE JEANNE (PATAILLOT) RONDOT FAMILY

Claude Francois Rondot was born January 17, 1795, in Val De Gouhenans, Athesans, Haute Saone, France. He was the son of Pierre and Jeanne Francoise (Bourcardey). Claude married Marie Jeanne Pataillot, the daughter of Jean Guillaume and Anne Baptiste (Belzingue), on January 18, 1820. In 1850 they emigrated from France through the Port of Havre and arrived on the *Gallia* on May 9, 1850, through the Port of New York. The ship's records indicate three children traveled with them: their daughter, Hortense, and two others whose relationship is unknown, Christian and Eugene. The family traveled to Stoney Point, Ontario, Canada, where sons John August and Charles Emile, who had emigrated from France in the 1840s, were married in June of 1850. Claude's sons, Charles Alexander and John Baptist, along with daughters, Isabelle and Justine, came to America on the ship *Lucania* in 1851.

Claude's Last Will and Testament, dated February 16, 1855, lists the following children as heirs: John Augustus (1821-1899), Charles Alexander (1822-1896), Charles Emile (1830-1918), John Baptist (born 1824), Hortense Julliard (1826-1901), and Justine Ternet (1828-1892).

Claude purchased 80 acres of land on August 3, 1850, in Perry Township. All of the children, except Charles Emile, eventually moved to Allen County.

John August married Dorothea Marie Blanchette (1830-1897) in Canada in June of 1850. In 1851 he bought 25 acres of land from his father and in June of 1856 he purchased a 40 acre farm in Jefferson Township. On April 30, 1863, they moved to Washington Township on a 75 farm. They raised a large family of seven sons and eight daughters.

Charles Alexander married Melitine Tournier in 1855 in the Fort Wayne Cathedral. He had purchased 20 acres of land from Claude in 1853. Charles and Melitine had a son and two daughters.

It is believed that John Baptist was never married. He worked as a farm hand in Jefferson Township and was last known as working for Joseph Fremion Brick Manufacturing Company per the 1880 census and Fort Wayne city directory.

Hortense married Francois Julliard in 1852 in Allen County. They had two daughters. After Francois' death in 1856, Hortense married Joseph Cochoit (1826-1902) in 1858 in the Fort Wayne Cathedral. They had two sons and two daughters.

Justine married Claude Francis Teraet (1819-1888) in Allen County in December of 1852. They raised a family of ten children.

Charles Emile married Sophia Dequindre in 1850. Sophia (1835-1890) was born in Belle Riviere, Ontario, Canada. They raised their family of 13 children in Ontario, Canada.

Through a family letter from John August to his brother Emile in Canada, it has been established that Marie died in 1854 and Claude in 1855 during the cholera scourge in Allen County, during the years of 1849-1856. Although no records have been located, it is presumed that they were buried in the old St. Vincent's Cemetery, in that portion taken over when the brick church was built about 1862.

Submitted by Angela Green

ROOP – ZIMMERMAN

Andrew Hollopeter (1777-1846) and Phebe Blatchford (1782-1842) left Pennsylvania for Seneca County, Ohio. Four of Andrew and Phebe's sons continued west to Allen County and settled in Cedar Creek Township. Many of these Hollopeters are buried in Old Leo Cemetery.

Abraham (1800-1869), oldest son of Andrew and Phebe Hollopeter, married Lydia Myers and had nine children: Jacob (1820-1870) married Eliza Hawkins, then Calista Roberts; John Wesley (1822-1893) married Mary Kaziah Zimmerman; Cyrus (1829-1900) married Lydia Conway; Mathias (1833-1898) married Susan Hannen, then Mary Ellen Stevick; Abel (1836-1906) married Malinda Herrin; and Israel (1840-1916) married Jemima Stevick. Nothing is known about Abraham and Lydia Hollopeter's three daughters, Elizabeth, Catherine and Margaret. The six sons of Abraham and Lydia had large families that were born and died in Allen County.

Andrew and Phebe Hollopeter's son, Wesley (1806-1873) married Rosanah Edmonds (1804-1872) and had at least four children: Elizabeth married George Swartz, Andrew married Nancy Hyatt, Enoch married Mary Stevick, and Emeline (1845-1880) married Samuel Zimmerman.

Andrew (1808-1892), the third Hollopeter son, married Catherine Edmonds and had at least five children. According to his obituary in Fort Wayne *Daily Gazette*, "Rev. Andrew Hollopeter, who has been a minister of the M.E. church for over sixty years, died near Leo, this county, on December 18, at the advanced age of 84 years." The fourth Hollopeter son to settle in Allen County was Isaiah (1822-1884) who married Sarah McWilliams and had at least four children.

The two Zimmermans who married Hollopeters were siblings, children of Rachel Roop and Andrew Zimmerman, grandchildren of. Fredrick Roop and Elizabeth Abbott of Huntingdon County, Pennsylvania. According to *Valley of the Upper Maumee River*, pp. 344 & 345, Samuel Zimmerman (1840-1920) served in Company C, 88th Indiana Infantry Regiment during the Civil War. He married Emeline Hollopeter on December 14, 1865 in Cedar Creek Township. The couple had five sons before her death. Samuel then married Emily (Teeple) Spuller, but there are no known children from the second marriage. Samuel was township assessor for four years and had a "good farm of over seventy-five acres, well improved with good buildings. He is one of the leading citizens of his township." Samuel's children were Charles Zimmerman who married Hattie M. Trease, daughter of John Trease (1848-1899) and his first wife, Amanda, on February 12, 1893 in Allen County; Simpson who died before his twentieth birthday; Waeley who died at age two; Dr. Harris Haskell Zimmerman (1871-1947) who married Hattie Douglas and practiced medicine in Red Bluff, California; and Avery who married Anna Blanche Barnhart in DeKalb County, Indiana, on December 28, 1901.

An interesting note: John L. Trease, father of Hattie, married a second time on December 10, 1885 in Allen County, to Roxie Belle Shannon, daughter of Boyd Gamble Shannon and Caroline Zimmerman. Caroline was Samuel Zimmerman's sister. John and Roxie had two children: George Trease (1886-1907) and Elsie Trease (1891-1960) who married William Wedler (1889-1966) on July 2, 1912 in Allen County.

Submitted by Karin King

THOMAS ROSEBERRY, SR.

Thomas Roseberry Sr. migrated from Ireland to Pennsylvania where he met and married Catharine Earhart; they were the submitter's great, great, great, great, grandparents. In time Thomas and Catharine, with son, Thomas Roseberry Jr., migrated from Pennsylvania to Ohio, and then, with many brothers and sisters, the family migrated from Ohio to Jefferson County, Indiana.

The children of the family matured, married and some migrated south and further west. Thomas Roseberry Jr., with wife Jane Neal Roseberry, migrated to Trimble County, Kentucky, from Jefferson County, Indiana, where they started their family, which included Rebecca Roseberry. Thomas and Jane's children matured, married and some migrated further south and west.

Rebecca Roseberry met and married Madison Barriger in Trimble County, Kentucky, and had two sons, submitter's great grandfather, Francis, and James.

Francis "Frank" M. Barriger migrated from Trimble County, Kentucky to Jefferson County, Indiana after the Civil War and married three times, having a total of twelve chldren from these unions. All three wives died young, near the age of 35, two wives of tuberculosis in Jefferson County, Indiana. It is the last union to Catharine "Kate" Caley Gaylord, that submitter's grandmother Clara Mae Barriger, their youngest child, was born in Madison, Jefferson County, Indiana. Just after Clara's birth, Frank died of heart problems; three years later Kate died of Tuberculosis.

Within two weeks of Kate's death, Clara and three of her siblings were sent to the Soldiers' and Sailors' orphanage in Knightstown, Henry County, Indiana. This orphanage was created to serve the orphaned children of the Civil War veterans. Clara Barriger was adopted out to a barren couple, Warren and Emma Evans Crum, who lived in Ridgeville, Randolph County, Indiana. Clara grew to a beautiful young lady and met Robert Barnes. They moved to Hanover, Jefferson County, Indiana, and their child, Dorothy Pearl Barriger was born. Clara met Roy Hardamon and had Virgina "Ginny" and Gerald "Pete" from this union. In time Clara moved back north to Dunkirk, Jay County, Indiana. Clara then met and married Donald Haffner.

Dorothy Pearl Barriger met Robert Irvin McCune in Dunkirk, Jay County, Indiana. They married, and had three children, Wanda Joy, Linda Lou and David Lee McCune.

In 1967 Wanda McCune met Lee LaVern Shultz in Dunkirk, Jay County, Indiana. Wanda and Lee married in 1968 in Dunkirk, and the couple then moved to Fort Wayne, Allen County, Indiana in 1969. Wanda and Lee Shultz had three children from this union, Michelle "Shellie" Lee, Jonathan "Jon" Brian, and Mitchell "Mitch" Wade. Shellie met and married Steven Mix in Fort Wayne. This union had two children, Britney Tacconi Mix and Alex Wayne Mix. Jon Shultz and Diana Honeick met and had two chilren together, Olivia and Jake Shultz. Mitch is engaged to Lisa Mauger; they are to marry September 16, 2006 in Fort Wayne, Allen County, Indiana.

Submitted by Wanda Shultz

MARVIN OTIS & LOIS F. ROSS FAMILY

Marvin was born October 17, 1934 in Coatesville, Indiana to Walter Lee Ross and Lena Burl (Hedge) Ross. Walter was born in Boone County in 1896. He was an army chef overseas in World War I. On returning from service Walter became a tenant farmer who later worked for Stewart-Warner in Indianapolis. He died in 1967 in Indianapolis at Veteran's Hospital. Lena was born in 1899 and grew up in Jamestown, Indiana graduating from North Salem High School. Lena bore nine children to Walter: seven sons---Wilmer, Buell, Delmus, Melvin, Marvin, Herschel and Robert; two daughters---Adalene (Ross) Alexander and Vera Jean (Ross) Clark. Lena died in 1971.

Marvin's grandfather, William Preston Ross, was born in Hendricks County in 1868 and died in 1906; and grandmother Anna (Zimmerman-Ross) Chambers died in 1954, age 80. Marvin's great grandfather, James Loaten Ross, was born in Madison County, Kentucky in 1837; James was wounded in the Civil War as a Union soldier.

Lena (Hedge) Ross' father, Alva Otis Hedge, was a farmer in Boone County, Indiana and died in 1951, age 78. Her mother Lottie Alice (Ferguson) Hedge was a descendant of John Ferguson who moved to Indiana from Virginia in the 1870s. Lottie Alice Hedge died in 1961, age 83.

Lois F. Ross' parents, Harold G. Griffey and Elizabeth Fern (Smith) Griffey, attended school and grew up in the Indianapolis area. Lois has two sisters---Frances (Griffey) Blackwell and Rosalee (Griffey) Bailey.

Marvin attended school in Fillmore, Indiana graduating from Fillmore High School in Fillmore's centennial year of 1952. Marvin earned both a bachelor's (1956) and master's (1958) degree from Indiana State University, Terre Haute. Lois graduated from Ben Davis High School, near Indianapolis, in 1955. She attended Lincoln Christian College in Lincoln, Illinois. Marvin and Lois were married October 22, 1960 in Indianapolis. Following their marriage Lois worked for American States Insurance Company and, later, was employed in sales by Sears.

Marvin and Lois Ross, Kerry and Alison

Marvin began his professional career as a teacher at Clinton High School and then at Maine Township High School, Des Plaines, Illinois before beginning an eleven year teaching assignment of mathematics and physical science in the Washington Township Schools, Marion, County. In 1971 Marvin became the first full time executive director of the Fort Wayne Education Association representing the teachers' union of some 1800 teachers, for the next 21 years, who were employed by the Fort Wayne Community Schools.

Following Marvin's retirement in 1992, the couple was very active from 1993 through 2003 with the Allen County National Day of Prayer Ministry. Marvin served as its coordinator for nine of these years. Besides multiple servant positions in the church, Marvin has a volunteer ministry of assisting needy, low-income individuals with Medicaid, food stamp and disability applications.

Marvin and Lois' family includes son Kerry J. Ross, who works at ARC and lives in Fort Wayne, and daughter Alison married to Mehmet Uyan who live in Tampa, Florida. Alison is a leasing coordinator for a major insurance company and Mehmet works in the restaurant business.

Submitted by Marvin O. Ross

MABEL (SHEEHAN) ROSSWURM

Mabel Sheehan was the scholar of the family. She went to the Stevenson one room school house in Jackson Township and Monroeville High School. Then she attended one year of college at Angola, Indiana, where she received her license to teach school. Mabel saw the first light of day on October 5, 1899. She was the first born of John L. and Bertha (Poorman) Sheehan. At this time they were living on the Lortie Road in northern Monroe Township.

After acquiring her license to teach, she lived and taught school in the Pleasant Township school system. She married Lester Rosswurm, of Monroeville, Indiana, in 1919 and gave up her career to become a homemaker and mother.

Of this union was born three daughters: Cecelia born May 22, 1921 married to Richard Hartman; Agatha born January 5, 1924 married to Parnell (Pete) Bales; Joan born June 16, 1925 married to Edward Kever. They lived most of their married life in the Fort Wayne-New Haven area. He worked on the Nickel Plate railroad for 41 years including several years as wreckmaster. She passed away on November 23, 1955 at the age of 56, of a cerebral hemorrhage. Her death was so sudden and a horrible shock to the family.

Joan and her family moved in with her father for a time. He lived on the Franke Road near Paulding Road.

A couple years after Mabel died, Les remarried Alma McCrae, a widow, and they had many happy years together. He suffered a long time with cancer until his death on September 18, 1973. He was 76 years old. Both Les and Mabel are buried in the Catholic Cemetery, Fort Wayne, Indiana.

Submitted by Roxanne Napier

JOHN WENDELDEAN & DORIS (DONLEY) ROTH FAMILY

The earliest known Roth ancestor is Jacob. He and his wife, Elizabeth Schantz, were the parents of five children born in France. The third of these children was Benedict, born in Brunstock, France, on June 1, 1822.

Benedict Roth immigrated to America through New York in 1849 and settled in Wayne County, Ohio. It took forty-two days on a sailboat to arrive in New York. He arrived with ninety-five cents to begin his farming career. Two years later he followed the Wabash and Erie Canal to Allen County, Indiana, in 1851.

Doris and Wendeldean Roth

On the farm near Grabill, Indiana, Benedict and his wife, Anna Sauder, raised fifteen children in a small log cabin. The beds were spread out in the evening and stacked on top of each other during the day to make room for housekeeping. This same log cabin remained on the family farm until 1998, when the family donated it to the Sauder Museum in Archbold, Ohio.

Benedict Roth's son, Simon, then assumed responsibility of the farm. He had three children. John, the only son, remained on the farm. After John's death, the farm was transferred to his only son, John Wendeldean Roth. Wendeldean passed away on September 17, 2002.

Wendeldean and Doris Donley were wed on November 22, 1959. They had three sons: Kevin, Kent, and Kraig. All of the sons still live on the "Hoosier Century" farmstead which has been in the same family for over one hundred years.

Wendeldean was very active in Rural Youth, attaining the position of state vice-president. He had a successful cattle breeding and leasing business. His interests were varied. He was a Republican precinct committeeman for many years and several times a delegate to the state convention. He was also a real estate broker and real estate investor. Wendeldean and Doris Roth managed the Grabill License Bureau for twenty years, from 1968 to 1988. They were active in the Grabill Missionary Church and volunteered at the Grabill County Fair.

Their three sons are all married and have children of their own. Most of the earliest ancestors are buried in the Yaggy Cemetery, next to the family farm. The Roth family is thankful to God for the rich heritage and blessings He has provided. One of the genealogical records ends with this conclusion: "Finally—my sincere wish and prayer is that the names of all those that appear on these pages shall also be found written in the Lamb's Book Of Life, Revelation 21:27."

Submitted by Kevin Roth

ALBERT WILLIAM & SARAH ANN (COOK) ROUSSEAU

The Albert William Rousseau family can trace its ancestry to Albert's great-great grandfather, Rueben Rousseau of Lyon, France, born in 1753. Rueben was a soldier under General Lafayette during the Revolution. After the war, Rueben and his two brothers, James and Hilliard, came to the United Colonies. The Rousseaus were Huguenots (French Protestants) which was a breakaway group from the Roman Catholic Church. They came to America to escape persecution from the State and the Church. They landed at Charleston, South Carolina in 1777 and migrated to North Carolina where they settled at Trap Hill in Wilkes County near Wilkesboro.

Reuben married and lived on a plantation in Wilkes County. He was a successful farmer and lived on the plantation until his death. David, son of Rueben and great grandfather of Albert, was born in 1779 in Wilkes County. He attended the local schools and as a young man took over his father's plantation. David married Nancy Shorer in 1801. Seven children were born of this marriage, one of whom was William, born in 1807. After Nancy Rousseau died, David lived with his daughter, Amelia. They later moved to Ohio and then to Indiana, traveling in covered wagons. The Rousseau family left the South because they were opposed to slavery.

David Rousseau arrived in Indiana in the early pioneer days (about 1830) and lived in Henry, Wells, Allen and Whitley counties. He was a typical pioneer: a man of great energy and sturdy integrity. He took great delight in hunting and fishing, a preference which seemed to be inherited by many of his descendants. He spent the final years of his life in Whitley County. He died in 1855.

One of David's sons was William, grandfather of Albert. He lived with his parents in Wilks County, North Carolina, and attended school there. Later he attended Western Reserve College in Cleveland, Ohio. All four of the college buildings were made of logs. William married Ruth McBride in 1833 in New Castle, Indiana. William and Ruth had 12 children. William devoted his attention principally to farming and cattle raising. He was also a carpenter and contractor. He is mentioned in the April-June issue of the *Old Fort News*, published by the Allen County Historical Society. In an article about the history of the years from 1827 to 1877, it is stated that William Rousseau marked his stock with a crop off the right ear and a swallow fork in the left ear. A photo is shown. "William and Ruth were folks of sterling character and were numbered among those who aided in the founding of the industrial and civic structures of Allen County," wrote their grandson, Albert W. Rousseau in a family history.

Albert W. Rousseau

William and Ruth's youngest child was James Harrison, father of Albert. He was born in 1854, one year before his father died. James loved music and traveled with a band of musicians for several years. He was accomplished at playing his coronet and violin, and he often played at dances as a member of the Aboite Township Band, which was organized in 1880 and numbered 15 musicians. He was also a member of the Old Aqueduct Club.

James married Anna Bell Cartwright, mother of Albert, in 1881. She attended schools in Fort Wayne and completed her education by attending Wayne Street Methodist Episcopal College, which later became Taylor Bible College. After graduation, she was hired as a teacher by Captain Kelsey, who had also attended the Methodist College and later became the superintendent of Allen County Schools. Anna's father, James Cartwright, operated a grocery store, and they lived on West Jefferson. Anna and James settled in Aboite township. One of their homes was located on Highway 24, and another was located on Covington Road, next to the Sycamore Hills golf course.

The children of James Harrison and Anna Cartwright Rousseau born at the Covington Road address were Edith Cattin (1882), Carl (1883-1883) and Nellie Lamle (1886).

James and Anna decided to move to South Dakota in 1885 where they homesteaded 160 acres. James liked to tell of his visits to Fort Yates and La Grace, where he saw the great Indian chief, Sitting Bull, and his band of Indians who were engaged in a war dance. James hunted and fished along the Missouri River. Because of the long, cold winters and hot, windy summers, James and Anna decided to move back to Indiana to the farm on Covington Road where their son, James, was born in 1887, followed by Albert William in 1891 and Ivory Robert in 1893.

The homestead was sold in 1895, and 300 acres were purchased on Huntington Road (Highway 24) near the town of Aboite. A large gravel pit was discovered on the land as well as two smaller ones. The timber was cut and sold, and some was used for ties for the interurban railway which was the Huntington, Wabash, Peru and Logansport run. Starting at the Whitley County Road, the farm was divided into nine small farms. During the years spent on this farm, three children were born: Mabel (1896-1896), Jessie Larkin Allegar (1898), and Felix (1900).

In 1904, James and Anna Rousseau bought the Lillie Homestead on St. Marys Avenue in

Fort Wayne. James then engaged in the real estate business. He died in 1936, and Anna died in 1946. Both had good health, many friends, and enjoyed many happy times with their family. Their grandchildren are: Carl, Paul and Nellie Cattin (Edith Cattin, mother), Susann McComb (James), Delilah Blaising, (I. Robert) Richard, Dr. John, Edwin (Albert) and Donna Irving (Felix).

Their son, Albert "Bert" William Rousseau, was born on the farm on Covington Road on July 21, 1891. He started school in a one room brick schoolhouse in Aboite Township. The building has been preserved. When he was 13, the family moved to St. Marys Avenue. He attended Rudisill School, Bloomingdale School and Jefferson School when it was first built. He also attended Fort Wayne High School, later known as Central High School. He then enrolled at International Business College.

Albert married Sarah Ann "Sadie" Cook in 1913 and four sons were born to them: Richard Albert (1914-1974), Donald Philip (1923-1928), John William (1925-1984), and Edwin James in 1933. John pursued a career in medicine, majoring in obstetrics and gynecology. Edwin pursued a career in real estate and government, serving 38 years during a 40 year span as a Fort Wayne city councilman, Allen County councilman and Allen County commissioner. Albert and Sarah's grandchildren: Elaine King, Yvonne Hawkins, Sarah Vaughn (children of Richard and Georgette Voirl) Carolyn Collins, James Rousseau, Richard Rousseau (children of John and Fahma North) and Mark Rousseau, Renee Rousseau, Denise VanderHagen, Suzanne Hausfeld (children of Edwin and Marilyn Johnson.) Albert and Sarah's great grandchildren are: Michelle, Brett and Ryan, children of Mark and Lynne Carter Rousseau; Joshua, (daughters Anikah, and Aubrey, wife Brenda) Joseph and Andrew Kearby, sons of Renee Rousseau and David Kearby; Lauren, Mitchell, Lynnel and Mya VanderHagen, children of Denise Roussseau and Mark VanderHagen; Anthony, Allison and Amy, children of Suzanne Rousseau and Michael Hausfeld. Other great grandchildren are: Amy King and Frank King (wife Angie, children Lydia and Isabelle); Chelsy Vaughn; Megan Collins; LeeAnne Rousseau Gogis (husband Gary and son Braydon), Daniel, Allison, and Matthew, children of James and Barbara Bryan Rousseau.

Albert knew early on that he wanted to be a businessman, and that he would need to earn and save some money before he could start out on his own. He worked at various jobs until 1922 when he and his brother, James, started an automobile agency in their own building at Fifth and Harrison Streets. They called it Rousseau Brothers. They repaired automobiles and took the Elgin franchise until the Elgin Company went broke. They sold Hudson and Essex from 1927 to 1930. In 1930, they signed a franchise with DeSoto Motor Corporation and were given nine counties. They agreed to retail automobiles in Allen County and wholesale in the other eight counties. This franchise was profitable, and they handled DeSoto and Plymouths until 1959. Albert Rousseau's partners were his brother James, until his death in 1948, his son Richard who came into the business in 1934, his friend, Edward Stouder, who started with him in 1938, and his son Edwin who came in the business in 1956. Bert led by example and was known for honest and fair treatment of his employees and customers. During the Depression, he was known to allow some of his customers to keep the cars he had sold them, and to pay him when they got a job.

Albert was a member of Sol. D. Bayless Masonic Lodge 359, Ancient Scottish Rite 32, Mizpah Shrine Temple of Fort Wayne and was a founding member of the Trinity United Methodist Church. He died in 1983 at the age of 92.

Submitted by Marilyn and Ed Rousseau

GEORGE & MARY (LOPSHIRE) RUCH FAMILY

In the IOOF Cemetery, in New Haven, Indiana, George and Mary Ruch and their children and grandchildren have found their final rest. They are visited each year by their great-grandchildren, and flags are left to honor those who fought in the Civil and First World War. Each year, too, their story is told to the younger ones in the family, who need to know, remember, and to share their history with their children in years to come.

George Ruch began his journey to this country with his parents, Adam and Sarah Ruch, and ten brothers and sisters from Alsace-Loraine, September 27, 1832. They traveled by wagon for two weeks to reach the ship, which took 36 days in crossing. Their provisions included sea biscuits, dried fruit, dried beef, beans, rice, barley, and coffee. They farmed for seven years in Stark County, Ohio, and then moved by wagon to Fort Wayne in 1839.

George Ruch 1826-1913

George Ruch married Mary Lopshire in Fort Wayne, July 23, 1846, and they had six children who lived. George served in the Civil War as a member of company G. 182nd Indiana Volunteers. He was a successful farmer in Jackson Township, Allen County, building a beautiful home on the corner of Morgan and Howe Roads. He established the Ruch School on his property in 1898. He died September 23, 1919, at the age of 87. His grandson, when asked how George Ruch had died, replied, "The corn picker got him." At the age of 87, he was still farming, and died from gangrene after his injury became severely infected.

George Ruch's daughter, Loretta May, married Arthur F. Meads, on October 15, 1891. Apparently she was not of legal age to be married, and the license shows an attached note stating: "Please let bearer have license for the marriage of Miss L. May Ruch to Mr. Arthur F. Meads and oblige." It_is signed by George Ruch, and dated, October 11, 1891.

Lloyd L. Meads was one of five children born to Loretta May Ruch and Arthur F. Meads. He married Elizabeth J. Arthur, on June 23, 1919, shortly after he returned from serving in the U.S. Army in France during World War One. They raised two daughters, Jean Eileen and Carol Ann Meads. Jean, who is now deceased, had four children and many grandchildren and great-grandchildren. Carol Ann married Paul N. Lewark on August 20, 1955, and recently celebrated 50 years of marriage. They have four children, eleven grandchildren, and two great-grandchildren.

The old letters, cards, and legal documents that tell the story of those who came before the Ruch family make one marvel at the hard choices that were made to leave what was known, to travel so very far, under often dangerous and extremely uncomfortable conditions, to what was unknown, to pursue a better life for their families. One is eternally grateful that they cared enough to record their memories, and to tell their stories to their children, who have told their children for many generations. They will never be forgotten, nor will the risks and hard work that was theirs be taken for granted.

Submitted by Carol Meads Lewark

LINDA LEE & JOSEPH D. RUFFOLO FAMILY

Joseph D. Ruffolo, born in Kenosha, Wisconsin May 9, 1941, met Linda Lee Parisi, born in Chicago Heights, Illinois December 24, 1941, while both were students at the University of Wisconsin (Madison) in1960. Linda and Joe both earned their Bachelor degrees from the University of Wisconsin in 1963 and 1964 respectively. In 1965 Joe served as a legislative assistant for the Department of Health, Education, and Welfare in Washington D.C. He returned to the University of Wisconsin to do graduate work while working part time for the Wisconsin State Department of Education.

Linda worked as a speech therapist in the public schools of Arlington Heights, Illinois from 1963-1965. She did some graduate work at Northwestern University in Evanston during that time and earned her Masters degree in Speech Pathology and Audiology from Illinois State University in June 1966. They were married July 16, 1966, and settled in Elmhurst, Illinois where Linda was employed by Elmhurst College as an Instructor of Speech and the Assistant Director of the Elmhurst College Speech Clinic. She worked there for five years and attained the rank of Assistant Professor. Joe was employed at Reynolds Metals in McCook, Illinois in Labor Relations.

In 1974 they moved to Fort Wayne with two children. Julie Kathleen was born April 8, 1971 while they lived in Elmhurst, and Joseph Donald II was born December 31, 1973 while they lived in Memphis, Tennessee. While they lived in Memphis, Joe was employed by Dobbs Houses, (restaurants and airline catering) a division of Squibb Corporation, as Vice President of Labor Relations. Linda was a full time mother while they lived in Memphis 1971-74.

Joe was hired by the corporate headquarters of North American Van Lines in Fort Wayne, then owned by PepsiCo, as Vice President of Administration in 1974. In the mid 1980s he was

The Linda Lee and Joseph D. Ruffolo Family, From Left: Joe II, Julie and Brian Gilpin, Linda and Joe

vice president of Relocation and International Services, initiating full service to Russia and China. In 1984 Joe attended the Harvard Advanced Management Program and also served as President of the American Movers Association. North American was sold to the Norfolk Southern Corporation in 1984. Joe served as President and CEO of NAVL from 1987-1993.

During the 31 years from their arrival in Fort Wayne to the documentation of this history Linda and Joe were involved in many aspects of Fort Wayne community life. When Joe retired from North American Van Lines in 1993 he started a business with Graham Richard called RUFFOLO RICHARD LLC. The mission of the firm was "to regain and retain local ownership of area companies" by sourcing capital for business owners. When Graham became mayor in 1999, Joe continued the firm with two new partners, Bix Benson, a former NBD Bank vice president, and Rick Keltsch, one of the second generation of owners of the long time locally owned Keltsch Brothers Pharmacies. Their business backgrounds complimented each other, and they became known as RUFFOLO BENSON LLC.

Joe and Linda and family are longtime members of St. Charles Catholic Church, the Summit Club and Fort Wayne Country Club.

Joe was a founder of TOWER BANK and has been instrumental in many local and regional business success stories. He served on Boards of three publicly traded companies: Tower Financial Corporation, founding director, Steel Dynamics, Inc. and Kitty Hawk Inc. He also served on the following private company Boards: Beltmann Transportation Group, Connor Corporation, DeKalb Plastics and SaniServe Inc. In addition Joe served as director on the boards of the following non-profit organizations: Parkview Hospital, Parkview Health, founding director, Fort Wayne-Allen County Economic Alliance, founding director, Northeast Indiana Innovation Center, founding director, the Fort Wayne Corporate Council, the Fort Wayne Philharmonic Board, the American Symphony Orchestra League, the Fort Wayne Museum of Art, Anthony Wayne Services, and the American Red Cross. He was a member of the Anthony Wayne Rotary Club, the Quest Club, and Business Forum (a past president). He was on the Mayor's Task Force for Juvenile Crime and Emergency Medical Response Services.

Linda worked as the Development Director of the McMillen Center for Health Education from 1992-1995 and as the Executive Director of Development for IPFW from 1992 through this documentation in 2005. She is a member of the Downtown Rotary Club and served on many fundraising and steering committees for non-profit boards. She was the Special Events Chair for Fort Wayne's Bicentennial in 1994 and the Millennium Celebration in 2000. She was a member of the St. Charles School Education committee and founder of its Music Booster Group. She was part of Snider High School PTA, planning committee. She served on the Advisory Boards for FAME, the Junior League and the Fort Wayne Community Schools Study Connection, for which she was a tutor since its inception through this writing. Linda was a Director and Officer for many of Fort Wayne's non-profit Boards including United Way, Arts United (chair 1992-94), the Fort Wayne Philharmonic, Fort Wayne Philharmonic Women's Committee (president 1983-84), Council on Equity, WBNI, PBS (chairman 2004-05), the Lincoln Museum (president 2002-2004), Hospice Home, Girl Scouts, Fort Wayne Museum of Art Alliance, Fort Wayne Ballet, and Allen County Courthouse Preservation Trust. She received the WANE TV 15 Who Care Award, in 1995 the Foellinger-Shoaff Award for Excellence, in recognition for her contributions to the Arts in Fort Wayne, in 2001 the Mike McClelland Volunteer Study Connection Award, in 2002 the Helene Foellinger Award and the Governor' s Award of distinction, Sagimore of the Wabash.

Daughter Julie is a graduate of St. Charles School, Snider High School, holds a Bachelor's degree from DePauw University in Greencastle, Indiana and a Master's from Loyola University in Chicago. On June 20, 1998 she married Brian Gilpin, son of Rosie and Paul Gilpin, owners of Gilpin IRONWORKS in Decatur, also longtime Fort Wayne residents. Julie and Brian live in Whitefish Bay, Wisconsin. Brian is a patent attorney and partner in the Milwaukee Law Firm of Godfrey and Kahn. He serves as a Board member of the Milwaukee Boy's and Girl's Club. Julie is a Legal Personnel and Recruitment Manager in the Human Resources Department of the Von Briesen and Roper Law Firm, also in Milwaukee. She has been a college district president for Kappa Alpha Theta since 1995 and is the 2005 President of Junior League in Milwaukee.

Henry H. Rush

Son, Joe II, also graduated from St. Charles Elementary School and Snider High School. He earned his Bachelor's degree from BROWN University in Providence, Rhode Island and his MBA from the Goizueta School of Business at EMORY University in Atlanta. He has held positions at CNN, Walt Disney, AOL, and is currently a Senior Director of Business Development for Nickelodeon online at Viacom in Manhattan, New York.

Submitted by Linda Lee and Joseph D. Ruffolo

HENRY H. RUSH FAMILY

Henry H. Rush settled in Allen County, Maumee Township, around 1881. He purchased 40 acres for farming at the corner of the Indiana-Ohio State Line and Woodburn Road. Henry moved to Allen County from Ohio. He married Evelyn Chaney, also from Ohio. Together they had three children, Nora, Clyde, and Margaret. Henry retired in 1915 and purchased Dr. A.P. Betts's home in Woodburn. Henry H. Rush was born in 1852 and died in 1929. Evelyn Chaney Rush was born in 1856 and died of typhoid fever in 1893.

Their first child, Nora Rush, was born May 6, 1883 and died June 24, 1969. She married Ellis Goff from Antwerp, Ohio on July 7, 1903. They had one daughter, Gaylen Irene Goff. Gaylen was born September 10, 1925. Gaylen Goff married John Stetler from Willshire, Ohio. They had a daughter named Debra Kim Stetler, born in Decatur, Indiana, Adams County on February 2, 1956. Debra Kim married Richard Eubank of Woodburn and had two children. Christy Lynn was born September 16, 1974, and Andrew J. was born May 8, 1979. Christy graduated from Ball State University with a degree in education. Christy married Michael Preston of Woodburn and Andrew married Janis Nieuwlandt of Harlan. Andrew works as an electrician. Andrew and Janis had Joselyn Irene on April 18, 2003.

Henry and Evelyn's second child was Clyde Rush. Clyde lived from 1887 to January 7, 1951. He enlisted in the marines, making a goodwill tour around the world from 1907-1909 under President Theodore Roosevelt. Upon his return, Clyde settled in the Fort Wayne area and became an iron worker. Later in his life he managed a bar in the Milner Hotel on Baker Street.

Henry and Evelyn's third child was Margaret Rush. She was born June 11, 1889 and died on October 11, 1985. She married Orville Woods of

Decendants of Henry H. Rush

Fort Wayne and moved to Toledo, Ohio. Margaret worked as a private music instructor. They had one daughter, Evelyn Jeanette Woods, born in September of 1918. Evelyn Woods graduated from Julliard School of Music in New York City. She married James Chavey of Detroit, Michigan and they had one son, James Chavey, born in 1942 and who died in July of 1960 in a car accident.

This family is proud to have lived in Allen County for six generations through Henry H. Rush, Nora Goff, Gaylen Stetler, Debra Kim Eubank, Andrew Eubank, and Joselyn Eubank!

Submitted by Gaylen Stetler

BLANE P. RYAN FAMILY

Blane Patrick Ryan was born December 17, 1957 in Fort Wayne, Indiana to Paul Joseph and Alice Catherine (Wilson) Ryan. Paul was employed as a police officer with the Fort Wayne Police Department, retiring in 1983 at the rank of lieutenant. He is deceased. Alice worked with Fort Wayne Community Schools as a school aide, retiring in 1995. Other children in the family are Mark Stephen born August 30, 1959, Anne Elizabeth born October 1, 1961, and John Leslie, born August 19, 1964.

Blane married Diane Carol Hoevel on May 30, 1981. She was born May 2, 1956 in Fort Wayne, Indiana to Howard Anthony and Georgian (Allgeier) Hoevel. Diane graduated from Bishop Luers High School in 1974 while Blane graduated from North Side High School in 1976. Both Blane and Diane graduated from Indiana University-Purdue University at Fort Wayne in 1981. Blane is currently employed at Fort Wayne Community Schools as a teacher. His current teaching assignment is at South Side High School. Diane is currently employed with General Electric at Fort Wayne in customer service. Their children are Colette Mary, born March 19, 1984, Eric Patrick born May 10, 1988, and Leslie Anne born December 23, 1991. They reside in Monroeville, Indiana where Blane is currently a member of the Monroeville Town Board. Blane is also currently a board member of the Allen County Fort Wayne Historical Society and is President of the Four President's Corners Historical Society. The Ryans are members of Saint Rose de Lima Catholic Church in Monroeville.

The Ryans came to Allen County from Warsaw, Indiana where Albert John Ryan was born to John and Mary (Rolston) Ryan. The Ryans operated a steam threshing business in the area between Warsaw and Etna Green, Indiana. Albert worked on the Pennsylvania Railroad and retired after 44 years. After World War I, Albert married Jane Loretta Kilkelly in Elmira, New York in 1919. They moved to Fort Wayne where Paul Joseph was born August 12, 1929.

Because of his service in France during World War I, Albert became interested in roses and became a member of the American Rose Society. He later served as a consultant and was instrumental in the development of Lakeside Rose Gardens in Fort Wayne.

The Wilsons came to Fort Wayne in the 1930s. Leslie Wilson was born in Russell Springs, Kentucky in May 1900. He graduated from Kentucky Normal College, later renamed Western Kentucky University, and Indiana School of Medicine. He married Mary Ann Eaton of Wheeler, Indiana. Their daughter, Alice Catherine, was born July 13, 1928 in Gary, Indiana. A pair of twins, Ralph Leslie and Mary Ann, were born in Dublin, Indiana but died soon after they were born. A son, Allen Dwayne Wilson was adopted in Richmond, Indiana in 1935. Leslie served his country as a surgeon in the United States Navy in World War II and later served as the first Chief of Surgical Services when the Veteran's Administration Hospital opened in Fort Wayne in 1953. Leslie was also a Mason while Mary was a member of the Order of the Eastern Star.

Submitted by Blane P. Ryan

PATRICK & NANCY ANN (DWYER) RYAN SR. FAMILY

Patrick Ryan, Sr. was married to Nancy Ann Dwyer in the Parish of Upper Church, County Tipperary, Ireland in 1833. They had five children: Patrick, Thomas, James, Mary and Margaret, born in the townland of Foilnaman and baptized in Upper Church parish. During the potato famine, they immigrated to Canada and lived there three years. By springtime 1851, the family arrived in Allen County, Indiana.

Patrick bought a forty-acre farm in Jefferson Township, section 20, at the corner of U.S. 30 and Ryan Road, the road being named after him. Another son, John, was born here in 1854. They raised cattle, hogs, chickens, grains, and vegetables and had a fruit orchard. An over abundance of eggs and butter was probably sold at market. Acres of woodland provided firewood and fencing. Patrick died September 8, 1884, at age 82. Nancy died November 8, 1897, at age 83. They are buried in St. Louis Besancon Cemetery.

Patrick Jr. was born March 31, 1834. He married Mary Jane Powers January 9, 1859, in the Methodist Episcopal Church in New Haven, Indiana. They had nine children: Albert, Elmer, Lillie, Freeman, Franklin, Harvey, Delia, Harry and Emma, five dying in infancy. Patrick became a naturalized citizen in 1856. He died at the home of a son on September 21, 1920, in Arcola, Indiana and is buried in I.O.O.F. Cemetery in New Haven with his wife.

Mary was baptized January 9, 1836. Nothing else is known of her.

Thomas was born April 7, 1838. He and Mary Broderick married January 20, 1862, at St. John the Baptist Catholic Church, New Haven, Indiana. They lived in Milan Township (post office Gar Creek). Of their nine children, three died in infancy. The surviving children were Patrick, John, Joseph, Anna, Mary, and Ellen. Thomas was naturalized in 1864. He died January 27, 1880 of typhoid fever and is buried in St. Louis Besancon Cemetery.

James, born June 23, 1840, served in the Civil War enlisting in the 30th Regiment, Company E, Infantry. After the war he married Catherine Shob/Schaab April 1, 1869. They had two daughters. He died February 15, 1873, daughter Anna died February 24, 1873, his wife died March 4, 1873 and daughter Mary died May 3, 1874. They are all buried at St. Louis Besancon Cemetery.

Margaret was born June 14, 1843. She married James Finan on March 22, 1862. They lived in Benton Township, Paulding County, Ohio, and had seven children: John, Patrick, Clara, Thomas, James, Eugene, and Mary. James died in 1873 and is buried in St. Louis Besancon Cemetery. Margaret never remarried. She died July 19, 1916, in Payne, Ohio and is buried in the Catholic Cemetery there.

John was born April 14, 1854. He inherited his father's farm and lived with his mother, caring for her until she died. John married Julia Dodane on April 9, 1893. They had five children: Edith, who became Sister M. Wilfreda, Julia, Lawrence, Agnes, and Leonard. John died of pneumonia December 20, 1943 and is buried at St. Louis Besancon Cemetery.

Submitted by Margery Graham

ROSE MARIE HART RYAN FAMILY

Rose Marie Hart Ryan was born on May 3, 1933 at St. Joseph Hospital in Fort Wayne, Indiana. Rose was the daughter of Hugh Patrick Hart and Hilda Laurine App. Rose can trace her family on the App side back to 1751 to her Great great great grandfather, Felix App of Ertingen, Germany. Felix and his wife Franziskd Figel had a son, Philipp App, born April 30, 1795 in Ertingen. Philipp's occupation was a weaver. He married Regina Baier on November 11,1823. Regina and Philipp had eleven children, most of whom died before their first birthdays. One child who lived was Mathias App, born February 13,1830 in Ertingen.

L to R: Rose Marie Hart Ryan, Mary Ellen Hart Schon, Hilda Laurine App Hart, Jane Frances Hart, Agnes Ann Hart, Martin Patrick Hart.

Mathias App learned the shoemaker trade at a young age in Germany. Then in 1852 he came to America, settling in Fort Wayne, Indiana. By 1860, he had established his own custom shoemaking business. His shops were located in several Calhoun street addresses, but eventually he bought land at 916 Calhoun Street, where he built his own building and remained in business there as App Shoe Store for over 50 years.

Mathias was an active member of St. Mary's Catholic Church. He married Rosina (Ketcher) Wagner on April 19, 1858. Rosina and Mathias had seven children. One son, Martin, joined him in his shoe business over the years. Martin was Rosina and Mathias' third child. He was born December 25,1863 in Fort Wayne, Indiana. Martin was a member of St. Mary's Catholic Church. Martin married Elizabeth Kramer on June 19, 1888. Martin and Elizabeth had six children. Their youngest child was Hilda Laurine App, born June 4, 1900. Hilda attended St. Mary's Catholic Elementary school and then attended Ladywood Academy in Chicago to study music and teaching. When she returned to Fort Wayne, she taught music at various schools in the Anthony Wayne Township District. Because her job required extensive traveling from school to school, her father Martin bought her one of the first Model T Fords in the area, and she became one of Fort Wayne's first women drivers. Later in life, Hilda taught fourth grade at St.Vincent Catholic School in Fort Wayne.

On February 16, 1931 Hilda married Hugh Patrick Hart. Hilda and Hugh had five children. They had one son, Martin Patrick Hart, born September 2,1934. Their four daughters were Agnes Ann Hart, born February 13,1932; Jane Frances Hart, born March 12,1936; Mary Ellen Hart Schon, born October 10,1937 and Rose Marie Hart Ryan, born May 3,1933 at St. Joseph Hospital in Fort Wayne. Rose was nicknamed "Poadie" by her older sister Agnes, who called her that because she couldn't pronounce "Rosie".

Rose Marie Hart attended St. Patrick's Catholic Church and elementary school in Fort Wayne. She went on to Central Catholic High School and St. Francis College, also in Fort Wayne. She worked before marriage at both Tokhiem and G.E. as a stenographer and secretary. Later, after her children were raised, she worked in the offices of St. Joseph Hospital School of Nursing. After retiring, she has spent several years as a volunteer reader for NEIRRS (Northeast Indiana Radio Reading Service). Rose married James Richard Ryan on October 3,1953 at St. Patricks Church in Fort Wayne. James and Rose had six children: Regina Marie Ryan Blanchette, born July 25,1954; Timothy James Ryan born July 20,1955; Rebecca Susan Ryan Laughlin, born September 11,1958; Kara Ann Ryan Slocum, born January 5,1963; Molly Kathleen Ryan Smethers, born December 4,1965 and Sean Hart Ryan, born July 27,1968.

Rose now has 20 grandchildren and continues to live in the Fort Wayne area with her husband of more than 50 years, James Ryan.

Submitted by Regina Blanchette

THOMAS LYNN RYAN FAMILY

Thomas (Tom) Lynn Ryan was born August 31, 1941, in Kokomo, Indiana (Howard County), brother to John Patrick Ryan, born September 26, 1933, and Roberta Ruth Ryan, born July 3, 1935. His parents were Robert Michael Ryan, Jr. born April 18, 1900, in Elwood, Indiana and Cora Estelle Hollingsworth, born November 12, 1904, in New London, Indiana. He was educated at Kokomo Public Schools and Indiana University, Bloomington, Indiana; Bachelor of Arts 1963, Doctor of Jurisprudence 1968.

Tom was married July 29, 1967, to Cecelia (Celie) Helen Seibert, who was born October 1, 1946, in Chicago, Illinois to Victor John Seibert, Sr., born October 6, 1921, in Tell City, Indiana, and Adele Kuczynski, born June 25, 1925, in Chicago, Illinois. Three children were born to Tom and Celie in Fort Wayne, Indiana; Lara Lynn Ryan on June 3, 1970, Kathryn (Kate) Lynne Ryan on August 13, 1975, and John (Jack) Michael Ryan on January 15, 1977. All three children of Tom and Celie graduated from Bishop Dwenger High School.

Lara graduated from Purdue University, West Lafayette, Indiana, in 1994 with a Bachelor of Science degree in Micro-Biology, Genetics, and Environmental Science, and joined Aluminum Corporation of America (ALCOA) in 1995.

Kate graduated from Indiana University, Bloomington, Indiana, in 1998 with a Bachelor of Arts in Education, studied in England, and on July 12, 2003, married David William Shively of Churubusco, Indiana. They have two children; Samantha Rose Mary, born November 16, 2003, and Olivia Cecelia, born October 13, 2005.

Jack enjoys a career in the United States Air Force. After enlisting in 1996 and while serving in England, he married Sonya Lorraine Ungermann on March 3, 2001, and has two children; Camryn Thomas, born October 17, 2001, and Alexander Paul, born February 2, 2004.

Celie graduated in 1969 from Indiana University, Bloomington, Indiana, with a Bachelor of Science in Education and, after raising their children, was employed as a teacher and human resources specialist for the city of Fort Wayne.

Tom was admitted to the Bar of the Indiana Supreme Court in 1968 and associated in private legal practice with Wyss, McCain, Mochamer, Roby, Ryan and Myers, 1800 Lincoln Bank Tower, Fort Wayne, Indiana, from 1969 to August, 1983, with a satellite office with Daniel A Roby, 420 East Eighth Street, Anderson, Indiana. He served as a Deputy Allen County Public Defender, 1973 to 1983, and had extensive trial experience in general, civil and criminal law and before the Indiana Court of Appeals, Indiana Supreme Court, Seventh Circuit Court of Appeals, and the Supreme Court of the United States.

His public service has been extensive: Investigator, Monroe County Prosecuting Attorney, 1966 to 1968; Deputy Prosecuting Attorney 1968 to 1969; Judge, Allen Circuit Court, by appointment of the Honorable Robert D. Orr, Governor of the State of Indiana on August 1,1983; three unopposed elections as a Republican candidate to six (6) year term January 1, 1985, expiring December 31, 1990; re-elected 1991 to 1996 and 1997 to 2002; Allen County Court House Preservation Trust, Inc., Incorporator and member of Board of Directors (1993-1994), President, Board of Directors (1994-1998); City of Fort Wayne Redevelopment Commission, Design Committee for Allen County Courthouse Green; Founder: Allen County Intensive Supervision, Home Detention and Community Service Programs; Allen County Community Corrections Advisory Board, co-chair (1999), chair (1985-1994), director (1994-present); Allen County Criminal Justice Task Force (1994-present); Alcohol Abuse Deterrent Program, Inc., founder and advisor to Board of Directors (1989-2002); One Church- One Offender, Inc., co-founder and advisor to Board of Directors (1991-2002); Allen County Bar Foundation, Inc., Board of Directors (1994-1997); sponsor: Lutheran Social Services' "Children Cope with Divorce" and "Transparenting."

He was also President, Allen County Old Records Commission; Indiana Trial Courts' Legislative Interim Study Commission (1989-1990); Governor's Task Force to Reduce Drunk Driving.

Judicial Conference of Indiana: Metropolitan Courts Committee (1984-1994), Alternative Dispute Resolution Committee (1994- present), Fourth District Representative (1994), sub-committee chair and coauthor of Indiana Supreme Court Rule 7, Standards of Conduct for Neutrals in Alternative Dispute Resolution, Chairman, Alternative Dispute Resolution Committee (1995-1996), Magistrates' Committee (1997-2002); Senior Judge Committee (2001-2002); Certified Civil and Family Relations Mediator; Pension Reform Committee (1993).

Indiana Commission on the Social Status of Black Males: Third Annual Conference (1996), Strengthening the Black Male in the Family and Community, Fourth Annual Conference (1997), Black Men Standing Tall in Troubled Times - Judicial Sentencing: Who Are the Victims.

Tom's continuing legal education activities have been: Co-author "The Guest Act and How to Get Around It" presented at Indiana Continuing Legal Education Forum (1981); "Personal Injury Trials in Indiana;" "Trial Practice and Strategy: Evidentiary Issues," Indiana Continuing Legal Education Forum, seminar faculty, "Trial Objections" (1994); "Tort Reform Administration (Nuts and Bolts)," Indiana Continuing Legal Education Forum seminar faculty, "Juristic Park - Allen County" (1995); Advanced Family Mediation Workshop, seminar faculty (1997-1998); Alternative Dispute Resolution video, "You Have a Choice," and brochure (2001).

His memberships, past and present have been: Indiana Judges Association, Indiana Judicial Conference, Indiana State Bar Association; Indiana Trial Lawyers Association, Membership Committee 1979- 1980, Legislative Committee 1981 -1983, Law Pac 1981-1983; Allen County Bar Foundation, Director 1994- 1997; Allen County Bar Association, Continuing Legal Education Committee, Gridiron, Judicial Liaison, Criminal Procedure Committee, Civil Procedure Committee, Alternative Dispute Resolution Committee advisor; Allen County Trial Lawyers Association; Association of Trial Lawyers of America. Also, Allen County Mental Health Association; Izaac Walton League; Cedar Creek Study Commission, Indiana Department of Natural Resources; Leo Lions' Club; Indiana Mock Trial Competition, Board of Governors (1994-1998), instructor (1993-1994), competition judge (1994); Judicial Associate Editor, Georgetown University, peer review, Courts, Health Science & the Law (1990).

Tom's legislation related activities have been: Member, Probation Services Study Committee (1999-), Legislative Interim Study Commission on Probation Services (1998-1999); Pilot for court-annexed mediation in Family Law (1998-1999); Allen County Circuit Court, Title IV-D Hearing Officer, (1995); Allen County Circuit Court Magistrate (1984); public defender expense recoupment and user fees (1985); intensive and electronic supervision and felony escape offenses for removal of electronic devices while in home detention (1988); bail reform and 10% cash bond to secure fines, court costs, restitution and attorney fees (1985); alcohol abuse deterrent program, (1988); joint legislative resolution establishing an interim study committee to regulate evidence and the forensic use of deoxyribonucleic acid (DNA) for identification in criminal and civil (paternity) litigation, (1991); automated case management; special judge and venue fees reform; Alternative Dispute Resolution.

He has been awarded: The Herbert Harley Award presented by the American Judicature

Society in recognition of services in promoting the effective administration of justice (2002); Certificate of Recognition presented by the Indiana Judges Association for excellence in public information and education in matters of concern regarding the Indiana Judiciary (2002); Certificate of Appreciation presented by the Indiana Supreme Court (2002); Certificate of Appreciation presented by the Board of the Alcohol Abuse Deterrent Program, Inc. (2001); Appreciation Award presented by the Indiana Commission on the Social Status of the Black Male (1996).

The Sagamore of the Wabash award was presented by the Honorable Frank O'Bannon, Governor of the State of Indiana, December, 2002, upon his retirement as Judge of the Allen Circuit Court on December 31, 2002.

Submitted by Thomas L. Ryan

LAWRENCE & IRENE (BUNNELL) SABLIC FAMILY

Lawrence Francis "Larry" Sablic was born in Fort Wayne, Indiana on July 28, 1924 to Louis and Anna (Schuster) Sablic. Larry had one sister, Mary Angeline (Hill). He attended St. Peter's Catholic grade school and Central Catholic and Central High Schools. He was a member of St. Peter's Catholic Church. Larry served in the Army Air Corp from 1944 to 1946, stationed at Murac Air Force Base in Murac, California. After being injured, Larry received an honorable medical discharge and returned to Fort Wayne. He became an apprentice with Keefer Printing Company. Larry worked as a printer until 1966, when he started working for Tonne Dairy, later purchased by Allen Dairy. He worked there until his retirement in 1986.

Larry and Irene Sablic with children, 1984.

Thelma Irene Bunnell was born on August 9, 1924 in Montgomery County, Indiana. Her parents were Jacob Wesley and Zetta Myrtle (Herron) Bunnell. Irene had five sisters and one adopted brother. A sixth sister died in infancy. She graduated from Wingate High School in Wingate, Indiana, in 1942. In 1944, Irene started work for Western Union in Anderson, Indiana. She transferred to Fort Wayne and worked from 1945-1959. Irene then worked for G.C. Murphy's Company from 1960 until 1970.

Larry met Irene on a Greyhound bus in route from Anderson, Indiana to Indianapolis in April, 1945. Irene traveled on to Crawfordsville, Indiana. The next day Irene was heading back to Anderson from Crawfordsville. When she got off to switch buses in Indianapolis, there stood Larry. This began their romance.

Larry and Irene were married on January 18, 1947, at St. Peter's Catholic Church. They have seven children Lawrence Jacob was born 1947. He first married Judith Theurer in 1972, their daughters are: Rhonda (married Jeff Griffin) and Michelle (married Lanny Mendenhall). He then married Patricia Christ in 1992, and has three stepchildren: Ann, Amy, and Andy.

Joseph Louis was born in 1949, married Joyce Felger in 1974, and their daughters are: Mandy (married Steve Cherifi) and Melissa (married Ryan Hess).

James Michael was born in 1954, married Patricia Waddell in 1985; he has a stepson, Brandon Hilt and daughter Christa.

Stephan Thomas was born in 1956, and married Susan Kinsey McIntosh in 1986; he has two stepsons: Dylan and Duncan McIntosh.

Rose Marie was born in 1958, and married Michael Bishop in 1978. Her stepsons are: Michael and Thomas and daughters: Rebecca (married Rick Ridenour), Stephanie, and Cynthia. Rose later had two additional children: Louis Sablic and Shirley Durnell.

Roberta Anna was born in 1961, married Donald Davis in 1984, and have three children: Kenneth, Benjamin, and Anna.

Rita Lynne was born in 1963, married Robert Peterson in 1985, and has three children: Heather, Jamie, and Matthew.

Larry and Irene have been members of the Disabled American Veterans and American Legion organizations for over 50 years. They both have served as past commanders several times at the DAV. They have volunteered many hours through various veterans' organizations.

Submitted by Roberta Davis

LOUIS (ALOJZ/LOJZO) SABLIC & ANNA ELIZABETH (SCHUSTER) SABLIC FAMILY

Alojz Sablic "Louis" was born June 21, 1986 in Kostrena, Croatia (formerly Fiume, Austria-Hungary). His parents were Franjo "Frank" and Ana (daughter of Petar Vranic) Sablic. Louis had two older sisters: Mihajla (1872-1939) and Vika (1883-1922). At the age of 17 Louis left Kostrena to immigrate to the United States.

On April 2, 1903 he set sail from Antwerp, Belgium on board the vessel SS Zeeland. He arrived at Ellis Island, New York on April 15, 1903. From New York he traveled to Plymouth, Indiana where he worked as a laborer. He submitted his application to become a United States citizen on April 24, 1917. He became a naturalized citizen on March 3, 1923. Although Louis and his family wrote letters, he never returned to Croatia or saw his mother or sisters again.

Anna Elizabeth Schuster was born on February 13, 1883 in LeMont, Illinois. Her parents were Lorenz "Lawrence" and Mary Angelina (Haluc) Schuster. Lorenz was born in Germany. Little is known about Mary Angelina.

Anna was baptized at St. Alphonsus Catholic Church, LeMont, Illinois. Her sponsors were Christopher and Elizabeth Hettinger. Anna had one sister, JoHanna Mary Schuster. The Schuster family moved to Yoder, Indiana around 1917.

In 1920, Louis moved to Fort Wayne, Indiana. Shortly afterward he married Anna Elizabeth Schuster on April 6, 1920 in St. Peter's Catholic Church. Reverend C. Thiele officiated. In 1925 Louis started work in the building maintenance department of International Harvester. He retired from Harvester in 1953.

Louis and Anna were members of St. Peter's Catholic Church and active in the Holy Name Society and the Third Order of St. Francis. They had two children: Mary Angeline, known as "Angeline", born on May 26, 1921 and Lawrence Francis "Larry", born on July 28, 1924.

Anna died on December 29, 1963 and Louis died on January 21, 1965. They are both buried in the Catholic Cemetery, Fort Wayne, Indiana

Her maternal aunt, Jo Hanna Mary Schuster, raised Angeline. Angeline married Vernon R Hill in 1944 in Fort Wayne, Indiana. They had two children: Mary Ann and John. Mary Ann married Paul Hibler and had three children: Mary Margaret, Ruth and Robert.

Louis and Anna Sablic, 1945

Larry attended St. Peter's Catholic grade school, Central Catholic and Central High Schools. He married Thelma Irene Bunnell on January 18, 1947, in St. Peter's Catholic Church. Larry and Irene had seven children: Lawrence Jacob, Joseph Louis, James Michael, Stephan Thomas, Rose Marie, Roberta Anna and Rita Lynne. They all grew up living in the home next to their grandparents and attended St. Peter's Catholic grade school.

Submitted by Roberta Davis

SACK FAMILY

On a trip to Germany in 1990 Jim Sack and his son, Graehm went to their "home" village of Arzberg in Oberfranken, Bavaria, Germany. It is a town of some 5,000 people within five miles of the Czech border northeast of Bayreuth.

His great grandparents had come from there in the 1850s. Georg Sack and his brother Andreas traveled first to Cincinnati, then to South Bend and on to Ligonier, northwest of Fort Wayne. Other brothers and cousins followed to South Bend, an enclave in America for many Arzbergers. In South Bend, Georg met and married a woman from his village, Wilhelmina Antoinette König. They would live and work in Ligonier as grocers, as would their son, William Frederick Sack, Jim's grandfather. They also had another son, Hermann, and a daughter, Clara. Clara would stay in Ligonier. Hermann would become a respected musician working in New York and other cities, before returning to Fort Wayne where he played piano at the old Van Orman Hotel.

William Frederick Sack would marry well. The grand-daughter of civil war hero, publisher, educator and state senator Col I.B. McDonald of Columbia City, daughter of a state senator and publisher, James McDonald, Hazel Brand McDonald would move with W. F. Sack to Ligonier where she would eventually become a leading Roosevelt era politician and city clerk of Ligonier for 12 years. Her son, James McDonald Sack was born in 1913. He also married up. In 1947 he met Ruth Elmore Bryant, the daughter of farmers from Lily, Kentucky, in Indianapolis where he worked for a trucking company. She was a beautician. They married and moved to Fort Wayne where he eventually went to work for Magnavox as assistant general traffic manager. She is strong woman and staunchly Republican echoing Eastern Kentucky's support of the Union and Lincoln during the Civil War. She would convince her husband to become a Republican, despite his staunchly Democratic mother.

James M. Sack and Ruth Bryant Sack would have three children, James, Jr., William Lee, and Muriel Louise. They lived first on Harrison Street south of Williams then moved to a duplex at 713 Edgewater. From there they moved to 5103 Forest Avenue where Jim's mother still lives. The children went to Brentwood School, Lakeside Junior High School and Snider High School. Jim completed his studies with a masters from Indiana Bloomington in Telecommunications; his sister earned a masters from St. Francis College in Music and his brother graduated from the Rocky Mountain School of Art.

In 1981, with his son's help, Jim founded Germanfest, in 1985 he founded the German Heritage Society and in 1990 started the sister city relationship with Gera, Germany. His son graduated from architectural school at the University of Illinois and works for Morrison, Kattman, Menze. He is married with daughter Vivian, son Henry and wife Wendy. He, like Jim's mother, is firmly Republican. Jim, like his grandmother, firmly Democratic. Jim's wife, Svetlana Antsulevich, was born in Russia and migrated here in 1999 after they had met on the internet and dated in Warsaw, Poland. They live at 902 West Rudisill Boulevard, on the street named for the man who made Fort Wayne a German city. From this German street in this German town they trace their roots back to 1386 in Arzberg.

Submitted by Jim Sack.

JOHN & LOUISA (WHITTERN) SALWAY

John and Louisa (Whittern) Salway, and two children, planned to set sail for Australia, but the boat had already sailed. They left Tauton, England by ship at South Hampton in 1839 and set sail for America. After six weeks on the ocean they arrived at New York City. They took a boat to Albany, New York and after traveling to various cities in the East and Midwest came to Indiana in 1868.

Lola M. and John R. Salway wed, June 24, 1945 and moved to the farm and into the farmhouse in Monroeville, Indiana. The farmhouse had been used to stable farm animals so the previous April they cleaned, painted and wallpapered the six rooms. They farmed the land with their two horses, Mack and Jack. There were no storm doors, storm windows or screens for the house. One horse put one foot in the kitchen door, while Lola was mopping the floor, but that was as far as he got. The house had no electricity or telephone. The only running water was you ran to get it, and pump it. The house was so cold in the winter the drinking water would freeze in the bucket. There was no bath, just a path.

The horses would go into the barn after working in the field and if the chickens had laid any eggs in the manger the horses would eat the eggs. A chicken house was added to the farm the following year. They started with four cows and some calves and soon had 12 head of cows that were milked by hand. Before they bought a milking machine they milked 22 cows by hand and sold 40 to 50 gallons of milk to the Pet Milk Company. The up to 30 dozen eggs the chickens laid were sold to a buyer who came to the house once a week. One summer over 2,000 bales of hay was baled and stored from the dirt floor to the roof of the barn.

The spring of 1947 brought electricity in the house, but whenever it would storm the power would go out and the kerosene lamps would be lit. A phone was installed in 1952 or 1953. 1957 was an eventful year with running water in the house, a water heater, clothes dryer and built-in kitchen cupboards. They added three rooms to the six-room farmhouse in 1961 to accommodate their growing family of six children. It was constructed using lumber from the farm. A second addition was added in 1980.

The home was always full of family, friends and Christ's love. John started driving a school bus in the mid 1950s for Hoagland School (later to be part of East Allen Schools) to supplement the farms earnings. Lola started driving for East Allen County schools in the mid 1960s. Both continued to drive the buses until they retired. John died Christmas day in 1982. Lola died July 11, 2001. Their children still own the farm.

Submitted by Sharon Johnson.

PAUL & JACQUELINE LOUISE SANDERS

Jacqueline Louise (Jackie Lou) Cline was born June 22,1945 in Adams County, Indiana, the daughter of Marion and Tabitha (Teeter) Cline. Marion, a native of Champaign County, Ohio, was the youngest child of John and Anna (Romine) Cline. Tabitha, a native of Adams County, Indiana, is the oldest daughter of John and Lucy (Decker) Teeter.

Paul and Jackie Sanders Wedding, June 27, 1970

Jackie grew up in Jay County and graduated from Poling High School in 1963. She came to Fort Wayne in 1966. She lived at the YWCA and attended Electronic Computer Programing Institute. She was employed by Waterfield Mortgage as a Data Processing Clerk 1967-1971. She left Waterfield in 1971 to be a stay at home mom, working part time at various locations in the data processing field. She and Paul Allen Sanders were married June 27, 1970 in Bryant, Indiana.

Paul was born January 18,1947 in Jay County, Indiana, the son of Meredith and Genevieve (Imel) Sanders. Meredith's parents were Ted and Gamet (Timmons) Sanders. Genevieve was the daughter of Russell and Marie (Hamish) Imel. Paul graduated form Portland High School in 1966. Shortly after graduation he was drafted by the US Army where he served with the 14th Combat Engineers during the Viet Nam war. He worked for United Parcel Service as a delivery driver, retiring in 1996 with thirty years of service.

Jackie was an active 4-H leader in Allen County for several years and is a member of the Mary Penrose Wayne chapter of the DAR. Paul is a member of the New Haven American Legion.

Their daughter, Norma Ann Sanders-Riley, was born October 28, 1971, in Allen County, Indiana. She was active in the Allen County 4-H program. She graduated from New Haven High School in 1990 where she participated in marching, concert and jazz band as well as ISMA contests. Norma married Steven Andrew Riley on February 11, 2002. They later divorced. She is employed by Terex Advance and is a student at Indiana Institute of Technology. She has two children, Kristofer Andrew Sanders, the son of Todd Andrew Reynolds, and Amethyst Dawn Sanders, the daughter of Michael Douglas Higgenbotham. Kristofer is a student at New Haven High School and Amethyst attends Central Lutheran School. They are active in Allen County 4-H and the McMillan summer sports programs.

Submitted by Paul and Jackie Sanders

SANDERSON FAMILY

The Sanderson family of Fort Wayne, Indiana has a rich history that dates back to 1890 when Patriarch Irven Sanderson of Paulding, Ohio married hometown sweetheart Sylvia Stopher. Soon after, Irven, independent and hard-working, left Paulding in search of prosperity, opportunity and independence. In early 1900, Irven and Sylvia found those qualities in Fort Wayne, where they started their own furnace company. In 1914, they gave birth to their only son, Ray E. Sanderson. With a successful business there and a young child, Irven and Sylvia had firmly established the Sanderson family roots in Fort Wayne.

In 1936, a young Ray fell in love with Jean Karn, the granddaughter of a prominent Fort Wayne family physician, Dr. Morse Harrod. Dr. Harrod lived on East Washington Boulevard, where he practiced medicine for most of his career. A traditional family, the Harrod's had three children, one of which was Camila, Jean's mother. Making Fort Wayne newspaper headlines, the then 18-year old Camila eloped with 21 year-old Sidney Karn, the manager of a local meat market. The article read, "Miss Harrod attended Sunday school as usual, but left after the service and went directly to the depot, where she was joined by Mr. Karn and tickets were purchased for Chicago, where the wedding was solemnized." The newlyweds returned to Fort Wayne to start a family, eventually welcoming two daughters, Jean and Alice. Sidney continued his career managing meat markets, a vocation he held until his death of influenza at age 43.

Morrie and Ann, 2004

Jean Elizabeth Karn, born in 1914, attended South Side High School and the International Business College. Working briefly for Wolf & Dessauer department store in downtown Fort Wayne, Jean was a volunteer for various organizations, including the Fort Wayne Women's Club and Parkview Hospital Whitecross Auxiliary. In 1936, she met and wed Ray E. Sanderson at the First Baptist Church in Fort Wayne.

Ray was a graduate of Central High School and the International Business College. After marrying Jean, he joined Fort Wayne's prominent Lupke & O'Brien Insurance Agency, where he grew professionally for nearly nine years before starting his own company in early 1946 with friend and colleague Robert O'Brien. The two opened O'Brien & Sanderson Insurance Agency, an independent insurance company that would eventually become one of the regions largest and most successful insurance agencies.

Ray, an amateur poet and lake enthusiast in his free time, also dedicated himself to his community. He volunteered as a Sunday school teacher and, together with O'Brien, founded the Fort Wayne Pony League, a baseball league for boys ages 13-15. On a personal and professional level, Ray enthusiastically supported youth baseball, contributing financially to area leagues and teams for years and often parlaying those relationships into lucrative business for the Agency. When O'Brien & Sanderson was sold to the Toledo-based Hylant Group in 2000, it earned the noble honor of being one of only two 50-year sponsors of a Fort Wayne little league team, which back in 1957 won the Little League World Series.

Ray and Jean started a family in 1938, welcoming the first of two sons, Ray Morse "Morrie", born that year, and then Jack Lee in 1945.

Jack and Morrie grew up on the south side of Fort Wayne, both graduates of South Side High School. The younger son, Jack, went on to earn a Business degree from Indiana University in Bloomington and upon graduation joined O'Brien & Sanderson as an Insurance Agent. After two years there Jack realized his interests lie in forensics. That career path started in Clear Lake, Indiana, where the Sanderson family had spent their summers and where Ray had founded the Clear Lake Yacht Club. Jack served as Chief of Police there for seven years, and then joined the Steuben County Sheriff's Department in Angola as Chief Detective. Jack left the Sheriff's Department to join Barker and Herbert Analytical Laboratories in New Haven, Indiana, where he was a forensic investigator for 11 years. By then an expert in the forensic engineering field, Jack's specialty was in gas and electrical appliances and how they cause fires. That led him to start Forensic Investigator, LLC in 1986 where he established himself as a renowned and respected expert, speaking on the topic at seminars throughout the world. His professional experience and travel afforded him exposure to a variety of activities that eventually turned in to hobbies, including photography, boating, sailing, travel, writing, and public speaking. In 1966, Jack married Kathryn H. Alexander and the two had a daughter, Stephanie Joy. He later married Mary Cahill, with whom he lives today in St. Joseph, Michigan. Daughter Stephanie, a former school teacher and now full-time mother, has three children, Tyler, Ethan and Owen, and lives in Park Ridge, Illinois, with her husband Jack Guest.

The older of Ray Sanderson's boys, Morrie, was a born leader, seeking leadership roles within his schools and in social groups. He served as president of his senior class at South Side High School, president of his fraternity (Theta Chi) at Bowling Green State University, and was recipient of the University's President Award as Outstanding Student of his 1960 graduation class. Upon graduation from Bowling Green State University, Morrie joined the U.S. Army and served in the Reserves as an Infantry First Lieutenant before returning to Fort Wayne to join his father's company. A young, eager Morrie held several different jobs at O'Brien & Sanderson, learning the business from his father and helping the agency to grow. In 1975, Ray retired and Morrie became President and Chief Executive Officer, a post he held until its sale to the Hylant Group in 2000.

Throughout his career, Morrie remained dedicated to the Fort Wayne community, serving in numerous leadership roles with area civic and professional organizations, including First Presbyterian Church, The Civic Theatre, Fort Wayne Insurance Association, Independent Insurers of Indiana, and the Fort Wayne Business Forum, a professional group that he helped found nearly 40 years ago. Dedicated to professional growth and economic development, the Business Forum remains a vital entity in the Fort Wayne business scene.

In 1962, Morrie met and married Ann Kay Edens. Ann was a graduate of South Side High School and Indiana University, earning her degree in Speech and Hearing Therapy and being awarded the Outstanding Senior in Speech & Hearing in 1961. She was president of her sorority (Alpha Omicron Pi) and upon graduation worked as a speech and hearing specialist in New Haven Public Schools before turning her attention to her family and her community. Channeling her energies to civic duty and motherhood, Ann assumed leadership roles with various non-profit organizations over a near 40-year period, including the Fort Wayne Museum of Art, Alliance, First Presbyterian Church, Junior League of Fort Wayne (awarded Sustainer of the Year) and as co-founder of Three Rivers Montessori School, a school that today is well-respected in Northeast Indiana. Earlier in their marriage, Ann and Morrie embraced yacht sailing in the Caribbean Sea as a hobby, spending nearly 10 years accruing valuable yachting skills and hundreds of cherished memories.

In 1964, Ann gave birth to John James Sanderson, the first of three children for Morrie and Ann. A South Side High School graduate, John moved to Boulder, Colorado to pursue a degree from the University of Colorado. He later returned to Fort Wayne and joined the family business at O'Brien & Sanderson as an automation and technology expert, shepherding the company's conversion to computer-based quotes and paperless processes. But Sandersons are entrepreneurial at heart, and John left O'Brien & Sanderson to parlay his computer savvy into a business. In 1998, John started TechServices, a Microsoft training company dedicated to providing technical services to other businesses. Meanwhile, John met and married Rebecca "Becky" Soracco. They have two daughters, Rachel Suzanne and Ella Marie, born in 2000 and 2003, respectively. John's experiences and successes while owning TechServices opened the door to an opportunity at Microsoft Corporation in Denver, Colorado, and in 2005 he joined Microsoft as a Developer (Tools) Sales Specialist.

Jack, Ray, Jean, and Morrie on Ray's 80th Birthday

Chris Allen, the second of Morrie and Ann's children, was born in 1966. Also a graduate of South Side High School, Chris attended Washington University in Saint Louis, earning a degree in French and Economic, with high honors. Chris studied abroad at the Ecole Europeenne des Affaires in Paris, France for a year and worked in Chicago and in Belgium before returning to Fort Wayne in 1989. He then began his career in property investment and real estate, ventures he continues today. Taking the lead from Morrie and recognizing the value of the Business Forum in the Fort Wayne business community, Chris and John co-founded The Leadership Forum, a group of young business leaders dedicated to the economic and professional growth of Fort Wayne and its leaders. Today, it remains an influential and dynamic group of young leaders in the area. Chris married Susan Coleman in 1995 and they had a daughter, Lauren Ashley, in 1996.

Jill, the youngest of the Morrie Sanderson children, was born in 1972. She attended Homestead High School and Culver Girls Academy, graduating from the latter. Following in her brother John's footsteps, she too followed a call west. Jill attended the University of Colorado and the University of Montana, studying Economics and Public Policy, and then joining John at TechServices as his office manager. In 2002, Jill returned to Fort Wayne where she was hired as an account executive at Hylant Group (previously O'Brien & Sanderson). Jill continues to pursue her hobbies and immerse herself in volunteer roles with the Fort Wayne Rescue Mission, Big Brothers/Big Sisters, and Third Thursdays @ Three (a professional women's networking group).

Ray Sanderson passed away in 2003 and Jean, now 91, lives in Northeast Fort Wayne. Morrie remains as Chief Operating Officer and Chairman of the Board of Hylant Group in Fort Wayne. Morrie and Ann share time between their Fort Wayne and Sarasota homes.

Submitted by Morrie Sanderson

SASSMANNSHAUSEN FAMILY

This account of the Walter B. Jr. and Lynn J. Sassmannshausen family actually began at Valparaiso University when the couple met at one of those ubiquitous mixers given for incoming freshmen in September of 1960. Walter, who has been called "Skipper" or as he reached adulthood, "Skip, a sophomore from Crystal Lake, Illinois, and Lynn, a freshman from Philadelphia, Pennsylvania, literally fell in love at first sight. They became engaged two weeks later, and married On January 25, 1964. To split the difference of geography between parents of the Midwest and the East, they decided to put down roots in Fort Wayne, Indiana, in February, 1964.

Both were trained in education, yet each started work in other areas. Lynn found employment at Lutheran Hospital in the Records Department. Skip worked for Lincoln National Life Insurance as a "home office medical underwriter", studying insurance medicine and rating policies.

Soon, however, Skip and Lynn moved back into the school setting with both teaching at Mount Calvary Lutheran School in Waynedale, Indiana. Lynn taught third and fourth grade, and Skip taught fifth and sixth grades. It goes without saying that the students involved all learned to spell "Sassmannshausen." This was a joyous time as a son, Jeffrey Walter, was born to the couple on November 27, 1966. The people of Mount Calvary became an extended family.

The Sassmannshausen Family

Lynn was a "stay-at-home" mom only a short time and went to work at a nursery school run by First Christian Union Church. The couple's second son, Gregory Martin, was born on March 10, 1971.

Skip became a social studies/English teacher at Ben F. Geyer Middle School, part of Fort Wayne Community Schools. He completed his Master's degree at St. Francis University. He continued his coaching activities that had included football, basketball, and track at Mount Calvary. At Geyer, he worked mainly with the football team. Skip also served as head of the English department and at another time, head of the Social Studies department. "Mr. S." taught at Geyer for 23 years, with a single year away while teaching at Miami Middle School.

After Greg's birth, Lynn returned to the Lutheran School System as a teacher at Emmanuel/St. Michael school. She received her Masters degree from Indiana University and served as a master teacher working with sixth, seventh, and eighth grade students.

Skip had taken a football coaching job at Concordia Lutheran High School and, several years later, went there to teach Psychology, Sociology, World Geography, and Honors Humanities. He also sponsored the African-American Club at the high school. He retired in 2002, after 37 years of teaching. In retirement, he volunteered as a consultant for three years for the Voice, Concordia Lutheran High School's student newspaper.

The Sassmannshausens had been active members of Emmanuel Lutheran Church since they had arrived in Fort Wayne in 1964. Both sons were baptized there, attended grade school there, and, in Jeff's case, married there.

Besides attending Emmanuel/St. Michael School, both boys graduated from Concordia Lutheran High School. Jeff received his undergraduate degree from Indiana University. Greg graduated from the University of Indianapolis. They received their Doctor of Medicine degrees from the Indiana University School of Medicine at Indianapolis. Both have returned to Fort Wayne to practice, Jeff as a dermatologist (Three Rivers Dermatology) and Greg as an orthopedic surgeon (Fort Wayne Orthopedics).

Dr. Jeff is married to Loretta (Baker) and has three children, Connor, Carsen, and Jacob. Dr. Greg is married to Jill (Bauer) and has two children, Hannah and Luke.

Through the years, Skip has been active in the Allen County-Fort Wayne Historical Society. In 1975, he served as the project co-coordinator for the visit of the American Freedom Train. He was one of the founders of the Fort Wayne Railroad Historical Society and the Three Rivers Railroad Heritage Council. He served of the Boards of Directors of Concordia Lutheran High School and the Baker Street Community Association. He was editor for publications of the Michigan State Trust for Railway Preservation and the Nickel Plate Road Historical and Technical Society. Skip served as member of the Board of Emmanuel Lutheran Church and as Congregational President.

Lynn served on many educational committees within the Lutheran School Community of Fort Wayne. She was a caring teacher with high expectations for her students and the talent to motivate them. She was an avid reader and had a special ministry of note and letter writing to people in medical, emotional, or family distress. She was a wonderful wife, mother, and homemaker who encouraged her family with love, intellect, and faith. She was unable to finish the 2003-2004 school year and died after a short battle with cancer on July 20, 2004.

Because of her example, this family continues to serve and witness in our community. To God alone be the Glory.

Submitted by Walter Sassmannshausen

GARL SATTERTHWAITE FAMILY

Garl Max Satterthwaite was born August 2, 1911, in Indianapolis, Indiana. His great-great grandparents, Benjamin Linton Satterthwaite, born July 23, 1800, and Ruth Evans, born September 13, 1802, came from New Jersey to Warren County, Ohio in the early 1800s with their parents. Benjamin and Ruth were married in 1822 and moved to Wayne County, Indiana in the 1820s. Ruth died in 1831 and Benjamin married Mary Lukens in 1832 and soon migrated to Huntington County with their three children. Ruth was the mother of Samuel Evans and Sarah Ann, and Mary was the mother of Elizabeth. Mary died in 1866 and Benjamin died in 1869 in Huntington County. Garl's great grandparents were Samuel Evans Satterthwaite, born May 25, 1825, in Warren County and Hannah Thomas, born August 27, 1839, in Grant County, Indiana. Hannah's grandfather, Jeremiah Cox (1763-1831) was one of the first settlers of Richmond, Wayne County and was a member of the convention that formed the first Constitution of the State of Indiana in 1816. Samuel and Hannah were married in 1859 in Grant County, Indiana, but lived their entire lives in Huntington County. Samuel died there in 1908, and Hannah died there in 1919. Samuel and Hannah were the last of a continuous line of Quakers in their families since the religion began in England about 1640. Samuel and Hannah had five boys and two girls.

Garl's grandfather, John Breckenridge Satterthwaite, was the fourth child of Samuel and Hannah and was born November 4, 1866, in Huntington

The Garl Satterthwaite Family

County. In 1887, John married Amanda Delilah Long, daughter of Lewis and Sarah Catherine Priddy Long. Amanda was born December 7, 1869, in Huntington County. John and Amanda had four boys and two girls. Their son, Frank, born in Huntington County, was Garl's father. Most of Frank's ancestors had been farmers in Ohio, Pennsylvania or New Jersey. Frank left the family farm and went to Indianapolis and began to work for the railroad as a Car Repairman. Two years later, he was promoted to Locomotive Fireman and then to Locomotive Engineer in 1919. In his first 25 years, he earned a total of about $55,000 or an average of just over $180 per week. Frank married Ethel Fornshell and had two children in Indianapolis. Garl, the subject of this sketch, was born August 2, 1911, and Maxine was born in a few years later. Before Garl, Frank had a son, Lawrence F. Satterthwaite, born in Huntington County and died in Florida in 2003. Frank died in 1967 and Ethel died in 1960. Maxine Kennedy is living in Florida. Frank and Ethel, along with his parents, his grandparents, and his great grandparents are all buried in the Mount Etna Cemetery in Huntington County.

Garl joined the Navy at age 16 and was given an honorary discharge after four years, in 1932. Garl married Mary Mildred Teachnor in Indianapolis on June 3, 1931, and by 1936, they had three children. These were the Depression years and the going was extremely difficult. The family moved many times. Garl Max Satterthwaite, Junior, better known as "Max" east of the Mississippi, Clyde Lee and Shirley Ann were all born in Indianapolis. In 1936, Garl was working for General Electric and the family was living in Fort Wayne. They rented a two story house on Van Buren Street just north of the railroad tracks. It is now an empty lot. Patty Lou was born while they lived on Van Buren. The Satterthwaite's then moved to another rented house around the corner on Jackson Street near the end of West Superior. Max, the oldest, still talks about the times he played nearby under the Sherman Boulevard Bridge and on the railroad trestle. Max and Clyde attended Washington Elementary School. By 1940, after several more moves to various locations back in Indianapolis, Garl returned to Fort Wayne to work at General Electric. They bought a home in Fort Wayne on Ethel Street, a dirt street on the boundary of the North East corner of town. Donald Ray was born a few years later. All the children went to Franklin grade school on Saint Mary's Street and four went to North Side High School, but Max went to Central High. Max took Purdue Extension classes in Fort Wayne and went on to graduate from Purdue University and University of Southern California.

Garl and Mary worked at General Electric for over twenty years. Garl had another short stint in the Navy, serving in the U.S. near the end of World War II. For recreation, Garl and Mary bowled regularly at the General Electric Employees Recreation Building, the family spent time at Lake Barbee during the summer two-week plant shutdown and regularly went to Indianapolis on weekend trips so the parents, grandparents and other relations could play penny-ante poker. After retirement, Garl and Mary moved to California and Arizona, but finally decided Fort Wayne was where they wanted to spend their final years. Garl died January 7, 1992 and Mary died December 20, 1995 and they are buried in Lindenwood Cemetery beside their son, Clyde. They have 12 grandchildren, 16 great grandchildren, and 2 great-great grandchildren. Garl "Max" now lives in Moorpark, California with his wife, Carol; Clyde died January 12, 1966 in North Carolina while on Marine Corp training; Shirley Moore and her husband, Gerry, live in Muskegon, Michigan; Patty Stauffer, and her husband, Bill, and Donald and his wife, Nancy, still live in Fort Wayne.

Submitted by Garl M. Satterthwaite

CARLTON JOSEPH SAUDER & M. JOANNE (MILLER) SAUDER

Carlton was born April 2, 1929, in the Methodist Hospital, Fort Wayne, Indiana. Carlton's parents were Jerry H. Sauder and Wilma Grabill Sauder. He was the first child born to this couple. Jerry Sauder owned Sauder's Farm Hatchery and Feed Mill. He also served as minister at Grabill Evangelical Mennonite Church. Wilma Sauder had been a teacher and was extremely active in both the church and the community. Carlton had two sisters. Kathryn Sauder Moore (married to Larry Moore of Harlan) and Carolyn Sauder Urich (married to Joe Urich from Bluffton, Ohio).

Carlton and Joanne Sauder

Carlton went to school in Leo all his primary and high school years. He graduated from Leo High School in 1947. Following high school, Carlton entered Bluffton College, Bluffton, Ohio, where he earned a B.A. in business and economics. He was graduated from Bluffton College in 1951. In the fall of 1951 Carlton enrolled at Purdue University for graduate work in animal nutrition. He spent one year at Purdue and then he was drafted into the U.S. Army in 1952.

Carlton entered the Army in August 1952. Following his basic training he attended Motion Picture School at Fort Monmouth, New Jersey. From there he was sent to Korea where he served for a year and a half with the 25th Infantry Division, Signal Corp Photo Unit. He returned to the states in the summer of 1954. Since that time he has worked for the family business, Sauder Feeds. Most of his professional life has been spent doing animal nutrition work for the family feed manufacturing business.

Carlton married M. Joanne Miller in 1952 just prior to his entering the Army. Joanne was born in Orville, Ohio, on October 23, 1932. She was the daughter of Ivan and Annabelle (Hartzler) Miller. In 1937 the family moved to northwestern Pennsylvania where her father was a large-scale potato grower. Joanne attended a one- room school in Beaverdam, Pennsylvania, where she was double promoted twice. She entered Corry High School at age 11, graduated from high school at age 15, and graduated from Bluffton College at age 19 in 1952. The couple met in college and married several weeks after her graduation in 1952. Joanne s B.A. degree was in English, Latin, and history. She later completed a M.S. degree in counseling from St. Francis College plus considerable graduate work. .

When Carlton returned from Korea the couple settled in Grabill, Indiana, where they have lived ever since. Carlton served on the Grabill Town Council, Grabill Chamber of Commerce, Cedar Creek Lions Club, and the Cedar Creek Township Advisory Board. He was Cedar Creek Township Trustee for one four-year term. He also served on the Allen County Plan Commission as well as the Allen County Board of Zoning Appeals. Carlton served for years as a Director of the Grabill Bank until his retirement in 2003. He has been an active member of Grabill Evangelical Mennonite Church all of his life.

Joanne taught school for 26 years in the East Allen County Schools. She taught at Leo High School and Village Woods Middle School. She transferred to Leo Elementary in 1979 where she piloted an elementary counseling program for East Allen County Schools. She retired from teaching in 1988. Joanne was the first woman to serve on the Grabill Town Council. She was President of the Council for 20 years. Joanne was on the Allen County Extension Board, and was appointed to the Allen County Solid Waste District. She taught Sunday school for decades at Grabill Evangelical Mennonite Church where she has been active. She was appointed to the Executive Committee for the Mennonite Central Committee, a church wide relief and development agency. This assignment required considerable international travel to developing countries. Joanne was elected to the Board of Trustees of Bluffton College in 1995. She now serves as Secretary of the Trustee Board.

The Sauders have two sons and three grandchildren. Their son, Jerry Ivan Sauder, graduated from Bluffton College where he met and married Kathy Sivey Sauder. Both Jerry and Kathy are involved in the management of Sauder Feeds, the family business celebrating 85 years of service in 2005. They have three children: Joshua, a Bluffton College graduate, now employed by Sauder Feeds; Maria Sauder (Ben) Klea, a student at IPFW, and Megan, a senior at Leo High School. Their son, James Miller Sauder, a Bluffton College graduate, lives with his partner, Paul Hogrefe, in Minneapolis where he is Director of Operations for Headwaters Foundation.

Submitted by Carlton Sauder

JERRY H. & WILMA GRABILL SAUDER FAMILY

Jerry H. Sauder (1898-1992) and Wilma Grabill (1900-1989) grew up on adjoining farms in Cedar Creek Township and attended the same one-room school. The Wabash Railroad and its railway station, built between their farms the year Wilma was born, was the eventual location of the town of Grabill. It was named for her father, Joseph Grabill.

Jerry and Wilma Sauder

At age 11, Jerry begged his parents for an incubator to hatch eggs. The young entrepreneur started a mail order business and in 1918 built a hatchery. He went to Bluffton College, Ohio, for a few business courses where he began a love of theology that led to a B.A., then a M.A. and B.D. from Witmarsum Theological Seminary. Jerry was asked to become pastor of the Grabill Mennonite Church, an unsalaried position he held for 23 years, performing 37 marriages. Wilma went to Tri State Teachers College and became a teacher in area one-room schools. She received a B.A. from Wheaton College.

Jerry and Wilma married in 1927 and continued graduate studies at Northwestern University and Chicago Divinity School. Responsibilities lured them back home where Jerry continued developing his business, building a feed mill in 1935, and pastoring his home church, while Wilma became a homemaker and mother of Carlton, Kathryn (Moore) and Carolyn (Urich).

The Saunders quietly modeled a strong sense of service and positive attitudes for their church and community. Wilma was a charter member of the GLC Club, Helping Hands, served as Sunday school teacher, 4-H leader, and on the Indiana State Board Citizenship Committee. Jerry was a charter member of the Cedar Creek Lions Club and Grabill Chamber of Commerce. As a 45-year member of the Bluffton College Board of Trustees, the Sauder Visual Arts Center at Bluffton College honors his name. In 1967 Jerry and Wilma donated the original Grabill barn for a community center. The center helped begin the Grabill Country Fair.

Submitted by Carlton Sauder

JAMES WILLIAM SAVAGE FAMILY

James William Savage was born in Dixon, Van Wert County, Ohio on April 14, 1888 to Thomas Jefferson Savage and Susan Amanda Snyder. Thomas married Susan on October 5, 1869. They had eight children: Celestia Ellen, Susan Estella, Otis Orrin, Carrie Belle, Mary Ella, Albert J., Harry Edison, and James William.

Susan died on September 22, 1888 in Van Wert County, Ohio and Thomas on September 14, 1923 in Fort Wayne, Allen County, Indiana. He was a farmer in Van Wert County Ohio.

James married Mary Stella Bollinger of Allen County, Indiana on September 23, 1911 in Eau Claire County, Wisconsin. Mary Stella was born to Isaac Bollinger and Susan Schmidt on August 26, 1891 and was one of nine children: Martin Theodore, Arthur Orlando, William Roscoe, Leona Leota, Oran Otis, Cora Levada, Ida May, Mary Stella, and Harry Wilson.

James and Mary had eleven children: Susie Phyllis Juanita, James Herbert, Herbert Milton, Czerney L., Darwin Stuart, Richard Gordon, Lome Verne, Maynard, Norma Valetta, Patricia Mercedes, and Dallas Quentin.

Mary Stella died on April 8, 1963 and James on June 21, 1980 in Fort Wayne. They are buried in Lehman Cemetery, Paine, Ohio. He was a tenant farmer in Allen County, Indiana and she was a homemaker.

Richard Gordon Savage was born on October 13, 1918 in Edgerton, Allen County, Indiana. He went to Milan Township School and worked on the farm his parents rented until he voluntarily joined the Air Force during World War II. He was an airplane mechanic in the European Theatre and was honorably discharged on August 29, 1945. He worked for the Indiana Air National Guard at Baer Field, Fort Wayne, Indiana for twenty-four years. He went on active duty in November 1961 during the Berlin Crisis, serving in Chamblee, France.

Richard Gordon Savage married his World War II sweetheart, Dorothy Louise Volmerding on September 23, 1945 (see Henry William Volmerding Family). Richard and Dorothy had two children: LouAnn Rae and Cheryl Kay.

LouAnn was born on May 30, 1948 in Fort Wayne. She went to school at Trinity Evangelical Lutheran, Concordia Lutheran High School, Indiana Business College, and graduated from MCC, Waco, Texas in 2005 with a teaching certificate. She married Donald L. Olson, Jr. on August 22, 1970 at Trinity Evangelical Lutheran Church. She and Reverend Olson live in Waco, Texas with their two adopted sons: Matthew William August and Jonathan William Andrew.

Cheryl was born on July 21, 1956 in Fort Wayne. She went to school at Trinity Evangelical Lutheran, Concordia Lutheran High School, Indiana Vocational Technical College, and graduated with a Bachelor's of Science Degree with an Accounting major from Indiana Purdue University, Fort Wayne, in 1991. She married Jerry N. Miller on August 29, 1981 at Trinity Evangelical Lutheran Church, Fort Wayne. She and Jerry live in Fort Wayne, with their two adopted children: Aaron Newton and Taylor Louise. Jerry is a HVAC Tech and Cheryl is a Business Manager. They are members of Trinity Lutheran Church.

Submitted by Cheryl Miller

NORMAN E. & KATHRYN L. SCHAEFER

Norman E. Schaefer was born April 21, 1923. His family left Germany and came to Allen County in the 1860s. Norman and his brother, Wayne Walter, were the grandsons of Ferdinand A. Schaefer and Sophia W. Kammeyer, and the sons of Walter C. Schaefer and Matilda M. Korn. Walter was an officer with the Fort Wayne Police Department. Norman married Kathryn Louisa Magley on July 27, 1946, at Forest Park Methodist Church. The Magley family emigrated from Switzerland in 1831, settling first in Columbus, Ohio, and then later moving to Whitley County, Indiana. Kathryn, born March 13, 1918, is the granddaughter of Benjamin Franklin Magley and Emma Catherine Kessie, and the daughter of Benjamin Harrison Magley and Bertha Eliza Hire. Ben and Bertha moved to Allen County in the 1920s. Bertha was a teacher in Thorncreek Township in Whitley County prior to moving to Fort Wayne. Ben was a farmer, sold International Harvester farm equipment, and briefly worked for the railroad while in Whitley County. After moving to Fort Wayne, he worked as an engineer at International Harvester and retired in 1955.

Kathryn, Norman, Elizabeth and Susan Schaefer

Norman attended St. John's Lutheran School as a beginning student. He completed his early education at Forest Park School and graduated from North Side High School in 1940. Kathryn attended James Smart School before graduating from South Side High School in 1936. Kathryn worked for Gilmartin Lumber Yard, Canfield Lumber, and International Harvester prior to marrying Norm. Norm served in World War II as a bombardier in the Army Air Force, worked as a driver for local dairies upon returning from military service, and retired from the Fort Wayne Fire Department after 32 years in 1980. He held various ranks in the Department, but was honored to serve as Assistant Chief in the 1960s when he helped lead the fight against the Wolf and Dessauer fire. He also worked several other major fires, such as the Broadway gas explosion, Maloley's Grocery on Creighton Avenue, downtown Trolly Bar, Sheraton Hotel, and the Rosemarie Hotel on the Landing. On days off from the FWFD, he worked for NuClean, the company he owned and operated. Kathryn "Kate" was the company bookkeeper, which allowed her to stay home while raising their daughters. During those same years, both Norm and Kate were actively involved with the local Democratic Party. In 1966, they purchased property at Lake George in Michigan where they spend several months each year. Norman and Kathryn are the parents of Elizabeth K. Racine and Susan A. Ross, both of Fort Wayne, grandparents of Molly E. Baumert, Matthew B. Young, and Adam D. Racine of the Fort Wayne area, and have two great-grandchildren.

Submitted by Susan A. Ross

RICHARD E. SCHEELE FAMILY

Richard "Dick" Scheele was the son of Marcella Drahot and Edwin F. Scheele. He was the third generation of Scheele presidents of Wm. Scheele and Sons, Company, Inc., Fort Wayne, Indiana. The beverage business was founded by his grandfather, William Scheele in 1893.

On May 6, 1950, Dick was married to Rosemary Reuss, daughter of Marie Kiley and John L. Reuss, president of Old Crown Brewery. It was said to be a "marriage of beverages."

Dick became president of Wm. Scheele and Sons when his father, Edwin F. Scheele passed away in August 1962. By this time, he already had eight children and two more were to follow.

Richard Scheele

In 1958, Dick purchased a large parcel of land west of the city, on Aboite Center Road, with hopes and dreams of building a family getaway. This dream became a reality, with the building of an A-frame house, barns, lake, and planting of hundreds of trees. Being the generous man that he was, this home provided swimming, fishing, horseback riding and cookouts enjoyed by family and friends. It became known as the "Scheele Farm" and was the site for Dick's annual employee picnic. The Scheele Farm was known and enjoyed by many generations in Fort Wayne.

Under Dick's direction, by the mid sixties, Scheele's bottling line included Pepsi, Teem, Suncrest and White Rock products. Soon other Mason's, Canada Dry and Nesbitt's products were added to the Pepsi Plant, located at 1207 N. Harrison Street.

Richard started a canning plant in 1969. Summit City Canning was located at 601 Louisedale Drive, Fort Wayne. In April of 1975, Dick sold the bottling and canning companies to RKO. At that time, the Pepsi plant was in the top ten Pepsi plants, per capita for franchises in the country.

Dick became a consultant for RICO and was in the final negotiations with Indiana Purdue University, Fort Wayne, to build an indoor iceskating rink when he passed away suddenly on July 13, 1975, at age 53.

He was involved in youth hockey, Pepsi, Komets, and President of the 100% Club. He supported the Philharmonic and Fort Wayne Follies. Dick was a member of the Fort Wayne Country Club, Elks Club, Navy Club and St. John the Baptist Church.

Dick had a great love of classic cars. In 1998, his 1930 LaSalle Model 340 Eight Coupe was donated to the Auburn Corde Duesenburg Museum. This classic car was a gift from his children, William, John, Mary (Russell), Sara, Patricia (Crawford), Thomas, Nora (Sunderland), Edwin, Stephen and the late Matthew Scheele, in memory of Richard and Rosemary Scheele. The sporty LaSalle took its place in the Gallery of Classics display on the museum's first floor.

Submitted by Mary Russell

GEORG & BABETTE SCHEIBENBERGER

In 1918, Georg Hans Scheibenberger married Babette Meringer. Georg was born May 22, 1893, in Porndorf, Bavaria, Germany. He was a workman, while Babette, daughter of Leonhard Meringer, from Koenigshofen, was a Hausfrau, a housewife. She was born September 22, 1893. Together they lived in Straubing, Germany. Georg joined the Kaiser's army during World War I and served during 1914-1917. He served in the cavalry and fought mostly in France. He was awarded the Iron Cross, Second Class, and several other medals.

After his discharge from the army, Babette and he lived in Ansbach, Germany, a town a few miles south of Nuremburg. On March 17, 1921, the couple's first son Karl Christian was born.

Post-World War I Germany was in chaos. Government was in a shambles, unemployment was high and the German economy was almost non-existent. The Deutschmark was devalued almost daily. It got so bad that when those fortunate enough to work were paid, their money was worthless. At one time it took a cart-full of Deutschmarks to buy a loaf of bread.

At this time, Georg, Babette and young Karl decided to leave Germany for the United States. In December 1923, they left Ansbach and traveled to the German port city of Bremen where they boarded the SS *America*. Their trip was paid for by an uncle, Martin Gospadarek, living in Fort Wayne. On December 13, 1923, they landed at Ellis Island, and went through the rigorous immigration process. Records reflect that upon their arrival at Ellis Island they had $50. They also misspelled Georg's last name listing it as "Schreibenberger."

The family traveled to Fort Wayne and Georg obtained a job at Fort Wayne Waste Paper Company, located at Columbia and Barr Street, the current sight of the Performing Arts Center. Georg was also active in the German American Legion, an organization of German World War I veterans, and the family regularly attended events at Germania Park.

On December 22, 1927, their second son, Robert George Scheibenberger, was born. Both Karl and Robert attended St. Paul's Lutheran School and graduated from North Side High School. Both worked at the United States Postal Service and retired from there.

Georg, Robert, Karl and Babette Scheibenberger, 1938.

Karl married Pauline Poorman, and Robert married Marilyn Rouch. Karl and Pauline had two sons, David and Daniel. Both are retired school teachers. Robert and Marilyn have two sons and twin daughters.

Their oldest son, Kenneth Robert, is a Judge of the Allen Superior Court. He is married to Susan Bunger, from Goshen, Indiana. They have a daughter Abigail Alice and a son Samuel Robert. Ken was a founder of the German Heritage Society and has served as its President since 1987. He is also active in the annual Germanfest celebration.

Son Timothy Lee is an industrial electrician and is married to Rena Wilson. Daughter Melinda Sue is married to Mark Smith. They have a daughter, Natalie. Daughter Laura Ann is married to Matthew Hillyard. They have two sons, Isaac and Zachary.

Babette Scheibenberger died in 1957 and Georg died in 1962.

Submitted by Ken Scheibenberger

LOIS IRENE SCHEIMANN

Lois Irene Scheimann was born in Fort Wayne on September 22, 1935, the second child of Harold Scheimann and Alice (Ross) Scheimann. Her older brother, Donald Harold, was born in 1933 and her younger sister Carol Alice, in 1938. Both the Ross and Scheimann families originated in Germany. The Scheimanns originally settled in the Decatur, Indiana, area in 1845 and moved to Allen County about 1900. The Ross family went from Germany to Minnesota then William Ross, Lois's grandfather, moved to Fort Wayne in 1925. Both families originally made their living in farming. William Ross became the manager of the kitchen at Concordia Senior College, later to become the Seminary.

Lois grew up in Fort Wayne, graduating from Bethlehem Lutheran School in 1948. She then went to Central High School, graduating in 1953. While in high school she was active in girl's athletics and student plays. She was voted Junior Prom Queen and, in her senior year, was voted Best Girl Citizen by the student body. She then studied nursing at Parkview Hospital and graduated in 1956 as a Registered Nurse. Her first job as a nurse was at the VA Hospital in Cincinnati, Ohio. She married Jack L. Gumbert on June 15, 1957. Between 1957 and 1961, she worked as a research assistant at the University of Cincinnati Medical School. After returning to Fort Wayne in 1967, she devoted her time to her family while Jack Sr. was in Vietnam (see history of Jack L. Gumbert, MD). After he returned and started a General Surgery practice, she remained active in bowling, golf and tennis and competed on Wildwood's Women's Traveling Tennis team. She served on many committees at the Fort Wayne Medical Society and is past president of the Parkview Medical Auxiliary. She is also one of the founding members of the Fort Wayne Zoo Auxilliary and past president of the Carroll High School PTO. She is one of the first women to be elected to the Gethsemane Lutheran Church Council, and while at that church, served on many of its committees.

All five of the children have gone to college and earned various degrees.

1. Jack L. Jr. has a Masters Degree in Military Science and has been in the Army as a career. He presently holds the rank of Lieutenant Colonel, and is the Professor of Military Science at Ohio State University.

2. Lori Irene has a Doctor of Education degree trom Indiana University and is presently the principal of Mount Vernon Intermediate School in Greenfield, Indiana.

3. Bradford Martin has a bachelor degree in psychology from Indiana University and is co-executive director of Step-Up Inc. of Indianapolis, Indiana.

4. Grant David attended Ball State University and is the owner of Cedar Canyon Construction Company of Huntertown, Indiana.

5. Joseph Vincent has a Master degree in Business Administration and works for the Renal Care Unit in Indianapolis, Indiana.

Lois and Jack live in Pine Valley where they are active in the club's activities. She is an avid gardener, golfer and enjoys fishing with Jack. She is also active at their present church, Praise Lutheran, where she serves as prayer chain co-coordinator.

Submitted by Jack Gumbert, M.D.

SCHINNERER FAMILY

This family story began years ago, in 1960, when Ken Schinnerer was born in Fort Wayne, Indiana at Parkview Hospital. His parents, Herb and Eloise Schinnerer, had built a one-story house with a full basement "out in the country" off Wheelock and St. Joe Roads in Allen County. At that time the area was very much considered "out in the country". Ken and his older brother and sister and younger sister grew up there and had many adventures, some probably not to the delight of their parents.

Kenton, Brenda and Kacy Schinnerer

Ken attended Holy Cross Lutheran School and then went to Concordia High School. He graduated in 1978. Later he went to four years of trade school to become a Licensed Journeyman Master Carpenter. He has become a very skilled and conscientious carpenter.

Brenda was born in 1961 at Parkview Hospital. Her parents were Lantz and Clarasee Bracken. During her early childhood, she grew up living in two houses in downtown Fort Wayne. In 1967 her parents built their dream house "out in the suburbs" between Stellhorn and Trier Roads. Her younger brother and sister helped the household keep things at a steady pace also. Brenda attended Washington Center School for kindergarten and Brentwood School in first and second grades, then to Croninger to finish grade school, seventh through ninth grades at Blackhawk, then high school at Snider. She graduated in 1979. She attended one year at I.U. Art School on Berry Street in Fort Wayne.

Ken and Brenda were married in May 1982 and have been married for 23 years. Their daughter, Kacy, was born in July 1992. She also was born at Parkview Hospital. She is such a blessing to her parents. Kacy attends Holy Cross School like her Dad but will be a Leo Lion for high school.

The family lives in a 1940s Sears kit house north of Fort Wayne in a little town called Leo. The house sits on some beautiful acreage that borders the St. Joe River Cedarville reservoir. On a full moon night the reflection on the water makes it look like a lake of liquid silver, or, on a cold winter's eve, you can hear the ice groan and moan and crack! It's "old man Joe" calling out to you. Living on the St. Joe River can be magical at times. They have lived here for 21½ years and truly love it. Their street is like the "Leave it to Beaver" neighborhood from the old TV show. Everyone knows each other and actually cares about each other's lives. Living in Allen County is nice. Where they live, they can get to most of Fort Wayne in 20 minutes or into Auburn, Indiana, in that same amount of time. There isn't much "out in the country" left anymore in our county due to all the construction going on, but if a person looks hard enough, "living out in the country" is still there. It's still in the hearts of the people. It's a nice place to be.

Submitted by Brenda S. Bracken Schinnerer

FAMILY OF RAMAS J. SCHLATTER

Ramas J. Schlatter (1901-1978) was the fourth son of Christian B. Schlatter (1861-1939), called "Huckleberry Chris" because he had a huckleberry patch, and to distinguish him from others named Christian in the family. Ramas' grandfather was Benjamin Schlatter, who came to Leo, Indiana, in 1853 from Alsace Lorraine.

Ramas married Rhoda Steiner on June 16, 1927. Rhoda (1902-2001) was the daughter of Eli and Emma Steiner. Ramas' siblings were Odie, Syntyche, Edward, Adam, Maggie, Mary and Philip.

Adam Schlatter, drafted during World War I, while in the service did some serious thinking about his relationship with God. At that time he was corresponding with Milly Stavenic from Mansfield, Ohio. These events led both Adam and Milly to make personal commitments to Jesus Christ as their Savior and to each other in marriage.

Tragedy struck the Schlatter family in 1930. Adam contracted lockjaw from a scratch on his forehead in July of 1930 and while in the hospital he had a near death experience. Milly, at his side, thought he had died. He revived for a time and shared with her and others about seeing his Savior, Jesus Christ. As a result of Adam's death, many things changed in the Schlatter family and influenced others. Edward, Ramas and his wife, Rhoda, Philip and his wife, Thelma, all com-

June 16, 1966,
Ramas and Rhoda Schlatter's 39th Anniversary

mitted their lives to Jesus Christ as their Savior and Lord.

Another change came to the life of Ramas because Milly could no longer stay on the farm after Adam died. Ramas and Rhoda and their young son, Donald, moved to the farm and Milly, with Ethelyn and Joan, moved to Ramas' previous home, where Victor was born.

Ramas Schlatter's children are Donald, Leon, Allen Jay, and Melba Jeanne.

Donald Christian married Janet Eikenberry on June 26, 1949. After teaching and missionary work in Alabama, Don and Janet went to the New Tribes Missions training camp in Fout Springs, California. There Don survived a forest fire that killed other New Tribes missionary candidates. Don, Janet and their first child, Rachel, went to Thailand, where they served for fifty-two years and translated the Bible into the Lawa language. Their children are Rachel (Steffen), Philip, Thomas, Joanna (Fama), and Mary (Aspinwall).

Leon Edwin married Jewel Miller on June 1, 1962, in Manaus, Brazil. Both had previously taught in Indiana. They served as school teachers in Brazil with New Tribes Missions as school teachers for 41 years. Their children are Sandra (Gutwein), Denise (Hohulin), Karen (Fontanilla) and Daniel.

Allen Jay married Carol Kiefer on January 29, 1956. Allen, also known as A.J., taught in the East Allen County school system for many years, farmed, and was the pastor at Westwood Fellowship in Woodburn. Their children are Mark, Stephen, Jana (Worthman), and Kurt.

Melba Jeanne married William Heinsman on November 3, 1956. They served in Taiwan with Team Radio as engineer and director for 35 years, broadcasting the gospel to mainline China. Their children are Kristen (Mante), Joseph, Ronald, Susan (Estell), and Randal.

Many of Ramas' grandchildren have served as missionaries, pastors, church workers, or teachers.

Submitted by Leon Schlatter

JOHANN WENDELIN SCHLEINKOFER & CHARITAS MATTES FAMILY

Johann Wendelin Schleinkofer was born in Ober Roden, Germany, on December 11, 1858, and died in Fort Wayne on November 23, 1933. He was the oldest child of Caspar Schleinkofer and Elizabeth Jäger. After fulfilling his obligation in the German army, he immigrated to Fort Wayne in March of 1882. Johann joined his cousin, Jacob Koehl who had immigrated to Fort Wayne in 1880. Peter Schleinkofer, Johann's youngest sibling also settled in the Fort Wayne area some years later.

Charitas Mattes was born in Trittenheim, Germany, on January 19, 1856, and died April 13, 1926, in Fort Wayne. She was the second of eight children born to Nicholas Josef Mattes and Anna Maria Kremer. Nicholas, Anna and at least six of their children came to Fort Wayne over a ten year period. Other children documented to have arrived here in Fort Wayne include Joseph, Nicholas, Jacob, Apollonia, and Catherine.

Johann and Charitas were married at St. Peter's on May 21, 1889. They are shown here in their wedding picture. They had four children: Anna (1891-1961), John (1893-1962), Leona (1895-1949), and Joseph (1897-1955). Johann worked with his two sons on the Pennsylvania railroad. Johann was a machinist, John a fireman, and Joseph a riveter.

Johann Schleinkofer and Charitas Mattes wedding picture.

The marriages and children for Charitas Mattes' siblings are as follows: Joseph Mattes married Anna Shiller. They had five children: Nicholas, Catherine, Frank, Joseph and Anna. Nicholas Mattes married Theresa Schaefer. They too had five children: Nicholas, Catherine, John, Agnes and Joseph. Jacob Mattes married Eva Lerch and had nine children: Joseph, Nicholas, Leonard, Apolina, Anna, George, Henry, John, and Jacob. Apollonia Mattes married Adam Kramer. She had seven children: Joseph, Nicholas, Maria, Eva, Agalla, Catherine, and Charitas. Catherine Mattes married John Rodermund and had four boys: John, Jacob, Joseph, and Nicholas.

Anna Schleinkofer married Everett Miller and had two sons. After serving in the military, John remained single. Leona married Fred Belger and had one daughter. Joseph Schleinkofer married Beatrice Wheeler, daughter of Homer Wheeler and Elizabeth Steele. Although Beatrice was from Missouri, her mother's ancestors (Steele/Anspaugh) had settled in Noble County, Indiana, years before. Beatrice and her descendants remain in Fort Wayne and the surrounding area.

Submitted by David Schleinkofer.

ALBERT & ANGELINE (CARANI) SCHMID

Albert Evans Schmid, Jr., was born in Knoxville, Tennessee. His parents were Albert Sr. and Bertha Floyd Schmid and he had two brothers, Richard Rudolph and William Floyd. After serving in the U.S. Navy Construction Battalion and USN ROTC, he received a B.S. in Electrical Engineering from the University of Tennessee. It was while attending Brown University in Providence, Rhode Island, that he met Angelina Jean Carani.

Angelina was the daughter of Anthony Carani and the former Helen Victoria Vanderberg. They had two sons, Paul and Anthony Jr., and a younger daughter Delores, in addition to Angelina.

After World War II, Albert and Angelina were married and returned to Knoxville, Tennessee, where he received his B.S.E.E. They moved to Maryland where he was employed by the U.S. Navy Ordnance Lab and completed the studies for a Doctorate in Electrical Engineering. In 1952 the family, including two daughters, moved from Greenbelt, Maryland, to Fort Wayne where Albert was to be employed by the Magnavox Company for thirty-six years. By 1956 another daughter, Rebecca Suzanne, and son, Albert III, completed the family.

At that time the family bought a house at 1802 Florida Drive which would be the family home forever.

The first daughter, Beverly Jean, was born in Knoxville, Tennessee, moving to Fort Wayne where she and the other children all attended Forest Park Elementary and Lakeside Junior High School. All graduated from North Side High School. Beverly received a teaching degree from Manchester College, and her Masters from Indiana University in Fort Wayne. She married Robert Stahly from Berne, who is now deceased. They had two daughters, Susan Marie and Michelle Lynn. Beverly continues to teach in the Fort Wayne Community Schools. Both Susan and Michelle received bachelors degrees at Indiana-Purdue in Fort Wayne. Susan married Michael Holbrook and they both are employed by Holbrook Trailer Transport Company. They have a son, Joshua and a daughter Abigail. Beverly's second daughter, Michelle, also teaches in Fort Wayne School System receiving her M.S. from St. Francis University in Fort Wayne. She is married to Stephen Shank, who is employed by Steel Dynamics. They have two sons, Steve Jr. and Stuart Ray.

Patricia Louise Oswald now teaches in the Los Angeles School System. She was born in Riverdale, Maryland, but moved here near the end of her first year. She attended Hillsdale College in Michigan and received her B.S. in Psychology and an associate degree in Mental Health from Purdue in Fort Wayne. She married Walter Rex Oswald and they have a son, Billy Rex, and a daughter, Angela Marie. Billy Rex works for Southwest Airlines and lives with his mother in Hermosa Beach, California. Angela works in Honolulu, Hawaii, and plans to attend the university there.

Both Albert III and Rebecca continue to live and work in Fort Wayne. They were both born here and have lived in the Lakeside neighborhood most of their lives.

Angelina died at almost seventy-five years having been the perfect wife and mother. She participated in all the children's activities, and was PTA president at all of their schools. During the ten years from 1978 until 1988 when she and Albert lived in California, she was active in the Rolling Hills Women's Club and also the Rolling Hills Estates Homeowners Association, serving as president of both. When Albert retired from Magnavox in Torrance, California, she wanted to return to Fort Wayne where most of her family lived. She enjoyed her life as mother, grandmother and great-grandmother.

Albert now shares his life with Elaine Bourie, a friend for more than fifty years. They enjoy living half time in New Haven, Indiana, and half time in Pinellas Park, Florida.

Submitted by Albert E. Schmid

DON J & PAMELA JEAN (ATKINS) SCHMIDT FAMILY

Don J Schmidt was born March 11, 1937, in Logansport, Indiana, to Helen Louise (Davis) and Donald Boetcher Schmidt. They also had Allen K. Schmidt and Sheila Faye Schmidt. Don J's maternal grandparents were Mildred (Yerkes) and Homer Davis of Walton, Indiana. His paternal grandparents were Clara (Boetcher) and Albert Jacob Schmidt of Logansport, who established the family business of Schmidt Plumbing and Heating in Logansport.

Don J, Pam, Kurt and Kraig Schmidt

Don J graduated from Logansport High School and Purdue University. He worked for Rea Magnet Wire in Lafayette, Indiana, taught mathematics at North Central High School in Indianapolis, Indiana, and was Admissions Counselor for Western Michigan University in Kalamazoo, Michigan, before becoming the Activities Director for Indiana University Purdue University at Fort Wayne, and moving to Fort Wayne in 1964. He joined the Manufacturing Technology Department in 1966, and is retiring in May 2005. He is a Fort Wayne City Councilman and has been on the council since 1971, having served as Council President four years. He is the longest serving elected official in the city of Fort Wayne's history, 34 years of dedicated service. He is a member of The Business Forum, is a 32nd degree Mason, a member of the Mizpah Shrine, and the Mizpah Shrine Band.

Don J was a passionate high school football and basketball referee for 50 years, having started while a sophomore at Purdue, and officiated the Indiana State Championship football game in 1974. He was also a circuit tennis player and traveled extensively to tournaments throughout the mid-western and southern states. He won the National Public Parks Doubles Tennis Tournament with Ed Foster of Niles, Michigan, in 1961. It was during the National Public Parks Tournament in Detroit in 1962, that he met his wife, Pam. Don J is the only Fort Wayne tennis player to ever win the Men's Singles City Championship in all three divisions, Open, Jr. Veterans, and Veterans in 1975, 1983, and 1960 respectively.

Pamela Jean (Atkins) Schmidt was born August 15, 1944, in Detroit, Michigan, to Ruby Doris (Wisehart) and Billy Ray Atkins, who was killed in Normandy, France, on July 27, 1944, just a few days before Pam was born. Her maternal grandparents were Zella Ray (Freeland) and William Harris Wisehart of Buchanan, Tennessee. Her paternal grandparents were Pauline (Outland) and Tommie Dee Atkins of Murray, Kentucky.

Pam graduated from Ferndale High School, Ferndale, Michigan, and Central Michigan University. She taught school in the primary grades, and then worked for Concordia Educational Foundation and Dr. Guenther Herzog at Concordia Lutheran High School.

She is a member of the Daughters of The American Revolution through her ancestor Patriot James Dunn Freeland's service from the state of North Carolina. She is a member of the United Daughters of The Confederacy through her ancestor Patriot Benjamin Laten Wisehart's service during the War Between the States from the state of Tennessee.

Pam was a member of Junior League, and Tri Kappa, and has served on the boards of The Historical Society, The Philharmonic Women's Committee, and Historic Landmarks of Indiana. She is currently serving on the boards of Science Central, Fort Wayne Sister Cities International, and the city of Fort Wayne's Historic Preservation Review Board.

Don J and Pam are members of Christ's Hope Ministries and Church.

They have two sons, Jason Kurt Schmidt, born March 23, 1969, at Lutheran Hospital in Fort Wayne, and Justin Kraig Schmidt, born July 20, 1975, at Lutheran Hospital in Fort Wayne.

Kurt graduated from Holy Cross Lutheran School, Concordia Lutheran High School and Purdue University with a degree in aeronautics, and is a commercial airline pilot. He has a graduate degree in horology from West Dean College, West Dean, England, and he is certified by the British Horological Institute. He is a 32nd degree Mason and a member of the Mizpah Shrine. He and Anna Maria Valente Pereira have two daughters, Lauren Alexandra, born January 16, 2000, and Reagan Elizabeth, born June 12, 2005, both in Mineola, New York.

Kraig graduated from Holy Cross Lutheran School, Concordia Lutheran High School, and Duke University with a degree in physics. He has a graduate degree in landscape architecture from the University of Virginia where he worked for two years. He is employed by EDAW, Landscape Architects, in Alexandria, Virginia, where he lives.

Submitted by Pam Schmidt

ROBERT & CAROLYN SCHMIDT

Two persons closely associated with Indiana's canals are Robert F. and Carolyn I. Schmidt. Both work diligently to build the Canal Society of Indiana (CSI) into a vibrant statewide historical organization that seeks to preserve Hoosier canal era history. For over a decade, Bob has been the president and Carolyn the editor. Both Bob, son of Erwin and Eloise Schmidt, and Carolyn, daughter of Henry and Estella Henze, were born in Evansville, Indiana, in 1943 and graduated from Reitz High School in 1961.

They were married on December 28, 1963. Bob received his B.A. degree in political science from DePauw University in Greencastle, Indiana. Carolyn graduated with a B.S. degree in elementary education from Indiana State University at Terre Haute, Indiana, and taught sixth grade in Greencastle. They moved to Fort Wayne in 1965, Bob with General Electric finance and Carolyn with Fort Wayne Community Schools where she taught fourth grade at Harmar school and received her Masters in education from St. Francis University. Job transfers with GE took them to Tell City, Indiana, where Carolyn taught first grade; Jonesboro, Arkansas, and then back to Fort Wayne in 1977.

Robert and Carolyn Schmidt

They reared their two sons, Greg born April 5, 1971, and Jeff born February 27, 1976, in southwest Allen County and participated in Boy Scouts, Carolyn as Den Mother and Bob as Scout Master. After General Electric, Bob worked for twelve years as a Prudential insurance agent. Carolyn became a full time volunteer for CSI. They attend Peace UCC in Aboite Township.

The Schmidts became interested in canals and were instrumental in saving the timber frame Gronauer lock from Interstate 469 bypass construction in 1991. It received national recognition as one of the few remaining wooden canal structures in Indiana. Its timbers were preserved in South Carolina and sent to the Indiana State Museum in Indianapolis. From then on, the society grew. Carolyn handles CSI's day-to-day business and publishes *The Hoosier Packet*, its news and journal. In May of 1999, they worked with the Forks of the Wabash, Inc. and the Indiana Dept. of Transportation in the excavation, study and removal of a canal floodgate, which released excess water from the Wabash & Erie Canal into Silver Creek near Huntington, Indiana. Portions of it are on display in the Canal Interpretive Center at Delphi, Indiana.

The Schmidts travel extensively to canal and historical sites throughout the U.S. and Canada. As authorities on Indiana's canals, they have amassed a comprehensive library of books, maps and old newspaper accounts and helped produce two videos about Indiana's canals. They plan many weekend canal site tours throughout the state and beyond for society members. In 2003 they led members on a three-day Erie Canal cruise in New York. Dressed in canal era clothing, they make numerous canal presentations to local groups and stimulate canal interest wherever they go. Bob is a director of the American Canal Society and Carolyn is on the board of the Maumee Valley Heritage Corridor.

Submitted by Robert and Carolyn Schmidt

ROBERT T. SCHOTT

Robert "Bob" T. Schott was born February 2, 1911, in Fort Wayne, Indiana, to August and Almeda Schott. The other children were Pauline born August 17, 1904, Velma born April 6, 1909, and Melvin born February 11, 1918. The family residence was at 1211 Taylor Street, near Broadway. Bob's first wife was Bernice Goddard who was born March 20, 1909, in Fort Wayne and died in 1976. They married May 12, 1934, and had two sons, Anthony, who died in infancy and Larry, born 1942. Larry, who served three terms in Germany and three terms in Vietnam, died October 9, 1993. Bob married his second wife, Nettie Larison Casper, March 20, 1977. Nettie was born August 22, 1912, at Plainfield, Indiana, to Shelton Myles and Bertha Lee Larison.

Robert, whose love of aviation began at an early age, began taking flying instructions at age 16 paying for lessons from his paper route earnings. He was a true aviation pioneer and is widely known as an aviator. Bob founded the Greater Fort Wayne Aviation Museum in 1984. In his later years he donated his lifetime collection of aviation memorabilia to the museum. As aviation editor for the Fort Wayne *News-Sentinel*, Bob wrote a daily and weekly column of aviation news. For six years Bob was the host of Plane Talk, the nation's first weekly aviation program on Fort Wayne radio station WOWO. In 1943 he organized the Fort Wayne Aero Club and was its first president. From 1942 to February 1945 Bob managed the Smith Field Municipal Airport. The first Airport Manager's Meeting was planned by Bob and held in the Anthony Hotel in 1944 with 164 participants from around the United States. It was a great success. In 1945 he moved to Cleveland where he became managing editor of Aviation Publications for Conover-Mast Publishing Company.

Bob is the author of the pilot's "Ten Commandments of Flying," and he authored the book *Copy Boy* about his life and aviation. He was also responsible for the "Flying Green Cross" which promotes safety among pilots and others working in aviation. Bob belonged to many organizations including his life membership of OX-5 Wing, charter membership of QB'S and associate member of Early Birds. He devoted many years of service to the Boy Scouts of America and was awarded "The Silver Beaver Award" for

Robert Schott with Captain Eddie Rickenbacher, President of Eastern Airlines at a National Safety Division meeting, held in Cleveland, Ohio

distinguished service to boyhood. He also held a Board of Directors position in the financial division of the Fort Wayne Area Council of Boy Scouts headquarters.

Mr. Schott was an elder of Emmaus Lutheran Church and chairman of the church's Men's Club. In 1954, he moved to LaGrange, Indiana, to become a retailer. He then entered the real estate business successfully and started his own real estate school. Here he joined Mt. Zion Lutheran Church and became a trustee. Bob was an active member of his church and supported their activities in any way possible.

Submitted by Mrs. Nettie Schott

JERRY SCHULTZ & DOLLY (JUNGELS) SCHULTZ FAMILY

Jerry and Dolly Schultz live on the northwest side of Fort Wayne and have been Allen County residents since 1972. Jerry Allen Schultz, one of five siblings, was born on February 13, 1948, in Laporte, Indiana, to Edward Kenneth Schultz and Ruth Earle Schultz of Medaryville, Indiana. Edward Schultz worked for The Gumz Farms in North Judson, Indiana, supervising migrant workers for more than thirty years. Ruth Schultz baked wedding and birthday cakes, and retired as a cook from the West Central High School system. Jerry Schultz graduated from Medaryville High School in 1966. Jerry's only sister, Becky Schultz Stiller, resides in Flora, Indiana, and his three brothers reside with their families as follows: Kenneth Schultz in E. Granby, Connecticut; Donald Schultz in Austin, Texas; and Raymond Schultz in Medaryville.

L to R: Standing: Alyssa, Katie, Jeff and Jodi Bryne, Dolly and Jerrry Schultz. Seated: Sheriden, Keith, Savannah, Misty and Corbin Wallin

Dolly Marie Jungels Schultz was born in West Liberty, Kentucky, on March 23, 1951, while her mother was attending the burial of her grandmother, Dollie Marie Stepp. Dolly is one of six children born to Fred Daniel Jungels and Phyllis Stepp Jungels of Medaryville, Indiana. She graduated with only eleven years of schooling from West Central High School as Student of the Year in 1968, receiving several awards for scholastic achievement. Dolly's sister, Kerri Jungels Hamilton lives in Allen County with her husband, Greg, and their two sons, Logan and Codey. Dolly's remaining two sisters, Carol Conley and Brenda Burge, reside in Medaryville along with their only surviving brother, Fred Michael Jungels, and their respective families. Dolly's brother, Daniel Jungels, died two days after his birth on March 6, 1952. Fred Jungels is one of seven children born to John Jungels and Goldie Fleming Jungels of Jasper County, Indiana. The John Jungels family is of German descent. The Goldie Fleming family is of Irish descent. Dolly's descendant, Ronald Fleming, immigrated from Ireland to America in 1766-67 when he was 23-24 years of age. His port of entry was Charles Town, South Carolina. He served in the Fifth Pennsylvania Regiment during the Revolutionary War under Brigadier General Anthony Wayne and was honorably discharged in the winter of 1780-81. Fred Jungels of Medaryville, Indiana, was honored for his long standing career as a heavy equipment operator working on major highways throughout Indiana for nearly forty years, including I-65, I-94, I-69 and U.S. 30 in Fort Wayne. When Dolly was a young girl, she remembers her father taking the family to see a new highway on which he was working called a "four leaf clover."

After graduation from Medaryville High School, Jerry Schultz served in the United States Air Force for four years, with a one year tour of duty in Vietnam as an aircraft mechanic at Ton San Nhut Air Base. Jerry and Dolly were married on November 23, 1968, in Medaryville three months prior to his departure for overseas duty. Following his honorable discharge, Jerry attended Nashville Auto-Diesel College in Nashville, Tennessee. Upon graduation from college, Jerry accepted a job at Ryder Truck Rental in Fort Wayne in 1972 as a diesel mechanic, where he has worked for more than thirty years.

In 1980 Dolly Schultz accepted a position as legal assistant to Attorney Daniel A. Roby of the Roby, Hood & Manges Law Firm where she has worked for more than twenty-five years.

Jerry and Dolly attend New Hope Baptist Church (formerly Fort Wayne Baptist Temple) where they have served for more than thirty-two years. Dolly has been the church pianist for more than thirty years and has directed several musical dramas for the church. Jerry and Dolly had four children, three daughters and a son: April Marie Schultz (born in Nashville, Tennessee, January 31, 1972, died on February 1, 1972); their son, born prematurely, died in Fort Wayne in June, 1976. Their two surviving daughters born in Fort Wayne are Jodi Lyn Schultz born March 30, 1975, and Misty Jill Schultz born June 29, 1978. Jodi and Misty are both graduates of Blackhawk Christian School.

Jodi Schultz married Jeffrey Scott Byrne of Pinckney, Michigan, on June 14, 1997, and they now reside in Alanson, Michigan. They have two daughters, Katie Lyn and Alyssa Anne. Jeffrey is a lineman for Consumers Energy in Cheboygan, Michigan, and Jodi is self-employed as assistant to BI Worldwide, event planners for Whirlpool.

Misty Schultz married William "Keith" Wallin of Fort Wayne on August 28, 1999, and resides with her family in Fort Wayne. Keith Wallin's father, Billy Wallin, was a retiree from Delta Airlines in Fort Wayne. They have two daughters and one son: Savannah Grace, William Corbin, and Sheriden Elise. Keith Wallin is a first shift supervisor at Ellison Bakery and Misty Wallin works for Petroleum Traders and New Hope Baptist Church in Fort Wayne.

Submitted by Jerry and Dolly Schultz

JULIA DOCTOR ROBY SCHULZ

Julia was born on November 23, 1928, in Marion Township, Allen County, Indiana. She is the daughter of Oscar Doctor and Anna Bradtmueller who had six children, Aaron, Clinton, Selma, Doris, Julia and Vesta. Julia was born in the same house where six generations of Doctors lived: Lewis, Oscar, Clinton, Alan, Brent and Brent's children.

Julia is a descendant of Heinrich Doctor who came to the United States in 1834 on the ship *Virginia* from Konigsberg, Germany. Heinrich's son George is her great grandfather. Heinrich and George purchased land in Marion Township in 1840 and 1850 respectively and Lewis purchased the land in 1872 where Julia was born. She was a member of Soest Emmanuel Lutheran Church where she was baptized and confirmed. She attended seven grades at the church school, eighth grade at Marion Township Poe School, and attended Hoagland High School.

Julia married Garland Gerald Roby in 1946. He was born in Larwill, and his parents were Garland Immanuel Roby and Adeline Anderson. He graduated from Central High School and the General Electric Apprentice School of Drafting. Garland served in the Air Force during World War II. He was a scout leader for many years. They had five children, Linda Leigh, Garland Dene, Gerald Lynn, John Francis and JoAnn Marie.

Linda married Larry Burns and Roger Butler and has one son. She is a Licensed Practical Nurse and has worked thirty-five years at Lutheran Homes.

Dene married Alice Maddox and Nancy Pierce Alberding. He has two children and four stepchildren. He has worked for Rea Magnet Wire for thirty-one years as a Maintenance Technician.

Gerald married Sandra Archer. They have five children. He has an Associate Degree in Electronics and presently works for Young's Florist.

John married Marianna Goodland and Judy Sellers. He has four children. He served thirteen years in the U.S. Army. John was an X-Ray Technician and now lives in Florida and has a boat restoration business.

JoAnn married Michael Pullen. They have three children and live in Columbia City. JoAnn

L to R: Lizette Rudy, JoAnn Pullen, John Roby, Edmund Schulz, Julia Schulz, Gerald Roby, D. Dene Roby, Linda Butler

is a Registered Nurse and works at Parkview Whitley County Hospital.

Garland died in a scouting accident in 1965.

Julia married again in 1970 to Edmund A. Schulz from Lorain, Ohio. He is an Electrical Engineer graduate from Purdue University. Ed retired from Indiana and Michigan Electric Company with thirty-nine years of service. He has one child, Ann Lizette. She has a business degree from Valparaiso University. Liz married John Rudy. They have one son and live in Illinois.

Julia was active for many years in P.T.A. and Home Demonstration Clubs. She is a charter member of American Quilters Society and Patchwork Artist Quilt Club, and is a member of Appleseed Quilters Guild. Julia's hobbies include quilting, genealogy, gardening, golf and bridge.

Submitted by Julia E. Schulz

SCHWARTZ FAMILY

A history of Allen County shows that in the fall of 1862, two members met at the home of Jacob Schwartz and organized the local Apostolic Christian Church which was established in Switzerland. A census from June 16, 1880 recorded Jacob Schwartz, born in Alsace Lorraine, and brother, Christian Schwartz, born 1857, residing on plats 85 and 86 on what is now Schwartz Road. Jacob's five-year-old daughter, Lola, also resided there. Jacob's wife, Katerina, died prior to the 1880 census. Oral history indicated the older family members arrived in Indiana via the Wabash-Erie Canal, which was constructed in the 1832-1853 era. Oral history also indicated that Christian Schwartz, whose farm on Schwartz Road included gravel deposits, tried to strike a deal with the Allen County Government. This proposal would have supplied gravel to pave Schwartz Road in exchange for tax payments.

Schwartz farm on the Schwartz Road

Christian Schwartz, 1857-1929, and Wilhelmina (Minnie Bertsch, born in Germany) had seven children:

Son, Aaron Schwartz (Sarah) owned a farm in Cedarville along the St. Joe River. The old barn was converted into a fellowship center and is used by the Leo Apostolic Christian Church.

Son, Jacob J. Schwartz, 1900-1988 (wife Frances) owned a farm northwest of Cedarville. Frances was a teacher at Leo School and recently celebrated her 97th birthday on October 3, 2004. She lives in Fort Wayne, Indiana.

Daughters, Leah Schwartz, 1899-1974, and Mary Schwartz, 1895-1972, lived on part of the original Schwartz homestead until the City of Fort Wayne created Cedarville Reservoir, which flooded the bottomland along the St. Joe River in the early 1950s. Then they moved to Leo, Indiana.

Son, Henry Schwartz (Frances) had two sons, Harry Schwartz (Kate) and Arthur 1923-2002 (Dutch). Henry and Frances lived in Grabill, Indiana and started the Schwartz Auto Company. Harry and Arthur continued to sell Fords and other automobiles in Grabill, Decatur and other locations. Harry's son, Bob Schwartz, continued the Schwartz Ford tradition in Peru, Indiana until recently. Their other son, Steven Schwartz, lives in Indianapolis. Daughters Rita Gabriel and Susan Vlk live in Fort Wayne. Art and Dutch had two sons and two daughters. Arthur Jr. lives in Upland, California; Allen Schwartz lives in Fort Wayne; Tracy died in 1954; and Amy Schwartz Kemery (Bruce) lives in Goshen, Indiana. Erne (Dutch) lives in Allen County.

Christian and Minnie's oldest daughter, Elizabeth, married George Stieglitz and lived in the Harlan, Indiana area with many descendants still living in Allen County.

Christian and Minnie Schwartz also had a son, Samuel Schwartz, 1897-1984 (Irene) who, in turn, had two sons, John C. Schwartz 1928-1998 (Janet Weida) and Samuel R. Schwartz 1934-present (Janet Kestner). John and Sam both graduated from Purdue University in 1956. John was a veteran of the Korean War. John's daughter, Jacqueline, is an instructor of preschool children and lives with her mother, Janet S. Schwartz in Fort Wayne. They own part of the original Schwartz farm. Samuel R. Schwartz retired from Parkview Hospital Laboratory in 1999 and his wife retired earlier from East Allen County School system as an elementary teacher. They live in Fort Wayne, have two daughters, Gretchen Gouloff (Mike) in Fort Wayne and Erin Hukill (Karl) in Dallas, Texas. There are four granddaughters, Ali and Anya of Fort Wayne and Demaree and Hannah in Dallas. Sam Schwartz owns the remainder of the original farm on Schwartz Road.

Submitted by Samuel R. Schwartz

LEE SCOLES FAMILY

It is almost impossible for any of us to imagine what it would be like to travel from Fort Wayne, Indiana, to San Francisco, California, starting on September 7, 1921, and returning on April 2, 1922. This is what Lee and Constance Scoles did with their 1916 Federal truck with the lettering, "LEE SCOLES MOVING & HAULING, Phone 1629." The truck chassis cost $3,000 and the material to convert it to a "house on wheels" cost $300. Warren G. Harding was President of the United States and prohibition was in full swing when he did this. Little did Scoles realize the impact he would have on the motor home industry as it is today. The fact that he built it in Fort Wayne (only 85 miles from Elkhart, which is considered by many as the recreational vehicle capital of the world) is amazing.

The party of 12 included Lee's wife, daughter, parents, sisters and brothers, traveling through Illinois, Missouri, Colorado (Pike's Peak), Wyoming (Yellowstone Park), Montana, Idaho, and Washington—then south through Oregon, California, Las Vegas, Nevada, Santa Fe, New Mexico, and the Mojave Desert.

The tires were made of solid rubber, eliminating flats, but making it easier to become bogged down in mud. Scoles became stuck in some Missouri mud and got out by driving a three-foot stake into the ground ahead of the truck and fastening a chain to the stake and the rear wheels. He made it across roads that would be considered impassable today.

Million-dollar RVs are basically the same today except that they have air conditioning, microwave ovens, TVs, back-up cameras, Global Positioning Systems, and more comforts of life. Lee's "rolling cottage" was 20 feet long and 6 feet wide. It had no glass windows—instead, the openings had screens to keep the bugs out and were covered with canvas to be rolled down during bad weather and at night. Remember that this was 85 years ago.

Arriving back in Fort Wayne, the family members returned to their homes, jobs, and schools. They never forgot their trip to the West using transportation that was a cross between a covered wagon and today's RV.

Submitted by Alice K. Worman

SCOTT FAMILY

The year was 1950 and John Wesley Scott (1922 to 1988) was currently working deep in the coalmine beneath Cumberland, Kentucky. When he was discharged from the Navy after World War II he returned home. He was drawn there because his mother, Bertha Smiddy (1899 to 1988) who married his father in 1921, still lived in Appalachia. He found work with the Peabody Coal Company. Like his father, John Dawson Scott (1898 to 1939), he was now working in the coalmines of southeastern Kentucky.

His grandfather, Nathan Scott (1853 to 1909) had worked in the mines in central Tennessee, but in part because of his health, his wife Mary Lou Prater (1866 to unknown) and he became caretaker of their own boarding house in Eastland, Tennessee.

John Wesley Scott's other grandfather, Sampson Smiddy (1865 to 1914) married Lucy Katherine Brooks (1871 to 1959). He was a bricklayer. His job was to help shear up the tunnel walls of the mines. He would occasionally work outside his hometown. He had been working in a coalmine in Royalton, Illinois, when there was an explosion. He died along with fifty-two other men.

John Dawson Scott died at forty-one years of Black Lung. Now John Wesley Scott was working at the same occupation. He was haunted by a few words spoken to him by his dad. His father talked about the hardships of working in the mines and he hoped his sons would not follow in his footsteps, yet that is where he found himself. He had a wife, Betty Augusta Fleischman (1925 to date) and a nine month old child, Rodney Dale

Scott (1949 to date) to support. Both Benham and Lynch, Kentucky, were company towns. The coal companies owned all the businesses and the homes where the workers lived. The only work in the area was mining, but at that moment John Scott laid his shovel down and started to walk out of the mine. It was the middle of the day and there was no system to bring just one person out of the mine. Every step he took was detached from the normal process of leaving the mine. By the time he reached the top of the shaft, men that he had been working with earlier were leaving for home.

When he reached Benham and his wife, he told her that he had quit. They had talked earlier. She knew that he was unhappy. Betty's brother, Carl Fleischman (1920 to 1982), lived in Fort Wayne, Indiana. He was an electrician and was working for Fruehauf Trailers. He had been encouraging them to come to Fort Wayne. Carl declared that there was plenty of work. John Scott had served as a welder aboard his ship in the Navy and he felt he had a marketable skill. They loaded up everything they had in the old Ford and headed north. In one fall day in 1950 the city of Fort Wayne grew by three.

John Wesley Scott 1944

John Scott worked in local factories and welding shops. Finally he took the test to be a Boilermaker. He spent the remainder of his years working as a Boilermaker out of his union hall. After Mark Wesley Scott (1955 to date), their second child, was born, Betty found employment working at Magnavox. She spent ten years working for that company. In 1968 John and Betty Scott moved to Clinton, Indiana. John was helping construct the Montezuma Nuclear Power Plant until it financially collapsed. They decided to stay in the area. Mark had gone with them.

Rodney Scott stayed in Fort Wayne. He married Vicki Jo Schwalm (1950 to date) when she was fifteen years old and he was sixteen. They had five children, two died at childbirth, but Jeffrey Eric Scott (1967 to date), Troy Dawson Scott, (1969 to date), and Tara Andreya Scott (1975 to date) had survived. Tara married Jamie Tyler Fruit (1971 to date). After eighteen years of marriage Vicki and Rodney divorced. Rodney Scott later married Becki Nadine Beal (1955 to date). After three years they were divorced, but John Wesley Scott II (1988 to date) was born from that relationship. Rodney Scott then married Jill Ann Yoder (1953 to date) and that relationship has continued. Rodney Scott completed four college degrees and has worked as a licensed therapist, administrator, and has taught college.

Mark Scott married Mary Lou Priest (1954 to date). They had one child Amy Jo Scott (1972 to date). Amy married Anthony Glen Kite (1970 to date). Mark worked light manufacturing and construction.

Submitted by Rodney Scott

KENNETH L. SCROGHAM

Kenneth LeRoy Scrogham was born July 11, 1937, in Fort Wayne, Indiana, to Vilas and Alice Caroline (Reinking) Scrogham. Vilas was born March 6, 1910, in Delavan, Illinois; he died August 23, 2004. Alice was born January 18, 1918, in Fort Wayne, Indiana.

Vilas, Ken's father, in addition to retiring from the Fort Wayne Police Department, owned the St. Mary's Mobile Home Court and engaged in other real estate ventures in Fort Wayne.

Kenneth is the oldest of four children. His siblings are Lynn Alan Scrogham, born October 5, 1941, Wayne Edward Scrogham, born January 26, 1943, and Nancy Kay Scrogham Gerow, born March 23, 1951.

Kenneth L. Scrogham, 1997

Ken graduated from South Side High School in 1955, prior to attending Indiana University. He graduated from IU with an AB in 1959. His education continued at Indiana University School of Law, Indianapolis. He was awarded his JD in 1965.

After returning to Fort Wayne, Ken entered private law practice. He has been in practice for more than forty years. During that time he spent sixteen and one-half years in public service: six years as Deputy Prosecutor, four years as Associate Fort Wayne City Attorney, and six and one-half years as attorney for the Allen County Welfare Department. The Indiana Bar Foundation admitted Ken as a Fellow in April, 1994.

Ken is a member of Indiana Wayne Lodge #14, Fraternal Order of Police. He is a member of Emmaus Lutheran Church and serves as Vice-President of the Congregation. He serves as the attorney on the Emmaus Lutheran Church Foundation.

On June 3, 1961, Ken and Janett Sue Habecker were married. Janett was born January 25, 1940, to Denton and Rachel Belle Harris Habecker. Their three children are Lorinda Noel Scrogham, born December 27, 1964, Susan Michelle Scrogham Jones (Jay), born December 25, 1965, and Ryan Kenneth Scrogham (Charmaine Keller), born December 26, 1967.

Ryan and Charmaine have three children: Audrey Lauren, born February 5, 1999, Elise Sophia, born March 21, 2001, and Brett Ryan, born February 13, 2003. They live in Greenwood, Indiana.

Ken's wife, Janett, died May 1, 1993. She is buried in Fort Wayne.

On September 9, 2000, Kenneth married Mary Carolyn Poe Menge. Mary is the daughter of Glenn William and Winifred Anderson Poe. She was born August 31, 1938 in Lima, Ohio. Her family moved to Fort Wayne in 1945 where her father, Glenn, had been transferred by the Soil Conservation Department.

Submitted by Kenneth L. Scrogham

JOHANN SEELIG & MARGARETHA NEIREITER SEELIG FAMILY

Johann Seelig was born January 23, 1827 in Fischborn, Hessen, Germany, and his wife Margaretha Neireiter was born August 23, 1831 in Sotzbach/Untersotzbach, Hessen. Johann Seelig's parents are unknown, but Margaretha's parents were Johann Neireiter and Maria Schmidt. Fischborn and Untersotzbach were small neighboring villages. It is most likely they shared a central church where the families met. Johann and Margaretha were married in Germany May 25, 1850, and their first five children were born in Untersotzbach. When baby Elizabeth was six months old and Henry was two years, six months, the family traveled to New York from Bremen on the Bremen Bark Cariolan, arriving December 5, 1860. They went a short time later to Fort Wayne, as John Seelig was listed as a laborer in the 1861 Fort Wayne City Directory. Why they chose to settle in Fort Wayne is unknown. There were no other Seelig families in the area. However, there were several Neireiter families.

Johann and Margaretha Seelig had nine children, seven of whom survived to adulthood. Margaretha, born April 7, 1851, married Benjamin Gutermuth. Anna, born June 6, 1853, married Henry Krauskopf. Henry, born January 12, 1858, married Maria Sophia Boerger. Elizabeth, born April 26, 1860, apparently never married. Conrad Seelig, born April 8, 1863, married Matilda Heth. John, born August 14, 1865, married Catherine Schmidt, and Carl, born March 25, 1870, married Rosa Hofer. The dates and places of birth of the children of John and Margaretha are found in the German records of Salem Reformed Church, Fort Wayne. The Seelig's were early members of this church, founded in 1868 by Boerger relatives, William and Rudolph Boerger, and Jacob Heth, Seelig relative, Conrad Neireiter and others.

By 1897, two of the children, Henry and Conrad Seelig, started the Seelig Brothers Grocery Store at 75 East Wayne Street, Fort Wayne. They operated this grocery store for more than twenty years.

Henry Seelig and his wife, Maria Sophia Boerger, daughter of William Boerger and Elizabeth Spring, had three daughters. Elma Elizabeth Seelig, born July 2, 1888, married Otto Kirsch of Decatur. Meta Elise Seelig, born September 29, 1889, married Walter Robinson, and Esther Margaret Emma Seelig, born March 3, 1898, married Frederick Edward Geiser.

Henry and Mary Seelig were married more than fifty years. They were married August 18, 1887 at Salem Reformed Church. They lived all of their married life in Fort Wayne. Henry died March 16, 1939 and Mary died January 7, 1941. They are buried in the Seelig plot, Section G, lots 49 and 50, Lindenwood Cemetery, Fort Wayne, with many of their descendants. The lot owners were John Seelig, Henry Seelig, Conrad Seelig, Benjamin Gutermuth, and Henry Krauskopf and the date purchased was August 30, 1898. There are more than twenty burials of members of these related families in this plot.

Submitted by Nancy L. Riffle

GLENN & VELMA SHANK

Glenn Shank was born on January 2, 1912, and Velma Tooman was born April 7, 1913 in Putnam County, Ohio. His stepmother, Hettie Shank, died on February 25,1977. His father, Cary Shank, died on February 15, 1960. Velma's mother was Mary Tooman, and her father was Guy Tooman. Glenn and Velma's early years were spent working on the family farms. They were high school sweethearts with only six students in their graduating class. Velma was promoted to Glenn's class, as she was the only student in her class. They both graduated in 1918 from Miller's High School in Putman County, Ohio.

They were married by a Justice of the Peace in Continental, Ohio, and moved to Indiana soon after their marriage. They stayed with relatives in Auburn, Indiana until they could find a farm to rent. It was a very difficult time; however, Glenn soon found a muck (black dirt) farm that they could rent near Auburn. Relatives assisted them by finding used furniture and loaning them the tools and equipment.

Glenn and Velma Shank

In 1939 they bought a farm on the Wood's Road near Huntertown. A new house was needed, so Glenn took the money they had saved and gave it to a builder in Huntertown named Harvey Green. He laid the money on the table, and Harvey counted it and thought he could use the money to build a new house. That house on Wood's Rd. still looks good today.

Glenn expanded crops grown to include carrots, beets, broccoli, and spinach. He trucked these vegetables to Saratoga, Indiana where they processed V-8 cocktail juice using German WWII prisoners. To make extra money, he would truck sacked potatoes in one-hundred pound bags to customers in southern Indiana. He would then return with a load of coal and sell this to neighbors. In this way, he paid for his gasoline for the trip. Gasoline was rationed and farmers would receive extra gas for their farming responsibilities.

In 1947 they bought the adjoining farm of 303 acres. Mint was one of the crops grown on this new farm. They raised peppermint and spearmint. It was cut, dried, pitched on a wagon, and hauled to huge mint vats, stamped in tightly, and then steam would be turned on. People would often stop to see the mint operation. The aroma of the mint oil was detected as far away as Huntertown. Velma would deliver two or three meals a day, because the boiler was always in danger of overheating. Glenn was often there eighteen hours a day.

The couple raised four children Jean, (August, 7, 1931- July 16, 2004) was married to Edward Ryan, Virginia, (March 8, 1934) married Roger Harrod, Gerrald (Bud), (July 27, 1937) married Sally Stonestreet, and Bob, (December 3, 1941-January 1, 2003) was married to Diane Gross. There are nineteen grandchildren, four great-grandchildren, and one great-great-grand child. Anthony Shank, son of Gerrald and Sally, is deceased, and Annie Ryan, daughter of Joe and Gail Ryan, is deceased. Forty-seven family members live on Wood and Hand Roads. The remaining family members live within ten miles.

Glenn always liked a challenge, so he ran for Township Trustee and won! He later became a School Board member. During his tenure on the School Board land was needed to build Carroll High School. The corporation bought forty acres of farmland on the Carroll Road. Many people thought the price was too high. He later received some interesting phone calls. As it turned out, the price was a bargain! On this land there is now located Carroll High School, the Freshman Academy, Hickory Center Elementary School, football fields, a track field, a cross country course, and tennis courts. There is also an Aquatic Center and storage buildings.

He served as past president of the Huntertown Lion's Club, and attended the Lion's Convention in Hawaii. He passed the Real Estate and Brokerage exam and became a Real Estate agent at age 65. He worked in Real Estate for ten years.

Velma passed away on July 3, 2002, at age 89. Glenn passed away on March 19, 2004, at age 91. They had 71 wonderful years together.

Submitted by Virginia Harrod

SHANNON/MCCRORY - ROOP CONNECTION

Caroline Zimmerman (1838-1915), third daughter of Rachel Roop and Andrew Zimmerman, married Boyd Shannon (1834-1901) in 1855 and had ten children before divorcing him and marrying James McCrory in 1877 (see *Valley of the Upper Maumee River,* a historical account of Allen County and the city of Fort Wayne, Indiana, Madison, WI; Publisher: Brant & Fuller, 1889, p. 345-346). Most of Caroline's children married in Allen County. The Shannon children were Victoria (1855-1932) married George Shirey on March 22, 1872; Ida married Nathan Thorpe; Samuel (1862-1944) married Martha Toler; Roxie Belle (1865-1932) married three times (first to Jerry Shirey, second to John Trease, third to Charles Nelson); Clara (1868-1944) married James Joseph Mayhew on December 14, 1890; Etta (1870-1898) married Daniel Butler on October 27, 1887; George (1875-1949) also married three times (first to Elinora Lorena, second to Esther (unknown) of Denmark, third to Margaret M. Smith). Rachel and Mary Shannon died before their second birthdays and are buried in Old Leo Cemetery. Nothing is known of what became of the tenth child, Cornelia Shannon.

Victoria and George Shirey had five children born in Cedar Creek Township: Harry married Anna Bahrdt; Charles (1878-1955) married Iva Robison; George (1883-1959) married Mabel Hoppel; Alva Cleveland (1885-1927) married Bessie Murinel/Mulrine; and Victoria (1893-1959) married David Wright, then Elmer Wetzel.

Samuel and Martha Shannon had eight children born in Allen County: Preston (1887-1974) married Jennie (unknown); Florence married Albin Johnson; Grover (1892-1969) married Vera Coleman, then Nina Jeffries; Raleigh (1895-1969) married first Naomi Golden, second Ethel Ramsey, third Genevieve Reason; Martha married Harry Worden; Harry (1901-1969) married Ruth (unknown); Ora (1901-1902); and Alton (1904-1976) married Rebecca (unknown). Seven of the Shannon children died in Fort Wayne, where they were lifelong residents. Raleigh died in South Bend.

Clara and James Mayhew only had one daughter, Ethel (1890-1961) who married Ward Hall (1885-1969) on February 21, 1908 in Allen County. Ethel and Ward Hall had five children: Orville (1909-1995), Joseph (1912-1994), Ward (1916-1975), Emma who died in Huntertown in 2004, and Robert (1931-1977). Both Ethel and Ward Hall are buried in Parker Cemetery, near Clara and James Mayhew.

Caroline Zimmerman's only child with James McCrory was Leonard Marion McCrory (1877-1964) who married Jane Valien on October 2, 1897. Leonard and Jane's daughter, Beatrice McCrory (1902-1995) married Albert Disler; both are buried in Greenlawn Memorial Park.

According to 1896 newspaper accounts, there was a sharp division between James McCrory's children by his first marriage with Margaretha Eichelberger and the second wife, Caroline Zimmerman. In May 1896, there was a "commission of lunacy" held, and in June, James McCrory was declared of unsound mind. On September 4, 1896, the *Fort Wayne News,* headlined: "TORE THE DEED - Sam McCrory Says His Stepmother Destroyed His Title To Property." Two months later, James McCrory died, and the land dispute continued for two years before the 320 acres called McCrory's subdivision was settled.

Submitted by Kathleen Bowsher

SHARPE FAMILY

Willie M. Sharpe and Audrey L. Howell were married August 7, 1964, at First Presbyterian Church's McMillen Chapel. (Audrey became an ordained Elder at First Presbyterian in January 1998). They met in July 1961 at Fort Wayne State School, where Audrey was a speech pathologist and Willie was a social worker. Descended from African slaves, he was born in GA; she in NC. They were educated in segregated schools of Georgia, North Carolina, and Delaware. Both received baccalaureate degrees from HBCUs, he from Morehouse College (1958); she from Hampton Institute (now University, 1960). Willie's MSW degree was earned at Atlanta University (1961). Audrey earned degrees at Northwestern University (MA, 1966) and Ball State University (Ed.D., 1980). They have one daughter, Kimberly Yvonne, born September 2, 1967. Kim attended Haley, Memorial Park and Snider. She graduated from Spelman College in 1989 and Indiana University (MSW) in 1994. She married Robert Davison, III of Columbus, Georgia in 1995. They have two children, Robert Austin, IV and Audra Nicole.

Wedding Day-L to R front: Dr. Joan Bodein, Maid of Honor, Bettye J. Walker, Audrey, Willie, Audrey's sister, Essie Howell Fountain, Willie's brother, and Best Man, Rudell Sharpe, Thelma Bower. Back: Dr. Vernon P. Bodein, Theodore Bower.

Both Audrey and Willie held memberships in community organizations and served on community boards. Audrey was the first black member of the Fort Wayne Junior League, a charter member of the Fort Wayne Alumnae Chapter, Delta Sigma Theta Sorority and a member of the 1986 class of Leadership Fort Wayne. They were both members of the Fair Housing Association and the NAACP. Willie served on the boards of Fort Wayne Philharmonic, Neighbors Inc., YMCA, Youth Bureau and ACEOC. Audrey served on the boards of Allen County Public Library, Park Commissioners, Big Brothers-Big Sisters, United Way, YWCA and McMillen Center for Health Education.

In 1974, Audrey became a Title I teacher/Program Coordinator in East Allen County Schools. Superintendent Daryl R. Yost appointed her assistant principal at Village Woods Junior-Senior High School in 1980 and principal at Village Elementary School in 1981, making her the district's first black administrator. Superintendent Michael Benway later provided leadership and mentorship, giving Audrey confidence to serve during the fractious desegregation crisis. She retired from EACS in 1998.

Willie worked at the Child Guidance Clinic, later the Mental Health Center and finally, Park Center, Inc., from 1962 until 1990, with a 1 1/2 year hiatus (1966-1968) to work as an Administrator at Boys' Training School, Whitmore Lake, Michigan. The first black professional employee of the Child Guidance Clinic, he became its Chief Psychiatric Social Worker. He was Coordinator of Special Services, then Associate Clinical Director at the Mental Health Center. At his retirement from Park Center, Willie was the Director of Quality Assurance. Following retirement, he took a part time position as QA Coordinator at Northeastern Center, Kendallville. Denied housing at the Centlivre Village Apartments and Parnell Park Apartments in 1964 because of their race, the Sharpes, in 1968, rented a townhouse at Parnell Park Apartments, without incident. In 1969, they became block busters in the Lake Forest subdivision. There was mild opposition from some neighbors, but no white flight. The Sharpes moved to Ellenwood, Georgia in 2001.

Submitted by Audry H. Sharpe

SHAW-MCDONALD FAMILY

In the summer of 1960, Eleanor Cecelia McDonald Shaw and her husband, Robert Stephen Shaw, moved to Fort Wayne, Indiana, (his family home for many years) from Hattiesburg, Mississippi, where they had recently graduated from the University of Southern Mississippi. They had been married the previous fall and were ready to set up housekeeping, expecting their first child.

Bob's mother's family lived in Chicago for many years. Just after her birth in 1904, her parents, Martin and Florence Draths, moved to Fort Wayne. The family lived near St. Peter's Catholic Church where the children attended school.

Bob's father, Orrice, was born on the family farm near Wabash, Indiana. He moved to Fort Wayne to work in business after attending Indiana Business College. In later years he founded the Optimist Club here.

The Shaw family, with four children, grew and prospered until the Depression. They moved away from Fort Wayne, and Bob was born in Grand Ledge, Michigan. They returned and he attended St. Jude School. Bob and his two brothers graduated from North Side High School and joined the Armed Services. Bob chose four years with the Air Force. He was stationed in the southern U.S. in Alabama, Mississippi and Laredo, Texas. It was while he was stationed at Keesler Air Force Base that he decided to attend college on his GI Bill. Bob and Eleanor met at the University of Southern Mississippi, formerly known as Mississippi Normal College for teachers. Bob was enrolled in the business program and Eleanor was in teacher training.

Eleanor's mother had been threatening to 'fix her up' with her friend's son from church who just returned from the service. After all, Eleanor was twenty years old by then! But when Eleanor brought Bob home, her mother was delighted that he was 'tall and had good teeth'. Only problem was-he was a Yankee!

Eleanor's mother was a Mouton whose ancestors were original Acadian settlers to Louisiana in the 1700s. Jean Mouton, Eleanor's third great-grandfather, fought in the American Revolution under the leadership of General Bernardo de Galvez in 1777.

Eleanor and Bob's three children, Timothy, Mark and Ann Marie, were all born in Fort Wayne. Mark and Ann and their families still live in Fort Wayne. Tim was killed in a tree climbing accident at age eight.

Eleanor taught at Snider High School for twenty-six years directing the publication of the yearbook and newspaper for twenty years while teaching classes in English Literature and Journalism and managing the staff photography room and computer equipment. Bob taught at International Business College, Indiana Vocational Technical College and Leo High School. After teaching, he continued full-time in real estate concentrating on income property management.

Bob and Eleanor have been married forty-five years and their hobbies are golfing, travel, and enjoying their three grandchildren. Bob also likes to do home improvement projects. Eleanor is a member of The Daughters of the American Revolution. Bob and Eleanor are members of St. Jude Catholic Church.

Submitted by Eleanor C. Shaw

CARL ALLEN SHEEHAN FAMILY

Carl Allen Sheehan was born in Madison Township on May 9, 1940. As was common in country living, he was born at home. He was the fourth child and third son of Irvin W. and Alberta R. Sheehan.

He spent his formative years on the family farm, helping with the animals, crops and harvesting. Living in the country, the children would ride their bicycles to each other's homes and play baseball, croquet, hide and seek and other games typical of the times.

He received his elementary education at St. Louis Catholic School, Besancon and graduated in 1959 from Hoagland High School. After graduation he joined his father in farming.

Katherine Ann Logan came into his life and on June 30, 1962, they were married at St. Patrick's Catholic Church in Fort Wayne, Indiana. Of this union, five children were born: Laura Ann on May 1, 1963, Corey Allen on November 16, 1964, Matthew Wayne on July 22, 1966, Brian Keith on July 10, 1968, and Jonathan Perry on September 8, 1975.

Their first home was an apartment in Monroeville, Indiana. They next moved to a farmhouse on Maples Road near the home where he grew up. Carl's father had died in 1961, and his mother was living alone in a big house, trying to take care of the farm, so Carl moved his family into his childhood home.

Katherine and Carl Sheehan

While living with his mother Alberta, she started dating a widower and former neighbor, William Gerardot, and married him in 1969. They moved into a small apartment in Fort Wayne, Indiana and Carl and Katherine purchased the farm from her. Alberta and Bill did not take to city living, so they put a mobile home on farm land he owned and moved about two miles from her former home.

Carl made farming his livelihood and expanded his farm operation by renting land in addition to what he owned. He added outbuildings to the property to house his growing hog operation. As with any farming operation there were good years and bad but they prevailed and prospered.

Kathy went to work for a decorator, sewing draperies and home accessories. In 1994 Kathy went into business for herself, working out of her home. After three years she outgrew her space in the home and an addition was added onto the garage for her workshop. Window Fashions by

Kathy's Sewing Inc. has expanded and now has three employees.

A recession hit the area in 1997-1999. Farm and hog prices were very depressed. After a vain struggle, Carl sold his hogs and farm equipment and sought other employment. He is employed by EMP-CO-OP.

Carl still lives in the area where his pioneer ancestors settled and lived, on the acreage owned by his father. The original house has been completely remodeled several times and many outdoor improvements have been made. The descendants of John William Sheehan and Bertha Poorman Sheehan hold a family reunion at his home each August. Between 100 and 150 descendants of John and Bertha attend.

Submitted by Carl Sheehan

DANIEL SHEEHAN & ELIZABETH HUTCHINSON FAMILY

Daniel Sheehan's father immigrated to the United States from Ireland, year unknown. Daniel (1796-1871) was born in Lancaster County, Pennsylvania and married Elizabeth Hutchinson (1802-1875) of Monongahela County, Pennsylvania. At one point they lived in Columbiana County, Ohio. They had eleven children: Sarah, John A., Matilda, Lydia, James, William II, Elizabeth, Joseph, Martha Jane, Margaret and Daniel Jr.

Daniel Sheehan

In 1845 the family, driving horses and wagons, settled in Allen County, Indiana near the town of Monroeville on the Ridge Road (U.S. 30). They pitched tents for living quarters as they built a log cabin residence. The family then consisted of eight children living at home. Two children had died in Ohio and a daughter had married and lived in New Haven.

Daniel was a hardy pioneer and farmer, an esteemed citizen and beloved father. He was a zealous member of the Presbyterian Church as was his wife and children. Daniel was born October 23, 1796 and died March 25, 1871. Elizabeth was born August 17, 1802 and died August 30, 1875. Both are buried in the Stephenson Cemetery.

Submitted by Kathy Sheehan

EUGENE IRVIN SHEEHAN FAMILY

Eugene Irvin Sheehan was born in 1933, the depths of the depression, to Irvin and Alberta (Geis) Sheehan. He was born at home in a farmhouse on the Snyder Road in Madison Township, Allen County, Indiana.

Eugene Sheehan

When he was three years old the family moved to Monroeville, Indiana. At age five the family moved to a farm on the Wilson Road in Jefferson Township and lived with his uncle, Richard Sheehan. The family made their last move to a farm Irvin purchased on the Grotrain Road in Madison Township, where he lived until he married.

Eugene attended St. Louis Besancon Catholic School for eight years and graduated from Hoagland High School. After completing his education, he worked at International Harvester until he was drafted into the Army. His basic training was at Camp Roberts, California. He was transferred to Camp Ord, California for several months, and then was shipped to Korea until discharged in April 1956. While in Korea he hunted pheasants to pass the time. Upon his discharge he returned to work at Harvester.

In 1956 he met and married Nancy Jean Ladd at St. John Lutheran Church, New Haven, Indiana. After several moves, they built a home on Nicole Lane in New Haven, Indiana where they now live. They have two daughters, Regina Rose, born July 11, 1959 and Jennifer Ann, born March 1, 1963. Three sons were stillborn. They are buried in the Catholic Cemetery, Fort Wayne, Indiana.

Also, in December 1956, he quit Harvester and went to work for Commonwealth Life Insurance Company for a year. He then started working with "Dutch" Oberley, an independent agent, selling property and casualty insurance. When Mr. Oberley died in 1959, Gene purchased the agency and went into business for himself.

Being self-employed allowed him the freedom to pursue many interests. He traveled and came to love the game of golf and became quite proficient at it even making a hole-in-one. He purchased a snowmobile and made many trips to northern Michigan, riding the trails for hours. Small game hunting with his father, brothers, and relatives was another fall and winter pastime. As he grew older he gave up hunting and the snowmobile and developed a fondness for bowling. Once he rolled a 762 series. He also likes euchre and pinochle.

His daughter, Regina, married Robert McLinden and they have three children: Kristina, David, and Michael. Kristy is married to Sam Cerillo and they have one son, Evan. David attends IPFW and Michael is a senior at New Haven High School. Jennifer has one son, Shane, and they make their home in Jeffersonville, Indiana. Shane is a freshman at Providence High School in Clarksville, Indiana.

Gene is now retired after approximately 50 years in the insurance industry.

Submitted by Eugene Sheehan

IRVIN WILLIAM SHEEHAN & ALBERTA REGINA GEIS FAMILY

Irvin William Sheehan (Irv) was born March 24, 1901, the second child and first son of John and Bertha Sheehan. He was born in a log cabin and spent his formative years in Monroe Township. He attended Stephenson School, a one-room schoolhouse.

Irish and fun loving, he met Alberta Geis at a Saturday dance. They were married January 22, 1929 at St. Rose Catholic Church, Monroeville.

Irvin worked for the Pennsylvania Railroad then the International Harvester Company. They made their first home in an apartment on Columbia Avenue in Fort Wayne, Indiana where their first child, Mary Angela was born. At this time, Irvin became very ill with a high fever and joint stiffness. He was in the hospital a month and was diagnosed with inflammatory rheumatism. This left him with a weakened heart.

The depression set in and being ill and unemployed the family moved to the Monroeville area, living with family, friends. Irvin worked odd jobs, even opening a pool hall with Alberta's brother, Joe Geis. During this time, Eugene (1930) and William Neal (1935) were born. In 1934 Irv was called back to work at Harvester.

Their next move was in with Irv's brother, Richard Sheehan. Like many rural homes, it had neither indoor plumbing nor electricity. It was installed while they lived there. After years of moving and struggling, the economy was starting to improve and Irvin purchased a farm in 1940 on the Grotrain Road. Here Carl and Nancy were born. He started farming his 56 acres, raising grain crops to sell and feed his livestock. He raised pigs and cows for meat and to sell. Alberta had a large garden and raised chickens. She did much preserving and jelly making. There was an orchard with apple, cherry, pear, and plum trees, and a big strawberry patch.

Alberta Geis Sheehan and Irvin Sheehan

The house was old with no modern amenities, so Irvin started remodeling doing most of the work himself with help from friends and relatives. It took three years but the results were well worth it. The family lived in the house while he did the work, living part of the time in the basement. When it rained, water would seep through the flooring above and get things wet. A real endurance test, but they prevailed.

Irv loved to hunt. On opening day of rabbit season, men would gather to hunt and the women brought food, cooked and socialized. He also enjoyed playing cards: pinochle, euchre and canasta. Bowling and Western movies were also favorite pastimes. He was a devoted, hard working family man and member of St. Rose Catholic Church, the Moose Lodge, union member and staunch Democrat.

His damaged, overworked heart gave out on September 29, 1961 and he died at the supper table.

After Irvin's death, Alberta continued to live on the farm. Eight years later, she married a widower and neighbor, William Jennings Gerardot. She sold the farm to her son, Carl, and moved several miles north on the Snyder Road. She died February 12, 1993. She and Irvin are buried in the Catholic Cemetery in Monroeville, Indiana.

Submitted by Andrew Lynn Houser

JOHN LAWRENCE SHEEHAN & BERTHA POORMAN FAMILY

John Lawrence Sheehan was the fourth child and first living son born to William II and Elizabeth Sheehan. He was born in Monroe Township, Allen County, Indiana, May 14, 1869. He married Bertha Poorman, a neighbor, February 23, 1899. Their first home was a log cabin on the Lortie Road. There, children Mabel, Irvin, Helene and Richard were born. Helene died in 1904 at the age of two.

John Lawrence Sheehan

They next moved to a home along U.S. 30 and Rebecca, Russell, Mary and Harold were born here. In the fall of 1918 John purchased the Sheehan homestead on the corner of Morgan Road and U.S. 30 where he had lived as a child. Here Isabel and Raymond were born.

John's entire life was spent along the Ridge Road. After being named U.S. 30, his sons helped lay the pavement for the new road using draft horses and manual labor. He was a hard working and successful farmer but the Great Depression devastated this family. They lost everything including the farm, forcing them to move east to a house along U.S. 30 near what was known as "The Red Ball Inn". In spite of their difficulties, being Irish, they were always a fun loving and close family. John died February 12, 1934 after a long illness of lung cancer.

After John died, Bertha along with children Richard, Isabel and Raymond, moved to a home near Monroeville. She developed liver cancer and died June 4, 1937. John and Bertha are buried in the I.O.O.F. Cemetery at the edge of Monroeville, Indiana.

Mabel married Lester Rosswurm from Monroeville. They had three daughters: Cecelia, Agatha and Joan. They lived in Fort Wayne, Indiana. Lester and Mabel are buried in the Fort Wayne Catholic Cemetery.

Richard Sheehan, known as "Daddy" never married. He lived in the Monroeville area all his life and was a farmer.

Rebecca married Robert Youse. They had no children. They eventually moved to Lake of the Woods, and Stroh, Indiana. They ran a restaurant and bar at each site.

Russell (Bud) married Dorothy Roemer and they had no children. He was a life long farmer and never moved from the Ridge Road/U.S. 30 area.

Mary married Merlin Dodane and they lived in Fort Wayne along with their two sons: Gordon and Lawrence.

Harold married Margaret Gepfert. They had four children: Bruce, Sandra, Danny Joe and Rebecca. They made their home in Fort Wayne, Indiana. After Margaret's death, he married Lavon Commet Geis.

Isabel married Lester Sheets from the Decatur area. They had three children: Gary, Peggy and Linda.

Raymond married while he was serving in the U.S. Army. He made his home in California.

Helene, Richard, Rebecca, Russell, Harold and Raymond are buried in the Monroeville I.O.O.F. Cemetery. Irvin is buried in St. Rose Catholic Cemetery, Monroeville. Mary is buried in St. Louis Catholic Church Cemetery along old U.S. 30. Mabel is buried in the Decatur, Indiana cemetery.

Submitted by Scott Eugene Houser

RAYMOND (PETE) SHEEHAN

Raymond Sheehan was the youngest of the ten children born to John L. and Bertha (Poorman) Sheehan. He was born April 23, 1921 in the "Big Square House on the Corner" of Morgan Road and U. S. 30, known as the old Sheehan place.

His schooling was obtained from a little brick schoolhouse in Jackson Township and the Monroeville High School in Monroeville, Indiana. His father died when he was thirteen and his mother, brother Richard, and sister Isabel, lived together in a red brick house on the Monroeville Road east of Monroeville. When he was seventeen his mother died and he took turns living with his brothers and sisters. He worked at the General Electric Company for a time while living with his sister, Mary.

Then he joined the Army and also married a woman named June. They had a little girl called Suzanne, born in 1945. He was discharged from the Army but couldn't seem to get himself settled. His marriage only lasted two years. Again he joined the Army making it his career, serving over twenty years, and was a World War II veteran. He married a Spanish lady from California named Edna. He stayed in California after retiring and that's where he died on July 1, 1972 of cirrhosis of the liver. He is buried in the I.O.O.F. Memorial Cemetery.

Mary Sheehan, Raymond's sister, was born April 11, 1910 and died February 12, 1946. She was only thirty-five years old and cancer was the cause. She was the seventh child and fourth daughter of John L. and Bertha (Poorman) Sheehan. Mary was born in Jackson Township along U.S. 30 and received her schooling from the Stevenson School and one year of high school at Monroeville.

Mary worked at the Dudlow Wire Company on Wall Street and also the General Electric Company in Fort Wayne as did her future husband, Merlin Dodane. He was also a native of Jackson Township, born in 1910. They were married in 1931 and always lived in Fort Wayne, Indiana. To this union were born two sons: Gordon born April 18, 1934, married Barbara Lauer; Lawrence born December 19, 1937, married Judith Weingartner.

Merlin remarried to have help caring for his young sons. Her name was Rose Barl, a spinster. In July 1952, Merlin died quite unexpectedly of a cerebal hemorrhage. Both are buried in the new section of St. Louis Besancon Cemetery.

Submitted by Judy Dodane

RICHARD (DADDY) SHEEHAN

Richard M. Sheehan was the fourth child of John L. and Bertha (Poorman) Sheehan. He was born on February 7, 1904 when the family was living on Lortie Road in a log cabin. He attended Stevenson School in the winter months when he couldn't work on the farm to help the family. Richard was the musician of the family. When he was about eight years old, he took piano lessons but the third time the teacher came, Richard ran out the door and that was the end of his piano lessons.

He worked on the neighboring farms and the Nickel Plate and Pennsylvania Railroads until 1930 then he worked at International Harvester for four years. Like his father and grandparents before him, he was a tiller of the soil with much experience behind him. After his father died, he took charge of the family that was still home, Mother, Isabel and Raymond. Having lost the Sheehan Homestead during the depression, they were living near the "Old Red Ball Inn" on U.S. 30 but soon moved to a farm east of Monroeville on Monroeville Road.

After his mother died and his sister married, he rented the Schodd farm on Wilson Road in Jefferson Township. There he lived for over twenty years. When the farm had to be sold to settle an estate, he moved to a little house in Townley. Shortly thereafter he moved a mile south on State Road 101 and stayed there until 1976. He retired in 1972 at the age of 68. He had had terrible back pain for years. He sold his farm equipment at public auction. Because of the fine condition he kept his equipment, Glenn Merica, the auctioneer, said his was the best sale he ever had for that size.

Being a bachelor all his life, he was tired of being lonely; his health was failing (he was diabetic) so with great excitement, in the fall of 1976, he bought a cute little house on Elm Street in Monroeville. He was beginning to neighbor and enjoyed going uptown to the restaurant. Then on November 9, 1976 he was on his way to see his brother, Harold, who was gravely ill with cancer when his brand new Ford developed a flat tire. He died in his car near New Haven of an apparent heart attack. He is buried next to his parents, grandparents and brother Raymond in the I.O.O.F. Memorial Cemetery, Monroeville, Indiana.

Submitted by Nathan Lothamer

RUSSELL (BUD) SHEEHAN

Russell Sheehan was the sixth child of John L. and Bertha (Poorman) Sheehan. He was born on July 10, 1908 in a house along U. S. 30 between Townley and the state line in Jackson Township, Allen County, Indiana. He lived his first ten years here with his many brothers and sisters, Mabel, Irvin, Richard, Rebecca, Mary and Harold. Isabel and Raymond were to join them later.

In company with his family, during the fall of 1918, Bud moved to the "Big Square House on the Corner". Known as the Sheehan place, this house still stands today at the corner of old U.S. 30 and Morgan Road.

Bud acquired his education from the Stevenson School, a little, red brick, one-room schoolhouse, so familiar in that era. This school was at the corner of Hoffman and Morgan Roads in Jackson Township.

After fourteen years of pleasant memories, again the family picked up and moved down the highway to yet another farm. The year was 1932 and in the depth of the depression. The farm had belonged to Bud's grandparents, William II and Rebecca (Jones) Sheehan.

By this time, Bud had grown to be quite a man. On December 23, 1933 he took as his wife, Miss Dorothy Roemer of New Haven. She was the daughter of Charles and Elizabeth Roemer, born July 15, 1910. They lived with his parents for a few years then rented a farm just west of Townley and stayed there twelve years until 1950 when they purchased a farm on U.S. 30 just a quarter of a mile from the Ohio state line.

Mr. Sheehan was a farmer all his life. He and his wife owned 260 acres of land plus sharecropped additional land in the area. He was respected in the area for his fine character and sound judgment. He was a patriotic citizen, taxpayer, and a member of St. Mark Lutheran Church. He had served jury duty on a murder trial, been assessor for a private estate worth millions and a loyal Democrat.

Bud Sheehan lived his entire life along the U.S. 30 highway between Townley and the state line. In fact, when he was fifteen, he worked to help pave it. At first it was stone and mud. After U.S. 30 was made into a dual super highway, the road is now called Lincoln Highway or old 30. He was quoted as saying, "I've lived my entire life along 30 and I plan to die here". That he did.

Russell (Bud) Sheehan died July 21, 1990 and was buried in Monroeville I.O.O.F. Cemetery. His wife Dorothy died August 28, 1990 from grief and was buried beside her husband.

Submitted by Kurt Lothamer

WILLIAM "NEAL" SHEEHAN FAMILY

On October 28, 1935, William Neal Sheehan was born to Irvin and Alberta (Geis) Sheehan in a farm house on Ternet Road about three-fourths of a mile south of Highway 30 near the village of Tillman in Jefferson Township of Allen County, Indiana. William "Neal" was the third child born to this couple, parents of five children. Older siblings were Mary Angela and Eugene Irvin, and the younger siblings were Carl Allen and Nancy Louise. The parents raised their family on a farm which they bought in 1941, located on the Grotrian Road, Monroeville, Indiana.

Sheehan Family 1985, Back: Susan Connors Sheehan, William Neal Sheehan. Front: Jeffery Neal Sheehan, Kristine Lynne Sheehan, Tracey Anne Sheehan

Neal attended St. Louis Besancon Catholic Grade School, New Haven, Indiana and graduated from Hoagland High School, Hoagland, Indiana. He worked at International Harvester in Fort Wayne from 1955 to 1968, with a military leave from 1956 to 1959. He also worked at Cooper Industrial Products in Auburn, Indiana for one year and at Hoosier Wire Die in Fort Wayne for two years. In 1971, he began working for the Norfolk Southern Railroad as an engineer and retired from that railroad in 1997.

Neal's military service includes the Air National Guard and Army. Neal was in the Air National Guard from 1953 until 1956, subsequently joining the Army. He took basic training at Fort Louis, Washington. He was then stationed at Fort Bragg, North Carolina where he served as a paratrooper with the 82nd Airborne Division.

On February 17, 1962, he married Susan Kay Connors, of New Haven, Indiana. Neal and Susan had three children; Jeffery Neal, Tracey Ann, and Kristine Lynn. All children were born in Fort Wayne, Allen County, Indiana.

Jeff went to Indiana-Purdue University, Fort Wayne, where he received a bachelor's degree in education. He has taught at Heritage High School, Hamilton High School, and presently at Eastern Green High School near Bloomington, Indiana, where he is also head football coach. He married Lisa Johnson of Fremont, Indiana. They were divorced in 1997. He has a daughter, Sydney, born in 2001.

Tracey was born on February 14, 1965. She was in the U.S. Air Force for four years, stationed in Louisiana, and then worked and served with the Air National Guard. Along with her avionics training in the Air Force and Air Guard, she obtained a bachelor's degree in business management from Indiana Technical College, Fort Wayne. While in the air force, Tracey married Joseph Clevinger in Fort Wayne on February 14, 1987, and they had a child, Savannah Marie Clevinger, born on December 27, 1987. They divorced in 1989. Tracy is employed by Fort Wayne Community Schools.

Kristine was born on June 17, 1967. She received a certificate in dental assisting from Indiana-Purdue, Fort Wayne. She married Mark Welty in December 1989, and they have two sons, Vince William, born December 12, 1990, and Jack David, born September 23, 1995. She also works for Fort Wayne Community Schools.

Neal and Susan are living their retirement years on Lake George, on the Indiana/Michigan state line.

Submitted by William Neal Sheehan

WILLIAM SHEEHAN II & REBECCA EMELINE JONES FAMILY

William Sheehan II was the sixth child and third son of Daniel and Elizabeth Hutchinson Sheehan. He was born June, 1, 1843. When William II was twelve years old, he traveled from Ohio with his family and settled in the wilderness across the state line, along a path which was called the Ridge Road. Today this area is Northern Jackson Township, Allen County, Indiana. This path became US 30, now called Lincoln Highway.

On July 3, 1862, he married Rebecca E. Jones. Rebecca was born in Harrison County, Ohio, on October 16, 1841. William served in the Civil War, enlisting in the 23rd Indiana Battery Light Artillery, attaining the rank of Corporal before his discharge in July 1865.

Of Irish descent, Mr. Sheehan, like his father and grandfather, was a tiller of the soil. He became quite successful clearing the land and farming. He built a grand home at the junction of Morgan Road and US 30 for his large family. This home is still standing in the same location. William and Rebecca had seven children: Elbert, Willa, Nettie, John Lawrence, Maude, Katherine, and Leonard.

William Sheehan II

John Lawrence married Bertha Poorman. Of this union were born ten children: Mabel, Irvin, Helen, Richard (Daddy), Rebecca, Russell (Bud), Mary, Harold, Isabel and Raymond (Pete).

Katherine married Dr. Charles Wybourn and moved to California. They had two sons, David and Robert.

As a young man, Leonard traveled to Missouri to work in a sawmill owned by a Mr. Mumma. He married Mr. Mumma's daughter, Pearl, and they were parents to eight children: Beatrice, Zenda, Maude, Martin, Jessie, Robert, Josie and Florence. When the forests of Missouri were no longer producing lumber and the industry declined, Leonard and his family moved back to Indiana.

Of their other children, Elbert died at birth. Willa, Nettie, and Maude never married. They lived together in New Haven, Indiana. Maude was a registered nurse, graduating from the Lutheran Hospital School of Nursing. Willa and Nettie were known to be seamstresses. All sewing was done by hand.

William died October, 12, 1904, and Rebecca died November 1, 1917. They are buried in I.O.O.F. Cemetery, Monroeville, Indiana.

Submitted by Bradley Houser

DONALD & MARY SHEETS FAMILY

Donald Duane Sheets was born to Arthur Kenneth Sheets and Ocie Mildred Hallock on November 17, 1930, in Werner, Dunn County, North Dakota. He moved to Allen County, Indiana from North Dakota with his parents, brother Lester, and sister Mildred on March 25, 1937.

Donald played tuba for the Gospel Temple band and trumpet for the Elmhurst High School band. The Gospel Temple Band played music for the radio program "Back Home Hour" with Bob Sievers, recorded at the Gospel Temple, and broadcast on WOWO. Donald attended Anthony Wayne Elementary School, graduated from Elmhurst High School in 1948, and from Jewelry College, Chicago, Illinois in 1951.

Donald married Mary Belle Crites February 1, 1951 in Fort Wayne. She was the daughter of Charles Bernice Crites and Ona Mae Hunter. The children of Charles Crites and Ona Hunter are Harwood Russell Crites, born October 1, 1919; Oneta Luiza Crites, born March 19, 1927; Mabel Gaynell Crites, born October 12, 1932; and Mary Belle Crites, born October 12, 1932 in Bloomfield, Green County, Indiana.

Mary Belle Crites moved to Fort Wayne in 1950 after graduation from Bloomfield High School. Mary lived with her sister, Oneta Crites, and Oneta' s husband, Marion Noel. Oneta and Marion Noel were attending Fort Wayne Bible College on Rudisill Boulevard in Fort Wayne, Indiana. Donald and Mary first met at Adams Lake when they were introduced by Gayle Sheets, Donald's cousin. Donald and Mary were married in 1951 in the Weddle home, by Dr. Forrest Weddle, Donald's second cousin, and European and Bible History Professor at Fort Wayne Bible College.

Donald and Mary were members of the Gospel Temple, and later Avalon Missionary Church. Their first home was on Ansley Drive, where Donald's parents, Ocie and Kenneth Sheets lived, and owned three properties. Donald used to ride his bike down Illinois Road, delivered the *News-Sentinel* newspaper, and mowed grass for homes on North Washington and Ardmore Roads. At the comer of Ansley Drive and Illinois Road was a family-owned grocery store where Donald, and later his daughters, would go to buy candy. Donald and Mary built a house in Ridgeway Addition, at the corner of Smith and Lower Huntington Roads in 1960. They purchased a home in Apache Junction, Arizona in 1997.

Donald worked at U.S. Rubber Company, and at Bowmar Instruments as an inspector, where he retired in 1993. Mary first worked at the Gospel Temple Bookstore, and then for Sears on Rudisill Boulevard. Mary graduated from Saint Francis College in 1966 with a degree in Elementary Education. She began teaching for Fort Wayne Community Schools in 1967 at Anthony Wayne Elementary School, and then taught at Maplewood Elementary School until 1995 where she retired after 30 years of teaching. The children of Mary and Donald Sheets are Benita Ann Sheets, and Barbara Marie Sheets.

Submitted by Donald Sheets

ISABEL (SHEEHAN) SHEETS

Isabel Sheehan was the fifth daughter and ninth child born to John L. and Bertha (Poorman) Sheehan on November 9, 1918, at the old Sheehan homestead on U.S. 30 and Morgan Road. She received her schooling at the Stevenson one-room school and Monroeville Schools. Most of her youth was spent along U.S. 30, until after her father died in 1934. Then, with her mother and two brothers, Richard "Daddy" and Raymond "Pete", she moved to a brick house east of Monroeville on the Monroeville Road. While living there her mother became seriously ill with cancer and she nursed and cared for her (Ironically, Isabel's daughter, Peggy, had to do the same for her when she developed cancer). She kept house for her brothers the first year after her mother's death in 1937.

On August 27, 1938 she married Lester E. Sheets from Decatur, Indiana. Uncle Lester Sheets was born August 27, 1916, the son Jesse and Addie Sheets. He was a mechanic for 16 years with the Clyde Butler Garage and in January of 1962 started his own mechanic business as owner and operator of the Sheets Garage. They were blessed with three children: Garry E. born August 24, 1940, married Judy Rawlings; Peggy born November 22, 1945, married David Gay; Linda, born September 28, 1955.

Decatur was their home for their entire married life and she was a housewife and homemaker. Both Les and Isabel were members of the Moose. Like her mother and two of her sisters she also had cancer and suffered a great deal before she died on June 2, 1967. She was only 48 years old. Les also developed cancer and passed away on July 27, 1970 at the age of 53. Both are buried in the Decatur Cemetery.

Submitted by Judith Sheets

KENNETH & OCIE SHEETS FAMILY

Arthur Kenneth Sheets was born September 1, 1904, to Frederic R. Sheets and Carrie Hineline in Porter County, Indiana, and died August 13, 1980, in Fort Wayne, Allen County, Indiana. Arthur Kenneth Sheets married Ocie Mildred Hallock July 15,1924 in Werner, Dunn County, North Dakota. She was the daughter of Claude C. Hallock and Ethel Card. Ocie was born May 23, 1902 in Nutwood, Warren County, Ohio, and died October 28, 1994 in Fort Wayne, Allen County, Indiana.

The Arthur Kenneth Sheets family moved to Fort Wayne on March 25, 1937. "Kenneth" had been a farmer in North Dakota. They farmed land that had been homesteaded by the Hallock family. Kenneth bought Ocie a horse that she named Tootsie. The land there was flat and treeless, and Ocie once said that she had to get used to living here with the trees and houses being so close together. The draught and grasshoppers in North Dakota caused poor farming for the family, and they moved to be by Kenneth's brothers, Virgil and Benjamin Sheets, who lived in Fort Wayne. Benjamin worked as an engineer for the Pennsylvania Railroad. Kenneth's first job in Fort Wayne was as a coal and ice deliveryman. Kenneth later worked as a machine operator for International Harvester, where he retired. He was known as "Red" because of his reddish blond hair.

Ocie graduated from high school in Werner, North Dakota, and studied to be a teacher at the Dickinson Normal School in North Dakota.

Back row, L to R: Marvin Steyer, Bryan Gripp, Derek Horres, Jeff Harris, Stephanie Homer, Damon Homer, Brian Harris Middle Row, L to R: Benita Steyer, Mary Sheets, Donald Sheets, Barbara Harris. Front row, L to R: Jennifer Steyer, Benjamin Steyer

The Kenneth and Ocie Sheets Family. L to R: Doris Sheets, Ocie Sheets, Lester Sheets, Kenneth Sheets, Mildred Mabee, Louis Mabee, Mary Sheets, Donald Sheets.

Ocie taught two terms of school in a one room schoolhouse south of Werner. Kenneth and Ocie met when she was a teacher, and he used to come and help her clean the schoolhouse at the end of the day. After they were married, Ocie had to quit teaching, because married women were not encouraged to teach. Students from Ocie's days of teaching kept in touch by letter years after the family moved to Indiana.

The children of Arthur Sheets and Ocie Hallock are Lester Kenneth Sheets, born September 25, 1926; Mildred Ethel Sheets, born July 17,1928; and Donald Duane Sheets, born November 17, 1930, all born in Werner, Dunn County, North Dakota. Lester Sheets married Doris Leedy, born December 17, 1928, on November 23, 1947, in Columbia City, Whitley County, Indiana. Mildred Sheets married Louis Mabee, born on October 11, 1923, on July 18, 1946 in Fort Wayne, Indiana. Donald Sheets married Mary Belle Crites born on October 12, 1932, on February 1, 1951 in Fort Wayne, Indiana.

Both Kenneth and Ocie were active members at the Gospel Temple where they both taught Sunday school classes, and Ocie was a member of a ladies group that made bandages for missionaries.

Submitted by Mary Sheets

EVELYN MUELLER & ELMER SHERBONDY

Evelyn Mueller (1916-) and Elmer Sherbondy (1915-1965) married in St. John's Lutheran Church, Fort Wayne, Indiana on December 27, 1941, had two children, Jeanette Evelyn Sherbondy (anthropology professor at Washington College, Chestertown, Maryland) and Don Owen Sherbondy (architect, owner of Sherbondy Art and Architecture, Phoenix, Arizona), and two granddaughters, Julieta Cristina Tord (former program director for Big Brothers Big Sisters of Central Maryland) (1967-) and Katelyn Rose Sherbondy (student of Arizona School for the Arts (1990-). The families of Elmer and Evelyn arrived in Allen County as early as the 1830s and as late as 1903 where they became farmers, workers, owners of small businesses, engineers, and teachers.

Elmer Walter Sherbondy trained at the General Electric Apprentice School as a draftsman and also studied at Purdue University extension. During the last six years of his life he helped create the integrated computer information processing system utilizing generic product drawings for the General Purpose Motor Engineering Department. His early death in 1965 unfortunately kept him from pursuing his passion for computer engineering. Elmer was a dedicated Boy Scout leader and an artistic photographer.

His ancestors were among the earliest to settle in Allen County. His mother's grandfather, Dietrich Gerke, along with most of his brothers and sisters, arrived in America between 1834-1838 from Bohmte, Hanover to establish farms in Adams and Allen Counties. On January 17, 1840 the Lutheran missionary, Friedrich Wyneken, married Dietrich Gerke to Agnes Elizabeth Trier, who was born in Erksdorf, Hesse-Darmstadt and came in 1836 to Fort Wayne with her parents who established a farm. Upon Dietricht's death Agnes married Christ Schaper, from Bueckeburg, Germany who carried on the farming.

Elmer Sherbondy's paternal ancestors first reached New England in the 17th century. His grandmother, Lusannah Richardson Miner, descended from Thomas Miner and Grace Palmer. Miner arrived in America from Chew Magna, Somerset, England in 1632 where he was an interpreter for the Indians. He settled in Massachusetss, then New London, Connecticut, and co-founded Stonington, Connecticut. Lusannah's grandfather, Samuel Amos Miner, arrived by canal in Fort Wayne in 1835 and took up farming in Whitley County on the land where the Miami Indian tribe continued to gather for its annual powwows. Lusannah Miner married Abraham M. Sherbondy on April 23, 1868 in Fort Wayne where Abraham worked as a carpenter and fireman for the railroads.

"Our best day!"
Evelyn and Elmer's Wedding
Photograph by Clevo Briscoe Graae (1940)

His ancestor, Jean Cherpantier, probably French, originally settled near Stroudsburg, Pennsylvania where he established farms and grist mills. He fought with the Pennsylvania Militia in the Revolutionary War. Abraham's grandfather, George Sherbondy, born on November 15, 1769, established a farm in Westmoreland County, near Smithton, Pennsylvania. When he died in 1817 his widow, Mary Sherbondy, left for Ohio and Indiana with some of her children. By 1850 her son Abraham J. Sherbondy was established as a farmer and constable in Fort Wayne and lived only four households away from Dietrich Gerke's farm. Sherbondy's grandsons became electrical engineers with the Pennsylavia Railroad in Fort Wayne. Elmer's father was Frank Pearl Sherbondy who volunteered in the war with Spain as a young man. He married Sophie Gerke on September 23, 1903. He worked as chief electrician of the Grand Rapids and Indiana Railroad before they returned to Fort Wayne where he established the Sherbondy Auto Electric Service on East Wayne Street.

In the 1850s Evelyn Mueller's maternal ancestors left Germany for Fort Wayne. Great grandfather Franz Rudolph Kabisch came from Zeitz, Saxony and great grandmother Katharina Ellet from Konigsberg, Hesse-Darmstadt; Evelyn's grandfather Heinrich Frech came from Ilsfeld, Besigheim, Württemberg and his wife Christina Roth from Baden, Bavaria. The Frech farm was in Aboite Township. Kabisch was a plasterer and butcherer (Kabisch Meat Market) on Fairfield Avenue. His son Rudy Kabisch was a tinner who married Emma Frech on April 20, 1892. Emma was an active member of the Women's Christian Temperance Union. Their daughter, Mabel Jeannette Kabisch, married Friedrich Wilhelm Mueller (Bill) who had come to Fort Wayne with his parents and siblings in 1903 from Dresden, Germany, aboard the ship *Saxonia*. Bill worked for forty-five years with General Electric where he retired as a specialist in advanced methods and equipment. Mabel dedicated her life to service through St. John's Church and the Veterans' Hospital. She loved painting and poetry.

Evelyn Marie Mueller was a born teacher. She studied piano and clarinet at the Fort Wayne School of Music, began teaching music while still a girl, and conducted the first orchestra for the Fort Wayne Civic Theater. She was a charter member of the Fort Wayne Philharmonic Society. She graduated from Ball State Teachers College in 1938 with a B.S. and taught in the Fort Wayne Community School System for twenty-five years until her retirement from Riverside School. She continued teaching until recently the Adult Bible class at Lutheran Church of Our Savior. A member of the Sigma Eta Fine Arts Sorority and the Delta Kappa Gamma Honorary Society for Teachers, Evelyn is an artist as well as musician. She plays piano, reads avidly, and writes beautiful letters in impeccable handwriting. She shared with her husband, children and grandchildren her love of knowledge, music, and beauty.

Submitted by Jeanette Sherbondy

JOHN KING SHERMAN & AUGUSTA HOWE (GREENER) SHERMAN

Both Augusta "Gussie" Howe Greener and John King Sherman were born in Columbus, Ohio. John King was born November 22, 1879 and was the seventh of eleven children. His father had fought in the Civil War with the Ohio regiment and became a doctor after the war. His mother was a homemaker.

Gussie's parents were both teachers of the deaf. Her mother had lost her hearing as a toddler in a scarlet fever epidemic in Wales. As there was a good deaf school in Ohio, and her father would be able to find work there as a metal worker, the family moved to America. Gussie's father had lost his hearing as a teenager after catching a bad ear infection after being dipped in dirty water. He met Gussie's mother at the school for the deaf. They had five children.

John and Gussie both graduated from Columbus High School in 1897 and from Ohio State University in 1901. He took a job as a civil engineer with the Pennsylvania Railroad,

a job he would keep until he retired. Gussie went on to get a Masters Degree from Gallaudet University in Washington D.C. and to teach at a deaf school in northern Wisconsin. They were married in 1906.

His job with the railroad required John Sherman to move his household several times, and the family spent many of their early years in different towns and cities in Indiana, Ohio, and Illinois, but finally settled in Fort Wayne, Indiana. Fort Wayne was an important place for the Pennsylvania Railroad because it had a roundhouse there where it could turn its engines around. They lived at 308 East Suttonfield Street, then moved to Braning Street. They lived on East Foster Parkway, then lastly on Fairfield Avenue. John was a Mason, and often attended meetings, while Gussie was a charter member of the Fort Wayne Women's Club, and an active member of the Garden Club. They often went to local club meetings of Ohio State Alumni. They were long-time members of Plymouth Congregational Church. They celebrated their 50th wedding anniversary at the Fort Wayne Women's Club.

All of their children studied at South Side High School in Fort Wayne. Their oldest son, John Jr., graduated from MIT and got a job with Proctor and Gamble. Their twin girls, Mary and Martha, received AB degrees from Radcliff College and became teachers and social workers. Their youngest son, David, graduated from Purdue University in Engineering and started working for U.S. Rubber.

After his retirement, John enjoyed having a big garden at his daughter Mary's home off West Hamilton Road. He and his wife were frequent patrons of the Southside Farmer's Market. Whenever the apple seller saw Gussie coming, he would get a dollar sack of apples bagged and ready for her.

John Sherman's scrapbooks are in the possession of the Allen County Fort Wayne Historical Society. During their lifetime, they were solid citizens of the community.

Submitted by Mary Willet

LYNN VICTOR SHIRK FAMILY

Lynn was born in Monroe, Indiana on September 24, 1903. He was one of seven boys born to Robert Lawton and Luella Virginia (Bouse) Shirk. Their children were Floyd, Carl, Bob, Ben, John, Lynn, and Kenneth.

Lynn was raised on an 80-acre farm and attended school in Monroe, graduating in 1922. He played basketball, and he was a star forward on the all-county team and in the all-district finals.

He was recruited to play football for the University of Illinois, but, when his father took sick, his brothers said he couldn't go. He had to stay home and help on the farm. However, he did play some semi-pro basketball for the Berne Athletic Club until moving to Florida with a brother in the construction business from 1923-1926. They built the first fire station in West Palm Beach.

Returning to Fort Wayne, Lynn worked at several fuel companies before ending up at Superior Coal Company in the 1930s. While working, he studied the production end and the heating engineering of the fuel business. He leased oil fields in West Texas, Oklahoma and other places,

Lynn and Thelma Shirk

wildcatting one of the largest fields in Illinois in 1952. He also started Superior's first fuel truck transport. He retired as vice president and general manager of Superior Fuel Company in 1973 after 46 years in the fuel oil business.

Lynn learned to fly his own plane and became a licensed pilot at Smith Field. He spent a month in Africa and Europe in 1972 searching for oil and uranium by air. Later he traveled to Ethiopia and Zaire in search of copper, gold, and silver. He also spent time out west in Arizona mining.

Lynn married on November 11, 1924 to Thelma Eliza Peterson, who was born on February 23, 1906 in Decatur, Indiana to Charles Ansel and Maude Thompson (Fuller) Peterson. Lynn and Thelma had one child, Jack Burton Shirk, born November 12, 1925, one grandchild, Gregory Lynn Shirk, born on August 19, 1950, and four great-grandchildren: Scott Robert, Stacy Marie, Natalie Lynn, and Matthew Dean. Lynn and Thelma were members of Simpson United Methodist Church. Politically he was identified with the Republican party.

Submitted by Greg Shirk

ELSIE & FOREST SHIVELY

The year was 1935 when Forest Shively, a plumber by trade, and his wife, Elsie, decided to purchase a farm of their own. Born on a farm on Illinois Road, Forest had never ventured far from home when he purchased 80 acres on Bass Road. Over the next few years the family prospered and the farm grew with the acquisition of an adjoining 40-acre parcel of land. A narrow gravel path separated the two parcels of land. The gravel path needed to be wider if the county was to call it a road, provide maintenance and enable school bus traffic. In the early 1940s, Saint Patrick's Church in Arcola persuaded the family to donate land sufficient to widen the road to meet requirements. This saved school buses and church parishioners several miles of driving on country roads. It is amazing how just 60 years ago people of different religious background could agree, with but a little talk and a friendly hand shake.

The farm was a good place. There was always plenty to eat. Each year a large vegetable garden was planted and harvested by the family members. Strawberries were picked and taken to the frozen food locker in Arcola for use the following winter. The farm raised corn and wheat for cash crop; oats and hay were grown for the animals.

Harvesting wheat was exciting. Neighbors formed a thrashing team where neighbor helped neighbor. A big thrashing machine was placed behind the barn. And there were wagons and tractors and horses. Young boys pumped drinking water for the men as well as for the horses. The ladies prepared big meals; the food just kept coming.

During summer months hay was dried and taken to the barn for winter feedings. Haying was a hot job for the people unlucky enough to work in the hayloft. Horses pulled hay from wagon to the haymow by a system of pulleys, ropes, and a hayfork. A rope that was used by family and neighbor children on which to swing still hangs in the barn.

Forest, Elsie, Kenny, Jerry, Joan Shively

For entertainment, there was a weekly free out-door movie by the railroad track in Arcola. When the train came through, off went the movie. Sometimes the old projector broke the film and we would go home without knowing if the good guys won. The farm on the Bass Road at the end of the Hamilton Road is still a working farm growing corn and soybeans. There are wonderful memories of Elsie and Forest Shively and the beautiful farm.

Submitted by Jerry Shively

WALLACE & SARAH SHIVELY

In the 1912 photo are Homer Diehl, age 15 and Forest Merrit Shively, age four. They were sons of Wallace Benjamin and Sarah Jane Shively who came to Allen County, Indiana in November of 1897. Wallace and Sarah, proud parents of their then year old son Homer, purchased a 120 acre farm located south of Illinois Road, half way between Hadley and Scott Roads. They purchased the farm from Eli and Caroline Wolf Diehl, parents of Sarah. Allen County records show the Diehls to be residents of Mahoning County, Ohio, and that 80 acres of the 120 acre farm sold to the younger family for 1,333 and one-third dollars on November 20, 1897. The picture of the house and barn was in a catalog distributed in the 1890s in the eastern

Homer Diehl (age 15)
Forest Merit Shively (age 4), 1912.

United States. The appearance of the barn and house remained essentially unchanged until recent years when it was sold to developers. Remnants of the barn and a wood shed can still be seen today as one drives along the newly developed housing area. The Diehl family, living in eastern Ohio, purchased this and a second property in Allen County.

A second daughter, Maddie Wolf, and her family, lived on the adjoining farm. The Wolf family returned to Ohio in the early 1900s to continue working in the family lumber business while the Shively family took roots in Aboite Township.

At this time, Aboite Township had only one-room school houses; two of them were located on Illinois Road. The Stouder School District No. 2 had 14 students in 1918-19. The school stood at the corner of Scott and Illinois Road; D. O. McComb was the superintendent. The second Aboite Township school on Illinois Road was Klaehn Public School which had 18 pupils in 1914. W.B. Shively was placed into teaching public school for several years; a hand held school bell remains in the family.

The family farm was a typical farm of the times. Money was made by harvesting timber from the area and shipping it east for use in manufacturing and construction industries. The family farmhouse was lit with gas lights, a real luxury for the early 1900s.

The family also lived in town during the winter. The children attended Jefferson School located at Jefferson and Fairfield Avenues, during winter months, while in fall and spring months they would attend the one-room school house. Illinois Road was a gravel road, and during the late 1920s, on a bright summer day a proud uncle would take niece and nephew for rides in his nice shiny car. Sometimes they would drive slowly (so as not to damage the car on the gravel roads) to the Allen-Whitley County Line Road and then to Dunfee for ice cream.

As the family grew, more land was purchased on the Illinois Road and Bass Road for family members. With the help of the Aboite Assessors Office, the Recorders Office and the public library, the dates and deeds of the property on Illinois Road were located. Many changes have taken place in Aboite Township since Wallace and Sarah Shively purchased their property through a catalog in the late 1800s.

Submitted by Joan LeGrand

**Due to publisher's error, please find a photo of the Shively homestead on page 760.*

ANGELA COCHOIT SHOULTS FAMILY

Angela Rose Cochoit was born on January 23, 1943, the daughter of Jules Emil and Edith Matilda (Sorg) Cochoit. Both the Cochoit and Sorg families were early settlers in Allen County, Indiana. She is a member of the First Families and Homesteaders of Allen County. Some of the other ancestral surnames of Allen County include Casso, Manier, Rondot, and Rauner.

Angela's parents moved to Pomona, California in 1947 where she and her brother, Jules, attended St. Joseph elementary school and graduated from Pomona Catholic High. Angela then received an Associate of Arts Degree from Mt. San Antonio College in 1962.

On August 1, 1964 Angela married Raymond Eugene Shoults who was born in San Bernardino, San Bernardino County, California. Raymond is the son of Raymond Eugene and Margaret Francis (Marshall) Stites. After the death of his father in

Raymond Eugene Shoults and Angela Rose Cochoit, 1964

1940, his mother married Richard Dean Shoults in 1942 and Raymond was adopted by his stepfather. Raymond graduated from Pomona High School in 1955 and worked in construction for a short time before going to work for the missile division of General Dynamics/Pomona. He was then called to active duty in the U.S. Navy and was stationed in Japan. After being discharged from the Navy, he then returned to work for General Dynamics/Pomona where Angela was employed as a secretary.

In 1965 they moved to the San Diego area of southern California where Raymond worked for Ryan Aeronautical Company. In 1972, the family moved to Omaha, Nebraska where Raymond had a top fuel dragster and Angela went to work for Pacesetter Corporation. In 1979 the family moved to Hanna, Wyoming where both Raymond and Angela worked for Arch Mineral Corporation, a coal mining company. Raymond was Maintenance Foreman and Angela was the secretary to the V.P. of the Western Division. After 10 years there, Raymond then went to work for Freeport Mc-Moran, a copper mining company based out of New Orleans, Louisiana. This venture took them overseas to the Indonesian Island of Irian Java for the next several years. Upon Raymond's retirement in 1996, they then returned to the wide open spaces of Wyoming where Raymond could enjoy hunting antelope, deer, and elk.

Raymond and Angela have two children: Richard Dean, II, who married Katherine M. Olson and has a daughter, Alexandra R.; and Corrine L., who married David O. Cotton and has two children, Jessica L. and Matthew D. Angela also raised her stepson. Randy D., who married Patricia M. Kinsella and has two children, Morgan M. and Adam P. Raymond also had a daughter, Rena A., who has five children: Erica Y., who married Jerry "Ryan" Farrar and has two sons, Christopher R. and Brandon J; Melissa E. and Domonique R. Gomez, and Gaberiel G. and Anthony M. Becerra.

Submitted by Angela Cochoit Shoults

DONALD & MARY SHUTT FAMILY

Donald Shutt was born in Normal, Illinois, and Mary Gensheimer was born in Bloomington, Illinois. They met through one of Donald's friends. Donald joined the U.S. Air Force in of January 1951 as the war in Korea was starting. After going through tech school in Cheyenne, Wyoming, he was assigned to Tinker Airforce Base in Oklahoma City, Oklahoma. At this time he went home and married Mary Gensheimer on November 24, 1951. They stayed there until January of 1952, at which time they moved to Kelly Field, at San Antonio, Texas.

Mary was pregnant with son, Joseph, and in August of 1952, Donald was sent to France. Joe was born September 15, a few hours before his Grandmother Shutt's and his father's birthdays on September 16. Donald returned on December 26, 1953 and was assigned to Smoky Hill Airforce Base, in Salina, Kansas. The family came home to Illinois in January 1955 and promptly moved to Fort Wayne, Indiana.

In Fort Wayne Donald got a job at International Harvester running a machine end milling axle ends. A week later two other companies where he had applied asked him to go to work for them. He went with Materials Handling Equipment Corporation, a branch of a South Bend company. He worked with forklift trucks, batteries and all the other products sold and serviced there. In 1972 Donald was advanced to a sales position selling and engineering all types of equipment, applying them to the work required. He retired from there on June 31, 1994, 39 1/2 years after he started.

Mary and Donald Shutt

During this time, the family continued to grow to nine children, two girls and seven boys: Joseph, Richard, Robert, Barbara, Thomas, Diana, Paul and Michael. They traveled from one coast to the other staying in campgrounds and pulling a fold-down trailer. During this time, Donald was also taking wedding photographs and doing some commercial work, taking photographs and processing them in his color darkroom.

In 1997 they built a new house Donald had designed in the addition named Hidden Hills Estates. In September, after getting a late start in May due to bad weather, they moved. By this time all of the children were married and starting their own families, and it was just Donald and Mary. They now have 23 grandchildren and one great grandchild, while expecting two more.

In April of 1998 Donald started the Three Rivers Woodworkers club. In the beginning there were six members, and now they have over sixty members. They meet the first Tuesday of the month, and lately have more people than chairs. The last meeting held at the Shutt house was on November 2, 2004. The meetings will now be held in an industrial building north of Huntertown.

Donald still designs and builds custom furniture and makes company brochures using his photography. Donald and Mary look forward to new challenges in the future.

Submitted by Donald Shutt

EDWARD LEROY SIEBER

Dr. Edward LeRoy Sieber came to Fort Wayne to start his dental practice in 1913. His first office was in the Central Building across from the Patterson Fletcher Building. His roots were with a large family on a farm near Camden, Indiana. He graduated from Indiana University with a B.S. degree in Chemistry in 1904. His bride, Bertha Johnston, born May 14, 1884, also grew up on a farm with a large family near Greenhill, Indiana. Her pet lamb yielded a beautiful white wool blanket. She attended Simmons College in Boston, Massachusetts. Bertha taught home economics at Kansas State Agricultural College were she met Roy, who was teaching Chemistry.

Bertha was called home to nurse her father, James Armstrong Johnston, who was a Civil War veteran. He was mustered into the military service in August 1862 for the term of three years in the 10th Light of Artillery Battery of Indiana Volunteers. LeRoy pursued further education at Northwestern University in Dentistry. Bertha promised to marry Roy by 1913, and she did, on December 31.

Dr. Edward LeRoy Sieber, dentist for forty years

They both joined Plymouth Congregational Church at the corner of Harrison and Jefferson Street. Roy served as a deacon and a Mason, and was a member of the Orchard Ridge Country Club. Bertha was also active at Plymouth where she was a member of Group Three. She was also a member of the Fort Wayne Women's Club and the A.A.U.W. as well as the Y.W.C.A.

Bertha and Roy became parents of two daughters, Mary Elizabeth and Elinor Johnston.

Elinor was married in October of 1940 to Lee B. Storms. They had a son, Charles Dirk Storms, who carried on the 100-year heritage of Red Spot Paint and Varnish Company in Evansville. Lee B. Storms died on a hunting trip. Elinor then met an married Charles Fox. After many years of happy traveling, Charles also passed away. Elinor then met and-married Tom Baker. She remained happily married until her death on May 2, 2003.

As a child, Mary Elizabeth attended open-air school which was located right where Plymouth Congregational Church is now. She would meet and marry Gathings Stewart on July 6, 1940. They had three children: James Gathings, John Edward, and Elizabeth Stewart Acton. Gathings was drafted into WW II and sent to Chicago University for one year of training in meteorology. Son, Jim, and Mary Lib, went home to her parents when Gathings received his first assignment to Dyersburg, Tennessee. Then Jim and his mother camp-followed on to San Angelo, Texas, Gathings home state. He was mustered out as a first lieutenant, and went back to the Lincoln Life Insurance Company in Fort Wayne as an actuary.

By May of 2000, Gathings and Mary Lib had eight grandchildren and four great grandchildren, two girls and two boys. Their son, Jim, is on the board of DePauw University. John Edward is currently Managing Director of Financial Reporting Advisors. Elizabeth is C.F.O. of Comerica Bank in Detroit, Michigan.

Gathings was a member of Quest Club, Rotary, a trail guide at Fox Island, and a Boy Scout leader for 20 years. He worked at Lincoln Life Insurance Company for 40 years where he became the president of the company.

Mary Lib was also a trail guide at Fox Island, a stitcher at Plymouth and Sanibel churches, and a docent at the Fort Wayne Art Museum. She also loved gardening and traveling. Their hobbies were lapidary, photography, and collecting Madonna's (because she loved being a mother).

At Indiana University, Mary Lib was a Kappa Kappa Gamma; later she was invited to Tri Kappa. She founded Evening Art League, and belonged to P.E.O., a women's reading club and an art appreciation group. She was President of her Plymouth Congregational Church guild, and her circle, Mary Lyon. Religious stitchery banners were part of her handy work for the Plymouth sanctuary and the Sanibel, Florida churches. In 1926, on her first train trip with Jeannette Kent, she purchased her first Madonna, a Guadalupe water bottle in California, leading to a collection of many purchased on her world travels. She gave a slide talk on the Madonnas 100 times. Her collection was added to Saint Francis University's Madonnas collection in 2002. She and Gathings were world travelers and able to visit many parts of the world during Gathings retirement.

Gathings died at Hospice in May of 2003. Mary Lib then moved to the Townehouse Retirement Center.

Submitted by Mary Lib Stewart

DIETRICH F. SIELING,

MAN DONATED PARK TO THE CITY

Submitter's great great grandfather, Dietrich F. Sieling, came over to this country from Germany sometime during 1883. Leaving from the port of Bremen, Germany he sailed on a ship named "The Hopsbunch". Not speaking any English upon his arrival, he quickly learned the language from a young girl named Ida Fiedler who was later to become his wife. Ida was living with her parents, William and Anna Fiedler, who were also German immigrants living in Fort Wayne. Being of German Lutheran background, she and Dietrich instantly became good friends and later fell in love and were married August 22, 1889 at Emmaus Lutheran Church located on 322 Broadway, Fort Wayne, Indiana. Dietrich and Ida had eight children named:

Bernard W. Sieling, born 1889, died 1944
Carl R. Sieling born 1893, died 1964
Louella Sieling born 1896, died 1983
Dietrick Sieling born 1897, died 1916
Albert Sieling born 1899, died 1968
Herman S. Sieling, born 1909, died 1959
Mayme Sieling, birth and death unknown
Theodore Sieling died in infancy

Dietrich, although an immigrant and living in a new country, was a very smart business man and soon became successful in the community. He owned not only his own grocery store and saloon, but also believed in acquiring real estate. It is said that at one time he owned approximately 25 properties. Being a kind and generous man, he gave each one of his children a house as a wedding present as soon as they were married.

Dietrich F. Sieling

Not only was he generous to his children, but he was very community minded and donated a parcel of land to the city with the provision that it be used as a city park. It is still in existence today and is known as Sieling Park. The park is located across the street from the beautiful Victorian style family home Dietrich and Ida lived in during their life together. Still standing majestically and proud at 2208 Wayne Trace in Fort Wayne, it has been designated as a historic site and is now known as the "Rose" house.

A proud American, Dietrich was the head of the Democratic party here in Fort Wayne, Indiana. Following his death in 1936, his obituary with photo appeared on the front page of the newspaper and was entitled "Prominent Fort Wayne business man died today." He is survived today by many descendants who still live in Fort Wayne. Among them are Valerie Sieling Tagtmeyer, Mr. Robert Heubner, Mr. Dick Sieling and several great great grandchildren. Dietrich is buried in the St. John's Lutheran Cemetery.

Submitted by Suzy Tagtmeyer Alexander, great great granddaughter

JOHN MANAHAN SIEMER

"ENGINEER JOHN"

John Manahan Siemer was born on September 17, 1922 in Mount Healthy, Ohio, to Carl George Siemer and Gladys Manahan Siemer. He was in the U.S. Army from November, 1942 to November, 1945. He served in England, France, Belgium and Germany during World War II.

Following the war, he attended the Cincinnati College of Music and became schooled as an announcer. He came to Fort. Wayne, Indiana, as a staff announcer at WKJG in the summer of 1953. In 1954, he became host of the "Cartoon Express", a children's TV cartoon show. Several years later it was changed to the Engineer John Show. All in all, it spanned a period

Engineer John Siemer

of 17 years, five days a week. Children were featured on the show daily. The children were glued to television in those days and today they still remember "Engineer John" and introduce their children to him. In 1972, he entered television advertising, retiring in 1989.

John Siemer is a member of the American Legion Post #296. He is also a member of the Maumee Masonic Lodge #725, the Fort Wayne Valley of the Scottish Rite and Mizpah Shrine of Fort Wayne, Indiana. He is retired and living in Fort. Wayne.

John and his wife, Ann, had three married children, one deceased.: Judith Ann Perillo, Christi Lynn Burns, and Dr. Mark Siemer. They have ten grandchildren and two great- grandchildren. John Siemer is active, enjoys golf, family, wife and friends. John and Ann are thankful for their life in Fort Wayne, Indiana.

Submitted by John M. Siemer

ERNEST G. & MARY M. (MURCHLAND) SINGER

Ernest Gilbert Singer was born April 23, 1894, in Dixon, Ohio, the son of Thomas E. and Lillie (Gilbert) Singer. Ernest graduated from high school in Van Wert, Ohio, in 1913 and received his law degree at Ohio Northern University in 1917. He was sworn in as a member of the Ohio State Bar on May 31, in Columbus, Ohio, and was honorably discharged from that post on August 11, 1917, as he went home to watch the outcome of the war.

Ernest married Mary Marguritte Murchland on November 10, 1917, and left the next day for the service. He attended Officers' Training School at Fort Benjamin Harrison and was sent to Fort Thomas, Kentucky. From there Ernest was sent to San Antonio, Texas/Kelly Field. He joined an aero machine gun squadron and was sent on to Tallifero Field, Fort Worth, Texas, for more schooling. His final stop was Carlstom Field, Arcadia, Florida, where he taught ground school to future pilots. Mary joined him in Florida in September 1918. She worked in an orange packing plant back when they used to wrap each orange in tissue.

After the war (discharged on March 13, 1919), Ernest never did practice law. He joined his brother-in-law in running the Reed-Singer Store in Dixon, Ohio. Ernest ran the "Huckster," selling vegetables, fruits, eggs, and chickens door-to-door. In 1924 Ernest and Mary moved to Fort Wayne. He was a streetcar conductor for awhile, and then worked at International Harvester Company in time study.

His wife, Mary Marguritte Murchland, was born July 15, 1900, in Monroe Township, Allen County, Indiana. Her parents were Abel and Jennie Erwin Murchland. The couple had three children: Norval Lee, born February 16, 1920; Byron Clayton, born June 21, 1924; and Aleta Rose, born October 31, 1927. The family moved to Monroeville when Aleta was one year old. The Singer home on Elm Street was remodeled by grandson, Ernest Gerardot, and is now the home of great great granddaughter, Amy and Jon Sorrell, and her family.

On July 23, 1936, Ernest had his first stroke. He died January 21, 1944, of another stroke. His final resting-place is in Monroeville Cemetery.

The eldest son, Norval, married Jean Parnin and had two children, Karen and Stephen. Upon retiring from the IHC Scout plant, Norval, Jean

Singer Family

and their daughter Karen, moved to Laramie, Wyoming. Norval died November 1, 1997.

Byron married Julia Miller and they had two children, Judith and Michael. Byron worked in sales most of his life and relocated to New York. He died July 24, 1971, and was buried in Monroeville Cemetery. Julia died in 1996.

Aleta married Leonard S. Gerardot on February 7, 1946, in California, while Leonard was in the Navy. (Leonard's parents were Charles and Ellen Cayot Gerardot.) They moved back to Monroeville, where they raised their 11 children: Jeanne Marie, Nora Louise, Lois Ann, Joyce Lynn, Jill Beth, Mary Ellen, Ernest Eugene, Jane Gayle, Lisa Kay, Mark Christopher, and Barry Allen. The couple now resides in Fort Wayne.

Mary Singer remarried on June 24, 1950, to Ralph Gerardot (born June 18, 1903), the older brother of Aleta's husband. Ralph died April 29, 1987, at the age of 82 and is buried at St. Louis Catholic Cemetery, Besancon, next to his first wife, Nora (who had died in 1929). Mary died January 22, 1989, at the age of 88. She is buried in the Monroeville Cemetery, along side Ernest.

Submitted by Amy and Jon Sorrell

SIZEMORE FAMILY

Julia Sizemore was the widow of Elbert Sizemore of Magoffin County, Kentucky, who died on October 31,1943. Soon after, Julia, with daughters Eulah and Daisy and sons Alfred and Wilfred, made their journey to Fort Wayne, Indiana, and settled for the most part in Allen County. Sons Kash and Leroy came to Fort Wayne later than the others because, at the time of the move, Leroy was working in the shipyards in Norfolk in the defense industry, and Kash was away in the Army.

Grief and need for healing may have been one reason they came to Indiana; economic opportunity was another. World War II was underway, and Fort Wayne was a major industry player.

Eulah was born September 16, 1908 and married William P. Joy. They lived on Huffman Street, and worked together at Saint Joseph Hospital and at several apartment communities. Bill died in December of 1965; Eulah died in March of 1999.

Leroy was born April 28, 1914. Leroy married Flora F. Estep. He worked at Peter Eckrich, and Flo worked at G.E.

Daisy was born on March 8, 1920, and was married to Lawrence G. Bauch. She was the Quality Control Inspector at the Horton Manufacturing Company. Lawrence also worked there before they marrried, but was called up to serve in the army in World War II. Daisy would also work at General Electric, Wayne Knitting Mills, Slicks Laundry, and Parkview Hospital.

Alfred was born on June 13,1926. He married Virginia, and worked at the J and B Tool and Die Company. He died in February of 1987. Alfred served in the armed forces in World War II.

Wilfred was born on June 13,1926. He married Joy, and worked at Horton Manufacturing Company. He later left Fort Wayne and settled in Georgia. Wilfred died in June of 2003.

Kash was married to Merle and worked at Dana, and Hickory Creek Apartments. He was the commander at the Waynedale Am Vets; he died in January 2002.

Submitted by Daisy Bauch

BENJAMIN WATSON SKELTON FAMILY

Benjamin Watson Skelton was born (1847-1921) to William and Elizabeth (Price). With his mother and wife, Nancy Collyer, they came to Fort Wayne from Ohio. They had eight children: Maud (1869) married William "Will" Watson (June 1873-1951). Edmond (May 1876 in Indiana), Benny W. (1878-1879), May (1880), Nattie (1883) married Albert Payne, Jr. in 1905, Lota "Lottie" Edith (1885) married Demons Fast in 1911, and Harrison (1888-1962 Marion, Indiana) married Margaret Stoltz in 1910. "B.W." owned the Star Grocery located at 254 Calhoun Street. Later, he also operated a candy factory. This family is buried at Lindenwood Cemetery.

Benjamin "Benny" Skelton married Edith Ecanbarger. They had two daughters, Jane Margaret (1915-1975 Battle Creek, Michigan) and Claire Mae (1919). After they separated, Benny and the girls lived with his parents. Benjamin Skelton died at the home of his daughter Jane Margaret Smith on Pittsburg Street.

Jane Margaret Skelton married Robert Firestine in 1934, and had daughter Joanna. In 1937, Jane Margaret married David Benjamin Smith (1912-1999) in Huntington County. They had daughters Sharon Smith-Bowser (1938) and Karen Lee Smith-

Top, Ben Skelton, 1912, Jefferson Street. Bottom, Claire and Jane Skelton.

Voirol (1939). There are six grandchildren. In 1958, Jane Margaret married Carl Bergstrom. They are buried in Rock Island National Cemetery, Illinois.

Claire Mae Skelton married on July 23, 1938, George Alvin "Al" Lewis. Al retired from General Electric in 1974. They had one son, Gerald (1941) and two grandchildren Dawn Lewis-Rice and Mathew Lewis.

Sara "Sadie" Ann McFerran was born (1873, Indiana-1945) to Milton and Eliza "Jane" (Rodabaugh McFerran). According to the census of 1880, they were living with their eight children in Bowling Green, Kentucky. Milton was a railroad engineer. Later, two children, Edward and Lucy were born, and both died as infants: After Kentucky, Milton (1841-1909) and Jane (1843-1924) moved their family to Fort Wayne and they died there.

The McFerran children were John A. (1866 Ohio), Sam (1867 Ohio), and George (1872 Ohio-1939) married Carrie Kaag in 1893. Next in the birth order, was "Sadie," Anna (1875 Indiana-1937) married Jack Davis but is buried under her maiden name, Benjamin (1876 Indiana-1913), Elizabeth "Lizzie" McFerran-Depner (1878 Kentucky), who lived in Kentucky and always wore White Shoulders perfume, and Jane Dulaney "Jennie"(1880 KY-1945), who married Henry Cohen in 1913.

In 1914, Lizzie had daughter Ruth Depner and Jennie had son Raymond Cohen. William and Sadie lived with Jennie on Harrison Boulevard., until they built a home on Arlington Avenue, one of the first to live there. Later, after losing the home on Arlington, William and Sadie moved to Monroe Street. Sadie died on Huestis Street in the home of her grand daughter, Jane Margaret Smith.

Submitted by Claire Skelton Lewis

SKELTON/DAWKINS FAMILY

The Howard E. Dawkins Sr., family history goes back to John Skelton and his wife, Jane Fearlamb. John was a Quaker who emigrated from England to Pennsylvania in the 1697. He married Jane Fearlamb, a Quaker from Mt. Mellac, Ireland. The property owned by John was in the Skelton family for 120 years.

One of their children, William, married a woman named Mary (unknown).

Another son, Alexander Skelton, married Rachel Maris, who was the great granddaughter of George Maris, a colonial judge in Does Run, Chester County, Pennsylvania. George brought his family and wife from England in 1693, after being confined in prison for six months for holding a Quaker meeting in his home. Alexander and Rachel's son, William, married Elizabeth Gerber, daughter of Jacob and Elizabeth Gerber. William built the first mill at Lumberton, in Bucks County, Pennsylvania, in 1758. When the building was torn down, the initials W.S. were found in the cement foundations. A man who had been deserted by his wife wrote on the mill *'Here Skelton lurks, and unkind refuge seeks. On Delawares doleful banks, between two awful peaks.'*

Joseph, William and Elizabeth's son, came to Ohio with several of his brothers and settled. Joseph was a wheelwright and farmer. He married Margaret Holm who was of Scottish heritage. Amelia C., their daughter, met and married John William Snyder of Bavarian heritage, the son of Moses and Leah (Fought) Snyder. They moved to Allen County, Indiana, from Williams County,

B. W. Skelton *Amelia C. Skelton*

Ohio. Their daughter, Ida Emmeline (Linney), married T. Ralph Dawkins, the grandson of Welsh immigrants from Kent, England. The author's father, Howard E. Dawkins Sr. was born from this union. He married Emma L. Ladig, of German and English descent and worked on his father's dairy farm, in a factory, as a real estate salesman, and as a conductor on the Norfolk and Western Railroad during his lifetime.

In Pennsylvania they were Quakers; in Ohio, Mennonites; and in Indiana, Methodist Episcopalians. They were mill builders and owners, farmers, wheelwrights, retail shop owners and school teachers. There is a great liking in the family for the names William, John, Alexander, Joseph, Aaron, Mary, Rachel, Sarah and Emmeline. At times it's very difficult to know of whom is being spoken.

Benjamin W. Skelton, Amelia's uncle and William and Elizabeth's son, served in the Civil War in Ohio and was very active in the GAR. He served as the head of the Republican Party in Allen County, and ran Star Grocery for a while. He was elected a judge in the Criminal Court of Allen County.

The Skeltons, as a family, were very family oriented. They displayed a love of books and learning, and followed a strict code of moral conduct and honor.

Submitted by Marcie Flennery

VINCENT ELLSWORTH & SHIRLEY POINSETT SLATER FAMILY

Vincent Ellsworth Slater was born August 25, 1913 in LeRaysville, New York to Harold and Martha Cool Slater. He had five siblings - Emma, Harriet, Stanley, Roxie Ellen and Frederick. Vincent first married Margaret Ellis August, 1944 in Florida while he was in the service. They had two children, Patricia Ann, born 1945, and Frederick born 1946. Patricia married Warren Nangle (both deceased) in 1966 and had one son, Michael Christopher Nangle Swift, who lives in Las Vegas, Nevada. Michael was adopted by Rob and Loyce Swift. Fred is a teacher in the Boston School System.

Vincent graduated from Orlando High School, Florida and Peabody Institute, Baltimore Maryland, and attended college at Wesminster Choir College, Princeton, New Jersey. He retired in 1984 from Plymouth Congregational United Church of Christ as organist/choir director. Prior to his Fort Wayne job, he had been employed as organist/choir director at Fourth Presbyterian Church in Chicago and Covenant Church, Detroit, Michigan.

Vincent married his second wife, Shirley Marie Poinsett, October 18,1959. Shirley was born December 8, 1931 to Peter and Ruth Davis Poinsett, also born in Fort Wayne, Indiana. She graduated from North Side High School in 1950. She worked as a secretary for Lincoln National Life Insurance Company, Capehart-Farnworth and Fruechtenicht Law Office. Shirley's hobbies are singing and genealogy, and she has helped with costumes for Plymouth Congregational UCC's annual Boar's Head Festival for 30 years.

Two children were born to Vincent and Shirley – Scott born September 23, 1960 and Stephen Vincent born October 4, 1968. Scott is single and has a bachelor's degree from SUNY, Binghamton, New York in Philsophy and Anthropology. He is currently working on his second master's at Ball State, Muncie, Indiana. Stephen married Cynthia Van Horn September 16, 2000. He is employed by Indiana Central Hardware Company in Indianapolis. They have a son, Quinton Joseph, born October 16, 2002. Cynthia is employed by an insurance company in Indianapolis.

Shirley Poinsett Slater and Vincent E. Slater, 2000

Shirley has one brother, Thomas Franklin Poinsett (born 1936) who married Anita Steel in New Haven, Indiana, in May, 1974. Thomas is retired from a career of typesetting, and lives near Auburn, Indiana. They have two daughters, Kimberly Sue, unmarried living near Los Angeles, California, and Michell who married Christiaan Martin and is living in Fort Wayne. Kim works out of her home as a graphics/web designer. Michell works for a business firm and Christiaan is in the computer business.

Shirley is fifth generation in Allen County, Indiana on her paternal side, the Rockhills and Poinsetts, who came to Allen County during the 1820s and 30s from New Jersey. Shirley's gr-gr-grandfather, Peter Poinsett and his son, John Stockton Poinsett, worked on the canals in Ohio and Indiana during the 1830s. Also on her paternal side, her grandmother Emma Eggiman Poinsett's grandfather, Anthony Eggiman, came to Allen County from Switzerland in 1837. Her mother Ruth's maternal line, the Rogges, came here from Prussia in 1860. Her mother's father, Frank Davis, came from Rushville, Indiana, in 1902 when he married her mother, Clara Rogge.

Submitted by Shirley and Vincent Slater

SLOFFER FAMILY

Aaron Sloffer I, was born in southern Germany ca 1776. Aaron spent twelve years in the Russian Army. He and his wife, Susanna, born ca 1782, came to the United States after Aaron Sloffer II was born in 1810. He applied for citizenship in Erie County, New York, on March 7, 1831 and was granted all the rights and privileges of a citizen of the U.S.A. on August 20, 1838. He bought land in Erie County, New York, 1843.

In the 1850 Federal Census of Lancaster Township, Erie County, New York, Aaron Sloffer I and his wife had in the household, Aaron Sloffer II and his wife Elizabeth (born, ca 1815, Baden, Germany). This younger couple had four children; Elizabeth, born 1836; William, born 1839; Aaron III, born 1842, and John, born 1846. Both Aaron I and Aaron II were farmers.

Sarah Jane Sloffer Bosler related that when the Sloffer family moved to Indiana, they traveled from Upper New York State on Lake Erie to Toledo, Ohio; they continued to Fort Wayne via the Maumee River.

Aaron and Suzanna Sloffer

Aaron Sloffer, II bought land August 6, 1857, in section 1, Eel River Township, Allen County, Indiana. The 1860 Federal Census of Eel River Township lists Aaron Sloffer II, his wife Elizabeth, their four children and Aaron's mother. Presumably Aaron Sloffer I died before the family moved to Indiana. The Allen County DAR cemetery records lists "Susanna Sloffer, wife of Aaron Sloffer, Sr., died February 27, 1865, age 83 years, 9 months, 3 days". The cemetery is in Huntertown, Indiana. Aaron II died before 1880 and Elizabeth died 1897.

Elizabeth Sloffer (1836-1921) married John George Heiber. They had eleven children and lived in Ari, Indiana. William Sloffer (1839-1865) married Rebecca Miller (1837-1923). Their children were William Henry (1861-1901) who married Alice Rich and Charles Wesley (1862-1939) married Edith Bowman. William and Alice had four daughters; Clara married Frank Weller, Ima married Frank Greenwell, Gladys married Ervin Wolf, and Lucille married Floyd Gause. Charles and Edith's children were Ivan Glen, who married Myrtle Zinn, Harlan Page, and Leah Elva who married Howard Hatch. Aaron Sloffer married December 29, 1861, Suzanna Miller (1835-1878). Aaron and Suzanna's children were Sarah Jane (1863-1943) married to Albertus Henry Bosler. Benjamin Franklin Sloffer (1865-1951) married Anna McCurdy and their sons were Burl and George. Jacob Isiah Sloffer (1869-1950) married Delia McCurdy; and they had a daughter Ava Marie. John Sloffer (1846-1919) married Rebecca Hutsell (1849-1932). Their children were Estella (1871-1905) married to Everett Montooth: Carl (1876-1966) married Alice Hatch, and Milo (1884-1974) married Bertha Dunten.

Additional information on Sarah Jane Sloffer can be found in the Bosler biography.

Submitted by Christina Bianski

EPHRAIM & MARSHA SMILEY, JR. FAMILY

Audrey and Ephraim Smiley, Sr. moved to Fort Wayne from Coy, Alabama, in the early 1950s, with their young children, Yvonne, Ephraim Jr., and Robert. After their move here, they had three more children, Sandra, I. Tim, and Walter. Ephraim Smiley retired from Slater Steel, while Audrey, primarily a homemaker, worked in later years as a seamstress. They celebrated their Golden Wedding Anniversary in 1998.

1994 South Side High School Graduation. Front: Jonathan Smiley, Christopher Smiley and Brian Smiley. Back: Ephraim Smiley Sr., E. Scott Smiley, Marsha and Ephraim Smiley, Jr.

Ephraim Smiley, Jr. wed Marsha Washington in a garden wedding ceremony in Lakeside Park, in 1974. Prior to a near fatal illness in 1987, Marsha worked as a medical assistance caseworker. Since 1992, Marsha has devoted herself to mentoring youth through literacy and history projects. In 1999, she founded "Spirit Flight", workshops for youth that interweave the study of virtues with African American achievement. Among the awards she has received for her work are a United Way "Doing Good Works" honor (1998); and a Literacy Star Award from the Literacy Alliance & Star Financial Bank (2002). Her most recent recognition was being an "International Women's Day" honoree (2005). Marsha earned her bachelor's degree from I.U.-Bloomington.

1998 Golden Wedding celebration. Front: Yvonne Cooley, Audrey and Ephraim Smiley, Sr. Back: Tim Smiley, Robert Smiley, Ephraim Smiley, Jr., Walter Smiley and Sandra Washington (Pratt).

Ephraim Jr. earned a degree in Sociology from Butler University in 1973. He is currently employed by Fort Wayne Community Schools. Some of his honors are: N.A.A.C.P. Wickliffe Community Service Award (1997), IPFW's "Great Men...Then & Now" Award (1999) James Yerger Humanitarian Award (2002), and Indiana Youth Investment Award (2004). For their work with youth, both he and Marsha received "Certificates of Recognition" in 2005, from the Mayor's Office.

In 1999, in collaboration with Anthony Truelove, the owner of Lafayette Bait & Tackle, Ephraim founded the Fort Wayne Community Fishing Club to mentor at risk youth. Ephraim has assisted with the Fort Wayne Park Board's summer gardening projects for youth, utilizing plows he crafted out of old bicycle parts. In addition to recycling, he began organic gardening over twenty-five years ago.

Marsha and Ephraim have four sons: E. Scott, Christopher, Jonathan, and Brian. Scott, a teacher at Paul Harding High School, graduated from South Side in 1994. He was given the honor of addressing his classmates at his commencement. He received the following awards: the Sertoma Award, the E. Wayne Scott Award, National Honor Society, Fort Wayne Alliance of Black School Educators Certificate for Outstanding Achievement, and was on the Northeast Indiana Boy's Basketball All-Academic Team. He was a member of South Side High School's 1993 semi-state basketball team. Scott graduated from Taylor University-Upland in 1999. His book of poetry, *Parole for the Soul* was set for publication in 2005.

Chris attended Bowling Green State University, as an art major. While at Harding High School, Chris excelled in both basketball and football. He was named to the AU-SAC basketball team in 1999 and quarterbacked Harding's 1997 semi-state football team.

While employed at Kingston, Jon has received several exemplary citations for his work. Ephraim and Marsha's youngest son, Brian, is an education major at the University of St. Francis. Brian, a 2004 graduate of Harding High School, was a recipient of the Scholar/Athlete Award of the National Football Foundation & College Hall of Fame, Student Honor Society of the National Urban League, First Team All-SAC Conference (2004), and twice named to the All-State offensive linemen teams. In his senior year, his team was State runner-up in the state football tournament.

Submitted by Marsha Smiley

ALVIN FRANK SMITH & BLANCHE IRENE JOHNSTON

Alvin Frank Smith was born August 4, 1902, and died April 16, 1986. Blanche Irene [Johnston] was born May 30, 1906, and died May 9, 1999. They were married March 14, 1925, and had two daughters, Alice Lucille [Fritz] born September 5, 1925, and Phyllis Irene [Arnold] born April 27, 1927 and died March 8, 1996.

They lived on the Smith homestead at 5215 Carroll Road in Eel River township. He was a school bus driver for Huntertown School for nineteen years, and worked at General Electric for nine years. He farmed and was a carpenter the rest of his life. Blanche was a homemaker, and a wonderful baker and good cook.

Alvin had a twin brother, Almon Fred. Blanche had a twin sister, Grace Ilene. Blanche and Grace married brothers.

After the death of Jeffery and Marilyn Arnold, their grandson bought the north 38 acres, and Richard and Alice Fritz's daughter bought the south 42 acres.

Submitted by Russell Ott

CHARLES M. SMITH

Charles M. Smith was born June 30, 1915, and Mary Virginia (White) Smith was born November 3, 1915, both born in Fort Wayne, Indiana. Charles went to Central High School and Virginia went to St. Mary's. Charles worked for Leland and Holsum bakeries. He went to Chicago Baking School for one year, and then moved back to Fort Wayne. He turned Catholic for Virginia, and they got married February 22, 1941.

He went back to Chicago to cake decorating school at Lambert College. By this time, Charles and Mary had two daughters, V. Carole (Smith) Beiswanger and Patricia L. (Smith) Alspaugh. Back in Fort Wayne in 1944, he started his own bakery, The Baker Boy Bake Shop, at 1638 Wells Street.

Charles and Mary had a son, Timothy C. Smith, and several years later another son, Donald J. Smith.

In the early 1950s he put in a coffee bar, the first coffee bar and bakery in Fort Wayne. Charles, Virginia and the four children ran the bakery until May 23, 1974 when they had a fire and the bakery was destroyed.

Submitted by Pat Alspaugh

JACOB SMITH FAMILY

The enclosed photo was obtained from the daughter of James L. Johnson, he a nephew of Enoch H. Smith. It shows the E.H. Smith family in front of their Smith Road home prior to moving into Yoder in 1917. As reported by B.J. Griswold in his early 1900 local histories, Enoch H. Smith was the manager of one of Yoder's grain elevators. Griswold also provided a bio of Mrs. Smith's parents, James T. and Margaret Herman Woods. Enoch Smith served for numerous years, including those during the depression, as township Trustee. His father, Finley Smith, and grandfather, Jacob Smith, had also served Pleasant Township in that same capacity, Jacob as the township's initial Trustee. In June 1851 Jacob presented a petition to the Allen County commissioners requesting that a road be built from the Plank Road (Bluffton Road), westward through Pleasant and Lafayette Townships to the county line. The petition was accepted, and that road, known today as Yoder Road, played a vital role in the development of the area, including the formation of the town of Sheldon, now Yoder.

In 1844, sisters Elizabeth and Mathilda First and their first-cousin, also an Elizabeth First, were led from Wayne County, Ohio to their new homelands in Pleasant Township by their husbands; Jacob Smith, Henry Casteel, and George Stonebrook, respectively. Henry Casteel and Jacob Smith were also first cousins; their mothers were the daughters of Philip and Elizabeth Stough Beerbower. These settled lands, were situated

E. H. Smith family in front of their Smith Road home

around the junction of sections 29, 30, 31, 32 and locally were called Smith Corners.

In 1881, a period of great religious revival, Jacob and Elizabeth Smith deeded a small tract of land legally described by the distance from Smith Corners and located on part of their 80-acre, section 31, tract for the formation of the Fair View Church of God. Across the road, the township school was often called the Smith School.

Jacob Smith (1813-1891) was born in Wayne County, Ohio to a German Lutheran family. He and older brother, Henry (1812-1863) were christened in 1814 in Jacob's Lutheran Church, Fayette County, Pennsylvania. Their great-grandfather, Philip Schmidt (1725-1814) wife, Barbara Markley (Merckle) Schmidt (1730-1818) and family settled there in 1767. They immigrated to this country in 1750 aboard the ship *The Edinburgh* and settled along Antietam Creek, in Frederick County, Maryland where ten of their thirteen children were born. Their eldest, Henry Smith (February 17, 1751 – May 10, 1838) participated in the Revolutionary War. His pension listed him as Indian Spy. Henry married Elizabeth Grovenstadt, and they raised eight children, including Elias (1789-1855), Jacob's father. After Elizabeth died August 10, 1796, Henry married Margaret Sheeter Stough, and they had five children. In 1813, Henry and Margaret signed Henry's pension lands over to his son, Elias Smith and wife, Elizabeth Beerbower (1790-1865). This 160 acre tract in Ohio's heartland, along with other adjoining tracts issued to Smith family members and in-laws, created what became referred to as the 'Smith Settlement' in early Wayne County, Ohio. The settlement was near the town of Apple Creek, which was often called Edinburgh.

Many ninth and tenth generation descendants of the Philip Smith family still reside within Pleasant Township of Allen County, Indiana.

Submitted by Thomas J. McGinnis, grandson to Enoch H. Smith

JAMES & SUSANNAH SMITH

James Smith was born in Ohio around 1809 according to Census records. On December 24,1830, Ohio State Marriage records show that he married Susannah Overly; she was the daughter of Martin and Polly (Welch) Overly. James and Susannah lived in Ohio until about 1847 mostly in Darke County. James and Susannah had fourteen children; eight of the children were born in Ohio, according to census records. The remaining six children were born in Indiana. They include Margaret born in 1831, Mary Ann born in 1832, Sarah born in 1834, William born in 1836, Brunson born in 1838, Charles born in 1840, Kisiah born in 1842, James W. born in 1843, Joseph born in 1847, Francis born in 1849, Susan born in 1850, Henry born in 1854, Martha born in 1857 and Barberry died as an infant, birth and death dates are unknown. From census information it becomes clear this Smith family had moved to Lafayette Township, Allen County, Indiana by the 1850 Federal Census . They settled on land that was patented to him by the government in Lafayette Township Section 24.

James Smith was a founding member of the United Brethren Evangelical Church in Nine Mile, Indiana in 1853. The church is presently known as Nine Mile United Methodist Church. Interesting details emerge about James Smith and other founding members in a historical overview written for the churches 100th anniversary which reads as follows: "THE HISTORY OF THE NINE MILE EVANGELICAL U. B. CHURCH - This church was organized at the home of John Miller by Rev. Casey with 16 charter members. Daniel and wife Lucy Ann Buskirk sold One acre of ground for $10.00 to the trustees of the United Brethren Church, who were Gabriel Miller, Benjamin C. Davis, James Smith, Thomas Overly and Charles Miller, on January 3, 1853. For a period of five years, the meetings were held at the homes of the various members, but in 1859, they erected a log church on the present grounds in section 7, Pleasant township."

Further research on all these families listed in this historical overview of the church show them in the 1850 Census in the area of Nine Mile, Indiana. James' wife was an Overly daughter, as stated in the above paragraph, and it is believed that Thomas Overly recorded in the historical overview is her brother. Martin and Polly had a son named Thomas born in 1809. These two families show up as neighbors in the 1850 Indiana Federal Census. It appears that both families are living on the property owned by James and Susannah.

The Smiths remain in Allen County for several generations. James Smith died in 1868 and is buried in the cemetery at the Nine Mile United Methodist Church, formerly known as the Nine Mile United Brethren Church, but not before several of his children. The family plot is in the northwest corner of the old part of the cemetery. The first Smith child who died was an infant named Barberry. This child was likely one of the first burials in the cemetery. According to church records and recorded tombstones, the first burial is in 1853. The child was likely born sometime between 1853 and 1855. Susanna would have several live births after this time. Her last live birth took place when she was 47 years old. I have been unable to find birth records for this child. This child's name appears on his father and mother tombstone in the cemetery. The stone is in several pieces and is difficult to read. The next child to be buried in this cemetery was Kisiah in 1861. She died at age 19. Charles died two years later. Charles and Kisiah's names appear on the same broken tombstone. There may also be an unnamed infant buried in this family plot too. Part of an infant stone remains and was recorded as a part of this plot in the transcription book.

Submitted by Janet Smith

JAMES W. SMITH FAMILY

James W. Smith was born in 1843 in Darke County, Ohio. He married Della Denney on March 10,1869. Della Denney was the daughter of Walter and Mary Denney who lived in Wells County, Indiana. James enlisted on the 19th of October 1864 in the Army. He listed his occupation at that time as farmer and stated that he was 21 years of age. He mustered out into the Indiana 142 infantry reporting to Nashville, Tennessee. He served until 1865 before returning to Indiana inflected with a chronic reoccurring dysentery ailment. He resumed farming living near Sheldon, Indiana (now Yoder). James W. and Della Smith had five children. They were William Francis, (1870), Alvin Oliver (1873), Della (1876), Dora (1877), and Francis Willard (1887). James died on February 5, 1915. Della was born in Brook, Virginia on May 12, 1845; she died in January, 1925.

William Francis, married Dessie Heckman on April 15,1905. They had two children: Virgil (1906) and Della (1910). Dessie (Heckman) Smith died prior to 1920. William F. is listed as a widower in the 1920 federal census; his mother is a widow and living with him and his two children in Pleasant Township.

Alvin Oliver Smith was born on December 18, 1873. He married Cora May Crites on December 24, 1892. Cora May Crites was the daughter of John H. and Amanda (McGoogan) Crites of Wells County. John H. Crites is the son of Jessie and Elizabeth (Meyers) Crites. Amanda McGoogan was the daughter of Hannah and William McGoogan from Wells County. Alvin and Cora Smith had two sons; Everett Alton Smith (August 16,1904) and James Fredrick Smith (1910). Alvin Smith ran a dairy farm and creamery in Allen County until 1919. The Alvin Smith family decided to move to the Flint, Michigan area to seek employment in the automotive industry. It was decided that Cora and Everett would travel to Flint using a motorcar. Alvin and Fred rode in a train car with the Smith family belongings. The family story states that "the dairy producing equipment and the Smith Cow would be included with the Smith belongings just in case the automotive industry opportunities did not pan out". The family settled on Term Street in Flint, Michigan; this area later became known as Burton, Michigan. Alvin Smith died of a brain aneurysm while working on the factory line in the Buick plant in Flint on January 19,1925. Cora married John Daly of Clio, Michigan after Alvin's death.

Della Smith married William Sparks. They had four children: Nora (1897), Talmadge (1898), Virgil J. (1901) and Alvin (1904).

Dora married William Harvey Jackson on June 30, 1893. They had two children: Oscar (1895) and Ruth (1903).

Francis Willard was born on January 7,1887 in Murray, Indiana located in Wells County. Frank married Arena May Straley on November 30, 1907. They had two children; James W. Smith (February 19, 1911) and Dorothy Smith.

Submitted by Janet Smith

LEO & DORTHY SMITH FAMILY

Leo and Dorthy Smith moved from Colin, near Churubusco, to a farm on Shoaff Road, four miles west of Huntertown, in the 1920s. On this 125 acre farm, they raised onions, potatoes, and peppermint on the muck bottom land. Leo built a peppermint still across the road from the dwellings, and had a contract with the Wrigley Gum factory in Michigan for the peppermint and spearmint oils. Wrigley would send inspectors to make sure the fields of mint were free of weeds.

Leo and Dorthy raised two daughters and five sons: Phyllis Smith Meyer (November 5, 1925), Marilyn Smith Waterson (October 6, 1927), Max Smith (February 16, 1929), Donald Smith (February 17, 1930-May 24, 1999), Roger Smith (January 21, 1932), David Smith (February 14, 1930), and Larry Smith (August 30, 1941).

Seated, Phyllis Smith Meyer, David, Dorthy, Leo, Larry and Marilyn Smith Waterson. Standing, Donald, Roger and Max Smith

Leo Smith was born on September 6, 1899 and died on September 28, 1970. Dorothy (Hively) Smith was born on January 2, 1902 and died on May 12, 1968.

Submitted by Max and Marilyn Waterson

LOUISE SMITH

Louise Smith was born in Allen County, Indiana May 6, 1851. She was one of ten children born to William Wilson Smith, born in Ohio in 1825 and Catherine Glock, born in Wertenberg, Germany in 1830. Of these ten children three died in infancy or as young children. Louise married Solomon J. Snider on March 17, 1878, in Allen County, Indiana. Solomon was born in Wells County in 1845 and was the son of Henry and Lurana (Morris) Snider. Louise and Solomon had two children, Chancellor Ferris, born in 1881, and Destina Elizabeth, born in 1885. In addition to those two children, she was the mother to Solomon's three children born to his first wife, Elizabeth Mallone, who was born in 1847 and died in 1875. Those children were Rufus Snider, born in 1870, Dr. William Snider and Etta May (Snider) Brown, born in 1872.

Solomon and Louise lived near Poe, Indiana, until 1904 when they bought land on the Pigeon River near White Pigeon, Michigan. They lived out their last years there. Solomon died on September 26, 1913 and Louise on October 8, 1913, within a month of each other. They are buried in White Pigeon, Michigan.

Chancellor Smith married Edna Irene Dunn in 1923 and they had one son, Jack, in 1924. Chancellor and Edna were divorced and he died in 1948. Jack Smith married and had four children.

Destina Smith married Daniel Maybee in 1908. He died of typhoid fever after seven months of marriage. Destina then married William Malone of LaGrange County in 1918. Destina had a total of six children: Virginia, Hazel, Bertha, Anna, Martin and Wayne. Virginia had three children, Hazel had two children, Bertha died in infancy, Anna had four children, Martin had one child and Wayne had none. Destina Malone died in 1955.

Submitted by Carol Haviland, great granddaughter of Louise Smith

SAMUEL CHALMER SMITH & IDA ALICE [BEAR]

Samuel Chalmer Smith (1874-1948) married Ida Alice Bear (1877-1940) on December 16, 1897. His parents were David Smith and Rebecca (Jones.) Her parents were Levi Bear and Anna (Kingdom).

Sam and Ida had ten sons: Ralph, David, twins Alvin and Almon, Raymond, Willard, Merle, Chalmer, Robert and Kenneth; and two daughters, Gladys (Delegrange) and Helen (Bucher).

On Feburary 23, 1943, the sons, along with father, appeared in the Roto Section of the Fort Wayne *News Sentinel*. Ten brothers all registered for war duty. Kenneth, the baby of the family, was in the Navy. All the family are now deceased except Robert who lives in Spencerville, Indiana.

Samuel was on the school board and is mentioned on the Huntertown School Plaque. Samuel and Ida sold the family farm to Alvin and Blanche Smith and Raymond and Grace Smith and moved to Emerson Avenue, Fort Wayne, Indiana.

Submitted by Judy Ott

WILLIAM WILSON SMITH

William Wilson Smith's grandfather, also named William, was born in England in 1740. He married a Scottish girl and they emigrated to Snow Hill, Maryland in 1773. There were two children born to this union, one died in infancy and was buried in England. William accompanied his parents to America and his occupation was as a clam gatherer and sailor. He married a girl from Maryland, moved to Circleville, Ohio, bought a 160 acre farm, and raised five children. Their son Thomas was born in 1802 and married Elizabeth Bitzer. To this union were born five children: William Wilson, Catherine, Mary, Isaac, and Thomas, Jr. Soon after the birth of the last child, Elizabeth died and was buried in Ohio. Thomas Sr. was a cooper by trade, and when good timber got scarce, he moved his family to Monmouth, Indiana, and married Charity.

William Wilson Smith was born on December 6, 1825 and was educated in the grammar schools of Ohio. He had the distinction of being the first public school teacher in Marion Township, Allen County, Indiana. The log schoolhouse stood on a three cornered plot of ground one-half mile northwest of the Poe-Hoagland road on US 27. The township paid him $24 a term, consisting of three months. While teaching school, he met and

then married Catherine (Glock) Smith, on March 28, 1850. She was born on January 31, 1830 in Wurttemberg, Germany, the daughter of Johann Suter and Louisa Hecht. Wilson saved enough money from his teaching profession to purchase an 80 acre farm on the Allen-Wells County line in Pleasant Township, one half mile east of State Road 1. They remained on that farm clearing, farming and teaching until 1863.

Wilson was appointed assessor of the township the first year of his arrival. At the same time the duties of the office were not burdensome, as there were only five persons in the township who possessed of a sufficient amount of property to render them subject to assessment. He sold this farm and purchased another farm one mile north of Echo on the Poe-Echo Road. While living on that farm he was elected Wells County commissioner. The farm was so low and wet that Wilson and Catherine could hardly raise enough to eat. In April of 1871 they sold the farm and purchased 108 acres on the Winchester Road. They remained on that farm until they passed away. Wilson died on May 18, 1903, and Catherine died December 6, 1901. Their remains were laid to rest in the Poe Cemetery. They were both charter members and active in the work of the Poe Methodist Church.

Ten children were born to their union: Louise married Solomon Snider; Marion married Mary Kansas Snider; Mary Elizabeth married Simon Somers; Ardella Evaline married Nathan Snider, brother to Solomon; Henry Isaac, an attorney in Fort Wayne, married Pearl America; Rosa Almina married William Dalman, and Jack Calvin never married. Three children died in infancy: Charles, Romanza, and William Frederick.

Submitted by Betty J. Sizemore

RUTHFORD E. & BERTHA H. (VOLLMAR) SMUTS HOMESTEAD

Ruthford and Bertha Smuts built their home in 1931, north of Zanesville, Indiana on Indianapolis Road, Lafayette Township. Ruthford was a school teacher and carpenter. Bertha was a mother and homemaker. They lived in Wells County and moved to Allen County as a requirement of his holding a teaching job at Elmhurst High School. There he taught manual arts and was coach of the girl's basketball team. He moved on to teach industrial arts at North Side High School.

Ruthford acquired a plot of ground to the south of where they had been living from a neighbor, Jack Caley. The cost of the land was for Ruthford to build Jack Caley a garage, a matter of bartering. The land was part of a cornfield. The house and garage were built with timber from a piano factory in Bluffton. Ruthford, his brother, Estal, and his father, Ira C. Smuts, built the house. The inside doors, flooring, and timbers were from the factory. The bricks and slate roof were from an old one room schoolhouse that they razed. New lumber was also used. The heating system was a large central wood and coal furnace located in the basement. There was a cistern built of bricks that furnished water for laundry and baths. The children helped carry drinking water from the neighbor's well until a well was drilled.

Over the years, Ruthford and Bertha planted over 400 trees that now surround the house and garage. The spruce at the northeast corner was a Christmas tree that had been decorated by the girls and was later planted in the spring.

Smuts Homestead

The family moved into their "new" home in late 1931 just in time for the arrival of their fifth daughter of six children (all girls)-Jeanette, Gene, Glenna, Barbara, Rosemary, and Sharon. Many happy hours were spent in that house with work, 4-H projects, softball games in the yard, cheerleading practice, and celebrations of graduation and weddings.

Bradley L. Cayot, grandson of the Smuts, bought the house in 1985. He put vinyl siding on it, removed the slate roof and hooked up to the Zanesville sewer system. He has since moved and sold the property to Nathan and Erica Hockemeyer in 2003.

The Smuts girls are Jeanette Oldfield (Floyd), Gene Geringer (Gerald), Glenna Cayot Guerin (Dale), Barbara Peterson (Ronald), Rosemary Kumfer (Robert), and Sharon Chilcote (Edwin). There are 25 grandchildren and fifteen great-grandchildren.

Submitted by Rosemary Smuts Kumfer

JACOB SNYDER FAMILY

Jacob (1805-1871) and Margaret (Riggle) Snyder moved from Ohio to Allen County, Springfield Township, Indiana, in 1846 farming 80 acres. Jacob Morrison (1845-1905), one of three sons, married Sarah Louise Horn from Harlan, Indiana. Later he married Almeda (Fleck) Ely and farmed property on Notestine Road in Saint Joseph Township. Jacob and Margaret are buried in Springfield Center Cemetery and Jacob Morrison and Sarah are buried at Viberg Cemetery. Reunion records show that Jacob Morrison Snyder's descendants faithfully attended annual reunions from 1912 through the late 1940s. Twenty-five to thirty-eight members attended on a regular basis. Most of the reunions were in Allen County. They even had business meetings and programs about father's duties to children.

George H, another son of Jacob M. Snyder, was born in December, 1866, grew up on the family farm, and was married to Carrie B. Douglass. They moved to Auburn and had five children. She died in childbirth when Irvin Leroy, the last child, was born.

George then married Lyda Fink, his housekeeper, in 1906. They moved to Reidmiller Avenue in Fort Wayne and George worked at General Electric as a machinist.

Irvin (1905-1954) and Lucille Dutton (1907-2004) were childhood sweethearts who lived near each other through high school. Irvin graduated from Central High School. Lucille attended Central also, but then graduated from the new South Side High School. They built their home at 3518 Gay Street and furnished it. Then they got married! They were members of Wayne Street Methodist Church at Wayne and Broadway. Irvin worked for A. H. Perfect, a food distributor, then sold John Hancock Life Insurance door to door. In his later years he was a payroll-timekeeper for International Harvester. In her later years, Lucille worked at Sears on Rudisill as the "candy lady".

George Snyder and his youngest son, Irvin, about 1907.

Irvin and Lucille's children, Charles Richard and Barbara Ann, were raised first on Gay Street and then later on Nuttman Avenue, both graduating from South Side High School. Charles(1931) worked at Lincoln Life Insurance Company, retiring at age 55. He is married to Ruth Carey. Barbara(1933) was married to Richard Emmett Hill (1930) in 1957. They are parents of two children, Timothy Richard, and Elizabeth Ann. Both Barbara and Richard have earned doctoral degrees and are Professors Emeriti from Purdue and Indiana Universities respectively, having retired from IPFW in 1991. In 1986, Timothy married Barbara J. Simonson. He is a professor at San Jose

George Snyder family group at a reunion near Grabill, Indiana. Irvin, Lucille and their two children are in the reunion picture. (circa 1940) Barbara is in the front row, lower right, and Charles Richard is in the front row, lower left.

State University in California. He and Barbara have two children, Griffin (seven) and Emily (four). In 1988, Elizabeth (Betsy) married Jay VanMarkwyk at First Presbyterian Church in Fort Wayne. Betsy is a speech pathologist and Jay is a chemist. They continue to enjoy living In Fort Wayne with their dog, Bailey.

Barbara's recent discovery that descendants now live in the same township as Jacob Morrison Snyder lived in the early 1900s is awesome.

Submitted by Barbara Snyder Hill

FREDERICK WILHELM SOEST

Frederick Soest came to the United States on October 15, 1836, from the state of Westphalia in Germany to New York on the ship *Howard*. He was twenty four years old and his occupation was a distiller. Frederick married Margaret Griebel on July 30, 1840 at St. Paul Lutheran Church in Fort Wayne, Indiana. He purchased land on the corner of Thompson and Emmanuel roads in Marion Township, Allen County from Frederick and Berdhardina Soest Lemkuhle and built a log house. Frederick and his family were members of the Lutheran Church. They had ten children, William, Katherina, Caroline, Louis, Christian, Mary, George and Julia. Two did not survive.

William married Louisa Bastian and operated a saw mill on Wayne Trace just south of the church.

Katherina married Mr. Schoppman.

Caroline married Conrad Ferber who operated the blacksmith shop on Wayne Trace which is across ftom the church. The shop is now displayed in the Allen County Historical Museum.

Louis married Karolyn Bastian. He operated a general store in which he ran the post office before house to house delivery. It was located next door to the Ferber's blacksmith shop. He was appointed Postmaster in 1889 which is how the name Soest became attached to the area.

Christian married Emma Schmidt.

Mary and George never married.

Taken in 1880s, Can only identify: seated L to R: first person – Mary Soest, second person – Julia Soest Doctor, seated extreme right – Caroline Soest Ferber

Julia married Lewis Doctor. They purchased a seventy acre farm on the southwest corner of Flatrock and Emmanuel roads in Marion Township. They cleared the trees to farm. They had a large orchard of fruit trees, berries and vegetables with which they supplied the Waltemath grocery store on Lafayette Street in Fort Wayne. They also supplied them with poultry, beef, pork and eggs. Lewis was overseer of a group of men who graveled the roads in the area. He and Louie Saalftank took care of the Soest Church cemetery for many years.

Frederick was naturalized July 8, 1843. He died September 15, 1882; Margaret died December 4, 1898. They were buried in the Soest cemetery.

Submitted by Linda L. Butler

GERALD H. SOMERS, MD FAMILY

Gerald Henry Somers, MD was born February 3, 1911 and was the son of Law Erskine Somers, Maryland, and Augusta M. Kroder, originally of Ossian, Indiana. Law Somers was a physician in Waynedale on Lower Huntington Road and, following Law's death in 1945, Gerald Somers returned from WWII and assumed his father's practice. The medical practice was moved to Physician's Plaza (a partnership that Gerald founded) on Brooklyn Avenue in the late 1950s. Gerald attended the University of Chicago, Butler and Indiana University.

Gerald H. Somers, MD

Gerald married Jane Rhue of Marion, Indiana on June 18, 1937. Jane was the daughter of John Alonzo Rhue and Mary Todd and was born on August 9, 1910. Gerald and Jane had five children: Mary (Molly), John Erskine, James Gerald, Jeffrey Rhue, and Jay Charles. Jay, who was born May 10, 1949, passed away in June 1949. Jane graduated from DePauw University and was a school teacher.

Gerald and Jane belonged to the First Presbyterian Church, Fort Wayne Country Club and Orchard Ridge Country Club. Gerald was the President of the Fort Wayne Medical Society. Jane was the President of the Medical Auxiliary, the Kappa Alumni, Tri-Kappa Charity, and the Women's Reading Club.

Gerald died May 14, 1969 and Jane lives in Angola, Indiana, where the Somers family has maintained a vacation home since 1947.

The Somers family lived at 227 West Fleming in the 1950s, and at 1253 West Rudisill in the late 1950s and 1960s. All four surviving children attended South Side High School where they were active in sports.

Molly Somers was born on June 9, 1940 and graduated from Northwestern and Washington State University with a Master's in English Literature. She married Gerald Schwartz of New York (born July 2, 1932) on October 19, 1964 and moved to Cullowhee, North Carolina, where they both taught at Western Carolina University. They have two children, Rebecca and William, plus six grandchildren.

John Somers was born on January 4, 1943 and graduated from DePauw and University of Chicago with an MBA in Finance. He married Cynthia Bauer of Hammond, Indiana, (born August 20, 1951) on July 17, 1971 and, after working in Chicago, Minneapolis and Ann Arbor; they relocated to Angola, Indiana. They had four children, Chris, Jeff, Michael and Mathew (Michael and Mathew are deceased) plus four grandchildren.

James Somers was born on October 22, 1943 and graduated from Parsons College and Bowling Green University with a Masters in Educational Psychology. He married Kathryn Bohnke of Monroeville, Indiana (born January 13, 1941) on June 6, 1964. Jim has been a school psychologist in Green Bay, Wisconsin, and Lansing, Michigan. They currently maintain a home in Angola. They have three children, Stephanie, Suzanne, and Scott, plus eight grandchildren.

Jeff Somers was born September 26, 1947 and graduated from Indiana University with a masters in social studies. He worked in Fort Wayne and Indianapolis with the State Mental Health System and then relocated to North Carolina where he works with the elderly.

Submitted by John E. Somers

HARLEY HOLMES SOMERS

Harley was born January 26, 1883 in Marion Township, Allen County, Indiana. He was born at home, the first child of Simon and Mary Elizabeth (Smith) Somers. A brother, Lucius Virgil, was born August 1, 1885. His early years were spent helping his father farm. He had a strong desire to learn and was an avid reader, receiving his education in the township schools and supplementing this with high school courses at Middletown.

After graduation, he began teaching school and taught for nine years at the Poe and Turner schools. In 1907 the students at Huntertown had run the teacher out, and Harley was called to teach there. He had no problems. He loved history, was a good debater, and all through his lifetime filled scrapbooks with pictures and stories about people and places in Marion and Pleasant Townships.

May 12, 1907 he married Etna Grace Trenary, and they had two children: Byron Trenary, born June 27, 1912, and Mary Ellen, born July 21, 1914.

Having a desire for business led him to assume the position of assistant cashier of the bank at Hoagland. He remained in this position for eight months gaining valuable experience.

Harley and Etna Grace Somers, 1922

Harley was instrumental in the organization of the Farmers State Bank in the town of Sheldon (Yoder). He was secretary-treasurer of this bank that opened for business October 22, 1910. Later he moved his family from Yoder to Fort Wayne where he built a home on South Seminole Circle, and later, another large home on the corner of South Seminole and Harrison.

For many years he was director of the National Farm Loan Association located on Court Street. He had purchased over three hundred acres of farmland in Pleasant Township and, in the mid 1940s, moved to the farm located west of Yoder on the Yoder road. He was well versed in farming and livestock, having learned from his father.

Harley and Grace were members of the Poe and Simpson Methodist churches. He was affiliated with the Scottish Rite, Shrine, Kiwanis and various other civic organizations. His politics were Republican, and he was known for maintaining an independent attitude and giving his support to the men and measures meeting the approval of his judgment.

Their son, Byron, married Catherine Staples on May 30, 1937 and served one term as a State Representative. Their daughter, Mary Ellen, married George Glass, an attorney in Fort Wayne, on April 16, 1938, and they had one daughter, Sandra (Robert) Houlihan. Harley died November 30, 1951, Grace died January 5, 1976, and they are buried in the Poe Cemetery, Poe, Indiana.

Submitted by Sandra Houlihan

LUCIUS VIRGIL SOMERS

Lucius was born August 1, 1885 in a two room house located on the Somers Road in Marion Township, Allen County, Indiana. He was the son of Simon Wesley and Mary Elizabeth (Smith) Somers. Lucius had one brother, Harley Holmes Somers, born January 26, 1883. At the age of seventeen Lucius began teaching school. He taught his first two years at the Bethel School located on Winchester Road south of Poe. The shell of the schoolhouse is still standing. The next six years he taught at the Poe School, one year in primary and five years in the upper grades. After Poe, he taught at the Turner School, and it was while teaching school at Poe that he met his future wife, Ethel Elizabeth Snider born October 29, 1890.

Ethel was the daughter of Preston H. and Matilda (Felger) Snider. Preston was a well-to-do landowner and farmer in Marion Township. Lucius and Ethel were married April 9, 1913 in the Poe Methodist Church, and were faithful members their entire life. Lucius taught Sunday School for more than sixty years, and Ethel was active in the ladies ministries. To this union were born two daughters, Matilda Elizabeth (Waldo) Herrmann and Catharine Louise (Franklin) Burns.

Lucius worked to help his father buy Henry Dirkson's River Farm on Hoagland Road now known as the Stone-Street Quarry. In 1909 Lucius hauled the first load of dirt out of the gravel pit with horse teams and wagons. This pit provided gravel for roads in Marion and neighboring townships. During his lifetime, he acquired and farmed approximately 600 acres. He was active in the affairs of the community, was a census taker in 1910 and wrote the Poe news for

Lucius and Ethel Somers, March of 1962

the Fort Wayne newspaper in the early 1900s. He served in the State Senate for twenty-six years serving on the Natural Resources, Conservation, and Public Policy Committees and was the Chairman of Agriculture. He was a member of the board of Parkview and Methodist Hospitals, a charter member of the Marion Township Farm Bureau and a director with the Association Life Insurance Company of Indianapolis.

Lucius was a conservative Republican, a man of integrity and once said, "I don't want to live and die and not have done something for my fellow man." He entered eternity April 28, 1975, and Ethel followed January 13, 1981. They are buried in the Poe Cemetery, Poe, Indiana.

After their deaths, their daughter Elizabeth, and husband Wally, moved to the Somers Farm to take over the management and oversee "Stone-Street". Both are still operating and in business today. Wally and Elizabeth have one daughter, Lucinda Goode. Catharine and Frank live in Brookhaven, Mississippi, and have two children, Jill (Robert) Logan and Franklin (Carol) Burns.

Submitted by Elizabeth Herrmann

NOAH SOMERS

Noah Somers was born March 26, 1812 in Shenandoah County, Virginia, the son of Barbara Sours and Philip Somers, Jr. He was the seventh child in a family of ten. His grandfather, Philip Somers, Sr., was born in Germany and settled in Shenandoah County, now Page County, Virginia, before 1767. Noah married on August 15, 1830, in Shenandoah County, Virginia, Nancy May McFarland, born about 1815, her parents not known. They attended the Christian Church near Luray, Virginia.

Their first four children were born in Virginia, and the fifth was born in Stark County, Ohio in 1849.

In 1850, Noah purchased land in Section 25 of Pleasant Township at the corner of Comer and Winchester Roads. He cleared and farmed this land, and also was a cooper by trade. He made sugar barrels, finding the material on his own land. Noah was 6' 1" and weighed 250 pounds, while Nancy weighed 100 pounds-but was known as the boss. Nancy was little but wiry and able to enter ground in a wilderness, and also make the long hard trip from Virginia to Indiana.

To this union seven known children were born. Harrison Edward married Elizabeth Roe. Jane A. married Preston Chapman, an undertaker in Poe. Theodore F. married Katherine Ward and moved to Iowa. Samuel Britel married Katherine Ward and moved to Sturgis, Michigan. Levi Leviticus married Harriet Ranney. Syndia A. married her first cousin, Peter Paul Somers, who died young, and she married, second, Samuel Reed. Auston, who died when 21 years old in 1879, is buried in the Bethel Cemetery in Marion Township.

The following stories were told by Charles Emerick and recorded by Harley Somers, Noah's great-grandson:

Noah Somers had the reputation of being the strongest man in the community. George Chapman also was a very strong man and had the reputation of being a good wrestler and fighter. During the course of typical log rolling work, Noah was found on one end of a log and George on the other. Approaching the pile, Noah raised his end of the log high and threw it under the other logs. This pushed the end held by Chapman back, throwing him down and angering him. Chapman immediately jumped up, approached Noah and declared that he could whip him any place and any time. Both of these men were influential members of the Little River Christian Church. Noah, realizing this, extended his hand and said, "Of course you can, brother Chapman." This ended the controversy, and they parted on good terms.

Noah and Nancy Somers, 1880

Another story: During the Civil War there was an organization in Marion and Pleasant townships known as the Knights of the Golden Circle, who were Southern sympathizers. Noah Somers was an ardent union man who furnished two sons for the union army. It was his habit to walk to the city of Fort Wayne. On one of these trips he passed the log home of Jacob Emerick. He was accosted by Emerick inquiring where he was going and at what time he expected to return. He was informed by Emerick that this organization intended to call upon him that evening and engage him in controversy which might result very unfavorable to him. Emerick advised him to return, say nothing, and above all things, to bolt his doors and stay at home, and if any disturbance was made, not to put in his appearance. That evening, members of this organization did call upon him and, on finding him in evidence, proceeded to steal his chickens; they killed or stole the whole flock. In after years, Noah often spoke of Jacob Emerick in endearing terms, saying that, although he was often under the influence of liquor, that he was a good man and a good neighbor.

Noah died November 22, 1883 and Nancy died in 1888. They are buried in the Bethel Cemetery south of Poe on the Winchester Road. Beside the cemetery stands the brick shell of the Bethel School where Noah's grandsons, Harley and Lucius Somers, both taught school.

Submitted by Rachel L. McNeezy

SIMON WESLEY SOMERS

Simon was born January 17, 1857 in Marion Township, Allen County, Indiana. He was the oldest child of Harrison Edward and Elizabeth (Roe) Somers. Harrison and Elizabeth had six other children, as follows: Olive Angeline married Reuben Wood, John William married Agnes Myers and Hettie Comer, Anna Albina married Elias Ake, Elmer Elsworth married Rhea Rogge, Charles Eugene married Mattie M. Philly, and Preston Harvey married Mary Belle Donnell.

Simon received his early education in the public schools of his community. As a young man, he worked on the home farm helping his father and later hired out to neighboring farms.

February 23, 1882 Simon married Mary Elizabeth (Smith) Somers, born December 21, 1854. Libby was the daughter of William Wilson and Catherine (Glock) Smith, and she taught school in Marion Township. In 1883 Simon purchased 40 acres in Marion Township and later added 104 acres of excellent farm land. This farm was located on the Somers Road in Marion Township, and the house and barn are still standing at this writing.

Simon and Mary Elizabeth (Smith) Somers

Simon and Mary had two sons, Harley Holmes born January 26, 1883, and Lucius Virgil born August 1, 1885.

In 1896 Simon rented the Hostmier Farm and, knowing that there was a large spring at the foot of the hill, he was satisfied that there was gravel in this land. He purchased the 65 acres from Henry Dirkson and proceeded to hunt for gravel, which he found in abundance, and thus opened the gravel pit. Simon, Harley and Lucius worked in this pit with hand scrappers day after day, around and around taking off the top dirt which was 18 inches to 4 feet in depth. This uncovered a vein of gravel some 22 feet thick. In 1908 four thousand yards were sold at 25 cents per yard. All the gravel was hauled away on wagons and shoveled by hand. Two or three shovels were worn out every year. The gravel was of the best quality, and thousands of yards were hauled away by horse teams from Madison, Marion and Pleasant Townships in Allen County, Root and Preble Townships in Adams County and Jefferson Township in Wells County. This pit furnished all the gravel for roads for a radius of ten miles in all directions. While digging the pit, many Indian relics were found, as the Indians had a camp on this ground in 1790. Today this pit is known as the "Stone-Street Quarry" located on the Hoagland Road.

Simon was a Republican, and they were faithful members of the Poe Methodist Church. He died December 13, 1944, and Libby died April 9, 1944.

Submitted by Scott W. Marquardt

JOHN BAPTIST SORDELET FAMILY

John Baptist Sordelet was born on December 27, 1873 in Jefferson Township, Allen County, Indiana. He married Melanie Jane "Emma" Kline on August 22, 1899 and died September 28, 1947 in Fort Wayne, Indiana. His parents, Jacques Sordelet and Augustine Huguenard, were born in Courchaton, Haute Saone, France. They left from Harve, France on the ship *Camille* and arrived at the Port of New York on May 1, 1847. They followed the Erie Canal to Buffalo, then on across Ohio to Indiana.

John and Emma farmed and worked in a grocery store in Jefferson Township until 1928 when they moved to Fort Wayne. John took a job at Tokheim and the children went together to buy their first home on Schele Street in 1936. The children remember him making a monthly visit to collect $10 for the mortgage. John was elected Wayne Township Assessor from 1932-1938. Both John and Emma are buried in the Catholic Cemetery.

Their children are Louis, 1900; Blanch, 1902; Mary, 1904; Leonard, 1906; Francis, 1908; Edward, 1911; Clara, 1914 and Norbert, 1917.

The grandchildren loved to play in Grandma Emma's grape arbor; better yet, they loved Grandma Sordelet's grape jam. After just getting up from the dinner table, the children claimed they were hungry so they could get a piece of bread with delicious grape jam. Grandma Emma enjoyed cooking chicken dinners at St. Andrew's Church.

Louis Nicholas Sordelet married Henrietta Brake on May 10, 1922 at St. Mary's Church in Fort Wayne, Indiana. Henrietta was the daughter of Ulrich Henry Brake, born in Esterwagen, Germany and Mary Francis Stewart. Louis attended elementary school in the little brick schoolhouse of Besancon, Indiana. When he was 16 years old, he enlisted in the Navy and served in France during WW I. After his return, he went to work at General Electric Company. Louis and Henrietta raised their family at 3015 Holton Avenue, and they attended St. Peter's Catholic Church. Louis died on July 17, 1983 and is buried in Leipsig, Ohio. Henrietta was a "kettler" at the knitting mill, mending runs in silk stockings. She was also an expert seamstress, making new clothes out of old ones. She was known for her blanket coats during their popularity. For entertainment during the depression, Louis and Henrietta would pack up the kids and go to friends to play cards. Henrietta died on Septemer 4, 1943 and is buried in the Catholic Cemetery, Fort Wayne.

Their children are Rita Mae, born 1923, Virginia, 1926 and Ruth in 1927. Rita married Clarence Elgain Stump on August 11, 1939. Elgain was born on November 12, 1916 in Clinton, Ohio, and died on May 9, 1993. Both Rita and Elgain loved gymnastics and were active in the Turners Club. Rita is a talented seamstress, painter and a member of the Artists Guild. Clarence built the family business, Quality Tool & Die. Their children are James, John, Kenneth, Donald, Mary and Andrew, all of Fort Wayne.

Submitted by Jeanne Stump

John Sordlet Family

JOHANN MELCHIOR SORG

Johann Melchior "John Michael" Sorg was born in Echardroth, Schluchtem, Hesse, Germany on November 21, 1809, the son of Johann Adam Sorg (1777-1845) and Elisabeth Bos. Oral family tradition relates that Melchior was a stowaway aboard the Brig Favourite which sailed from Bremen to America and arrived at New York City on June 18, 1834. It is believed that the family followed the waterways to Detroit, Michigan, where they purchased oxen, wagons, rifles, and supplies to travel to Fort Wayne. Here they purchased sections of virgin farmland southeast of Fort Wayne from the U.S. government for $1.25 per acre.

The threat of Indians was a constant source of fear. One story concerning a confrontation between the Indians and J. Melchior Sorg has been recorded. After buying his farm in the summer of 1834, J. Melchior Sorg proceeded to clear some land and build a cabin. A few days after his arrival, he was chopping down trees when three Indians silently appeared from the surrounding forest. The Indians quietly sat down on the log that he was chopping, took out their pipes, and motioned for tobacco. Being a smoker, he gave them some of his tobacco. After the Indians filled their pipes, they disappeared back into the forest. The next two days the same Indians returned and again requested tobacco from him, and he gave them some. Then on the fourth day, the Indians arrived with a large pipe. They motioned to Melchior and he filled the pipe with all the tobacco that he was carrying. As he watched, the Indians proceeded to smoke the big pipe one at a time, only taking three puffs each

Johann Melchior Sorg, 1809-1890

time. They then handed the pipe to Melchior, who also took three puffs from it. The Indian pipe was passed around three times and three puffs were taken each time by each man. Afterwards, the three Indians departed back into the woods. A few days later these same Indians returned with a side of venison for Melchior and then regularly brought fresh meat for him and his family. Thus, Melchior's kindness and friendliness to his native neighbors was reciprocated, and the peace pipe was smoked at least once by a German immigrant.

Johann Melchior married Theresa Bauer on January 9, 1837 in Fort Wayne. Theresa died on March 30, 1855 leaving him with seven children: Joseph Louis, who married Mary Hoevel; John "George", who married Mary Johanna "Mary Jane" Rauner; Theodore, who married Margaret Herber and Catherine Bestues; John M., who married Barbara Gaul; Peter; Anthony David, who married Faronica Elizabeth Schmidt; and Julianna.

On July 9, 1855 he married Barbara Lauer. Six children were then born: Katherine, who married William Suelzer; Christina Wilhelmina, who joined a religious order and was known as Sister Modesta; Charles, who married Mary Fox; Johann Melchior, Jr., who married Susan H. Bubb; Henry, who married Francis Anna (Fuchs) Fox; and Josepha.

Johann Melchior died in Fort Wayne, Indiana on March 15, 1890.

Submitted by Tom Wolfcale

JOHN MICHAEL SORG FAMILY

John Michael Sorg was born August 30, 1875 in Pleasant Township, Allen County, Indiana. On October 12, 1897 he married Mary Margaret McLaughlin in St. Peter's Catholic Church. Mary was born February 12, 1875 in Jefferson Township, Whitley County, Indiana. Her parents were James and Mary "Caroline" (Hinen) McLaughlin, early settlers in Whitley County.

John spent most of his life farming and then later worked for the General Electric Company from which he retired in 1939. John died on July 2, 1955, and Mary continued to live at their residence at 425 West DeWald Street, in Fort Wayne until her death on January 5, 1966.

They were preceded in death by one daughter, Edna Catherine, in 1908. Their other nine children were: Alfred John, who married Elizabeth Miller and were the parents of Mary, Donald A., and Joseph E.; Irene Alice who married Clarence Oser and were the parents of one daughter, Marie; Oscar William (Brother Rembert, C.S.C. of the Order of the Holy Cross); Estella Francis who married Glenn O. Wolfcale and were the parents of James F. and Thomas O.; Agnes Rosella who married Glen E. Ulrey and were the parents of Roberta C; Mary Josephine (Sister Marguerite Mary of the Sisters of Providence); Edith Matilda who married Jules E. Cochoit and were the parents of Jules E. and Angela R.; Clara Alvera who married Anthony Lauer and were the parents of David and Anthony E., Jr.; and Velma Celeste who married Paul Witte and were the parents of Darla, Lawrence A., and Jean.

John Michael was the son of John "George" Sorg, born September 18, 1841 in Marion Township, Allen County, Indiana. J. George was educated in the public and parochial schools of Allen County and was employed in the carpenter's

John M. Sorg Family, 1930. Back: Agnes, Alfred, Edith, Oscar, Estrlla Middle: Irene, Mary, Clara Front: John Michael, Velma, Mary

trade for some time. He eventually inherited a tract of one hundred acres from his father, Johann Melchior, and thereafter devoted himself exclusively to farming. On November 4, 1873, J. George married Mary Johanna (Mary Jane) Rauner, the daughter of Lambert and Theresa (Bush) Rauner. Mary Jane was born August 7, 1856 in Orange County, New York. They were the parents of twelve children: Theresa (1873-1941) who married Frank Steinacker; John Michael (1875-1955); Bernhard G. (1877-1939) who married Matilda VanAllen; Anthony A. (1881-1941) who married Margaret F. Noonan; Lambert J. who married Ethel E. (Unk); Catherine M. who married Frank Lahrman; Ferdinand S. (who died at the age of fourteen years); Daniel; Francis M. (1891-1959) who married Louis Wilkie; Andrew G.; Roman H.; and Robert F. (1898-1945) who was a Shipfitter Second Class in the U.S. Navy. J. George died on the home farm on December 17, 1903 and Mary Jane died in 1917.

Submitted by Jim Wolfcale

MONTE WALTER & KAREN SUE SCHINGS SOUTHWARD FAMILY

Monte Walter Southward was born in Crawford County, Ohio to Henry Jackson and Lucille Southward. Monte grew up and lived 50 years of his life along the Lincoln Highway "U.S. Route 30" in Wyandot County, Ohio, on his parents farm, which is still owned and occupied by the family. In 1974 Monte married Karen Sue Schings whose parents are Charles and Lucille Lowmaster Schings. They are parents of two children: Greg, who resides in New Jersey and Monica who resides on the home place in Ohio. Monte has four children from his previous marriage: Justin, Upper Sandusky, Ohio; Jeff, New Orleans, Louisiana; Jodi, Upper Sandusky, Ohio; one son, Jack, is deceased; six grandchildren and one great grandchild.

Monte and Karen owned and operated Auto Parts stores in Bucyrus, Lima, Mansfield, Marion, Sandusky, Sidney, Springfield, Tiffin and Upper Sandusky, Ohio for over 30 years.

Monte and Karen moved to Aboite Township, Allen County, Indiana in 2003. Monte and Karen are not the first of his family to settle here. A great aunt, Nancy Southward Alspaugh, born in 1865, Wyandot County, Ohio, lived here for several years on Maysville Road, Fort Wayne, Indiana. Nancy was the youngest daughter of John S. and Mary Benjamin Southward, great-great grandparents of Monte. Nancy passed away June 15, 1943, and is buried in Prairie Grove cemetery in Wayne Township.

Squire Elijah Benjamin, born in Athens County, Ohio October 7, 1810, was one of the first settlers of Largo, Wabash County, Indiana in the year 1834. His parents were Nathan and Mary Nulton Benjamin, gr.gr.gr.gr. grandparents of Monte. Elijah is great uncle to Nancy and gr-gr-gr great uncle to Monte. Squire Elijah was contracted in 1833 to cut and lay stone for the locks in Fort Wayne on the Wabash and Erie Canal. Mr. Benjamin worked several years as a stone mason contractor on the canal.

Monte's gr.gr.gr.gr grandparents, Sebastian and Mary Guy Southward,

Monte W. and Karen S. Schings Southward Family

came to Pike County, Ohio from White Post, Virginia in 1807. Their son Henry married Catherine Nixon, daughter of John and Ruth Nixon, in Ross County, Ohio and migrated north to what is now Wyandot County, Ohio in 1823, first settling near the town of McCutchenville, then later moving to Richland Township near the town of Wharton, Ohio where he passed away in 1881.

Submitted by Monte & Karen Southward

NEIL & DIANA SOWARDS FAMILY

Neil Sowards first visited Fort Wayne in 1959 as he and a friend proceeded on a canoe trip from Toledo, Ohio to New Orleans. He never dreamed he would some day live in Fort Wayne and make a life here.

Neil and Diana Sowards came to Fort Wayne in 1966 when he began a job as Christian Education Minister at First Baptist Church. Their two children, Rinda (Batenich), who was adopted in 1967 and was a Korean-American, and David, both attended public schools and graduated from South Side High School. Diana worked at Lutheran Hospital.

In 1972, Neil went into the full time coin business, attending coin shows every weekend and conducting a mail order business. He developed a business in tokens, foreign coins and notes, obsolete paper money, including broken banknotes, stock certificates and checks. He edited *The Handbook of Check Collecting* in 1975 and wrote a column for *The Banknote Reporter* for several years.

Sensing a need for more male oriented shopping at Glenbrook Square, in 1976 he and

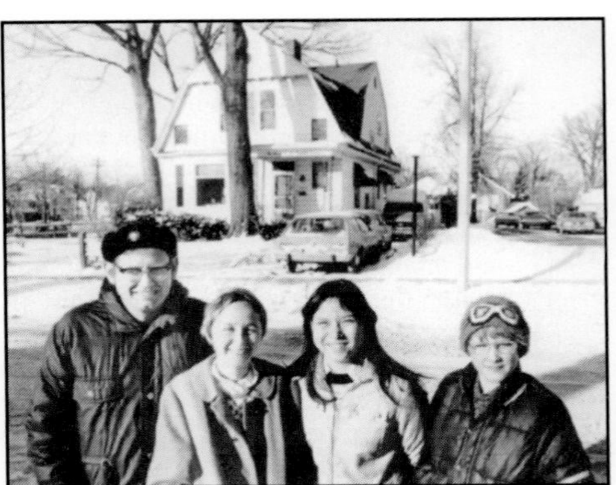

Neil, Diana, Rinda, David Sowards, Newspaper Picture 1978

partner, Barry Krumlauf, opened A-Z Coins, Inc. (later changed to A-Z Coins and Stamps, Inc.) which is still one of the few local enterprises in Glenbrook.

In 1982 Neil and Diana donated materials for the Baker's House at Historic Fort Wayne, and they and volunteers built it and furnished it. He also served as Treasurer and Board member for Historic Fort Wayne at this time.

Starting in 1985, after a very moving visit to Burma where his parents had served as missionaries, Neil and Diana began Friends of Burma, an organization which promotes education, microcredit, and humanitarian aid. Through Friends of Burma they have helped build six buildings, four community libraries, and given scholarships to over 600 students a year in Burma in honor of his parents, and helped fourteen students study in America. Through the following years they have devoted a majority of their time to promoting these projects and teaching business in Burma. In addition, they have aided many Burmese refugees who came to Fort Wayne from 1990 on, culminating in a Burmese population of between 1500 and 2000 in 2004.

In 2002 Neil received an honorary Doctor of Divinity degree from Myanmar Institute of Theology in Rangoon, honoring his many years of service.

Since 1968, the family has observed the many changes to the Lutheran Hospital neighborhood where they lived, from the days of boys serenading the Lutheran Nursing School students, to the building of the new Duemling Clinic and its subsequent dormancy, to the razing of the multiple hospital buildings, to the development of the beautiful Lutheran Park.

Submitted by Neil and Diana Sowards

PHILLIP SOWERS FAMI1Y

Phillip Sowers was born in Ohio and migrated to Indiana where he married Amanda Harriet Yeakey.

They had six children, and among them were Frank Sowers, born 1854, who married Sarah Hilkert, and Alice S. Sowers, born 1855, who married Issac Fredson.

Their daughter, Ella Estelle Sowers, was born September 23, 1865 in Noble County, Indiana, and died December 21, 1962 in Butler, DeKalb County, Indiana. Ella Estelle Sowers married, first, William Riley Fike in Noble County, Indiana. In his fiftieth year, William

Left to Right, unknown, unknown, Ella and Jeff Fike

commited suicide in his garage while Ella was preparing breakfast. William was born April 9, 1856 in Michigan, and died April 19, 1906 in DeKalb County, Indiana. William was a great judge of good horse flesh, and always had fine horses on his farm. Ella later married William's brother, Jefferson. Jefferson was born in 1861 in Michigan, and died in 1936 in Indiana. Both William and Jefferson Fike were the sons of Elias Fike and Lois Sprague who married in St. Joseph County, Michigan, October 16, 1851.

William and Ella had five sons, of which we have information about four: Raymond was born near Kendallville, Noble County, Indiana, and he married first, Tracy L. Treesh; second, he married Edith Pearl Firestone on December 25, 1910 in DeKalb County, Indiana. Harry was born March 25, 1891 in Noble County, Indiana, and he married Ethel Mae Treesh on April 26, 1922. Howard was born April 9, 1895, and he married Ruth May Christlieb on December 20, 1921. Arthur Sr. was born May 30, 1898 in DeKalb County, Indiana, and he married Elva M. Harter May 20, 1922 in Coldwater, Michigan.

In an article printed in the Auburn Newspaper, DeKalb County, Indiana, Ella was named as winning the title of the oldest living settler. "Auburn Woman, 95 is oldest settler. Ella Fike repeats at 1960 Fair. An Auburn woman, Mrs. Ella Fike, of 810 North Van Buren Street, Auburn, Indiana, came downtown Saturday afternoon to register, for the second consecutive year as the oldest settler at the 1960 DeKalb County Free Fall Fair. Mrs. Fike, age 95, was born September 23, 1865. She won her first crown as the oldest settler to register."

Then two years later at age 97 Ella is called home to be at the side of our L ord. The obituary in the Auburn newspaper of DeKalb County, Indiana states. "Auburn woman dies at the age of 97. Mrs. Ella E. Fike of 816 North Van Buren Street had been a nursing home Patient for more than a year. Mrs. Ella E. Fike died at the age of 97 years at the Sheehy Nursing Home in Butler at 8:25 a.m. Friday from complications of advanced age. Mrs Fike had been in failing health for the past two years and entered the nursing home June 16, 1961. She had resided in Auburn for 12 years."

Other persons mentioned in this submission are Roy Sowers, born January 18, 1908, who married Vernie Russell, and Martha A. Sowers, who married George D. Leighty.

Submitted by Cheryl Green

MARTIN SPANLEY FAMILY

Martin Spanley (Mathias Spanle) was born January 23, 1824 in Lacherhof, Wurttemberg, Germany and baptized in the Catholic parish of Dunningen the next day. When Martin was a young man, his parents, Karl Spanle and Theresia Borrhe, died. At age 23, he left for America from the port of Le Harve on March 27, 1847. Two months later, on May 28, he arrived at the Port of New York. His journey brought him to Fort Wayne, Indiana and within seven weeks he was married to Brigitta Stern on July 5, 1847 at the Cathedral of the Immaculate Conception. Brigitta was the daughter of Bernard Stern and Mary Haig. She and Martin had four sons. The first two, Edward and Carl, died as infants. Martin was born January 25, 1851. Francis Xavier was born July 9, 1853. The German parishioners of the Cathedral wanted a German language church. When St. Mary's Catholic Church was formed, Martin and Brigitta were charter members.

Frank Spanley and Elizabeth Keintz, 1885

Martin became a naturalized citizen in 1849. He served jury duty, voted, and performed civic duties. His forty-acre farm in section sixteen of Wayne Township was purchased at a sheriff's sale. The family resided in a log cabin until Martin's death. His first occupation was distiller, then farmer, and he raised cattle, marking them with a triangular hole and a slit in the under part of each ear. At night the cows were brought into the cabin for protection against wolf attacks, and the animals helped keep the cabin warm. Twenty years after he settled in Allen County, Martin's two nephews, Lewis P. and Joseph Spanley, came to Fort Wayne. Martin died in 1887 and Brigitta died in 1910. Both are buried in the Catholic Cemetery.

Martin Spanley Jr. married Sophia Gebhard in 1879. They had three children, Charles A., and twins, Mary J. and Bernard J. Spanley. Martin and Sophia are buried in the Catholic Cemetery.

Frank X. Spanley married a neighbor girl, Elizabeth Keintz, October 27, 1885. They had ten children, Walter J., John, Cecelia E., Mathias F., Edna M., Elizabeth B., twins Eleanor M. and Loretta T., Helen J., and Lucille A. Spanley. Frank inherited the farm near Ardmore Avenue with the stipulation that he would care for his mother until her death. He built a second story on the cabin to make room for his large family. Brigitta only spoke German, so the grandchildren were raised bi-lingual. After farming a few years, the family moved into the city to 1307 Scott Avenue, bringing a pet dog, Pete the buggy horse and Charlie the plow horse. The animals were almost lost in a barn fire at the new residence. Frank worked for the Electric Works. Their next home was at 1019 Lafayette Street, a house with enough room for family, several boarders and the family piano. Music and dancing were favorite pastimes.

Frank died June 25, 1929, seven months after his wife. Elizabeth died November 15, 1928. Both are buried in the Catholic Cemetery.

Submitted by Carol Quickery

JOHN SPILLSON

Good food prepared and served properly in a congenial atmosphere was a very serious matter to John Spillson, creator and owner of Café Johnell, one of the finest restaurants in the area for over thirty years.

John Spillson

John was born on March 2, 1921, literally in a cafeteria in Monroe, Michigan, the son of Cleo and Nicholas Spillson. He had a sister Grace, and a brother, Achilles. The family lived in Monroe and later in Detroit. John served in the Merchant Marines between 1941 and 1943. After discharge, John moved to Fort Wayne where his father had once owned the Berghoff Gardens. Here he met and married Jayne Howell; their children were Kala, Nike, John, Mark and Nick.

In November of 1956 John borrowed $600 from John Eschoff and Wimpy Rodenbeck to open a chicken and rib carry-out. He later converted the business to a pizza carryout where he was known to have the greatest pizza in town. In the early 1960s John remodeled the restaurant as a café that featured French foods and wines. Jayne was responsible for the plush décor of the rooms. In the beginning friends loaned them original paintings, then gradually they replaced them with replicas, then with originals of their own.

From the beginning they drew people from cities and towns outside Fort Wayne. Among the many famous people who dined at the restaurant were the King of Norway, President Nixon, and sportscaster Chris Schenkel. The hallmark of fine dining at Café Johnell was a leisurely meal with friends or loved ones, good conversation, and fine wine to set the mood. The restaurant received many awards, and was written up in the Wall Street Journal.

John's knowledge of fine wine grew over the years, as did his culinary talents. Spillson tried to travel in Europe every year to look for new ideas, and created many of his own dishes. His daughter, Nike, trained at the Cordon Bleu School in Paris, and became the chef in charge of the kitchen. John was active in the day to day operation of the restaurant until his death in 1995, when Nike took over and ran the business for a time.

Over the years, John continued to find new ways to present cuisine and still keep the prices down, doing it all within the framework of his "Three P's," punctuality, preparedness and perfection. His goal from the beginning was simple: good food, good service. And everyone who dined at this very famous restaurant over the years would agree that he met his goal.

Submitted by Mark Spillson and Margaret Eckrich

DELBERT SPRINGER FAMILY

Delbert Ferdinand Springer was born June 7, 1933 in Allen County. He died March 2, 1985.

His father was Adrian Michael Springer born January 23, 1907, in Wells County. He died February 1, 1958. Adrian worked as a carpenter for John R. Worthman in Fort Wayne, Indiana. His mother was Dorothy (Leaming). She was born April 24, 1915, and died July 9, 1975. Dorothy was a member of the American Legion Post 241 Auxiliary in Fort Wayne. He had one brother, Edward Gordon. Edward was Dorothy's son from her first marriage. Adrian never adopted Edward, but Edward took the Springer name.

Delbert attended Elmhurst High School. He was in the Navy during the Korean War. He served on the USS Valley Forge, and was honorably discharged on April 1, 1960. Delbert retired from Interstate Freight Systems in 1979. He then worked for Zeiss Security as a security guard.

Delbert married Margery (Bower) on December 27, 1958. They had three children. Jennifer Lyn was born on August 28, 1959. She graduated from South Side High School in 1977. She married Robert Pierce in 1979 and they had a daughter named Jenemarie, born March 1, 1980. They divorced in 1983. Jenny then married Tom Hakes on January 15, 1988, and they have three children:

Brandy Rose born July 8, 1990

Allison Jewel born August 5, 1991

Arron Jason born July 9, 1994

Jenny is a Fort Wayne Community Schools bus driver and Tom works at the State School.

Deidre Ann was born May 23, 1963. She graduated from Northrop in 1981. Deidre married Ed Wolfe in 1981 and they later divorced in 1988. She then married John Wayer on September 16, 1989. They have one son, Jonathon Wayer, born October 24, 1995. Dee and John divorced in 1999. Dee married Donald Britton on December 29, 2001. They are both employed at Tetapak in Fort Wayne, Indiana.

Delbert Franklin was born October 27, 1965. He graduated from North Side High School in 1984. He married Lisa (Klinger) on May 28, 1988. They have one son, Nathaniel Matthew, born April 18, 1996. Delbert works at Autoliv and Lisa works at Nietert Insurance.

Submitted by Lisa Springer

WILHELM GOTTLIEB STAHL – DORATHA SCHOENE (AMERICANIZED TO SHANE) FAMILY

Wilhelm was born in the Village of Hohenhaslach, Germany on September 21, 1862. He sailed from Breman, Germany on January 5, 1874, arrived in New York U.S.A. in February 1874, and came directly to Fort Wayne, Indiana. His naturalization took place in Fort Wayne, Indiana on May 29, 1886.

He was a U.S. Mail carrier and a charter member of the National Association of Letter Carriers branch #116, Fort Wayne, Indiana. He was a secretary for the Moose Lodge, Fort Wayne. He also was a custodian at the South Side High School.

Wilhelm married Doratha on December 8, 1886. They had five children. The first was stillborn; the others were:

1. Inez, married George Hermans, (no children) lived in Fort Wayne, Indiana.

2. Esther, married William Fry, (no children) lived in Zion, Illinois.

3. Earl, married Anna Weikel (no children) lived in Fort Wayne and Angola, Indiana

4. Karl F. (Earl's twin) Toolmaker at G.E. married Marcella Nichter. They had three sons, Thomas, James, and William.

Thomas K. married Jean Krause (deceased). Thomas and Jean were both school teachers. Thomas also was a Postmaster in Virginia. They had two children, Kim M. who has one son, Karl M. who has one daughter. Thomas K. is re-married and lives in Florida.

James R. married Patricia J. Sheets. James was a Fort Wayne Police Officer (retired) and Patricia was a U.S. Postal Clerk and Nurse (retired). They have four children, Daniel E., Ronald L, Bruce R., and Julie C. Daniel E. is married to Janet Bollenbacher. Daniel is a plumber. Ronald L. married Linda Hause (divorced). Ronald is a automotive painter and auto damage estimator. They have a son and a daughter. Bruce R. married Nancy Trevino (divorced). Bruce is a Fort Wayne Firefighter. They have a son and daughter. Bruce is remarried to Kim Long and has one stepson. Julie C. (Ortiz) married Meliton Ortiz. Julie works for American Electric Power in the Printing Services Department; they have three daughters. All of the James R. Stahl family live in Allen County, Fort Wayne, Indiana.

William P. married Virginia Southworth (divorced). William was a plumber in California (retired) they have a son and a daughter. William is re-married to Pam Kruger and lives in Nevada.

Submited by James R. Stahl

The James R. Stahl Family. L to R: Bruce, Ronald, Julie, Patricia, Daniel, James

ORPHIA ANN STAYER FAMILY

Orphia Ann Stayer was born on May 31, 1938, in Angola, Indiana, and she died on June 11, 2001, in Fort Wayne, Allen County, Indiana. Ann's parents were James Stayer and Velma Kathern Smith. James and Velma were married on March 6, 1948. James was born on October 18, 1913, and Velma was born on October 22, 1917, at Fort Madison, Lee County, Iowa, and died on March 9, 2002.

Ann Stayer married Wayne Merle Fike on June 30, 1956, in Auburn, DeKalb County, Indiana. Wayne was born on March 26, 1937, in Noble County, Indiana. Wayne drove a semi filled with chickens from the Fort Wayne area to Ohio and also drove a cement mixer. Later he obtained a job at Dana Corporation in Fort Wayne, Allen County, Indiana. Ann worked for Magnavox in the office, later resigning to take care of her family. Wayne and Ann had six children: Christopher Allen, Cheryl Ann, Larry Wayne, Cynthia Kay, Catherine May, and Carla Jo. All the children graduated from high school and married in Fort Wayne, Allen County, Indiana.

Orphia Ann Stayer Family

Christopher Allen married Tammie M. Boissnet on August 6, 1977, and they had two children, Jessica Marie and Christopher James.

Cheryl Ann married Russell Wayne Green on May 27, 1978, and they had two children, Kristina Ann and Nicholas Wayne in Michigan. Kristina Ann married Brandon Linnabury in Jackson, Michigan.

Larry Wayne was born on March 16, 1960, in Auburn, DeKalb County, Indiana, and died on July 6, 1962, in Auburn, DeKalb County, Indiana.

Cynthia Kay married Scott Sower on July 1, 1978, and they had two sons Dominque and Derrick.

Catherine May married Matthew Blaine Halferty on July 19, 1986, and they had three children: Darby Logan, Delena Christan, and Dalton Jermiah.

Carla Jo married Sherman Gayheart, Jr., on November 21, 1987, and they had one daughter, Brittney.

Submitted by Carla Gayheart

PAUL & RUTH STEINER FAMILY

Paul Andrew Steiner was born on February 17, 1929, near Woodburn, Indiana. His great-great-grandfather, John Steiner, was born in Alsace, France where he was conscripted into Napoleon's army. Because he was a Mennonite, he escaped into Switzerland and then emigrated to Kitchener, Ontario, Canada in the early 1800s. He later settled in Wayne County, Ohio, and then to Allen County, Ohio, where he bought a 240 acre farm from the government for $1.25 an acre.

Later, Paul's grandfather, Paul Abraham Steiner and his wife, Magdalena Gerig Steiner, who came from Grabill, settled on a farm near Woodburn, a hundred years ago. Paul's father, Eli Gerig Steiner, married Emma Yaggy, the daughter of Andrew and Lydia Gerig Yaggy. Andrew's son, Jesse, also farmed near Woodburn. The Yaggy family originally came from Alsace, France

Paul and Ruth Steiner

Eli and Emma Steiner's children, in addition to Paul, are Phyllis McCoy, Wilma Petersen, Richard Steiner, Carolyn Rowell, and Sharon Connor. Eli was a farmer, a businessman, and later a pastor and denomination leader with the Evangelical Mennonite Church, now called Fellowship of Evangelical Churches, headquartered in Fort Wayne. He graduated from the Fort Wayne Bible Institute.

Paul and Ruth's children are Nancy Keller, BS-RN, Mark, MBA, JD, Jonathan, MBA, and David Steiner, JD. They have eleven grandchildren, eight grandsons and three granddaughters.

While attending Taylor University, Upland, Paul met his wife, Ruth Edna Henry, of East Orange, New Jersey. She is the daughter of Israel Howard Henry, an electrical engineer, and Ruth Edna Sharretts, a nurse. Ruth Steiner is a direct descendant of the Sharretts, who were among the first settlers of Staten Island. Through her father, she is a direct descendant of patriot Patrick Henry. Paul and Ruth were married September 1, 1950, after his graduation from Taylor. Ruth graduated one year later with a degree in Home Economics Education. After a year of social work, they moved to Bluffton, Ohio, where he entered the family feed and grain business. Paul and his father were also partners in a mineral feed supplement business and a lumber yard, of which Paul later became sole owner and manager. In 1964, he sold the lumber yard and moved to Fort Wayne, where he joined the Brotherhood Mutual Insurance Company. In 1971, he became president and several years later was elected chairman of the board. He retired in 1994. The company became a major insurer of churches and related ministries.

Paul attributes whatever success he has had in business and leadership to the early influence of his father, a good work ethic, innate business instincts, and God's guidance and blessing. He served on numerous non-profit organization boards, many as president or board chairman. These included chairman of the board of the National Association of Mutual Insurance Companies and of the Fort Wayne Bible College/Summit Christian College, now Taylor University. He served as president of the Fort Wayne Rotary Club and the Fort Wayne Rescue Mission. He was also a trustee of the American Bible Society.

Submitted by Paul A. Steiner

PHILLIP JAMES & KATHLEEN ANN (HALE) STEWART FAMILY

Phillip James Stewart was born August 22, 1972, in Fort Wayne, Indiana, to Wesley Clark Stewart (born November 20, 1943, in New Haven, Indiana) and Nancy Lynn Waterson (born August 25, 1953, in Fort Wayne, Indiana). Phillip grew up in Fort Wayne with his sister, Brandy Marie Bock (born May 26, 1975, in Fort Wayne, Indiana). He graduated from North Side High School in June of 1991. He enlisted in the United States Marine Corps, serving from June 1991 to June 1995. Phillip was stationed at Camp Pendleton, California, as an infantryman in Alpha Company, 1st Battalion, 4th Marine Regiment, 1st Marine Division. During his time of service, he was deployed overseas on two separate six month Western Pacific deployments aboard the USS Ogden LPD 5 and the USS Cleveland LPD 7. Phillip had attained the rank of corporal and, upon his discharge, he returned to Fort Wayne and enrolled as a student at Indiana-Purdue University, Fort Wayne. Phillip was employed by Allen County for six years. He then applied to the Fort Wayne Fire Department in 2001 and attended the Fire Academy in 2002, and was officially hired as a firefighter on September 13, 2002. On April 21, 2004, Phillip started working part-time as an ER Tech at Lutheran Hospital. Phillip is a member of the Republican Party, National Rifle Association, American Legion Post #47, and the Marine Corps League. Phillip's interests are politics, history, genealogy, camping and basketball.

Kathleen Ann (Hale) Stewart was born December 17, 1972, in Fort Wayne, Indiana, to Jeffery Kent Hale (born September 30, 1948, in Noblesville, Indiana) and Frances Margaret Vodde (born May 15, 1950, in Fort Wayne, Indiana). Kathleen grew up in Fort Wayne with her

Stewart Family,
Phillip, Kathleen, Madelyn, Gillian, Owen

sister, Christine Marie (Hale) Douglas (born April 19, 1970), and two brothers, Andrew Nathan Hale (born November 10, 1980) and Patrick Ryan Hale (February 25, 1985). All of Kathleen's siblings were born in Fort Wayne, Indiana. She graduated from North Side High School in June of 1991. Kathleen attended Indiana-Purdue University Fort Wayne and earned an Associate's Degree in Organizational Leadership and Supervision from Purdue University. Kathleen was employed with Lincoln National Life (Fort Wayne) for nine years.

Kathleen and Phillip met while students at North Side High School and were set up by a friend of Phillip's after Phillip had expressed interest in Kathleen. They began dating in the latter part of their senior year. In early 1993, Kathleen moved to Oceanside, California, to live with Phillip. They eloped to Las Vegas, Clark County, Nevada, on March 6, 1993.

Phillip and Kathleen Stewart have three children: Madelyn Olivia (September 8, 1996), Gillian Makenzie (March 6, 2000), and Owen Alexander (July 12, 2004). All of their children were born in Fort Wayne at Parkview Memorial Hospital. The Stewart family are members of Saint Jude Catholic Church in Fort Wayne. The Stewart family resides at 2821 Hazelwood Avenue on the northeast side of Fort Wayne.

Phillip Stewart is a descendant of William Watterson (1806 - 1892), a farmer, and Frances Shively (1813 - 1854), who traveled by canal boat [via the Erie Canal] to Allen County, Indiana from Washington, Pennsylvania. William Watterson purchased eighty acres (Section 21, Township. 32, North Range 11) in Eel River Township (near Watterson Road and Wesley Chapel Road) from his brother Thomas Wiley Watterson in 1847 for the sum of five hundred dollars. Thomas Watterson had purchased the land on June 2, 1835, from the U.S. Government, and the land patent was signed by President Andrew Jackson on April 5, 1836.

Submitted by Phillip Stewart

MARVIN & BENITA STEYER FAMILY

Marvin Raymond Steyer was born on January 26, 1956, in Lima, Allen County, Ohio to Mary Margaret Wiechart, daughter of Gregory Wiechart and Dorothy Baldauf, and her husband, Wilfred John Steyer, son of Albert John Steyer and Frances Lauretta Lenhart.

Children of Wilfred and Mary Steyer are: Jean Ann Steyer, born June 15, 1951; Lois Marie Steyer, born March 16, 1953; and Martha Kay and Marvin Ray, twins born January 26, 1956, all born in Lima, Allen County, Ohio.

The Wilfred and Mary Steyer family lived on the Wiechart family homestead near Middlepoint, in Van Wert County, Ohio. Mary was born in the farmhouse which was built by her parents, Dorothy Baldauf and Gregory Wiechart. The original barn burned down to the ground when Mary was a young girl, and the "chicken coop" was built and used for the wedding reception held when Wilfred and Mary were married September 10, 1949. Wilfred farmed and worked at Aeroquip, in Van Wert, Ohio, where he retired. Mary worked at the Middlepoint grain elevator as a bookkeeper. Mary graduated from Indiana Business College in Fort Wayne. Wilfred Steyer died October 19, 2001, in Lima, Ohio, and is buried in Delphos, Ohio. The Wilfred and Mary Steyer family were members of St. John Catholic Church, Delphos, Ohio.

Marvin graduated from St. John Catholic High School in 1974, and from Ohio State University, Columbus, Ohio with a degree in Industrial Arts Education in 1981. Marvin worked as a teacher for the Ohio State School for the Blind, and as a tool salesman. He moved to Fort Wayne, Allen County, Indiana in 1992. Marvin married Benita Ann Sheets on June 11, 1994, in Fort Wayne, Indiana.

The Marvin and Benita Steyer Family. L to R: Bryan Gripp, Marvin Steyer, Jennifer Steyer, Benita Steyer, Benjamin Steyer

Benita Sheets was born May 15, 1952, to Donald Duane Sheets and Mary Belle Crites at Lutheran Hospital, in Fort Wayne, Indiana. Benita graduated from Elmhurst High School in 1970, and from Purdue University, West Lafayette, Indiana, in 1973 with a degree in Home Economics Education. She has worked as a social worker and a teacher for the State of Indiana, a retail store manager, and as a teacher at the Braille Institute in California. She was the President of the Zeta Tau Alpha, Fort Wayne, Indiana, Alumnae Chapter, and President of the Seton Society ladies group at St. Elizabeth Ann Seton Church. Benita had one adopted son, Bryan Wesley Gripp, born June 6, 1985, in Olney, Richland County, Illinois. Bryan graduated from Homestead High School in 2004. The children of Marvin and Benita Steyer are: Jennifer Ann Marie Steyer and Benjamin Ray Steyer. The family are members of St. Elizabeth Ann Seton Church. Their home is located in Aboite Township, Allen County, Indiana.

Submitted by Marvin and Benita Steyer

HAROLD STITH & HANA LEE BRYANT-STITH

"There's no shame in working with your hands, but it is important to acquire a trade that you can depend on to make a living," said Harold Stith, founder and owner of Stith Plumbing & Heating Company, Inc.

Stith knows about hard work and low pay, but the sacrifices are worth it when the goal is to attain a position of master of one's craft.

In 1965, Stith founded his business after having worked as a plumber for white firms as far back as the 1950s. He worked his way up through the ranks as apprentice, journeyman and master plumber before becoming owner of his own business that served a 99% white clientele. He plumbed many of Fort Wayne's well-known buildings.

Born in Virginia, he was raised in Englewood, New Jersey, and, while in his teens, his family moved to New York City. Shortly after the family moved to the city, Stith joined the U.S. Army. He served in the army from 1942 until 1946, in the Pacific Theater of War.

While in the service he met a gentleman who had worked with Joe Louis, the famous African-American Boxer. Through his contact with Mr. Merritt, he became interested in prize fighting and began training. When time and circumstances permitted, he began doing exhibition fights, to entertain the service men, on land, on sea and from island to island. Immediately he established himself as a promising fighter, as he defeated challenger after challenger.

After he was discharged from the army, Stith went into professional boxing and fought out of Newark, New Jersey, for three years. He had a colorful and promising fighting career, having had 119 professional fights, winning 103, and 70 of these by knockout. At one time he was a challenger for the Light-weight Division. In 1950, Stith had an unfortunate accident, an artery muscle was cut through at the base of his right thumb and he lost the complete use of his thumb. In almost a twinkle of the eye, his boxing career was ended.

In the meantime, he had met and married Hana Stith and he enrolled in the New York School of Industrial Technology to study Electrical Engineering. In August of 1950, the Stith's came to Fort Wayne on a short vacation. However, Harold looked around and saw the grass was greener in Indiana than in New York and decided to stay. Within three weeks he had found a job at General Electric, where he worked for seven years. But in the meantime he worked at odd jobs; plumbing was the kind of work that he really liked to do and came to him easily.

In 1957, Stith was laid off from General Electric and decided to seek work in the field of plumbing. He walked the town over, putting in application after application for plumbing work, only to be turned down again and again. Finally, after being rejected by major concerns in Fort Wayne, he was hired by H.B. Shank and Sons.

Grateful for the job, he accepted the most difficult and dirtiest jobs in the field. He was hired to do the rough-ins, which consisted of the digging and underground work. He worked in the most adverse conditions in all kinds of weather. He knew that if he was to become a master plumber he had to serve four years as an apprentice and three years as a Journeyman.

During his nine year tenure at Shank's, Stith learned about the heating and plumbing business. When he left Shank, he joined the Plumbers & Steamfitters Union Local #166, as the first black member of the union.

Harold went to work for Schwegman Whittee, where he began working on commercial and industrial jobs. He later transferred to W.P. McDonald, where he worked on large commercial jobs. He helped to plumb Parkview Memorial Hospital, Memorial Park Middle School, the Fort Wayne State Development Center and the Allen County Public Library. Working for McDonald provided him with a wealth of experience. It was while working for McDonald, that Stith finally received his Master's License. When Stith called McDonald to give him a two weeks notice that he was leaving, he was told, "You're fired, you don't quit me."

Stith had taken the test for his license two times and each time he was told that he had failed. Failure meant that he could not take the test again for six months. After he failed the second time, he asked to see his paper. He had difficulty in getting the test, but, when he did, he found that some of the answers checked wrong were not. He hired an attorney and threatened to sue the city. The compromise was that he be allowed to take the test a third time. He did and he passed.

After being licensed, he opened his own business and the jobs rolled in; 99% were from white customers and firms. Those jobs included working with Architectural Builders, doing exclusive houses in Pine Valley, Woodview Manor Apartments, Indiana Construction Company, Portland Indiana Apartments, the Edsall House, the Veterans Hospital, Dawn Doughnuts, Sunoco Gas Stations, McDonald's in Fort Wayne and Lima, Grissom Air Force Base, sewage treatment plants, and others too numerous to name.

Stith never had a business loan; he paid as he grew, buying only what he could pay for. At one time he had four trucks and five full time employees. He hired both black and white plumbers. Some of the leading white plumbers in the city got their start with Stith. There were times when there was no money left for him, but his bills and men were paid on time.

Through his 37 years of business, he gained a reputation of being one of the best and fairest businessmen in the profession. He donated his service to those who could not pay and needed help, especially the elderly. Stith plumbed some of the black churches in Fort Wayne for the cost of materials only, and, at times, he ended up paying for the material. He was generous in sponsoring activities and sports team for youth, buying uniforms and paying for trips. For over 20 years he worked with a local boxing club, training youth and providing financial assistance.

Stith retired in 2003, after reaching his 80th birthday. He is still semi-active in the community; he is a member of the South Side Kiwanis Club, and meets with them weekly. He believes when opportunity knocks, one must answer - life is just what you make it and his life has been good.

HANA LEE BRYANT-STITH

Hana L. Stith is a native of Fort Wayne, Indiana. She attended Justin N. Study, Washington Junior High, and graduated from Central High School. She attended Wilberforce University and graduated from St. Francis College, where she received both her B.S. and Masters Degrees. She continued advanced education at Ball State, Indiana Wesleyan, IPFW and received certification in Guidance and Counseling from Purdue University.

Hana was the first African-American teacher hired at McCulloch School, in 1960, where she taught for 17 years. She was a classroom teacher for 22 years and 14 years as a Title 1 Teacher, sometime servicing three schools. She spent most of her teaching career teaching in inner-city schools, where she felt she was needed most. She retired from FWCS in 1996 after 36 years of service.

Hana has been active in community affairs for many years and served on local commissions and boards for 22 years. She was the first lady to serve on the Redevelopment Commission, where she served for 12 years, under four mayors. She served on the Metropolitan Human Relations Commission for four years and, following that, the Board of Safety for six years. She was a volunteer docent at the Lincoln Museum for three years and has been active in the local NAACP for many years.

She developed an interest and fondness for African American History in 1966 through her teaching at McCulloch School. In 1975, she and another teacher started research on a Black History Project for the city by working with the Allen County Historical Museum, for the country's Bicentennial Celebration. For 25 years she collected and documented information on local history. In 1998 an African American Historical Society was formed, with Stith serving as temporary chairperson. In 1999, she founded a home for the African/African American Historical Society Museum, at 436 East Douglas Avenue. On February 1, 2000, the museum opened. The museum has been well received, supported and attended. It has become one of Fort Wayne's newest and most exciting attractions. Hana serves as the president of the Society, a docent, curator and general manager of the museum.

Hana has received many awards. Among her most cherished are Sagamore of the Wabash, Weisser Park Youth Center Award, the Mugluma International for Africa Inc. Award, Alpha Phi Alpha Fraternity Humanitarian Award, the Elizabeth Dobyness Award and the Concerned Christians Award.

Mrs. Stith is a lifelong member of Turner Chapel African Methodist Episcopal Church, the first African American Church in Fort Wayne. She has served in numerous capacities in her church.

She and Harold have one daughter, Robin Stith, an attorney, and a granddaughter, Hanani.

Submitted by Hana Stith

WILLIAM & ANNA STOHLMANN

William Adolph Stohlmann was born on November 3, 1878, in St. Louis, Missouri, to Leopold Stohlmann, (February 6, 1845-November 17, 1912), and Elizabeth (Boien), (April 18, 1856-March 10, 1898). Leopold and Elizabeth came to America from the Netherlands and were married in New Hanover, Monroe County, St. Louis, Missouri, on November 10, 1878. They later moved to North Dakota. They had eight children:

Louisa C., born August 16, 1874, died October 4, 1935. Henry, born May 27, 1877, died June 11, 1877. William A., born November 3, 1878, died January 18, 1957. Louis F., born March 6, 1882, died March 14, 1958. Katy, born April 17, 1890, died July 20, 1935. Charles, born March 10, 1893, died June 13, 1966. Emma, born May 31, 1895. Maggie, born August 11, 1897, died July 21, 1898.

William moved to St. Louis, Missouri, with brothers and sisters after their mother died of blood poisoning in North Dakota. His father, Leopold, took his team of horses to help build the Canadian railroad. He died from an accident building the railroad, and is buried in Weymuth, Canada, Saskatchewan Province.

Anna Hattie Hildebrandt's parents lived in St. Louis. Anna was born on January 20, 1886, in Hamburg, Germany. Her father came to America in 1891, and her mother arrived with the children in 1893 from Hamburg. Anna's father, William Fredrick Hildebrandt, was a cabinet maker in St. Louis. Her mother, Bertha Charlotte (Lietz) Hildebrandt, was born in 1856, and died in 1934. They are buried in Lake Village, Indiana. Their children were Charles, Anna Hattie, Frank, Hulda, and William. The children were all born in Germany.

William and Anna Stohlmann

William Adolph Stohlmann was Anna's ice delivery man. Anna and William fell in love and were married in St. Louis on July 11, 1905. They later moved with their first three children to Lake Village, Indiana, to work on Governor McCray's cattle farm. Three other children were born there. They then moved to Fort Wayne, Indiana, near Lafayette Township, and farmed. In later years they moved to Huntertown, Indiana, on the Anson Dunten farm, and then the Elbridge Tucker farm on Gump Road, east of Route 27. They later moved to the New Haven and Leo area on Route 37. Their farm became the addition of Maplewood Downs. On this farm they would bring their cattle across Highway 37 and up a lane to the barn. It was a long and muddy trip during the winter and spring months. Anna died October 11, 1947, on this farm, at 62 years old, and is buried along with William at Prairie Grove Cemetery, Waynedale, Indiana. William died on January 18, 1957.

The children of Anna and William are:

1. Walter Louis, who was born on April 12, 1906, in St. Louis, Missouri. He died on June 12, 1932 in the Lutheran Hospital from cancer, and is buried in Prairie Grove Cemetery, Waynedale, Indiana.

2. Alice Catherine was born on May 20, 1907, in St. Louis, Missouri. She died on June 26, 1960, in Orlando, Florida. She married Paul Altman from Huntington, Indiana. Their children were Barbara Altman, August 15, 1931, to November 6, 1977, and Neil Robert October 20, 1933, born in Allen County, Fort Wayne, Indiana. Upon Alice's death in Orlando, Paul remarried Gladys (last name unknown), and is buried in Orlando, Florida.

3. Helen Adeline was born on October 22, 1910, in St. Louis, Missouri. She died July 13, 1991, and is buried in Cedar Chapel Cemetery,

Garrett, Indiana. She married Taft Heffelfinger November 23, 1932, in Huntertown, Indiana. Their children are Richard Lionel, February 14, 1934, and Shirley Ann, March 9, 1935. Taft died on June 13, 1985, and is buried in Cedar Chapel Cemetery with Helen.

4. Edward August was born on December 28, 1916 in Lake Village, Indiana. He married Vonita Schultz, and their children are Connie Lucille, March 14, 1938-March 6, 2005; Caroline Marcile, August 3, 1941, Duane Alan, March 5, 1949, and Joyce Elaine, June 20, 1956. Ed died on April 21, 1982. Ed and Vonita are buried in Albion, Indiana.

5. Norma Loretta was born on February 13, 1918 in Lake Village, Indiana. She died on March 26, 1982, and is buried in Dearborn, Michigan. Her son by her first marriage to Patrick Wood is Patrick David, born July 20, 1955. Her second marriage was to Frank Rauchman of Dearborn, Michigan. No children were born of this marriage.

6. William L. was born on March 6, 1920, in Lake Village, Indiana. He died on October 11, 1977, in Fort Wayne, Indiana. He married Jocile Davison on April 19, 1947. Jocile was born on June 28, 1918, in Markle, Indiana. They had two children, Cheryl Ann August 21, 1950, and William L. June 12, 1955. William is buried in Markle, Indiana. William worked for the League for the Blind in Fort Wayne.

7. Bernice Clarice was born March 25, 1922, in Morocca, Indiana. She married George Myron in Fort Wayne, Indiana, and had two children, JoAnn, March 21, 1944, and Floyd Scott, July 23, 1956, in Dayton, Ohio. George died in Dayton, Ohio. He was an engineer at Wright Patterson Air Force Base.

8. Robert James was born on August 6, 1924, in Zanesville, Indiana. He died on July 8, 1973 in Bowman-Gray Hospital, Winston-Salem, North Carolina, of cancer. He is buried in Mooresville, North Carolina. He worked overseas for 13 years in Africa. He also worked on the Trans-Am Highway in Bolivia. He was sent to Vietnam and was in charge of all supplies brought into Vietnam during the war. He became a supervisor of building bridges for the American government in Tanzania. He was on his way back from a vacation in Fiji when he became ill on the ship. He had four children by his first marriage to Jean Miller of Leo, Indiana. They are Michael Robert, July 3, 1947, Richard Gene, March 30, 1951, Donna Marie, September 6, 1953, and James Eugene, September 19, 1957. The children were born in Apopka, Florida. He married his second wife, Lynda, in Vietnam. She was a nurse in the battlefields.

Submitted by Shirley Underwood

ADOLPH STOLTE FAMILY

Our German ancestor, Adolph Stolte, was born in 1832 on the Kötter farm in Wester Township, near the village of Ladbergen, in the state of North Rhine-Westphalia, Germany. Adolph's parents, Herman Heinrich Stolte, born 1795, and Anna Christina Elizabeth Hemmer, born 1797, were married in the Protestant Church in Ladbergen in 1825. Anna was the daughter of Anna Christina Elizabeth Kötter and Heinrich Wilhelm Hemmer of the nearby Hemmer farm. German 19th century farms included tenant farm families who were usually related to the landowners.

A story told from ancient times is that on the Hemmer farm there was once a holy place of the Germanic God Thor. The name Hemmer arose from the connection with the hammer of this god. The name Kötter means a farmer who takes care of livestock. "Stolte" is a derivation from the Danish world "stolt", which means "proud" in English. "Stolte" then means "the proud". This is a very old tradition in Scandinavian languages to make names out of descriptive adjectives.

During Adolph's life, much of the area was still covered with heath land and wilderness. The land formed from the retreating glacier is similar to the land around Fort Wayne.

Adolph Stolte

Adolph and his family worked the poor, sandy soil. They grew rye, barley and buckwheat; raised livestock; tended beehives; gathered wild food in the common land; raised flax and wove fine linen; harvested bark for tannic acid; dug peat for fuel while wearing wooden shoes.

In 1842, common lands were divided up and assigned to landowners. The cottage industry of linen weaving brought in less and less money. In June of 1844, a hailstorm destroyed all of their crops, leaving only potatoes.

Travel agents from Bremen came to Ladbergen. In 1844, 104 people immigrated. Adolph, his brothers, Heinrich and William, and his sisters, Sophie and Elizabeth, took a Weser River boat to Bremen, where they boarded a steamship for America. They then came to Indianapolis, Indiana.

Adolph's mother, Anna Christina, immigrated to Indianapolis four years after her husband Herman Heinrich Stolte's death in 1850. Herman, who served in the Prussian Army for seven years, had been taken prisoner for about six months during the Franco-Prussian war.

Adolph's younger cousin, Fritz Kötter, immigrated to the United States in 1864 to avoid being drafted into the army. He settled on a farm near New Knoxville, Ohio. Fritz Kötter's great-grandson is Astronaut Neil Armstrong, the first man to walk on the moon. Coincidently, the Müenster-Osnabrück International Airport is located on the site of the Kötter farm in Wester Township.

Adolph's sister, Elizabeth, married H. Kruse in Indianapolis. His sister, Sophia, married Richard Brocking. His sister, Christina, married Rudolph Rögge and stayed in Westphalia. His younger brother, Heinrich (Henry), clerked in Indianapolis and saved money to travel to Colorado and Montana; then returned to Indianapolis and opened a grocery store. His brother, William, married and also opened a grocery in Indianapolis.

In 1857, Adolph married Elizabeth Peters, who was born in 1834 in Minden, Germany. They came to Fort Wayne and homesteaded the farm in Williams Township on the southeast corner of Hillegas and Goshen Road in the 1860s. Their six children are Fred W., Leonard, Charles, Frank, George and Elizabeth.

Two sisters, Margaret and Betty Oehler, from Maples, Indiana, married brothers Fred W. and Charles. Charles, a coachman and boilermaker at Bass Foundry, rode a bicycle to work every day of his working life. Fred W. and Margaret opened a grocery store on West Main Street where O'Sullivan's Italian Pub is today. They lived upstairs above the store with their three children, Matilda, Suzanne and Fred L. During "The Flood of 1913," Fred W. descended the stairway and was surprised! He walked into the floodwater that filled his store.

Fred W. built the home at 924 Columbia Avenue, where he occasionally played the fiddle at family gatherings. He was a deputy sheriff of Allen County and an automobile salesman at the Schiefer Auto Company on the corner of Washington and Clay Streets. A story he loved to tell was of the time he and his friend was driving his new Model-A Ford from Waterloo to Auburn. They came up over a hill and hit a cow. The toolbox flew up, stuck to the ceiling, the lid fell open, and it was raining monkey wrenches!

Leonard Stolte, "The Colonel", a successful farmer, married Gertrude Ludnick and had eight children: Albert, Herbert, John, Donald, Eugene, Marie, Elisabeth and Ruth. Leonard attended Indiana Business College, opened a school supply store and organized a WPA road construction program. He became a township trustee, a school superintendent and a member of St. John's Reformed Church. Why was he called "The Colonel"? Because he called everyone else "Colonel."

Frank moved to Lansing, Michigan, and went into the automobile business. The youngest sibling, Elizabeth, never married and stayed on the homestead with her parents.

The family attended St. John's Evangelical United Church of Christ at Washington and Webster Street It was jokingly said that the reason why Uncle George carried his rifle to church was "he wanted make sure he was gonna get what he was praying for." George had a farm on the California Road and was elected to the state legislature.

Fred W. Stolte's daughter, Suzanne, taught at Rudisill School, then went on to teach at Columbia University in New York. She married Dr. Richard Linton, a bacteriologist from Harvard. The couple lived in India, where Dr. Linton conducted research for a cure of malaria. Their daughter, Jennifer, tells vivid stories about her childhood in India. She loved to ride her pony, "Hagi" over the Himalayan foothills of Kashmir.

Dr. Jennifer Linton remembers Aunt Matilda Philley, "A truly gracious and loving human being and a lovely looking woman. After her husband,

Ross, died in his early forties, she was invited to come to India with my parents and me. She accepted, and, after a year, she and I returned to the U.S. (Nyack, New York), where I could resume my schooling. She remained with us throughout my high school years, as my mother had become ill."

"Matilda enjoyed singing and music and she taught me to dance. She was a second mother to me: sharing her joy of living with everyone who had the blessing of knowing her."

Fred W.'s son, Fred Leonard Stolte, returned from service in the Army in WWI, attended Tri-State University in Angola and worked at Auburn Cord. In 1920 he married Dorothy Osborn, who taught at a one-room school near Montpelier, Ohio. Dorothy was the daughter of Euretta Preston and Morrison Osborn, who came down the Erie Canal from New England and settled in Williams County, Ohio. Dorothy and Fred had two sons: Fred Osborn born in 1921 and David K. born in 1923.

Fred and Dorothy moved to Fort Wayne. Fred was employed at the National Mill and Supply Company. Dorothy worked in the hosiery department at Wolf & Dessauer. Dorothy's flair for fashion design led to a career as a stylist for the Wayne Knitting Mills.

While traveling for Wayne Knitting, Dorothy obtained recipes from hotel chefs. After they retired, she enjoyed cooking family dinners at their wooded property in Hillsdale County, Michigan. Dorothy loved to watch the sunset make a candlelight effect, flickering through the darkening woods.

Fred grew a garden and preserved the wildlife on the property. In the early spring he tapped the sugar maples to make syrup with the help of his sons, Fred and David.

Fred Osborn Stolte married (Beulah) Ann Brooks in 1947. Fred O.'s father, who worked at the United State Post Office, introduced them when Ann was employed in an office at the Federal Building on Harrison Street when the main USPS was still there. Ann came from Ohio and attended Indiana Business College. She was born in 1925 in Porter County, New York, on a farm near Lake Ontario. Orphaned at age four, then adopted by the Brooks family near Payne, Ohio, Ann was happily reunited with her sisters in the early 1970s. Her families are the Farrell's and Gordon's of Paulding, Ohio.

Fred O. served in the Marine Corp in WWII, fought in the Battle of Midway in the Pacific, and remained close to his Marine buddies throughout his life. After studying engineering at Indiana Tech, he drafted plans for Eckrich and Magnavox. As a consultant engineer, he developed an IBM typewriter ("the battleship of typewriters"), a Xerox copier, a radio worn on the inside of a helmet, heating and cooling systems, and a Whirlpool refrigerator with the water dispenser on the door.

Fred and Ann raised their three children: Fred Brooks, Carol Sue and Thomas D. in Lake Township, Allen County, Indiana. The house on O'Day Road overlooks a restored wetland.

Sources:

Ladbergen, Friedrich Saatkamp, 1985, available from the New Knoxville, OH Historical Society, New Knoxville, OH 45871.

Commemorative Biographical Record of Prominent Men of Indianapolis, J.H. Beers & Co, 1908.

Pictorial History of Fort Wayne Indiana, B.J. Griswold, 1917.

A videotape of Fred O. Stolte and Jennifer Linton looking at family photographs, 1996.

The German Space Society, Muenster, Germany, provided information about Neil Armstrong and the Kötter farm.

*The inspiration for this writing came from a 2004 trip to Ladbergen, by Jennifer Linton and Carol Stolte Spallone.

Submitted by Carol Stolte Spallone

CHARLES LEWIS & PRISCILLA FRIEBURGER STRACK FAMILY

Charles L. Strack was born "Carl" Strack to Charles R. Strack and Maude Amon, April 27, 1897. His great-grand mother was the daughter of Maria Theresa "LaBlonde" Richardville. Charles, a Miami Indian, was born on the Richardville Reserve in the house still standing at Bluffton and Winchester Road in Fort Wayne, Indiana. His mother died when Charles was nine years old, and he was sent to St. Joseph's Catholic orphanage in Lafayette, Indiana.

Priscilla Leota Frieburger was born in Yoder, Indiana on May 13, 1900, to John Freiburger and Mary Miner. She was the youngest of 13 children. Priscilla was schooled at St. Catherine's Academy in Fort Wayne, Indiana. Priscilla's elder brother, Rev. Edward Frieburger, was the orphanage director where Charles lived. Priscilla and Charles became adolescent friends and developed a deep regard for each other.

Charles entered the United States Navy in July 26, 1918, and served his country as a Native American during WW I. He served his country, even though Native American people did not have status as American citizens. It was not until 1924 that Native People were granted American citizenship by an act of Congress.

Charles and Priscilla married in November of 1920 at St. Patrick Catholic Church, Fort Wayne. They lived on a farm near Arcola, Indiana and raised eight children. All of their children, James, Robert, Mary, Godfroy (Cap), Catherine, Charles (Tony), Edward, and Priscilla graduated from Central Catholic High School in Fort Wayne. Charles and Priscilla Strack celebrated their 50th wedding anniversary in 1970. Their legacy includes 43 grandchildren and 85 great-grandchildren.

Submitted by Laura Nagy

STRACK/SWENDA

The Miami people believe that they were created in Indiana – that is the story of the origin of "the people" in Indiana and what follows is a continuation of that story.

Ackenaqua is the father of several children, including Chief Little Turtle and Tacumwah. Tacumwah was in charge of the only portage that linked an all water route from the St. Lawrence Seaway to the Gulf of Mexico and was located in the Fort Wayne area. Tacumwah married Antoine Joseph Drouet deRichardville. Their children included Jean Baptiste Richardville. He was educated in both the Miami and European cultures. He spoke Miami, French and English. He fought in several battles under the leadership of his uncle, Little Turtle. He was chief of the Miami and negotiated with the United States until his death in 1841. Indiana's "ethnic cleansing", or Miami Indian Removal, took place in 1846, but many Richardville relatives were allowed to stay in Indiana.

Richardville's children included Lablonde Tahkonzahqua Richardville (1792-1854). Her children included Mongosequah, aka Archangel (1826-1885), who married James R. Godfroy, aka Sahcoquah (1820-1894). They had Mary Godfroy, aka Sahcochequah (1840-1883). Mary Godfroy married Charles F. Strack (1832-). They were the parents of Charles R. Strack, aka Kikongdagah (1871-1920). He married Maude Amann (1872-1908) and they had Charles Lewis (1897-1973), Eva (1899-1923), John (1899-1955), Violet (1903-1940), and George (1905-). Charles Lewis (aka Carl) Strack married Priscilla Leota Freiburger (1900-1993). They were the parents of James Lyle (born 1922), Robert Eugene (1923-1997), Godfrey Francis (born 1924), Mary Maude (born 1926), Catherine Mae (born 1928), Charles Richard (born 1931), Edward Joseph (born 1935), and Priscilla Anne (born 1940).

Robert Tippmann, Jr., and his wife, Dani; Robert III and his wife Katrina, Robert IV, Aden, Joseph and his wife Heather, Blake, Ingrid, Michael, David, Brittney Schoenle, Mary, Gloria and Gabriel Tippmann

Mary Maude Strack married Joseph J. Swenda (1927- 1992) on October 22, 1949 in St. Patrick's Catholic Church in Arcola, Indiana. They had Patricia Rosemary (born 1953), Dani Michelle (born 1959) and Kristina Melody (born 1961). Dani Michelle married Robert Thomas Tippmann, Jr. (born 1959) on September 22, 1979 in St. Patrick's Catholic Church, Arcola, Indiana. They currently live in Columbia City, Indiana and are the parents of Robert Thomas, III (born 1980), Joseph Daniel (born 1981), Blake Adam (born 1981), Ingrid Ann (born 1983), Michael Xavier (born 1981), David Anthony (born 1985), Mary Regina (born 1987), Gregory James (born 1989), Gloria Archangel Alaankahanihsaata (born 1996) and Gabriel Christopher (born 2000).

Robert Tippmann, Jr. is president of Tippmann Heating and Air Conditioning, LLC, serving northern Indiana.

Robert Thomas Tippmann III married Katrina M. VanSumeran on January 18, 2003, at St. Therese's Catholic Church, Waynedale, Indiana. They had Robert Thomas IV (born 2002) and Aden Nathaniel (born 2004).

Joseph Daniel married Heather Michelle Nancarrow on September 4, 2004, at Our Lady of Good Hope, Fort Wayne, Indiana.

Joseph Daniel Tippmann, Blake Adam Tippmann and Michael Xavier Tippmann served in the U.S. Marines.

Submitted by Dani Tippmann

LUTHER GEORGE & ARLENE ANN (LYTAL) STRASEN FAMILY

Luther George Strasen was born on September 22, 1933, in Nagercoil, Tamil Nadu, fifteen miles from the southern tip of India, the son of missionary parents who went to India in 1921. He is a fourth generation pastor in the Lutheran Church-Missouri Synod. His great-grandfather, Karl Johann (John) Strasen, born in Buetzow, Mecklenburg-Schwerin, Germany, on May 30, 1827, came to America in 1846 and was one of the first six graduates of Concordia Theological Seminary that had started in Fort Wayne, Indiana. In 1849, Karl John married Rosine Auguste Mueller, who was born April 10,1831, in Planena bei Halle in Prussia. As a teen-ager, she had come to St. Louis with her parents, who, because of religious oppression, left Germany in what is known in The Lutheran Church-Missouri Synod as the "Saxon Immigration."

Luther's grandfather, Henry Strasen was born on February 7, 1869, in Watertown, Wisconsin, where his father was serving a parish. In 1892, he married Martha Wichmann, who was born on November 14, 1871, in Farmers Retreat, Indiana, where her father was a pastor. Luther's father, Bernhard Theodore Strasen, was born November 3, 1898, in Janesville, Minnesota, the town of his father's first parish.

Luther's mother, Henriette Ida Julia (Ziegfeld) Strasen, was born on January 11, 1894, in German Village, the old section of Columbus, Ohio. Her grandfather, Carl Ziegfeld, was born in Jemgung, Grand Duchy of Oldenburg, Germany, on April 16, 1822. One of his brothers, Florenz, was the grandfather of the American showman Florenz Ziegfeld. Carl Ziegfeld moved to Holland and there, in 1849, married Elizabeth Vrind, who was born February 8, 1827. Henriette's father, Frederick Ziegfeld, was born on June 19, 1860, and traveled from Holland to Columbus, Ohio, with his family in 1868. In 1884, Frederick married Pauline Horst, who was born on April 29, 1859 in Peru, Indiana.

Henriette Ziegfeld met Bernhard Strasen just before they boarded the ship which took them to India, where she would be an educational worker and he a missionary for The Lutheran Church-Missouri Synod. They were married on June 27, 1923, and had six children while in India; three daughters, Pauline, Ruth, and Elizabeth, and then three sons, Theodore, David, and Luther.

In India, Luther attended a school for missionary children and came to the United States with his parents in 1945. He was in the eighth grade at St. John's Lutheran School, Elgin, Illinois, and then enrolled at Concordia High School and Junior College, Fort Wayne, Indiana. While in high school he met Arlene Ann Lytal, who was born in Fort Wayne on November 22, 1934.

Arlene's father, Dale Lytal, was born on September 27, 1907, at Burr Oak, Indiana. Dale's grandfather, Benjamin Lytal, was born in 1822 in Canton, Ohio. He married Susannah Shively, who was born on May 20, 1826. Their son, Isaac, was born in Canton, Ohio, on February 27, 1861. The family moved to Kosciusko County, Indiana, and Isaac Lytal married Elnora Ritchhart, who was born on December 25, 1872, in Pierceton, Indiana. Isaac's family, including Dale Lytal, finally settled in Fort Wayne.

Arlene's mother, Hilda (Eisberg) Lytal, was born on October 15, 1910, in a home near Bass Street on the west side of Fort Wayne. Hilda's grandparents were Ferdinand and Carolyn (Bodeker) Eisberg, both born in Germany. Hilda's father, William Eisberg, was born in Hanover, Germany, on October 1, 1875 and, after coming to Fort Wayne, was the coachman for John Bass, who owned Bass Foundry. At the Bass mansion, now on the University of St. Francis campus, he met Josephine Vine, the cook, who was born in Bellevue, Ohio, on December 28, 1884, and they were married in 1904. Hilda recounted how she and the Bass children "ice skated" on the ballroom floor by strapping large tablespoons to their shoes. Members of both the Lytal and Eisberg families worked at General Electric and Dale Lytal and Hilda Eisberg met there. They were married on May 4, 1929, at Suburban Bethlehem Lutheran Church, five miles northeast of Fort Wayne, and had two children, Arlene and James.

Luther and Arlene Strasen Family at Michael and Michele Strasen wedding, May 21, 1994. (l-r) Catherine and Michael Gastineau, Treva and Timothy Strasen, Michele and Michael Strasen, Arlene and Luther Strasen, Sarah and Robert Jacobs, Laura and Craig Stephens.

Luther graduated from Concordia Junior College in 1953 and proceeded to Concordia Seminary in St. Louis, Missouri, where he finished his college and seminary years in 1958. Arlene attended Emmaus Lutheran School and graduated from Concordia High School in 1953. She enrolled in the Lutheran Hospital School of Nursing, Fort Wayne, graduated in 1956, and worked one year for Dr. Francis Land. Luther and Arlene were married on June 29, 1957, at Emmaus Lutheran Church, Fort Wayne, and lived in St. Louis during Luther's final seminary year. His first parish, where he was ordained as a pastor in the Lutheran Church-Missouri Synod, was at St. Martin Lutheran Church, Clintonville, Wisconsin, from 1958-1962. From 1962-1968 he was the pastor of Concordia Lutheran Church, Greenwood, Indiana. In 1968, the family moved to Fort Wayne, where Luther served Peace Lutheran Church for 28 years. Arlene began employment at Lutheran Hospital in 1969 and they both retired in 1996.

They have five children: Timothy, born August 16, 1958, and married to Treva Yeager (children:Wyatt and Kyle); Sarah (March 14, 1960), married to Robert Jacobs (Andrea, Jonathan, Catherine); Catherine (December 1, 1961), married to Michael Gastineau (Mitchell, Claire, Philip, Connor); Laura (July 2, 1964), married to Craig Stephens (August, Jared); and Michael (July 18, 1966), married to Michele Maddox (Benjamin, Spencer, Madelyn).

Submitted by Luther Strasen

ELAINE TATE TRUCKENBROD (MRS. IVAN D. STRONG)

Elaine, the third daughter of Edmund and Neva Jay Truckenbrod (Tate) was born May 11, 1928, in Mendota Illinois. Her father was a jeweler and watch maker in the family store. After the stock market crash of 1929, he moved his young family to Chicago in late 1931, where he was allowed to set up a small table in a barber shop to repair watches and jewelry. In October 1941, he borrowed $500 from an uncle and opened his jewelry store on Chicago's south side.

Elaine and Ivan Strong

Living in that area, Elaine graduated from South Shore High School in 1945. That fall she enrolled in the Chicago Academy of Fine Arts, which offered a one-time opportunity to complete four years of art courses in an accelerated two year program. Upon completion and graduation, Elaine accepted a position in the art department of Messengers Corporation in Chicago, which had its headquarters in Auburn, Indiana. Later that year, the company moved its art department back to Auburn and Elaine made the move also.

While living in Auburn, she was introduced to a young man, who had an eight year old daughter from a previous marriage. Ivan was the first son of Willard and Irene Strong of rural Dekalb County. Ivan, his brother, and two sisters all attended Leo High School, where he graduated in 1935. Shortly after graduation, Ivan went to work for the B & O Railroad. On January 1, 1949, Ivan and

Elaine were married in Chicago and then lived in Auburn for a short time. In November of 1954, they purchased a small home in Apple Acres, one of the first subdivisions to Leo, Indiana. Their three younger children grew up there and graduated from Leo High School. Paul, born in April 1950, now resides in Weatherford, Texas with his wife Sally. He has a grown son living in San Jose, California. Dail, born in January 1952, lives with her husband, Robert, and teenage daughter in Leo. She has a grown daughter who lives with her husband and two young children in Fort Wayne. Lara Lee, born in July 1953, now lives with her mother and is her full-time care giver.

In 1968, Elaine joined TOPS (Take Off Pounds Sensibly) and in 1969 was appointed to be a supervisor over several chapters overseas. Three years later she was promoted to Regional Director. Upon her retirement in 1989, Elaine had directed chapters in thirteen states, as well as chapters in over thirty countries around the globe.

After Ivan passed away in January of 1995, Elaine had a small home, that she designed, built in Apple Acres, across the street from their first home in Leo.

Historical note: When visiting her Aunt Mary in Virginia, Elaine noticed a small table among other beautiful antiques, some over 150 years old. She noticed that it looked like unfinished oak wood and asked her aunt if there was a story concerning the table. Her aunt told her that about nine generations ago, her Uncle John Tate served as a courier for General Washington during the War of Independence. Late in the war, John was killed by the enemy while on one of his courier runs. When the war was over, General Washington visited John's widow near the family farm in Moccasin Valley where John Tate was buried. The general expressed to her his appreciation for John's services. Washington presented her with his campaign table. The table was folded and had legs bundled in such a way so it could be carried on horseback. That same table has remained in the Tate family ever since.

Submitted by Elaine Strong

STUART FAMILY

FROM ARKANSAS TO INDIANA

Samuel and Gladys Stuart migrated to Indiana from the Little Rock-Fulton, Arkansas, area during World War I. When Samuel Stuart tried to re-register for the draft, he was told, "We don't need you people!" Not long afterwards he was hired by Joslyn Steel Mill, (later to become Slater Steel). He worked there until hired by the Fort Wayne Police Department (FWPD) in 1926. In the early years he could not arrest any white people; he had to call the station and request a white officer. Art Williams was the first black policeman, Oliver Lee was the second and Samuel Stuart was the third. No more blacks were hired until after World War II. One early mayor was quite an alcoholic, and it was our father's job to take him home. Promotion in the FWPD was strictly political. Dad retired after 41 years of service.

Growing up in Fort Wayne was difficult in the 30s and 40s and 50s if you were black. There was always racial hostility present, some blatant, some subtle. Blacks were expected to "stay in their place." Whites wouldn't sit next to a black person on the bus or streetcar. If there was an empty seat next to a white person, they would move towards the aisle in an attempt to discourage you from sitting next to them. Most restaurants would not serve you; all of the movie theaters made blacks sit in the balcony. Only one of the two public swimming pools allowed blacks, and then only on a segregated basis. The roller skating rinks were segregated. Blacks could only skate on certain days. Many white physicians and dentists would not treat you. The YMCA was segregated. Police frequently harassed blacks and whites, particularly when they were of opposite sexes. I personally witnessed Judge W.O. Hughes and Judge Shannon castigate blacks and whites in courts about "race mixing" and "staying in their place." Even the school system practiced their own brand of discrimination.

My sister Eloise returned to Fort Wayne after graduating from Hampton Institute with a degree in education in 1941. The Superintendent, Merle J. Abbot, refused to talk to her about employment. His secretary delivered his message, "We don't hire colored people." If black and white students were too friendly at high school functions, especially dancing together, they were summoned to the principal's office and read the "riot act." Upon entering high school, black students were routinely enrolled in general studies, home economics or shop courses (manual training or vocational ed). My parents, both of them, had to come to high school and demand that my brother, Samuel Stuart Jr., be allowed to enroll in college prep studies. He became the first black valedictorian in 1941. I had to do the same thing in 1945 when I wanted to change to college prep classes. The guidance counselor told me "you're not going to college!"

The hospitals were segregated. Patient rooms were segregated when I returned to Fort Wayne after college, dental school and the military. There was still a fair amount of blatant racial hostility present throughout Fort Wayne. Lindenwood Cemetery had a separate section for African-Americans. The manager said to me, "You people would feel more comfortable being buried together." Subtle, but clear, patterns of prejudice were obvious in housing, employment and public accommodations. Many times I heard "Oh, excuse me I didn't see you." "Were you next?" "I'm sorry but that house was just sold" etc., etc. Even the Fort Wayne Urban League, which was partially funded by United Way, was coaxed to "go slow" by the white power structure. "Paternalistic Segregation" I called it.

In 1963 I went to Lakeside Golf Course to play golf and was told by the manager that in order to play golf I had to submit an application and I would be notified when it had been approved by the board. In those days blacks and whites worked in teams to prove that discrimination existed.

My teammate, who was white, appeared shortly and was given immediate access to the golf course. I hired an attorney, Larry Burke, to sue the golf course. My attorney found that a law against this kind of segregation had been on the books since 1933. The Lakeside Golf Course was fined $300.00; as a result of this lawsuit other public golf courses in Fort Wayne were integrated.

I recall many experiences of segregation in my lifetime, far too numerous to record here. It seems my entire life has been made up of one incident of discrimination after another. The struggle continues. Discrimination/Racism has evolved to a state of near invisibility, but it is not dead.

Written by Dr. Bernard K. Stuart, and submitted, after his death, by his sister, Catherine Wilhelmenia Hayden

JACOB AUGUSTUS STUART

(1831 -1909)

Born in Perry County, Ohio, on May 7, 1831, Jacob Augustus Stuart was the son of William and Mary Groves Stuart. There were seven other children in the family: Sara (Mrs. Levi Small), James, Samuel, Jane (Mrs. Jacob Groves), Mary Ann (Mrs. Perry Dawley), Thomas, and William, who remained in their home county while Jacob moved on to Indiana ,where he married Asenath Kinsey in DeKalb County October 12, 1867.

When Asenath died, leaving Jacob with two small children, Thomas Wilbur and Edward Lincoln, he took the children back to Hocking County to live with his sister-in-law while the Stuart brothers served in the Civil War in Company D, 17th Ohio Volunteer Infantry.

When the war ended, Jacob and his two sons moved to Aboite Center Road, Allen County, Indiana, where he met and married Minerva Jeffries, daughter of Robert and Nancy Stott Jeffries on March 11, 1866. From this marriage were four children, Carrie (Mrs. Charles Decker), Mary (Mrs. Jule Jeanmougin), Ferguson and Jesse. Jacob died April 8, 1915 in Fort Wayne and is buried in Lindenwood Cemetery with his wife, Minerva, who died November 22, 1908. According to her obituary, Minerva was a great gardener and known for her beautiful flowers on Liberty Mills Road.

Four Generations of Stuart: Thomas Wilbur, Jacob Augustus, Lawrence, Thomas William

Thomas Wilbur, the oldest son of Jacob, was born January 11, 1859, and married Christina Swinehart November 27, 1884.They had three children: Ethel May, who died young., Lawrence Earl, and Daisie Arvilla (Mrs. Edgar Johnson).

Lawrence Stuart was born June 15, 1887, in Sherman County, Kansas, while his parents tried homesteading in the west. He later married on June 28, 1913, to Bessie Marie Wood. Their son,Thomas William, was born August 8, 1914. He is seen in the four generation photo. Their other children were Kenneth Earl and Richard Lawrence. Lawrence Stuart was killed in a pedestrian accident in Kendallville on August 27, 1966.

Submited by Jean Decker Allread

PHILIP GENE & DORCAS ELISE (RINGENBERG) STUCKEY FAMILY

Philip Gene Stuckey was born January 1, 1943, in Leo, Indiana, to Dale and Virginia (Stucky) Stuckey. His four siblings are Janice (Stuckey) Roth, Patricia (Stuckey) Gudakunst, Thomas Stuckey and Jon Stuckey. Philip's father, Dale, was born August 5, 1918, the sixth of seven children born to Frank and Mary Stuckey of Leo, Indiana. Dale was a farmer and served in World War II with the U.S. Army. Dale's father, Frank, was the son of Fanny (Schlatter) and Joe Stuckey. Philip's mother, Virginia, was born May 24, 1921, in Fort Wayne, Indiana, to Leo and Ruth (Stauffer) Stucky. Leo was from the Berne, Indiana, area and Ruth was from Bluffton, Ohio. They met when they were both students at Bluffton College. Virginia had one brother, who died as a child.

Phil and Dorcas Stuckey

Dorcas Elise (Ringenberg) Stuckey was born February 23, 1943, in Fort Wayne, Indiana, to Loyal and Rhoda (Roth) Ringenberg. She is the youngest of three children born to Loyal and Rhoda. Her siblings are M. Lenore (Ringenberg) Chernenko and William Carey Ringenberg. Dorcas' father, Loyal, was born February 3, 1904, in Leo, Indiana. He was the sixth of eight children born to Peter and Anna (Gerig) Ringenberg. Loyal was a minister ordained by the Missionary Church, a teacher, a writer and a missionary in Taiwan. Loyal's father, Peter, was brought to America by his father, Peter Ringenberg, from Leissigen, Switzerland, in 1870, after his mother, Susan Gutner Ringenberg, died. Dorcas' mother, Rhoda Roth Ringenberg, was the tenth child born to David and Magdalena (Goldsmith) Roth on November 12, 1903, in Harlan, Indiana. Magdalena's father was the first pastor of the Grabill Missionary Church in 1901, where Phil and Dorcas were married in 1964, and have been longtime members.

Phil and Dorcas both graduated from Leo High School in 1961. Phil received his teacher's degree from Ball State University and taught Industrial Tech for East Allen County Schools for 33 years—three years at New Haven High School and 30 years at his alma mater, Leo High School. Dorcas also attended Ball State University and did secretarial work and worked in food service for 21 years at Leo High School. Their family includes three children: Kim Renee Horn and husband Patrick, Doug Stuckey and wife Regina, and Scott Stuckey and wife Regan. They also have eight grandchildren: Mitchell, Taylor, and Christopher Horn; Isaac and McKennah Stuckey; Caroline and Lea Stuckey; and Jenna (Roschi) Coram. Phil and Dorcas have lived all of their married life in the same home on St. Joe Road near Grabill, Indiana, the location of their church and an area that is rich with their family heritage.

Submitted by Phil and Dorcas Stuckey

JAMES & JEANNE STUMP FAMILY

James Elgain Stump (born on August 28, 1941), son of Clarance Elgain Stump and Rita Mae Sordelet, was raised in Fort Wayne. He was a Senior Leader at Franke Day Camp under founder Dennis Gerloch, who taught him love of the outdoors. In elementary school at St. Peters, he really enjoyed scouting, proud that he was elected by his peers to Order of the Arrow at Camp Big Island, in 1952. He earned money to buy his first typewriter in 1955 by selling doughnuts door to door for Karen's Kitchen. He graduated in 1964 from Indiana University, Bloomington, with a BS in Accounting. Jim became a Certified Public Accountant; he returned to Fort Wayne from Dayton in 1968 and was a Trust Tax Officer for the Lincoln National Bank. He joined his partners in a CPA firm in 1968 and was named one of the "Top 50 CPAs in America" in 1984 by Money Magazine. He retired from BKD, LLP (George S. Olive CPAs) in 2001 and rejoined the trust department of the now Wells Fargo Bank.

Jim's civic activities include participation on boards of local arts organizations, as well as early childhood and special education. He is involved in his Scottish heritage and participates in Clan Mackenzie activities. Jim shares his wife, Jeanne's passion for cats and dogs and loves the mountains, camping, hiking, and reading. Jim loves to learn new things; he is a member of the Quest Club.

Jim and Jeanne Stump, 2004

His children, from his first marriage, are Michael Elgain (1963), married to Robyn Amstutz; David Malvan (1965); and Juliana Mary (1967), married to Alan Bengs. Mike is a roofer for CMS in Fort Wayne. Juli and Alan are parents of Mackenzie Edith (2001) and Dashel Martin (2003). Juli is a student counselor with Indiana Institute of Technology. David is a journeyman tool & die maker at the Stump family business, Quality Tool Company, Inc. His son is Kevin Joseph Stump (1988).

Jim married Jeanne (Laitas) Gaskill on April 21, 1990. Jeanne (born January 8, 1948) to Walter Laitas and Elizabeth Rooker, grew up in Metamora, Illinois. She graduated from Elmhurst College, Elmhurst, Illinois, with a major in elementary education. She later became certified in Early Childhood Education; in 1983, she earned her Masters in Early Childhood/Special Education. She enjoyed teaching special children in local schools until 1999, when her genealogy hobby became a new career. Jeanne earned her certification as a professional genealogist in 2001. She was inducted as a Fellow of the Society of Antiquaries, Scotland, and was asked to be the genealogist for Clan Mackenzie of America. She is on the board of the Allen County Genealogical Society. She specializes in Lithuanian research, (her father's ancestry) and visited family in Lithuania. Jeanne's passions are caring for orphaned kittens, pets, knitting and reading.

Her children, from a previous marriage, are Dawn Elisa (1973) and Keith Michael (1975). Elisa, married to Jason Bennett, graduated from the University of Iowa and Indiana University Law School, Indianapolis. She is an attorney with Hogan, Dirig and Bennett in Fort Wayne. Keith received his BA from Ball State University, and MS from Northern Illinois University. He is a hydro-geochemist with the URS Corporation in Indianapolis, Indiana.

Submitted by Jim Stump

JOHN L. STUMP FAMILY

John Louis Stump was born January 15, 1943, in Fort Wayne, Indiana, to Clarence Elgain Stump, Jr. and Rita Mae Sordelet. Clarence Jr. moved to Allen County, Indiana, in 1925 along with his father, Clarence E. Stump, Sr. and mother, Lou Effie (Taylor) Stump. When International Harvester moved from Akron, Ohio, to Fort Wayne, the Stump family moved from the Akron area with the company.

Isaac W. Taylor, father of Lou Effie Stump, fought for the Union cavalry in the Missouri theatre during the American Civil War. He participated in the battle of Prairie Grove, Arkansas, and mustered out at the war's end with an honorable discharge in 1865. Lou Effie Stump was a pioneer, having moved in a covered wagon with her family to Oklahoma Indian Territory after the Civil War. She grew up with religion and was a member of the Women's Christian Temperance Union (WCTU).

Rita Mae Sordelet and her two sisters, Virginia and Ruth Ann, resided in Allen County from birth. The girls' father, Louis N. Sordelet, joined the navy during World War I, was stationed in France, and was honorable discharged in 1918. He married Henrietta Blake in 1922. Louis was

John and Denise (Rohrs) Stump, 1999

a career General Electric employee, retiring as a general foreman.

Clarence Stump, Jr. was a journeyman tool and die maker and a majority owner of Quality Tool Company, Inc. During World War II, Clarence Elgain Stump, Jr., worked in the war-related defense industry as a tool and die maker with a mandatory government exemption. Married in 1939, six children were born to Clarence E. and Rita M. Stump; James. E., John L., Kenneth J., Donald, E., Mary K. and Andrew G. James graduated with a BS in 1963 from Indiana University and is a CPA working in the banking industry. John graduated with a BSME from Purdue in 1967 and a MSME from Northwestern in 1969 and is a part owner of Quality Tool Company Inc., designers and builders of tooling for the manufacturing industry. Kenneth is a journeyman toolmaker, working at Quality Tool Company, Inc. Donald graduated with a BS from Indiana University in 1975 and is a journeyman toolmaker working at LH Carbide Die Company. Mary is a journeyman toolmaker working at Quality Tool Company, Inc. Andrew is a journeyman toolmaker, having worked at Quality Tool Company, Inc. and Benteler Tool and Die, but is disabled due to an old injury from a motorcycle accident.

John Stump married Nancy J. Baron, August 28, 1965 and their union produced two children, Louis F. Stump and Charles E. Stump. Both Louis and Charles are employed at Quality Tool Company, Inc. Louis and Charles' maternal grandparents are Frank B. Baron and Helen nee Miller. Frank and Helen were born and raised in Fort Wayne Indiana., They were married in 1938.

John Stump married Denise J. Rohrs, August 20, 1993. Denise, the oldest, is followed by Dennis, Colleen, Eric, Bruce, Brian, and Linda, the children of Duane and Gertrude "Trudy" Cook Rohrs, both from the Hicksville, Ohio, area, who married in 1949. Duane retired as a foreman from Dana Corporation in Fort Wayne, and Trudy, as a nurse, from the Fort Wayne State Developmental Center.

The Stump family is proud to be part of the Allen County industrial network. Three generations have worked in the tool and die industry and they look forward to all challenges in the future for the fourth generation.

Submitted by John L. Stump

JOSHUA SUMMERS & ALITHA (JUDD) SUMMERS FAMILY

Joshua Summers was born in Shenandoah County (now Page County), Virginia in the Hawksbill Creek area near Luray ca. 1782, the son of Phillip and Susanna Summers. The spelling of the family name depends on whether you use the English spelling Summers or the German spelling Somers. This family's ancestry is German, but some of Joshua and Alitha's sons used the English spelling and some used the German spelling. Joshua's brothers were: Phillip Jr., John, Joseph, and Michael; his sisters were Barbara Printz, Eve Avery, Elizabeth Shank, Magdalena Horde, Sally Printz, Mrs. Brubaker, and Mrs. Welsh.

Joshua married Alitha Judd, in Shenandoah County, Virginia, on August 8, 1806. She was born in Virginia ca. 1780, daughter of Michael and Mary (Wolfe) Judd. Joshua and Alitha, with some of their younger children, came to Allen County, Indiana, from Virginia in 1840 where they purchased 160 acres of land in Marion Township. Some members of the family had come to Allen County earlier. Joshua Summers was a farmer.

Joshua Summers did not live very long in Allen County; he died on November 11, 1841, and is buried in the old Bethel Cemetery, south of Poe on Winchester Road in Allen County. His wife lived to December 30, 1870, when she joined him in Bethel Cemetery.

Joshua and Alitha (Judd) Summers had 13 known children, all born in Virginia, probably Shenandoah County. The oldest appears to be Polly, born ca. 1808, married Michael Rock, and lived in Adams County, Indiana. Next was Isaac, born ca 1810, married Anne Cecil, and lived in Wells County, Indiana He later moved to Tennessee. Mary was born ca. 1811, married Christian Comer, and lived in Wells County, Indiana. Sarah was born in 1813, married James Comer, and lived in Allen County, Indiana. Next was Abraham, born 1814, married Mary A. Shenk, and lived in Adams and Wells Counties, Indiana. Jacob was born in 1816, married Catherine Boyce first, and then Phoebe Ann (Sturgeon) Lucas; he lived in Wells County, Indiana. Rebecca was born in 1818, married Christian Judd, and lived in Stark County, Ohio. William, born 1819, married Emeline Rock, and lived in Allen and Wells County, Indiana. Anna, born 1822, married Andrew Lipes, and lived in Allen County, Indiana. Andrew was born in 1825, married Rebecca Lipes, then Maria McKessick, and last, Rhoda Smith; he lived in Allen County, Indiana. Julia Ann, born ca. 1826, married William Jobs, and lived in Allen County, Indiana. Joseph was born in 1830, married Francis Sommers, then Victoria Sommers, and lived in Allen and Wells Counties, Indiana. Elizabeth, born ca. 1833, married William Claus, then Richard Short, and lived in Adams County, Indiana.

Many descendents of this family still reside in the Allen, Adams, and Wells County area today but other members of this family live nationwide.

Submitted by Charles Myers

LEONARD ORLANDO SUMNEY FAMILY

Leonard Orlando Sumney was the first-born child of Mary Ann (Steiner) Lugibill and Daniel Oscar Sumney, born November 14, 1897, on a farm near Bluffton, Ohio. He graduated from Bluffton High School.

The first Sumney of record in the United States, Isaac Sumney, the founder of Sumneytown, Pennsylvania, just north of Philadelphia, was born about 1710. Isaac was a Huguenot. His father may have been Jean Somaine, a Huguenot galley slave, who was ordered to leave his native country within fifteen days after being released by order of Louis XIV of France.

Isaac Sumney, who married Magdalena, had five children. He was an innkeeper, owning and operating the Sumneytown Hotel. The stage coaches and Conestoga wagons stopped there, and Indian emissaries and officials of the frontier passed through and made acquaintances with Sumney. He moved to Philadelphia after the Revolutionary War and continued in the hotel business until his death. Isaac Sumney was buried July 19, 1781, most likely in what is now Franklin Square in Philadelphia.

Leonard and Ercel Sumney

Seven generations later, after some family members had migrated to Ohio, Leonard Sumney continued the westward migration, arriving in Allen County, Indiana, in the spring of 1920. He had driven a team of horses from Bluffton, Ohio, delivering them to an uncle near Woodburn.

Attending church in Grabill, Leonard met, and later married, on November 9, 1922, Ercel Leona Klopfenstein, daughter of Oliver L. and Mary Anna (Witmer) Klopfenstein. To this union were born four children: Marguerite Jean, Marceil Joan, Roland Leon, and Sharon Lou Sumney. All of these children were graduates of the Leo schools and obtained degrees in higher education.

Leonard, a man with many talents and abilities, was a farmer, hauled milk to Allen Dairy in Fort Wayne, partnered in another small dairy in Grabill, was a substitute mail carrier, a blacksmith, and a welder. During World War II, being too old to be drafted, he helped with the war effort as a welder, helping build army trucks for Truck Engineering in Fort Wayne. Later, when manufacturers had not yet converted their production lines from military to civilian needs and farmers could not buy new machinery, he built multitudes of farm wagons, tractors, buck rakes, and other farm machinery.

Leonard and Ercel Sumney lived their entire adult life in Allen County, Indiana, and were lifelong members of the Grabill Evangelical Mennonite Church, where he held various positions of leadership over the years. Leonard passed away on February 15, 1975, at age 77, and Ercel lived nearly 96 years until July 19, 1998.

Marguerite Jean Sumney married Albert Ray Carver and lived in Spring Green, Wisconsin, where they raised five children. Marceil Joan Sumney married Thomas Keith Zehr and bore four children while living in Fort Wayne. After Thomas passed away, Marceil later married Richard (Dick) Kryder, of Leo, Indiana. Roland Leon Sumney married Carol Louise Stump, of Mishawaka, Indiana, and they live in Fort Wayne. They have five children. Sharon Lou Sumney married Jon David vonGunten and they live in Fort Wayne and have three children.

Submitted by Roland Sumney

ROLAND LEON SUMNEY FAMILY

Roland Leon Sumney was born January 19, 1933, to Leonard Orlando and Ercel Leona Sumney in a farmhouse on the Leo-Grabill road in Allen County, Indiana. Sisters Marguerite Jean and Marceil Joan preceded him in birth. Another sister, Sharon Lou, followed later.

Roland attended the Leo schools, graduating in 1951. When drafted into the army during the Korean War, he served in Korea in a medical battalion until his discharge. Roland then resumed his formal education at Taylor University, Upland, Indiana, receiving his bachelor's degree in business administration.

On August 30, 1958, he married Carol Louise Stump of Mishawaka, Indiana, daughter of Robert and Bessie Stump. Carol graduated from Parkview Memorial Hospital School of Nursing in Fort Wayne as a registered nurse and spent many years working in local physician's offices. Their five children, Mark, Lora, Todd, Carrie, and Carla, all graduated from Northrop High School in Fort Wayne, and Taylor University in Upland, Indiana.

Roland started his business career on February 2, 1959, at Brotherhood Mutual Insurance Company, Fort Wayne, Indiana, a property and casualty insurance company that insures churches throughout the United States. He retired as vice-president corporate secretary, having served more than 39 years. He continues to serve on the company's board of directors.

When living in Grabill, Roland and Carol were active leaders in the Grabill Evangelical Mennonite Church. After moving to Fort Wayne in 1966, they became active members of Brookside Community Church.

Mark Alan Sumney, born November 18, 1959, received his degree in business administration and a certificate in church music. Mark is employed as emcee/worship leader manager for the Billy Graham Training Center at The Cove in Ashville, North Carolina. His wife, Tracy Lynna Herter of Dowagiac, Michigan, earned her bachelor's degree in psychology from Anderson University, Anderson, Indiana, and is home schooling their three children.

Lora Kay Sumney, born December 14, 1962, received her degree in social work. She married Kenneth Edward Wilkinson of Chicago, Illinois. Lora is mother to three children and is a secretary at Northrop High School. Ken has a master's degree in recreation from Indiana University and is director of parks and recreation in New Haven, Indiana.

Todd Michael Sumney, born February 6, 1965, married Kari Ann Boyd of Scottsdale, Arizona, They have two sons. Having received his degree in business administration, Todd is owner of an advertising firm in Scottsdale and Kari assists in the business.

Carrie Lynn and Carla Marie Sumney are twin girls, born March 2, 1972. Carrie's degree is in health and physical education and she teaches at Center Grove Middle School, south of Indianapolis. After receiving her degree in psychology, Carla Marie achieved a masters degree in public administration from Indiana University and is director of human resources at Paragon Medical in Pierceton, Indiana. Her husband, Timothy James Nussbaum, has a masters degree in marriage and family counseling from Saint Francis University, Fort Wayne. Tim serves as director of corporate services at the Otis R. Bowen Center in Warsaw, Indiana.

Submitted by Lora Wilkinson

DANIEL & ANNA (STANTON) SWANK

Daniel Swank and Anna Stanton, daughter of Peter and Freelive Stanton, were married in Wayne County, Ohio, on January 17, 1858. Shortly after their marriage, they moved to Allen County and settled in Pleasant Township on 80 acres of ground, one fourth mile south of Winters Road on the west side of Bluffton Road.

Eleven children were born to Daniel and Anna, nine boys and one girl survived; a baby daughter died in infancy. Their children were: Alonzo, July 14, 1863 (married Blanch Carson); Manilus, February 21, 1860 (Mary Preble); Irving, August 26, 1858 -May 24, 1917 (Mary Ross); Mason, September 26, 1866 (Margaret Dishong); Stephen, November 2, 1872 (Ida Lamay); Thomas, 1870 (Lena Smith); Wesley, 1876 (Cora Dishong); Edward, January 16, 1879 (Elizabetha Madden); Grover, November 27, 1884 (Goldia Weist); and Flora, March 3, 1882 (Stephen Kinerk). In their later years, Daniel and Anna moved to Fort Wayne and lived their final years on Vesely Avenue, directly behind Halls Restaurant.

Daniel and Anna Swank

Edward, the eighth son, married Elizabetha Madden, daughter of Dennis and Mary Madden, on November 26, 1902, and lived on the home place, where their eight children were born. Several years later they purchased a farm around the corner on Winters Road.

Edward and Elizabetha's children: a daughter (April 28, 1904 -April 29, 1904) buried on the Swank farm; Leslie Edwin (January 17, 1907 - December 17, 1944); Howard (September 15, 1909 - June 18, 2000); Gerald Arnold (February 15, 1912 - February 23, 1912) buried on the Swank farm; Helen Grace (August 15, 1913); Edith Catherine (January 10, 1917); Robert Christopher (May 11, 1919); Elise Mae (August 1, 1922).

Edward and Elizabetha's son Robert married Alma Smith (born September 1, 1923) on August 23, 1941. Robert served in World War II in the Army Air Force as a chief mechanic. After the war he worked for John Dehner as a heavy equipment operator.

Robert and Alma lived and farmed on Winters road until 1995, when Fort Wayne International Airport bought the ground for expansion and the new air traffic control tower. From there they moved to Wells County, where they both still live.

On June 2, 1962, Bob and Alma's daughter Joyce, (born November 11, 1942) married Norman Bauermeister at Bethlehem Lutheran Church, Ossian, Indiana. They make their home in Wells County, where they farm 400 acres and Norman was a partner in Bauermeister Builders home construction company.

Norman and Joyce's family consists of two daughters, Brenda (born January 4, 1964) and Jodi (November 3, 1967). Both girls graduated from Purdue University and now live in Allen County. Brenda and her husband Dr. Alan Stephens, along with their three children, Zachary, Tyler and Erin, live in Aboite Township. Jodi and her daughter, Kaylee, live in Wayne Township

Submitted by Alma Swank

HAROLD JUNIOR & ELAINE (RUSWINKLE) SWEET FAMILY

Harold Junior Sweet was born in Paulding County, Ohio, on August 10, 1929, at his grandparents' home in Antwerp, Ohio. He was brought back to Woodburn, where his parents were residents and where he has lived for 75 years.

Harold Junior was born to Harold Ray and Mildred (Ruppert) Sweet. Harold Ray was born on April 24, 1908, to Thomas Walter and Julia (Burrier) Sweet. Mildred was born on September 23, 1905, to Oscar and Mary Rebecca (Billman) Ruppert. Harold Ray and Mildred were married on February 2, 1927, in Allen County, Indiana. Harold Ray died on March 27, 1979, and Mildred died on December 5, 1980.

Thomas Walter Sweet, Harold Junior's grandfather, was born September 20, 1883, to Daniel and Mary Ann (Foster) Sweet. His grandmother, Julia (Burrier) Sweet, was born February 15, 1885. Thomas and Julia were married on June 25, 1907. Thomas died in 1923 and Julia in January 1965.

Daniel Sweet, Harold Junior's great-grandfather, was born in 1847 to John Nelson and Mary (Shaffer) Sweet. His great-grandmother, Mary Ann (Foster) Sweet, was the daughter of Edward and Anna (Simmons) Foster. Edward Foster was the first justice of the peace, from 1873-1879, in Maumee Township, Woodburn, Indiana. Daniel and Mary Ann were married on November 28, 1882, in Allen County, Indiana. Daniel died in 1926 and Mary Ann in 1888.

John Nelson Sweet, Harold Junior's great-great-grandfather, was born to William and Elizabeth (Tyler) Sweet in 1808. John's wife, Mary (Shaffer) Sweet, was born in 1818 in Pennsylvania. John was one of the first settlers in Maumee Township. He died in 1866 and Mary on September 23, 1898.

Elaine and Harold J. Sweet, March 17, 2005

Harold Junior's great-great-great grandfather, William Sweet, was born in 1782. William's wife, Elizabeth (Tyler) Sweet was born in 1781 in Rhode Island. He was one of the first settlers in Springfield Township, along with Ezra May and Isaac Hall.

Harold Junior Sweet graduated from Woodburn High School in 1947. He served in the army during the Korean War from 1951-1952, as a corporal in the 25th Infantry Division, 27th Regiment, L Company. His unit defended Heartbreak Ridge in the spring of 1952. He was first scout and messenger during radio silence on night patrols. Harold married Elaine Ruswinkel on May 4, 1963, at Zion Lutheran Church, Luckey, Ohio. Elaine was born on November 3, 1937, in Luckey, Ohio, to Franklin E. and Frieda L. (Rife) Ruswinkel. After the wedding, she moved to Woodburn, Indiana, where Harold was employed at Woodburn Die for 35 years. He retired on January 31, 1999.

Harold and Elaine Sweet's daughter, Cheryl, was born on December 2, 1964. She married William Walker on September 15, 1985, and they have a daughter, Brittanie Nicole Walker, born on September 15, 1989.

Harold is a member of the V.F.W. and the New Haven Eagles and is an avid fisherman. Elaine is a member of the Daughters of Union Veterans, Otis Tent 54. They both are members of the Woodburn Community Historical Society.

Submitted by Elaine Sweeet

SWEET - WATERSON

Francis sweet, son of John and Judith Sweet, was born July 28, 1806, near Jonesboro, Tennessee. His ancestors came to America in 1636 and were leading people in the Massachusetts Bay Colony. In 1808, John moved his family to Miami County, Ohio. Francis was a carpenter and farmer. On December 13, 1827, he married Abigail Hammond, daughter of Louis and Nancy Buffington Hammond. She was born May 27, 1810, in Abbeyville District, South Carolina. They settled in Troy, Ohio. In 1836, Francis purchased forty acres of land in Lake Township near Arcola, Indiana. There he was a farmer, postmaster, and Justice of the Peace. They were the parents of ten children. Abigail died August 13, 1865 in Allen County, Indiana. Francis married Hannah Peabody in 1867. He died March 25, 1884, in Columbia City, Indiana. They are buried in Lake Chapel Methodist Church Cemetery, Allen County, Indiana.

Their oldest daughter, Elmira, was born August 7, 1828, in Ohio. Upon the death of her first husband in 1854, she married William Waterson, a widower and farmer, on April 26, 1855. He was the son of James and Jane Waterson. William was born November 18, 1806, in Armstrong County, Pennsylvania. His first wife, Frances Shively, had died September 27, 1854, in Eel River Township, Allen County, Indiana. They were the parents of ten children. William and Elmira had four children. William died May 30, 1892. Elmira died July 24, 1877. They are buried in Eel River Cemetery, Allen County, Indiana.

David Watterson was born June 15, 1857, in Eel River Township, Allen County, Indiana, and was employed by several railroads. He married Anna Maxwell, daughter of John and Margaret Maxwell, December 13, 1877. Anna was born May 2, 1861, in Eel River Township. They had two children. David died January 31, 1925. Anna died May 18, 1935. They are buried in Lindenwood Cemetery, Fort Wayne, Indiana.

Charles Watterson was born April 25, 1878, in Churubusco, Indiana, and was an employee of the Nickel Plate and B & O Railroads. He married Catherine Holzhauer, daughter of Cornelius and Elizabeth Schneider Holzhauer, March 29, 1900, in Bellevue, Ohio. Catherine was born October 7, 1881, in Germany. They had two sons. Charles died in a train accident in Mark Center, Ohio March 12, 1905. Catherine married Jacob Feichter on December 31, 1909. She died October 24, 1939. They are buried in Lindenwood Cemetery.

Clarence Watterson was born November 29, 1900, in Fort Wayne, Indiana. He served in the 42nd Rainbow Division as a messenger during World War I. He retired from General Electric. On August 16, 1919, he married Stella Wies, daughter of Jesse and Barbara Sorg Wies. She was born August 26, 1901, in Fort Wayne, Indiana. They had three children. Clarence died January 13, 1984. Stella died April 30, 1990. They are buried in Lindenwood Cemetery.

Josie Watterson was born August 3, 1920, in Fort Wayne, Indiana. She married James Schroff, son of Edward and Marie Wilkinson Schroff, January 20, 1938. James was born September 16, 1917, in Cumberland, Maryland and was employed by Home Telephone, later known as General Telephone. They had three children. James died April 24, 1986. Josie died June 10, 2004. They are buried in LaGrange, Indiana.

David Schroff was born August 15, 1941, in Fort Wayne, Indiana. He was employed at General Electric, retiring in 1997. On February 26, 1965, he married Judith Pio, daughter of George and Rosalie Rumpsa Pio. She was born October 17, 1944, in Minneapolis, Minnesota. They're the parents of Stephanie and Mark and grandparents of two. They've lived in Eel River Township since 1966.

Submitted by Judith Schroff

MARY STRACK SWENDA

Mary Strack was born May 16, 1926, at home on Juliette Avenue in Fort Wayne, Indiana, and at four years of age moved to a 20 acre farm on State Road 14. It was the Depression. Reared by her mother, Priscilla Freiburger, the youngest of 13, and her father, Charles L. Strack, a Miami Indian who was orphaned at eleven years of age, Mary's family met many challenges and grew up with a lot of love. They were taught never to lie, cheat or steal. She attended St. Joseph's Catholic Grade School and Central Catholic High School in Fort Wayne, Indiana. Mary worked at the General Electric in Fort Wayne for nine years.

Left to Right, Dani, Mary, Joseph, Krisi, Patti

Her older brothers were drafted in World War II. So her family moved to Arcola, on an 80 acre farm. Mary's brother got a one year deferment. The war ended during that year, but he still was drafted. Mary met her husband, Joseph Swenda, when her brother wanted his guitar brought to the army base at Little Rock, Arkansas.

Mary took her mother and the guitar to her brother. After mass they went to the day room. There she met Joseph Swenda and he asked her brother, "Can I buy her a Coke?" Joseph bought the Coke, and three years later, on October 22, 1949, Mary and Joseph were married.

Joseph was a welder at the American Hoist and Derrick and they had three lovely daughters. They purchased a farm on Bass Road in 1949, where they built their home, and it continues as the family farm.

Mary drove a school bus for Fort Wayne Community Schools for 31 and a half years. Joseph left for heaven on March 31, 1992. Mary retired in 1998. Her girls, Patricia, Dani, and Kristina grew up and had children of their own.

Mary was awarded the Sagamore of the Wabash because she was a very special mother.

Submitted by Mary M. Swenda

CHARLES FRANKLIN & HANNAH ALBINA (BELLIS) TATMAN

Charles Franklin Tatman was born April 25, 1866, in Leesburg, Union County, Ohio. He died on November 10, 1957, in Jackson, Michigan. He married Hannah Albina Bellis on May 3, 1889, in Paulding County, Ohio. They lived in Allen County, Indiana

The ten children of Charles and Hannah Albina Tatman were: William Elsworth, born February 20, 1891, in Baldwin, Jackson Township, Allen County, Indiana, and died on July 1, 1971. He is buried at the IOOF Cemetery, New Haven, Indiana. He married Elizabeth Ellen McCormick, May 14, 1912, in Besancon, Allen County, Indiana.

Orpha May Ellen, born September 11, 1892, in Allen County, Indiana and died December 9, 1976, in Jackson, Michigan. She married Joseph Nathanial Hay, September 22, 1908, in Allen County, Indiana.

Grace Elizabeth, born September 23, 1894, in Allen County, Indiana, and died September 12, 1996, in Jackson, Michigan is buried at Woodlawn Cemetery, Jackson, Michigan. She

Family of Charles and Hannah Bellis Tatman, 1899. William, Grace, Charles, Orpha, Louis and Hannah

married Floyd Ort on January 24, 1910, and then Charles Hicks.

Louis Merton, born on January 6, 1897, in Allen County, Indiana, and died on October 27, 1972, in Jackson, Michigan, is buried at Hillcrest Cemetery, Jackson, Michigan. He married Nina Pernell on November 1, 1916, and then Ruth Niddiate.

Daisy Muriel, born on July 9, 1900, in Marion, Grant County, Indiana, and died on September 18, 1989, in Fort Wayne, is buried at Covington Memorial Cemetery, Fort Wayne, Indiana. She married Charles Gibson,on November 27, 1914, in Monroeville, Allen County, Indiana.

Alfred Rosevelt, born on January 5, 1903, in Allen County, Indiana and died on June 29, 1986, in Fort Wayne, Indiana. He married Hazel Grotrain, on June 5, 1927, in Fort Wayne, Indiana.

Velma Olive, born on February 7, 1905, in Monroeville, Allen County, Indiana, and died on December 24, 1995, in Jackson Michigan. She married Leon Clarence Kitzmiller on March 22, 1923, in Fort Wayne, Indiana.

Myrtle Dora, born on April 18, 1907, in Allen County, Indiana, and died on September 21, 1990, in Jackson, Michigan, and is buried at Hillcrest Memorial Park, Jackson, Michigan. She married Wallace Ellis on February 27, 1924, in Jackson, Michigan.

Richard Arnold, born on March 22, 1909, in Allen County, and died on October 26, 1985, in Jackson, Michigan. He married Beulah Watts on August 5, 1931, in Jackson, Michigan, and then Doris Diver, in Jackson, Michigan.

Leona Mae, born on February 8, 1912, in Allen County, Indiana, and died on May 14, 1989, in Jackson, Michigan, is buried at Hillcrest Cemetery, Jackson, Michigan. She married Clarence Gumper on August 12, 1933.

Submitted by Loretta Brady

NEIL A. & LOIS A. (GERARDOT) TERNET

Neil Alan Ternet and Lois Ann Gerardot were wed August 6, 1971, in St. Rose de Lima Catholic Church, Monroeville, Indiana. They had attended the same grade school, high school, and church, but never really dated until the summer of 1969.

Neil Alan Ternet was born May 28, 1952, in Fort Wayne, Indiana, to Gerald F. and Jane (Berg) Ternet. Neil was the youngest son of seven children. His siblings included Gerald D., Michael, Terry, Thomas, Sandra, and Candace. His father "Pinch" was a farmer and ran a small backhoe service, which included digging local graves. His mother is a housewife and a fine seamstress. The family grew up on a farm in Jackson Township until moving to Monroeville in 1971 with their two daughters.

Neil attended Jackson Grade School until the fourth grade, when he transferred to St. Joseph Grade School in Monroeville. His high school years were spent at Monroeville High School and Heritage High School, where he graduated in 1970. Neil served his toolmaker apprenticeship with General Electric Company. He was later employed by International Harvester. Currently he is a machinist/mechanic for B. F. Goodrich, with 22 years service.

Lois was born June 24, 1951, in Fort Wayne, the third eldest daughter of Leonard S. and Aleta R. (Singer) Gerardot. Her siblings include Jeanne, Nora, Joyce, Jill, Mary, Ernest, Jane, Lisa, Mary, and Barry. Her father was a machinist by trade and retired from B. F. Goodrich Tire Company. He was also a U.S. Navy veteran of WWII. Her mother was a homemaker, an excellent cook, and a seamstress. The family home was at 112 Central Avenue in Monroeville.

Lois and Neil Ternet

Lois attended St. Joseph Grade School, Monroeville High School, and later Heritage High School, where she graduated in the first class of 1969. She went on to further her studies at IPFW and received a MHT degree from Purdue. Her employment has included parts manager at Northway Chrysler Plymouth and parts scheduler and expediter at International Harvester Company. Currently, Lois is the editor of *The Monroeville News*, a weekly newspaper, and works part-time in the office at Meyer Auto. She has also volunteered as an EMT with the Monroeville EMS since 1976.

Neil and Lois have two children: Amy Lyn (born November 12, 1976) and Nicholas Alan (born March 24, 1979). They grew up in Jackson Township, rural Monroeville, and graduated from Heritage High School. Amy married Jon Sorrell in 1994. They have two children: Atticus Christopher (May 6, 1995) and Iris Catherine (March 24, 2001). Amy graduated from I.U. with an English and Journalism degree in secondary education. She is a teacher.

After high school, their son, Nicholas, took some college courses at IPFW, but found the skilled trade schooling more to his liking. He is employed as a mechanic/electrician at B. F. Goodrich and is married to Jennifer Klima (2002).

Submitted by Lois and Neil Ternet

THOMPSON-LAPP

Records of Jeremiah Thompson, of possible Irish descent, go back to the 1860s in Fort Wayne. Jeremiah married Susan Briggs, who it appears was the widow of a Mr. Weeks. One can only surmise that the father of Jeremiah might have come to Fort Wayne as a railroad worker, as that was a common reason for Irish immigrants to come to Fort Wayne at that time. Among Jeremiah and Susan's children was William Wilber Thompson (1867-1946), who married Mattie Kuntz. The family lived near and attended St. Patrick Catholic Church. Circa 1900, William and Mattie built a new house at 1530 Sherman Boulevard. This house would eventually play a central role in the lives of their descendants. William and Mattie had five children: Edith (1891-1970), Erin (circa 1893-1919), Kenneth (1897-1969), Rosella (1898-1974), and Neil (1908-1972).

Children of William and Mattie Thompson, circa 1915

Erin left the house to marry Herman Hilker. They had one son, also named Herman. Kenneth also moved out when he married Agnes Zentner (1897-1971), a Fort Wayne dress designer. The couple had two daughters and two sons. Likewise, Rosella moved out when she married Herb Meier and had a son and a daughter before Herb passed away. As a young widow, she married Charlie Auer and they had a son and a daughter. But it was the oldest daughter, Edith, and youngest son, Neil, who would continue to reside in the family homestead for years to come. In 1916, Edith married Fredrick (Fred) Lapp (1889-1956). Fred's family belonged to Emmaus Lutheran Church on Broadway. His father had come from Hessen Kassel in Germany. Fred's mother's maiden name was Stellhorn. Fred and Edith purchased William and Mattie's home on Sherman Boulevard after Mattie had passed away. William continued to live in the house as the "grandfather" until his death in 1946, when he was hit by a car as he disembarked from the bus at Sherman and Hoffman Street. Fred and Edith had a large family with three sons (Eugene, Eldon, Dale) and seven daughters (Joan Lapp, Thelma Ringler, Maxine Poinsatte, Jean Shomey, Ruth Wyss, Carolyn Lapp and Mary Schuckle). Eugene perished in the 1918 flu epidemic. Joan died of a fever at age of three and a half. All of the children attended Precious Blood Catholic School a few blocks away. Fred was a respected engineer on the Nickel Plate railroad.

Neil also continued to live in the house as the "uncle" for a number of years while Edith

Thompson-Lapp Homestead, 1530 Sherman Blvd.

and Fred were raising their children. Neil, who studied music at the Julliard School in New York, was an accomplished pianist and was the organist at St. Patrick's Catholic Church. Eventually Neil would move from the house when he married Collette Schnurr (1906-1983). They had three sons and one daughter.

Although the house was quite full, with mother, father, grandfather, uncle and all the children, there was always enough food to share with the hobos who would come to the back door during the Great Depression. 1530 Sherman Blvd was marked with an "X" on the sidewalk, as many houses were, as a sign that this was place where the hungry could be fed.

In the 1960s, Edith and her daughter, Carolyn, a teacher at Bishop Luers High School, lived in the house, until Edith passed away in 1970. The Thompson-Lapp Homestead was then occupied in the 1970s by Edith and Fred's granddaughter (great-granddaughter of William and Mattie), Kristine Poinsatte, and her husband, John Szczepanski, a naturalized U.S. citizen, who was born in Leyden, Holland. Later, in the early 1980s, the house was occupied by Eugene Poinsatte, the great-grandson of William and Mattie. In the 1990s, James Wall, the great-great-grandson of William and Mattie, lived in the venerable old house on Sherman Boulevard.

William and Mattie would likely be quite surprised, yet proud, that their "new" home continues in the family 100 years later.

Submitted by Richard Poinsatte

REV. RALPH & GLENDIA THORNTON

Ralph and Glendia (Parker) Thornton are residents of Fort Wayne. They reside on Fairfield Avenue. The Thorntons are both natives of Oklahoma; Ralph was born in 1940 in Leedey and Glendia was born in 1945 in Oklahoma City.

Ralph noticed Glendia when she walked by the gas station where he was an attendant. He asked another guy there who she was. The other guy dared Glendia to call Ralph and she did. The rest was history for the Harding High School student and the sophomore at the University of Oklahoma. They were married on March 24, 1961, in Gainsville,Texas.

Both were in school at Oklahoma City, where Ralph was studying for the ministry. His first church assignment was in Shawnee, Oklahoma. He was there for six years, and they then moved to Witchita for the next nine years. The decision was then made to enroll in seminary at Findlay College in Ohio.

After three years in Ohio, he accepted an assignment at the Zanesville Church of God, situated on the Allen-Wells County Line in Zanesville, Indiana. It was 1991 when they moved to Zanesville, where they served until 1997.

The Thorntons are the parents of two sons. Joe Lyman Thornton was born in December, 1961, and he passed away in July, 2005. His widow, Catrina lives in Huntington. Robert E. Lynn Thornton was born in February, 1964, and he lives with his wife Mary in Racine, Wisconsin. Robert and Mary are also from Oklahoma; Robert came to Zanesville in 1993 to become Zanesville's first Town Marshall. They have two daughters; Mrs. Floyd (Bobbie) Robbins lives in Bluffton. She has a step-daughter, Tina Robbins, and two sons, Robert and Michael. Kari Ann Schultz lives in Colorado Springs, Colorado and she has a son Brendon.

Glendia and Ralph Thornton

Ralph and Glendia both work for WalMart at Apple Glenn. Ralph is in automotive and Glendia is in sporting goods. Ralph enjoys all kinds of cars and collects models of them. Glendia loves cats; besides the three that make their home with the Thorntons, she collects everything cats. She also loves dolls and doll houses.

They spend their spare hours visiting with friends and family.

Submitted by Glendia Thornton

LAURENCE & MARY TIPPMANN FAMILY

Laurence Tippmann was born in 1909 to Joseph and Margaret Tippmann in Connellsville, Pennsylvania. Joseph Tippmann's father, a German immigrant, had a large family of 13 children and operated a brewery in Connellsville. Joseph's wife, Margaret Donegan, was the daughter of Irish immigrants.

In 1926, Joseph and Margaret Tippmann moved from Connellsville, Pennsylvania, to Gary, Indiana, to seek a better life for their five children. In Gary, Joseph Tippmann used his skills as a plumber, tinsmith, and refrigeration technician to make a living during the Depression. Laurence, the oldest son, learning from his father, worked as a refrigerator repairman and developed skills as a salesman.

Mary Cross was the daughter of Irish Canadian immigrants, Robert Cross and Catherine Dempsey, who migrated to Chicago from Quebec City, Canada, and eventually to Gary, Indiana. Mary and Laurence met in Gary and married in 1931. In 1936 they visited Fort Wayne. They liked the clean air and friendly people and decided to move here with their three children. They packed the car, drove to Fort Wayne, and rented a house on Pontiac Street. In the next six years Laurence's parents and his three brothers and his sister and her husband and four children also moved to Fort Wayne.

Before World War II, Laurence worked as a salesman and worked with his father building freezers for grocery stores. During the war he worked on the railroad and after the war he returned to sales, until 1951, when he built a shop and launched his own business, the Tippmann Engineering Company. By 1951 the family had grown to 16 children. Of the 16 children, 15 are now married with families. Larry, the oldest son, is a priest.

From 1941 to 1951 the family had to struggle constantly to make ends meet. The family can thank the generosity of St. Jude Grade School and Central Catholic High School, and especially the Sisters of Providence nuns, who educated the entire family at St. Jude and Central Catholic High School, St. Joseph Hospital and the doctors who provided affordable medical care (13 children born there), and individuals like the small grocery store owner, Art Wiesenberg, who graciously extended credit to the family to buy groceries.

It was in 1941 that the family moved to 3316 East State Street, where the number of children grew from 6 to 16. It is now hard to imagine 18 people living in a six room house with one bathroom and about 1,000 feet of living space. The house was crowded, but there was plenty of room outside, with endless games of football, basketball, kick the can, etc. There were horses, sled hills, ice skating and, in the summer, playing in the woods or swimming all day at the beach. There were hilarious and memorable incidents, such as Mom's reaction when they brought a horse, into the house, and the night the triplet sisters were born.

The descendants of Laurence and Mary Tippmann comprise probably the largest extended family in Allen County. As of September 2005, Laurence, who died in 1984, and Mary, who died in 1970, have had 16 children, 135 grandchildren, 378 great-grandchildren and 11 great-great-grandchildren for a total of 540 descendants. (This does not include 118 spouses.) Of the 540 descendants, 524 are now living and, of these, 477 (91 percent) live in the Fort Wayne area. (In addition to the descendants of Laurence and Mary Tippmann, there are the spouses and descendants of Laurence's brothers, Vincent Otto Tippmann and Henry Tippmann, and the descendants of his sister Eleanor Galloway, many of whom live in the Fort Wayne area).

Mary & Laurence Tippmann

Beginning with the Tippmann Engineering Company in 1951, Tippmann family members have engaged in a large number of business enterprises, providing jobs and livelihoods to hundreds of Allen County residents. These business enterprises, of which there are now well over 60, include cold storage warehouses in Allen County and throughout the country, construction companies, real estate and property management companies, manufacturing (ovens, refrigeration equipment, paintball guns and sewing machines, etc.) landscaping, and a variety of service companies. The family members own and manage large commercial buildings, such as the Fort Wayne Lincoln Tower and industrial and residential real estate.

In addition to business and commerce, the Tippmann family members have taken an active role in charitable enterprises. They have sponsored and supported charitable organizations, such as the Franciscan Center, which provides food and services to the needy, Vincent House, which provides housing and social services to the homeless, Matthew 25 Health and Dental Clinic, the Rose Home for homeless women, and St. Andrews Center drug rehabilitation program for men. Also, the Mary Cross Tippmann Foundation and the Charlie Tippmann Foundation support charitable projects both in Allen County and worldwide.

In addition to local charitable work and financial support, Tippmann family members have generously supported Catholic Relief Services with contributions for famine and disaster relief and have continued to support religious organizations and relief missions in such places as Bangladesh, Africa, Honduras, and Mexico City.

Over the past 69 years the Laurence and Mary Tippmann extended family has grown and prospered greatly from living in Fort Wayne and Allen County and, in turn, continues to support the community in business and charitable enterprises.

Submitted by Donald Tippmann, Ed. D.

FRED W. TOENGES FAMILY

In 1861 Frederick William Toenges was born in Uchte Pro Hanover Ki, Slozenan. He immigrated from Germany in 1878 to the U.S. He first settled in the Decatur, Indiana, area and worked on a farm. Because the farmers needed his experience as a shoe cobbler, he spent most of his time plying this trade.

He moved to Fort Wayne because he knew he could be more successful working as a shoe cobbler in a larger town. He opened his own store in 1891 on Maumee Avenue. He married Elise Boesse in 1886 and had nine children and one adopted one. The first child was a son, John, born in 1888. The other children were Walter, Arthur, Hilda, Luella, Linda, Alma, Paul, Edna and Velma.

John Toenges had three daughters, Mildred, Vera and Ruth. Mildren's children are Ron, Marilyn and Richard Schroeder. Vera's children are Jim, Lynn, Fred and Steve Auman. Ruth's children are Freya, John, May, and Dianna Michels.

Walter Toenges had one daughter.

Arthur Toenges had a son Frederick (Fred) and a daughter, Jane. Fred had four children, Heather, Holly, Fred William, and Ross. Jane had four children, Robert, Janet, Sharon, and Joe Douglas.

Fred W. Toenges Family

Hilda Toenges has three sons, Elmer, Erwin and Paul Hoerner. Elmer was killed in the invasion of Normandy during WW II.

Luella Toenges had two children, Dorthy and Richard Nord.

Alma Toenges had two children, Margaret and Wilford Hanover.

Linda Toenges did not have any children; she was married to George Skinnel.

Paul Toenges had a son, Harold, and he had five children, Gary, Deane, Gregory, Alan, and Tammy Sue.

Edna had four children, Betty and Marcie by her first husband, and Theya and Tom Heckman.

Velma Toenges had a son and a daughter.

John and Arthur joined their father in the shoe business, and they incorporated the business, F. W. Toenges and Sons, Inc. in 1917. After John's death in 1946, Arthur's son, Fred, started working in the store. In 1964, Fred purchased the business from his father, and has enabled the family business to continue for the last 114 years. Fred's son, Ross, who graduated from Purdue and Northwestern Medical School of Orthotics and Prosthetics, is carrying on the family business.

Submitted by Fred Toenges

GEORGE W. TOWNSEND FAMILY

George William Townsend was born March 28, 1922, in Fort Wayne, Indiana, to Clarence and Etta (Falls) Townsend. He attended school in Jefferson Township. He married Margaret Beck on June 26, 1942, in Allen County. Margaret was the daughter of Alvin Chance and Golda (Dunlap) Beck.

On October 5, 1942, he enlisted in the Army. In 1943, he was stationed at Kelly Field in San Antonio, Texas, and, by 1944, he was in the Western Pacific with the 497th Bombardment Group. He was an airplane sheet metal worker and spent time on Guam, Tinnian, and Saipan. While he was in the Pacific, Margaret and her mother worked two different shifts at a plant making bullets for the war. After the War, he went into the Air National Guard. In 1950 he was recalled to active duty and was sent to Scott Air Force Base in Illinois and Luke Air Force Base in Phoenix, Arizona. He went back to the Air National Guard. In 1961 he was again called to active duty and sent to Germany and France. He retired in 1982 from the Air Guard as a Master Sergeant.

George Townsend in uniform

George owned a heating and air conditioning business, G. Townsend & Son. There were four children: Susan, Nancy, Richard, and George, Jr. He died May 20, 1994, and is buried at Covington Memorial Gardens.

George's father, Clarence William Townsend, was born January 23, 1894, in Jackson Township. Clarence married Etta Gertrude Falls on January 28, 1913. They were married at St. Louis Catholic Church at Besancon. Etta was born in Jackson Township. Clarence and Etta had three children: Edwin Clarence, Marietta Agnes, and George William. Clarence retired in 1958 from the Centlivre Brewery. On the 71st anniversary of her wedding, Etta remembered that it had started snowing and by the time they came out of the church, the snow was up to her ankles, and she had no boots. The reception was at the Townsend farm on Paulding Road. Clarence died May 6, 1966, and Etta died April 19, 1984. They are buried at the I.O.O.F. Cemetery in New Haven.

Clarence's father, William N. Townsend, was born November 27, 1863. He married Anna A. Ryan on April 28, 1892. Anna was born November 11, 1873, in Milan Township. Their only child was Clarence William. William had a farm in Jefferson Township. Anna was of Irish heritage and was a very good seamstress, who made clothes for many in her family. She also made the cakes for the reception for her son's wedding. Anna died October 10, 1924, and William died September 15, 1930. They are buried at the I.O.O.F. Cemetery in New Haven.

William's father, George W. Townsend, was born November 6, 1841, in Adams Township to Peter and Esther (Neal) Townsend. He married Josephine Cecilia Gladieux on August 23, 1860,

George, Edwin, Etta, Marietta, and Clarence Townsend

Anna, Clarence and William Townsend

in Allen County. Josephine was born in Vellescot, France, on April 2, 1841. Her parents, Jean Pierre and Rosalie (Rossat) Gladieux, brought her to the U.S. when she was three years old and settled in Stark County, Ohio, before coming to Besancon, Indiana. George and Josephine's children were Cecilia, William, George, Jr. and Louise. They were members of the St. Louis Catholic Church at Besancon. They built their house on U.S. 30 (then Ridge Road) about 1871. They celebrated their golden wedding anniversary August 23, 1910, with a large party of 250 guests at their farm. "The afternoon was spent in a most enjoyable manner. Speaking, singing, piano solos, also a good old-fashioned platform dance," according to the newspaper article. George died March 26, 1911, and Josephine on October 12, 1919. They are both buried at the I.O.O.F. Cemetery in New Haven.

George's father, Peter, was born October 5, 1816, in Warren County, Ohio, to Joseph and Barbara (Studebaker) Townsend. Peter married Esther Neal on January 4, 1841, in Neave Township, Darke County, Ohio. They had two children, George William and Barbara Ann. Esther was only 36 years old when she died in 1855. Peter than married her sister, Sarah Ann, on March 24, 1859, in Allen County. They had five more children: Caleb, Adema, Amanda, William Tecumseh Sherman, and Ulysses Grant. Peter was a farmer in Jefferson Township. Peter died Mar. 20, 1875, and Sarah died in 1882. They are both buried at the I.O.O.F. Cemetery in New Haven.

Peter's father, Joseph (1780 – 1843), was born in Newbury District, South Carolina. Joseph married Barbara Studebaker (1788 – 1875) on May 29, 1806, in Warren County, Ohio. Their children were Minerva, George, Rachel, Jonathan, James, and Peter. Joseph and Barbara both died in Jefferson Township and are buried at the I.O.O.F. Cemetery in New Haven.

Joseph's parents, William (1759 – 1824) and Margaret (1760 – 1845), lived in Darke County,

George, Jr., George, Cecilia, William, Josephine and Louise Townsend

Ohio. Their children were John, Joseph, Mary, Elizabeth, Eli, James, William, Jr. and Jonathan. William was buried at the Martin Cemetery in Greenville Township in Darke County when he died there. His son Joseph moved to Allen County, Indiana, where he built a mill on Townsend Creek about 1827. His land was near Route 30. On March 9, 1840, James filed a partition suit in Darke County against his mother. After that suit was settled September 5, 1843, Margaret moved to Indiana with Joseph. She was buried on the old Miller farm in Allen County. The cemetery was later destroyed and her remains were moved to the I.O.O.F. Cemetery in New Haven.

Submitted by Susan Townsend Downey

GERALD DEAN & DORIS MARILYN BEAN TRAINER

Dean Trainer was born July 9, 1911, and Doris Bean Trainer was born February 15, 1915, in Blue Mound, Illinois. They had two sons; H. Stuart Trainer, born June 9, 1935, at Blue Mound, Illinois and David D., born November 24, 1936, at Decatur, Illinois.

Dean Trainer worked for Shell Company before and during WWII. He was transferred to Fort Wayne in 1947. Sons Stuart and David both graduated from Elmhurst High School.

L to R: Stuart, Dean, Doris, and David Trainer

Dean and Doris leased a Shell Oil Company Service Station and started in business at the Bluffton Road and Lower Huntington Road in the Waynedale area. Waynedale Shell Service expanded numerous times in the following 48 years. Stuart and David joined the business full time when they graduated from high school in 1953 and 1954.They attended many schools and clinics to upgrade themselves.

Stuart married Sarah (Sue) Lammiman, born December 9, 1936, at the Waynedale United Methodist Church, August 15, 1959. They have two children, Mark Alan, born December 11, 1960, and Ann M., born October 31, 1963. Both children graduated from Indiana University. While Stuart worked in the family business, Sue was a nurse R.N. She graduated from Parkview School of Nursing in 1959. Stuart was active in the Waynedale Methodist Church and Waynedale Masonic Lodge #739, and master of the lodge in 1966. Sue was active in Waynedale Methodist Church and Tri Kappa Sorority. Sue Trainer's parents are Charles H. Lammiman, born March 24, 1904, in Monroe, Indiana, and Madelene Havice, born December 14, 1902, in Wren, Ohio. Sue had a sister, Nancy, who taught over 40 years in Fort Wayne. She married John Webb in 1955, and they had one daughter, Janet, born March 14, 1961.

David married Norma Jane Bricker September 14, 1957. Daughter Cheryl Ann, was born March 12, 1959; Gregory Scott, born March 13, 1962; and Lisa Renee, born October 6, 1964. Norma Bricker Trainer was born in Muncie, January 1. 1938. Her father, Charles Bricker, from Wabash, moved to Fort Wayne in the early 1940s. Norma has a sister, Betty (Riley) Bricker, and brothers Dale Bricker and Calvin Bricker of Fort Wayne. Norma's mother was Buelah Lehman Bricker of Fort Wayne. Cheryl Trainer graduated from Indiana University. Greg and Lisa Trainer graduated from Purdue. David and Norma were affiliated with the First Assembly of God Church, Fort Wayne.

Dean Trainer died February 1968. Stuart, David, and Doris took over the business and changed the name to Trainer Service Center, Inc. Business flourished for many years thereafter. Doris Trainer died in 1981. They had 48 years of business, dealing honestly and with integrity with the public. Stuart and David sold the property in February 1997 and closed the business.

Submitted by David D. Trainer

CHARLES TAYLOR & IZORA (JOHNSON) TREVEY

On a farm in Pleasant Center Township of Allen County, Charles Taylor Trevey, a son of John Joseph and Mary Velma (Snider) Trevey, was bom December 23, 1861, and grew to adulthood. Meanwhile, Izora Johnson started life September 21, 1869, on a farm bordering the Allen-Wells County Line Road.

Of Izora's childhood little is known, except that her father built a dolly cradle for her and that she and her immediate family lived near many Johnson relatives in the southwest corner of Allen County. During her early years, grandparents Noah and Sarah (Thomas) Johnson were next-door neighbors. Great-grandmother Rebecca (Baxter) Johnson lived only one mile away. With Johnson farms sprinkled throughout the area, Izora was rich in relatives. However, before she was ten, her parents, Emmitt Enos and Emma Catherine (Smetzer) Johnson, moved to the Village of Sheldon.

It so happened that Charles Taylor Trevey also went to Sheldon and taught school there. He and Izora met and married on September 4, 1887. Their first son, Sylva Clayton, was born in Sheldon. Izora was expecting a second baby when tragedy struck: Sylva died suddenly and was buried in the Old Ossian Cemetery. Four months later, on May 24, 1890, Ralph Emerson Trevey was born.

By then, Izora's parents had moved from Sheldon to Fort Wayne. Charles and Izora, with little Ralph, followed their example. Another son, Gail, was born on November 23, 1897. For the first time there were two little boys in the home, but for less than two years. Gail choked on the sheath of a hickory nut and, in spite of surgical efforts to save his life, died September 19, 1899.

This heartbreaking event turned Charles to alcohol. Then, on November 29, 1899, Mary Catherine, their only daughter, was born prematurely. She weighed one and one-half pounds. For six weeks, in the room with the base burner, family members, including Grandma Mary Trevey, carried the baby on a pillow, because she seemed too fragile to hold any other way. The tender care worked and the infant prospered.

However, more sorrow was in store for Charles and Izora. On April 14, 1900, her thirteen-year-old brother, Ray, fell from his bicycle, was run over by a street car and died. Then, on September 24, 1901, Izora had a son who was stillborn. Her mother died in 1905 and her grandfather, Noah Johnson, in 1907.

Charles and Izora built a house at 921 Saint Mary's Avenue. From there she worked as a very skillful seamstress. Charles was employed by Standard Oil Company and Wayne Knitting Mills. Izora's excellent taste resulted in an attractively furnished home and her goal was the purchase of a piano for their daughter. On February 28, 1908, Izora suddenly collapsed and died. After her funeral, Ralph was sent to live with his Grandfather Emmitt, Mary Catherine was whisked away to Laketon to stay with Johnson relatives, and Charles went away "for the cure" of his alcoholism.

Charles Taylor and Izora (Johnson) Trevey, circa 1890

When he returned, Charles took Mary Catherine to live with his sister, Emma (Trevey) Moses, and her family on Taylor Street near Broadway. Every work day, Charles walked from there to the Wayne Knitting Mills and back again, saving the nickel streetcar fare until he had enough money to grant Izora's wish. He bought a brand new Packard Piano for Mary Catherine and she studied with Alma Miller. Years later, several descendants of Charles and Izora learned to play piano on that upright instrument.

On November 17, 1910, Charles and Mary Jane McDowell were married in Hillsdale, Michigan. He contracted tuberculosis and died October 24, 1919. Charles and Izora are buried in Lindenwood Cemetery, near two of their children and also near Izora's parents and siblings.

Izora Johnson's lineage goes back through Emmitt Enos, to Noah, to James, to Solomon Johnson's wife, Fanny Warne, whose father, Joseph Warne, fought in the American Revolution. Also, Izora's paternal grandmother, Sarah (Thomas) Johnson, traces through Enos Thomas to Seth Thomas and Martha Kirk, then through Martha to Joseph Kirk, to John Kirk (born 1660 at Alfreton in Derbyshire, England), and to Godfrey Kirk.

Submitted by Linda Sue Lauer

JOHN JOSEPH & MARY VELMA (SNIDER) TREVEY

John Joseph Trevey was the youngest of the six children of Jacob Trevey and Mary McCartney. Mary Velma Snider was the youngest of the eight children of Philip Snider and Nancy Dolman. The families owned adjoining farms in Botetourt County, Virginia, and when John Joseph was twenty and Mary Velma was eighteen, in November of 1846, they married.

This couple traveled from Virginia to Allen County, Indiana, in an ox-drawn covered wagon over corduroy roads. The trip occurred between the taking of the 1850 Census in the Western District of Botetourt County in mid-August and the death, on November 24, 1851, of the daughter they had named after Mary Velma.

It seems that Philip Snider may have encouraged his sister, Mary, and her husband, to join him in Allen County. Philip had walked here from Botetourt County, Virginia, in 1848. Later he walked back to Botetourt, purchased a team of horses, and brought two other sisters, Christina and Sarah, to Allen County. The three are listed together in Madison Township in the 1850 Census. Eventually, all of Philip's siblings, except one, moved to Indiana; and all but two of those chose Allen County.

The purchase of a farm in Pleasant Township by John Joseph and Mary Velma (Snider) Trevey was recorded on July 10, 1852. Their home still stands on Pleasant Center Road, but the logs have been covered with clapboards and additions have been made to the structure. The house is still occupied and the land is farmed.

Seven of their eight children were reared in the farmhouse. They were: John William, (little Mary Velma died before reaching her first birthday), James Lewis, Harvey Clark, Sarah Jane, Charles Taylor, Emma, and Benjamin Franklin. All were married and remained in the area. They gave a total of 18 grandchildren to their parents.

John Joseph and Mary Velma (Snider) Trevey, circa 1872

In 1867, John Joseph and Mary Velma Trevey sold "in consideration of one dollar" a half-acre of their land and a Disciples of Christ Church was built there. The church bordered the road; the farmhouse was far behind at the end of a long lane. On the other side of Pleasant Center Road, Mary Velma's sister, now Sarah (Snider) Fisher, and her husband allowed the construction of Pleasant Township School #6, a one-room school, which was used until the mid 1930s. Both the church and the school are now gone and the lands reverted to the heirs.

Of the death of John Joseph Trevey, it is said that he worked on his farm on December 15, 1874, came to the house for his noon meal, after which he stood up and dropped dead of a heart attack. Mary Velma was still living on the farm at the turn of the century. Her youngest son, Benjamin Franklin Trevey, his wife and their two children, were with her. At the time of her death, April 30, 1915, she was living with her daughter, Emma (Trevey) Moses, in Fort Wayne. Mary Velma was almost 88 years old. She had been a widow for 41 years, had watched three children die, and had only 11 of her 18 grandchildren still living.

John Joseph and Mary Velma (Snider) Trevey are buried in Williamsport Cemetery, Poe, Indiana, only a few miles from their farm.

Submitted by Helen May Wise

MELVIN EVERETT & PATRICIA ANN (FLOSENZIER) TREVEY FAMILY

Melvin Everett Trevey was born July 21, 1921, at 625 Huffman Street, Fort Wayne, Indiana to Albert Russell Trevey (born June 23, 1873, died November 17,1957) and Ethel Etta Knisely (born August 7,1892, died March 1, 1980). Ethel was born to David Scott Knisely and Mary Etta Martz in Allen County, Ohio. Albert married Ethel on January 25, 1911. They had a daughter Georgia Evelyn Trevey (born January 17, 1915, died October 19, 1991) who did not marry and had no children.

About 1922, Melvin's family built and moved to a new house at 1628 Barthold Street. Albert and his cousin Frank Fisher built a garage for the Treveys' first automobile, an Overland Touring Car, replaced by a new 1925 Overland Sedan. The Treveys bought a 40 acre farm at 11003 Illinois Road. Albert took a leave of absence for health reasons from General Electric and they lived on the farm from May to August in 1926. Albert loved farm life and Melvin recalls many pleasant and interesting events the short time they lived there. The Treveys moved back to Fort Wayne to a new house at 3919 Fairfield Avenue, due to the Illinois Road being paved. Albert was laid off from GE during the Great Depression. Ethel took in laundries, working hard and long to keep things going. Ethel was a great cook and the family ate well during the Depression. Albert

1949. First row: William Everett Trevey, Second Row: Patricia Ann Flosenzier Trevey, Melvin Everett Trevey

worked at General Electric 23 and a half years, retiring in 1938.

Albert Russell Trevey was born to John William Trevey and Rachel C. Fell. John William Trevey was born October 16, 1847, in Botecourt County,Virginia, to John Joseph Trevey (born March 17, 1826, died December 15, 1874) and Mary Velma Snider (born May 18, 1828, died April 30, 1915). Rachel C. Fell (born June 4, 1846) to John Christian Fell (born in Sindringen, Wurttemberg, Germany, on September 22, 1811, died March18, 1897) and Elizabeth Harris (born 1826, died December 19, 1895).

John Christian Fell came to Cleveland, Ohio, about 1833 and eventually to Allen County, Indiana. The John Joseph Treveys, in 1850-51, with their young son John William, traveled over corduroy roads in an ox-drawn wagon to Allen County, Indiana. In 1852, the Treveys bought 160 acres on Pleasant Center Road, Pleasant Township, Allen County. John William Trevey operated a tile mill on or near the farm

On September 8, 1903, John W. and Rachel C. Trevey purchased the brick house and lot known as 426 West Fourth Street, Fort Wayne, Indiana, which was their last residence. The abstract for the property is a history in itself, with data from 1568. John W. died suddenly in his chair the evening of November 25, 1925. Rachel died in 1930.

John William and Rachel C. had two other sons, James Frederick Trevey (born December 5, 1870, died in 1946) and George M. Dallas (born October 8, 1876). In 1912, James F. married Lillie B. Liggett (1879-1966).

Melvin Everett Trevey graduated from Harrison Hill in 1934 and South Side in 1939. Melvin started employment at International Harvester Company's Fort Wayne plant in the cost department on July 17, 1939. He enlisted in the U. S. Army, 134th Ordnance Maintenance Battalion, 12th Armored Divison on July 20, 1942. After basic training at Camp Perry, Ohio, the unit moved to Camp Campbell, Kentucky. Melvin was sergeant major of the 134th and departed the U.S. for the European Theater on September 20, 1944, on a British ship, the Empress of Australia, which was captured in World War I from Germany. That ship sank shortly thereafter. The 12th Armored Division arrived in England, crossed the English Channel, and engaged in combat in France, Belgium, Holland and Germany, being a part of the Third and Seventh Armies. After the cessation of hostilities, Melvin transferred to the Production Control Unit, European Theater of Operations, and lived in the Grand Hotel, in Heidelberg, Germany. Melvin later discovered he was only 40 miles from his great-great-grandparents Fell farm. Melvin departed Europe at Bremerhaven, Germany, January 3, 1946, and arrived in the U.S.A. on January 16, 1946, and was honorably discharged from service at Camp Atterbury, Indiana, January 21, 1946. He returned to Fort Wayne and continued employment with International Harvester Company in February of 1946.

On August 3, 1946, Melvin married Patricia Ann Flosenzier (born September 27, 1925) in Indianapolis, Indiana. Patricia attended Harrison Hill School and graduated from South Side High School in 1943. During World War II, Patricia worked at the GE supercharger plant and was active in the USO. In 1945, Patricia graduated from M Dowel School of Design and lived in Greenwich Village, New York City.

William Everertt Trevey, their only child, was born May 28, 1947, at the Lutheran Hospital in Fort Wayne. William graduated from Ohio State University in 1971. William married Karen Ann Healy July 25, 1997, and they currently work and live in Huntsville, Alabama. They have no children.

Melvin and Patricia started marriage at 3919 Fairfield Avenue, and then moved to a new home at 4840 Bowser Avenue. In 1955, they built a new home at 1919 Sundown Lane on land purchased from Molley Trick. Patricia was secretary to Lester Grile, the superintendent of the Fort Wayne Community Schools. Melvin was promoted and transferred to the IH Springfield Plants, Springfield, Ohio, in 1960.

While in Springfield, the Treveys lived at 340 South Bird Road and 120 Ardmore Avenue. In 1963, they purchased a house at 2625 Casey Drive and lived there until Melvin retired from International Harvester as supervisor of internal control on October 28, 1978. During the 1970s they successfully showed Weimaraners in many different cities.

They moved to Fort Myers, Florida, their current residence, on July 27, 1981. Upon moving to Fort Myers, Melvin and Patricia joined the Fort Myers Track Club and Melvin ran many 5K and 10K road races. Melvin and Patricia also volunteered for seven years at the Fort Myers Community Hospital, Melvin as head of volunteers in the emergency room and Patricia as a patient representative. Patricia is a life member of the Women's Symphony Society and one of her highlights was chairperson of a luau, complete with fire & hula dancers, celebrating the 25th year of the Symphony Society. 400 people attended the gala affair under the stars.

Patricia is a member of the DAR. Melvin is a life member of the 12th Armored Division Association and Veterans of Foreign Wars Post 10097 and a member of the American Legion Post 247. Melvin was a member of the Dayton Chapter of Internal Auditors and the National Association of Accountants while working at IH in Ohio. Melvin and Patricia traveled extensively, seeing most of the states in the U.S. and for years vacationed at the Disney complex in Florida. In 1984 Melvin started a second career as a musician, playing keyboards at many gigs for dancing and listening, currently still performing in 2005.

Submitted by Melvin E. Trevey

TSULEFF FAMILY

Maria Tsuleff is a third generation American on her father's side of the family. Both sets of her great grandparents came from the area in Eastern Europe known as Macedonia.

War in Macedonia, left George Tsuleff's family in poverty and danger. He saw other members of his family killed in their own front yards. In 1915 he left his wife and two sons in Vishini, Macedonia and traveled by ship to New York City, and on to Fort Wayne where others from his village had already found success.

Upon his arrival, George lived with several other Macedonian men; communal living allowed them to save money to bring their families over. They worked at a traction (light) company factory. One by one they purchased businesses, such as groceries, bakeries, and restaurants.

George and Turpa (Prestonaras) Tsuleff

Spiro and Todorka (Spasov) Christ

Nicholas and Virginia (Christ) Tsuleff

Back: Scott and Jenny Tsuleff; Front: Maria, Brittany, Zachary

George purchased a grocery and meat market on the corner of Smith and Buchanan Streets. His wife, Turpa (nee Prestonaras), and sons Thomas (age 12) and Peter (age 10) came by ship in 1923, and they lived above the store. Nicholas George was born there in 1924. Peter died on May 31, 1932, from acute kidney disease. Thomas married and had three children; he died on November 21,

1945. Nicholas married Virginia Christ, daughter of Spiro and Todorka Spasov.

Spiro Christ, born 1882, was also from Vishini, the son of Krusto and Syltana Paliganoff. War and poverty forced his family to seek work outside Madedonia. Each year, Spiro, his father and brothers, went to Asia Minor to cut trees. When Spiro was fifteen, he refused to return home at the end of the job and never saw his family again. He worked his way to America, leaving on a ship from Constantinople (Istanbul), Turkey in 1906. He changed his name to Christ when he came to America. He eventually bought a bakery in Fort Wayne on South Clinton, and lived in a small apartment above the store.

Todorka Spasov, born September 21, 1897, to Demitre and Petra Spasov, came from Bulgaria to America to visit her sister in 1922. Her father was a chef for King Boris in Sophia, Bulgaria. During her visit, a marriage was arranged between her and Spiro Christ. After little courting, they were married in the home of her sister, Vasilka George, on Sandpoint Road on February 4, 1923. It ended up being quite a love match. Spiro died in November 23, 1957, at the age of 75. Todorka never remarried. She died in 1998 at the age of 101. They had three daughters: Eleanor (married Joseph Moricz), Virginia, and La Verne (married Alex Tsiguloff).

Virginia Christ married Nicholas Tsuleff on October 9, 1955, in Saint Nicholas Eastern Orthodox Church. They had two sons: Scott Christ, (born May 23, 1958) and Steven Christ (born June 19, 1962). Scott married Jenneth Crandall on August 15, 1982, in Fremont, Indiana. They had three children: Brittany Leigh (born 1985), Maria Elizabeth, the author of this piece (born 1987), and Zachary Crandall (born 1991). Scott was well known as a radio personality on WBCL and WMEE.

Submitted by Maria Tsuleff

LAURIE GENSHEIMER TUCCO

Laurie Gensheimer was born on January 4, 1961, in Allen County in Fort Wayne, Indiana. She was the third child born and has one older brother, David, one older sister, Debbie, one younger sister, Janine, one younger brother, Patrick. She truly experienced being the middle child. Her parents were Robert and Maurine (Hartman) Gensheimer. Maurine was an Allen County native and Bob moved here in January, 1955 from Bloomington, Illinois. Her parents are still residents of Allen County today. Laurie attended Ball State University and received her bachelor's degree in Fashion Merchandising and Marketing in 1983. She married Matthew Tucco on June 6, 1987, at St. Henry's Catholic Church in Fort Wayne. Matt and Laurie currently reside in Fishers, Indiana, with their two sons, Joseph and Nicholas. Matt is a business owner of Advanced Copy Products and Laurie sells residential real estate for her company, Tucco Realty. Laurie and her family enjoy coming back to Fort Wayne for family reunions and family gatherings. Laurie has a collection of wedding photos of her relatives on display in her foyer. She would like to submit this photo and newspaper article of her great-grandmother, Frances Schmidt. Here is the wedding announcement that was published in The Fort Wayne *Daily News* on Wednesday, February 6, 1907:

Matt, Laurie, Nicky & Joey Tucco

Frances Schmidt in her wedding gown

"This morning at 9 o'clock St. Peter's Catholic Church was the scene of a very pretty wedding ceremony. The Reverend Fathers Delaney and Mungovan, of St. Patrick's Church officiating. The bride was beautiful in her dainty wedding gown, a white lace robe over ivory white taffeta. The veil which enveloped the costume was caught on the coiffure by a cluster of swansonia. The bride was attended by Miss Elizabeth Ahern, who wore a pretty toilet of white silk. She carried a cluster of bride roses. The groomsman was Mr. George Sarrazen. The many friends of the bride and groom were ushered to their seats by Messrs. Jefferson Delagrange, Edward Reinhart and Louis Otten. As the bridal party entered the wedding march from Lohengrin was played, and for the recessional the Mendelssohn march was played. Immediately after the wedding ceremony the bridal party were served breakfast at the future home of the couple, 1913 Hanna Street. The groom is a son of Mr. J. H. Hartman, the well known South Hanna Street grocer."

Clem Hartman, Laurie's great-grandfather and husband of Frances Schmidt, started out as a bookkeeper in his father's grocery business. He later ran the store. Clem owned property around town. Frances outlived Clem by almost 40 years, and continued to collect rent after his death. She received rent money from Wolf and Dessauer's warehouse, on the corner of Washington and Clinton Streets, until 1965, when she sold it. She never had a traditional job, but made a living off of the rent money that she collected from her various properties around town.

Submitted by Debra Wolfe

CLAIR & ANITA (VONDERAU) TUSTISON FAMILY

On September 26, 1936, Anita Vonderau and Clair Tustison said their vows in St. Peter's Lutheran Church, 7710 East State Blvd, with Rev. Henry Abram officiating. At the time of their marriage both were working, Anita at Brewer Motors Inc. of New Haven as a bookkeeper, and Clair as a salesman for John Wilding Paper Company. Clair soon took a new job with John Wilding that caused the family, who had deep roots in Allen County, to move across the state to Fulton County, Indiana. The couple settled in Rochester where they had three children: Joan Sue on June 9, 1938, Gary Von on May 23, 1941, and Kaye Lyn on April 15, 1943. Clair continued to do well in his sales job and the family soon moved to DeKalb County, Indiana. There, in Garrett, Anita gave birth to their last child, Neil Ray on April 20, 1946.

Anita Eleanor Susan Vonderau was the first of three children born to Jacob Heinrich Albert, known as Albert, and Eleanor, nee Proschel, Vonderau in Thurman, Allen County, Indiana, on March 06, 1912. Anita grew up as the elder daughter on the family farm, which was nestled among the farms of her uncles and grandparents. She had a wonderful childhood, learning all about animal husbandry, as well as how to manage a house. Anita grew up in the heady days of the twenties and learned the advantages of a farm community during the early thirties.

Clair was the fourth child born to Vere Courtney and Ada Mae, nee Humbarger, Tustison. Clair was born on January 10, 1913, in New Haven. This was the year of the big Maumee River flood. He had an older sister, two older brothers and a younger sister, all of whom were born in New Haven. Clair grew up in the city, where his father was the clerk-treasurer, and along with his older brothers enjoyed the advantages of the small city lifestyle.

Anita and Clair Tustison

Anita and Clair both graduated from New Haven High School where Clair and his brother, Lyle, were a part of the 1929-30 Allen County championship basketball team. This team won the third straight Allen County Championship for the Bulldogs of New Haven, and they became the first county school to beat a Fort Wayne city team. Clair also played the male lead in the three-act senior comedy "Sunshine Lane". After high school Anita attended and graduated from the International Business College in Fort Wayne.

Clair became manager of the Millcraft Paper Company in Fort Wayne and the family moved back to that city in 1946. The children were raised in Fort Wayne. Clair died on February 10, 1952, at age 39. He is buried in the IOOF Cemetery in New Haven. Anita raised the children by herself, working primarily at the Millcraft Paper Company. Anita died February 15, 1994, at age 81. She is buried in the IOOF cemetery next to Clair.

Submitted by Gary V. Tustison

CYRUS AND SARAH (ACTON) TUSTISON FAMILY

Cyrus and Sarah, nee Acton, Tustison were married by Reverend M. Layman in Allen County on December 29, 1863. Sebastian Tustison, Cyrus' uncle, a famous hunting guide in Indiana and Ohio, was a witness to this marriage. Interestingly, both Cyrus and Sarah were born in Morrow County, Ohio. Sarah was born September 6, 1843, and still lived in Morrow County at the time of their marriage. Cyrus was born September 20, 1837, but his family had moved to Defiance County, Ohio, when he was seven years old. Cyrus' family moved again, in 1861, to Allen County, Indiana, when Cyrus was a strapping twenty-three year old. At twenty-five, Cyrus was married and supported his family primarily by his carpentry work, but also by helping farmers during planting and harvesting.

Cyrus Tustison.

Cyrus and Sarah had eight children, all born in Allen County:

Margaret Ellen born January 13, 1865, married John W. Harrington June 2, 1887.

Mary Catherine born May 15, 1869, married Herschel A. Long January 27, 1890.

John Gabriel born October 1, 1871, married Hattie (Harriett) Guebard February 3, 1897.

Oliver Acton born October 27, 1874, married Iva H. Peeper.

Lee Adrian born April 22, 1878, married Katie Ethel Hatfield December 25, 1918.

Bertha Maude born October 11, 1881, married Byron Thimlar May 15, 1900.

Vere Courtney born January 23, 1885, married Ada Mae Humbarger September 11, 1907.

William Nelson born December 27, 1886; do not know of a marriage.

Cyrus' father, Nelson Tustison Jr., was the second child of Nelson Sr. He was born in Philadelphia, Pennsylvania, and came west to Crawford County, Ohio, with his mother, father, uncle, and three brothers in 1817, at the tender age of five. Cyrus' mother, Useby Phoebe Cox, was raised in Crawford County, Ohio, on a farm near the Tustison Farm. The Tustison and Cox families became very close, with three Tustison brothers marrying three Cox sisters!

Cyrus died on March 13, 1888, leaving Sarah with four children under ten years of age. Sarah was a loving mother, who single-handedly raised all of the children and lived to see them grow up. Two of her children passed away before her; Mary died in childbirth at age thirty-one, and John died at twenty-nine years of age. Sarah passed away on February 19, 1918.

Submitted by Neil Tustison

NELSON JR. & USEBY (COX) TUSTISON FAMILY

Nelson Tustison Jr. and Useby, nee Cox, were married on July 20, 1834, in Crawford County, Ohio. Both families were farmers and lived near each other in Crawford County. The families were very close, with three Tustison brothers marrying three Cox sisters. Both families had moved into North-Central Ohio between 1818 and 1825, so they had established profitable farms by the 1830s.

Nelson's mother, Jane, nee Brown, Tustison was born in Philadelphia on October 26, 1790, of English parents. Nelson's father, Nelson Tustison Sr., was born in 1786. The earliest document concerning Nelson Sr., is a Seaman's Protection paper signed on May 12, 1809. This was a certificate issued to United States seamen to prove they were United States citizens if stopped by a British warship at sea.

A Lutheran minister married Jane and Nelson Sr. on August 11, 1810. Nelson Jr., the couple's second child, was born on September 12, 1812. The Philadelphia City Directory of 1813 lists Nelson Sr.'s occupation as "catgut maker," so it appears he left the sea to settle down. This was a busy time in Philadelphia, as well as the fledging United States, and Nelson Sr. enlisted in the Pennsylvania Volunteers on Sept. 8, 1814, to defend Philadelphia from British invaders.

Soon after the peace, Nelson Sr., who had shown he was an accomplished sailor, soldier, and musician, decided it was time to move west, away from the crowded city. The Tustison family, which had now grown to five children, four boys and a baby girl, along with the family of Jane's brother, Joseph Brown, started out for Ohio in 1818.

Useby's parents were married in Coshocton County, Ohio. John Martin Cox emigrated from Germany, but his future wife, Rebecca Hull, was already living in Coshocton County when he arrived. After their marriage, and some time after the Nelson Tustison family had arrived in Crawford County, John and Rebecca Cox bought their farmland in Crawford County.

Nelson Jr. and Useby spent the first ten years of their marriage farming in Crawford County, near their parents. Their first child, Delilah, was born on November 11, 1835, Cyrus entered the world on September 20, 1837, and Oliver was born on April 7, 1840. Nelson Sr. passed away on August 30, 1841 and was buried in the family graveyard in Crawford County.

The family of Nelson and Useby continued to grow with the birth of their second girl, Alvira, on October 28, 1841. By 1844, Nelson Jr. and Useby determined they needed a larger farm and moved to Defiance County, Ohio. The family spent the next seventeen years in the Hicksville area. They didn't realize it at the time, but they became a magnet for the some of the younger Tustison brothers. Approximately one year after they moved, Washington Tustison, who married Useby's sister, Catherine Cox, in Crawford County, Ohio, in 1845, moved nearby to the southeastern corner of DeKalb County, Indiana. On January 20, 1847, Charles William, the couple's fifth child, was born. In 1849, Charles Tustison, who married Useby's sister, Sarah, in 1835 in Crawford County, moved to Defiance County, Ohio.

The growth of the Tustison families in Defiance County, Ohio, and DeKalb County, Indiana, continued into 1849, when Sebastian Tustison, moved his family to DeKalb County, Indiana. Now all four brothers lived very close to each other, and did so for some time.

Useby gave birth to Mathias M., the couple's sixth child on July 8, 1852. Their first child, Delilah married Hezekiah Loveland in 1854 and started farming just down the road in Scipio Township, Allen County, Indiana. Useby gave birth to a son, John, on April 5, 1855. Nelson and Useby experienced their first loss of a child when Charles William, then ten years old, died on August 10, 1857. Three years later Useby gave birth to the couple's last child, Bertha, on April 12, 1860.

In April of 1861, Nelson bought the Southeast fractional quarter of Section 2, Township 30, Range 13, equal to about 100 acres, from James and William S. Reid. The family moved soon after to Adams Township, Allen County, Indiana where Nelson and Useby lived until their deaths.

In 1872-1873, a series of tragedies struck the Nelson Tustison family. Their son Oliver's first daughter, three-month-old Ina A. died in April 1872. Twenty-year-old Mathias, their sixth child, died on October 3 of that year and four months later, on February 7, 1873, thirty-one year old Alvira, their fourth child, died. Useby died on February 15, 1873. On February 21, 1873, just six days after his wife and 12 days after his daughter, Alvira, Nelson Jr. died. The inscription on the obelisk at the family gravesite in the IOOF Cemetery in New Haven reads: "Our Father, Mother & Sister are gone, They lay beneath the sod, Dear parents though we miss you much, We know you rest with God."

Submitted by Gail Robinson

VERE COURTNEY & ADA MAE (HUMBARGER) TUSTISON FAMILY

Vere Courtney and Ada Mae, nee Humbarger, were married by Reverend J.L. Hutchins on September 11, 1907, at the home of Vere's mother in New Haven. Vere was a New Haven boy born on January 23, 1885, the seventh child of Cyrus and Sarah, nee Acton, Tustison. Ada was also a Hoosier, born on January 8, 1886, in DeKalb County, Indiana. She was the second child of Charles Peter and Alma M., nee Elsea, Humbarger. Ada's family moved to Hicksville, Ohio, when she was six years old. Ada graduated from Hicksville High School, and soon after came to work in New Haven, where she met Vere and fell in love. At the time of their marriage, Vere was a wood turner at the local baseball bat manufacturing company. About eight years into their marriage, Vere won his first election as New Haven Clerk-Treasurer, a position he held for the next 27 years.

Vere and Ada had a loving home and raised five children in New Haven, three boys, sandwiched by two girls. Bertha Mildred, their first child, was born on July 9, 1908. Norbert Lynn was born on April 21, 1910, followed by Forest Lyle on June 26, 1911, and Clair Vaughn on January 10, 1913. Glenna Mae, the baby of the family, was born on September 5, 1926. All three boys played basketball and during their tenure the New Haven Bulldogs won the Allen County Championship three years in a row. Glenna attended all the games and became the family cheerleader.

Ada and Vere Tustison

Vere Tustison had deep roots in Allen County. His grandparents, Useby Phoebe, nee Cox, and Nelson Tustison Jr., came to Adams Township, Allen County in 1861 from Defiance County, Ohio. Vere's father, Cyrus, though born in Morrow County, Ohio, came with the family to Indiana. He was twenty-three when he moved, and it was in Allen County that he met and married Sarah Acton.

The young Vere Tustison family first lived in a homestead "between the railroad tracks" in New Haven, just down the street from Cyrus and Sarah. As things improved, they moved to South Street and finally, in 1918, after the war, to the house on Green Street.

Vere enjoyed playing the guitar for the New Haven Band and through this became active in other community affairs. He backed into politics when he was asked to be the recorder for the town of New Haven because of his good handwriting. As the town grew, Vere became the Clerk-Treasurer (an elected position) and the unofficial "Mayor" of New Haven. This meant he was responsible for making sure that everything needing to get done got done. He became involved with everything that needed a boost, but the thing he was most proud of was helping to start the library. He held the job of Clerk-Treasurer for so long that, in 1942, the Democratic Party told him the job was his for life!

Vere died on December 23, 1943. Ada died on March 18, 1960. Both Vere and Ada are buried in the IOOF Cemetery in New Haven.

Submitted by Holly Snodgrass

FRANK M. UEBER FAMILY

Frank Michael Ueber was born in Herbolzheim, Germany, on October 5, 1862, to Franz Karl and Anastacia (Lamminger) Ueber. When he was nine years old, he, his parents, and his twelve-year-old brother, Joseph, came to America aboard the S. S. Rhein and arrived in New York on March 25, 1872. They settled on a farm in Noble County, Indiana, near the town of Ege. At that time, Franz Karl's brother, Ludwig, his wife, Amelia (Pfister) Ueber, and children were living in the nearby Avilla area.

On November 23, 1882, Frank married Magdalena Gramlich in the Immaculate Conception Catholic Church in Ege, Indiana. They lived for the next 24 years in Noble County, Indiana. They raised eleven children: John D., Julia (Emma), Charles, Herman, Anthony, Anna, Rose, Lawrence, Joseph A., Isabel, and Alma.

In 1907, the family moved to a two-story home at 2522 Oliver Street in Fort Wayne, Indiana, so the older boys could find work. They were members of St. Peter's Catholic Church and the younger children went to that parish's grade school. Frank worked at various jobs at the Pennsylvania Company and S. F. Bowser Company. Magdalena died in 1920 at the age of 52. Frank lived at the Oliver Street home until 1934, after which he lived with his son, Lawrence, and wife, Marie.

In his retirement years, he sharpened lawnmowers and spent many summers at the Sylvan Lake summer home of his son, John, and wife.

John D. married Rosa Bender. In the mid 1920s he became president of Hercules Coal Company on Miner Street.

Julia E. married Charles J. Freiburger. He was in the furnace and sheet metal business and also served as Allen County Commissioner. They raised thirteen children.

Charles worked at Fort Wayne Electric Company and General Electric and married Esther Minnich. They raised nine children.

Herman worked as a baker and married Julia Alter. They had five children.

Anthony (Tony) was a Fort Wayne policeman and married Angela Kiep. They raised three children.

Anna worked for a candy company as a young girl, married James A. Basil, and lived in Chicago. They had two children.

Seated: Rose, Frank M., Alma, Magdalena, and Julia; Standing: Anna, Charles, Lawrence, Isabel, John, Joseph, Anthony, and Herman Ueber.

Rose became a nurse, graduating in the first nursing class of St. Joseph Hospital, where she worked. She married John McCarthy. They had one daughter.

Lawrence was a public accountant. He married Marie Weidner. He enjoyed deer hunting in Michigan with brothers, Tony and Joe, as well as fishing on Indiana lakes.

Joseph A. was a salesman for Fort Wayne Dairy Equipment Company and married Marie Blank. They raised three children. The family spent summer weekends at their cottage on Lake of the Woods in Lagrange County. They enjoyed ice fishing and ice skating there in the winter.

Isabel married Jacob (Jack) Renner and died at the early age of 21.

Alma married Thomas Sanders, who died in 1932. Her second husband, Carl Marx, was an attorney, and they lived in Chicago.

Frank Michael Ueber died in 1940 at the age of 77. He and Magdalena are buried in the Catholic Cemetery, Fort Wayne, Indiana, as are all their children, with the exception of Anna and Alma, who are buried in Chicago, Illinois.

Submitted by Stephen Ueber

EDWARD J. & DOROTHY MAY BLAIR UHL FAMILY

Edward J. Uhl was the third child in a family of nine children born to John and Johana Sophia Puchta Uhl. Edward (aka E.J.) was born on March 14, 1878, in Delphos, Ohio. His father, John, had been born in Germany; his mother, Sophia, was born in Venedocia, Ohio. John and Sophia were married July 30, 1872. Their first five children, John, Margaret, Edward J., Henry Louis, and Frank Joseph were born in Delphos, Ohio. Their next four children, Kathryn, Annie Elizabeth, Albert, and Mary Frances, were born in Venedocia, Ohio.

When he was 26-years old, Edward married Dorothy May Blair (June 1, 1904). Edward and his brother, Henry, ran a grocery store in Venedocia, Ohio, until approximately 1911. During this time, four children were born to Edward and Dorothy – Lester, Gilbert, Margaret, and Marvin. In 1911, Edward moved his growing family to Pennfield, Michigan, where daughter, Pauline was born. Then a job on the Nickle Plate Railroad brought the family to Fort Wayne, Indiana, about 1918, where twins, Gerald and Geraldine

Edward J. and Dorothy May Blair Wedding Picture

Edward J. Uhl

were born. Edward worked for the railroad until 1929, sold insurance for a few years, and then worked at Allied Feed Mills until his retirement.

The family was quite musically inclined. Edward played the mandolin, Dorothy played the pump organ. Lester became a full-time musician playing piano and organ with the Earl Gardner Band in Fort Wayne. Pauline and Geraldine played piano and organ and also sang for church and family activities. Marvin played the harmonica and Hohner button accordion. The family lived at 738 Runnion Avenue and many of the family members worked within walking distance of their home (Allied Mills, Fort Wayne Knitting Mills, and Fort Wayne Tailoring Co.). Often family members would bring friends home over lunch periods and everyone would enjoy singing and instrumental music.

Dorothy died unexpectedly in 1931. Edward continued to live on Runnion Avenue until his death in 1958.

His daughter, Pauline and husband, Dick Gillie, lived in the house on Runnion Ave. until Pauline's death in 1980. They had one daughter, Patricia Gillie Piper, who now lives in Peru, Indiana.

Geraldine married Warren Hockaday; they lived in Chicago, Garrett, and retired in Wisconsin. Their one son, Michael, is a teacher in Fort Wayne Community Schools. He is an excellent musician and is a member of the Junk Yard Band.

Gerald married Mable Springer. They had two daughters – LuAnn Uhl Nash and Barbara Uhl Stanski, both living in Fort Wayne. Gerald and Mable lived on Indiana Ave.; he retired from General Electric Co.

Lester never married.

Margaret lived in Cleveland for many years. She married William Rahn and they later moved to Florida. They had no children.

Marvin married Helen Koppenhofer and they had two daughters and one son. Marvin worked for Fort Wayne Tailoring Co. until it went out of business. Their daughters are Mary Ellen Uhl Day, who lives on the Wells/Allen County Line, close to Zanesville, and Betty Lou Uhl Knox Barry, who lives in Fort Wayne. Their son, Edward Jay, is deceased.

Submitted by Mary E. Day

Edward Uhl and his family – 1953 Pauline, Margaret, Lester, Edward J., Gerald, Geraldine, Marvin

MARVIN & HELEN KOPPENHOFER UHL

On January 20, 1910, Marvin Edward Uhl was born in Venedocia, Ohio, to Edward J. and Dorothy May Blair Uhl. Marvin was the fourth child in the family. Around 1913, Ed took a job on the railroad, which brought the family to Fort Wayne, Indiana. Their home at 738 Runyan Street was where Marvin and his brothers grew up.

Marvin's family was quite musically inclined and Marvin taught himself to play the harmonica and the Hohner button accordion. As a teen-ager, he would frequently play his harmonica as he rode the bus around town. His sisters would sit in another part of the bus so no one would know Marvin was their brother.

Around 1929, Marvin met a girl at a dance at Trier Park. Her name was Helen Emma Koppenhofer and she had come to Fort Wayne from her family home in Ohio, working at the Dudlo Plant. They were married in 1932. Marvin worked as an order marker, cutter, and pattern maker at the Fort Wayne Tailoring Company, until it closed in the mid 1960s.

Marvin and Helen Uhl Wedding Picture

Mary Ellen, Eddie, Betty Lou Uhl in 1943

While the family lived on Anderson Avenue, three children were born: Mary Ellen, 1935; Elizabeth Louise (Betty Lou), 1937; Edward Jay (Eddie), 1942. The family then moved to 4540 Avondale Drive, and in 1947, moved to 3112 Smith Street.

Shortly after Eddie's birth, he was diagnosed with Downes Syndrome. It was estimated by doctors he would have a short life span, perhaps 18 years. Eddie was a happy, healthy child and Helen was a stay-at-home mother who took good care of her family. When the "Johnny Appleseed School" was established, Eddie was one of the first students registered. Helen took him to school and brought him home each day, traveling by bus. The Appleseed School later changed to the Association for Retarded Citizens (ARC). Eddie worked at the ARC Workshop until his death at age 54.

Mary Ellen married Melvin Day and they have four sons: Mark Alan, 1956; Michael Eugene, 1957; Matthew Lynn, 1959; and Mitchell Dean, 1965. Mary Ellen and Mel, Michael's family, and Matthew's family all presently live in Wells County near Zanesville, Mark and his family live south of Joliet, Illinois, and Mitchell and his wife live just outside of Detroit, Michigan.

Betty Lou married James Knox and has two sons: Charles Eugene, 1957, and David Ryan, 1959. Betty Lou and James Knox were divorced and she married Theodore Barry in 1977. They have had a counseling business in downtown Fort Wayne. Chuck and David both have businesses in Fort Wayne; David and his family live in Leo.

Marvin provided accordion music at the weddings of several of his grandsons. He died in 1980. Helen and Eddie moved to an apartment shortly after his death. The two of them rode the bus and walked wherever they wanted to go, contributing to their good health for many years. Eddie died at age 54 in 1996, and Helen died at age 96 in 1998.

Submitted by Betty Barry

HARRY & BLANCHE UNDERWOOD FAMILY

Harry Ben Underwood was born February 24, 1887, in Butler County, Ohio, to Daniel Edwin Underwood and Mary Ann Smith. Blanche Underwood was born on December 3, 1896 to Nettie Lyons and Carl Fritz in Milton, Indiana. Harry and Blanche were married on June 24, 1914 in Fort Wayne, Indiana. They raised their children as follows in Fort Wayne:

1. Benjamin Leon, born August 16, 1916, died January 17, 2002 in New York City.

2. Alice May, born July 15, 1918, married Everett Morning on October 1, 1935. Everett died February 13, 1967. Married, second, Ralph Hageman June 18, 1984, died February 24, 1991. The children of Everett and Alice are: Marjorie Mae, born July 2, 1936, died October 30, 1937 of spinal meningitis; James A., born November 28, 1938; Mary Alice, born May 16, 1940; Ronald A., born May 10, 1942; Jerome A., born September 11, 1943; Judith A., born September 22, 1947, and Barbara A., born January 23, 1949.

3. Mary Jane, born May 10, 1921, married Robert Palmer, died February 24, 2003. They had two daughters, Sandra, born February 7, 1947, and Cheryl, born August 5, 1953.

4. Charles Edward, born July 25, 1923, married Delores June Wills March 6, 1943. The children of Charles and June are: Suzanne, born March 20, 1945; Bonnie Mae, born August 1, 1946; June Ellen, born September 4, 1947; Richard Charles, born June 23, 1953; Thomas Edward, born September 13, 1957; and Lori Beth, born February 3, 1970.

5. Hugh Franklin, born December 21, 1925, married Shirley Heffelfinger on November 25, 1959. The children of Hugh and Shirley are: Cathy Lynn, born September 6, 1961; Scott Paul, born November 18, 1962; Hugh Brian, born May 13, 1964; and Sue Ann, born August 21, 1965.

Harry and Blanche Underwood

6. Nina Ruth, born May 14, 1928, married William Hoover on March 21, 1946. Their children are: William Lynn, born July 15, 1947; Ruth Ann, born December 13, 1948; Marcia, born July 17, 1950; Linda, born November 22, 1952; Thomas, born June 6, 1956; Karen, born July 24, 1957; Susan, born December 17, 1959; and David, born April 24, 1960.

7. Harry Wayne, born August 11, 1930, died September 16, 1930.

8. Paul Eugene, born September 15, 1931, married Victoria Turpchinoff on June 7, 1953, died June 24, 2001. The children of Paul and Victoria are: Steven Lawrence, born April 14, 1954; Thomas Alan, born October 25, 1956; John William, born August 25, 1959; James Edward, born September 27, 1961; Paul Michael, born March 16, 1967.

9. Lois Ann, born May 26, 1933, married Donald Yoder.

10. Jeanice Pearl, born December 7, 1937, married David Irvene on June 7, 1986. Her children from a previous marriage: Carmen, born June 21, 1957; Tina Hayden, born May 22, 1965; and Dennis Hayden, born January 1, 1967

Harry Underwood died November 11, 1965, and Blanche died May 16, 1987, in Fort Wayne, Indiana. They are buried in Praire Grove Cemetery along with their infant son, Harry Wayne, and their son, Benjamin Leon. Harry worked for General Electric for over forty years. He was a member of the National Guard, and served in the Mexican Conflict in 1918.

Submitted by Shirley Underwood

KONRAD MORBECK LARS & SARA LYNN (AYRES) URBERG FAMILY

Konrad Morbeck Lars Urberg was born October 29, 1971, in Fort Wayne, Indiana to S.S. and Patricia Haraldson Urberg. S.S. and Patricia moved to Fort Wayne in 1970 to serve Bethany Lutheran Church on Engle Road. S.S. retired from Bethany after 26 years. Konrad has three sisters: Dagny of Freeport, Illinois, who is married to Thompson Brandt; Ingrid of Camrose, Alberta, Canada; and Ragna of Fort Wayne. Dagny and Thompson Brandt have two children, Kristin and Carsten.

Sara Lynn Ayres was born November 29, 1971 in Fort Wayne, Indiana, to Donald Allen Ayres and Kathleen Johnson Ayres. Donald was born and raised in Fort Wayne. He is the President and owner of Don Ayres Pontiac, Inc. Kathleen moved to Fort Wayne from Lima, Ohio, in 1941 as an infant. She is a retired Fort Wayne Community Schools teacher. Her parents, Michael Thomas and Kathryn Sealts Johnson, relocated to Fort Wayne for Michael to work in advertising for *The Journal-Gazette*. Kathleen has five siblings: Michael Thomas (Tom,) Robert, Brice, Joan, and Jeannette (Kandy). Sara has one sister, Alison Kay, of Fort Wayne, who is married to Mark Birkmeier. She is a teacher at Bunche Montessori School. Mark is a civil engineer with Primco. They have a son, Paul Alexander.

Konrad and Sara married June 7, 1997, at Saint Paul's Lutheran Church on Barr Street. Sara and Konrad graduated from Concordia Lutheran High School, where they met. Konrad graduated from Luther College in Decorah, Iowa, and Indiana University School of Law. He is an attorney at Christoff and Christoff Attorneys. Sara graduated from Duke University and The Krannert Graduate School of Management at Purdue University. She also graduated from the NADA Dealer Candidate Academy. Sara is Vice President of Don Ayres Pontiac-GMC-Honda which her father, Donald, founded in 1970. Sara and Konrad have a daughter, Kristina Caroline, born November 6, 2002. They are members of Saint Paul's Lutheran Church and live in Aboite Township.

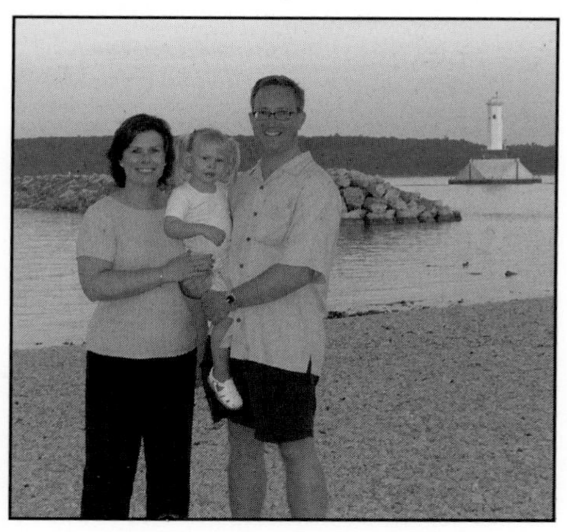

Konrad, Sara, and Kristina Caroline Urberg

Sara's ancestors on her father's side have a fairly long history in Allen County. Donald Ayres' great grandfather, George Welker, came to Fort Wayne from Baltimore, Maryland, around 1870. He was a furniture maker. George married Lillian Friday and had a son, George H. in 1886. George H. had a sister, Ada. George H. was a watch maker and later a foreman at General Electric. He married Esther Gick and had a daughter, Ada Minnie Lillian, May 28, 1928. Ada had two siblings: Paul and Geraldine. Ada married Paul Franklin Ayres. They had a son, Donald Allen, April 1, 1943. Donald has a brother, Paul, Jr. Donald Ayres' paternal grandfather, Asa Ayres, came to Fort Wayne from Virginia in 1908 to work on the Pennsylvania Railroad. He married Ethel Jones, who was from Pleasant Mills, Indiana. They had a son, Paul Franklin Ayres, on June 11, 1911. Paul had four siblings: Carl, George, Virginia, and Arlie. Paul worked in the engineering department of International Harvester for 44 years.

Submitted by Sara Urberg

SAMUEL & IDA VAN BUSKIRK FAMILY

Samuel Orien Van Buskirk was born on his family's farm on December 31, 1881 in Madison Township, Allen County. His parents were John W. and Matilda E. (Edwards) Van Buskirk. Samuel's grandfather, Jacob, first came to northern Indiana from Carroll County, Ohio, in 1848 and settled in Adams County. Samuels's father, John W., moved to Madison Township, Allen County in 1866 to be raised by relatives after the death of his father, Jacob. The family can trace their genealogy back to Laurens Andriesen Van Buskirk, who emigrated from Holland and settled in New Amsterdam (New York) in 1654.

Samuel and Ida Van Buskirk, children: Loyd, Helen and Mary

Ida Sophia Bitner was born on April 13, 1881, on her family's farm in Adams County. Her parents, Herman and Louisa Bitner (Buettner), were German Lutheran immigrant farmers.

Samuel and Ida first met at a barn dance and were later married on March 20, 1903, at the Methodist Church in Monroeville. They had three children: Loyd Franklin, Helen Louise, and Mary Matilda.

Samuel was a talented individual and moved his family around a lot due to his talent at refurbishing older homes. He also built several homes in Fort Wayne and Monroeville. His first job was as an engineer/conductor for the Interurban Belt Line. This was the line that went between Warsaw, Fort Wayne, and Lima, Ohio. He was a trained barber and barbered periodically throughout his life. He was a photographer for a short period of time in Ossian. He also ran the Van's Home Store and the Van's Grocery Store both in Monroeville. He always believed that you had to take a chance in order to be successful in life.

Loyd Van Buskirk graduated from the Indianapolis School of Embalming in 1928. During his life he worked as an embalmer at the Scheuman, Van Buskirk, and Schanee Funeral Homes. He also worked at the Van's Home Store and the Van's Shoe Store, in Monroeville.

Helen Van Buskirk graduated from Ball State Teacher's College in 1933. She first worked as a teacher in a one-room schoolhouse near the Fort Wayne airport. She then worked at Monroeville School as a first grade teacher. Later in life, she was instrumental in starting the first kindergarten in Monroeville. She also worked at the Van's Home Store in Monroeville.

Mary Van Buskirk graduated from the Fort Wayne International Business College in 1935. She first started a ladies notions shop in Monroeville called Mi-Ladies Shoppe. She later worked for Wolf and Dessauers Department Store and L.S. Aryes. She also worked at the Van's Home Store.

Samuel and Ida Van Buskirk were humble and loving individuals whose lives revolved around the church and their family. They were Methodists and lived their lives according to the teachings of Christ. They are remembered for their kindness, generosity, and wisdom. Their descendents in the area are inspired by their example and faith.

Submitted by Sally Van Buskirk Huebner

VANHOOZEN FAMILY

The first reported white settlers in Aboite Township arrived from Maryland in 1833. Jesse Vermilyn and his family came about the same time. His son, Jesse Vermilyn, was the first white baby born in Aboite Township and he died in the fall of 1833, the same year he was born. Nathaniel (Nate) VanHoozen, also spelled VanHuesen, arrived in Aboite Township in 1833, from the Syracuse area in New York State. He was a young man 17 or 18 years of age. One family story relates that he came to Aboite Township to work on the Wabash Erie Canal and helped Jesse Vermilyn clear land and make bricks for the Vermilyn home, which overlooked the canal. The home served as an Inn for travelers as well as a post office.

Nathaniel VanHoozen

The Indian Removal Act began in 1832 and unclaimed land was available for the white settlers. The land was a forest of trees and wild animals; Indians were still roaming the area. Nathaniel informed his brother-in-law, William Hamilton (who was married to Nate's sister Joanna) of the work and opportunities of the Aboite area. William and Joanna were both born and raised in the Syracuse, New York, area. Nathaniel lived with the Hamiltons until he purchased land and built a log cabin in 1842. Nathaniel's frame home was built later, one half mile west of the Hamilton Road on the north side of the Aboite Center Road. Nathaniel and William cleared the land for farming and raised domestic animals.

Nathaniel, at age 30, married Sarah Fulk, age 18, on April 2, 1846. They had six children born in Aboite Township: (l) Hannah, born in 1848, married Jacob Taylor and moved to Ohio; (2) Printha, born in 1850, married Tom Smith and moved to Hutchinson, Kansas, no children; 3) George, born in 1852, married Ruth Kelsey and owned a farm just north of his father's farm on Covington road. They had four children, Russell, Loree, Ethel, Donald; (4) John, born in 1854, married Alice Kelsey, a sister to Ruth. They had three children, Claude, Rosmond and Edith, who died before adulthood. Alice died at an early age, leaving the children without a mother; (5) Henry, born in 1857, married Eleta Hays Simonton. They had two children, Clifton M. VanHoozen and Doris Delvin; (6) Sarah, born in 1860, did not marry.

Sarah Fulk VanHoozen died of small pox and was buried on the family farm; later her remains were moved to the Bullard Cemetery near Sleepy Hollow Drive. Maria S. Hancock Rye was the second wife of Nathaniel and they had two children; (1). Susan, married Frank Parnin and they had two children, Doris and Ross. (2) William Nathaniel married Frank Parnin's sister, Helen; they had one son, Glenn.

Nathaniel's sister, Joanna, married William Hamilton and they had six children. Three died before adulthood. The two daughters married and moved out of Allen County; the son, William A., was given land by his father and later bought land in Aboite Township. He married Barbara Scott, and they had ten children, all born in Aboite Township. Many of Nathaniel's descendants lived in Aboite Township and at present time the seventh generation is residing in the Township.

Henry, George, and John have descendants living in the Fort Wayne area. Nathaniel and Maria are buried in Lindenwood Cemetery. The Hamiltons are also in Lindenwood Cemetery in Fort Wayne.

VanHoozen Park is located on the south side of Aboite Center Road, between Homestead and Hamilton Roads. The park was dedicated August 2001, a tribute to the VanHoozen family who helped develop Aboite Township into the beautiful, prosperous community that it is today. Family members were involved in developing the school system from one-room schools into the Southwest Allen County Schools, which is Aboite and Lafayette Townships. Ronald VanHoozen, like his father Clifton and grandfather Henry, has lived in Aboite Township all his life. He has served as township trustee, township assessor, and SWAC school board.

Submitted by Ronald VanHoozen

RICHARD VER WIEBE FAMILY

Richard and Carol Ver Wiebe moved to Fort Wayne in 1958. Dick began the practice of law with Solly Frankenstein and Carol joined the staff of the society department of the *Journal Gazette*.

Dick remained in general trial practice for the following 20 years. In 1979 he became a federal administrative law judge under Health and Human Services, hearing Social Security appeals.

He worked with the Fort Wayne Community Forum in 1960 and was active in the formation in 1961 of the Allen County chapter of the Indiana Civil Liberties Union, serving as chair of its first steering committee. In 1966, he served as the first president of the People's Forum, a group established to combat extremism. He was also a founding board member of Switchboard, which began in 1970 and is now part of United Way, and was instrumental in organizing the northeast Indiana chapter of Planned Parenthood.

Richard Ver Wiebe Family 1986

Carol retired from the *Journal Gazette* in 1960 to raise a family. During these early retirement years she served as president of the Unitarian Universalist Congregation of Fort Wayne, Fort Wayne Allen County League of Women Voters, and the Membership Activities Council of the Fort Wayne Museum of Art.

Together, Dick and Carol were on founding boards for Fort Wayne Cinema Center and Friends of the Allen County Public Library. Carol served two early terms as president of Cinema Center.

Both plunged into Fort Wayne's lively arts community. Dick has won four Anthony Awards from Fort Wayne Civic Theatre and has appeared on stage at Arena Dinner Theatre, First Presbyterian Theater and various small theaters around town. Dick began his participation with the Philharmonic Chorus in 1959 and has done solo work and narration with the Fort Wayne Philharmonic Orchestra. He appeared with local opera companies and in musical productions at the Foellinger Theater in Franke Park. In addition to performing, Dick served on the Fine Arts Foundation board from 1972-1983. He was a member of the Civic Theater board. He is heard on WBNI and his program, "Best Seat in the House" has been broadcast weekly since 1978.

Carol was also involved with WBNI before her retirement in 1996. She served as director of development for 13 years, adding duties as assistant general manager in 1987.

Dick is a life-long Hoosier, born and raised in West Lafayette and a graduate of Purdue. His law degree is from IU Bloomington. He met Carol, a graduate of the University of Washington School of Journalism, while serving in the Army during the Korean war.

The Ver Wiebes have two children, both graduates of Elmhurst High School. Ann graduated from Kalamazoo College. She has a master's degree in arts administration and is on the staff of public radio station WKSU in Kent, Ohio. Richard Jr. graduated from Indiana University Bloomington, has master degrees in American studies and education and teaches history in Syracuse, New York. He and his wife, Nisha Gupta, have two daughters, Avalon and Mandala Kiara.

Submitted by Richard and Carol Ver Wiebe

DONNA NAHRWOLD VOLDERING FAMILY

Christian Nahrwold Sr. was born April 6, 1808, in Prussia. He left Bremen, Germany, when he was 32, and arrived in New York on April 15, 1840. He became an American citizen on October 5, 1842, giving up allegiance to King Wilhelm. Reportedly, he married Louise Bleeke, although this has not been proved. Christian Nahrwold Sr. died March 27, 1863, in America.

His son, Christian Nahrwold Jr., was born November 6, 1852. He married Julia Kipp, who died March 4, 1941. The couple's oldest son, August H., was born January 13, 1881, on a farm near Friedheim. The family attended the Lutheran church in Friedheim. When August was 13, his father, Christian Jr., died of Bright's disease (a disease of the kidneys) on November 11, 1894. August Nahrwold was a building contractor, owner of a small grocery store and a carpenter, among other things. August married Selma K. Ehrman on October 18, 1903. Selma Ehrman was born March 21, 1883, and was a maid for Judge Heaton. Selma's mother was Caroline Bleeke; the first Bleekes were a prominent family who founded the Bleeke settlement off Highway 101, south of Monroeville. Selma bore seven children, the sixth of whom was Norwin William Nahrwold, born June 7, 1915. Selma Ehrman Nahrwold died September 29, 1965. August Nahrwold died in February 1969. They were members of Zion Lutheran Church, 2313 S. Hanna Street. Norwin Nahrwold married Dorothy Elizabeth Zaugg on October 14, 1939. Dorothy was born June 23, 1916, and died November 1, 2004. Norwin and Dorothy had four children, the third of whom was the author, Donna Jean Nahrwold Volmerding.

The August Nahrwold family Front row: August, Delores, Norwin and Selma. Back row: Clarence, Chester, Delores, Harold and Herbert.

The Nahrwolds were members of Redeemer Lutheran Church on Rudisill Boulevard until 1952, when they joined Bethlehem Lutheran Church, mostly because Bethlehem had a Christian day school.

Norv worked at International Harvester from age 19 until his retirement in 1977. He was the supervisor of data processing for many years. Dorothy worked at Sears, Roebuck and Co. in the phone catalog sales department for a few years, until she retired in 1977.

Dorothy's parents were Oliver Leander Zaugg, born December 2, 1878, and Mary or Marie Bittner Zaugg, born April 24, 1888. Marie (the preferred name) grew up in the Bleeke church area and knew Selma Ehrman as a schoolgirl, although Selma was five years older. Selma and Marie were delighted when their children married. Marie taught Sunday School at Redeemer for twenty years. She also worked in a restaurant for awhile, and took in laundry and ironing for extra money. Marie and Oliver married May 5, 1907. Oliver was a painter who goldleafed the steeple cross on Emmaus Lutheran Church, 2322 Broadway. He also painted a life-size picture of the Good Shepherd at First Missionary Church on Rudisill Boulevard. Oliver Zaugg died November 9, 1957; Marie Bittner Zaugg died December 16, 1968. Marie's parents were Herman and Louisa (Roth) Bittner. Oliver's parents were Peter and Louise (Wabley) Zaugg.

Submitted by Donna Nahrwold Volmerding

HENRY WILLIAM VOLMERDING FAMILY

Henry William Volmerding was born on March 7, 1869, in Fort Wayne, Allen County, Indiana, to Friedrich Wilhelm Vollmerding and Sophia Meinzen, both of Hanover, Germany. Henry was the only child. Friedrich died on July 28, 1878, in Fort Wayne. He and Sophia are buried in the Old Concordia Cemetery. He was a carpenter and she was a homemaker.

Henry married Louise Ida Muller of Marshall, Calhoun County, Michigan, on May 12, 1898, in St. Paul's Lutheran Church in Fort Wayne. Louise was born to Gottlieb Muller of Strasburg, Germany, and Anna Julie of Brumberg, Germany, on January 19, 1877 and was one of five children: Emily, Pauline, Clara Muller, Louise Ida, and Frank Muller.

Gottlieb died on October 13, 1911, and Anna died on February 4, 1898, in Fort Wayne. They are buried in Lindenwood Cemetery. He was a logger and she was a homemaker.

Henry and Louise had eight children: Richard Henry, Hulda Sophia, Henry William Jr., Albert, Gertrude Pauline, Lillian Ann, Fredrick Gottlieb, and Dorothy Louise.

Henry died on June 27, 1962, and Louise on December 20, 1962, in Fort Wayne. They are buried in Lindenwood Cemetery. He was a union painter and was also actively involved in the Fort Wayne Maennerchor. Louise was a homemaker. Henry and Louise were founding members of Trinity Evangelical Lutheran Church in Fort Wayne.

Dorothy was born on July 12, 1921, in Fort Wayne, Indiana. She went to school at Trinity Evangelical Lutheran, Central High School. She did not graduate from high school, but received her GED at the age of seventy-two.

Dorothy Louise married Richard Gordon Savage, her World War II sweetheart, on September 23, 1945, at Trinity Evangelical Lutheran Church, Fort Wayne (see James William Savage family). She became a homemaker after her marriage.

Submitted by Dorothy L. Savage

ALBERT & ELEANOR (PROSCHEL) VONDERAU FAMILY

Albert and Eleanor were married on November 24, 1910, in St. Peter's Lutheran Church on the Maysville Road. Albert had looked forward to this day, building Eleanor a new house on his 66 acres on Thurman Road. Soon after the marriage he would complete the farm by building a barn, chicken house, pig house, and corn/grain storage bin. Albert and Eleanor lived on the farm until their deaths, (enhancing/expanding it each year) making it a prosperous place to live.

Albert and Eleanor had three children. Their first child, Anita Eleanor Susan, was born on March 6, 1912, in Milan Township. Anita was named for her two aunts, one on each side of the family- what a way to keep peace! Eleanor then gave birth to fraternal twins! Frederick and Florence were born January 21, 1915, in Milan Township. All the children were raised on the farm; and they continued to visit the homestead into their adult years, teaching their children the lessons of their childhood.

In the early days Albert farmed exclusively with horses. He kept the last two horses until they died, remembering all the work they had done, and used them when the ground was too wet for a tractor or to pull a stump. Albert was a man of his time, advancing from horsepower to the use of a tractor. Living within the larger community, the brothers and uncles shared in the harvesting of the crops and the women created fantastic feasts on these occasions. Albert and his brother, Paul, continued their pursuit of technology, bringing one of the first steam-powered threshers into Allen County.

Albert and Eleanor Vonderau

Jacob Heinrich Albert was born in St. Joe Township on December 31, 1884, in his father's (Johann Frederick Vonderau) house on Parent Road. Albert was the second of seven children - five boys, and two girls. Eleanor Proschel was born on March 21, 1885, near Rochester, Minnesota. Eleanor came to Allen County as a young lady, visiting a cousin on what was then Thurman Road (now Schwartz Road). She stayed, soon met Albert, and the couple fell in love. Eleanor brought her beloved piano to their home, where it was enjoyed by several generations.

Albert Vonderau's father, Johann Friedrick "Frederick" Vonderau, was one of 14 children, and five of them became farmers in Allen County. Albert grew up in this community of Vonderaus and later became a part of the larger community, along with his brothers who lived on nearby farms of their own: Paul Herrmann born July 8,1883, Georg Christian born November 19, 1888, and Oscar born November 17, 1897. Albert became a prosperous dairyman and a farmer who was very active in the community. He served as board secretary and board member of Allen County Dairy, Director of Echo Life Insurance Co., Director of The New Haven-Thurman Equity Exchange, active in the Lutheran Hospital Association, on the board of the Parkview Hospital, and a member of the New Haven Chamber of Commerce.

Eleanor passed away in 1946, and Albert died on October 20, 1958. Both are interred in St. Peter's Cemetery.

Submitted by Joan Poling

FREDERICK & MAREA (EICKHOFF) VONDERAU FAMILY

Johann Friedrick "Frederick" Vonderau and Marea Elenora Eickhoff were married on August 27, 1882, by Reverend H. Kühn in Indianapolis, Indiana. As was sometimes the custom in those days, Frederick's mother, Anna Margaretha (nee Kern), asked the church for locations where there might be eligible young women. Frederick and his brother were sent to Indianapolis from Allen County. It was during this visit that Frederick met Marea. After a courtship, the couple were married in Indianapolis and moved back to St. Joe Township in Allen County.

Frederick and Marea settled down to farming and raising children. They had seven children, five boys and two girls. Paul Herrmann Friedrick Wilhelm was the first child born to the couple, on July 8, 1883, in St. Joe Township. Jacob Heinrich Albert was the second child, born on December 31, 1884. Augusta Louise Anna, their first girl, was added to the family on September 24, 1886. Following the pattern of boy, boy, girl, Kasper Georg Christian was born on November 19, 1888, followed by Edward Friedrick Wilhelm on January 2, 1892, and Eleanora Margaretha Charlotte on January 23, 1895. Finally, the baby of the family, Oscar, was born on November 17, 1897. The boys became farmers in the area, and the girls married and moved to town.

Marea Vonderau and Freidrick Vanderau

The family attended St. Peter's Lutheran Church on State Street. In April, 2005, this church published a paperback book, 1855-2005 "150 Years of God's Grace." This book contains a picture of Frederick and his siblings taken for their mother at the time of his father's funeral in 1914. The book also contains Oscar's historical perspective of St. Peter's Church entitled "As I recall.."

Frederick, the seventh child of Johann Jacob and Anna Margaretha (the first Hoosier in the family) was born on March 28, 1857, in St. Joe Township. The senior Vonderaus started their family in Union County, Ohio, where they were married on December 28, 1845. The first six children were born in Union County, Ohio, and the last seven in Allen County, Indiana. Frederick's father, Johann Jacob, entered the United States on July 5, 1842, having sailed across the Atlantic on the ship "London." Jacob spent some time in Pennsylvania with his elder brother, and then traveled to Union County, Ohio, where he met and married Margaretha. Both of Frederick's parents were from Germany.

Marea was born November 13, 1857, to Henry Eickhoff and Charlotte (nee Elbrecht) in Indianapolis, Marion County, Indiana.

Frederick was a very successful farmer and was able to help his children get a good start on life. In addition to farming, Frederick was involved with threshing and owned a sawmill. Frederick was a director of the New Haven State Bank since its inception.

Frederick died at 57 years of age on July 2, 1914, and is buried in St. Peter's Cemetery. Marea lived on the family farm until her death on April 8, 1940. She is buried next to her husband.

Submitted by Amy Groce

JACOB & ANNA (KERN) VONDERAU FAMILY

Johann Jacob and Anna Margaretha were married by the Reverend Adam Ernst in St. John's Lutheran Church in Union County, Ohio, on December 28, 1845. They moved to Allen County in late 1856, settling in a rented house in St. Joe Township.

Jacob was born in Ernsthofen, Hessen-Darmstadt, Germany, on December 8, 1819. He was the tenth child of Johann Jacob and Anna Bärbel (nee Krämer). Jacob emigrated from Germany, landing at New York on July 5, 1842. His older brother had sailed to the United States with several other families from Ernsthofen in August 1838. Those families traveled from New York to take employment near the town of Carlisle, Pennsylvania. Young Jacob traveled by himself, having become interested in the United States through correspondence with his older brother. In autumn of 1842 the twenty-two year old arrived in Carlisle. Jacob had been apprenticed as a tailor in Germany and started working in this capacity for Johann Jacob Weidmann. Jacob Weidmann's brother, Johann Ludwig Weidmann, had moved from Pennsylvania to Union County, Ohio. Again it seems correspondence caught the eye and ear of young Jacob, and by 1844 he traveled to Marysville, Union County, Ohio to work with Johann Ludwig Weidmann. It was here he was to find his bride. Johann Jacob became a naturalized United States citizen in September, 1848.

Anna Margaretha Kern was born January 7, 1827, in Klein-Weisach, Franconia, Germany. We do not know what path her family took to arrive in Union County, Ohio, but they were there for some time before Jacob Vonderau arrived. Anna's parents were Johann Michael and Anna Margaretha (nee Koerner) Kern. The Kerns also moved from Marysville, Union County, Ohio to Allen County, Indiana. Anna's younger sister, Susanna, married the Reverend Sihler on June 8, 1846, at St. John's Lutheran Church in Union County. At that time he was the Pastor of St. Paul's Lutheran Church in Fort Wayne.

Jacob and Anna had 14 children, seven were born in Union County, Ohio, and seven were born in Allen County, Indiana. The children were: 1) Susanna Dorothea Sybilla born November 8, 1846; 2) Michael Caspar born March 6, 1848; 3) Peter Wilhelm born April 3, 1850 - Peter is buried in St. John's Cemetery; 4) Peter Wilhelm born June 30, 1851; 5) Elisabetha Catharina born March 3, 1853; 6) Georg Michael Herrmann born February 11, 1855; 7) Johann Friedrick born March 28, 1857; 8) Johann Georg Jacob born March 15, 1859; 9) Johann Friedrick Conrad born March 11, 1861; 10) Anna Margaretha Elizabeth Wilhelmina born June 28, 1863; 11) Johann Georg Christian born May 16, 1866; 12) Marie born April 1, 1868 - Marie is buried in St. Peter's Cemetery; 13) Johann Martin Ludwig born March 7, 1870; 14) Paul Anton Gottlieb born December 13, 1872 – Paul is buried in St. Peter's Cemetery.

Jacob died on October 28, 1897, and Anna passed away on February 27, 1908. Both are buried in St. Peter's Cemetery.

Submitted by Jill Cox

VONDERAU FAMILY

Does this picture of the big red barn with the US flag painted on it seem familiar? You would have seen it from Interstate 469, between US 24 and Indiana SR 37 east of Fort Wayne, just where Parent Road is cut off by Interstate 469. This farm lies west of Interstate 469 and south of Parent Road, in Milan Township. During the Christmas season you may have also seen a tractor and windmill outlined in lights. Vonderaus have owned this just under hundred acres farm since 1902.

Vonderau Barn

The first generation owner, Fred, sold it to son, Paul, in 1914, and he sold to son, Robert, in 1962,who still owns it and lives there. This farm is located in the old Lake Maumee bottom, has good loam soil, and has always produced well.

This branch of the Vonderau family came to this area in about 1860, from the vicinity of Pomeroy, Ohio. Paul and his wife, Emma Rosebrock, lived the entire seventy years of their married life here, raising five children.

Paul always had a crop and livestock operation, for many years raising purebred Scotch shorthorn cattle. He also operated a portable saw mill, and a large threshing rig. One of the old farmsteads from which they sawed native timber is still to be seen on SR 37, now home to the Galbraith Nursery. Once, when they had the saw mill set up near the Maumee River, there was an overnight flash flood and most of the logs floated away. Only a few were retrieved.

It was Robert Vonderau's good fortune to work with the threshing rig for some years. His job was to supply water for the steam engine which powered the threshing machine which used over 1000 gallons of water and two tons of coal on an average day. He has lots of memories of the long hot days, the good food, all manner of problems, the large loads of grain, and the huge straw stacks. This was the time of neighbor helping neighbor through the good years and the not so good years.

During World War II, Robert served with the Air Force for four years in the South Pacific. He took over the management of the farm in the early 1950s, and phased out the livestock when he established a plumbing and heating service in 1960. He continued to operate the farm until about 1990.

Fourth generation son, Marshall, and family make the old brick farmhouse their home, and daughter, Elaine, also lives close by in a new home. They and their children graduated from Woodlan High School, and all are doing well in their chosen vocations.

Robert was a pilot for many years, and enjoyed flying friends and fellow Kiwanis members to many places.

So much has changed on the farm, from horses for power to diesel tractors, two row farm equipment to twelve, livestock and fenced fields to all one unfenced plot, cultivating and hoeing for weed control to chemicals, new genetic seeds and greater yields. But higher input costs, higher land values, less profit.

Many of the farms in the immediate area have been lost to commercial and residential development. The lights of the nearest shopping mall burn brightly just over a mile away. Good farmland and homes of fine old families have been lost to suburban sprawl.

Robert and his wife, Henrietta, still live there on Parent Road. She is retired from East Allen County Schools with 45 years of teaching. They can watch the unbelievable amount of commerce pass close by on Interstate 469 (600 trucks per hour), and on the Norfolk and Southern Railroad (50 trains a day).

The various generations of Vonderau have been active members of St. Peters Lutheran Church and local civic groups. For the past hundred years the Vonderau family has taken good care of this farm, and it has been good to them.

Robert O. Vonderau

JOSEPH J. & MARY ANN (ALLGEIER) VOORS FAMILY

The first of the Voors family arrived in Fort Wayne in 1843. Bernard Voors had left his ancestral home in Hanover, Prussia (Germany), sailing from Bremen on the ship Pauline. He bought 117 acres (at $7.50 an acre) in what is now the northeast part of Fort Wayne. Since then, the Voors family branched out in many directions.

Joseph John "Joe" Voors, Jr., born April 26, 1917, was the son of Joseph J. Voors, Sr., and Charlotte Clausmeier. He had four brothers and one sister: William J., John E., Richard L., Charles, and Helen (Roy). Joe started grade school at the Cathedral, and in 1929, his family joined the new St. Jude church and school. He graduated from Central Catholic High School and moved on to St. Joseph College, Rensselaer, where he earned a bachelor's degree. He also received a degree from Indiana Business School in Fort Wayne.

During World War II, Joe served in the Army Quartermaster Corps for four years. He returned

Joseph J. Voors II and Mary Ann Allgeier Voors

to Fort Wayne to join his father at Voors Coal Co., with offices on Main Street. Eventually, Joe owned Ace Coal Co., located on Wayne Trace. In 1954, when most heating changed to gas and oil, he joined Parrot Meat Packing as personnel director until he retired in 1982. Joe was always active in sports, mainly basketball and softball, pitching the church league championship game for the St. Jude's softball team at age 65. He also served his church as trustee, parish council member, choir member and usher, before his death on July 12, 1985.

On October 4, 1944, while still in the Army, Joe married Mary Ann Allgeier, daughter of Henry G. Allgeier, Jr., and Marie Hartman. Henry Allgeier was an officer of the Lincoln National Bank. Marie Hartman had been secretary to Bert Griswold at the time he authored the 1917 history of Fort Wayne. Mary Ann was born June 24, 1921. She was the first female graduate of the new Central Catholic High School in 1939 (the first graduating class after the merger of Central Catholic High School for boys and St. Augustine's Academy for girls.) She worked at Lincoln National Life Insurance Company from 1939 until 1944, when she was required to leave employment because she got married.

Joe and Mary Ann are the parents of Katherine A. Underhill (Sam), a long-time employee of Parkview Hospital; Joseph J. III (Mary Daly), vice president of the retirement division with Prudential Finance: and Michael H., professor of Fine Arts at East Carolina University. Joe and Mary Ann are grandparents of Nicholas and Anthony Miller, and Jennifer, Joseph E., Daniel J., and Shannon Voors.

Submitted by Mary Ann Voors

PHILIP & ELIZABETH (CARTEAUX) WALDORF FAMILY

Philip Robert Waldorf was born March 13, 1969, in Fort Wayne, Indiana, to Michael Robert and Jenna Louise (Wyatt) Waldorf. Philip's great-great-grandfather, James Louis Wyatt, was born in 1858 in LaOtto, Indiana, to Shedrick Bostic and Lucinda (Pellet) Wyatt. James married Joanna Hall, made their home in LaOtto, Indiana, and had two sons and two daughters. James was widely recognized as one of the pioneer insurance men of Noble, LaGrange, Steuben, and DeKalb counties and served in that occupation for 56 years. He was a member of the Emmanuel Lutheran Church in LaOtto. His wife Joanna died in 1923 and in 1927 he moved to Fort Wayne to be close to his children. He died of pneumonia on April 12, 1943, at the home of his daughter, Georgianna Wyatt Simon. His other children were Dr. James Louis Wyatt, Jr., Robert H. Wyatt and Nellie Wyatt Weaver Erickson.

Dr. James L. Wyatt, Jr., Philip's great-grandfather, was born April 15, 1893, in LaOtto, Indiana. He married Mildred Charlotta Mumaw on January 26, 1914, in Sturgis, Michigan, and, after graduating from the Indiana University medical school in 1923, moved back to Fort Wayne with his wife and son, James Louis Wyatt III. Dr. Wyatt served on the surgical staff at St. Joseph Hospital and the visiting staffs at Lutheran and Parkview Hospitals. He was later installed as president of the Indiana Section of the American College of Surgeons. James and Mildred had a second child, Joan Louise Wyatt Fackler Gerberding, born March 25, 1932. The Wyatt's were all members of Trinity English Lutheran Church in Fort Wayne. Mildred died in 1946. Dr. Wyatt died of a heart attack at his home on February 27, 1961, and was fondly remembered by many of the physicians in Fort Wayne.

Dr. James Louis Wyatt III was born June 25, 1915, in Edon, Ohio. His twin brother, Richard Jacob Wyatt, died at birth. He graduated from Indiana University and received his medical degree in 1934 from Loyola University, Chicago. He married June Light in June 1938, in Bloomington, Indiana, and later moved back to Fort Wayne to start a family. James and June had three children, James Louis Wyatt IV, Jon Light Wyatt, and Jenna Louise Wyatt, Philip's mother. Dr. Wyatt was a fellow of the International College of Surgeons and a member of the American Society of Surgeons, the Allen County Medical Society and the Indiana State Medical Society. Dr. Wyatt died of a coronary on June 23, 1976, at Lutheran Hospital.

The Philip Waldorf Family, Philip, Elizabeth, Megan (6) and Philip (3), January, 2005

Jenna Louise Wyatt was born February 5, 1948, in Fort Wayne. She graduated from South Side High School in 1966 and attended Parsons College, Iowa, and Indiana-Purdue University in Fort Wayne. She married Michael Robert Waldorf, who was born March 17, 1954, in Columbus, Ohio. They had two children, Philip Robert Waldorf and Joshua Wesley Waldorf. Joshua was born July 17, 1982, and died several hours after birth due to polycystic kidney disease.

Philip Waldorf graduated from Homestead High School in 1987 and attended Broward Community College, Fort Lauderdale, Florida, and Indiana-Purdue University, Fort Wayne. Philip married Elizabeth Marie Carteaux on August 28,

1993, in Fort Wayne and they have two children, Megan Marie Waldorf, born October 27, 1998, and Philip Robert Wesley Waldorf, born May 17, 2001. Elizabeth Waldorf was born January 5, 1969, in Fort Wayne to Robert and Donna Carteaux. She graduated from Bishop Dwenger High School in 1987, attended Indiana-Purdue University in Fort Wayne and is employed by Verizon. Philip is currently a stay-at-home dad and substitute preschool teacher. The Waldorf family attends Trinity English Lutheran Church, where Philip and his children are fourth and fifth generation members, respectively. Philip continues to share his time with Trinity Church by serving on the Children's Faith Education Committee, Mission and Outreach Committee, Global Mission Committee, Preschool Advisory Board, and is a past member of Church Council. He also serves as a eucharistic minister, Sunday School teacher, and dramatist.

Submitted by Philip Waldorf

DALE G. & DOROTHY M. (SMITH) WALDROP FAMILY

Dale G. Waldrop was born on June 28, 1911, in Edgerton, Indiana, to George G. Waldrop and Edith M. Anspach. Dale was the sixth of their children. Lela G. Waldrop, wife of August W. Rime was the oldest, followed by Gerald W. Waldrop, husband of Elsie L. Linnemeier, Kenneth A. Waldrop, husband of Vera E. Stevens, Wayne D. Waldrop, husband of Ruth F. Carrier, Ruth B. Waldrop, wife of Arthur D. Kapp, Donald E. Waldrop, husband of Frances Berg, Mary E. (Betty) Waldrop, wife of Donald L. Comer, Robert Waldrop, husband of Helen J. Marshand, and George G. Waldrop, husband of Phyllis Strasser. Dale's family lines trace directly back to England and General Robert E. Lee.

Dorothy (Smith) and Dale Waldrop

Dale moved to Fort Wayne, Indiana, with his family in 1918 and remained there until his death at age 84, in 1995. He attended South Side High School where he earned an art scholarship. Dale and Dorothy owned and operated their own grocery called Oxford Market from 1949 until 1955, when they both went to work at Roger's Market. He worked for Roger's until he retired after 32 years of service. Dale was an assistant manager. He also served with the Indiana National Guard and was an award-winning bowler and city champion. He always had a sincere smile, a handshake and a story for everyone.

Dorothy M. Smith became Dale's wife on October 24, 1936, in Fort Wayne Indiana. Dorothy was born on August 15, 1915, in Roanoke, Indiana, to Archie M. Smith and Eva May Runyan. Dorothy was the oldest of five children. Following, in order, are Earl E. Smith, husband of Mary C. Buchanan, Mildred M. Smith, wife of Ira E. Crandal, Lloyd Dale Smith, husband of Edith Shivley and Phyllis J. Smith, wife of Ronald D. Egolf. Dorothy enjoyed many clubs and organizations with her friends and was active in her children's lives. She was a loyal friend to all. She obtained tuition for Beauty College by selling a cow that she raised, and held a beauty license until her death in 1999 at age 84. Dorothy is a first cousin five times removed to President Abraham Lincoln.

Dale and "Dotty" attended South Wayne Baptist Church for over 50 years. Together they enjoyed playing cards, traveling, gardening, fishing, bowling, and life at the lake. Their children are: Barbara J. Waldrop, wife of Steven T. Arnett, John W. Waldrop, husband of Sandra L. Huff, and Cynthia S. Waldrop, wife of Phillip L. Charais.

Submitted by Phillip L. Charais

ROSELLA CAROLINE PARISOT WALL

Rosella was born June 6, 1898 and died 95 years later on March 1, 1993, both in Fort Wayne. There is no record of her birth. In her long life, she never drank or smoked. She only drove once and hit a parked car. She only voted twice. The first was for Al Smith in 1928 because he was the first Catholic to run for President, and the other was against her husband, Herb, who lost his bid for City Council. She was a very religious woman who received all six sacraments at St. Patrick Catholic Church. She prayed three times a day, did crossword puzzles, and liked to watch TV. She was a seamstress her whole life until she was forced to stop in her mid 80s due to arthritis. Her philosophy was "enjoy your youth." Rosella predicted her death every year for her last twenty. Her prediction finally came true when she died of complications from a broken hip, presumably a pulmonary embolism. Her two last wishes were to be "thrown in the ground" the day after her death because "no one wants to look at a shriveled up old lady," and no drinking during or after her funeral. She got her wishes.

Ruth Caroline Parisot Wall

Her parents were Joseph Alexander Parisot and Mary Josephine Treuchet, both born and buried in Fort Wayne. Joseph's parents were Jean Baptiste Joseph Parisot, born in Villafans, France, and Mary Reichardt, who was born in Germany. Mary Reichardt was disowned from her Lutheran family for marrying a Catholic. Joseph was mustered into the Civil War February 3, 1864, in Fort Wayne to Company C, 44th Regiment of the Indiana Volunteers by Sergeant Samuel Sweet. Mary's parents were Celestin N. Treuchet and Josephine Elion (Alion), both from Goa, France,

Rosella met her husband, Herbert Conrad Wall, ten days before they married. They had four children, Herbert Jr., Rita, Leonard Alexander "Bud," and Carl Allen "Butch." Rita died at age five from meningitis. Herb was born in San Francisco on March 9, 1892, to Charles J. from Munich, Germany, and Regina Hartman from Fort Wayne. Regina was the daughter of Herman Hartman, one of the Fathers of the City. Herb was one of the original salesmen of Motorola's first products, a car radio. He owned and operated Wall Electronics, a Motorola dealership, at 241-243 Pearl Street until his death March 14th, 1959. The dealership went to his sons, then eventually to Carl, who lost it to poor management in 1971.

Her sons, Herb and Bud, both served in WWII, and Carl served in the Korean Conflict. Carl was the first in her family to receive a college degree, graduating from Indiana University in 1951. Herb Jr. had three children, Barbara Ann, Carolyn Jane, and Lori Ann. Bud had five children, John Herbert, Leonard Alexander, II, Caryl Ann, Rita Ann, and Patricia Ann. Carl had four children, Gregory Conrad, Lisa Ellen, David Joseph, and Jennifer Ann.

Submitted by Gregory Wall

ORREN ALBERT & DELORIS MAY (GEETING) WARE FAMILY

Orren was born May 27, 1930, on Freedom Street in Huntington, Huntington County, Indiana. He and his wife, Deloris, are the parents of Connie Denihan (Timothy), referenced in this book. His great great grandparents, Philip and Martha "Patsy" (Mayo) Ware were married in Patrick County, Virginia, on October 1, 1797, by Rev. Isaac Adams. Philip's father, Samuel Ware, had to sign the marriage record. Martha's parents were Williamson and Hannah (Phillips) Mayo. Philip was a private in the War of 1812 under Capt. Samuel Caldwell. Philip then moved to Cabell County, Virginia, before 1819 and to Johnson County, Indiana, about October 27, 1820, and was one of the original land purchasers. Philip died there on May 6, 1835. Philip and Martha had six known children (William R., Samuel, Sarah, Jennie Jane, James, Elizabeth), Samuel being Orren's great grandfather.

Samuel Ware was born February 2, 1801, and was married twice. He had 13 children. By his first wife (Mary Stowers-married September 22, 1824 in Johnson County, Indiana), they were: Greenville, James, William Riley, Elizabeth Jane, Martha Ann, Ann Eliza. Mary's parents were Travis and Elizabeth (Blankenship) Stowers. His children by his second wife (Prudence Monroe-married August 7, 1842 in Warren County, Indiana, by Edward Mace) were: Lydia Ellen, Philip Lee, Mary Ann, Thomas Jefferson, Sarah Jane, David,

Orren Albert Ware family, Thanksgiving 2004. Back Row, l to r: Orren A. Ware, Jennifer M. Watkins, Derek A. Ness, Timothy J. Denihan. Middle Row, l to r: Deloris M. Ware, Meredith E. Watkins, Angela M. Ness holding Nathaniel O. Ness, Richard C. Ness. Front Row l to r: Carol A. Ness with Kaitlyn N. Ness in front, Connie S. Denihan, Marcia K. Watkins.

and John Wesley. Samuel and Prudence moved to Fulton County, Indiana, about 1848 where their last four children were born, and where he died April 5, 1859, before his youngest son was two years old. Samuel was a school teacher.

Orren's grandfather, John Wesley, was born July 19, 1857, and married Paulina Rebecca Hizer May 27, 1880, in Fulton County, Indiana. They had nine children: (Charles Daniel, Bertha Pearl, Herman Wesley, Maude Matilda, Walter Aaron, Elmer Ira, Albert Earl, Loyd Alva, and Ray Samuel). Paulina's parents were Aaron and Matilda Ann (Smith) Hizer. John and his family moved to Wexford County, Michigan, in 1908 where they worked on a potato farm. They moved to Huntington County, Indiana, in 1912 where he died July 1, 1940.

Submitted by Timothy and Connie Denihan

HENRY W. & FRANCIS A. WARFIELD

In 1904, Henry William Warfield moved from Peoria, Illinois, to Fort Wayne, Indiana, where his first cousin lived. His paternal cousin was William E. Warfield, land owner and educator. Uncle Will came to Fort Wayne in the early 1890s. Henry had lived in Peoria, Illinois, with his first wife and his three children. The marriage ended in divorce. Henry was born in Henderson, Kentucky in the 1860s. There is limited information concerning his parents, brothers and sisters.

Francis Alice Henderson was the daughter of Rev. and Mrs. Alexander Henderson of Van Wert, Ohio. She was born in 1880. She was the youngest child and had four brothers, Matthew, Mark, Luke, and John, and two sisters, Nell and Carolyn. Frances moved to Defiance, Ohio, in 1904, lived there for a short time, then moved to Fort Wayne in late 1904 with her sister Nell. She met and married Henry in 1905. To this union was born one daughter, Delia Mae and four sons, Charles William, John Henry, James Richard, and Donald Leonard Warfield.

Frances Alice Warfield joined a small group of Baptists under the leadership of Rev. Graham Jordan. The small group met in homes and in space donated by white landowners in the area. Henry and other men from the construction trades helped to build the Mount Olive Baptist Church at 421 E. Brackenridge Street. Frances was a member of the Missionary Society.

Henry and Frances Warfield's daughter, Delia Mae, married Seno Edgar Brown of Paulding, Ohio. Seno Brown was a farmer on his father's land. His father and mother owned extensive land in Paulding County around Paulding, Ohio. Later he got a job at Joslyn Steel Mill in Fort Wayne. Their children: Seno Edgar Brown Jr., Dolores Elizabeth, and Delia Mae Brown.

Charles William Warfield married Caroline Walters. They had one daughter, Jean Eloise. Charles second marriage was to Margaruite Eunice Edwards. Born to this union were four daughters: Audrey Nouvella, Consuella Joan, Camilla Elinore, and Beatrice Frances, and two sons, Charles William Jr. and Roger Ray Warfield. Charles Warfield was the handler of horses at the Brown Trucking Company and later drove trucks for this same company for a period of fifty years.

Henry W. and Francis A. Warfield

John Henry Warfield was married three times. His first wife was Helen Kelly. His second wife was Mildred Jackson from Newark, New Jersey, and his third wife was May Alice Watts. He had no children. John Henry worked at International Harvester as a laborer.

Donald Leonard Warfield died in 1918 at 18 months old during the whooping cough epidemic after the flood.

James Richard Warfield married Camilla Phoenix of Finley, Ohio. Born to this union were five daughters: Wallace Juana, Joyce Eloise, Beverly Joan, Camilla Elinore, and Lois Ilene. Also four sons: Carlos Laverne, James Richard and two who died in infancy. James Richard attended Taylor University at Upland, Indiana. After graduation he worked for the International Harvester Company, and retired in the late 1900s.

This covers the first three generation of Henry W. Warfield's family in Allen County, Fort Wayne, Indiana. There are now six generations living in the area and other parts of the U.S.A., such as Saginaw, Michigan, Oakland, California, Mandesto, California, Denver, Colorado, Roanoke, Indiana, Indianapolis, Indiana, Bloomington, Indiana, and Peoria, Illinois.

Submitted by Dolores E. Brown Greene Cansler

HARRY & JUANITA MAE (MCDUFFEE) WARNER FAMILY

Harry Warner was born August 13, 1918, in Perry Township, Allen County. His parents were Lincoln and Olive (Hursh) Warner, On October 2, 1948, he was married to Juanita Mae McDuffee, who was born May 18, 1924, in Eel River Township, Allen County. Her parents were Milton H. and Aldia E. (Disler) McDuffee. On August 30, 1950 a daughter, Rebecca Ann was born and on June 4, 1952 a son, Dale Harry, was born.

Harry attended a one-room grade school, until the sixth grade, at Thomas School, Cedar Creek Township, then Huntertown Elementary School in Perry Township, and graduated from Huntertown High School in 1937. He worked at Holben's Garage in Auburn, Indiana, before joining the Army Air Corps in December of 1939. He served overseas in the South Pacific, from January 1942 until July 1945. Following his discharge, he worked at Dana Corporation in Fort Wayne, Indiana, 34 and a half years, retiring in August of 1981. Harry passed away July 13, 1999, and is buried in Eel River Cemetery in Allen County, near Churubusco.

Juanita attended school all 12 years at Leo Elementary and High School, graduating in April 1942. She was employed at Fort Wayne National Bank, beginning in May 1942, both full and part-time, until her retirement in January 1937.

Their daughter, Rebecca, graduated from Manchester College in 1972 and married Charles Wayne Morris on June 16, 1973. They have three children - Kara Lyn, born August 16, 1976; Kyle Warner, born October 9, 1979; and Ryan Wayne, born March 11, 1983. Rebecca teaches third grade at Huntertown Elementary School and Charles is an engineer at Navistar in Fort Wayne, Indiana.

Harry and Juanita's son Dale graduated from Manchester College in 1974 and married Jody Lee Snyder on June 4, 1983. They have two children, Joshua Dale born January 28, 1986 and Jennifer Joy born January 3, 1988. Dale is an engineer at Verizon in Fort Wayne, Indiana, and Jody is a speech and hearing specialist at Cedarville-Leo Schools.

Harry and Juanita Warner lived at 3610 Hollopeter Road, Huntertown, Indiana, in Perry

Front, Jennifer, Harry, Juanita, Dale and Joshua Warner. Back, Ryan, Kyle and Kara Morris, Rebecca (Warner) Morris, Charles Morris, Jody (Snyder) Warner

Township, their entire married life. Their travels during their marriage took them to all 50 states, as well as Australia, New Zealand and Central Europe, Some of their trips were to Air Force Reunions, held annually in different parts of the United States. The trip to Australia was sponsored by the Air Force group, going back to Townsville, where the group was stationed during World War II.

Harry and Juanita celebrated their Golden Wedding on October 2, 1998, with an open-house, hosted by their children and grandchildren, at Agape Church of the Brethren near Fort Wayne, Indiana, where the entire family are members.

Juanita resides in the family home on Hollopeter Road, Perry Township, Allen County.

Submitted by Juanita Warner

HAROLD MAX & MARILYN JEAN (SMITH) WATERSON FAMILY

Harold "Max" Waterson was born on July 12, 1926, on a farm on the Eby Road, east of St. Joe Road in Allen County. His father, Clarence Waterson (1876-1950), had purchased the farm just before the Great Depression, a cloddy, clay 40 acre farm off of which he made a living, using two or three horses to plow and work the ground. He was married to Eva (Gump) (1885-1972).

Clarence was returning to the area where he was born, one of the sons of Samuel K. Watterson (the name was then spelled with two "t"s) (1837-1926) and Ann Elizabeth McKee (1859-1926). Samuel Watterson's farm was in Eel River Township, located on the Watterson Road just west of Wesley Chapel Road. Wesley Chapel United Methodist Church was built on the corner of the farm and Samuel and his father-in-law, John McKee, preached there for several years.

Clarence was making hay in the summer of 1938 and, since he didn't have much to cut that year, didn't think he had to replace the trip rope on the hay fork in the bank barn. As he was tripping a load of hay from the fork, the trip rope broke and Clarence lost his balance, fell off the load of hay onto the wooden floor of the bank barn, injuring his back and neck. He spent most of the rest of the summer in the Fort Wayne Methodist Hospital (then located on Lewis Street), lying in bed, his head suspended with a strap, which was attached to the top of the bed, under his chin and neck, waiting for his neck and back to heal. It was a hot summer and there was no air-conditioning in the hospital.

In 1939, the family moved off the farm to a house in Huntertown. Clarence's wife, Eva, also had close relatives around Huntertown. Clarence and Eva Waterson raised four children, three daughters and one son. The children walked to the one-room Blume School located on the southeast comer of St. Joe and Flutter Roads.

Velva (1908-1985), who married Philemon Smith, after going through eight grades went to work at General Electric in Fort Wayne and helped support the family during the Depression.

The other two girls, Edna (1920-1973) and Zelma (1922 - 1977), who married Freeman Goodyear, graduated from Leo High School.

Harold "Max" (1926) was drafted into the U.S. Army during World War II and was able to complete only half of his senior year at Huntertown High School. Max served in the army from January 25, 1945, to August 28, 1946, on Iwo Jima and on Oahu, Hawaii, receiving his honorable discharge as a sergeant. On June 29, 1947, he married Marilyn Jean Smith, the daughter of Leo and Dorothy Smith of Eel River Township. They have two children: Vickie Sue (1953), married to David Gillett and living in Lakeland, Florida, and Rickie Lynn (1956), married to Vicki Friskney, living in Albion, Indiana.

Max and Marilyn Waterson

Max recalls the house he grew up in as a "Sears and Roebuck house." There were two of such Sears houses built in Huntertown. If one were to look at an old Sears catalogue, the ad for them could be seen, all pre-cut and ready to assemble. Max and Marilyn have lived most of their married life in and around Huntertown, except for nine years when they lived on a lake-side house on Big Turkey Lake in Steuben County. In 1951, the Watersons laid out one of the sub-divisions in Huntertown, east and south of Hunter Street. Max worked at Dana in Fort Wayne in management and then, for 36 years, as an electrician, retiring in 1982. Their grandchildren are: Matthew D. Gillett (1972), married to Liz, living in Marietta, Georgia; Joshua D. Gillett (1974), living in Tampa, Florida; and Tracy Waterson (1976), married to Kevin Strater, living in Albion, Indiana.

Submitted by Harold (Max) and Marilyn Jean (Smith) Waterson

RAYMOND RICHARD WATKINS & VIRGINIA LOUISE VOSBURGH FAMILY

Raymond Richard Watkins, born August 24, 1932, in Scenery Hill, Pennsylvania, is the son of Elva Fremont and Emma Barnhart Watkins. The Watkins family descends from Thomas Watkins, who settled in Washington County, Pennsylvania, in 1820. Ray is one of nine children. Edith (Richard Hanson) lives in Punta Gorda Florida. Fremont Jr. (Sara Jane Matthews), Phyllis (Lloyd Kinder), Donald (Regina Bengal), Gerald (Joanne Nyswander), and Delbert all live in Washington County, Pennsylvania. Geraldine (Kenneth Bedillion) died in 1977 and Clifford (Dorothy Briggs) died in 1999. Raymond came to Allen County in 1951 to go to school.

Virginia Vosburgh Watkins was born in Fort Wayne, Indiana, December 3, 1936, the daughter of Eldon James and Ida Richardson Vosburgh, who came to Allen County from Clayton, Michigan.

Eldon went to college at Tri State College in Angola, where he received a degree in electrical engineering, and then went to work for GE in Fort Wayne. Virginia lived in the Southwood Park area and attended Harrison Hill Elementary School and South Side High School, where she graduated as salutatorian of the class of 1954.

Raymond met Virginia at First Methodist Church, where they both attended the youth group. They were married in the church on November 25, 1954. Raymond worked at GE, where he was Manager of Shop Operations and Acting Plant Manager in the Hermetic Motor Dept. He retired in 1992 with 40 years of service. Virginia was a pension consultant at Fort Wayne National Bank, Lincoln National Life Insurance Company, and Buck Consultants. She also retired in 1992 and they winter in Port Charlotte, Florida.

Raymond and Virginia Vosburgh Watkins Family, October 16, 2004

They have four children: Michael Raymond, born October 7, 1955, was married first to Janice Lash, was divorced and then married Gail Wilibey on February 12, 1994, in Fort Wayne. He is a vice president at New York Life. Dennis David, born May 17, 1958, was married to Julie Miller Desmond, is divorced, lives in Huntington County, and is employed in maintenance at Perfection Biscuit Company. Cynthia Kay, married to Stuart Barnes, is employed at Waterfield Mortgage. Eric Eldon, was married to Jacquelyn Johns, November 18, 1989, in Fort Walton Beach, Florida, and is a lieutenant colonel in the Air Force, currently stationed in Tucson, Arizona.

The Vosburghs descend from Abraham Pieterse Vosburgh, who was in Albany, New York, in 1649, through his son Jacob. James Robison Vosburgh came to Branch County, Michigan, in 1850 from Niagara County, New York. Family names include Van Alstyne, Warren, Washburn, Robison, Ripley, Mack, Mosher, and Anderson.

Ida Richardson's parents were William J. and Nettie Coleman Richardson. Both the Richardson's and Coleman's were in this country in the 1640s and the Richardsons settled in Fulton County, Ohio in the 1850s. Family names include Combs, Whiting, Taylor, Pearson, Riggs, Godfrey, Johnson, and Belden (Belding). At least seven from these families were patriots in the American Revolutionary War, including Capt. James Robison and two Thomas Richardsons, a father and son.

Submitted by Virginia Watkins

VESSIE WEAVER

It was 1920 and the trip to Fort Wayne from Howard County, Indiana, was long for the Weaver family. Vessie Weaver and her husband, Ernest, and seven children arrived to live in a rented home. It didn't take long for the property to take on a healthy glow. A large garden with plenty of vegetables and beautiful flowers soon made the property a perfect place to raise the happy Weaver children. The older girls were soon students at Central High School, while the younger children attended the old Lincoln School. In 1925, the eighth child was born and soon after that Vessie and her eight children were alone to take care of themselves. Phil, now age 80 and the last of the family, lives in Ann Arbor and Florida.

Vessie knew that with everyone pulling together all eight of her children would one day graduate from high school. Some went on to business schools and colleges. Vessie was proud that her children achieved their goals in education. Her knowledge of gardening and cooking qualified her to become the cook for the children's school. She could be seen carrying a large kettle of beans or potatoes from her kitchen to the Lincoln School, located then at the corner of California and Lincoln highways. A cow provided the family with milk and they had a pony for the children to enjoy.

Vessie was the leader of the local 4-H club and taught the girls to sew their own clothes. They exhibited their sewing and gardening at the county fair and were rewarded with blue ribbons and dress revue winners for their outstanding skills. The older girls worked at the dime stores in downtown Fort Wayne while attending school. The boys were caddies at the Elks County Club. Golfing was a favorite sport for the family because golf club members would give the Weaver boys old golf clubs. Everyone practiced the game out in the cow pasture until they earned enough money to play on a real golf course.

Vessie Weaver and Children. Front: Bernice Jamison, Velma Voige, Elaine Griffis, Vessie Weaver. Back: Philip Weaver, Damon Weaver, Elsie Shively, Ralph and Richard Weaver.

With everyone pooling their money and doing whatever they could to help, the family thrived. Then World War II came. One by one the stars began to be added to the service banner that Vessie so proudly hung in the front window of her living room. During the war, families displayed a banner having a white background ringed in red and showing a blue star for each member serving his country. Vessie's banner had four blue stars, plus a gold star in the middle. She had given her country her eldest son to keep her nation free. An officer and a pilot in the Army Air Corp, Ralph died in combat at age 34.

At the age of 96, Vessie often took morning walks, did dishes and a little cooking. She left a family of five living children, 20 grandchildren, and 32 great grandchildren.

Submitted by Joan LeGrand

DONALD ALLEN & JOANNE ALICE PARSON WEBER FAMILY

Donald Allen Weber was born April 18, 1938, at St. Joseph Hospital in Fort Wayne. His parents were both Fort Wayne natives. George Anthony Weber was born January 24, 1914, the youngest of twelve children born to Frank Weber and Christina Stein. George's wife, LaDonna Marie Wiseley, was born June 2, 1916, the second of four children of Walter Alfred Wiseley and Ruth Anna Marie Kallen. Walter was born in Wapakoneta, Ohio, the son of Amos Wiseley and Emma Swim. Ruth Anna Marie Kallen was the youngest daughter of Peter Kallen and Johanna Katherine Mansdorfer.

Captain Donald A. Weber, Fort Wayne Fire Department 1972.

Donald attended Frances Slocum and Holy Cross Grade Schools, Forest Park Junior High, and graduated from North Side High School in 1956. On August 27, 1956, Donald enlisted in the United States Navy. After graduation from Boot Camp at Great Lakes, he attended Machinist Mate School and then went on board the D.S.S. Passumpsic AO-1O7, where he spent the next three and one half years touring the Pacific Ocean. By August 27, 1960, Donald had earned the rank of Second Class Petty Officer and received an Honorable Discharge. Donald married Joanne Alice Parson on September 2, 1961, in Paulding, Ohio. Joanne was the daughter of Lloyd Parks Parson and Allie Lunette Schifferly.

Don was accepted on the Fort Wayne Fire Department October 15, 1962, where he served until April of 1983. He served as Captain at Fire Station Number Eight on Fairfield Avenue from 1973 to 1976. He was placed on a medical pension in 1983 by the City of Fort Wayne.

Donald started his own business as a photographer, taking pictures of school children. In 1983, he became the first Executive Director of the Fort Wayne Firefighters Museum, holding that title until 1986. He was the scoutmaster of Troop 317 at Riverside School for eight years. In his final year as scoutmaster, the troop went to the Filmont Scout Ranch in New Mexico for a twelve day hiking trip.

Donald and Joanne were blessed with four children, all four who still live in the Fort Wayne area.

Joseph Anthony Weber was born February 10, 1962. He graduated from Purdue University, West Lafayette and works at Franklin Electric in Bluffton, Indiana. Joe married Jodi Ann Steele on July 29, 1989. They have two children, Jared Anthony, born June 21, 1999, and Jadyn Ann, born October 7, 2004.

Christina Marie Weber was born June 18, 1963. She graduated from Purdue University, Fort Wayne and works at Lutheran Hospital as a Registered Nurse. Tina married Frank Vincent Paladino August 20, 1988. They have three children, Kaitlyn Marie born June 11, 1990, Jessica Elizabeth born September 15, 1992, and Rebecca Joanne born December 18, 1994.

Kathleen Sue Weber was born July 31, 1964. She graduated from Purdue University, Fort Wayne and works at Parkview Hospital as a Registered Nurse. Kathy married Randall Lee Zion October 25, 1985. They have three children, David Lee born April 25, 1986, Rachel Elizabeth born November 8, 1990, and Matthew John born January 2, 1995.

Andrew Allen Weber was born February 19, 1969. Andy enlisted in the United States Navy, serving six years as a Nuclear Reactor Operator, four on board the U.S.S. Abraham Lincoln CVN-72 during the first Gulf War. Andy married Mamie Lee Kirtley in Idaho Falls, Idaho, on December 27, 1991. They are the parents of five sons: Jacob Allen, born March 9, 1993, Nicholas Charles, born July 3, 1996, Daniel Joseph, born July 11, 1997, Thomas Donald, born December 5, 1999 and Samuel Lee, born March 21, 2003.

Joanne Alice Parson Weber filed a petition for dissolution of marriage in Allen Superior Court and was granted same on February 19, 2002.

Submitted by Andrew A. Weber

JOHN WEBER & CATHERINE KRETZ OFENLOCH FAMILY

John Weber was born in Germany on January 1826. He sailed from Havre to New York, arriving April 26, 1852 on the ship St. George. His uncle, John Mohr, was here in Fort Wayne and owned a shoe store. John was a shoemaker by trade.

He married Anna Maria Hergenroether August 4, 1853. They had four children, but only John Jr. lived to be an adult. Anna died in 1862, and John married Catherine Kretz Ofenloch April 12, 1863.

Barbara Clara was born April 2, 1864, and died May 31, 1888.

Frank was born October 20, 1866. He married Christina Stein, daughter of John Joseph and Catherine Schramm Stein, at St Mary's Catholic Church November 7, 1889. Frank and Christina had twelve children. Frank was a cigar maker at Berndt's Rusty Cigar Factory. The children were born at 122 (1404) Maumee. The family then moved to 2021 East Washington Street. Their first child, John Frank, born July 22, 1889, died

L-R seated: John Weber Jr., John Weber Sr., Catherine Kretz Ofenloch Weber. Standing in rear L-R: Frank Weber, Barbara Weber.

of burns by scalding at the age of two. 2) Joseph Edward was born November 4, 1890, and served in the Army during World War I. He worked at the Berghoff Brewery. 3) Catherine Gertrude was born July 22, 1892, and worked at the Rub-No-More Soap Factory. She married Frank Perley Miller and had four sons, Richard Frank, Daniel Martin, Edward Paul, and Raymond Joseph. 4) Peter Bernard was born April 17, 1894, died at four years of age. 5) George Robert was born April 5, 1896, and died at two years old. 6) John Theodore was born November 13, 1897, and worked for the Pennsylvania Railroad. He married Margaret Catherine Kloss in Chicago. They lived in Chicago and raised seven children: twins, Margaret Helen and Ruth Catherine, John Joseph, Mary Delphine, Evelyn Helen, Lois Gertrude, and Daniel Joseph. 7) Martin Frank was born September 2, 1899, was a millwright. He worked at the Handle Factory and Berghoff Brewery. Mart married Olive Ione Ludwig of Paulding, Ohio. They raised one daughter, Mary Olive. 8) Paul Peter was born August 12, 1901,

L-R: LaDonna Marie Wiseley Weber and George Anthony Weber, June 2, 1937.

served in the Navy and worked at the Berghoff Brewery. He married Catherine Henrietta Kloss in Chicago; she was the sister of his brother John's wife. They had four children, Catherine Ann, Rita Marie, Nancy Louise, and James Paul. 9) Mary Delphine was born October 27, 1903, and married Herbert James (Bill) Bauer on April 6, 1921. They had four children, Dorothy Delphine, Herbert Martin (Bud), Carol Ann, and Barbara Jean. 10) Frank Joseph was born January 10, 1907; he was a bookkeeper at General Electric and died at age 24. 11) Mary Cecilia was born December 31, 1910, and worked at Wolf & Dessauer's. She married Ashley John Parquette and they had two sons, George Ashley and Richard Ashley. Mary Cecilia Weber Parquette, the sole survivor of the twelve Weber children, lives in Fort Wayne. 12) George Anthony was born January 24, 1914, and attended St. Mary's School and Central High. He worked at the Berghoff Brewery, delivering beer by horse drawn wagon until motorized trucks. George married LaDonna Marie Wiseley, daughter of Walter Alfred and Ruth Anna Marie Kallen Wiseley, on June 2, 1937, at St. Mary's Catholic Church in the rectory. They raised two sons, Donald Allen and Richard Walter, and a daughter, Sue Ann. George was drafted into the U.S. Army and served in France and Germany during World War II. Returning home, he was one of many veterans hired by the Fort Wayne Fire Department. Hired on July 7, 1945, he served twenty-five years in the department before retiring in 1970. LaDonna died on June 15, 1974. George died September 8, 1981. They are buried in St. John's Cemetery on Engle Road.

Submitted by Donald A. Weber

JOHN BERNARD WEBER

John Bernard Weber, Sr. was born in Schwarzenholz, Saarland, Germany, on March 30, 1827. He came to the United States in 1856 and lived in Decatur, Indiana, with his brother Simon. John married Mary Magdalena Sorg, a native of Germany, in Wayne County, Ohio, on April 2, 1857. Their nine children were born in Decatur, Indiana, Adams County.

John Bernard Weber established the Weber Sales and Livery Stable in Decatur, Indiana. He moved to Fort Wayne, Indiana, Allen County in 1887. John and his family lived at 226 Main Street in a sturdy brick house built in the 1850s. He built the Weber Sales Business there. The business occupied a large brick building that extended from West Main Street to Pearl Street.

The business specialized in wholesale trading of horses and wagon mules. Frequent large shipments were made to eastern and foreign markets. One of their best customers was John Wannamacher of Wannamacher's Department Stores in Philadelphia, Pennsylvania. The Weber Business provided horses for most of the larger city fire departments and the United States Army.

John Bernard Weber and Mary Magdalena Weber, 50th Wedding, 1907

John Bernard Weber, Sr. ran the business with his sons, Noah J. Weber of Allen County and John B. Weber, Jr. of Adams County, as well as his grandson, Leo John Weber, of Adams County. His daughter, Lena Weber of Fort Wayne, kept the business' books.

The family of John Bernard Weber and his wife Mary Magdalena were numbered among the most popular and best known people in Allen County. They celebrated their 50th wedding anniversary in 1907. Mary Magdalena Weber died on April 24, 1912. John Bernard Weber, Sr. died on April 16, 1917.

Submitted by great, great, granddaughter, Ellen Colchin White

LEO J. WEBER, VETERAN HORSEMAN

Leo John Weber was a veteran horseman and a member of a pioneer Fort Wayne family. His family was identified with the horse and mule business in Fort Wayne and throughout northern Indiana for more than 100 years. Leo Weber operated the Indian Village Riding Academy at 1501 Bluffton Road, starting in 1933. The brick riding stable still stands on the bank of the St. Mary's River across from Foster Park. The horses waded through the shallows of the St. Mary's River and went down the bridle paths at Foster Park. Later, Leo moved the academy to South Fairfield Avenue, using the opposite end of Foster Park with its bridle paths.

During World War I, Leo Weber bought thousands of horses for the United States Government for use in the army cavalry and artillery units. He also supplied horses for the famous Black Horse Troop of the Culver Military Academy. Leo went to France after enlisting in the United States Army in 1918. He served in Europe from 1918 to 1919.

Leo John Weber, 1935

Leo's grandfather, John Bernard Weber Sr., and Leo's father, John Bernard Weber Jr., had the Weber Sales and Livery Stable at 226 West Main Street. It occupied a large brick building extending from West Main Street through to Pearl Street. The business, a well known landmark in Fort Wayne, was established in 1887 and was conducted by the grandfather, father, and several uncles.

Leo Weber was regarded as an outstanding equine authority and exhibited gaited horses, hunters, and jumpers at many horse shows in the midwest. He presided as horse show judge on many occasions. Leo was born in Decatur, Indiana. (Adams County) on December 17, 1888. He married Adda Anne Lafferty, a 1919 Lutheran Hospital Nurses Training School graduate, in 1921. They had four daughters: Patricia, Harriet, Margaret, and Elizabeth. Adda died in 1938, and.

Leo Weber died of a heart attack in 1950 in his Allen County home on South Calhoun Street.

Patricia married Buster L. Baker and now lives in Forest Grove, Oregon. Harriet married Richard L. Bouillon and she died in 1961. Margaret married Max E. Colchin and she lives in Fort Wayne, Indiana. Elizabeth originally married Anthony J. Faurote, and later Wayne Smith. They now live in Wellington, Florida.

Submitted by Margaret A. Weber Colchin

CHARLES WEEKS

In 1759, Charles Weeks was born in Hampshire County, Virginia (now West Virginia). Charles served under the immediate command of General George Washington as a 2nd Lieutenant in 1779.

Charles, along with his brother James, settled in Shelby County, Ohio around 1817. In 1822, Charles Weeks with sons Charles Jr. and Martin, came to Adams Township, Allen County, Indiana settling on the Maumee River. There were eight original settlers. The area is north of the cloverleaf toward New Haven. Charles Weeks, Sr. served on the first grand jury of Allen County in 1824 and again in 1825.

Martin Weeks purchased land from John B. Bouri in the southeast portion of Adams Township in 1830. Martin was the neighborhood "bad man". He was hostile, violent, and an alcoholic. He later experienced a change of heart and became a Baptist minister.

Charles Weeks, Jr. married in 1831 to Mary Crow. They settled around Huntertown. He was the first postmaster. He later perished in a fire.

James Weeks purchased land from Samuel Lil.

Burt Weeks was a son of William Weeks, who fought in the Civil War.

Submitted by Sandy Bates

WEHRENBERG

The family name is Wehrenberg. Henry Christian Wehrenberg, and a friend, from Stylburg, Germany in 1870, stowed away on a sailing vessel to America, arriving in New York when Henry was eighteen years old. His future wife, Wilhemine Albersmeyer, sailed to America several years later with her mother and six siblings. In New York, Henry worked in the construction business, mainly as a brick mason. He had already earned his apprenticeship. After a couple of years, he drifted to Fort Wayne. He met Wilhemine, and they were married. They began to raise their family on Lewis Street, then moved to Madison Street. They called that street "Catechism Row," as it was down from St. Paul's Lutheran Church. Their neighbors were the Dryers, Rodenbecks, Bickels, Koenigs, Krudops, Hitzemans, and the whole Niemeyer tribe. The Catholics lived on the south side of Madison and the Lutherans lived on the north side. The youngest male offspring of Henry and Wilhemine, Alfred, remembers the kids liked to pelt each other with apple cores and walnuts, and all kinds of things.

There were five children in the family: Fred, Paul, Henry, Wilma, and, Al. Their father died when Al was sixteen, and, their mother died when Al was eighteen. After his mother died, Al lived with his sister and her husband, Walter Helmke, a couple of years, still on Madison Street.

L-R: Al, Paul, Wilma, young Henry, Fred Wehrenberg

After the senior Henry had been in Fort Wayne for a couple of years and had become a citizen, he learned a little more English. He formed a partnership with his friend Bueschіng. They became Wehrenberg and Buesching Contracting Co. The Wehrenberg and Buesching families were joined when Paul married Ella Buesching. Charles Buesching, Ella's brother, would become president of Lincoln National Bank.

Henry also started a lumber business. He was one of the earliest owners of a chain of businesses. There was Standard Lumber Co. in Fort Wayne, and New Haven Lumber Co., and lumber companies in Monroeville, Geneva, Grabill, and Spencerville. He owned all those companies. Mostly, they took the name of the town where they were.

Eldest son Fred went through St. Paul Lutheran School and had some years at Fort Wayne High School. He had been self taught by working with his father in the lumber business. He took over when his father passed away. Next youngest, Paul, was in the construction business, as well as the younger Henry. Fred's eldest son Fritz continued in the lumber business until he retired and went to manage a Lutheran hospital in Monrovia, Liberia. The younger Henry's son, Henry, worked for the state highway department.

Only daughter, Wilma, married Walter E. Helmke before her parents died, living next door to her parents on Madison St. Wilma attended Luther Institute in its early years. Walter went away to Indiana University Law School. From an offspring of theirs, their only son, Walter P., one of his three children, one of two sons, would become one of Fort Wayne's honorable mayors, Paul Helmke.

Wehrenberg Family Legacy, Valparaiso University: The Wehrenberg family was very important in gaining a Lutheran university, Valparaiso. Henry and Fred Wehrenberg worked with Henry Moellering to take over Indiana Normal College, which was near bankruptcy. In 1926, Wilhemine and Henry made the bold decision to invest in the future of their family, higher education, and the church. St. Paul's Lutheran Church had a leading part in acquiring the physical properties of the university and setting up the academic program. One of four primary organizers, Henry and Wilhemine pledged a substantial portion towards the total amount campaign required to purchase the then closed and bankrupt Valparaiso University. Their dream was to see Valparaiso University, founded in the Lutheran heritage, become a leading institution of higher education. A residency hall, built in 1951, named Wehrenberg Hall in honor of the family, is there. A number of thet hird generation Wehrenbergs went there. Third generation Fritz Wehrenberg, wife Dolores Busse W., and all six offspring graduated from Valparaiso University. That is just one branch of Wehrenbergs that attended and, as well, graduated from VU.

Alfred attended Valparaiso University and came back to live in Fort Wayne. It was the Depression years, and his first job out of town was with the forest service Conservation Corp. He was lucky enough to get in with the C. C. C. program, and was sent all over the state of Indiana doing a variety of jobs. Later he was in southern Indiana for a while, meeting his wife, Velma Parker, running a dress shop in Evansville, eventually marrying in Tell City.

St. Paul Lutheran Church was a very much integrated part of the Wehrenberg family life, on a number of levels. A major one including the rebuilding after the church fire of 1903. Senior Henry Wehrenberg was always very proud of the schools and other buildings he had constructed around Fort Wayne. What he was most proud of was the building of St. Paul Lutheran Church. After the fire had destroyed the church in 1903, he was hired to help rebuild the church. Two sons, Henry and Paul, worked with him on this job. It was a brick building and they were brick masons. He always mentioned that it was a great pleasure that he was allowed to do this.

Submitted by Ruth (Rhodes) Snyder, the eldest grandchild of 12, of Fred Wehrenberg.

PAUL ANTHONY & FRANCES (HOLTHOUSE) WEHRLE

Frances Virginia Holthouse was born August 2, 1915, to Clarence and Alma (Starost) Holthouse in Decatur, Indiana. She married Paul Anthony Wehrle on November 21, 1940 at St. Joseph Church on Brooklyn Avenue, Fort Wayne.

Paul Anthony Wehrle was born August 23, 1915, in Fort Wayne to Carl and Caroline (Huhn) Wehrle. Carl Wehrle was born in Freiburg, Germany, and emigrated with his parents, Michael and Josephine (Zimmerman) Wehrle in the 1880s. After settling briefly near Payne, Ohio, Michael and Josephine moved to Fort Wayne with their family in the 1890s. Caroline Huhn was born in Fort Wayne to Frederick Huhn, a stonecutter, and Mary (Kress) Huhn, who had was in Fort Wayne in 1860. Her parents, Eustach Kress and Catherine (Auth) Kress were married at St. Mary's Catholic Church in Fort Wayne in 1858.

Wherle Tavern, 1911.
Behind bar, L to R: Adolph Wehrle, Carl Wehrle

Michael and Josephine (Zimmerman) Wehrle had the following children: Adolph, Mary, Amelia "Molly", Emil, Rose, William, Caroline, and Carl.

Michael Wehrle and his sons (including Carl) opened a tavern in the 1900 block of Fairfield Avenue shortly after their arrival in Fort Wayne, and lived next door. Carl Wehrle married twice. His first wife, Elizabeth Schenk, died, leaving Carl with five small children: Josephine (married August Becker); Mary, Agnes (married Robert Mensing); Margaret (married John Roehling), and Carl Anthony, Jr. (married Esther Wieseman, Annabelle Donovan). After Elizabeth's death, Carl married Caroline Mary Huhn. Their children were Robert Joseph (married Helen Eber); William Jasper (married Margaret Bennett); and Paul Anthony (married Frances Holthouse).

The Wehrle Tavern was converted into a bakery business during the years of Prohibition. It re-opened as a tavern when the amendment was repealed. Paul and Frances (Holthouse) Wehrle continued to run the Wehrle Tavern until the early 1980s.

Paul and Frances Wehrle had seven children, five surviving to adulthood. They are:

Rita Jane (1942), married Robert W. Quinn Jr.; children: Angela, Gregory, Jeffrey, Daniel, Katharine, and Elizabeth.

Barbara Ann (1946), married Paul Brubaker; children: Paul, Lori, and Michael James.

Paul Anthony (1948-2004), married Sally Green; children: Damien Green, Nathan Green Wehrle.

Kathleen Jo (1952), married Terry Cunningham; children: John, Benjamin, Matthew and Katherine.

Jon Thomas (1954), married Kathleen Wiltshire; children: Samuel and Rachel.

Submitted by Daniel Quinn

FRED WEIBEL FAMILY

Fred Weibel Sr. was born on September 21, 1821, in Baebtin, Canton Basil, Switzerland. Anna Marie Barbara Touman was born February 22, 1822, also in Switzerland. Fred Sr, and Anna Marie came to the United States between 1849 and 1851. It is suggested that they arrived on their own boat. The Weibels left Switzerland due to the political aftermath of the Swiss Civil War of 1847.

Fred Jr. was born on April 23, 1851, in Lafayette Township in Allen County, Indiana. He was the first American-born Weibel and the first son of Frederick and Anna Marie. Daughters, Margarete and Louisa, were born in Switzerland. Son John (1856-1938), and daughter Lydia, were born after the family settled in Allen County. Fred Sr. was a successful farmer near Nine Mile. However, the promise of free land lured the Weibels to eastern Kansas prior to the January 16, 1865, birth of their son Edward. Fred Sr. and Anna Marie (Mary) remained in Eudora Township, Douglas County, Kansas. Anna Marie died there in 1888 and Fred Sr. on April 28, 1899.

Fred Jr. returned to Allen County and married Leah Sarah Voltz on July 30, 1876. Leah was the daughter of Christian Voltz (1820-1899), another Lafayette Township pioneer, and Anna Seegram (circa 1820-1863). Fred Jr. and Leah had six children: William (1878-1934), George (1880-1931), John (Jack) (1882-1962), Anna May (1883-1928), Charles (Charley) (1886-1983), and Pearly (1893-1896).

The Fred Weibel, Jr. Family, 1910. Seated: Fred Weibel and Leah. Standing: William, George, Charles, John and Anne.

Fred Jr. started a profitable well drilling business in Lafayette Township before relocating his family to Fort Wayne in 1896, where he purchased a home at 479 Broadway. and opened a shop at 18 Harrison Street. His sons joined the growing family business. By 1902, Fred was a respected Fort Wayne businessman who won a bid to drill the second largest well in Fort Wayne. In 1907, he was awarded a contract to drill an artesian well for a new Fort Wayne Hotel. Later in life, Fred Jr. and his son-in-law, J. Fred Geiger, opened a grocery store at 836 East Wayne Street. Both families lived at 518 Organ Avenue. Fred Jr. died on November 24, 1922, and Leah, June 19, 1926. They are buried in Prairie Grove Cemetery.

In 1900, son William, a steamfitter, married Olive Ake, daughter of Elias (1857-1944) and Anna Summers (1861-1933). In 1906, George married Edna A. Lehman (1885-1908) then moved to Denver, Colorado, due to Edna's poor health. After Edna's death, George started a Denver plumbing and heating business. He was killed when a boiler exploded. Annie married J. Fred Geiger (1882-1973) prior to 1908 in Indianapolis and eventually returned to Fort Wayne. In November 1908, John (Jack) married Edith Emma Lee (1885-1950), daughter of Jeffrey Lee (1860-1922) and Lizzie Stellhorn (1855-1908). Also a steamfitter, Jack relocated to Detroit in 1910 and then to went Chicago in 1932 to work at the World's Fair. In 1936, Jack opened the Weibel Heating Company. In 1909, Charley married Alma Schnitker (1887-1986), daughter of Christian Schnitker (1859-1958) and Omelia Krannichfeld (1861-1923). Charley was a route salesman for the Perfection Biscuit Company of Fort Wayne for 32 years.

Several great-grandchildren of William, Anna, and Charley remain in the greater Fort Wayne area.

Submitted by Dennis J. Cotter

HERBERT & LORRAINE WEIER FAMILY HISTORY

Herbert and Lorraine Weier moved to Fort Wayne, Indiana in the spring of 1958. They were married on August 26, 1956, at Westminster Presbyterian Church in Peoria, Illinois.

Herbert and Lorraine Weier

Herbert was born October 13, 1931 in Cook County, Illinois, to Herbert and Emily (Cillian) Weier. He attended the Chicago Public Schools and graduated from Austin High School in 1950. He was a member of the Trinity Evangelical United Brethren Church in Chicago, Illinois.

Lorraine was born December 28, 1931, in Tazewell County, Illinois to Silas and Hannah (Holliger) Hofmann. She attended public schools in Deer Creek Township and graduated from Deer Creek-Mackinaw High School in 1949. She was a member of the Presbyterian Church in Washington, Illinois. Both Herbert and Lorraine attended Blackburn College in Carlinville, Illinois.

Herbert enlisted in the United States Navy in 1952 during the Korean Conflict. At the time of his discharge in 1956, he had achieved the rank of First Class Petty Officer. Lorraine received an Associate in Arts Degree from Blackburn College, Carlinville, Illinois in 1951. In 1953 she received a Bachelor of Science Degree, cum laude, from the University of Illinois. She was employed by The Commonwealth Edison Company in 12 northern Illinois counties in the Sales Promotion Department.

In 1955 Lorraine was selected by the Illinois State 4-H Foundation as a delegate on the International 4-H Exchange Program. The assignment was to The Netherlands. After completion of the program's obligations, she was employed by the McClean County, Illinois Home Economics Extension Service, and later by the University of Illinois in the production of a daily radio program that was distributed throughout the State of Illinois.

After their marriage, Herbert and Lorraine moved to Fort Wayne, Indiana, where Herbert attended the Indiana Institute of Technology. After graduation in Electrical Engineering in 1963, he was employed by The Magnavox Company in Fort Wayne until his retirement in 1990.

In 1958, Lorraine was employed by the Garret-Keyser-Butler School Corporation in Garrett, Indiana. Later employment included Volunteer Coordinator and Public Relations Director for the Allen County Economic Opportunity Council and lecturer in Nutrition and Wellness for St. Vincent's Hospital Wellness Centers in Indianapolis, Indiana.

Both Herbert and Lorraine were active at The First Presbyterian Church as Youth Advisors, officers, committee members and theater volunteers.

Both were active in the formation of the West Central Neighborhood Association and in its services to the community. Both served United Way Organizations on boards and committees. Herbert and Lorraine were docents at the Fort Wayne Museum of Art and served The Center for Nonviolence as committee and panel members. Both were active volunteers for the Northeast Indiana Radio Reading Service for sight impaired persons.

Locally, Herbert and Lorraine were members and supporters of The United Way of Allen County and Arts United of Greater Fort Wayne. They were supporters of local, national and international environmental organizations, including The Nature Conservancy, ACRES, and The Friends of the Parks of Fort Wayne and Allen County.

Submitted by Herbert and Lorraine Weier

DOUGLAS HALE SR. & CANDY KAMPHUES WELLMAN

Douglas Hale Wellman was born to Francis and Eugenia Wellman on March 15, 1951. He was their third child. He attended school at Franklin Elementary, Franke Park Elementary, Franklin Junior High School, and graduated from Northside High School in 1969. He attended IU-Purdue in Fort Wayne, Indiana, for one year.

His wife, Candy Kamphues, was born on February 27, 1952, in Fort Wayne to Scott and Opal Banning Kamphues. She attended elementary school at Slocum Junior High School at Lakeside and graduated from Northside High School in 1970. Candy was the second of three children, the other two, a sister, Marilyn born in 1948, and a brother, Ricky born in 1953; both died in infancy.

Doug and Candy met while attending Northside High School and were married on August 15, 1970 in St. Matthews Lutheran Church.

Doug went to work for Norfolk & Western Railroad in October of 1970 and took a leave of absence in February, 1971, to enlist in the United States Air Force. He served as a B-52 / Kcl35 mechanic while stationed at Ellsworth Air Force Base near Rapid City, South Dakota. While Doug and Candy were living in South Dakota they had Douglas Jr., born on April 11, 1972, and Scott Francis, born on May 11, 1973.

Douglas and Candy Wellman

On March 26, 1974, Doug was reassigned to The Indiana Air National Guard at Baer Field air base and worked as a mechanic on F-lOOs. He completed his military service in March, 1976. While serving in the Air National Guard, he returned to work at Norfolk & Western.

On January 26, 1976, Matthew was born, followed by Heidi Ann on October 16, 1978. Then, on April 5, 1981, Holly Suzanne was born. Doug and Candy moved into the Brookside Parkerdale Addition in 1977 and remained there.

Candy was a full time mother and housewife and enjoyed crocheting, and doing other arts and crafts. She became a lover of boxer dogs, after having two as family pets. Doug and Candy continue to attend St. Matthew's Lutheran, where they were married.

Their oldest son, Doug Jr., served in the U.S. Army and became an over the road truck driver. Their second son, Scott, attended St. Paul Tech and became a drafter and designer. He also took animation training. Heidi attended International Business College and became a graphic designer. Their youngest daughter, Holly, attended Purdue, became a registered nurse, and worked at Lutheran Hospital in Fort Wayne.

Doug is very interested in history, political science, the creation-science-evolution controversy, and is an avid fisherman. He also enjoys hunting and writing. He regularly writes guest columns for the *Fort Wayne News-Sentinel*.

Doug joined the Anthony Halberstadt Chapter, Sons of the American Revolution, in 2001 and served as Secretary-Treasurer until 2004; he now serves as President. He is also a member of the National Rifle Association.

Submitted by Douglas H. Wellman

FRANCIS A. & EUGENIA W. WELLMAN

Francis Wellman was born to Selden and Edna Wellman in Naperville, Illinois, on May 24, 1914. He was their second child. He went to Bloomingdale Elementary School and attended Central High School and graduated from Northside High School in 1933. He served in the Civilian Conservation Corps in the Mammoth Cave National Park area and in southern Indiana. He worked off and on for General Electric, and finally hired out on The Nickel Plate Road in 1940. The Nickel Plate Road was bought by the Norfolk & Western in 1964. Francis retired in 1976. Francis' grandfather, Jerome Wellman, was born in La Fountaine, Indiana, to Moses Wellman and Emily Memphis Hale Wellman. Moses' grandfather, Rudolph Wellman, fought in the Revolutionary War.

Francis' mother, Edna, died of cancer in 1943. His father, Selden, died in 1960. Both are buried in Lindenwood Cemetery, with grandfather, Jerome Wellman, and Jerome's daughter, Bertha Wellman Welch.

Moses Wellman is buried in the Hale Family Cemetery in La Fountaine, Indiana. Moses' father, Samuel, and his wife, Jane Coffee Wellman, are buried in the HalfAcre-Long Cemetery in Wabash County. Samuel's father, Rudolph, is buried in Little Crabapple Cemetery near St. Clairesville, Ohio.

As of 2005 Francis, age 91, was residing in Fort Wayne with his wife Eugenia.

Eugenia was born to Archibald Spoerhase and Elsie Matsanke Spoerhase on July 27, 1916. She attended Anthony Wayne Elementary School and graduated from Elmhurst High School in 1934.

Francis and Eugenia were married on October 22, 1938, in Trinity English Lutheran Church in Fort Wayne, Indiana. They raised five children: Ronald Francis, born June 12, 1941; Jerome David born July 24, 1943; Douglas Hale born March 15, 1951; Marcia Diane born December 6, 1952; and Linda Sue born July 20, 1960.

Francis A. and Eugenia W. Wellman

As of 2005 they had 14 grandchildren and five great-grandchildren.

They were charter members of St. Matthew's Lutheran Church which was started in the old Wells Street Theater in Fort Wayne in 1953. St. Matthew's later moved to a chapel on Irene Court and then finally to its present location on Goshen Road in 1960.

Eugenia's mother, Elsie Matsanke, emigrated from Russia to the U.S. in 1912. She fled the Bolshevik Revolution with her youngest brother, Alfonz Matsanke. She spoke several languages fluently and taught herself English. She met and married Archibald Spoerhase on October 16, 1915. Elsie' father and four of her brothers were Lutheran ministers in Russia.

Archibald's father and mother emigrated to the U.S. from Germany.

Francis and Eugenia both enjoyed fishing. Francis was an excellent checker and ping pong player as well. Francis was also very much interested in Bible study and history. Francis and Eugenia made their home in Jerome Wellman's edition on the north side of Fort Wayne which was initially purchased by Francis' grandfather, Jerome. They were still residing there as of 2005.

Submitted by Francis Wellman

JOHN WENDLING & ALICE BURNS FAMILY

John Wendling was born August 13, 1909, in Freidorf, Hungary, the first child and only son of Johann Wendling and Katherine Muhlroth. John's paternal grandparents were Karl Wendling and Eva Weisgerber and his maternal grandparents were Kristof Muhlroth and Margaret Huy. On July 12, 1912, with the ensuing war approaching, Johann departed from Cuxhaven, Germany for America, on the Kaiserin Auguste Victoria and arrived at Ellis Island on July 22, 1912. He then sought employment as a cabinet maker in Chicago. Nine months later, John, age two and a half, also journeyed with his mother, Katherine, and younger sister, Barbara, on the U.S. President Grant and arrived at Ellis Island on April 2, 1913. They then were reunited with their husband/father in Chicago, Illinois. Another

Wendling family: John (son), Johann (father), Barbara (daughter), Katherine (daughter) and Katerine (mother). 1918

Alice (Burns) Wendling and John Wendling. Wedding picture, May 4, 1935.

child, Katherine, was born December 27, 1916, in Chicago. Johann and Katherine's original intent was to remain in America for three years and then return; however, they chose to remain.

The voyage was harsh crossing the Atlantic. One story told of John almost being blown overboard, until a cousin grabbed him and pulled him back. This cousin was Katherine Albrecht, traveling with her mother, Elizabeth, who was a sister to Katherine (Muhlroth) Wendling.

After arriving at Ellis Island, young John was almost denied permission to enter because he had an eye infection, but, after much pleading by his mother, permission was granted for them to continue on to Chicago.

While growing up in Chicago, John attended LeMoyne Grade School and spent his youth delivering groceries, selling newspapers on the street corner at nine years of age and later ushered at the Uptown theater. He attended Lane Technical School and was active in their R.O.T.C. program, graduating January 27, 1928, with the rank of major. In his early twenties, recalling those cold Chicago winters, he would often buy the remaining newspapers from the corner newsstand so the young paperboy could return home. Catching a streetcar, he would distribute a paper on each seat.

John began working for Victor Manufacturing and Gasket Company in Chicago, Illinois. Then, after a lay-off from National Engineering in Chicago, his mother, Katherine, who was a friend of Frank Freimann's mother, advised him that there was an opportunity at the Magnavox Company in Fort Wayne, Indiana. John was hired and eventually became a senior mechanical engineer, and during his employment of over 40 years was granted two patents. The first patent was awarded on June 10, 1958, for a floating stop switch mechanism. The second patent was granted November 17, 1959, for an extendible antenna used on sonobuoys, which the navy used to detect hostile submarine presence. He was also instrumental in setting up the speaker system atop the Lincoln Tower in Fort Wayne that broadcast Christmas carols in the 1950s and 60s. His skills were also utilized in the original model train exhibit in the Museum of Science and Industry in Chicago.

John Wendling met his future wife, Alice Burns, at Magnavox. She was one of ten children of Edward and Anna Burns, born in Fort Wayne, where she attended McCulloch Grade School and later St. Andrew's Academy. As a young adult, she worked for Dudlow Manufacturing, Phelps Dodge, and Steinite, which later became Magnavox. Finding a reason to visit the area where she was testing equipment at Magnavox, John used a grinder, directing some sparks in her direction to capture her attention. Deliberately meeting her at the water fountain, he asked for her phone number on three separate occasions.

Following a courtship and engagement, John and Alice were married in St. Andrew's Catholic Church on May 10, 1935. Their marriage of 61 years included five children; John Edward (Joyce Felger-deceased) (Candace Cohen); Thomas Francis (Susan Platt-deceased) (Ila Crupe); Sharon Ann (Thomas O'Keefe); Marilyn Katherine (Robert Walker); and William Michael (Louise Dwire).

Alice spent her life as a devoted wife, mother, and grandmother, enjoying the family gatherings, baking, and taking trips with her daughters. John and Alice both enjoyed dancing and some of their favorite memories were of the Aragon Ballroom in Chicago. John retired from the Magnavox Company in 1974 with over 40 years of service. Their retirement years included short trips and country rides on Sunday.

John was self taught in many fields. Gathering his knowledge from books, he produced his own photo developing lab, repaired radios for extra income, and wired electricity in his home. He was extremely interested in anything electronic, built his own greenhouse, cultivated his own garden, which included numerous vegetables and berries, tended to seven fruit trees, raised rabbits, and built a 60 room martin house. John enjoyed bowling in a weekly league and would often invite several of his fellow employees to his home for frequent games of ping pong.

John and Alice were blessed with 17 grandchildren and several great-grandchildren. They both lived to be 87 years old. John died in 1996 and Alice died in 1999.

Submitted by John Wendling

DONN PAUL & DIANE MUELLER WERLING FAMILY

Donn was born October 14, 1945, to Paul and Lydia (Rebber) Werling on their 1850s farm on Moeller Road in Adams Township. Two miles east on Werling Road, Donn's great-grandfather, Heinrich, pioneered in the 1860s after emigrating from Lambsheim, Germany, in 1841. His Rebber ancestors came from near Hanover, Germany, in c. 1850. Grandmother was the daughter of the Rev. S.F. Stock, a pioneer Lutheran minister, who helped to found Woodburn and Gar Creek Lutheran Churches and the Lutheran Hospital. Diane's ancestors came from Switzerland and Saxony in Germany. Her grandmother, Delphia Kernen, lived to be a 100 and was once roasted on radio and in person for her many loves, including gardening and her many grandchildren. Her mother, Carlene, chaired the Fort Wayne children's garden show for many years.

Their only child, Benjamin Paul, was born, January 23, 1979, when Diane was the famous lighthouse keeper of the Grosse Point lighthouse in Evanston, Illinois. Their preservation and interpretation of the lighthouse appeared in the *Chicago Tribune*, *Preservation*

Ben, Donn and Diane Werling

Magazine of the National Trust, as well as the Armed Forces papers around the world.

Donn was subsequently director of the Henry Ford Estate for nearly twenty years, during which time his restoration work of the mansion and Jens Jensen landscapes appeared in three national cable shows, including "America's Castles" and House and Garden on A&E, as well as in the *Detroit News and Free Press* and *Preservation Magazine* of the National Trust for Historic Preservation.

Donn and Diane founded the Great Lakes Lighthouse Keepers Association and have helped it grow to a national leader in lighthouse preservation. Their family musical group, Sweetwater Journey, has made six recordings and performed throughout the Great Lakes region. Donn has composed over a 100 ballads, Diane plays the banjo and piano, and Ben plays the cello and harmonica. *Lakes and Lighthouses* and *Henry Ford a Hearthside Perspective* (book) both won national awards for excellence in interpreting our nation's heritage.

Presently, Donn is director of the Allen County Fort Wayne Historical Society, and they live on the same ancestral farm where he was born. Diane is director of the nascent Two Trees Memorial Arboretum which works to preserve and beautify the open space of Allen County while, at the same time, encrypting in its landscape the Gospel message of forgiveness and eternal life.

A retirement community, TurnPointe Woods, is being developed on the back half of their farm, while the historic 1895 house and associate historic structures are being preserved and restored for Arboretum purposes.

Benjamin Paul is a graduate of Luther College, B.A. and Cornell U., M.S. and is currently a doctoral student in entomology at the University of Wisconsin, Madison.

Following is the refrain of a ballad that chronicles the immigration of Germans to our region:

Friedheim II stands for peaceful home the second time around

For just like our forebears of old we seek new freedom's ground

We're looking for freedom to live and grow. Freedom for body and soul

Together we'll mine the Son's free gold working for Friedheim II-donn werling, 1978

Submitted by Donn Werling

HENRY WESSELS FAMILY

Henry (1845-1936) and Mary Wessels (1857-1932) came to Allen County, Indiana, in 1910, and bought a 160 acre farm on Butt Road in

Wessles Family

Lake Township. It was located one mile east of the Whitley County line between U.S. #30 (now Washington Center Road extended) and what is now new #30. They came from Blackford County, Indiana with seven of their eight children. Of German descent, Henry's father emigrated in 1836. His sons, J. Joseph (1885-1964) and Frank Wessels (1887-1968) farmed the "home place" from 1910 until it was sold in 1972 to Jim and Maxine Poinsette and their daughter Elaine and her husband Joe Hilger move in there. Twenty acres of that farm had been sold by Wessels to Frank Butts, whose farm adjoined that one.

Joe and Frank Wessels bought an 80 acre farm across from Lake Everett on Butt Road in 1919, and sold it in 1943. Joe had married in 1925, and he and his wife Jane and their daughters Mary Anne, Adelaide (1928-1946), Betty, and Patricia farmed there until 1943, when they moved back to the "home place".

Joe was involved in community, township, and county conservation and agricultural activities: Lake Township Advisory Board, Farm Bureau, Agricultural Adjustment Association, and he was a charter member of the Allen Dairy Company and Producer's Marketing. His wife Jane, formerly a registered nurse from Indianapolis, was always there when anyone in the neighborhood needed nursing care.

The Wessels family were members of St. Patrick's Catholic Church at Arcola from 1910 until Jane died in 1974. Mary Anne (Mrs. Frank Brown), Betty, (Mrs. Bernard Richardville) and Patricia, (Mrs. Lloyd Ness) were each married there. They had gone to St. Patrick's Grade School and Arcola High School. Over the years, family members who died were buried in the St. Patrick's Cemetery, which was on Bass Road south of Arcola.

Over the years, life on the farm changed from crop rotation, raising a variety of animals to provide manure for fertilizer and food, using work horses and a tractor for power, with much manual labor, to using chemical fertilizer, pesticides, herbicides, and a combine for the wheat and oats instead of the binder. Corn was picked with a machine instead of husked, cut and shocked. The "Threshing Ring," with neighboring friends working together to help each other, was gone. An oil furnace replaced cutting down trees from the woods for the stoves.

The Wessels family milked cows, sold Grade A milk, and raised chickens to sell eggs as cash crops. They had a milk house with a cold water tank to hold the ten gallon cans of milk before it was picked up by the milkman in his truck, and a milking parlor with a cement floor so the manure could be cleaned out daily. During WWII they raised fields of tomatoes and sugar beets also. Mexican workers came to harvest the tomatoes. It was hard work, but it was a good life.

Submitted by Mary Anne Brown

JOHN MARC WHEAT

John Marc Wheat is a sixth-generation Hoosier, born in Fort Wayne on October 22, 1964, to Thomas Earl Wheat (born May 28, 1936 in Allen County) and Suzanne Louise Morris (born May 28, 1943 in Fort Wayne, died November 20, 2001 in Beaufort, South Carolina). Land records indicate that the Reverend Thomas Wheat (1789-1860), a Methodist "circuit rider" and founder of the Indiana Wheat line, was in Fort Wayne as early as August 20, 1838.

Since August 2003, Marc has served as Staff Director and Chief Counsel of the Subcommittee on Criminal Justice, Drug Policy, & Human Resources, chaired by Congressman Mark Souder (R-Indiana). The Subcommittee's primary focus is on the $12.4 billion drug control budget. Marc first met Congressman Souder in 1987 when Marc worked for Congressman Dennis Hastert (now Speaker of the House of Representatives) and Souder worked for then Congressman (later Senator) Dan Coats.

Wedding photo of Edward L. Morris and Anna E. Karst, who resided at 442 West Butler in Fort Wayne until Anna's death in 1968

Before joining the Subcommittee, Marc served in President George W. Bush's Administration as the Senior Advisor for Senate Affairs at the U.S. Department of State during the fighting in Afghanistan and Iraq. His responsibilities were focused on enacting the Bush Administration's diplomatic and reconstruction priorities through the $16 billion Foreign Operations Appropriations bill.

Prior to joining the State Department a month after 9/11, he had been Counsel to the House Energy and Commerce Committee since June 1995, focusing on health care and bioethics.

Before attending law school, Wheat was the Director of Tax and Budget Policy for Citizens for a Sound Economy. While at CSE, Wheat's Porkbusters Coalition introduced President George H. W. Bush's 98 rescissions in March 1992, and succeeded in the elimination of $8.1 billion of wasteful spending, the largest such rescission since 1982. Wheat's Porkbusters Coalition was

Marc, Marie, and Benjamin Wheat, inaugural night, January 20, 2005

the subject of *Adventures in Porkland*, a book by *Washington Post* reporter Brian Kelly and illustrated by political cartoonist Pat Oliphant.

Prior to joining CSE, Marc worked for Congressman Dennis Hastert (R-Illinois) for three years. As the congressman's Senior Legislative Assistant, Marc focused on repealing the Social Security earnings limit (later the 7th pledge in the Contract With America).

He married Nancy Marie Gilliland (born August 21, 1969 in Greenville, South Carolina) on May 22, 1993. She is the daughter of James Milton Gilliland (born February 17, 1945) and Josie Virginia Petty (born September 7, 1947).

Marie G. Wheat serves as an appointee in the Bush Administration as the Chief of Staff and Chief Operating Officer of the Peace Corps, having most recently served as Chief of Staff to Congressman Jim DeMint (R-South Carolina). Previously, she was the Staff Director for the Senate Subcommittee on Oversight of Government Management, Restructuring, and the District of Columbia, chaired by Senator Sam Brownback (R-Kansas).

Prior to her time in the Senate, she was Legislative Director to Rep. Steve Largent (ROK) concentrating on tax, budget, energy and health issues. She was featured in National Journal's "Tracking the Rising Stars" at the beginning of the 104th Congress and has been a guest on radio and television shows, including C-Span's Washington Journal, NET's Business Week, Colombian National Radio, as well as others.

Marie first came to Capitol Hill to serve Rep. John Kasich (R-OH) as an analyst on the House Budget Committee, where she handled taxes, regulatory issues, government reform, and abolition of the Interstate Commerce Commission. Before working for Congress, she was the Policy Analyst for James C. Miller III, Budget Director for President Reagan, while he served as Chairman of the Board at Citizens for a Sound Economy. She also worked at the Strom Thurmond Institute in her home state of South Carolina before coming to Washington.

Marc received his B.A. degree (majoring in Spanish) from the University of Illinois at Urbana-Champaign in 1987, and his J.D. in the Corporate and Securities Specialty Track at George Mason University School of Law. Marie received a B.A. in Economics and Political Science from Clemson University.

Marc is First Vice President of the Memorial Foundation of the Germanna Colonies in Virginia, Chairman of Oakseed Ministries, and is a member of the Society of the Cincinnati. Marie is Chairman of the Board of Rockville Pregnancy Center.

The Wheats have two children: Benjamin Patterson (born March 14, 2004) and Laura Elizabeth (expected in August 2005).

Sources: *Who's Who in America* (57th edition), and *Who's Who in the World* (20th edition).

Submitted by Marc and Marie Wheat

WILLIAM WHITE FAMILY

William White lived at 811 East Wayne Street with his beloved wife, Anna Beatrice Rutherford White, in Fort Wayne, Indiana, for over 45 years. They had met in Atlanta, Georgia, while he attended Morehouse College and as she studied domestic science at Spelman College, next door. After Anna, known as "BB", was diagnosed with a degenerative hearing problem, Spellman College requested that she remain at the school as a cook. Shortly thereafter, her services were requested as a domestic worker by a family in New Jersey. They were cousins of the Rockefellers. Later, William and Anna "BB" married in New York, and then moved to Fort Wayne. BB's sister, Cordelia, and her husband, Alfred Lester, had moved here to follow his railroad work.

William and BB produced William Rutherford White in 1919. Sarah Grace was born two years later. They both graduated from Harmar Elementary and Central High Schools. William's mother sought legal assistance and won a case for him to become the first black student at the Fort Wayne Art School. He also attended John Herron Art Institute in Indianapolis, Indiana. Then he joined the Army and served in World War II. Upon return, he married Alice Ruth Greene in 1946. They produced a daughter, Sandra Marie White, in 1947.

Sandra Marie White

William Rutherford White's sister, Sarah Grace, received her Bachelor's degree from Indiana University and her Master's in Social Work from Atlanta University in Georgia. In Chicago, she retired after decades of service as Senior Supervisor at an adoption agency and as a Grant Specialist for Region V.

Sandra Marie White, daughter of Alice and William, is also an artist like her father. He mentored her in examples, such as his portraits of Abraham Lincoln, John F. Kennedy, Robert Kennedy, and Martin Luther King-called "Where did our dreams go?" 10,000 copies of it were reproduced. Her mother, Alice, supported both artists' aspirations while faithfully employed at General Electric over thirty-one years. She had graduated from Central High School and attended Indiana University. She sang in the choir at Turner Chapel African Methodist Episcopal Church over fifty years. Meanwhile, Sandra attended Harmar Elementary and graduated from Central High School. She won five art scholarships and received a degree from Indiana University in Commercial Art. In 2005, Sandra was selected for inclusion in *Who's Who in America*. Pending is a nomination for inclusion for 2006 in *Who's Who in American Women*. Sandra is also a former College of the Scriptures student of Louisville, Kentucky. She is a missionary member of Turner Chapel A.M.E. Church and has done volunteerism extensively during the past sixteen years of physical disability.

Sandra and Sarah Grace are the only known survivors of William and Anna White.

Submitted by Sandra M. White

WIEHE FAMILY

120 YEARS, FIVE GENERATIONS, LAKE TOWNSHIP

Ferdinand Wiehe, a German immigrant, came to the United States in 1871 at the age of 19 with, as it was told through the years, $5 in his pocket and an admonition from his father as he was leaving Germany to "stay close to the church." By 1885 he had acquired a wife Sophia (Prange), also a German immigrant, and a family which he brought down the Old Trail Road, at that time a very apt description of the (now) Leesburg Road, to the newly purchased farm at the corner of Leesburg and Flaugh Roads, five miles northwest of Fort Wayne.

Adjacent to the farm stands the Suburban Bethlehem Lutheran church from whose bell tower still rings the original old church bell. Ferdinand Wiehe brought that bell from the railroad station in Fort Wayne in 1903, by horse and wagon, to the church, of which he was an early member. It has rung and is destined to continue its well loved peal over the farm and surrounding countryside for the Sunday services, weddings, baptisms and funerals of past generations and generations yet to come. The bell was transferred from the old original church to the newly built church in 1979; it strikes a gentle note of remembrance in the present day farm owners as it rings each day at noon and six in the evening.

Paul Wiehe, the grandson of Ferdinand, together with his wife Olga, were married in 1953 and raised four children in the old original brick farmhouse built by Grandfather Ferdinand Wiehe, making a total of twelve children which "this ole house" has seen through the generations. They are the six children of Ferdinand and Sophia: Ferdinand, Sophia (Knake), Theodore, William, Berth (Kruse) and Henry; the two children of Henry Wiehe (youngest child of Ferdinand) and his wife Julia (Rodenbeck): Eleanor (Wiehe) Bradtmueller and Paul Wiehe; the four children of Paul and Olga Wiehe: Ann (Wiehe) Rhodes, John, William and James. A story told these four great-grandchildren of Ferdinand was that when the house was built in 1902 the basements of that day were dug out by hand. When great-grandfather, who was only five feet, three inches tall, was able to stand up comfortably with room to

Wiehe Family

spare, they stopped digging. This was of very limited interest to the boys, as they all grew to well beyond six feet tall by young manhood and were forced to walk well bent over when they needed to walk in the basement.

Paul and Olga Wiehe built a new home across the road from the old house and incorporated into the new home bricks from the old house and the old dinner bell which had called the family members of past generations in from the fields. A remembered story was that the horses knew the meaning of the bell's ringing and would simply "take off" for the barn upon hearing it, knowing that it was time for oats and rest in the cool, dark barn. The fifth generation grandkids now still love to give the bell rope a pull or two.

Today the farm acreage is rented to a friend and neighbor, Jim Braun. The house still remains in productive use, as it has for years been rented to a succession of Concordia Seminary ministerial students and their families. The farm is registered as an Indiana Hoosier Homestead farm, that is, farms that have been in the same family for 100 years or more, and in this year of 2005, now marks its 120th year.

Olga Wiehe's three sons say they want to extend it for at least another generation, and now all live in three homes on the farm itself. They are: oldest son John and wife Jane (Schwehn-Roehm), children Zachary, Daniel, Dustin and Brooke; middle son Bill (William) and wife Jennifer (Doehrmann) and son Jarod; and youngest son Jim (James). Very frequent visitors to great-great grandfather's home place are Olga's daughter Ann, her husband Steve Rhodes and their daughter Christina. And so, five generations now. Paul, Olga's beloved husband of 50 years, passed away in 2003, but she still lives on the farm to carry on with her family very near.

Submitted by Olga Wiehe, farm owner

WILL FAMILY

Donald Will grew up on a farm near Chickasaw, Ohio. He opened his first jewelry store in 1959, in Versailles, Ohio, after serving in the army during World War II and working for a jeweler in a neighboring community.

In his early 30s at the time, he sold the family home to raise start-up capital for his first store and moved with his wife, Doris, and six children into an apartment above it.

Will's family and business grew. They moved to Fort Wayne in 1964, and opened a store in Southgate Plaza. They closed that store in 1971 after opening a store in Georgetown Square Shopping Center.

Don and Doris had ten children – seven boys and three girls – Darrell, Dana, Diane, Denise, Daniel, Darren, Dale, Dean, Douglas and Dixie. All of them eventually expressed an interest in working in the business.

To accommodate that interest, the family expanded its retailing, opening a second store in Englewood, Colorado in 1980, and a third store in Fort Wayne at Sleepy Hollow Professional Offices. They later opened their fourth store in 1998 in Woodland Plaza.

Will Family

The children were required to formally study an aspect of the jewelry business before going to work for Will Jewelers, and similar educational standards were required of employees hired outside the family. The firm now employs seventeen, with Darrell Will as president, Darren Will as vice-president, Dixie Clark as secretary and Denise Copper as treasurer.

Submitted by Dawn Will

CATHERINE ELIZABETH (ORMSBY) WILLIAMS

Catherine Elizabeth "Betty" Ormsby was born in Darke County, Ohio, on December 17, 1935. Her parents were Argus Luster (1894-1967) and Edna Chloe Mann Ormsby (1914-2003). Betty's siblings are Judith Elaine Ormsby Richter (born January 10, 1941) and Nancy Lou Ormsby Henninger (born June 24, 1942).

Betty came to Fort Wayne when she was about one year old and now resides in New Haven. She attended Justin Study Elementary, Washington Middle School and graduated from South Side High School in 1954. When she was ten years old, she took lessons on the Hawaiian guitar and performed in many local recitals. In high school, she was a majorette and in the Outgoing Choir.

Philip Jerome Wilson and Catherine Ormsby were married in 1955 and six children were born, all in Fort Wayne. Phil and Betty were later divorced. The following are their children.

Philip Jerome (Jerry) Wilson, II was born September 8, 1955, and married Connie Rae Crewdson on November 30, 1985. Jerry is self-employed at P. J. Entertainment and Connie has retired from Lincoln Life Insurance. They have three children: Philip Jerome (PJ), III, born January 7, 1987; Kaitlyn Elizabeth Wilson, born January 11, 1988; Nicholas Andrew, born January 16, 1990. They presently live near Huntertown, Indiana.

Catherine Elizabeth "Betty" (Ormsby) Williams, 1997

Catherine Jo Wilson was born January 21, 1957 and married Gary David Piatt on June 9, 1984. Currently they both work for Northwest Allen County School System, with Gary teaching engineering technology and Cathy is an instructional aid. Previously Cathy worked as a dental laboratory technician for 20 years. Cathy brought two children to this marriage: Lyndsy Ann Wilson Piatt, born June 16, 1978, and Matthew David Wilson Piatt, born August 26, 1979. In 1985, Gary adopted Lyndsy and Matthew. Matthew has a son, Kyle Thomas Piatt, born September 21, 1999, and Lyndsy has a son, Hunter Thomas Piatt, born December 30, 2004. Gary and Cathy live in northwest Allen County, near Carroll High School.

Cynthia Marie Wilson was born May 10, 1958, and married Kent Allan "Norm" Hesterman, October 29, 1983. Cynthia is a physical education teacher at Northwest Allen County Schools and previously taught in the Catholic school system. Kent works at Starcraft Marine in Topeka, Indiana. Their children are Luke Allan, born June 13, 1985; Neil Thomas, born October 3, 1988; and Hannah Marie born December 8, 1993. They presently live north of Huntertown.

Steven Robert Wilson, born June 21, 1961, was killed in an automobile accident on December 12, 1980. He is buried in Fort Wayne Catholic Cemetery. His love, Lisa Marie McCoy, is still in touch with the family.

Lisa Kay Wilson was born May 12, 1963, (a twin) and married Muneer Humdi Abe Samra on July 1, 1982; they were divorced in 1988. Their son is Omar Muneer Abu Samra, born May 9, 1987. Lisa lives near New Haven.

The youngest daughter, Lori Ann Wilson, was born May 12, 1963, (a twin) and married Thomas Carl Fisher, September 21, 1993. They have two children, Megan Marie, born January 4, 1995, and Jacob Thomas, born October 1, 1997. Lori now lives in New Haven.

Betty then married Francis William Merritt in August 8, 1968 and Melissa Diane Merritt was born on July 23, 1971. Francis died on January 21, 2003, in Fort Wayne.

Their daughter, Melissa, married Todd Douglas Zimmerman on October 14, 2004. She works at Perfection Bakery in marketing and Todd is employed at American Electric Power. They have two daughters: Chloe Elle, born June 19, 2002, and Emma Marie, born December 31, 2004. They live in the northeast part of Fort Wayne.

Betty worked at the Carpenter's Local Union from 1977-1989 and is currently working at Verizon. She enjoys gardening and her backyard is the envy of the neighborhood, with many flower gardens and also a vegetable garden. She enjoys sitting on her deck and crocheting, having made afghans for all of her grandchildren and most of her great nephews and nieces. She thoroughly enjoys spending time with her grandchildren and great-grandchildren, and attending school functions and ball games. She is planning to retire in 2006 in order to have more time to do the fun things in her life.

Betty married Kenneth Alan Williams on October 14, 1989. They currently reside in New Haven, Indiana

Submitted by Betty Williams

GREGG ROBERT WILLIAMSON FAMILY

Gregg Robert Williamson was born at Witman Memorial Hospital, Lebanon, Boone County, Indiana, on September 27, 1957. He is the son of Robert Merle Williamson and Joan Elizabeth Heidenreich. At the time of his birth, his family resided in Lizton, Hendricks County, Indiana. He has two older sisters, Cheryl Lynn George of Greencastle, Putnam County, Indiana, and Pamela Sue Coers of Danville, Hendricks County, Indiana. Gregg has a younger brother, John Bradley Williamson, who lives in Clinton Falls, Putnam County, Indiana.

In 1967, Gregg and his family moved to Speedway, Marion County, Indiana, a suburb of Indianapolis. He graduated from Speedway High School in 1976. Immediately after high school, Gregg served a full-time religious mission for the Church of Jesus of Latter-day Saints (Mormon) in the Colorado-Wyoming area. On December 28, 1978, he married Dena Gale Durrett.

Gregg and Dena Williamson

Dena was born in Portales, New Mexico, on January 16, 1961, the daughter of Jerry Dean Durrett and Gayla Hibbits. She has an older brother, Gary Dean Durrett, of Gilbert, Arizona. Dena's father was a geophysicist employed in the petroleum industry and she grew up around the world in locations including, California, Indonesia, Denmark, England, and Colorado.

Gregg and Dena were married in Mesa, Arizona. Gregg attended Ball State University in Muncie, Indiana, until 1980, when he entered the U.S. Army, during which time he was assigned to Fort Wainwright, Alaska and Fort Campbell, Kentucky where he served as legal clerk. While stationed in Alaska, Gregg earned an Associate of Applied Science degree in para-professional counseling. After a brief break in service, during which time he earned a Bachelor of Science in history from Ball State, he returned to active duty in the U.S. Army Reserve, with assignments in Indiana, Utah and Wisconsin. During his service in the army he served as an administrative supervisor and later a supply sergeant. Gregg completed his final tour of duty with the military in Fort Wayne, Indiana. During that assignment he enrolled in graduate school at Indiana University. He took classes at the campus in Fort Wayne and Indianapolis and earned his Masters of Library Science in December 2001.

Upon graduation, Gregg was hired as the first manager of the new William H. Willennar Genealogy Center, a service of the Eckhart Public Library in Auburn, Indiana. Dena works as an acquisitions clerk for the Historical Genealogy Department of the Allen County Public Library. Gregg and Dena have three children, Brittney Anne, born January 20, 1980, Robert Alexander, born June 24, 1981, and Michael Allen, born March 25, 1983. Gregg enjoys public service and held several adult leadership positions in both Boy Scouts and Cub Scouts, including Scoutmaster, Cubmaster, Troop Committee Chairman and District Committee Member. He earned the Eagle Scout award as a youth and the District Award of Merit as an adult.

Gregg and Dena continue to attend and serve in the Church of Jesus Christ of Latter-day Saints, attending a Fort Wayne congregation. Gregg also is a member of the DeKalb County Indiana Genealogy Society, serving as an officer and as editor of that organization's quarterly newsletter.

Submitted by Dena Williamson

GENOIS WILSON

FIREFIGHTER

A courageous, pioneering spirit driven by deep caring and passion for the safety of children.

It was 1952 in Holly Grove, Arkansas. Her mother couldn't hear her screams, as she died from smoke inhalation. Her hand-sewn cotton shirt dress was caught on the door of a wood burning stove after casting a log inside to keep the fire burning. She died from excessive inhalation of creosote, a poison from burning wood. She was three years old. Genois Young, her younger sister, was one year old.

In 1953, Leonard and Bernadine Young, father and mother, gathered their children and moved north, hoping for better housing, schools, employment and a brighter future. Settling in Fort Wayne, Indiana, the family initially moved in with their cousins, the Springer family. Later they got their own house and the family grew to eight children. Genois spent most of her childhood with her seven other siblings. Her father worked at General Electric. Her mother worked at the Sherman White Company. Genois graduated from Central High School in 196S, ranking ninth in a class of 200. She was accepted at Indiana Purdue University at Fort Wayne (IPFW) and majored in sociology.

Genois Wilson

Genois never forgot her older sister. She learned of her short life during the very brief times her mother would speak of her. She often wondered what she would have been like had she lived. She often thought about the tragedy of her death and about how many other families suffered losses from similar deadly, but preventable, accidents.

During college, Genois was uncertain about what she would choose for a career. She was very moved by people who worked out their passions doing good things for others. She knew deep inside that, whatever she chose to do with her life, somehow she would be in a position to help others. While on an internship, Genois worked on a survey project which brought her to the home of a white lady named Charlotte, on Maumee Avenue. She invited Genois and a survey teammate in and began sharing what she was doing with her life. Charlotte was inviting children in the neighborhood inside (for cookies and milk) into her living room after school. In the next room Charlotte showed them a home-made altar she constructed, adorned with crosses and burning candles. Charlotte prayed earnestly (every day) for the safety of each child. Charlotte's self made ministry made such a deep impression on Genois that she committed in her heart that one day she would devote herself to a worthy cause, like Charlotte had.

Genois was the first in her family to graduate from college with a bachelor's degree in 1974. She was faced with the ordeal of choosing a career and finding a job in it. She had no idea what it would be. She was married, and had become a single mom to son, Marlin. Hank Sanders, a police detective, was recruiting on campus for police officer candidates and encouraged her to take the public safety exam so she could qualify to work as a police officer. Genois had no special inclination for police work. After Hank's much urging, she decided to take the test to please Hank. Genois passed the test and was hired to work in the emergency dispatch area of the Department of Public Safety in 1975. She was assigned to direct emergency vehicles on the best routes to locations where citizens were in critical need of help. She was the first female ever to work in the department. She donned a police department man's shirt, with a clip on tie, and strapped on a .38 caliber gun and reported to work on the third shift.

Genois liked the idea of doing something to help people who were in the midst of emergencies. She wanted to do the best job she could, so she drove the entire city and surrounding area several times. Genois learned every main street, side street, and back alley so she could guide emergency vehicles by phone on the shortest route to get to people in critical need.

After four years of dispatch work, Genois realized she was not fulfilled. There was something more she knew she had to do with her life.

Then one day in 1979, Fire Chief Tom Loraine came unexpectedly to see her. He invited her to join the fire department. He told her they had a new position in fire prevention and he thought she would be perfect for it. The sparks, lights, and sirens in Genois spirit began to go on. She would soon find her heart's devotion; serving to aid the plight of children, to protect them, and to teach them how to be safe, especially in a fire.

Genois endured ten weeks of rigorous training, the same as every firefighter must complete. She wrestled with masks, dirty spray hoses, ladders, hoisted heavy equipment, and learned to start fires, control them, and put them out. It was a test of physical strength. She had to learn to fight fires without a mask so she would know how to survive from the victim's point of view. Her small body frame and height did not compare to the other men in training with her. She finished all requirements for active firefighting duty and became the first woman firefighter in Allen County. In 1979, however, women were not placed in firehouses for on-call fire emergency duty. Genois was assigned to the fire prevention department and she was delighted. She studied at the National Fire Academy in Maryland. Upon her return, Genois became increasingly aware of the lack of fire prevention education readily available for children. One of Genois's first projects was to teach fire safety to pre-schoolers, the first program of its kind for such a young age group. She also initiated a fire safety program for hearing- impaired persons.

Genois designed and implemented educational training programs for public citizens, in general. She extended her reach by developing an "in-service" training program to teach firefighters to teach others about fire prevention. As a result, she developed a team of trained firefighters who worked year round teaching fire prevention in elementary schools.

Over the next several years Genois developed the most successful fire prevention education program in the history of the Fort Wayne Fire Department. She launched the slogan "Stop, Drop and Roll" to remind children quickly what they should do if their clothing caught fire. The program was taught in every school in the city. Firefighters went to the schools in their fire trucks and uniforms to teach the children the curriculum developed by Genois. The program was so successful it opened the door for Genois to help design and implement another major project, the Fire and Police Safety Village. The Village is a realistic model of the city of Fort Wayne, built on the scale of a child. Life-like fire and police emergencies can be simulated there and the child can safely experience what actually happens in a real emergency or disaster.

By 1987, Genois was simply obsessed with executing a comprehensive program to educate every child in Allen County in fire prevention and how to be safe if caught in a fire. She was appointed Fire Education Director and continued to expand prevention programs to community organizations and local businesses.

During her career, Genois was the recipient of numerous community service awards. Among them were the Jaycees Outstanding Firefighter Award, the City of Fort Wayne Certificate of Commendation Award, YWCA Women of Achievement Award, Phiio Farnsworth Award, Fort Wayne Community Television Center Award, American Legion Indiana Firefighter of the Year Award, and Public Safety First Ladies of Fort Wayne Award. In 2002, Genois was featured on the History-Makers Television Documentary, a national program to document the accomplishments of history-makers in local communities.

In 1995, after 20 years of service in fire prevention, Genois retired, leaving a legacy of educational fire prevention programs and curriculums, an in-service training program to teach firefighters how to deliver fire prevention education to children and the general public, and the Fire and Police Safety "Survive Alive" Village for Allen County. Genois remembers the life long determination of her parents, the encouragement of her pastor, the devotion of "Charlotte," and the words of her sixth grade teacher, Dr. Verna Adams: "You can do anything." She knows now that her big sister's short life was not in vain. Through it she discovered the calling of her life and did her job well.

Genois Wilson is currently working as a probation officer in Allen Superior Court.

Submitted by Genois Wilson

AMOS & MARY WINDSOR FAMILY

Amos Windsor was the youngest son of Isaac and Anne/Nancy (Riley) Windsor of Yadkin County, North Carolina. He married Mary McDaniel and they, with at least two children, emigrated from Virginia to Rush County, Indiana, before 1840.

On October 6, 1848, Amos purchased 80 acres in southern Allen County, Indiana, from the U.S. Government. This parcel is in Section 34, Lafayette Township, just northeast of Zanesville, and remained undivided in recent years.

In 1850, Amos and Mary (McDaniel) Windsor had five children in their household: Aquilla, William R., Frances, Elizabeth A., and Mary M., while the eldest, Judah, had remained in Rush County to marry John Bitner. Aquilla Windsor married Eleanor Bell in 1853, and they lived in Union Township, Wells County, until their deaths. Aquilla was living with a daughter, Laura Griffith, in 1910 at age 80.

Frances Windsor married Elihu S. Wells, whose family was in Rush County, Indiana. The writer has not traced the other siblings.

Mary Windsor died in Allen County in 1855. Amos married again in 1857, to Ann Senner/Sonner of Wells County. The family was in Lafayette Township, Allen County, until after 1860 and then Amos and Ann relocated to Benton Harbor, Michigan by 1870. Amos died in 1873, age 72.

Amos and Mary (McDaniel) Windsor's first daughter, Judah, was born in 1827 in Grayson County, Virginia. The family then came to Indiana and lived approximately ten years in Rush County, where Judah remained to marry in 1848 when the rest of her family moved to Allen County. She and John Bitner had thirteen children, including John Jr., who married Permelia McBride.

The eldest child of John and Permelia (McBride) Bitner was Lula Inez, who married Robert K. Sharp. The fifth of their eight children was Helen, who married Howard H. Smith in 1928. They had two sons, Donald E. and Wm. Robert.

Donald E. Smith was born in 1931 on the Sharp farms, in a house on the Henry/Rush County line. He lived most of his early life, from age three to 18, in Knightstown, Indiana. Graduating from Knightstown High School in 1949, he entered the F. W. Woolworth Co. store management-training program.

However, when awarded a scholarship to attend Wabash College, Crawfordsville, Indiana, he enrolled at the college in 1950 and graduated in 1954.

While attending Wabash College, Donald joined the U.S. 5th Army Reserve and served three years in a counter intelligence prisoner of war interrogation unit during the Korean War. The unit was to be called to active duty if East Germany volunteered its German-speaking troops to fight U.S. troops in Korea. A cease-fire was declared in the summer of 1953, leaving him eligible for an honorable Army discharge. In the summer of 1954 he enlisted in the two year Air Force Pilot Training program. His first year was spent training in different models of single engine aircraft in Texas, Florida, and Arizona before serving out his final year in finance at Bakalar Air Force Base, Columbus, Indiana.

While stationed at Marianna, Florida, Donald married Gretel Heinzerling in 1954. Donald and Gretel have four children: S. Adrienne Winkler, Howard E. Smith, Sarah L. Smith and Emily C. Smith. They have ten grandchildren.

Upon discharge from the Air Force in August 1956, Donald and Gretel moved to Garrett, DeKalb County, Indiana, where Donald took employment as advertising manager, sports editor and feature writer of the *Garrett Clipper* newspaper.

Donald spent seven years at the newspaper before becoming a sales engineer for Electric Motors and Specialties in Garrett and for Morrill Motors in Fort Wayne. The two affiliated corporations also had four satellite plants manufacturing motors in Tennessee and Virginia. The motors were used in commercial and residential refrigeration appliances. Donald retired in 1996 as 1st Corporate Vice President of Electric Motors and Specialties. He earlier had held the positions of sales manager and vice president of sales & marketing.

As an avocation, for ten years after leaving the Air Force, Donald gave flight instruction for Auburn Airways, Consolidated Airways and for Airgo Smith Field in Allen County. His leisure activity has been tennis. Donald is a member of Wildwood Racquet Club in Fort Wayne, plays at several courts in DeKalb County, and for nine years has been part of the Greater Garrett Community Tennis Association volunteer group, providing a summer tennis program for youth and adults. He also is a board member of Fort Wayne's Midwest Wheel Chair Sports Foundation.

The families of five children of Isaac and Nancy (Riley) Windsor of Yadkin County, North Carolina immigrated to Indiana in the middle 1800s. Amos and Mary (McDaniel) Windsor have been described above. Enos and Nancy (Jones) Windsor moved to Wayne County and then he re-settled in Preble County, Ohio. James Riley Windsor's widow, Susannah (Minish) Windsor, brought their children to Hancock County. Aquilla Windsor's widow, Elizabeth (?) (Minish) Windsor, came to Wayne County with their four daughters. And some of Daniel and Sarah (Arnold) Windsor's children settled in Henry County.

Submitted by Gretel Smith

AMOS & EMMA SWIM WISELEY FAMILY

Amos Wiseley and Emma Swim shared the same birthday, April 17, 1861. They were born and raised next door to each other in Botkins, Shelby County, Ohio. Amos was the youngest of fifteen children of Allen and Mary Gilmore Wiseley. Emma was the daughter of George W. and Mary Ann Stout Swim.

Amos and Emma Swim Wiseley were married February 27, 1881, at Wapakoneta, Ohio. They had four children: Florence May Wiseley was born May 12, 1883. She died age two years, six months. Pearl Mable was born June 18, 1886, and died at the age of eight months. Both are buried at Wapakoneta. Walter Alfred Wiseley was born February 17, 1891, and Lillian Maud Wiseley was born in April of 1897. Amos and Emma moved to New Haven around 1900, where Amos was caretaker at the I.O.O.F Cemetery. Amos died January 23, 1926, and Emma died September 3, 1939. Both are buried at the I.O.O.F Cemetery in New Haven.

Emma (Swim) and Amos Wiseley, February 27, 1881

Lillian Wiseley married Isaac Nickelson November 16, 1921. They lived most of their married life in Grass Creek, Indiana.

Walter Alfred Wiseley worked in New Haven and Fort Wayne as a waiter in restaurants. He married Ruth Anna Marie Kallen, daughter of Peter and Johanna Mansdorfer Kallen, at St. John's Evangelical Lutheran Church on April 15, 1914. They had four children. Charles Walter Wiseley was born January 21, 1915 and died the same day; LaDonna Marie Wiseley was born June 2, 1916; Allen Henry Wiseley was born September 10, 1919; and Walter Emil (Dude) Wiseley was born November 21, 1920. Walt and Ruth lived in the Hungry Hills neighborhood in the northwest part of Fort Wayne. They lived at 1416 St. Mary's, 1512 High, 1937 Spring Street, and in two different houses on Hinton Drive, 1639 and 1646. Walt worked for the Kroger Company as a meat cutter, retiring in 1956 after forty-seven years. In June of 1956, they moved to Ontario, California. A few years later they moved to a mobile home park in La Verne, California. On April 15, 1964, they celebrated their 50th Wedding anniversary with their family. Walter died June 11, 1968, and Ruth died June 17, 1983. They are buried in Bellevue Cemetery in Ontario, California.

Children L-R: LaDonna Marie Wiseley, Walter Emil Wiseley, Allen Henry Wiseley. Adults: Walter Alfred and Ruth Anna Marie (Kallen) Wiseley.

LaDonna Marie Wiseley married George Anthony Weber, son of Frank and Christina Stein Weber, on June 2, 1937, at St. Mary's Church. They had three children: Donald Allen, Richard Walter, and Sue Ann Weber.

Allen Henry Wiseley joined the United States Navy in 1937. He was a veteran of World War II and the Korean War. He married Mary Elizabeth Bracewell, September 27, 1941. They had four children; Ruth Marie, Allen Henry II, Charles Walter, and Michael Donald. Allen died September 1, 1980.

Walter Emil Wiseley enlisted in the United States Navy during World War II. Dude married Betty Maxine McHenry on December 18, 1945 in Fort Wayne, Indiana. They had two children; Sandra Kay and Deanna Ruth. Walter "Dude" Wiseley died July 18, 1985.

Submitted by Christina M. Paladino

SAFARA A. WITMER

Safara A. Witmer was born in Grabill, Indiana, on January 31, 1899, being the second child of Samuel C. Witmer and Ida B. Gerig Witmer. Safara received his elementary and high school education in the public schools of Springfield Township and the City of Fort Wayne. In 1922 he graduated from the Fort Wayne Bible Training School, later the Fort Wayne Bible College, and presently the Fort Wayne campus of Taylor University. Safara subsequently devoted most of his adult years to the Bible College, serving in various capacities.

Safara was married to Edith McLean on February 28, 1924. Edith was a native of Scotland, and after emigrating with her parents to Canada, enrolled at the Bible Training School in 1919, where she later met Safara.

Safara was invited to join the faculty of the Bible College in the mid 1920s, beginning an affiliation that lasted more than 30 years. That affiliation was interrupted briefly on several occasions by leave of absence to continue his higher education, to serve as an Army Chaplain during World War II, and to engage in the ministry.

Chaplain Safara Witmer and wife, Edith

Safara was awarded the A.B. degree by Taylor University in 1929, the M.A. degree by Winona Lake School of Theology in 1937, and the Ph.D. degree by the University of Chicago in 1951. In 1949 Wheaton College awarded him the honorary degree of Doctor of Laws.

During the 1930s he served several years as minister of the First Missionary Church of Fort Wayne. He subsequently returned to the Bible College to serve as Dean of Students until 1942, when he became an Army Chaplain and served two years on active duty in that role during WWII. He then returned to the Bible College in 1944, when he was appointed to the office of President of the Bible College, a position that he held until 1958. In that year he resigned his office of President of the College, and became Executive Director of the Accrediting Association of Bible Institutes and Bible Colleges, an organization of which he had a leading role in founding several years earlier. He served in that capacity until his untimely death on September 11, 1962. His many years of service to the Bible College, now the Fort Wayne campus of Taylor University, are memorialized in the Witmer Hall, completed and dedicated in 1970, which houses both administrative offices and classrooms.

Safara enjoyed several hobbies during his life, among them photography and the study of astronomy.

Safara and Edith were the parents of two children, Evangeline N., born March 6, 1926, and Ruth E., born February 1, 1931. Evangeline passed away on June 26, 1951. Ruth and her husband, Dr. Ian H. Cook, reside in Fort Wayne, where Ian still is engaged in the medical practice of general surgery, now with the United States Veterans Hospital.

Submitted by Christine Gerig,
written by Wayne Witmer

ERWIN F. & EILEEN RUTH (BIEBERICH) WITTE FAMILY

Erwin F. Witte was born November 30,1926 near Monroeville, Indiana, to Paul and Clara (Bohnke) Witte. He graduated from Ossian High School in April 1945; he served in the U.S.Army in 1945 -1946 and worked at International

Harvester/Navistar for 37 years. Erwin had three brothers, Carl, Hilbert, and Paul R. Witte.

On April 23, 1949, he married Eileen Bieberich, who was born November 8, 1927, in Fort Wayne Indiana, the daughter of Edwin and Luella (Young) Bieberich.. Their marriage was blessed with three sons, Dennis Erwin, born August 26, 1951; Kenneth Lee, born February 14,1954; and Robert Alan born August 8, 1956, all born in Fort Wayne, Indiana.

Dennis, Kenneth and Robert Witte graduated from St. Peter's Lutheran Grade School and Concordia Lutheran High School in Fort Wayne, Indiana.

Dennis went on to study at Concordia University, River Forest, Illinois and graduated in 1972. He has been on the Concordia University-River Forest staff since then, presently serving as vice president of Information Services. On August 26,1972, he married Marcia Wachtel (September 30, 1951) daughter of Kenneth and Betty Wachtel of Altamont, Illinois. Dennis and Marcia have two sons, Mark Kenneth (November 18, 1980) and David Robert (May 12, 1983). Mark and David graduated from Glenbard High School, Lombard, Illinois. Mark is enrolled at Concordia Theological Seminary, Fort Wayne, Indiana. On August 16, 2003, Mark married Sarah Kem (August 17, 1980), they are parents of Luke David (December 10, 2004). David is attending Concordia University, River Forest, Illinois.

Kenneth went on to study at Concordia University, River Forest, Illinois, and graduated in 1976. He taught at Lutheran High North, in Mount Clemens, Michigan, Concordia University at Mequon, Wisconsin, and is presently teaching at Sheboygan Lutheran High School, Sheboygan, Wisconsin. Kenneth married Cynthia Lubner, daughter of Mark and Bernice Lubner of Fredonia, Wisconsin, on July 15, 2000, in Fredonia, Wisconsin. They have two children, Katelyn Rose (July 5, 2001) and Matthew Luke (June 10, 2003)

Erwin and Eileen Witte 50th Wedding Anniversary, April 23, 1999. Front: Erwin and Eileen Witte, Back: Robert, Kenneth, Dennis Witte

Robert graduated from Purdue University in 1978 with a degree in electrical engineering. Following graduation he went to work for Hewlett Packard and worked for them until 1999. At that time his division left Hewlett Packard and formed Agilent Laboratories. He presently works for Agilent Laboratories in Monument, Colorado. On May 27, 1978, he married Joyce Selking (February 19, 1956) daughter of Albert and Elsie Selking of Fort Wayne, Indiana.. Bob and Joyce have two daughters, Sara (April 7, 1984) and Rachel (September 29,1986) Sara is attending Colorado University, Boulder, Colorado. Rachel graduated from Lewis Palmer High School, Monument, Colorado, in May, 2005.

Submitted by Erwin F. and Eileen Witte

SAMUEL WOLF

FORT WAYNE BUSINESSMAN & COMMUNITY LEADER

Samuel Wolf was born in Fort Wayne, Indiana, on January 25,1868. He was the youngest son of Abraham Wolf and Helena Stein.

Abraham arrived in New York from St. Grethens, Germany in 1853 at the age of 23, and applied for citizenship in Allen County, Indiana, in 1857. Abraham was a kosher butcher, with a shop and home at the corner of Main and Webster Streets. The home address was 259 West Main Street. Abraham and Helena had five children, all born in Fort Wayne: Minna, Flora Wolf Greenebaum, who died along with her baby in childbirth at the age of 21, Leopold, Sarah Wolf Beck, and Samuel. Abraham died of stomach cancer on August 5, 1905, in Fort Wayne.

Samuel Wolf, Wolf & Dessauer's Department Store, born 1868, died 1960

Wolf and Dessauer's Department Store, Fort Wayne

Wolf and Dessauer's on left, 1930s

Parents of Samuel Wolf. Abraham Wolf, born 1830 in St. Grethens Germany, died June 15, 1905 in Fort Wayne. Helena Stein Wolf, born 1834, died June 20, 1916 in Fort Wayne.

Samuel Wolf, the youngest son, attended Jefferson School. He worked in political clerkships for a while, but was finally told by his father, Abraham, that he would have to find gainful employment. He then went to work for the Louis Wolf Dry Goods Store, and when Louis Wolf retired Sam purchased the inventory and the building. Eventually, Samuel borrowed $5,000 from his father to enlarge that store and purchase new inventory.

He ran an ad in a trade journal looking for an investor and Myron Dessauer read this, came to Fort Wayne, invested another $5,000, and the two men became partners in the Wolf and Dessauer Store.

They soon outgrew the Louis Wolf building and opened a larger store. The new department store opened on April 15th, 1886. This store was prosperous and well received. They again outgrew their facility, and in 1919 they opened a new building at the corner of Calhoun and Washington Streets. The new store was much larger and offered more services, such as a beautiful eating area, exercise rooms for the employees, and an employee cafeteria.

Samuel served on many boards and committees, including The National Aeronautic Association of the U.S.A., the Morris Plan Bank, the Standard Discount Corporation, the Board of Park Commissioners, and the Board of Public Welfare. He was also a Director of the Lincoln National Life Insurance Company and the Anthony Wayne Bank. He also served as president of several corporations, including the Fort Wayne Hotel Corporation and the Jefferson Realty Corporation. Samuel also served as the head of the Democratic Party of Allen County.

Samuel married Mary Ann (Mamie) Wertheimer of Ligonier, Indiana. They had one daughter, Dorothy Rose. Dorothy married David Samuel Hutner, who with his brother founded Hutner's Mens Wear Store and the Hutner's Paris stores in Fort Wayne. The Hutner children, grandchildren and great-grandchildren still reside in Fort Wayne.

As a young man, Samuel pitched in the first baseball game under lights in Fort Wayne and enjoyed baseball all his life. Samuel Wolf died in Fort Wayne in 1960 at the age of 92.

Submitted by Robert Hutner

W. PAUL WOLF FAMILY

W. Paul Wolf's great-great-grandparents, Christian (born on September 6, 1803, died on

W. Paul Wolf Family

January 30, 1851) and Dorothea (Fink) Wolf, (born on February 3, 1811, died on April 2, 1888), lived in Lautenbach, Wurttemberg, Germany. They had eight children: Friedericka (1832-1912) married George Griebel of Soest, eight miles south of Fort Wayne, and had five children; Johann Christian (1833-1880) married and lived in Lansing, Michigan, had four children, and fought in the Civil War; Marie Dorothea (born 1835) married John Felger of Soest and had seven children; Gottlieb Johann (born 1837) married Mary Berkes. They lived on a farm two miles NW of Avilla and had four children; Jakob Frederick (born 1839) married, lived in Lansing, and fought in the Civil War; Catherine Caroline (born 1843) married Kendallville watchmaker, John Bittekoffer, and had six children; Christianna Louise (1846-1936) married Gottfried Ernest Spiegel on May 27, 1867, in St. John's Evangelical Lutheran Church, Fort Wayne, and had six children; Carolina (1849-1910) married Johann Gehring, lived on a DeKalb County farm east of Kendallville, and had eight children.

After her husband died in 1851, Dorothea Wolf and eight children began their journey to America by walking across France to board ship in Le Havre. The sailing vessel took 70 days to cross the ocean, including 21 days sitting on the high sea with no wind. Their passport was issued July 28, 1852, at Weiblingen, Wurttemberg, Germany. They came to Fort Wayne by the canal system, and first lived in the home of a brother-in-law, Johann George Wolf and his wife.

Johann and his wife came to America in 1846 as one of the first of eleven German students sent over through Rev. Loehe, a missionary, to be assigned to the ministry, or to be German Lutheran school teachers. Johann George Wolf was the first German school teacher at St. Paul's Lutheran Church. He died on May 6, 1862, during the cholera epidemic and is buried in Concordia Lutheran Cemetery. The school children, with congregations help, had a marker placed at his grave. Johann's wife and three children later moved to St. Louis, Missouri, and began baking the communion wafers for the Lutheran churches.

Dorethea Wolf and family settled near Avilla, 22 miles north of Fort Wayne. It was quite a wilderness at that time. They lived in a log cabin and helped clear the land and build roads. She died at age 77 on Easter Sunday night, April 2, 1888, at the home of her son, Gottlieb Johann Wolf. Dorethea is buried in the Lutheran Cemetery.

Great-grandfather, Gottlieb Johann Wolf, (born on September 7, 1837) married Mary Berkes, and was an Avilla, Indiana farmer. They had four children: William, Fred, George, and John Wolf. Grandfather, William Wolf, married Margaret Hess and owned three farms. They had seven children: Ella, Emma, Charles, Walter, Ervin, Nora, and Clara Wolf.

On June 19, 1924, Ervin William Wolf married Gladys Slofer, a grade school teacher. They had four children: Mary Louise, Marjorie, Paul, and Erma Lee. Ervin used his dump truck to help build State Road 8 at Albion, and Gladys once taught school in an unheated basement of a general store in Swan, Indiana. Ervin was the first Wolf family member who did not farm. He owned the E.W.Wolf General Store in Avilla. He also served three years as an Allen Township, Noble County Constable. His duties ranged from catching horse thieves to keeping peace.

Paul was born November 2, 1931, at his parent's North Main Street home in Avilla. During grade school age he would do any available work: collect milkweed pods for the World War II Defense Dept, deliver Post Office telegrams on his bicycle, and weed onions on hot muck land at ten cents an hour for ten hour days. He worked at his father's store for 35 cents per week.

Following Paul's 1950 high school graduation, his father gave him $500 towards college education. He studied accounting at International Business College, with studies later continued at Maryland and Indiana Universities. During the Korean War, he served with the U.S. Air Force Director of Intelligence division, assigned to the National Security Agency (NSA), Washington D.C., in crypto intelligence.

He commenced his banking career in 1956-1957 with Avilla Bank, and in 1957-60 with the Indiana Department of Financial Institutions as a commercial bank examiner. During a 1957 bank examination of First State Bank of Hoagland, Paul discovered a Wolf family relative in Martin A. Griebel, the bank president. He joined Home Loan Bank on July 1, 1960 as Assistant Secretary-Treasurer. On May 8, 1961, at age 29, he was the youngest person to be appointed to a local bank board of directors. Paul became President of Home Loan Bank in January, 1970, and Chairman of the Board in 1991, both positions held until his October 15, 1999 retirement.

During his Home Loan Bank tenure, he discovered area relative Margaret Spiegel (died November 17, 1998), a former North Side High School teacher and then Snider High School dean of girls, who retired in 1974. Also, Dr. Frances Krauskopf, history professor for the University of St. Francis. She retired in 1982 with 17 years of service.

Paul married Carolyn Parker on December 19, 1959, sharing a family of three: Susan (married Keith Gotsch), Paul William (married Caren Meyer), and John Ervin Wolf. He then married Carolyn Stradley on May 15, 1988, adding stepson Mark to his family. His six grandchildren are Megan, Mitchell, and Mallory Gotsch; and Paul Michael, William Trevor, and Cameron Wolf. Paul served eight years as vice chairman of the seven member banking board of the Indiana Department of Financial Institutions. He also served on the Indiana Economic Development Council Board and its Executive Committee, and 17 years on the University of St. Francis Citizens' Board.

Paul is President of the Associated Churches Foundation Board and a board member of The Community Foundation of Greater Fort Wayne. He previously served on the 216 E. Washington Boulevard. Foundation, Inc. Board.

Submitted by W. Paul Wolf

DEBRA GENSHEIMER WOLFE

Debra Gensheimer Wolfe was born on May 29, 1959, in Fort Wayne, Indiana. Debra, the daughter of Maurine (Hartman) and Robert Gensheimer, has lived almost all of her life in Fort Wayne. She graduated from Bishop Luers High School in 1977, and earned a degree as a Radiologic Technologist at Saint Joseph Hospital in 1979. She is currently employed at Parkview North Hospital as a certified X-Ray Technologist and Computed Tomography Technologist. Debra married Robert Wolfe, of Fort Wayne, on June 19, 1981. Their daughter Elizabeth was born May 19, 1983. Twins, Justin and Kristen, were born December 24. 1985.

Debra's hobby is genealogy. This is a story of Debra's great great-great grandfather Herman Hartman. Hartman is a German name that means "brave man". Hartman was originally spelled Hartmann. This is an obituary that Debra found in the *Fort Wayne Sentinel* dated January 24, 1896.

HERMAN HARTMAN.

A Pioneer Business Man, Called Away.

One of the Fathers of the City and a Prominent Figure in Her History Summoned By the Grim Reaper.

Fort Wayne has lost another pioneer in the person of Herman Hartman, who passed away last evening at the residence of his son, J. H. (Hobby) Hartman, (1921 South Hanna) corner of Hanna and Wallace Streets. The deceased had been in the enjoyment of excellent health all his life, and up to a few days ago was in the possession of all his faculties. Old age, however, was causing gradual decay of the vital powers, and for a few days past the infirmities have advanced rapidly, and the venerable old gentleman was finally laid with the friends of his youth who had preceded him to the other shore. Herman Hartman was born in the year

Herman and Anna Ricter Hartman c. 1890

Elizabeth, Bob, Deb, Kristen and Justin Wolfe

1822 at Amelshern, near Muester, Westphalia (a providence of Germany), and spent his early days in agricultural pursuits. At the age of twenty-two he came to America, and at first settled in Peru, where he engaged in the brewing business. He was married in 1852 to Miss Anna Richter of Fort Wayne, and the following year he moved to the small town and established the first brewery, which was situated on East Washington street (on the south side between Lafayette and Clay), and which was known for years as Hartman Brewery. He built up a large trade, and his brewery grew to large proportions. He continued the business until 1872, when he sold out and retired from active life, to enjoy a well earned rest. May 5, 1895, the partner of his journey through life was called away, and since that time he had but waited a similar call, which came last night. Five children and ten grandchildren survive him. The only member of his immediate family who is left is his sister, Mrs. Schierman (Scherman), of 422 East Washington Street. The children are: John Hubert (Hobby) Hartman of this city, the well known grocer, with whom the old gentleman made his home; Mrs. Theresa Peters and Mrs. Regina Wall, of San Francisco; Mrs. Anna Kulm, of Hopland, California, and Sister Nicolina, of the order of Notre Dame, of Teutopolis, Illinois. The deceased was a member of St. Mary's Benevolent society, of St. Mary's Catholic Church, of which institution he was one of the founders. He was also a member of the Allen County Old Settler's Society, and was a regular attendant at all of the meetings of the pioneers. At these gathering, his flow of quaint German humor, undimmed by age, and his fond reminisces made him a general favorite. His life long honesty and integrity secured for him the respect of all with whom he came in contact during his long life and his never failing good humor made him liked by young and old. Time of funeral is Saturday afternoon at 1 o'clock at St. Peter's Catholic Church.

Submitted by Debra Wolfe

RICHARD WILLIAM WOLFE & CATHERINE KAVERMAN FAMILY

Richard Wolfe was born on October 6, 1923, in Fort Wayne, Indiana. He was the oldest child of Leo John Wolfe and Ursula Frances Inderrieden. His sister, Martha Jane Wolfe, was born on June 22, 1927. Richard's father, Leo, was born in Earlington, Kentucky, on September 17, 1893. Richard's mother, Ursula, was born on January 1, 1894, in Fort Loramie, Ohio. Richard's father, Leo, moved to Fort Wayne after World War I to find work. He first worked at a bakery as a baker until it closed. Leo went back to Fort Loramie, Ohio to marry Ursula Inderrieden on November 24, 1922. Leo and Ursula Wolfe then relocated in Fort Wayne. Leo went to work at Holsum bakery until he retired.

Wolfe family in front of G & W Radiator

Richard spent the first four years of school at St. Peters and the next four years at James Smart Grade School. He went to Central High School and graduated in 1943. Richard William Wolfe married Ann Catherine Kaverman on November 25, 1950, at St. Peter's Catholic Church in Fort Wayne. Ann was born in Delphos, Ohio, on April 25, 1923. She is the oldest child of Otto David Kaverman and Edith Ann Kehres. Otto was born on December 5, 1889, in Delphos, Ohio. Edith was born on October 3, 1894, in Ottoville, Ohio. Otto Kaverman and Edith Kehres were married on June 6, 1922, in Delphos, Ohio. Ann has one brother, Tom, who was born on March 11, 1931. Ann lived on the family farm until she moved to Fort Wayne to attend the Saint Joseph's School of Nursing. She graduated in 1944. Ann has remained friends all of her life with some of her nursing school classmates. Richard started an automotive repair business with his partner, Richard Gfell, in 1950, called Park-View Texaco. This service station was located at 2125 Maumee, the northwest corner of Maumee and Glasgow, right across from Memorial Park. Dick Wolfe and Dick Gfell relocated to 2229 South Anthony in 1957. They opened a new Phillips 66 station and called the business Gfell and Wolfe. They had a big grand opening with Ann Colone, clowns, and balloons. Five years later they started repairing radiators and renamed the business G & W Radiator. They pumped gas for many years and serviced cars. Dick and Ann had four children. They are: Richard, Robert, James and Thomas. The four boys grew up into the automotive trade and worked at the station with their father. Dick Senior retired in 1985 and Dick, Bob, and Tom took over the business.

On August 6, 2004, the brothers closed the business to pursue other business interests.

Submitted by Richard Wolfe

WOODS & WILCOXSON

The town of Yoder, which used to be called Sheldon, is in Pleasant Township in southern Allen County. This area became the home of George W. Woods, Sr. (1812-1881) and his wife Charlotte Violet Richey (1816-1890). They moved from Wayne County, Ohio, where they were married in 1833, to Pleasant Township by 1850. George and Charlotte, along with many of their numerous descendants, are buried in Oak Lawn Cemetery in the town of Ossian, which is near Yoder.

The nine children of George Woods and Charlotte Richey were Samuel, James T., John B., Alexander, Elizabeth (Mrs. Ben Kumfer), Milton, Mary "Jane" (Mrs. Allen Bushee), George Jr., and Jacob, all of whom married and raised families nearby. Their son, Alexander "Pard" Woods, was born September 15, 1841, in Wayne County, Ohio. He died in 1910 after being struck by an interurban car in Yoder. Alexander married Minerva "Elizabeth" Huss (1839-1916). She was the daughter of Abraham Huss and Nancy "Jane" Bodle.

Alexander and Minerva Woods were the parents of three children, Francis Meredith, Cora May (Mrs. Otto Fusselman), and Bessie Idel (Mrs. Harlan Brown). The son, Francis Meredith "Frank" Woods, was born July 11, 1863, in Pleasant Township and died July 8, 1936, at the family farm in Yoder. He married Edith Nancy Wilcoxson, born March 17, 1869, in Wells County and died on July 6, 1967, age 98. She was the daughter of Meredith Wilcoxson and Nancy Powell.

Meredith Wilcoxson was born in 1830 in North Carolina and died January 20, 1901, in Yoder. He was the son of Jesse Wilcoxson and Sarah Elizabeth Denney, who were married in Wilkes County, North Carolina and moved to Wells County before 1850. Jesse Wilcoxson is believed to be the great grandson of Sarah Boone, the sister to the legendary Daniel Boone. Meredith married Nancy Powell on March 17, 1853, in Wells County. Nancy was the daughter of Mason Powell and Clara "Clarissa" Brown, who were married in Wilkes County, North Carolina, and moved before 1840 to Wells County. The children of Meredith and Nancy Powell Wilcoxson were Mary Ann (Mrs. Robert McBride), Sarah "Jane" (Mrs. Henry Golliver), Adam, Daniel Boone, and Edith (Mrs. Frank Woods). After Nancy's death, Meredith married Anna Golliver and had six more children, Fanny, Elizabeth, Jacob, Malissa, Harry, and Floyd.

Frank Woods and Edith Wilcoxson Woods raised twelve children on their farm in Yoder. They were Ethel (Mrs. John Wilson/Mrs. Freeman Evans), Jesse, Otto, Vernie (Mrs. Homer Krauter), Edna (Mrs. John Archbold), Ahdelia "Dee" (Mrs. William Kline), Annie (Mrs. William Johnson), Ronald, Al, Helen (Mrs. Donald List), Glenna (Mrs. Henry Clark), and Art.

The Woods and Wilcoxson families were among the first settlers of the farmlands near Yoder and many of their descendants still reside near that area to date.

Submitted by Cindy Cadwallader

STEPHEN H. & MARSHA J. (RINGENBERG) WRIGHT FAMILY

Stephen Harlan Wright was born in Fort Wayne, Indiana, on December 6, 1948. Stephen's parents, John Harlan Wright (1919) and his mother, Helen R. Lower Wright (1917), were originally from Peoria, Illinois. They moved to Fort Wayne when J. Harlan, who had been working as a draftsman at Caterpillar, felt called into full-time ministry and came to study at Fort Wayne Bible College.

Stephen and his sister, Martha Roselle Wright (1954-2001), enjoyed their childhood as PKs

Stephen H. Wright family -- Jaala, Joshua, Jairus, Marsha, Jonathan, Joseph, and Stephen

(preacher's kids) in Auburn, Indiana, and Pandora, Ohio. The family returned to Fort Wayne when J. Harlan became Alumni Coordinator for Fort Wayne Bible College. Stephen graduated from South Side High School in 1968 and attended Fort Wayne Bible College for one year. He was active in the Holton Avenue Missionary Church.

Marsha Jane Ringenberg was born in Fort Wayne on September 17, 1947. Her parents lived in Grabill, where her father, Morris J. Ringenberg (1916-2003), was an officer in the Grabill Bank, and her mother, Margaret Ray Ringenberg (1921), was a pilot and flight instructor. Marsha was active in Girl Scouting, music, and earned her pilot's license at the age of seventeen.

After graduating from Leo High School in 1965, Marsha enrolled in Fort Wayne Bible College as a music education major. There she traveled with musical teams that often were accompanied by the alumni coordinator, Rev. J. Harlan Wright. One day he was able to introduce Marsha to his son, Stephen.

After graduating from college in 1970, Marsha became a junior high music teacher in the Fort Wayne Community Schools. She also started directing the choir at her home church, Grabill Missionary Church. Stephen and Marsha were married on July 29, 1972, and in 1974 she earned her Masters in Fine Arts in Music Education from Ball State University. In 1975 Marsha joined the staff of Grabill Missionary Church in music and worship ministries.

Stephen and Marsha have five children: Jonathan Alan (1975), Joseph David (1977), Joshua Peter (1979), Jairus Stephen (1980), and Jaala Joy (1983.) Marsha has continued at Grabill Missionary Church and Stephen is employed as a driver for USF Holland. Jonathan was married to Rebecca Lynn Clark (1976) and they are the parents of Isaac David Wright (2004).

Submitted by Marsha J. Wright

DALE L. WUTHRICH FAMILY

The Dale L. Wuthrich family moved to Allen County in the summer of 1949. A good job at the Hobby House Restaurant in downtown Fort Wayne lured Dale away from feedmill work in Milford, Indiana. Dale's parents hailed from a Swiss-German area of Europe, arriving in the U.S. when they were children. His wife Betty (Striggle) was raised on a farm in Whitley County.

Jane Wuthrich was two and her brother Timothy was six months when the family moved into the house on Prospect Avenue near North Side High School. Jane's wedding was in that house on November 11, 1967; she married Vaughn H. Smith from Muncie, Indiana. Also in 1967, Timothy married Stephanie Brickley. A few years later, with his wife and three children, he moved to Kalamazoo, Michigan, accepting work as a computer programmer. Dale's wife, Betty, continued to live in the house after Dale's death in 1979. Jane never lived more than 45 minutes from the house; not too many people stay in their hometown area, but Jane is glad she is one of them. The picture included with this history was taken in the family's living room the day of Jane's graduation from North Side High School in 1964.

Dale Wuthrich Family. Tim, Jane, Dale, Betty, 1964

The 1950s were a good time to grow up in the city of Fort Wayne. Of course, every Sunday the family attended The First Church of God together. The Wuthrich children played at the park with no need to worry that any stranger would harm them. One of their favorite places was Franke Park, with the trails and the zoo. School fieldtrips to downtown Fort Wayne included visiting the top of the Lincoln Tower, the tallest building in town at that time. A family tradition was viewing the lighted Christmas decorations at Wolf & Dessauers and The Grand Leader. A special treat was enjoying fresh donuts at the Murphey's store. As of 2005, Murphey's donut machine is still making donuts at Cindy's Diner downtown.

Another of the family's favorite places was Gardner's drive-in restaurant. The young ladies who were "car hops" actually came out to your car and took your order—no unintelligible speaker phones in those days! The Lunchbox Cafe on Maplecrest Road still serves Gardners-style hamburgers and onion rings. It is quite possible that Gardner's smooth Frosty malts were the inspiration for the Frosty that Dave Thomas made famous at the Wendy's Restaurants. Dale worked with Dave at The Hobby House for many years (before Wendy's of course).

Dale and his family vacationed almost every year. They traveled to every state east of the Mississippi. It was fun to visit the Great Smokey Mountains or the beaches of Lake Michigan, but it was always good to come home to Allen County and their own little place in the world. Jane (Wuthrich) Jantzen agrees with these words she once read: "As for traveling, when I was home I was in a better place."

Submitted by Jane Ann (Wuthrich) (Smith) Jantzen

FREDRICK & POLLYANNA WYMER

Pollyanna Edwards was born in Wells County on January 24, 1962. She was the third child of Kenneth and Melba Edwards. In 1973, she moved with her parents to Zanesville in Allen County. Pollyanna graduated from Homestead High School and Ivy Tech's Culinary Arts School. She Married Stephen Bennett in 1982. They had three children: Brock Bennett (born in1983) married Richelle Best, and they have a son Logan (born in 2004); Brice Bennett (born in1985) married Melissa Burk, and they have a daughter Maci (born in 2005); Baili Bennett (born in 1988) is still at home. Pollyanna was divorced in 1998, and in July, 2003, married Fredrick Wymer.

Fredrick Wymer was born in Carson City, Michigan, on October 7,1957. He was the third child of Wallace and Lilly Wymer of Ithaca, Michigan. Fred graduated from Ithaca High School in 1976 and I.T.T. Technical Institute, Fort Wayne, in 1978. He married Sheryl Harden in 1980. They had two children: Matthew Wymer (born in 1983) is a student at IPFW in Fort Wayne, majoring in computer science; Lisa Wymer (born in 1986) is a freshman at Ball State University. Both are Homestead High School graduates. Sheryl and Fredrick were divorced in 2002.

Brock, Brice, and Baili Bennett were all home schooled by their mother. Brock graduated from Huntington College in 2003, with honors, at age 20, and is now employed at Wabash Alloys in Wabash Indiana. Brice graduated from Taylor University, Fort Wayne, in 2005 with a degree in ministry, at age 20, and is now employed at Peytons in Bluffton awaiting a job opening in his career field. Baili is a part time student at Taylor University in Fort Wayne. At 16, Baili is a home schooled senior.

Fred and Polly Wymer Family. Back: Logan, Brock, Richelle Bennett, Fred and Polly Wymer, Melissa, Brice and Maci Bennett. Front: Baili Bennett, Matt and Lisa Wymer

Polly is a stay at home mom, who also buys, fixes up, rents and sells properties. Fred is an electrician and also aids in their real estate business.

During their first marriages, both Fred and Polly lived in Windfall Estates addition just north of Zanesville in Lafayette Township. After their divorces, and subsequent marriage in 2003, they reside in Union township, Wells County. They love having family get-togethers in Indiana and Michigan and spending time with their children and grandchildren.

Submitted by Pollyanna Wymer

BERNARD FRANCIS WYSS

Bernard (Ben) was born in Marion Township, Allen County, on May 9, 1893, to John B. and Margaret G. Wyss. He attended Saint Joseph's Catholic Grade School, Hessen Cassel. Ben worked on his parent's farm on South Anthony Extended, before joining the Army on July 20, 1917. He was in Battery B, 150th U. S. Field Artillery. During World War I, he served in Baccarat, Champagne Marne, Aisne Marne, Saint Mihiel, Woevre, Meuse Argonne, France and in the army of occupation. He was honorably discharged at Camp Zachary Taylor in Kentucky on May 10, 1919.

Ben Wyss

Franz Joseph and Anna Mary Zuber Wyss

Frank J. Wyss

Frank J. Wyss

Anna Mary Zuber Wyss

Children of Franz Joseph and Anna Mary Wyss. Row 1, L to R: Elizabeth (Wyss) Hake, Mary (Wyss) Herber, Gertrude (Wyss) Hoffman. Row 2, L to R: Frank Wyss, John B. Wyss, Nicholas J. Wyss, Phillip Wyss, William Wyss

On October 17, 1922, Ben married schoolmate, Edna Bobay at Saint Joseph's Catholic Church, Hessen Cassel. Their first daughter, Clara Margaret, was born on May 30, 1924, and the next year, the family moved to Columbus, Ohio, where Ben began a job with the Pennsylvania Railroad as a machinist, a job he held for over 40 years. Their second daughter, Mary Catherine, was born on November 11, 1928.

On June 1, 1946, Clara Margaret married James G. Smith and they had one son, Robert. Clara Margaret Smith died on February 21, 2001, in Lakeland, Florida. On June 12, 1948, Mary Catherine married Wesley Belcher and they had three children, Steven, Sharon, and Susan.

Ben died on August 10, 1984. Edna died on August 18, 1972.

Submitted by Mary Catherine Belcher

WYSS FAMILY

Francis/Franz Joseph Wyss was born on May 11, 1826, to Nickolas and Elizabeth Wyss; Anna Mary Zuber was born on February 2, 1831, to Nickolas and Mary Zuber, both in Guensberg in Canton Soloturn, Switzerland. There they grew up, were sent to school, and worked on the little farms with their parents. Later, Francis Joseph served in the Swiss Army. He learned the tailor trade and followed it until he left Switzerland.

Francis Joseph Wyss and Anna Mary Zuber were married on June 11, 1850, and lived in Guensberg for nearly two years. Their first child, a son, was born in 1851. Soon they decided to leave Switzerland and seek a home in the New World. In March 1852, with their baby boy, they left Guensberg, accompanied by Francis Joseph's only brother, Hironimus; Anna Mary's brother, Urs; and cousin Pantalion; and their families, making a group of about fourteen. They traveled by stagecoach drawn by horses to Basel, a day's journey, stopping only to change horses. From Basel, they traveled by rail to Manheim, Germany, and on to Cologne, where they remained one day. Here they visited the Cologne Cathedral, known as the most magnificent church in the world. At Cologne they boarded a riverboat going down the Rhine to the seaport of Breman. There they boarded a sailing ship. At times the storms were so severe that the passengers had to sit on the floor and hold on to something fastened to the floor or wall to prevent them from being thrown down. One night they thought surely they would sink, but in the morning the sea was calm.

Early in May, fifty-nine days after setting sail, the boat arrived in New York, where another boy was born to Francis Joseph and Anna Mary. A few days later they started west by rail. At Schenectady their elder son died and was buried there.

From Schenectady they went to Buffalo. There they boarded a horse-powered boat which took them to Toledo. From Toledo, they came down the Wabash Canal to Antwerp, Ohio, on a boat pulled by mules walking on a towpath beside the canal.

At Antwerp, they visited two brothers of Anna Mary, who had come to America about ten years previously. There the second son died and was buried. From Antwerp, they traveled to Fort Wayne, Indiana, where Francis Joseph bought a farm from Christ Kleber/Klebor, an uncle of the late Christ Kleber of Hessen Cassel.

There they and Hironimus lived. It was an eighty-acre farm with a two-room, one-story log cabin in a four-acre clearing. They had no furniture, slept on straw ticks on the floor, and used their travel chests for tables and chairs until they made furniture. On February 1, 1854, another son, Frank, was born. In the fall of 1855 twin boys were born; they both died during the following year. In five years Francis and Anna Mary traveled thousands of miles, set up a new home, and lost four infant sons.

A few years later Anna Mary's brother and sister-in-law at Antwerp, the Zubers, became ill with typhoid fever and died, leaving eight children. Five of the children, ranging from four months to sixteen years of age, came to live with Francis Joseph and Anna Marie until they were old enough to go to work in the city.

The family continued working hard on the farm. Francis was one of the farmers assisting in the building of the Pennsylvania Railroad. In addition to their son, Frank, Francis and Anna Mary had eight more children: John was born August 5, 1857; Nicholas was born February 3, 1860; Elizabeth was born March 28, 1862; Philip was born December 23, 1864; Mary was born March 22, 1867; Gerhard was born March 10, 1869; William was born August 2, 1872; and Gertrude was born September 9, 1875. In April 1879 Hironimus died. In April 1896 son, Gerhard died.

On June 11, 1900, Francis Joseph and Anna Mary celebrated their Golden Wedding Anniversary. In 1910, at their sixtieth anniversary, in attendance were 200 relatives and friends; they had sixty-three grandchildren living. The day began with a nuptial Mass at St. Joseph's Church at Hessen Cassel, followed by a reception at their home. Anna Mary died May 1, 1911, and Francis Joseph died on August 22 of the same year.

Note from Mary Elizabeth Wyss: This story taken in part from information compiled by Frank J. Wyss in 1936 at the age of 82 years. The Wyss Family Tree of all eight children was donated to the Genealogy Department, Fort Wayne Public Library

Submitted by Mary Elizabeth Wyss, Margaret Wyss Knouff, and David D. Rohyans

FRANK & AGNES GIBSON WYSS FAMILY

Frank Joseph, lived and farmed in Marion Township. He was the son of Francis Joseph and Anna Mary (Zuber) Wyss, whose story can be found in this volume. He was born February 1, 1854, in Marion Township. He married Agnes J. Gibson, "the girl next door." She was the daughter of David and Lucy Farrel Gibson, born April 12, 1866. Frank and Agnes Gibson Wyss were married at St. Joseph Hessen Cassel on May 6, 1884. In the early 1900s, Frank and Agnes built a new farm house, located at 12535 South Anthony extended. Their children were: Charlotte (Lottie) (April 19, 1885 - December 6, 1977) married John Beckman in 1912; Celestine (January 11, 1889 - July 18, 1961) married Cecilia Suelzer on September 24, 1919; Gertrude (Stella) (March 10, 1892 - July 18, 1978) married John Zuber on September 18, 1917; Francis (March 1, 1894 - December 19, 1982) was a member of the Congregation of the Holy Cross and was a missionary priest in India and Pakistan; Edward (January 9, 1896 - September 16, 1901); Aloysius (March 10, 1898 - October 14, 1979) married Edith Prior on January 9, 1943; Clarence (May 8, 1900 - June 20, 1980) married Colette Fetter on June 19, 1929; Viola (May 19, 1902 - November 18, 1987) married Richard Paul Rohyans on September 1, 1927; Verba (May 23, 1906 - April 30, 2002); Frances (December 1886 - 1887); Henry (November 1887).

Frank and Agnes Gibson Wyss, May 6, 1934, 50th Wedding Anniversary

Frank and Agnes Wyss Family, 50th Wedding Anniversary. L to R: Front row, Lottie Beckman, Frank Wyss, Agnes Wyss, Verba Wyss. Back Row, L to R: Stella Zuber, Celestine Wyss, Rev. Frank Wyss C.S.C., Aloysius Wyss, Clarence Wyss, Viola Rohyans

Frank and Agnes believed in education and sent their boys to Central Catholic High School at Cathedral Square in Fort Wayne, Indiana, and Verba attended a Catholic girls academy. They took the interurban to and from school. Frank and Agnes lived and farmed in Marion Township until 1921, when they moved to Fort Wayne and he worked in carpentry.

Frank and Agnes celebrated 64 years of marriage and had 22 living grandchildren. Frank died February 17, 1949, and Agnes died July 30, 1948.

Resources: Frank J. Wyss to daughter Gertrude (Stella) Wyss Zuber in 1935.

Pictorial History Fort Wayne, Indiana, by B. J. Griswold Volume 2.

Wyss Family History by Rita Wyss Mac Bain, granddaughter of Frank and Agnes Wyss.

David D. Rohyans and Margaret Rohyans Rorick, grandchildren of Frank and Agnes Wyss.

St. Joseph Catholic Church, Hessen Cassel, Records.

Typed by Sally Rorick Still, great granddaughter of Frank and Agnes Wyss, and submitted by David D. Rohyans

HENRY E. WYSS

Henry Edward Wyss was born on July 25, 1900, in a log house on a farm six miles south of Fort Wayne on South Anthony Extended. His parents were John Bernard and Margaret Gertrude (Beckman) Wyss. He was the eighth child of a total of 13 children. He spent his formative years on the farm, learning a strong work ethic, which he passed on to his children and grandchildren. He was a lifelong resident of Allen County, except for a year at the age of 21 when he lived in Eagle Rock, California, and worked at a knitting mill in Glendale.

Upon returning to Allen County, he began working at the Wayne Knitting Mill, where he made Belle Sharmeer hosiery. One woman, who worked as a finisher, commented that she always knew when she received Henry's work it would be well done with no mistakes. He stayed at that job until 1953, when the factory was moved to Tennessee. He then worked at Kresge Warehouse for twelve years and retired for the first time at age 65. He worked at Rogers' Market on Fairfield Avenue, where he cleaned, stocked shelves, and toted groceries. At the same time, he established his own landscaping business, charging his clients $3.50 per hour. He took a lot of pride in his work and was seen in many yards in the Southwood Park area of town, maintaining and beautifying the lawns. He continued both of these occupations for the next thirteen years, when he retired once again.

In 1928, Henry married Gertrude Bridget Reilly, daughter of Agnes and Michael Reilly, at St. Patrick's Catholic Church in Fort Wayne. Their children are Mary Katherine (Houser), Robert Henry, James Nicholas (deceased), Rosaline Marie (O'Keefe), and Margaret Mary (Knouff). They lived on Pasadena Drive for 24 years until 1961, when Gertrude died of cancer at the age of 55. Two years later Henry married Hester (Martz) Barkley at St. Mary's Catholic Church in Decatur. They lived in the house on Pasadena until 1987, when they sold it to Henry's granddaughter, and she continues to live there with her family.

During World War II, Henry was an Air Raid Warden, taking that job very seriously. For many

Henry E. Wyss

years he was a Democratic Precinct Committeeman. He was adamant about the duty of voting in every election, as he felt it was a privilege no one should ever disregard. Henry was a member of the Foster Park Lions Club from 1969 to 1991 and maintained perfect attendance each year. In 1978 he was on the Board of Directors. Every year, between Thanksgiving and Christmas, he sold Christmas trees for their fund raiser at their tree lot on Bluffton Road. In all kinds of weather he was a dependable, hard worker who became fondly known as "Mr. Christmas Trees."

Henry was a faithful member of St. John the Baptist Catholic Church on Fairfield Avenue, where he served as a usher for over 40 years. At the time of his death in 1991, Henry had 19 grandchildren and 16 great-grandchildren, all of whom where greatly influenced by his deep faith in God and his assurance of his eternal reward in heaven.

Submitted by Rosie O'Keefe

JOHN BERNARD WYSS

John, born August 5, 1857, was the fourth son of Franz J. Wyss and Anna Mary Zuber, Allen County pioneers and farmers. Franz and Anna were married in Guensberg, the Canton Solothun, Switzerland on June 11, 1850. After a long and hard journey, via an Erie Canal towboat in 1852, they settled in Allen County. They settled on eighty acres just east of the Nine Mile house in Marion Township. It was in 1883 that John B. acquired his own land in Marion Township and began farming.

On June 1, 1886, John B. Wyss married Margaret G. Beckman, daughter of Fred Beckman and Catharine Rake, in Marion Township, Allen County. They lived in an ancient log cabin for thirteen years before they built their modern farm home in which they lived ever since. The main crops raised on the farm were corn and soybeans. For their family table they raised milk cows, pigs, and chickens, along with a variety of vegetables from Mrs. Wyss' s large garden.

Within this union, thirteen children were born to them: Clara C., born April 27, 1887; George R., born December 6, 1889; Rose, born June 27, 1891; Bernard F., born May 9, 1893; John F., born January 16, 1895; Rosella (Sister Agnetis), born November 6, 1896; Bertha (Sister Rosaline), born October 11, 1898; Henry Edward, born July 25, 1900; Albert, born May 30, 1902; Florence H., born December 27, 1903; Marie, born May 23, 1906; Mable M., born May 6, 1908; and the youngest child, Walter W., born May 12, 1910. Mr. and Mrs. Wyss

Mr. and Mrs. John B. Wyss and thirteen children in front of the Wyss homestead, 1915

Bernard Wyss Homestead, owned by the same family for over 100 years, Marion Township, Allen County

were members of St. Joseph's Catholic Church, Hessen Cassel, and their children attended the parish school.

John B. Wyss's political life began in 1900 when a group of neighbors gathered at his home and guaranteed him the Democratic nomination as trustee of Marion Township in Allen County. He agreed and was duly elected. One of his first endeavors was to lay 16,000 yards of gravel on roads, which were in bad condition. His attention, as trustee, then turned to the problem of low attendance at nine rural schools. He eliminated four of the nine schools and paid the parents a small sum to transport their children to the remaining schoolhouses.

In the years to follow, Mr. Wyss became a member of the Township Advisory Board, the Allen County Board of Commissioners and Allen County Council. He also was elected to a two-year term to the House of Representatives of Indiana in 1915. It was in Indianapolis that John Bernard Wyss fought a tough political battle. He sought to amend the Barrett assessment law. His bill passed the House, but lost in the Senate. Later the bill was reconsidered and won by one vote. The then Governor Ralston failed to sign it, and it became a law without his signature.

Though Mr. Wyss left a lasting impression in Indianapolis, it was in Allen County that he accomplished much that he set out to do. His progressive ideas were usually fought bitterly by opposition, according to those who watched him during twenty years in that government body. Because many believed him to be 'right and honest,' his projects were usually adopted. One of those progressive ideas was building public restrooms at the courthouse.

As a member of the Allen County Board of Commissioners from 1907 to 1913, he led a drive to replace 65 wooden culverts with cement ones and to build seven river bridges. Elected to the County Council in 1918, he was the only Democrat to gain an office in Allen County in a "Republican year". He was offered the chairmanship of that body, but declined the position to devote his energies on behalf of the Tuberculosis Hospital and the County Infirmary. With the exception of the first four years, John B. Wyss was elected by his fellow councilmen to be their chairman during the entire period of his service with that body. In 1934, Mr. Wyss was re-elected to the council for his fifth term, at the age of 77 years. On Aug 5, 1937, John B. Wyss was celebrating his 80th birthday while serving as the chairman of the Allen County Council. He retired from active political life in 1938.

Between the years 1937 and 1945 he was a member of the Allen County Public Library Board, helping to provide a thorough and complete library service for the public and parochial school children in rural schools. John B. Wyss retained a keen interest in civic affairs until his death on December 15, 1947.

Submitted by Mary K. Houser

CORNELIUS YANT

Cornelius Yant was a blacksmith and farmer, and a pioneer of Aboite Township. He was born November 29, 1829, and died August 19, 1908. Cornelius Yant, a hard working man, was born in Starke County, Ohio, before coming to Indiana and settling in Aboite Township, Allen County, at the age of eight. His father was Frederick Yant and his mother was Rachel Baer of Pennsylvania and Ohio, respectively. He spent most of his time in the blacksmith shop from early morning to late evening. He was well known and a highly respected resident. His wife, Hannah, and he lived off the Liberty Mills Road by the corner of Homestead Road and had five children; Mrs. Abbie Weichselfelder, of Palo Alto California, Mrs. Minnie Shuman of Ardmore, Oklahoma, Mrs. Viola Coleman, and Ms. Ella Yant and son Marion Edward Jackson Yant of Fort Wayne, Indiana.

His wife was Hannah Hickox, and she was born in Mercer County, Pennsylvania. She was born August 20, 1837, and died February 4, 1926. According to the obituary, she fainted and drowned in a bathtub at the home of her daughter, Mrs. Viola Coleman, 808 Grace Avenue, Fort Wayne. She was a member of the Methodist Church.

Submitted by Joyce Kammeyer

DONALD H. YANT

60 years later, 2nd Lt. DONALD H. YANT, LONG LOST CREWMEMBER HONORED

Sixty years after the plane explosion that killed 2nd Lt. Donald H. Yant his sacrifice was honored. He died in a crash on Guam in a B-29 bomber that blew up due to engine failure in the morning of May 11, 1945 shortly after taking off on the south runway of the north field, en route to an undisclosed mission in the combat zone. The aircraft crashed into the ocean, killing all eleven aboard. The May 11, 2005, memorial had full military rites at Andersen Air Force Base. After contacting the Department of Defense and the Guam Historical Society, the efforts by both the military and Guam's civil government resulted in the staging of the memorial service. A floral wreath and momument were lowered into the blue seas where the bodies are buried at sea. Military service members were moved by the ceremonies, and glad to have their chance to recognize the efforts of comrades of long ago.

Donald Yant was the son of Marion and Ida Blanch Mertz Yant of Fort Wayne and a graduate of South Side High School 1943. Donald Yant was associated with his brother in the plumbing business in Fort Wayne at Yant Plumbing & Heating, which was owned by his brother. Kenneth Yant, of New Haven, Indiana. Donald Yant was born August 10, 1925 and died May 11, 1945 in service to his country in Guam, Marianas Ialands.

Submitted by Joyce Kammeyer

KENNETH MARION YANT

An accomplished plumber, Kenneth M. Yant learned the plumbing trade working at the old Methodist Hospital on Lewis Street in Fort Wayne. He started his own business, Yant Plumbing and Heating, in 1941, and it is in business today and run by his son, David Yant. Mr. Yant was a hard working plumber and he had a heart of gold. He did many wonderful things in his lifetime. He was born May 16, 1906, and died May 8, 1971. He was on the trustee board of the New Haven Methodist Church and gave his tithe to accomplish the mission of Jesus Christ in the community. Kenneth Yant married Esther Bandelier on August 1, 1928. Esther was born July 7, 1907, and died February 2, 1995. They had four children: Edith M. Yant Liao, A. Wesley Yant, Joyce Yant Hetrick-Kammeyer, and David Yant.

Esther was the seventh child of Emmett Bandelier and Mary Adams Bandelier. She loved to ride horseback, and she would ride from New Haven to Monroeville, Indiana. You could see her long red hair flowing in the wind as she rode her horse. Everyone noted the beautiful young lady on the horse with the red hair. She always loved animals, and she always had a barnyard full of sheep, a pony or two, chickens, dogs, and several cats. Everyone knew where the farm was at New Haven, with the big red barn on the corner of Hartzell Road and Parrott Road.

The graduates at New Haven High School played a joke and came and took two sheep and put them in the school cafeteria. When the cooks of the school came in they called the office and said, "Where did these little lambs come from?" One of the boys who had taken the lambs loved one little pet lamb so much that he offered to keep it, and Esther Yant said "OK". She loved her Lord Jesus Christ and was a member of the New Haven Methodist Church. On behalf of the Bandelier family, Emmett and Mary Bandelier gave the big church leaded glass windows on the east side of the church as a memorial. A plaque is placed there stating the gift from the family. Esther's lucky number was seven: she was born the seventh child, the seventh month, seventh day, and seventh year. She was truly a "Child of God" being blessed and loving her Lord. Esther and her mother, Mary Adams Bandelier, had the first women's circle in the home at 206 Hartzell Road, New Haven, for New Haven United Methodist Church. Mary Bandelier felt the ladies of the church needed an outlet and believed women need Christian friends to communicate their faith and grow together as a group in love.

Submitted by David Yant

LEON YOUNGPETER FAMILY

Leon A. Youngpeter and family came to Fort Wayne, Indiana, from Decatur, Indiana, in 1962, when Leon became the head basketball coach at Central Catholic High School, where his teams won Sectional and Regional titles in 1968, and a Sectional title in 1969. He had coached previously at Dayton Chaminade High School and St. Joseph's High School in Decatur, Indiana.

Leon, born in 1935, in the village of Landeck, Ohio, and his wife, (Helen) Diane Griffis, born in 1936, in Delphos, Ohio, were married on September 3, 1956, in St. John the Evangelist Catholic Church in Delphos, Ohio. Their parents were Clarence and Alma (Schirack) Youngpeter and Richard and Helen (Fleming) Griffis. Leon coached and taught at Central Catholic High School until 1970, when he began an administrative career with Fort Wayne Community Schools at R. Nelson Snider High School. Leon left FWCS in 1975 to become Principal at Homestead High School and returned to FWCS to become Assistant Principal at Northrop High School in 1979. The next year he went to R. Nelson Snider High School as Assistant Principal and remained there until his retirement in 1998. While at R. Nelson Snider High School, Leon was instrumental in getting the students involved in the Christmas Food Box program through St. Mary's Church Soup Kitchen. Since the late 1980s this program has grown to include other schools and organizations under Leon's leadership.

Leon earned degrees from the University of Dayton and St. Francis College (now the University of St. Francis) and administrative certification from Purdue University at Fort Wayne. Diane earned an AS degree in Accounting from Indiana University at Fort Wayne.

The Youngpeter family joined St. Andrew's Catholic Church upon their arrival in Fort Wayne and later joined St. Jude Catholic Church after moving to the Lakeside area in 1965. The children attended St. Jude School Grade School. The children are: Paul Scott, born 1958; Julia Lynn (Steven) Myers, born 1959; Jill Ann (Matthew) Brown, born 1960; Mary Diane, born 1963; Janet Rose (Andreas) Schwarz, born 1964; Karen Marie (James R) Ridenour, born 1965; and David Leon, born 1976. The three older children were born in Dayton, Ohio, and the other four in Fort Wayne. Paul graduated from Bishop Dwenger High School and the other children are alumni of North Side High School.

Submited by Leon Youngpeter

REBECCA (SHEEHAN) YOUSE

Rebecca (Becky) Sheehan was the most sophisticated and independent of the ten children born to John L. and Bertha (Poorman) Sheehan. She was the fifth child, born in May of 1906. She lived on U.S. 30 and attended eight years at the red brick, one room Stevenson schoolhouse, the corner of Hoffman and Morgan Roads. At the age of 16 or 17 she ventured out on her own. She took a room in Fort Wayne at O'Briens and went to work at the General Electric. While working there she lost two fingers in a punch press.

She always dressed in the finest clothes, and she never had a red hair out of place. She was so beautiful. She married a fellow employee of G.E., Robert Youse, from the Hoagland and Monroeville areas and operated various taverns during their married life, one at Hoagland, Indiana, another at the Lake-of-the-Woods near Stroh, Indiana, and the last one was at Elmira at Big Turkey Lake.

Becky died on July 4, 1959, after an extended illness with cancer. Robert remarried a woman name Helen, and he died in 1962. Both Becky and Bob were buried at the IOOF Memorial Cemetery, Monroeville, Indiana.

Submitted by Roxanne Napier

NICKOLAS & MARY ZUBER

Nickolas and Mary Zuber and their children were born and grew up in Gunsberg, Canton Soloturn, Switzerland. The parents died in Switzerland. The children of Nickolas and Mary Zuber were Urs Zuber; Anna Mary Zuber, who was born February 2, 1831, and was married in Switzerland to Francis Joseph Wyss, born May 11, 1826; and Joseph Zuber. Anna Zuber Wyss, Francis Wyss, Urs Zuber and other family members left Switzerland in March 1852, and journeyed to Fort Wayne to join other family members.

Zuber Family, Back Row, Ivy Kitty May Zuber Beerman, Harry Zuber, Anna Zuber Harp, and Dude Zuber. Front Row, Lucinda Koehler Zuber, Emma Zuber Davidson, William Zuber

A son, name unknown, lived in Antwerp.

Joseph Zuber, born February 10, 1814, died May 19, 1856, married Elizabeth Offalker in Switzerland. Joseph, Elizabeth, and another Zuber brother immigrated to the United States in 1841. They traveled by stagecoach to Basel and from Basel they went by rail to Manheim, Germany, to Cologne. At Cologne they boarded a riverboat going down the Rhine to Bremen. There they boarded a sailing ship, arriving in New York 59 days later. From Schenectady they went to Buffalo and Toledo, then down the Wabash Canal to Antwerp, Ohio.

In May 1885, Joseph and Elizabeth became ill with typhoid fever and died, leaving eight children. Neighbors raised the three older sons, Jon, Joseph, and Francis until the three boys joined the army during the Civil War. The five younger children, from four months to sixteen years of age, came to Allen County and lived near Hessen Cassel with their Aunt Anna Mary and Uncle Francis Joseph Wyss.

The children of Joseph and Elizabeth were:

Jon B. (September 9, 1838-June 17, 1922) married Julia Kauffer on October 12, 1861, in Antwerp Ohio.

Joseph (April 17, 1843-April 18, 1907) married Louisa Raymond of Mt. Etna Ohio.

Francis (August 13, 1844-December 12, 1929) married Anna Elizabeth Kauffman on August 11, 1872.

Elizabeth (1840-1865) married Jacob Weiss on July 25, 1865, in Fort Wayne.

David (August 31, 1849-December 18, 1911) married Susan C.

Mary (1847-1865) married Leonard Lang on July 27, 1865, in Fort Wayne.

Rosette (1851- August 24, 1852).

William D. (1853-1927) married Lucinda Koehler in Fort Wayne on July 4, 1877. Lucinda's parents were Michael Koehler (October 15, 1824-March 30, 1881) and Catherine Keifer (October 15, 1829-September 7, 1886) both of Fort Wayne. William went to work in Fort Wayne for the Koehler Brickyard-Lumber Company. He fell in love with the owner's daughter, Lucinda, but the parents forbad them to marry because of religion. They married and Lucinda was disowned. William continued to work for the company, but the family had nothing to do with their daughter and her five children.

Andrew F. (Dude) Zuber (November 11, 1877-May 15, 1944) married Dora "Doddie" Corville and they had one son.

Anna Rosetta Zuber (November 7, 1879-April 29, 1959) married Albert Frank Harp and had three children.

Ivy Kitty May Zuber (December 12, 1985-August 19, 1958) married Charles (Jon) Beerman and had six children.

Emma Zuber (September 11, 1892-June 28, 1958) married Elmer C. Davidson; they had no children.

Harry Zuber married Winnifred (Winnie) Meese and had seven children.

Submitted by Kirt Clark

WILLIAM CHARLES ZWICK & CAROLINE SCHAMERLOH ZWICK FAMILY

William Charles Zwick was born in Adams County, Indiana, on August 10, 1882. He was a descendant of Prussian immigrants who came to America in the first half of the 19th century and settled in Adams County.

Caroline Schamerloh Zwick was born in Allen County, Indiana on May 15, 1881. She was descended from immigrants who came to

Mr. And Mrs. William C. Zwick, 1903.

The Zwick Family, c. 1921.
From left to right: Louise, Catherine, William, Walter, Ruth, Caroline, Benjamin, and Irving

America from the village of Buchholz, Westphalia, Germany, in the middle of the 19th century.

William and Caroline were married on November 18, 1903. They had six children: Walter Henry, born November 15, 1904; Benjamin Frederick, born September 10, 1906; Louise Wilhelmina, born August 16, 1908; Irving Albert, born May 18, 1910; Catherine Louise, born July 29, 1912; and Ruth Marie Wilhelmina born July 24, 1916. Their descendants are listed at the end of this document.

William and Caroline, or Will and Lena, as they were known to their friends, settled in Fort Wayne shortly after their marriage. By 1906, they were living at 441 East Lewis Street and Will's occupation at that time was "stationary engineer." In 1909, they moved to 1221 Archer Avenue.

On December 4, 1906, Will was appointed to the position of Patrolman with the Fort Wayne Police Department. He was promoted to Sergeant on January 15, 1915. It was during his tenure as sergeant that Will was engaged in a violent gun battle in which both he and his assailant emptied their weapons at each other and Will succeeded in shooting off his assailant's trigger finger. On January 8, 1922, Will was promoted to the rank of Captain of Police, which was the second ranking command position in the Fort Wayne Police Department. In the newspaper article reporting his promotion he is described as one of the most popular of the non-commissioned officers.

On August 17, 1927, Will was forced to resign from the Fort Wayne Police Department on disability because of a paralytic stroke. He died on February 2, 1928.

As a result of Will's death, it was necessary for Lena to go to work outside of the home. She worked as a presser at Pollak Brothers, which was a dressmaking firm that was located at Main and Maiden Lane. She retired from Pollak Brothers in 1947. In 1945, Lena's grandson, William C. Lee, came to live with her and lived with her until he completed college and married. Lena continued to live at 1221 Archer Avenue until the early 1960s, when she moved to the Northcrest Apartments. She lived her final years with her daughter and son-in-law Louise and Robert Ramsey. She died on July 31, 1972. She was a wonderful person. Truly the salt of the earth.

Descendants of William Charles and Caroline Schamerloh Zwick

Walter Henry Edward Zwick

Walter Henry Edward Zwick (November 15, 1904-February 7, 1994) married Marilyn Kirby (death date: March 10, 1999) on May 31, 1934. They had no children and are both buried in Portland, Oregon.

Benjamin Frederick Zwick

Benjamin Frederick Zwick (September 10, 1906-August 21, 1971) had no children. He was married to Alice Tigges, 1929-1930. They divorced. He married, second, Inez Swain on March 20, 1935. He and Inez are buried in Greenlawn Cemetery, Fort Wayne.

Louise Wilhelmina Zwick

Louise Wilhelmina Zwick (August 16, 1908-February 1, 1999) married Robert Ramsey (February 15, 1909-January 23, 1979) on August 27, 1927. They are both buried in Greenlawn Cemetery Fort Wayne. Their children were Charlotte and Patricia Ann.

Charlotte Ramsey (born November 21, 1928) married Gale Mulles (born January 14, 1927) on April 14, 1946. Their children were Richard and Rebecca Ann. Richard Mulles was born November 9, 1946, married first, Mary Baker, on April 6, 1968. They had a daughter, Samantha Ann Mulles, born December 25, 1968. They divorced, and Richard married second, in 1972, Sharon Elton. They divorced, and he married, third, on October 21, 1989, Valerie Troutman (born October 23, 1949). Rebecca Ann Mulles (born December 2, 1948) married Robert Lawson on September 21, 1968. They divorced, and she married, second, Howard Freese (born October 10, 1938), on October 9, 1977. Rebecca and Howard had two children: David Andrew, born May 29, 1978; and Heather Lyn, born January 7, 1980.

William C. Zwick,
Captain Fort Wayne Police Department, 1922.

Patricia Ann Ramsey (born March 13, 1930) married Henry Hartman (May 9, 1925-March 29,

2004) on September 24, 1949. Their children are Daniel John and Joseph Edward.

Daniel John (born October 5, 1956) married Lori Ferguson on May 19, 1979. They divorced, and he married second, on June 28, 1997, Tammy Holden. They are divorced.

Joseph Edward was born on June 14, 1960, and died October 7, 1995.

Irving Albert Zwick

Irving Albert Zwick (May 18, 1910-August 15, 1984) married Margaret O'Neal (December 12-1914-April 6, 2005) on September 22, 1940. Irving is buried at Veterans Administration National Center, White City, Oregon. They were the parents of Walter Frederick (born May 8, 1941), who resides in London, England. He married Katherine Rhoda Sanderson (born February 7, 1941) on August 31, 1963. Their children are Karen Lalonde and Linda Kelsey.Karen Lalonde (born October 17, 1969) married John Lachlan MacLachlan (born April 19, 1964) on July 29, 2000. Linda Kelsey was born April 29, 1972.

Catherine Louise Zwick

Catherine Louise Zwick (July 29, 1912-August 15, 1941) married Russell Lee (June 29, 1910-January 8, 1987) on May 29, 1935. They had one son, William Charles Lee (born February 2, 1938) who married Judith Bash (born June 2, 1937) on September 19, 1959. William Charles and Judith had three children, Catherine Louise, Mark Robert, and Richard Russell.

Catherine Louise Lee was born November 18, 1960.

Mark Robert, born August 18, 1962, married Jan Chalupny (born March 10, 1962) on June 18, 1993. They had two children, Katherine Fiona Chalupny Lee,born March 18, 1995; and Caroline Willa Chalupny Lee, born August 1, 1998.

Richard Russell Lee was born May 31, 1971.

Ruth Marie Wilhelmina Zwick

Ruth Marie Wilhelmina Zwick (July 24, 1916-March 4, 1947) married John Lingo on November 9, 1946.

Submitted by William C. Lee

Paul Knafel Family. Top, left to right: Sandra, Wanda, Betty. Seated: (Senora) Sue Cain, Paul Knafel, and DeElda. 1988. See page 555 for the Knafel family biography.

Wallace & Sarah Shively house and barn on Illinois Road. The picture is from a real estate catalog in the 1890's. See page 696 for the Shivley family biography.

Fran Allison and Velma Kaade, Parade of Homes, September 1960. See page 544 for Kaade/Keen family biography.

Junior Acheivement, July 1959. L to R: Willis Martin, a past president, and Bob Kaade, current president, honoring Paul Clarke, immediate past president. See page 544 for Kaade/Keen family biography.

Index

A

C

D

E

I

J

K

L

M

N

O

P

S

T

U

X

Y

Z

Family Record

Name	Birth		Death	
	Date	Place	Date	Place

Family Tree

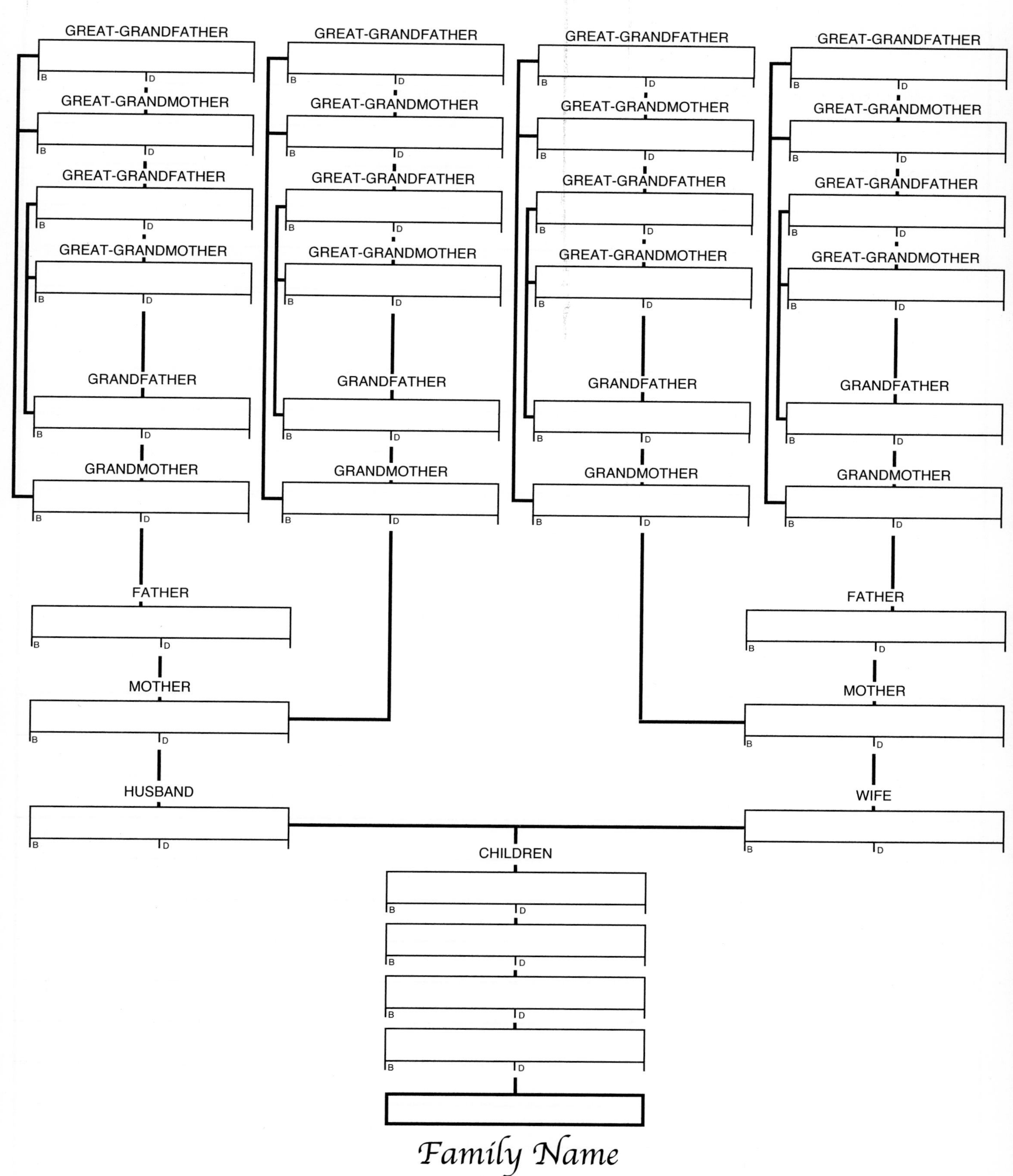

Family Name

Notes